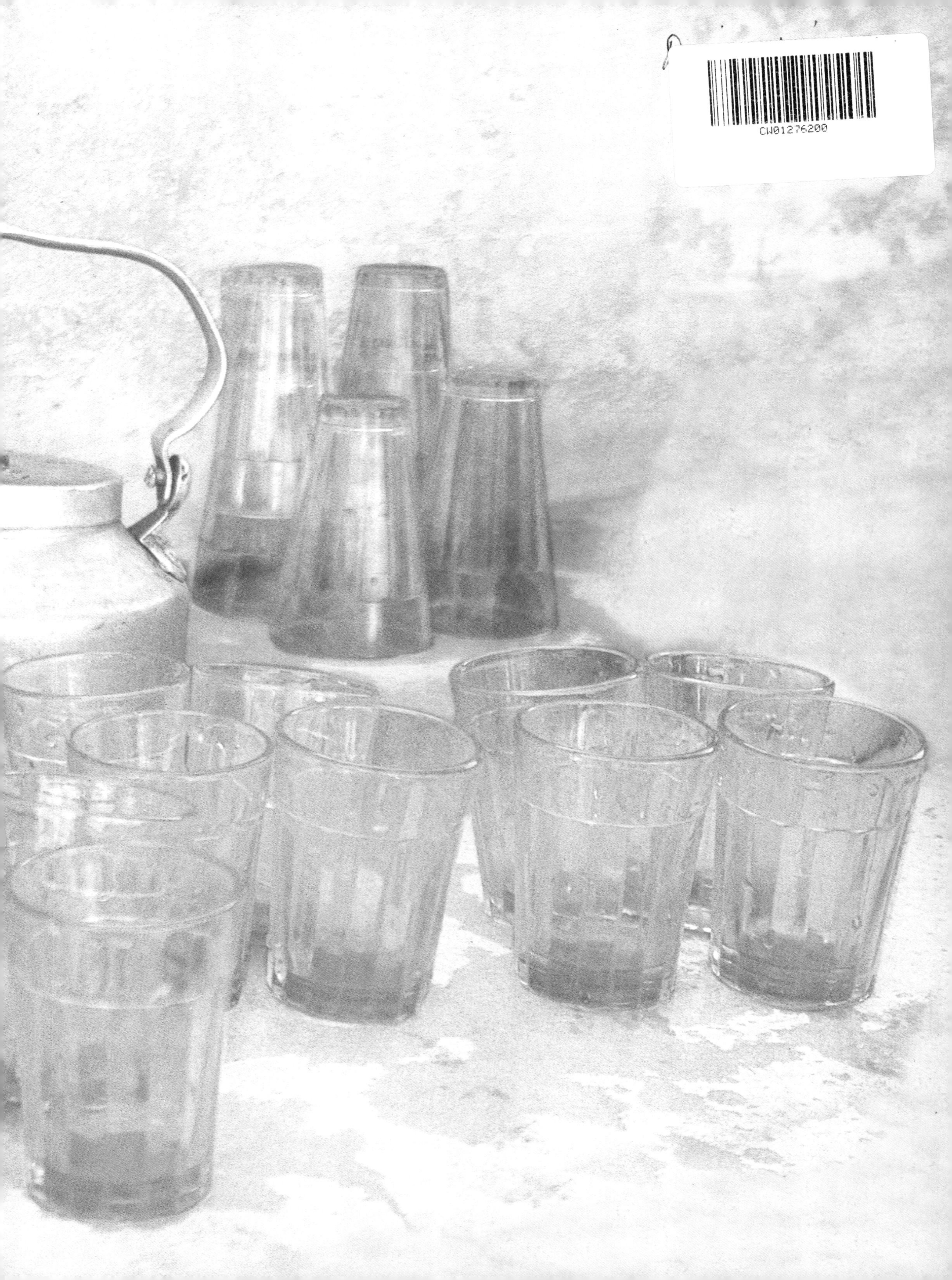

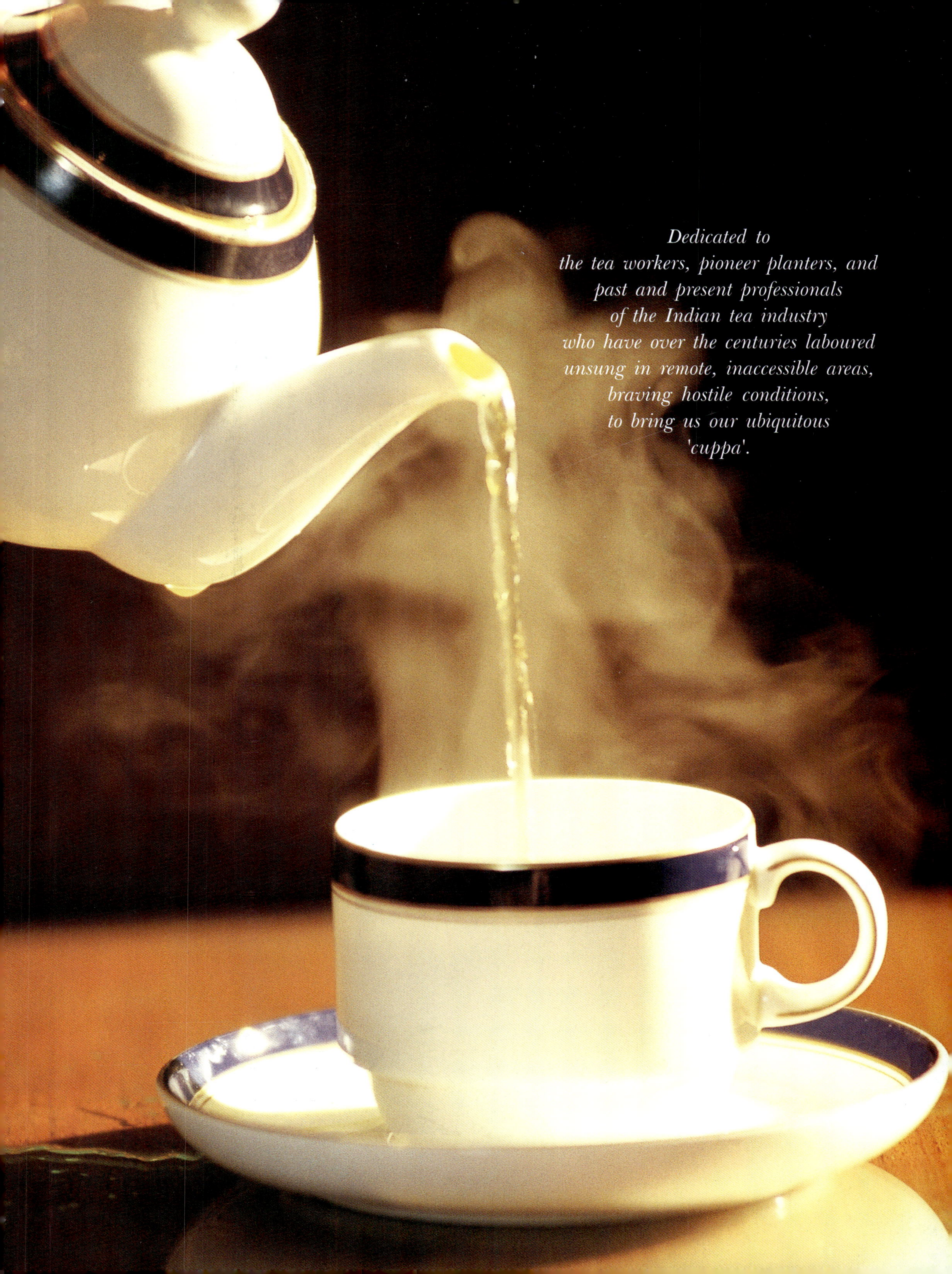

Dedicated to
the tea workers, pioneer planters, and
past and present professionals
of the Indian tea industry
who have over the centuries laboured
unsung in remote, inaccessible areas,
braving hostile conditions,
to bring us our ubiquitous
'cuppa'.

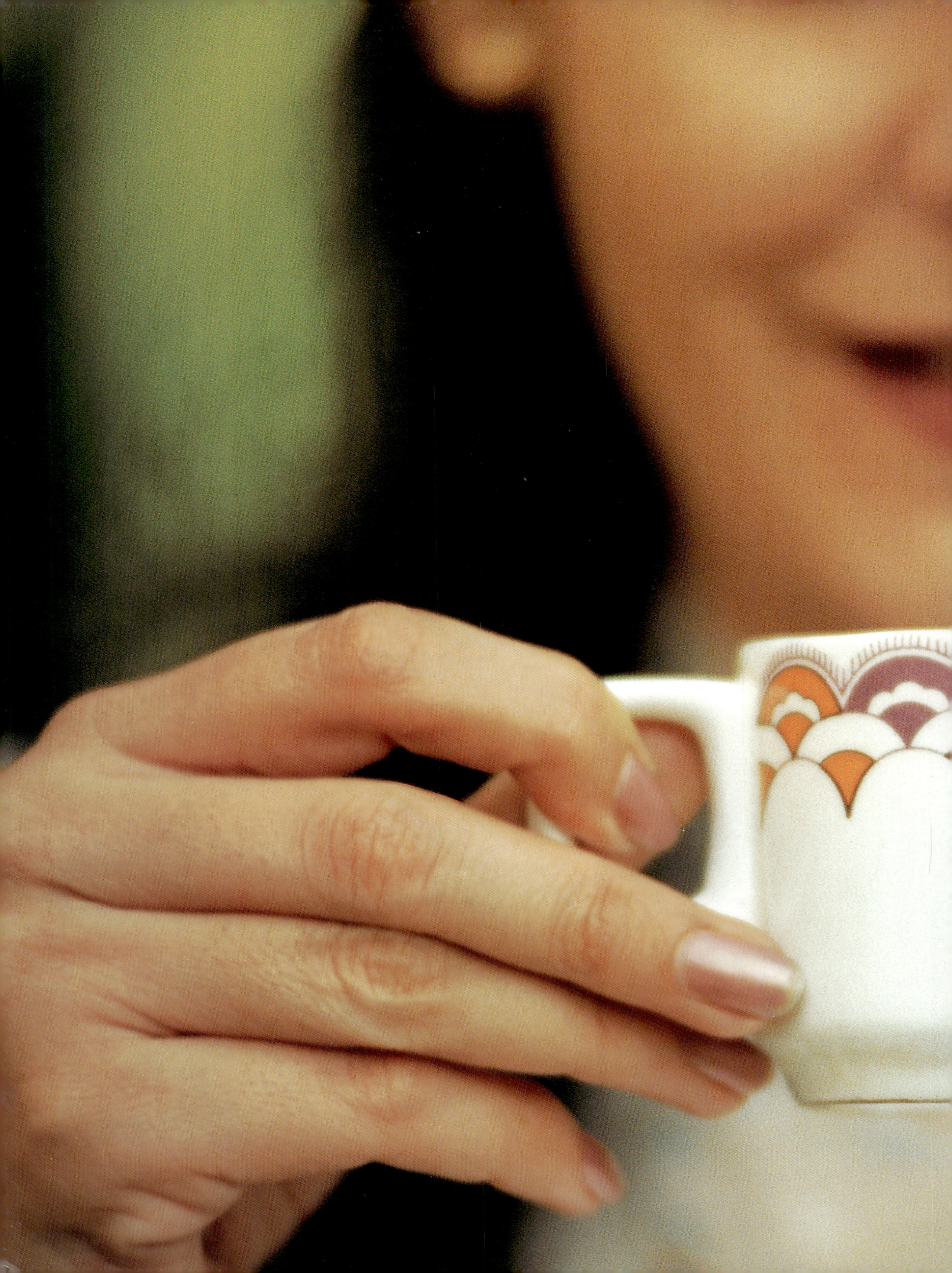

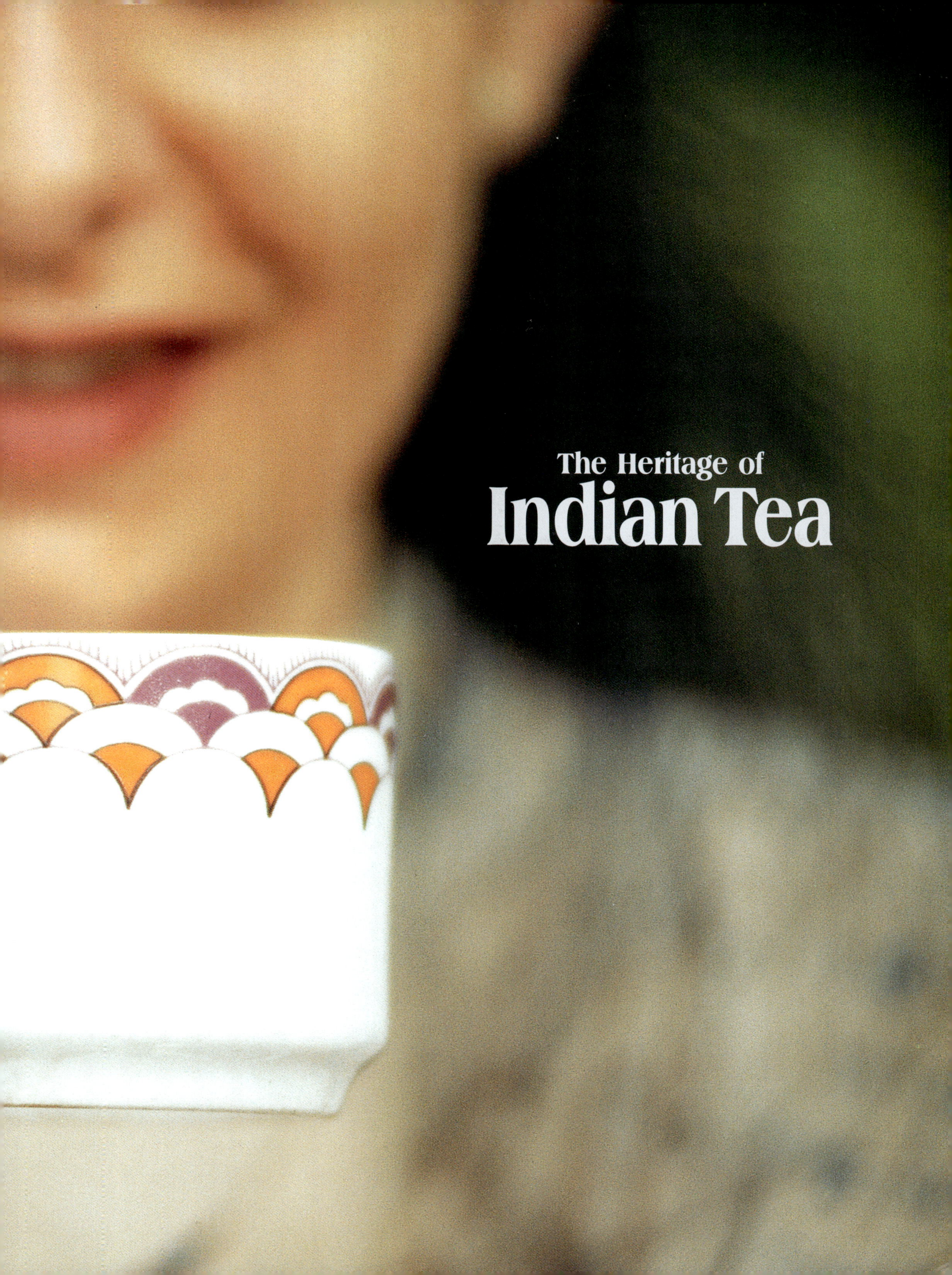

The Heritage of Indian Tea

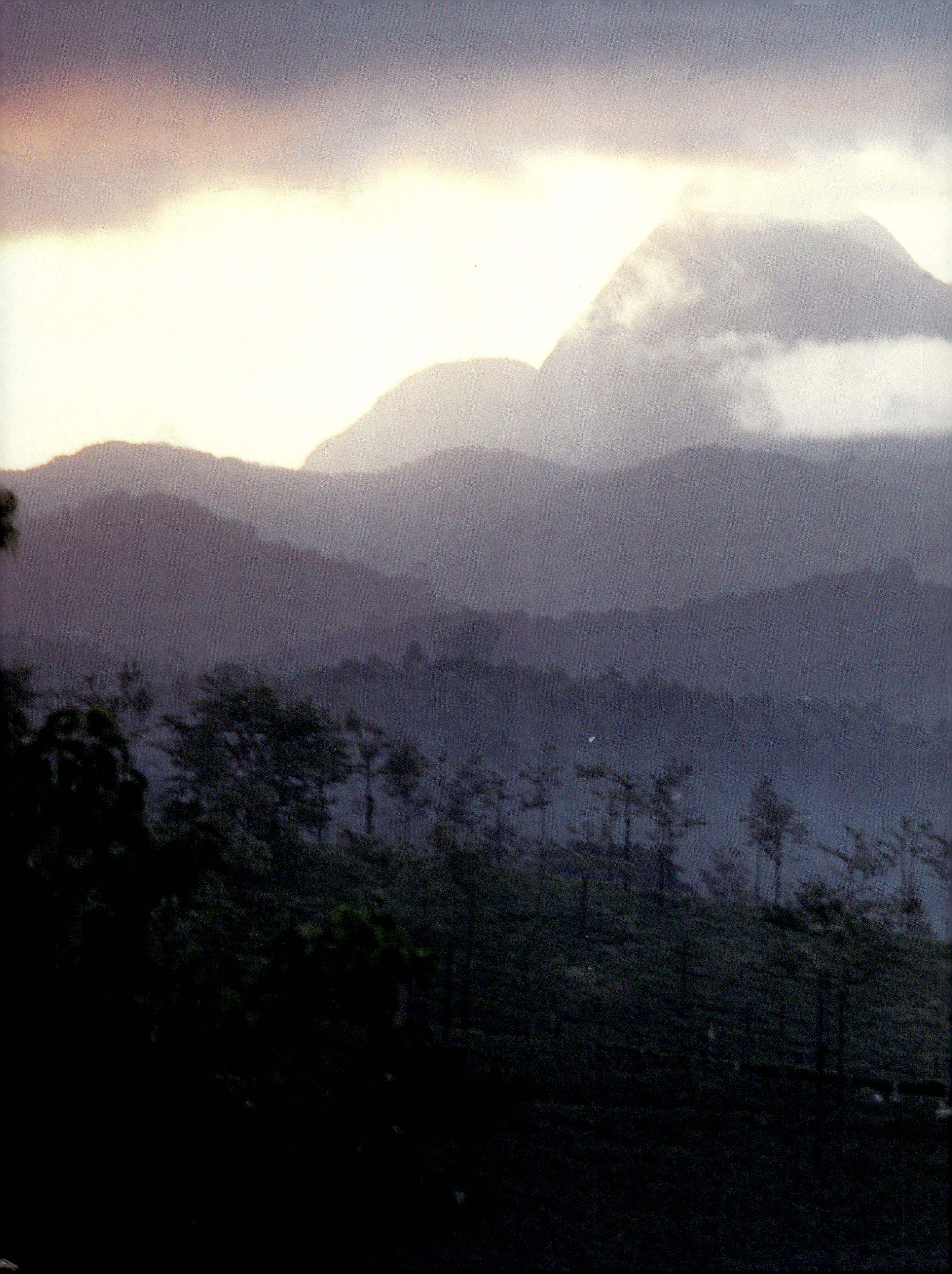

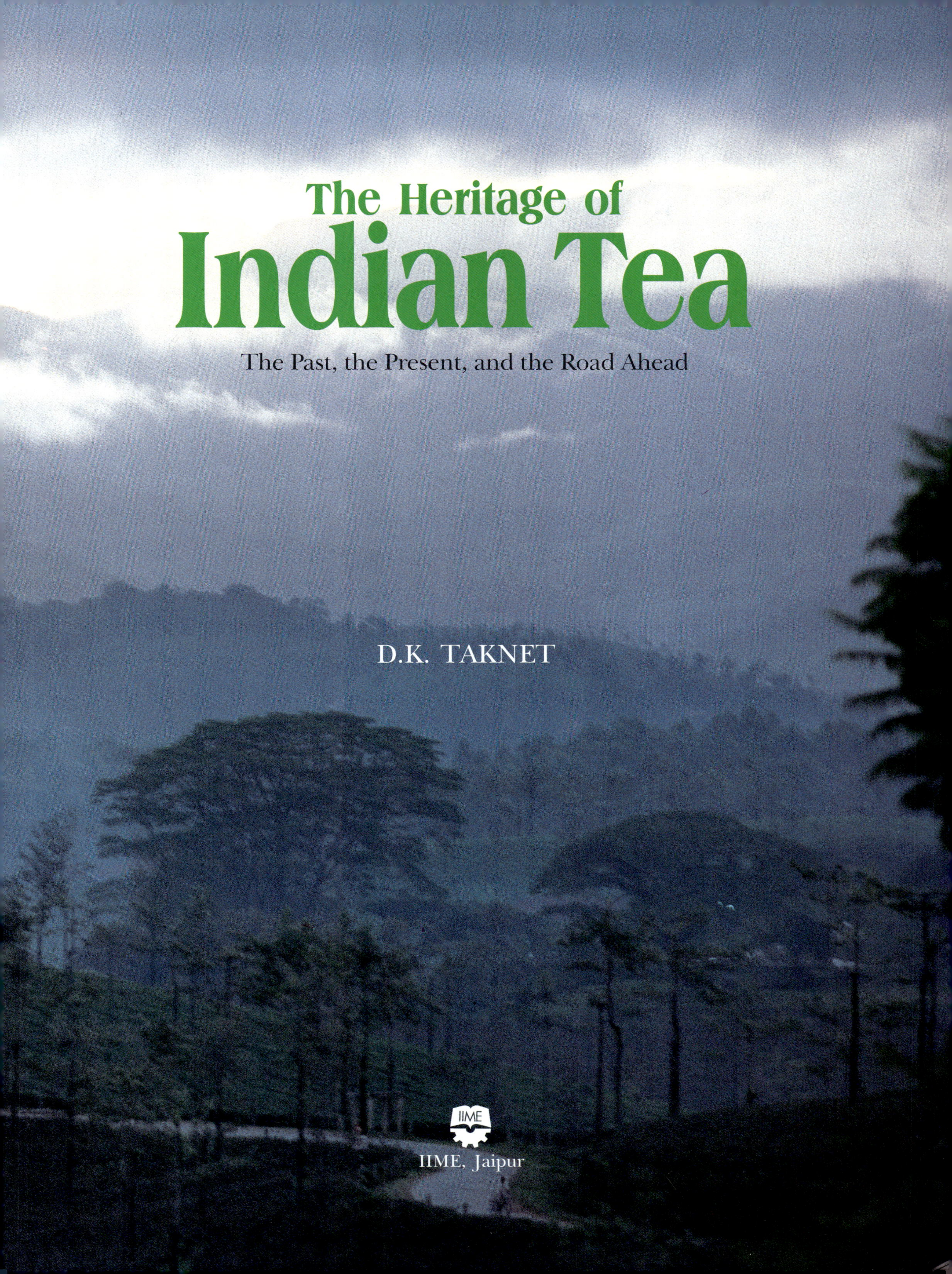

The Heritage of

Indian Tea

The Past, the Present, and the Road Ahead

D.K. TAKNET

IIME, Jaipur

Indian Institute of Marwari Entrepreneurship
1, Mahatma Gandhi Marg, Jhalana Institutional Area
Jaipur 302 004
Tel: 0091-141-703093-94/620535
Fax: 0091-141-620111
E-mail: iime1@sancharnet.in
            iime_delhi@hotmail.com

First published by IIME 2002

© D.K. Taknet 2002
E-mail: dk_taknet@hotmail.com

ISBN 81-85878-01-3

Picture research by
Sujata Taknet

Designed by
Gopi Gajwani

Computer concepts by
Rajesh Kudiwal

Printed in India by
Ajanta Offset & Packagings Ltd., New Delhi

This study was undertaken on behalf of and supported by the University Grants Commission, Ministry of Human Resource Development, Government of India, New Delhi.

This book is sold subject to the condition that it shall not, by way of trade or otherwise, be lent, resold, hired out, or otherwise circulated without the publisher's prior written consent in any form of binding or cover other than that in which it is published and without a similar condition including this condition being imposed on the subsequent purchaser and without limiting the rights under copyright reserved above, no part of this publication may be reproduced, stored or introduced into a retrieval system, or transmitted in any form or by any means (electronic, mechanical, photocopying, recording or otherwise), without the prior written permission of both the copyright owner and the above-mentioned publisher.

Contents

Foreword   9

Preface   11

1 THE PIONEERING YEARS   15

2 TRADITION OF SERVICE   45

3 PARTNERS IN PROGRESS   95

4 WHERE TEA IS A WAY OF LIFE   123

5 COMMITMENT TO TEA AND ASSAM   155

6 FACING THE FUTURE   189

A Calendar of Indian Tea   245

All for a Cup of Tea   247

Bibliography   251

Index   258

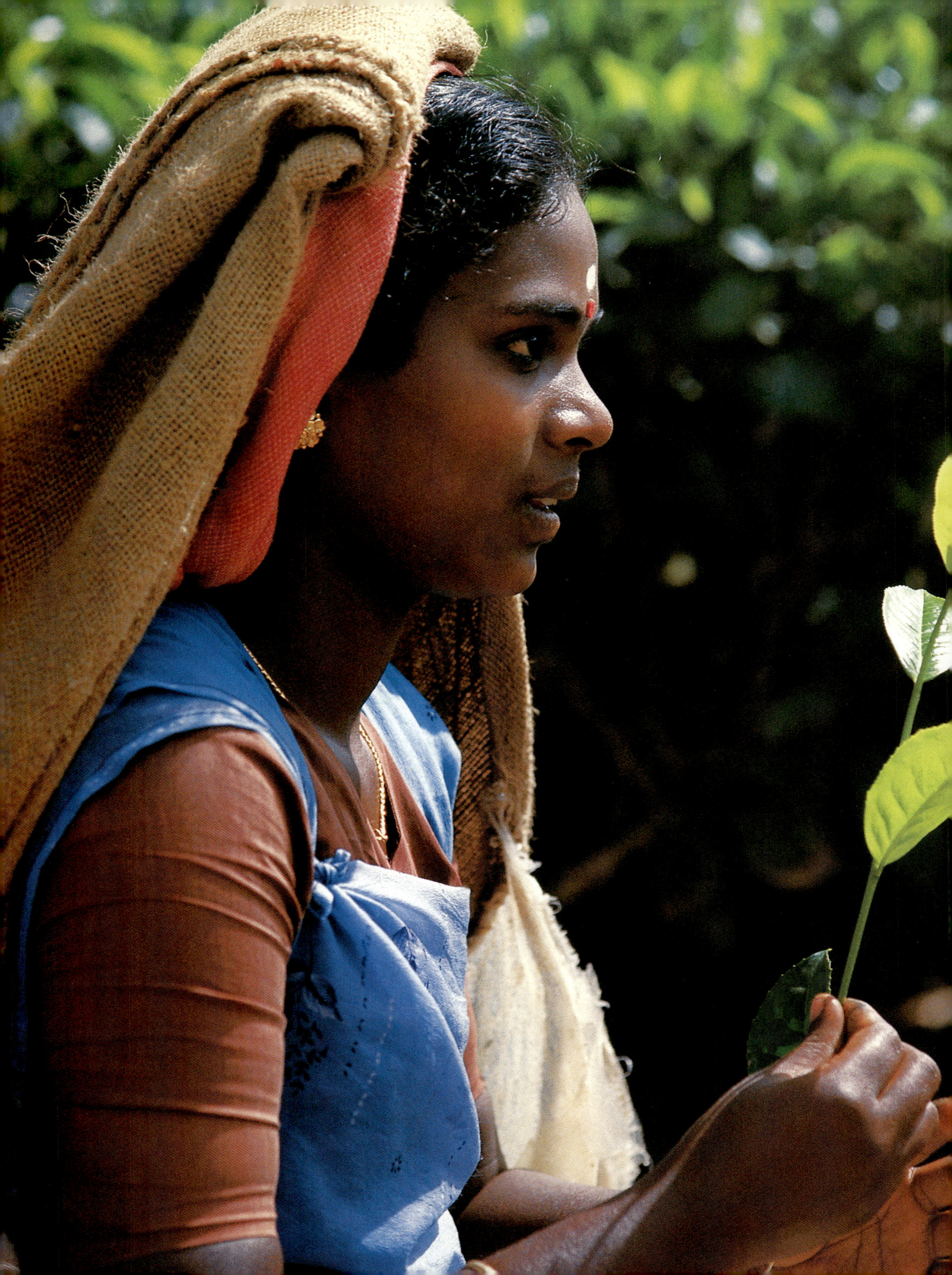

Foreword

India is the largest producer of tea in the world and among the world's largest exporters. Few people, however, realize the crucial role of tea in the Indian economy. The industry is one of the largest and most enlightened employers in the country, particularly of women and the underprivileged in less developed areas. Few are aware of the enormous scale, depth, and breadth of the developmental role the tea industry has played wherever tea is grown in India, be it in the once inhospitable North-East or the Nilgiris in the South.

The Indian tea industry has long needed a publication to document its traditions and contribution, which are more than a century old. Dr D.K. Taknet's book is a well-researched and insightful effort at providing a holistic perspective of the industry. This research study is extremely interesting because of its style and rare pictures. In addition to a brief survey of the history of Indian tea and vignettes of life on the tea estate, it is concerned, in particular, with the developmental role the Indian tea industry has played.

Overall, the work provides a well-rounded picture of the Indian tea industry: how it came into being, and what it means to India, the Indian economy, and the Indian people. Significant among the questions it raises are what the future holds, and whether the industry will successfully face the challenges ahead and retain its pre-eminent position in the world. The reader will, I am confident, get considerable value from the book's account of the manner in which the Indian tea industry has preserved its values and its rich heritage.

Mumbai
8 May 2002

Ratan N. Tata
Chairman
Tata Industries Ltd

Top: Tea service sahib style!

Facing page : Intense concentration! A tea worker contemplates a tea twig.

Following spread : An artist's impression of a flowering twig of tea.

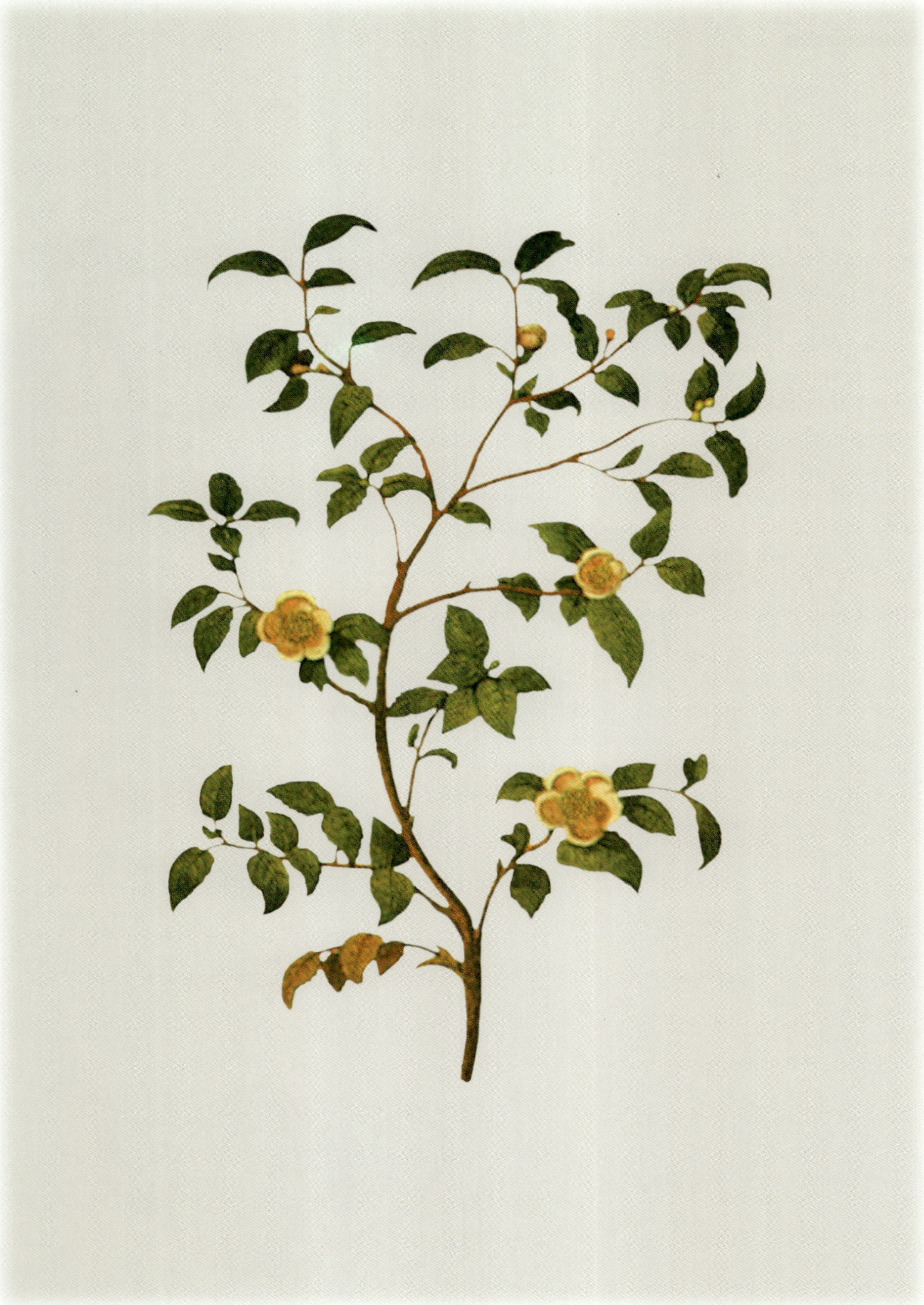

Preface

As a nation we can be justifiably proud of the notable achievements of the Indian tea industry. Its significance is immense and its impact multidimensional. The industry has, over the years, been making continuing and conscious efforts to play a constructive social role commensurate with its position as a major player in the Indian economy.

Once a British-dominated industry, it began to gradually change hands after 1947 when doyens of the Indian business community took over its reins and made its functioning transparent and well organized. This book attempts to provide readers with an insight into the history of the Indian tea industry, its major role in the Indian economy, global presence, and its conscious commitment to welfare activities for the benefit of people living in and around the tea estates.

The subject is vast simply because the tea industry is spread over a huge geographical area. Given the range and scope of the welfare programmes undertaken by the industry, it has not been possible to allude to all that the industry has done for the people of tea-growing areas and their respective states. What has been possible, however, is to demonstrate that in tea there is an industry of which we can all be legitimately proud.

The book also brings to the reader a profile of the Williamson Magor group which has not restricted its business philosophy merely to production and profit. Rather, it has actively associated itself with improving the lives of its employees and the wider public, and indeed other tea estates, by consciously allocating resources, skills, and talent with the aim of spreading prosperity. It is deeply committed to the overall development of tea and to see its institutions grow and prosper for the betterment of the industry.

However, notwithstanding its distinctive identity, it represents the values and culture of the tea industry as a whole. What is found in Williamson Magor in a heightened form is also shared by other leading tea companies with some exceptions, ironically, among others, those estates controlled and run by state governments.

The study outlines the dangers lurking on the horizon, and the many challenges facing the Indian tea industry. The rise of militancy in the north-east and the ongoing financial crisis are the twin dangers that are posing a serious threat to its very existence. It is ironical that an industry whose role in the socio–economic development of the country has been much larger than that of any other, is taxed much more than those producing other commodities with much less to show in terms of social awareness.

For a number of years the industry has been unable to generate sufficient resources to plough back into the gardens, undertake long-term developmental investment, and meet the challenges posed by new competitors and new technologies or, for that matter, develop dynamic and new marketing strategies. In consequence, slowly but inexorably, Indian tea is losing ground in the international market and its buoyancy in the domestic market. Upgradation of research facilities, existing factories, and plantations is desperately needed if the industry is to regain its competitive edge. The danger, the study indicates, is real, and remedial measures need to be taken urgently, for otherwise the industry will end up as a part of our glorious past rather than being a living, dynamic presence in our emerging future.

The world of tea with its unique aroma and graceful ethos was completely new and fascinating for me. The colourful history of Indian tea and its wonderful people with their variegated activities is remarkable and endlessly engrossing. To be able to speak in the tea idiom in the course of conducting interviews during the past four years, I had to travel over 400,000 km, a distance equal to travelling nearly five times around the world. I spent 400 days on the road on my way to interviewing over 2000 people directly or indirectly associated with tea, ranging from chairmen emeritus in lofty company boardrooms to the lowly tea pluckers on far-flung tea estates in Assam and south India where tea starts its journey to the world's teacups.

People from diverse backgrounds, with the common thread of tea running through their lives, poured out their hearts. From the old guard and the brown sahibs to today's young and professional tea estate managers, everybody had fascinating tea stories to tell, replete with previously unsuspected facts, anecdotes, opinions, and vignettes, providing dramatic insights into the tea industry. I have benefited immensely from the tea people who have inspired, guided, and taught me. I would like to thank them as they have played an integral role in advancing my understanding and research.

In order to write this book I had, in addition, to pore over approximately 10,000 sheets of interview transcripts and notes from field visits and personal records, and letters running to over 12,000 pages, together with other data including official records, reports, journals, periodicals, company balance sheets, annual reports, previous publications from the nineteenth to the twenty-first centuries by planters, tea experts, corporate executives, tea companies, associations, and the like. It was a truly mammoth task to distil the essence from my researches to fit into the limited space available to me. All in all, it has been personally a very enriching trip down the tea lane.

This study was undertaken on behalf of and supported by the University Grants Commission, Ministry of Human Resource Development, Government of India, New Delhi. I would like to express a special word of thanks for all the support extended by the Commission.

Sincere thanks are also due to Tarun Gogoi, chief minister of Assam, Prafulla Kumar Mahanta, the former chief minister of Assam, and Gunin Hazarika, the former minister of industries, and the officers of the Assam government, P.K. Bora, Jatin Hazarika, H.N. Das, P.R. Doley, and S.S. Hojai, for providing valuable information. I am grateful to Priyaranjan Das Munshi, Paban Singh Ghatowar, and M.C. Khandiat, and also to Aveek Sarkar, Harsh Goenka, Raghu Mody, A. Mazumdar, and A.N. Haksar for interacting and frankly exchanging their views with me.

I am indebted to the Williamson Magor group and its chairman, B.M. Khaitan, and his wife Shanti Khaitan, for their support. I am grateful to their sons Deepak, Aditya, and other executives of the group who spared so much of their valuable time to provide insights into the Williamson Magor saga and the tea industry as a whole.

My warm thanks to the tea people of various tea companies and associations for providing information on various aspects of the industry, although one aspect of the industry on which inadequate data is available is the welfare projects of the tea gardens. Interaction with them proved to be very illuminating. Among them are R.K. Krishna Kumar, R.S. Jhawar, S.M. Kidwai, Homi R. Khusrokhan, P. Siganporia, P.G. Sandys-Lumsdaine, J.M. Trinick, the late Mumtaz Ahmad, Bharat Bajoria, H.P. Barooah, Mahadeo Jalan, G.D. Kothari, C.K. Dhanuka, K.S. David, Ashok Lohia, D. Atal, N.K. Kejriwal, M.D. Kanoi, Y.K. Daga, D.P. Bagrodia, K.K. Saharia, M.L. Jalan, Krishan Katyal, Om Kaul, Dushyant Singh, and S.N. Singh.

The active support of I.L. Lewis, J. Simrany, Nazeeb Arif, D. Chakrabarti, R. Das, P.K. Bhattacharjee, Robin Borthakur, S.P. Verma, D. Bora, Bamin Dutta, Biresh Paul, Gita Narrayani, Chandan Mukherjee, S.P. Dua, S.L. Sharma, R.K. Chandak was of immense help in the completion of this study and has been much appreciated. I wish to acknowledge leading auctioneers like Krishan Katyal, Om Kaul, V. Dudeja, and others for their assistance, and I am specially indebted to planters and others who provided such a wealth of information. I must also record my warm appreciation of the efficient and ungrudging support of Om Arora, Asha Kiran, C.L. Kataria, Priya Sinha, S. Mahadevan, Siddharth Mukherjee, Anjana Chatterjee, Caroline McDermott, Aloka Sen, Subhash Garg, Harekrishna Das, Jagdish Joshi, Leeladhar Sharma, Mahesh Joshi, Akhilesh, Naveen Mathur, Sushil Pasricha, and Milan Bhattacharya for their untiring efforts and timely feedback.

My thanks to Adil Tyabji not only for editing the book and also providing other constructive suggestions. I warmly acknowledge the assistance of Veena Baswani, A.L. Roongta, Inder Sawhney, Umesh Anand, Pramesh Ratnakar, Neeraj Mehrotra, and Tapas Das with the manuscript.

I am grateful to Rajesh who slaved over my PC for the past four years at all hours, ensuring that the thousands of words and figures marched in the desired order and sequence. He conjured up endless printouts without a trace of irritation. I salute his sincere endeavours.

My special thanks to Gopi Gajwani, an artist of eminence, who coordinated the design of this book with a talented team. I am specially indebted to G.P. Todi, chairman and managing director, Ajanta Offset, New Delhi for his invaluable personal and sustained efforts to achieve the highest quality printing standards.

Finally, I owe a deep debt of gratitude to my wife Sujata who has been a constant source of strength and encouragement as co-traveller, interviewer, and keen observer. She has been a paragon of patience and dedication, helping in creative development and refining the ideas, concepts, and framework, and scrupulously examining the manuscript to offer valuable critical suggestions. The love and enthusiasm of my son Devashish has always inspired and rejuvenated me. He put up with many long and lonely evenings to enable me to complete this study. They are truly the wind beneath my wings, and I could never have flown without them.

I sincerely hope this book will help in generating a new broad-based understanding and appreciation of the Indian tea industry's proactive developmental role, its triumphs and perils, and at the same time, it will interest all those associated with tea who have the well-being of the industry close at heart.

New Delhi
May 2002   D.K. TAKNET

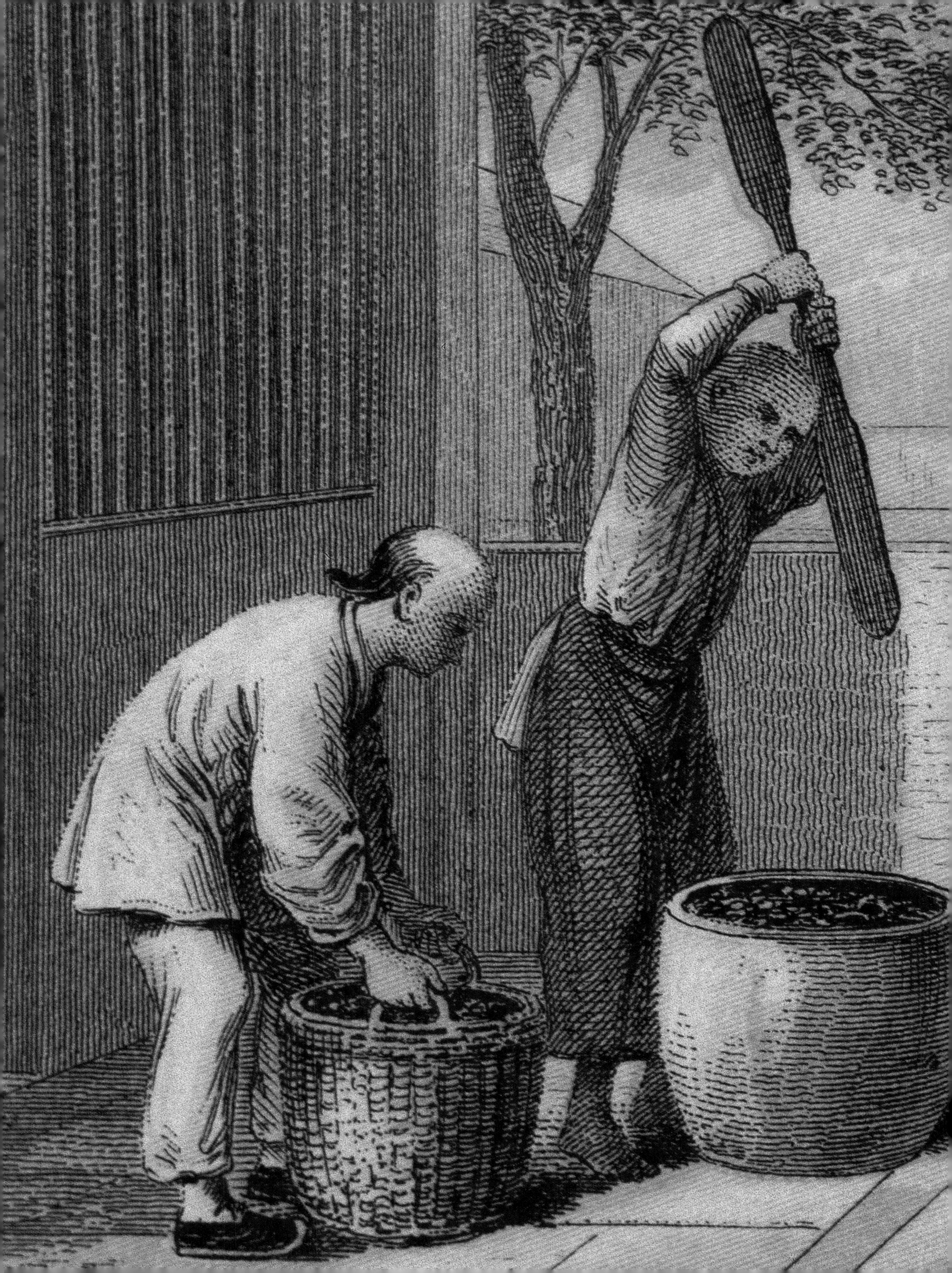

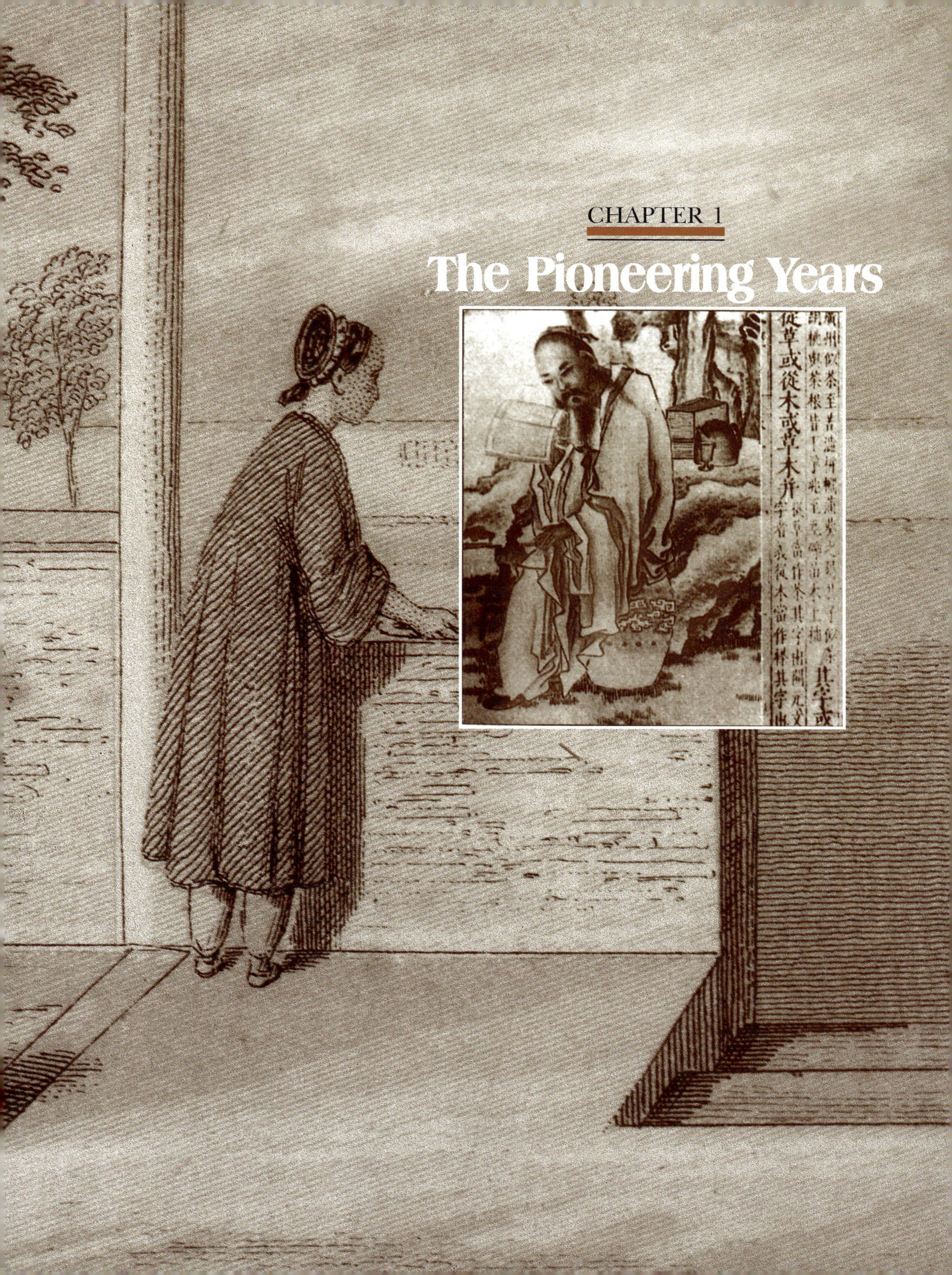

CHAPTER 1

The Pioneering Years

Top left: Utamaro, Courtesan Okita of Naniwa-ya Tea-house. *Top right:* A nineteenth-century painting of a servant carrying tea. *Left below:* Coolies transporting tea to the staging post at Palumpore (c. 1883).

Preceding spread: Tea has been drunk longest in China and Japan where it has played an important role in social life: processing small twisted tea in China (c. 1840). *Inset:* Lu Yu, the author of *Ch'a Ching*.

16 | THE HERITAGE OF INDIAN TEA

Tea has brought cheer to people across the world for over 4500 years. The ancient Chinese first drank it for its medicinal value, and later, from the third century onwards, as a refreshing beverage. Japan was the only other country where the growing and drinking of tea took early root, the Japanese raising tea-drinking to a fine art in their tea ceremonies. The popularity of tea spread to other parts of the world after the seventeenth century.

In England, tea received royal patronage when King Charles II married the Portuguese princess Catherine of Braganza, who was an inveterate tea-drinker. Britain was engaged in a war with France between 1756 and 1763, and obliged to levy several taxes to maintain its standing army in America. Following protests by the colonists, the British government withdrew all the taxes except that on tea. This did not appease the colonists, who boarded a ship in Boston harbour loaded with chests of tea, and threw them overboard into the sea as a protest to proclaim that there could be no taxation without representation in the British parliament. This event was described then and ever after as the Boston Tea Party.

The Boston Tea Party fracas led to the American Revolution and the declaration of American Independence in 1773. Thus it was that tea played a key role in altering the course of history! Through the centuries, tea has also symbolized warmth, friendship, mutual respect, and caring. Ralph Waldo Emerson wrote in the eighteenth century, 'There is a great deal of poetry and fine sentiments in a chest of tea'.

Today tea is the reigning beverage in over 45 countries and is consumed in over 115 countries around the globe. The Irish are the world's largest consumers, each person on an average consuming eight cups a day. However, the largest producer and overall the greatest consumer is India, where, at any time and anywhere, *chai* is an essential part of daily life.

Top: Portuguese princess Catherine of Braganza who introduced the English court to the social etiquette of tea drinking. *Middle:* The Boston Tea Party. *Below:* Russian tea drinkers with a samovar.

THE PIONEERING YEARS | 17

Top: Charles Alexander Bruce, the Father of Indian tea. *Below:* Darjeeling planter, mid-1860s.

Pioneering Initiatives

The year was 1823. Robert Bruce, a Scottish trader and explorer, visited Rangpur, the Ahom capital in Upper Assam. He had journeyed many times to these frontiers, but this particular foray had a very special purpose. He planned to meet Bessa Gaum, the chief of the Singhpo, one of the principal indigenous tribes of the Indian north-east, in connection with tea.

Bruce had learnt from a native nobleman, Maniram Datta Barua, that the Singhpo grew a variety of tea unknown to the rest of the world. If all that he had wanted was samples of the plants and seeds, he could have obtained them from just about any tribal contact. Bruce, however, wanted much more: the friendship of the Singhpo tribe and long-term access to the areas where the tea grew. If this was good tea, Assam could rival China, and Bruce sensed that he was on the threshold of something really big.

His meeting with the Singhpo chief inspired further hope. The brew from the plant did very closely resemble tea, and Bruce was permitted to carry away plants and seeds. This magnanimous gesture by the tribe opened Assam's doors to an industry that would sustain it for generations to come. Long after that happened—indeed, to this day—growing tea is the mainstay of Assam's economy. Bruce was an adventurous pioneer who sensed that history could be made, though he had no inkling of the remarkable consequences his initiative would have. Other Europeans followed him. He died in 1824 soon after his meeting with the Singhpo chief.

His younger brother, Charles Alexander Bruce, collected the tea plants and despatched them to David Scott, the governor-general's agent in Assam. The plants were then sent to Dr N. Wallich, superintendent of the Calcutta Botanical Garden, who declared they were not genuine tea! The indigenous Assam tea plant had to wait for another decade for recognition.

In 1833 the East India Company's monopoly of the Chinese trade came to an end. The British government decided to initiate tea-planting in India on a war footing. On 1 February 1834, Lord Bentinck, as governor general, set up the historic Tea Committee with George James Gordon as its secretary. The Tea Committee sent out a circular asking where tea could be grown. Captain F. Jenkins, based in Assam, responded by saying that Assam was ideal for tea cultivation.

His assistant, Lieutenant Charlton, collected the indigenous tea plants and sent them to Calcutta. Dr Wallich now pronounced Charlton's samples to be genuine tea, 'not different from the plant of China'. Jenkins and Charlton were awarded gold medals by the Agricultural and Horticultural Society of

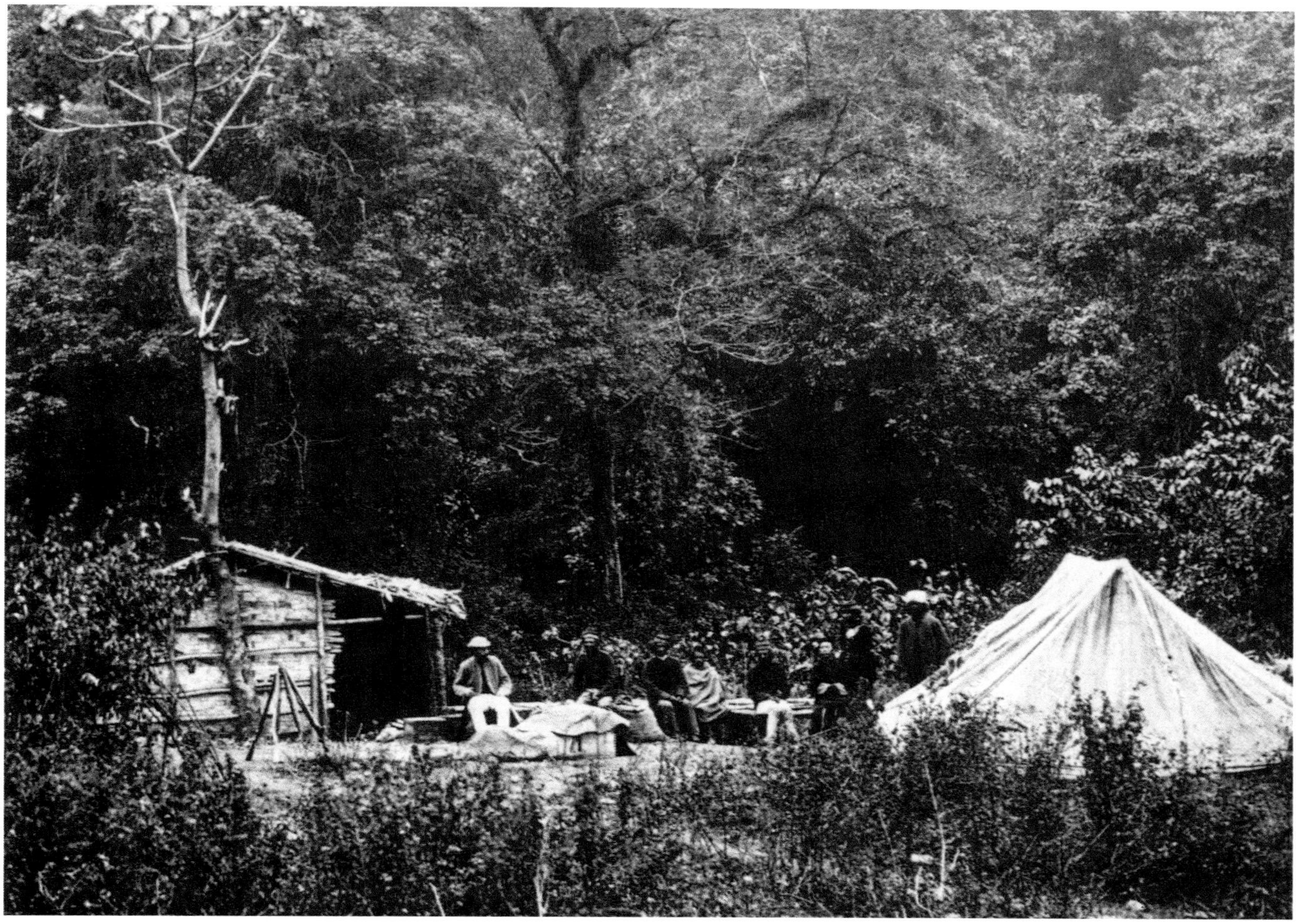

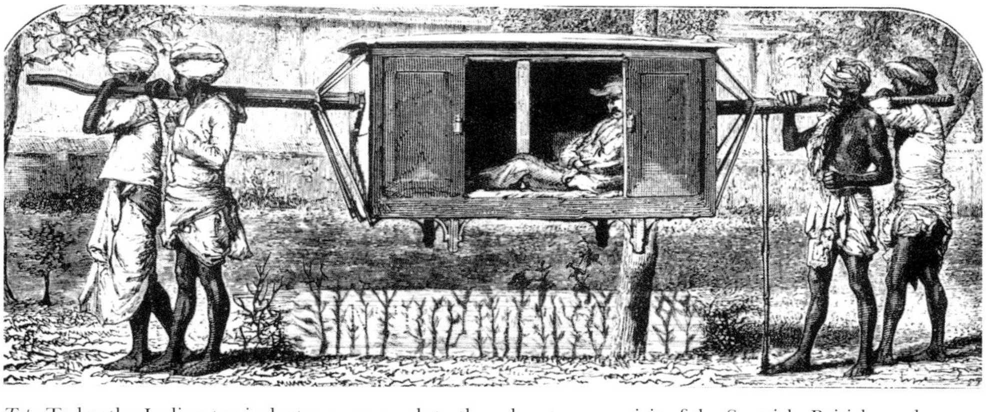

Top: Today the Indian tea industry owes much to the adventurous spirit of the Scottish, British, and Indian pioneers who braved dense jungles, disease-bearing insects, and prowling beasts of prey to grow tea in Assam. Here, a group of pioneers bivouac in a forest with their boxes of multifarious equipment and supplies, including rifles to protect themselves from the depredations of wild animals.
Below: Borne aloft! The palanquin was frequently used by planters to travel in the foothills.

Bengal while Charles Alexander Bruce was unceremoniously ignored.

In 1835, the Tea Committee appointed a Scientific Commission to select appropriate sites for planting tea, and Assam was again found to be the most suitable. The committee, however, decided that the Chinese plant and not the 'degraded Assam plant' should be used. The Tea Committee's secretary, Gordon, returned from a trip to China armed with tea seeds which were raised in nurseries in Calcutta. Young bushes raised in these nurseries were sent to Charles Alexander Bruce. He dutifully started several plantations with them in Chubwa. The Chinese plants proved to be a terrible disaster because they cross-pollinated with the native plant and produced a hybrid that would torment planters for many years to come.

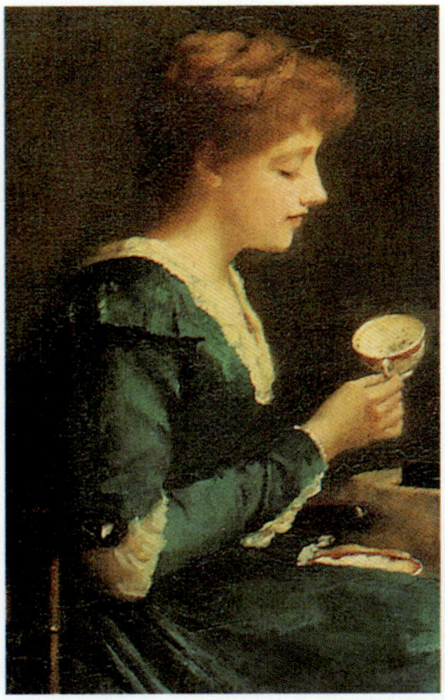

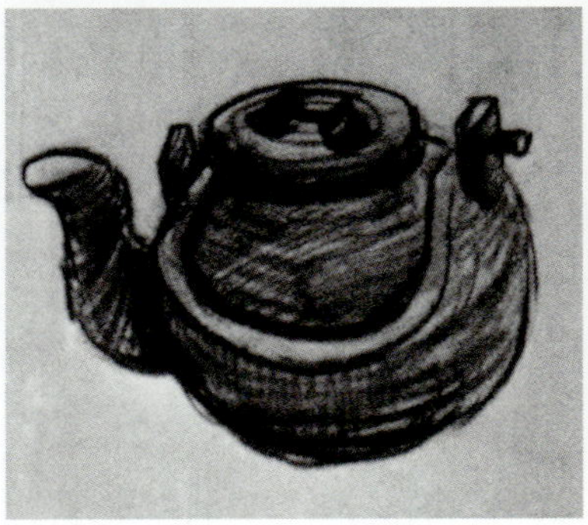

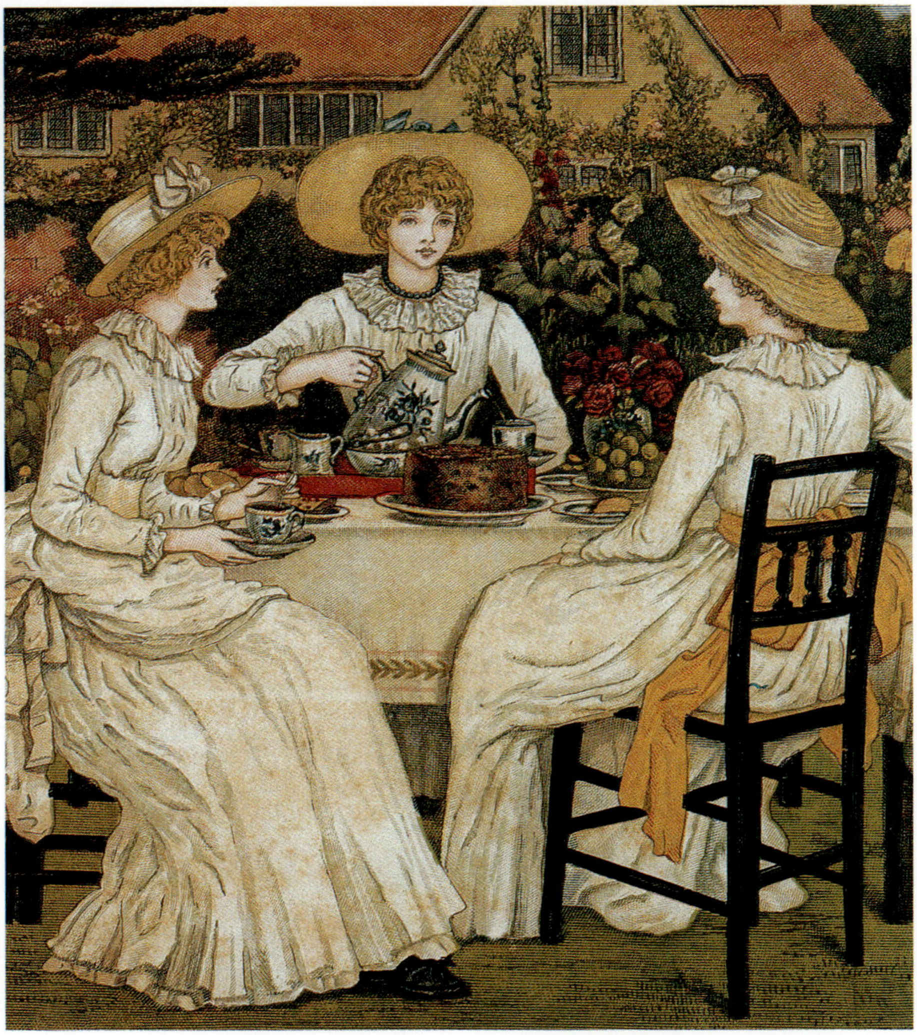

Top left and below right: The age-old and graceful custom of afternoon tea, generally served at five o'clock, remains an ideal way of entertaining friends and acquaintances. Henry James wrote, 'There are few hours in life more agreeable than the hour dedicated to the ceremony known as afternoon tea.' *Below left:* Drawing of a kettle by Vincent van Gogh.

The Breakthrough

Bruce did not give up. He set up a nursery at Sadiya consisting entirely of native bushes, and these survived. With the help of Chinese workmen, whom Gordon had sent to Assam, he managed to quietly despatch a small sample of manufactured tea grown from the local Assamese plant to the Tea Committee in 1836. The first samples were approved by the viceroy, Lord Auckland. Experts pronounced their verdict: it was of good quality.

In 1837, Bruce despatched another consignment of 46 chests of tea made entirely from the leaves of the Assamese bush to the Tea Committee. After removing a portion that had spoilt in transit, 350 pounds in eight chests were sent to the London auctions on 8 May 1838. This historic consignment was auctioned in London on 10 January 1839 and generated great excitement and patriotic fervour. Bruce had shown the way!

The Assam Company

The East India Company was the first to develop plantations in north-east India. In 1839, the Bengal Tea Association was set up in Calcutta. Private enterprise needed no further incentive and stepped into the nascent industry. In 1839, the first company for growing and making tea in India, Assam Company, was set up. Shares worth 500,000 pounds were floated, and such was the euphoria generated that they were immediately snapped up. In 1840, the government handed over almost all its tea holding to the company, and the latter, in addition, leased large tracts of land under the Assam Wasteland Rules of 1838.

From the outset the company was bedevilled by shortage of labour and technical expertise. Despite the poor performance of the Chinese plant, Assam Company still grew it and employed Chinese methods of cultivation and manufacture. The expenses were exorbitant and the actual production insignificant. The company slipped into the red, and by 1843 was facing bankruptcy and liquidation. A saviour, in the form of Henry Burking Young from Calcutta, revived it in 1847, and Stephen Mornay took charge in Assam. Together they improved cultivation, streamlined the company's finances, and within five years they were a success story.

In May 1855, indigenous tea bushes were first discovered in Cachar district of Assam. The very next year proprietary gardens were established there. Tea cultivation spread to Tripura, Sylhet, and Chittagong. Jorehaut Tea Company followed in the footsteps of Assam Company and was incorporated on 29 June 1859. By 1859 there were nearly 50 tea gardens in Assam. Seeds and saplings

Top: A sketch of Ging Tea Garden, Darjeeling. *Middle:* Weighing the tea leaves for payment of tea workers. *Below:* A country-made revolving sieve to separate the finer tea leaves.

Top: Withering house. *Middle:* The interior of a tea-house. *Below:* The traditional method of rolling the leaf by hand.

were also planted in Kumaon, Dehra Dun, Kangra, Kullu, and Garhwal on an experimental basis.

By 1862, the tea industry in Assam comprised 160 gardens owned by 57 private and five public companies. In 1868 the government appointed a commission to enquire into all aspects of the industry, and expressed the view that it was basically sound. The total amount of capital invested in the industry increased from less than £ 1 m. in 1872 to £ 14 m. within three decades. In 1881, the Indian Tea Association was founded to represent north Indian planters, and in 1893 the United Planters' Association of Southern India was set up to represent those in the south.

Tea Travels

All was not, however, lost for the Chinese tea bush. It was found suitable for Darjeeling. In 1841, Dr A. Campbell brought Chinese tea seeds from Kumaon and planted them in his garden in Darjeeling town. Commercial cultivation began around 1852–3. By 1874, there were 113 tea gardens in Darjeeling district alone. This inspired planters to try out tea cultivation in the Terai region. James White set up the first Terai plantation called Champta in 1862. Planting was then extended to the Dooars, but the Assamese tea bush proved more suited to this region. Gazeldubi was the first Dooars garden, and by 1876 the area boasted 13 plantations, which in 1877 led the British to set up the Dooars Tea Planters' Association.

In the south, the pioneers cleared the forests to grow crops, and following much experimentation, finally settled on tea. In the process they faced much hardship, combating disease, the depredations of wild animals, and a chronic shortage of capital. They were, however, enterprising and determined men who shrugged off these adversities and persevered. James Finlay & Co. was the first to attempt tea cultivation in the high ranges of Kerala. The hills of Kerala, especially Munnar, are now home to the highest teas grown in the world. The specific geographical conditions and the height of the plantations make the tea unique. Tea was planted over the graveyard of coffee. Miles and miles of coffee plantations had been infested with 'leaf rust'. Mann was the first planter to manufacture Nilgiri teas. He started a tea plantation near Coonoor in 1854, which is now known as Coonoor Tea Estate. Around this time, another planter, Rae, set up Dunsandle Estate near Kulhatty. Following their success, other planters in the Nilgiris began to follow suit in 1859.

The Nilgiris or the Blue Mountains, popularly known as the 'Queen of the Hills', are situated at the tri-junction of Tamil Nadu, Karnataka, and Kerala.

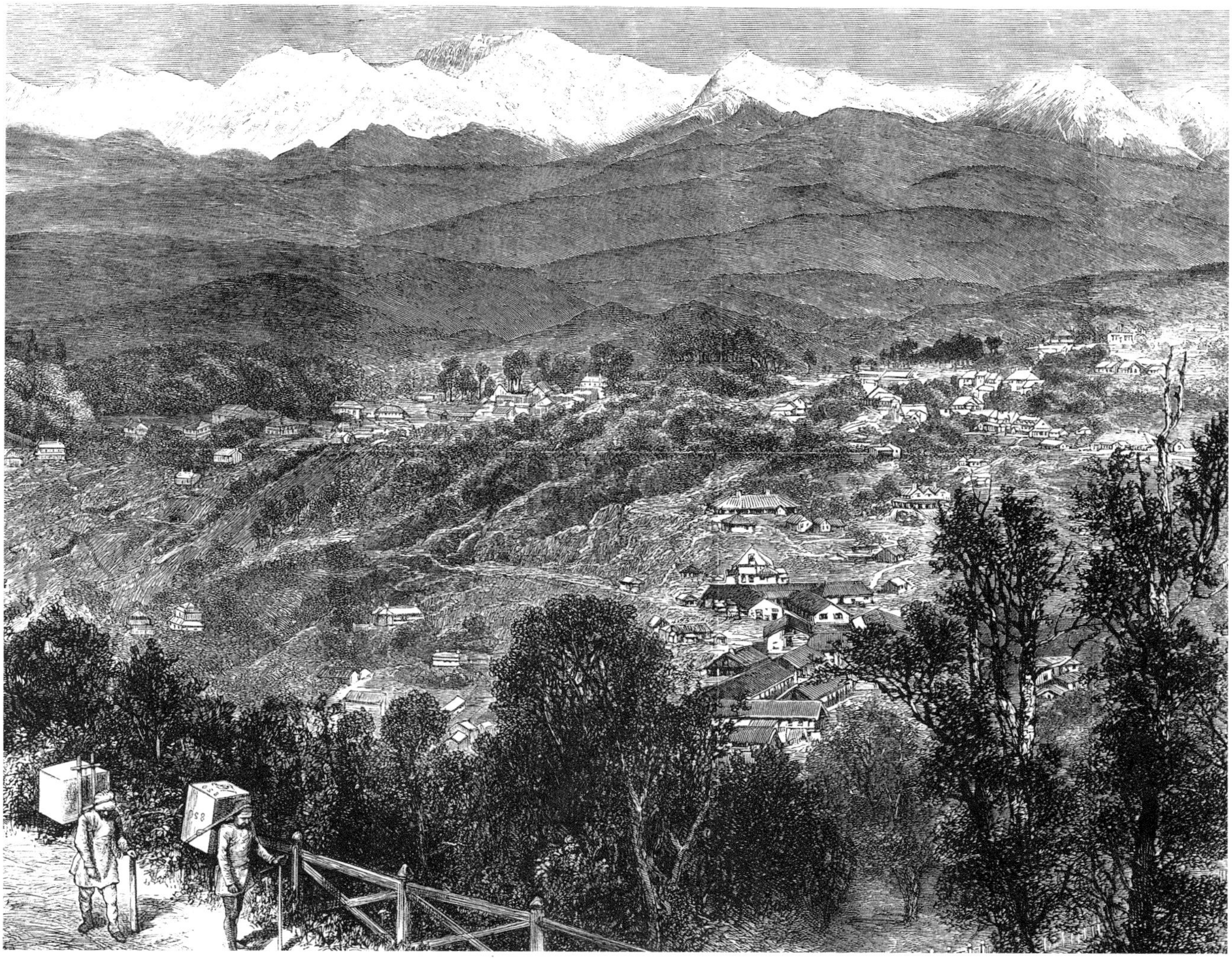

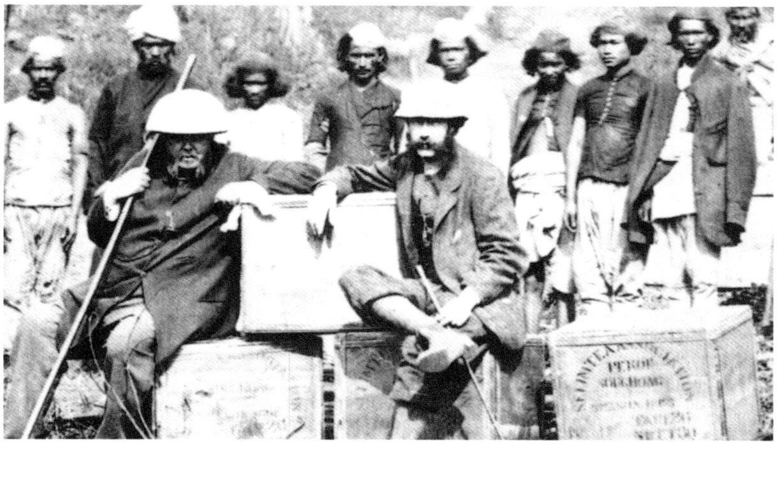

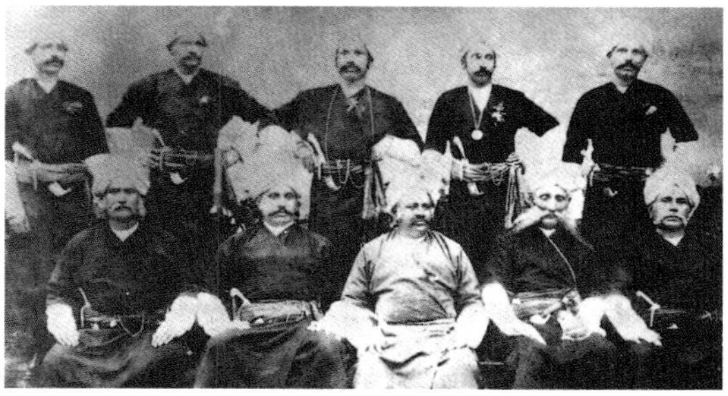

Top: A view of a south Darjeeling town with wild tea bushes. Most of the tea gardens are situated slightly below the town, which itself is at 7,400 ft.
Below left: The pioneer planters and tea workers.
Below right: The pioneers who met the Viceroy in Bangalore in November 1895.

Top: Painting of buffalo hunting in the high, dense grasslands in Assam.
Below: Painting of an Assamese gentleman with a Meree woman. The principal occupation of these quiet, tolerant, and industrious people is animal husbandry.

The region is well known for a concentration of 80 native plant species, which is a rare occurence in nature. Notwithstanding this, southern tea production stagnated for a long time, gathering momentum only in the early twentieth century. Today, the total cultivated area of the Nilgiris is 77,469 ha of which 69.5 per cent is under tea. Most south Indian tea is grown in the hilly regions of Tamil Nadu, Kerala, and Karnataka states, but the bulk of Indian tea comes from the eastern and north-eastern parts of the country where tea estates are mostly located in the plains.

The Early Entrepreneurs

The role played by the pioneers of tea prior to Independence is a saga of courage, entrepreneurship, and determination. Sir Percival Griffiths, in his *History of the Indian Tea Industry* (London, 1967)—considered to be one of the best accounts of the early years—described the first planters as having had 'to hew their way through trackless jungles to cope with disease and the ravages of wild beasts, to recruit and maintain the morale of the workers from distant provinces, and last, but not least, to learn the technique of tea cultivation and manufacture'.

There were dense, impenetrable tropical forests. Herds of wild elephants tramped right across the young tea bushes. There were no means of transport

and communication. Right up to the late nineteenth century, people in Assam travelled mostly by boat up and down the mighty Brahmaputra river. The pioneers and local inhabitants played a major role in building roads, bridges, and other infrastructural facilities in the tea-producing areas.

The Plantation Inquiry Commission mentioned in its report that the tea-planting industry had played a valuable part in opening up and developing what were previously inaccessible jungles and forests. Doing business in Assam has entailed tackling the challenge of backwardness. Assam is a microcosm of the problems relating to the environment, health, employment, habitat, gender inequality, and ethnic unrest that afflict the country as a whole.

Maniram Dewan, the prime minister of the last Ahom king, Purandhar Singha, was the first Indian to grow tea on a commercial basis in Assam. He was followed by Rosheswar Barua, who established six tea estates. Many other Indian planters followed their lead. Among them, some noteworthy names were Bistooram Barooah, Kaliprasad Chaliha, Hemadhar Barua, Rai Bahadur Jagannath Barua, Rai Bahadur Krishnakant Barua, Colonel Sibram Bora, Sarbananda Borkakoti, Rai Bahadur Bisturam Barua, Rai Bahadur Sib Prasad Barua, Rai Bahadur Debi Charan Barua, Ganga Gobind Phukan, Malbhog Barua, Narayan Bezbarua, Ghanshyam Barua, Radhakanta Handique, and Narayan Bedia.

Top: Pioneer Assam planters who assembled at Dibrugarh to form the Assam Tea Planters' Association.
Below: Maniram Dewan was the first Indian to grow tea on a commercial basis in Assam. He was later hanged by the British in 1857 for his part in the Mutiny.

Top: A sketch of a wealthy shopkeeper in Assam known as a *kyah*. *Kyah*s also served as moneylenders and supplied foodgrains and other necessary goods of daily consumption to the tea gardens, and their descendants continue to do so. *Below:* A sketch of a bullock cart. *Jahan na pahunche belgadi, vahan pahunche Marwari.*

Facing page top: An old steamer on the Brahmaputra river. This was the principal means of transporting tea and travellers during the early days. *Below:* A planter with his car battling the rough terrain on Assam Trunk Road which links lower and upper Assam.

From faraway Rajasthan, the land of heat and dust, came the Marwaris who found their leafy fortunes in tea cultivation. In 1819, Navrangrai, the father of Harbilash Agrawal, migrated from Churu and settled in Tezpur. A few years later he was joined by a stream of traders. They braved immense hardship, but battled on and built their businesses from scratch. From Tezpur the Marwaris spread into Dibrugarh around 1825, and Harbilash Agrawal set up Tamboolbari Tea Estate there. Snehiram Lohia started as a trader in Tinsukhia and later became a leading tea planter.

The Marwaris travelled across rough mountainous terrain, often on foot. There were no transport facilities and it used to be said: *Jahan na pahunche belgadi, vahan pahunche Marwari* (the Marwari can even reach a place which is inaccessible to a bullock cart). Innumerable Marwaris succumbed to illness and lack of medical care. They had to rely on their own intelligence and skill to develop plantations, clearing the jungles and identifying the soil best suited to tea. So expert did they become that very soon European and other Indian planters began to seek their advice.

The former chief commissioner of Assam, R.H. Keating, commented : 'The Assamese with their subsistence economy were not interested in large trade and industry in 1874. Hence, the Marwaris were allowed to facilitate commercial transactions with Bengal. Later, a large number of Marwaris took over trade and business and benefited immensely.' According to the 1881 census, there were 2400 Marwaris living in Assam. Many of them were moneylenders or worked as traders supplying foodgrains to the tea estates. The *Census Report, 1921*, notes that 'Wholesale and important retail trade is in the hands of men of Rajputana and of Eastern Bengal'.

Later the Marwaris even began buying out British plantations. Their role in the development of Assam was quite significant, and was highlighted by the first Congress chief minister of Assam, Gopinath Bordoloi, 'I always praise the unremitting efforts of the Marwaris which have resulted in making Assam a prosperous place worth living in. They have performed a great service for Assam and the Assamese masses.' Bordoloi added, 'The credit for changing the face of Guwahati, Noganva, Jorhat, Dhubri, Gowalpada, Shivasagar, Dibrugarh, Lakhimpur, and other cities situated on the banks of the Brahmaputra goes to the Marwaris who came to Assam in the last century and settled here. Likewise, they deserve the credit for bringing prosperity to Shillong, Dimapur, Kohima, Tinsukhia, Digboi, and Imphal.'

Building a Communications Network

Communications are the lifeline of an industry. No credit is too great for the enterprising planters who braved elephants and other grave hazards to grow tea in the wilds, for Assam then was a maze of dense tropical forests. The only way to travel was by slow boats crawling up and down the mighty Brahmaputra. In 1834, members of a tea committee took four months to reach Upper Assam from Calcutta by boat. Between 1848 and 1853 a regular steamer service was established between Guwahati and Dibrugarh. Rapid expansion and development of the transport network was a landmark in the history of the tea industry. Later, the planters organized themselves into the Assam Valley Tea Association with their headquarters at Kokilamukh near Jorhat, and set up a tea-rate road fund to finance the construction of infrastructural facilities like roads and bridges.

The North Trunk Road was realigned from Tezpur to Mangaldai in order to link it further to the Dooars. The Assam Trunk Road, which links lower and

Top and middle: The pioneer planters and tea garden workers, toiling in taxing conditions, have created an infrastructure of bridges, roads, and railways in the tea-growing areas.
Below: The Manipur road, a spectacular engineering feat achieved by the tea community. It proved crucially important for the military operations in 1941–2 in Assam.

upper Assam, was constructed. Gardens situated on the southern bank of the Brahmaputra are all linked to this road. The planters lent their weight to the people of Assam to lobby the government and got a bridge built over the Brahmaputra at Pandu.

During the Second World War, Cooch Behar was connected to Joghighopa by rail, road, and bridge. The planters built a network of link roads, and being members of local development boards, got money sanctioned for its maintenance. The Indian Tea Association, and later the Assam Branch Indian Tea Association, were formed to look after the interests of the industry. No Tea Board existed then. Soon these associations became important vehicles for social upliftment.

The first passenger train, called Dibru Sadiya, chugged out from Dibrugarh on 16 July 1883 for Makum. It was owned and run by the Assam Railway and Trading Company which had, inter alia, business interests in tea, coal, and timber. Later, the extension of the railway link from Calcutta to Tinsukhia was also undertaken by the tea planters.

A few years later, the train was extended to Saikhowa Ghat and Tipongpani Colliery. The three-mile Jorhat State Railway followed. It was built by the state government for the convenience of the numerous tea gardens in Jorhat. The 20-mile Tezpur–Balipara Light Railway came next. Half the share capital was owned by tea companies, and the Tezpur Local Board subsidized one-fourth

28 | THE HERITAGE OF INDIAN TEA

the cost. By 1903, 715 miles of railways had been constructed at an estimated investment of Rs 95 m. The result was that it now took planters only three days to reach Calcutta.

After the Second World War, the tea estates developed airstrips, and today Assam has more airfields than any other state in India. This network of roads, bridges, and airstrips has proved to be invaluable. They were used by the British during the Second World War and by the Indian Army in later years during the wars with China and Pakistan.

In 1941, the Japanese wrought havoc in south-east Asia, and by February 1942 Rangoon was threatened. The million-strong Indian minority decided to leave for home. Some left by sea for Chittagong while others took the long and arduous route to Manipur and Assam. Slowly the stream of battered refugees, without any transport, food, or shelter, began to swell. After the fall of Malaya and Burma, every hour counted for the defence of India. The army demanded roads which were non-existent. It was then that an appeal was made to the tea industry in Assam to offer relief and succour to the refugees fleeing Burma.

In response to this a chain of staging camps headed by planters and their wives was set up by the industry between the Burmese border and the Indian railheads. They distributed rations, provided medical help and shelter. Shoulder to shoulder, the planters also helped in constructing single track railways, numerous army camps, and several airfields. In 1944, as a result of a strong armoured attack by the Allies through Manipur, Burma was recaptured. The planters did a memorable job and received letters of appreciation from the British cabinet, the viceroy Field-Marshal Wavell, and Lord Louis Mountbatten.

The infrastructure created by the pioneers became the foundation for the urbanization of Assam. Most of the towns in upper Assam are located within the tea estates or on land adjoining tea gardens. Towns like Jorhat, Tezpur, Dibrugarh, Tinsukhia, and Makum burgeoned as the demand for Indian tea in Britain began to spiral. While in 1866 only 4 per cent of British tea imports were from India, by 1903 this percentage had climbed to 59.

Ancillary industries, such as warehousing, transport, and retailing, were set up. Tea machinery began to be manufactured. Today, Assam is known not only for its tea but also for producing tea machinery which is exported all over the world. In 1912, the Tocklai Experimental Research Station, the largest such research centre in the world, was set up, and since then has contributed greatly to research and development efforts.

Top: The first part of the journey up to the tea-growing areas in the hills in southern India begins by boat. *Middle:* A sketch of an early model of Jackson's cross-action roller. *Below:* Sorting by machinery: from the earliest days India has been known worldwide for its production of innovative tea machinery.

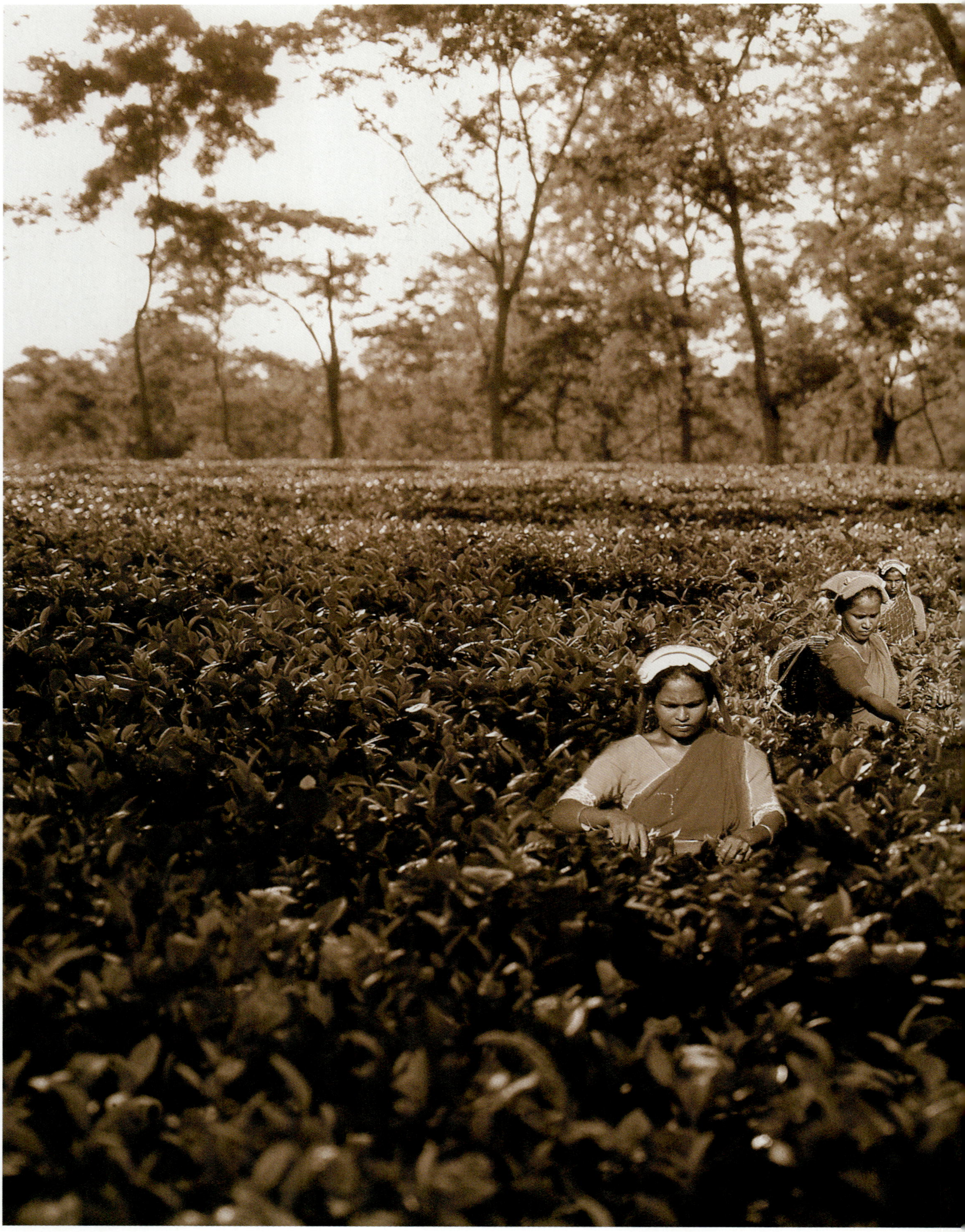

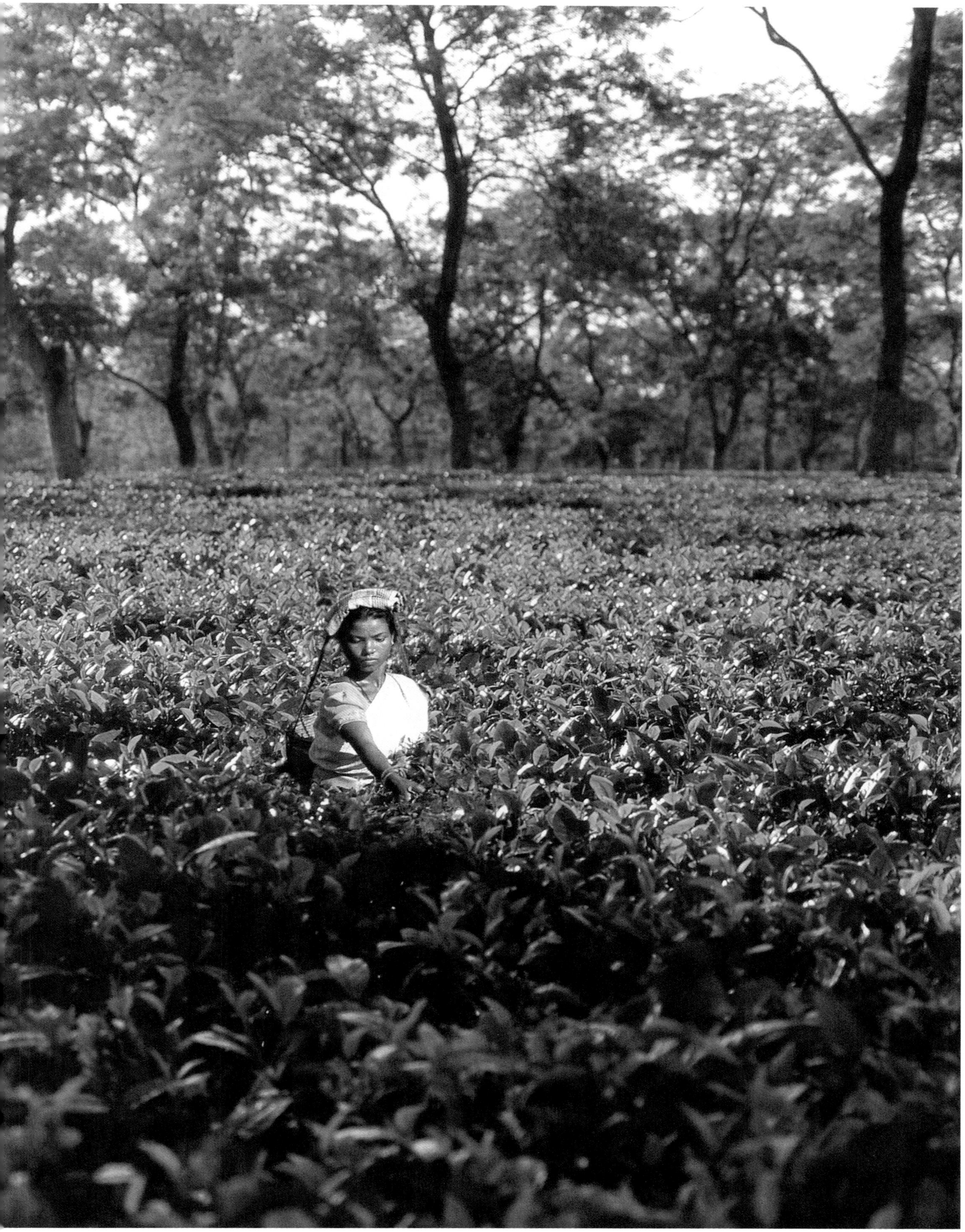

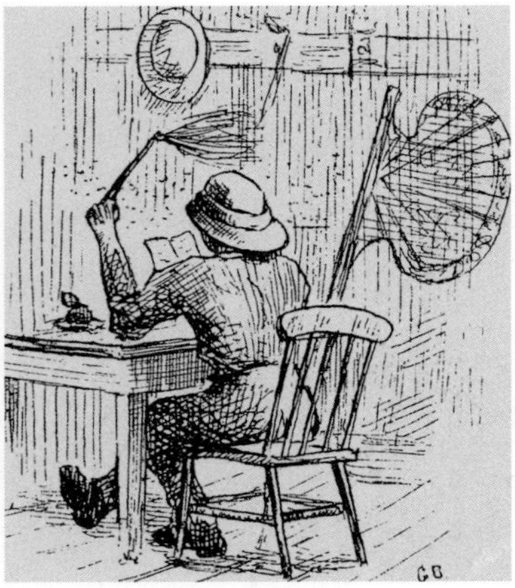

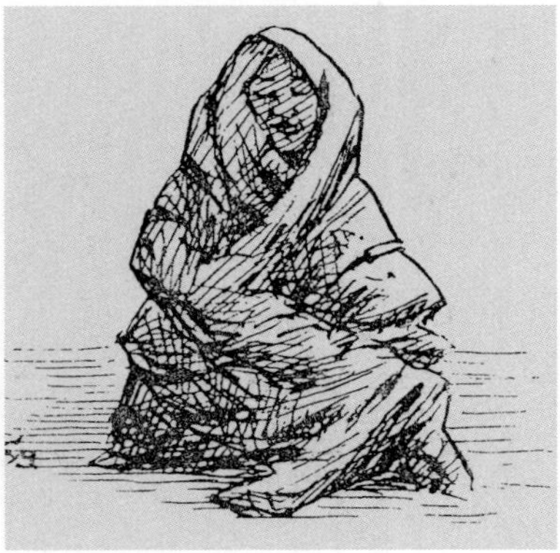

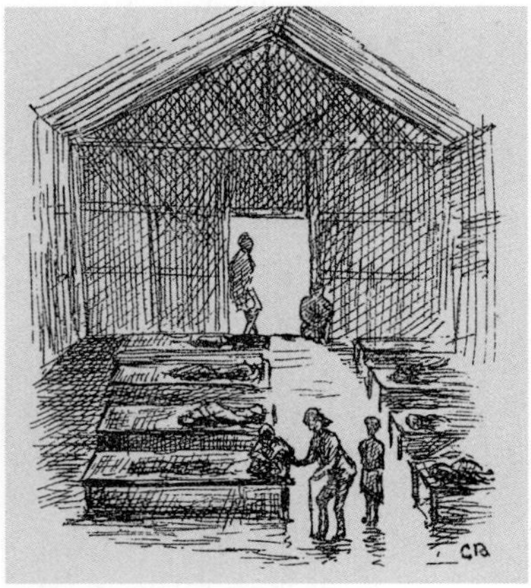

Top: In the early days mosquitoes posed a great threat to the health of tea workers and planters. *Middle:* An ailing worker. *Below:* Sick coolies in a hospital.

Preceding spread: Toil amidst splendour: tea leaves and buds being plucked in the magnificent environs of a tea garden.

Creating a Nurturing Infrastructure

Individual planters made enduring contributions in building up the social infrastructure and took a keen interest in rescue operations during natural calamities. Perhaps the first welfare project undertaken by the Indian tea industry was the establishment of the Prince of Wales Technical School.

In 1858, George Williamson, founder of Williamson Magor, bought two tea gardens called Cinnamara and Senglung in Sonari, Assam, which had belonged to Maniram Dewan, Assam's first Indian tea planter (Dewan had been hanged by the British for taking part in the Mutiny and his estates had been sold at a throwaway price). Williamson sold these gardens two years later and, through a will dated 23 February 1865, donated about £ 10,000 for opening libraries and schools in the Jorhat and Golaghat areas. This was among the earliest instances of a planter wishing to give something back to the land that had brought him prosperity. An Assamese businessman, Bholanath Barua, donated a lakh of rupees to one of these schools which enabled its upgradation, and it was then renamed Prince of Wales Technical School.

There were no hospitals or doctors in those early days: people in droves died of malaria and kala-azar. Hookworm infestation was a common disease affecting the tea workers. Planters learnt some basic elements of health care: they carried their own medicine chests, using them to cure their own workers. An early planter, E.G. Fley, wrote, 'When I was an assistant it was my duty to administer the medicines to all sick workers who were brought to me by the line chowkidar. With the aid of Dr Goodeve's book I did my best. The specifics were quinine, chlorodyne and castor oil ... naturally, the mortality on the gardens was of very high percentage.'

It was the planter Dr John Berry White who realized the need for a medical school. At one time kala-azar killed one-third of the population in Nagaon district. White donated his entire savings of Rs 50,000 to start the Berry White Medical School at Dibrugarh, and trained hundreds of pharmacists and compounders. The school he founded is today known as Assam Medical College.

In 1895, the Indian Tea Association and its Assam branch financed research on kala-azar, malaria, and hookworm at the School of Tropical Medicine and Hygiene, Calcutta. An injection to counter kala-azar was discovered by Dr U.N. Brahmachari, and thenceforth the disease was no longer fatal. Malaria was endemic in Assam. In 1904 the Association helped the government to set up a Malaria Commission and financed research on the mosquito. Dr Ramsay of Labac Tea Estate identified the female anopheles mosquito as

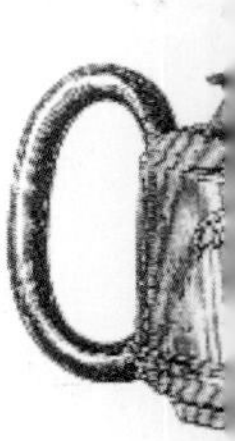

Top left: Planters in a Darjeeling plantation supervising plucking operations.
Top right: A tea estate manager conducts a medical inspection of the labour line.
Middle: A tea worker. *Below:* George Williamson, founder of Williamson Magor, was among the earliest planters wishing to give something back to the land.

the principal carrier of malaria and recommended the first anti-malarial measures: covering drains and growing trees around ponds to bring a halt to the propagation of mosquitoes.

In 1906, Pasteur Institute was founded in Shillong to produce medicines against rabies, with the Association lending a helping hand. Today, Pasteur Institute produces a range of vaccines and is a centre of pathological and microbiological research. The campaign against the mosquito gathered momentum when Ross Institute of Tropical Hygiene was established at Jorhat in 1930. The institute trained estate medical staff in spraying chemicals and larvicides and within fifteen years malaria was contained. The National Malarial Eradication Programme took over, but the gardens continued to lend support the government effort.

Remarkable foresight and innovation was shown in introducing family

Top: Hanumanbux Kanoi, the largest individual tea producer in India.

Facing page: A painting of workers plucking tea.

welfare practices as early as 1950. Dr Charles Emmette of Mariani Medical Practice and Dr Ian Gilroy of Ross Institute worked out the programmes, and doctors introduced workers to technology for birth control. Some tea gardens even offered a 'no-birth bonus'. Extensive immunization was carried out, and paramedical staff was trained. Efforts were made to provide safe drinking water and construct toilets.

The tea industry has a history of providing food security to its workers. As the estates are located in remote areas, the provision of food is an important part of estate management. Food has always been subsidized to protect workers against price increases. In 1951, when there were no stocks of food in the government godowns, the Indian Tea Association and its Assam Branch hired old Dakota planes and roped in private airlines such as Jamair, Skyplayers, and Kalinga to airlift food for the workers. That single airlift operation cost them the equivalent of Rs 260 m. in today's terms.

The planters were fully alive to their responsibilities towards the upliftment of the people of Assam. The gardens of Hanuman Bux Kanoi, the largest individual tea producer in India, were known for high quality bushes, cleanliness, up-to-date machines, and a well-trained labour force. The Kanois made a major contribution to education, founding Dibrugarh High School, Kanoi College, Manohari Devi Kanoi Girls' College, Kanoi Law College Auditorium, and many other educational institutions in Dibrugarh, especially encouraging the education of girls. The Assam government recognized his great contribution by declaring his death anniversary, 19 April, a state holiday.

Other leading families like the Bagrias, Bagrodias, Baruas, Bedias, Berias, Bezbaruas, Boras, Chalihas, Chokhanis, Jalans, Kaseras, Kedias, Khemanis, Lohias, Modis, and Saharias have helped the local inhabitants in a number of ways and have been intimately involved with local social life. There are Marwari families in most villages of Assam. The place where they live and work is called a *gola*, and serves as a kind of welfare centre that provides solutions for local problems. People go to the *gola* when they are in need of help, be it money or a safe place to leave their children.

If there is a marriage in a Marwari family, a majority of the guests are likely to be Assamese, and even the invitation cards will have been printed in Assamese. H.K. Barpujari, a well known writer from north-east India, has said : 'The Marwaris patronize local institutions and donate liberally.' A resident of Dibrugarh shares this perspective of the industry's role: 'We have been fully dependent on tea planters from foodgrains to our livelihood. They have never disappointed us in the hour of any need.'

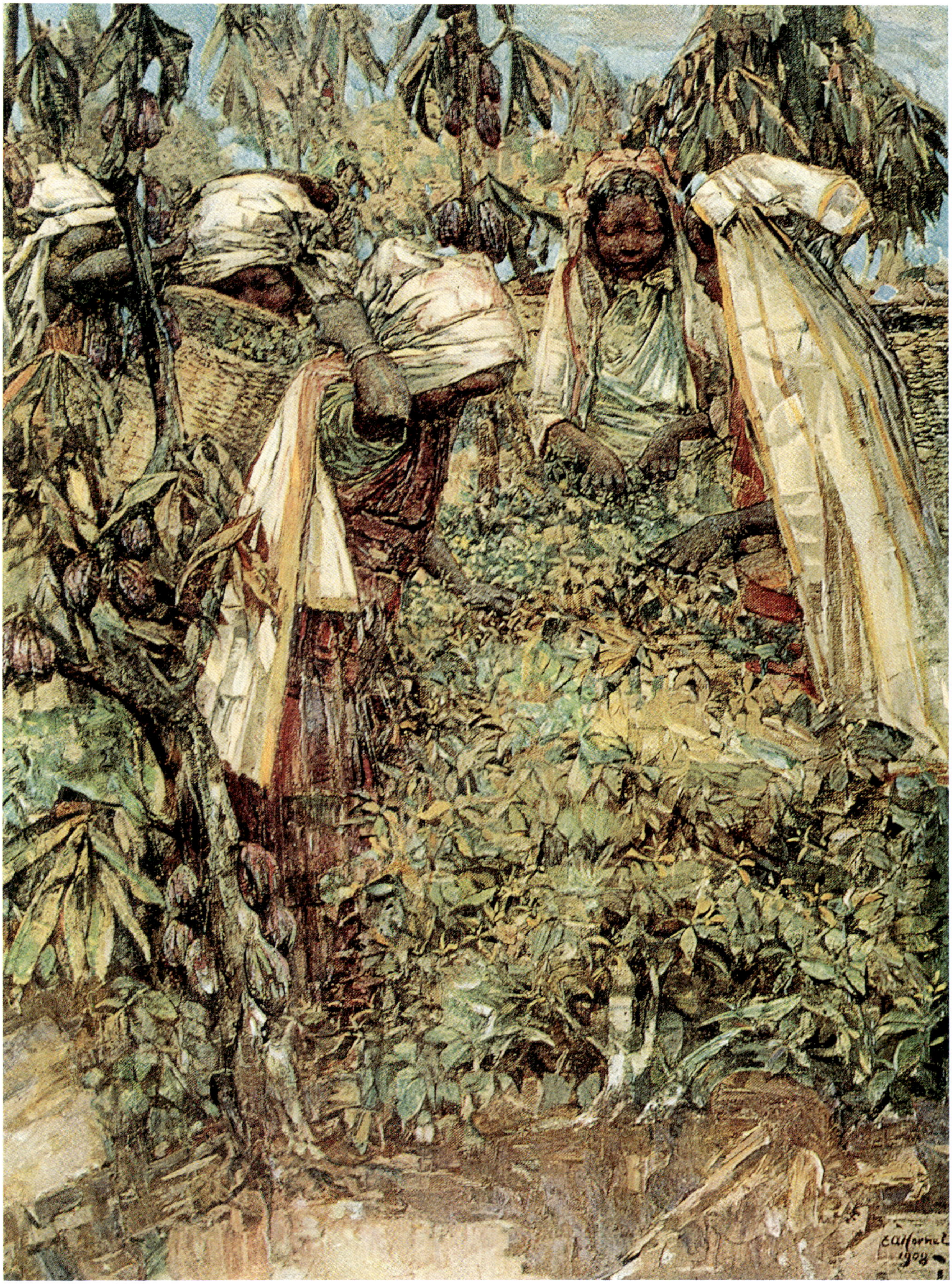

Top and middle: Mahatma Gandhi and Jawaharlal Nehru visited Assam during the freedom movement. *Below:* Surabala Bordoloi receiving the Bharat Ratna award from K.R. Narayanan, president of India, on behalf of her late husband Lokpriya Gopinath Bordoloi.

Facing page: Colour woodblock print of a geisha greeted by a young maidservant with a cup of green tea as she emerges from a summer bath.

Raising the Indian Tricolour

Tea played a significant role in the freedom movement in Assam, and was directly involved in it through Jyotiprasad Agarwala and Bimala Prosad Chaliha. During the freedom movement, many Congress leaders, such as Gopinath Bordoloi, Tarunram Phukan, Nabin Chandra Bordoloi, Kuladhar Chaliha, Jadav Prasad Chaliha, Prafulla Chandra Borooah, Bishnuram Medhi, were associated with tea. They sacrificed much for the country and often had to suffer imprisonment.

A number of Assamese leaders greatly depended upon the support of the tea gardens. During the national freedom movement, Mahatma Gandhi and other national leaders lived at planters' houses. Many planters helped the movement financially and actively participated in it. When Jamnalal Bajaj was on tour in Assam in 1921, numerous planters boycotted foreign goods, setting them afire, their wives too participating actively in the movement. According to Tarun Gogoi, chief minister of Assam, innumerable tea workers themselves participated in the freedom movement, some even sacrificing their lives to the cause.

Prior to Independence, several public welfare institutions were established by the planters. Kishanlall Agarwala, owner of four tea estates, Pipritola, Gangabari, Malkhowa, and Rajgarh, made considerable donations to schools and colleges, and set up a blood bank and an eye hospital at St Luke Hospital in Tinsukhia. J.B. College of Jorhat was built on land donated by Jagannath Barua, Assam's first graduate tea planter.

Murlidhor Jalan built a new township known as Jalannagar near Dibrugarh. Bishnu Ram Barooah and Prasanna Baruah of Jorhat, Nilambar Dutta and Rohini Baruah of Dibrugarh, Someswar Baruah of Tinsukhia and Ghanshyam Baruah of Golaghat were all philanthropists who devoted much of their time and resources to the welfare of the people of Assam.

After Independence, the tea business gradually began to pass into the hands of Indian businessmen. The Marwaris and others took over many tea estates from the Europeans and contributed to the development of the tea industry by adopting modern techniques in the cultivation and manufacture of tea. The Khaitans, Birlas, Goenkas, Pauls, Jajodias, Dhanukas, Jalans, Poddars, Sethias, Kotharis, Lohias, Saharias, Berias, and Ruias also became major producers of Assam tea. Today, 90 per cent of the tea industry is owned by Indians, and of this the share of the Marwaris is nearly 80 per cent.

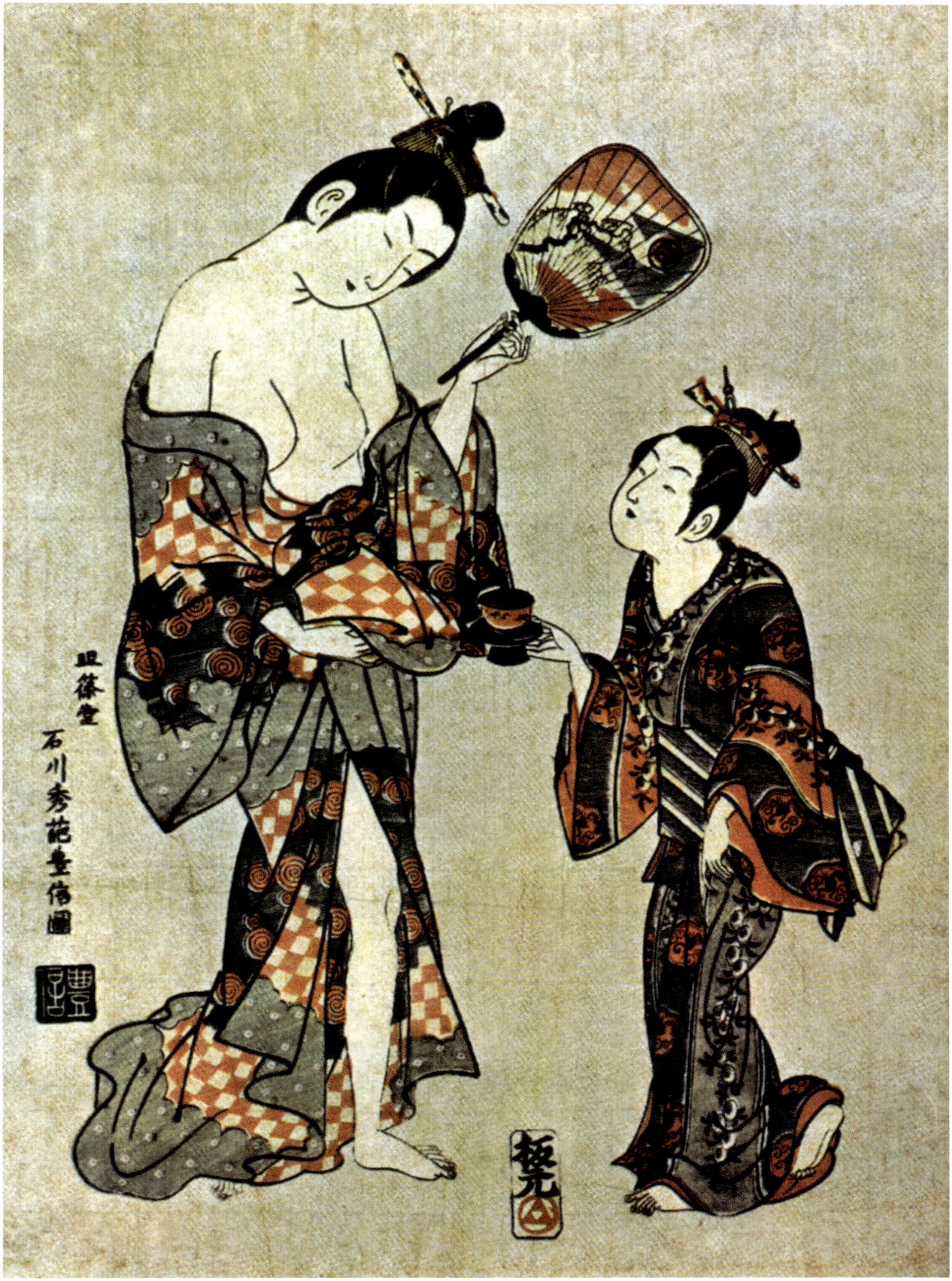
明篠堂
石川秀葩豊信圖
板元

Top left: A sketch of a *burra* sahib, known in the old days as the *mai–baap* of tea workers. *Top right:* Partners in a unique work culture: *burra* sahib discussing the work programme with his assistants over cups of tea. This is in the continuing tradition of passing on age-old traditions, values, and practices to the next generation.

Burra Sahib: A Forgotten Tale

To the city dweller, the life of a tea estate manager is a world apart. Imagine being paid to work amidst resplendent, mist-clad mountains and valleys!

In reality the story is not quite so idyllic! A day in the life of a tea estate manager in the remote valleys of Assam is one of intense stress and hard work from daybreak to nightfall, sometimes stretching into the early hours of the following day. It is a challenging assignment, and every cup of good quality tea reflects the sacrifice, values, traditions, and determination of an unsung manager.

Looking after production requires a thorough knowledge of the processes of manufacturing tea; at the same time, administrative work is equally important. District officials have to be dealt with, government laws and regulations need to be interpreted. The manager deals with over 26 different laws relating to tea-growing and manufacturing. He must know how to strike a balance between the gardens, the office, and the factory.

It is his brief to look after the interests of the company as well as keep the workers contented and motivated. In the old days, the manager was known as *mai–baap* and used to act as adviser, arbitrator, and magistrate, often settling disputes between groups of workers, families, and even between husband and wife! Even today his interaction continues beyond working hours : as the workers are residents of the estate, it is his responsibility to ensure peaceful coexistence.

Today, a manager is being constantly evaluated and must demonstrate leadership qualities. He must be willing to listen to problems and find solutions to them. A human touch is imperative so that the power that goes with his position is respected by the workers and other estate staff.

An average day begins as early as 6.00 a.m. with a quick check of the garden and the factory, after which a load of paperwork awaits his attention at the office. The first consultation of the day is held with the assistant managers and head clerk, when tasks are assigned to various groups.

Then the manager goes to the garden to oversee the operations there. The sirdar, or head of the labour force, briefs him on the latest developments. A second visit is paid to the garden and the factory in the afternoon. Though work at the garden stops at sundown, the manager must formulate his plans for the day ahead. There may sometimes be an emergency that requires immediate attention, whatever the hour. In addition, there are social commitments to be fulfilled, such as presiding over or attending school and sports functions in the neighbourhood. In days gone by, the manager was a *burra* sahib, who was also expected to be a good rider and marksman. Then the major qualifications when he joined were a sense of adventure and sound common sense.

When the tea gardens had British managers, the memsahib had a major role to play. She hosted lavish parties, and it was around her that all the activities at the *burra* bungalow revolved. Today, the manager's wife still has an important role to play, but she is expected to spend much of her time engaged in projects for the welfare of the workers in the garden and people in the neighbouring villages. She forms part of the Mahila Samitis and Mothers' Clubs where women are encouraged to take to vocational activities and improve hygiene and child-rearing practices.

Today, life in the gardens is very different to what it was during the Raj. The change in ethos has changed the style of living. Everything appears to be more businesslike. Most of the recruits to the gardens today are engineers, agriculture graduates, or computer professionals. Many women hold the position of manager and undertake the responsibilities that go with it with great diligence and efficiency.

It is a lonely life for the manager of an estate. Stripped of the old flourishes of the British Raj, not much luxury awaits the newcomer in the profession today. There are new tensions, such as threats from extremists and undue influence exerted by local authorities. That notwithstanding, the new breed of manager takes it all in his stride. The *burra* sahib of yesteryears has become the professional of today with the capacity to deal with a vast range of issues and problems.

Top left: The master of all he surveys: a planter on a round of a tea garden.
Top right: Burra sahibs were traditionally fond of sports. Here, one enjoys a round of golf. *Below:* Ladies leading the way: tea ladies play an important role in message the tea culture of commitment to welfare.

THE PIONEERING YEARS | 39

Top: The *burra* bungalows are known for their architectural distinction and graceful and unique lifestyle. Today, these bungalows are a focus of the tea community's celebrations.

Facing page: A tea lady takes shelter behind her cup of tea. Although, over the past two decades, the lifestyle has changed as a consequence of the improved infrastructure and communications in the tea-growing areas, the core values and traditions remain unaltered.

Following spread: Nature's splendour: a breathtaking view of a lush green garden in Assam. Assam is by far the largest tea-producing area in the world and has over 2000 gardens, some of them extending over 2000 acres. Assam contributes over 50 per cent of India's total tea production of 855 m. kg which is celebrated for its rich, full-bodied, bright liquor. Assam teas are brown with golden leaves, and are also known as 'orange'. The first flush has a rich and fresh aroma; the second produces the famous 'tippy teas'.

The *Burra* Bungalow

The *burra* bungalow is the most attractive part of a tea estate. That is where the manager lives and all activity centres around it. Most bungalows were built some 65 years ago. They usually sprawl over 6000 sq ft and have four or five, and occasionally even eight, bedrooms. Company visitors and other guests are generally accommodated at the *burra* bungalow for want of suitable alternative accommodation. High ceilings, several acres of garden, and a veranda with a slanting roof on the periphery are other standard features, as is a panoramic view of the surrounding garden.

The kitchen is situated at a distance from the bungalow, and the cooks, in line with tradition, tend to prefer preparing continental food. There is a large retinue of servants to maintain the bungalow. The head servant is known as the bearer, orderly, or butler. Senior and trustworthy servants who can be relied upon to take good care of the *burra* sahib and memsahib are entrusted with this position. All the skills of the *paniwala*, the *jharoowala*, the *polishwala*, and the gardener, along with a small platoon of other servants, are put into effect to ensure that the *burra* bungalow is perfectly maintained and exudes style and elegance.

Life on an estate has changed since the time of the British, but the *burra* bungalow has survived. Its sprawl is perhaps one of the few luxuries that the modern manager enjoys amidst the many tensions that he has to cope with. In contrast to the past, the manager has ceased to be a distant and awesome figure. He has to be accessible to the workers and local people who often congregate at the *burra* bungalow to celebrate festivals and other important local events. All in all, the institution of the *burra* bungalow is symbolic of the changing times and aspirations.

THE HERITAGE OF INDIAN TEA

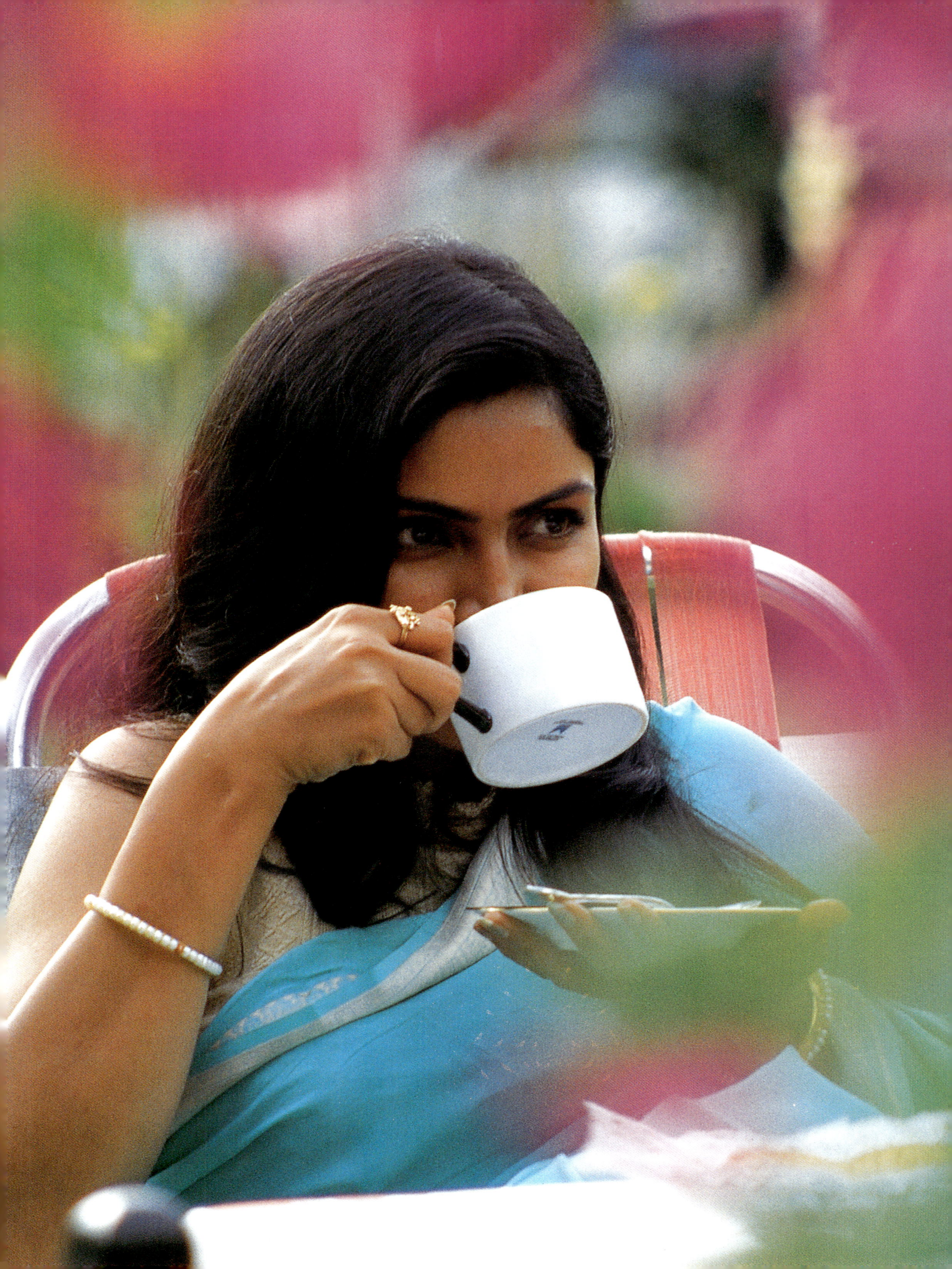

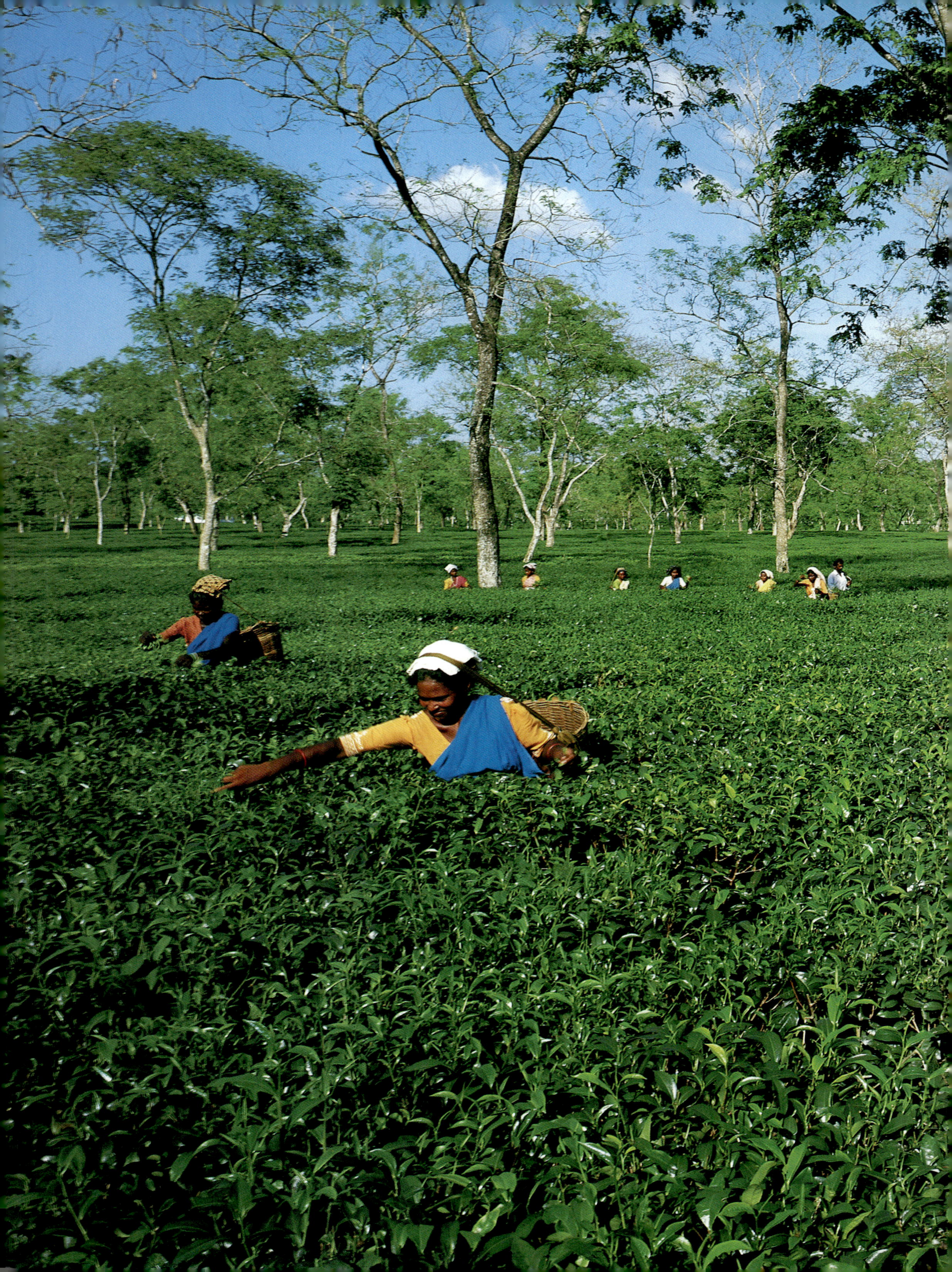

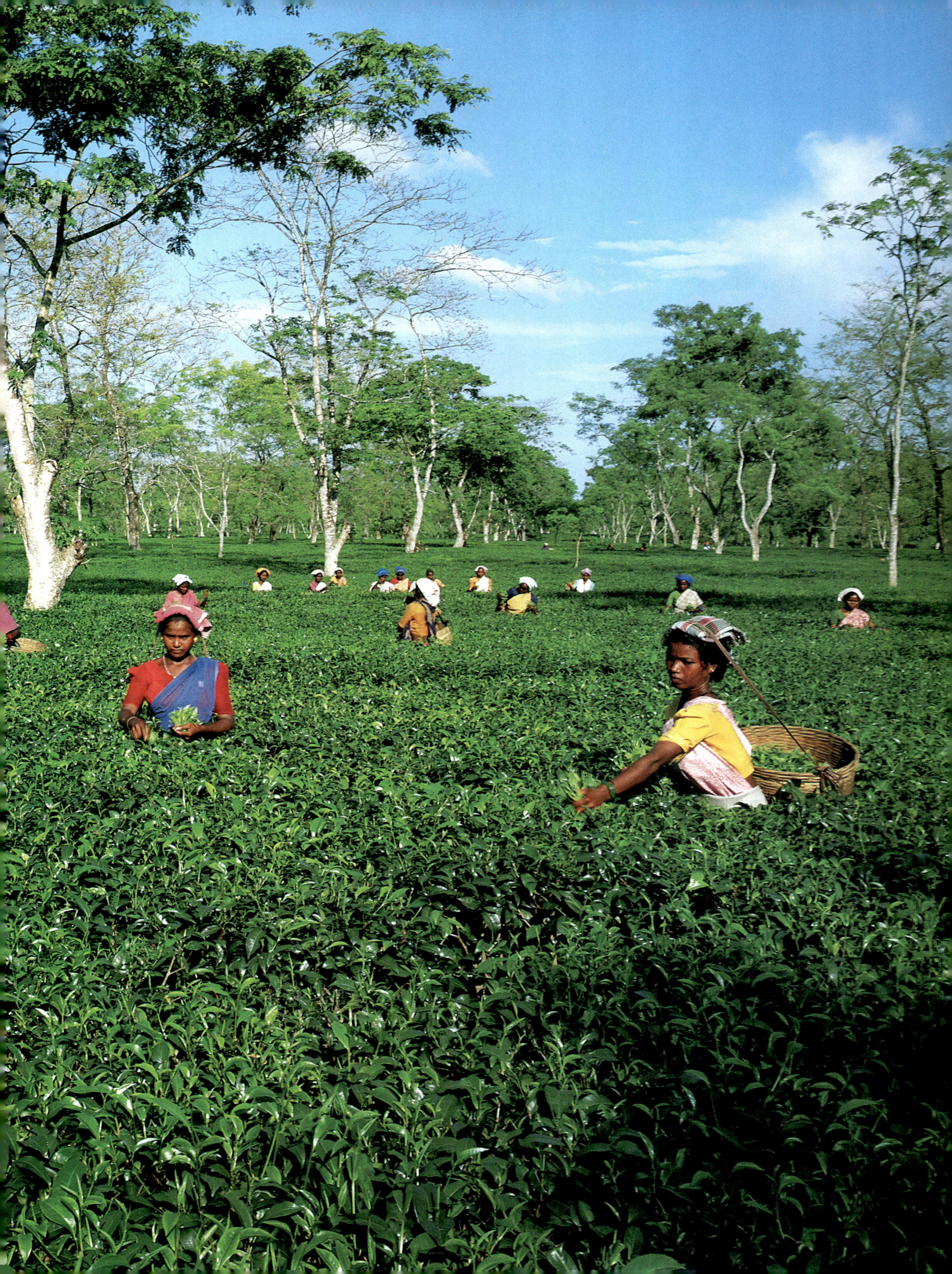

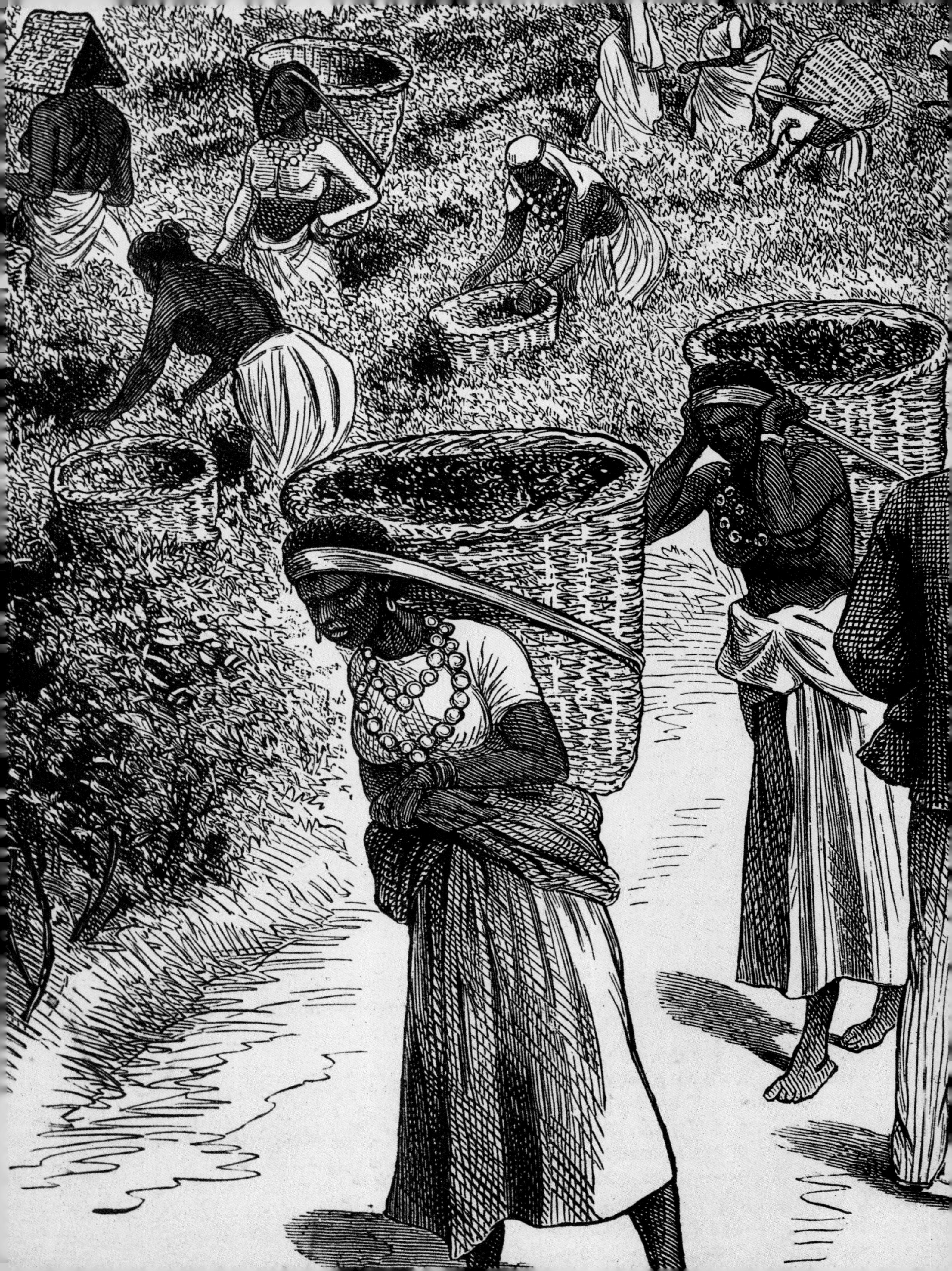

CHAPTER 2

Tradition of Service

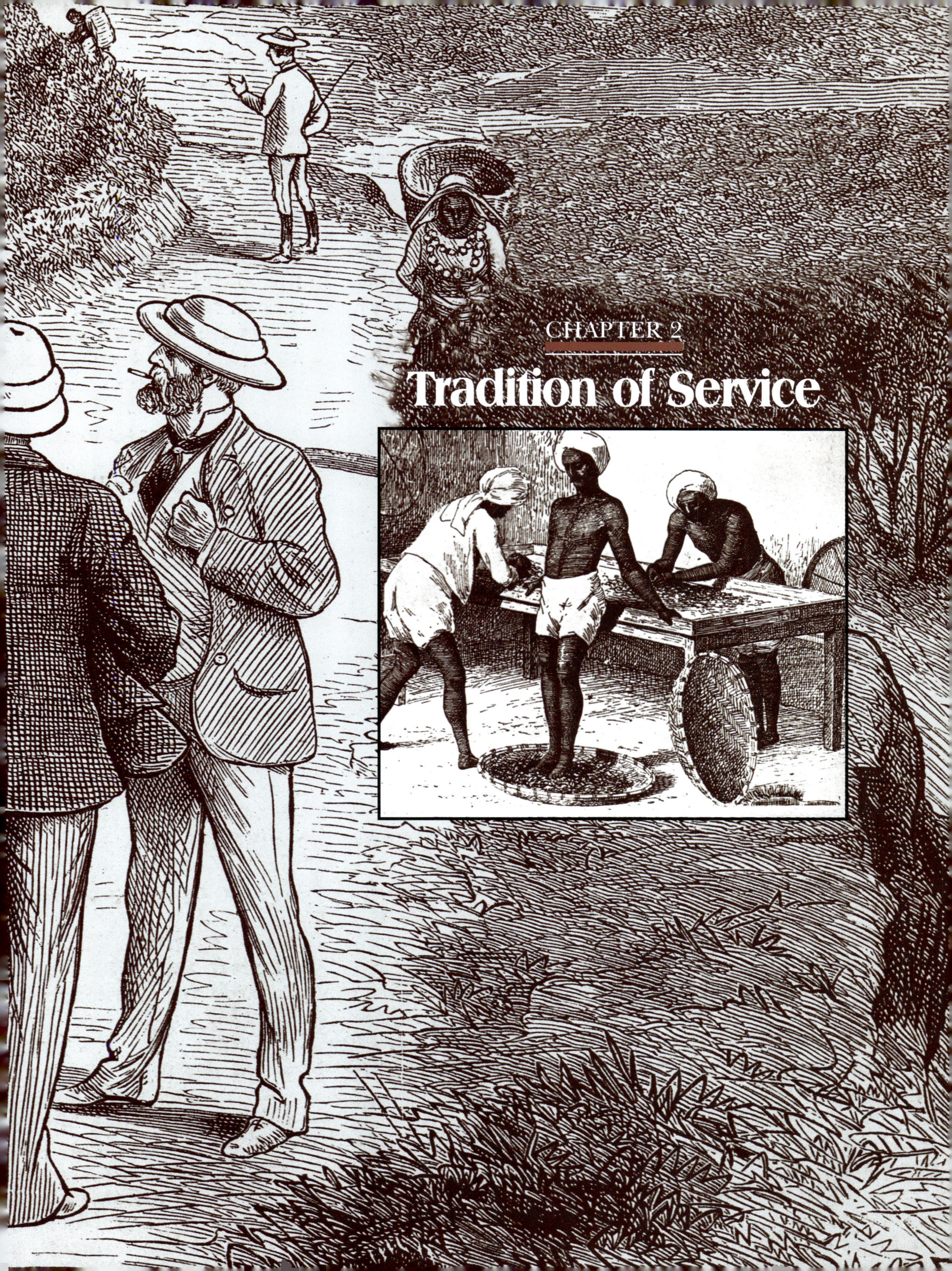

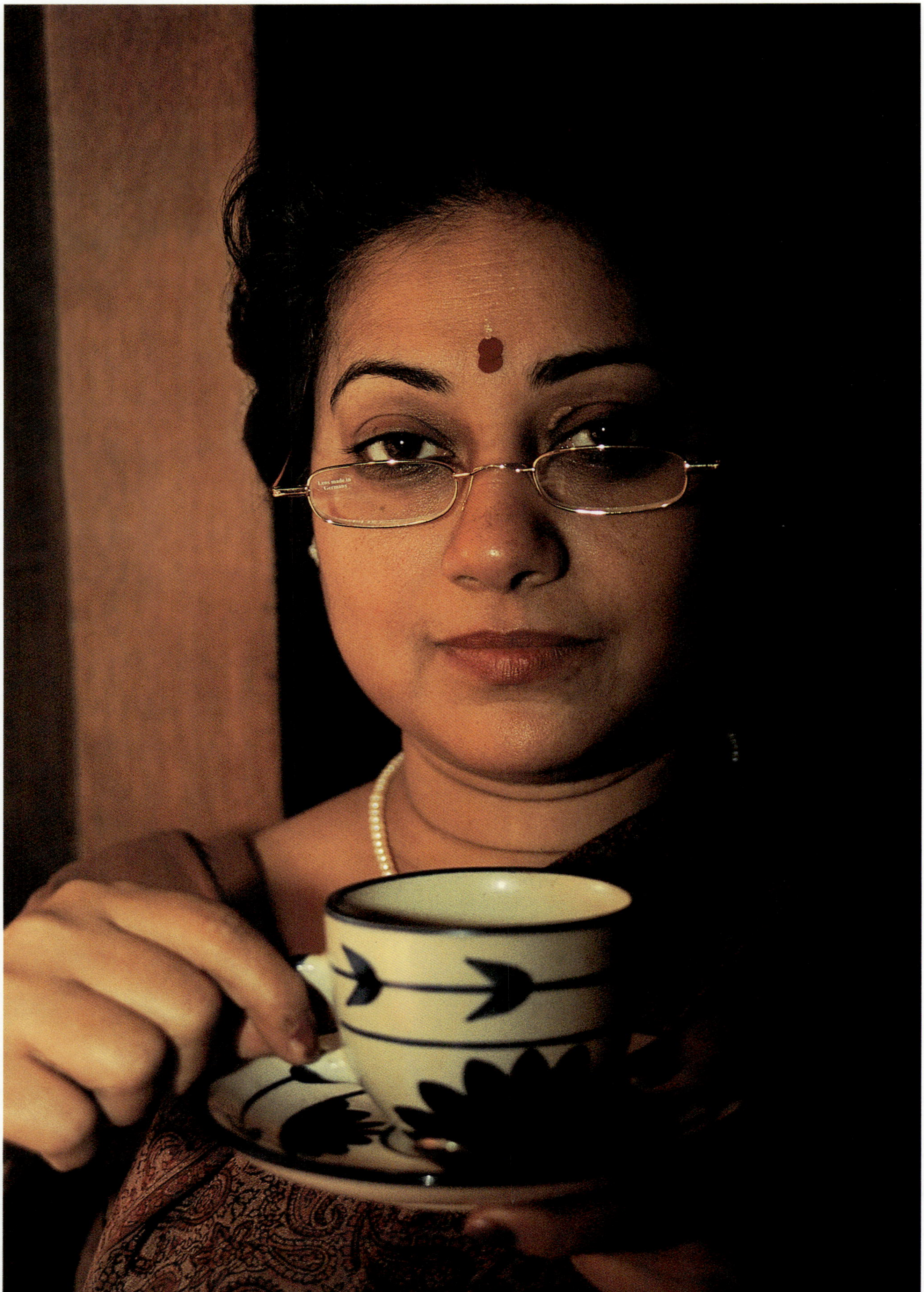
Lens made in
Germany

Alexandra Stoddard wrote, 'The art of tea is a spiritual force for us to share'. Over the years the Indian tea industry has shared its prosperity and made contributions to the social, economic, and cultural development of tea-growing areas. Its numerous associations contribute funds to educational institutions, hospitals, dispensaries, temples, sports and cultural complexes. A wide range of sporting and cultural events are sponsored by them. They have contributed sizeably to higher education and technical and agricultural training with the aim of upgrading the employability of the local people. All these contributions are in addition to the statutory obligations enjoined upon the companies.

Bharat Bajoria, chairman of the Indian Tea Association, says, 'A large number of school buildings are named after erstwhile managers or superintendents who have built them. Even today if there is a *shaadi* or *shradh* or some other social function, the water tanker and all the other infrastructure necessary will come from a neighbouring garden. The industry has undertaken massive development work in and around tea estates.'

Appreciating the tea industry's efforts and keenness to accelerate the pace of development, the late Hiteswar Saikia, former chief minister of Assam, said on 29 February 1992, 'We can't have some islands of progress and plenty amidst oceans of poverty and backwardness. The colonial legacy of diverting resources from the state and turning a blind eye to her development is, as a matter of fact, a thing of the past ... It is a matter of satisfaction that not only individual tea estates, but the tea industry as a whole has, of late, demonstrated a great measure of enthusiasm in taking up welfare schemes. This is indeed a welcome development.'

Many tea estates have received awards for their services to the community. In 1995, Koomber Tea Co. Ltd, a part of the Goodricke group of companies, was awarded the Worldaware Business Award for social progress. The judge for the award commented: 'Koomber is seen locally as a very good employer, and it evidently has a long-standing commitment to supporting local people ... An excellent example of long-term commitment to successful commercial activity coupled with responsibility towards the local community.' The tea industry has thus not only made pioneering efforts for the development of its tea estates, but participated actively in the development of nearby areas.

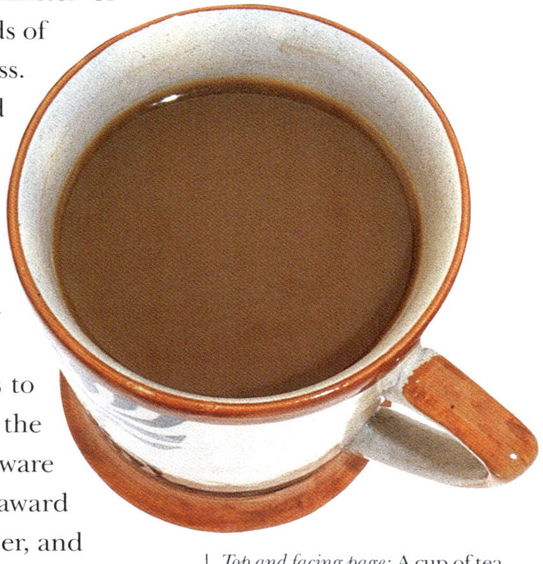

Top and facing page: A cup of tea with its long, fascinating, and romantic history, has become an essential part of everyday life.

Preceding spread: A sketch of tea plucking in Bengal. *Inset:* The old method of rolling the leaf by hand and foot.

Top: An aerial view of Assam Valley School, the largest school in north-east India.
Below: Students of Assam Valley School in the library.

Facing page: Tea workers' children wending their way to school in Darjeeling.

Education for All

From the era of saint Sankaradeva and his disciple Madhavdeva, Assamese literature has been popular amongst the people. Tea has always played an active role in encouraging literature and strengthening the basic structure of education in Assam. Today, the tea industry is assisting and building schools, colleges, libraries, cultural and sports complexes in an effort at promoting education. Tea companies have, in addition, actively encouraged literature.

Contribution to the promotion of education dates back to the time of George Williamson, who helped in opening libraries and a school at Jorhat and Golaghat which was later known as the Prince of Wales Technical School. H.K. Barpujari, historian of repute, has noted: 'Technical education in Assam was represented by the Williamson Artisan School, Dibrugarh.' Later this school was closed and scholarships were introduced for railway trainees who were called Williamson apprentices. Today, Williamson Magor provides financial assistance to many schools and colleges, which include Bardubi High School, Margherita Public Higher Secondary School, Bokial Teen Ali High School, Mahadeo Agarwalla High School, Doom Dooma College, Mariani College, Darrang Women's College, Rangapara College, Tyagbir College, Bokagam Library, and Moran College. Apart from these activities, Hunwal Tea Estate has released land for the Mariani Town Committee.

In line with its commitment to the improvement of educational facilities in the remote north-eastern states of the country, the Williamson Magor group spent Rs 400 m. in setting up Assam Valley School in Tezpur on a campus of 275 acres. It is a co-educational and fully residential school which is surrounded by beautiful tea gardens and spectacular snow-clad mountains. This school is among the best in the country given its distinctive features and novel concept of education. It serves the entire country, only 25 per cent of its students coming from families in the industry. In the words of D. Summerscale, former headmaster of Westminster School, a premier school in the United Kingdom, 'Schools in our country envy Assam Valley School'.

Every year Williamson Magor scholarships are awarded to meritorious students from Assam to pursue studies at premier institutions of higher education. Six students are awarded scholarships annually, and these encompass undergraduate courses in engineering such as electronics and telecommunications, computer science, agricultural engineering, and textile technology. Postgraduate fellowships are given for business management and medical science courses. Williamson Magor has also organized several lectures in Guwahati to enrich the intellectual life of Assam.

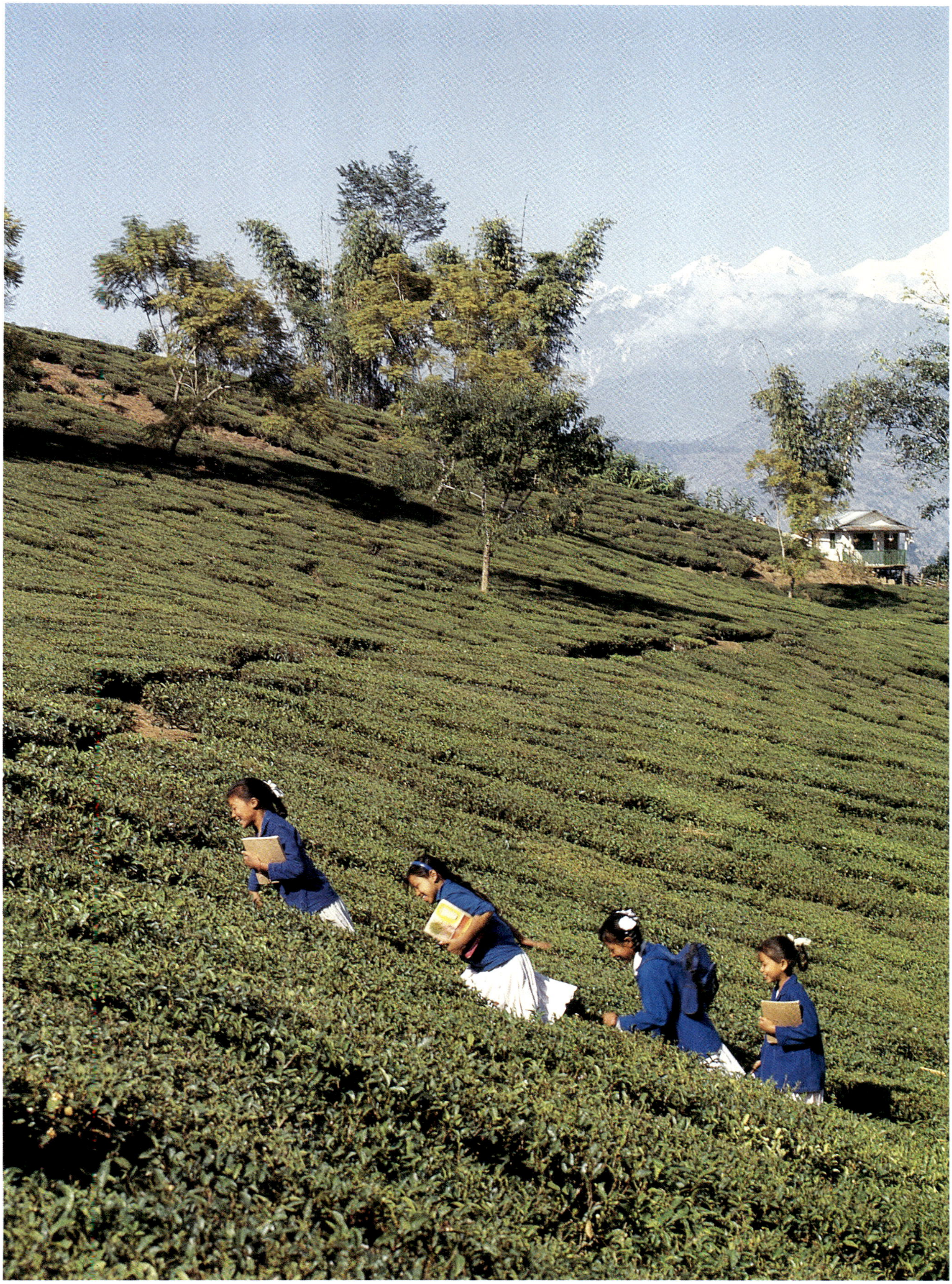

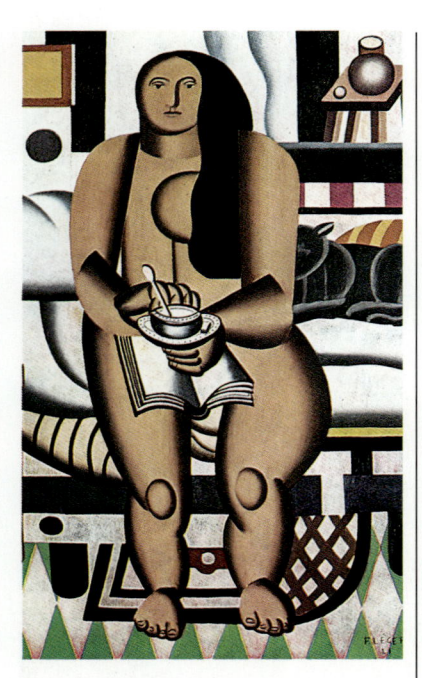

Top: A section from a painting by Fernand Léger, French artist, 1881–1955.

Facing page: A cup of tea is a wonderfully refreshing and stimulating beverage. Over 2.5 m tons of tea are produced annually throughout the world generating business worth 3 bn dollars a year. Today, over 3 bn cups of tea are drunk around the world every day.

When the then chief minister of Assam, Prafulla Kumar Mahanta, laid the foundation stone of Bidhi Vidya Bhawan set up by the Law Faculty of Guwahati University, the Williamson Magor Education Trust underwrote the entire construction cost of the building. On that occasion, the chief minister said, in appreciation of the Trust's generous gesture, that the importance of legal education had grown with the new globalized lifestyle. A permanent building for the law faculty had been a long-felt need. 'The setting up of this facility will usher in a new era of higher legal education and research which is an integral part of governance of the state.' Mahanta added, 'The trust has specifically worked for the development of education and culture in our state.'

The group's generosity has extended beyond the borders of Assam too and often provided financial support to encourage literacy through a range of educational institutions. Indeed, it has promoted countrywide education through Vivekananda Kendras, the Ramakrishna Mission, and other educational societies. Most of them are located in rural areas and tribal belts where children from the deprived sections of society are educated. Ramgarh Vikas Trust and Gram Bharati Vidya Peeth, Kothayari, were among the institutions generously assisted. The group, in association with other corporates, has promoted the International Management Institute, New Delhi, which has become one of the premier management institutes in the country.

Assam Company, the world's first tea company, has spent money liberally on setting up educational centres and providing employment opportunities and scholarships to the local youth. Bearing in mind the need for cutting-edge technologies on the plantations, it has endowed a professional chair at Assam Agricultural University. It has also contributed to the Spastic Society of Assam, the Jerai Anchalik Sports Association, and the All-Assam Lawn Tennis Association. The tea companies of the Apeejay Surrendra group have constructed schools at Suffry, Lankashi, Makum, and Kharjan, and set up a school transport system. The Goodricke group funded the construction of the high school at Amgoorie town.

Nurturing Talent

In keeping with national aspirations, the tea industry is laying greater and greater emphasis on improving the quality of primary and higher education and giving it the highest priority in their developmental programmes. Brooke Bond Lipton (India) Ltd has contributed to Hoonlal Higher Secondary School

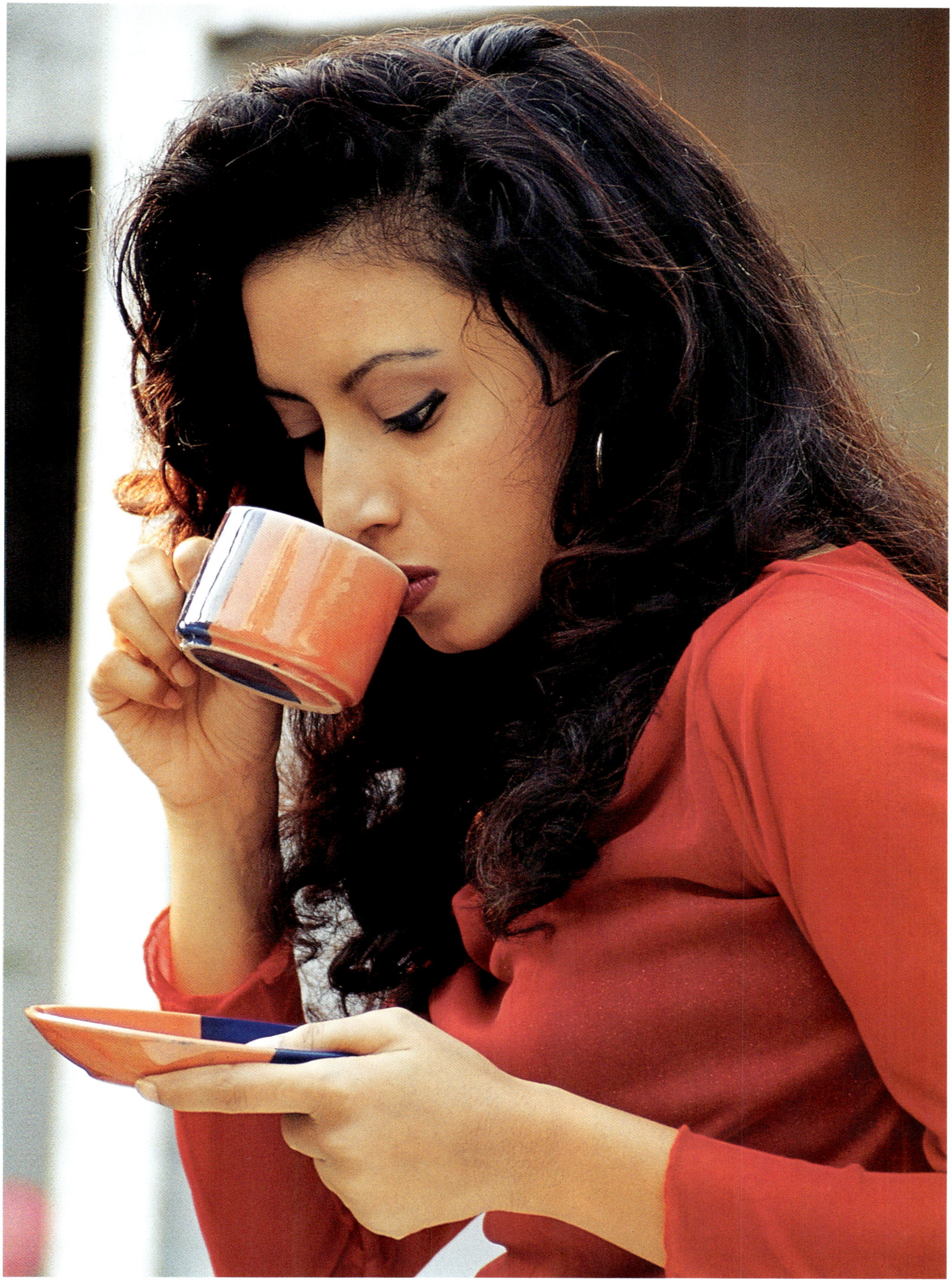

and Doom Dooma College. It has also assisted the Kasturba Welfare Centre, and opened a centre for handicapped children. The company has, in addition, adopted a village, Shantipur, for agronomical development. S. Sharma, a senior executive, however, adds, 'Yet we have to do a great deal more to fulfil our social obligations'.

H.P. Barooah, a dedicated and veteran planter from Assam, and the chairman of B&A Plantations and Industries Ltd, said: 'Kamal Kumari Foundation was set up in 1980 in memory of my mother who was an enterprising Assamese lady planter. She devoted herself to social work, founding several cultural and religious organizations.' This foundation awards scholarships to young talented students of Assam, enabling them to study at prestigious institutions in the country.

The Kamal Kumari Awards were started by the foundation in 1990 to promote excellence in science, technology, and the arts. Every year the foundation honours a group or an individual for outstanding contribution to literature, education, the fine arts and performing arts. Other activities include building and renovating public facilities, medical aid, and the promotion of literature and culture in Assam. The Murlidhor Jalan Foundation and the Assam Branch Indian Tea Association have set up a Nucleus Internet Centre at Dibrugarh University.

Keeping pace with the others, Rossell Industries Ltd, which recently merged with Hindustan Lever Ltd, has constructed buildings for schools at Panitola, Nalani, Daisajan, Chabua, and Bokel, and provided land for several schools and colleges. It has also supported seven girls' schools. At Jayshree Tea's Sholayar and Kallyar estates, four primary schools and one middle-level school function from buildings on the estates. Washabarie, Mohurgong, and Gulma Tea Estates have built over 15 schools in and around their gardens and maintain churches, temples, and hospitals.

Assam Company sponsors a Children's Science Congress and has endowed a professional chair at Assam Agricultural University at Jorhat. Dipak Tanti, the son of a worker on a Goodricke garden, was assisted in his ambition to become a doctor. He now works for the company. Goodricke also helps the mentally challenged through the Goodricke School for Special Children at Siliguri, and contributes to Interlink, an organization that sponsors cultural activities for handicapped children. Its managing director, K.S. David, says, 'Compassion, concern, and caring are as important as the bottom-line on the balance sheet, and this unique corporate character of Goodricke comes from being a part of the Camellia group'.

Top: Tea became a grand tradition in India from the eighteenth century. Every cup continues a long and hallowed tradition.

Facing page: Dolly Roy, perhaps the first woman tea taster in India, recounted what her mentor had once told her: 'Dress it [tea] up as if it were a bride.'

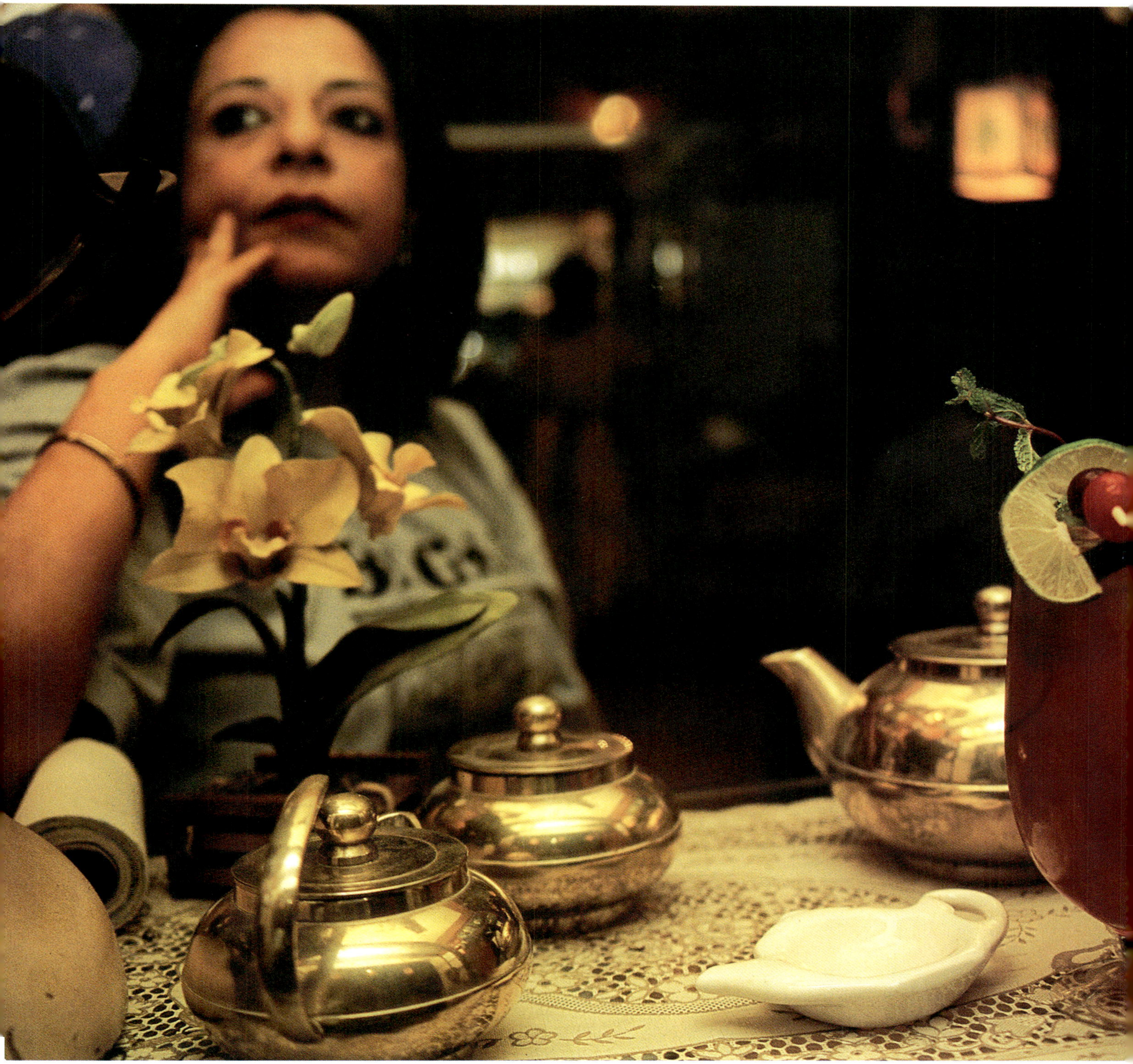

Top: Plucker at work in a plantation in Assam. Women pluckers form 50 per cent of the Indian tea industry's workforce. An average plucker harvests nearly 30 kg a day. The Indian tea industry is predominantly labour-intensive and employs over 1.1 m. workers directly from far-flung, remote, and backward areas which makes it the second largest employer in the country. It cares for these workers and their 5 m. dependants from generation to generation. *Centre spread:* Let's relax!

Tata Tea Ltd, the world's largest integrated tea company's adult education, family planning, health education, and pre-school education facilities are well known. It runs 230 adult literacy centres for workers and their dependants in its north India plantations. The company has set up self-employment training schemes for the dependants of workers in Assam and the Dooars. A vocational training institute at Rowta, located in a backward area, teaches unemployed people carpentry, motor mechanics, television and radio repair. A trade centre at Chubwa provides instruction in welding and tailoring. Prinson Daimari, one of the trainees, feels that the centre serves not merely as a training institute but a place where youngsters can learn the proper utilization of time, discipline, and teamwork. Most of the trainees feel that the centre contributes a great deal in preparing them for life and in cultivating time-tested values. The company has also opened an Industrial Training Institute at Rowta Charali in Darrang district in Assam for tribal youth and assisted Dibrugarh University in setting up a computing centre by providing computers, printers, furniture, etc.

The South India Plantation Division of Tata Tea Ltd set up a welfare complex known as Srishti at Nullatanni Estate in Kerala. It comprises three units, namely Dare, Athulya, and Aranya, for rehabilitation of handicapped children and youth. Children learn to make envelopes, jute bags, and registers, and these goods are in turn bought by the company for its own use. It also set up three vocational training-cum-production centres for handicapped persons at Rungamuttee, Dam Dim, and Nowera Nuddy in the Dooars. Tata Tea Ltd was awarded the FICCI Award 1997–8 for its outstanding achievement in training and placement of persons with disability. Even a small project like the Chittavurrai Estate community hall has its own significance. Thavasilingam, a link worker, says that the community hall has been of tremendous benefit to the local people as an essential component of much-needed social infrastructure. According to R.K. Krishna Kumar, vice-chairman, Tata Tea Ltd and a distinguished tea man: 'All these are symbolic of our deep and firm commitment to welfare as one of the core policies of the company. We at Tata Tea are acutely conscious of the fact that more needs to be done in so many areas.'

Top: Tata Tea Ltd being awarded the FICCI Award for corporate initiative in the field of training and placement of the disabled by Atal Behari Vajpayee, prime minister of India, in New Delhi on 24 December 1998. *Below:* Ratan Tata, chairman of Tata Tea Ltd, being received by R.K. Krishna Kumar and M.H. Ashraff on his visit to Munnar.

Following spread: An aerial view of lush green plantations in the Nilgiris in southern India, exuding an old world charm that is stubbornly reclusive. The productivity of the gardens of this region is 2300 kg per ha, the highest in the country. The tranquil environs of these uniquely beautiful gardens offer an ideal escape from the constraints of civilization.

A TRADITION OF SERVICE | 55

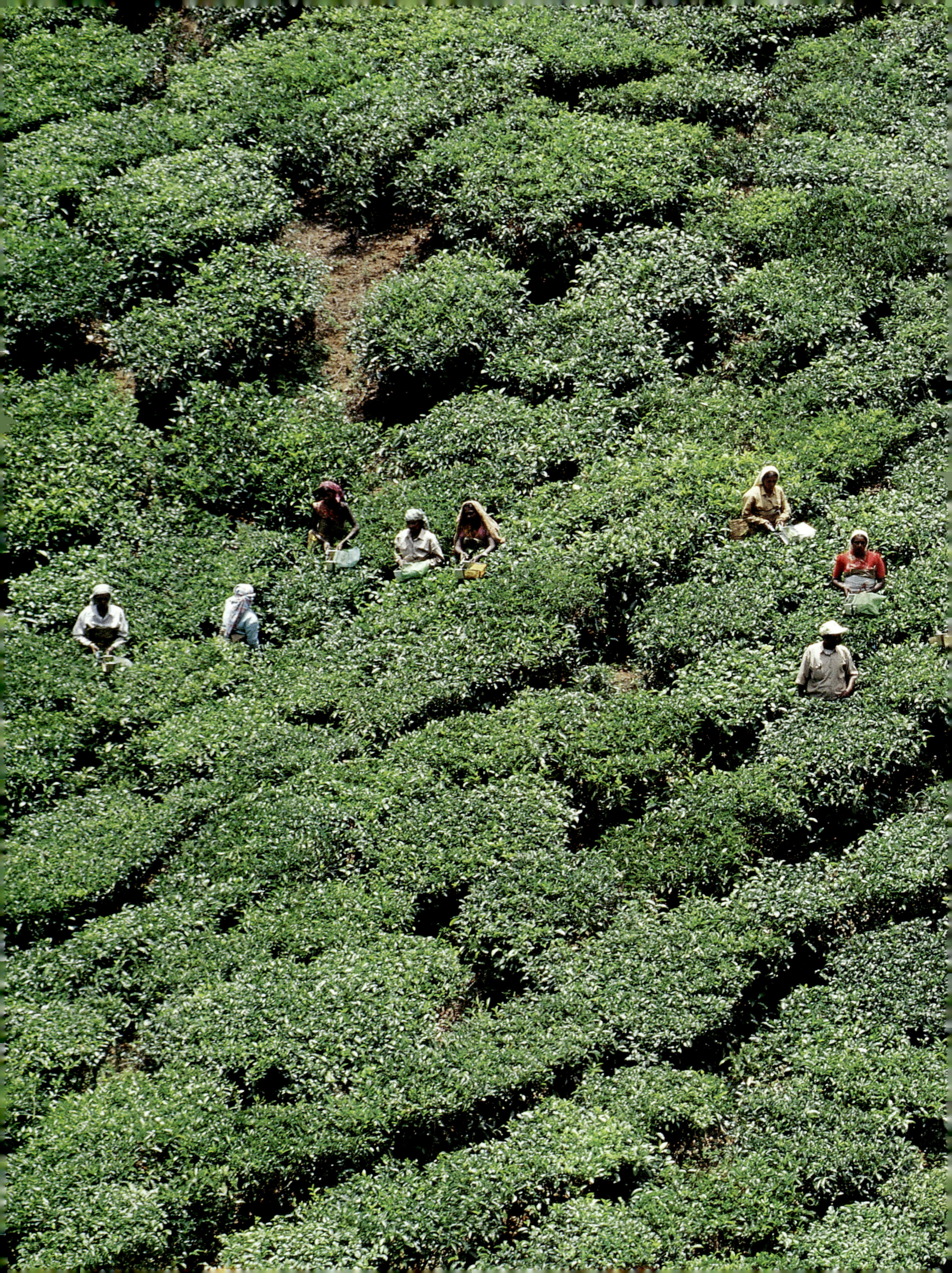

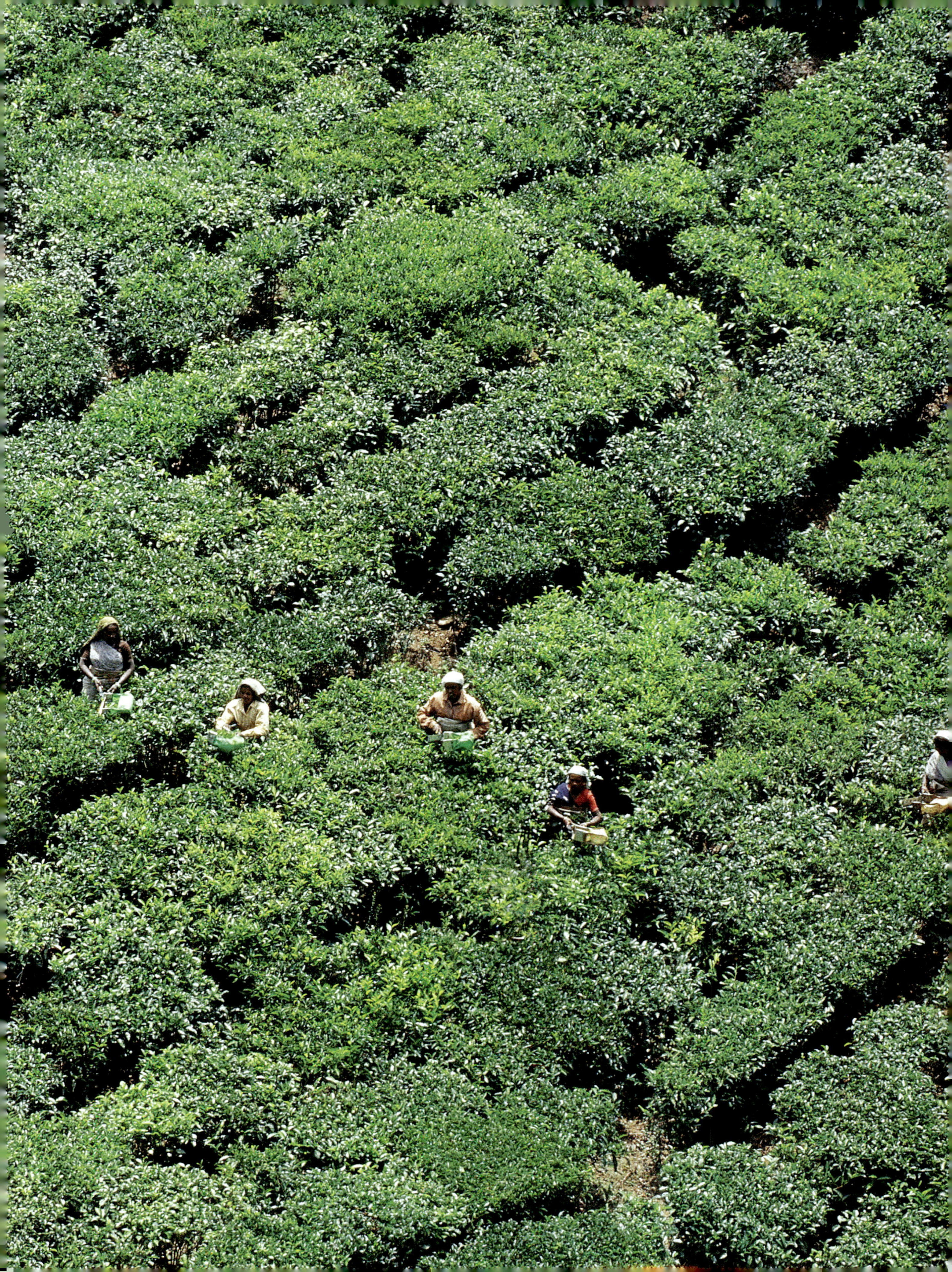

Top: The universal language of art is thought-provoking: *A Woman with a Kettle* by Vincent van Gogh, October 1882.

Facing page: A section of an oil painting by Vincent van Gogh, 1885.

Cultural Promotion

Encouraging the Assamese people's appreciation of their own rich cultural heritage, the Williamson Magor Education Trust instituted the Assam Valley Literary Award, which incidentally coincided with the Biswanath Chariali session of Asam Sahitya Sabha. Prof. J. Das, former president of Asam Sahitya Sabha, a premier organization devoted to the enrichment of Assamese literature, says that Williamson Magor performed a great service by instituting a literary award.

Its aim is to create a better society by encouraging creative literature which upholds human values and dignity. The award is conferred every year on a living creative writer in the Assamese language whose works represent a significant contribution to society. It consists of a cash award of rupees two lakhs, a citation, and a trophy custom-designed by Shobha Brahma, a renowned artist of Assam. Prominent Assamese literateurs who have received this award include Bhabendra Nath Saikia (1990), Homen Borgohain (1991), Syed Abdul Malik (1992), Navakanta Barua (1993), Prof. Jogesh Das (1994), Saurabh Kumar Chaliha (1995), Umakanta Sarma (1996), Nilmani Phookan (1997), Mahim Bora (1998), Ajit Barua (1999), and Hiren Bhattacharjya (2000).

The Williamson Magor Education Trust has also been associated with various literary bodies like Asam Sahitya Sabha and Bodo Sahitya Sabha in publishing books. It encourages regional literature and folk culture in an effort to preserve the literary heritage of Assam. Books by writers from the tea community on the language and culture of tribals have also been published by Asam Sahitya Sabha with the support of the group. Some other books published by the Trust in Assamese and the Bodo and Korbi languages are *Some Assamese Proverbs* (1980), *Chah Majdoor Asomia Sabda Aru Khondobakya Sombhar* (1990), *Chah Majdoor Samaj Aru Sanskriti* (1990), *Jwhwlao Dwimalu* (1991), *Lam Kirtan* (1991), and *Chinta Kosh* (1992).

The Trust has distributed a large number of books to a range of libraries and built a Sahitya Sora at Margherita. Since 1980, it has also taken up the publication of translations of works by eminent authors and winners of the Assam Valley Literary Award in collaboration with the Sahitya Academy. A book entitled *Twilight*, translations of Homen Borgohain's novels *Astorag* and *Longing for Sunshine*, and a translation of the Syed Abdul Malik's *Suruj Mukhir Swapna* are among these.

Releasing the book entitled *Asomiya Shityar Chaneki* on 16 March 2001, Prafulla Kumar Mahanta, then chief minister of Assam, commented, 'The Williamson Magor Education Trust, in association with Asam Sahitya Sabha, Bodo Sahitya Sabha, and other organizations, has published valuable and

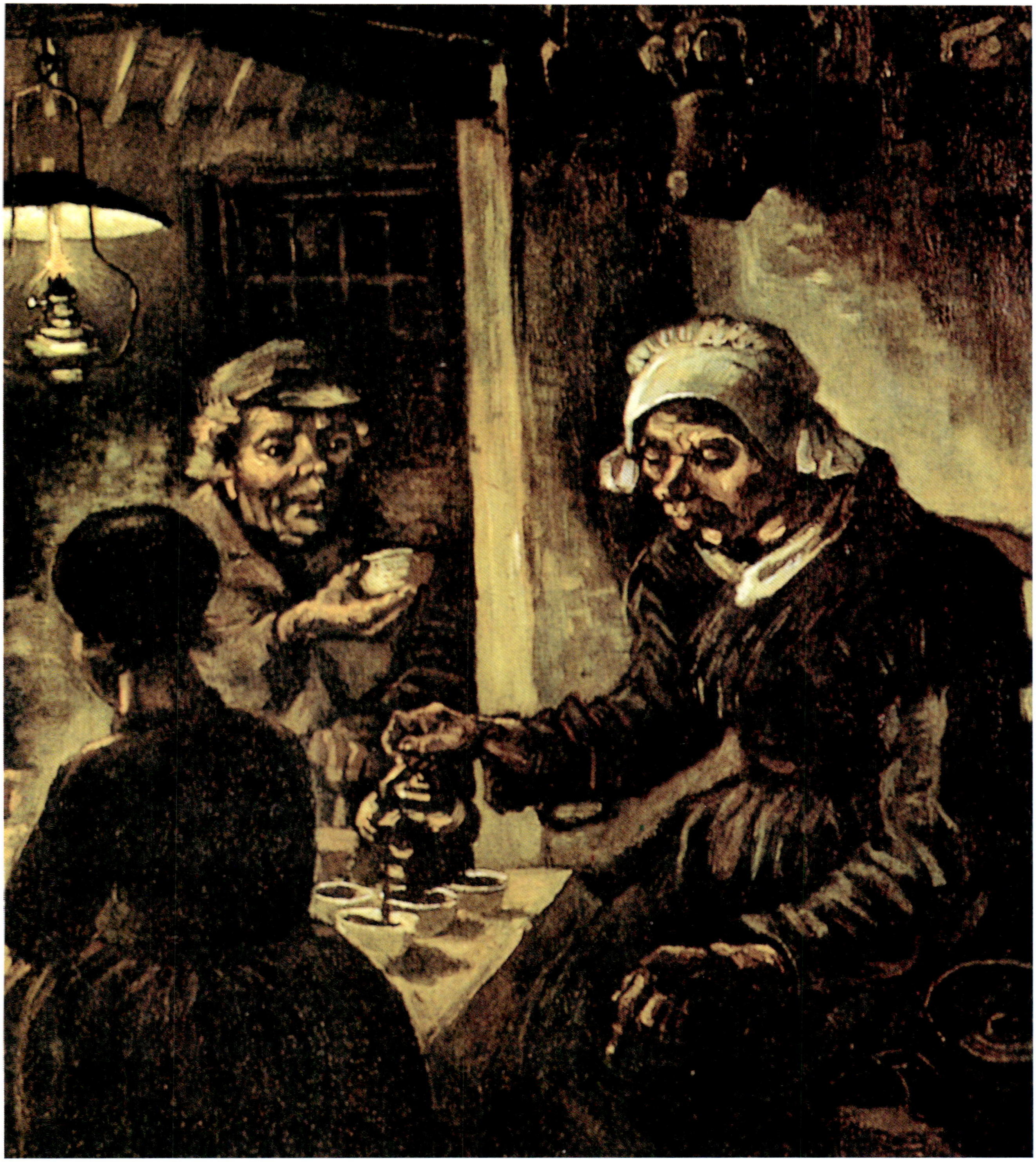

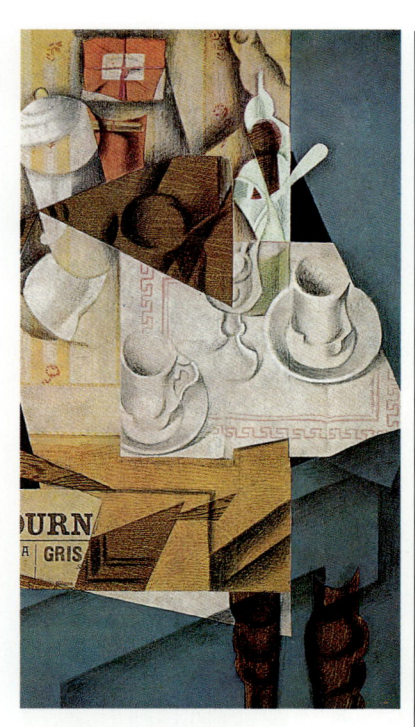

A section from a painting by Spanish artist Juan Gris, 1914.

rare books for the preservation of Assam's traditional culture and literature. In addition, the Trust has translated into English, books by renowned authors for readers in other parts of our country and abroad. This has encouraged us all. Such efforts are really praiseworthy.'

The group has given another enduring gift to Guwahati in the form of the Williamson Magor Hall, which is fully air-conditioned with a seating capacity of 250. The conference hall, situated on the second floor and decorated with cane-crafted linings from Tripura, provides breathtaking views of the Brahmaputra, and is of historic significance as the first meeting of Vivekananda Kendra was held there. Today, the Williamson Magor Hall is the centre of all cultural and intellectual events in Guwahati.

In the sphere of religion, a beautiful Tirupati Balaji temple now adorns the outskirts of Guwahati. The story of the construction of this temple began with a visit by B.M. Khaitan to Kanchipuram. The Shankaracharya discussed with him the idea of the construction of a temple in Guwahati. His idea was enthusiastically welcomed by industrialists and institutions. The Williamson Magor group supported the initiative to build the temple and the Assam government donated eight bighas of land. A temple architect of international renown, Ganapathi Sathapathy, prepared the plan for the temple while Larsen & Toubro Ltd constructed the basic structure for it in 1995. The Kumbhabishekam (Pranapratistha) was performed on 4 June 1998 in the presence of the Shankaracharya.

The entrance has been constructed in a grand and imposing style with gateways surmounted by *gopuram*s, characteristic of south Indian temples. The main gate is handcrafted. It is 40 ft high, topped with a 70 ft *gopuram*. Lord Ganeshji graces the entrance, and Lord Balaji is the principal deity of the temple. The latter's statue, 11 ft in height, carved out of a single block of granite weighing four tonnes, was crafted in Kanchipuram. Another temple is dedicated to Goddess Padmavati and Goddess Mahalakshmi, the consort of Balaji. Padmavati's temple has been built at some distance bearing in view the practice in Tirupati of not housing Balaji and Padmavati in the same room. Other temples dedicated to Durga, Ganesha, and Garuda have also been built.

The temple has become a major tourist attraction and a centre for the exchange of ideas and cultural interchange between the peoples of south and north-eastern India. It is not just an enduring symbol of a rich architectural and cultural heritage but also serves as a spiritual meeting-ground between diverse people promoting national integration.

The celebrated artist, Meera Mukherjee, sculpted a magnificent statue of the Buddha which Goodricke acquired and maintains. In addition, the Apeejay Surrendra group has provided assistance to Vivekananda Rock Memorial and Vivekananda Kendra's Cultural Research Library at Guwahati. Even in Calcutta, Goodricke has made a major contribution by buying Tagore Hall, a nineteenth-century historical building, which it is converting into an art gallery with free space for training young artists.

A magnificent statue of the Buddha created by the famous sculptor Meera Mukherjee.

A TRADITION OF SERVICE | 61

From the early days the tea estates have patronized a number of sports, and especially encouraged talented and promising youngsters.

Patronage to Sport

The Goodricke East India Golf Championship is a popular event. Goodricke also sponsors the largest open chess tournament in Asia, in which Grandmasters from all over the world participate, and has also set up the Goodricke Chess Academy. Tennis player Leander Paes was supported by the company during the early phase of his career.

Williamson Magor has always supported sports in a major way and contributed generously to the construction of a stadium in Tinsukhia, Upper Assam. Besides this, the Williamson Magor Football Academy was set up at Monabarie. The Academy's team is amongst the four best in Assam, and its players have represented the state at the national level. Rossell Industries Ltd has supported sports in the form of Jorhat Sports Club and Guwahati Sports Association. Brooke Bond Lipton (India) Ltd has financially assisted the Assam Table Tennis Association, Doom Dooma Sports Association, Upper Assam Golf Association, and the Tea Sports Control Board of Assam.

A tea estate's well-equipped hospital that caters to the health-care of the workforce and local population in the area.

Towards Better Health

The hope is that good health will become the birthright of many more people and that the industry's healing touch will, to some extent, help to dispel the blight of disease that looms large over the tea-growing areas. Tea estates permit local people to use their medical facilities at their in-house dispensaries and garden hospitals which, in the case of most of the leading companies, are extraordinarily well equipped.

In south India, Tata Tea's General Hospital at Munnar in Kerala has twice been rated the best industrial hospital in India. In 1984, an innovative community development and social welfare programme instituted by the hospital promoted safe hospital deliveries for pregnant women, and as a result maternal mortality was reduced to zero by 1990. The programme provides medical care, complete immunization coverage, and encourages breast feeding. It was subsequently extended, free of cost, to the Muthuvan tribals known as *kudi*s who live on the periphery of the tea estates. Tribals were

A plucker in Assam performs the gesture of plucking the uppermost leaf gently, skilfully, and gracefully, tossing the leaves over her shoulders into the wicker basket on her back. A plucker works for eight hours a day in hot and uncomfortably humid conditions. It's rarely a man's job in India. Indian tea is an industry of Rs 60 bn and generates an income and livelihood for nearly 20 m. people.

trained as barefoot doctors and given access to education. The hospital was awarded the FICCI award for family planning in 1989 and declared the best industrial hospital by the Bombay Management Association in 1991.

Tata Tea's estate hospitals are also widely recognized as 'baby-friendly'. Selected permanent workers of the tea estates serve as link workers to disseminate health information and motivate people to participate in community initiatives. Of these, 60 per cent are women. Interestingly, all welfare initiatives are coordinated and supervised by the estate-level welfare committees. The company takes serious action against any tea estate manager seen to be lagging behind in social welfare measures. 'We are all proud of our rich legacy, heritage and caring attitude. Now our company uniquely conducts a welfare audit that evaluates the success of the various human welfare activities we engage in to improve the quality of life in and around our estates in both the north and south India plantation divisions,' said soft-spoken Homi R. Khusrokhan, managing director of Tata Tea Ltd. These audits evaluate existing welfare schemes and help in improving facilities provided by the tea estates.

It has built over 36 hospitals and dispensaries, and has helped initiate sundry projects for the upliftment of tribal-dominated areas in Assam. Its multi-speciality Referral Hospital and Research Centre at Chubwa in Upper Assam is a showcase of state-of-the-art medical technology. The hospital is the focal point of the company's existing medical network in Assam, and has an outreach service that provides primary health care to local people free of cost. Eye and laproscopic sterilization camps have been organized, and these have benefited over 25,000 people.

Severe epidemics of malaria often convulse Assam. Tata Tea's malaria outreach programme has organized camps in the Suhagpur and Naukata areas. It also assists in preventive measures and supplements the government's infrastructure by providing defogging machines. The company took Lifeline Express, a mobile hospital fitted within a rail compartment, to Nalbari and provided medical and surgical facilities to nearly 500 villages. Wheelchairs, crutches, and hearing aids were distributed free. It also helped set up Sri Shankaradeva Netralaya in Guwahati to provide quality eye care. This is supported by other members of the Indian Tea Association. P. Siganporia, deputy managing director of Tata Tea Ltd, says, 'It is providing the finest community development and social welfare services to local inhabitants'.

The Goodricke group has set up a group referral hospital at Aibheel which caters both to employees and the public of the Dooars. Jayshree Tea, owned by B.K. Birla, runs B.P. Kedia Central Hospital at Cachar and Sholayar Garden Hospital in the south. AFT Industries Ltd, owned by the Surrendra Paul family, has built a medical research centre at Londsoal and commissioned a group hospital at its Empire Plantations. It runs a mobile clinic that delivers primary health care to villages around Londsoal. Besides this, it organizes eye camps at Singlo and Budlapara estates. Considerable attention is also paid to the enhancement of health facilities in and around the tea gardens, and medical and other assistance is provided to those affected by floods. Moran Tea has never failed to provide food, medicines, and other succour to flood-affected people in Assam.

In addition to the statutory requirements of a hospital on each estate, the Williamson Magor group runs six central hospitals at Phulbari, Monabarie, Pareery, Dirial, Margherita, and Chuapara. These hospitals are fully equipped

Top: A referral hospital at Aibheel which caters both to the employees and the public of the Dooars. *Below:* A view of Phulbari Central Hospital. It is fully equipped and is run by a team of enthusiastic, qualified doctors with specialists in every field.

A TRADITION OF SERVICE | 65

Top: Chai is a ritual in India: a piping hot cup of *chai* accompanying the morning shave is a relaxing way to start the day.

Facing page: Chai! Chai! echoes through streets and market places where mobile *chai* wallahs peddle tea in glasses, kettles, or samovars.

Following spread: Chai is brewed everywhere, be it a village or city: *chai* ready to serve!

and are run by enthusiastic qualified doctors and specialists. These facilities are continually being upgraded. The medical adviser, Dr S.B. Mor, says, 'All the garden and central hospitals are upgraded almost every year, and we are constantly adding something new. Whenever we mention any new item of equipment, the group sanctions its purchase in the belief that medical concerns should not have to wait. This provides us with great moral support and a will to do things. That is how we progress rapidly.' The hospitals of the group are actively involved in promoting family welfare and educating workers and villagers about healthier and smaller families. Children are immunized against tuberculosis, diphtheria, tetanus, whooping cough, polio, and measles.

A diagnostic centre has been established by it at Paneery Tea Estate where 18,000 to 22,000 patients, mostly from the scheduled castes and scheduled tribes, are treated annually free of cost. Doctors are available from morning to evening to treat patients. In view of the backwardness of the Mangaldai area, the group holds medical camps where basic facilities are provided, apart from anti-malarial measures and the like. C.K. Barua, a resident of the Assamese *basti*, adjoining Paneery Tea Estate, unequivocally expressed his feelings, 'Magor hospital does a lot to make us healthy without discriminating between garden staff and the poor villager. In the absence of a government hospital, it is a real godsend for us.'

Medicines are supplied free to the remotest villages through well-equipped mobile vans. The individual tea estates have shown interest in providing equipment and medical facilities to the remotest areas of Assam. Nya Gogra Tea Estate of Gohpur has donated medical equipment to the Gohpur public health centre. The chief medical and health officer, Nagaon, has expressed gratitude to the group for providing an ambulance for the benefit of the people of the isolated Kuthori area.

Keyhung, Dirial, and Attareekhat tea estates of George Williamson (Assam) Ltd have demonstrated an interest in promoting health. Keyhung Tea Estate has set up a Mothers' Club, for which 21 women, 10 each from Laipuli and Kakogen divisions with a team leader called *gramsevika*, have been selected. Each member has been given charge of 40 houses and provides advice on hygiene, nutrition, and birth control. Clubs such as these help in providing valuable services to the local inhabitants. The scene is altogether different in smaller gardens, many of which have provided insufficient health care facilities to their workforce. This resulted, for instance, in a gastroenteritis epidemic in some gardens in 1998. The tea associations have taken remedial action against gardens which are not health conscious.

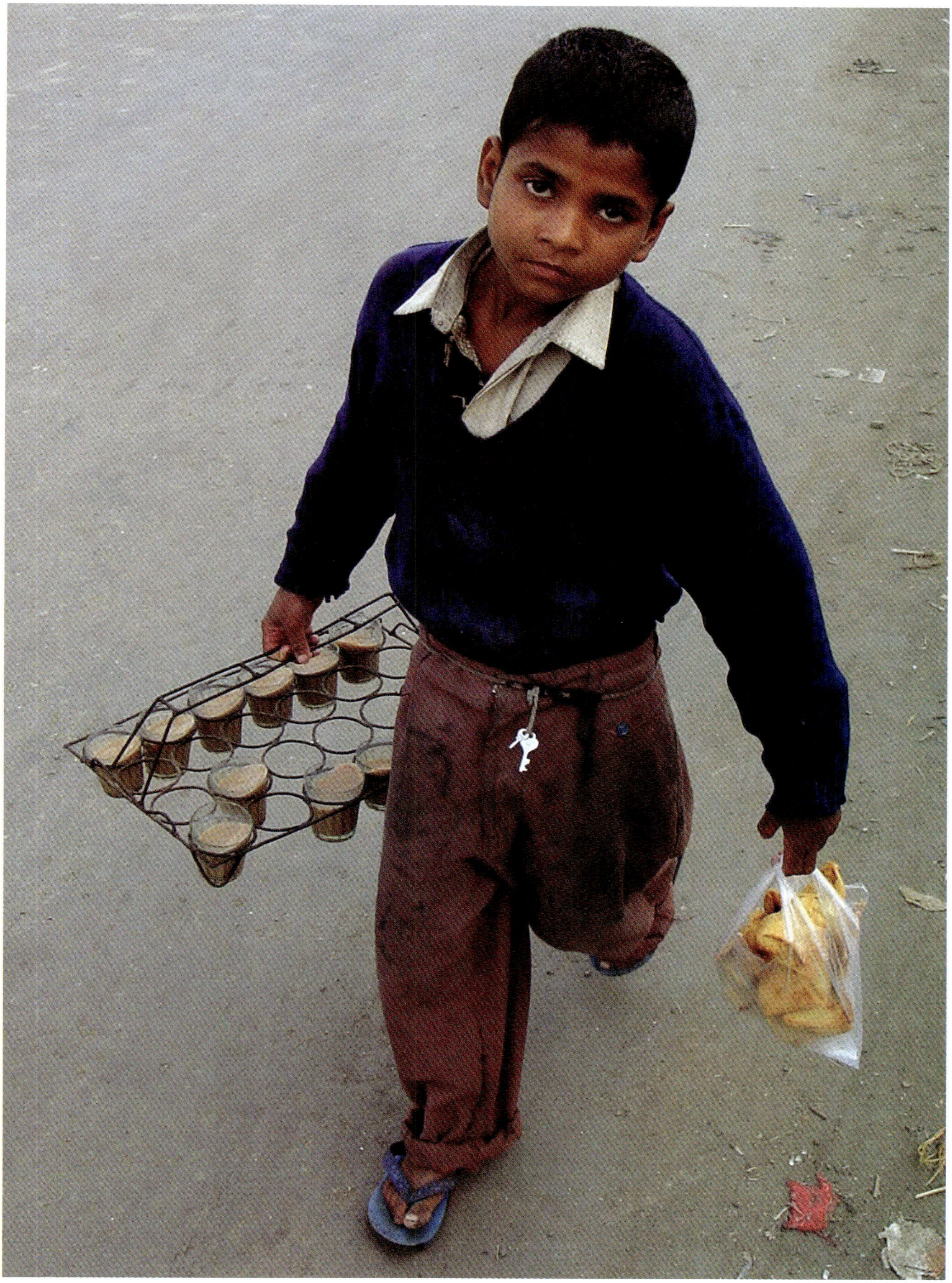

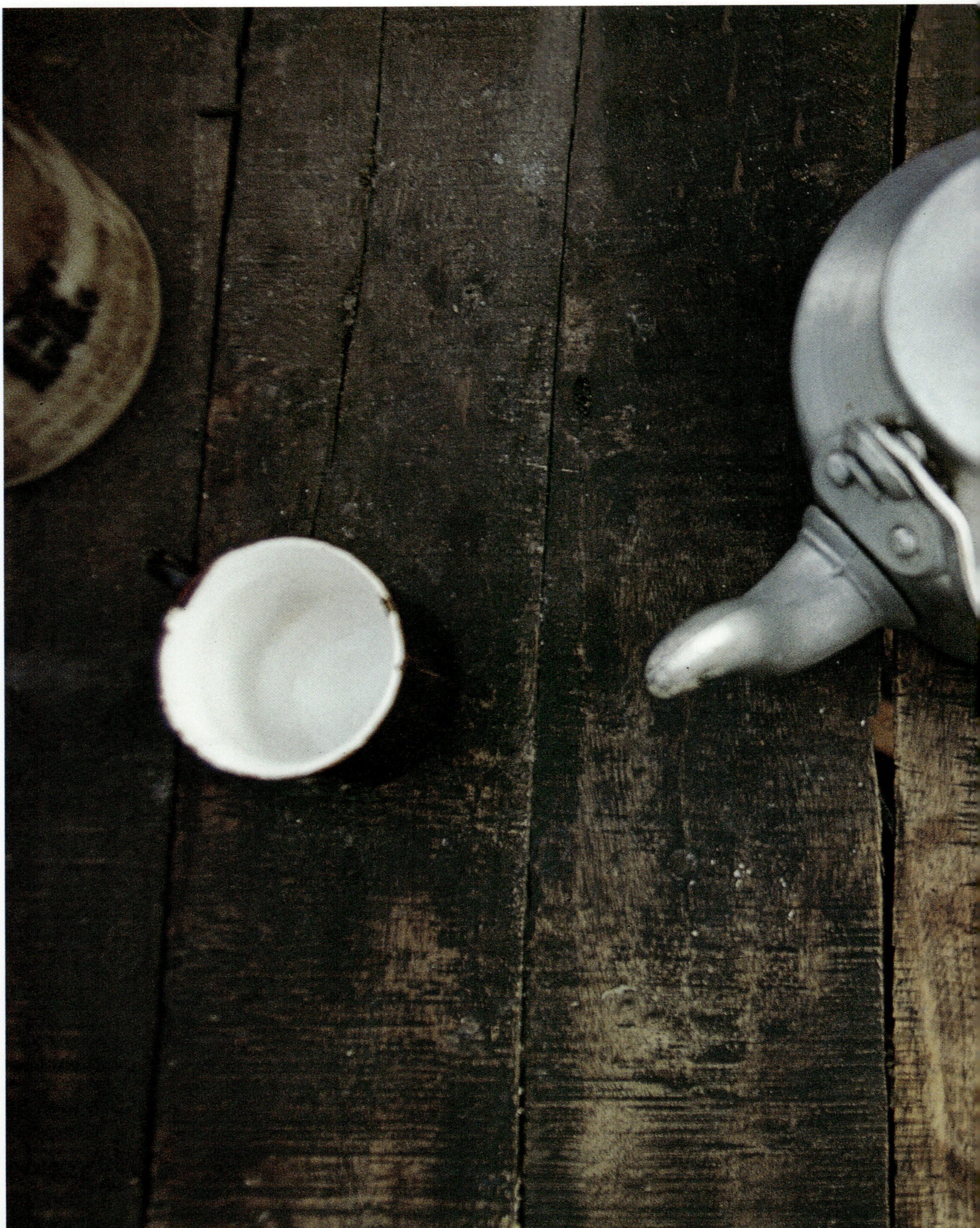

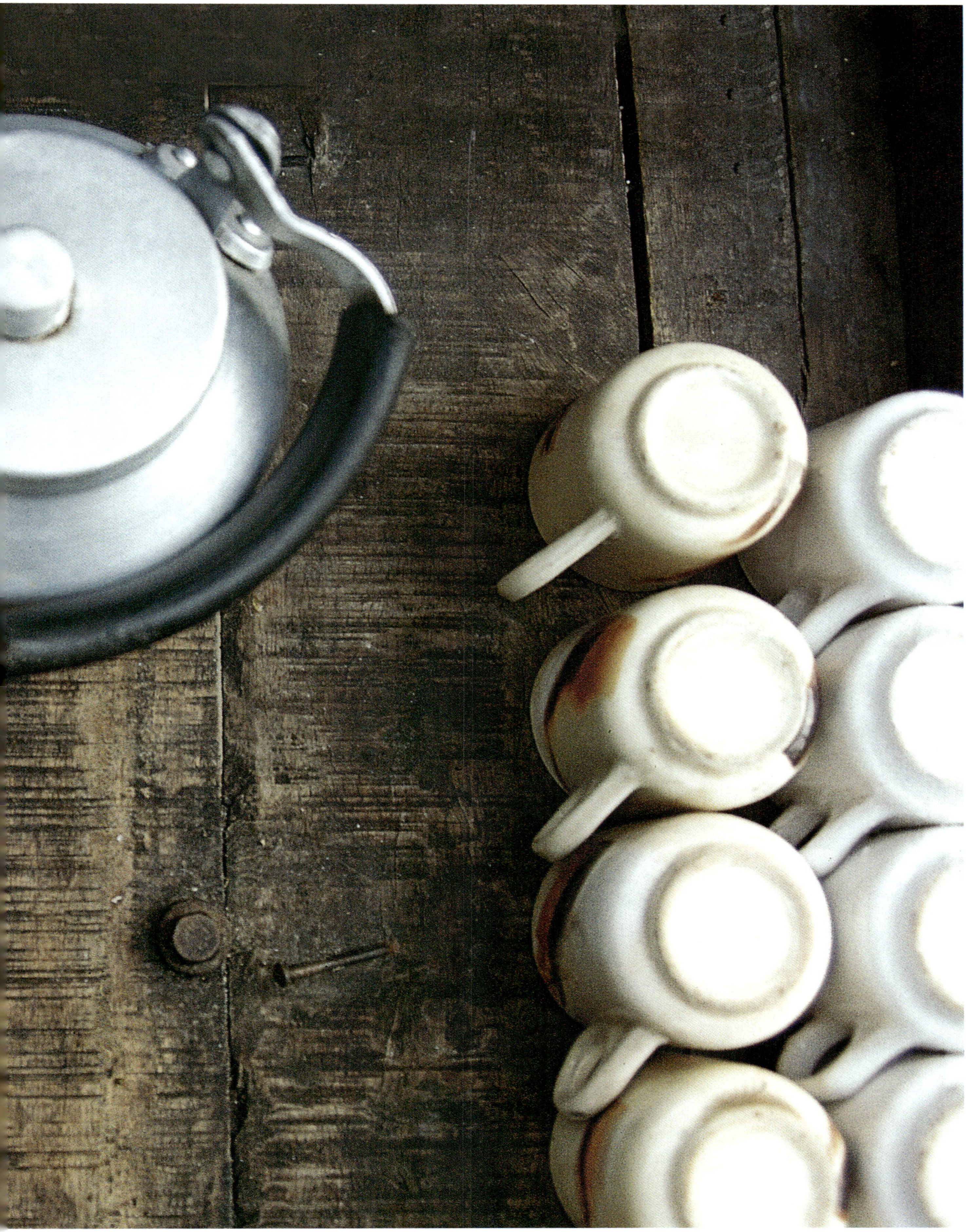

Many tea companies support local farmers in tea-growing areas to improve their yields through transfer of modern farming technologies. In addition, several agricultural projects have been introduced to educate and enable small farmers to undertake multiple-cropping and yield-enhancement-farming practices.

Towards Technology

Tata Tea Ltd has introduced a lab-to-land programme to transfer new farming technologies from laboratories to the fields to enable small and marginal farmers to improve yields and generate additional income. According to Ratan Tata, chairman, Tata Tea Ltd, 'The lab-to-land programme implemented in collaboration with Assam Agriculture University is aimed at educating farmers about modern farming techniques and thereby helping them to improve the yields from their land.'

Pramod of Midhkhat village in the Teok region said, 'I was given good quality seeds and pesticides as a result of which my harvest of paddy increased and we could have two to three crops in one year which was not so earlier. This has resulted in substantial financial gains.' Simultaneously, the company also provides technical know-how together with fertilizers, pesticides, seeds, and sprayers, and already over 3900 families have benefited from this scheme. Dr M.K. Sadhu of Calcutta University wrote in his evaluation report: 'It is being carried out by 18 tea estates of Tata Tea Ltd, extending from Nahortoli in upper Assam to Lamabari on the north bank, thus covering almost the entire state of Assam ... there is praiseworthy and exemplary cooperation between industry and an educational institution.'

For several decades the tea industry has empowered thousands of people by imparting different forms of training in various skills. Efforts are now focused on making these programmes more holistic and development oriented. Tata Tea's Tea Estate Area Community Uplift Programme works in collaboration with Rashtriya Gramin Vikas Nidhi of the Industrial Development Bank of India. Under this programme, self-employment schemes involving poultry farms, fisheries, and piggeries have been initiated for rural communities, especially the Bodos.

A local proverb states: 'The house of a thatcher always leaks. The child of a weaver always wears torn clothes.' In 1995 the Williamson Magor group turned this proverb on its head by promoting the Bodo Handloom Scheme for Bodo weaver women in its estates in Darrang district. Its aim is to make Bodo women happier, more self-confident, and self-sufficient, as this will eventually serve to spread prosperity across a large area of Assam. The idea was that it would not only raise the living standards and dignity of the Bodo women weavers of traditional handloom fabrics, but also generate a sense of gender-equality.

The group set up a number of weaving centres close to the houses of weavers so that self-employed women could look after their homes and, at the

A number of planters have concerns that extend beyond commerce and have introduced several self-employment schemes for the betterment of the rural communities, contributing their skills and expertise to help neighbouring communities become self-sufficient and enhance the quality of their lives.

An old lady drinks masala chai, the most popular form of tea in India. It is best made from Assam CTC tea by boiling the tea leaves with milk, sugar, ginger, and cardamom.

same time, generate income. It has proved an immense boon to Bodo women who have traditionally excelled in handloom weaving and the production of handicrafts. The Bodo women acquiesce: 'This income has enhanced our prestige in the eyes of our husbands, and now they give us equal treatment.' Hundreds of Bodo women are beneficiaries of the scheme. Amir Ahsan, former senior manager, Borengajuli Tea Estate, who supported this scheme, says about its impact: 'Today it leads to greater monetary benefits and empowerment of the Bodo woman who contributes to her household income. Now she doesn't have to go and ask her husband for money, so she's becoming more and more self-reliant. Most of them have started sending their children to school because they are able to pay for their uniforms and books.' Through the group's consistent, coordinated, and energetic efforts, today Bodo women are heading from darkness to light, from dependence to self-reliance.

Dirial Tea Estate of George Williamson (Assam) Ltd provides weaving, knitting, and cutting lessons to all the girls in the neighbouring areas to enable them to be self-reliant. It has also introduced a 'self-help banking system' to eradicate moneylenders. Through other vocational training centres of various companies, countless youth from backward areas have been imparted marketable skills. In order to increase and upgrade employment opportunities, the Assam Branch Indian Tea Association has given Rs 2,80,457 to government agencies to set up three vocational centres and two farm machinery centres in the Assam valley. The tea estates have also allotted surplus land fit for tea cultivation to educated but unemployed youth. In addition, three vocational centres have been set up in the Dooars region.

The South India Plantation Division of Tata Tea runs four technical training schools in the high ranges of south India and a school in tailoring for girls at its Vellonie Estate. Another of its schools in Kerala provides excellent subsidized education. Scholarships are also available to outstanding students. It annually conducts one of the most popular tournaments in the district, namely the Finlay Football Inter-estate Tournament in Munnar. Tata Tea also promotes the Bharat Scouts and Guides movement in its tea estates, a rare example in the corporate world. 'Our people located in remote areas of the country lead a lonely life, yet despite this handicap they contribute immensely not just to the company's bottom line, but substantially also to the social issues in their areas. This is indeed commendable. Even the wives of our management staff contribute significantly to the society in which they live and work,' says Homi R. Khusrokhan, managing director, Tata Tea Ltd. 'We are grateful to them for taking time off from their busy schedules for community development programmes.'

A Silent Agrarian Revolution

Assam remained untouched by the green revolution, and although Assam's soil is fertile, ironically the state is a major importer of foodgrains. Low farm productivity is a major contributor to poverty. Over 80 per cent of the rural population in Assam is dependent on agriculture for their livelihood. A vast majority of farmers practise monocropping, with rice as the principal crop and very low productivity levels. Particular attention is being paid to rice cultivation, as rice occupies 70 per cent of the total cropped area with an average yield of a lowly 1345 kg per ha. The majority of farmers being small, they are not able to increase production due to a lack of purchasing power. The tea industry believes that there is a great deal of potential for increasing agricultural production. Therefore, the Assam Branch Indian Tea Association, as well as some of the leading tea companies, have undertaken over 17 agricultural projects in various parts of Assam to educate and enable farmers to adopt multiple-cropping and yield-enhancement programmes, and have encouraged entrepreneurship.

Dr D.N. Chakravati, a noted agriculturist said, 'When tea planters of Assam were talking about agriculture, Williamson Magor was the only group that came forward generously to initiate the project on agriculture. Their response was very instantaneous and positive.' Beginning with the cultivation of the sunflower, the group has participated actively in providing technical know-how and agricultural inputs for tea-growing to the local farmers.

Williamson Magor & Co. Ltd has undertaken agricultural development programmes in Assam which were started from the *kharif* season of 1998 in Balipara and the Biswanath–Charali area and implemented through a Guwahati based non-governmental organization called Bureau of Integrated

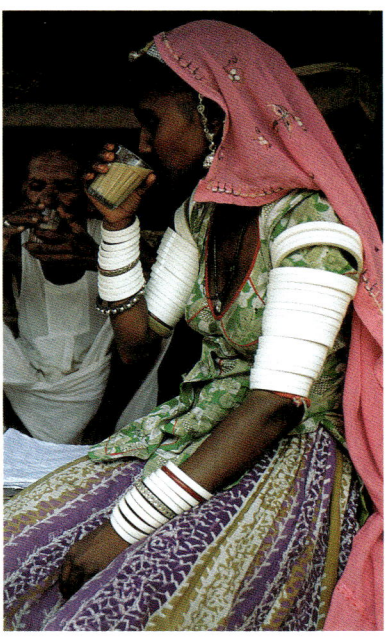

Top left: Tea is a priority regardless of age. A young boy emerges from the water to serve tea to customers. Sixty-seven per cent of rural households in India drink tea. *Top right: Chai* is an essential part of Indian life, enjoyed from the early morning to late into the night.

The perfect brew for the man in the street.

Rural Development. The Bureau selected 62 farmers from 4 villages through local bodies and officials. The inputs, such as seeds of the Bahadur variety, fertilizers, and pesticides were supplied to them at half the actual cost. A series of time-bound training programmes were conducted to equip the farmers to adopt suitable methods of cultivation. These efforts led to an increase in the average yield of 5.4 m.t. per ha, the highest being 7.5 m.t. per ha which exceeded the state average three- or fourfold, benefiting, inter alia, many young farmers. A similar programme was sponsored by the group for 41 farmers selected from the villages of Bokagaon and Barpatgaon. The response to this initiative was overwhelming, and requests are pouring in for more such projects. 'All this shows our firm commitment to share prosperity with the neighbourhood,' says S.N. Singh, former planter of Williamson Magor.

Dhunseri Tea & Industries Ltd and Tezpore Tea Co. Ltd too have implemented an agricultural development programme which has won over the hearts of impoverished Bodo peasants living 150 miles from Guwahati near their estates at Bettybari, Darrang district. The companies began the programme by sponsoring a non-governmental organization called Chah Udyog Gramin Krishi Vikas Samiti, which has helped farmers to diversify crops and increase yields. It also helped them sell their produce at a better price, and provided transport and tractors. The spirit of self-help so fostered motivated the farmers of Onthaibari, which means stony land, to diversify from paddy to wheat, build a road and a water channel. About 60 per cent of the farmers now earn enough to save.

The Samiti has also undertaken a project to introduce horticulture and agro-based units. It has already covered an area of 1245.39 ha in 140 villages, benefiting nearly 1800 families. Prafulla Kumar Mahanta, then chief minister of Assam, said, 'What the two tea companies have been doing so far for the development of agriculture in the rural areas in and around their plantations is praiseworthy and worth emulating'. The owner of these two companies, C.K. Dhanuka, is contemplating the initiation of even more innovative projects for the people of Assam: 'Our companies have a clear policy for innovative welfare schemes, and we always encourage our managers and non-governmental organizations by providing sufficient finances and organizational infrastructure for community development.'

George Williamson (Assam) Ltd is engaged in helping the villages of Suklai, Rajagurh, and Khagrabari in growing tea and its maintenance, harvesting it, and then purchasing leaf at competitive prices. It has also helped villagers around the tea estates in land preparation for the cultivation of paddy and pulses. Tractors and implements are being provided too in order to introduce modern farming methods to help improve the yield.

The Indian Tea Association has formed a society, Gramin Krishi Unnayan Prakalpa, at its Assam Branch, for developing the rural economy by undertaking several agricultural projects in Assam. The Rural Agricultural Development Project of the Association was inaugurated at Paneery under Mangaldai circle on 12 February 2000 by the late Bineswar Brahma, president, Bodo Sahitya Sabha. The activities under the project are monitored by the respective members of the circle of the Assam Branch Indian Tea Association. Prakalpa has already set up 10 agricultural centres and is planning to establish 16 agricultural extension centres equipped with specialized personnel to provide agricultural inputs to villagers.

Gunin Hazarika, then Assam's industry and commerce minister, had words of high praise for the agricultural projects. 'I am happy to say that these efforts have enhanced the productivity and yield of several crops benefiting farmers ... Similarly, the Association has extended support to farmers to take to non-traditional items such as sunflower and high-yielding potato seeds,' he said at the 110th annual general meeting organized by the Assam Branch Indian Tea Association on 22 January 2000 at Thakurbari Club in Tezpur.

Top: The glasses and a kettle foreground an artistic landscape.

Following spread: A panoramic view of a tea estate in the Nilgiris, southern India. In this area of undulating hilly landscapes, tea is grown at heights of 1000 m to 2500 m. The flavour and fragrance of teas grown here are the result of the high elevation of the area. In the Nilgiris, the appearance of each garden is different, determined by its location and topography. Isolated as they are, the tea people in the estates have forged a common bond and live together in a spirit of harmony and comradeship.

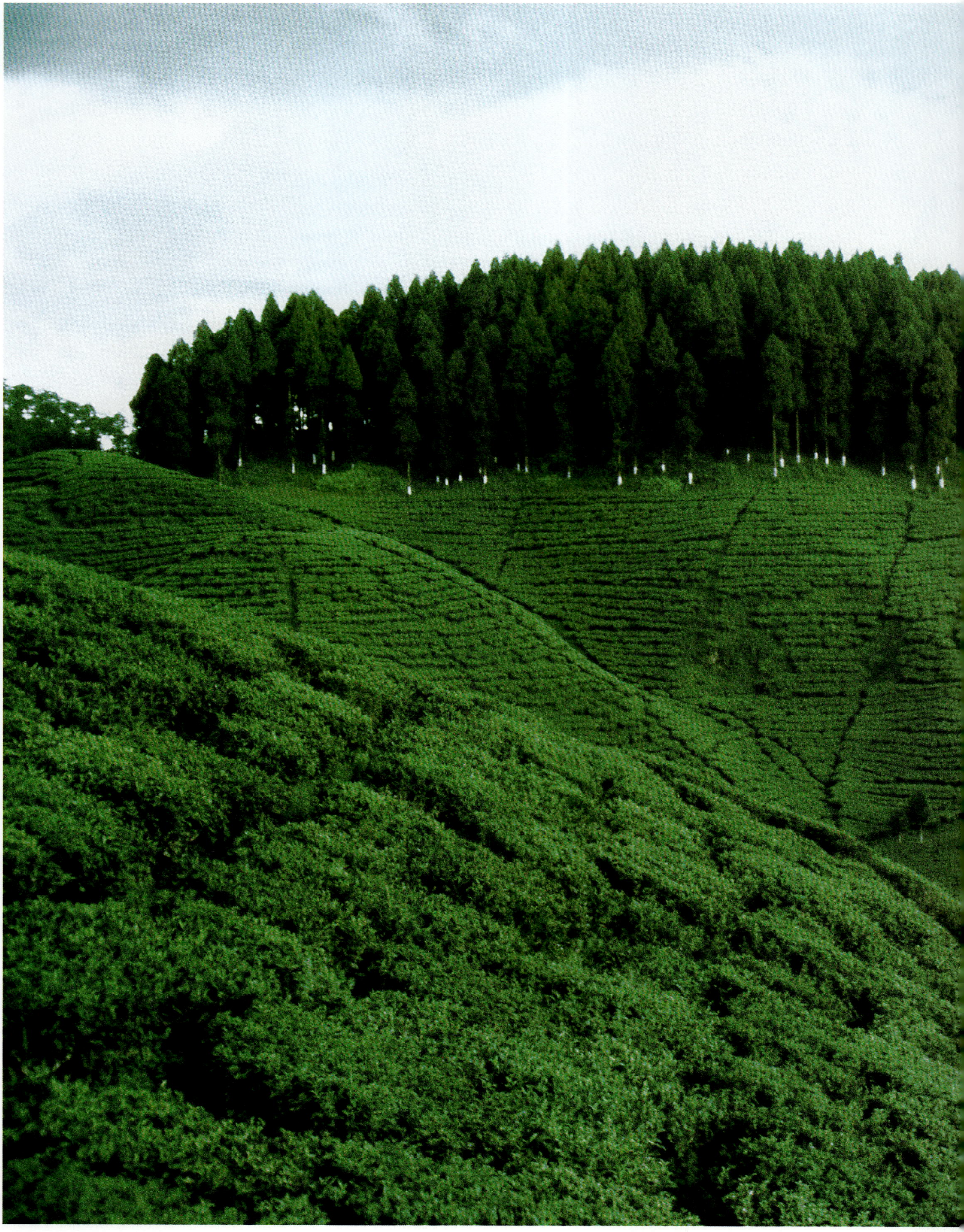

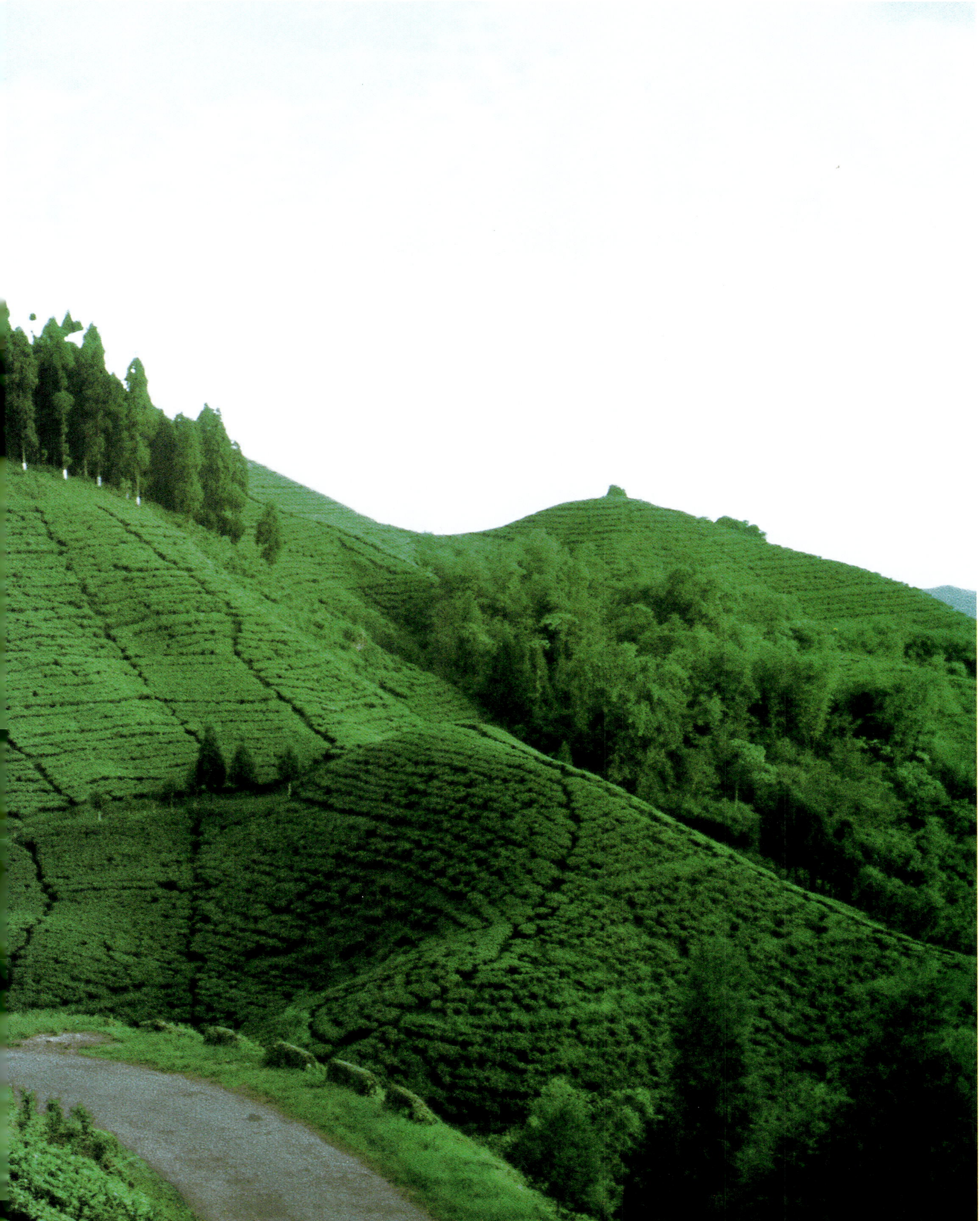

Top left, right, and below: Conserve to preserve: where protection of wildlife is a way of life.

Protection of Wildlife and Ecology

Protection of Assam's wildlife and ecology has been a traditional concern for the tea estates, and planters from very early times showed great interest in this. Venison used to be sold openly in markets and elephants were killed for their ivory. Planters demanded a sanctuary for the rhino, an end to the killing of deer, and closed seasons for hunting.

In the old days, in Hathikuli Tea Estate located near Kaziranga National Park, the estate's manager used to watch over the animals through a powerful telescope perched strategically on his veranda. To this day managers continue that tradition. On the north bank of the Brahmaputra, planter John Oliver founded the Assam Valley Wildlife Preservation Society with the help of his employer Williamson Magor. They bred species threatened with extinction, such as the white-winged wood duck and the pygmy hog at the Bordubi, Attareekhat, and Mangaldai tea estates.

Tata Tea Ltd, supported by many other tea companies, set up Rhino Foundation to protect the one-horned rhino at Kaziranga National Park. In the high ranges of Kerala, Tata Tea has adopted a strategy of joint management in preserving the famous Eravikulam National Park in active collaboration with the forest department of Kerala. It also supports High Range Wildlife and Environment Preservation Association for comprehensive environmental management and sustainable development. The association employs 12 Muthuvan watchers for environment preservation and wildlife protection. Its latest achievement is the formation of the Munnar Development Core Committee which comprises representatives of the environmental stakeholders in the region.

The land under the control of Tata Tea is studded with large tracts of Shola forests, and these are well protected. It has also taken a keen interest in energy conservation and adopted proactive measures to motivate people to assist in conservation in the high ranges. Ratan Tata says, 'To encourage the youth to take up nature conservation activities, the company has sponsored the setting up of Kanan Devan Nature Clubs in women's colleges in Kerala which have already done commendable work on environmental protection and nature conservation'.

The tea industry provides a non-polluting atmosphere and is eco-friendly, providing protection against soil erosion and encouraging biodiversity. In Assam, forests have been decimated over the past 35 years. A tea plantation is a good replacement though it cannot match the long-lasting beneficial effects of a natural forest. Tea bushes greatly enhance the water-holding capacity of the soil and provide shade in and around the estates. In view of the multiplicity of problems relating to soil and land resources, the need to improve soil health and increase the productivity of the land has received close attention from the tea estates. They have undertaken an integrated afforestation programme in order to preserve and enhance the ecological balance of the regions in which they are active. With the current trend towards organic tea, greater and greater attention is being devoted to repairing and conserving the soil spectrum.

Many tea estates have distributed fruit saplings to workers and farmers living around their estates to improve their health and the contiguous environment. Chuapara Tea Estate has grown saplings of various fruit trees and distributed them free of cost to neighbouring villages. This will improve the nutritional content of the villagers' diet and also provide them with the means of earning an additional income. Soom Tea Estate has planted over 30,000 trees to help preserve the environment and the general ecology of the estate and surrounding areas.

The Williamson Magor group has undertaken flood control measures in Assam to reduce soil erosion, and to make use of the otherwise wasted water flows for irrigation. Baghjan Tea Estate has planted fruit trees along the river banks of Dangari river, thereby helping in reducing soil erosion. A 300 m long spur has been constructed to divert the Dangari river back to its original course, thereby stopping it from eroding areas planted with tea and occupied by villagers.

Top: A Muthuvan watcher with her child. Traditionally, the Muthuvans have a concern for the environment and wildlife preservation. *Below:* The Muthuvan headman standing in front of his cottage which is called *a kudi*.

Top left: A tea kettle impatiently awaits a tea enthusiast. *Top right:* From tea pan to glass to mouth is a smooth and flowing cycle.

Facing page: Earthenware for the earthy drink.

The Dufflaghur Tea Estate flood control works is situated on the Tabang and Singhlijan rivers was set up by constructing large spurs on the banks of the Buri Dehing river in upper Assam, Nonio river in lower Assam, and Pana river in the Dooars in West Bengal. It has constructed a bund on the bank of the river Brahmajan which was diverted to its old course by dredging for one kilometre and constructing spurs in the breached areas. Dirok Tea Estate took up the diversion of the Singhlijan river to its old course and constructed a bund to protect villages from floods. Through these voluntary projects, the estates have succeeded in their endeavour to achieve the twin objectives of preventing substantial erosion, as well as diverting the turbulent water flows for much-needed irrigation purposes.

Several companies are moving away from packing tea in wooden chests to using jute sacks instead. Tea companies have begun avoiding the use of harmful pesticides and chemical fertilizers for their tea bushes both because of long-term soil productivity and the fact that some Western consumers have begun to demand organic and environmentally friendly products. The Goodricke group has banned the use of any chemicals on its Darjeeling estates and phased out pesticides from its Assam plantations. It has graduated from ISO 9002 to the current international standard, Hazard Analysis Critical Control Point, which certifies that the product is totally safe for human consumption in all respects. The group's Castleton Tea Estate has become the world's first to receive the ISO 9002 certification, and its Darjeeling tea has been certified as organic by the international Swiss organization VSBLO (now known as IMO). Many tea estates and tea plants of the Goodricke group operate an environmental management system which complies with the requirements of ISO 14001 and BS EN ISO 9002. Tata Tea uses only agro-chemicals that have been approved for use in the fields by the Environmental Protection Agency of the USA and the Central Insecticides Board of India.

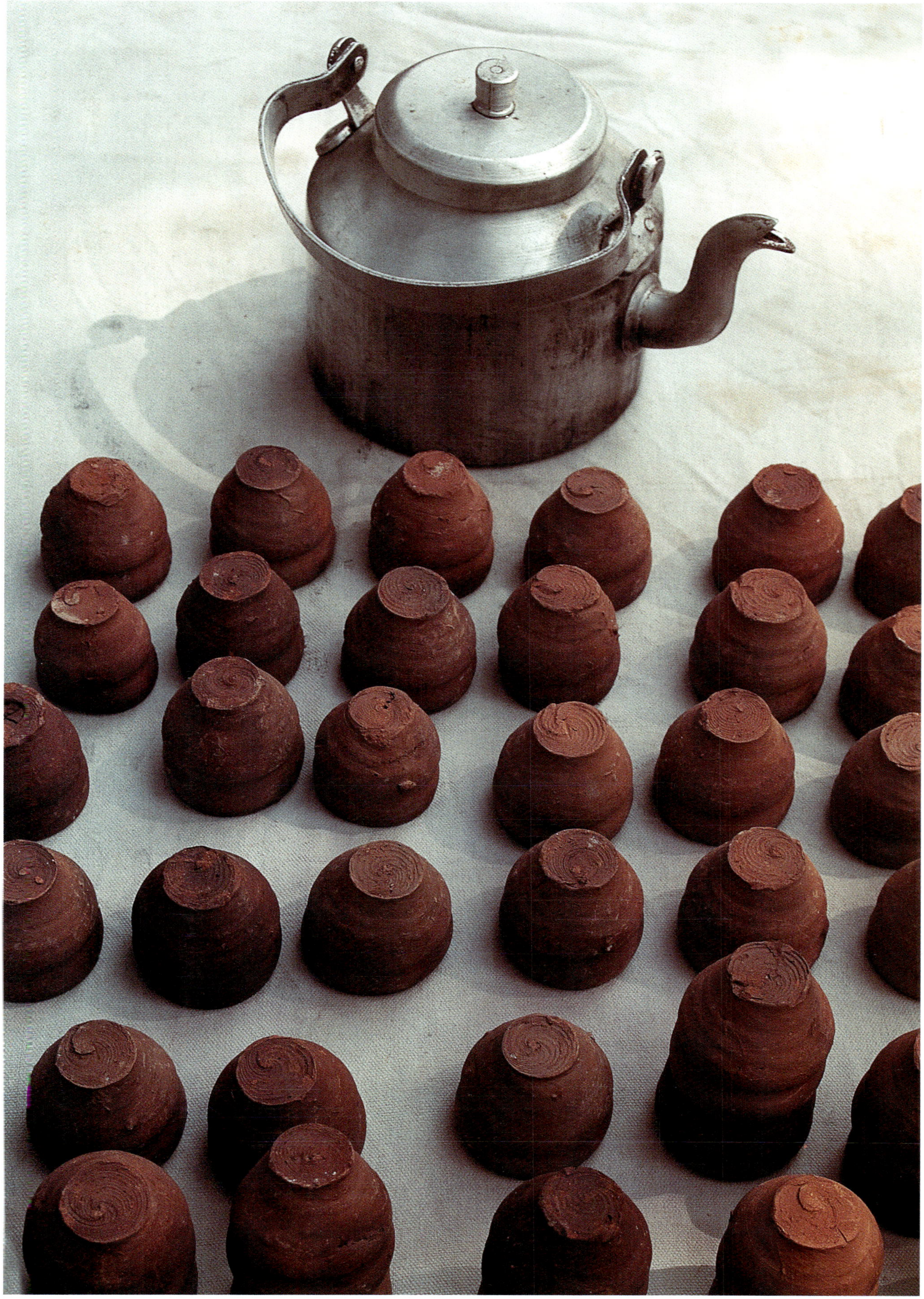

Top: Pencil and black chalk drawing by Vincent van Gogh, November 1882. *Below:* Pen and water colour drawing by Vincent van Gogh, September 1881.

Continuing Welfare in Testing Times

All this notwithstanding, by the 1980s tea estates began to face rough weather on their home turf. The fallout of the agitation against foreigners launched by the All Assam Students' Union and the rise of terrorism in the state found tea estates at the receiving end of local ire. Several charges were levelled against them. The industry was accused of not fulfilling its social obligations to the people of Assam and of siphoning money out of the state. Tea garden managers found themselves working in a tense environment, often contending with extortion, kidnapping, and even murder. This crippled the economy and paralysed the entire system. It is laudable that even under such dangerous and trying circumstances, they continue to work unremittingly.

When Surrendra Paul, owner of AFT Industries Ltd, a tea major in Assam, was gunned down by terrorists on 9 April 1990, the industry reacted with shock and horror. Tea mandarins realized that their contribution to Assam's development had gone unnoticed and unrecognized as they had worked behind the scenes and not highlighted their socio–economic contributions, traditionally shying away from publicity. In the process they had allowed many undeserved, adverse reports and criticism to go unchallenged.

They also realized that as their social work had been scattered and uncoordinated, it had not received the public recognition it deserved. The former chairman of the Indian Tea Association and managing director of Warren Tea Ltd, V.K. Goenka, says, 'Whether there are natural calamities or even if there are no natural calamities, we help as much as possible but we never want to get any publicity because we are not doing it for the sake of any commercial returns'.

According to R.K. Krishna Kumar, former chairman, Indian Tea Association and the CCPA, an ardent supporter of the welfare of tea-growing areas, 'The situation in Assam highlights the problem in different parts of India: the need for more active involvement in development. Insularity has been our major weakness. In public perception, the plantation units are seen as islands of affluence in the midst of rural poverty ... society expects industry to perform a large role, an activist role, in development, transcending the boundaries of their own gardens or industrial units.'

A Historic Resolution

Although the tea industry began social welfare work prior to Independence, it was only after Independence that this began to gather momentum and was systematically organized by tea companies and associations. D. Prakash, chairman, Assam Branch Indian Tea Association, mentioned in the course of a speech he delivered at the 198th annual general meeting of the Association on 5 December 1987, 'We have fully identified ourselves with the problems of the state and have been trying to bring about a change in the quality of life of the people'.

In order to set the record straight, the members of the Assam Branch Indian Tea Association passed a historic resolution. At an extraordinary general meeting held at Dibrugarh on 21 May 1990, the Association decided to streamline its social welfare activities, diversify into rural development, and create a special fund for social welfare projects. Since then, the Association has mobilized and spent massive resources on various developmental activities through its zones and circles.

Today the government of Assam recognizes the value of the Association's advice on virtually all matters, whether relating to social welfare or policies relating to tea. As the Association expanded during the past few years, it decided to work in tandem with the government and to coordinate its activities with it. A standing committee was set up, headed by the chief secretary of Assam, to identify areas of cooperation.

The former additional secretary-general of the Assam Branch Indian Tea Association, P.K. Bhattacharjee, highlighted the industry's close relationship with the government when he pointed out that the government involved the industry and its association in discussions on all matters of any significance. This really came home to him when he was obliged to absent himself from a meeting and sent a letter of regret. At the following meeting an explanation for his absence was demanded, whereupon he was obliged to confess to the minister that he had not realized till then how important his presence at the meeting was regarded as being.

It is noticeable that several government-owned tea estates are not as productive and have not been undertaking the community welfare work expected of them. It is unfortunate that from 1994 onwards, a number of the member gardens have not contributed to the social welfare fund of the Assam Branch Indian Tea Association, with some large companies not having paid their annual subscription for as long as the past three years. The Association is therefore finding it difficult to run its welfare projects. Every day there are

Top: Black chalk with wash drawing of a peasant woman by Vincent van Gogh, May 1885. *Below:* Lithograph of a section of a painting by Vincent van Gogh, April 1885.

Tea is an ideal social drink: light and refreshing.

new proposals for development work which cannot be taken up for want of contributions from members.

The Association is well organized and has infrastructure at the grass-root level throughout Assam. Its circles organize monthly meetings where all the tea estates managers meet and discuss important issues relating to the industry, including social welfare work, the latter accounting for about 30 per cent of its time. Social welfare activities have been categorized into different segments, such as education, sports, health, agriculture, the arts, flood and drought relief, tourism, and any other activity or initiative that needs to be coordinated with the state government.

Since 1989, the Association has spent over Rs 80 m. on welfare under various developmental heads through subscription from its member estates, and undertaken over 200 major projects. The highest investments have been in Guwahati, Sonitpur district, and Tinsukhia. Every year the mighty Brahmaputra causes floods and erosion. The Association has extended substantial relief to the affected people of the region in the form of supply of foodgrains, provision of medical facilities, and erection of temporary shelters in various parts of Assam.

Inaugurating Golaghat Civil Hospital on 29 September 1993, the late Hiteshwar Saikia, former chief minister of Assam, remarked, 'The manner in which the Assam Branch Indian Tea Association has stepped forward to supplement the government's effort is laudable'. He referred to the fact that the Association had spent nearly Rs 30 m. on social welfare, of which over Rs 4 m. had been allocated to improving medical facilities in the state. 'In fact their contribution to areas of social benefit is simply splendid.'

He pointed out that the Association had spent Rs 10.6 m. on new and improved educational facilities, Rs 4.33 m. on developing the infrastructure for sports, and another Rs 2.5 m. on preserving Assam's art and culture. 'The list is endless, but what is even more praiseworthy is that even during the period of insecurity this Association was not deterred from carrying out its activities aimed at social benefit. Of late, the Association has embarked on projects of agricultural development in the rural areas. This will benefit the people of Assam in general, and the rural population in particular, as over 80 per cent of Assam's population is rural based.'

Many schools and colleges have been built by the Association. The arts have received their due. Jorhat Theatre and Nazira Natya Mandir have been financed, and the Assam Cultural Complex, a centre for the performing arts, was built at a cost of Rs 100 m. Two major indoor sports stadiums have been built, one at Cotton College, Guwahati's premier college, and the other at the Nehru Stadium complex. In its centenary year the Assam Branch Indian Tea Association constructed bus shelters in tea-growing areas, a waiting hall at Jorhat Civil Hospital, and a public park at Tezpur in memory of Charles Alexander Bruce, father of the tea industry.

Now tea companies and other organizations in Assam have drawn up a blueprint for the economic development of the state entitled 'Insurgence to Resurgence' prepared under the auspices of the North-East Chamber of Commerce and Industry.

A cup of *chai* in the morning in conjunction with the newspaper is a relaxing way to start the day.

Increasing Scope

The Consultative Committee of Plantation Associations, consisting of nine tea associations from Assam, the Dooars, Darjeeling district, and southern India, has implemented several development programmes. The North–Eastern Tea Association, Tea Association of India, United Planters' Association of Southern India, Assam Tea Planters' Association, Bharatiya Cha Parishad, Dooars Branch Indian Tea Association, Indian Tea Planters' Association, Darjeeling Tea Planters' Association, Terai Indian Planters' Association, and Kangra Valley Small Tea Planters' Association have contributed on an ongoing basis to the betterment of the lives of the local people. All the tea estates are members of one or other of these producers' associations, but not all of them have been actively involved with the communities in their area of operations. Although many associations claim that all their members have been actively involved in development initiatives, they have little to show in concrete terms of the initiatives undertaken by them.

Crumbling towns are being given a facelift. The North-Eastern Tea Association, for instance, has concentrated its energies on Golaghat town's inadequate infrastructure. It has provided street lights, beautified the local park, and built a new Harijan Community Hall. The Association gave money to the cash-strapped local municipal corporation and has offered to clear the streets of garbage. The district administration is undertaking a project called 'People Project Golaghat 2000' to improve basic amenities, to which the Association has lent financial support.

The Tea Association of India spends Rs 2 m. annually on several welfare projects, and these include the conversion of *kuchha* schools into *pucca* ones and digging deep shaft wells. It has also contributed to the chief minister's relief fund and renovated many old educational institutions. Besides this, various cultural organizations, such as the Sahitya Sammelan, are assisted by

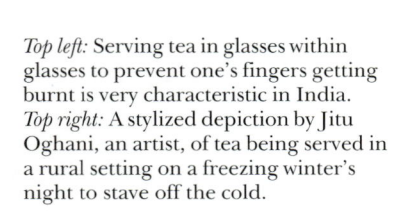

the Association. Asam Sahitya Sabha and Sibsagar Natya Mandir at Dibrugarh have been supported by it. The association has also assisted Cachar Cancer Hospital, Cachar Tea Garden Wholesale Cooperative, and even financed dustbins and street lighting for Jorhat.

The Indian Council of Agricultural Research, government of India, started setting up Krishi Vigyan Kendras to increase rural income and employment by improving farming practices under the aegis of this association in 1983. Farmers and young people are taught how to cultivate crops, principally tea. The best Krishi Vigyan Kendra award was awarded to the Krishi Vigyan Kendra of the United Planters' Association of Southern India during 1996–7. The Association has also implemented a few small grower enhancement schemes sanctioned by the government of India. Sundry agencies have sponsored the Association's programmes, and now there is a need for a coordinated and comprehensive plan of development.

The Bharatiya Cha Parishad's secretary, S.P. Verma, says that proprietary gardens actively participate in social welfare activities. Ranjit Chaliha, a former chairman of the Parishad, adds, 'Although their production base was small, many local Indian tea planters have made significant contributions to the growth of the tea industry in Assam in particular and to Assamese society in general'. The

Top left: Serving tea in glasses within glasses to prevent one's fingers getting burnt is very characteristic in India.
Top right: A stylized depiction by Jitu Oghani, an artist, of tea being served in a rural setting on a freezing winter's night to stave off the cold.

86 | THE HERITAGE OF INDIAN TEA

promotion of education, health, and sports is a priority for the Parishad.

Mahadeo Jalan, former chairman of the Parishad, mentions, 'The local planters have done good work in the field of education over the past 100 years. Most of the old private educational institutions belong to them. They know the local sentiment and have done a great deal of public welfare work around their tea estates. Even today they are contributing immensely to several welfare activities.' A well known tea planter, the late Bimala Prosad Chaliha, when he was chief minister of Assam, took the initiative to set up the Guwahati Tea Auction Centre.

Jyoti Prasad Agarwala, Parbati Prasad Barua, and Rohini Kumar Baruah have produced Assamese literature, films, songs, plays, etc. They have also financially assisted many public institutions. The Jalans of Dibrugarh have donated land for Dibrugarh Medical College. Many other colleges like the Dr J.K. Saikia Homeo College, Kanoi College, Devicharan Baruah Girls' College, Chandra Kamal Bezbaruah College, N.N. Saikia College, Jogananda Deva Goswami College, and Devraj Rai College were established by local planters.

Empowerment of Women

Dense jungles, tea estates, and a meandering Teesta make up the Dooars valley where the lower Himalayan hills and the north Bengal plains meet. Frequently, wild elephants can be seen tramping through tea gardens. Located east of Kalimpong, in Jalpaiguri district of West Bengal, the Dooars is the second largest tea-producing area in India with about 154 tea gardens. The Dooars Branch Indian Tea Association has helped to organize seminars on industry and employment at Jalpaiguri Engineering College, and supported schemes for handicapped people and the elderly.

India is afflicted by an ever-increasing population which has created socio–economic and environmental problems. Although India cannot follow the Chinese way of family planning, it is clear that something must be done to control the population. The Association has implemented an innovative family welfare programme combining environmental sanitation, parasite control, and people's participation. The Family Welfare Education Programme was started in 1982. At the initial stage managers, trade unions, and the medical staff were motivated. A mobile education unit explained the value and methods of family planning to workers and promoted it amongst them.

However, workers still opted for terminal methods: contraception did not gather momentum and there was very little community participation. The programme was re-tailored on the basis of greater feedback. Chojiro Kuni, an

Top: Oh how delicious! *Below:* Two Naga women in Kohima, Nagaland, join in the fun.

Top: Chai is popular everywhere at any time, regardless of the weather. It is flavoured with spices and mixed with piping hot milk.

Facing page: Picture of patience: plucking tea requires patience, skill, and nimble fingers which race swiftly over two leaves and a bud.

expert on environment, sanitation, and parasite control, who works for a Japanese organization for integrated cooperation in family planning, has been greatly impressed with the project as it is now constituted.

The project received support from the United Nations Children's Fund, the United Nations Population Fund, and the Ministry of Health and Family Planning, and was implemented from 1992 covering about 450,000 workers in 125 gardens. The aim of the initiative was to strengthen the health infrastructure, and in order to achieve this project implementation group was set up at Binnaguri, the Association's headquarters.

An area supervisor was appointed for each sub-district, and in every garden women volunteers, selected from amongst the workers, were trained. They were organized into Mothers' Clubs and given uniforms. About 119 Mothers' Clubs have been trained in health and family welfare. They play a key role because they deal directly with workers, motivating and educating them. Information, education, and communication are the principal components of the project, with films, posters, charts, seminars, and group meetings being used as facilitators. Everyone has been roped in.

The Dooars Branch Indian Tea Association is continuing this project supported by its own resources and some additional financial assistance from the Tea Board of India. The greatest achievement of the project has been the establishment of Mothers' Clubs in all the gardens. Each club comprises 20 women trained in immunization, mother and child care, and health and hygiene, and aims at spreading the message of good health and better living amongst tea labourers and their dependants. Indeed, these clubs have even successfully discouraged vendors from selling alcohol, a major achievement. This is truly a process of empowerment of women and offers the promise of a better future for tea workers in general. Keeping in view the achievements of this project, the tea industry has now decided to extend the concept of Mothers' Clubs to Assam too.

Traditionally, community welfare was limited to charity or donations. There has now been a shift towards planned change, with the tea industry acting as facilitator. Tarun Gogoi, chief minister of Assam says, 'We appreciate and compliment the industry's work in health, education, literature, technology, etc. ... In fact it plays an important role in organizing welfare activities in the state in a range of areas but it should play a much larger role in socio–economic development by diversifying into other areas as they have the resources, rural infrastructure, and technical expertise to do so.' P.K. Bora, the chief secretary, adds, 'the industry should harness its

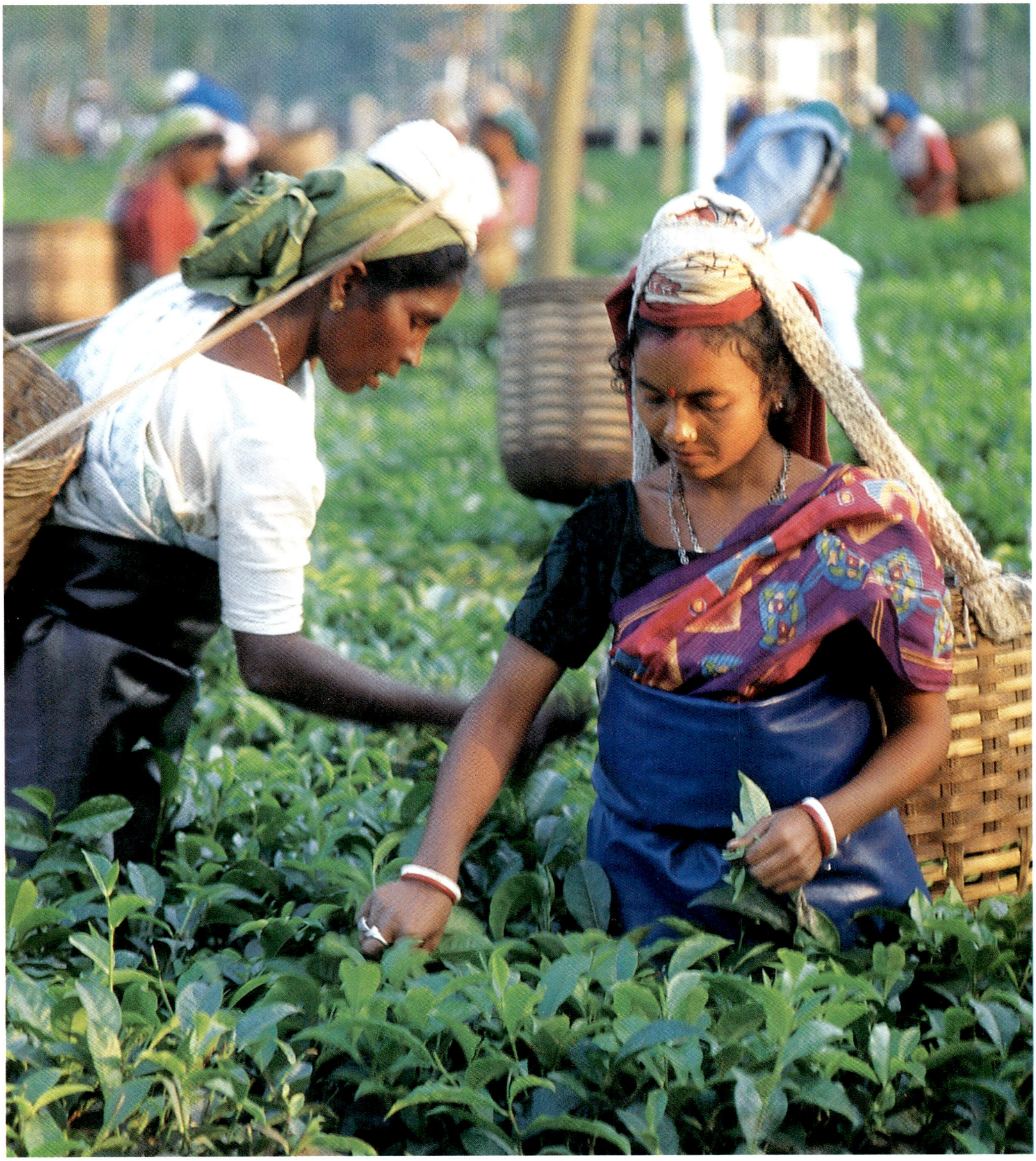

Top: Over the centuries, tea has symbolized warmth and mutual respect.

Facing page: Behind bars! The tea pan fumes tantalizingly while customers must impatiently await their turn across the wire netting.

Following spread: A Darjeeling tea garden nestling in the foothills of a snow-covered Himalayan range. Accounts of the remarkable beauty of the gardens here have spread for and wide. In this region there are 86 gardens where tea grows at altitudes ranging from 610 to 2134 m on steep slopes which provide ideal natural drainage. This, coupled with the intermittent cloud and sunshine, combine to impart a unique character and 'muscatel' flavour, producing the world's finest teas with the most delicate flavours. A large tea garden is often self-reliant in terms of housing, schools, dispensaries, recreational facilities, and places of worship.

collective wisdom and take a major initiative in investing and re-investing in the state's industries and its social infrastructure for mutual prosperity and thereby build up a long-standing relationship.'

A Heritage to Cherish

The industry owes a debt to society which it can repay by active participation in community development and redoubling its commitments. It is therefore time for the industry to organize itself to face the challenges of the future in order to be able to continue to play an expanding role in the socio–economic development process, thereby helping to improve the quality of life of hundreds of millions of people in and around tea-growing areas of the country. People have great expectations from the industry, and it is therefore up to it to take the necessary steps to meet these. Fifteen per cent of what it spends goes into labour welfare. It is this that makes life within the tea estates so much better and more prosperous than that in the surrounding areas, and is precisely why a tea plantation has often been described as an island of prosperity afloat amidst a sea of backwardness. This dichotomy has led to tension between tea gardens and their neighbours. Local society expects the estate to transform their lives as well. Assam Branch Indian Tea Association's former chairman, Vijay Mehra, reiterates the tea industry's commitment to the people of Assam, 'We have always given due weightage to local sentiment'.

Needless to say, the development of the tea industry has been inextricably linked with the socio–economic development of the tea-growing areas. It is, therefore, also time to look back and make new resolutions for the future. As R.K. Krishna Kumar enthusiastically puts it, 'A deep and more constructive involvement in the development of the community at large is now clearly expected from us. We must respond to this challenge in a constructive manner if we are to ensure that we retain and heighten the goodwill and support of the community without which our operations can well become untenable.'

The tea industry has given much to the tea-producing states but much more remains to be done in terms of true participation and involvement in social change. A genuine spirit of trusteeship on the part of the tea industry can bring about a socio–economic revolution that will truly fulfil the aspirations of the people.

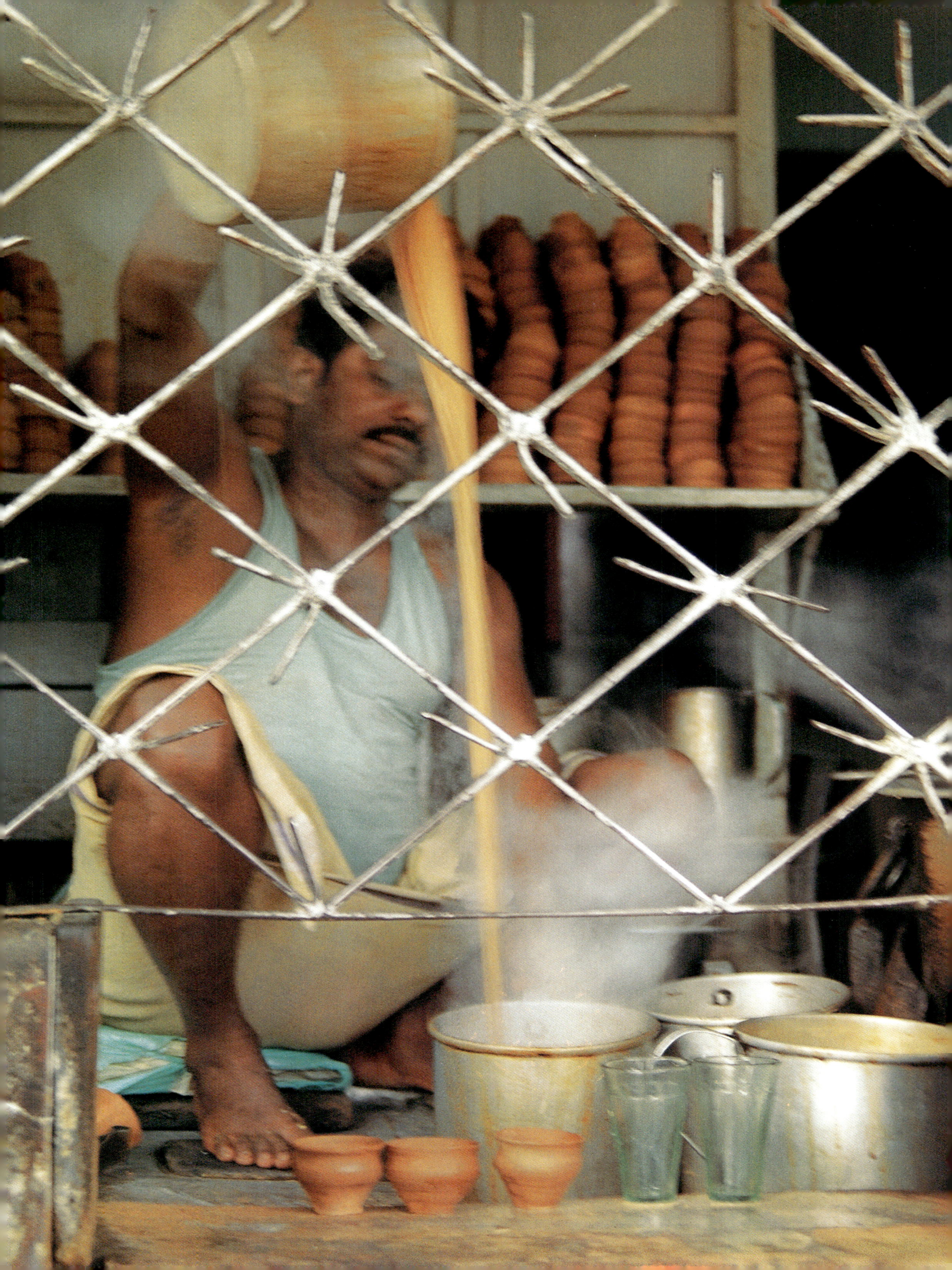

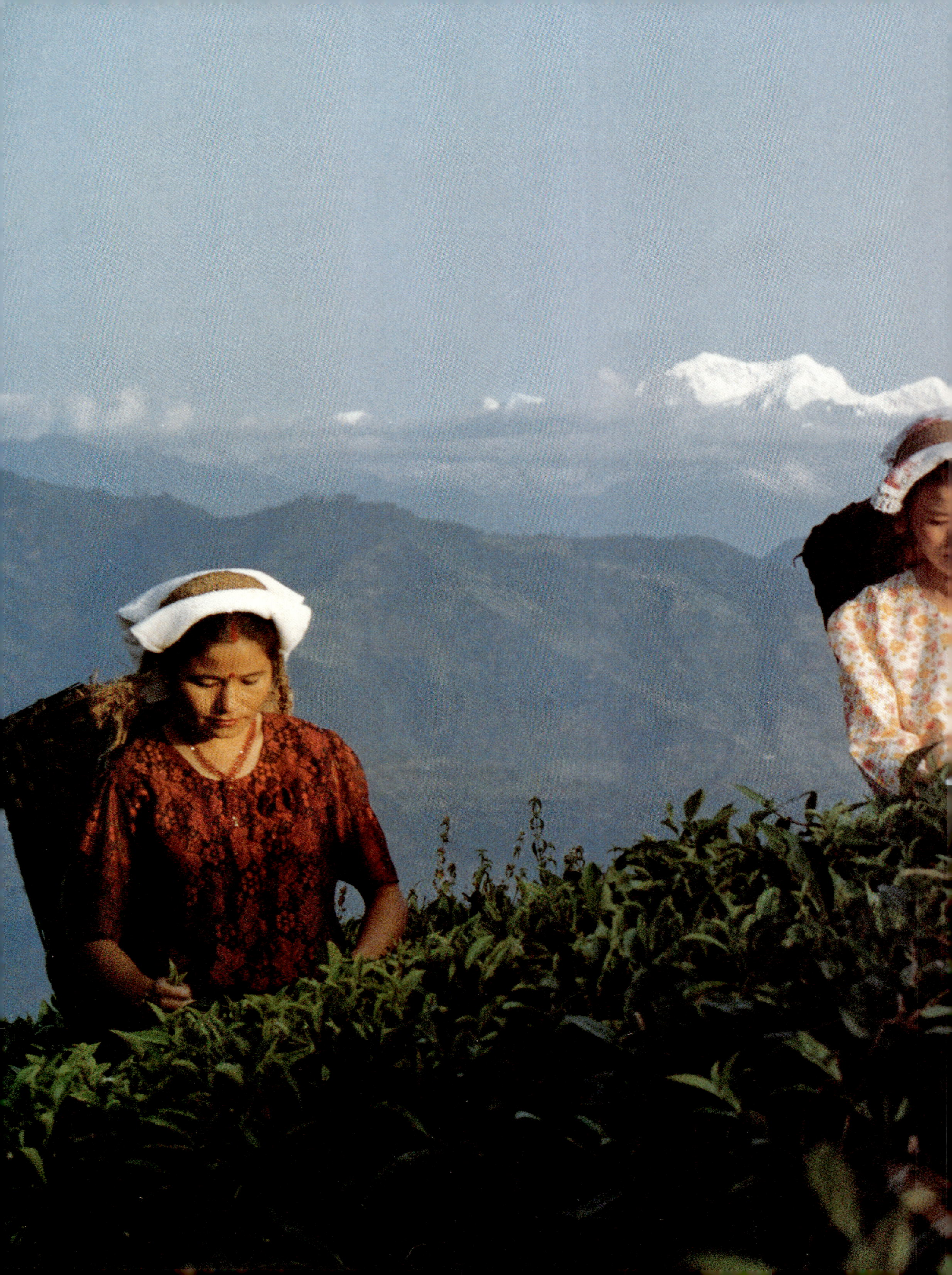

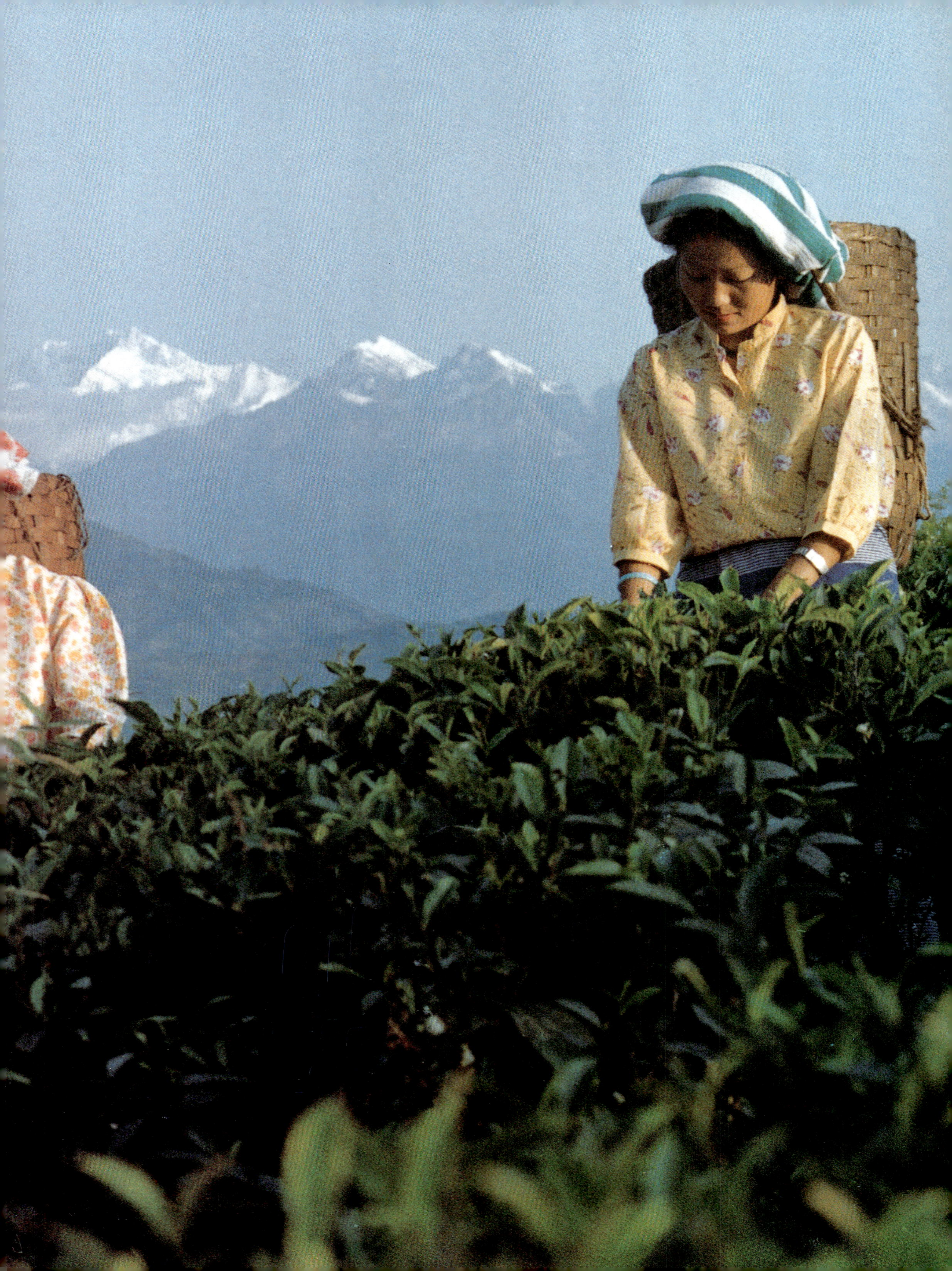

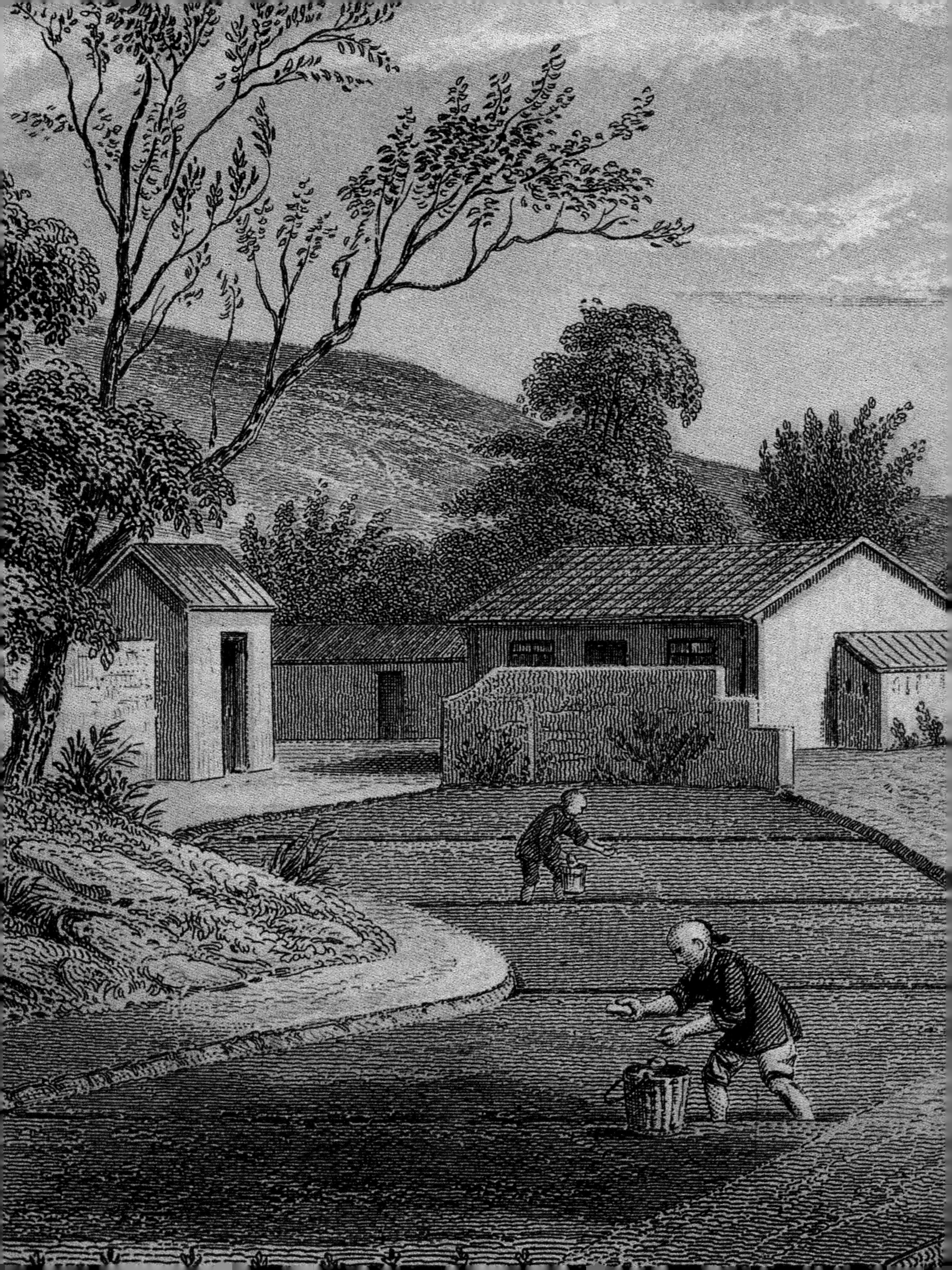

CHAPTER 3

Partners in Progress

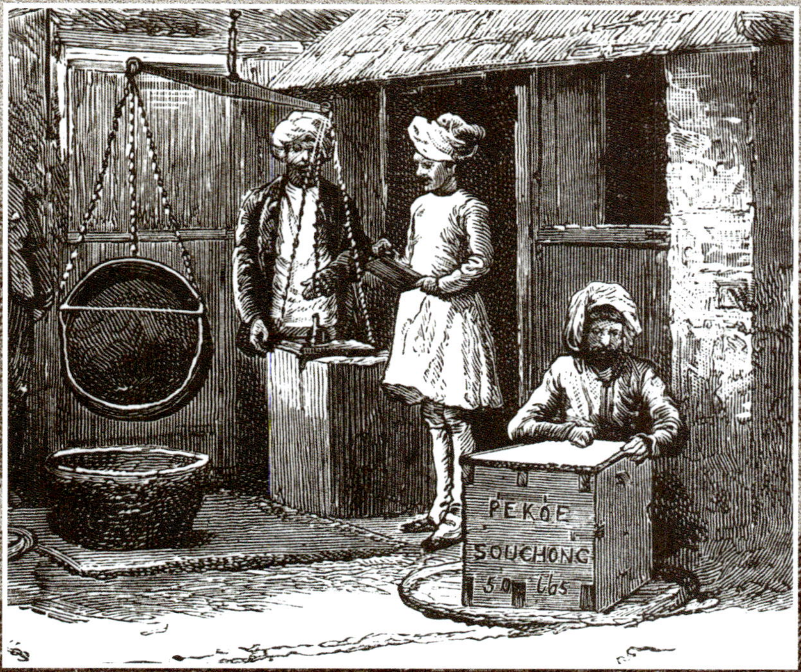
PEKOE
SOUCHONG
50 lbs

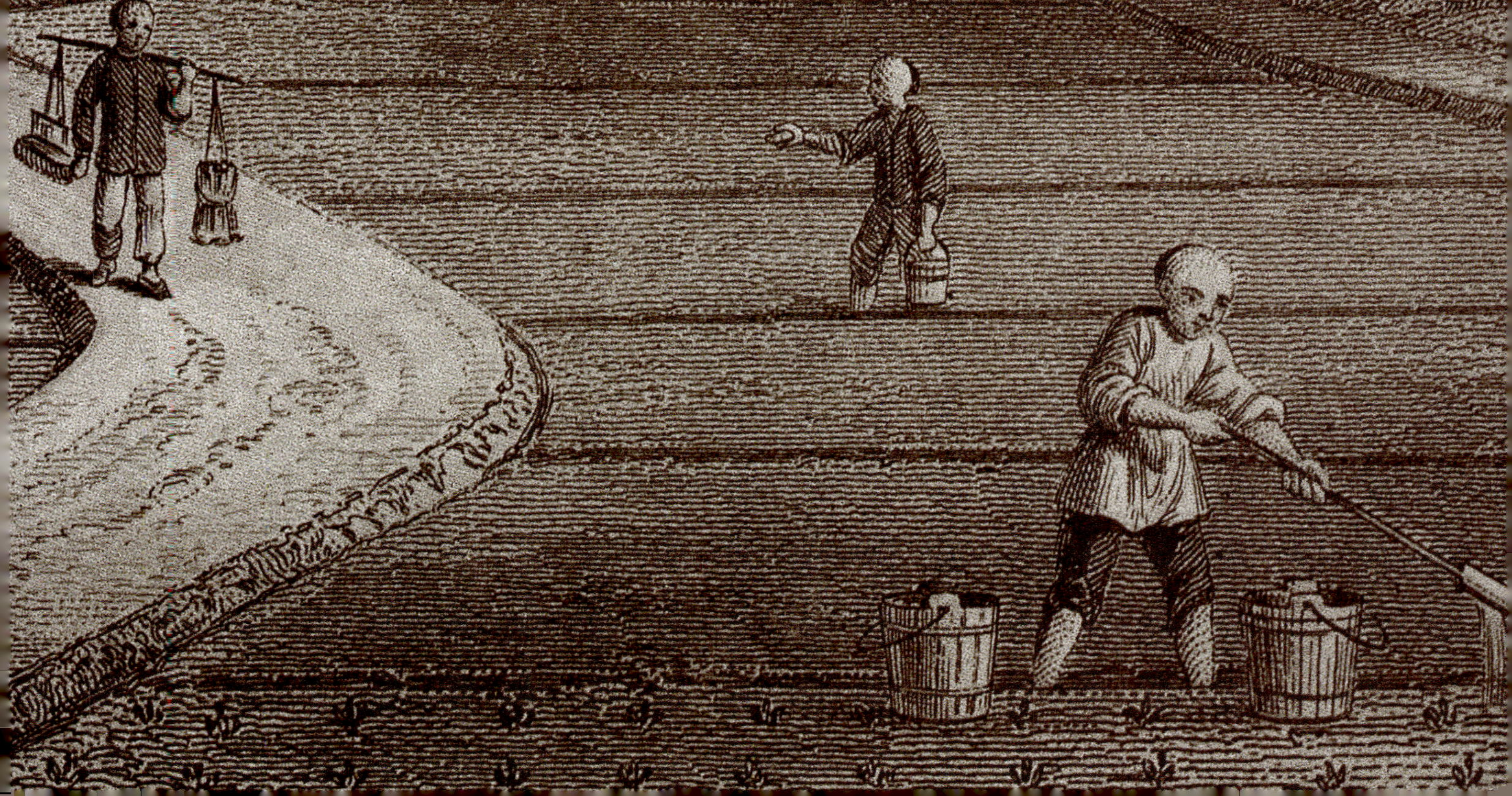

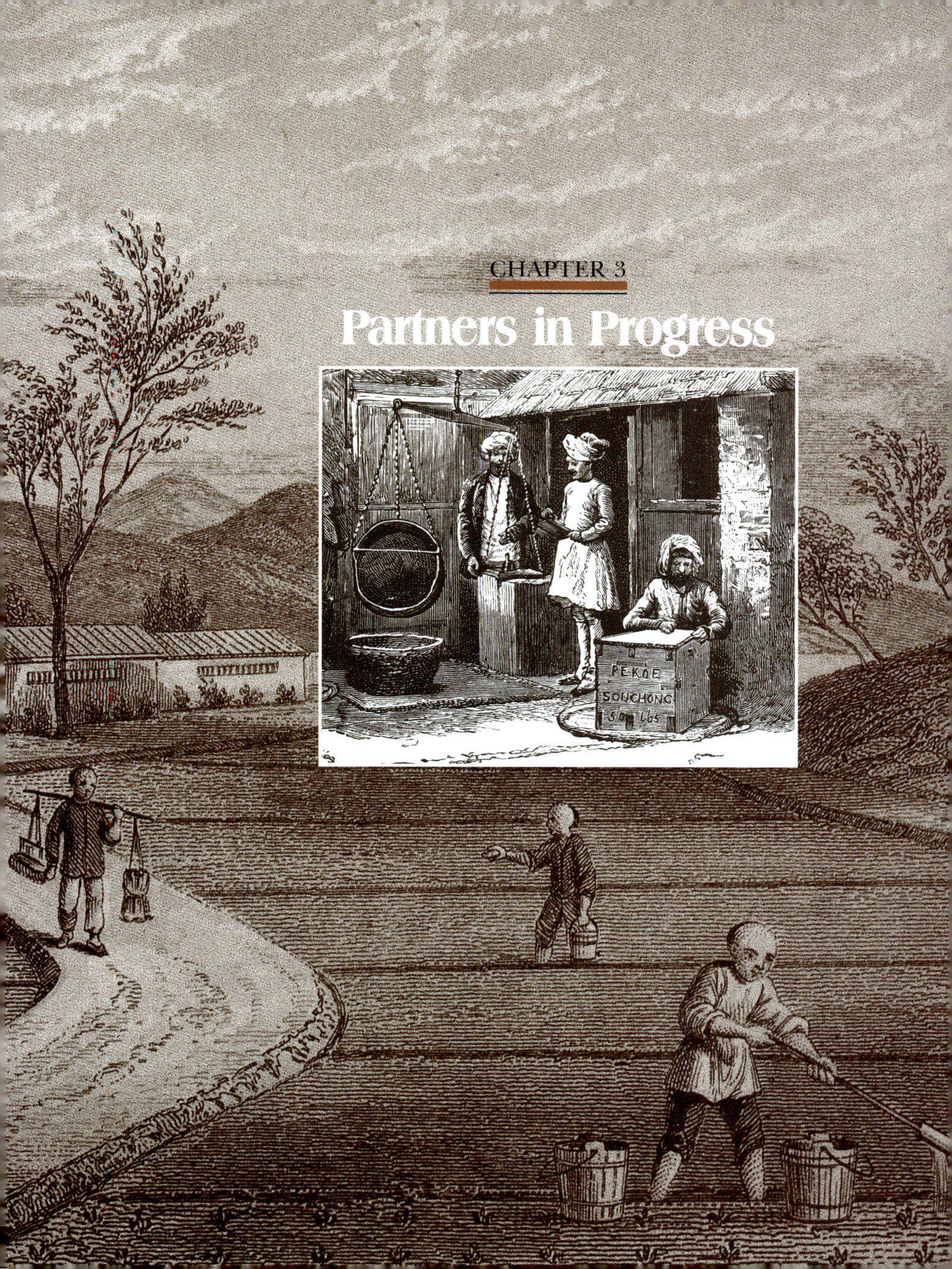

The tea industry has for long been seized of the need to help local people with livelihood programmes, and has shared its knowledge about tea cultivation with small farmers and young unemployed people. Today, the tea industry supports over 91,000 small tea growers in the north-east, West Bengal, Himachal Pradesh, and the south. About 221 'bought leaf' factories and 17 cooperative factories cater to small growers.

Concern for Small Tea Growers

The industry nurtures small tea growers by helping them to acquire technical know-how, offering capital intensive manufacturing facilities, and helping to market their produce. Earlier, this practice was mostly confined to south India and Himachal Pradesh, but since 1989 it has firmly established itself in north-east India too. The average yield of this sector is quite low in comparison to that of the organized sector. The industry believes that given adequate inputs in the form of quality, technical expertise, and finance, this sector holds tremendous growth potential.

The contribution of this segment is very significant in the south Indian tea industry. Small tea growers have existed in south India since 1931. B.K. Nandi Gowder was the first to set up a factory in the small-grower sector around 1935. The United Planters' Association of Southern India has played a vital role in supporting them by supplying tea plants and technical expertise free of cost. Today, the number of small tea farmers has increased to nearly 60,000, a membership twice that of the large tea corporates in the United Planters' Association of Southern India.

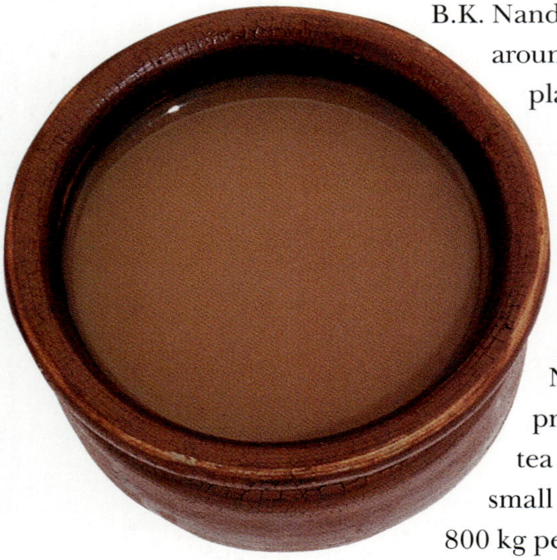

The Nilgiri region is the largest small-grower's region in the country, covering around 30,000 ha in over 600 hamlets of the Nilgiris. This segment contributes 22.5 per cent of the total production of the south, and in the Nilgiri region its share of the total tea production is 52 per cent. The average productivity level of the small growers has, through concerted efforts, been enhanced from 800 kg per ha in 1982 to 2000 kg per ha in 1999. The Krishi Vigyan Kendra is implementing a number of tea development programmes for small growers to increase their productivity and quality with the support of the Indian Council of Agricultural Research and the Tea Board of India.

Facing page: A painting by Jogen Chowdhury, renowned artist from Calcutta.

Preceding spread: Drawing of a panoramic view of tea cultivation. *Inset:* Weighing and packing tea in India (c. 1883).

The Tamil Nadu state government has been assisting the cooperatives and the processing units managed by small tea growers. Highlighting the

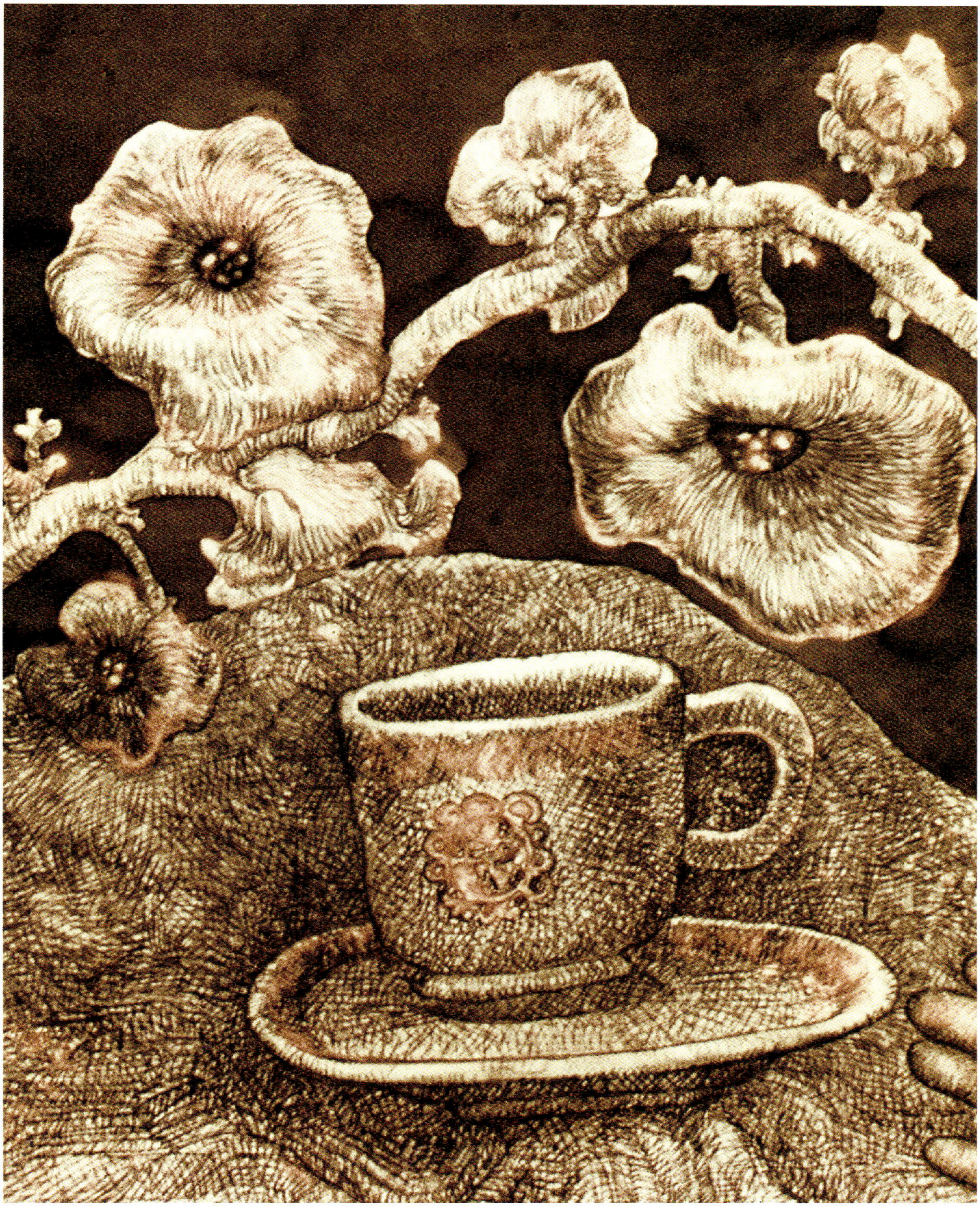

A small tea grower, his factory and house in his tea garden in the Nilgiris, the largest and most prosperous small tea grower's region in the country. Today, the number of such growers has increased to nearly 60,000 covering around 30,000 ha, encompassing over 600 hamlets of the Nilgiris in southern India.

growing prosperity among small growers, Dr S. Ramu, senior scientist and head, Krishi Vigyan Kendra, says, 'The economy has improved so much. Even their living standards have gone up and their lifestyle has changed. They have started living in *pucca* houses equipped with a range of domestic gadgets and also own cars; their children are being educated in convent schools. Earlier there was an occasional convent school or two, but now even small places have a number of English medium schools.'

The Tea Board of India has pitched in too. It is implementing a scheme for the overall development of the small tea growers which provides them with loans or subsidies to set up tea plantations in new areas. It also imparts training on modern aspects of tea cultivation and manufacture, supply of materials and other inputs, organizes field and factory tours, and the like. Karbi Anglong, North Cachar Hills, Kokrajhar, Nalbari, and Barpeta are some of the places that are being promoted as ideal new areas. As land is scarce, the Tea Board of India intends to club together several plots of 25–30 ha into tea-growing cooperatives. Interested farmers are provided with training on all aspects of tea cultivation.

Top left: Small tea growers at work. They grow about 90 m. kg of average quality tea. *Top right:* Happy plucker returning after a day's work with the day's 'catch' on her back.

As a consequence, in the north-east, tea cultivation is generating an income for three million people and becoming a popular career choice for young people. There are now some 25,000 small tea growers with almost 1.2 m. ha under tea production and produce approximately 46 m. kg of tea. With financial assistance from the North-Eastern Development Finance Corporation, some of them have even started their own companies with processing factories. According to Hemanta Gohain, general secretary of the All Assam Small Tea Growers' Association, they have transformed the rural economy during the last decade. The small growers have not only made a profit for themselves, but have opened up an income-generating avenue for their 30,000 direct employees and also contributed towards welfare activities.

Robin Borthakur, secretary, Assam Branch Indian Tea Association, describes how the industry has been assisting this segment: 'We have been giving them technical guidance and have organized training camps for small tea growers. In certain cases, we have ploughed their land free of cost and given them plants, given them cartons of tea bushes, etc. to enable them to plant them themselves. We are even buying tea leaves from them.'

The result is that tea is becoming a peasant crop with thousands of farmers giving up paddy cultivation to grow tea on every inch of available land. 'People have even started growing tea in their courtyards,' says Rajen Kalita, a small tea grower from Jorhat. An investment of approximately Rs 80,000 to Rs 100,000 per ha is needed, and on an average, tea cultivated on a hectare of land produces 15,000–18,000 kg of tea leaves. These are then sold to large gardens at a price ranging between Rs 12–15 per kg. 'I have become quite well off after cultivating tea as the returns are good,' adds Gopal Sharma, a small tea grower from Assam.

PARTNERS IN PROGRESS

Top: We care, so we share: small tea growers have been helped by the Tea Board of India, tea associations, and leading tea companies in conducting soil surveys, nursery development, and planting. They have been educated from the field to factory level to produce better quality tea. *Below:* Small growers and villagers watching a pruning demonstration conducted by the Tea Board of India under its Tea Quality Upgradation Programme.

Challenges Confronting Small Growers

The unfortunate thing is that there is no monitoring of the produce of small tea growers. They grow about 90 m. kg of average quality tea, and the poor quality of their produce has become a serious problem for the industry. It is felt that this aspect is being neglected by small tea growers desperate to increase production. According to a leading tea auctioneer, 'Presently, small tea growers are continuing to make easy money and are not bothered about quality standards. Most of them believe in short-term benefits. They should learn a lesson from their counterparts in Kenya who are known for producing the best quality tea.' He adds, 'It is a matter of grave concern and a warning to the industry. We are already seeing the effect of poor quality on the south Indian tea markets and also in some parts of north India. Indian tea has always been known the world over for its distinguished flavour and strength, a reputation built up painstakingly over many decades.'

In the south, the Tea Board of India has sponsored the Tea Quality Upgradation Programme to educate small tea growers to produce better quality tea. Many programmes have been launched under this project ranging from the field to factory level. The plucking and pruning standards required to improve quality have been set out and processing methods in manufacturing have also been streamlined and fine-tuned. The fifteen-day training course includes field trips, cultivation on demonstration plots and nurseries, and information on crop diversification.

Agricultural experts regularly visit 200 contiguous villages where tea is grown. During their interaction they educate the growers on new technology and better agricultural practices to improve their produce. As a result, they are able to garner higher returns, apart from reaching a large market even while lacking any major infrastructure. Over 20,000 small tea growers have benefited from this programme. M. Nanjan, director, Bikkatty Industrial Cooperative Tea Factory, says, 'We are in the twenty-first century. Quality upgradation is essential as almost all the countries in the world, including India, have signed the World Trade Organization agreement, so we have no option but to upgrade our quality of tea in order to survive in the future. This programme has made a huge difference by creating awareness amongst us.' The Tea Board of India should register both small tea growers and 'bought leaf' factories, and the sale of green leaf should be allowed only after production of valid registration certificates.

Another major problem the tea estates are facing is that of green leaf theft. Highlighting this problem, S.S. Sindhu, chairman, Assam Branch Indian

The higher harvesting and pruning standards required to improve quality have been introduced, and processing methods in manufacturing have also been fine-tuned.

Tea Association, mentioned at the 110th annual general meeting, 'This problem is becoming more and more complex by the day. Various methods have been tried by the tea gardens in close collaboration with the police and district administration to put a stop to this menace, but no success has so far been achieved. The thieves not only steal the green leaves, but also seriously damage the bushes. So much so, that from bushes with a deep skiff or light prune, it becomes difficult to even obtain leaves for tipping at the start of the season. Moreover, this problem is leading inexorably towards an outbreak of serious clashes between the garden workers and the villagers in the not too distant future. The only solution appears to be securely fencing the more vulnerable sections of the gardens, and this has already been done by some enterprising garden owners and companies.'

Such theft should of course be checked by the state government through the introduction of a system of proper regulation. Assam's former industry and commerce minister, Gunin Hazarika, is himself concerned: 'Our government is fully seized of the problem, though I am aware that the measures adopted by the district authorities so far are not foolproof. In this connection ... the government is examining the suggestions put forward by different organizations to evolve a mechanism that can weed out this menace.' R.S. Jhawar suggests that better coordination and planning between the small tea growers and the principal producers is essential to find a solution to this problem and sustain Assam's reputation as a producer of quality tea.

Top: Senior tea executives keep abreast of the latest technological and scientific developments in field and factory management and enforce a rigorous quality regimen. These have earned Indian planters a reputation throughout the world. *Below:* R.K. Krishna Kumar, vice chairman, Tata Tea Ltd, and chairman of the Tetley group, is a visionary: an articulate and dedicated tea man who has shown the way to the industry through the Tetley acquisition. He also became the first Indian to receive the global honour 'Tea Man of the Year' in 1998.

Partners in Strength

Today, Indian entrepreneurship in the tea industry is widely acknowledged, not only because of its quality tea but also the commitment quotient and overall quality of its human resources. It has put in a great deal of effort into human resource development, and the results are way ahead of those in most other industries in India. Welfare activities and the appointment and training of personnel has been so spectacular that other tea-producing countries have begun to look towards India for expertise.

Indian planters are today consultants to a number of countries. The World Bank has been sending Indian planters to various parts of the world, including East Africa, Malawi, Tanzania, and Mauritius to act as such. Sri Lanka too has invited and acknowledged the expertise of Indian planters in finding solutions to problems of low yield and inappropriate manufacturing technology. In this way, the human resource development of the Indian tea industry has earned an enviable reputation throughout the world. It is worth mentioning that R.K. Krishna Kumar was conferred the 'Tea Man of the Year' award for 1998 by the *Tea and Coffee Journal* of New York for his distinguished services to the industry. He ably represented its concerns and successes at national and international levels.

In addition, the Indian Institute of Plantation Management was set up in Bangalore to train managerial staff in practising management in the context of plantation industries in the modern free trade era. Its director, Subhash Sharma, says that there were three distinct and overlapping eras, namely, the romantic, the scientific, and that of globalization. 'Management education for planters has acquired greater importance in the current scenario of liberalization and globalization. It is in this context that our institute has emerged as a pioneering organization, providing management education and research inputs to the plantation community.'

The industry makes it a point to foster its employees' growth. The managers and workers are well paid and looked after by the plantation industry, and every facility is provided to enable them to lead comfortable lives; indeed, often the terms and facilities provided are superior to those in other industries. They have forged mutual bonds and live together in perfect harmony. The tea estates are like large, close-knit families, and every tea worker is well cared for by the industry.

Miles of green tea bushes provide a clean and healthy environment for workers. Within the estate, workers and their families are provided with free housing, medical facilities, education, and transport for their children, subsidized food, recreational facilities, and other fringe benefits. Almost 50 per cent of the workforce consists of women who earn the same wages as men. The Plantations Labour Act gave tea workers the same benefits as industrial labour. In addition, there are a number of non-statutory welfare amenities provided voluntarily by most tea estates. The quality of life of the tea plantation workers is thus far higher than that of their counterparts in other industries in India in terms of wages and other benefits. Social overhead costs, a relevant indicator, are the highest in India at around US $ 0.75 per kg as against $ 0.43 in Kenya, $ 0.15 in Malawi, and $ 0.64 in Sri Lanka.

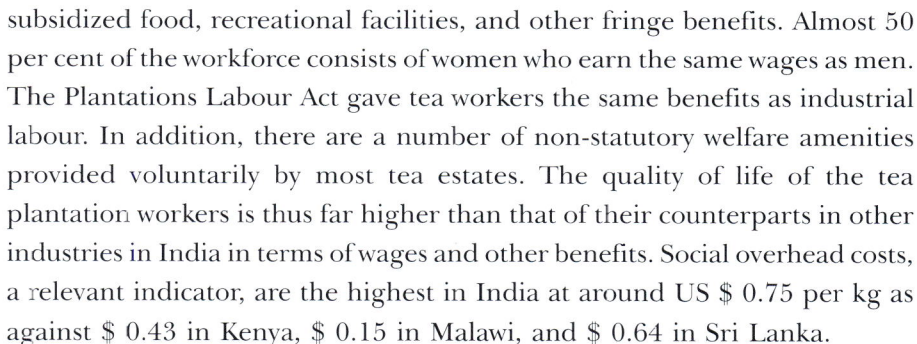

The image of the hungry, sick, and exploited worker therefore belongs to history. There is a stark difference between the living conditions of the early workers who laboured on tea plantations and those who work there now. When tea plantations were set up in Assam during the 1830s, planters realized that they needed a huge labour force that would settle on the estates.

The first batch of workers was recruited by Assam Company in 1841 from the Chhotanagpur area of Bihar. They were transported there in horrifying conditions, and many died of cholera on the way. There was no legislation to enforce their rights. The government enacted the Free Contractors System in 1859, but this just gave license to unscrupulous contractors. Most recruits were Adivasis from Bihar, Madhya Pradesh, and Orissa. Contractors, called 'coolie catchers' because of their brutality, lured tribals to the estates. Many of them went singing songs to Assam like: *Chal mini Asom jibo, Deshe baro dukhre, Asom deshere mini, Cha bagan hariyal* (My love, let us go to Assam; there is so much sorrow at home. In Assam, my love, there are lush green tea gardens).

Top left: Skilful plucking produces the finest brew. *Top right:* Deepika Medappa, a woman planter in Munnar. Tata Tea Ltd was perhaps the first Indian company to recruit women planters.

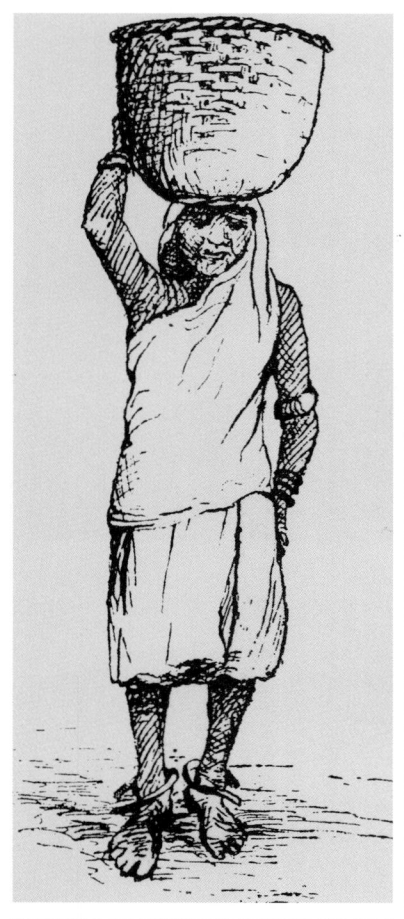

Sketches of plantation life in British India: *Top left:* Plucker carrying leaves in Assam. *Top right:* The coolie lines. *Below left:* Naga woman plucker. *Below right:* Plucking the leaf in a garden.

The songs were sweet but the ground reality altogether different. Many of the recruits either died on the way or on the estates. No amenities, such as health care or housing, were provided to them, and they were forced to work inhuman hours on the estate. Under these miserable conditions many fell victim to malaria and other tropical diseases. The Tea District Emigration Act of 1868 gave rise to the first batch of legally recognized labour, but tales of brutality continued to abound.

Shortage of labour often goaded managers and their sirdars to overwork labour. The minimum wage was Rs 3, an amount that looked after the essential needs of a family of four, but the workers' living conditions left a great deal to be desired. The planters themselves lived in 'primitive living quarters, where disease vied with discomfort, making life arduous ...', according to an early history of James Finlay & Co.

Sir Henry Cotton, chief commissioner of Assam, did take up the cause of the tea worker, but the government overruled him, pointing out that 'half a million migrants from the poorest class of India are indebted to the industry for a much more liberal supply of food than they could have expected from their own homes'. The Indian National Congress honoured Cotton with the presidentship of the party in 1904.

104 | THE HERITAGE OF INDIAN TEA

NAHORTOLI TEA ESTATE

Managing from the heart: glimpses of the comfortable lives led by tea workers and their dependants. *Top left:* A workers' colony. *Top right:* A worker's house. *Below:* A worker's family watching TV.

Towards a Better Life

Living conditions began to improve over time in tandem with the upswing in the fortunes of the tea industry. The Assam Labour Enquiry Committee of 1921–2 reported, 'most gardens are equipped with an ample supply of medical and surgical appliances, and on large estates the expenditure on hospitals and medical stores is a very considerable item ... many hospitals in the Assam valley fulfil all modern requirements and leave nothing to be desired'. In 1931, the Royal Commission on Labour appointed by the British government claimed that the tea plantations had already introduced voluntary welfare measures and planters were increasing the minimum wages. However, the overall conditions of tea labourers were not as good as was claimed.

Jawaharlal Nehru visited some tea gardens, and wrote prior to Independence: 'I must say that most of these gardens in the upper valley looked clean and efficient, more so than the gardens of Ceylon. But the shine of the shoe is not the test of its fit or the comfort it gives to the wearer. I suppose the garden labourers are not looked upon as the wearers of the shoe in question. But I was more interested in them than in the quality of the tea produced or the dividends of the companies.'

In 1946, the Labour Investigation Committee stated that because of the war, wages had not kept pace with living costs. It recommended improvements in working and living conditions. After Independence, the Indian government set up the Industrial Committee on Plantations to frame a labour code to regulate the employment conditions of workers. Based on its recommendations, the Plantations Labour Act was enacted on 1 September 1954.

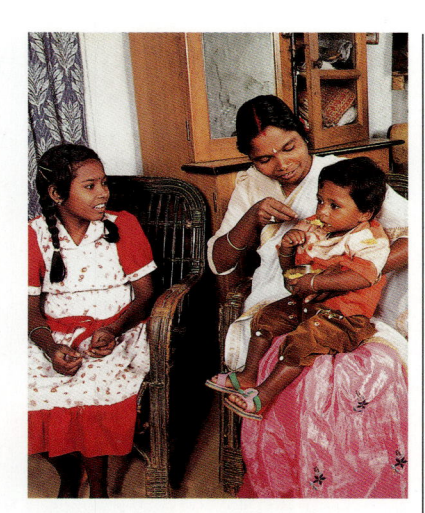

A tea worker in a happy frame of mind feeding her child.

Today, tea garden workers, both permanent and temporary, number 0.6 m. in Assam alone, 0.3 m. in West Bengal, 0.02 m. in the rest of north India, and another 0.25 m. in south India. The tea industry cares for the workers and their families from generation to generation. In Assam alone it pays Rs 1.65 bn a year as cash wages; Rs 160 m. towards plucking incentives; Rs 627 m. as provident fund, gratuity, earned leave wages, sick leave, and bonus; and Rs 624 m. towards food subsidy, firewood, housing, medical facilities, dry tea, protective clothing, and entertainment facilities. The Plantations Labour Act requires estates employing over a thousand workers to maintain a hospital, and a few of these are examples of excellence. The smaller estates have group hospitals. The infant mortality rate, death rate, and maternity death rate in the gardens of Assam are much lower than the national average. Appreciating the industry's role in Assam, Tarun Gogoi said, 'It's a labour-intensive industry and has played a significant part in the welfare and economy of the state. Even so, there is still a lot of scope for improvement in the working conditions of the labourers employed.'

The southern Indian tea industry provides clean, three-room apartments to its workers equipped with gas stoves, television sets, medical care, education for children, and other facilities. With the spread of education, tea workers' children are now not often keen to work in the tea gardens, migrating instead to urban areas to work in offices. Some have even obtained employment in tea garden offices, while others have become welfare officers, assistant managers, and managers.

The United Planters' Association of Southern India formulated a voluntary health package called the Comprehensive Labour Welfare Scheme about a decade and a half ago. It covers all aspects of total health care for plantation workers. The birth rate in the estates registered a drop from 42 per 1000 population to 21, while the infant mortality rate declined from 119 per 1000 live births to 48.

The United Planters' Association of Southern India reports that no medical facility is beyond a distance of 2 km from the workplace. Most estates have an ambulance service that links up with the garden dispensary. The principal problem today is poor diet and ignorance. About 40 to 55 per cent of the people approach hospitals for treatment of respiratory ailments; another 18 to 25 per cent suffer from waterborne stomach ailments. Tata Tea Ltd was the first tea company to promote the smokeless chullah amongst its women workers. Trees to provide firewood for women are grown on the company's estates. In estates where potable water has been made available, the ratio of stomach ailments has declined. Hospital births are encouraged. Family welfare programmes have taught the labourers to reduce the size of their families. Immunization coverage is 100 per cent in most gardens. Both birth and death rates and maternal mortality rates are lower than the national average.

Protective clothing is provided to workers engaged in spraying operations. Tata Tea Ltd has screened women workers for cervical cancer in its Kerala estates and helped them to get treatment. Health and safety is at the top of the Unilever agenda, and as a result no accidents have occurred in their factories. The tea industry continues to subsidize food-grains supplied to workers at rates prevalent as far back as 1951, the price charged being approximately 50 paise per kg of rice and wheat.

The Plantations Labour Act requires every estate where 50 or more women are employed to have a crèche. Almost all estates have crèches, and primary schools for the very young. Estates usually provide transport to children who have to travel to school. Many tea companies have opened special schools for handicapped children, and vocational centres where they can be trained to earn an income. For adults, there are literacy centres. Vocational training courses offer employment options to workers' children.

Canteens and recreation facilities are provided. The United Planters' Association of Southern India, for instance, reports that Ladies' Clubs have been set up for women workers. Free housing, equipped with individual toilets, is provided to workers, and surplus land is being given to them for growing food-grains. Every worker's home boasts a tiny plot where vegetables can be grown or poultry raised. Link workers spread health messages and ensure that latrines and drains are clean. Demonstrations of the preparation of food from local crops has improved nutritional standards. Unfortunately, complete details of the welfare activities of gardens are not available with the association. The need for improvement however remains and not all the gardens have all these facilities.

Over half the cost of production constitutes wages and welfare expenses. However, unless wages are related to productivity, the industry will not be able to sustain such high expenditure. The tea estates and trade unions have to step in to save workers from liquor consumption as it has destroyed the social fabric of the tea workers' lives.

Top: Adding more to life: a concern for tea workers' children. Other gardens have to catch up to match these standards.

Following spread: Pluckers holding long bamboo staves in southern India. These staves, sometimes used in gardens, are placed vertically at a given height known as the 'marker', indicating the level below which leaves are not to be plucked.

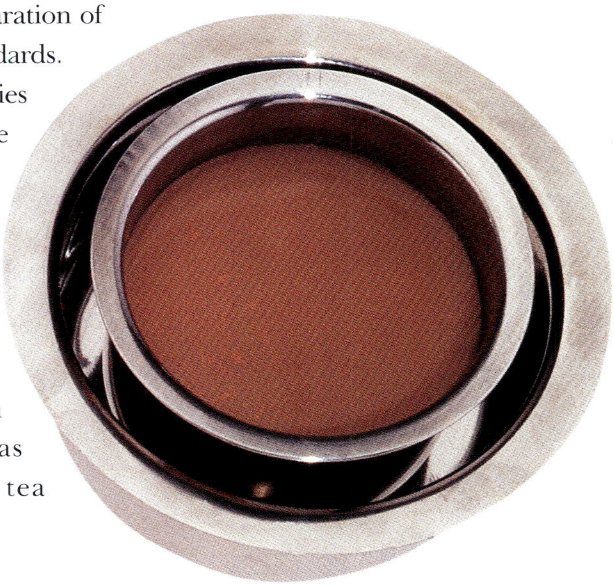

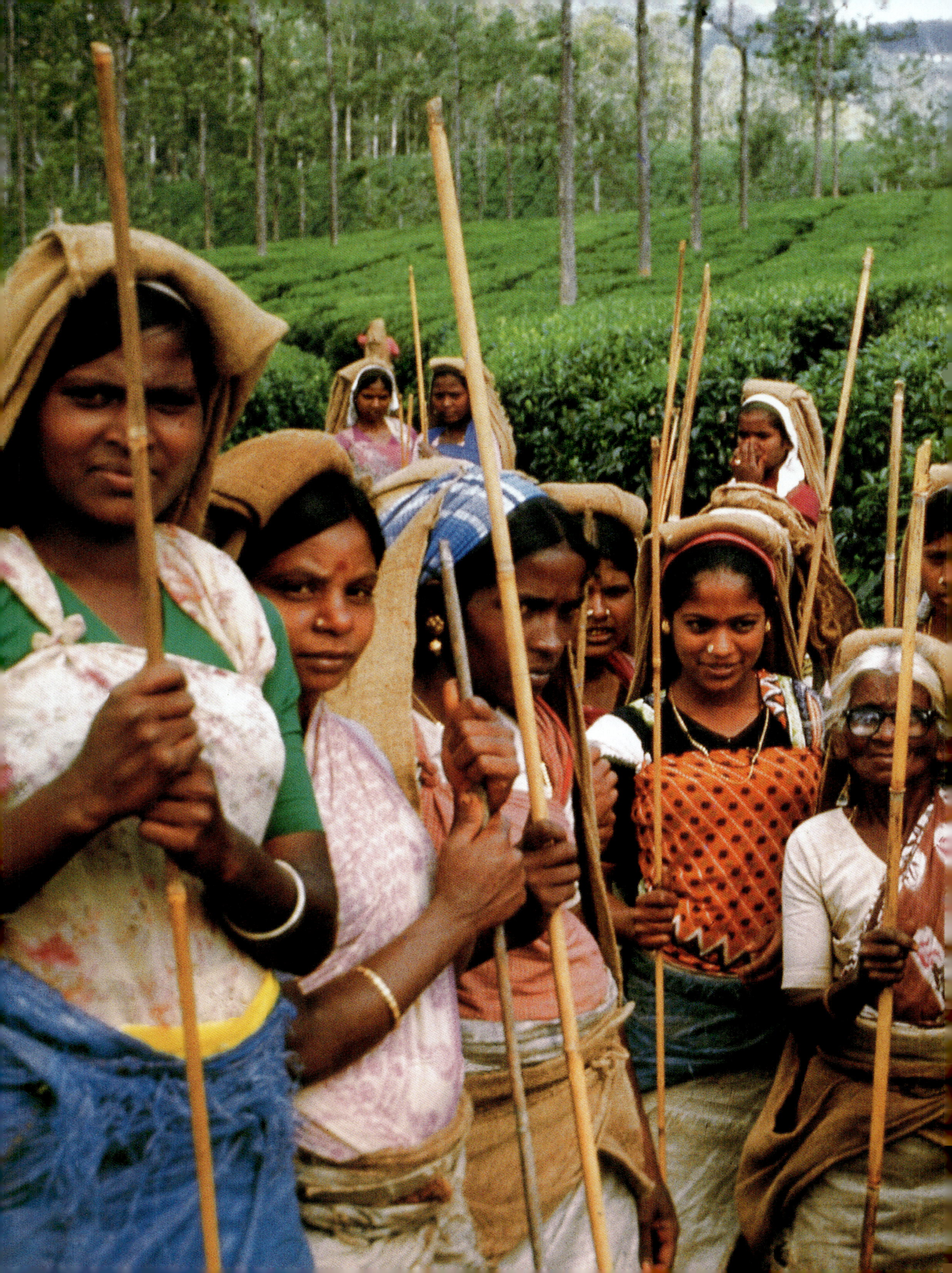

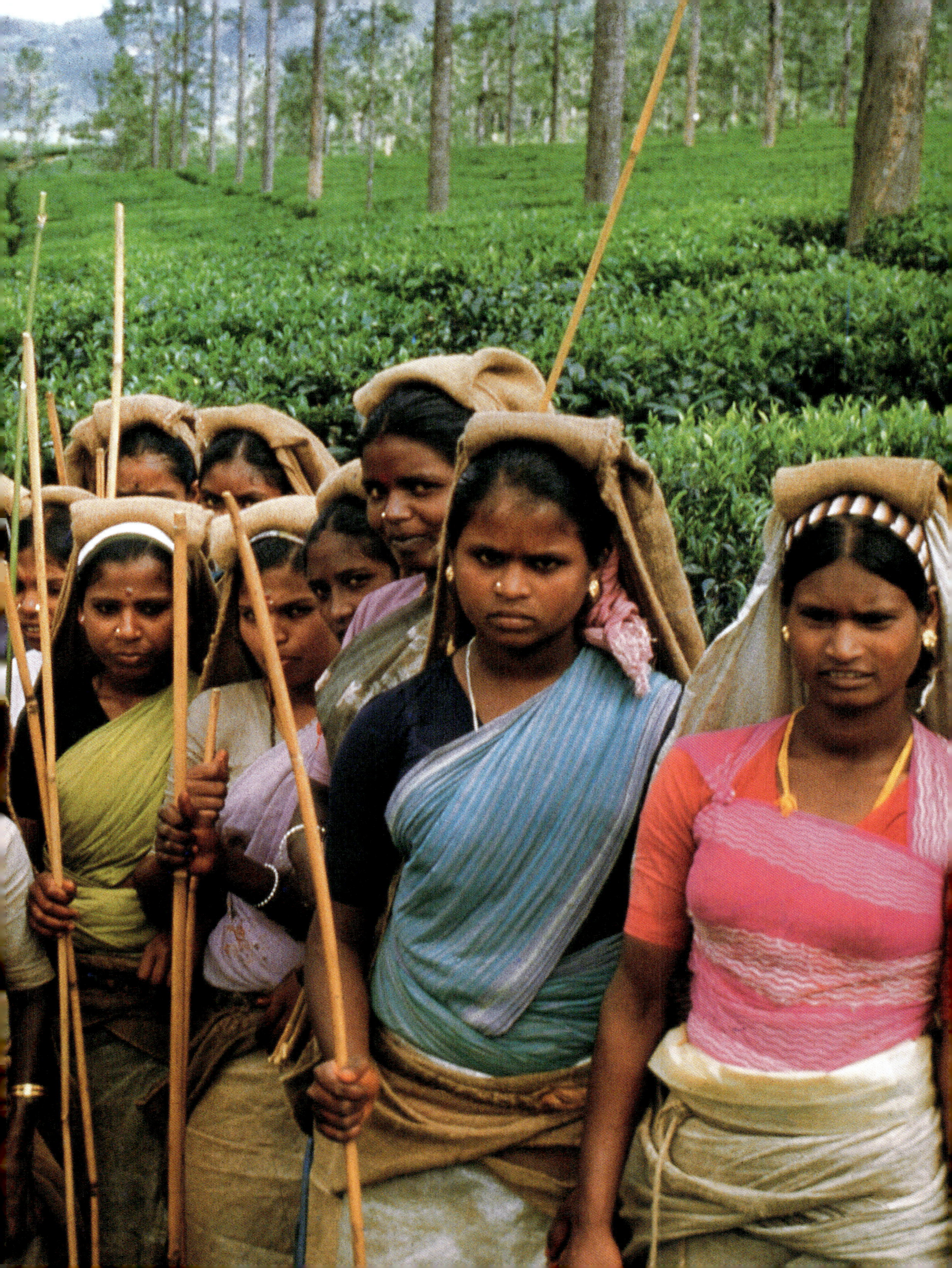

Top left: A woman plucker eagerly awaiting her colleagues' arrival for lunch.
Top right: In tune with nature: a lush green tea garden in Assam. Shade trees and pluckers always present a pretty sight. Shade trees are still considered necessary, and protect the tea bushes from intense sunlight.

Organized Representation

Nearly every worker belongs to a trade union and enjoys the benefit of virtually all the labour laws that cover industrial workers. Unions wield power and are well organized. There are four major trade unions in Assam, all affiliated to the Indian National Trade Union Congress. These are the Assam Cha Mazdoor Sangha, Assam Cha Karamchari Sangha, Cachar Cha Shramic Union, and Indian Tea Employees' Union. A few other unions commanding limited membership are affiliated to the Hind Mazdoor Sabha and All India Trade Union Congress. Revision of wage rates and conditions of service are determined through collective bargaining.

Disputes, if any, are settled by the industry through harmonious negotiations with the unstinted cooperation of the trade unions who are themselves believers in the philosophy: 'Prosper and share the prosperity with the workers.' According to M.C. Khandiat, general secretary, Assam Cha Mazdoor Sangha, 'There are a few companies like Magor and Tatas. If you sign any agreement with them, they will definitely execute it and will give good feedback and get the problems sorted out.' A. Bhattacharjee of the

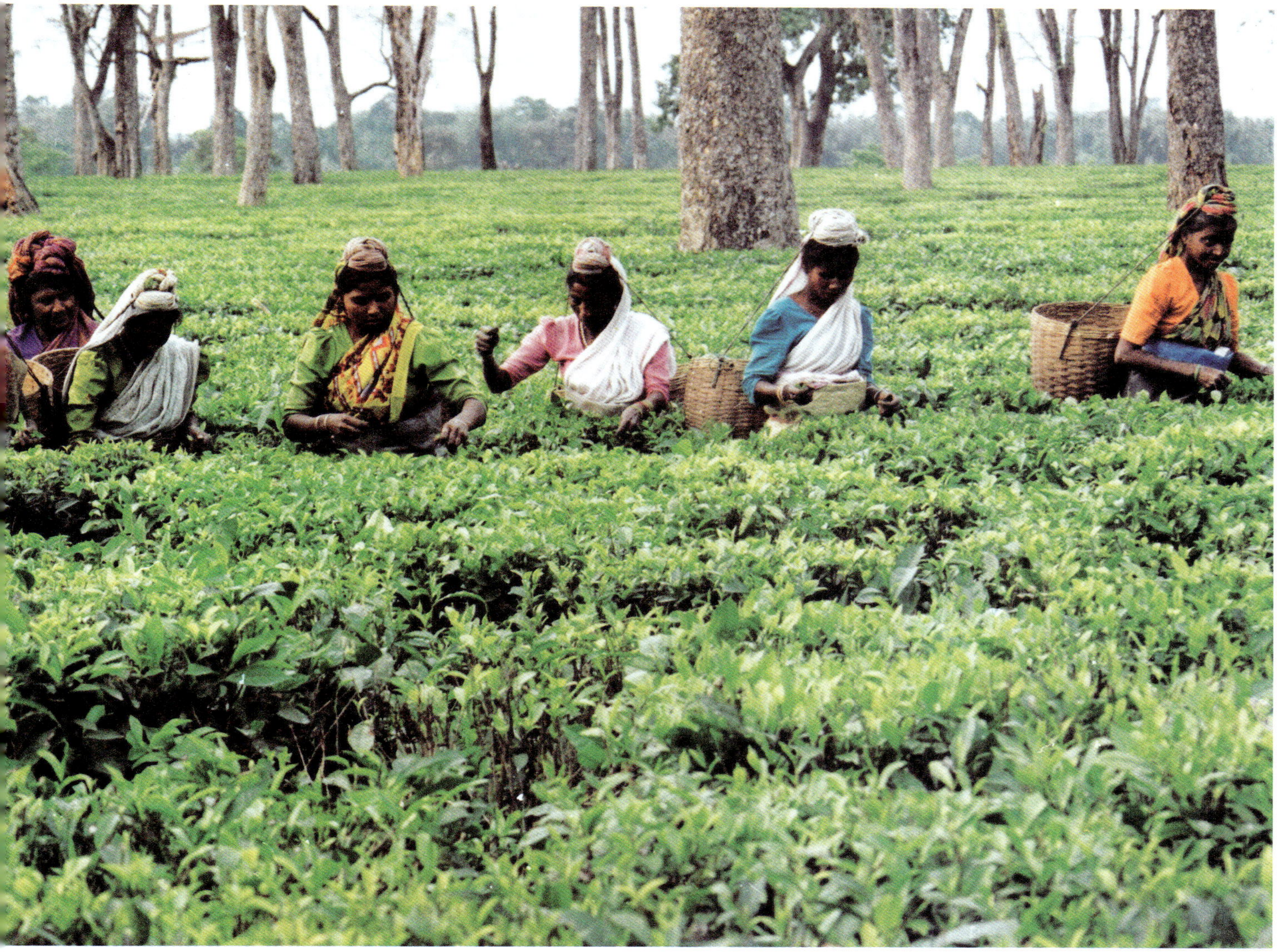

Assam Cha Karamchari Sangh avers: 'We have proper industrial relations with the industry. The overall condition of the labour is good, but much remains to be done and not all gardens have a good record.'

Speaking at the 108th annual general meeting of the Assam Branch Indian Tea Association, its chairman, R.A. Nyss, pointed out, 'So far as labour housing is concerned, although our record is quite enviable, yet we have not been able to provide 100 per cent standard *pucca* houses everywhere along with the attendant facilities'. P.K. Bhattacharjee accepts it is unfortunate that there are still a few gardens that are not fulfilling statutory obligations. This brings a bad name to the industry.

'We always advise our members to properly implement labour welfare legislation. If there is any violation or a case of persecution of a manager for pursuing welfare measures rather than his defence, we invariably advise him to go ahead and implement them. We regularly organize conferences and seminars to motivate planters to put better labour welfare measures into place,' explains Robin Borthakur, secretary, Assam Branch Indian Tea Association. In the opinion of V.K. Goenka, chairman, Warren Tea: 'We must

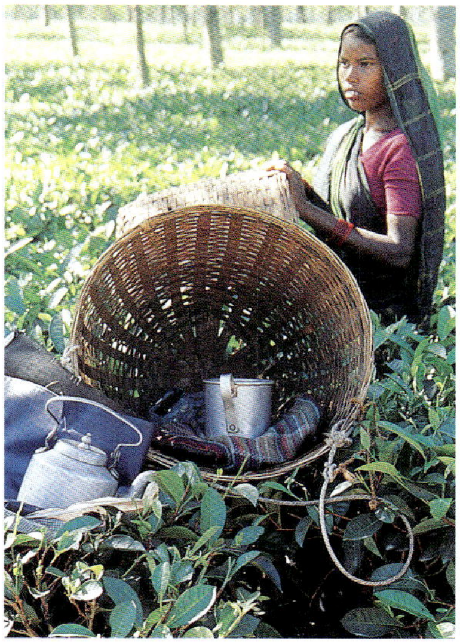

An aluminium mug is an essential part of a tea worker's kit, used for drinking *laal chai* and water: a plucker during a lunch break with a basket, mug, and kettle.

understand that a happy workforce is essential for the improvement of the industry. To this end we have to plough back a substantial part of our earnings to create a good working environment in the gardens.'

Today, descendants of the labourers who came from Orissa, Bihar, Madhya Pradesh, and Andhra Pradesh constitute an important segment of the population of the state and are known as tea tribes. Barki Prasad Telenga, Rameshwar Dhanowar, Dileshwar Tanti, Chatragopal Karmakar, all former labour ministers, A.P. Sarwan, a former chief secretary of Assam, and Paban Singh Ghatowar, former union minister of state, are members of these. The tea tribes vote and are represented in the state assembly and in parliament.

Although plantation workers are covered by a plethora of legislations enacted by central and state governments covering all aspects relating to their welfare, the Indian tea industry still provides some non-statutory benefits to the plantation workers, such as collective bargaining and the existence of industry-wide settlements which cover not only wages but the entire gamut of service conditions. In the south, the industry enjoys a good rapport with the labour unions. Despite the presence of a multi-union set-up, all the unions have been cooperative on all industry-wide issues. Peter Mathias, chairman, Karnataka Planters' Association, says, 'In a recent crisis, the tea workers came forward voluntarily to support the industry. They have shown solidarity with the industry which is quite encouraging.'

The Indian tea industry has a second dimension aside from being the producer of a commodity, as the generator of a unique culture reflected in the tea estates. Right from the outset the tea industry welcomed workers' families on the estates, and workers came from different parts of the country. Although the people of the tea gardens are somewhat isolated, they have forged bonds with the local people in their hinterland. Today, after a long process of living together, intermarrying, and sharing customs and festivals, cultural integration has been almost total. Be it the tribal Jhumur dance or the Assamese Bihu festival, all the workers and planters join in as one large intercultural mix.

Recently, the government of India's Ministry of Labour published a pamphlet entitled '20-point Programme: Progress of Implementation', which listed the welfare measures necessary and the progress made in their implementation. The government said that it had implemented four points while the tea industry had implemented all the twenty welfare measures and gone beyond them. This testifies that the tea industry has made the workers its partners in progress, equitably sharing profits with them.

Top and below: A large number of tea gardens demonstrate an equal concern for the entertainment of the workforce.

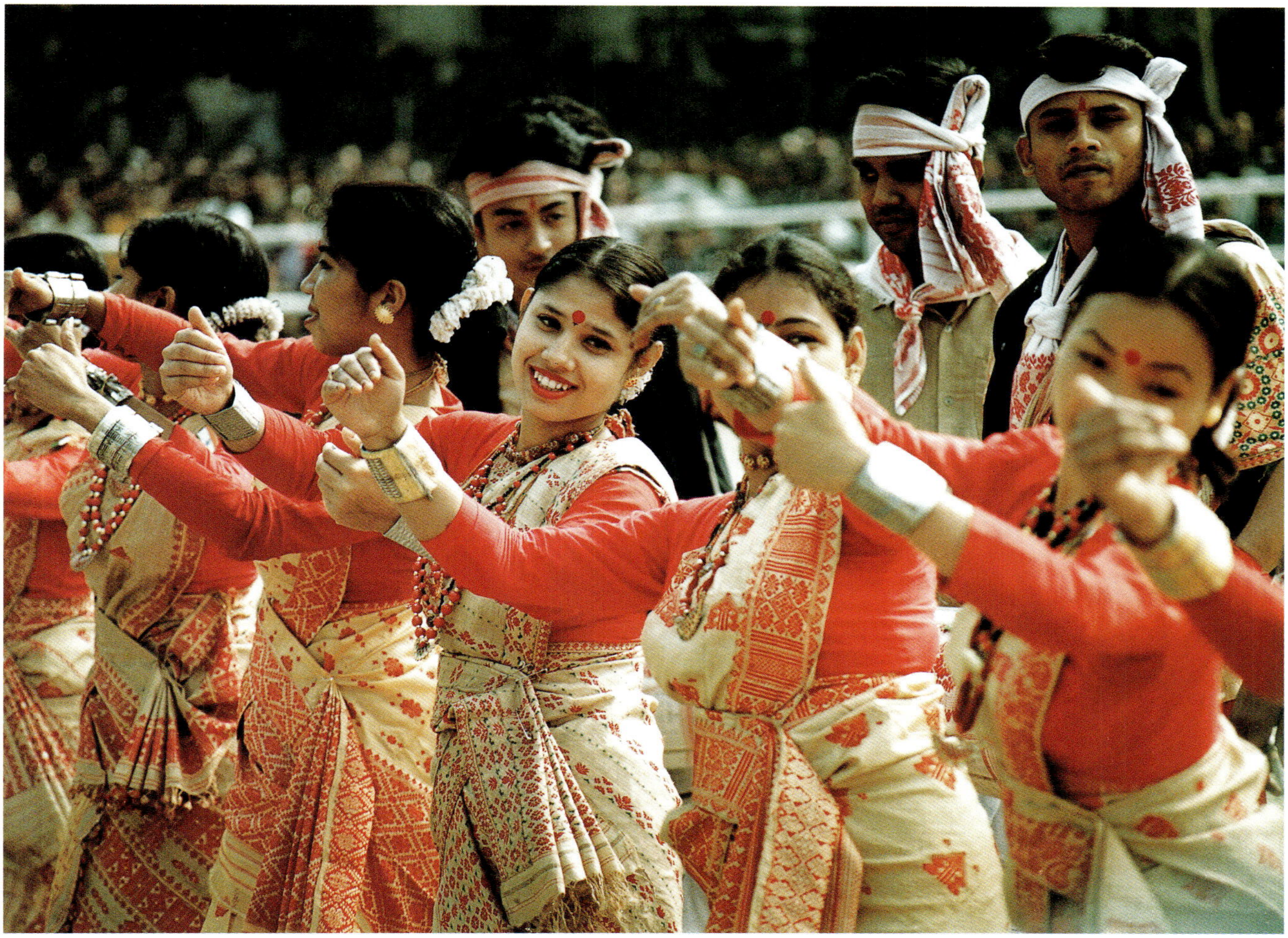

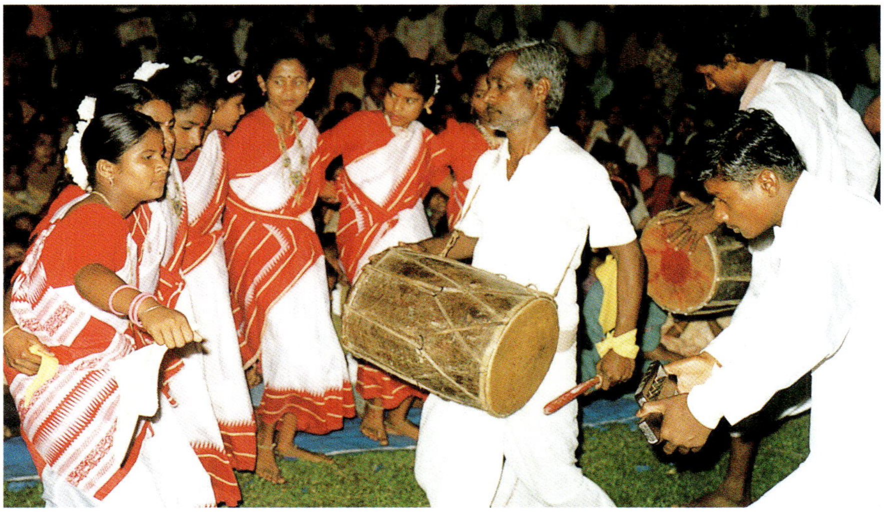

Top and below: Colours of life: festivals are an integral part of Indian culture. Men and women, in vibrant attire, participate in Bihu, an Assamese folk dance, and Jhumur, a tribal folk dance. These traditional dances are promoted by most gardens with an annual cultural programme.

The joys of work: picking fresh tea leaves and buds in Assam.

Insurgence to Resurgence

The tea industry's significance in the Indian economy is immense. The hard numbers are mind-boggling. Today, India has approximately 38,000 tea gardens spread over 435,000 ha. Assam has become the largest tea-producing area in the world and Guwahati is the world's largest CTC tea auction centre. South India's productivity, which at 2300 kg per ha is even higher than that of Kenya, is the highest in the country. Some estates have even achieved over 5000 kg tea per hectare per year. Also, the improvement in the yield has been much more rapid in the south.

The Indian tea crop was 5 m. kg in 1905, and by 1998 production had increased to 870 m. kg. Due to adverse climatic conditions in 1999, the output dropped to 806 m. kg. In 1999, the consumption and export of Indian tea was 638 m. kg and 190 m. kg respectively. In 2000, India produced 835 m. kg tea and by 2001 production had increased to 855 m. kg, and domestic consumption is expected to rise to 673 m. kg, up from 653 m. kg last year. In 2001, tea export is expected to rise 7 per cent to 215 m. kg from 201 m. kg in 2000. Since Independence, production has grown over 190 per cent while the land area has only increased by 38 per cent. India's share in the world tea market has fallen from 45 per cent in 1951 to around 28 per cent today. In the eighties, tea was one of India's largest foreign exchange earners; in the mid-nineties, it accounted for only 1.2 per cent of export earnings.

The tea plantations, accounting for 8 per cent of the total cultivable land, are estimated to contribute 2 per cent of the national agricultural income. Tea supports over 2 per cent of the Indian population. Unlike some of the other export-oriented industries, it has few import requirements.

The gentle aroma of Indian tea signals the start of another day around the world. Tea, however, is not just another habit but a Rs 60 bn plantation industry equivalent to 0.5 per cent of the gross domestic product. Tea is also a major source of revenue for the central and state governments. The annual contribution to taxes and duties is approximately Rs 11 bn. The industry contributes approximately Rs 20 bn in foreign exchange from exports to over 75 countries. The contribution of the tea industry to the national exchequer is thus significant and its impact multi-dimensional, bringing remote areas into the mainstream of development.

The industry generates income and livelihood for nearly 20 m. people besides its own labour force. This makes it the second largest employer in India. Per hectare, tea directly employs 2.5 persons in comparison to 1.38

persons in the agricultural sector as a whole. The industry generates employment amounting to 700 person-days per year per hectare, which cannot be matched by any other agro-industry. The employment is family-based and therefore, on an average, it supports 5 m. dependants over and above its own workforce.

The vast majority of workers employed on the tea estates belong to the socially and economically deprived sections of society, and a majority of them are women. Tea has the reputation of being the largest employer of women workers in India, and they receive equal pay for equal work.

The tea industry is a model for efficient utilization of land and the application of technology to growing an agricultural crop. Tea also generates employment in various other sectors such as road construction, transportation, warehousing, plywood, aluminium foil, paper, cardboard, fertilizer, coal, iron, and steel. Its role in the socio-economic development of the country has been widely recognized. This is much larger than that of any other industry and yet tea is taxed at a much higher rate than any other commodities of daily use.

Top: The highest quality tea is the product of fine plucking. *Below:* A basket of tea leaves slung over a plucker's back.

PARTNERS IN PROGRESS | 115

Women workers in British India:
Top: Women pluckers waiting for their harvest to be weighed. *Below:* Weighing the leaf and hand sorting.

Women in Tea

The tea industry has always depended on women, given their skill in plucking the leaves from the tea bush. Fifty per cent of the pluckers on a garden are women. They perform some very important tasks with great sincerity and application under very harsh and taxing climatic and environmental conditions.

Employment of women for harvesting tea has evolved as a general practice not only in India but also in other tea-producing countries. Of a total of 1.1 m. workers permanently employed in the industry, women account for about half a million. Plucking tea requires patience, skill, and nimble fingers which race swiftly over two leaves and a bud. The job can be monotonous and back-breaking, but tea pluckers undertake it with dedication and fortitude, working eight-hour shifts beginning at 8 a.m.

A woman plucker has a strenuous working day which begins at 5 a.m. She first collects water for cooking and washing. She makes tea/lunch for the household by 6.30 a.m., bathes the children and readies them for school, does her morning chores like cleaning the house, feeding the pets, and by 8.00 a.m. she is in the garden for plucking. Normally, by the time she returns, it is 4.30 p.m. She washes the family's dirty clothes, locks up the cow in its shed, and then settles down to cook the evening meal for the family. By the time dinner is over and she has washed the dishes, it is 9.00 p.m. By then she is too exhausted to do anything other than fall asleep instantly for tomorrow is yet another very strenuous day.

Pluckers are organized into groups under a sirdar. During the harvesting season they put in longer hours of work so that they can earn an incentive wage called a *ticca*. Most pluckers are Adivasis from Bengal, Orissa, and Madhya Pradesh. The social welfare programmes undertaken by their employers are gradually changing their low status within their community. The wives of tea planters today ensure there is no neglect of the diseased and the distressed. They take personal care of children in the crèches and pre-primary schools, patients in hospitals, and homes for the disabled. They are engaged in helping the blind and the spastic community to become self-reliant. The tea ladies also demonstrate a concern for the welfare of the local people.

Tea society is heterogeneous and pluckers have economic independence: they are members of trade unions, and some of them have even become trade union leaders. In earlier times, women were mostly employed as tea pluckers, but now also work as managers, tea tasters, supervisors, and union leaders. Tata Tea Ltd recruited seven women assistant managers some years ago. Their success has paved the way for others. M.H. Ashraff, former executive director, Tata Tea Ltd, says : 'The plantation industry was the last bastion of male chauvinism so far as managerial staff were concerned. We decided that we would give an equal opportunity to girls for the post of estate assistant managers ... we are not at all surprised to find that they have fitted in perfectly with plantation life and have been able to carry out their duties as efficiently as their male counterparts.'

The new crop of managers, such as Anshu Meshack, Sanskriti Dwivedi, and Babini Uthapa are undaunted by their long hours of work and their isolated lifestyle. Riding up steep slopes on flimsy bikes, they instruct workers and stop by to chat with them. The job profile includes supervision, organization of workers' schedules, labour management, field rounds, and factory duties. Women managers bring a different kind of empathy to the job. Productivity has increased too. Daisy Brahmalahan is posted at Majuli Tea Estate in the heart of Bodoland. Last year, the estate posted a record production of 50,000 kg in a single day.

The Tata Administrative Services has a fair sprinkling of women in the tea business. Abanti Sankaranarayanan is brand manager of Tata Tea Ltd (north India plantation division); Indrani Ghosh is a taster checking tea leaves for their freshness, body, and strength; and there is Mansweta Sengupta, a deputy manager with the company's community development and social welfare programme.

Mahatma Gandhi believed that women were unaware of their own power, but the Indian tea industry realized their potential and provided a good environment with plenty of opportunities: *Top left:* Pluckers packing freshly picked leaves into nylon bags. *Top right:* During a fine plucking, two leaves and a bud are harvested. *Below left:* The joy of communion: Daisy Brahmalahan, assistant manager, with a plucker. *Below right:* Indrani Ghosh, tea taster.

PARTNERS IN PROGRESS | 117

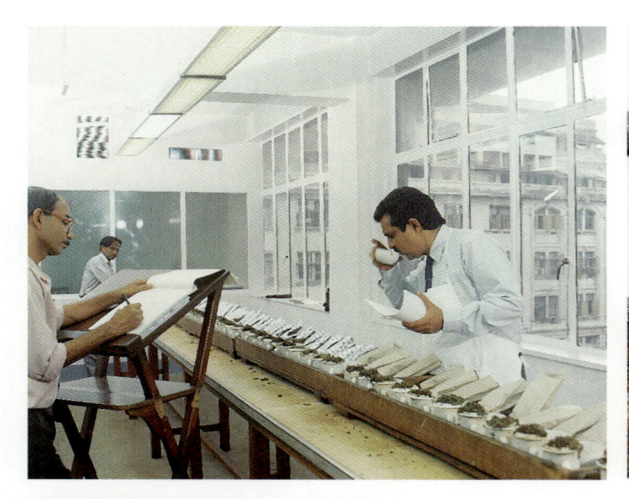

Top left, right and below: Tea tasters at work. A single sip is sufficient to convey where the tea has been grown, the way it was plucked, manufactured, and its market worth.

Facing page: Tea and serious conversation go hand in hand in a setting of extreme opulence at Samode Palace, Jaipur.

Following spread: Together we can achieve! Pluckers at work in a picturesque garden with rich vegetation in the Assam.

The Tea Taster

The tea taster has specialized skills and senses developed over the years which make it possible for him to trace the antecedents of tea leaves, the garden they come from, the conditions in which they were plucked, and the like. He must be equipped with expertise in the various processes of tea manufacture and the preferences and biases of the world tea market. He requires an encyclopaedic palate-memory and experience, and a long association with a wide range of teas. The tea taster is thus the key agent who helps the producer to improve the quality of the tea he grows.

A taster works in a room that is well lit but shielded from sunlight and shadow. Samples of tea are brewed. A quarter *tola* of each sample is infused in four ounces of boiling water for five or six minutes, depending on the taster's preference. The liquor is then poured out into clean porcelain cups so that its colour can be observed, and often milk is added to evaluate the colour more accurately. The taster takes a spoonful of the liquor and rolls it around in his mouth for a few seconds, and then spits it out. During this brief exercise he is able to evaluate its flavour, briskness, strengths and defects. A tea taster generally tastes up to a 1000 cups a day.

Strength and flavour are prerequisites of a good tea. These come from the thickness, briskness, and pungency of the tea liquor. Assam tea is renowned for the high level of all these qualities. The pungency of the flavour depends on the soil and the area where it has been grown, and a tea taster is able to distinguish this.

The palate of the taster, who is familiar with the preferences of the various markets, determines the price of a particular consignment of tea. Today, there is no substitute for a tea taster, and no computer can serve as a substitute for the taster's palate.

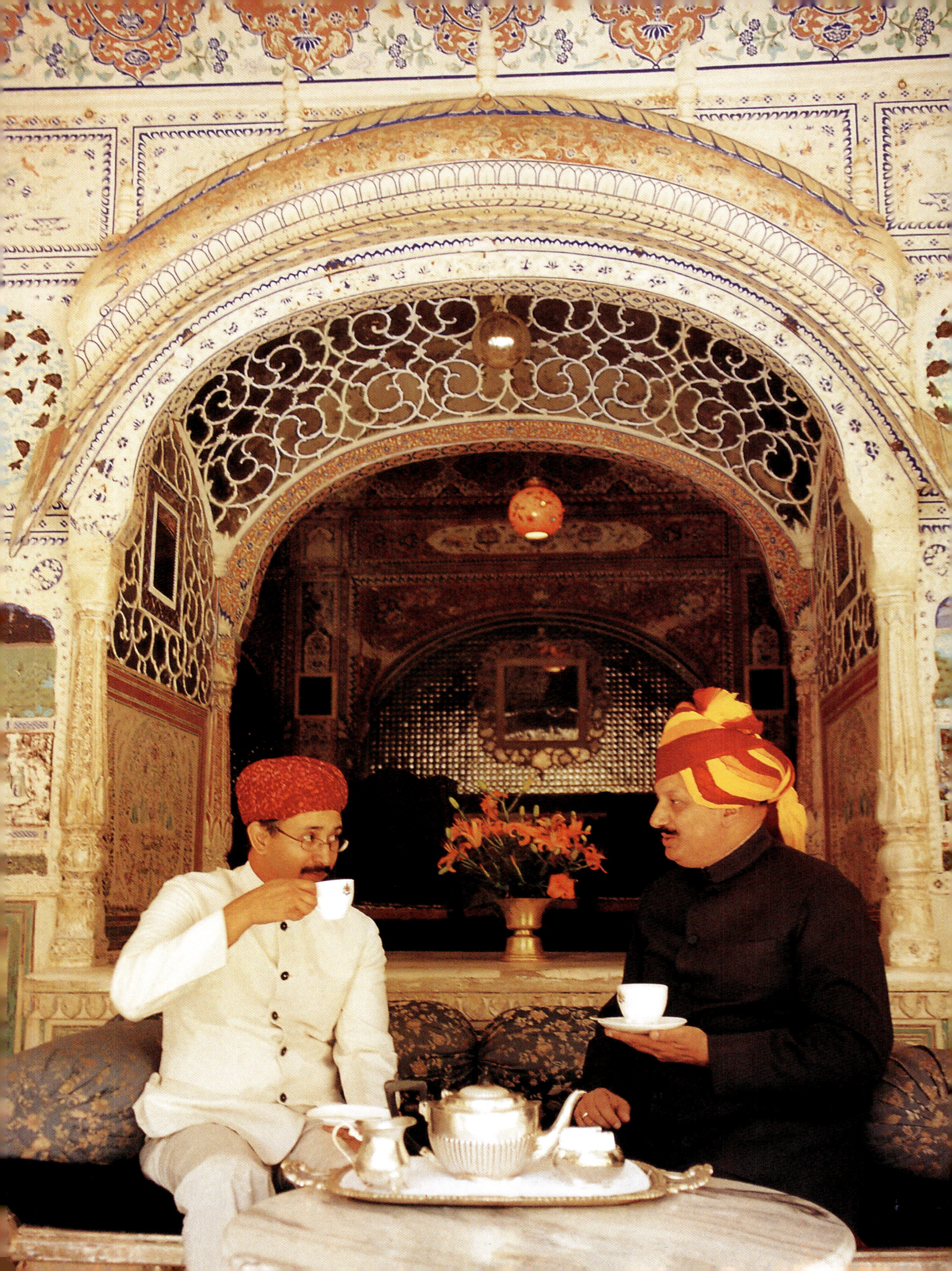

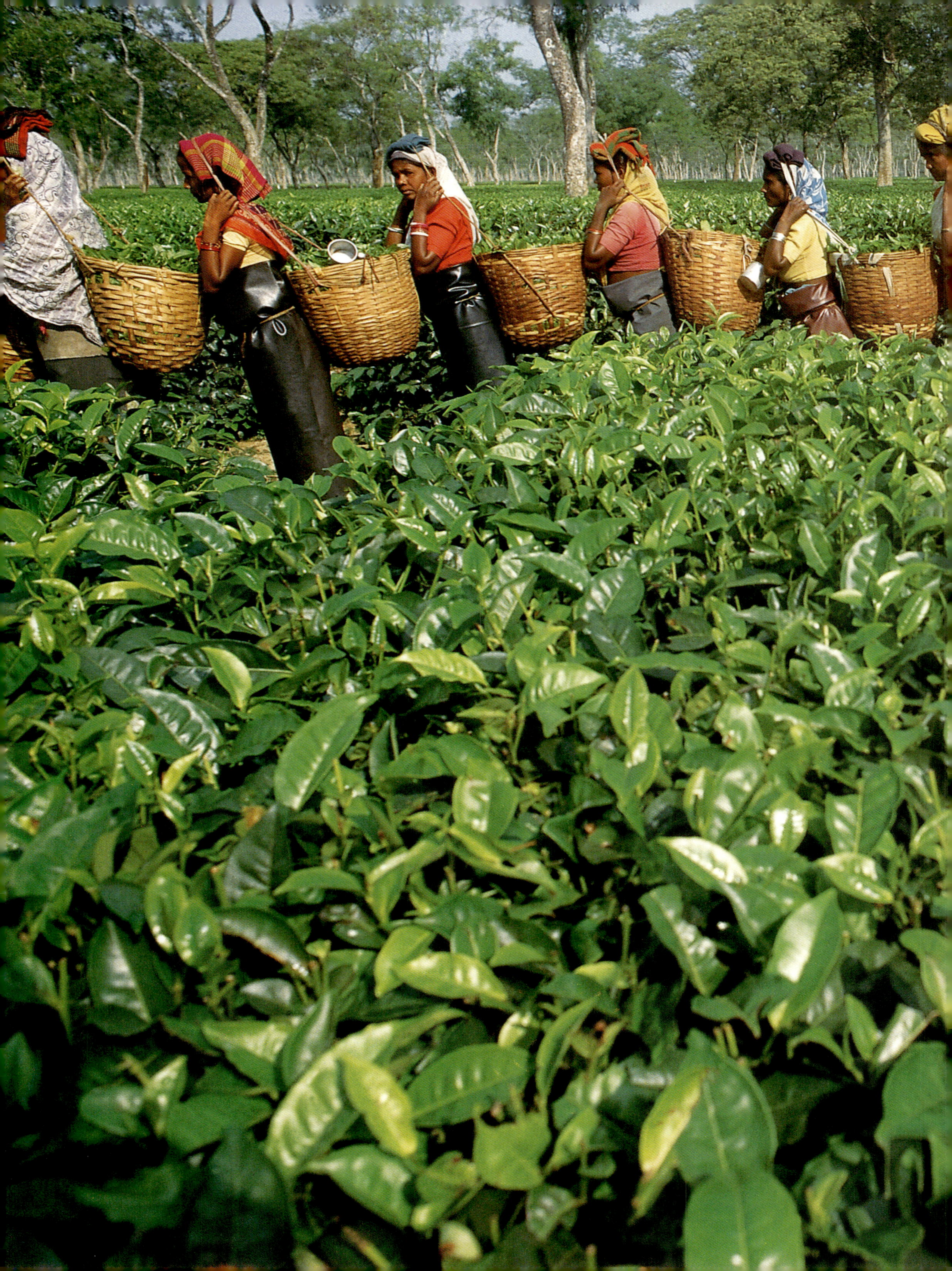

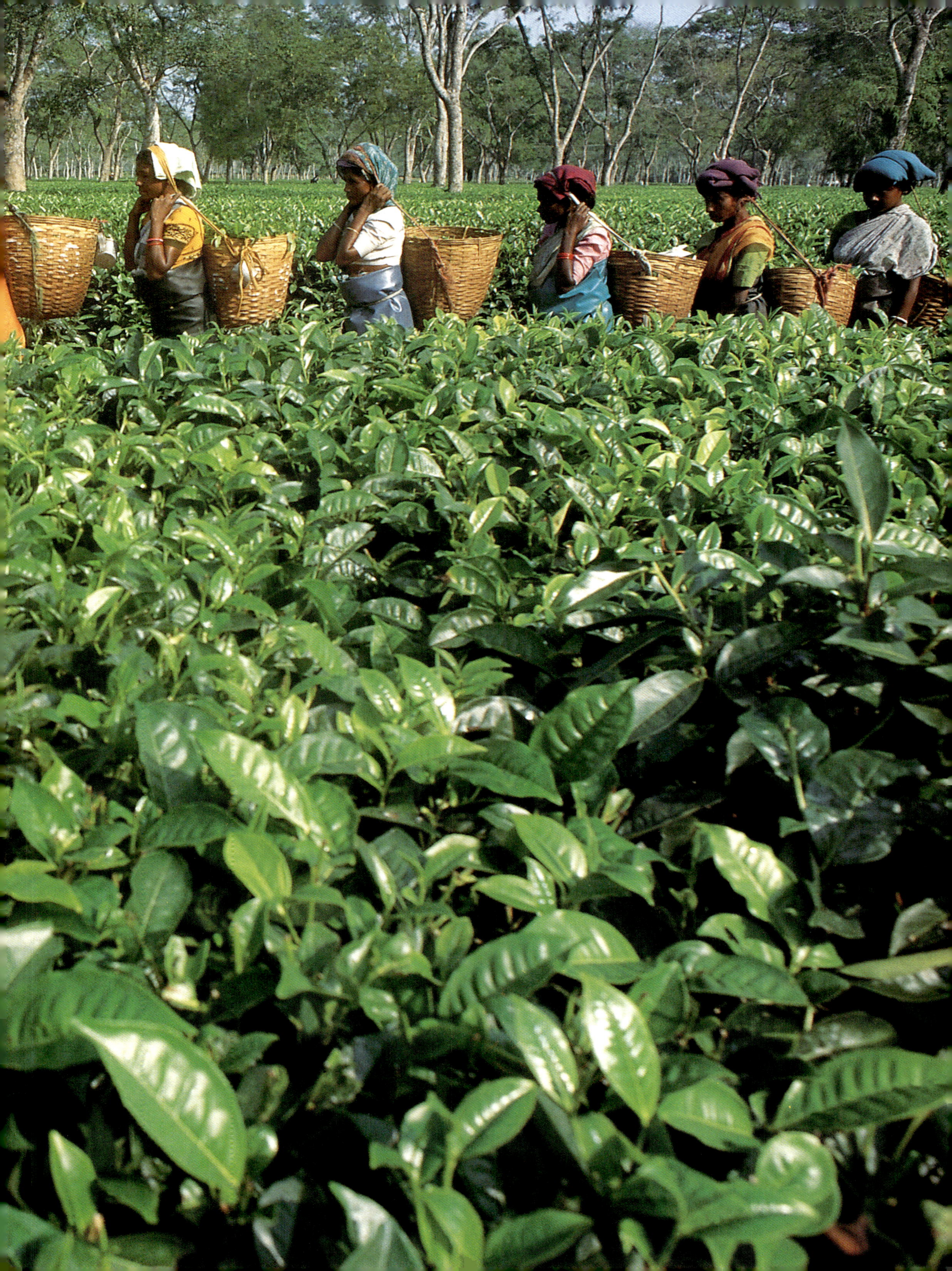

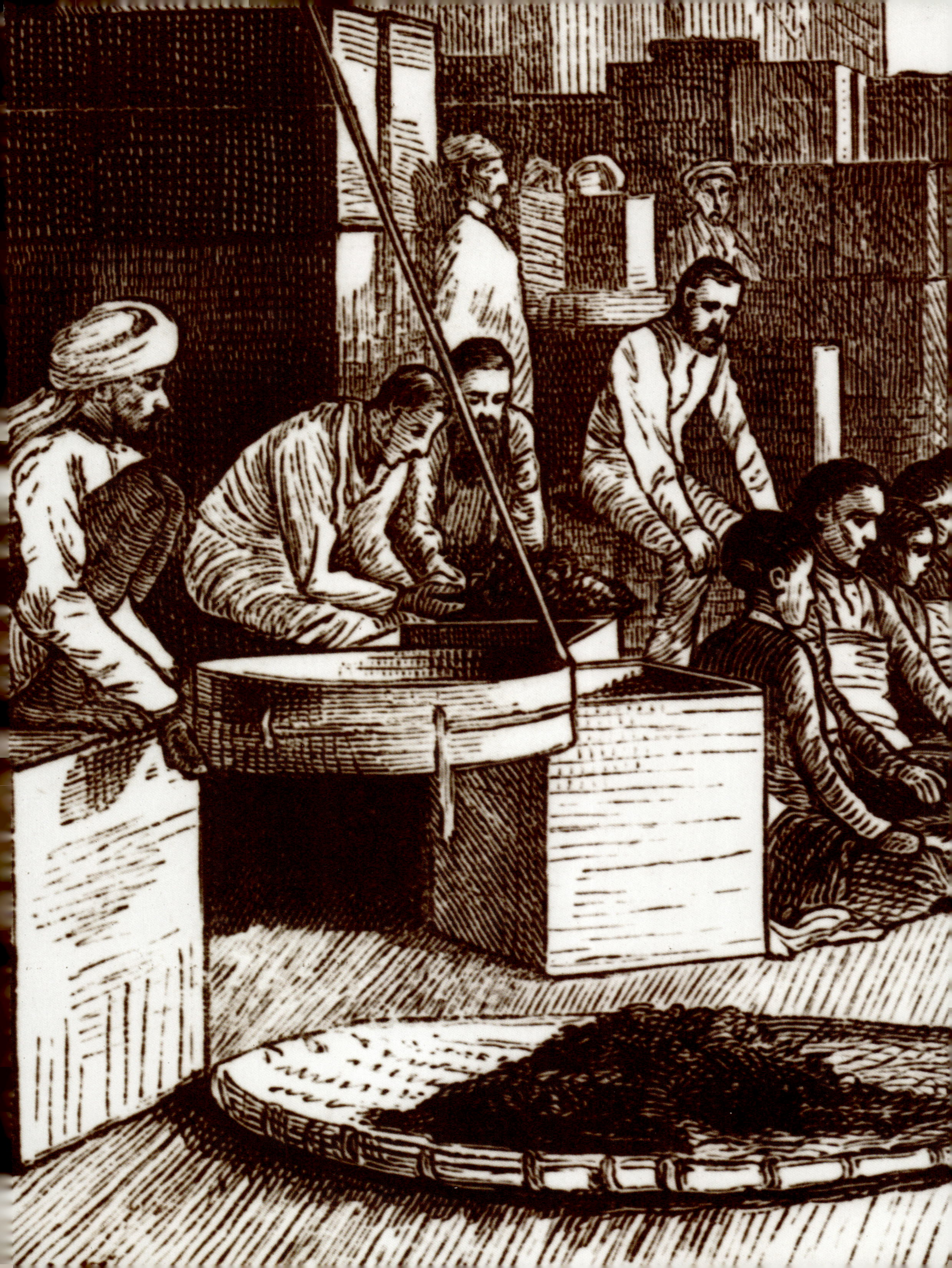

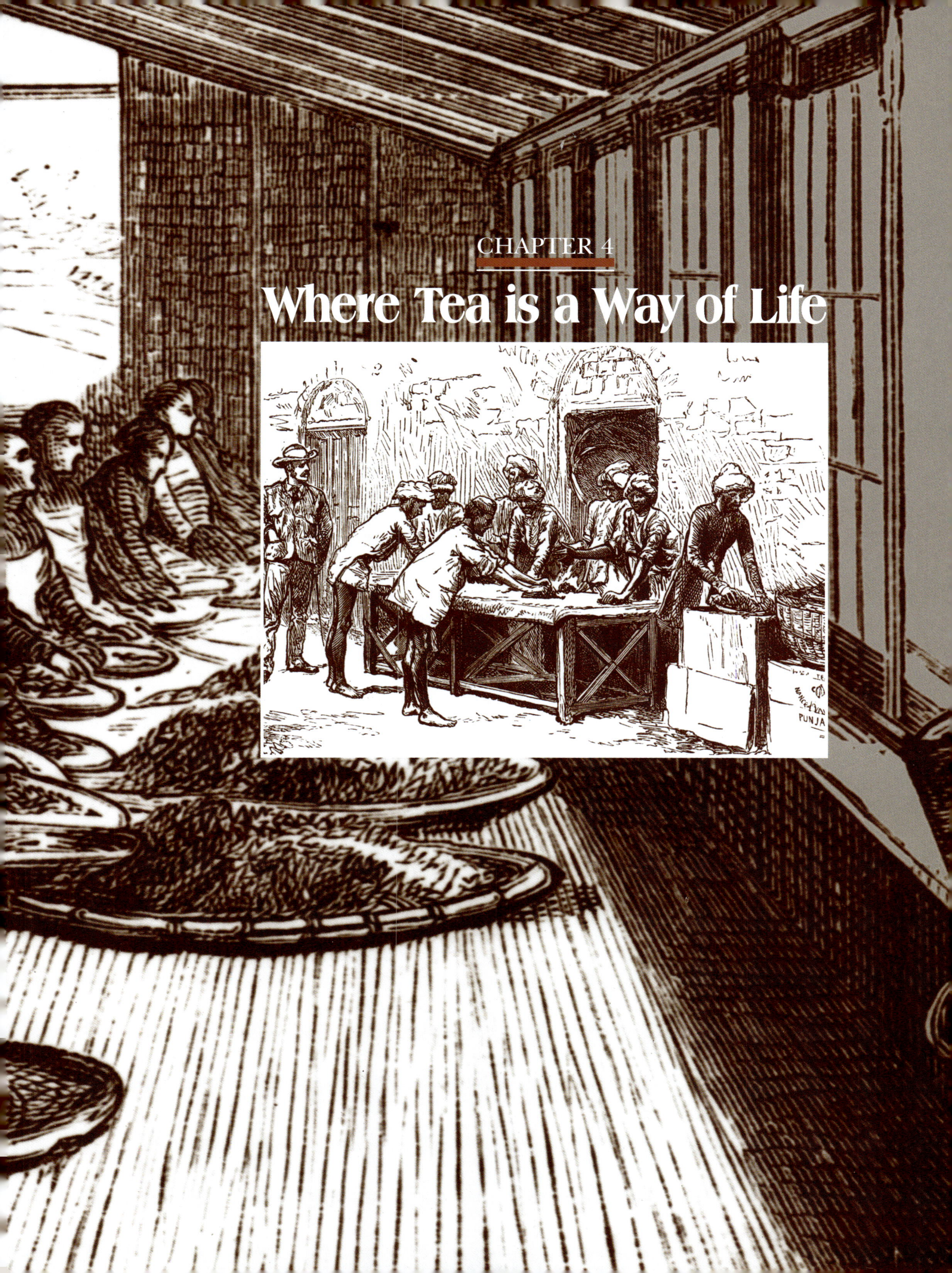

CHAPTER 4

Where Tea is a Way of Life

art of the élite group of the largest producers of the best-quality tea on the planet, and the largest exporters of some of the finest teas in the world, the Williamson Magor group's story is indeed unique. With 133 years of rich experience in the tea business, the group is today looked upon as much more than just a business enterprise. It is acknowledged as a long-standing Indian institution; a corporate role model embodying steadfast commitment to quality and a profound humanitarian concern.

The story of the Williamson Magor group, with its rich cast of characters, its ups and downs, its triumphs and tragedies, is a microcosm of the story of tea in Assam and indeed in the country as a whole. The group has been a partner in the country's progress for over a century now. When India wanted to extend her hospitality internationally, it came forward to offer the best quality tea. Personifying the cup that cheers, Williamson Magor's is an invigorating tale replete with romance and human warmth.

A Memorable Heritage

The Williamson Magor story began in 1868 when two young and enterprising Englishmen, James Hay Williamson and Richard Manuel Blamey Magor, got together at the Great Eastern Hotel in Calcutta and signed a partnership deed in April 1869. Over the following few decades, while remaining almost exclusively in the hands of the Williamson and Magor families, the company consolidated its position, expanding through mergers. Running the tea estates was left to the visiting agent, and the partners generally came to India only in winter, for a couple of months, for a leisurely trip around Assam.

A period of consolidation of Williamson Magor's position in the tea world began with the recruitment of young blood: O.J. Roy and Patrick Hay Williamson. O.J. Roy was the son of James E. Roy of Duncan Macneill who had been on friendly terms with Stephen Anderson for many years. Patrick Hay Williamson was the son of R.L. Williamson and, consequently, the grandson of James Hay Williamson, one of the founders of Williamson Magor.

Patrick Hay Williamson was widely known as Pat Williamson, and his stylish and lavish lifestyle earned him the sobriquet 'the last of the nabobs'. His business acumen was worthy of emulation. Pat Williamson played a memorable role in helping the Assamese tea estates during the Chinese invasion. On the business side, his greatest achievement was the smooth transition of the British partnership of Williamson Magor into the Indian company of Williamson Magor & Co. Ltd.

Top: A late eighteenth-century painting of a British family in India partaking of afternoon tea.
Middle: J.H. Williamson, R.M.B. Magor
Below: Pat Williamson

Preceding spread: A sketch of tea withering in a factory. *Inset:* Rolling the leaves by hand.

Making Waves

Independence in 1947 ushered in dramatic changes in the tea industry. Industrial giants moved into the large tea estates vacated by their European owners. These Indian entrepreneurs improved the quality and distribution networks by introducing technological changes. More importantly, the managing agency system that had been in vogue during the time of the British, gradually began to come apart in the late fifties and early sixties, and was finally abolished in 1968.

It was a time when fortunes were being made and lost. 'There is a tide in the affairs of men,' Shakespeare pointed out in *Julius Caesar*, 'which if taken at the flood leads to fortune.' One man who was able to ride the wave of success and fortune was B.M. Khaitan, and from the sixties the story of Williamson Magor is inextricably linked with him.

Britishers, who fondly referred to B.M. Khaitan as 'Birju', realized his business acumen in 1954 when he helped Williamson Magor at a critical juncture. Bishnauth Tea Co., Williamson Magor's flagship company, faced the threat of falling into the hands of Balmukund Bajoria who had accumulated a threatening 25 per cent of its shares, one per cent short of a controlling stake. To buy out Balmukund Bajoria required a lot of money which was available neither in London nor in Calcutta. Had Bishnauth been lost, it would have sent the signal that Williamson Magor was not strong enough to protect its company. Birju salvaged the situation, his family providing the money required to be paid to Bajoria.

Birju frequently proved to be the saviour of the firm, and Pat Williamson was instrumental in appointing him managing director on 18 January 1964. After Pat Williamson died in 1965, B.M. Khaitan became the chairman of Williamson Magor in 1966, and with it earned the affectionate appellation BM. The event made news not just as another takeover of an industrial institution of Anglo-India, but also because of the deep underlying friendship and mutual regard shared by two individuals drawn from such completely disparate societies.

BM virtually turned the company around single-handed and soon established a reputation for total integrity and reliability. The managerial staff of the 'British' company were soon to find that their terms of employment and pay packets were improved considerably under the Indian chairman, a trend that has continued to this day. In the coming years, some of the most prestigious British tea companies would seek out BM as a partner or as the preferred choice for sale of their tea estates.

Top: B.M. Khaitan, a living legend, renowned for his sterling contribution to the Indian tea industry and great commitment to social and employee welfare. *Below:* The silent poetry of a cup and ornate teapot symbolizing companionship.

WHERE TEA IS A WAY OF LIFE

Tea, with its lively blend of taste and strength, creates a social bond.

Laying the Foundation

The Khaitans trace their lineage to a distinguished family, originally from Rajasthan. BM, the family patriarch, took over the reins of the company and firmly steered it to impressive growth in partnership with the Magor family based in the UK. During the foundation stone-laying ceremony of Assam Valley School, R.B. Magor remarked that it was unusual for an English family to still be in business in India after so many years, and that this had only been possible because of his happy association with his friend Birju.

From behind the scenes, his wife Shanti, the consummate homemaker who always helps others, evidently played a major part in the eventual success of the Khaitans' association with the Magors. They have three children: Deepak (1955), married to Yashodhara Goenka; Divya (1966), married to Sandeep Jalan; and Aditya (1968), married to Kavita Ruia. Today, members of the Khaitan family are at the helm of the group.

A Time for Cheer

Notwithstanding the growing menace of Naxalism in West Bengal, in December 1968 the management decided to celebrate Williamson Magor's centenary in style, believing it would cheer up everyone; and indeed it did. Williamson Magor invited all the planters in Assam, a number of overseas guests and retired planters with their wives, and for four days the entire Williamson Magor family celebrated with gusto, attending parties, cocktails, and dinners, along with boat cruises, taking pride in what they had created. The centenary also marked the official opening of Four Mangoe Lane, the group's current headquarters. Incidentally, to this day no one knows how the 'e' attached itself to 'Mango'!

Earlier, on 24 January 1966, while laying the foundation stone of the building, R.B. Magor had said, 'It has been a privilege to work with our new *burra* sahib and friend Birju Khaitan, and although he has only recently ascended to the *gaddi* of Williamson Magor & Co. Ltd, all of us who have worked with him realize how singularly lucky and fortunate we are that, after Pat Williamson's untimely death, we have such a worthy chief. He is very well suited to carry on the firm's traditions and to expand our interests in the years to come, and thus ensure our employees' future prosperity.'

Magor's words proved to be prophetic. In the momentous years following the centenary, the group has moved from strength to strength, building upon its traditions and corporate culture, and striving for the prosperity of its employees and shareholders, and the larger community enfolding the tea industry.

Mergers and Acquisitions

Over the years the Williamson Magor group has built up an enviable track record of negotiated mergers, acquisitions, and takeovers. BM says, 'The expansion of our entire business has been from the sixties, as one merger followed another in quick succession, including the merger of all the tea companies. We didn't enter much into greenfield areas except in one or two cases for, during the eighties, mergers were the only way of expanding rapidly because putting up a greenfield project takes not less than seven years.' The merger of Macneill & Barry took place in January 1975 to form Macneill & Magor Ltd, and when many other tea companies merged with it, the company's name was changed to Williamson Magor & Co. Ltd on 12 May 1992.

In 1985, Williamson Magor acquired India Foils Ltd with which it had a close relationship as the latter made the aluminium lining for its tea chests from Alcan, and later sold it to Sterlite industries owned by the Agarwalas. The next major step was to buy the tea companies within the McLeod Russel group with the help of the Gutheries, a prominent tea family in the UK. The McLeod Russel acquisition made Williamson Magor the world's largest private tea producer. However, it was the 1994 acquisition of 51.3 per cent holding of Union Carbide India Ltd, now known as Eveready Industries (India) Ltd, that catapulted the group into the big league and on to the media centre stage. The group dedicated this deal 'To Calcutta with love'.

Williamson Magor celebrated its 125th anniversary in February 1994, organizing a grand function. Befitting its culture, the celebration was a great occasion to cheer up everyone with golf, races, dances, and cocktails in an elegant environment. Lunch was organized at the Calcutta Club for two thousand people. It was not just a group function but was attended by leading personalities from Calcutta. The chief ministers of West Bengal and Assam were also present and blessed the group's prosperity and its inclination to develop their states.

Under the visionary leadership of the Khaitans, the Williamson Magor group has today grown into a large conglomerate. Its track record is marked by a spirit of dynamism, discipline, hard work, and a tenacious and relentless commitment to excellence. With its policy of progressive diversification, it has been pushing back the frontiers in tea, batteries, and information technology. However, notwithstanding the diversification, tea continues to be the group's central concern. Although the group recently disposed of a few of its tea estates in line with its ongoing road map for restructuring, it still owns 29 tea gardens in Assam and the Dooars, and produces nearly 35–8 m. kg of tea per year.

When tired or stressed, a cup of steaming tea refreshes, revives, and relaxes.

Tea is a shared culture irrespective of the individual's social or economic standing.

The boards of Eveready Industries (India) Ltd and Bishnauth Tea Co. Ltd have also agreed to the proposed merger of the two companies. In their opinion, this will consolidate and strengthen the entire tea operations of the two companies under one umbrella and enable the company to expand into the value added packet tea segment where Eveready Industries (India) Ltd has already carved out a niche for itself. The group has emerged as one of the largest producers of tea in the world, exporting over 11 m. kg in the face of stiff international competition, and has earned a very well-deserved international reputation for consistent quality and rock-solid reliability.

Core Values and Culture

The Williamson Magor saga of success is based on certain core values and corporate culture developed by its chairman. Underlying this is a firm belief that teamwork and motivation rooted in fairness are the key to success in business. The group sets benchmarks for itself in these areas and strives to achieve them, believing in seeking the active participation of everyone in decision-making rather than relying on the imposition of central diktats. Quality, productivity, and optimal utilization of resources, human and material, woven around the concept of the welfare of the community as a whole is central to the management's philosophy.

However, it is more than just sound business practices that contribute to its success story. BM's fundamental insight, that tea is not just a commodity but a way of life, has been internalized by the group as a whole. He firmly believes that business cannot sustain growth unless there is perfect harmony among the owners, managers, workers, and the government.

More than most others, the group understands and lives by the principle that, in the final analysis, the quality of tea will always be an eloquent testimony to the well-being and efforts of those associated with its production. With this in view, over the years, the group has consciously associated itself with the life and problems of its employees and the contiguous communities by utilizing its resources, skills, and talent to the development of human resources.

Says Aveek Sarkar, owner of a leading newspaper, the *Telegraph* : 'The group has earned itself a very high reputation because it has involved itself in a lot of welfare activities without seeking personal publicity.' Its penchant for maintaining a low profile has earned for it the confidence of the central and state governments, the public

and private sectors, its share holders, as well as the Reserve Bank of India and other financial institutions.

The Williamson Magor group enjoys a reputation for financial probity. It always tries to keep on optimal terms with the government, financial institutions, banks, creditors, and other stakeholders. D. Pal Choudhary, senior accounts manager, Williamson Magor & Co. Ltd, explains, 'It is group policy that government taxes and dues should be paid honestly as and when they become due'. S.K. Nigam, chairperson, Central Board of Direct Taxes, Department of Revenue, Ministry of Finance, government of India, conferred the Rashtriya Samman on B.M. Khaitan on 7 April 2000 for being one of the highest tax payers during the assessment years 1994–5 to 1998–9.

The group never actively seeks leadership roles in business, social, cultural, and sports organizations; rather, the opportunities come their way in the natural order of things. Whenever anybody from the group has headed an organization or association, it is by consensus or by invitation. Innumerable such examples abound, as in the cases of International Chamber of Commerce, Indian Chamber of Commerce, Bengal Chamber of Commerce and Industry, and the Indian Tea Association. 'All this business of throwing a hat into the ring is alien to Williamson Magor's corporate culture. These jobs come by consensus and invitation; when any member of Williamson Magor moves out and becomes the president of any chamber or association, he does not have just Williamson Magor in mind, he has to think of the entire

Top: Art has no language and yet successfully communicates with its audience: a famous painting entitled *That Unending Story* by Rameshwar Broota, a well known Indian artist. *Below:* The essence is the delicate flavour and aroma.

WHERE TEA IS A WAY OF LIFE | 129

Top left: Ramashankar Singh, the oldest employee of Williamson Magor, says that the tie that binds him to the company is not just the good salary and the manifold facilities, but above all its healthy and motivating environment and the dignified treatment extended to employees. *Top right:* Executives enjoying a cup of tea in a familial atmosphere in the penthouse at Four Mangoe Lane, Calcutta.

industry. His whole focus becomes much wider,' said the late Mumtaz Ahmad, former chairman of the Indian Tea Association.

Corporate culture plays a crucial role in economic performance, and is an important factor in determining the success of a company. The group's corporate culture has been nurtured for decades. Its salient features are fairness in dealing with and excellence in human resources, focus on consistent quality, research and development, and a concept of public welfare.

Williamson Magor is a professionally run conglomerate with a family atmosphere. Its culture includes the following tenets: to run its business as efficiently as possible, be competitive, make enough money not only to plough back into the business but also to serve in equal measure the interests of the various stakeholders, and support cultural, educational, and welfare activities, particularly in the states of Assam and West Bengal. A central pillar in the group's philosophy is employee welfare both in monetary terms and at the human level. A reason why it is able to hold on to its employees is that besides compensating them well monetarily, they also enjoy a large measure of independence and scope for creativity.

Citing an example, A. Monem, vice-president of the sales division of Williamson Magor, relates, 'I come from a family of tea planters, tea owners ... and I think you have to be in love with tea and there is a sense of security when you know the man

130 | THE HERITAGE OF INDIAN TEA

Top left: Nurturing change through human assets: senior planters sharing their experience about the art of producing quality tea. High quality teas are increasingly in demand among the the Indian middle class and export markets. *Top right:* R.S. Jhawar, executive director of Eveready Industries (India) Ltd and former chairman of the Indian Tea Association, is widely known for his energetic promotion of the tea culture.

running the company is in love with tea himself. It's a company run by a family of tea lovers and professionals in a family-like manner.'

Loyalty and Commitment

The rise of militancy in Assam has thrown up unforeseen challenges for the management. The isolated tea gardens have been soft targets for militants, and kidnapping of managers for ransom has become commonplace. G.P. Barua elaborates, 'So the whole atmosphere was tense as the group's managers worked in remote areas. At that time their only beacon of light was the chairman. They felt that even if something happened to them the *burra* sahib would take care of the family.'

A few armed extremists entered the bungalow of Tarun Bordoloi, senior manager of Hunwal Tea Estate, and took him to his office. One of them stood at the door with an AK-47, while another was near a phone. They told him that they were from the United Liberation Front of Asom and asked him to forward a demand letter of Rs 15 lakhs to the company. Later, the chairman called from Calcutta and spoke to him and members of his famiily. Bordoloi realized that the chairman was acutely concerned about his safety; indeed, more so than even some members of his own family. The chairman assured his wife, 'Nothing is more important to me than your husband's life and I'll ensure he is safe'. He also told his wife, 'If there is anything we can do to give you a sense of security let me know'. Every possible measure was then taken to safeguard him and his family.

In February 1990 the killing of D.K. Choudhary, manager of Romai Tea Estate, by militants came as a great shock. The management decided to continue paying the salary and emoluments that Choudhary had been receiving to his wife. The education of his children was ensured, and later his son was employed as an assistant manager. In April 1992, militants picked up Subir Ray, manager of Dimakusi garden located in Udalguri subdivision of Darrang district. The management spared no effort and eventually managed to get Ray safely back to his family. There have been several other similar examples of the caring attitude and generosity of spirit, as in the case of the untimely demise of P. Bajaj and Ranjan Mukerji. This protective attitude has earned the company the loyalty of all its executives.

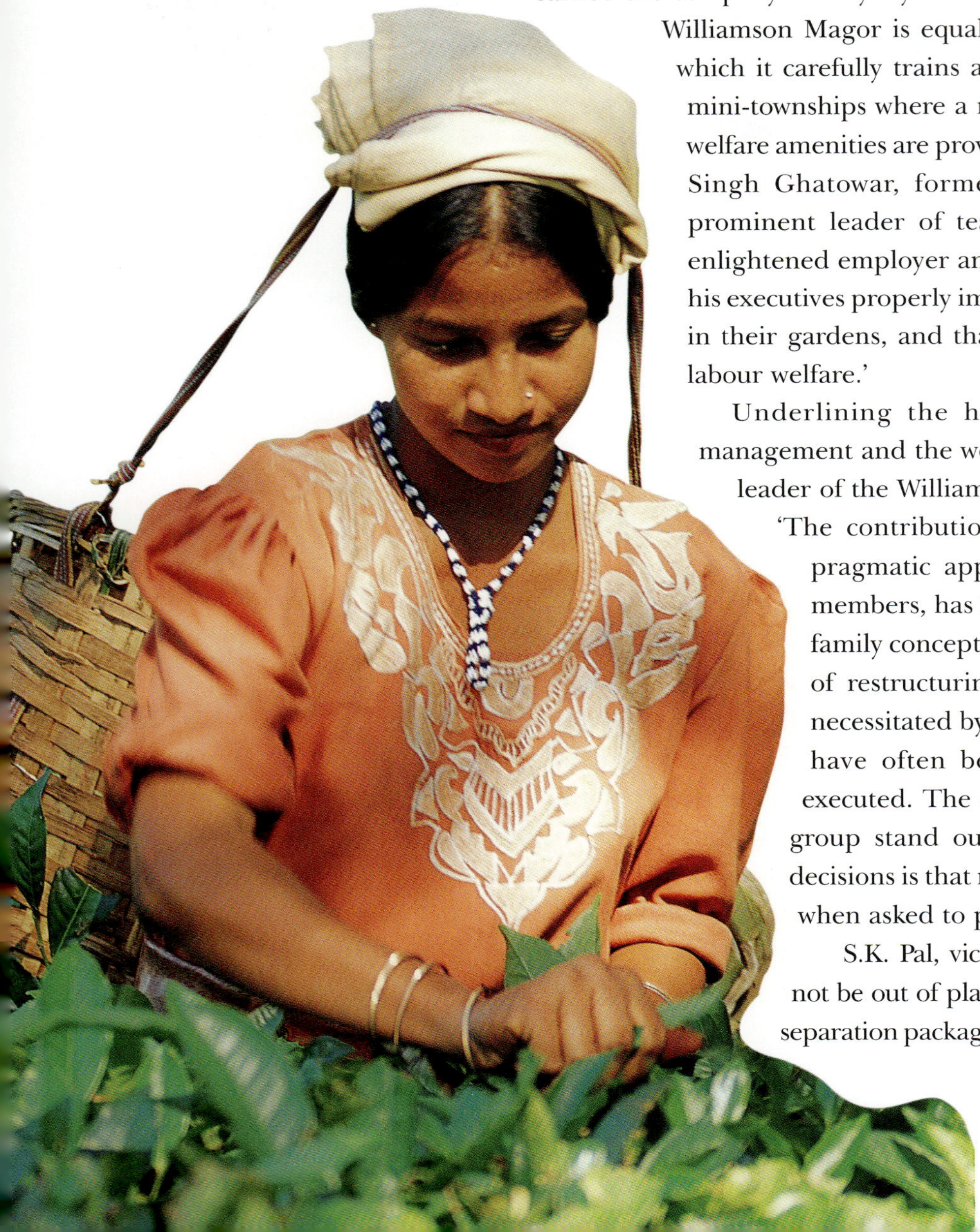

Williamson Magor is equally solicitous about the labour force which it carefully trains and nurtures. Its tea estates are like mini-townships where a number of additional, non-statutory welfare amenities are provided voluntarily. According to Paban Singh Ghatowar, former union minister of state and a prominent leader of tea workers, 'Its chairman is a very enlightened employer and takes personal interest to see that his executives properly implement the labour welfare activities in their gardens, and that's why it is rated high in terms of labour welfare.'

Underlining the healthy relationship between the management and the workers, Subrata Narayan Maitra, the leader of the Williamson Magor Workmen's Union, says: 'The contribution of the management, with their pragmatic approach towards the welfare of staff members, has helped us a lot in building up a one-family concept.' The group has undergone its share of restructuring, reorganizing, and shedding fat necessitated by business compulsions. Such actions have often been undertaken and meticulously executed. The one thing, however, that makes this group stand out even while taking hard business decisions is that no employee ever got a raw deal even when asked to part company.

S.K. Pal, vice-president (HRD), confirms, 'It may not be out of place to mention here that the voluntary separation package offered to its employees in the recent

An extensive and well-coordinated replantation and reinvestment programme is the key to success: *Top left:* Young tea plants are grown in the shade of a garden nursery in Assam. *Top right:* A tea worker tending to seedlings with care.

Facing page: Picture perfect: a woman plucker's deft touch.

past has become a benchmark for many companies who have followed suit and have been successful in their mission'. Even when an employee parts company, he never hesitates to come back in the event of his requiring any assistance, and generally such help is willingly provided.

A Tradition of Excellence

At the Williamson Magor group the loyalty generated by its commitment to fairness is testified to by the extensive plantation programme and high quality standards it is able to maintain. 'From 1968 onwards, we went in for extensive replanting of its tea gardens. The replanting project continued for seven years, covering about 1000 to 1500 acres a year, which has yielded rich dividends in terms of larger yields and lower costs,' says Deepak Khaitan, managing director of the group. It has a very careful programme of investment year on year, to develop better systems and improve discipline in the gardens and factories. Its agricultural and technical experts have changed the face of the estates and factories to such a degree that virtually every factory in the tea gardens has been completely dismantled and reconstructed.

Development of the tea estates receives the utmost priority, and the group has reinvested over Rs 2.5 bn over the past five years. In the plantation area, massive improvement of the drainage system, roads, and bridges was effected. Large replanting programmes were undertaken each year by

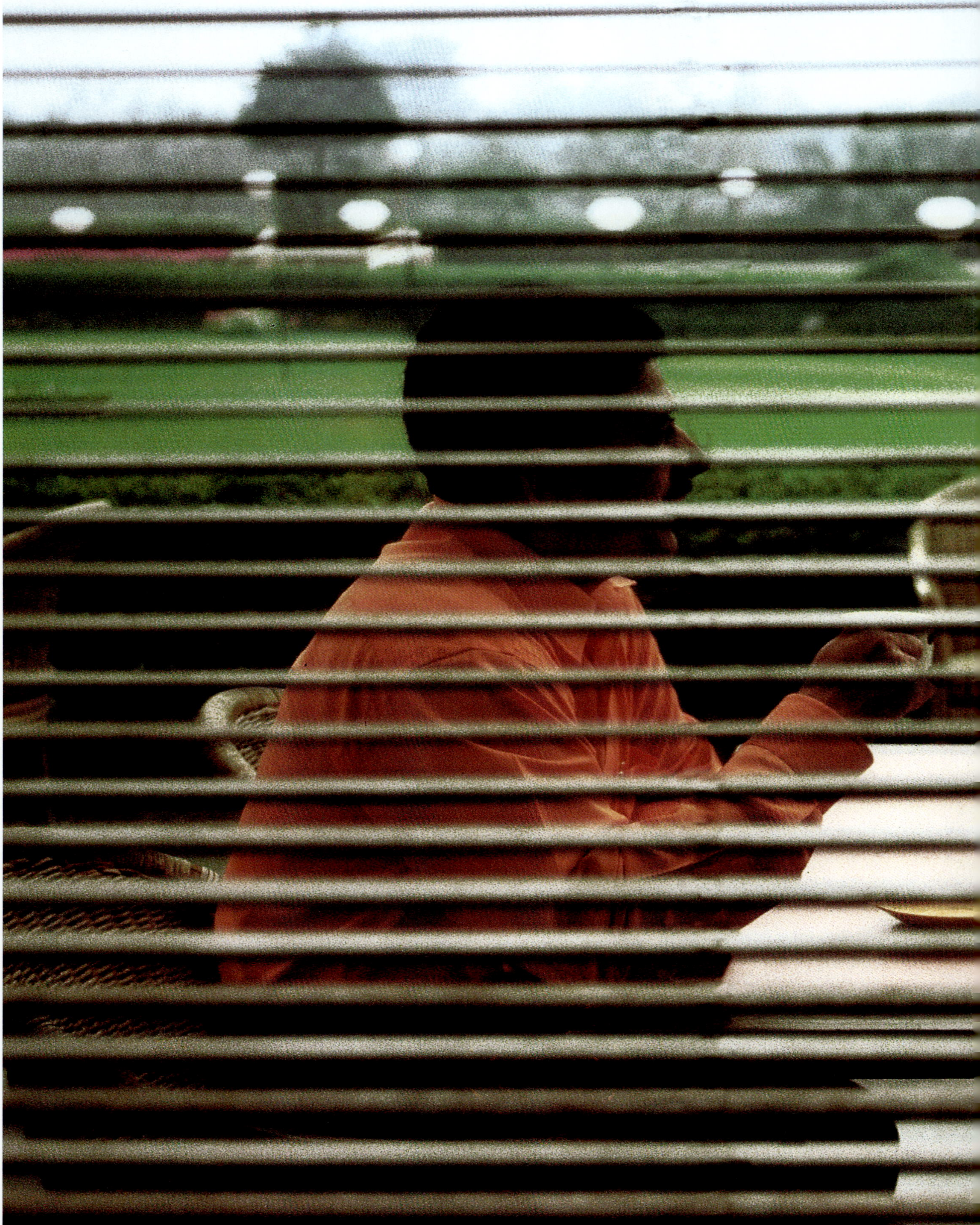

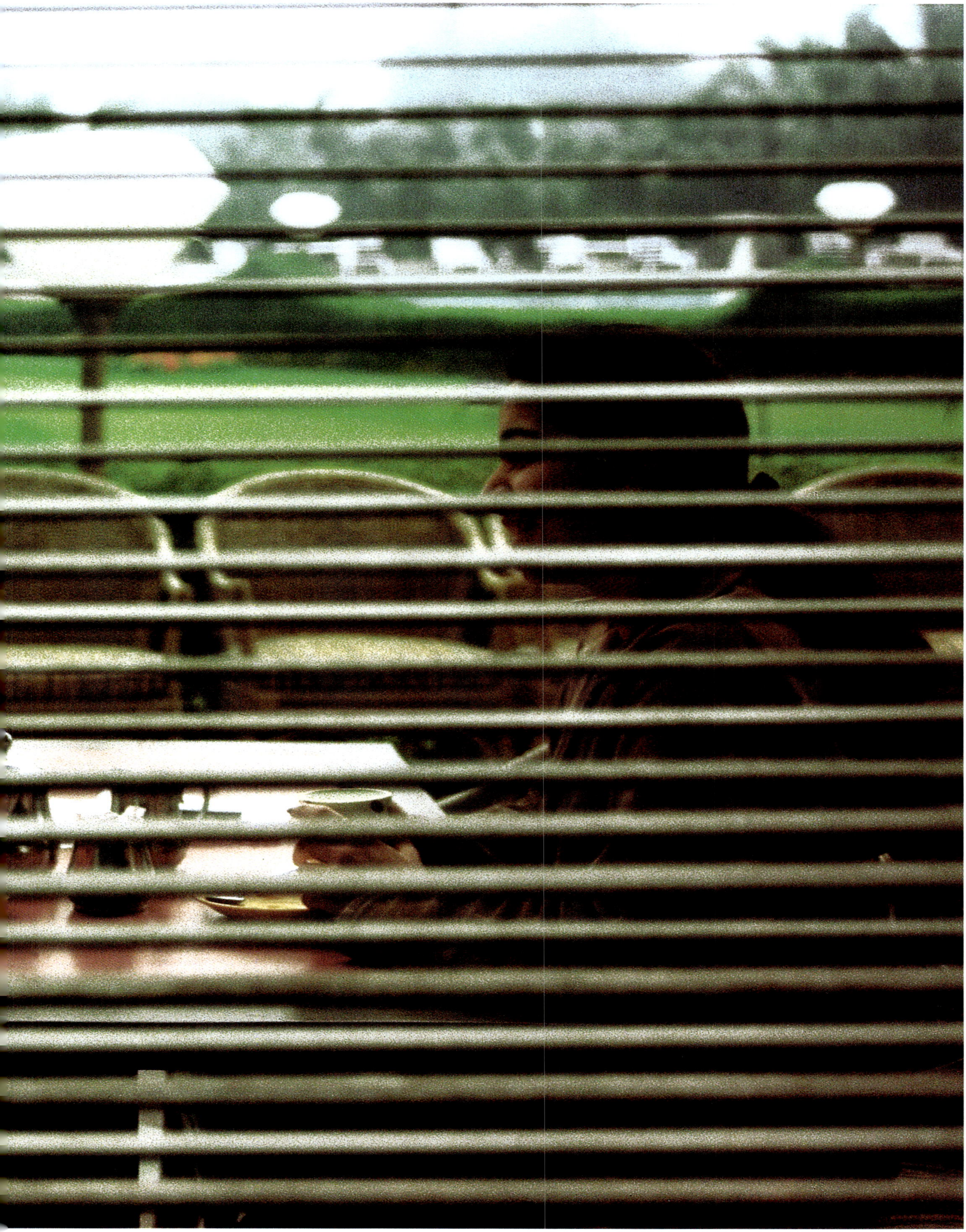

Top: Tea plants have to be carefully tended to produce quality teas.
Below: The quest for modern agricultural practices is ceaseless.

Preceding spread: A leisurely afternoon exchange over cups of tea.

uprooting the unproductive tea sections in order to pre-empt future loss of crop. The basic concern from field to factory is to ensure not just higher production but also better quality while remaining in touch with emerging trends in the industry. That is why overseas buyers respect the group's philosophy of development with its concentration on consistent quality.

By consciously adopting a policy of keeping abreast of the latest technological and scientific developments in the fields of agriculture and biotechnology, and by enforcing a rigorous quality regimen, the Williamson Magor group continues to retain its leadership position in tea.

Research and Development a Priority

A research and development focus has provided strong scientific support to the group's quantitative growth with continuing enhancement in the quality of the product. It would be pertinent here to recall that many years ago it was George Williamson who introduced a new methodology for the production of tea in Assam that was very different from the traditional method developed in China. That tradition of innovation not only continues but has been greatly intensified.

The research and development policy keeps the group's long-term interests in view and believes in anticipating the needs of the future. It is committed to modernization and encourages it in every field. While it sponsors research related to crop improvement and the important area of control of white ants,

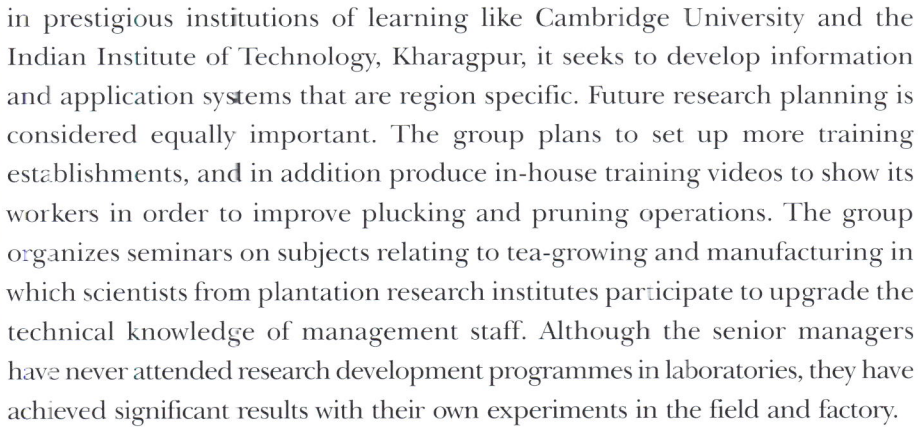

in prestigious institutions of learning like Cambridge University and the Indian Institute of Technology, Kharagpur, it seeks to develop information and application systems that are region specific. Future research planning is considered equally important. The group plans to set up more training establishments, and in addition produce in-house training videos to show its workers in order to improve plucking and pruning operations. The group organizes seminars on subjects relating to tea-growing and manufacturing in which scientists from plantation research institutes participate to upgrade the technical knowledge of management staff. Although the senior managers have never attended research development programmes in laboratories, they have achieved significant results with their own experiments in the field and factory.

Research activities received a boost when the management appointed Dr W. Hadfield, a renowned agronomist from Cambridge, as consultant to review its existing agronomic policies. He has been visiting the group's tea estates since 1991–2, providing detailed reports on their yield patterns. The implementation of the recommendations of its research and development department has begun paying rich dividends in terms of improved quality and enhanced production efficiencies. The yield increases are closely linked to effective pest control and irrigation practices.

Williamson Magor has extended considerable support to the Tea Research Association since its inception, with senior members of the group having acted

Top left: The path of innovation: a modern way of transporting the harvest on an elevated monorail and ropeway which helps in minimizing transportation time and retaining the freshness of the tea leaves.
Top right: A blend of the collective wisdom of planters and modern advances has introduced many path-breaking practices in planting, cultivating, and manufacturing.

A moment of reflection and togetherness over cups of tea.

as members of its Council of Management. Apart from this, many tea estate managers have actively participated in various expert committees in Assam and the Dooars. The management has also permitted the Association to carry out many experiments on the group's tea estates and, indeed, initiated some of these.

Innovation and Modernization

Innovation, expansion, and modernization are of course integral to corporate success. This has meant ongoing research into production systems and processing methods to enhance the quality of the products for consumers. The managers of the tea estates strictly adhere to their manual, literally treating it as their Bible. It contains detailed instructions on matters relating to the field, factory, stores, accounts, and other related topics, to running the garden and factory employing the best and most efficient means. The standing instructions also cover policy statements for managers. The manual has been compiled on the basis of the collective wisdom of planters accumulated over more than a century. The group has switched from seeds to clonal planting and has developed twelve new clones. It has developed proper tracks, drainage, and nurseries, and adopted a policy of uprooting tea bushes over 50 years old: this puts the estates of the group far ahead of the competition. Overseas buyers are provided with the facility of independently auditing the Williamson Magor tea estates.

Managers have deployed modern agricultural practices, using the latest scientific methodology and technology with a long-term perspective. Williamson Magor can claim well-deserved credit for introducing many path-breaking practices and constantly improving processes in the tea industry. It has contributed many new techniques in planting, cultivating, and manufacturing which have now been adopted by the entire industry: one such example is the drier and the dehumidification plant. The group has created and gifted to the tea industry the withering system and fermenting units. Williamson Magor's J.M. Trinick introduced the 'Trinick Sorter' and Probir Das invented the 'Probir Weigher' which are now used by most of the industry's tea estates.

The group has replaced cane baskets with nylon bags for carrying leaf, developed enclosed withering troughs, Jumbo CTCs, the Vibro Fluid Bed Drier, and was among the first to use computers to record the weight of leaf and in the field, electronic bird repellers; it devised the Sinar moisture meter (a system for continuous sorting), the miracle mill-dust collecting system, and the Thermax OBT-75 burner. It has also developed a system for vacuum packing of bulk tea to enable it to retain its freshness over a longer period. All these developments in Williamson Magor have undoubtedly benefited the tea industry as a whole in the form of demonstration effect.

Shehzad
The cup that cheers in ornate porcelain. It concentrates the mind, quenches thirst, and has health-sustaining qualities.

Excellence the Watchword

The workforce takes immense pride in producing the finest teas, and consistent quality has been the group's watchword for over a century. In its broadest sense, the term 'quality', in tea, is used as a description of all the characteristics on the basis of which a tea acquires its market value, namely, appearance and cup character: in other words, liquoring qualities such as colour, brightness, strength, briskness, and aroma. The percentage of good teas produced by the group is so high that they are considered a benchmark for judging quality teas. To sustain such quality standards year after year, great commitment and skill are necessary.

After all, as John Ruskin said, 'Quality is never an accident. It is always the result of intelligent effort. There must be the will to produce a superior thing.' The Bukhial, Hunwal, Partabghur, Dekorai, Pabhoi, Tezpore, Gogra, Margharita, and Namdang tea estates of the group have been assessed as providing teas which fall into the premier market segment and have been designated their preferred tea suppliers by Premier Beverages Ltd, UK.

At the heart of quality tea is the natural leaf. The tea needs to be carefully nurtured and tended, from the initial planting of the seed to the final packaging of the tea leaves. Today, the group's tea estates are far in advance

of their competitors in terms of every aspect of making quality teas. This has meant that it continues to produce some of the world's finest teas.

J.M. Trinick, an internationally renowned tea taster, concludes, 'Williamson Magor is producing the best quality tea in the world and exports more teas from India than anyone else, and is therefore better known internationally. I don't think there is any buyer in the world who is not aware of Williamson Magor and its reputation.' Errol O'Brien, former senior tea buyer of Tea Trading Corporation of India, tells how he bought quality tea for a special occasion. 'In June 1981, the Indian Tea Board in London had requested the Tea Trading Corporation of India to provide a black, well-curled Assam tea filled with tips and with a good strong liquor to supply tea for a special caddy to commemorate the marriage of Prince Charles and Lady Diana. The caddies were to be prepared and marketed by Martin Gill of London Herb & Spice Co. In order to procure a suitable Assam tea for the royal blend, I contacted Michael Rome of Williamson Magor, and he provided me with an excellent invoice of tippy teas from one of the company's prime properties. These were the teas that went into the souvenir caddies. Within a week of the marriage, the caddies were a sell-out.'

Top: 'A cup of tea' is a common phrase at any time in any language, in any country.

Facing page: A portrait of a woman holding a cup of tea by Johann Heinrich Tischbein (c. 1756). In the words of Henry Fielding, 'Love and scandal are the best sweeteners of tea'.

Consistent Quality

The group has created a culture in which innovative professionalism earns both respect and reward. The fact is that it has over the years not only been able to maintain high standards of quality but has also pioneered new innovations and techniques on a regular basis. This reveals the importance of organizational culture as a prerequisite for innovative practice. The knowledge and expertise gained over the years in tea has been utilized to design, develop, and install integrated quantity and quality improvement programmes.

According to Tushar Kanti Dhar, a former senior manager of Bukhial Tea Estate, 'For quality control we have to take a lot of care from plantation to plucking, manufacturing to packaging, paying full attention to even the minutest details. We call it "A to Z care" for quality.' The human factor is paramount in establishing and maintaining quality standards. At all times, employees need to ensure that production is geared to suit the type of green leaf being harvested and to meet the various market requirements, including price.

On the tea estates it takes years to train the managerial, field, and factory staff who will in turn gradually motivate the workers. A very strict disciplinary regime has to be followed by managers and workers at all times to ensure that the right leaves are plucked and the most efficient machines are utilized in the

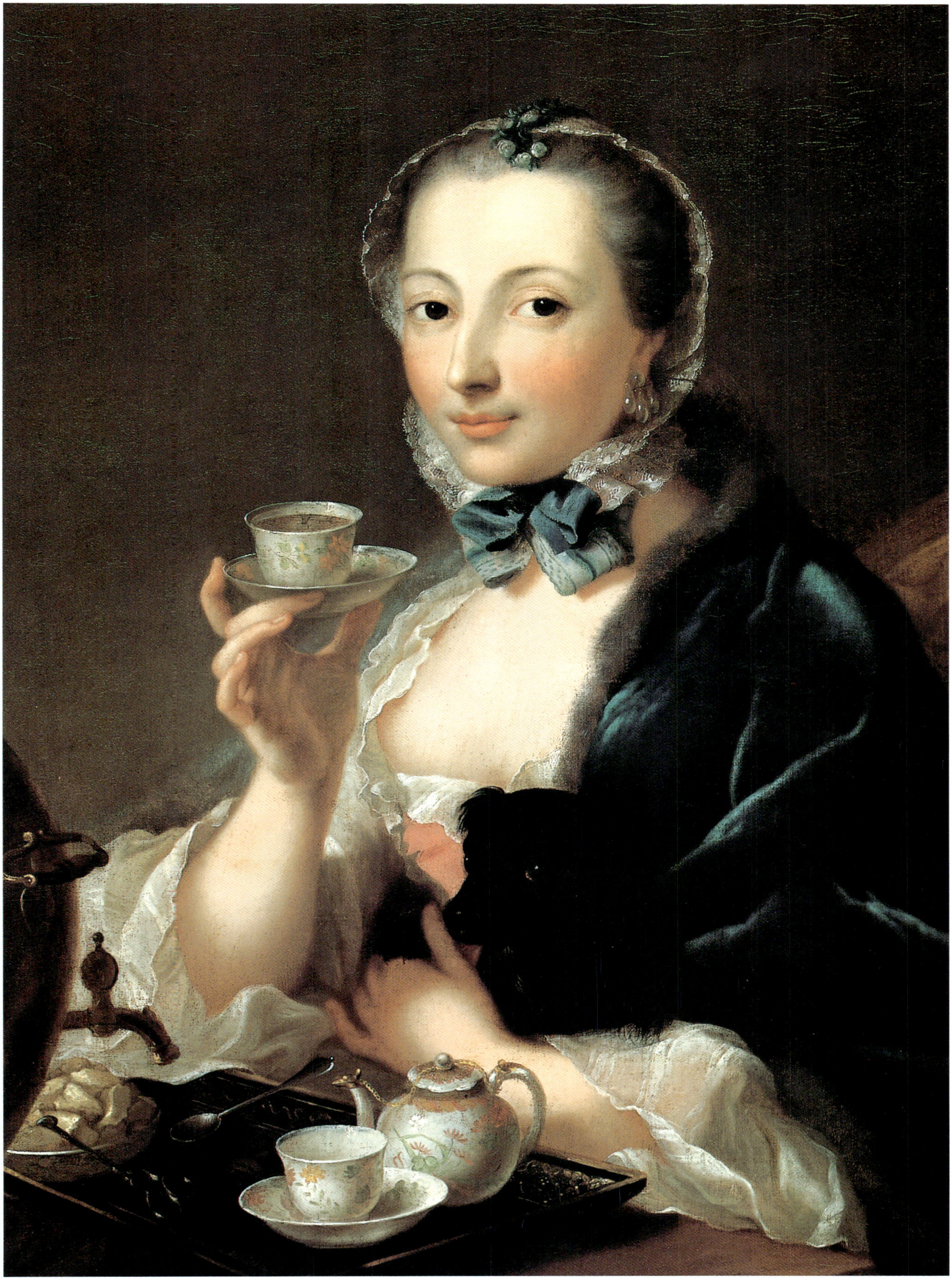

A masterly oil painting by Arpita Singh, distinguished Indian artist. Okakura Kakuza wrote that like art, tea has its periods and its schools. Its evolution may be roughly divided into three principal stages: boiled tea, whipped tea, and seeped tea. Ours conforms to the last of these phases.

factories. The advisers of the group supervise the entire process, keeping a watchful eye on the minutest details. Quality performance also needs to be regularly monitored through quality evaluation reports by experts. As a natural corollary, the vast tea gardens have been maintained in prime condition by the planters over decades.

The tea estate managers of the group are always keen to interact with overseas buyers. 'They are ever willing and eager to show off the new things that are happening on the estate; very proud to show us around, and Premier functionaries are delighted to go out there and see these things in action. In that way our relationship is completely different from that a normal buyer has with the growers, because the average person's attitude is to go to an estate for two to three hours and then move on to the next. A Premier executive, on the other hand, stays around chatting, looking, inspecting everything, and that can only come about from years of trust that we have built up with Williamson Magor,' says Philip Mumby, former chief buyer of Premier Beverages Ltd, UK, a leading British tea-packaging company.

These efforts have obviously borne fruit, as the chairman of J. Thomas & Co. Pvt Ltd, the country's oldest and the world's largest tea broker, wrote to the group, 'During the non-quality period, your tea has been of a very high standard. Teas were brisk, full with brightness, and generally well above the standard produced by other major groups.' Many domestic and overseas tea blenders use Williamson Magor teas as an essential component for their blend throughout the year. Similarly, the managing director, Carritt Moran & Co. Pvt. Ltd, wrote in April 1991, 'The excellent quality of teas made by your group has received overwhelming support both from the internal and export sections of the trade'.

Perhaps the most significant testimony to the consistent quality of the teas supplied overseas is that many buyers have been buying tea from Williamson Magor for over a hundred years. Said a buyer from Rotterdam, 'What is amazing is not just quality, but the consistent quality that Williamson Magor is able to deliver ... it is like a Rolls Royce amongst teas'. The tea factories of the group are known for hygiene and automation. There is no tea lying around on the floor of the factories, otherwise a common sight in the industry. Controlled by machines, the manufacturing process takes place under the best hygienic conditions, with every precaution taken to ensure safety. According to A. Monem, 'We invite our customers to visit our gardens and factories to get a first-hand experience of the high standards of cleanliness and hygienic conditions that are maintained by us, and these have resulted in the group's highest exports sale of over 20 m. kg during 2000'.

Williamson Magor tea has introduced a radically new method of packaging that preserves the full freshness of the tea all the way from the estate until it is finally packed for the consumer. In 1987 Williamson Magor conducted experimental trials in Assam using vacuum packing as a method of eliminating even the slightest loss of liquoring characteristics during transit and storage. The success of these trials led to two vacuum packing machines being installed in Assam and in Kenya. Today, of course, vacuum packaging is common practice.

Top: Tea plays an important part in the lifestyle of young people too.

Following spread: Chai-wala in the maidan adjacent to Victoria Memorial in Calcutta. The man in the street enjoys the fragrance of his carefully brewed, constantly steaming *chai* stored in an aluminium or brass kettle.

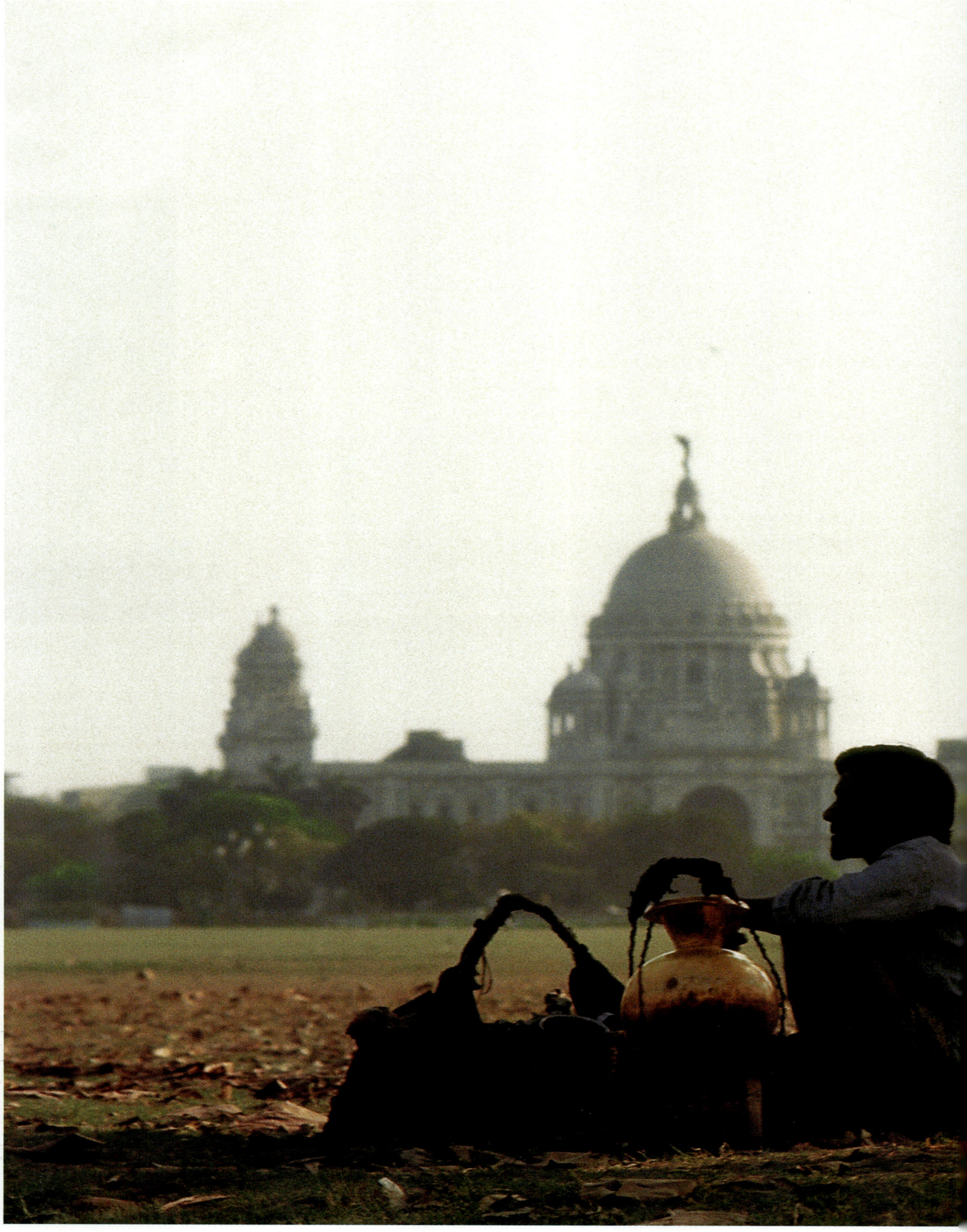

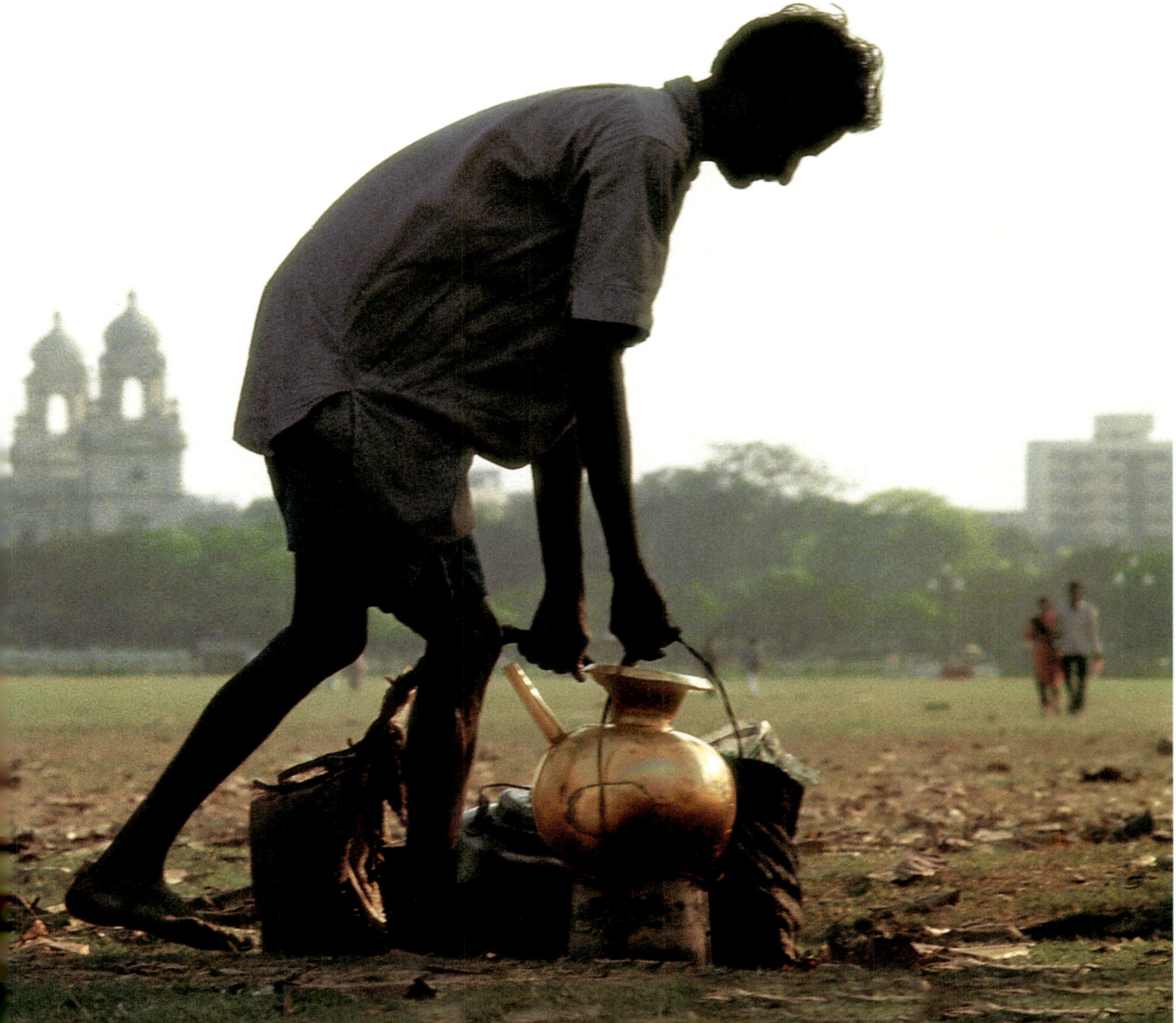

Top: Iced tea is a wonderfully refreshing summer drink, and makes for elegant cocktails. It was first introduced by an Englishman, Richard Blechynden, at the St Louis Fair in 1904. Now urban youngsters are developing a taste for it. Hindustan Lever Ltd is among the leading companies to have launched iced tea with their Lipton Ice tea brand.

Facing page: A painting by James Joseph Jacques Tissot, a famous French artist (c. 1847).

Human Welfare a Cornerstone

Williamson Magor's corporate philosophy is firmly rooted in the understanding that business must always have a human face. This is demonstrated by its pursuit of sustainable development as a natural and integral part of its management culture. The management believes in being proactive in implementing responsible developmental projects and in supplementing governmental efforts in areas of national interest such as the environment and biodiversity conservation. The *Isa Upanishad* says: 'Create wealth by ethical means and enjoy it by giving', and that is precisely what the management seeks to put into practice. The group has contributed substantially towards the social, economic, and cultural development of West Bengal with the aim of improving the quality of life of the people. From renovating cemeteries to working in alliance with the Indian Chamber of Commerce, from helping the West Bengal government dig tubewells in rural districts to nurturing and sustaining golf and polo, the group has always been ready with a helping hand whenever and wherever required.

Williamson Magor works closely with reputed business organizations, in the process often giving an added dimension to their welfare programmes. The chairman and several directors of the group have provided dynamic leadership to many business organizations, keeping the interests of both the organization and the nation in the forefront. Chief among these are the International Chamber of Commerce, Indian Chamber of Commerce, Indian Tea Association, and the Bengal Chamber of Commerce and Industry. The group has also contributed generously and participated actively in the various social welfare projects undertaken by the Indian Chamber of Commerce. It has been the moving force in the adoption of a cluster of villages by the Chamber. A number of activities in the villages were funded by the group, thereby enabling the Chamber to fulfil its social agenda.

As a tea group, for Williamson Magor the east naturally meant the north-east as a whole, and it worked hard to evolve a consensus that the Chamber ought to gear itself to seek to resolve the problems of the long-neglected north-eastern region. As the Williamson Magor chairman once said: 'After all, India's eastern region does not end with Cooch Behar district of West Bengal! There are seven more states to the east. The Chamber must play a greater role to ensure that the part of the country where the sun rises first should now also see its long overdue sunrise of prosperity.'

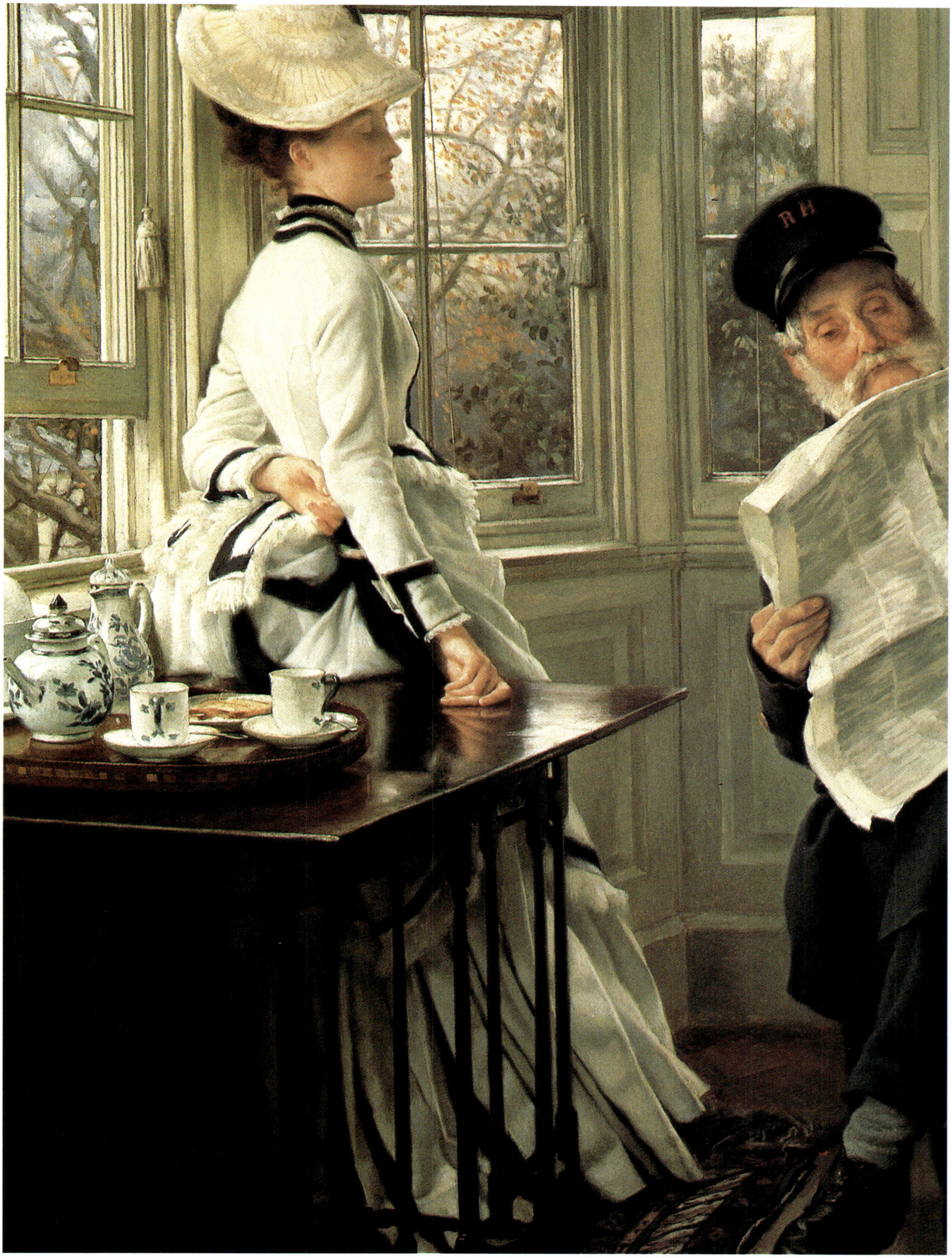
RH

Victoria Memorial, with its grand façade, is one of Calcutta's important heritage sites. Calcutta has always attracted the tea people who have involved themselves in its cultural life in a variety of ways.

Besides its long association with business associations and the north-eastern region, the Williamson Magor group has had a close relationship with Calcutta's diverse developmental activities. It has been in the forefront in the affairs of the city and has repeatedly shown its concern for the cultural and social environment. The tercentenary of Calcutta was marked by major celebrations. This provided the group with an ideal opportunity to express its commitment to the city that has played a major role in its destiny. Calcutta renewed itself with great vigour, and Williamson Magor played a prominent role in making the city proud of its history and showing it in its true colours to visitors as well as its own citizens. As part of the tercentenary celebrations, the group helped in the restoration and renovation of major historical landmarks like the Victoria Memorial, St John's Church, Job Charnock's Mausoleum, and St Andrew's Church. The entire air-conditioning work of the Calcutta Tercentenary Gallery of the Victoria Memorial was undertaken by Williamson Magor. The gallery was inaugurated on 19 April 1992 by the then chief minister of West Bengal, Jyoti Basu.

Williamson Magor supported various tournaments in Calcutta, contributing its mite towards making it a sporting and health-conscious city. It has been a major sponsor of polo since the days when Pat Williamson was the president of the Calcutta Polo Club. The polo ground at the centre of the

Satyajit Ray, the internationally acclaimed film maker, enjoying one of nature's greatest gifts.

racecourse is appropriately named after him. The management has also sponsored individual polo players like Manupal Godara. The Royal Calcutta Turf Club, the Royal Calcutta Golf Club, and Calcutta Polo Club feel that the Williamson Magor group has functioned as an umbrella that has protected them from problematic downpours. Its companies have sponsored polo, golf, racing, football, hockey, cricket, tennis, squash, and badminton.

Any visionary who has the welfare of the people at heart would give education the first priority because, without basic learning and skills, it is not possible to compete in a fast-changing world. Literacy has to be the first priority in any scheme of things, and it is the investment in this that eventually yields returns both to the individual and society at large. The Williamson Magor group's contribution to education and vocational training has been wide-ranging.

It has always been concerned with the overall development of educational institutions. In Calcutta it has taken a personal interest in institutions like Shikshayatan, Loreto College, and St Xavier's School and College. Fr P.C. Mathew, the principal of St Xavier's College, talks about the role Williamson Magor played in the 125-year celebration of the school. 'We contacted many people for help. Williamson Magor's chairman was the only one to say, "No, you don't have to come over. I will come over". And then he comes and tells us, "Father, you just tell us what you want and we will provide

WHERE TEA IS A WAY OF LIFE | 149

it ...'" Williamson Magor's assistance enabled St Xavier's to establish the first educational computer centre in Calcutta.' They have even helped with the library, audio-visual equipment, and the renovation of the auditorium. In addition, liberal assistance has been provided to prestigious educational institutions like the International Management Institute, New Delhi; Indian Institute of Plantation Management, Bangalore; Gram Bharati Vidyapeeth Kothayari, Sikar, among others.

Williamson Magor believes that it can sustain growth only in a growing environment; that it cannot insulate itself from its immediate surroundings and needs to assimilate itself culturally and socially with its working environment. Says its chairman, 'Whenever there is an opportunity for social welfare, we like to be associated with it. The desire is always there; there may sometimes be an insufficiency of resources but we certainly try to extend all the support possible within the means available.'

Today, the Williamson Magor group is actively contributing to the socio–economic upliftment of people, though silently and without any fanfare. It follows the advice of the *Bhagawad Gita*, which says that a gift is good which is made to one from whom no return is expected, in the conviction that to give to a worthy person is one's duty. This is a basic principle adopted by them. In BM's words: 'We consider ourselves custodians, expecting nothing in return. Pour a bucket of water at the base of a tree and move on, not caring about how juicy the fruits will be. You will have done your bit.'

A dynamic chairman invariably stamps his personality on the organization he leads, and this has never been truer than in the case of Williamson Magor where BM's personality and philosophy are sharply etched in every sphere of its working. A deeply religious man, BM himself always attributes his enormous business success to the generosity of God. 'We are no more than instruments in divine hands. Nothing happens of our own volition. All is God's grace. All that we have earned and spent is only a benediction from above. We are only instruments fulfilling the Divine Will. God has given us all we have and we spend it as He wills and will continue to do so as long as we have anything left with us.'

The Williamson Magor group can understandably take pride in its past achievements. It is fully equipped to meet the challenges of the future with conviction and nurtures the belief that change for the sake of change is as dangerous as blind loyalty to the past. Its well-conceived blend of continuity and innovation marks the difference between a mere legal corporate entity and one that is geared towards striving for higher performance, while simultaneously exceeding expectations in its role as a responsible corporate citizen.

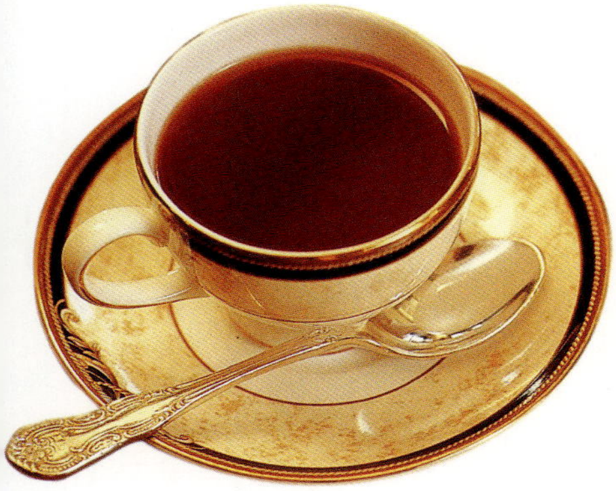

Top: 'Better to be deprived of food for three days than of tea for one.' (Ancient Chinese proverb.)

Facing page: A painting by Reggianini Vittorio (b. 1858) of afternoon tea, a custom that has been popular worldwide over the centuries.

Following spread: Rawal Raghavendra Singh and Lalit Singh Sisodia receiving regal service in the royal suite of Samode Palace.

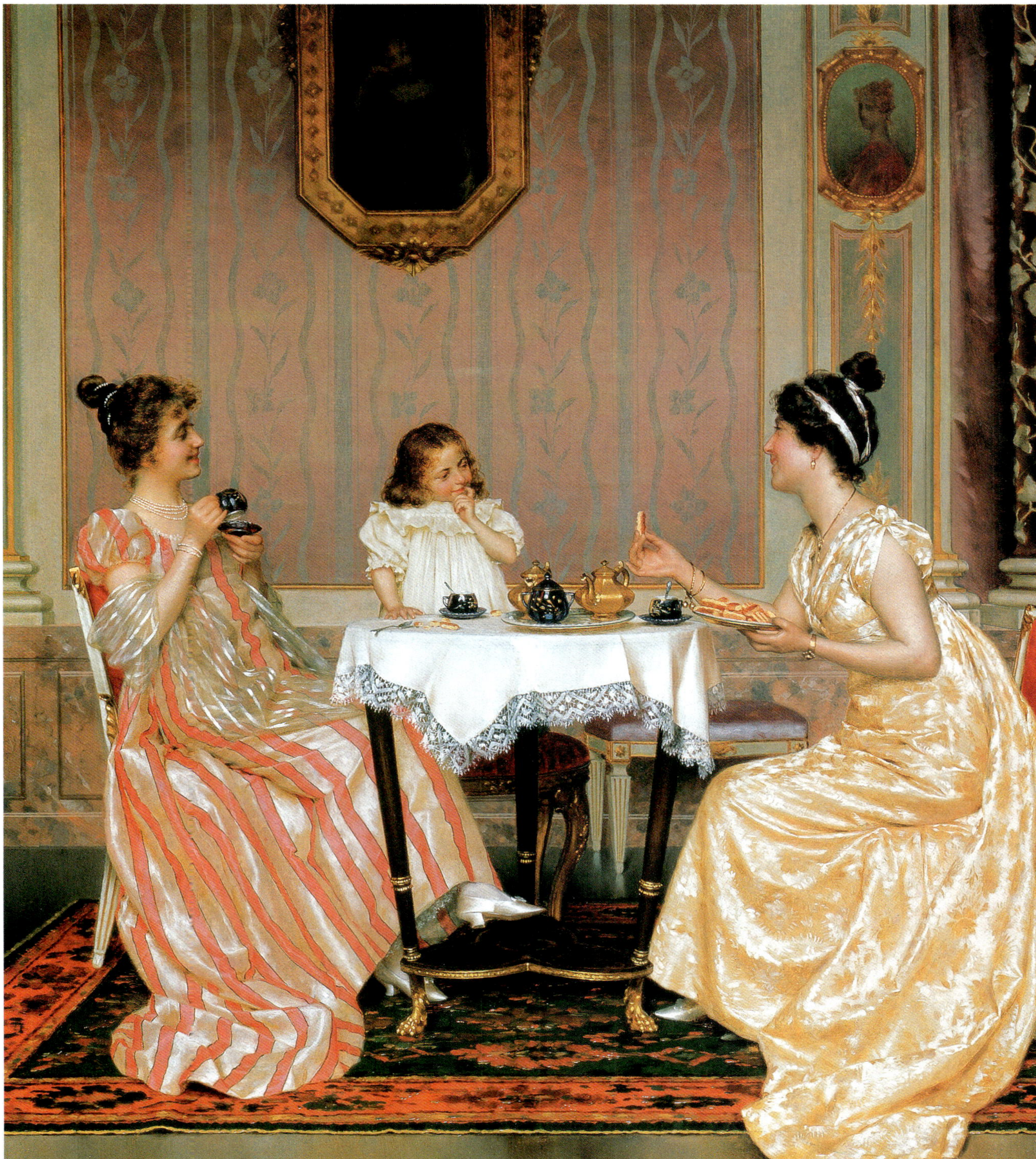

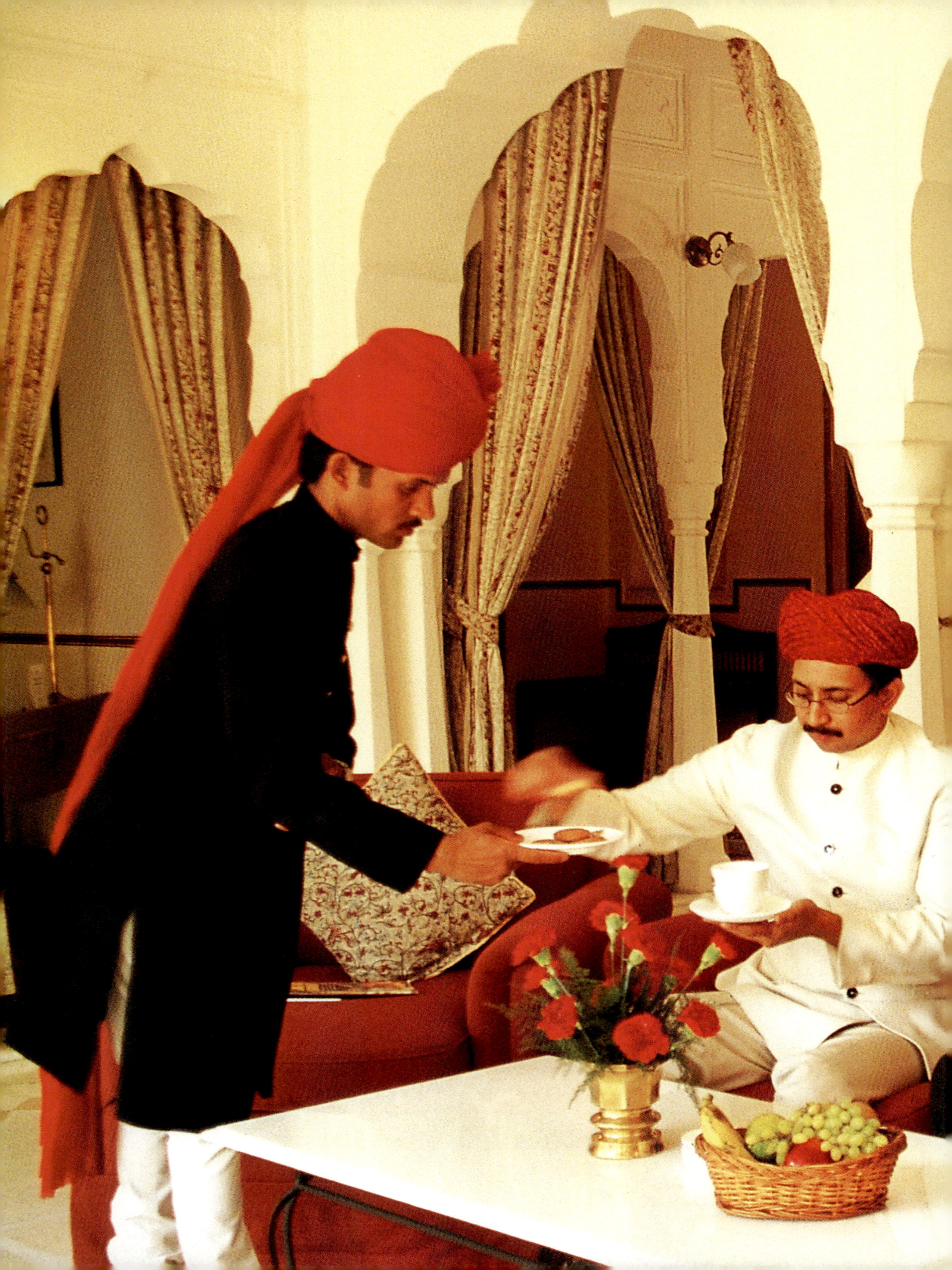

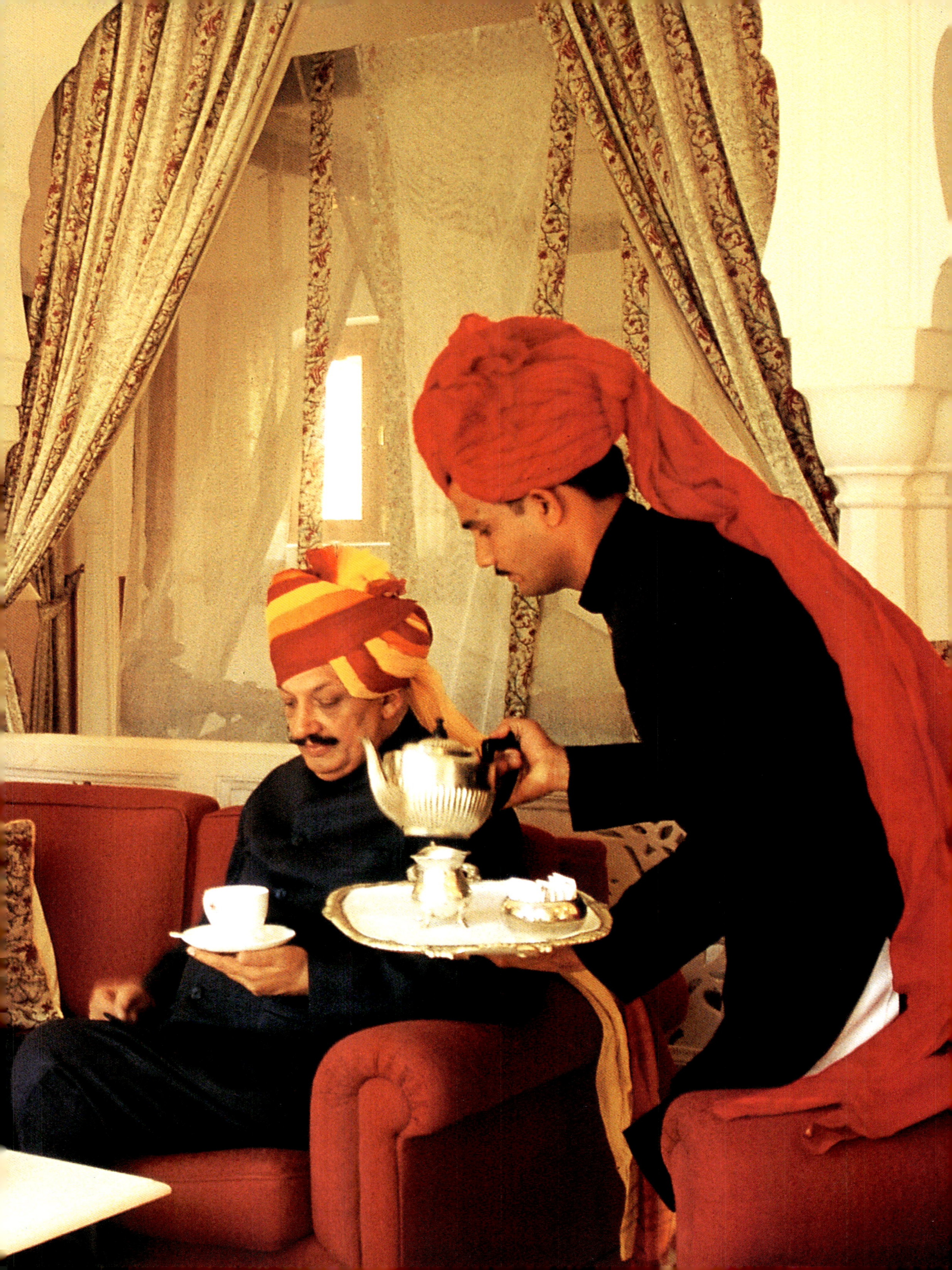

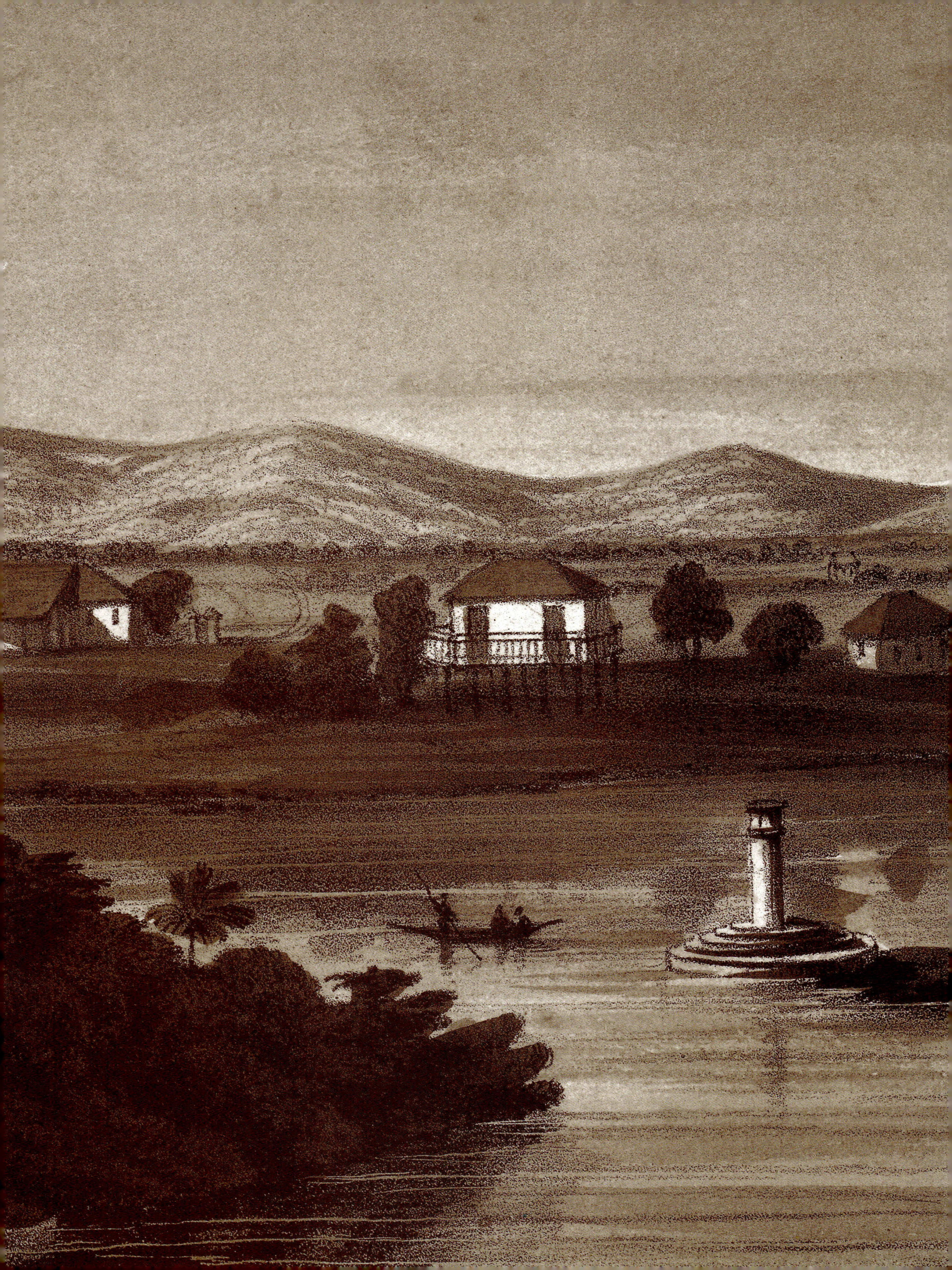

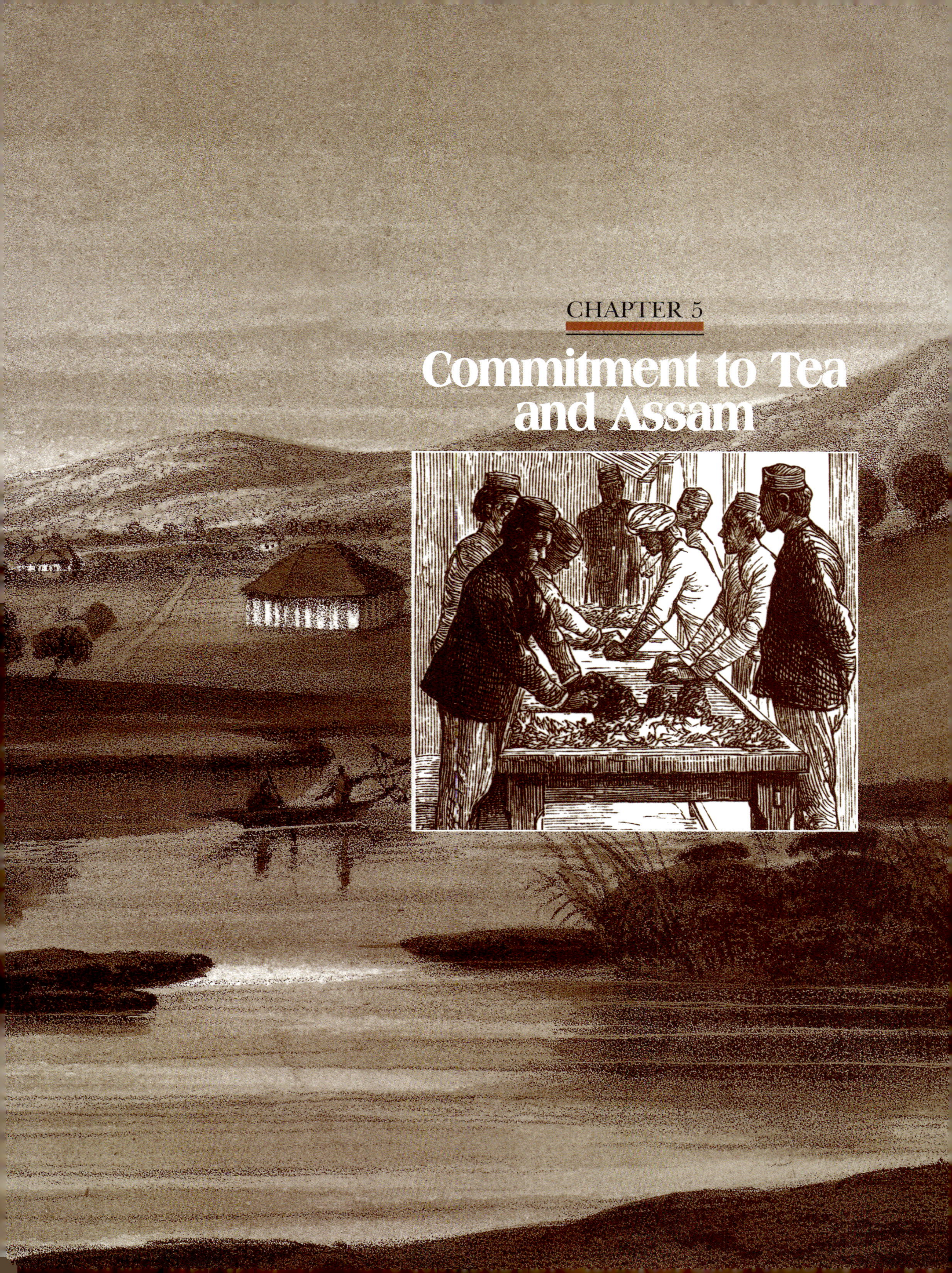

CHAPTER 5

Commitment to Tea and Assam

Those who love the colour green and all that it signifies, love the seven sisters of the north-east of India and the mother state, Assam, the gateway to the entire region. The north-east is bounded by Myanmar in the east, Tibet and Bhutan to the north, and Bangladesh to the south and east. A narrow land corridor, known as the chicken's neck, in parts as narrow as 20 km, connects the region to the mainland. Assam itself comprises valleys, the principal among which has been carved out over millennia by the majestic Brahmaputra river. Second in importance is Barak valley to the south-east of the state.

Ranging from the wild, dark, and deep green of primeval forest to the wet, gleaming green of the swamps, and the orderly, undulating green of the tea gardens, green, with all its infinite varieties of shades and hues, dominates the Assamese landscape. Largely isolated from mainstream India, Assam has retained its aura of natural freshness together with its rich and varied wildlife. Elephants, the famous one-horned rhino, and swamp deer share the habitat with wild buffalo and tiger. Enchanted by its beauty, Mahatma Gandhi wrote in *Young India*, 'Assam is a land of magnificent vegetation. Some of the river scenery is hard to beat throughout the world'. Similarly, Jawaharlal Nehru called Assam the land of tea: 'I loved the uncommon combination of semi-tropical scenery and snow-topped mountains with a noble river running between them'.

Right: Reading the tea leaves in order to set high standards.

Facing page: The path of progress: a plucker arriving at a tea garden.

Preceding spread: An illustrative view of Guwahati (c. 1847).
Inset: Rolling tea by hand.

156 | THE HERITAGE OF INDIAN TEA

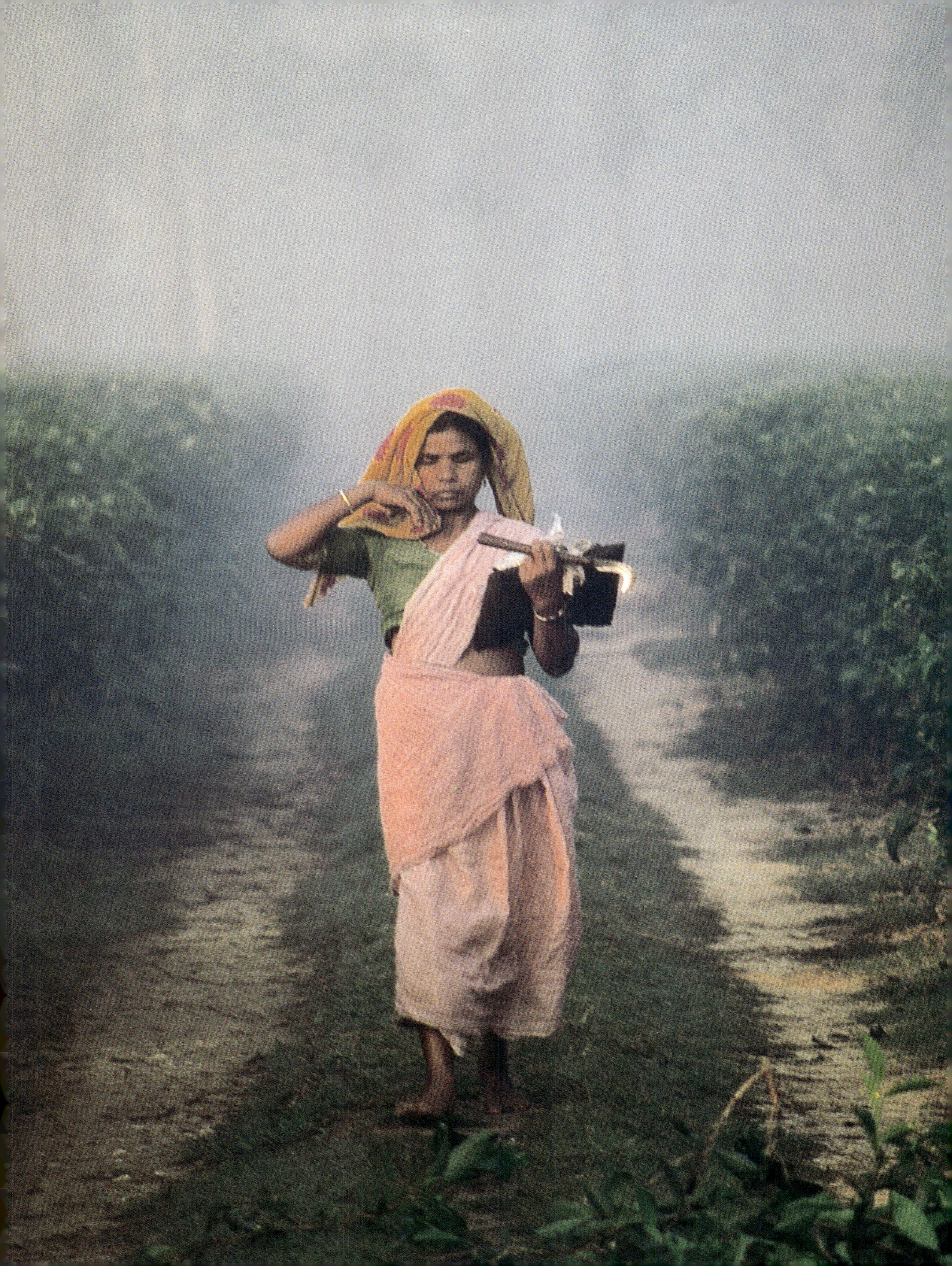

Tea gardens bloom with a variety of flowers in a sea of greenery, presenting a spectacle of colour and splendour.

Economic Re-engineering

The majestic Brahmaputra charts its course through the state, and its many tributaries provide a perennial source of water, Assam's life-blood, with its many uses: of sustaining life, travel, transport, irrigation, and power. An intrinsic part of the larger, dynamic Brahmaputra–Yangtze–Mekong economic region, the state is the gateway that links India to east and south-east Asia. Rich in natural resources, the state abounds in fossil fuels, a range of minerals, forests, fertile soils, and hydel resources.

While nature has been generous to Assam, history has not been equally so. It was ruled by the Ahoms between the thirteenth and nineteenth centuries until the arrival of the British. Assam is an ethnic melting pot where over 300 distinct communities have lived together over the centuries. It is the home of many colourful cultures and has welcomed followers of diverse faiths and people speaking a variety of different languages. This diversity makes governance difficult.

For Assam, 1947 proved to be a catastrophic year. India's partition triggered both seclusion and alienation from the Indian mainland. Internally too, the reorganization of old Assam and its division into five states resulted in a tragic erosion of age-old bonds, with multiple divisions along ethnic and regional lines shaping the political climate. Intrinsically a part of the neglected north-east, Assam, like the other seven sister states has, for decades now, suffered the violence, strife, and law and order problems that accompany the rise of separatist movements. As if this was not bad enough, the state has also had to bear the brunt of illegal immigration from neighbouring Bangladesh and Myanmar.

The recently established North-East Chamber of Commerce and Industry has spelt out the scope and prospects of the proposed 'economic re-engineering'. There are ample opportunities for all-round development in many sectors like agriculture, power, food processing, tourism, and information technology. The tea, oil, and other industries have been a beacon of hope, both sustaining and nurturing Assam. Indeed, tea and Assam are inseparable. Guwahati has emerged as the largest and busiest tea auction centre in the country. The tea research centre at Tocklai is known throughout the world for its pioneering and innovative work. The Inland Container Depot, Amingaon, was set up at the initiative of the tea industry to boost exports.

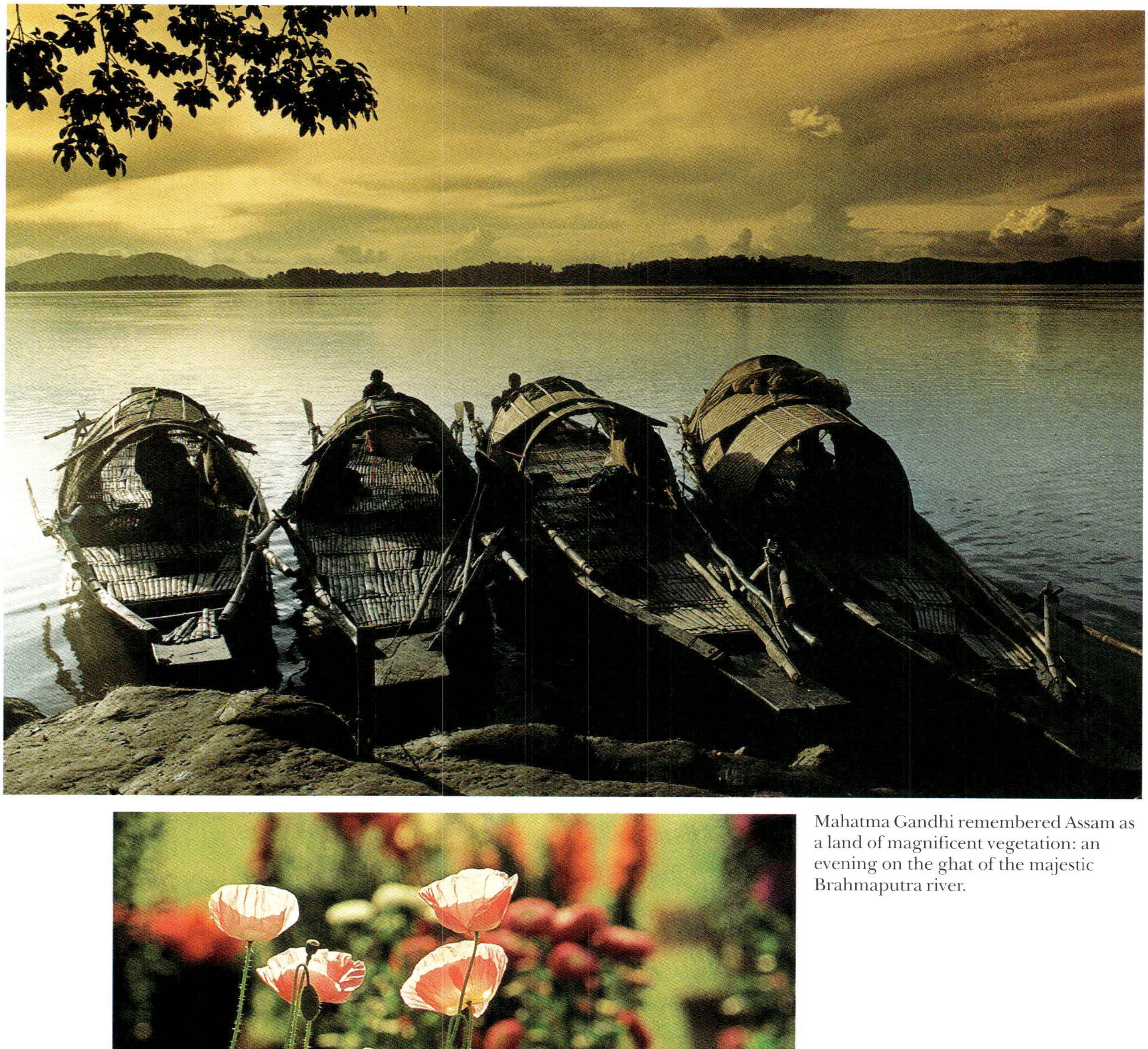

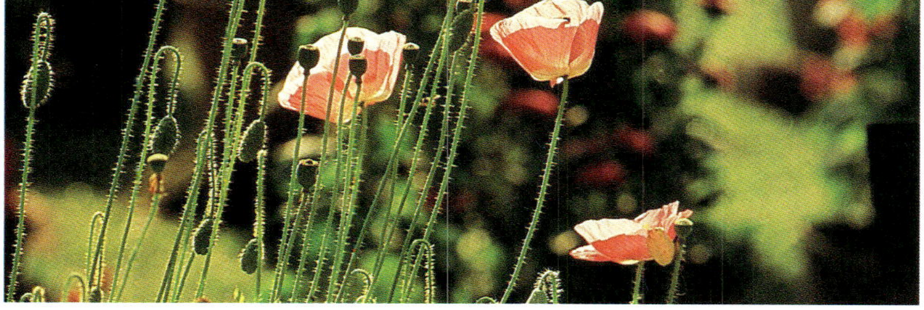

Mahatma Gandhi remembered Assam as a land of magnificent vegetation: an evening on the ghat of the majestic Brahmaputra river.

Top: The Indian rope trick? No, just the art of pouring tea.

Centre below: Made for each other! A tea kettle heating over a *chullah*.

Facing page: The strainer plays its part as tea cups await their turn.

Profitable Growth for All

The tea industry has brought prosperity to several areas which are not only relatively backward, but positively inaccessible to any other major economic activity. By far the largest tea-producing area in the world, Assam contributes over 50 per cent of India's total tea production. Tea contributes about 27 per cent of the state's revenue. It also brings in over Rs 20 bn into the state economy. The tea industry feeds nearly 11 per cent of the 27 m. population of Assam and contributes Rs 14.5 bn to the state as agricultural income tax, cess on green leaf, land revenue, and sales tax.

A vast majority of the industry's total expenditure is incurred and retained in Assam. According to T.R. Swaminathan, former director of the Williamson Magor group, 'Today, and indeed over the past 10 years, almost 90 per cent of the industry's total input costs are incurred within the state. There are a lot of local purchases and tea gardens can literally be run from Assam without any Calcutta support.' Almost 93 per cent of industrial requirements are met locally. The tea estates together spend a large sum a day on procuring stores and consumables from the local market: items like electric poles, hume pipes, fencing posts; agricultural tools like pruning knifes and hoes; items like umbrellas, blankets, chappals, medicines; office supplies; vehicle and tea machinery maintenance; communication services, and a number of other such items and services.

The reality is that over 50 per cent of the people employed in the tea estates belong to Assam. The industry's need for inputs, transport, tea machines, and warehousing is providing employment to innumerable people. It has also helped large numbers of local vendors, small-scale entrepreneurs, and a variety of ancillary industries, such as plywood, sawmill, and transport services that have come into being and thrive. Tea towns have witnessed great prosperity through the various welfare projects undertaken by the industry for the benefit of people living in and around the tea estates. Notwithstanding heavy odds, tea companies are using their resources as well as managerial and technological skills in helping people and spreading prosperity which is principally the responsibility of the government.

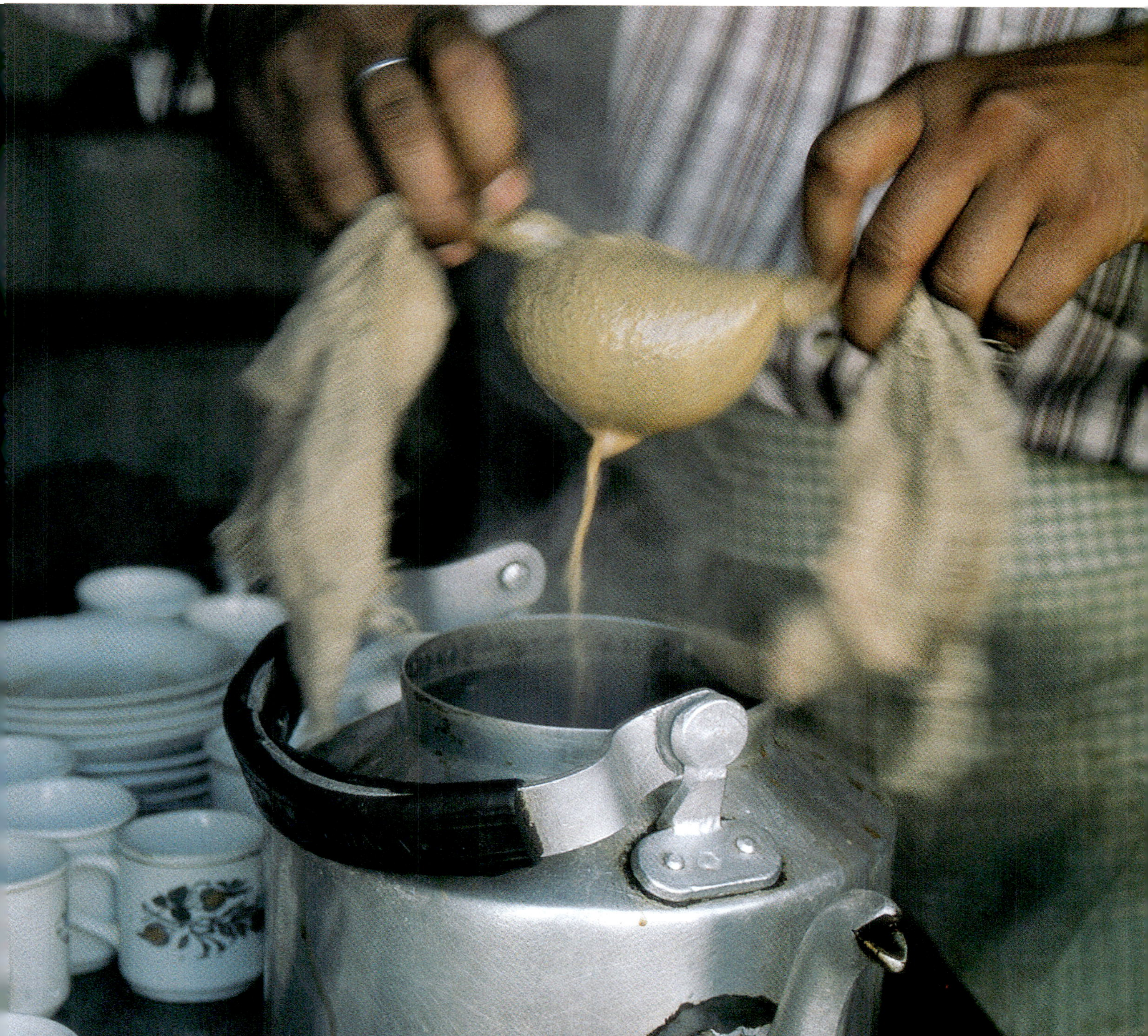

Top: Throughout India tea shops are popular, and there people drink *chai* in different forms and in a variety of utensils.

Facing page: Tea has a unique effect on social customs all over the world and is drunk by all shades of people with a variety of lifestyles. 'Dolly's Tea Shop,' Calcutta, provides a stylish ambience for the invigorating drink.

Inspiring Leadership

Undeniably, Williamson Magor's contributions to Assam are significant, but what is equally so is the way in which they have been achieved. The group's chairman and senior executives are irrevocably committed to the cause of both tea and Assam. There is no doubt about the motivation underlying the group's welfare programme as well as the motives and the attitude of the employees who implement it. All of them draw inspiration from a passionate, heartfelt concern for the land.

B.M. Khaitan feels a very special bond with Assam. As he says, 'You cannot wipe off over 50 years of life just because you have diversified into other areas. In the group there is always a warm and caring feeling for Assam. We know this is where we started from; and we would like to be able to give something back ... and yes, there is always so much more to do.'

Naturally, the unfolding scenario is a cause for concern. 'One cannot help but think and worry about Assam. There has been neglect in the past. Things are falling apart: there is so much violence these days, and yet it used to be so peaceful, so beautiful. It is getting torn apart, and my heart bleeds for it. Therefore, whatever one does, one feels one has not done enough. I do not know what the future holds, but I only hope that better sense prevails.'

The group's efforts and contributions have been recognized and appreciated. P.K. Mahanta, then chief minister, remarked that Williamson Magor's investment in business and social welfare should be emulated as a benchmark. He added, 'B.M. Khaitan is an open-hearted man. He always says his company is keen on doing something for Assam. I have realized through experience that whatever he says comes from his heart and is very true.'

In addition to building institutions and operating community development projects through trusts, Williamson Magor has encouraged individual companies and gardens in initiating and supporting their own diverse and wide-ranging public welfare programmes. This approach has ensured that its initiatives have the maximum possible reach and impact not only in relation to the workers, but the entire neighbourhood.

Soon after becoming chairman of Williamson Magor, on the occasion of the official opening at Four Mangoe Lane on 6 December 1968, BM assured the entire tea industry that he would continue to maintain a progressive outlook and would share his know-how with others, and cooperate with other agencies in a constant quest for newer and better methods of making tea and protecting the interests of the industry.

The years have proved BM to be a man of his word. His sincere and

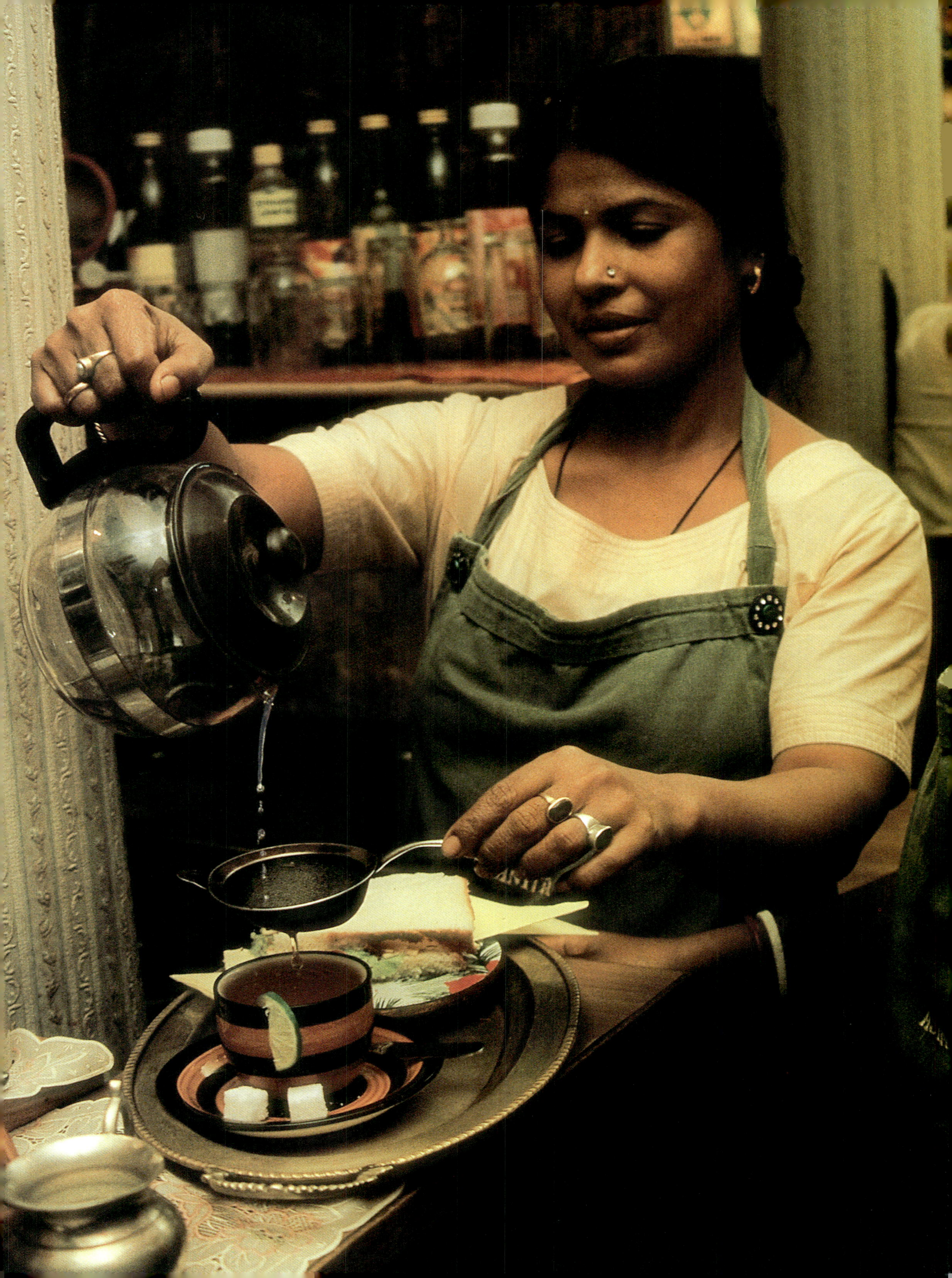

transparent commitment to the tea industry has resulted in his winning the trust and respect of the tea fraternity. D. Atal, former chairman of the Indian Tea Association, said: 'I have had on numerous occasions the benefit of BM's wise counsel in determining the best course of action for the tea industry. Whenever I have approached him to sort out a matter relating to tea, I received a very good response from him. He would always say, "Tell me if there is anything we can do to support the industry".'

All his life, BM has never held back from wholeheartedly tackling the problems afflicting the tea industry, and has gone out of his way to seek redressal. Paban Singh Ghatowar, former union minister of state, recalls the occasions when he had to interact with him. 'On a few occasions I have interacted with BM. He has talked about the general health of the tea industry, and I have seen him taking a lot of interest in the overall development and well-being of the industry; and he sometimes expresses his concern about the difficulties it is facing. He is totally involved with the industry.' What does BM feel about it? 'Tea is life for me: without tea I cannot think of anything.'

In cold climates, as in the hilly areas, tea is truly a blessing. *Top*: A man enjoys his cup of tea as his kettle boils merrily over the fire to provide as many more cups as he may require to fortify himself against the cold.
Below: A Kashmiri woman and her daughter sit behind a samovar drinking *kahawa* tea known for its flavour and aroma.

Facing page: Sharing multiplies the pleasure: hill people relaxing over *chai*.

Promoting Tea

Deeply committed as it is to the overall development of Assam, the Williamson Magor group has played a visionary role in promoting the interests of the tea industry, rightly believing that Assam and tea are interdependent; that they share a common destiny. At Williamson Magor it has always been clearly understood that the fortunes of tea and Assam are interlinked, and that if the tea industry prospers, so will Assam. The group has always taken the lead in persuading the government to reduce the crippling burden of taxes imposed on the industry, and been at the forefront in presenting the industry's problems to the latter and seeking their redressal through relentless effort.

When the government of India set up a committee headed by an eminent economist, Dr L.C. Jain, to prepare a blueprint for the economic development of Assam, the chairman of Williamson Magor wrote to him on 30 March 1996, drawing his attention to the crippling impact of the budget on the tea industry. He pointed out that the withdrawal of Section 32 AB and the investment deposit scheme had created a far more negative impact than the benefits provided by the reduction in corporate tax. BM's contention was that while corporate tax had been reduced by 10 per cent, the overall tax payable had increased by 10 per cent. 'This is due to the dual taxation imposed on the tea industry by the centre and the state, the tax rate being as high as 83 per cent for Assam.' His consistent efforts to achieve a reduction of the tax on tea in

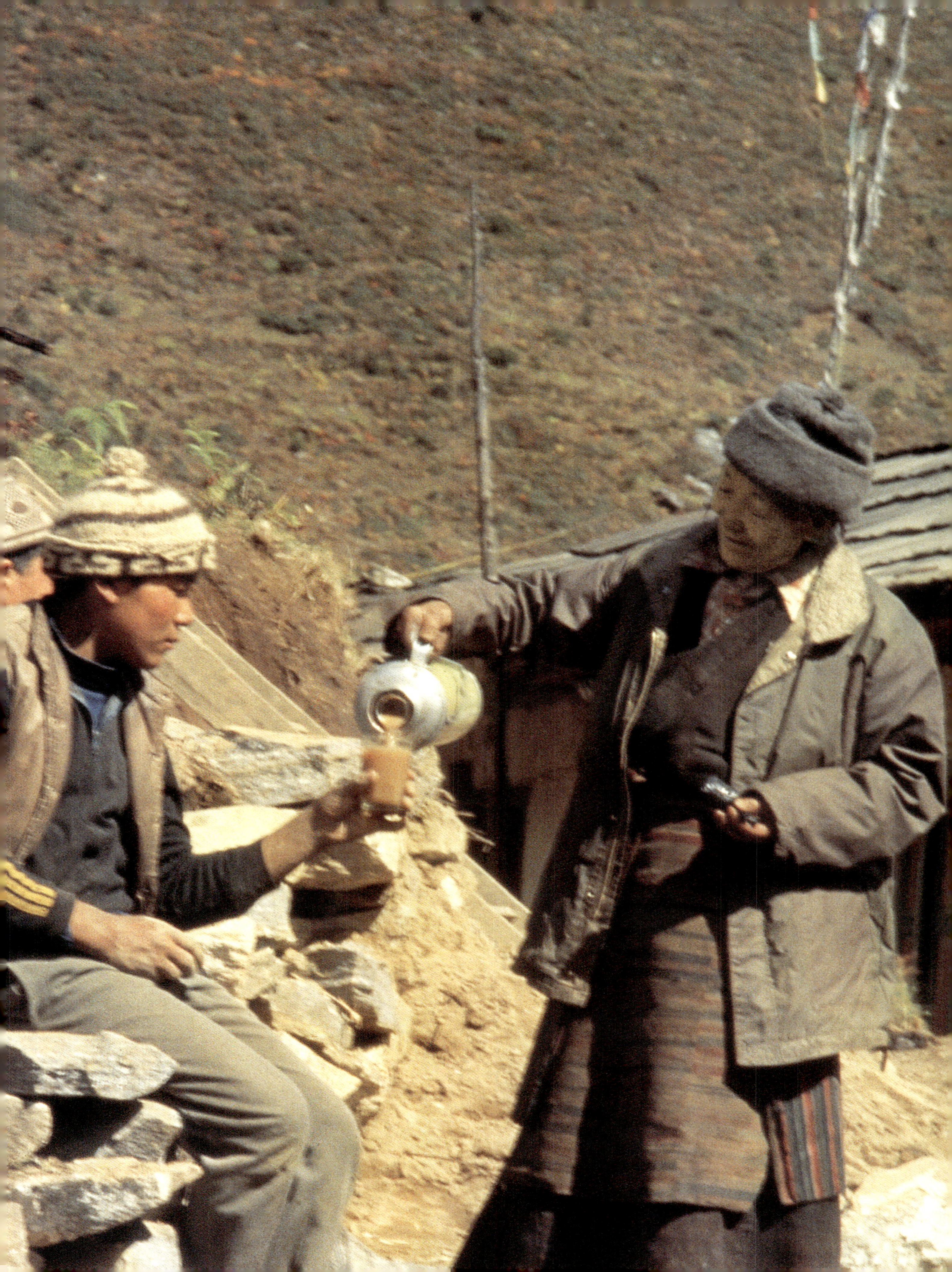

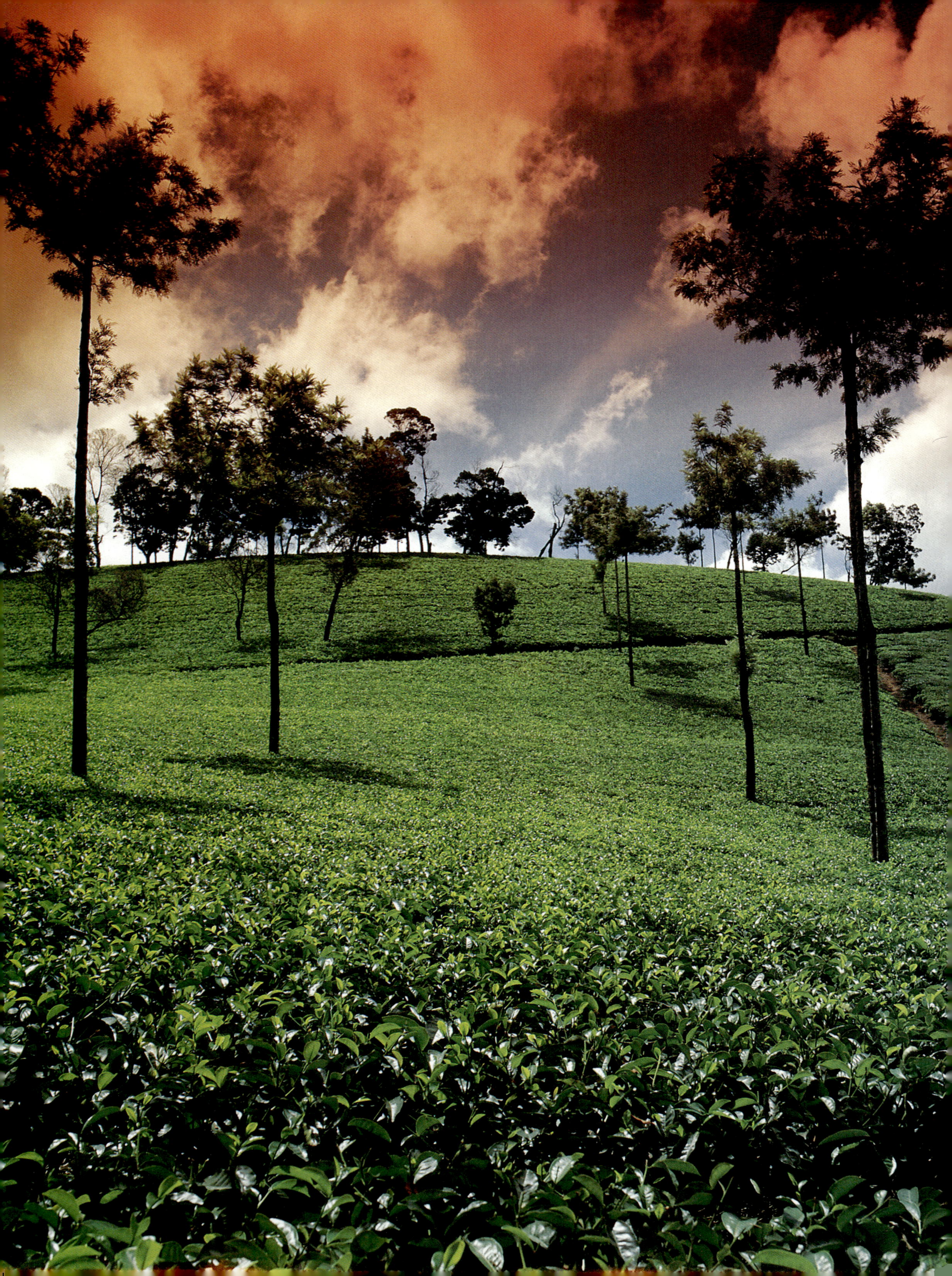

Assam state were eventually to have an effect on the government. He assured the then chief minister, 'You reduce the tax and I assure you that government revenue will not fall'.

Efforts spanning 15 years to get the taxes reduced finally bore fruit in 1993. The government took him at his word and reduced agricultural income tax from 75 to 60 per cent. Commenting on the 20 per cent deduction for development purposes, R.B. Magor wrote to BM on 14 September 1993: 'It is a great achievement and we and the entire tea industry are in your debt.' Later, the government of West Bengal also reduced the tax.

The Williamson Magor group has always supported various business and research organizations of the Indian tea industry. It has also invested a lot of time and resources in enhancing their efficiency and image. Many senior executives of Williamson Magor have headed the Indian Tea Association and made notable contributions to the cause of the tea industry. Among them, A.G. Watson (1892), G.G. Anderson (1898–9), R.L. Williamson (1908), A.D. Gordon (1913, 1916–17, 1920, 1924, 1928), K.B. Miller (1934), E.H. Hannay, OBE (1966), and K.M. Kidwai (1972–3) are some names to reckon with.

The late Mumtaz Ahmad enjoyed an impeccable reputation in the tea industry. 'Mumtaz Ahmad is a doyen of the tea industry. It is a token of the appreciation of the producers and traders for you, Mumtaz, that your name has been suggested for inclusion in the national level council, although no alphabets have been mentioned after your name to describe your position in the industry,' said Dinesh Singh, union commerce minister, at the National Tea Seminar in Coonoor on 6 September 1989. Ahmad was also the chairman of the Indian Tea Association in 1984. His tenure was aptly described as a tumultuous year for the tea industry in the country.

In the words of Mumtaz Ahmad, 'The realization of a higher unit value for our tea meant for India and other tea-producing countries a twenty-year-old dream came true. It also meant that the hard and intensive work put in by the Food and Agricultural Organization and the governments of the tea-producing countries, including India, all working jointly and towards the same purpose, had borne fruit.' He added, 'We were therefore so pleasantly surprised when the export duty was removed. It was reduced to Rs 2 per kg in September 1978, and was abolished completely in February 1979.' Mumtaz always fought for the tea industry. 'Whatever little success I have had during my tenure is on account of my credibility and the full support of the Williamson Magor group,' he said.

Top: Plucking leaves with a gentle touch: this function is generally performed over fifty thousand times a day by a single worker.

Facing page: Camellia sinensis lives in an earthly paradise: a majestic tea garden in southern India blessed by colourful clouds and the hymns of the wind. The setting sun paints the sky in a riot of colours, creating an iridescence in the sky. Such eye-catchingly beautiful gardens have inspired poets, photographers, and writers to great heights of creativity.

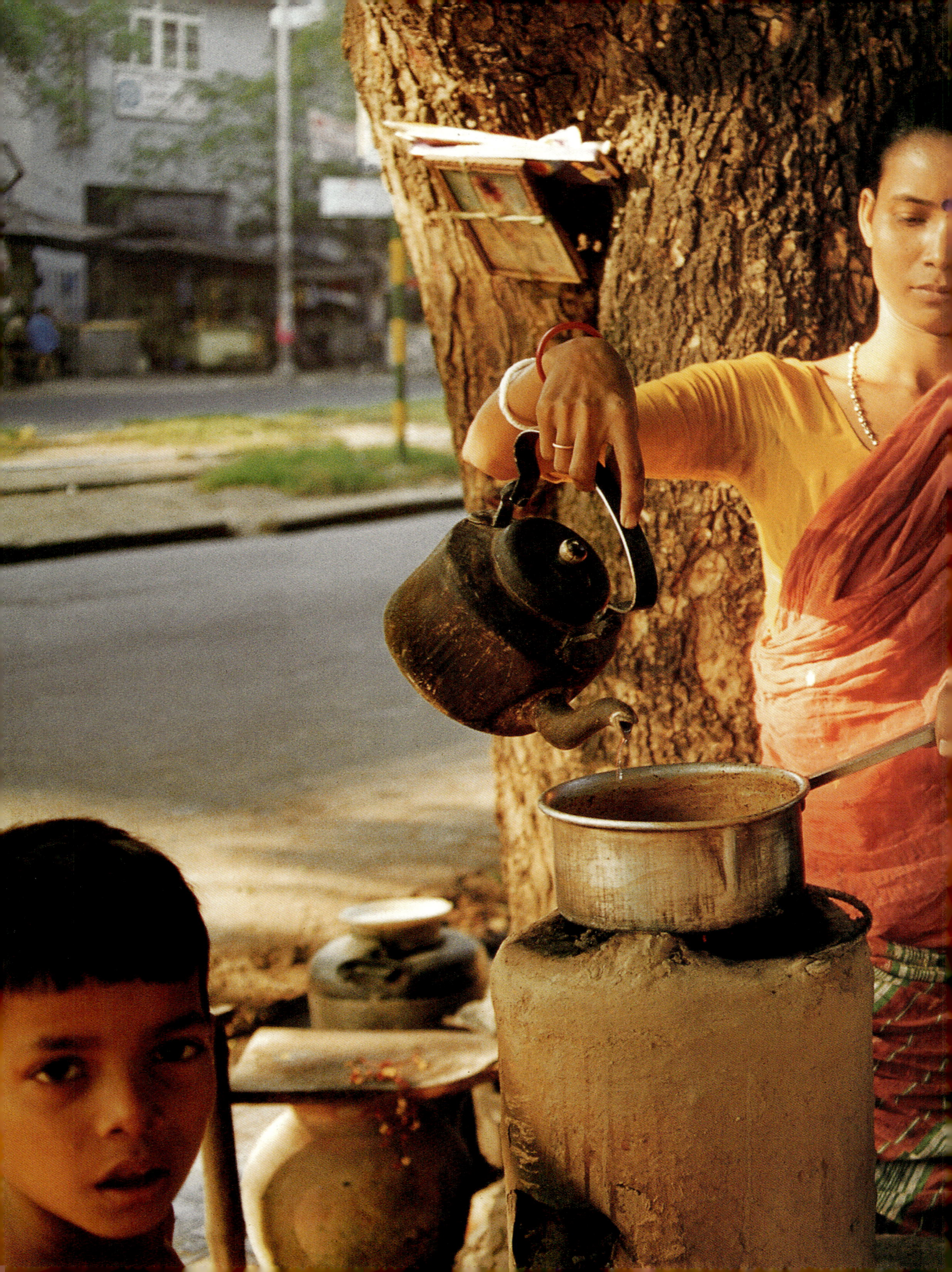

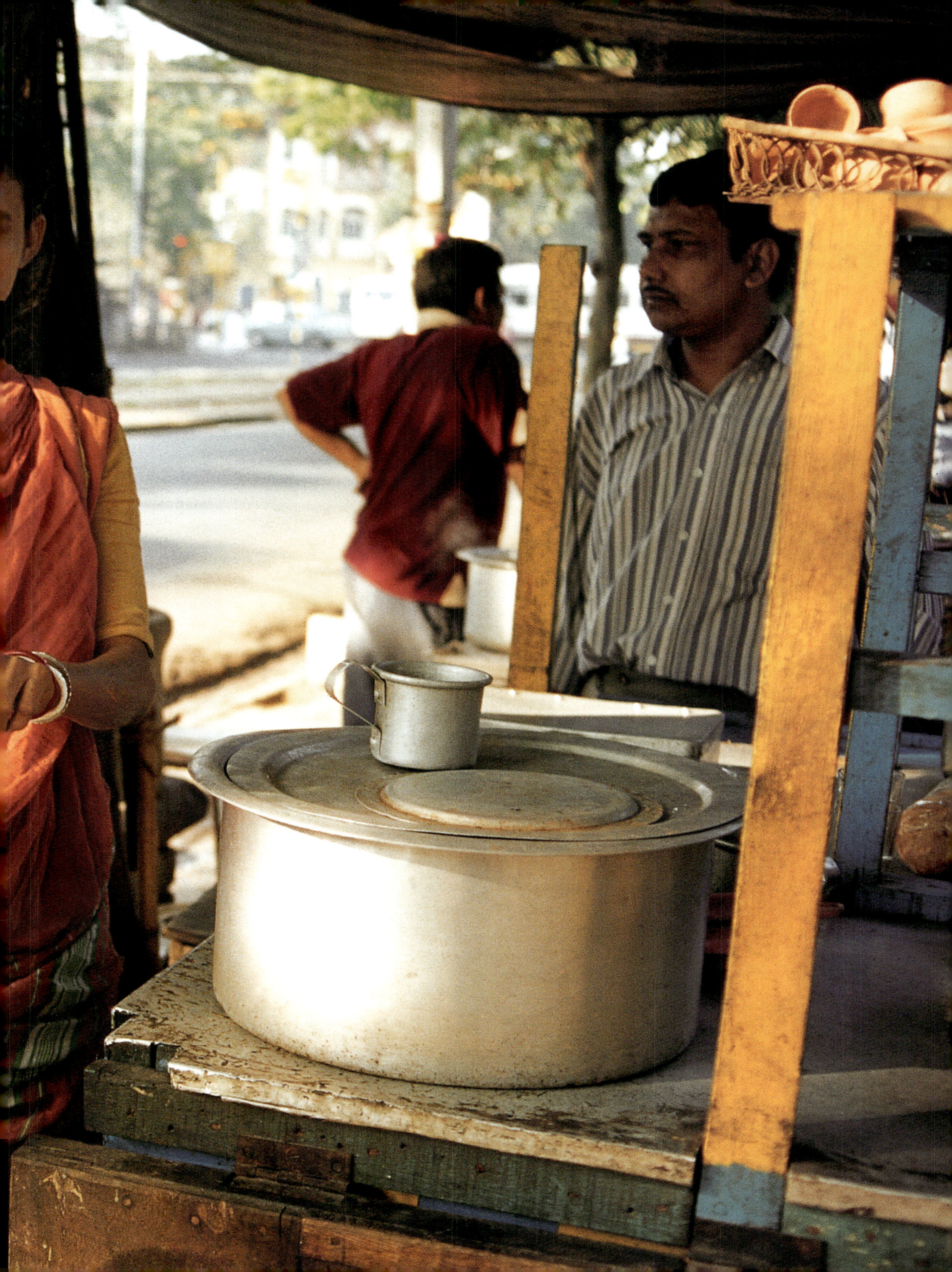

Top left: A heavy beard and moustache is no barrier to the enjoyment of *chai* in *desi* style in Rajasthan. *Top right:* A Muslim relishing the goodness of *chai* in the company of a friend.

Facing page: Bubbling over with a fragrant aroma ...

Preceding spread: Roadside tea shops are popular everywhere: a *chai-wali* making a cup of tea in Calcutta where tea and gossip go hand in hand.

R.L. Rikhye was the chairman of the Indian Tea Association in 1985–6 when the government introduced an export price policy under which Indian tea was priced out of the international market, leading to inordinate delays in supply. In consequence, the industry lost most of its export market in the United States. Rikhye took up the issue with the Ministry of Finance which took a decision to withdraw the minimum export price policy. Credit goes to Rikhye too for motivating the government to reduce the rate of interest on borrowings from financial institutions. He also successfully conducted mutually beneficial negotiations with the various unions regarding wage agreements in relation to tea workers.

A Noteworthy Contribution

R.S. Jhawar's initiatives and drive in the Indian Tea Association have been widely recognized. The Association has, under his leadership, taken fresh initiatives that have impacted export promotion, government relations, price stabilization, and improved interaction among various sections of its membership. As chairman of the Consultative Committee of Plantation Associations, the apex body of tea producers in India, Jhawar has promoted consensus building within the industry on vital issues. These efforts have had the full support of Four Mangoe Lane.

170 | THE HERITAGE OF INDIAN TEA

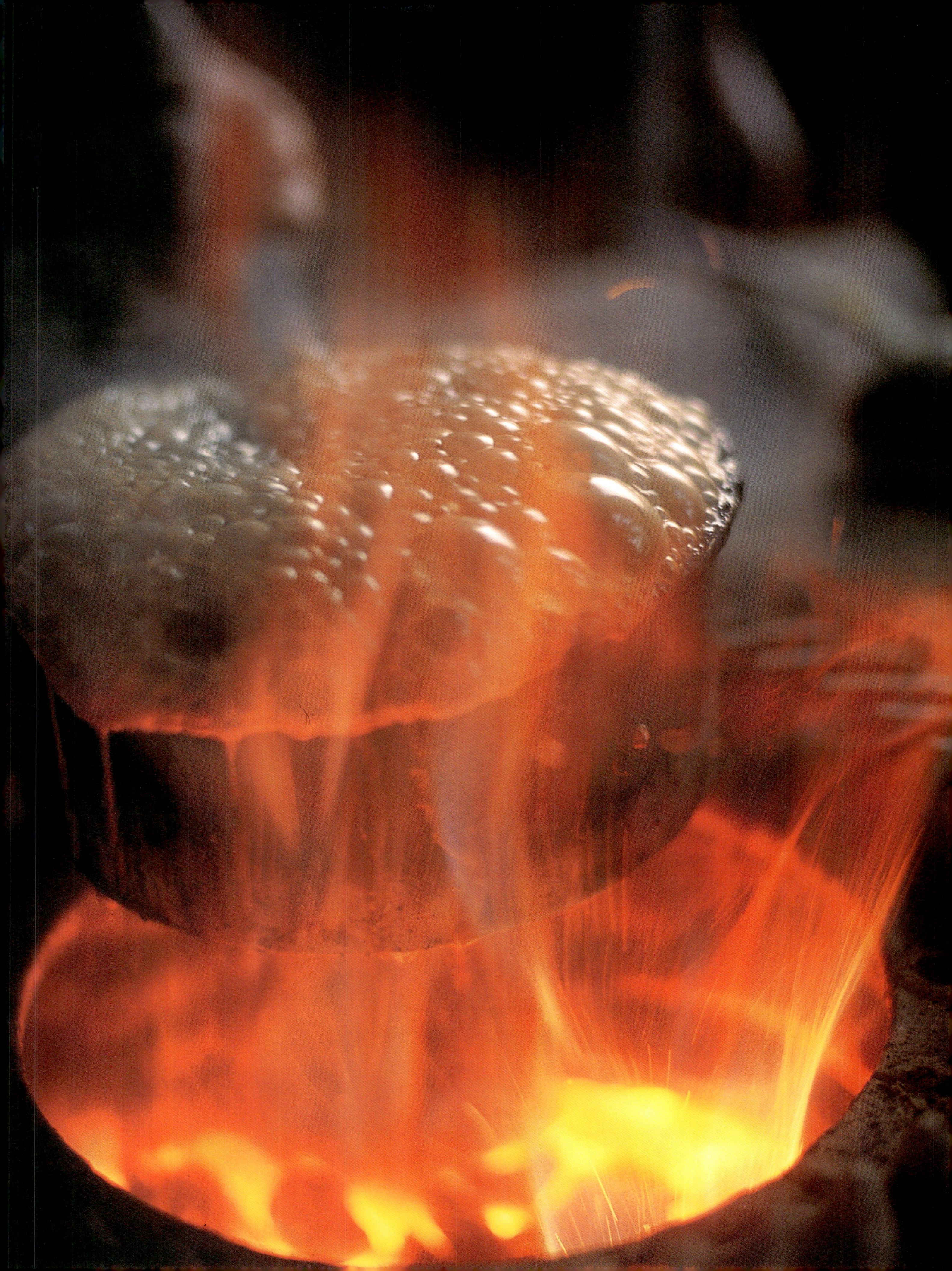

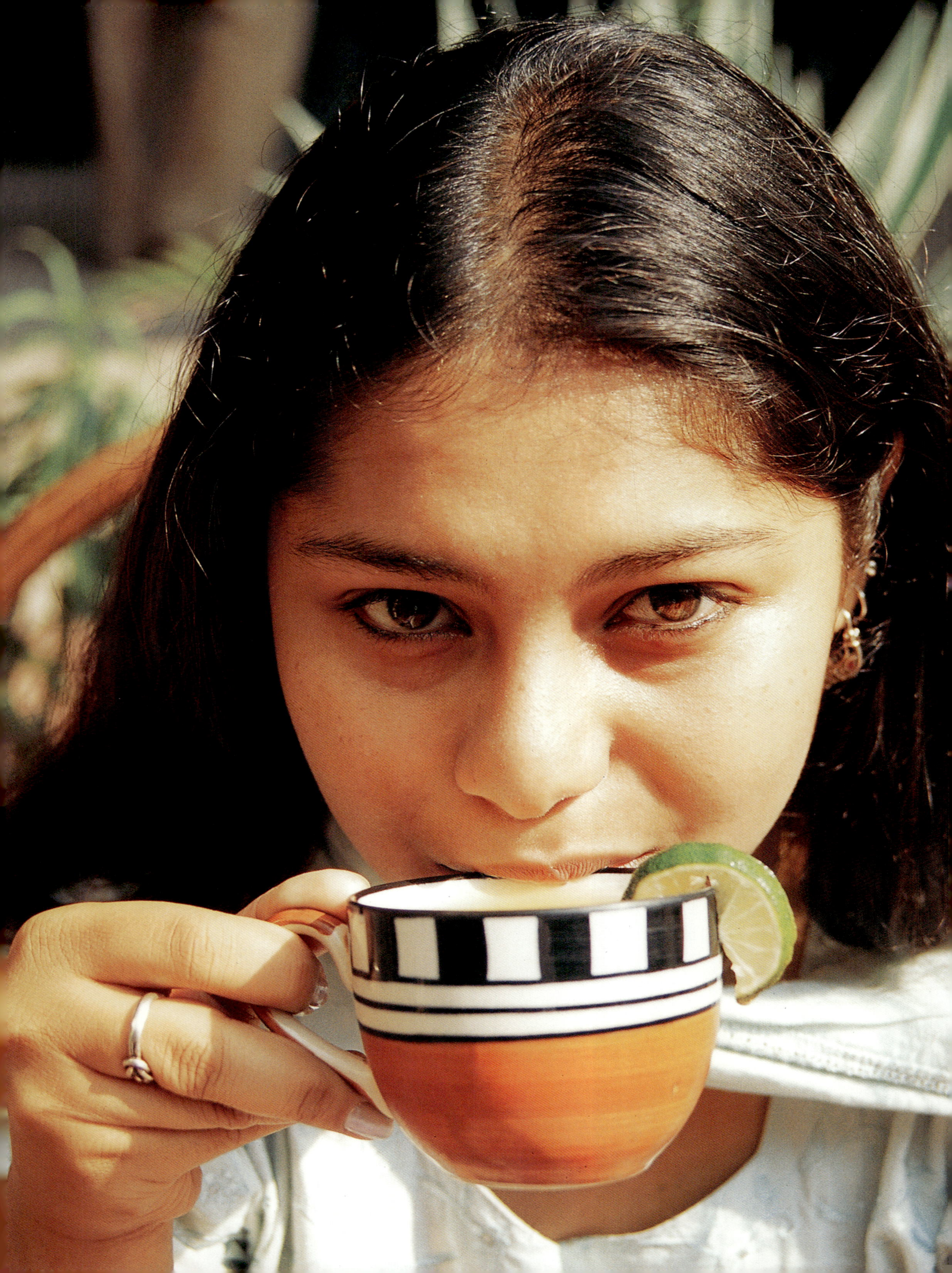

It was the Association's vision that led to the India International Millennium Tea Convention in New Delhi in March 2000. It was attended by 800 delegates, including 150 international participants from a range of countries. It was the largest convention ever held in the world to consider issues relating to tea and human health, and not only helped in improving the image of Indian tea, but also led to the promotion of tea as a health beverage on the basis of the findings of research conducted by eminent scientists and research scholars.

As chairman of the Indian Tea Association, Jhawar has attended a number of conferences and symposia all over the world and made sustained efforts to improve the image of Indian tea and to enhance its status in the world market. An aggressive export marketing effort was subsequently launched by the Indian Tea Association to increase India's share of the international market. These vigorous efforts resulted in a better image for Indian tea and a slight improvement in India's exports to the USA, UAE, several other Middle-Eastern countries, and Pakistan.

Keeping in view the emerging scenario of a progressive dismantlement of import barriers, the Association mounted strong representations to the commerce and finance ministries to institute appropriate tariff safeguards to provide a level playing field for the industry. As a result of these efforts the basic customs duty on import of tea was raised initially from 15 to 35 per cent, and, thereafter, the budget proposals for 2001–2 provided for a further enhancement from 35 to 70 per cent.

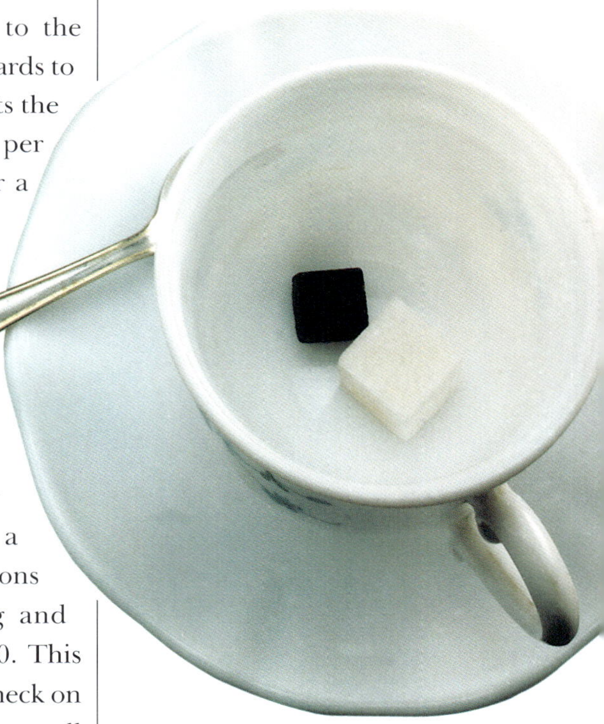

The contentious issue of sampling costs involved in sales through auctions was taken up by the Association with the Tea Board of India. After protracted discussions among representatives of the trade, and the Tea Board of India's strong and proactive mediation, a revised set of sampling norms was announced. These norms are expected to significantly reduce outflow of free samples to the trade and thereby improve the efficiency of sales through the auction system. In a significant move, the Consultative Committee of Plantation Associations unanimously decided to temporarily cease plucking and manufacture in north India from 12 December 2000. This step was taken to control production and to keep a check on the availability of poor quality teas in the market as well as to arrest any further downslide in prices, although both operations were resumed in March 2001 and had only a marginal impact on tea prices.

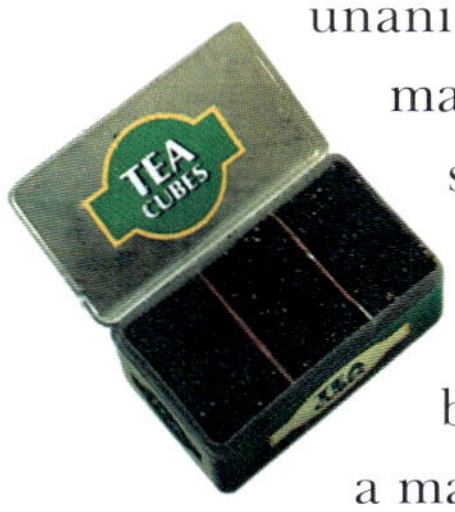
TEA
CUBES

Top: Tea cubes are becoming more popular by the day.

Facing page: Tea is moving with the times: a young girl enjoying lemon tea.

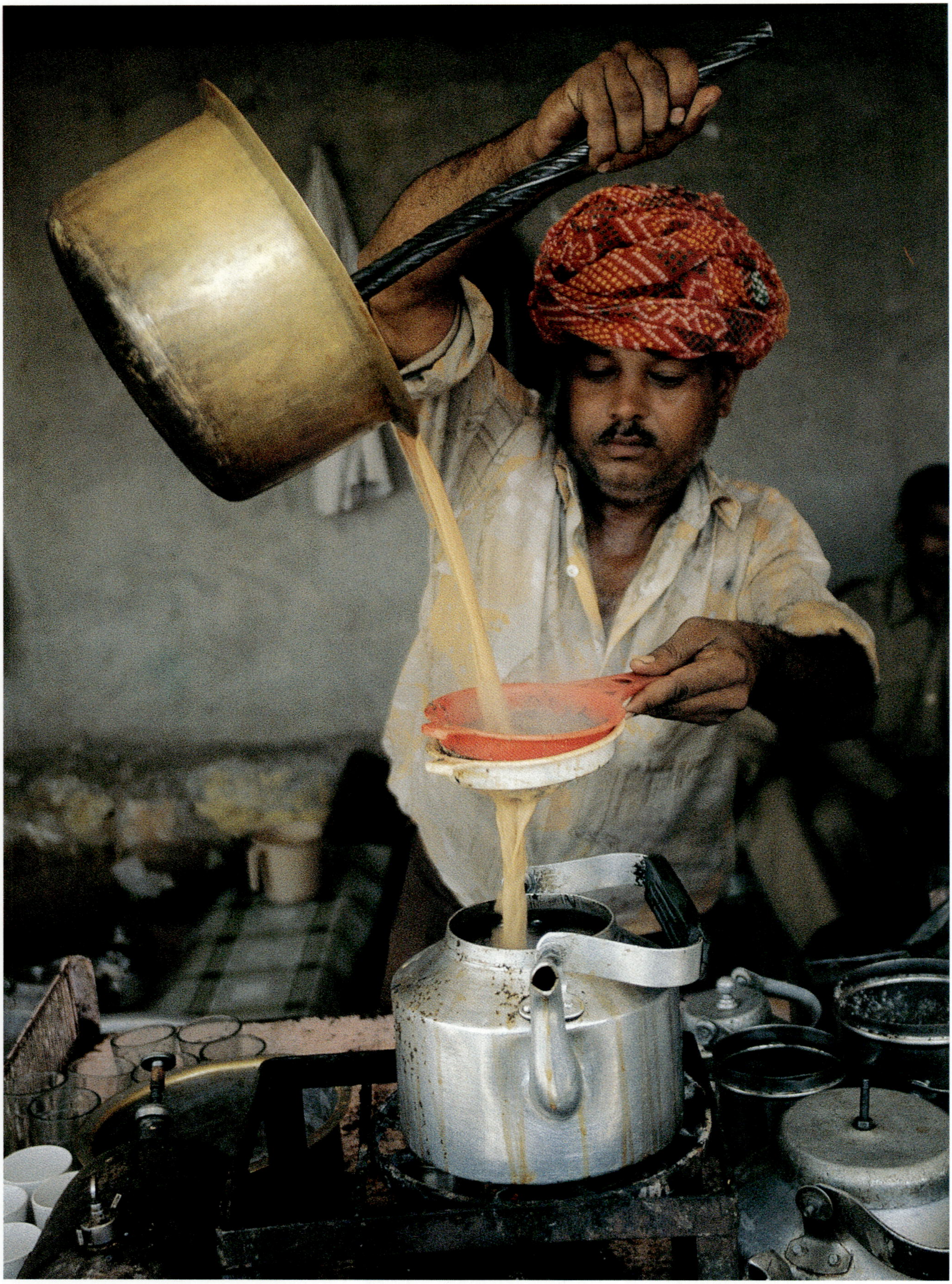

Hand in Hand

Several contentious issues with the Assam government were resolved during the first year of Jhawar's tenure as chairman of the Association. The Association negotiated with the government on the proposal to raise land revenue. In the eventual settlement the rates were much lower than those originally proposed by the government. The latter has, in principle, agreed to fund 49 per cent of the major items of expenditure on research and development conducted by the Tea Research Association. Negotiations were held with the Assam Cha Mazdoor Sangha on the long-standing issue of wages for the weekly day of rest and a settlement was arrived at. To resolve the growing problem of unemployment, the plantation industry has agreed to provide permanent jobs to 10,000 people.

The tea industry has been facing difficult times from early 1999 with tea prices showing a downward trend and a decline in production. Exports have also fallen. The very real problems faced by the industry have come home to the union government which recently allowed flexibility in the auction system, increased the customs duty on imported tea, and enhanced the allowance under section 33 AB. To achieve this the Indian Tea Association played an important role in appropriately presenting the case and lobbying with the central government on these issues.

Appreciating Jhawar's tenure in the Indian Tea Association, Prabir Sengupta, union commerce secretary, wrote to him on 30 July 2001, 'I must commend you for the very sincere efforts that you have made for the promotion of the interests of the tea industry as also the perseverance with which you articulated the issues.' L.V. Saptharishi, additional secretary, added, 'You facilitated our task by maintaining an excellent rapport with us and giving us feedback on all the important developments affecting the interests of the tea industry.'

Four Mangoe Lane provides approximately one-third of the budget of the Assam Branch Indian Tea Association, and more importantly, permits its senior tea planters to work for the organization. M.L. Rome (1970), T.N. Barooah (1979 & 1980), G.F. Simpson (1981), D. Prakash (1987), Mandhata Singh (1989), Wazir Khan (1992–3), T.C. Bordoloi (1995–6), and A.N. Zaman (1996–7) have provided dynamic leadership and implemented several welfare projects in Assam. Besides this, Williamson Magor executives have been untiring in their efforts towards ensuring the prosperity of the Indian tea industry by actively participating in the proceedings of various associations and research centres as members of the general committee and the sundry sub-committees.

Top: Tea is also associated with travel. *Garam chai* provides solace to the weary traveller. *Below:* Every city or town has its own popular tea shops where people relax momentarily over a cup of tea, and have their own unique ways of cooling it.

Facing page: Would you like some tea? Every *chai-wala* has his own way of brewing *chai* in India with its own unique flavour and strength.

Following spread: Drinking tea outdoors is natural for Indians: no matter what the hardships ahead, *garam chai* never fails to evoke a satisfied smile.

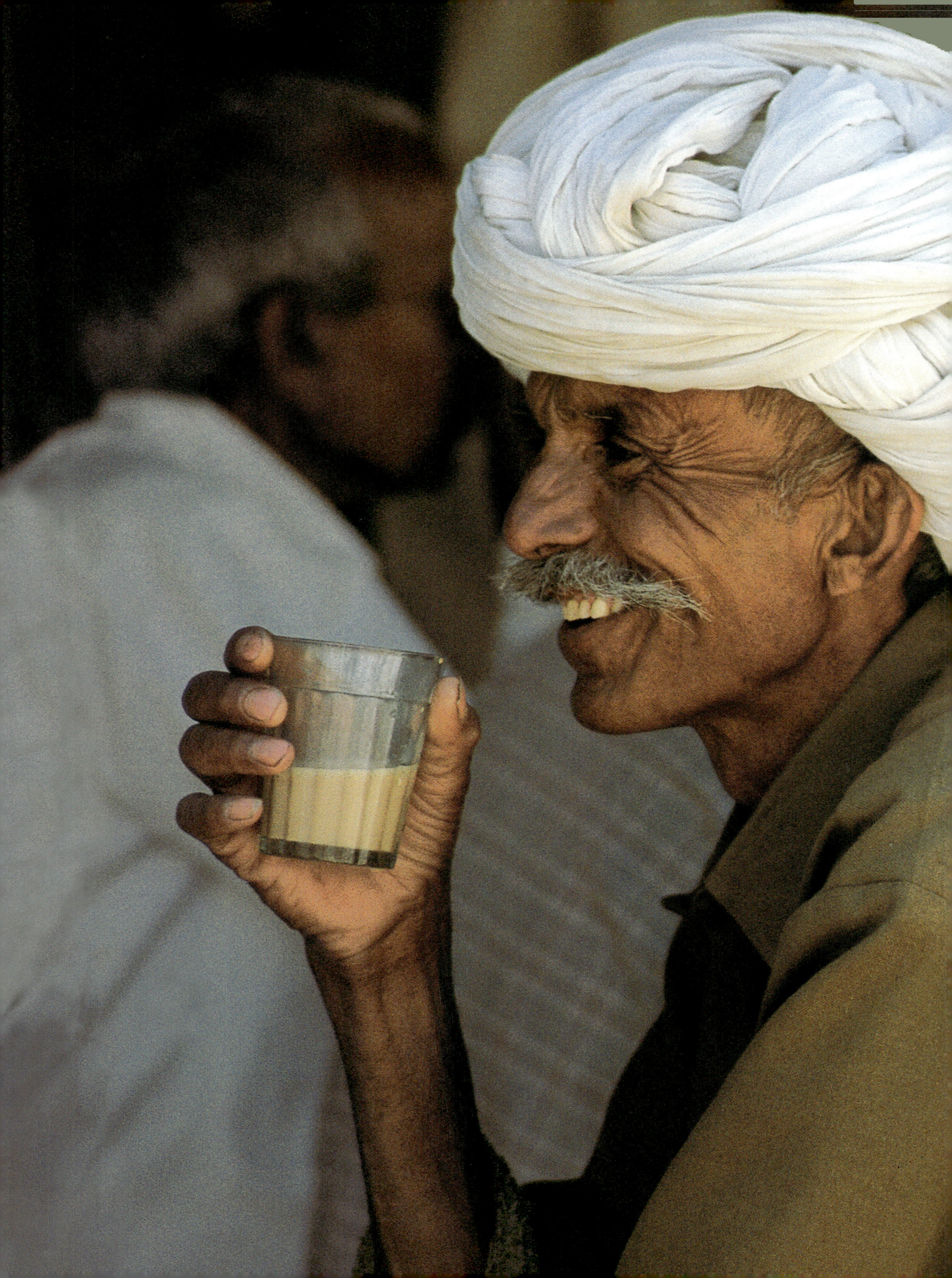

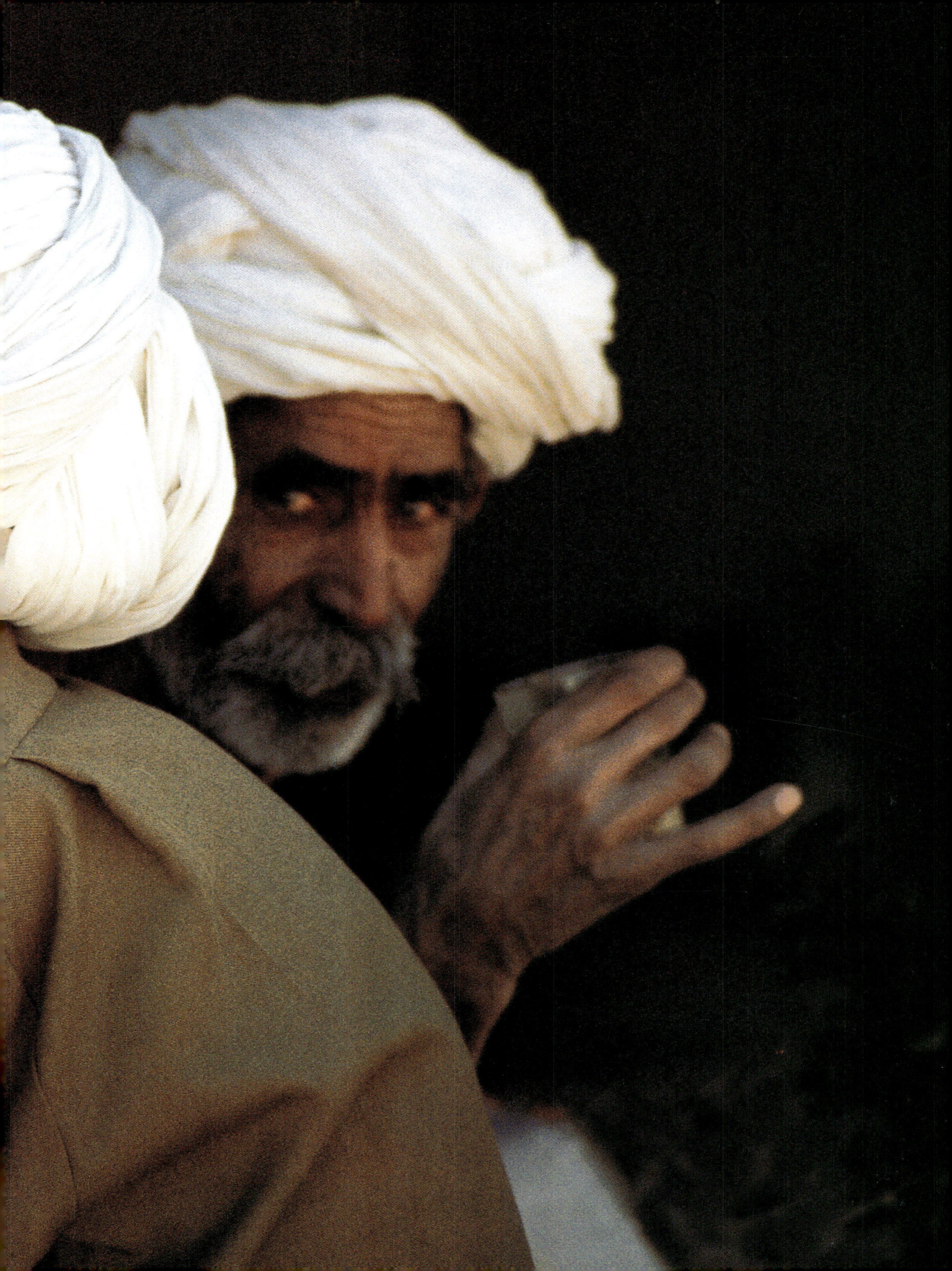

Top: Pluckers are habituated to working on steep mountain slopes to give us our morning cup of tea.

Facing page: Nature lends her finery to a tea garden in Munnar. Mountains, waterfalls, clouds, and greenery all catch a breath amidst the tranquillity of nature.

The Williamson Magor group was actively involved in the setting up of an Inland Container Depot in Assam. R.L. Rikhye was sent to UK and other countries to study the conditions of the ports. This initial exercise resulted in timely completion of the project, and now the group provides 75 per cent of the cargo for movement from the depot. The Guwahati Tea Auction Centre is also supported by the group, as is the Assam Branch Indian Tea Association which continues to promote the development of villages in the vicinity by disseminating expertise in agricultural practices.

Oasis of Prosperity

While concerning itself with the protection of the interests of the industry as a whole, the Williamson Magor group has taken particular care of its own gardens and workers. Its gardens are special places, and apart from the various facilities provided, boast a unique atmosphere. Shanti Khaitan describes it thus, 'It is like a great big family. People are always interested in each other and what they can do for one another.' As the tea gardens are often located

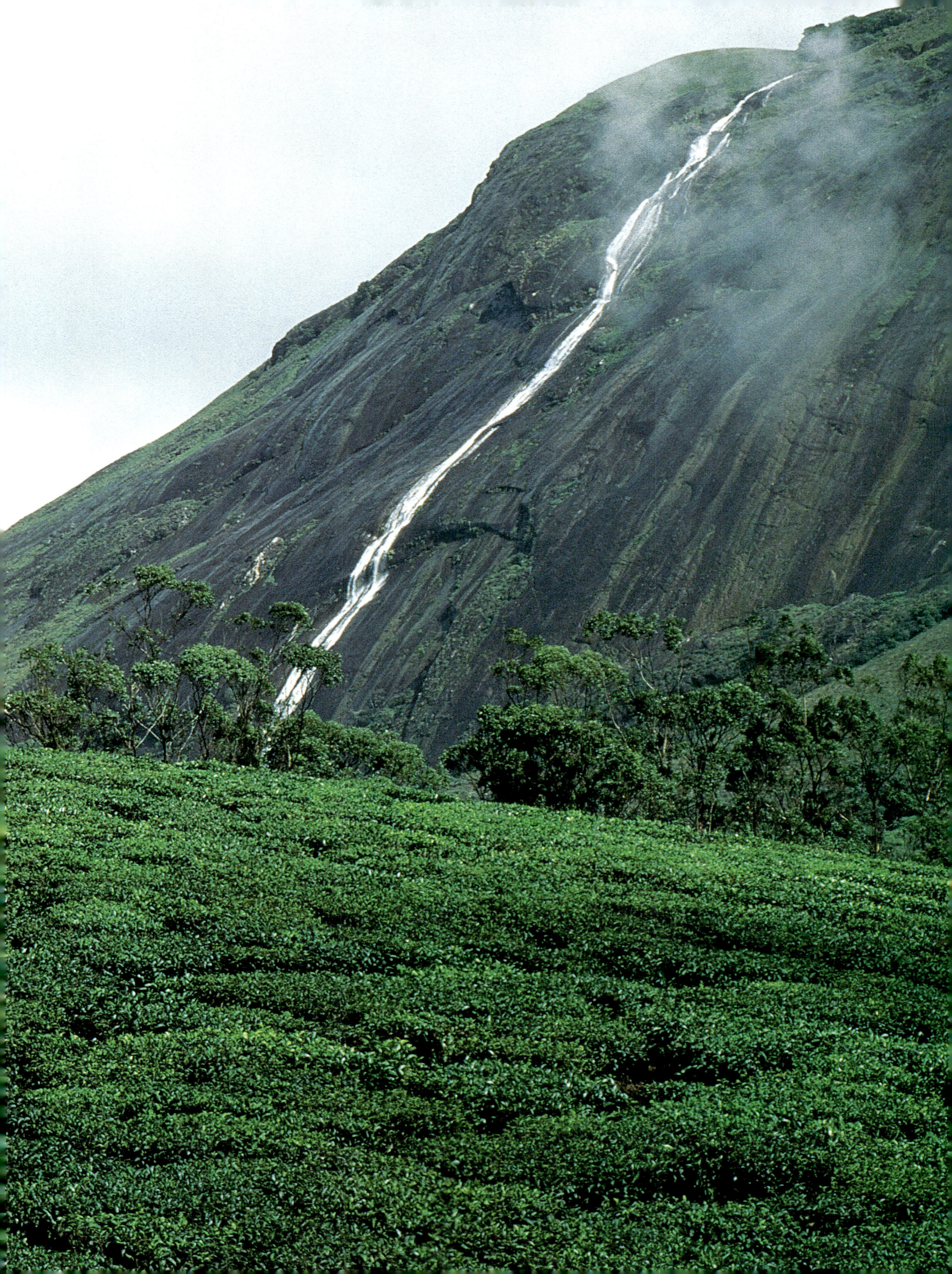

Top: Darjeeling pluckers arriving at a tea garden shrouded by the morning mist.

Facing page: Women pluckers in Assam are impatient to start their day's routine. Large shade trees is an essential feature of Assam gardens.

Following spread: After a tiring day, pluckers leave the garden with their pickings for respite at home.

in remote and backward regions, their air of prosperity and well-being make them stand out as isolated oases of privilege in an otherwise desolate landscape. This naturally triggers both resentment and envy.

Williamson Magor was quick to recognize this problem, avers its chairman. 'A tea garden today has become like an oasis among the villages. The worker is well looked after, he has access to good hospitals, he gets food at a concessional price, he gets wages coming every day, and his standard of living and everything is far better than his neighbour's. This leads to problems.'

As far as the group is concerned, the solution to this particular problem is simple: 'We want to spread more and more prosperity around,' says BM, and that is exactly what the group has done. The entire top management shares this spirit of trying to contribute at the human level too; it believes in growing tea not just for profits but for 'something more'.

At Williamson Magor, many unsung but crucially important welfare initiatives emerge at the level of the garden manager and are implemented within the tea estate itself. The company recognizes that a manager on the tea garden is often considered to be a benefactor, and as a benefactor he is bound to develop a concern and affection for those around him who are dependent on him. 'Running a tea garden,' says Aditya Khaitan perceptively, 'epitomizes everything that life has to offer.'

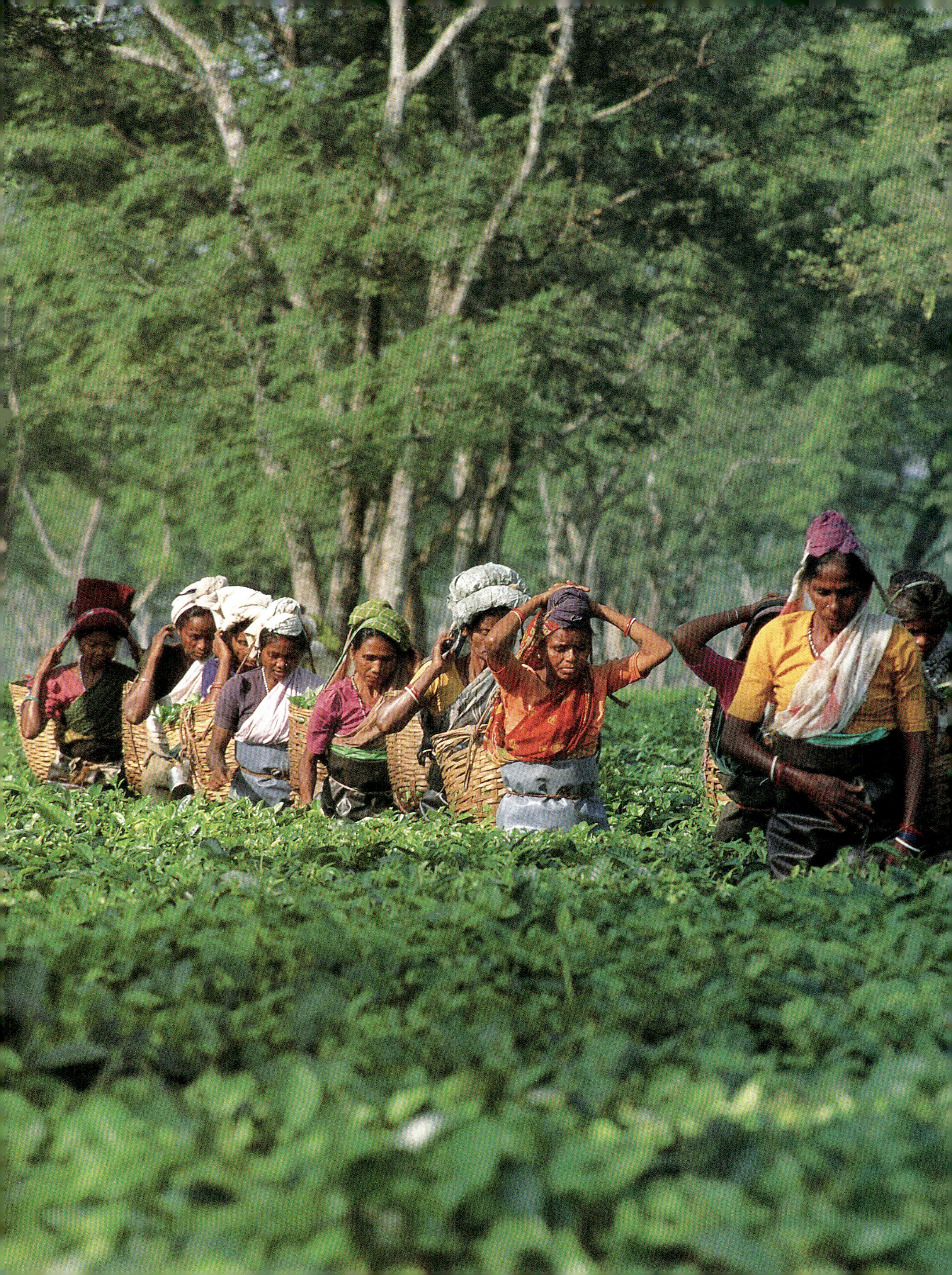

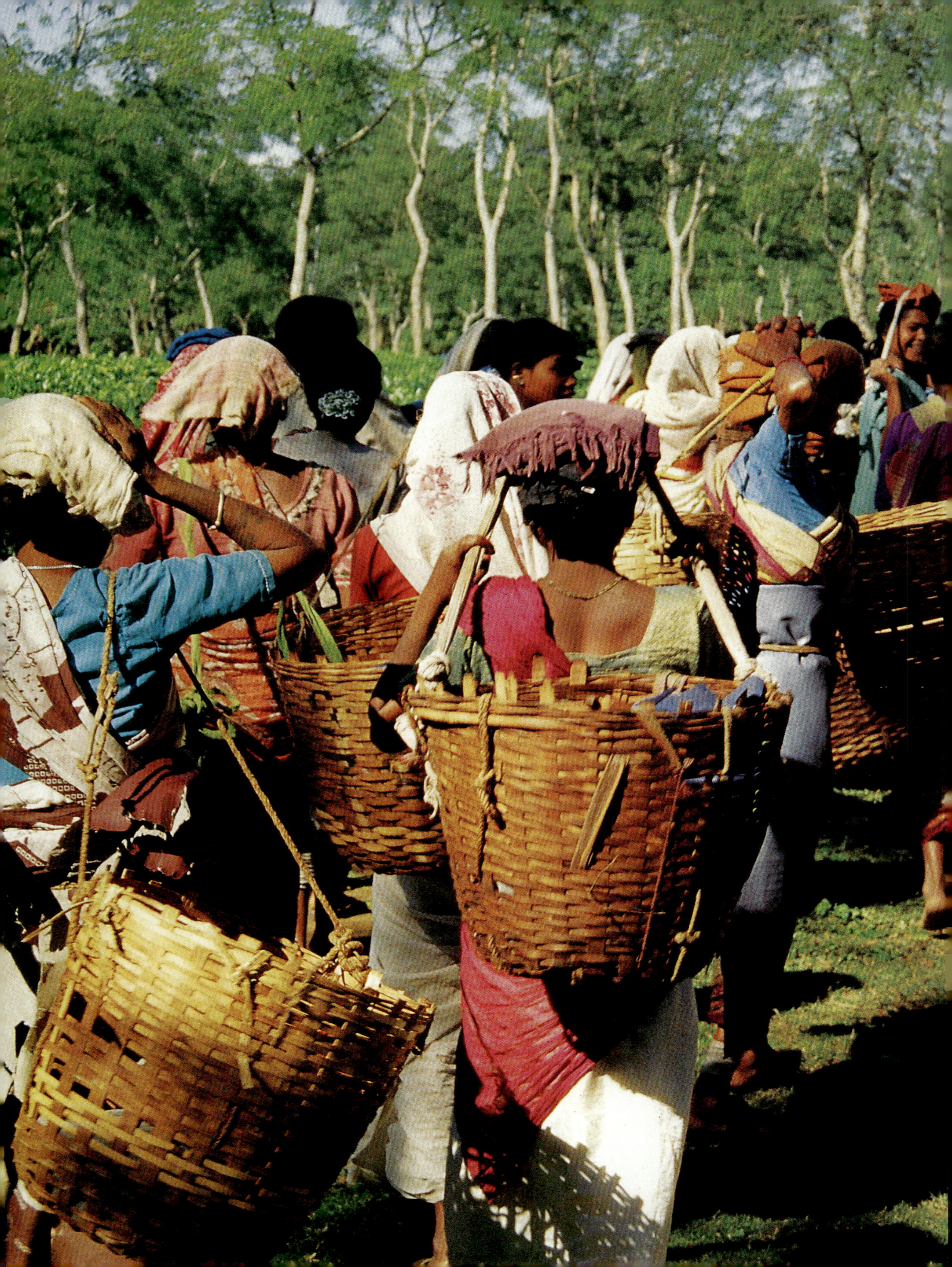

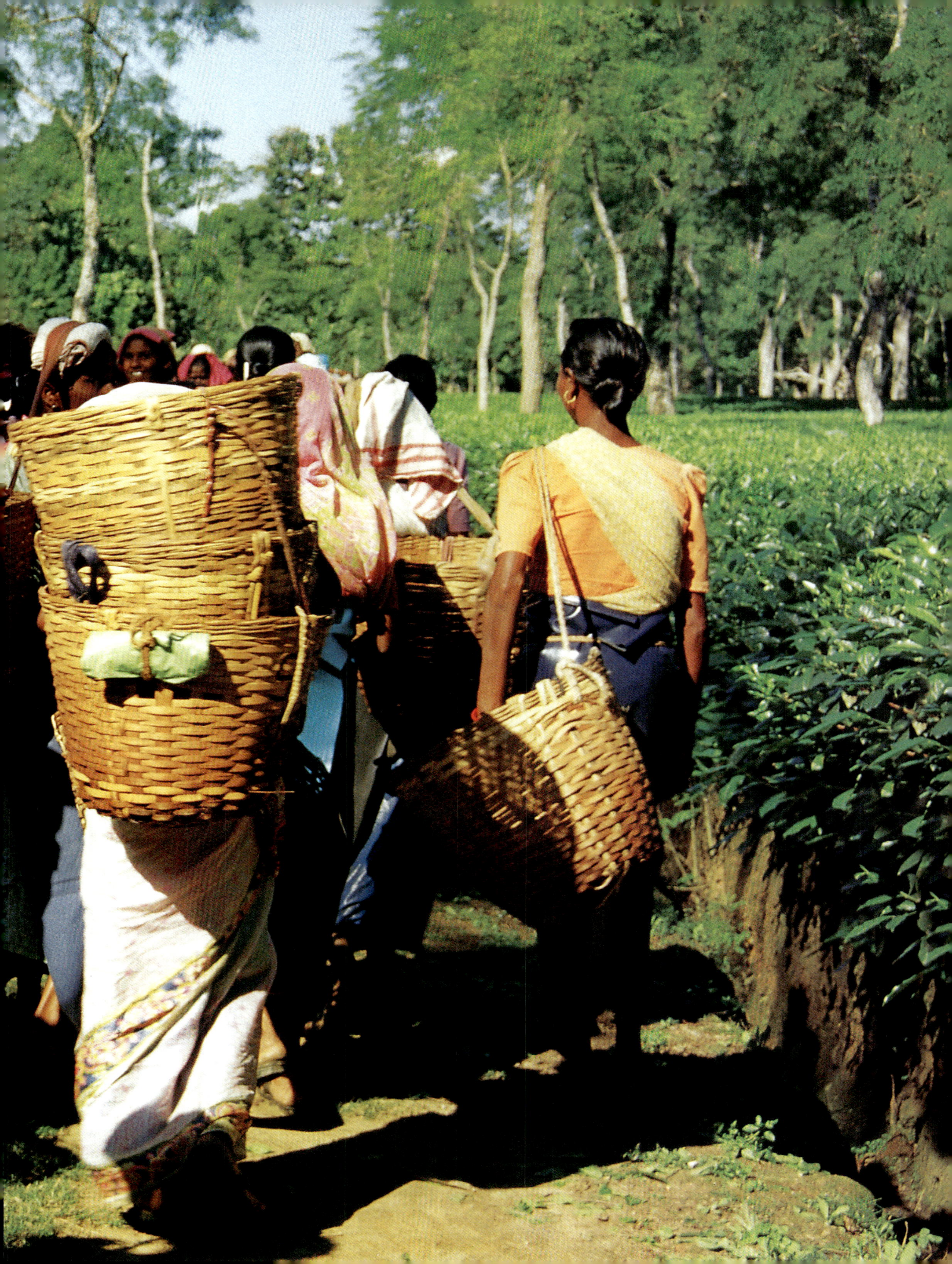

Looking to the Future

The B.M. Khaitan and R.B. Magor saga dates back to the sixties. Together they established the Williamson Magor brand that has had a well-earned reputation for decades as a producer of quality teas. Over the years, the Khaitans and the Magors have managed their tea business with single-minded dedication and produced top-quality teas that find a ready market with discerning buyers all over the world.

Their partnership has produced a titan in the tea industry, yet many readers will be unaware that the tea gardens of this group have all along been three distinct entities: the Bishnauth Tea Company and McLeod Russel owned by the Khaitans and George Williamson (Assam) Ltd owned by the Magors.

To ensure that the future of this partnership does not run into problems, the two families recently decided that the time had come to effect an amicable parting of ways. What with the opening up of the economy and the World Trade Organization regime coming into force, this independence will ensure consolidation of their individual operations and pave the way to strengthening their individual companies, enabling them to face future challenges and exploit new opportunities.

George Williamson (Assam) Ltd will own and run its 17 gardens in Assam which have an annual production of 19.50 m. kg. The Khaitans will continue to own and run their tea gardens that have existed under the banner of Bishnauth Tea Company and McLeod Russel. Both these companies are now part of Eveready Industries (India) Ltd. The total tea production under the control of the Khaitans will be 35–8 m. kg per annum.

The corporate headquarters of the Khaitans continues to be located at Four Mangoe Lane at Calcutta while George Williamson (Assam) Ltd will relocate itself elsewhere in the city. Division of assets both at Calcutta and the plantations, including manpower, has been mutually worked out without a hitch. The Khaitans have generously cooperated with the Magors, and George Williamson (Assam) Ltd was till recently functioning from the seventh floor of Four Mangoe Lane and availing of the group's facilities.

The parting of ways with the Magors will make the Khaitan group leaner and fitter, and prepare the ground for modern management of its assets. Now, with greater senior management focus through the freeing up of managerial resources from George Williamson (Assam) Ltd, new marketing initiatives, and the promotion of the packet tea business on the back of steady domestic demand with the backing of their prime quality tea-producing gardens, the Khaitans have much to look ahead to.

Flavour, strength, sweetness, colour, and aroma characterize the cup that cheers.

Earlier, the Magors were the sole selling agents for the group's teas in London. After their planned demerger from Eveready, the Khaitans' consolidated tea business should be well positioned for the road ahead. In batteries, the principal concern is to cut costs. However, with Eveready enjoying an overwhelming brand recall of over 80 per cent, a leading market share of 43 per cent in the Indian battery market, and enjoying initial success in exploring overseas markets with the Lava brand, the Khaitans are better placed than any other Indian company for a future in the battery business. 'We are the first Indian company to sell our batteries in the US,' says an excited Deepak Khaitan, who looks after Eveready Industries (India) Ltd. Engineering firms owned by the Khaitans have done well with restructuring. Macneill Engineering Co., McNally Bharat, and Worthington Pumps have a combined turnover of Rs 3.8 bn with reasonable profits.

The group's restructuring has been on the advice of Mckinsey and Ernst & Young. This involves selling off uneconomic tea gardens, possible disposal of profit-making engineering companies, and unlocking value in major, surplus, real estate assets. This will help the Khaitans shrug off any debt overhangs. All in all, the family seems set to conquer further frontiers in the new millennium.

Top: Tea, beauty, and elegance in perfect harmony: an oil painting by James Joseph Jacques Tissot (c. 1875–8).

Following spread: A majestic and magnetic tea garden of Munnar. Munnar is predominantly a tea area, and its great natural beauty endows it with great popularity, particularly amongst the tea community. Eleanor, the newly wed bride of planter Henry Knight, came to Munnar and, fascinated by it, exclaimed to her husband, 'Wherever I die, bury me here'.

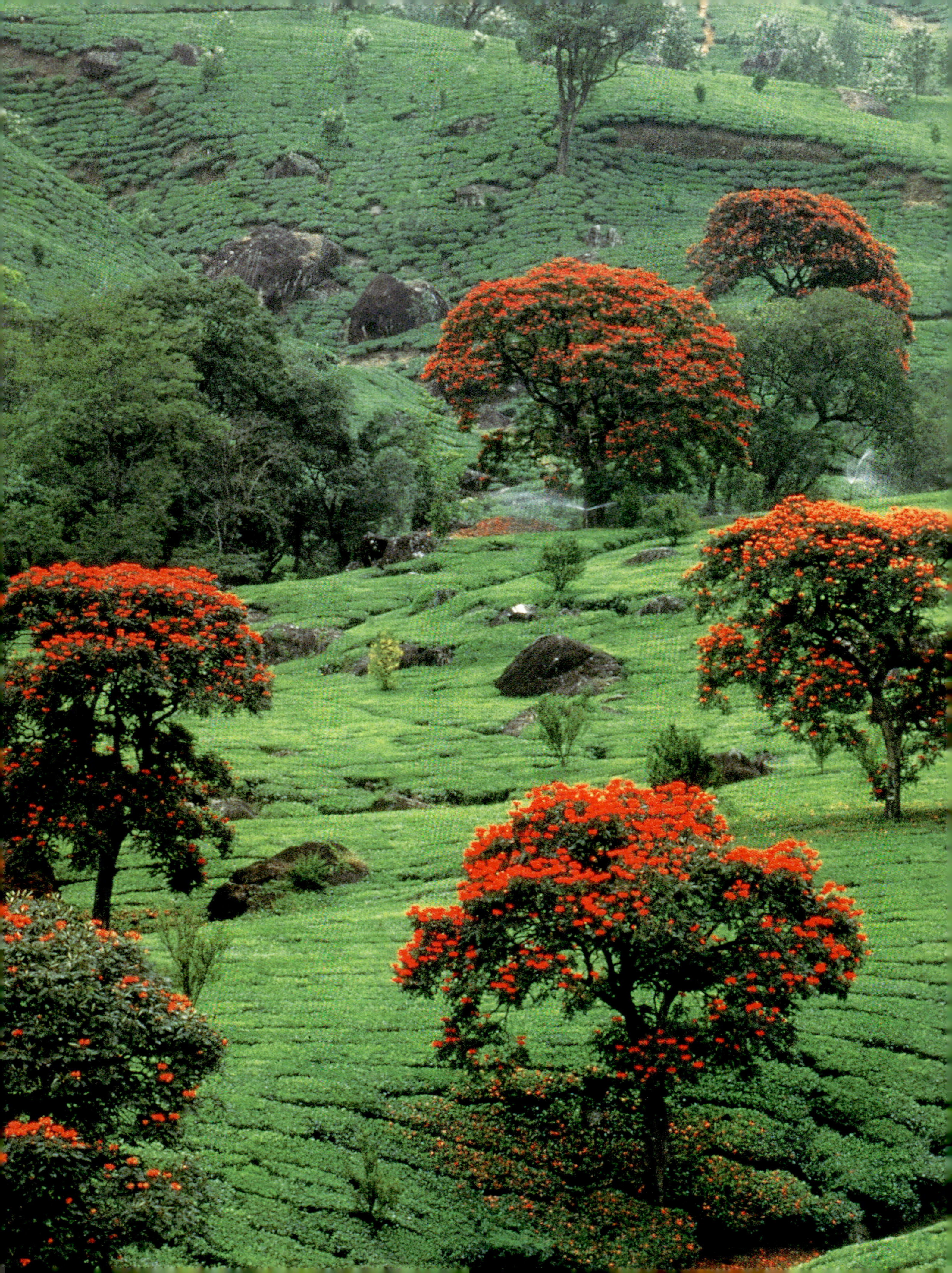

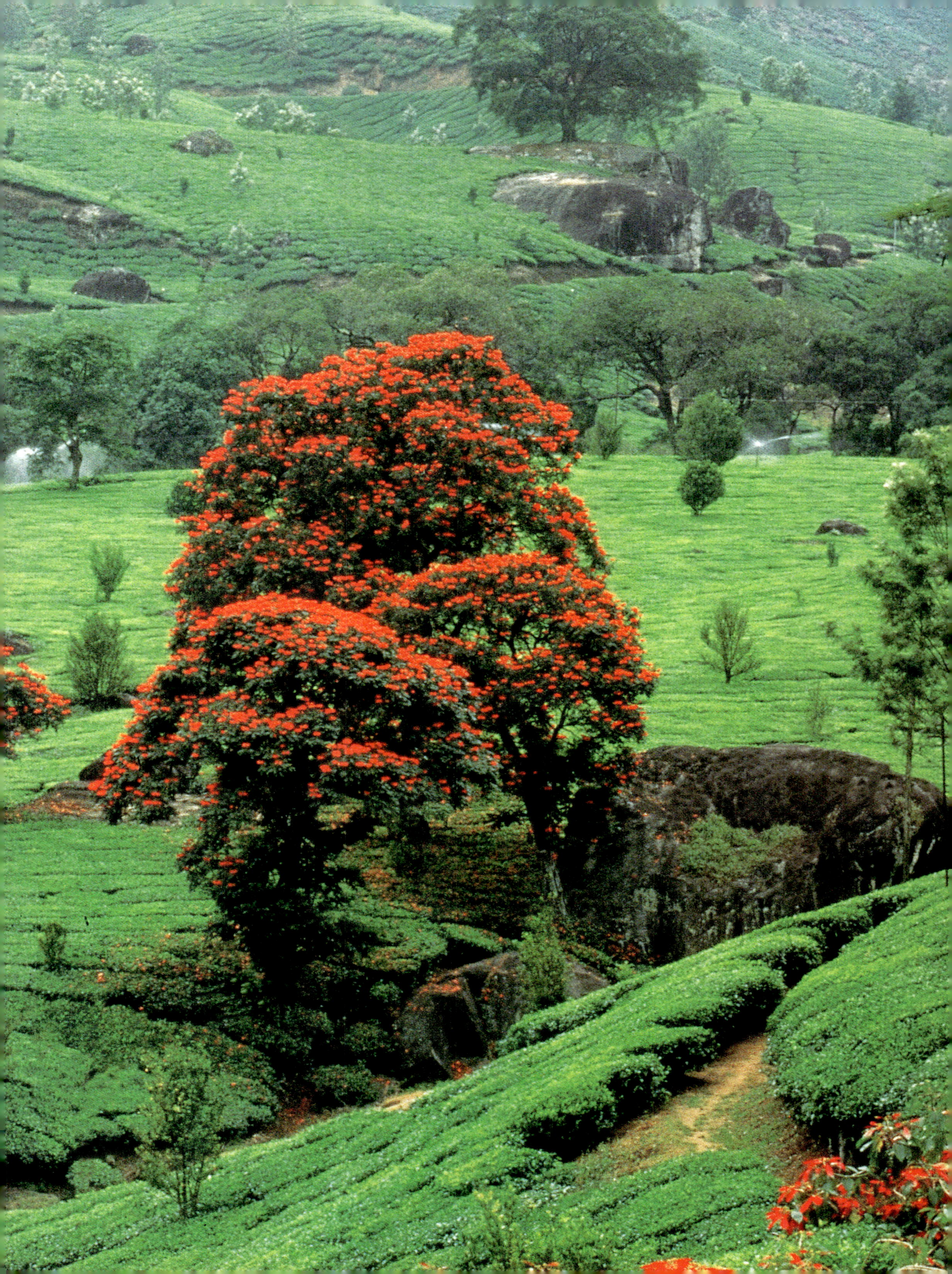

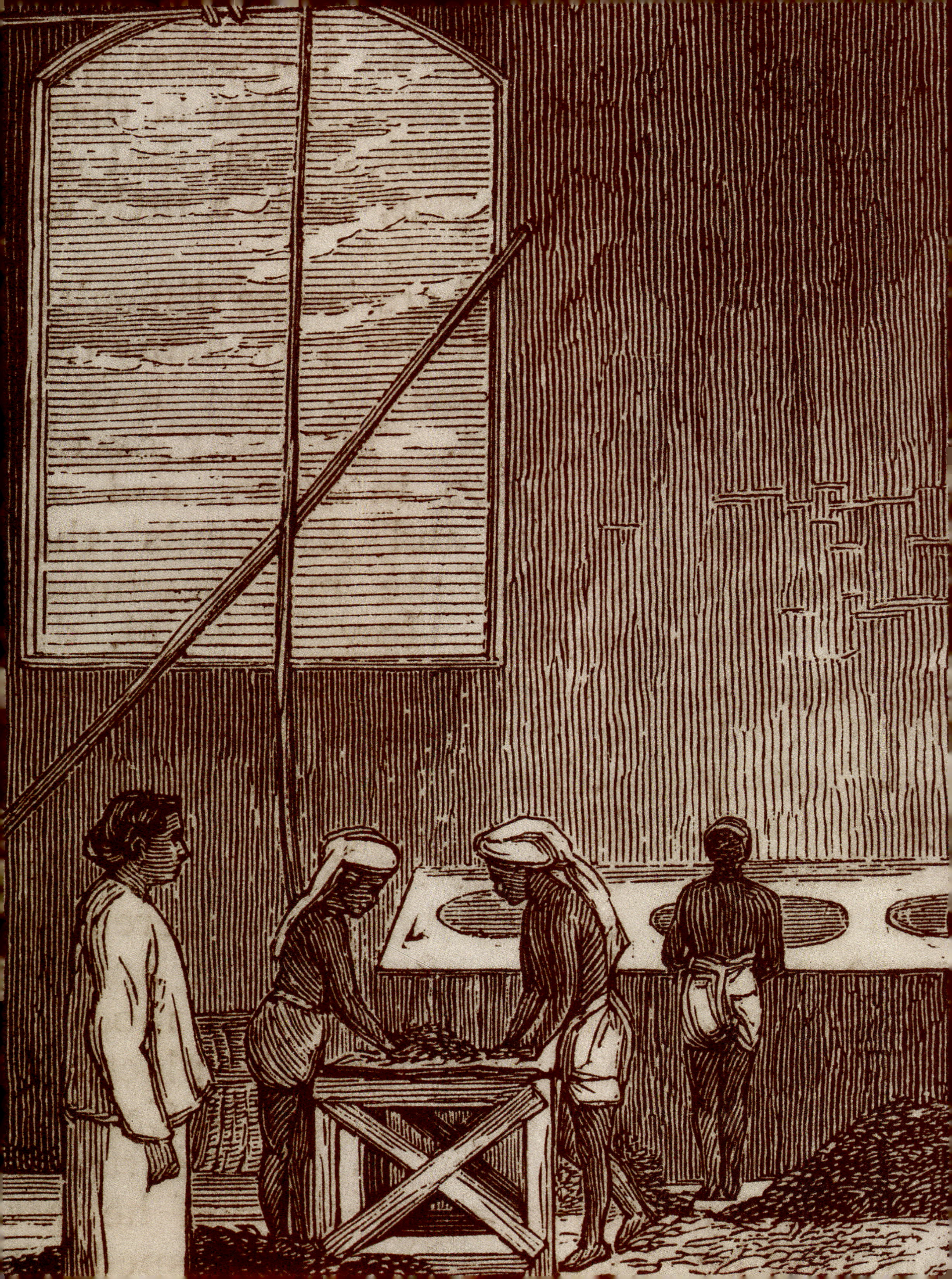

CHAPTER 6

Facing the Future

Coca Cola was looking for a new beverage for the Chinese market. It came up with one made from brewed tea leaves and called it Tiamyudi, which means 'heaven and earth'. It is a bottled drink and is available in both sweetened and unsweetened forms. Each year, some such unique inspiration adopts tea and radically changes its image, offering it to millions of new consumers across the globe. Tea is iced, flavoured, mixed with herbs. It is grown organically and accepted as a health drink. Billions of dollars are spent in researching formulations and building brands. The traditional cup that cheers is ceaselessly reinvented for the Americans, Europeans, and Asians who are taking to it in increasing numbers. It is this millennium challenge that faces Indian tea producers. Sadly, far from being able to invent and create new beverages or experiment with existing ones, they are burdened with taxes, political uncertainties, infrastructure costs, and the menacing shadow of terrorism. The result is that the Indian tea industry has little energy left for the many battles it should be fighting in the global market place.

India remains the world's largest producer of tea, but each year a little of its international presence is lost to leaner and meaner competition. The bill for the modernization of the tea industry is likely to run into several tens of billions of rupees. However, when companies have to shoulder all manner of burdens, and this includes providing for their own protection, unheard of in other industries, there is no money left for growth plans. Thus, while the international market for tea grows, Indian producers are compelled to constantly keep looking inward and worry about their domestic problems. Uppermost amongst their concerns is the overbearing role of the government, because it eats into the efficiencies of businesses.

Top: The new and the old: iced tea, a new innovation to compete in the soft-drinks market, alongside a traditional, ornate cup.

Facing page: An artist relaxing in contemplation over a cup of tea.

Preceding spread: The interior of a tea-house. *Inset:* sunrise in a plantation.

190 | THE HERITAGE OF INDIAN TEA

Upsetting the Apple-cart

The prevalent consensus among the tea people seems to be that if left alone by the government and provided with a level playing field, the tea industry will do well by the government, the community, and the workers. Short-sighted and ad hoc policy-making is merely upsetting the apple-cart. Relieved from undue tinkering with internal functioning best regulated by the market, the industry will satisfactorily achieve its production and export targets, and provide foreign exchange besides feeding its people and taking care of the rural community as it has been doing for the past 75 years.

What the tea industry does for communities in and around its gardens is incredible. Apart from various welfare activities and employment, it supplies rice and wheat flour at approximately 50 paise per kg, not only to the 1.1 m. people who work for it permanently but also to their dependants numbering over 5 m. An amazing figure of nearly 2 per cent of the Indian population is supported by the tea industry together with its associated and ancillary activities in distribution, retailing, warehousing, tea shops, etc. In the event of any national calamity, the tea industry always provides aid to the limit of its over-taxed abilities. This is unparalleled in India. It also pays a wide range of exorbitant taxes. The result is that the industry is more preoccupied with coping with these pressures than in challenging the cutting edge of commercial competition.

The cost of producing tea in India has been rising steadily, profits have been declining, and the vitally needed reinvestment is slowing down. Rather than aggressively pursuing a larger share of a growing international market, Indian producers have to content themselves with mainly selling at home. While it is true that a healthy domestic market is essential to support exports, this should not be allowed to become a substitute for a vigorous international presence.

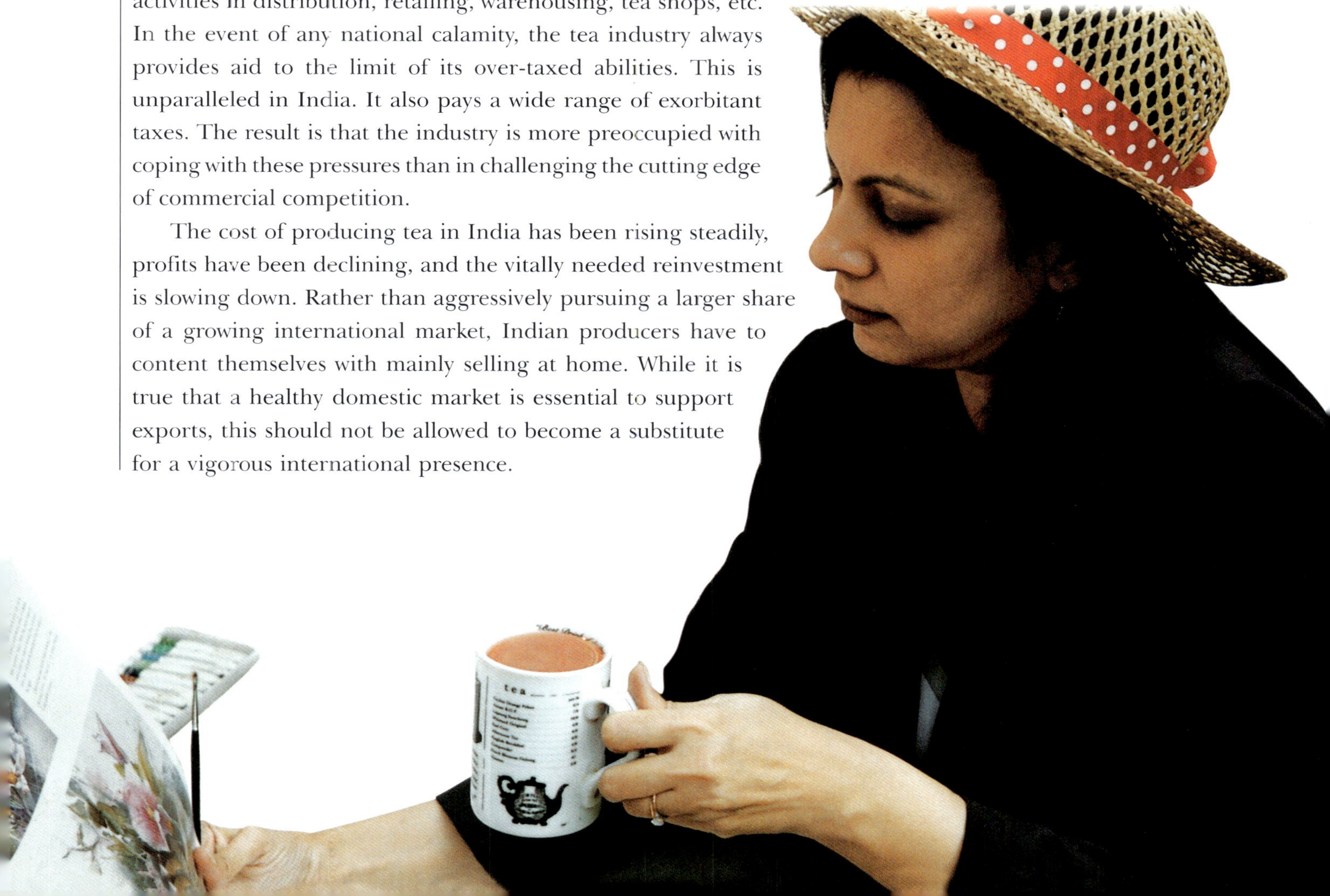
tea

RANGO
DOUBLE DIAMOND
DOUBLE DIAMOND

Top left: Chai-making is an exacting process. Each infusion has its own character and secret. Poor preparation can ruin its flavour and taste: a tea stall at a railway station. *Top right:* A tea retailer who sells loose and packaged tea. Buyers can now choose from the wide range of brands available in the market. The domestic market is worth Rs 33.9 bn. *Below:* Porters relaxing over tea after a gruelling day.

Expanding the Domestic Market

That is however precisely what is happening. Indian tea now has its strongest presence in India, when at one time it dominated world markets. Industrialization, urbanization, and the development of agriculture keep expanding the domestic market. Domestic tea consumption, which was 562 m. kg in 1995, increased to 653 m. kg in 2000. Today, the total domestic market is approximately Rs 33.9 bn of which Hindustan Lever Ltd, regional players, and Tata Tea Ltd have shares of 36.2 per cent, 23.7 per cent, and 20.1 per cent respectively. The growth rate has declined from 2.5 per cent to 1.8 per cent over the past five years due to shifting consumer preferences: tea has been losing ground to colas and ASDs.

Although India is the world's largest producer of tea, its per capita consumption of tea remains among the lowest in the world: just 0.63 kg per capita compared to Ireland's per capita of 2.78 kg. Therefore, there is an urgent need for promotion of tea by the government in collaboration with the industry. An aggressive promotional campaign, using the health platform, will definitely boost tea consumption in the domestic and international markets. The promotion of tea in India should be based on two themes: 'Tea is good for health', and 'Tea is the beverage for the youth'. The Tea Board of India has been quick to realize this and has launched a campaign '*piyo* more *chai*' in association with the industry to encourage domestic consumption by focusing on its 'miraculous' properties. It will also highlight that drinking tea keeps one healthy and lowers the risk of heart disease, cancer, and the like. Bharat Bajoria, chairman, Consultative Committee of Plantation Associations, said, 'Through this campaign we are trying to address this issue as tea is also good for health'. N.K. Das, chairman, Tea Board of India, too said that the government supported the campaign and would like the benefits and pleasures of tea-drinking to spread to everyone. For the export market, the industry is keen to improve the quality of the product and will soon chart out a focused action plan.

The Indian Tea Association is also implementing a mid-term strategy for the industry in consultation with Accenture, the multinational consulting major. Tapas Das, additional secretary-general, Indian Tea Association, adds, 'No doubt a strong and vibrant internal market will create the necessary synergies for an expanding export market'.

The rural market accounts for 60 per cent of consumption and the urban market, 40 per cent. The states with the highest per capita consumption are either tea producers, such as Assam, Kerala, and West Bengal, or those which have high per capita income levels like Maharashtra, Gujarat, and Punjab. Over 30 per cent of domestic sales are accounted for by Maharashtra, Gujarat, and Rajasthan. There are many strong local players who understand local taste and market their own local brands like Girnar, Wagh Bakri, and the like.

About 70 per cent of the consumers in the south and 90 per cent of those in the north drink tea twice a day. About 98 per cent of tea drinkers make tea by boiling it with water, milk, and sugar. Only 6 per cent tea drinkers in urban areas drink brewed tea. About 50 per cent of India's tea consumers like to drink tea outside the home. That is why tea shops are so popular. Taste, aroma, strength, and freshness are much sought after; price, colour of leaf, brand name, and packaging are less important. Indians like their tea straight. Only two per cent of consumers like tea flavoured with cardamom or ginger. Indians largely drink black tea or CTC. In the north, leaf tea is popular and in the south, tea dust.

Hindustan Lever Ltd is known for consistency with a standard quality, and is India's largest exporter of tea in terms of value. Its seven brands — Red Label, Taj Mahal, Taaza, A1, 3 Roses, Super Dust, and Top Star — count among India's top 10 packaged tea brands. It is also known for its packaging innovation and for launching Lipton Ice tea in the country.

With tariff barriers being lifted, tea producers are gearing themselves to face competition from cheaper tea imports. Sri Lankan tea is expected to throw a challenge. Tea pundits believe that imports will turn the heat on the smaller producers, especially small tea growers in the south. Blending Indian tea with cheaper imported teas for export will lower the quality of Indian teas and deal a major blow to the image being nurtured by the tea majors of India as the home of high quality teas. In the opinion of G.P. Goenka: 'Quality improvement and getting yields up substantially should be high on all producers' agenda ... Each producer must chalk out survival plans for himself.'

Top: Traditions of tea-making: an old man preparing tea aboard a boat in Calcutta.
Below: The fine art of tea-making is universally appreciated.

3-50
3-50
2-50
1-50
5-00
3-00
7-00
3-00

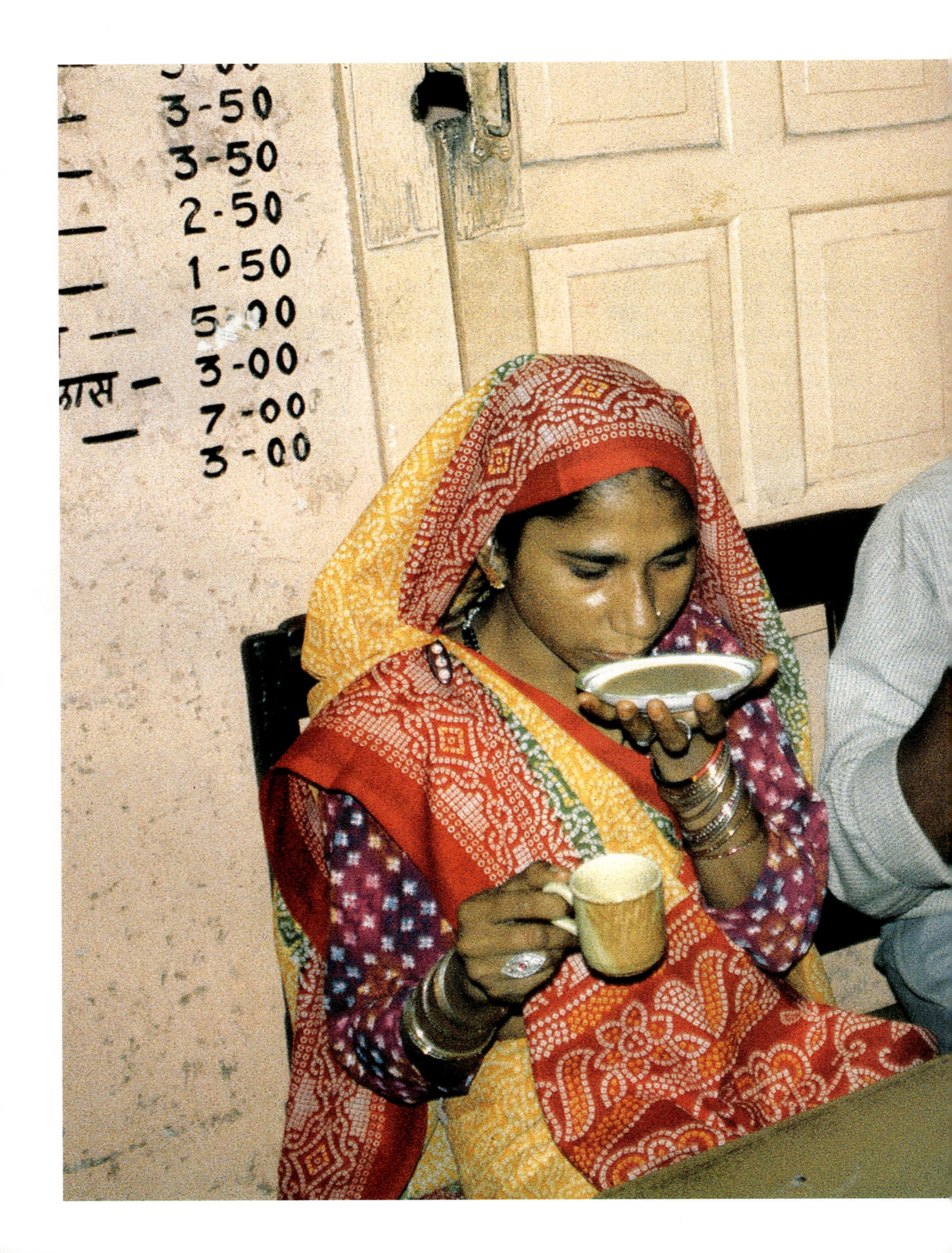

ास -

the campaign and would like the benefits and pleasures of tea-drinking to spread to everyone. For the export market, the industry is keen to improve the quality of the product and will soon chart out a focused action plan.

The Indian Tea Association is also implementing a mid-term strategy for the industry in consultation with Accenture, the multinational consulting major. Tapas Das, additional secretary-general, Indian Tea Association, adds, 'No doubt a strong and vibrant internal market will create the necessary synergies for an expanding export market'.

The rural market accounts for 60 per cent of consumption and the urban market, 40 per cent. The states with the highest per capita consumption are either tea producers, such as Assam, Kerala, and West Bengal, or those which have high per capita income levels like Maharashtra, Gujarat, and Punjab. Over 30 per cent of domestic sales are accounted for by Maharashtra, Gujarat, and Rajasthan. There are many strong local players who understand local taste and market their own local brands like Girnar, Wagh Bakri, and the like.

About 70 per cent of the consumers in the south and 90 per cent of those in the north drink tea twice a day. About 98 per cent of tea drinkers make tea by boiling it with water, milk, and sugar. Only 6 per cent tea drinkers in urban areas drink brewed tea. About 50 per cent of India's tea consumers like to drink tea outside the home. That is why tea shops are so popular. Taste, aroma, strength, and freshness are much sought after; price, colour of leaf, brand name, and packaging are less important. Indians like their tea straight. Only two per cent of consumers like tea flavoured with cardamom or ginger. Indians largely drink black tea or CTC. In the north, leaf tea is popular and in the south, tea dust.

Hindustan Lever Ltd is known for consistency with a standard quality, and is India's largest exporter of tea in terms of value. Its seven brands — Red Label, Taj Mahal, Taaza, A1, 3 Roses, Super Dust, and Top Star — count among India's top 10 packaged tea brands. It is also known for its packaging innovation and for launching Lipton Ice tea in the country.

With tariff barriers being lifted, tea producers are gearing themselves to face competition from cheaper tea imports. Sri Lankan tea is expected to throw a challenge. Tea pundits believe that imports will turn the heat on the smaller producers, especially small tea growers in the south. Blending Indian tea with cheaper imported teas for export will lower the quality of Indian teas and deal a major blow to the image being nurtured by the tea majors of India as the home of high quality teas. In the opinion of G.P. Goenka: 'Quality improvement and getting yields up substantially should be high on all producers' agenda ... Each producer must chalk out survival plans for himself.'

Top: Traditions of tea-making: an old man preparing tea aboard a boat in Calcutta.
Below: The fine art of tea-making is universally appreciated.

Experimenting with Variety

A strategic shift towards selling tea as a young person's drink is directed at acquiring a share of the cold drinks' market. Youngsters have moved towards the more vibrant colas. To regain lost ground and its market share, tea must be promoted as a fun drink. According to S. Ravindranath, head, beverages, of Hindustan Lever Ltd, 'We are looking at the soft beverages segment to target the youth'. Other new products are also being promoted and new strategies adopted. 'The tea industry has to go in for product innovation,' says D.P. Maheshwari, chairman of the Planters' Association of Tamil Nadu. 'It is the absence of value addition that has adversely affected Indian tea.'

Hindustan Lever, for instance, is marketing Lipton Tiger to low income consumers in rural and urban markets. It is moving away from selling tea purely as a home-consumption item, and currently vending machines powered by solar energy are being put through their paces.

The Williamson Magor group has been successful with its Tez, Premium Gold, and Jago brands in the domestic market and now plans a new concept brand 'Greendale', being developed by Paris-based strategic marketing guru and designer Shombit Sengupta. G.P. Goenka's Duncans Industries Ltd is keen to increase its share of the market and its annual production by acquiring new gardens. Its major brands include Double Diamond and Sargam. Tata Tea Ltd is one of the largest tea marketing companies in the world. It has 53 estates spread across 26,000 ha in Assam, West Bengal, Tamil Nadu, and Kerala, and produces over 60 m. kg of tea each year. The company operates a 100 per cent-owned instant tea export-oriented unit, the largest such facility outside the US. It is the second largest seller of packet tea in India. It launched its Agni, Chakra Gold, Gemini, and Kannan Devan brands after studying regional preferences. Homi R. Khusrokhan says, 'We will strengthen our regional focus while seeking a larger national share'. Tata Tea Ltd intends to achieve acceptance of tea as an FMCG product, as do other large corporates. Although finance is a constraint, the tea majors have ambitions of becoming multinationals after strengthening their domestic base. The Tetley takeover worth £ 271 m. by Tata Tea Ltd is the first of its kind in the history of corporate takeovers by any Indian company.

The Need of the Hour

Indian tea is valued for its aroma and strength. India has to produce more tea quickly and efficiently without compromising on quality. Since Independence, production has increased steadily. This is a tribute to the industry, but it is not good enough. In Kenya, the cost of producing a kilogramme of tea is Rs 30, but in India it is Rs 50. The average Indian productivity is about 1869 kg per ha while Kenya's is nearly 2507 kg. New markets have to be explored and a basket of teas invented to tempt younger consumers. Over the past few years there appears to be global over-supply. Better price realization for tea therefore critically depends on increasing market share through better productivity and also creating a niche in the value added segment through product innovation.

Research, money, and vision are needed. Besides this, efforts towards production innovations and value addition would also be helpful. When tea plants age they produce fewer leaves. In India, 38 per cent of the tea bushes are over 50 years old. In the north-east, 35 per cent of the bushes are over 50 years old. Darjeeling is the worst off with about 75 per cent of its bushes over 50 years old. Replantation, rejuvenation, and extension of tea cultivation can improve yields. Replantation means a major loss of production because it takes six to seven years before the new tea bush bears usable leaves, if one takes into account the two years that the soil must be left fallow for rejuvenation. Methods have to be found to reduce soil erosion in the process of uprooting bushes for replantation and to shorten the gestation period of new tea bushes in order to reduce crop losses.

Planters carry out replantation with clones which yield about 5000 kg per ha. Tea research has yet to identify a 'golden' clone that will yield several times the current yield. Research in biotechnology is urgently needed. Besides, global warming and changes in weather patterns mean that tea producers will need to rely on genetic engineering to find tea plants resistant to drought, waterlogging, and seasonal dormancy.

Rejuvenation of plantations takes place through pruning, infilling, and using good plant material. Research on better agricultural practices that will rejuvenate and repair the soil is necessary. The Darjeeling tea plantations have suffered because of old tea bushes, high cost of inputs: specifically pesticides and low labour productivity. When 'self-sustainable farming' based on the use of organic manures and biological control of pests started nearly 15 years ago, the Goodricke group and Ambootia led the way by switching to organic farming of Darjeeling tea. Though the initial cost is high, expenses

Top and facing page: The dark green tea leaves are processed in a variety of ways to produce tea with different flavours. A selection of the finest Indian teas.

Following spread: A family enjoying their tea in a typical Indian restaurant. Today, domestic tea consumption in India is approximately 650 m. kg.

3-50
3-50
2-50
1-50
5-00
３-00
ास — 3-00
7-00
3-00

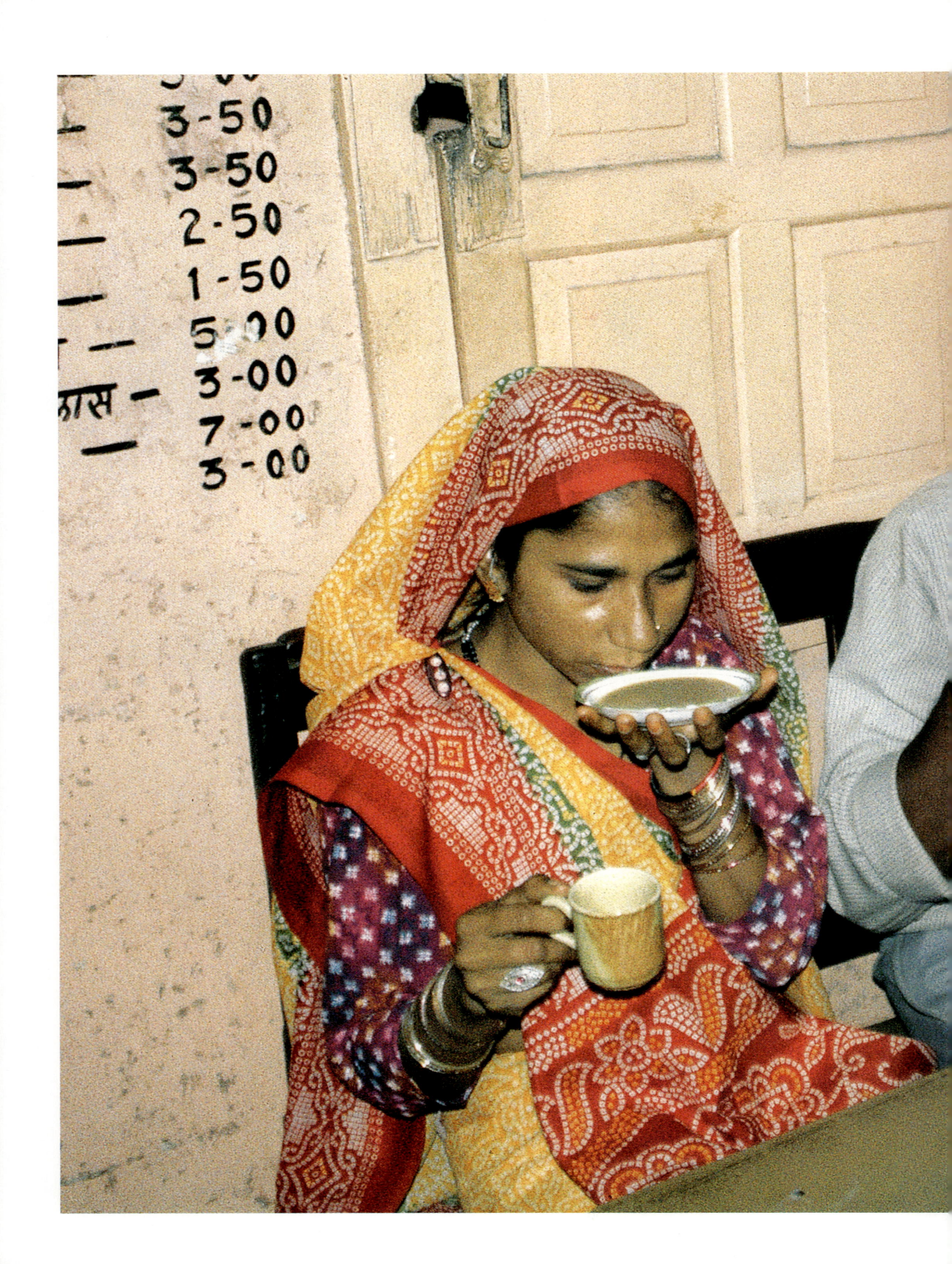

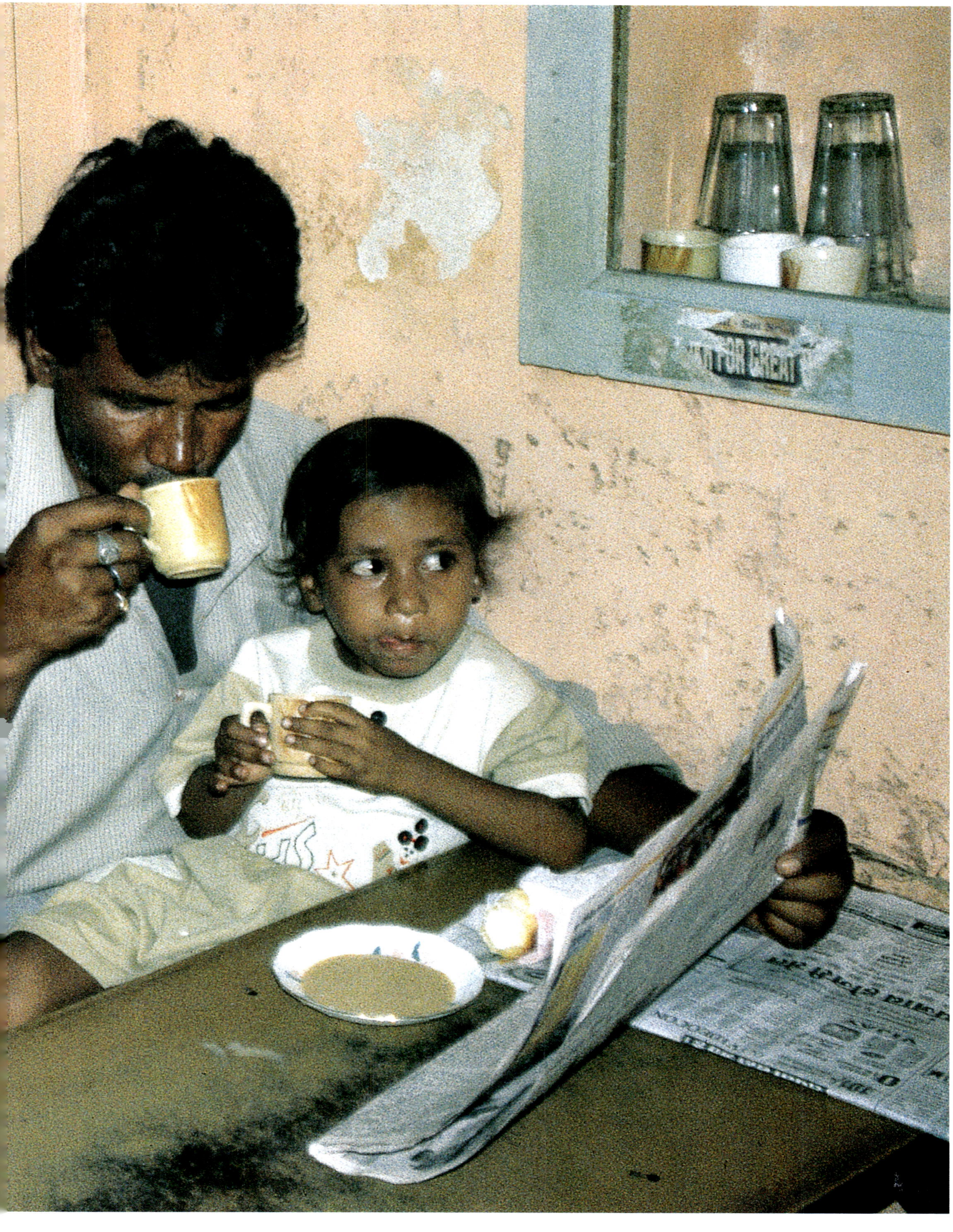

level out and yields increase significantly. The conversion to organic farming leads to substantial production loss at the outset. It takes around eight years for a garden converting to organic farming to return to normal production levels. Goodricke bought Dooteriah as a 'sick' garden in 1988 and by 1997 it became one of the four bio-gardens of the group in Darjeeling. Its tea yield is lower than the average productivity but the production loss is more than made up by higher price realizations. A small amount of organic tea is also produced in southern India and Assam, but as the premiums for organic tea in the world market are getting squeezed, further conversion to organic farming in Darjeeling has stopped.

An additional 2 m. ha need to be brought under tea cultivation. Economic clusters of small tea growers, armed with technical skill and institutional support, can increase yields, but new states should also be surveyed for extension of cultivation.

Although tea manufacture has undergone tremendous modernization and mechanization, the control of process parameters is still carried out manually, and electronic controls were never tried seriously, probably due to apprehensions about their performance in the dusty and humid environment of a tea factory. Studies on the employment of electronic controls and automation have shown significant results in capacity utilization, quality control, and optimization of fuel consumption. There is an urgent need to adopt electronic controls and automation in all the process variables, manual operations, and generation of on-line reports. Recently, a few companies and research institutions have started showing interest in this relatively neglected area.

SAN-CHA
Rare Darjeeling Tea
by Aap ki pasand
Officially Certified Darjeeling by Tea Board India

Today, India exports the finest teas colourfully packaged in art silk, embroidered velvet, rosewood tea boxes, brass cans, and the like. Attractive packaging has done much to lure buyers all over the world.

Studying the Import–Export Market

The CIS countries, Pakistan, the UK, Egypt, and the USA together account for half of the world's total imports. The entry of imported tea has catalyzed local producers to transform themselves into value aspirants. International benchmarking and branding have suddenly become assets. It is predicted that in a few years' time, four or five brands will dominate the Indian market and smaller brands will either be acquired by larger companies or find themselves edged out. It is the packet tea segment which is becoming popular, and Hindustan Lever Ltd has already captured 32 per cent of this. Tata Tea Ltd has its sights on a 21 per cent share. Tea bags and value added teas occupy a niche market, which is growing as the Indian consumer becomes more sophisticated and quality conscious.

With the Free Trade Agreement among the SAARC countries coming into effect, and further removal of all quantitative restrictions on the import of tea into India from the following year, the tea markets will become much more competitive as the cost of imported teas will be very low. There is a possibility of a bilateral arrangement between India and Egypt to neutralize the duty advantage being enjoyed by the African tea-producing countries. The import of tea also brings down Indian standards. Tea which is brought in for blending and re-export, is not always of good quality and hurts the image of Indian tea in the international market. Last year, 12 m. kg of tea were imported; a year earlier the figure was 8 m. The industry hopes that qualitative restrictions and higher import duties will correct the situation. Now the Tea Board of India has taken a decision to monitor and inspect all imports to maintain standards, and declared that teas that do not conform to the quality standards will not be imported.

Stagnating Exports

After passing through the romantic and scientific era, the Indian tea industry now faces new challenges arising out of liberalization and globalization. India's share has continuously declined in the global tea export market despite a steady increase in production. It is not a healthy sign that India's export figures are stagnating while the global market in tea is expanding. In 1951, India produced 285 m. kg of tea and exported 206 m. In 1998, India produced a record 870 m. kg and exported just 210 m. During 1999, India was able to export only 192 m. kg with an aggregate value of Rs 19 bn, as opposed to 806 m. kg of total production volume. In 2000, the tea export volume touched 201 m. kg with a total domestic production of 846 m. kg. In 2001, tea production has surpassed 855 m. kg. The major exporters of teas in terms of volume, supplying around 78 per cent of the world's imports, have been Sri Lanka, Kenya, China, India, and Indonesia. Sri Lanka is now the leading exporter, followed by Kenya. There are younger rivals like Argentina, Uganda, Turkey, and Vietnam waiting in the wings.

Even as Indian companies contend with low profitability and depressed prices, their competitors in other countries have shown that they can raise production, cut back on costs, and yet ensure better quality. All this has been possible because of the relaxed regulatory environment in which they function and do business. It has helped them to go out and explore new markets, and the result has been that last year Kenya and Sri Lanka exported 90 per cent of their production.

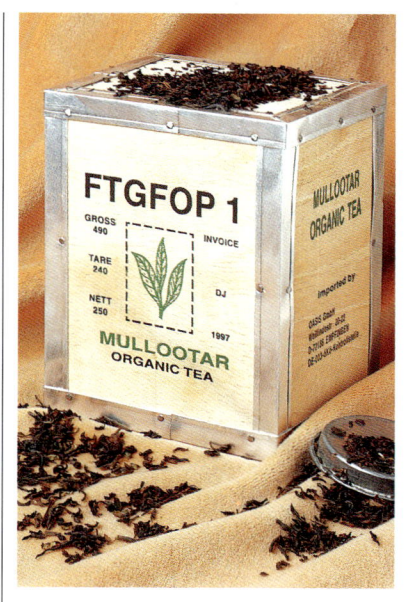

Indian tea companies have a very wide range of tea brands comprising numerous varieties of Indian tea grown in the various tea-growing regions of the country.

For a good brew, the water quality is as important as the tea leaves. An elegant tea set adds a touch of class.

There is, therefore, need for detailed research into the latest production and marketing trends worldwide. The government has to encourage this introspection with the right incentives because, in this era of globalization, India needs to be aggressive in carving out the share of world trade it deserves. Tea is a strong Indian product, with Assam and Darjeeling being associated with high value. It is important that this advantage, built over the centuries, is not frittered away. The ground reality is that while an exporter like Sri Lanka consistently invests huge sums in the promotion of its tea, the Tea Board of India spends virtually nothing.

The Indian share of world production of tea has fallen from about 42 per cent in 1951 to 28 per cent today; percentage share is declining but in terms of volume it remains at 200 m. kg. Its share of world exports fell from 45 per cent in 1951 to 33 per cent in 1970, and is 28 per cent today. With the changes in global markets, new tea producers have made an impressive entry. While India's value added tea exports to total exports ratio remains stagnant, international marketeers have many mantras to offer. New images are constructed around tea drinks through sophisticated advertising and innovative marketing techniques. The Coca Cola cold drink, made from brewed tea leaves and launched in China, has many appealing ingredients, not least among them its name, Tiamyudi.

Branding and Quality

A strong brand name helps. Products are linked to countries. France is famous for wines and the Swiss for cheese and chocolates. 'Branding is essential for value addition. Packet tea is not only convenient but also ensures against the addition of spurious elements. Moreover, brands can also be created to suit particular tastes. However, companies must ensure that brands are built around quality and standards are maintained,' says Roshan L. Joseph, director, Eveready Industries (India) Ltd. The Japanese, supported by their government, worked tirelessly after the Second World War to give their products an image of reliability and quality. The Goodricke group and Ambootia, producers of organically grown Darjeeling tea, have applied for protection of trademarks under geographical appellations.

K.S. David, managing director of the Goodricke group, opines: 'The task before the industry is to find new avenues of marketing. We should stop selling and start marketing. Tea is a lifestyle product and should be sold as such. It caters to every taste and every pocket, and in that sense is a leveller. We at Goodricke, for instance, try and emphasize the quality of the good life associated with tea. The packaging and branding and product quality are all tailored together to reflect this graciousness.'

The East African tea producers, Kenya and Malawi, are strengthening their positions. They have a small domestic market and focus on exports. Favourable internal tax rates and an expanding acreage of young tea bushes are helping them to beat the competition. The Chinese, on the other hand, have increased production of black tea, principally for export. They overturned India's prime position in the Australian market in the 1980s and then went on to capture markets in Morocco, New Zealand, France, and Spain. A controlled economy in those years enabled them to dump tea at prices 20 per cent below those of Indian tea.

Despite their initial run of success, the Chinese may find it difficult to beat the competition in the long term. Chinese authorities are worried about the declining quality of their tea. Unfavourable weather, lack of investment, small-scale production without adequate quality control, has led to the 'sale of fake and shoddy products by illegal traders', reports the *Tea and Coffee Trade Journal*. An inspection carried out by the Chinese government in 1998 found that tea samples were unhygienic and suffused with DDT. In February 1999, strict controls on agricultural pesticides were prescribed.

China recently announced that it will start growing tea without using chemical fertilizers and pesticides. Having chosen Yunnan, the country's largest tea-growing province, for growing organic tea, the Chinese government is planning to create a dedicated organic tea plantation on 6667 ha, targeting an eventual production of 4 m. kg as opposed to India's present annual output of nearly 1 m. kg from the organic tea-producing gardens of the Darjeeling hills. A point of view in the industry holds that the recent export setback in Europe, particularly in Germany, with its extremely stringent chemical residue norms for tea, is the key to the Chinese decision. Be that as it may, fresh concerns have arisen among Indian organic tea producers who are already being squeezed by growing buyer resistance to high premiums on chemical-free tea in a limited organic tea market comprising some European countries and Japan. Currently, Indian organic tea producers face competition from their Nepalese counterparts due to the latter's lower cost of production and the resultant discounted prices. The Goodricke group, India's largest producer of organic tea, is of the view that China will be a big threat to their dominance of the world organic tea market, and that the only recourse for Indian exporters is conversion to organic farming and growing organic teas in virgin lands, both of which are expensive and time-consuming processes.

Top: What a wonderful aroma!

Following spread: Good morning! invariably begins with a cup of tea and the newspaper.

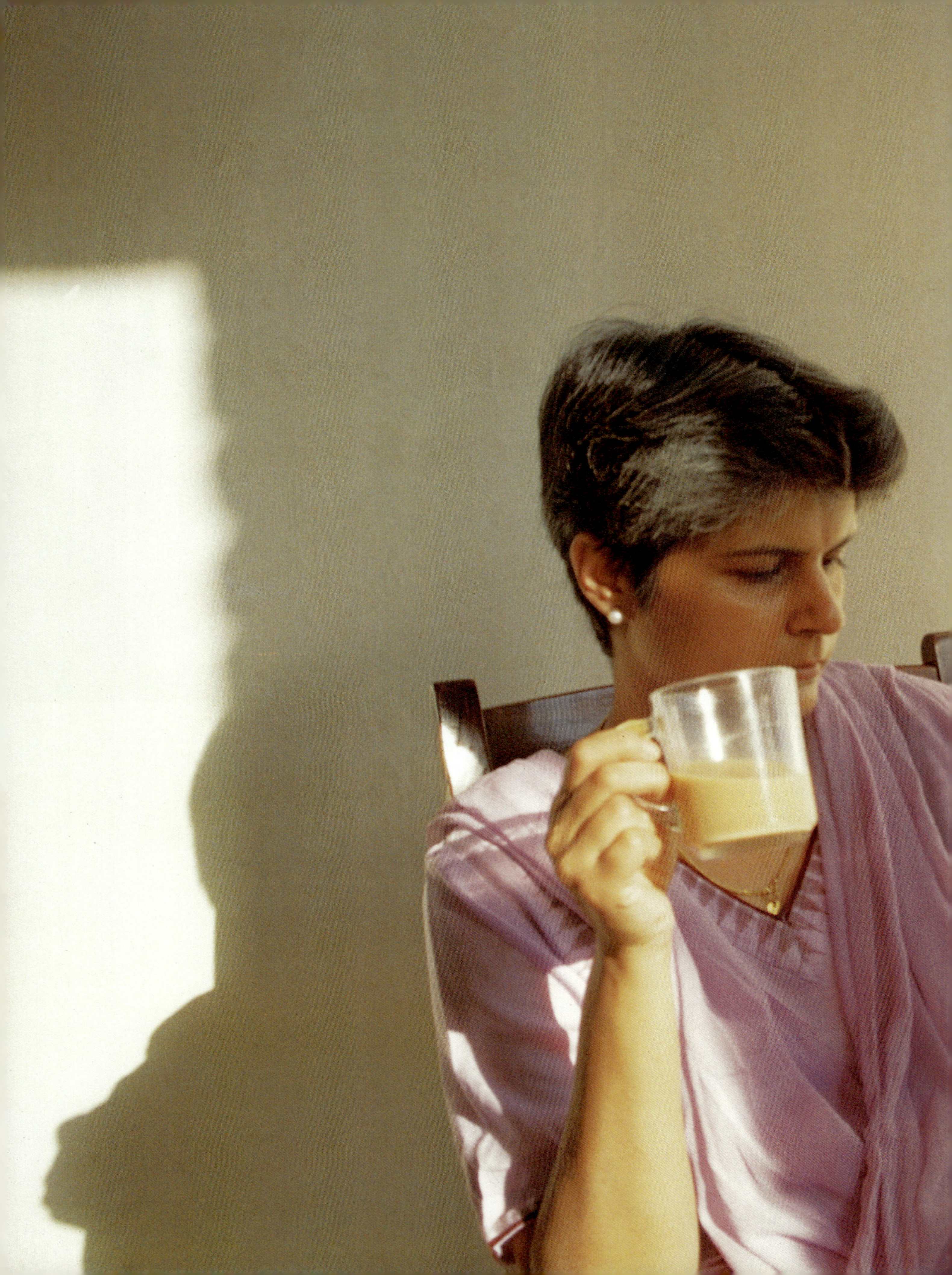

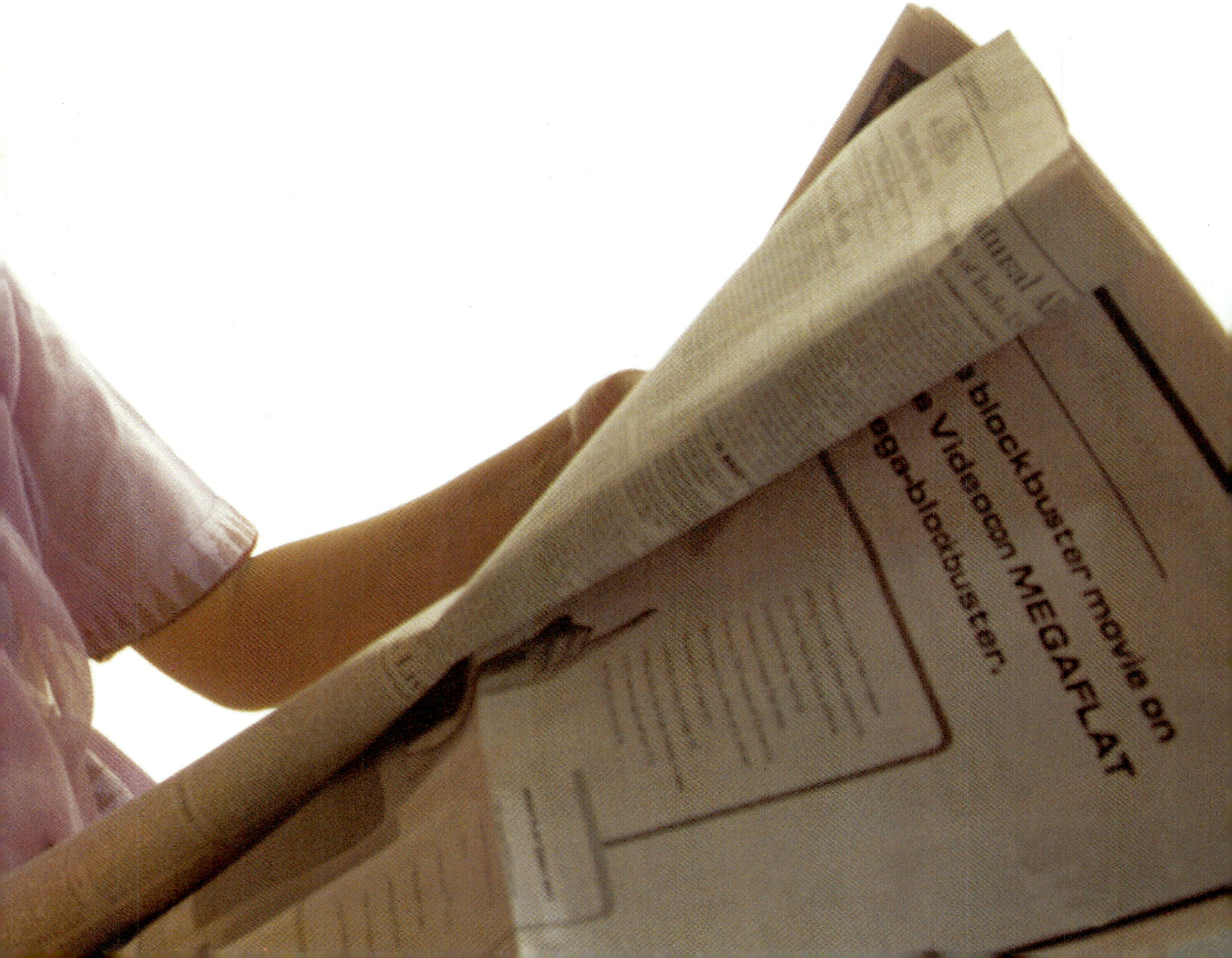
blockbuster movie on
Videocon MEGAFLAT
ega-blockbuster.

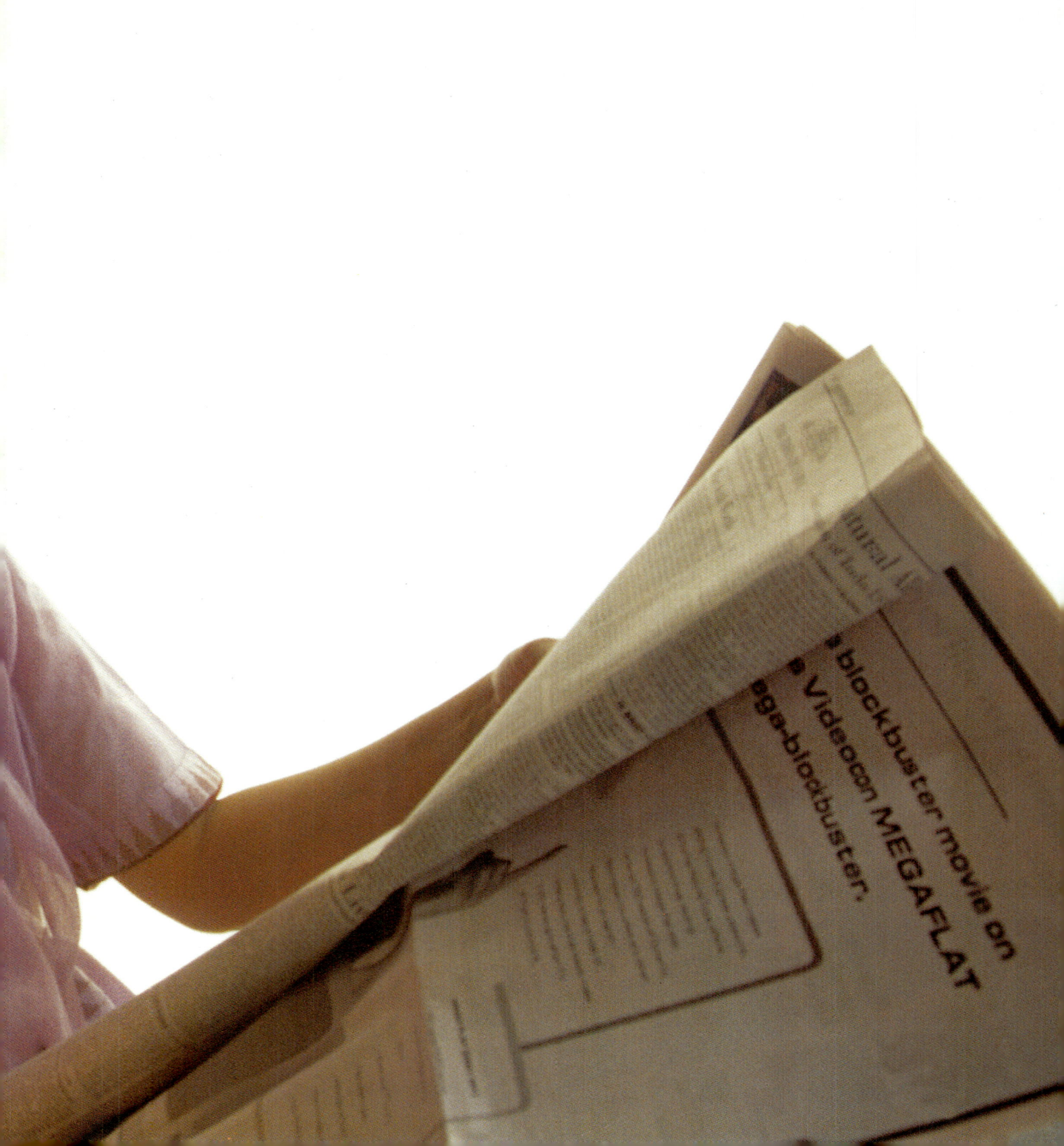

Top: Tea time folks!: the younger generation has not fallen behind in its enjoyment of tea. *Below right:* Buyers are offered a variety of brands with attractive packages to choose from.

Indian tea reaches nearly eighty countries across the globe. Internationally, the principal buyers are the CIS countries and the UK. Pakistan is the third largest buyer followed by the US, Egypt, and Japan. The imposition of an export duty by the Indian government on its own tea helped East-African producers to undercut Indian tea. Tea is an essential commodity in India and the government was concerned about protecting local consumers from a price hike.

Apart from Russia, India needs to make special efforts to export tea to some other CIS countries like Ukraine, Kazakhistan, and Uzbekistan. The Indian Tea Association is in touch with tea associations in these countries, and there are exporters who are planning to send delegations to them in a bid to build commercial relations based on quality. Recently, an Indian company, J.V. Gokal & Co. Ltd, was awarded 'Product of the Year-2000' by the Kazakhistan Institute of Food Industry for the high quality and consistency of its 'Assam' brand tea.

Pakistan is a good market for tea. The annual consumption of tea in Pakistan is over 150 m. kg. In India, per capita consumption is 0.58 kg but in Pakistan it is 1 kg. Pakistan buys its tea mostly from Kenya and has recently bought 0.8 m. kg from India after a delegation headed by the chairman of the Tea Board of India visited Pakistan. Though there was much backslapping about this 'breakthrough', the truth is that India has been selling tea quietly to Pakistan over the years.

The US, Canada, and the Middle East are markets where consumption of Indian tea is being promoted. Though 110 m. lb of black tea is imported into the US annually, India's share is only 3 m. lb. India's lead in growing tea organically is proving to be an advantage. Thomas J. Lipton, which controls 50 per cent of the market, has introduced higher quality Indian tea, anticipating an upward trend in tea-drinking. Tea salons have been promoting tea-drinking, and Chado in Beverly Hills, Los Angeles carries 250 varieties of tea, including Indian tea. Tiazzi, a drink which combines fruit juice with tea, is making waves. This drink is being marketed by Kraft Foods and Starbucks.

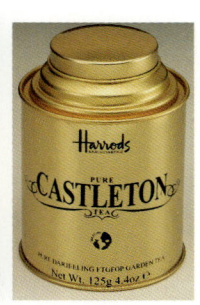

Promotion and Marketing

In tomorrow's global village, information technology will be one of the primary conduits for the promotion and sale of tea. Forrester Research estimates that by 2003 as much as five per cent of all global sales and services could be via the Internet. Online auctions and trading are major marketing tools. They can discover new tea markets, spread tea information to consumers, and increase distribution. 'We will use the Net a great deal more to get closer to our customers. Buyers can bid on the Net and you only have to look at our new website, www.wmtea.com, to see how serious we are,' says Deepak Khaitan. A new dimension has thus been added by e-commerce and the Internet, and we can only hope that the broking community will rise to meet these new challenges. The signs of this are propitious.

The Baglas of Hanuman Tea have introduced www.teauction.com, and are confident of becoming global players. They have entered into an agreement with Forbes & Walker, one of the top tea-broking houses located in Colombo. Teauction.com was set to hold the first cyber auction in Colombo in association with its joint venture partner, Forbes & Walker. It will also be the first in the business of online tea trade in Sri Lanka. The Baglas are also planning to set up similar joint ventures in Bangladesh. Ayush Bagla says that they are routing almost 26 m. kg of tea through their site, private sales, and affiliate broking firms; this saves on the warehousing costs of the clients. Satyam Infoway Ltd, India's premier Internet and e-commerce solutions provider, has also launched www.teawebex.com. The portal is the first site to offer digital catalogues with valuation, the latest selling price of tea, news and market reports, and comprehensive information about the industry.

The industry needs to upgrade its technology and invest more in the development of human resources. There should be greater exposure to modern management techniques and the productivity of workers has to increase. Adding to the costs and delays are poor transport and telecommunications in the north-east. Power cuts plague tea factories, even while natural gas from Assam's gas- and oilfields is wasted through flaring. The dark shadow of the 'babu armed with red tape' continues to haunt tea estate managers. Unproductive paperwork results in a criminal wastage of valuable time.

Top: Innovative ideas are urgently required to boost the marketing of Indian tea around the globe. Zakir Hussain, a brand ambassador for Taj Mahal Tea, enjoying a cup.
Below: A vivacious woman follows suit.

Top: The auction system continues to be the principal channel for marketing tea as it has been for centuries. Recent changes will provide the system with greater flexibility and transparency.

Facing page: 'Polly put the kettle on we'll all have tea' (Charles Dickens). India is well known for its numerous varieties of quality teas, and equally so for its variety of methods of making tea. There is often a fireplace to keep tea on the boil.

The slam of a hammer has decided the price of tea for over a century. Historically, the majority of the world's tea produce has been marketed through the auction system. Even today, about 85 per cent of the total world tea production is traded through auctions. Tea-growing nations have found the tea auction system ideally suited to the sale of the product, and today thirteen auction centres exist, all in the countries of origin. Seven of them are in India, the largest tea producer in the world.

Recognizing the obvious merits of the tea auction system, the government of India introduced the Tea Marketing (Control) Order, 1984. Till recently there was an obligation on the producers to route 75 per cent of their produce for sale through the auction system. The union commerce ministry withdrew this order in January 2001. This will provide flexibility, making the auction system more vibrant and transparent. It will also lead to better valuation of teas, both within and outside the auction system, as all the sales outlets will compete with one another.

Reacting to this, R.S. Jhawar said that the withdrawal of this order means that the system is becoming one of the options for selling teas, though the bulk of tea producers will continue to depend on the auctions as there is no other system that offers hassle-free payments. Umang Kanoria, president, Tea Association of India, feels that the existing auction system has been doing yeoman service to the industry and will continue to do so.

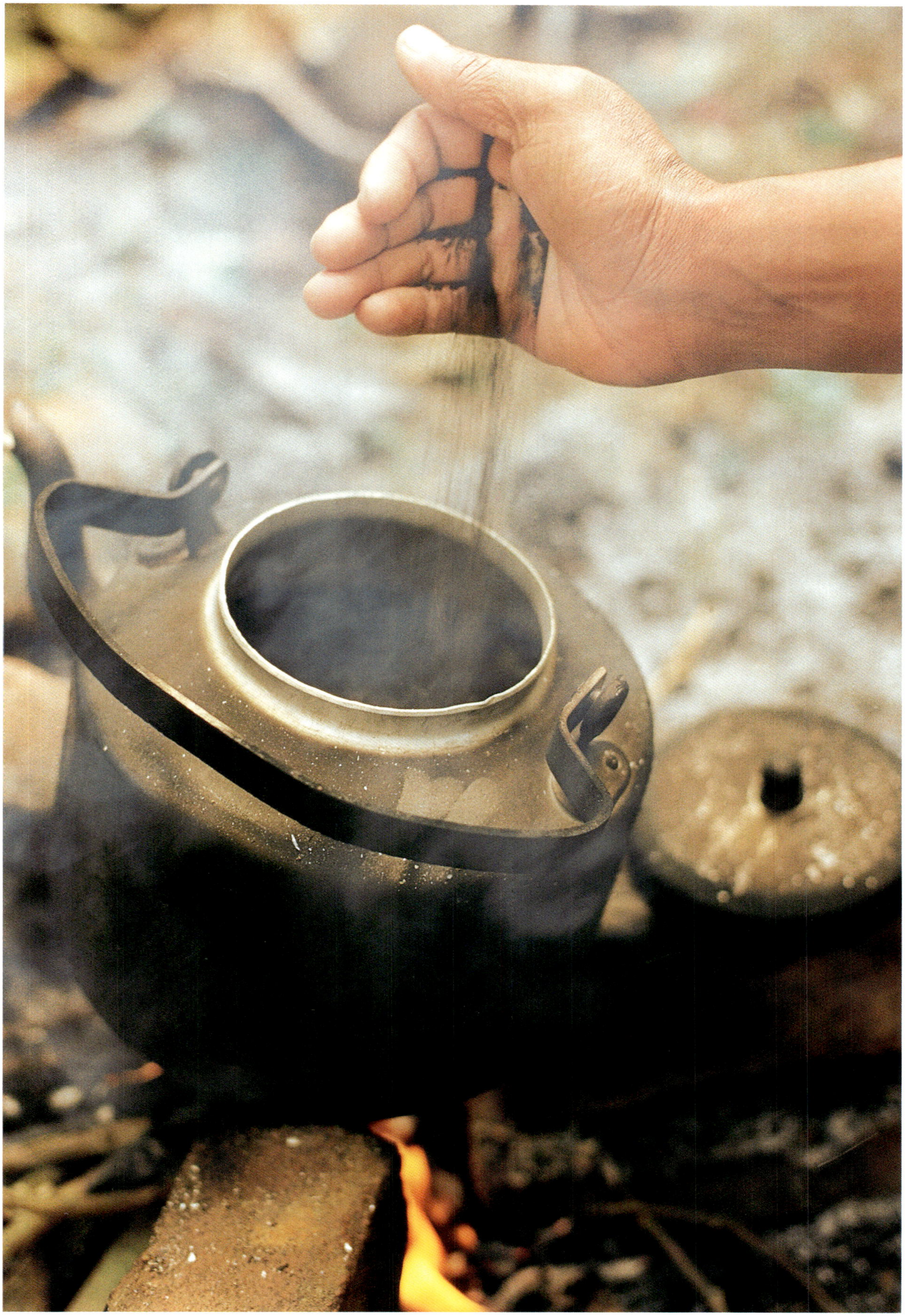

This natural brew is a good way of fostering fellowship and nurturing friendships.

Trends indicate that in the near future most tea will be sold from its home turf. Tea auctions in London, that began on 10 January 1839, making it the world's oldest auction centre, were discontinued in June 1998 bringing to a close a historic chapter. Over the years, offerings at this historic auction were becoming sparser and sparser. Tea is now auctioned in the tea-producing countries where buyers seem to prefer doing business. That being the case, local auction centres are becoming international.

Calcutta was chosen because it has a port, good banking services and communications. It is also close to Assam, the Dooars, and Darjeeling. Cochin, Mombasa, and Colombo were also selected as auction centres for similar reasons. Then Guwahati, Siliguri, Coonoor, and Coimbatore became auction centres because they were in close proximity to tea-production areas, and, therefore, sending tea to auctions was inexpensive and producers had better control. These centres are flourishing today.

In India, buyers have been purchasing tea from private dealers and paying higher prices. Major producers are selling directly to consumers. The cost of running an auction house is increasing and yet brokers receive a commission of only one per cent from the producers and very little from the buyers. The London auction has been bypassed and replaced by direct exports to wholesalers or blenders. The tea auction system has served the industry well and is fair and transparent. Research indicates that the principal problem is a critical poverty of scientific market intelligence, especially where overseas buyers are concerned. Tea exporters do not have their finger on the pulse of global bazaars. The best-informed person is the foreign buyer or blender–packer, who keeps a tab on auction prices internationally and is ever alert to demand–supply configurations.

For exporters, the best strategy is to treat the foreign buyer or blender–packer as a friend. Tea sales benefit them and promotional campaigns abroad cannot work without their participation. Global markets are battlefields where fortunes built on taste fluctuate according to season.

The Cup that Cheers and Cures

Tea is known the world over as a drink that brings hearts and minds together. It is now being promoted as the health beverage of the future and a range of tea brands claiming particular medicinal properties are available in the market.

Meanwhile, changes are taking place in positioning tea as more than just a beverage. The tea world has started promoting tea as a health drink, in tune with the twenty-first century, but the message must be based on sound scientific data so that it can counter challenges from other beverages, especially carbonated drinks and coffee. Scholars, scientists, and many research institutions in several countries have been researching the qualities of tea as a health beverage. Over the past 15 years, several research studies have been published on the impact of tea on health. It became such an important issue that the first international conference on the health benefits of tea was organized in France, and later in 1998 the second International Scientific Symposium on Tea and Human Health was organized in Washington.

American, Chinese, and Japanese scientists are unanimous that, apart from being a stimulant and a refreshing beverage, tea has many beneficial effects on health, one among them a contribution to longevity. Polyphenol

Top: The essence of tea lies in its flavour and colour after it has been brewed.
Centre: There is a tea superstition that bubbles on tea denote kisses.

gives tea superior antioxidant properties that help in preventing and controlling several chronic diseases like cancer, hypertension, kidney stones, eye problems, and even diabetes. It is also helpful as an anti-bacterial germicide for dental caries, liver toxicity, and regulation of intestinal flora.

Tea modulates chemotherapy when administered to cancer patients. It enhances the tumour-inhibiting effects of doxorubicin, and it has been found that an amino acid present both in black and green tea enhances the inhibition of liver metastasis induced by doxorubicin.

Tea liquor contains both vitamins and minerals. Dr John Weisburger, director emeritus of the American Health Foundation, has said that three or four cups of tea a day could provide protection against heart diseases and various forms of cancer. Other studies have shown that antioxidants present in green tea might retard the onset of arthritis. A recent study at the Antioxidant Research Centre in London, published in *Free Radical Research*, highlighted that the antioxidants in two cups of tea equal those in seven glasses of orange juice or twenty glasses of apple juice.

The beneficial effects of tea for human health and longevity are gradually beginning to emerge from worldwide research. The Brooke Bond Tea & Health Information Centre, the first centre of its kind in the world, was set up in Bangalore by Hindustan Lever Ltd to collate the latest scientific data from across the globe on the health benefits of tea. Today, tea is poised to become the health drink of the future.

Cheers to *Chai*!

The Indian palate has defined tea in a special way. Tea leaves, spices, milk, and sugar are boiled together. The best cup of *chai* made in this way is available in private homes, especially in the north. The spices used vary from region to region and among households in India. The commonest are cardamom, cinnamon, ginger, cloves, and pepper. Drinking *chai* is a part of life in India, and most Indians are amazed at all the current fuss in the West. Many foreigners have left India with fond *chai*-drinking memories and experiences. Today, even tea parlours are gaining in popularity. Sanjay Kapur's 'Aap ki Pasand' in New Delhi and 'Dolly's Tea Shop' in Calcutta are leading ones, providing consumers with tea of varying flavours and aroma in an ideal environment redolent with the tea culture.

Indian *chai* produces a warming, soothing effect, acts as a natural digestive aid, and induces a wonderful sense of well-being. Great *chai* can often be had in Indian restaurants, but making your own *chai* provides particular

satisfaction, and for this Indian grocers carry a variety of *chai* masala mixes. Here are some Indian recipes for tea as *chai*: *Ginger tea:* Popular in north India, specially in winter, it is taken with milk. It is good for the throat and serves to treat ordinary colds and fevers. *Cardamom tea:* Naturally flavoured with a fruity aroma, it is good for the digestive system and effective in treating headaches. Should be had plain or with a dash of milk. *Cinnamon tea*: Popular among coffee drinkers, taken without milk, it is good for the nervous system and memory. *Masala tea:* The most popular of all, it is based on strong Assam tea and a blend of many Indian spices added to milk. Ideal for breakfast and very rejuvenating. *Rose tea:* It has a gentle flavour with a sweet fragrance from a blend of Darjeeling leaves and rose petals. It is recommended for curing constipation. *Earl Grey tea:* Popular around the world for its delicate liquor and exceptional fragrance, it is flavoured with an extract of Bergamot.

We seek no earthly treasures, grant us just our morning cup of tea!

FACING THE FUTURE | 211

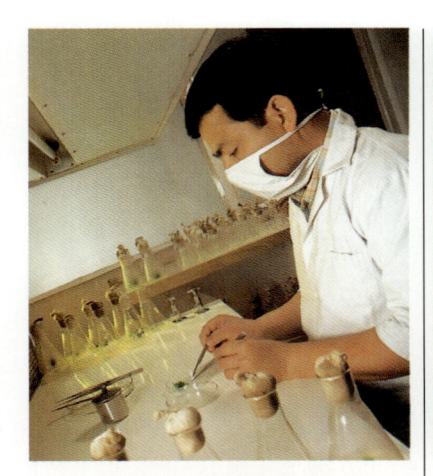

An eagle eye for quality:
Top left: Biotechnology in the service of tea.
Top right: A modern instant tea plant.
Below: Tea plant in a test tube.

Quest for Quality

Apart from the variety of ways in which tea is prepared in India, Indian tea, whether from Assam or Darjeeling, with a wide range of varieties and grades, is globally perceived to be of distinctive quality. To further buttress this perception, Indian companies have been proactive in obtaining ISO ratings for their gardens and factories, and over eight factories have been certified as such. Parry Agro's Mayura was the world's first ISO 9002 CTC tea factory. A few gardens of Duncan, Andrew Yule, and Hanuman Tea have also received ISO 9002. Mim is the single Darjeeling tea estate which has received ISO 14000 for environmental standards. Peter Leggatt, chairman, Goodricke group, said on receiving the ISO mark, 'The ISO award for the company demonstrates to buyers worldwide that Indian tea remains the world leader in quality and excellence—so important at a time when Western consumers are becoming more demanding of safe, environmentally friendly products'. Some tea factories have started using completely computerized machinery to ensure quality and hygiene. India has set high quality standards in tea production, which are above the international ISO 3720 standard.

The Tea Board of India has gone to the extent of approaching the quality assurance services of Australia and the Technical Food Insurance Spectrum of the US to provide assistance to Indian companies in the implementation of international quality standards. The former chairman of the Tea Board of India, S.S. Ahuja, said, 'There can be no compromise on quality as overseas markets are becoming increasingly quality conscious'. The Board declared 2000 as the year of quality, exports, productivity, and sustainable growth. Besides this, the Board has vigorously promoted and strengthened the Assam, Nilgiris, and Darjeeling logos.

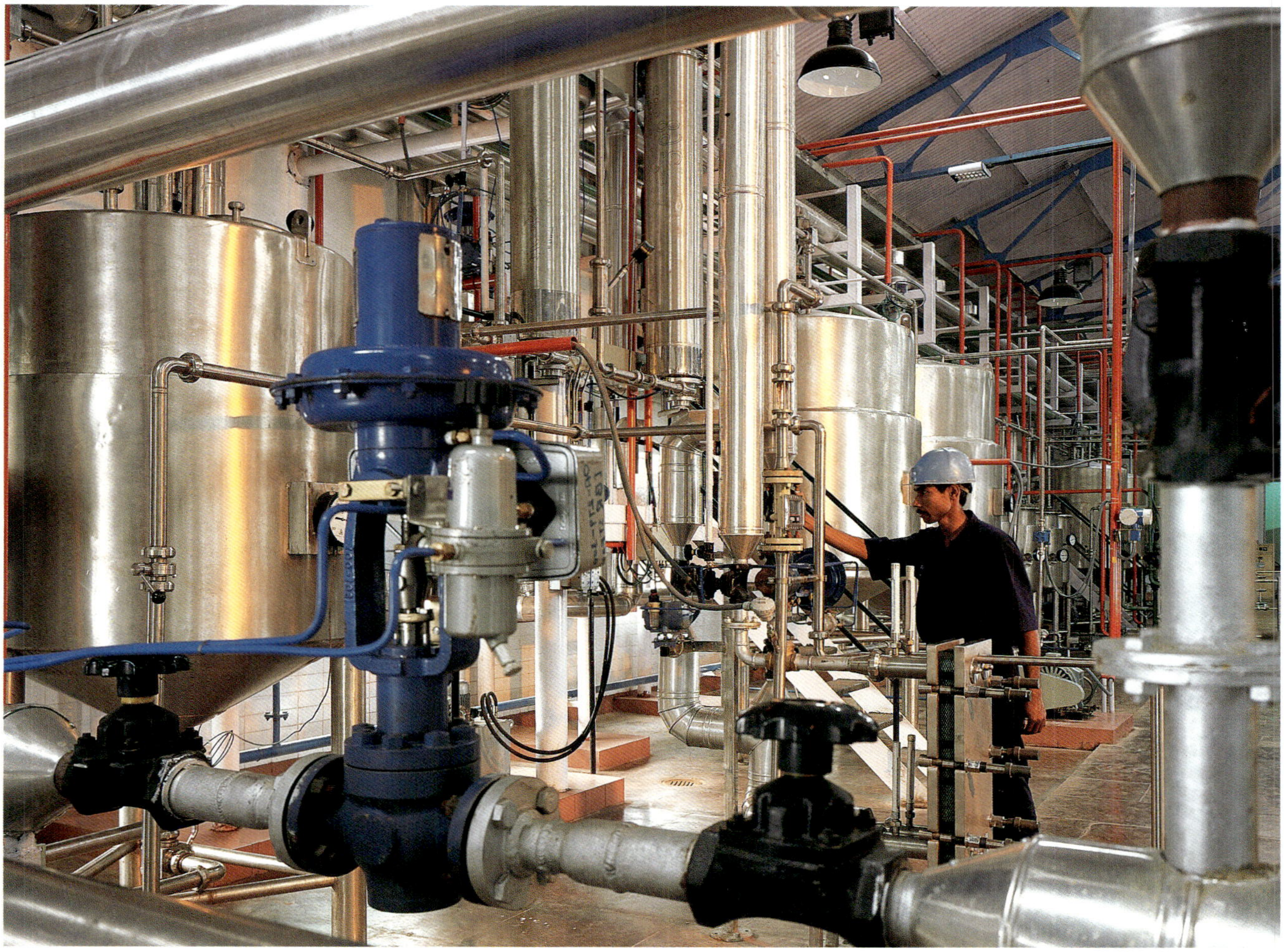

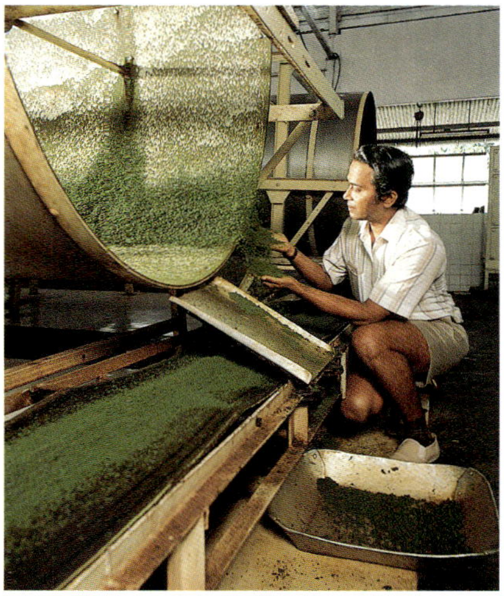

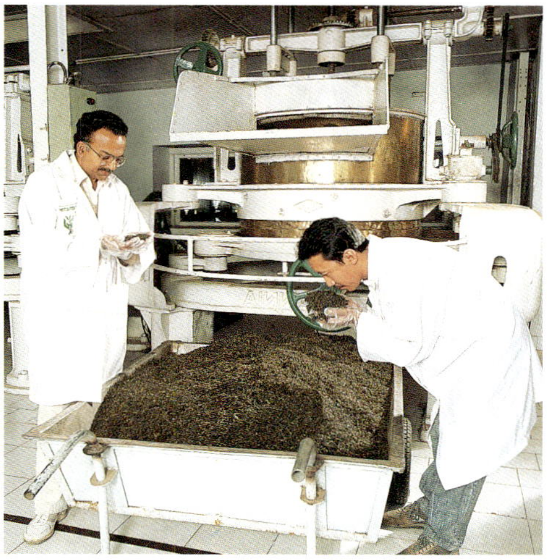

Top, below left and right: Growth horizons for the new millennium: the Indian tea industry places great store on research and development, quality control, and hygiene.

Following spread: Oil painting by August Haerning (b. 1874) of a tea party in the charming environs in which it has been grown.

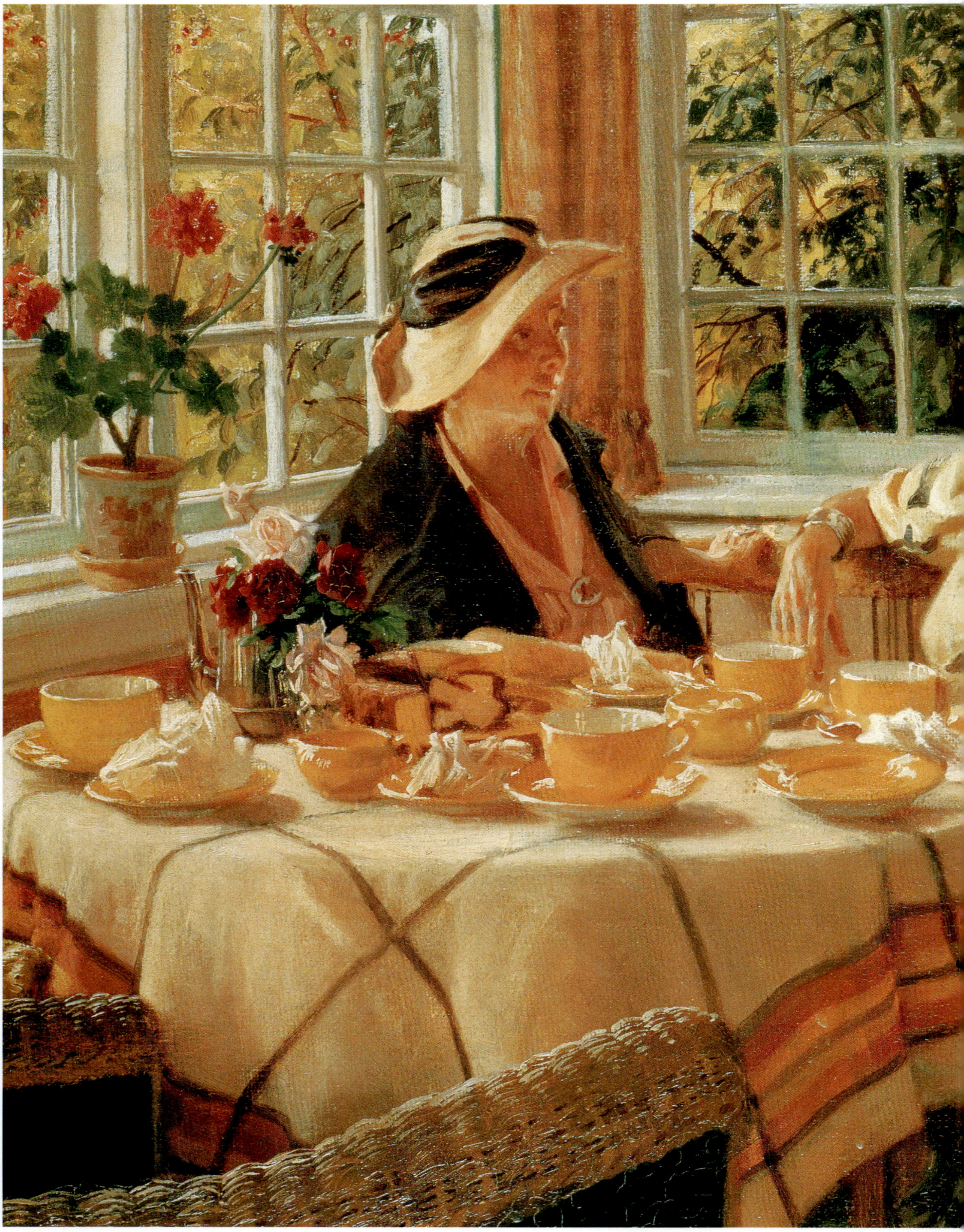

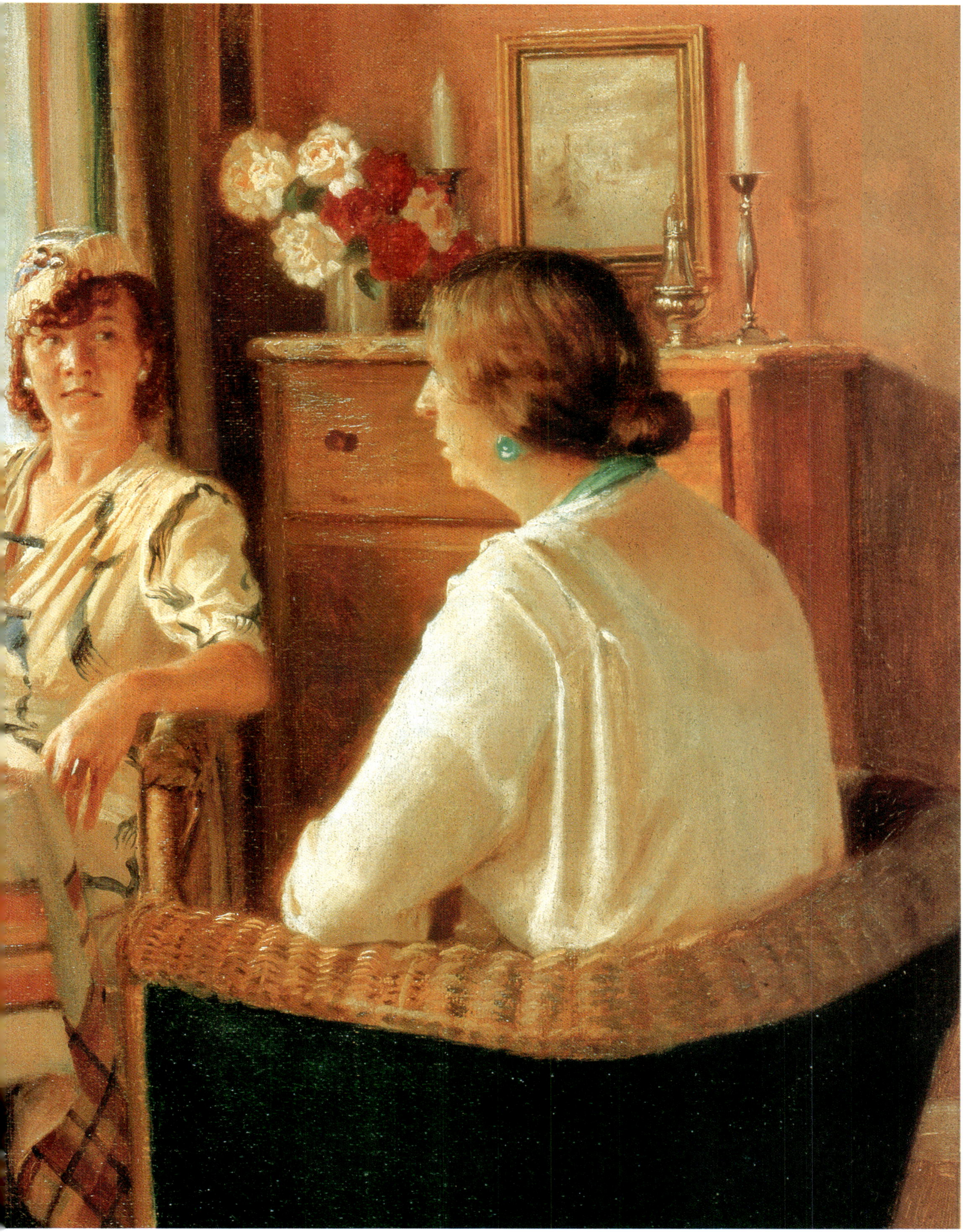

Logos and Flavours

Assam is the world's single largest tea-growing region, and tea from there has been called 'a cup of gold'. Any quality blend is incomplete without a substantial percentage of Assam tea. There are two 'flushes' of Assam tea: the first produces teas of great delicacy with a mildly astringent taste, but it is the second flush with its fuller, richer aroma that is most eagerly awaited because the addition of a small quantity of it can lend lustre to any blend. The Tea Board of India has created a logo to testify that a particular tea is a genuine product of the Assam tea gardens.

The Nilgiris or the Blue Mountains are situated in southern India, and tea is grown there at higher elevations. The conditions prevalent favour a fine flavour and a brisk liquor. This unique blend of fragrance and briskness makes Nilgiri tea amongst the best in the world. The Tea Board of India logo for Nilgiri tea depicts pure fragrance.

Darjeeling tea is nature's gift to the Himalayan region of north-east India. The distinctive, exclusive, and rare character of Darjeeling tea, which has made it a household name across the world, is the result of several geographical factors. Although Darjeeling produces 10 to 11 m. kg annually, it is alleged that the total quantity of tea sold as 'Darjeeling' in the global market is over 40 m. kg. To protect this valuable tea from imitation, the Tea Board of India has developed a logo emphasizing its gentle fragrance. This ensures that the prices consumers pay are for the genuine leaf.

Champagne in a Hot Pot

The flavour of a cup of tea is always welcome, but when it is from Darjeeling, the pleasure is manifold. Tea from this mountain-clad region of north Bengal is a rare blend that cannot be replicated anywhere else in the world : kissed by the mist, hymns of the wind, blessings of blue sky ... Given its unique flavour and quality, it is called the Champagne of Tea. As Champagne is to France, so Darjeeling is to India. Its uniqueness, based on geographical conditions and an image of excellence built over the years, has an enormous cachet and value.

A few years ago, Darjeeling tea made it to the *Guinness Book of World Records* for the highest price per kilogramme paid for tea. Its Castleton tea estate sold tea at Rs 13,011 per kg in 1992, thereby establishing a world record. Connoisseurs the world over are anxious to procure the finest Darjeeling tea. Supermarkets and fashionable stores in the leading tea-consuming countries prominently display invoices from Darjeeling estates.

Top, middle and above: The Tea Board of India has introduced Assam, Nilgiri, and Darjeeling logos to testify to the genuine quality of the product.
Below: A plucker in a Darjeeling tea estate.

Harrods in London has a specialized tea counter where the most expensive Darjeeling, Assam, and Nilgiri tea in the world is available.

The story of Darjeeling tea started 150 years ago when a civil surgeon by the name of Dr A. Campbell planted tea seeds in his garden. The first commercial tea gardens were started by the British at Tukvar, Steinthal, and Aloobari. Darjeeling Tea Company was established in 1864 with four gardens. By 1866, Darjeeling had 39 gardens.

Today, there are 86 tea gardens covering 19,000 ha. The Darjeeling tea gardens are situated at elevations of 610 to 2134 m on steep slopes that provide ideal natural drainage for the generous rainfall the district receives. This, coupled with intermittent cloud and sunshine, combine to impart to Darjeeling tea its unique flavour. The tea is light in colour with a noticeable astringency. The teas produced at the beginning of the season, known as the 'first flush', have a mildly astringent taste, are very clear and lively, and are noted for their exquisite delicacy. The later 'second flush' teas are the ones most prized by tea connoisseurs. The brew from them is slightly darker and has a fuller, richer aroma.

Darjeeling tea, which enjoys an established premium market, represents just over one per cent of all the tea India produces, but its turnover exceeds the revenue generated by tourism in this area. It employs over 52,000 people on a permanent basis, while a further 15,000 are engaged during the plucking season. Over 60 per cent of the workforce consists of women. Such a labour-intensive structure, together with the popularity of the beverage and its worldwide recognition, are reasons enough to regard Darjeeling tea as a national asset, to be nurtured and preserved so long as drinking tea remains a daily ritual.

Research and Development

Every asset has to be carefully nurtured. India has commanded a position of leadership in the quantity and quality of its tea output among the tea-producing countries in the world due to its long running research endeavours. The role of research is immense for two principal reasons. First, the tea industry combines roles in agriculture, manufacturing, and marketing. Second, tea is grown in varying terrains and climatic conditions which have a bearing on cost, quality, and yield.

Leading tea companies have their own research programmes. The saga of research and development began in 1824 when the first specimens of indigenous tea plants from Assam were given to Dr N. Wallich for scientific

Top: Kashmiris are fond of tea flavoured with cardamon seeds and crushed almonds: a Kashmiri woman carrying a samovar of tea. *Below:* The popular saffron tea of Kashmir has a rich, heightened flavour.

Top and facing page: Behind the scenes preparations are afoot. In the West, tea was for long the pre-rogative of the upper classes but in India *chai* plays important role in the lives of all classes of people.

Following spread: Regal confabulations over cups of tea amidst the ornate and luxurious interiors of Nayala House, Jaipur.

study. He visited Assam after undertaking a boat journey of over four months and submitted his report in 1835. Several other scientists, like Dr W. Griffith and Dr J. McLelland, were also associated with tea research.

The Indian Tea Association was closely associated with the scientific study of tea in Assam, but the industry as a whole was involved for the first time when James Buckingham of Amgooria Tea Estate asked for the views of planters on the special qualities of *Albizzia stipulata*. The planters' replies were published by the Indian Tea Association in 1885.

The Association established a Scientific Research Organization in 1899 which was the precursor of the Tocklai Experimental Research Station founded in 1911. This organization conducted useful research in the introduction of scientific methods into tea cultivation. It was followed by a scientific department set up by the United Planters' Association of Southern India in 1909.

Harold H. Mann, a well known agricultural scientist, was appointed in 1900 to conduct research on methods of growing and making tea. He set up a scientific station at Heelekah Tea Estate near Moriani, and recommended the use of oil cakes and cowdung to energize the exhausted soil. Mann discovered that waterlogging was responsible for greatly reducing the quality of the soil, and therefore suggested proper drainage. His efforts led to a full-fledged research station, conducting studies on the cultivation of tea, being set up in Tocklai in 1911.

The Tocklai Experimental Research Station, established by P.H. Carpenter and supported by an entomologist and a mycologist, is today the largest organization conducting research on tea in the world, and some revolutionary methods of manufacturing tea have been developed there. Its activities cover all aspects of tea cultivation and manufacture. Its principal achievements have been the development of high-yielding varieties of the tea plant, effective pest control, better drainage systems and techniques of cultivation. The dimensions of research have widened steadily with increasing needs.

In 1938, an advisory department was set up with the aim of transferring technology to members of the Indian Tea Association. On 1 January 1964, the Tea Research Association was formed to take over the management of the Tocklai Experimental Research Station in order to enable all the tea gardens, irrespective of their membership of the Indian Tea Association, to avail themselves of its services.

Credit for increasing production must also go to the United Planters' Association of Southern India. An institution for research in tea was set up in Devashola in 1926 and transferred to the Annamalais in 1964. It has grown into a fully-fledged Tea Research Foundation with its Tea Research Institute in Valparai. It has regional centres in Gudalur, Coonoor in Tamil Nadu; Munnar, Meppadi, and Vandiperiyar in Kerala; and also Durgadabetta in Karnataka. It has made breakthroughs in pest and weed control, zinc deficiency, and optimization of tipping. The Darjeeling Tea Research Centre has even researched traditional operations like pruning and plucking, but its emphasis has been on agro-technology to improve productivity and the quality of tea. The Tea Research Association's long-term objectives are to increase the yield and make more cups available per kilogramme of tea. In keeping with global trends, it has also become important to grow tea without using chemical fertilizers and pesticides. This requires maintenance of the delicate balance of nature and is possible only through innovative research.

Besides this, upgradation of existing factories and plantations is necessary. Concerted efforts, which have yet to be made in this direction, are urgently required so that the production of tea can be increased along with enhanced quality.

FACING THE FUTURE | 219

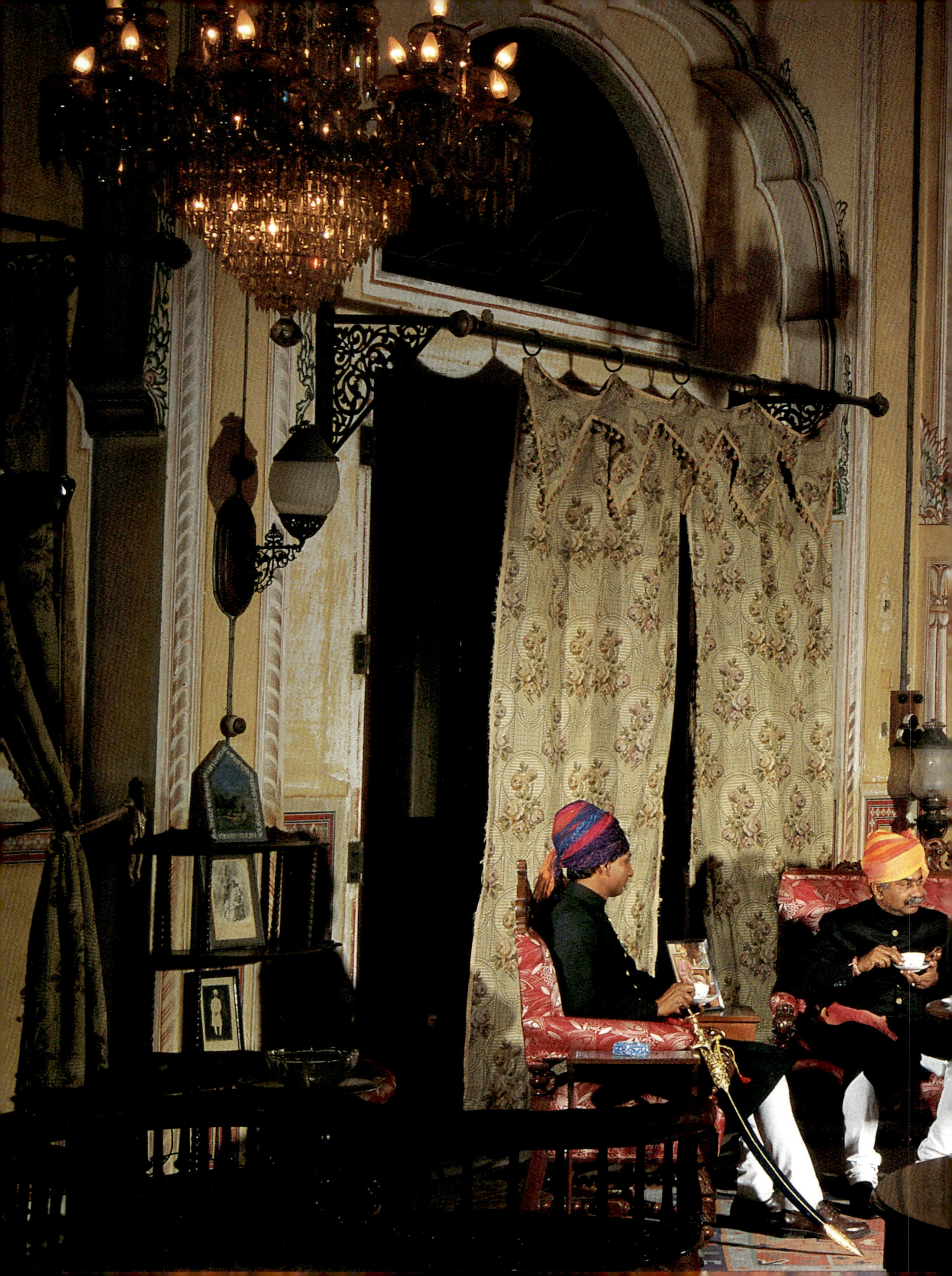

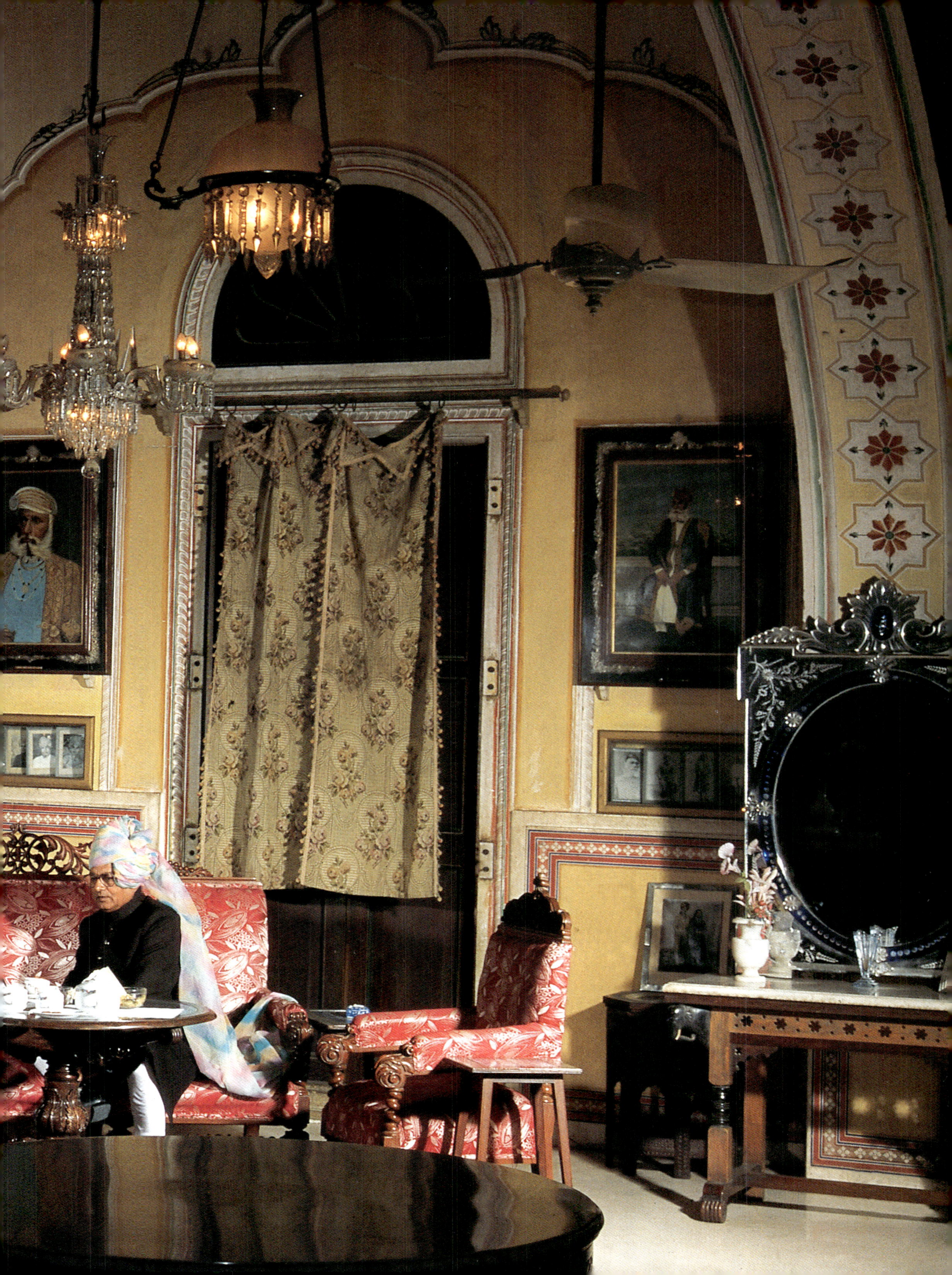

Top and below: Future challenges: in Assam, floods and militancy pose major threats to the tea industry.

Facing page: Nature's miracle: a path to heaven through a tea garden of southern India which reflects majesty and splendour clothed in nature's resplendent shades.

Fighting Floods

Nature's role cannot be ignored. In Assam, floods threaten the existence of tea bushes. About 40 per cent of the area under tea cultivation in Assam has been seriously affected by waterlogging. The Brahmaputra river is the second greatest bearer of silt in the world. The beds of the Barak and the Brahmaputra have risen along with those of their tributaries. In consequence, floods have increased in frequency and spread to new areas, and the water table has risen throughout the region. Rainwater collects in this salty soil because there is no method of draining it away; the tender roots of tea bushes get submerged in it and absorb the nutrients from the soil, and the plants consequently cease to flush out the water. As the water table falls during winter, the plants lose their absorptive root system and suffer instead from drought. As a result, tea and other plants can die of rot and suffocation.

Large parts of the tea estates of upper Assam, agricultural land, and forests have been eroded. About 50,000 ha of marginal land with the tea estates, which have a production potential of 100 m. kg of tea at a conservative estimate, can be brought under tea cultivation if the drainage system is improved. Tea scientist D.N. Baruah, former adviser to the Tea Research Association, and B.C. Borbora of the Tocklai Experimental Research Station, suggest dredging the rivers, planting trees in the catchment areas, and constructing dams as possible solutions. The annual flooding of the Brahmaputra and its tributaries also remains a major cause for concern. The industry has made several representations to the central and state governments on this score, but the problems of erosion and flooding have yet to be addressed.

Beneath the Shadow of the Gun

Another major setback has been the rise of militancy, which has adversely affected reinvestment in the tea industry and its production. The United Liberation Front of Asom and other extremist groups in Assam have been playing havoc with the tea industry. Although neighbouring West Bengal has been relatively peaceful, the recent movements of the Kamatapuri Liberation Army and the Kamatapuri People's Party, together with the dacoities committed in the Dooars and North Bengal, have aroused fears about the emergence of an Assam-type situation. The lack of protection for the plantation industry placed it at the mercy of extremists. Sheer helplessness forced some tea estates to pay ransom or protection money.

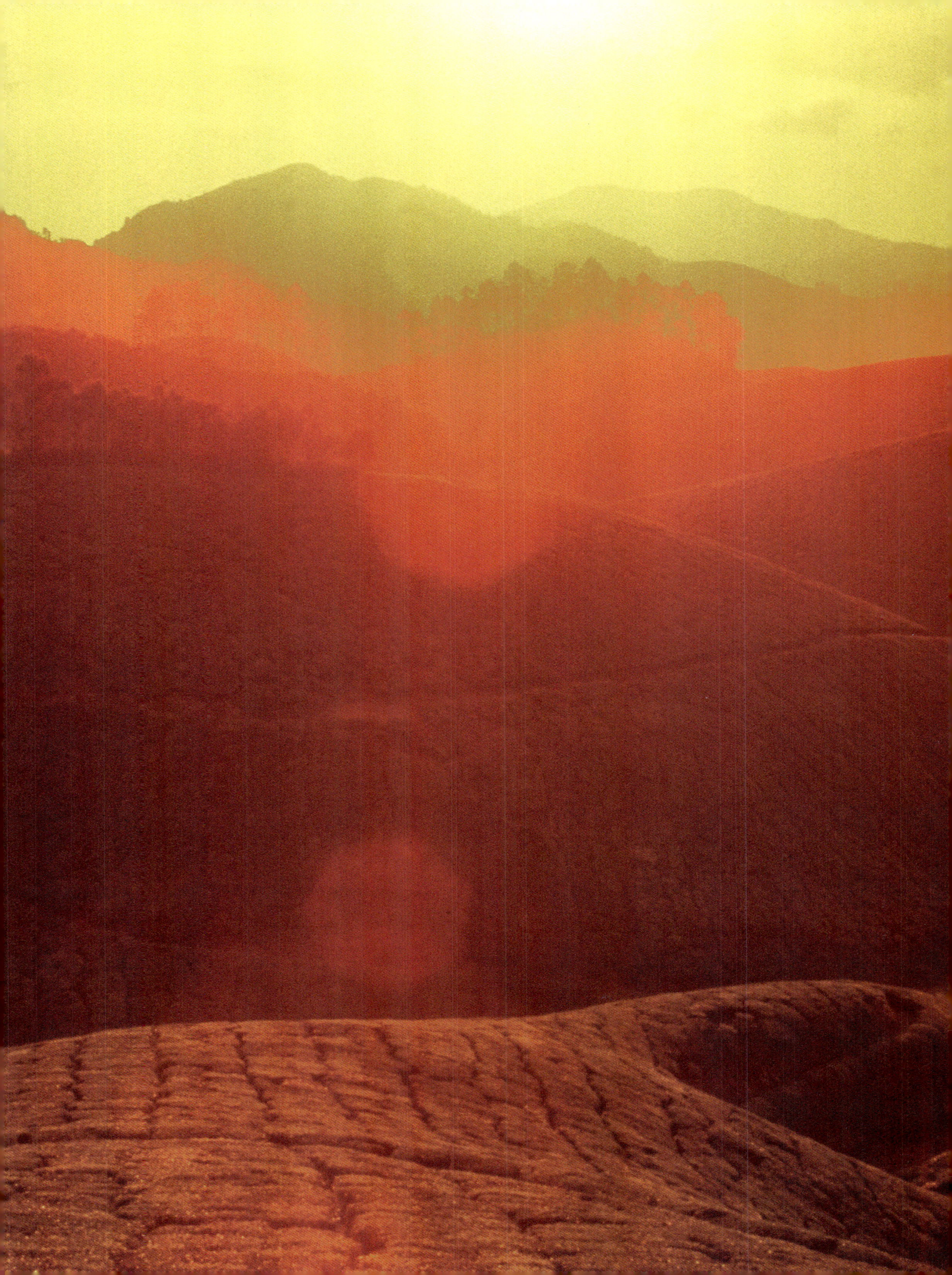

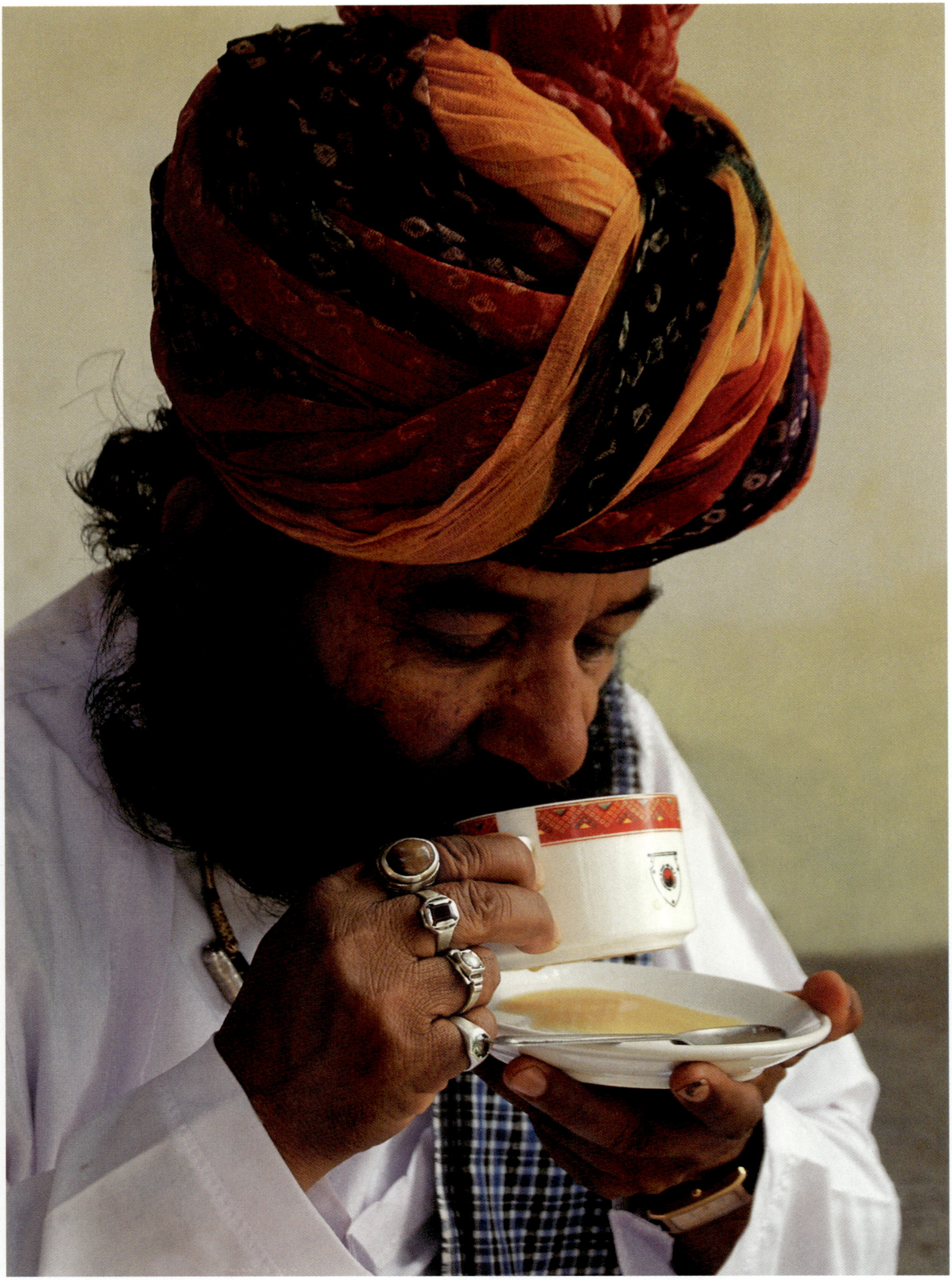

Today, in India's private sector, tea is the only industry which spends several millions of rupees on its own protection every year. The Assam Tea Plantation Force was created on 20 October 1993 through a Memorandum of Understanding between the state government and the Indian Tea Association. The militants' depredations have been relentless, and it is a miracle that the tea industry in the state has survived.

Living continually under the shadow of the gun, the industry was in deep trouble during the prolonged agitation against foreign nationals. Later, United Liberation Front of Asom extremists indulged in killings, kidnappings, and extortions. Bodo militants and the National Socialist Council of Nagaland also joined them. Since 1990, about 12 tea personnel have been killed and another 40 kidnapped and later released. Hindustan Lever Ltd, a subsidiary of Unilever of London, decided not to pay ransom to extremists and simply evacuated its entire managerial staff and their families to Calcutta. They returned later when the situation permitted. On another occasion the company also pulled Brooke Bond and Lipton out of the auctions as a gesture of protest.

'Tea gardens are still receiving extortion notices with demands for huge amounts of money,' according to a senior tea planter. As if that was not enough, the United Liberation Front of Asom has even warned tea companies in Assam against setting up social organizations. The situation was so bad a decade ago that eminent journalist Arun Shourie had to cancel his visit to the state. 'No one brings good news from Assam,' said Shourie in his message to the students of Cotton College, while expressing his inability to attend the seminar organized by the college's Students' Union on 25 January 1990.

Several Assamese writers who are concerned about militancy in Assam feel that terrorism has led to a bad work culture in the state. Participating in a debate once, Sahitya Akademi Award winner Nagen Saikia said, 'Revolution through killings and bullets can never be supported by any writer or artist because all imaginative people are creative only because they love human beings' Keshab Mahanta, a poet and lyricist, also condemned the violence unleashed by the United Liberation Front of Asom and other extremist groups. Last year's Akademi award winner Chandroprasad Saikia said that no one 'supports terrorism. Assam should be known as the land of Saint Sankardev, not of terrorism.'

The roots of militancy in Assam date back to the mid-1980s when the agitation against foreigners ended with the conclusion of the Assam accord

Top: Tea time! in oil.

Facing page: A distinguished traditional musician from Rajasthan relishes his tea.

Will formidable taxes lead to prohibitive prices and add to the number of empty glasses?!

between the All Assam Students' Union and the Rajiv Gandhi government in 1985. The Asom Gana Parishad was elected to power with the enthusiastic support of the people. However, a section of students who had supported the agitation broke away and formed the United Liberation Front of Asom by forging links with extremist groups.

According to P.K. Bora, the chief secretary, government of Assam, 'The government has dealt firmly with the situation and taken decisive steps to maintain peace and order by setting up a unified command structure involving the army, state police, and paramilitary forces'. Tarun Gogoi, the chief minister of Assam, has asked the central government for talks with the militants as part of his government's proposed political initiative to tackle insurgency as a substitute to an elusive military solution. It is clear that there is an urgent need for both the central and the state governments to work together to bring militancy to an end and bring peace and prosperity to the state. The tea industry has already started its efforts towards ushering in an era of peace and prosperity. Through its initiatives, many young members of the United Liberation Front of Asom have started a new life in agriculture, dairy farming, raising poultry, and even as small tea growers.

Crippled by Taxes

The Indian tea industry is burdened with cumbersome taxes which have weakened its competitive edge in world markets. High taxation wipes out a major percentage of profits. The result is that the industry is not in a position to plough back funds for long-term development. There is an urgent need to examine the tax structure and rationalize it.

B.M. Khaitan wrote to L.C. Jain, member, Planning Commission, 'It is imperative that the tax structure is modified and the fiscal levies of the kind recently imposed on green leaf removed. The tea companies do not ask for special treatment but submit that our rate of taxation should be brought on par with other industries. This will leave some funds with us which could be ploughed back into the development of the tea estates and for investment in other industries which can be situated in Assam'. S.M. Kidwai, former managing director of Tata Tea Ltd, says, 'The greatest hindrance to the growth of tea is the various taxes'.

The P.C. Barooah Committee on the tea industry set up by the government of India has observed, 'When taxation exceeds a certain level it tends to become counter-productive; it does not leave enough to undertake further development and creates in the producer a lack of confidence in the

future to undertake development, even on borrowed finance. This is exactly the position we find in the tea industry today ... We would, therefore, urge the government to take a more realistic view and adopt a more rational and equitable fiscal policy to enable the industry to undertake badly needed renovation, modernization, rehabilitation, and development.'

The tea industry is heavily taxed both by the union and state governments in the states where tea is grown. Forty per cent of the industry's income is subjected to central income tax. The remaining 60 per cent invites agricultural income tax in the states. This is a huge burden, and much in excess of what other industries have to bear. Incentives under the Central Income Tax Act are available to tea companies on only 40 per cent of their income. There are other burdens, such as green leaf tax, sales tax, and land revenue, and a cess of 30 paise per kilogramme payable to the Tea Board of India. Another sad reality faced by the industry is that if a tea company has gardens in more than one state, the prevailing taxation system does not permit it to set off agricultural losses in one state against profits made in another—an option available to most other industries.

An evocation of the current plight of the Indian tea industry: an empty tea cup with leaves swept by the wind.

Under Section 80 HHC of the Income Tax Act, 1961, deduction in relation to export profits is allowed from business income. Now, in the case of tea, this is applicable to only 40 per cent of the income that falls within the purview of the Centre, and what is worse is that this provision is applicable with retrospective effect from 1 April 1992. This discriminates between mere merchant–exporters and the companies that actually grow and export tea, the former being able to claim a deduction of 100 per cent of their income. Implementation of the provision with retrospective effect is especially unfair because tea producers, who are also exporters and have been claiming full deduction up to now, are faced with the prospect of their entire tax planning being thrown completely out of gear.

Tea is listed as an essential commodity, yet a central excise duty of Rs 2 per kg on bulk tea has been imposed which is a cruel addition to the already burgeoning costs of the industry. Its withdrawal will provide partial but immediate relief. Recently the Tea Board of India too has recommended the abolition of the excise duty on tea. Additional resources need to be made available to the industry to enable them to uproot and replant uneconomic sections of tea plantations which will in the long run enhance the productivity and competitiveness of the Indian tea industry.

The central government should consider providing an interest subsidy from banks on loans availed for replantation which will constitute a nominal

Top: Those who produce tea, also enjoy its flavour and aroma with salt.
Centre: Tools of the trade: accessories used by tea workers.

annual liability. In addition, interest-free loans should be provided for the purchase of orthodox machinery.

The profits of the tea industry before tax are not particularly high and, indeed, have been declining. In consequence, the industry pays shareholders less than other industries do, severely damaging their ability to raise fresh equity capital through the capital markets. This further constrains their ability to add debt in times of need and their debt–equity ratio becomes harder to maintain at a reasonable level, thus increasing their perceived risk profile. At the same time, companies have invested almost all their profits in capital expenditure in order to remain competitive. The fiscal and non-fiscal policies of the central government in areas of production, trade, and prices have been major dampeners in the industry's growth. Producers say that India has always been perceived as an unreliable supplier in global markets, and that this is the result of the fiscal and non-fiscal interventions by the government which wipe out a major share of their profits.

Financial Crunch

The tea industry faces a severe monetary crunch. Mumtaz Ahmad, who was one of the most eloquent and respected spokesmen of the industry, said that he was once asked by an eminent person, 'I agree that you have the infrastructure : you have the manpower, the research, and, what is more, the will-power and determination to continue to grow. But have you the finance?' Ahmad's prompt and revealing answer was, 'Yes we have, but the money is not with us; it is with the government. I am here referring to the various duties and taxes that tea is subjected to before we are left with any money to develop and grow.'

Just how heavy is the tax burden that the states place on the tea industry? Here is the example of Assam. Under the 1922 act, agricultural income tax in Assam was levied at a flat rate of four annas to the rupee. In 1993–4, it rose by 60 per cent. The result is that the tea industry currently contributes as much as 27 per cent of the total tax revenue of the government of Assam. In addition, the industry pays excise duty and a central cess on tea. There is a green leaf cess levied in Assam and West Bengal. Land revenue is paid all over. There are, in addition, sales and panchayati taxes, not to speak of the high labour welfare costs.

One of the important tax concessions that the industry has sought relates to replantation. When bushes are planted afresh, there is a sharp drop in revenue and income. Currently, there is a subsidy that only partially covers

the cost of replantation. It would be much more practical to introduce a provision in the Income Tax Act, 1961 to allow a weighted deduction of 140 per cent on expenditure incurred on replanting. The more replanting there is, the greater the long-run potential for increase in production.

The industry's fortunes are cyclical and depend heavily on the erratic rains. The boom spells in 1954, 1977, 1988, and 1998 were followed by depressions that lasted much longer. During boom periods, taxes rise but they do not fall during a depression. This is especially problematic for tea because its depressions last longer than its boom periods.

Heavy taxation prevents the industry from making vital investments in machinery and production processes. For instance, there is a growing market for tea bags internationally. Machines and paper for making tea bags have to be imported. There used to be a concessional import duty of 15 per cent on machines which was raised to 35 per cent, and then scrapped altogether in 1994. Now a duty of 20 per cent is paid with the result that tea companies pay 5 per cent more than they did in 1990. Similarly, filter paper has to be imported and invites a duty. The import duties on both these products are in sharp contrast to the subsidy on imports provided by a competitor like Sri Lanka to its tea-bag exporters.

As Mumtaz Ahmad put it, the tax burdens are all the more unfair because the tea industry contributes significantly to the development of rural areas. His suggestion was that the Centre and the states should sit together and work out a uniform policy on agricultural income. 'What hurts us greatly is the higher tax burden borne by the tea industry in comparison to that borne by other industries. As things stand at the moment, the tea industry has a legitimate grievance that they alone are accorded discriminatory treatment.'

Rationalizing the Fiscal Policy

In recent years international competitors like Sri Lanka and Kenya have undertaken suitable tariff restructuring. In India, on an average, agricultural tax is 50 per cent, while manufacturing or corporation tax is 38.5 per cent. In Sri Lanka these are 15 per cent and 30 per cent, respectively. In Kenya, agricultural tax, the only component of taxation on the tea industry, is 32.5 per cent. There is no income tax in Indonesia. In India there are some indirect taxes as well. The tax component in India works out to roughly 56 per cent of the profits of tea-producing units. Compared to this, Kenyan producers are subjected to a total tax of 32.5 per cent, while the Sri Lankan producers pay only a paltry 8 per cent. As a result, the Kenyan and Sri Lankan producers

Refreshing draughts, different receptacles.

Calcuttans love a steaming *bhar* (small clay cups) of *cha* which is kept continually hot in large aluminium or brass kettles and mugs. The *bhar* can be disposed of after the tea has been consumed.

have huge post-tax disposable incomes, which are ploughed back profitably. In contrast, Indian producers share little of this comfort. The exchequer, at best, makes some Rs 900–1000 m. from tea excise. If this is abolished, the industry will make higher profits, which would increase the direct tax element.

Despite the recommendations of various commissions and committees appointed by the government of India and repeated representations by the industry, tax levels have not been appropriately scaled down. This has weakened the competitiveness of the industry in global markets.

The Union budget of 2001–2 provided some relief to the Indian tea industry: the Union finance minister increased the customs duty as well as developmental allowances on tea. This provided an impetus for the growth and development of the industry by encouraging upgradation of production technology necessary for fighting competition in the global market.

'We welcome the increase in customs duty on import of tea from 35 to 70 per cent. This is in consonance with the government's policy of ensuring that there are adequate safeguards after the quantitative restrictions are dismantled. Enhancement of allowance under Section 33 AB from 20 per cent to 40 per cent will enable the industry to substantially step up its developmental activities by way of replantation, rejuvenation, and modernization, and will provide a strong foundation to the tea industry, not only to sustain growth, but also measure up to challenges in the post-World Trade Organization era,' remarked R.S. Jhawar, former chairman of the Indian Tea Association. The recent Union budget of 2002–3 has halved the excise duty from Rs 1 per kg and enhanced the duty on tea imports to 100 per cent from 70 per cent earlier. While these changes have been welcomed by the industry, how effective they will be in tiding it out of its current recession remains in doubt. Many had expected the excise duty to be abolished altogether. Many other suggestions made by the industry were, sadly, not implemented.

Today, there is an urgent and imperative need to review and rationalize the existing fiscal and non-fiscal policies of the Centre and state governments, and for greater coordination between the Centre and the tea-growing states for an equitable tax regime that will permit the tea industry to develop.

Danger Signs

Currently, the Indian tea industry is facing very rough times. Low prices, cheap imports, and stiff competition from other beverages has resulted in a year that has been dubbed as one of the worst in the industry's history. The situation has taken a turn for the worse since 1998, eroding the profitability

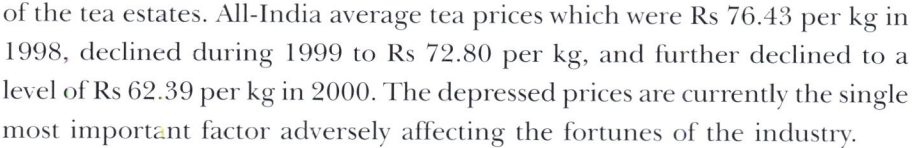

of the tea estates. All-India average tea prices which were Rs 76.43 per kg in 1998, declined during 1999 to Rs 72.80 per kg, and further declined to a level of Rs 62.39 per kg in 2000. The depressed prices are currently the single most important factor adversely affecting the fortunes of the industry.

Besides this, the industry has been under severe cost pressures. Over the past two years, direct labour wages have increased by 36 per cent; cost of the foodgrains subsidy to workers by 30 per cent; fertilizer prices by 24 per cent; input costs have risen by 106 per cent; and transportation costs are up by 77 per cent. To sum up, since 1998, the cost per kilogramme of tea has risen by Rs 12.25 and the average impact of decreases in price and increases in cost is Rs 26.25 per kg. D. Chakrabarti, secretary-general, Indian Tea Association, feels that the situation is extremely critical, with the ruling prices being, in many cases, below the cost of production, and unless prices improve, prospects of which appear dim, a number of estates may have to close down. Tea estates in the Dooars, Tripura, and some parts of Assam are in bad shape. 'The very survival of the industry could be at risk due to crashing tea prices,' says D. Bora, secretary of the Assam Tea Planters' Association. In the south, the situation is worse. Ullas Menon, secretary-general, United Planters' Association of Southern India, says that several estates are not in a position to remit the statutory provident fund contributions in time and there is considerable delay.

Top left and right: 'The essence of the enjoyment of tea lies in an appreciation of its colour, fragrance, and flavour, and the principles of preparation are refinement, dryness, and cleanliness' (Chalu of Cai Xiang, 1012–67).

Following spread: Although a relatively inexpensive beverage, some self-control must be exercised given its hold on the people: a popular tea shop in Calcutta.

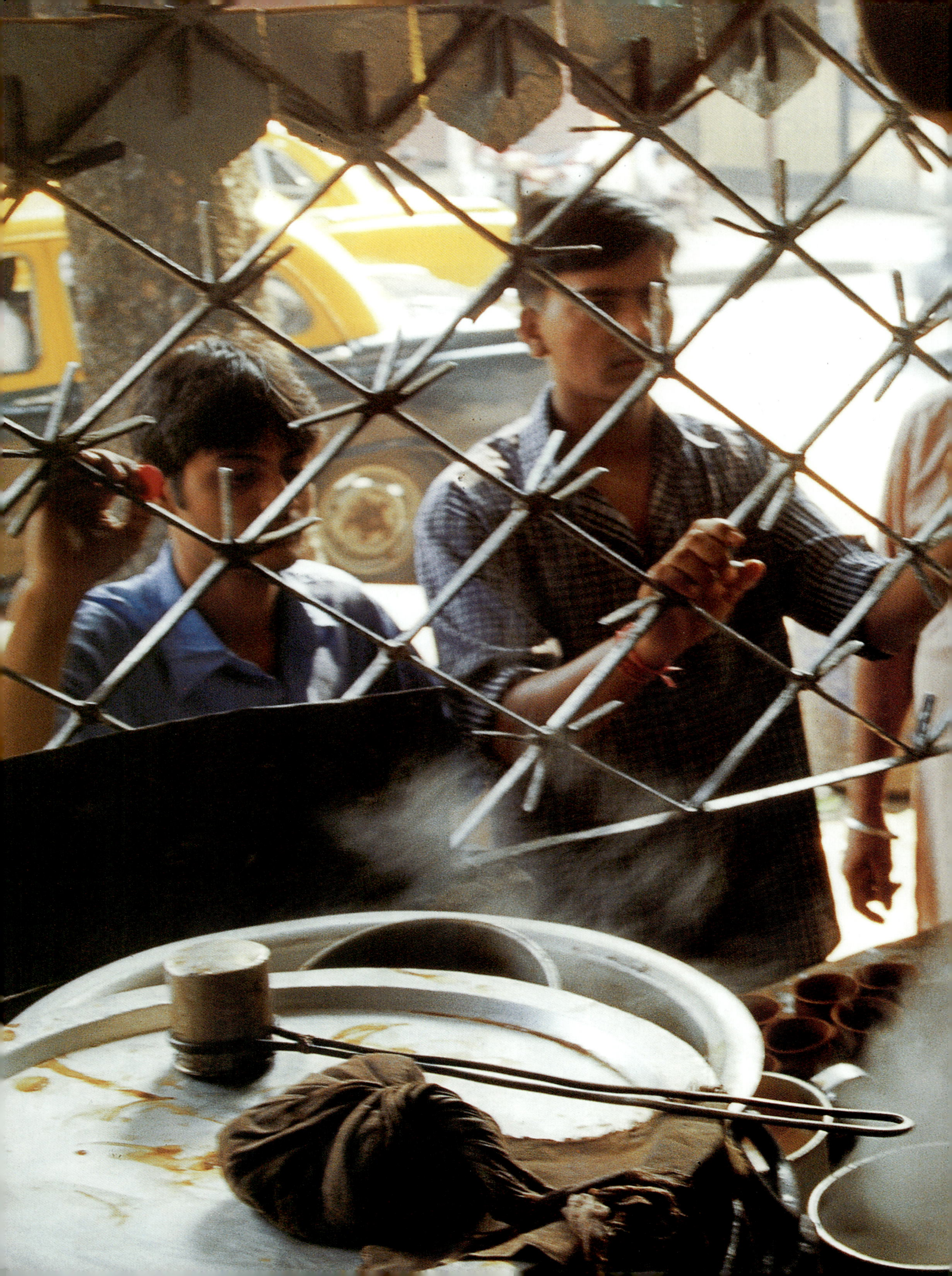

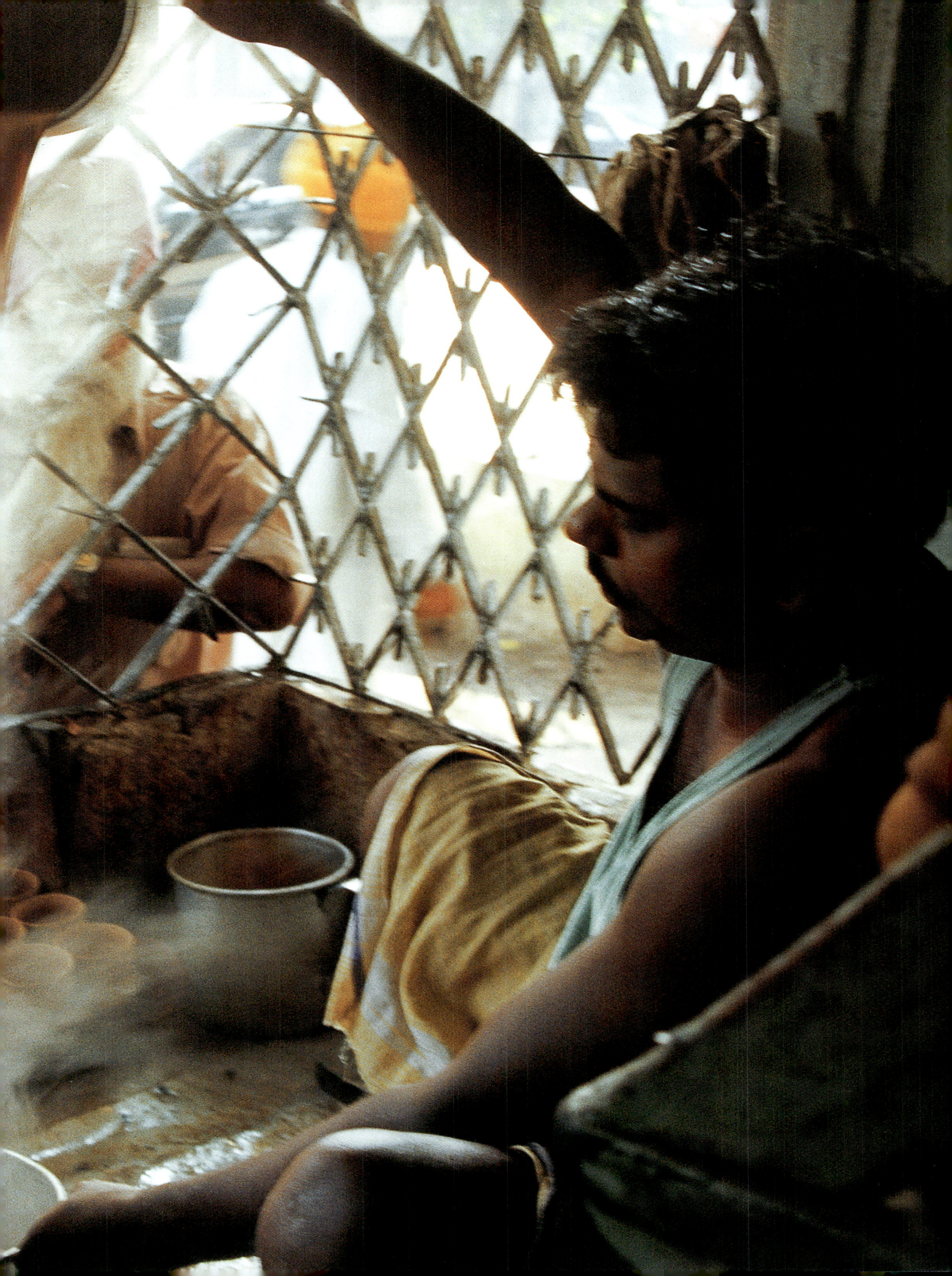

The plight of the tea producers has worsened since mid-1999 when the average price of tea started falling. Exports had not shown the requisite increase because Indian tea was being priced out of the market by other countries that were selling their product at much lower prices. Tea experts believe that the industry is approaching a situation like that of 1952, and that there is a dire need for far-sighted and proactive measures to tide over the crisis facing it. They even doubt the economic viability of growing tea in the near future under the present constraints. The morale of tea companies is low. The performance of recent years has been much below expectations and there is little sign of the business gathering momentum. To top it all, there is also the threat of unrestricted imports. The cost of production keeps rising, but the price at which tea is sold does not keep pace with such increases. According to Prafulla Goradia, 'Price is problem number one of tea. Over the last 60 years, inflation is estimated to have increased the general price level by 150 times in India while the wholesale or auction prices of the tea have appreciated only about 25 times.'

The southern tea industry is in the throes of a crisis, and falling prices have put most north Indian tea producers on a slow growth path. If gardens and factories close down, and tea workers and their families are thrown out of employment, there will be a serious law and order situation. Tea producers willy-nilly soldier on with heavy borrowings, but this cannot continue indefinitely and some sectors of the industry have already started tottering. So critical has the situation become that it is acutely necessary for the finance ministry to intervene immediately with both short- and long-term strategies to bail out the industry with fiscal concessions that will provide it with some respite; otherwise the country's oldest organized industry is likely to collapse, leaving the millions of people dependent on it in the lurch. R.K. Krishna Kumar optimistically believes that 'Indian tea has faced crises before and has come out stronger. I believe that if we are willing to undertake major restructuring of our industry's cost structure, we will come out of the present crisis as well.'

Deny me not, oh Lord!
my morning cup of tea.

Making its Voice Heard

To prevent such a catastrophe, the genuine demands of the industry have not been addressed. The tea industry's insularity has perhaps been its greatest weakness. Working in remote, isolated parts of India, far away from the hubbub of the metros, the industry is often unable to make its presence felt in the urban-oriented corridors of power. Once, in an introspective mood, the late Mumtaz Ahmed remarked that perhaps the locational isolation at times

There is nothing like a cup of tea to break the monotony of a business meeting and bring a smile to concentrated faces.

made them lose touch with the outside world and engendered a certain degree of insularity. This, in turn, perhaps made them exaggerate their unflattering self-image. They tended to forget that their industry has unfolded the most amazing success story of the century: one of progress without profits.

In a democracy it is essential that correct messages enter the political system. The tea industry has to emerge from its shell and share its performance, problems, and future prospects with society at large. This will undoubtedly help to clear the prevailing misconceptions and generate a new understanding of its proactive developmental role. Where the sugar and cotton industries have been successful in getting themselves heard in parliament, tea, despite the contribution that it makes to the economy, has failed to do so. To retain its pre-eminence and to keep its image intact, it is necessary to have a strong information base.

Paban Singh Ghatowar, former union minister of state and member of parliament from Assam, is of the view that, 'Even the people coming from tea-

Tea is an any time beverage, be it morning or evening, the workplace or the home.

growing areas are not aware of what the tea industry is doing, what its difficulties are, and what the industry wants to achieve in future for the prosperity of the country. If there is a debate in parliament, you will not find much material on this industry.' According to Prafulla Goradia, a man of letters, 'It is largely a gentleman's profession. Nevertheless, the tea fraternity continues to be publicity-shy. Shed this shyness, become bolder, and tell the world in general and Indians in particular what enormous services and pleasure the gardens and their bushes provide to them.'

At the time of the Union budget, other industries, through their associations, call meetings of members of parliament and brief them about their problems and demands. The tea industry makes representations to the government but does nothing to ensure that politicians speak for it. According to H.P. Barooah, 'Unfortunately we are introverts in this industry; we do not go and try to make one of our tea industrialists a minister, nor do we go and call on a minister or member of parliament every time we are in Delhi unless one is representing the tea association'.

The many contributions made by the tea industry constitute a story rarely told or understood. 'One of the problems ... is widespread ignorance in Delhi about tea and the tea industry,' said Abid Hussain, former member of the planning commission and commerce secretary, government of India. C.K. Dhanuka, vice-chairman of the Indian Tea Association and president of the Indian Chamber of Commerce, concurs: 'Yes I think there is a point in it because tea always seems to be the concern only of the gentleman farmer. There is a lacuna in the system and therefore tea has ended up with very little visual presence and very little support in Delhi.'

A Plea for a Dynamic Policy Initiative

Although the industry has taken several steps for its revival, such as enhancement of productivity, improvement in quality, and cost competitiveness, a campaign for generic promotion in the domestic market and enhancement in volume and price realization of tea exports is necessary. The government has to give the tea industry more space within which to shape its own future. If this does not happen quickly, Indian tea will run the risk of sinking permanently into a morass of problems and lose whatever residual advantage it now enjoys in the world market. Therefore, suitable strategies and a proper agenda need to be evolved to give Indian tea the fillip necessary to raise it once more to its erstwhile paramount position.

There is no alternative but for the central and state governments, the Tea Board of India, tea producers, research associations, workers, the trade unions, and local communities to work together to achieve common goals. As tea makes a significant contribution to the economy and the local communities, such cooperation can only be in the interest of the country. Better packaging, brand-building, promotion of tea as a generic beverage and a health drink, the opening up of new markets, research and development are just some of the goals that need to be urgently addressed.

The wide-ranging and significant contributions that the tea industry makes, as examined in the foregoing pages, to the gross domestic product, to exports, to the provision of mass employment, to the economic and social development of the states in which it operates, gives it a strong claim for special consideration by our planners, policy-makers, and administrators. The prosperity of millions is linked to its continuing health and growth. It is therefore imperative that a cohesive and long-term approach be adopted so that the Indian tea industry once more scales the heights it enjoyed as a world leader in tea, quantitatively, qualitatively, and in terms of competitiveness.

Top: The stylish but packed tea rooms of the Taj during the afternoon when tea is served with delicious snacks.

Following spread: For the genteel upper class, relaxing on a traditional *jhoola* and exchanging confidences or having a tête-à-tête with a cup of tea is a keenly awaited 5:00 p.m. ritual.

FACING THE FUTURE | 237

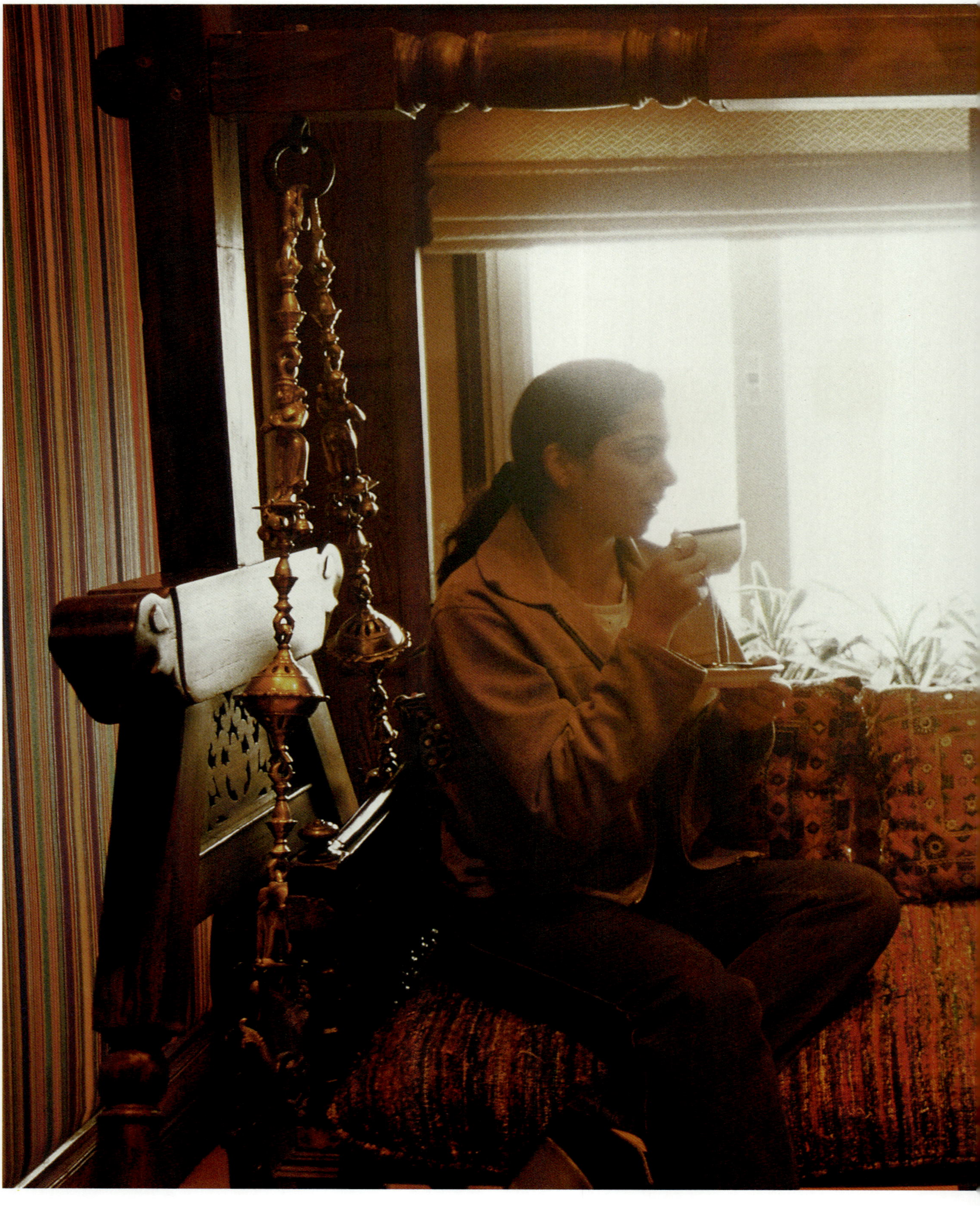

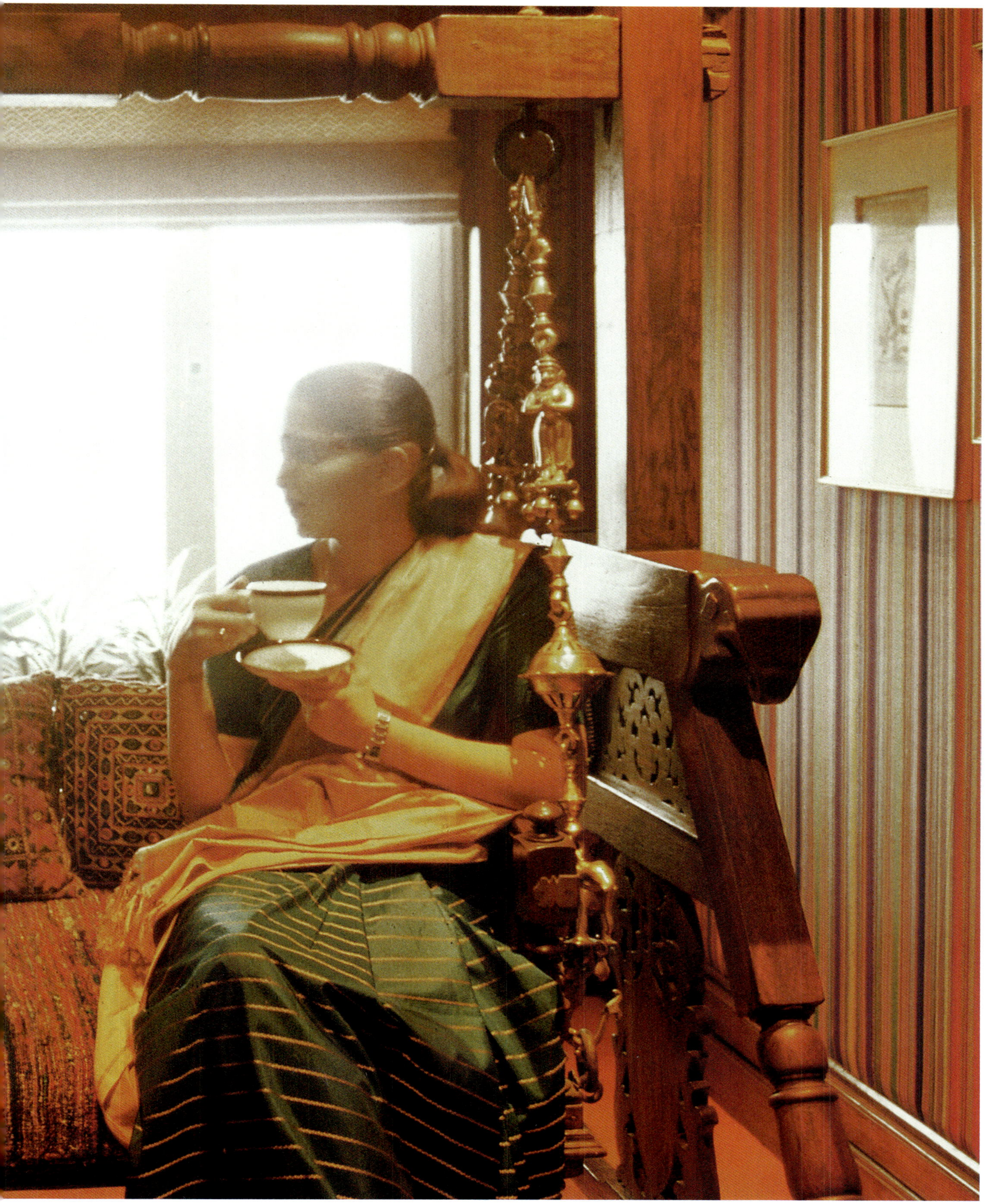

We reap what we sow

The man riding the motor cycle braked suddenly. He had seen Amir Ahsan, senior manager of Dirai Tea Estate. He got off the bike, went running up to the manager and, in front of everyone, touched his feet and invited him over for lunch.

At lunch, Debjyoti Baruah's entire family—his mother, his five brothers, their wives and children—were there to greet the man who had helped transform their lives. As soon as Amir Ahsan arrived with his family, the five brothers reverently touched his feet. The mother, with tears in her eyes, presented him with a beautiful shawl which she had personally woven for him. Lunch itself was an elaborate affair with all the *bahu*s hovering around the guest, offering him first this, and then that, ensuring that there was always enough on his plate to demonstrate that he was a guest who was loved and honoured in that household.

Then suddenly, in the midst of the meal, the mother looked at the guest and said, 'It is all because of you. Because of you we are happy and together. You gave my children back; back to me,' she said.

She was referring to the dark shadow of militancy which, not so long ago, had threatened to engulf the family. Debjyoti, unemployed, alienated, was flirting with the United Liberation Front of Asom and terrorism. He would swagger into the market and everyone would sort of move away.

It was Amir Ahsan, tea estate manager of the Williamson Magor group, who intervened. He spoke to Debjyoti and offered to help, making it clear that he would not be giving him any money. 'Money,' he told Debjyoti, 'never puts a person right. It is only when you become self-reliant and have work to do that you learn the worth of money and become a better human being.'

Instead, he helped the Bodo to acquire five hectares of land. He had the soil analysed at the Tocklai Experimental Research Station and advised the family how they could go about planting tea and other crops. He gave them cuttings, showed them how to set up a nursery, and the techniques that are involved in raising a plant. He told them how to irrigate and look after their crop. Debjyoti was always there at the farm from morning till evening, working.

Now, three years later, surrounded by his family, Debjyoti told the former manager, 'Sir we have named the farm after you. *Hamar ghar aur garden dono hare-bhare hain.*' Today Debjyoti enjoys the fruit of his labour, proudly holding his head high.

Tea and Tourism

Misty mountains, exotic birds, wild elephants and waterfalls ... quaint towns, cobbled streets, churches, and bazaars : experience a slice of history. Tea gardens are a world apart.

Assam's Barak and Brahmaputra valleys produce over 50 per cent of India's finest tea. The estates in the Brahmaputra valley share their periphery with Kaziranga National Park. Planters discovered Kaziranga and brought it to the attention of conservationists. It is now a reserved forest providing protection to the one-horned rhino and the white-browed gibbon, India's only ape. About 304 bird species, including the Bengal Pelican, an endangered species, live in the park's grasslands.

Happy Valley Tea Estate in Darjeeling is one of the gardens which a tourist can visit and watch tea being manufactured. The town is located 2134 m above sea level. Darjeeling's antique toy like train is the best way to travel up to the town. Introduced in 1878, the train winds its way past tea gardens and terraced rice fields before chugging up to Ghoom, the highest rail station in the world. Here you can watch Tiger Hill's special sunset. The Natural History Museum located here has a collection of 2000 species of orchids, birds, and animals.

The highest racecourse in the world is situated at Lebong, about 8 km from Darjeeling. East of Kalimpong, following the Teesta river to the Dooars, is a dense jungle. There is a wildlife sanctuary at Jaldapara and adventure sports are popular. Kangra Valley in Himachal Pradesh mainly grows green tea for Afghanistan. There are fruit orchards, waterfalls, pine-covered trails, and a hang-gliding site called Billing located here. Kangra boasts of many ancient temples and paintings.

The Nilgiri mountains in south India are still haunted by the British Raj: old clubs, churches, and cemeteries dot them. Ooty's Hunt Club has portraits of bygone hunters gazing down solemnly. The game of snooker was born at the Ooty Club on a sultry afternoon in 1875. Sir Winston Churchill was refused entry to this club because he wasn't senior enough in the army. Marquis Tweedale founded the Botanical Garden in these blue mountains in the 1860s. The Nilgiris still have rich flora: the *kurinji* flower, for instance, which blossoms only once in twelve years.

The Indira Gandhi Wildlife Sanctuary is located in the Annamalais or Elephant Hills. The lion-tailed monkey and the black eagle live here. About 1200 ha are under tea cultivation in these hills. The principal town, Vaparai, has the oldest club in Tamil Nadu. Some of the highest tea estates in the world are located in Kerala's high ranges: the Munnar Hills. Eravikulam National Park is also located here, and is home to the Nilgiri Tahr, a rare mountain goat. The Thekkady Wildlife Sanctuary is about 190 km from Kochi. Vandiperiyar has some of India's oldest plantations and is located 20 km away.

Top and below: Tea-growing areas are as fascinating as any other tourist destination, offering panoramic views, picturesque locales, and a pleasant climate. There are in addition many wild animals and birds in the vicinity as an additional lure for tourists.

Following spread: Women pluckers returning home in southern India.

FACING THE FUTURE | 241

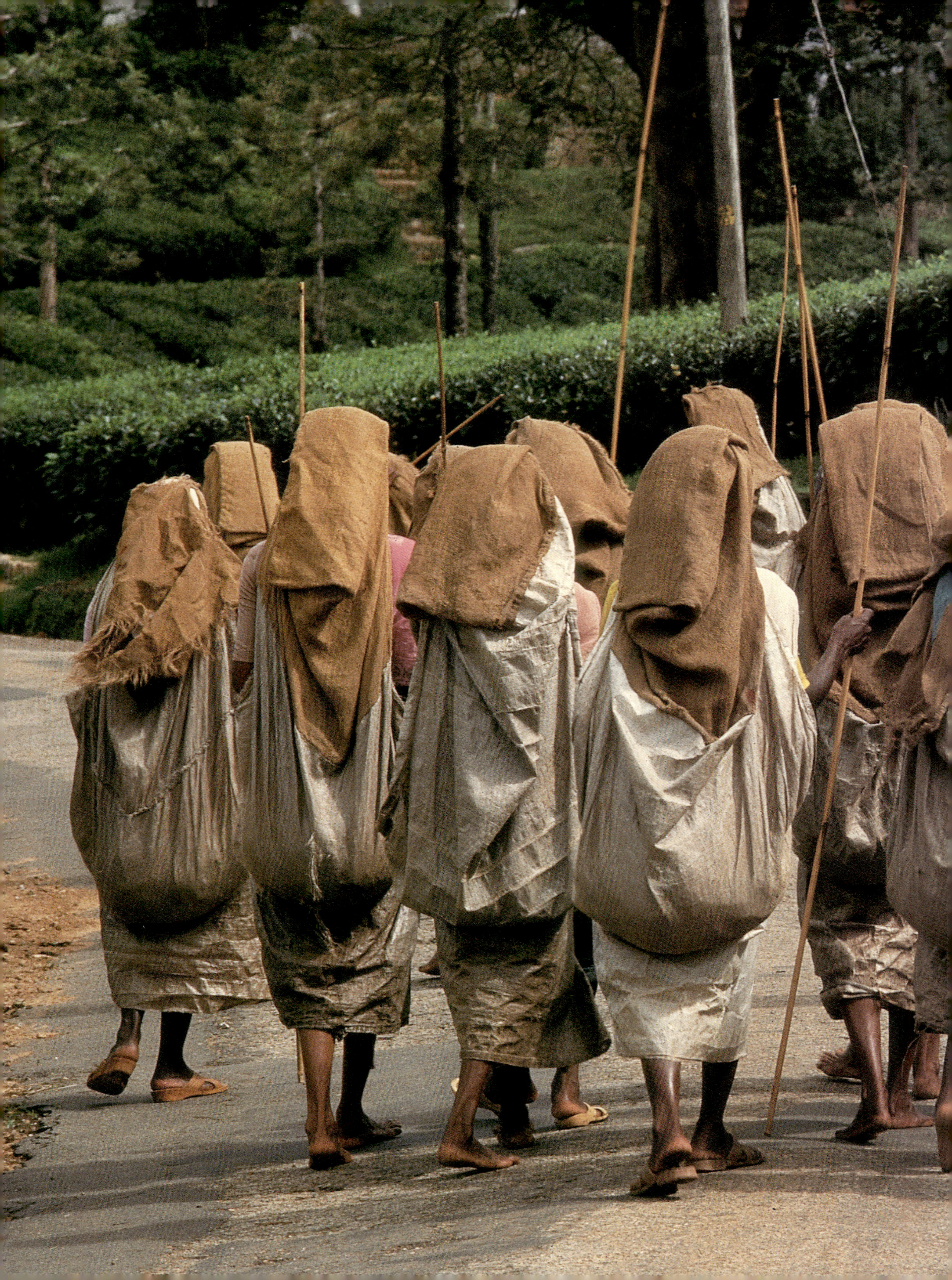

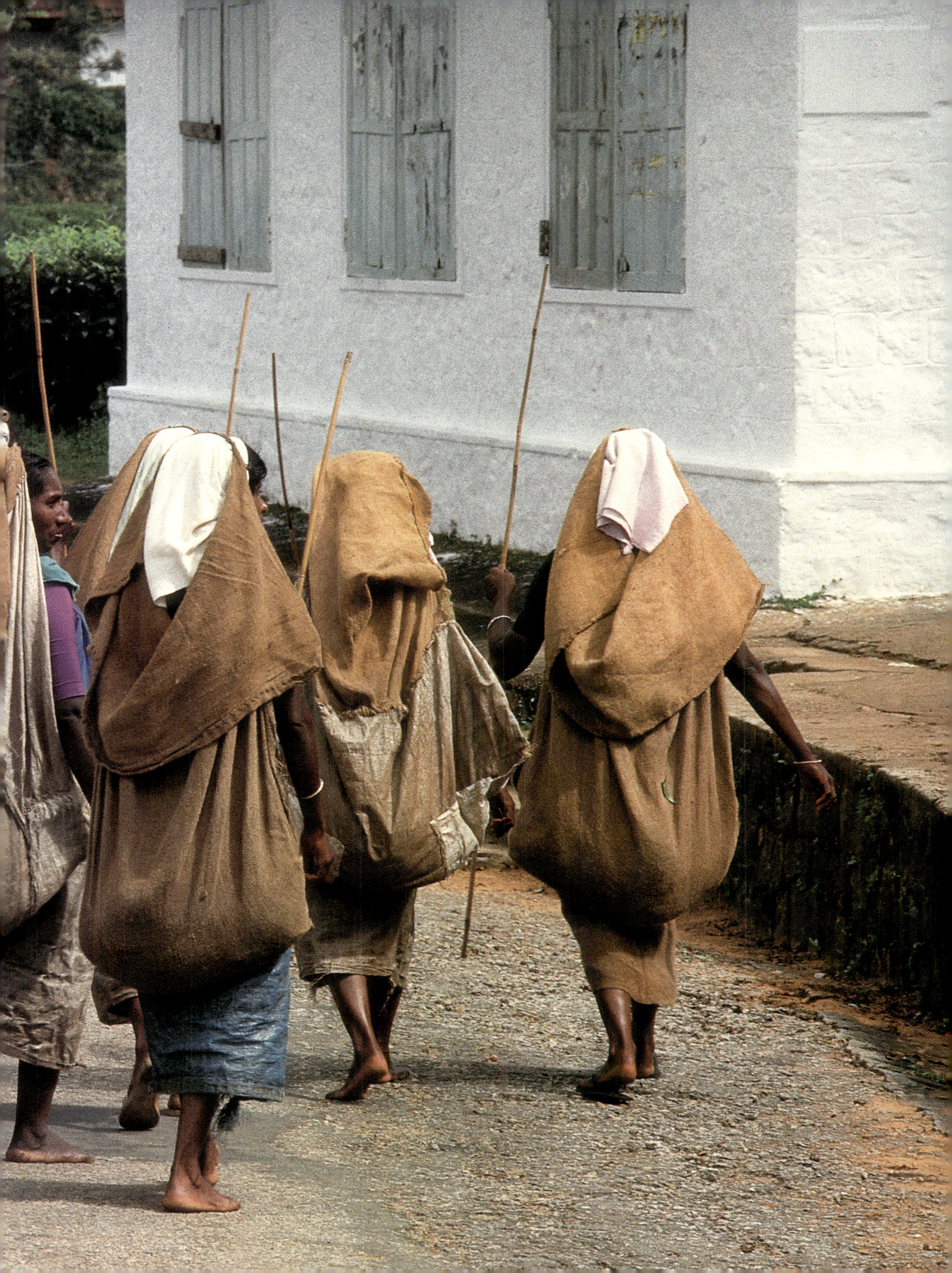

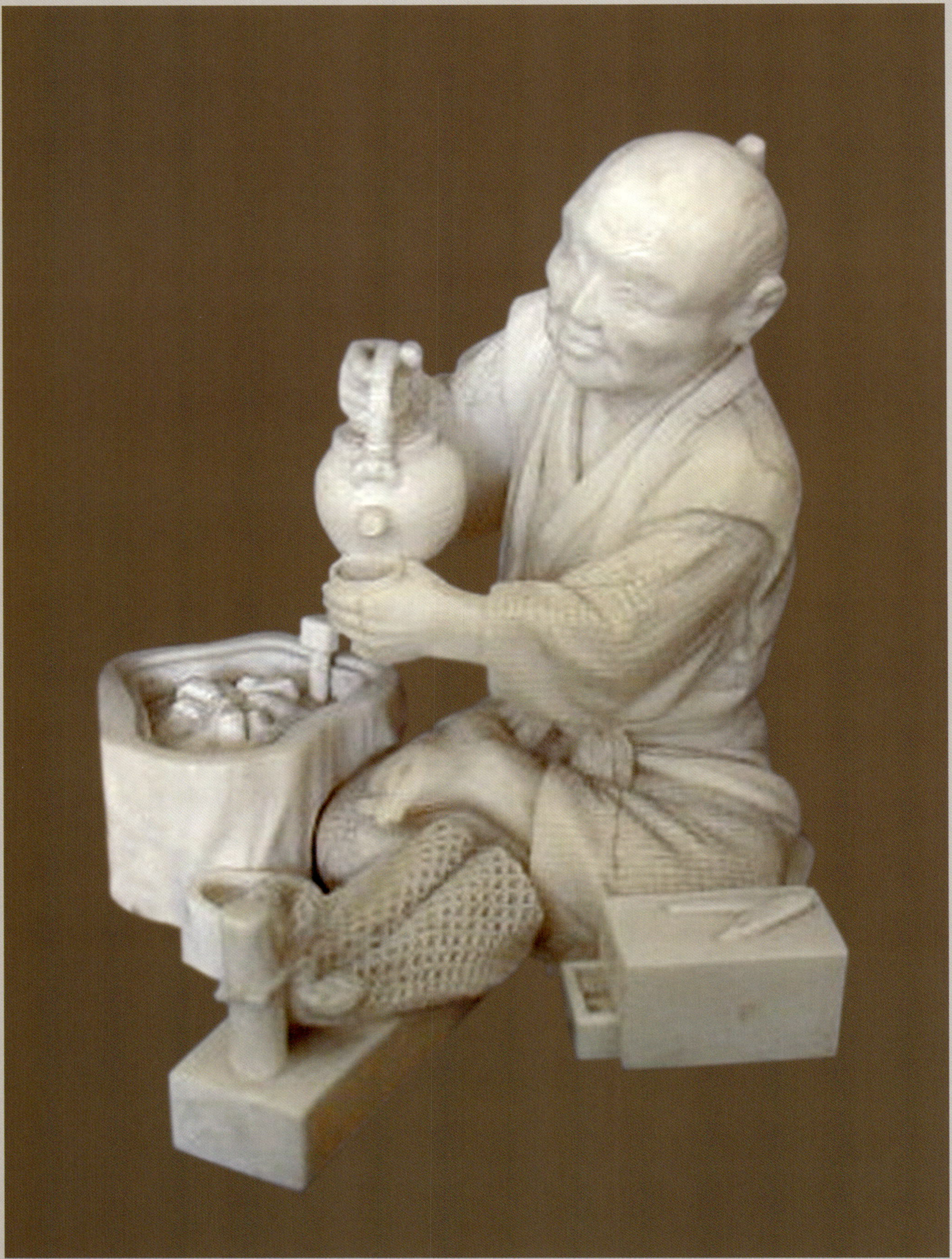

A traditional Japanese figure of a man grinding tea in a mortar with pestle.

A Calendar of Indian Tea

2737 BC	Discovery of tea by Emperor Shen Nung.
780 BC	The first book on tea written by Lu Yu.
AD 6	Tea enters Japan.
729	Emperor Shomu serves tea to Buddhist monks in Japan.
805	Dengyo Daishi, a monk, brings the first tea seeds from China to Japan.
1610	First tea sample reaches the Netherlands.
1618	First tea reaches Russia as a gift from the Chinese to Tsar Alexis.
1669	The first tea shipment to England by the East India Company.
1700	Chinese tea became the first internationally traded commodity.
1773	The famous Boston Tea Party.
1804	First London Tea Room opened.
1821–4	Burmese rule in Assam, with puppet Ahom monarch Jogeswar Singha.
1823	Birth of Indian tea. Robert Bruce discovers wild tea in Assam.
1824	British conquest of lower Assam.
1825	British conquest of upper Assam.
1826	24 February, Treaty of Yandobo, on the basis of which the king of Burma ceded Assam to the British.
1832	Tea planted in India for the first time by Dr A. Christie in the Nilgiris.
1833–8	Purandar Singha ruled in Upper Assam as a tributary prince.
1834	First Tea Committee appointed by Lord Bentinck, governor general of India.
1835	Tea first planted commercially in India.
1838	The first consignment of Assam tea exported to England.
1839	Assam Company, the first company to grow and manufacture tea in India; the first tea consignment auctioned in London; formation of the Bengal Tea Association.
1841	Dr A. Campbell buys China tea seeds and plants them in his garden in Darjeeling; the first batch of workers recruited by Assam Company.
1854	First tea plantation trials in the Nilgiris.
1855	Tea bushes discovered in Cachar district of Assam.
1856	Tea cultivation expanded to the Nilgiris and Kerala.
1859	The Jorehaut Tea Company incorporated.
1861	The first tea auction held by J. Thomas & Co., today the world's largest tea broker.
1869	The opening of the Suez Canal, a landmark in the growth of the Indian tea industry.
1872	First mechanical tea roller introduced by a certain William Jackson in Jorhat.
1876	The first Indian-owned tea estate established.
1877	Dooars Tea Planters' Association set up.
1881	Indian Tea Association formed.
1883	First Tea Cess and promotion; the first passenger train, Dibru Sadiya, chugs out from Dibrugarh.
1888	Import of Indian tea into Britain exceeds that of China.
1891	For the first time India exports a million pounds of tea; Nilgiri Planters' Association founded.
1892	Formation of the Darjeeling Tea Planters' Association.
1893	The United Planters' Association of Southern India founded.
1896	Indian Tea Cess Committee formed and Planters' Enquiry Committee appointed.
1897	US Tea Act to ensure quality standards of all tea imported into the United States.
1900	Indian Tea Association establishes a scientific department.
1902	A few varieties of tea grown in south India are sold in Calcutta.
1903	Indian Tea Cess Act comes into force.
1906	*The Planters' Chronicle* commences publication. The Pasteur Institute founded at Shillong to produce medicine to combat rabies.
1907	Import and re-export of tea.
1908	The tea bag invented in the United States.
1909	United Planters' Association of Southern India establishes a scientific department.
1912	The Tocklai Experimental Research Station set up.
1915	Formation of the Indian Tea Planters' Association.
1921	The Assam Labour Enquiry Committee set up.
1922	Factories Act becomes applicable to tea estates.
1925	Ross Institute, a local research centre, established.

1928	First indication of the slump that is to follow.
1929	Crash of the American stock market and the depression that followed.
1930	Small tea growers begin planting in the Nilgiris.
1931	The Royal Commission on Labour appointed by the government.
1932	Introduction of CTC manufacturing machines.
1933	Indian Tea Control Bill introduced; formation of Assam Tea Planters' Association.
1934	The first time a joint promotional campaign is organized by India, Ceylon (Sri Lanka), and Java.
1935	International Tea Market Expansion Board established.
1944	For the first time excise duty becomes leviable on tea.
1946	Blister blight threatens tea.
1947	ESUSI becomes the first registered trade union in the Indian tea industry; export duty raised.
1948	Royal Commission on Industrial Labour.
1950	D.C. Kothari elected the first Indian president of United Planters' Association of Southern India.
1951	Plantations Labour Act passed.
1952	Tea Act introduced.
1953	Tea Board of India founded.
1954	Plantations Labour Act brought into force. A boom year for tea.
1956	Formation of the Consultative Committee of Tea Producers' Association and Tea Association of India; formation of Bharatiya Cha Parishad.
1961	Dooars Tea Research Institute founded.
1963	Coonoor Auction Centre started.
1964	The Tea Finance Committee set up by the government of India; Tea Research Association formed.
1967	P.C. Barooah Committee on the tea industry set up.
1968	Instant tea comes into being; crude fibre for CTC teas.
1971	United Planters' Association of Southern India's Comprehensive Labour Welfare Scheme implemented.
1973	First National Seminar on tea organized by the Consultative Committee of Plantation Associations in New Delhi.
1975	Equal Remuneration Act. Plantations, the first to implement it.
1976	For the first time Pakistan buys Indian tea; Second National Seminar on tea organized by the Consultative Committee of Plantation Associations in New Delhi, inaugurated by Fakhruddin Ali Ahmed, the then president of India.
1978	Tea declared an essential commodity; the Direct Taxes Committee (Choksi Committee) set up by the government of India.
1980	Coimbatore auctions.
1981	Formation of North-Eastern Tea Association; a national meeting on tea to discuss tax on tea; an international seminar on tea organized in Calcutta on the occasion of the Centenary of the Indian Tea Association.
1983	United Planters' Association of Southern India's Krishi Vigyan Kendra programme starts.
1984	Record year of tea production for the industry; Third National Seminar on Tea organized by the Consultative Committee of Plantation Associations.
1987	National Conference on Tea Productivity and Development organized by the Tea Board of India in Calcutta.
1990	For the first time the element of productivity is introduced in a wage agreement; Surrendra Paul, owner of AFT Industries, gunned down by terrorists.
1991	The Chelliah Committee on Tax Reforms.
1993	United Planters' Association of Southern India centenary celebrations.
1995	Assam Valley School, the single largest project of the tea industry in Assam, established.
1999	World's largest tea party in Hong Kong attended by 4950 guests; the Plantation Inquiry Commission.
2000	India International Millennium Tea Convention organized by the Consultative Committee of Plantation Associations in New Delhi.
2001	Government decision to withdraw Tea Market (Control) Order, 1984; Union government increases import protection on tea and enhances development allowance in the Union budget of 2001–2.

All For a Cup of Tea

Time for you and time for me,
And time yet for a hundred indecisions,
And for a hundred visions and revisions,
Before the taking of a toast and tea.

T.S. ELIOT

Tea pot is on, the cups are waiting,
Favourite chairs anticipating,
No matter what I have to do,
My friend there's always time for you.

ANONYMOUS

There is a great deal of poetry and fine
sentiment in a chest of tea.

RALPH WALDO EMERSON

Where there's tea, there's hope.

SIR ARTHUR PINERO

The spirit of the tea beverage is one of peace,
comfort, refinement ...

ARTHUR GRAY

The mere chink of cups and saucers turns
the mind to happy repose.

GEORGE GISSIE

Every nation in creation has its favourite drink,
France is famous for her wine, it's beer in Germany.
Turkey loves her coffee, and they serve it blacker
than ink; Russians love their vodka,
England loves her tea.

JOHN BALDREY

Let others sing the praise of wine
Let others deem it joy divine
Its fleeting bliss shall never be mine
Give me a cup of tea.

ANONYMOUS

Tea is drunk to forget the din of the world.

T'IEN YIHENG

I got nasty habits: I take tea at three.

MICK JAGGER

The first cup moistens my lips and throat.
The second shatters my loneliness.
The third causes the wrongs of life to fade
gently from my recollection.
The fourth purifies my soul.
The fifth lifts me
to the realms of the unwinking gods.

CHINESE MYSTIC POET, T'ANG DYNASTY

Tea tempers the spirit and harmonizes the mind,
dispels lassitude and relieves fatigue,
awakens thought and prevents drowsiness,
lightens up or refreshes the body,
and clears the perceptive faculties.

CONFUCIUS, 551–479 BC

The effect of tea is cooling and as a beverage
it is most suitable. It is especially fitting for
persons of self-restraint and inner worth.

LU YU, CH'A CHING (715–803)

The flavour of Zen and the flavour of tea is the same.

JAPANESE PROVERB

Better to be deprived of food for three days
than of tea for one.

ANCIENT CHINESE PROVERB

The essence of the enjoyment of tea lies
in appreciation of its colour, fragrance and flavour,
and the principles of preparation are refinement,
dryness and cleanliness.

CHALU OF CAI XIANG (1012–67)

*Tea with us became more than an idealization
of the form of drinking; it is a religion
of the art of life.*

OKAKURA'S *THE BOOK OF TEA*

*Tea! thou soft, sober, sage and venerable liquid;
thou female tongue-running, smile-smoothing,
heart-opening, wink-tippling cordial,
to whose glorious insipidity I owe the happiest
moments of my life, let me fall prostrate.*

COLLEY CIBBER (1671–1757)

Love and scandal are the best sweeteners of tea.

HENRY FIELDING

*Thank God for tea!
What would the world do without tea?
... I am glad I was not born before tea.*

SIDNEY SMITH (1775–1834)

*We had a kettle; we let it leak.
Our not repairing it made it worse.
We haven't had any tea for a week.
The bottom is out of the universe!*

RUDYARD KIPLING

*Tea, though ridiculed by those who are naturally coarse
in their nervous sensibilities, ...
will always be the favourite beverage of the intellectual.*

THOMAS DE QUINCY

*Polly put the kettle on,
we'll all have tea.*

CHARLES DICKENS

*If you are cold, tea will warm you;
if you are too heated, it will cool you;
if you are depressed it will cheer you;
if you are excited, it will calm you.*

WILLIAM GLADSTONE

*I must drink lots of tea or I cannot work.
Tea unleashes the potential which slumbers
in the depth of my soul.*

LEO TOLSTOY

The blessed drink of early morning tea.

JAN STRUTHER

*It has been well said that tea is suggestive
of a thousand wants, from which spring the
decencies and luxuries of civilizations.*

AGNES REPPLIER

*Tea is the beverage of ceremonious people,
and like the dense monsoon rains,
it is both calming and stimulating,
encouraging conversation and relaxation ...
ideas and traditions seep slowly
in its steamy transparence.*

PASCAL BRUKHER

*The naming of teas is a difficult matter,
it isn't just one of your everyday games.
Some might think you mad as a hatter,
should you tell them each goes by several names.
For starters each tea in this world must belong
to the families Black or Green or Oolong;
then look more closely at these family trees,
some include Indian along with Chinese.*

T.S. ELIOT

The cup that cheers but does not inebriate.

WILLIAM COWPER

*There are few hours in life more agreeable
than the hour dedicated to the ceremony
known as afternoon tea.*

HENRY JAMES

*An all-embracing aspect of tea is its
central place in the cultures of
countries that adopt it.
Whether at a Japanese tea ceremony,
in a Bedouin tent, in an urban cafe
or the hot tea shop outside,
the preparation and taking of
tea is an essential and
characteristic part of society's life.
Other drinks—beer, wine, coffee—have had
less impact on manners, on hospitality,
on the ways in which people come together
and drink together. It is not beer that draws
people to pubs, but the promise of alcohol;
not the drink but the intoxication.
Tea, as its lovers know only too well,
needs no such lure. It is the epitome of hospitality
and politeness: the real cup that cheers.*

SERANA HARDY

*There is no trouble so great or grave that cannot
be much diminished by a nice cup of tea.*

BERNARD-PAUL HEROUX

*Here, thou great Anna! Whom three realms obey,
Does sometimes counsel take
And sometimes tea.*

ALEXANDER POPE

*Steam rises from a cup of tea and we are wrapped
in history, inhaling ancient times and lands,
comfort of ages in our hands.*

FAITH GREENBOWL

*Tea's proper use is to amuse the idle,
and relax the studious, and dilute the
full meals of those who cannot use exercise,
and will not use abstinence.*

SAMUEL JOHNSON

*In my own hands I hold a bowl of tea;
I see all of nature represented in
its green colour.
Closing my eyes I find green mountains
and pure water within my own heart.
Silently sitting alone and drinking tea,
I feel these become a part of me.*

SOSHITSU SEN

*Banking is business, oil is industry,
tea and coffee are trades, but the tea trade
in particular has always had a special
aristocratic position in the world of
buying and selling.*

EDWARD BRAMAH

*Come, oh come, Yea tea-thirsty
restless ones; the kettle boils,
bubbles, and sings, musically.*

RABINDRANATH TAGORE

*I want not wealth, nor earthly treasures
Nor fame, esteem as others crave;
Let my fate ordain for me
My morning cup of tea
Nicely made for me.
Don't deny me, O my Lord
My morning cup of tea.*

DWIJENDRALAL ROY

*A woman is like a teabag. It's only when
she's in hot water that
you realize how strong she is.*

NANCY REGAN

*The history of tea in India is a glorious
record of continuous development of one of
our foremost industries and a valuable national asset.*

SANJIVA REDDY

*Tea is not a mere commodity for us.
It is heritage based on values and culture,
full of sentiments and commitments.*

B.M. KHAITAN

*Tea is not a product, it's a practice.
What the Asians call the 'Way'.*

JAMES NORWOOD PRATT

*Tea is a healthy drink with a lot of style about it.
It can well set the pace for the day and
unlike carbonated drinks, does not leave
a damaging impact on the body.*

N.K. DAS

*The growing and making of tea seemed to us
to be one of those occupations that call forth
the best in people, giving meaning to their work
and peace to their lives. It's a great business.
I'm fortunate to be a part of it.*

PETER LEGGATT

*It is a culture—a culture steeped in history,
and a history replete with highlights
of development and contribution to
economic growth and social progress.*

R.S. JHAWAR

*We should tell the world that tea is good
but Indian tea is the best.*

B.R. SHAH

*Teaism is truly a way of life which one
can only experience when you make a tea garden
your home and each one in it becomes part of
your own extended family.*

NEENA ROY CHOWDHURY

*Tea is not just a business,
but it's a matter of social philosophy and
a way of life for Assamese society.*

G.P. BARUA

*Tea contains health promoting ingredients,
lowering the risk of heart disease,
stroke and cancer.*

DR JOHN WEISBURGER

*Tea is one of the richest natural sources of
antioxidants...
We should not create an impression that
tea is a medicine or a magic bullet.
It should be part of our diet.*

P.R. KRISHNASWAMY

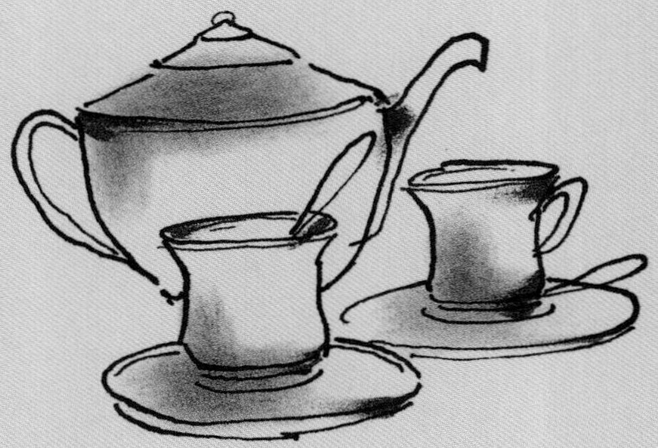

Bibliography

A. OFFICIAL RECORDS AND REPORTS

Allen, B.C., *Assam District Gazetteers*, Vol.II, Sibsagar, 1905; Vol.VIII, 1905.

Assam Pradesh Congress Committee Papers, 1930–47, Congress Bhavan, Guwahati.

Assam Secretariat Files in the State Archives of Assam, Shillong.

A.S.S.U. and A.A.G.S.P., 'Save Assam Today to Save India Tomorrow: An Appeal from People of Assam', Guwahati, 1980.

Census of India, *District Census Handbook*, Goalpara, Lakhimpur, Nowgang, Sibsagar, Assam, 1961.

Government of Assam, *Annual Reports on Immigration in Assam*, Shillong, 1876–91.

_____, *Economic Survey of Assam*, (1971).

Government of India, *Barooah Committee Report on Tea*, New Delhi, 1969.

Pakyntein E.H., *Census of India, 1961*, Vol.III, Assam Part 1-A: General Report, 1964B.

Plantation Labour Act, 1 September 1954.

Proceedings of the Assam Legislative Assembly (various years).

Proceedings of the 52nd Annual Tea Convention, 26-9 Oct. 1997.

Report of the Ad Hoc Committee on Tea, Calcutta, 1950.

Report of the Assam Labour Enquiry Committee (1921–22), Shillong, 1922.

Report of the Committee on Tea Auctions, Government of India, New Delhi, 1951.

Report of the Dooars Enquiry Committee, 1911.

Report of the General Committee, Indian Tea Association, 1983.

Report of the Official Team on the Tea Industry, New Delhi, 1952.

Report of the P.C. Barooah Committee on the Tea Industry, 1968.

Report of the Plantation Enquiry Commission, Part I—Tea, New Delhi, 1956.

Report of the Royal Commission on Labour, 1931.

Report of the Task Force on Tea Industry, Vols. I & II, 1973–4.

Report of the Tea Finance Committee, New Delhi, 1964.

Report of the Working Group on Finance for Tea Industry, Bombay, 1972.

Report on Financial & Costs Survey of Tea Industry, 1963–65, Calcutta, 1971.

Report on the Labour Condition in the Tea Plantations and Tea Factories in India, 1961.

Standards of Medical Care for Tea Plantations in India, Government of India, 1947.

Survey of Tea Plantation and Labour in Darjeeling Hills, Tea Board of India, 1963.

Tea Directory, Tea Board of India, Calcutta, 1970.

Tea Statistics, 1970–1, 1973–4 & 1985–6, Calcutta.

20-Point Programme: Progress of Implementation, Ministry of Labour, Government of India.

39th Annual Report, Tea Board of India, 1992–3.

B. JOURNALS, PERIODICALS, AND NEWSPAPERS

Assam Review & Tea News, Vol. 85, No.10, Dec. 1997; No.11, Jan. 1997.

_____, July 1975, Nov. 1986, & Jan. 1987, Assam Review Publishing Co., Calcutta.

Baruah, Srinath, 'Unemployed Problem in Assam and Employment Pattern in North East Frontier Railways', *North East Quarterly*, Vol.I: 3–4 Feb.–March 1983.

Business Standard, special feature on 'Tea Industry', May 1991.

Contemporary Tea Times, Sept. & Oct. 1999.

Dewan, Maniram, 'Native Account of Washing for Gold in Assam', *J.A.S.B.*, July, 1838.

Hussain, Monirul, 'Tribal Movement for Autonomous State in Assam', *Economic and Political Weekly*, Vol. 22:32, 8 Aug. 1987.

Kakati, Satish Chandra, 'The Role of Tribals in the Freedom Movement', *Assam Tribune*, 15 Aug. 1988.

Mann, H.H., 'An Early History of the Tea Industry in India', *Assam Review*, Sept. 1934.

Mazumdar, Swaraj, '150 Years of Indian Tea', *Amrit Bazar Patrika*, Calcutta, 24 Jan. 1985.

Misra, Tilottoma, 'Assam: A Colonial Hinterland', *Economic and Political Weekly*, Vol.15:32, 9 Aug. 1980.

N.E. Plantation News, July 1981, Jorhat, Assam.

Omvedt, Gail, 'Aspects of the Assamese Problems', *Frontier*, Vol.12:41, 7 June 1980.

Phukon, Jagdish, 'First Indian Tea Planter was a Freedom Fighter', *Assam Tribune*, Guwahati, 19 Dec. 1986.

Planters' Chronicle, 'Focus: Future of Tea Industry', Aug. 1996.

_______, 'Focus on Social Responsibilities', April 1995.

_______, 'Focus on Welfare', July 1988.

Taknet, D.K., 'The Marwaris: Merchants to the Nation', *Business India*, 10 April–3 May 1987.

_______, 'Their Success Has Become a Legend Now', *The Economic Times*, New Delhi, 30 March 1995.

Tea International, The journal of the world tea trade, Issue 6, Sept.–Oct. 1994.

Tea Market Annual Report and Statistics, 1996–7 and 1997–8, J. Thomas & Co. (Pvt) Ltd.

Tea & Coffee Trade Journal, 'Indian Tea and the Rajasthan Marwaris', Vol.169, No.10, Oct. 1997.

Venkata Ram, C.S., 'Tea Industry in South India', *Science Today*, 1978.

C. SPEECHES, DOCUMENTS, AND PUBLICATIONS OF TEA COMPANIES, ASSOCIATIONS, AND ORGANIZATIONS

Address by A. Ramesh Rao at the 102nd annual conference of the United Planters' Association of Southern India on 12 Sept. 1995.

Address by B.M. Khaitan at a felicitation reception for Jyoti Basu and Buddhadeb Bhattacharya in Calcutta on 8 Nov. 2000.

Address by B.M. Khaitan, president, Indian National Committee of the International Chamber of Commerce in Calcutta on 12–13 Nov. 1987.

Address by L.N. Bezbarua, president, Asam Sahitya Sabha Annual Session of 1924, Asam Sahitya Sabha, Jorhat, 1924.

Address by M. Ahmad, chairman, Indian Tea Association, at the annual general meeting held at Calcutta on 8 April 1978 and 15 April 1979.

Address by M. Ahmad, chairman, Indian Tea Association, at the annual general meeting of Assam Branch of Indian Tea Association on 10 Dec. 1977, 4 Feb. 1978, 8 Dec. 1978, and 12 Jan. 1979.

Address by Prof. Nagen Saikia, president, Asam Sahitya Sabha, at the Sixty–Third Session on 8 March 1997.

Address by R.A. Nyss, chairman, Assam Branch of Indian Tea Association, at the annual general meeting held at Jorhat on 21 Feb. 1998.

Address by R.L. Rikhye, chairman, Indian Tea Association, at the annual general meeting held at Calcutta on 17 May 1986 and 4 April 1987.

Address by R.S. Jhawar, chairman, Indian Tea Association, at the annual general meeting held at Calcutta on 5 May 2000.

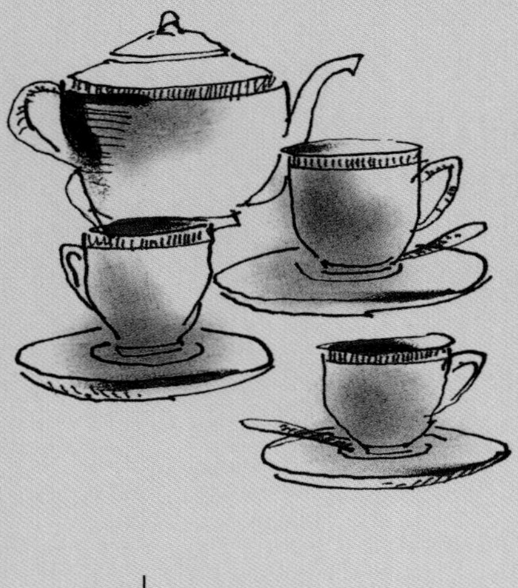

Address by R.S. Jhawar, chairman, Indian Tea Association, at the India International Millennium Tea Convention held at New Delhi on 22 March 2000.

Address by Ranjit Chaliha, chairman, Bhartiya Cha Parishad, at its annual general meeting held at Dibrugarh on 5 April 1980 and 16 May 1998.

Address by S.S. Sindhu, chairman, Assam Branch of Indian Tea Association, at the annual general meeting held at Tezpur on 22 Jan. 2000.

Address by T.C. Bordoloi, chairman, Assam Branch of Indian Tea Association, at the annual general meeting held at Dibrugarh on 9 March 1996.

Address by B.M. Khaitan at the official opening of Four Mangoe Lane at Calcutta on 6 Dec. 1968.

Address by B.M. Khaitan, president, Indian Chamber of Commerce, at the first quarterly general meeting held at Calcutta on 26 July 1973.

Address by B.M. Khaitan, president, Indian Chamber of Commerce, at the second quarterly general meeting held at Calcutta on 9 Nov. 1973.

Address by B.M. Khaitan, president, Indian Chamber of Commerce, at the third quarterly general meeting held at Calcutta on 15 Feb. 1974.

Address by B.M. Khaitan, president, Indian Chamber of Commerce, at the annual general meeting held at Calcutta on 18 April 1974.

Address by B.M. Khaitan, chairman, Diamond Jubilee Committee of Indian Chamber of Commerce, on 7 Dec. 1985.

Address by B.M. Khaitan, president, Indian National Committee of the International Chamber of Commerce, at the annual general meeting held at New Delhi on 23 Dec. 1987.

Address by B.M. Khaitan at the foundation stone laying ceremony of Assam Valley School on 11 Feb. 1990.

Address by B.M. Khaitan at the inauguration of New Universal Foil Rolling Mill at Kamarhati on 5 March 1997.

Address by Deepak Khaitan, president, Indian Chamber of Commerce, at the seminar on Industrial Opportunities in West Bengal at Oberoi Grand, Calcutta, on 11 Feb. 1992.

Address by Deepak Khaitan, president, Indian Chamber of Commerce, at the annual general meeting held at Calcutta on 22 Dec. 1992.

Speech of Hiteswar Saikia, chief minister of Assam, at the 102nd annual general meeting of Assam Branch Indian Tea Association at Cinnamara, 29 Feb. 1992.

Speech of Prafulla Kumar Mahanta, chief minister of Assam, at the annual general meeting of Assam Branch Indian Tea Association, 27 Feb. 1999.

Speech of Prafulla Kumar Mahanta, chief minister of Assam, at the 100th annual general meeting of Assam Branch Indian Tea Association at Dibrugarh, 16 Dec. 1989.

Annual Reports, Indian Tea Association, Calcutta, (various years).

Annual Reports, United Planters Association of Southern India from 1893.

Annual Reports, brochures, and leaflets of various tea companies and associations.

Asam Sahitya Sabha, Memorandum to the Home Minister on foreign national issue, Jorhat, 1980.

Assam Branch Indian Tea Associations's various office files.

Assam Tea Planters' Association, Golden Jubilee Souvenir, 1986.

Bose, Sanat Kumar, *Capital and Labour in the Indian Tea Industry*, All India Trade Union Congress, Bombay, 1954.

Centenary Souvenir (1881–1981), Indian Tea Association.

Centenary Souvenir of Assam Branch Indian Tea Association (1889–1989), Guwahati.

Centenary Volume of the Assam Railways and Trading Co. Ltd. (1881–1981).

BIBLIOGRAPHY | 253

Consultative Committee of Plantation Associations, *A Blueprint for the Development of the Tea Industry in India*, Calcutta, 1983.

Guha Thakurta, J., 'Role of Women in Indian Tea Industry', Jan. 1986, *TAI News Letter*, Tea Association of India, Calcutta.

J. Thomas & Co. Pvt Ltd, *Tea Statistics*, 1998.

Jhawar, R.S., 'Tea & Human Health: From Laboratory Studies to Creating Public Awareness', 23 Nov. 2000.

Kankani, N.C., 'Tea Production', Paper presented in National Seminar on Tea, 25 Aug. 1988, Tea Board, India.

National Seminar on Tea: Proceedings, Vigyan Bhawan, New Delhi, 1984.

Observations of B.M. Khaitan, chairman, Indian Chamber of Commerce Task Force, in the presence of the governor of West Bengal in Calcutta, 28 March 2000.

Planting in Nilgiris, Nilgiri Planters' Association 75th Anniversary Souvenir, 1966.

Sardar, Bidyut, *Tea in India*, Consultative Committee of Plantation Associations, Calcutta, 1984.

Tanna K.J., *Plantation in Nilgiris*, Glen Morgan Estate, Nilgiri, 1969.

Tata Tea Samachar, Vol.1, No.2, July–Sept. 1999 and April–June 2000.

Taten, Vol.II, No.2; Vol.VI, No.3; and Vol.IX, No.1.

Tea Budget Memorandums submitted by Indian Tea Association to government of India and government of Assam.

Tea Digest, published by the Calcutta Tea Traders Association, Calcutta, 1975.

Tea Time, 'Tax on Tea', Vol.II, No.VI, June 1991.

_____, 'The Kanoi Saga: Import and Perish', Vol.V, No.3, March 1994.

Tea Today, 'Flood Control in Assam', Vol.17, No.3 & 4, 1996.

United Planters' Association of Southern India, *Comprehensive Labour Welfare Scheme*.

_____, *Year Book* and *Annual Report*, 1980.

WM Times, Inaugural issue, the house journal of Williamson Magor's tea division, March 2000.

D. SELECTED INTERVIEWS

Ahmad, Mumtaz, former chairman, Indian Tea Association, 15 Oct. 1996 and 26 Sept. 1997, Calcutta.

Ahsan, Amir, senior manager, Borengajuli Tea Estate, 5 Dec. 1996.

Atal, D., former chairman, Indian Tea Association, 28 June 1995, Calcutta.

Barooah, H.P., chairman, B&A Plantations & Industries Ltd, 19 June 1996, Calcutta.

Barua, G.P., former vice-president, McLeod Russel (India) Ltd, 6 April 1995, Calcutta.

Bhattacharjee, P.K., former additional secretary-general, Assam Branch Indian Tea Association, 23 Nov. 1998 and 21 April 1999, Guwahati.

Bora, P.K., chief secretary, government of Assam, 26 Nov. 2001, Guwahati.

Borthakur, Robin, secretary, Assam Branch Indian Tea Association, 16 Dec. 2000, Guwahati.

Carling, D.P.K., headmaster, Assam Valley School, 10 June 1997, Calcutta.

Chakrabarti, D., secretary-general, Indian Tea Association, 18 Dec. 2000, Calcutta.

Chakravati, Dr. D.N., president, Bureau of Integrated Rural Development, 27 Nov. 1998, Guwahati.

Daga, Y.K., chairman, Darjeeling Tea Planters' Association, 4 March 1997, Calcutta.

Das, Prof. Jogesh, former president, Asam Sahitya Sabha, 24 May 1995, Guwahati.

Das, R., former secretary-general, Indian Tea Association, 25 April 1999.

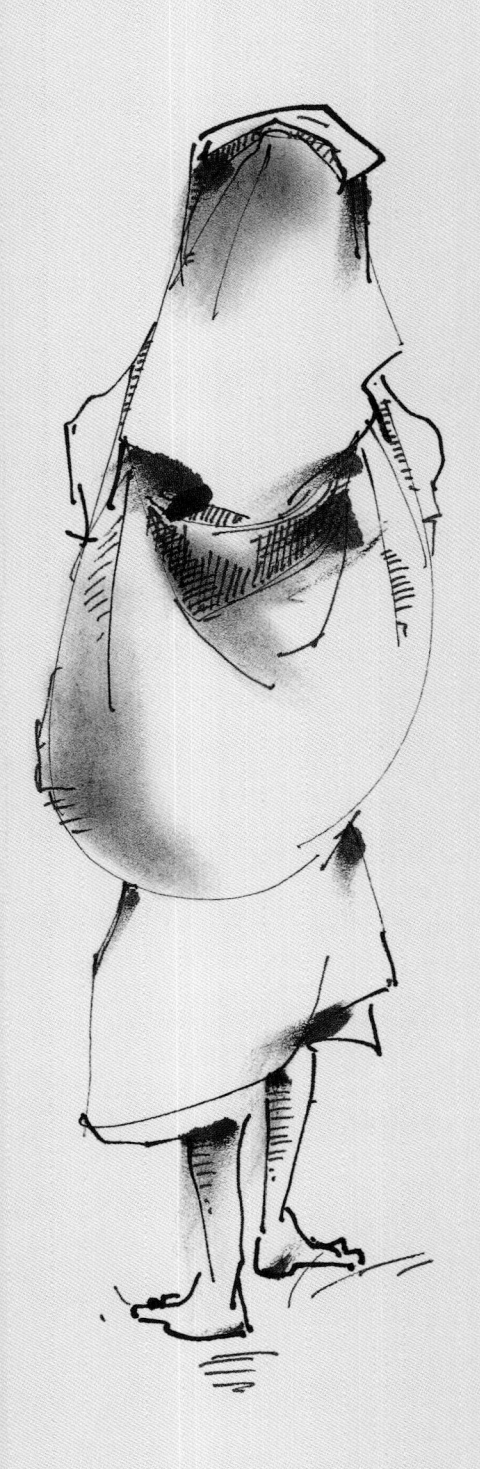

Das, Tapas, additional secretary-general, Indian Tea Association, 18 Dec. 2000, Calcutta.
Dhanuka, C.K., vice-chairman, Indian Tea Association, 10 Oct. 1996, Calcutta.
Dutta, Bamin, secretary, Darjeeling Tea Planters' Association, 9 Dec. 1996, Darjeeling.
Ghatowar, Paban Singh, former union minister of state, Goverment of India 5 March 1997, New Delhi.
Goenka, V.K., managing director, Warren Tea Ltd, 12 Oct. 1998, Calcutta.
Gogoi, Tarun, chief minister, Assam, 28 Nov. 2001, Guwahati.
Hazarika, Gunin, industry and commerce minister of Assam, 26 Nov. 1998, Guwahati.
Jalan, Mahadeo, former chairman, Bhartiya Cha Parishad, 27 June 1995 and 14 April 1999, Dibrugarh.
Jhawar, R.S., senior executive, Williamson Magor group, 24 Aug. 1996, Calcutta.
Khaitan, Aditya, director, Williamson Magor group, 14 Oct. and 8 Nov. 1996, Calcutta.
Khaitan, B.M., chairman, Williamson Magor group, 17 Oct. 1998; 1 March, and 5 May 2000, Calcutta.
Khaitan, Deepak, managing director, Williamson Magor group, 28 Oct. 1996, Calcutta.
Khaitan, Shanti, 1 March 2000, Calcutta.
Khandiat, M.C., general-secretary, Assam Cha Mazdoor Sangha, 25 Nov. 1998, Dibrugarh.
Khusrokhan, Homi R., managing director, Tata Tea Ltd, 20 Nov. 2001, Calcutta
Kidwai, S.M., former managing director, Tata Tea Ltd, 26 June 1995 and 25 April 1999, Calcutta.
Kumar, R.K. Krishna, vice-chairman, Tata Tea Ltd, 26 Dec. 2001, Mumbai.
Monem, A., vice-president, sales division, Williamson Magor group, 1 Aug. 1996, Calcutta.
Mor, Dr S.B., medical adviser, Williamson Magor group, 19 Dec. 2000, Calcutta.
Rikhye, R.L., chairman, Indian Tea Association, 16 Oct. 1997, Calcutta.
Sandys-Lumsdaine, P.G, 19 July 1996, Newbury, Berkshire, UK.
Sarkar, Aveek, *Telegraph*, 18 April 1996, Calcutta.
Siganporia, P., joint managing director, Tata Tea Ltd, 23 Nov. 2001, Calcutta.
Trinick, J.M., tea taster & manufacturing adviser, Williamson Magor group, 29 May 1996 and 20 May 2000, Calcutta.
Verma, S.P., secretary, Bhartiya Cha Parishad, 25 Nov. 1998, Dibrugarh.

E. SELECTED BOOKS

Acharyya, N.N., *The History of Medieval Assam*, Guwahati, 1966.
Agarwala, Jyotiprasad, *Chandrakumar Agarwala* (Assamese), Guwahati, 1967.
Antrobus, H.A., *A History of the Assam Company (1839–1953)*, Edinburgh, 1957.
_____, *A History of the Jorhat Tea Company Ltd. (1859–1946)*, London, 1948.
Awasthi, R.C., *Economics of Tea Industry in India*, Guwahati, 1975.
Bagchi, A.K., *Private Investment in India (1900–1939)*, Orient Longman.
Baildon, Samuel, *The Tea Industry in India*, 1882.
Bald, C., *Indian Tea — Its Culture and Manufacture*, Calcutta, 1922.
Barpujari, H.K. (ed.), *Political History of Assam (1826–1919)*, Vol.I, Guwahati.
_____, *Assam in the Days of the Company (1826–1858)*, Guwahati, 1963.
_____, *Comprehensive History of Assam*, Vol.5, Guwahati, 1993.
Barua, B.K., *A Cultural History of Assam*, Vol.1, 1954.
Barua, Harendranath (ed.), *Bharatar Mukti Yunjat Jiivanii* (Assamese), Guwahati, 1972.

Barua, Hem, *The Red River and the Blue Hill*, Guwahati, 1962.
Barua, Prafullachandra, *Uttamchandra Baruvar Jiivanii* (Assamese), Guwahati, 1962.
Barua, U.N., *A Glimpse of Assam*, 1946.
Basu, N.K., *Assam in the Ahom Age (1228–1826)*, Calcutta, 1970.
Basu, N.N., *The Tea Act 1953*, Calcutta, 1995.
Bezbarua, Lakshminath, *Mor Jivan Sonvaran* (Assamese), Jorhat, 1961.
Bhattacharya, Narendrakumar, *Karmayogii Bhuban Gagai* (Assamese), Sibsagar, 1956.
Bhattacharyya, J.B., *Cachar Under British Rule in North-East India*, New Delhi, 1977.
Bhuyan, S.K., *A Chronicle of Assam (1681–1826)*, 1933.
Bishop, S.O., *Sketches in Assam*, Calcutta, 1885.
Blofeld, John, *The Chinese Art of Tea*, Boston, 1985.
Bordoloi, Gopinath, *Gandhiji* (Assamese), Guwahati, 1969.
Butler, John, *Travels and Adventures in the Province of Assam*, London, 1855.
Chakravorty, Birendra Chandra, *British Relations with the Hill Tribes of Assam Since 1858*, 1964.
Chatterji, S.K., *The Place of Assam in the History and Civilization of India*, Guwahati University, Guwahati, 1970.
Das, R.K., *Plantation Labour in India*, Calcutta, 1931.
Deka, P., *Industrial Development in North East India*, Guwahati, 1987.
Dhar, P.K., *The Economy of Assam*, Bijini, Assam, 1988.
Dudeja, Vijay, *Spotlights on Tea*, Calcutta, 1990.
Dusinberre, Deke, (trans.), *The Book of Tea*, Italy.
Dutt, K.N., *Landmarks of the Freedom Struggle in Assam*, Guwahati, 1958.
Dutta, Arup Kumar, *Cha Garam! The Tea Story*, Guwahati, 1992.
Dutta, Debabrata, *History of Assam*, Calcutta, 1989.
Edgar, J.W., *Papers Regarding the Tea Industry in Bengal*, Calcutta, 1873.
ESRA, *Growth and Potential of Tea Industry in India*, Economic and Scientific Research Association, Calcutta, 1983.
Evans, John C., *Tea in China: The History of China's National Drink*, New York, 1992.
Forrest, D.M., *A Hundred Years of Ceylon Tea*, London, 1967.
Forrest, Denys, *Tea for the British: Social and Economic History of a Famous Trade*, London, 1973.
Frith, W.G.C., *The Royal Calcutta Turf Club*, Calcutta, 1976.
Gait, E.A., *History of Assam*, Guwahati, 1963.
Gawthropp, W.R., *The Story of the Assam Railways & Trading Co. Ltd (1881–1891)*, 1851.
Ghose, M.N., *Religious Beliefs of the Assamese People*, Shillong, 1896.
Gokhale, Nitin A., *The Hot Brew — The Assam Tea Industry's Most Turbulent Decade (1987–1997)*, Guwahati, 1998.
Goswami, P.C., *Economic Development of Assam*, Bombay, 1963.
Griffiths, Sir Percival, *History of the Indian Tea Industry*, London, 1967.
Guha, Amalendu, *Planter-Raj to Swaraj: Freedom Struggle and Electoral Politics in Assam (1826–1947)*, New Delhi, 1971.
Gupta, Sujoy, *Four Mangoe Lane — The First Address for Tea*, New Delhi, 2001.
Harler, C.R., *Tea Growing*, London, 1968.
History of James Finlay and Company, 1750-1950.

Jhawar, R.S., *Tea — The Universal Health Drink*, Calcutta, 2000.
Kumar, Ashok, et al. (eds.), *Darjeeling Tea*, Darjeeling Planters' Association, Calcutta, 1997.
Lahon, N.L.T., *Election Politics in Assam*, Guwahati, 1987.
Magor, R.B., *Boxwalla*, UK, 1997.
Majumdar, D.N., *Races and Culture of India*, Bombay, 1961.
Manoharan, S., *Indian Tea — A Strategy for Development*, New Delhi, 1974.
Marx, K. and F. Engels, *The First Indian War of Independence (1857–1859)*, Moscow, 1978.
Mills, A.J. Moffatt, *Report on the Province of Assam*, Calcutta, 1854.
Misra, Sibranjan, *Tea Industry in India*, New Delhi, 1986.
Mitra, Rajendra Lal, *Agni Purana*, Calcutta, 1873–9.
Moitra, M.C., *New Dimension of Tea — Its Projection in the 21st Century*, 1991.
Murty, T.S., *Assam: The Difficult Years: A Study of Political Development in 1979–83*, New Delhi, 1983.
Namboodiry, Udayan, *St. Xavier's — The Making of a Calcutta Institute*, New Delhi, 1995.
Nath, R.M., *The Background of Assamese Culture*, Guwahati, 1948.
Patten, M., *The Complete Book of Tea*, London, 1989.
Phukan, A.R. Dhekial, *Plea for Assam and Assamese*, 1855.
Pratt, James Norwood, *New Tea Lover's Treasury*, San Francisco CA, 1999.
Pugh, Peter, *Stuck to Tea*, UK, 1991.
Reade, Arthur, *Tea and Tea Drinking*, London, 1884.
Saikia, Nagen (ed.), *Assam Bandhu 1885–86*, Guwahati, 1984.
Samuel, Baildon, *The Tea Industry in India*, W.H. Allen & Co., London, 1882.
Sarkar, Gautam K., *The World Tea Economy*, New Delhi, 1972.
Sarma, B., *The Rebellion of 1857 vis-a-vis Assam*, 1958.
Sastri, R.S. and T.G. Sastri, *Arthasastra of Kautilya*, Mysore, 1958.
Sen, B.M. and R.C. Goffin, *Stories from Assam History*, Calcutta, 1923.
Sharma, Lakheshwar, *Shri Kanoi — Abhinandan Grantha* (Hindi), Dibrugarh, 1961.
Stern, N.H., *An Appraisal of Tea Production on Small Holdings in Kenya*, Paris, 1972.
Taknet, D.K., *Industrial Entrepreneurship of Shekhawati Marwaris*, Jaipur, 1987.
_____, *Marwari Samaj*, Jaipur, 1990.
_____, *Marwari Samaj Aur Brajmohan Birla*, New Delhi, 1993.
_____, *B.M. Birla — A Great Visionary*, New Delhi, 1996.
Ukers, W.H., *All About Tea*, Vol.1 & 2, New York, 1934.

Index

AFT Industries Ltd, 65, 82, 246
Agarwala, Jyoti Prasad, 36, 87
Agarwala, Kishanlall, 36
Agrawal, Harbilash, 26
Agrawal, Navrangrai, 26
Agricultural and Horticultural Society of Bengal, 18-19
Ahmad, Mumtaz, 129, 167, 228, 229, 234, 252, 254
Ahsan, Amir, 72, 240, 254
Ahuja, S.S., 212
All-Assam Lawn Tennis Association, 50
All Assam Small Tea Growers' Association, 99
All Assam Students' Union, 82, 226
All India Trade Union Congress, 110, 253
Ambootia, 195, 200
American Health Foundation, 210
American Revolution, 17
Amgooria Tea Estate, 218
Anderson, G.G., 167
Anderson, Stephen, 124
Andrew Yule, 212
Apeejay Surrendra Group, 50, 61
Assam Sahitya Sabha, 58, 86, 252, 253, 254
Ashraff, M.H., 55,116
Asom Gana Parishad, 226
Assam Agricultural University, 50, 52, 70
Assam Branch Indian Tea Association, 28, 32, 34, 52, 72, 73, 75, 83, 84, 85, 90, 99, 100–1, 111, 175, 178, 251, 252, 253, 254
Assam Cha Karamchari Sangha, 110
Assam Cha Mazdoor Sangha, 110, 175
Assam Company, 20, 21, 50, 52, 103
Assam Cultural Complex, 84
Assam Labour Enquiry Committee, 105
Assam Medical College, 32
Assam Railway and Trading Company, 28
Assam Table Tennis Association, 62
Assam Tea Plantation Force, 225
Assam Tea Planters' Association, 231, 246
Assam Valley Literary Award, 58
Assam Valley School, 48, 126, 246, 253
Assam Valley Tea Association, 27
Assam Valley Wildlife Preservation Society, 78
Atal, D., 164, 254
Attareekhat Tea Estate, 66, 78

B&A Plantations and Industries Ltd, 52
B.P. Kedia Central Hospital, 65
Baghjan Tea Estate, 79
Bagla, Ayush, 205
Bagrias, 34
Bajaj, Jamnalal, 36
Bajaj, P., 132
Bajoria, Balmukund, 125

Bajoria, Bharat, 47, 192
Bardubi High School, 48
Barooah, Bishnu Ram, 36
Barooah, Bistooram, 25
Barooah, H.P., 52, 236, 254
Barooah, T.N., 175
Barpujari, H.K., 34, 48
Barua, Ajit, 58
Barua, Bholanath, 32
Barua, C.K., 66
Barua, Ghanshyam, 25
Barua, G.P., 131, 250, 254
Barua, Hemadhar, 25
Barua, Malbhog, 25
Barua, Maniram Dutta, 18
Barua, Navakanta, 58
Barua, Parbati Prasad, 87
Barua, Rai Bahadur Bisturam, 25
Barua, Rai Bahadur Debi Charan, 25
Barua, Rai Bahadur Jagannath, 25
Barua, Rai Bahadur Krishnakant, 25
Barua, Rai Bahadur Sib Prasad, 25
Barua, Rosheswar, 25
Baruah, Debjyoti, 238
Baruah, D.N., 222
Baruah, Ghanshyam, 36
Baruah, Prasanna, 36
Baruah, Rohini Kumar, 87
Baruah, Someswar, 36
Basu, Jyoti, 148, 252
Bedia, Narayan, 25
Bengal Chamber of Commerce and Industry, 129, 146
Bengal Tea Association, 21, 245
Bentinck, Lord, 18, 245
Berias, 34, 36
Berry White Medical School, 32
Bezbarua, Narayan, 25
Bezbarua, L.N., 252
Bharat Scouts and Guides Movement, 72
Bharatiya Cha Parishad, 85, 86, 87, 246, 253, 255
Bhattacharjee, A., 110
Bhattacharjee, P.K., 83, 111, 254
Bhattacharya, Buddhadeb, 252
Bidhi Vidya Bhawan, 50
Birla, B.K., 65
Bishnauth Tea Co. Ltd, 125, 128, 184
Bodo Handloom Scheme, 71
Bodo Sahitya Sabha, 58, 75
Bokagam Library, 48
Bokial Teen Ali High School, 48
Bombay Management Association, 64
Bora, Col. Sibram, 25
Bora, D., 231
Bora, Mahim, 58
Bora, P.K., 88, 226, 254
Borbora, B.C., 222
Bordoloi, Gopinath, 26, 36

Bordoloi, Nabin Chandra, 36
Bordoloi, Surabala, 36
Bordoloi, T.C., 131, 175, 253
Bordubi Tea Estate, 78
Borengajuli Tea Estate, 72, 254
Borkakoti, Sarbananda, 25
Borooah, Prafulla Chandra, 36
Borthakur, Robin, 99, 111, 254
Boston Tea Party, 17, 245
Brahmalahan, Daisy, 117
Brahma, Bineswar, 75
Brahma, Shobha, 58
Brahmachari, Dr U.N., 32
Brooke Bond Lipton (India) Ltd, 50, 62, 225
Brooke Bond Tea & Health Information Centre, 210
Broota, Rameshwar, 129
Bruce, Charles Alexander, 18, 20, 21, 85
Bruce, Robert, 18, 245
Bukhial Tea Estate, 139, 140
Bureau of Integrated Rural Development, 73, 255

Cachar Cancer Hospital, 86
Cachar Cha Shramic Union, 110
Cachar Tea Garden Wholesale Cooperative, 86
Calcutta Botanical Garden, 18
Calcutta Polo Club, 148, 149
Calcutta Tercentenary Gallery, 148
Cambridge University, 137
Camellia Group, 52
Campbell, Dr A., 22, 217
Carpenter, P.H., 218
Carritt Moran & Co. Pvt. Ltd, 143
Castleton Tea Estate, 80
Catherine of Braganza, 17
Central Board of Direct Taxes, 129
Central Income Tax Act, 227
Central Insecticides Board of India, 80
Chah Udyog Gramin Krishi Vikas Samiti, 74, 75
Chakrabarti, D., 231, 254
Chakravati, Dr D.N., 73, 254
Chaliha, Bimala Prosad, 36, 87
Chaliha, Jadav Prasad, 36
Chaliha, Kaliprasad, 25
Chaliha, Kuladhar, 36
Chaliha, Ranjit, 86, 253
Chaliha, Saurabh Kumar, 58
Chandra Kamal Bezbaruah College, 87
Charles II, King, 17
Charles, Prince, 140
Charlton, Lieutenant, 18
Children's Science Congress, 52
Choudhary, D.K., 132
Choudhary, D. Pal, 129
Chowdhury, Jogen, 96

258 | INDEX

Chuapara Tea Estate, 66
Comprehensive Labour Welfare Scheme, 106, 246
Consultative Committee of Plantation Associations, 82, 85, 170, 173, 192, 253
Cotton College, 84, 225
Cotton, Sir Henry, 104

Daga, Y.K., 252
Daimari, Prinson, 54
Darjeeling Tea Planters' Association, 85, 245, 254, 255
Darjeeling Tea Company, 217
Darjeeling Tea Research Centre, 219
Darrang Women's College, 48
Das, Prof. Jogesh, 58, 254
Das, N.K., 192, 250
Das, Probir, 139
Das, R., 255
Das, Tapas, 193, 255
David, K.S., 52, 200
Dekorai Tea Estate,139
Devicharan Baruah Girls' College, 87
Devraj Rai College, 87
Dewan, Maniram, 25, 32,252
Dhanowar, Rameshwar, 112
Dhanuka, C.K., 75, 236, 255
Dhanukas, 36
Dhar, Tushar Kanti, 140
Dhunseri Tea & Industries Ltd, 74
Diana, Princess, 140
Dibrugarh Medical College, 87
Dibrugarh University, 52, 54
Dimakusi Garden, 132
Dirai Tea Estate, 240
Dirial Tea , 66, 72
Dirok Tea Estate, 80
Dooars Branch Indian Tea Association, 85, 87, 88
Dooars Tea Planter's Association, 22,245
Doom Dooma College, 48, 52
Doom Dooma Tea Association, 62
Dufflaghur Tea Estate, 80
Duncans Industries Ltd, 194, 212, 230
Dunsandle Estate, 22
Dutta, Nilambar, 36
Dwivedi, Sanskriti, 116

East India Company, 18, 21
Emerson, Ralph Waldo, 17,247
Emmette, Dr Charles, 34
Empire Plantations, 65
Environmental Protection Agency of USA, 80
Eravikulam National Park, 78
Ernst & Young, 185
Eveready Industries (India) Ltd, 127, 128, 131, 184, 185, 200

Family Welfare Education Programme, 87
FICCI, 55, 64
Finlay Football Inter-estate Tournament, 72
Fley, E.G., 32
Forbes & Walker, 205
Forrester Research, 205
Four Mangoe Lane, 126, 130, 162, 170, 175, 184, 253

Gandhi, Mahatma, 36, 117, 156, 159
Gandhi, Rajiv, 225
Gangabari Tea Estate, 36
George Williamson (Assam) Ltd, 66, 72, 75, 136, 184, 255
Ghatowar, Paban Singh, 112,132, 164, 235, 255
Ghose, Indrani, 117
Gill, Martin, 140
Gilroy, Dr Ian, 34
Ging Tea Garden, 21
Godara,Manupal, 149
Goenka, G.P., 193, 194
Goenka, V.K., 82, 111, 255
Goenkas, 36
Gogh,Vincent van, 20, 58, 82, 83
Gogoi, Tarun, 36, 88, 106, 226, 255
Gogra Tea Estate, 139
Gohain, Hemanta, 99
Golaghat Civil Hospital, 84
Goodricke Chess Academy, 62
Goodricke, East India Golf Championship, 62
Goodricke Group, 47, 61, 64, 80, 195, 198, 200, 201, 212, 248
Goodricke School for Special Children, 52
Goradia, Prafulla, 234, 236
Gordon, A.D., 167
Gordon, George James, 18, 20, 21
Gramin Krishi Unnayan Prakalpa, 75
Griffith, Dr. W., 218
Griffiths, Sir Percival, 24
Guha, Thakurta, J., 252
Guwahati Sports Association, 62
Guwahati Tea Auction Centre, 87, 178

Hadfield, Dr W., 137
Handique, Radhakanta, 25
Hanuman Tea, 205, 212
Hannay, E.H., 167
Happy Valley Tea Estate, 240
Harijan Community Hall, 85
Hathikula Tea Estate, 78
Hazarika, Gunin, 75, 101, 255
High Range Wildlife & Environment Preservation Association, 78
Hind Mazdoor Sabha, 110
Hindustan Lever Ltd, 52, 146, 192, 193, 194, 198, 210, 225

Hoonlal Higher Secondary School, 50
Hunwal Tea Estate, 48, 131, 139
Hussain, Abid, 236
Hussain, Zakir, 205

India International Millennium Tea Convention, 173, 246, 253
Indian Chamber of Commerce, 129, 146, 236, 253
Indian Council of Agricultural Research, 86, 96
Indian Institute of Plantation Management, 102, 150
Indian Institute of Technology, 136
Indian National Trade Union Congress, 110
Indian Tea Association, 22, 28, 32, 34, 47, 64, 75, 82, 129, 130, 131, 146, 164, 167, 170, 173, 175, 193, 204, 218, 225, 230, 231, 236, 245, 246, 252, 253, 254, 255
Indian Tea Employees Union, 110
Indian Tea Planters' Association, 85
Indira Gandhi Wildlife Sanctuary, 239
Industrial Committee on Plantations, 105
Industrial Development Bank of India, 71
Industrial Training Institute, 54
Inland Container Depot, 158, 178
International Chamber of Commerce, 129, 146, 252, 253
International Management Institute, 50, 150

Jain, L.C., 164, 226
Jajodias, 36
Jalan, Mahadeo, 87, 255
Jalan, Murlidhor, 36
Jalan, Sandeep, 126
Jalans, 34, 36, 87
Jalpaiguri Engineering College, 87
James Finlay & Co., 22, 104
James, Henry, 20, 248
Jayshree Tea, 52, 64
J.B. College, 36
Jenkins, Captain F., 18
Jerai Anchalik Sports Association, 50
Jhawar, R.S., 101, 131, 170, 173, 175, 206, 230, 250, 253, 254, 255
Job Charnock's Mausoleum, 148
Jogananda Deva Goswami College, 87
Jorehaut Tea Company, 21, 245
Jorhat Civil Hospital, 85
Jorhat Sports Club, 62
Jorhat Theatre, 84
Joseph, Roshan Lal, 200
J. Thomas & Co. Pvt Ltd, 143, 245, 254
Jumbo CTC, 139
J.V. Gokal & Co. Ltd, 204

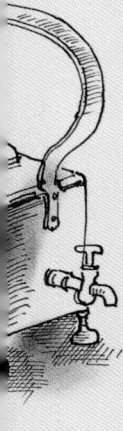

Kakuza, Okakura, 142
Kalita, Rajen, 99
Kamal Kumari Awards, 52
Kamal Kumari Foundation, 52
Kamatapuri Liberation Army, 222
Kanan Devan Nature Clubs, 79
Kangra Valley Small Tea Planters' Association, 85
Kanoi College, 34, 87
Kanoi, Hanuman Bux, 34
Kanoi Law College Auditorium, 34
Kanoria, Umang, 206
Kapur, Sanjay, 118, 210
Karmakar, Chatragopal, 112
Karnataka Planters' Association, 112
Kaseras, 34
Kasturba Welfare Centre, 52
Kaziranga National Park, 78, 239
Keating, R.H., 26
Kedias, 34
Keyhung Tea Estate, 66
Khaitan, Aditya, 126, 180, 255
Khaitan, B.M., 60, 125, 126, 127, 128, 129, 150, 162, 164, 167, 180, 184, 226, 250, 252, 253, 254, 255
Khaitan, Deepak, 126, 133, 185, 205, 253, 255
Khaitan, Divya, 126
Khaitan, Kavita, 126
Khaitan, Shanti, 126, 178, 255
Khaitan, Yashodhara, 126
Khaitans, 36, 126, 127, 184, 185
Khan, Wazir, 175
Khandiat, M.C., 110, 255
Khemanis, 34
Khusrokhan, Homi R., 64, 72, 194, 255
Kidwai, K.M., 167
Kidwai, S.M., 226, 255
Knight, Eleanor, 185
Knight, Henry, 185
Koomber Tea Co. Ltd, 47
Kothari, D.C, 246
Kotharis, 36
Kraft Foods Starbucks, 204
Krishi Vigyan Kendra, 86, 96, 98, 246
Krishnaswamy, P.R., 250
Kumar, R.K. Krishna, 55, 82, 90, 102, 234, 255

Labour Investigation Committee, 105
Law Faculty of Guwahati University, 50
Leggatt, Peter, 212, 250
Lipton, Thomas J., 204
Lohia, Snehiram, 26
Lohias, 34, 36
London Herb & Spice Co., 140
Loreto College, 149

Macneill & Barry, 127
Macneill & Magor Ltd, 127

Macneill Engineering Co., 185
Magor, R.B., 126, 167, 184
Magor, Richard Manuel Blamey, 124
Magors, 126, 184, 185
Mahadeo Agarwalla High School, 48
Mahanta, Keshab, 225
Mahanta, Prafulla Kumar, 50, 58, 75, 162, 251
Maheshwari, D.P., 194
Mahila Samiti, 39
Maitra, Subrata Narayan, 132
Majuli Tea Estate, 117
Malik, Syed Abdul, 58
Malkhowa Tea Estate, 36
Mangaldai Tea Estate, 78
Mann, Harold H., 218, 252
Margherita Public Higher Secondary School, 48
Margharita Tea Estate, 139
Mariani College, 48
Mathias, Peter, 112
Mathew, Fr P.C., 149
McKinsey, 185
McLelland, Dr J., 218
McLeod Russel, 127, 184
McNally Bharat, 185
Medhi, Bishnuram, 36
Mehra, Vijay, 90
Menon, Ullas, 231
Meshack, Anshu, 116
Miller, K.B., 167
Ministry of Finance, 129, 170
Ministry of Labour, 112, 251
Modis, 34
Mohurgong Tea Estate, 52
Monem, A., 130, 143, 255
Mor, Dr S.B., 66, 255
Moran College, 48
Moran Tea Co. Ltd, 65
Mornay, Stephen, 21
Mothers' Clubs, 39, 66, 88, 167,
Mountbatten, Lord Louis, 29
Mukerjee, Ranjan, 132
Mukherji, Meera, 61
Mumby, Philip, 142
Munnar Development Care Committee, 79
Murlidhor Jalan Foundation, 52

N.N. Saikia College, 87
Nanjan, M., 100
Narayanan, K.R., 36
National Socialist Council of Nagaland, 225
Natrajan, G., 255
Natural History Museum, 239
Navrangrai, 26
Nazira Natya Mandir, 84
Nehru, Jawaharlal, 36, 105, 156
Nehru Stadium Complex, 84
Nigam, S.K., 129

Nilgiri Planters' Association, 245
North-East Chamber of Commerce and Industry, 85, 158
North-Eastern Development Finance Corporation, 99
North-Eastern Tea Association, 85, 246
Nucleus Internet Centre, 52
Nullatanni Estate, 55
Nya Gogra Tea Estate, 66
Nyss, R.A., 111, 252

O'Brien, Errol, 140
Oliver, John, 78

Pal, S.K., 132
Paneery Central Hospital, 66
Paneery Tea Estate, 66
Parry Agro, 212
Pasteur Institute, 33, 245
Paul, Surrendra, 65, 82
Pauls, 36
P.C. Barooah Committee, 226, 246, 251
People Project Golaghat 2000, 85
Phookan, Nilmani, 58
Phukan, Ganga Gobind, 25
Phukan, Tarunram, 36
Phulbari Central Hospital, 65, 66, 67
Pipritola Tea Estate, 36,
Planning Commission, 226
Plantation Inquiry Commission, 25, 245, 251
Plantation Labour Act, 103, 105, 106, 107, 246, 251
Planters' Association of Tamil Nadu, 194
Poddars, 36
Prakash, D., 83, 175
Pratt, James Norwood, 250
Premier Beverages Ltd, 139, 143
Prince of Wales Technical School, 32, 48
Pugh, Peter, 254

Rajgarh Tea Estate, 36
Ramgarh Vikas Trust, 50
Ramsay, Dr, 32
Ramu, Dr S., 98
Rangapara College, 48
Rao, Ramesh, 250
Rashtriya Gramin Vikas Nidhi, 71
Ravindranath, S., 194
Ray, Subir, 132
Reserve Bank of India, 128
Rhino Foundation, 78
Rikhye, R.L., 170, 178, 253, 255
Rome, M.L., 140, 175
Ross Institute of Tropical Hygiene, 33, 34
Rossell Industries Ltd, 52, 62
Roy, Dolly, 52, 162
Roy, James E., 124

Roy, O.J., 124
Royal Calcutta Golf Club, 149
Royal Calcutta Turf Club, 149
Royal Commission on Labour, 105, 246, 251
Ruias, 36
Rural Agricultural Development Project, 75
Ruskin, John, 139

SAARC, 199
Sadhu, Dr M.K., 70
Saharias, 34, 36
Sahitya Academy, 58, 225
Sahitya Sammelan, 85
Sahitya Sora, 58
Saikia, Chandroprasad, 225
Saikia, Hiteshwar, 47, 84
Saikia, Prof. Nagen, 225, 252
Sandys-Lumsdaine, P.G., 253
Sankaranarayanan, Abanti, 117
Saptharishi, L.V., 175
Sarkar, Aveek, 128, 255
Sarma, Umakanta, 58
Sarwan, A.P., 112
Sathapaty, Ganapathy, 60
Satyam Infosys Ltd, 205
Scientific Research Organization, 218
Scott, David, 18
Second International Scientific Symposium on Tea, 209
Sengupta, Mansweta, 117
Sengupta, Prabir, 175
Sengupta, Shombit, 194
Sethias, 36
Shah, B.R., 250
Sharma, Gopal, 99
Sharma, S., 52
Sharma, Subhash, 102
Shikshayatan, 149
Sholayar Garden Hospital, 66
Shourie, Arun, 225
Sibsagar Natya Mandir, 86
Siganporia, P., 64, 255
Simpson, G.F., 175
Sinar Moisture Meter, 139
Sindhu, S.S., 100, 253
Singh, Arpita, 142
Singh, Mandhata, 175
Singh, Ramashankar, 130
Singh, S.N., 74
Singha, Purandhar, 25, 245
Singhpo, 18
Soom Tea Estate, 79
South India Plantation Division of Tata Tea, 55, 72

Spastic Society of Assam, 50
Sri Shankaradeva Netralaya, 64
Srishti, 55
St Andrew's Church, 148
St John's Church, 148
St Luke Hospital, 36
St Xavier's College, 149, 150
St Xavier's School, 149
Sterlite Industries, 127
Summerscale, D., 48
Swaminathan, T.R., 160

Tagore Hall, 61
Tamboolbari Tea Estate, 26
Tanti, Dileshwar, 112
Tanti, Dipak, 52
Tata Administrative Services, 117
Tata, Ratan, 55, 70, 79
Tata Tea Ltd, 54, 55, 63, 64, 70, 72, 78, 79, 80, 102, 103, 106, 107, 110, 116, 117, 192, 194, 198, 226, 255
Tea Association of India, 85, 206, 246
Tea Board of India, 88, 96, 98, 100, 140, 173, 192, 199, 200, 204, 212, 216, 227, 237, 246, 251
Tea Committee, 18, 20, 21, 245
Tea Estate Area Community Uplift Programme, 71
Tea Marketing (Control) Order, 206, 246
Tea Quality Upgradation Programme, 100
Tea Research Association, 137, 175, 218, 219, 222, 246
Tea Research Foundation, 219
Tea Research Institute, 219
Tea Sports Control Board of Assam, 62
Tea Trading Corporation of India, 140
Technical Food Insurance Spectrum, 212
Telenga, Barki Prasad, 112
Terai Indian Planters' Association, 85
Tezpore Tea Company Ltd, 74
Thakurbari Club, 75
Thekkady Wildlife Sanctuary, 239
Thermax OBT-75, 139
Tiamyudi, 190
Tiazzi, 204
Tirupati Balaji Temple, 60
Tocklai Experimental Research Station, 29, 218, 222, 240, 245
Trinick Sorter, 139
Trinick, J.M., 139, 140, 255
Tyagbir College, 48

Union Carbide (India) Ltd, 127

United Liberation Front of Asom, 131, 222, 225, 226, 240
United Nations Children's Fund, 88
United Nations Population Fund, 88
United Planters' Association of Southern India, 22, 85, 86, 96, 106, 107, 218, 231, 245, 246, 253, 254
Upper Assam Golf Association, 62
Uthapa, Babini, 117

Vajpayee, Atal Behari, 55
Vellonie Tea Estate, 72
Verma, S.P., 86, 255
Vibro Fluid Bed Drier, 139
Victoria Memorial, 143, 148
Vivekanand Rock Memorial, 61
Vivekananda Kendra's Cultural Research Library, 50, 60
VSBLO, 80

Wallich, N., 18, 217
Warren Tea Ltd, 82, 111, 255
Washabarie Tea Estate, 52
Watson, A.G., 167
Wavell, Field Marshal, Viceroy, 29
White, James, 22
White, Dr John Berry, 32
Williamson Artisan School, 48
Williamson, George, 32, 33, 48, 136
Williamson, James Hay, 124
Williamson Magor & Co. Ltd, 73, 124, 126, 127
Williamson Magor Education Trust, 50, 58, 60
Williamson Magor Football Academy, 62
Williamson Magor Group, 32, 33, 48, 60, 62, 65, 71, 73, 74, 78, 79, 110, 124–30, 134–135, 141, 147, 160, 162, 164, 167, 175, 178, 180, 194, 240, 255
Williamson Magor Hall, 60
Williamson Magor Hospital, 66
Williamson Magor Scholarship, 48
Williamson Magor Workmen's Union, 132
Williamson, Patrick Hay, 124, 125, 126, 148, 149
Williamson, R.L., 124, 167
World Bank, 102
World Trade Organization, 100, 184
Worthington Pumps, 185

Young, Henry Burking, 21
Yu, Lu, 16, 245, 247

Zaman, A.N., 175

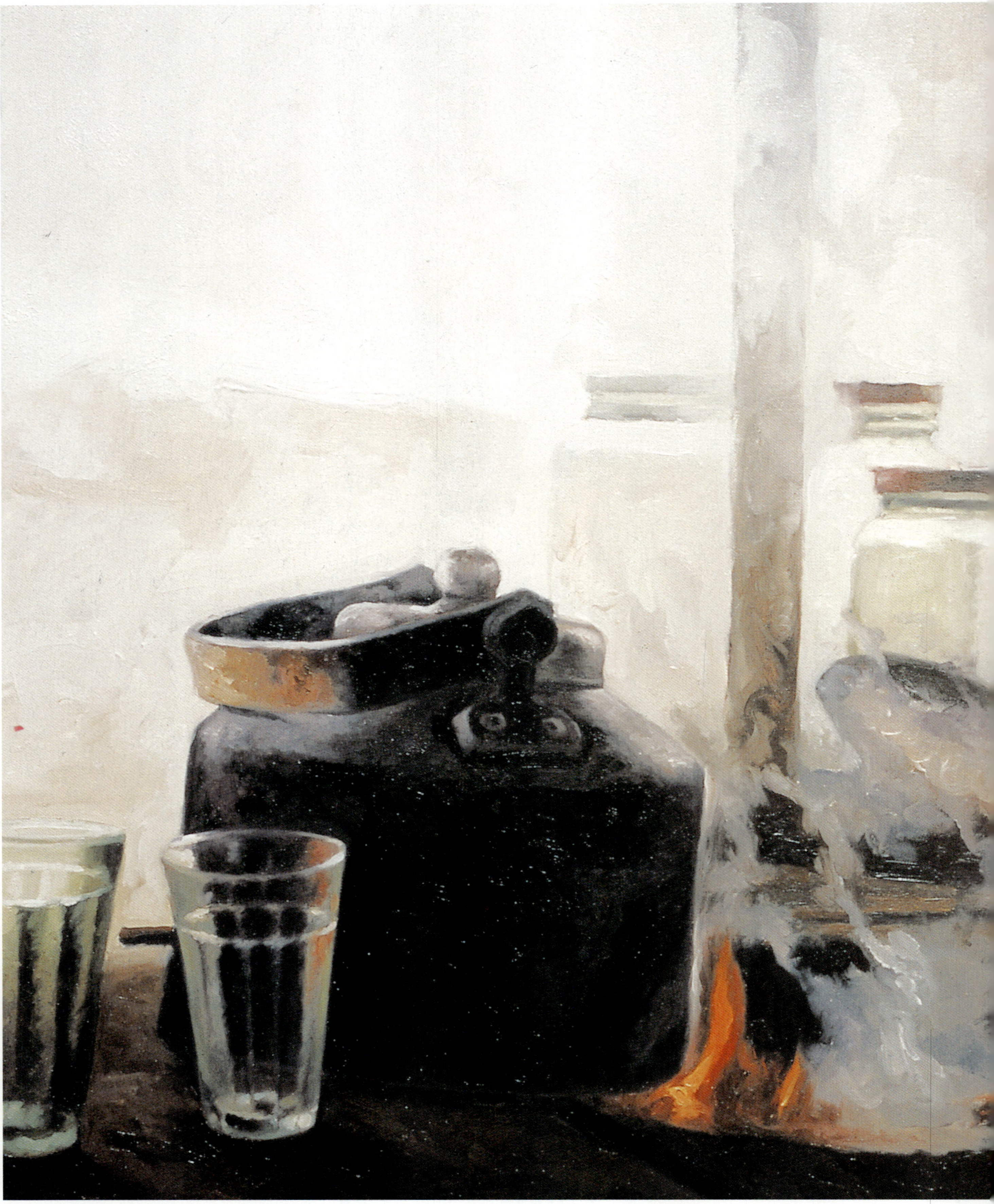

An artistic impression of a tea shop by Sanjay Bhattacharjyya

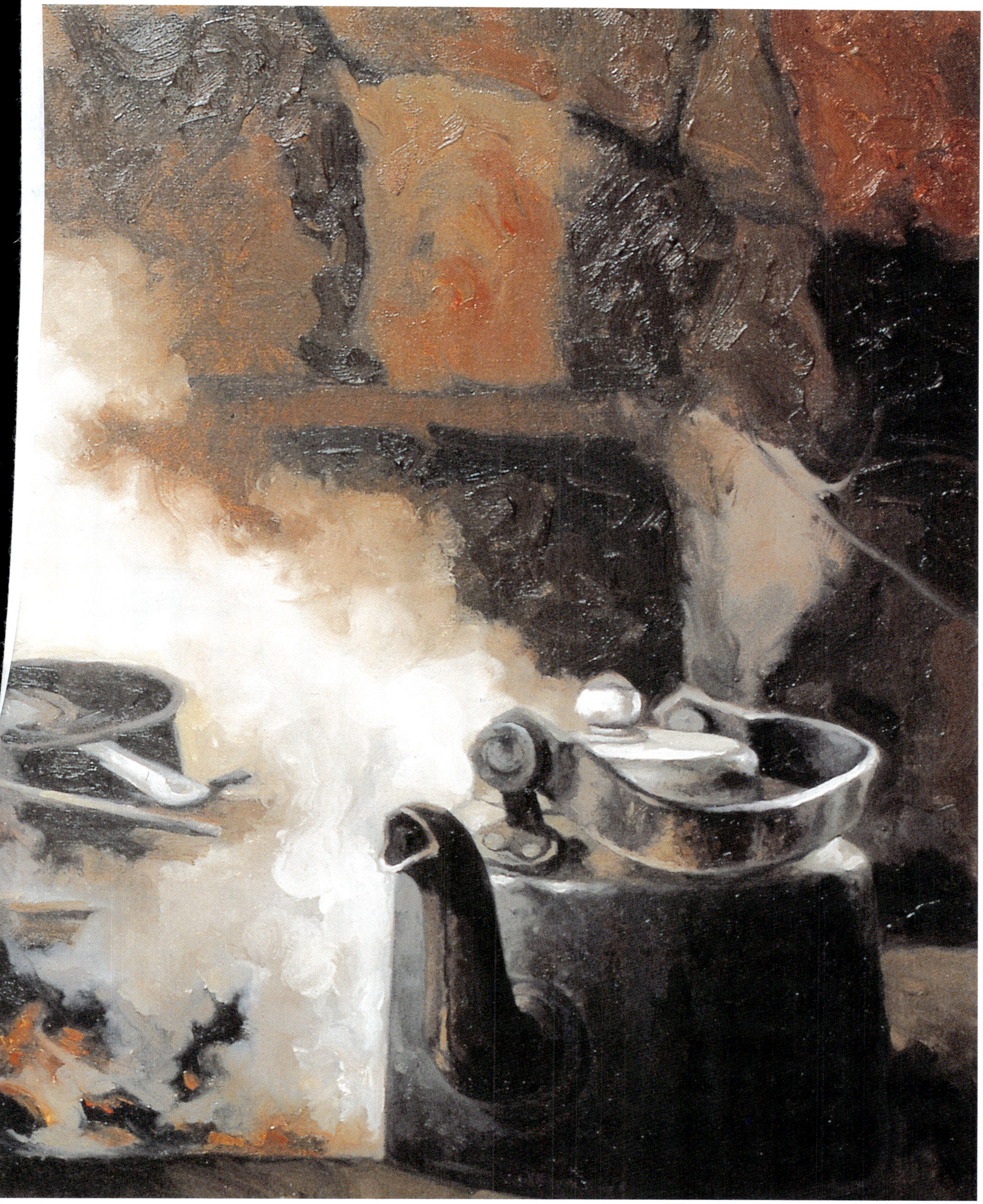

Photo Credits

The publisher and author thanks the relevant photographers, individuals, organizations, and tea companies for their kind permission to reproduce the photographs in this book, details of which are provided below. Their courtesy is gratefully acknowledged. The publishers have done their utmost to clear copyright with all the relevant copyright holders traceable, and in the event of any omissions deeply regret the lapse. In the event of any being pointed out, they will be glad to add them in any future editions.

Jacket (front) Business History Museum-IIME (BHM-IIME), (back) Joginder Chawla; pp.1–3 IHCL; pp. 4–5 Joginder Chawla; pp.6–7 IHCL; p.8 Joginder Chawla; p.10 Ann Ronan/Image Select; pp.14—15 Mary Evans Picture Library; p.16 (top right) Aaron/DR; p.17 (top) Edward Bramah Tea and Coffee Museum; p.18 (below) Royal Geographical Society; p.19 (top) Royal Geographical Society; p.20 (left top) The Bridgeman Art Library, (below right) Mary Evans Picture Library, (below left) Vincent van Gogh Foundation; p.21 (top) The Graphic, (middle and below) George M. Barker; p.22 (top and middle) George M. Barker, (below) Davidson Co. Ltd; p.23 (top) The Graphic, (below right) S. Muthiah, (below left) Royal Geographical Society; p.24 (top and below) Smith, Elder and Co.; p.26 (top) George M. Barker; p.27 (top) Sir Percival Griffiths; p.28 (top) The Graphic; p.29 (middle and below) The Graphic; p.30–1 BHM-IIME; p.32 George M. Barker; p.33 (top left) Royal Geographical Society (top right and middle) The Graphic; p.35 Mary Evans Picture Library; p.36 (below) TTL; p.38 (top left) George M. Barker, (top right) Mansell Collection; p.39 (top left and right) WMG, (below) R.R. Konwar; pp.40–3 BHM-IIME; pp.44–5 The Graphic; p.46 BHM-IIME/P.K. Paul; p.48 WMG; p.49 GG; p.50 Fernand Léger; p.51 Kamal Kumar; p.53 BHM-IIME/P.K. Paul; p.54 BHM-IIME; p.55 (top and below) TTL; pp.58–9 Vincent van Gogh Foundation; p.60 Juan Gris; pp.61–3 GG; p.64 WMG; p.65(top) GG, (below) WMG; p.66 BHM-IIME; p.67 R.R. Konwar; pp.68–9 Gopi Gajwani; p.70 WMG; p.71 GG; pp.72–4 BHM-IIME; p.75 R.R. Konwar; pp.76–7 Joginder Chawla; p.78 (top left and below) WMG, (top right) R.R. Konwar; p.79 TTL; pp.80–1 BHM-IIME/Gopi Gajwani; pp.82–3 Vincent van Gogh Foundation; p.84 Subhash Bhargava; p.85 Dindodia Picture Agency; p.86 Jitu Oghani /Pankaj Madhok; p.87 (below) R.R. Konwar; pp.88–91 BHM-IIME; pp.92–3 GG; pp.94–5 Mary Evans Picture Library; p.97 Heart; pp.98–9 BHM-IIME; p.103 (left) BHM-IIME, (right) TTL; p.104 (top left, below and right) George M. Barker, (right below) The Graphic; p.105 (top left and below) TTL, (top right) WMG; p.106 TTL; pp.108–9 Joginder Chawla; pp.110–1 BHM-IIME; p.112 GG; p.113 R.R. Konwar; pp.114–5 BHM-IIME; p.117 (below left and right) TTL; p.118 (left) K. Katyal, (right) Sanjay Kapur; 119 BHM-IIME/R. Chauhan; pp.120–1 BHM-IIME; p.129 (top) Rameshwar Broota; p.130 WMG/P.K. Paul; pp.131–3 BHM-IIME; pp.134–5 Gopi Gajwani/IHCL; pp.136–7 WMG; p.138 BHM-IIME/Gopi Gajwani/IHCL; p.139 P.K. Paul; p.141 Johann Heinrich Tischbein; p.142 Heart; pp.144–5 Gopi Gajwani; p.146 IHCL; p.147 James J.J.Tissot; p.149 Gopi Gajwani; p.151 Christie's Images, London/The Bridgeman Art Library; pp.152–3 BHM-IIME/R. Chauhan; pp.154–5 Smith, Elder and Co.; pp.156–7 BHM-IIME; p.158 (below) Dindodia Picture Agency; p.159 (top) R.R. Konwar; pp.161–3 BHM-IIME; p.164 (top) Dindodia Picture Agency, (below) R. Khullar; p.165 Dindodia Picture Agency; pp.168–77 BHM-IIME; p.179 Dindodia Picture Agency; pp.180–3 BHM-IIME; p.185 Private Collection Christie's Images/The Bridgeman Art Library; pp.186–7 Dindodia Picture Agency; p.191 J. Thomas & Co. Ltd; p.192 BHM-IIME; p.193 (top) BHM-IIME; (below) HLL; pp.194–7 BHM-IIME; p.198 Sanjay Kapur; p.199 GG; pp.202–3 Gopi Gajwani; p.204 (top) Dindodia Picture Agency, (below) GG; p.205 (top) HLL, (below) TTL; p.207 BHM-IIME; p.209 BHM-IIME/Gopi Gajwani/IHCL; pp.210–1 BHM-IIME; p.212 (top left and below) TTL, (top right) GG; p.213 (top and below right) GG, (below left) TTL; pp.214–5 Christie's Images, London/The Bridgeman Art Library; p.216 Tea Board of India, (below) GG; p.217 R. Khullar; p.218 BHM-IIME, p. 219 (top) Gopi Gajwani/BHM-IIME; pp.220–1 Anadi/Dushyant Singh; p.222 (top) R.R. Konwar, (below) Kamal Kumar; p.223 Dindodia Picture Agency; p.224 BHM-IIME/L.S. Tak/Ramji Vyas; p.225 Toulouse-Lautre; p.226 R.R. Konwar; p.227 BHM-IIME/Gopi Gajwani; pp.228–33 BHM-IIME; p.235 BHM-IIME/Gopi Gajwani/IHCL; pp.236–9 Gopi Gajwani/BHM-IIME; p.241 (top) GG; pp.242–3 Joginder Chawla; p.244 JCollector (Geri Servi); pp.246–61 Gopi Gajwani; pp.262–3 Sanjay Bhattacharjyya.

A NEW ESSAY UPON
TEA

ADDRESSED TO
THE MEDICAL PROFESSION

WHEREIN ARE SHOWN

I

A Part of its History

II

Its Effect on the Human Frame

III

The Rules for Choosing and Serving
what is best.

LONDON
MCMXXXVI

JOHN COAKLEY
LETTSOM

DEDICATION

To John Coakley Lettsom, M.D., F.R.S.,
*who published the first important
Medical treatise in English
on tea-drinking, in 1772.*

> When any sick to me apply,
> I physics, bleeds and sweats 'em;
> If after that they choose to die,
> What's that to me, I. Lettsom.

He dressed simply in the Quaker fashion—probably 'marone light mixture or bright snuff, pea-green or peach-bloom'—this discreet and successful physician of the eighteenth century. Walking through drab streets to his practice in Bloomsbury or in the City, visiting the elegant houses of his rich patients, Lettsom is a figure of his age.

The mark of his enterprise remains in many branches of his profession, both as practising physician, social worker and writer. He founded the

Medical Society of London and became a fellow of the Royal Society. He inaugurated Dispensaries for the poor; he spurred on prison reform, fostered the Royal Humane Society, and was the father of open-air sanatoria.

Such activities were, however, extra to the enormous practice which, at the height of his fame, brought him an income of £12,000 a year—at that time a fortune and the equivalent of at least twice as much to-day.

Lettsom was at his wisest and his wittiest in a treatise written originally for his M.D.—'Observationes ad vires Theae pertinentes'. Perhaps no ambitious young doctor of to-day would take tea as the subject of his thesis, but in Lettsom's time 'this exotic shrub' had a profound interest for medical men and laymen. Thanks to smuggling and the coffee-house, tea drinking was becoming increasingly popular. Was it a pernicious habit or a delightful and safe social relaxation? The question agitated all society, and, in particular, all Quakerdom.

John Wesley was an antagonist of tea; James Hanway, a philanthropist who, besides introducing the umbrella, bore all the marks of the Salvation Army man, was another; while Johnson and Goldsmith took up the cudgels in tea's defence. Strange anomaly in an age of intemperance! But to the nonconformist conscience tea was then a needless self-indulgence, while to Johnson, that 'Colossus of the caddy', it was a strict necessity.

The moment was opportune for Lettsom, ever a good publicist, to revise and print in English his medical observations on tea-drinking.

One feels in reading these that practically everything there is to be said about tea from the medical standpoint was said and extremely well said nearly two centuries ago under much the same conditions of controversy as exist to-day!

* * *

'The accounts which have been given of the virtues and efficacy of Tea, are in general so contradictory and void of true medical observation, that it seemed no improper subject for a candid discussion.'
Preface to Lettsom's Treatise

Although slightly flavoured by botanical enthusiasms and couched in the sonorous phrases of the original Latin, Lettsom's Treatise reflects the modern medical attitude to tea—neither that of a 'partial advocate' nor 'passionate accuser'.

'As the custom of drinking Tea is become universal,' he says, 'every person may be considered a judge of its effects, at least so far as concerns his own health; but as the constitutions of mankind are as various as the individuals, the effects of this infusion must be different also, which is the reason that so many opinions have prevailed upon the subject.'

And: 'Many persons who have once conceived a prejudice against it, suffer it to influence their judgement too far, and condemn the custom as universally pernicious. Others, who are no less biased on the other extreme, would make their own private experience a standard for the general, and ascribe the most extensive virtues to this infusion. This contrariety of opinion has been particularly maintained among physicians, which will ever be the case, while mere suppositions are placed in the room of experiments and facts impartially related.'

His conclusion is that to the strong vigorous man 'in firm health' tea can do nothing but good—may, indeed, be preferable to any other regale, but to the tender, delicate and enfeebled who lack appetite and exercise, it may be lowering.

Lettsom proved for himself the antiseptic and astringent power of tea; its capacity for producing 'watchfulness in some conditions'; its association with nervous disorders though not as their cause, and its too prolific use among the poorer people.

Never pedantic, never narrowed to the limits of a single experiment, he draws on human nature for his conclusions on tea and draws with common sense.

He ends this eminently sane discourse thus: 'So far, therefore, Tea, if not drank too hot, nor in too great quantities, is perhaps preferable to any other vegetable infusion we know. And if we take into consideration likewise, its known enlivening energy, it will appear that our attachment to Tea, is not merely from its being costly or fashionable, but from its superiority in taste and effects to most other vegetables.'

Boundless wisdom! We end in the hope that what follows may contribute somewhat to the practical Lettsom's store 'of facts impartially related'.

The quotations on pages 5 and 6 are from Lettsom's Treatise: 'The Natural History of the Tea Tree with Observations on the Medical Qualities of Tea and Effects of Tea-drinking'.

I. A PART OF ITS HISTORY

TCHA When I drink tea, I am conscious of peace.
The cool breath of heaven rises in my
sleeves and blows my cares away.
Old Chinese Poem

SINCE the mists of antiquity opened in 2700 B.C. on the Chinaman Shenung—said to have been the first teacher of medicine—tea has been at least semi-medicinal. In those dim days, and ever after among the Chinese, it was regarded as an antiseptic for brackish drinking-water and as a stimulant of the highest order.

There has always been dispute over the original home of tea—India or China. Hindu legend ascribes discovery to an ascetic who, by its heaven-sent help, kept a nine years' vow of sleeplessness and afterwards carried it to China. Be that as it may, we know for certain that the Chinese were the first tea-drinkers, venerating the cup of tea and surrounding it with poetry and ceremonial since the fourth century.

Japan followed suit, in the six hundreds, with her 'honourable five o'clock tea'; wild Tartar horsemen boiled a kettle on the plains; Persian grandees partook of 'Tcha', and Thibetan Lhamas gave enormous tea-parties long before tea had been dreamed of in other lands.

LONDON'S COFFEE-HOUSES

Tea came to England in the middle of the seventeenth century and many are the stories which survive of

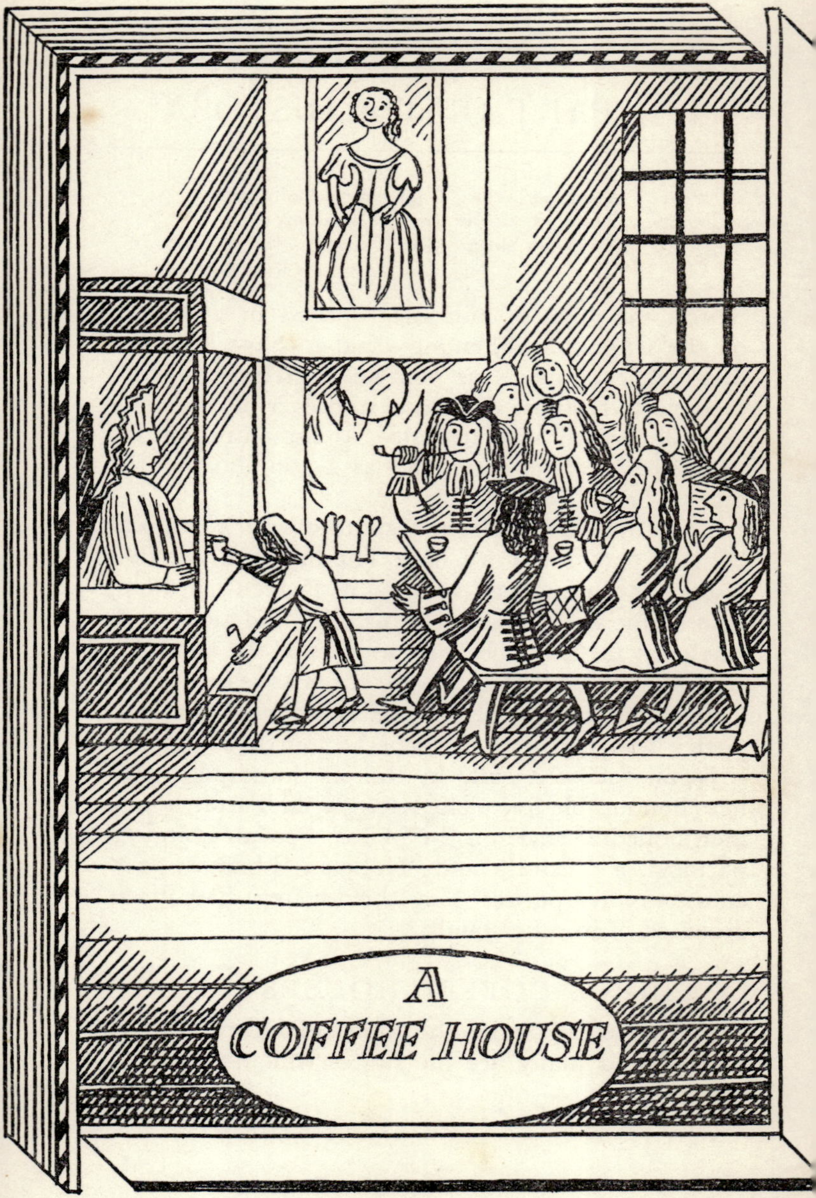
A
COFFEE HOUSE

the treatment it at first received. Some spread the stewed leaves on bread, others 'encouraged' the infusion with beaten eggs, or served it as a boiled vegetable. But the real entrée of tea as a beverage was made in the convivial and democratic coffee-house which, by the end of the seventeenth century, and all through the eighteenth century, was such a feature of social and political life.

Here for 2d. a man could buy a cup of tea, look at his newspaper, scan the witty pages of *The Spectator*, and listen to the giants of the day 'tossing their minds'. Here Pepys and Dryden, Steele and Addison, Pope, Swift, and Dr. Johnson in turn sipped the 'fragrant cups' side by side with barristers and clergy and country attorneys come to London to do their business. So in an age of heavy drinking, and in the predecessor of the masculine club, tea gained its first popularity.

SMUGGLING

But for the majority of people tea still remained a luxury, and with good reason. In 1689 heavy duties were introduced which put a premium on the poor man's tea-drinking. To get their tea—Englishmen smuggled. Through four reigns the whisper of muffled oars was heard along the coasts. From the Isle of Man to Porthcothan Bay, from Galloway to Langston Point, 'all the lively young men' were employed in this recognized industry. Many a cave and hiding place for unlawful tea-chests is still remembered among the rocky coves of Devon, Dorset and Cornwall. Inland in quiet villages more than one tombstone commemorates some unlucky tea-smuggler who died by the exciseman's bullet. But—the Englishman held fast to his own. Slowly and secretly the tea-pot crept into scores of cottage kitchens.

'THE EXCELLENT AND BY ALL PHYSITIANS APPROVED DRINK . . . TAY'

The more tea became fashionable the more it became a subject of controversy. On the one hand there were champions who extolled it for everything from weak eyes to scurvy. Foremost among these was Dr. Cornelius Bontekoe who recommended from 12 cups a day to 200 for the seasoned drinker! Soon, to stem the flow of panegyric, appeared the famous Lettsom with his impartial treatise on 'this distinguished vegetable'. It is very noticeable that the early literature of tea, and even the advertisements for it, had a strong medical flavour. As in the East, so in the West, men noticed 'Tea removeth lassitude, vanquisheth heavy dreams, easeth the frame and strengtheneth the memory. . . . It is of great avail to men of corpulent bodies and to such as eat much flesh. It clears a dull head, and maketh the frame active and lusty'. There is no doubt that this clarifying power of tea was a splendid antidote to the gross high feeding of eighteenth-century England.

A STORM IN A TEA-CUP

But by the latter half of the century, Methodist worthies, smug philanthropists, and even Society, had entered the tea-fight. Rich men begrudged poor men the watery luxury of tea, and all Nonconformity

A little tea, one leaf I did not steal,
For guiltless bloodshed I to God appeal;
Put Tea in one scale, human blood in t'other,
And think what 'tis to slay a harmless brother.

Epitaph in a Dorset churchyard to a tea-smuggler shot by a Revenue Officer, 1765

was ally, condemning in particular that 'clandestine commerce'—smuggling.

Into this breach leaped Johnson. What man better qualified to be protagonist of tea than he, who in defending it, described himself: 'a hardened and shameless tea-drinker, who has for 20 years diluted his meals with only the infusion of this fascinating plant, whose kettle has scarcely time to cool, who with Tea amuses the evening, with Tea solaces the midnights, and with Tea welcomes the morning'. As Boswell says: Johnson's answer 'to the violent attack upon that elegant and popular beverage shows how well a man of genius can write upon the slightest subject when he writes *con amore*'.

Publicity—even if controversial—sells the goods, and innocent tea went on its way rejoicing. Tea-gardens followed on the heels of coffee houses; the blue-stockings began their sway—their quality of tea and conversation equally excellent; royalty took tea; tea-table prattle changed to scandal; poets sang of tea, and tea made its début on the stage.

CLIPPERS

At the dawn of the nineteenth century, when duties were at last lowered, demand began to grow at such a pace that a special fleet of merchantmen was needed to cope with it. Fast clippers, built for speed alone, raced back from the East to be the first with fragrant cargoes for the London market and fetch the highest prices. For a brief space these gallant clippers made the tea trade famous until, with the opening of the Suez Canal, and the coming of the steamer, their friendly rivalry died out.

ENTER INDIA

Up till now 'the China drink' had held the field, but just at the moment when the public was crying out for tea, the wild indigenous shrub of Assam showed its head. Treated with scorn to begin with, 'Thea Assamica' soon began to prove itself superior to Chinese rivals. In 1836 the first sample of this tea

By 1870 the racing tea-clipper was doomed —steamers superseded 'Thermopolæ' and 'Ariel', 'Taiping' and 'Cutty Sark'

from India reached London where, sold at auction, it realized from 16s. to 34s. a pound. Disturbed Chinese merchants called their teas 'Assam Pekoe Souchong' in the vain hope of securing the same excellent prices as the Indian trade!

Following suit to India, Ceylon started cultivation. Soon this plucky little island, which had been brought to the verge of ruin by the failure of its coffee plantations, was producing acres of its own delicious, aromatic tea. Netherlands East Indies are also to-day great tea producers.

'ANY INTERFERENCE WITH ITS CONSUMPTION WOULD WRECK AN EMPIRE'—AUGUSTINE BIRRELL

As if to make up for lost centuries, a great industry began to spring up from the moment Indian teas arrived on the market—bringing prosperity to millions and a tea-pot into every British home and in many homes in all parts of the world. Tea became the darling of the great temperance societies, made fun of by Dickens, with his young women 'swelling wisibly' by their ninth cup at teetotal meetings. The hissing urn called the gentlemen from their post-prandial port to hand the ladies cups of tea and little hot cakes and buns and to nibble and sip and indulge in lively conversation.

All through demure and prosperous Victorian days, when every Empire enterprise seemed cast for success, the tea industry grew and boomed until now in Great Britain alone we consume 450,000,000 lb. a year—almost ten pounds a head.

Over a million acres are under Empire Tea, approximately 650,000,000 lb. are produced each year, and thousands of British subjects employed in the varied stages between tea garden and tea caddy.

A MYTH DISPELLED

'I am glad I was not born before tea', said Sydney Smith. It is a charming and gracious idea that women, and women alone, preside over the tea table. But tea itself, since it first found its way into a cup, has been as much a masculine as a feminine drink. From the day of the Ming Dynasty with its 'egg-shell' porcelain till the day of the British working man with his dixie, men have drunk tea and spoken in praise of it. To the wits of the coffee-houses and the men of fashion and learning in the eighteenth century —Dr. Johnson and his quart pot in the van—tea was a 'sober, sage and venerable drink'. To the great Victorian writers—Lamb, De Quincey, Hazlitt and Coleridge among them—it was 'the beverage of the intelligence'.

And men of action, though saying less about tea, have been no less prodigal in their use of it. Cobden and Palmerston drank gallons, and Gladstone took it bitter, strong, and even cold, at every opportunity. In the Peninsular War, Wellington made tea an essential of his commissariat, and Wolseley supplied scalding draughts to famished Crimean troops. In the last war, was not a really good R.T.O. the man who at every *Halte Repas* provided boiling water for tea?

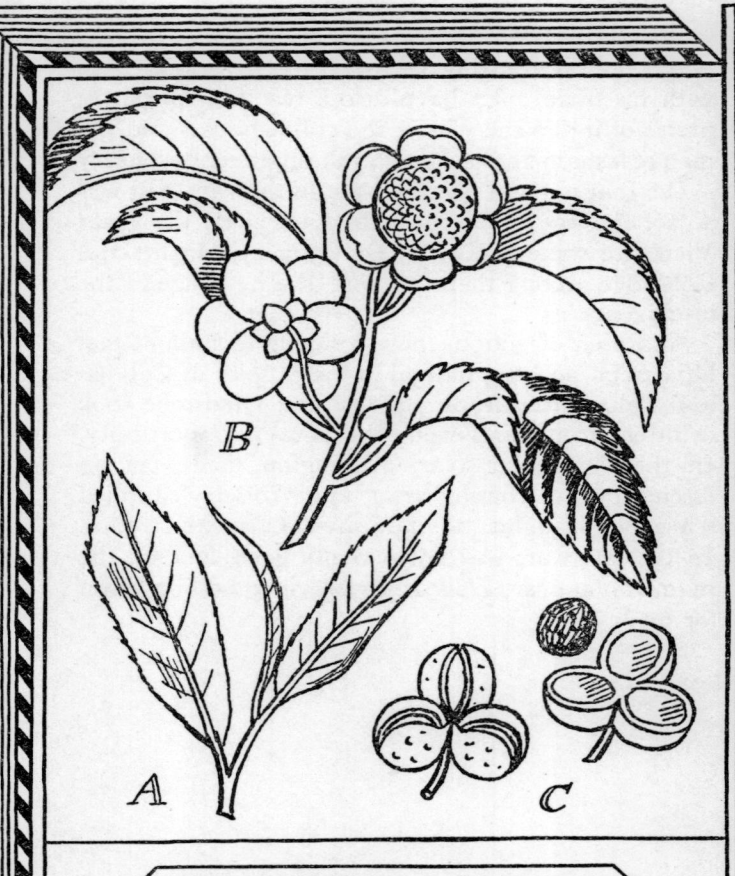

CAMELLIA THEA
(ASSAMICA)

(A) Plucking shoot about 7 days old
(B) Flower
(C) Fruit, showing cross section with seed

EXTRACT from review of this booklet in BRITISH MEDICAL JOURNAL:

> '. . . But in spite of its (tea) great social importance, we have still relatively little information regarding the effects produced on the body by tea-drinking. . . .'

HITHERTO the statement made by the *British Medical Journal* has been true, but members of the Medical profession will now find, if they will peruse Part II of this booklet (page 19), that this defect has at least partially been remedied, for they will find there the results of recent research on a scientific basis upon the effect on the human frame of a cup of tea.

II. ITS EFFECT ON THE HUMAN FRAME

THE CONSTITUENTS AND PHYSIOLOGICAL EFFECTS OF A CUP OF TEA

IN the last forty years the controversy which had been waged through the eighteenth and nineteenth centuries became changed in character. From being concerned with tea *qua* tea, it developed into a rivalry, stimulated by commercial interests, between different kinds of teas. Into the discussion both the chemist and the doctor were drawn. Argument centred in particular on the pharmacology of tea—and its chemical composition. Elaborate tests and analyses were undertaken, and minute and unimportant differences in the composition of teas came to be exaggerated.

In the light of modern knowledge, the premise on which argument was based appears to be uncertain or even false. Such experiment as had been carried out had been centred on the pharmacological effects of certain constituents of tea as shown in the laboratory rather than on clinical and laboratory experiment with tea in the form in which it is drunk, namely, the cup of tea. The time, therefore, is opportune for an unbiassed and scientifically founded statement of the ingredients which are contained in tea, their pharmacological action and the consideration of the nature of tea tannin, about which so much misunderstanding seems to exist.

COMPOSITION OF TEA

The amount of solid material dissolved out of the leaves when tea is made is extremely small, so that from the point of view of nutrient value tea taken without milk or sugar may be considered merely as water. There are, however, certain soluble bodies in the leaves such as tea-tannin, theine or, as it is commonly called, caffeine, important mineral salts and volatile oils; the last named, though they are present only in very small quantities, may have an appreciable influence on the palate and on the function of the digestive and nervous system.

The physiological action on the human body of an infusion of tea when compared with hot water depends almost entirely on the tea-tannin, the caffeine, and the volatile oils which this beverage contains. To appreciate the effect that tea may have on the body, it is important that the essential action of these substances should be understood.

(1) CAFFEINE

Caffeine is contained in both tea and coffee in very small quantities and is the body to which the stimulating effects of these beverages are due.

The stimulating action of caffeine is exerted chiefly on the nervous system. It increases what may be called nervous alacrity, decreases nervous fatigue, and, while its influence prevails, improves the capacity both for mental and physical work. Physiological experiments have shown that after the administration of caffeine in amounts of 5 to 10 grains, the time occupied by nervous processes is shortened and reflex excitability is increased. Caffeine stimulates the heart through the cardiac centre and probably has a direct action as well. The increased force and frequency of the heart action when caffeine is given in large doses may induce a profuse flow of urine and aid in the removal of waste products.

(2) VOLATILE OILS

The volatile oils in tea have not as yet been fully investigated. They are known to act as cerebral and cardiac stimulants. They are present only in minute quantities and contain some 50 per cent. of a furfurol alcohol, with minute quantities of valerianic acid, phenol, pyridine, and nitrogenous aromatic substances.

The pharmacological effect of tea oils *per se* has been shown to be local irritation and reflex stimulation, as in the case of condiments.

(3) TANNIN
CHEMICAL RELATIONSHIP OF TEA TANNIN AND OTHER TANNINS

The bulk of evidence points conclusively to the fact that Tea Tannin is a separate entity, and certainly is not the same as the British Pharmacopœia tannic acid.

In discussing the action of tea in the alimentary tract, it is common for critics of the beverage to refer to tannin as though it were a single substance instead of a large group of widely different substances. Present-day chemists use the term as a generic one to denote a large body of substances, which have certain properties in common. Tannins are vegetable substances occurring in the higher plants. They are found in the bark of some plants, in the wood, leaf or pods of others. They are mostly uncrystallizable colloidal substances, soluble in water, slightly acidic, and showing astringent properties. They precipitate gelatine from solution and form insoluble compounds with gelatine-yielding tissues, a property which enables some of them to convert hide into leather.

The tannins are a very heterogeneous class of chemical substances, but in general have been primarily divided into two main groups based on the fact that on dry distillation tannin materials give either derivatives of gallic acids or catechol. The tannin of the Pharmacopæia, usually called "Acid tannicum", is a pyrogallic tannin. It is moderately strong as an acid. In regard to the tea tannin, on the other hand, it has for many years been generally recognized as a substance quite different from the B.P. Ac. Tannicum in action and constitution, but around which much discussion has centred as to whether it is a pyrogallic or a catechol tannin. The most recent researches of Maitland (*Analyst*, 1936, 61, p. 228) and, to a certain extent, Nierenstein (*Analyst* 1936, 61, p. 294), however, seem to indicate that tea tannin is a combination of gallic acid on a basic catechol group. It is a much weaker acid than the gallic acid. Evidence that the strong gallic derivatives used commercially for tannin have fundamentally a quite different formula construction, has also been put forward.

Acidum Tannicum is about twenty-five times stronger as an acid than tea tannin. Both these acidities, however, are weak compared with that of the stomach juice, which shows a pH value of about 1·5.

It is perhaps not so well appreciated as it should be that, as is shown in the following table, many beverages besides tea depend for their palatability on the presence of tannin; for instance, beer (hops), cider, wines and cocoa.

	TANNIN grams per 100 c.c.
Tea (5 minutes' infusion)	0.26
Beer	minute trace (0.01 or under)
Cider	0.05—0.50
Wines	0.01 up to 0.34
Cocoa (7.5 grams with 100 c.c. water)	0.36

Tea-tannin causes the pungency and gives taste to the tea. It is considered an astringent, the action of which is purely localized. Its pharmacological effect is due to its precipitation of albumen and other proteins. It may be said to exhibit the chief properties of tannin, except that it has no true tanning power. However, such clinical experiments as have been undertaken tend to suggest that, whereas acidum Tannicum has an astringent action and medically is used for this purpose, tea-tannin has a very much milder effect.

The amount of caffeine and tea-tannin in tea is quite small. Normally, a teacupful of ordinary strength infused for five minutes contains about one grain of caffeine and twice as much tea-tannin. Indian and Ceylon teas are somewhat richer in all the chief ingredients than China teas. Green tea is richer in tea-tannin than black tea, but the amount of caffeine in the two is almost the same. The chief difference between black and green tea is that the former is fermented whereas the latter is not. One of the main results of fermentation is to render the tannin less soluble, so that an infusion of green tea contains more unchanged tea-tannin than an infusion of black tea.

THE IMPORTANCE OF INFUSION

Although tea varies in character as regards its chemical constituents, the composition of the infusion is of much greater practical importance than that of the leaves from which it is made. If tea is infused for five minutes, about one-eighth of the weight of the leaf goes in solution; if it is infused for ten minutes about one-third becomes dissolved. In making a large cupful of tea ($\frac{3}{4}$ pint) about $\frac{1}{8}$ oz. of dried leaf usually is employed, and a cupful of such tea contains in solution about 15 grains of solid matter. The bulk of this is made up of gummy matters and extractives, the most important ingredients being caffeine and tea-tannin.

The caffeine is so soluble that it is practically all dissolved out of the leaf immediately infusion has begun. With tea-tannin this is not the case. Experimental work by Hughes, Hale-White, Dittman, Hutchison, and many others has shown that the longer tea is infused the higher is the proportion of tea-tannin content that is dissolved out.

THE EFFECT ON THE DIGESTION OF A CUP OF TEA

A study of the literature on Tea had made it apparent that although, in the past, extensive

A warning. In 1524 two Persian Doctors who had dared to impugn coffee as injurious to health were hanged by the Sultan's order!

laboratory investigations had been undertaken at various times, little scientific work had been done to elucidate the problems associated with the cup of tea.

In consequence, a special investigation was recently undertaken to study the effect that the drinking of tea has on man. One of its special objects was to find out if the cup of tea, as usually drunk with milk and sugar, was harmful to the individual. The detail of the scheme was drawn up with the particular purpose of providing evidence for or against the harmlessness of tea-drinking rather than for a portrayal of any good or pleasurable effects that tea may have on the individual. It was realized at the outset that the investigation, which was intended to be of short duration and relatively simple in nature, would be of more value if it provided evidence for the harmlessness of tea by giving negative results, or for its harmfulness by producing positive unpleasant results, than by giving positive information as to its beneficial and pleasurable effects.

The scheme submitted for the investigation was divided into two parts; the first was to be clinical in character and to be concerned with the detailed study of the individual before and after drinking a cup of tea. It was to be concerned with the effects on the human body of tea of several kinds made in different ways and taken in varying amounts. Also, it was to compare the effect on digestion of tea with that of some of its individual components such as caffeine and tannin, and with other beverages such as hot water, milk and coffee. The second part was to be a laboratory investigation in which the composition of tea, the analysis of different teas, and the effects of their various components on the stomach juices *in vitro* were to be studied. In both parts of the investigation particular attention was given to the belief that tea is harmful on account of its tannin content.

CLINICAL INVESTIGATION

A series of observations and tests were made on a group of individuals consisting of young men and women in normal health. They were kept under detailed observation and their food and drink was carefully controlled. Standard quantities of tea and other fluids were given them. A careful note was made in every instance of the presence or absence of certain well-defined subjective signs or symptoms noted by the subject of the experiment and of certain objective signs noted by the investigator. In addition, radiographic examination of the gastro-intestinal tract was made with special reference to the emptying time of the stomach after taking different beverages. An analysis of the results of these observations showed that generally hot water was drunk without causing discomfort; when caffeine alone or B.P. tannin alone was added to the water and the mixture drunk, marked discomfort and sickness ensued. When both caffeine and B.P. tannin were added to hot water, however, no discomfort followed.

Tea, made rather stronger than is usually taken, infused 3 minutes, and drunk without the addition of milk, caused no discomfort when good quality was used, but if poor quality tea was used, slight discomfort followed.

When milk and sugar were added to a 3-minute infusion of any of the teas which were tested, no unpleasant symptoms followed.

When a 10-minute infusion of any of the teas was drunk without milk, complaint was generally made of marked discomfort. The discomfort was less, however, with good quality tea than with poor quality. On adding milk and sugar to the 10-minute infusion, no complaint was made after drinking good quality tea.

In summarizing briefly the results of these observations, one may state that the addition of milk and sugar allayed any unpleasant effects of any tea even when an excessive infusion of 10 minutes was drunk. A pure 3-minute infusion of tea could be drunk without causing symptoms. Good quality Indian-Ceylon and good quality China tea reacted on the individuals in quite similar ways.

LABORATORY INVESTIGATION

This investigation was undertaken:

(1) To compare the effects of different kinds of tea on the digestive ferments.

(2) To study the effect of the addition of milk to tea, and to find out if any changes resulting from the effect of tea on the digestive ferments were altered or modified by the addition of milk.

It was found that the effect of tea on salivary (diastatic) digestion was extremely small when the laboratory experiments copied accurately the alkalinity of the salivary juices. That is, if there was a sufficient amount of sodium bicarbonate present, no effects were noted. If not buffered to alkalinity in this way a small decrease in diastatic activity was noted in quantitive relationship to the tannin present. Caffeine was found to produce no changes. Milk (a substance containing the amphoteric proteins) acted as buffering agent in maintaining alkalinity as does sodium bicarbonate, and being a protein forms an insoluble compound with tannin if the pH becomes on the unfavourable acid side.

Five points were derived from the study of the effect of tea on gastric (peptic) digestion:

(1) Tea-tannin had a definite effect in reducing peptic digestion.
(2) This was a function of the quantity of the tea-tannin present.
(3) It was entirely subjective to the acidity and buffering properties present in the mixtures.
(4) It was very satisfactorily countered by the addition of milk to the tea.
(5) It was only within the range of acidity of the normal fasting stomach that tea-tannin had the above effect.

In vivo, when the stomach is stimulated, the acidity is raised and the deleterious effects, if any, of the tea-tannin become negligible and absent. The astringent action of tea *per se* is sufficient *in vivo* to stimulate the gastric mucosa, thus to raise the acidity beyond the danger point of tea-tannin.

In the study of the effect of tea on the pancreatic (lipolytic) digestion, no changes were noted if the solutions were kept well buffered to alkalinity. Lipase splits fat into glycerin and acid. If the latter was sufficient to produce acidity of the whole solution, the tannin from the tea became effective in destroying or inhibiting the lipolytic action of the enzymes. Milk was found to act as a buffering agent, as in the salivary digestive experiments.

The conclusions that were drawn from the laboratory experiments were that tea without milk, or other food, under certain conditions, may definitely affect the digestive processes. These conditions but rarely occur in healthy persons. Milk is found to be a completely satisfactory antidote.

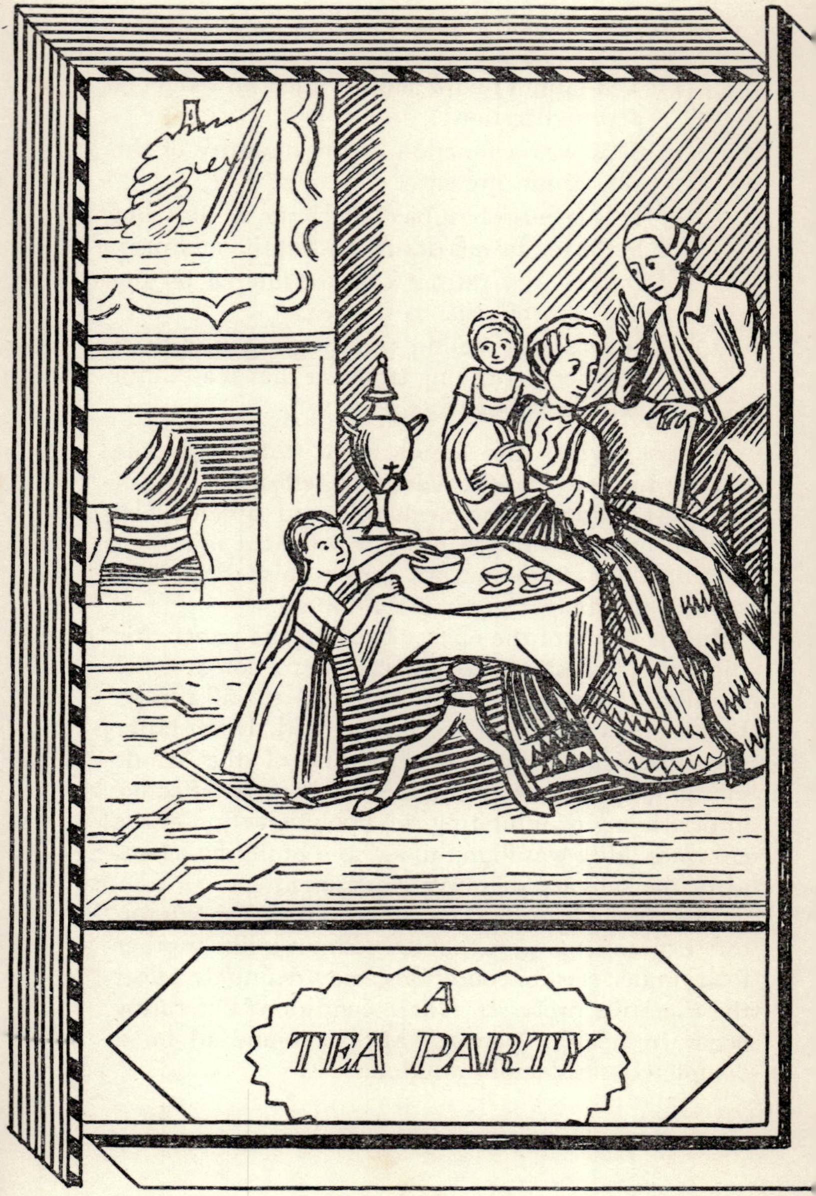
A
TEA PARTY

CONCLUSIONS SUMMARIZED

It was concluded from the study that tea-drinking is harmless. The clinical observations show that the cup of tea as normally drunk has no ill effects on the human body. The laboratory tests link up intimately with the clinical observations. They indicate that under certain laboratory conditions tea may have definitely deleterious effects on the digestive processes, but when the laboratory conditions copy closely those that are present in normal, healthy persons, these effects do not arise.

In health, when the stomach is stimulated, the acidity is raised, and any harmful effects that the tea may have become negligible or absent. The astringent action of tea *per se* is sufficient *in vivo* to stimulate the gastric secretions and thus to raise the acidity beyond the danger point of tannin, remembering that tea-tannin bears no close relation either in its composition or action to the Tannic acid of the Pharmacopœia.

Further, under all the clinical and laboratory conditions that have been investigated, the unpleasant effects that occurred when certain teas were improperly prepared have been nullified by the addition of milk.

The practical inferences which may be drawn from the clinical and laboratory observations and experiments which have been undertaken show that tea as it is normally drunk is not harmful.

In conclusion, both clinical and laboratory investigations bring out the fact that such few ill-effects as may occur from tea-drinking are the result of excessive consumption and bad preparation.

Finally, certain points of immediate interest will be tabulated:

(1) Good tea, properly made, is in every way harmless.

(2) Poor tea, badly made, may have slightly unpleasant effects.

(3) Good India, Ceylon or Java-Sumatra tea produces no other symptoms and signs and no more harmful effects than does good China tea.

(4) If milk is added to the cup of tea, even the effects of excessive consumption and bad preparation are counteracted.

From the foregoing it will be realized that there is no need for a Doctor to delete tea from any patient's diet, providing it is taken in the ways recommended here. Tea does not harm the human frame; and in good tea you have the very best of its refreshing qualities.

The erroneous impression that good tea properly made may be harmful to the digestion owing to its tannin content has recently gained considerable ground owing to the claims made on behalf of some packet teas that they are 'tanninless'. On this point, however, the report in the *Lancet* of February 15th, 1936, of a communication by Mr. H. H. Bagnall, B.Sc., F.I.C., City Analyst of Birmingham, made at the meeting of the Society of Public Analysts at Burlington House on February 5th, 1936, deserves particular attention.

At this meeting Mr. Ainsworth Mitchell, D.Sc., F.I.C., read a communication from Mr. H. H. Bagnall, B.Sc., F.I.C., City Analyst of Birmingham, in which he spoke of the results of his analyses of a number of packet teas whose wrappers bore various claims, mainly in the direction of preventing or curing digestive disorders because of the absence from the teas of tannin. In every case those claims were unsupported by scientific fact. In the alleged tannin-free teas he found from 9.9 to 16.4 per cent of tannin, the average of a series being 12.5 per cent. Two China teas contained 8.6 per cent of tannin. In many cases a representation to the firms of the error in the claims made resulted in modification of the wording on the packets.

This report shows that in the packets analysed by Mr. Bagnall the tannin content was the same as the average tannin content of ordinary teas of the same class, e.g. Indian or China. Mr. Bagnall obviously does not profess to have made an exhaustive examination of every type of tea for which 'tanninless' claims are made, and it may be, therefore, that there are some such teas not analysed by him which have a lower tannin content than those which he analysed, but the results of his examination clearly show that discrimination should be exercised in accepting the claims of so-called 'tanninless' teas and the implied suggestion that ordinary tea has by comparison a high tannin content and is on that account harmful to the digestion. It is to be hoped that those who prefer a cup of ordinary tea will feel reassured as to their being able to enjoy it without the smallest fear of any harmful effects.

REFERENCES

The Lancet, August 1st, 1908. 'A Controversy about Tea', page 325.

Hutchison, R. 'Food and the Principles of Dietetics', Edward Arnold & Co., 1933.

The Lancet, ii, 1911, page 1573.

Bannister, Cantor Lectures, 1890.

Schumburg, Archiv. f. Anat. und Physiol., 1899. Sup. Bd. 289.

Cushny, 'Pharmacology and Therapeutics of the Action of Drugs'. 8th Edition, J. & A. Churchill.

'The Chemistry and Pharmacology of a Cup of Tea', Carpenter and Harler.

Indian Tea Association *Quarterly Journal*, Part I, 1932.

The Lancet, Feb. 15, 1936. Tea and Coffee, page 387.

Analyst, 1936. Vol. 61.

Report of Clinical and Laboratory Investigations on Tea, 1934, prepared for the Empire Tea Market Expansion Board.

III. THE RULES FOR CHOOSING AND SERVING WHAT IS BEST

TEA MANUFACTURE

TEA, whether green or black, is made from new young shoots consisting of leaves and buds that have just grown and are only a few days old.

In making green tea these young shoots are rapidly heated and then twisted and dried. But in order to make black tea, a more complicated process of manufacture has to be followed. The young shoots are first spread out on racks or trays so that they may become partially dry and flaccid like a kid glove. When they have attained this condition, the shoots are rolled by machines so that the leaves are twisted in the same way as a spill of paper. In this process, some of the juice is squeezed on to the outside of the leaves. The twisted shoots are then spread out in a cool place in contact with the air so that the juices may absorb oxygen. During this process—which is controlled by enzymes—the juices of the leaf become coloured and the shoots take on the coppery-red look of a new penny. Next—the shoots are collected and quickly heated and dried. At this stage the tea becomes black, resuming its reddish colour again on being wetted with water. The shoots being dry, the sorting of the tea into grades is carried out. Unopened buds—which are now often of a golden colour—together with the youngest leaves,

History often omits to record that Dr. Johnson was, like most English people of his century, a connoisseur of quality and correct making. Here is a supposed portrait, after Zoffany, of the great man taking his dish of tea by the riverside with the Garricks.

are separated to form the finest grades. The older leaves form the lower grades. In some cases grades are made up of twisted but unbroken leaves, but in other cases the leaves are broken. Whole leaf and broken teas are used both for the finest and the poorer quality teas.

'LIE' TEA

In early days, tea was made in large quantities and drawn off, like beer, as required. An impost of 8d.

a gallon was levied on this draught tea, and 'ill-disposed traders' took every opportunity of making it go farther by adulteration. In the reigns of the first three Georges laws were passed against this practice, but by Queen Victoria's time fresh legislation was necessary. The collection of used tea-leaves from hotels and restaurants had become quite a thriving industry; factories existed for dyeing and drying the remains and turning them, with the help of horse-chestnut foliage, blacklead and indigo, into new tea at 20s. a pound. The Chinese, too, were adepts at imitations of tea. The hands of many Eastern workmen grew green from mixing 'Lie' tea —for which leaves were 'faced' with a mixture of Prussian blue and gypsom.

To-day, however, adulteration is a thing of the past and tea is a pure product. The standards observed by world-producers are very high, and as an additional safeguard every single consignment coming into any British port is strictly examined by the Customs.

GOOD TEA

Perhaps we are not quite so discerning as past generations as to the rival merits of Orange Pekoe, Bohea and Souchong. But in actual fact the finest tea in the world is within reach of everyone's purse to-day. The production and blending of quality teas has been brought to a fine art. For a few shillings extra on the annual budget, the poorest household can secure the best quality India, Ceylon or Java-Sumatra tea. It is an axiom of the tea-trade that the better the tea the better it is for you, and the more

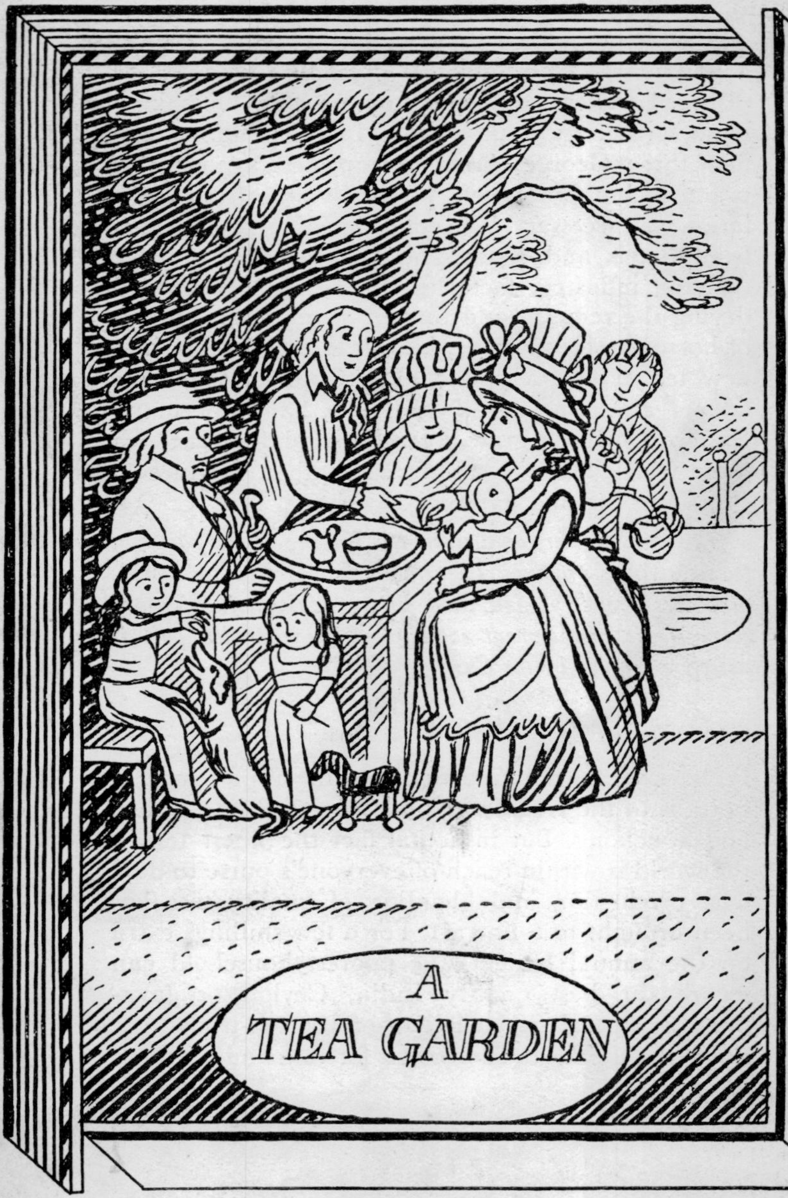
A
TEA GARDEN

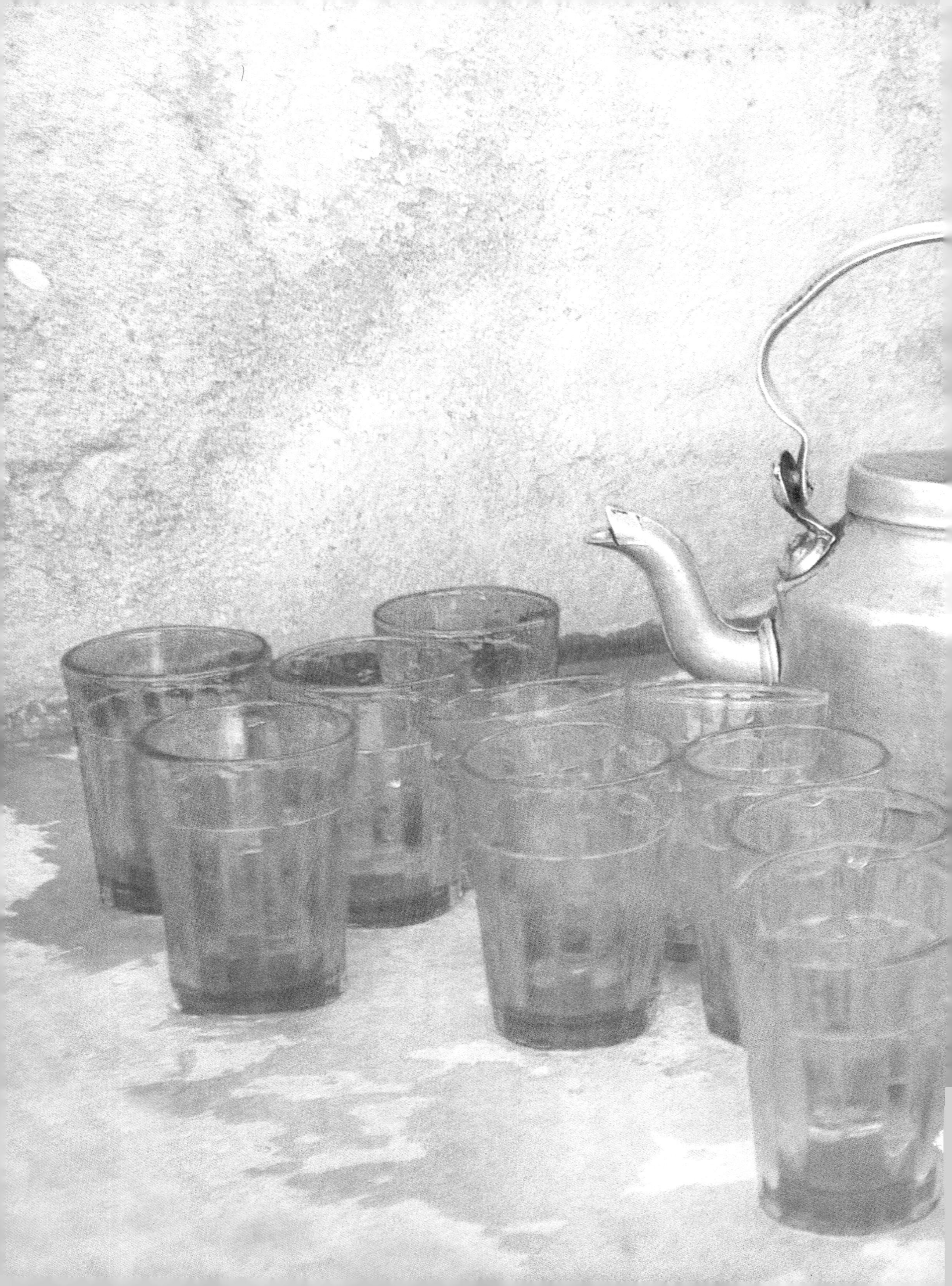

BY APPOINTMENT TO HER MAJESTY THE QUEEN
BL CARS LIMITED · BIRMINGHAM
MANUFACTURERS OF ROVER CARS, LAND-ROVERS,
RANGE ROVERS AND AUSTIN CARS

BY APPOINTMENT TO HER MAJESTY QUEEN ELIZABETH
THE QUEEN MOTHER
BL CARS LIMITED · COVENTRY AND BIRMINGHAM
MANUFACTURERS OF DAIMLER, JAGUAR AND ROVER CARS
AND LAND-ROVERS

BY APPOINTMENT
TO H R H THE PRINCE OF WALES
LAND ROVER LIMITED · SOLIHULL
MANUFACTURERS OF MOTOR VEHICLES

LAND ROVER
Series 2 & 2A

REPAIR OPERATION MANUAL

AKM8159

Published by
Land Rover Ltd
A Managing Agent for Land Rover UK Limited
PUBLICATION No. AKM8159 (EDITION 1)

Land Rover Limited
Lode Lane
Solihull
West Midlands
B92 8NW
England

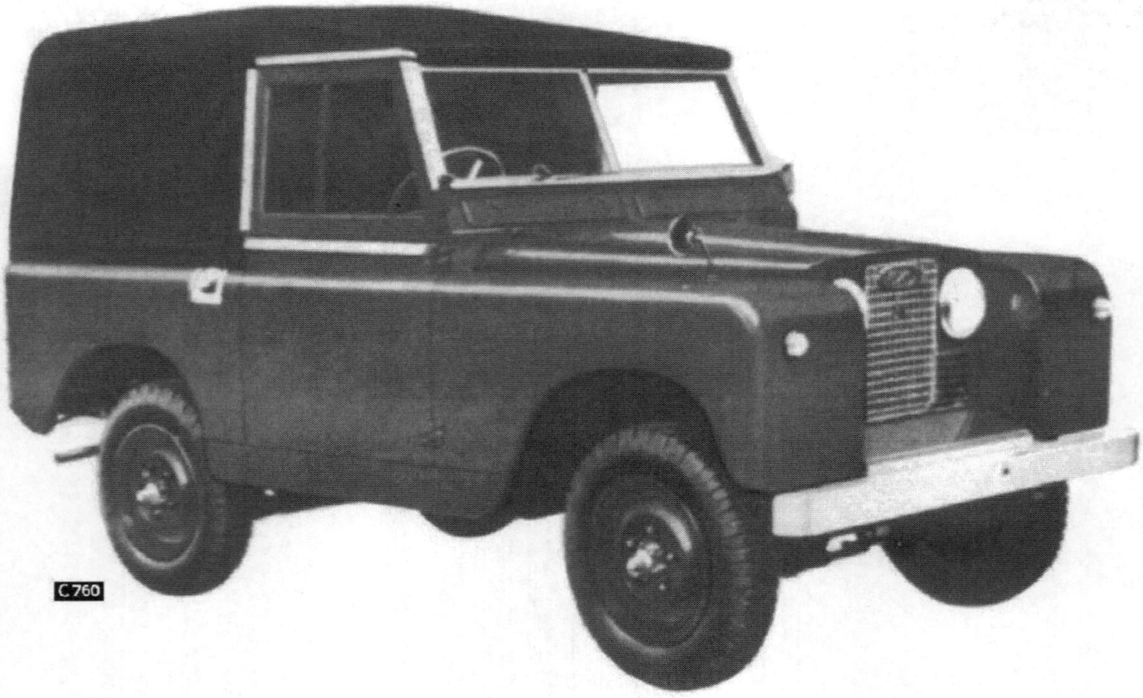
C760

LAND-ROVER 88

(88 inch—2,23 m—wheel base)

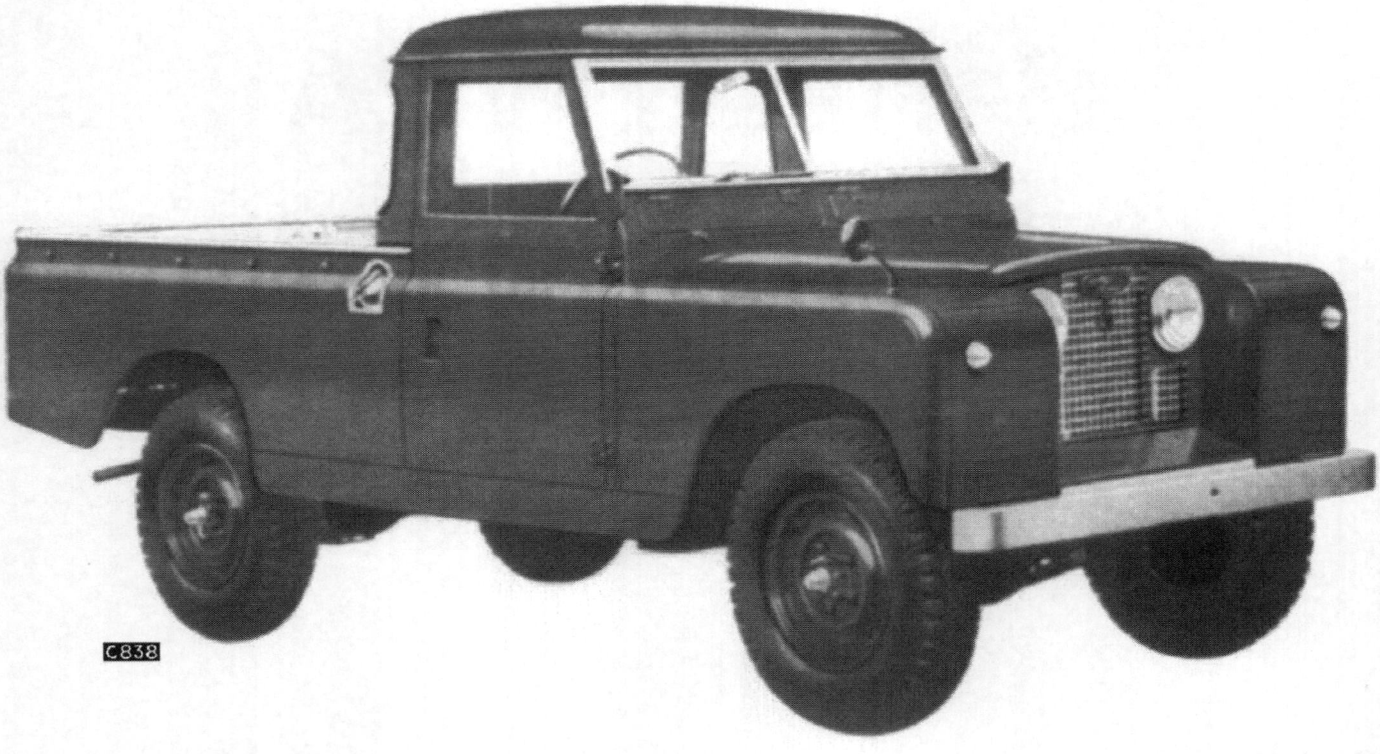
C838

LAND-ROVER 109

(109 inch—2,76 m—wheel base)

The two models shown are typical examples of their range, which are produced with a wide choice of body designs

CONTENTS

	Section	Page
Commencing Vehicle Numbers		4
Introduction		5
Engine - 2¼ Litre Petrol	A-1	6
Engine - 2¼ Litre Diesel	A-2	56
Engine - 2.6 Litre Petrol	A-3	105
Clutch Units	B	148
Gearbox	C	162
Propeller Shafts	D	204
Rear Axle and Suspension	E	208
Front Axle and Suspension	F	233
Steering and Linkage	G	253
Brake System	H	273
Chassis	J	318
Cooling System	K	320
Fuel System	L	328
Exhaust System	M	369
Electrical Equipment	N	373
Instruments and Controls	P	423
Body	Q	434
Wheels and Types	R	462
Lubricants and Services Materials	X	465
Tools	Z	466
Detailed Alphabetical Index		471

COMMENCING VEHICLE NUMBERS

PETROL MODELS, 4 CYLINDER—2¼ LITRE ENGINE

	1958 109 Series II	1959 88 Series II	1960 88 Series II	1961 88 Series II	88 Series IIA
Home, RHStg		141900001	141000001	141100001	24100001A
Export, RHStg		142900001	142000001	142100001	24200001A
Export, RHStg, CKD		143900001	143000001	143100001	24300001A
Export, LHStg		144900001	144000001	144100001	24400001A
Export, LHStg, CKD		145900001	145000001	145100001	24500001A

	1958 109 Series II	1959 109 Series II	1960 109 Series II	1961 109 Series II	109 Series IIA
Home, RHStg	151800001	151900001	151000001	151100001	25100001A
Export, RHStg	152800001	152900001	152000001	152100001	25200001A
Export, RHStg, CKD	153800001	153900001	153000001	153100001	25300001A
Export, LHStg	154800001	154900001	154000001	154100001	25400001A
Export, LHStg, CKD	155800001	155900001	155000001	155100001	25500001A

	Series IIA
Home, RHStg, 88 Station Wagon	31500001B
Export, RHStg, 88 Station Wagon	31600001B
Export, RHStg, CKD, 88 Station Wagon	31700001B
Export, LHStg, 88 Station Wagon	31800001B
Export, LHStg, CKD, 88 Station Wagon	31900001B

From March 1965 onwards. Vehicle numbers prior to this date are the same as for 88

	1959 Series II	1960 Series II	1961 Series II	Series IIA
Home, RHStg, 109 Station Wagon	161900001	161000001	161100001	26100001A
Export, RHStg, 109 Station Wagon	162900001	162000001	162100001	26200001A
Export, RHStg, CKD, 109 Station Wagon	163900001	163000001	163100001	26300001A
Export, LHStg, 109 Station Wagon	164900001	164000001	164100001	26400001A
Export, LHStg, CKD, 109 Station Wagon	165900001	165000001	165100001	26500001A

PETROL MODELS, 6 CYLINDER—2.6 LITRE ENGINE

	109 Series IIA
Home, RHStg	34500001D
Export, RHStg	34600001D
Export, RHStg, CKD	34700001D
Export, LHStg	34800001D
Export, LHStg, CKD	34900001D

	Series IIA
Home, RHStg, 109 Station Wagon	35000001D
Export, RHStg, 109 Station Wagon	35100001D
Export, RHStg, CKD, 109 Station Wagon	35200001D
Export, LHStg, 109 Station Wagon	35300001D
Export, LHStg, CKD, 109 Station Wagon	35400001D

DIESEL MODELS, 4 CYLINDER—2¼ LITRE ENGINE

	88 Series IIA
Home, RHStg	27100001A
Export, RHStg	27200001A
Export, RHStg, CKD	27300001A
Export, LHStg	27400001A
Export, LHStg, CKD	27500001A

	109 Series IIA
Home, RHStg	27600001A
Export, RHStg	27700001A
Export, RHStg, CKD	27800001A
Export, LHStg	27900001A
Export, LHStg, CKD	28000001A

	Series IIA
Home, RHStg, 88 Station Wagon	32000001B
Export, RHStg, 88 Station Wagon	32100001B
Export, RHStg, CKD, 88 Station Wagon	32200001B
Export, LHStg, 88 Station Wagon	32300001B
Export, LHStg, CKD, 88 Station Wagon	32400001B

From March 1965 onwards. Vehicle numbers prior to this date are the same as for 88

	Series IIA
Home, RHStg, 109 Station Wagon	28100001A
Export, RHStg, 109 Station Wagon	28200001A
Export, RHStg, CKD, 109 Station Wagon	28300001A
Export, LHStg, 109 Station Wagon	28400001A
Export, LHStg, CKD, 109 Station Wagon	28500001A

LOCATION OF CAR AND UNIT NUMBERS

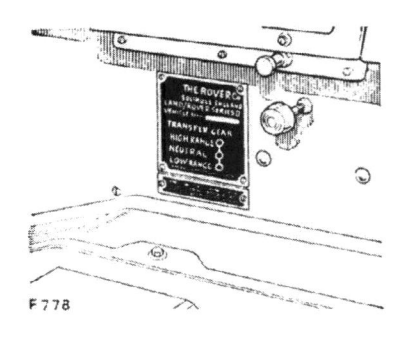

F778

Vehicle and chassis number

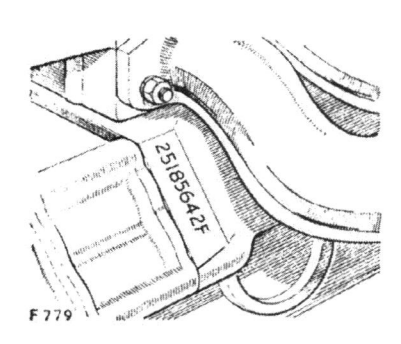

F779

Engine number

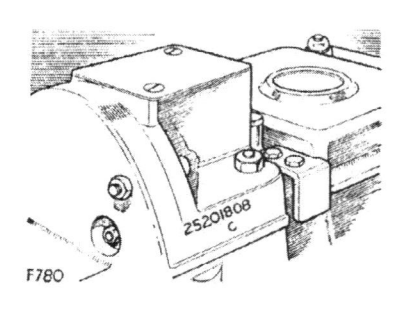

F780

Gearbox number

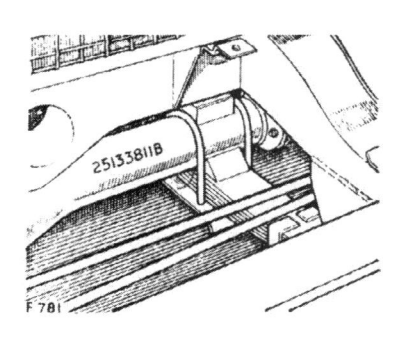

F781

Front and rear axle number

INTRODUCTION

This Manual covers all overhaul and repair procedures for the "basic" Land-Rover; briefly described below, but does not include the use and overhaul of "Optional extra equipment", which is the subject of a separate publication.

The "basic" Land-Rover is produced in two wheel base lengths, 88 inch and 109 inch (2,23 m and 2,76 m), with a choice of three engine types; 2¼ litre - four cylinder Petrol and Diesel and 2.6 litre - six cylinder Petrol. Other equipment, including fuel system, electrical equipment, drive units brakes and body vary according to model and choice.

Identification of a particular model can be made by referring to the vehicle number and the chart on the following page. The Vehicle number is stamped on a plate mounted inside the driving compartment.

Although the Manual applies specifically to Bonneted Control models, most of the overhaul procedures also apply to Forward Control models when the units are removed from the vehicle.

Layout of the Workshop Manual

This Workshop Manual is designed to assist those responsible for the maintenance and overhaul of the Land-Rover. The subject matter is sectionalised as detailed in the General Index, and the pages are numbered within those sections. A further sub-index will be found at the beginning of each section.

Operating instructions and details of routine maintenance will be found in the Owner's Instruction and Maintenance Manuals, a copy of each will be found in the literature pack supplied with the car.

As the Manual covers both Home and Export models, reference is made throughout the text to the 'left-hand' (LH) and 'right-hand' (RH) sides of the vehicle, rather than to 'near-side' and 'off-side'. The 'left-hand side' is that to the left hand when the vehicle is viewed from the rear; similarly, 'left-hand steering' (LHStg) models are those having the driving controls on the left-hand side, again when the vehicle is viewed from the rear.

Measurements

All measurements are given in Imperial measure with US and metric equivalents added where possible, but in certain cases this is not practicable and the Imperial figure must be used.

Workshop technique

When undertaking any overhaul operation, it is advisable to follow a standard technique. which will ultimately save both time and trouble. Prior to dismantling, the unit should be thoroughly cleaned externally and, as the stripping progresses, components washed in paraffin or petrol before setting out in order on a large drip tray. Small parts, such as nuts and bolts, should be placed in boxes to prevent loss, and shims attached to their respective components to facilitate assembly. All joint washers, lockers, tab washers and split pins must be renewed on assembly.

When the unit is finally rebuilt, use only the recommended lubricants. See Section X.

Operation times

These are not included in this Manual and are the subject of a separate publication.

Workshop tools

In order to assist the operator when following details given in this Manual, a list of the tools required for the operation has been included.

In addition, details of any special tools which are necessary, are included in the heading of the operation for which they are required. See also Section Z.

This new edition incorporates all applicable workshop information appertaining to the Land-Rover circulated by means of Land-Rover Service News Letters up to Vol. 3, No. 2.

Section A1—Land-Rover

SECTION A1—2¼ LITRE PETROL ENGINE

INDEX TO OPERATIONS—SECTION A1

Note: A comprehensive detailed index is included at the end of this manual

Description of Listed Operations	Operation Number	
	Remove/Refit	Overhaul
Bonnet panel	A1-1	—
Air cleaner—remove, clean and refit	A1-2	—
Radiator and grille panel assembly	A1-3	—
Front floor	A1-4	—
Engine	A1-5	—
Carburetter	A1-6	Section L
Inlet and exhaust manifolds	A1-7	A1-8
Starter motor	A1-9	Section N
Dynamo	A1-10	Section N
Water pump	A1-11	Section K
Thermostat housing	A1-12	Section K
Fuel pump	A1-13	Section L
Cylinder head	A1-14	—
Engine side covers	A1-15	—
Oil filter, external, to replace element	A1-16	A1-16
Oil filter, external	A1-17	—
Ignition timing procedure	A1-18	Section N
Distributor and drive gears	A1-19	—
Tappet adjustment	A1-20	A1-21
Valve gear, rocker shaft and push rods	A1-22	A1-23
Tappet assemblies	A1-24	—
Engine front cover and oil seal	A1-25	—
Timing chain tensioner	A1-26	—
Timing gears and chain, including valve timing	A1-27	—
Crankcase sump	A1-28	A1-30
Oil pump	A1-29	Section B
Clutch assembly and flywheel	A1-31	—
Rear main bearing oil seal and flywheel housing ..	A1-32	—
Pistons and connecting rods	A1-33	A1-34
Crankshaft and main bearings	A1-35	A1-36
Camshaft	A1-37	—
Cylinder block and camshaft bearings	A1-38	A1-38
Reclamation of flywheel	A1-31	A1-39

Section A1—Land-Rover ENGINE—2¼ LITRE PETROL

This Section concerns remove, refit and overhaul procedures for the 2¼ litre petrol engine.

When carrying out a complete engine overhaul, the section can be worked straight through in the order presented.

Alternatively, the individual operations which form the greater percentage of maintenance work undertaken by Distributors and Dealers, are detailed under appropriate headings, and will be found to be complete in themselves.

Some operations are marked with an asterisk * to indicate that they can be carried out with the engine installed. In all other cases it is necessary to remove the engine unit in order to carry out the work detailed.

Where LH (left-hand) or RH (right-hand) appears in the text, this indicates RH or LH side of vehicle or engine when viewed from the rear.

Brief description of engine

The cylinder block is of cast iron. Re-boring is permitted up to a maximum of .040 in. (1,0 mm) oversize above the standard bore size of 3.562 in. (90,49 mm). Further reclamation is obtained by fitting cylinder liners and boring out to standard bore size. Liners may be re-bored up to .010 in. (0,25 mm) oversize.

The crankshaft is supported by three bearings. The thrust is taken by the centre bearing. The bearings are white-metal lined steel shells.

The camshaft is supported by four bearings and actuates roller type cam followers operating valve rockers through push rods, and lead/tin plated bronze slides. Adjustment is made on the adjusting screws on valve rockers. The bearings are white-metal lined steel shells.

The camshaft is chain driven and a chain tensioner is fitted.

The engine is lubricated by a pressure fed oil system which incorporates a pump located in the crankcase sump and an external full flow oil filter.

Engine component dimensions are provided in the Detail Data at the end of this Section.

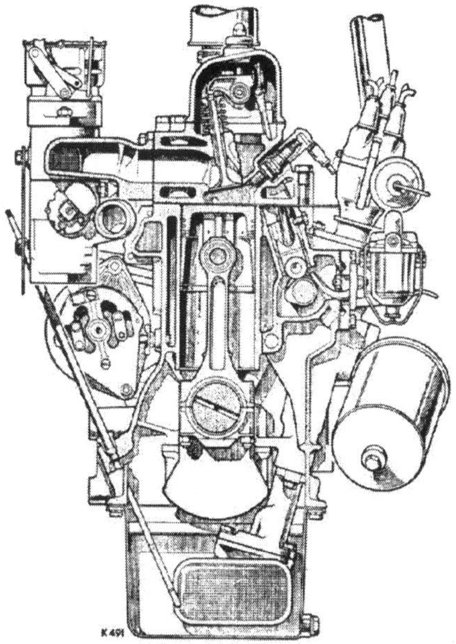

ENGINE—2¼ LITRE PETROL

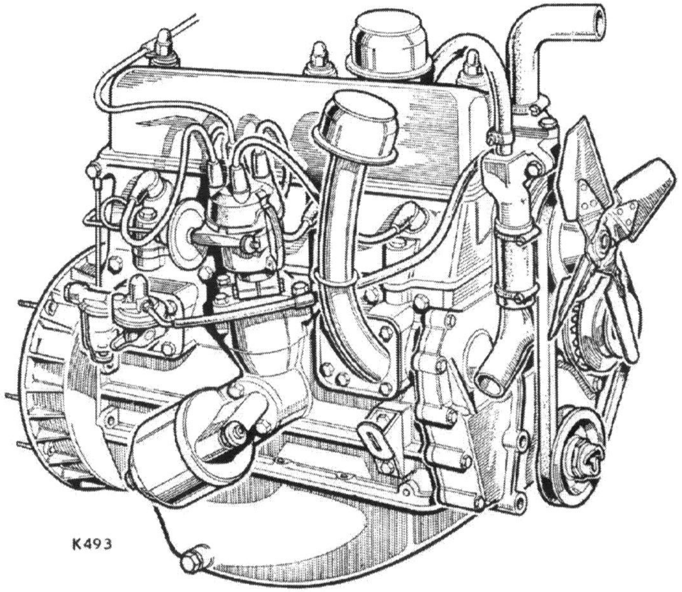

General view of engine, RH side

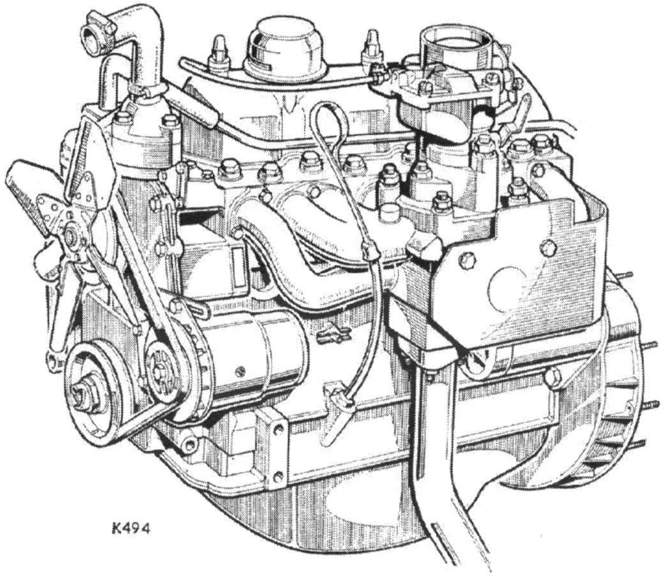

General view of engine, LH side

Cross-section view of engine

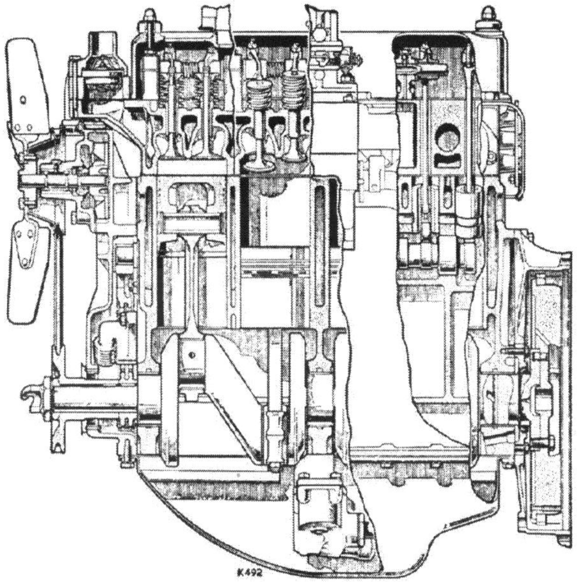

Longitudinal section of engine

ENGINE—2¼ LITRE PETROL — Section A1—Land-Rover

*Bonnet panel, remove and refit—Operation A1-1

Workshop hand tools:
Screwdriver (medium), Pliers

To remove
1. Remove the spare wheel from the bonnet panel, if fitted.
2. Remove fixings at prop rod and bonnet hinge.
3. Remove bonnet panel.

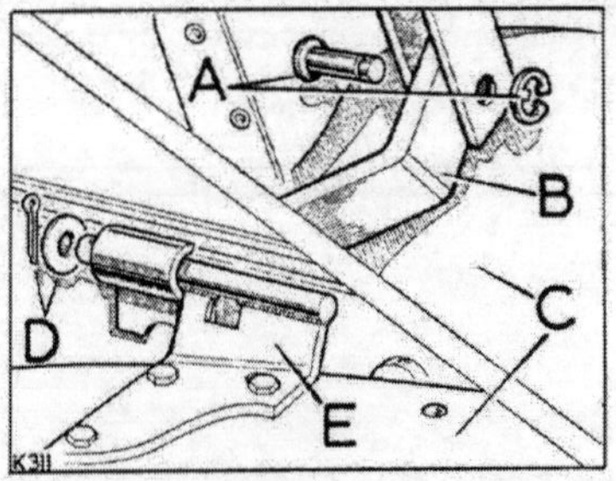

To refit
1. Refit the bonnet panel, using suitable coverings on the wings to avoid damage to paintwork.
2. Refit the spare wheel, if fitted, to bonnet panel.

Fig. A1-1. Fixings at bonnet panel
A—Prop rod fixings
B—Bonnet prop rod
C—Bonnet panel
D—Bonnet hinge fixings, RH side only
E—Bonnet hinge

*Air cleaner, remove, clean and refit—Operation A1-2

Workshop hand tools:
Spanner sizes: 7/16 in. AF open ended
Screwdriver (medium)

To remove
1. Lift and prop bonnet.
2. Remove air intake elbow from carburetter.
3. Slacken the fixings and move aside the retaining strap.
4. Remove air cleaner complete with hose and elbow.

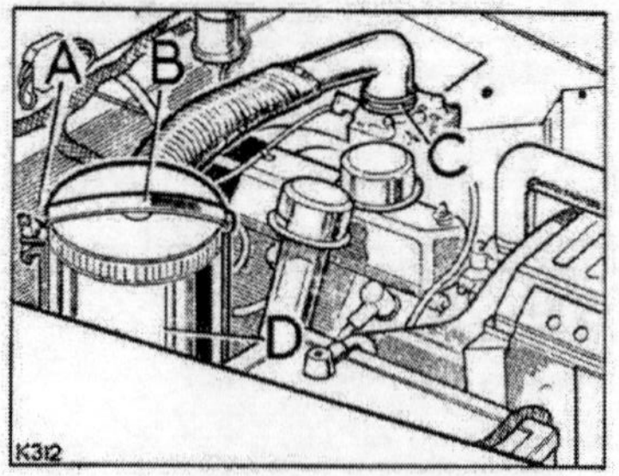

Fig. A1-2. Air cleaner and elbow fixings
A—Retaining strap fixings
B—Air cleaner retaining strap
C—Elbow fixings at carburetter
D—Air cleaner

To dismantle and clean
1. Separate the air cleaner body assembly from the oil container, retained by clips.
2. Drain the oil and withdraw the wire mesh unit.
3. Wash all components in clean fuel.

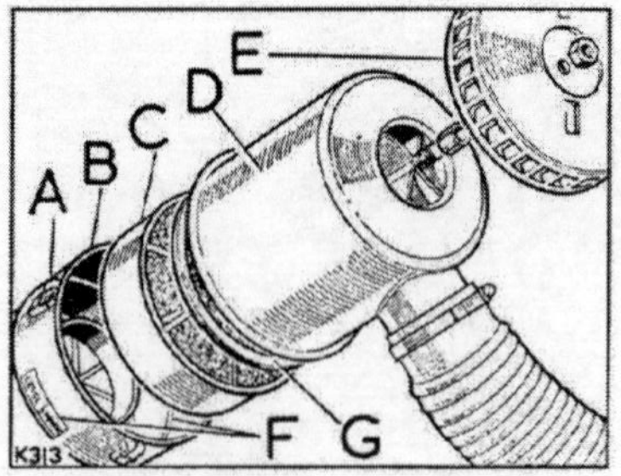

To assemble
1. Fill the oil container with clean engine oil to the oil level mark on the container. See Fig. A1-3.
2. Reverse the dismantling procedure, fitting a new sealing washer between the oil container and the air cleaner body.

To refit
1. Refit the air cleaner and hose; if necessary, reposition the air cleaner body relative to the oil container to prevent the hinged clips from fouling on the retaining strap supports when fitted.
2. When fitting the elbow to the carburetter, ensure that the sealing sleeve is fitted correctly on to the carburetter before tightening clip.

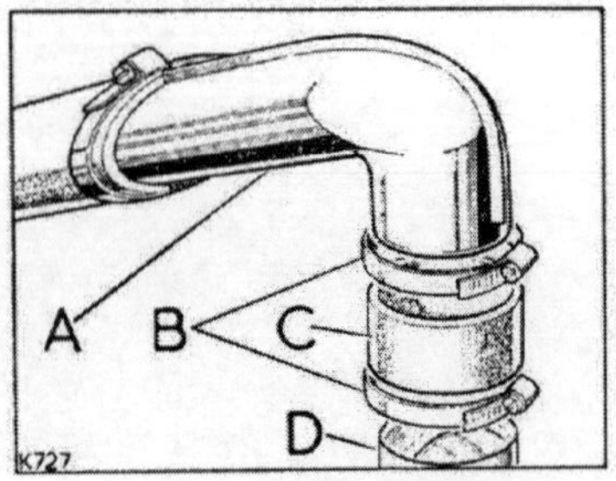

Fig. A1-3. Exploded view of air cleaner
A—Hinged clips
B—Oil container
C—Wire mesh unit
D—Air cleaner and mesh assembly
E—Air intake cap and fixings
F—Oil level mark
G—Sealing washer

Fig. A1-4. Air intake elbow details
A—Elbow
B—Fixing clips
C—Sealing sleeve
D—Carburetter air intake

Operations marked with an asterisk (*) can be carried out with the engine installed in the vehicle

ENGINE—2¼ LITRE PETROL

*Radiator and grille panel assembly, remove and refit—Operation A1-3

Workshop hand tools:
Spanner sizes: 7/16 in. x 1/2 in. AF open ended, 2 off, 2 BA open ended
Screwdriver (medium), Pliers

To remove

1. Remove bonnet panel. Operation A1-1.
2. Disconnect battery leads.
3. Remove front apron panel.

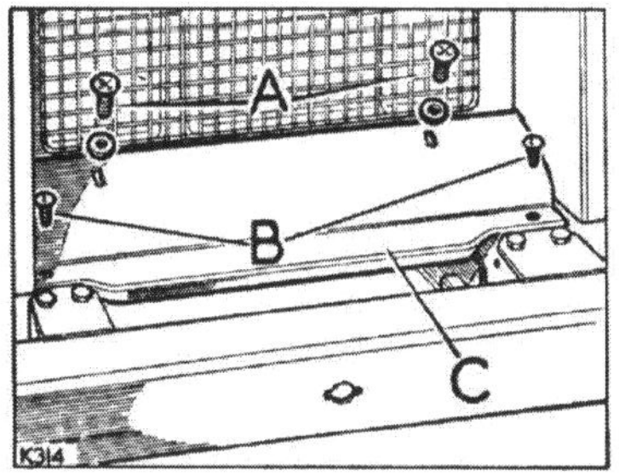

Fig. A1-5. Apron panel fixings

A—Fixings at cross member brackets
B—Fixings at side members
C—Apron panel

4. Remove nameplate and radiator grille.

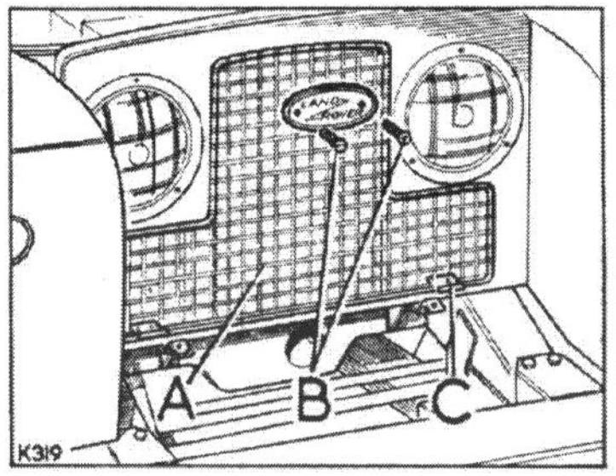

Fig. A1-6. Radiator grille fixings

A—Radiator grille
B—Fixings for nameplate and grille
C—Support brackets

5. Remove radiator cap, drain off coolant.

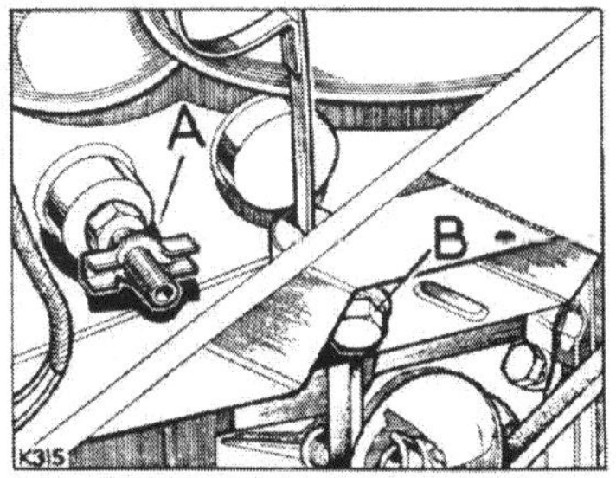

Operations marked with an asterisk (*) can be carried out with the engine installed in the vehicle

Fig. A1-7. Coolant drain points location

A—At engine block
B—At radiator

6. Remove the shroud from the radiator fan cowl.

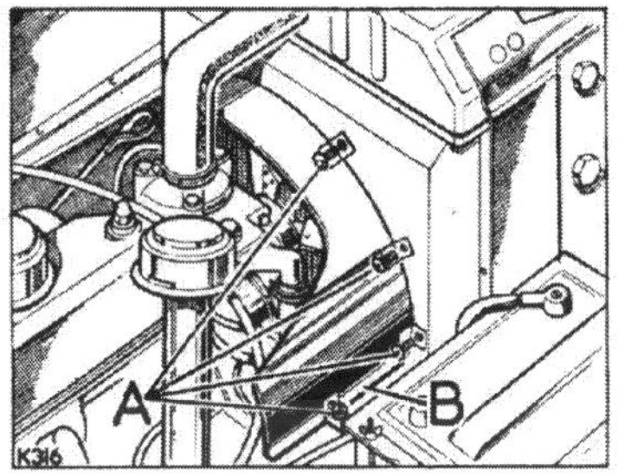

Fig. A1-8. Fan shroud fixings

A—Fixings for shroud
B—Fan shroud

7. Slacken the fixings and detach the radiator coolant hoses.
8. Remove the fan blades fixings and lower fan blades to rest on lower part of fan cowl. Remove the fan blades to rest on lower part of fan cowl. Remove the fan blades when access is obtained during grille panel removal.

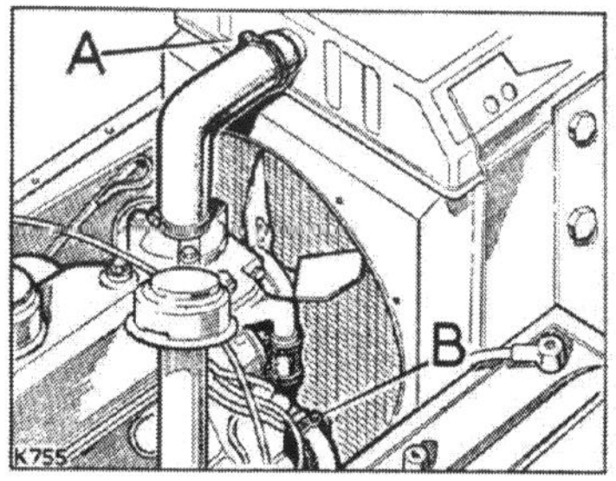

Fig. A1-9. Radiator hose fixings

A—Fixings at top hose
B—Fixings at bottom hose

9. Disconnect the electrical leads for the front lamps at the snap connectors and earth terminal. Withdraw leads clear of grille panel.

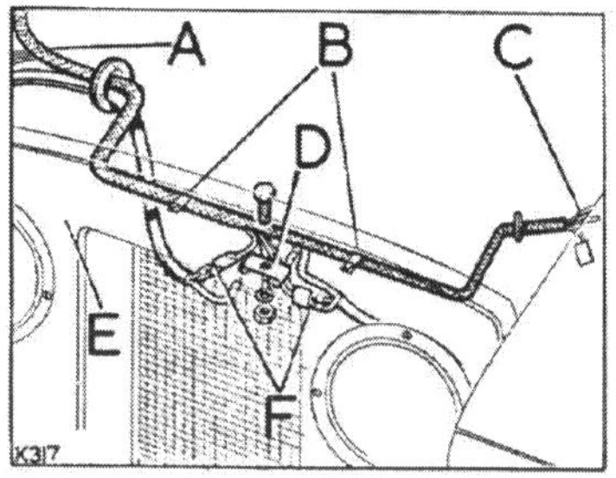

Fig. A1-10. Front lamps electrical leads

A—Electrical leads harness
B—Cable clips for harness
C—Wing lamp leads snap connectors
D—Earth connection
E—Grille panel
F—Headlamp leads snap connectors

10. Remove the grille panel to front wings fixings, the securing nuts and washers are located in the respective wheelarches.

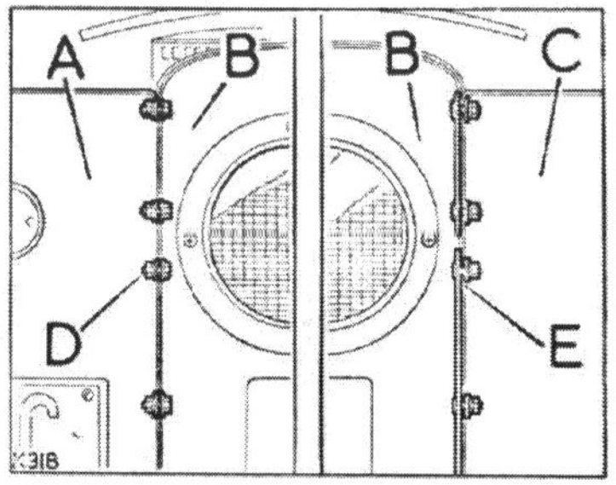

ENGINE—2¼ LITRE PETROL

Operation A1-3—continued

Fig. A1-11. Radiator grille panel fixings

A—Front wing, RH side
B—Radiator grille panel
C—Front wing, LH side
D—Fixings at RH side
E—Fixings at LH side

11. Remove the grille panel fixings at the brackets on the chassis cross member.

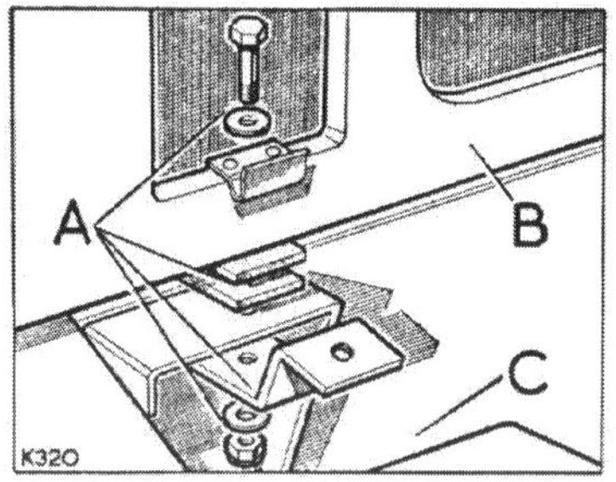

Fig. A1-12. Fixings at chassis cross member

A—Panel fixings
B—Radiator grille panel
C—Chassis cross member

12. Carefully withdraw the assembly and the previously released fan blades from the engine compartment.

To refit

1. Position the radiator and grille panel assembly on to the vehicle. Fit the fan blades to the fan pulley before engaging the grille panel fixings. See Figs. A1-11 and A1-12 for fixings details.

ENGINE—2¼ LITRE PETROL

Operation A1-3—continued

2. Refit the electrical leads through the grille panel grommets and make the electrical connections at the snap connectors and earth terminal, referring to the appropriate circuit diagram, Section N.

3. Refill the engine coolant system, allowing a full flow through the drain taps before closing them. See Fig. A1-7 for coolant drain taps location. Fill the radiator header tank to within ½ in. to ¾ in. (12 mm to 19 mm) below the bottom of the filler neck.

4. Refit the front apron panel and reconnect the battery leads.

5. Refit the bonnet panel. Operation A1-1.

COOLANT SYSTEM
Bonneted Control Model, 2¼ Litre Petrol

Capacity	Imperial Unit	US Unit	Litres	Antifreeze	Frost Precaution
88	18 pints	21¾ pints	10.25	33⅓%	—25°F / —32°C
109	18 pints	21¾ pints	10.25	33⅓%	—25°F / —32°C

---

*Front floor, remove and refit—Operation A1-4

Workshop hand tools:
Spanner sizes: ⁷⁄₁₆ in. AF, ⁷⁄₁₆ in. BSF open end, ⁷⁄₁₆ in. AF socket
Screwdriver (medium)

To remove

1. Unscrew the knob and locknut from the transfer gear lever.
2. Remove the fixings and withdraw the dust cover from the transfer gear lever.
3. Unscrew the knob and locknut from the four-wheel drive lever, and withdraw the spring and ferrule.
4. Remove both halves of the front floor board.
5. Remove the gearbox tunnel cover.
6. Remove the gearbox tunnel front panel.

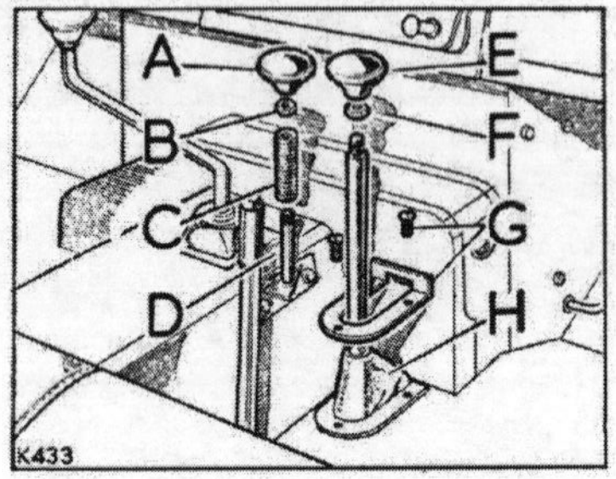

Fig. A1-13. Four wheel drive and transfer levers
A—Knob, four-wheel drive lever E—Knob, transfer gear lever
B—Locknut for knob F—Locknut for knob
C—Spring G—Fixings for dust cover
D—Ferrule H—Dust cover

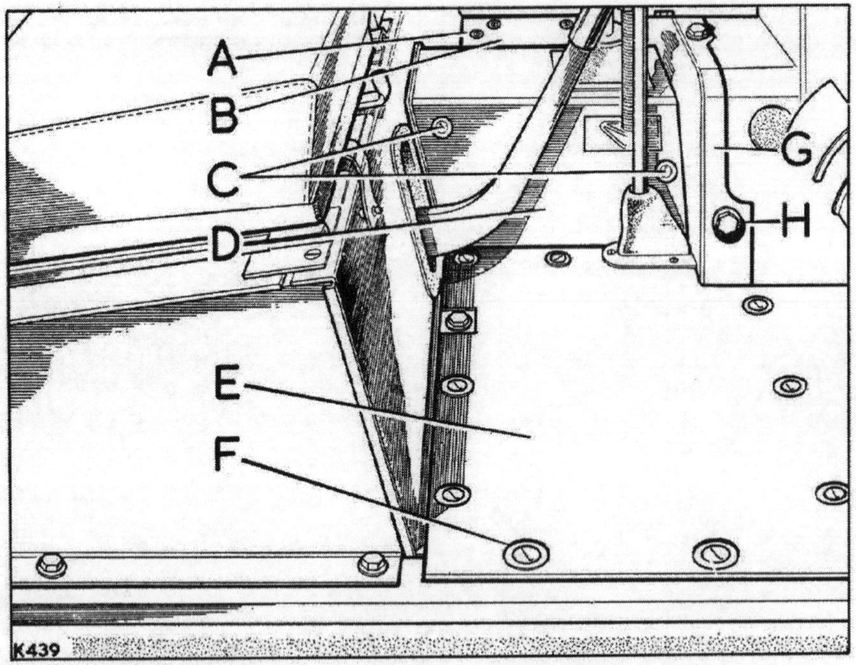

Fig. A1-14. Front floor
A—Fixings (9 off), left-hand floor board E—Floor board, right-hand
B—Floor board, left-hand F—Fixings (12 off), right-hand floor board
C—Fixings (4 off), tunnel cover G—Front panel for gearbox tunnel cover
D—Gearbox tunnel cover H—Fixings (4 off), front panel

Operations marked with an asterisk (*) can be carried out with the engine installed in the vehicle

ENGINE—2¼ LITRE PETROL

Operation A1-4—continued

To refit

1. Reverse the removal procedure, using waterproof sealant between the joint flanges of the front floor and the chassis. A suitable sealant is 'Sealastrip', manufactured by Expandite Ltd., Chase Road, London NW10, England.

2. Adjust the four-wheel drive lever during assembly, as follows: Fit the ferrule, spring and locknut to the lever, depress the lever and adjust the locknut until the compressed spring length is 2 5/16 in. − 1/16 in. (58 mm −1 mm), then fit the knob and tighten the locknut.

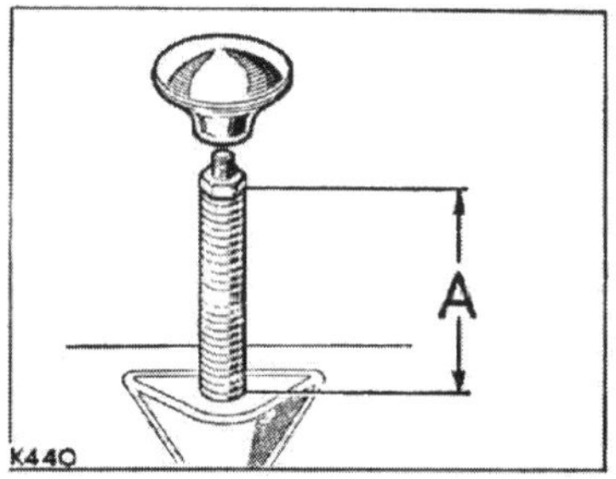

Fig. A1-15. Adjusting four-wheel drive control lever
A—2 5/16 in. −1/16 in. (58 mm −1 mm)

ENGINE—2¼ LITRE PETROL

Engine, remove and refit—Operation A1-5

Workshop hand tools:
Spanner sizes: 7/16 in. x 1/2 in. AF (2 off) open end
9/16 in., 11/16 in. AF open end
7/8 in. AF ring
7/16 in., 9/16 in. AF socket
5/16 in., 3/8 in. BSF open end
2 BA open end
Pliers, Screwdriver (medium)

Special tools:
Lifting sling for engine, Part No. 600963

To remove

1. Remove the bonnet panel. Operation A1-1.
2. Remove air cleaner. Operation A1-2.
3. Remove radiator and grille panel complete. Operation A1-3.
4. Remove the front floor. Operation A1-4.
5. Disconnect the following items at the left-hand side of the engine:
   (a) Front exhaust pipe. Fig. A1-27 refers.
   (b) Heater hoses if fitted.
   (c) Carburetter linkage at ball joint.
   (d) Cold start inner and outer cables at carburetter.
   (e) Distributor leads at ignition coil.
   (f) Engine earth cable. Fig. A1-25 refers.
   (g) Engine mounting rubber upper fixing. Fig. A1-19 refers.

6. Disconnect the following items at the right-hand side of the engine:
   (a) Fuel inlet pipe at fuel pump.
   (b) Battery lead at clip adjacent to fuel pump.
   (c) Starter motor leads at dash panel.
   (d) Dynamo leads at voltage regulator.
   (e) Engine electrical leads at snap connectors adjacent to dash. Fig. A1-21 refers.
   (f) Release disconnected cables from retaining clips at dash panel.
   (g) Release speedometer drive cable from cable clip. If necessary, disconnect the vacuum pipe from the distributor to free the drive cable during engine removal.
   (h) Engine mounting rubber upper fixing. Fig. A1-19 refers.

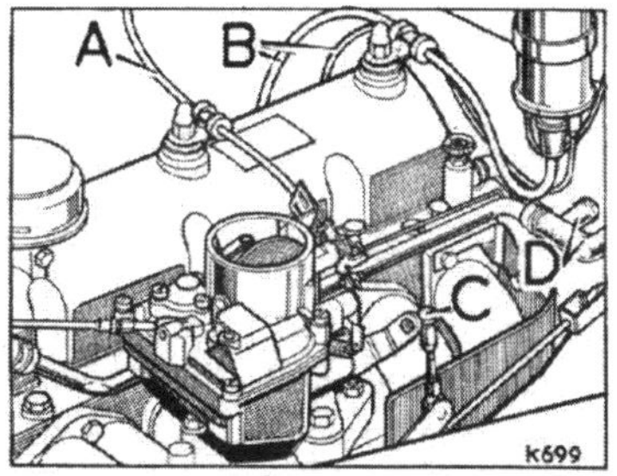

Fig. A1-16. View of engine compartment, LH side
A—Cold start cable
B—Distributor leads
C—Carburetter linkage ball joint
D—Heater hoses, if fitted

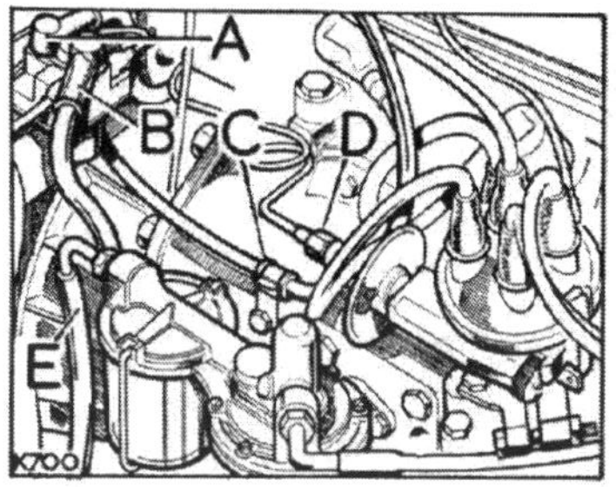

Fig. A1-17. View of engine compartment, RH side, with air cleaner removed
A—Starter leads
B—Battery lead
C—Speedometer drive cable clip
D—Vacuum pipe to distributor
E—Fuel inlet pipe

7. Fit suitable lifting equipment and support the engine weight.

ENGINE—2¼ LITRE PETROL   Section A1—Land-Rover

Operation A1-5—continued

At RH side—remove support bracket fixings as the lower centre fixing on RH suspension rubber is inaccessible when fitted.

9. Lift the engine sufficient to withdraw the LH side suspension rubber and the RH side suspension rubber and bracket complete, then lower engine to its original position to maintain alignment with the gearbox.

10. Remove the fixings securing the bell housing to the flywheel housing.

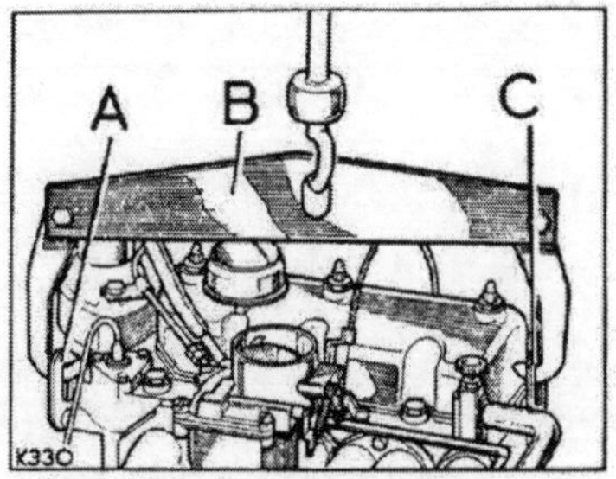

Fig. A1-18. Engine lifting sling in position

A—Front lifting bracket.
B—Lifting sling, Part No. 600963
C—Rear lifting bracket

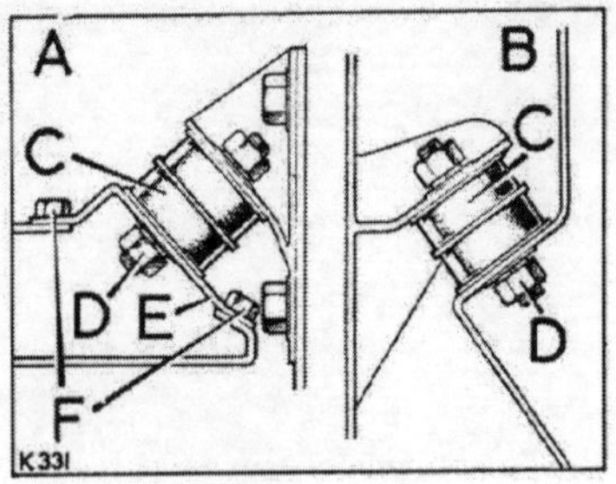

Fig. A1-19. Engine front mounting details

A—LH side mounting
B—RH side mounting
C—Suspension rubbers
D—Lower centre fixing
E—Support bracket at RH side fixing
F—Support bracket fixings

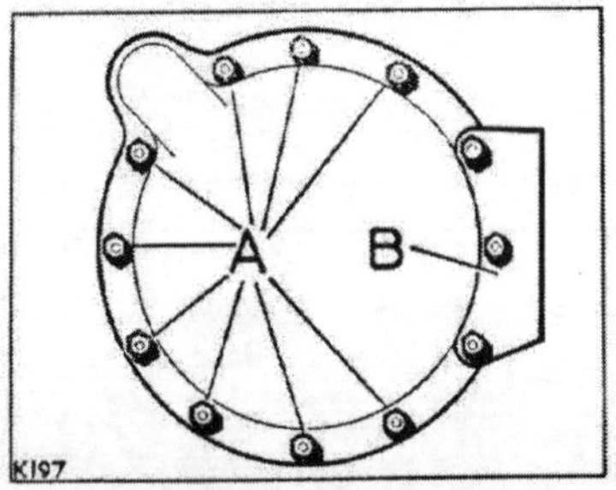

Fig. A1-20. Location of bell housing fixings, view from cab

A—Fixings, bell housing to engine
B—Fixings, clutch slave cylinder mounting

11. Support the gearbox assembly, using a suitable packing block or a jack.

12. Pull the engine forward sufficient to disengage the drive from the gearbox. Ensure that all cables, pipes, etc. are clear then hoist the engine from the vehicle.

Note: Where replacement of engine mounting feet is necessary, if using spring washers in place of the previously used lockplates on the engine mounting feet to cylinder block fixings, torque load the fixings to 80 lb ft.

Section A1—Land-Rover   ENGINE—2¼ LITRE PETROL

Operation A1-5—continued

To refit

1. Engage a gear to prevent gearshaft rotation. Offer engine to gearbox. It may be necessary to rotate the engine sufficient to align the gearbox primary pinion with the clutch plate splines. When aligned, push the engine fully to the rear and secure the bell housing to the flywheel housing, tightening the fixings evenly.

2. Lift the engine sufficient to remove the packing or jack from beneath the gearbox and insert the engine front mounting rubbers.

3. Lower the engine and fit the upper and lower fixings to the engine mountings. Fig. A1-19 refers.

4. Remove the engine lifting sling.

5. Secure the speedometer drive cable in the cable clip adjacent to the fuel pump.

6. Connect the engine electrical leads at the snap connectors at rear RH side of engine compartment.

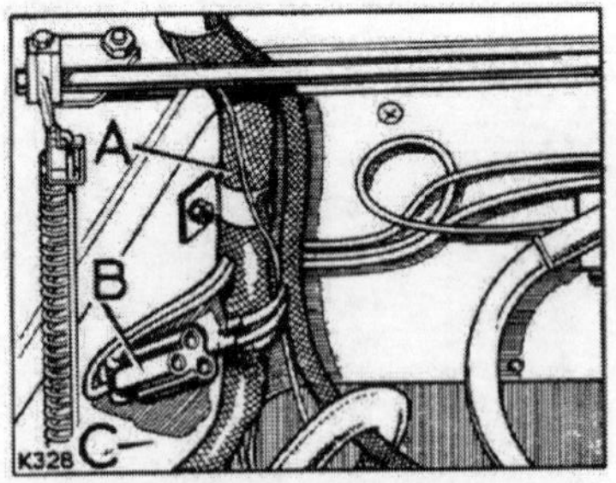

Fig. A1-21. Location of snap connectors

A—Engine compartment harness
B—Snap connectors for oil pressure light, choke warning light and coolant temperature gauge
C—Dash panel, RH side engine compartment

7. Connect the fuel inlet pipe to the fuel pump and secure the battery lead in the adjacent cable clip.

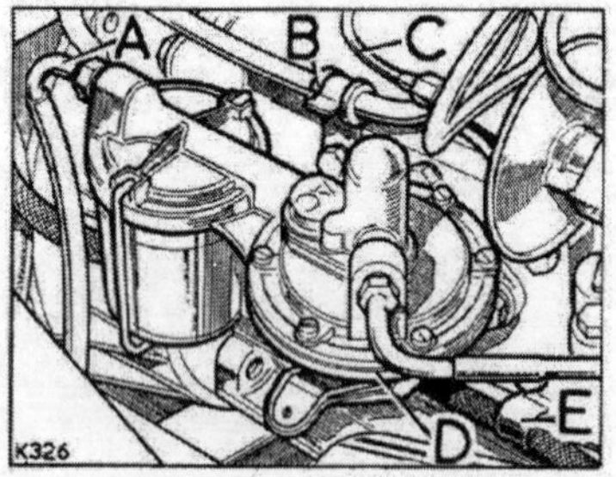

Fig. A1-22. Fuel pump location, RH side engine block

A—Fuel inlet pipe
B—Speedometer cable clip
C—Distributor vacuum pipe, refit if previously disconnected
D—Fuel pump
E—Battery lead clip

8. Connect the dynamo and starter motor leads at dash panel. Figs. A1-17 and A1-23 refer.

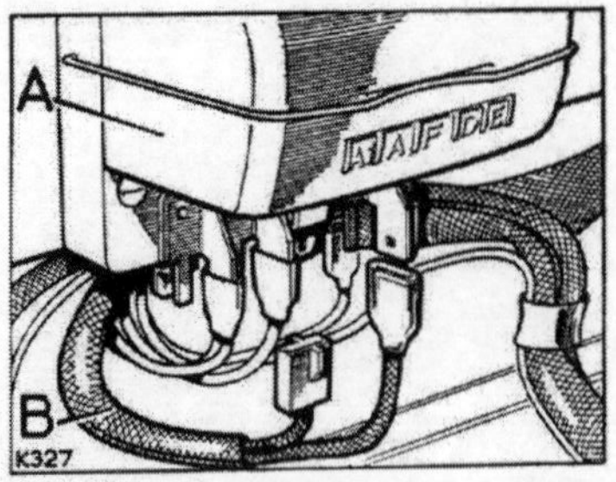

Fig. A1-23. Electrical leads at dash panel, RH side

A—Voltage regulator
B—Dynamo feed leads

ENGINE—2¼ LITRE PETROL

Operation A1-5—continued

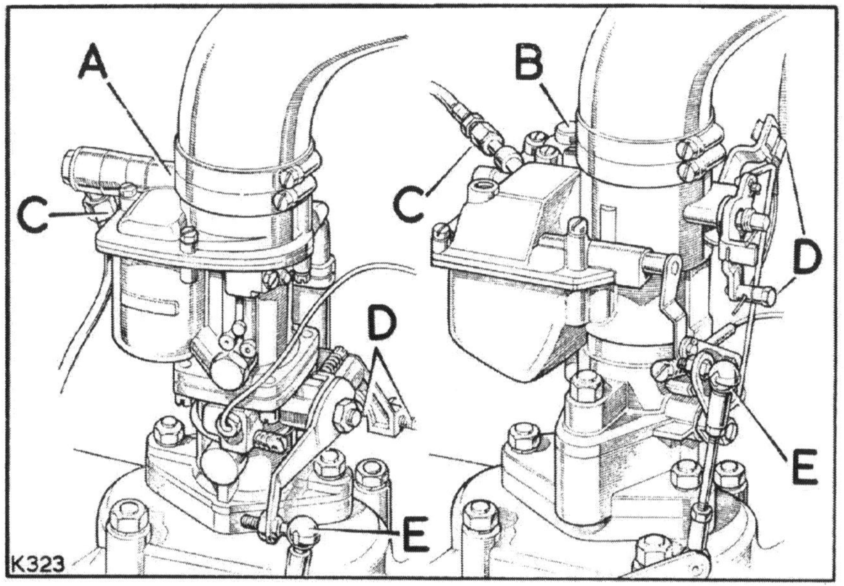

9. Connect the carburetter linkage.
10. Connect the engine earth cable.
11. Connect the distributor leads at the ignition coil.
12. Connect the heater hoses, if fitted, in engine compartment.
13. Connect the front exhaust pipe to the exhaust manifold.
14. Refit the front floor. Operation A1-4.
15. Refit the radiator and grille panel. Operation A1-3.
16. Refit the air cleaner. Operation A1-2.
17. Refit the bonnet panel. Operation A1-1.

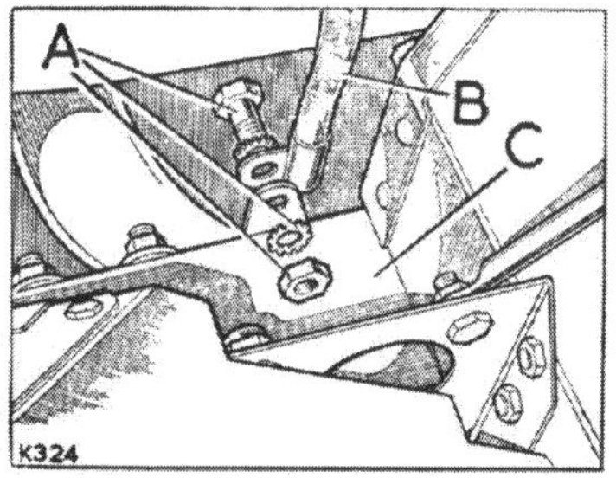

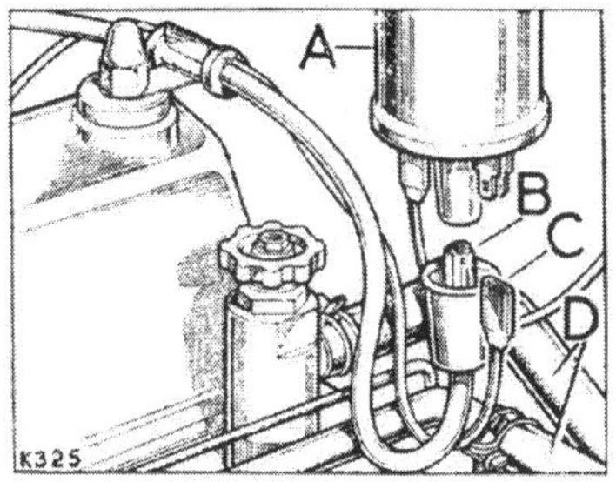

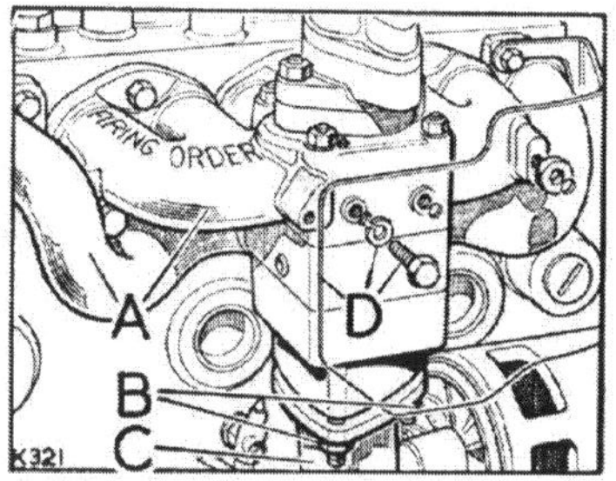

Fig. A1-24. Carburetter linkage

A—Carburetter, Solex type
B—Carburetter, Zenith type
C—Fuel inlet connection
D—Fixing, cold start inner and outer cable
E—Throttle linkage ball joint

Fig. A1-25. Earth cable location

A—Earth cable fixings
B—Earth cable
C—Chassis LH side member

Fig. A1-26. Ignition coil and heater hoses, LH side

A—Ignition coil
B—High tension lead
C—Low tension lead
D—Heater hoses

Fig. A1-27. Front exhaust pipe fixings

A—Exhaust manifold
B—Fixings for front exhaust pipe
C—Front exhaust pipe
D—Heat shield and fixings, if fitted

ENGINE—2¼ LITRE PETROL

*Carburetter, remove and refit—Operation A1-6

(For overhaul information, Section L refers)

Workshop hand tools:
Spanner sizes: 2 BA, 7/16 in. Whitworth, 7/16 in. AF open ended

To remove

1. Lift and prop bonnet panel.
2. Disconnect battery.
3. Disconnect controls at RH side of carburetter.

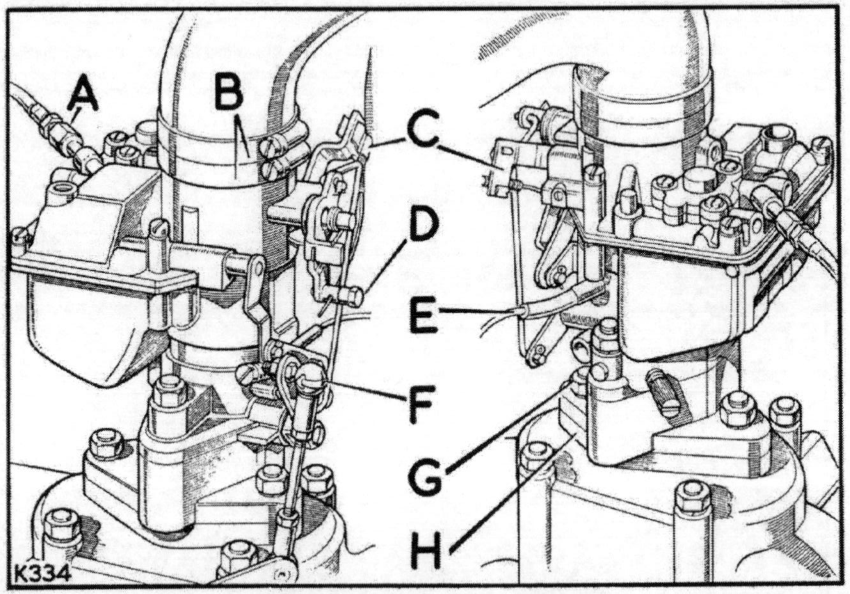

Fig. A1-28. Zenith carburetter, where fitted

A—Fuel inlet connection
B—Air inlet hose clips
C—Fixing for cold start outer cable
D—Fixing for cold start inner cable
E—Vacuum pipe
F—Throttle linkage
G—Fixings
H—Adaptor and joint washers

Operation A1-6—*continued*

4. Disconnect air intake connection, and the carburetter controls at LH side.
5. Remove fixings and lift off carburetter, adaptor piece and joint washers.

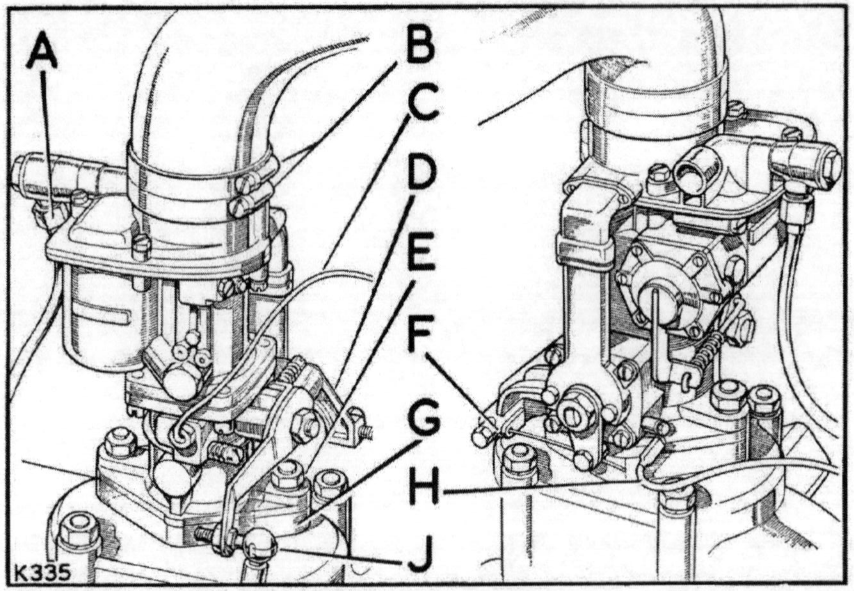

Fig. A1-29. Solex carburetter, where fitted

A—Fuel inlet connection
B—Air intake connection
C—Vacuum pipe to distributor
D—Cold start inner cable
E—Carburetter fixings
F—Cold start outer cable
G—Carburetter adaptor piece and joint gaskets
H—Feed lead for heater, where fitted
J—Throttle linkage ball joint

To refit

1. Refit carburetter, manifold adaptor and joint washers.
2. Reconnect all carburetter linkage. See Fig. A1-28 and Fig. A1-29. When the cold start cable is connected, check that the maximum travel on the carburetter linkage is obtainable in both directions.
3. Refit battery leads and close bonnet panel.

Operations marked with an asterisk (*) can be carried out with the engine installed in the vehicle

ENGINE—2¼ LITRE PETROL   Section A1—Land-Rover

*Inlet and exhaust manifold, remove and refit—Operation A1-7

(For overhaul information, Operation A1-8 refers)

Workshop hand tools:
Spanner sizes: 2 BA, 5/16 in. Whit, ½ in. AF, 7/16 in. AF open end, ¼ in. AF socket
Screwdriver (medium), Pliers

Special tools:
Torque wrench

To remove
1. Remove bonnet panel. Operation A1-1.
2. Remove carburetter. Operation A1-6.
3. Remove the exhaust heat shield if fitted.
4. Disconnect front exhaust pipe from manifold.

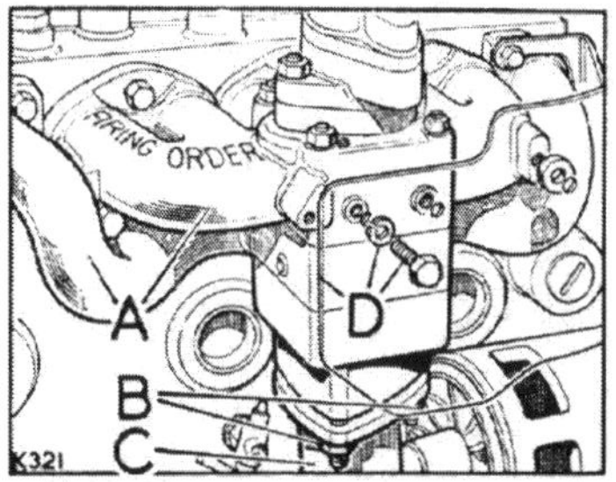

Fig. A1-30. Front exhaust pipe fixings
A—Exhaust manifold
B—Fixings for front exhaust pipe
C—Front exhaust pipe
D—Heat shield and fixings, if fitted

5. Remove fixings and withdraw inlet and exhaust manifolds complete. Remove joint washer.

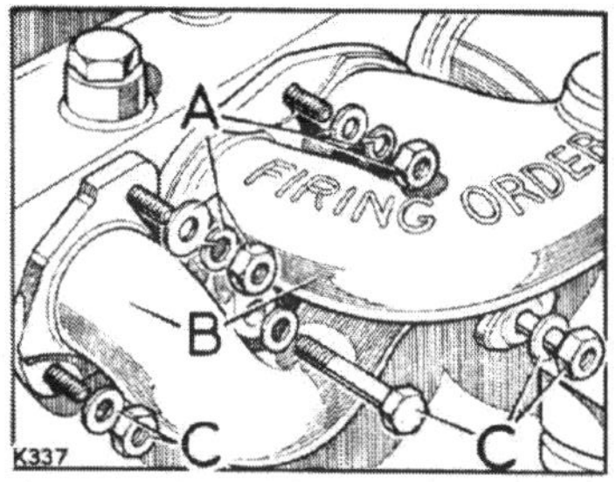

Fig. A1-31. Manifold fixings to cylinder head
A—Upper fixings
B—Manifolds assembly
C—Lower fixings

To refit

Note: Where a replacement joint washer is required, early and late types are available; the early type is a one-piece washer for both inlet and exhaust manifolds, the late type washers (2 off) are for the inlet manifold only with the exhaust manifold and cylinder head in metal-to-metal contact. For replacement purposes use joint washers of the type originally fitted to the particular engine.

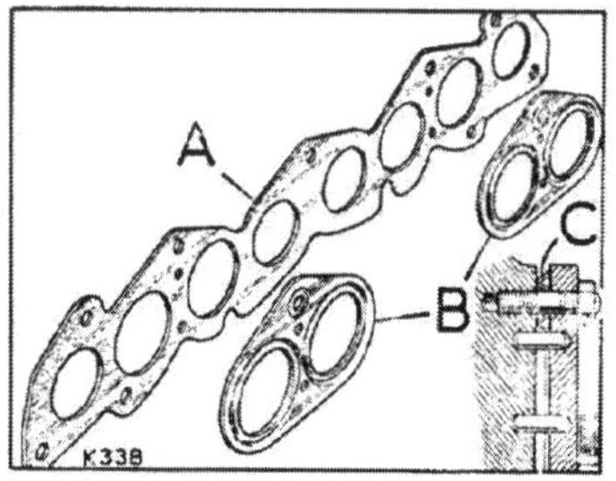

Fig. A1-32. Manifold joint washers
A—Early type, for inlet and exhaust manifold
B—Late type, for inlet manifold only
C—Position of raised portion, when fitted

1. When fitting the late type joint washers proceed as follows:
   (a) Tighten the inlet manifold to exhaust manifold fixings to 17 lb ft (2,3 mkg) torque load then slacken off slightly.
   (b) With the raised rings on the inlet manifold joint washer toward the cylinder head, fit the joint washer and manifolds complete and tighten the fixings.
   (c) Finally, retighten the inlet manifold to exhaust manifold fixings to 17 lb ft (2,3 mkg) torque load.

ENGINE—2¼ LITRE PETROL   Section A1—Land-Rover

Operation A1-7—continued

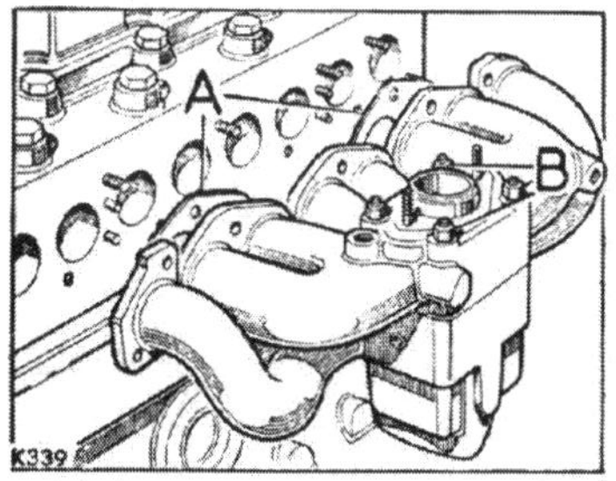

2. Refit the front exhaust pipe, see Fig. A1-30.
3. Refit the carburetter and bonnet panel, Operations A1-6 and A1-1 respectively.

Fig. A1-33. Refitting inlet and exhaust manifolds
A—Joint washers, late type shown. Position washer with raised rings towards cylinder head
B—Fixings, inlet manifold to exhaust manifold

Operations marked with an asterisk (*) can be carried out with the engine installed in the vehicle

ENGINE—2¼ LITRE PETROL

Inlet and exhaust manifold, overhaul—Operation A1-8

(For removing and refitting instructions, Operation A1-7 refers)

Workshop hand tools:
Spanner sizes: ½ in. AF ring, 2 BA open ended
Screwdriver (medium)

To dismantle

1. Separate the exhaust manifold assembly from the inlet manifold.

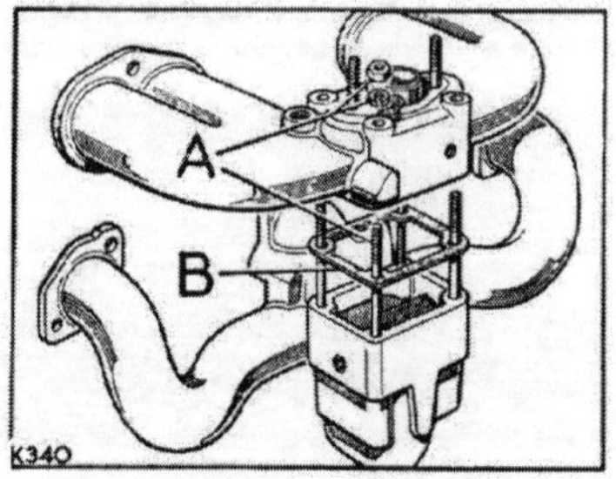

Fig. A1-34. Separating the manifolds

A—Fixings, exhaust manifold to inlet manifold
B—Joint washer

2. Clean the component parts, using clean fuel.
3. Examine joint faces for damage, examine the exhaust manifold for cracks.

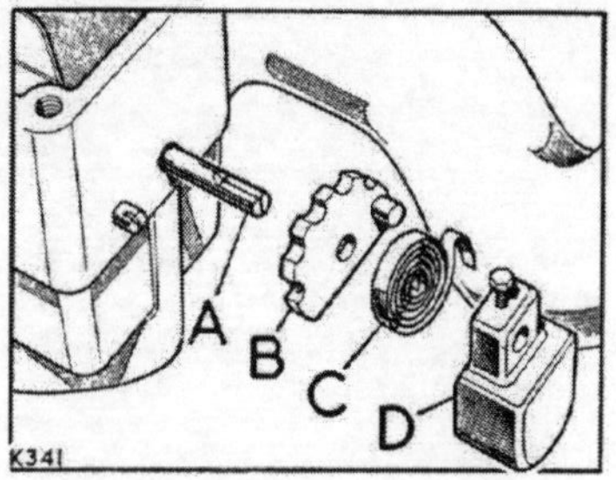

Fig. A1-35. 'Hot spot' components

A—Butterfly spindle, slotted to retain spring inner end
B—Adjusting plate and pin for spring outer end location
C—Bi-metal spring
D—Counterbalance weight and fixing

4. Examine the bi-metal spring attached to the exhaust manifold butterfly spindle. If the spring is sound, no further dismantling is necessary. If spring replacement is required, slacken the counterbalance weight fixing and remove the 'hot spot' components from the butterfly spindle.

To assemble

1. If removed, refit the 'hot spot' components to the exhaust manifold and adjust as follows:
   (a) Remove the retaining set screw.
   (b) Turn the adjusting plate until the counterbalance weight is just supported by the spring. Do not over-tension the spring otherwise the 'hot spot' flap in the exhaust manifold will not close during engine running.
   (c) Replace the retaining screw, selecting the appropriate serration in the adjusting plate, and tighten.

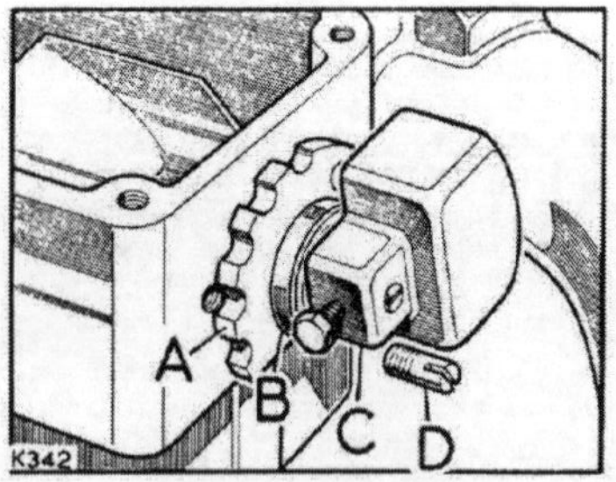

Fig. A1-36. Adjusting the 'hot spot' components

A—Serrated adjusting plate
B—Bi-metal spring
C—Counterbalance weight
D—Retaining set screw

2. Fit the inlet manifold to the exhaust manifold, referring to Fig. A1-34. Do not fully tighten the inlet manifold to exhaust manifold fixings until the assembly is refitted to engine, as described in Operation A1-7.

ENGINE—2¼ LITRE PETROL

*Starter motor, remove and refit—Operation A1-9

(For overhaul instructions, Section N refers)

Workshop hand tools:
Spanner sizes: ⁷⁄₁₆ in. AF open end, ⅝ in. BSF open end
Screwdriver (medium), Pliers

To remove

1. Remove the bonnet panel. Operation A1-1.
2. Disconnect the battery leads.
3. Remove the exhaust heat shield, if fitted.

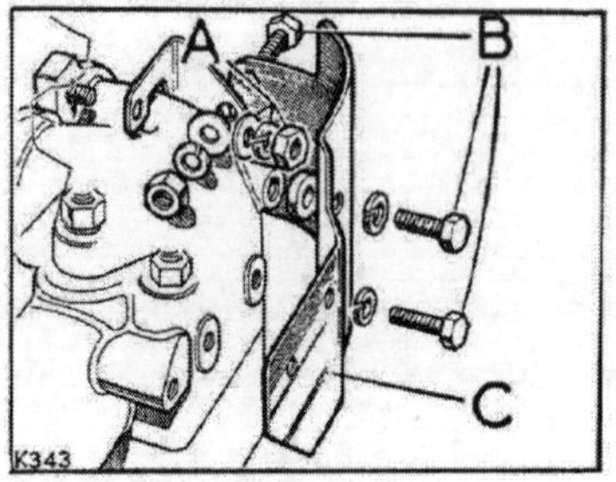

Fig. A1-37. Heat shield and fixings

A—At cylinder block
B—At exhaust manifold
C—Heat shield

4. Disconnect electrical lead at starter terminal, remove fixings at engine and withdraw starter. If necessary, disconnect the front exhaust pipe at the manifold to facilitate starter withdrawal.

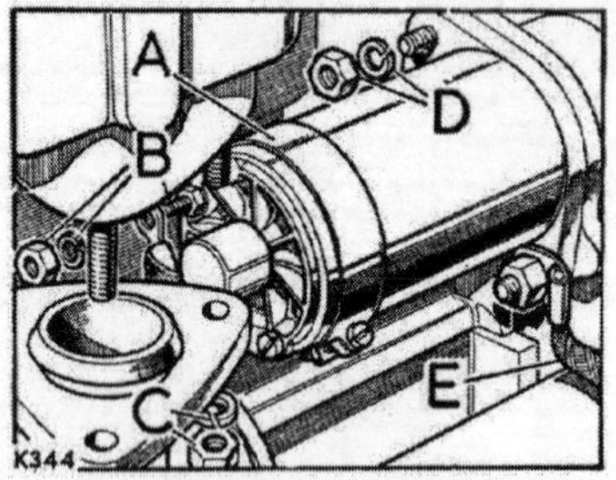

Fig. A1-38. Starter motor and front exhaust fixings

A—Starter motor
B—Electrical lead and fixing
C—Front exhaust pipe fixings
D—Fixings at engine
E—Earth strap, if fitted

To refit

1. Refit the starter motor and the exhaust heat shield, if fitted, referring to Fig. A1-38 and A1-37 respectively for details of connections and fixings.
2. Connect the battery leads.
3. Refit the bonnet panel. Operation A1-1.

Operations marked with an asterisk (*) can be carried out with the engine installed in the vehicle

ENGINE—2¼ LITRE PETROL

*Dynamo, remove and refit—Operation A1-10

(For overhaul Instructions, Section N refers)

Workshop hand tools:
Spanner sizes: ½ in. AF open end, ½ in. AF ring
Screwdriver (medium), Pliers

To remove

1. Remove bonnet panel. Operation A1-1.
2. Disconnect battery leads.
3. Remove dynamo electrical leads, slacken dynamo fixings and withdraw fan belt from dynamo pulley.
4. Remove fixings and withdraw dynamo.

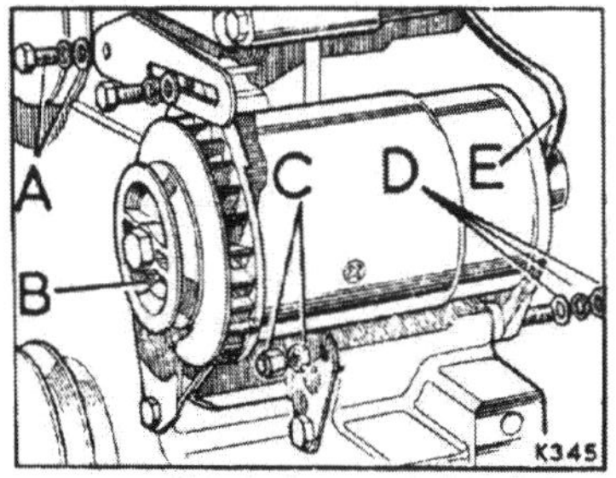

Fig. A1-39. View of dynamo and fixings

A—At adjusting bracket
B—Fan belt pulley
C—At front support
D—At rear support
E—Electrical leads at dynamo terminals

To refit

1. Refit the dynamo; reset the fan belt tension and fully tighten the dynamo fixings. The tension is correct when the fan belt can be depressed $\frac{5}{16}$ in. to $\frac{7}{16}$ in. (8 mm to 11 mm) by thumb pressure applied midway between the fan pulley and crankshaft pulley.
2. Refit the battery leads.
3. Refit the bonnet panel. Operation A1-1.

ENGINE—2¼ LITRE PETROL

*Water pump, remove and refit—Operation A1-11

(For overhaul Information, Section K refers)

Workshop hand tools:
Spanner sizes: $\frac{7}{16}$ in. AF open end, ½ in. AF ring
Screwdriver (medium), Pliers

To remove

1. Remove bonnet panel. Operation A1-1.
2. Remove radiator filler cap and drain coolant.

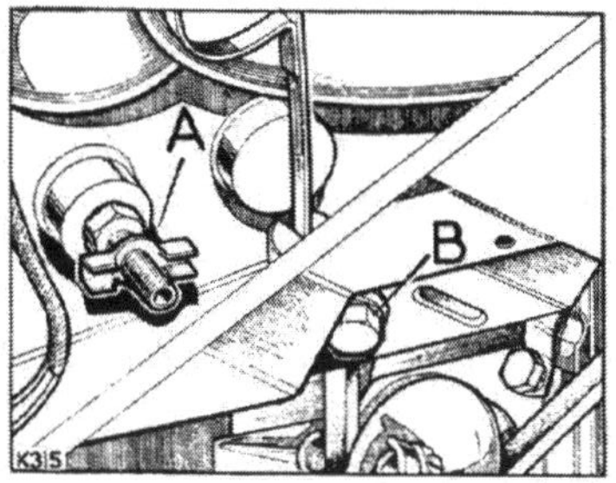

Fig. A1-40. Coolant drain taps location

A—Cylinder block drain
B—Radiator drain

3. Remove the shroud from the radiator fan cowl.

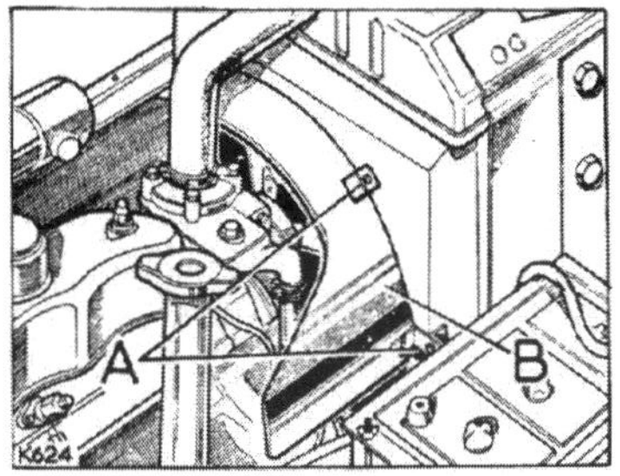

Fig. A1-41. Fan cowl shroud fixings

A—Fixings at fan cowl
B—Fan cowl shroud

4. Slacken dynamo fixings and remove fan belt; remove dynamo adjusting link to gain access to water pump fixings.

Fig. A1-42. Adjusting link and fan fixings

A—Fan blades fixings
B—Adjusting link fixings
C—Move dynamo clear of water pump fixings

5. Remove fan blades and fan pulley.

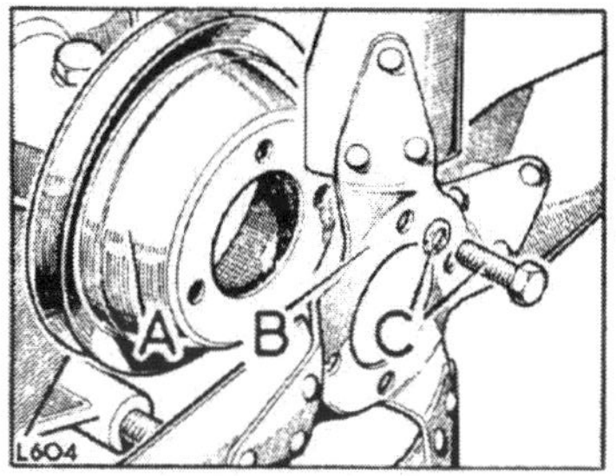

Fig. A1-43. Fixings for fan and pulley

A—Fan pulley, withdraw with fan blades
B—Fan blades, remove from vehicle or lower to rest on fan cowl
C—Fan blades fixings

6. Detach the radiator bottom hose and the by-pass hose from the water pump.

Operations marked with an asterisk (*) can be carried out with the engine installed in the vehicle

ENGINE—2¼ LITRE PETROL

Operation A1-11—continued

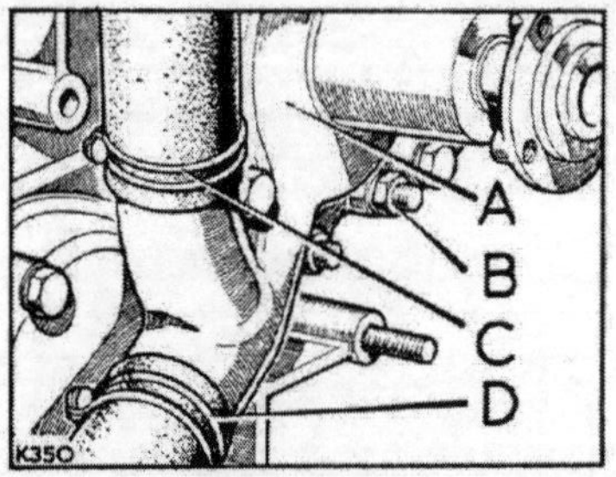

2. Refit the water pump and connect the coolant hoses, referring to Fig. A1-44. The water pump ⅞ in. UNF fixing bolts are of differing lengths and care should be taken to locate them correctly.
3. Refit the fan pulley, fan blades and dynamo, referring to Figs. A1-43 and A1-42 as necessary.
4. Reset the fan belt tension and fully tighten the dynamo fixings. The tension is correct when the fan belt can be depressed ⅜ in. to ⁷⁄₁₆ in. (8 mm to 11 mm) by thumb pressure applied midway between the fan pulley and crankshaft pulley.
5. Refit the fan cowl shroud, referring to Fig. A1-41.
6. Refill the engine coolant system. Allow a full flow of coolant through the drain taps before closing them.

COOLANT SYSTEM
Bonneted Control Model, 2¼ Litre Petrol

Capacity	Imperial Unit	US Unit	Litres	Antifreeze	Frost Precaution
88	18 pints	21¼ pints	10.25	33⅓%	−25°F / −32°C
109	18 pints	21¼ pints	10.25	33⅓%	−25°F / −32°C

7. Refit the bonnet panel, Operation A1-1.

Fig. A1-44. Water pump and hose fixings
A—Water pump
B—Water pump fixings
C—At by-pass hose
D—At radiator bottom hose

7. Remove fixings and withdraw water pump and gasket.

To refit
1. Smear general purpose grease on both sides of the joint washer and position on front cover joint face.

ENGINE—2¼ LITRE PETROL

*Thermostat and housing, remove and refit—Operation A1-12
(For thermostat overhaul information, Section K refers)

Workshop hand tools:
Spanner sizes: ⁷⁄₁₆ in. AF ring
Screwdriver (medium)

To remove
1. Lift and prop bonnet.
2. Remove radiator cap and partially drain coolant.
3. Disconnect top hose/s and remove by-pass pipe fixings.
4. Remove thermostat housing fixings and withdraw housing and outlet pipe complete. Remove joint washer.
5. Separate housing from outlet pipe and withdraw thermostat and joint washer.

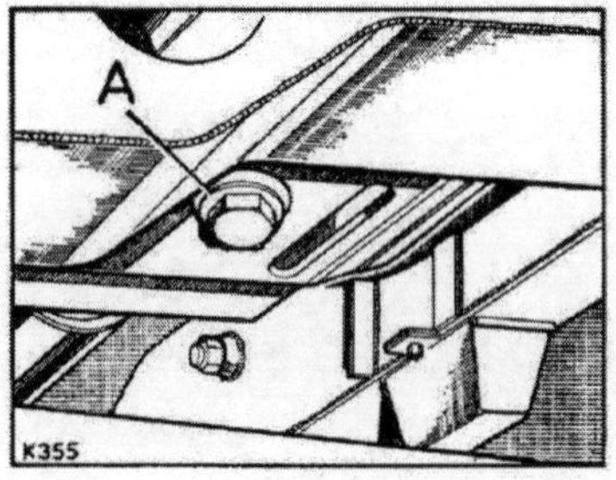

To refit
1. Smear general purpose grease on both sides of the joint washers.
2. Fit the thermostat into the housing and position on the engine.
3. Assemble the outlet pipe and joint washer to the thermostat housing. Fit all fixings and connect the coolant hoses, referring to Fig. A1-46.
4. Refill the coolant system as necessary, allowing a full flow through the radiator drain tap before closing it.

COOLANT SYSTEM
Bonneted Control Model, 2¼ Litre Petrol

Capacity	Imperial Unit	US Unit	Litres	Antifreeze	Frost Precaution
88	18 pints	21¼ pints	10.25	33⅓%	−25°F / −32°C
109	18 pints	21¼ pints	10.25	33⅓%	−25°F / −32°C

5. Refit the radiator cap and close the bonnet.

Fig. A1-45. Radiator drain location
A—Radiator drain plug

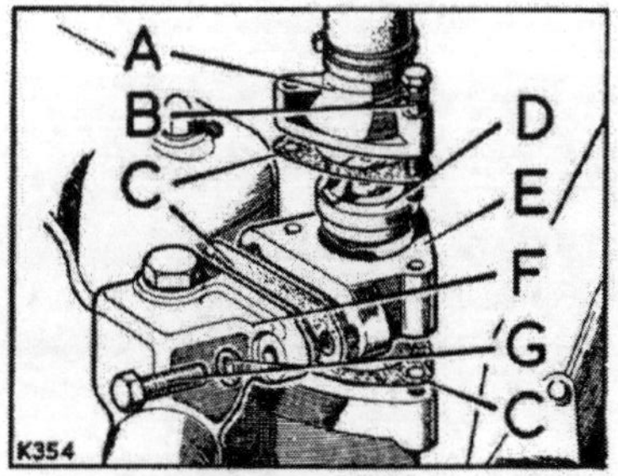

Fig. A1-46. Thermostat housing fixings
A—Outlet pipe
B—Fixings
C—Joint washer
D—Thermostat
E—Thermostat housing
F—By-pass pipe
G—Fixings

Operations marked with an asterisk (*) can be carried out with the engine installed in the vehicle

ENGINE—2¼ LITRE PETROL Section A1—Land-Rover

*Fuel pump, remove and refit—Operation A1-13

(For overhaul Information, Section L refers)

Workshop hand tools:
Spanner sizes: 11/16 in. AF, ½ in. AF open end, ½ in. AF socket
Screwdriver (medium), Pliers

To remove

1. Remove bonnet panel. Operation A1-1.
2. Remove air cleaner. Operation A1-2.
3. Disconnect fuel pipes at fuel pump.
4. Remove the fixings and withdraw the pump and rear cover complete.

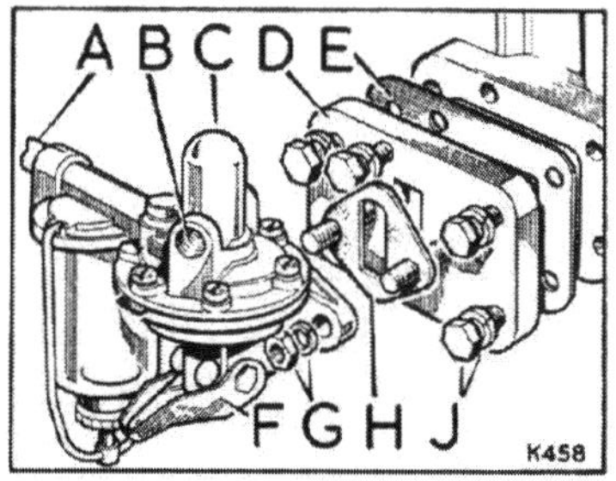

To refit

1. Fit the fuel pump to the cover.
2. Smear general purpose grease on both sides of the joint washer.
3. Refit the fuel pump and joint washer and connect the fuel pipes.
4. Prime the fuel pump by operating the hand prime lever until no resistance is felt.
5. Refit air cleaner. Operation A1-2.
6. Refit bonnet panel. Operation A1-1.

Fig. A1-47. Fuel pump location and fixings

A—Fuel inlet pipe
B—Fuel outlet pipe
C—Fuel pump
D—Side cover
E—Joint washer for side cover
F—Hand prime lever
G—Pump fixings
H—Joint washer
J—Fixings for side cover

5. If required, remove the fuel pump from the rear cover.

Section A1—Land-Rover ENGINE—2¼ LITRE PETROL

*Engine side covers, remove and refit—Operation A1-14

Workshop hand tools:
Spanner sizes: 11/16 in. AF, ½ in. AF open ended, ½ in. AF socket
Screwdriver (medium), Pliers

To remove

1. Remove bonnet panel. Operation A1-1.
2. Remove air cleaner. Operation A1-2.
3. Remove the fixings at the front side cover and withdraw the side cover and oil filler pipe complete with baffle and joint washers.
4. Disconnect the fuel inlet and outlet pipes at the fuel pump, remove the fixings at the rear side cover and withdraw the cover and fuel pump complete.

To refit

1. Refit the front side cover. When fitting the fixings, first engage the tapping nearest to the oil filler pipe, otherwise subsequent access for this fixing will be restricted.
2. Refit the rear side cover and fuel pump and connect the fuel pipes. Prime the fuel system by operating the hand prime lever until no resistance is felt. See Fig. A1-49 for location of hand prime lever.
3. Refit the air cleaner. Operation A1-2.
4. Refit the bonnet panel. Operation A1-1.

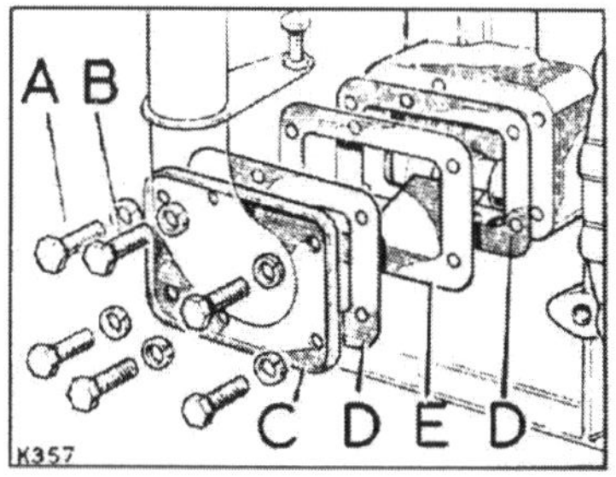

Fig. A1-48. View of front side cover

A—Fixings for side cover
B—Fit this bolt first when refitting
C—Filler pipe and side cover
D—Joint washers
E—Baffle

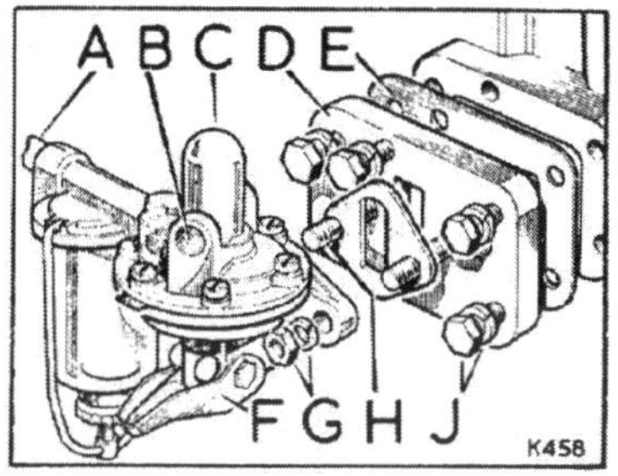

Fig. A1-49. View of rear side cover

A—Fuel inlet pipe
B—Fuel outlet pipe
C—Fuel pump
D—Side cover
E—Joint washer for side cover
F—Hand prime lever
G—Pump fixings
H—Joint washer
J—Fixings for side cover

Operations marked with an asterisk (*) can be carried out with the engine installed in the vehicle

ENGINE—2¼ LITRE PETROL

*Oil filter, external, replace element—Operation A1-15

Workshop hand tools:
Spanner sizes: ⅝ in. AF socket

Element, to remove

1. Position a suitable waste oil receptacle under the filter.
2. Remove the centre fixing from the filter.
3. Remove filter body and allow oil to drain.
4. Remove sealing ring from filter cap.
5. Remove filter element.

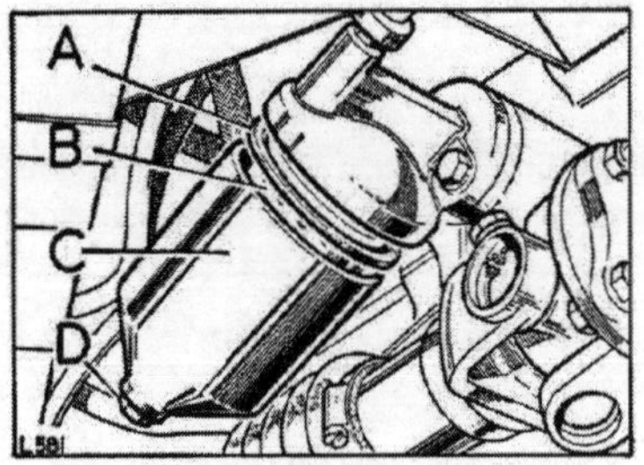

Fig. A1-50. View of oil filter

A—Sealing ring
B—Element
C—Filter body
D—Filter centre fixing

6. Wash metal components, using clean fuel.

Element, to refit

1. Fit the new element to the filter body and refit body to cap. Ensure filter body is fully home on to sealing ring in filter cap. See Fig. A1-50.
2. Replenish the engine lubricating oil.
3. Check the sump oil level after a short engine run and top-up as necessary.

ENGINE LUBRICANT CAPACITY
Bonneted Control Model, 2¼ Litre Petrol

		Capacity	Imperial Unit	US Unit	Litres
88	Engine	11 pints	11 pints	13 pints	6.0
	Filter	¾ pint	1½ pints	1.8 pints	0.85
	Engine and Filter	11¾ pints	12½ pints	14.8 pints	6.85
109	Engine	11 pints	11 pints	13 pints	6.0
	Filter	¾ pint	1½ pints	1.8 pints	0.85
	Engine and Filter	11¾ pints	12½ pints	14.8 pints	6.85

COOLANT SYSTEM

---

*Oil filter, external, remove, overhaul and refit—Operation A1-16

Workshop hand tools:
Spanner sizes: ⅝ in. AF, 1⅛ in. AF socket, 7/16 in. BSF open end

To remove

1. Lift and prop bonnet.
2. Detach oil pressure switch lead.
3. Remove the fixings and withdraw the oil filter and joint washer.

Fig. A1-51. Oil filter fixings

A—Fixings, filter to engine, RH side
B—Oil pressure switch lead

To overhaul

1. Drain off oil.
2. Remove the centre fixing at the filter base and dismantle the filter assembly.
3. Wash the components in clean fuel and inspect for general condition.
4. Replace the sealing washer and filter element.
5. Refit the oil pressure switch.
6. Refit the sealing washer to the filter cover and place the filter element in the filter body.

To refit

1. Smear general purpose grease on to both sides of the joint washer.
2. Refit the filter body to the top cover ensuring that the body seats correctly on to the sealing washer.
3. Refit the assembled filter to the engine, referring to Fig. A1-51.
4. Connect the oil pressure switch lead and close the bonnet.
5. Check the sump oil level after a short engine run and top-up as necessary to the 'high' mark on the oil level dipstick.

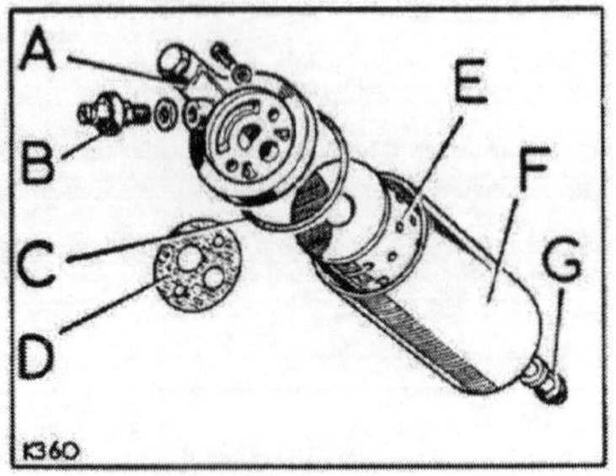

Fig. A1-52. Exploded view of oil filter

A—Top cover
B—Oil pressure switch
C—Sealing washer
D—Joint washer
E—Element
F—Container
G—Centre fixing

ENGINE LUBRICANT CAPACITY
Bonneted Control Model, 2¼ Litre Petrol

		Capacity	Imperial Unit	US Unit	Litres
88	Engine	11 pints	11 pints	13 pints	6.0
	Filter	¾ pint	1½ pints	1.8 pints	0.85
	Engine and Filter	11¾ pints	12½ pints	14.8 pints	6.85
109	Engine	11 pints	11 pints	13 pints	6.0
	Filter	¾ pint	1½ pints	1.8 pints	0.85
	Engine and Filter	11¾ pints	12½ pints	14.8 pints	6.85

Operations marked with an asterisk (*) can be carried out with the engine installed in the vehicle

ENGINE—2¼ LITRE PETROL

*Ignition timing procedure—Operation A1-17

Workshop hand tools:
Spanner sizes: 7/16 in. AF open end
Screwdriver (medium), Pliers

Special tools:
Suitable test lamp—12 volt—and leads

Note: Timing pointer position differs between early and late engines. Fig. Nos. A1-53 and A1-54 refer.

Procedure

1. Remove bonnet panel. Operation A1-1.

2. **Engines with timing pointer on flywheel housing**—rotate the crankshaft in direction of rotation until the appropriate timing mark on the flywheel is aligned with the timing pointer and the distributor rotor is at No. 1 cylinder firing position.

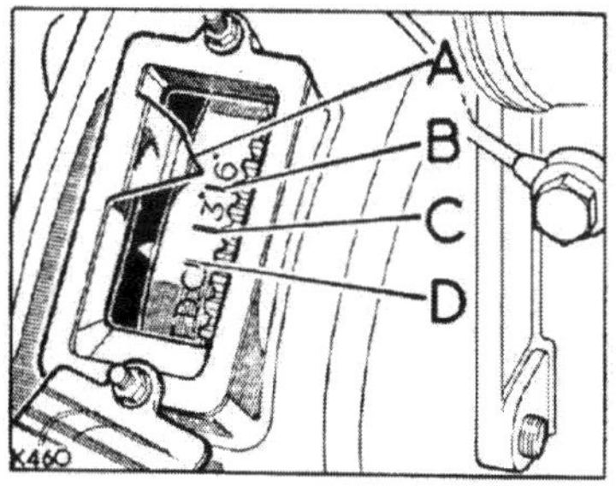

Fig. A1-53. Timing pointer on flywheel housing
A—Timing pointer
B—6° mark, align when using 90-96 octane fuel
C—3° mark, align when using 80-85 octane fuel
D—TDC mark, align when using 74-76 octane fuel

3. **Engines with timing pointer on front cover bracket**—rotate the crankshaft in direction of rotation until the timing mark on the crankshaft pulley is aligned with the appropriate tongue on the timing pointer and the distributor rotor is at No. 1 cylinder firing position.

4. Slacken the pinch bolt in base of distributor body and rotate the distributor in opposite direction to arrow on rotor arm until the contact breaker points are just opening with the cam follower on the leading side of the cam. Re-tighten the pinch bolt.

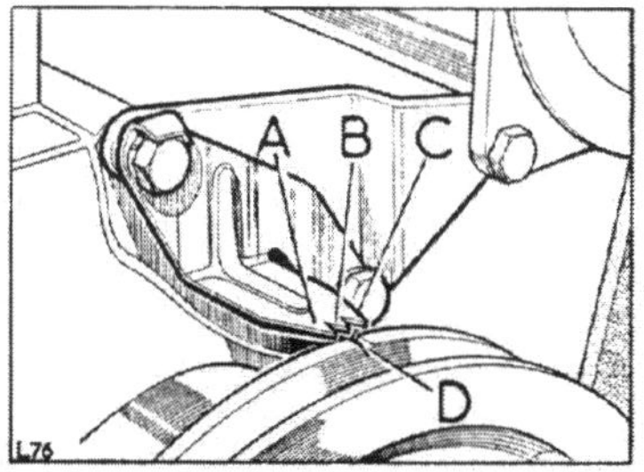

Fig. A1-54. Timing pointer on front cover
A—6° tongue, align when using 90-96 octane fuel
B—3° tongue, align when using 80-85 octane fuel
C—TDC tongue, align when using 74-76 octane fuel
D—Mark on crankshaft pulley, align with appropriate tongue

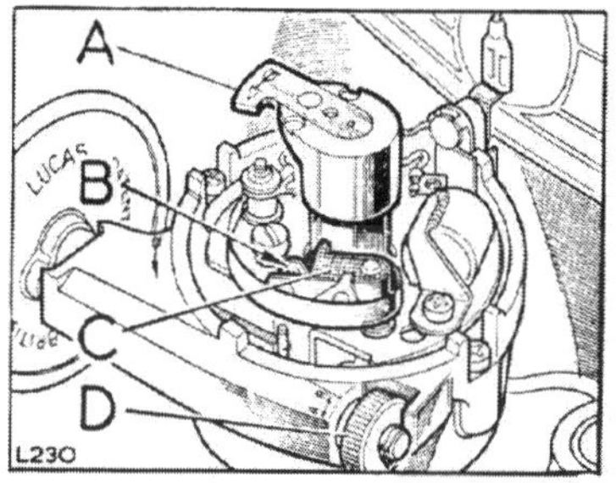

Fig. A1-55. View of distributor
A—Rotor arm
B—Contact breaker points
C—Cam follower
D—Vernier screw adjuster

Operation A1-17—continued

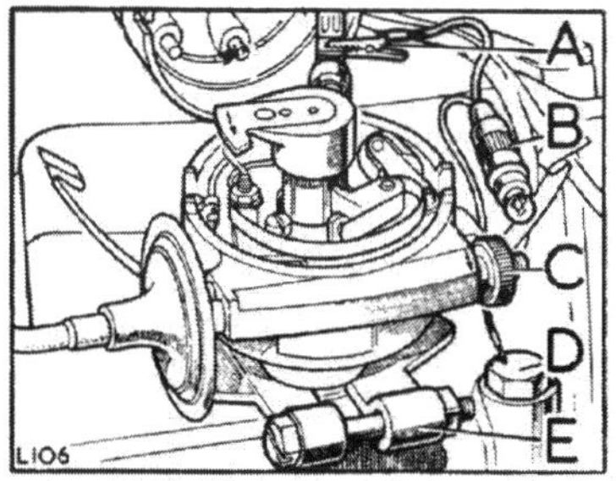

5. Connect one lead of a 12 volt test lamp to the distributor LT terminal and the other one to a good earth on engine. Switch ignition 'on' and turn the crankshaft two revolutions in direction of rotation. The bulb should light as the timing pointer comes into alignment with the appropriate mark. See paragraphs 2 and 3.

6. Adjust as required by slackening the pinch bolt and turning the distributor bodily, or for fine adjustment, by means of the vernier screw.

7. When satisfactory, remove the test lamp and leads and refit the distributor cap.

8. Refit the inspection cover to the flywheel housing, where applicable.

9. Refit the bonnet panel. Operation A1-1.

Fig. A1-56. Test lamp in position
A—LT terminal at distributor
B—Test lamp
C—Vernier screw adjuster
D—Suitable earth
E—Pinch bolt

Operations marked with an asterisk (*) can be carried out with the engine installed in the vehicle

ENGINE—2¼ LITRE PETROL   Section A1—Land-Rover

*Distributor and driving gear, remove and refit—Operation A1-18

(For overhaul Instructions, Section N refers)

Workshop hand tools:
Spanner sizes: ⅜ in. AF, ½ in. AF, ⁷⁄₁₆ in. AF open end, ⅝ in. AF socket
Pliers (snipe nosed), Screwdriver (small), Screwdriver (medium)

To remove

1. Remove bonnet panel. Operation A1-1.
2. Remove air cleaner. Operation A1-2.
3. Remove external oil filter. Operation A1-16.
4. Disconnect battery.
5. Disconnect distributor leads and vacuum pipe.

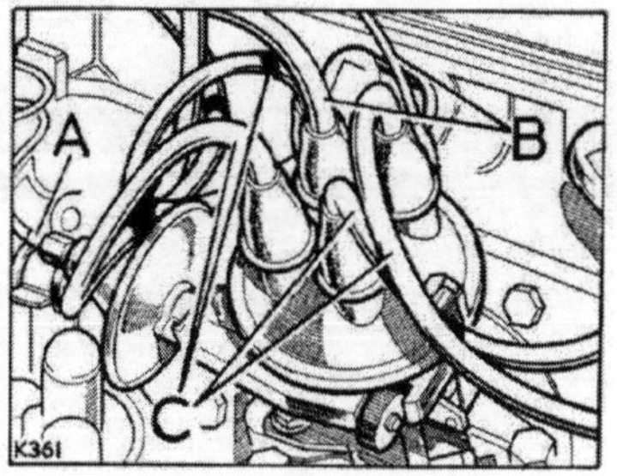

Fig. A1-57. Distributor connections
A—Vacuum pipe
B—High tension and low tension leads, disconnect at distributor
C—Ignition leads, disconnect at sparking plugs

6. Disconnect vacuum pipe; remove fixings and withdraw distributor and adaptor from engine.
7. Lift the short drive shaft coupling from the vertical drive gear, remove the locating grub screw and withdraw the vertical drive gear assembly using suitable pliers.

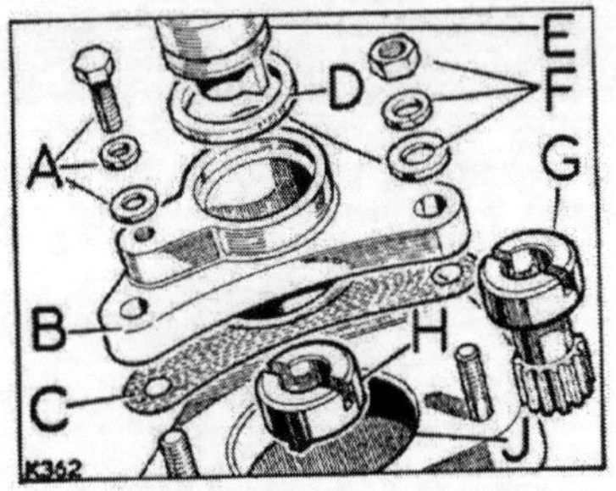

To refit

1. **Engines with timing pointer on flywheel housing.** Rotate the crankshaft until the appropriate timing mark on the flywheel is aligned with the timing pointer and both valves on No. 1 cylinder are fully closed. See Fig. A1-60.

Fig. A1-58. Distributor removal
A—Distributor fixings
B—Distributor adaptor
C—Joint washer
D—Cork washer
E—Distributor
F—Adaptor fixings
G—Top drive shaft, early engines
H—Drive shaft coupling, later engines
J—Vertical drive gear housing

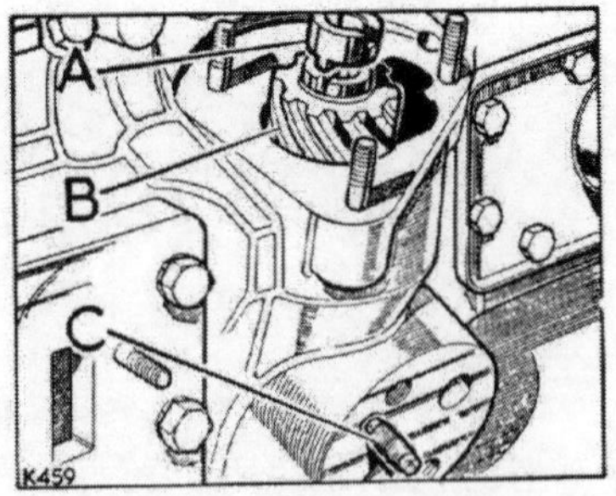

Fig. A1-59. Distributor drive gear details
A—Drive shaft coupling
B—Vertical drive gear assembly
C—Locating grub screw at tapping in oil filter location face

Operation A1-18—continued

2. **Engines with timing pointer on front cover bracket.** Rotate the crankshaft until the timing mark on the crankshaft pulley is aligned with the appropriate tongue on the timing pointer and both valves on No. 1 cylinder are fully closed.

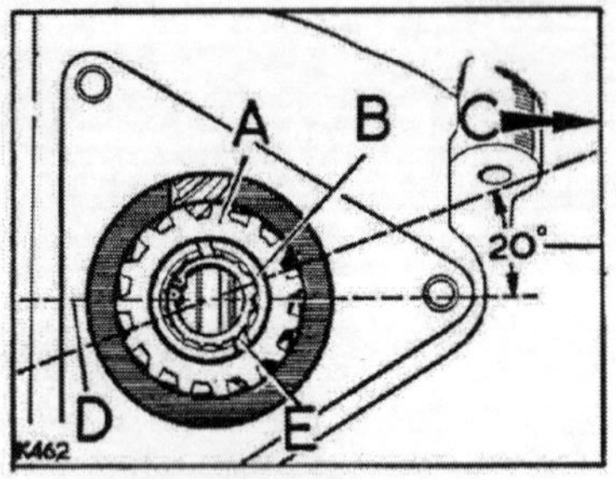

Fig. A1-62. Fitting vertical drive gear
A—Vertical drive gear
B—Master spline for locating drive shaft, early engines
C—To front of engine
D—Line parallel with engine centre line
E—Offset slot for use with later type drive shaft coupling

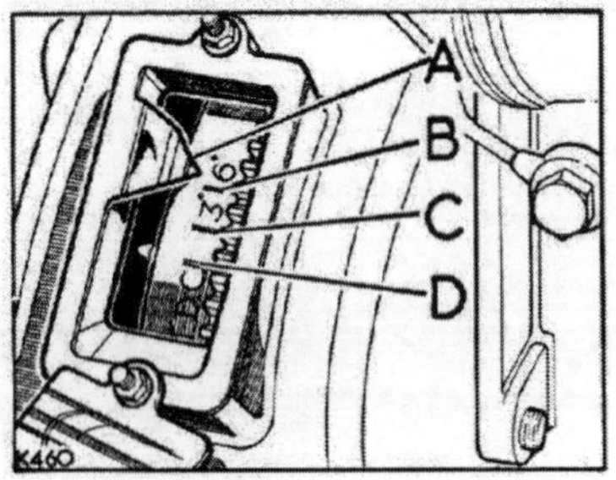

Fig. A1-60. Timing pointer on flywheel housing
A—Timing pointer
B—6° mark, align when using 90-96 octane fuel
C—3° mark, align when using 80-85 octane fuel
D—TDC mark, align when using 74-76 octane fuel

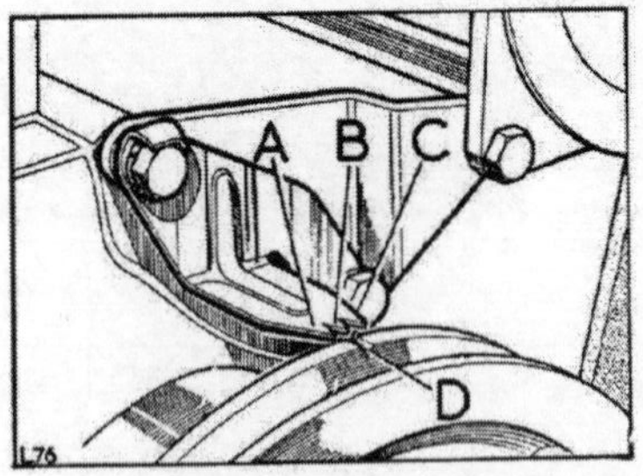

Fig. A1-61. Timing pointer on front cover
A—6° tongue, align when using 90-96 octane fuel
B—3° tongue, align when using 80-85 octane fuel
C—TDC tongue, align when using 74-76 octane fuel
D—Mark on crankshaft pulley, align with appropriate tongue

Continue for all engines:

3. Insert the vertical drive shaft assembly so that when fully engaged, the master spline is pointing toward No. 1 cylinder. See Fig. A1-62.
4. Locate the small hole in the vertical drive gear bush through the oil filter location face, and fit the grub screw. Fig. A1-59 refers.

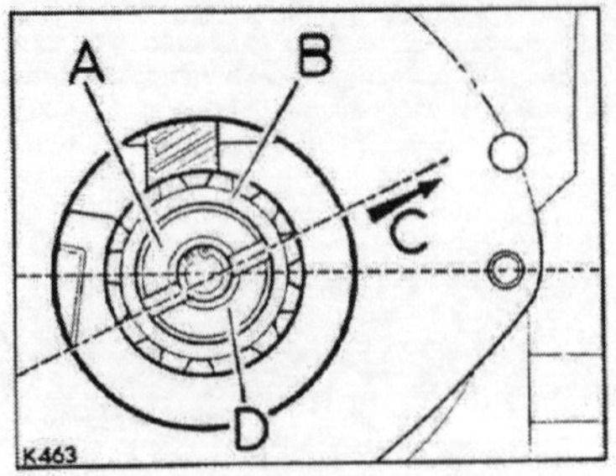

Fig. A1-63. Fitting drive coupling
A—Top drive coupling
B—Vertical drive gear
C—No. 1 cylinder
D—Narrow segment of coupling

Operations marked with an asterisk (*) can be carried out with the engine installed in the vehicle

ENGINE—2¼ LITRE PETROL

Operation A1-18—continued

5. Fit the short distributor drive shaft coupling to the vertical drive gear with the narrow segment toward the RH side of engine and the slot toward No. 1. cylinder.

6. Fit the distributor adaptor plate and joint washer and locate the cork washer in the recess.

7. Adjust the distributor contact breaker gap to .014 in. to .016 in. (0,35 mm to 0,40 mm) and set the octane selector so that the fourth line from LH side on calibrated slide is against the face of the distributor body casing.

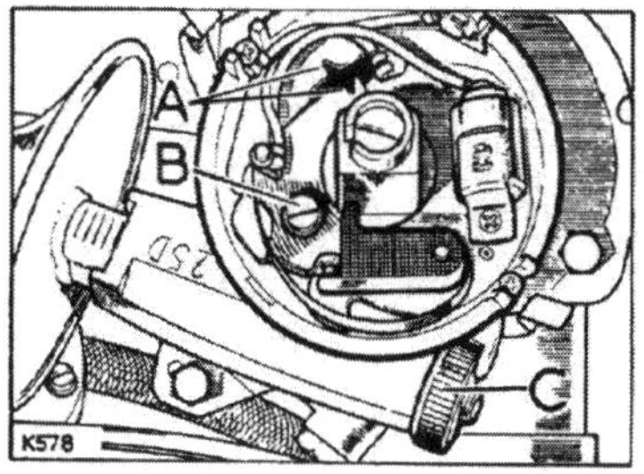

8. Offer up the distributor to the engine with the rotor arm in the No. 1 cylinder firing position. With the vacuum unit facing rearward, the narrow segment of the distributor shaft should be toward the RH side of the vehicle and the dog pointing toward No. 1 cylinder. The drive shaft will then engage correctly with the drive shaft coupling at engine. See Fig. A1-63.

Fig. A1-64. Distributor settings

A—Adjust here to set gap
B—Locking screw for gap setting
C—Adjuster screw

9. Fit the distributor to the mounting adaptor plate Fig. A1-58 refers.

10. Carry out the ignition timing procedure detailed in Operation A1-17.

11. Refit the distributor cap.

12. Refit the vacuum pipe and distributor leads, referring to Fig. A1-57.

13. Connect the battery leads.

14. Refit the external oil filter. Operation A1-16.

15. Refit the air cleaner and bonnet panel, Operations A1-2 and A1-1 respectively.

16. Replenish the engine lubricating oil as necessary after a short engine run.

ENGINE LUBRICANT CAPACITY
Bonneted Control Model, 2¼ Litre Petrol

		Capacity	Imperial Unit	US Unit	Litres
88	Engine		11 pints	13 pints	6,0
	Filter		1½ pints	1,8 pints	0,85
	Engine and Filter		12½ pints	14,8 pints	6,85
109	Engine		11 pints	13 pints	6,0
	Filter		1½ pints	1,8 pints	0,85
	Engine and Filter		12½ pints	14,8 pints	6,85

---

*Tappet adjustment—Operation A1-19

Workshop hand tools:
Spanner sizes: ½ in. AF ring
Screwdriver (medium), Feeler gauges, Pliers

Tappets, to adjust

1. Remove the bonnet panel. Operation A1-1.
2. Remove the air cleaner. Operation A1-2.
3. Remove the engine top cover.

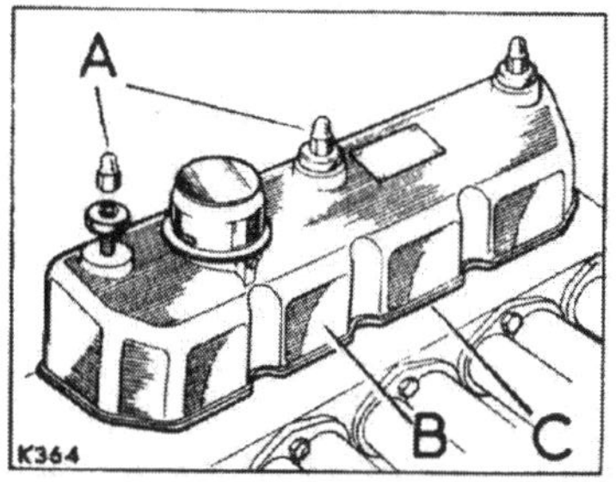

Fig. A1-65. Engine top cover

A—Fixings for top cover
B—Top cover
C—Joint washer

4. Set the tappet clearances to .010 in. (0,25 mm) for all valves.

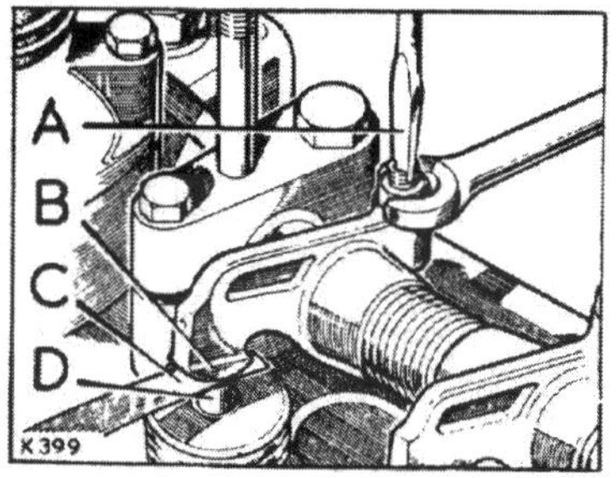

The tappet setting is most easily carried out in the following sequence, No. 1 tappet being at the front of the engine:

Set No. 1 tappet clearance with No. 8 valve fully open.
Set No. 3 tappet clearance with No. 6 valve fully open.
Set No. 5 tappet clearance with No. 4 valve fully open.
Set No. 2 tappet clearance with No. 7 valve fully open.
Set No. 8 tappet clearance with No. 1 valve fully open.
Set No. 6 tappet clearance with No. 3 valve fully open.
Set No. 4 tappet clearance with No. 5 valve fully open.
Set No. 7 tappet clearance with No. 2 valve fully open.

5. Recheck tappet clearances with locknuts fully tightened.

6. Refit the engine top cover, referring to Fig. A1-65.

7. Refit the air cleaner and bonnet panel. Operations A1-2 and A1-1 respectively.

Fig. A1-66. Setting tappet clearances

A—Screwdriver
B—Rocker pad
C—Feeler gauge
D—Valve stem

Operations marked with an asterisk (*) can be carried out with the engine installed in the vehicle

ENGINE—2¼ LITRE PETROL   Section A1—Land-Rover   ENGINE—2¼ LITRE PETROL

*Valve gear, rocker shaft and push rods, remove and refit—Operation A1-20

(For overhaul instructions, Operation A1-21 refers)

Workshop hand tools:
Spanner sizes; ½ in. AF ring, ⅜ in. AF socket
Screwdriver (medium), Pliers

Special tools:
Torque wrench

Operation A1-20—continued

To remove

1. Remove bonnet panel. Operation A1-1.
2. Remove air cleaner. Operation A1-2.
3. Remove engine top cover.

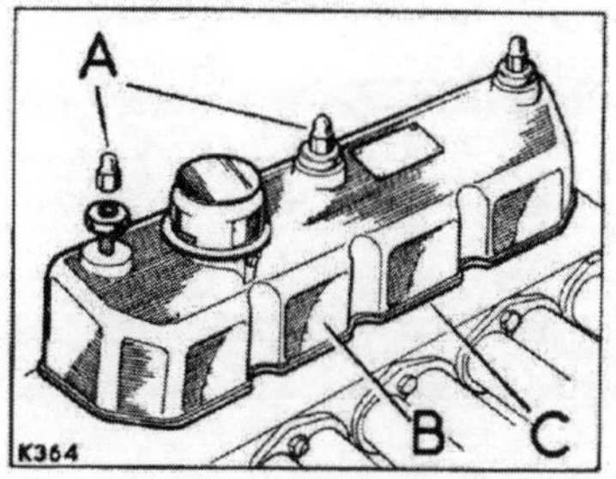

Fig. A1-67. Engine top cover
A—Fixings   B—Top cover
C—Joint washer

4. Slacken locknuts and turn tappet adjusting screws to disengage from push rods.
5. Remove fixings from rocker shaft support brackets. Do not remove shaft assembly at this stage.

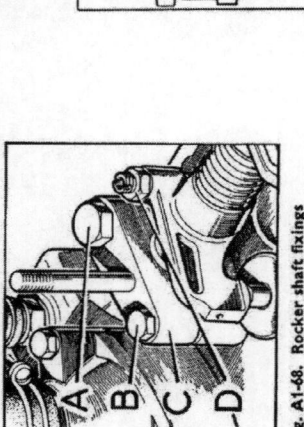

Fig. A1-68. Rocker shaft fixings
A—Fixings, brackets to engine
B—Fixings, shaft to brackets
C—Rocker brackets
D—Tappet locknuts and adjusting screws

6. Withdraw the rocker shaft assembly complete, using the engine top cover secured inverted to the rocker bracket studs to retain the assembly.
7. Withdraw the tappet push rods and retain them in numbered sequence related to the tappet served.

To refit

1. Fit the tappet push rods to their original bores. Ensure the push rods are bottomed in the spherical seat in the cylinder head and gasket.
2. Clean the rocker shaft assembly fixing bolt threads of deposits which could become trapped between the cylinder head and gasket.
3. Fit the rocker shaft assembly, located by spigots. Tighten the fixings as follows:
   ½ in. UNF bolts to 65 lb ft (8,9 mkg) torque load.
   ⅝ in. UNF bolts to 18 lb ft (2,4 mkg) torque load.
4. Check tighten all ½ in. UNF cylinder head fixings, in the order shown, to a torque load of 65 lb ft (8,9 mkg).

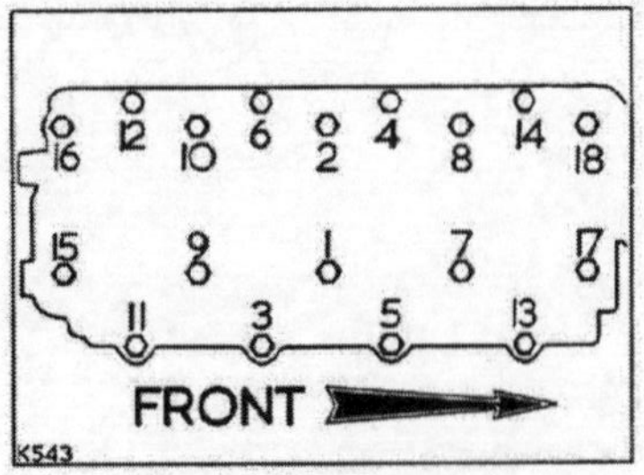

Fig. A1-69. Order of tightening cylinder head fixings

5. Fit the tappet screw locknuts and set the tappet clearances to .010 in. (0,25 mm) (with the locknuts tightened) in the following sequence:
   Set No. 1 tappet with No. 8 valve fully open.
   Set No. 3 tappet with No. 6 valve fully open.
   Set No. 5 tappet with No. 4 valve fully open.
   Set No. 2 tappet with No. 7 valve fully open.
   Set No. 8 tappet with No. 1 valve fully open.
   Set No. 6 tappet with No. 3 valve fully open.
   Set No. 4 tappet with No. 5 valve fully open.
   Set No. 7 tappet with No. 2 valve fully open.
6. Refit the engine top cover.
7. Refit the air cleaner and bonnet panel. Operations A1-2 and A1-1 respectively.

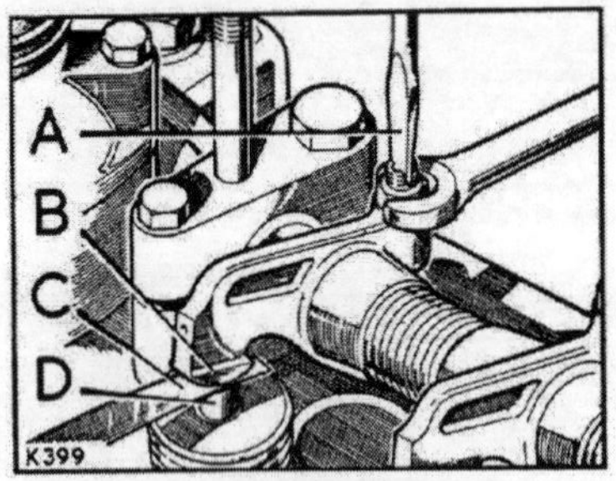

Fig. A1-70. Adjusting tappets
A—Screwdriver
B—Rocker pad
C—Feeler gauge
D—Valve stem

Operations marked with an asterisk (*) can be carried out with the engine installed in the vehicle

ENGINE—2¼ LITRE PETROL — Section A1—Land-Rover

*Valve gear and rocker shaft, overhaul—Operation A1-21

(For removal and refitting instructions, Operation A1-20 refers)

Workshop hand tools:
Spanner sizes: ½ in., 7/16 in. AF ring
Screwdriver (medium)

To dismantle

1. Remove the tappet adjusting screws from the valve rockers.
2. Withdraw the valve gear from the rocker shaft.

Inspection

1. Rocker brackets. Ensure the oil feed holes are clear. Inspect the locating dowel spigots; the spigots must be undamaged to ensure a correct fit on the locating dowels in the cylinder head.

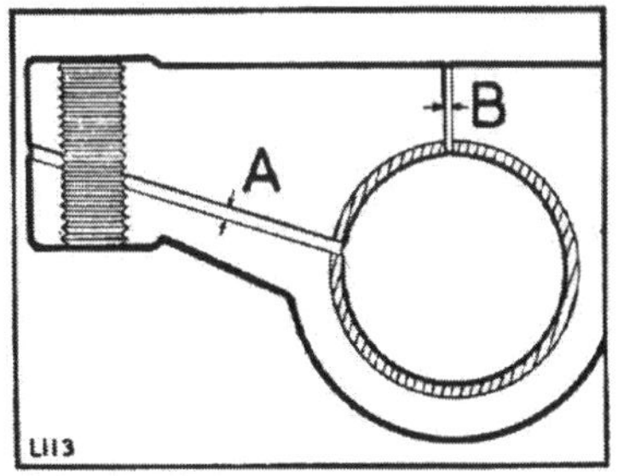

2. Valve rockers. Visually inspect the rocker bushes for wear. If necessary, press replacement bushes into the rockers and ream to 0.530 in. +0.001 in. (13,5 mm +0,02 mm).

Fig. A1-71. Sectioned view of valve rocker

A—Oil feed drilling for tappet adjusting screw
B—Oil outlet drilling for splash lubrication

Note: The oil holes in the rocker bushes are pre-drilled and must be aligned with the oil holes in the valve rocker when assembled.

Check that all oil passage drillings are clear.

3. Tappet adjusting screws and locknuts. Examine threads for damage. Check that the oil relief drilling is clear.

4. Inspect the rocker shaft for wear and scores; check that the oil feed holes are clear.

5. Examine the rocker shaft springs, spacing washers and the locating screw for soundness and general condition.

To assemble

1. Fit an intermediate rocker bracket to the rocker shaft and engage the locating screw through the bracket and into the larger hole in the shaft.

2. Continue assembly, referring to Fig. A1-72 and note the assembled position for the spacing washers and the handed valve rockers.

3. Refit the tappet adjusting screws to the valve rockers. Fit the locknuts.

4. Refit to engine as detailed in Operation A1-20.

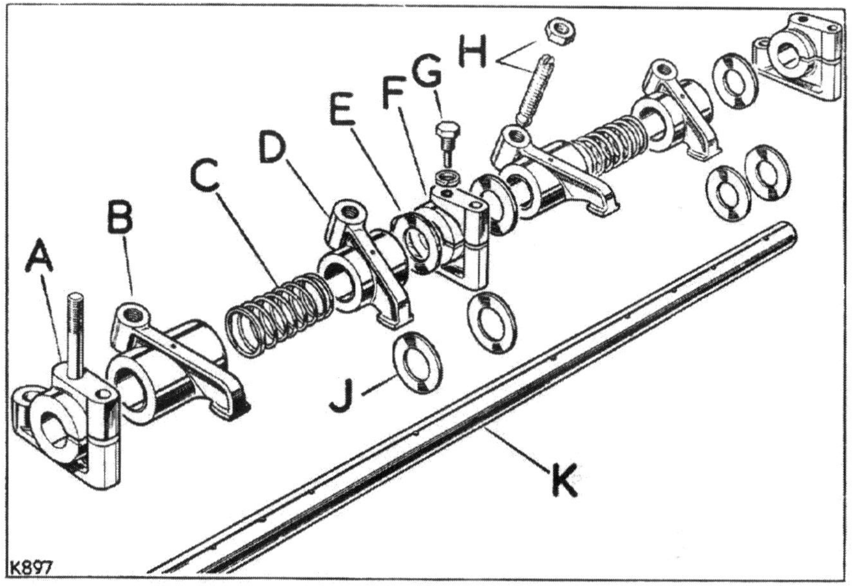

Fig. A1-72. Valve gear and rocker shaft arrangement

A—Rocker brackets. Front, centre and rear brackets carry studs for top cover fixings
B—Exhaust valve rockers (4 off)
C—Rocker shaft springs (4 off)
D—Inlet valve rockers (4 off)
E—Spacing washers (6 off)
F—Intermediate rocker bracket (2 off)
G—Locating screw for rocker shaft (2 off on early models)
H—Tappet screws adjacent to larger fixing holes in brackets
J—Spacing washers for diesel models. Not applicable for petrol models
K—Valve rocker shaft (2 off on early models)

Operations marked with an asterisk (*) can be carried out with the engine installed in the vehicle

ENGINE—2¼ LITRE PETROL   Section A1—Land-Rover

*Cylinder head, remove and refit—Operation A1-22

(For overhaul instructions, Operation A1-23 refers)

Workshop hand tools:
Spanner sizes: 7/16 in., 1/2 in., 5/8 in., 7/8 in. AF open end
7/16 in., 1/2 in., 9/16 in., 3/4 in. AF socket
7/16 in., 5/8 in. BSF open end
2 BA open end
14 mm box spanner
Screwdriver (medium), Pliers

Special tools:
Torque wrench

To remove

1. Remove bonnet panel. Operation A1-1.
2. Remove air cleaner. Operation A1-2.
3. Disconnect battery leads.
4. Remove engine top cover.

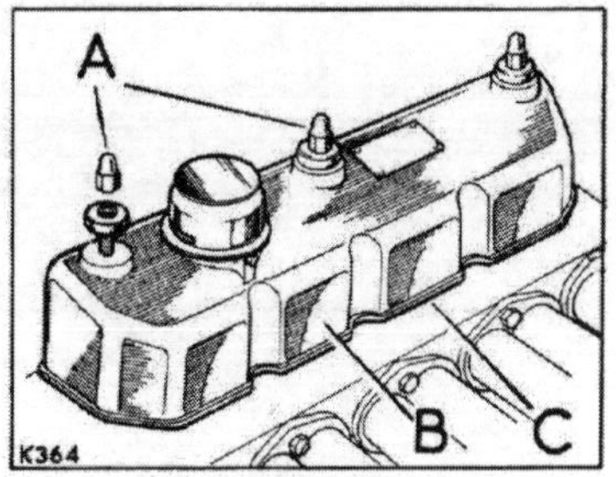

Fig. A1-73. Engine top cover
A—Top cover fixings
B—Top cover
C—Joint washer

5. Remove radiator filler cap and drain coolant.

Fig. A1-74. Coolant system drain points
A—At engine block
B—At radiator block

6. Disconnect or remove the following components at the RH side of engine:
   (a) Disconnect the vacuum pipe at distributor.
   (b) Disconnect the distributor leads at the ignition coil and sparking plugs.
   (c) Remove the sparking plugs.
   (d) Remove the fan cowl shroud.
   (e) Disconnect oil gallery pipe.
   (f) Disconnect the coolant by-pass hose.

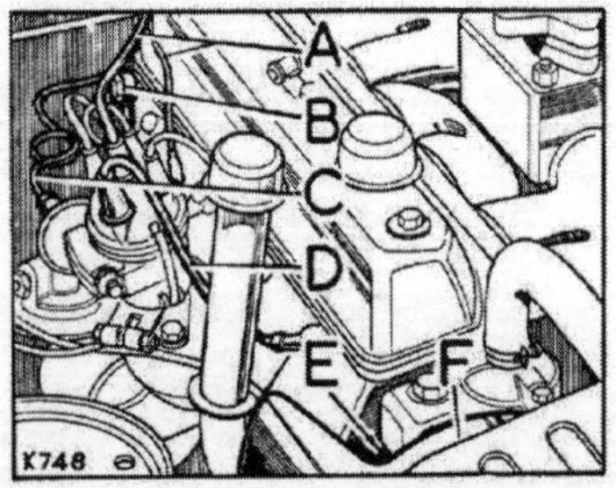

Fig. A1-75. View of engine compartment, RH side
A—Distributor leads to ignition coil
B—Oil gallery pipe
C—Distributor vacuum pipe
D—Distributor leads to sparking plugs
E—Coolant by-pass hose
F—Fan cowl shroud

7. Disconnect or remove the following components at the LH side of engine:
   (a) Disconnect coolant hose/s at thermostat housing.
   (b) Disconnect accelerator linkage at ball joint at carburetter.
   (c) Disconnect cold start inner and outer cables at carburetter.

Operations marked with an asterisk (*) can be carried out with the engine installed in the vehicle

---

Section A1—Land-Rover   ENGINE—2¼ LITRE PETROL

Operation A1-22—continued

   (d) Disconnect the fuel inlet pipe at carburetter and release from clip on engine.
   (e) Disconnect front exhaust pipe at exhaust manifold, removing heat shield if necessary to gain access.

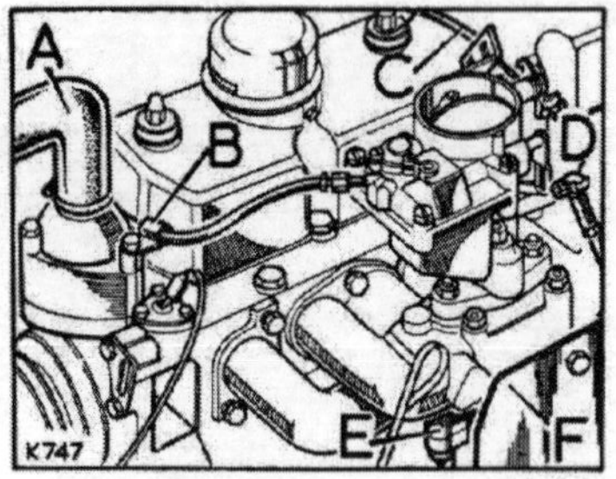

Fig. A1-76. View of engine compartment, LH side
A—Coolant hose/s at thermostat housing
B—Fuel inlet pipe clip
C—Cold start cables
D—Carburetter ball joint
E—Front exhaust pipe
F—Heat shield, if fitted

8. Remove the valve rocker shaft assembly and retain as an assembly.
9. Slacken evenly and remove the remaining fixings (Fig. A1-77 refers) and withdraw the cylinder head and joint gasket.

To refit

1. To aid subsequent alignment, smear clean engine oil on the cylinder block and cylinder head gasket joint faces. Position the joint gasket on the block with the lettering 'PETROL' uppermost.
2. Position cylinder head on joint gasket. Clean all deposits from fixing bolt threads and engage all fixings except those also used to secure the rocker shaft assembly.
3. Place the push rods into position and ensure that they bottom correctly into the spherical seats in the tappet slides.
4. Fit the rocker shaft assembly and engage the fixings.

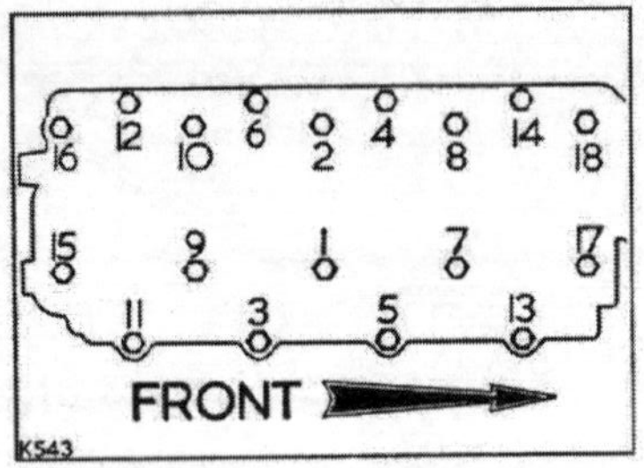

Fig. A1-77. Order of tightening cylinder head fixings

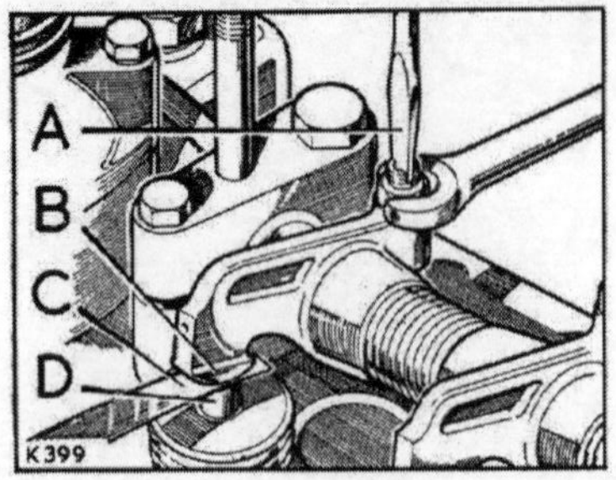

Fig. A1-78. Setting tappet clearances
A—Screwdriver
B—Rocker pad
C—Feeler gauge
D—Valve stem

ENGINE—2¼ LITRE PETROL

Operation A1-22—continued

5. Tighten the cylinder head and rocker shaft fixings in the order shown as follows:
   ½ in. UNF bolts—65 lb ft (8,9 mkg) torque load.
   ⁷⁄₁₆ in. UNF bolts—18 lb ft (2,4 mkg) torque load

6. Set the tappet clearances to .010 in. (0,25 mm) for all valves.

   The tappet setting is most easily carried out in the following sequence, No. 1 tappet being at the front of the engine:

   Set No. 1 tappet clearance with No. 8 valve fully open.
   Set No. 3 tappet clearance with No. 6 valve fully open.
   Set No. 5 tappet clearance with No. 4 valve fully open.
   Set No. 2 tappet clearance with No. 7 valve fully open.
   Set No. 8 tappet clearance with No. 1 valve fully open.
   Set No. 6 tappet clearance with No. 3 valve fully open.
   Set No. 4 tappet clearance with No. 5 valve fully open.
   Set No. 7 tappet clearance with No. 2 valve fully open.

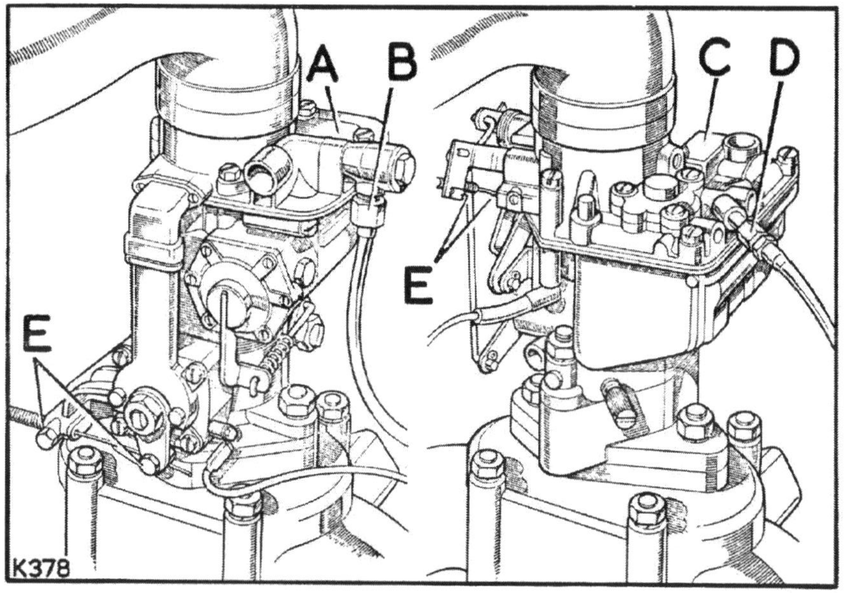

Fig. A1-79. Location of carburetter controls and heater hoses

A—Carburetter, Solex (where fitted)
B—Fuel inlet connection
C—Carburetter, Zenith (where fitted)
D—Fuel inlet connection
E—Cold start control; inner and outer cable fixings, Zenith carburetter

Operation A1-22—continued

7. Refit the engine top cover, referring to Fig. A1-73.
8. Fit the front exhaust pipe to the manifold and, where applicable, refit the exhaust heat shield.

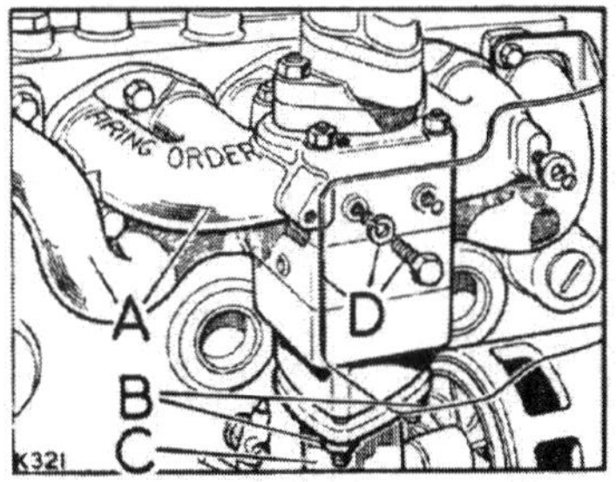

Fig. A1-80. Front exhaust pipe fixings

A—Exhaust manifold
B—Fixings for front exhaust pipe
C—Front exhaust pipe
D—Heat shield and fixings, if fitted

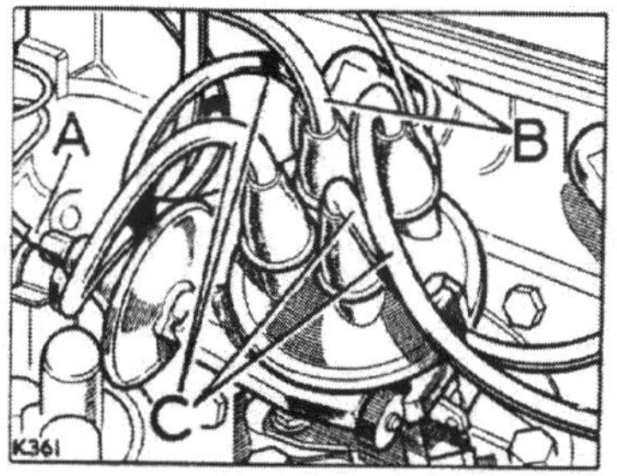

9. Connect fuel inlet pipe at carburetter and retain pipe length in retaining clip at engine.
10. Connect the carburetter controls and, if fitted, the heater hoses.
11. Fit the fan cowl shroud and connect coolant hoses at thermostat housing. See Fig. A1-75.
12. Refit sparking plugs and connect oil gallery pipe.
13. Connect distributor leads and vacuum pipe.
14. Refill coolant system, allowing a full flow through the coolant drain taps before closing them.

COOLANT SYSTEM
Bonneted Control Model, 2¼ Litre Petrol

Capacity	Imperial Unit	US Unit	Litres	Antifreeze	Frost Precaution
88	18 pints	21¼ pints	10,25	33⅓%	−25°F −32°C
109	18 pints	21¼ pints	10,25	33⅓%	−25°F −32°C

15. Connect battery leads.
16. Refit air cleaner. Operation A1-2.
17. Refit the bonnet panel. Operation A1-1.
18. After the initial engine run, that is with the engine at normal running temperature, check the cylinder head fixings to the correct torque load with the sparking plugs removed.

Fig. A1-81. Distributor connections

A—Vacuum pipe
B—High tension and low tension leads, connect at ignition coil
C—Ignition leads, connect at sparking plugs

ENGINE—2¼ LITRE PETROL

*Cylinder head, overhaul and decarbonize—Operation A1-23

(For removal and refitting instructions, Operation A1-22 refers)

Workshop hand tools:
Spanner sizes: ½ in., ⅞ in. AF open end
½ in. AF socket
½ BA open end
5/16 In. Whit open end
7/16 in. AF ring
Screwdriver (medium), Pliers, 1 lb hammer

Special tools:
Part No. 276102—Valve spring compressor
Part No. 274400—Inlet valve guide removal tool
Part No. 274401—Exhaust valve guide removal tool
Part No. 600959—Exhaust valve guide replacement tool
Part No. 601508—Inlet valve guide replacement tool
Torque wrench

To dismantle and overhaul

1. Remove the inlet and exhaust manifold assembly.
2. Remove the thermostat housing complete. Operation A1-7.
3. Remove the valve assemblies and retain components in related sets.

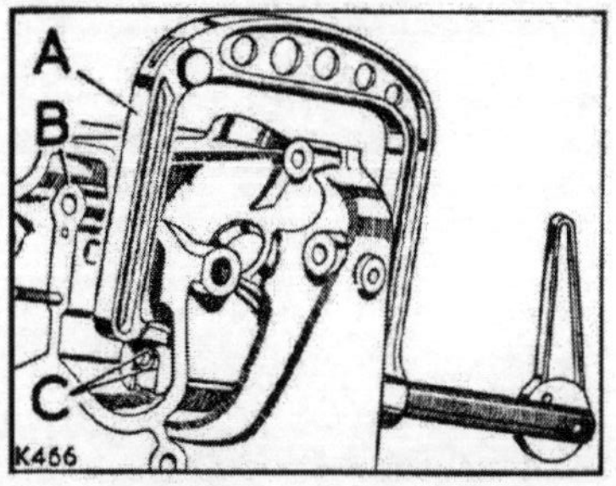

Fig. A1-82. Valve assemblies
A Special tool, Part No. 276102
B—Cylinder head
C—Split cones, remove before releasing special tool

4. Remove the oil seals from the valve guides.
5. Remove carbon deposits from the valve seats, combustion chambers, valves and also from the piston crowns, using suitable scrapers, abrasive cloth and a wire brush. Take care to prevent dislodged deposits from entering oilways and coolant passages.
6. Clean combustion deposits from valve guide bores.

7. Reface the valves: inlet valves 30°—¼°; exhaust valves 45°—¼°, using suitable grinding equipment, or replace as necessary. The valve faces should be flat and not distorted. Use a straight-edge to visually check.

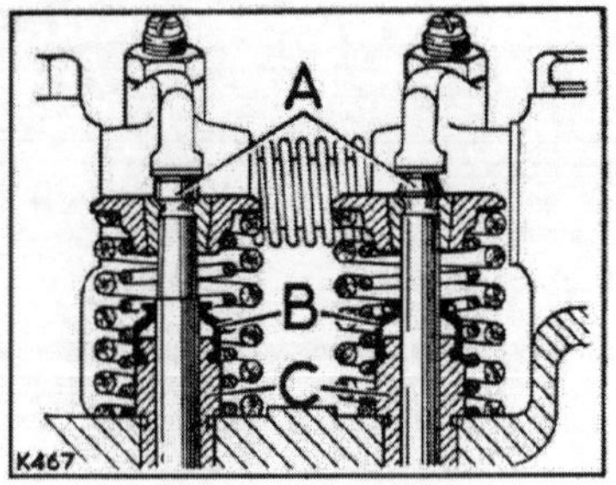

Fig. A1-83. Valve guides and oil seals arrangement
A—Valves
B—Oil seals, latest type shown seating externally on valve guides
C—Valve guides; early type have internal groove for oil seals

8. Check fit of valve stems in respective valve guides. If clearance is excessive, remove the guides, using the special drifts, Part No. 274401 for exhaust valve guides, Part No. 274400 for inlet valve guides.
9. Where replacement valve guides are to be fitted, lubricate the guides and their housing bores and drift into position using the special drift, Part No. 601508 for inlet valve guides, and special drift, Part No. 600959 for exhaust valve guides. Recheck the valve stem fit in the guide, paragraph 8 refers.

The special drifts are so formed to avoid damage to the valve guides.

10. Reface the valve seats in the cylinder head, using suitable equipment. Valve seat angle: 30° for inlet, 45° for exhaust.

Operation A1-23—continued

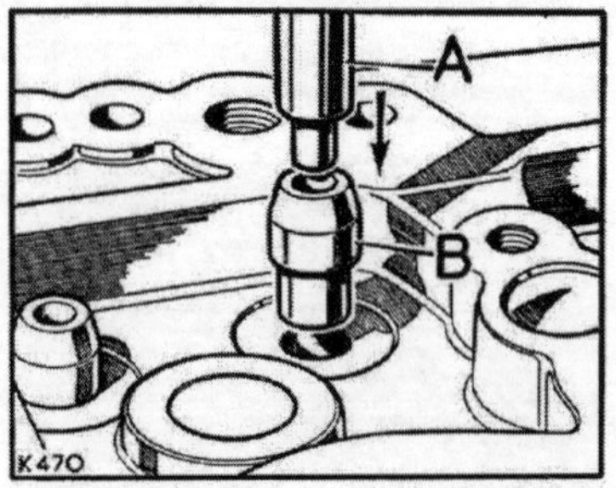

Fig. A1-84. Fitting replacement valve guides
A—Special tool   B—Valve guide

11. Inspect the valve springs which are provided as paired assemblies. The springs must be an interference fit with each other.
12. Inspect the valve split cones and valve spring caps for general condition.
13. Inspect the cylinder head for damage to threads.

To assemble

1. Assemble the oil seals to the valve guides.
2. Lubricate the valve stems and fit the valves to their respective valve guides.
3. Fit the valve springs and spring caps and, using the special tool, Part No. 276102, compress the springs and fit the split cones to the valve stem waists. Fig. A1-82 refers.
4. Remove the compression tool and ensure the assemblies are seated by tapping sharply on each valve stem end, using a hide mallet.
5. Complete the assembly by fitting the thermostat housing, Operation A1-12, and the manifolds assembly, Operation A1-7.

Operations marked with an asterisk (*) can be carried out with the engine installed in the vehicle

ENGINE—2¼ LITRE PETROL

*Tappet assemblies, remove and refit—Operation A1-24

Workshop hand tools:
Spanner sizes: ⅜ in. AF open ended, ½ in. AF ring
Pliers (cutting), Screwdriver (medium), Feeler gauges

Special tools:
Torque wrench
Part No. 530101—Tappet guide removal tool

To remove

1. Remove bonnet panel. Operation A1-1.
2. Remove air cleaner. Operation A1-2.
3. Disconnect battery.
4. Remove valve gear, rocker shaft and push rods. Operation A1-20.
5. Remove cylinder head. Operation A1-22.
6. Remove tappet guide locating bolts at RH side of engine block.
7. Remove the tappet slides, leaving the guides in position to retain the rollers and ensure that they do not fall behind the camshaft. Remove the rollers, using a local made spring clip.

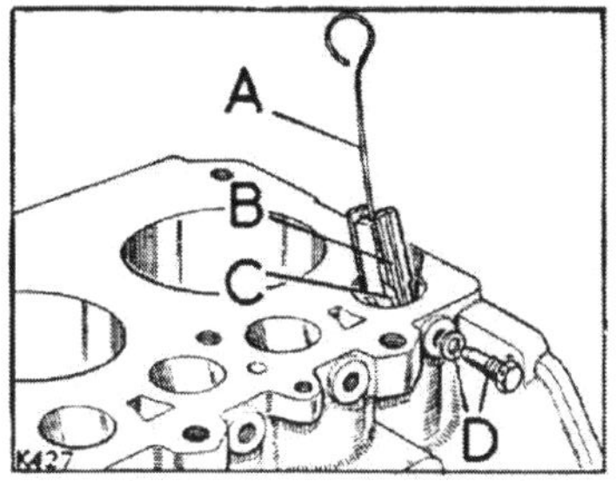

Fig. A1-85. Removing tappets and rollers
A—Spring clip
B—Tappet slide
C—Tappet roller
D—Locating screw and washer

8. Remove the tappet guides. The use of special tool, Part No. 530101 as illustrated will facilitate this procedure if the guides are difficult to remove by hand.

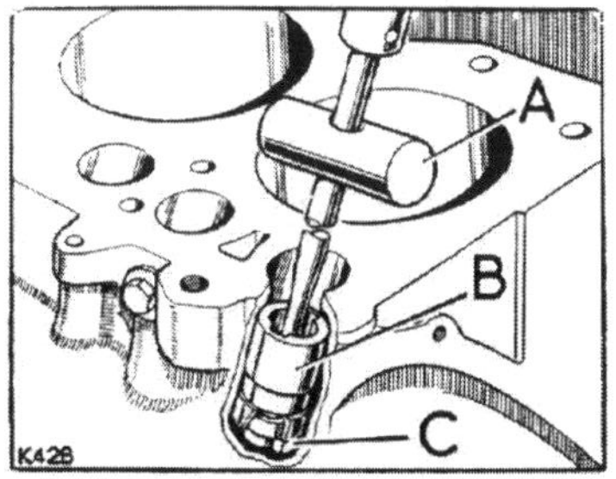

Fig. A1-86. Removing tappet guides
A—Special tool, Part No. 530101
B—Tappet guide
C—Extractor adaptor, part of special tool, Part No. 530101

9. It is advisable to retain the tappet guides, guides and rollers as related sets.

To refit

1. Fit the tappet guides and engage the locating bolts sufficient to retain the guides.

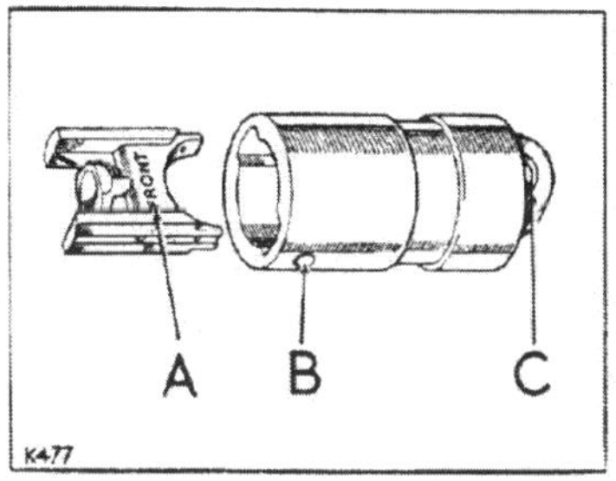

Fig. A1-87. Tappet slides and rollers
A—Letters 'FRONT' on slide to be toward front of engine
B—Hole for locating bolt
C—Larger chamfer on roller to be towards front of engine

Operation A1-24—continued

2. Fit the tappet slides and rollers, positioning the components relative to the front of the engine as illustrated in Fig. A1-87.
3. Tighten the locating bolts and lock together in pairs, using suitable gauge soft iron wire.
4. Smear clean engine oil on the cylinder block and cylinder head gasket joint faces to aid subsequent alignment of bolt holes. Position the gasket on the block with the lettering 'PETROL' uppermost.
5. Position the cylinder head on to the gasket. Clean all deposits from fixing bolt threads and engage the fixings.
6. Refit the tappet push rods to their original bores. Ensure that they bottom correctly into the spherical seats.
7. Clean the rocker shaft fixing bolt threads of all deposits; fit the rocker shaft assembly and engage the fixings.
8. Tighten the cylinder head and rocker shaft fixings in the order shown as follows:
   ½ in. UNF bolts—65 lb ft (8,9 mkg) torque load.
   ⁷⁄₁₆ in. UNF bolts—18 lb ft (2,4 mkg) torque load.
9. Set the tappet clearances to .010 in. (0,25 mm) for each valve.

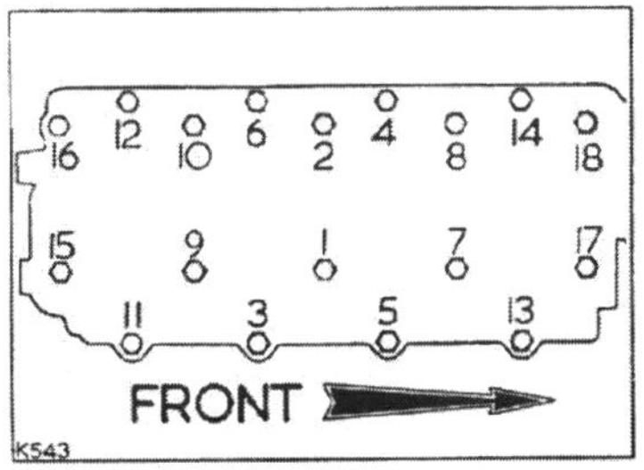

Fig. A1-88. Order of tightening cylinder head fixings

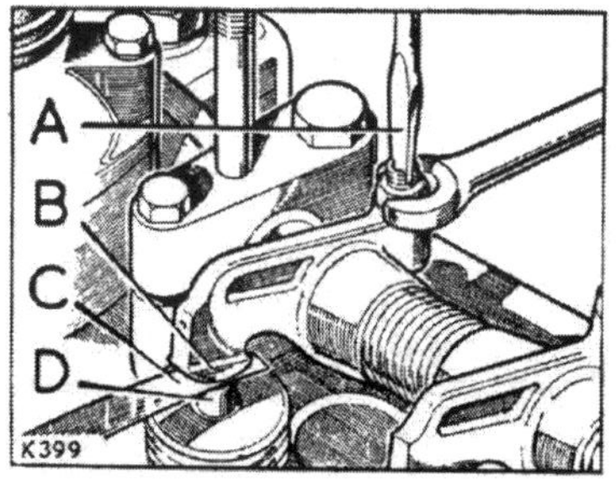

Fig. A1-89. Setting tappet clearances
A—Screwdriver   B—Rocker pad
C—Feeler gauge   D—Valve stem

The tappet setting is most easily carried out in the following sequence, No. 1 tappet being at the front of the engine:

Set No. 1 tappet clearance with No. 8 valve fully open.
Set No. 3 tappet clearance with No. 6 valve fully open.
Set No. 5 tappet clearance with No. 4 valve fully open.
Set No. 2 tappet clearance with No. 7 valve fully open.
Set No. 8 tappet clearance with No. 1 valve fully open.
Set No. 6 tappet clearance with No. 3 valve fully open.
Set No. 4 tappet clearance with No. 5 valve fully open.
Set No. 7 tappet clearance with No. 2 valve fully open.

10. Refit the engine top cover.
11. Complete refitting the cylinder head details, referring to Operation A1-22.
12. Refill the engine coolant system.

Operations marked with an asterisk (*) can be carried out with the engine installed in the vehicle

ENGINE—2¼ LITRE PETROL
Section A1—Land-Rover

Operation A1-24—continued

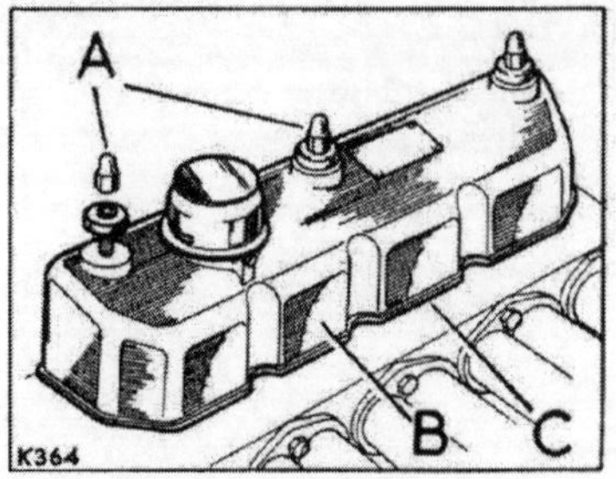

13. Connect the battery leads.
14. Refit the air cleaner. Operation A1-2.
15. Refit the bonnet panel. Operation A1-1.
16. After the initial engine run, that is with the engine at normal running temperature, check the cylinder head fixings to the correct torque load with the sparking plugs removed.

Fig. A1-90. Engine top cover

A—Fixings B—Top cover C—Joint washer

COOLANT SYSTEM
Bonneted Control Model, 2¼ Litre Petrol

Capacity	Imperial Unit	US Unit	Litres	Antifreeze	Frost Precaution
88	18 pints	21¾ pints	10.25	33⅓%	−25°F −32°C
109	18 pints	21¾ pints	10.25	33⅓%	−25°F −32°C

Section A1—Land-Rover
ENGINE—2¼ LITRE PETROL

*Engine front cover and oil seal, remove and refit—Operation A1-25

Workshop hand tools:
Spanner sizes: 2 BA open end, ¼ in. AF socket ½ in. AF, ⅞ in. AF open ended Screwdriver (medium), Pliers

Special tools:
Part No. 530102—Spanner for starter dog

To remove
1. Remove bonnet. Operation A1-1.
2. Remove radiator and grille panel. Operation A1-3.
3. Slacken dynamo fixings and remove fan belt.
4. Remove dynamo adjusting link to gain access to front cover fixings.
5. Remove the starter dog and fan belt driving pulley.
6. Separate the by-pass pipe from the thermostat housing.
7. Remove the front cover fixings, including those at sump front flange.
8. Remove the front cover and joint gaskets.

Oil seal
If a replacement oil seal is required, proceed as follows:

1. Carefully lever the oil seal metal casing away from the housing bore sufficient to collapse the seal and allow its removal. Use a screwdriver or suitable metal strip as a lever.
2. Apply a thin coating of suitable jointing compound, such as Hylomar SQ 32M, to the oil seal metal surfaces.

Fig. A1-91. Dynamo fixings
A—Adjusting link fixings
B—Fan belt pulley
C—At front support
D—At rear support
E—Electrical leads at dynamo

Fig. A1-92. Fan belt driving pulley fixings
A—Special tool. Part No. 530102 for starter dog
B—Starter dog
C—Lock plate
D—Fan belt driving pulley, key located

Fig. A1-93. Oil seal removal
A—Oil seal, shown collapsed
B—Suitable lever
C—Front cover inner face

3. Locate the oil seal squarely in the housing bore with the garter spring toward the operator and press fully in.

Operations marked with an asterisk (*) can be carried out with the engine installed in the vehicle

ENGINE—2¼ LITRE PETROL

Operation A1-25—continued

Front cover, to refit

1. It is of advantage temporarily to remove the fixing stud from the cylinder block front face. This will enable the front cover to be lifted sufficient to clear the edge of the sump gasket when offering the front cover to the engine.

2. Smear general purpose grease on both sides of the front cover and water inlet joint washers.

3. Continue the refitting by reversing the removal procedure, noting that the front cover is located to the cylinder block by dowels. Fig. A1-94 refers.

4. Refit the fixing stud if previously removed, from the front of the engine.

5. Fit the by-pass pipe to thermostat housing fixings. Fig. A1-94 refers.

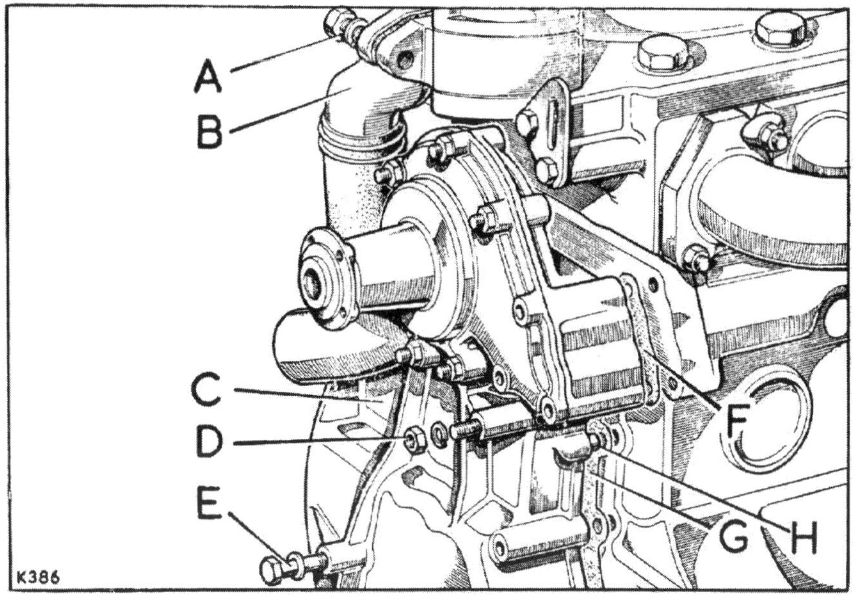

6. Fit the starter dog and fan belt driving pulley. Fig. A1-92 refers. The correct torque loading for the starter dog is 150 lb ft (20,5 mkg).

7. Fit the dynamo adjusting link, Fig. A1-91 refers. Set the fan belt tension to 7/16 in. to 7/16 in. (8 mm to 11 mm), checked by thumb pressure applied to the fan belt between the fan pulley and crankshaft pulley, when finally tightening the dynamo fixings.

8. Refit the radiator grille panel. Operation A1-3 and refill the coolant system.

9. Refit the bonnet panel. Operation A1-1.

COOLANT SYSTEM
Bonneted Control Model, 2¼ Litre Petrol

	Capacity	Imperial Unit	US Unit	Litres	Antifreeze	Frost Precaution
88	18 pints	18 pints	21¾ pints	10,25	33½%	−25°F −32°C
109	18 pints	18 pints	21¾ pints	10,25	33½%	−25°F −32°C

Fig. A1-94. Front cover and bracket fixings

A—Fixings for by-pass pipe
B—By-pass pipe
C—Front cover complete with water pump
D—Dynamo link fixing
E—Front cover fixings
F—Joint washer at water inlet
G—Joint washer
H—Locating dowels (2 off)

ENGINE—2¼ LITRE PETROL

*Timing chain tensioner, remove, inspect and refit—Operation A1-26

Workshop hand tools:
Spanner sizes: ½ in. AF, ⅜ in. AF socket, ⁷⁄₁₆ in. x ½ in. AF open end (2 off), 2 BA open end
Screwdriver (medium), Pliers

To remove

1. Remove bonnet panel. Operation A1-1.
2. Remove radiator and grille panel. Operation A1-3.

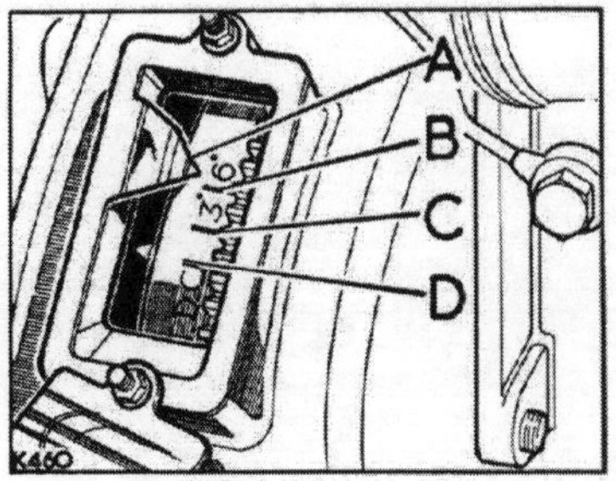

Fig. A1-95. Timing marks on flywheel, early engines
A—Timing pointer
B—6° mark, align when using 90-96 octane fuel
C—3° mark, align when using 80-85 octane fuel
D—TDC mark, align when using 74-76 octane fuel

3. Turn the crankshaft in the direction of rotation until the timing marks are aligned as illustrated.
4. Remove engine front cover. Operation A1-25.
5. Remove the fixings and withdraw the tensioner ratchet and spring from the piston housing.
6. Remove the piston housing fixings, compress the tensioner spring by hand and withdraw the tensioner arrangement complete.

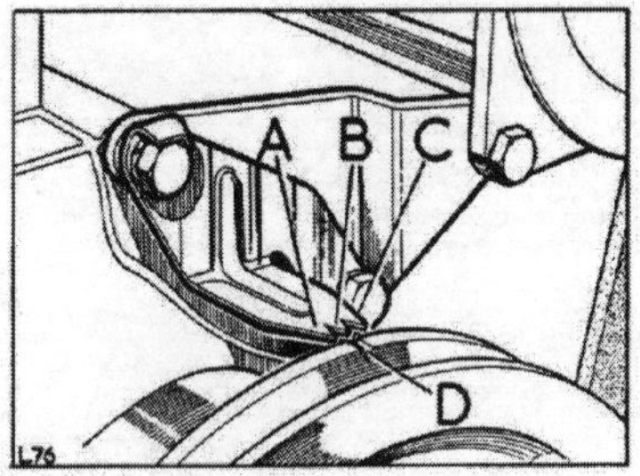

To dismantle and inspect

1. Remove the non-return valve ball, spring and plug from the piston housing.

Fig. A1-96. Timing marks at front cover
A—6° tongue, align when using 90-96 octane fuel
B—3° tongue, align when using 80-85 octane fuel
C—TDC tongue, align when using 74-76 octane fuel
D—Mark on crankshaft pulley, align with appropriate tongue

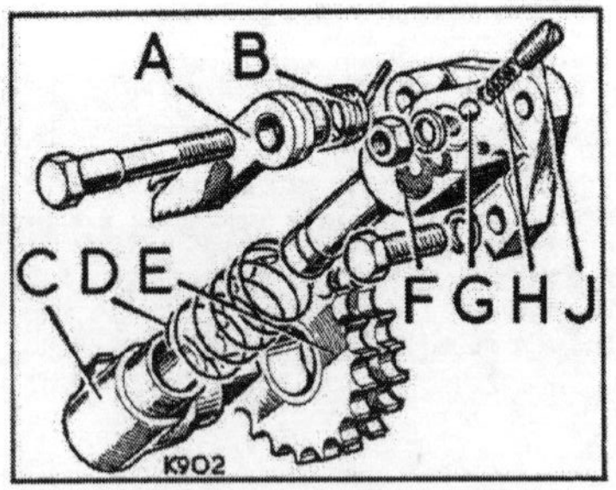

Fig. A1-97. Timing chain tensioner details
A—Ratchet
B—Ratchet spring
C—Cylinder
D—Chain tensioner spring
E—Idler wheel
F—Piston
G—Non-return ball valve
H—Spring for ball valve
J—Spring retainer plug

Operations marked with an asterisk (*) can be carried out with the engine installed in the vehicle

Operation A1-26—continued

2. Clean the components, using clean fuel.
3. Replace piston and housing if unduly worn.
4. If the tensioner cylinder bush is unduly worn, the cylinder and bush complete must be renewed.
5. Replace the idler wheel and ratchet arm if the bushes are unduly worn.
6. Inspect the rubber pad on the chain vibration damper on the engine block and replace if grooved.
7. Ensure that all oil passage drillings are clear.

To assemble

1. Refit the non-return valve ball, spring and plug to the piston housing. Fig. A1-97 refers.

To refit

1. Assemble together the piston housing, tensioner spring, cylinder and idler wheel. Compress the assembly against the tensioner spring.
2. Offer up the assembly to the engine, locating the piston housing on the dowels and the cylinder spigot in the location slot.
3. Fit the ratchet and spring and allow the idler wheel to take up the timing chain slack.

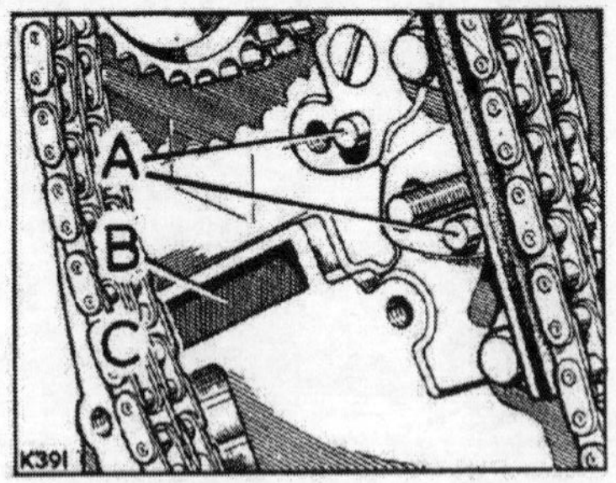

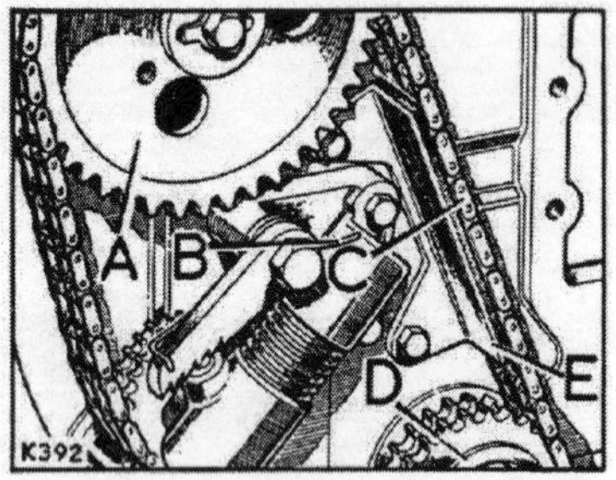

Fig. A1-99. Timing chain and chainwheels arrangement
A—Camshaft chainwheel
B—Ratchet spring
C—Timing chain, no slack at this side
D—Crankshaft chainwheel
E—Vibration damper

4. If necessary, adjust the position of the chain vibration damper to allow .010 in. (0.25 mm) maximum clearance between the timing chain and the vibration pad.
5. Temporarily refit the front cover and ensure that the timing marks are still correctly aligned at the flywheel or front cover as applicable. Figs. A1-95 and A1-96 refer. Then, providing the camshaft has not been rotated, this will ensure that the engine valve timing has not been inadvertently disturbed. If there is any doubt, check as detailed in 'Valve timing procedure', Operation A1-27.
6. Refit the engine front cover. Operation A1-25.
7. Refit the radiator grille panel, Operation A1-3, and refill the coolant system.
8. Refit the bonnet panel. Operation A1-1.

Fig. A1-98. Timing chain tensioner location details
A—Piston housing location dowels
B—Location slot for cylinder
C—Timing chain

COOLANT SYSTEM
Bonneted Control Model, 2¼ Litre Petrol

	Imperial Unit	US Unit	Litres	Antifreeze	Frost Precaution
Capacity	18 pints	21¼ pints	10.25	33⅓%	−25°F −32°C
88	18 pints	21¼ pints	10.25	33⅓%	−25°F
109	18 pints	21¼ pints	10.25	33⅓%	−32°C

ENGINE—2¼ LITRE PETROL

*Timing gears and chain, remove and refit—Operation A1-27

This operation includes valve timing procedure

Workshop hand tools:
Spanner sizes: ⅞ in. x ½ in. AF open end (2 off)
½ in. AF, ⅝ in. AF socket
½ BA open end
Screwdriver (medium), Pliers

Special tools:
Part No. 507231—Chainwheel extractor
Dial test Indicator and bracket

To remove

1. Remove bonnet panel. Operation A1-1.
2. Remove radiator and grille panel. Operation A1-3.
3. Remove the engine front cover. Operation A1-25.
4. Remove timing chain tensioner. Operation A1-26.
5. Lift off the timing chain and remove the chain-wheels, using special extractor tool, Part No. 507231 to withdraw the camshaft chainwheel.

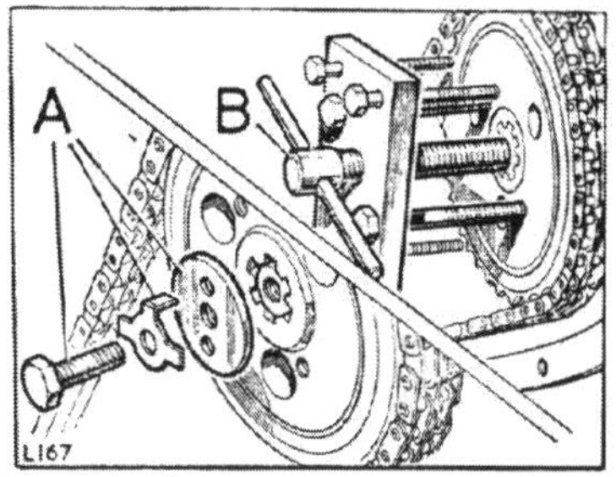

Fig. A1-100. Removing camshaft chainwheel
A—Camshaft chainwheel fixings
B—Extractor, Part No. 507231

6. Inspect the chainwheels and timing chain for damage and general condition.

To refit and set valve timing—engines with timing pointer on flywheel housing

1. Remove the engine top cover.

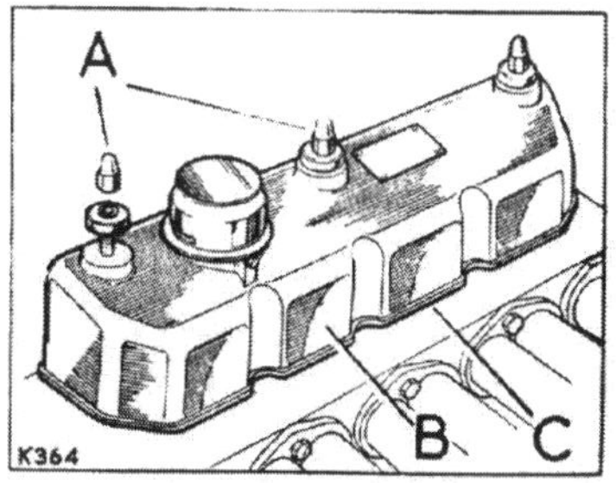

Fig. A1-101. Engine top cover
A—Fixings for top cover
B—Top cover
C—Joint washer

2. Remove the inspection cover plate from the flywheel housing.
3. Fit the crankshaft chainwheel, key located, larger shoulder first.
4. Turn the crankshaft in direction of rotation until the EP mark on flywheel is in line with timing pointer.

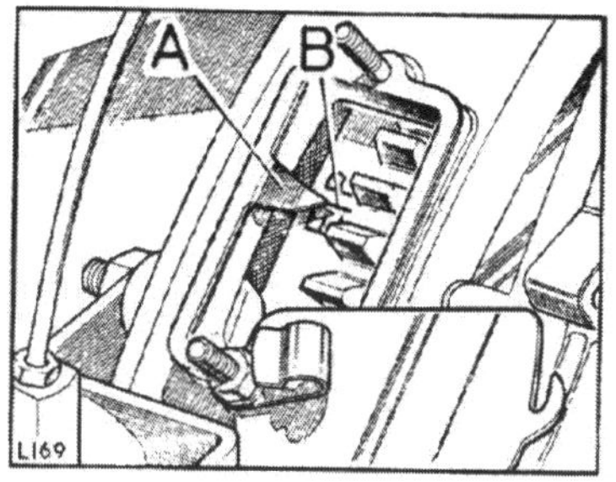

Fig. A1-102. Timing marks
A—Pointer at flywheel housing
B—EP mark on flywheel

Operations marked with an asterisk (*) can be carried out with the engine installed in the vehicle

---

Operation A1-27—continued

5. Fit the camshaft chainwheel on to the camshaft splines. Do not lock the fixings at this stage.
6. Rotate the camshaft until No. 1 cylinder exhaust valve is fully closed and set the tappet clearance to .010 in. (0.25 mm).

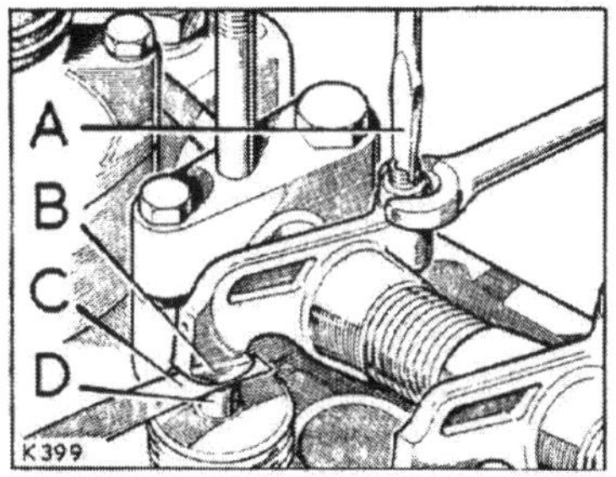

Fig. A1-103. Adjusting tappets
A—Screwdriver   C—Feeler gauge
B—Rocker pad   D—Valve stem

7. Fit a dial test indicator so that the 'fully open' position of the valve can be ascertained.

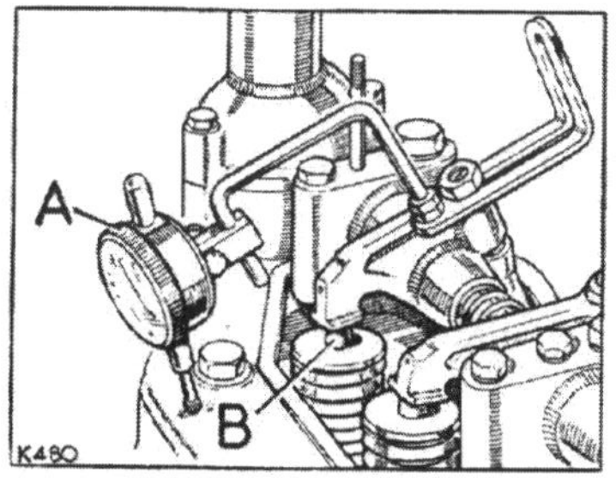

Fig. A1-104. Dial test Indicator in position
A—Dial test indicator
B—No. 1 cylinder exhaust valve

8. Turn the camshaft in direction of rotation until the rocker pad has nearly opened the valve fully. Stop camshaft rotation and suitably mark the chainwheel and the timing casing relative to each other.
9. Note the reading on the dial test indicator then further turn the camshaft in direction of rotation until the dial test indicator needle has reached the same position as previously noted. Stop rotation of camshaft.
10. Suitably mark the chainwheel adjacent to the mark previously made on the timing casing, then make a third mark to bisect the angle between the two previously made marks.

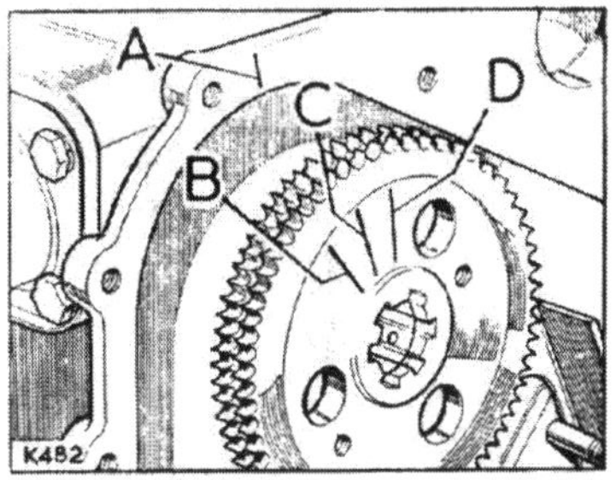

Fig. A1-105. Chainwheel marking
A—Mark previously made on timing casing
B—Second mark on chainwheel
C—Mark between two previously made marks on chainwheel
D—Mark first made on chainwheel

11. Turn the camshaft against the direction of rotation and align the third (middle) mark with the mark on the timing casing.
No. 1 exhaust valve is now fully open.
12. Fit the timing chain to the chainwheels with 'no slack' on the driving side.

If the chain is slack when fitted it is necessary to reposition the camshaft chainwheel on the camshaft splines which are off-set to allow for this adjustment. It will then be advisable to re-check the valve timing. Lock the camshaft chainwheel fixings when satisfactory.

ENGINE—2¼ LITRE PETROL

Operation A1-27—continued

13. Refit the inspection cover to the flywheel housing.
14. Refit the remaining components as detailed under "To rebuild" at the end of this Operation.

To refit and set valve timing—engines with timing pointer on engine front cover

1. Fit the crankshaft chainwheel, key located, larger shoulder first.
2. Rotate the crankshaft until the keyway in the crankshaft front end is vertical in relation to the cylinder bore. No. 1 cylinder piston is now at top dead centre, that is, at the position required for valve timing.

Fig. A1-106. Crankshaft, front end
A—Key for chainwheel in vertical position

3. Fit the camshaft chainwheel, using keyway marked 'P', and rotate the chainwheel until the groove marked 'P' is in line with the centre of the tapped hole as illustrated.
4. Fit the crankshaft chainwheel, locating on the key.
5. With the camshaft chainwheel positioned with the groove marked 'P' aligned with the tapped hole and with the crankshaft chainwheel keyway positioned vertical, fit the timing chain. There must be no slack chain on the driving side.

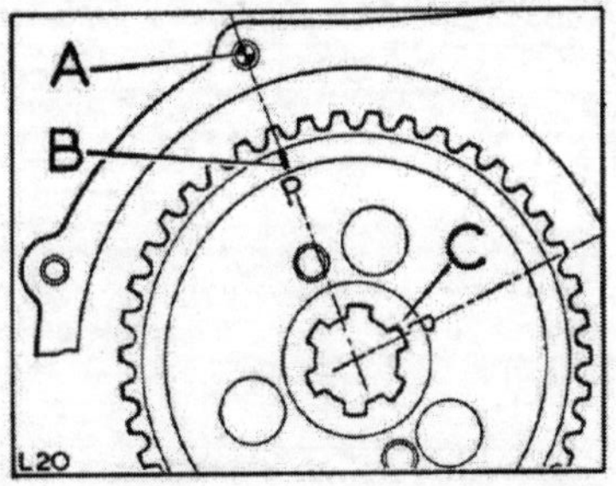

Fig. A1-107. Camshaft chainwheel in position
A—Tapped hole in cylinder block front face
B—Groove marked 'P' in line with centre of tapped hole
C—Fit spline marked 'P' on to camshaft key

6. With the chainwheels set in the above relationship, the valve timing is now correct. Lock the camshaft chainwheel fixings.

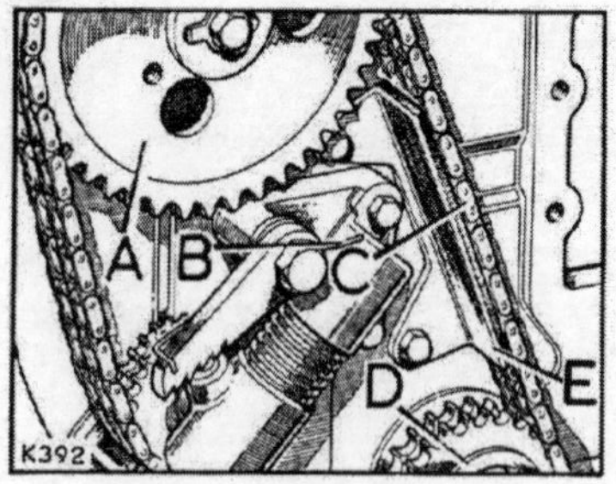

Fig. A1-108. Chainwheels fitted
A—Camshaft chainwheel
B—Ratchet spring
C—Ensure that there is 'no slack' at driving side of chain
D—Crankshaft chainwheel
E—Vibration damper

To rebuild

1. Refit the engine top cover. Fig. A1-101 refers.
2. Refit the timing chain tensioner. Operation A1-26.
3. Refit the engine front cover. Operation A1-25.
4. Refit the radiator grille panel. Operation A1-3.
5. Refill the engine coolant system, allowing a full flow through the coolant drain taps before closing them.
6. Refit the bonnet panel. Operation A1-1.

COOLANT SYSTEM
Bonneted Control Model, 2¼ Litre Petrol

	Capacity	Imperial Unit	US Unit	Litres	Antifreeze	Frost Precaution
88	18 pints	18 pints	21½ pints	10,25	33⅓%	−25°F −32°C
109	18 pints	18 pints	21½ pints	10,25	33⅓%	−25°F −32°C

ENGINE—2¼ LITRE PETROL

*Crankcase sump, remove and refit—Operation A1-28

Workshop hand tools:
Spanner sizes: ½ in. AF ring, 7/16 in. BSF socket

To remove

1. Drain off the engine lubricating oil.
2. Remove the fixings, lower and withdraw the sump.

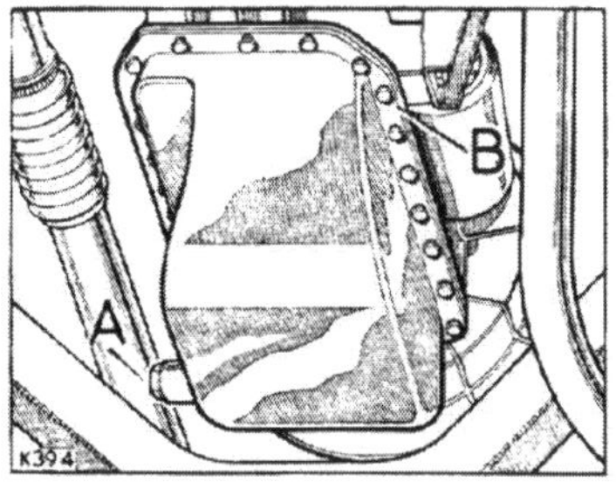

Fig. A1-109. View of crankcase sump

A—Drain plug   B—Sump fixings

To refit

1. Fit a new joint washer and reverse the removal procedure.
2. Replenish engine lubricating oil to 'high' mark on dipstick and check level after engine run.

ENGINE LUBRICANT CAPACITY
Bonneted Control Model, 2¼ Litre Petrol

		Capacity	Imperial Unit	US Unit	Litres
88	Engine	11 pints	11 pints	13 pints	6.0
	Filter	1½ pints	1¼ pints	1.8 pints	0.85
	Engine and Filter	12½ pints	12¼ pints	14.8 pints	6.85
109	Engine	11 pints	11 pints	13 pints	6.0
	Filter	1½ pints	1¼ pints	1.8 pints	0.85
	Engine and Filter	12½ pints	12¼ pints	14.8 pints	6.85

*Oil pump, remove and refit—Operation A1-29

(For overhaul Instructions Operation A1-30 refers)

Workshop hand tools:
Spanner sizes: ½ in. AF, 7/16 in. BSF socket, ½ in. AF ring

To remove

1. Remove crankcase sump. Operation A1-28.
2. Remove the oil pump fixings and withdraw the assembly complete with drive shaft.

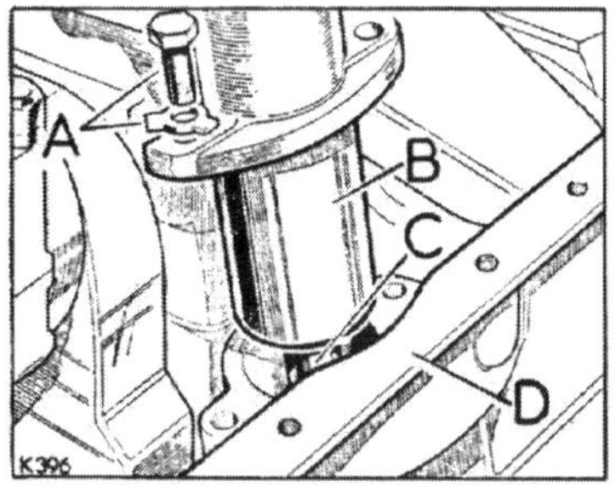

Fig. A1-110. Oil pump and drive shaft

A—Fixings
B—Oil pump
C—Drive shaft, longer splines engaged in pump
D—Sump joint face

To refit

1. Offer up the pump and drive shaft and engage the drive splines at the engine. Fit the fixings and secure.
2. Fit the crankcase sump and joint gasket.
3. Fill sump with clean oil to 'high' mark on dipstick. Check level and add oil if necessary after engine run.

ENGINE LUBRICANT CAPACITY
Bonneted Control Model, 2¼ Litre Petrol

		Capacity	Imperial Unit	US Unit	Litres
88	Engine	11 pints	11 pints	13 pints	6.0
	Filter	1½ pints	1¼ pints	1.8 pints	0.85
	Engine and Filter	12½ pints	12¼ pints	14.8 pints	6.85
109	Engine	11 pints	11 pints	13 pints	6.0
	Filter	1½ pints	1¼ pints	1.8 pints	0.85
	Engine and Filter	12½ pints	12¼ pints	14.8 pints	6.85

Operations marked with an asterisk (*) can be carried out with the engine installed in the vehicle

ENGINE—2¼ LITRE PETROL

*Oil pump, overhaul—Operation A1-30

(For removal and refitting instructions, Operation A1-29 refers)

Workshop hand tools:
Spanner sizes: ⁷⁄₁₆ in. AF, ½ in. AF socket, 1⅛ in. AF open end
¼ lb Hammer, Flat ended drift, Feeler gauges

To dismantle

1. Unscrew the union nut and withdraw filter from pump.
2. Remove the fixings and withdraw the cover from the body.
3. Withdraw the oil pump gears.
4. Remove the oil pressure relief valve components.
5. Clean all components and inspect for general condition.
6. Check the radial clearance and end-float of the gears as illustrated.
7. If necessary the idler gear bush may be renewed. Press the new bush into the gear, drill the lubrication hole .125 in. (3,175 mm) and ream the bush to .5 in. (12,7 mm).

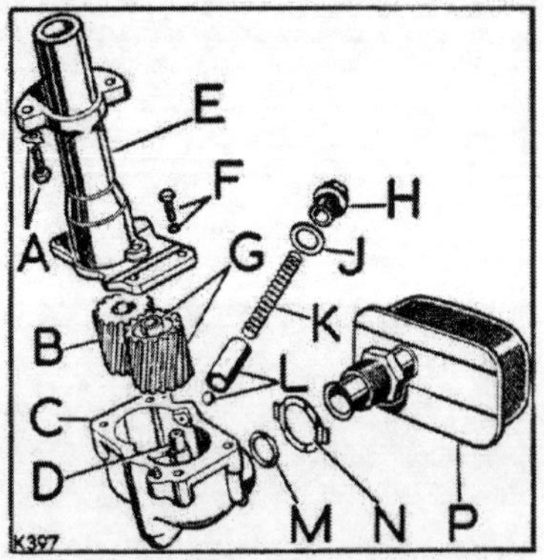

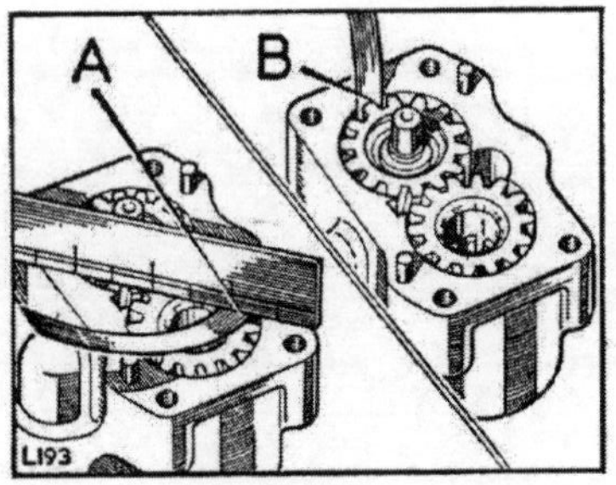

Fig. A1-112. Checking clearance of oil pump gears

A—Drive gear (steel)
B—Idler gear (aluminium)

8. Inspect the pressure relief valve ball seating and renovate, if necessary, using a locally manufactured lapping tool as illustrated.
9. The lapping tool may be installed in a drilling machine or hand brace and the ball seating refaced, using coarse grinding paste. The tool may then be removed and used to 'hand lap' the ball seating with fine grinding paste to a good finish. The seat must then be thoroughly cleaned.

Clearances:

End-float, steel gear .. .002 in. (0,05 mm) to .005 in. (0,12 mm)
End-float, aluminium gear .003 in. (0,07 mm) to .006 in. (0,15 mm)
Radial clearance of gears .001 in. to .004 in. (0,02 mm to 0,10 mm)
Backlash of gears.. .. .006 in. to .012 in. (0,15 mm to 0,28 mm)

Fig. A1-111. Exploded view of oil pump

A—Fixings, oil pump to cylinder block
B—Pump drive gear
C—Pump body
D—Idler gear spindle
E—Pump cover and shaft housing
F—Fixings, cover to body
G—Idler gear and bush assembly
H—Threaded plug
J—Washer
K—Spring
L—Relief valve ball and plunger
M—Sealing ring
N—Lockwasher
P—Oil filter

Operations marked with an asterisk (*) can be carried out with the engine installed in the vehicle

Operation A1-30—continued

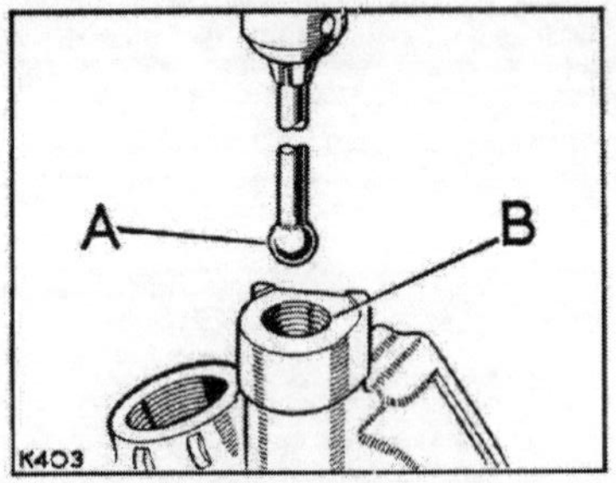

Fig. A1-113. Lapping tool for ball valve seat

A—Steel ball, Rover Part No. 3748, soldered to suitable tubing
B—Relief valve housing bore

To assemble

1. Fit the pump gears to the body, with the plain portion of the drive gear bore uppermost.
2. Smear the joint faces with suitable jointing compound and fit the pump cover to the pump body, locating on the dowels.
3. Assemble the pressure relief valve components to the housing bore. When fitting the plunger, insert the end with the integral ball seating first.
4. Fit the oil filter to the pump.
5. Position the filter such that it will be square to the sump baffle plate when fitted and secure with the lockwasher.

ENGINE—2¼ LITRE PETROL

*Clutch assembly and flywheel, remove and refit—Operation A1-31

(For overhaul instructions, Section B refers. For flywheel data see Engine detail data at end of this Section)

Workshop hand tools:
Spanner sizes: ½ in. AF, ⅝ in. AF open end, ⅝ in. AF socket
⅞ in. AF open end, ⅞ in. AF socket
⁷⁄₁₆ in. BSF open end
1 lb hammer, Small chisel

Special tools:
Part No. 605022—Clutch plate alignment gauge
Torque wrench
Dial test Indicator

To remove

Note: If it is required to remove the clutch only, it is not necessary to remove the clutch seat base nor completely remove the gearbox. Proceed with the gearbox removal, Operation C1-3, but only withdraw the gearbox rearward approximately 5 in. (127 mm), to give access to the clutch fixings.

1. Remove the front floor. Operation A1-4.
2. Remove the gearbox complete, as detailed in Section C.
3. Mark the position of the clutch assembly cover plate in relation to the flywheel. The marks are for use during subsequent refitting, when, with the marks aligned, the original balance condition will be regained.
4. Remove the fixings and withdraw the clutch assembly from the flywheel. Withdraw the clutch plate which is released during this procedure.
5. Remove the fixings and withdraw the flywheel.

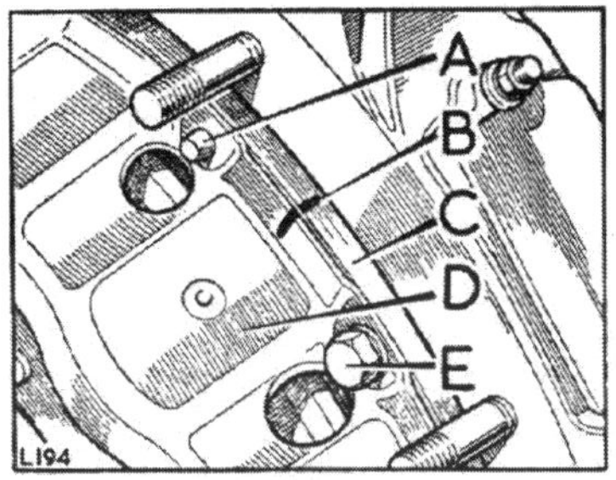

Fig. A1-114. Clutch assembly fixings

A—Locating dowel
B—Suitably mark clutch cover relative to flywheel
C—Flywheel
D—Clutch assembly
E—Fixings for clutch (6 off)

Operation A1-31—continued

To refit

1. Fit the flywheel to the crankshaft and tighten the fixings to 60 lb ft to 65 lb ft (8,5 mkg to 9 mkg) torque load. Do not lock the fixings at this stage.
2. Check the run-out on the flywheel face as illustrated. The run-out must not exceed .002 in. (0,05 mm).
3. Lock the flywheel fixings.
4. Offer the clutch driven plate to the primary shaft and ensure that it will slide easily on all the splines.
5. Place the driven plate in position on the flywheel with the longer end of the central boss away from the engine.
6. Centralise the driven plate with the flywheel, using a slave primary shaft or the special centralising tool, Part No. 605022.
7. Offer up the clutch assembly to the flywheel, aligning the previously made relationship markings. Fig. A1-114 refers.
8. Fit the fixings and tighten evenly one turn at a time, using diagonal selection to avoid distortion of the clutch cover, to 22 lb ft to 25 lb ft (3,0 mkg to 3,5 mkg) torque load.
9. Lock the clutch assembly fixings where applicable.
10. Remove the centralising tool or slave shaft.
11. Refit the gearbox as detailed in Section C.
12. Check and set the clutch pedal adjustment as detailed in Section B.
13. Refit the front floor. Operation A1-4.

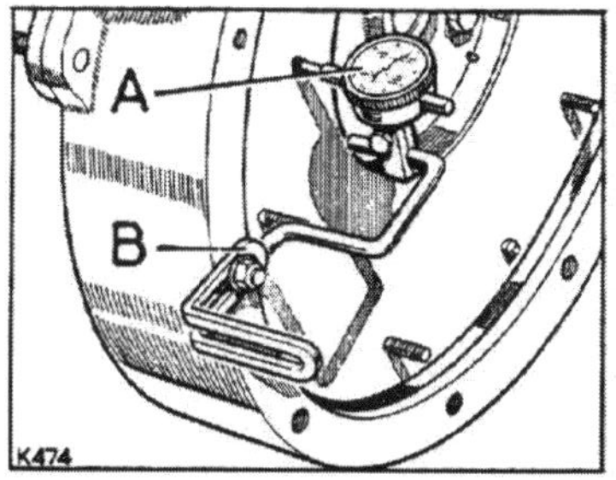

Fig. A1-115. Checking run-out on flywheel face

A—Dial test indicator
B—Suitable bracket

Fig. A1-116. Centralising clutch driven plate

A—Flywheel
B—Flywheel fixings
C—Driven plate
D—Centralising tool or slave primary shaft

Operations marked with an asterisk (*) can be carried out with the engine installed in the vehicle

ENGINE—2¼ LITRE PETROL

*Rear main bearing oil seal and flywheel housing, remove and refit—Operation A1-32

Workshop hand tools:
Spanner sizes: 7/16 in. AF, 7/16 in. AF open end
5/8 in. BSF, 7/16 in. BSF open end
7/16 in. AF, 1/2 in. AF, 9/16 in. AF, 5/8 in. AF, 1 1/16 in. AF socket
1/4 in. AF ring
7/16 in. BSF socket
Screwdriver (medium), Pliers, snipe nosed
1 lb hammer, Small chisel, Feeler gauges

Special tools:
Part No. 600963—Engine lifting sling
Part No. 270304—Guides for rear main bearing oil seal (2 off)
Part No. 605022—Clutch plate alignment gauge
Torque wrench

To remove

1. Remove bonnet panel. Operation A1-1.
2. Remove the front floor. Operation A1-4.
3. Remove gearbox assembly. Section C.
4. Remove the starter motor. Operation A1-9.
5. Remove the crankcase sump. Operation A1-28.
6. Remove the clutch assembly and flywheel. Operation A1-31.
7. Fit suitable lifting equipment and support the engine weight.

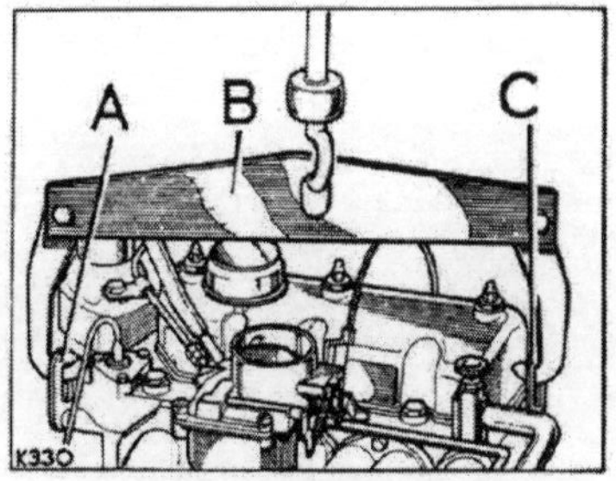

Fig. A1-117. Lifting sling in position
A—Front lifting bracket
B—Engine lifting sling, Part No. 600963, engaged in lifting brackets
C—Rear lifting bracket

8. Remove the packing piece from between the flywheel housing and the chassis cross-member, previously fitted during gearbox removal.
9. Remove the fixings and withdraw the flywheel housing. Remove the oil sealing ring.

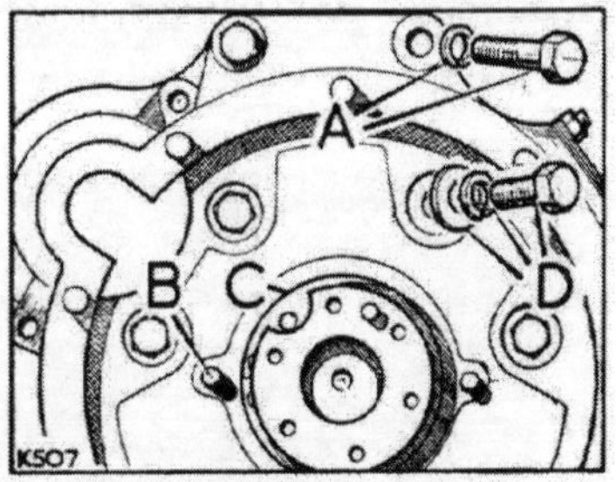

Fig. A1-118. Flywheel housing fixings
A—Fixings at flange
B—Locating dowels
C—Oil seal in recess
D—Fixings in counter-bores

10. Remove the rear bearing cap.
11. Remove the fixings and detach the two halves of the rear main bearing retainer from the cylinder block and rear bearing cap respectively. The halves are dowel located.

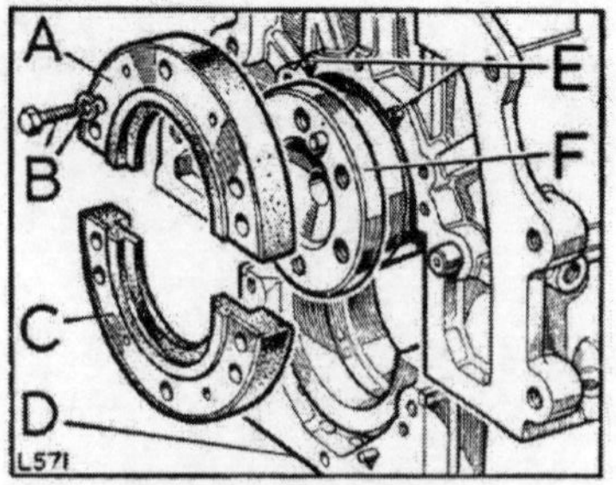

Fig. A1-119. Seal retainer fixings
A—Seal retainer upper half
B—Fixings for seal retainer
C—Seal retainer lower half
D—Rear main bearing cap
E—Locating dowels
F—Crankshaft flange, rotate to align cut-out with fixings

12. Remove the oil seal from the crankshaft.

Rear main bearing oil seal, to refit

1. Assemble the garter spring on the oil seal journal of the crankshaft, laying the spring around the journal, with the hook and the eye adjacent to one another, then insert the hook into the eye. See Fig. A1-121. Care must be taken to ensure that during this operation the spring is not stretched at all.

   The spring should be moved along the journal until it is against the thrower flange.

2. Apply Silicone Grease MS4 to the crankshaft oil seal journal and to both sides of the split oil seal sealing lip.

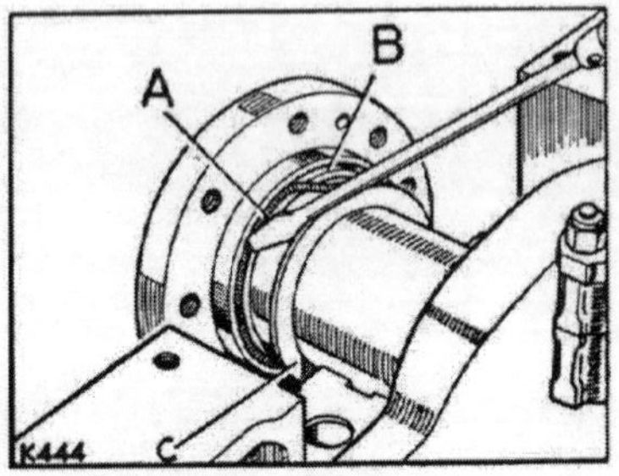

Fig. A1-121. Fitting garter spring to recess
A—Garter spring
B—Oil seal recess for garter spring
C—Thrower flange

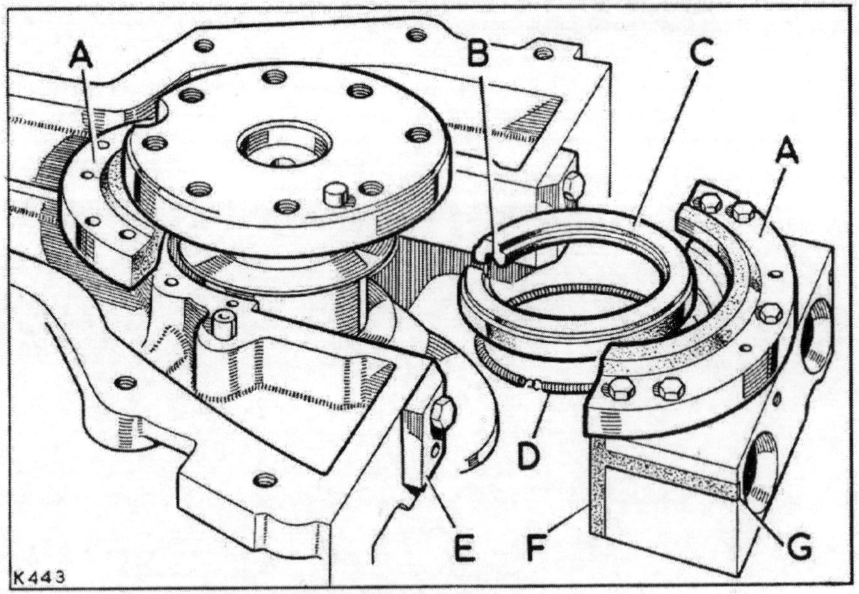

Fig. A1-120. Oil seal details
A—Retainer halves
B—Split line of seal to be towards top of engine
C—Split oil seal
D—Garter spring, hook and eye to be midway between split and hinge of oil seal when fitted
E—Guides, Part No. 270304, for rear main bearing cap 'T' seals
F—Trim these edges before fitting to avoid seal folding up when fitting
G—Trim these ends when cap is fitted to allow 1/32 in. (0.8 mm) protrusion

Operations marked with an asterisk (*) can be carried out with the engine installed in the vehicle

Operation A1-32—continued

Open the split seal sufficiently to allow it to be fitted over the crankshaft oil seal journal. Recess in oil seal must be towards thrower flange and garter spring.

The oil seal must not be repeatedly fitted and removed from the crankshaft, as this can damage the sealing lip.

3. Ensure that the hook and eye of the garter spring are located mid-way between the split and hinge of the oil seal. Then, using a small screwdriver or similar tool, gently ease the spring into the recess in the oil seal.

4. Rotate the oil seal until the split in the cylinder head and in its approximate running position on the journal; this position is important.

Apply Hylomar SQ32M sealing compound to the seal diameter of the two half plates, using either an applicator or a brush.

Important: Do not degrease the half seal plates with trichlorethylene, but wipe clean with a dry cloth prior to applying the Hylomar.

5. Fit one half of the oil seal retainer on to the crankcase dowels. The oil seal should be compressed to assist assembly, also ensure that it is correctly located in the retainer recess. Bolt the retainer to the crankcase, leaving the two bolts adjacent to the split line finger-tight, fully tighten the remaining three bolts. In order to fit the bolt it will be necessary to hold the seal so that it does not rotate with the crankshaft.

6. Bolt the other half of the oil seal retainer on to the main bearing cap, in the same way. Apply Silicone grease MS4 to the 'T' seals and fit them to the main bearing cap. The cap must be off the crankcase for these operations. Trim the edges of the 'T' seals as illustrated to prevent them from fouling the cylinder block when fitted.

7. Fit the main bearing cap with the seal retainer, bearing shell and 'T' seals to the crankcase until there is a ¹⁄₃₂ in. (0,8 mm) gap between the cap and crankcase. Use the guides, Part No. 270304 to feed the 'T' seals past the crankcase edges, see Fig. A1-120.

8. Ensure that the seal remains correctly located in the retainer recess.

9. Pull the cap down slowly, ensuring there is no buckling of the split seal or misalignment of the butt joint.

10. Tighten the cap bolts to 85 lb ft (11,5 mkg) torque load and recheck that the seal is located correctly in the housing.

11. Finally tighten the bolts securing the retainer halves. Turn the bolt heads so that the hexagon corners will not foul the flywheel housing seal when fitting.

Flywheel housing, to refit

12. Replace the oil seal in the flywheel housing recess and fit the housing to the cylinder block. Fig. A1-118 refers.

13. Refit the clutch and flywheel. Operation A1-31.

14. Refit the crankcase sump. Operation A1-28. During this procedure trim the ends of the rear main bearing 'T' seals to allow approximately ¹⁄₃₂ in. (0,8 mm) protrusion from the rear bearing cap face. Fig. A1-120 refers.

15. Refit the starter motor. Operation A1-9.

16. Refit the gearbox, as described in Section C, and remove the engine lifting equipment.

17. Refit the front floor. Operation A1-4.

18. Replenish engine lubricating oil as necessary.

ENGINE LUBRICANT CAPACITY
Bonnated Control Model, 2¼ Litre Petrol

	Capacity	Imperial Unit	US Unit	Litres
88	Engine	11 pints	13 pints	6,0
	Filter	1½ pints	1,8 pints	0,85
	Engine and Filter	12½ pints	14,8 pints	6,85
109	Engine	11 pints	13 pints	6,0
	Filter	1½ pints	1,8 pints	0,85
	Engine and Filter	12½ pints	14,8 pints	6,85

19. Refit the bonnet panel. Operation A1-1.

---

*Pistons and connecting rods, remove and refit—Operation A1-33

(For overhaul instructions, Operation A1-34 refers)

Workshop hand tools:
Spanner sizes: ⁷⁄₁₆ in. AF, ½ in. AF, ⁹⁄₁₆ in. AF, ¾ in. AF sockets
¼ in. AF, ⁷⁄₁₆ in. AF, ⅜ in. AF, ⅝ in. AF, ¾ in. AF open end
⅞ in. AF ring
⅜ in. BSF, ⅝ in. BSF open end
14 mm plug spanner
Screwdriver (medium), Pliers

Special tools:
Torque wrench

To remove

1. Remove the bonnet panel. Operation A1-1.
2. Remove the air cleaner. Operation A1-2.
3. Remove the valve gear and rocker shaft. Operation A1-20.
4. Remove the cylinder head. Operation A1-22.
5. Remove the crankcase sump. Operation A1-28.
6. With two pistons at bottom dead centre (BDC) remove the connecting rod cap fixings.
7. Remove the caps and withdraw the connecting rod bearing halves. Retain the caps and bearings in related sets.

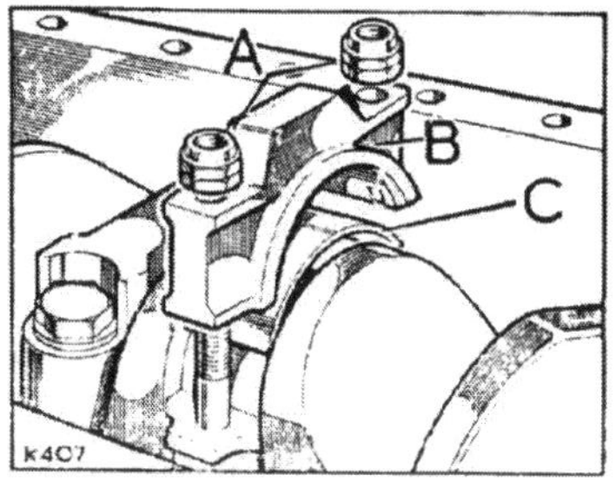

Fig. A1-122. Connecting rod big-end details
A—Fixings for connecting rod caps
B—Connecting rod caps
C—Connecting rod bearing lower half

8. Withdraw the pistons and attached connecting rods from the top of the bore.
9. Position the remaining pistons at BDC and repeat the removal procedure.
10. Retain the removed components in related sets.

To refit

Note: If replacement components are to be fitted, the checks detailed in 'overhaul—Operation A1-34' must be carried out as necessary.

1. Position the crankshaft with two crank pins at BDC and insert the appropriate pistons and attached connecting rods (oil hole toward camshaft) into the cylinder bores, from the top of the cylinder block, using a suitable piston ring clamp.

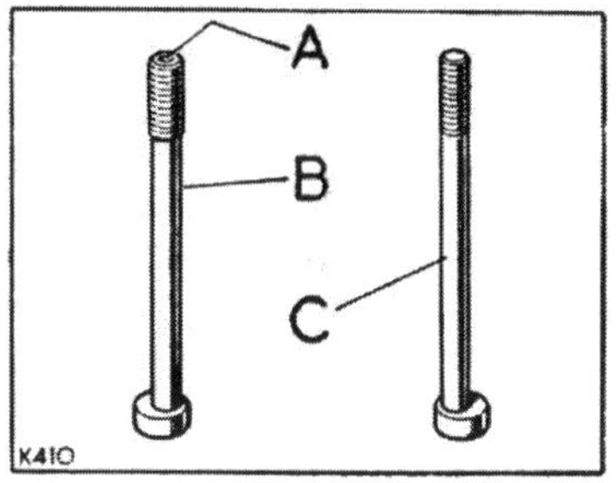

Fig. A1-123. Identification of connecting rod fixing bolts
A—Drilled point to identify rolled threads
B—Bolts with rolled threads
C—Bolts with machined threads

2. Lubricate the journals and bearing halves and fit the appropriate bearing halves to the connecting rods and caps.
3. Fit the connecting rod caps and new fixing nuts. Tighten the fixings to 35 lb ft (4,9 mkg) for bolts with machined threads and 25 lb ft (3,5 mkg) for bolts with rolled threads, referring to the illustration Fig. A1-123 for identification of threads.

Operations marked with an asterisk (*) can be carried out with the engine installed in the vehicle

ENGINE—2¼ LITRE PETROL

Operation A1-33—continued

4. Repeat the procedure to fit the remaining piston assemblies.
5. Refit the crankcase sump. Operation A1-28.
6. Refit the cylinder head. Operation A1-22.
7. Refit the valve gear and rocker shaft. Operation A1-20.
8. Set the tappet clearances as detailed in Operation A1-19.
9. Refill the engine coolant system.

COOLANT SYSTEM
Bonneted Control Model, 2¼ Litre Petrol

	Capacity	Imperial Unit	US Unit	Litres	Antifreeze	Frost Precaution
88	18 pints	18 pints	21½ pints	10,25	33½%	−25°F / −32°C
109	18 pints	18 pints	21½ pints	10,25	33½%	−25°F / −32°C

10. Replenish the engine lubrication system.

ENGINE LUBRICANT CAPACITY
Bonneted Control Model, 2¼ Litre Petrol

		Imperial Unit	US Unit	Litres
88	Engine	11 pints	13 pints	6,0
	Filter	1½ pints	1,8 pints	0,85
	Engine and Filter	12½ pints	14,8 pints	6,85
109	Engine	11 pints	13 pints	6,0
	Filter	1½ pints	1,8 pints	0,85
	Engine and Filter	12½ pints	14,8 pints	6,85

11. Refit the bonnet panel. Operation A1-1.

ENGINE—2¼ LITRE PETROL

Pistons and connecting rods, overhaul—Operation A1-34
(For removal and refitting instructions, Operation A1-33 refers)

Workshop hand tools:
Spanner sizes: ⅞ in. AF socket
Circlip pliers, Feeler gauge

Special tools:
Torque wrench
Part No. 605238—'Plastigage' strip
Piston ring clamp

To dismantle

Note: During the following procedures retain all components in related sets to facilitate subsequent assembly.

1. Remove the piston rings using suitable expanding pliers.
2. Remove circlips and withdraw gudgeon pins. Where piston crowns are marked with an 'X', withdraw the gudgeon pin toward the 'X' side. Removal of gudgeon pins is facilitated if the piston is first warmed to 55°C (131°F) approximately.

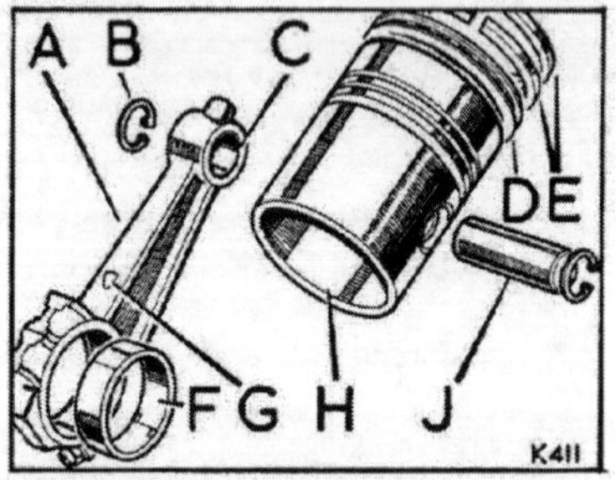

Fig. A1-124. Exploded view of piston and connecting rod
A—Connecting rod assembly
B—Retaining circlips for gudgeon pin
C—Connecting rod bush
D—Scraper ring
E—Compression rings
F—Bearing halves
G—Oil spray hole
H—Piston
J—Gudgeon pin

3. Clean all components and inspect for damage and general condition.

Checking piston clearance in cylinder bore

1. Insert a long .0025 in. (0,063 mm) feeler gauge down the RH side of the cylinder bore. Insert the correct piston inverted into the cylinder bore. Position the gudgeon pin bore parallel with the centre line of the engine.

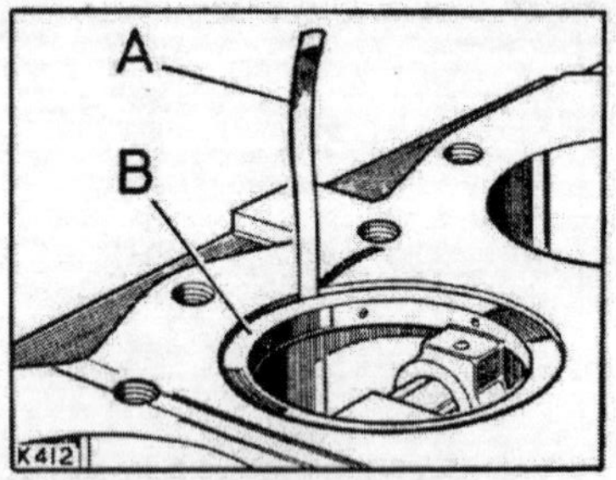

Fig. A1-125. Checking piston clearance
A—Feeler gauge
B—Piston in cylinder bore

2. Push the piston down the cylinder until the piston skirt reaches its tightest point in the bore. At this point withdraw the feeler gauge—a steady resistance should be felt. If necessary, select pistons from the range available until this check is satisfactory.

3. Graded pistons of standard size are available for replacement purposes. The grade letter which is stamped on the piston crown represents a diameter dimension as follows:

Grade letter	Cylinder bore diameter
'Z'	Nominal to plus .0002 in. (0,005 mm) above nominal.
'A'	.0002 in. to .0004 in. (0,005 mm to 0,01 mm) above nominal
'B'	.0004 in. to .0006 in. (0,01 mm to 0,015 mm) above nominal.
'C'	.0006 in. to .0008 in. (0,015 mm to 0,02 mm) above nominal.
'D'	.0008 in. to .0010 in. (0,02 mm to 0,025 mm) above nominal.

The original grade letter of the cylinder bore will be found stamped on the cylinder block adjacent to the respective cylinder bore.

Operations marked with an asterisk (*) can be carried out with the engine installed in the vehicle

ENGINE—2¼ LITRE PETROL

Operation A1-34—continued

Where cylinder reboring is necessary, oversize pistons are available for replacement purposes. Refer to Operation A1-38 for cylinder bore overhaul details.

Checking piston ring clearance

1. Check the piston ring gaps in the cylinder bores using a slave piston as illustrated to keep the rings square in the bore.

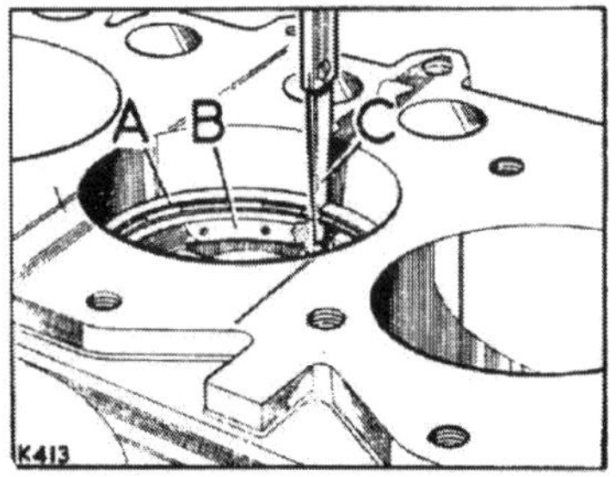

Fig. A1-126. Checking piston ring gap
A—Piston ring
B—Slave piston
C—Gap to be .015 in. to .020 in. (0,38 mm to 0,5 mm) for all rings

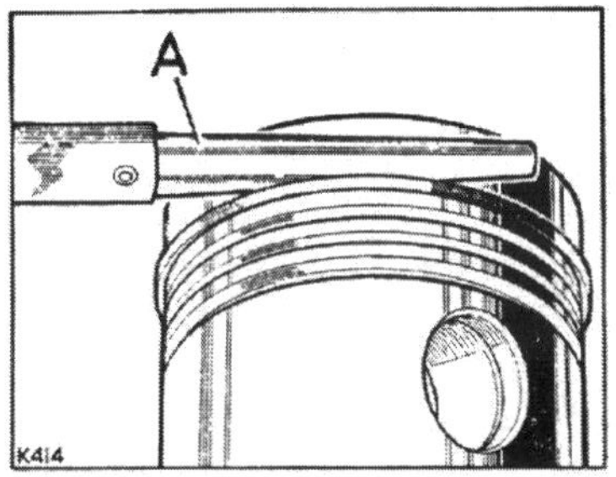

Fig. A1-127. Checking ring clearance in groove
A—Side clearance for compression rings to be .0018 in. to .0038 in. (0,046 mm to 0,097 mm)
Side clearance for scraper rings to be .0015 in. to .0035 in. (0,038 mm to 0,089 mm)

2. Check the piston ring clearance in the piston grooves as shown. Fit the two compression rings with the sides marked 'T' or 'Top' uppermost. The scraper ring may be fitted either way.

Connecting rod checks

1. Measure the gudgeon pin fit in the connecting rod bush. The required fitted clearance is .0003 in. to .0005 in. (0,007 mm to 0,012 mm) giving an easy sliding fit when cold and dry. A replacement bush must be reamed when fitted to obtain this clearance. Ensure that the pre-drilled oil hole is aligned with the connecting rod oil hole when pressing in a replacement bush.

2. Check the gudgeon pin diameter relative to the piston bore. The required interference fit is zero to .0002 in. (0,005 mm).

3. Fit each connecting rod to a suitable test fixture and check for twist and malalignment.

Connecting rod bearing cap checks

1. Select the correct cap for each connecting rod as denoted by the number stamped near the joint faces. This number also indicates the crankshaft journal to which it must be fitted.

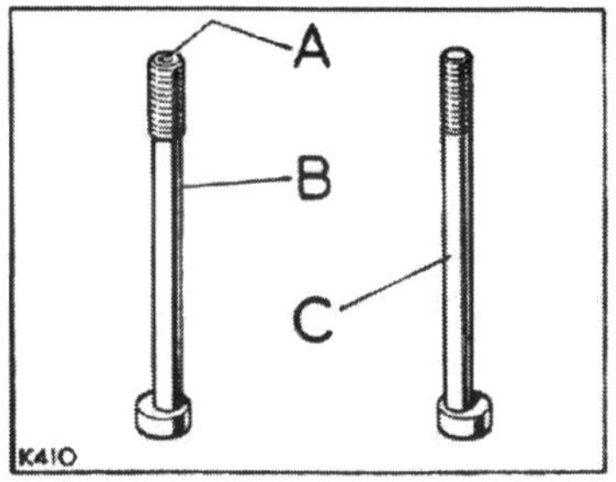

Fig. A1-128. Connecting rod cap fixings identification
A—Drilled point
B—Rolled threads
C—Machined threads

2. Assemble the caps, less bearing halves, to the respective connecting rods.

3. Tighten the fixings to 35 lb ft (4,9 mkg) for bolts with machined threads; tighten to 25 lb ft (3,5 mkg) for bolts with rolled threads, identified by a drill point at nut end.

4. Slacken off one fixing and check that there is no clearance at the joint face. If there is clearance then the assemblies must be replaced.

Connecting rod bearing nip

1. Fit the bearing halves. Torque tighten the fixings then slacken one fixing as before and check the clearance between the joint faces. The clearance must be .002 in. to .004 in. (0,05 mm to 0,10 mm).

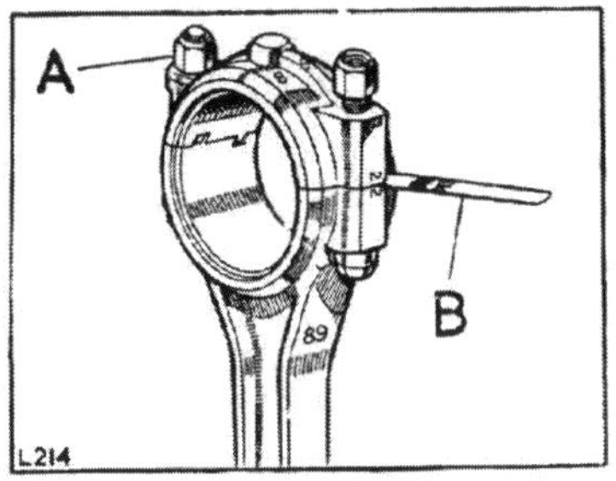

Fig. A1-129. Checking connecting rod bearing nip
A—Fixing, torque loaded
B—Feeler gauge

The bearing nip can be corrected by selective assembly of the bearing shells; these are available in slightly varying thicknesses. Do not file or machine the caps or connecting rods to vary the bearing nip.

2. Assemble each connecting rod assembly to its respective crankshaft journal and repeat the connecting rod bearing nip check. Again the clearance between the connecting rod and cap must be .002 in. to .004 in. (0,05 mm to 0,10 mm).

Alternatively, use 'Plastigage' strip inserted between the connecting rod bearings and the crankshaft journals. This method will indicate the actual clearance between the bearings and the journals and must be .001 in. to .0025 in. (0,025 mm to 0,063 mm) with the fixings torque loaded as in the alternative method.

'Plastigage' is available under Rover Part No. 605238. Remove all traces of 'Plastigage' from the components after use.

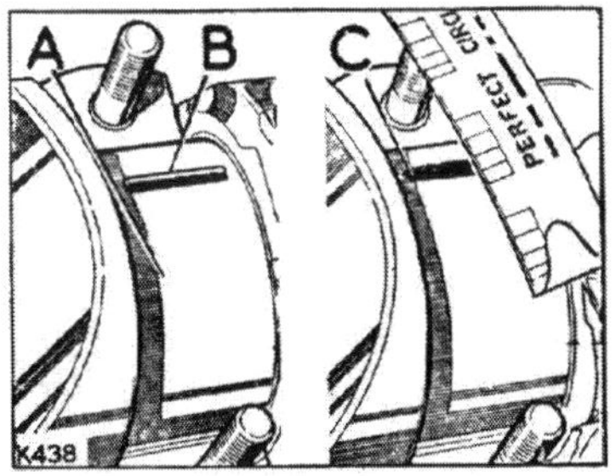

Fig. A1-130. Checking connecting rod and bearing clearance, using 'Plastigage'
A—Journal for connecting rod
B—Initial position of 'Plastigage'
C—Flattened 'Plastigage', do not remove until width has been measured against graduated scale on 'Plastigage' packet

3. Make a final check to prove the bearing clearance, using a .0025 in. (0,063 mm) shim paper. The connecting rod should resist rotation when the shim paper is fitted between the journal and one half of the bearing shell and move freely by hand with the shim paper removed.

Connecting rod end-float check

1. Check the connecting rod end-float using a feeler gauge inserted between the end face of the rod and the journal shoulder.

The end-float should be .007 in. to .011 in. (0,20 mm to 0,30 mm).

2. Remove the connecting rods from the crankshaft and retain all parts as related sets.

ENGINE—2¼ LITRE PETROL

Crankshaft and main bearings, remove and refit—Operation A1-35

(For overhaul instructions, Operation A1-36 refers)

Special tools:
Part No. 600963—Engine lifting sling
Part No. 270304—Guides for rear main bearing oil seal (2 off)
Part No. 605022—Clutch plate alignment gauge
Torque wrench

Workshop hand tools:
Spanner sizes: ⅞ in. AF, ⅞ in. AF, ¾ in. AF, ⅝ in. AF open end ⅞ in. AF, ⅝ in. AF, ½ in. AF, ½ in. AF, ⁷⁄₁₆ in. AF socket, ⅜ in. BSF, ⁷⁄₁₆ in. BSF open ¼ in. BSF socket
⅜ in. AF, ⅞ in. AF ring
1 lb hammer, Small chisel, Feeler gauges

To remove

1. Remove bonnet panel. Operation A1-1.
2. Remove air cleaner. Operation A1-2.
3. Remove radiator and grille panel complete. Operation A1-3.
4. Remove front floor. Operation A1-4.
5. Remove engine from vehicle. Operation A1-5.
6. Remove crankcase sump. Operation A1-28.
7. Fit the engine to a suitable stand.
8. Remove oil pump. Operation A1-29.
9. Remove engine front cover. Operation A1-25.
10. Remove timing chain and tensioner. Operation A1-26.
11. Remove clutch and flywheel. Operation A1-31.
12. Remove flywheel housing. Operation A1-32.
13. Remove the connecting rod caps and bearing lower halves. Retain as related sets.
14. Remove the main bearing caps and lift crankshaft clear. Retain the bearing halves and caps in related sets.
15. Remove the oil seal from the crankshaft.
16. Remove the seal retainer halves, Fig. A1-133 refers.

To refit

1. Where replacement components are to be fitted, the relevant checks detailed in Operation A1-36 must be carried out.
2. Assemble the crankshaft to the engine and insert the bearing upper halves, located by tongues, to the crankcase.
3. Position a thrust washer at each side of the centre bearing shell. The thrust washer thicknesses must agree within .003 in. (0.07 mm).
4. Position the bearing lower halves on to the front and centre bearing caps and fit the caps.
5. Assemble the garter spring on the oil seal journal of the crankshaft as illustrated, by laying the spring around the journal, this will bring the two ends, the hook and the eye, adjacent to one another, then insert the hook into the eye. Care must be taken to ensure that during this operation the spring is not stretched at all.

    The spring should be moved along the journal until it is against the thrower flange.

6. Apply Silicone Grease MS4 to the crankshaft oil seal journal and to both sides of the split oil seal sealing lip.

    Open the split sufficiently to allow it to be fitted over the crankshaft oil seal journal. Recess in oil seal must be towards thrower flange and garter spring.

    The oil seal must not be repeatedly fitted and removed from the crankshaft, as this can damage the sealing lip.

Fig. A1-132. Crankshaft main bearing caps
A—Bearing lower half
B—Fixings, bearing caps to cylinder block
C—Bearing cap
D—Thrust washer positioned each side of centre bearing upper half

---

Operation A1-34—continued

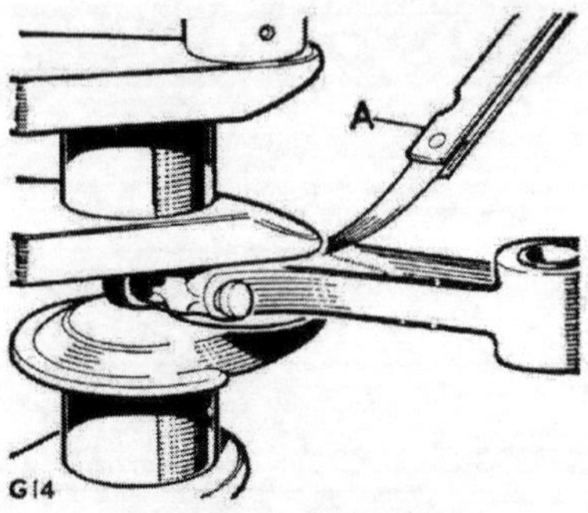

To assemble

1. Assemble the pistons to the respective connecting rods. When refitted, the 'X' mark on the piston crown (where applicable) is to be toward the front of the engine, and the oil spray hole in the connecting rod toward the camshaft.
2. With the pistons warmed to approximately 55°C (132°F), fit the gudgeon pins (from the 'X' side) and retaining circlips.
3. Position the previously fitted piston rings so that the ring gaps are adjacent to the gudgeon pin bore on alternate sides of the piston and do not coincide.

Fig. A1-131. End-float check
A—Feeler gauge

Operation A1-35—continued

7. Rotate the oil seal until the split is on the vertical axis pointing towards the cylinder head and in its approximate running position on the journal; this position is important.

   Apply Hylomar SQ32M sealing compound to the seal diameter of the two half plates, using either an applicator or a brush.

   Important: Do not degrease the half seal plates with trichlorethylene, but wipe clean with a dry cloth prior to applying the Hylomar.

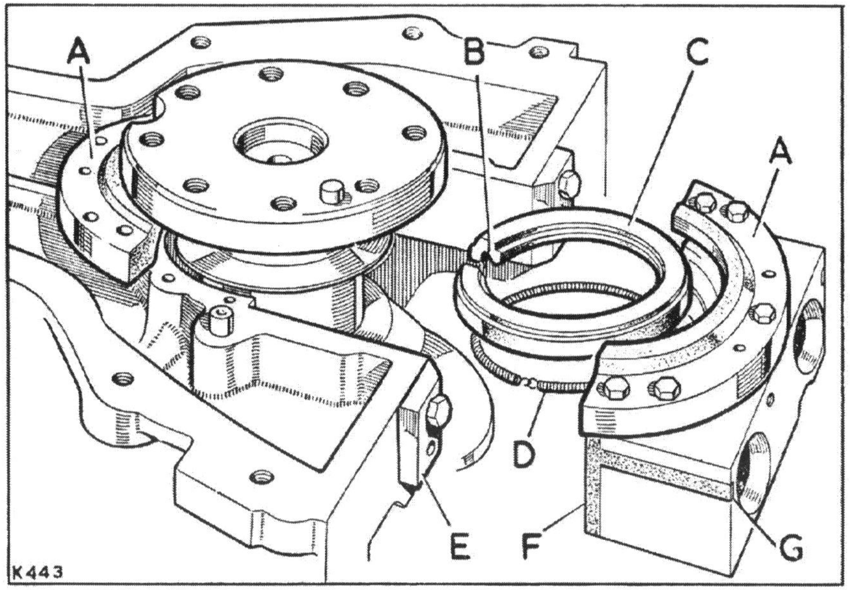

Fig. A1-133. Oil seal details

A—Retainer halves
B—Split line of seal to be towards top of engine when fitted
C—Split oil seal
D—Garter spring, hook and eye to be midway between split and hinge of oil seal when fitted
E—Guides, Part No. 270304, for rear main bearing cap 'T' seals
F—Trim these edges before fitting cap to prevent seal from folding
G—Trim these ends when cap is fitted to allow 1/32 in. (0.8 mm) protrusion

Operation A1-35—continued

8. Fit one half of the oil seal retainer on to the crankcase dowels. The oil seal should be compressed to assist assembly, also ensure that it is correctly located in the retainer recess. Bolt the retainer to the crankcase, leaving the two bolts adjacent to the split line finger-tight, fully tighten the remaining three bolts. In order to fit the bolt it will be necessary to rotate the crankshaft; it is essential to hold the seal so that it does not rotate with the crankshaft.

9. Bolt the other half of the oil seal retainer on to the main bearing cap, in the same way. Apply Silicone grease MS4 to the 'T' seals and fit them to the main bearing cap. The cap must be off the crankcase for these operations.

   Trim the edges of the 'T' seals as shown to prevent them from fouling the cylinder block when fitted.

10. Fit the main bearing cap with the seal retainer, bearing shell and 'T' seals to the crankcase, until there is a 1/32 in. (0.8 mm) gap between the cap and crankcase.

11. Ensure that the seal is located in the retainer recess.

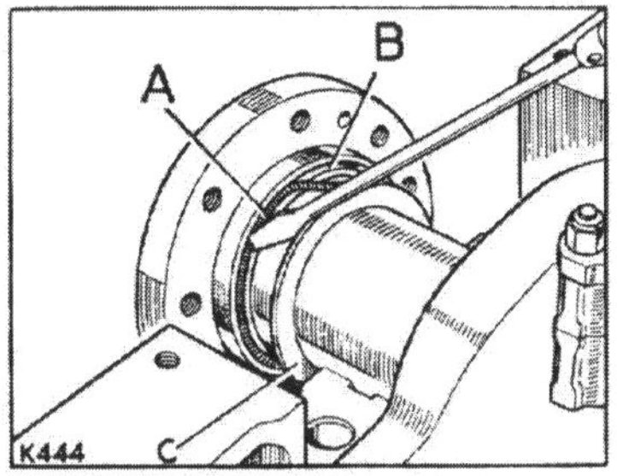

Fig. A1-134. Fitting garter spring

A—Garter spring
B—Oil seal recess for garter spring
C—Thrower flange

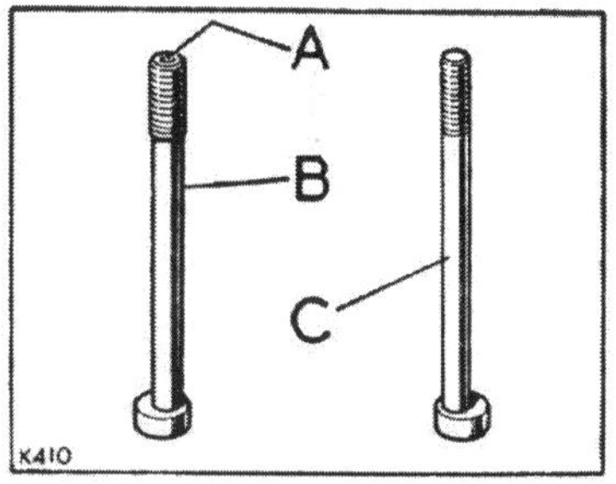

12. Pull down the cap slowly, ensuring there is no buckling of the split seal or misalignment of the butt joint.

13. Tighten all the bearing cap fixings to a torque loading of 85 lb ft (11,75 mkg).

14. Fit the appropriate bearing shells to the connecting rod caps, ensure that the upper and lower shells are correctly located by their tongues and fit the caps to the appropriate connecting rods. Use new fixing nuts and tighten the fixings to 35 lb ft (4,9 mkg) for bolts with machined threads and 25 lb ft (3,5 mkg) for bolts with rolled threads, referring to Fig. A1-135 for identification.

Fig. A1-135. Identification of connecting rod bolts

A—Drilled point to identify rolled threads
B—Bolts with rolled threads
C—Bolts with machined threads

15. Refit the flywheel housing. Operation A1-31.
16. Refit the clutch and flywheel. Operation A1-32.
17. Refit the timing chain and tensioner. Operation A1-26.
18. Carry out the valve timing procedure as detailed in Operation A1-27.
19. Refit the engine front cover. Operation A1-25.

ENGINE—2¼ LITRE PETROL

Operation A1-35—continued

20. Refit the oil pump. Operation A1-29.
21. Remove the engine from the stand, using suitable lifting equipment.
22. Refit the crankcase sump. Operation A1-28.
23. Refit engine to vehicle. Operation A1-5.
24. Refit front floor. Operation A1-4.
25. Refit the radiator and grille panel. Operation A1-3.
26. Refit the air cleaner. Operation A1-2.
27. Refit the bonnet panel. Operation A1-1.

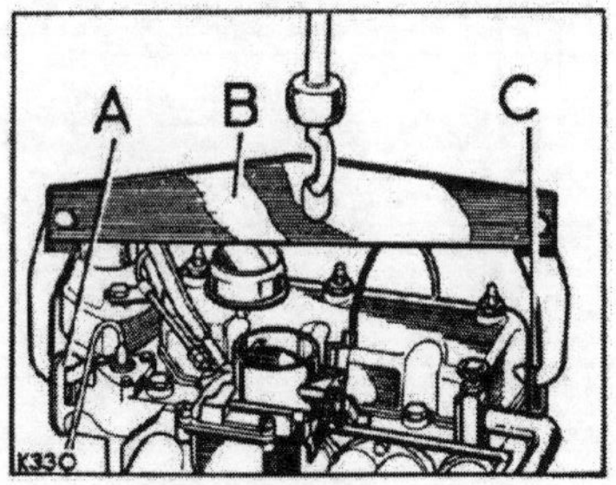

Fig. A1-136. Engine lifting sling in position

A—Front lifting bracket
B—Lifting sling, Part No. 600963
C—Rear lifting bracket

Crankshaft and main bearings, overhaul—Operation A1-36

(For removal and refitting details, Operation A1-35 refers)

Workshop hand tools:
Spanner sizes: ⅞ in. AF open end
1 1/16 in. AF socket
Screwdriver (medium), Screwdriver (small)
Feeler gauges

Special tools:
Torque wrench
Dial test Indicator
Part No. 60S238—'Plastigage' strip

Fig. A1-137. Main bearing cap location details

A—Bearing lower half
B—Fixings, bearing cap to cylinder block
C—Bearing cap
D—Thrust washer at each side of centre bearing upper half

To overhaul

1. Inspect all components for damage and general condition.
2. The crankshaft journals should be closely inspected for wear or damage, and the crankpins also checked for ovality.
3. Check for general condition of main bearing cap locating dowels, dowel spigots and surrounding areas.
4. With the crankshaft removed, check the main bearings for fit in the housings, as follows: fit the front bearing cap, less the shell bearings, to the correct location.
5. Fit and tighten the main bearing bolts to 85 lb ft (11,75 mkg).
6. Slacken one bolt and check that there is no clearance between the two faces. Clearance here indicates that the cap has been filed or is damaged and it will be necessary to replace the complete cylinder block.
7. If satisfactory, fit the main bearings and repeat the above check. The clearance at the face should now be .004 in to .006 in. (0,10 mm to 0,15 mm) and is achieved by selective assembly of the shells.

Fig. A1-138. Checking main bearing nip

A—Set bolt, slack
B—Main bearing cap
C—Feeler gauge
D—Set bolt, tightened

8. Repeat the procedure and check the remaining bearings and caps.
9. When the bearing nip has been checked, remove the caps and bearing shell bottom halves. Position a standard size thrust washer at each side of centre bearing shell—top half, and fit the crankshaft.

The thrust washer thicknesses must agree within .003 in. (0,08 mm).

10. Mount a dial test indicator, then check and note the crankshaft end-float reading which should be .002 in. to .006 in. (0,05 mm to 0,15 mm).
If the crankshaft end-float reading obtained is not within the limits, fit suitable oversize thrust washers. The variation of thrust washer thickness at each side must not exceed .003 in. (0,08 mm) to ensure that the crankshaft remains centralised.
11. When satisfactory, check the crankshaft for freedom of rotation. Fitting a .0025 in. (0,06 mm) feeler paper between a main bearing and the journal should cause resistance to rotation: the crankshaft should be free to rotate by hand with the feeler paper removed.

ENGINE—2¼ LITRE PETROL

Operation A1-36—continued

12. The running clearance between the bearings and the crankshaft journals should be .001 in. to .0025 in. (0.02 mm to 0.06 mm). An alternative method of checking the clearance is by using 'Plastigage' strip, available under Rover Part No. 605238, as illustrated.

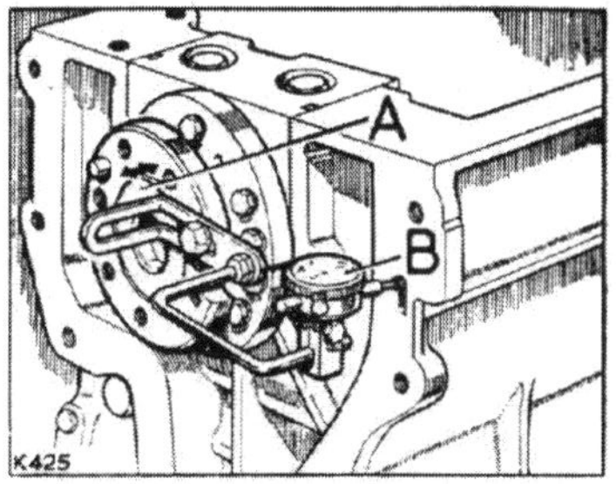

Fig. A1-139. Checking crankshaft end-float

A—Lever crankshaft fully forward then fully to rear
B—Dial test indicator

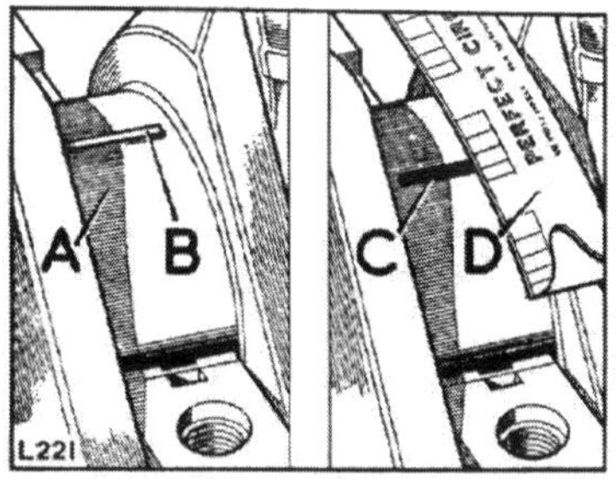

Fig. A1-140. Use of 'Plastigage' strip to measure bearing clearance

A—Main bearing journal
B—Initial position of 'Plastigage'
C—Flattened 'Plastigage', do not remove until measured against scale
D—Graduated scale on 'Plastigage' packet

*Camshaft, remove and refit—Operation A1-37

(For camshaft bearing overhaul information, Operation A1-38 refers)

Workshop hand tools:
Spanner sizes: ¼ in. x 7/16 in. AF (2 off), ⅜ in. AF open end
½ in. AF, ⅝ in. AF, ¾ in. AF socket
¾ in. AF ring
¼ in. BSF, ⅜ in. BSF open
1/16 in. BSF open end
2 BA open end
Screwdriver (small), Screwdriver (medium), Pliers (snipe nose), Feeler gauges

Special tools:
Part No. 530102—Spanner for starter dog
Torque wrench
Part No. 507231—Extractor for camshaft chainwheel
12 v test lamp
Part No. 530101—Extractor for tappet guides and camshaft

To remove

1. Remove bonnet panel. Operation A1-1.
2. Remove air cleaner. Operation A1-2.
3. Remove radiator and grille panel. Operation A1-3.
4. Remove the external oil filter. Operation A1-16.
5. Remove the distributor and drive gear. Operation A1-18.
6. Remove valve gear and rocker shaft assembly. Operation A1-20.
7. Remove cylinder head. Operation A1-22.
8. Remove engine front cover. Operation A1-25.
9. Remove timing chain tensioner. Operation A1-26.
10. Remove tappet locating bolts at RH side of engine block. Do not remove tappet guide at this stage.
11. Remove the tappet slides leaving the guides in position to retain the tappet rollers and ensure that they do not fall behind the camshaft. Remove the rollers, using a local made spring clip.
12. Remove the tappet guides. The use of special tool, Part No. 530101 as illustrated, will facilitate this procedure if the guides are difficult to remove by hand.

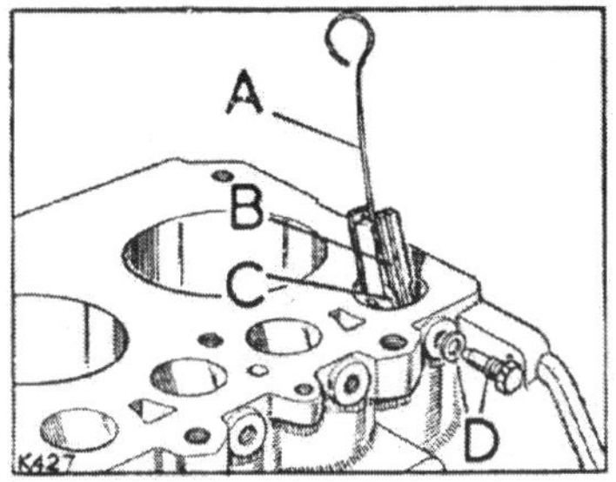

Fig. A1-141. Removing tappets and rollers

A—Spring clip
B—Tappet slide
C—Tappet roller
D—Tappet guide locating bolt

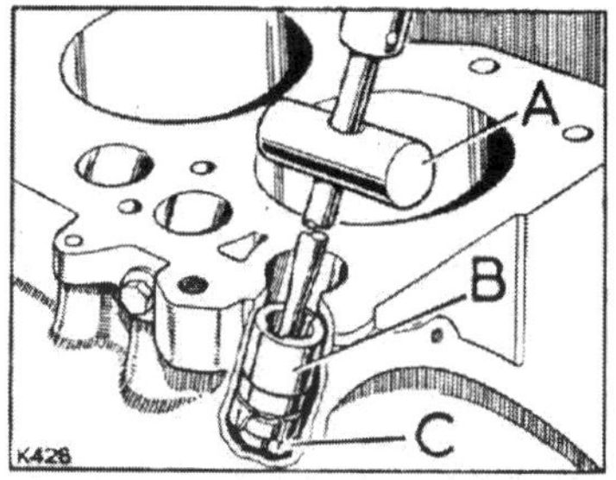

Fig. A1-142. Removing tappet guides

A—Special tool, Part No. 530101
B—Tappet guide
C—Extractor adaptor, part of special tool, Part No. 530101

Operations marked with an asterisk (*) can be carried out with the engine installed in the vehicle

ENGINE—2¼ LITRE PETROL

Operation A1-37—continued

13. Withdraw the distributor drive shaft then remove the locating grub screw and withdraw the vertical drive shaft gear.

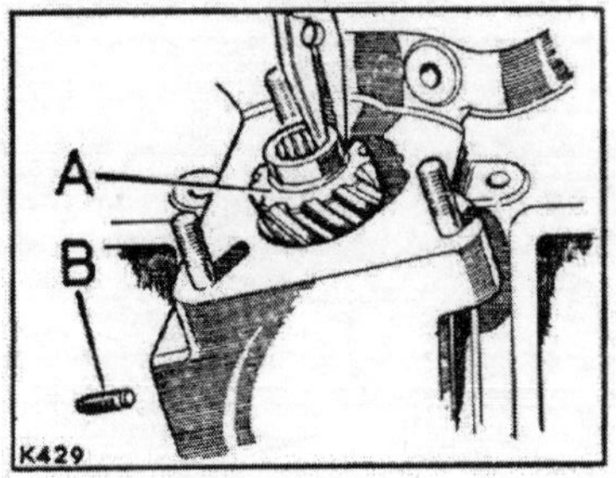

Fig. A1-143. Removing the vertical drive shaft gear

A—Vertical drive shaft gear
B—Locating grub screw in external oil filter joint face

14. Withdraw the timing chain and remove the camshaft chainwheel.

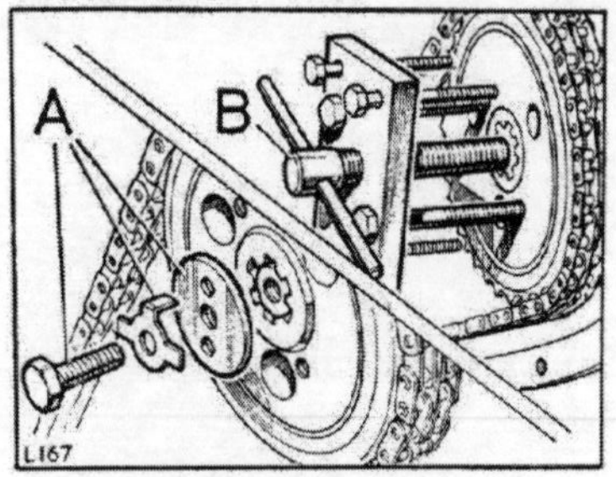

Fig. A1-144. Camshaft chainwheel

A—Fixings, chainwheel to camshaft
B—Use of special extractor, Part No. 507231 facilitates chainwheel removal

15. Remove the thrust plate and withdraw the camshaft, using special tool, Part No. 530101 or a slave bolt.

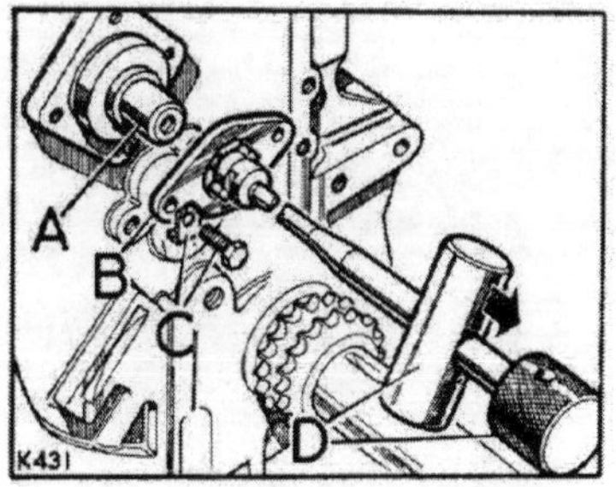

Fig. A1-145. Removing the camshaft

A—Camshaft
B—Thrust plate
C—Fixings, thrust plate to cylinder block
D—Special tool, Part No. 530101 in position

Note: Camshaft bearing removing, refitting and overhaul details are included in 'Cylinder block overhaul, Operation A1-38' as a reaming procedure is required with the engine removed.

To refit:

1. Insert the camshaft, keyed end to front of engine, and fit the thrust plate. Do not lock the fixings at this stage.

2. Fit the chainwheel to the camshaft and check the camshaft end-float which must be .0025 in. to .0055 in. (0,06 mm to 0,13 mm).

Operation A1-37—continued

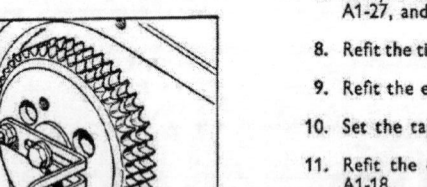

Fig. A1-146. Camshaft end-float check

The end-float is adjusted by thrust plate selection.

3. When satisfactory, remove the chainwheel and lock the thrust plate fixings with the lock tabs. Refit the camshaft chainwheel, Fig. A1-145 refers.

4. Refit the tappets assemblies, see Figs. A1-142 and A1-141.

5. Refit the cylinder head. Operation A1-22.

6. Refit the valve gear and rocker shaft assembly. Operation A1-20.

7. Carry out the valve timing procedure. Operation A1-27, and refit the timing chain.

8. Refit the timing chain tensioner. Operation A1-26.

9. Refit the engine front cover. Operation A1-25.

10. Set the tappet clearances. Operation A1-19.

11. Refit the distributor and drive gear. Operation A1-18.

12. Set the ignition timing. Operation A1-17.

13. Refit the radiator and grille panel assembly. Operation A1-3.

14. Refit the air cleaner. Operation A1-2.

15. Replenish the engine lubricating oil.

ENGINE LUBRICANT CAPACITY
Bonneted Control Model, 2¼ Litre Petrol

		Capacity	Imperial Unit	US Unit	Litres
88	Engine	...	11 pints	13 pints	6,0
	Filter		1½ pints	1.8 pints	0,85
	Engine and Filter		12½ pints	14.8 pints	6,85
109	Engine	...	11 pints	13 pints	6,0
	Filter		1½ pints	1.8 pints	0,85
	Engine and Filter		12½ pints	14.8 pints	6,85

16. Refit the bonnet panel. Operation A1-1.

ENGINE—2¼ LITRE PETROL

Cylinder block and camshaft bearings, overhaul—Operation A1-38

Workshop hand tools:
Screwdriver (medium)
Mallet (hide faced)
Spanner size: $\frac{7}{16}$ in. AF open end

Special tools:
Part No. 274394—Guide plug
Part No. 274389—Reamer for bearings

Method 'A'
Part No. 274388—Bearing drift
Part No. 274385—Guide tube for front bearings
Part No. 274382—Bearing fitting bar
Part No. 274383—Spacer
Part No. 274384—Spigot
Part No. 274386—Guide tool for rear bearings
Part No. 531760—Adaptor

Method 'B'
Part No. 274388—Bearing drift
Part No. 531760—Adaptor
or:
Part No. 605975—Bearing drift and adaptor complete

Carry out the engine removal and dismantling work previously detailed as necessary until only the camshaft bearings remain in the cylinder block.

Camshaft bearings, to replace

Note: Two methods of replacing the bearings are detailed. Use Method 'A' if the full range of special tools is held; Method 'B' uses a simplified tooling procedure.

Method 'A', to replace bearings

1. When new camshaft bearings are to be fitted, the front and front intermediate bearings must be removed and new ones fitted **before** removing the rear bearings.

2. Unscrew the 3½ in. (88 mm) long stud from the joint face at front of cylinder block and remove the bearing cover at rear of cylinder block.

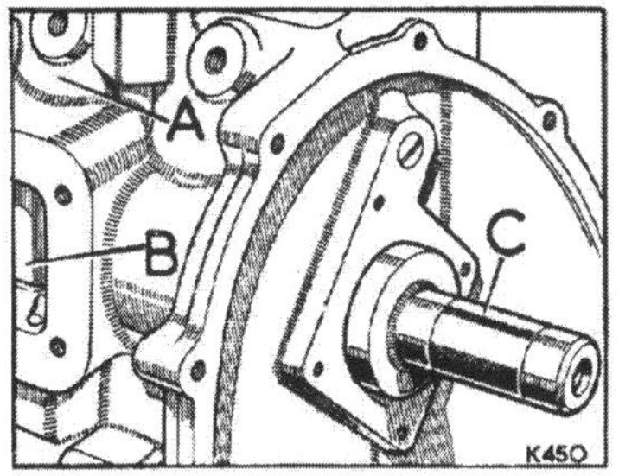

Fig. A1-147. Driving out the front bearings
A—Cylinder block
B—Front tappet chamber
C—Special tool, Part No. 274388

Operation A1-38—continued

3. Drive out the front and front intermediate bearings, using special tool, Part No. 274388.

4. Withdraw the front bearing from the vacant front side cover aperture. Collapse the front intermediate bearing and withdraw from the distributor drive chamber.

5. Fit new front and front intermediate bearings, **before** removing the rear bearings with drift.

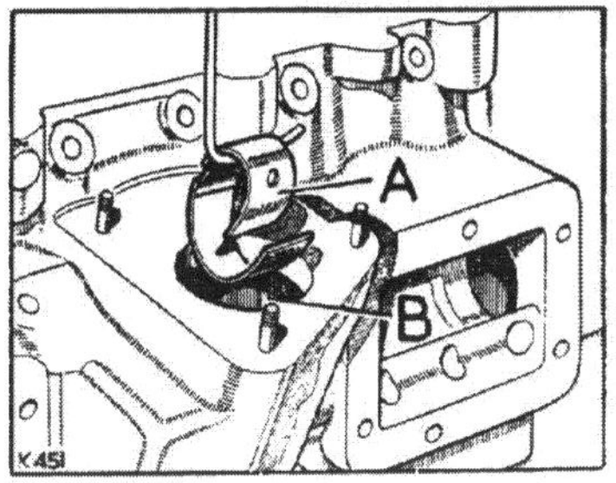

Fig. A1-148. Front intermediate bearing removal
A—Collapsed bearing
B—Distributor drive chamber

6. Fit a guide tool, Part No. 274385, into the two **old** rearmost bearings with the part of flange marked 'TOP' uppermost, then insert end cover set bolts loosely for location purposes. Position a new front bearing on to the handle end of bearing fitting bar, Part No. 274382, and locate by means of the peg and semi-circular cut-out, then slide a spacer, Part No. 274383, on to the fitting bar and engage the locating shoulder.
Note: The front bearing is wider and has an extra oil drilling.

7. Place a new bearing on spigot, Part No. 274384, and position it inside the foremost tappet chamber with the bearing nearest the front intermediate housing.

8. Insert the bearing fitting bar into the front bearing housing and feed the spigot on to the bar; withdraw the spigot handle. Turn the spigot to engage the locating shoulder. Turn the bar inward, then press the fitting bar inward, turning as necessary to engage the bar slot with the peg in guide tube.

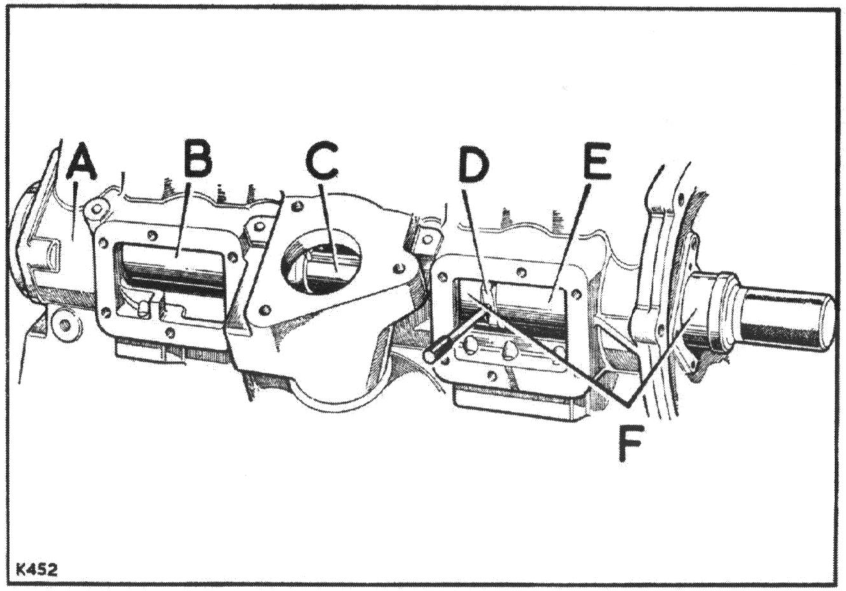

Fig. A1-149. Fitting camshaft front bearings
A—Cylinder block
B—Guide tube
C—Bearing fitting bar
D—Spigot
E—Spacer
F—New bearings

9. When the fitting bar has been pressed in as far as possible by hand, ensure that all locating points are properly engaged, then drive the bearings into position with a hide-faced hammer.

10. The bearings must now be aligned with the oil holes, proceed as follows:

Partially withdraw bearing fitting bar and remove spigot, Part No. 274384. Slide adaptor, Part No. 531760, on to bar and re-insert bar and drive in until flange of bar abuts on cylinder block. This will align the oil holes on the intermediate bearing.

Withdraw bar and adaptor and remove spacer, then refit adaptor, Part No. 531760, and align front bearing oil holes by gently tapping tool as required.

11. Remove the bearing fitting tools and check the oil holes for alignment.

12. Remove the two rearmost bearings and fit new camshaft rear bearings in the same manner as for front bearings, but remove the spacer from fitting bar and use guide tool, Part No. 274386, instead of the guide tube used when fitting front bearings.

Method 'B', to replace bearings

1. Using special tool, Part No. 274388, or Part No. 605975 (less the adaptor), drift out all the bearings. The two centre bearings can be drifted into the distributor drive chamber and collapsed to enable withdrawal.

Note that the two centre and the rear bearing are of the same width, whereas the front bearing is wider and has an additional oil feed hole.

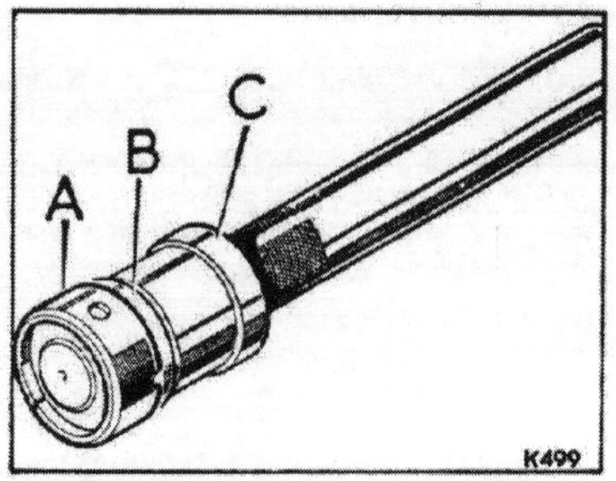

Fig. A1-150. Replacing camshaft bearings

A—Camshaft bearing
B—Adaptor
C—Drift, Part No. 274388 or Part No. 605975.

2. To fit the new bearings, the drift, Part No. 274388 and special adaptor, Part No. 531760 or the drift and adaptor complete, Part No. 605975 are required. Proceed as follows:

(a) With the cylinder block vertical, rear face down, place a new shell bearing into the front camshaft chamber and position it so that it is above the second bearing housing, counting from the front of the block. The chamfer on the bearing edge must be towards the housing bore, and the oil hole in the bearing must be aligned with the innermost oil feed drilling in the housing bore. Accuracy is essential otherwise misalignment of the oil holes may result and once the bearing is in place it cannot be rotated to correct any error. Pencil marks on the bearing outer diameter and the cylinder block adjacent to the housing will assist in checking alignment.

(b) Having visually aligned the bearing, carefully place inside it the special adaptor, Part No. 531760 or Part No. 605975.

(c) Maintain the bearing in a level position. Pass the drift through the front bearing housing into the camshaft chamber so that it rests on top of the adaptor. Commence drifting the bearing into the block. Ensure that the bearing is not drifted in too far, and that the oil feed holes are correctly aligned.

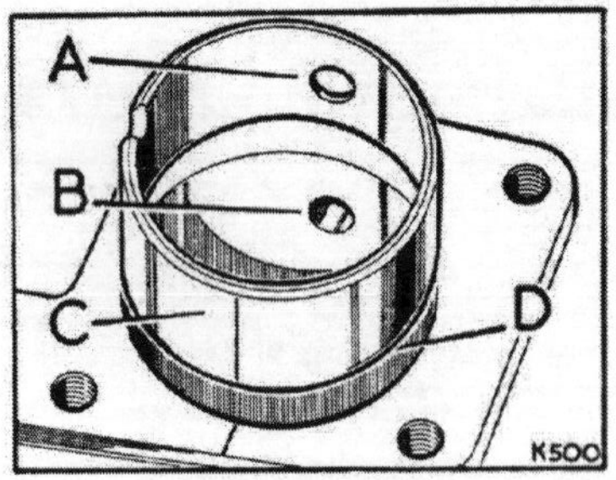

Fig. A1-151. Aligning oil holes

A—Oil hole in bearing
B—Oil feed hole in block
C—Pencil marks
D—Chamfer on leading edge

3. Repeat the operation for the front bearing. Note that the front bearing is wider and has a small hole in addition to the large oil feed hole. This small hole aligns with a vertical drilling in the block, which in turn feeds a horizontal drilling for the tappet mechanism. Drift this bearing in so that the outer edge is just below the machined surface of the front face. This is to ensure that when the camshaft thrust plate is fitted it will not stand proud on the bearing edge.

4. Turn over the cylinder block so that the rear face is uppermost, and drift in the two remaining narrow bearings in the manner described in para. 2.

5. Retain the cylinder block in the vertical position, front face downwards, in readiness for the reamering operation.

Reamering the bearings

1. Locate a guide plug, Part No. 274394, in the new front camshaft bearing and locate, using the endplate screws. Do not tighten these screws until the reamer, Part No. 274389, is put into position and the guide collar immediately in front of the cutter is entered into the rearmost bearing, which is first to be cut. This precaution is to ensure correct alignment of the reamer. Before commencing the reamering operation it is necessary to turn the engine block to a vertical position, front end facing downwards, in order that the weight of the reamer will assist in the cutting operation. As each bearing is cut the reamer should be held steady by the operator whilst an assistant, using a high pressure airline, blows away the white metal cuttings, before allowing the reamer to enter the next bearing.

2. After the rearmost and the two intermediate bearings have been cut, remove the guide plug, Part No. 274394, before cutting the foremost bearing. Remove the reamer handle and bolt, and carefully remove the reamer, turning it in the same direction as for cutting. Care must be taken

Operation A1-38—continued

to prevent the reamer damaging the foremost bearing as the reamer is removed.

No lubricant is necessary for the reaming operation, best results are obtained when the bearings are cut dry.

3. Remove the plugs from the ends of oil gallery passage and clean the gallery and oil feed passages to camshaft and crankshaft bearings, using compressed air. Refit the plugs and lock in position. The hexagon-headed plugs at the rear of the block should have new washers fitted, and their threads coated with a suitable jointing compound.

The cylinder block must be thoroughly cleaned at this stage.

Cylinder bores

1. The bores may be reclaimed by machining up to .040 in. (1,0 mm) maximum oversize, replacement pistons being available in oversize increments of .010 in., .020 in., .030 in. and .040 in. (0,25 mm, 0,5 mm, 0,76 mm and 1,0 mm).

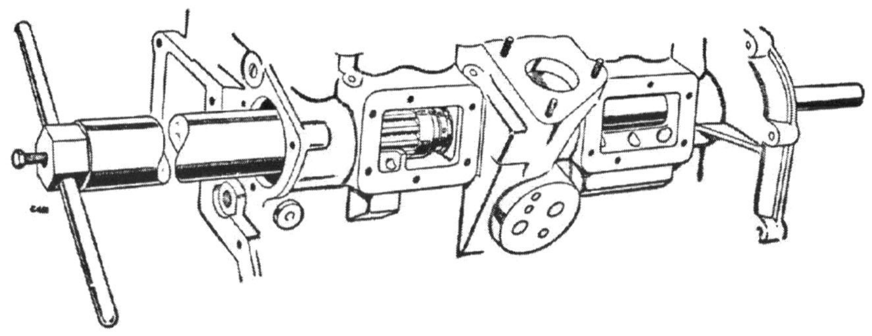

2. Where the maximum permitted boring tolerance is not sufficient to reclaim the bores, cylinder liners may be fitted.

3. Fitting the cylinder liners conforms to normal practice. Machine the cylinder block bores to 3.7175 in. +.0005 in. (94,4245 mm +0,0127 mm). This will provide the liner with a .003 in. to .0045 in. (0,0762 mm to 0,1143 mm) interference fit.

4. Press the liners into the cylinder block. The liners must not be proud of, or more than .010 in. (0,254 mm) below, the top face of the cylinder block. Cylinder liners should then be bored out to standard size, that is 3.562 in. (90,47 mm). Liners may be rebored .010 in. (0,254 mm) oversize.

5. Before reassembly, deglaze the cylinder bores using suitable honing equipment or suitable fine grade abrasive cloth.

When the overhaul is completed, rebuild the engine by reversing the removal procedure. In addition, carry out the following procedures at the appropriate stage of rebuild:

Valve timing procedure. Operation A1-27.
Tappet adjustment. Operation A1-19.
Ignition timing procedure. Operation A1-17.

Also replenish the engine lubrication system and engine coolant system.

Fig. A1-152. Reamering camshaft bearings. (Engine must be in vertical position)

ENGINE—2¼ LITRE PETROL

Reclamation of flywheel and starter ring—Operation A1-39

(For Flywheel remove and refit instructions, Operation A1-31 refers)

Wear or scoring on the flywheel pressure face

1. Remove the clutch bolts and dowels from the flywheel.
2. Check the thickness of the flywheel before commencing machining, as it may have been previously machined.
   The maximum amount of metal which may be removed from the flywheel face is .030 in. (0,76 mm). If the face is not satisfactory after machining to these limits, the flywheel must be scrapped. See chart below.
3. Machine the whole pressure face, not merely inside the bolts and dowels, until the score marks are removed.

Starter ring excessively worn or damaged

Petrol models

1. Remove the scrap starter ring by securing the flywheel in a vice fitted with jaw protectors, then drill a $\frac{5}{32}$ in. (4 mm) diameter hole axially between the root of any one tooth and the inner diameter of the starter ring sufficiently deep to weaken the ring. Care must be taken to prevent the drill entering the flywheel.
2. Place a chisel immediately above the drilled hole, and strike it sharply.

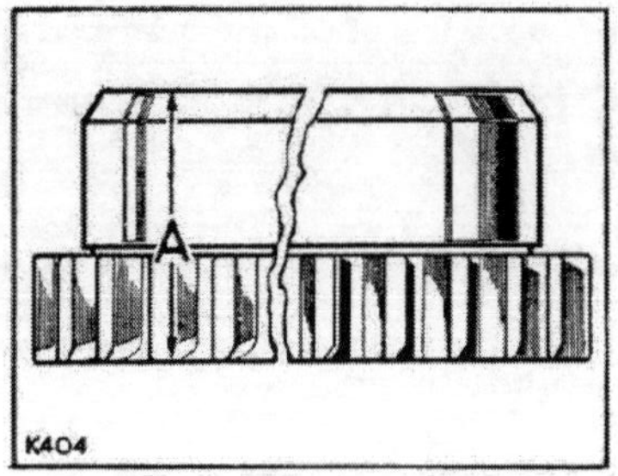

   Important: The starter ring will normally split harmlessly but on remote occasions rings have been known to fly asunder when split; it is therefore important that the operator should take suitable precautions. For instance, a cloth may be laid over the upper part of the starter ring.

3. Heat the starter ring uniformly to between 220°C and 225°C but do not exceed the higher temperature.
4. With the flywheel placed on a suitably flat surface, position the ring on to the flywheel with the square edge of the teeth against the flange.

   There should be a clearance of $\frac{1}{16}$ in. to $\frac{1}{8}$ in. (1,5 mm to 3 mm) between the inner diameter of ring and flywheel if the temperature is correct. Press the starter ring firmly against the flange until the ring contracts sufficiently to grip the flywheel.

5. Allow the flywheel assembly to cool gradually; do not hasten cooling in any way and thereby avoid the setting up of internal stresses in the ring which may cause fracture or failure in some respect.

Fig. A1-153. Machining flywheel
A—Minimum thickness after refacing

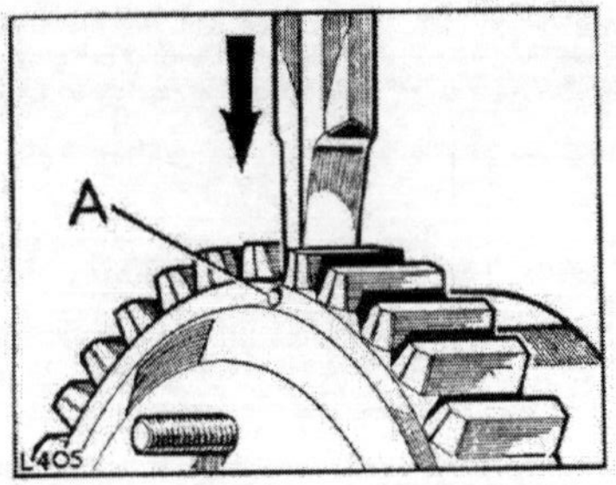

Fig. A1-154. Removing an unserviceable starter ring
A—Drilled hole

Models	Flywheel Part Number	Ring Gear Part Number	Dimension 'A' Minimum thickness after refacing	Flywheel Part Number when re-conditioned	Remarks
Series II and IIA 2¼ litre Petrol models up to engine suffix 'E'. (Two dowel hole type)	247991 (Can be replaced by 600243)	506799	1.373 in. (35,0 mm)	530514 (Can be replaced by 600540)	Cast-iron flywheel. Detachable ring gear fitted as original equipment. No machining necessary other than for refacing.
Series IIA 2¼ litre Petrol models. Engine suffix 'F' onwards. (Four dowel hole type)	600243 (Will replace 247991 and 536882)	506799	1.373 in. (35,0 mm)	600540 (Will replace 530514 and 600244)	Cast-iron flywheel. Detachable ring gear fitted as original equipment. No machining necessary other than for refacing. Dowels are not fitted, but are supplied loose so that they may be assembled to suit the type of clutch fitted.

ENGINE—2¼ LITRE PETROL

Fault diagnosis—Engine, 2¼ litre Petrol

Symptom	Possible cause	Investigation	Remedy
A—Engine fails to rotate when attempting to start	Incorrect starting procedure	Follow procedure as described in Owner's Instruction Manual	
	Battery leads loose or terminals corroded	Check for condition of leads and terminals	Clean and tighten as necessary
	Battery discharged	Check and remedy as described in Section N	
	Starter solenoid malfunction	Link battery feed to starter feed thus by-passing solenoid	
	Starter motor inoperative	If lights dim when starter switch is operated, the starter pinion may be jammed in the flywheel starter ring	Free the starter by removing the protection cap and turning the squared end of the starter armature clockwise
		Check for loose or dirty connections and for soundness of leads	Clean and tighten at terminals. Replace lead as necessary
		Depress switch on engine compartment dash panel to connect battery feed to starter	If starter then rotates engine, replace the ignition switch. If starter remains inoperative, refer to Section N
B—Engine rotates but fails to start	Starter motor speed too low	Check battery leads at terminals	Clean and tighten as necessary
		Check state of battery charge. Section N	When refitting a recharged or replacement battery, check the voltage regulator output setting, Section N. Check also the fan belt tension
	Faulty ignition system	Remove a sparking plug lead and hold lead end ¼ in. (6 mm) approximately from engine block. With Ignition 'ON', depress starter solenoid switch and check that an easily visible blue spark jumps the gap between plug lead and engine	If no spark or if spark is weak or yellowish, check the ignition system as described in Section N
		If the spark appears adequate, remove the sparking plugs	Clean the plugs and reset the plug gaps, Section N. Replace if necessary
	Fuel system defects	With the engine cold, remove fuel inlet pipe at carburetter, operate priming lever at pump and check for full bore fuel flow	If fuel flow is unsatisfactory, refer to Section L
		If flow is satisfactory, ensure that carburetter float chamber fuel level is satisfactory	If float chamber level is too low, refer to Section L for carburetter float needle checks
	Incorrect 'hot spot' adjustment	This setting if incorrect may prevent the engine from starting when hot, due to excessive vapourising of fuel in manifold	Reset 'hot spot' components with engine cold. Ensure bi-metal spring is in good condition, replace if necessary
C—Engine starts but immediately stops	Faulty electrical connections	Check ignition circuits, leads and terminals for possible loose or defective connections as described in Section N	
	Insufficient fuel supply	Carry out the checks and remedies listed under 'Fuel system defects', paragraph B	

Fault diagnosis—Engine—2¼ litre Petrol—continued

Symptom	Possible cause	Investigation	Remedy
D—Engine fails to idle	Carburetter setting faulty	Adjust throttle stop screw on carburetter until engine will run with screw on stop. If engine idle speed is then too high, check the carburetter settings as described in Section L	
	Faulty fuel pump	Carry out the checks and remedies listed under 'Fuel system defects', paragraph B	
	Ignition system faults	Check electrical leads insulation and terminal connections	Clean and tighten terminals. Replace leads if necessary
		Carry out the checks listed under 'Faulty ignition system', paragraph B, to check the sparking plugs and their electrical feed	
	Battery charge too low	Check if lamps brightness varies with engine speed	Carry out the checks listed under 'Battery discharged' Section N
		Check fan belt tension setting, Section A1	Reset to correct tension and recharge battery from external supply or by a long period of engine running in daylight
	Incorrect ignition timing	Adjust throttle stop screw on carburetter until engine will idle without stopping. Rotate vernier adjuster on distributor through advance and retard range. If the engine speed increases at a new vernier position, then the original ignition setting is incorrect for the fuel grade in use	Reset ignition timing to the correct setting for the fuel grade in use
	Valve operation defective	Remove engine top cover and check tappet clearances	Reset clearances
		Check for defective valve springs	Replace as pairs
		Rotate engine, using starting handle, and check for valves sticking open	Carry out engine decarbonise and top overhaul procedure
		Check for worn valves and valve guides	Replace as necessary
	Faulty cylinder head gasket	Check for leaks across sealing areas	Replace as necessary
	Exhaust system faulty	Examine for possible restrictions	Remove restriction. Replace components as necessary
E—Engine misfires on acceleration	Distributor operation faulty	Check condition of contact breaker points. Check gap: .014 in. to .016 in. (0.35 mm to 0.40 mm)	Reface points and reset gap, or replace points if badly worn or pitted
	Coil or condenser faulty	Check by substituting serviceable components	Replace unserviceable components

ENGINE—2¼ LITRE PETROL

Fault diagnosis—Engine—2¼ litre Petrol—continued

Symptom	Possible cause	Investigation	Remedy
E—Engine misfires on acceleration—cont	Sparking plugs faulty	Remove sparking plugs, check for carbon deposits. Check electrode gap. Visually examine for signs of cracked insulation	If sparking plugs appear otherwise serviceable, clean off all deposits and reset the gap as described in Section N
	Carburetter operation faulty	Check for restrictions in carburetter fuel passages	Clean out passages as described in Section L
		Check carburetter accelerator pump diaphragm and linkage, where applicable. Check carburetter control settings	Check carburetter as described in Section L
	Faulty distributor operation	Check condition and setting of distributor contact breaker points	Clean points and stone flat. Reset gap to .014 in. to .016 in. (0.35 mm to 0.40 mm)
	Ignition coil or distributor condenser faulty	Check by substituting new components	Replace as necessary, referring to Section M
F—Engine backfires	Air leakage	Check exhaust system and ensure joints are sound; check components for damage and cracks	Tighten joints or replace components as necessary
	Internal leakage	Excessively worn valve guides and valves may allow crankcase fumes to enter exhaust system	Carry out cylinder head overhaul procedure
	Ignition system defect	Check electrical leads, insulation and terminal connections	Clean and tighten terminals. Replace leads if necessary
		Check condition of sparking plugs, insulation and electrode gap	Reset or replace as necessary Section N
		Check if ignition timing setting is too retarded	Reset timing
	Carburetter defect	Check jets for any restriction which may cause a too weak mixture. Check mixture control setting	Check carburetter settings and clean out passages if necessary, Section L
	Valve operation incorrect	Check valve timing	Reset timing if necessary. Ensure that timing chain tensioner is free to operate, ensure that timing chain has no slack on driving side
		Check tappet clearances	Reset clearances
		Check for valves sticking open	Carry out engine decarbonise procedure
		Check for badly seating valves	Carry out cylinder head overhaul procedure
G—Engine knocks	Ignition system defects	Check condition of sparking plugs	Reset or replace as necessary, Section N
		Check if ignition timing is too advanced	Reset ignition timing to the correct setting for the fuel grade in use
		Check operation of distributor advance and retard mechanism, Section N	

Fault diagnosis—Engine—2¼ litre Petrol—continued

Symptom	Possible cause	Investigation	Remedy
G—Engine knocks—cont	Fuel system defects	Check setting of mixture control screw	Reset control screw as described in Section L
		Check grade of fuel in use is suitable	Rotate octane selector on distributor. If engine knock stops, fuel in use is not correct for the ignition timing setting
	Valves operation incorrect	Check tappet clearances	Reset
		Check valve timing	Reset
	Wear in engine	Check pistons and bearings	Overhaul as necessary
	Excessive carbon deposits	Remove cylinder head and check for deposits in combustion chamber areas	Remove carbon deposits
	Excessively weak mixture	Check setting of mixture control screw	Adjust control screw as detailed in Section L
H—Engine 'spits back' through carburetter		Check for air leakage into fuel induction system	Tighten fixings or replace components as necessary
J—Engine runs erratically	Ignition timing incorrect	With engine running, rotate vernier adjuster at distributor through advance and retard range. If engine runs smoothly at a new position then the original ignition timing is incorrect for the fuel in use	Reset ignition timing to the correct setting for the fuel in use
	Fuel system defect	Check for restriction in fuel supply and for fuel pump malfunction, Section L	
	Electrical system defects	Check for faulty electrical connections	Clean and tighten at terminals. Replace leads if insulation is not sound
		Check condition of sparking plugs	Clean and reset electrode gap. Replace plugs as necessary, Section N
		Check battery connections and state of battery charge	Clean and tighten connections. Recharge battery if necessary, Section N
		Check that vacuum pipe connection at distributor is sound	Rectify as necessary
	Valves operation incorrect	Check distributor operation as described in Section N	
		Check tappet clearances	Reset
		Check for valve sticking open. Check also for broken or defective valve springs	Carry out cylinder head overhaul procedure
		Remove cylinder head and check for worn valves and valve guides. Examine cylinder head gasket for signs of leakage across th sealing areas	Carry out the cylinder head overhaul procedure
	Exhaust system defects	Check for damage, cracks and ensure joints are tight	Rectify or replace components as necessary, Section M

Fault diagnosis—Engine—2¼ litre Petrol—continued

Symptom	Possible cause	Investigation	Remedy
K—Lack of power	Ignition system defect	Check condition of sparking plugs, insulation and electrode gap	Clean and reset electrode gap. Replace plugs if otherwise faulty
		Check distributor advance and retard mechanism, as detailed in Section N	Replace as necessary, referring to Section N
		Check for faulty coil, condenser or battery by substituting serviceable components	
		Check ignition timing	Reset
	Poor engine compression	If the compression pressure is appreciably less than the figure quoted in the 'Data' section, the piston rings may be worn or the valve seating poor	Carry out the applicable overhaul procedures
	Clutch slip	If vehicle road speed does not respond adequately to engine speed increases during normal travel, clutch slip may be taking place	Carry out the fault diagnosis procedure described in Section B
	Fuel system defect	Check fuel system for external leakage. Check fuel tank filler breather is clear. Check for restrictions in fuel system, indicated by low fuel level in float chamber	Rectify as described in Section L
	Exhaust system faulty	Check for damage, holes and cracks	Replace components as necessary, Section M
	Brakes 'binding'	Check as detailed in Section H	
L—Engine stalls	Fuel system defects	Check the carburetter control screw settings. Ensure throttle stop and mixture settings are correct.	Reset as necessary, Section L
		Check for restriction or foreign matter in fuel system	Rectify as detailed in Section L
	Ignition system defects	Check distributor contact breaker points and gap setting	Clean points and reset gap. Replace points as necessary, Section N
		Check condition of sparking plugs, electrode gap and also examine insulation	Clean plugs and reset gaps as necessary, Section N. Replace plugs as necessary
		Check operation of ignition coil and distributor condenser by substituting serviceable components	Replace as necessary, Section N
	Valve operation faulty	Check tappet clearances	Reset as necessary
M—Noisy valve mechanism	Valve operation incorrect	Check for excessive tappet clearances	Reset
		Rotate engine and check for sticking valves, and broken or defective valve springs. Check for excessively worn components	Carry out cylinder head overhaul procedure. Replace valve springs

Fault diagnosis—Engine—2¼ litre Petrol—continued

Symptom	Possible cause	Investigation	Remedy
N—Main bearing rattle	Low oil pressure	Refer to paragraph P for checks and remedy	
	Component or assembly defects	Check if main bearing cap fixings are loose	Tighten to correct torque loading
		Check bearing clearance. Examine bearings and crankshaft for wear	Carry out the overhaul procedure
P—Low oil pressure	Insufficient oil supply	Check at engine dipstick	Replenish sump with correct grade lubricating oil, Section X refers
	External leakage	Check engine for oil leaks. Ensure oil pressure switch joint washer is sound	Rectify as necessary
	Oil pump operation faulty	Check the oil pump intake filter for restriction	Remove foreign matter if necessary. Clean filter in clean fuel
		Check for wear in pump gears assembly	Carry out the oil pump overhaul procedure
		Check for foreign matter on ball valve seat	Clean and refit
	Oil pressure relief valve malfunction	Relief valve plunger sticking	Clean and ensure smooth operation before refitting
		Check that oil pump body joint fixings are tight	Tighten fixings
		Relief valve spring weak. Check by substitution of serviceable spring	Replace spring
	Excessively worn bearings	Check bearing clearances at main journals, connecting rod big ends and camshaft as necessary	Replace the bearings, referring to the appropriate overhaul procedure
Q—Oil pressure warning light remains 'ON', with engine running	Low oil pressure	Refer to paragraph P for checks and remedy	
	Oil pressure switch unserviceable	Check by substitution of serviceable component	Replace switch
	Electrical fault	Check circuit connections and leads	Rectify poor connections or replace leads as applicable
R—Warning light fails to glow with engine stopped and ignition switch 'ON'		Check warning lamp bulb by substitution of serviceable bulb	Replace bulb
		Check oil pressure switch by substitution of a serviceable switch	Replace switch
		Check electrical circuit	Rectify poor connections or replace leads as applicable

ENGINE—2¼ LITRE PETROL

GENERAL DATA

Capacity (piston displacement)	2286 cc (140 cu in.)
Number of cylinders	4
Bore	3.562 in. (90,47 mm)
Stroke	3.5 in. (88,8 mm)
Compression ratio	7:1 or 8:1
BHP at 4,250 rpm	77 81.
BMEP	7:1 134 lb./sq. in. (9,4 kg./cm²) at 2,500 rpm
	8:1 137 lb./sq. in. (9,6 kg./cm²) at 2,500 rpm
Maximum torque	7:1 124 lb./ft. (17 mkg) at 2,500 rpm
Firing order	1—3—4—2
Piston speed at 4,280 rpm	2,500 ft./min. (12,6 m./sec)
Compression pressure (at starter motor cranking speed, with engine hot)	7:1 145 lb./sq. in. (10,2 kg./cm²)
	8:1 160–170 lb./sq. in. (11,2–11,9 kg./cm²)

DETAIL DATA

Camshaft

Journal diameter	1.842 in.—.001 (26,70 mm—0,025)
Clearance in bearing	.001 to .002 in. (0,02 to 0,05 mm)
End-float	.0025 to .0055 in. (0,06 to 0,14 mm)
Cam lift—inlet	.257 in. (6,53 mm)
Cam lift—exhaust	.257 in. (6,53 mm)

Camshaft bearings

Type	Split, steel backed, white metal lined
Internal diameter (line-reamed in position)	1.843 in. +.0005 (46,8 mm + 0,012)

Connecting rods

Bearing fit on crankpin	.001 to .0025 in. (0,025 to 0,063 mm)
Bearing nip	.002 to .004 in. (0,05 to 0,10 mm)
End-float at big-end	.007 to .011 in. (0,20 to 0,30 mm)
Gudgeon pin bush, fit in small-end	.001 to .003 in. (0,02 to 0,76 mm) interference
Gudgeon pin bush internal diameter—reamed in position	1.000 in. +.0003 (25,4 mm +0,008)
Fit of gudgeon pin in bush	.0003 to .0005 in. (0,007 to 0,012 mm) clearance

Crankshaft

Journal diameter	2.5 in.—.0005 (63,5 mm—0,012)
Crankpin diameter:	
Early models	2.126 in.—.001 (53,9 mm—0,025)
Late models	2.312 in. (58,7 mm)
End-float (controlled by thrust washers at centre bearing)	.002 to .006 in. (0,05 to 0,15 mm)

Regrind sizes:

Undersize	Journal dia.	Crankpin dia.
.010 in. (0,25 mm)	2.490 in. (63,24 mm)	2.302 in. (58,47 mm)
.020 in. (0,50 mm)	2.480 in. (62,99 mm)	2.292 in. (58,22 mm)
.030 in. (0,76 mm)	2.470 in. (62,73 mm)	2.282 in. (57,96 mm)
.040 in. (1,01 mm)	2.460 in. (62,48 mm)	2.272 in. (57,70 mm)

Flywheel

Number of teeth	97
Thickness at pressure face	1.250 to 1.226 in. (31,75 to 31,14 mm)
Maximum permissible run-out on flywheel face	.002 in. (0,05 mm)
Primary pinion bush—fit in flywheel	.001 to .003 in. (0,02 to 0,07 mm)
Internal diameter—reamed in position	.878 in. +.0005 in. (22,3 +0,013 mm)
Fit of shaft in bush	.001 to .003 in. (0,025 to 0,076 mm)
Maximum refacing depth	.030 in. (0,76 mm)
Minimum overall thickness after grinding	1.485 in. (37,7 mm)

Engine timing markings

Early engines	Timing marks and pointer at flywheel
Later engines	Valve timing marks at timing chain wheels
	Ignition timing mark on crankshaft pulley, timing pointer at engine front cover
TDC (74–76 octane fuel)	When opposite pointer, No. 1 piston is at top dead centre
3° BTDC (80–85 octane fuel)	When opposite pointer, indicates firing point of
6° BTDC (90–96 octane fuel)	No. 1 cylinder when both valves are closed

Gudgeon pin

Fit in piston	Zero to .0002 in. (0,005 mm) interference
Fit in connecting rod bush	.0003 to .0005 in. (0,007 to 0,012 mm) clearance

Main bearings

Clearances on crankshaft journal	.001 to .0025 in. (0,02 to 0,06 mm)
Bearing nip	.004 to .006 in. (0,10 to 0,15 mm)

Pistons

Type	Light alloy, tin plated, flat top
Clearance in bore, measured at bottom of skirt at right angles to gudgeon pin	.0019 to .0023 in. (0,048 to 0,058 mm)
Clearance in bore, measured at top of skirt at right angles to gudgeon pin	.003 to .004 in (0,08 to 0,10 mm)
Fit of gudgeon pin in piston	Zero to .0002 in. (0,005 mm) interference
Gudgeon pin bore	.9998 in. +.0002 (25,37 mm +0,005)

Piston rings

Compression (2)

Type	Taper periphery
Gap in bore	.015 to .020 in. (0,38 to 0,50 mm)
Clearance in groove	.0018 to .0038 in. (0,046 to 0,097 mm)

Scraper

Type	Slotted, square friction edge
Gap in bore	.015 to .020 in. (0,38 to 0,50 mm)
Clearance in groove	.0015 to .0035 in. (0,038 to 0,089 mm)

Rocker gear

Bush internal diameter, reamed in position	.53 in. +.001 (13,4 mm +0,02)
Shaft clearance in rocker bush	.0005 to .0015 in. (0,013 to 0,038 mm)

Section A1—Land-Rover

ENGINE—2¼ LITRE PETROL

Tappet clearance	.010 in. (0,25 mm) hot or cold
Timing chain tensioner	
Fit of bush in cylinder	.003 to .005 in. (0,07 to 0,12 mm) Interference
Fit of bush in idler wheel	.001 to .003 in. (0,02 to 0,07 mm) Interference
Fit of idler wheel on steel shaft	.001 to .003 in. (0,02 to 0,07 mm) clearance
Fit of piston in cylinder bush	.0003 to .0013 in. (0,008 to 0,033 mm) clearance
Thrust bearings, crankshaft	
Type	Semi-circular, steel back, tin plated on friction surface
Standard size, total thickness	.093 in.—.002 (2,362 mm—0,05)
Oversizes	.0025 in. (0,06 mm); .005 in. (0,12 mm); .0075 in. (0,18 mm); .010 in. (0,25 mm)
Valves	
Inlet valve	
Diameter (stem)	.3112 in.—.0005 (7,9 mm—0,013 mm)
Face angle	30°—¼
Exhaust valve	
Diameter (stem)	.3415—.0005 (8,67 mm—0,013)
Face angle	45°—¼
Fit of inlet valves in guide	.001 to .003 in. (0,02 to 0,07 mm)
Fit of exhaust valves in guide	.0023 to .0038 in. (0,096 to 0,058 mm)
Valve seat	
Seat angle—inlet	30°
Seat angle—exhaust	45°
Valve guides	
Inlet guide bore size, after fitting	.3125 in.+.0015 (7,93 mm+0,04)
Exhaust guide bore size, after fitting	.3435 in.+.0015 (8,73 mm+0,04)
Valve springs	
Early type	
Inner	
Length—free	1.61 in. (40,89 mm)
Length under 17.5 lb. (7,9 kg) load	1.38 in. (35,1 mm)
Outer	
Length—free	1.76 in. (44,9 mm)
Length under 46 lb. (21 kg) load	1.50 in. (38,3 mm)
Later type	
Inner	
Length—free	1.680 in. (42,67 mm)
Length under 17.7 lb. (8,0 kg) load	1.462 in. (37,13 mm)
Outer	
Length—free	1.822 in. (46,28 mm)
Length under 46 lb. (21 kg) load	1.587 in. (40,3 mm)

ENGINE—2¼ LITRE PETROL

Valve timing	
Inlet opens	6° BTDC
Inlet closes	52° ABDC
Inlet peak	113°
Exhaust opens	34° BBDC
Exhaust closes	24° ATDC
Exhaust peak	95°
Vertical drive shaft gear	
Backlash	.006 to .010 in. (0,15 to 0,25 mm)
Internal diameter of bush	1.063 in.+.001 (27,0 mm+0,02)
Fit of gear in bush	.001 to .003 in. (0,02 to 0,07 mm) clearance
Oil pump, early type	
Type	Spur gear
Drive	Splined shaft from camshaft skew gear
End-float of gears	.002 to .005 in. (0,025 to 0,12 mm)
Radial clearance of gears	.0005 to .002 in. (0,012 to 0,050 mm)
Backlash of gears	.004 to .008 in. (0,10 to 0,20 mm)
Oil pump, late type	
Type	Skew gear
Drive	Splined shaft from camshaft skew gear
End-float of gears:	
Steel gear	.002 in. (0,05 mm) to .005 in. (0,12 mm)
Aluminium gear	.003 in. (0,07 mm) to .006 in. (0,15 mm)
Radial clearance of gears	.001 to .004 in. (0,02 to 0,102 mm)
Backlash of gears	.006 to .012 in. (0,14 to 0,28 mm)
Oil pressure, engine warm	
2,000 rpm	45 to 65 lb./sq. in. (3,16 to 4,57 kg cm²)
Oil pressure relief valve	
Type	Non-adjustable
Relief valve spring:	
Free length	2.670 in. (67,82 mm)
Compressed length at 5.7 lb. (2.58 kg) load	2.45 in. (61,23 mm)

SECTION A2—2¼ LITRE DIESEL ENGINE

INDEX TO OPERATIONS

Note: A comprehensive, detailed index is included at the end of this Manual

Description of Listed Operations	Operation Number Remove/Refit	Operation Number Overhaul
Bonnet panel	A2-1	—
Air cleaner	A2-2	—
Radiator and grille panel assembly	A2-3	—
Front floor	A2-4	—
Engine	A2-5	—
Fuel injectors	A2-6	Section L
Fuel filter, replace element	A2-7	—
Inlet and exhaust manifolds	A2-8	—
Starter motor	A2-9	Section N
Dynamo	A2-10	Section N
Water pump	A2-11	Section K
Thermostat and housing	A2-12	Section K
Fuel pump	A2-13	Section L
Engine side covers	A2-14	—
Oil filter, external, replace element	A2-15	—
Oil filter, external	A2-16	A2-16
Distributor pump	A2-17	—
Distributor pump drive gears	A2-18	—
Tappet adjustment	A2-19	—
Valve gear, rocker shaft and push rods	A2-20	A2-21
Cylinder head	A2-22	A2-23
Tappet assemblies	A2-24	—
Engine front cover and oil seal	A2-25	—
Timing chain tensioner	A2-26	—
Timing gears and chain, including valve timing procedure	A2-27	—
Crankcase sump	A2-28	—
Oil pump	A2-29	A2-30
Clutch assembly and flywheel	A2-31	Section B
Rear main bearing oil seal and flywheel housing	A2-32	—
Pistons and connecting rods	A2-33	A2-34
Crankshaft and main bearings	A2-35	A2-36
Camshaft	A2-37	—
Cylinder block and camshaft bearings	—	A2-38
Flywheel reclamation	A2-31	A2-39

This Section concerns remove, refit and overhaul procedures for the 2¼ litre diesel engine.

When carrying out a complete engine overhaul, the section can be worked straight through in the order presented.

Alternatively, the individual operations which form the greater percentage of maintenance work undertaken by Distributors and Dealers, are detailed under appropriate headings, and will be found to be complete in themselves.

Some operations are marked with an asterisk * to indicate that they can be carried out with the engine installed. In all other cases it is necessary to remove the engine unit in order to carry out the work detailed.

Where LH (left-hand) or RH (right-hand) appear in the text this indicates LH or RH side of vehicle or engine when viewed from rear.

Brief description of engine

The cylinder block is of cast iron. Re-boring is permitted up to a maximum of .040 in. (1,0 mm) oversize above the standard bore size of 3.562 in. (90,49 mm). Further reclamation is obtained by fitting cylinder liners and boring out to standard bore size. Re-boring of cylinder liners is permitted up to .010 in. (0,25 mm).

The crankshaft is supported by three bearings. The thrust is taken by the centre bearing. The bearings are steel shells lined with copper lead tin plating.

The camshaft is supported by four bearings and actuates roller type cam followers operating valve rockers through push rods, and lead/tin plated bronze slides. Adjustment is made on the adjusting screws on valve rockers. The bearings are white-metal lined steel shells.

The camshaft is chain driven and a chain tensioner is fitted.

The engine is lubricated by a pressure fed oil system which incorporates a pump located in the crankcase sump and an external full flow oil filter.

Engine component dimensions are provided in the Detail Data at the end of this Section.

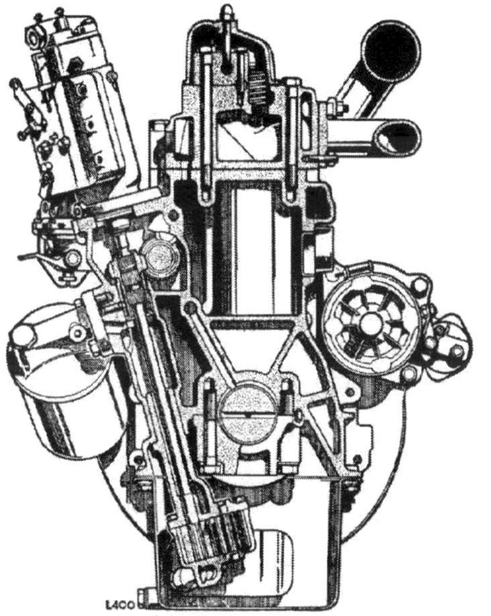

Page 4-A2　Section A2—Land-Rover

ENGINE—2¼ LITRE DIESEL

Cross-section view of engine

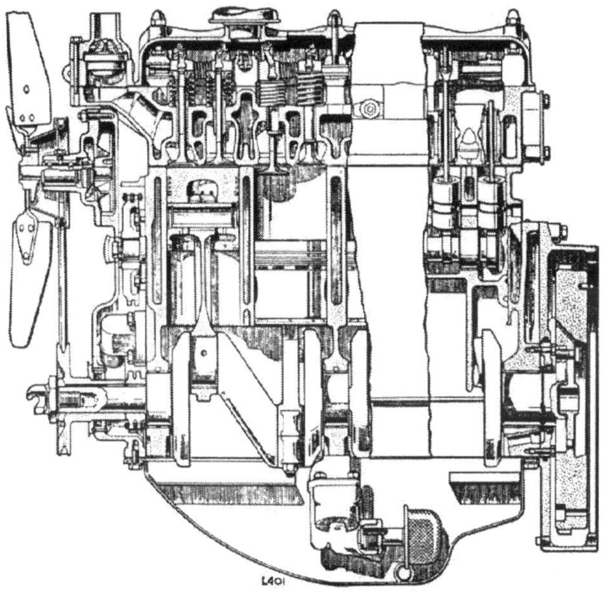

Longitudinal view of engine

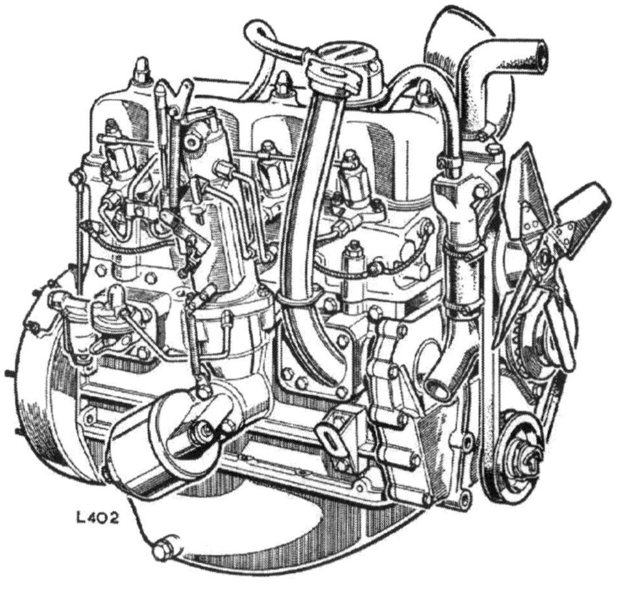

Section A2—Land-Rover　Page 5-A2

ENGINE—2¼ LITRE DIESEL

General view of engine, RH side

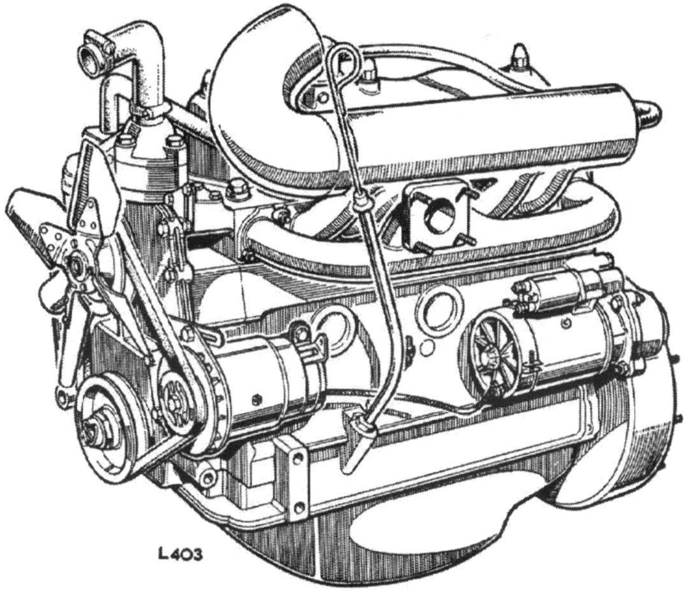

General view of engine, LH side

ENGINE—2¼ LITRE DIESEL   Section A2—Land-Rover

*Bonnet panel, remove and refit—Operation A2-1

Workshop hand tools:
Screwdriver (medium), Pliers

To remove

1. Remove the spare wheel from the bonnet panel, if fitted.
2. Remove fixings at prop rod and bonnet hinge.

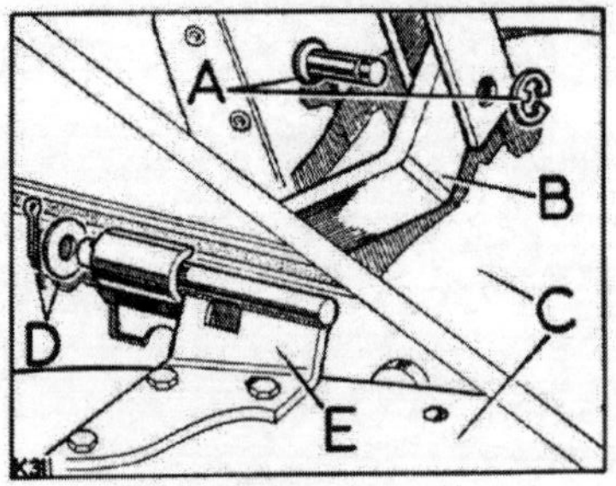

Fig. A2-1. Fixings at bonnet panel

A—Prop rod fixings
B—Bonnet prop rod
C—Bonnet panel
D—Bonnet hinge fixings, RH side only
E—Bonnet hinge

3. Remove bonnet panel.

To refit

1. Refit the bonnet panel, using suitable coverings on the wings to avoid damage to paintwork.
2. Refit the spare wheel, if fitted, to bonnet panel.

Section A2—Land-Rover   ENGINE—2¼ LITRE DIESEL

*Air cleaner, remove, clean and refit—Operation A2-2

Workshop hand tools:
Spanner sizes: 7/16 In. AF open ended
Screwdriver (medium)

To remove

1. Lift and prop bonnet.
2. Remove air intake hose from inlet manifold.

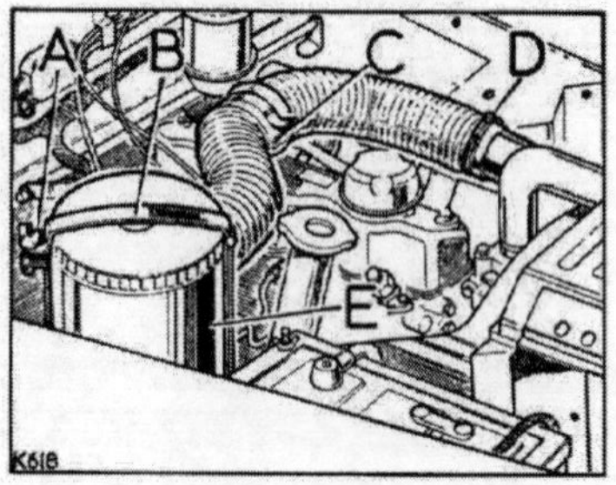

Fig. A2-2. Air cleaner and hose fixings

A—Retaining strap fixings
B—Air cleaner retaining strap
C—Hose support clip
D—Air cleaner hose fixings
E—Air cleaner

3. Slacken the fixings and move aside the retaining strap.
4. Remove air cleaner complete with hose.

To dismantle and clean

1. Separate the air cleaner body assembly from the oil container, retained by clips.
2. Drain the oil and withdraw the wire mesh unit.

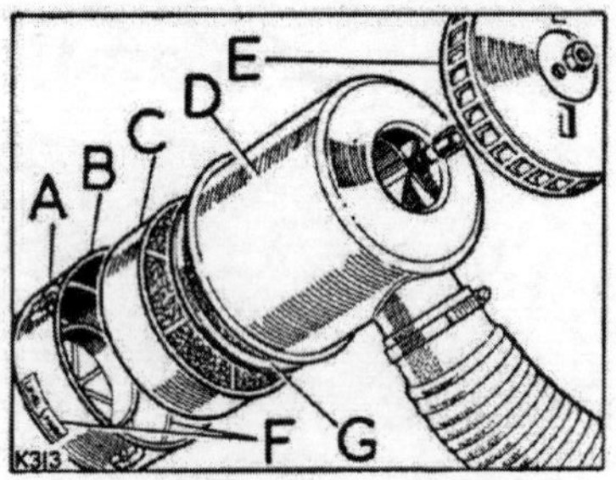

Fig. A2-3. Exploded view of air cleaner

A—Hinged clips
B—Oil container
C—Wire mesh unit
D—Air cleaner and mesh assembly
E—Air intake cap and fixing
F—Oil level mark
G—Sealing washer

3. Wash all components in clean fuel.

To assemble

1. Fill the oil container with clean engine oil to the oil level mark on the container. See Fig. A2-3.
2. Reverse the dismantling procedure, fitting a new sealing washer between the oil container and the air cleaner body.

To refit

1. Refit air cleaner and hose, if necessary, reposition the air cleaner body relative to the oil container to prevent the hinged clips from fouling on the retaining strap supports when fitted.

Operations marked with an asterisk (*) can be carried out with the engine installed in the vehicle

ENGINE—2¼ LITRE DIESEL

*Radiator and grille panel assembly, remove and refit—Operation A2-3

Workshop hand tools:
Spanner sizes: 7/16 in. x ½ in. AF open ended, 2 off, 2 BA open ended
Screwdriver (medium), Pliers

To remove
1. Remove bonnet. Operation A2-1.
2. Disconnect battery leads.
3. Remove front apron panel.

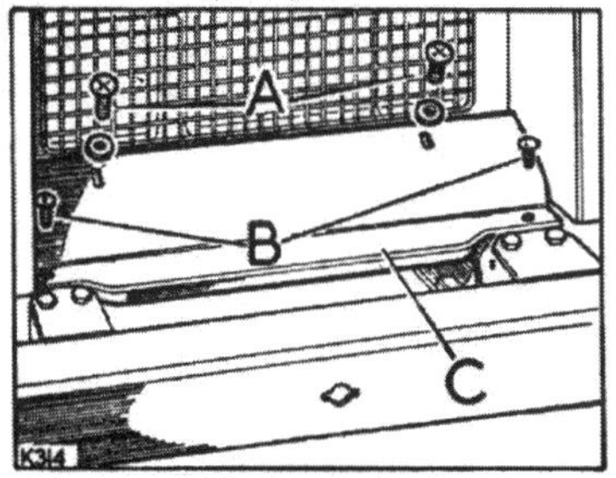

Fig. A2-4. Apron panel fixings
A—Fixings at cross member brackets
B—Fixings at side members
C—Apron panel

4. Remove nameplate and radiator grille.

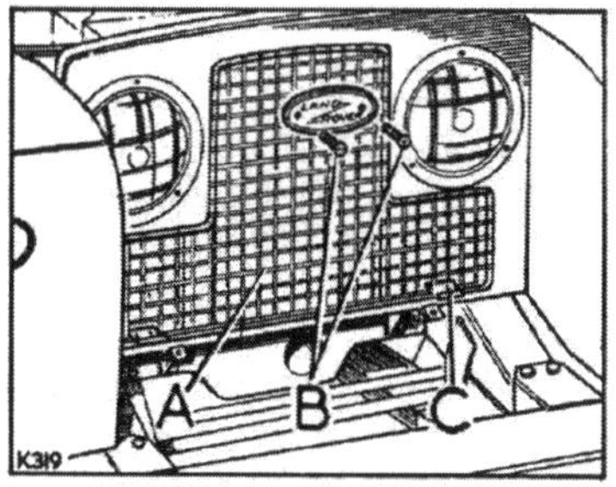

Fig. A2-5. Radiator grille fixings
A—Radiator grille
B—Fixings for nameplate and grille
C—Support brackets

5. Remove radiator cap, drain off coolant.

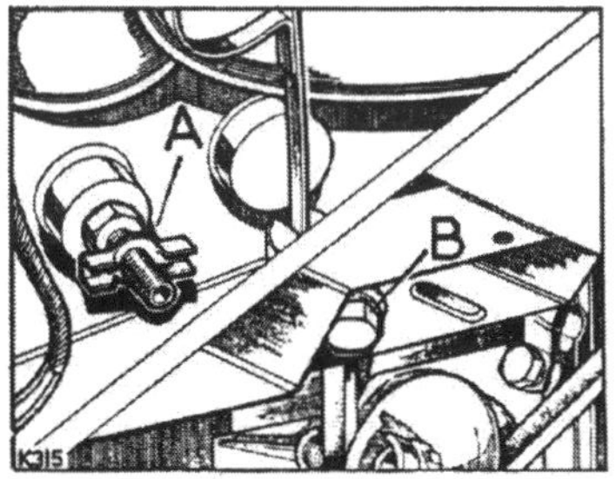

Fig. A2-6. Coolant drain points location
A—At engine block   B—At radiator

6. Remove shroud from radiator fan cowl.

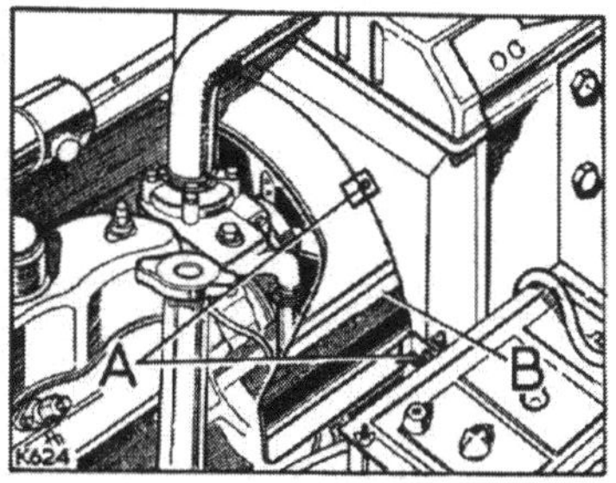

Fig. A2-7. Fan shroud fixings
A—Fixings for fan shroud
B—Fan shroud

7. Slacken fixings and detach radiator coolant hoses.

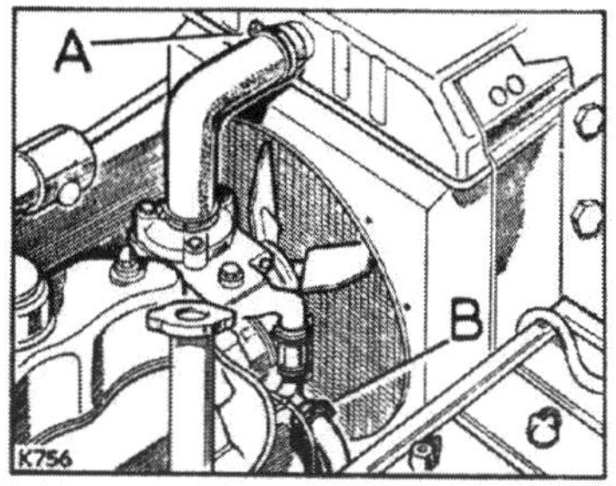

Fig. A2-8. Coolant hose fixings
A—Fixings at top hose
B—Fixings at bottom hose

8. Remove the fan blades fixings and lower the fan blades to rest on lower part of fan cowl. Remove the fan blades when access is obtained during grille panel removal.

9. Disconnect the electrical leads for the front lamps at the snap connectors and earth terminal. Withdraw harness clear from grille panel.

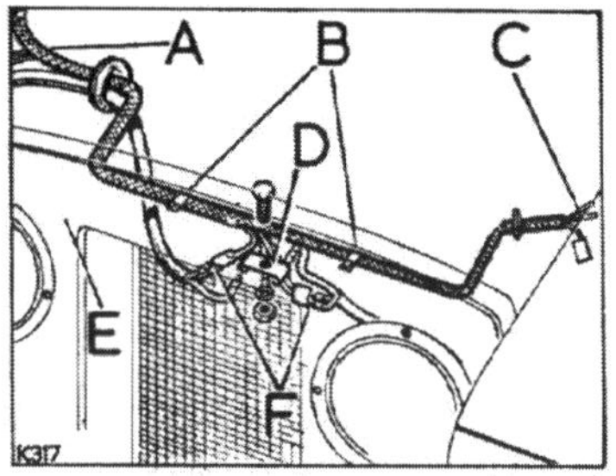

Fig. A2-9. Front lamps electrical leads
A—Electrical leads
B—Cable clips
C—Winglamp leads snap connectors
D—Earth connections
E—Grille panel
F—Headlamp leads snap connectors

10. Remove the grille panel to front wings fixings, the securing nuts and washers are located in the respective wheelarches.

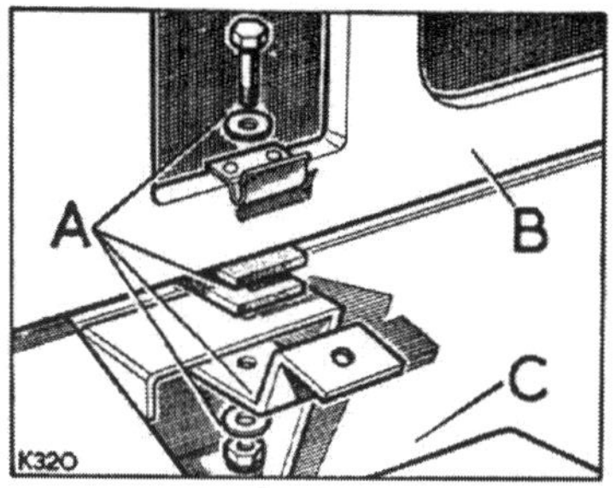

11. Remove the grille panel fixings at the brackets on the chassis cross member.

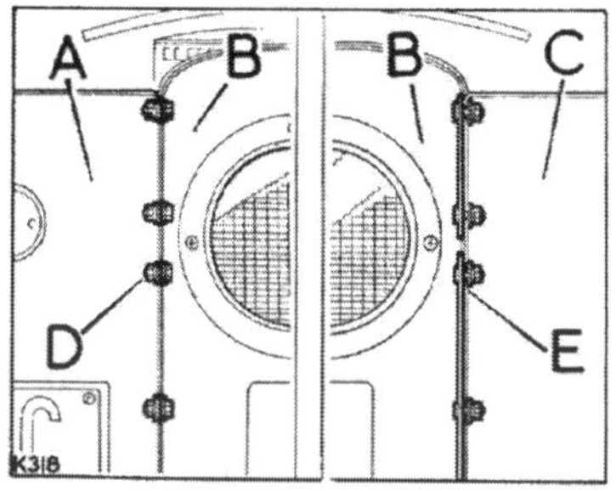

Fig. A2-10. Radiator grille panel fixings
A—Front wing, RH side
B—Radiator grille panel
C—Front wing, LH side
D—Fixings at RH side
E—Fixings at LH side

12. Carefully withdraw the assembly and the previously released fan blades from the engine compartment.

Fig. A2-11. Fixings at chassis cross member
A—Panel fixings
B—Radiator grille panel
C—Chassis cross member

Operations marked with an asterisk (*) can be carried out with the engine installed in the vehicle

ENGINE—2¼ LITRE DIESEL

Operation A2-3—continued

To refit

1. Refit the radiator grille and radiator complete on to the vehicle. Fit the fan blades to the fan pulley before engaging the grille panel fixings.

2. Refit the electrical leads through the grille panel grommets and make the electrical connections at the snap connectors and earth terminal, referring to Fig. A2-9 and the appropriate circuit diagram, if necessary, in Section N.

3. Connect the coolant hoses and replenish the engine coolant system, allowing a free flow through the drain taps before closing them. Fig. A2-6 refers. Fill the radiator header tank to within ½ in. to ¾ in. (12 mm to 19 mm) below the bottom of the filler neck.

4. Refit the fan cowl shroud, Fig. A2-7 refers.

COOLANT SYSTEM
Bonneted Control Model, 2¼ Litre Diesel

	Capacity	Imperial Unit	US Unit	Litres	Antifreeze	Frost Precaution
88	17½ pints	17½ pints	21 pints	10,0	33⅓%	−25°F −32°C
109	17½ pints	17½ pints	21 pints	10,0	33⅓%	−25°F −32°C

4. Refit the front apron panel. Fig. A2-4 refers.
5. Connect battery lead.
6. Refit the bonnet panel. Operation A2-1.

*Front floor, remove and refit—Operation A2-4

Workshop hand tools:
Spanner sizes: 7/16 in. AF, 7/16 in. BSF open end, 7/16 in. AF socket
Screwdriver (medium)

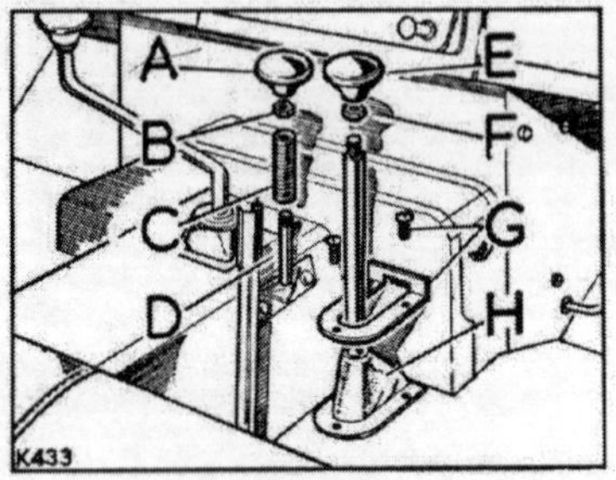

Fig. A2-12. Four-wheel drive and transfer levers
A—Knob, four-wheel drive lever
B—Locknut for knob
C—Spring
D—Ferrule
E—Knob, transfer gear lever
F—Locknut for knob
G—Fixings for dust cover
H—Dust cover

To remove

1. Unscrew the knob and locknut from the transfer gear lever.
2. Remove the fixings and withdraw the dust cover from the transfer gear lever.
3. Unscrew the knob and locknut from the four-wheel drive lever, and withdraw the spring and ferrule.
4. Remove both halves of the front floor board.
5. Remove the gearbox tunnel cover.
6. Remove the gearbox tunnel front panel.

Operations marked with an asterisk (*) can be carried out with the engine installed in the vehicle

ENGINE—2¼ LITRE DIESEL

Operation A2-4—continued

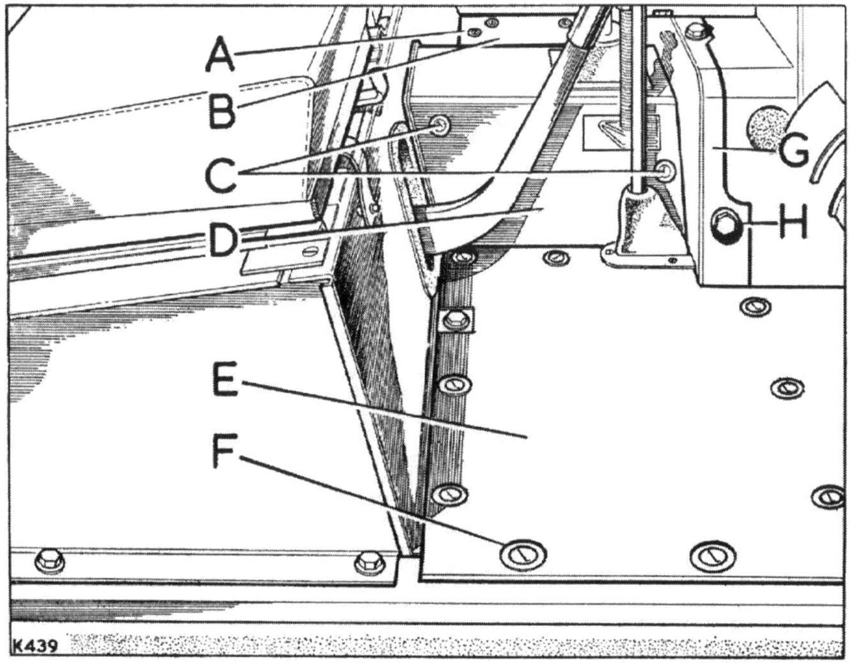

Fig. A2-13. Front floor

A—Fixings (9 off), left-hand floor board
B—Floor board, left-hand
C—Fixings (4 off), tunnel cover
D—Gearbox tunnel cover
E—Floor board, right-hand
F—Fixings (12 off), right-hand floor board
G—Front panel for gearbox tunnel cover
H—Fixings (4 off), front panel

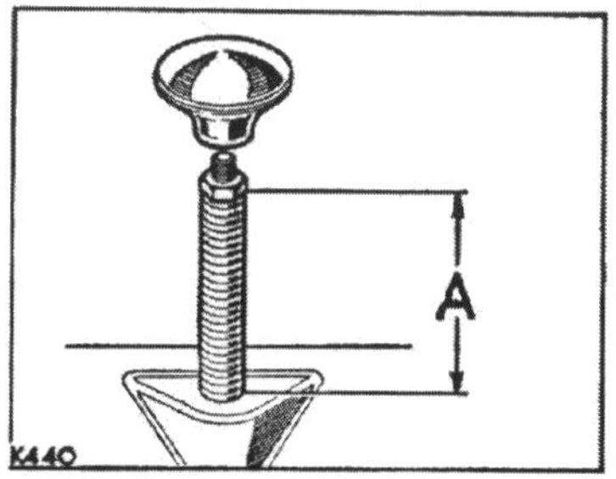

Fig. A2-14. Adjusting four-wheel drive control lever

A—2 7/16 in. − 1/16 in. (58 mm −1 mm)

To refit

1. Reverse the removal procedure, using waterproof sealant between the joint flanges of the front floor and the chassis. A suitable sealant is 'Sealastrip', manufactured by Expandite Ltd., Chase Road, London NW10.

2. Adjust the four-wheel drive lever during assembly, as follows. Fit the ferrule, spring and locknut to the lever, depress the lever and adjust the locknut until the compressed spring length is 2 7/16 in. − 1/16 in. (58 mm −1 mm), then fit the knob and tighten the locknut.

ENGINE—2¼ LITRE DIESEL

Engine, remove and refit—Operation A2-5

Special tools:
Lifting sling for engine, Part No. 600963

Workshop hand tools:
Spanner sizes: 7/16 in. x ½ in. AF (2 off) open end
⅝ in. AF, ½ in. AF, 11/16 in. AF open end
7/16 in. AF, ⅝ in. AF ring
½ in. AF, 7/16 in. AF socket
7/16 in. BSF, ⅜ in. BSF open end
2 BA open end
Pliers, Screwdriver (medium)

To remove

1. Remove the bonnet panel. Operation A2-1.
2. Disconnect the battery earth lead.
3. Remove the air cleaner. Operation A2-2.
4. Remove radiator and grille panel. Operation A2-3.
5. Remove the front floor. Operation A2-4.
6. Disconnect the following items at the left-hand side of the engine; refer to Fig. A2-15 for location details:
   (a) Front exhaust pipe at manifold.
   (b) Heater hoses, if fitted.
   (c) Starter motor leads.
   (d) Dynamo leads.
   (e) Engine earth cable.

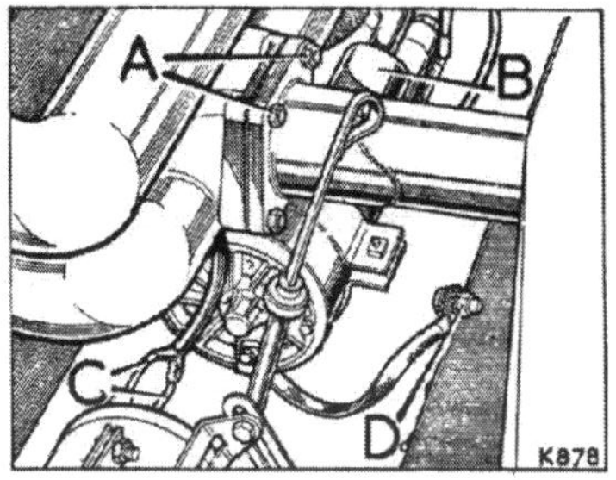

Fig. A2-15. View of engine, LH side

A—Front exhaust pipe fixings
B—Disconnect leads at solenoid
C—Dynamo leads
D—Engine earth cable fixings

7. Disconnect the following items at the right-hand side of the engine; refer to Fig. A2-16 for location details:
   (a) Electrical feed to heater plugs.
   (b) Fuel pipe to fuel pump.
   (c) Fuel pipe from spill pipe to fuel filter.
   (d) Oil pressure switch lead from external oil filter.
   (e) Accelerator linkage at fuel distributor pump.

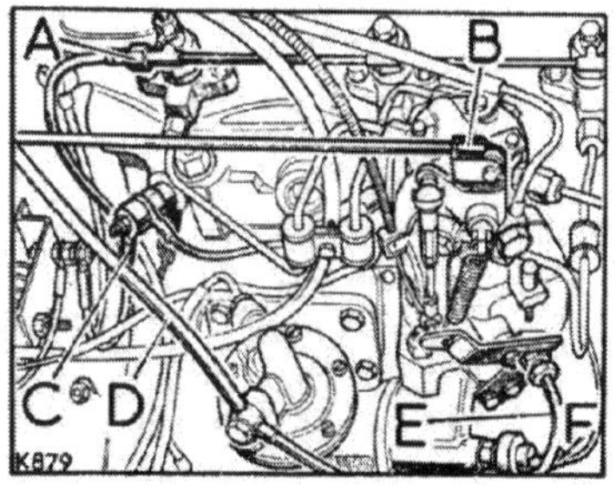

Fig. A2-16. View of engine, RH side

A—Fixing for spill pipe return
B—Disconnect accelerator linkage at clip
C—Electrical feed to heater plugs
D—Fuel pipe to fuel pump
E—Fuel return pipe
F—Oil pressure switch lead

8. Remove the engine mounting upper fixings.

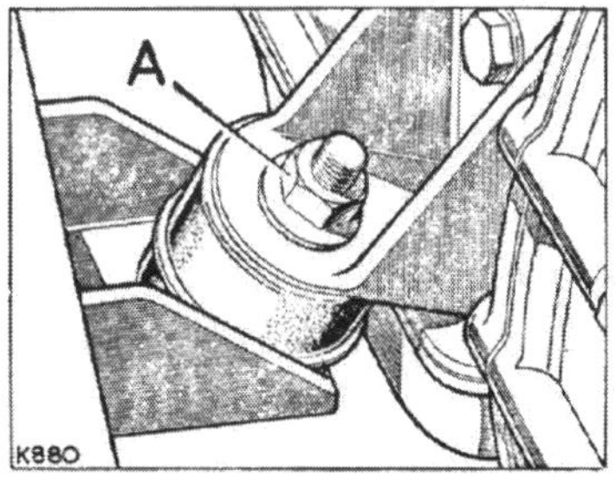

Fig. A2-17. Engine mounting, RH side shown

A—Upper fixings

ENGINE—2¼ LITRE DIESEL

Operation A2-5—continued

9. Fit a suitable lifting sling and support the engine weight.

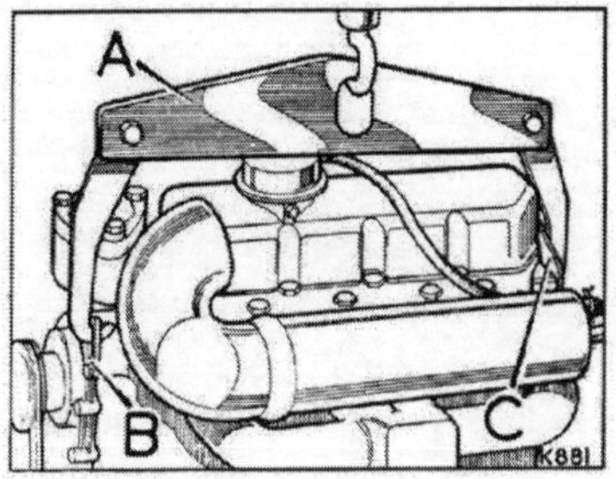

10. Remove the engine front mounting rubbers as follows:
    At LH side: remove lower centre fixing from suspension rubber and withdraw rubber.
    At RH side: remove support bracket fixings and withdraw the bracket and suspension rubber.

11. Lower the engine to regain alignment with the gearbox. Support the gearbox weight, using a suitable jack or packing block, and remove the bell housing to flywheel housing fixings.

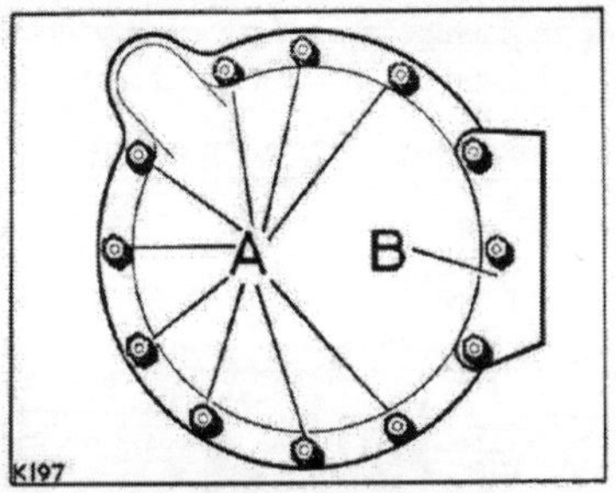

12. Pull the engine forward sufficient to disengage the drive from the gearbox. Ensure that all cables, pipes, etc. are clear then hoist the engine from the vehicle.

To refit

1. Engage any gear to prevent gear shaft rotation. Offer engine to gearbox. It may be necessary to rotate the engine sufficient to align the gearbox primary pinion with the clutch plate splines. When aligned, push the engine fully to the rear and secure the bell housing to the flywheel housing, tightening the fixings evenly. Fig. A2-20 refers.

2. Lift the engine sufficient to remove the packing or jack from beneath the gearbox and insert the engine front suspension rubbers. Fig. A2-19 refers.

3. Lower the engine and fit the suspension rubber fixings.

4. Remove the engine lifting sling.

5. Refit the engine earth cable.

6. Refit the dynamo electrical leads.

7. Refit the starter motor leads.

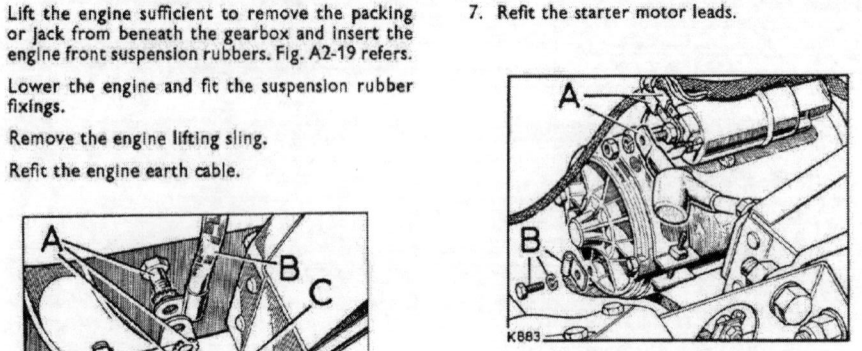

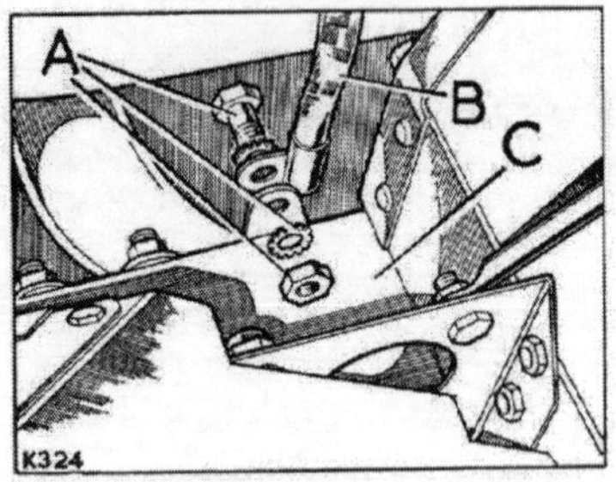

8. Reconnect the heater hoses, if fitted.

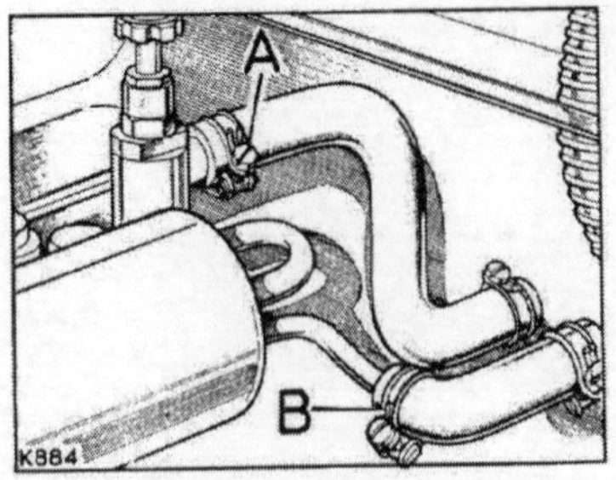

Fig. A2-18. Engine lifting sling in position
A—Engine lifting sling, Part No. 600963
B—Engine lifting bracket, front
C—Engine lifting bracket, rear

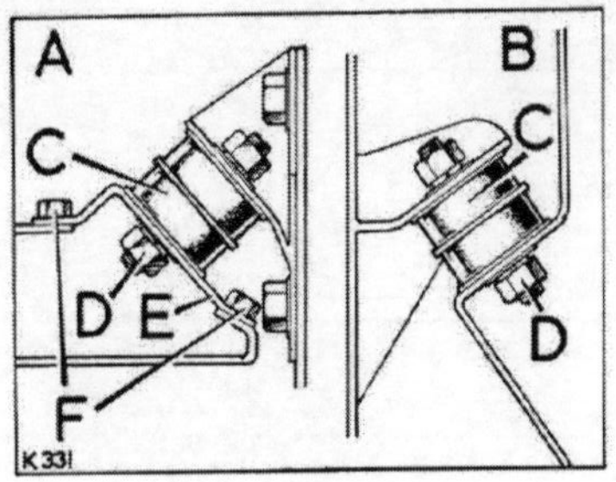

Fig. A2-19. Engine front mounting details
A—RH side mounting
B—LH side mounting
C—Suspension rubbers
D—Lower centre fixing
E—Support bracket at RH side fixing
F—Support bracket fixings

Fig. A2-20. Bell housing fixings
A—Fixings at bell housing
B—Fixings at clutch slave cylinder mounting

Fig. A2-21. Engine earth cable
A—Fixings
B—Earth cable
C—Chassis side member

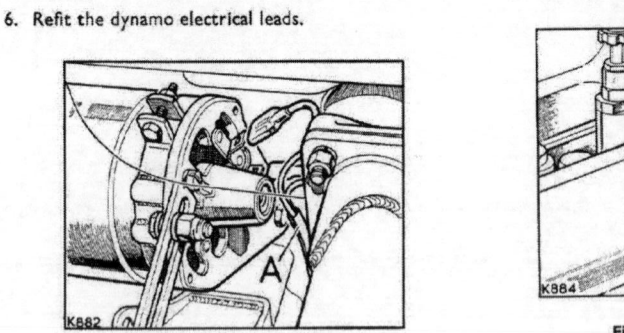

Fig. A2-22. Dynamo electrical leads
A—Leads with push-on connectors

Fig. A2-23. Starter motor leads
A—Leads to solenoid terminals
B—Earth cable fixings

Fig. A2-24. Heater hoses
A—At control tap
B—At by-pass pipe

ENGINE—2¼ LITRE DIESEL

Operation A2-5—continued

9. Refit the front exhaust pipe to the manifold.

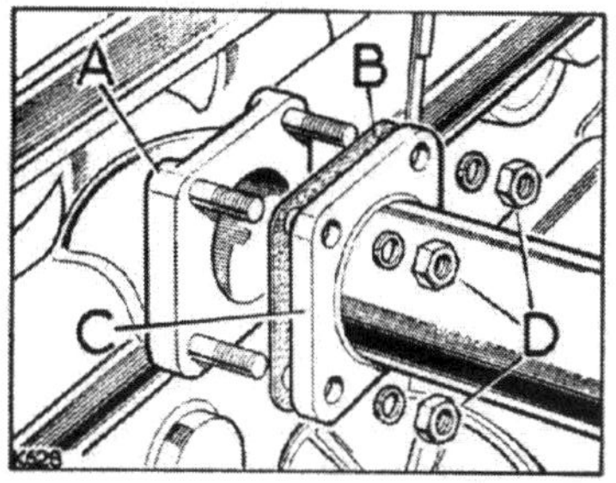

Fig. A2-25. Front exhaust pipe

A—Exhaust manifold
B—Joint washer
C—Front exhaust pipe
D—Fixings

10. Reconnect the electrical feed to the heater plugs.

Fig. A2-26. Heater plug feed

A—Electrical feed lead
B—Fixings

11. Refit the fuel pipe to the fuel pump and the spill return pipe from the filter.

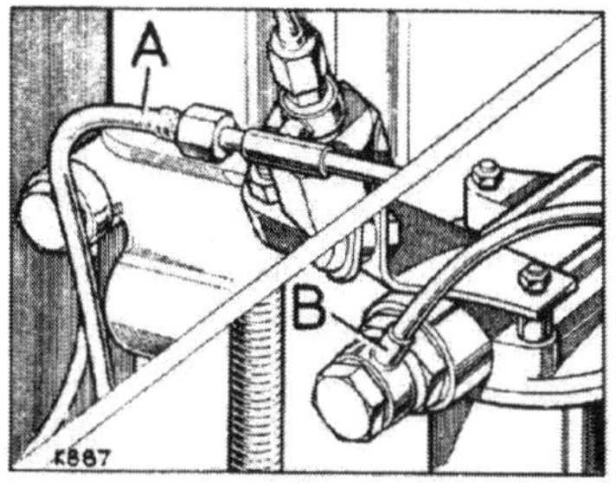

Fig. A2-27. Fuel pipes at pump and spill pipe

A—Spill return pipe to filter
B—Fuel inlet to pump

12. Reconnect the oil pressure switch lead to the external oil filter.

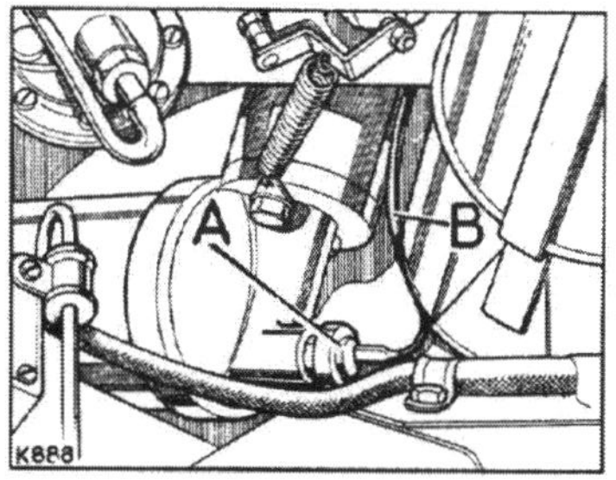

Fig. A2-28. Oil pressure switch lead

A—Oil filter terminal
B—Switch lead

13. Reconnect the accelerator linkage at the fuel distributor pump.

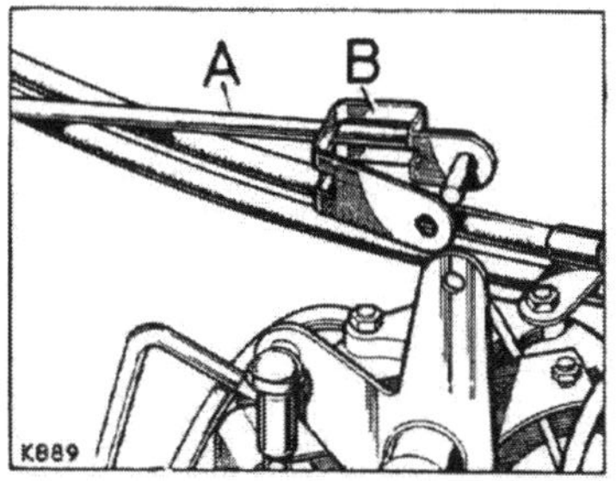

Fig. A2-29. Accelerator linkage at pump

A—Accelerator linkage
B—Spring clip

14. Refit the front floor. Operation A2-4.

15. Refit the radiator and grille panel. Operation A2-3, and refill the engine coolant system.

COOLANT SYSTEM
Bonneted Control Model, 2¼ Litre Diesel

Capacity	Imperial Unit	US Unit	Litres	Antifreeze	Frost Precaution
88	17½ pints	21 pints	10,0	33⅓%	−25°F −32°C
109	17½ pints	21 pints	10,0	33⅓%	−25°F −32°C

16. Prime the fuel system as described in Section L.
17. Refit the air cleaner. Operation A2-2.
18. Reconnect the battery earth lead.
19. Refit the bonnet panel. Operation A2-1.

ENGINE—2¼ LITRE DIESEL

*Fuel injectors, remove and refit—Operation A2-6

(For overhaul Instructions, Section L refers)

Workshop hand tools:
Spanner sizes: ½ in. x 7/16 in. AF open end (2 off)
7/16 in. AF, ⅝ in. AF open end
⅞ in. AF socket
Screwdriver (medium), Pliers

Special tools:
Torque wrench

To remove

1. Remove the bonnet panel. Operation A2-1.
2. Remove the air cleaner. Operation A2-2.
3. Slacken the injector fuel pipes at the distributor pump and disconnect at the injectors.
4. Disconnect the fuel spill pipe and slacken the spill pipe fixings at the injectors.

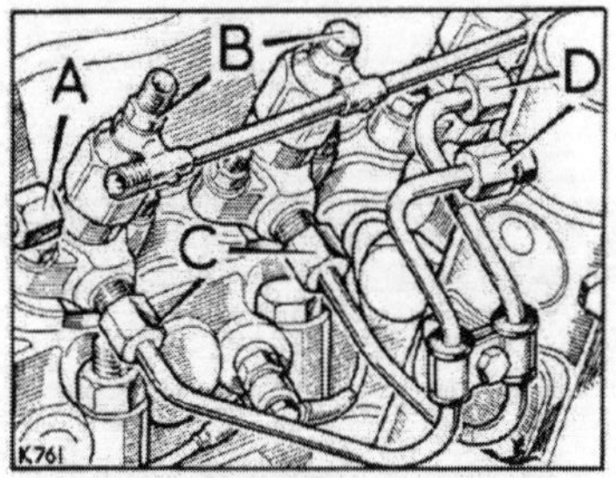

Fig. A2-30. Injector fuel pipes arrangement
A—Disconnect spill pipe here
B—Slacken spill pipe fixings at injectors
C—Disconnect pipes at injectors (4 off)
D—Slacken pipes at distributor pump (4 off)

5. Remove the fixings retaining the injectors and withdraw the injectors from the engine, complete with spill pipe.

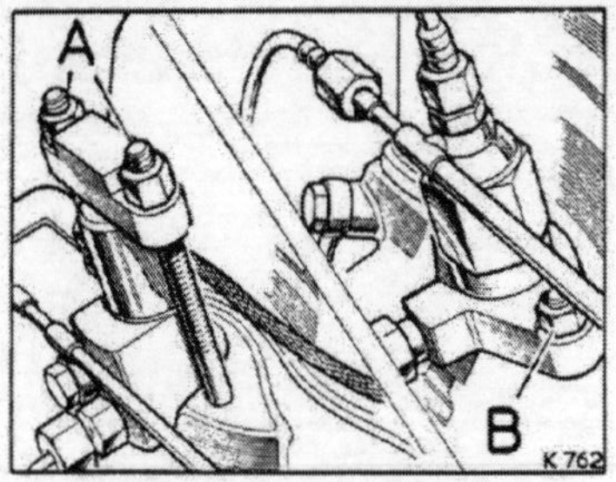

6. Take care to avoid damage to the needle valves which protrude from the injector faces. Immerse the components in clean fuel pending overhaul or refitting.

7. Remove the steel sealing washers from the injector housing bores. The remaining sealing washers (copper) are normally withdrawn with the injectors, ensure that they are not left behind in the bores.

To refit

1. Refit the new steel sealing washers into the injector bores, with the raised corrugation uppermost.

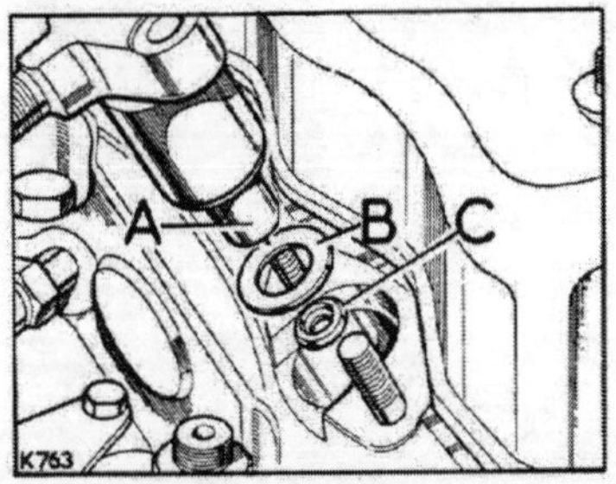

Fig. A2-32. Injector sealing washers arrangement
A—Injector
B—Copper sealing washer
C—Corrugated sealing washer

2. Refit the injectors and new copper sealing washers.
3. Fit the injector fixings and tighten evenly to a torque load of 6 lb ft to 8 lb ft (0.8 mkg to 1.0 mkg), Fig. A2-31 refers. **Do not overtighten the fixings.**
4. Refit the fuel pipes to the injectors and tighten at the distributor pump. Fig. A2-30 refers.
5. Refit the fuel spill pipe and tighten the spill pipe fixings at the injectors.
6. Prime the fuel system as described in Section L.
7. Refit the air cleaner. Operation A2-2.
8. Refit the bonnet panel. Operation A2-1.

Fig. A2-31. Fuel injector fixings
A—Early type. fixings at clamp bars
B—Later type, fixings at injector flanges

---

*Fuel filter, to replace element—Operation A2-7

Workshop hand tools:
Spanner size: ⅞ in. AF

To replace element

1. Lift and prop bonnet panel.
2. Support element holder and unscrew the special bolt on the top of the filter, the element holder can now be removed.

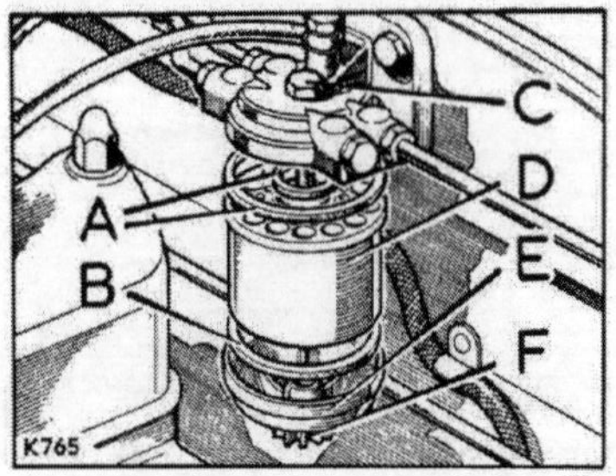

Fig. A2-33. Fuel filter, located on engine dash panel
A—Upper sealing washers
B—Lower sealing washer for element holder
C—Retaining bolt
D—Element
E—Element holder
F—Drain plug

3. Remove and discard the used element.
4. Wash the element holder in petrol or fuel oil.
5. Renew both the large sealing washer and the small sealing washer in the filter top, also renew the large sealing washer in the element holder.
6. Push new element on to filter top spigot with the perforated holes in the element to the top.
7. Fit the element holder to the bottom of the element, and secure with the special bolt.
8. Repeat the procedure on the second filter on twin filter systems.
9. Prime the system and check for fuel leaks, referring to Section L.
10. Close bonnet panel.

Operations marked with an asterisk (*) can be carried out with the vehicle installed in the engine

Operations marked with an asterisk (*) can be carried out with the engine installed in the vehicle

ENGINE—2¼ LITRE DIESEL

*Inlet and exhaust manifolds, remove and refit—Operation A2-8

Workshop hand tools:
Spanner sizes: ½ in. AF ring, ⅜ in. AF open end, ½ in. AF socket
Screwdriver (medium)

To remove

1. Remove bonnet panel. Operation A2-1.
2. Disconnect the air cleaner hose at inlet manifold and the engine breather pipe if fitted.

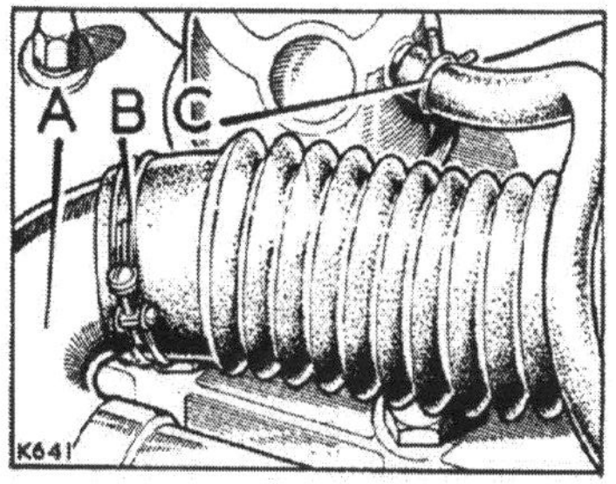

Fig. A2-34. Inlet manifold connections

A—Inlet manifold
B—Air cleaner hose fixing
C—Breather pipe fixing

3. Disconnect front exhaust pipe at manifold.

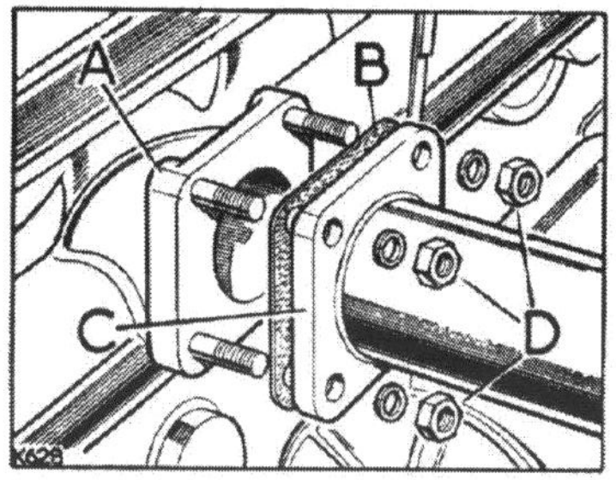

Fig. A2-35. Exhaust pipe fixings

A—Exhaust manifold
B—Joint washer
C—Front exhaust pipe
D—Fixings

4. Withdraw the oil level dipstick, remove the fixings and withdraw the manifolds.

Fig. A2-36. Manifolds fixings

A—Inlet manifold
B—Joint washer
C—Exhaust manifold
D—Lower fixings (5 off)
E—Upper fixings (4 off)

To refit

1. Fit the joint washer and position the exhaust manifold on the studs.
2. Position the inlet manifold and fit the clamp plates to the upper fixings to secure the two manifolds. Do not fully tighten at this stage.
3. Fit the remaining fixings to the lower studs and tighten all fixings evenly. Refit exhaust pipe.
4. Refit the inlet manifold connections, referring to Fig. A2-34.
5. Refit the bonnet panel. Operation A2-1.

*Starter motor, remove and refit—Operation A2-9

(For overhaul instructions, Section N refers)

Workshop hand tools:
Spanner sizes: ½ in. AF, ⁷⁄₁₆ in. AF, ⅝ in. AF, ¹¹⁄₁₆ in. AF open end
Screwdriver (medium), Pliers

To remove

1. Remove bonnet panel. Operation A2-1.
2. Disconnect battery.
3. Disconnect electrical leads.

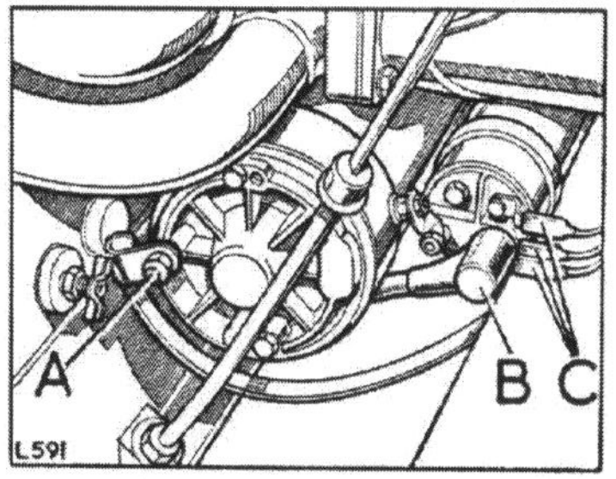

Fig. A2-37. Electrical leads at starter

A—Earth strap terminal
B—Withdraw rubber boot for access to lead
C—Push-on type connectors

4. Remove fixings at engine and withdraw starter.

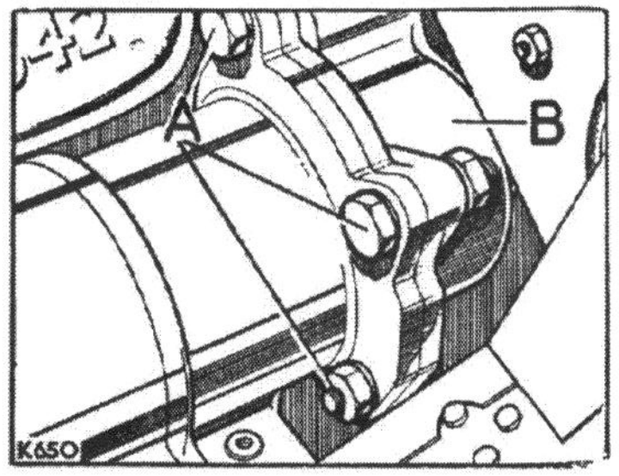

Fig. A2-38. Starter motor fixings

A—Fixings
B—Flywheel housing (LH side)

To refit

1. Reverse the removal procedure.

Operations marked with an asterisk (*) can be carried out with the engine installed in the vehicle

ENGINE—2¼ LITRE DIESEL

Section A2—Land-Rover

*Dynamo, remove and refit—Operation A2-10

(For overhaul instructions, Section N refers)

Workshop hand tools:
Spanner sizes: ½ in. AF open end, ½ in. AF socket, ⅜ in. AF ring Screwdriver (medium), Pliers

To remove

1. Remove bonnet panel. Operation A2-1.
2. Disconnect battery leads.
3. Remove dynamo leads and slacken the adjusting link fixings at front and rear.
4. Slacken the special stud fixings at the rear of the dynamo and the support bracket fixings at the front.
5. Move the dynamo toward the engine and remove the fan belt from the dynamo pulley.
6. Remove the slackened fixings and withdraw the dynamo.

Fig. A2-39. View of dynamo and fixings

A—Adjusting link fixing, front
B—Adjusting link fixing, rear
C—Dynamo leads
D—Fixings at front support
E—Fixings at special stud

To refit

1. With the special stud and packing washers in position, offer the dynamo to the engine. Adjust the packing thickness, if necessary, to allow the dynamo pulley to align with the crank and fan pulley when fitted.
2. Fit the remaining fixings. Do not fully tighten at this stage.
3. Fit the fan belt and adjust the tension to ⅞ in. to ⅞ in. (8 mm to 11 mm) measured by thumb pressure applied to the belt between the crankshaft pulley and the fan pulley. Fully tighten all fixings.
4. Refit the dynamo electrical leads.
5. Connect the battery lead.
6. Refit the bonnet panel. Operation A2-1.

*Water pump, remove and refit—Operation A2-11

(For overhaul information, Section K refers)

Workshop hand tools:
Spanner sizes: ⅞ in. AF open end, ⅜ in. AF ring Screwdriver (medium), Pliers

To remove

1. Remove bonnet panel. Operation A2-1.
2. Remove radiator filler cap and drain coolant.

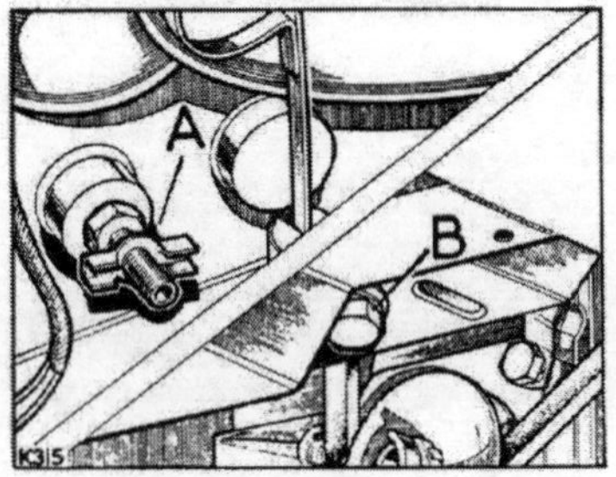

Fig. A2-40. Coolant drain points location

A—Cylinder block drain point
B—Radiator drain point

3. Remove the shroud from the radiator fan cowl.

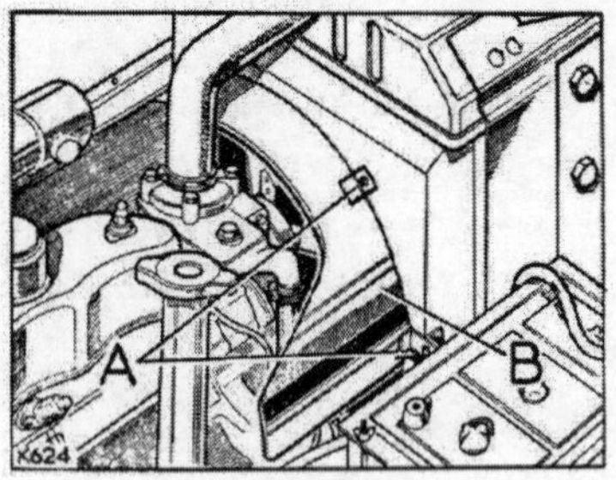

Fig. A2-41. Fan cowl shroud fixings

A—Fixings at fan cowl
B—Shroud

4. Slacken dynamo fixings and remove dynamo adjusting link to gain access to water pump fixings.

Fig. A2-42. Dynamo fixings

A—Adjusting link fixings, front
B—Adjusting link fixing, rear
C—Dynamo leads (reference only)
D—Fixings at front support
E—Fixings at special stud

5. Remove fan blades and fan pulley.

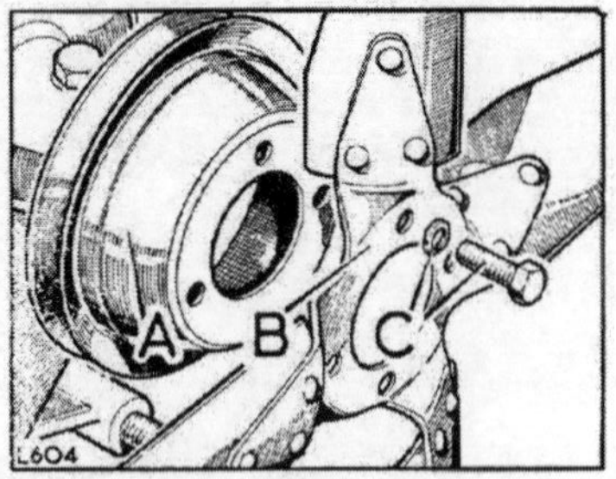

Fig. A2-43. Fixings for fan and pulley

A—Fan pulley, withdraw with fan blades
B—Fan blades, remove from vehicle or lower to rest on fan cowl
C—Fan blades fixings

Operations marked with an asterisk (*) can be carried out with the engine installed in the vehicle

ENGINE—2¼ LITRE DIESEL

Operation A2-11—continued

6. Detach the radiator bottom hose and the by-pass hose from the water pump.

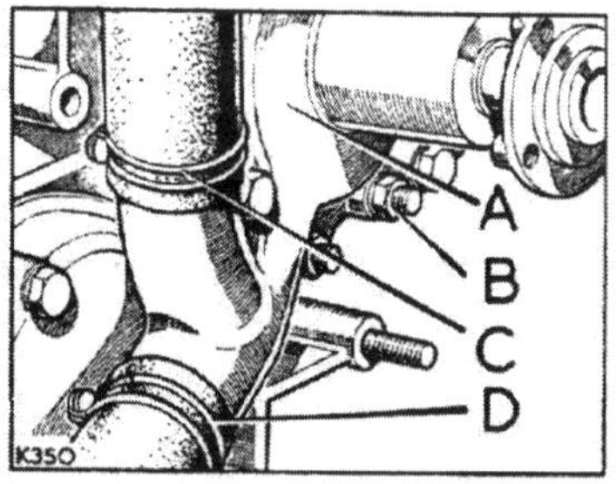

Fig. A2-44. Water pump and hose fixings
A—Water pump
B—Fixings
C—At by-pass hose
D—At radiator bottom hose

7. Remove fixings and withdraw water pump and gasket.

To refit

1. Smear general purpose grease on both sides of the joint washer and position on front cover joint face.
2. Complete the refitting by reversing the removal procedure.
3. Before finally tightening the dynamo fixings, set the fan belt tension. The tension is correct when the belt can be depressed ⁷⁄₁₆ in. to ⁷⁄₁₆ in. (8 mm to 11 mm) by thumb pressure applied between the fan pulley and crankshaft pulley.
4. Refill the engine coolant system.

COOLANT SYSTEM
Bonneted Control Model, 2¼ Litre Diesel

	Capacity	Imperial Unit	US Unit	Litres	Antifreeze	Frost Precaution
88	17½ pints	17½ pints	21 pints	10.0	33⅓%	−25°F −32°C
109	17½ pints	17½ pints	21 pints	10.0	33⅓%	−25°F −32°C

5. Refit the bonnet panel. Operation A2-1.

ENGINE—2¼ LITRE DIESEL

*Thermostat and housing, remove and refit—Operation A2-12

(For thermostat overhaul Information, Section K refers)

Workshop hand tools:
Spanner sizes: ⁷⁄₁₆ in. AF ring
Screwdriver (medium)

To remove

1. Lift and prop bonnet.
2. Remove radiator cap and partially drain coolant.

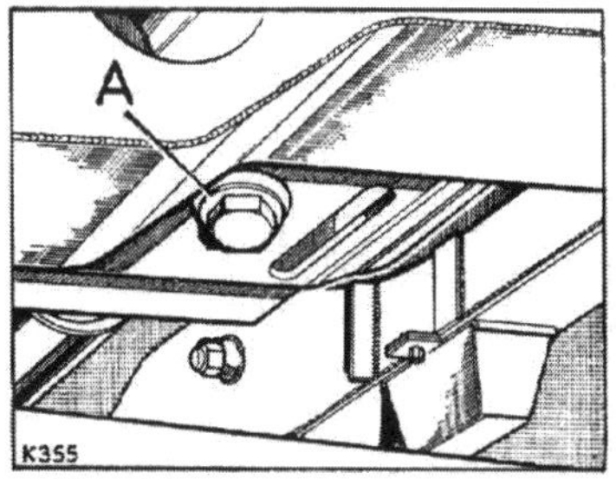

Fig. A2-45. Radiator drain location
A—Radiator drain plug

3. Disconnect top hose/s and remove by-pass pipe fixings.
4. Remove thermostat housing fixings and withdraw housing and outlet pipe complete. Remove joint washer.

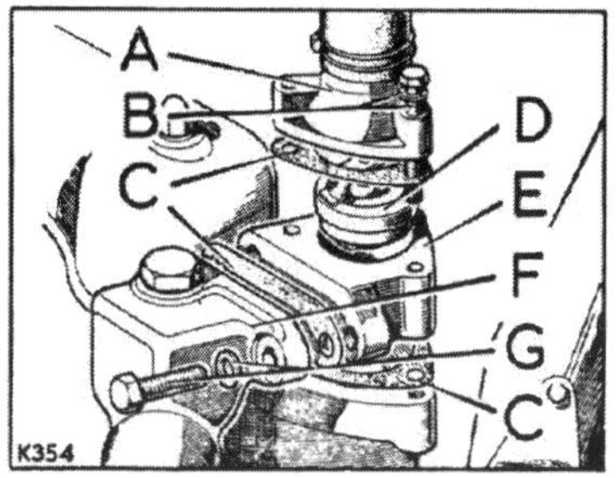

Fig. A2-46. Thermostat housing fixings
A—Outlet pipe
B—Fixings
C—Joint washers
D—Thermostat
E—Thermostat housing
F—By-pass pipe
G—Fixings

5. Separate housing from outlet pipe and withdraw thermostat and joint washer.

To refit

1. Smear general purpose grease on both sides of the joint washers.
2. Fit the thermostat into the housing and position on the engine.
3. Assemble the outlet pipe and joint washer to the thermostat housing and fit the fixings.
4. Complete refitting by reversing the removal procedure. Refill coolant system as necessary.

COOLANT SYSTEM
Bonneted Control Model, 2¼ Litre Diesel

	Capacity	Imperial Unit	US Unit	Litres	Antifreeze	Frost Precaution
88	17½ pints	17½ pints	21 pints	10.0	33⅓%	−25°F −32°C
109	17½ pints	17½ pints	21 pints	10.0	33⅓%	−25°F −32°C

Operations marked with an asterisk (*) can be carried out with the engine installed in the vehicle

ENGINE—2¼ LITRE DIESEL

*Fuel pump, remove and refit—Operation A2-13

(For overhaul information, Section L refers)

Workshop hand tools:
Spanner sizes: 1¼ in. AF open end, ½ in. AF open end, ⅜ in. AF socket
Screwdriver (medium), Pliers

To remove

1. Remove bonnet panel. Operation A2-1.
2. Remove air cleaner. Operation A2-2.
3. Disconnect fuel pipes at fuel pump.
4. Remove the fixings and withdraw the pump and side cover complete.
5. If required, remove the fuel pump from the side cover.

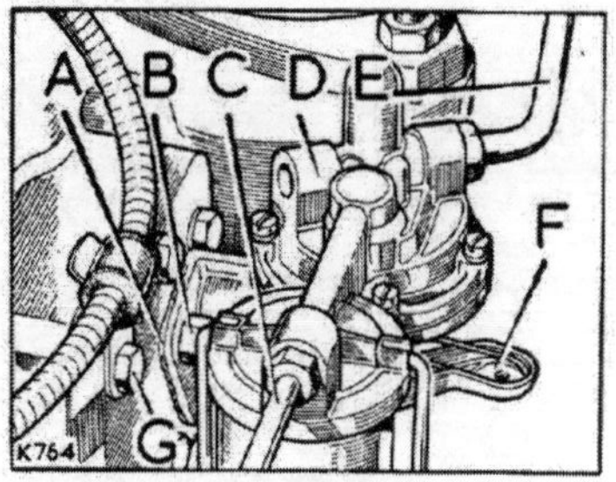

To refit

1. Refit pump to cover.
2. Smear general purpose grease on both sides of the joint washer.
3. Refit the fuel pump and joint washer and connect the fuel pipes.
4. Prime the fuel pump by operating the hand prime lever until no resistance is felt.
5. Release the air vent screws on the fuel distributor casing (Operation A2-17 refers) and operate the pump hand prime lever until the fuel flow from the vent screws is free of air. Close the vent screws.
6. Refit the air cleaner. Operation A2-2.
7. Refit the bonnet panel. Operation A2-1.

Fig. A2-47. Fuel pump location and fixings

A—Joint washer
B—Pump fixings
C—Fuel inlet pipe
D—Fuel pump
E—Fuel outlet pipe
F—Hand prime lever
G—Side cover fixings

*Engine side covers, remove and refit—Operation A2-14

Workshop hand tools:
Spanner sizes: 1¼ in. AF, ½ in. AF open ended, ⅜ in. AF socket
Screwdriver (medium), Pliers

To remove

1. Remove bonnet panel. Operation A2-1.
2. Remove air cleaner. Operation A2-2.
3. Remove the fixings at the front side cover and withdraw the side cover and oil filler pipe complete with baffle and joint washers.
4. Disconnect the fuel inlet and outlet pipes at the fuel pump, remove the fixings at the rear side cover and withdraw the cover and fuel pump complete.

To refit

1. Reverse the removal procedure. When fitting the front cover fixings, first engage the tapping nearest to the filler pipe, otherwise subsequent access for this fixing will be restricted. Also, align the timing pointer with the timing mark scribed on the fuel distributor pump flange (later engines).
2. Refit the air cleaner. Operation A2-2.
3. Refit the bonnet panel. Operation A2-1.

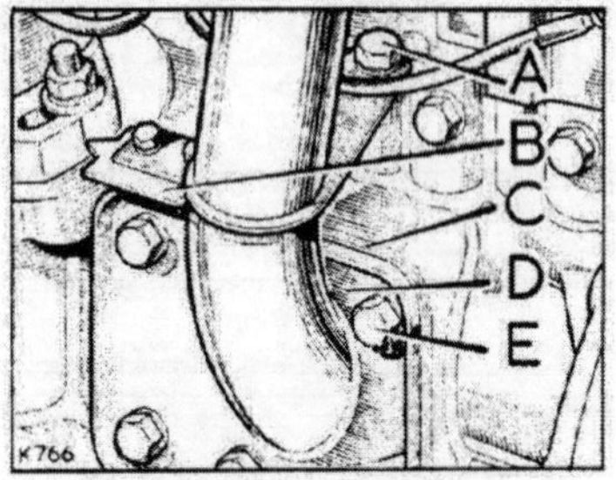

Fig. A2-48. View of front side cover

A—Fixings for filler pipe bracket
B—Distributor pump timing pointer; later engines
C—Joint washers and baffle plate
D—Filler pipe and side cover
E—Fixings for side cover

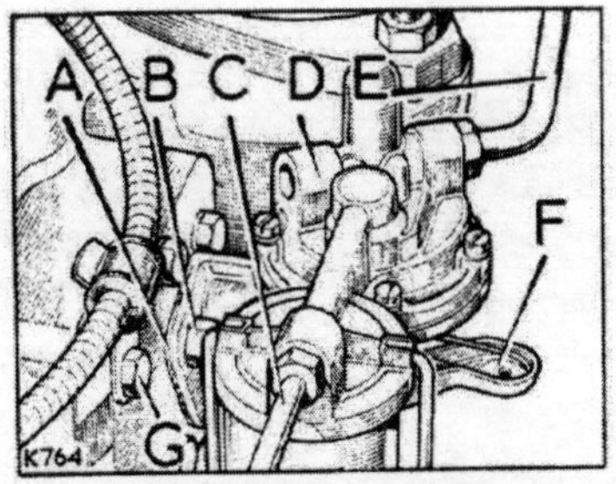

Fig. A2-49. View of rear side cover

A—Pump joint washer (reference only)
B—Pump fixings (reference only)
C—Fuel inlet pipe
D—Fuel pump
E—Fuel outlet pipe
F—Hand prime lever
G—Side cover fixings (6 off)

Operations marked with an asterisk (*) can be carried out with the engine installed in the vehicle

*Oil filter, external, replace element—Operation A2-15

Workshop hand tools:
Spanner sizes: ⅝ in. AF socket

Procedure

1. Position a suitable waste oil receptacle under the filter.
2. From under the vehicle, remove the centre fixing from the filter.
3. Remove filter and allow oil to drain.
4. Remove sealing ring from filter cap.
5. Replace filter element.
6. Fit the new element to the filter body and refit body to cap. Ensure filter body is fully home on to sealing ring in filter cap.
7. Replenish the engine lubricating oil.
8. Check the sump oil level after a short engine run and top-up as necessary.

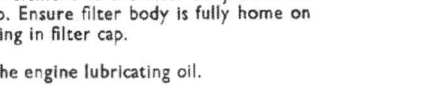

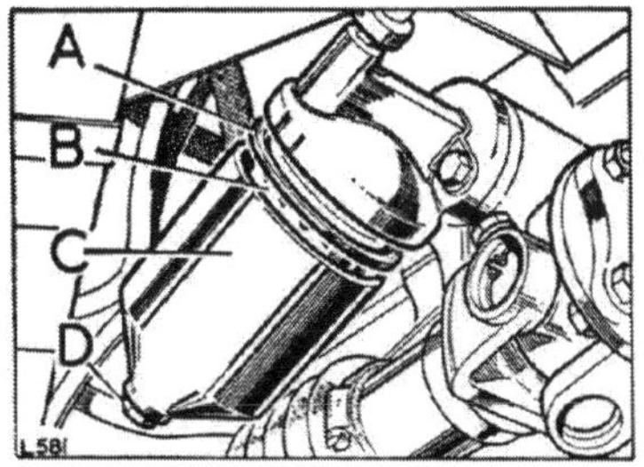

ENGINE LUBRICANT CAPACITY
Bonneted Control Model, 2¼ Litre Diesel

		Capacity	Imperial Unit	US Unit	Litres
88	Engine	11 pints	11 pints	13 pints	6.0
	Filter	1½ pints	1½ pints	1.8 pints	0.85
	Engine and Filter	12½ pints	12½ pints	14.8 pints	6.85
109	Engine	11 pints	11 pints	13 pints	6.0
	Filter	1½ pints	1½ pints	1.8 pints	0.85
	Engine and Filter	12½ pints	12½ pints	14.8 pints	6.85

Fig. A2-50. View of oil filter
A—Sealing ring
B—Element
C—Container
D—Fixing for container

---

*Oil filter, external, remove, overhaul and refit—Operation A2-16

Workshop hand tools:
Spanner sizes: ⅝ in. AF, 1⅛ in. AF socket, 7/16 in. BSF open end

To remove

1. Lift and prop bonnet.
2. Detach oil pressure switch lead.
3. Remove the fixings and withdraw the oil filter and joint washer.

Fig. A2-51. Oil filter fixings
A—Fixings, filter to engine, RH side
B—Oil pressure switch lead

To overhaul

1. Drain off oil.
2. Remove the centre fixing at the filter base and dismantle the filter assembly.
3. Wash the components in clean fuel and inspect for general condition.
4. Replace the sealing washer and filter element.
5. Reverse the dismantling procedure.

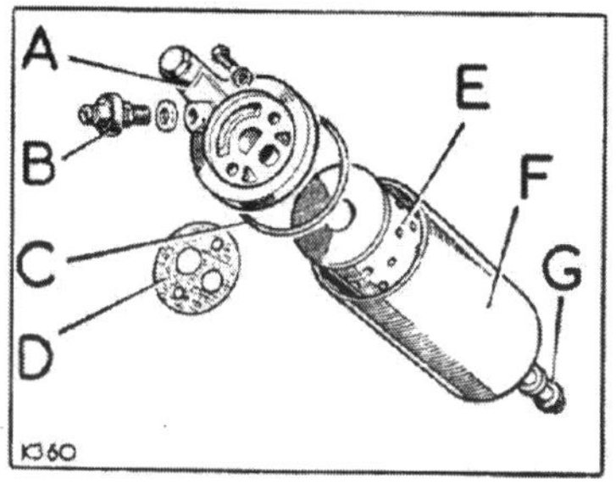

To refit

1. Smear general purpose grease on to both sides of the joint washer.
2. Refit filter body to top cover, ensuring that the body seats correctly on to the sealing ring.
3. Refit the assembled filter to the engine, Fig. A2-51 refers, and connect the oil pressure switch lead.
4. Replenish the engine lubricating oil and top-up as necessary after a short engine run.

ENGINE LUBRICANT CAPACITY
Bonneted Control Model, 2¼ Litre Diesel

		Capacity	Imperial Unit	US Unit	Litres
88	Engine	11 pints	11 pints	13 pints	6.0
	Filter	1½ pints	1½ pints	1.8 pints	0.85
	Engine and Filter	12½ pints	12½ pints	14.8 pints	6.85
109	Engine	11 pints	11 pints	13 pints	6.0
	Filter	1½ pints	1½ pints	1.8 pints	0.85
	Engine and Filter	12½ pints	12½ pints	14.8 pints	6.85

5. Close the bonnet panel.

Fig. A2-52. Exploded view of oil filters
A—Top cover
B—Oil pressure switch
C—Sealing washer
D—Joint washer
E—Element
F—Container
G—Centre fixing

Operations marked with an asterisk (*) can be carried out with the engine installed in the vehicle

ENGINE—2¼ LITRE DIESEL

*Distributor pump, remove and refit—Operation A2-17

This Operation includes distributor pump timing procedure

Workshop hand tools:
Spanner sizes: ⅝ in. AF, ⁹⁄₁₆ in. AF, ⁷⁄₁₆ in. AF, ⅝ in. AF, ½ in. AF, ⁷⁄₁₆ in. AF open end ½ in. AF socket

Special tools:
Part No. 605863—Timing gauge for use with later type distributor pump

To remove

1. Remove the bonnet panel. Operation A2-1.
2. Disconnect the battery earth lead.
3. Remove the air cleaner. Operation A2-2.
4. Disconnect the engine stop cable and stop spring.
5. Disconnect the accelerator linkage at the securing clip.
6. Slacken the fuel inlet pipes at the injectors and disconnect all the fuel pipes at the distributor pump.
7. Remove the fixings at the distributor pump base, lift pump from engine.

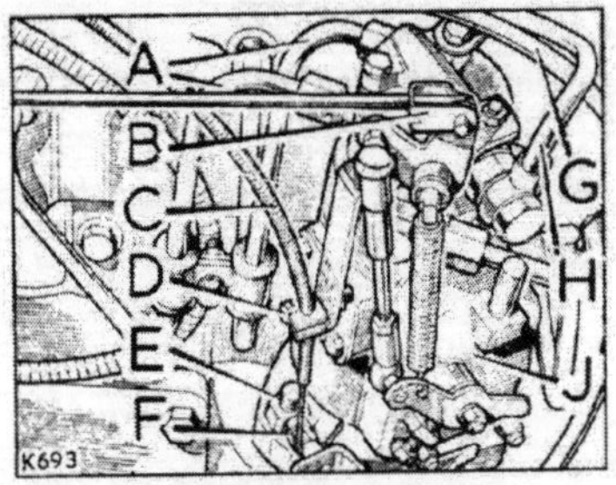

To refit and set pump timing

1. Remove the engine top cover.

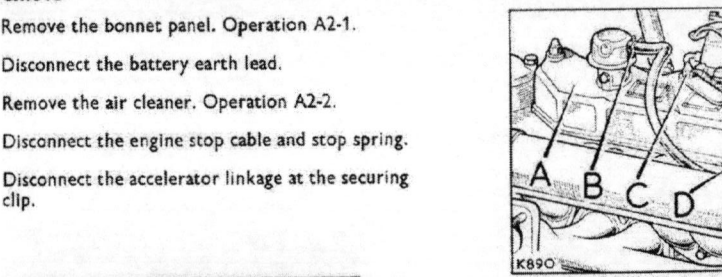

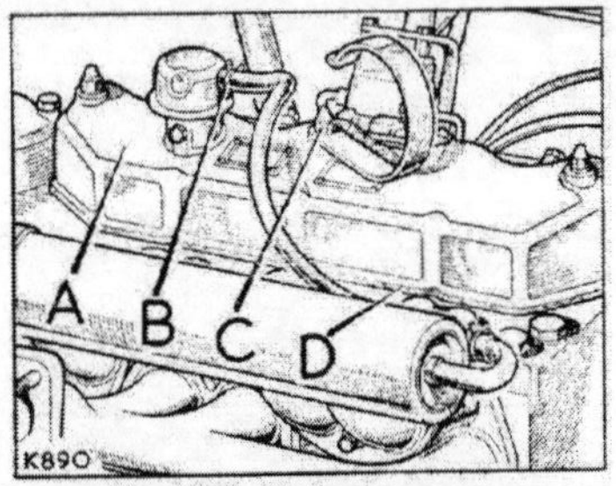

Operations marked with an asterisk (*) can be carried out with the engine installed in the vehicle

Fig. A2-53. View of distributor pump
A—Injector pipes
B—Accelerator linkage clip
C—Engine stop cable
D—Outer cable fixing
E—Pump fixings (3 off)
F—Inner cable fixing
G—Fuel outlet pipe
H—Fuel inlet pipe
J—Distributor pump

Fig. A2-54. Engine top cover
A—Top cover   B—Breather hose fixing
C—Fixings (3 off)   D—Joint washer

Distributor pump timing procedures

1. The following procedures for distributor pump timing concern early and late type pumps. Early type pumps have internal timing marks viewed through an inspection aperture, the timing mark on the pump rotor is to be aligned with the mark scribed on the round edged circlip or with the straight edge of the circlip, depending on the type fitted.

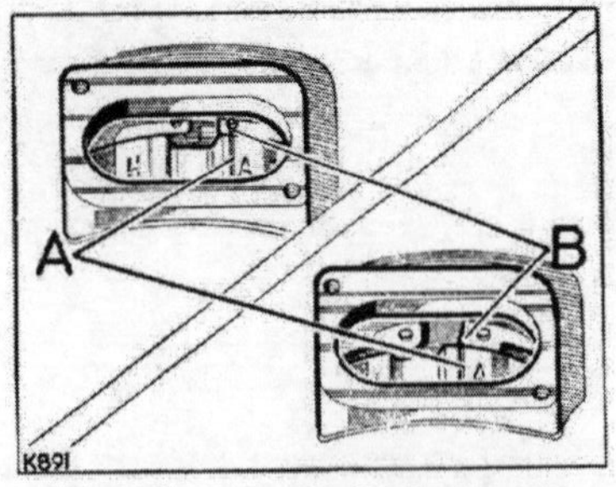

Fig. A2-55. Early type distributor pumps
A—Timing mark on pump rotor
B—Scribed mark or straight edge as applicable

2. Later type pumps, identified by the DPA No. 3248760 marked on the manufacturer's label, have an external timing mark on the pump mounting flange which, used in conjunction with an engine mounted timing pointer, allows the pump timing to be set without the need to remove the inspection cover from the pump.

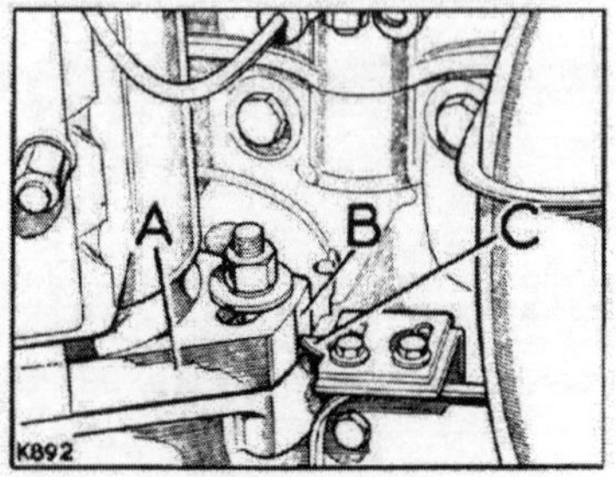

Fig. A2-56. Later type distributor pump
A—Pump mounting flange
B—Timing mark
C—Timing pointer

Setting flywheel position, early and late type pumps

1. Turn the crankshaft in direction of rotation until both valves on No. 1 cylinder are fully closed (indicated by clearance between the rocker pads and valve stems) and No. 1 piston on compression stroke.

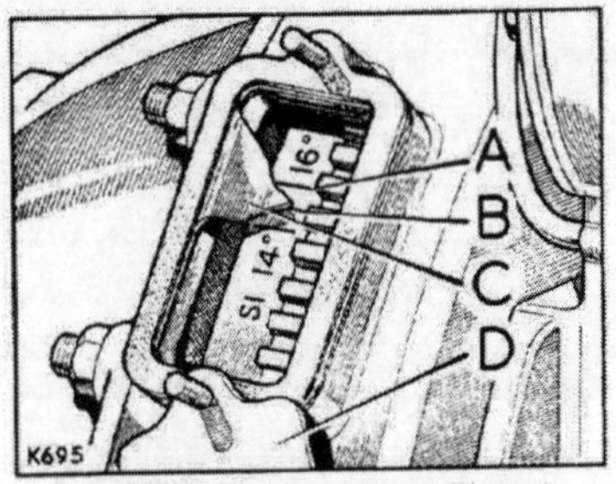

Fig. A2-57. Timing marks at flywheel
A—16° mark on flywheel, for use with early type pumps
B—15° mark on flywheel, for use with later type pumps
C—Timing pointer
D—Inspection cover on flywheel housing

2. Continue to turn the crankshaft slowly until the applicable timing mark (see Fig. A2-57) is aligned with the timing pointer on the flywheel housing. If a 15° mark (for later pumps) is not provided, make a suitable mark midway between the 14° and 16° marks.

If the engine is inadvertently turned too far and the timing mark passes the pointer, do not turn the flywheel back but instead repeat the foregoing procedure.

3. Ensure that the vertical drive gear master spline is correctly positioned.

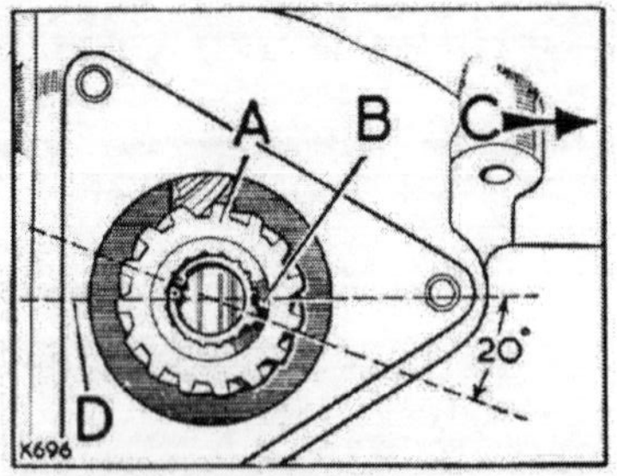

Fig. A2-58. Vertical drive gear correctly positioned
A—Vertical drive gear
B—Master spline to be at 20° angle to engine centre line
C—Front of engine
D—Line parallel with engine centre line

4. With the engine set as described, the distributor pump may now be fitted and correctly aligned with the applicable timing marks as follows:

Distributor pump timing, pumps with internal timing marks (early type pumps, 16° setting)

1. Fit the short drive shaft to the vertical drive shaft gear, narrow portion nearest to the camshaft. If a splined type drive shaft is being used, fit the chamfered end first and engage the master splines.

ENGINE—2¼ LITRE DIESEL

Operation A2-17—continued

2. Remove the inspection cover from the side of the fuel distributor pump. Rotate the spindle of the pump until the line marked 'A' on the driving plate aligns with the timing circlip mark. See the illustration for the early and late types of circlip.

3. Offer the distributor pump to the engine and engage the pump drive. Fit the pump fixings and tighten sufficient to prevent the pump from rocking sideways but allowing rotational movement. Observe the timing marks through the inspection window and make any necessary final adjustment to align the marks by turning the pump body in the required direction. When turning the pump body in the direction of the direction of rotation, hold the drive plate against the backlash, which exists between the vertical drive shaft gear and the camshaft gear, causing any error.

   Note: Any error of a given width on the pump marking will be 12 times that width if transferred to the flywheel.

4. When the marks are correctly aligned, fully tighten the three securing nuts. Recheck the timing by turning the crankshaft in the direction of rotation until both valves of No. 1 cylinder are closed and the piston is ascending the bore on the compression stroke. Ensure that the timing line adjacent to letter 'A' on the driving plate is in alignment with the circlip mark, according to type, and that the 16° mark on the flywheel is exactly in line with the timing pointer, as previously illustrated in Fig. A2-57.

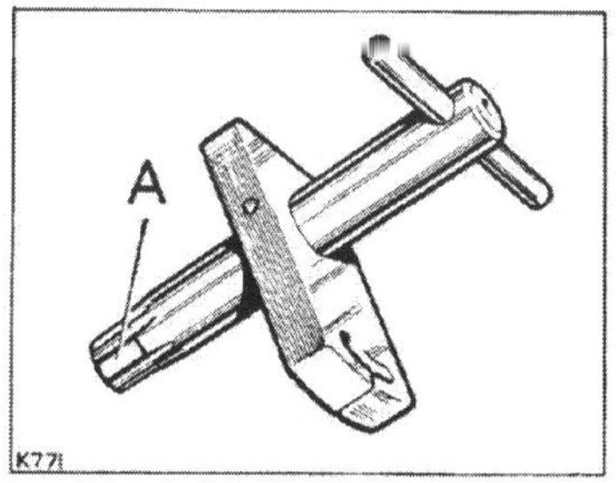

Fig. A2-59. Timing gauge, Part No. 605863

A—Master spline

Distributor pump timing, pumps with external timing mark (later type pumps, 15° setting)

1. Offer up the timing gauge, Part No. 605863, to the vertical drive gear, aligning the master splines.

2. Insert the timing gauge into the driving gear, then twist gauge in a clockwise direction to take up backlash and any wear in the gears. Hold in this position, then, if necessary, slacken off bolts retaining timing pointer on side of cylinder block. Adjust pointer so that it coincides with the line on timing gauge.

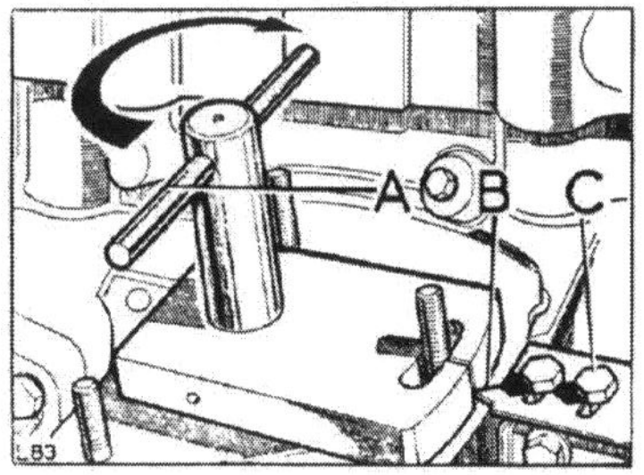

Fig. A2-60. Timing gauge located in driving gear

A—Timing gauge in position
B—Timing pointer adjusted so that point coincides with line on gauge
C—Bolts retaining timing pointer

3. Remove timing gauge and insert the short drive shaft, located by master spline.

4. Rotate driving gear on distributor pump so that master spline lines up with master spline on driving gear.

   Then offer pump to engine, ensuring that the timing mark on the pump flange coincides with the timing pointer.

5. When the distributor pump is timed as detailed above, that is, with the timing pointer on the engine altered to take up backlash and wear on the gears, the distributor pump timing is at the optimum position.

ENGINE—2¼ LITRE DIESEL

Operation A2-17—continued

3. When the fuel flow is free of air, close the air vent screws.

4. Refit the engine top cover, Fig. A2-54 refers.

5. Continue the procedure by setting the distributor pump control screws. Before starting the engine to set the screws, crank the engine, using the starter motor, and bleed the distributor pump to injectors fuel line by slackening off one injector feed pipe. Allow fuel to flow until air-free then retighten pipe.

Setting the distributor pump control screws

On distributor pumps with the maximum output control screw sealed, the control screw setting must not be altered. Adjustment is allowed to the slow-running control screw only.

However, when a new or reconditioned distributor pump is to be fitted, it will be found that the slow-running control screw is loosely attached to the distributor pump and that the maximum output control screw is not sealed.

It is necessary, therefore, after the distributor pump has been assembled to the engine, first to fit the slow-running control screw and then adjust both screws as detailed below.

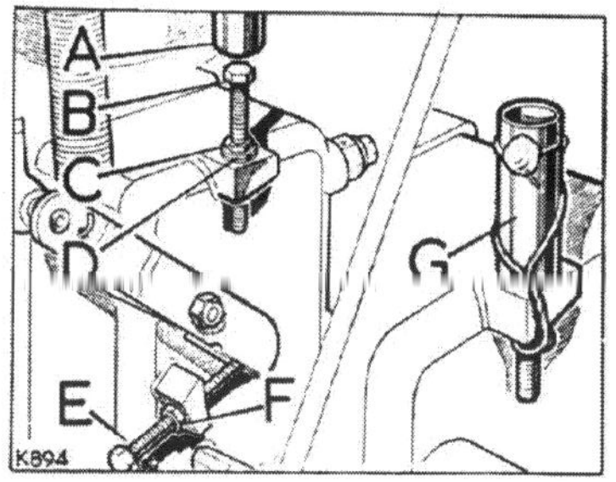

Fig. A2-63. Distributor pump control screws

A—Screw collar
B—Maximum output control screw
C—Locknut
D—Screw retainer for collar
E—Slow running control screw
F—Locknut
G—Screw collar shown lockwired after setting

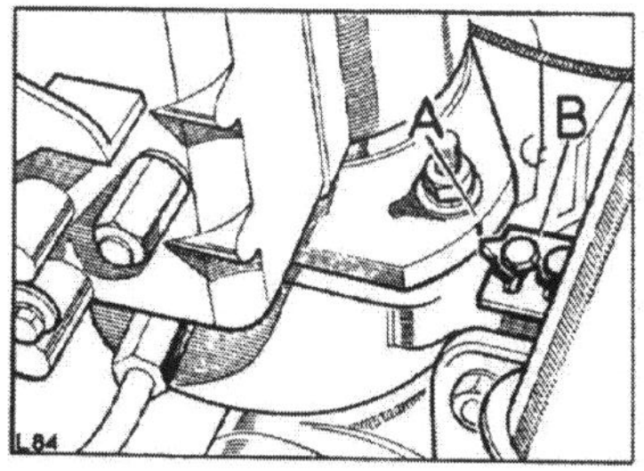

Fig. A2-61. Distributor pump correctly timed

A—Timing mark on distributor pump
B—Timing pointer

Distributor pump refitting continued, early and later type pumps

1. Connect the fuel pipes, accelerator linkage and stop cables, Fig. A2-53 refers, and check the controls for full movement.

2. Release the air vent screws on the distributor pump casing, (see Fig. A2-62) and operate the hand priming lever at the base of the fuel pump. This will cause fuel to flow through the air vents orifices.

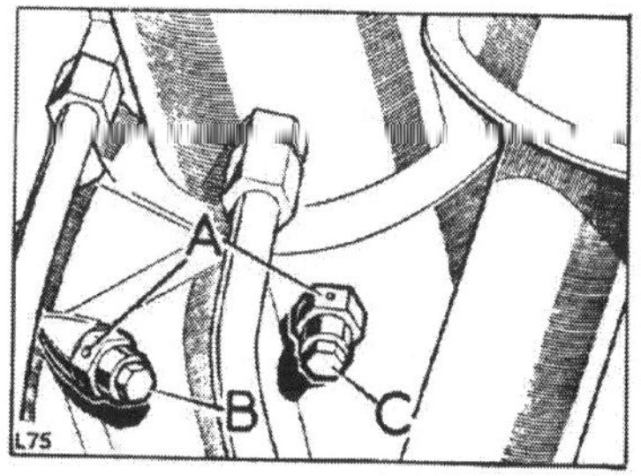

Fig. A2-62. Priming the fuel system

A—Fuel orifice
B—Air vent screw on distributor body
C—Air vent screw on distributor control cover

ENGINE—2¼ LITRE DIESEL

Operation A2-17—continued

1. Slow-running control screw

Adjust the control screw until the engine slow-running speed is 590 ± 20 rpm. This may be checked using a suitable revolution counter, or by adjusting the control screw until the lowest engine speed consistent with smooth, even running is achieved.

2. To adjust the slow-running control screw, proceed as follows:

(a) Check engine speed with revolution counter.

(b) Slacken adjusting screw locknut and screw inwards to increase speed and outwards to decrease.

(c) When a slow-running speed of 590 ± 20 rpm has been obtained, tighten locknut.

(d) Remove revolution counter.

3. Maximum output control screw

Adjust the control screw, where necessary, until the engine maximum speed is 4200 ± 20 rpm. This may be checked using a suitable revolution counter, or by road test; the road speed equivalent of 4200 rpm being 48 mph (77 kph) in third gear. When maximum engine speed of 4200 ± 20 rpm has been obtained, tighten locknut, replace adjusting screw collar, wire and seal screw collar as shown at Fig. A2-63.

When satisfactory, refit the engine air cleaner, Operation A2-2 and the bonnet panel, Operation A2-1.

---

*Distributor pump drive gears, remove and refit—Operation A2-18

Special tools:
Part No. 605863—Timing gauge for use with later type distributor pump

Workshop hand tools:
Spanner sizes: ⅜ in. AF, 7/16 in. AF, ½ in. AF, ⅝ in. AF, ¾ in. AF, 7/16 in. AF open end
⅜ in. AF socket, 7/16 in. BSF open end
Screwdriver (medium), Pliers (long nosed)

To remove

1. Remove bonnet panel. Operation A2-1.
2. Remove air cleaner. Operation A2-2.
3. Remove the external oil filter. Operation A2-16.
4. Remove the distributor pump and short drive shaft. Operation A2-17.
5. Remove the drive gear bush locating screw and withdraw the vertical drive gear, using long-nosed pliers.

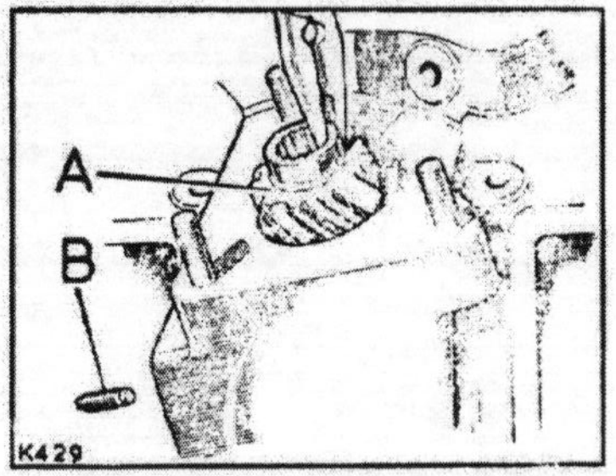

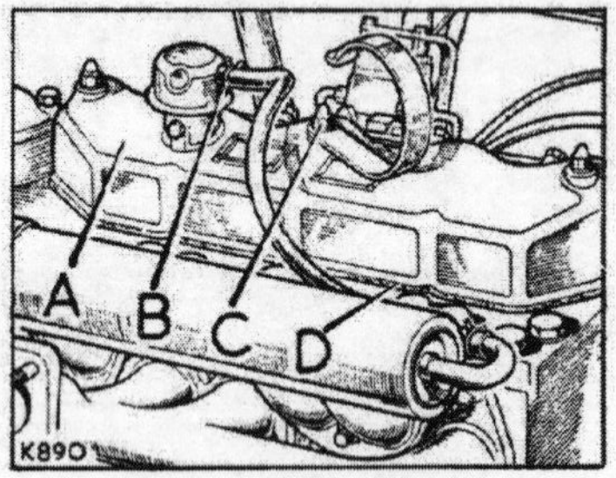

Fig. A2-65. Engine top cover
A—Top cover
B—Breather hose fixings
C—Fixings
D—Joint washer

Fig. A2-64. Vertical drive shaft gear
A—Vertical drive shaft gear
B—Locating screw housed in tapping at external oil filter locating face

To refit

Note: Distributor pump timing depends upon the vertical drive gear master spline being correctly positioned relative to the flywheel.

Therefore the following procedures to establish this position must be carried out methodically and accurately.

1. Remove the engine top cover.
2. Turn the crankshaft in the direction of rotation until both valves on No. 1 cylinder are fully closed (indicated by clearance between the rocker pads and the valve stems).
3. Continue to turn the crankshaft slowly until the appropriate timing mark on the flywheel is aligned with the timing pointer on the flywheel housing. This must be done carefully. If the flywheel is inadvertently turned too far and the timing mark goes past the pointer, do not turn the flywheel back, but repeat the above operation.

Ensure that a correct line of vision is taken when lining up the timing marks. An incorrect line of vision can result in the timing being 1° to 2° out.

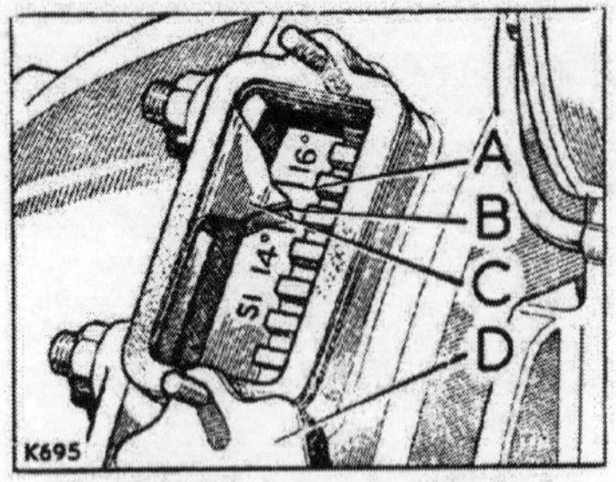

Fig. A2-66. Timing marks at flywheel
A—16° mark on flywheel, for early type pumps
B—15° mark on flywheel, for late type pumps
C—Timing pointer
D—Inspection cover on flywheel housing

Operations marked with an asterisk (*) can be carried out with the engine installed in the vehicle

ENGINE—2¼ LITRE DIESEL

Operation A2-18—continued

4. Insert the vertical drive gear assembly into the distributor drive housing and engage the gear on the camshaft. When fitted, the vertical drive gear master spline must be positioned as shown in Fig. A2-67 and the locating screw hole in the drive gear bush must be aligned with the locating screw tapping in the oil filter mounting face.

   As the bush cannot be easily turned when fitted, to align the master spline and bush correctly may require some trial and error fitting.

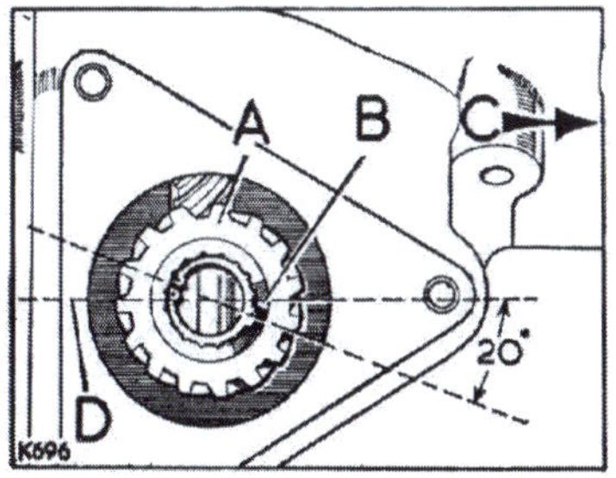

Fig. A2-67. Vertical drive gear correctly positioned

A—Vertical drive gear
B—Master spline to be at 20° angle to engine centre line
C—Front of engine
D—Line parallel with engine centre line

5. When the correct position is attained, secure the vertical drive shaft assembly by fitting a new special locating screw in the threaded hole of the block, so that the end of the screw locates the drive gear bush.

   The special screw has a nylon peg fitted, which, when the screw is in position, acts as a locking device. Do not use the original screw under any circumstances.

6. Refit the distributor pump and short drive shaft and carry out the distributor pump timing procedure. Operation A2-17.
7. Refit the external oil filter. Operation A2-16.
8. Refit the air cleaner. Operation A2-2.
9. Refit the bonnet panel. Operation A2-1.

*Tappet adjustment—Operation A2-19

Workshop hand tools:
Spanner sizes: ½ in. AF ring
Screwdriver (medium), Feeler gauges, Pliers

Tappets, to adjust

1. Remove the bonnet panel. Operation A2-1.
2. Remove the air cleaner. Operation A2-2.
3. Remove the engine top cover.

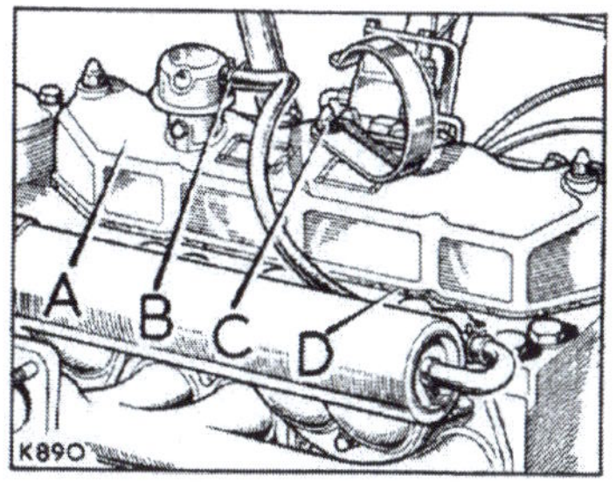

Fig. A2-68. Engine top cover

A—Top cover
B—Breather hose fixings
C—Fixings for top cover
D—Joint washer

4. Set the tappet clearances to .010 in. (0,25 mm) for all valves.

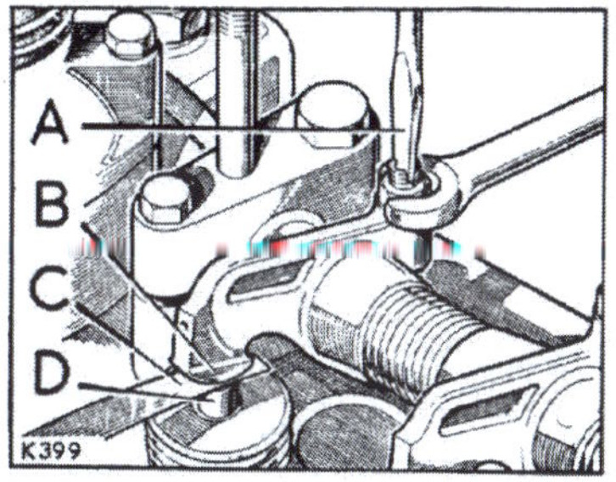

Fig. A2-69. Setting tappet clearances

A—Screwdriver
B—Rocker pad
C—Feeler gauge
D—Valve stem

The tappet setting is most easily carried out in the following sequence, No. 1 tappet being at the front of the engine:

Set No. 1 tappet clearance with No. 8 valve fully open.
Set No. 3 tappet clearance with No. 6 valve fully open.
Set No. 5 tappet clearance with No. 4 valve fully open.
Set No. 2 tappet clearance with No. 7 valve fully open.
Set No. 8 tappet clearance with No. 1 valve fully open.
Set No. 6 tappet clearance with No. 3 valve fully open.
Set No. 4 tappet clearance with No. 5 valve fully open.
Set No. 7 tappet clearance with No. 2 valve fully open.

5. Recheck the clearances with the tappet locknuts fully tightened.
6. Refit the engine top cover, Fig. A2-68 refers.
7. Refit the air cleaner. Operation A2-2.
8. Refit the bonnet panel. Operation A2-1.

*Operations marked with an asterisk (*) can be carried out with the engine installed in the vehicle

ENGINE—2¼ LITRE DIESEL

*Valve gear, rocker shaft and push rods, remove and refit—Operation A2-20

(For overhaul instructions, Operation A2-21 refers)

Workshop hand tools:
Spanner sizes: ½ in. AF ring, ¾ in. AF socket
Screwdriver (medium), Pliers

Special tools:
Torque wrench

To remove

1. Remove bonnet panel. Operation A2-1.
2. Remove air cleaner. Operation A2-2.
3. Remove engine top cover.

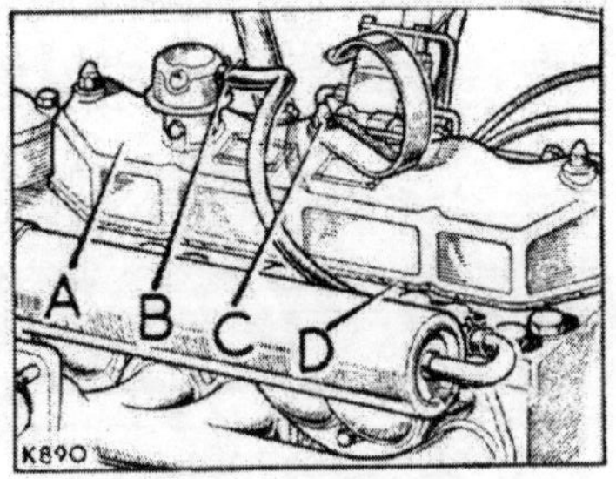

4. Slacken locknuts and turn tappet adjusting screws to disengage from push rods.

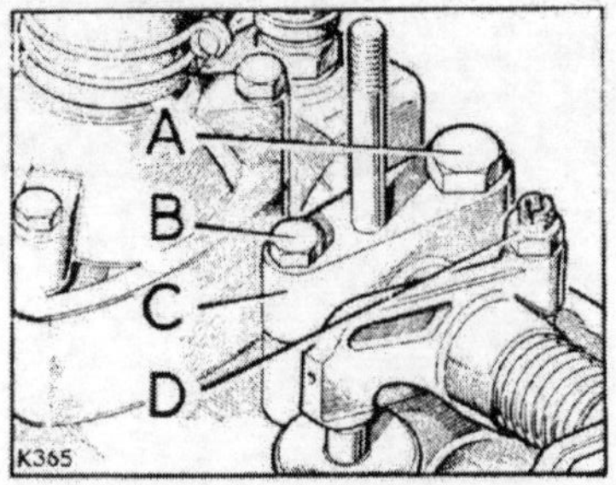

5. Remove fixings from rocker shaft support brackets. Do not remove shaft assembly at this stage.

6. Invert the engine top cover and secure it to the studs on the rocker brackets. Withdraw the rocker shaft assembly complete, using the engine top cover to retain the assembly.

7. Withdraw the tappet pushrods and retain them in numbered sequence related to the tappet served.

To refit

1. Fit the tappet push rods to their original bores.

2. Clean the rocker shaft fixing bolt threads of deposits which could become trapped between the cylinder head and gasket.

3. Fit the rocker shaft assembly, located by spigots on the rocker brackets. First engage the smaller fixings, then the larger fixings. Tighten the fixings as follows:
   ½ in. UNF bolts to 90 lb ft (12.5 mkg) torque load.
   ⅜ in. UNF bolts to 18 lb ft (2.4 mkg) torque load.

4. Check tighten all cylinder head ½ in. UNF fixings, in the order shown, to a torque load of 90 lb ft (12.5 mkg).

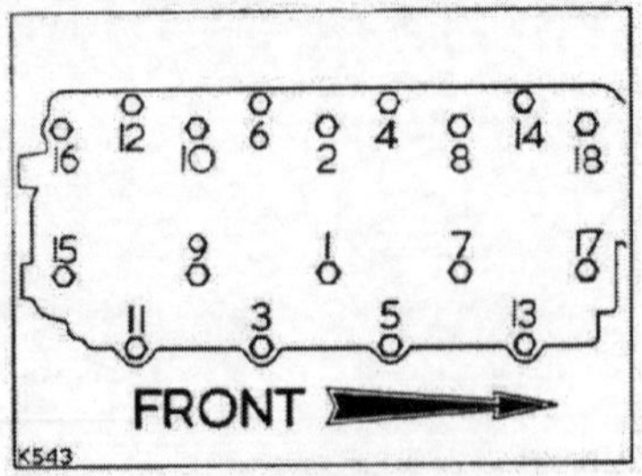

Fig. A2-70. Engine top cover
A—Top cover
B—Breather hose fixings
C—Fixings
D—Joint washer

Fig. A2-71. Rocker shaft fixings
A—Larger fixings, brackets to engine (5 off)
B—Smaller fixings, shaft to brackets (5 off)
C—Rocker brackets
D—Tappet locknuts and adjusting screws

Fig. A2-72. Order of tightening cylinder head fixings

Operation A2-20—continued

5. Fit the tappet screw locknuts and set the tappet clearances to .010 in. (0.25 mm) for all valves.

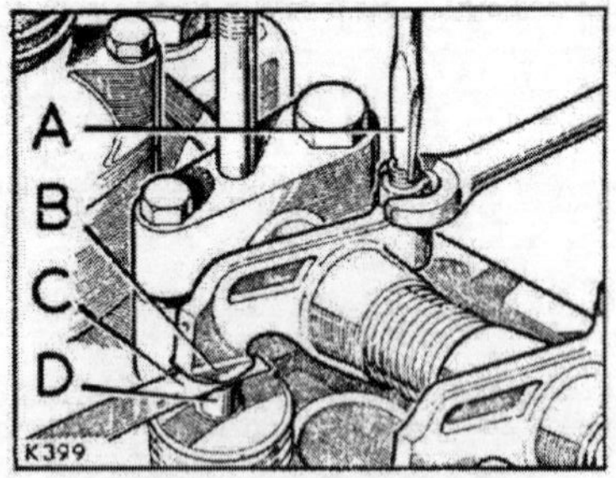

Fig. A2-73. Setting tappet clearances
A—Screwdriver   C—Feeler gauge
B—Rocker pad   D—Valve stem

The tappet setting is most easily carried out in the following sequence, No. 1 tappet being at the front of the engine:

Set No. 1 tappet with No. 8 valve fully open.
Set No. 3 tappet with No. 6 valve fully open.
Set No. 5 tappet with No. 4 valve fully open.
Set No. 2 tappet with No. 7 valve fully open.
Set No. 8 tappet with No. 1 valve fully open.
Set No. 6 tappet with No. 3 valve fully open.
Set No. 4 tappet with No. 5 valve fully open.
Set No. 7 tappet with No. 2 valve fully open.

6. Refit the air cleaner. Operation A2-2.

7. Run the engine until hot then check tighten all of the cylinder head ½ in. UNF fixings to the correct torque loading of 90 lb ft (12.5 mkg). This will necessitate removal of the fuel injectors in order to gain access to all the fixings unless a special cranked adaptor is used. Fuel injector removal and refitting is described in Operation A2-6.

8. Refit the engine top cover, Fig. A2-70 refers.

9. Refit the bonnet panel. Operation A2-1.

Operations marked with an asterisk (*) can be carried out with the engine installed in the vehicle

ENGINE—2¼ LITRE DIESEL

*Valve gear and rocker shaft, overhaul—Operation A2-21

(For removal and refitting instructions, Operation A2-20 refers)

Workshop hand tools:
Spanner sizes: ½ in. AF, ⅞ in. ⁷⁄₁₆ in. AF ring
Screwdriver (medium)

To dismantle

1. Remove the tappet adjusting screws from the valve rockers.
2. Withdraw the valve gear from the rocker shaft.

Inspection

1. Rocker brackets. Ensure the oil feed holes are clear. Inspect the locating dowel spigots; the spigots must be undamaged to ensure a correct fit on the locating dowels in the cylinder head.
2. Valve rockers. Visually inspect the rocker bushes for wear. If necessary, press replacement bushes into the rockers and ream to 0.530 in. + 0.001 in. (13,5 mm + 0,02 mm).

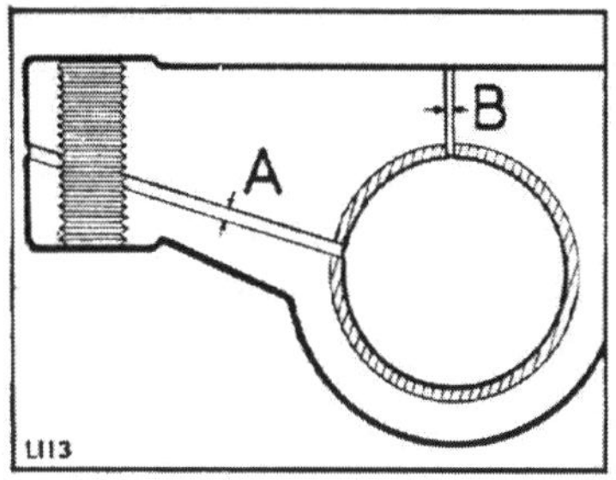

   Note: The oil holes in the rocker bushes are pre-drilled and must be aligned with the oil holes in the valve rocker during fitting.

   Check that all oil passage drillings are clear.

3. Tappet adjusting screws and locknuts. Examine threads for damage. Check that the oil relief drilling is clear.
4. Inspect the rocker shaft for wear and scores; check that the oil feed holes are clear.
5. Examine the rocker shaft springs, spacing washers and the locating screw for soundness and general condition.

To assemble

1. Fit an intermediate rocker bracket to the rocker shaft and engage the locating screw through the bracket and into the larger hole in the shaft.
2. Continue assembly by fitting the illustration and the valve gear and rockers. Refer to the illustration and note the assembled position for the spacing washers and the handed valve rockers.
3. Refit the tappet adjusting screws and locknuts.
4. To refit the valve gear and rocker shaft assembly, refer to Operation A2-20.

Fig. A2-74. Sectioned view of valve rocker

A—Oil feed drilling for tappet adjusting screw
B—Oil outlet drilling for splash lubrication

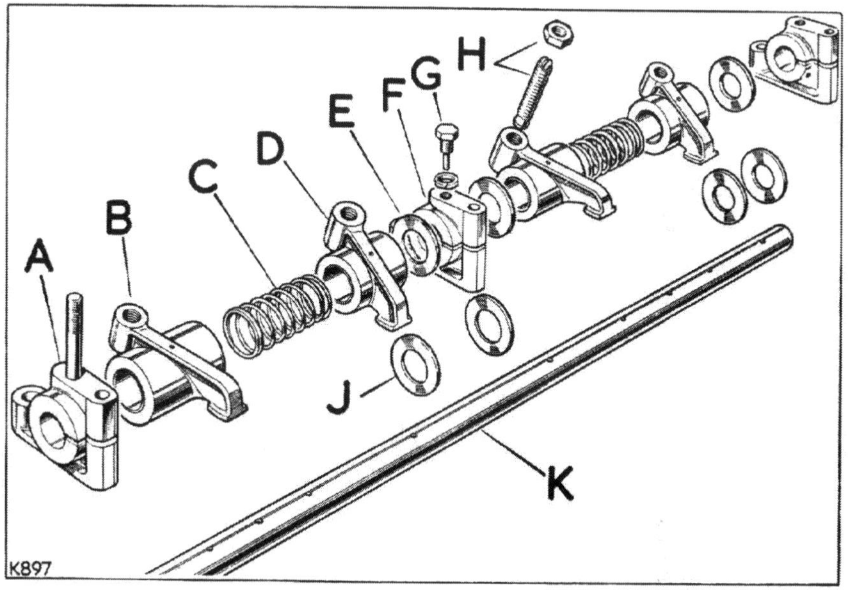

Fig. A2-75. Valve gear and rocker shaft arrangement

A—Rocker brackets. Front, centre and rear brackets carry studs for top cover fixings
B—Exhaust valve rockers (4 off)
C—Rocker shaft springs
D—Inlet valve rockers (4 off)
E—Spacing washers (6 off thick, petrol models only)
F—Intermediate rocker bracket (2 off)
G—Locating screw for rocker shaft (2 off on early models)
H—Tappet screws adjacent to larger fixing holes in brackets
J—Spacing washers (8 off, thin)
K—Valve rocker shaft (2 off on early models)

Operations marked with an asterisk (*) can be carried out with the engine installed in the vehicle

ENGINE—2¼ LITRE DIESEL

*Cylinder head, remove and refit—Operation A2-22

(For overhaul information, Operation A2-23 refers)

Workshop hand tools:
Spanner sizes: ⁷⁄₁₆ in. AF, ½ in. AF, ⅜ in. AF, ⁹⁄₁₆ in. AF, ⁷⁄₁₆ in. AF open end, ⅝ in. AF, ½ in. AF, ⁷⁄₁₆ in. AF, ⅝ in. AF, ¾ in. AF sockets
2 BA open end

Screwdriver (medium), Pliers

Special tools:
Torque wrench

To remove

1. Remove the bonnet panel. Operation A2-1.
2. Remove air cleaner. Operation A2-2.
3. Disconnect the battery earth lead.
4. Remove the engine top cover.

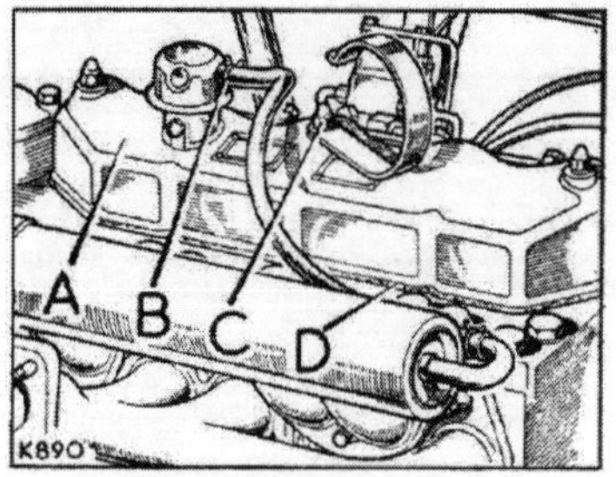

Fig. A2-76. Engine top cover
A—Top cover
B—Breather hose fixings
C—Top cover fixings
D—Joint washer

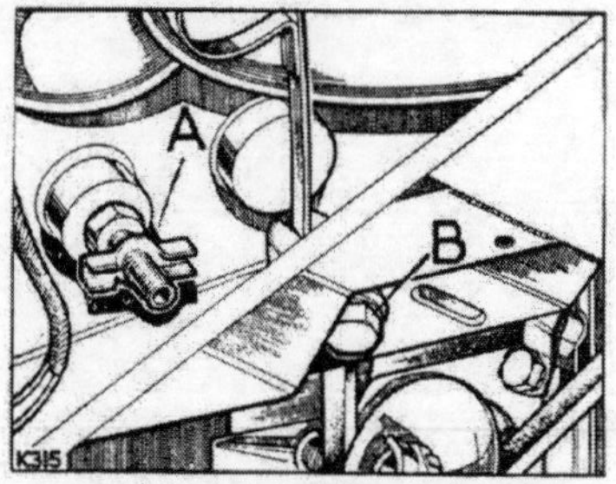

Fig. A2-77. Coolant system drain points
A—At engine block
B—At radiator block

5. Remove radiator filler cap and drain the engine coolant.
6. Continue the procedure with the following components, referring to Fig. A2-78 for location details:
   (a) Disconnect fuel return pipe at injector spill pipe.
   (b) Disconnect oil gallery pipe at upper fixing.
   (c) Disconnect heater plugs electrical feed lead.

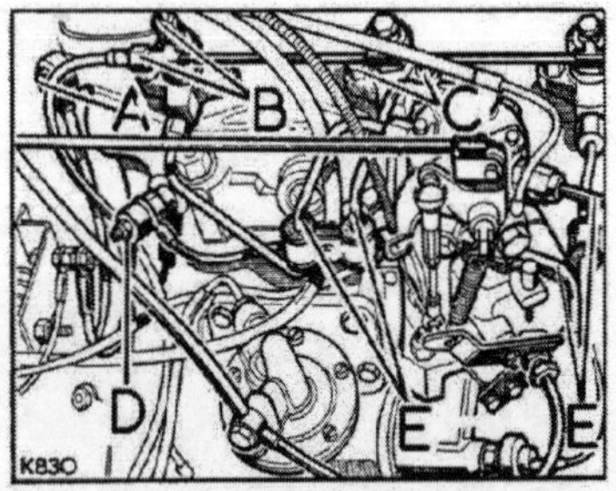

Fig. A2-78. View of engine, RH side, rear
A—Oil gallery pipe upper fixing
B—Fuel spill pipe connections
C—Fuel injector fixing
D—Electrical feed for heater plugs
E—Fuel injector feed pipes

7. Carry out the following procedure at the LH side of the engine.
   (a) Disconnect front exhaust pipe from manifold.
   (b) Disconnect heater hoses, if fitted.

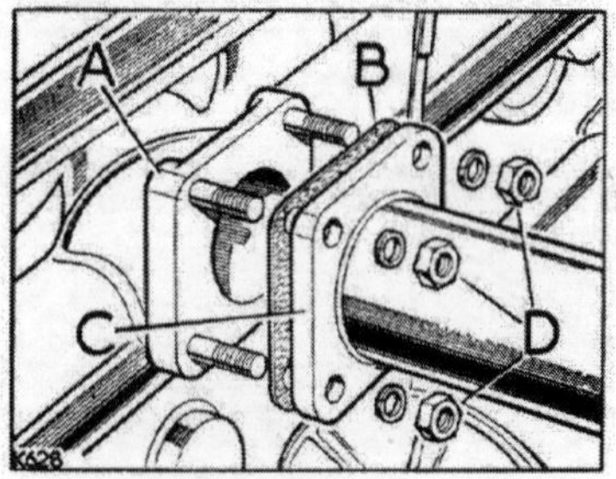

Fig. A2-79. Front exhaust pipe
A—Exhaust manifold
B—Joint washer
C—Front exhaust pipe
D—Front exhaust pipe fixings

8. At RH side of engine carry out the following procedure, referring to Fig. A2-80 for location details:
   (a) Disconnect radiator top coolant hose.

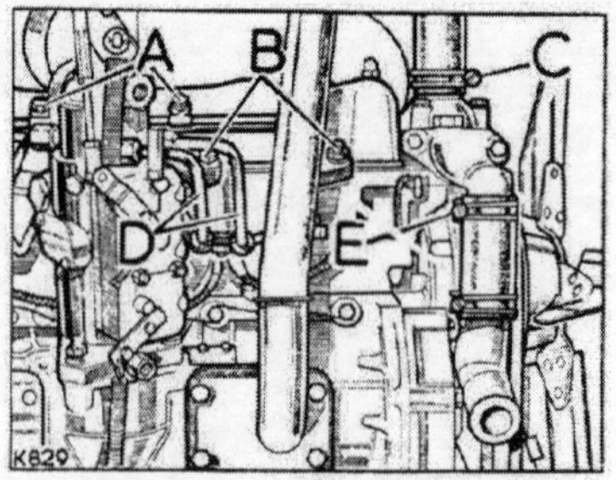

Fig. A2-80. View of engine, RH side, front
A—Fuel spill pipe fixings
B—Fuel injector fixings, later type shown. Early types are secured with clamp bars
C—Radiator top hose fixings
D—Fuel injector feed pipes
E—By-pass hose fixings

   (b) Disconnect coolant by-pass pipe.
   (c) Slacken fuel injector feed pipes at distributor pump and disconnect at fuel injectors.
   (d) Slacken fuel spill pipe fixings at fuel injectors.
   (e) Remove the fixings and withdraw the fuel injectors (attached together by the fuel spill pipe) and sealing washers (8 off) from the engine.
   Take care to avoid damage to the needle valves protruding from the injectors. Immerse the injectors in clean fuel pending refitting.

9. Fit inverted top cover to rocker bracket studs, remove assembly complete using top cover as a retainer.
10. Remove the tappet push rods and retain in numbered sequence related to valve served.

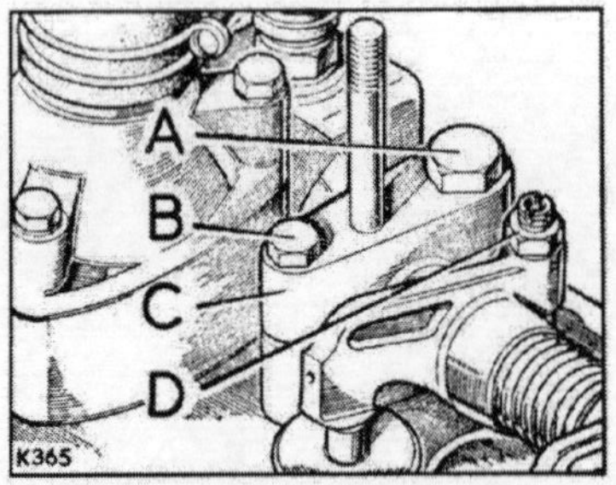

Fig. A2-81. Rocker shaft assembly
A—Larger fixings, brackets and cylinder head to engine
B—Smaller fixings, brackets to cylinder head
C—Rocker brackets
D—Slacken locknuts and adjusting screws

11. Slacken evenly and remove the remaining fixings and withdraw the cylinder head and joint gasket.

Operations marked with an asterisk (*) can be carried out with the engine installed in the vehicle

Operation A2-22—continued

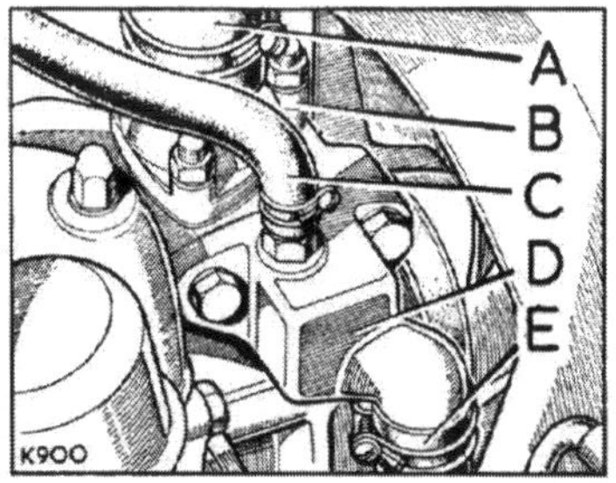

To refit

1. Thinly coat the cylinder head gasket with suitable jointing compound such as Hylomar SQ32M. Position the gasket, lettering 'DIESEL' uppermost, on the cylinder block.
2. Position the cylinder head on the gasket and engage the fixings. Do not fully tighten at this stage.
3. Insert the push rods into their parent tappet seats.
4. Refit the valve rocker shaft assembly, located by dowels. Do not fully tighten the fixings at this stage.
5. Tighten the cylinder head ½ in. UNF fixings to a torque load of 90 lb ft (12,5 mkg) in the order shown.

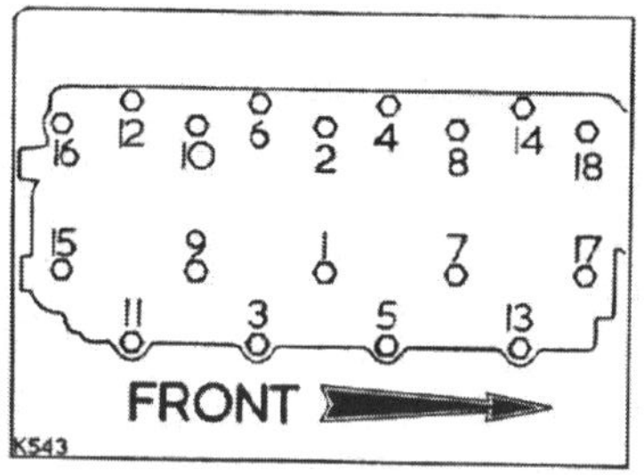

Fig. A2-82. Order of tightening cylinder head fixings

6. Tighten the 5/16 in. UNF fixings securing the valve rocker shaft assembly to a torque loading of 18 lb ft (2,4 mkg), turning down the fixings evenly before final tightening.
7. Refit the fuel injectors, ensuring that the injector sealing washers are correctly fitted as illustrated. Tighten the injector fixings at the clamp bar (early types) or injector mounting flange (later types) to 6 lb ft to 8 lb ft (0,8 mkg to 1,0 mkg). Tighten evenly to avoid distortion and **do not overtighten**.

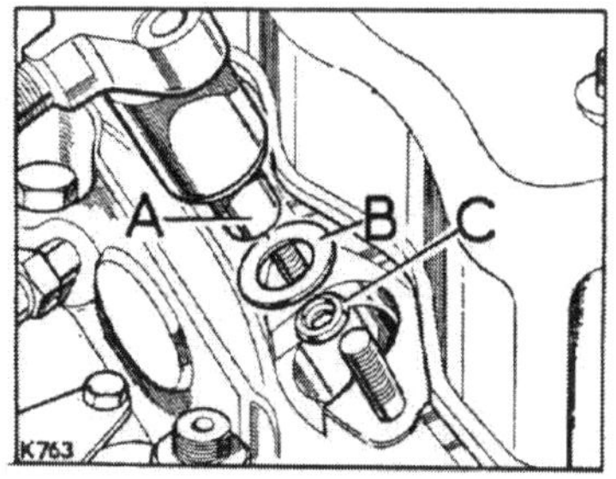

Fig. A2-83. Fitting fuel injectors

A—Injector
B—Copper sealing washer
C—Steel washer, fitted with raised portion uppermost

8. Tighten the injector spill pipe at the banjo fixings, connect the injector feed pipes and the pipe from the fuel filter.

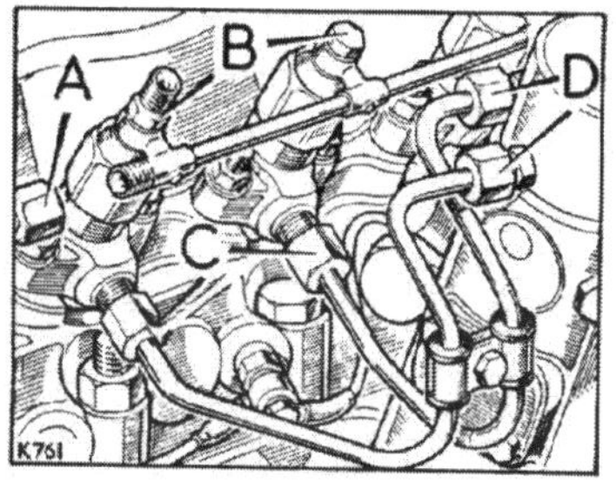

Fig. A2-84. Fuel pipes at injectors

A—From fuel filter
B—Spill pipe banjo fixings
C—To injectors (4 off)
D—From fuel distributor pump

9. Refit the heater hoses, if fitted.
10. Connect coolant hoses at radiator and by-pass pipe.

Fig. A2-85. Coolant hoses

A—Radiator top hose
B—Thermostat housing
C—Heater hose, if fitted
D—By-pass pipe
E—By-pass hose

11. Replenish the engine coolant system. Allow a full flow of coolant through the drain taps before closing them. See Fig. A2-77.
12. Set the tappet clearances. Operation A2-19.
13. Refit the front exhaust pipe, Fig. A2-79 refers.

COOLANT SYSTEM
Bonneted Control Model, 2¼ Litre Diesel

	Capacity	Imperial Unit	US Unit	Litres	Antifreeze	Frost Precaution
88	17½ pints	17½ pints	21 pints	10,0	33⅓%	−25°F −32°C
109	17½ pints	17½ pints	21 pints	10,0	33⅓%	−25°F −32°C

14. Refit the engine top cover, Fig. A2-76 refers.
15. Connect the battery earth lead.
16. Refit the air cleaner. Operation A2-2.
17. Refit the bonnet panel. Operation A2-1.

Note: It is most important that the cylinder head fixings torque loading be checked and if necessary reset after the next engine run and with the engine thoroughly warm.

This will entail removal of fuel injectors unless a special cranked adaptor spanner is used on the fixings adjacent to the injectors. Failure to do so may cause stresses to the cylinder head leading to cylinder head cracking.

ENGINE—2¼ LITRE DIESEL   Section A2—Land-Rover

*Cylinder head, overhaul and decarbonize—Operation A2-23

(For removal and refitting instructions, Operation A2-22 refers)

Workshop hand tools:
Spanner sizes: ½ in. AF, ⅞ in. AF open end
½ in. AF socket
2 BA open end
⅝ in. Whit open end
⅞ in. AF ring
Screwdriver (medium), Pliers, 1 lb hammer

Special tools:
Valve spring compresser tool, Part No. 276102
Inlet valve guide removal tool, Part No. 274400
Exhaust valve guide removal tool, Part No. 274401
Exhaust valve guide replacement tool, Part No. 600959
Inlet valve guide replacement tool, Part No. 601508
Exhaust seat insert replacement tool, Part No. 530625
Push rod tube replacement tool, Part No. 274399

1. Remove the inlet and exhaust manifolds. Operation A2-8.

2. Remove the thermostat housing. Operation A2-12.

Valves, springs and guides

1. Using a valve spring compressing tool, Part No. 276102, remove the valve assemblies and retain in related sets.

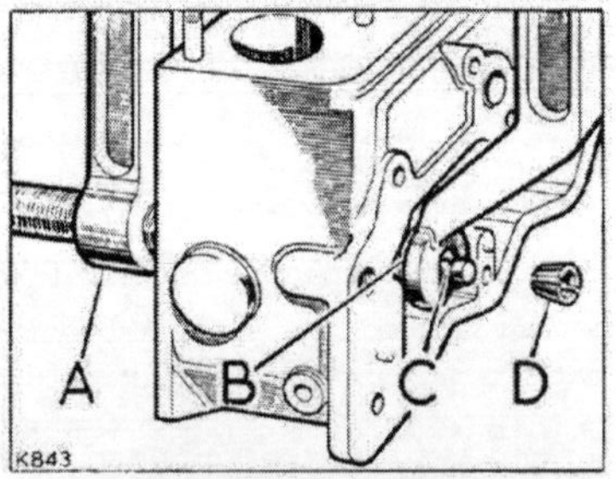

Fig. A2-86. Valve assemblies removal
A—Special tool, Part No. 276102, cam operated
B—Valve spring compressed to release split cones
C—Valve stem
D—Split cones, remove before releasing special tool

2. Remove the oil seals from the valve guides.

3. Remove carbon deposits from the valve seats, combustion chambers, valves and also from the piston crowns, using suitable scrapers, abrasive cloth and a wire brush. Take care to prevent dislodged deposits from entering oilways and coolant passages.

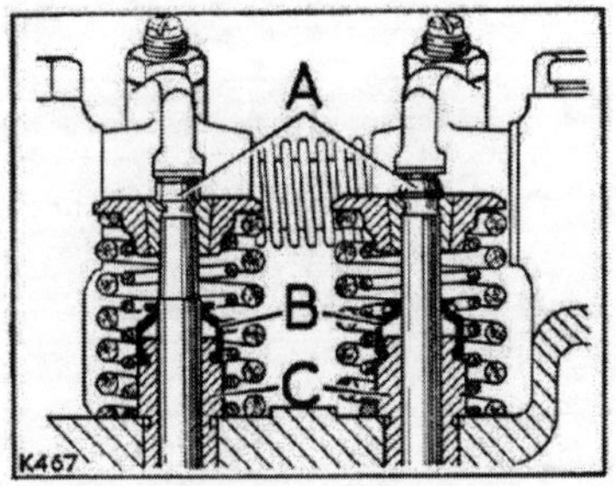

Fig. A2-87. Valve guides and oil seals arrangement
A—Valves
B—Oil seals
C—Late type guides shown

4. Clean the combustion deposits from valve guide bores.

5. Check the fit of the valve guides by inserting the valve stems into their respective guide bores, there should be running clearance but no excessive side-float (see Data for dimensions). If the valve guides are to be replaced, they must be drifted out, using the special tools, Part No. 274400 for inlet guides, Part No. 274401 for exhaust guides.

6. Lubricate the replacement valve guides and their housing bores.

7. Fit the replacement guides to the cylinder head using special drift, Part No. 600959, for exhaust valve guides and special drift, Part No. 601508, for inlet valve guides.

   (a) Early type guides (with internal seating for valve stem oil seals), have three packing washers under the exhaust guide head and two packing washers under the inlet guide head.

The special drifts are so formed to avoid damage to the seal guides. Recheck the valve stem fit, see paragraph 5.

8. Examine the valve springs assemblies. An assembly consists of two springs, the inner spring being an interference fit in the outer spring. If the inner spring is loose, replace the assembly complete.

Replacement valve springs should be fitted as follows:

The correct springs for use with the later type valve guides (see Fig. A2-87) are identified with a red stripe painted on the spring coils.

It is permissible to use the later springs on earlier type valve guides provided that the packing washers are removed from under the valve guide heads and the springs are fitted as sets. However, it is recommended that where new springs are to be fitted, earlier type valve guides and the exhaust valves be replaced by the later types. Conversion kits comprising valve guides, exhaust valves and valve springs are available from the Parts Department.

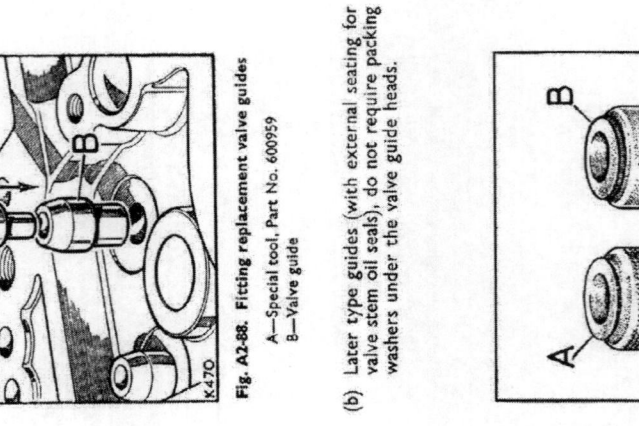

Fig. A2-88. Fitting replacement valve guides
A—Special tool, Part No. 600959
B—Valve guide

(b) Later type guides (with external seating for valve stem oil seals), do not require packing washers under the valve guide heads.

9. If it is necessary to renew the exhaust valve seat inserts, proceed as follows:

Using a suitable parallel-sided grinding stone, which must be held in the chuck of a bench drill, carefully grind away the insert in one place until only a thin portion remains. Masking the area suitably to prevent fragments flying about, gently tap the thin part of the insert in order to break it into small pieces. Remove the broken parts.

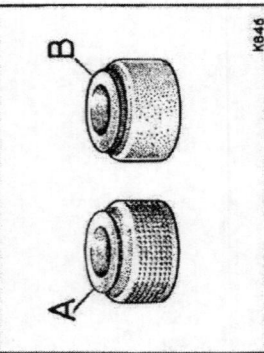

Fig. A2-89. Later type valve guide seals
A—Seal for exhaust valve guide
B—Seal for inlet valve guide

10. For the next part of the operation it is necessary to have the valve guides removed. Clean the seat recess carefully. Obtain a suitable bolt and nut to use in conjunction with a special tool, Part No. 530625, which is a fitting tool for the exhaust seat insert. Using the bolt and fitting tool as illustrated, gently pull the new insert into the seat recess.

Operations marked with an asterisk (*) can be carried out with the engine installed in the vehicle

ENGINE—2¼ LITRE DIESEL

Operation A2-23—continued

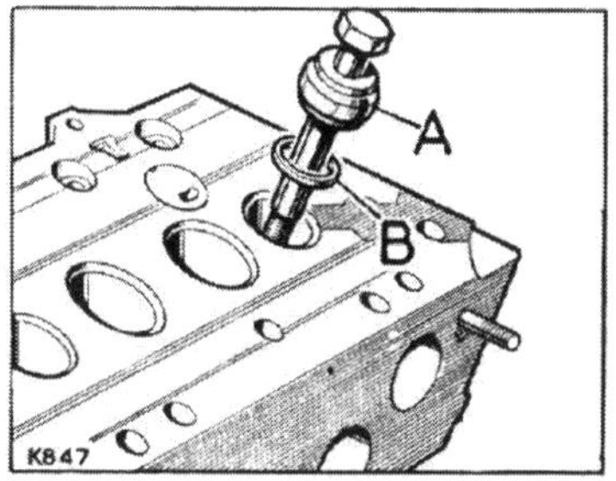

Fig. A2-90. Fitting valve seat insert
A—Special tool, Part No. 530625
B—Seat insert

11. It is not necessary to heat the cylinder head or freeze the insert for this operation, but light taps on the bolt head may be required to ensure that the insert enters smoothly. Once the insert is fully in place, carefully press in the guide as previously detailed.

Valve seats, to reface

1. Reface the valve seats, using suitable cutting or grinding tools. Both inlet and exhaust seat angles are 45°.
2. Using a small amount of grinding paste, lap the valves to their respective seats. Seat tightness is of prime importance, particularly on the 2¼ litre diesel, where the compression ratio is 23.0:1.
3. When lapping is completed, carefully clean off all traces of paste. Ensure that valves are retained in their respective fitting order.

Push rod tubes

1. For routine cylinder head overhaul it is not normally necessary to remove the push rod tubes.

Should it be necessary to renew the tubes, drift out the old ones using special tool, Part No. 274399. When the tubes are removed they are scrap and new ones must be fitted.

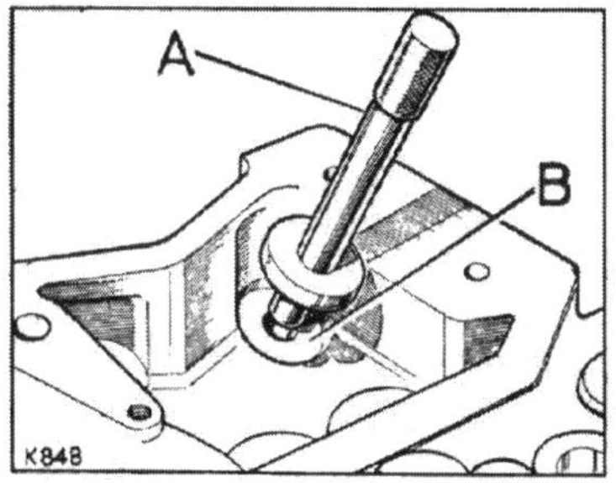

Fig. A2-91. Removing push rod tubes
A—Removal drift, Part No. 274399
B—Push rod tube

2. New tubes complete with new sealing rings should be smeared with Silicone MS4 Compound and pressed into the head, from the head face.

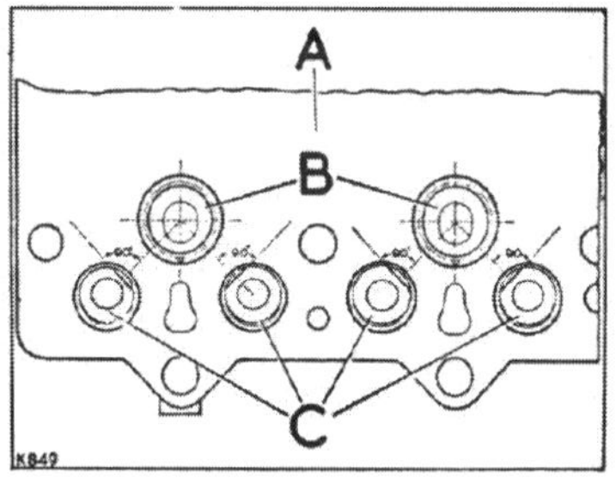

Fig. A2-92. Correct position of push rod tubes in relation to hot plugs
A—Cylinder head
B—Hot plug (combustion chamber)
C—Push rod tubes

Ensure that the chamfers on the tubes and cylinder head are in full contact and that the 'flat' of the tube is at right-angles to a line drawn between the centre of the push rod tube and the centre of the hot plug, as illustrated. Failure to fit the tubes correctly will result in restriction of coolant flow around the hot plugs.

Hot plugs (combustion chamber) and injector shrouds

When carrying out normal top overhaul work on the cylinder it is not necessary to remove either the injector shrouds or the hot plugs.

Small surface cracks in the hot plug, extending from the opening to approximately 5/16 in. (8.0 mm) in length can be ignored. However if any severe cracks appear on the face of the hot plug, closely inspect the cylinder head for signs of cracks, particularly between inlet and exhaust valve seats. Such cracking indicates that the engine has overheated, usually through lack of coolant, and the cylinder head should be scrapped.

1. To remove the hot plug insert a thin soft metal drift through the injector shroud throat and tap

the hot plug from the inside. Once removed, the hot plug is scrap, because the drifting operation will damage the pegs inside. The greatest care should be taken to avoid damaging the injector shroud. Should the shroud become damaged, drift the shroud out towards the injector bore, using a suitable round-ended drift.

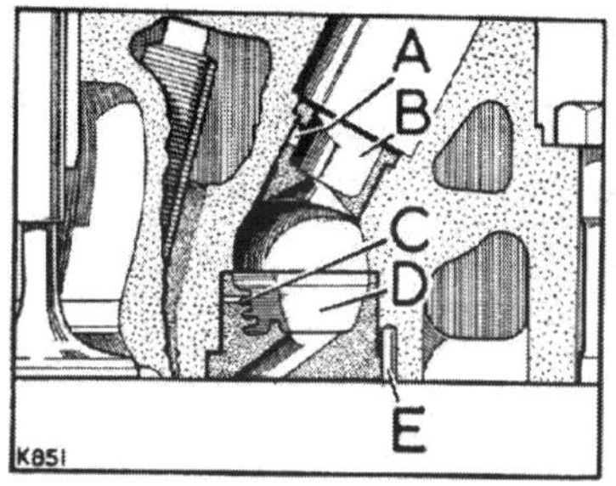

2. Thoroughly clean out the combustion chamber. The hole in the side of the injector shroud is for manufacturing purposes only, but at the same time can be used as a guide when refitting the shroud.

3. Smear a little oil on the shroud and insert into the cylinder head with the hole pointing towards the centre of the cylinder head, and drift into position, using tool, Part No. 274399.

4. The hot plugs must now be replaced by tapping gently into position with a hide-faced hammer. When fitted they must be checked with a clock gauge to ensure that they do not protrude above the level of the cylinder head face more than .001 in. (0,025 mm) and are not recessed below the level of the cylinder head face more than .002 in. (0,05 mm).
If the hot plugs are loose in the cylinder head they may be retained with a little grease.
The fitment of wooden plugs in the injector nozzle apertures will be found advantageous at this stage, to prevent entry of dirt into the combustion chamber.

Fig. A2-93. Cross-section view of injector shroud and hot plug
A—Position hole toward cylinder head centre line when refitting
B—Injector shroud
C—Swirl holes in hot plug
D—Hot plug
E—Locating peg

To assemble

1. Assemble the oil seals to the valve guides, Fig. A2-87 refers.
2. Lubricate the valve stems and fit the valves to their respective valve guides.
3. Fit the valve springs and spring caps and, using the special tool, Part No. 276102, compress the springs and fit the split cones to the valve stem waists, Fig. A2-86 refers.
4. Remove the compression tool and ensure that the assemblies are seated by tapping sharply on each valve stem end, using a hide-faced mallet.
5. Complete the assembly by refitting the thermostat housing, Operation A2-12, and the manifolds, Operation A2-8.

ENGINE—2¼ LITRE DIESEL

*Tappet assemblies, remove and refit—Operation A2-24

Workshop hand tools:
Spanner sizes: ½ in. AF open ended, ½ in. AF ring
Pliers (cutting), Screwdriver (medium), Feeler gauges

Special tools:
Torque wrench
Tappet guide removal tool, Part No. 530101

To remove

1. Remove bonnet panel. Operation A2-1.
2. Remove air cleaner. Operation A2-2.
3. Disconnect battery.
4. Remove valve gear, rocker shaft and push rods. Operation A2-20.
5. Remove cylinder head. Operation A2-22.
6. Cut the lockwire and slacken the tappet guide locating bolts at RH side of engine block.

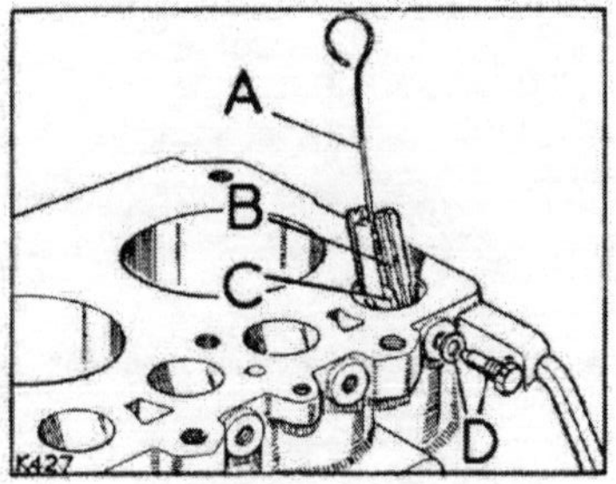

Fig. A2-94. Removing tappets and rollers
A—Spring clip
B—Tappet slide
C—Tappet roller
D—Tappet guide locating bolts

7. Remove the tappet slides, leaving the guides in position to retain the rollers. Remove the rollers using a locally made spring clip. Take care to avoid dropping the rollers behind the camshaft.
8. Remove the tappet guides and locating bolts. The use of the special tool, Part No. 530101, as illustrated will facilitate this procedure if the guides are difficult to remove by hand.
9. It is advisable to retain the tappet slides, guides and rollers as related sets.

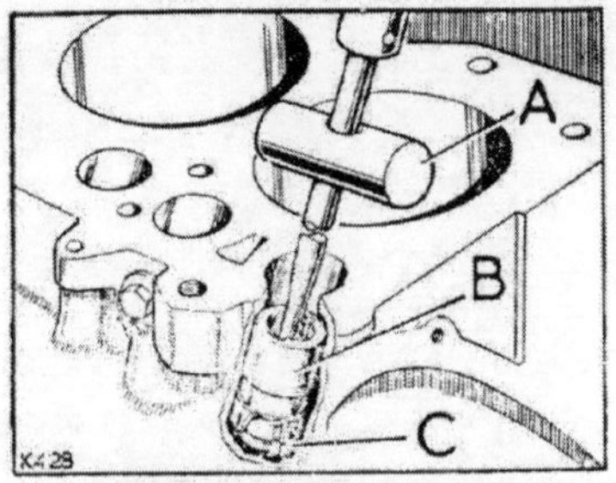

Fig. A2-95. Removing tappet guides
A—Special tool, Part No. 530101
B—Tappet guide
C—Extractor adaptor, part of special tool, Part No. 530101

To refit

1. Fit the tappet guides and engage the locating bolts sufficient to retain the guides.

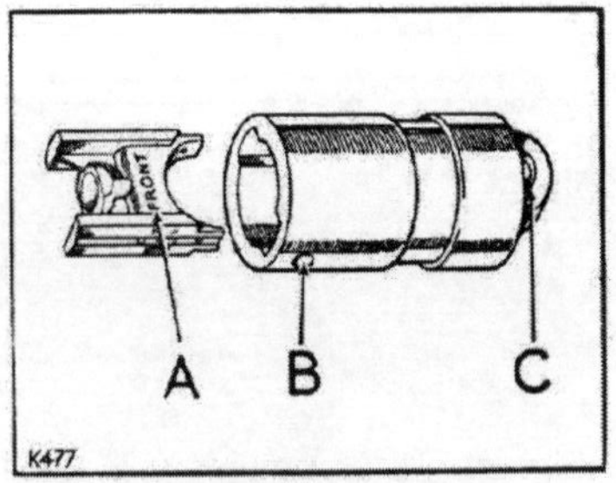

Fig. A2-96. Tappet slides and rollers
A—Letters "FRONT" on slide to be toward front of engine
B—Tappet guide bolt location hole
C—Larger chamfer on roller to be toward front of engine. Latest type roller shown

Operation A2-24—continued

2. Fit the tappet slides and rollers, positioning the components correctly relative to the front of the engine as illustrated.
3. Tighten the locating bolts and lock together in pairs, using suitable gauge soft iron wire.
4. Fit a replacement gasket, lightly coated with suitable jointing compound such as Hylomar SQ32M, and refit the cylinder head by reversing the removal procedure. Engage the fixings but do not fully tighten.
5. Refit the valve gear, rocker shaft and push rods by reversing the removal procedure. Engage the fixings but do not fully tighten at this stage.
6. Tighten the cylinder head and rocker shaft fixings, in the order shown as follows:
   ½ in. UNF bolts—90 lb ft (12,5 mkg) torque load.
   ⅝ in. UNF bolts—18 lb ft (2,4 mkg) torque load.

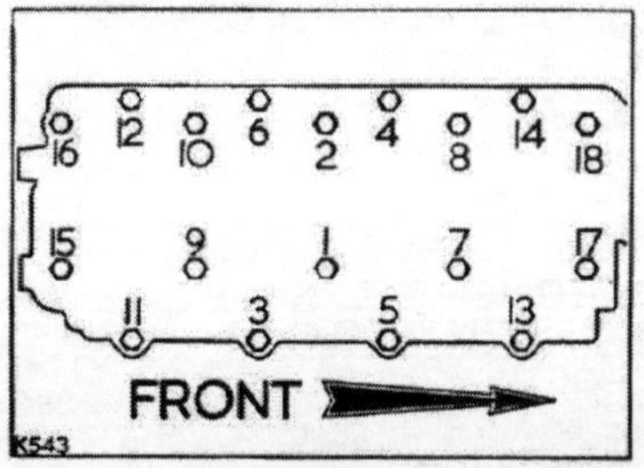

Fig. A2-97. Order of tightening cylinder head fixings

7. Set the tappet clearances to .010 in. (0,25 mm) for each valve.

   The tappet setting is most easily carried out in the following sequence, No. 1 tappet being at the front of the engine:
   Set No. 1 tappet clearance with No. 8 valve fully open.
   Set No. 3 tappet clearance with No. 6 valve fully open.
   Set No. 5 tappet clearance with No. 4 valve fully open.
   Set No. 2 tappet clearance with No. 7 valve fully open.
   Set No. 8 tappet clearance with No. 1 valve fully open.
   Set No. 6 tappet clearance with No. 3 valve fully open.
   Set No. 4 tappet clearance with No. 5 valve fully open.
   Set No. 7 tappet clearance with No. 2 valve fully open.

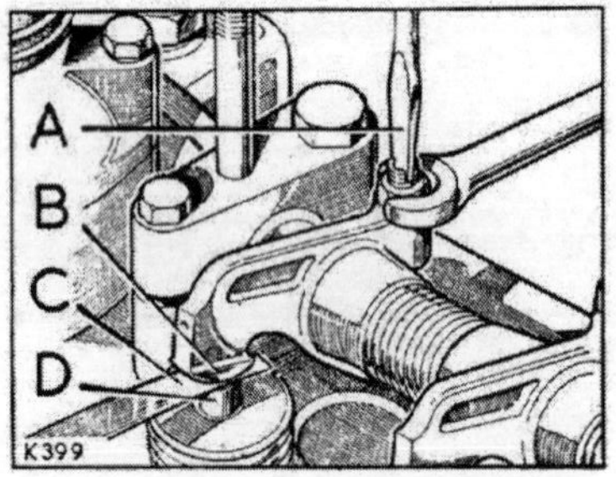

Fig. A2-98. Setting tappet clearances
A—Screwdriver   C—Feeler gauge
B—Rocker pad   D—Valve stem

8. Refit the air cleaner. Operation A2-2.
9. Refit the battery lead.

   Note: It is most important that the cylinder head fixings torque loading be checked and, if necessary, reset after an engine run, that is with the engine hot. This will entail removal of the fuel injectors to obtain full access to the cylinder head fixings.

10. Refill the engine coolant system.

COOLANT SYSTEM
Bonneted Control Model, 2¼ Litre Diesel

Capacity	Imperial Unit	US Unit	Litres	Antifreeze	Frost Precaution
88	17½ pints	21 pints	10,0	33⅓%	−25°F −32°C
109	17½ pints	21 pints	10,0	33⅓%	−25°F −32°C

11. Refit the bonnet panel. Operation A2-1.

Operations marked with an asterisk (*) can be carried out with the engine installed in the vehicle

ENGINE—2¼ LITRE DIESEL

*Engine front cover and oil seal, remove and refit—Operation A2-25

Workshop hand tools:
Spanner sizes: 2 BA open end
⅜ in. AF socket
⅜ in. AF, ⁷⁄₁₆ in. AF open ended
Screwdriver (medium), Pliers

Special tools:
Spanner for starter dog, Part No. 530102

To remove

1. Remove bonnet. Operation A2-1.

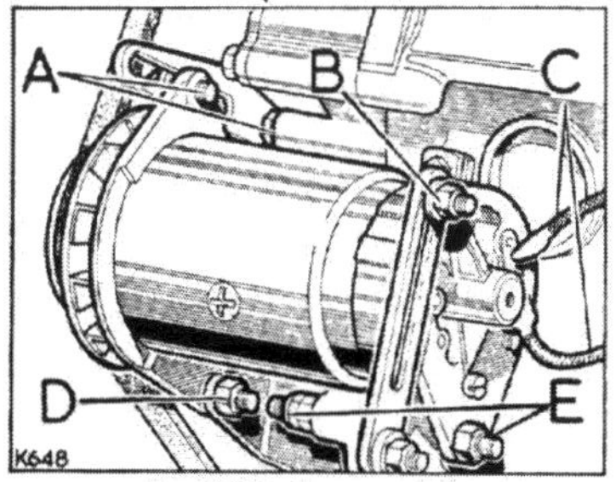

Fig. A2-99. Dynamo fixings
A—Adjusting link fixings, front
B—Adjusting link fixing, rear
C—Dynamo leads
D—Fixings at front support
E—Fixings at special stud

2. Remove radiator and grille panel. Operation A2-3.

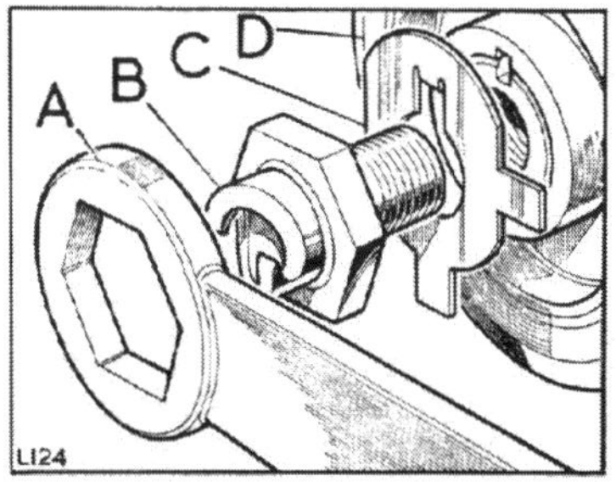

Fig. A2-100. Fan belt driving pulley fixings
A—Special tool, Part No. 530102, for starter dog
B—Starter dog
C—Lock plate
D—Fan belt driving pulley, key located

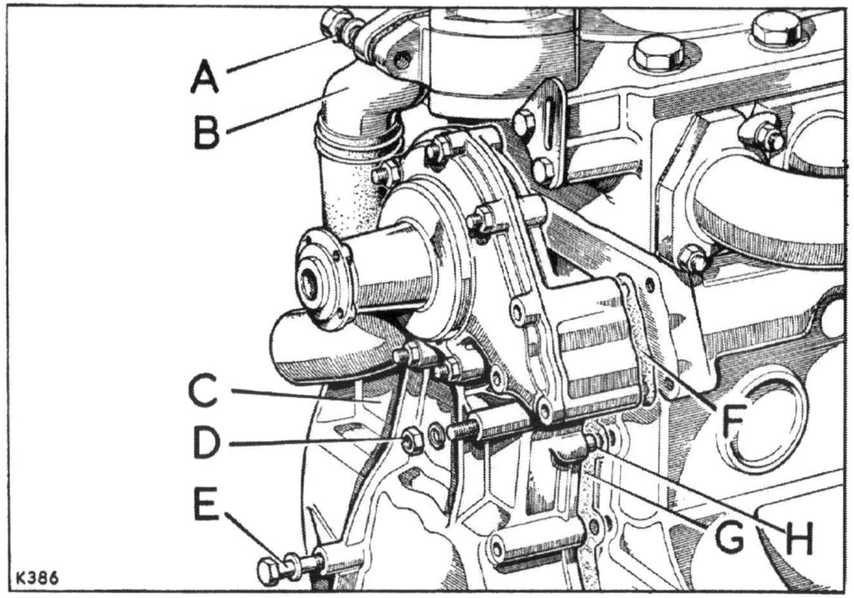

Fig. A2-101. Front cover and bracket fixings
A—Fixings   C—Front cover   E—Front cover fixings   G—Joint washer
B—By-pass pipe and joint washer   D—Dynamo link fixings   F—Joint washer   H—Locating dowels (2 off)

Operations marked with an asterisk (*) can be carried out with the engine installed in the vehicle.

3. Slacken dynamo fixings and remove fan belt.
4. Remove dynamo adjusting link.
5. Remove the starter dog and fan belt driving pulley.
6. Remove the fan blades and fan pulley.
7. Separate the by-pass pipe from the thermostat housing.
8. Remove the front cover fixings, including those at the sump front flange.
9. Remove the front cover and water inlet joint gaskets.

Oil seal

If a replacement oil seal is required, proceed as follows:

1. Carefully lever the oil seal metal casing away from the housing bore sufficient to collapse the seal and allow its removal. Use a screwdriver or suitable metal strip as a lever.

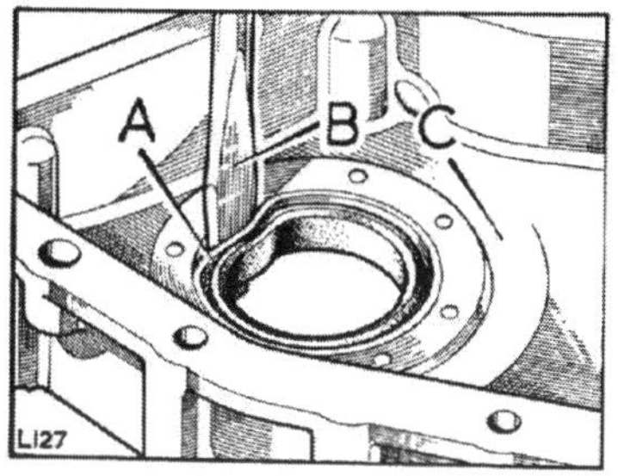

Fig. A2-102. Oil seal removal
A—Oil seal, shown collapsed
B—Suitable lever
C—Front cover inner face

Oil seal, to fit

1. Apply a thin coating of suitable jointing compound such as Hylomar SQ 32M, to the oil seal metal surfaces.
2. Locate the oil seal squarely in the housing bore with the garter spring toward the operator and press fully in.

Operation A2-25—continued

Front cover, to refit

1. It is of advantage temporarily to remove the fixing stud from the cylinder block front face. This will enable the front cover to be lifted sufficient to clear the edge of the sump gasket when offering the front cover to the engine.
2. Smear general purpose grease on both sides of the front cover and water inlet joint washers.
3. Continue the refitting by reversing the removal procedure, noting that the front cover is located to the cylinder block by dowels, Fig. A2-101 refers.
4. Refit the fixing stud, if previously removed, from the front of the engine.
5. Refit the fan blades and pulley.
6. Fit the starter dog and pulley, Fig. A2-100 refers. The correct torque loading for the starter dog is 150 lb ft (20,5 mkg).
7. Complete the refitting by reversing the removal procedure for the remaining items. Set the fan belt tension to ⁵⁄₁₆ in. to ⁷⁄₁₆ in. (8 mm to 11 mm), checked by thumb pressure applied to the fan belt between the fan pulley and crankshaft pulley when finally tightening the dynamo fixings.
8. Refill the engine coolant system.

COOLANT SYSTEM
Bonneted Control Model, 2¼ Litre Diesel

	Capacity	Imperial Unit	US Unit	Litres	Antifreeze	Frost Precaution
88	17½ pints	17½ pints	21 pints	10,0	33⅓%	−25°F −32°C
109	17½ pints	17½ pints	21 pints	10,0	33⅓%	−25°F −32°C

ENGINE—2¼ LITRE DIESEL

*Timing chain tensioner, remove, inspect and refit—Operation A2-26

Spanner sizes: ½ in. AF, ⅝ in. AF socket, 7/16 in. x ½ in. AF open end (2 off), 2 BA open end

Workshop hand tools:
Screwdriver (medium), Pliers

To remove

1. Remove bonnet panel. Operation A2-1.
2. Remove radiator and grille panel. Operation A2-3.
3. Turn the crankshaft in the direction of rotation until the timing marks are aligned as illustrated.

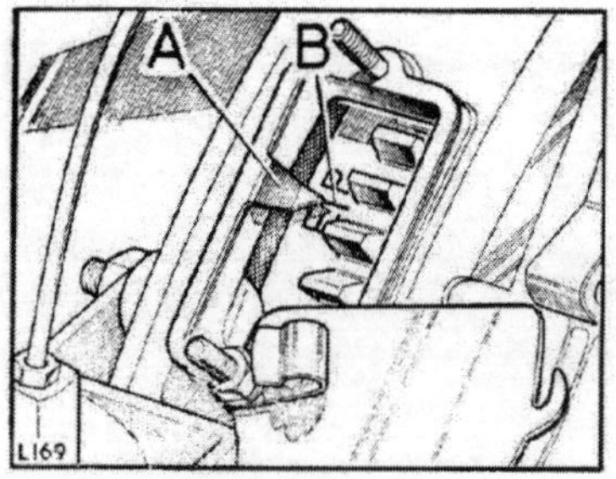

Fig. A2-103. Timing marks

A—Timing pointer
B—Align mark on flywheel with pointer in bell housing aperture

4. Remove engine front cover. Operation A2-25.
5. Remove the fixings and withdraw the piston housing ratchet and spring from the piston housing.
6. Remove the piston housing fixings, compress the tensioner spring by hand and withdraw the tensioner arrangement complete.

To dismantle and inspect

1. Remove the non-return valve ball and retainer from the piston housing.
2. Clean the components, using clean fuel.
3. Replace piston and housing if unduly worn.
4. If tensioner cylinder bush is unduly worn, the cylinder and bush complete must be renewed.
5. Replace the idler wheel and ratchet arm if the bushes are unduly worn.

6. Inspect the rubber pad on the chain vibration damper on the engine block and replace if grooved.

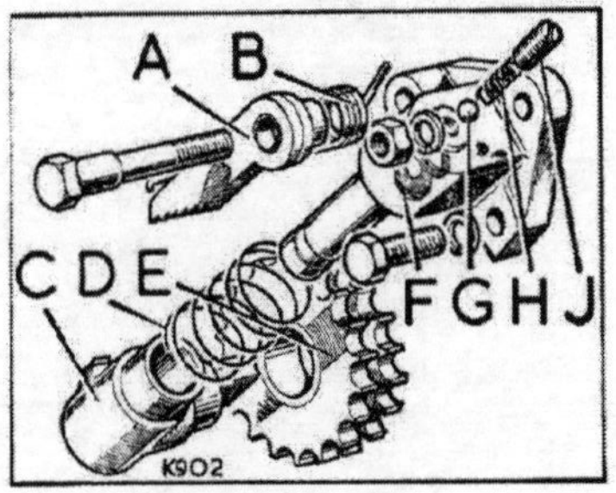

Fig. A2-104. Timing chain tensioner details

A—Ratchet
B—Ratchet spring
C—Cylinder
D—Chain tensioner spring
E—Idler wheel
F—Piston
G—Non-return ball valve
H—Spring retainer
J—Plug

7. Ensure that all oil passage drillings are clear.

To assemble

1. Reverse the removal procedure.

To refit

1. Assemble together the piston housing, tensioner spring, cylinder and idler wheel. Compress the assembly against the tensioner spring.
2. Offer up the assembly to the engine, locating the piston housing on the dowels and the cylinder spigot on the location slot.
3. Fit the ratchet and spring and allow the idler wheel to take up the timing chain slack.

Operation A2-26—continued

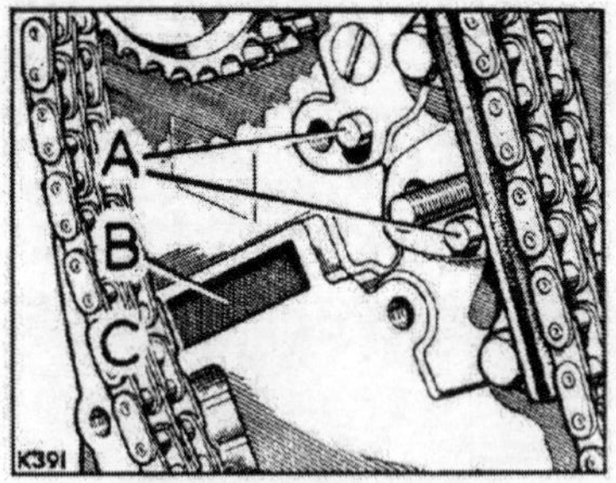

Fig. A2-105. Timing chain tensioner location details

A—Piston housing location dowels
B—Location slot for cylinder
C—Timing chain

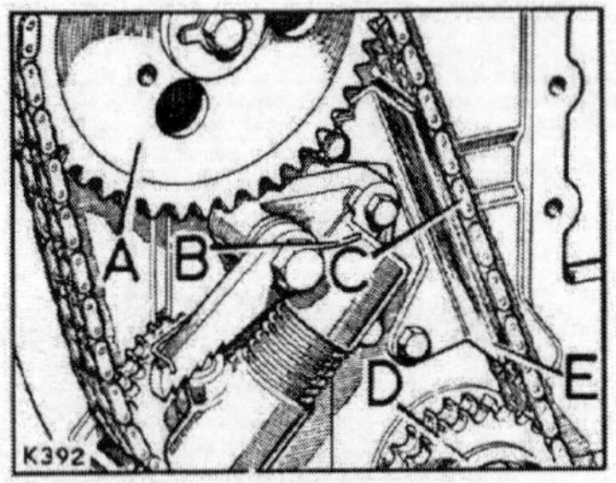

Fig. A2-106. Timing chain and chainwheel arrangement

A—Camshaft chainwheel
B—Ratchet spring
C—Timing chain, 'no slack' at this side
D—Crankshaft chainwheel
E—Vibration damper

4. Refit the front cover. Operation A2-25.
5. Ensure that the timing marks are still correctly aligned at the flywheel. Then providing the camshaft has not been rotated this will ensure that the engine valve timing has not been inadvertently disturbed. If there is any doubt, check as detailed in valve timing procedure, Operation A2-27.
6. Complete the refitting by reversing the removal procedure.
7. Refill the engine coolant system.

COOLANT SYSTEM
Bonneted Control Model, 2¼ Litre Diesel

Capacity	Imperial Unit	US Unit	Litres	Antifreeze	Frost Precaution
88	17½ pints	21 pints	10,0	33⅓%	−25°F −32°C
109	17½ pints	21 pints	10,0	33⅓%	−25°F −32°C

Operations marked with an asterisk (*) can be carried out with the engine installed in the vehicle

ENGINE—2¼ LITRE DIESEL

*Timing gears and chain, remove and refit—Operation A2-27

This Operation includes valve timing procedure

Workshop hand tools:
Spanner sizes: 7/16 in. x ½ in. AF open end (2 off)
½ in. AF, ⅝ in. AF socket
2 BA open end
Screwdriver (medium), Pliers

Special tools:
Chainwheel extractor, Part No. 507231
Dial test indicator and bracket

To remove

1. Remove bonnet panel. Operation A2-1.
2. Remove radiator and grille panel. Operation A2-3.
3. Remove the engine front cover. Operation A2-25.
4. Remove timing chain tensioner. Operation A2-26.
5. Lift off the timing chain and remove the chainwheels, using special extractor tool, Part No. 507231, to withdraw the camshaft chainwheel.

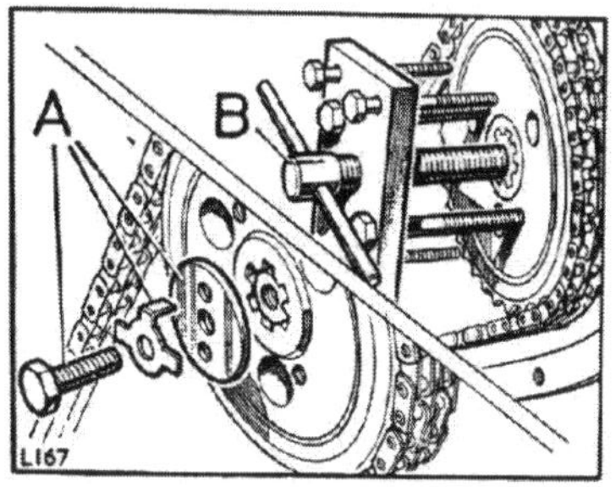

Fig. A2-107. Chainwheels and fixings
A—Camshaft chainwheel fixings
B—Extractor, Part No. 507231

6. Inspect the chainwheels and timing chain for damage and general condition.

To refit and set valve timing

1. Remove the engine top cover.
2. Remove the Inspection cover plate from the flywheel housing.
3. Fit the crankshaft chainwheel, key located.

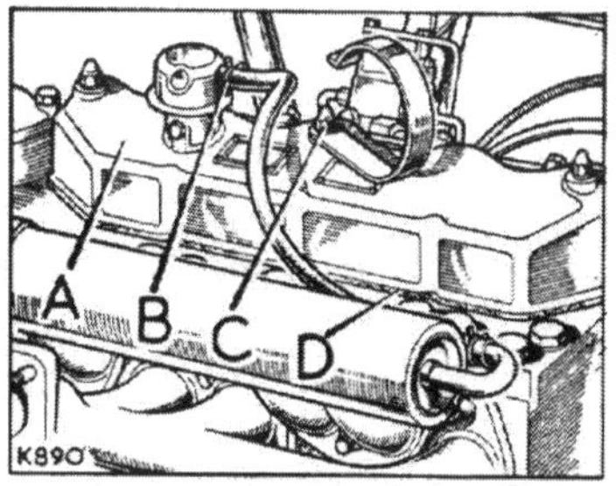

Fig. A2-108. Top cover
A—Top cover
B—Breather hose fixings
C—Fixings for top cover
D—Joint washer

4. Turn the crankshaft in direction of rotation until the EP mark on flywheel is in line with timing pointer.
5. Fit the camshaft chainwheel on to the camshaft splines. Do not lock the fixings at this stage.

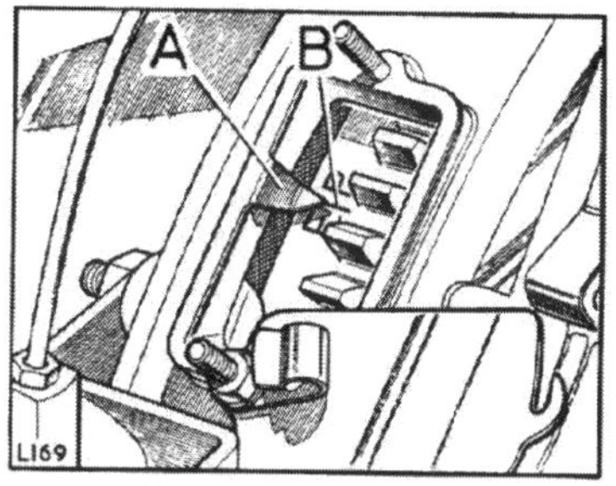

Fig. A2-109. Timing marks
A—Pointer at flywheel housing
B—EP mark on flywheel

6. Rotate the camshaft until No. 1 cylinder exhaust valve is fully closed and set the tappet clearance to .010 in. (0,25 mm).

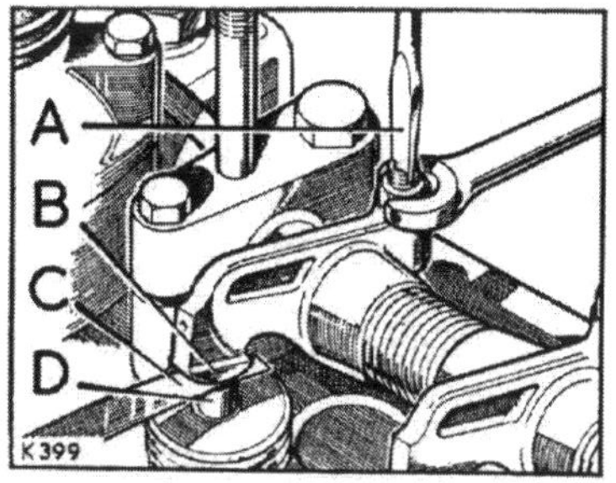

Fig. A2-110. Adjusting tappet
A—Screwdriver C—Feeler gauge
B—Rocker pad   D—Valve stem

7. Fit a dial test indicator so that the 'fully open' position of the valve can be ascertained.

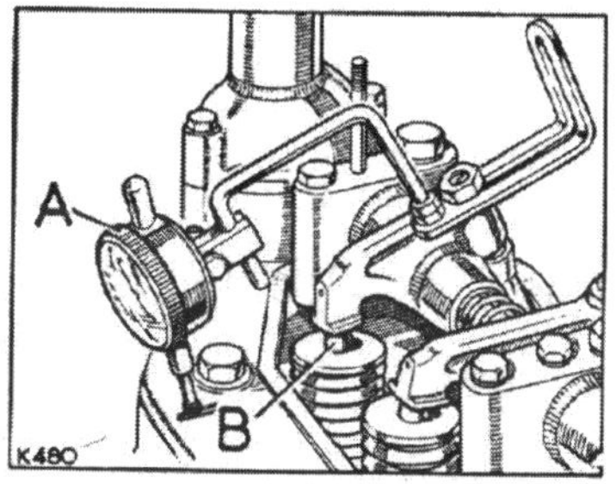

Fig. A2-111. Dial test indicator in position
A—Dial test indicator
B—No. 1 cylinder exhaust valve

8. Turn the camshaft in direction of rotation until the rocker pad has nearly opened the valve fully. Stop camshaft rotation and suitably mark the chainwheel and the timing casing relative to each other.

Operation A2-27—continued

9. Note the reading on the dial test indicator then further turn the camshaft in direction of rotation until the dial test indicator needle has reached the same position as previously noted. Stop rotation of camshaft.

10. Suitably mark the chainwheel adjacent to the mark previously made on the timing casing, then make a third mark to bisect the angle between the two previously made marks.

Fig. A2-112. Chainwheel marking—Stage II
A—Mark on timing casing
B—Second mark on chainwheel
C—Mark between two previously made marks on chainwheel
D—Mark first made on chainwheel

11. Turn the camshaft against the direction of rotation and align the third (middle) mark with the mark on the timing casing. No. 1 exhaust valve is now fully open.

12. Fit the timing chain to the chainwheels with 'no slack' on the driving side.

If the chain is slack when fitted it is necessary to reposition the camshaft chainwheel on the camshaft splines which are off-set to allow for this adjustment. It will then be advisable to recheck the valve timing. Lock the camshaft chainwheel fixings when satisfactory.

13. Refit the timing chain tensioner. Operation A2-26.

Operations marked with an asterisk (*) can be carried out with the engine installed in the vehicle

Operation A2-27—continued

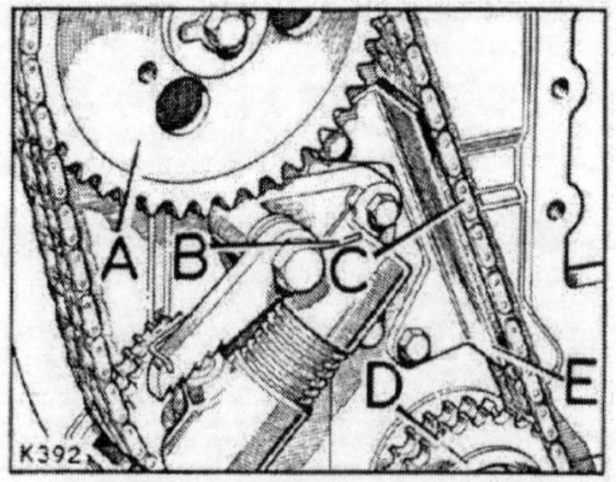

Fig. A2-113. Fitting the timing chain

A—Camshaft chainwheel
B—Ratchet spring
C—Timing chain, 'no slack' at this side
D—Crankshaft chainwheel
E—Vibration damper

14. Refit the engine front cover. Operation A2-25.
15. Refit the radiator and grille panel. Operation A2-3.
16. Refill the engine coolant system, allowing a full flow through the coolant drain taps before closing them.

COOLANT SYSTEM
Bonneted Control Model, 2¼ Litre Diesel

	Capacity	Imperial Unit	US Unit	Litres	Antifreeze	Frost Precaution
88	17¾ pints	17¾ pints	21 pints	10.0	33⅓%	−25°F −32°C
109	17¾ pints	17¾ pints	21 pints	10.0	33⅓%	−25°F −32°C

17. Refit the bonnet panel. Operation A2-1.

*Crankcase sump, remove and refit—Operation A2-28

Workshop hand tools:
Spanner sizes: ½ in. AF ring, ⁷⁄₁₆ in. BSF socket

To remove
1. Drain off the engine lubricating oil.
2. Remove the fixings, lower and withdraw the sump.

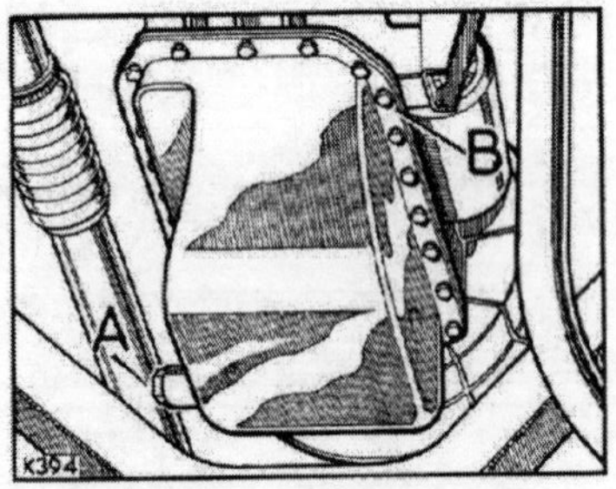

Fig. A2-114. View of crankcase sump

A—Drain plug   B—Sump fixings

To refit
1. Fit a new joint washer and reverse the removal procedure.
2. Replenish engine lubricating oil to 'high' mark on dipstick and check level after engine run.

ENGINE LUBRICANT CAPACITY
Bonneted Control Model, 2¼ Litre Diesel

	Capacity	Imperial Unit	US Unit	Litres
88	Engine	11 pints	13 pints	6.0
	Filter	1¼ pints	1.8 pints	0.85
	Engine and Filter	12¼ pints	14.8 pints	6.85
109	Engine	11 pints	13 pints	6.0
	Filter	1¼ pints	1.8 pints	0.85
	Engine and Filter	12¼ pints	14.8 pints	6.85

Operations marked with an asterisk (*) can be carried out with the engine installed in the vehicle

ENGINE—2¼ LITRE DIESEL

*Oil pump, remove and refit—Operation A2-29

(For overhaul instructions, Operation A2-30 refers)

Workshop hand tools:
Spanner sizes: ½ in. AF socket, ⁷⁄₁₆ in. BSF socket, ¼ in. AF ring

To remove

1. Remove crankcase sump. Operation A2-28.
2. Remove the oil pump assembly complete with drive shaft.

To refit

1. Offer up the pump and drive shaft and engage the drive splines at the engine. Fit the fixings and secure.
2. Fit the crankcase sump and joint gasket.
3. Fill sump with clean oil to 'high' mark on dipstick. Check level and add oil if necessary after engine run.

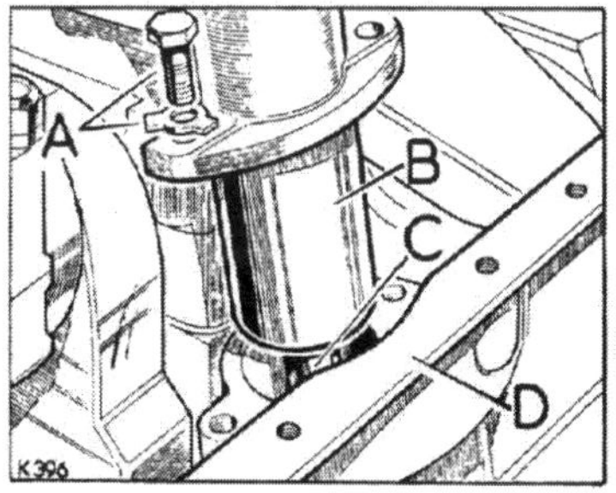

Fig. A2-115. Oil pump and drive shaft
A—Fixings
B—Oil pump
C—Drive shaft, longer splines engaged in pump
D—Sump joint face

ENGINE LUBRICANT CAPACITY
Bonneted Control Model, 2¼ Litre Diesel

		Capacity	Imperial Unit	US Unit	Litres
88	Engine		11 pints	13 pints	6.0
	Filter		1½ pints	1.8 pints	0.85
	Engine and Filter		12½ pints	14.8 pints	6.85
109	Engine		11 pints	13 pints	6.0
	Filter		1½ pints	1.8 pints	0.85
	Engine and Filter		12½ pints	14.8 pints	6.85

---

*Oil pump, overhaul—Operation A2-30

(For removal and refitting instructions, Operation A2-29 refers)

Workshop hand tools:
Spanner sizes: ⁷⁄₁₆ in. AF, ⅝ in. AF socket, 1⅛ in. AF open end ¼ lb Hammer, Flat ended drift, Feeler gauges

To dismantle

1. Unscrew the union nut and withdraw filter from pump.
2. Remove the fixings and withdraw the cover from the body.

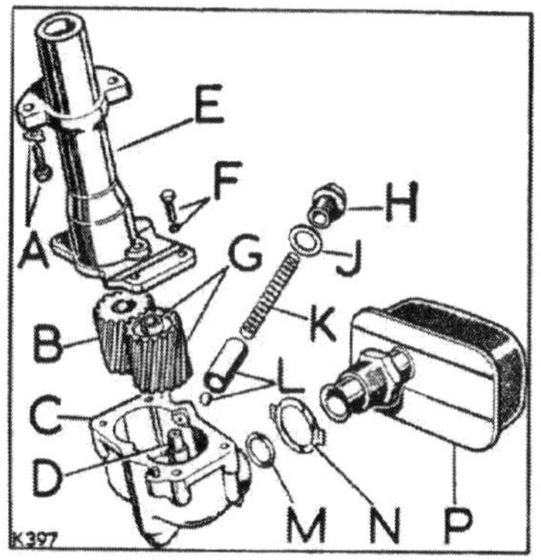

Fig. A2-116. View of oil pump
A—Fixings, oil pump to cylinder block
B—Drive gear
C—Oil pump body
D—Spindle for idler gear
E—Pump cover and shaft housing
F—Fixings, cover to body
G—Idler gear and bush assembly
H—Plug
J—Washer
K—Spring
L—Relief valve ball and plunger
M—Sealing ring
N—Lockwasher
P—Oil filter

3. Withdraw the oil pump gears.
4. Remove the oil pressure relief valve components.
5. Clean all components and inspect for general condition.
6. Check the radial clearance and end-float of the gears as illustrated.

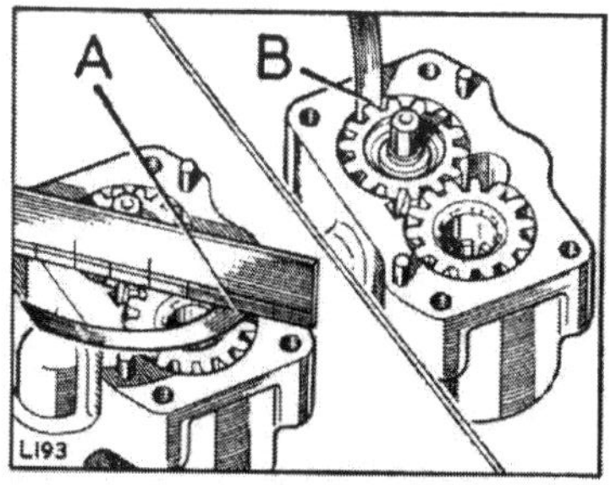

Fig. A2-117. Checking clearance of oil pump gears
A—Checking end-float
B—Checking radial clearance

Clearances

End-float, steel gear	..	.002 in. (0,05 mm) to .005 in. (0,13 mm)
End-float, aluminium gear		.003 in. (0,07 mm) to .006 in. (0,15 mm)
Radial clearance of gears	..	.001 in. (0,02 mm) to .004 in. (0,10 mm)
Backlash of gears	..	.006 in. (0,15 mm) to .012 in. (0,30 mm)

7. If necessary the idler gear bush may be renewed. Press the new bush into the gear, drill the lubrication hole .125 in. (3,175 mm) and ream the bush to .5 in. (12,7 mm).
8. Inspect the pressure relief valve ball seating and renovate, if necessary, using a locally manufactured lapping tool as illustrated.
9. The lapping tool may be installed in a drilling machine or hand brace and the ball seating refaced, using coarse grinding paste. The tool may then be removed and used to 'hand lap' the ball seating with fine grinding paste to a good finish. The seat must then be thoroughly cleaned.

Operations marked with an asterisk (*) can be carried out with the engine installed in the vehicle

ENGINE—2¼ LITRE DIESEL　　Section A2—Land-Rover

Operation A2-30—continued

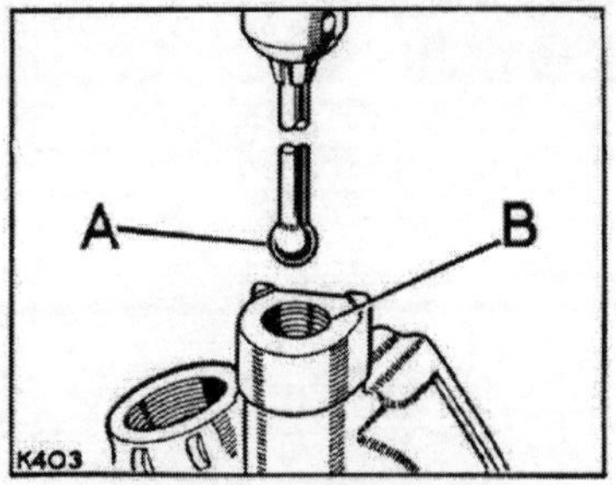

To assemble

1. Fit the pump gears to the body with the plain portion of the drive gear centre bore uppermost.
2. Smear the joint faces with suitable jointing compound and fit the pump cover to the pump body, locating on the dowels.
3. Assemble the pressure relief valve components to the housing bore. Keep the bore vertical until the ball valve is retained. When fitting the plunger, insert the end with the integral ball seating first.
4. Fit the oil filter to the pump.
5. Position the filter such that it will be square to the sump baffle plate when fitted and secure with the lockwasher.

Fig. A2-118. Lapping tool for ball valve seat

A—Steel ball, Rover Part No. 3748, soldered to suitable tubing
B—Relief valve housing

Section A2—Land-Rover　　ENGINE—2¼ LITRE DIESEL

*Clutch assembly and flywheel, remove and refit—Operation A2-31

(For overhaul instructions, Section B refers. For flywheel data see Engine detail data at end of this Section)

Workshop hand tools:
Spanner sizes: ½ in. AF, ⁷⁄₁₆ in. AF, ⅝ in. AF socket
⁷⁄₁₆ in. AF open end
⁷⁄₁₆ in. BSF open end
1 lb Hammer, Small chisel, Feeler gauge

Special tools:
Clutch plate alignment gauge, Part No. 605022
Torque wrench

To remove

Note: If it is required to remove the clutch only, it is not necessary to remove the seat base nor completely remove the gearbox. Proceed with the gearbox removal, Operation C1-3, but only withdraw the gearbox rearward approximately 5 in. (127 mm), to give access to the clutch fixings.

1. Remove the front floor. Operation A2-4.
2. Remove the gearbox complete, as detailed in Section C.

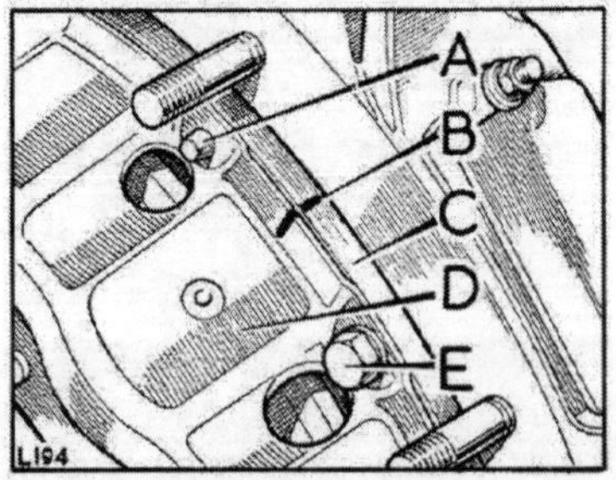

Fig. A2-119. Clutch assembly fixings

A—Locating dowel
B—Suitably mark clutch cover relative to flywheel
C—Flywheel
D—Clutch assembly
E—Fixings for clutch (6 off)

3. Mark the position of the clutch assembly cover plate in relation to the flywheel. The marks are for use during subsequent refitting, when, with the marks aligned, the original balance condition will be regained.
4. Remove the fixings and withdraw the clutch assembly from the flywheel. Withdraw the clutch plate which is released during this procedure.
5. Remove the fixings and withdraw the flywheel.

To refit

1. Fit the flywheel to the crankshaft and tighten the fixings to 60 lb ft to 65 lb ft (8,5 mkg to 9,0 mkg) torque load. Do not lock the fixings at this stage.
2. Check the run-out on the flywheel face as illustrated. The run-out must not exceed .002 in. (0,05 mm).

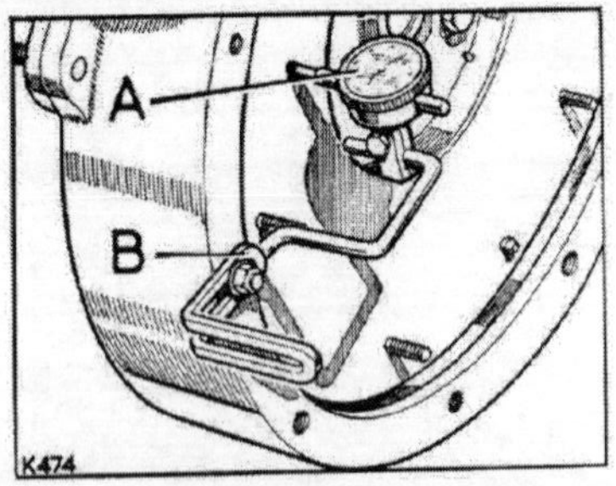

Fig. A2-120. Checking run-out on flywheel face

A—Dial test indicator
B—Suitable bracket

3. Lock the flywheel fixings.
4. Offer the clutch driven plate to the primary shaft and ensure that it will slide easily on all the splines.
5. Place the driven plate in position on the flywheel with the longer end of the central boss away from the engine.
6. Centralise the driven plate with the flywheel, using a slave primary shaft or the special centralising tool, Part No. 605022.

Operations marked with an asterisk (*) can be carried out with the engine installed in the vehicle

Section A2—Land-Rover

ENGINE—2¼ LITRE DIESEL

*Rear main bearing oil seal and flywheel housing, remove and refit—Operation A2-32

Workshop hand tools:
Spanner sizes: 7/16 in. AF, 1/2 in. AF open end
  1/4 in. BSF, 7/16 in. BSF open end
  1/2 in. AF, 9/16 in. AF, 5/8 in. AF, 3/4 in. AF,
  7/8 in. AF, 15/16 in. AF socket
  3/8 in. AF ring, 7/16 in. BSF socket
Screwdriver (medium), Pliers (snipe nosed),
1 lb Hammer, Small chisel, Feeler gauges

Special tools:
Engine lifting sling, Part No. 600963
Guides for rear main bearing oil seal, Part No. 270304 (2 off)
Clutch plate alignment gauge, Part No. 605022
Torque wrench

To remove

1. Remove bonnet panel. Operation A2-1.
2. Remove the front floor. Operation A2-4.
3. Remove gearbox assembly. Section C.
4. Remove the starter motor. Operation A2-9.
5. Remove the crankcase sump. Operation A2-28.
6. Remove the clutch assembly and flywheel Operation A2-31.
7. Fit suitable lifting equipment and support the engine weight.

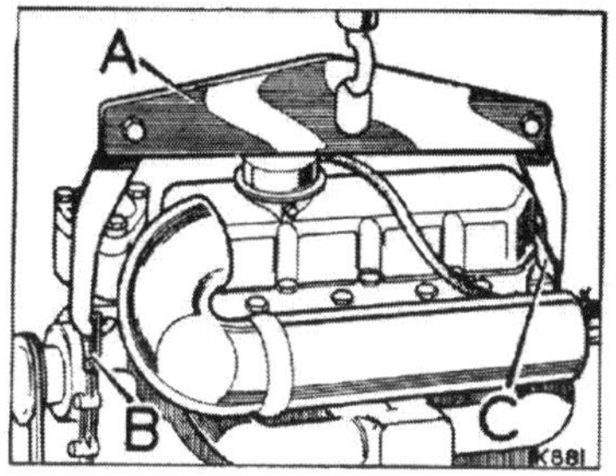

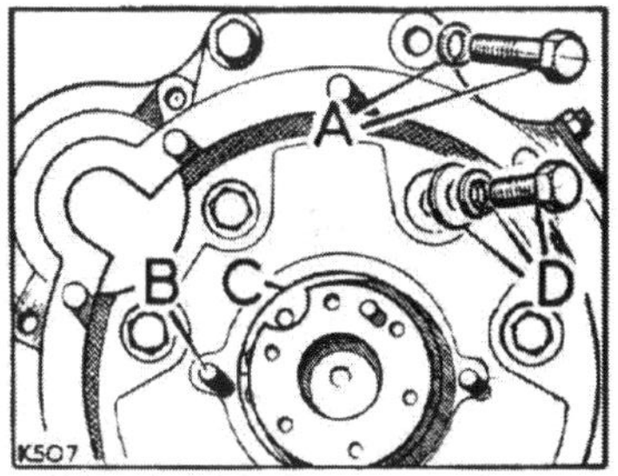

Fig. A2-123. Flywheel housing fixings
A—Fixings at flange
B—Locating dowels
C—Oil seal in recess
D—Fixings in counterbores

Fig. A2-122. Lifting sling in position
A—Engine lifting sling, Part No. 600963, engaged in lifting brackets
B—Front lifting bracket
C—Rear lifting bracket

Fig. A2-124. Seal retainer fixings
A—Seal retainer upper half
B—Fixings for seal retainer
C—Seal retainer lower half
D—Rear main bearing cap
E—Locating dowels
F—Crankshaft flange, rotate to align cut-out with fixings

8. Remove the packing piece from between the flywheel housing and the chassis cross member, previously fitted during gearbox removal.
9. Remove the fixings and withdraw the flywheel housing. Remove the oil seal.

Operations marked with an asterisk (*) can be carried out with the engine installed in the vehicle

---

ENGINE—2¼ LITRE DIESEL

Section A2—Land-Rover

Operation A2-31—continued

7. Offer up the clutch assembly to the flywheel, aligning the previously made relationship markings.
8. Fit the fixings and tighten evenly one turn at a time to 22 lb ft to 25 lb ft (3,0 mkg to 3,5 mkg) torque load, using diagonal selection to avoid distortion of the clutch cover.
9. Lock the clutch fixings.
10. Remove the centralising tool or slave shaft.
11. Refit the gearbox—see Section C.
12. Refit the front floor. Operation A2-4.
13. Check and set the clutch pedal adjustment as detailed in Section B.

Fig. A2-121. Centralising clutch driven plate
A—Flywheel
B—Flywheel fixings
C—Driven plate
D—Centralising tool or slave primary shaft

ENGINE—2¼ LITRE DIESEL

Operation A2-32—continued

10. Remove the rear bearing cap.

11. Remove the fixings and detach the two halves of the rear main bearing retainer from the cylinder block and rear bearing cap respectively. The halves are dowel located.

12. Remove the oil seal from the crankshaft.

Rear main bearing oil seal, to refit

1. Assemble the garter spring on the oil seal journal of the crankshaft, by laying the spring around the journal, this will bring the two ends, the hook and the eye, adjacent to one another, then insert the hook into the eye. Care must be taken to ensure that during this operation the spring is not stretched at all.

The spring should be moved along the journal until it is against the thrower flange.

2. Apply Silicone Grease MS4 to the crankshaft oil seal journal and to both sides of the split oil seal sealing lip.

Open the split seal sufficiently to allow it to be fitted over the crankshaft oil seal journal. Recess in oil seal must be towards thrower flange and garter spring.

The oil seal must not be repeatedly fitted and removed from the crankshaft, as this can damage the sealing lip.

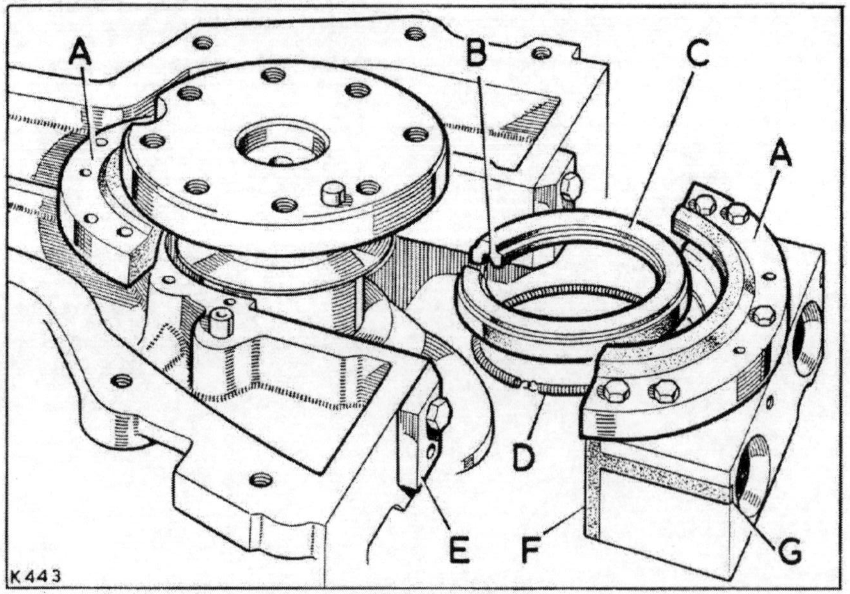

Fig. A2-125. Oil seal details

A—Retainer halves
B—Split line of seal to be toward top of engine
C—Split oil seal
D—Garter spring, hook and eye to be midway between split and hinge of oil seal when fitted
E—Guides, Part No. 270304, for rear main bearing cap "T" seals
F—Trim these edges before fitting to prevent fouling on block
G—Trim these ends when cap is fitted to engine to allow 1/32 in. (0,8 mm) protrusion

Operation A2-32—continued

6. Bolt the other half of the oil seal retainer on to the main bearing cap, in the same way. Apply Silicone grease MS4 to the 'T' seals and fit them to the main bearing cap. The cap must be off the crankcase for these operations.

Trim the edges of the 'T' seals as illustrated in Fig. A2-125 to prevent them from fouling the cylinder block when fitted.

7. Fit the main bearing cap with the seal retainer, bearing shell and 'T' seals to the crankcase until there is approximately 1/32 in. (0,8 mm) clearance between the cap and crankcase. Use the guides, Part No. 270304, as illustrated to feed the 'T' seals past the edges of the crankcase. Remove the guides after fitting the cap.

8. Ensure that the seal is located in the retainer recess.

9. Pull down the cap slowly, ensuring there is no buckling of the split seal or misalignment of the butt joint.

Tighten the cap bolts to 100 lb ft (13,8 mkg) torque and re-check that the seal is located correctly in the housing.

10. Finally tighten the bolts securing the retainer halves. Turn the bolt heads so that the hexagon corners will not foul the flywheel housing seal when fitting.

Flywheel housing, to refit

11. Replace the oil seal in the flywheel housing recess and fit the housing to the cylinder block. Fig. A2-123 refers.

12. Refit the crankcase sump. Operation A2-28. When fitting the crankcase sump, trim the ends of the rear main bearing oil seal 'T' seals to allow approximately 1/32 in. (0,8 mm) protrusion from the rear bearing cap face. Fig. A2-125 refers.

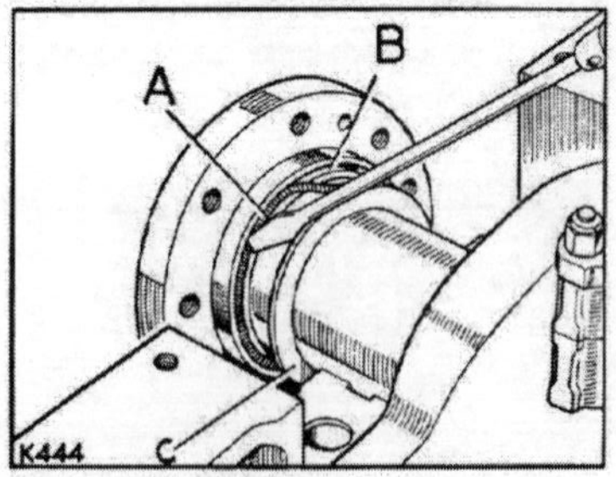

Fig. A2-126. Fitting garter spring to recess

A—Garter spring
B—Oil seal recess for garter spring
C—Thrower flange

3. Ensure that the hook and eye of the garter spring are located midway between the split and hinge of the oil seal. Then, using a small screwdriver or similar tool, gently ease the spring into the recess in the oil seal.

4. Rotate the oil seal until the split is on the vertical axis pointing towards the cylinder head and in its approximate running position on the journal; this position is important.

Apply Hylomar SQ32M sealing compound to the seal diameter of the two half plates, using either an applicator or a brush.

Important: Do not degrease the half seal plates with trichlorethylene, but wipe clean with a dry cloth prior to applying the Hylomar.

5. Fit one half of the oil seal retainer on to the crankcase dowels. The oil seal should be compressed to assist assembly, also ensure that it is correctly located in the retainer recess. Bolt the retainer to the crankcase, leaving the two bolts adjacent to the split line finger-tight, fully tighten the remaining three bolts. In order to fit the bolt it will be necessary to rotate the crankshaft; it is essential to hold the seal so that it does not rotate with the crankshaft.

ENGINE—2¼ LITRE DIESEL

Operation A2-32—continued

13. Refit the gearbox. See Section C.
14. Refit the starter motor. Operation A2-9.
15. Refit the front floor. Operation A2-4.
16. Replenish engine lubricating oil as necessary.
17. Refit the bonnet panel. Operation A2-1.

ENGINE LUBRICANT CAPACITY
Bonneted Control Model, 2¼ Litre Diesel

		Capacity	Imperial Unit	US Unit	Litres
88	Engine	11 pints	11 pints	13 pints	6.0
	Filter	1½ pints	1½ pints	1.8 pints	0.85
	Engine and Filter	12½ pints	12½ pints	14.8 pints	6.85
109	Engine	11 pints	11 pints	13 pints	6.0
	Filter	1½ pints	1½ pints	1.8 pints	0.85
	Engine and Filter	12½ pints	12½ pints	14.8 pints	6.85

*Pistons and connecting rods, remove and refit—Operation A2-33

(for overhaul instructions, Operation A2-34 refers)

Special tools:
Torque wrench

Workshop hand tools:
Spanner sizes: 7/16 in. AF, ½ in. AF, 9/16 in. AF, ⅝ in. AF sockets
¼ in. AF, 7/16 in. AF, ½ in. AF, 9/16 in. AF, ⅝ in. AF open end
5/16 in. AF ring
7/16 in. BSF, ⅜ in. BSF open end
14 mm plug spanner

Screwdriver (medium), Pliers

To remove

1. Remove the bonnet panel. Operation A2-1.
2. Remove the air cleaner. Operation A2-2.
3. Remove the valve gear and rocker shaft. Operation A2-20.
4. Remove the cylinder head. Operation A2-22.
5. Remove the crankcase sump. Operation A2-28.
6. With two pistons at bottom dead centre (BDC) remove the connecting rod cap fixings.
7. Remove the caps and withdraw the connecting rod bearing halves. Retain the caps and bearings in related sets.
8. Withdraw the pistons and attached connecting rods from the top of the bore.
9. Position the remaining pistons at BDC and repeat the removal procedure.
10. Retain the removed components in related sets.

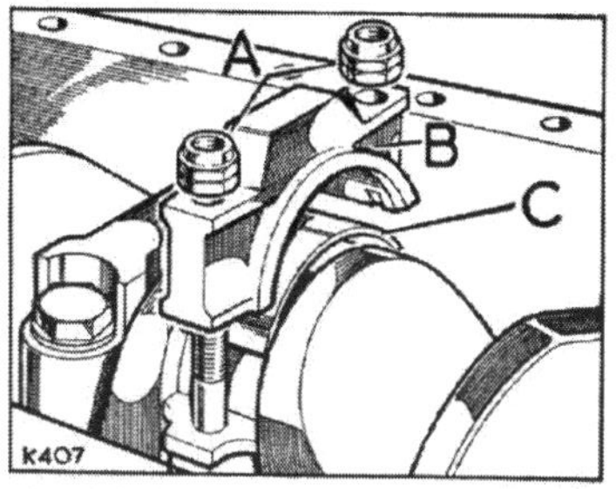

To refit

Note: If replacement components are to be fitted, the checks detailed in overhaul, Operation A2-34, must be carried out as necessary.

1. Position the crankshaft with two crank pins at BDC and insert the appropriate pistons and attached connecting rods into the cylinder bores from the top of the cylinder block, using a suitable piston ring clamp. Position the oil hole in connecting rod toward camshaft side of engine.
2. Lubricate the journals and bearing halves and fit the appropriate bearing halves to the connecting rods and caps, Fig. A2-127 refers.
3. Fit the connecting rod caps and new fixing nuts. Tighten the fixings to 25 lb ft (3.5 mkg).
4. Repeat the procedure to refit the remaining two assemblies.
5. Refit the crankcase sump. Operation A2-28.
6. Refit the cylinder head. Operation A2-22.
7. Refit the valve gear and rocker shaft. Operation A2-20.
8. Set the tappet clearances, Operation A2-19, and refit the top cover.
9. Refit the air cleaner. Operation A2-2.

Fig. A2-127. Connecting rod big-end details
A—Fixings for connecting rod cap
B—Connecting rod cap
C—Connecting rod bearing lower half

Operations marked with an asterisk (*) can be carried out with the engine installed in the vehicle

ENGINE—2¼ LITRE DIESEL

Pistons and connecting rods, overhaul—Operation A2-34

(For removal and refitting Instructions, Operation A2-33 refers)

Special tools:
Torque wrench
'Plastigage' strip, Part No. 605238
Piston ring clamp

Workshop hand tools:
Spanner sizes: ⅞ in. AF socket
Circlip pliers, Feeler gauge

To dismantle

Note: During the following procedures retain all components in related sets to facilitate subsequent assembly.

1. Remove the piston rings using suitable expanding pliers.

2. Remove circlips and withdraw gudgeon pins. Withdraw the pins toward the 'X' mark on the piston crown where so marked. Removal of gudgeon pins is facilitated if the piston is first warmed to 55°C (131°F) approximately.

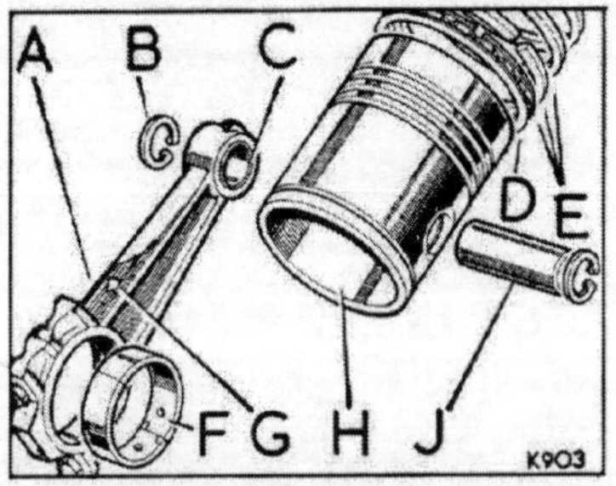

3. Clean all components and inspect for damage and general condition.

Fig. A2-128. Exploded view of piston and connecting rod

A—Connecting rod assembly
B—Retaining circlips for gudgeon pin
C—Connecting rod bush
D—Scraper ring
E—Compression rings
F—Bearing halves
G—Oil spray hole
H—Piston
J—Gudgeon pin

Checking piston clearance in cylinder bore

1. Insert a long .004 in. (0,10 mm) feeler gauge down the RH side of the cylinder bore, insert the correct piston inverted into the cylinder bore. Position the gudgeon pin bore parallel with the centre line of the engine.

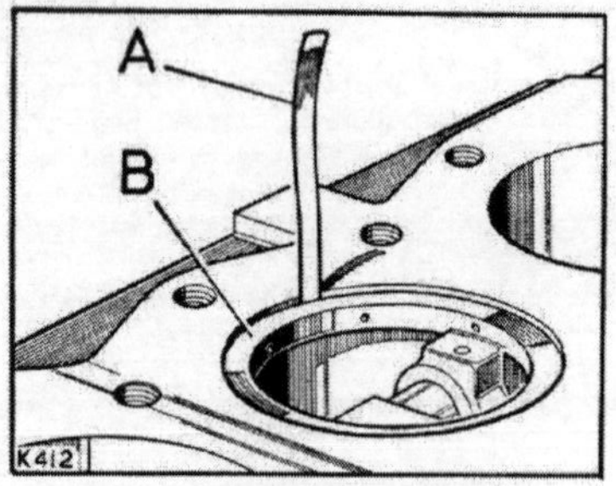

Fig. A2-129. Checking piston clearance

A—Feeler gauge
B—Piston in cylinder bore

2. Push the piston down the cylinder until the piston skirt reaches its tightest point in the bore. At this point withdraw the feeler gauge—a steady resistance should be felt. If necessary, select pistons from the range available until this check is satisfactory.

Pistons for the 2¼ litre diesel engine are available in the standard size only in two diameters, that is small diameter identified by the letters 'ZAB' stamped on the piston crown; and large diameter identified by the letters 'BCD'. The difference between the two diameters is .0005 in. (0,012 mm).

The letters 'L' and 'H' which follow the diameter letters represent a difference in height between the gudgeon pin centre and the piston crown. All service replacement pistons will be type 'L' and these must be used where the 'H' type pistons were fitted as original equipment.

The cylinder block has each bore diameter identified by a letter stamped adjacent to the bore on the manifold side of the cylinder block, just above the water gallery casting.

Operation A2-33—continued

10. Refill the engine coolant system.

COOLANT SYSTEM
Bonneted Control Model, 2¼ Litre Diesel

Capacity	Imperial Unit	US Unit	Litres	Antifreeze	Frost Precaution
17½ pints	17½ pints	21 pints	10,0	33⅓%	−25°F −32°C
17½ pints	17½ pints	21 pints	10,0	33⅓%	−25°F −32°C

11. Replenish the engine lubrication system.

ENGINE LUBRICANT CAPACITY
Bonneted Control Model, 2¼ Litre Diesel

	Capacity	Imperial Unit	US Unit	Litres
88	Engine	11 pints	13 pints	6,0
	Filter	1½ pints	1.8 pints	0,85
	Engine and Filter	12½ pints	14.8 pints	6,85
109	Engine	11 pints	13 pints	6,0
	Filter	1½ pints	1.8 pints	0,85
	Engine and Filter	12½ pints	14.8 pints	6,85

12. Refit the bonnet panel. Operation A2-1.

ENGINE—2¼ LITRE DIESEL

Operation A2-34—continued

The diameter letters represent a difference in bore diameter of .0002 in. (0,005 mm) as shown below:

Grade letter	Cylinder bore diameter
'Z'	Nominal to plus .0002 in. (0,005 mm) above nominal.
'A'	.0002 in. to .0004 in. (0,005 to 0,01 mm) above nominal.
'B'	.0004 in. to .0006 in. (0,01 mm to 0,015 mm) above nominal.
'C'	.0006 in. to .0008 in. (0,015 mm to 0,02 mm) above nominal.
'D'	.0008 in. to .0010 in. (0,02 mm to 0,025 mm) above nominal.

When fitting new pistons to a cylinder block the appropriate piston diameter should be selected:

Use small diameter (ZAB/L) pistons in bores stamped 'Z', 'A' or 'B'.

Use larger diameter (BCD/L) pistons in bores stamped 'B', 'C' or 'D'.

When replacement standard size pistons are fitted to an engine which has been in service, it is of course necessary to check each individual cylinder bore and fit the appropriate size of piston as required.

Any cylinder block carrying the grade letters 'ZZ' indicate that in this particular case the bore diameter is between the nominal size and minus .0002 in. (0,005 mm). However as blocks marked in this manner are the exception rather than the rule, 'ZZ' grade pistons are not available, and in the case of a small mileage engine with negligible bore wear requiring a new piston a grade 'ZAB' would be suitable, subject to the normal checks being carried out.

Pistons are also supplied by the Parts Department the following oversize dimensions:

(a) Oversize .010 in. (0,254 mm).
(b) Oversize .020 in. (0,508 mm).
(c) Oversize .030 in. (0,762 mm).
(d) Oversize .040 in. (1,016 mm).

Small and large diameter gradings do not apply to oversize pistons.

Checking piston ring gap in bore

1. Check the piston ring gaps in the cylinder bores using a slave piston as illustrated to keep the rings square in the bore.

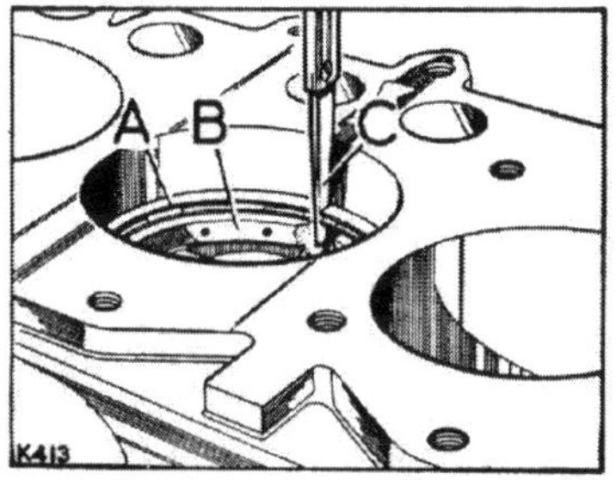

Fig. A2-130. Checking piston ring gap

A—Piston ring
B—Slave piston used to keep rings square
C—Feeler gauge

The piston ring gaps must be as follows when fitted:

(a) Upper compression ring (chromed): .014 in. to .019 in. (0,35 mm to 0,50 mm).
(b) Middle and lower compression rings: .010 in. to .015 in. (0,25 mm to 0,38 mm).
(c) Scraper ring (early type one-piece): .010 in. to .015 in. (0,25 mm to 0,38 mm).
(d) Scraper ring (later type three-piece), upper and lower rail: .015 in. to .045 in. (0,38 mm to 1,14 mm).

ENGINE—2¼ LITRE DIESEL

Operation A2-34—continued

Checking ring clearance in piston groove

1. Fit the piston rings to the piston and check the clearances in the respective grooves as illustrated.

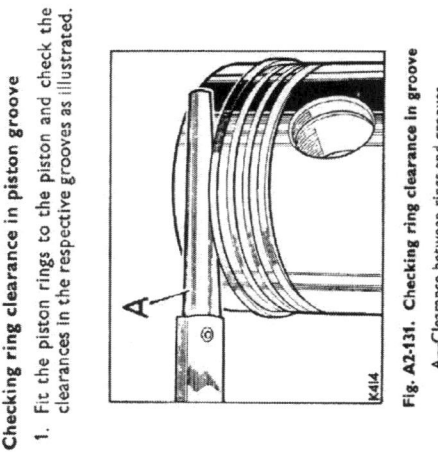

Fig. A2-131. Checking ring clearance in groove

A—Clearance between rings and grooves to be .0025 in. to .0045 in. (0,06 mm to 0,11 mm)

Note: With the latest type scraper ring, clearance between the rings and grooves to be .0015 in. to .0025 in. (0,038 mm to 0,064 mm).

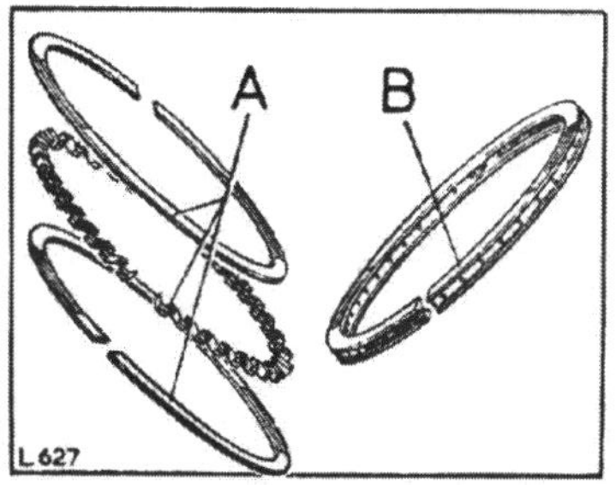

The top compression ring is chromium-plated and may be fitted either way, whereas the second and third compression rings are bevel-edged and must be fitted with the side marked 'T' or 'Top' uppermost.

The oil scraper ring fitted on earlier engines as original equipment may also be fitted either way. The second scraper ring groove below the gudgeon pin is left empty on production. This groove can be used to carry another scraper ring if necessary.

The later type three-piece scraper ring, which may be fitted to replace earlier one-piece scraper rings, is fitted as follows:

(a) The three-piece oil control ring must be fitted to the upper scraper ring groove only. No machining is necessary to the groove. The lower groove below the gudgeon pin must not be used.

(b) The two chrome-plated rails of the ring assembly should be checked for ring gap in the normal way. The gap is .015 in. to .045 in. (0,38 mm to 1,14 mm).

(c) Wind a rail on to the piston skirt, just below the upper scraper ring groove.

(d) Place the expander in the groove with its ends butted, in line with the gudgeon pin bore. Great care must be taken to ensure the ends of the expander do not overlap, and to facilitate this, the ends have been coloured white and green so that they can easily be seen. **Both coloured ends must be visible.**

(e) Fit the lower rail into the groove, beside the expander. The ring gap should be situated approximately 1.0 in. (25,4 mm) to the left of the coloured butted ends of the expander.

(f) Do not, at this stage, push the back of the expander into the groove. Wind the other rail down over the bands into the scraper groove on the upper side of the expander with the gap of the rail situated approximately 1.0 in. (25,4 mm) to the right of the coloured butted ends of the expander.

Fig. A2-132. Early and late type scraper rings

A—Later type ring, three-piece. Fitted to upper groove (above gudgeon pin) only
B—Early type ring, one-piece. Can be fitted to upper and lower scraper ring grooves

ENGINE—2¼ LITRE DIESEL

Operation A2-34—continued

(g) Work the back of the expander down into the groove between the rails previously fitted. Centralise the ring on the piston, but do not move the assembly more than is necessary. The ring will now be complete in the groove, and although it may feel somewhat stiff to move in the groove, this can be ignored.

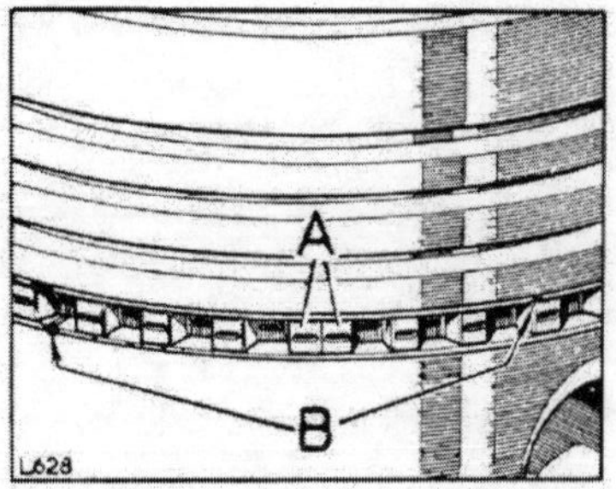

Fig. A2-133. Later type oil scraper ring fitted
A—Coloured ends butting, not overlapped
B—Gaps in upper and lower rails

Gudgeon pin checks

1. Measure the gudgeon pin fit in the connecting rod bush. The required fitted clearance is .001 in. (0,025 mm) maximum giving an easy sliding fit when cold and dry. A replacement bush must be reamed when fitted to obtain this clearance. Ensure that the pre-drilled oil hole in the bush is aligned with the connecting rod oil hole when pressing in a replacement bush.

2. Check the gudgeon pin diameter relative to the piston bores. The required interference fit is zero to .0002 in. (0,005 mm) which will give an easy hand fit with the piston warmed to 49° to 60°C.

3. Fit each connecting rod to a suitable test fixture and check for twist and mal-alignment.

Connecting rod bearing cap checks

1. Select the correct cap for each connecting rod as denoted by the number stamped near the joint faces. This number also indicates the crankshaft journal to which it must be fitted.

2. Assemble the caps, less bearing halves, to the respective connecting rods.

3. Tighten the fixings to 25 lb ft (4,9 mkg).

4. Slacken off one fixing and check that there is no clearance at the joint face. If there is clearance then the assemblies must be replaced.

5. Repeat the check on the other side of the assembly.

Connecting rod bearing nip

1. Fit the bearing halves. Torque tighten the fixings then slacken one fixing as before and check the clearance between the joint faces. The clearance must be .002 in. to .004 in. (0,0 mm to 0,10 mm).

   The bearing nip can be corrected by selective assembly of the bearing shells; these are available in slightly varying thicknesses. Do not file or machine the caps or connecting rods to vary the bearing nip.

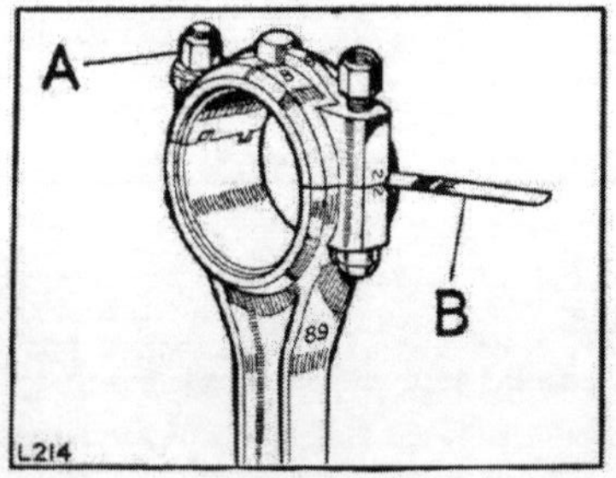

Fig. A2-134. Checking connecting rod bearing nip
A—Fixing, torque loaded
B—Feeler gauge

2. Assemble each connecting rod assembly to its respective crankshaft journal and repeat the connecting rod bearing nip check. Again the clearance between the connecting rod and cap must be .002 in. to .004 in. (0,05 mm to 0,10 mm).

   Alternatively, use 'Plastigage' strip inserted between the connecting rod bearings and the crankshaft journals. This method will indicate the actual clearance between the bearings and the journals and must be .001 in. to .0025 in. (0,025 mm to 0,063 mm) with the fixings torque loaded as in the alternative method.

Operation A2-34—continued

'Plastigage' is available under Rover Part No. 605238. Remove all traces of 'Plastigage' from the components after use.

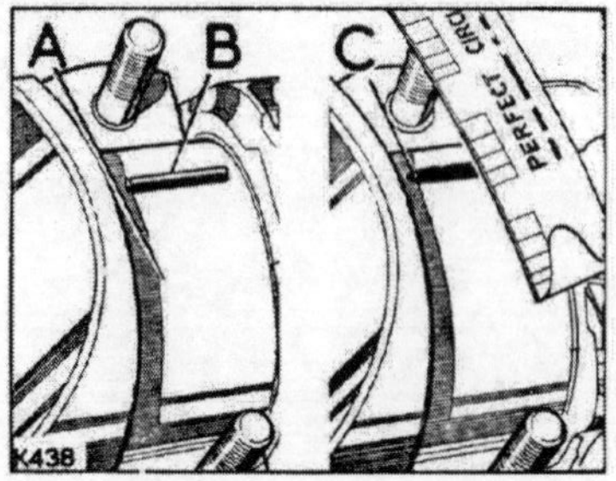

Fig. A2-135. Checking connecting rod and bearing clearance, using 'Plastigage'
A—Journal for connecting rod
B—Initial position of 'Plastigage'
C—Flattened 'Plastigage', do not remove until width has been measured against scale on packet

3. Make final check to prove the bearing clearance, using a .0025 in. (0,063 mm) shim paper. The connecting rod should resist rotation when the shim paper is fitted between the journal and one half of the bearing shell and move freely by hand with the shim paper removed.

Connecting rod end-float check

1. Check the connecting rod end-float using a feeler gauge inserted between the end face of the rod and the journal shoulder.

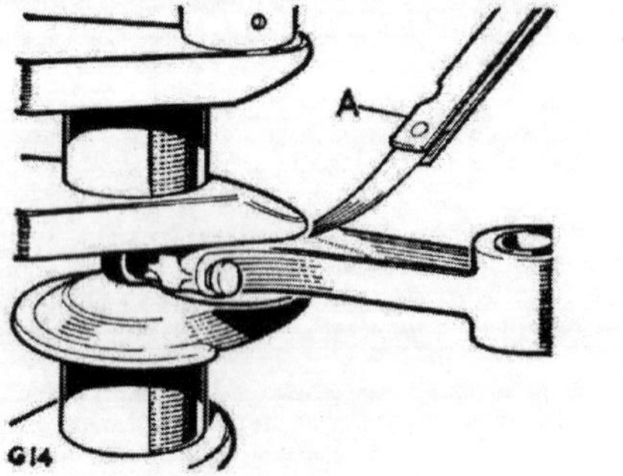

Fig. A2-136. End-float check
A—Feeler gauge B—Connecting rod
C—Journal shoulder

The end-float should be .007 in. to .011 in. (0,20 mm to 0,30 mm).

2. Remove the connecting rods from the crankshaft and retain all parts as related sets.

To assemble

1. Assemble the pistons to the respective connecting rods. Position the point of the 'V'-shaped recess in the piston crown toward the oil spray hole side of the connecting rod.

2. With the pistons warmed to approximately 55°C (132°F), fit the gudgeon pins and retaining circlips. Where the piston crowns are marked with an 'X', enter the gudgeon pin from the 'X' side.

3. Position the previously fitted piston rings so that the ring gaps are adjacent to the gudgeon pin bore on alternate sides of the piston and do not coincide.

ENGINE—2¼ LITRE DIESEL

Section A2—Land-Rover

Crankshaft and main bearings, remove and refit—Operation A2-35

Workshop hand tools:
Spanner sizes: 9/16 in. AF, 7/16 in. AF, 1/2 in. AF open end
7/16 in. AF, 1/2 in. AF, 9/16 in. AF, 5/8 in. AF, 13/16 in. AF socket
5/16 in. BSF, 3/8 in. BSF open end
3/8 in. BSF socket
1/2 in. AF, 9/16 in. AF ring
1 lb Hammer, Small chisel, Feeler gauges

Special tools:
Engine lifting sling, Part No. 600963
Guides for rear main bearing oil seal, Part No. 270304 (2 off)
Clutch plate alignment gauge, Part No. 605022
Torque wrench

To remove

1. Remove the bonnet panel. Operation A2-1.
2. Remove the air cleaner. Operation A2-2.
3. Remove the radiator and grille panel. Operation A2-3.
4. Remove the front floor. Operation A2-4.
5. Remove the engine from the vehicle. Operation A2-5.
6. Remove the engine front cover. Operation A2-25.
7. Remove the timing chain and tensioner. Operation A2-26.
8. Remove the crankcase sump. Operation A2-28.
9. Fit the engine to a suitable stand.
10. Remove the oil pump. Operation A2-29.
11. Remove the clutch and flywheel. Operation A2-31.
12. Remove the flywheel housing. Operation A2-32.
13. Remove the connecting rod caps and bearing lower halves and retain as related sets.

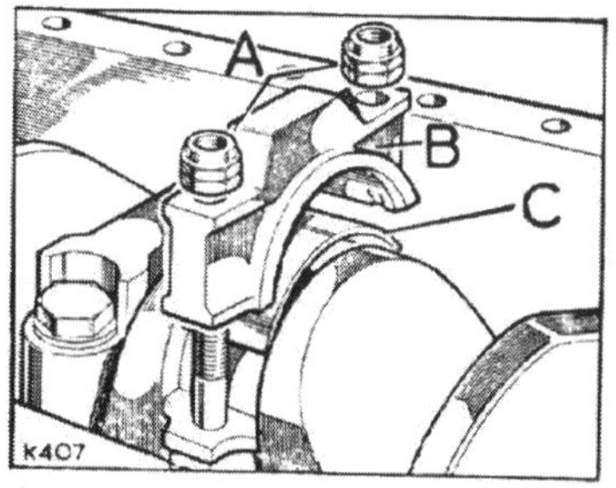

Fig. A2-137. Connecting rod big-end details
A—Fixings for connecting rod caps
B—Connecting rod caps
C—Connecting rod bearing lower half

14. Remove the main bearing caps and lift the crankshaft clear. Retain the bearing halves and caps in related sets.

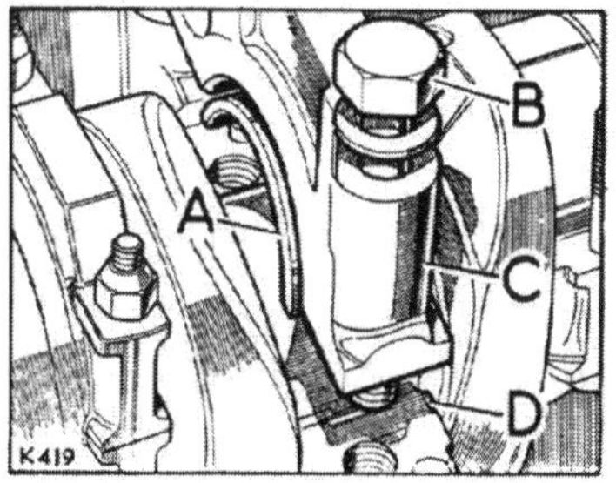

Fig. A2-138. Crankshaft main bearing caps
A—Bearing lower half
B—Fixings, bearing cap to cylinder block
C—Bearing cap
D—Thrust washer positioned each side of centre bearing upper half

15. Remove the oil seal from the crankshaft.
16. Remove the seal retainer halves, Fig. A2-139 refers.

To refit

1. Where replacement components are to be fitted, the relevant checks detailed in Operation A2-36 must be carried out.
2. Position the crankshaft bearing upper halves to the engine, locating the bearing tongues into the recesses provided.
3. Assemble the crankshaft to the engine and insert the thrust washers at each side of the centre bearing shell with unplated faces toward cylinder block. The thrust washer thicknesses must agree within .003 in. (0.07 mm).
4. Position the bearing lower halves on to the front and centre bearing caps and fit the caps. Do not fully tighten the fixings at this stage.

Operation A2-35—continued

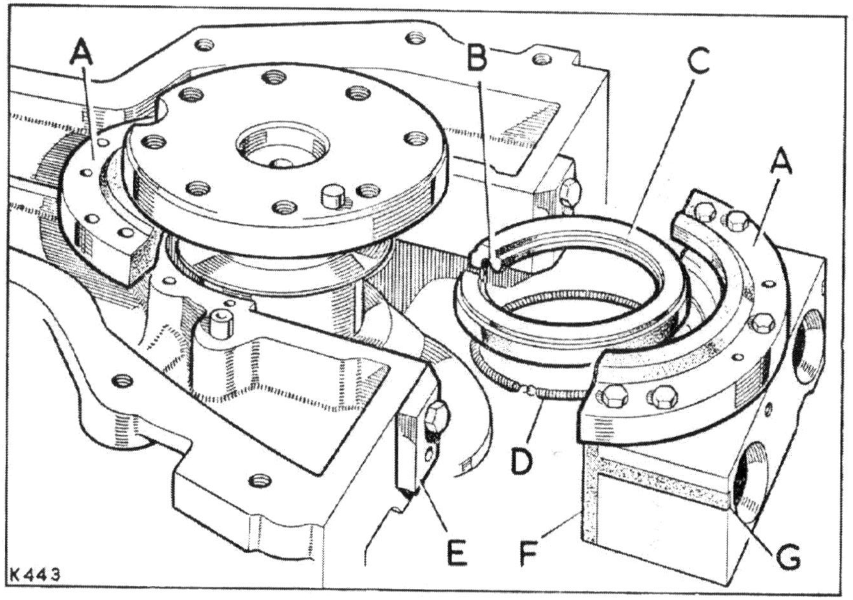

Fig. A2-139. Oil seal details

A—Retainer halves
B—Split line of seal to be toward top of engine when fitted
C—Split oil seal
D—Garter spring, hook and eye to be midway between split and hinge of oil seal when fitted
E—Guides, Part No. 270304, for rear main bearing cap "T" seals
F—Trim these edges before fitting to engine to prevent seals from folding
G—Trim these ends to allow 1/32 in. (0.8 mm) protrusion when cap is fitted to engine

5. With the crankshaft in the engine, assemble the garter spring on the oil seal journal of the crankshaft, by laying the spring around the journal, this will bring the two ends, the hook and the eye, adjacent to one another, then insert the hook into the eye. Care must be taken to ensure that during this operation the spring is not stretched at all. The spring should be moved along the journal until it is against the thrower flange.

6. Apply Silicone Grease MS4 to the crankshaft oil seal journal and to both sides of the split oil seal sealing lip.
   Open the split sufficiently to allow it to be fitted over the crankshaft oil seal journal. Recess in oil seal must be towards thrower flange and garter spring.
   The oil seal must not be repeatedly fitted and removed from the crankshaft, as this can damage the sealing lip.

ENGINE—2¼ LITRE DIESEL

Operation A2-35—continued

to the main bearing cap. The cap must be off the crankcase for these operations.

Trim the edges of the 'T' seals as shown to prevent them fouling the cylinder block when fitted.

10. Fit the main bearing cap with the seal retainer, bearing shell and 'T' seals to the crankcase, see Fig. A2-139, until there is a 1/32 in. (0,8 mm) gap between the cap and crankcase.

11. Ensure that the seal is located in the retainer recess.

12. Pull down the cap slowly, ensuring there is no buckling of the split seal or misalignment of the butt joint.

13. Tighten all the bearing cap fixings to a torque loading of 100 lb ft (13,8 mkg).

14. Refit the flywheel housing. Operation A2-32.

15. Refit the clutch and flywheel. Operation A2-31.

16. Refit the oil pump. Operation A2-29.

17. Remove the engine from the stand and refit the sump. Operation A2-28.

18. Refit the engine to the vehicle. Operation A2-5.

19. Carry out the valve timing procedure. Operation A2-27.

20. Refit the timing chain and tensioner. Operation A2-26.

21. Refit the engine front cover. Operation A2-25.

22. Refit the front floor. Operation A2-4.

23. Refit the radiator and grille panel. Operation A2-3.

24. Refit the air cleaner. Operation A2-2.

25. Refill engine coolant system.

COOLANT SYSTEM
Bonneted Control Model, 2¼ Litre Diesel

	Capacity	Imperial Unit	US Unit	Litres	Antifreeze	Frost Precaution
88	17½ pints	17½ pints	21 pints	10,0	33⅓%	−25°F / −32°C
109	17½ pints	17½ pints	21 pints	10,0	33⅓%	−25°F / −32°C

26. Replenish the engine lubricating oil.

ENGINE LUBRICANT CAPACITY
Bonneted Control Model, 2¼ Litre Diesel

		Capacity	Imperial Unit	US Unit	Litres
88	Engine		11 pints	13 pints	6,0
	Filter		1½ pints	1,8 pints	0,85
	Engine and Filter		12½ pints	14,8 pints	6,85
109	Engine		11 pints	13 pints	6,0
	Filter		1½ pints	1,8 pints	0,85
	Engine and Filter		12½ pints	14,8 pints	6,85

27. Refit the bonnet panel. Operation A2-1.

Operation A2-35—continued

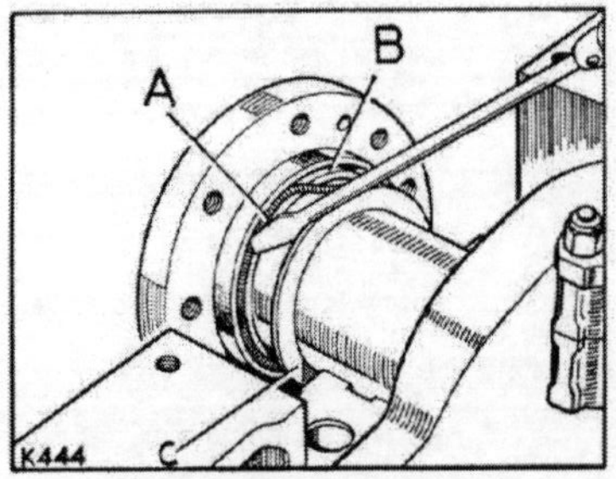

Fig. A2-140. Fitting garter spring

A—Garter spring
B—Oil seal recess for garter spring
C—Thrower flange

7. Rotate the oil seal until the split is on the vertical axis pointing towards the cylinder head and in its approximate running position on the journal; this position is important.

Apply Hylomar SQ32M sealing compound to the seal diameter of the two half plates, using either an applicator or a brush.

Important: Do not degrease the half seal plates with trichlorethylene, but wipe clean with a dry cloth prior to applying the Hylomar.

8. Fit one half of the oil seal retainer on to the crankcase dowels. The oil seal should be compressed to assist assembly, also ensure that it is correctly located in the retainer recess. Bolt the retainer to the crankcase, leaving the two bolts adjacent to the split line finger-tight, fully tighten the remaining three bolts. In order to fit the bolt it will be necessary to rotate the crankshaft; it is essential to hold the seal so that it does not rotate with the crankshaft.

9. Bolt the other half of the oil seal retainer on to the main bearing cap, in the same way. Apply Silicone grease MS4 to the 'T' seals and fit them

ENGINE—2¼ LITRE DIESEL

Crankshaft and main bearings, to check—Operation A2-36

(For removing and refitting details, Operation A2-35 refers)

Workshop hand tools:
Spanner sizes: ⁷⁄₁₆ in. AF open end
1¹⁄₁₆ in. AF socket
Screwdriver (medium), Screwdriver (small),
Feeler gauges

Special tools:
Torque wrench
Dial test indicator
'Plastigage' strip for use on checking bearing clearance, Part No. 605238

To overhaul

1. Inspect all components for damage and general condition.

2. Check for crankshaft journal ovality, or excessive scoring. Crankshafts may be reground in .010 in. (0,25 mm) stages to .040 in. (1,0 mm) undersize.

   Bearing sets in .010 in. (0,25 mm) stages are supplied by the Parts Department. These sets include crankshaft thrust washers and connecting rod bearings.

3. Extreme care must be taken when regrinding 2¼ litre Diesel crankshaft journals, to ensure that a .150 in. (3,8 mm) radius is maintained on the journal sides as shown in the illustration.

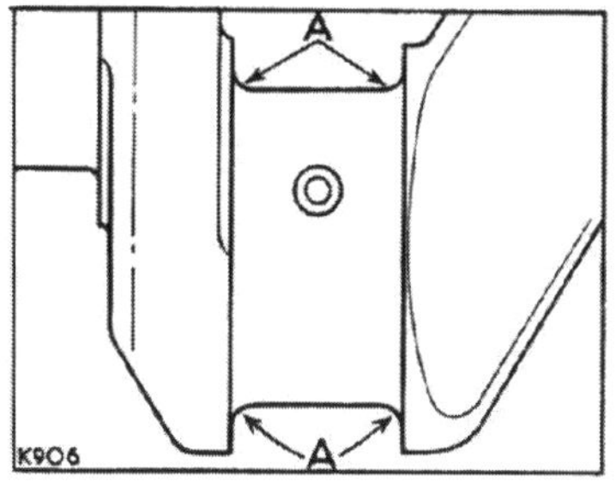

Fig. A2-141. Crankshaft journal radius
A—Maintain a radius of .150 in. (3,8 mm)

4. The crankshaft journals should be closely inspected for wear and damage and the crankpins checked for ovality.

5. Check for general condition of main bearing cap location dowels, dowel spigots and surrounding areas.

6. With the crankshaft removed, check the main bearings fit in the housings as follows:

   (a) Fit the front bearing cap, less the shell bearings, to the correct location.

   (b) Fit and tighten the cap fixings to a torque loading of 100 lb ft (13,8 mkg).

   (c) Slacken one fixing and check that there is no clearance between the cap and cylinder block faces. Clearance here indicates that the cap has been filed or damaged and it will be necessary to replace the complete cylinder block.

7. Check for clearance on the other side of the cap and block assembly, repeating the foregoing procedure.

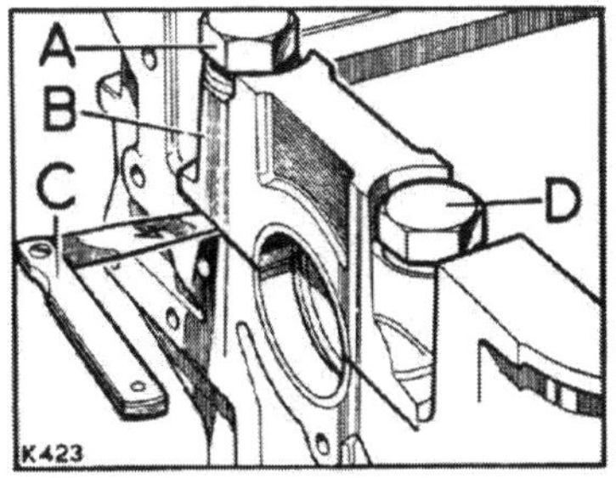

Fig. A2-142. Checking main bearing nip
A—Slackened fixing
B—Main bearing cap
C—Feeler gauge
D—Tightened fixing

8. When satisfactory, fit the main bearings and repeat the foregoing procedure. The clearance at the face should now be .004 in. to .006 in. (0,10 mm to 0,15 mm) and may be achieved by selective assembly of the bearing shells.

9. Repeat the procedure and check the remaining bearings and caps.

10. The running clearance between the bearings and the crankshaft journals should be .001 in. to .0020 in. (0,02 mm to 0,05 mm). An alternative method of checking the clearance is by using 'Plastigage' strip, available under Rover Part No. 605238, as illustrated.

11. When the bearing nip has been checked, remove the caps and bearing shell bottom halves. Position a standard size thrust bearing at each side of centre bearing shell—top halves—and fit the crankshaft. Fit the thrust washers with the unplated faces toward the cylinder block. Lubricate the crankshaft journals, using clean engine oil.

    The thrust washer thicknesses must agree within .003 in. (0,07 mm).

12. Mount a dial test indicator, then check and note the crankshaft end-float reading which should be .002 in. to .006 in. (0,05 mm to 0,15 mm).

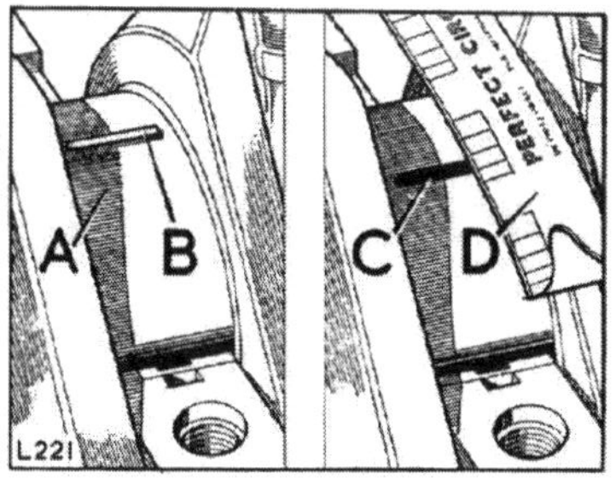

Fig. A2-143. Use of 'Plastigage' strip to measure bearing clearance
A—Main bearing journal
B—Initial position of 'Plastigage'
C—Flattened 'Plastigage', do not remove until measured against scale
D—Graduated scale on 'Plastigage' packet

If the crankshaft end-float reading obtained is not within the limits, fit suitable thrust washers from the range available. The variation of thrust washer thickness at each side must not exceed .003 in. (0,08 mm) to ensure that the crankshaft remains centralised.

13. When satisfactory, check the crankshaft for freedom of rotation. Fitting a .0025 in. (0,06 mm) feeler paper between a main bearing and the journal should cause resistance to rotation; the crankshaft should be free to rotate by hand with the feeler paper removed.

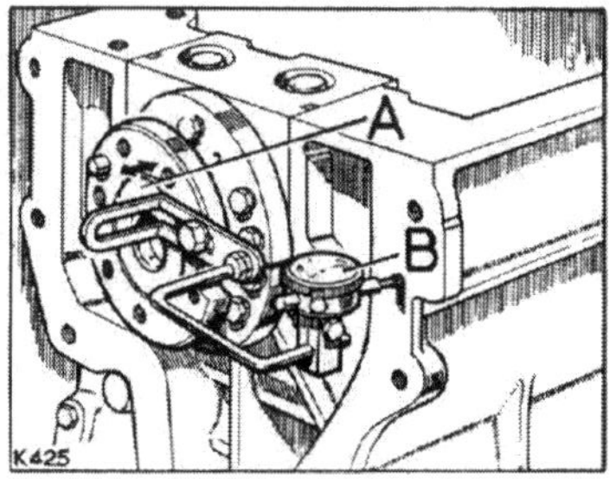

Fig. A2-144. Checking crankshaft end-float
A—Lever crankshaft fully forward, then fully to rear, to check total end-float
B—Dial test indicator

ENGINE—2¼ LITRE DIESEL   Section A2—Land-Rover   Section A2—Land-Rover   ENGINE—2¼ LITRE DIESEL

*Camshaft, remove and refit—Operation A2-37

(For camshaft bearing overhaul information, Operation A2-38 refers)

Operation A2-37—continued

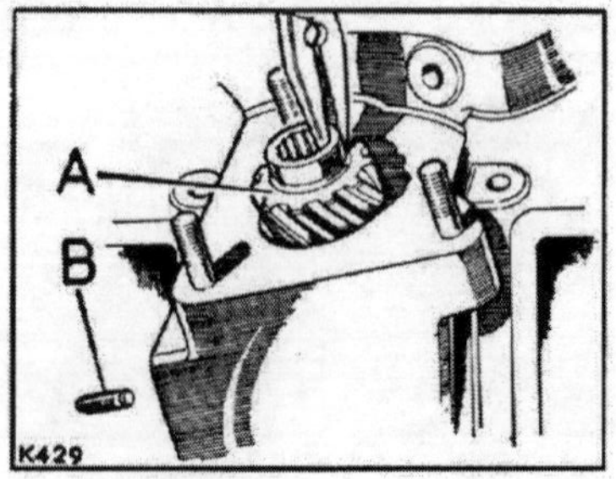

Workshop hand tools:
Spanner sizes: ½ in. x ⁷⁄₁₆ in. AF (2 off), ⅜ in. AF open end
½ in. AF, ⅝ in. AF, ¾ in. AF socket
⁷⁄₁₆ in. AF ring
¼ in. BSF, ⅜ in. BSF open end

Screwdriver (medium), Screwdriver (small), Pliers (long nosed), Feeler gauges

Special tools:
Extractor for camshaft chainwheel, Part No. 507231
Extractor, Part No. 530101
Torque wrench

To remove

1. Remove bonnet panel. Operation A2-1.
2. Remove the air cleaner. Operation A2-2.
3. Remove the radiator and grille panel. Operation A2-3.
4. Remove the external oil filter. Operation A2-16.
5. Remove the fuel distributor pump. Operation A2-17.
6. Remove the distributor pump drive gears. Operation A2-18.
7. Remove the valve gear and rocker shaft. Operation A2-20.
8. Remove the cylinder head. Operation A2-22.
9. Remove the engine front cover. Operation A2-25.
10. Remove the timing chain tensioner. Operation A2-26.
11. Remove tappet locating bolts at RH side of engine block. Do not remove tappet guide at this stage.

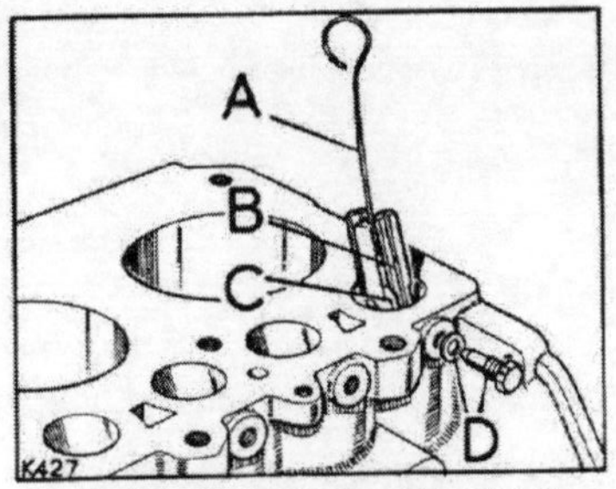

Fig. A2-145. Removing tappets and rollers
A—Spring clip
B—Tappet slide
C—Tappet roller
D—Tappet guide locating bolts

12. Remove the tappet slides and withdraw the tappet rollers, using a locally made spring clip. On early type only the tappet rollers are withdrawn complete with the tappet slides.
13. Remove the tappet guides. The use of special tool, Part No. 530101 as illustrated, will facilitate this procedure if the guides are difficult to remove by hand.

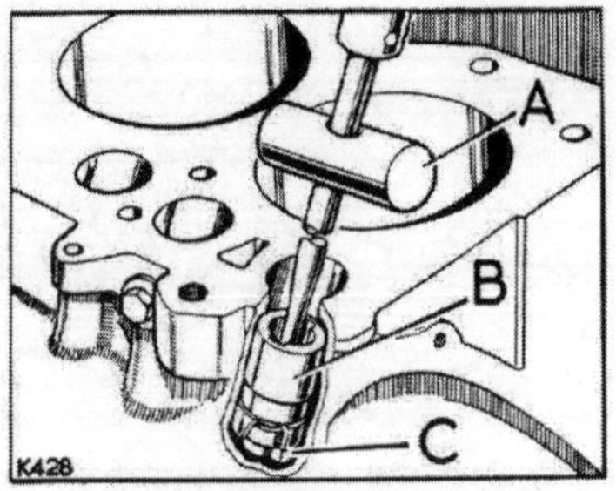

Fig. A2-146. Removing tappet guides
A—Special tool, Part No. 530101
B—Tappet guide
C—Extractor adaptor, part of special tool, Part No. 530101

14. Withdraw the distributor drive shaft then remove the locating grub screw and withdraw the vertical drive shaft gear.
15. Withdraw the timing chain and remove the camshaft chainwheel.
16. Remove the thrust plate and withdraw the camshaft, using special tool, Part No. 530101 or a slave bolt.
17. Camshaft bearing removing, refitting and overhaul details are included in 'Cylinder block overhaul, Operation A2-38' as a reaming procedure is required with the engine removed.

Fig. A2-147. Removing the vertical drive shaft gear
A—Vertical drive shaft gear
B—Locating grub screw in external oil filter joint face

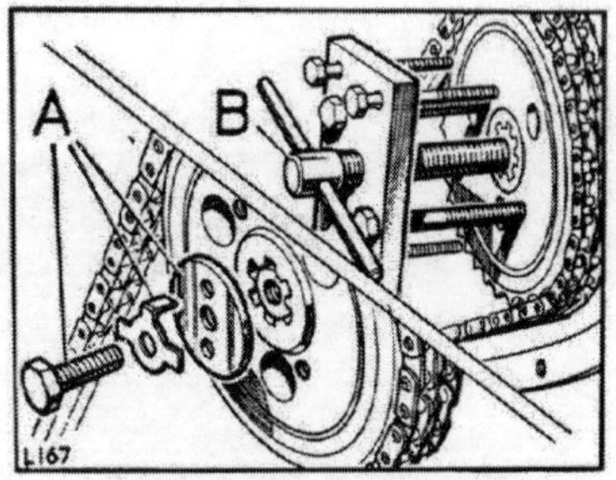

Fig. A2-148. Camshaft chainwheel
A—Fixings, chainwheel to camshaft.
B—Use of special extractor, Part No. 507231, facilitates chainwheel removal

To refit

1. Insert the camshaft, keyed end to front of engine, and fit the thrust plate. Do not lock the fixings at this stage.

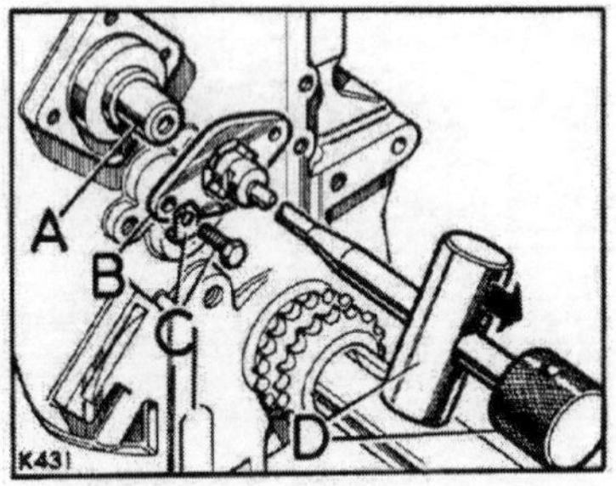

Fig. A2-149. Removing the camshaft
A—Camshaft
B—Thrust plate
C—Fixings, thrust plate to cylinder block
D—Special tool, Part No. 530101, in position

2. Fit the chainwheel to the camshaft and check the camshaft end-float which must be .0025 in. to .0055 in. (0,06 mm to 0,13 mm). Refer to Fig. A2-149. Remove the chainwheel, lock the thrust plate fixings, Fig. A2-149 refers, and refit the chainwheel.

The end-float is adjusted by thrust plate selection.

3. When satisfactory, remove the chainwheel, lock the thrust plate fixings, Fig. A2-149 refers, and refit the chainwheel.
4. Refit the tappet assemblies, referring to Fig. A2-145 and Fig. A2-146.
5. Refit the cylinder head. Operation A2-22.
6. Refit the valve gear and rocker shaft. Operation A2-20.
7. Carry out the valve timing procedure. Operation A2-27.
8. Refit the timing chain tensioner. Operation A2-26.

Operations marked with an asterisk (*) can be carried out with the engine installed in the vehicle

ENGINE—2¼ LITRE DIESEL

Operation A2-37—continued

9. Refit the engine front cover. Operation A2-25.
10. Refit the fuel distributor pump drive gears. Operation A2-17.
11. Refit the fuel distributor pump and carry out the distributor timing procedure. Operation A2-16.
12. Refit the external oil filter. Operation A2-3.
13. Refit the radiator and grille panel. Operation A2-3.
14. Refit the air cleaner. Operation A2-2.
15. Replenish the engine lubricating oil.

ENGINE LUBRICANT CAPACITY
Bonneted Control Model, 2¼ Litre Diesel

	Capacity	Imperial Unit	US Unit	Litres
88	Engine	11 pints	13 pints	6.0
	Filter	1½ pints	1.8 pints	0.85
	Engine and Filter	12½ pints	14.8 pints	6.85
109	Engine	11 pints	13 pints	6.0
	Filter	1½ pints	1.8 pints	0.85
	Engine and Filter	12½ pints	14.8 pints	6.85

16. Refill the engine coolant system.

COOLANT SYSTEM
Bonneted Control Model, 2¼ Litre Diesel

	Capacity	Imperial Unit	US Unit	Litres	Antifreeze	Frost Precaution
88	17½ pints	17½ pints	21 pints	10.0	33⅓%	−25°F / −32°C
109	17½ pints	17½ pints	21 pints	10.0	33⅓%	−25°F / −32°C

17. Refit the bonnet panel. Operation A2-1.

Fig. A2-150. Camshaft end-float check

Cylinder block and camshaft bearings, overhaul—Operation A2-38

Workshop hand tools:
Spanner sizes: ¼ in. x ₇⁄₁₆ in. AF (2 off), ½ in. AF, ₇⁄₁₆ in. AF, ⅝ in. AF, ⅞ in. AF, ⁹⁄₁₆ in. AF open end
₇⁄₁₆ in. AF, ½ in. AF, ⁹⁄₁₆ in. AF socket
⅜ in. AF, ½ in. AF, ⁹⁄₁₆ in. AF, ₁₃⁄₁₆ in. BSF
₇⁄₁₆ in. BSF, ½ in. BSF, ⅝ in. BSF open end
₇⁄₁₆ in. BSF socket
Screwdriver (medium), Screwdriver (small), Pliers (long nosed), Feeler gauges, 1 lb Hammer, Chisel (small)

Special tools:
Camshaft bearing overhaul tools:
Guide plug, Part No. 274394
Reamer for bearings, Part No. 274389

Method 'A' (see text)
Bearing drift, Part No. 274388
Guide tube for front bearings, Part No. 274385
Bearing fitting bar, Part No. 274382
Spacer, Part No. 274383
Spigot, Part No. 274384
Guide tool for rear bearings, Part No. 274386
Adaptor, Part No. 531760

Method 'B' (see text)
Bearing drift, Part No. 274388
Adaptor, Part No. 531760
or
Bearing drift and adaptor complete, Part No. 605975

To remove

Carry out the engine removal and dismantling work previously detailed as necessary until only the camshaft bearings remain in the cylinder block.

Camshaft bearings, to replace

Note: When new camshaft bearings are to be fitted, the front and front intermediate bearings must be removed and new ones fitted **before** removing the rear bearings.

Two methods of replacing the bearings are detailed. Use Method 'A' if the full range of special tools is held; Method 'B' uses a simplified tooling procedure.

Method 'A', to replace bearings

1. Unscrew the 3½ in. (88 mm) long stud from the joint face at front of cylinder block and remove the bearing cover at rear of cylinder block.

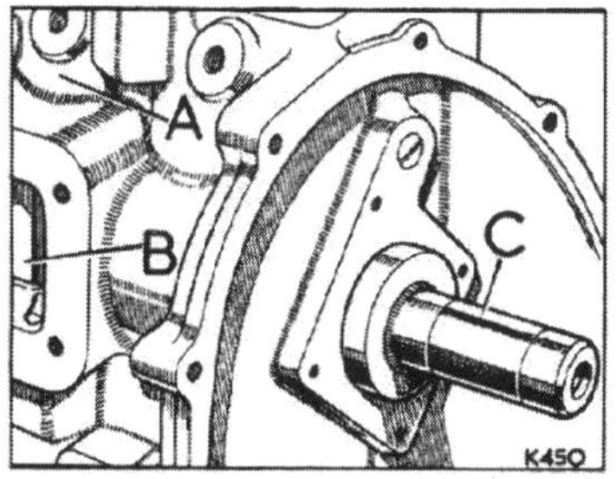

Fig. A2-151. Driving out the front bearings
A—Cylinder block
B—Front tappet chamber
C—Special tool, Part No. 274388

2. Drive out the front and front intermediate bearings, using the special tool, Part No. 274388.
3. Withdraw the front bearing from the vacant front side cover aperture. Collapse the front intermediate bearing and withdraw from the distributor drive chamber.
4. Fit new front and front intermediate bearings, **before** removing the rear bearings with drift.
5. Fit a guide tool, Part No. 274385, into the two old rearmost bearings with the part of flange marked 'TOP' uppermost, then insert end cover set bolts loosely for location purposes. Position a new front bearing on to the handle end of bearing fitting bar, Part No. 274382, and locate by means of the peg and semi-circular cut-out, then slide a spacer, Part No. 274383, on to the fitting bar and engage the locating shoulder.

Note: The front bearing is wider and has an extra oil passage drilling.

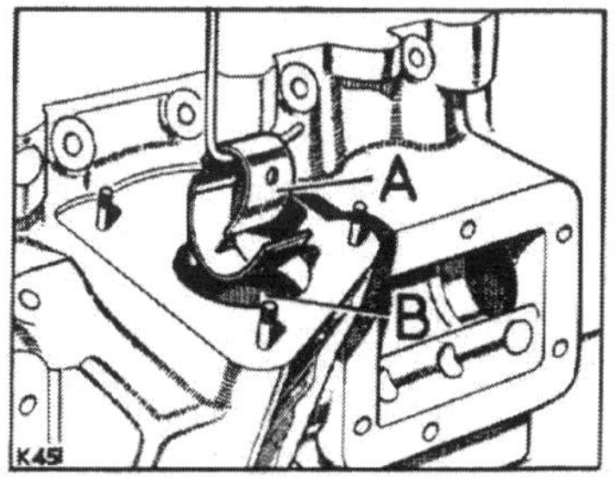

Fig. A2-152. Front intermediate bearing removal
A—Collapsed bearing
B—Distributor drive chamber

ENGINE—2¼ LITRE DIESEL

Operation A2-38—continued

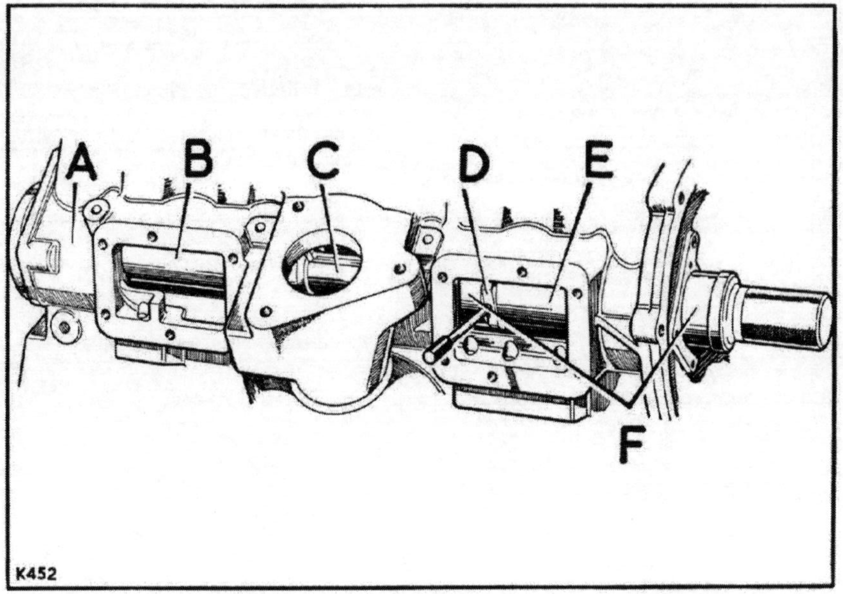

Fig. A2·153. Fitting camshaft front bearings

A—Cylinder block
B—Guide tube
C—Bearing fitting bar
D—Spigot
E—Spacer
F—New bearings

6. Place a new bearing on spigot, Part No. 274384, and position it inside the foremost tappet chamber with the bearing nearest the front intermediate housing.

7. Insert the bearing fitting bar and feed the spigot on to the bearing housing and withdraw the spigot handle. Turn the spigot to engage the locating shoulder in the spacer, then press the fitting bar inward, turning as necessary to engage the bar slot with the peg in guide tube.

8. When the fitting bar has been pressed in as far as possible by hand, ensure that all locating points are properly engaged, then drive the bearings into position with a hide-faced hammer.

9. The bearings must now be aligned with the oil holes, proceed as follows:

Partially withdraw bearing fitting bar and remove spigot, Part No. 274384. Slide adaptor, Part No. 531760, on to bar and re-insert bar and drive in until flange of bar abuts on cylinder block. This will align the oil holes on the intermediate bearing.

Withdraw bar and adaptor and remove spacer, then refit adaptor, Part No. 531760, and align front bearing oil holes by gently tapping tool as required.

10. Remove the bearing fitting tools and check the oil holes for alignment.

11. Remove the two rearmost bearings and fit new camshaft rear bearings in the same manner as for front bearings, but remove the spacer from fitting bar and use guide tool, Part No. 274386, instead of the guide tube used when fitting front bearings.

Operation A2-38—continued

Method 'B', to replace bearings

1. Using special tool, Part No. 274388, or Part No. 605975 (less the adaptor), drift out all the bearings. The two centre bearings can be drifted into the distributor drive chamber and collapsed to enable withdrawal. Note that the two centre and the rear bearings are the same width, whereas the front bearing is wider and has an additional oil feed hole.

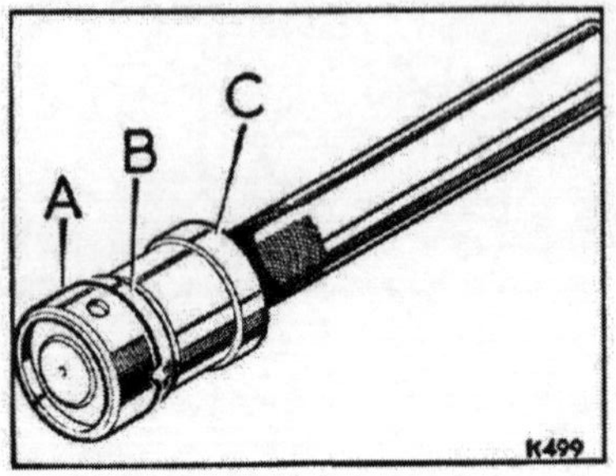

Fig. A2·154. Replacing camshaft bearings

A—Camshaft bearing
B—Adaptor
C—Drift

2. To fit the new bearings, the drift, Part No. 274388, and special adaptor, Part No. 531760, or the drift and adaptor complete, Part No. 605975, are required. Proceed as follows:

(a) With the cylinder block vertical, rear face down, place a new shell bearing into the front camshaft chamber and position it so that it is above the second bearing housing, counting from the front of the block. The chamfer on the bearing edge must be towards the housing bore, and the oil hole in the bearing must be aligned with the innermost oil feed drilling in the housing bore. Accuracy is essential otherwise misalignment of the oil holes may result and once the bearing is in place it cannot be rotated to correct any error. Pencil marks on the bearing outer diameter and the cylinder block adjacent to the housing will assist in checking alignment.

(b) Having visually aligned the bearing, carefully place inside it the special adaptor, Part No. 531760, or Part No. 605975.

(c) Maintain the bearing in a level position. Pass the drift, through the front bearing housing into the camshaft chamber so that it rests on top of the adaptor. Commence drifting the bearing into the block. Ensure that the bearing is not drifted in too far, so that the oil feed holes are correctly aligned.

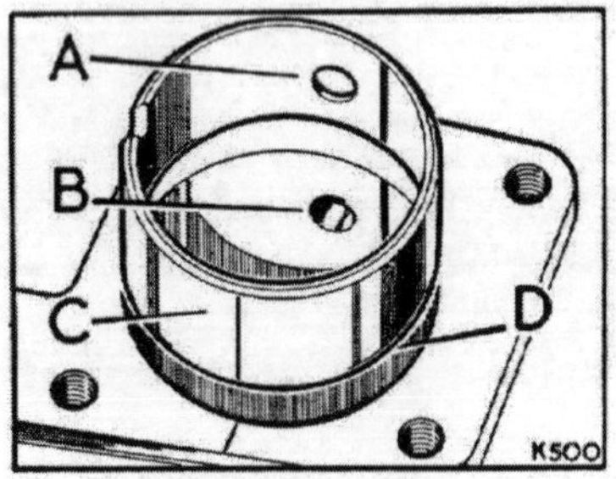

Fig. A2·155. Aligning oil holes

A—Oil hole in bearing
B—Oil feed hole in block
C—Pencil marks
D—Chamfer on leading edge

3. Repeat the operation for the front bearing. Note that the front bearing is wider and has a small hole in addition to the large oil feed hole. This small hole aligns with a vertical drilling in the block, which in turn feeds a horizontal drilling for the tappet mechanism. Drift this bearing in so that the outer edge is just below the machined surface of the front face. This is to ensure that when the camshaft thrust plate is fitted it will not stand proud on the bearing edge.

4. Turn over the cylinder block so that the rear face is uppermost, and drift in the two remaining narrow bearings in the manner described in para. 2.

5. Retain the cylinder block in the vertical position, front face downwards, in readiness for the reaming operation.

Operation A2-38—continued

Reamering the bearings

1. Locate a guide plug, Part No. 274394, in the new front camshaft bearing and locate, using the endplate screws. Do not tighten these screws until the reamer, Part No. 274389, is put into position and the guide collar immediately in front of the cutter is entered into the rearmost bearing, which is first to be cut. This precaution is to ensure correct alignment of the reamer. Before commencing the reamering operation it is necessary to turn the engine block to a vertical position, front end facing downwards, in order that the weight of the reamer will assist in the cutting operation. As each bearing is cut the reamer should be held steady by the operator whilst an assistant, using a high pressure airline, blows away the white metal cuttings, before allowing the reamer to enter the next bearing.

2. After the rearmost and the two intermediate bearings have been cut, remove the guide plug, Part No. 274394, before cutting the foremost bearing. Remove the reamer handle and bolt, and carefully remove the reamer, turning it in the same direction as for cutting. Care must be taken to prevent the reamer damaging the foremost bearing as the reamer is removed.

No lubricant is necessary for the reamering operation, best results are obtained when the bearings are cut dry.

3. Remove the plugs from the ends of oil gallery passage and clean the gallery and oil feed passages to camshaft and crankshaft bearings, using compressed air. Refit the plugs and lock in position. **The cylinder block must be thoroughly cleaned at this stage.**

Cylinder bores

1. The bores may be reclaimed by machining up to .040 in. (1,0 mm) maximum oversize, replacement pistons being available in oversize increments of .010 in., .020 in., .030 in. and .040 in. (0,25 mm, 0,5 mm, 0,76 mm and 1,0 mm).

2. Where the maximum permitted boring tolerance is not sufficient to reclaim the bores, cylinder liners may be fitted.

Fitting the cylinder liners conforms to normal practice. Machine the cylinder block bores to 3.7175 in. +.0005 in. (94,4245 mm + 0,0127 mm). This will provide the liner with a .003 in. to .0045 in. (0,067 mm. to 0,0114 mm) interference fit.

3. Press the liners into the cylinder block. The liners must not be proud of, or more than .002 in. (0,05 mm) below, the top face of the cylinder block. Cylinder liners should then be bored out to standard size, that is, 3.562 in. (90,47 mm) minimum. Liners may be re-bored .010 in. (0,254 mm) oversize.

Before reassembly, deglaze the cylinder bores using suitable honing equipment and finally using fine grade abrasive cloth.

When the overhaul is completed, rebuild the engine as follows:

1. Refit the camshaft. Operation A2-37.
2. Refit the crankshaft. Operation A2-35.
3. Refit the pistons and connecting rods. Operation A2-33.
4. Refit the flywheel housing. Operation A2-32.
5. Refit the clutch assembly and flywheel. Operation A2-31.
6. Refit the oil pump. Operation A2-29.
7. Refit the crankcase sump. Operation A2-28.
8. Refit the tappet assemblies. Operation A2-24.
9. Refit the cylinder head. Operation A2-22.
10. Refit the valve gear and rocker shaft. Operation A2-20.
11. Next refit the timing gears and chain and carry out the valve timing procedure. Operation A2-27.
12. Refit the timing chain tensioner. Operation A2-26.
13. Refit the engine front cover. Operation A2-25.
14. Refit the fuel distributor pump drive gears. Operation A2-18.
15. Next refit the fuel distributor pump and carry out the pump timing procedure. Operation A2-17.
16. Refit the external oil filter. Operation A2-16.
17. Refit the engine side covers. Operation A2-14.
18. Refit the starter motor. Operation A2-9.
19. Refit the engine to the vehicle. Operation A2-5 and replenish the lubricating oil.

ENGINE LUBRICANT CAPACITY
Bonneted Control Model, 2¼ Litre Diesel

		Capacity	Imperial Unit	US Unit	Litres
88	Engine		11 pints	13 pints	6,0
	Filter		1¼ pints	1,8 pints	0,85
	Engine and Filter		12¼ pints	14.8 pints	6,85
109	Engine		11 pints	13 pints	6,0
	Filter		1¼ pints	1,8 pints	0,85
	Engine and Filter		12¼ pints	14.8 pints	6,85

20. Refit the front floor. Operation A2-4.
21. Refit the radiator and grille panel. Operation A2-3 and refill the coolant system.

COOLANT SYSTEM
Bonneted Control Model, 2¼ Litre Diesel

	Capacity	Imperial Unit	US Unit	Litres	Antifreeze	Frost Precaution
88		17½ pints	21 pints	10,0	33⅓%	−25°F / −32°C
109		17½ pints	21 pints	10,0	33⅓%	−25°F / −32°C

22. Refit the air cleaner. Operation A2-2.
23. Refit the bonnet panel. Operation A2-1.

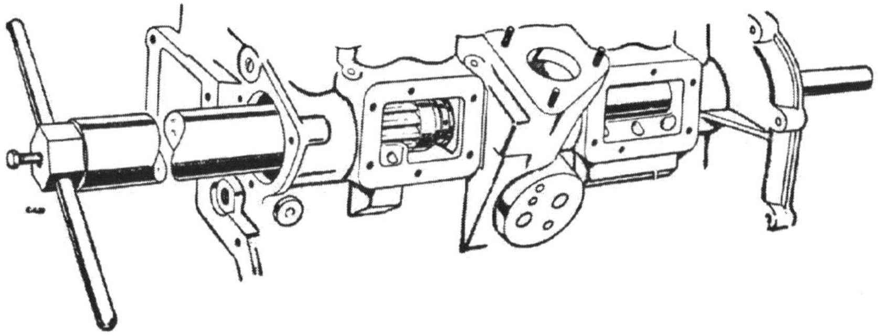

Fig. A2-156. Reamering camshaft bearings (Engine must be in vertical position)

Reclamation of flywheel and starter ring—Operation A2-39

(For Flywheel remove and refit instructions, Operation A2-31 refers)

Wear or scoring on the flywheel pressure face

1. Remove the clutch bolts and dowels from the flywheel.
2. Check the thickness of the flywheel before commencing machining, as it may have been machined previously.

   The maximum amount of metal which may be removed from the flywheel face is .030 in. (0,76 mm). If the face is not satisfactory after machining to these limits, the flywheel must be scrapped. See following chart.
3. Machine the **whole** pressure face, not merely inside the bolts and dowels, until the score marks are removed.

Starter ring excessively worn or damaged

If the starter ring is bolted to the flywheel proceed as follows:

1. Remove the clutch bolts, dowels and primary pinion bush.
2. Machine the flywheel teeth off flush and turn the gear ring spigot to the dimensions given in the following chart.
3. Fit the ring gear to the flywheel, using the original clutch cover fixing bolts. (These bolts should be a tight fit in the flywheel, and must be replaced if in poor condition).
4. Replace the dowel and renew the primary pinion bush if necessary.

If the starter ring is shrunk on to the flywheel, proceed as follows:

1. Remove the scrap starter ring by securing the flywheel in a vice fitted with jaw protectors, then drill a $\frac{3}{16}$ in. (4 mm) diameter hole axially between the root of any one tooth and the inner diameter of the starter ring sufficiently deep to weaken the ring. Care must be taken to prevent the drill entering the flywheel.
2. Place a chisel immediately above the drilled hole, and strike it sharply.

   Important: The starter ring will normally split harmlessly but on remote occasions rings have been known to fly asunder when split; it is therefore important that the operator should take suitable precautions. For instance, a cloth may be laid over the upper part of the starter ring.
3. Heat the starter ring uniformly to between 220°C and 225°C but do not exceed the higher temperature.

A
L405

Fig. A2-157. Removing an unserviceable starter ring

A—Drilled hole

Operation A2-39—*continued*

4. With the flywheel placed on a suitably flat surface, position the ring on to the flywheel with the square edge of the teeth against the flange.

   There should be a clearance of $\frac{1}{16}$ in. to $\frac{1}{8}$ in. (1,5 mm to 3 mm) between the inner diameter of ring and flywheel if the temperature is correct. Press the starter ring firmly against the flange until the ring contracts sufficiently to grip the flywheel.
5. Allow the flywheel assembly to cool gradually; do not hasten cooling in any way and thereby avoid the setting up of internal stresses in the ring which may cause fracture or failure in some respect.

B
D
A
C
L406

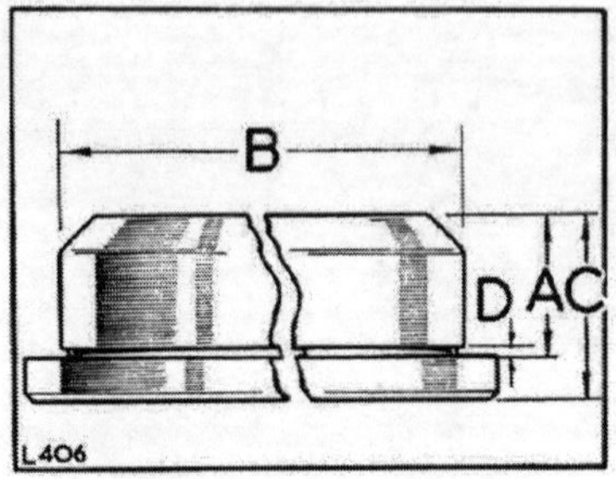

Fig. A2-158. Flywheel reconditioning

A—Depth of spigot
B—Spigot diameter
C—Minimum thickness after refacing
D—Undercut

Models	Flywheel Part Number	Ring Gear Part No.	Dimension 'A' Depth of Spigot	Dimension 'B' Spigot Diameter	Dimension 'C' Minimum thickness after refacing	Dimension 'D' Undercut	Flywheel Part Number when re-conditioned	Remarks
Series IIA 2¼ litre Diesel models (Two dowel hole type)	516082 (Can be replaced by 546519)	510489	.750 in. (19,0 mm)	9.562 in. (242,9 mm)	1.454 in. (36,9 mm)	.062 in. x .031 in. (1,60 x 0,80 mm) deep	524638 (Can be replaced by 549544)	Steel flywheel. Machine from crankshaft flange side
Series IIA 2¼ litre Diesel models (Four dowel hole type)	546519 (Will replace 516082)	510489	.750 in. (19,0 mm)	9.562 in. (242,9 mm)	1.454 in. (36,9 mm)	.062 in. x .031 in. (1,60 x 0,80 mm) deep	549544 (Will replace 524638)	Steel flywheel. Machine from crankshaft flange side. When fitting this flywheel with a diaphragmspringtype clutch it is necessary to remove one dowel and fit two dowels in the same way as detailed for Petrol models.
Series IIA 2¼ litre Diesel models (Multi-purpose, two and four dowel accommodation)	566852 (Will replace 516082 and 546519	568431	—	—	1.454 in. (36,9 mm)	—	Non-available	Cast-iron flywheel. Detachable ring gear fitted as original equipment. No machining necessary other than for refacing.

ENGINE—2¼ LITRE DIESEL

Fault diagnosis—Engine, 2¼ litre Diesel

Symptom	Possible cause	Investigation	Remedy
A—Engine fails to rotate when attempting to start	Incorrect starting procedure	Follow procedure as described in Owner's Instruction Manual	
	Battery leads loose or terminals corroded	Check for condition of leads and terminals	Clean and tighten as necessary
	Battery discharged	Check as detailed in Section N	
	Starter motor inoperative	Check for loose or dirty connections and for soundness of leads	Clean and tighten at terminals. Replace leads as necessary
		Check starter motor for malfunction, Section N	
B—Engine rotates but fails to start	Starter motor speed too low	Check battery leads at terminals	Clean and tighten as necessary
		Check state of batteries charge. Section N	When refitting a recharged or replacement battery, check the voltage regulator output setting, Section N. Check also the fan belt tension
	Heater plug operation faulty	Check electrical leads to and between heater plugs. If leads sound and connections good, refer to Section N for heater plugs defects location	
		Check that fuel is reaching injectors, Section L	
	Fuel system defects	Check condition and setting of injector nozzles, Section L	
	Insufficient compression in cylinders	Check tappet clearances	Reset as necessary
		Check tighten the injector fixings and heater plugs in case of external leakage	Tighten to the correct torque loading
		Rotate engine, using starting handle, and check for valves sticking open and for defective valve springs	Carry out the cylinder head overhaul procedure
		Check tighten cylinder head fixings to the correct torque loading	Tighten in the correct sequence
		Remove cylinder head and check cylinder head gasket, valve seats, valve springs, pistons and piston rings for wear	Rectify or replace as necessary
C—Engine starts but immediately stops	Fuel system defect	Check for fuel starvation as described in Section L	
D—Engine fails to idle	Fuel system defects	Check setting of slow-running control screw	Reset as necessary
		Check injector nozzle setting. Check injector nozzle auxiliary spray hole for blockage	Refer to Section L
	Incorrect tappet clearance	Check and reset as necessary	
	Insufficient compression in cylinders	Check and remedy as described in paragraph B	

Fault diagnosis—Engine—2¼ litre Diesel—continued

Symptom	Possible cause	Investigation	Remedy
E—Reduced power and rough running	Faulty valve operation	Check tappet clearances	Reset
		Remove top cover and check for defective valve springs	Replace in pairs
		Check valves for signs of overheating	Replace as necessary
	Fuel system defects	Check for fuel starvation at injector nozzles as described in Section L	
		Check injector nozzle valve seating is correct. Ensure sealing washers are in place and sound	Rectify or replace as necessary
		Check injector nozzles for signs of overheating	Refer to Section L
		Check tighten injectors to correct torque loading	Tighten as necessary
		Check fuel injector pump timing	Reset as necessary
	Compression uneven	Check and remedy as listed under 'Insufficient compression in cylinders', paragraph B	
F—Engine overheating	Defective cooling system	Refer to 'Fault diagnosis', Section K	
	Defective lubrication system	Check and remedy as described under 'Low oil pressure', paragraph G	
	Fuel system defects	Check for restricted fuel supply to fuel injectors	Refer to Section L
		Check for defective fuel Injector nozzles	Refer to Section L
		Check for incorrect fuel injector pump timing	Reset as necessary
G—Low oil pressure	Insufficient oil supply	Check at engine dipstick	Replenish sump with correct grade lubricating oil, Section X refers
	External leakage	Check engine for oil leaks. Ensure oil pressure switch joint washer is sound	Rectify as necessary
	Oil pump operation faulty	Check the oil pump intake filter for restriction	Remove foreign matter if necessary. Clean filter in clean fuel
		Check for wear in pump gears assembly	Carry out the oil pump overhaul procedure
	Oil pressure relief valve malfunction	Check for foreign matter on ball valve seat	Clean and refit
		Relief valve plunger sticking	Clean and ensure smooth operation before refitting
		Check that oil pump body joint fixings are tight	Tighten fixings
		Relief valve spring weak. Check by substitution of serviceable spring	Replace spring

Fault diagnosis—Engine—2¼ litre Diesel—continued

Symptom	Possible cause	Investigation	Remedy
G—Low oil pressure—cont.	Excessively worn bearings	Check bearing clearances at main journals, connecting rod big ends and camshaft as necessary	Replace bearings, referring to the appropriate overhaul procedure
H—Oil pressure warning light remains 'ON', with engine running	Low oil pressure	Refer to paragraph G for checks and remedy	
	Oil pressure switch unserviceable	Check by substitution of serviceable component	Replace switch
	Electrical fault	Check circuit	Rectify poor connections or replace leads as applicable
J—Warning light fails to glow with engine stopped and ignition switch 'ON'		Check warning lamp bulb by substitution of serviceable bulb	Replace bulb
		Check oil pressure switch by substitution of a serviceable switch	Replace switch
		Check electrical circuit	Rectify poor connections or replace leads as applicable
K—Noisy valve mechanism	Valve operation incorrect	Check for excessive tappet clearances	Reset
		Rotate engine and check for sticking valves and broken or defective valve springs. Check for excessively worn components	Carry out cylinder head overhaul procedure. Replace valve springs
L—Main bearing rattle	Low oil pressure	Refer to paragraph G for checks and remedy	
	Component or assembly defects	Check if main bearing cap fixings are loose	Tighten to correct torque loading
		Check bearing clearance. Examine bearings and crankshaft for wear	Carry out the overhaul procedure
M—Black smoke issues from exhaust	Fuel system defects	Check for defective fuel injection nozzles as described in Section L	Reset injectors (Section L) or replace as necessary
		Check for incorrect fuel injector pump timing	Reset timing
N—White vapour issues from exhaust	Internal coolant leakage	Check for coolant leakage into combustion chamber. Do not confuse with vapour apparent immediately after starting, caused by condensation in exhaust system	Rectify as necessary
	Fuel system defects	Check as described in Para. M	
	Insufficient compression in cylinders	Check as described in Para. B	

Fault diagnosis—Engine—2¼ litre Diesel—continued

Symptom	Possible cause	Investigation	Remedy
P—Blue smoke issues from exhaust	Engine burning oil	Check for blocked or overfilled air cleaner	Rectify as necessary
		Check tappet clearances	Reset as necessary
		Run engine with exhaust manifold removed. Smoke from individual cylinders may indicate a faulty injector	Refer to Section L
		Check for incorrect pump timing. Check that pump drive gear locating screw is not worn or loose	Reset or rectify as necessary
		Check cylinder compression pressures	Carry out the overhaul procedures on cylinder head and piston rings as necessary

ENGINE 2¼ LITRE DIESEL

GENERAL DATA

Capacity (piston displacement)	2286 cc (139.5 cu. in.)
Number of cylinders	4
Bore	3.562 in. (90,49 mm)
Stroke	3.5 in. (88,9 mm)
Compression ratio	23 to 1
BHP	62 at 4,000 rpm
BMEP	111 lb. sq. in. (7,8 kg/cm²) at 1,750 rpm
Maximum torque	103 lb. ft. (14,00 mkg) at 1,750 rpm
Firing order	1—3—4—2
Piston speed at 4,000 rpm	2,333 ft./min.

DETAIL DATA

Camshaft
Journal diameter	1.842 in.—.001 in. (46,8 mm—0,02 mm)
Clearance in bearing	.001 in. to .002 in. (0,02 mm to 0,05 mm)
End-float	.0025 in to .0055 in. (0,06 mm to 0,13 mm)
Cam lift—inlet	.262 in. (6,65 mm)
Cam lift—exhaust	.279 in. (7,10 mm)

Camshaft bearing
Type	Split—steel backed, white metal lined
Internal diameter (line reamed in position)	1.843 in.+.0005 in. (46,81 mm+0,012 mm)

Connecting rods
Bearing fit on crankpin	.001 in. to .0025 in. (0,02 mm to 0,06 mm) clearance
Bearing nip	.002 in. to .004 in. (0,05 mm to 0,10 mm)
End-float at big-end	.007 in. to .011 in. (0,20 mm to 0,30 mm)
Gudgeon pin bush fit in small end	.002 in. to .004 in. (0,05 mm to 0,10 mm) interference
Gudgeon pin bush internal diameter—reamed in position	1.1875 in.+.0005 in. (30,15 mm+0,012 mm)
Fit of gudgeon pin in bush	.0002 in. to .0008 in. (0,005 mm to 0,02 mm) clearance

Crankshaft
Journal diameter	2.5 in.—.001 in. (63,5 mm—0,02 mm)
Crankpin diameter	2.313 in.—.001 in. (51,6 mm—0,02 mm)
End-float (controlled by thrust washers at centre bearings	.002 in. to .006 in. (0,05 mm to 0,15 mm)

Regrind sizes:

Undersize	Journal dia.	Crankpin dia.
.010 in. (0,25 mm)	2.490 in. (63,24 mm)	2.303 in. (58,49 mm)
.020 in. (0,50 mm)	2.480 in. (62,99 mm)	2.293 in. (58,24 mm)
.030 in. (0,76 mm)	2.470 in. (62,73 mm)	2.283 in. (57,98 mm)
.040 in. (1,01 mm)	2.460 in. (62,48 mm)	2.273 in. (57,73 mm)

Flywheel
Number of teeth	100
Thickness	1.484 in. (38 mm)
Maximum permissible run-out on flywheel face	.002 in. (0,05 mm)
Maximum refacing depth	.030 in. (0,76 mm)
Minimum thickness after grinding	1.454 in. (36,9 mm)

Markings
TDC	When opposite pointer, No. 1 piston is at top dead centre
EP	When opposite pointer, No. 1 exhaust valve should be fully open
16° mark (up to engine suffix K)	
15° mark (from engine suffix L)	When opposite pointer, with both valves on No. 1 cylinder closed, indicates start of injection

ENGINE 2¼ LITRE DIESEL—continued

DETAIL DATA—continued

Primary pinion bush:
Fit in flywheel	.001 in. to .003 in. (0,02 mm to 0,07 mm) interference
Internal diameter—reamed in position	.878 in.+.0005 in. (22,3 mm+0,013 mm)
Fit of shaft in bush	.001 in. to .0035 in. (0,02 mm to 0,08 mm) clearance

Gudgeon pin
Fit in piston	Zero to .0002 in. (0,005 mm) interference
Fit in connecting rod bush	.0002 in. to .0008 in. (0,005 mm to 0,02 mm) clearance

Injection pump
Type	Distributor, self-governing
Injection takes place	16° (engines up to suffix K)
Injection takes place	15° (engines from suffix 'L' onwards)
Injector Type	CAV Pintaux
Nozzle size	BDNO/SP6209

Main bearings
Clearance on crankshaft journal	.001 in. to .002 in. (0,02 mm to 0,05 mm)
Bearing nip	.004 in. to .006 in. (0,10 mm to 0,15 mm)

Oil pump
Type	Skew gear
Drive	Splined shaft from camshaft skew gear
End float of gears:	
Steel gear	.002 in. to .005 in. (0,05 mm to 0,13 mm)
Aluminium gear	.003 in. to .006 in. (0,07 mm to 0,15 mm)
Radial clearance of gears	.001 in. to .004 in. (0,02 mm to 0,010 mm)
Backlash of gears	.006 in. to .012 in. (0,15 mm to 0,30 mm)

Oil pressure, engine warm
At 2,000 rpm	45 to 65 lb sq in. (3,16 to 4,56 kg/cm²)

Oil pressure relief valve
Type	Non-adjustable
Relief valve spring	
Free length	2.670 in. (67,82 mm)
Compressed length at 5.7 lb (2,58 kg) load	2.45 in. (61,23 mm)

Pistons
Type	Light alloy, with swirl-inducing recess in crown
Clearance in bore, measured at bottom of skirt at right angles to gudgeon pin	.004 in. to .005 in. (0,10 mm to 0,12 mm)
Fit of gudgeon pin in piston	Zero to .0002 in. (0,005 mm) interference
Gudgeon pin bore	1.187 in.+.0005 in. (30,14 mm+0,012 mm)

Piston rings

Compression No. 1
Type	Square friction edge—chromium plated
Gap in bore	.014 in. to .019 in. (0,40 mm to 0,50 mm)
Clearance in groove	.0025 in. to .0045 in. (0,06 mm to 0,114 mm)

Compression—Nos. 2 and 3
Type	Bevelled friction edge. Marked 'T' on upper side
Gap in bore	.010 in. to .015 in. (0,25 mm to 0,40 mm)
Clearance in groove	.0025 in. to .0045 in. (0,06 mm to 0,114 mm)

Scraper No. 4
Early type, one piece	Slotted, square friction edge, double landed
Gap in bore	.010 in. to .015 in. (0,25 mm to 0,40 mm)
Clearance in groove	.0025 in. to .0045 in. (0,06 mm to 0,114 mm)

ENGINE 2¼ LITRE DIESEL

DETAIL DATA—continued

Scraper No. 4
Later type, three piece .. .. .. Expander and rails
Gap in bore .. .. .015 in. to .045 in. (0,38 mm to 1,14 mm)
Clearance in groove .. .. .. .0015 in. to .0025 in. (0,038 mm to 0,064 mm)

Push-rod tubes
Fit in cylinder head .. .. .. .0005 in. to .002 in. (0,01 mm to 0,05 mm) interference on large diameter.
Full contact fit at chamfered edges of tube and cylinder head

Rocker gear
Bush internal diameter (reamed in position) .. .530 in.+.001 in. (13,4 mm+0,02 mm)
Shaft clearance in rocker bush .. .. .0005 in. to .0025 in. (0,0127 mm to 0,062 mm)
Tappet clearance .. .. .010 in. (0,25 mm) hot or cold

Timing chain tensioner
Fit of bush in cylinder .. .. .. .003 in. to .005 in. (0,07 mm to 0,12 mm) interference
Fit of bush in idler wheel .. .. .. .001 in. to .003 in. (0,02 mm to 0,07 mm) clearance
Fit of idler wheel on stub shaft .. .. .001 in. to .003 in. (0,02 mm to 0,07 mm) clearance
Fit of piston in cylinder bush .. .. .0003 in. to .0015 in. (0,008 mm to 0,038 mm) clearance

Thrust bearings, crankshaft
Type .. .. Semi-circular, steel back, tin plated on friction surface
Standard size, total thickness .. .. .093 in.—.002 in.; .005 in. (2,36 mm—0,05 mm)
Oversizes .. .. .0025 in. (0,06 mm); .005 in. (0,12 mm); .0075 in. (0,18 mm); .010 in. (0,25 mm)

Valves
Inlet valve
 Diameter (stem) .. .. .3112 in.—.0005 in. (7,90 mm—0,013 mm)
 Face angle .. .. 45°—¼°
Exhaust valve
 Diameter (stem) .. .. .3415 in.—.0005 in. (8,67 mm—0,013 mm)
 Face angle .. .. 45°—¼°
Fit of inlet valves in guides .. .. .. .0013 in. to .003 in. (0,033 mm to 0,07 mm) clearance
Fit of exhaust valves in guides .. .. .0023 in. to .0038 in. (0,058 mm to 0,096 mm) clearance
Valve seat
 Seat angle (inlet and exhaust) .. .. 45°+¼°

Valve springs
Early type:
 Inner
  Length—free .. .. 1.61 in. (40,9 mm)
  Length under 12 lb (5,44 kgs) load .. 1.454 in. (36,9 mm)
 Outer
  Length—free .. .. 1.768 in. (44,9 mm)
  Length under 33 lb (14,96 kgs) load .. 1.579 in. (40,1 mm)
Later type:
 Inner
  Length—free .. .. 1.680 in. (42,67 mm)
  Length under 18 lb (8,0 kgs) load .. 1.466 in. (37,23 mm)
 Outer
  Length—free .. .. 1.822 in. (46,28 mm)
  Length under 47 lb (20,9 kgs) load .. 1.587 in. (40,3 mm)

ENGINE 2¼ LITRE DIESEL

DETAIL DATA—continued

Valve timing
Inlet opens .. .. 16° BTDC
Inlet closes .. .. 42° ABDC
Inlet peak .. .. 103° ATDC
Exhaust opens .. .. 51° BBDC
Exhaust closes .. .. 13° ATDC
Exhaust peak .. .. 109° BTDC

Vertical drive shaft gear
Backlash .. .. .006 in. to .010 in. (0,15 mm to 0,25 mm)
Internal diameter of bush .. .. 1.00 in.+.001 in. (25,4 mm+0,02 mm)
Fit of gear in bush .. .. .. .001 in. to .003 in. (0,02 mm to 0,07 mm) clearance

Vibration damper (early models)
Fit of bushes in flywheel and back plate .. .002 in. to .004 in. (0,05 mm to 0,10 mm)
Internal diameter of bushes (reamed in position) 1.917 in.+.001 in. (48,7 mm+0,02 mm)
Fit of bushes on driving flange .. .. .001 in. to .003 in. (0,02 mm to 0,07 mm) clearance
Maximum permissible run-out of flywheel .. .002 in. (0,05 mm)

SECTION A3—2.6 LITRE PETROL ENGINE

INDEX

Note: A comprehensive detailed index is included at the end of this manual

Description of Listed Operations	Remove/Refit	Overhaul
Bonnet panel	A3-1	—
Air cleaner—remove, clean and refit	A3-2	—
Radiator and grille panel assembly	A3-3	—
Gearbox tunnel and front panel	A3-4	—
Engine	A3-5	—
Carburetter	A3-6	Section L
Oil pressure switch	A3-7	Section N
Exhaust manifold	A3-8	—
Starter motor	A3-9	—
Dynamo or alternator	A3-10	Section N
Water pump	A3-11	Section N
Thermostat	A3-12	Section K
Rocker oil feed pipe	A3-13	Section K
Engine breather box	A3-14	—
External oil filter, replace element	A3-15	—
External oil filter	A3-16	—
Ignition timing procedure	A3-17	—
Distributor	A3-18	Section N
Tappet adjustment	A3-19	—
Top rockers and shafts	A3-20	—
Cylinder head	A3-21	A3-22
Engine front cover and oil seal	A3-23	—
Timing chain tensioner	A3-24	—
Timing gears and chain, including valve timing procedure	A3-25	—
Side rockers and shafts	A3-26	—
Crankcase sump and oil strainer	A3-27	A3-29
Oil pump and drive shaft	A3-28	Section B
Clutch assembly and flywheel	A3-30	—
Rear main bearing oil seal and flywheel housing	A3-31	—
Pistons and connecting rods	A3-32	A3-33
Crankshaft and main bearings	A3-34	A3-35
Camshaft and bearings	A3-36	—
Cylinder block	—	A3-37
Reclamation of flywheel	A3-30	A3-38

This Section concerns remove, refit and overhaul procedures for the 2.6 litre petrol engine.

When carrying out a complete engine overhaul, the section can be worked straight through in the order presented. Alternatively, the individual operations which form the greater part of maintenance work undertaken by Distributors and Dealers and which are detailed under the appropriate headings will be found to be complete in themselves.

Some operations are marked with an asterisk (*) to indicate that they can be carried out with the engine installed. In all other cases it is necessary to remove the engine unit in order to carry out the work detailed.

Where LH (left-hand) or RH (right-hand) appears in the text this indicates LH or RH side of vehicle or engine when viewed from the rear.

Brief description of engine

The engine is a six-cylinder unit with the block cast integrally with the crankcase, having a bore of 3.063 in. (77,8 mm), a stroke of 3.625 in. (92,075 mm) and a capacity of 160.3 cu. in. (2,625 cc).

An aluminium alloy cylinder head which is inclined on the cylinder block gives high-efficiency combustion chambers. Overhead inlet and inclined side exhaust valves are fitted, and the pistons are of inverted 'V' shape on the crown to conform to the special combustion chamber shape.

The camshaft is driven by a double roller chain which has a hydraulically operated tensioner. The seven-bearing crankshaft is fitted with a torsional vibration damper.

Lubrication is by a large capacity oil pump which delivers oil under pressure throughout the engine and a full-flow oil filter is fitted.

Full engine data is to be found in the Detail Data provided at the end of this Section.

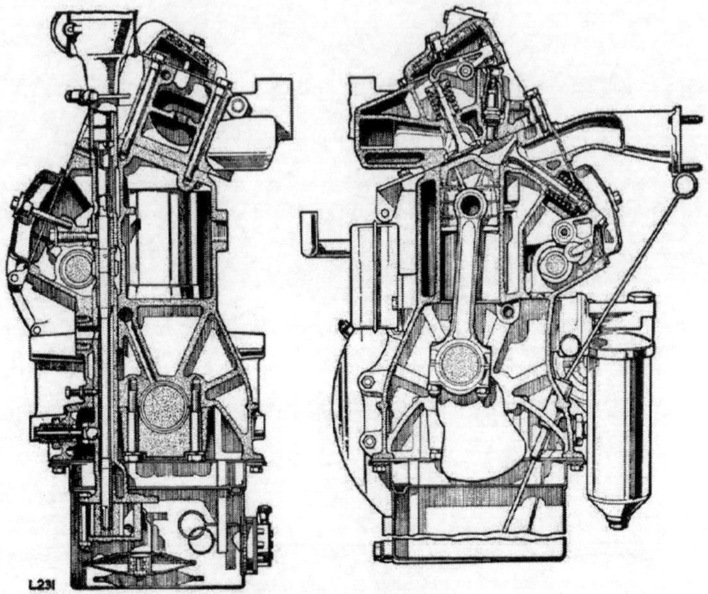

ENGINE—2.6 LITRE PETROL

Cross-section view of engine

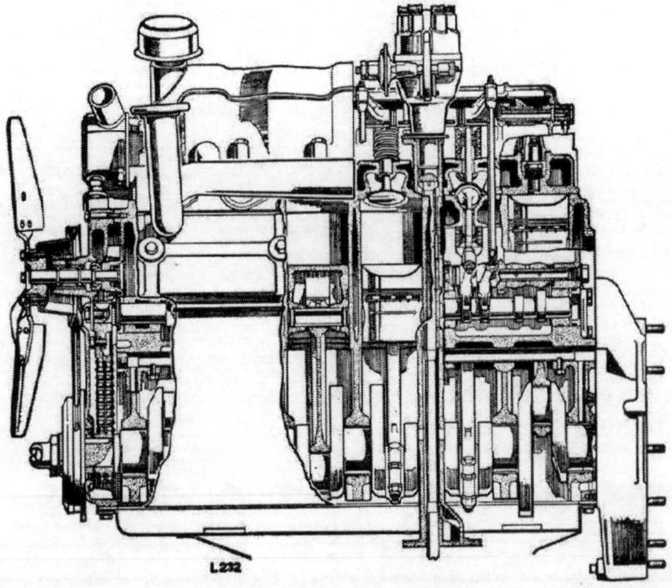

Longitudinal section of engine

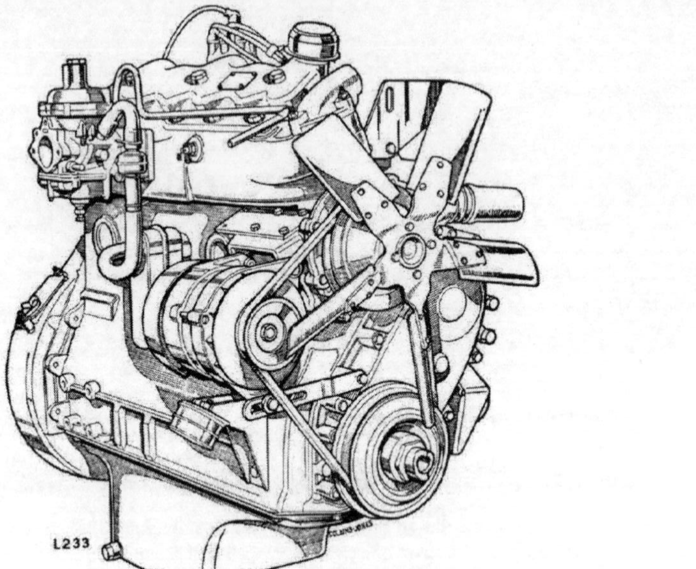

General view of engine, RH side

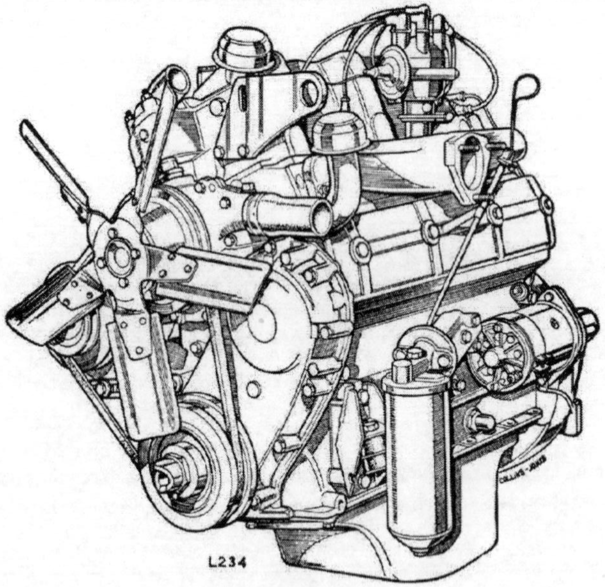

General view of engine, LH side

ENGINE—2.6 LITRE PETROL

*Bonnet panel, remove and refit—Operation A3-1

Workshop hand tools:
Screwdriver (medium), Pliers

To remove

1. Remove the spare wheel from the bonnet panel, if fitted.
2. Remove fixings at prop rod and bonnet hinge.
3. Remove bonnet panel.

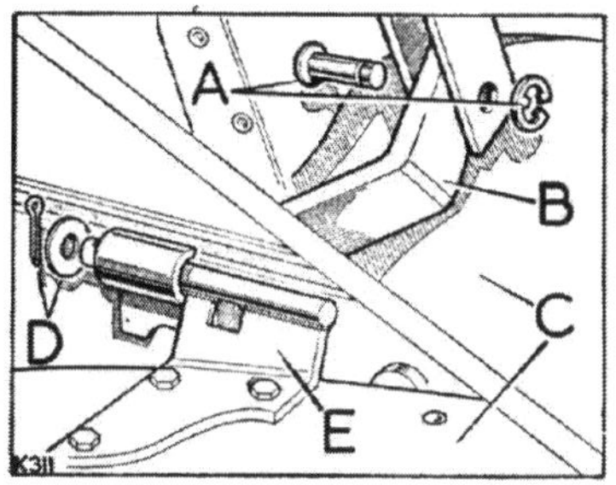

To refit

1. Refit the bonnet panel, using suitable coverings on the wings to avoid damage to paintwork.
2. Refit the spare wheel, if fitted, to bonnet panel.

Fig. A3-1. Fixings at bonnet panel

A—Prop rod fixings
B—Bonnet prop rod
C—Bonnet panel
D—Bonnet hinge fixings, RH side only
E—Bonnet hinge

*Air cleaner, remove, clean and refit—Operation A3-2

Workshop hand tools:
Spanner sizes: $\frac{7}{16}$ in. AF open ended
Screwdriver (medium)

To remove

1. Lift and prop bonnet.
2. Remove air intake hose from carburetter inlet.
3. Slacken the fixings and move aside the retaining strap.
4. Remove air cleaner complete with hose.

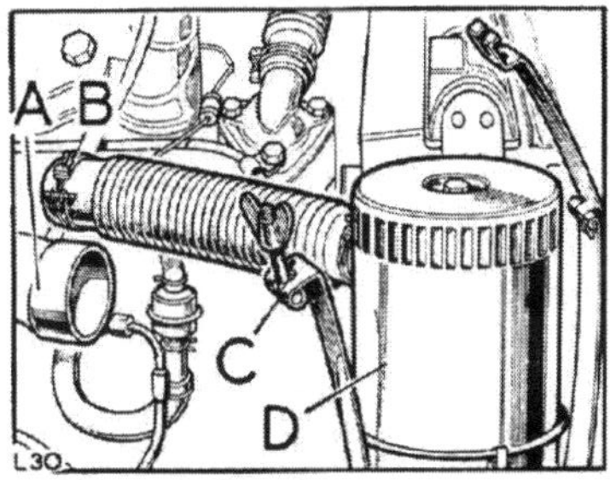

Fig. A3-2. Air cleaner and hose fixings

A—Carburetter inlet
B—Hose fixings
C—Retaining strap fixings
D—Air cleaner

To dismantle and clean

1. Separate the air cleaner body assembly from the oil container, retained by clips.
2. Drain the oil and withdraw the wire mesh unit.
3. Wash all components in clean fuel.

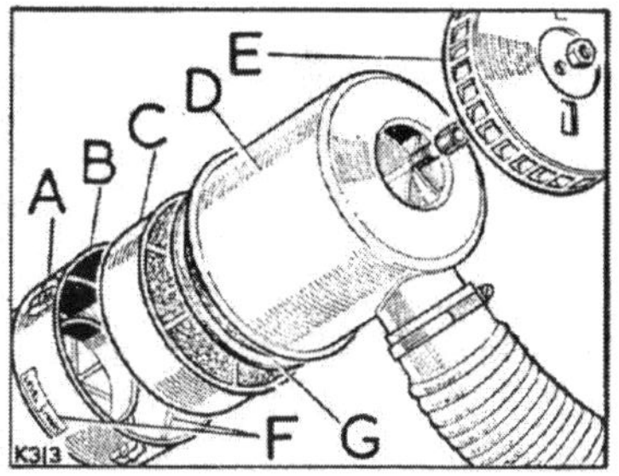

Fig. A3-3. Exploded view of air cleaner

A—Hinged clips
B—Oil container
C—Wire mesh unit
D—Air cleaner and mesh assembly
E—Air intake cap and fixing
F—Oil level mark
G—Sealing washer

To assemble

1. Fill the oil container with clean engine oil to the oil level mark on the container. See Fig. A3-3.
2. Reverse the dismantling procedure, fitting a new sealing washer between the oil container and the air cleaner body.

To refit

1. Refit air cleaner and hose, if necessary reposition the air cleaner body relative to the oil container to prevent the hinged clips from fouling on the retaining strap supports when fitted.

Operations marked with an asterisk (*) can be carried out with the engine installed in the vehicle

ENGINE—2.6 LITRE PETROL Section A3—Land-Rover

*Radiator and grille panel assembly, remove and refit—Operation A3-3

Workshop hand tools:

Spanner sizes: $\frac{7}{16}$ in. x $\frac{1}{2}$ in. AF open ended, 2 off, 2 BA open ended
Screwdriver (medium), Pliers

To remove

1. Remove bonnet. Operation A3-1.
2. Disconnect battery leads.
3. Remove front apron panel.

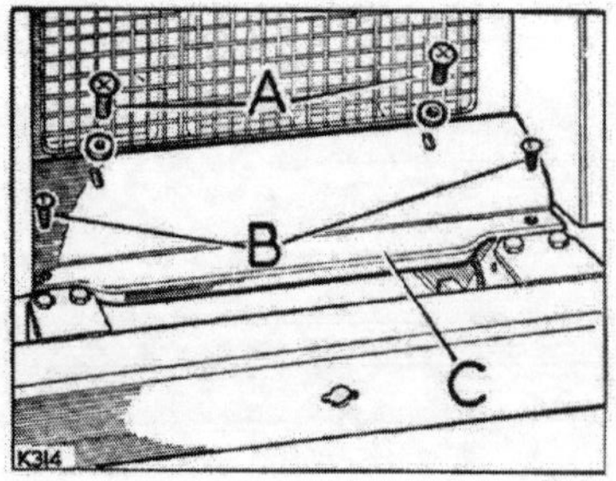

Fig. A3-4. Apron panel fixings

A—Fixings at cross member brackets
B—Fixings at side members
C—Apron panel

4. Remove nameplate and radiator grille.

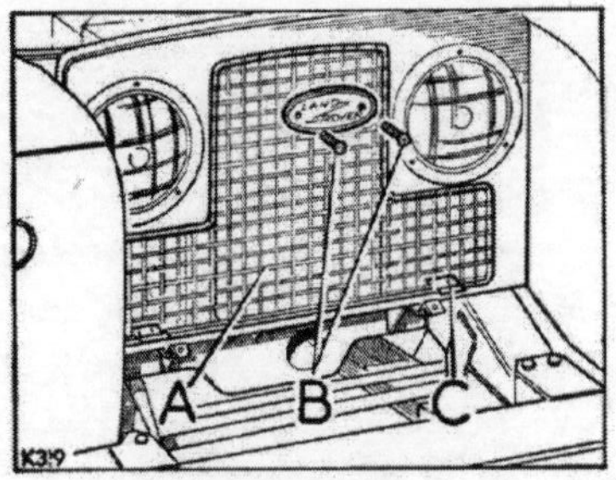

Fig. A3-5. Radiator grille fixings

A—Radiator grille
B—Fixings for nameplate and grille
C—Support brackets

5. Remove radiator cap, drain off coolant.

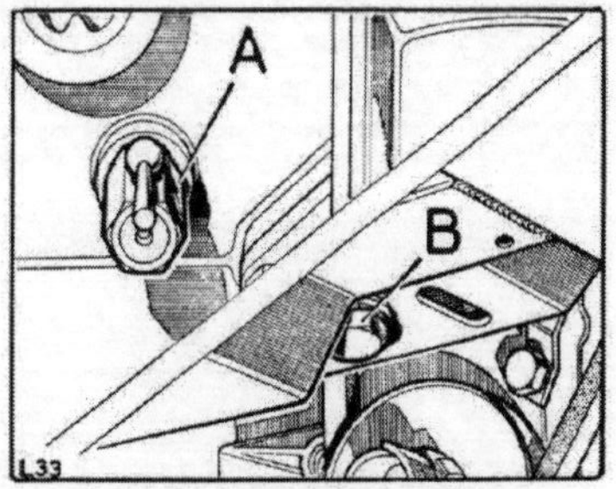

Fig. A3-6. Coolant drain taps location

A—At engine block, RH side
B—At radiator

6. Remove shroud from radiator fan cowl.

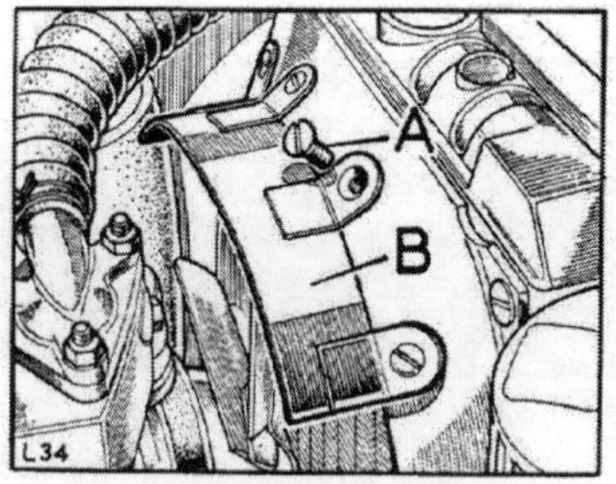

Fig. A3-7. Fan shroud fixings

A—Fixings for fan shroud
B—Fan shroud

7. Slacken fixings and detach radiator coolant hoses.
8. Remove the fan blades fixings and lower the fan blades to rest on lower part of fan cowl. Remove the fan blades when access is obtained during grille panel removal.

Operations marked with an asterisk (*) can be carried out with the engine installed in the vehicle

---

ENGINE—2.6 LITRE PETROL Section A3—Land-Rover

Operation A3-3—continued

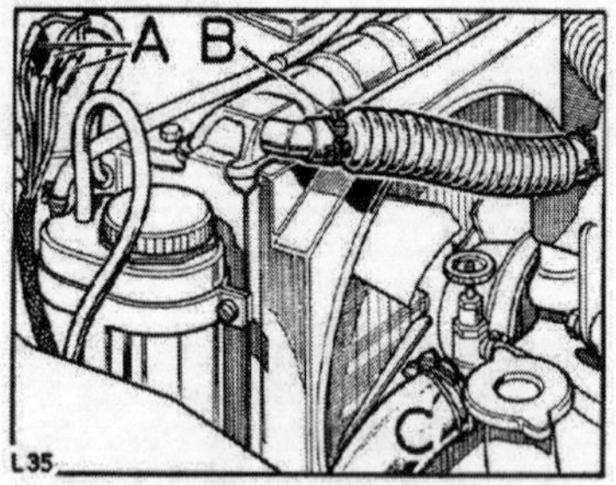

Fig. A3-8. Coolant hose and leads connectors

A—Snap connectors (3 off each side of vehicle)
B—Fixings at top hose
C—Fixings at bottom hose

9. Disconnect the electrical leads for the front lamps at the snap connectors.
10. Remove the grille panel to front wings fixings, the securing nuts and washers are located in the respective wheelarches.
11. Remove the grille panel fixings at the brackets on the chassis cross member.

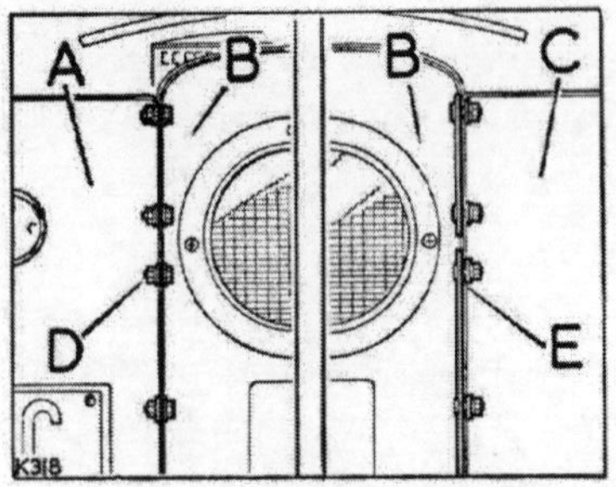

Fig. A3-9. Radiator grille panel fixings

A—Front wing, RH side
B—Radiator grille panel
C—Front wing, LH side
D—Fixings at wheelarch, RH
E—Fixings at wheelarch, LH

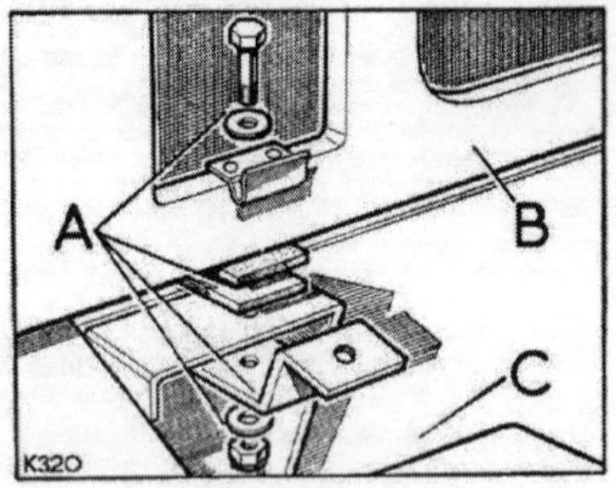

Fig. A3-10. Fixings at chassis cross member

A—Panel fixings
B—Radiator grille panel
C—Chassis cross member

12. Carefully withdraw the assembly and the previously released fan blades from the engine compartment.

To refit

1. Refit the radiator grille and radiator complete on to the vehicle. Fit the fan blades to the fan pulley before engaging the grille panel fixings. See Figs. A3-10 and A3-9 for fixings details.
2. Make the electrical connections at the snap connectors, referring to Fig. A3-8 and the appropriate circuit diagram, if necessary, in Section N.
3. Connect the coolant hoses and replenish the engine coolant system, allowing a free flow through the drain taps before closing them. Fig. A3-8 refers. Fill the radiator header tank to within $\frac{1}{2}$ in. to $\frac{3}{4}$ in. (12 mm to 19 mm) below the bottom of the filler neck.

Coolant system capacity
Bonneted Control Model, 2.6 Litre Petrol

Imperial Pints	U.S. Pints	Litres	Antifreeze	Frost Precaution
20	24	11.2	33⅓%	—32°C (—25°F)

4. Refit the front apron panel. Fig. A3-4 refers.
5. Connect battery lead.
6. Refit the bonnet panel. Operation A3-1.

ENGINE—2.6 LITRE PETROL

*Gearbox tunnel and front panel, remove and refit—Operation A3-4

Workshop hand tools:
Spanner sizes: 7/16 in. AF, 1/2 in. AF, 7/16 in. BSF open end, 7/16 in. AF Screwdriver (medium)

To remove

1. Unscrew the knob and locknut from the transfer gear lever.
2. Remove the fixings and withdraw the dust cover from the transfer gear lever.
3. Unscrew the knob and locknut from the four-wheel drive lever, and withdraw the spring and ferrule.
4. Remove the gearbox tunnel cover.
5. Remove the gearbox tunnel front panel.

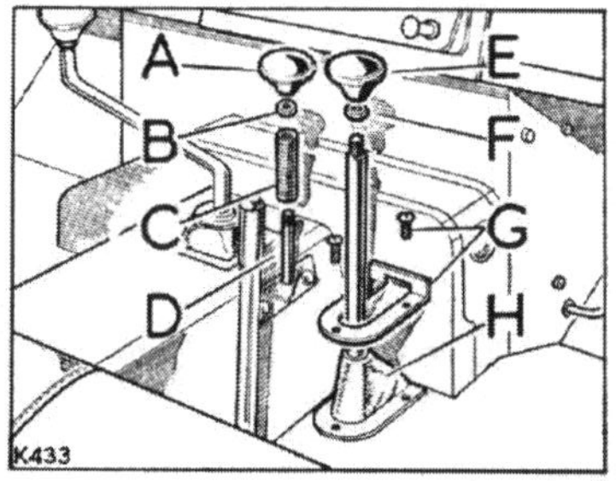

To refit

1. Reverse the removal procedure, using waterproof sealant between the joint flanges of the front floor and the chassis. A suitable sealant is 'Sealastrip', manufactured by Expandite Ltd., Chase Road, London NW10, England.
2. Adjust the four-wheel drive lever during assembly as follows: Fit the ferrule, spring and locknut to the lever, depress the lever and adjust the lock-nut until the compressed spring length is 2 5/16 in. — 1/16 in. (58 mm — 1 mm), then fit the knob and tighten the locknut.

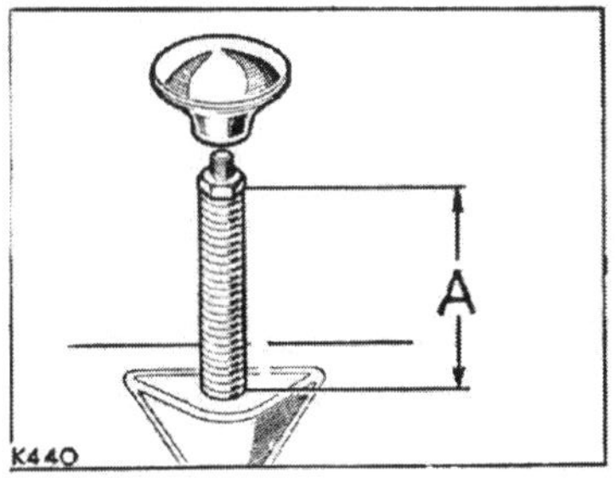

Fig. A3-13. Adjusting four-wheel drive control lever

A—2 5/16 in.— 1/16 in. (58 mm — 1 mm)

Fig. A3-11. Four wheel drive and transfer levers

A—Knob, four-wheel drive lever
B—Locknut for knob
C—Spring
D—Ferrule
E—Knob, transfer gear lever
F—Locknut for knob
G—Fixings for dust cover
H—Dust cover

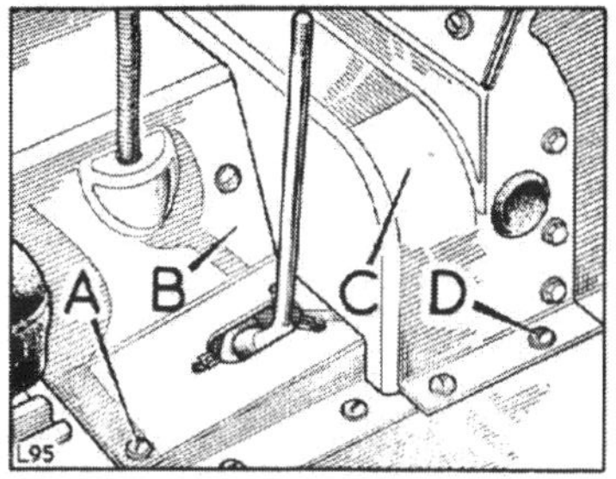

A3-12. Front floor

A—Fixings, tunnel cover (9 off)
B—Gearbox tunnel cover
C—Front panel for gearbox tunnel cover
D—Fixings, front panel (15 off)

ENGINE—2.6 LITRE PETROL

Engine, remove and refit—Operation A3-5

Workshop hand tools:
Spanner sizes: 7/16 in., 1/2 in., 9/16 in., 15/16 in. AF
3/8 in., 7/16 in., 1/2 in., 5/8 in. BSF
3/8 in. Whit, 1/4 in. BSF

Special tools:
Engine sling, Part No. 600963

To remove

1. Remove bonnet panel. Operation A3-1.
2. Remove air cleaner. Operation A3-2.
3. Remove radiator and grille panel. Operation A3-3.
4. Remove the gearbox cover. Operation A3-4.
5. Disconnect the following items at the left-hand side of the engine; refer to Fig. A3-14 for location of items:
   (a) Front exhaust pipe from manifold.
   (b) Exhaust heat shield.
   (c) Starter motor leads
   (d) Oil pressure switch lead
   (e) Engine earth cable at chassis side member.

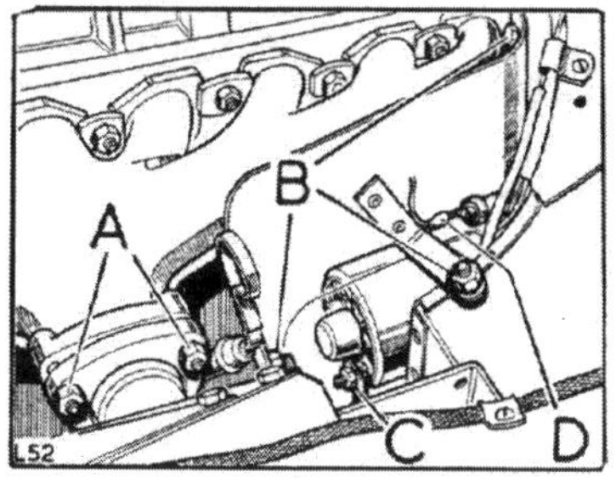

Fig. A3-14. View of engine, LH side

A—Front exhaust pipe fixings
B—Exhaust heat shield fixings
C—Starter motor leads
D—Oil pressure switch lead

   (f) Dynamo leads.
   (g) Hose at brake servo unit.
   (h) Fuel feed pipe at carburetter
   (i) Cold start control cable.

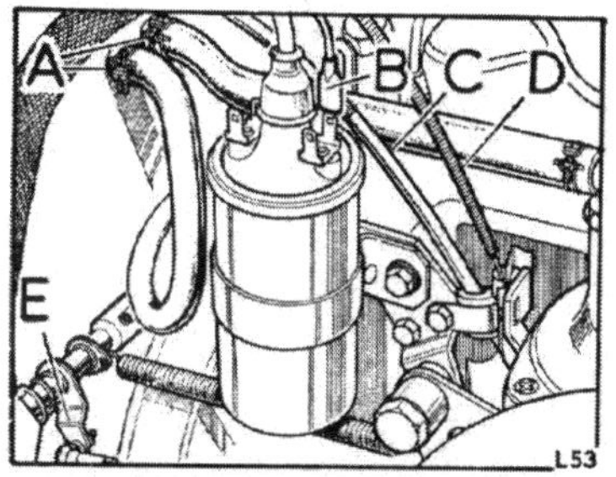

Fig. A3-15. View of engine, RH side, front

A—Heater hoses
B—Switch lead
C—Speedometer cable
D—Cold start control cable
E—Accelerator linkage, spring loaded

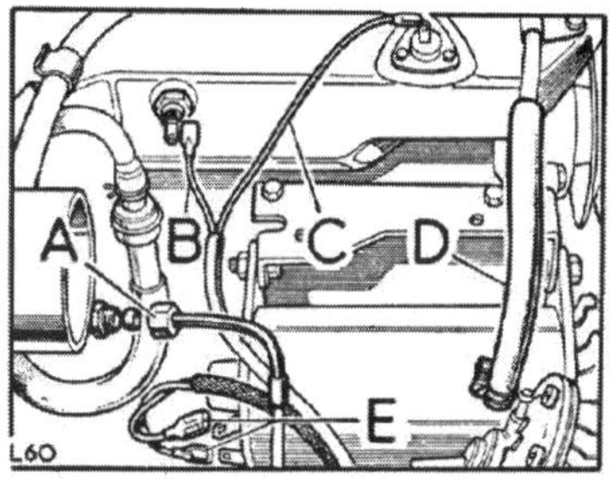

6. Disconnect the following items at the right hand side of the engine, refer to Fig. A3-15 and A3-16 for location of items.
   (a) Heater hoses
   (b) Switch lead at ignition coil.
   (c) Accelerator linkage at dash panel.
   (d) Speedometer cable at engine block clips.
   (e) Leads for cold start and coolant temperature indicators.

Fig. A3-16. View of engine, RH side, rear

A—Fuel feed pipe
B—Cold start warning light lead
C—Coolant temperature lead
D—Servo unit hose
E—Dynamo leads

Operations marked with an asterisk (*) can be carried out with the engine installed in the vehicle

ENGINE—2.6 LITRE PETROL

Operation A3-5—continued

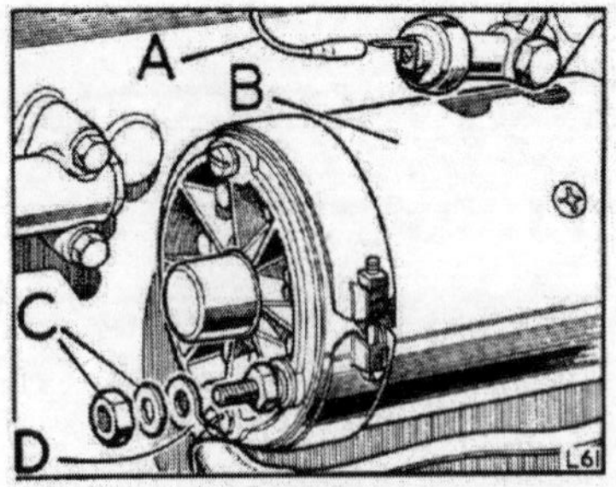

7. Remove the engine front mountings upper and lower fixings.

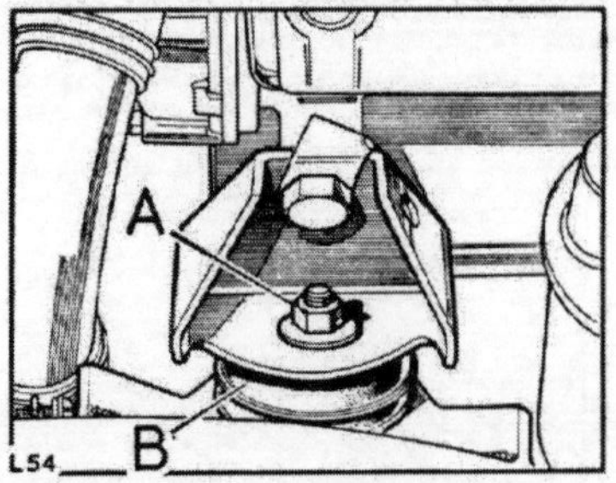

Fig. A3-17. Front mountings arrangement (2 off)
A—Upper fixing
B—Suspension rubber with integral studs

8. Fit a suitable lifting sling and support the engine weight.

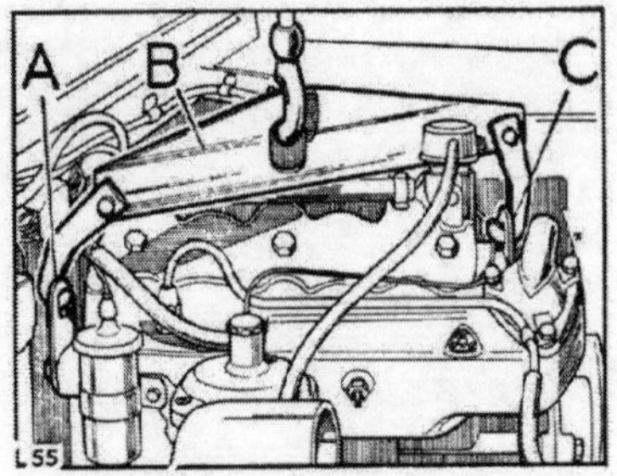

Fig. A3-18. Engine lifting sling in position
A—Rear lifting bracket
B—Sling, Part No. 600963
C—Front lifting bracket

9. Support the gearbox, using suitable packing blocks or a jack, and remove the bell housing to flywheel housing fixings.

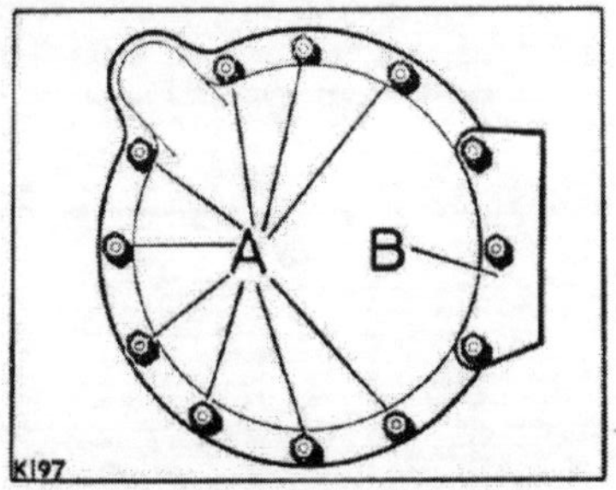

Fig. A3-19. Bell housing fixings
A—Fixings, bell housing to engine
B—Fixings, clutch slave cylinder mounting

10. Pull the engine forward sufficient to disengage the drive from the gearbox. Ensure that all cables, pipes, etc. are clear then hoist the engine from the vehicle.

To refit

1. Engage a gear to prevent gearshaft rotation and offer the engine to the gearbox. If necessary, rotate the engine sufficient to align the gearbox primary pinion with the clutch plate splines. When aligned, push the engine fully to the rear and secure the bell housing to the flywheel housing, tightening the fixings evenly.
2. Lift the engine sufficient to remove the packing or jack from beneath the gearbox and insert the engine front mounting rubbers.
3. Lower the engine and fit the upper and lower fixings to the engine. Fig. A3-17 refers.
4. Remove the engine lifting sling.
5. At the left hand side of the engine refit the electrical leads to the starter motor and oil pressure switch.

Fig. A3-20. Starter motor and oil pressure switch
A—Oil pressure switch lead
B—Starter motor
C—Starter motor lead and fixings
D—Protection cover and feed lead

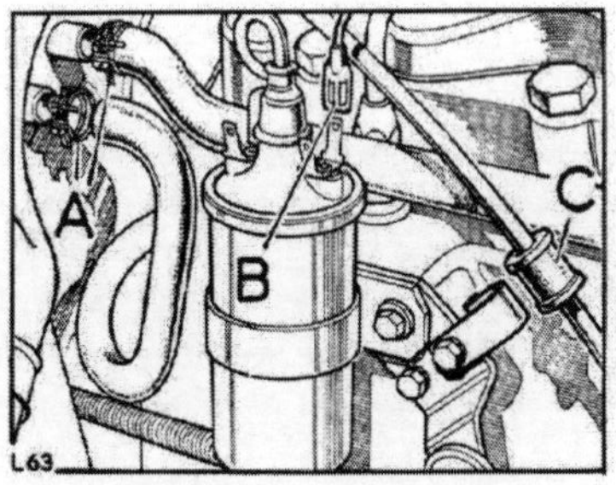

6. Refit the exhaust heat shield, if applicable, and fit the front exhaust pipe to the manifold. Fig. A3-14 refers.
7. At the right hand side of the engine refit the switch lead to the ignition coil, connect the heater hoses and secure the speedometer drive cable in the upper clip.
8. Reconnect the accelerator linkage at the dash panel and engage the speedometer drive cable in the adjacent clip.

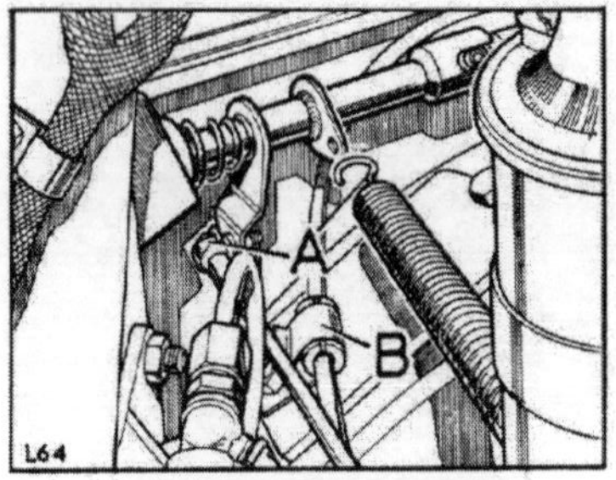

Fig. A3-21. Ignition coil and heater hoses
A—Heater hose fixings
B—Switch lead
C—Clip for speedometer cable

Fig. A3-22. Accelerator linkage
A—Spring loaded linkage
B—Clip for speedometer cable

9. Refit the leads to the cold start and coolant temperature indicators and to the dynamo, referring to Fig. A3-16 for details.
10. Refit the fuel inlet pipe and the cold start control cables at the carburetter.
11. Refit the gearbox covers. Operation A3-4.
12. Refit the radiator and grille panel assembly and replenish the coolant system. Operation A3-3.
13. Refit the air cleaner. Operation A3-2.
14. Refit the bonnet panel. Operation A3-1.

ENGINE—2.6 LITRE PETROL

*Carburetter, remove and refit—Operation A3-6

(For overhaul procedures, Section L refers)

Spanner sizes—Zenith carburetter: 7/16 in., 1/2 in. AF open end, 2 BA open end

Workshop hand tools:
Spanner sizes—SU carburetter: 3/8 in., 7/16 in., 1/2 in., 3/4 in. AF open end, 2 BA, 4 BA open end
Screwdriver, small

To remove

1. Lift and prop bonnet.
2. Remove the air cleaner. Operation A3-2.
3. Where a Zenith carburetter is fitted, disconnect the items indicated on Fig. A3-23.
4. Where an SU carburetter is fitted, disconnect the items indicated on Fig. A3-24.
5. Remove the fixings and withdraw the carburetter.

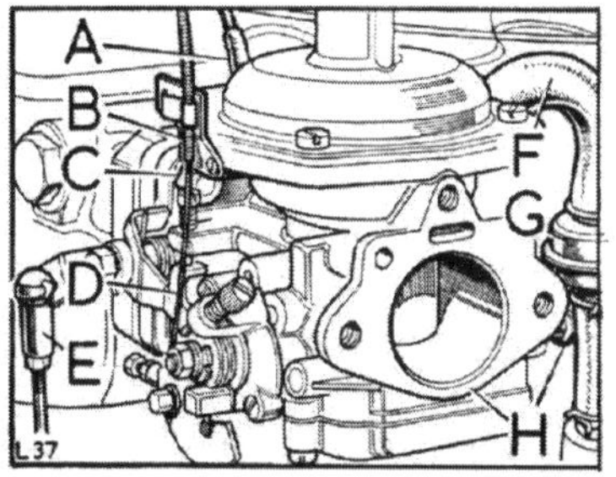

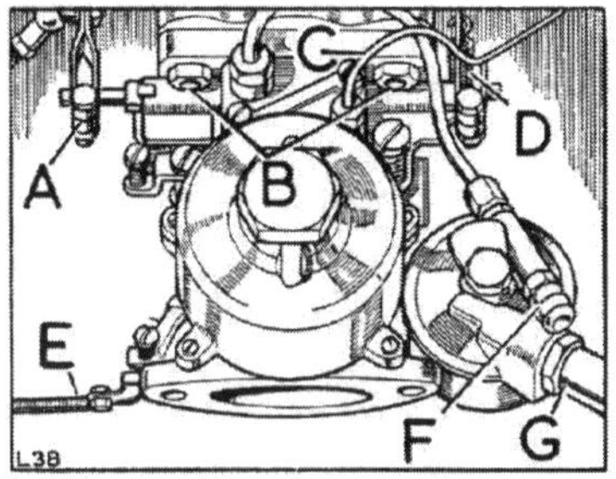

Fig. A3-23. View of Zenith carburetter

A—Vacuum pipe
B—Cold start outer cable and fixing
C—Fixings, carburetter to cylinder head
D—Cold start inner cable
E—Throttle linkage ball joint
F—Breather filter hose
G—Breather filter, withdraw hose at carburetter
H—Fuel inlet pipe

Fig. A3-24. View of SU carburetter

A—Throttle linkage
B—Fixings, carburetter to engine
C—Vacuum pipe
D—Throttle return spring
E—Cold start cable
F—Economiser hose
G—Fuel inlet pipe

To refit

1. Ensure that the carburetter and cylinder head-joint faces are clean.
2. Refit the carburetter, referring to Fig. A3-23 or Fig. A3-24 as appropriate.
3. Adjust the cold start control as described in Section L.
4. If necessary, adjust and tune the carburetter as described in Section L.

*Oil pressure warning light switch, remove and refit—Operation A3-7

Workshop hand tools:
Spanner size: 1/2 in. AF

Oil pressure switch, remove and refit

1. The oil pressure switch is screwed into the oil supply pipe from the cylinder block to the cylinder head.

   Its function is to cause the oil warning light to operate if the oil pressure drops below 8 to 10 lb/sq in. (0,6 to 0,7 kg/cm²).

2. Lift and prop bonnet.

3. The switch can be removed from the union by disconnecting the electrical connection and using a 1/2 in. AF spanner to unscrew the complete unit.

4. If a faulty switch is suspected, it can be checked by substitution or by temporarily fitting a pressure gauge in its place.

5. When replacing the switch, fit a new sealing washer.

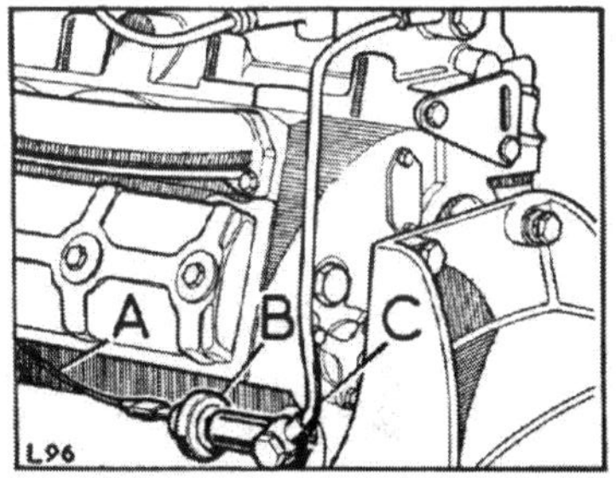

Fig. A3-25. Rocker oil feed pipe and oil pressure switch

A—Electrical lead
B—Oil pressure switch
C—Rocker oil feed pipe

Operations marked with an asterisk (*) can be carried out with the engine installed in the vehicle

ENGINE—2.6 LITRE PETROL   Section A3—Land-Rover

*Exhaust manifold, remove and refit—Operation A3-8

Workshop hand tools:
Spanner sizes: ½ in., 7/16 in. AF open end

To remove
1. Lift and prop bonnet.
2. Remove the exhaust heat shield, if fitted.
3. Remove the fixings and withdraw the manifold from the engine.

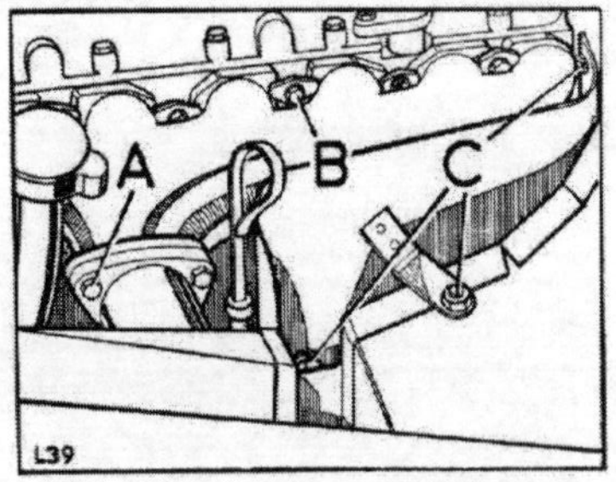

To refit
1. Refit the exhaust manifold and joint washers, and the heat shield if fitted.
2. Tighten the fixings evenly to avoid distortion.
3. Close the bonnet panel.

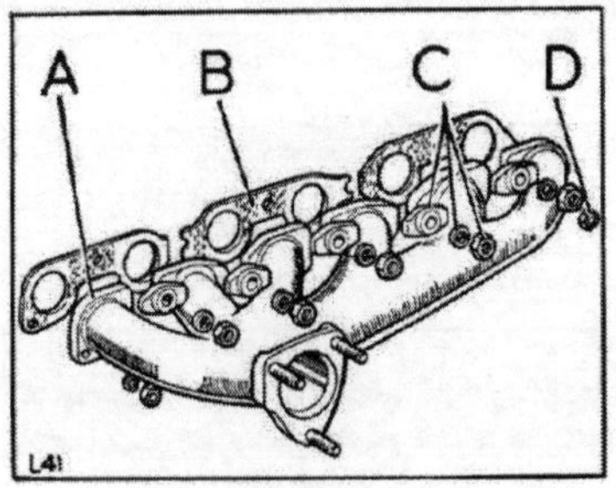

Fig. A3-26. Exhaust manifold fixings
A—Front exhaust pipe fixings
B—Manifold fixings
C—Heat shield fixings

Fig. A3-27. Exhaust manifold arrangement
A—Exhaust manifold
B—Joint washers
C—Upper fixings
D—Lower fixings

Section A3—Land-Rover   ENGINE—2.6 LITRE PETROL

*Starter motor, to remove and refit—Operation A3-9

(For starter motor overhaul procedures, Section N refers)

Workshop hand tools:
Spanner sizes: 7/16 in. AF, ¼ in. Whit

Starter, remove
1. Remove the bonnet panel. Operation A3-1.
2. Disconnect the battery leads.
3. Disconnect wiring from starter to solenoid.
4. Remove starter motor, secured by two fixings.

Note: It may be necessary to remove heat shield to facilitate starter removal.

Starter, refit
1. Reverse removal procedure and connect wiring.
2. Check operation of starter motor.
3. Refit bonnet panel. Operation A3-1.

Fig. A3-28. Starter motor fixings
A—Starter fixings
B—Earth strap
C—Electrical lead cover

Operations marked with an asterisk (*) can be carried out with the engine installed in the vehicle

ENGINE—2.6 LITRE PETROL

*Dynamo or alternator, to remove and refit—Operation A3-10

(For overhaul procedures, Section N refers)

Workshop hand tools:
Spanner sizes: ½ in. AF, 7/16 in. AF, 5/16 in. AF, ¼ in. BSF

DYNAMO

To remove

1. Lift and prop bonnet panel.
2. Disconnect the dynamo wiring and slacken the dynamo fixings.
3. Push the dynamo towards the engine and disengage the driving belt from the dynamo pulley.
4. Remove all fixings and withdraw dynamo.

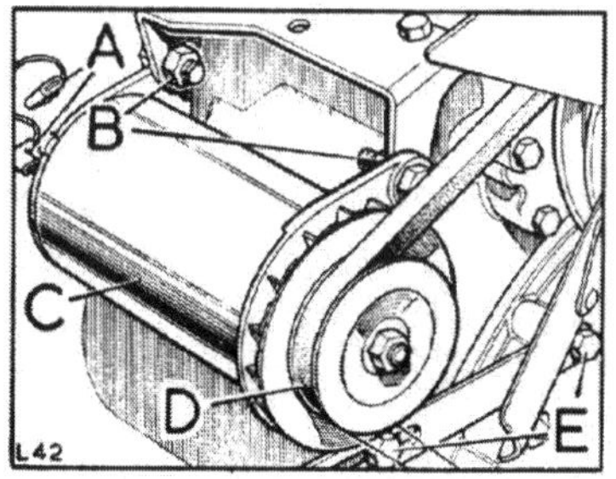

Fig. A3-29. Dynamo and fixings

A—Electrical lead terminals
B—Fixings at mounting bracket
C—Dynamo
D—Fan belt
E—Fixings at adjusting bracket

To refit

1. Offer the dynamo to mounting bracket and align the bolt holes. Secure with bolts and self-locking nuts.
2. Check the alignment of the dynamo and vibration damper pulleys, correct if necessary by adjusting the dynamo top mounting bracket on the engine. Failure to align pulleys will cause premature belt wear.
3. Pivot the dynamo inwards and fit driving belt.
4. Fit the lower securing bolt to the dynamo adjusting link. Do not tighten.
5. Adjust the belt to the correct tension. Fan belt tension: 5/16 in. to 7/16 in. (8,0 mm to 11,0 mm). Check by thumb pressure between the pulleys.
6. Connect wiring in accordance with the appropriate circuit diagram, Section N, and reconnect the battery leads.
7. Close the bonnet.

ALTERNATOR
Remove and refit

The procedure is similar to that for dynamo remove and refit, reference being made to Fig. A3-30.

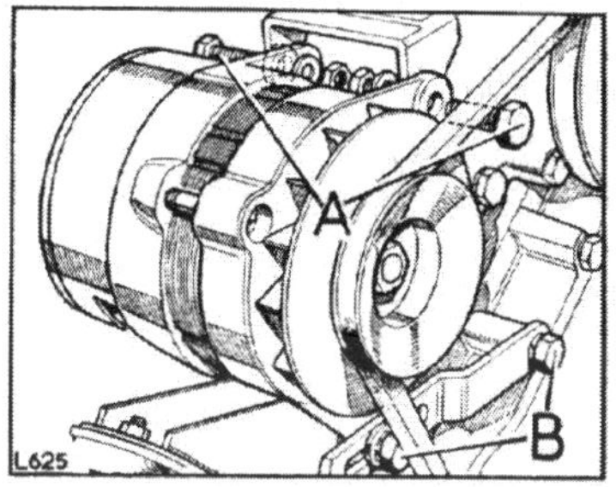

Fig. A3-30. Alternator and fixings

A—Mounting bracket fixings
B—Adjusting link fixings

*Water pump, remove and refit—Operation A3-11

(For overhaul information, Section K refers)

Workshop hand tools:
Spanner sizes: 7/16 in. AF open end, ½ in. AF ring Screwdriver (medium), Pliers

To remove

1. Remove bonnet panel. Operation A3-1.
2. Remove radiator filler cap and drain coolant.

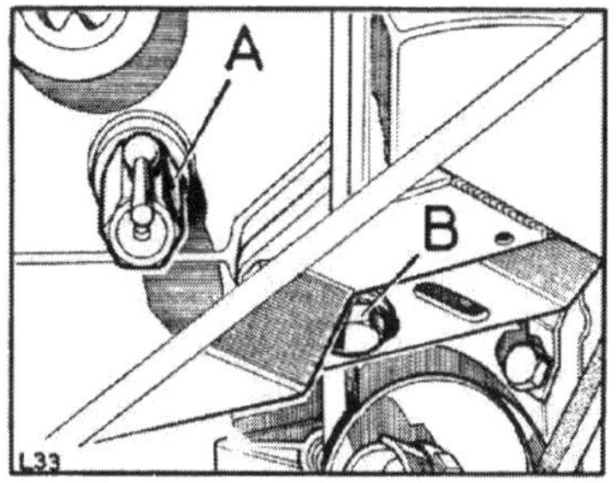

A3-31. Coolant drain taps location

A—Cylinder block drain
B—Radiator drain

3. Remove the shroud from the radiator fan cowl.

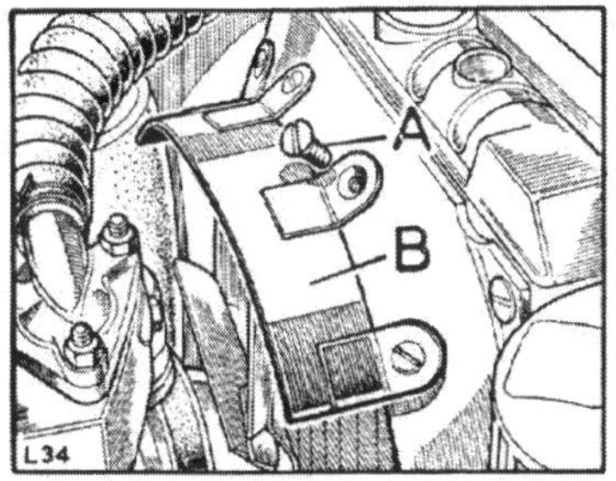

Fig. A3-32. Fan cowl shroud fixings

A—Fixings at fan cowl
B—Shroud

4. Slacken dynamo fixings and remove fan belt.

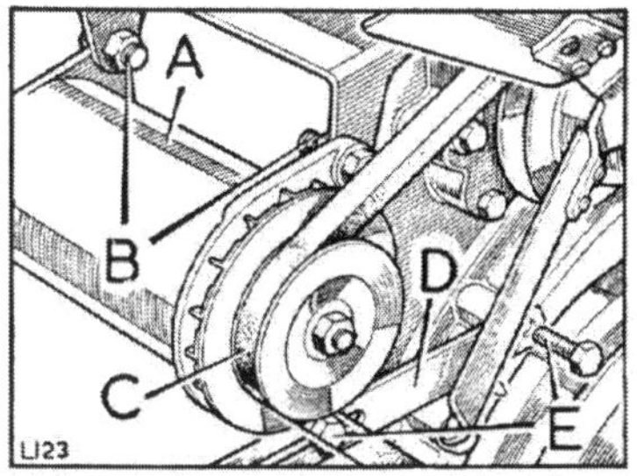

Fig. A3-33. Dynamo fixings

A—Dynamo
B—Fixings
C—Fan belt
D—Adjusting link
E—Adjusting link fixings

5. Remove fan blades, packing piece and fan pulley.

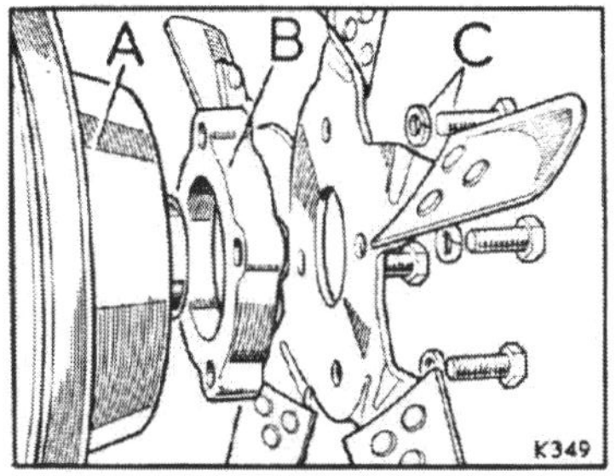

Fig. A3-34. Fixings for fan and pulley

A—Fan pulley, withdraw with fan blades
B—Distance piece
C—Fan blades fixings

Operations marked with an asterisk (*) can be carried out with the engine installed in the vehicle

ENGINE—2.6 LITRE PETROL

Operation A3-11—continued

6. Detach the radiator bottom hose and the heater hose if fitted.

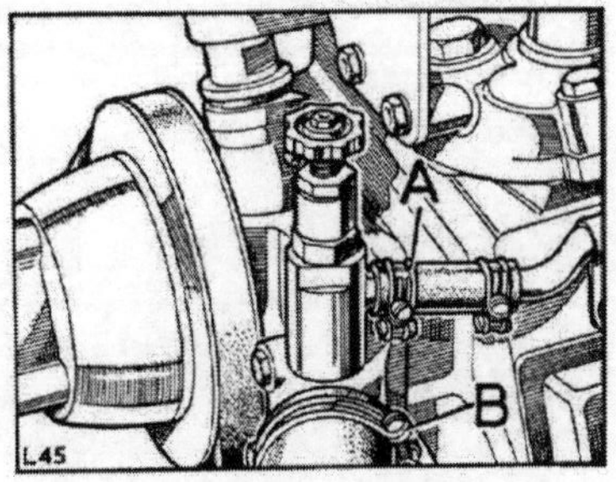

Fig. A3-35. Water pump hose fixings

A—At heater hose
B—At radiator bottom hose

7. Remove fixings and withdraw water pump, tilting the pump upwards off the locating dowels. This will compress the 'O' ring at the pump by-pass outlet and allow the pump to be withdrawn. Remove the joint washer.

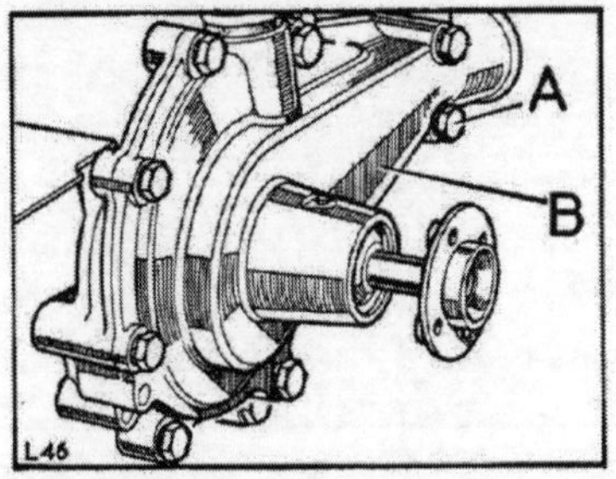

Fig. A3-36. Location of water pump fixings

A—Fixings   B—Water pump

Operation A3-11—continued

To refit:

1. Ensure that the fitting faces of water pump and cylinder block are clean.
2. Lightly grease a new joint washer and position it on the cylinder block.
3. Lightly smear a new 'O' ring with Silicone Compound MS4 and position it on pump by-pass outlet.

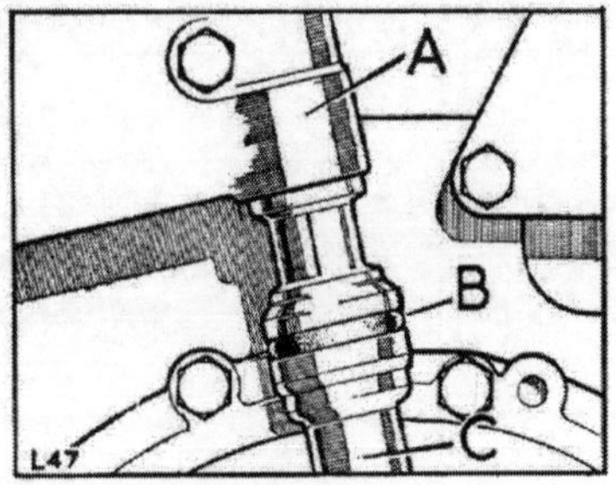

Fig. A3-37. Seal between cylinder head and water pump

A—Cylinder head, thermostat housing
B—Rubber 'O' ring
C—Water pump

4. Then fit water pump to cylinder block by tilting it on to the dowels, ensuring that the 'O' ring is not dislodged. Secure pump with the fixings, referring to Fig. A3-36 for location details.

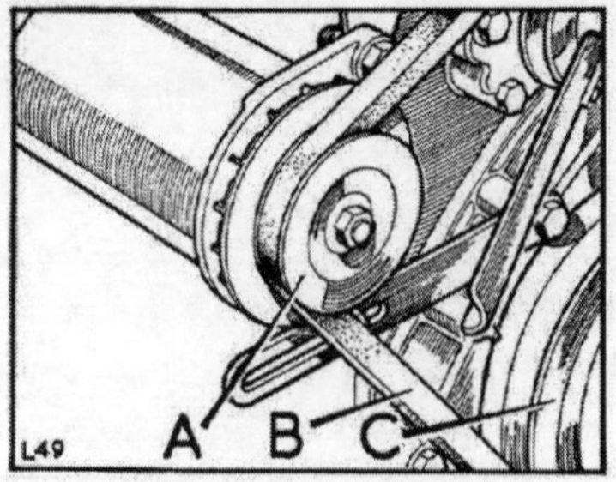

5. Fit the water outlet and heater hoses to the pump.
6. Refit the packing piece, fan pulley, fan blades and fan belt.
7. Adjust the fan belt to the correct tension. Fan belt tension: $\frac{5}{16}$ in. to $\frac{7}{16}$ in. (8 mm to 11 mm). Check by thumb pressure between the pulleys.

Fig. A3-38. Checking fan belt tension

A—Dynamo pulley
B—Thumb pressure applied midway between the pulleys
C—Crankshaft pulley

8. Refill the engine coolant system and replace the radiator cap.

Coolant system capacity
Bonneted Control Model, 2.6 Litre Petrol

Imperial Pints	U.S. Pints	Litres	Antifreeze	Frost Precaution
20	24	11.2	33⅓%	−32°C (−25°F)

9. Refit the bonnet panel. Operation A3-1.

ENGINE—2.6 LITRE PETROL

*Thermostat, to renew—Operation A3-12

(For overhaul details, Section K refers)

Workshop hand tools:
Spanner size: $\frac{7}{16}$ in. AF
Screwdriver, medium

To remove

1. Lift and prop bonnet.
2. Drain off coolant at radiator.

Fig. A3-39. Radiator drain point
A—Drain point   B—Radiator

3. Remove outlet pipe from the cylinder head
4. Lift out the thermostat and joint washers.

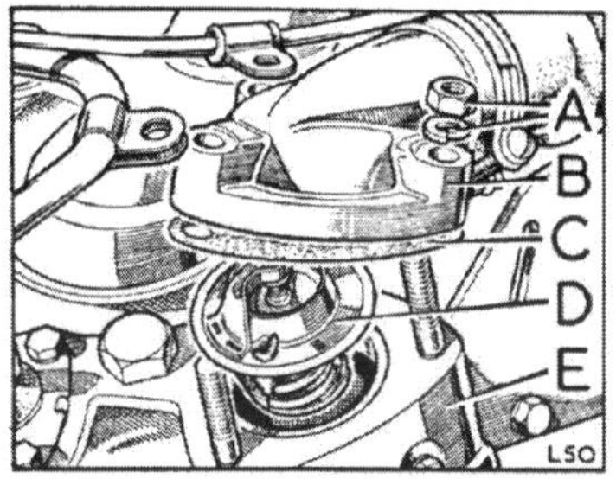

Fig. A3-40. Removing thermostat
A—Outlet pipe fixings
B—Outlet pipe
C—Joint washer
D—Thermostat
E—Cylinder block

To refit

1. Fit a new thermostat complete with new joint washers.
2. Reverse removal procedure.
3. Top up the coolant and check for leaks.

Coolant system capacity
Bonneted Control Model, 2.6 Litre Petrol

Imperial Pints	U.S. Pints	Litres	Antifreeze	Frost Precaution
20	24	11.2	33⅓%	—32°C (—25°F)

*Rocker oil feed pipe, remove and refit—Operation A3-13

Workshop hand tools:
Spanner sizes: $\frac{5}{8}$ in. AF, $\frac{7}{16}$ in. BSF

To remove

1. Lift and prop bonnet panel.
2. Disconnect wiring from oil pressure switch.
3. Remove banjo bolt fixing oil pipe to cylinder block, and remove heat shield if required.
4. Remove banjo bolt fixing oil pipe to cylinder head.
5. If required, remove oil pressure switch.

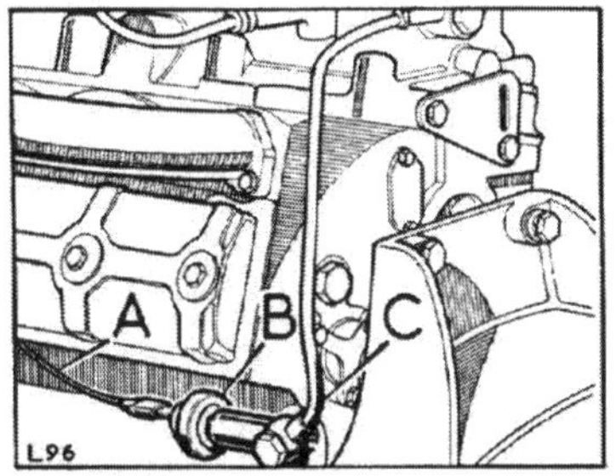

Fig. A3-41. Oil pressure switch and rocker oil feed pipe
A—Electrical lead
B—Oil pressure switch
C—Rocker oil feed pipe

Oil pipe, refit

1. Renew joint washers as required and ensure that a meter plug is fitted to the top banjo union.
2. Reverse removal procedure.

Operations marked with an asterisk (*) can be carried out with the engine installed in the vehicle

ENGINE—2.6 LITRE PETROL

*Engine breather box and filter, remove and refit—Operation A3-14

Workshop hand tools:
Spanner sizes: 7/16 in., 1/2 in. AF open end
Screwdriver, medium; Pliers

1. Remove the bonnet panel. Operation A3-1.
2. Remove the air cleaner, Operation A3-2, to obtain access.
3. Withdraw the filter hose from the carburetter.
4. Remove the fixings and withdraw the breather box from the engine. Discard the joint washer.

Fig. A3-42. Breather box and filter layout
A—Filter hose
B—Engine breather filter
C—Breather box
D—Breather box fixings

5. Withdraw the hoses from the breather box and filter.

Inspection

1. Wash the filter and breather box in clean fuel to remove all deposits.
2. Examine the components and hoses for damage and general condition. Allow the components to dry before refitting.

To refit

1. Smear general purpose grease on both sides of the new joint washer.
2. Fit the breather box and joint washer to the engine.
3. Fit the hoses to the filter.
4. Fit the hose free ends to the breather box and carburetter.

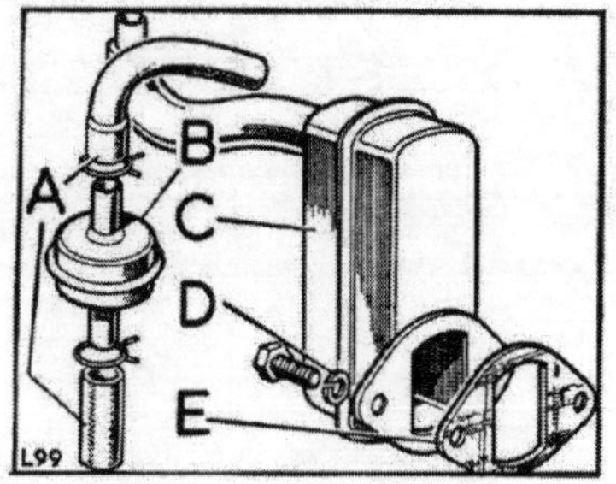

Fig. A3-43. Filter arrangement
A—Hoses   D—Fixings for box
B—Filter   E—Joint washer
C—Breather box

5. Refit the air cleaner. Operation A3-2.
6. Replace the bonnet panel. Operation A3-1.

*Oil filter, external, replace element—Operation A3-15

Workshop hand tools:
Spanner sizes: 3/8 in. AF socket

Procedure

1. Position a suitable waste oil receptacle under the filter.
2. Remove the centre fixing from the filter.
3. Remove filter bowl and allow oil to drain.
4. Remove sealing ring from filter cap.
5. Wash the components using clean fuel.
6. Replace filter element and sealing ring.

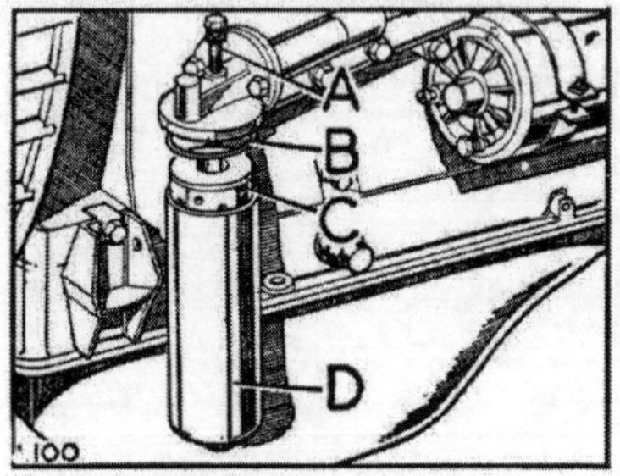

Fig. A3-44. View of oil filter
A—Filter centre fixing   C—Element
B—Sealing ring   D—Filter body

7. Fit the new element to the filter body and refit body to cap. Ensure filter body is fully home on to sealing ring in filter cap.
8. Replenish the engine lubricating oil.
9. Check the sump oil level after a short engine run and top-up as necessary.

Engine lubricant capacity
Bonneted Control Model, 2.6 Litre Petrol

	Imperial Pint	U.S. Pint	Litre
Engine	12	14.4	6.25
Filter	1	1.2	0.5
Total	13	15.6	6.75

ENGINE—2.6 LITRE PETROL

*Oil filter, external, remove, overhaul and refit—Operation A3-16

Workshop hand tools:
Spanner sizes: ⅝ in. AF, 1⅛ in. AF socket, ⅝ in. BSF open end

To remove
1. Lift and prop bonnet.
2. Detach oil pressure switch lead.
3. Remove the fixings and withdraw the oil filter and joint washer.

To overhaul
1. Drain off oil.
2. Remove the centre fixing and dismantle the filter assembly.
3. Wash the components in clean fuel and inspect for general condition.
4. Replace the sealing washer and filter element.
5. Reverse the dismantling procedure

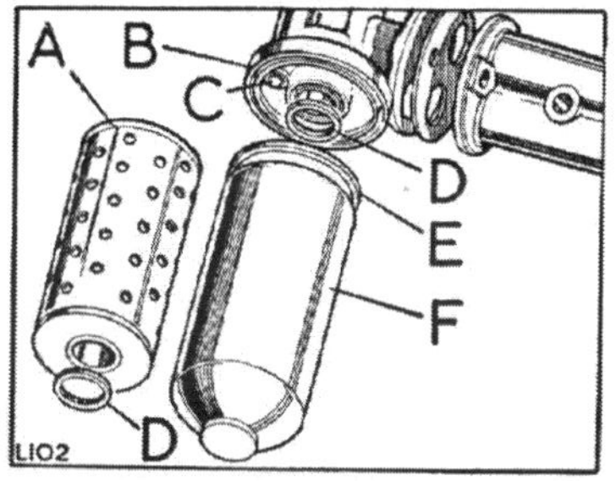

To refit
1. Assemble the element and seals to the filter body.
2. Refit filter body to top cover, ensuring that the body seats correctly on to the sealing ring.
3. Refit the assembled filter to the engine. Fig. A3-45 refers.
4. Replenish the engine lubricating oil and top-up as necessary after a short engine run.
5. Close the bonnet panel.

Engine lubricant capacity
Bonneted Control Model, 2.6 Litre Petrol

		Imperial Pint	U.S. Pint	Litre
Engine	.. ..	12	14.4	6.25
Filter	.. ..	1	1.2	0.5
	Total	13	15.6	6.75

Fig. A3-45. Oil filter fixings
A—Fixings, adaptor to block
B—Fixings, filter to adaptor

Fig. A3-46. Exploded view of oil filter
A—Element
B—Top cover
C—Pressure relief valve ball
D—Sealing washer for element
E—Sealing washer, large
F—Container

*Ignition timing procedure—Operation A3-17

Workshop hand tools:
⅞ in. AF open end, ½ in. Whit open end Screwdriver (medium), Pliers

Special tools:
12 volt test lamp and leads

The following information concerns engines with 7.0:1 and 7.8:1 compression ratios for which the ignition settings differ. The engine compression ratio is indicated by the commencing three digits of the engine number stamped on the upper LH side of the engine block adjacent to the manifold front fixings.

Compression ratio	Engine numbers commence with
7.0:1	346
7.8:1	345

The required ignition settings for the different engines are given in the 'Procedure' section which follows:

In addition, the timing marks location varies as follows:

Early engines: timing marks appear on flywheel.
Later engines: timing marks appear on crankshaft pulley.

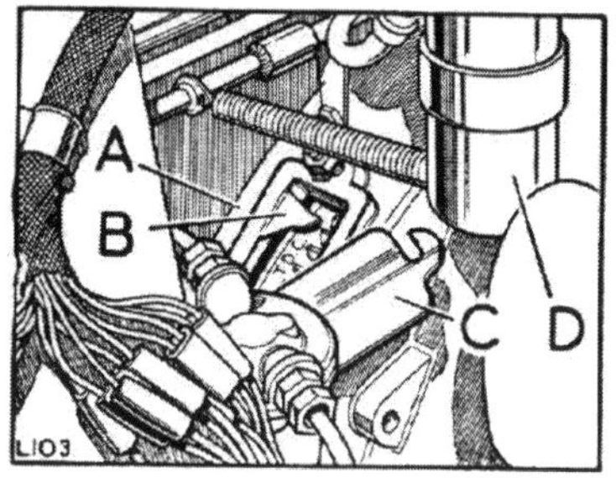

Fig. A3-47. Location of timing pointer, early engines
A—Flywheel housing
B—Timing pointer
C—Timing aperture cover
D—Ignition coil (reference only)

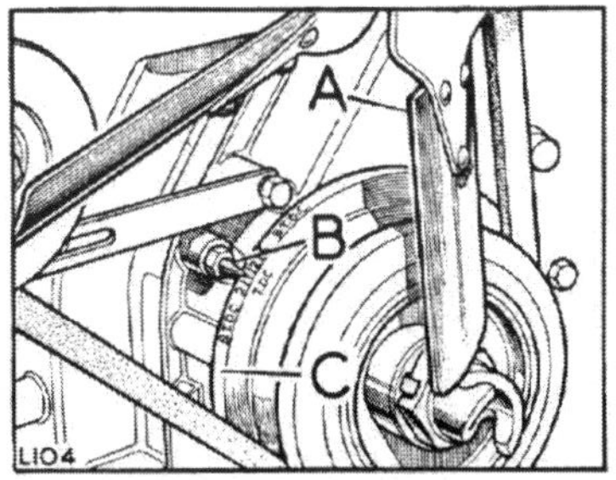

Fig. A3-48. Location of timing pointer, later engines
A—Fan
B—Timing pointer at front cover
C—Crankshaft pulley

Procedure
1. Remove bonnet panel. Operation A3-1.
2. Remove the distributor cap then rotate the engine in direction of rotation until the appropriate timing mark is aligned with the pointer and the distributor rotor is at No. 1 cylinder firing position.

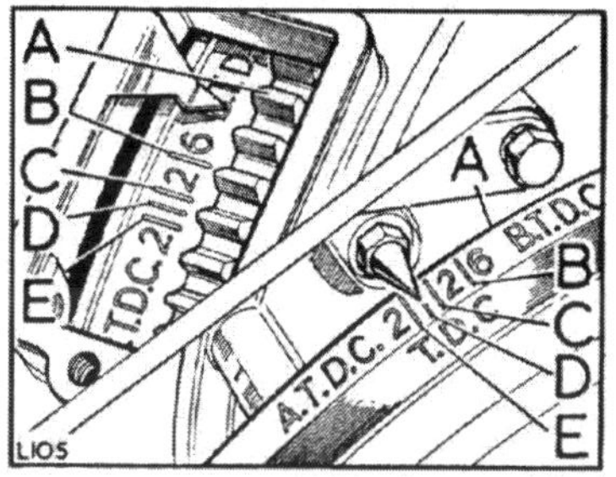

Fig. A3-49. Timing marks and fuel octane applications
A—Crankshaft pulley or flywheel, as applicable
B—6° BTDC mark for special market engines only (8.8:1 compression ratio and using 95 octane fuel)
C—2° BTDC mark for use on 7.0:1 engines using 83 octane fuel
D—TDC mark for use on 7.0:1 engines using 80 octane fuel
E—2° ATDC mark for use on 7.0:1 engines using 78 octane fuel and also on 7.8:1 engines using 90 octane fuel.

Operations marked with an asterisk (*) can be carried out with the engine installed in the vehicle

ENGINE—2.6 LITRE PETROL   Section A3—Land-Rover

Operation A3-17—continued

Note: If the use of lower octane fuels on 7.8:1 engines is unavoidable, the ignition setting may be retarded as required to a maximum of 6° ATDC. For example, for fuel of octane number 85 (which is the lowest operable octane number for the engine) the 6° ATDC setting may be used and is established by using the existing markings as a guide.

3. Slacken the pinch bolt in base of distributor body and rotate the distributor in opposite direction to arrow on rotor arm until the contact breaker points are just opening with the cam follower on the leading side of the cam. Re-tighten the pinch bolt.

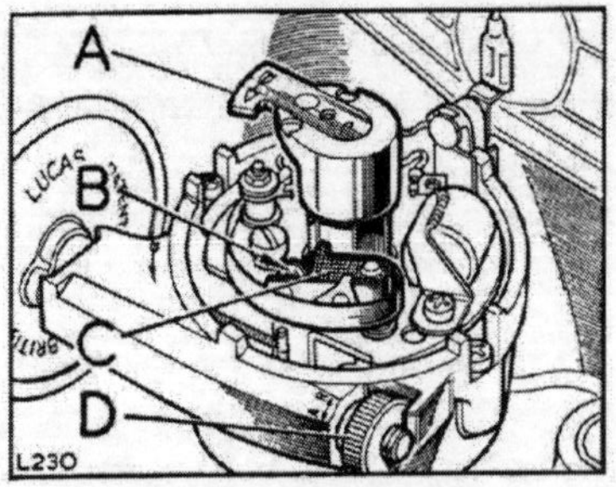

Fig. A3-50. View of distributor

A—Rotor arm
B—Contact breaker points
C—Cam follower
D—Vernier screw adjuster

Fig. A3-51. Test lamp in position

A—LT terminal at distributor
B—Test lamp
C—Vernier screw adjuster
D—Suitable earth
E—Pinch bolt

4. Connect one lead of a 12 volt test lamp to the distributor LT terminal and the other one to a good earth on engine. Switch ignition 'on' and turn the crankshaft two revolutions in direction of rotation. The bulb should light as the timing pointer comes into alignment with the appropriate mark. See paragraph 2.

5. Adjust as required by slackening the pinch bolt and turning the distributor bodily, or for fine adjustment, by means of the vernier screw.

6. When satisfactory, remove the test lamp and leads and refit the distributor cap.

7. Refit the inspection cover to the flywheel housing, where applicable.

8. Refit the bonnet panel. Operation A3-1.

Section A3—Land-Rover   ENGINE—2.6 LITRE PETROL

*Distributor and HT leads, remove and refit—Operation A3-18

(For overhaul procedures, Section N refers)

Workshop hand tools:
Spanner sizes: $\frac{7}{16}$ in. AF, open end, $\frac{7}{8}$ in. AF open end

To remove

1. Lift and prop bonnet panel.
2. Disconnect vacuum pipe at distributor.
3. Remove leads at sparking plugs.
4. Disconnect the low tension and high tension leads.
5. Remove the distributor fixings and withdraw the distributor from the drive shaft housing.
6. If required, lift out the short drive shaft from the housing.

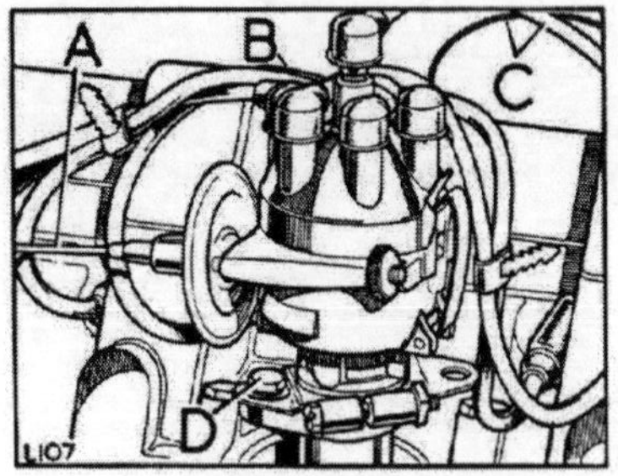

To refit

1. If removed, refit the short drive shaft into the distributor housing to engage the offset drive in the distributor gear shaft.
2. Where a replacement distributor is to be fitted, check the contact breaker gap and reset if necessary to .014 in. to .016 in. (0.35 mm to 0.40 mm). Set the octane selector, using the knurled adjuster so that the fourth line of the calibrated slide is against the distributor body casing.
3. Turn the distributor drive shaft to align with the offset drive in the short drive shaft.
4. Refit the distributor to the engine.
5. Check and if necessary reset the ignition timing as described in Operation A3-17.
6. Close the bonnet.

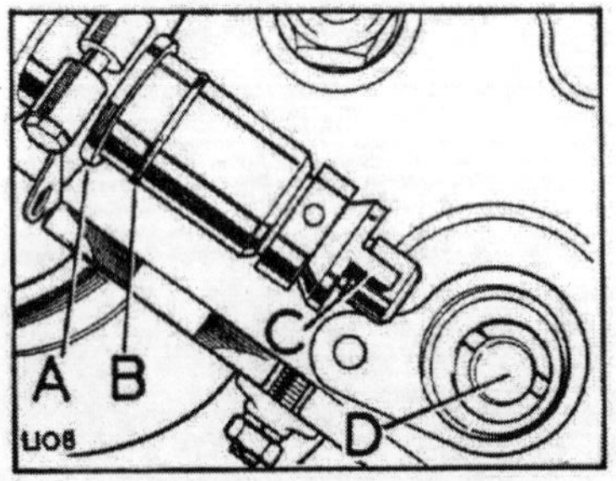

Fig. A3-52. Distributor location and fixings

A—Vacuum pipe
B—Sparking plug leads
C—HT and LT leads
D—Distributor fixing

Fig. A3-53. Distributor refitting

A—Cork seal
B—'O' ring seal
C—Offset drive to align with engine drive
D—Offset drive at engine

Operations marked with an asterisk (*) can be carried out with the engine installed in the vehicle

ENGINE—2.6 LITRE PETROL

*Tappet adjustment—Operation A3-19

Workshop hand tools:
Spanner size: ½ in. AF open end
Screwdriver (medium), Feeler gauges

1. Lift and prop bonnet.
2. Remove the air cleaner. Operation A3-2.
3. Remove the side and top rocker covers.
4. Turn the crank in the direction of rotation until number six inlet valve (counting from the front of the engine) is fully open, that is, with the valve spring fully compressed. In this position the tappet for number one inlet valve is on the dwell of the cam.
5. Slacken the tappet locknut, then rotate the adjusting screw until there is .006 in. (0,15 mm) clearance between rocker and valve stem when checked with a feeler gauge. Ensure all clearance is taken up at the push rod ends. Tighten locknut and recheck clearance.

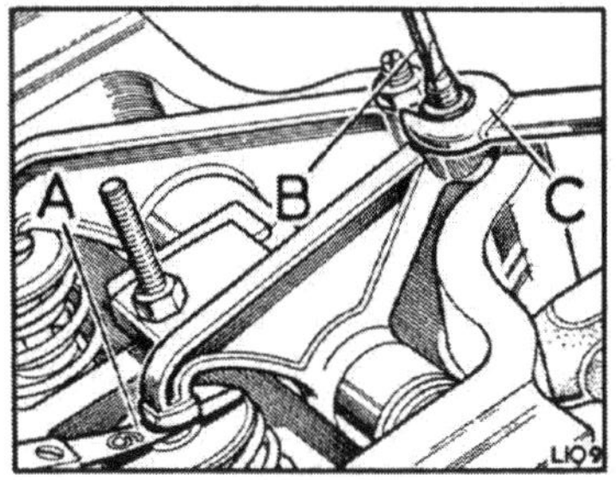

Fig. A3-54. Adjusting tappets, inlet valves
A—Feeler gauge
B—Screwdriver
C—Tappet spanner

6. Set the remaining inlet tappets referring to the sequence table which appears in the next column.

7. Adjust the exhaust valves in a similar manner using a .010 in. (0,25 mm) feeler gauge.

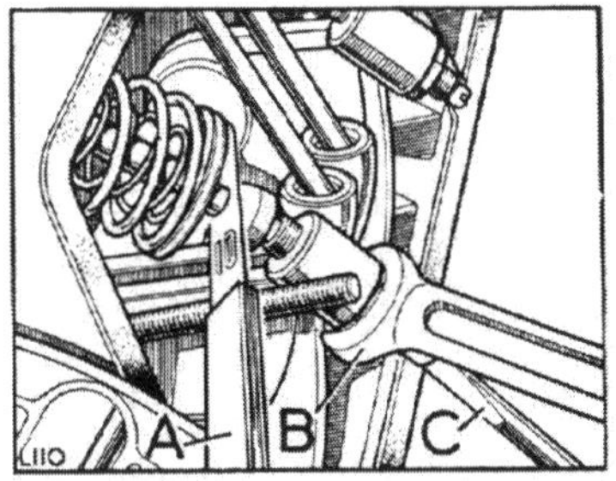

Fig. A3-55. Adjusting tappets, exhaust valves
A—Feeler gauge
B—Tappet spanner
C—Screwdriver

Tappet clearance:
Inlet valves .006 in. (0,15 mm).
Exhaust valves .010 in. (0,25 mm).
Set No. 1 tappet with No. 6 valve fully open
Set No. 2 tappet with No. 5 valve fully open
Set No. 3 tappet with No. 4 valve fully open
Set No. 4 tappet with No. 3 valve fully open
Set No. 5 tappet with No. 2 valve fully open
Set No. 6 tappet with No. 1 valve fully open

8. Check and if necessary reset the inlet valve tappet clearances with the engine at normal running temperature.
9. Close the bonnet.

*Top rockers and shafts, remove and refit—Operation A3-20

Workshop hand tools:
½ in. AF, ¾ in. AF open end, 1⅛ in. AF
Feeler gauges. Screwdriver (medium)

Special tools:
Part No. 262749, special tool for extracting rocker shafts

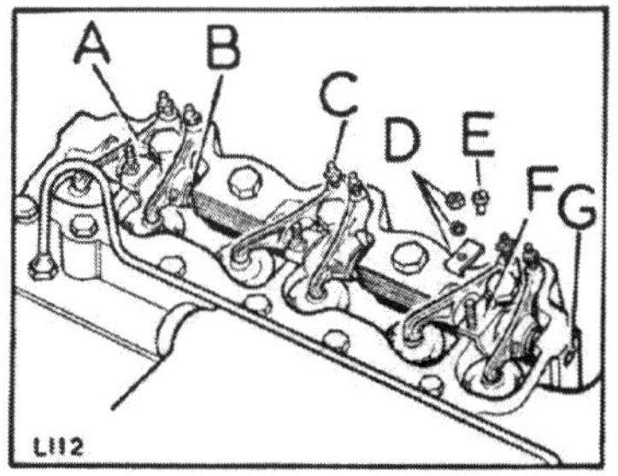

Fig. A3-57. Top rocker assembly
A—Rocker levers
B—Rocker springs (6 off)
C—Tappet adjusting screws
D—Spacer block fixings
E—Shaft locating screws (3 off)
F—Spacer blocks (3 off)
G—Tapping for end plug

Top rocker shafts and rockers, to fit

Rocker bushes must be a press fit in the rockers, and rotate freely on the shafts when fitted; the bushes must be pressed in .010 to .020 in. (0,25 to 0,50 mm) below the thrust face of the rocker. After fitting the bushes drill the two oil holes through each bush; ream in position to .50 in. +.001 (12,5 mm +0,025).

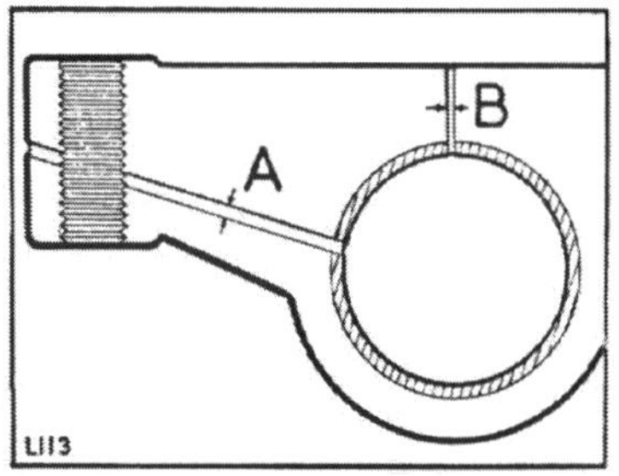

1. Remove the bonnet panel. Operation A3-1.
2. Remove the radiator and grille panel. Operation A3-3.
3. Remove the distributor cap, and sparking plug leads Release the HT lead from the ignition coil and place the distributor cap and lead assembly aside.
4. Remove the engine breather filter from the top rocker cover.
5. Remove the three sleeve nuts and sealing washers securing the top rocker cover, lift off the cover and gasket.

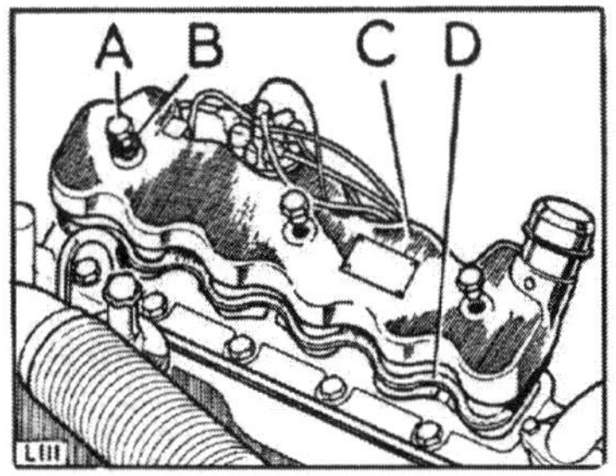

Fig. A3-56. Top rocker cover
A—Sleeve nut
B—Sealing washer
C—Rocker cover
D—Gasket

6. Slacken the tappet adjusting screws right back.
7. Remove the rocker shaft end plug and sealing washer from the front of the cylinder head.
8. Remove the three nuts, shakeproof washers and retaining plates securing the rocker spacers.
9. Remove the three locating screws securing front and rear rocker shafts.
10. Extract the front and rear rocker shafts, using special tool, Part No. 262749 and lift out the rocker levers, springs and spacers from the cylinder head as they are released.

Fig. A3-58. Drilling rocker shaft bush
A—Oil hole ⅜ in. (2,8 mm) diameter
B—Oil hole 1/16 in. (1,6 mm) diameter

Operations marked with an asterisk (*) can be carried out with the engine installed in the vehicle

ENGINE—2.6 LITRE PETROL   Section A3—Land-Rover

Operation A3-20—continued

Refit the rockers and shafts by reversing the removal procedure. Fig. A3-59 refers.

The rocker shafts must be replaced with the oil holes facing away from the inlet valves. A suitable mark made on the shaft end relating to the oil holes position will facilitate correct alignment.

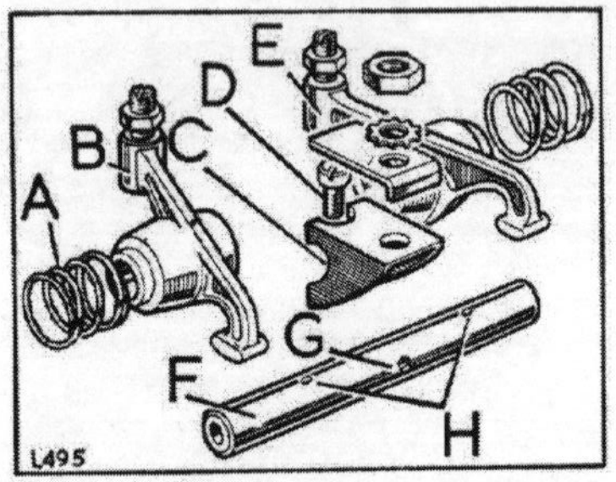

Fig. A3-59. Arrangement of top rocker assembly showing front shaft

A—Spring
B—Rocker arm (left-handed) and tappet screw
C—Spacer block
D—Locating screw
E—Rocker arm (right-handed)
F—Rocker shaft. Front (shorter) shaft shown; rear (longer) shaft arrangement is similar, but is fitted with tapped hole toward front
G—Tapped hole for locating screw
H—Plain holes, to be positioned away from valves when shaft is fitted

---

Section A3—Land-Rover   ENGINE—2.6 LITRE PETROL

*Cylinder head, remove and refit—Operation A3-21

(For cylinder head overhaul details, Operation A3-22 refers)

Workshop hand tools:
Spanner sizes: $\frac{7}{16}$ in., $\frac{1}{2}$ in., $\frac{9}{16}$ in., $\frac{5}{8}$ in., $\frac{3}{4}$ in., $\frac{7}{8}$ in. AF sockets
Screwdriver (medium), Pliers

Special tools:
Torque wrench

To remove

1. Remove the bonnet panel. Operation A3-1.
2. Remove the air cleaner. Operation A3-2.
3. Drain the coolant from the radiator and engine block.

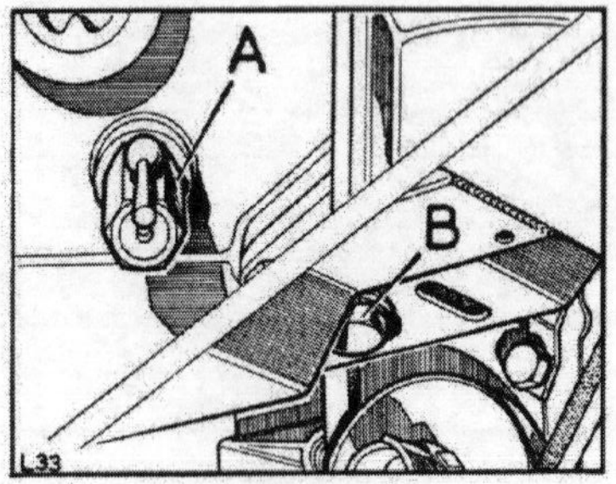

Fig. A3-60. Coolant drain taps location

A—At engine block, RH side
B—At radiator

4. Remove the carburetter. Operation A3-6.
5. Disconnect the control rods, bell-crank to cross-shaft.

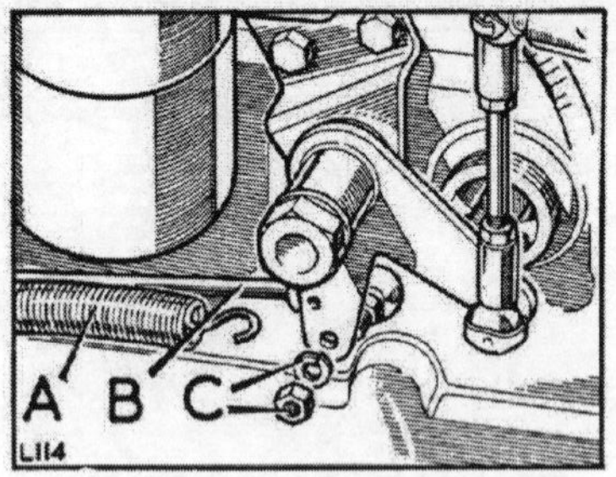

Fig. A3-61. Throttle linkage

A—Return spring
B—Control rod, cross shaft to bell crank
C—Fixings

6. Remove the distributor. Operation A3-18.
7. Disconnect the rocker feed oil pipe at rear of cylinder head.

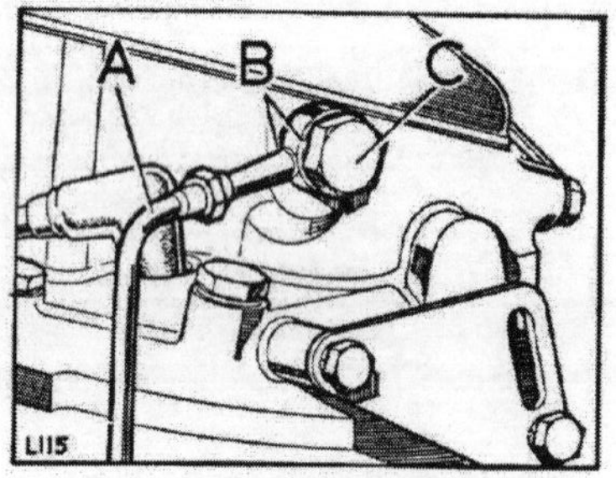

Fig. A3-62. Rocker oil feed upper fixings

A—Oil feed pipe
B—Joint washer
C—Banjo bolt and meter plug

8. Disconnect the mixture control warning light and coolant temperature transmitter leads at the cylinder head, RH side.

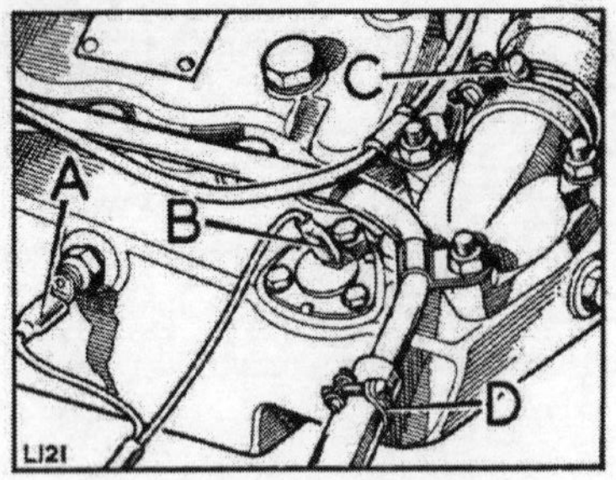

Fig. A3-63. Cylinder head, RH side

A—Mixture control warning light lead
B—Coolant temperature transmitter lead
C—Radiator top hose
D—Servo brake hose

Operations marked with an asterisk (*) can be carried out with the engine installed in the vehicle

ENGINE—2.6 LITRE PETROL

Operation A3-21—continued

9. Disconnect the servo brake pipe.
10. Disconnect the radiator top hose. Where fitted, release the clip on the short by-pass hose between cylinder head and water pump.
11. Remove the top rocker cover and slack off the tappets.

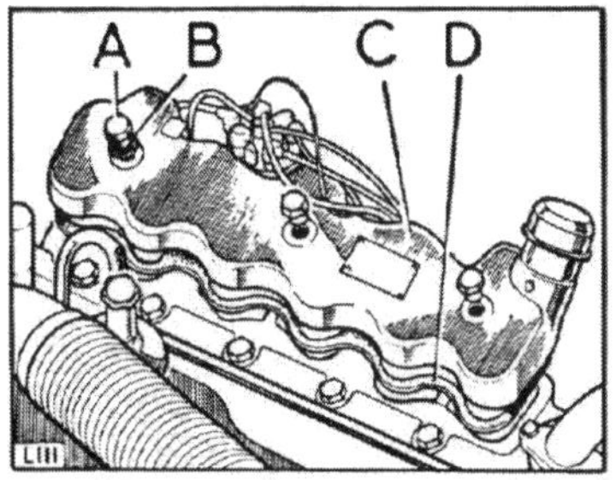

Fig. A3-64. Top rocker cover

A—Sleeve nut
B—Sealing washer
C—Rocker cover
D—Joint gasket

12. Slacken the cylinder head fixings evenly and remove them. Fig. A3-67 refers.

    Lift off the cylinder head and discard the head gasket and the 'O' ring seal from between the cylinder head and water pump.

13. Withdraw the push rods and retain in sequence related to the tappet served.

To refit

1. Remove side rocker cover. If necessary, remove the engine oil level dipstick and tube to allow rocker cover withdrawal.
2. Replace the push rods in their original positions.
3. Smear a new cylinder head gasket with oil and place on the face of the cylinder block, with the side marked 'this side up' uppermost.
4. Use two old cylinder head bolts with their heads sawn off to locate the gasket and head. Cut a screwdriver slot across the diameter of the bolts to facilitate removal when the cylinder head is in position.

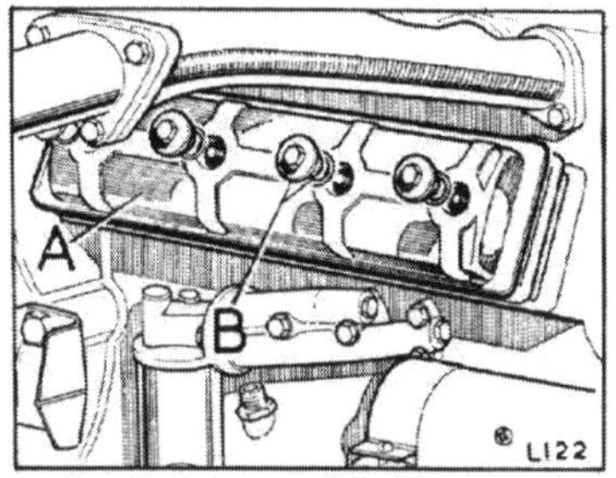

Fig. A3-65. Side rocker cover

A—Side cover   B—Fixings

5. Position the cylinder head on to the block; as this is being done connect the by-pass hose or sealing washer to the cylinder head.
6. Check that the push rods are seating correctly.

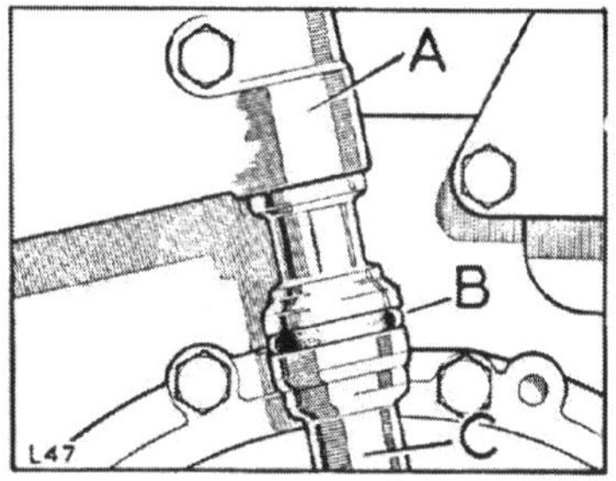

Fig. A3-66. Seal between head and pump

A—Cylinder head, thermostat housing
B—Rubber 'O' ring
C—Water pump

7. Tighten the cylinder head bolts in order shown and to the following torques:
   (a) Bolts 'A'   ..   50 lb ft (7 mkg)
   (b) Bolts 'B'   ..   30 lb ft (4 mkg)

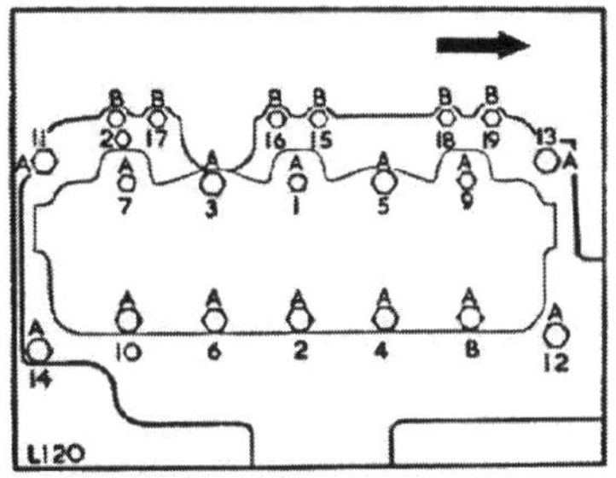

Fig. A3-67. Order of tightening cylinder head bolts

8. Adjust the tappets. Operation A3-19.
9. Refit the side rocker cover and top rocker cover.
10. Refit the coolant hose, electrical leads and servo pipe. Fig. A3-63 refers.
11. Replenish the coolant system.
12. Refit the distributor. Operation A3-18.
13. Refit the carburetter. Operation A3-6.
14. Reconnect the throttle linkage, Fig. A3-61 refers
15. Refit the air cleaner. Operation A3-2.
16. Refit the bonnet panel. Operation A3-1.
17. With the engine hot after the initial engine run, recheck the cylinder head fixings torque loadings and reset as necessary.
18. Check and reset tappet clearances as necessary Operation A3-19.

Coolant system capacity
Bonneted Control Model, 2.6 Litre Petrol

Imperial Pints	U.S. Pints	Litres	Antifreeze	Frost Precaution
20	24	11.2	33%	—32°C (—25°F)

ENGINE—2.6 LITRE PETROL

*Engine, to decarbonise and top overhaul—Operation A3-22

Workshop hand tools:
Spanner sizes: $\frac{7}{16}$ in. AF, $\frac{1}{2}$ in. AF, $\frac{5}{8}$ in. AF, 2 BA
Sparking plug spanner
Screwdrivers (medium and large)
Pliers

Special tools:
Torque wrench, Feeler gauges
Extractor (Part No. 262749) for rocker shaft
Valve spring compressor (Part No. 276102)
Valve guide removal drift (Part No. 274401)
Valve guide refitting drift (Part No. 600959)
Protection plate, insert removal (Part No. 263050)
Valve seat insert tool (Part No. 530625)

A decarbonising gasket set is available

1. Remove the bonnet panel. Operation A3-1.
2. Remove the air cleaner. Operation A3-2.
3. Drain the coolant from the radiator and engine block.
4. Remove the carburetter. Operation A3-6.
5. Disconnect the control rod, bell crank to cross-shaft.
6. Remove the distributor. Operation A3-18.
7. Remove the sparking plugs.
8. Remove the cylinder head. Operation A3-21.
9. Remove the water outlet pipe and withdraw the thermostat.

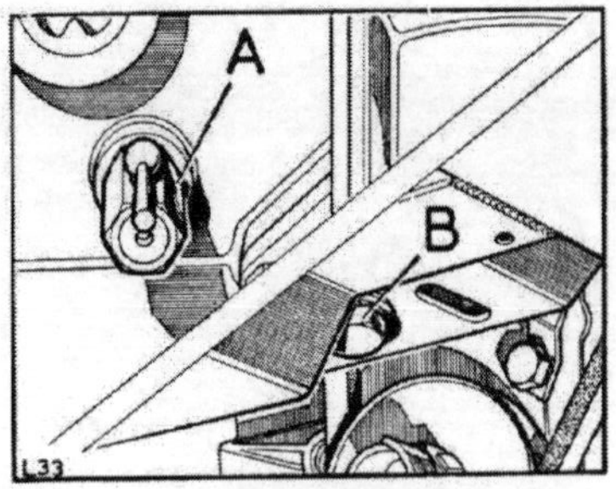

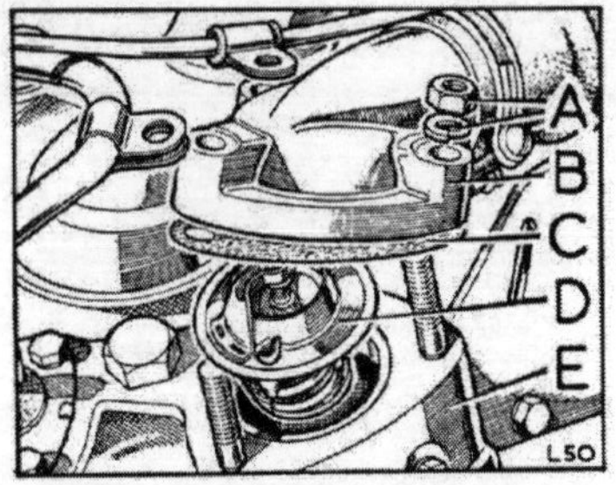

Fig. A3-68. Coolant drain taps location
A—At engine block, RH side
B—At radiator

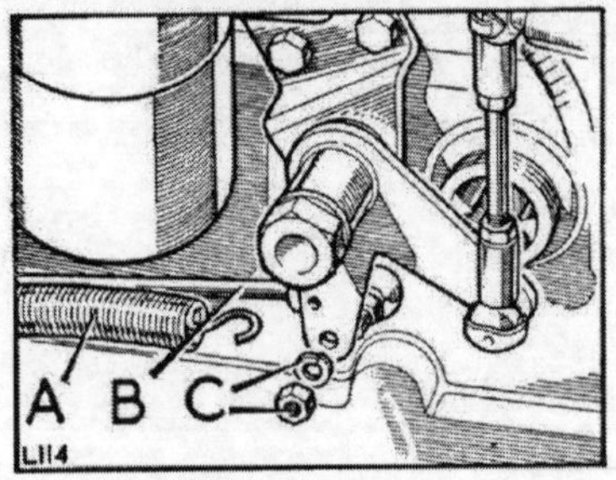

Fig. A3-69. Throttle linkage
A—Return spring
B—Control rod, cross shaft to bell crank
C—Fixings

Operations marked with an asterisk (*) can be carried out with the engine installed in the vehicle

ENGINE—2.6 LITRE PETROL

Operation A3-22—continued

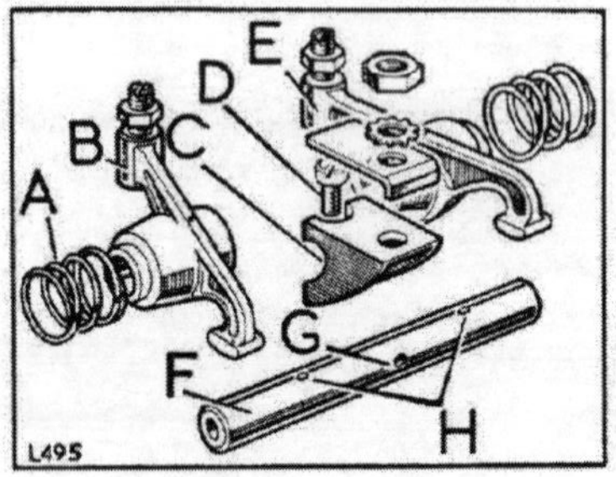

10. Remove the rocker shaft assembly complete from the cylinder head.
11. Mark the inlet valves to ensure they are refitted in their original positions.
12. Compress the valve springs, using valve spring compressor Part No. 276102). Remove split cones and withdraw valves. Remove compressor and lift off valves. Retain the springs in pairs, they are selected to ensure an interference fit.
13. Carefully remove the combustion deposits from the cylinder head and valve ports and the piston crowns.
14. If necessary, remove the inlet valve seat insert by carefully grinding the seat insert away; when thin enough, the insert can be prised out.
15. If necessary, remove the inlet valve guides, first removing the oil seals, using drift (Part No. 274401).

Fig. A3-70. Removing thermostat
A—Outlet pipe fixings
B—Outlet pipe
C—Joint washer
D—Thermostat
E—Cylinder block

Fig. A3-71. Arrangement of top rocker assembly showing front shaft
A—Spring
B—Rocker arm (left-handed) and tappet screw
C—Spacer block
D—Locating screw
E—Rocker arm (right-handed)
F—Rocker shaft. Front (shorter) shaft shown; rear (longer) shaft arrangement is similar, but is fitted with tapped hole toward front
G—Tapped hole for locating screw
H—Plain holes, to be positioned away from valves when shaft is fitted

Cylinder head, assemble

1. Where it is necessary to fit new inlet valve seat inserts to the cylinder head, heat the head evenly for a few minutes to approximately 150°F (65°C), the temperature of a normal degreaser, enter the seat squarely into the cylinder head recess, which must be thoroughly clean, and press into position.
2. Valve guides, to refit: replace the steel shim washer on the new valve guides.
   Lubricate the inlet valve guides and carefully drift them into position, using drift (Part No. 600959). Offer the valves to the guides and ensure they are a satisfactory fit with running clearance but no excessive side-float.
3. Use the valve guide as a pilot and cut the valve seat to 30°.

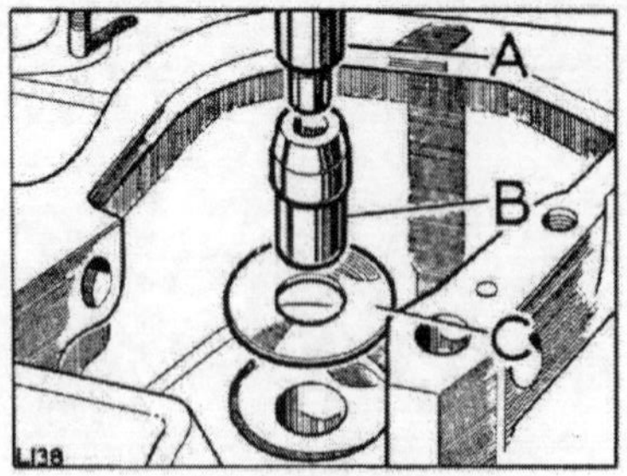

Fig. A3-72. Compressing the inlet valve springs
A—Split cones
B—Waisted recess for cones
C—Special tool. Part No. 276102

Fig. A3-73. Fitting inlet valve guide
A—Assembly drift
B—Inlet valve guide
C—Support washer

ENGINE—2.6 LITRE PETROL

Operation A3-22—continued

4. Face the inlet valves to 30° and lap each valve into its respective seat. The valve end face must be flat when visually checked using a straight edge.

5. Wash each valve seat, port and guide with clean paraffin.

6. It is important that new rubber 'O' rings are fitted to each inlet valve guide after all the lapping and preparatory work has been finished. This will ensure that once fitted the valve is not withdrawn through the bore of the seal, thus destroying the seal.

7. Lightly oil the valve stem and locate each inlet valve into its respective seat. Using the compressing tool (Part No. 276102), fit the spring assemblies, caps and split cones.

8. Replace the complete top rocker shaft assembly and fixings. Fig. A3-71 refers.

9. The cylinder head is now ready for reassembly and should be placed to one side until the cylinder block and exhaust valves have received attention.

Exhaust valves, overhaul

1. Remove the exhaust manifold and withdraw the gaskets.

2. Remove the side rocker cover and joint washer

3. Mark the exhaust valves for refitting in correct sequence.

4. Slacken the tappet adjusting screws right off and set each rocker back on its cam.

5. Compress the valve springs, using valve spring compressor (Part No. 276102). Remove split cones and withdraw valves. Remove compressor and lift out valves. Retain the springs in pairs; they are selected to ensure an interference fit.

6. Remove the combustion deposits from the valves and ports.

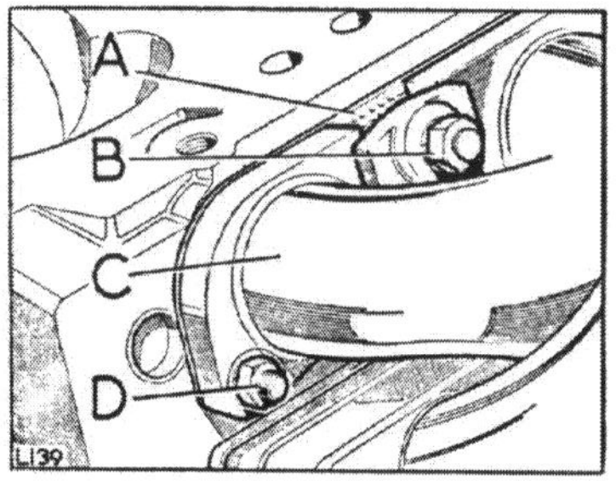

Fig. A3-74. Exhaust manifold fixings

A—Gaskets (3 off)
B—Top fixings (5 off)
C—Manifold
D—Lower fixings (2 off)

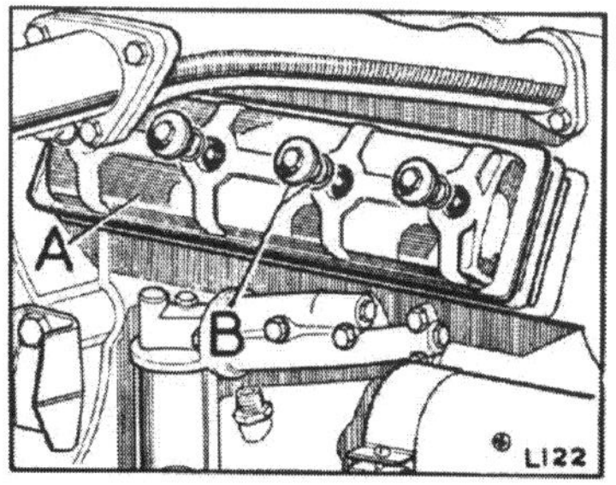

Fig. A3-75. Side rocker cover

A—Rocker cover   B—Fixings

Operation A3-22—continued

Note: If valve seat inserts or valve guides are to be removed, first remove the side rockers and shafts, Operation A3-26, to obtain access.

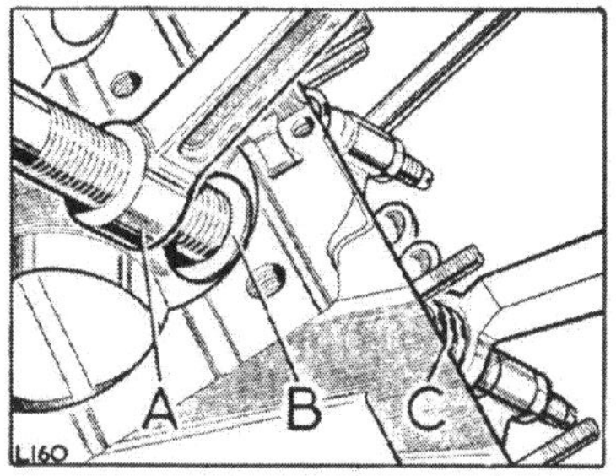

Fig. A3-76. Compressing exhaust valve springs

A—Special tool, Part No. 276102
B—Valve head
C—Valve spring

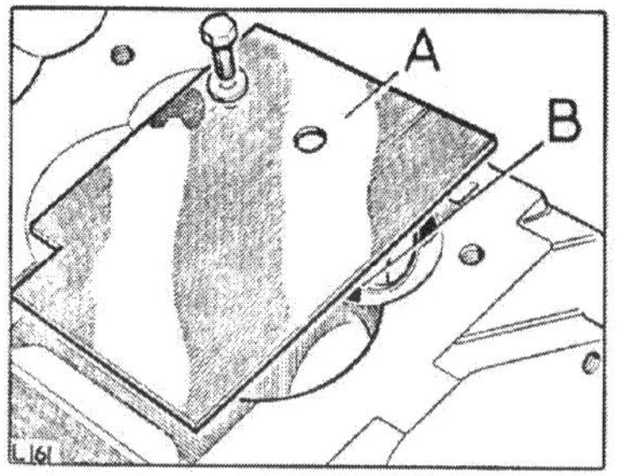

Fig. A3-77. Special protection plate

A—Protection plate, Part No. 263050
B—Exhaust valve seat insert

7. If necessary, remove the valve seat inserts. Owing to the extreme hardness of the seat inserts, great care must be taken during the removal operation to prevent possible injury from flying fragments. A cutting stone should be used, in order to reduce the insert to a minimum thickness, before attempting to break the seat with a chisel. When grinding, take care to avoid damage to the cylinder block.

8. After grinding the seat inserts, secure a protection plate (Part No. 263050) over the cylinder block face and break the seat insert with a suitable chisel applied through the hole in the plate.

9. If necessary, the exhaust valve guides can be drifted out, using a drift (Part No. 274401), as illustrated.

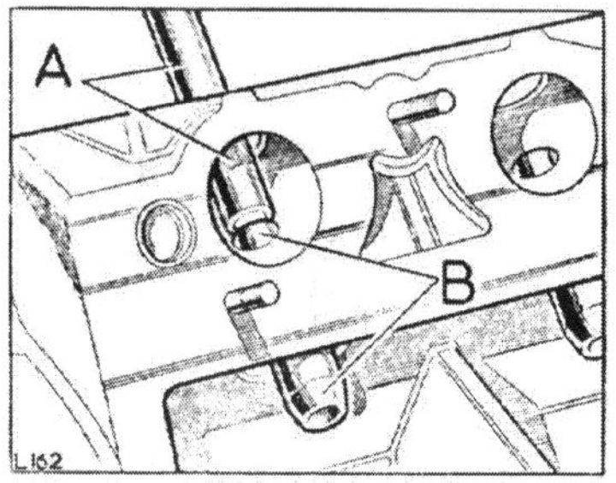

Fig. A3-78. Removing exhaust valve guide with drift

A—Drift   B—Valve guide

Exhaust valves, seats and guides, refit

1. If new exhaust seat inserts are to be fitted, clean the seat recess and pull the new insert into position, using a special tool (Part No. 530625). It is not necessary to heat the block or freeze the insert, but light taps on the tool may be required to ensure that the insert enters smoothly. Continue precautions against fragmentation by fitting the protection plate (Part No. 263050) and leaving it in position for a few minutes, as the insert may shatter.

2. Lubricate the exhaust valve guides and carefully drift them into position, using drift (Part No. 600959).

ENGINE—2.6 LITRE PETROL

Operation A3-22—continued

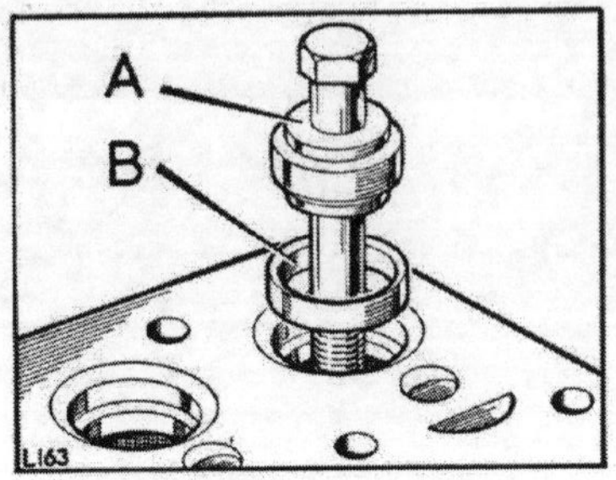

To assemble

1. Refit the side rockers and shafts, Operation A3-26, if previously removed.
2. Fit the cylinder head. Operation A3-21.
3. Adjust the tappets. Operation A3-19.
4. Fit the exhaust manifold, Fig. A3-74 refers.
5. Fit the distributor. Operation A3-18.
6. Fit the carburetter. Operation A3-6.
7. Reconnect the throttle linkage, Fig. A3-69 refers.
8. Refit the sparking plugs.
9. Refit the air cleaner. Operation A3-2.
10. Replenish the coolant system.

Coolant system capacity
Bonneted Control Model, 2.6 Litre Petrol

Imperial Pints	U.S. Pints	Litres	Antifreeze	Frost Precaution
20	24	11,2	33⅓%	—32°C (—25°F)

Fig. A3-79. Fitting exhaust valve seat
A—Insert tool, Part No. 530625
B—Valve seat

3. Use the valve guide as a pilot and cut the valve seat to 46°.
4. Face the exhaust valves to 45° and lap each valve into its respective seat, using suitable equipment.
5. Wash each valve, seat, port and guide with clean paraffin.
6. Lightly oil valve stem and locate the valves into their respective guides. Using the compressor tool (Part No. 276102), fit the spring assemblies, caps and split cones.

ENGINE—2.6 LITRE PETROL

*Engine front cover and oil seal, remove and refit—Operation A3-23

Workshop hand tools:
Spanner sizes: ⅞ in. x ½ in. AF open (2 off) ¼ in. AF socket, 2 BA open end Screwdriver (medium), Pliers

Special Tools:
Part No. 530102, starter dog spanner

To remove

1. Remove the bonnet panel. Operation A3-1.
2. Remove the air cleaner. Operation A3-2.
3. Remove the radiator and grille panel. Operation A3-3.
4. Slacken the dynamo and adjusting link fixings and remove the fan belt. Remove the adjusting link to gain access to the front cover fixings.
5. Remove fan blades, distance piece and fan pulley.
6. Remove the starting dog, using special tool, Part No. 530102, and withdraw the key located pulley from the crankshaft.

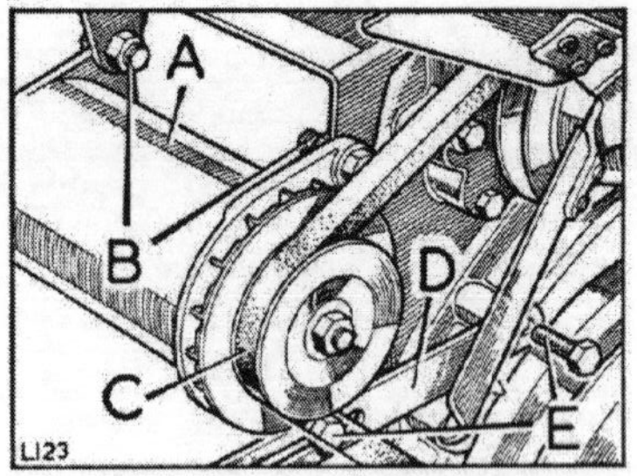

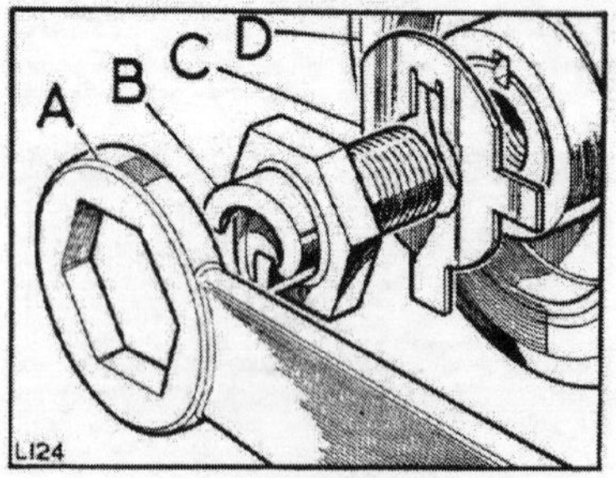

Fig. A3-80. Dynamo adjusting link fixings
A—Dynamo   D—Adjusting link
B—Dynamo fixings   E—Fixings
C—Fan belt

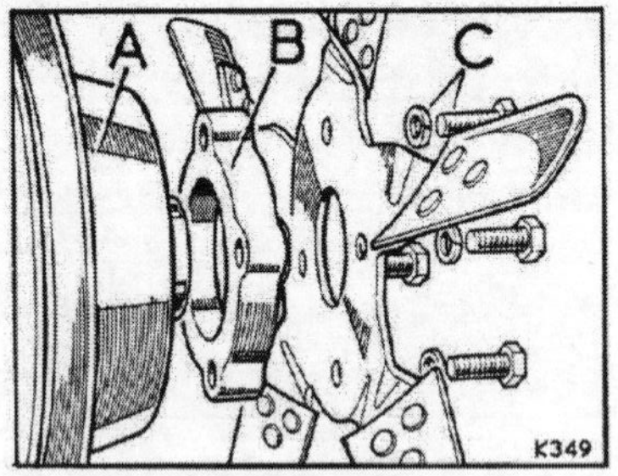

Fig. A3-81. Fan blades fixings
A—Fan pulley
B—Distance piece
C—Fan fixings

Fig. A3-82. Starter dog and pulley fixings
A—Special tool, Part No. 530102
B—Starter dog
C—Starter dog lock plate
D—Crankshaft pulley

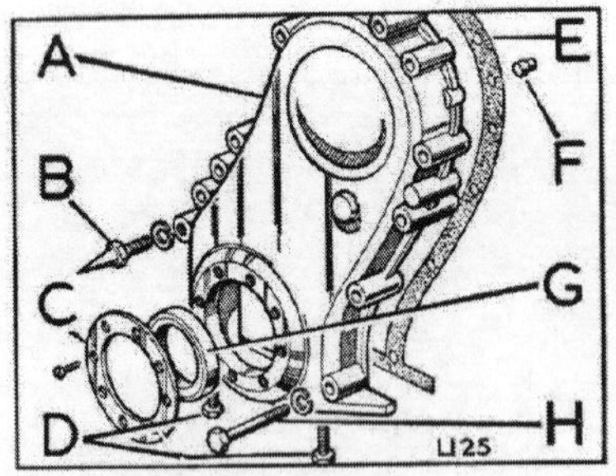

Fig. A3-83. Front cover fixings
A—Front cover
B—Timing pointer
C—Mud excluder, fixed by drive screws.
D—Fixings at sump
E—Joint washer
F—Locating dowel
G—Oil seal
H—Fixings at front of engine

Operations marked with an asterisk (*) can be carried out with the engine installed in the vehicle

ENGINE—2.6 LITRE PETROL

Operation A3-23—continued

7. Remove the fixings and withdraw the front cover and joint washer from the engine.
8. If required remove the oil thrower retained by the crankshaft key.

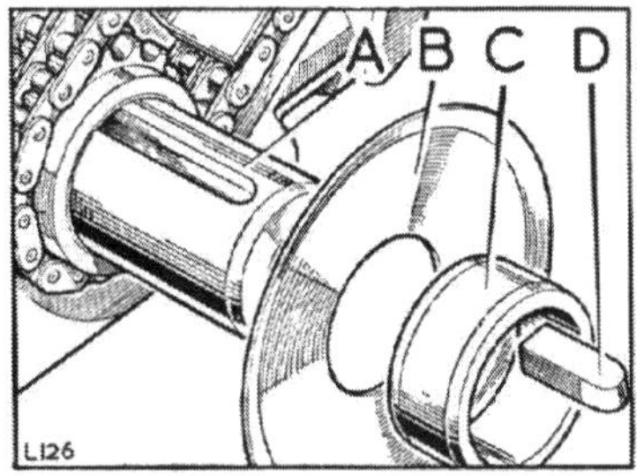

Fig. A3-84. Oil thrower details

A—Crankshaft
B—Oil thrower
C—Oil seal ring
D—Key on crankshaft

Oil seal

If a replacement oil seal is required, proceed as follows:

1. Carefully lever the oil seal metal casing away from the housing bore sufficient to collapse the seal and allow its removal. Use a screwdriver or suitable metal strip as a lever.
2. Apply a thin coating of suitable jointing compound such as Hylomar SQ32M, to the new oil seal metal surfaces.

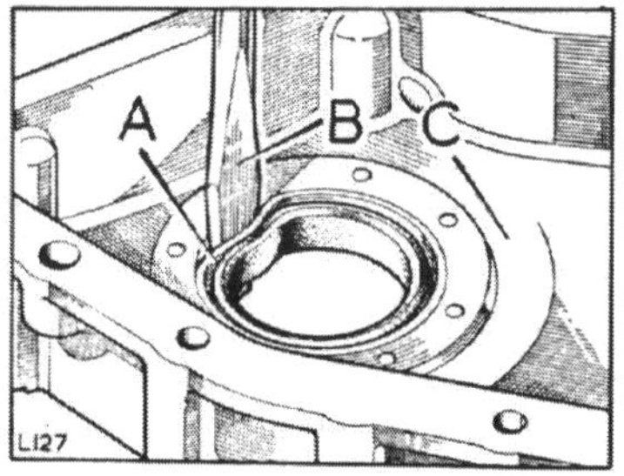

Fig. A3-85. Oil seal removal

A—Oil seal, shown collapsed
B—Suitable lever
C—Front cover

3. Locate the oil seal squarely in the housing bore with garter spring toward operator and press fully in.

To refit

1. If previously removed, fit the oil thrower (concave face toward the front) and oil sealring on to the crankshaft and refit the crankshaft key, Fig. A3-84 refers.
2. Smear general purpose grease on to both sides of the joint washer and position on the engine front cover joint face.
3. Fit the front cover and secure, Fig. A3-82 refers for fixings.
4. Fit the crankshaft pulley, key located, and starter dog. The correct torque loading for the starter dog is 200 lb ft (27,5 mkg). Secure with a new lockplate. Fig. A3-83 refers.
5. Fit the fan blades, pulley and distance piece.
6. Fit the dynamo adjusting link, fit the fan belt and set the fan belt tension. The tension is correct when there is $\frac{5}{16}$ in. to $\frac{7}{16}$ in. (8 mm to 11 mm) free movement, measured as illustrated. Tighten the dynamo fixings and recheck the tension.

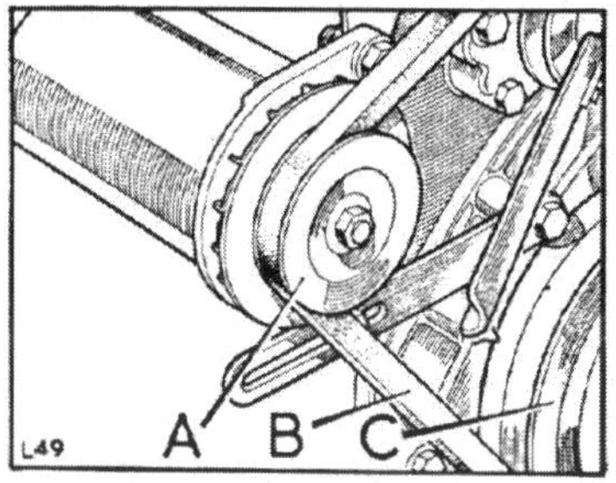

Fig. A3-86. Checking fan belt tension

A—Dynamo pulley
B—Thumb pressure applied midway between the pulleys
C—Crankshaft pulley

7. Refit the radiator and grille panel, Operation A3-3, positioning the fan blades to avoid damage to the radiator block.
8. Refit the air cleaner, Operation A3-2.
9. Refit the bonnet panel, Operation A3-1.

ENGINE—2.6 LITRE PETROL

*Timing chain tensioner, remove and refit—Operation A3-24

Workshop hand tools:
Spanner sizes: $\frac{7}{16}$ in. AF, $\frac{1}{2}$ in. AF open end
$\frac{1}{8}$ in. (3 mm) Allen key

To remove

1. Remove the bonnet panel. Operation A3-1.
2. Remove the air cleaner. Operation A3-2.
3. Remove the radiator grille panel. Operation A3-3.
4. Remove the engine front cover. Operation A3-23.

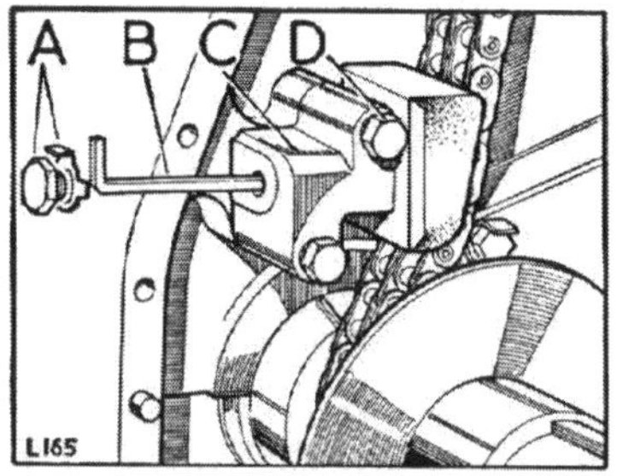

Fig. A3-87. Tensioner and adjuster fixings

A—Retainer plug and tab washer
B—Allen key
C—Chain tensioner
D—Fixings for retaining tensioner to engine

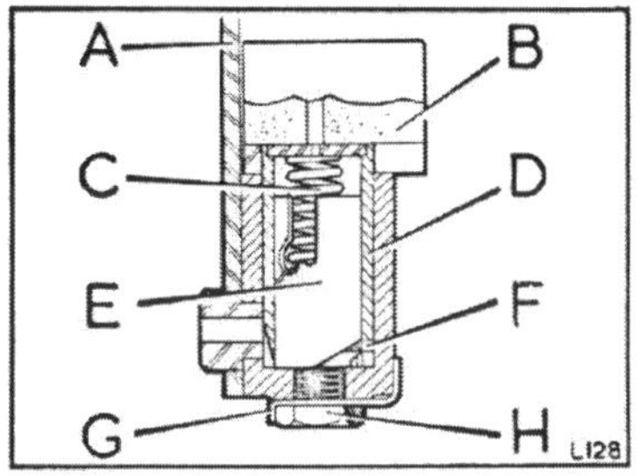

5. Remove the tensioner adjuster plug. Using a $\frac{1}{8}$ in. (3 mm) Allen key, turn the adjuster clockwise until the adjuster retracts into the body, thus relieving the spring loading on the tensioner.
6. Remove the fixings and withdraw the tensioner assembly from the engine.
7. If required, dismantle the assembly by withdrawing the tensioner body from the pad assembly, then turn the adjuster anti-clockwise and allow it to withdraw under spring pressure.
8. Check parts for wear and replace as necessary.

Fig. A3-88. Cross-section view of tensioner arrangement

A—Mounting plate
B—Tensioner pad
C—Tension spring
D—Plunger
E—Adjuster cylinder
F—Limiter peg
G—Tabwasher
H—Plug

To refit

1. If previously dismantled, assemble the spring and adjuster to the tensioner pad bore and turn in fully until retained by the peg in the bore.

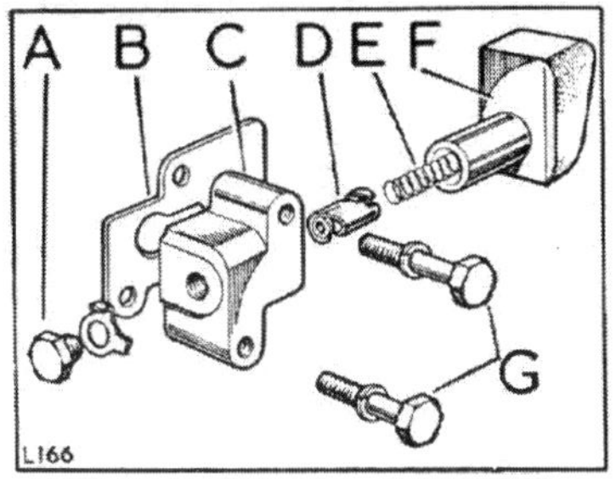

Fig. A3-89. Tensioner arrangement

A—Plug for adjuster tapping
B—Mounting plate
C—Tensioner body
D—Adjuster
E—Spring
F—Tensioner pad
G—Body fixings

2. Fit the tensioner body to the assembled pad, spring and adjuster.
3. Position the mounting plate on the assembly and offer the assembly to the engine, locating on the dowel.
4. Secure with the fixings, Fig. A3-89.

Operations marked with an asterisk (*) can be carried out with the engine installed in the vehicle

ENGINE—2.6 LITRE PETROL Section A3—Land-Rover

Operation A3-24—continued

5. Turn the Allen key in a clockwise direction until the rubber head of the tensioner moves forward under spring pressure against the timing chain. Do not attempt to force the rubber head on to the chain by external pressure and do not turn the Allen key anti-clockwise.

6. Fit the plug and lock tab to the base of the tensioner.

7. Refit the engine front cover. Operation A3-23
8. Refit the radiator and grille panel. Operation A3-3.
9. Refit the air cleaner. Operation A3-2.
10. Refit the bonnet panel A3-1.

Section A3—Land-Rover ENGINE—2.6 LITRE PETROL

*Timing gears and chain, remove and refit—Operation A3-25

(This operation includes valve timing procedure)

Workshop hand tools:
Spanner sizes: $\frac{7}{16}$ in. x $\frac{1}{4}$ in. AF (2 off)
$\frac{1}{2}$ in. AF, $\frac{5}{8}$ in. AF socket
$\frac{2}{2}$ BA open end
Screwdriver (medium), Pliers

Special tools:
Part No. 507231, Chainwheel extractor
Dial test indicator and bracket

To remove

1. Remove the bonnet panel. Operation A3-1.
2. Remove the air cleaner. Operation A3-2.
3. Remove the radiator and grille panel. Operation A3-3.
4. Remove the engine front cover. Operation A3-23.
5. Remove the timing chain tensioner. Operation A3-24.
6. Remove the chainwheels, using special extractor Part No. 507231 to withdraw the camshaft chainwheel, and lift off the timing chain.
7. Inspect the components for damage and general condition.

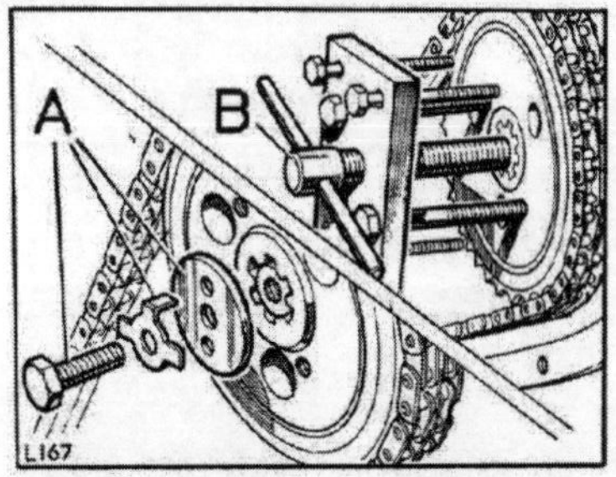

Note: There are two types of camshaft chain wheel in use, a two piece unit consisting of a hub and wheel secured together by three bolts and lock plates, and a later type chainwheel manufactured in one piece used in conjunction with a modified crankshaft chainwheel. Where required, the later type chainwheels may be fitted to early engines (providing they are fitted as a pair) and the valve timing procedure simplified as described in the relevant part of the following 'Procedure'.

Valve timing procedure

In addition to the differing chainwheels in use, the valve timing procedure is also affected by the location of the timing marks on the engine. On early engines, the exhaust peak (EP) mark is located on the flywheel, on later engines it is located on the crankshaft pulley.

To refit and set valve timing—engines with timing pointer on flywheel housing and two piece camshaft chainwheel.

1. Remove engine side rocker cover.

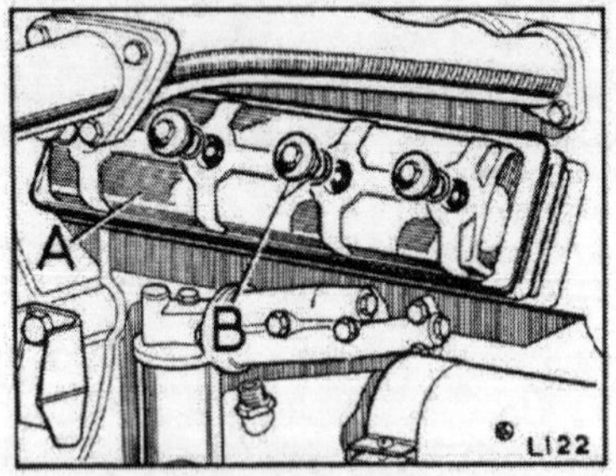

Fig. A3-91. Engine side rocker cover fixings
A—Side cover   B—Fixings

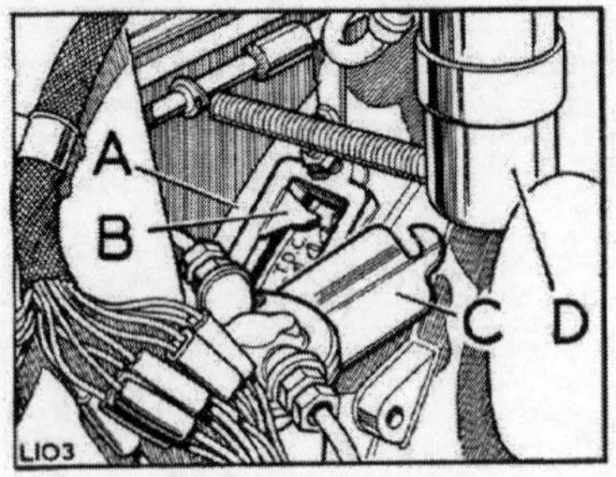

Fig. A3-90. Removing camshaft chainwheel
A—Chainwheel fixings   B—Extractor

Fig. A3-92. Timing pointer location, early engines
A—Flywheel housing
B—Timing pointer
C—Cover plate
D—Ignition coil (reference only)

Operations marked with an asterisk (*) can be carried out with the engine installed in the vehicle

ENGINE—2.6 LITRE PETROL

Operation A3-25—continued

2. Remove the inspection cover plate from the flywheel housing.
3. Fit the crankshaft chainwheel, key located.
4. Turn the crankshaft in direction of rotation until the EP mark on flywheel is in line with timing pointer.

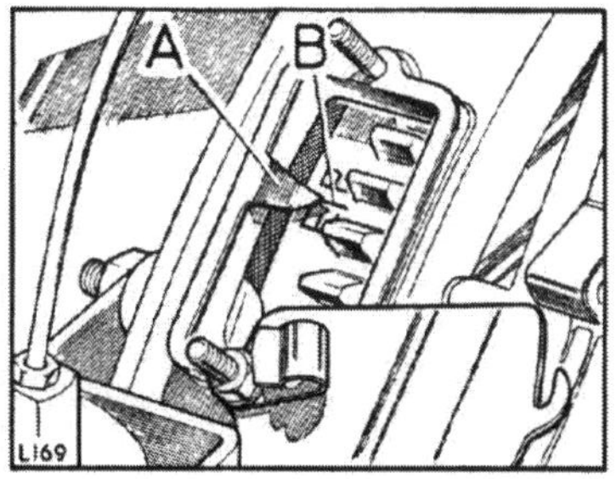

Fig. A3-93. Timing marks
A—Pointer at flywheel housing
B—EP mark on flywheel

5. Fit the camshaft chainwheel and hub assembly on to the camshaft splines. Do not lock the fixings at this stage.

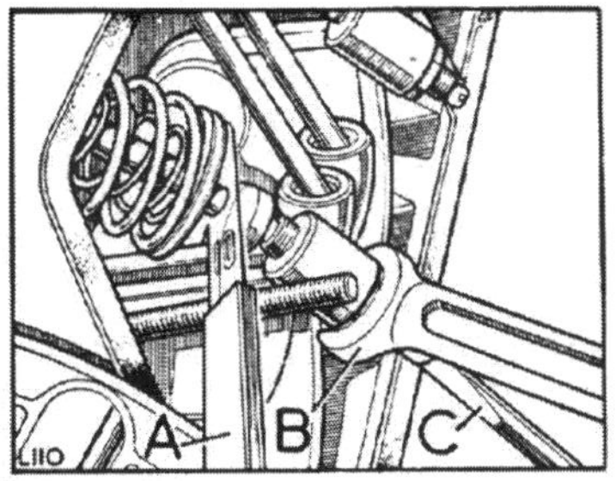

Fig. A3-94. Adjusting tappets
A—Feeler gauge
B—Tappet spanner
C—Screwdriver

6. Rotate the camshaft until No. 1 cylinder exhaust valve is fully closed and set the tappet clearance to .010 in. (0,25 mm).
7. Fit a dial test indicator so that the 'fully open' position of the valve can be ascertained.
8. Turn the camshaft in direction of rotation until the rocker pad has nearly opened the valve fully. Stop camshaft rotation and suitably mark the chainwheel and the timing casing relative to each other.
9. Note the reading on the dial test indicator then further turn the camshaft in direction of rotation until the dial test indicator needle has reached the same position as previously noted. Stop rotation of camshaft.

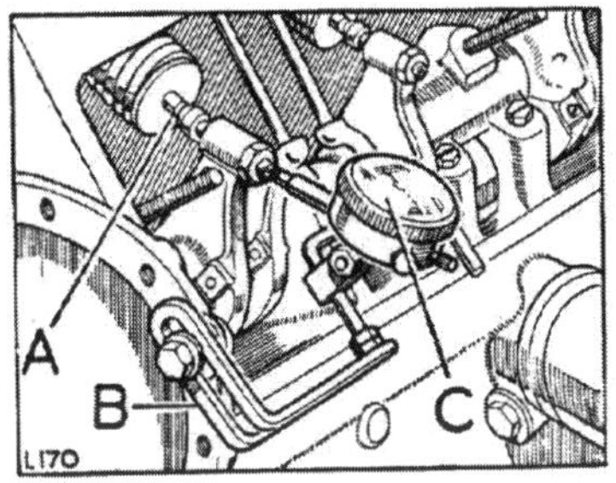

Fig. A3-95. Dial test indicator in position
A—No. 1 cylinder exhaust valve
B—Mounting bracket
C—Dial test indicator

10. Suitably mark the chainwheel adjacent to the mark previously made on the timing casing, then make a third mark to bisect the angle between the two previously made marks.
11. Turn the camshaft against the direction of rotation and align the third (middle) mark with the mark on the timing casing.

Fig. A3-96. Chainwheel marking
A—Second mark on chainwheel
B—Mark between two previously made
C—Mark first made on chainwheel
D—Mark on timing casing

No. 1 exhaust valve is now fully open.

12. Fit the timing chain to the camshaft chainwheel, locate the crankshaft chainwheel on the chain and push the chainwheels home.

It is of the utmost importance that the driving side of the chain is tight to maintain correct valve timing. In order to achieve this condition, additional fixing holes are provided in the camshaft chainwheel which allow the chainwheel to be fitted in alternative positions, one of which will give the required condition.

Further adjustment can be obtained by removing the chainwheel from the hub and repositioning the chainwheel on the camshaft splines. If adjustment is necessary, the greatest care must be taken when removing and refitting the chain and chainwheel, to avoid disturbing the crankshaft and the camshaft.

13. When the valve timing and the driving side of the chain are correctly set, lock the camshaft chainwheel fixings.
14. Recheck the valve timing to ensure that it is correct and has not been disturbed during adjustment or assembly.
15. Refit the inspection cover to the flywheel housing.

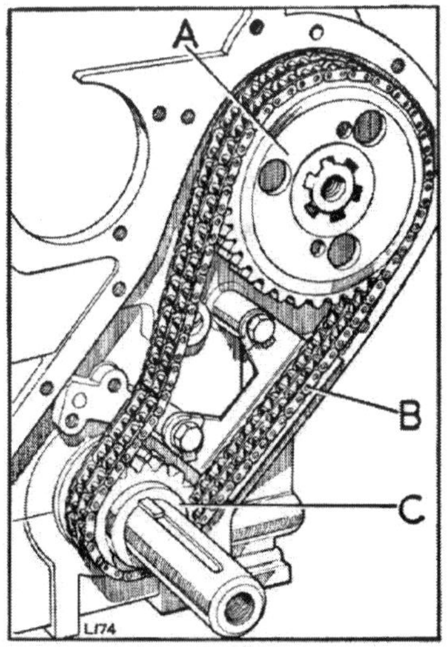

Fig. A3-97. Fitting the timing chain
A—Camshaft chainwheel
B—Timing chain—'no slack' at this side
C—Crankshaft chainwheel

16. Refit the remaining components as detailed under 'To rebuild' at the end of this Operation.

To refit and set valve timing—engines with timing pointer on engine front cover and with the modified chainwheels.

1. Rotate the crankshaft until the keyway in the crankshaft front end is vertical in relation to the cylinder bore. No. 1 cylinder piston is now at top dead centre, that is, at the position required for valve timing.
2. Fit the camshaft chainwheel, using keyway marked 'P', and rotate the chainwheel until the groove marked 'A' is in line with the centre of the tapped hole as illustrated.

ENGINE—2.6 LITRE PETROL   Section A3—Land-Rover

Operation A3-25—*continued*

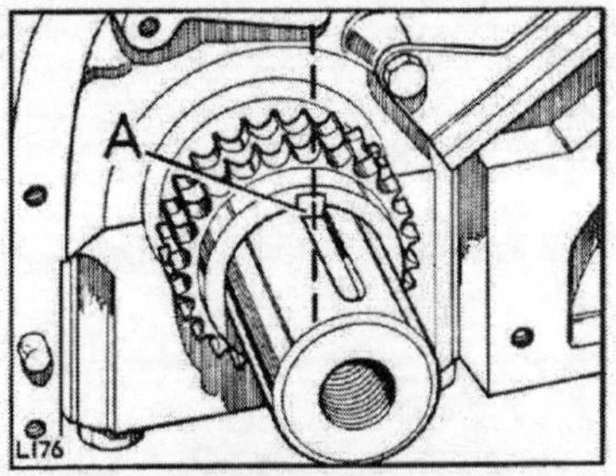

3. With the camshaft chainwheel positioned with the groove marked 'A' aligned with the tapped hole and with the crankshaft chainwheel keyway positioned vertical, fit the timing chain by carefully removing the chainwheels, fitting the chain then fitting the assembly to the engine. Take care not to disturb the chainwheel relative positions. When fitted, there must be no slack chain on the driving side. Fig. A3-97 refers.

4. With the chainwheels set in the above relationship, the valve timing is now correct. Lock the camshaft chainwheel fixings.

To rebuild

1. Refit the timing chain tensioner. Operation A3-24.
2. Refit the engine front cover. Operation A3-23.
3. Refit the radiator grille panel. Operation A3-3.
4. Refill the engine coolant system, allowing a full flow through the coolant drain taps before closing them.

Coolant system capacity
Bonneted Control Model, 2.6 Litre Petrol

Imperial Pints	U.S. Pints	Litres	Antifreeze	Frost Precaution
20	24	11.2	33⅓%	−32°C (−25°F)

5. Refit the side rocker cover. Fig. A3-91 refers.
6. Refit the air cleaner. Operation A3-2.
7. Refit the bonnet panel. Operation A3-1.
8. After a short engine run, carry out tappet adjustment (Operation A3-19) if necessary.

Fig. A3-98. Crankshaft, front end
A—Key for chainwheel in vertical position

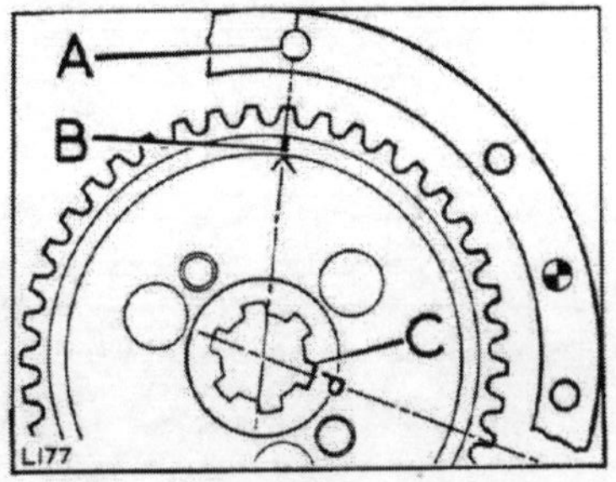

Fig. A3-99. Camshaft chainwheel in position
A—Tapped hole in cylinder block front face
B—Groove marked 'A' in line with centre of tapped hole
C—Fit chainwheel spline marked 'P' on to camshaft key

Section A3—Land-Rover   ENGINE—2.6 LITRE PETROL

*Side rockers and shafts, to remove and refit—Operation A3-26

Special tools:
Extractor (Part No. 262749)
Allen key, ⅛ in. (3 mm)
Spanner for starter dog (Part No. 530102)
Dial test indicator
Bracket for dial test indicator (Part No. 530106)

Workshop hand tools:
Spanner sizes: ⁷⁄₁₆ in. AF, ½ in. AF, ⁹⁄₁₆ in. AF, ¾ in. AF, 2BA Small adjustable ⅛ in. Whit
Screwdriver, medium
Pliers, pointed-nose

To remove

1. Remove the bonnet panel. Operation A3-1.
2. Remove the radiator and grille panel. Operation A3-3.
3. Remove the exhaust manifold. Operation A3-8.
4. Remove the engine front cover. Operation A3-23.
5. Remove the timing chain tensioner. Operation A3-24.
6. Remove the timing gears and chain. Operation A3-25.
7. Remove the top rocker cover and slacken the tappet adjusting screws right back.

Fig. A3-101. Side rockers and tappets
A—Tappet adjusting screws and locknuts
B—Side rocker cover
C—Fixings for side rocker cover

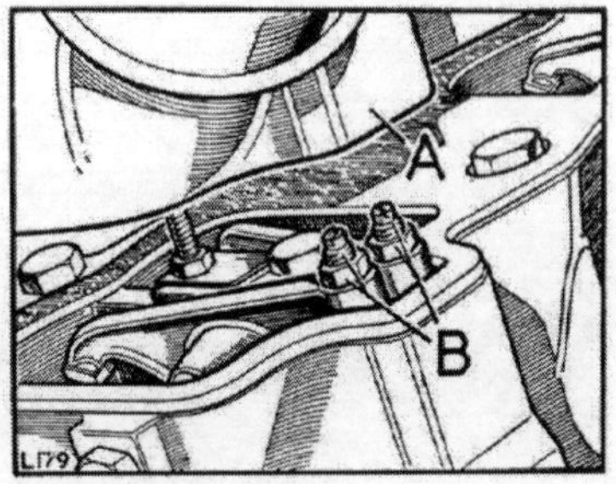

Fig. A3-100. Top rockers and tappets
A—Top rocker cover
B—Tappet adjusting screws and locknuts

8. Remove the side rocker cover and slacken the tappet adjusting screws right back.
9. Remove the end plug from the front end of the rocker shaft.
10. Remove the two locating screws securing front and rear rocker shafts.
11. Remove the oil feed bolt locating the distributor housing to allow removal of the shaft.

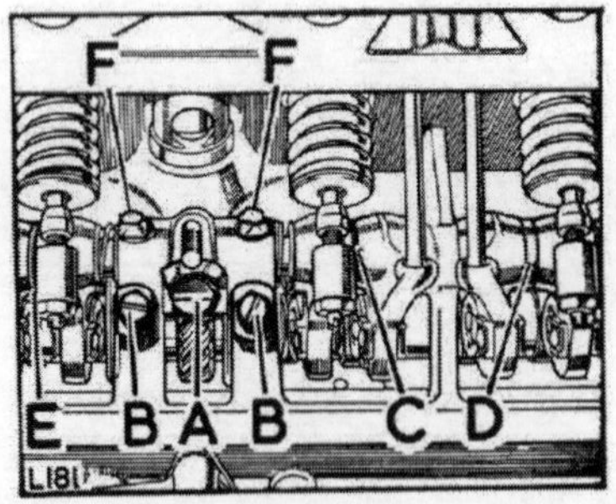

Fig. A3-102. Camshaft and rocker shaft locating screws
A—Oil feed locating bolt
B—Camshaft bearing locating screws
C—Spacing washer, thin
D—Spacing washer, thick
E—Spacing washer, medium
F—Rocker shaft locating screws

*Operations marked with an asterisk (*) can be carried out with the engine installed in the vehicle.

ENGINE—2.6 LITRE PETROL

Operation A3-26—continued

12. Extract the front and rear rocker shafts, using special extractor tool (Part No. 262749).

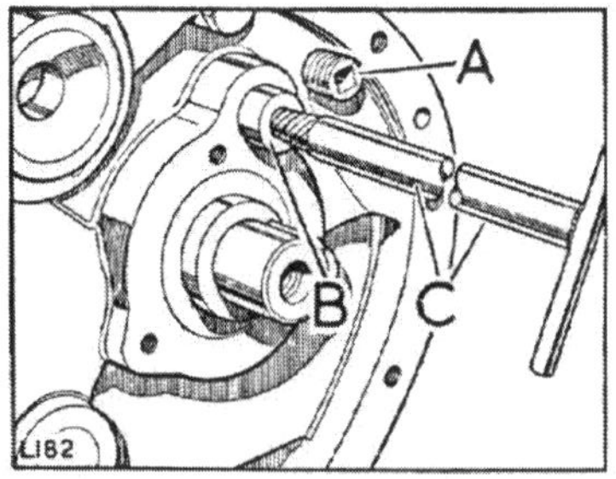

Fig. A3-103. Extractor, rocker shaft
A—Plug   B—Rocker shaft   C—Extractor

13. Remove exhaust valve rockers, inlet cam followers, springs and spacers. Note the sequence of assembly. Push rods should be lifted clear of the rockers as they are removed.

To refit

Note: Before refitting, fit a suitable slave bolt and packing washer into the tapped hole at front end of camshaft. This will enable the camshaft to be rotated as required from the rocker assembly being fitted.

1. Replace the rear rockers, cam followers, springs, spacers and shims in the order removed. Fig. A3-104 refers.
2. Feed the rear rocker shaft through the rockers, followers, etc. Ensure that the locating screw hole in the shaft is to the front; use the extractor tool to align the hole with the hole in the block.
3. Secure the shaft with the locating screw and lock washer.
4. Fit the front rocker assembly, in the order removed. Fig. A3-104.

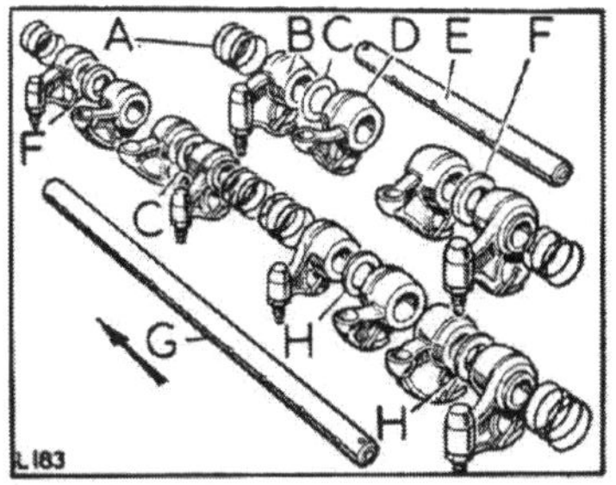

Fig. A3-104. Arrangement of side rocker components
A—Rocker springs (6 off)
B—Rocker with tappet screw (6 off)
C—Spacing washer, thin
D—Rocker for push rod (6 off)
E—Rear shaft (short)
F—Spacing washer, thick
G—Front shaft (longer)
H—Spacing washer, medium
Arrow indicates front of engine

5. Feed the front rocker shaft through the rockers, followers, etc. Ensure that the locating screw hole in the shaft is to the rear and in line with the hole in the block. Secure with locating screw and lock or spring washer.
6. Ensure that the inlet push rods are in position.
7. Replace the end plug.
8. Refit the timing gears and chain and carry out the valve timing procedure. Operation A3-25.
9. Refit the timing chain tensioner. Operation A3-24.
10. Refit the engine front cover. Operation A3-23.
11. Adjust the tappets. Operation A3-19.
12. Refit the side and top rocker covers.
13. Refit the exhaust manifold. Operation A3-8.
14. Refit the radiator and grille panel and replenish the coolant. Operation A3-3.
15. Refit the bonnet panel. Operation A3-1.

*Sump and internal oil strainer, to remove and refit—Operation A3-27

Workshop hand tools:
Spanner sizes: 7/16 in. AF, 1/2 in. AF, 5/8 in. AF
Pliers, long-nosed

Sump and internal oil strainer, remove

1. Lift and prop bonnet.
2. Drain engine oil.
3. Remove dipstick.
4. Remove the fixings securing sump to cylinder block.

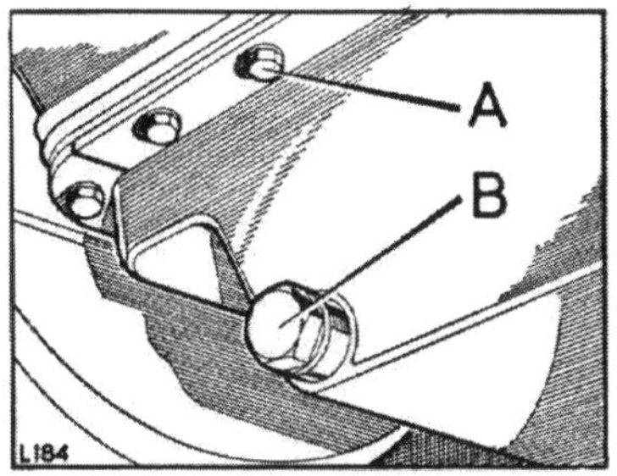

Fig. A3-105. Sump fixings
A—Sump fixings
B—Sump drain plug

5. Lower the sump carefully to clear oil strainer and remove.
6. Remove joint washer.
7. Remove oil strainer from pump.
8. Wash all components using clean fuel.

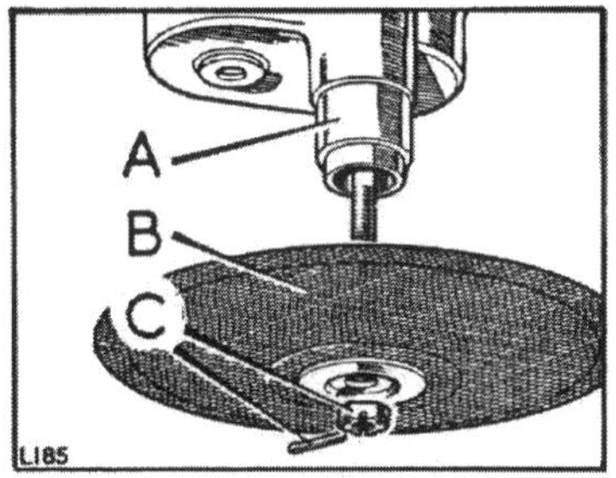

Fig. A3-106. Oil pump strainer
A—Oil pump
B—Strainer
C—Strainer fixings

Sump and internal oil strainer, refit

1. Reverse removal procedure.
2. Use new sump joint washer.
3. Ensure that the two set bolts (7/16 in. UNC) are fitted to the timing cover.
4. Refill the engine to the correct level with the recommended grade of lubricant.

Engine lubricant capacity
Bonneted Control Model, 2.6 Litre Petrol

	Imperial Pint	U.S. Pint	Litre
Engine	12	14.4	6.25
Filter	1	1.2	0.5
Total	13	15.6	6.75

5. Run the engine and check for oil leaks.

Operations marked with an asterisk (*) can be carried out with the engine installed in the vehicle

ENGINE—2.6 LITRE PETROL   Section A3—Land-Rover

*Oil pump and drive shaft, to remove and refit—Operation A3-28

(For oil pump overhaul, Operation A3-29 refers)

Workshop hand tools:
Spanner sizes: ½ in. AF, ⅝ in. AF, ¾ in. AF open end

Special tools:
12 volt test lamp

To remove

1. Remove bonnet panel. Operation A3-1.
2. Remove the distributor and short drive shaft. Operation A3-18.
3. Remove the crankcase sump. Operation A3-27.
4. Remove the non-adjustable oil pressure relief valve. Take care to retain the steel ball which is released during this procedure.

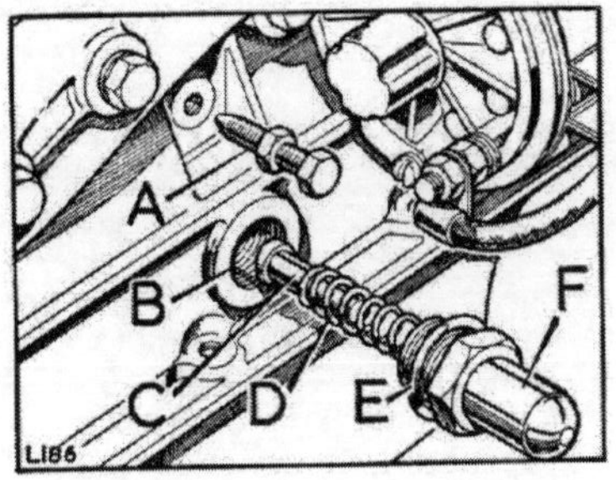

Fig. A3-107. Oil pressure relief valve details

A—Oil pump locating screw
B—Housing for relief valve at RH side of engine block
C—Plunger
D—Spring
E—Joint washer
F—Retaining cap

5. Remove the oil pump locating screw and withdraw the oil pump and strainer assembly from the engine.
6. Remove the side rocker cover.

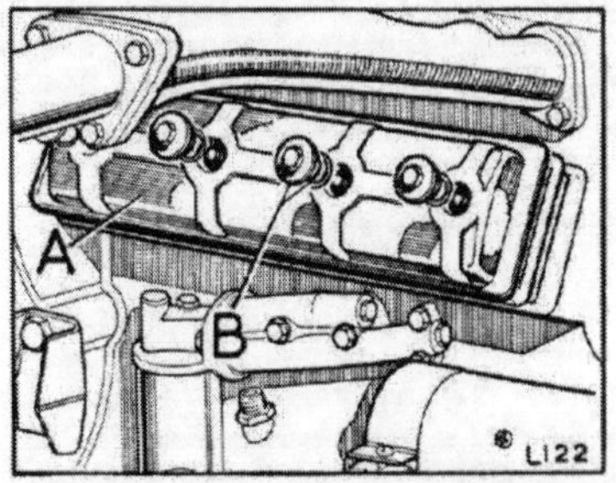

Fig. A3-108. Side rocker cover details

A—Side rocker cover
B—Cover fixings

7. Remove the oil feed bolt and lock washer locating the distributor housing inside rocker chamber.

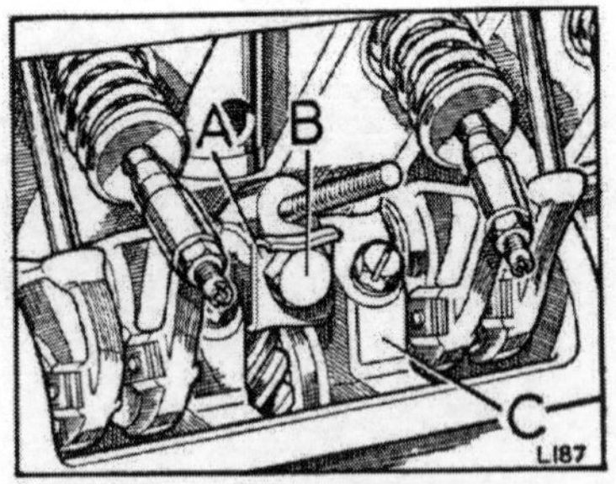

Fig. A3-109. Distributor housing locating bolt

A—Lock washer
B—Oil feed and locating bolt
C—Side rocker chamber

8. Lift out the distributor housing and withdraw the oil pump and distributor gear drive shaft toward the cylinder head.

Section A3—Land-Rover   ENGINE—2.6 LITRE PETROL

Operation A3-28—continued

To refit

1. Offer oil pump to housing, align pressure relief valve housing and the locating screw bore with the respective tappings in the engine block and fit the locating screw and locknut. Fig. A3-107 refers.
2. Fit the relief valve components to the pump, referring to Fig. A3-107 for assembly detail.
3. Rotate the engine in direction of rotation until the TDC mark on the flywheel or crankshaft pulley, as applicable, aligns with the timing pointer with both valves on No. 1 cylinder fully closed (i.e. No. 1 cylinder commencing firing stroke).

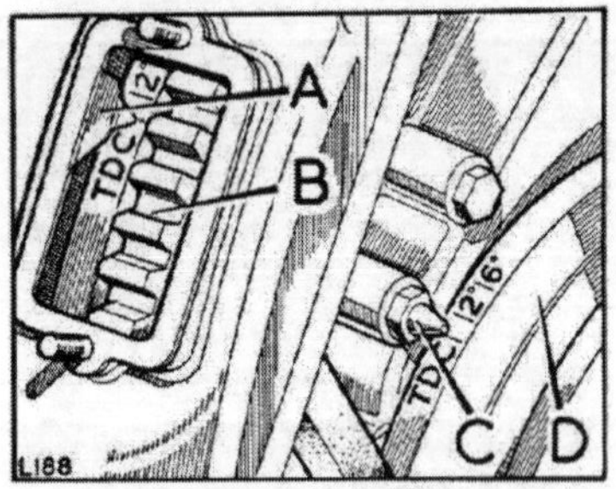

Fig. A3-110. TDC mark aligned with pointer

A—Timing pointer, early engines
B—Flywheel
C—Timing pointer, later engines
D—Crankshaft pulley

4. Fit the oil pump and distributor gear drive shaft to the engine with the lower splines engaged in the oil pump, and the skew gear engaged with the camshaft.
5. Turn the drive shaft using a suitable screwdriver, until the offset drive slot in the end of the shaft is positioned as illustrated in Fig. A3-111.
6. Fit the distributor housing to the engine and locate and secure with the oil feed bolt and lock washer. Fig. A3-109 refers.
7. Insert the short drive shaft, engaging the offset drive in the end of the main shaft.

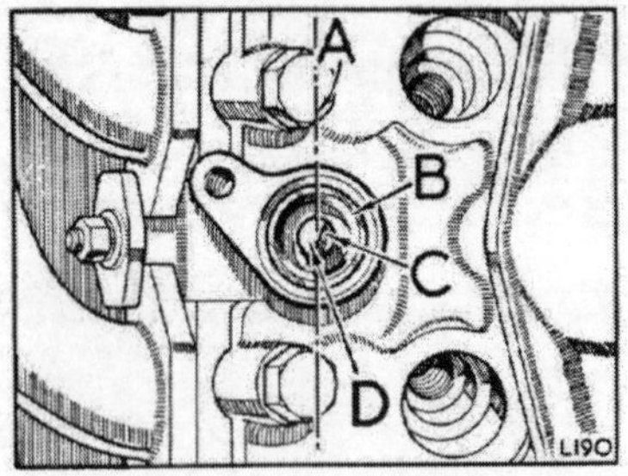

Fig. A3-111. Position of drive slot in gear shaft

A—Parallel with centre line through engine
B—Distributor housing
C—Drive slot
D—Larger segment of drive

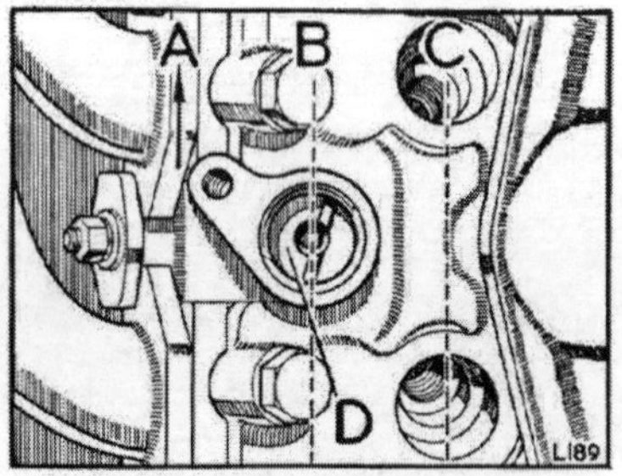

Fig. A3-112. Short drive shaft in position

A—Front of engine
B—Centre line parallel with line through plug holes
C—Centre line through spark plug holes
D—Larger segment of drive

8. Align the offset dog on the distributor shaft with the offset slot in the short drive shaft and fit distributor. The distributor rotor arm should now be in the No. 1 cylinder firing position and the distributor vacuum unit toward the front of the engine.

Operations marked with an asterisk (*) can be carried out with the engine installed in the vehicle

Page 52-A3 — Page 53-A3

ENGINE—2.6 LITRE PETROL

Operation A3-28—continued

9. Refit the rocker side cover. Fig A3-108 refers.
10. Carry out the ignition timing procedure. Operation A3-17.
11. Refit the crankcase sump and replenish the engine lubricating oil. Operation A3-27.
12. Refit the bonnet panel. Operation A3-1.

ENGINE—2.6 LITRE PETROL

Oil pump, to overhaul—Operation A3-29

(For oil pump removal, Operation A3-28 refers)

Workshop hand tools:
Spanner sizes: $\frac{7}{16}$ in. AF, $\frac{1}{2}$ in. AF
Straight edge, Feeler gauges

Oil pump, strip

1. Remove the oil pump strainer, secured by a castle nut and split pin.
2. Remove the oil pump cover, secured by four bolts and spring washers.
3. Lift out the gears, if necessary drive out the bush in the idler gear.
4. Remove the idler gear spindle, which is screwed into the cover. If necessary, drive out the bush at the top of the oil pump body.

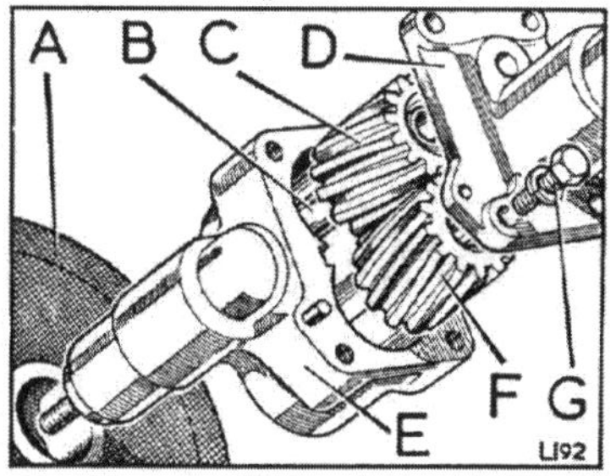

Fig. A3-113. Exploded view of oil pump

A—Strainer
B—Idler gear spindle
C—Idler gear and bush assembly
D—Oil pump cover
E—Oil pump body
F—Driving gear
G—Pump cover fixings

5. Clean all parts, examine for wear and renew as necessary.

Oil pump, rebuild

1. If removed, press a new bush into the body and ream in position to .5625 in. plus .001 in. (14,28 mm plus 0,02 mm). Ensure correct alignment with the bore at the bottom end of the pump body, and the bush should be a light drive fit.
2. If removed, press a new bush in the idler gear. Drill the $\frac{1}{8}$ in. (3,0 mm) oilway and ream in position to .500 in. plus .001 in. (12,7 mm plus 0,02 mm).
3. If removed, replace the idler gear spindle.
4. Refit the gears and check tolerances as follows:
   (a) Check the radial clearance, which should be .001 to .004 in. (0,02 to 0,10 mm).
   (b) Check the backlash between gears, which should be .008 to .012 in. (0,20 to 0,30 mm).
   (c) Check the end-float of the gears:
       Steel .002 to .005 in. (0,05 to 0,12 mm)
       Aluminium .003 to .006 in. (0,07 to 0,15 mm)
       Renew parts as necessary. If the clearances are incorrect, oil flow will be insufficient.

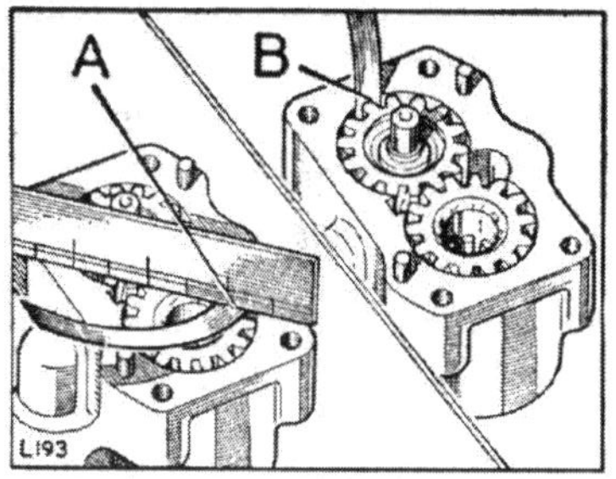

Fig. A3-114. Checking clearance of oil pump gears

A—Checking end-float
B—Checking radial clearance

5. When the tolerances are correct, fit the idler gear to the spindle. Mesh the driving gear (steel) with the idler gear, inserting the splined end of the gear first.
6. Fit the housing to the pump cover, renewing the locknuts.
7. Fit the oil strainer.

ENGINE—2.6 LITRE PETROL   Section A3—Land-Rover

*Clutch assembly and flywheel, remove and refit—Operation A3-30

(For overhaul instructions, Section B refers. For flywheel data see Engine detail data at end of this Section)

Workshop hand tools:
Spanner sizes: ½ in. AF, ⅝ in. AF socket
⁷⁄₁₆ in. AF open end, ⅞ in. AF socket
⁷⁄₁₆ in. BSF open end
1 lb hammer, Small chisel

Special tools:
Part No. 605022—Clutch plate alignment gauge
Torque wrench
Dial test indicator

To remove

Note: If it is required to remove the clutch only, it is not necessary to remove the seat base nor completely remove the gearbox. Proceed with the gearbox removal, Operation C1-3, but only withdraw the gearbox rearward approximately 5 in (127 mm), to give access to the clutch fixings.

1. Remove the gearbox tunnel and front panel, Operation A3-4.
2. Remove the gearbox complete, as detailed in Section C.
3. Remove the starter motor, Operation A3-9, to facilitate subsequent procedure.
4. Mark the position of the clutch assembly cover plate in relation to the flywheel. The marks are for use during subsequent refitting, when, with the marks aligned, the original balance condition will be regained.
5. Remove the fixings and withdraw the clutch assembly from the flywheel. Withdraw the clutch plate which is released during this procedure.

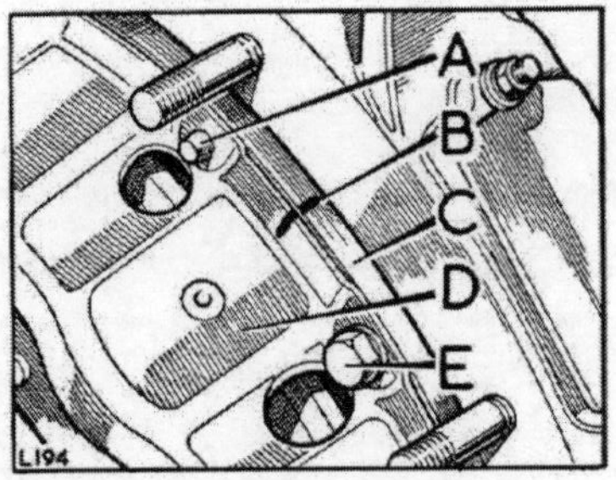

Fig. A3-115. Clutch assembly fixings
A—Locating dowels
B—Suitably mark clutch cover relative to flywheel
C—Flywheel
D—Clutch assembly
E—Fixings for clutch (6 off)

6. Remove the fixings and withdraw the flywheel.

To refit

1. Fit the flywheel to the crankshaft and tighten the fixings to 60 lb ft to 65 lb ft (8,5 mkg to 9,0 mkg) torque load. Do not lock the fixings at this stage.
2. Check the run-out on the flywheel face as illustrated. The run-out must not exceed .002 in. (0,05 mm).

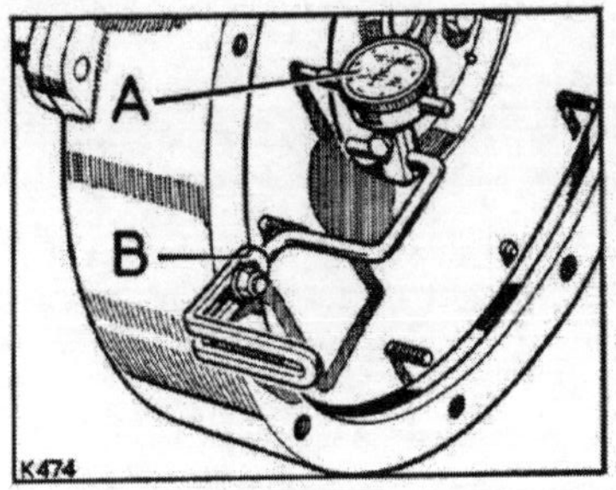

Fig. A3-116. Checking run-out on flywheel face
A—Dial test indicator
B—Suitable bracket

3. Lock the flywheel fixings.
4. Offer the clutch driven plate to the primary shaft and ensure that it will slide easily on all the splines.
5. Place the driven plate in position on the flywheel with the longer end of the central boss away from the engine.
6. Centralise the driven plate with the flywheel, using a slave primary shaft or the special centralising tool, Part No. 605022.
7. Offer up the clutch assembly to the flywheel, aligning the previously made relationship markings. Fig. A3-115 refers.
8. Fit the fixings and tighten evenly one turn at a time to 22 lb ft to 25 lb ft (3,0 mkg to 3,5 mkg) torque load, using diagonal selection to avoid distortion of the clutch cover.

Operation A3-30—continued

Fig. A3-117. Centralising clutch driven plate
A—Flywheel
B—Flywheel fixings
C—Driven plate
D—Centralising tool or slave primary shaft

9. Lock the clutch assembly fixings.
10. Remove the centralising tool or slave shaft.
11. Refit the starter motor, Operation A3-9.
12. Refit the gearbox as detailed in Section C.
13. Check and set the clutch pedal adjustment as detailed in Section B.
14. Refit the gearbox tunnel and front panel. Operation A3-4.

Operations marked with an asterisk (*) can be carried out with the engine installed in the vehicle

ENGINE—2.6 LITRE PETROL

*Rear main bearing oil seal and flywheel housing, remove and refit—Operation A3-31

Workshop hand tools:
Spanner sizes: 7/16 in. AF, 9/16 in. AF open end
5/8 in. BSF, 7/16 in. BSF open end
7/16 in. AF, 1/2 in. AF, 9/16 in. AF, 5/8 in. AF, 13/16 in. AF socket, 1/2 in. AF ring
1/4 in. BSF socket
Screwdriver (medium), Pliers, snipe nosed
1 lb hammer, Small chisel, Feeler gauges

Special tools:
Part No. 600963—Engine lifting sling
Part No. 270304—Guides for rear main bearing oil seal (2 off)
Part No. 605022—Clutch plate alignment gauge
Torque wrench

To remove

1. Remove bonnet panel. Operation A3-1.
2. Remove the gearbox tunnel and front cover. Operation A3-4.
3. Remove gearbox assembly. Section C.
4. Remove the starter motor. Operation A3-9.
5. Remove the crankcase sump. Operation A3-27.
6. Remove the clutch assembly and flywheel. Operation A3-30.
7. Fit suitable lifting equipment and support the engine weight.
8. Remove the packing piece from between the flywheel housing and the chassis cross-member, previously fitted during gearbox removal.
9. Remove the fixings and withdraw the flywheel housing. Remove the oil sealing ring.

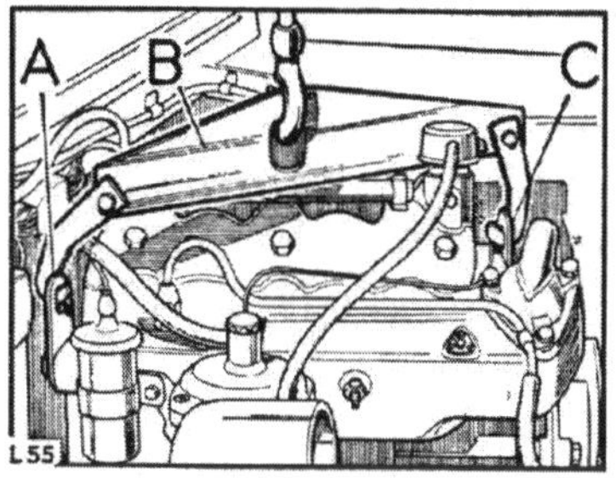

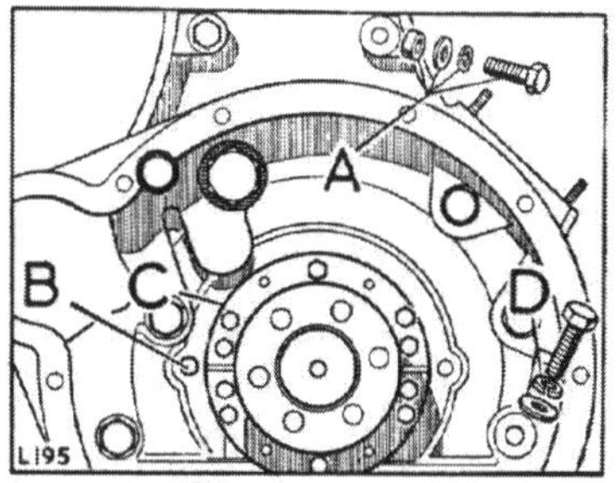

Fig. A3-118. Lifting sling in position
A—Rear lifting bracket
B—Engine lifting sling, Part No. 600963, engaged in lifting brackets
C—Front lifting bracket

Fig. A3-119. Flywheel housing fixings
A—Fixings at flange
B—Locating dowels
C—Oil seal in recess
D—Fixings in counterbores

10. Remove the rear bearing cap.
11. Remove the fixings and detach the two halves of the rear main bearing oil seal retainer from the cylinder block and rear bearing cap respectively. The halves are dowel located.

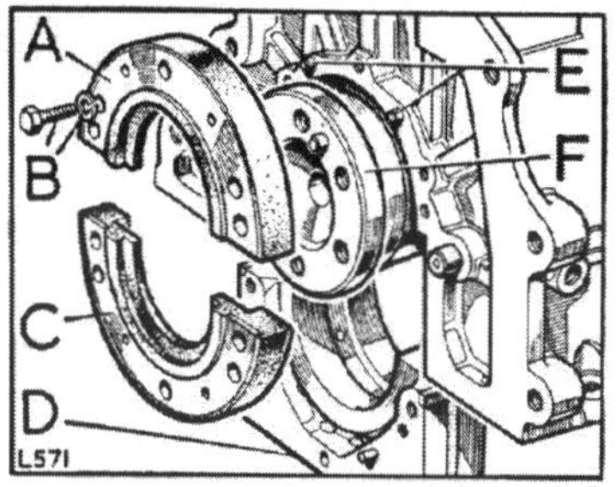

Fig. A3-120. Seal retainer fixings
A—Seal retainer upper half
B—Fixings for seal retainers
C—Seal retainer lower half
D—Rear main bearing cap
E—Locating dowels
F—Crankshaft flange

Operations marked with an asterisk (*) can be carried out with the engine installed in the vehicle

---

Operation A3-31—continued

12. Remove the oil seal from the crankshaft. Fig. A3-122 refers.

Rear main bearing oil seal, to refit

1. Assemble the garter spring on the oil seal journal of the crankshaft, laying the spring around the journal, with the hook and the eye adjacent to one another, then insert the hook into the eye. See Fig. A3-121. Care must be taken to ensure that during this operation the spring is not stretched at all.

The spring should be moved along the journal until it is against the thrower flange.

2. Apply Silicone Grease MS4 (provided in the replacement oil seal kit) to the crankshaft oil seal journal and to both sides of the split oil seal sealing lip.

Open the split seal sufficiently to allow it to be fitted over the crankshaft oil seal journal. Recess in oil seal must be towards thrower flange and garter spring.

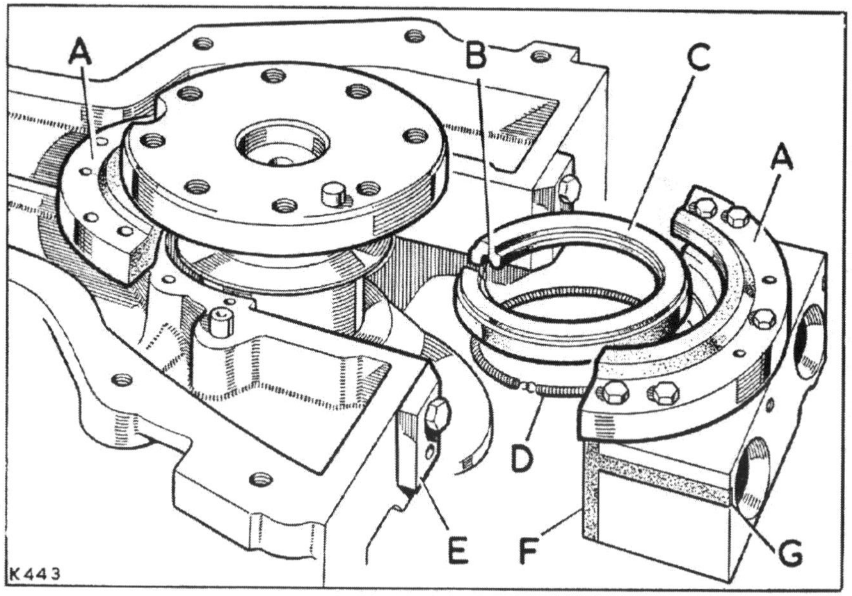

Fig. A3-121. Oil seal details
A—Retainer halves
B—Split line of seal to be towards top of engine
C—Split oil seal
D—Garter spring, hook and eye to be midway between split and hinge of oil seal when fitted
E—Guides, Part No. 270304, for rear main bearing cap 'T' seals
F—Trim these edges before fitting to avoid foul on seating radius
G—Trim these ends to allow 1/32 in. (0,8 mm) protrusion when cap is fitted

ENGINE—2.6 LITRE PETROL

Operation A3-31—continued

The oil seal must not be repeatedly fitted and removed from the crankshaft, as this can damage the sealing lip.

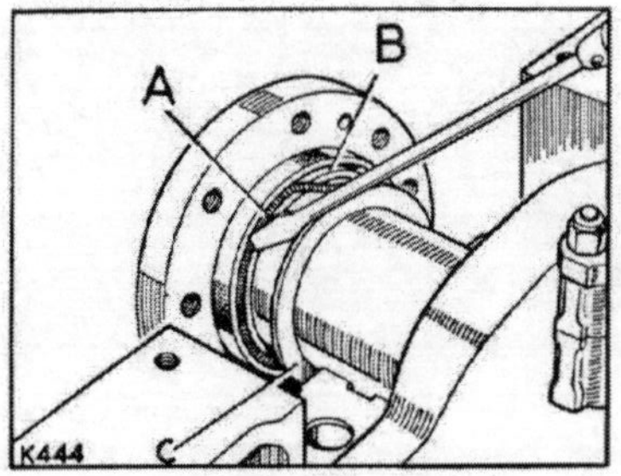

Fig. A3-122. Fitting garter spring to recess

A—Garter spring
B—Oil seal recess for garter spring
C—Thrower flange

3. Ensure that the hook and eye of the garter spring are located mid-way between the split and hinge of the oil seal. Then, using a small screwdriver or similar tool, gently ease the spring into the recess in the oil seal.

4. Rotate the oil seal until the split is on the vertical axis pointing towards the cylinder head and in its approximate running position on the journal; this position is important.

 Apply Hylomar SQ32M sealing compound to the seal diameter of the two half plates, using either an applicator or a brush.

 Important: Do not degrease the half seal plates with trichlorethylene, but wipe clean with a dry cloth prior to applying the Hylomar.

5. Fit one half of the oil seal retainer on to the crankcase dowels. The oil seal should be compressed to assist assembly, also ensure that it is correctly located in the retainer recess. Bolt the retainer to the crankcase, do not fully tighten the fixings at this stage. In order to fit the bolt it

will be necessary to rotate the crankshaft; it is essential to hold the seal so that it does not rotate with the crankshaft.

6. Bolt the other half of the oil seal retainer on to the main bearing cap, in the same way. Apply Silicone grease MS4 to the "T" seals and fit them to the main bearing cap. The cap must be off the crankcase for these operations. Trim the edges of the "T" seals as illustrated to prevent them from fouling the cylinder block when fitted.

7. Fit the main bearing cap with the seal retainer, bearing shell and "T" seals to the crankcase until there is a 1/32 in. (0,8 mm) gap between the cap and crankcase. Use the guides, Part No. 270304 to feed the "T" seals past the crankcase edges, see Fig. A3-121.

8. Ensure that the seal remains correctly located in the retainer recess.

9. Pull the cap down slowly, ensuring there is no buckling of the split seal or misalignment of the butt joint.

10. Tighten the cap bolts to 75 lb ft (10 mkg) torque load and recheck that the seal is located correctly in the housing.

11. Finally tighten the bolts securing the retainer halves. Turn the bolt heads so that the hexagon corners will not foul the flywheel housing seal when fitting.

Flywheel housing, to refit

12. Replace the oil seal in the flywheel housing recess and fit the housing to the cylinder block. Fig. A3-119 refers.

13. Refit the clutch and flywheel. Operation A3-30.

14. Refit the crankcase sump. Operation A3-27. During this procedure trim the ends of the rear main bearing "T" seals to allow approximately 1/32 in. (0,8 mm) protrusion from the rear bearing cap face. Fig. A3-121 refers.

15. Refit the starter motor. Operation A3-9.

16. Refit the gearbox, as described in Section C, and remove the engine lifting equipment.

17. Refit the front floor. Operation A3-4.

18. Replenish engine lubricating oil as necessary.

19. Refit the bonnet panel. Operation A3-1.

Engine lubricant capacity
Bonneted Control Model, 2.6 Litre Petrol

	Imperial Pint	U.S. Pint	Litre
Engine	12	14.4	6.25
Filter	1	1.2	0.5
Total	13	15.6	6.75

ENGINE—2.6 LITRE PETROL

*Pistons and connecting rods, remove and refit—Operation A3-32

(For overhaul instructions, Operation A3-33 refers)

Workshop hand tools:
Spanner sizes: 7/16 in. AF, 1/2 in. AF, 9/16 in. AF, 3/4 in. AF sockets
1/2 in. AF, 7/16 in. AF, 3/8 in. AF, 5/8 in. AF, 3/4 in. AF open end, 1/2 in. AF ring
7/16 in. BSF, 3/8 in. BSF open end
14 mm plug spanner

Screwdriver (medium), Pliers

Special tools:
Torque wrench

To remove

1. Remove the bonnet panel. Operation A3-1.
2. Remove the air cleaner. Operation A3-2.
3. Remove the cylinder head. Operation A3-21.
4. Remove the crankcase sump. Operation A3-27.
5. With two pistons at bottom dead centre (BDC) remove the connecting rod cap fixings.
6. Remove the caps and withdraw the connecting rod bearing halves. Retain the caps and bearings in related sets.

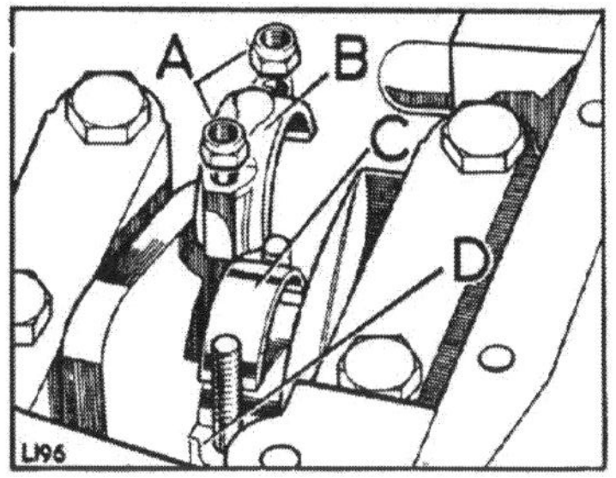

Fig. A3-123. Connecting rod big-end details
A—Fixings for connecting rod cap
B—Connecting rod cap
C—Connecting rod bearing lower half
D—Connecting rod big-end

7. Withdraw the pistons and attached connecting rods from the top of the bore.
8. Position the remaining pistons at BDC and repeat the removal procedure.
9. Retain the removed components in related sets.

To refit

Note: If replacement components are to be fitted, the checks detailed in 'overhaul'—Operation A3-33' must be carried out as necessary.

1. Position the piston rings so that the piston rings end gaps do not align with each other or with the gudgeon pin bore in the piston.
2. Position the crankshaft with two crank pins at BDC and insert the appropriate pistons and attached connecting rods into the cylinder bores, from the top of the cylinder block, using a suitable piston ring clamp.

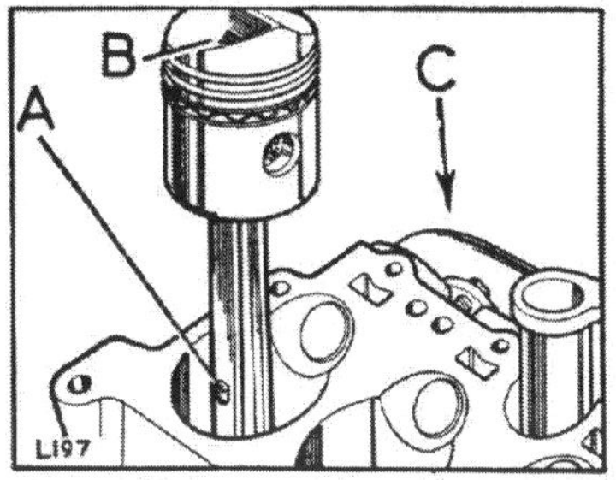

Fig. A3-124. Refitting pistons and connecting rods
A—Oil hole in connecting rod positioned away from camshaft side of engine
B—Flat on piston crown positioned away from camshaft
C—Camshaft side of block

3. Lubricate the journals and bearing halves and fit the appropriate bearing halves to the connecting rods and caps.

4. Fit the connecting rod caps and new fixing nuts with the locating tongues on the upper and lower bearing halves at the same side of the connecting rod. Tighten the fixings to 20 lb ft (2,8 mkg).

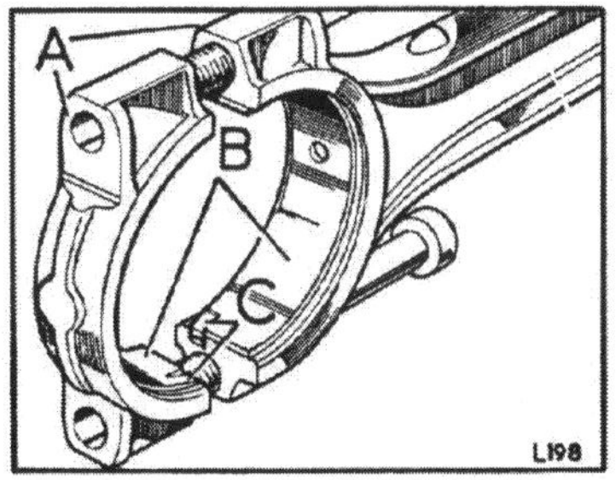

Fig. A3-125. Connecting rod big-ends
A—Cap and connecting rod, check cylinder bore identity numbers correspond
B—Bearing halves located by tongues
C—Tongues are positioned at same side of connecting rod

5. Repeat the procedure to fit the remaining piston assemblies.
6. Refit the crankcase sump. Operation A3-27.
7. Refit the cylinder head. Operation A3-21.
8. Set the tappet clearances as detailed in Operation A3-19.
9. Refill the engine coolant system.

Coolant system capacity
Bonneted Control Model, 2.6 Litre Petrol

Imperial Pints	U.S. Pints	Litres	Antifreeze	Frost Precaution
20	24	11.2	33⅓%	—32°C (—25°F)

10. Replenish the engine lubrication system.

Engine lubricant capacity
Bonneted Control Model, 2.6 Litre Petrol

	Imperial Pint	U.S. Pint	Litre
Engine	12	14.4	6.25
Filter	1	1.2	0.5
Total	13	15.6	6.75

11. Refit the bonnet panel. Operation A3-1.

Operations marked with an asterisk (*) can be carried out with the engine installed in the vehicle

ENGINE—2.6 LITRE PETROL

Pistons and connecting rods, overhaul—Operation A3-33

(For removal and refitting instructions, Operation A3-32 refers)

Workshop hand tools:
Spanner sizes: ⅞ in. AF socket
Circlip pliers, Feeler gauges

Special tools:
Torque wrench
Part No. 605238—'Plastigage' strip
Piston ring clamp

To dismantle

Note: During the following procedures retain all components in related sets to facilitate subsequent assembly.

1. Remove the piston rings using suitable expanding pliers.
2. Remove circlips and withdraw gudgeon pins. Where piston crowns are marked with an 'X', withdraw the gudgeon pin toward the 'X' side.

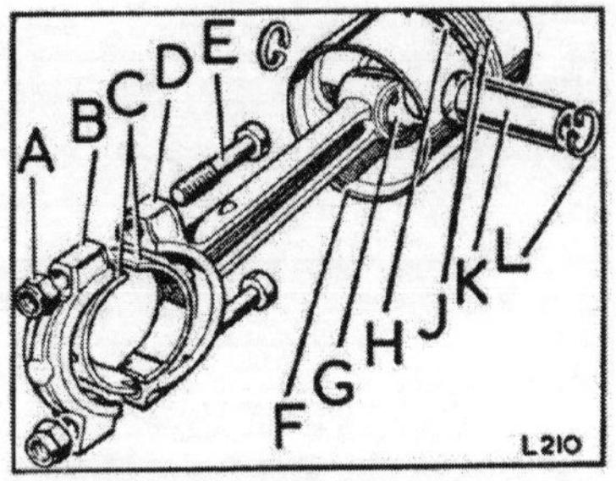

Fig. A3-126. Exploded view of piston and connecting rod

A—Connecting rod cap fixings
B—Connecting rod cap
C—Bearing halves
D—Connecting rod
E—Fixing bolts
F—Piston
G—Gudgeon pin bush
H—Scraper ring
J—Compression rings
K—Gudgeon pin
L—Retaining circlips for gudgeon pin

Pistons, check

1. New piston assemblies are available for replacement purposes in standard diameter and by .010 in. (0,25 mm) oversizes up to .040 in. (1 mm).
2. Standard size pistons are graded in diameter size differences of .0002 in. (0,005 mm). This grading does not apply to oversize pistons. The grade letter which is stamped on the piston crown represents a diameter dimension as follows:

Grade letter	Cylinder bore diameter
'Z'	Nominal to plus .0002 in. (0,005 mm) above nominal.
'A'	.0002 in. to .0004 in. (0,005 mm to 0,01 mm) above nominal.
'B'	.0004 in. to .0006 in. (0,01 mm to 0,015 mm) above nominal.
'C'	.0006 in. to .0008 in. (0,015 mm to 0,02 mm) above nominal.
'D'	.0008 in. to .0010 in. (0,02 mm to 0,025 mm) above nominal.

3. When fitting standard pistons in a comparatively new engine, a graded piston, corresponding to the piston removed, should be fitted. However, a check must still be made to ensure that the clearance falls within the limits laid down.

4. For example: If the vehicle has done little mileage and there is no appreciable bore wear, a graded piston of the same size as that taken out should be used; however, if a certain amount of bore wear is apparent, it may be necessary to fit a piston two or three grades larger than the one removed. In the case of a top-limit piston fitted as original equipment, it may be necessary to rebore to the first oversize to obtain the correct piston fit.

5. The grade size of any particular bore is also stamped on the cylinder block exhaust manifold face, using the same letters as stamped on the piston crown.

6. When fitting pistons, standard or oversize, into a new or rebored cylinder block, the clearance should be checked as follows:
   (a) Clearance in the bore, measured at the bottom of the piston skirt at right angles to the gudgeon pin — .002 to .0025 in. (0,05 to 0,06 mm).
   (b) Clearance in the bore, measured at the top of the piston skirt at right angles to the gudgeon pin — .003 to .0035 in. (0,08 to 0,09 mm).

Operations marked with an asterisk (*) can be carried out with the engine installed in the vehicle

Operation A3-33—continued

In the absence of other suitable measuring instruments a long feeler, .0035 in. (0,09 mm) thick, may be used. Insert the feeler against the thrust side of the bore, as illustrated, with the piston located crown downward. The piston should become a tight fit when the top of the skirt (immediately below the scraper ring groove) enters the bore. Pistons to be checked without the piston rings fitted.

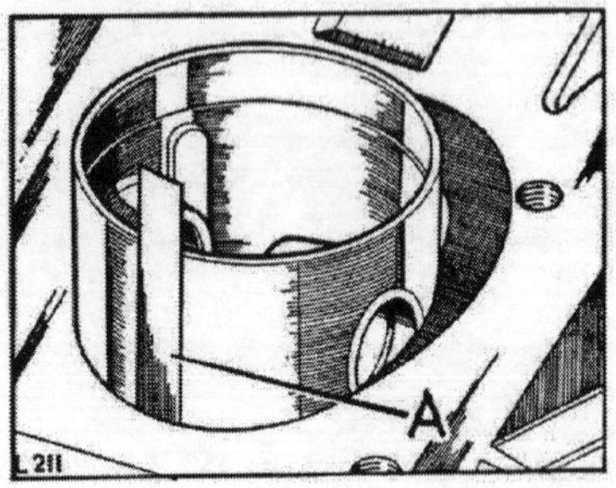

Using a feeler gauge, measure the ring gap, which should be:

| Compression rings | .015 to .020 in. (0,4 to 0,5 mm) |
| Scraper ring | .015 to .033 in. (0,4 to 0,8 mm) |

If necessary, use a very fine-cut flat file and carefully increase the gap as required.

Compression rings are marked 'TOP' on one face and must be fitted accordingly.

8. Check piston ring side clearance in piston groove, which should be:

| Compression ring | .0018 to .0038 in. (0,05 to 0,09 mm) |
| Scraper ring | .002 to .004 in. (0,05 to 0,10 mm) |

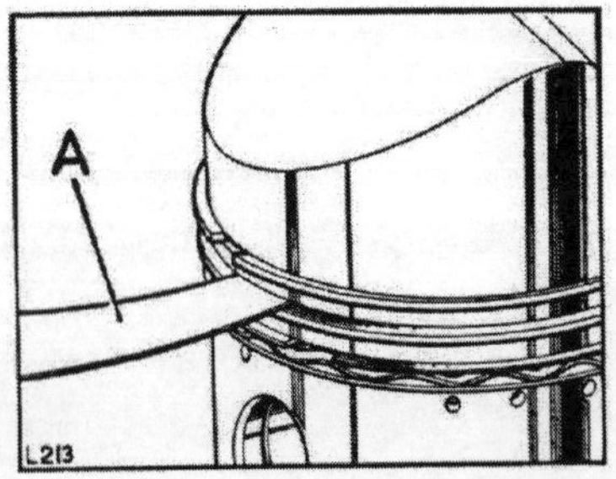

Fig. A3-127. Checking piston clearance with feeler gauge
A—Feeler gauge

7. To check new piston rings, support the ring in the bore with a slave piston.

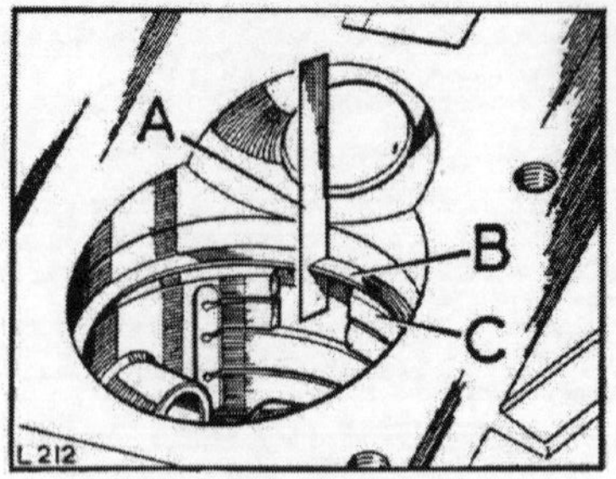

Fig. A3-128. Checking piston ring gap
A—Feeler gauge
B—Piston ring
C—Slave piston

Fig. A3-129. Checking ring clearance in groove
A—Feeler gauge

Connecting rods, check

1. Check connecting rod alignment with a suitable alignment jig.
2. Check that the connecting rods and caps have not been filed.
   (a) Select the correct cap for each connecting rod as denoted by the number stamped on the joint faces. This number also indicates the crankpin to which it must be fitted.
   Assemble the connecting rods, less shell bearings, with corresponding numbers together.

ENGINE—2.6 LITRE PETROL

Operation A3-33—continued

(b) Tighten the securing nuts to the correct torque, then slacken one of them right off and check that there is no clearance at the joint face. A clearance indicates that the rods or caps have been filed and the complete connecting rod must be replaced.

Tightening torque for connecting rod bolts:
20 lb ft (2,8 mkg).

New bolts and self-locking nuts must be used for final assembly. Use the original bolts and nuts for checking purposes.

Check the bearing nip as follows:

(a) Fit the bearing shells and tighten both nuts to correct torque. Slacken one nut right off and check the nip with a feeler gauge, as illustrated. Clearance should be .002 to .004 in. (0,05 to 0,10 mm).

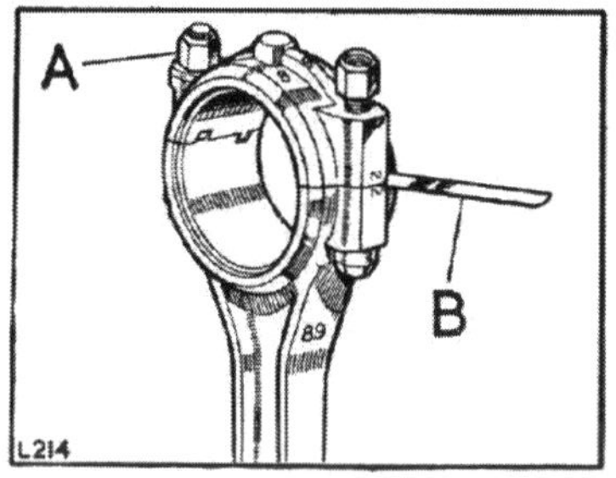

Fig. A3-130. Checking big-end bearing nip

A—Fixing, torque loaded
B—Feeler gauge

(b) Select bearing shells to give correct nip.

(c) Assemble each connecting rod assembly to its respective crankshaft journal and repeat the connecting rod bearing nip check. Again the clearance between the connecting rod and cap must be .002 in. to .004 in. (0,05 mm to 0,10 mm).

Alternatively, use 'Plastigage' strip inserted between the connecting rod bearings and the crankshaft journals. This method will indicate the actual clearance between the bearings and the journals and must be .001 in. to .0025 in. (0,025 mm to 0,063 mm) with the fixings torque loaded as in the alternative method.

'Plastigage' is available under Rover Part No. 605238. Remove all traces of 'Plastigage' from the components after use.

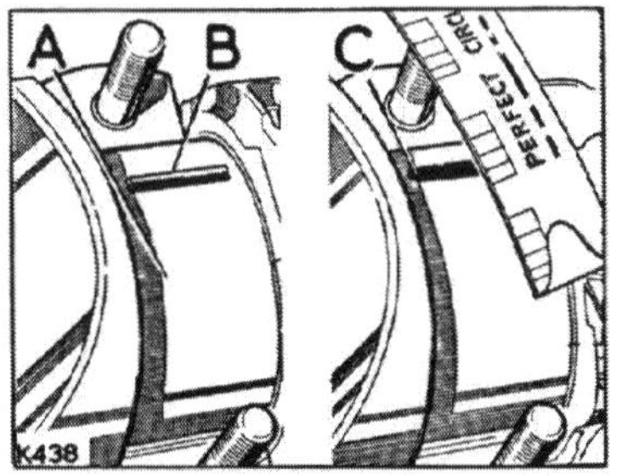

Fig. A3-131. Checking connecting rod and bearing clearance, using 'Plastigage'

A—Journal for connecting rod
B—Initial position of 'Plastigage'
C—Flattened 'Plastigage', do not remove until width has been measured against graduated scale on packet

3. To check big-end side clearance, assemble connecting rods to respective crankpins. Insert a feeler gauge between the end face of the rod and the crankpin shoulder.

Side clearance should be .006 in. to .015 in. (0,15 mm to 0,38 mm).

4. Remove connecting rods from crankpins. Ensure the bearing shells are kept with respective rods.

Fitting pistons to connecting rods

1. The gudgeon pin should be a good hand push fit into the piston bore at a temperature of 50° to 70°F (10° to 21°C) and should not fall out of the piston under its own weight.

2. If it is necessary to replace the gudgeon pin bush, this must be done with the aid of a power press. Ensure that the oil hole in the bearing exactly coincides with the hole in the connecting rod. The bush should be a .001 to .003 in. (0,025 to 0,076 mm) interference fit in the connecting rod. Hone the bush when fitted to the connecting rod to internal diameter .8755 in.—.0005 in. (22,24—0,0127 mm). Ensure correct alignment is maintained whilst honing.

3. Fit a new circlip in the side of the piston opposite the 'X'.

Place the connecting rod into the piston, ensuring spray hole in connecting rod is to the same side as the bore number stamped on the piston crown, thrust side.

On new pistons the machined section of the piston crown goes to the same side as the spray hole in the connecting rod Fig. A3-124 refers. Line up the connecting rod with the gudgeon pin and push pin into position. Fit second new circlip.

ENGINE—2.6 LITRE PETROL

Crankshaft and main bearings, remove and refit—Operation A3-34

(For overhaul instructions, Operation A3-35 refers)

Workshop hand tools:
Spanner sizes: $\frac{7}{16}$ in. AF, $\frac{9}{16}$ in. AF, $\frac{11}{16}$ in. AF open end $\frac{13}{16}$ in. AF, $\frac{1}{2}$ in. AF, $\frac{5}{8}$ in. AF, $\frac{7}{8}$ in. AF
$\frac{5}{16}$ in. BSF, $\frac{7}{16}$ in BSF open end
$\frac{7}{16}$ in. BSF socket
$\frac{1}{2}$ in. AF, $\frac{9}{16}$ in. AF ring
1 lb hammer, small chisel, Feeler gauges

Special tools:
Part No. 600963—Engine lifting sling
Part No. 270304—Guides for rear main bearing oil seal (2 off)
Part No. 605022—Clutch: plate alignment gauge
Torque wrench

To remove

1. Remove bonnet panel. Operation A3-1.
2. Remove air cleaner. Operation A3-2.
3. Remove radiator and grille panel complete. Operation A3-3.
4. Remove front floor. Operation A3-4.
5. Remove engine from vehicle. Operation A3-5.
6. Remove crankcase sump. Operation A3-27.
7. Fit the engine to a suitable stand.
8. Remove oil pump. Operation A3-28.
9. Remove engine front cover. Operation A3-23.
10. Remove timing chain and tensioner. Operation A3-24.
11. Remove clutch and flywheel. Operation A3-30.
12. Remove flywheel housing. Operation A3-31.
13. Remove the connecting rod caps and bearing lower halves. Retain as related sets.
14. Remove the main bearing caps and lift crankshaft clear. Retain the bearing halves and caps in related sets.
15. Remove the oil seal from the crankshaft.
16. Remove the seal retainer halves.

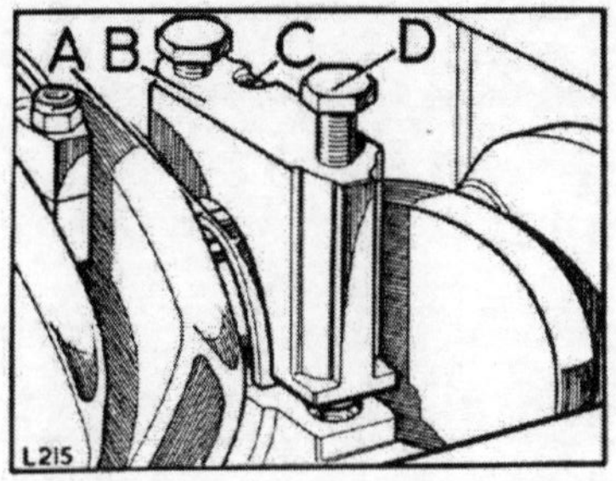

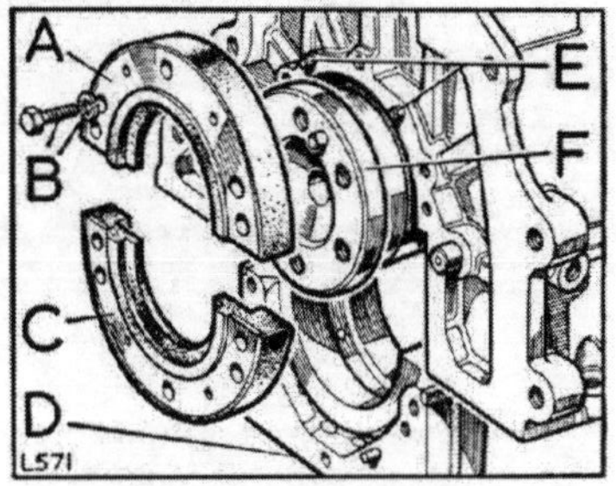

Fig. A3-132. Crankshaft main bearing caps
A—Bearing lower half
B—Bearing cap
C—Letter 'F' toward front of engine when refitting
D—Fixings, bearing cap to cylinder block

Fig. A3-133. Oil seal retainers
A—Seal retainer upper half
B—Seal retainer fixings
C—Seal retainer lower half
D—Rear main bearing cap
E—Locating dowels
F—Crankshaft flange

To refit

1. Where replacement components are to be fitted, the relevant checks detailed in Operation A3-35 must be carried out.
2. Assemble the crankshaft to the engine and insert the bearing upper halves, located by tongues, to the crankcase.
3. Position a thrust washer at each side of the rear upper bearing shell. The thrust washer thicknesses must agree within .003 in. (0,08 mm).
4. Position the bearing lower halves on to the front and centre bearing caps and fit the caps.

Operation A3-34—continued

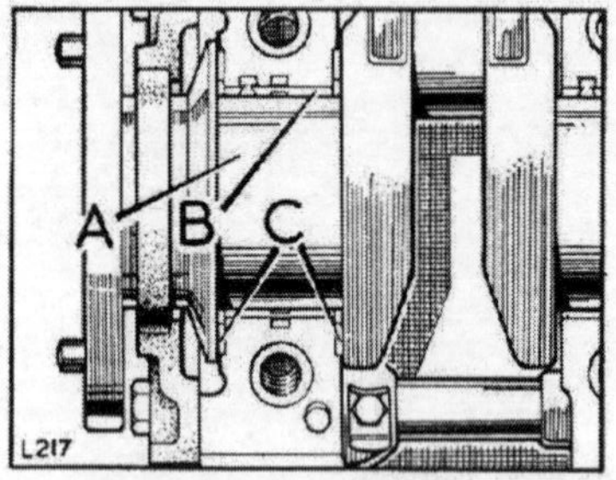

5. Assemble the garter spring on the oil seal journal of the crankshaft as illustrated, by laying the spring around the journal, this will bring the two ends, the hook and the eye, adjacent to one another, then insert the hook into the eye. Care must be taken to ensure that during this operation the spring is not stretched at all.

   The spring should be moved along the journal until it is against the thrower flange.

6. Apply Silicone Grease MS4 to the crankshaft oil seal journal and to both sides of the split oil seal sealing lip.

   Open the split sufficiently to allow it to be fitted over the crankshaft oil seal journal. Recess in oil seal must be towards thrower flange and garter spring.

   The oil seal must not be repeatedly fitted and removed from the crankshaft, as this can damage the sealing lip.

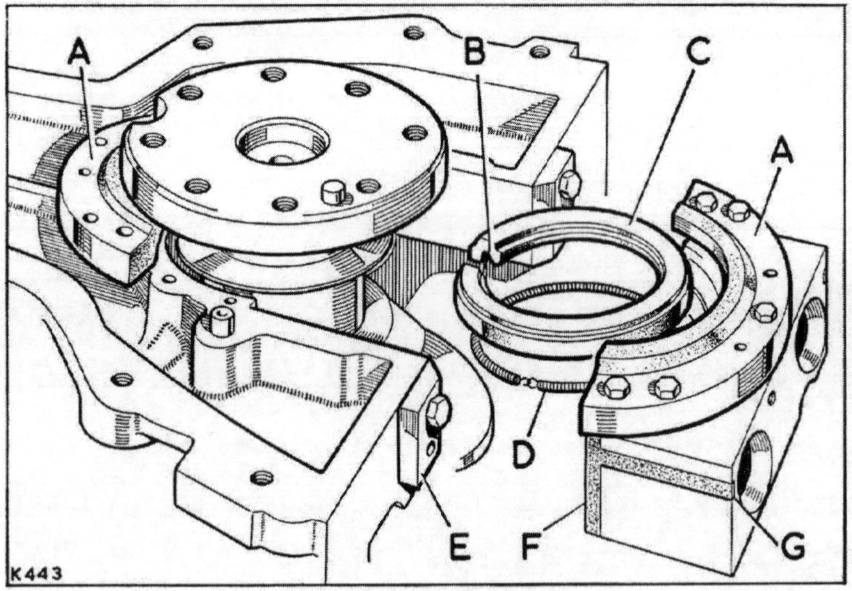

Fig. A3-134. Thrust washer and bearing location
A—Crankshaft journal, lubricate with clean oil
B—Bearing with tongue located
C—Thrust washers, grooved (soft metal) faces toward crankshaft web

Fig. A3-135. Oil seal details
A—Retainer halves
B—Split line of seal to be towards top of engine when fitted
C—Split oil seal
D—Garter-spring, hook and eye to be midway between split and hinge of oil seal when fitted
E—Guides, Part No. 270304, for rear main bearing cap 'T' seals
F—Trim these edges before fitting to avoid foul on seating radius
G—Trim these ends to allow $\frac{1}{32}$ in. (0,8 mm) protrusion when cap is fitted to engine

ENGINE—2.6 LITRE PETROL

Operation A3-34—continued

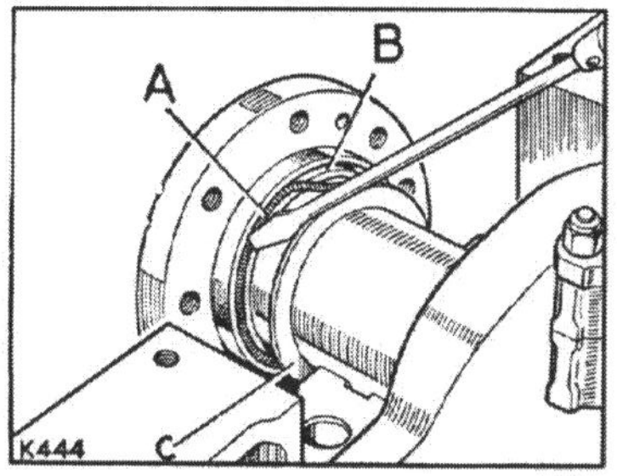

13. Tighten the seal retainer halves fixings and position the corners of the fixing heads so that they will not foul the flywheel housing oil seal when subsequently fitted.
14. Tighten all the main bearing cap fixings to a torque loading of 75 lb ft (10,0 mkg).
15. Fit the appropriate bearing shells to the connecting rod caps, ensure that the upper and lower shells are correctly located by their tongues and fit the caps to the appropriate connecting rods. Use new fixing nuts and tighten the fixings to 20 lb ft (2,8 mkg).
16. Refit the flywheel housing. Operation A3-31.
17. Refit the clutch and flywheel. Operation A3-30.
18. Refit the timing chain and tensioner. Operation A3-24.
19. Carry out the valve timing procedure as detailed in Operation A3-25.
20. Refit the engine front cover. Operation A3-23.
21. Refit the oil pump. Operation A3-28.
22. Remove the engine from the stand, using suitable lifting equipment.

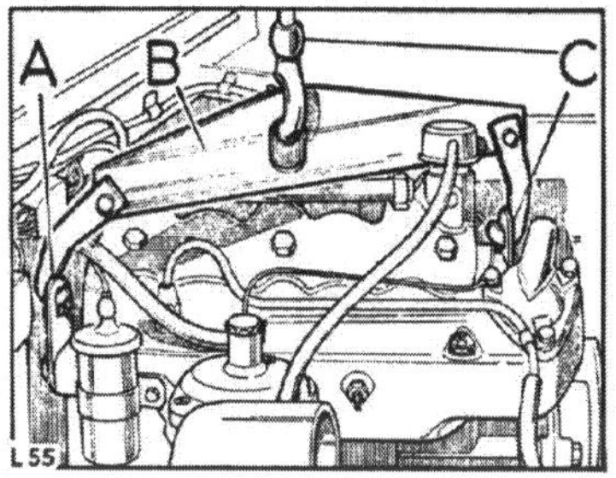

Fig. A3-137. Engine lifting sling in position
A—Rear lifting bracket
B—Lifting sling, Part No. 600963
C—Front lifting bracket

23. Refit the crankcase sump. Operation A3-27.
24. Refit engine to vehicle. Operation A3-5.
25. Refit the front floor. Operation A3-4.
26. Refit the radiator and grille panel. Operation A3-3.
27. Refit the air cleaner. Operation A3-2.
28. Refit the bonnet panel. Operation A3-1.

Fig. A3-136. Fitting garter spring
A—Garter spring
B—Oil seal recess for garter spring
C—Thrower flange

7. Rotate the oil seal until the split is on the vertical axis pointing towards the cylinder head and in its approximate running position on the journal; this position is important.
   Apply Hylomar SQ32M sealing compound to the seal diameter of the two half plates, using either an applicator or a brush.
   Important: Do not degrease the half seal plates with trichlorethylene, but wipe clean with a dry cloth prior to applying the Hylomar.
8. Fit one half of the oil seal retainer on to the crankcase dowels. The oil seal should be compressed to assist assembly, also ensure that it is correctly located in the retainer recess. Bolt the retainer to the crankcase, do not fully tighten the fixings at this stage. In order to hold the seal in position, bolt the other half of the oil seal retainer on to the main bearing cap, in the same way. Apply Silicone grease MS4 to the 'T' seals and fit them to the main bearing cap. The cap must be off the crankcase for these operations.
   Trim the edges of the 'T' seals as shown to prevent them from fouling the cylinder block when fitted.
9. Fit the main bearing cap with the seal retainer, bearing shell and 'T' seals to the crankcase, until there is a $\frac{1}{32}$ in. (0,8 mm) gap between the cap and crankcase.
10. Ensure that the seal is located in the retainer recess.
11. Pull down the cap slowly, ensuring there is no buckling of the split seal or misalignment of the butt joint.

Crankshaft and main bearings, to check—Operation A3-35

(For removal and refitting details, Operation A3-34 refers)

Workshop hand tools:
Spanner sizes: $\frac{7}{8}$ in. AF open end
$1\frac{1}{8}$ in. AF socket
Screwdriver (medium), Screwdriver (small),
Feeler gauges

Special tools:
Torque wrench
Dial test indicator
Part No. 605238—'Plastigage' strip

To overhaul

1. Inspect all components for damage and general condition.
2. The crankshaft journals should be closely inspected for wear or damage, and the crankpins also checked for ovality.
3. Check for general condition of main bearing cap locating dowels, dowel spigots and surrounding areas.

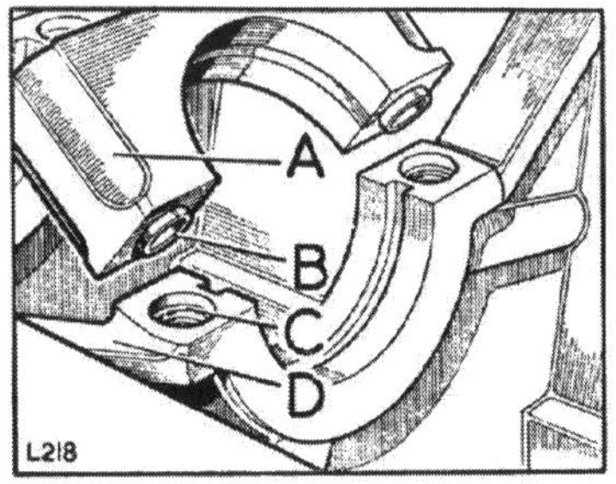

A3-138. Main bearing cap location details
A—Main bearing cap
B—Dowel spigots
C—Spigot locating bores
D—Cylinder block

4. With the crankshaft removed, check the main bearings for fit in the housings, as follows: fit the front bearing cap, less the shell bearings, to the correct location.
5. Fit and tighten the main bearing bolts to 75 lb ft (10,0 mkg).
6. Slacken one bolt and check that there is no clearance between the two faces. Clearance here indicates that the cap has been filed or is damaged and it will be necessary to replace the complete cylinder block.
7. If satisfactory, fit the main bearings and repeat the above check. The clearance at the face should now be .004 in. to .006 in. (0,10 mm to 0,15 mm) and is achieved by selective assembly of the shells.

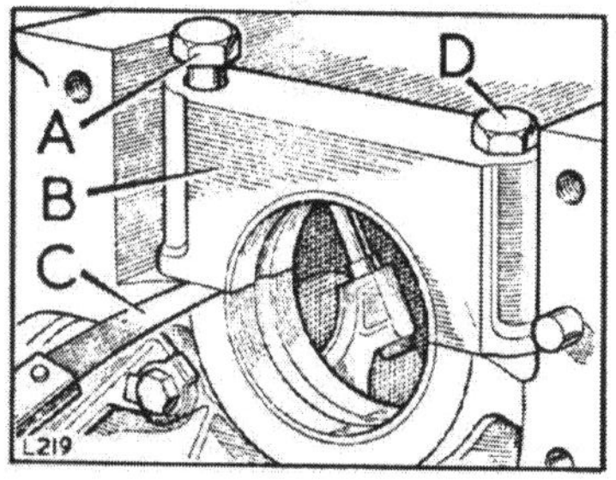

Fig. A3-139. Checking main bearing nip
A—Set bolt, slack
B—Bearing cap
C—Feeler gauge
D—Set bolt, tightened

8. Repeat the procedure and check the remaining bearings and caps.
9. When the bearing nip has been checked, remove the caps and bearing shell bottom halves. Position a standard size thrust washer at each side of rear bearing shell—top half, and fit the crankshaft.
   The thrust washer thicknesses must agree within .003 in. (0,08 mm).
10. Tighten the main bearing caps to 75 lb ft (10,0 mkg) torque load.
11. Mount a dial test indicator, then, using a suitable lever, check and note the crankshaft end-float reading which should be .002 in. to .006 in. (0,05 mm to 0,15 mm).
    If the crankshaft end-float reading obtained is not within the limits, fit suitable oversize thrust washers. The variation of thrust washer thickness at each side must not exceed .003 in. (0,08 mm) to ensure that the crankshaft remains centralised.

ENGINE—2.6 LITRE PETROL

Operation A3-35—continued

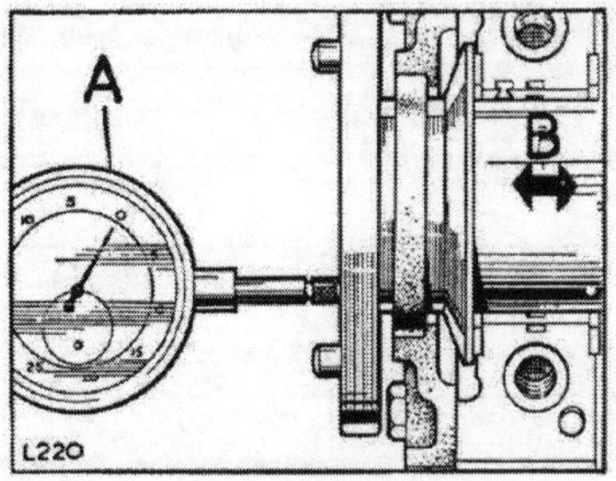

Fig. A3-140. Checking crankshaft end-float

A—Dial test indicator
B—Lever crankshaft fully forward then fully to rear

12. When satisfactory, check the crankshaft for freedom of rotation. Fitting a .0025 in. (0,06 mm) feeler paper between a main bearing and the journal should cause resistance to rotation; the crankshaft should be free to rotate by hand with the feeler paper removed.

13. The running clearance between the bearings and the crankshaft journals should be .0006 in. to .002 in. (0,015 mm to 0,05 mm). An alternative method of checking the clearance is by using 'Plastigage' strip, available under Rover Part No. 605238, as illustrated.

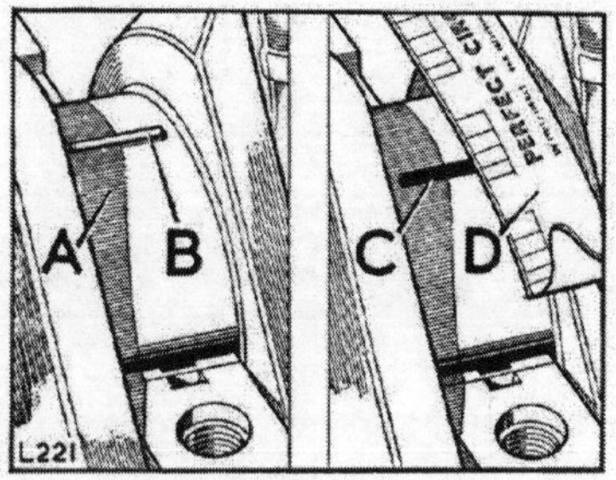

Fig. A3-141. Use of 'Plastigage' strip to measure bearing clearance

A—Main bearing journal
B—Initial position of 'Plastigage'
C—Flattened 'Plastigage', do not remove until measured against scale
D—Graduated scale on 'Plastigage' packet

*Camshaft and bearings, remove and refit—Operation A3-36

Workshop hand tools:
Spanner sizes: 7/16 in. AF, 1/2 in. AF, 9/16 in. AF, 3/4 in. AF open end 1/2 in. AF socket, 1/8 in. Whit open end 3/8 in. (3 mm) Allen key
Screwdriver (medium), Pliers

Special tools:
Part No. 262749—Extractor for shafts
Part No. 530102—Spanner for starter dog
Dial test indicator and bracket
Part No. 507231—Extractor for chain wheel
Part No. 530101—Extractor for camshaft

Note: This operation includes removal of the camshaft bearings with the exception of the rearmost bearing, the cover for which can only be removed with the flywheel housing removed.

To remove

1. Remove the bonnet panel. Operation A3-1.
2. Remove the air cleaner. Operation A3-2.
3. Remove the radiator and grille panel. Operation A3-3.
4. Remove the exhaust manifold. Operation A3-8.
5. Remove the engine front cover. Operation A3-23.
6. Remove the timing chain tensioner. Operation A3-24.
7. Remove the camshaft chainwheel and timing chain. Operation A3-25.
8. Remove the camshaft thrust plate.
9. Remove the side rockers and shafts. Operation A3-26.

Fig. A3-142. Thrust plate and fixings

A—Camshaft
B—Thrust plate
C—Fixings

10. Remove the distributor and short drive shaft, Operation A3-18, and withdraw the vertical drive gear assembly.
11. Remove the camshaft bearings locating screws.
12. Withdraw the camshaft, using the special tool, Part No. 530101, until the bearings are clear of their housings.

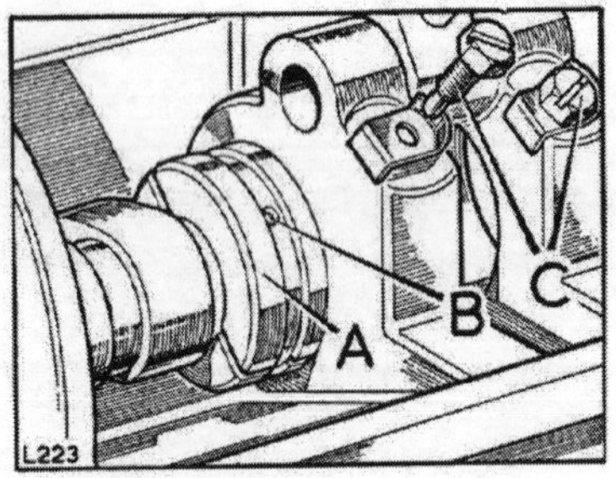

Fig. A3-143. Camshaft bearing location

A—Camshaft bearing (6 off)
B—Holes for locating screws
C—Locating screws

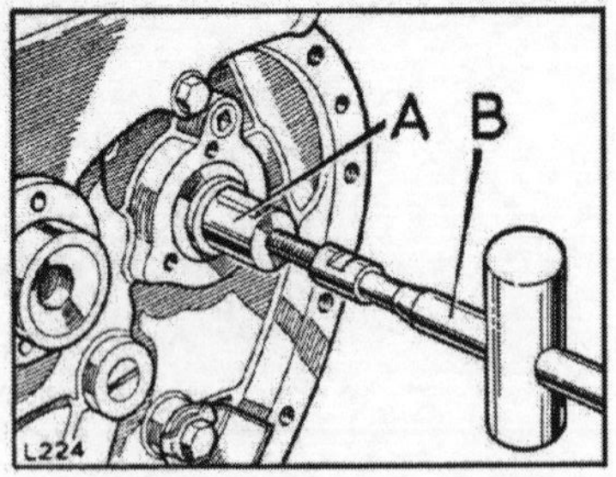

Fig. A3-144. Extractor for camshaft
A—Camshaft   B—Extractor

Operations marked with an asterisk (*) can be carried out with the engine installed in the vehicle

ENGINE—2.6 LITRE PETROL

Operation A3-36—continued

13. Where two housings are close together, it will be advantageous to pass the rearmost bearing through both housings, before removal. The camshaft bearings are easily removed, being of the split type. With the bearings removed, pull the camshaft clear of the engine.

14. Keep the bearings in the correct pairs as indicated by the numbers stamped on the end face; these bearings are of soft material and care should be taken to avoid damage, should it be necessary to refit the originals.

To refit

1. Before attempting to fit the camshaft bearings to the cylinder block, ensure that the bearing halves fit together correctly on the dowels by checking that no light is visible between the joint faces.

2. The bearings must be fitted dry and should be a hand push fit in the cylinder block; they must always be renewed in paired halves and the numbers stamped on one of the end faces of the bearing halves must be adjacent.

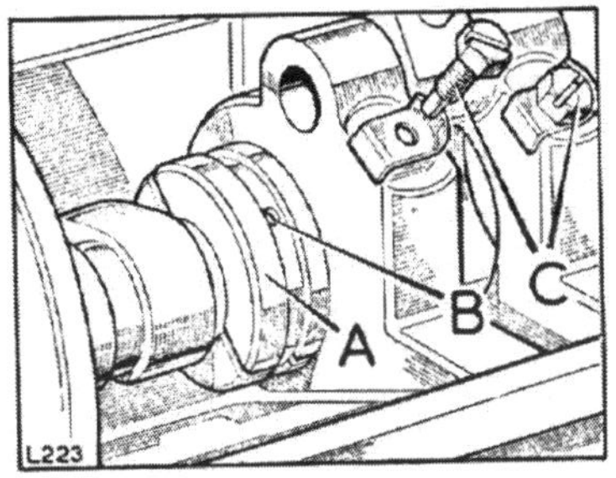

Fig. A3-145. Camshaft bearing location

A—Camshaft bearing
B—Locating screw hole
C—Locating screws and lockplates

3. When fitting the bearings to the camshaft housing, align the locating screw holes in the bearings with the corresponding holes in the housings.

4. Insert the camshaft partly into the cylinder block, allowing the distributor and oil pump drive gear to pass through the first and second intermediate housing webs. Assemble the bearings on to their respective journals on the camshaft. Ensure that the dowelled joint faces are tightly fitted together and the locating holes in the bearings are in line with the holes in the housing webs.

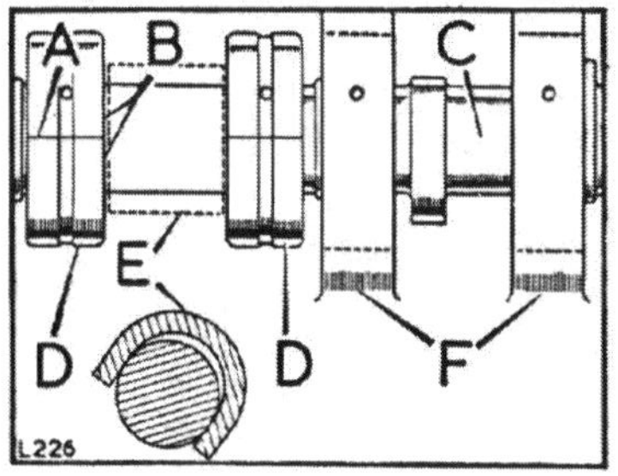

Fig. A3-146. Camshaft fitting with distance piece

A—No gap here when fitted
B—Faces with numbers to be adjacent
C—Camshaft
D—Bearings, intermediate
E—Distance piece
F—Bearing housings

5. Place a suitable distance piece (Fig. A3-146 refers) between the first and second intermediate bearings. The width of the distance piece to be approximately the distance between the bearing housings but allowing sufficient clearance for withdrawal.

6. With all the bearings in place and correctly aligned and using a plastic-faced mallet, gently tap the camshaft rearwards until the bearings are fully home in their respective housings and the locating holes are aligned. Remove the distance piece.

7. Before fitting the locating set bolts to the bearings and housings, squirt engine oil down the holes to lubricate the bearings. Fit the locating set bolts and spring washers.

ENGINE—2.6 LITRE PETROL

Operation A3-36—continued

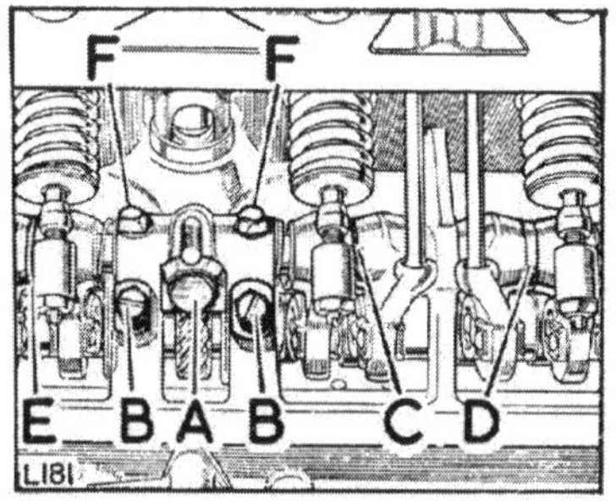

Fig. A3-147. Camshaft and bearing refitting

A—Oil feed locating bolt
B—Camshaft bearing locating screw
C—Spacing washer, thin
D—Spacing washer, thick
E—Spacing washer, medium
F—Rocker shaft locating screws

8. Fit the camshaft thrust plate and camshaft hub, noting any alignment marks made previously. The camshaft should have .0045 to .0065 in. (0.11 to 0.16 mm) end-float measured between the hub and the thrust plate. A new thrust plate must be fitted where the end-float is in excess of these tolerances.

9. Temporarily remove the camshaft chainwheel and refit the side rocker shafts, Operation A3-26.

10. Fit the camshaft chainwheel and carry out the valve timing procedure, Operation A3-25.

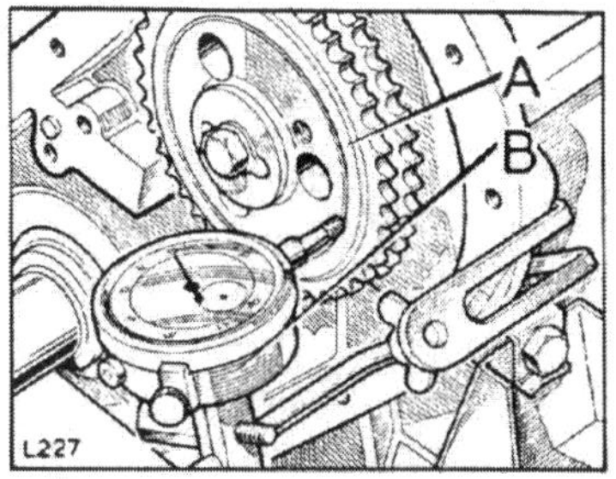

Fig. A3-148. Camshaft chainwheel end-float

A—Camshaft chainwheel
B—Dial test indicator

11. Fit the timing chain tensioner, Operation A3-24.

12. Fit the engine front cover, Operation A3-23.

13. Fit the vertical drive gear assembly, Operation A3-28.

14. Fit the distributor, Operation A3-18.

15. Carry out ignition timing procedure, Operation A3-17.

16. Reverse removal procedure for remaining items.

17. Fill radiator with coolant, anti-freeze in winter. Capacity: 20 Imperial pints (24 U.S. pints, 11,2 litres).

18. Run engine and check for oil and water leaks. Carry out any adjustments required.

ENGINE—2.6 LITRE PETROL

Cylinder block, to overhaul—Operation A3-37

Special tools:
Reboring jig block (Part No. 261288)
Cylinder liner press block (Part No. 246650)
Extractor (Part No. 262749)

Carry out the engine removal and dismantling work previously detailed as necessary until the cylinder block only remains

Cylinder block, preparation

1. Clean out the main oil gallery and all oilways; renew all blanking plugs.
2. If necessary, remove the oil gallery pipe from the block by using extractor (Part No. 262749).
3. Clean out the water gallery and water jacket.

Cylinder block, checks

1. Examine the block for cracks and distortion of machined faces.
2. The cylinder block must be checked by first assembling the crankshaft bearing caps (without the bearing shells) to the crankcase. Ensure correct location by means of the dowels. Bearing caps are numbered in their respective order from the front of the engine.
3. Tighten both securing bolts for each cap to 75 lb/ft (10,0 mkg). Slacken one bolt of each pair right off. There should be no clearance at the joint face. **If there is clearance, this indicates that the caps have been filed. The cylinder block is scrap and must be replaced.**
4. Check for stripped threads and general damage to cylinder block.
5. Measure the amount of wear in each cylinder bore.

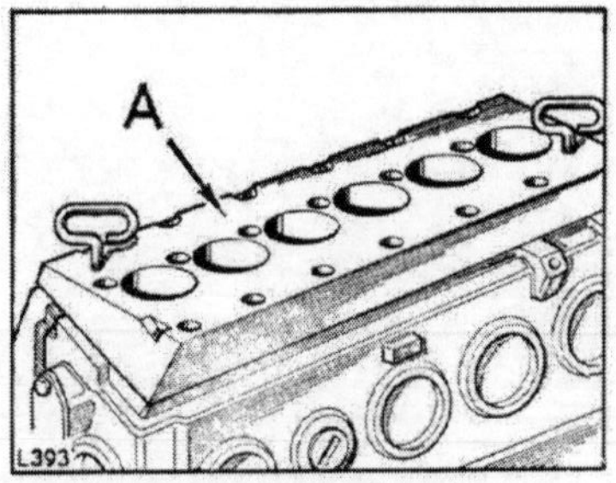

Fig. A3-149. Jig block for reboring
A—Jig block, Part No. 261288

Reboring

1. Although the cylinder head is inclined at an angle of 22°, standard boring equipment can be used in conjunction with a special jig block (Part No. 261288).

Cylinder liners

1. Cylinder liners may be fitted; note the following points:
   (a) Machine the cylinder block bores to 3.200 in. plus .001 in. (81,28 mm plus 0,025 mm). This gives an interference fit of .003 to .004 in. (0,07 to 0,10 mm).
   (b) Prior to pressing in the liner, allowance must be made for twist up to 3/16 in. (5 mm) clockwise. To facilitate realignment should the liner not be positioned correctly at the first attempt, scribe lines down the sides of the liner from the two peaks, and make corresponding marks on the cylinder block.
   (c) Press in the liner, using a special press block (Part No. 246650), until the top edge is level with the bottom of the exhaust valve pocket. Blend to the shape of the cylinder block.

Bore to the selected diameter to suit pistons. Liners may only be bored to suit standard or .010 in. (0,25 mm) oversize pistons. For piston selection see Operation A3-33.

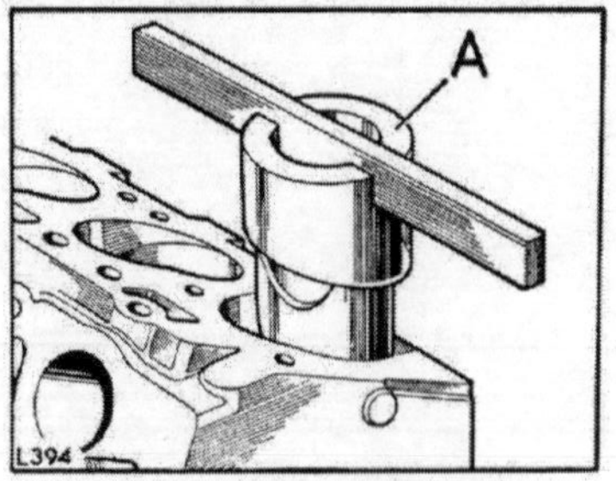

Fig. A3-150. Fitting a cylinder liner
A—Press block, Part No. 246650

Reclamation of flywheel and starter ring—Operation A3-38

Wear or scoring on the flywheel pressure face

1. Remove the clutch bolts and dowels from the flywheel.
2. Check the thickness of the flywheel before commencing machining, as it may have been previously machined.
   The maximum amount of metal which may be removed from the flywheel face is .030 in. (0,76 mm). If the face is not satisfactory after machining to these limits, the flywheel must be scrapped. See chart below.
3. Machine the **whole** pressure face, not merely inside the bolts and dowels, until the score marks are removed.

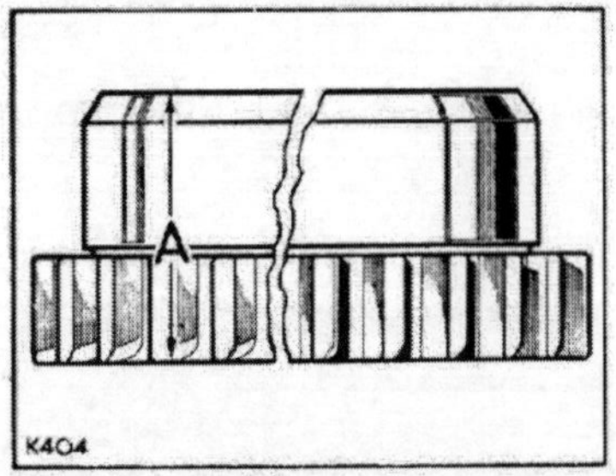

Fig. A3-151. Machining flywheel
A—Minimum thickness after refacing

Starter ring excessively worn or damaged

Petrol models

1. Remove the scrap starter ring by securing the flywheel in a vice fitted with jaw protectors, then drill a 5/32 in. (4 mm) diameter hole axially between the root of any one tooth and the inner diameter of the starter ring 5/32 in. (4 mm) deep. Care must be taken to prevent the drill entering the flywheel.

Important Note: The starter ring will normally split harmlessly but on remote occasions rings have been known to fly asunder when split; it is therefore important that the operator should take suitable precautions. For instance a cloth may be laid over the upper part of the starter ring.

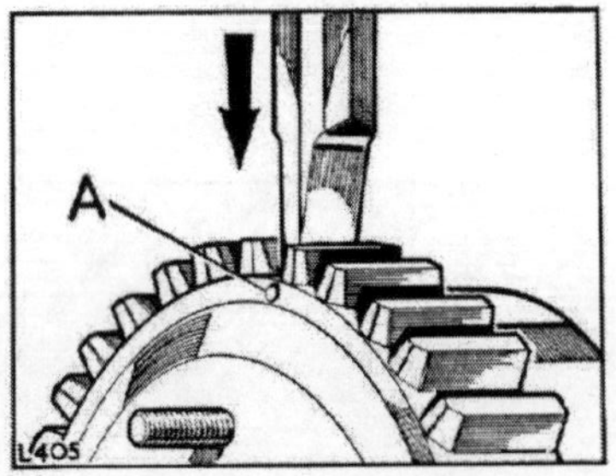

Fig. A3-152. Removing an unserviceable starter ring
A—Drilled hole

Models	Flywheel Part Number	Ring Gear Part Number	Dimension 'A' Minimum thickness after refacing	Flywheel Part Number when re-conditioned	Remarks
2.6 litre Petrol models	541760	506799	1.204 in. (30,5 mm)	600537	Cast-iron flywheel. Detachable ring gear fitted as original equipment. No machining necessary other than for refacing.

Operation A3-38—continued

2. Place a chisel immediately above the drilled hole, and strike it sharply.

3. Heat the starter ring uniformly to between 220°C and 225°C but do not exceed the higher temperature.

4. With the flywheel placed on a suitably flat surface, position the ring on to the flywheel with the square edge of the teeth against the flange.

There should be a clearance of $\frac{1}{16}$ in. to $\frac{1}{8}$ in. (1,5 mm to 3 mm) between the inner diameter of ring and flywheel if the temperature is correct. Press the starter ring firmly against the flange until the ring contracts sufficiently to grip the flywheel.

5. Allow the flywheel assembly to cool gradually; do not hasten cooling in any way and thereby avoid the setting up of internal stresses in the ring which may cause fracture or failure in some respect.

Fault diagnosis—Engine—2.6 litre Petrol

Symptom	Possible cause	Investigation	Remedy
A—Engine fails to rotate when attempting to start	Incorrect starting procedure	Follow procedure as described in Owner's Instruction Manual	
	Battery leads loose or terminals corroded	Check for condition of leads and terminals	Clean and tighten as necessary
	Battery discharged	Check and remedy as described in Section N	
	Starter motor inoperative	If lights dim when starter switch is operated, the starter pinion may be jammed in the flywheel starter ring	Free the starter by removing the protection cap and turning the squared end of the starter armature clockwise
		Check for loose or dirty connections and for soundness of leads	Clean and tighten at terminals. Replace leads as necessary
		Depress switch on engine compartment dash panel to connect battery feed to starter	If starter then rotates engine, replace the ignition switch. If starter remains inoperative, refer to Section N
B—Engine rotates but fails to start	Starter motor speed too low	Check battery leads at terminals	Clean and tighten as necessary
		Check state of battery charge. Section N	When refitting a recharged or replacement battery, check the voltage regulator output setting, Section N. Check also the fan belt tension
	Faulty ignition system	Remove a sparking plug lead and hold lead end $\frac{1}{4}$ in. (6 mm) approximately from engine block. With ignition "ON", depress starter solenoid switch and check that an easily visible blue spark jumps the gap between plug lead and engine	If no spark or if spark is weak or yellowish, check the ignition system as described in Section N
		If the spark appears adequate, remove the sparking plugs	Clean the plugs and reset the plug gaps, Section N. Replace if necessary
	Fuel system defects	With the engine cold, remove fuel inlet pipe at carburetter, operate priming lever at pump and check for full bore fuel flow	If fuel flow is unsatisfactory refer to Section L
		If flow is satisfactory, ensure that carburetter float chamber fuel level is satisfactory	If float chamber level is too low, refer to Section L for carburetter float needle checks
C—Engine starts but immediately stops	Faulty electrical connections	Check ignition circuits leads and terminals for possible loose or defective connections, as described in Section N	
	Insufficient fuel supply	Carry out the checks and remedies listed under 'Fuel system defects', paragraph B	
D—Engine fails to idle	Carburetter setting faulty	Adjust throttle stop screw on carburetter until engine will run with lever on stop. If engine idle speed is then too high, check the carburetter settings as described in Section L	

ENGINE—2.6 LITRE PETROL

Fault diagnosis—Engine—2.6 litre Petrol—continued

Symptom	Possible cause	Investigation	Remedy
D—Engine fails to idle—cont.	Faulty fuel pump	Carry out the checks and remedies listed under 'Fuel system defects', paragraph B	
	Ignition system faults	Check electrical leads insulation and terminal connections	Clean and tighten terminals. Replace leads if necessary
		Carry out the checks listed under 'Faulty ignition system', paragraph B, to check the sparking plugs and their electrical feed	
	Battery charge too low	Check if lamps brightness varies with engine speed	Carry out the checks listed under 'Battery discharged, charge low'. Section N
		Check fan belt tension setting	Reset to correct tension and recharge battery from external supply or by a long period of engine running in daylight
	Incorrect ignition timing	Adjust throttle stop screw on carburetter until engine will idle without stopping. Rotate vernier adjuster on distributor through advance and retard range. If the engine speed increases at a new vernier position, then the original ignition setting is incorrect for the fuel grade in use	Reset ignition timing to the correct setting for the fuel grade in use
	Valve operation defective	Remove engine top cover and check tappet clearances	Reset clearances
		Check for defective valve springs	Replace as pairs
		Rotate engine, using starting handle, and check for valves sticking open	Carry out engine decarbonise and top overhaul procedure
		Check for worn valves and valve guides	Replace as necessary
	Faulty cylinder head gasket	Check for leaks across sealing areas	Replace gasket
	Exhaust system faulty	Examine for possible restrictions	Remove restriction. Replace components as necessary
E—Engine misfires on acceleration	Distributor operation faulty	Check condition of contact breaker points. Check gap: .014 in. to .016 in. (0.35 mm to 0.40 mm)	Reface points and reset gap or replace points if badly worn or pitted
	Coil or condenser faulty	Check by substituting serviceable components	Replace unserviceable components
	Sparking plugs faulty	Remove sparking plugs, check for carbon deposits. Check electrode gap. Visually examine for signs of cracked insulation	If sparking plugs appear otherwise serviceable, clean off all deposits and reset the gap to .029 to .032 in. (0.75 to 0.8 mm.)
	Carburetter operation faulty	Check for restrictions in carburetter fuel passages	Clean out passages as described in Section L

Fault diagnosis—Engine—2.6 litre Petrol—continued

Symptom	Possible cause	Investigation	Remedy
E—Engine misfires on acceleration—cont.	Carburetter operation faulty—cont.	Check carburetter accelerator pump diaphragm and linkage, where applicable. Check carburetter control settings	Check carburetter as described in Section L
F—Engine backfires	Air leakage	Tighten exhaust system and ensure joints are sound; check components for damage and cracks	Tighten joints or replace components as necessary. Section M
	Internal leakage	Excessively worn valve guides and valves may allow crankcase fumes to enter exhaust system	Carry out cylinder head overhaul procedure
	Ignition system defect	Check electrical leads, insulation and terminal connections	Clean and tighten terminals. Replace leads if necessary
		Check condition of sparking plugs, insulation and electrode gap	Reset or replace as necessary, Section N
		Check if ignition timing setting is too retarded	Reset timing
	Carburetter defect	Check jets for any restriction which may cause a too weak mixture. Check mixture control setting	Check carburetter settings and clean out passages if necessary. Section L
	Valve operation incorrect	Check valve timing. Section A1	Reset timing if necessary. Ensure that timing chain tensioner is free to operate, ensure that timing chain has no slack on driving side
		Check tappet clearances	Reset clearances
		Check for valves sticking open	Carry out engine decarbonise procedure
		Check for badly seating valves	Carry out cylinder head overhaul procedure
G—Engine knocks	Ignition system defects	Check condition of sparking plugs	Reset or replace as necessary, Section N
		Check if ignition timing is too advanced	Reset ignition timing to the correct setting for the fuel grade in use
		Check operation of distributor advance and retard mechanism, Section N	
	Fuel system defects	Check setting of mixture control screw	Reset control screw as described in Section L
		Check grade of fuel in use is suitable	Rotate octane selector on distributor. If engine knock stops, fuel in use is not correct for the ignition timing setting

Fault diagnosis—Engine—2.6 litre Petrol—continued

Symptom	Possible cause	Investigation	Remedy
G—Engine knocks—cont.	Valves operation incorrect	Check tappet clearances	Reset clearances
		Check valve timing	Reset timing
	Wear in engine	Check pistons and bearings	Overhaul as necessary
	Excessive carbon deposits	Remove cylinder head and check for deposits in combustion chamber areas	Remove carbon deposits
H—Engine 'spits back' through carburetter	Excessively weak mixture	Check setting of mixture control screw	Adjust control screw as detailed in Section L
		Check for air leakage into fuel induction system	Tighten fixings or replace components as necessary
J—Engine runs erratically	Ignition timing incorrect	With engine running, rotate vernier adjuster at distributor through advance and retard range. If engine runs smoothly at a new position, then the original ignition timing is incorrect for the fuel grade in use	Reset ignition timing to the correct setting for the fuel in use
	Fuel system defect	Check for restriction in fuel supply and for fuel pump malfunction, Section L	
	Electrical system defects	Check for faulty electrical connections	Clean and tighten at terminals. Replace leads if insulation is not sound
		Check condition of sparking plugs	Clean and reset electrode gap. Replace plugs as necessary, Section N
		Check battery connections and state of battery charge	Clean and tighten connections. Recharge battery if necessary, Section N
		Check that vacuum pipe connection at distributor is sound	Rectify as necessary
		Check distributor operation as described in Section N	
	Valves operation incorrect	Check tappet clearances	Reset clearances
		Check for valves sticking open. Check also for broken or defective valve spings	Carry out cylinder head overhaul procedure
		Remove cylinder head and check for worn valves and valve guides. Examine cylinder head gasket for signs of leakage across the sealing areas	Carry out the cylinder head overhaul procedure
	Exhaust system defects	Check for damage, cracks and ensure joints are tight	Rectify or replace components as necessary, Section N
K—Lack of power	Ignition system defect	Check condition of sparking plugs, insulation and electrode gap	Clean and reset electrode gap. Replace plugs if otherwise faulty
		Check distributor advance and retard mechanism as detailed in Section N	

Fault diagnosis—Engine—2.6 litre Petrol—continued

Symptom	Possible cause	Investigation	Remedy
K—Lack of power—cont.	Ignition system defect—cont.	Check for faulty coil, condenser or battery by substituting serviceable components	Replace as necessary, referring to Section N
		Check ignition timing	Reset timing
	Poor engine compression	If the compression pressure is appreciably less than the figure quoted in the 'Data' section, the piston rings may be worn or the valve seating poor	Carry out the applicable overhaul procedures
	Clutch slip	If vehicle road speed does not respond adequately to engine speed increases during normal travel, clutch slip may be taking place	Carry out the fault diagnosis procedure described in Section B
	Fuel system defect	Check fuel system for external leakage. Check fuel tank filler breather is clear. Check for restrictions in fuel system, indicated by low fuel level in float chamber	Rectify as described in Section L
	Exhaust system faulty	Check for damage, holes and cracks	Replace components as necessary, Section M
	Brakes 'binding'	Check as detailed in Section H	Reset as necessary, Section L
	Fuel system defects	Check the carburetter control screw settings. Ensure throttle stop and mixture settings are correct	
L—Engine stalls		Check for restriction or foreign matter in fuel system	Rectify as detailed in Section L
	Ignition system defects	Check distributor contact breaker points and gap setting	Clean points and reset gap. Replace points as necessary, Section N
		Check condition of sparking plugs electrode gap and also examine insulation	Clean plugs and reset gaps as necessary, Section N. Replace plugs as necessary
		Check operation of ignition coil and distributor condenser by substituting serviceable components	Replace as necessary, Section N
	Valve operation faulty	Check tappet clearances	Reset as necessary
M—Noisy valve mechanism	Valve operation incorrect	Check for excessive tappet clearances	Reset clearances
		Rotate engine and check for sticking valves and broken or defective valve springs. Check for excessively worn components	Carry out cylinder head overhaul procedure. Replace valve springs
N—Main bearing rattle	Low oil pressure	Refer to paragraph P for checks and remedy	
		Check if main bearing cap fixings are loose	Tighten to correct torque loading
	Component or assembly defects	Check bearing clearance. Examine bearings and crankshaft for wear.	Carry out the overhaul procedure

ENGINE—2.6 LITRE PETROL

Fault diagnosis—Engine—2.6 litre Petrol—continued

Symptom	Possible cause	Investigation	Remedy
P—Low oil pressure	Insufficient oil supply	Check engine dipstick	Replenish sump with correct grade lubricating oil, Section X refers
	External leakage	Check engine for oil leaks. Ensure oil pressure switch joint washer is sound	Rectify as necessary
	Oil pump operation faulty	Check the oil pump intake filter for restriction	Remove foreign matter if necessary. Clean filter in clean fuel
		Check for wear in pump gears assembly	Carry out the oil pump overhaul procedure
	Oil pressure relief valve malfunction	Check for foreign matter on ball valve seat	Clean and refit
		Relief valve plunger sticking	Clean and ensure smooth operation before refitting
		Check that oil pump body joint fixings are tight	Tighten fixings
		Relief valve spring weak. Check by substitution of serviceable spring	Replace spring
	Excessively worn bearings	Check bearing clearances at main journals, connecting rod big ends and camshaft as necessary	Replace the bearings, referring to the appropriate overhaul procedure
Q—Oil pressure warning light remains 'ON', with engine running	Low oil pressure	Refer to paragraph P for checks and remedy	
	Oil pressure switch unserviceable	Check by substitution of serviceable component	Replace switch
	Electrical fault	Check circuit	Rectify poor connections or replace leads as applicable
R—Warning light fails to glow with engine stopped and ignition switch 'ON'		Check warning lamp bulb by substitution of serviceable bulb	Replace bulb
		Check oil pressure switch by substitution of a serviceable switch	Replace switch
		Check electrical circuit	Rectify poor connections or replace leads as applicable

ENGINE—2.6 LITRE PETROL

GENERAL DATA

Capacity (piston displacement)	2625 cc (160.3 cu in.)
Number of cylinders	6
Bore	3.063 in. (77,8 mm)
Stroke	3.625 in. (92,075 mm)
Compression ratio	7:1 or 7.8:1
BHP at 4,500 rpm	90 95
BMEP at 1,750 rpm	7:1 122 lb sq in. (8,57 kg cm²)
	7.8:1 127 lb sq in. (8,92 kg cm²)
Maximum torque	7:1 132 lb ft (18 mkg) at 1,500 rpm
	7.8:1 134 lb ft (18,5 mkg) at 1,750 rpm
Firing order	1—5—3—6—2—4
Piston speed at 4,500 rpm	2,719 ft/min (826 m/min)
Compression pressure (at starter motor cranking speed, with engine hot)	7:1 140 lb sq in. (9,84 kg cm²)
	7.8:1 170 to 175 lb sq in (11,95 to 12,3 kg cm²)

DETAIL DATA

Camshaft

Journal diameter	.999 in. (25,38 mm)
Clearance in bearing	.001 to .0025 in. (0,02 to 0,06 mm)
End-float	.0045 to .0065 in. (0,114 to 0,165 mm)
Cam lift—inlet	.374 in. (9,5 mm)
Cam lift—exhaust	.403 in. (10,2 mm)

Camshaft bearings

Type	Split Mazac. Six off
Internal diameter (line-reamed in position)	1.0 in. (25,4 mm)

Connecting rods

Bearing fit on crankpin	.001 to .002 in. (0,025 to 0,05 mm)
Bearing nip	.002 to .004 in. (0,05 to 0,10 mm)
End-float at big-end	.006 to .015 in. (0,15 to 0,38 mm)
Gudgeon pin bush, fit in small-end	.001 to .003 in. (0,02 to 0,76 mm) interference
Gudgeon pin bush internal diameter—reamed in position	.8755 in.—.0005 in. (22,24 mm—0,0127 mm)
Fit of gudgeon pin in bush	.0002 in. to .0006 in. (0,005 mm to 0,015 mm) clearance

Crankshaft

Journal diameter	2.6245 in.—.0005 in. (67,0 mm—0,0127 mm)
Crankpin diameter	1.875 in.+.00075 in. (47,63 mm+0,018 mm)
End-float (controlled by thrust washers at rear main bearing)	.002 in. to .006 in. (0,05 mm to 0,15 mm)
Regrind permissible by .010 in. (0,254 mm) stages to	Journal dia. 2.584 in. (65,63 mm) Crankpin dia. 1.835 in. (46,6 mm)

ENGINE—2.6 LITRE PETROL

Flywheel
Number of teeth 97
Thickness .. .. 1.250 in. to 1.226 in. (31,75 mm to 31,14 mm)
Maximum permissible run-out on flywheel face .. .002 in. (0,05 mm)
Primary pinion bush—fit in flywheel .. .. .001 in. to .003 in. (0,02 mm to 0,07 mm)
Internal diameter—reamed in position .. .. .878 in. +.0005 in. (22,3 mm +0,013 mm)
Fit of shaft in bush .. .. .001 in. to .003 in. (0,025 mm to 0,076 mm)
Maximum refacing depth .. .. .. .030 in. (0,76 mm)
Minimum overall thickness after grinding .. 1.204 in (30,5 mm)

Engine timing markings
Early engines .. .. Timing marks and pointer at flywheel
Later engines .. .. Valve timing marks at timing chain wheels Ignition timing marks on crankshaft pulley, timing pointer at engine front cover

TDC for 7:1 engines using 80 octane fuel .. When opposite pointer, No. 1 piston is at top dead centre

6° BTDC for 8.8:1 engines using 95 octane fuel
2° BTDC for 7:1 engines using 83 octane fuel
2° ATDC for 7:1 engines using 78 octane fuel
and 7.8:1 engines using 90 octane fuel } When opposite pointer, indicates firing point of No. 1 cylinder when both valves are closed

EP .. .. Exhaust peak. Align with pointer to set engine for valve timing

Gudgeon pin
Fit in piston .. .. Push fit with piston warmed to 60°F (15°C)
Fit in connecting rod bush .. .. .. .0002 in. to .0006 in. (0,005 mm to 0,015 mm) clearance

Main bearings
Clearances on crankshaft journal .. .. .0006 in. to .002 in. (0,015 mm to 0,05 mm)
Bearing nip .. .. .004 in. to .006 in. (0,10 mm to 0,15 mm)

Pistons
Type .. .. Aluminium alloy, tin plated; pent roof type
Clearance in bore, measured at bottom of skirt at right angles to gudgeon pin .. .. .002 in. to .0025 in. (0,05 mm to 0,062 mm)
Clearance in bore, measured at top of skirt at right angles to gudgeon pin .. .. .003 in. to .0035 in. (0,08 mm to 0,089 mm)

Piston rings
Compression (2)
Type .. .. Taper periphery
Gap in bore .. .. .015 in. to .020 in. (0,38 mm to 0,50 mm)
Clearance in groove .. .. .0018 in. to .0038 in. (0,046 mm to 0,097 mm)
Scraper
Type .. .. Duaflex 61
Gap in bore .. .. .015 in. to .033 in. (0,38 mm to 0,83 mm)
Clearance in groove .. .. .002 in. to .004 in. (0,05 mm to 0,10 mm)

ENGINE—2.6 LITRE PETROL

Tappet clearance
Exhaust valves .. .. .010 in. (0,25 mm) hot or cold
Inlet valves .. .. .006 in. (0,15 mm) with engine at running temperature

Timing chain
Chain type .. .. Duplex pre-stretched endless
Pitch .. .. .375 in. (9,52 mm)
Chain tensioner .. .. Hydraulic self-adjusting (Renolds type SCD)

Thrust bearings, crankshaft
Type .. .. Semi-circular, steel back, tin plated on friction surface
Standard size, total thickness .. .. .. .093 in.—.002 in. (2,362 mm—0,05 mm)
Oversizes .. .. .0025 in. (0,06 mm); .005 in. (0,12 mm);
.0075 in. (0,18 mm); .010 in. (0,25 mm);
.0125 in. (0,316 mm)

Valves
Inlet valve
Diameter (stem) .. .. .3425 in.—.0005 in. (8,6995 mm—0,0127 mm)
Face angle .. .. 30°¼
Exhaust valve
Diameter (stem) .. .. .3425 in.—.0005 in. (8,6995 mm—0,0127 mm)
Face angle .. .. 45°¼
Fit of inlet valves in guide .. .. .. .0013 in. to .003 in. (0,033 mm to 0,07 mm)
Fit of exhaust valves in guide .. .. .. .0013 in. to .003 in. (0,033 mm to 0,07 mm)

Valve seat inserts
Fit of inlet seat insert in cylinder head .. .. .0034 in. to .0045 in. (0,086 mm to 0,114 mm) interference
Fit of exhaust seat insert in cylinder block .. .0034 in. to .007 in. (0,086 mm to 0,178 mm) interference
Seat angle—inlet .. .. 30°
Seat angle—exhaust .. .. 45°
Seat mean diameter—inlet .. .. .. 1.2645 in. (32 mm)
Seat mean diameter—exhaust .. .. .. 1.7415 in. (44 mm)

ENGINE—2.6 LITRE PETROL

Valve springs
Inlet
  Inner
    Length—free .. .. .. 1.703 in. (43,26 mm)
  Outer
    Length—free .. .. .. 1.960 in. (49,8 mm)
Exhaust
  Inner
    Length—free .. .. .. 1.703 in. (43,26 mm)
  Outer
    Length—free .. .. .. 1.861 in. (47,26 mm)

Valve guides
Bore size, after fitting .. .. .3455 in.—.0022 in. (8,7757 mm—0,056 mm)
Oil seal .. .. .. 'O' ring fitted in internal groove
Guide length
  Inlet .. .. .. 1.5 in. (38,10 mm)
  Exhaust .. .. .. 2.25 in. (57,15 mm)
Fit in cylinder head/block
  Inlet .. .. .. .0024 in. to .0035 in. (0,06 mm to 0,09 mm)
  Exhaust .. .. .. .0014 in. to .0025 in. (0,035 mm to 0,063 mm)

Valve timing
Inlet opens .. .. .. 12° BTDC
Inlet closes .. .. .. 46° ABDC
Duration .. .. .. 238°
Exhaust opens .. .. .. 47° BBDC
Exhaust closes .. .. .. 17° ATDC
Duration .. .. .. 244°

Oil pump
Type .. .. .. Spur gear
Drive .. .. .. Splined shaft from camshaft skew gear
End-float of gears:
  Steel gear .. .. .. .002 in. (0,05 mm) to .005 in. (0,12 mm)
  Aluminium gear .. .. .. .003 in. (0,07 mm) to .006 in. (0,15 mm)
Radial clearance of gears .. .. .001 in. to .004 in. (0,02 mm to 0,102 mm)
Backlash of gears .. .. .. .008 in. to .012 in. (0,20 mm to 0,28 mm)

Oil pressure, engine warm
At 2,000 rpm .. .. .. 40 to 50 lb/sq in. (3,16 to 4,57 kg cm²)

Oil pressure relief valve
Type .. .. .. Non-adjustable
Relief valve spring:
  Free length .. .. .. 3.425 in. (87,0 mm)
  Compressed length at 17.5 lb (7,9 kg) load .. 1.990 in. (50,55 mm)

SECTION B—CLUTCH UNITS

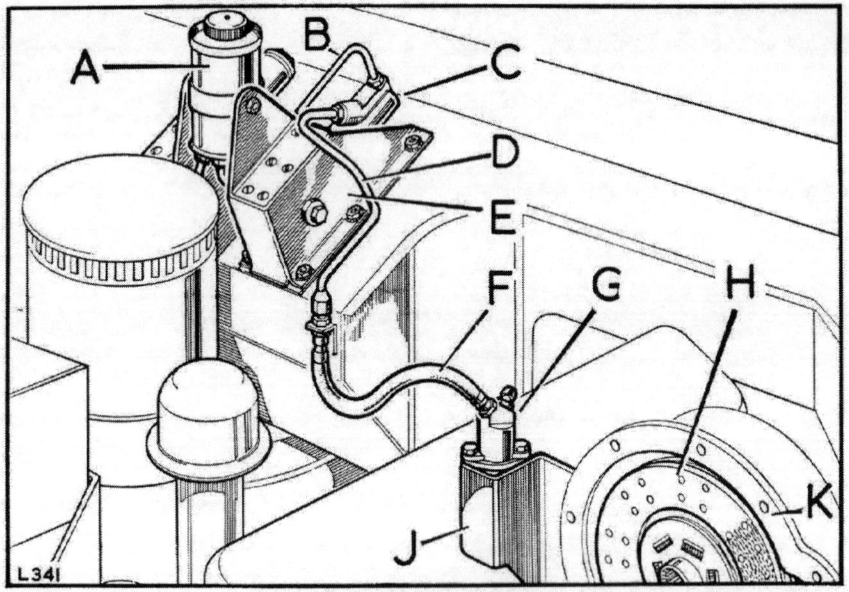

Fig. B1-1. Layout of clutch system

A—Hydraulic fluid reservoir (where fitted separate from master cylinder)
B—Fluid inlet pipe from reservoir
C—Master cylinder
D—Fluid outlet pipe
E—Clutch pedal bracket
F—Flexible hose
G—Slave cylinder
H—Clutch assembly
J—Slave cylinder bracket
K—Bell housing

CLUTCH UNITS

INDEX—CLUTCH UNITS

Note: A comprehensive, detailed index is included at the end of this manual.

Description	Operation Number	
	Remove/Refit	Overhaul
Clutch assembly and flywheel	Section A	B-1
*Clutch withdrawal race housing	B-2	B-2
Clutch slave cylinder assembly	B-3	B-4
Clutch master cylinder	B-5	B-6
Clutch pedal, bracket and reservoir	B-7	—
Bleeding the hydraulic system	B-8	—
Clutch linkage and pedal, to adjust	B-9	—

*This heading and operation number is for reference purposes only. The relevant information is provided in Section C—Gearbox.

Brief description of clutch system and operation

A Borg and Beck single dry plate clutch with hydraulically operated control mechanism is used.

Two types of clutch unit are in use, either a 9½ in. diameter diaphragm type, or a 9 in. coil spring type.

The hydraulic operating mechanism consists of a ¾ in. (19 mm) bore master cylinder which is mechanically attached directly to the clutch pedal and is connected by hydraulic piping to the slave cylinder.

The hydraulic fluid reservoir may be integral with the master cylinder or mounted separately.

A mechanical linkage connects the slave cylinder to the clutch withdrawal unit which utilises a thrust ball race. The withdrawal unit housing is attached to the gearbox and is automatically lubricated by gearbox oil.

Take precautions to keep all components scrupulously clean when carrying out any work on the hydraulic system.

Use only the recommended hydraulic fluid as specified in Section X.

CLUTCH UNITS

Key to Fig. B1-2. Early and late type clutch assemblies

1. Flywheel housing
2. Stud fixing flywheel housing to bell housing
3. Stud fixing inspection cover
4. Stud for starter motor
5. Sealing ring for flywheel housing
6. Inspection cover plate (early type engines)
7. Joint washer for cover plate
8. Nut fixing cover plate
9. Bolt ⎫
10. Bolt ⎬ Fixing flywheel housing to cylinder block
11. Spring washer ⎪
12. Plain washer ⎭
13. Indicator for engine timing (early type engines)
14. Drain plug for housing
15. Stowage bracket for drain plug. On later engines the plug is stowed in a blind tapping in the flywheel housing
16. Flywheel assembly
17. Dowel locating clutch cover plate
18. Bush for primary pinion
19. Special fitting bolt fixing clutch cover plate, applicable to certain models only. See Parts Catalogue
20. Set bolt ⎫ Fixing clutch cover plate
21. Spring washer ⎭
22. Locker ⎫ Fixing flywheel to crankshaft
23. Special set bolt ⎭
24. Cover plate for coil spring type clutch
25. Pressure plate
26. Release lever
27. Strut for release lever
28. Eyebolt and nut for release lever
29. Pin for release lever
30. Anti-rattle spring for release lever
31. Clutch coil spring (9 off)
32. Clutch driven plate
33. Diaphragm spring type clutch, fitted to 2.6 litre engines and later 2¼ litre Diesel engines. Optional equipment on 2¼ litre petrol engines.
34. Clutch driven plate

Fig. B1-2. Early and late type clutch assemblies

CLUTCH UNITS

Clutch unit and flywheel, to overhaul—Operation B1-1

(For removing and refitting details, Section A refers)

Workshop hand tools:

Spanner sizes: 11/16 in. AF socket
Screwdriver (medium)

Special tools:

Socket wrench, Part No. 530103 clutch setting gauge, suitable press and wooden support blocks, suitable rivetting tool and 5/32 in. (4 mm) twist drill as required

COIL SPRING TYPE CLUTCH

Clutch unit, to dismantle

1. Suitably mark the cover plate, pressure plate lugs and release levers, so that they may be assembled in the same relative position in order to retain the original balance.

2. Place the cover assembly under a press with the pressure plate resting on wooden blocks, so arranged that the cover can move downwards when pressure is applied. Place a block of wood across the top of the cover, resting on the spring bosses.

3. Press the cover downwards and remove the three release lever adjusting nuts; slowly release the pressure to prevent the clutch springs from flying out.

4. Lift off the cover and withdraw the clutch springs.

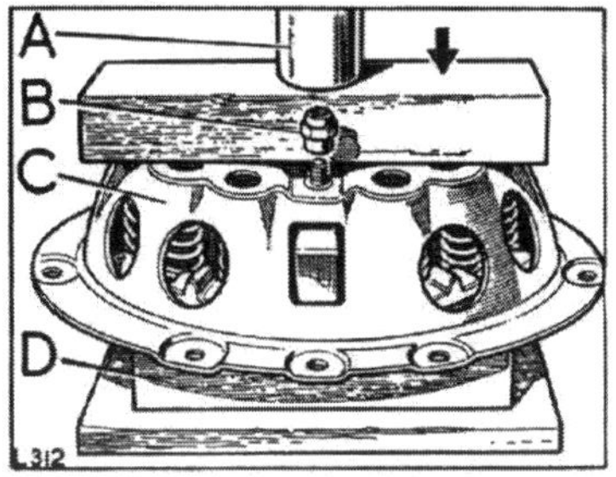

5. Remove each release lever by holding the lever and eyebolt between fingers and thumb, so that the inner end of the lever and the threaded end of the eyebolt are as near together as possible, keeping the release lever pin in position in the lever. Lift the strut over the ridge on the lever and remove the eyebolt and release lever from the pressure plate.

Fig. B1-3. Removing clutch cover plate

A—Suitable press
B—Release lever adjusting nuts
C—Clutch cover
D—Support blocks

6. Withdraw the anti-rattle springs from the clutch cover.

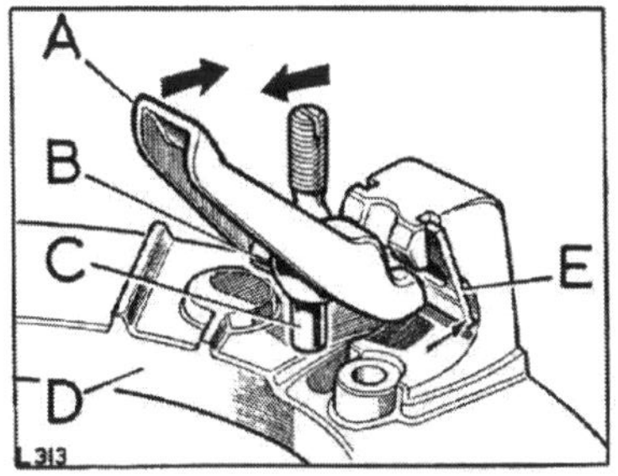

Fig. B1-4. Release levers removal

A—Release lever
B—Release lever pin
C—Eyebolt
D—Pressure plate
E—Strut

Inspection

1. Pressure plate

Examine the pressure plate for signs of scoring or burning, and regrind if necessary. Refer to the Data pages for dimensions. The thickness of the plate is measured from the pressure face to the underside of the operating lugs, as illustrated

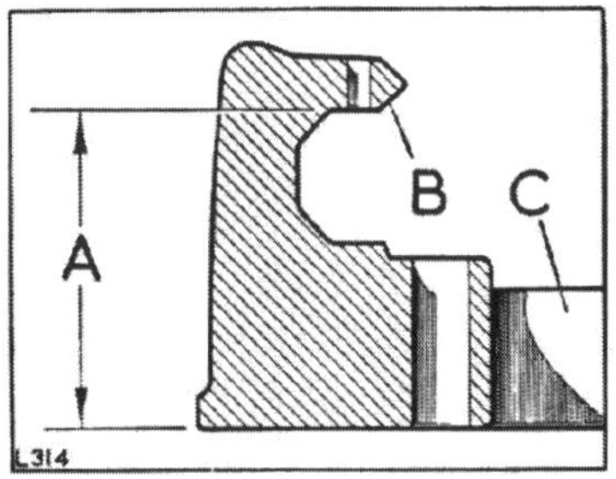

Fig. B1-5. Checking pressure plate dimension

A—Thickness dimension measured here
B—Pressure plate lug
C—Pressure plate

Operation B1-1—continued

Discard the plate if it still shows signs of wear after grinding. Serious shortening of the effective life of the clutch unit will result if the limit for regrinding is exceeded.

The thickness of the pressure plate must always be measured from the underside of the same operating lug and the amount skimmed off the plate stamped on the side of the lug in question.

(b) Replace the primary pinion bush in the flywheel, if necessary, and ream to .878 in. +.0005 in. (22.30 mm +0.0127 mm) when fitted. If time allows, soak the replacement bush in clean engine oil for 24 hours before fitting.

Clutch driven plate

1. Examine the clutch driven plate for wear and signs of oil contamination. Examine all rivets for pulling and distortion, the friction lining rivets must be below the friction surface. If oil contamination is present on the friction linings or if they are appreciably worn, replace the clutch driven plate assembly complete or alternatively, replace the friction linings as follows:

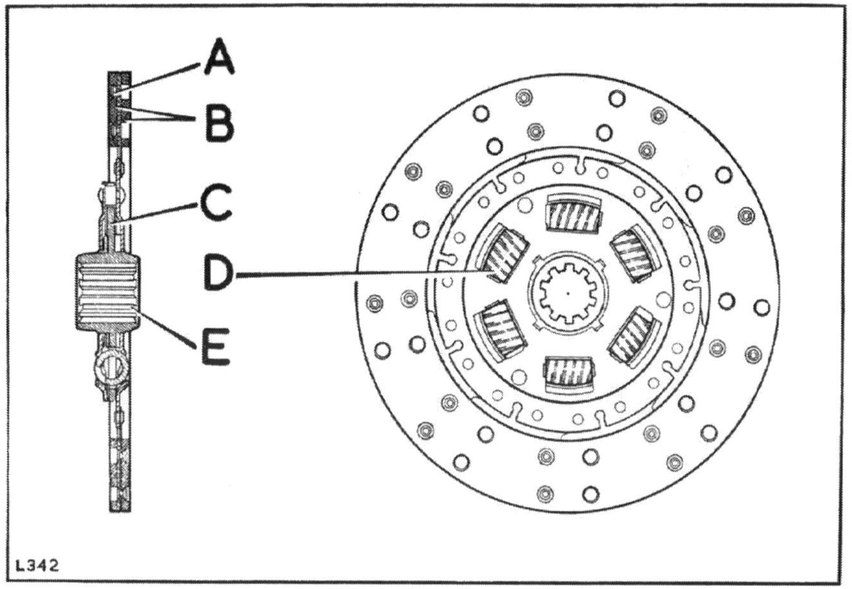

2. Flywheel

(a) If the flywheel is excessively worn it must be renewed or refaced. The refacing procedure is detailed in Section A.

Fig. B1-6. Clutch driven plate

A—Securing rivets (38 off) Rivet heads to be below friction surface
B—Friction linings
C—Examine centre plate and segments for cracks and distortion
D—Visually check damper springs for damage and soundness
E—Examine splines for damage and wear

/ # CLUTCH UNITS

Operation B1-1—continued

Driven plate, to reline

(a) Drill out the retaining rivets, using a 5/32 in. (4 mm) drill inserted through the clearance hole in the opposite lining; each rivet attaches one facing only. The rivets must not be punched out, as serious deformation of the plate would thereby result.

(b) Thoroughly examine the segments for cracks; renew as necessary.

(c) Place one facing in position with the countersunk holes coinciding with the ones located on the crown or longer side of each segment.

(d) Insert the rivets with their heads in the countersunk holes of the facing and roll the shanks over securely against the segments. If a rolling tool is not available, a blunt-ended centre punch will prove satisfactory.

(e) Secure the second facing on the opposite side of the plate in a similar manner, matching the countersunk holes with the remaining holes in the segments. The rivet heads should always face outwards.

(f) Mount the plate on a suitable mandrel between centres and check for run-out as near the edge as possible; if the error is more than .010 in. (0,25 mm), press over the high spots until the plate is true within this figure.

Clutch springs

Check the clutch springs in accordance with the data given at the end of this Section and renew as necessary.

To rebuild

1. A very slight smear of high melting-point grease should be applied to the following parts during assembly:
   Release lever pins, contact faces of struts, eyebolt seats in cover, drive lug sides on the pressure plate and the plain end of the eyebolts.
2. Fit the lever pin to the release lever.
3. Fit the eyebolt and pin into the release lever.
4. Hold the threaded end of the eyebolt and the inner end of the lever as close together as possible.

5. Fit the release lever strut to the release lever lug on the pressure plate and swivel the lower edge away from the eyebolt locating hole in the pressure plate. Hold the strut in this position. Fig. B1-4 refers.

6. Offer the eyebolt and release lever to the pressure plate, engaging the eyebolt plain end into the hole provided.

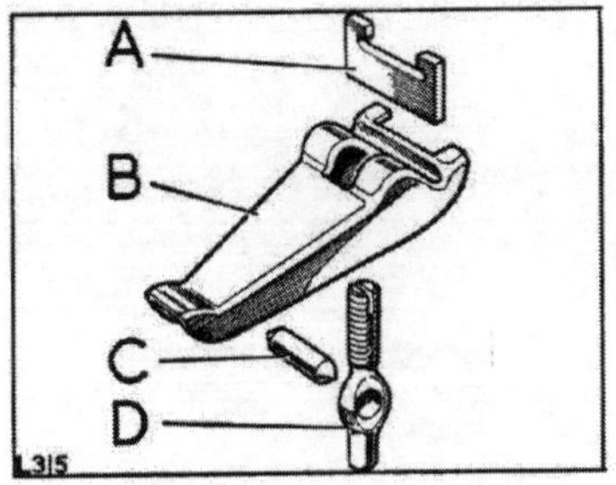

Fig. B1-7. Release lever and eyebolt arrangement
A—Strut C—Pin for eyebolt
B—Release lever D—Eyebolt

7. Move the strut in its slots and engage the strut lower edge into the recess formed in the release lever.

8. Release the lever and eyebolt. They are now retained to the pressure plate.

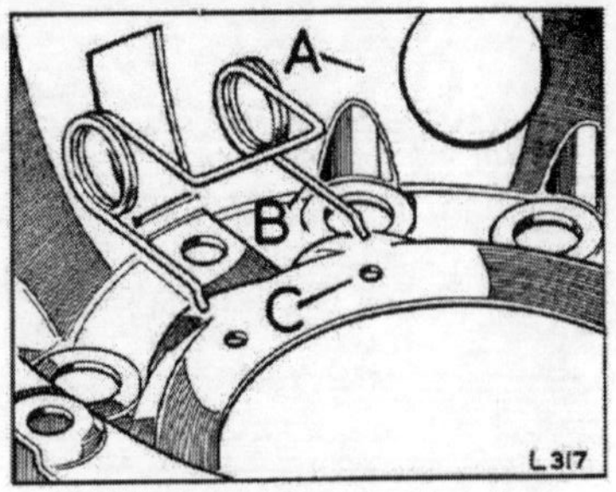

Fig. B1-8. Fitting Anti-rattle springs
A—Clutch cover
B—Anti-rattle springs
C—Location holes for springs

Operation B1-1—continued

9. Fit the remaining two release levers in a similar manner.

10. Engage the anti-rattle springs into the holes provided in the clutch cover plate.

11. Place the pressure plate on the wooden blocks under the press and arrange the thrust springs in a vertical position on the plate, seating them on the bosses provided. Lay the cover over the assembled parts, ensuring that the tops of the thrust springs are directly under the seats in the cover.

12. Ensure that the machined portions of the pressure plate lugs are under the slots in the cover and that the parts marked before dismantling are in their correct relative positions.

13. Place the block of wood across the cover, resting it on the spring bosses, and depress the cover, guiding the eyebolts and pressure plate lugs through the holes in the cover.

14. Screw the adjusting nuts on the eyebolts and operate the clutch a few times by means of the press, to ensure that the working parts have settled into their correct positions.

15. Next, adjust the release levers.

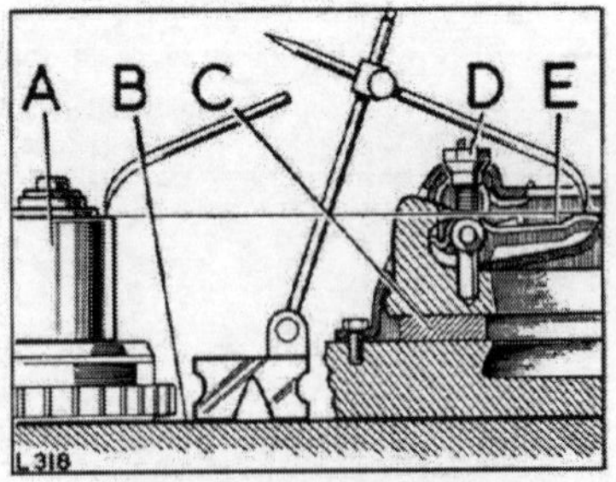

Adjusting release levers

This adjustment must be carried out before the clutch is refitted to the engine, and will always be necessary after complete stripping of the unit, or if any new parts have been fitted.

1. The setting of the clutch release levers is checked, using 3/8 in. (9,5 mm) distance pieces in place of the driven plate. The levers must be adjusted to a dimension of 1.655 in. (42 mm) from the flywheel face, with a maximum of .010 in. (0,25 mm) difference in height between the three levers.

2. Place the flywheel on a surface plate and set the scribe to 1.655 in. (42 mm) from the flywheel face, using gauge Part No. 530103.

3. Place the three distance pieces on the flywheel in place of the driven plate.

4. Fit the cover assembly to the flywheel by tightening all six securing nuts a turn at a time by diagonal selection, until the unit is fully secured.

5. Check the height of each operating lever and adjust as necessary, by turning the adjustment nut until the top of the lever is exactly level with the scribe. Adjust the two other levers in a similar manner.

6. Secure the adjusting nuts by staking.

DIAPHRAGM TYPE CLUTCH

Overhaul procedures for the diaphragm type clutch assembly are as follows:

(a) Clutch unit—no dismantling or overhaul are permissible. Replace the unit complete where necessary.

(b) Flywheel—overhaul as described for the coil spring type clutch flywheel.

(c) Clutch driven plate—overhaul as described for the coil spring type clutch driven plate.

Fig. B1-9. Setting the release levers
A—Gauge, Part No. 530103
B—Surface plate
C—Distance pieces, 3/8 in. (9,5 mm)
D—Adjustment nut for lever
E—Release lever

Clutch withdrawal race housing assembly—Operation B1-2

For remove, overhaul and refit details refer to Section C—Gearbox

CLUTCH UNITS

Clutch slave cylinder, remove and refit—Operation B1-3

Workshop hand tools:
Spanner sizes: ½ in. AF, ⅜ in. AF, ⁷⁄₁₆ in. BSF open end, ⁷⁄₁₆ in. AF socket
Screwdriver (medium), Long nosed pliers

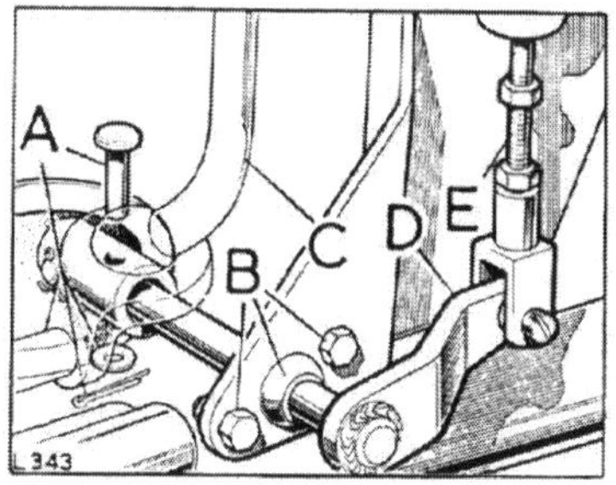

Fig. B1-10. View of operating shafts
A—Fixings, clutch shaft lever to connecting tube
B—Spherical bearing and fixings
C—Transfer gear lever, shown 'ghosted' for clarity
D—Operating lever
E—Slave cylinder push rod

To remove

1. Remove the front floor or gearbox tunnel, as applicable, to gain access to the bell housing. This procedure is described in Section A.
2. Slacken the hydraulic fluid inlet pipe at the slave cylinder. Fig. B1-11 refers.
3. Remove the operating lever return spring, if fitted.
4. Remove the clevis pin securing the clutch shaft operating lever to the cross-shaft connecting tube.
5. Rotate the clutch shaft operating lever and withdraw the push rod from the slave cylinder; if necessary, slacken the spherical bearing fixings to facilitate lever rotation.

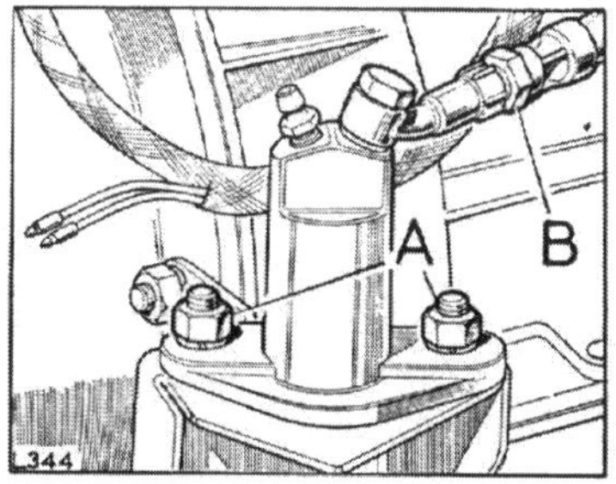

Fig. B1-11. Slave cylinder fixings (latest type cylinder shown)
A—Fixings at support bracket
B—Fluid inlet pipe

6. Remove the fixings and withdraw the slave cylinder from the support bracket.
7. Position a clean container under the slave cylinder and remove the cylinder from the hydraulic fluid inlet pipe.

Clutch slave cylinder, to overhaul—Operation B1-4

Workshop hand tools:
Spanner size: ⁷⁄₁₆ in. AF
Circlip Pliers

To dismantle

1. Withdraw the dust cover from the end of the slave cylinder and remove the exposed circlip.
2. Hold the fingers over the cylinder bore, apply a low air pressure to the fluid inlet tapping and expel the assembled piston from the bore.

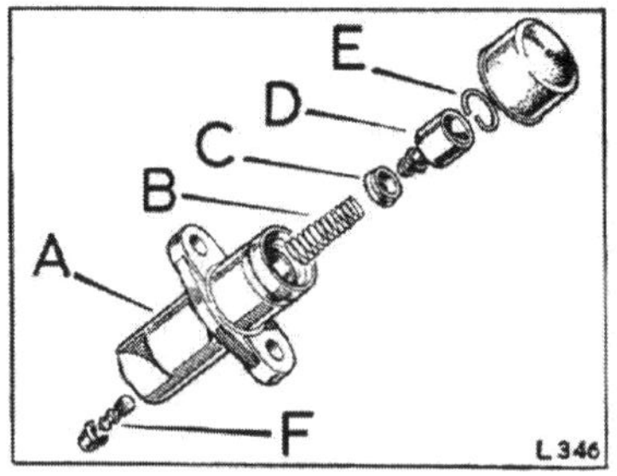

Fig. B1-12. Exploded view of slave cylinder
A—Slave cylinder   D—Piston
B—Spring   E—Circlip
C—Piston seal   F—Bleed union

3. Remove the spring and seal from the piston.
4. Clean all components in Girling cleaning fluid and allow to dry.

Overhaul

1. Examine the cylinder bore and the piston and ensure that they are free from corrosion, scores and ridges. Replace faulty components.
2. Replace the seals and dust cover with those provided in the slave cylinder overhaul kit.
3. Where applicable, replace the ball valve in the bleed union. Do not overtighten the bleed valve when refitting.

To assemble

1. Lubricate the seals, using Castrol-Girling Rubber Grease, and the remaining internal components using Castrol-Girling Brake and Clutch Fluid.
2. Fit the seal, flat side first, to the piston and locate the spring smaller end on to the piston spigot.
3. Enter the piston assembly, spring first, into the cylinder bore and secure with the circlip.
4. Refit the dust cover.

To refit

1. Fit the hydraulic fluid inlet pipe to the slave cylinder. Do not fully tighten at this stage.
2. Fit the slave cylinder to the support bracket.
3. Enter the push rod into the slave cylinder to engage the seating in the piston crown. If previously slackened, tighten the spherical bearing fixings.
4. Align the holes in the clutch shaft operating lever and the cross-shaft connecting tube and fit the clevis pin to secure the components, Fig. B1-10 refers.
5. Refit the operating lever return spring, where applicable.
6. Finally tighten the fluid inlet pipe.
7. Refit the front floor or gearbox tunnel as applicable, Section A.
8. Bleed the hydraulic system of air. Operation B-8.

CLUTCH UNITS

Clutch master cylinder, to remove and refit—Operation B1-5

(For overhaul details, Operation B1-6 refers)

Workshop hand tools:
Spanner sizes: $\frac{7}{16}$ in. AF, $\frac{1}{2}$ in. AF open end, $\frac{1}{2}$ in. AF socket
Screwdriver (medium), Pliers

To remove

1. Remove the bonnet panel. Section A.
2. **LH Steering models**
   (a) Remove the left-hand front wing as described in Section R.
   (b) Disconnect the hydraulic fluid pipes at the master cylinder.
   (c) Disconnect the fluid reservoir fixings where applicable.
   (d) Remove the clutch pedal bracket fixings (from inside the vehicle cab) and remove the clutch pedal, bracket and master cylinder complete. Fig. B1-13. refers.
   (e) Continue removal procedure from paragraph 4 onward.
3. **RH Steering models**
   (a) Disconnect the hydraulic fluid pipes at the master cylinder.
   (b) Disconnect the fluid reservoir fixings where applicable.

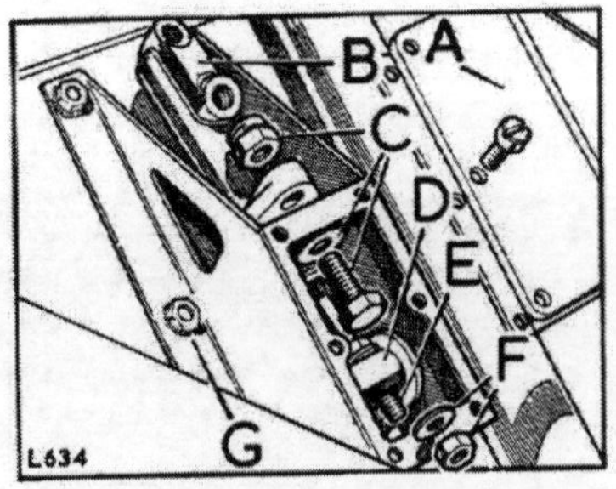

Fig. B1-13. View of master cylinder and mounting bracket
A—Bracket top cover, gasket and fixings
B—Master cylinder
C—Master cylinder fixings
D—Trunnion distance piece
E—Push rod
F—Push rod end fixing
G—Pedal bracket

4. Remove the top cover and gasket from the clutch pedal bracket.
5. Remove the master cylinder plunger end fixing at the pedal trunnion.
6. Remove the fixings and withdraw the master cylinder from the mounting bracket.

To refit

1. Fit the master cylinder to the pedal bracket, engaging the cylinder push rod into the hole provided in the pedal trunnion.
2. Fit the push rod end fixing.
3. **LH Steering models**
   Fit the pedal, bracket and master cylinder complete to the vehicle.
4. Fit the hydraulic fluid pipe/s.
5. Bleed the hydraulic system. Operation B-8.
6. Adjust the clutch pedal height and linkage travel. Operation B-9.
7. Fit the top cover plate and gasket to the pedal bracket and refit the fluid reservoir, where applicable.
8. **LH Steering models**
   Fit the LH front wing. Section R.
9. Refit the bonnet panel. Section A.

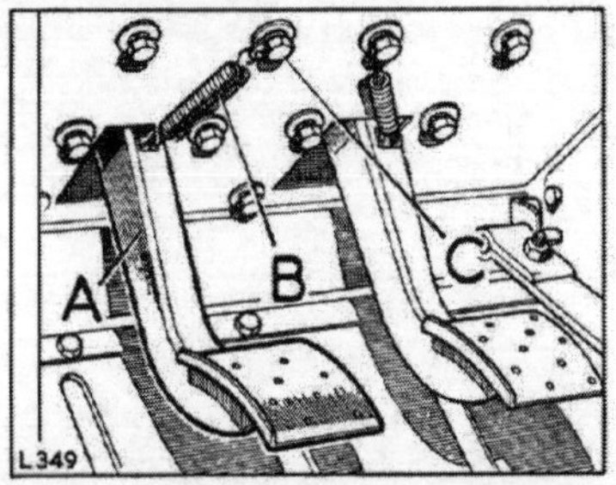

Clutch master cylinder, to overhaul—Operation B1-6

(For removal and refitting details, Operation B1-5 refers)

Workshop hand tools:
Spanner sizes: $\frac{1}{4}$ in. AF open end
Screwdriver (small), Pliers (snipe nosed)

There are two types of master cylinder in use. One type has a hydraulic fluid reservoir as an integral part of the cylinder and therefore has no fluid inlet tapping.

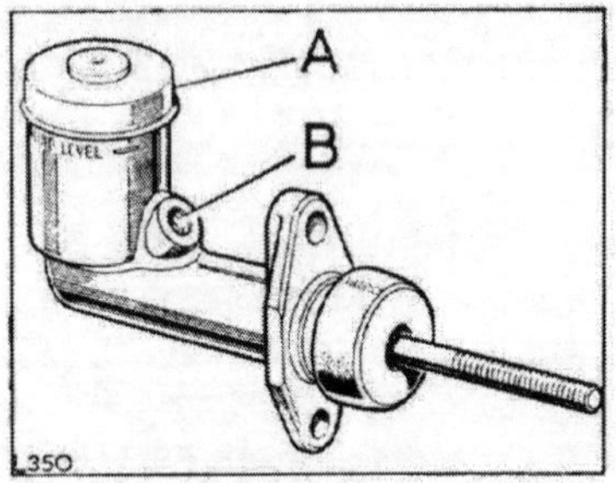

Fig. B1-15. Master cylinder with integral reservoir
A—Fluid reservoir cap
B—Fluid outlet tapping

The other type master cylinder is fed from an external hydraulic fluid reservoir and therefore an inlet pipe connection is provided.

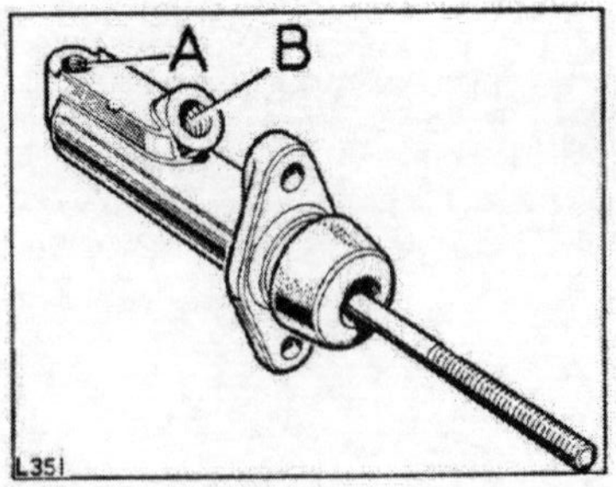

Fig. B1-16. Master cylinder for use with external reservoir
A—Fluid inlet tapping
B—Fluid outlet tapping

The method of operation, the internal components and the overhaul procedures are identical for both types.

Fig. B1-14. Clutch pedal bracket fixings, LHStg model shown
A—Clutch pedal
B—Pedal return spring
C—Bracket fixings (6 off)

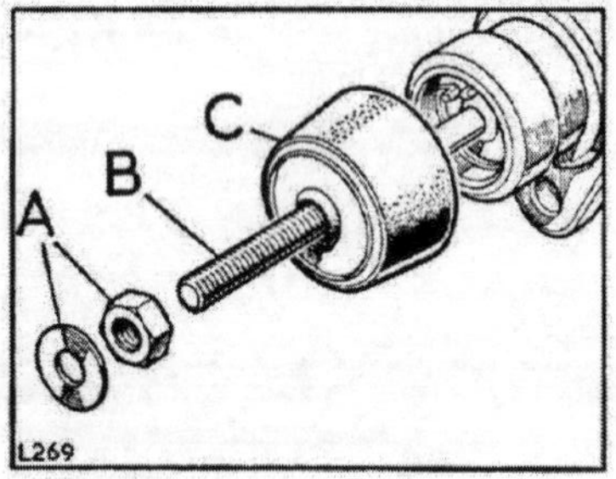

Fig. B1-17. Push rod end details
A—Locknut and washer
B—Push rod
C—Rubber cover

To dismantle

1. Remove the plain washer, nut and rubber cover from the push rod.
2. Remove the circlip and withdraw the push rod and retaining washer.

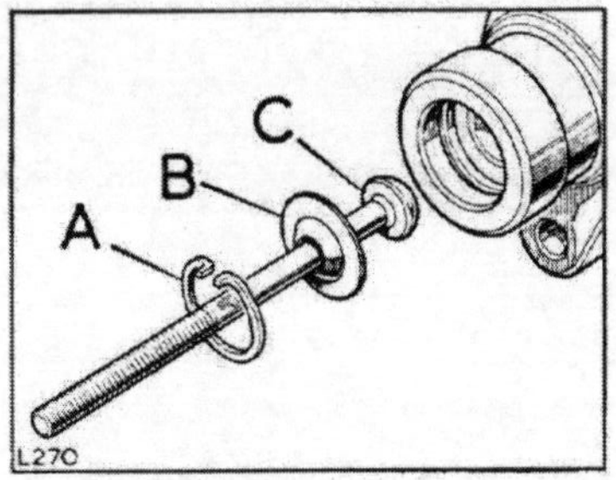

Fig. B1-18. Push rod fixings
A—Circlip
B—Retaining washer
C—Push rod

3. Withdraw the piston assembly from the master cylinder. If necessary, apply a low air pressure to the outlet port to expel the piston.

CLUTCH UNITS

Operation B1-6—continued

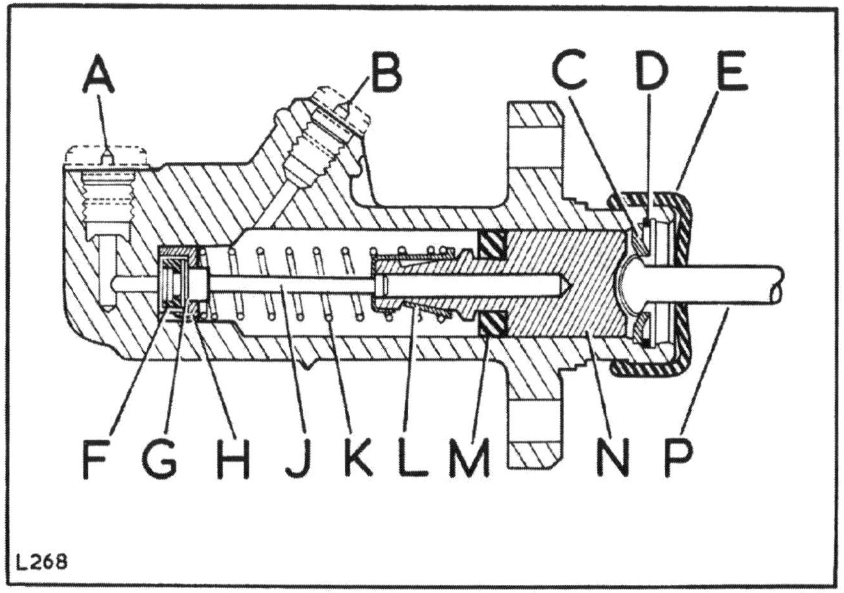

Fig. B1-19. Sectioned view of master cylinder

A—Inlet port
B—Outlet port
C—Spring washer
D—Circlip
E—Dust cover
F—Valve seal
G—Spring washer
H—Valve spacer
J—Valve stem
K—Return spring
L—Spring retainer
M—Piston seal
N—Piston
P—Push rod

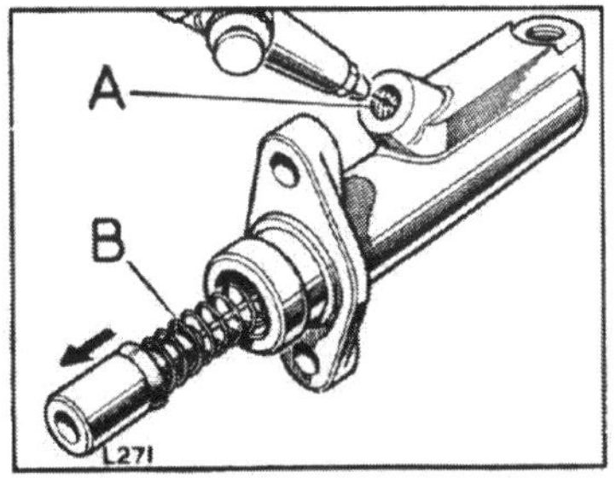

Fig. B1-20. Withdrawing piston assembly

A—Apply low air pressure to outlet port
B—Piston assembly

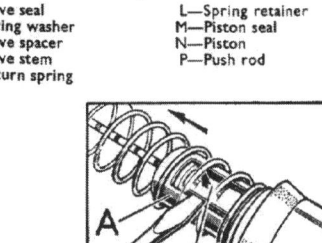

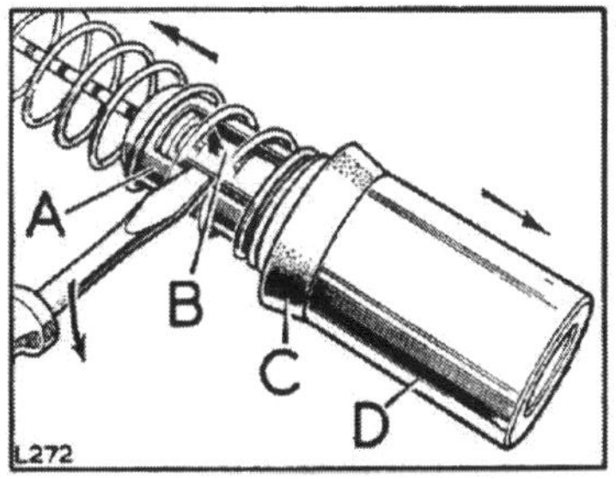

Fig. B1-21. Removing piston

A—Spring retainer
B—Locking prong
C—Seal for piston
D—Piston

Operation B1-6—continued

4. Prise the locking prong of the spring retainer clear of the piston shoulder and withdraw the piston. Remove the piston seal.

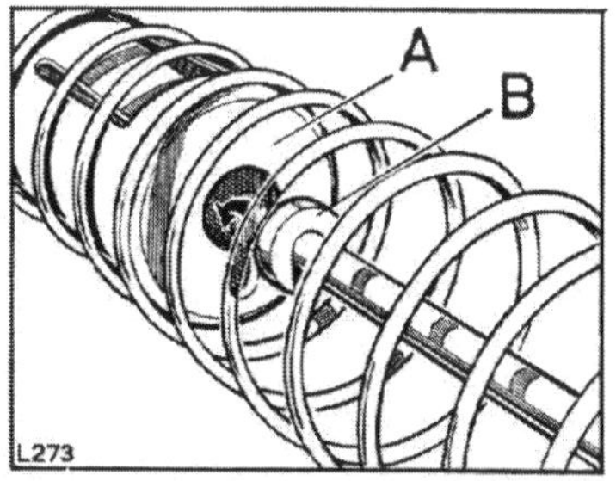

Fig. B1-22. Valve stem to spring retainer location

A—Spring retainer
B—Valve stem

5. Compress the spring and position the valve stem to align with the larger hole in the spring retainer. Withdraw the spring and retainer.

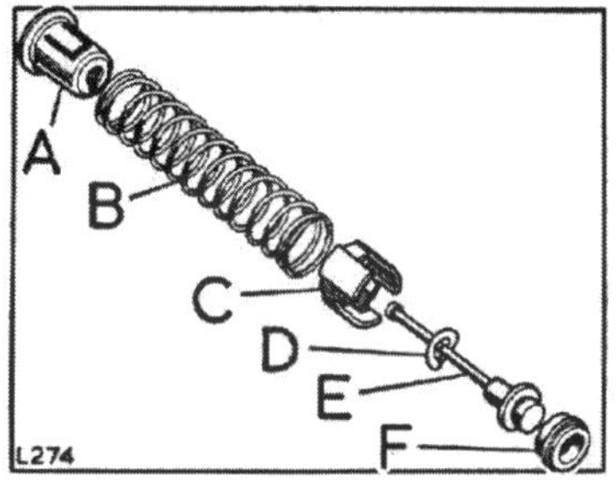

Fig. B1-23. Spring and valve assembly

A—Spring retainer
B—Spring
C—Valve spacer
D—Spring washer
E—Valve stem
F—Valve seal

6. Slide the valve spacer over the valve stem. Remove the special spring washer and valve seal from the stem.

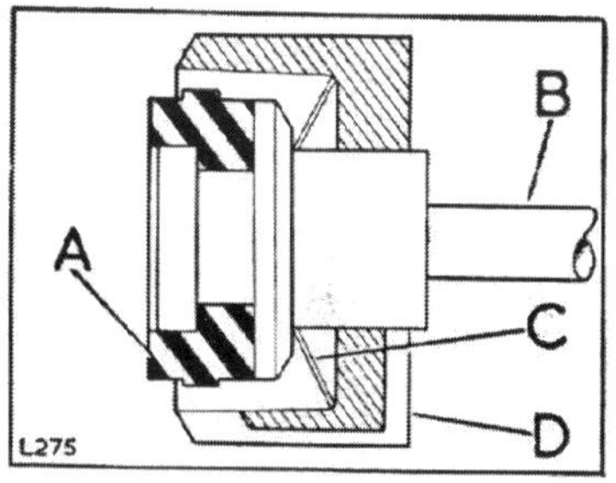

Fig. B1-24. Valve assembly

A—Valve seal
B—Valve stem
C—Spring washer
D—Valve spacer

Inspection

1. Clean all components in Girling cleaning fluid and allow to dry.

2. Examine the cylinder bore and piston, ensure that they are smooth to the touch with no corrosion, score marks or ridges. If there is any doubt, fit new replacements.

3. The seals and dust cover should be replaced with new components. These items are all included in the master cylinder overhaul kit.

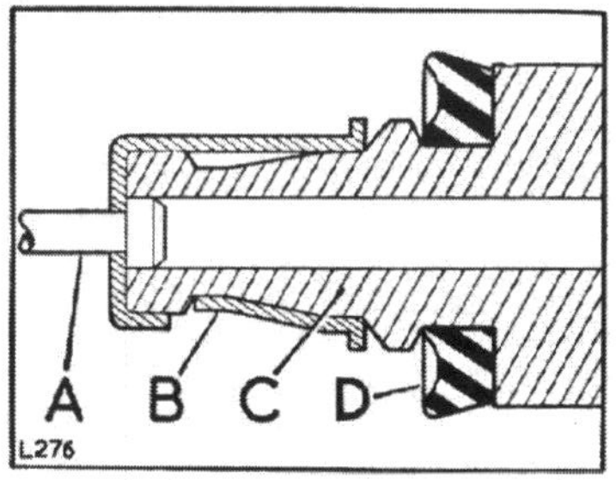

Fig. B1-25. Piston and spring retainer

A—Valve stem
B—Prong in engaged position
C—Piston
D—Seal

CLUTCH UNITS

Operation B1-6—continued

To assemble

1. Smear the seals with Castrol-Girling Rubber Grease and the remaining internal items with Castrol-Girling Brake and Clutch Fluid.

2. Fit the valve seal, flat side first, to the end of the valve stem.

3. Place the spring washer, domed side first, over the small end of the valve stem, then fit the valve spacer, legs first, and the coil spring.

4. Insert the retainer into the spring and compress until the stem passes through the keyhole and is engaged in the centre, see Fig. B1-25.

5. Fit the seal, large diameter last, to the piston.

6. Insert the piston into the spring retainer and engage the locking prong.

7. Smear the piston with Castrol-Girling Rubber Grease and insert the assembly, valve end first, into the cylinder.

8. Fit the push rod, retaining washer and circlip.

9. Smear liberally the inside of the dust cover with Castrol-Girling Rubber Grease and fit the cover over the push rod and cylinder.

10. Fit the adjuster nut and washer to the push rod.

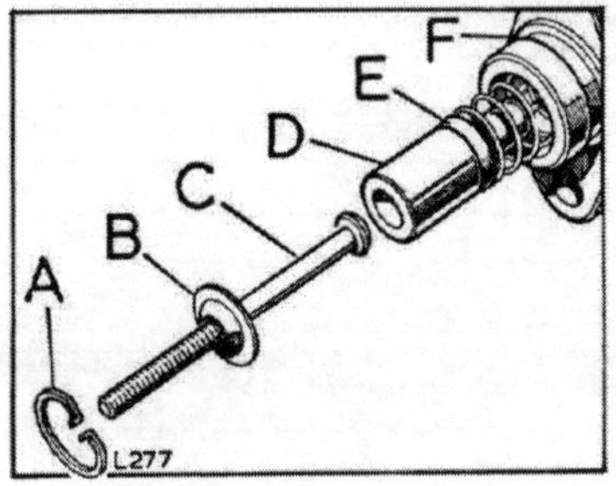

Fig. B1-26. Piston and push rod assembly
A—Circlip
B—Retaining washer, concave face toward push rod head
C—Push rod
D—Piston
E—Seal for piston
F—Cylinder

Clutch pedal and bracket, remove and refit—Operation B1-7

This operation includes removal and refitting of the bracket mounted hydraulic fluid reservoir, where fitted

Workshop hand tools:
Spanner sizes: $\frac{7}{16}$ in. AF, $\frac{1}{2}$ in. AF open end, $\frac{1}{2}$ in. AF socket
Screwdriver (medium), Pliers

To remove

Fluid reservoir

1. Remove the bonnet panel. Section A.
2. Disconnect the fluid pipes at the reservoir.
3. Remove the fixings and withdraw the reservoir complete with mounting clip.

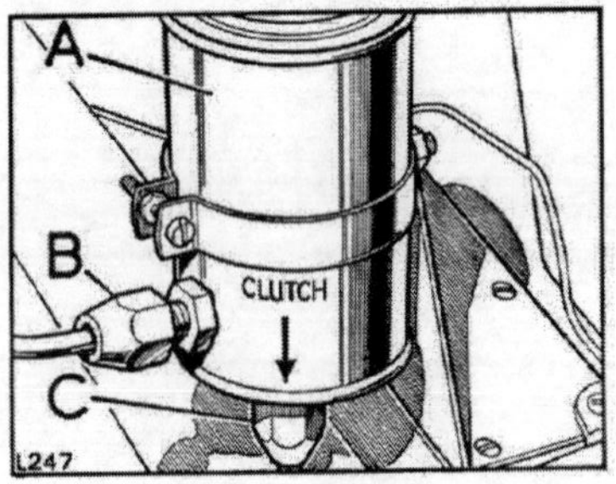

Fig. B1-27. Bracket mounted fluid reservoir
A—Fluid reservoir
B—Brake fluid pipe
C—Clutch fluid pipe

Clutch pedal and bracket

Note: For LH Steering models, first remove the LH front wing. Section R.

1. Disconnect the fluid outlet pipe (and inlet pipe where applicable) at the master cylinder.
2. Remove the clutch pedal bracket fixings (from inside the vehicle cab) and remove the bracket complete with pedal and master cylinder.

Clutch pedal and bracket, to dismantle

1. Remove the cover plate and gasket from the clutch pedal bracket.
2. Remove the fixing from the end of the master cylinder push rod.
3. Remove the locating pin and withdraw the pedal shaft securing the pedal to the bracket. Withdraw the pedal.

4. The pedal bushes may be renewed, if necessary.

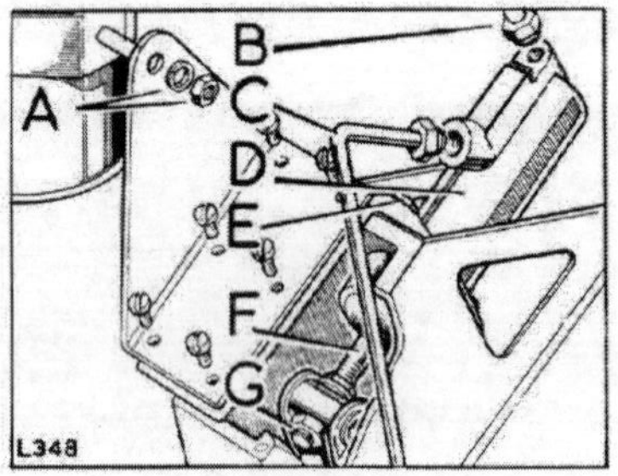

Fig. B1-28. View of master cylinder and mounting bracket
A—Bracket top cover, gasket and fixings
B—Fluid inlet pipe, where applicable
C—Fluid outlet pipe
D—Master cylinder
E—Master cylinder fixings
F—Push rod
G—Push rod end fixing

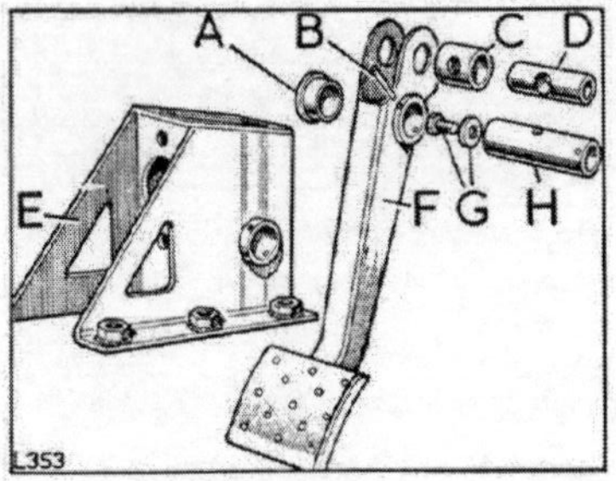

Fig. B1-29. Clutch pedal details
A—Pedal bush
B—Locating pin
C—Trunnion distance piece
D—Pedal trunnion
E—Pedal bracket
F—Clutch pedal
G—Oil plug and joint washer
H—Pedal shaft

CLUTCH UNITS

Operation B1-7—continued

To assemble and refit

1. Remove the oil plug and washer from the pedal shaft. Fill the shaft bore with clean engine oil and also lubricate the pedal trunnion and distance piece. Refit the oil plug and washer.
2. Fit the pedal to the bracket and secure with the pedal shaft. Fit the locating pin to the pedal shaft and bracket.
3. Engage the master cylinder push rod into the hole provided in the pedal trunnion and fit the end fixing.
4. Fit the assembled pedal bracket to the vehicle.
5. Fit the fluid pipe/s to the master cylinder. Fig. B1-28 refers.
6. If previously removed, fit the fluid reservoir.
7. Fit the fluid pipes to the reservoir. Fig. B1-27 refers.
8. Bleed the brakes hydraulic system, Section H, where a common fluid reservoir is used.
9. Bleed the clutch hydraulic system. Operation B1-8.
10. Adjust the clutch pedal height and linkage travel. Operation B1-9.
11. Fit the top cover plate and gasket to the pedal bracket.
12. Where removed, fit the front wing. Section R.
13. Fit the bonnet panel. Section A.

Fig. B1-30. Fixings for reservoir
A—Reservoir and clamp
B—Mounting bracket
C—Fixings

Hydraulic system, to bleed—Operation B1-8

Workshop hand tools:
Spanner sizes: $\frac{7}{16}$ in. AF, $\frac{7}{16}$ in. BSF open end, $\frac{7}{16}$ in. AF socket
Length of suitable tubing, Clean jar, Screwdriver (medium)

If the level of fluid in the reservoir is allowed to fall too low, or if any section of the clutch pipe line has been disconnected, air may enter the hydraulic system. This will result in incorrect clutch operation which may take the form of clutch judder and snatch. To rectify this, the air must be expelled by bleeding the hydraulic system.

During the procedure, the fluid in the reservoir must be continually replenished to prevent further air from being introduced into the system.

The correct fluid level for the different type reservoirs is as follows:

(a) **Reservoir integral with master cylinder**
Keep fluid level with marking on side of reservoir.

(b) **Separate combined fluid reservoir serving brake and clutch systems**
Keep fluid level above the top of the inner (clutch) reservoir.

Use only the recommended type of hydraulic fluid. Section X refers.

Procedure

1. Remove the front floor or gearbox tunnel, as applicable, to gain access to the slave cylinder on the bell housing. This procedure is described in Section A.
2. Attach a length of rubber tubing to the slave cylinder bleed screw and place the lower end of the tube in a glass jar containing a small amount of fluid.
3. Slacken the bleed screw and pump the clutch pedal, pausing at each end of each stroke, until the fluid issuing from the tube shows no signs of air bubbles when the tube is held below the surface of the fluid in the jar.

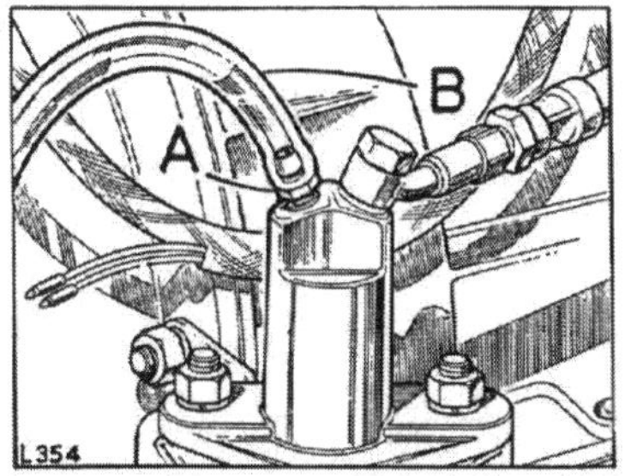

Fig. B1-31. View of slave cylinder
A—Bleed screw   B—Suitable tubing

4. Holding the tube under the fluid surface, tighten the bleed screw when commencing a pedal stroke.
5. When satisfactory, refit the front floor or gearbox tunnel as applicable. Section A.

CLUTCH UNITS

Clutch linkage and pedal travel adjustment—Operation B1-9

Workshop hand tools:

Spanner sizes: 7/16 in. AF, 1/2 in. AF open end

The following information concerns early and late type clutches.

Late models have a hydrostatic clutch, that is, clutch mechanism which requires no adjustment for the life of the clutch plate.

Models with the latest type clutch mechanism can be easily identified as follows:

(a) The support bracket for clutch slave cylinder on early models encloses the cylinder; on late models the cylinder is exposed.

(b) The operating lever on early models is straight, but on late models it is cranked.

(c) Return spring is not fitted to the operating lever on late models.

All these differences are clearly shown at Figs. B1-32 and B1-33.

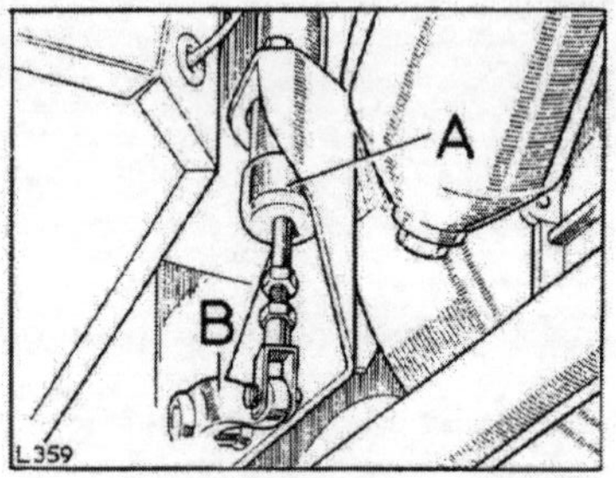

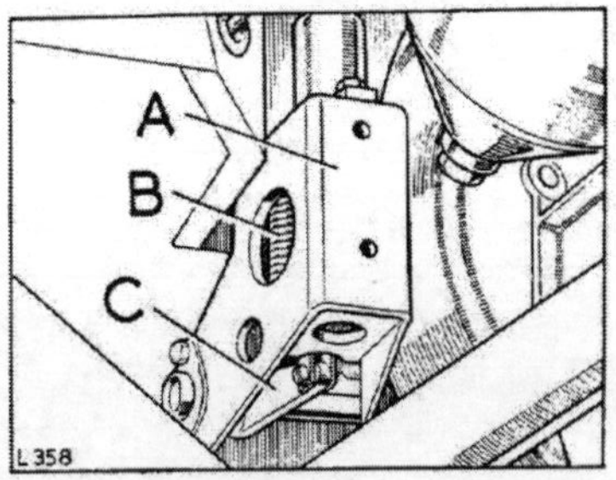

Fig. B1-32. Early type clutch mechanism
A—Support bracket enclosing slave cylinder
B—Return spring for operating lever
C—Straight operating lever

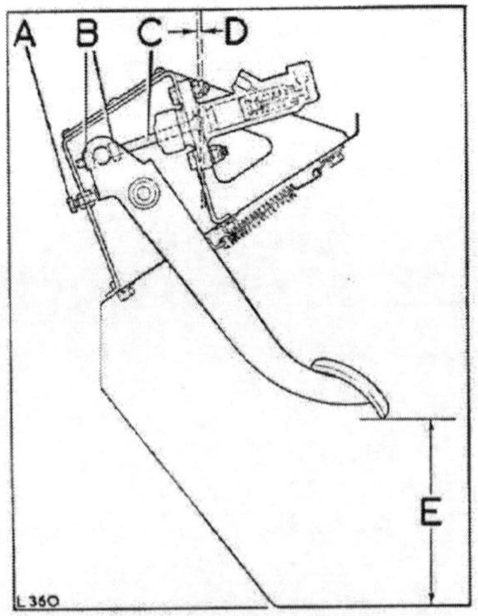

Fig. B1-33. Late type clutch mechanism
A—Exposed slave cylinder
B—Cranked operating rod

Fig. B1-34. Clutch linkage setting
A—Pedal position setting bolt
B—Master cylinder push rod locknuts
C—Master cylinder push rod
D—Free play 1/16 in. (1.5 mm)
E—Models with non-hydrostatic clutch mechanism: 6 1/4 in. (158 mm)
Models with hydrostatic clutch mechanism: 5 1/2 in. (140 mm)

Procedure

Pedal position, to adjust—All models

The lock-stop bolt located in the pedal bracket back plate, should not be disturbed, but in the event of this being absolutely necessary, it must be reset as follows: See Fig. B1-34.

1. Support the pedal pad at the correct height from the toe-board, and screw in bolt A until it touches the pedal shaft stop plate. Tighten the locknut.

Operation B1-9—continued

Master cylinder free play, to adjust—Early models. Fig. B1-34 refers

1. Check the free play D in the master cylinder push rod C which should be 1/16 in. (1.5 mm) at the push rod and is felt as approximately 5/16 in. (8 mm) at the pedal pad; if it is less than the given figure:

2. Slacken off locknut B and rotate the push rod C with the fingers, until the correct movement has been attained.

Pedal free play, to adjust—Early models

1. Slacken the push rod locknut, at the slave cylinder. See Fig. B1-35.

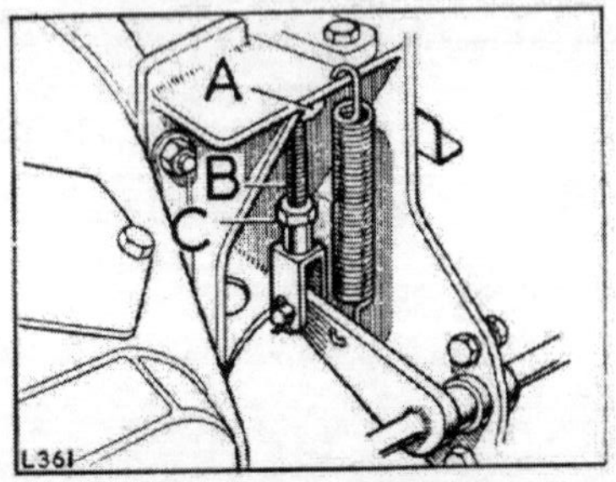

Fig. B1-35. Clutch adjustment
A—Slave cylinder
B—Push rod
C—Locknut for push rod

2. Adjust the push rod by rotating until the total free movement at the pedal is 1 1/2 in. (38 mm).

The total free play is felt in two stages:

(a) Light movement of approximately 5/16 in. (8 mm), which takes up the master cylinder free play against the pedal return spring.

(b) Slightly heavier movement which should be approximately 1 3/16 in. (30 mm) which takes up the slave cylinder free play through the hydraulic system and against the slave cylinder return spring.

3. Secure with the lock nut.

Hydrostatic clutch mechanism—Late models

1. The hydrostatic clutch operating mechanism is correctly set on initial assembly, to give approximately 5/16 in. (8 mm) free movement at the pedal pad and requires no adjustment throughout the life of the clutch plate, providing that no part or parts of the clutch assembly have been removed or replaced.

Important: Do not 'ride' the clutch as immediately the 5/16 in. (8 mm) free movement is taken up, the clutch mechanism begins to operate and premature clutch plate wear will result.

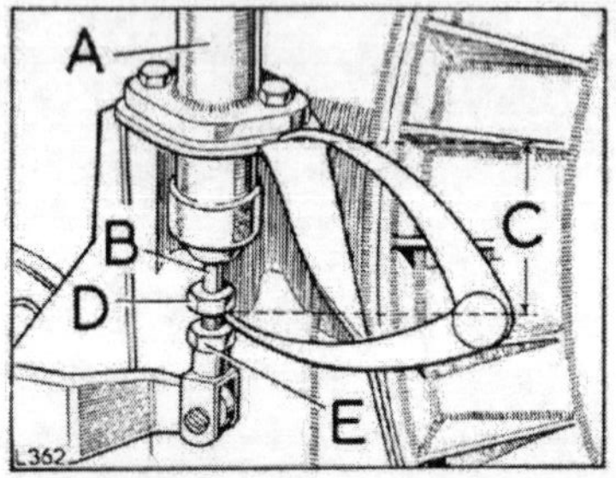

Fig. B1-36. Setting hydrostatic clutch linkage, Method A
A—Slave cylinder
B—Push rod
C—2 7/8 in. (73.4 mm). Check dimension with calipers as shown
D—Nut must be at end of push rod thread
E—Lock nut for push rod

2. Should a new clutch plate have been fitted, or a clutch assembly, clutch pressure plate, clutch slave cylinder, support bracket for cylinder or flywheel have been removed and replaced, it becomes necessary to re-set the free movement at the pedal pad as follows:

(a) If necessary bleed system Operation B1-8, then hold operating lever on the clutch cross-shaft down and ensure there is no free movement or backlash in the clutch withdrawal mechanism.

CLUTCH UNITS

Operation B1-9—continued

To adjust, Method A

(b) Adjust the push rod if necessary by slackening off lock nut 'E', and rotating push rod with the fingers to give dimension 'C' as shown in Fig. B1-36. Do not adjust nut 'D' to obtain this figure. Nut 'D' must always be tightened to the end of the push rod thread.

To adjust, Method B

(c) Fully depress clutch pedal and withdraw rubber boot on cylinder. Then adjust push rod until there is approximately ⅛ in. (3 mm) clearance between bottom of piston and circlip. See Fig. B1-37.

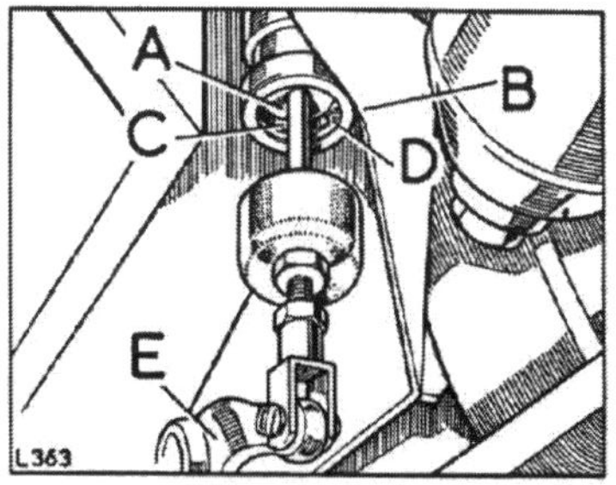

Fig. B1-37. Setting hydrostatic clutch, Method B

A—Piston
B—Exposed slave cylinder
C—⅛ in. (3 mm)
D—Circlip
E—Cranked operating rod

CLUTCH UNIT

Fault diagnosis—Clutch unit

Symptom	Possible cause	Investigation	Remedy
A—Grabbing clutch (Harsh engagement from standing start, often followed by clutch judder)	Operating mechanism faulty	Check operating levers for wear and binding which usually indicates a binding withdrawal race thrust bearing	Free off bearing, Section C. Replace levers as necessary
		Check clutch pedal for sticking	Free off pedal and check for damaged and distorted parts including return spring. Replace as necessary
		Check release lever adjustment	Reset as necessary
	Clutch unit faults	Check for oil on friction faces	Clean off metal faces. Replace driven plate. Rectify oil leak
		Note: The flywheel housing drain plug is for use when the vehicle is operating in deep mud or water. At all other times the plug should be removed from the drain tapping and stowed	
		Check clutch plates and flywheel run-out. Check flywheel for wear. Check also for glazing on driven plate linings	Reclaim or replace as applicable clutch plates, Section B, flywheel, Section A
		Check for driven plate hub splines sticking on pinion shaft	Free driven plate and check for wear and distortion. Check pinion shaft for wear
		Check for broken or weak pressure springs. Check torque damper springs in clutch driven plate	Replace as necessary
	Engine mountings faults	Check for damaged or deteriorated engine mountings. Check fixings for looseness	Replace or tighten as applicable
	Faulty driving technique	Ensure that when operating the clutch, this is done fully and as quickly as is consistent with normal driving requirements. Do not increase engine speed with clutch partially engaged	In operator's hands
B—Slipping clutch (Indicated by vehicle road speed not responding adequately to engine speed increases)	Operating mechanism setting incorrect (coil spring type units)	Check setting of clutch adjustment	Reset as necessary
	Operating mechanism faulty	Check for binding withdrawal lever	Free lever and check for wear and distortion
		Check clutch pedal for insufficient free movement	Adjust pedal setting
		Check for binding on clutch pedal moving parts	Rectify or replace parts
	Clutch unit faults	Check for oil on friction faces	Clean off metal faces. Replace driven plate. Rectify oil leak
		Note: The flywheel housing drain plug is for use when the vehicle is operating in deep mud or water. At all other times the plug should be removed from the drain tapping and stowed	
		Check for broken or weak pressure springs	Replace as necessary

CLUTCH UNIT

Fault diagnosis—Clutch unit—continued

Symptom	Possible cause	Investigation	Remedy
B—Slipping clutch—cont	Clutch unit faults—cont.	Check clutch plates and flywheel for wear and distortion	Reclaim or replace as applicable clutch plates, Section B, flywheel, Section A
		Check clutch driven plate for fractures and distortion. Damage may be caused by accidental loading during assembly of gearbox to engine. Always support gearbox weight during refitting	Replace driven plate and check mating components for damage
C—Dragging or spinning clutch (A spinning clutch results in initial gear crashing on engagement from a standing start. Normal gear engagement is possible if a suitable pause is made between depressing the clutch pedal and engaging the gear. A dragging clutch results in gear crashing regardless of the time taken for the gear engagement procedure)	Operating mechanism setting incorrect or faulty	Check setting of clutch adjustment if applicable (coil spring type unit)	Reset as necessary
		Check pedal adjustment setting	Reset as necessary
		Check master cylinder push-rod free movement setting	Reset as necessary
		Check clutch withdrawal sleeve for sticking	Rectify. Examine mating surfaces for scores and wear. Replace as necessary
	Clutch unit faults	Check as described under 'Clutch unit faults'. Paragraph B.	
		Check for primary pinion bush binding	Rectify or replace as necessary
		Check clutch driven plate hub for binding on primary pinion splines. Check for too thick friction linings. Ensure linings are sound	Replace as necessary
		Check for distorted clutch pressure plate and clutch cover	Replace as applicable
		Check for foreign matter in clutch unit	Clean and replace components as applicable
	Hydraulic system defects	Check fluid level in reservoir	Replenish as necessary
		Check for air in the system by bleeding	
D—Rattling clutch	Operating mechanism faults	Check for defective pedal return spring	Replace
		Check for defective operating lever return spring, where applicable	Replace
		Check linkage settings	Reset as necessary
	Clutch unit faults	Check for damaged pressure plate	Rectify or replace as applicable
		Check splines on clutch driven plate and primary pinion shaft for wear	Replace as necessary clutch plate, Section B, primary pinion, Section C

Fault diagnosis—Clutch unit—continued

Symptom	Possible cause	Investigation	Remedy
D—Rattling clutch—cont	Clutch unit faults—cont.	Check clutch driven plate for loose or broken springs and for warping	Replace driven plate
		Check for wear in the clutch withdrawal mechanism	Refer to Section C
		Check for worn primary pinion bush	Replace, Section A
E—Squeaking clutch	Primary pinion bush fault	Check for bush binding on primary shaft or turning in flywheel	Replace, Section A
F—Vibrating clutch or clutch judder (often preceded by clutch grab)	Clutch unit faults	Check the clutch driven plate for distortion and damage and for loose or broken torque springs	Replace driven plate
		Check for oil and other foreign matter on the clutch friction linings	Replace driven plate and clean related parts
		Note: The flywheel housing drain plug is for use when the vehicle is operating in deep mud or water. At all other times the plug should be removed from the drain tapping and stowed	
		Check for incorrectly fitted clutch pressure plate	Dismantle from clutch and refit, where applicable
		Check that contact witness on friction linings is evenly distributed	Replace driven plate as necessary
		Check for loose flywheel fixings.	Tighten to correct torque loading, Section A. Check flywheel run-out
	Defects other than in clutch unit	Check for loose engine mountings	Tighten
		Check for worn propeller shaft universal joints	Refer to Section D
		Check for bent primary pinion shaft	Refer to Section C
G—Stiff clutch operation	Operating linkage fault	Check for damaged moving parts in operating linkage	Replace as necessary
		Lubricate linkage and recheck operation	
H—Clutch knocks	Clutch unit fault	Check for worn clutch driven plate hub splines	Replace driven plate
	Primary pinion bush	Check for wear in bush	Replace as necessary
J—Fractured clutch plate	Incorrect fitting method	Damage may be caused by accidental loading during fitting. Always support gearbox weight during fitting.	Replace driven plate. Check mating components for damage
		Refer to Owner's Instruction Manual for permissible loads details	
K—Excessive lining wear	Overloading vehicle		
	Slipping clutch	Check as described under 'Slipping clutch'. Refer to Paragraph B.	

Section B—Land-Rover — CLUTCH UNITS

GENERAL DATA

Clutch, coil spring type

Type	Single dry plate, 9 in. (230 mm) diameter. Borg and Beck A6 type
Operation:	
Later type	Hydraulic (hydrostatic)
Early type	Non-hydrostatic
Engine applicability	2¼ litre diesel (early models), 2¼ litre petrol

Clutch, diaphragm spring type

Type	Single dry plate, 9½ in. (241 mm) diameter. Borg and Beck DS type
Operation	Hydraulic (hydrostatic)
Engine applicability	2.6 litre petrol, 2¼ litre diesel (later models), 2¼ litre petrol (optional)

Thrust springs (coil spring type clutch)

Number off	9
Free length (2¼ litre petrol)	2.680 in. (68 mm)
Free length (2¼ litre diesel)	2.688 in. (68.5 mm)
Working length	1.688 in. (43 mm)
Load at working length	135–145 lb (61–65 kg)
Colour identification	Yellow and light green paint (early 2¼ litre petrol)
	Yellow and green paint (early 2¼ litre diesel)
	Black paint (all later models)

Pressure plate

Re-grinding limit	.010 in. (0.25 mm) undersize
Minimum thickness	1.531 in. (39 mm)

Operating levers

Height from flywheel face using ⅜ in. (9.5 mm) distance piece in place of the driven plate: 1.655 in. (42 mm)

Driven plate

Diameter, coil spring type clutch	9 in. (230 mm)
Diameter, diaphragm spring type clutch	9½ in. (241 mm)
Thickness of plate, new	.330 in. (8.38 mm)
Maximum permissible wear	.120 in. (3 mm)
Damper springs identification colours:	
2¼ litre petrol	
9 in. plate	3 off buff or white; 3 off light green
9½ in. plate	6 off green
2¼ litre diesel	
9 in. plate	3 off dark grey; 3 off light green
9½ in. plate	6 off green
2.6 litre petrol	
9½ in. plate	3 off dark grey; 3 off light green

CLUTCH UNITS

Withdrawal mechanism

Clearance of flanged bushes on cross-shaft	.001 in. to .003 in. (0,02 mm to 0,07 mm)
Clearance of LH bush on cross-shaft	.004 in. to .006 in. (0,102 mm to 0,14 mm)
Clearance of bush on withdrawal sleeve	.003 in. to .006 in. (0,07 mm to 0,15 mm)

Clutch pedal unit

Fit of bush on pedal shaft	.001 in. to .003 in. (0,02 mm to 0,07 mm) clearance
Bush reamed bore	.750 in. (20 mm)

Master cylinder

Type	Girling cv
Bore	¾ in. (19 mm)
Stroke	1⅜ in. (35 mm)
Push-rod free movement	1/16 in. (1,5 mm)

Slave cylinder

Type	Girling
Bore	⅞ in. (22 mm)

SECTION C—GEARBOX

INDEX—GEARBOX

Note: A comprehensive, detailed index is included at the end of this manual.

Description	Operation No.
Exploded views and detail description	
General description and operation	
Seat base	
MAIN GEARBOX	
Bell housing	1
Clutch withdrawal unit	3
Gearbox casing, rear bearings and oil seal	16—17
Gear change lever	14—15
Layshaft and gears	24—25
Lubrication	11—12
Mainshaft and gears	20—21
Primary pinion	2
Selector shafts and forks	22—23
Reverse gear wheels	17
Reverse stop, main gear change lever	18—19
TRANSFER BOX	25
Bearing housing, mainshaft rear	13
Intermediate shaft	7—8—8A
Intermediate gear	8—8—8A
Lubrication	7—8—8A
Mainshaft gear for transfer box	7—8—8A
Rear output shaft and flange	2
Speedometer drive and housing	22
Transfer gears, high and low	8—8—8A
Transfer gearchange lever	5—6
Transmission brake	7
FRONT OUTPUT SHAFT HOUSING	4
Four wheel drive change lever	9—10
Front output shaft and flange	10
Lubrication	10
Selector shaft, four wheel drive	2
Selector shaft, transfer gears	8—8—8A
	10
	7—8—8A
	10

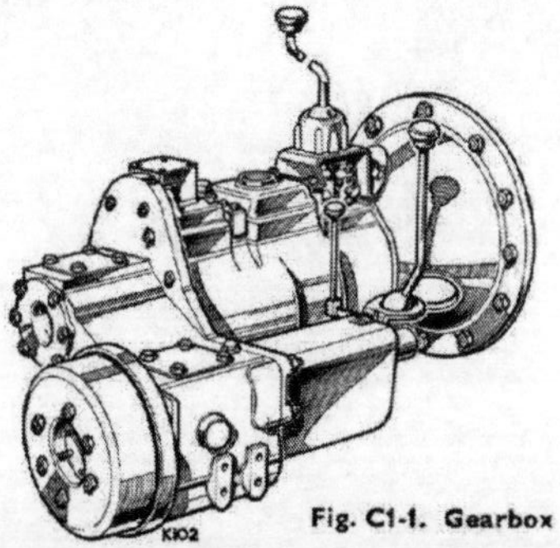

Fig. C1-1. Gearbox

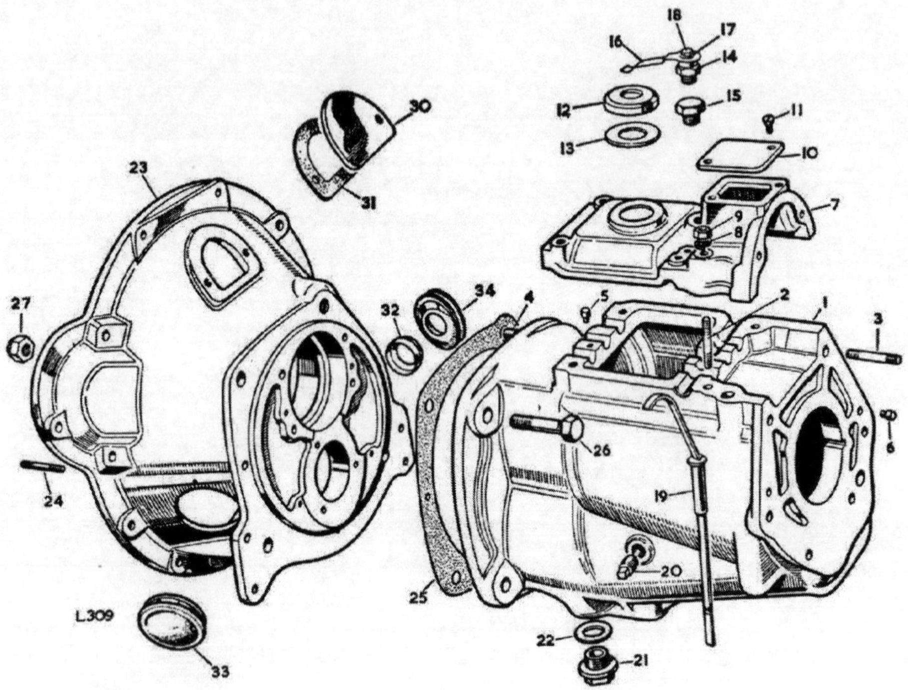

Fig. C1-2. Layout of the gearbox unit casings

1. Gearbox casing assembly
2. Stud or bolt for top cover and gear change plate
3. Stud, short, for transfer casing
4. Stud for bell housing
5. Dowel locating top cover
6. Dowel locating transfer casing
7. Top cover for gearbox
8-9. Fixings for top cover, used with stud
10. Inspection cover plate for selectors
11. Set screw fixing cover plate
12. Oil filler cap
13. Joint washer for cap
14. Plug for retaining spring and cap } late gearboxes
15. Plug retaining selector spring (late gearboxes)
16. Retaining spring for cap (early gearboxes)
17-18. Fixings for spring } early gearboxes
19. Oil level dipstick
20. Oil level filler plug
21. Drain plug for gearbox
22. Washer for plug
23. Bell housing assembly
24. Stud for withdrawal race housing
25. Joint washer, bell housing to gearbox
26-27. Fixings for gearbox casing
31. Top cover for bell housing
32. Rubber seal for top cover
33. Centre for dust cover (early gearboxes)
34. Grommet for bell housing hole
35. Grommet for bell housing shaft

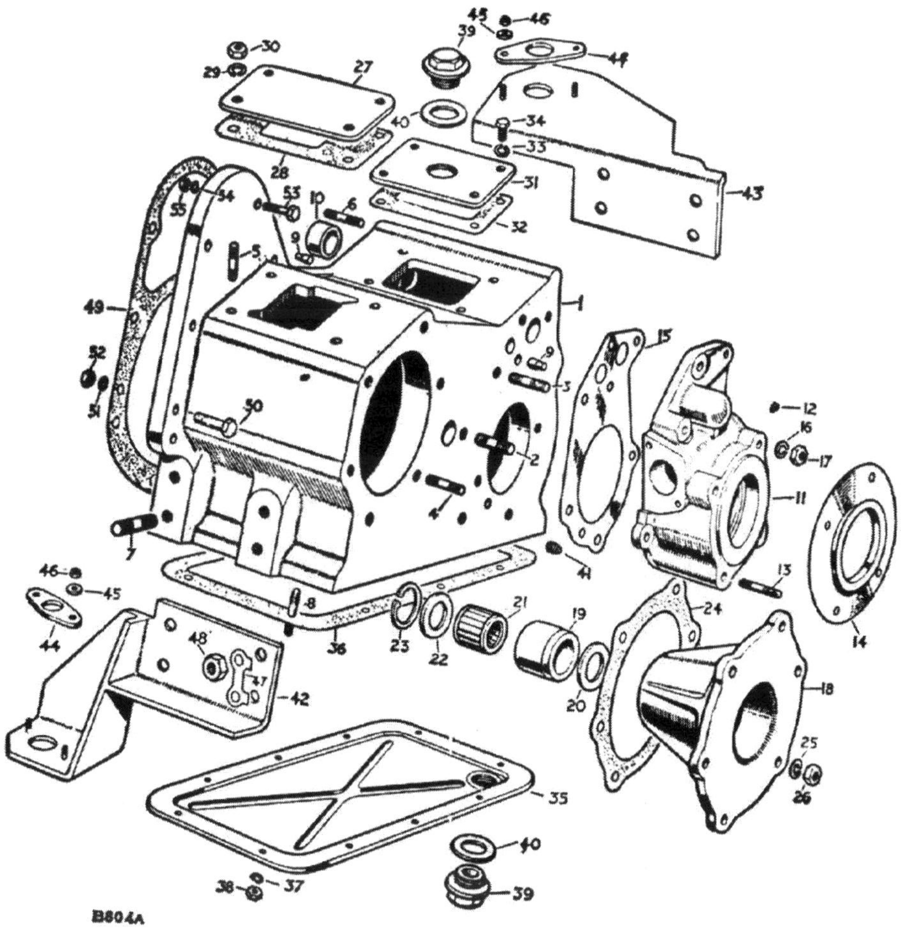

GEARBOX

Key to illustration of gearbox casings

1. Transfer box casing assembly
2. Stud for intermediate shaft
3. Stud for speedometer housing, short
4. Stud for mainshaft housing
5. Stud for top cover plate
6. Stud, short, for transfer shaft housing
7. Stud for engine mounting
8. Stud for bottom cover
9. Dowel locating speedometer housing
10. Bush for shaft guide (early gearboxes)
11. Housing assembly for speedometer pinion
12. Insert for pinion
13. Stud for transmission brake
14. Mudshield or oil catcher and joint washer for housing
15. Shim for speedometer pinion housing
16–17. Fixings for housing
18. Housing assembly, rear mainshaft bearing
19. Bush for housing
20. Retaining plate, inner
21. Bearing for mainshaft
22. Retaining plate, outer
23. Circlip fixing bearing
24. Joint washer for bearing housing
25–26. Fixings for housing
27. Cover plate for P.T.O. selector
28. Joint washer for cover plate
29–30. Fixings for cover plate
31. Cover plate for transfer gear change
32. Joint washer for cover plate
33–34. Fixings for plate
35. Cover plate, bottom, for transfer box
36. Joint washer for bottom cover
37–38. Fixings for cover
39. Plug, top and bottom (top plug, early gearboxes)
40. Joint washer for plug
41. Oil level plug
42. Rear mounting foot LH
43. Rear mounting foot RH
44. Adjuster for mounting foot ⎫
45. Plain washer   For early
46. Self-locking nut ⎬ adjuster   gearboxes
47–48. Fixings for feet
49. Joint washer, transfer box to gearbox
50–52. Fixings for transfer box
53–55. Fixings for transfer box

Fig. C1-3. Layout of the gearbox unit casings

Key to illustration of gearbox shafts and gears

1. Primary pinion and constant gear
2. Shield for primary pinion
3. Ball bearing for primary pinion
4–5. Fixings for bearing
6–8. Fixings for bearing
9. Layshaft
10. Mainshaft
11. Peg for 2nd gear thrust washer
12. Peg for mainshaft distance sleeve
13. Thrust washer for 2nd speed gear
14. 1st speed layshaft gear
15. 1st speed mainshaft gear
16. 2nd speed layshaft and mainshaft gear
17. Split ring for 2nd speed layshaft gear (early gearboxes)
18. 3rd speed layshaft and mainshaft gear
19. Distance sleeve for mainshaft
20. Thrust washer for 3rd speed mainshaft gear
21. Spring ring fixing 2nd and 3rd mainshaft gears
22. Sleeve for layshaft
23. Bearing for layshaft, front
24–26. Fixings for bearing to layshaft
27. Bearing plate assembly for layshaft
28. Stud for bearing cap
29. Distance piece for layshaft
30. Retaining plate for layshaft front bearing
31–32. Fixings for cap and bearing
33. Bearing for layshaft, rear
34. Synchronising clutch
35. Detent spring for clutch
36. Roller bearing for mainshaft
37. Ball bearing for mainshaft
38. Housing for mainshaft bearing, rear
39. Peg, housing to casing
40. Circlip, bearing to housing
41. Circlip, housing to casing
42. Oil seal for rear of mainshaft
43. Oil thrower for mainshaft
44. Distance piece, rear of mainshaft
45. Mainshaft gear for transfer box
46–47. Fixings for gear
48. Shaft for reverse gear
49. Reverse wheel assembly
50. Bush for reverse wheel
51. Gear, intermediate
52. Roller bearing for intermediate gear
53. Thrust washer for intermediate gear
54. Shim for intermediate gear
55. Shaft for intermediate gear
56. Sealing ring for intermediate gear
57. Retaining plate for shaft
58–59. Fixings for plate
60. Low gear wheel
61. High gear wheel
62. Output shaft, rear drive
63. Thrust washer for high gear wheel
64. Circlip fixing washer to shaft
65. Bearing for output shaft, front
66. Circlip fixing bearing to case
67. Bearing for output shaft, rear
68. Oil seal for output shaft
69. Speedometer worm complete
70. Flange for output shaft, rear drive
71. Mudshield for flange
72. Fitting bolt for brake drum
73. Retaining flange for brake drum bolts
74. Fitting bolt for propeller shaft
75. Circlip retaining bolts and flange
76–78. Fixings for flange
79. Speedometer pinion
80. Retaining plate for pinion
81. Screw fixing plate to housing
82. Sleeve for pinion
83. Sealing ring for sleeve
84. Joint washer for sleeve
85. Oil seal for pinion

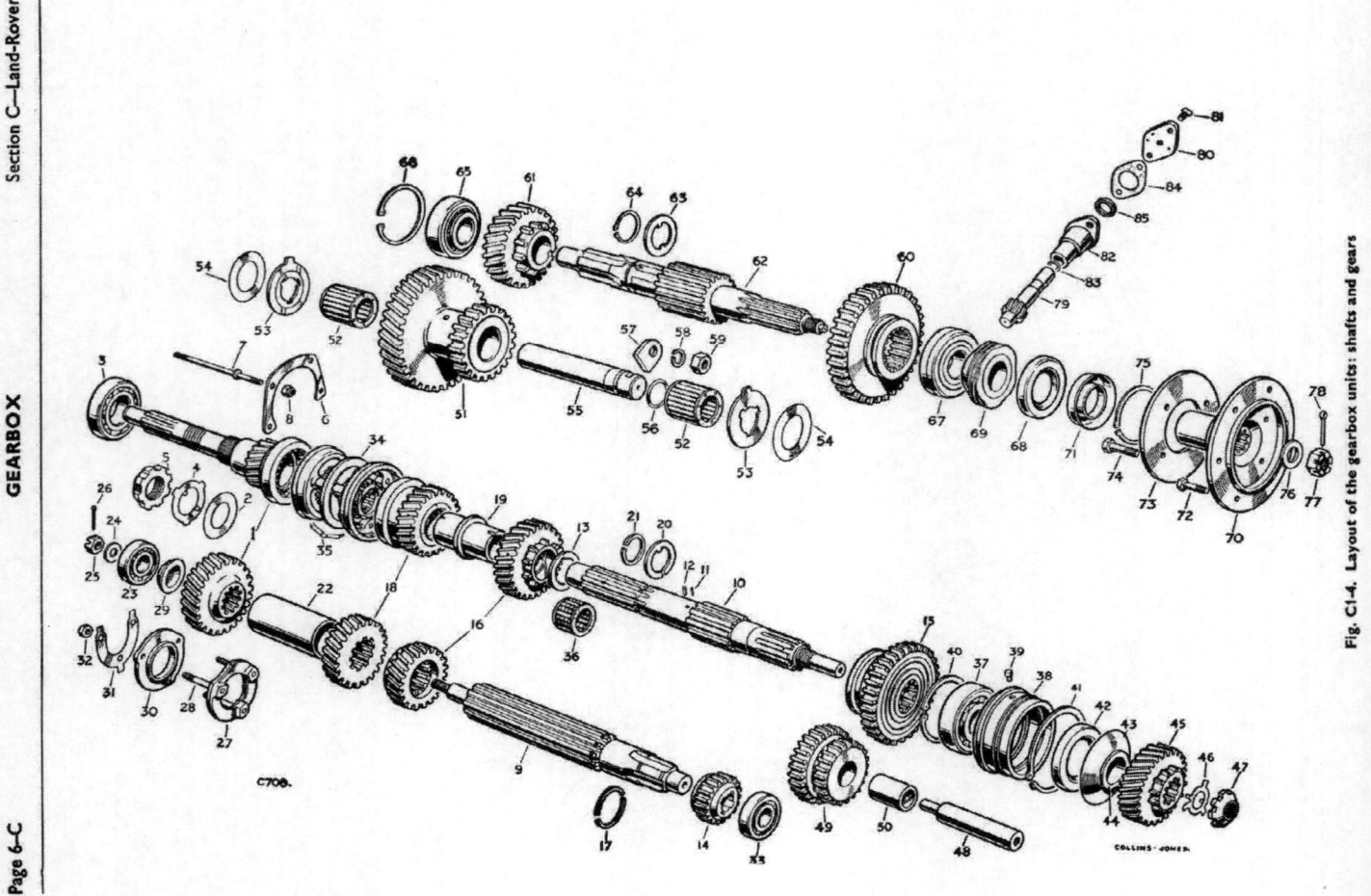

Fig. C1-4. Layout of the gearbox units: shafts and gears

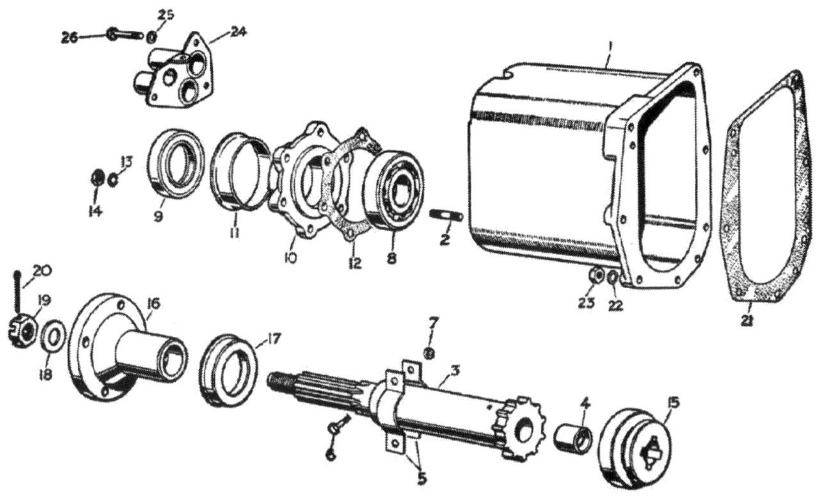

GEARBOX

Key to illustration of four wheel drive, transfer gear controls and front output shaft housing

1. Output shaft housing assembly
2. Stud for oil seal retainer
3. Front output shaft assembly
4. Bush for shaft
5. Oil thrower for output shaft
6–7. Fixings for oil thrower
8. Bearing for front output shaft
9. Oil seal for shaft
10. Retainer for oil seal
11. Mudshield for retainer
12. Joint washer for retainer
13–14. Fixings for retainer
15. Locking dog, four wheel drive
16. Flange for transfer shaft
17. Mudshield for flange
18–20. Fixings for flange
21. Joint washer for transfer housing
22–23. Fixings for housing
24. Dust cover plate for selector shafts
25–26. Fixings for dust cover

1. Selector shaft, four wheel drive
2. Selector fork complete, four wheel drive
3. Bush for selector fork
4. Spring for selector fork
5. Block for selector shaft
6–8. Fixings for block
9. Selector shaft, transfer gear change
10. Sealing ring for transfer gear change shaft
11. Selector fork, transfer gear change
12. Set bolt fixing fork
13. Distance tube for transfer selector shaft
14. Locating bush for selector shaft spring
15. Spring for gear change selector shaft
16. Connector, gear change to pivot shaft
17. Block for selector shaft
18–20. Fixings for block
21. Pivot shaft for selector shafts
22. Coupling, selector shafts to pivot
23–25. Fixings for coupling
26–27. Fixings for pivot shaft
28. Plunger for transfer selector shaft
29. Spring for plunger
30. Plug
31. Link for selector shaft
32–33. Fixings for link
34. Lever assembly, four wheel drive
35. Bush for lever
36. Special bolt, lever to housing
37. Locking pin, four wheel drive lever
38. Sealing ring, four wheel drive locking pin
39–40. Fixings for locking pin
41. Selector rod, four wheel drive
42. Clevis complete for rod
43. Split pin for clevis
44. Spring for selector rod
45. Special bush for spring
46. Control knob for rod
47. Locknut for knob and clevis
48. Transfer gear change lever complete
49. Spring for transfer gear change lever
50. Knob for gear change lever
51. Locknut for knob
52. Bracket for gear change lever
53. Distance piece for bracket
54–56. Fixings for bracket
57–58. Fixings for gear lever

Fig. C1-5. Layout of the gearbox unit: four wheel drive, front output shaft and housing

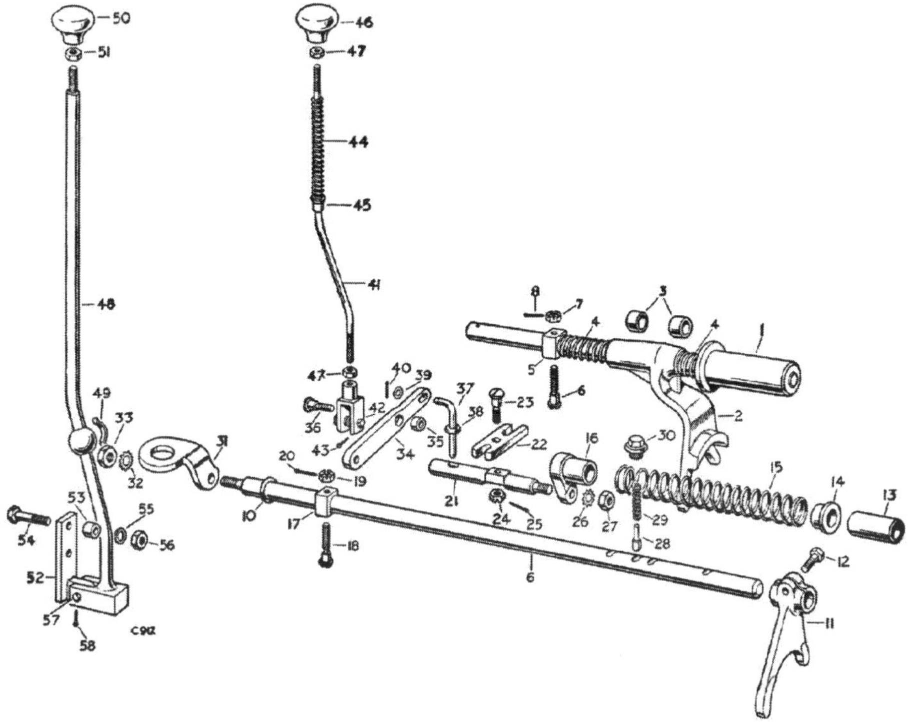

Fig. C1-6. Layout of the gearbox unit: four wheel drive and transfer gear controls

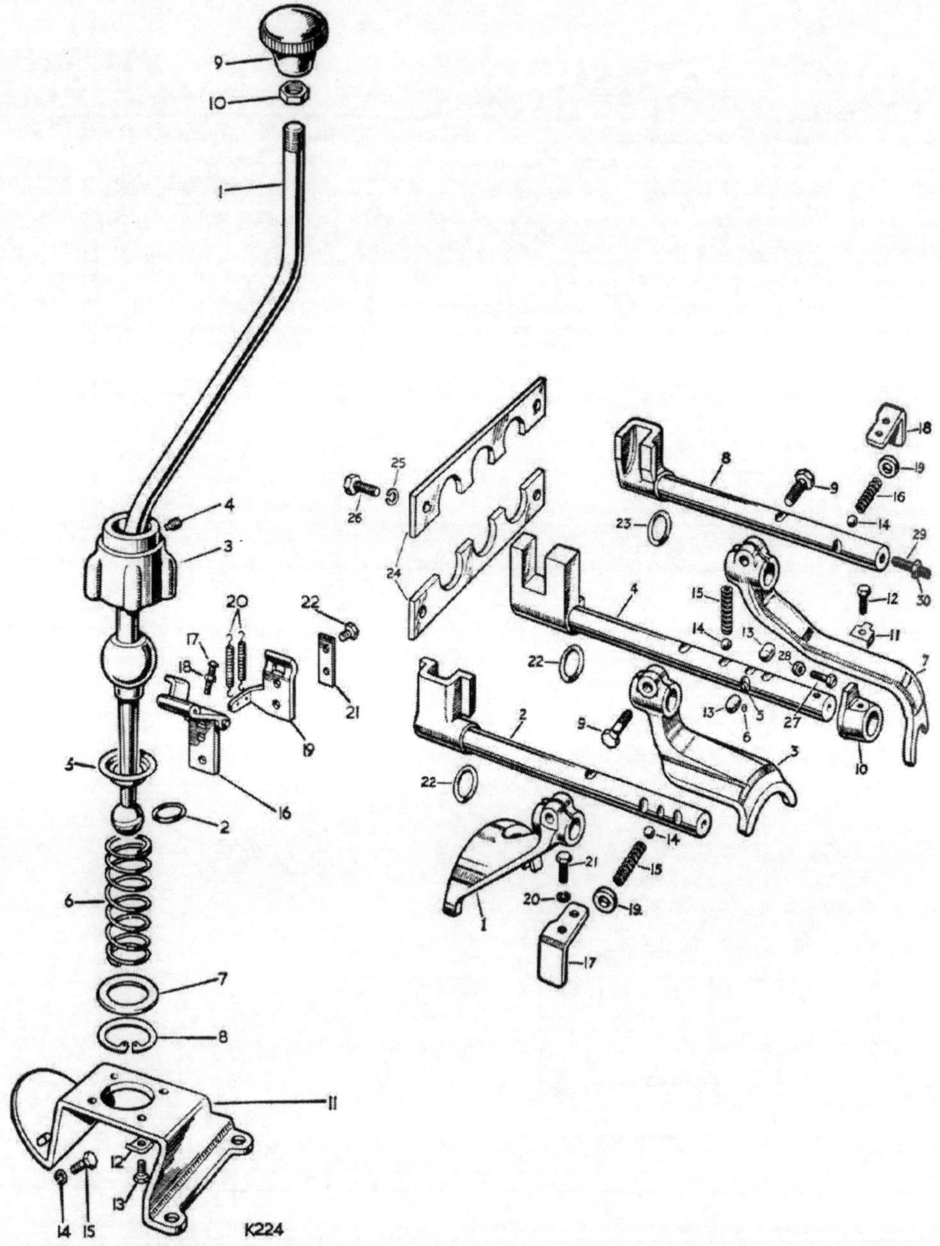

Section C—Land-Rover

GEARBOX

Key to illustration of the main gear change lever and selectors

Main gear change lever:

1. Gear change lever
2. O-ring for lever
3. Housing for lever
4. Locating pin for lever ball
5. Spherical seat for gear lever
6. Retaining spring for lever
7. Retaining plate for spring
8. Circlip fixing retaining plate
9. Knob for lever
10. Locknut for knob
11. Mounting plate for gear change
12-13. Fixings for housing
14-15. Fixings for mounting plate
16. Reverse stop hinge complete
17. Adjusting screw ⎱ For hinge
18. Locknut ⎰
19. Bracket for reverse stop spring
20. Spring for reverse stop
21-22. Fixings for hinge and bracket

Gear selectors:

1. Selector fork, 3rd and 4th speed
2. Shaft for fork, 3rd and 4th speed
3. Selector fork, 1st and 2nd speed
4. Shaft assembly for fork, 1st and 2nd speed
5. Interlocking pin
6. Peg fixing interlocking pin
7. Selector fork, reverse
8. Shaft for fork, reverse
9. Set bolt fixing forks to shafts
10. Stop for 2nd speed
11-12. Fixings for stop
13. Interlocking plunger
14. Steel ball for selectors
15. Selector spring, forward
16. Selector spring, reverse
17. Retaining plate LH ⎱ For selector
18. Retaining plate RH ⎰ springs, side
19. Rubber grommet
20-21. Fixings for retaining plates
22. Seal for selector shafts
23. Seal for reverse shaft
24. Retaining plate for sealing ring
25-26. Fixings for retaining plate
27. Set bolt ⎱ In cover for
28. Locknut ⎰ 2nd gear stop
29. Adjustable stop for reverse selector shaft
30. Locknut for stop

Fig. C1-7. Layout of the gearbox unit: main gear change lever and selectors

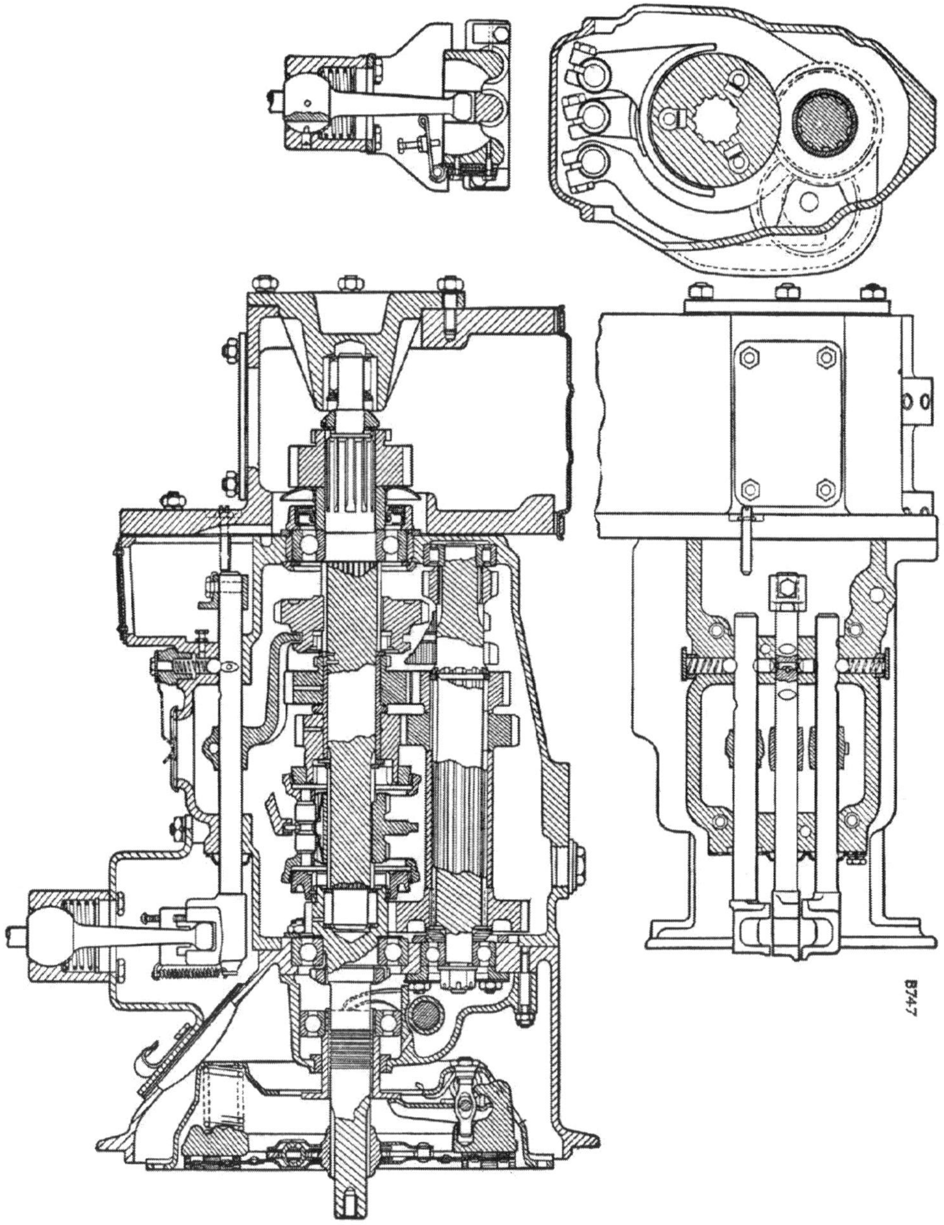

Page 13-C

Section C—Land-Rover

GEARBOX

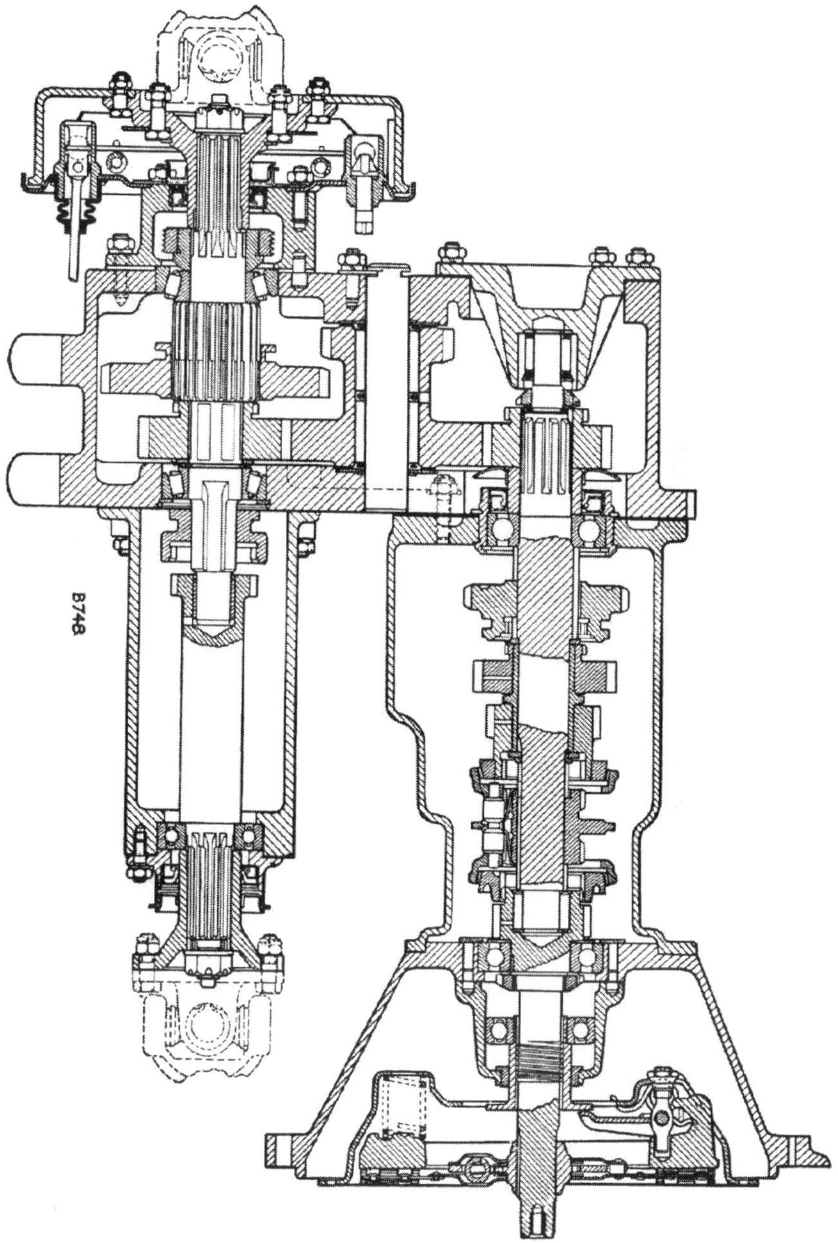

Fig. C1-9. Cross-section of gear box unit: plan

Page 12-C

Section C—Land-Rover

GEARBOX

Fig. C1-8. Cross-section of gearbox unit: elevation

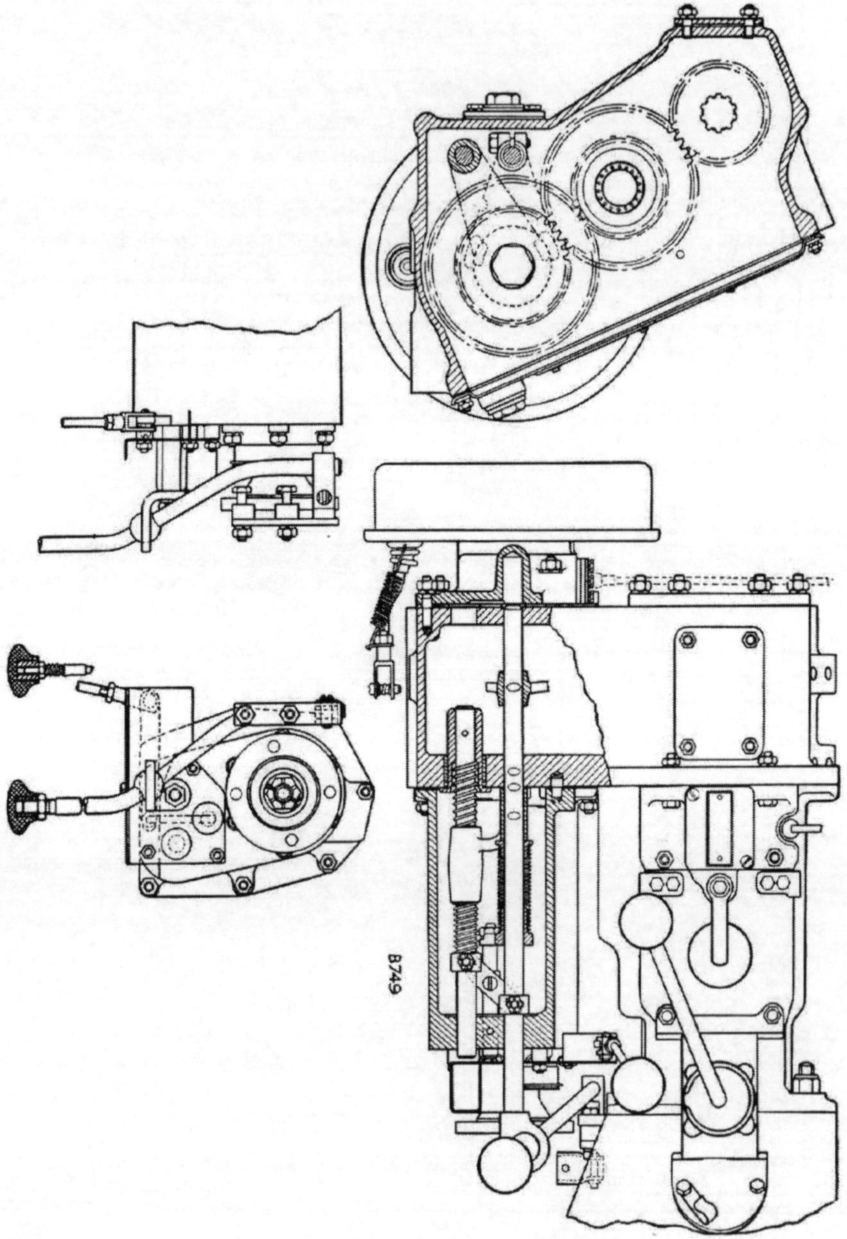

GEARBOX DESCRIPTION AND OPERATION

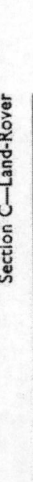

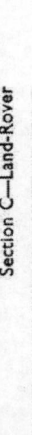

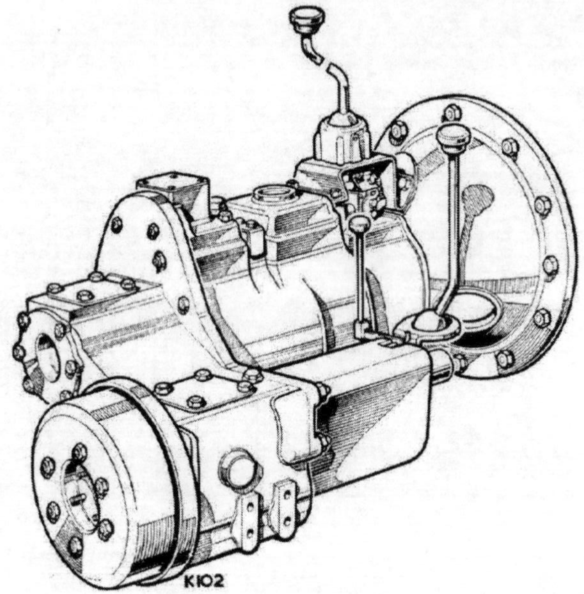

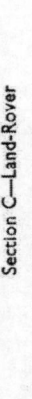

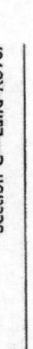

Fig. C1-11. Gearbox assembly complete

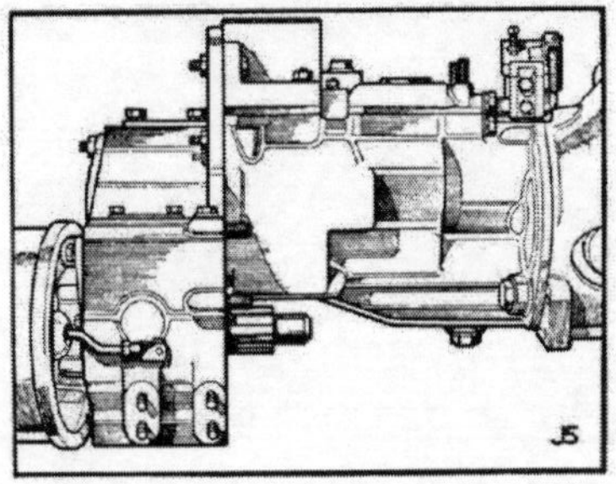

Fig. C1-13. Transfer box, secured to rear of main gearbox

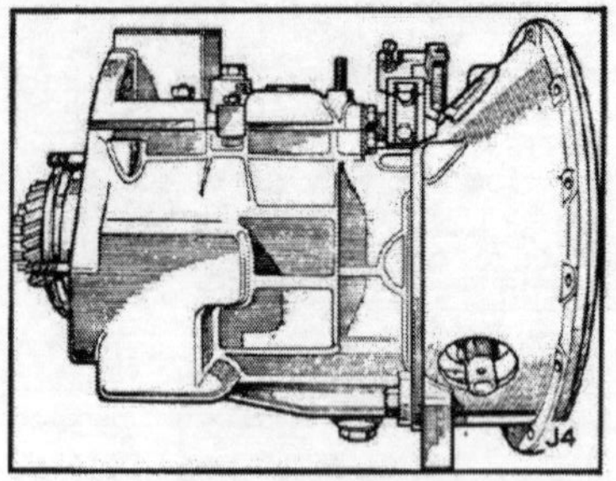

Fig. C1-12. Main gearbox unit

To the rear end of the main gearbox is attached the second unit, a two speed transfer box; high or low range can be selected by the transfer gear lever which has a red knob. Use of these two ratios give a total of eight forward gears and two reverse.

1. Description

The Land-Rover gearbox comprises three units. One, a main gearbox, which has four forward speeds and one reverse.

The gears are selected by the main lever which has a black knob.

Fig. C1-10. Cross-section of gearbox unit: controls

GEARBOX

The third unit is the four wheel drive selection mechanism attached to the front of the transfer box. Use of the lever with the yellow knob enables four wheel drive to be selected in high range. When low range is engaged by means of the transfer gear lever (red knob), four wheel drive is automatically selected through the same mechanism.

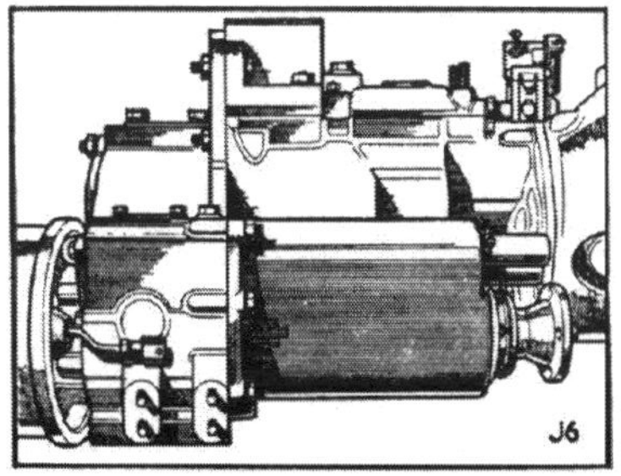

Fig. C1-14. Four wheel drive output housing secured to the front of the transfer box

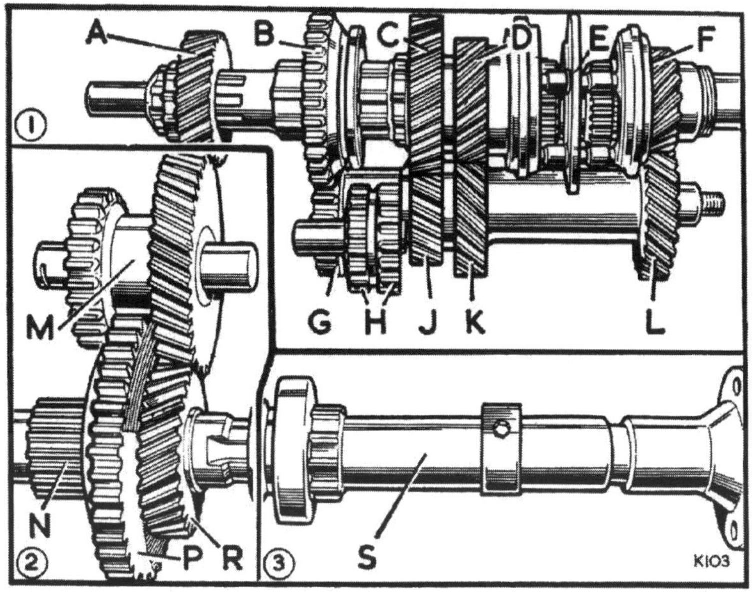

Fig. C1-15. Arrangement of gears

1—Main gear box 2—Transfer box 3—Four wheel drive output shaft

A—Mainshaft gear for transfer box
B—First speed mainshaft gear
C—Second speed mainshaft gear
D—Third speed mainshaft gear
E—Synchronising clutch
F—Primary pinion
G—First speed layshaft gear
H—Reverse gear
J—Second speed layshaft gear
K—Third speed layshaft gear
L—Constant gear
M—Intermediate gear
N—Output shaft, two wheel drive
P—Low gear wheel
R—High gear wheel
S—Output shaft, four wheel drive

2. Operation

Power flow 1st, 2nd and 3rd gear, high range two wheel drive. Input from the engine is via the primary pinion and constant gear to the layshaft, through layshaft to main shaft gears depending on gear selected, to main shaft gear in transfer box. Then through the intermediate gear to high gear wheel and output to rear axle only. The power flow in 2nd and 3rd follows the same general pattern, except that the 2nd and 3rd main shaft gears will be selected.

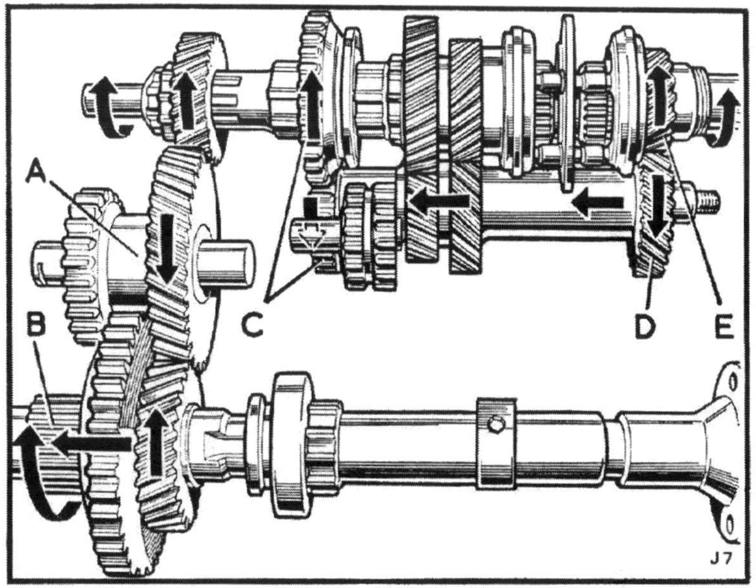

Fig. C1-16. Power flow with first gear engaged, high ratio, two wheel drive

A—Intermediate gear B—Output to rear axle C—Layshaft and mainshaft first gears D—Constant gear E—Primary pinion

Section C—Land-Rover GEARBOX

Power flow, top gear, high range, two wheel drive. In this case input is direct from primary pinion to main shaft gear for transfer box. Then through the intermediate gear to high gear wheel and output to rear axle only.

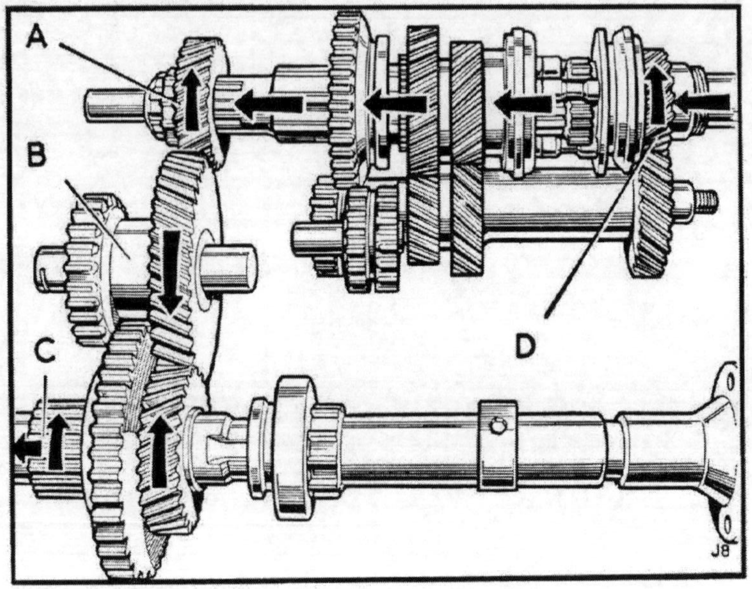

Fig. C1-17. Power flow with top gear engaged, high ratio, two wheel drive

A—Mainshaft gear B—Intermediate gear C—Output to rear axle D—Primary pinion

GEARBOX Section C—Land-Rover

Power flow, low range, four wheel drive. Input from the engine is via the primary pinion and constant gear to the layshaft, through layshaft to mainshaft gears depending on gear selected to main shaft gear for transfer box. Then through the intermediate gear to low gear wheel and with locking dog for four wheel drive engaged, output to both front and rear axles.

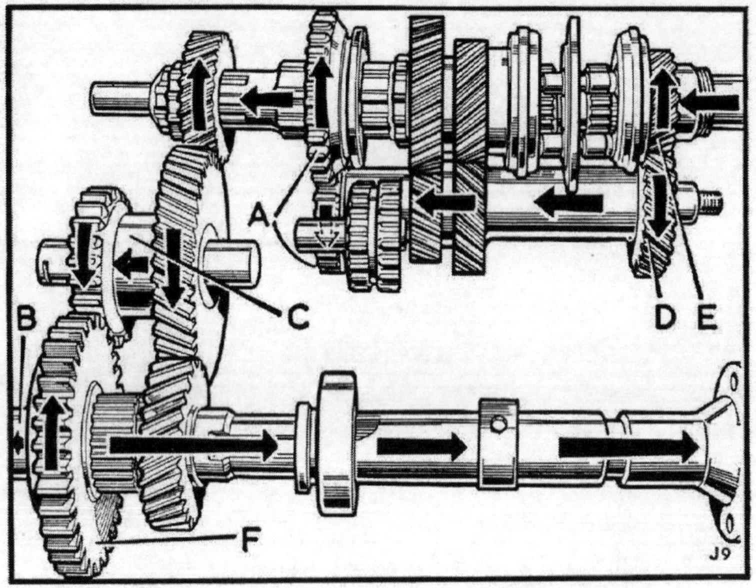

Fig. C1-18. Power flow with first gear engaged, low ratio, four wheel drive

A—Layshaft and mainshaft first gears C—Intermediate gear E—Primary pinion
B—Output to rear axle D—Constant gear F—Low gear wheel

170

GEARBOX

Power flow reverse gear, high range, two wheel drive.

Input from the engine is via the primary pinion and constant gear to the layshaft, through the layshaft to reverse idler, from reverse idler to mainshaft, this reverses direction of rotation of gears through transfer box. High or low range, two or four wheel drive can be selected as described previously.

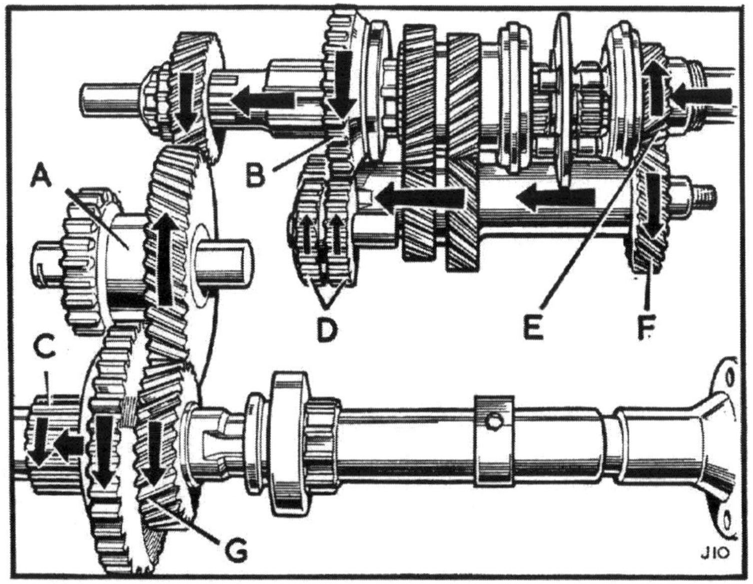

Fig. C1-19. Power flow with reverse gear engaged, high ratio, two wheel drive

A—Intermediate gear
B—Mainshaft first gear
C—Output to rear axle
D—Reverse idler
E—Primary pinion
F—Layshaft constant gear
G—High gear wheel

Seat base, remove and refit—Operation C1-1

Workshop hand tools:
Spanner sizes: $\frac{7}{16}$ in. AF, $\frac{9}{16}$ in. AF open end

To remove

1. Remove the front floor. Operation A1-4.
2. Lift out the seat cushions.
3. Release the seat squab retaining straps from the support rail.

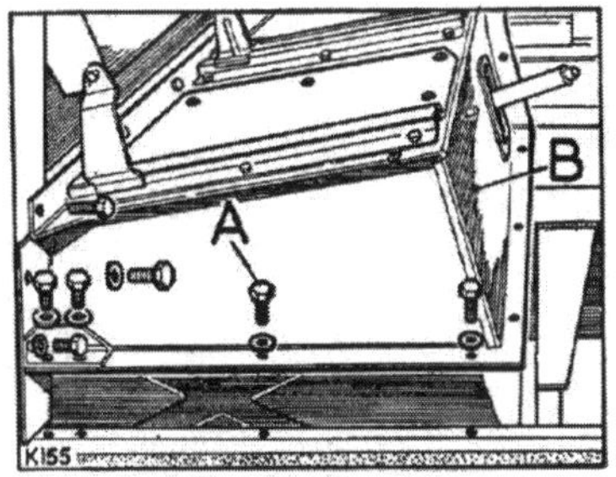

Fig. C1-20. Seat base
A—Fixings (23 off)   B—Seat base

4. From under the vehicle, remove the two nuts and spring washers securing the hand brake lever to the chassis.

   Note: The foregoing operation facilitates seat base removal by allowing the hand brake lever to be manoeuvred, but is not necessary on early models fitted with a short horizontal hand brake lever.

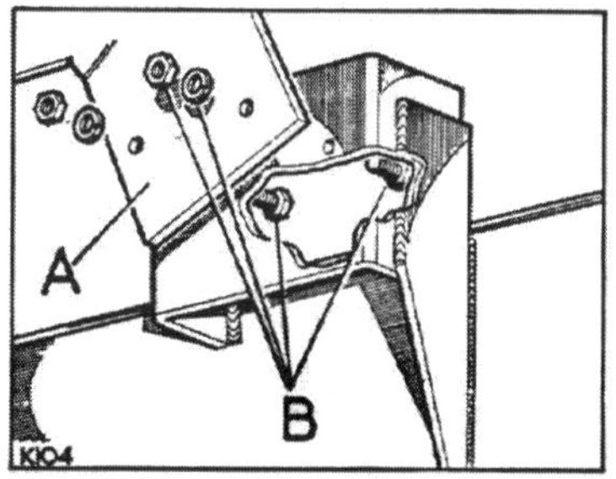

Fig. C1-21. Hand brake lever fixings
A—Mounting bracket for hand brake lever
B—Fixings, hand brake lever to chassis

5. Remove the seat base fixings.
6. Lift out the seat base complete, manoeuvring the hand brake lever through the aperture in the base front.

To refit

Reverse the removal procedure, using waterproof sealant between the joint flanges of the seat base and body. A suitable sealant is 'Sealastrip' manufactured by Expandite Ltd, Chase Road, London, NW 10.

Adjust the four wheel drive control lever. Operation A1-4.

GEARBOX

*Gearbox lubrication, draining and refilling—Operation C1-2

Workshop hand tools:
Spanner sizes: ½ in. AF, 11/16 in. AF open end

For the purpose of lubrication, the gearbox assembly is divided into two units. The main gearbox and clutch withdrawal mechanism are lubricated as one unit, and the transfer box and four wheel drive output shaft housing are lubricated as a separate unit.

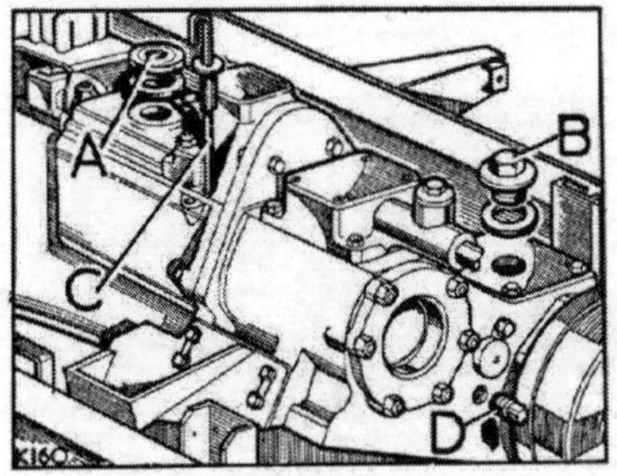

To drain

1. Place a suitable container beneath the gearbox.
2. Remove the drain plugs from the main gearbox and the transfer box.
3. Allow all the oil to drain, then replace both plugs together with joint washers.

To top up or refill

1. Remove the filler cap and/or plugs, as applicable.
2. Using the correct grade of lubricating oil, see Section X, fill the main gearbox to the 'H' mark on the dipstick or to the level plug hole, as applicable. Fill the transfer box to the level plug hole. Replace the dipstick and the filler and level plugs.

Capacities

Main gearbox: 2½ imperial pints, 3 U.S. pints, 1.5 litres.
Transfer box: 4½ imperial pints, 5¼ U.S. pints, 2.5 litres.

Gearbox breather

A breather hole is incorporated in the inspection cover for the selector shaft stops. The one breather hole provides for the complete gearbox assembly through internal communicating passages.

Ensure that the breather hole is clear, a blocked breather could cause failure of the gearbox oil seals.

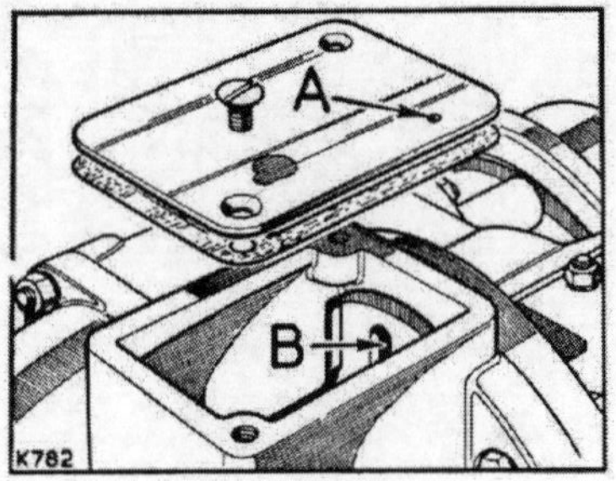

Fig. C1-22. Oil filler and level plugs (early gearboxes)
A—Filler cap, main gearbox section
B—Filler plug, transfer box section
C—Oil level dipstick, main gearbox
D—Oil level plug, transfer box

Fig. C1-23. Oil filler/level plugs (latest gearboxes) and drain plugs for all gearboxes
A—Filler level/plug main gearbox section
B—Filler level/plug, transfer box section
C—Drain plug, main gearbox section
D—Drain plug, transfer gearbox section

Fig. C1-24. Gearbox breather
A—Breather hole
B—Passage to transfer box

GEARBOX

Gearbox assembly complete, remove and refit—Operation C1-3

Workshop hand tools:
Spanner sizes:
2 BA, ½ in. BSF, 7/16 in. BSF, ⅜ in. BSF, ⅞ in. AF sockets, ⅜ in. AF, 7/16 in. AF open end
Pliers

To remove

1. Remove the front floor, Operation A1-4.
2. Remove the seat base, Operation C1-1.
3. Drain the gearbox lubricating oil. Operation C1-2.

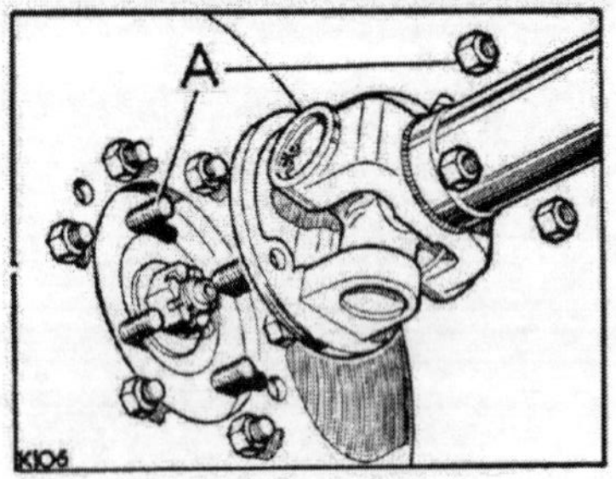

Fig. C1-25. Propeller shaft for rear axle
A—Fixings at coupling flanges

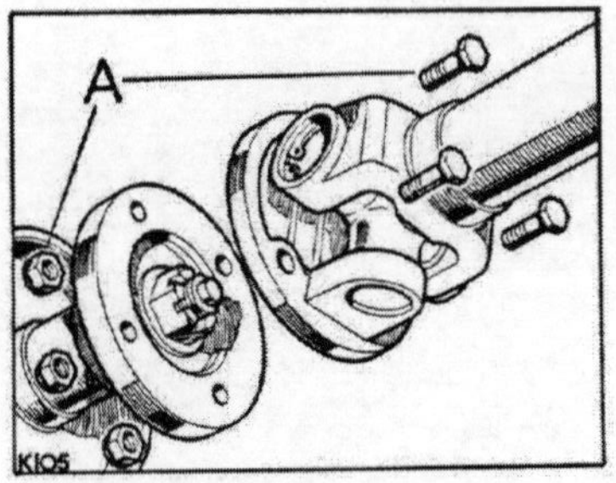

Fig. C1-26. Propeller shaft for front axle
A—Fixings at gearbox coupling flange

Note: If the vehicle is fitted with any optional equipment driven from the gearbox, it must be disconnected at the gearbox. Refer to separate publication for details of optional equipment.

4. Disconnect the rear propeller shaft and move it clear of the gearbox.
5. Disconnect the front propeller shaft from the gearbox.

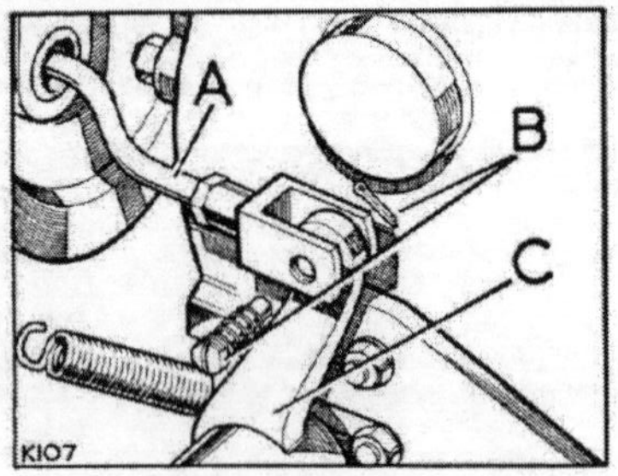

Fig. C1-27. Transmission brake
A—Expander rod
B—Fixings, expander rod to relay lever
C—Relay lever

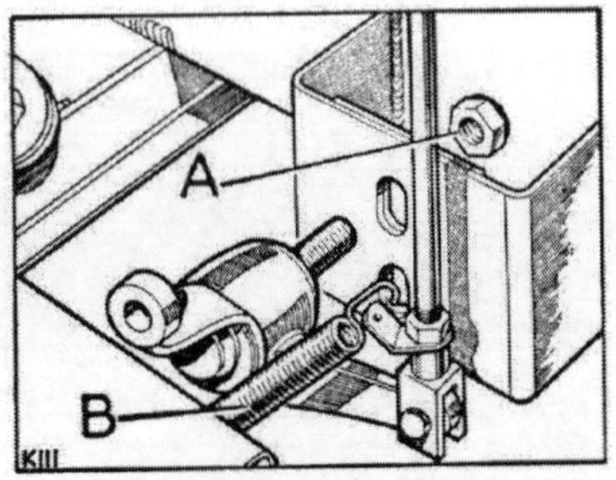

6. Disconnect the hand brake expander rod from the relay lever.

Fig. C1-28. Transmission brake lever and relay lever fixings
A—Fixings, relay mechanism to chassis
B—Return spring, transmission brake

7. Remove the transmission brake lever and relay mechanism.
8. LHStg models only. Remove the brake lever crossshaft.
9. Disconnect the speedometer cable from the gearbox.

Operations marked with an asterisk (*) can be carried out with the gearbox installed in the vehicle

GEARBOX

Operation C1-3—continued

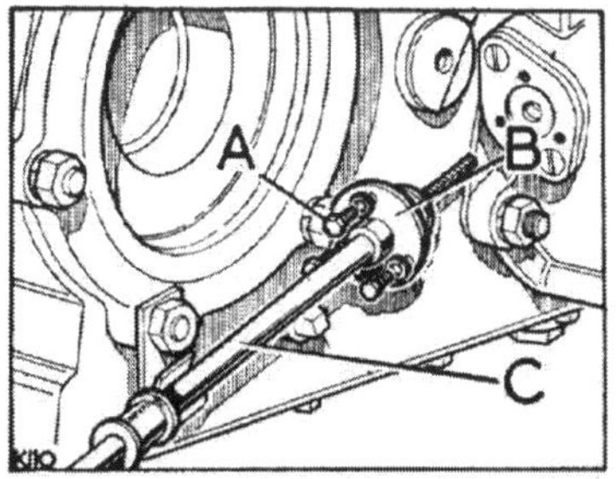

Fig. C1-29. Speedometer cable connection at gearbox

A—Fixings, speedometer cable to gearbox
B—Retaining plate for cable
C—Speedometer cable

Note: On certain models, the engine exhaust pipe is located above the gearbox left hand rear mounting, and where applicable, the exhaust pipe must be moved clear. Also check the location of the engine earth strap, on certain models it is fitted between the gearbox and chassis and must therefore be disconnected.

10. Remove the fixings from two rear mountings for the gearbox.

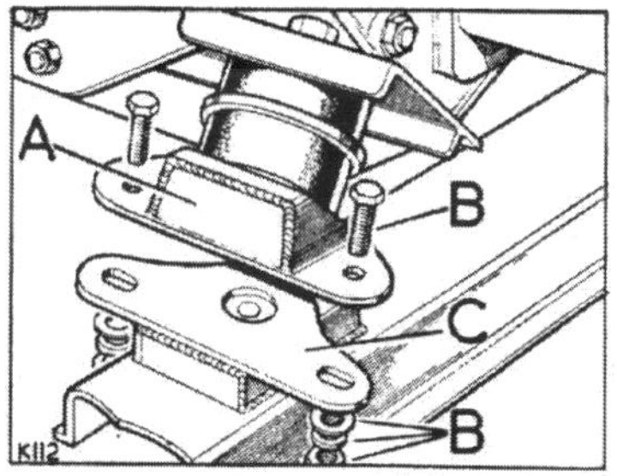

Fig. C1-30. Gearbox rear mountings

A—Rear mounting
B—Fixings, rear mounting to chassis
C—Chassis

Note: On certain models, a tie rod is fitted between the gearbox and chassis, and where applicable, release the bracket at the bell housing and move the tie rod clear.

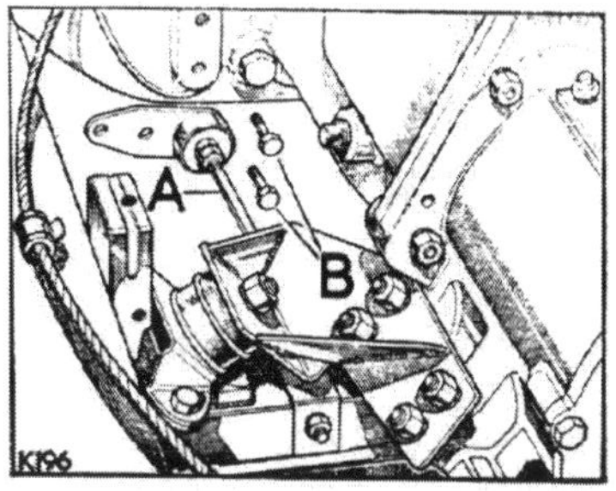

Fig. C1-31. Gearbox tie rod

A—Tie rod assembly
B—Fixings tie rod to bell housing

11. Disconnect the clutch cross-shaft.

12. Release the bracket for the clutch slave cylinder from the bell housing. Withdraw the slave cylinder, bracket and cross-shaft assembly, and retain the assembly at the side of the engine without straining the flexible pipe.

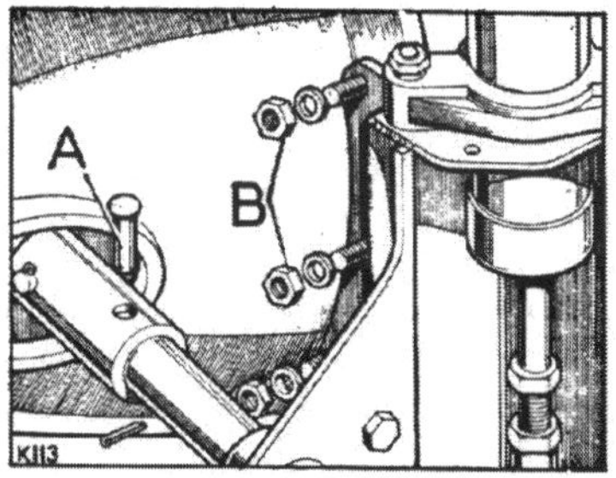

Fig. C1-32. Clutch cross-shaft and slave cylinder

A—Fixings, cross-shaft to connecting tube
B—Fixings, slave cylinder to bell housing

Operation C1-3—continued

13. Jack up the rear of the engine sufficient to insert a 1 inch (25 mm) thick block of wood between the flywheel housing and chassis, to retain the engine position when the gearbox is removed.

14. Place a suitable sling around the gearbox and tension it sufficient to take the weight.

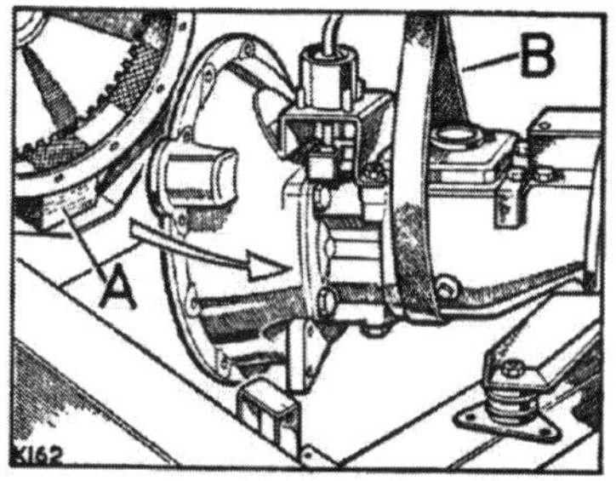

Fig. C1-33. Removing the gearbox

A—Wood block supporting engine
B—Sling

15. Remove the remaining nine nuts and plain washers securing the bell housing to the flywheel housing.

16. Carefully withdraw the gearbox rearwards clear of the clutch and lift from the vehicle.

To refit

1. Engage 4th gear and check that the primary pinion can be rotated by turning the transmission brake drum.

2. Place a suitable sling around the gearbox and lower it into position, carefully aligning the spline location between the primary pinion and clutch.

3. Secure the gearbox to the engine using nine of the bell housing fixings, leaving the three for the clutch slave cylinder mounting till later.

4. Locate the clutch slave cylinder, bracket and cross-shaft assembly in position and attach the cross-shaft to the connecting tube, then secure the slave cylinder bracket to the bell housing.

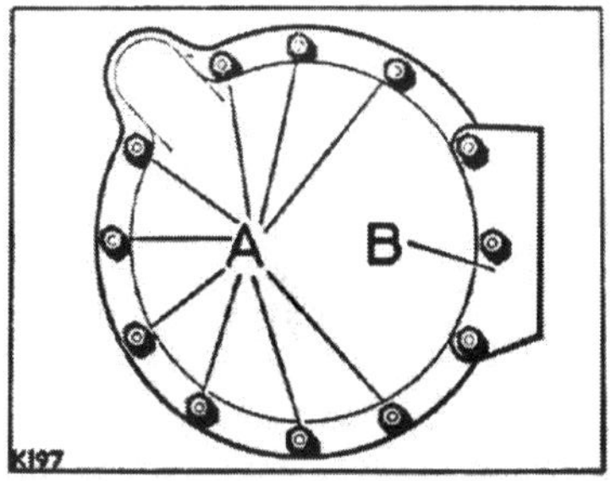

Fig. C1-34. Bell housing fixings

A—Fixings, bell housing to engine
B—Fixings, clutch slave cylinder mounting

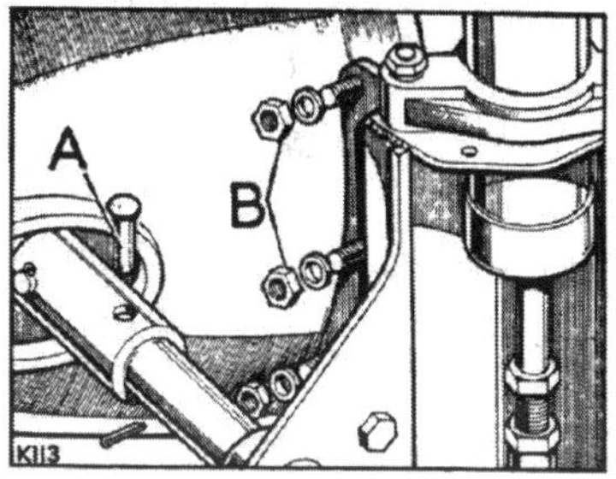

Fig. C1-35. Clutch cross-shaft and slave cylinder

A—Fixings, cross-shaft to connecting tube
B—Fixings, slave cylinder to bell housing

5. Jack up the rear end of the engine sufficient to remove the block of wood previously fitted between the flywheel housing and chassis.

6. Secure the gearbox rear mountings.

GEARBOX

Operation C1-3—continued

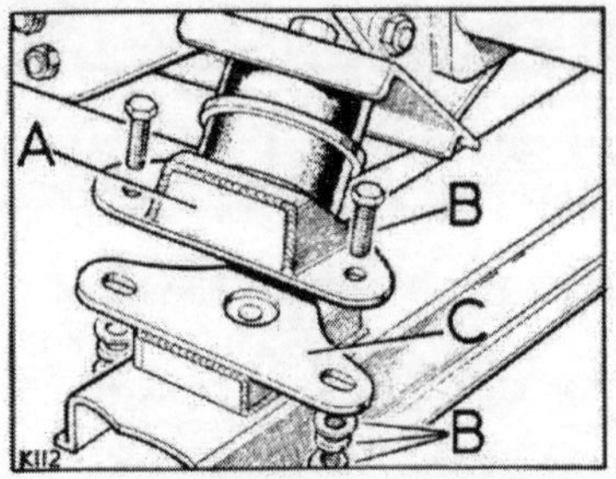

10. LHStg models only. Fit the hand brake cross-shaft.
11. Fit the hand brake lever and relay mechanism, see Fig. C1-28.
12. Connect the hand brake expander rod to the relay lever, see Fig. C1-27.
13. Reconnect the front propeller shaft, see Fig. C1-26.
14. Fit the rear propeller shaft.
15. Complete the reassembly by reversing the removal procedure.
16. Check and replenish the gearbox lubricating oil. Also ensure that the gearbox breather is clear, Operation C1-2.
17. Check and adjust the transmission brake. See Section H.
18. If necessary bleed the clutch system and adjust the pedal movement. See Section B.
19. Adjust the four wheel drive control lever. Operation A1-4.

Fig. C1-36. Gearbox rear mountings

A—Rear mounting
B—Fixings, rear mountings to chassis
C—Chassis

7. If removed, fit the tie rod between the bell housing and chassis, see Fig. C1-31.
8. If removed, refit the exhaust pipe.
9. Connect the speedometer cable to the gearbox, see Fig. C1-29.

GEARBOX

*Transmission brake, remove and refit—Operation C1-4

(For overhaul Instructions, refer to section H)

Workshop hand tools:
Spanner sizes: ⅜ in. BSF, ⅝ in. BSF sockets, $\frac{7}{16}$ in. AF open end
Pliers

To remove

1. Drain the lubricating oil from the transfer box. Operation C1-2.
2. Disconnect the rear propeller shaft, and move it clear of the transmission brake.

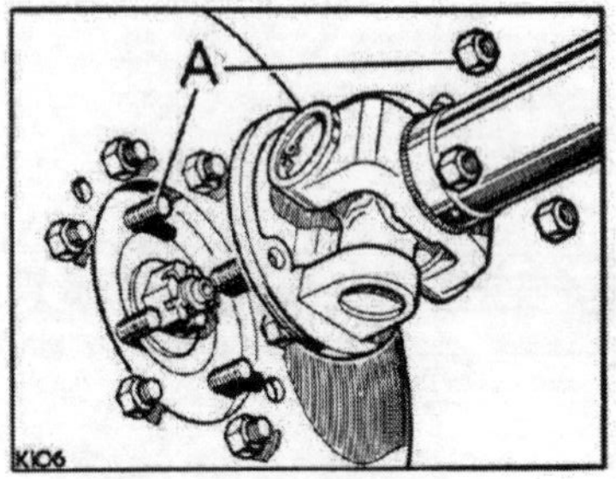

Fig. C1-37. Propeller shaft for rear axle

A—Fixings at coupling flanges

3. Disconnect the hand brake expander rod from the relay lever, and slacken the brake adjuster.

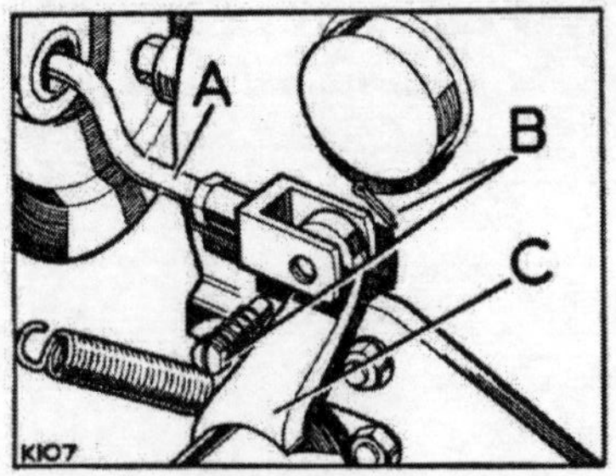

Fig. C1-38. Coupling, relay lever to expander rod

A—Expander rod
B—Fixings, expander rod to relay lever
C—Relay lever

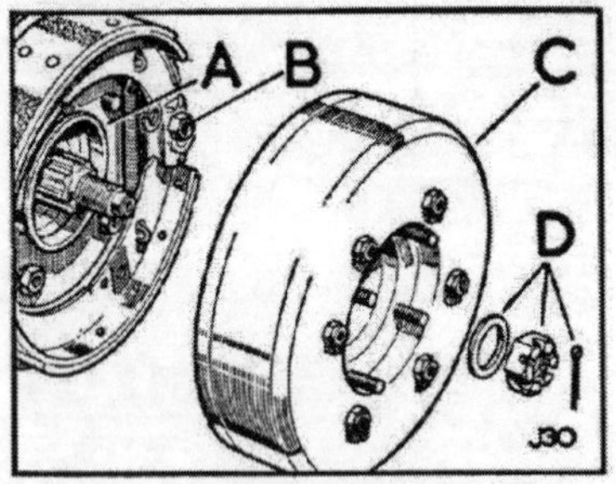

Fig. C1-39. Output drive flange and brake drum

A—Brake anchor plate
B—Fixings, brake anchor plate
C—Output flange and brake drum assembly
D—Fixings, output flange and brake drum

4. Remove the output flange and brake drum assembly.
5. Remove the brake anchor plate together with the oil catcher, or mud shield, as applicable.

Note: The oil catcher and joint washer prevent any oil leakage from the speedometer drive housing reaching the transmission brake, and can be fitted to earlier gearboxes in place of the joint washer inner member.

To refit

1. If an oil catcher is fitted, apply jointing compound to both sides of the joint washer.

Operations marked with an asterisk (*) can be carried out with the gearbox installed in the vehicle

GEARBOX

Operation C1-4—continued

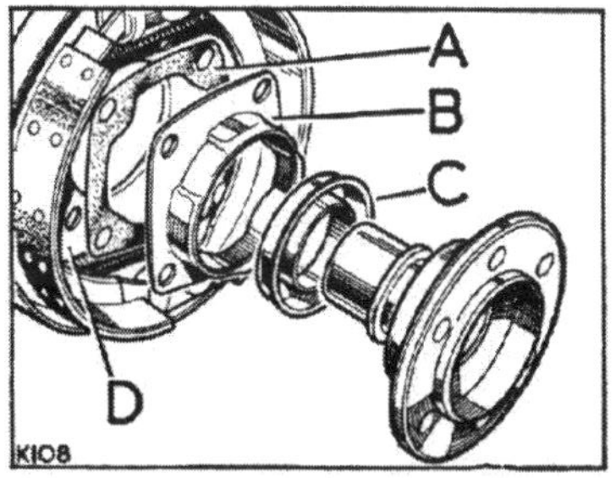

2. Fit the brake anchor plate and connect the expander rod to the relay lever.
3. Fit the output flange and brake drum. The output flange securing nut is tightened to a torque figure of 85 lb/ft (11.75 mkg).
4. Adjust the transmission brake, see Section H.
5. Fit the propeller shaft.
6. Replenish the transfer box lubricating oil. Operation C1-2.

Fig. C1-40. Oil catcher for transmission brake

A—Joint washer for oil catcher
B—Oil catcher
C—Mud shield for flange
D—Brake anchor plate

*Speedometer drive housing, remove and refit—Operation C1-5

(For overhaul instructions, Operation C1-6 refers)

Workshop hand tools:
Spanner sizes: 2 BA, ⅜ in. BSF sockets

To remove

1. Remove the transmission brake. Operation C1-4.
2. Disconnect the speedometer cable from the gearbox.
3. Remove the speedometer drive housing complete with shims.
4. Withdraw the speedometer drive worm.

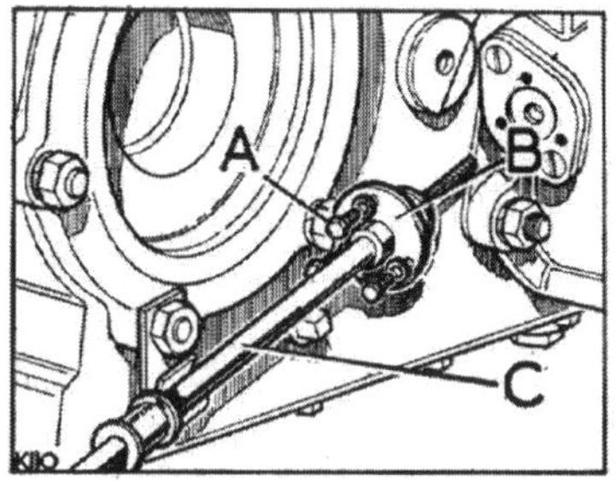

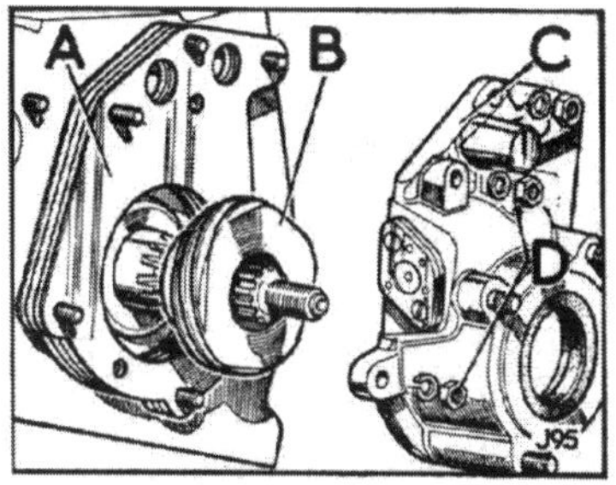

Fig. C1-41. Speedometer cable connection at gearbox

A—Fixings, speedometer cable to gearbox
B—Retaining plate for cable
C—Speedometer cable

Fig. C1-42. Speedometer drive assembly

A—Shims
B—Drive worm
C—Speedometer drive housing
D—Fixings, speedometer drive housing to transfer box

To refit

Reverse the removal procedure.

Check and if necessary, replenish the gearbox lubricating oil. Operation C1-2.

Operations marked with an asterisk (*) can be carried out with the gearbox installed in the vehicle

GEARBOX

*Speedometer drive housing, overhaul—Operation C1-6

(For removal and refitting instructions, Operation C1-5 refers)

Workshop hand tools
Screwdriver (medium)

To dismantle

1. Remove the speedometer pinion.

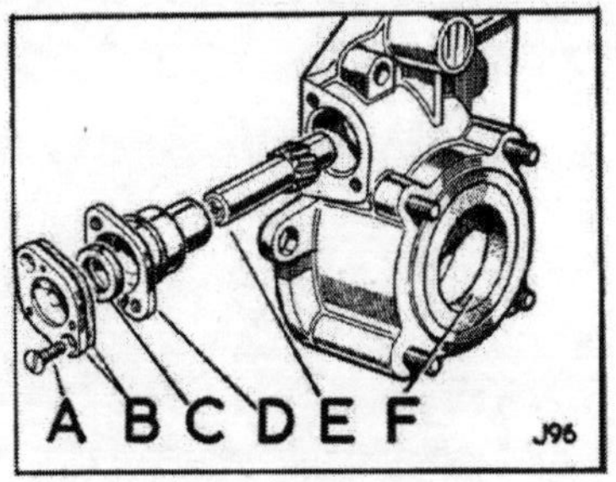

Fig. C1-43. Speedometer drive and housing
A—Fixings, pinion retaining plate
B—Retaining plate and gasket
C—Oil seal for pinion
D—Sleeve for pinion
E—Speedometer pinion
F—Oil seal for output shaft

2. Remove the oil seal and rubber 'O' ring from the sleeve.
3. Remove the output shaft oil seal from the speedometer housing.

Inspection

Examine the pinion teeth and the speedometer drive worm for wear.

Check the sleeve which should be a slide fit on the pinion.

To assemble

1. Fit the oil seal, lipped side inwards, and 'O' ring to the sleeve.
2. Fit the pinion and sleeve, ensuring that the relieved face on the sleeve will be towards the speedometer drive worm when assembled.

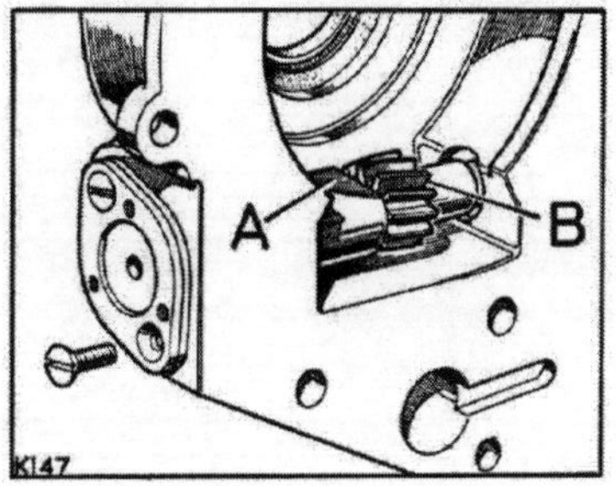

Fig. C1-44. Alignment of sleeve for pinion
A—Relieved face on sleeve
B—Drive worm

3. Fit the output shaft oil seal, lipped side inward, using jointing compound on the seal outer diameter. The housing may be warmed to facilitate assembly.

*Transfer box, remove and refit—Operation C1-7

(For overhaul instructions, Operation C1-8 refers)

Workshop hand tools:
Spanner sizes: ½ in. AF, ⅞ in. AF, 1½ in. AF open end
2 BA, ¼ in. BSF, ⅝ in. BSF, ⅜ in. BSF sockets
Pliers

Special tools:
Tool for withdrawing intermediate shaft,
Part Number 605862

To remove

1. Remove the front floor. Operation A1-4.
2. Remove the seat base. Operation C1-1.
3. Drain the gearbox lubricating oil. Operation C1-2.
4. Remove the transmission brake. Operation C1-4.

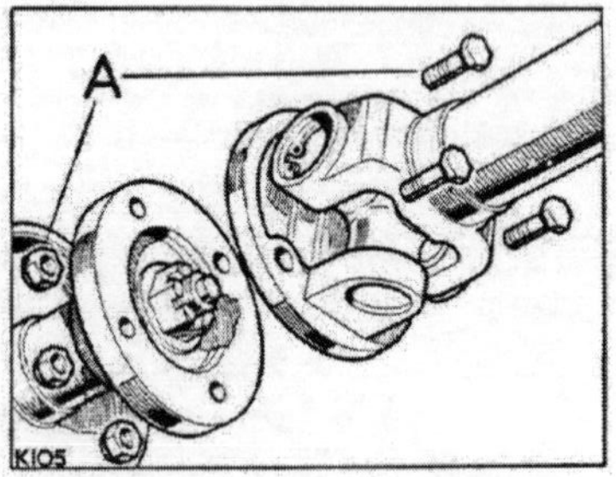

Fig. C1-45. Propeller shaft for front axle
A—Fixings at gearbox coupling flange

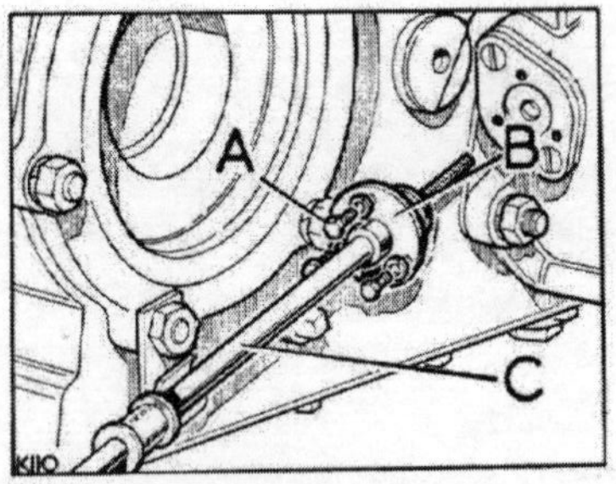

5. Disconnect the front propeller shaft from the gearbox.

Fig. C1-46. Speedometer cable connection at gearbox
A—Fixings, speedometer cable to gearbox
B—Retaining plate for cable
C—Speedometer cable

6. Disconnect the speedometer cable from the gearbox.
7. Disconnect the transfer gear lever from the bracket at the bell housing, withdraw the lever, taking care to retain the spring strip, located between the lever ball and link.

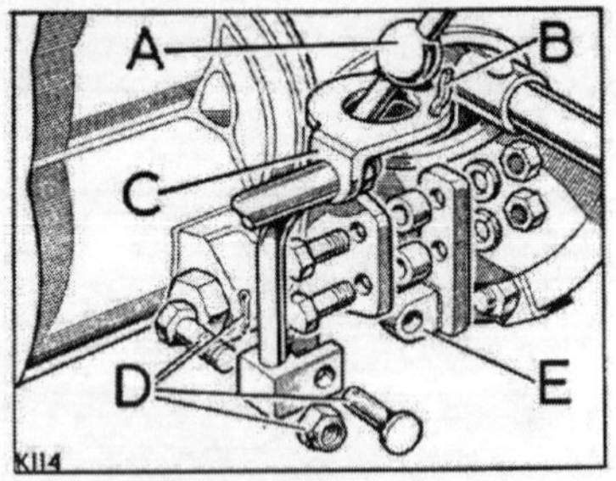

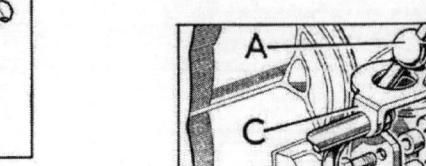

Fig. C1-47. Transfer gear lever
A—Transfer gear lever
B—Spring, lever ball to gearbox link
C—Link, for lever
D—Alternative fixings, lever to bell housing
E—Bracket, lever to bell housing

Note: If the vehicle is fitted with any optional equipment driven from the transfer box, it must be disconnected at the transfer box. Refer to separate publication for details of optional equipment.

8. Remove the hand brake lever and relay mechanism.
9. LHStg models only. Remove the hand brake cross-shaft.

Note: On certain models, the engine exhaust pipe is located above the gearbox left hand rear mounting, and where applicable, the exhaust pipe must be moved clear. Also check the location of the engine earth strap, on certain models it is fitted between the gearbox and chassis and must therefore be disconnected.

Operations marked with an asterisk (*) can be carried out with the gearbox installed in the vehicle

GEARBOX

Operation C1-7—continued

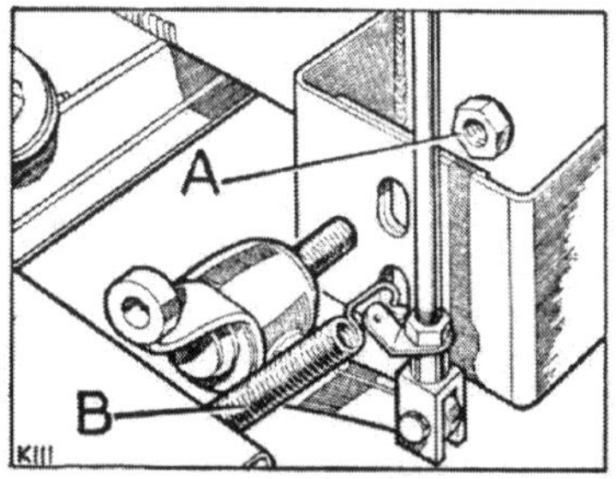

Fig. C1-48. Hand brake lever and relay lever fixings
A—Fixings, relay mechanism to chassis
B—Return spring, hand brake

10. Remove the fixings from the two rear mountings for the gearbox.

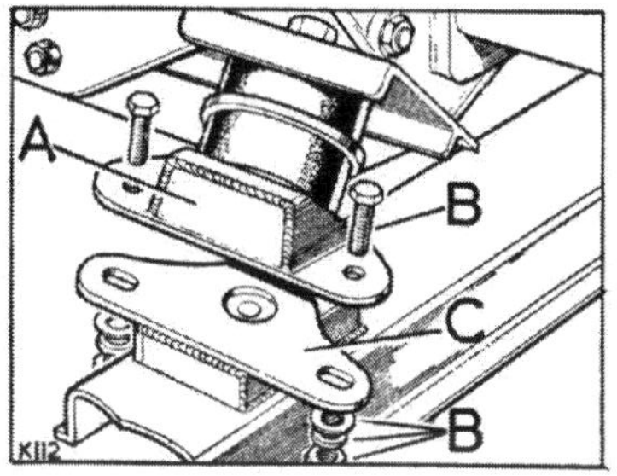

11. Jack-up the rear of the engine sufficient to insert a 1 in. (25 mm) thick block of wood between the flywheel housing and the chassis to support the gearbox.

12. Remove the bottom cover plate and gasket from the transfer box.

13. Remove the mainshaft rear bearing housing, or if fitted, the power take off drive unit.

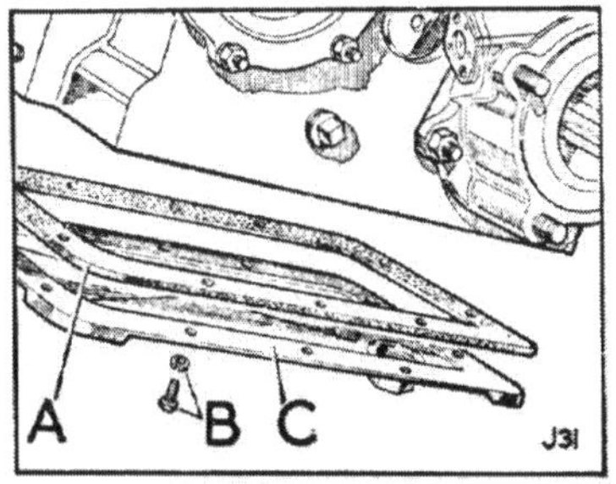

Fig. C1-49. Gearbox rear mountings
A—Rear mounting
B—Fixings, rear mountings to chassis
C—Chassis

Fig. C1-50. Transfer box bottom cover plate
A—Gasket for cover plate
B—Fixings (10 off) bottom cover plate to transfer box
C—Bottom cover plate

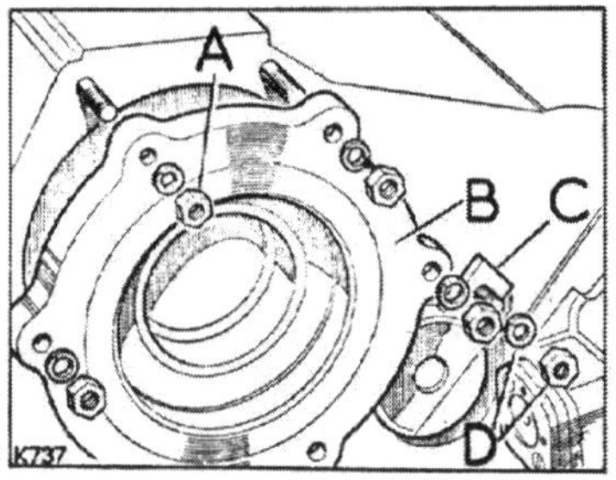

Fig. C1-51. Mainshaft rear bearing housing
A—Fixings for housing
B—Housing
C—Retaining plate, intermediate shaft
D—Fixings, retaining plate

14. Remove the fixings from the retaining plate for the intermediate shaft.

15. Support the intermediate gear by hand while using special tool Part No. 605862, to withdraw the intermediate shaft complete with retaining plate and oil seal 'O' ring. Withdraw the intermediate gear through the bottom of the casing; taking care not to let the roller bearings fall from the gear.

Operation C1-7—continued

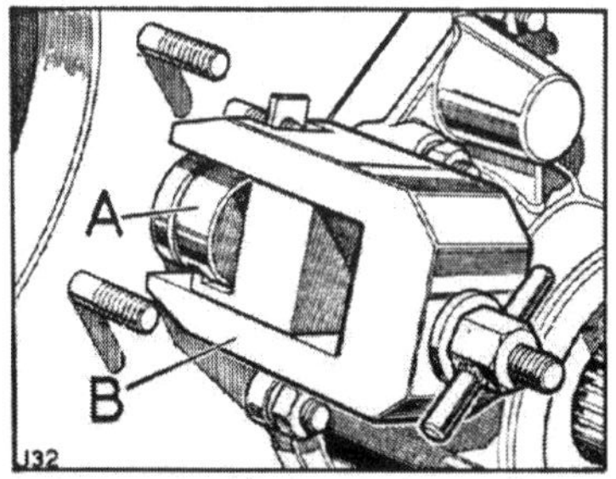

Fig. C1-52. Removing intermediate gear
A—Intermediate shaft
B—Special tool Part No. 605862

16. Remove the thrust washers and if fitted, shims, located between each end of the intermediate gear and casing.

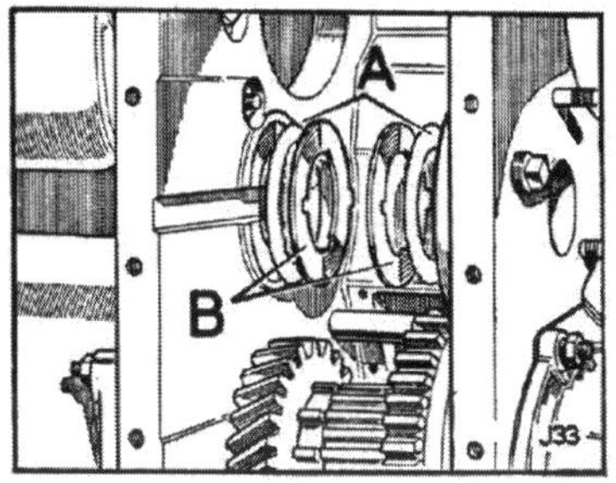

Fig. C1-53. Thrust washers and shims, intermediate gear
A—Shims   B—Thrust washers

17. Release the fixings and withdraw the transfer box and joint washer from the main gearbox, retained by dowel locations.

To refit

1. Smear both sides of the joint washer with general purpose grease and place it in position on the main gearbox.

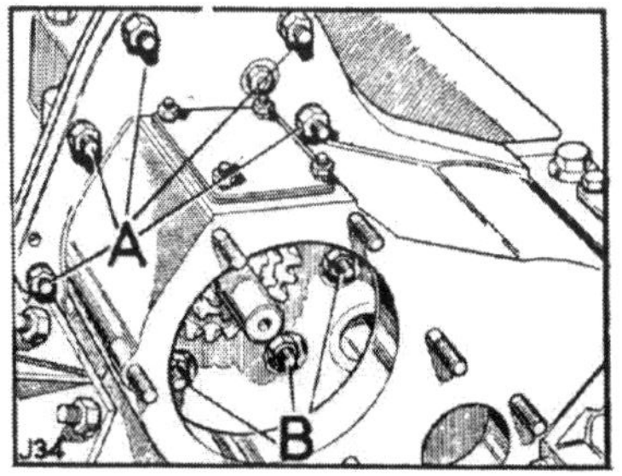

Fig. C1-54. Fixings, transfer box to main gearbox
A—External fixings (5 off)
B—Internal fixings (3 off)

2. Fit the transfer box to the main gearbox, engaging the dowel locations.

3. Fit any shims for the intermediate gear, between the thrust washers and the casing, ensuring that the thrust washer bronze faces are towards the intermediate gear. Use a little general purpose grease to retain in position, see Fig. C1-53.

Note: If the intermediate gear, bearings or thrust washers have been renewed, the gear end-float must be checked and adjusted, as described under 'Transfer box overhaul'.

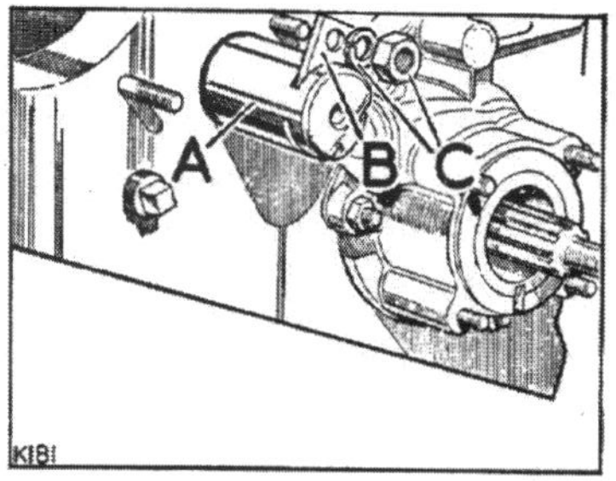

Fig. C1-55. Fitting intermediate shaft
A—Intermediate shaft
B—Retaining plate
C—Fixings for retaining plate

GEARBOX

Operation C1-7—continued

4. Locate the intermediate gear, complete with roller bearings, in position in mesh with the high and low gear wheels.
5. Fit the intermediate shaft, together with its oil seal 'O' ring and retaining plate, through the casing, shims, thrust washers and intermediate gear, tapping it lightly home when the spigoted end of the shaft engages its location in the front of the casing. The shaft **must** be a light tap fit.
6. Secure the retaining plate in position.
7. Fit the mainshaft rear bearing housing, see Fig. C1-51.
8. Fit the bottom cover plate and gasket, using jointing compound on both sides of the gasket, see Fig. C1-50.
9. Remove the support block from between the flywheel housing and the chassis, and secure the gearbox rear mountings, see Fig. C1-49.
10. If removed, refit the exhaust pipe.
11. LHStg models only. Fit the hand brake cross-shaft.
12. Fit the hand brake lever and relay mechanism, see Fig. C1-48.
13. Fit the transfer gear lever, and ensure that the link securing nut is tight.
14. Connect the speedometer cable to the gearbox, see Fig. C1-46.
15. Connect the front propeller shaft to the gearbox, see Fig. C1-45.
16. Fit the transmission brake. Operation C1-4.
17. Fit the rear propeller shaft.
18. Check and replenish the gearbox lubricating oil. Operation C1-2.
19. If the transfer box is of the all helical type, see Operation C1-8A, check and, if necessary, adjust the transfer travel stop, see Operation C1-9.
20. Fit the seat base. Operation C1-1.
21. Fit the front floor, Operation A1-4.

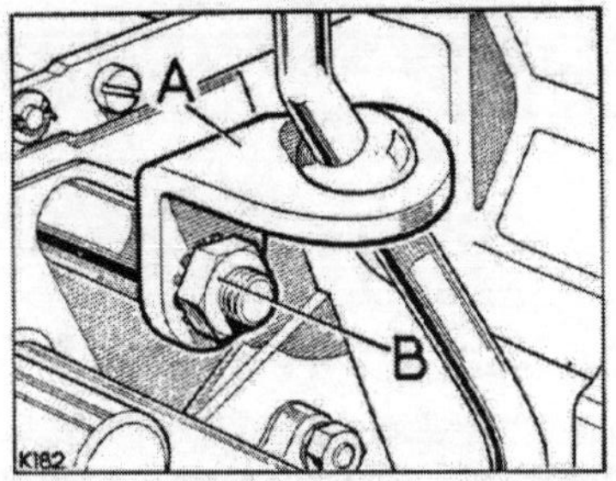

Fig. C1-56. Link for transfer selector shaft
A—Link   B—Fixings

---

*Transfer box, helical and spur gear type, overhaul—Operation C1-8
(For removal and refitting instructions, Operation C1-7 refers)

Workshop hand tools:
Spanner sizes: ⅜ in. BSF open end
Mallet, Circlip pliers, Feeler gauges, Spring balance

Special tools:
Tool for protecting output shaft, Part No. 243241

General

There are two types of transfer box in use, one utilises a helical and spur gear arrangement, while the other is of all helical design. The only visible external difference is a selector shaft adjuster, fitted to the front output shaft housing on the all helical box only. For overhaul instructions for the all helical type transfer box, Operation C1-8A refers.

To dismantle

1. Remove the front output shaft housing, Operation C1-9, and the speedometer drive housing, Operation C1-5. Refer to separate instructions for overhaul details of these two items.
2. Remove the circlip retaining the front bearing outer race.

Fig. C1-57. Circlip for front bearing
A—Circlip
B—Front bearing
C—Output shaft

3. Using a mallet, drive the output shaft rearwards to remove the rear bearing outer race. Ensure that the output shaft splines do not contact the casing and cause damage.
4. Fit protection cap Part No. 243241, over the threaded end of the output shaft, and drive the shaft forward as far as possible, then slide the packing piece between the rollers of the front bearing and the outer race.

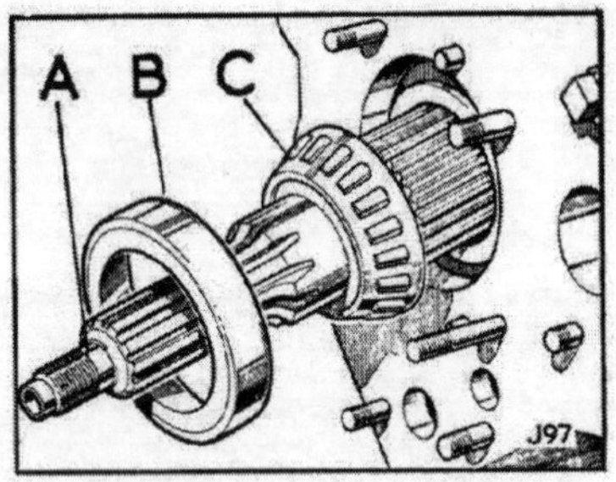

Fig. C1-58. Rear bearing for output shaft
A—Output shaft
B—Rear bearing outer race
C—Rear bearing

Note: A packing piece can be made from a scrap bearing outer race, with the outer diameter reduced to give clearance in the transfer box and suitably slotted to fit over the shaft.

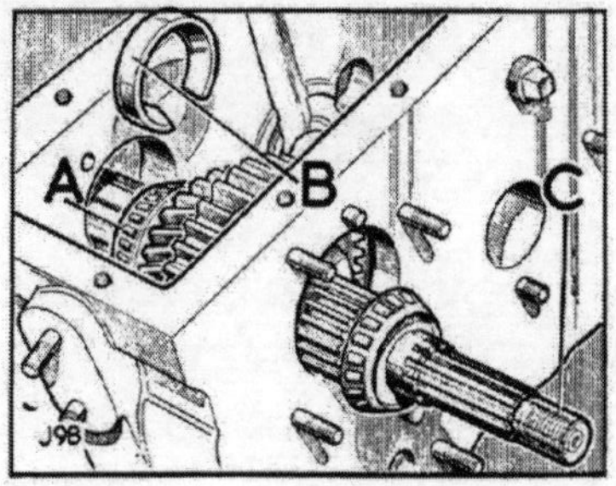

Fig. C1-59. Packing piece for bearing outer race
A—Front bearing
B—Packing piece
C—Protection cap

Operations marked with an asterisk (*) can be carried out with the gearbox installed in the vehicle

Section C—Land-Rover

GEARBOX

Operation C1-8—continued

5. With the packing piece in position, drive the shaft forward to remove the front bearing outer race.

6. Place pads of rag in position to protect the transfer box bearing bores during the following operations.

7. Using a suitable mild steel bar with a chisel end, drive the front bearing from the output shaft.

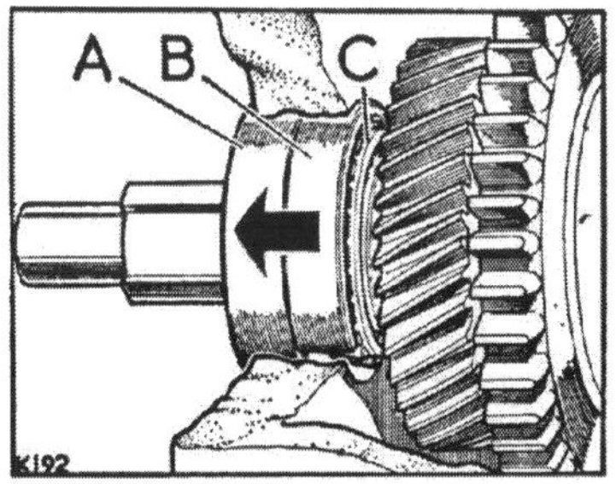

Fig. C1-60. Removing bearing outer race
A—Outer race
B—Packing piece
C—Front bearing

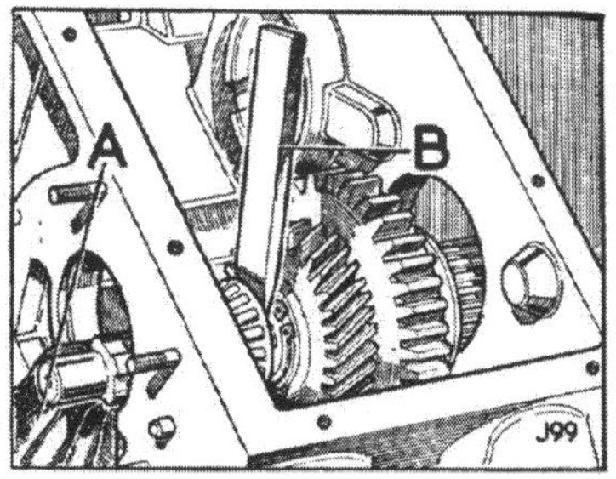

Fig. C1-61. Removing front bearing
A—Soft rag to protect casing
B—Mild steel, chisel edged drift

8. Remove the circlip and thrust washer from the output shaft, withdraw the shaft through the gears and remove the gears through the bottom of the casing.

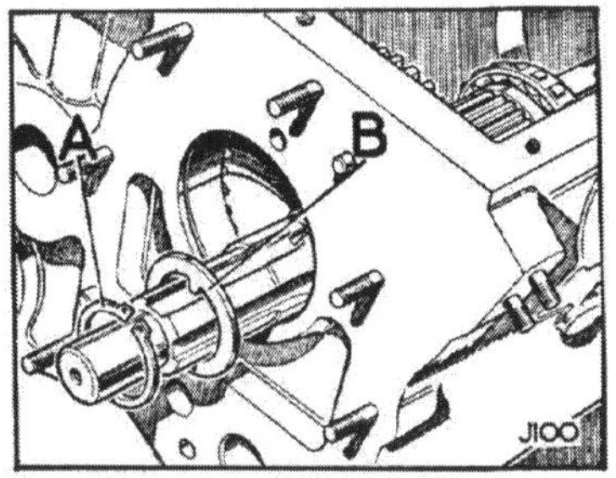

Fig. C1-62. Fixings, output shaft gears
A—Circlip, retaining thrust washer
B—Thrust washer for high speed gear

9. Extract or press the rear bearing from the output shaft.

Note: The low speed gear is strong enough to be used as a press block for the removal of the rear bearing.

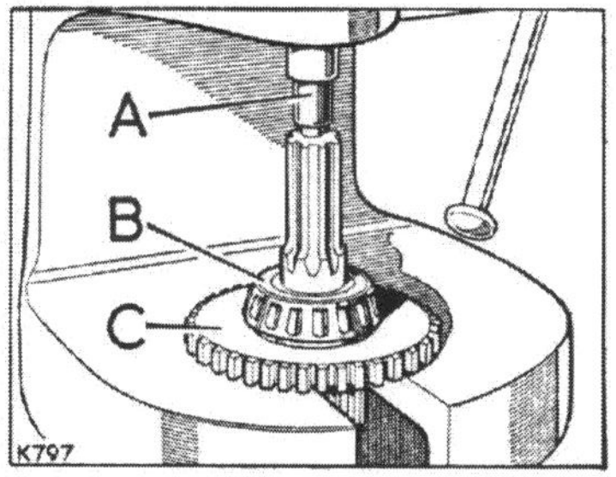

Fig. C1-63. Pressing off rear bearing
A—Protection cap
B—Rear bearing
C—Low speed gear

GEARBOX

Operation C1-8—continued

10. Remove the circlip, retaining plate and roller bearing from the mainshaft rear bearing housing.

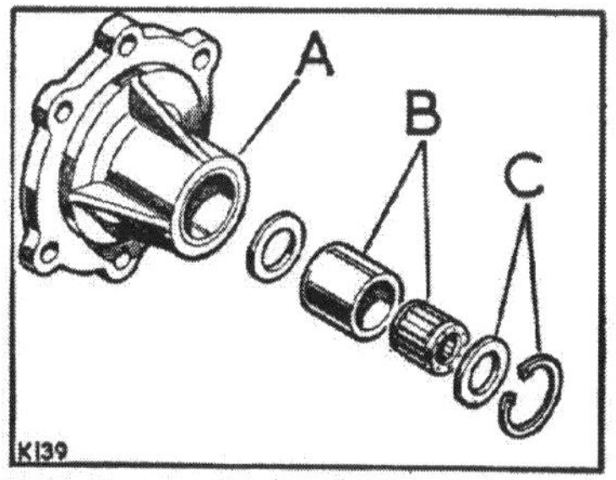

Fig. C1-64. Rear bearing housing for gearbox mainshaft
A—Bearing housing
B—Roller bearing
C—Fixings, bearing to housing

11. Remove the rear drive output flange from the transmission brake drum. Prise off the mud shield and remove the flange fixings.

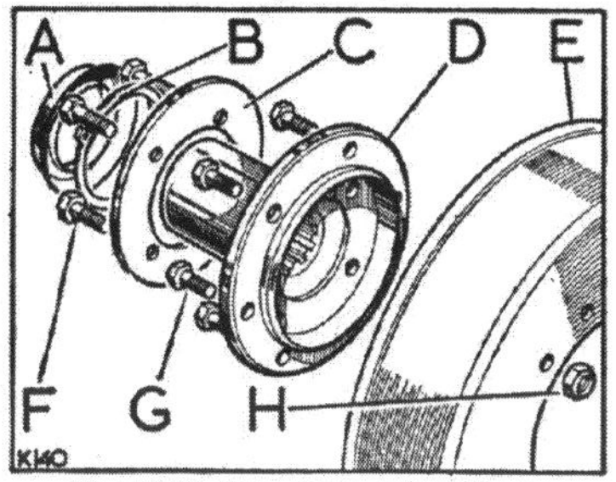

Fig. C1-65. Rear drive output flange
A—Mud shield
B—Circlip, retainer propeller shaft bolts
C—Retaining plate, drum bolts
D—Output flange
E—Drum, transmission brake
F—Fitting bolts, propeller shaft
G—Fitting bolt for brake drum
H—Nuts for brake drum bolts

Inspection

Renew any components which show obvious wear or damage. Check the condition of the shaft splines for the low gear wheel, it is important that the spline corners are not worn.

Note that the low gear wheel is a loose fit on the shaft, this allows the gear to tilt in operation, causing the spline edges at the annular groove to bite on the splines of the low speed gear, locking it in position.

Early transfer boxes are fitted with a bush for the selector shaft guide, the bush is pressed in and reamed to 1.148 in. (29,17 mm).

Examine the sleeve of the output flange for damage which could cause failure of the oil seal.

Pre-assembly check

1. Fit the high gear wheel on to the output shaft, followed by the thrust washer and circlip.

2. Place a suitable piece of tube over the shaft and push the circlip towards the gear to produce minimum gear end float. Maintaining this condition, check the end float between the gear and the shaft, this must be .006 in. to .008 in. (0,15 mm to 0,20 mm), under these conditions.

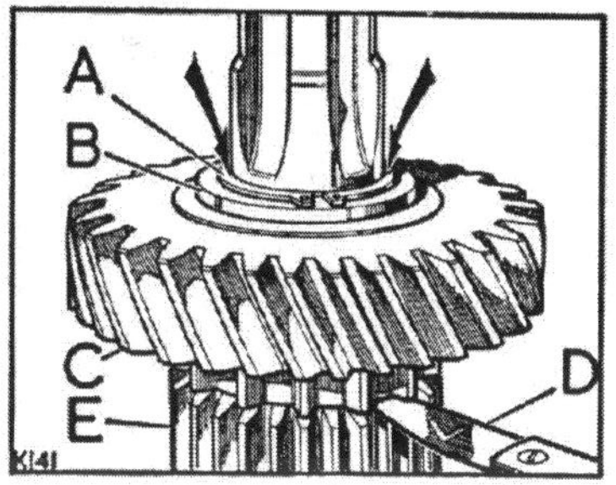

Fig. C1-66. End-float check, high gear wheel
A—Circlip   D—Feeler gauges
B—Thrust washer E—Output shaft
C—High gear wheel

3. Adjustment of the high gear wheel end float is made by reducing the thickness of the thrust washer, or fitting a new thrust washer, as required. If fitting a new thrust washer fails to reduce the end float to the required limits, replace the shaft and/or gear.

To assemble

1. Assemble the high and low gear wheels and the output shaft into the transfer box.

GEARBOX

Operation C1-8—continued

4. Fit the rear bearing outer race.

5. Using the protection cap, Part No. 243241, over the threaded end of the output shaft, drive the shaft forward until the front bearing is hard against the circlip. Then lightly tap the rear bearing outer race further in to remove all end float from the output shaft without introducing pre-load.

6. Set the output shaft bearing pre-load as follows:—

    (a) Fit the speedometer housing, without any shims, and loosely retain with nuts and spring washers.

    (b) Measure the rolling resistance of the output shaft, using a nylon cord attached to a spring balance. Coil the cord around the low gear wheel selector groove and note the measurement recorded on the spring balance required to rotate the output shaft after having overcome inertia. Ensure that the cord does not slip, giving a false reading.

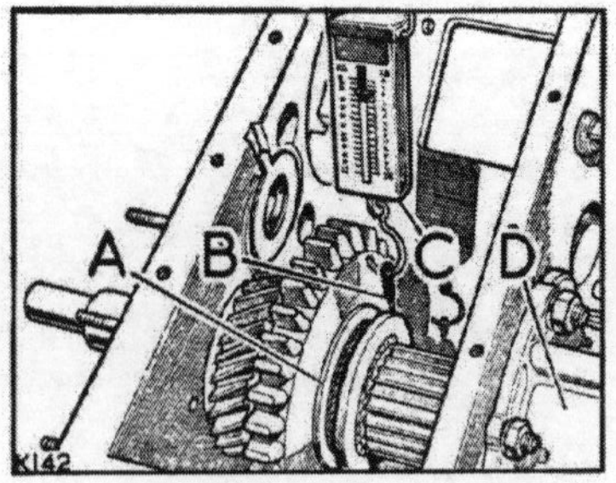

Fig. C1-69. Checking output shaft bearing pre-load

A—Low gear wheel selector groove
B—Nylon cord
C—Spring balance
D—Speedometer housing

(c) Bearing pre-load is correct when a figure of 2 to 4 lbs (0,9 to 1,8 kg) is recorded on the spring balance. Adjustment is made by tightening the speedometer housing securing nuts, progressively and evenly.

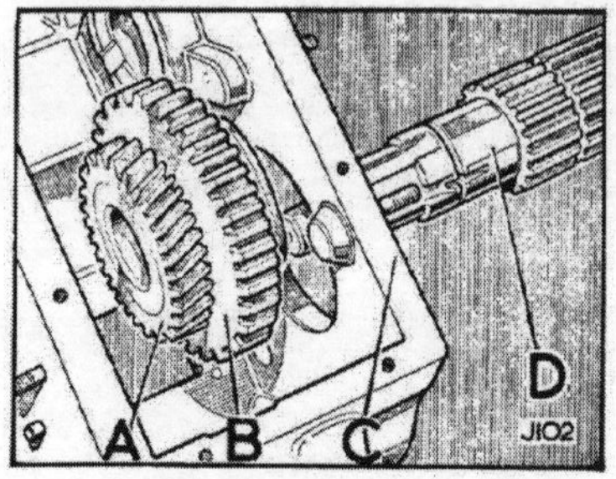

Fig. C1-67. Fitting output shaft and gears

A—High gear wheel
B—Low gear wheel
C—Rear face of transfer box
D—Output shaft

2. Fit the thrust washer, determined during the pre-assembly check, to the output shaft and secure, using a new circlip.

3. Use pads of rag to protect the two roller bearings bearing bores, and drive the two roller bearings on to the output shaft. Fit the front bearing outer race and secure with a circlip.

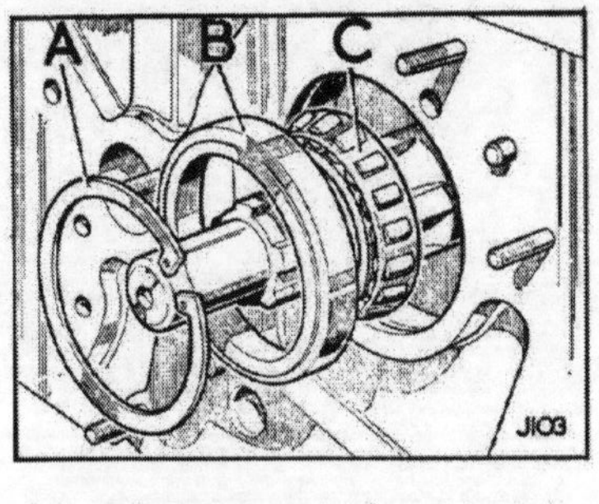

Fig. C1-68. Front bearing for output shaft

A—Circlip
B—Bearing outer race
C—Roller bearing

Operation C1-8—continued

(d) When the bearing pre-load is correct, ensure that the clearance gap between the speedometer housing and the transfer box is evenly disposed, using feeler gauges. The measured clearance obtained, is equal to the thickness of shims required for subsequent assembly between the speedometer housing and transfer box to maintain correct bearing pre-load.

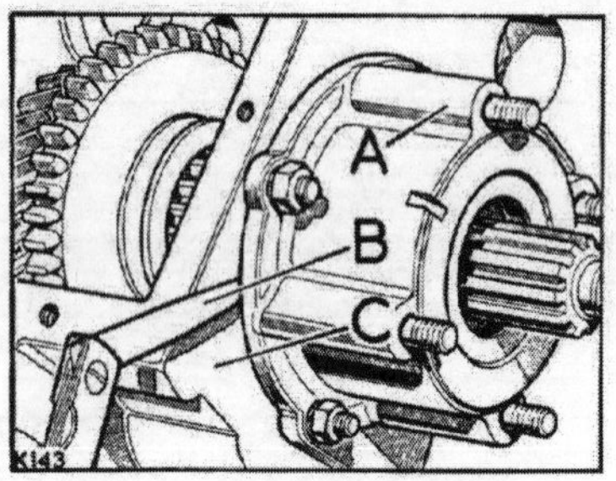

Fig. C1-70. Determining shims for speedometer housing

A—Speedometer housing
B—Feeler gauge
C—Transfer box

(e) Withdraw the spring balance and nylon cord from the low gear wheel, and remove the speedometer housing from the transfer box.

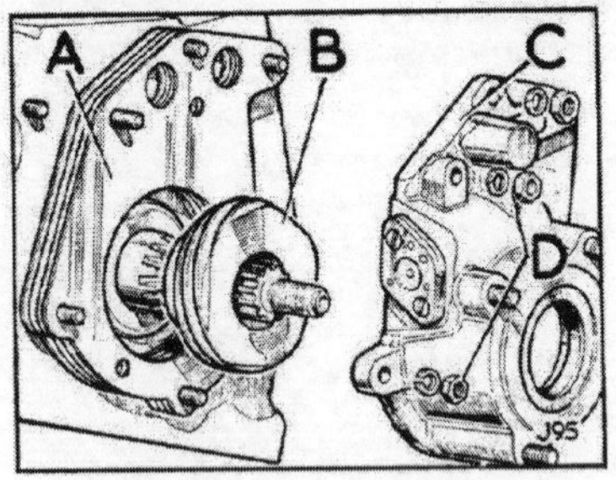

Fig. C1-71. Speedometer drive assembly

A—Shims
B—Drive worm
C—Speedometer drive housing
D—Fixings, speedometer housing

7. Using the determined thickness of shims, fit the speedometer drive worm and housing.

8. Determine the intermediate gear end float as follows:—

    (a) Place the two thrust washers for the intermediate gear in position in the transfer box and retain with a film of grease. The washers must be fitted with the bronze faces inward and located in the casing by their tabs.

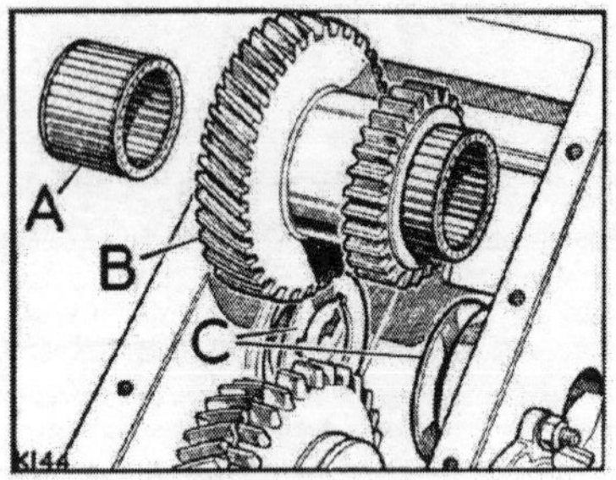

Fig. C1-72. Intermediate gear assembly

A—Roller bearings
B—Intermediate gear
C—Thrust washers

(b) Locate the intermediate gear, complete with roller bearings, in position in mesh with the high and low gear wheels.

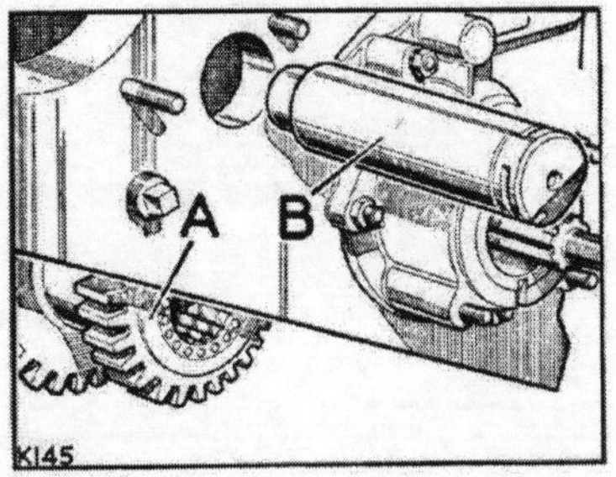

Fig. C1-73. Intermediate shaft assembly

A—Intermediate gear   B—Intermediate shaft

Operation C1-8—continued

(c) Fit the intermediate shaft through the casing, thrust washers and intermediate gear, tapping it lightly home when the spigotted end of the shaft engages its location in the front of the casing. The shaft must be a light tap fit.

(d) Using feeler gauges, check the end float of the intermediate gear, this must be .004 in. to .008 in. (0,10 mm to 0,20 mm). Adjustment is made by grinding the steel face of the thrust washers to increase end float, or by fitting shims, available in .010 in (0,25 mm) thickness, between the thrust washers and the casing to reduce end float.

(e) When the intermediate gear end float is correct, remove the intermediate shaft and gear, and place aside for subsequent assembly after the transfer box has been fitted to the main gearbox.

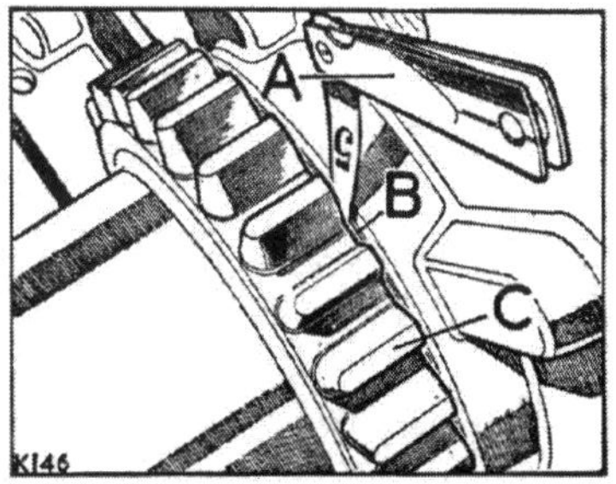

Fig. C1-74. Checking intermediate gear end-float

A—Feeler gauge
B—Thrust washer
C—Intermediate gear

9. Re-assemble the rear bearing housing and the output drive flange by reversing the removal procedure.

---

*Transfer box (all helical gear type), overhaul—Operation C1-8A

(For removal and refitting instructions, Operation C1-7 refers)

Workshop hand tools:
Spanner sizes: ⅜ in. BSF open end
Mallet, Circlip pliers, Feeler gauges, Spring balance

Special tools:
Tool for protecting output shaft, Part No. 243241

General

There are two types of transfer box in use, one utilises a helical and spur gear arrangement, while the other is of all helical design. The only visible external difference is a selector shaft adjuster, fitted to the front output shaft housing on the all helical box only. For overhaul instructions of the helical and spur gear type transfer box, Operation C1-8 refers.

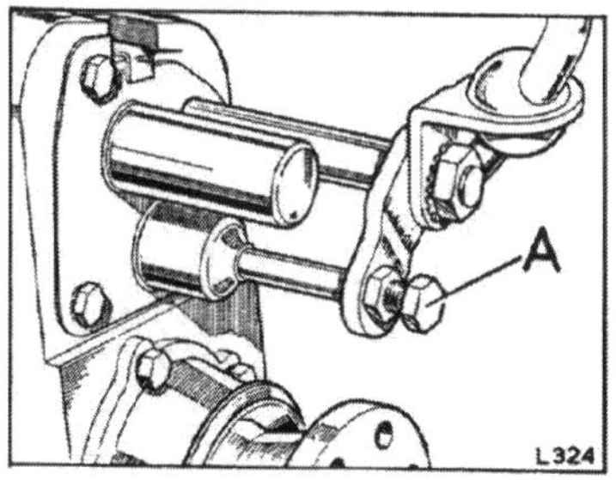

Fig. C1-75. Identification of all helical type transfer box

A—Adjuster for selector shaft stop

To dismantle

1. Remove the front output shaft housing, Operation C1-9, and the speedometer drive housing, Operation C1-5. Refer to separate instructions for overhaul details of these two items.

2. Remove the circlip retaining the front bearing outer race.

3. Place two ⅝ in. (16 mm) diameter distance pieces between the rear face of the low gear wheel and the transfer box.

4. Retaining the distance pieces in position, use a soft mallet to drive the shaft rearwards until the low gear wheel just abuts the distance pieces.

5. Insert a mild steel chisel between the bush for the high gear wheel and the front bearing and prize the bearing outward approximately ¼ in. (6 mm).

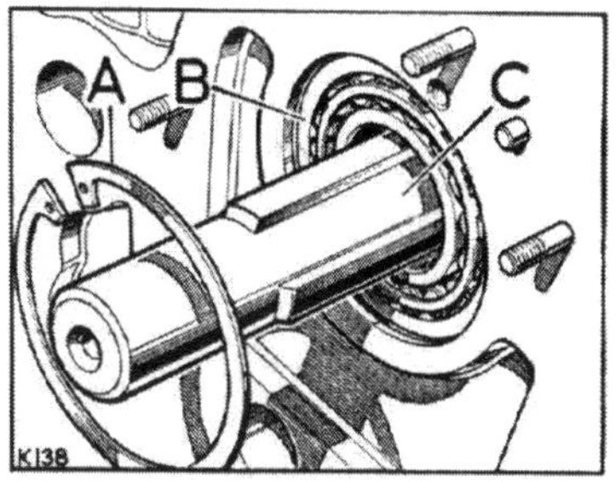

Fig. C1-76. Circlip for front bearing

A—Circlip
B—Front bearing
C—Output shaft

6. Part the change speed inner member and high gear wheel by hand and rotate the output shaft to locate the position of the shaft peg.

Fig. C1-77. Location of distance pieces

A—Distance pieces

Operations marked with an asterisk (*) can be carried out with the gearbox installed in the vehicle

GEARBOX

Section C—Land-Rover

Operation C1-8A—continued

7. Using a suitable piece of wire, locate the slot in the high gear wheel thrust washer over the peg in the output shaft.

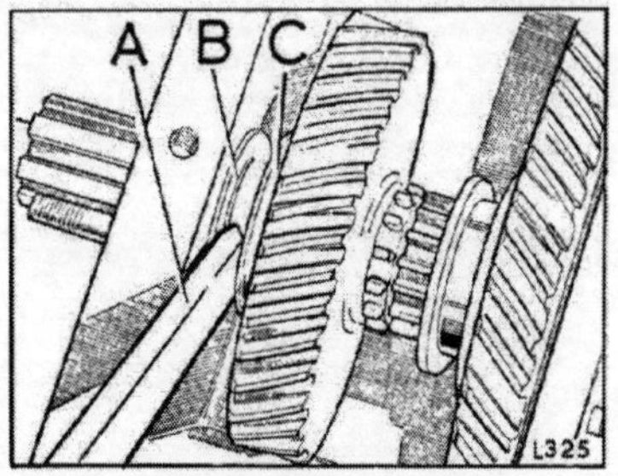

Fig. C1-78. Moving front bearing
A—Mild steel chisel
B—Front bearing
C—Bush for high gear wheel

Fig. C1-79. Locating the output shaft peg
A—Outer member for transfer change speed
B—Inner member for transfer change speed
C—Peg for output shaft
D—Thrust washer for high gear wheel

Note: The space shown between the change speed outer member and the high gear wheel has been exaggerated for clarity.

Operation C1-8A—continued

8. Retaining the distance pieces in position, use a soft-face mallet to drive the shaft rearwards until it can be withdrawn by hand complete with roller bearing, thrust washer and two locating pegs.

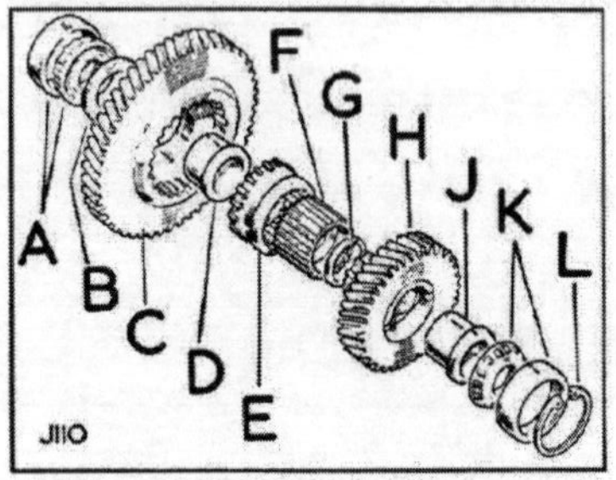

Note: If difficulty is experienced in carrying out items 4 to 7, it is permissible to ignore these items and proceed directly with item 8, but this will almost certainly sheer the locating pegs fitted in the output shaft, the sheered pegs must then be removed and new replacements fitted before assembly.

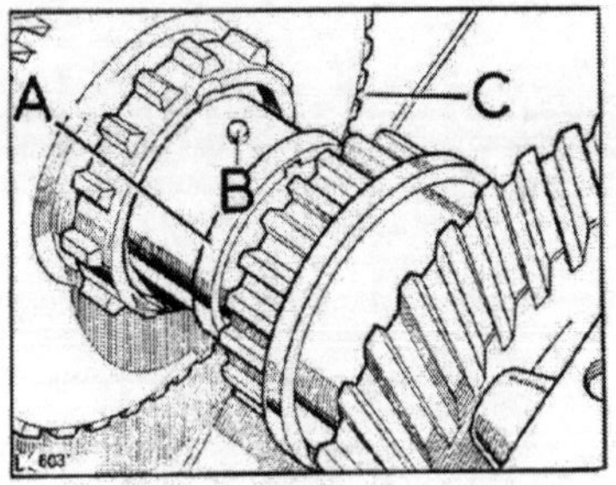

Fig. C1-80. Positioning thrust washer
A—Thrust washer for high gear wheel
B—Peg for output shaft
C—High gear wheel

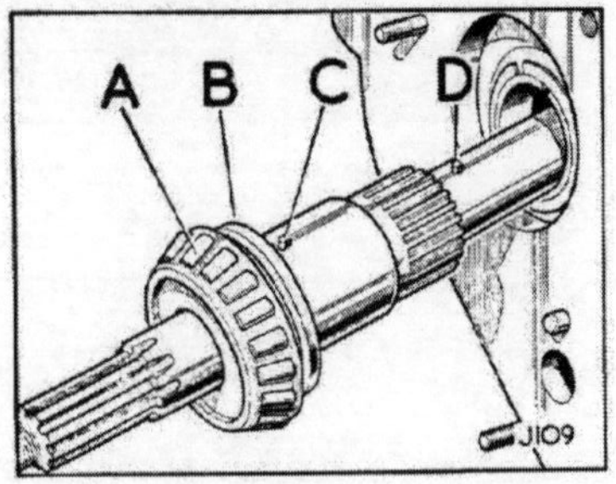

Fig. C1-81. Removing output shaft
A—Rear roller bearing
B—Thrust washer for low gear
C—Peg, outer, for output shaft
D—Peg, inner, for output shaft

Fig. C1-82. High and low speed gear assembly
A—Bearing for output shaft, rear
B—Thrust washer for low gear wheel
C—Low gear wheel
D—Bush for low gear wheel
E—Outer member for transfer change speed
F—Inner member for transfer change speed
G—Thrust washer for high gear wheel
H—High gear wheel
J—Bush for high gear wheel
K—Bearing for output shaft, front
L—Circlip fixing bearing

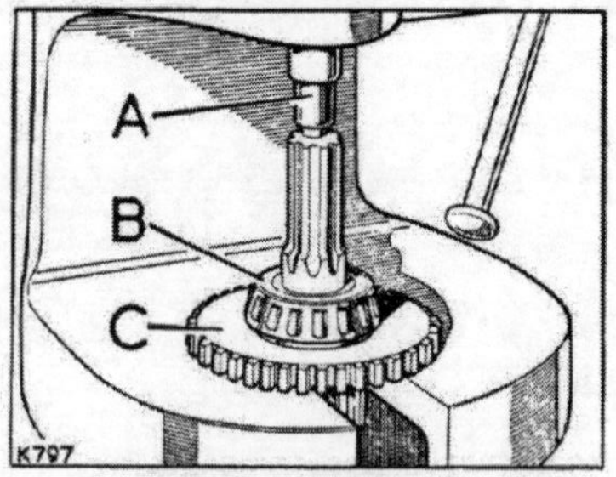

Operation C1-8A—continued

9. Withdraw the high and low speed gear assembly together with the front bearing from the transfer box.

10. Press the rear bearing and thrust washer from the output shaft.

   Note: The low speed gear is strong enough to be used as a press block for removal of the rear bearing.

11. Press the front bearing outer race from the transfer box.

12. Remove the circlip, retaining plate and roller bearing from the mainshaft rear bearing housing.

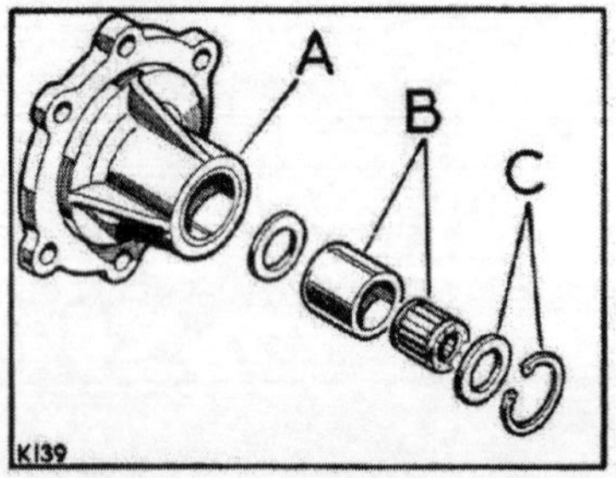

Fig. C1-83. Pressing off rear bearing
A—Protection cap
B—Rear bearing
C—Low gear wheel

Fig. C1-84. Rear bearing housing for gearbox mainshaft
A—Bearing housing
B—Roller bearing
C—Fixings, bearing to housing

Inspection

Renew any components which show obvious wear or damage.

The steel thrust washer for the high gear wheel and the two locating pegs in the output shaft must be in good condition. New locating pegs are 5/32 in. (3,96 mm) diameter by .656 in. (16,66 mm) long.

If necessary renew the oilite bush in the transfer casing, which carries the transfer selector shaft. This bush is an interference fit in the casing, and must be reamed to 1.148 in. (29,17 mm) after fitting.

Operation C1-8A—continued

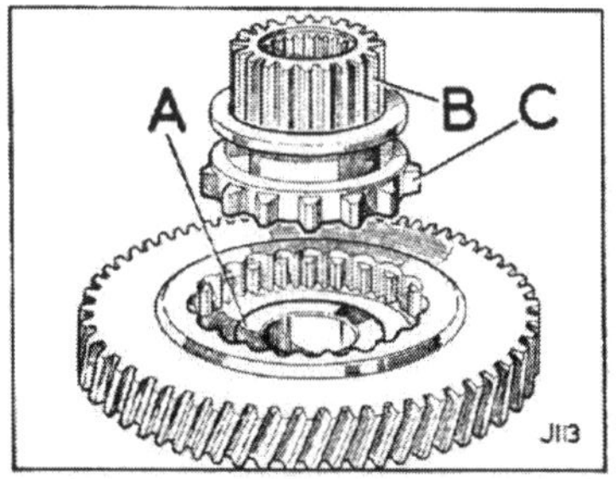

Pre-assembly check

1. Fit the steel thrust washer and the rear bearing on to the rear of the output shaft.
2. Fit the low gear wheel complete with bush on to the output shaft to abut with the steel thrust washer.

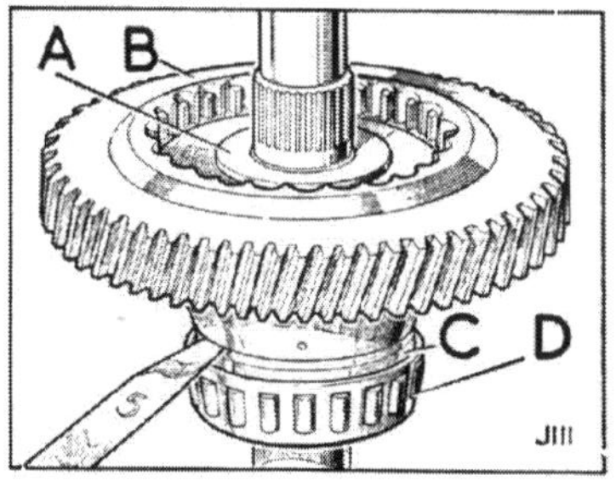

Fig. C1-85. Checking low gear end-float

A—Bush for low gear wheel
B—Low gear wheel
C—Steel thrust washer
D—Rear bearing for output shaft

3. Hold the bush in firm contact with the steel thrust washer and check the end-float of the low gear wheel, which must be .002 in. to .009 in. (0,05 mm to 0,22 mm).
4. Remove the low gear wheel from the shaft, and replace the centre bush. Fit the change speed inner member, the thrust washer for the high gear wheel and the high gear wheel complete with bush.
5. Hold the bush for the high gear wheel in firm contact with the thrust washer and check the end-float of the high gear wheel, which must be .005 in. to .022 in. (0,12 mm to 0,55 mm).
6. Excessive end-float on either gear wheel may be rectified by carefully rubbing down the end of the respective bush, using fine emery cloth and a face plate. Insufficient end-float can be rectified by fitting a new bush, followed by a further end-float check and rubbing down as necessary.

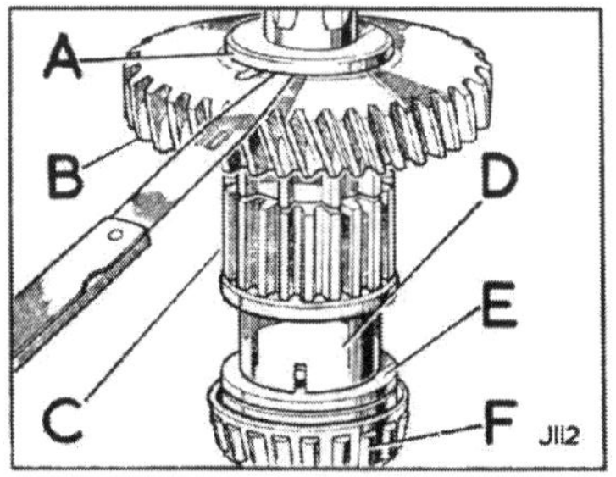

Fig. C1-86. Checking high gear end-float

A—Bush for high gear wheel
B—High gear wheel
C—Change speed inner member
D—Bush for low gear wheel
E—Steel thrust washer
F—Rear bearing for output shaft

7. Remove all the components from the shaft except the steel thrust washer and rear bearing inner member, ready to proceed with final assembly of the transfer box.

To assemble

1. The steel thrust washer, and the inner member of the rear roller bearing, should be in position on the output shaft. Ensure that the two steel location pegs are fitted to the shaft.
2. Fit the bush to the low speed gear wheel, in the correct direction.
3. Place the change speed inner and outer members against the thrust side of the bush. The recessed side of the inner member should be towards the bush, and the teeth on the outer member should be in mesh with the internal teeth of the gear wheel.
4. Place the high gear wheel, minus its centre bush, in position on the assembly with the dog teeth abutting the change speed outer member.
5. Lower the complete assembly into position in the transfer box, with the low speed gear wheel to the rear.

Fig. C1-87. Assembly of gear prior to fitting in box

A—Bush for low gear wheel
B—Change speed inner member
C—Change speed outer member

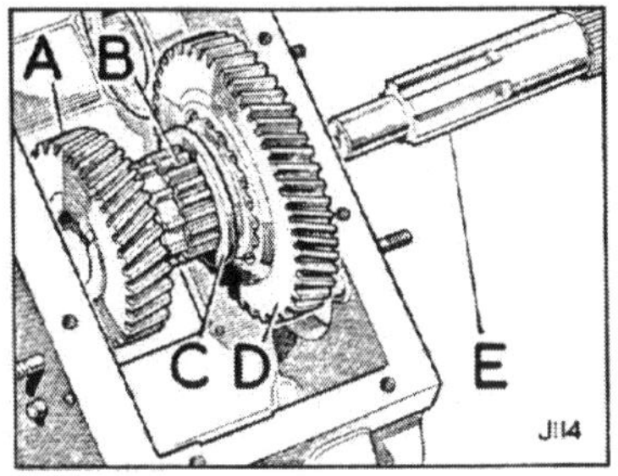

Fig. C1-88. Fitting output shaft to high and low gear assembly

A—High gear wheel
B—Change speed inner member
C—Change speed outer member
D—Low gear wheel
E—Output shaft

6. Carefully push the output shaft through the assembly and into position, from the rear, ensuring that the low speed gear wheel bush locates on the peg in the shaft, and that the splines of the change speed inner member are located on the shaft splines.
7. Slide the thrust washer for the high gear wheel over the front of the shaft and through the centre of the high speed gear, taking care to ensure that the washer slides over the peg and is located in the recess on the gear change inner member. Fit the bush through the high speed gear wheel and locate it also on the peg.
8. Turn the casing on its side with the rear face downwards and with the output shaft threaded end, resting on the bench, drift the front taper roller bearing on to the shaft. Take precautions to protect the thread against damage and make sure that the gears do not separate while the roller bearing is being fitted otherwise the bushes may become dislodged from the pegs on the shaft.

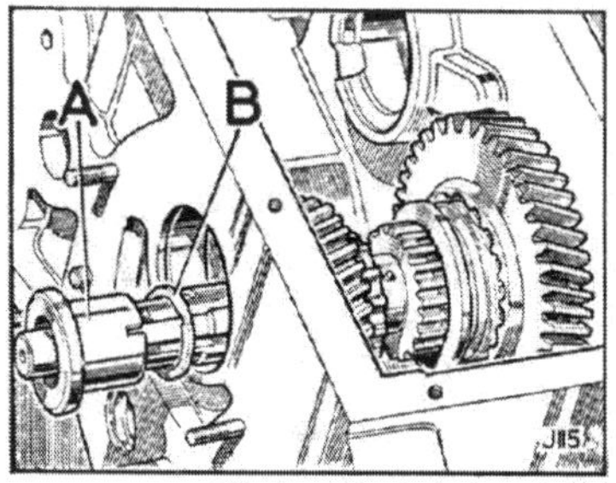

Fig. C1-89. Fitting thrust washer and bush to high gear wheel

A—Bush for high gear wheel
B—Thrust washer for high gear wheel

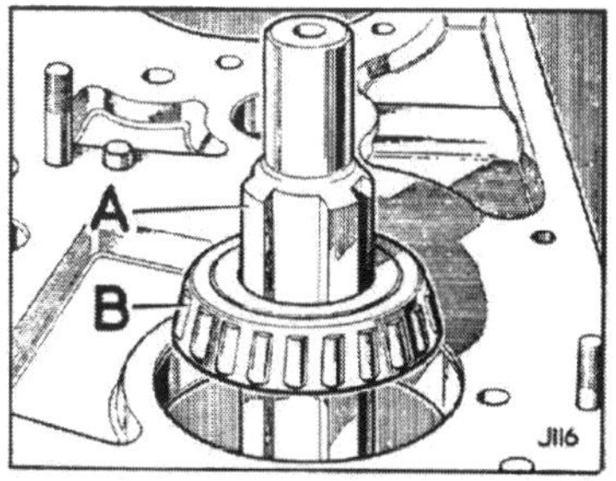

Fig. C1-90. Fitting front bearing

A—Output shaft
B—Front roller bearing

GEARBOX — Section C — Land-Rover

Operation C1-8A—continued

9. With the assembly held in the same position, drive the front bearing outer race into the housing and fit the circlip.

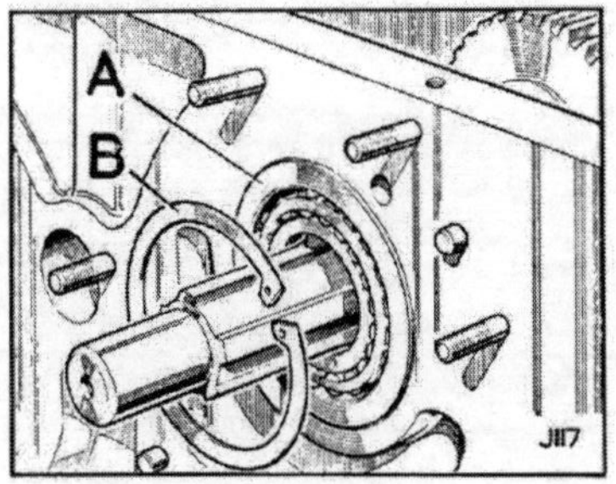

Fig. C1-91. Fitting front bearing outer race
A—Outer race for front bearing
B—Circlip for outer race

10. Fit the rear bearing outer race.

11. Using the protection cap, Part No. 243241, over the threaded end of the output shaft, drive the shaft forward until the front bearing is hard against the circlip. Then lightly tap the rear bearing outer race further in to remove all end-float from the output shaft without introducing pre-load.

12. Set the output shaft bearing pre-load as follows:

    (a) Fit the speedometer housing, without any shims, and loosely retain with nuts and spring washers.

    (b) Measure the rolling resistance of the output shaft, using a nylon cord attached to a spring balance. Coil the cord around the low gear wheel selector groove and note the measurement recorded on the spring balance required to rotate the output shaft after having overcome inertia. Ensure that the cord does not slip, giving a false reading.

    (c) Bearing pre-load is correct when a figure of 2 lbs to 4 lbs (0,9 kg to 1,8 kg) is recorded on the spring balance. Adjustment is made by tightening the speedometer housing securing nuts, progressively and evenly.

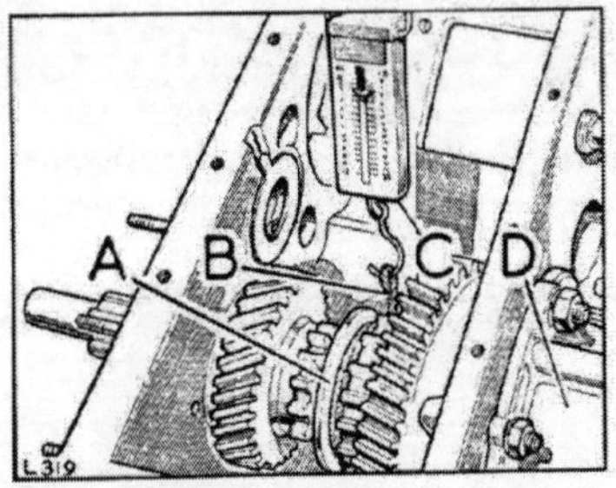

Fig. C1-92. Checking output shaft bearing pre-load
A—Low gear wheel selector groove
B—Nylon cord
C—Spring balance
D—Speedometer housing

    (d) When the bearing pre-load is correct, ensure that the clearance gap between the speedometer housing and the transfer box is evenly disposed, using feeler gauges. The measured clearance obtained, is equal to the thickness of shims required for subsequent assembly between the speedometer housing and transfer box to maintain correct bearing pre-load.

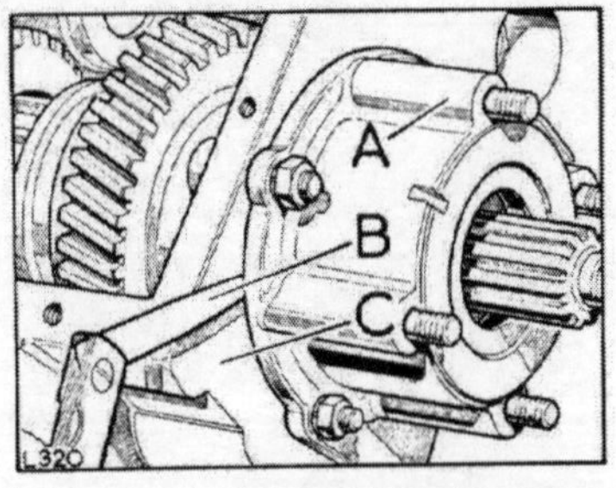

Fig. C1-93. Determining shims for speedometer housing
A—Speedometer housing
B—Feeler gauge
C—Transfer box

    (e) Withdraw the spring balance and nylon cord from the low gear wheel, and remove the speedometer housing from the transfer box.

13. Using the determined thickness of shims, fit the speedometer drive worm and housing.

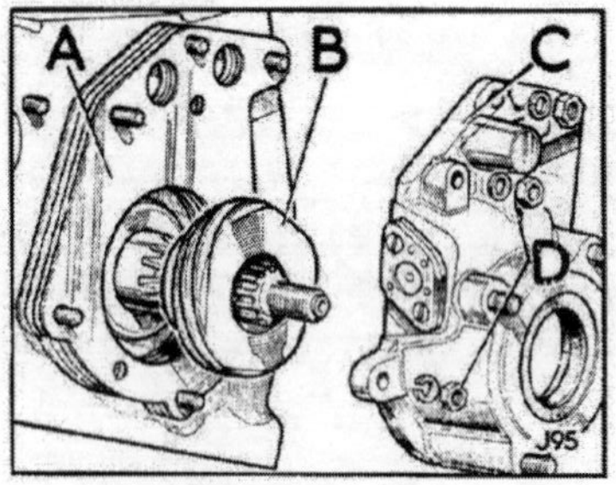

Fig. C1-94. Speedometer drive assembly
A—Shims
B—Drive worm
C—Speedometer drive housing
D—Fixings, speedometer housing

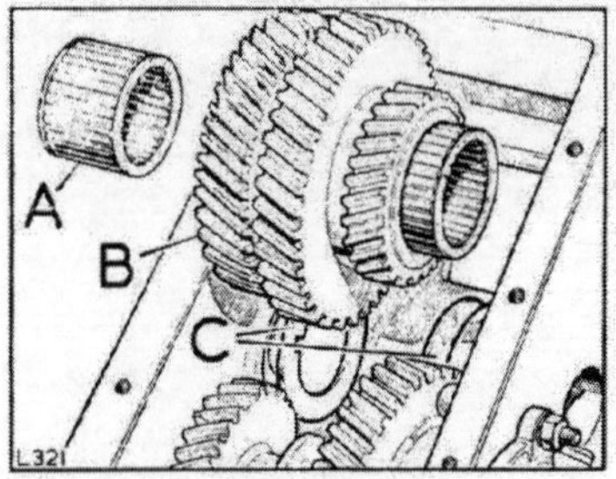

Fig. C1-95. Intermediate gear assembly
A—Roller bearings
B—Intermediate gear
C—Thrust washers

    (a) Place the two thrust washers for the intermediate gear in position in the transfer box and retain with a film of grease. The washers must be fitted with the bronze faces inward and located in the casing by their tabs.

    (b) Locate the intermediate gear, complete with roller bearings, in position in mesh with the high and low gear wheels.

    (c) Fit the intermediate shaft through the casing, thrust washers and intermediate gear, tapping it lightly home when the spigoted end of the shaft engages its location in the front of the casing. The shaft must be a light tap fit.

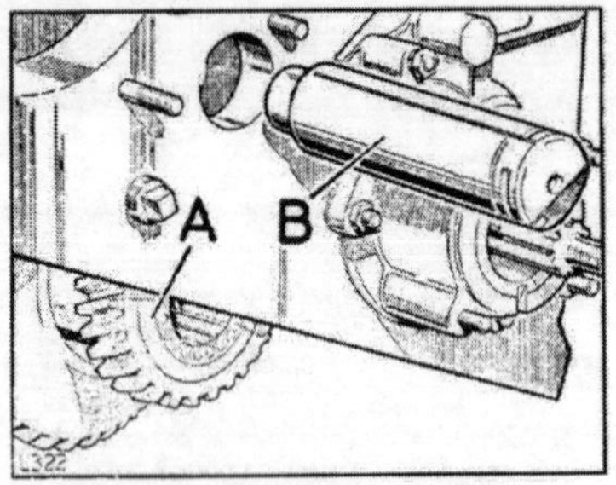

Fig. C1-96. Intermediate shaft assembly
A—Intermediate gear
B—Intermediate shaft

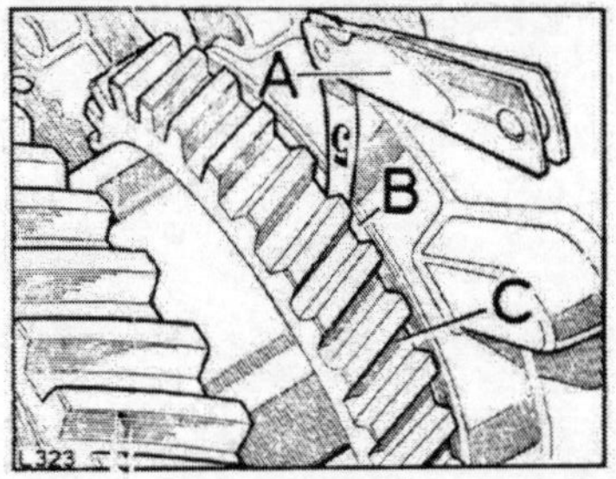

Fig. C1-97. Checking intermediate gear end-float
A—Feeler gauge
B—Thrust washer
C—Intermediate gear

14. Determine the intermediate gear end-float as follows:

Operation C1-8A—continued

(d) Using feeler gauges, check the end-float of the intermediate gear, this must be .004 in. to .008 in. (0,10 mm to 0,20 mm). Adjustment is made by grinding the steel face of the thrust washers to increase end-float, or by fitting shims, available in .010 in. (0,25 mm) thickness, between the thrust washers and the casing to reduce end-float.

(e) When the intermediate gear end-float correct, remove the intermediate shaft and gear, and place aside for subsequent assembly after the transfer box has been fitted to the main gearbox.

15. Reassemble the rear bearing housing and the output drive flange by reversing the removal procedure.

16. Adjust the transfer travel stop after fitting the front output shaft housing to the transfer box, see Operation C1-9.

*Front output shaft housing, remove and refit—Operation C1-9

(For overhaul instructions, Operation C1-10 refers)

Workshop hand tools:

Spanner sizes: 7/16 in. open end, 1/4 in. BSF, 5/16 in. BSF, 3/8 in. BSF socket

To remove

1. Remove the front floor. Operation A1-4.
2. Remove the seat base. Operation C1-1.
3. Drain the gearbox lubricating oil. Operation C1-2.
4. Remove the transmission brake. Operation C1-4.
5. Remove the transfer box. Operation C1-7.
6. Remove the transfer gear selector shaft plunger.
7. Remove the top cover from the transfer box.
8. Remove the pinch bolt from the transfer selector fork.
9. Remove the front output shaft housing from the transfer box, taking care to catch the four wheel drive locking dog which will be released.
10. Withdraw the loose selector fork from the transfer box.

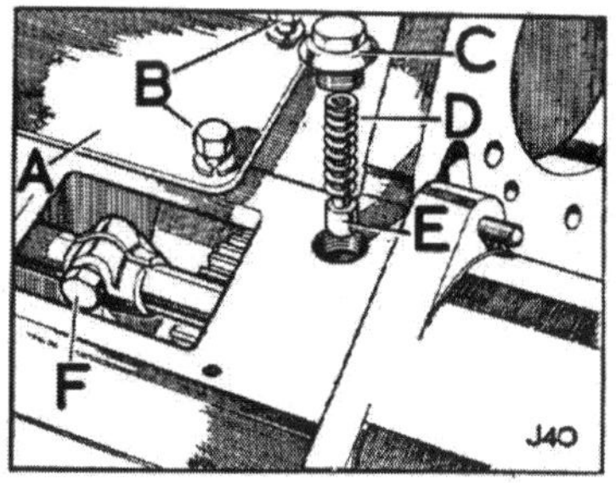

Fig. C1-98. Transfer gear selector

A—Top cover, transfer box
B—Fixings, top cover
C—Plug for plunger
D—Spring for plunger
E—Plunger, transfer selector shaft
F—Pinch bolt securing selector fork

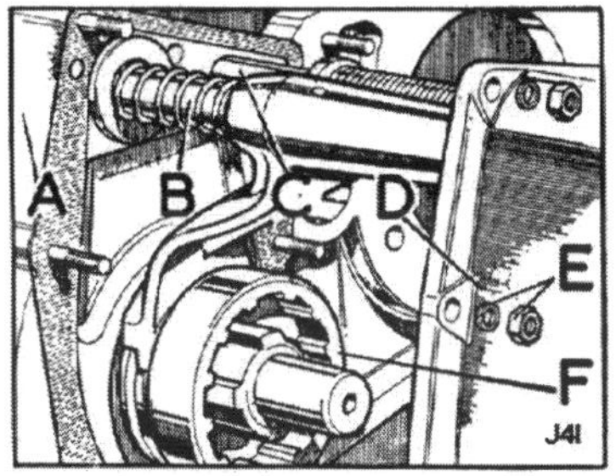

To refit

If the selector shafts have been removed, refer to Operation C1-10 for refitting procedure.

1. Place the transfer gear selector fork in position, with the threaded side of the pinch bolt hole towards the centre of the transfer box.
2. Smear both sides of the joint washer with a general purpose grease and place in position on the transfer box.
3. Offer the output shaft housing to the transfer box, carefully locating the transfer gear selector shaft through the selector fork.

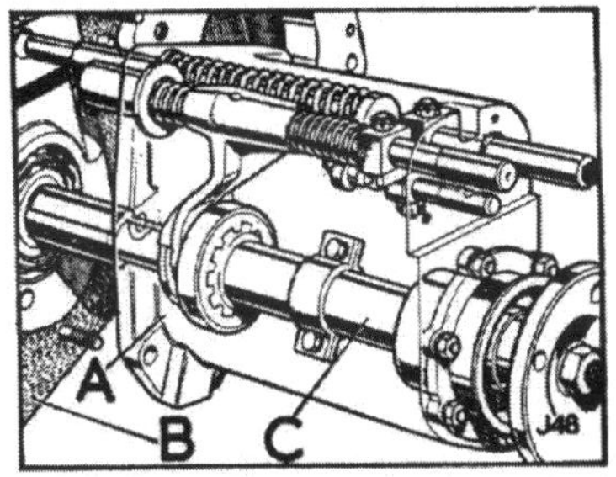

Fig. C1-99. Fixings for front output shaft housing

A—Transfer box
B—Selector shaft and fork, four wheel drive
C—Selector shaft and fork, transfer gear
D—Front output shaft housing
E—Fixings (7 off), front output shaft housing to transfer box
F—Locking dog, four wheel drive

Fig. C1-100. Offering front output shaft housing to transfer box

A—Transfer box
B—Joint washer
C—Front output shaft housing assembly

Operations marked with an asterisk (*) can be carried out with the gearbox installed in the vehicle

GEARBOX

Operation C1-9—continued

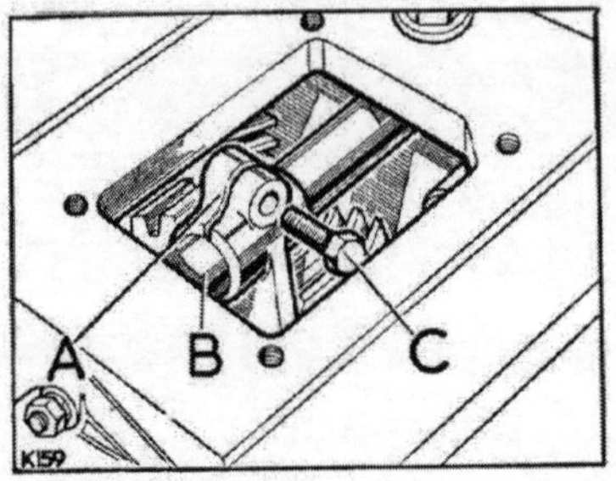

Fig. C1-101. Transfer gear selector fork assembly
A—Selector fork
B—Selector shaft
C—Pinch bolt

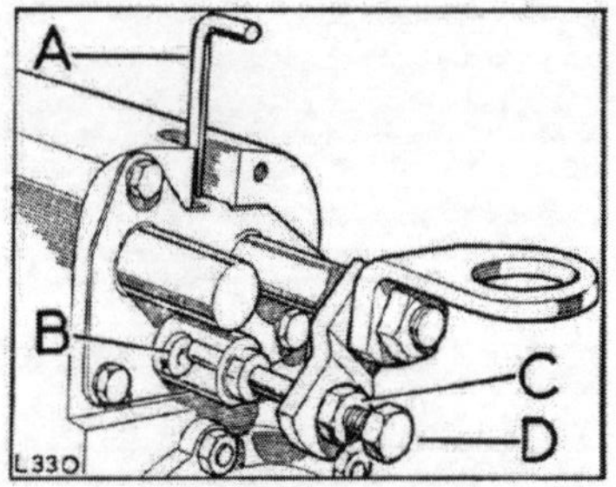

4. Complete the refitting by reversing the removal procedure. Ensure that the selector fork pinch bolt engages the groove in the selector shaft.

5. If the transfer box is of the all helical type, see Operation C1-8A, adjust the transfer travel stop as follows:
   Engage four wheel drive, low ratio, and check the fit of the four wheel drive locking pin in the pivot shaft. The pin must be an easy slide fit, if necessary, adjust the stop bolt to obtain this condition, then tighten the locknut to secure the stop bolt.

Fig. C1-102. Adjusting the transfer travel stop
A—Four wheel drive locking pin
B—Pivot shaft
C—Locknut
D—Adjuster bolt

6. Check and replenish the gearbox lubricating oil. Operation C1-2.

7. Adjust the four wheel drive control lever. Operation A1-4.

---

*Front output shaft housing, overhaul—Operation C1-10

(For removal and refitting instructions, Operation C1-9 refers)

Workshop hand tools:
Spanner sizes: 7/16 in. BSF, 3/8 in. BSF open end, 3/8 in. BSF socket. Screwdriver (medium), Mallet

To dismantle
To dismantle housing

1. Remove the link from the transfer gear selector shaft.
2. Remove the four wheel drive control lever.

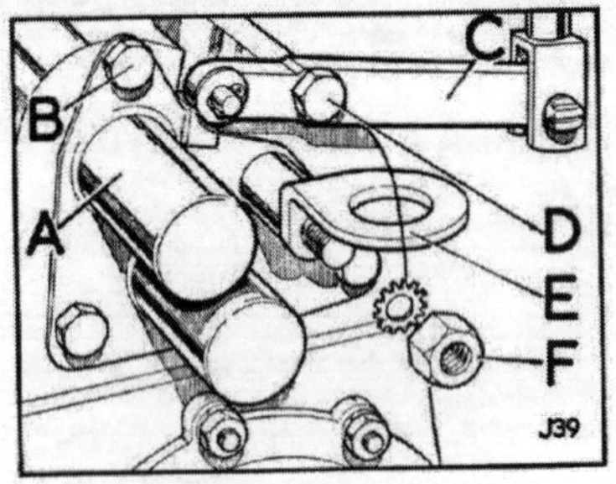

Fig. C1-103. Gear selector controls
A—Dust cover, selector shafts
B—Cover fixings
C—Selector lever, four wheel drive
D—Lever fixings
E—Link, transfer gear lever
F—Link fixings

3. Remove the selector shaft dust cover.
4. Withdraw the selector shaft assemblies and the four wheel drive locking dog from the housing.

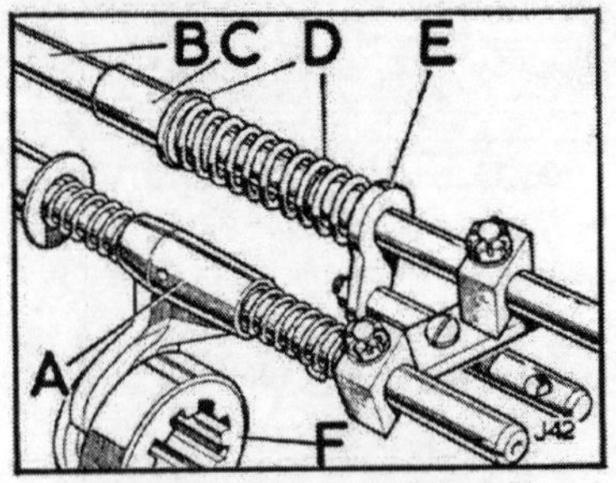

Fig. C1-104. Selector shaft assembly
A—Selector shaft, four wheel drive
B—Selector shaft, transfer gear
C—Distance tube
D—Locating bush and spring for selector fork
E—Gearchange pivot shaft assembly
F—Locking dog, four wheel drive

5. Remove the flange from the front output shaft.
6. Remove the oil seal retainer and gasket and press out the oil seal.

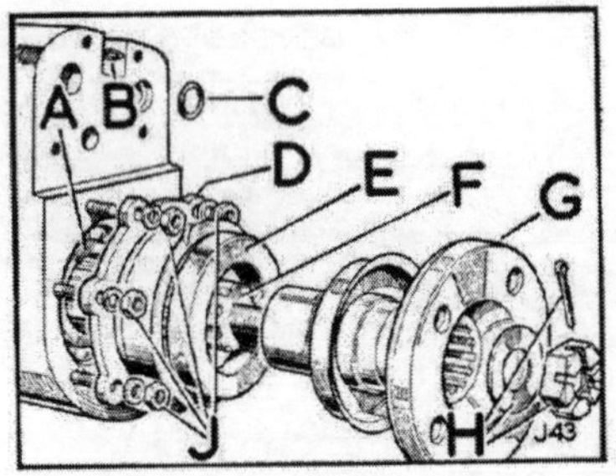

Fig. C1-105. Oil seal and flange for front output shaft
A—Bearing for output shaft
B—Sealing ring for four wheel drive locking pin
C—Sealing ring for transfer gear selector shaft
D—Retainer for oil seal
E—Oil seal
F—Output shaft
G—Flange for output shaft
H—Fixings, output flange
J—Fixings, oil seal retainer

7. Remove the front output shaft from the housing then press out the bearing.
8. Remove the sealing rings for the four wheel drive locking pin and the transfer gear shaft.

To dismantle four wheel drive selector shaft

9. Remove block from the selector shaft and withdraw the fork and springs.

Operations marked with an asterisk (*) can be carried out with the gearbox installed in the vehicle

GEARBOX

Operation C1-10—continued

13. Remove the coupling from the pivot shaft.

To dismantle front output shaft

14. Remove the two self-locking nuts and lift the two halves of the oil thrower from the shaft.

Inspection

Renew any components which show obvious wear or damage. Examine the bush in the four wheel drive control lever and replace if necessary.

Examine the four wheel drive selector fork and bushes, and renew as necessary. New bushes must be pressed flush with the end faces of the fork boss, and reamed in position to .6255 in. $\pm$ .0005 in. (15,887 mm $\pm$ 0,012 mm) diameter, and must be a sliding fit on the selector shaft.

Check the four wheel drive selector shaft springs, the free length should be 2.75 in. (69,8 mm).

Check the transfer gear selector shaft spring, the free length should be 7.156 in. (181,76 mm).

Examine the bush in the rear end of the front output shaft. The bush must be a sliding fit on the front end of the transfer box output shaft and must be firmly retained in its bore. If bush replacement is necessary, press the new bush flush with the end of the shaft and ream in position to .8755 in. $\pm$ .0005 in (22,2 mm $\pm$ 0,013 mm) diameter.

To assemble front output shaft

1. Fit the oil thrower to the front output shaft.

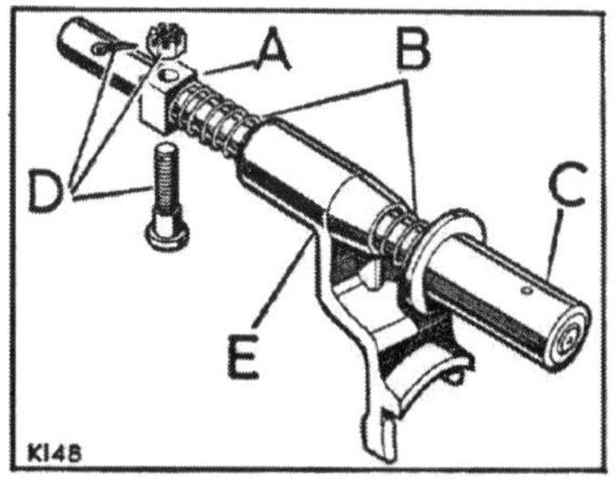

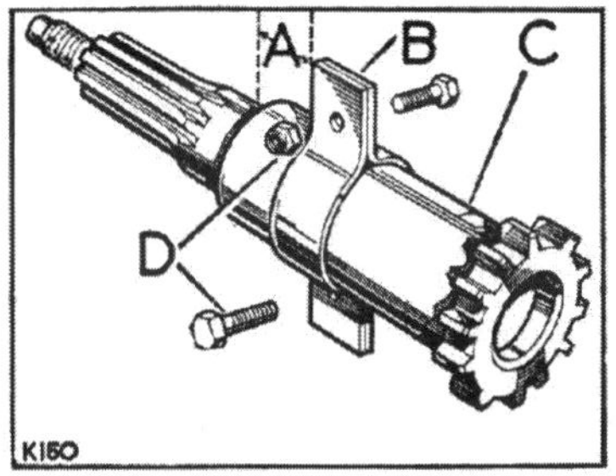

Fig. C1-106. Four wheel drive selector shaft

A—Block
B—Springs
C—Selector shaft
D—Fixings for block
E—Selector fork

To dismantle transfer gear selector shaft

10. Slide the distance tube, bush, spring and pivot shaft assembly from the selector shaft.
11. Remove the block.
12. Remove the connector from the pivot shaft.

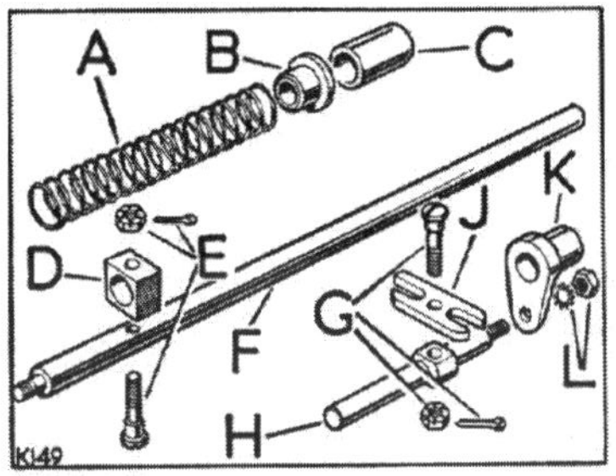

Fig. C1-107. Transfer gear selector shaft

A—Spring
B—Bush, spring location
C—Distance tube
D—Block
E—Fixings for block
F—Selector shaft
G—Fixings for coupling
H—Pivot shaft
J—Coupling, selector shafts
K—Connector, pivot shaft to selector shaft
L—Fixings, connector to pivot shaft

Fig. C1-108. Oil thrower location

A—1 inch $\pm \frac{1}{32}$ in. (25,4 mm $\pm$ 0,75 mm)
B—Oil thrower
C—Front output shaft
D—Fixings oil thrower

Operation C1-10—continued

To assemble transfer gear selector shaft

2. Fit the connector to the pivot shaft noting the relationship of the countersink in the hole at the other end of the shaft. Do not fully tighten the fixings at this stage.
3. Fit the coupling to the pivot shaft locating the extended arm correctly, as illustrated.

Fig. C1-109. Pivot shaft assembly

A—Nut and shakeproof washer
B—Connector
C—Extended arm of coupling
D—Special screw
E—Castle nut and split pin
F—Pivot shaft

4. Fit the block to the transfer gear selector shaft locating the fixings so that the nut and split pin are on the same side of the shaft as the plunger grooves.

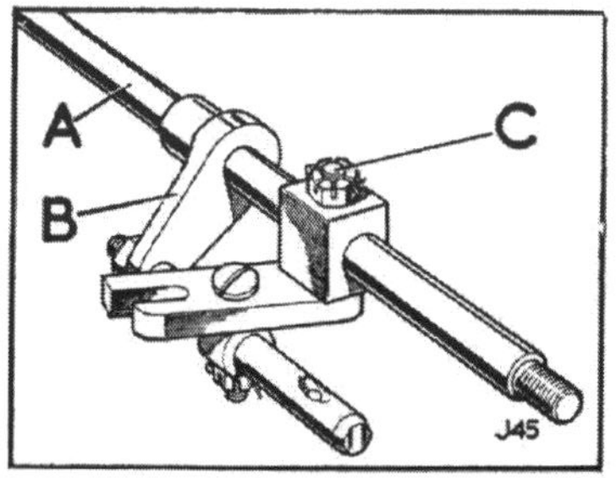

Fig. C1-110. Assembly of selector and pivot shafts

A—Transfer selector shaft
B—Connector
C—Special screw, securing block

5. Locate the pivot shaft assembly in position on the transfer gear selector shaft engaging the coupling with the special screw.
6. Fit the spring, locating bush and distance tube on to the selector shaft.

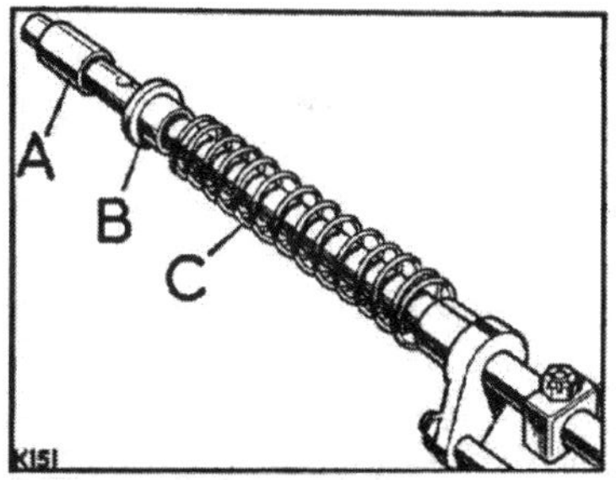

Fig. C1-111. Transfer gear selector shaft assembly

A—Distance tube
B—Bush, spring location
C—Spring

To assemble four wheel drive selector shaft

7. Fit the springs and selector fork to the shaft. Note that the two springs are identical and are interchangeable.

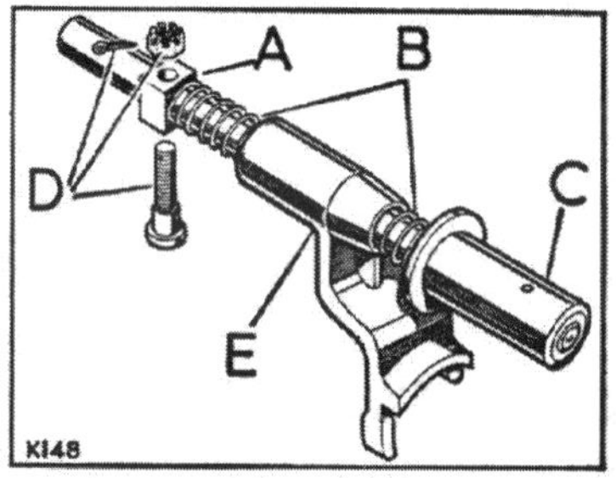

Fig. C1-112. Four wheel drive selector shaft assembly

A—Block
B—Springs
C—Selector shaft
D—Fixings for block
E—Selector fork

8. Fit the block to the selector shaft.

GEARBOX

Operation C1-10—continued

To assemble housing

9. Fit the oil seal for the front output shaft, lipped side inward, into the retainer, with a smear of sealant on the seal outside diameter.

10. Press the bearing into the housing.

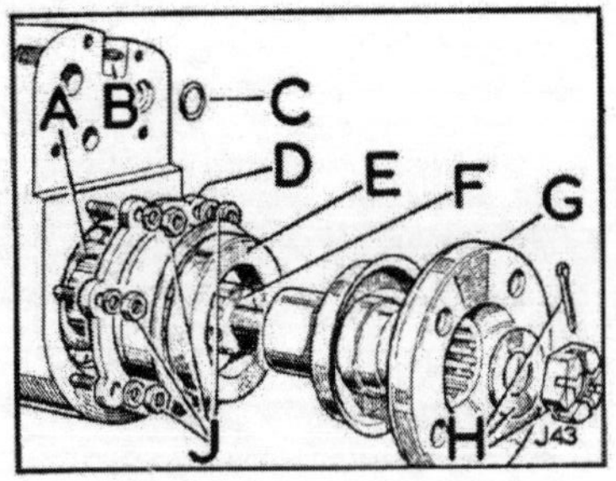

Fig. C1-113. Oil seal and flange for front output shaft

A—Bearing for output shaft
B—Sealing ring, four wheel drive locking pin
C—Sealing ring, transfer gear selector shaft
D—Retainer for oil seal
E—Oil seal
F—Output shaft
G—Flange for output shaft
H—Fixings, output flange
J—Fixings, oil seal retainer

11. Smear both sides of the joint washer with general purpose grease, and fit the oil seal retainer and joint washer to the housing.

12. Fit the front output shaft.

13. If the mud shield has been removed, refit it, dished side first, to the output flange. Fit the flange to the output shaft and tighten the securing nut to a torque figure of 85 lb ft (11.75 mkg).

Pre-alignment of selector shafts

14. Locate the two selector shafts together by engaging the coupling with the special screws.

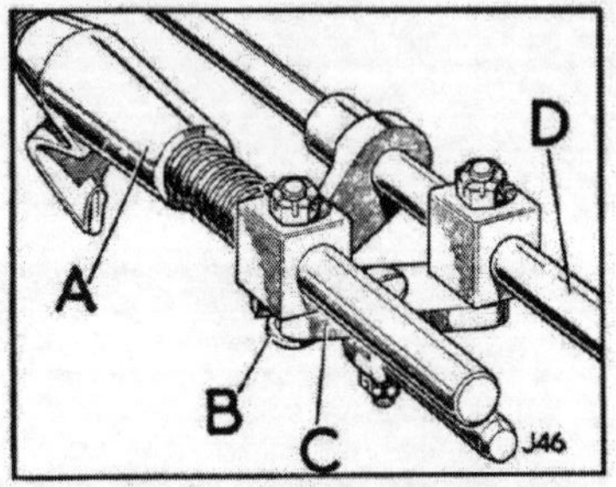

Fig. C1-114. Assembly of selector shafts

A—Four wheel drive selector shaft
B—Special screw
C—Coupling
D—Transfer gear selector shaft

15. Locate the selector shaft assembly into the front face of the output shaft housing, and fit the four wheel drive locking pin, engaging it in the countersunk hole in the pivot shaft. This will ensure correct radial alignment of the pivot shaft to the connector.

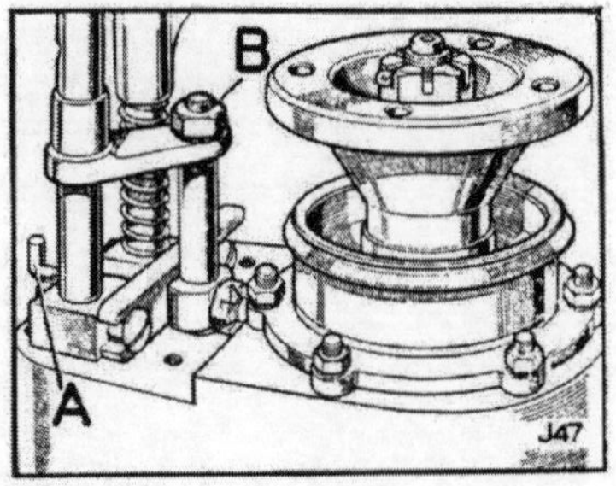

Fig. C1-115. Pre-alignment of selector shafts

A—Four wheel drive locking pin
B—Nut fixing connector to pivot shaft

16. Fully tighten the nut to secure the connector to the pivot shaft.

Operation C1-10—continued

17. Remove the locking pin and withdraw the selector shafts as one unit, then without disturbing their alignment, engage them into their correct location in the output shaft housing, while at the same time fitting the four wheel drive locking dog over the output shaft and into the selector fork.

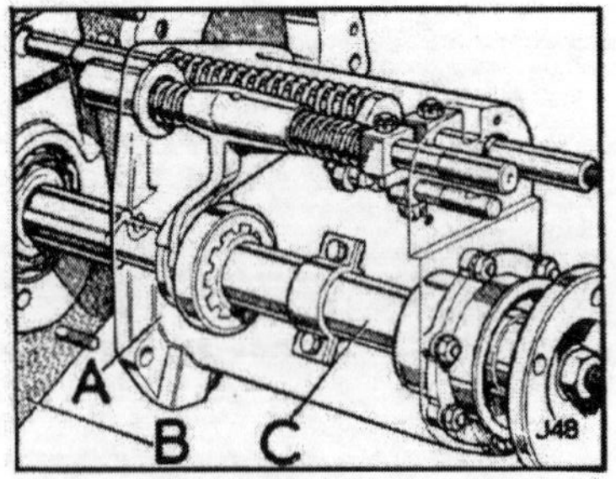

Fig. C1-116. Front output shaft housing

A—Transfer box
B—Joint washer
C—Front output shaft housing assembly

Note: If convenient, it will be advantageous at this stage to fit the front output shaft housing to the transfer box. Operation C1-9.

18. Fit the sealing rings for the transfer gear selector shaft and the four wheel drive locking pin.

19. Fit the selector shaft dust cover, using Bostik sealant on the joint face.

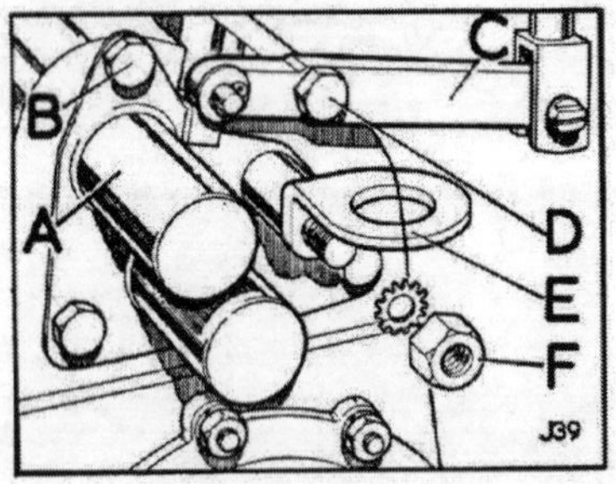

Fig. C1-117. Gear selector controls

A—Dust cover, selector shafts
B—Cover fixings
C—Selector lever, four wheel drive
D—Lever fixings
E—Link, transfer gear lever
F—Link fixings

20. Fit the link to the selector shaft, but do not fully tighten the fixing at this stage.

21. Fit the four wheel drive locking pin and control lever.

GEARBOX

*Main gear change lever, remove and refit—Operation C1-11

(For overhaul instructions, Operation C1-12 refers)

Workshop hand tools:
Spanner sizes: ½ in. BSF, $\frac{7}{16}$ in. AF open end

To remove

1. Remove the front floor complete. Operation A1-4.
2. Remove the main gear change lever complete.
3. To prevent loss, lift off the top cover plate and rubber seal from the bell housing.

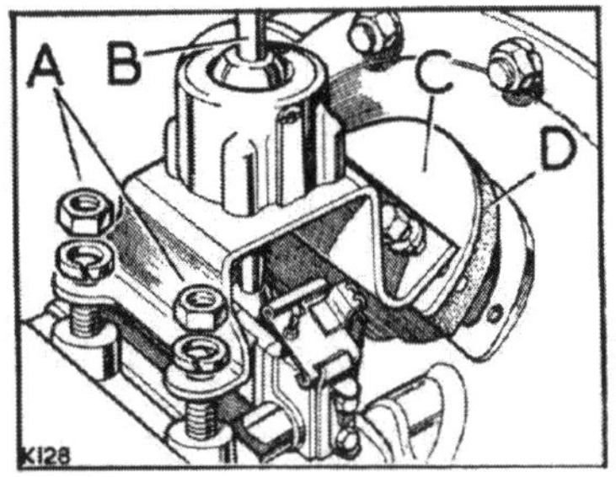

Fig. C1-118. Main gear change lever mounting
A—Fixings, main gear change lever
B—Main gear change lever
C—Top cover plate, bell housing
D—Rubber seal, top cover plate

To refit

Reverse the removal procedure, noting that a retaining clip for the speedometer cable locates under the head of the front left hand gear change lever securing bolt.

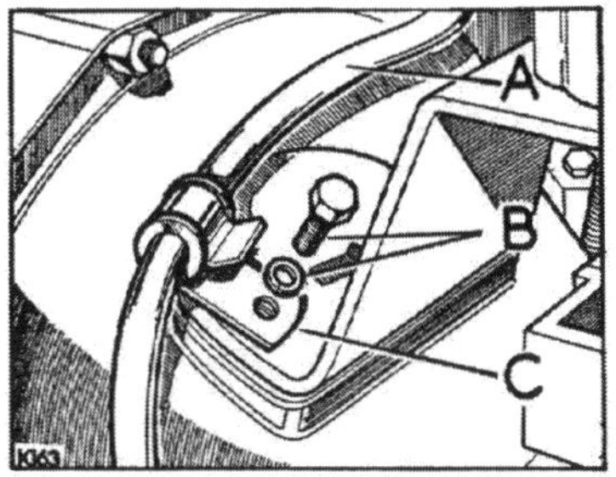

Fig. C1-119. Clip for speedometer cable
A—Speedometer cable
B—Fixing, cable clip
C—Clip for cable

Adjust the four wheel drive control lever, Operation A1-4.

---

*Main gear change lever, overhaul—Operation C1-12

(For removal and refitting instructions, Operation C1-11 refers)

Workshop hand tools:
Spanner sizes: ½ in. Whitworth socket, ⅜ in. BSF open end
Circlip pliers, Screwdriver (small), Mallet

To dismantle

1. Remove the lever housing from the mounting plate.

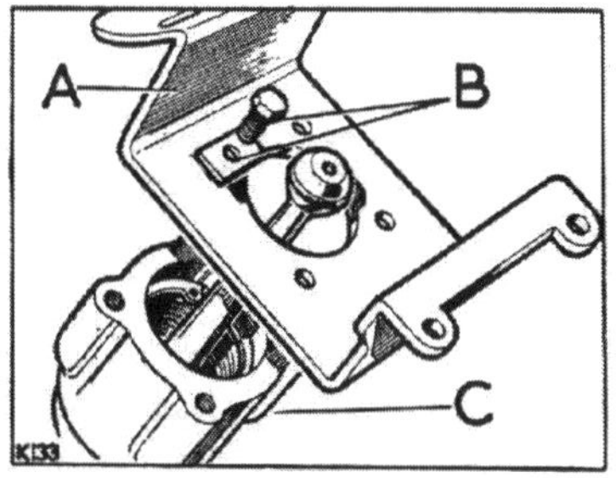

Fig. C1-120. Mounting for gear change lever
A—Mounting plate
B—Fixings, lever housing to mounting plate
C—Lever housing

2. Remove the circlip from the lever housing and withdraw the retaining plate, spring, spherical seat and gear change lever.

3. Remove the lever ball locating pin from the housing.

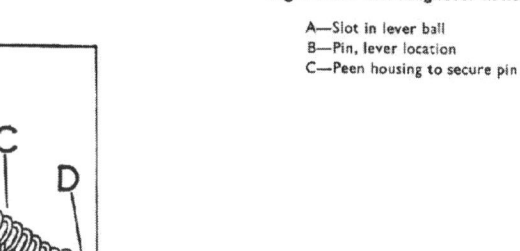

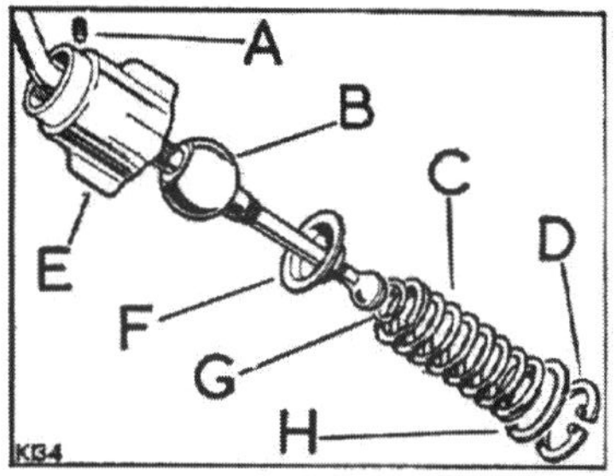

Fig. C1-121. Housing for gear change lever
A—Pin, locating lever ball
B—Gear change lever
C—Spring
D—Circlip
E—Housing for lever
F—Spherical seat
G—Rubber 'O' ring
H—Retaining plate

Inspection

Examine the components visually and renew any that show obvious wear or damage.

To assemble

Reverse the dismantling procedure.

When fitting the lever locating pin, ensure it engages the slot in the lever ball, then secure by peening.

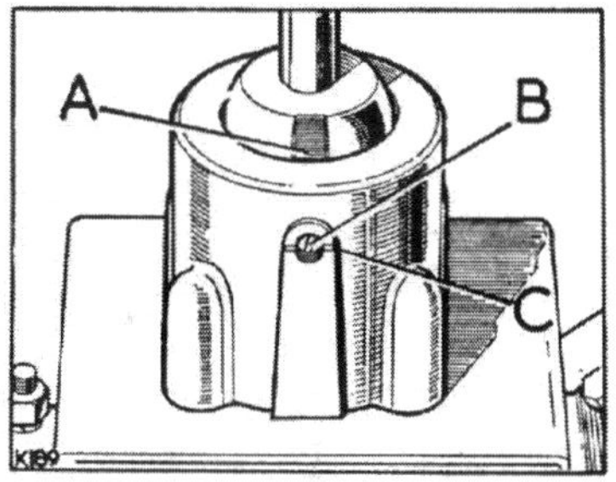

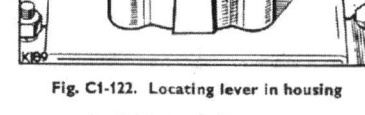

Fig. C1-122. Locating lever in housing
A—Slot in lever ball
B—Pin, lever location
C—Peen housing to secure pin

Operations marked with an asterisk (*) can be carried out with the gearbox installed in the vehicle

GEARBOX   Section C—Land-Rover

*Reverse stop main gear change lever, remove, refit and adjust—Operation C1-13

Workshop hand tools:
Spanner size: 2 BA open end
Screwdriver (small)

To remove
1. Remove the front floor. Operation A1-4.
2. Remove the hinge adjuster.

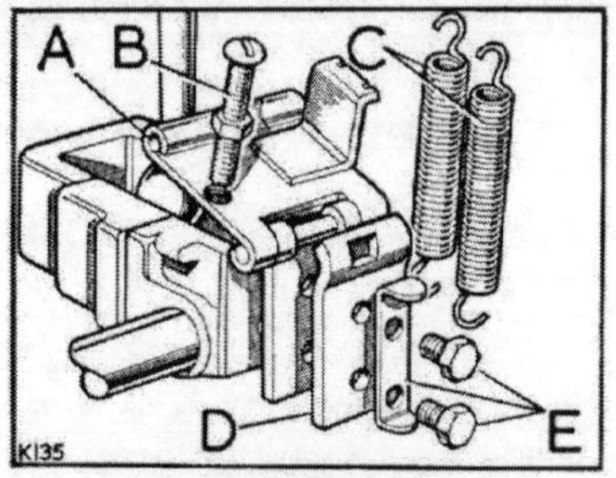

To adjust
1. Release the fixings and slide the reverse stop inspection cover up the four wheel drive selector lever.

   Note: If the gear box cover does not incorporate an inspection cover, then the adjustment must be carried out before the gearbox cover is fitted.

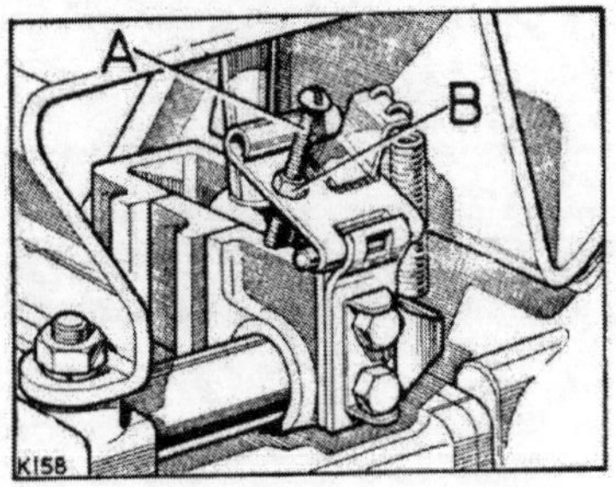

2. Adjust the screw so that the hinge rides easily up the gear lever when reverse gear is selected, while at the same time appreciable resistance is felt on moving the gear lever to the reverse position.

3. Ensure that 1st gear engages correctly. If there is any tendency to simultaneously engage reverse gear, readjust the reverse stop.

Fig. C1-123. Reverse stop assembly

A—Hinge, reverse stop
B—Adjuster, hinge
C—Springs, reverse stop
D—Bracket for springs
E—Fixings, hinge and bracket to selector shaft

Fig. C1-124. Adjusting the reserving stop
A—Adjusting screw   B—Locknut

3. Remove the hinge and bracket from the reverse selector shaft.
4. Detach the two springs.

To refit
Reverse the removal procedure. Adjust the reverse stop before fitting the front floor.

Adjust the four wheel drive control lever. Operation A1-4.

Section C—Land-Rover   GEARBOX

Clutch withdrawal unit, remove and refit—Operation C1-14

(For overhaul Instructions, Operation C1-15 refers)

Workshop hand tools:
Spanner sizes: ½ in. BSF, 5/16 in. BSF sockets
Pliers

To remove
1. Remove the front floor. Operation A1-4.
2. Remove the seat base. Operation C1-1.
3. Drain the gearbox lubricating oil. Operation C1-2.
4. Remove the gearbox assembly complete. Operation C1-3.
5. Remove the cross-shaft connecting tube from the clutch withdrawal unit.

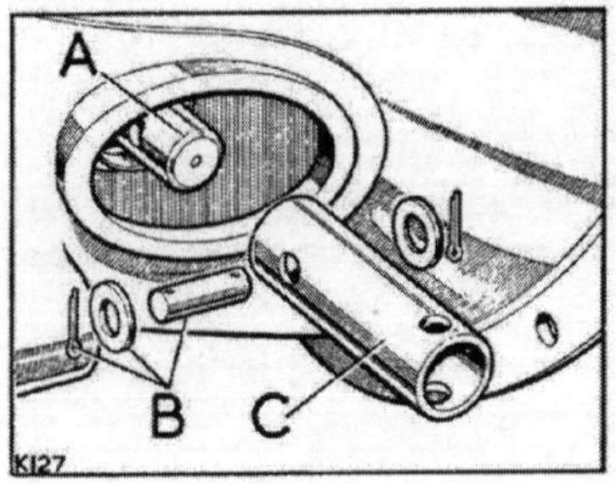

Fig. C1-125. Connecting tube for clutch cross-shaft
A—Clutch withdrawal unit
B—Fixings, connecting tube to clutch withdrawal unit
C—Connecting tube

6. Remove the clutch withdrawal unit.

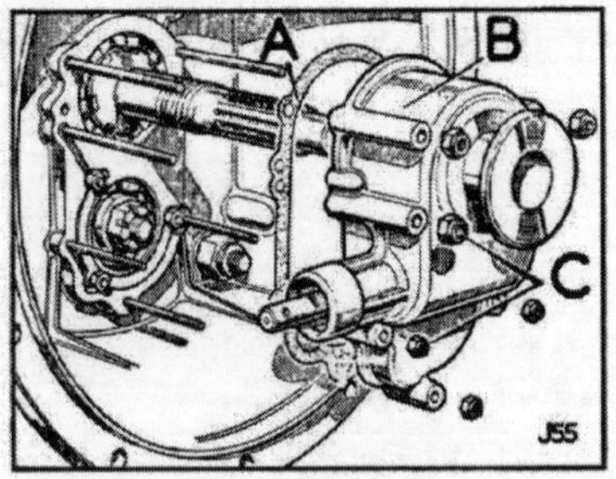

Fig. C1-126. Clutch withdrawal unit
A—Joint washer, clutch withdrawal unit to bell housing
B—Clutch withdrawal unit
C—Fixings, clutch withdrawal unit to bell housing

To refit
1. Smear both sides of the joint washer with a general purpose grease and place in position on the bell housing.
2. Reverse the removal procedure, using 'Bostik' adhesive to attach the rubber grommet to the clutch withdrawal unit and the bell housing. Tighten the ¼ in. BSF nuts to a torque figure of 10 lb ft (1,4 mkg). Tighten the 7/16 in. BSF nuts to a torque figure of 15 lb ft (2,0 mkg).

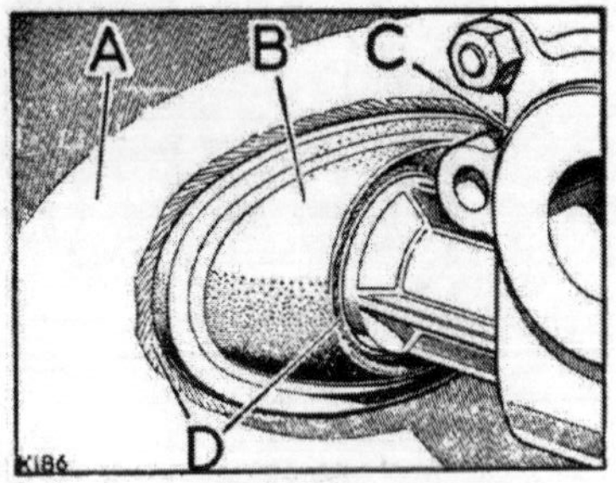

Fig. C1-127. Grommet for clutch withdrawal unit
A—Bell housing
B—Rubber grommet
C—Clutch withdrawal unit
D—Adhere in position

3. If necessary, bleed the clutch system and adjust the pedal movement. See Section B.
4. Check, and if necessary, replenish the gearbox lubricating oil. Operation C1-2.
5. Adjust the four wheel drive control lever. Operation A1-4.

*Operations marked with an asterisk (*) can be carried out with the gearbox installed In the vehicle

GEARBOX

Clutch withdrawal unit, overhaul—Operation C1-15

(For removal and refitting instructions, Operation C1-14 refers)

Workshop hand tools:
Spanner sizes: ⅜ in BSF open end
Mallet

To dismantle

1. Remove the cross-shaft cover plate.
2. Drive out the cross-shaft from right to left, this will also release the operating fork, thrust washer and thrust spring.
3. Press the withdrawal sleeve from the bearing.
4. Remove the cross-shaft oil seal.
5. Press out the cross-shaft bushes and the withdrawal sleeve bush.

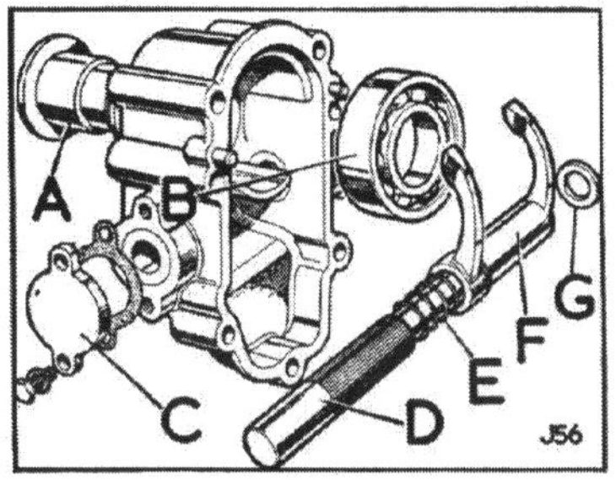

Inspection

Renew any components which show obvious wear or damage.

All bushes must be a press fit in the housing and a sliding fit on the cross-shaft or withdrawal sleeve.

Ensure that the oil scroll machined on the primary pinion is not damaged, a faulty scroll may result in oil reaching the clutch, causing slip.

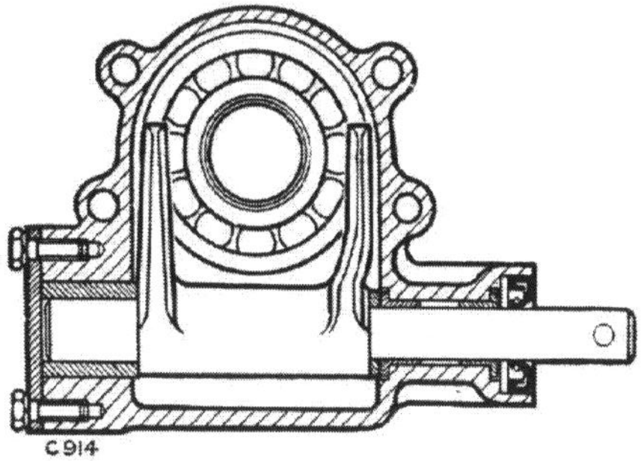

Fig. C1-128. Clutch withdrawal unit

A—Clutch withdrawal sleeve
B—Thrust bearing for withdrawal sleeve
C—Cover plate for cross-shaft
D—Cross-shaft
E—Spring for operating fork
F—Operating fork
G—Thrust washer for cross-shaft

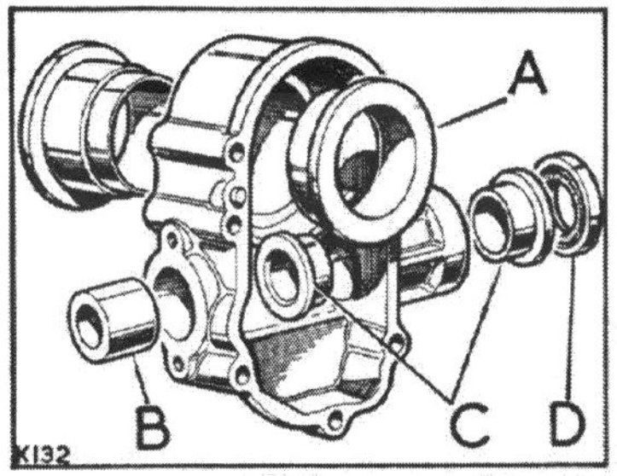

Fig. C1-129. Bushes and oil seal for withdrawal housing

A—Bush, clutch withdrawal sleeve
B—Bush, cross-shaft, right-hand side
C—Bush, cross-shaft, left-hand side
D—Oil seal

Fig. C1-130. Cross-section of withdrawal mechanism

To assemble

1. Fit the bushes for the cross-shaft and withdrawal sleeve to the housing.

    The plain bush for the cross-shaft must be reamered to .751 in. + .001 in. (19,0754 mm + 0,0254 mm) after fitting.

    The flanged bushes for the cross-shaft must be reamered to .6257 in. + .001 in. (15,8928 mm + 0,0254 mm) after fitting.

    The bush for the withdrawal sleeve must be reamered to 1.625 in. + .002 in. (41,2650 mm + 0,0508 mm) after fitting.

2. Fit the withdrawal sleeve and thrust bearing.

Operation C1-15—continued

3. Fit the oil seal, knife edge inwards.
4. Place the withdrawal fork, thrust washer and spring in position.
5. Place a ⁷⁄₁₆ in. (11 mm) diameter bar between the withdrawal sleeve and the housing, to give the required position of the withdrawal fork when the cross shaft is inserted.
6. Ensure the withdrawal fork is in contact with the bearing, and the ⁷⁄₁₆ in. (11 mm) diameter bar is trapped between the withdrawal sleeve and the housing, then insert the cross-shaft, with linkage connecting drilling in line with the withdrawal sleeve.
7. Fit the cover plate and joint washer.

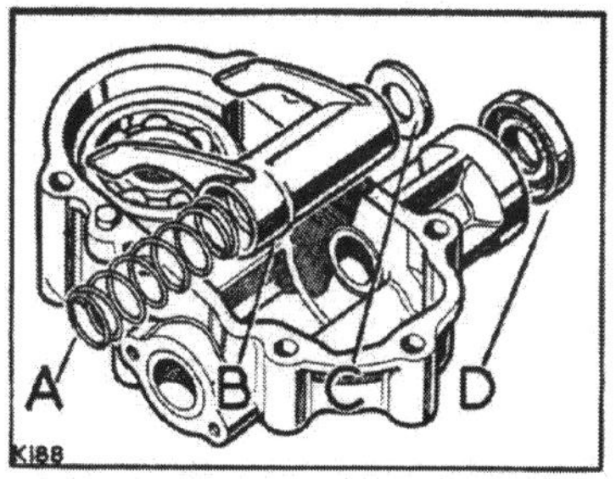

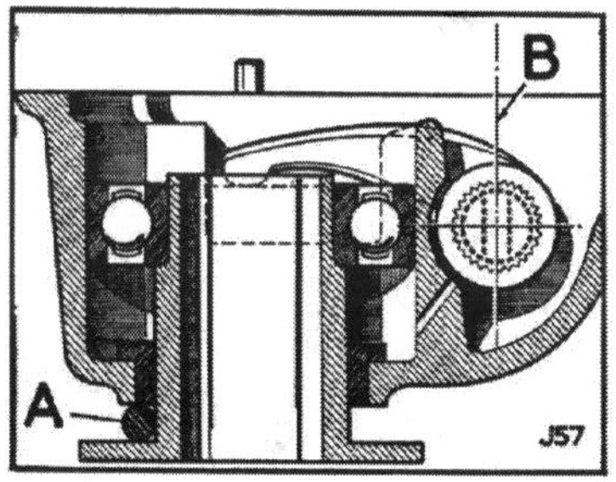

Fig. C1-131. Fitting withdrawal fork

A—Spring   C—Thrust washer
B—Withdrawal fork   D—Oil seal

Fig. C1-132. Setting clutch withdrawal mechanism

A—⁷⁄₁₆ in. (11 mm) diameter bar
B—Connecting drilling in line with withdrawal sleeve

GEARBOX

Bell housing, remove and refit—Operation C1-16

(For overhaul instructions, Operation C1-17 refers)

Workshop hand tools:
Spanner sizes: ½ in. BSF, ⁹⁄₁₆ in. BSF sockets

To remove

1. Remove the front floor. Operation A1-4.
2. Remove the seat base. Operation C1-1.
3. Drain the gearbox lubricating oil. Operation C1-2.
4. Remove the gearbox assembly complete. Operation C1-3.
5. Remove the main gearchange lever. Operation C1-11.
6. Remove the clutch withdrawal unit. Operation C1-14.
7. Disconnect the transfer gear lever from the bracket at the bell housing, withdraw the lever, taking care to retain the spring strip located between the lever ball and link.
8. Fully adjust the transmission brake to lock 'hard on'.
9. Select any gear and remove the split pin, nut and washer securing the gearbox layshaft. DO NOT remove the special nut from the primary pinion.

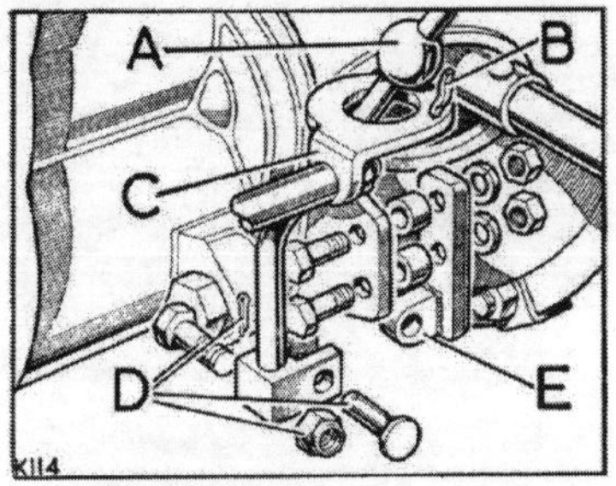

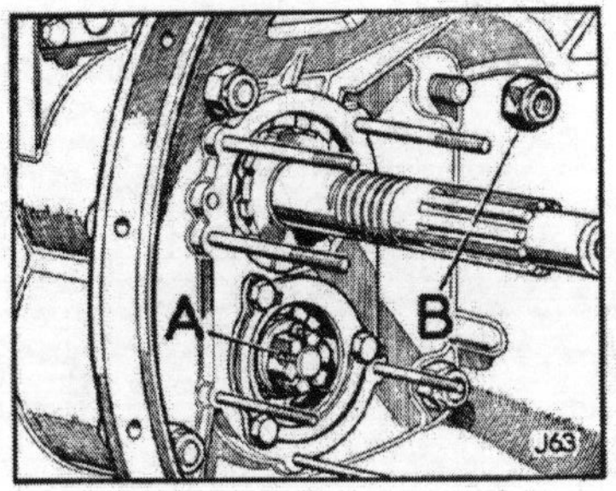

Fig. C1-133. Transfer gear lever
A—Transfer gear lever
B—Spring, lever ball to link
C—Link for lever
D—Alternative fixings, lever to bell housing
E—Bracket, lever to bell housing

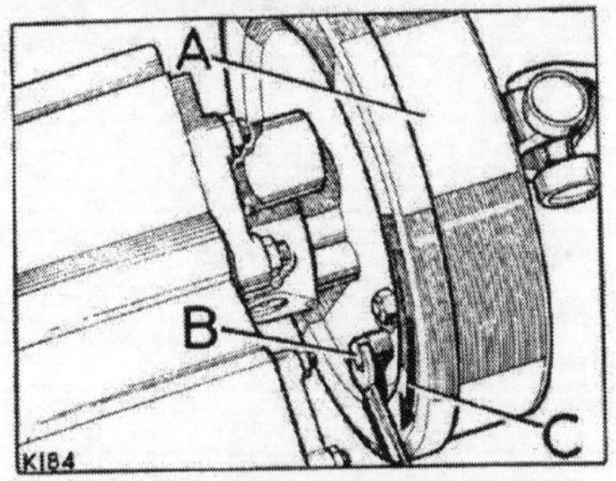

Fig. C1-134. Locking transmission brake
A—Transmission brake
B—Brake adjuster
C—Adjust as indicated to lock 'hard on'

GEARBOX

Operation C1-16—continued

10. Remove the bell housing fixings. Hold the layshaft depressed fully rearwards and ease the housing from the gearbox, taking care to catch the constant gear and conical distance piece which will be released.

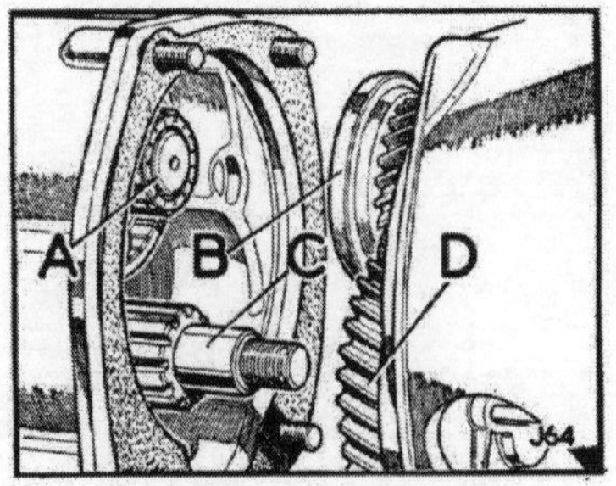

Fig. C1-135. Bell housing fixings
A—Fixings, gearbox layshaft
B—Fixings (4 off) bell housing to main gearbox

Fig. C1-136. Bell housing location
A—Gearbox mainshaft   C—Gearbox layshaft
B—Primary pinion   D—Constant gear

To refit

Note: Two of the bell housing to gearbox securing bolts are special fitted bolts, and must be positioned diagonally opposite.

1. Smear both sides of the joint washer with a general purpose grease and place in position on the gearbox.
2. Ensure that the roller bearing for the primary pinion is in position, then locate the conical distance piece and constant gear in place, in mesh with the primary pinion, on the rear face of the bell housing.

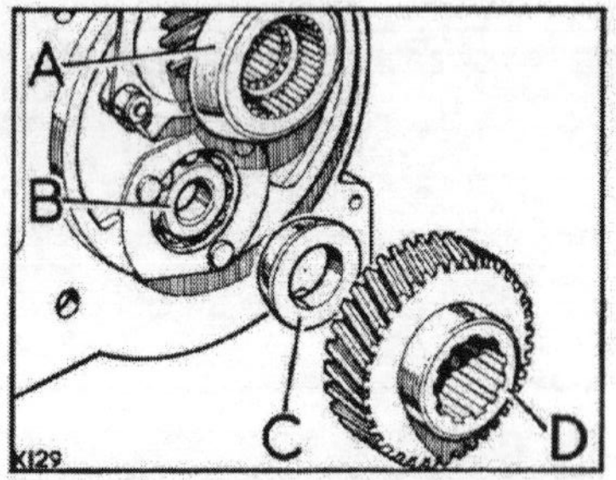

Fig. C1-137. Location of conical distance piece
A—Primary pinion   C—Conical distance piece
B—Bearing for layshaft D—Constant gear

3. Retain the constant gear and conical distance piece in position, by holding through the layshaft bearing, from the inside of the bell housing, then offer the bell housing to the gearbox, using special care to align the constant gear with the splines on the layshaft.
4. Complete the reassembly by reversing the removal procedure. The layshaft securing nut must be tightened to a torque figure of 75 lb ft (10,0 mkg).
5. Check and replenish the gearbox lubricating oil. Operation C1-2.
6. Adjust the transmission brake.
7. Adjust the four wheel drive control lever. Operation A1-4.

GEARBOX

Bell housing, overhaul—Operation C1-17

(For removal and refitting instructions, Operation C1-16 refers)

Workshop hand tools:
Spanner sizes: 7/16 in. BSF ring spanner, 1/2 in. AF socket
Mallet, Punch

To dismantle

1. Remove the retainer and bearing plate, then press the layshaft bearing from the bell housing.

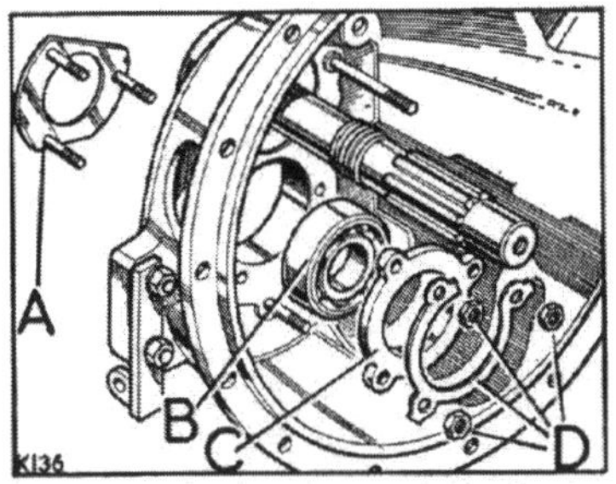

Fig. C1-138. Layshaft bearing

A—Retainer for bearing
B—Bearing for layshaft
C—Retaining plate for bearing
D—Fixings, bearing retainer

2. Remove the fixings and press the primary pinion and bearing assembly from the bell housing.

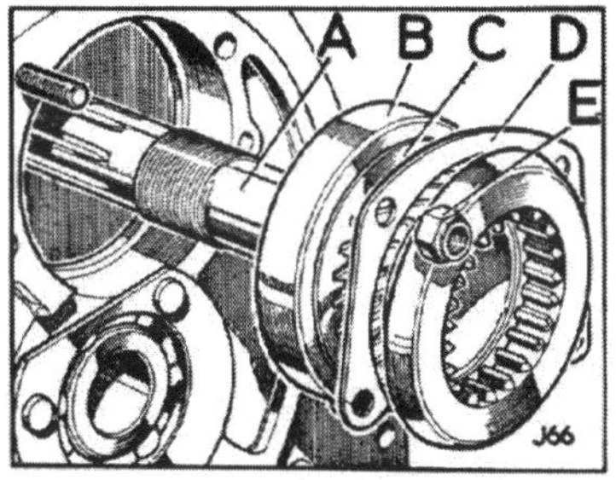

Fig. C1-139. Primary pinion and bearing assembly

A—Primary pinion
B—Bearing for pinion
C—Shield for pinion
D—Retaining plate for pinion
E—Fixings, retaining plate

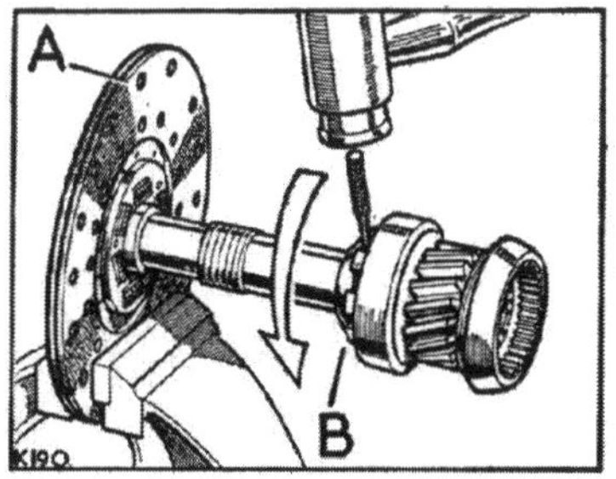

Operation C1-17—continued

Fig. C1-140. Removing nut from primary pinion

A—Old clutch plate
B—Unscrew nut as indicated

3. Remove the special LEFT HAND THREAD nut from the primary pinion.

   Note: An old clutch plate or gearbox output flange secured in a vice, can be used to hold the primary pinion while removing the nut.

4. Press the bearing and shield from the primary pinion.

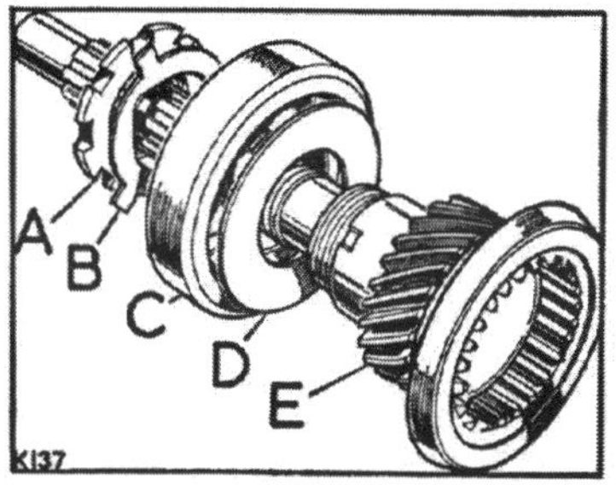

Fig. C1-141. Primary pinion assembly

A—Special nut, LEFT HAND THREAD
B—Lock washer
C—Bearing for primary pinion
D—Shield for primary pinion
E—Primary pinion

Inspection

Renew any components which show obvious wear or damage. Renew the lockwasher for the special LH thread nut. Ensure that the oil scroll machined on the primary pinion is not damaged, a faulty scroll may result in oil reaching the clutch, causing slip, check that the clutch plate slides freely on the primary pinion splined shaft.

To assemble

1. Fit the shield for the primary pinion in place, with the dished side towards the pinion.
2. Press the bearing on to the primary pinion.
3. Fit the lockwasher and special LEFT-HAND THREAD nut, tighten the nut and engage the lockwasher, see Figs. C1-141 and C1-140.
4. Press the primary pinion and bearing assembly into the bell housing, and secure the fixings, see Fig. C1-139.
5. Press the layshaft bearing into the bell housing, and secure the fixings, see Fig. C1-138.

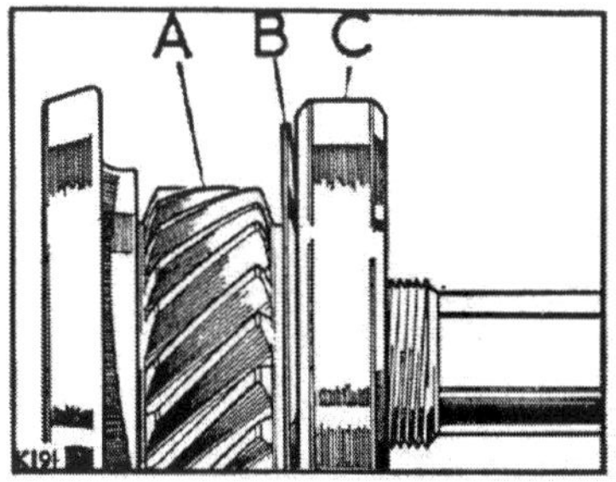

Fig. C1-142. Correct location of dished shield

A—Primary pinion
B—Dished edge of shield
C—Bearing

GEARBOX

*Gear selector shafts, remove, refit and adjust—Operation C1-18

(For overhaul instructions, Operation C1-19 refers)

Workshop hand tools:
Spanner sizes: 2 BA, ¼ in. BSF, ⁷⁄₁₆ in. BSF, ⅜ in. BSF open end
Screwdriver (medium)

To remove

1. Remove the front floor. Operation A1-4.
2. Remove the seat base. Operation C1-1.
3. Remove the main gear change lever. Operation C1-11.
4. Remove the three selector springs and pack the drillings in the top cover with grease, to prevent the selector balls from falling into the gearbox when the cover is removed.
5. Remove the top cover from the gearbox and collect the three selector balls.
6. Select first gear. Remove the reverse gear selector shaft by lifting and turning the shaft through approximately a quarter of a turn to the left. Lift the interlocking plunger from the top of the gearbox.

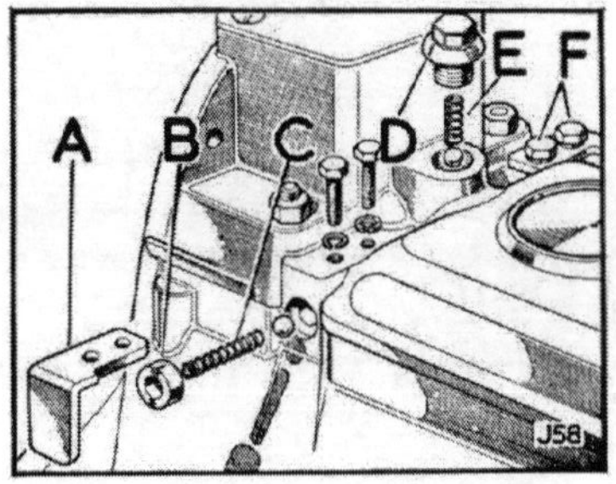

Fig. C1-143. Selector springs and balls
A—Retainer plate
B—Rubber sealing grommet
C—Spring reverse selector shaft
D—Plug
E—Spring, 1st-2nd selector shaft
F—Fixings, 3rd-4th selector spring

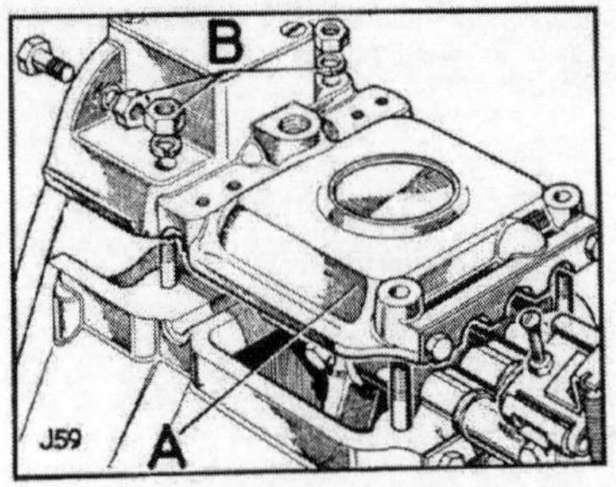

Fig. C1-144. Gearbox top cover
A—Top cover
B—Fixings, top cover to gearbox and transfer box

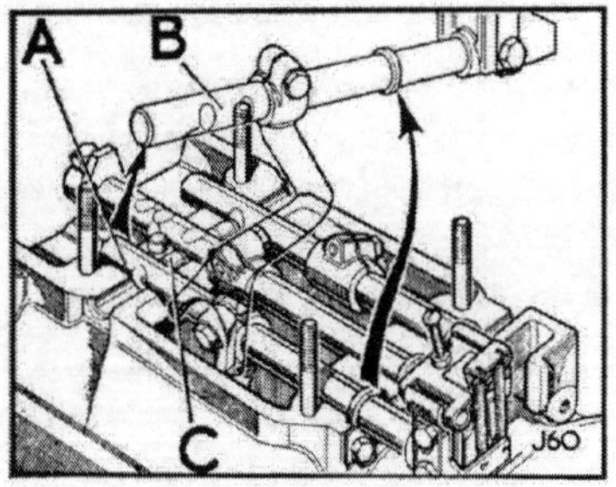

Fig. C1-145. Removing reverse gear selector shaft
A—Reverse selector shaft in position
B—Method of removal
C—Interlocking plunger

7. Move the 1st-2nd speed selector shaft into the 2nd gear position, that is to the front, then lift it clear. Lift the interlocking plunger from the top of the gearbox.

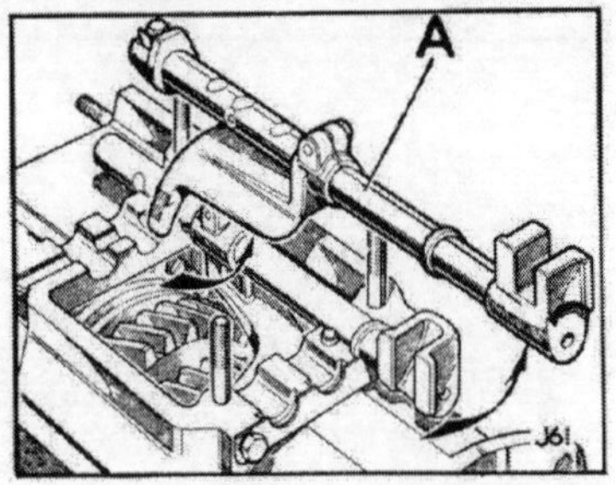

Fig. C1-146. Removing 1st-2nd speed selector shaft
A—Selector shaft, 1st-2nd speed

8. Move the 3rd-4th selector shaft into the 3rd gear position, that is to the rear, then lift it clear.

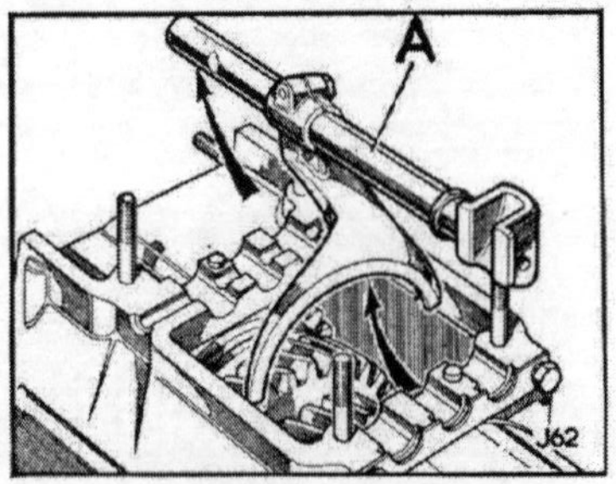

Fig. C1-147. Removing 3rd-4th selector shaft
A—Selector shaft, 3rd-4th speed

Operation C1-18—continued

To refit

1. Move the inner member of the synchromesh unit into the third gear position (fully rearwards), and fit the 3rd-4th selector shaft and fork. Ensure that the shaft seal is located in the groove casing.

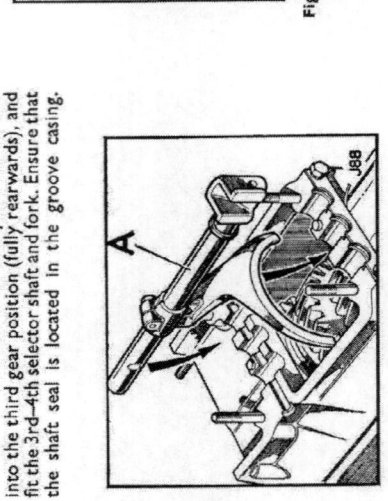

Fig. C1-148. Fitting 3rd-4th selector shaft
A—Selector shaft, 3rd-4th speed

2. Move the inner member of the 3rd-top synchromesh unit to the neutral position, and engage second gear, that is, move the 1st-2nd speed gear fully rearwards. Fit the 1st-2nd selector shaft and fork, locating the seal correctly.

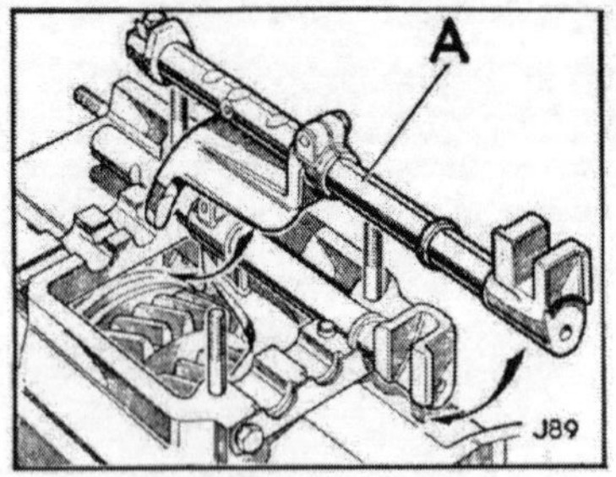

Fig. C1-149. Fitting 1st-2nd selector shaft
A—Selector shaft, 1st-2nd speed

3. Move the 1st-2nd selector shaft into the first gear position, that is, fully rearward, also move the reverse idler gear fully forward, then fit the reverse gear selector shaft by reversing the removal procedure.

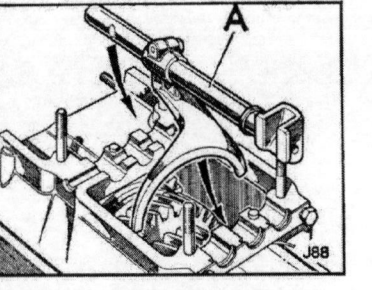

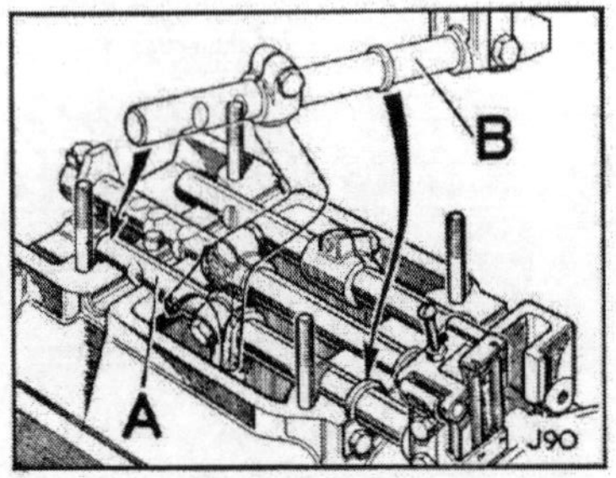

Fig. C1-150. Fitting the reverse gear selector shaft
A—Reverse selector shaft in position
B—Method of fitting

4. Place all selectors in the neutral position and fit the interlocking plungers.
5. Fit the gearbox top cover, selector balls, springs, rubber seals and retainers. Note that the reverse selector detent spring is stronger, being of slightly thicker material. Also the cut-away top edge of the retaining plates must face towards the front of the gearbox.

Operations marked with an asterisk (*) can be carried out with the gearbox installed in the vehicle

GEARBOX

Section C—Land-Rover

Operation C1-18—continued

Fig. C1-151. Selector shafts and plungers

A—Interlocking plungers

5. Check the operation of all three selector shafts.

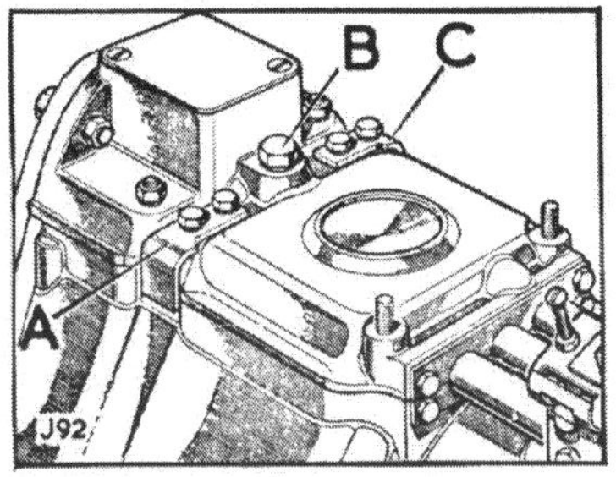

Fig. C1-152. Gearbox top cover

A—Retaining plate, reverse gear selector spring and ball
B—Retaining plug, 1st-2nd speed selector spring and ball
C—Retaining plate, 3rd-top speed selector spring and ball

7. Select 2nd gear and adjust the second speed stop bolt so that there is .002 in. (0,05 mm) clearance between the bolt head and the stop on the selector shaft, tighten the locknut.

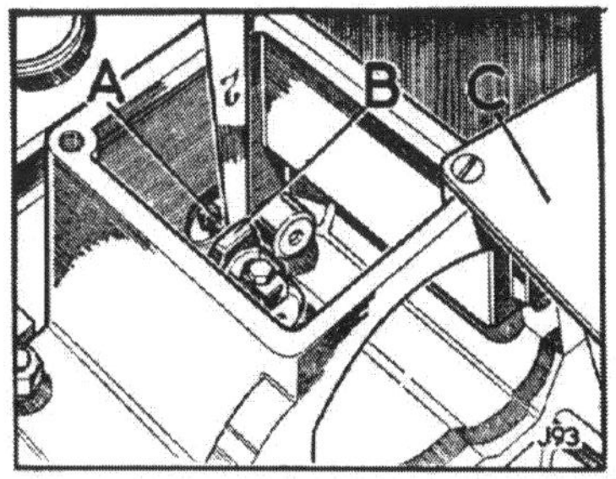

Fig. C1-153. Adjusting 2nd speed stop bolt

A—Set bolt and locknut for 2nd speed stop
B—Stop for 2nd gear
C—Inspection cover

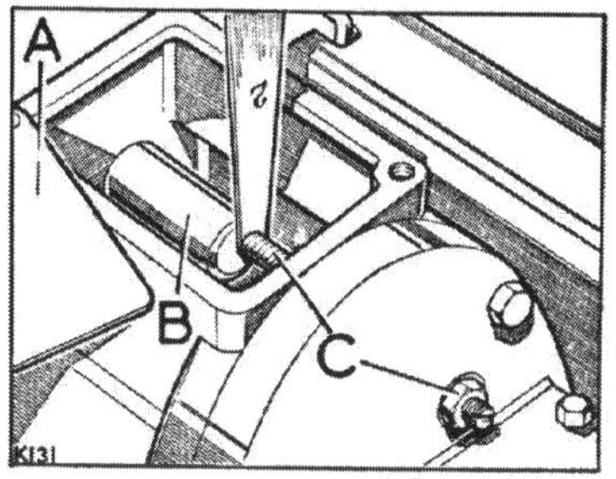

8. Select reverse gear and adjust the reverse gear stop bolt so that there is .002 in. (0,05 mm) clearance between the selector shaft and the end of the bolt, tighten the locknut.

Fig. C1-154. Adjusting reverse gear stop bolt

A—Inspection cover
B—Reverse gear selector shaft
C—Set bolt and locknut for second speed stop

Note: If the transfer box has been removed from the main gearbox, the foregoing adjustment must be carried out after the transfer box has been refitted.

9. Complete the re-assembly by reversing the removal procedure.

10. Adjust the four wheel drive control lever, Operation A1-4.

---

*Gear selector shafts, overhaul—Operation C1-19

(For removal and refitting instructions, Operation C1-18 refers)

Workshop hand tools:
Spanner sizes: ½ in. BSF, 7/16 in. BSF open end

To dismantle

1. Remove the stop from the reverse selector shaft, Operation C1-13.
2. Remove the stop from the 1st-2nd gear selector shaft.
3. Remove the forks and seals from the selector shafts.

Inspection

Examine the components visually and renew any that show obvious wear or damage.

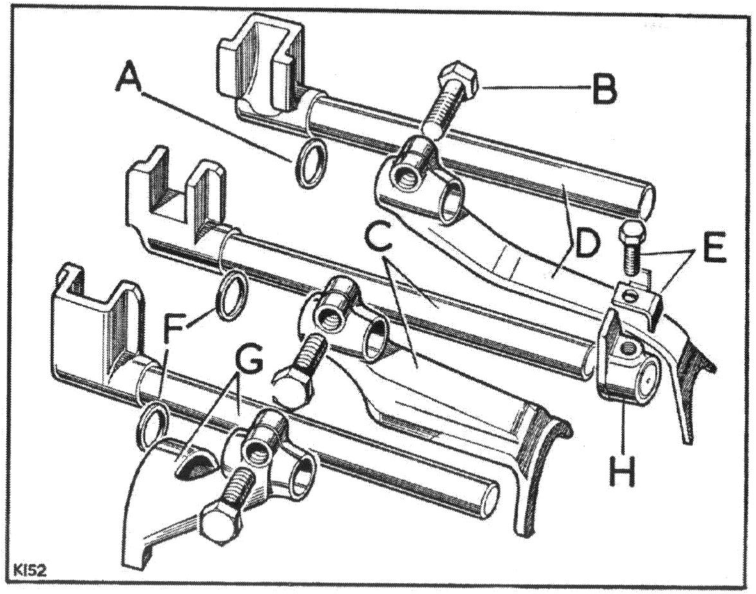

Fig. C1-155. Selector Shafts

A—Seal, reverse gear selector shaft
B—Fixing, selector fork
C—1st-2nd gear selector shaft and fork
D—Reverse gear selector shaft and fork
E—Fixings, 1st-2nd stop
F—Seal, forward selector shafts
G—3rd-4th gear selector shaft and fork
H—Stop, 1st-2nd gear selector shaft

Operations marked with an asterisk (*) can be carried out with the gearbox installed in the vehicle

GEARBOX

Operation C1-19—continued

To re-assemble

1. Fit the sealing rings to the selector shafts, noting that the bore of the seal is tapered and the thinner edge must face towards the front of the gearbox. Also the seal for the reverse shaft differs in size from the other two.

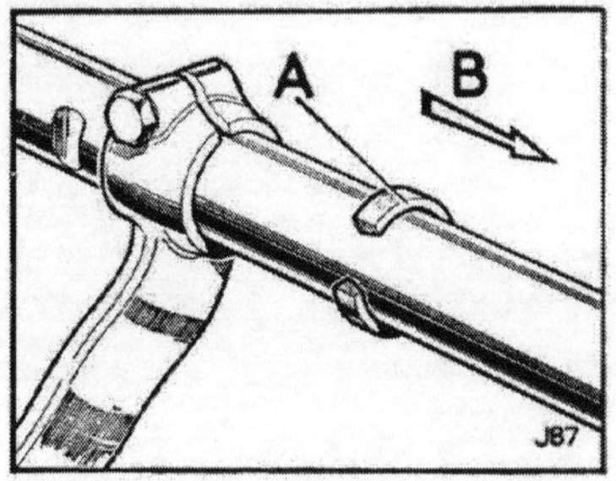

Fig. C1-156. Selector shaft seal location
A—Thin edge of seal
B—To front of gearbox

2. Fit the selector forks to their shafts. Align the selector fork pinch bolt holes with the groove in the top of the shaft, and in the case of the 1st–2nd gear selector shaft, the groove nearest the front.

Note: There is radial movement between the selector fork and shaft before the pinch bolt is tightened, and the fork should be secured in the mid-position.

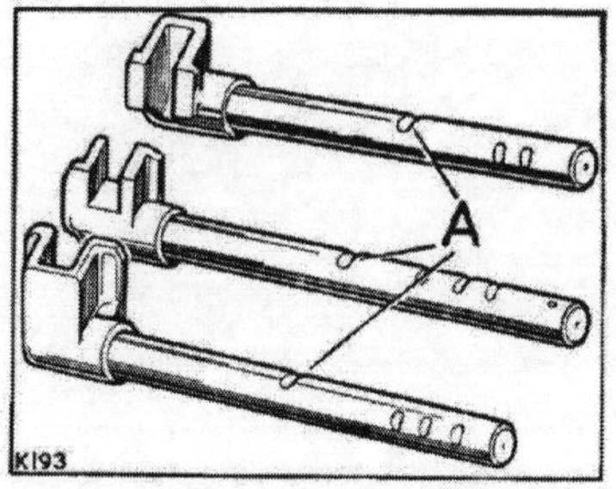

Fig. C1-157. Location of selector forks on shafts
A—Grooves for selector fork pinch bolts

3. Fit the stop to the 1st-2nd gear selector shaft.
4. Fit the stop to the reverse selector shaft. Operation C1-13.

Gearbox layshaft, remove and refit—Operation C1-20

(For overhaul instructions, Operation C1-21 refers)

To remove

1. Remove the front floor. Operation A1-4.
2. Remove the seat base. Operation C1-1.
3. Drain the gearbox lubricating oil. Operation C1-2.
4. Remove the gearbox assembly complete. Operation C1-3.
5. Remove the main gear change lever. Operation C1-11.
6. Remove the clutch withdrawal unit. Operation C1-14.
7. Remove the bell housing. Operation C1-16.
8. Withdraw the synchronising clutch unit from the mainshaft then withdraw the layshaft assembly from the gearbox.

Refer to Operation C1-25 for removal of the layshaft rear bearing outer race.

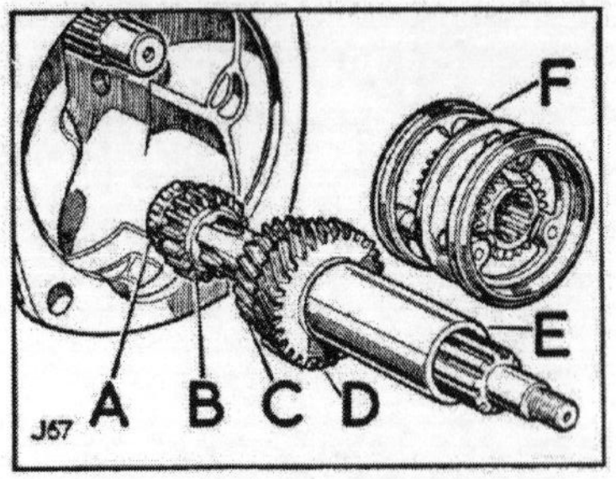

Fig. C1-158. Layshaft and synchronising clutch
A—Rear bearing for layshaft
B—1st speed layshaft gear
C—2nd speed layshaft gear
D—3rd speed layshaft gear
E—Sleeve for layshaft
F—Synchronising clutch

To refit

Note: If any layshaft components have been renewed, the checks described under 'Gearbox layshaft overhaul', must be carried out.

1. Insert the assembled layshaft into the gearbox, locating the gear into its outer race.
2. Fit the synchronising clutch to the mainshaft with the recessed end of the inner member toward the third speed gear.
3. Place the bell housing joint washer in position.
4. Ensure that the roller bearing for the primary pinion is in position, then locate the conical distance piece and constant gear in place, in mesh with the primary pinion, on the rear face of the bell housing.

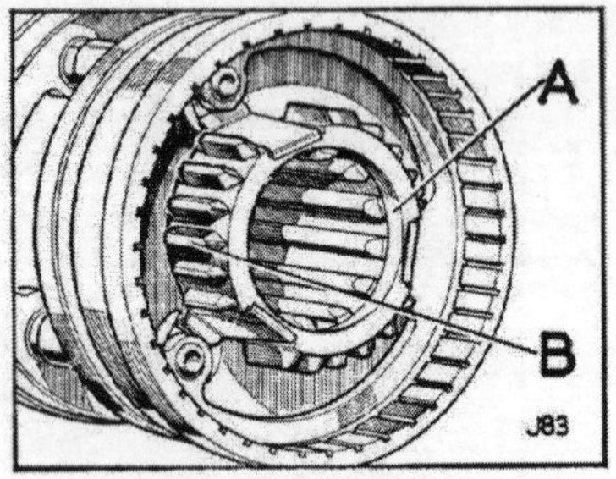

Fig. C1-159. Synchronising clutch
A—Recess on inner splines
B—Thicker teeth

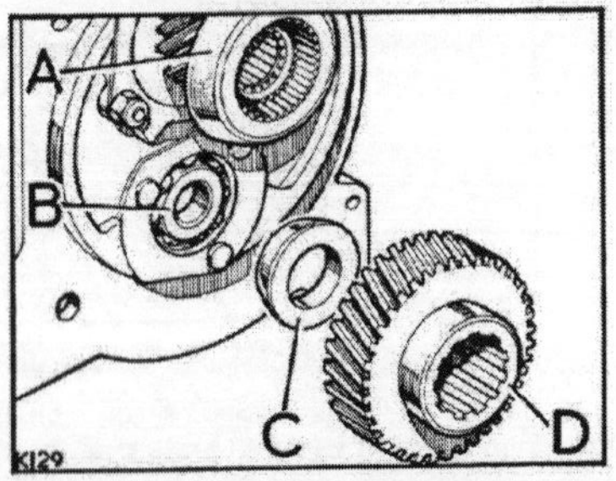

Fig. C1-160. Location of conical distance piece
A—Primary pinion
B—Bearing for layshaft
C—Conical distance piece
D—Constant gear

5. Retain the constant gear and conical distance piece in position, by holding through the layshaft bearing from inside the bell housing, then offer the bell housing to the gearbox, using special care to align the constant gear with the splines on the layshaft.
6. Complete the re-assembly by reversing the removal procedure.
   The layshaft securing nut must be tightened to a torque figure of 75 lb ft (10,0 mkg).
   Adjust the transmission brake.
   Check and replenish the gearbox lubricating oil. Operation C1-2.
   Adjust the four wheel drive control lever. Operation A1-4.

GEARBOX

Gearbox layshaft, overhaul—Operation C1-21

(For removal and refitting instructions, Operation C1-20 refers)

Workshop hand tools:
Spanner size: 1⅛ in. AF

1. Withdraw the sleeve and the 2nd and 3rd speed gears from the layshaft.

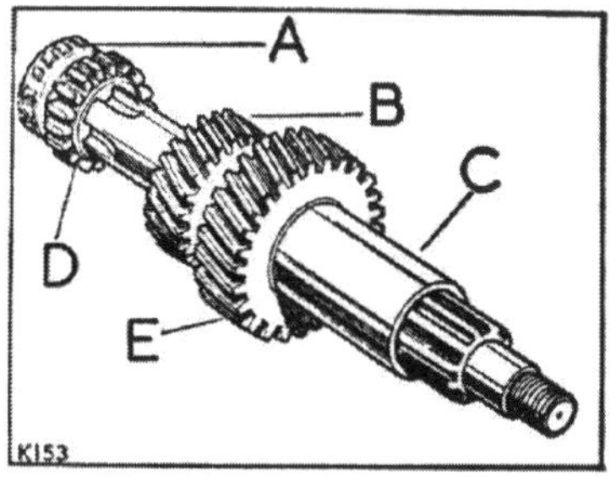

Fig. C1-161. Layshaft assembly

A—Rear bearing for layshaft
B—2nd speed gear
C—Sleeve for layshaft
D—1st speed gear
E—3rd speed gear

2. Press the first speed gear and bearing from the layshaft.

Refer to Operation C1-25 for removal of the layshaft rear bearing outer race.

Inspection

Examine the components visually for wear or damage.

To assemble, including tolerance checks

1. Fit the 1st speed gear, chamfered side of teeth first, on to the layshaft.
2. Press the layshaft rear bearing on to the shaft to abut with the 1st speed gear.

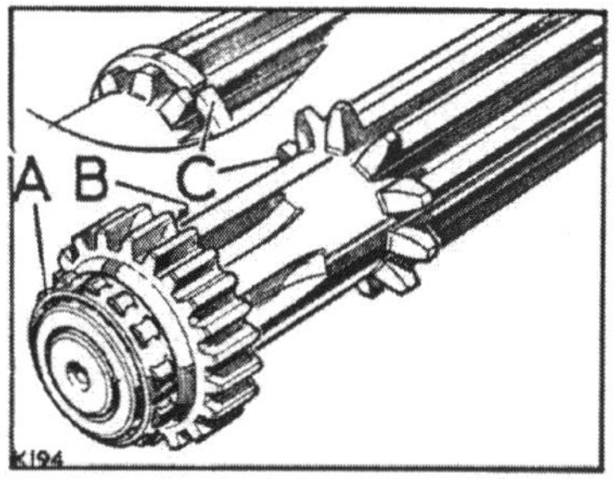

Fig. C1-162. Layshaft rear bearing and 1st speed gear

A—Bearing
B—Chamfered teeth on 1st speed gear
C—Integral shoulder (or split ring on early shafts) for 2nd speed gear location

Operation C1-21—continued

3. Early type layshafts, fit the split ring for the 2nd speed gear to the groove in the shaft.

   Note: Later type shafts are provided with a shoulder in place of the split ring.

4. Fit the 2nd speed gear, recessed side first, and locate it over the split ring or shaft shoulder, as applicable.

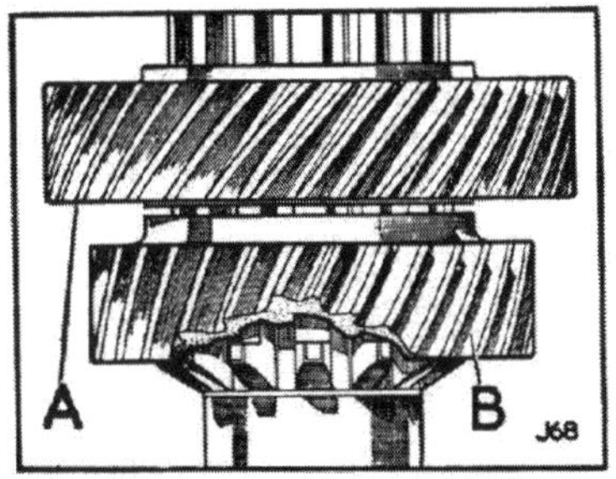

Fig. C1-163. 2nd and 3rd speed gear location

A—3rd speed gear   B—2nd speed gear

5. Fit the 3rd speed gear, narrow shoulder side first, then fit the sleeve to the layshaft.
6. Place the conical distance piece and constant gear in position, in mesh with the primary pinion on the rear face of the bell housing.
7. Locate the layshaft in position on the bell housing and secure with the plain washer and castle nut.

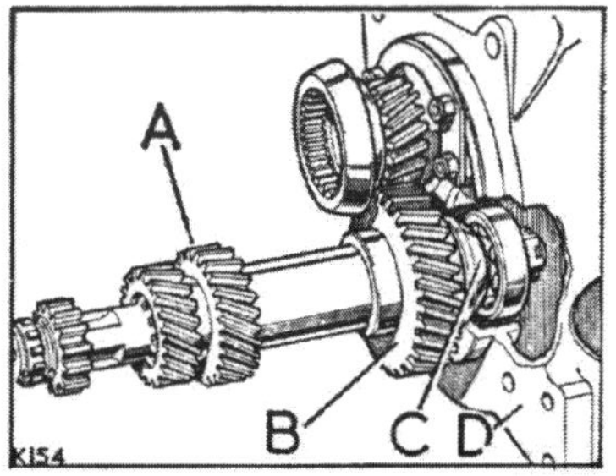

Fig. C1-164. Layshaft pre-assembly check

A—Layshaft
B—Constant gear
C—Conical distance piece
D—Bell housing

8. Ensure that the layshaft assembly is locked up tightly and that the gears are not tilted by excessive run-out, either on their faces or those of the distance piece. The gears must not have any end float on the shaft, if end float is present, fit a new sleeve and re-check.

9. Remove the layshaft assembly from the bell housing.

Important. When fitting the layshaft into the gearbox, carry out the following check after fitting the bell housing, but before fitting the layshaft securing nut.

1. Check that the layshaft has a definite but minimum end float.
2. If no end float is present, dismantle the assembly and fit a thinner conical distance piece, these are available in a range of thicknesses.

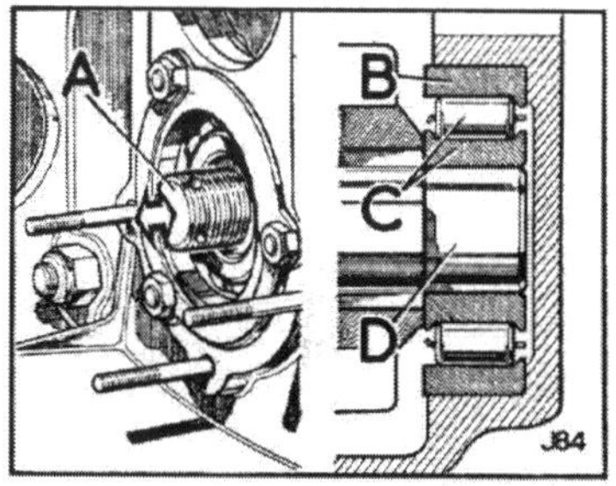

Fig. C1-165. Layshaft end float check

A—Move layshaft as indicated to check for minimum end float
B—Outer race, layshaft rear bearing
C—Roller bearing and inner race correctly located in outer race
D—Layshaft, rear end

Note: Layshaft end float is necessary to ensure that the rear bearing locates correctly within its outer race, and is not pressing hard against the lip at the rear of the outer race.

GEARBOX

Gearbox mainshaft, remove and refit—Operation C1-22

(For overhaul Instructions, Operation C1-23 refers)

Workshop hand tools:
Spanner size: ⅜ in. BSF socket
Mallet

Special tools:
Tool for mainshaft rear nut, Part No. 600300

To remove

1. Remove the front floor. Operation A1-4.
2. Remove the seat base. Operation C1-1.
3. Drain the gearbox lubricating oil. Operation C1-2.
4. Remove the gearbox assembly complete. Operation C1-3.
5. Remove the main gear change lever. Operation C1-11.
6. Remove the clutch withdrawal unit. Operation C1-14.
7. Remove the bell housing. Operation C1-16.
8. Remove the selector shafts. Operation C1-18.
9. Remove the layshaft. Operation C1-20.
10. Remove the rear bearing housing from the transfer box.

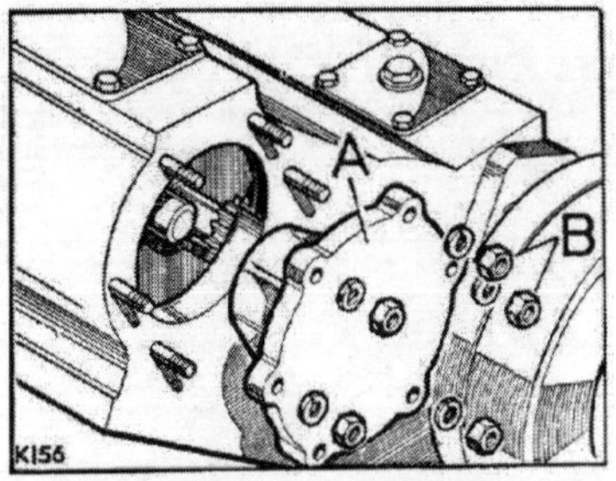

Fig. C1-166. Rear bearing housing
A—Bearing housing   B—Fixings

Fig. C1-167. Removing transfer gear securing nut
A—Mainshaft gear for transfer box
B—Lockwasher
C—Special nut
D—Special tool, Part Number 600300

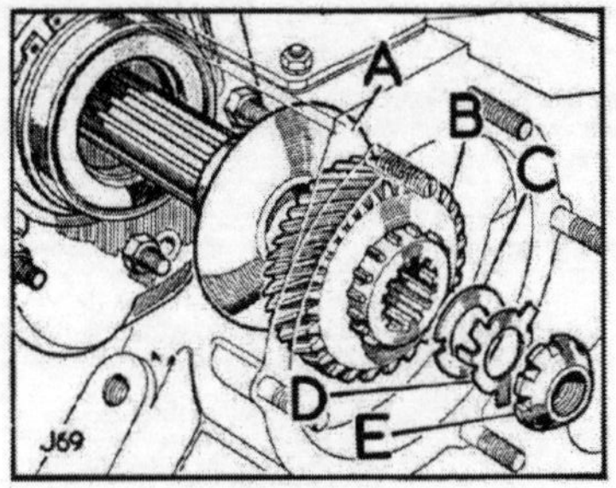

11. Using special tool, Part No. 600300, remove the mainshaft gear for transfer box.
12. Drive the mainshaft out from the gearbox.

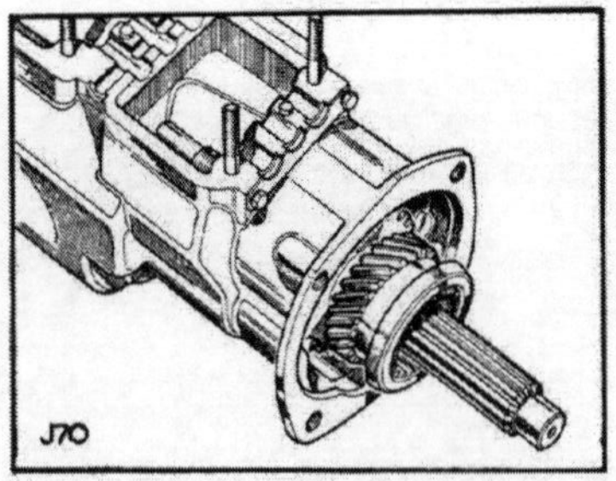

Fig. C1-168. Mainshaft gear for transfer box
A—Oil thrower
B—Mainshaft gear
C—Shim washer
D—Lockwasher
E—Special nut

Fig. C1-169. Removing mainshaft from gearbox

To refit

Note: If any mainshaft components have been renewed, the checks described under 'Gearbox mainshaft overhaul' must be carried out.

1. Place the oil thrower in position, locating the sleeve into the gearbox oil seal.
2. Locate the assembled mainshaft into the gearbox and drive into position.
3. Fit the mainshaft transfer gear, and engage the lockwasher to secure the special nut.
4. Complete the re-assembly by reversing the removal procedure.
5. Replenish the gearbox lubricating oil. Operation C1-2.
6. Adjust the four wheel drive control lever. Operation A1-4.

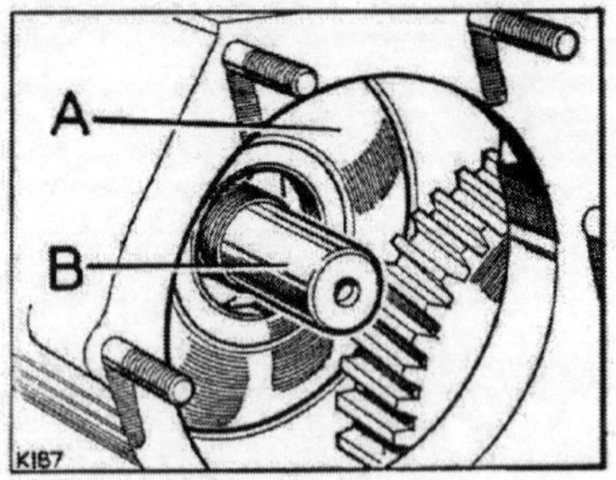

Fig. C1-170. Fitting the gearbox mainshaft
A—Oil thrower   B—Main shaft

Operation C1-22—continued

GEARBOX

Gearbox mainshaft, overhaul—Operation C1-23

(For removal and refitting instructions, Operation C1-22 refers)

Workshop hand tools:
Screwdriver (small), Feeler gauges

To dismantle

1. Withdraw the first speed gear.

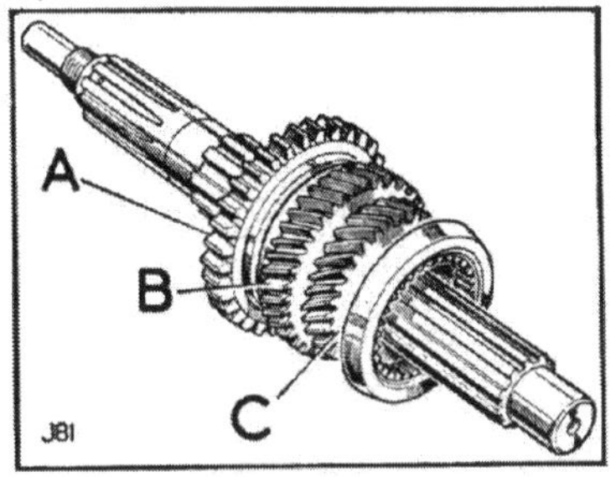

Fig. C1-171. Mainshaft assembly

A—1st speed gear
B—2nd speed gear
C—3rd speed gear

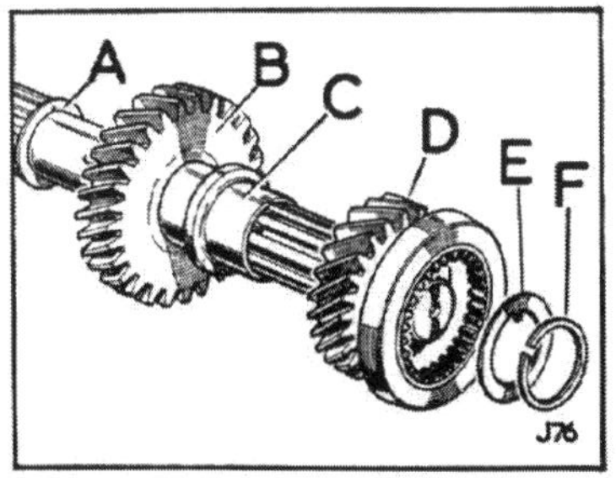

2. Prise the spring ring from the groove in the mainshaft, and withdraw the thrust washer, third speed gear, distance sleeve and second speed gear.

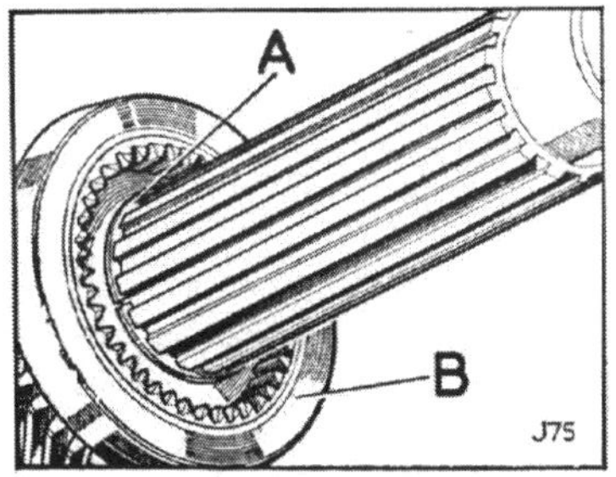

Fig. C1-172. Location of spring ring

A—Spring ring retaining mainshaft gears
B—3rd speed gear

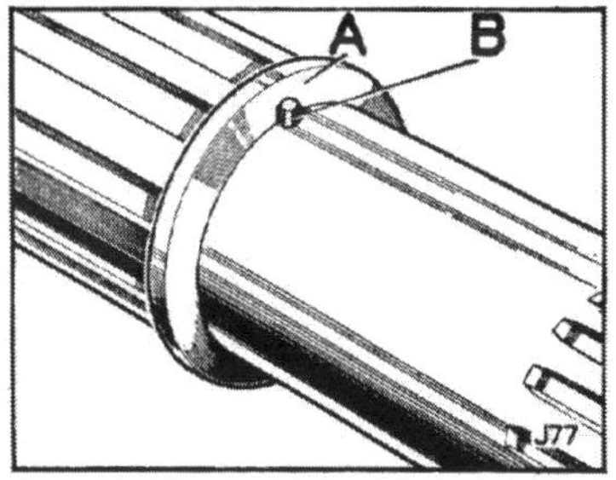

Fig. C1-173. Mainshaft components

A—Thrust washer, 2nd speed gear
B—2nd speed gear
C—Distance sleeve
D—3rd speed gear
E—Thrust washer, 3rd speed gear
F—Spring ring

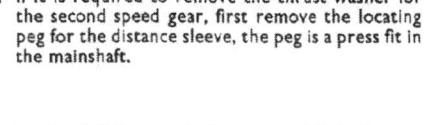

3. If it is required to remove the thrust washer for the second speed gear, first remove the locating peg for the distance sleeve, the peg is a press fit in the mainshaft.

Fig. C1-174. Thrust washer for 2nd speed gear

A—Thrust washer
B—Peg for distance sleeve

Operation C1-23—continued

Inspection

1. Examine all components for wear or damage.
2. Discard the mainshaft spring ring. Use a new replacement on assembly.
3. Check the synchronising clutch for wear, the detent springs can be replaced if required.
4. Examine the distance sleeve for the mainshaft. A new sleeve manufactured from improved material has been introduced and is fully interchangeable with the earlier type. The new sleeve can be identified by a small annular groove cut in the outside diameter of the central flange, the earlier sleeve has a plain flange.

It is recommended that only the new type sleeves are fitted as replacements, and early type sleeves should be discarded.

To assemble, including tolerance checks

1. If the thrust washer for the second speed gear has been removed from the mainshaft, place the washer in position, engaging it over its locating peg, but do not fit the locating peg for the distance sleeve at this stage.

2. Fit the second speed gear, dog coupling side last, to the end of the distance sleeve with the larger slot.

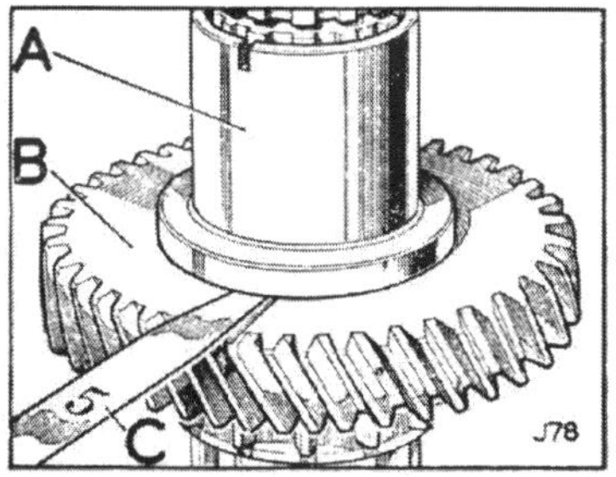

Fig. C1-175. End float check, 2nd speed gear

A—Distance sleeve
B—2nd speed gear
C—Feeler gauge

3. Slide the gear and sleeve assembly on to the mainshaft to abut with the thrust washer, then holding the sleeve hard against the thrust washer, check the end float of the second speed gear, this must be .004 in. to .007 in. (0,10 mm to 0,18 mm).

   Note: The end float of the second and the third speed gears is controlled by the length of the distance sleeve. With a new sleeve, the clearance may be excessive and can be corrected by rubbing down the end face of the sleeve on a face plate and emery cloth, ensuring that the applicable end of the sleeve is rubbed down. In the event of insufficient clearance, a new sleeve must be fitted.

4. Retain the second speed gear and distance sleeve on the mainshaft and fit the third speed gear and thrust washer. Hold the thrust washer hard against the sleeve and check the end-float of the third speed gear, this must be .004 in. to .007 in. (0,10 mm to 0,18 mm). End float adjustment is as already described.

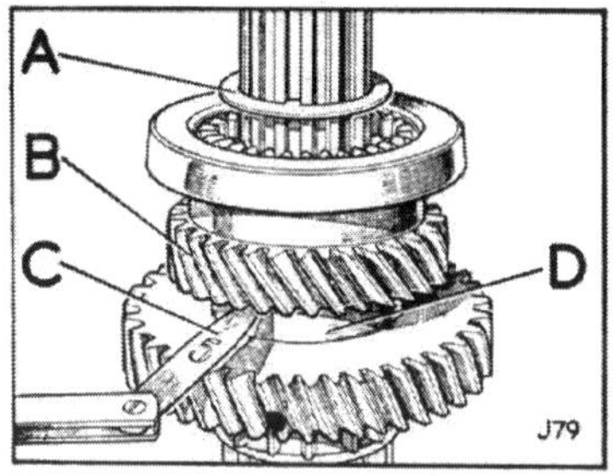

Fig. C1-176. End float check, 3rd speed gear

A—Thrust washer   C—Feeler gauge
B—Third speed gear   D—Distance sleeve

5. Remove the gears and distance sleeve from the mainshaft and refit the thrust washers and distance sleeve only, retain in position with the old spring ring.

6. Check the end float of the distance sleeve, this must be .001 in. to .008 in. (0,03 mm to 0,20 mm). Adjustment is made by changing either of the thrust washers which are available in a range of thicknesses.

GEARBOX

Operation C1-23—continued

7. When the end float of the mainshaft gears and distance piece are correct, remove the spring ring, thrust washer for third speed gear and the distance sleeve. If removed, fit the distance sleeve locating peg to the mainshaft, ensuring that the thrust washer for the second speed gear is engaged on its locating peg.

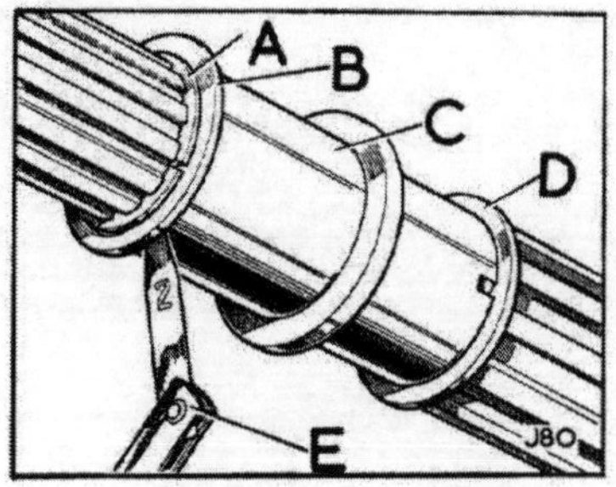

8. Fit the second speed gear, distance sleeve, third speed gear and thrust washer to the mainshaft, retain with a new spring ring. DO NOT use an old spring ring.

9. Fit the first speed gear on to the mainshaft, engaging the second speed gear dog clutch.

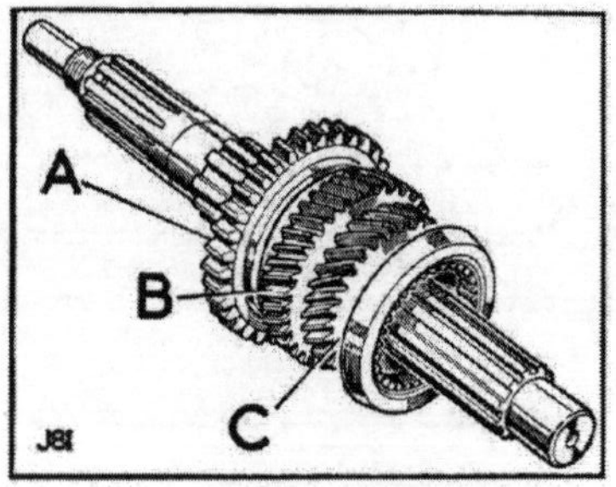

Fig. C1-177. End float check, distance sleeve

A—Spring ring
B—Thrust washer, 3rd speed gear
C—Distance sleeve
D—Thrust washer, 2nd speed gear
E—Feeler gauge

Fig. C1-178. Mainshaft assembly

A—1st speed gear
B—2nd speed gear
C—3rd speed gear

Gearbox main casing and reverse gear, remove and refit—Operation C1-24

(For overhaul instructions, Operation C1-25 refers)

Note: If it is required to change the rear main oil seal only, it is not necessary to completely dismantle the gearbox. The oil seal is accessible after removing the intermediate gear and the mainshaft gear from the transfer box, see Operations C1-7 and C1-22 for details.

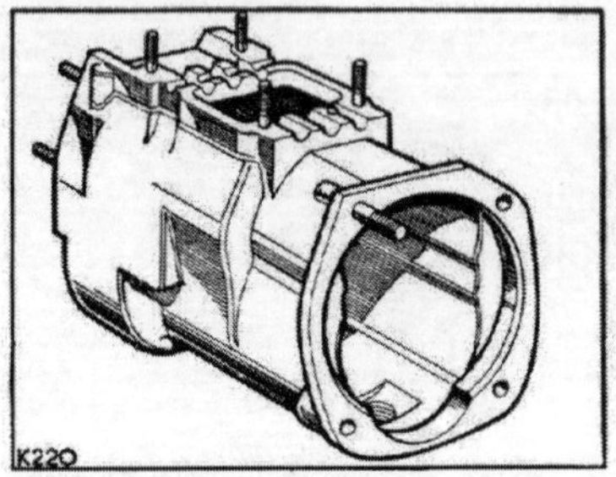

Fig. C1-179. Gearbox main casing

To remove

1. Remove the front floor. Operation A1-4.
2. Remove the seat base. Operation C1-1.
3. Drain the gearbox lubricating oil. Operation C1-2.
4. Remove the gearbox assembly complete. Operation C1-4.
5. Remove the transmission brake. Operation C1-7.
6. Remove the transfer box. Operation C1-7.
7. Remove the main gear change lever. Operation C1-11.
8. Remove the clutch withdrawal unit. Operation C1-14.
9. Remove the bell housing. Operation C1-16.
10. Remove the selector shafts. Operation C1-18.
11. Remove the layshaft. Operation C1-20.
12. Remove the mainshaft. Operation C1-22.

Upon completing the foregoing operations, the gearbox main casing is automatically released and can be dismantled as described under 'overhaul', Operation C1-25.

To refit

Reverse the removal procedure.
Replenish the gearbox lubricating oil. Operation C1-2.
Adjust the four wheel drive control lever. Operation A1-4.

GEARBOX

Gearbox main casing and reverse gear, overhaul—Operation C1-25

(For removal and refitting instructions, Operation C1-24 refers)

Workshop hand tools:
Circlip pliers, Mallet

To dismantle

1. Prise the oil seal from the rear of the mainshaft bearing housing.

2. Remove the circlip retaining the bearing housing to the rear face of the gearbox.

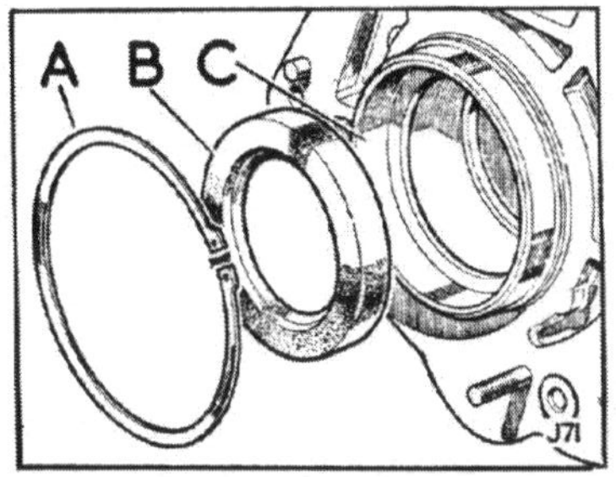

Fig. C1-180. Mainshaft rear oil seal

A—Circlip, retaining housing
B—Oil seal
C—Housing, mainshaft bearing and oil seal

3. Press out the housing, complete with bearing, in a forward direction.

4. Remove the circlip and press the mainshaft rear bearing from the housing.

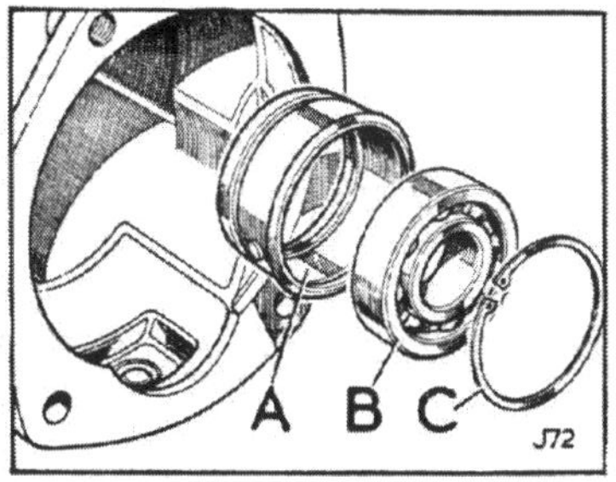

Fig. C1-181. Mainshaft rear bearing

A—Housing, rear bearing
B—Bearing
C—Circlip, retaining bearing

5. Warm the gearbox case and drive out the reverse gear shaft from inside the case. Lift out the reverse wheel assembly.

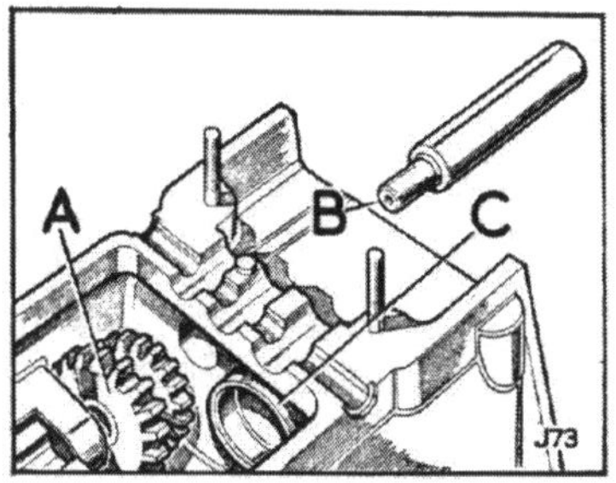

Fig. C1-182. Reverse gear and layshaft bearing

A—Reverse wheel assembly
B—Shaft, reverse wheels
C—Outer race, layshaft rear bearing

6. Warm the gearbox case, and tap the rear face with a mallet to free the layshaft bearing outer race.

Note: If any difficulty is experienced in removing the outer race, an alternative method is to use a mandrel, approximately 12 in. long (300 mm) by 1¹¹⁄₁₆ in. (43,50 mm) diameter, so that it is a tight fit in the outer race. Warm the gearbox case and outer race, keep the mandrel as cool as possible. With the casing warm, insert the mandrel into the outer race, which will shrink on to the mandrel, and withdraw easily.

7. The remaining oil drain and filler plugs, studs, dowels and retaining plate for selector shaft oil seals, can be removed as required.

Inspection

1. Check all components for wear or damage.

2. Ensure that the two dowels in the gearbox top face, and the two dowels in the rear face, are secure.

Operation C1-25—continued

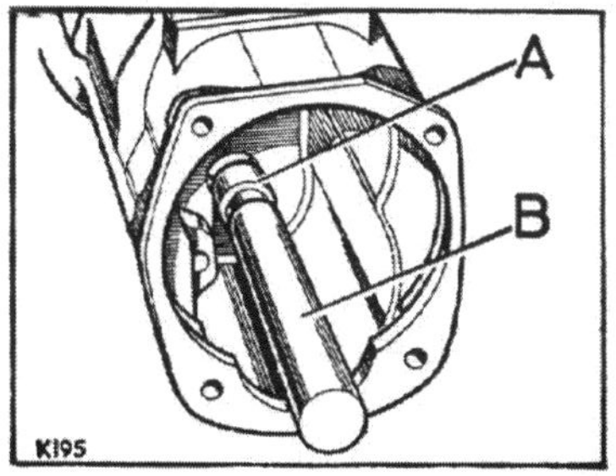

Fig. C1-183. Alternative method of removing layshaft rear bearing outer race

A—Bearing outer race B—Mandrel

3. Check the bush in the reverse wheel assembly. If a new bush is required it must be secured by peening after being pressed into position, and then reamed to .8125 in. +.001 in. (20,637 mm ± 0,025 mm) diameter.

Note that the latest type reverse gear assemblies incorporate lubrication oilways to prevent the possibility of reverse gear seizure, when reverse gear is engaged for prolonged periods.

Early gearboxes can be modified by fitting the latest type reverse gear, bush and shaft.

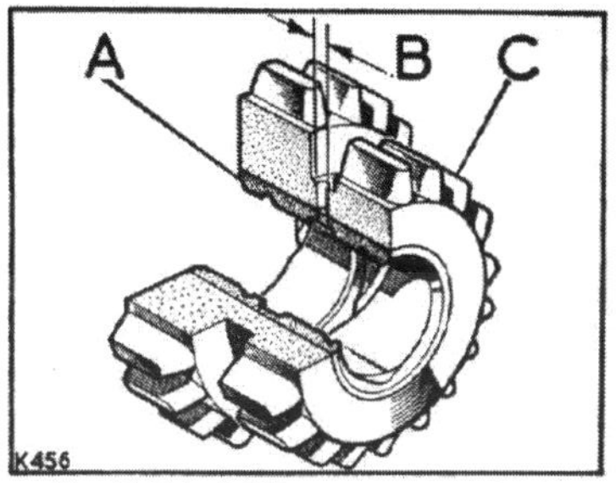

Fig. C1-184. Drilling reverse gear bush

A—Bush.
B—.125 in. (3,18 mm) diameter hole
C—Reverse gear wheel

Important: When fitting the latest type bush to the latest type gear, after reaming and peening as already described, drill a .125 in. (3,18 mm) diameter hole through the bush, using the existing hole in the gear as a pilot. Afterwards remove all fraze from the bore.

To assemble

1. Press the layshaft rear bearing outer race, lipped edge first, into the gearbox case.

2. Fit the reverse wheel assembly, with the small gear to the rear of the gearbox, then press the reverse shaft, small end first, into position until it is flush with the rear face of the gearbox.

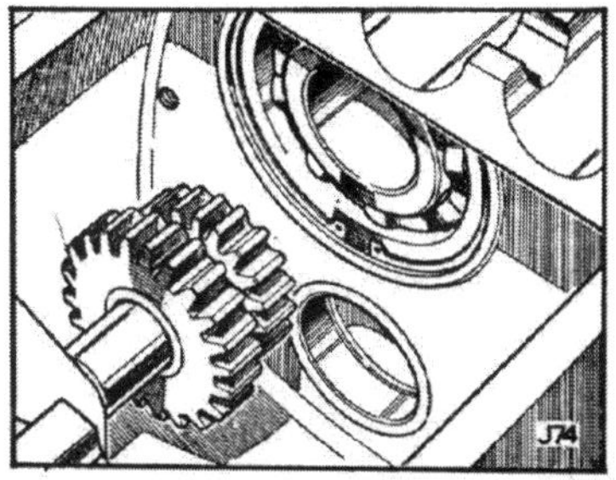

Fig. C1-185. Reverse gear and rear bearings

3. Press the mainshaft rear bearing into the housing and retain with a circlip.

4. Fit the mainshaft rear oil seal, lipped side first, into the bearing housing.

5. Check the bearing housing for method of location, see Fig. C1-181. Early type housings are peg located, latest type housings have a plain location and are retained with Loctite.

Early type: Locate the mainshaft bearing housing inside the gearbox and press it into position, ensuring that the peg location between the bearing housing and gearbox case is aligned.

Latest type: Smear the outside diameter of the bearing housing with Loctite Retaining Compound (Grade AAV), and press it into position.

Note that the gearbox should not be filled with lubricating oil or used for twenty-four hours, to allow the Loctite to fully cure.

6. Fit the retaining circlip to the groove in the bearing housing where it protrudes through the rear face of the gearbox.

GEARBOX

Fault diagnosis—Gearbox

Symptom	Possible cause	Investigation	Remedy
Gearbox noisy in neutral	Insufficient oil in gearbox	Check oil levels	Replenish
	Incorrect grade of lubricating oil	SAE 90 EP See Section X	Drain and replenish with correct grade
	Primary pinion bearing worn	Remove bell housing and check bearing	Fit new bearing
	Constant mesh gears incorrectly matched or badly worn	Remove bell housing and check constant gears	Fit a new matched pair of gears
	Layshaft bearings worn	Remove bell housing and check layshaft front bearing	Fit new bearing
		Remove layshaft and check rear bearing	Fit new bearing
Gearbox noisy in gear	Worn speedometer gear	Remove speedometer drive housing from gearbox and check worm and pinion	Fit new worm and pinion
Gearbox noisy in all gears except top (4th)	Constant gears worn or incorrectly matched, or layshaft bearings worn	Remove bell housing and check constant gears and layshaft bearings	Fit new matched pair of constant gears or layshaft bearings as required
Gearbox noisy in one particular gear only	Worn or damaged gears	Dismantle gearbox and check gears	Fit new gears as necessary
Gearbox noisy in all gears	Worn primary pinion or mainshaft bearings	Remove bell housing and check primary pinion and bearing	Fit new matched pair of constant gears and/or primary pinion bearing as required
		Dismantle gearbox and check mainshaft bearings and gear teeth	Fit new bearings and/or gears as required
Oil leaks from gearbox	Gearbox over-filled with lubricating oil	Remove level plugs	Rectify oil level with vehicle standing on level floor
	Loose or damaged drain or level plugs	Check drain and level plugs. Ensure that joint washer for drain plug is in place and is in good condition	Tighten plugs. If damaged, fit new plugs and joint washer as required
	Joint washers damaged, incorrectly fitted or missing	Determine point of leak, see exploded views in Section C for location of joint washers, and dismantle as necessary	Fit new joint washer with general purpose grease smeared on both sides
	Oil seals damaged or incorrectly fitted	Determine point of leak, see exploded views in Section C for location of oil seals, and dismantle as necessary	Fit new oil seal with 'Hylomar' SQ32M sealing compound smeared on the outside diameter
	Cracked or broken gearbox casings	Clean and examine casings	Fit new casings
Difficulty in engaging forward gears	Incorrect adjustment of gear change mechanism	Check adjustments, Operation C1-13 and C1-18	Adjust as necessary
	Clutch spinning or dragging	Check clutch adjustment. See Section B	Adjust as necessary
	Clutch plate sticking on the pinion shaft	Remove gearbox and clutch, check splines on clutch plate and pinion shaft	Fit new clutch plate and/or new matched pair of constant gears

Fault diagnosis—Gearbox—continued

Symptom	Possible cause	Investigation	Remedy
Difficulty in engaging reverse gear	Incorrect adjustment of selector stops	Check adjustments, Operation C1-13 and C1-18	Adjust as necessary
	Bush loose in gear	Remove reverse gear	Fit latest type reverse gear and shaft, see Operation C1-25
	Reverse gear seized on shaft	Remove reverse gear	
Difficulty in disengaging forward gears	Synchromesh unit faulty	Remove bell housing and check synchromesh unit	Fit new springs or synchromesh unit complete
	Distorted or damaged mainshaft splines	Remove mainshaft and check splines	Fit new mainshaft
Difficulty in disengaging reverse gear	Reverse gear seized on shaft	Remove reverse gear	Fit latest type reverse gear and shaft, see Operation C1-25
Gear lever going into reverse too easily and not into first	Incorrect adjustment of reverse stop	Check adjustment, Operation C1-13	Adjust as necessary
Transfer of oil between gearbox and transfer gear	Worn oil seal in gearbox	Remove the transfer box, mainshaft transfer gear and oil thrower, and check oil seal in gearbox	Fit new oil seal with 'Hylomar' SQ32M sealing compound on the outside diameter
Transfer of oil between gearbox and clutch	Worn oil seal or damaged joint washer in clutch withdrawal unit	Remove clutch withdrawal unit and check joint washer and cross-shaft oil seal	Fit new joint washer and oil seal with 'Hylomar' SQ32M sealing compound smeared on the outside diameter
Jumping out of high transfer	Incorrectly fitted rubber boot at transfer gear lever	Check that rubber boot is not tensioned when in high transfer	Reposition rubber boot
	Weak or broken selector spring	Remove plug and spring from top of transfer box and check spring	Fit new spring
Jumping out of low transfer	Incorrectly fitted rubber boot at transfer gear lever	Check that rubber boot is not tensioned when in low transfer	Reposition rubber boot
	Weak or broken selector spring	Remove plug and spring from top of transfer box and check spring	Fit new spring
	Excessive end-float of intermediate gear	Remove the bottom cover plate from the transfer box and check intermediate gear end-float: .004 in. to .008 in. (0,10 mm to 0,20 mm)	Adjust as required, Operation C1-8.
	Transfer selector fork incorrectly assembled	Remove the top cover from the transfer box and check that fork has threaded side of pinch bolt hole towards centre of box	Remove front output shaft housing and refit fork correctly
Transfer box noisy	Insufficient oil in transfer box	Check oil level	Replenish
	Incorrect grade of lubricating oil	SAE 90 EP See Section X	Drain and replenish with correct grade
	Excessive end-float of intermediate gear	Remove the bottom cover plate from the transfer box and check intermediate gear end-float: .004 in. to .008 in. (0,10 mm to 0,20 mm)	Adjust as required, Operation C1-8

Fault diagnosis—Gearbox—*continued*

Symptom	Possible cause	Investigation	Remedy
	End float of output shaft	Disconnect both propeller shafts from gearbox and check output shaft for end-float	Remove all end-float by setting the output shaft bearing pre-load, Operation C1-8
	Worn bearings	Remove transfer box and dismantle	Fit new bearings
Cannot engage four-wheel drive	Locking pin seized in casing	Remove floor panel and check operation of selector rod, lever and locking pin	Rectify or fit new locking pin
	Broken selector shaft spring	Remove and dismantle front output shaft housing	Clean and fit new parts as required
	Selector shafts sticking in bores of casing	Remove and dismantle front output shaft housing	Clean and fit new parts as required
Cannot disengage four-wheel drive	Spring for selector rod broken, missing or incorrectly adjusted	Check spring at selector rod (yellow knob)	Fit new spring and/or adjust, Operation A1-4
	Broken selector shaft spring	Remove and dismantle front output shaft housing	Clean and fit new parts as required
	Selector shafts sticking in bores	Remove and dismantle front output shaft housing	Clean and fit new parts as required
	Incorrect or excessively worn tyres, varying particularly between front and rear	Check tyres for type and condition	Tyres of same type and similar condition must be fitted to all four wheels

General Data

Main gearbox

Type	Four speed and reverse
Oil capacity	2½ pints (1,5 litres)
Early models: Dipstick position	LH rear of casing
Late models: Oil level plug	LH side of casing

Gear ratios:

	Up to gearbox suffix 'B'	From gearbox suffix 'C' onward
Top	1:1	1:1
Third	1.377:1	1.50:1
Second	2.043:1	2.22:1
First	2.996:1	3.60:1
Reverse	2.547:1	3.02:1

Transfer gearbox:

Type	Two-speed gear in main gearbox output, in unit with main gearbox
Oil capacity	4½ pints (2,5 litres)

Gear ratios:

	Up to gearbox suffix 'B'	From gearbox suffix 'C' onward
High	1.148:1	1.148:1
Low	2.888:1	2.350:1

Overall gear ratios: Up to gearbox suffix 'B'

Main gearbox	Transfer box	
	High ratio	Low ratio
Top gear	5.396	13.578
Third gear	7.435	18.707
Second gear	11.026	27.742
First gear	16.171	40.688
Reverse gear	13.745	34.585

Overall gear ratios: From gearbox suffix 'C' onward

Main gearbox	Transfer box	
	High ratio	Low ratio
Top gear	5.396	13.578
Third gear	7.435	18.707
Second gear	11.026	27.742
First gear	16.171	40.688
Reverse gear	13.745	34.585

Overall gear ratios: With special all helical transfer box

Fitted as standard equipment on 109, 1 ton model, optional on others

Main gearbox	Transfer box	
	High ratio	Low ratio
Top gear	7.19:1	15.4:1
Third gear	10.8:1	23.1:1
Second gear	15.96:1	34.1:1
First gear	25.9:1	55.3:1
Reverse gear	21.7:1	46.4:1

Front axle drive:

Type	Dog clutch in transfer box
To engage	Depress yellow knob on gearbox cover
To disengage	Automatic by selecting low transfer, then reverting to high transfer. Automatically engaged on selection of low transfer

GEARBOX

General Data—continued

Speedometer drive:
Ratio 2.2:1
Position .. .. At rear of transfer box

Transmission brake:
Type .. .. Mechanical. (See Section H). On transfer box output shaft

Detail Data

Main gearbox
Reverse gear bush:
 Reamed bore .. .. .8125 in. + .001 in. (20,637 mm + 0,0254 mm)
Mainshaft bush:
 Fit in gears .. .. .0025 in. to .0035 in. (0,0635 mm to 0,0889 mm)
 Fit on shaft .. .. Zero to .001 in. (Zero to 0,0254 mm)
 End-float .. .. .001 in. to .008 in. (0,0254 mm to 0,20 mm)
2nd and 3rd speed gears:
 End-float on distance sleeve .. .. .004 in. to .007 in. (0,10 mm to 0,18 mm)
Synchronising clutch-load .. .. .. 15 lb. to 20 lb (6,5 kg to 9 kg)
2nd gear stop:
 Adjustment .. .. .002 in. (0,05 mm) clearance
Reverse gear stop:
 Adjustment .. .. .002 in. (0,05 mm) clearance

Transfer gearbox:
Dog clutch selector shaft bush:
 Reamed bore .. .. 1.148 in. —.001 in. (29,17 mm —0,025 mm)
Output shaft front and rear bearings:
 End-float .. .. Zero
 Pre-load .. .. 2 lb to 4 lb (0.28 kg to 0.55 kg)
High-speed gear:
 End-float .. .. .004 in. to .008 in. (0,10 mm to 0,20 mm) (after adjusting output shaft end-float)
Intermediate gear:
 End float .. .. .004 in. to .008 in. (0,10 mm to 0,20 mm)

All helical transfer box, as above with the following exceptions:
Low speed gear:
 End-float .. .. .002 in. to .009 in. (0,05 mm to 0,23 mm)
High-speed gear:
 End-float .. .. .005 in. to .022 in. (0,12 mm to 0,57 mm)

Front output shaft housing assembly
Transfer selector shaft, spring:
 Free length .. .. 7.156 in. (181,76 mm)
 Length in position .. .. .. 3.875 in. (98,43 mm)
 Load in position .. .. .. 24 lb (10,89 kg)
Dog clutch selector springs:
 Free length .. .. 2.75 in. (69,8 mm)
 Solid length .. .. .64 in. (16,2 mm)
 Maximum load .. .. .. 13 lb (5,9 kg)

204

SECTION D—PROPELLER SHAFTS

INDEX—PROPELLER SHAFTS

Note: A comprehensive, detailed Index is included at the end of this manual

Description	Operation No.
	At beginning of section
Exploded view and description	2–3
FRONT PROPELLER SHAFT	
Lubrication	1
Sliding joint	3
Universal joints	3
REAR PROPELLER SHAFT	2–3
Lubrication	1
Sliding joint	3
Universal joints	3
FAULT DIAGNOSIS	At end of section
DATA	At end of section

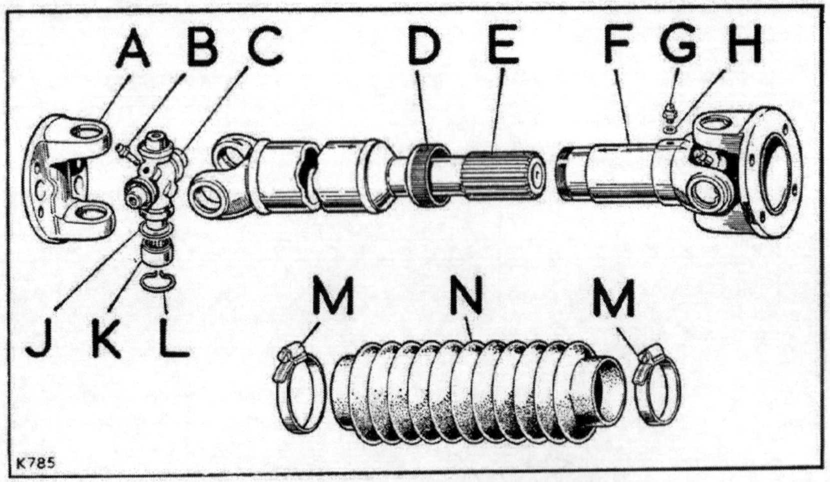

Fig. D1-1. Exploded view of propeller shaft

A—Flanged yoke
B—Grease nipple for universal joint
C—Journal for bearings
D—Dust cap
E—Splined shaft
F—Splined sleeve
G—Grease nipple for splined joint
H—Washer for nipple
J—Seal for journal bearing
K—Needle roller bearing assembly
L—Circlip retaining bearing
M—Clips fixing rubber grommet
N—Rubber grommet for sliding joint

PROPELLER SHAFTS

Lubrication, propeller shafts (front and rear axle drives)—Operation D1-1

Workshop hand tools:
Grease gun

Universal joints

1. Using the correct grade of grease, see Section X, apply grease at the lubrication nipples fitted to the universal joints at both ends of the propeller shaft.

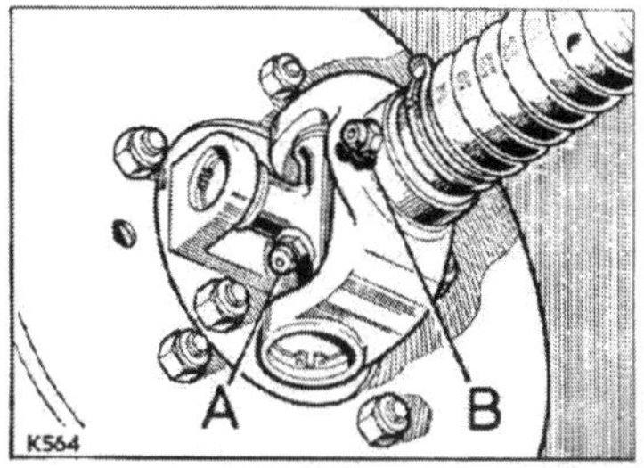

Fig. D1-2. Lubricating points for propeller shafts
A—Nipple for universal joint
B—Nipple for sliding joint

Sliding joints

1. Using the correct grade of grease, apply grease at the lubrication nipple fitted to the splined sleeve.

   Note: If the propeller shaft is fitted with a plug at the sliding joint lubrication point, replace the plug with a lubrication nipple.

   Important: If the propeller shafts are lubricated while they are removed from the vehicle, compress the sliding joint to avoid overfilling, then apply grease.

Propeller shafts (front and rear axle drives), remove and refit—Operation D1-2

(for overhaul instructions, Operation D1-3 refers)

Workshop hand tools:
Spanner sizes: $\frac{7}{16}$ in. AF open end and ring

To remove

1. Jack up the front or rear of the vehicle as applicable, until the wheels are just clear of the floor.
2. Disconnect the propeller shaft from the final drive unit.
3. Disconnect the propeller shaft from the transfer box or front output shaft housing, as applicable.
4. Withdraw the propeller shaft from under the vehicle.

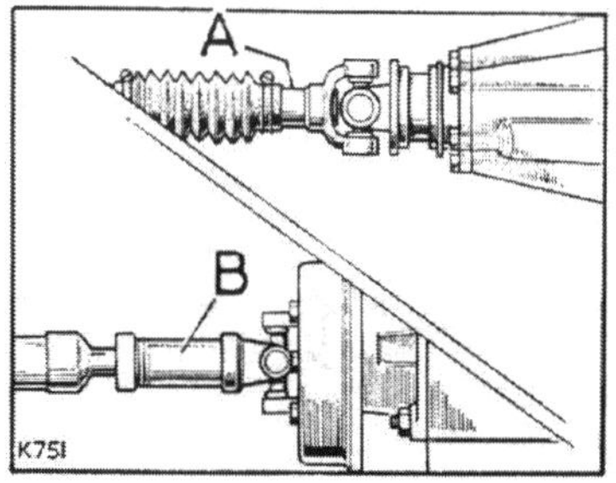

Fig. D1-4. Propeller shaft location
A—Sleeve end of front propeller shaft
B—Sleeve end of rear propeller shaft

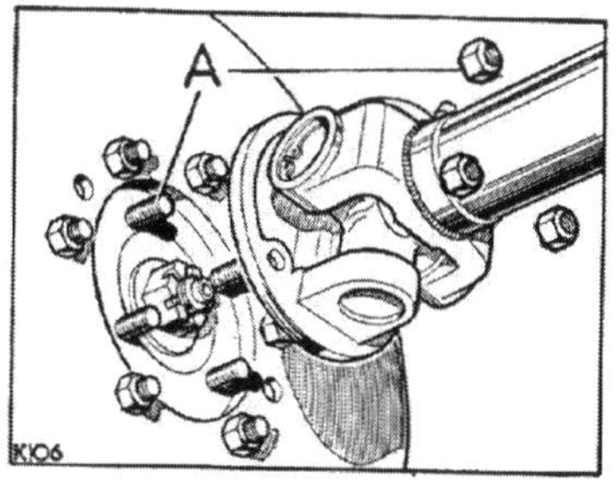

Fig. D1-3. Propeller shaft location
(Coupling at gearbox rear output flange illustrated)
A—Fixings at coupling flanges

To refit

1. Locate the propeller shaft in position. Ensure that the registers on the coupling flanges engage, and that the joint faces bed down correctly all round.
2. Secure the propeller shaft to the gearbox output flange. Tighten the nuts evenly.
3. Secure the propeller shaft to the final drive input flange, with the nuts behind the input flange. Tighten the nuts evenly.
4. Lower the vehicle to the floor.

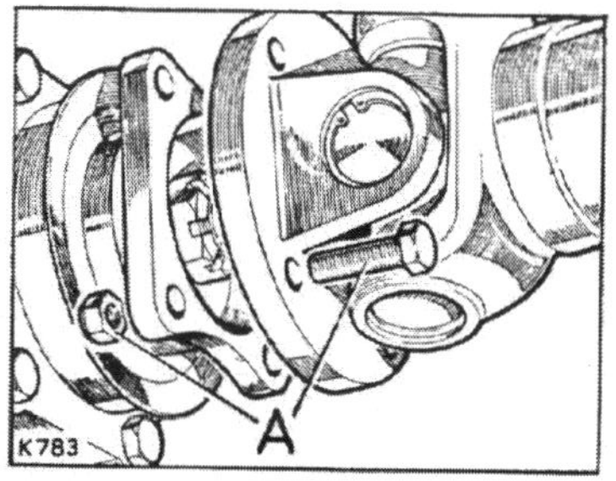

Fig. D1-5. Propeller shaft coupling to final drive unit
A—Fixings at coupling flanges

Note: The front propeller shaft should be fitted with the sleeve end (short end) towards the front axle. The rear propeller shaft should be fitted with the sleeve end towards the gearbox.

PROPELLER SHAFTS

Propeller shafts (front and rear axle drives), overhaul—Operation D1-3

(For removal and refitting instructions, Operation D1-2 refers)

Workshop hand tools:
Screwdriver, circlip pliers, mallet, brass drift, dial test indicator

To dismantle

1. If fitted, unscrew the two hose clips and slide the rubber grommet up the shaft.

   Important: Before dismantling the propeller shaft, ensure that the alignment marks on the splined sleeve and splined shaft are clearly visible. If necessary, make new alignment marks, as the propeller shaft must be re-assembled in its original location, to maintain the balanced setting.

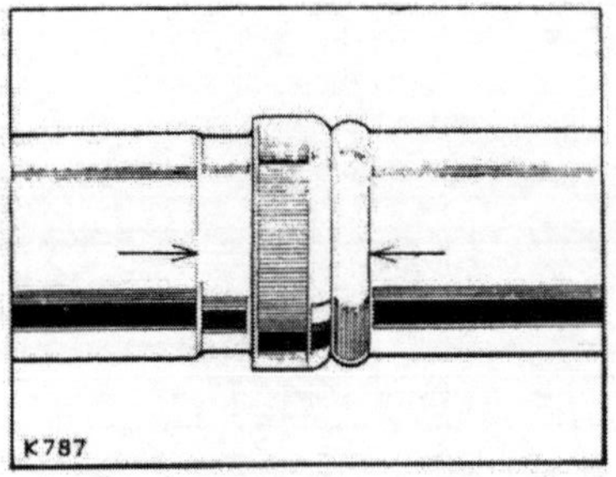

2. Unscrew the dust cap and withdraw the sliding joint from the splined shaft.

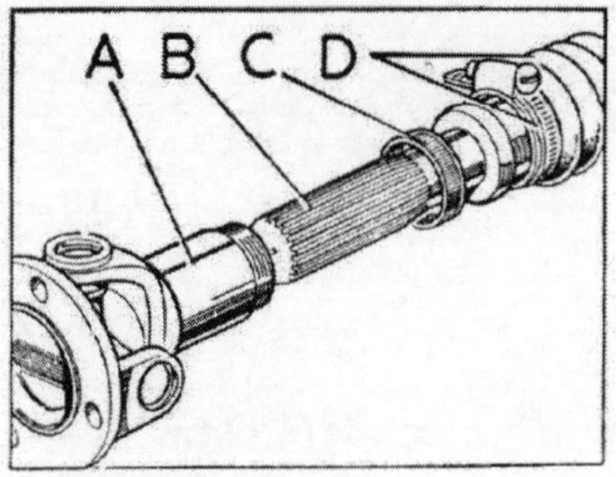

Fig. D1-7. Sliding joint for propeller shaft
A—Splined sleeve
B—Splined shaft
C—Dust cap
D—Rubber grommet and clips

Fig. D1-6. Alignment marks between splined sleeve and shaft

3. Dismantle each universal joint as follows:
   Clean the enamel and dirt from the four circlips and the tops of the bearing races.
4. Remove the circlips.

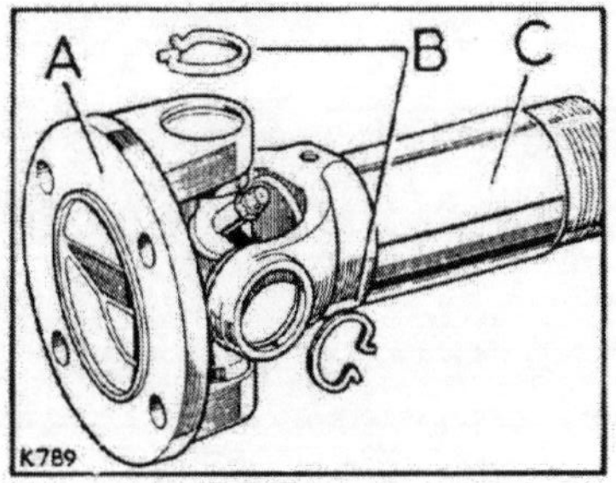

Fig. D1-8. Universal joint
A—Flange yoke
B—Circlips
C—Shaft yoke

5. Hold the joint with one of the splined sleeve (or shaft) yoke lugs uppermost and tap the radius of the yoke lightly with a soft-nosed hammer. The top bearing should then begin to emerge from the yoke.

   Note: If necessary, remove the grease nipple from universal joint to facilitate bearing removal.

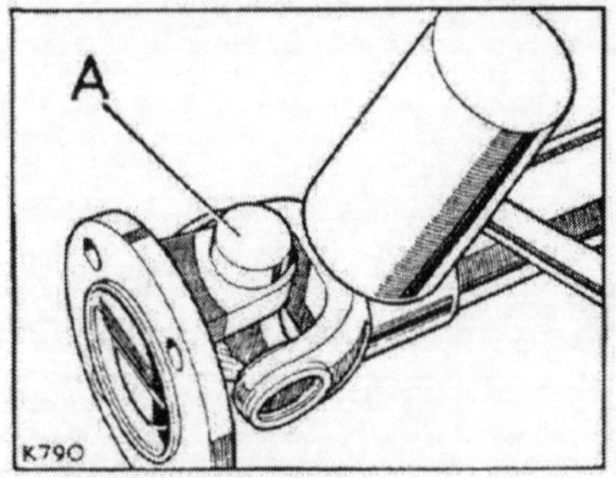

Fig. D1-9. First stage of yoke bearing removal
A—Bearing emerging

Operation D1-3—*continued*

6. Turn the joint over and withdraw the bearing. Always remove a bearing downwards, to avoid dropping the needle rollers. It may be necessary to tap the bearing race from the inside with a small drift; in such cases, care should be taken to prevent damage to the bearing race.

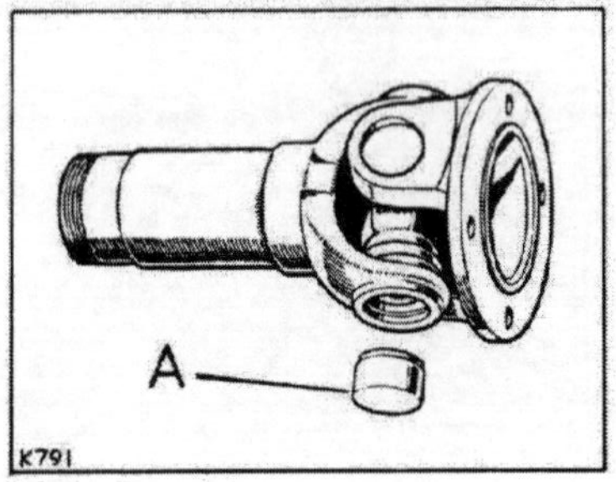

Fig. D1-10. Second stage of yoke bearing removal
A—Bearing withdrawn

7. Repeat the foregoing operations for the opposite bearing.
8. The splined sleeve (or shaft) yoke can now be removed.

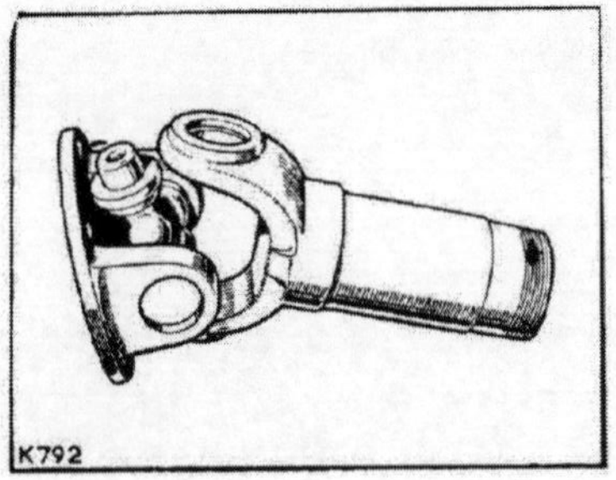

Fig. D1-11. Removing the splined sleeve or shaft

9. Rest the flange yoke on a short piece of tubing of suitable diameter (slightly larger than the bearing race) and drive out the two remaining bearings, using a brass drift.

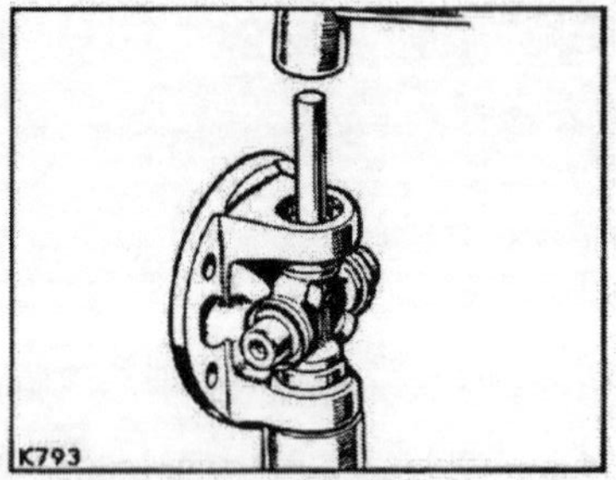

Fig. D1-12. Removing the flange yoke

Inspection

1. Examine all components for obvious wear or damage.
2. If the journal or bearings for the universal joint show any signs of wear, load markings or distortion, they must be renewed complete. Replacement journal assemblies comprise a spider complete with oil seals and four bearings.
3. In the event of wear taking place in any of the eight yoke cross holes, rendering them oval, a new propeller shaft complete must be fitted.
4. Temporarily assemble the splined sleeve and shaft with the alignment marks located directly opposite. Then using a dial test indicator, located on the outside diameter of the shaft splines, check the circumferential movement between the sleeve and shaft. The maximum permissible movement is .004 in. (1,0 mm). If wear beyond this limit has taken place, a new propeller shaft complete must be fitted.

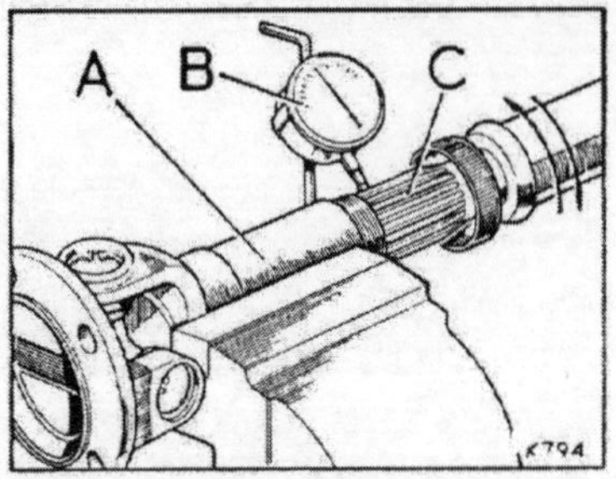

Fig. D1-13. Checking circumferential movement
A—Splined sleeve
B—Dial test indicator
C—Splined shaft

PROPELLER SHAFTS

Fault diagnosis—Propeller shafts

Symptom	Possible cause	Investigation	Remedy
Vibrating propeller shaft	Fixings loose	Check fixings at gearbox and differential coupling flanges	Tighten the fixings evenly and securely
	Incorrectly assembled propeller shaft	Check alignment of balance marks	Reassemble propeller shaft correctly aligned
	Worn needle roller bearings	Check bearings at both universal joints	Fit new bearings
	Worn splines	Remove propeller shaft and check splines with dial test indicator, Operation D1·3	Fit new propeller shaft complete
	Shaft out of balance	If the foregoing checks fail to produce a remedy	Fit new propeller shaft complete
Noisy universal joints	Lack of lubrication		Lubricate propeller shaft, Operation D1-1
	Fixing loose	Check fixings at gearbox and final drive coupling flanges	Tighten the fixings evenly and securely
	Worn needle roller bearings	Check bearings at both universal joints	Fit new bearings
	Worn splines	Remove propeller shaft and check splines with dial test indicator, Operation D1·3	Fit new propeller shaft complete

---

Operation D1-3—continued

To assemble

1. Assemble the needle rollers in the bearing races, if necessary using a smear of vaseline to retain them in place. About half fill the races with a recommended grease.

2. Insert the journal in the flange yoke holes and, using a brass drift slightly smaller in diameter than the hole in the yoke, lightly tap the first bearing into position, and retain with a circlip. It is essential that the bearing races be a *light drive fit* in the yoke trunnions.

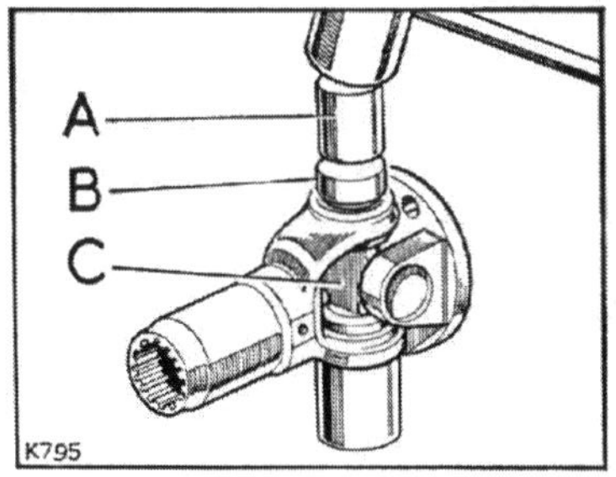

Fig. D1-14. Replacing a yoke bearing

A—Drift
B—Yoke bearing
C—Journal

3. Repeat the foregoing operations for the other three bearings comprising the universal joint.

4. Ensure that all four circlips are firmly located in their grooves. If the joint appears to bind, tap the yoke ears lightly with a soft mallet.

5. Where applicable, slide the rubber grommet and hose clips on to the shaft.

6. Liberally smear the splines of the shaft and sleeve with grease and assemble the propeller shaft, ensuring that the alignment marks on the shaft and sleeve are in line.

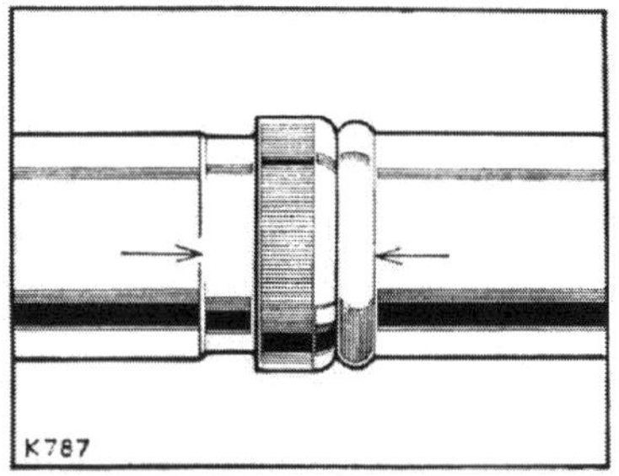

Fig. D1-15. Alignment marks between splined sleeve and shaft

7. If applicable, place rubber grommet in position and secure hose clips with 180° to each other to maintain balance.

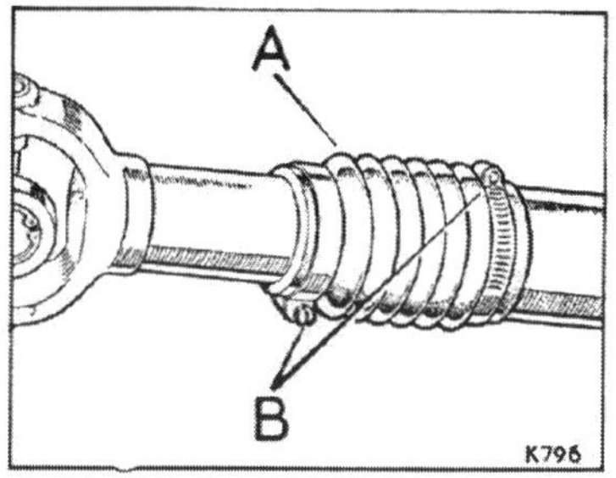

Fig. D1-16. Rubber grommet in position on shaft

A—Rubber grommet
B—Hose clips at 180° to each other

8. Lubricate the propeller shaft. Operation D1-1.

PROPELLER SHAFTS

GENERAL DATA

88 in.
Type .. .. :: Hardy Spicer needle bearing
Tubular shaft:
  Diameter .. .. :: 2 in. (50,8 mm)
  Wall thickness .. .. :: 3/32 in. (2,4 mm)
Overall length (face to face in neutral position):
  Front axle drive .. .. :: 23.812 in. (654 mm)
  Rear axle drive .. .. :: 21.812 in. (554 mm)
Lubricant .. .. :: Grease

109 in. 2¼ litre engine
Type .. .. :: Hardy Spicer needle bearing
Tubular shaft:
  Diameter .. .. :: 2 in. (50,8 mm)
  Wall thickness .. .. :: 3/32 in. (2,4 mm)
Overall length (face to face in neutral position):
  Front axle drive .. .. :: 23.812 in. (654 mm)
  Rear axle drive .. .. :: 42.812 in. (1,087 mm)
Lubricant .. .. :: Grease

109 in. 2.6 litre engine
Type .. .. :: Hardy Spicer needle bearing
Tubular shaft:
  Diameter .. .. :: 2 in. (50,8 mm)
  Wall thickness .. .. :: 3/32 in. (2,4 mm)
Overall length (face to face in neutral position):
  Front axle drive .. .. :: 27.312 in. (694 mm)
  Rear axle drive .. .. :: 39.312 in. (999 mm)
Lubricant .. .. :: Grease

SECTION E—REAR AXLE AND SUSPENSION

There are two entirely different types of differential in use. The majority of vehicles are fitted with Rover type units, but certain vehicles, including the One Ton Land-Rover and other models built to special order or specification, are fitted with units of ENV manufacture, this usually applies to the rear axle only. When carrying out any work or ordering parts for differentials, care must be taken to correctly identify the type of unit concerned.

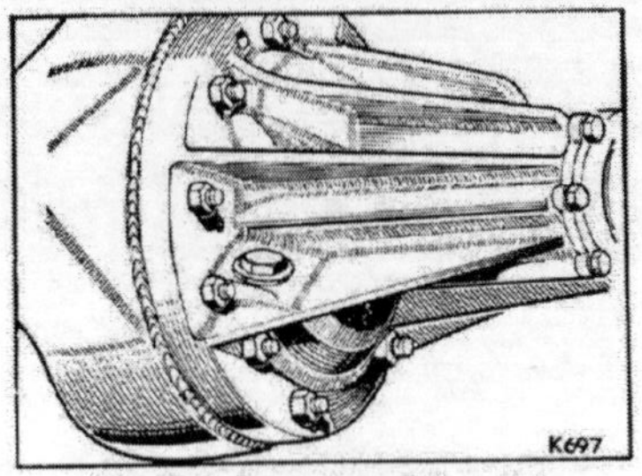

Fig. E1-1. Rover type differential

Fig. E1-2. ENV type differential

INDEX—REAR AXLE AND SUSPENSION

Note: A comprehensive, detailed index is included at the end of this manual

Description	Operation No.
Exploded views and description	At beginning of section
WHEEL HUBS	
Bearing adjustment	4
Bearing sleeve (stub axle)	5–6
Brake anchor plate	5
Driving member for hub	2–3–3A
Hub and bearings	5–6
Lubrication	1
Oil seal for driving member	3–3A
Oil seal for hub bearings	6
REAR SUSPENSION	
Bump stop rubber	11
Check straps for axle	8
Road springs	9–10
Shackle pins and bushes	9–10
Shock absorbers	7
DIFFERENTIAL	
Crown wheel and pinion	14–14A
Differential	14–14A
Lubrication	1–1A
Oil seal for bevel pinion case	12–12A
REAR AXLE	
Axle assembly	16
Axle case	15
Breather for axle case	15
Check strap for axle	8
Half shafts	2–3–3A
Lubrication	1
Oil seal for half shaft	3–3A
FAULT DIAGNOSIS	
DATA	At end of section

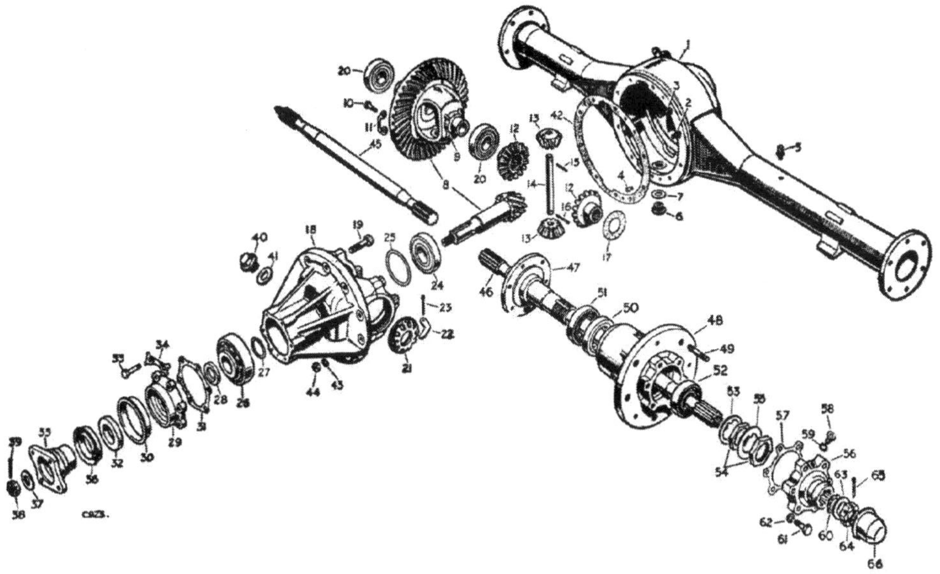

REAR AXLE AND SUSPENSION

Fig. E1-3. Layout of rear axle

1	Rear axle casing
2-3	Bolts fixing differential
4	Dowel locating differential
5	Breather
6-7	Oil drain plug
8	Crownwheel and bevel pinion
9	Differential casing
10-11	Fixings for crownwheel
12	Differential wheel
13	Differential pinion
14	Spindle for pinions
15-16	Fixings for spindle
17	Thrust washer for differential
18	Bevel pinion housing
19	Bolt fixing bearing cap
20	Roller bearings for differential
21	Serrated nut
22	Lock tab } For bearing adjustment
23	Split pin
24	Bearing for bevel pinion, pinion end
25	Shims for bearing adjustment, pinion end
26	Bearing for bevel pinion, flange end
27	Shims for bearing adjustment, flange end
28	Washer for bearing
29	Retainer for oil seal
30	Mudshield for retainer
31	Joint washer for retainer
32	Oil seal for pinion
33-34	Fixings for retainer
35	Driving flange
36	Dust shield for driving flange
37-39	Fixings for driving flange
40-41	Oil filler plug and washer
42	Joint washer for differential
43-44	Fixings for differential
45	Axle shaft, RH
46	Axle shaft, LH
47	Rear hub bearing sleeve
48	Rear hub assembly
49	Stud for road wheel
50	Hub bearing, inner
51	Oil seal for inner bearing
52	Hub bearing, outer
53-55	Fixings for hub bearing
56	Driving member for rear hub
57	Joint washer for driving member
58	Filler plug for hub driving member
59	Joint washer for filler plug
60	Oil seal for rear axle shaft
61-62	Fixings—driving member to rear hub
63-65	Fixings—axle shaft to driving member
66	Hub cap, rear

Lubrication, rear axle (differential and hubs)—Operation E1-1

(Vehicles fitted with ENV differential, Operation E1-1A refers)

Workshop hand tools:
Spanner sizes: ¾ in. AF open end

Final drive unit

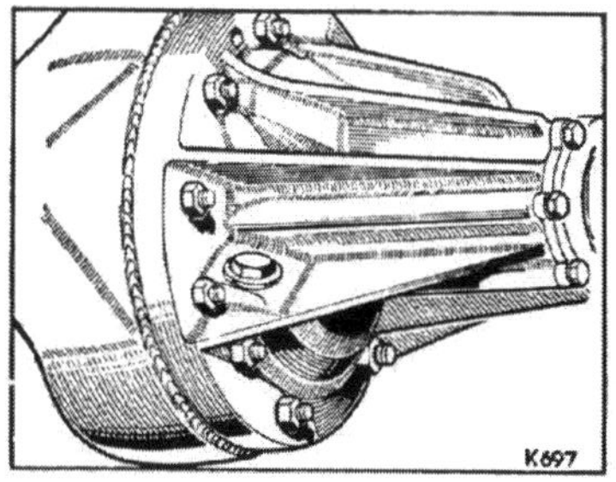

Fig. E1-4. Rover type differential

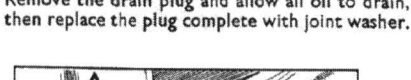

To drain

1. Place a suitable container beneath the differential.
2. Remove the drain plug and allow all oil to drain, then replace the plug complete with joint washer.

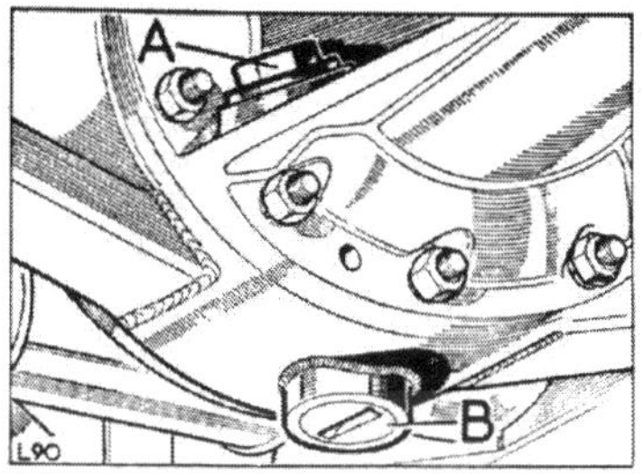

Fig. E1-5. Oil filler and drain plugs
A—Oil filler/level plug
B—Oil drain plug

To refill or top-up

1. Remove the oil filler/level plug.
2. Using the correct grade oil, see Section X, fill the final drive unit to the bottom of the filler plug hole.
3. Fit the oil filler/level plug complete with joint washer.

Capacity: 3 Imperial pints, 3¾ US pints, 1.75 litres.

Hubs

Note: There are two lubricating mediums in use, early hubs are oil filled, while later hubs are grease packed. The grease packed hubs provide an additional means of preventing oil leakage from the final drive unit, and it is recommended that the earlier, oil filled hubs are changed to grease lubrication, this can most conveniently be done during overhaul when the hubs are dismantled and all components are clean and free from oil.

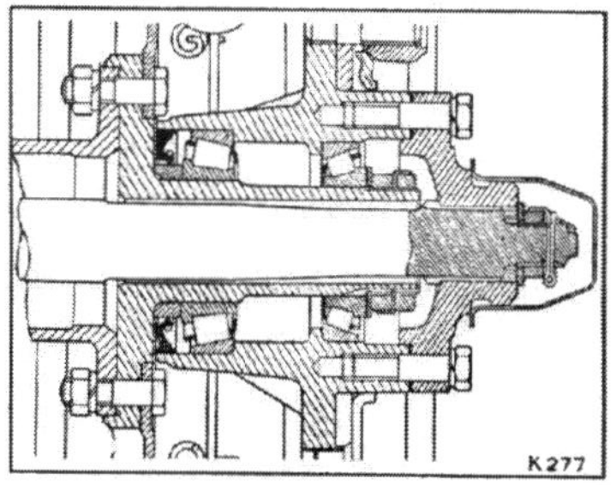

Fig. E1-6. Cross-section of hub

Where oil leakage is experienced on vehicles fitted with the earlier type hub, it is necessary to take the following action to grease-pack the hub.

1. Remove hub from vehicle, discard oil seal and thoroughly clean all parts.
2. Check bearings for wear and replace as required.
3. Pack both bearings with grease; also load area between bearings, leaving sufficient space for the bearing sleeve.
4. Fit new oil seal.
5. Assemble hub, at the same time applying grease between hub and hub driving member.
6. Check the end-float of the hub. Operation E1-4.
7. Do not attempt to fill hub by inserting grease through the oil filler plug in the hub driving member as there is a danger of over-filling and thereby forcing oil out through the oil seal and so on to the brake shoes.

Note: Lubrication instructions for grease filled hubs are similar to the foregoing, and are included in the operation dealing with hub overhaul.

REAR AXLE AND SUSPENSION

Lubrication, ENV differential—Operation E1-1A

(For instructions covering lubrication of wheel hubs, Operation E1-1 refers)

Workshop hand tools:
Spanner sizes: $\frac{9}{16}$ In. AF open end

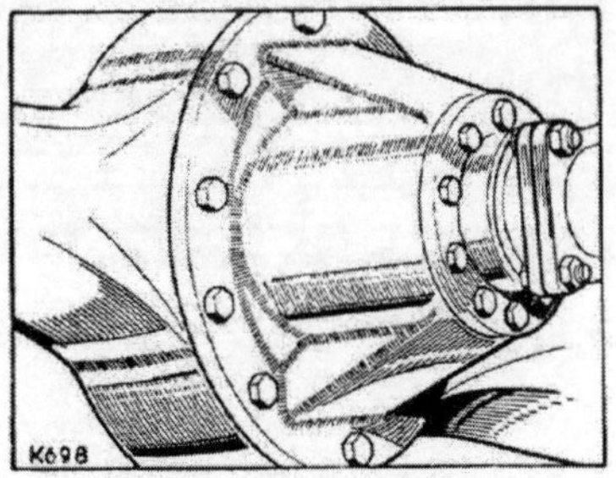

To fill or top up

1. Remove the oil filler/level plug.
2. Using the correct grade oil, see Section X, fill the differential to the bottom of the filler plug hole.
3. Fit the oil filler/level plug complete with joint washer.

Capacity: 2½ Imperial pints, 3.1 US pints, 1,4 litres.

To drain

1. Place a suitable container beneath the differential.
2. Remove the drain plug and allow all oil to drain, then replace the plug complete with joint washer.

Fig. E1-7. ENV type differential

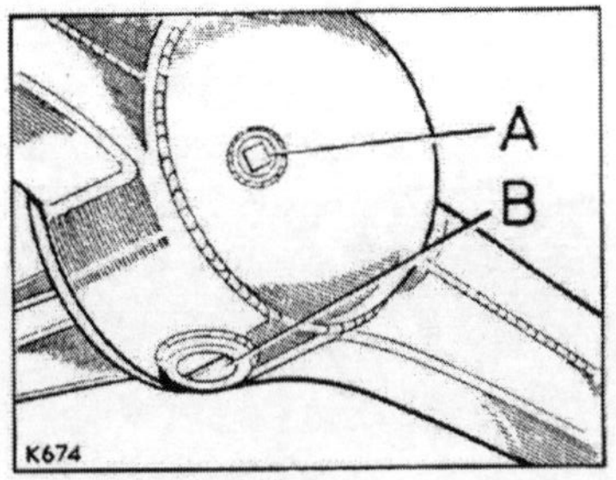

Fig. E1-8. Oil filler and drain plugs
A—Oil filler/level plug
B—Oil drain plug

Rear axle half shafts, remove and refit—Operation E1-2

(For overhaul instructions, Operation E1-3 refers)
(For removal, refitting and overhaul instructions of ENV type half shafts, Operation E1-3A refers)

Workshop hand tools:
Spanner sizes: ⅜ In. BSF socket

To remove

1. Remove the driving member fixings and withdraw the axle half shaft. Note that the driving member is spigotted into the hub and may be initially tight.

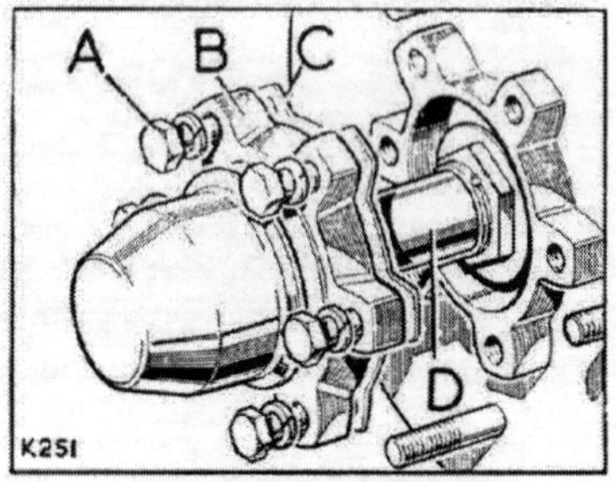

To refit

1. Smear both sides of the joint washer with general purpose grease and place it in position on the hub.
2. If the hub is grease lubricated, see Operation E1-1 (E1-1A), ensure that the space in the end of the hub and driving member is packed with grease.
3. Fit the axle half shaft, carefully engaging the splines into the differential. Tighten the securing bolts to a torque figure of 28 lb ft (3,9 mkg).
4. Check, and if necessary, replenish the rear axle lubricating oil. Operation E1-1 (E1-1A).
5. If the hubs are oil lubricated and it is not convenient to change to grease, remove the socket head oil filler plug from the driving member, and top-up the hub with ⅓ pint (0,190 litre) of oil of the same grade as that for the final drive unit, see Section X.

Fig. E1-9. Rear axle half shaft
A—Fixings, driving member
B—Driving member
C—Joint washer
D—Axle half shaft

REAR AXLE AND SUSPENSION

Rear axle half shafts, overhaul—Operation E1-3

(For removal and refitting instructions, Operation E1-2 refers)
(For overhaul instructions for ENV type half shafts, Operation E1-3A refers)

Workshop hand tools:
Spanner sizes: ⅝ in. BSF open end
Pliers, Screwdriver (large)

To dismantle

1. Prise off the hub cap.
2. Remove the driving member.
3. Withdraw felt oil seal from driving member.

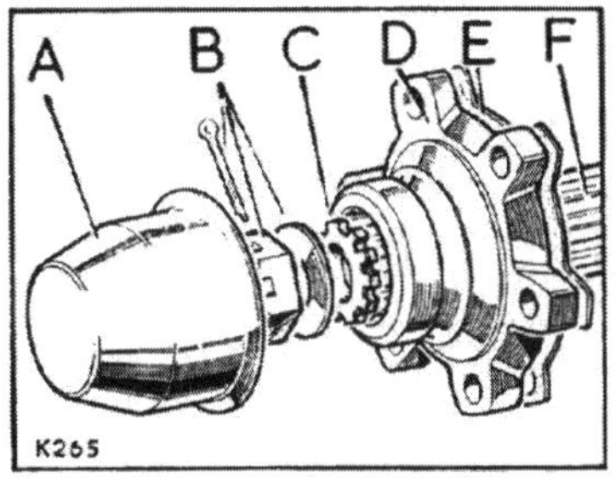

Fig. E1-10. Rear axle half shaft

A—Hub cap
B—Fixings, driving member to axle half shaft
C—Oil seal
D—Driving member
E—Joint washer
F—Axle half shafts

Inspection

1. Examine all components for obvious wear or damage.

To assemble

1. Fit the driving member to the half shaft, ensuring that the oil seal is fitted with the rubber side facing outward, see Fig. E1-11.
2. Tighten the driving member securing nut to a torque figure of 10 to 15 lb ft (1,4 to 2,0 mkg) and lock with a new split pin.

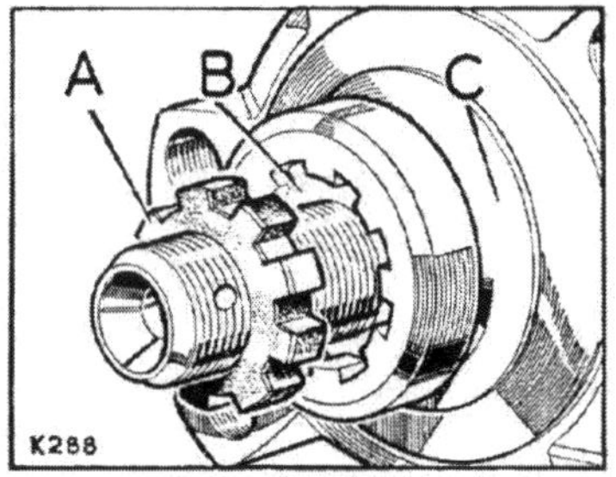

Fig. E1-11. Oil seal for driving member

A—Rubber face of seal
B—Axle half shaft
C—Driving member

3. Fit the hub cap, this must be a firm push fit.

ENV Rear axle half shafts, to remove, refit and overhaul—Operation E1-3A

(For removal and refitting instructions, Operation E1-2 refers)

Workshop hand tools:
Spanner sizes: ⁷⁄₁₆ in. AF, ⅝ in. BSF open end
Circlip pliers, Screwdriver (large)

To dismantle

1. Slacken the fixings at the rear road wheel.
2. Jack up the rear of the vehicle.
3. Remove the rear road wheel.
4. Remove the brake drum, disconnect the brake pipe at the anchor plate and remove the fixings between the anchor plate and axle case, see Operation E1-5 items 3, 4, 7 and 8, then withdraw the hub and half shaft assembly complete from the axle.
5. Remove the driving member fixings.
6. Prise off the hub cap.
7. Remove the circlip from the outer end of the half shaft and withdraw the driving member and half shaft from the hub.

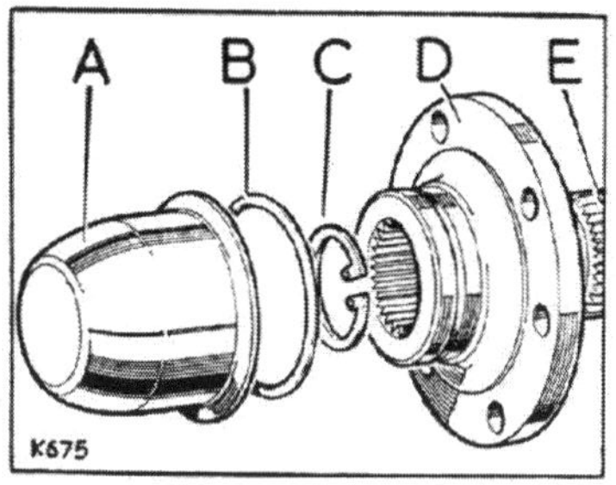

Fig. E1-12. ENV rear axle half shaft

A—Hub cap
B—Oil seal 'O' ring
C—Circlip
D—Driving member
E—Axle half shaft

Inspection

1. Examine all components for obvious wear or damage.

To assemble

1. Fit the driving member and axle half shaft to the hub.
2. Retain the half shaft and driving member assembly with a circlip, and secure the driving member to the hub.
3. Fit the oil seal 'O' ring and hub cap, this must be a firm push fit.
4. Complete the re-assembly by reversing the removal procedure, see Operation E1-5 items 1, 2, 3, 6 and 9. Bleed and adjust the brakes (Section H).
5. Check and, if necessary, replenish the rear axle lubricating oil, Operation E1-1A.

Note: Early half shafts have a second circlip fitted behind the driving member, this can be removed as necessary.

REAR AXLE AND SUSPENSION

Section E—Land-Rover

Hub bearings, to adjust—Operation E1-4

(For removal, refitting and overhaul instructions, Operations E1-5 and E1-6 refer)

Workshop hand tools:
Spanner sizes: ¾ in. BSF, ⁷⁄₁₆ in. BSF,
Screwdriver (medium),
Mallet, Circlip pliers, Dial Test Indicator

Special tools:
Spanner for hub bearing nuts, Part No. 606435 (see Section Z for illustration)

Adjustment procedure

1. Rover type axles—Remove the axle half shaft. Operation E1-2.
2. ENV type axles—Prize off the axle half shaft cap, remove the circlip from the axle half shaft and the fixings from the driving member, then withdraw the driving member from the hub.
3. Slacken the fixings at the rear road wheel.
4. Jack up the rear of the vehicle.
5. Remove the rear road wheel.
6. Fully slacken the rear brake shoe adjusters to ensure that the brake linings are clear of the drum.
7. Remove the rear brake drum.
   Note: If any difficulty is experienced in withdrawing the brake drum, fit one of the extractor drum fixing screws into the extractor hole, and tighten the screw while using a mallet to dislodge the drum.
8. Remove the locknut and washer from the hub.

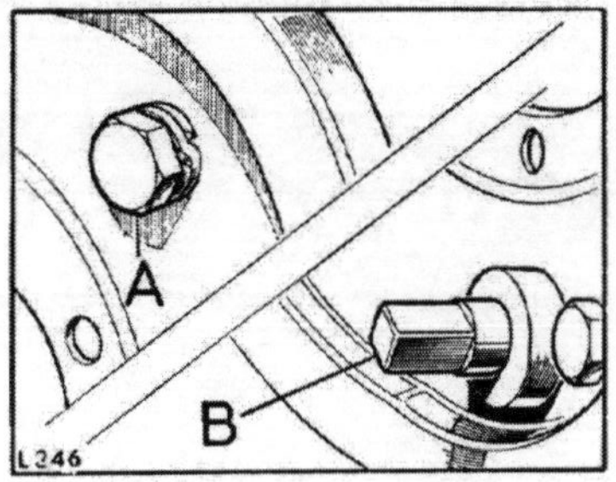

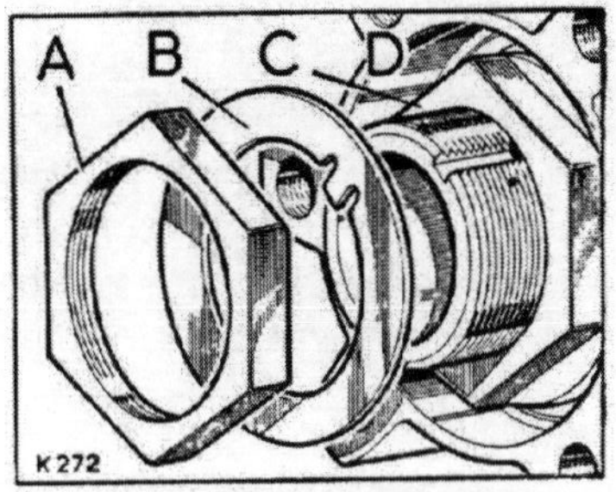

Fig. E1-13. Rear brake shoe adjuster (two variations in use)
A—Snail cam type
B—Fulcrum type

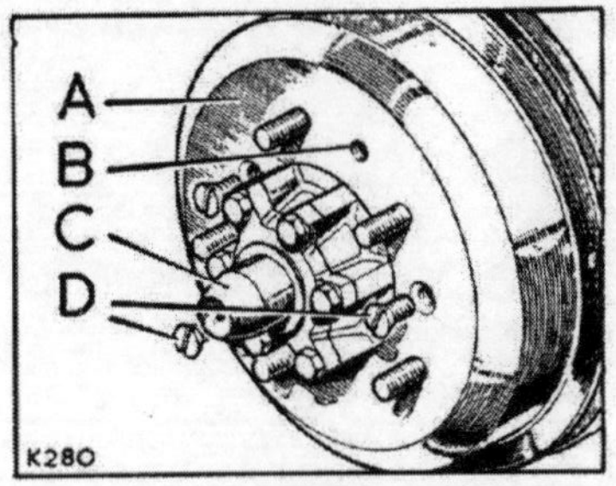

Fig. E1-14. Removing brake drum
A—Brake drum
B—Extractor hole
C—Hub
D—Fixings, drum to hub

Fig. E1-15. Hub bearing fixings
A—Locknut
B—Lockwasher
C—Nut for bearing adjustment
D—Hub

9. Spin the hub vigorously, causing the bearing rollers to settle in the tapered races, producing maximum end-float conditions.
10. Tighten the adjuster nut sufficient only to take up any obvious end-float.
    Note: It is necessary to spin the hub every time before checking the end-float, as moving the hub laterally will resettle the rollers, affecting the measurable end-float.
11. Fit the lockwasher and nut, tighten the nut but do not engage the lockwasher.
12. Using a dial test Indicator, check the end-float of the hub, which must be .004 in. to .006 in. (0,10 mm to 0,15 mm). See Fig. E1-16.
13. If the hub end-float is not within the permitted limits, remove the locknut and washer, and readjust the inner nut. Fit the lockwasher, tighten the locknut and recheck the end-float.

Operation E1-4—continued

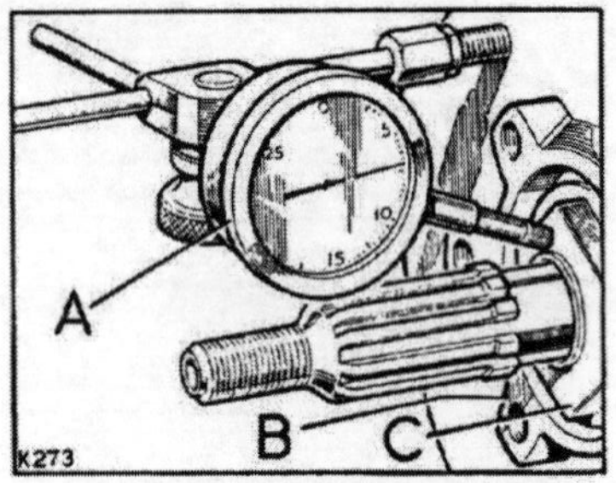

Fig. E1-16. Checking hub end-float
(Front hub illustrated, use same method for rear)
A—Dial test Indicator
B—Hub
C—Bearing locknut

14. When the end-float is correct, engage the lockwasher.
15. Complete the reassembly by reversing the removal procedure.
16. Adjust the brakes (Section H).
17. If the hubs are oil lubricated, replenish the lubricating oil. Operation E1-1 (E1-1A).

Section E—Land-Rover REAR AXLE AND SUSPENSION

Rear hubs, brake anchor plate and bearing sleeve, remove and refit—Operation E1-5

(For overhaul instructions, Operation E1-6 refers)

Workshop hand tools:
Spanner sizes : $\frac{7}{16}$ in. BSF, $\frac{7}{16}$ in. AF open end, $\frac{3}{8}$ in. BSF Circlip pliers, Screwdriver (large), Mallet

Special tools:
Spanner for hub bearing nuts, Part No. 606435 (see Section Z for Illustration)

To remove rear hub

1. Rover type axles—Remove the axle half shaft. Operation E1-2.
2. ENV type axles—Prize off the hub cap, remove the circlip from the axle half shaft and the fixings from the driving member, then withdraw the driving member from the hub.
3. Slacken the fixings at the rear road wheel, jack up the rear of the vehicle and remove the wheel.
4. Fully slacken the rear brake shoe adjuster to ensure that the brake linings are clear of the drum.

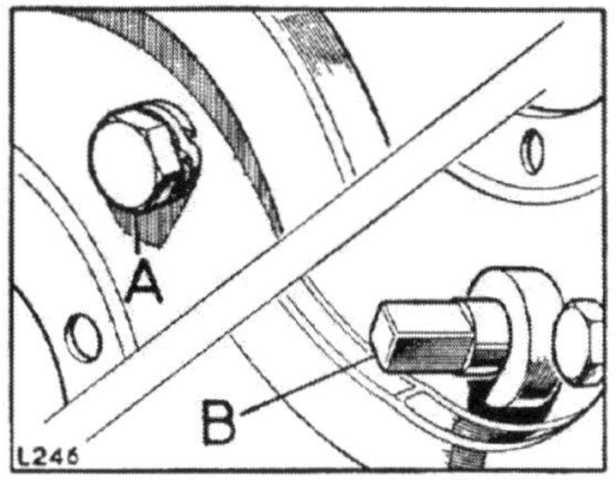

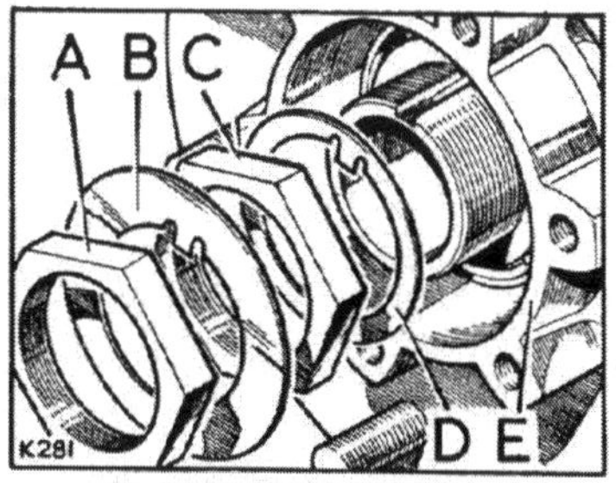

Fig. E1-19. Hub bearing fixings
A—Locknut
B—Lockwasher
C—Adjuster nut
D—Key washer
E—Hub

5. Remove the rear brake drum.
   Note: If any difficulty is experienced in withdrawing the brake drum, fit one of the extractor drum fixing screws into the extractor hole, and tighten the screw while using a mallet to dislodge the drum.

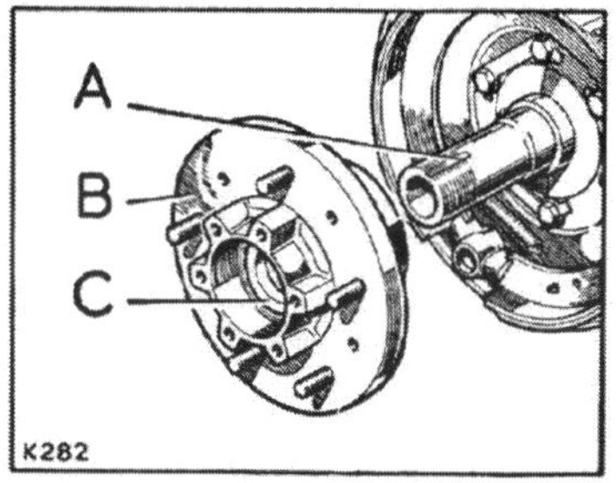

Fig. E1-17. Brake shoe adjusters (two variations in use)
A—Snail cam type
B—Fulcrum type

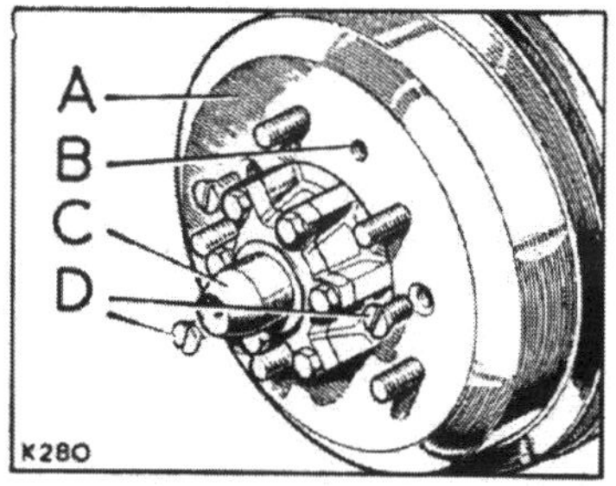

Fig. E1-18. Removing brake drum
A—Brake drum
B—Extractor hole
C—Hub
D—Fixings, drum to hub

Fig. E1-20. Removing rear hub and bearing assembly
A—Bearing sleeve
B—Hub
C—Outer bearing for hub

6. Remove the rear hub bearing fixings.
7. Hold the outer roller bearing in position and withdraw the hub and bearing assembly complete.

REAR AXLE AND SUSPENSION Section E—Land-Rover

Operation E1-5—continued

To remove brake anchor plate and bearing sleeve

8. Disconnect the brake pipe at the rear of the brake anchor plate, then depress the brake pedal, and wedge it in that position, to prevent further leakage of brake fluid. When depressing the brake pedal, take precautions to avoid fluid spillage.
9. Remove the brake anchor plate and withdraw the bearing sleeve.

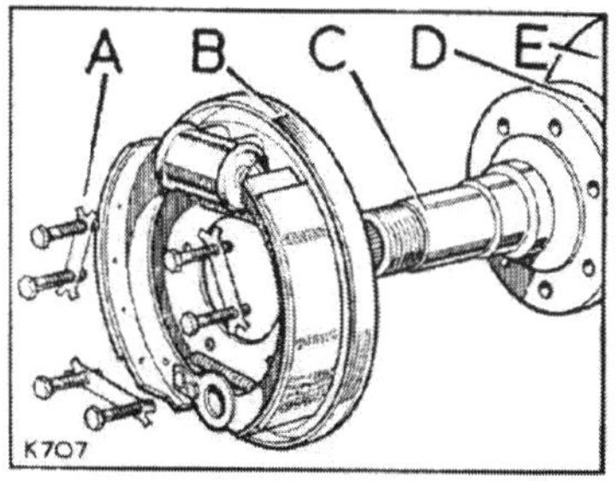

Fig. E1-21. Rear brake anchor plate and bearing sleeve
(typical brake plate illustrated)
A—Fixings, brake anchor plate and bearing sleeve to axle case
B—Brake anchor plate
C—Sleeve for hub bearings
D—Joint washer
E—Axle case

To refit brake anchor plate and bearing sleeve

1. Smear both sides of the joint washer with general purpose grease, and place it in position on the rear face of the hub bearing sleeve.
2. Position the hub bearing sleeve on the axle case, with the keyway at the top, then fit the brake anchor plate with the brake pipe connection located at the top. Ensure that cut-away in back plates face inwards.

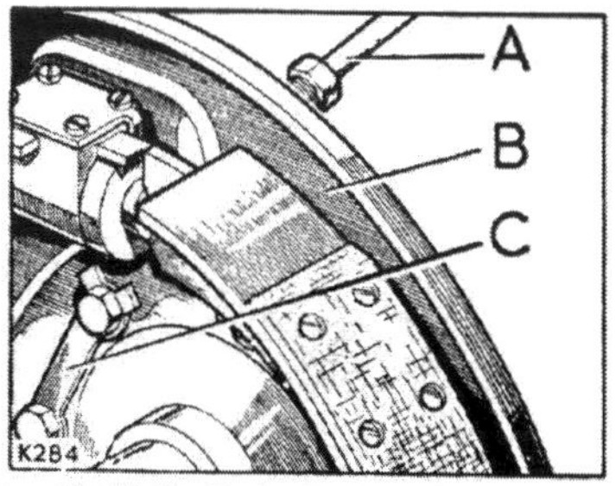

Fig. E1-22. Fitting brake anchor plate
A—Brake pipe connection at top
B—Brake anchor plate
C—Cut-away side of lockwasher facing inward

3. Connect the brake pipe at the rear of the brake anchor plate.

To refit rear hubs

4. Hold the outer roller bearing in position and slide the hub and bearing assembly onto the bearing sleeve.
5. Fit the key washer and bearing adjusting nut, then adjust the bearing end-float. Operation E1-4.
6. Fit the brake drum.
7. Complete the re-assembly by reversing the removal procedure.
8. Replenish the rear axle lubricating oil. Operation E1-1 (E1-1A).
9. Bleed and adjust the brakes. (Section H).

REAR AXLE AND SUSPENSION

Rear hubs and bearing sleeve, overhaul—Operation E1-6

(For removal and refitting instructions, Operation E1-5 refers)
(For overhaul of brake anchor plate, refer to Section H)

Workshop hand tools:
Screwdriver (medium), Mallet

To dismantle

1. Withdraw the outer roller bearing.
2. Prise out the oil seal and withdraw the inner roller bearing.
3. Press the bearing outer races from the hub.
4. If it is required to remove the inner bearing distance piece from the sleeve, it must be shattered, using extreme care to avoid damaging the sleeve.

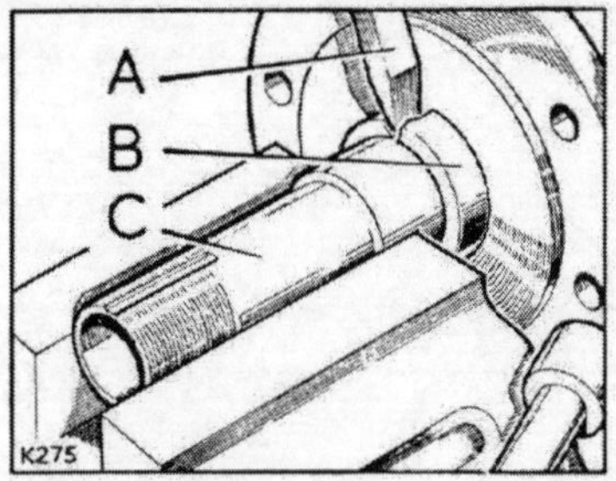

Inspection

1. Examine all components for obvious wear or damage.
2. Check the outside diameter of the inner bearing distance piece, this must not show any signs of damage or roughness as it forms the inner seat for the oil seal. The distance piece should be a press fit on the stub axle. Any clearance between these two parts will allow oil to leak past on to the brake linings.
3. The hub bearings must be a *press fit* in the hub and a *sliding fit* on the sleeve.

To assemble

1. Press the bearing outer races, wide side first, into the hub, ensuring that they abut the locating shoulders.
2. Using the correct grade of grease, see Section X, fully pack the inner roller bearing and place it in its outer race.
3. Smear the outside diameter of the oil seal with jointing compound, and press it into the hub, lipped side inward, until it is flush with the rear face of the hub. DO NOT press the seal below the rear face of the hub, or it may fail to locate its inner seat correctly, resulting in an oil leak which could contaminate the brake linings.
4. Pack the centre of the hub with the correct grade of grease, leaving sufficient space for the bearing sleeve.
5. Fully pack the outer roller bearing with the correct grade of grease, and place it in its outer race.

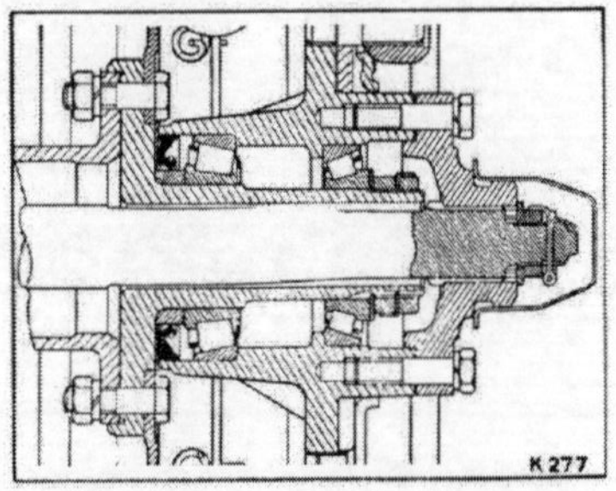

   Note: When fitting the hub to the axle, check the axle case breather (see Operation E1-15), a blocked breather could cause failure of the oil seals fitted in the hubs.

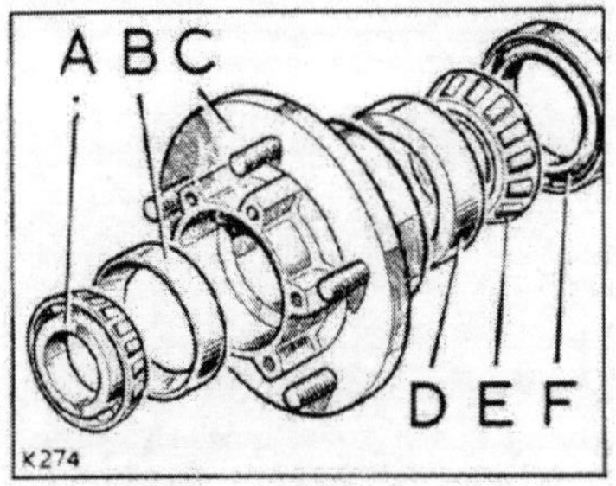

Fig. E1-23. Rear hub and bearings

A—Outer roller bearing
B—Outer race for outer bearing
C—Hub
D—Outer race for inner bearing
E—Inner roller bearing
F—Oil seal

Fig. E1-24. Removing inner bearing distance piece

A—Use chisel to shatter
B—Distance piece (shattered)
C—Sleeve for hub bearings

Fig. E1-25. Cross-section of rear hub

REAR AXLE AND SUSPENSION

Rear shock absorbers, remove and refit—Operation E1-7

Workshop hand tools:
Spanner sizes: 11/16 in. AF, 3/4 in. AF open end, 3/8 in. AF socket
Pliers, Screwdriver (medium)

To remove
1. Slacken the fixings at the rear road wheel.
2. Jack up the rear of the vehicle and support on stands.
3. Remove the rear road wheel.
4. Remove the rear shock absorber.

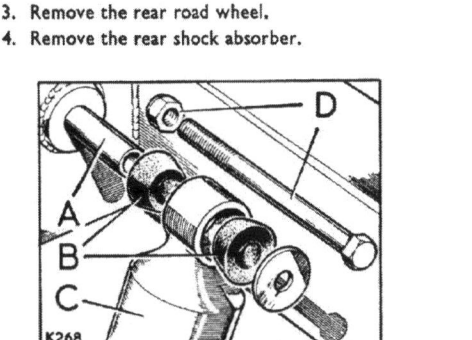

2. The shock absorber incorporates differential damping, having greater resistance on the extension stroke. Check the operation, by extending and compressing the shock absorber, there must be a uniform resistance throughout the length of the stroke. If the resistance is erratic or weak, fit a new shock absorber.

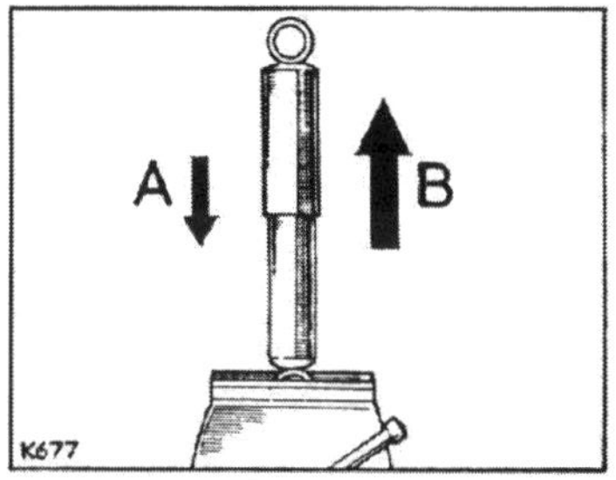

Fig. E1-28. Checking shock absorber
A—Compression stroke, light resistance
B—Extension stroke, heavy resistance

To refit
1. Fit the shock absorber in position.
2. Fully tighten the shock absorber fixings to ensure correct pre-load of the mounting rubbers. Where the fixing is made by split pin, the pre-load of the mounting rubbers is pre-determined by the position of the split pin.
3. Fit the road wheel.

Fig. E1-26. Shock absorber top fixing
A—Chassis
B—Rubbers
C—Shock absorber
D—Fixings

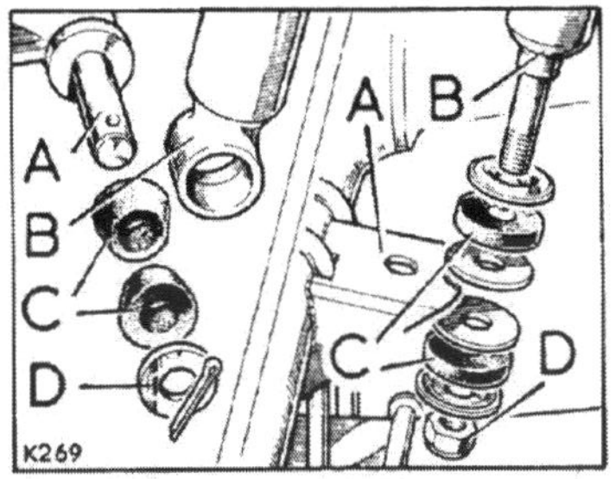

Fig. E1-27. Shock absorber bottom fixings (alternative types in use)
A—Chassis
B—Shock absorber
C—Rubbers
D—Fixings

To check operation of shock absorber
1. Secure the shock absorber vertically in a vice by holding the bottom fixing between the jaws.

Rear axle check strap, remove and refit—Operation E1-8

Workshop hand tools:
Spanner sizes: 7/16 in. AF open end, 7/16 in. AF socket

To remove
1. Slacken the fixings at the road wheel.
2. Jack up the vehicle and support on stands.
3. Remove the road wheel.
4. Support the rear axle with a jack.
5. Remove the axle check strap.

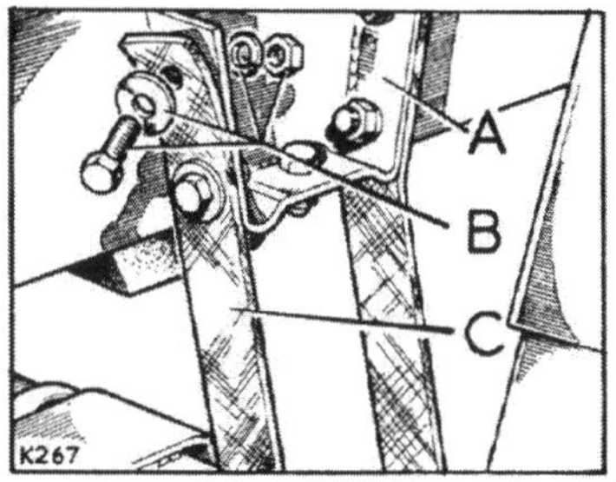

Fig. E1-29. Check strap for axle
A—Chassis
B—Fixings, check strap to chassis
C—Check strap

To refit
1. Fit the axle check strap, ensuring that the strap is located between the brake shield and the axle.

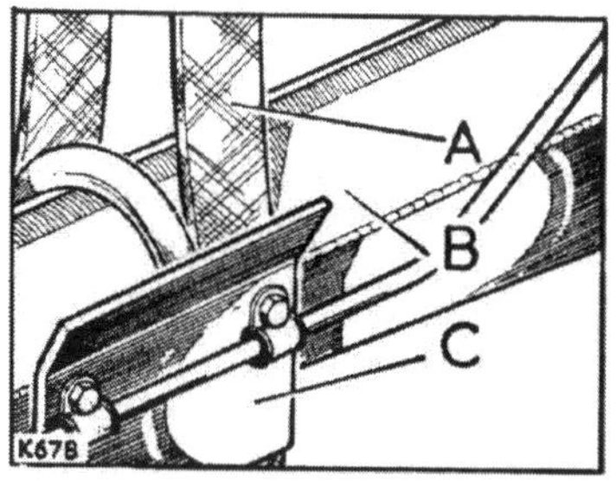

Fig. E1-30. Check strap location
A—Check strap
B—Rear axle
C—Shield for brake pipe

2. Fit the road wheel.

REAR AXLE AND SUSPENSION

Rear road springs, remove and refit—Operation E1-9

(For overhaul instructions Operation E1-10 refers)

Workshop hand tools:
Spanner sizes: $\frac{7}{16}$ in. BSF, $\frac{1}{2}$ in. AF, $\frac{7}{8}$ in. AF sockets
Mallet

IMPORTANT

The driver side and passenger side rear springs are not interchangeable, the free camber of the driver's side spring being greater to compensate for the extra weight (driver, etc.) carried on that side of the vehicle.

Note: To assist in identifying spring types, the Part No. is stencilled on the top face and stamped on the under face of one of the leaves.

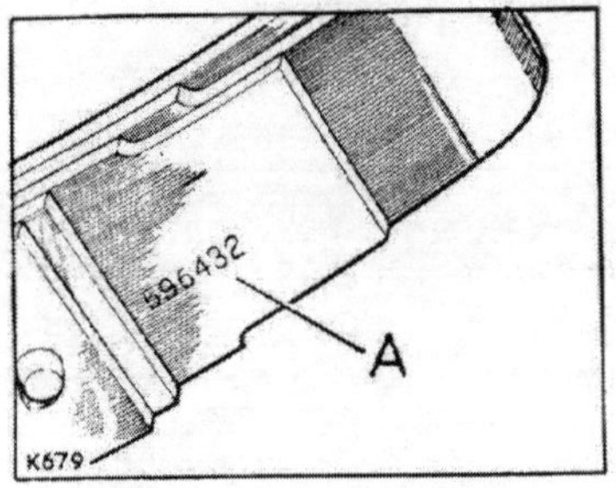

Fig. E1-31. Spring identification
A—Part No. stamped on spring

To remove

1. Jack up the vehicle and support it on jacking stands.
2. Remove the rear wheel.
3. Support the rear axle with a jack.
4. Remove the four nuts and two lockplates securing the spring to the axle.

   Note: On certain models, the rear shock absorbers are attached to the spring bottom plate, and where applicable, allow the plate to hang on the shock absorber boss.
   On all models, the brake pipe shields will remain in position, clipped to the pipe.

5. Remove the self-locking nut from the shackle pin in each spring eye.
6. Remove the shackle pin from the rear end of the spring, the pin is threaded into the inner shackle plate.
7. Remove the shackle pin from the front end of the spring.
8. Remove the road spring complete.

Fig. E1-32. Rear road spring and axle
A—Rear road spring
B—Bottom plate for spring
C—Fixings, bottom plate to 'U' bolts

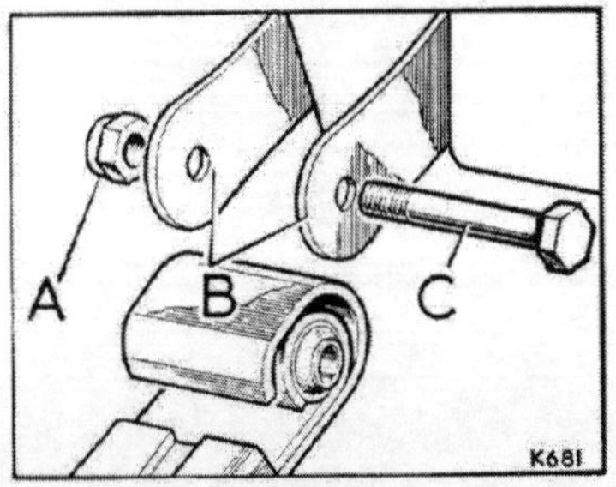

Fig. E1-33. Rear fixings for road spring
A—Self-locking nut
B—Shackle plates
C—Shackle pin

To refit

1. Slacken the shackle pin securing the shackle plates to the chassis.
2. Fit the road spring in position, secure 'U' bolts but do not fully tighten the shackle pins and locking nuts at this stage.
3. Lower the vehicle to the ground and move vehicle bodily backward and forward to settle the springs. Tighten the shackle pins and locking nuts. If the shackle pins and locking nuts are tightened prior to lowering the vehicle to the ground, premature failure of the bushes will occur.

Rear road springs, overhaul—Operation E1-10

(For removal and refitting instructions, Operation E1-9 refers)

Workshop hand tools:
Spanner sizes: $\frac{7}{16}$ in. BSF, $\frac{3}{8}$ in. BSF open end, $\frac{11}{16}$ in. AF, $\frac{7}{8}$ in. AF sockets
Screwdriver (large), Mallet, Hack-saw

To dismantle

1. Remove the fixings from the leaf clips, which may be bolts and nuts, and/or long screws threaded into the leaf clips.

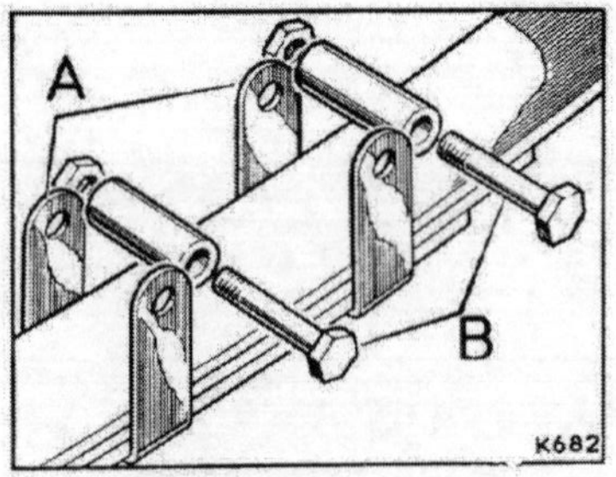

Fig. E1-34. Spring leaf clips
A—Leaf clips   B—Fixings

2. Remove the centre bolt and nut to release the spring leaves.
3. Press out the bushes from each end of the spring.

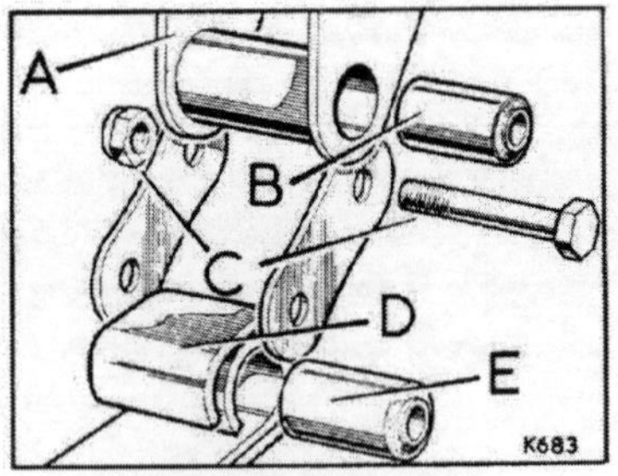

Fig. E1-35. Bushes for spring
A—Chassis
B—Bush for chassis
C—Shackle plates and fixings
D—Spring
E—Bush for spring

4. Remove the self-locking nut from the shackle pin securing the shackle plates to the chassis frame. Unscrew the pin from the inner shackle plate and remove it, together with the two plates.

5. If necessary, remove the shackle bush from the chassis frame bracket with the aid of a tubular drift or suitable extractor; if the bush disintegrates, leaving the outer casing in the chassis frame bracket, it should be carefully sawn through with a hack-saw to facilitate removal. DO NOT saw the chassis bracket.

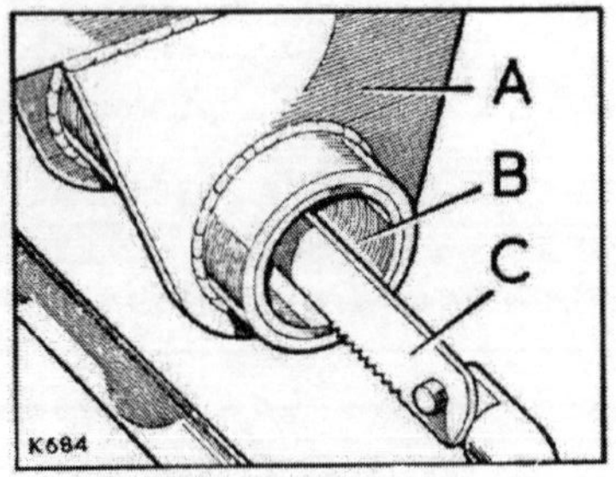

Fig. E1-36. Removing bush outer case
A—Chassis frame bracket
B—Bush outer case
C—Hack-saw with blade inverted

Inspection

1. Clean (or preferably degrease) the leaves; carefully examine them for signs of failure cracks. Only the main and second leaves are supplied as replacement, so that should any other leaf be faulty, the complete spring must be renewed.
2. The recambering of road springs is not advised, but if no alternative is possible, the spring should be reset, if necessary, either to a new spring or to the dimensions included in the data section.

To assemble

1. If removed, fit the shackle bush to the chassis frame bracket. The bush must be a drive fit.
2. Grease each leaf with graphite grease and reassemble the spring by fitting the centre bolt and leaf clips; fit the spring bushes, which must be a press fit.
3. Fit the shackle plates to the chassis frame, but do not fully tighten the fixings until the spring is refitted to the vehicle.

REAR AXLE AND SUSPENSION

Bump stop rubber, remove and refit—Operation E1-11

Workshop hand tools:
Spanner sizes: 7/16 in. AF open end, 7/16 in. AF socket

To remove

1. Slacken the fixings at the road wheel.
2. Jack up the vehicle and support on stands.
3. Remove the road wheel.
4. Remove the bump stop rubber secured to the underside of the chassis member.

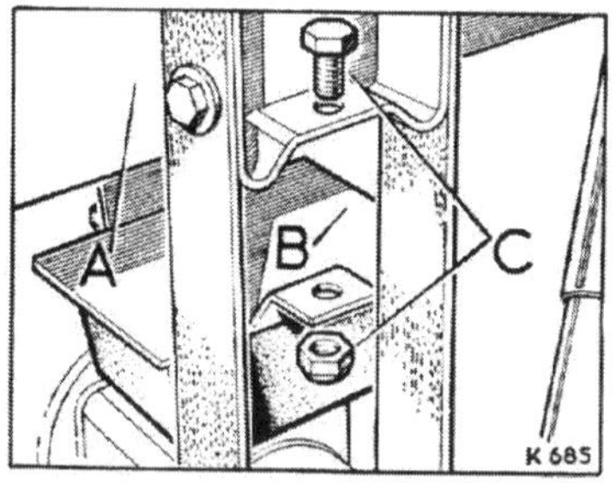

To refit

1. Fit the bump stop rubber, tightening the fixings evenly.
2. Fit the road wheel.

Fig. E1-37. Bump stop rubber

A—Chassis   B—Bump rubber   C—Fixings

Oil seal for bevel pinion case, remove and refit—Operation E1-12

Workshop hand tools:
Spanner sizes: 7/16 in. AF, 7/16 in. AF, 3/4 in. AF open end, 1 in. AF socket

To remove

1. Drain the lubricating oil from the differential Operation E1-1 (E1-1A).
2. Disconnect the rear propeller shaft and move it clear of the differential.

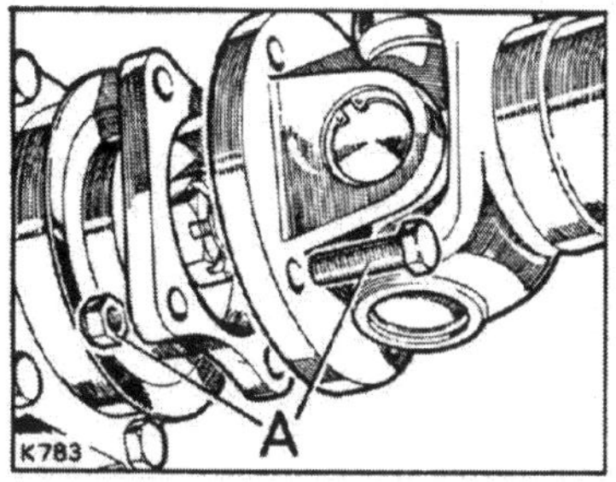

Fig. E1-38. Propeller shaft for rear axle

A—Fixings at coupling flanges

3. Remove the driving flange from the bevel pinion shaft.
4. Remove the oil seal retainer and joint washer, taking care not to dislodge the thick distance washer for the flange end bearing.

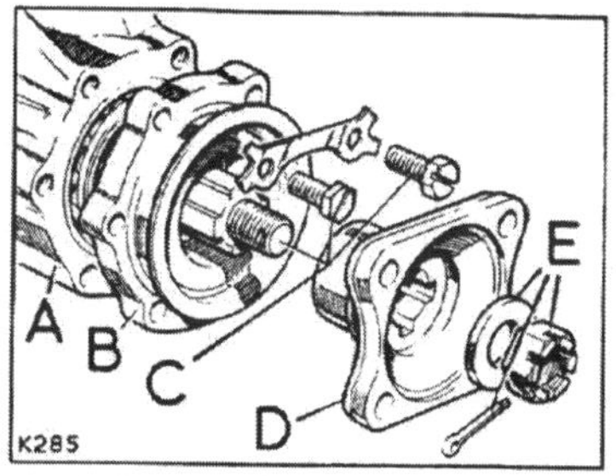

Fig. E1-39. Driving flange and oil seal retainer

A—Bevel pinion housing
B—Oil seal retainer
C—Fixings, oil seal retainer
D—Driving flange for bevel pinion
E—Fixings, bevel pinion driving flange

5. Press the oil seal from the retainer.

To refit

1. Warm the oil seal retainer to facilitate fitting the seal, smear the outside diameter of the seal with jointing compound and fit it, lipped side inward, into the retainer.

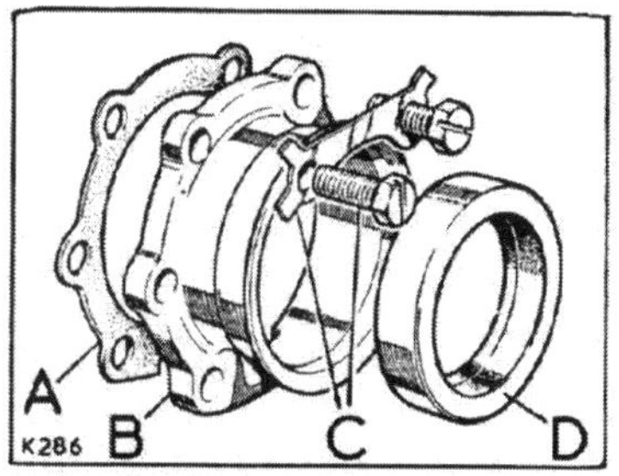

Fig. E1-40. Oil seal retainer

A—Joint washer
B—Retainer for oil seal
C—Fixings, oil seal retainer
D—Oil seal

2. Using a new joint washer, smear both sides with a jointing compound and fit the oil seal retainer, ensuring that the oilways in the bevel pinion housing, oil seal retainer and joint washer are aligned. Engage the locking plates.

   Note: Before fitting the driving flange, examine the outside diameter for roughness or damage which may have caused failure of the original seal, and rectify or renew as necessary.

3. Fit the driving flange to the bevel pinion, and tighten the securing nut to a torque figure of 85 lb ft (11,75 mkg).
4. Fit the propeller shaft.
5. Replenish the differential lubricating oil. Operation E1-1 (E1-1A).
6. Ensure that the axle case breather is clear (see Operation E1-15), a blocked breather could cause failure of the oil seals fitted in the axle assembly.

REAR AXLE AND SUSPENSION — Section E—Land-Rover

Oil seal for ENV bevel pinion housing, remove and refit—Operation E1-12A

Workshop hand tools:
Spanner sizes: ⅞ in. AF open end, ⅞ in. BSF socket
Screwdriver (medium)

To remove

1. Drain the lubricating oil from the differential. Operation E1-1 (E1-1A).
2. Disconnect rear propeller shaft and move it clear of differential.

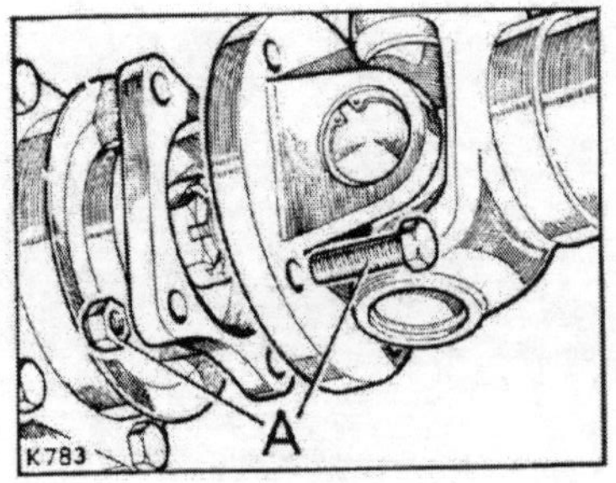

Fig. E1-41. Propeller shaft for rear axle
A—Fixings at coupling flanges

3. Remove the driving flange from the bevel pinion shaft.
4. Prise the oil seal from the bevel pinion housing.

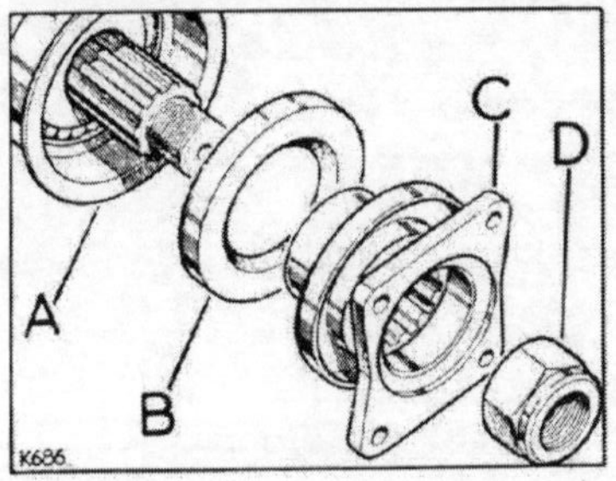

Fig. E1-42. Oil seal for bevel pinion
A—Bevel pinion housing
B—Oil seal
C—Driving flange
D—Fixings for driving flange

To refit

1. Smear the outside diameter of the oil seal with jointing compound and fit it, lipped side inward, into the bevel pinion housing.

   Note: Before fitting the driving flange, examine the outside diameter for roughness or damage which may have caused failure of the original seal, and rectify or renew as necessary.

2. Fit the driving flange to the bevel pinion, and tighten the securing nut to a torque figure of 100 to 120 lb ft (14 to 16 mkg).
3. Fit the propeller shaft.
4. Replenish the differential lubricating oil. Operation E1-1 (E1-1A).
5. Ensure that the axle case breather is clear (see Operation E1-15), a blocked breather could cause failure of the oil seals fitted in the axle assembly.

Differential, remove and refit—Operation E1-13

(For overhaul instructions, Operation E1-14 (E1-14A) refers)

Workshop hand tools:
Spanner sizes: ⅞ in. BSF socket, ⅞ in. AF open end

To remove

1. Drain the lubricating oil from the rear axle. Operation E1-1 (E1-1A).
2. Remove the axle half shafts, Operation E1-2 or E1-3A, as applicable. Note that it is only necessary to withdraw the half shafts sufficient to be clear of the differential.
3. Disconnect the rear propeller shaft and move it clear of the differential.

Fig. E1-43. Propeller shaft for rear axle
A—Fixings at coupling flanges

4. Remove the differential.

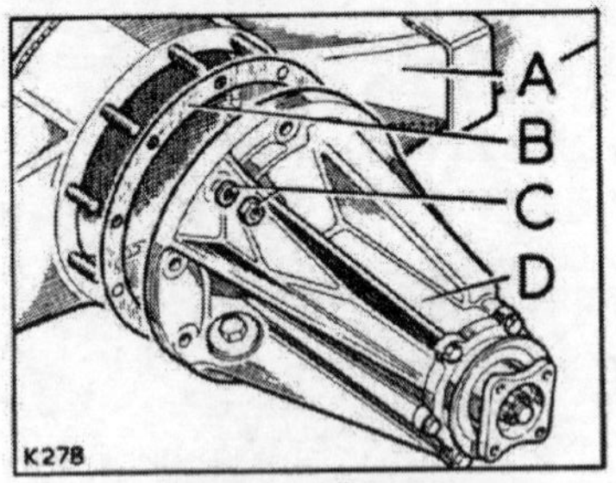

Fig. E1-44. Differential
A—Rear axle case
B—Joint washer
C—Fixings, bevel pinion housing to axle case
D—Bevel pinion housing

To refit

1. Smear general purpose grease on both sides of the joint washer for the differential and place it in position on the axle case.
2. Fit the differential.
3. Fit the propeller shaft.
4. Fit the axle half shafts. Operation E1-2, or E1-3A as applicable.
5. Replenish the rear axle lubricating oil. Operation E1-1 (E1-1A).

218

REAR AXLE AND SUSPENSION

Differential, to overhaul—Operation E1-14

(For removal and refitting Instructions, Operation E1-13 refers)

Workshop hand tools:
Spanner sizes: ½ in BSF open end
⅜ in. BSF, ⁷⁄₁₆ in. BSF, ⅝ in. BSF sockets
Pliers, Screwdriver (medium), Feeler Gauges,
Dial Test Indicator, Torque Wrench,
Spring Balance, Micrometer

Special tools:
262757	Bearing extractor
530105	Differential spanner
262761	Height gauge for
600299	differential pinion.
601998	1 off, as required.
605004	(See text)
606012	Dummy bearing, suffix 'B' axles
606019	Dummy bearing, suffix 'A' axles
530106	Bracket for Dial Test Indicator

Before commencing this operation, verify unit type. See Operation E1-14A.

Important note: During dismantling it is essential that all components are marked in their original position and relative to other components, so that if original components are refitted, their initial setting is maintained.

To dismantle

1. Remove the bearing caps.
2. Remove the serrated nuts.

Fig. E1-45. Bearing caps and adjusters
A—Fixings, bearing caps
B—Locker, bearing adjuster
C—Bearing cap
D—Serrated nuts

3. Withdraw the crown wheel and differential assembly.
4. Remove the bevel pinion driving flange and withdraw the pinion from the housing.
5. Withdraw the shims from the bevel pinion and extract, or drift off the roller bearing.
6. Remove the oil seal retainer and press out the seal.

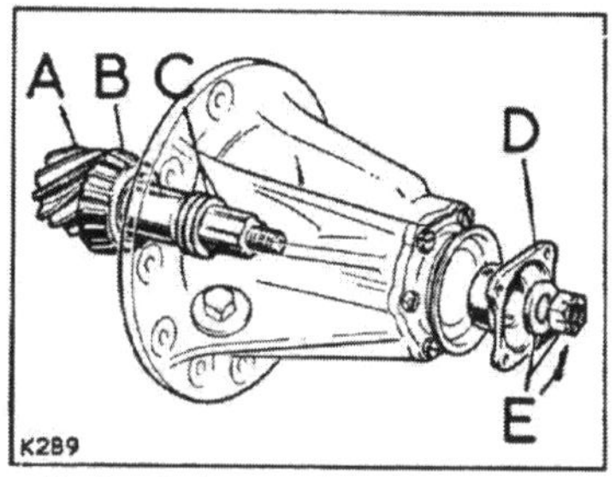

Fig. E1-46. Bevel pinion and driving flange
A—Bevel pinion
B—Roller bearing
C—Shims
D—Driving flange
E—Fixings, driving flange

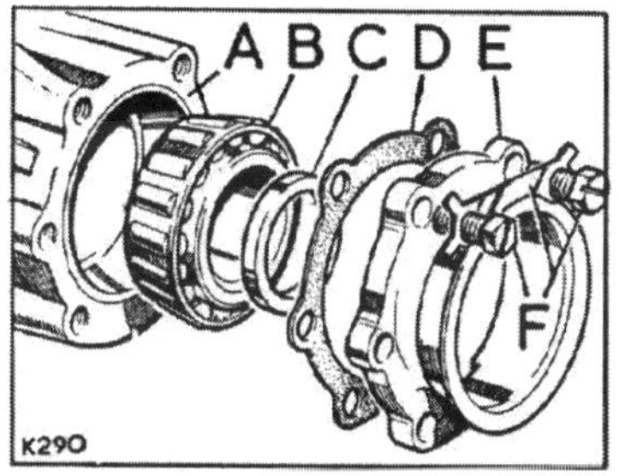

Fig. E1-47. Oil seal retainer and bearing
A—Bevel pinion housing
B—Roller bearing
C—Distance washer
D—Joint washer
E—Oil seal retainer
F—Fixings, oil seal retainer

Operation E1-14—continued

7. Withdraw the distance washer and roller bearing from the bevel pinion housing.
8. Press both bearing outer races from the bevel pinion housing, using special tool, Part Number 262757, to remove the pinion end outer race together with its shims.

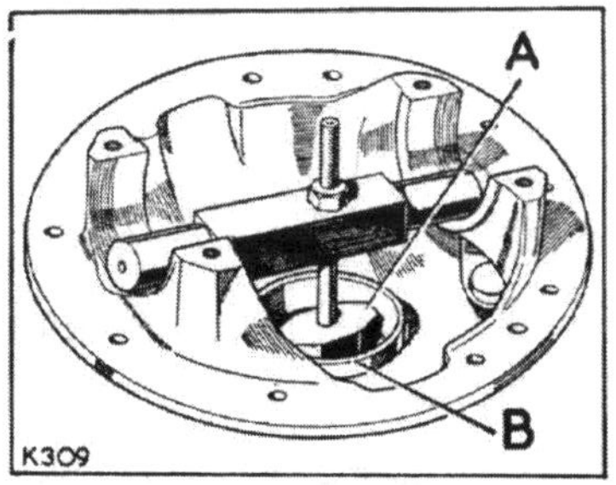

Fig. E1-48. Pressing out pinion end bearing outer race
A—Special tool, Part No. 262757
B—Bearing outer race

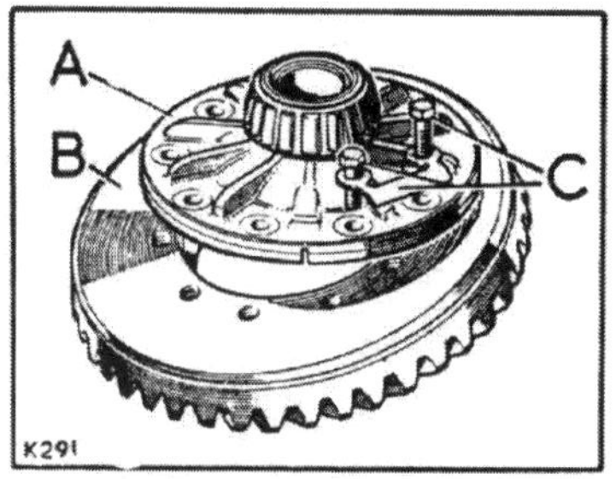

Fig. E1-49. Crownwheel fixings
A—Differential case
B—Crownwheel
C—Fixings

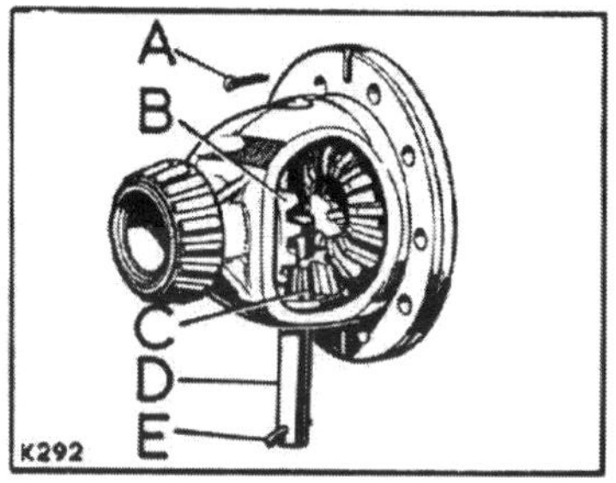

Fig. E1-50. Spindle for differential pinions
A—Split pin
B—Differential wheels
C—Differential pinions
D—Spindle
E—Plain pin

CAUTION: Before using special tool, Part Number 262757, ensure that projections on the extractor bar fit the cast slots at the rear of the bearing outer race. If necessary, grind the projections until a sliding fit is obtained, otherwise the bevel pinion housing may be damaged.

9. Remove the crown wheel from the differential case.
10. Remove the spindle from the differential pinions, rotate the differential wheels to release the pinions, then lift out the differential wheels together with their thrust washers. See Fig. E1-51.
11. Extract the roller bearings from the differential case.

REAR AXLE AND SUSPENSION

Operation E1-14—continued

Crownwheel and pinion is only supplied as a matched set, and MUST NOT be interchanged separately.

Bevel pinion housing and bearing caps are matched sets, and MUST NOT be interchanged separately.

Check the differential pinion seatings in the differential case. The spherical seats must finish flush, without any step or recess due to wear. If a step is present, it must be ground away to prevent the pinion teeth rubbing the casing.

Pre-assembly checks
Bevel pinion height setting

The bevel pinion height is adjusted by shimming between the pinion end bearing outer race and the pinion case. The outer race must be a press fit in the pinion case and should not be used while determining shimming. For the purpose of bevel pinion height setting, a loose fitting dummy bearing should be used in place of the pinion end bearing. Dummy bearings are available as follows: Part Number 606019 for use with suffix 'A' axles and Part Number 606012 for use with suffix 'B' axles.

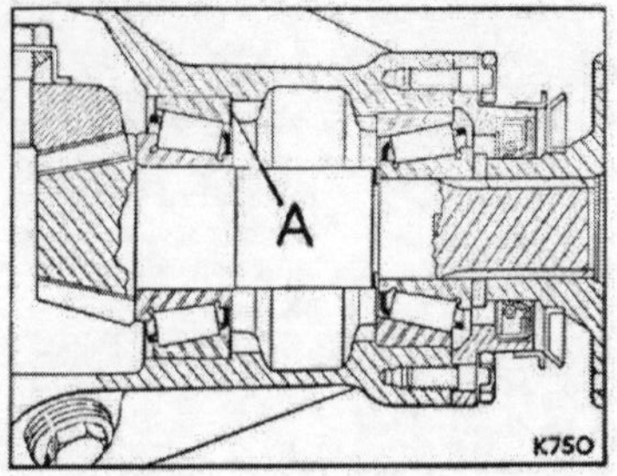

Fig. E1-53. Bevel pinion height adjustment shims

A—Shims

The dimensional difference between the width of the real bearing and the dummy bearing must be measured and taken into account when calculating shim thickness required.

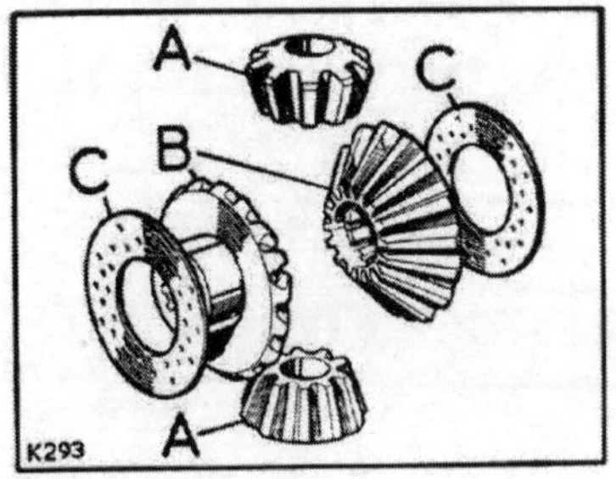

Fig. E1-51. Differential pinions and wheels

A—Differential pinions
B—Differential wheels
C—Thrust washers, differential wheels

Inspection

Examine all components for obvious wear or damage.

All bearings must be a press fit, except the flange end bevel pinion bearing, which must be a slide fit on the shaft.

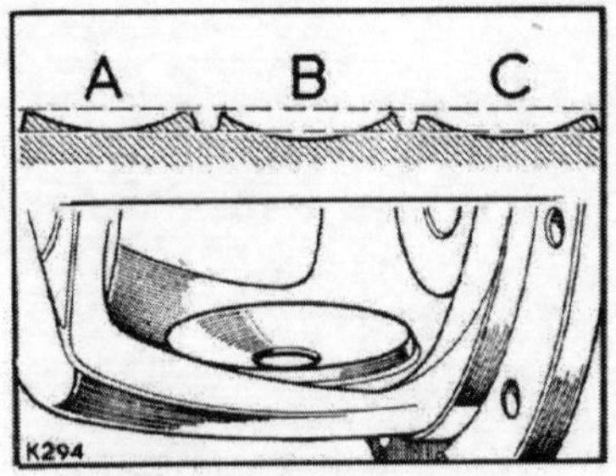

Fig. E1-52. Differential pinion seats

A—Seat as new
B—Recessed seat
C—Seat reclaimed by grinding

Operation E1-14—continued

1. Clean all traces of oil and grease from the bearing to be fitted to the pinion end of the bevel pinion shaft.

2. Measure and record the difference in width between the pinion end bearing and the dummy bearing. Make a number of checks at different points to ensure accuracy.

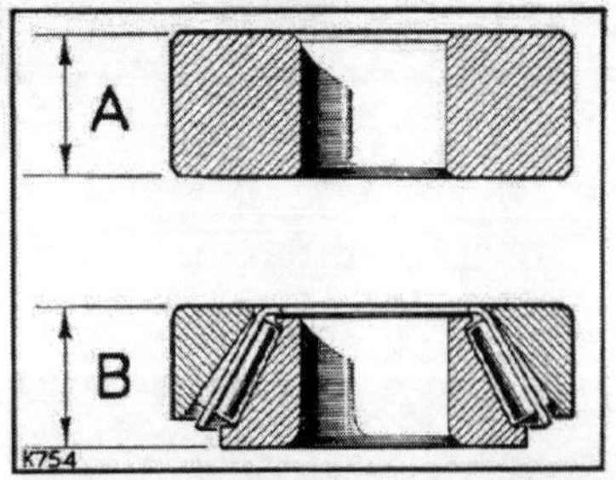

Fig. E1-54. Comparing real bearing with dummy bearing

A—Width of dummy bearing
B—Check real bearing width from inner race to outer race

3. Subtract .002 in. (0,05 mm) from the bearing difference dimension already obtained and recorded, to allow for bearing creep which will take place on final assembly when the bearing pre-load is set.

4. Press the flange end bearing outer race into the pinion case.

5. Fit the dummy bearing to the bevel pinion shaft and locate the shaft into the pinion case. DO NOT fit any shims at this stage.

6. Place the flange end roller bearing and distance washer on to the pinion shaft.

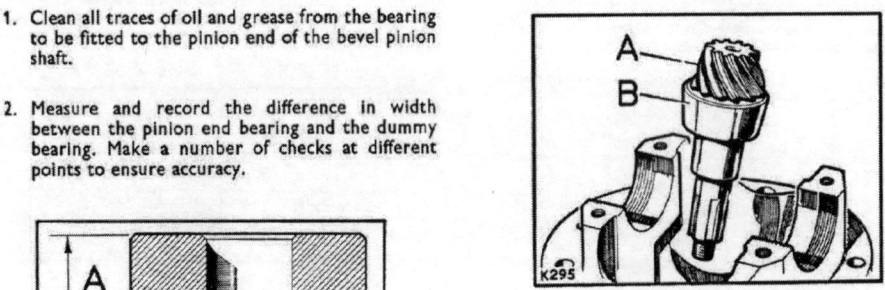

Fig. E1-55. Dummy bearing for bevel pinion

A—Bevel pinion
B—Dummy bearing

7. Deliberately omitting the oil seal and retainer, fit the driving flange and tighten the securing nut until the bevel pinion is stiff to turn, this will ensure that all clearance is removed without damaging the bearing.

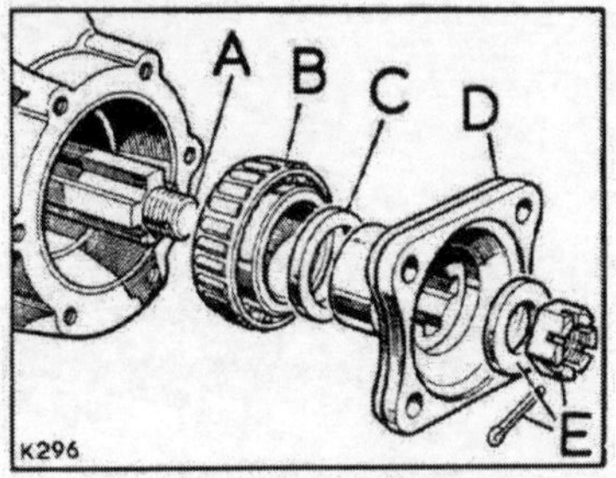

Fig. E1-56. Pinion driving flange

A—Pinion shaft
B—Roller bearing
C—Distance washer
D—Driving flange
E—Fixings, driving flange

Operation E1-14—continued

8. Locate the pinion height gauge into the pinion housing and secure with the bearing caps.

   Note: There are four variations of height gauge in use, and either one may be used.

9. Place the slip gauge on to the pinion face and, while held firmly in position, use feeler gauges to measure the clearance between the height gauge and the slip gauge, note the dimension obtained.

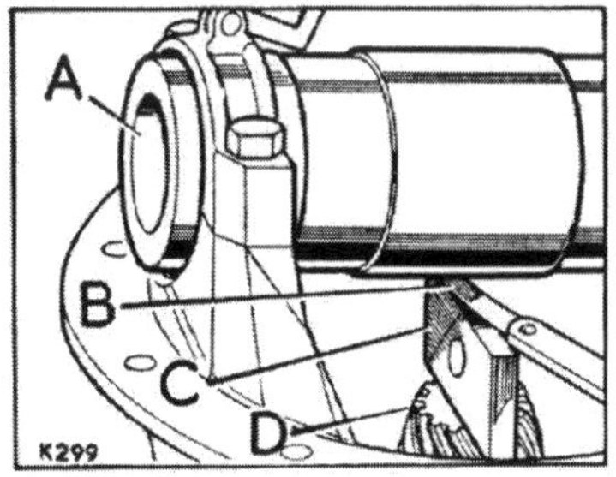

Fig. E1-57. Checking pinion height

A—Height gauge
B—Feeler gauge
C—Slip gauge
D—Pinion

10. Remove the height gauge, and check the markings on the pinion face. In addition to the production batch number which will be found on the face of all pinions, there may also be a pinion height dimension, which can be ±.005 in. (±0,12 mm). There may also be a further dimension, prefixed with the letter H or HD indicating 'head depth', this can be zero to —.004 in. (zero — 0,10 mm). These dimensions must be taken into account when setting the pinion height, regardless of which type of pinion height gauge is being used. Where a pinion has no dimensional marking, use the pinion height '0' and head depth '0' when referring to the following charts.

Fig. E1-58. Pinion height and head depth markings

A—Batch number
B—Height dimension
C—Head depth dimension

Illustration shows batch number, +1 pinion height indicating +.001 in. (0,02 mm) pinion height and HD-2 indicating —.002 in. (0,05 mm) head depth.

Chart A. To be used with height gauges, Part Nos. 601998, 262761 and 600299:

Final feeler gauge clearance

Pinion height markings	in. .012	mm 0,30	in. .011	mm 0,27	in. .010	mm 0,25	in. .009	mm 0,22	in. .008	mm 0,20	in. .007	mm 0,17	in. .006	mm 0,15	in. .005	mm 0,12	in. .004	mm 0,10	in. .003	mm 0,07	in. .008	mm 0,20
+5	.012	0,30	.011	0,27	.010	0,25	.009	0,22	.008	0,20	.007	0,17	.006	0,15	.005	0,12	.004	0,10	.003	0,07	.008	0,20
+4	.011	0,27	.010	0,25	.009	0,22	.008	0,20	.007	0,17	.006	0,15	.005	0,12	.004	0,10	.003	0,07	.002	0,05	.007	0,17
+3	.010	0,25	.009	0,22	.008	0,20	.007	0,17	.006	0,15	.005	0,12	.004	0,10	.003	0,07	.002	0,05	.001	0,02	.006	0,15
+2	.009	0,22	.008	0,20	.007	0,17	.006	0,15	.005	0,12	.004	0,10	.003	0,07	.002	0,05	.001	0,02	.000	0,00	.005	0,12
+1	.008	0,20	.007	0,17	.006	0,15	.005	0,12	.004	0,10	.003	0,07	.002	0,05	.001	0,02	.000	0,00	.001 * 0,02	.004	0,10
0	.007	0,17	.006	0,15	.005	0,12	.004	0,10	.003	0,07	.002	0,05	.001	0,02	.000	0,00	.001 * 0,02	.002 * 0,05	.003	0,07
—1	.006	0,15	.005	0,12	.004	0,10	.003	0,07	.002	0,05	.001	0,02	.000	0,00	.001 * 0,02	.002 * 0,05			.002	0,05
—2	.005	0,12	.004	0,10	.003	0,07	.002	0,05	.001	0,02	.000	0,00	.001 * 0,02							.001	0,02
—3	.004	0,10	.003	0,07	.002	0,05	.001	0,02	.000	0,00	.001 * 0,02									.000	0,00
—4	.003	0,07	.002	0,05	.001	0,02	.000	0,00	.001 * 0,02												
—5	.002	0,05	.001	0,02	.000	0,00	.001 * 0,02														

Head depth (H or HD) markings: —1 —2 0

Any pinion marking dimensions falling within the space marked with an asterisk (*) add the figure shown to the initial measurement taken between height gauge and slip gauge.

Operation E1-14—continued

Chart B. To be used with height gauge, Part No. 605004:

Final feeler gauge clearance

Pinion height markings	in. .020	mm 0,50	in. .019	mm 0,48	in. .018	mm 0,45	in. .017	mm 0,43	in. .016	mm 0,40
+5	.020	0,50	.019	0,48	.018	0,45	.017	0,43	.016	0,40
+4	.019	0,48	.018	0,45	.017	0,43	.016	0,40	.015	0,38
+3	.018	0,45	.017	0,43	.016	0,40	.015	0,38	.014	0,35
+2	.017	0,43	.016	0,40	.015	0,38	.014	0,35	.013	0,33
+1	.016	0,40	.015	0,38	.014	0,35	.013	0,33	.012	0,30
0	.015	0,38	.014	0,35	.013	0,33	.012	0,30	.011	0,27
—1	.014	0,35	.013	0,33	.012	0,30	.011	0,27	.010	0,25
—2	.013	0,33	.012	0,30	.011	0,27	.010	0,25	.009	0,22
—3	.012	0,30	.011	0,27	.010	0,25	.009	0,22	.008	0,20
—4	.011	0,27	.010	0,25	.009	0,22	.008	0,20	.007	0,17
—5	.010	0,25	.009	0,22	.008	0,20	.007	0,17	.006	0,15

Head depth (H or HD) markings: —3 —2 —1 0

11. From the height gauge dimension previously recorded, subtract the figure obtained from the applicable chart, then from the result, subtract the amended bearing difference dimension (difference between width of real bearing and dummy bearing, minus .002 in. (0,05 mm). The final result is equal to the thickness of shims required between the pinion end bearing outer race and the pinion case.

The following is an example of the recommended method of calculating shims for setting the bevel pinion height. The figures quoted are examples only, and must not be regarded as applicable.

Width of pinion end bearing	..	1.156 in. (29,36 mm)
Width of dummy bearing	..	1.152 in. (29,26 mm)
Difference		.004 in. (0,10 mm)
Subtract .002 in. for bearing pre-load	..	.002 in. (0,05 mm)
Amended bearing difference	..	.002 in. (0,05 mm)
Pinion height gauge clearance		.042 in. (1,06 mm)

Assuming pinion markings as illustrated and Chart A applicable:

Subtract chart reading	..	.006 in. (0,15 mm)
		.036 in. (0,91 mm)
Subtract amended bearing difference	..	.002 in. (0,05 mm)
Thickness of shims required between pinion end bearing outer race and pinion case		.034 in. (0,86 mm)
		.034 in. (0,86 mm)

Bevel pinion bearing pre-load

1. Press the pinion end bearing outer race, together with the shims previously determined for pinion height setting, into the pinion case. See Fig. E1-60.

2. Press the pinion end roller bearing on to the pinion shaft. See Fig. E1-61.

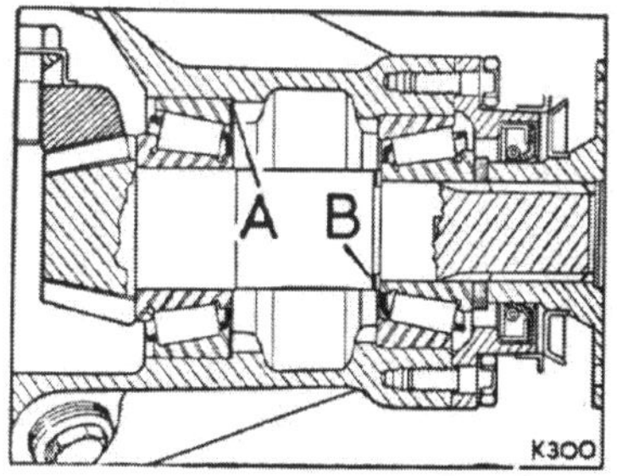

Fig. E1-59. Bevel pinion adjustment shims

A—Shims, pinion height adjustment
B—Shims bearing pre-load adjustment

REAR AXLE AND SUSPENSION

Operation E1-14—continued

Note: Axles up to serial number with suffix 'A' use shims ranging from .003 in. (0,076 mm) to .020 in. (0,5 mm) which must have special support washers fitted at each end. Axles from suffix 'B' onwards use shims ranging from .072 in. (1,82 mm) to .081 in. (2,05 mm) in place of the support washers. If the shims have been mislaid, use new shims of at least .020 in. (0,5 mm) thickness for suffix 'A' axles, and .180 in. (4,57 mm) for suffix 'B' axles.

4. Place the flange end roller bearing and distance washer on to the pinion shaft. See Fig. E1-66.

5. Deliberately omitting the oil seal and retainer, fit the driving flange and tighten the securing nut to 85 lb ft (11,75 mkg) torque loading.

6. Check the bevel pinion bearing pre-load by measuring the rolling resistance of the pinion shaft, using a nylon cord attached to a spring balance. Tie the cord to the driving flange, then coil it around the hub of the flange and note the measurement recorded on the spring balance required to rotate the pinion shaft, after having overcome inertia. Bearing pre-load is correct when a figure of 7 to 12 lb (3,2 to 4,5 kg) is recorded on the spring balance.

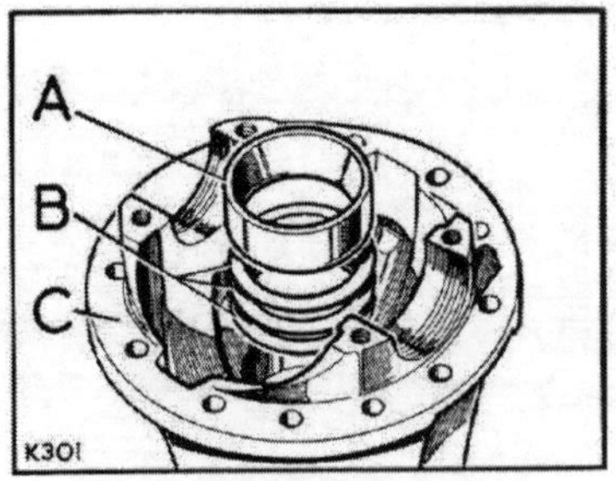

Fig. E1-60. Bearing outer race, pinion end
A—Outer race
B—Shims
C—Pinion case

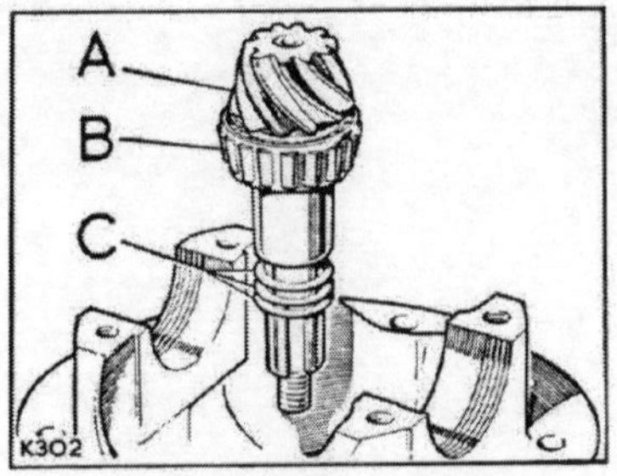

Fig. E1-61. Pinion assembly
A—Pinion shaft
B—Roller bearing, pinion end
C—Shims

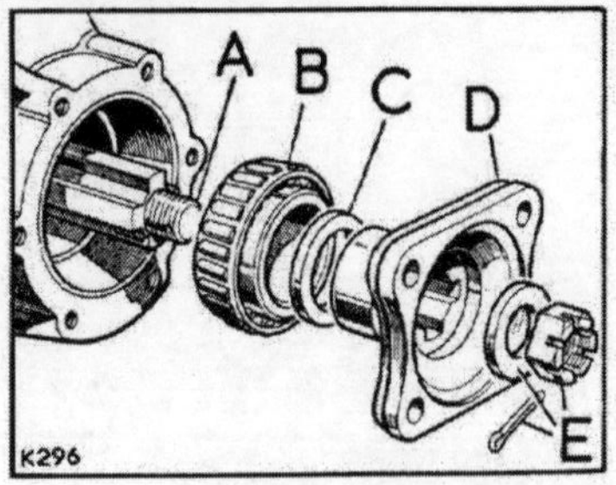

Fig. E1-62. Pinion driving flange
A—Pinion shaft
B—Roller bearing
C—Distance washer
D—Driving flange
E—Fixings, driving flange

Operation E1-14—continued

Adjustment can be made by changing the shims located on the pinion shaft between the bearings, shims are available in a range of thicknesses. Thicker shimming will reduce bearing pre-load, thinner shimming will increase pre-load.

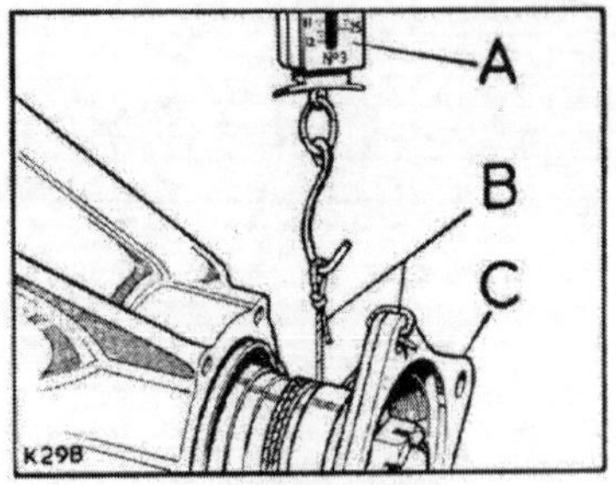

Fig. E1-63. Checking bevel pinion bearing pre-load
A—Spring balance
B—Nylon cord
C—Driving flange

7. When the bevel pinion bearing pre-load is correct reposition the pinion height gauge and check that the clearance between the height gauge and slip gauge agrees with the figure obtained from the chart ±.001 in. (±0,02 mm). Should adjustment be necessary, add or subtract shims beneath the pinion end bearing outer race, then reset the bevel pinion bearing pre-load.

When the bevel pinion height and bearing pre-load is correct, remove the driving flange and place aside for subsequent assembly.

Differential wheel and pinion backlash

1. Place a thrust washer in position on the rear face of each differential wheel.

2. Locate the two differential wheels and thrust washers into the differential case.

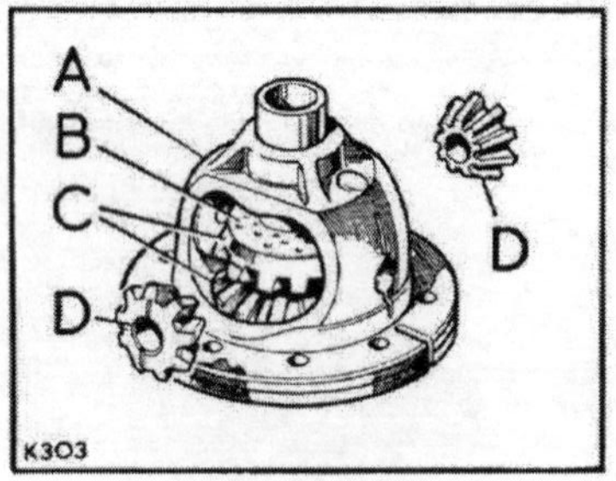

Fig. E1-64. Differential assembly
A—Differential case
B—Thrust washer
C—Differential wheels
D—Differential pinions

3. Insert the differential pinions through the two apertures in the case, at exactly opposite points, then rotate the wheel and pinion assembly to align the holes in the pinions and case for the pinion spindle.

Note: If original components are being refitted, ensure that the wheel and pinion assembly is in its original position before fitting the spindle.

4. Ensure that the plain pin is secure in the pinion spindle, then fit the spindle to the differential assembly.

5. Check for backlash between the differential wheels and pinions, a manual check is sufficient, no actual measuring is necessary. There must be a definite backlash, but this must be the minimum obtainable consistent with smooth running wheels and pinions. Adjustment can be made by changing the thrust washers for the differential wheels, which are available in a range of thicknesses.

REAR AXLE AND SUSPENSION

Operation E1-14—continued

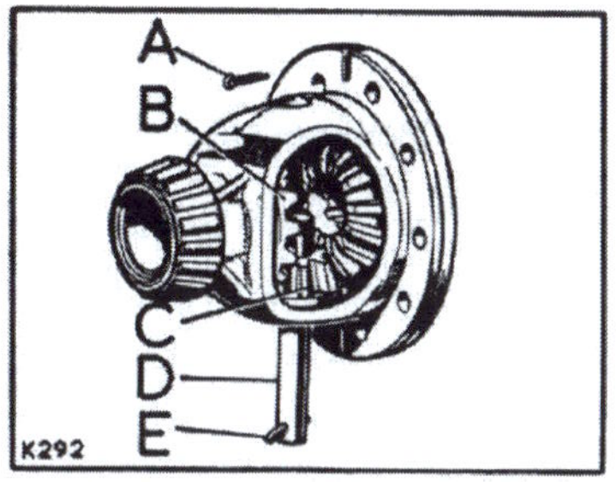

Fig. E1-65. Spindle for differential pinions
A—Split pin
B—Differential wheels
C—Differential pinions
D—Spindle
E—Plain pin

have a .375 in. (9,5 mm) diameter shank, and must be tightened to a torque figure of 35 lb ft (4,8 mkg). Tighten the bolts evenly to avoid distortion.

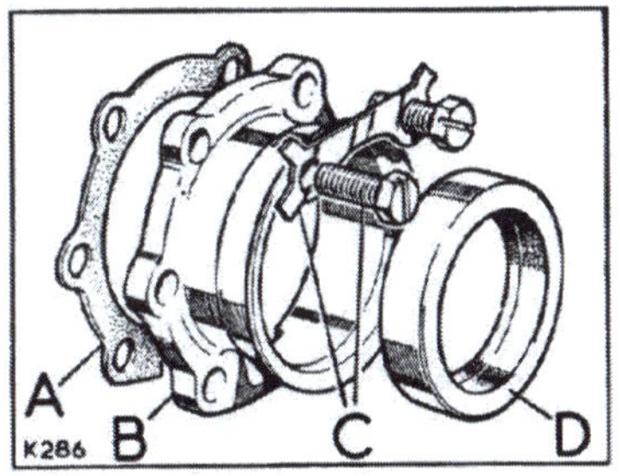

To assemble

1. Warm the retainer for the pinion case oil seal, smear the outside diameter of the seal with jointing compound and fit it, lipped side inward, into the retainer.

2. Smear both sides of the joint washer with jointing compound and place it in position on the oil seal retainer. Fit the oil seal retainer to the pinion case, ensuring that the oilways in the bevel pinion housing, oil seal retainer and joint washer are aligned.

3. Fit the driving flange to the bevel pinion, and tighten the securing nut to a torque figure of 85 lb ft (11,75 mkg).

4. Align the crownwheel with the differential case and secure in position, noting that two of the securing bolts are fitted diametrically opposite and must be tightened to a torque figure of 45 lb ft (6,2 mkg). The remainder of the bolts

Fig. E1-66. Oil seal retainer
A—Joint washer
B—Retainer for oil seal
C—Fixings, oil seal retainer
D—Oil seal

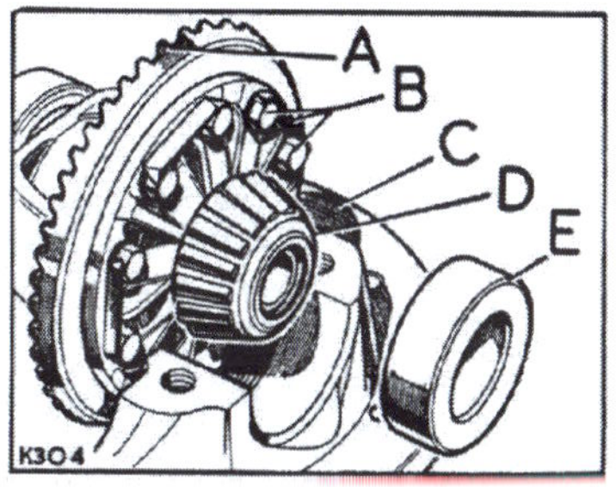

Fig. E1-67. Crownwheel assembly
A—Crownwheel
B—Fixings, crownwheel to differential case
C—Bevel pinion case
D—Roller bearing
E—Bearing outer race

Operation E1-14—continued

5. Fit the taper roller bearings, wide side first, to each side of the differential case.

6. Place the bearing outer races in position on the differential assembly and locate the assembly into the bevel pinion housing.

7. Fit the two serrated nuts and bearing caps to their respective sides of the bevel pinion housing. Tighten the bearing cap securing bolts firmly, but not fully.

8. Using special tool, Part Number 530105, tighten both serrated nuts to remove all bearing end-float without introducing pre-load.

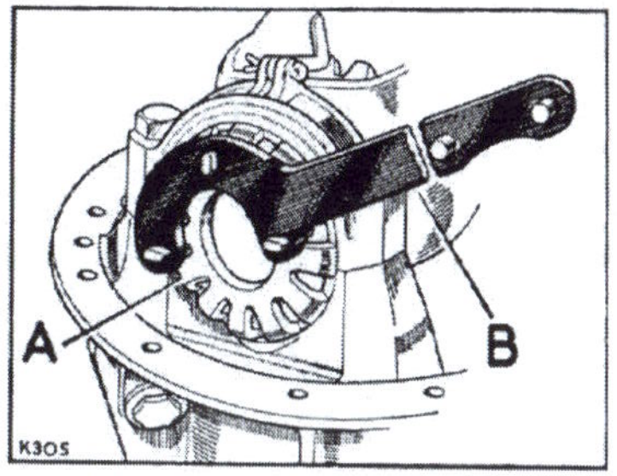

Fig. E1-68. Adjusting serrated nuts
A—Serrated nut
B—Special tool Part No. 530105

9. Using a dial test indicator, measure the run-out on the rear face of the crownwheel, this must not exceed .004 in. (0,10 mm). If excessive run-out is recorded, the crownwheel and differential must be removed from the bevel pinion housing, and the crownwheel repositioned on the differential case. Re-assemble and recheck. If necessary, this procedure must be repeated until the run-out is correct.

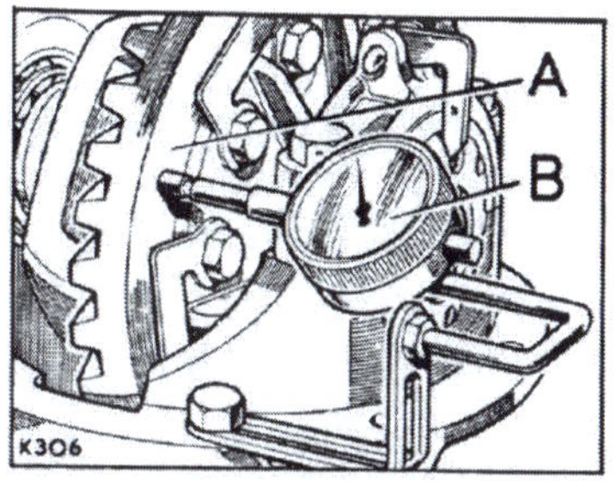

Fig. E1-69. Checking crownwheel run-out
A—Rear face of crownwheel
B—Dial test indicator

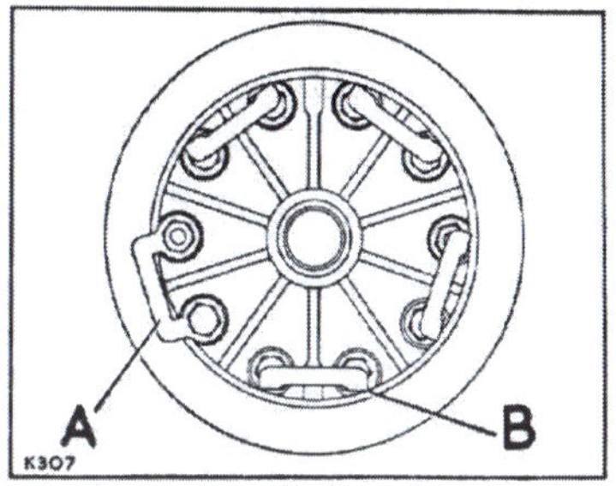

10. When the crownwheel run-out is correct, ensure that the lockplates are fully engaged over the crownwheel securing bolts.

Fig. E1-70. Engaging crownwheel lock plates
A—Lockplates before engagement
B—Lockplates engaged

11. Using a dial test indicator, check the crownwheel to bevel pinion backlash. This must be .008 in. to .010 in. (0,20 mm to 0,25 mm). Where necessary, adjust the crownwheel backlash by alternately slackening and tightening the serrated nuts until the backlash is correct.

REAR AXLE AND SUSPENSION

Operation E1-14—continued

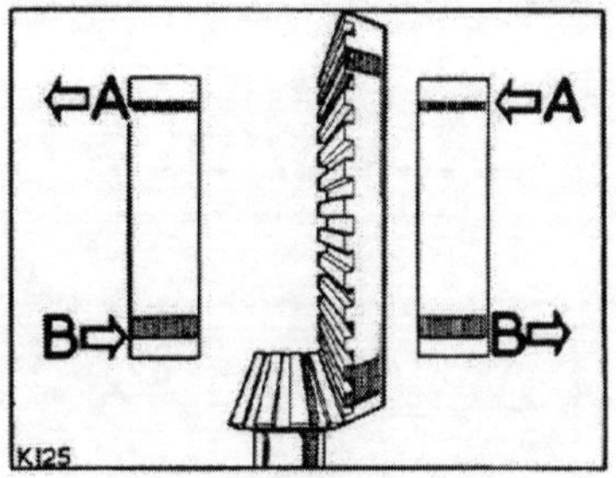

Fig. E1-71. Adjusting crownwheel to bevel pinion backlash

A—Move serrated nuts as indicated to reduce backlash
B—Move serrated nuts as indicated to increase backlash

12. With the backlash correct and no bearing end-float or pre-load, tighten both serrated nuts by half a serration only, to pre-load the taper roller bearings.

13. Engage the lockers into the serrated nuts. If either locker is not opposite a serration, bend it to fit the nearest serration in the anti-clockwise direction.

14. Fully tighten the bearing cap securing bolts to a torque figure of 60 lb ft (8,3 mkg), and wire-lock, together with the locker for the serrated nut.

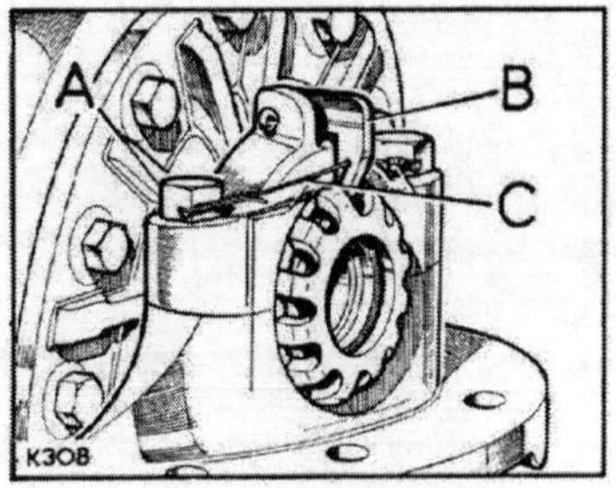

Fig. E1-72. Wire locking

A—Bolts securing bearing caps
B—Locker for serrated nut
C—Locking wire

Note: When refitting the differential, ensure that the axle case breather is clear (see Operation E1-15), a blocked breather could cause failure of the oil seals fitted in the axle assembly.

This page intentionally left blank

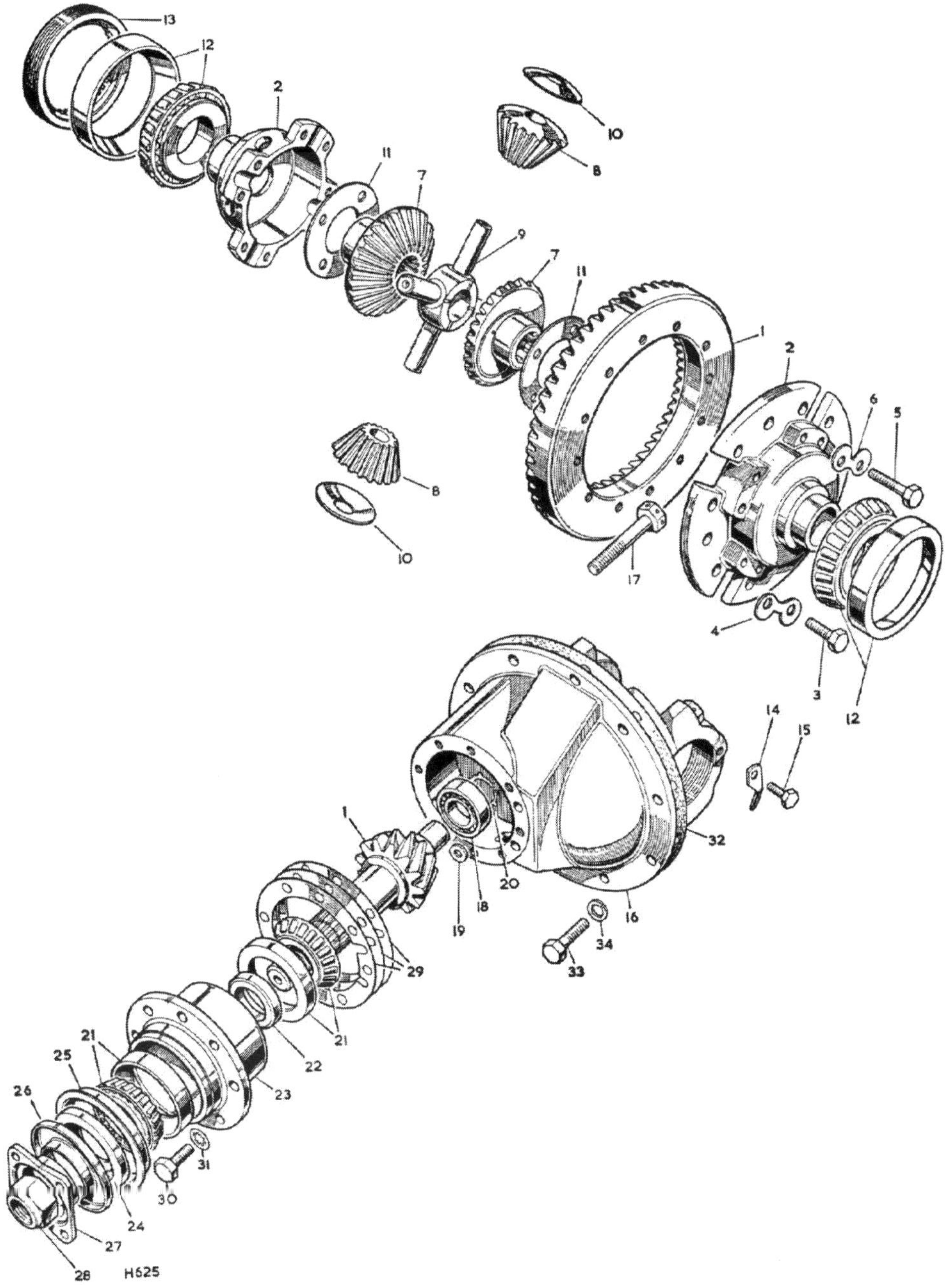

Section E—Land-Rover REAR AXLE AND SUSPENSION

Key to illustration of ENV differential

1. Crownwheel and bevel pinion
2. Differential casing
3. Set bolt ($\frac{7}{16}$ in. UNF × 1 in. long) } Fixing crownwheel to differential
4. Locking plate
5. Set bolt ($\frac{7}{16}$ in. UNF × 1$\frac{3}{4}$ in. long) } Fixing differential case halves together
6. Locking plate
7. Differential wheel
8. Differential pinion
9. Spindle for pinions
10. Spherical washer, differential pinion
11. Washer, differential wheel
12. Taper roller bearing for differential
13. Adjuster, differential bearings
14. Locking plate } For bearing adjuster
15. Set bolt
16. Nose piece complete with bearing caps
17. Special bolt fixing bearing cap
18. Bearing for bevel pinion, nose end
19. Retaining washer
20. Circlip
21. Bearing for bevel pinion
22. Spacer for bearing adjustment
23. Bevel pinion housing
24. Oil seal for pinion
25. Mudshield for bevel pinion housing
26. Mudshield for driving flange
27. Driving flange for bevel pinion
28. Special nut fixing driving flange
29. Shim, bevel pinion to crownwheel engagement
30. Set bolt } Fixing pinion housing to nose piece
31. Shakeproof washer
32. Joint washer, differential to axle casing
33. Set bolt } Fixing differential to axle casing
34. Spring washer

Fig. E1-73. Differential, ENV type

REAR AXLE AND SUSPENSION

ENV Differential, to overhaul—Operation E1-14A

(For removal and refitting instructions, Operation E1-13 refers)

Workshop hand tools:
Spanner sizes: $\frac{7}{16}$ in. AF, $\frac{1}{2}$ in. AF, $\frac{9}{16}$ in. AF, $\frac{5}{8}$ in. AF, $\frac{13}{16}$ in. AF, $\frac{7}{8}$ in. BSF sockets
Pliers, Mallet, Dial Test Indicator, Spring Balance, 1 in. Micrometer, Two $\frac{7}{16}$ in. diameter Whitworth Bolts threaded $2\frac{1}{4}$ in., Engineers Marking Blue, Torque Wrench

Special tools:
Tool for bearing adjustment, Part Number 600970

Important note: During dismantling it is essential that all components are marked in their original position and relative to other components, so that if original components are refitted, their initial setting will be maintained.

To dismantle

1. Slacken both bearing caps, then using special tool, Part No. 600970, slacken both bearing adjusters.
2. Remove bearing caps and adjusters.

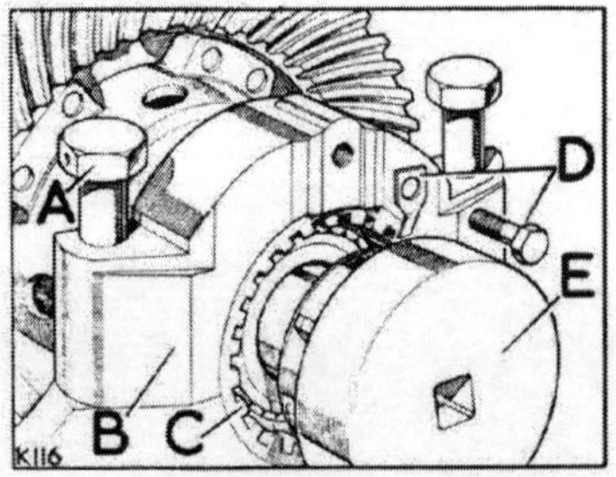

Fig. E1-74. Bearing caps and adjusters

A—Fixings, bearing caps
B—Bearing cap
C—Bearing adjuster
E—Special tool, Part No. 600970

3. Pass a suitable bar through the differential case and carefully lift the differential from the nose piece.
4. Remove the fixings from the bevel pinion housing and extract the housing from the nose piece, using the two extractor holes which are tapped $\frac{7}{16}$ in. Whitworth.

   Note and retain the shims fitted between the bevel pinion housing and the nose piece.

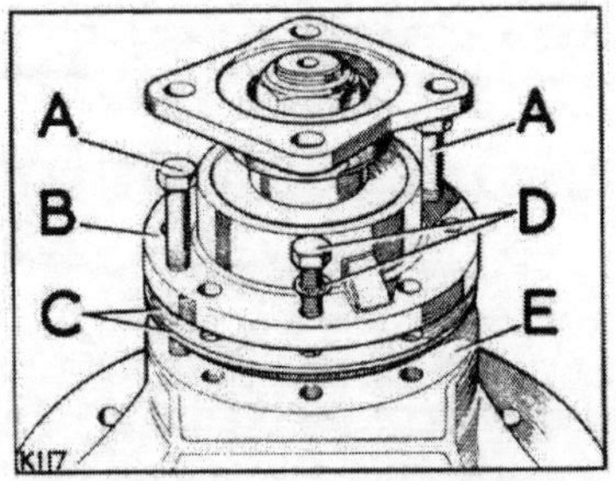

Fig. E1-75. Bevel pinion housing removal

A—Extractor bolts ($\frac{7}{16}$ in. Whitworth)
B—Bevel pinion housing
C—Shims
D—Fixings, bevel pinion housing to nose piece
E—Nose piece

5. Remove the rivet and washer retaining the bevel pinion nose end bearing and press the bearing from the nose piece.

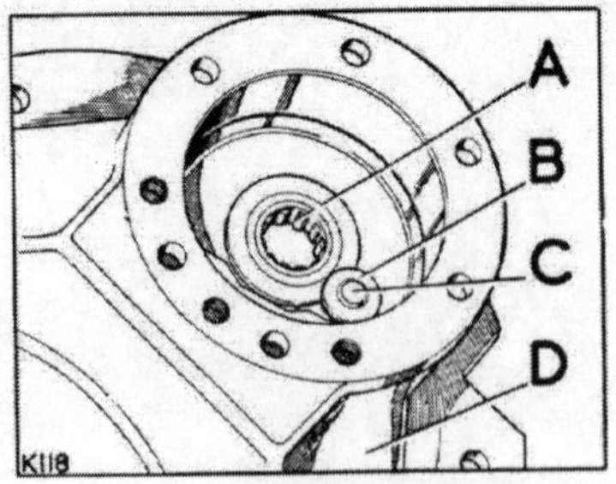

Fig. E1-76. Bearing in nose piece for bevel pinion

A—Bearing, bevel pinion nose end
B—Washer, retaining bearing
C—Rivet, retaining washer
D—Nose piece

6. Remove the driving flange from the bevel pinion.
7. Press the bevel pinion complete with bearing end spacer from the housing.
8. Remove the oil seal, taper roller bearing and two bearing outer races from the bevel pinion housing. If required, remove the mudshields from the pinion housing and driving flange.

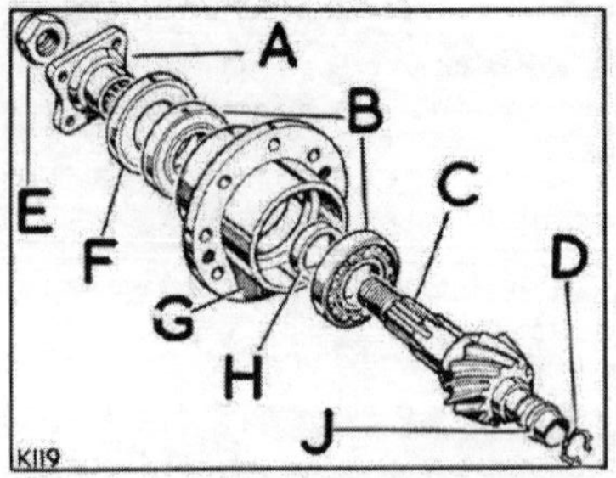

Fig. E1-77. Bevel pinion, bearings and housing

A—Driving flange
B—Roller bearings
C—Bevel pinion
D—Circlip, retaining inner race
E—Fixing, driving flange to bevel pinion
F—Oil seal
G—Bevel pinion housing
H—Spacer
J—Inner race, nose bearing

9. Remove spacer and roller bearing from the bevel pinion shaft also remove the circlip and inner race for nose bearing.
10. Remove the crownwheel from the differential housing.
11. Extract the two roller bearings from the outside of differential casing.
12. Separate the differential casing halves and withdraw the differential pinion assembly and the two differential wheels.

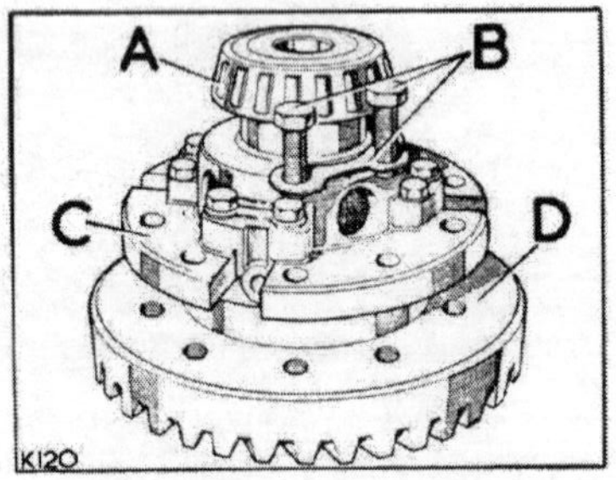

Fig. E1-78. Crownwheel and differential case

A—Roller bearings for differential case
B—Fixings (outer ring of bolts) crownwheel to differential housing
C—Differential case
D—Crownwheel

13. Withdraw the spherical washers and differential pinions from the spindle.
14. Withdraw the washers for the differential wheels, these may be adhering to the wheels or may remain in the casing halves.

Inspection

Inspect all components for wear or damage and renew as necessary.

The self-locking nut securing the bevel pinion driving flange must be a tight fit on the thread, if not, use a new nut.

If either the crownwheel or bevel pinion is worn or damaged, they can only be replaced as a pair.

Renew all lockplates.

REAR AXLE AND SUSPENSION

Operation E1-14A—continued

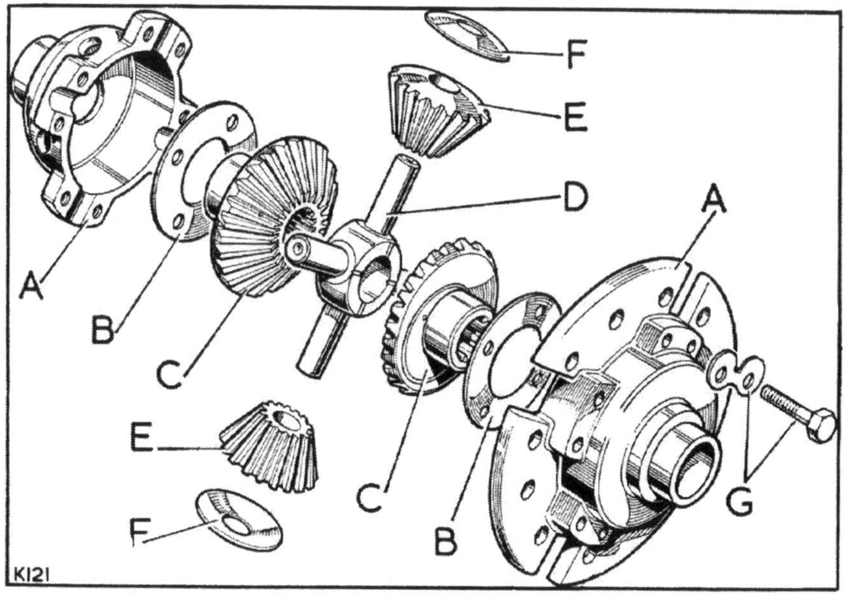

Fig. E1-79. Differential assembly

A—Differential casing
B—Washer, differential wheel
C—Differential wheel
D—Spindle for pinions
E—Differential pinions
F—Spherical washers, differential pinions
G—Fixings, differential casing halves

To re-assemble

During the re-assembly, it is of the utmost importance that all original components are refitted in their original positions in accordance with the alignment marks made during dismantling.

1. Fit the bevel pinion nose roller bearing into the nose piece and secure with a washer and rivet. See Fig. E1-76.

2. Fit the washers and differential wheels to their respective case halves.

3. Assemble the differential pinions and spherical washers to the spindle, and locate the assembly into the smaller differential case half. See Fig. E1-79.

Operation E1-14A—continued

4. Align the differential case halves and secure together, tighten the securing bolts to a torque figure of 50 to 60 lbs ft (7,0 to 0,8 mkg) then engage the lock plates.

5. Align the crownwheel with the differential case and secure in position. Tighten the securing bolts to a torque figure of 60 to 70 lbs ft (8,0 to 10,0 mkg) but do not engage the lock plates at this stage. See Fig. E1-78.

6. Fit a taper roller bearing, wide side first, to each side of the differential casing.

7. Place the bearing outer races in position on the differential assembly and locate the assembly into the nose piece.

8. Fit the two bearing adjusters and end caps to their respective sides of the nose piece, tighten bearing cap securing bolts firmly but not fully. See Fig. E1-74.

9. Tighten both bearing adjusters to remove all end-float without introducing bearing pre-load.

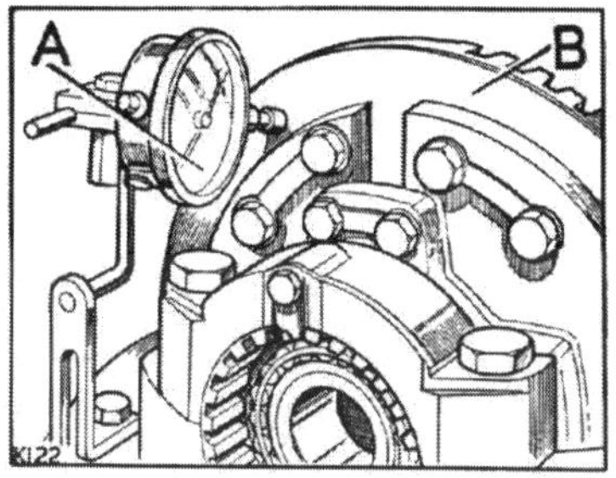

Fig. E1-80. Checking crownwheel run-out
A—Dial test indicator
B—Rear face of crownwheel

10. Using a dial test indicator, measure the run-out on the rear face of the crownwheel, this must not exceed .003 in. (0,08 mm). If excessive run-out is recorded, the crownwheel and differential assembly must be removed from the nose piece, and the crownwheel re-positioned on the differential case. Re-assemble and recheck, if necessary this procedure must be repeated until the run-out is correct.

11. Engage the lock plates on the crownwheel securing bolts.

12. Fit the inner race and circlip to the nose end of the bevel pinion.

13. Press the taper roller bearing, wide side first, on to the bevel pinion shaft to abut with the pinion.

14. Fit the two bearing outer races, wide side first, into the bevel pinion housing. If removed, fit the mudshields to the pinion housing and driving flange. See Fig. E1-77.

15. Locate the bevel pinion into its housing and fit the bearing spacer and second roller taper bearing.

16. Fit the driving flange to the bevel pinion and tighten the securing nut to a torque figure of 100 to 120 lbs ft (14 to 16 mkg).

Note: The pinion oil seal is deliberately omitted at this stage.

17. Check the bevel pinion bearing pre-load by measuring the rolling resistance of the bearing housing, using a nylon cord attached to a spring balance. Tie the cord to the housing flange, and coil it round the bearing housing, not the flange, and note the measurement recorded on the spring balance required to rotate the housing after having overcome inertia. Bearing pre-load is correct when a figure of 4½ to 9 lbs (2 to 4 kg) is recorded on the spring balance. Adjustment can be made by changing the bearing spacer which is available in a range of thicknesses. A thicker spacer will reduce the bearing pre-load, a thinner spacer will increase the bearing pre-load.

18. When the bevel pinion bearing pre-load is correct, remove the driving flange, smear the outside of the oil seal with jointing compound and fit the oil seal to the housing, then refit the driving flange and tighten the securing nut to a torque figure of 100 to 120 lb ft (14 to 16 mkg).

REAR AXLE AND SUSPENSION

Operation E1-14A—continued

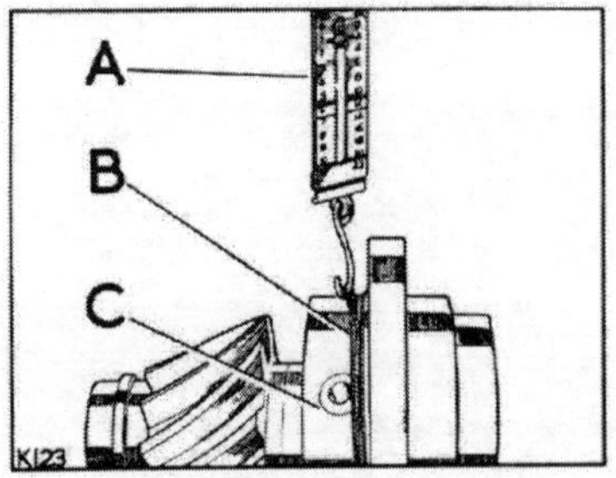

Fig. E1-81. Checking bevel pinion bearing pre-load

A—Spring balance
B—Nylon cord
C—Bearing housing

19. Fit the bevel pinion housing complete with shims to the nose piece, carefully aligning the oilways in the housing, shims and nose piece. Tighten the housing securing bolts to a torque figure of 40 to 50 lb ft (5.5 to 7.0 mkg).

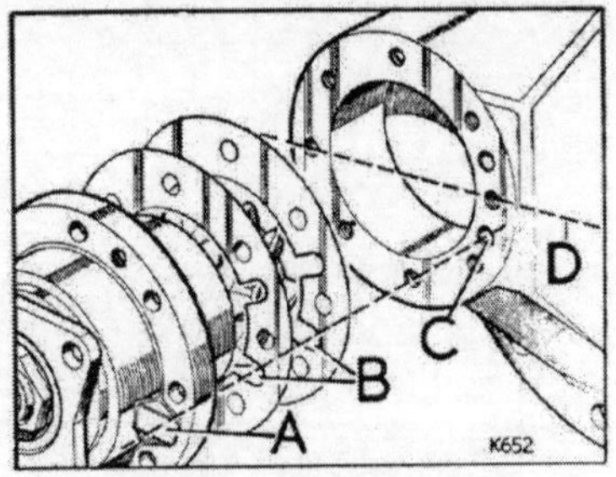

Fig. E1-82. Alignment of oilways

A—Oilway in nose piece
B—Oilway in shims
C—Oilway in bevel pinion housing
D—Horizontal centre line

Fig. E1-83. Checking crownwheel backlash

A—Periphery of crownwheel teeth
B—Dial test indicator

20. Using the dial test indicator, check the crownwheel to bevel pinion backlash. This must be between .006 in. to .009 in. (0.15 mm to 0.23 mm). Where necessary adjust the crownwheel backlash by alternately slackening and tightening the bearing adjusters until the backlash is correct.

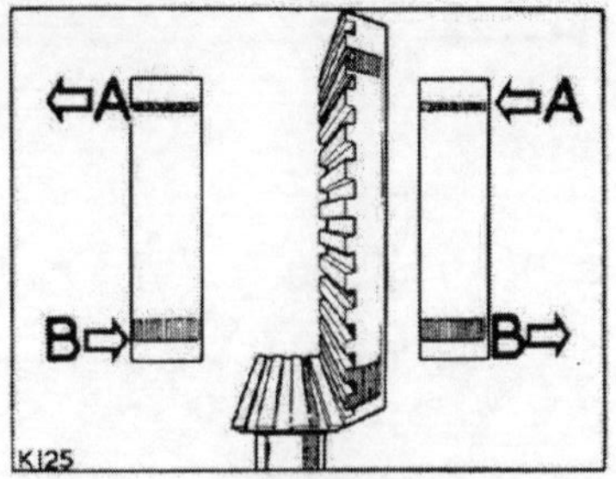

Fig. E1-84. Adjusting crownwheel to bevel pinion backlash

A—Move adjusters as indicated to reduce backlash
B—Move adjusters as indicated to increase backlash

21. Check the bevel pinion to crownwheel engagement, using Engineers Blue on the crownwheel teeth and rotate to obtain a reading. Correct engagement will give a mid-tooth reading. If a reading at the tooth root or crown is produced, this can be corrected by adjusting the shim thickness between the bevel pinion housing and the nose piece, any adjustment made to the shim thickness must be followed by a check and re-adjustment of the crownwheel to bevel pinion backlash.

22. When the bevel pinion to crownwheel engagement and backlash are correct, tighten both bearing adjusters by one serration to pre-load the roller bearings. Fully tighten the bearing cap bolts to a torque figure of 80 to 100 lb ft (11.0 to 14.0 mkg) and secure with locking wire. Fit the locking plates to secure both bearing adjusters.

Note: When refitting the differential, ensure that the axle case breather is clear (see Operation E1-15), a blocked breather could cause failure of the oil seals fitted to the axle assembly.

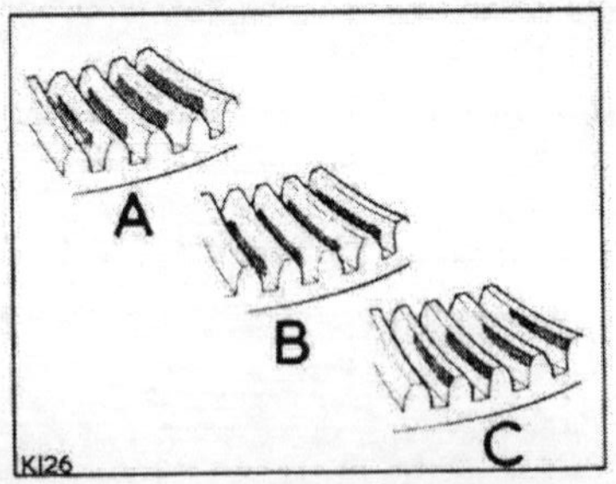

Fig. E1-85. Checking bevel pinion to crownwheel engagement

A—Position of marking shows correct engagement
B—Excessive engagement, increase shim thickness
C—Insufficient engagement, reduce shim thickness

REAR AXLE AND SUSPENSION

Rear axle case, remove and refit—Operation E1-15

Workshop hand tools:
Spanner sizes: $\frac{7}{16}$ in. BSF, $\frac{7}{16}$ in. AF, $\frac{9}{16}$ in. AF, $\frac{11}{16}$ in. AF, $\frac{3}{4}$ in. AF open end
$\frac{3}{8}$ in. BSF, $\frac{7}{16}$ in. BSF, $\frac{9}{16}$ in. BSF, $\frac{5}{8}$ in. AF, 2 in. AF sockets
Pliers, Screwdriver (medium)

To remove

1. Drain the rear axle lubricating oil. Operation E1-1 (E1-1A).
2. Remove the rear axle half shafts. Operation E1-2 or E1-3A, as applicable.
3. Remove the rear hubs. Operation E1-5.
   Note: It is not necessary to remove the hub bearing fixings, the hub, bearing sleeve and brake anchor plate can be removed as one unit.
4. Remove the rear shock absorbers. Operation E1-7.
   Note: If the shock absorber lower fixing is secured to the bottom plate for the 'U' bolts, it can be left in place, but the upper fixing must be slackened to prevent damaging the mounting rubbers when pivoting the shock absorber and bottom plate clear of the road spring.
5. Remove the differential. Operation E1-13.
6. Disconnect the rear brake pipe at the connection with the flexible pipe and withdraw the flexible pipe from the chassis bracket, then depress the brake pedal, and wedge it in that position, to prevent further leakage of brake fluid. When depressing the brake pedal, take precautions to avoid fluid spillage.

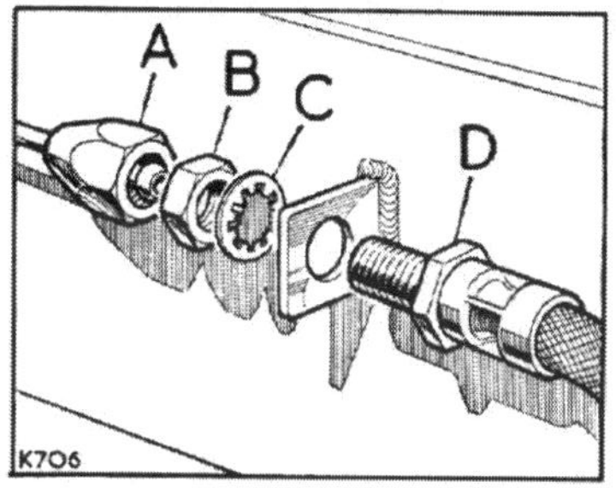

Fig. E1-86. Rear brake pipe connection

A—Pipe from master cylinder
B—Locknut
C—Shakeproof washer
D—Union and flexible brake pipe

7. Release the rear brake clips from the shields at each end of the axle case.

8. Remove the large hose clip securing the brake pipe to the rear axle case, release the T-piece from the bracket above the rear axle case and withdraw the rear brake pipe assembly from the vehicle.

Fig. E1-87. Brake pipe shield clips

A—Shield for brake pipe
B—Clips, brake pipe to shield
C—Fixings, clips to shield

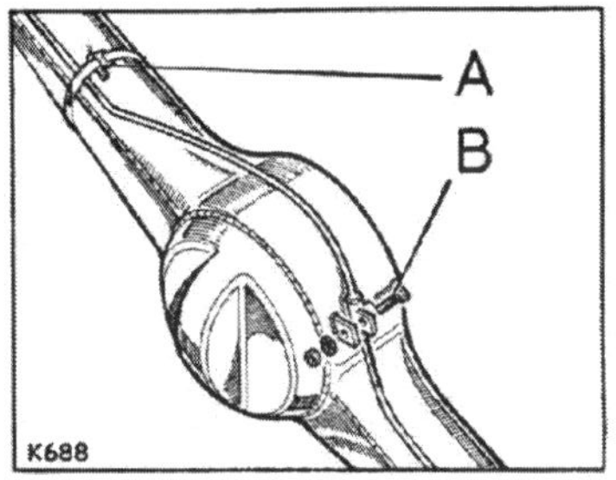

Fig. E1-88. Brake pipe clips at rear axle

A—Hose clip
B—Fixings for T-piece

9. Support the rear axle with a jack and disconnect one end of each check strap.

Operation E1-15—continued

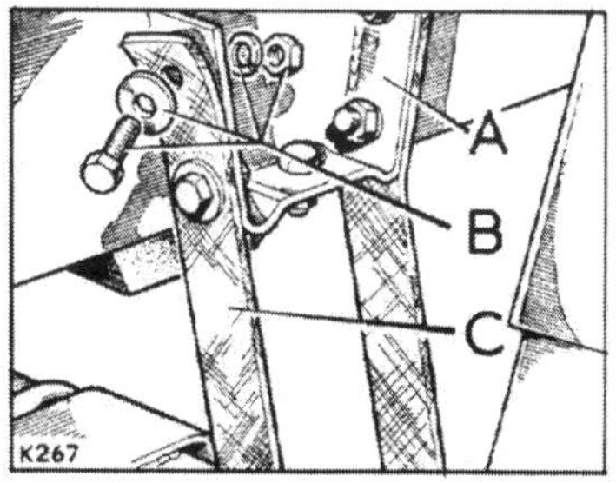

Fig. E1-89. Check strap for axle

A—Chassis
B—Fixings, check strap to chassis
C—Check strap

10. Remove the four 'U' bolts, and withdraw the axle case from the vehicle.

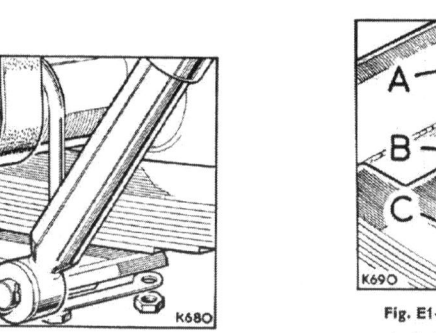

Fig. E1-90. Axle 'U' bolts

A—Road spring
B—Bottom plate
C—Fixings for 'U' bolts

To refit

1. Before fitting the axle case, ensure that the breather is clear, a blocked breather could cause failure of the final drive oil seals.

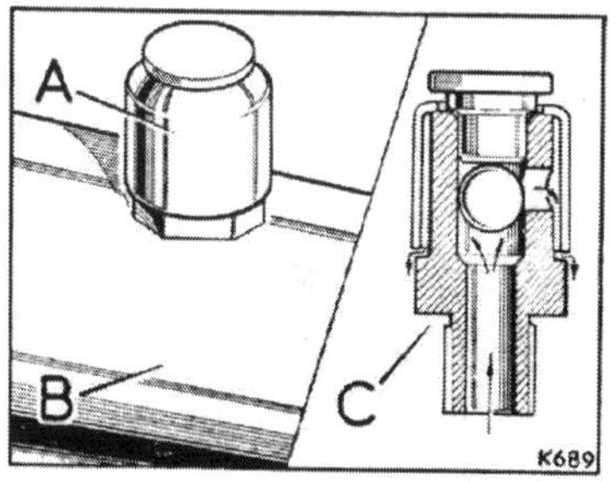

Fig. E1-91. Breather for axle case

A—Breather
B—Axle case
C—Flow through breather

2. Place the brake pipe shields in position on the road springs.

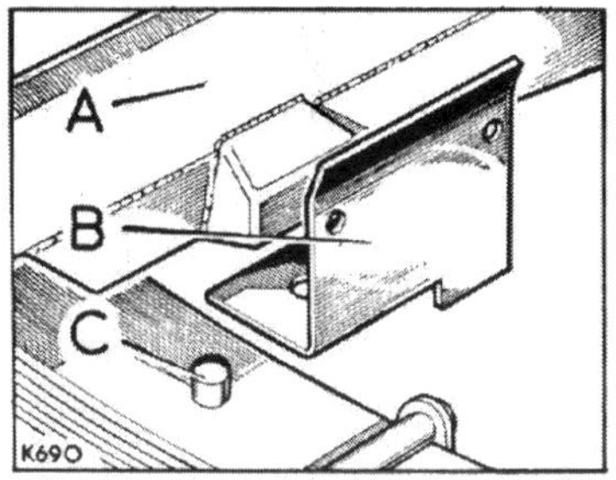

Fig. E1-92. Brake pipe shield location

A—Axle
B—Shield, with off-set toward centre of vehicle
C—Centre bolt for road spring

3. Locate the axle case in position on the road springs.
4. Fit the bottom plate and axle 'U' bolts and engage the lock plates.
5. Jack up the rear axle sufficient to fit the check straps. Ensure that the strap is located between the brake shield and the axle.

REAR AXLE AND SUSPENSION

Operation E1-15—continued

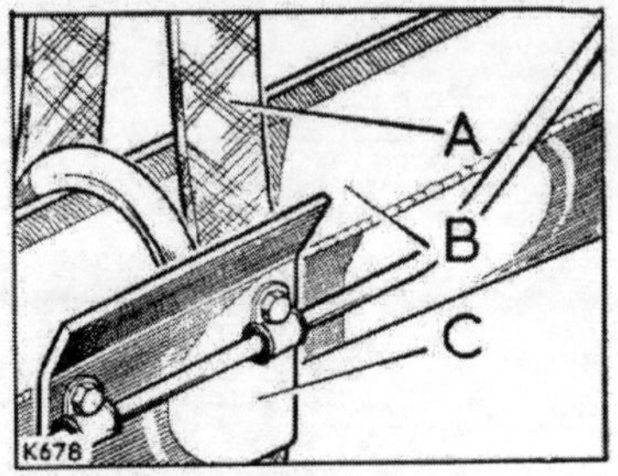

6. Fit the rear brake pipe to the axle case, connect the flexible pipe to the main pipe and secure the clipping. See Figs. E1-86, E1-87 and E1-88.
7. Fit the differential. Operation E1-13.
8. Fit the shock absorbers. Operation E1-7.
9. Fit the rear hubs and adjust the hub bearings Operations E1-5 and E1-4.
10. Fit the rear axle half shafts. Operation E1-2 or E1-3A, as applicable.
11. Replenish the rear axle lubricating oil. Operation E1-1 (E1-1A).
12. Bleed and adjust the brakes. (Section H).

Fig. E1-93. Check strap location
A—Check strap
B—Rear axle
C—Shield for brake pipe

Rear axle assembly, to remove and refit—Operation E1-16

Workshop hand tools:

Spanner sizes: $\frac{3}{8}$ in. BSF, $\frac{9}{16}$ in. AF, $\frac{5}{8}$ in. AF, $\frac{11}{16}$ in. AF, $\frac{3}{4}$ in. AF open end $\frac{7}{16}$ in. BSF, $\frac{7}{16}$ in. AF, $\frac{9}{16}$ in. AF, $\frac{5}{8}$ in. AF, $\frac{13}{16}$ in. AF, $\frac{7}{8}$ in. AF sockets
Pliers, Screwdriver, Mallet

To remove

1. Slacken the fixings at both rear road wheels.
2. Jack up the rear of the vehicle and support on stands.
3. Remove both rear road wheels.
4. Disconnect the rear propeller shaft and move it clear of the final drive unit.

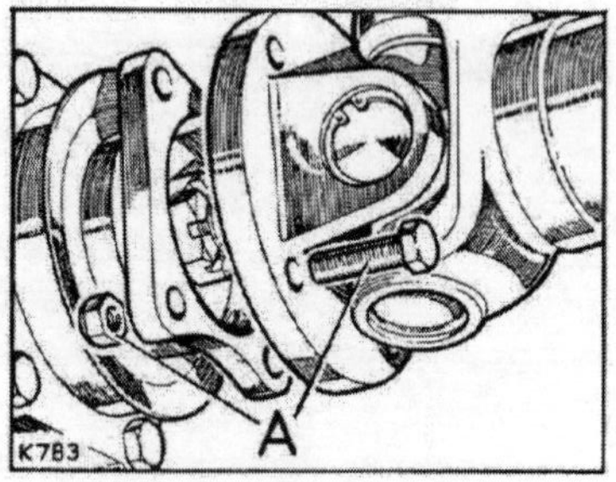

Fig. E1-94. Propeller shaft for rear axle
A—Fixings at coupling flanges

5. Disconnect the rear brake pipe at the connection with the flexible pipe and withdraw the flexible pipe from chassis bracket, then depress the brake pedal, and wedge it in that position, to prevent further leakage of brake fluid. When depressing the brake pedal take precautions to avoid fluid spillage.

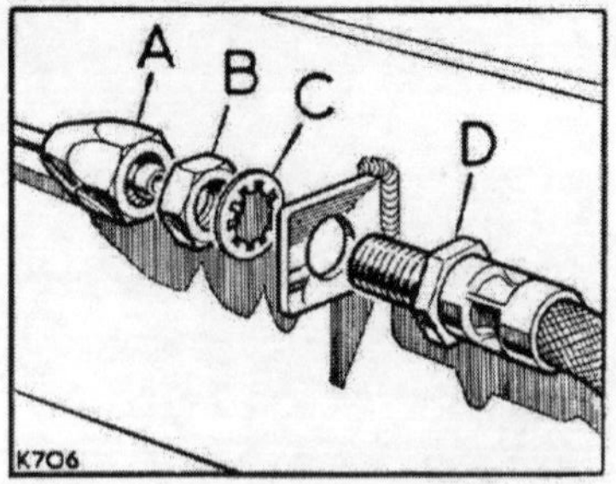

Fig. E1-95. Rear brake pipe connection
A—Pipe from master cylinder
B—Locknut
C—Shakeproof washer
D—Union and flexible brake pipe

6. Support the rear axle with a jack and disconnect one end of each check strap.

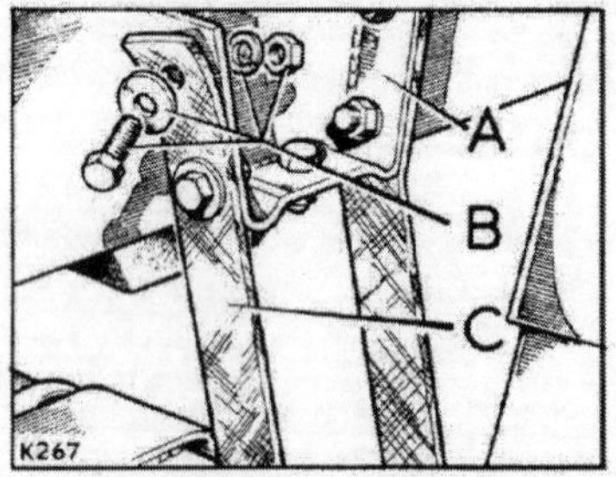

Fig. E1-96. Check strap for axle
A—Chassis
B—Fixings, check strap to chassis
C—Check strap

7. Remove both rear shock absorbers.

   Note: If the shock absorber lower fixing is secured to the bottom plate for the axle 'U'-bolts, it can be left in place, but the upper fixing must be slackened to prevent damaging the mounting rubbers when pivoting the shock absorber and bottom plate clear of the road spring.

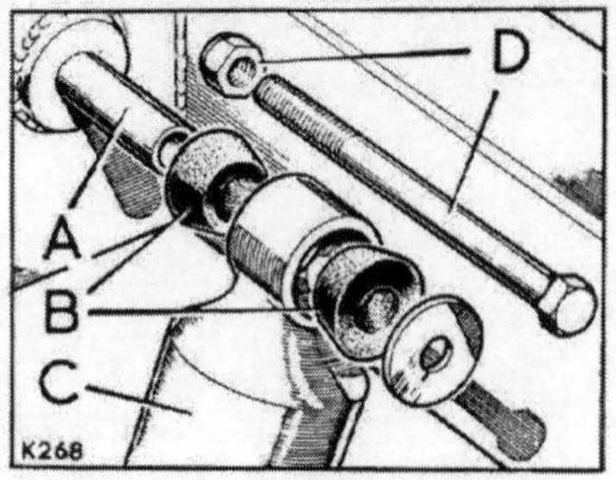

Fig. E1-97. Shock absorber top fixings
A—Chassis
B—Rubbers
C—Shock absorber
D—Fixings

REAR AXLE AND SUSPENSION

Operation E1-16—continued

8. Release the rear brake pipe clips from the shields at each end of the axle case.

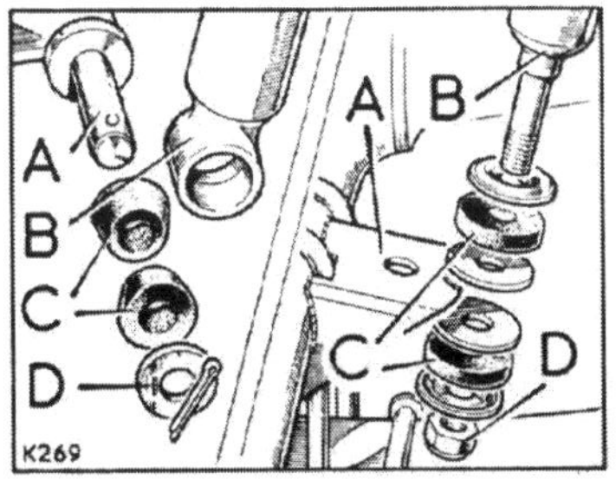

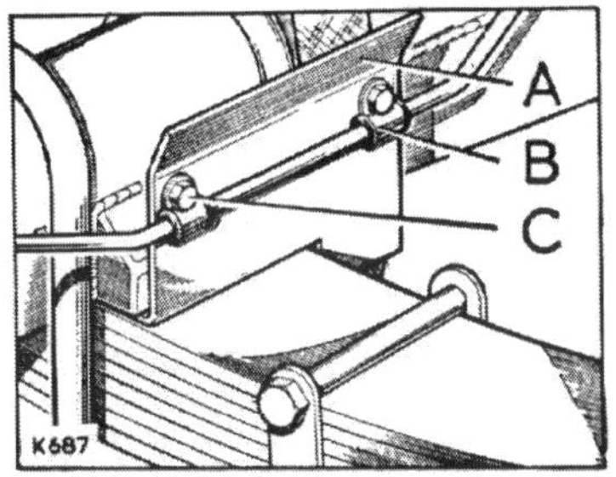

Fig. E1-98. Shock absorber bottom fixings (alternative types in use)
A—Chassis
B—Shock absorber
C—Rubbers
D—Fixings

Fig. E1-99. Brake pipe shield clips
A—Shield for brake pipe
B—Clips, brake pipe to shield
C—Fixings, clips to shield

9. Remove the four 'U' bolts from the axle.

Fig. E1-100. Axle 'U' bolts
A—Road spring
B—Bottom plate
C—Fixings for 'U' bolts

10. Support the rear axle with a jack, slacken all six shackle pins at the rear road springs, then remove the two rear shackle pins, noting that they are threaded into the inner shackle plates.

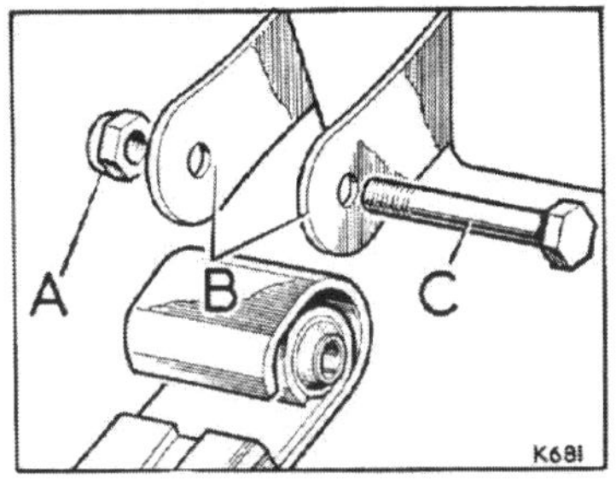

Fig. E1-101. Rear fixings for road spring
A—Self-locking nut
B—Shackle plates
C—Shackle pin

11. Lower the jack and withdraw the axle from under the vehicle.

Operation E1-16—continued

To refit

1. Place the axle on a jack and position under the vehicle.

2. Using a second jack, raise each road spring in turn and connect the rear ends of the springs to the chassis, but DO NOT tighten the shackle pins and locknuts at this stage.

3. Lift each end of the axle in turn, and locate the brake pipe shields in place.

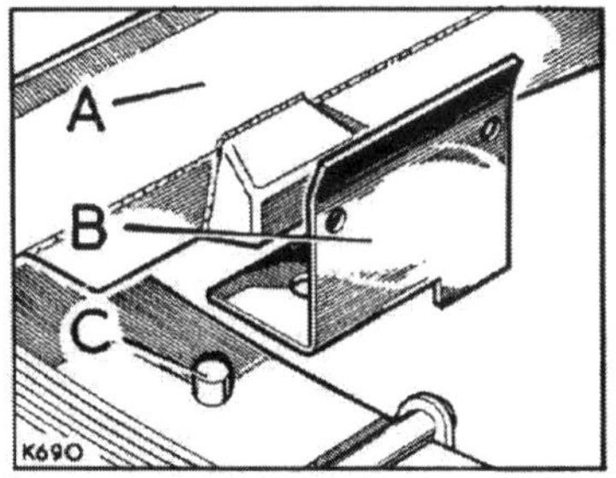

Fig. E1-102. Brake pipe shield location
A—Axle
B—Shield, with off-set toward centre of vehicle
C—Centre bolt for road spring

4. Fit the bottom plate and axle 'U' bolts and engage the lock plates.

5. Jack up the rear axle sufficient to fit the check straps.

6. Fit the rear shock absorbers.

7. Connect the rear brake pipe at the coupling with the flexible pipe. Secure the brake pipe clips to the shields.

8. Fit the rear propeller shaft.

9. Fit the rear road wheels.

10. Lower the vehicle to the ground and move vehicle bodily backward and forward to settle the springs. Tighten all six shackle pins and locknuts.

    Note: If the shackle pins and locknuts are tightened prior to lowering the vehicle to the ground, premature failure of the spring bushes will occur.

11. Check, and if necessary, replenish the rear axle lubricating oil. Operation E1-1 (E1-1A). (Section H.)

12. Bleed and adjust the brakes.

REAR AXLE AND SUSPENSION

Fault diagnosis—Rear axle and suspension

Symptom	Possible cause	Investigation	Remedy
Oil leaks	Loose or missing drain and filler plugs	Check oil drain and filler plugs at differential	Fit new joint washers and tighten plugs
	Damaged joint washers	Determine point of leak and dismantle as necessary	Fit new joint washers with both sides smeared with general purpose grease
	Oil seals damaged or incorrectly fitted	Determine point of leak, see exploded view of axle for location of oil seals and dismantle as necessary	Fit new oil seal with 'Hylomar' SQ32M sealing compound smeared on the outside diameter
Excessive tyre wear	Incorrect tyre pressures	Check tyre pressures, see Section R	Adjust as necessary
	Eccentric wheels and tyres	Check tyre concentricity line, check wheel pressings for damage or distortion	Rectify or renew
	Harsh or unequal brakes	Check brake adjustment, Section H	Adjust as necessary
	Wheels cambered	Check for settled road springs, damage to rear suspension and axle unit	Fit new parts as required
	Failure to rotate tyres		Change position of tyres, including spare, see Section R
	Fast cornering		} In the hands of the operator
	Sustained high-speed driving		
Rear end noisy	Hydraulic damper	Check damper mounting bushes for wear	Fit new bushes. If the damper itself is noisy, renew
		Check hydraulic damping, Operation E1-7	Fit new damper
	Looseness in rear suspension	Check all mountings for wear and security	Fit new parts as required. Securely tighten mountings
	Hub bearings incorrectly adjusted or worn	Check bearings for wear and adjustment	Fit new bearings and/or adjust
	Differential lubrication level too low or incorrect grade	Check lubrication level and grade	Replenish with correct grade of lubricating oil, see Section X
	Differential worn	Remove differential and check	Overhaul differential
	Propeller shaft worn		See Section D

GENERAL DATA

Axle type	Fully floating
Oil capacity:	
With Rover type differential	3 Imperial pints, 3¾ US pints, 1,75 litres
With ENV type differential	2½ Imperial pints, 3.1 US pints, 1,4 litres
Hub bearing lubrication:	
Early models	Oil—⅓ Imperial pint, 0,19 litres
Latest models	Grease
Final drive	Spiral bevel
Ratio	4.7 : 1

DETAIL DATA

Rear hub assembly:

Rear hub end-float	.004 in. to .006 in. (0,10 mm to 0,16 mm)
Clearance of hub bearings on hub bearing sleeve	.0002 in. to .0012 in. (0,005 mm to 0,030 mm)
Fit of hub inner bearing in hub	.001 in. to .003 in. (0,025 mm to 0,075 mm) interference
Fit of hub outer bearing in hub	.0005 in. to .0025 in. (0,030 mm to 0,0635 mm) interference

Differential assembly

Rover type:

Pinion teeth	10
Crown wheel teeth	47
Ratio	4.7:1
Backlash: crown wheel to pinion	.008 in. to .010 in. (0,20 mm to 0,25 mm) at the tightest point
Crown wheel bearing pre-load	.005 in. (0,12 mm)
Crown wheel run-out, maximum permitted when assembled	.004 in. (0,10 mm)
Bevel pinion bearing pre-load	7 lb to 12 lb (3,2 kg to 4,5 kg)
Backlash: differential wheels to differential pinions	Minimum but definite backlash
Distance from crown wheel axis to pinion face	3.000 in. to 3.002 in. (76,20 mm to 76,25 mm)

ENV type:

Pinion teeth	10
Crown wheel teeth	47
Ratio	4.7:1
Backlash: crown wheel to pinion	.006 in. to .009 in. (0,15 mm to 0,23 mm)
Crown wheel bearing pre-load	.002 in. to .004 in. (0,05 mm to 0,10 mm)
Crown wheel run-out, maximum permitted when assembled	.003 in. (0,08 mm)
Bevel pinion bearing pre-load	4½ lb to 9 lb (2 kg to 4 kg)

REAR AXLE AND SUSPENSION

Road springs (Refer to Section F for front road spring data)

	Driver's side	Passenger's side
88, Petrol, rear		
Number of leaves	11	11
Width of leaves	2½ in. (63,5 mm)	2½ in. (63,5 mm)
Static load (vehicle unladen)	690 lb (313 kg)	580 lb (263 kg)
Camber under static load	3¼ in. (82,6 mm)	3¼ in. (82,6 mm)
Free camber	7.42 in. (188,5 mm)	6.75 in. (171,5 mm)
88, Diesel, rear		
Number of leaves	11	11
Width of leaves	2½ in. (63,5 mm)	2½ in. (63,5 mm)
Static load (vehicle unladen)	690 lb (313 kg)	580 lb (263 kg)
Camber under static load	3¼ in. (82,6 mm)	3¼ in. (82,6 mm)
Free camber	7.42 in. (188,5 mm)	6.75 in. (171,5 mm)
109, Petrol, rear		
Number of leaves	10	10
Width of leaves	2½ in. (63,5 mm)	2½ in. (63,5 mm)
Static load (vehicle unladen)	1020 lb (463 kg)	860 lb (390 kg)
Camber under static load	2 in. (50 mm)	2 in. (50 mm)
Free camber	9¼ in. (235 mm)	8.2 in. (208 mm)
109, Diesel, rear		
Number of leaves	10	10
Width of leaves	2½ in. (63,5 mm)	2½ in. (63,5 mm)
Static load (vehicle unladen)	1020 lb (463 kg)	860 lb (390 kg)
Camber under static load	2 in. (50 mm)	2 in. (50 mm)
Free camber	9¼ in. (235 mm)	8.2 in. (208 mm)

Hydraulic dampers:
- Type .. Telescopic, double acting
- Mounting .. Rubber bushes

SECTION F—FRONT AXLE AND SUSPENSION

INDEX—FRONT AXLE AND SUSPENSION

Note: A comprehensive, detailed index is included at the end of this manual

Description	Operation Number
Exploded views and description	At beginning of Section
WHEEL HUBS	
Bearing adjustment	3
Brake anchor plate	4
Driving member for hub	6 and 7
Hub and bearings	4 and 5
Lubrication	1
Oil seal for driving member	7
Oil seal for hub bearings	5
Stub axle	4 and 5
SWIVEL PIN HOUSINGS	
Lubrication	9 and 10
Oil seal for swivel pin housing	1
Swivel pins, bush and bearing	8
FRONT SUSPENSION	
Bump stop rubber	10
Road springs	14
Shackle pins and bushes	12 and 13
Shock absorbers	12 and 13
DIFFERENTIAL	
Crown wheel and pinion	11
Differential	16-17
Lubrication	17
Oil seal for bevel pinion case	(See Section E)
FRONT AXLE	
Axle assembly	17
Axle case	1
Breather for axle case	15
Half shafts	(See Section E)
Lubrication	19
Oil seal for half shafts	18
Steering stop adjustment	18
	6 and 7
	1
	7 and 18
	2
FAULT DIAGNOSIS	
DATA	At end of Section

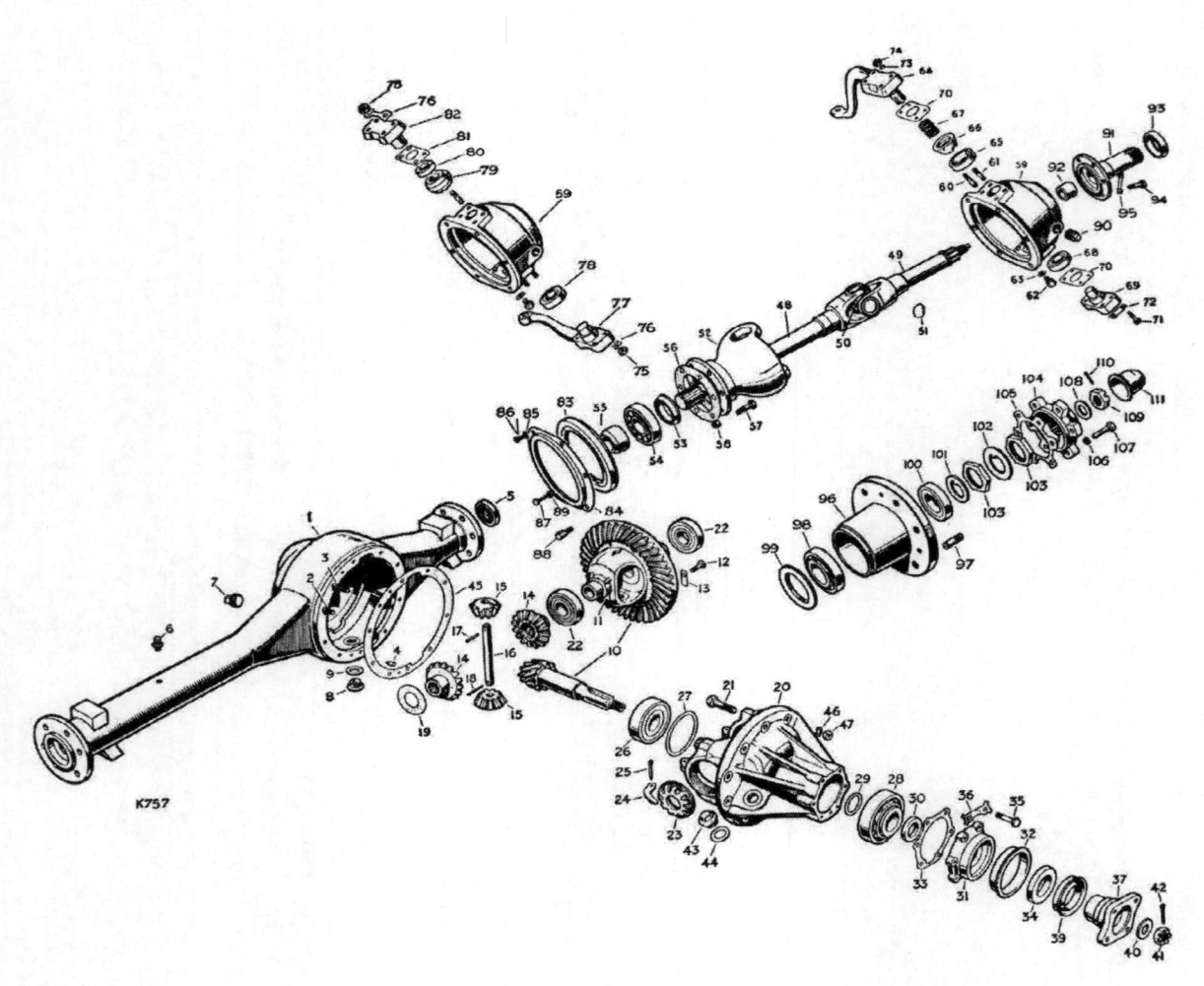

FRONT AXLE AND SUSPENSION

Key to Fig. F1-1. Exploded view of front axle

No.	Description	No.	Description
1	Axle casing complete	57–58	Fixings, housing to front axle casing
2–3	Fixings, bevel pinion housing to axle casing	59	Housing assembly for swivel pin
4	Dowel, locating housing	60	Special stud for steering lever and bracket
5	Oil seal, in casing	61	Stud for steering lever
6	Breather	62–63	Drain plug and joint washer
7	Oil filler plug	64	Swivel pin and steering lever
8–9	Drain plug and joint washer	65	Cone seat for swivel pin, top ⎫ early
10	Crownwheel and bevel pinion	66	Cone bearing for swivel pin, top ⎬ type
11	Differential casing	67	Spring for cone bearing
12	Set bolt	68	Bearing for swivel pin, bottom
13	Locker (double type)	69	Swivel pin and bracket
14	Differential wheel	70	Shim, for swivel pin bearing
15	Differential pinion	71–74	Fixings, swivel pin to swivel pin housings
16	Spindle for pinion		
17	Plain pin ⎫ For	75–76	Fixings, swivel pins to swivel pin housings
18	Split pin ⎭ spindle		
19	Thrust washer	77	Swivel pin and steering lever
20	Bevel pinion housing	78	Bearing for bottom swivel pin ⎫ latest
21	Special bolt, fixing bearing cap	79	Bush for top swivel pin ⎬ type
22	Taper roller bearing for differential	80	Thrust washer for bush
23–24	Bearing adjustment	81	Shim for top swivel pin
25	Split pin, fixing lock tab	82	Swivel pin and bracket
26	Bearing for bevel pinion, pinion end	83	Oil seal for swivel pin bearing housing
27	Shim, bearing adjustment, pinion end	84	Retainer for oil seal
28	Bearing for bevel pinion, flange end	85–89	Fixings, retainer and lock stop plate to swivel pin housing
29	Shim, bearing adjustment, flange end		
30	Washer for pinion bearing	90	Oil filler plug for swivel pin housing
31	Retainer for oil seal	91	Stub axle assembly
32	Mudshield for retainer	92	Bush for driving shaft, early models only
33	Joint washer for oil seal retainer	93	Distance piece for inner bearing
34	Oil seal for pinion	94–95	Fixings, stub axle to swivel pin housing
35–36	Fixings, oil seal retainer	96	Front hub assembly
37	Driving flange	97	Stud for road wheel
39	Mudshield for driving flange	98	Bearing for front hub, inner
40–42	Fixings for flange	99	Oil seal for inner bearing
43–44	Oil filler plug and joint washer	100	Bearing for front hub
45	Joint washer, differential to axle casing	101	Keywasher ⎫ Fixing
46–47	Fixings, differential to axle casing	102	Locker ⎬ front hub
48	Half shaft	103	Special nut ⎭ bearing
49	Stub shaft	104	Driving member for front hub
50	Journal assembly	105	Joint washer for driving member
51	Circlip for journal	106–107	Fixings, driving member to front hub
52	Housing for swivel pin bearing	108	Plain washer ⎫ Fixing
53	Distance piece for bearing	109	Slotted nut ⎬ driving member
54	Bearing for half shaft	110	Split pin ⎪ to
55	Retaining collar for bearing	111	Hub cap, front ⎭ driving shaft
56	Joint washer for housing		

Fig. F1-1. Exploded view of front axle

FRONT AXLE AND SUSPENSION

Lubrication, front axle (differential, swivel pin housings and hubs)—Operation F1-1

Workshop hand tools:
Spanner sizes: $\frac{7}{16}$ in. BSF, $\frac{1}{2}$ in. AF, $\frac{7}{16}$ in. AF open end

Hubs

Front hub lubrication is exactly the same as described for the rear, Section E, Operation E1-1.

Differential

To drain

1. Place a suitable container beneath the differential.
2. Remove the drain plug and allow all oil to drain, then replace the plug complete with joint washer.

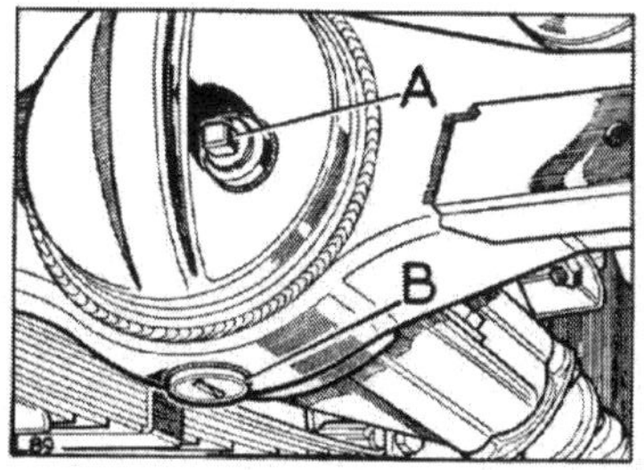

Fig. F1-2. Oil filler and drain plugs
A—Oil filler/level plug
B—Drain plug

Note: The plug fitted at the rear of the front axle should be disregarded.

To refill or top-up

1. Remove the oil filler/level plug.
2. Using the correct grade oil, see Section X, fill the differential to the bottom of the filler plug hole.
3. Fit the oil filler/level plug complete with joint washer.

Capacity

3 Imperial pints; 3½ US pints; 1.7 litres.

Swivel pin housings

To drain

1. Place a suitable container beneath the swivel pin housing.
2. Remove the drain plug and allow all oil to drain, then replace the plug complete with joint washer.

Fig. F1-3. Oil filler and drain plugs
A—Oil filler/level plug
B—Drain plug

To fill or top-up

1. Remove the oil filler/level plug.
2. Using the correct grade of oil, see Section X, fill the swivel pin housing to the bottom of the filler plug hole.
3. Fit the oil filler/level plug.

Capacity

1 Imperial pint; 1.2 US pints; 0.5 litre.

Steering lock stop, to adjust—Operation F1-2

Workshop hand tools:
Spanner sizes: $\frac{7}{16}$ in. AF open end

To adjust

1. Slacken the stop bolt locknuts.
2. Adjust the stop bolts so that the distance from the head of the bolt to the face of the oil seal retainer is ½ in. (12.5 mm).
3. Tighten the locknuts.
4. Check the steering at full lock, and ensure that the road wheel tyres do not foul any chassis components.

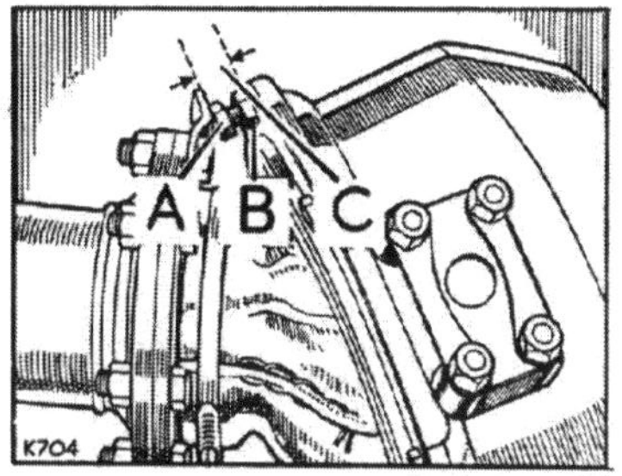

Fig. F1-4. Adjusting the lock stop bolt
A—Lock stop bolt
B—Locknut
C—Distance between head of bolt and oil seal retainer—½ in. (12.5 mm)

FRONT AXLE AND SUSPENSION

Section F—Land-Rover

Hub bearings, to adjust—Operation F1-3

(For removal, refitting and overhaul instructions, Operations F1-4 and F1-5 refer)

Workshop hand tools:
Spanner sizes; ¾ in. BSF, ⅝ in. BSF
Pliers, Screwdriver

Special Tools:
Spanner for hub bearing nuts,
Part No. 606435
(see Section Z for illustration)

To adjust

1. Slacken the fixings at the front road wheel.
2. Jack up the front of the vehicle.
3. Remove the front road wheel.
4. Fully slacken the front brake shoe adjusters to ensure that the brake linings are clear of the drum.
5. Remove the front brake drum.
   Note: If any difficulty is experienced in withdrawing the brake drum, fit one of the drum fixing screws into the extractor hole, and tighten the screw while using a mallet to dislodge the drum.
6. Prise off the hub cap.
7. Remove the driving member from the axle stub shaft and hub.

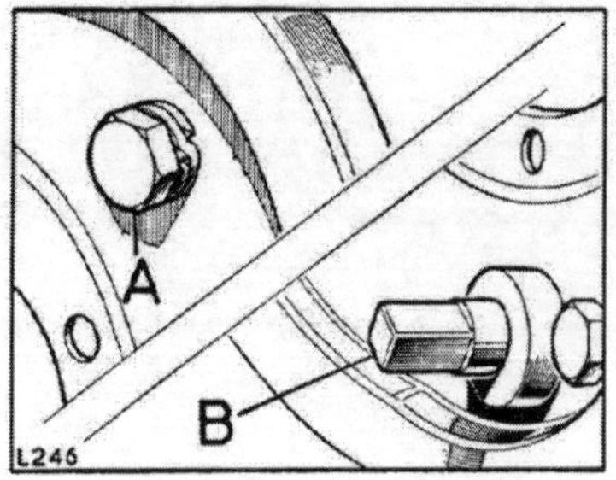

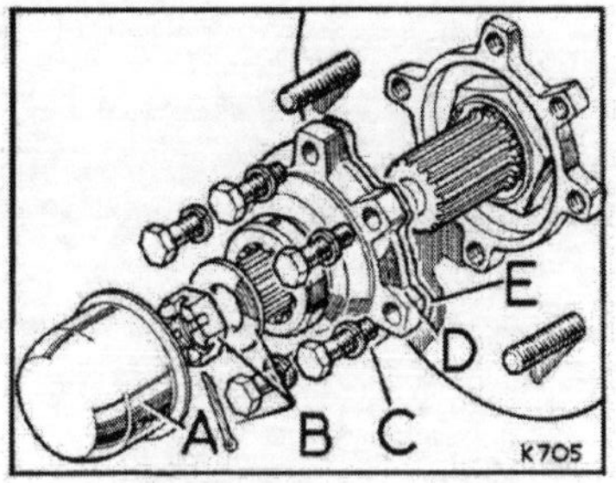

Fig. F1-5. Front brake shoe adjuster (two variations in use)
A—Small cam type
B—Fulcrum type

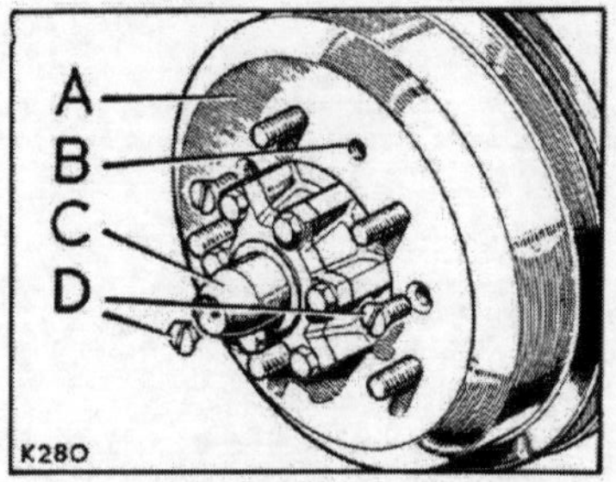

Fig. F1-6. Removing brake drum
A—Brake drum
B—Extractor hole
C—Hub
D—Fixings, drum to hub

Operation F1-3—continued

8. Remove the locknut and washer from the hub.
9. Spin the hub vigorously, causing the bearing rollers to settle in the tapered races, producing maximum end-float conditions.
10. Tighten the adjuster nut sufficient only, to take up any obvious end-float.
    Note: It is necessary to spin the hub every time before checking the end-float, as moving the hub laterally will resettle the rollers, affecting the measurable end-float.
11. Fit the lockwasher and nut, tighten the nut but do not engage the lockwasher.
12. Using a dial test indicator, check the end-float of the hub, which must be .004 in. to .006 in. (0.10 mm to 0,15 mm).
13. If the hub end-float is not within the permitted limits, remove the locknut and washer, and readjust the inner nut. Fit the lockwasher, tighten the locknut and recheck the end-float.
14. When the end-float is correct, engage the lockwasher.
15. Using a new joint washer and felt oil seal, fit the driving member to the hub and stub shaft, ensuring that the oil seal is fitted with the rubber side facing outward. Tighten the driving member securing bolts to a torque figure of 28 lb ft (3,9 mkg). Tighten the stub shaft securing nut to a torque figure of 10 lb ft to 15 lb ft (1,4 mkg to 2,0 mkg) and secure with a new split pin.
16. Complete the reassembly by reversing the removal procedure.
17. Adjust the brakes. (Section H.)
18. If the hubs are oil lubricated, replenish the lubricating oil. Operation F1-1.

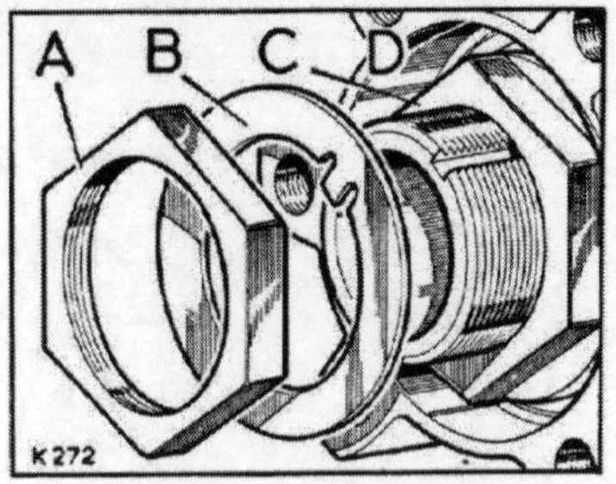

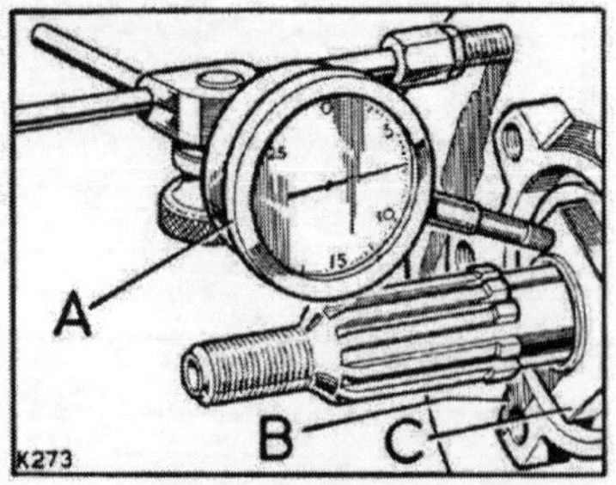

Fig. F1-7. Driving member for hub
A—Hub cap
B—Fixings, driving member to axle stub shaft
C—Fixings, driving member to hub
D—Driving member
E—Joint washer

Fig. F1-8. Hub bearing fixings
A—Locknut
B—Lockwasher
C—Nut for bearing adjustment
D—Hub

Fig. F1-9. Checking hub end-float
A—Dial test indicator
B—Hub
C—Bearing locknut

FRONT AXLE AND SUSPENSION

Front hubs, brake anchor plate and stub axle, remove and refit—Operation F1-4

(For overhaul instructions, Operation F1-5 refers)

Workshop hand tools:
Spanner sizes: ¼ in. BSF, ⁷⁄₁₆ in. BSF, ⁷⁄₈ in. AF, ⅝ in. AF open end, ⅜ in. BSF, ⅝ in. BSF Pliers, Screwdriver (large)

Special tools:
Spanner for hub bearing nuts, Part No. 606435
(see Section Z for illustration)

To remove front hub

1. Drain the lubricating oil from the swivel pin housing, Operation F1-1.
2. Slacken the fixings at the front road wheels.
3. Jack up the front of the vehicle and remove the front road wheels.
4. Fully slacken the front brake shoe adjusters to ensure that the brake linings are clear of the drum.

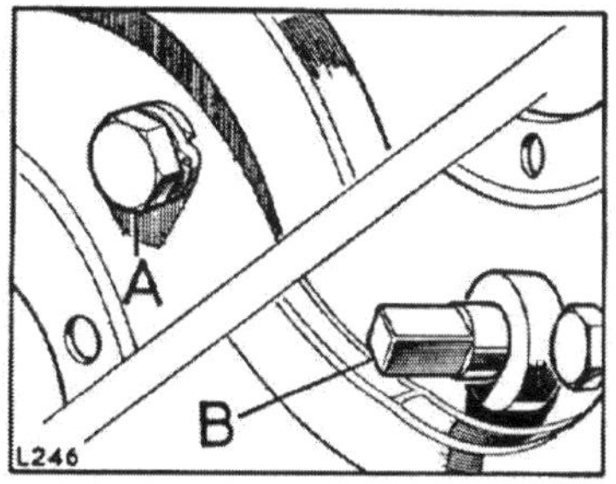

Fig. F1-10. Front brake shoe adjuster (two variations in use)
A—Snail cam type
B—Fulcrum type

5. Remove the front brake drum.

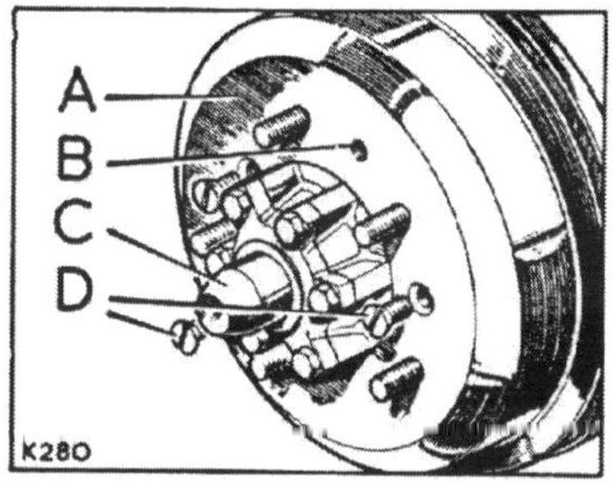

Fig. F1-11. Removing brake drum
A—Brake drum
B—Extractor hole
C—Hub
D—Fixings, drum to hub

Note: If any difficulty is experienced in withdrawing the brake drum, fit one of the drum fixing screws into the extractor hole, and tighten the screw while using a mallet to dislodge the drum.

6. Prise off the hub cap.
7. Remove the driving member from the axle stub shaft and the hub.

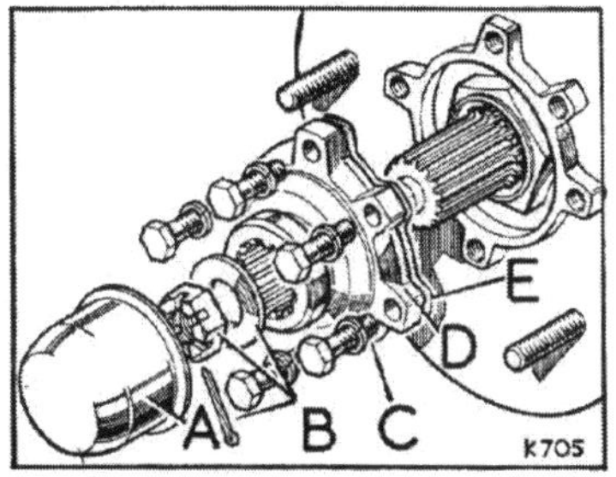

Fig. F1-12. Driving member for hub
A—Hub cap
B—Fixings, driving member to axle stub shaft
C—Fixings, driving member to hub
D—Driving member
E—Joint washer

8. Remove the front hub fixings.

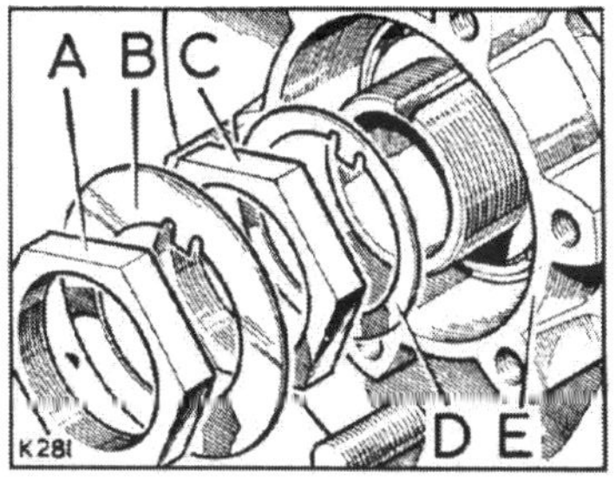

Fig. F1-13. Hub bearing fixings
A—Locknut   B—Lock washer
C—Adjuster nut   D—Key washer
E—Hub

Operation F1-4—continued

9. Hold the outer roller bearing in position and withdraw the hub and bearing assembly complete.

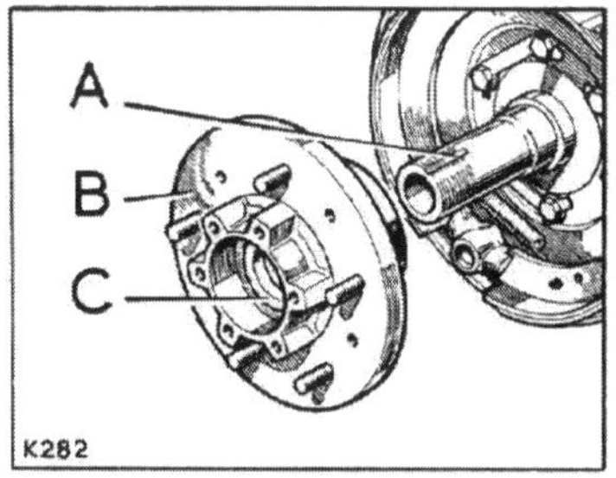

Fig. F1-14. Removing front hub and bearing assembly
A—Stub axle
B—Hub
C—Outer bearing for hub

To remove brake anchor plate and stub axle

10. Disconnect the front brake pipe at the connection with the flexible pipe, one each side of the vehicle, and withdraw the flexible pipe from the chassis bracket. Then, wedge the brake pedal and depress it in that position, to prevent further leakage of brake fluid. When depressing the brake pedal, take precautions to avoid fluid spillage.

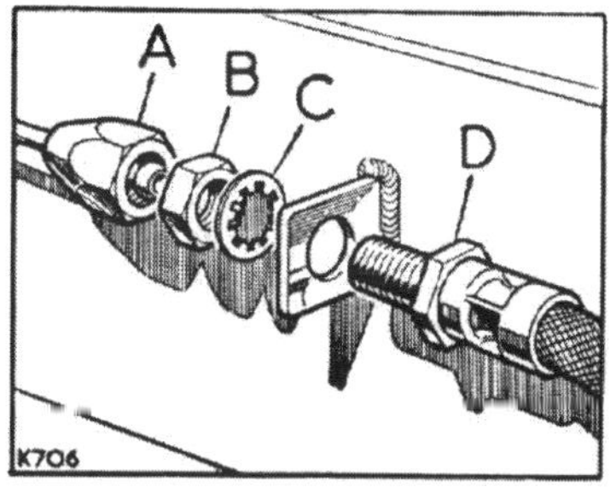

Fig. F1-15. Front brake pipe connection
A—Pipe from master cylinder
B—Locknut
C—Shakeproof washer
D—Flexible brake pipe

11. Remove the brake anchor plate and withdraw the stub axle.

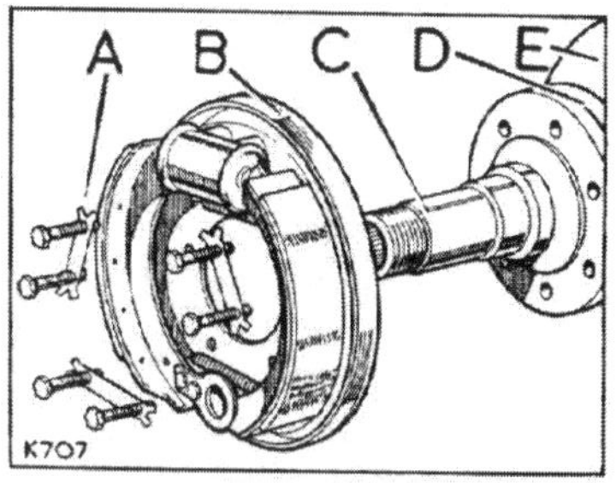

Fig. F1-16. Front brake anchor plate and stub axle (typical brake plate illustrated)
A—Fixings, brake anchor plate and stub axle to swivel pin housing
B—Brake anchor plate
C—Stub axle
D—Joint washer
E—Swivel pin housing

To refit stub axle and brake anchor plate

1. Smear both sides of the joint washer with general purpose grease, and place it in position on the rear face of the stub axle.
2. Position the stub axle, with the keyway at the top, on the swivel pin housing, then fit the brake anchor plate with the brake hose connection at the top. Ensure that the cut-away in the lock plates face inward.

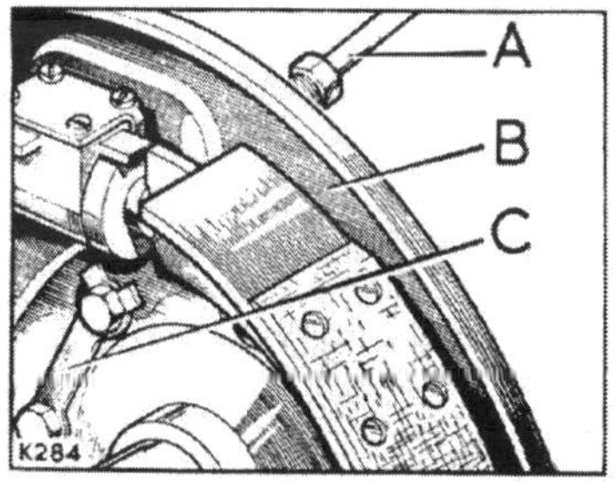

Fig. F1-17. Fitting brake anchor plate
A—Brake hose connection at top
B—Brake anchor plate
C—Cut away side of lockwasher facing inward

FRONT AXLE AND SUSPENSION

Operation F1-4—continued

3. Connect the front brake pipes at the coupling with the flexible pipes.

To refit front hub

4. Hold the outer roller bearing in position and slide the hub and bearing assembly on to the bearing sleeve.
5. Fit the key washer and bearing adjusting nut, then adjust the bearing end-float. Operation F1-3.
6. Complete the reassembly by reversing the removal procedure ensuring that the felt oil seal for the hub driving member is fitted with the rubber side facing outward.

Tighten the driving member securing bolts to a torque figure of 28 lb ft (3,9 mkg). Tighten the stub shaft securing nut to a torque figure of 10 lb ft to 15 lb ft (1,4 mkg to 2,0 mkg) and secure with a new split pin.

7. Bleed and adjust the brakes.
8. Replenish the front axle and swivel pin housing lubricating oil. Operation F1-1.

Front hubs and stub axles, overhaul—Operation F1-5

(For removal and refitting Instructions, Operation F1-4 refers)
(For overhaul of brake anchor plate, Section H refers)

Workshop hand tools:
Screwdriver (medium), Mallet

To dismantle

1. Withdraw the outer roller bearing.
2. Prise out the oil seal and withdraw the inner roller bearing.

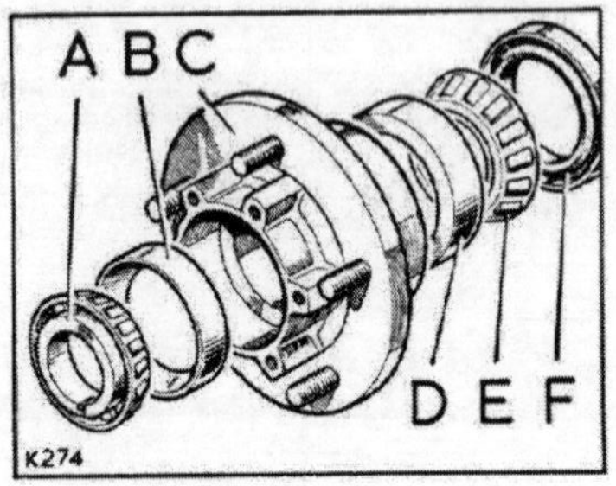

Fig. F1-18. Front hub and bearings
A—Outer roller bearing
B—Outer race for outer bearing
C—Hub
D—Outer race for inner bearing
E—Inner roller bearing
F—Oil seal

3. Press the bearing outer races from the hub.
4. If it is required to remove the inner bearing distance piece from the stub axle, it must be shattered, using extreme care to avoid damaging the axle.

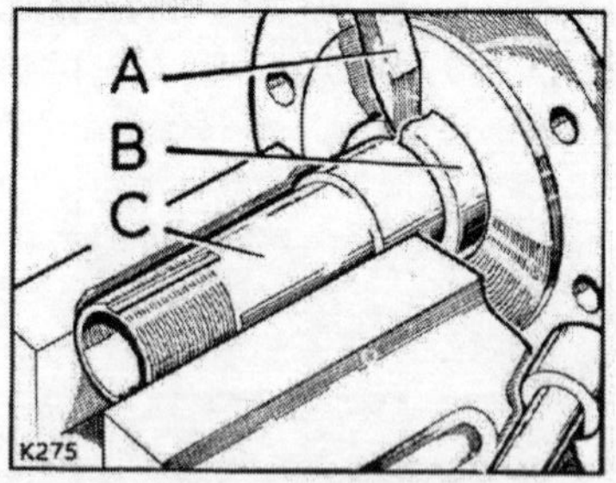

Inspection

1. Examine all components for obvious wear or damage.
2. Check the outside diameter of the inner bearing distance piece, this must not show any signs of damage or roughness as it forms the inner seat for the oil seal. The distance piece should be a press fit on the stub axle. Any clearance between these two parts will allow oil to leak past on to the brake linings.
3. The hub bearings must be a press fit in the hub and a sliding fit on the stub axle.

Note: Early stub axles are fitted with a bush at the inner end, which is reamered, after fitting, to 1.250 in. +.004 in. (31,75 mm +0,10 mm). If the bush is worn or damaged, a new replacement should be fitted and reamered in position. Latest type stub axles are of a strengthened design and are not fitted with a bush. The stub axle and half shaft should be examined for wear or damage, and replacements made accordingly. The latest type stub axle is interchangeable with the early type, deleting the bush.

To assemble

1. Press the bearing outer races, wide side first, into the hub, ensuring that they abut the locating shoulders.
2. Using the correct grade of grease, see Section X, fully pack the inner roller bearing and place it in its outer race.
3. Smear the outside diameter of the oil seal with jointing compound, and press it into the hub, lipped side inward, until it is flush with the rear face of the hub. DO NOT press the seal below the rear face of the hub, or it may fail to locate its inner seat correctly, resulting in an oil leak which could contaminate the brake linings.
4. Pack the centre of the hub with the correct grade of grease, leaving sufficient space for the bearing sleeve.

Fig. F1-19. Removing inner bearing distance piece
A—Use chisel to shatter
B—Distance piece (shattered)
C—Sleeve for hub bearings

Section F—Land-Rover FRONT AXLE AND SUPPENSION

Operation F1-5—continued

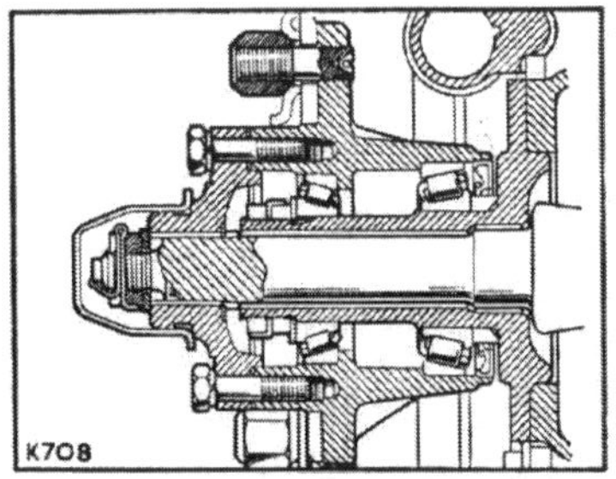

5. Fully pack the outer roller bearing with the correct grade of grease, and place it in its outer race.

   Note: When fitting the hub to the axle, ensure that the axle case breather is clear (see Operation F1-18), a blocked breather could cause failure of the oil seal fitted in the hub.

Fig. F1-20. Cross-section of front hub

Section F—Land-Rover FRONT AXLE AND SUSPENSION

Axle half shaft complete, remove and refit—Operation F1-6

(For overhaul instructions, Operation F1-7 refers)

Workshop hand tools:

Spanner sizes: ½ in. BSF, ½ in. BSF, $\frac{7}{16}$ in. BSF, $\frac{7}{16}$ in. AF, $\frac{5}{8}$ in. AF open end ½ in. BSF, $\frac{5}{8}$ in. BSF, 2 in. AF sockets

To remove

1. Drain the lubricating oil from the front axle and swivel pin housing. Operation F1-1.

2. Remove the front hub, brake anchor plate, and stub axle. Operation F1-4.

   Note: To avoid the necessity of bleeding the brakes on reassembly, DO NOT disconnect the brake pipes, after removing the anchor plate fixings, suspend the plate without straining the flexible pipe.

3. Withdraw the axle half shaft complete.

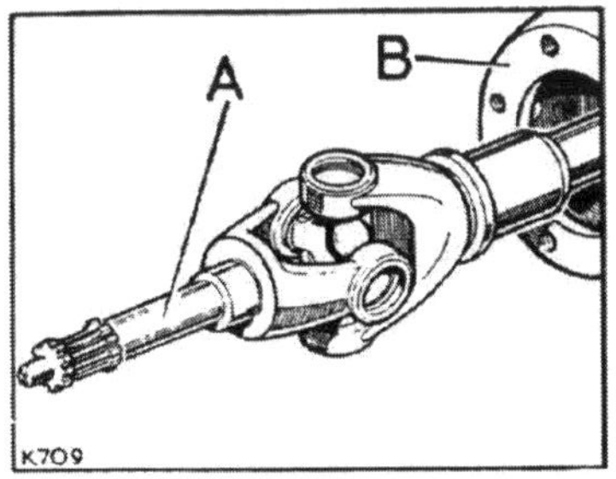

Fig. F1-21. Axle half shaft

A—Axle half shaft complete
B—Swivel pin housing

To refit

1. Using extreme care to avoid damaging the oil seal in the end of the axle case, fit the axle half shaft, long end first, into the swivel pin housing and axle case, carefully engaging the splines on the half shaft into the final drive unit.

2. Rotate the axle half shaft and check that there is a minimum clearance of .050 in. (1.2 mm) between the stub and half shaft yoke ears and the swivel pin end faces. Carry out this check at the top and bottom swivel pins when the yokes are at an angle, with the chamfered radius closest to the swivel pin end face.

   If the clearance is insufficient, increase the chamfer on the radius of the yokes.

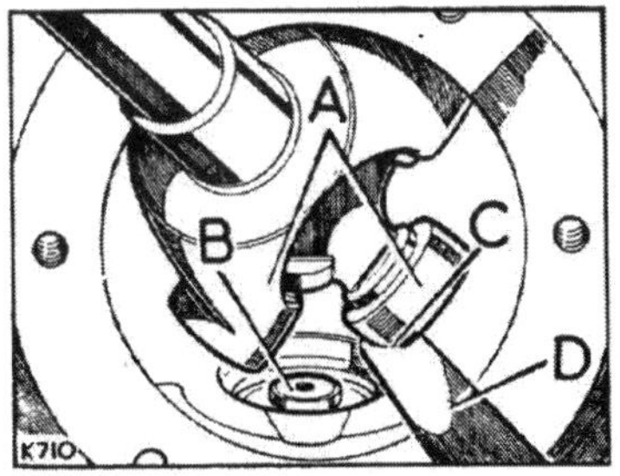

Fig. F1-22. Checking clearance between half shaft yokes and swivel pins

A—Half shaft yokes
B—Bottom swivel pin
C—Chamfered yoke radius
D—Feeler gauges .050 in. (1.2 mm) minimum

3. Fit the stub axle, brake anchor plate and front hub. Operations F1-4 and F1-3.

4. Replenish the front axle lubricating oil. Operation F1-1.

5. Bleed and adjust the brakes. (Section H).

FRONT AXLE AND SUSPENSION

Axle half shaft complete, to overhaul—Operation F1-7

(For removal and refitting instructions, Operation F1-6 refers)

Workshop hand tools:
Circlip pliers, Mallet, Brass drift

Special tools:
Hub removal tool and adaptor kit, Part No. 275870

To dismantle universal joint

1. Remove the circlips from the universal joint.

2. With one of the stub shaft yoke lugs uppermost tap the radius of the yoke lightly with a soft-nosed mallet.

   The top bearing should then begin to emerge from the yoke.

3. Turn the joint over and withdraw the bearing.

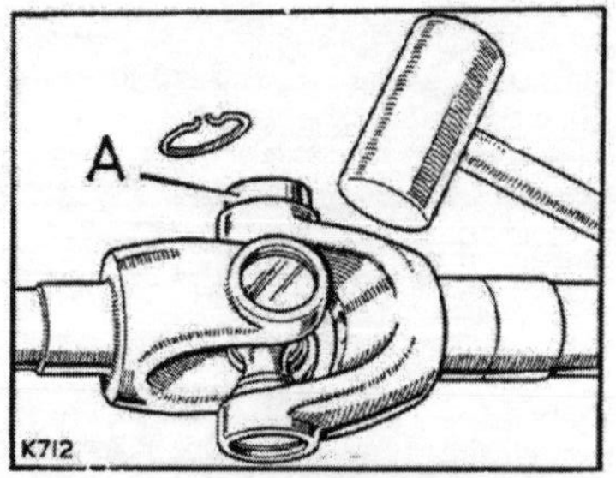

   Always remove a bearing downwards, to avoid dropping the needle rollers.

4. Repeat the foregoing operations for the opposite bearing.

5. Part the stub shaft from the spider journals.

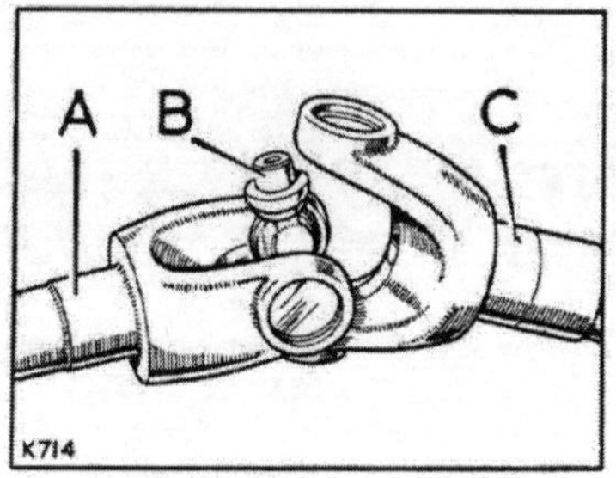

Fig. F1-23. First stage of yoke bearing removal
A—Bearing emerging

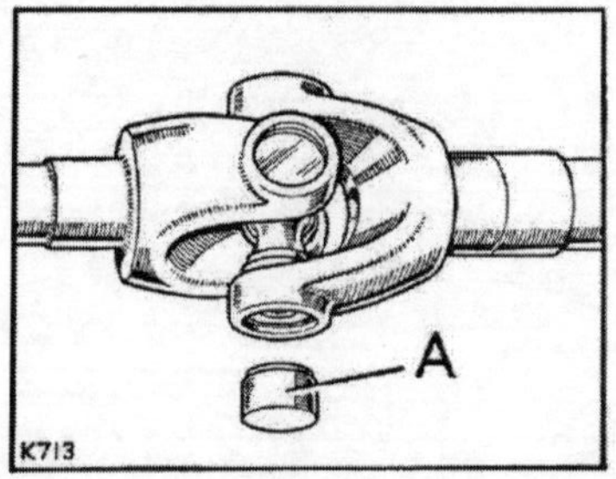

Fig. F1-24. Second stage of yoke bearing removal
A—Bearing withdrawn

Fig. F1-25. Removing the stub shaft
A—Stub shaft   B—Journal   C—Half shaft

6. Remove the half shaft bearings in the same manner as already described for the stub shaft.

To dismantle half shaft

1. Using special tool, hub removal tool and adaptor kit, Part No. 275870, clamp the extractor firmly in a vice.

2. Position the appropriate adaptors on the end of the axle shaft and insert into the extractor.

3. Secure the shaft to the extractor, using adaptor No. 5.

4. The shaft may now be forced out of the collar by screwing in the ram.

Operation F1-7—continued

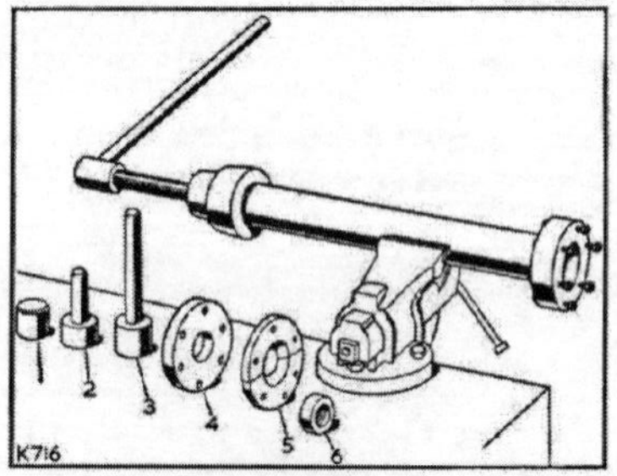

2. If the journal or bearings for the universal joint show any signs of wear, load markings or distortion, they must be renewed complete.

3. The bearing races should be a light drive fit in the yoke trunnions.

4. In the event of wear taking place in any of the four yoke cross holes, rendering them oval, a new stub shaft or half shaft must be fitted.

5. The bearing inner race must be a light press fit on the axle half shaft.

To assemble half shaft

1. Fit the conical distance piece over the half shaft with the internal chamfer to the radius on the shaft.

2. Place the roller race inner member and a new retaining collar over the half shaft with the chamfer towards the splined end; stand the shaft on end on a block of hard wood.

3. Bolt adaptor No. 4 to the tool with the recess towards the collar.

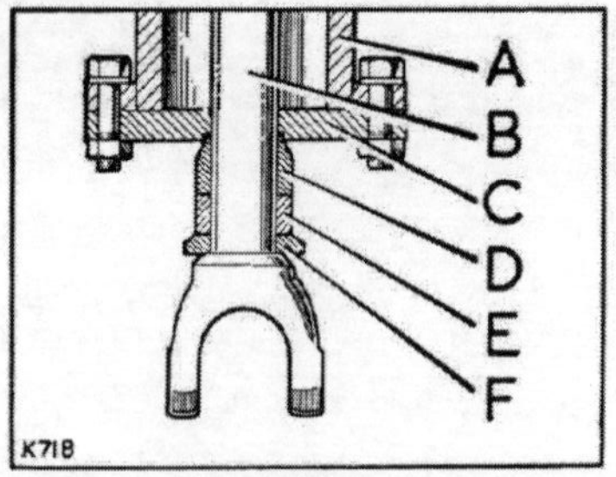

Fig. F1-26. Hub removal tool and adaptor kit (Part No. 275870)

5. After removal, discard the retaining collar. Use a new collar on assembly.

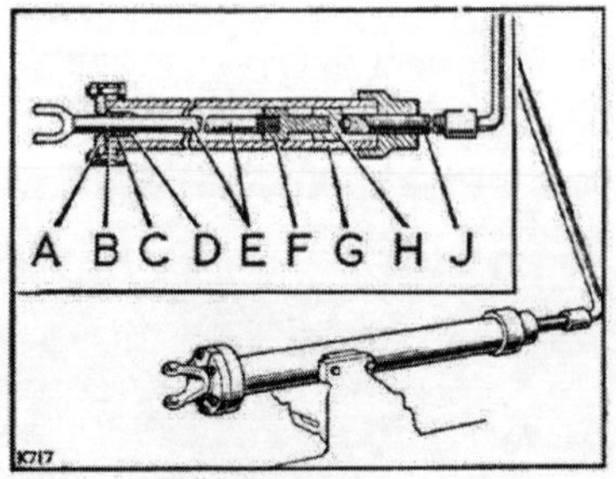

Fig. F1-27. Using special tool, Part No. 275870, to dismantle axle half shaft
A—Adaptor No. 5
B—Conical distance piece
C—Bearing inner race
D—Retaining collar
E—Axle half shaft
F—Adaptor No. 2 or 3, as applicable
G—Hub removal tool
H—Adaptor No. 1
J—Ram

Fig. F1-28. Special tool, Part No. 275870, assembled to axle half shaft
A—Hub removal tool
B—Axle half shaft
C—Adaptor No. 4
D—Retaining collar
E—Bearing inner race
F—Conical distance piece

Inspection

1. Examine all components for obvious wear or damage.

FRONT AXLE AND SUSPENSION

Operation F1-7—continued

4. The weight of the extractor is such that it may now be used as a ram to drive the collar on to the shaft.

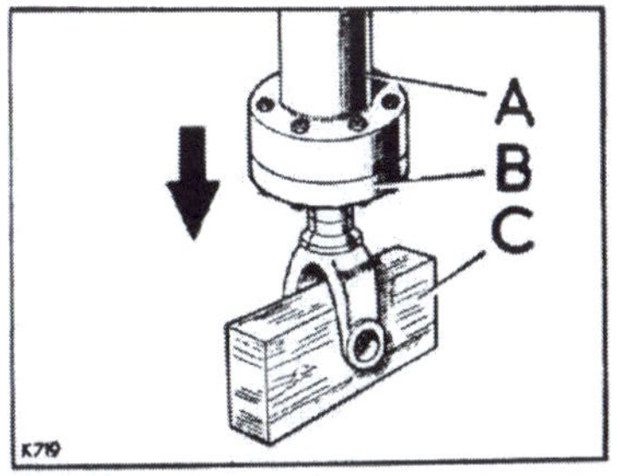

Fig. F1-29. Extractor used as a ram to drive collar on to axle shaft

A—Extractor (hub removal tool)
B—Adaptor
C—Hardwood block

To assemble universal joint

1. Assemble the needle rollers in the bearing races, if necessary using a smear of vaseline to retain them in place.

2. Insert the journal in the stub shaft yoke holes, and using a brass drift slightly smaller in diameter than the hole in the yoke, lightly tap the first bearing into position, and retain with a circlip.

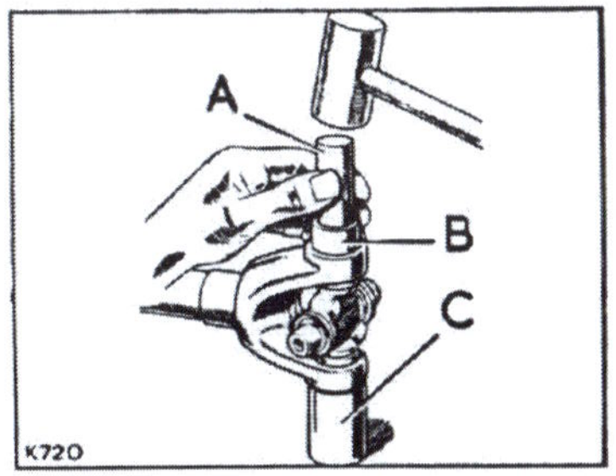

Fig. F1-30. Replacing a yoke bearing

A—Brass drift   B—Yoke bearing
C—Support

3. Repeat the foregoing operations for the other three bearings.

4. Ensure that the universal joint moves freely. If the joint appears to bind, hold one shaft so that the joint hangs free and tap the yoke ears lightly with a mallet.

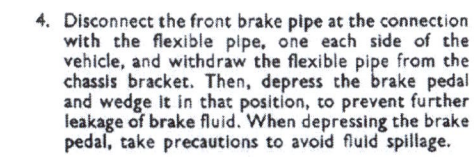

5. Check that all four circlips are firmly located in their grooves.

Oil seals for swivel pin housing and axle case, remove and refit—Operation F1-8

(For overhaul Instructions, Operation F1-10 refers)

Workshop hand tools:
Spanner sizes: ¼ in. BSF, ⅜ in. BSF, ½ in. BSF, 7/16 in. AF, ½ in. AF, ⅝ in. AF open end
Screwdriver (medium), Pliers

Special tools:
Extractor for steering ball joints, Part No. 600590

To remove

1. Drain the lubricating oil from front axle and swivel pin housing. Operation F1-1.

2. Slacken the fixings at the front road wheel.

3. Jack up the front of the vehicle and remove the road wheel.

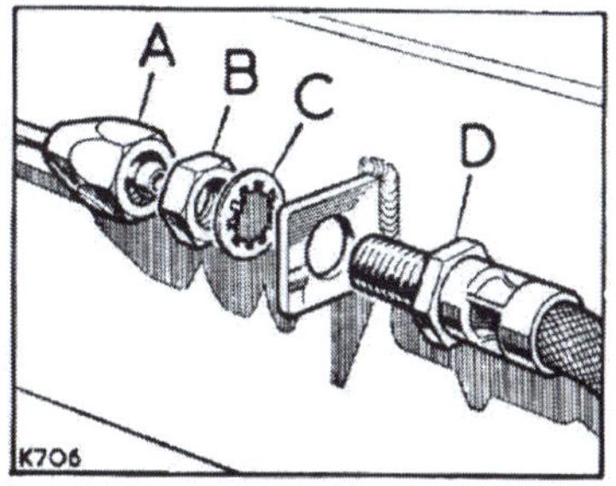

4. Disconnect the front brake pipe at the connection with the flexible pipe, one each side of the vehicle, and withdraw the flexible pipe from the chassis bracket. Then, depress the brake pedal and wedge it in that position, to prevent further leakage of brake fluid. When depressing the brake pedal, take precautions to avoid fluid spillage.

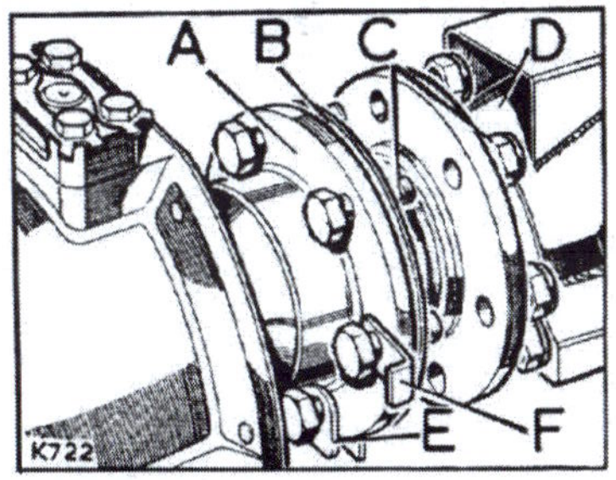

Fig. F1-31. Front brake pipe connection

A—Pipe from master cylinder
B—Locknut
C—Shakeproof washer
D—Flexible brake pipe

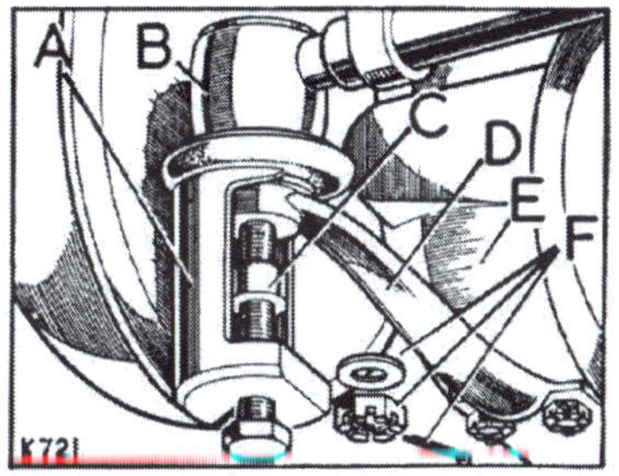

Fig. F1-32. Steering track rod and drag link connections

A—Special tool, Part No. 600590
B—Ball joint
C—Thread protection cap, part of 600590
D—Steering lever
E—Swivel pin housing
F—Fixings, ball joint to steering lever

Fig. F1-33. Swivel pin to axle case location

A—Swivel pin housing
B—Joint washer
C—Fixings, swivel pin housing to axle case
D—Axle case
E—Location stop for jack (RH side only)
F—Lock stop plate

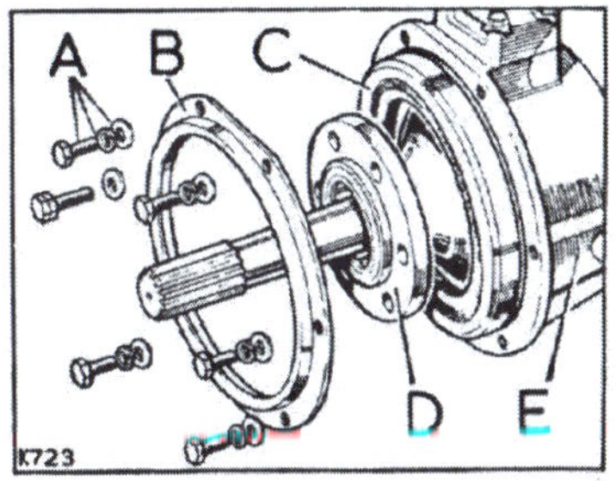

Fig. F1-34. Oil seal for swivel pin housing

A—Fixings (6 off) oil seal retainer to swivel pin housing
B—Oil seal retainer
C—Oil seal
D—Swivel pin bearing housing
E—Swivel pin housing

FRONT AXLE AND SUSPENSION

Operation F1-8—continued

5. Disconnect the steering drag link and track rod as applicable, using special tool, Part No. 600590 to extract the ball joints.
6. Remove the fixings between the swivel pin housing and the axle case, noting the steering lock stop plate, and on the right-hand side only, the jack location stop plate.
7. Withdraw the swivel pin housing, axle half shaft and front hub assembly complete.
8. Remove the oil seal retainer from the swivel pin housing.
9. Prise the oil seal from the swivel pin housing.
10. Prise the oil seal from the axle case.

To refit

1. Pack the swivel pin housing oil seal with heavy grease, and fit the oil seal and its retainer to the swivel pin housing, locating the steering stop adjustment bolt in the forwardmost hole.

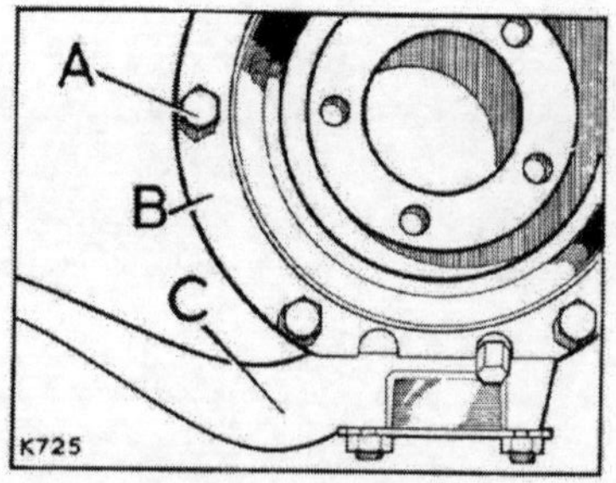

Fig. F1-35. Location of steering stop adjustment bolt
  A—Bolt for steering stop adjustment
  B—Retainer for oil seal
  C—Steering lever

2. Check that the oil seal wipes the full surface of the bearing housing and adjust the position, if necessary, by slackening off the retaining bolts and resetting the seal.

Operation F1-8—continued

3. Smear jointing compound on the outside diameter of the oil seal for the axle case. Fit the oil seal, lipped side inward, into the axle case, flush with the recessed end.

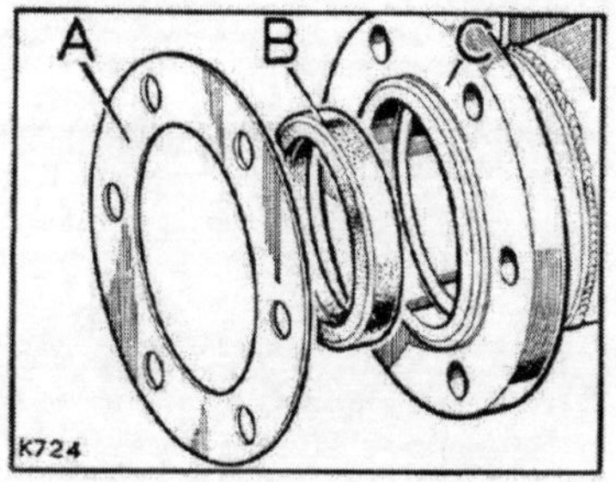

Fig. F1-36. Oil seal and joint washer for axle case
  A—Joint washer   B—Oil seal
  C—Axle case

4. Smear both sides of the joint washer with general purpose grease and place it in position on the axle case.
5. Offer the swivel pin housing and hub assembly to the axle case, carefully engaging the splines on the half shaft into the final drive unit.

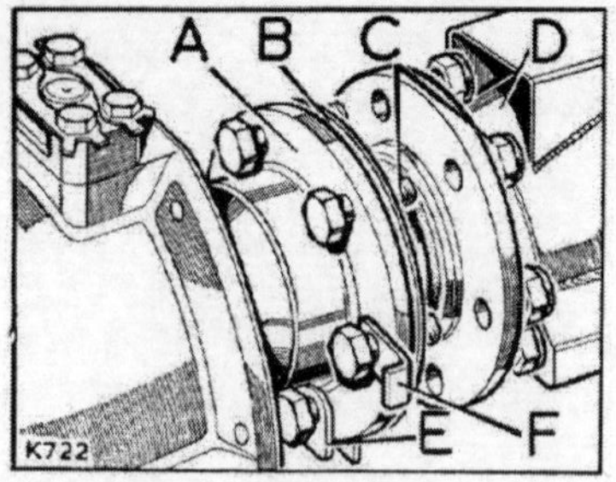

Fig. F1-37. Swivel pin housing to axle case location
  A—Swivel pin housing
  B—Joint washer
  C—Fixings, swivel pin housing to axle case
  D—Axle case
  E—Location stop for jack (RH side only)
  F—Lock stop plate

6. Secure the swivel pin housing to the axle case.
7. Connect the steering drag link and track rod, as applicable. Tighten the ball joint fixing nuts to a torque figure of 30 lb ft (4,0 mkg).
8. Connect the front brake pipe at the coupling with the flexible pipes.
9. Bleed and adjust the brakes. See Section H.
10. Replenish the front axle lubricating oil. Operation F1-1.
11. Fit the road wheels.
12. Check, and if necessary, adjust the steering stop.
13. Ensure that the axle case breather is clear (see Operation F1-18), a blocked breather could cause failure of the oil seals fitted in the axle case and swivel pin housing.

FRONT AXLE AND SUSPENSION

Swivel pin housing, remove and refit—Operation F1-9

(For overhaul instructions, Operation F1-10 refers)

Workshop hand tools:

Spanner sizes: ¼ in. BSF, ⅜ in. BSF, ⁷⁄₁₆ in. BSF, ½ in. AF, ⁹⁄₁₆ in. AF, ⁷⁄₁₆ in. AF open end ⅝ in. BSF, ⁵⁄₈ in. BSF, 2 in. AF sockets

Special tools:

Extractor for steering ball joints, Part No. 600590

To remove

1. Drain the lubricating oil from the front axle and swivel pin housing. Operation F1-1.
2. Remove the front hub, brake anchor plate, and stub axle. Operation F1-4.

   Note: To avoid the necessity of bleeding the brakes on reassembly, DO NOT disconnect the brake pipes, after removing the anchor plate fixings, suspend the plate without straining the flexible pipe.

3. Withdraw the axle half shaft complete.

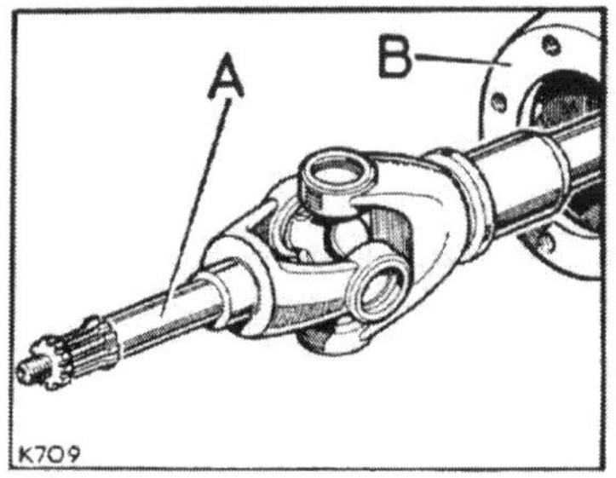

Fig. F1-38. Axle half shaft
A—Axle half shaft complete
B—Swivel pin housing

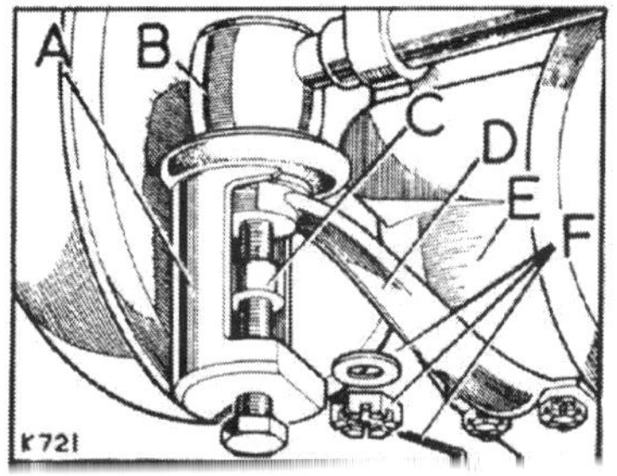

Fig. F1-39. Steering track rod and drag link connections
A—Special tool, Part No. 600590
B—Ball joint
C—Thread protection cap, part of 600590
D—Steering lever
E—Swivel pin housing
F—Fixings, ball joint to steering lever

4. Disconnect the steering drag link and track rod as required, using special tool, Part No. 600590, to extract the ball joints.

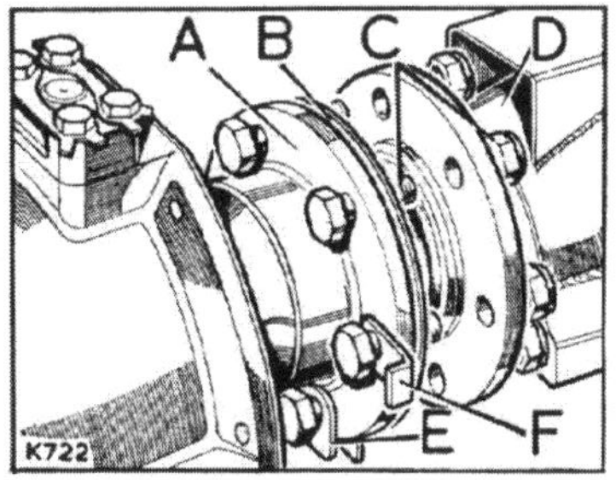

Fig. F1-40. Swivel pin housing to axle case location
A—Swivel pin housing
B—Joint washer
C—Fixings, swivel pin housing to axle case
D—Axle case
E—Location stop for jack (RH side only)
F—Lock stop plate

5. Remove the fixings between the swivel pin housing and the axle case, noting the steering lock stop plate, and on the right-hand side only, the jack location stop plate.

6. Withdraw the swivel pin housing complete with the joint washer.

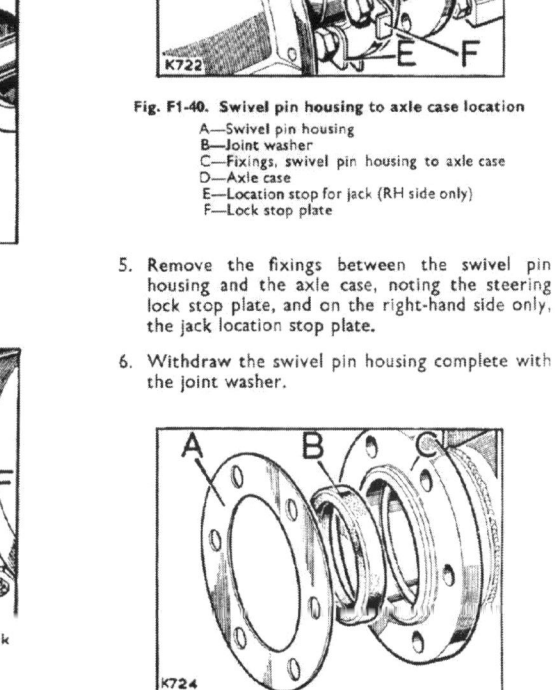

Fig. F1-41. Oil seal and joint washer for axle case
A—Joint washer B—Oil seal
C—Axle case

Operation F1-9—continued

To refit

1. Before fitting the swivel pin housing, examine the oil seal fitted in the end of the axle case and if necessary, fit a new replacement.
2. Smear both sides of the joint washer with general purpose grease and place it in position on the axle case.
3. Fit the swivel pin housing to the axle case.
4. Connect the steering track rod and drag link, as applicable. Tighten the ball joint fixing nuts to a torque figure of 30 lb ft (4,0 mkg).
5. Fit the axle half shaft, long end first, into the swivel pin housing and axle case, carefully engaging the splines on the half shaft into the final drive unit.
6. Fit the stub axle, brake anchor plate and front hub. Operations F1-4 and F1-3.
7. Replenish the front axle lubricating oil. Operation F1-1.
8. Bleed and adjust the brakes. (Section H).
9. Check, and if necessary, adjust the steering stop. Operation F1-2.

FRONT AXLE AND SUSPENSION

Swivel pin housing, to overhaul—Operation F1-10

(For removal and refitting instructions, Operation F1-9 refers)

Workshop hand tools:
Spanner sizes: ¼ in. BSF open end, ⅞ in. BSF socket
Screwdriver (medium), Mallet, Spring balance

General

Design modifications incorporated in the swivel pin housings have resulted in two main variations of swivel pin assemblies, as illustrated. Care should be taken to identify the type fitted and refer to the relative instructions.

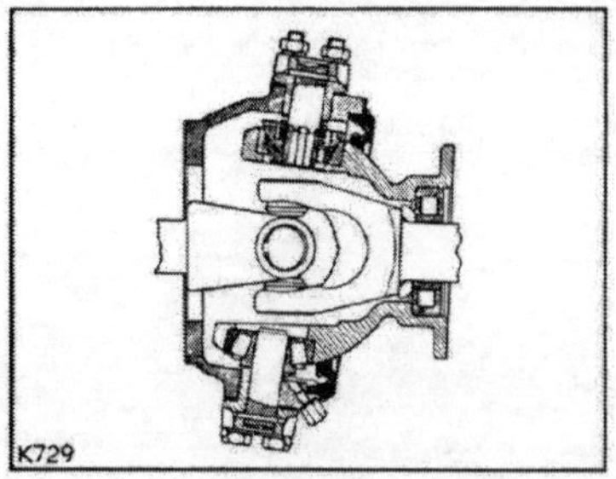

The parts supplied can be easily fitted to any existing Land-Rover from 1954 onwards by removing the existing swivel pin, coil spring, cone and cone seat and fitting in their place the new swivel pin and swivel pin bearing housing and bush.

From axles numbered:

141107339 88 RHD
141104520 88 LHD
151108875 109 RHD
154103275 109 LHD onwards

the steering levers are fitted to the bottom of the swivel housings with the ball joints above the levers.

Fig. F1-42. Cross-section of early type swivel pin housing with spring-loaded damper

Swivel pin conversion from spring-loaded damper to Railko bush type

The Railko bush type of steering damping gives very considerable improvement over the coil spring type; this applies particularly where there is any tendency to wheel wobble.

Owners of Land-Rovers who may be operating their vehicles under adverse conditions, may wish to take advantage of improved steering damping.

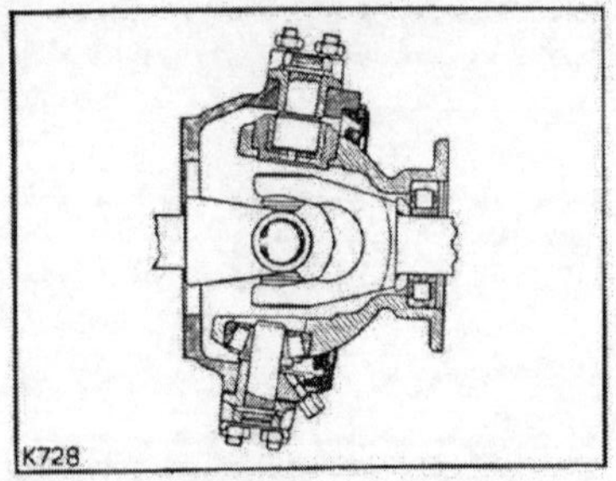

A swivel pin conversion kit, which is complete with detailed fitting instructions, is available under Part No. 532268.

Fig. F1-43. Cross-section of latest type swivel pin housing with Railko bush type friction damper

Swivel pin and steering levers are not interchangeable as individual items; they can, however, be fitted in pairs provided either the swivel pin housing complete is changed for the latest type, or studs are fitted in the bottom position of the existing swivel pin housing. Studs required are 6 off 508152, 2 off 508153. It is most important that the latest type steering levers are not fitted to an early type housing in the lower position with the existing bolts; the studs detailed above including the special fitting studs 508153 must be fitted. This prevents any tendency for movement between lever and housing which could give rise to premature breakage of the bolts with the possibility of serious damage.

Early type swivel pin housing with spring-loaded damper

To dismantle

1. Remove the oil seal retainer.
2. Prise the oil seal from the swivel pin housing.

Fig. F1-44. Early type pendant ball joint

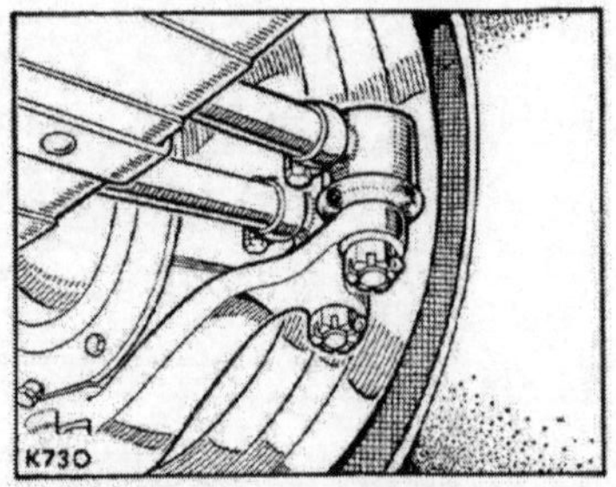

Fig. F1-45. Late type non-pendant ball joint

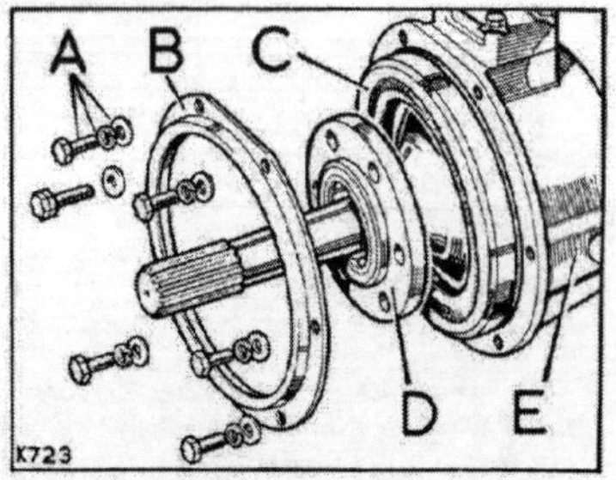

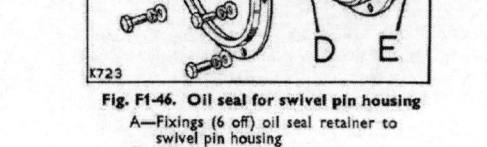

Fig. F1-46. Oil seal for swivel pin retainer
A—Fixings (6 off) oil seal retainer to swivel pin housing
B—Oil seal retainer
C—Oil seal
D—Swivel pin bearing housing
E—Swivel pin housing

3. Remove the swivel pin and steering lever assembly from the swivel pin housing together with the shims, which should be preserved. Remove the cone bearing spring.
4. Remove the swivel pin and bracket assembly from the swivel pin housing together with the shims, which should be preserved.
5. Part the swivel pin and swivel pin bearing housings and remove the roller race inner member and the cone bearing.

Operation F1-10—continued

6. Drive out the race outer member and the cone seat from the swivel pin bearing housing.

Inspection

1. Examine the bottom taper roller race and swivel pin for wear and renew as necessary. The bearing should be a *light press fit* in the housing and a *light push fit* on the swivel pin. If a new bearing race is slack in the housing, the housing must be renewed; if it is slack on the swivel pin, the swivel pin assembly must be renewed.

2. Examine the upper cone seat and swivel pin for wear and roughness and rectify as necessary. The cone seat should be a *light press fit* in the housing; if a new cone seat is slack in the housing, the housing must be renewed.

3. If the swivel pins are worn, new replacements can be fitted as follows:

    (a) Thoroughly clean the boss of the steering lever or bracket with paraffin and a wire brush.
    (b) Drill out the grooved pin by means of a ⅛ in. (3,17 mm) drill.
    (c) Place the steering lever or bracket upon a solid base, i.e., between the jaws of a vice, and drive out the swivel pin from the lever or bracket boss by means of a brass drift.
    (d) **Top swivel pin only.** Fit the new pin, by positioning its splines in relation to the track rod lever as shown, that is with a splined groove placed in line with the longitudinal axis of the track rod lever. This is very important as it ensures that the cone is located correctly.

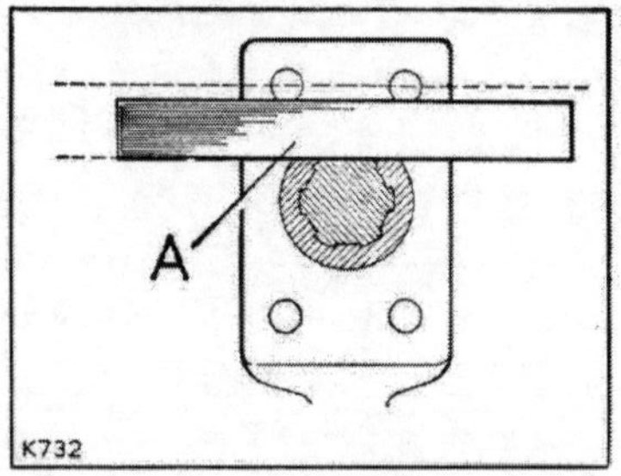

Fig. F1-47. Setting the top swivel pin
A—Straight edge

FRONT AXLE AND SUSPENSION

Operation F1-10—continued

(e) Press the pin squarely into the lever or bracket.

(f) Drill the lever or bracket boss and swivel pin with a $\frac{5}{32}$ in. (4 mm) drill and insert a $\frac{3}{32}$ in. grooved pin.

4. Examine the cone bearing for wear or roughness and rectify or renew as necessary.

5. Examine the surface of the swivel pin bearing housing for signs of corrosion or damage, and renew it if necessary.

To assemble

1. Press the roller bearing for the axle half shaft into the swivel pin bearing housing.

2. Press the taper roller bearing outer race, wide side first, into the bottom of the swivel pin bearing housing and place the roller bearing in position.

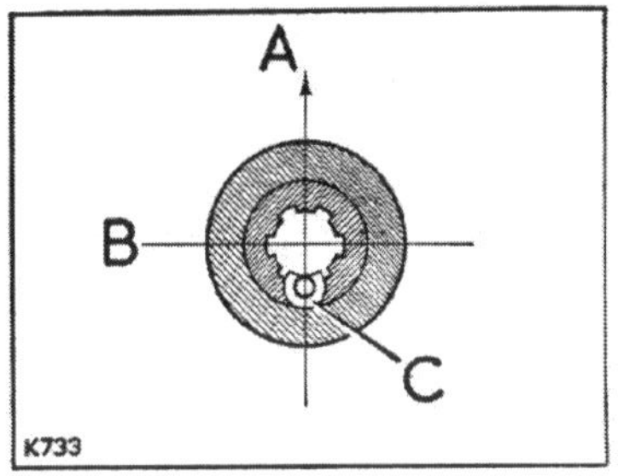

Fig. F1-48. Setting the cone bearing

A—Front of vehicle
B—Centre line of front axle
C—Vertical oil hole

3. Insert the cone bearing after smearing with oil, with the vertical oil hole in the bearing towards the rear of the vehicle.

4. Insert the race inner member, and holding it in position, offer the swivel pin housing to the bearing housing.

5. Smear the mating surfaces with suitable sealing compound and replace the swivel pin and bracket assembly at the bottom of the swivel pin housing, together with the shims removed on stripping, to the value of .040 in. (1,0 mm); tighten down. Sharply tap the assembly to ensure positive seating and again check the tightness of the securing nuts.

6. Insert the cone spring in the top bearing.

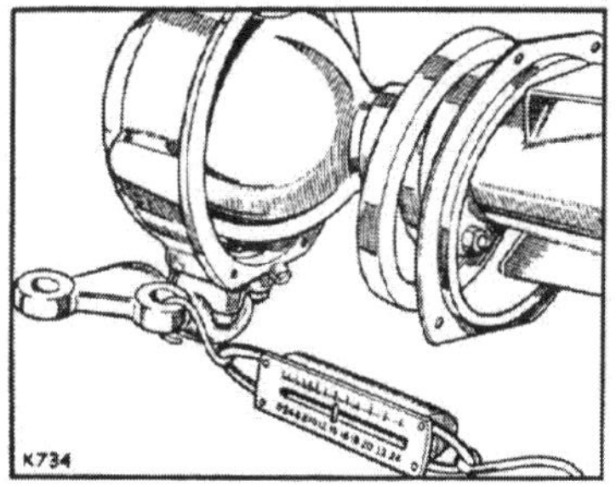

Fig. F1-49. Checking swivel pin housing resistance to rotation

Note: The swivel pins can be checked when in position on the axle, but the oil seal must be withdrawn as illustrated.

7. Fit the swivel pin and steering lever assembly to the swivel pin housing, fitting the shims removed on stripping to the value of .040 in. (1,0 mm). Note that the double steering lever is fitted to the LH assembly on RHStg models and to the RH assembly on LHStg vehicles.

8. Tighten the top swivel pin fixing nuts evenly and securely, but do not engage the lockplates.

9. Hold the swivel pin bearing housing by clamping the flange in a vice fitted with soft jaws, or temporarily, fit the swivel pin housing to the axle case.

10. Using a spring balance attached to the steering lever at the track rod connecting eye, measure the resistance to rotation of the swivel pin housing, which must be 14 lb to 16 lb (6,3 kg to 7,3 kg) after having overcome inertia. Adjust as necessary by adding or subtracting shims at the top only, until the correct resistance figure is obtained.

11. Engage the lockplates at the swivel pin fixing nuts.

12. Pack the swivel pin housing oil seal with heavy grease, and fit the seal and its retainer to the swivel pin housing, locating the steering stop adjustment bolt in the forwardmost hole.

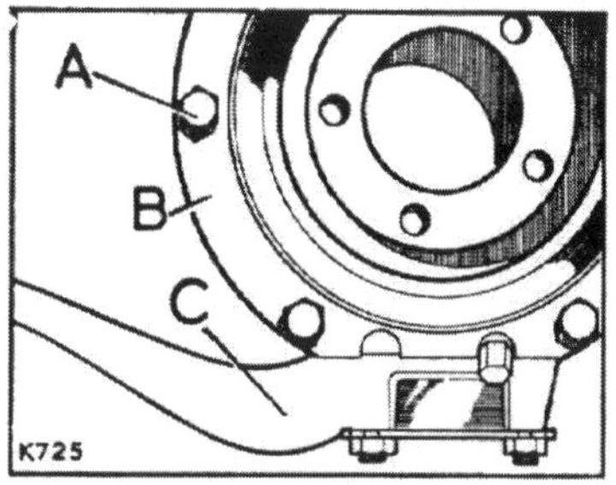

Fig. F1-50. Location of steering stop adjustment bolt

A—Bolt for steering stop adjustment
B—Retainer for oil seal
C—Steering lever

13. Check that the oil seal wipes the full surface of the bearing housing and adjust the position, if necessary, by slackening off the retainer bolts and resetting the seal.

Latest type swivel pin housing with Railko bush type damper
To dismantle

1. Remove the oil seal retainer.

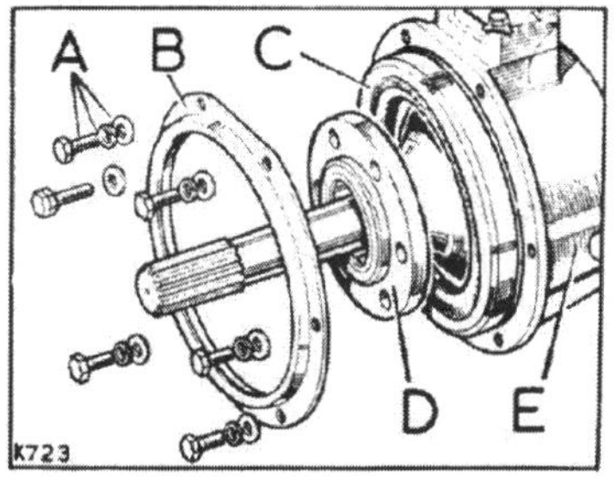

Fig. F1-51. Oil seal for swivel pin housing

A—Fixings (6 off) oil seal retainer to bearing housing
B—Oil seal retainer
C—Oil seal for bearing housing
D—Swivel pin bearing housing
E—Swivel pin housing

2. Prise the bearing housing oil seal from the swivel pin housing.

3. Remove the swivel pin end bracket and steering lever.

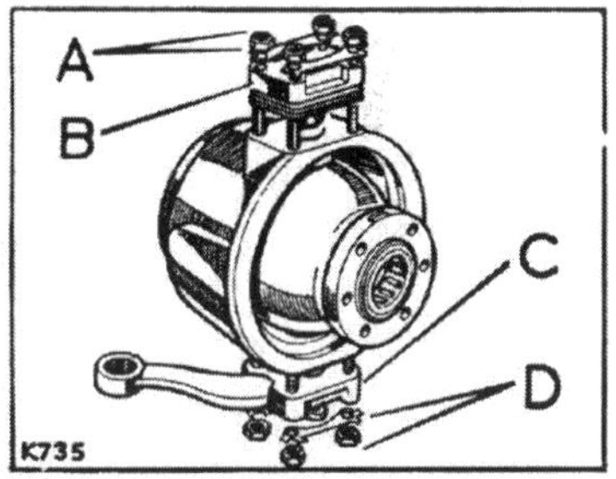

Fig. F1-52. Swivel pin end cap and steering lever

A—Fixings for end cap
B—End cap and swivel pin
C—Steering lever and swivel pin
D—Fixings for steering lever

4. Withdraw the swivel pin bearing housing complete with bearings.

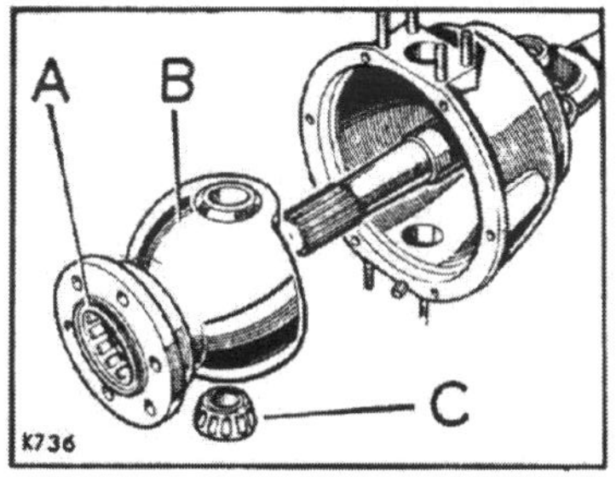

Fig. F1-53. Swivel pin bearing housing

A—Roller bearing for axle half shaft
B—Bearing housing
C—Taper roller bearings for bottom swivel pin

FRONT AXLE AND SUSPENSION

Operation F1-10—continued

5. Press the bush and bearings from the swivel pin bearing housing, as required.

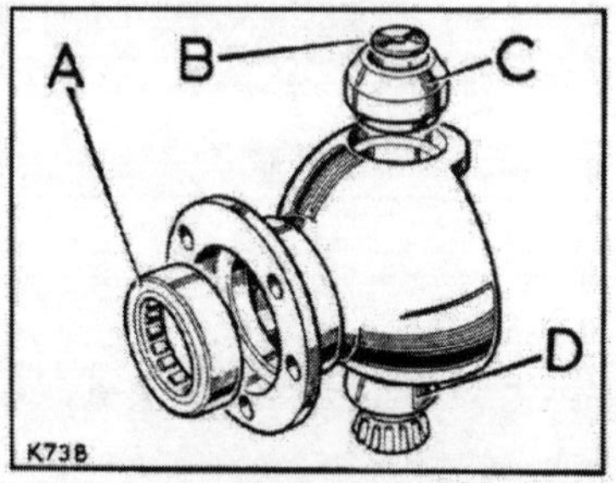

Fig. F1-54. Bush and bearings for swivel pin housing

A—Roller bearing for axle half shaft
B—Thrust washer for top swivel pin (early models)
C—Railko bush for top swivel pin
D—Outer race for bottom swivel pin bearing

6. On early models, withdraw the thrust washer from the bush for the top swivel pin. Later models have a modified bush which does not have a separate thrust washer.

Inspection

1. Examine all components for obvious wear or damage.

2. The taper roller bearing must be a light push fit on the bottom swivel pin, if a new bearing is a loose fit, the swivel pin assembly must be renewed.

3. The Railko bush must be a light push fit on the top swivel pin, if a new bush is a loose fit, the swivel pin assembly must be renewed. It is important to note that these bushes and thrust washers should not be washed in any type of cleaning fluid, otherwise there is a danger that the damping characteristics of the material will be adversely affected.

4. Examine the surface of the swivel pin bearing housing for signs of corrosion or damage, and renew if necessary.

Operation F1-10—continued

To assemble

1. Using the same oil as recommended for the swivel pin housing (see Section X), thoroughly lubricate the internal diameter of the Railko bush.

2. Press the roller bearing for the axle half shaft into the swivel pin bearing housing.

3. Press the Railko bush into the top of the bearing housing, and the taper bearing outer race, wide edge first, into the bottom of the housing. Take care to correctly identify the bush and bearing locations, noting that the top of the housing is narrower, as illustrated.

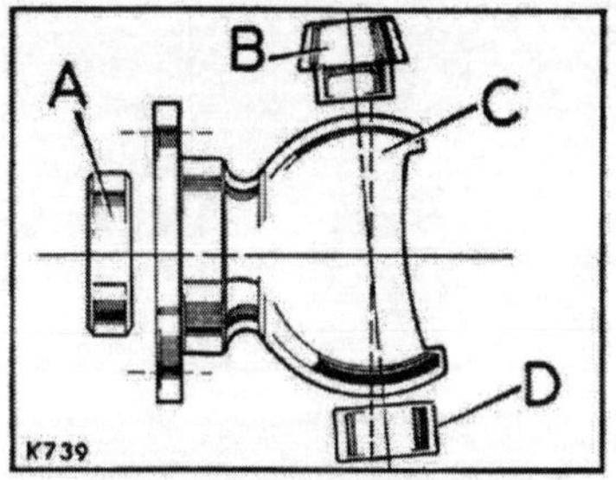

Fig. F1-55. Bush and bearing locations

A—Roller bearing for axle half shaft
B—Railko bush
C—Top of housing
D—Outer race for taper roller bearing

4. If the early type Railko bush is fitted, place the thrust washer in the bush.

5. Place the taper roller bearing in position in the bottom of the swivel pin bearing housing, and locate the bearing housing into the swivel pin housing.

6. Fit a rubber 'O' ring to the steering lever and swivel pin assembly, smear the mating surfaces of the swivel pin and housing with jointing compound, fit the steering lever ensuring that it faces forward (away from the oil filler/level plug), then secure and engage the lock plates.

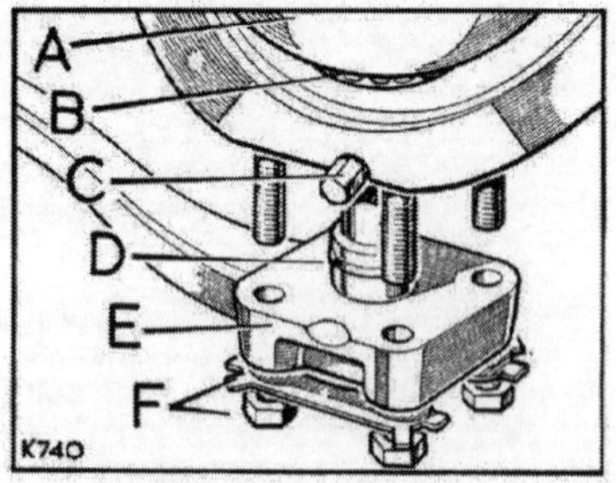

Fig. F1-56. Steering lever and swivel pin assembly

A—Swivel pin bearing housing
B—Taper roller bearing
C—Drain plug for swivel pin housing
D—Rubber 'O' ring
E—Steering lever and swivel pin assembly
F—Fixings for steering lever

Note: The double steering lever is fitted to the LH assembly on RHStg models and to the RH assembly on LHStg models.

7. Fit the swivel pin and bracket assembly to the top of the swivel pin housing, fitting the shims removed during dismanting to the value of .040 in. (1,0 mm). Tighten the fixings bolts evenly and securely, but do not engage the lock plates at this stage.

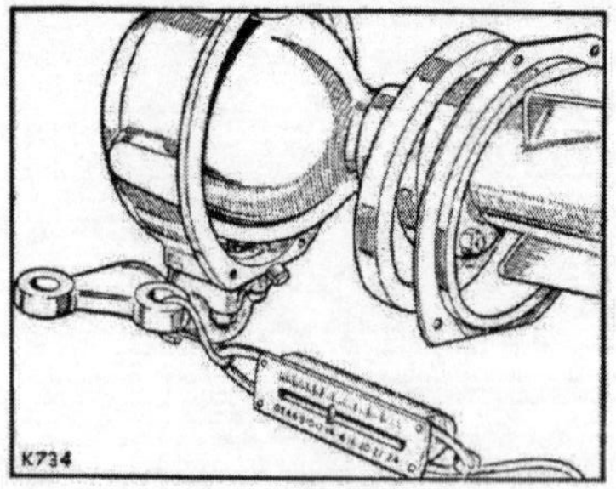

Fig. F1-57. Checking swivel pin housing resistance to rotation

8. Hold the swivel pin bearing housing by clamping the flange in a vice fitted with soft jaws, or temporarily fit the swivel pin housing to the axle case.

9. Using a spring balance attached to the steering lever at the track rod connecting eye, measure the resistance to rotation of the swivel pin housing, which must be 12 lb to 14 lb (5,4 kg to 6,3 kg) after having overcome inertia. Adjust as necessary by adding or subtracting shims under the swivel pin bracket until the correct resistance figure is obtained.

10. Engage the lockplates at the swivel pin fixing nuts.

11. Pack the swivel pin housing oil seal with heavy grease, and fit the seal and its retainer to the swivel pin housing, locating the steering stop adjustment bolt in the forwardmost hole.

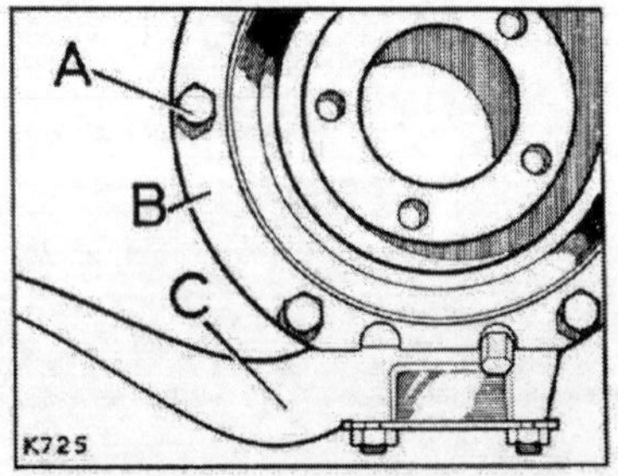

Fig. F1-58. Location of steering stop adjustment bolt

A—Bolt for steering stop adjustment
B—Retainer for oil seal
C—Steering lever

12. Check that the oil seal wipes the full surface of the bearing housing and adjust the position, if necessary, by slackening off the retainer bolts and resetting the seal.

Note: When refitting the swivel pin housing to the axle, ensure that the axle case breather is clear (see Operation F1-18), a blocked breather could cause failure of the oil seal fitted in the swivel pin housing.

Section F—Land-Rover FRONT AXLE AND SUSPENSION

Front shock absorbers, remove and refit—Operation F1-11

Refer to Section E. Operation E1-7

The instructions for this operation are similar to those for Operation E1-7 except that references to rear axle and suspension components should be read as front.

Front road springs, remove and refit—Operation F1-12

(For overhaul instructions, Operation F1-13 (E1-10) refers)

Refer to Section E. Operation E1-9

The instructions for this operation are similar to those for Operation E1-9 except that references to rear axle and suspension components should be read as front. Also, disregard reference to brake pipe shields.

Front road springs, overhaul—Operation F1-13

Refer to Section E. Operation E1-10

The instructions for this operation are similar to those for Operation E1-10 except that references to rear axle and suspension components should be read as front.

Bump stop rubber, remove and refit—Operation F1-14

Refer to Section E. Operation E1-11

The instructions for this operation are similar to those for Operation E1-11 except that references to rear axle and suspension components should be read as front.

Oil seal for bevel pinion case, remove and refit—Operation F1-15

Refer to Section E. Operation E1-12

The instructions for this operation are similar to those for Operation E1-12 except that references to rear axle components should be read as front.

Differential, remove and refit—Operation F1-16

(For overhaul instructions, Operation F1-17 (E1-14) refers)

Workshop hand tools:
Spanner sizes: $\frac{3}{8}$ in. BSF, $\frac{7}{16}$ in. BSF, $\frac{7}{16}$ in. AF, $\frac{9}{16}$ in. AF, $\frac{5}{8}$ in. AF open end

Special tools:
Extractor for steering ball joints, Part No. 600590

To remove

1. Drain the lubricating oil from the differential. Operation F1-1.
2. Slacken the fixings at the front road wheels.
3. Jack up the front of the vehicle and support on stands.
4. Remove the front road wheels.
5. Disconnect the front brake pipes at the connections with the flexible pipes, one each side of the vehicle, and withdraw the flexible pipes from the chassis brackets. Then, depress the brake pedal and wedge it in that position, to prevent further leakage of brake fluid. When depressing brake pedal, take precautions to avoid fluid spillage.
6. Disconnect the steering track rod and drag link, using special tool, Part No. 600590, to extract the ball joints.
7. Remove the fixings between the swivel pin housings and the axle case, noting the steering lock stop plate, and on the right-hand side only, the jack location stop plate.

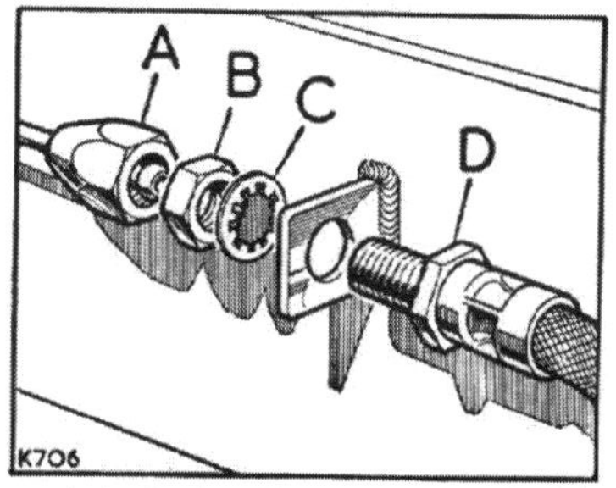

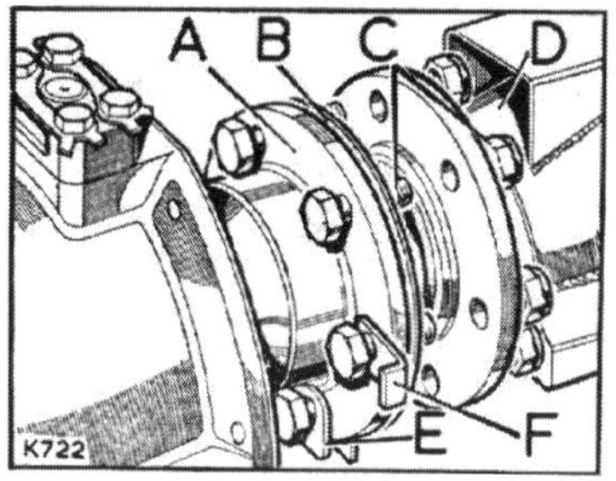

Fig. F1-59. Front brake pipe connections
A—Pipe from master cylinder
B—Locknut
C—Shakeproof washer
D—Flexible brake pipe

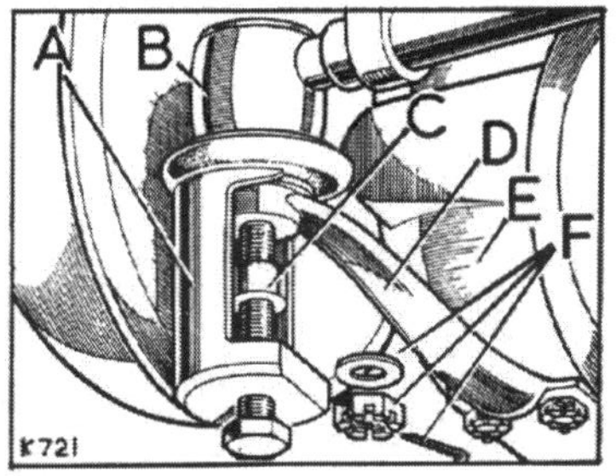

Fig. F1-60. Steering track rod and drag link connections
A—Special tool, Part No. 600590
B—Ball joint
C—Thread protection cap, part of 600590
D—Steering lever
E—Swivel pin housing
F—Fixings, ball joint to steering lever

Fig. F1-61. Swivel pin to axle case location
A—Swivel pin housing
B—Joint washer
C—Fixings, swivel pin housing to axle case
D—Axle case
E—Location stop for jack (RH side only)
F—Lock stop plate

8. Withdraw the swivel pin housing, axle half shaft and front hub assembly.
9. Disconnect the prop shaft and move it clear of the differential.
10. Remove the differential.

FRONT AXLE AND SUSPENSION Section F—Land-Rover

Operation F1-16—continued

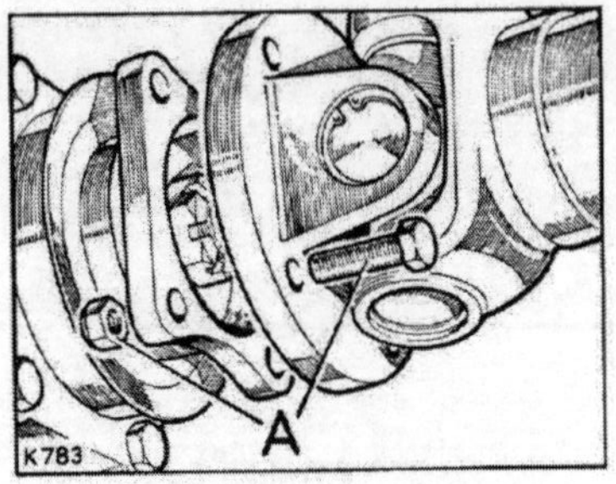

3. Smear general purpose grease on both sides of the joint washers for the axle case ends, and place in position on the axle case.

4. Offer the swivel pin housing and hub assemblies, each in turn, to the axle case, carefully engaging the splines on the half shaft into the final drive unit.

5. Secure the swivel pin housings to the axle case.

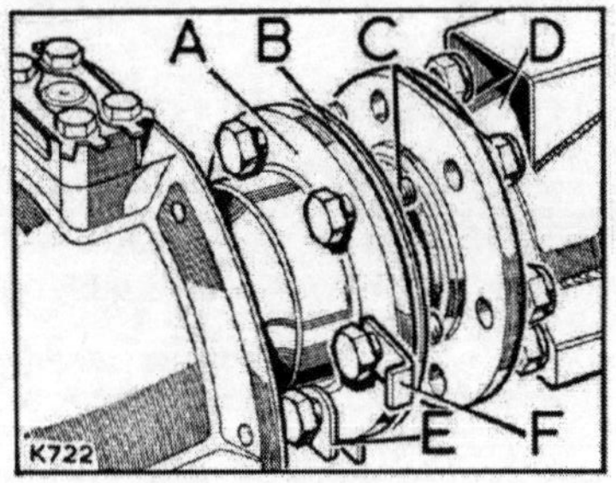

Fig. F1-64. Swivel pin housing to axle case location

A—Swivel pin housing
B—Joint washer
C—Fixings, swivel pin housing to axle case
D—Axle case
E—Location stop for jack (RH side only)
F—Lock stop plate

6. Connect the steering track rod and drag link. Tighten the ball joint fixing nuts to a torque figure of 30 lb ft (4,0 mkg).

7. Connect the front brake pipes at the couplings with the flexible pipes.

8. Bleed and adjust the brakes.

9. Replenish the front axle lubricating oil. Operation F1-1.

10. Fit the road wheels.

11. Check, and if necessary, adjust the steering stop.

Fig. F1-62. Propeller shaft for front axle

A—Fixings at coupling flange

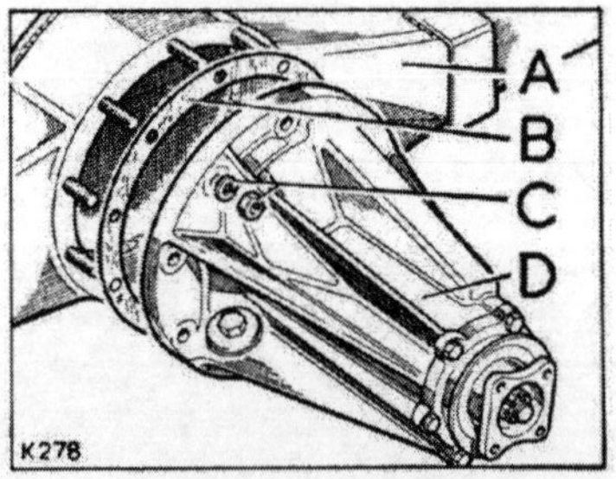

Fig. F1-63. Differential

A—Front axle case
B—Joint washer
C—Fixings, bevel pinion housing
D—Bevel pinion housing

To refit

1. Smear general purpose grease on both sides of the joint washer for the differential, and fit the joint washer and differential to the axle case.

2. Reconnect the front propeller shaft.

FRONT AXLE AND SUSPENSION

Differential, overhaul—Operation F1-17

(For removal and refitting instructions, Operation F1-16 refers)

Refer to Section E. Operation E1-14

The instructions for this operation are the same as those for Operation E1-14.

Section F—Land-Rover

FRONT AXLE AND SUSPENSION

Front axle case, remove and refit—Operation F1-18

Workshop hand tools:
Spanner sizes: $\frac{3}{8}$ in. BSF, $\frac{7}{16}$ in. BSF, $\frac{7}{16}$ in. AF, $\frac{9}{16}$ in. AF, $\frac{5}{8}$ in. AF open end
Pliers

To remove

1. Drain the lubricating oil from the differential. Operation F1-1.
2. Remove the differential. Operation F1-16.
3. Remove the four 'U'-bolts, and withdraw the axle case from the vehicle.

Fig. F1-65. Fixings for 'U'-bolts

Note: 'U'-bolt fixings are similar for front and rear axles, illustration shows rear axle.
A—Road spring   B—Bottom plate
C—Fixings for 'U'-bolts

To refit

1. Before fitting the axle case, ensure that the breather is clear, a blocked breather could cause failure of the oil seals in the axle case and final drive unit.

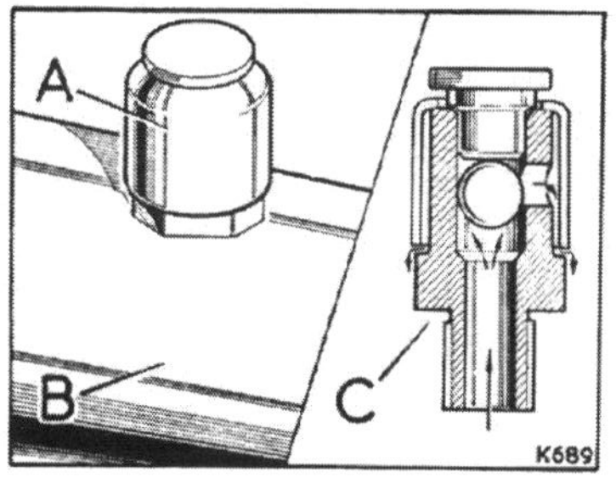

Fig. F1-66. Breather for axle case
A—Breather
B—Axle case
C—Flow through breather

2. Examine the oil seals fitted in the ends of the axle case and fit new replacements if necessary. If a new axle case is being fitted, new oil seals must be fitted.

When fitting new oil seals, smear the outside diameter of the seal with jointing compound, and fit the seal, lipped side inward, into the axle case, flush with the recessed end.

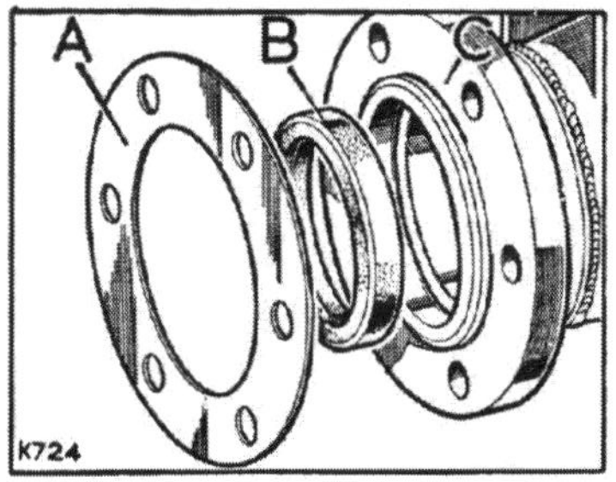

Fig. F1-67. Oil seal and joint washer for axle case
A—Joint washer   B—Oil seal
C—Axle case

3. Locate the axle case in position on the road springs.
4. Fit the axle 'U'-bolts and engage the lock plates.
5. Refit the differential. Operation F1-16.
6. Replenish the front axle lubricating oil. Operation F1-1.
7. Bleed and adjust the brakes. (Section H).
8. Check, and if necessary, adjust the steering stop. Operation F1-2.

Section F—Land-Rover

FRONT AXLE AND SUSPENSION

Front axle assembly, to remove and refit—Operation F1-19

Workshop hand tools:
Spanner sizes: $\frac{7}{16}$ in. BSF, $\frac{9}{16}$ in. AF, $\frac{5}{8}$ in. AF, $\frac{13}{16}$ in. AF, $\frac{7}{8}$ in. AF open end
Pliers, Mallet, Screwdriver (medium)

Special tools:
Extractor for steering ball joints, Part No. 600590

To remove

1. Slacken the fixings at both front road wheels.
2. Jack up the front of the vehicle and support on stands.
3. Remove both front road wheels.
4. Disconnect the front propeller shaft from the final drive unit.

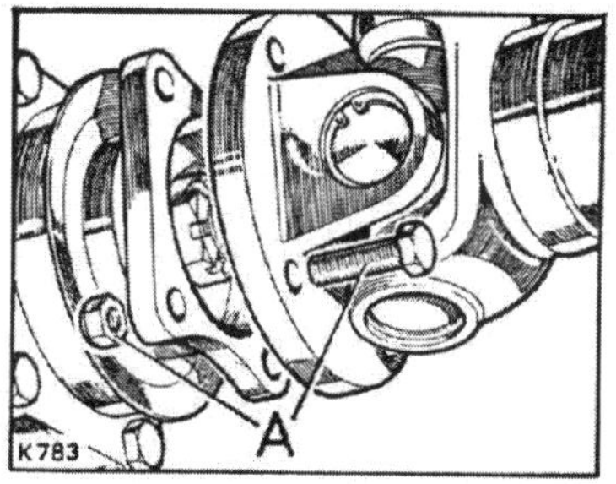

Fig. F1-68. Propeller shaft for front axle
A—Fixings at coupling flanges

5. Disconnect the front brake pipes at their connections with the flexible pipes each side of the vehicle, and withdraw the flexible pipes from the chassis brackets. Then, depress the brake pedal,

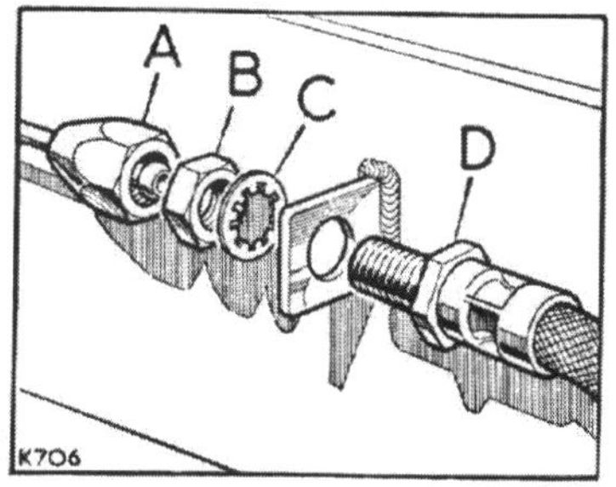

Fig. F1-69. Front brake pipe connection
A—Pipe from master cylinder
B—Locknut
C—Shakeproof washer
D—Flexible brake pipe

and wedge it in that position, to prevent further leakage of brake fluid. When depressing the brake pedal, take precautions to avoid fluid spillage.

6. Disconnect the steering drag link from the lower relay lever, using special tool, Part No. 600590, to extract the ball joints.

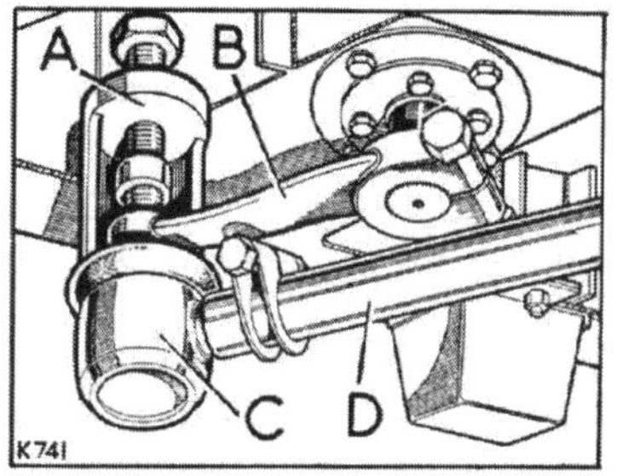

Fig. F1-70. Steering relay connection
A—Special tool, Part No. 600590
B—Lower relay lever
C—Ball joint
D—Steering drag link

7. Disconnect the lower ends of the shock absorbers from the road spring bottom plates.

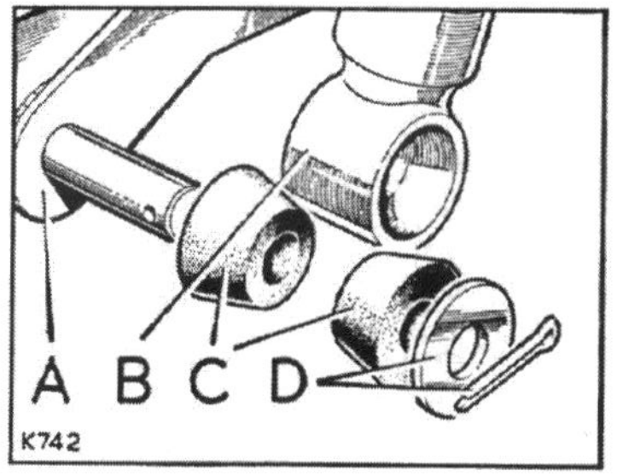

Fig. F1-71. Shock absorber, lower end fixing
A—Bottom plate for spring
B—Shock absorber
C—Rubbers
D—Fixings

FRONT AXLE AND SUSPENSION

Section F—Land-Rover

Operation F1-19—continued

8. Remove the four 'U'-bolts from the axle.

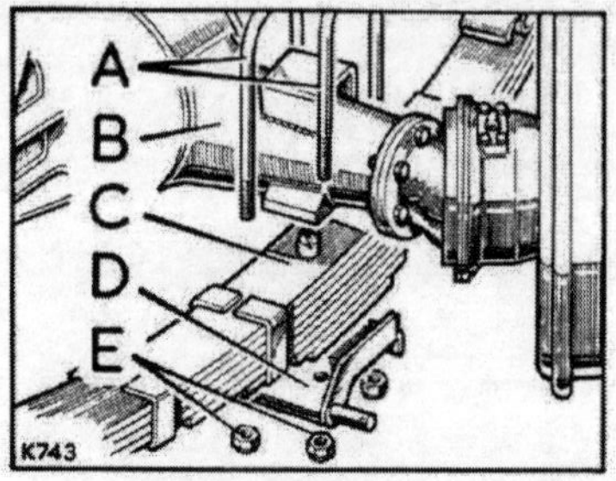

Fig. F1-72. Axle 'U'-bolts
A—'U'-bolts C—Road spring
B—Front axle D—Bottom plate
E—Fixings for 'U'-bolts

9. Support the front axle with a jack, slacken all six shackle pins at the front road springs, then remove the two front pins.

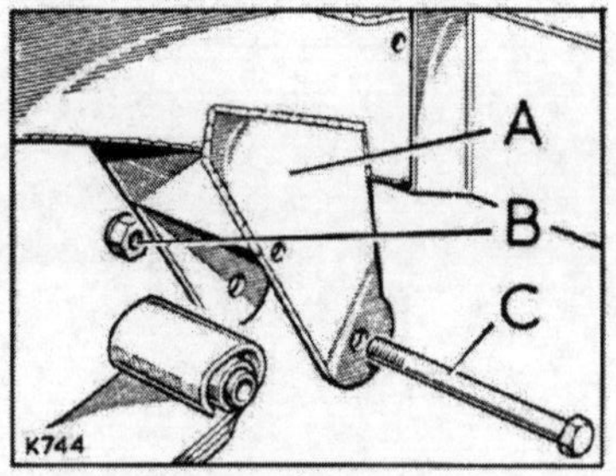

Fig. F1-73. Front fixing for road spring
A—Chassis bracket
B—Self-locking nut
C—Shackle pin

10. Lower the jack and withdraw the axle from under the vehicle.

To refit

1. Place the axle on a jack and position under the vehicle.
2. Using a second jack, raise each road spring in turn and connect the front ends of the springs to the chassis, but DO NOT tighten the shackle pins and locknuts at this stage.
3. Fit the axle 'U'-bolts and engage the lock plates.
4. Secure the shock absorber bottom fixings.
5. Connect the steering drag link to the lower relay lever. Tighten the ball joint fixing nut to a torque figure of 30 lb ft (4,0 mkg).
6. Connect the front brake pipes at the coupling with the flexible pipes.
7. Fit the front propeller shaft.
8. Fit the front road wheels.
9. Lower the vehicle to the ground and move vehicle bodily backward and forward to settle the springs, then tighten all six shackle pins and locknuts.

   Note: If the shackle pins and locknuts are tightened prior to lowering the vehicle to the ground, premature failure of the spring bushes will occur.

10. Bleed and adjust the brakes.
11. Replenish the front axle lubricating oil. Operation F1-1.
12. Check, and if necessary, adjust the steering stop.

Fault diagnosis—Front axle and suspension

Steering kick and wheel wobble

A certain amount of wheel kick must be expected over rough surfaces, but if this becomes excessive or if actual wheel wobble is experienced, the following checks must be carried out. Only after these checks have failed to reveal the cause should the swivel pin damping be checked.

1. Ensure that the bolts securing the steering box to its mounting bracket, and the bolts securing the bracket to the frame are tight. Also ensure that the steering box stiffener bracket is fitted.
2. Check the steering box adjustment, Operation G1-8.
3. Check the nut securing the drop arm to the rocker shaft and nuts securing ball joints to track rod and steering arms for tightness.
4. Check the ball joints for alignment and wear. Adjust or renew as necessary.
5. Check the relay top and bottom lever clamp bolt for tightness and check for wear at lever and shaft splines. Rectify any play in the relay unit.
6. The bolts securing the relay to the chassis must be checked for tightness, also the four bolts at the bottom plate for the relay. Check the bolt flanges for cracking and check the fit of the bottom of the relay in the spigot, this must be firm.
7. The nuts and studs securing the steering levers must be checked, and ensure that the one special 'fitting' stud on each side is a tight fit and that it positively locates the arm.
8. Check shock absorber action—replace if weak. Examine the rubber bushes and replace as necessary. Check road spring shackle pins and bushes for wear, check tightness of 'U' bolts. Ensure that the spring location bolt has not sheared and that its seating hole is not elongated.
9. Check all the spring leaves, either side of the centre bolt, for breakage.
10. Check the swivel pin damping (poundage figure), Operation F1-10, and adjust as necessary.
11. Check for badly or unevenly worn tyres. Similar tread pattern tyres should be fitted. Check the tyre pressures, Section R. Check the front wheel alignment, Operation G1-2.
12. While the vehicle is on a ramp or pit, examine the chassis members and axle casings for accident damage.

FRONT AXLE AND SUSPENSION

Fault diagnosis—Front axle and suspension—continued

Symptom	Possible cause	Investigation	Remedy
Vehicle pulls to one side	Incorrect camber	Check for settled road springs, worn shackle bushes or damage to front axle unit	Renew parts as necessary
	Incorrect or unequal castor or swivel pin inclination	Check front wheel alignment. Check for settled road springs or damage to front axle unit	Adjust wheel alignment and/or fit new parts as required
	Uneven tyre pressures or worn tyres	Check tyre pressures and/or wear condition, Section R	Fit new tyres and/or adjust pressures
	Dragging brake	Check brake adjustment, Section H	Adjust brakes
	Swivel pin tight	Dismantle and check swivel pins	Fit new parts as required, lubricate swivel pins on assembly
	Tight or dirty front wheel bearings	Remove hubs and check bearings	Fit new parts as required, pack hubs with fresh grease, refit and adjust hubs
	Incorrect toe-in of front wheels	Check wheel alignment, Operation G1-2	Adjust as necessary
Vehicle wanders	Incorrect tyre pressures or worn tyres	Check tyre pressures and wear condition, see Section R	Fit new tyres and/or adjust pressures
	Loose axle 'U' bolts	Check 'U' bolt fixings	Securely tighten
	Incorrect toe-in of front wheels	Check wheel alignment, Operation G1-2	Adjust as necessary
	Tight steering box	Check adjustment, Operation G1-8	Adjust as necessary
	Worn front wheel bearings	Check front hub bearings and adjustment	Renew and/or adjust hub bearings as necessary
	Worn swivel pins and bearings	Dismantle swivel pin housings	Fit new parts as required, lubricate swivel pins on assembly
	Incorrect castor	Check for settled road springs, damage to front suspension and axle unit	Fit new parts as required
	Bent or broken chassis	Check alignment of chassis, Section J	Repair or replace chassis
Wheel wobble	(See notes preceding fault finding chart)		
	Steering column loose at dash	Check fixings	Securely tighten
	Incorrect tyre pressures or worn tyres	Check tyre pressures and wear condition	Fit new tyres and/or adjust pressures
	Eccentric wheels and tyres	Check the tyre concentricity line. Check wheel pressings for damage or distortion	Rectify or renew
	Worn or loose hub bearings	Check bearings and adjustment	Renew and/or adjust hub bearings as necessary
	Worn swivel pins and bearings	Dismantle swivel pin housings	Fit new parts as required, lubricate swivel pins on assembly
	Insufficient damping at swivel pins	Check poundage figure, Operation P1-10	Adjust as necessary
	Insufficient damping at relay unit	Dismantle relay unit	Fit new parts as required

Fault diagnosis—Front axle and suspension—continued

Symptom	Possible cause	Investigation	Remedy
	Loose engine mountings	Check fixings	Securely tighten
	Worn universal joint at axle half shaft	Remove axle half shafts and check	Overhaul universal joints
	Incorrect castor	Check for settled road springs, damage to front suspension and axle unit	Fit new parts as required
Excessive tyre wear	Incorrect tyre pressures	Check tyre pressures, see Section R	Adjust as necessary
	Incorrect toe-in of front wheels	Check wheel alignment, Operation G1-2	Adjust as necessary
	Harsh or unequal brakes	Check brake adjustment, Section H	Adjust as necessary
	Worn swivel pins	Jack up front of vehicle and check swivel pins	Overhaul swivel pin housings
	Eccentric wheels and tyres	Check tyre concentricity line. Check wheel pressings for damage or distortion	Rectify or renew
	Incorrect camber	Check for settled road springs, damage to front suspension and axle unit	Fit new parts as required
	Failure to rotate tyres		Change position of tyres, including spare, see Section R
	Fast cornering		In the hands of the operator
	Sustained high-speed driving		
Front end noisy	Hydraulic damper	Check damper mounting bushes for wear	Fit new bushes. If the damper itself is noisy, renew
		Check hydraulic damping, Operation E1-7	Fit new damper
	Worn swivel pins	Jack up front of vehicle and check swivel pins	Overhaul swivel pin housings
	Looseness in front suspension	Check all mountings for wear and security. Check wheel alignment	Fit new parts as required, securely tighten mounting, adjust wheel alignment
	Differential lubrication level too low or incorrect grade	Check lubrication level and grade	Replenish with correct grade of lubricating oil, see Section X
	Differential worn	Remove differential and check	Overhaul differential
	Propeller shaft		See Section D
Oil leaks	Loose or missing drain and filler plugs	Check oil drain and filler plugs at steering box, relay unit, swivel pin housing and differential	Fit new joint washers where applicable and tighten plugs
	Damaged joint washers	Determine point of leak, see exploded view of axle for location of joint washers and dismantle as necessary	Fit new joint washers with both sides smeared with general purpose grease
	Oil seals damaged or incorrectly fitted	Determine point of leak, see exploded view of axle for location of oil seals and dismantle as necessary	Fit new oil seal with 'Hylomar' SQ32M sealing compound smeared on the outside diameter

GENERAL DATA

Axle type .. .. Fully floating

Oil capacity:

Differential: Rover type	3 Imperial pints, $3\frac{1}{2}$ US pints, 1,75 litres
ENV type	$2\frac{5}{8}$ Imperial pints, 3.1 US pints, 1,4 litres
Swivel pin housing	1 Imperial pint, 1.2 US pints, 0,5 litre

Hub bearing lubrication:

Early models	Oil—$\frac{1}{3}$ Imperial pint, 0,19 litre
Latest models	Grease
Final drive	Spiral bevel
Ratio	4.7:1

Angularity of universal joint on full lock:

Inner wheel	26°
Outer wheel	24° 30′

DETAIL DATA

Front hub and stub axle assembly:

Front hub end-float	.004 in. to .006 in. (0,10 mm to 0,16 mm)
Clearance of hub bearings on hub bearing sleeve	.0002 in. to .0012 in. (0,005 mm to 0,030 mm)
Fit of hub inner bearing in hub	.001 in. to .003 in. (0,025 mm to 0,075 mm) interference
Fit of hub outer bearing in hub	.0005 in. to .0025 in. (0,030 mm to 0,0635 mm) interference
Clearance between stub shaft and stub axle bush (early models only)	.020 in. to .028 in. (0,50 mm to 0,70 mm)
Stub axle bush bore	1.250 in. + .004 in. (31,75 mm + 0,10 mm)

Swivel pin setting:

Coil spring type	Resistance of 14 lb to 16 lb (6,3 kg to 7,3 kg) at steering lever eye
Railko bush type	Resistance of 12 lb to 14 lb (5,4 kg to 6,3 kg) at steering lever eye
Clearance between stub and half shaft yoke lugs and swivel pin end faces	.050 in. (1,27 mm)
Cone spring:	
Number of working coils	3
Free length	1.150 in. ± .010 in. (29,2 mm ± 0,25 mm)
Length in position	.687 in. (17,4 mm)
Rate	660 lb/in. (7,5 mkg)
Fit of retaining collar on shaft	.001 in. (0,025 mm) interference (selective assembly)

Differential assembly (Refer to Section E for differential data)

Road springs (Refer to Section E for rear road spring data)

	Driver's side	Passenger's side
88, Petrol, front		
Number of leaves	9	9
Width of leaves	$2\frac{1}{2}$ in. (63,5 mm)	$2\frac{1}{2}$ in. (63,5 mm)
Static load (vehicle unladen)	636 lb (288,5 kg)	490 lb (222,3 kg)
Camber under static load	$2\frac{15}{16}$ in. (74,6 mm)	$2\frac{15}{16}$ in. (74,6 mm)
Free camber	6.080 in. (154,4 mm)	5.330 in. (135,4 mm
88, Diesel, front		
Number of leaves	11	11
Width of leaves	$2\frac{1}{2}$ in. (63,5 mm)	$2\frac{1}{2}$ in. (63,5 mm)
Static load (vehicle unladen)	750 lb (340 kg)	750 lb (340 kg)
Camber under static load	$2\frac{7}{8}$ in. (73,02 mm)	$2\frac{3}{8}$ in. (60,3 mm)
Free camber	$5\frac{5}{8}$ in. (143 mm)	$5\frac{1}{8}$ in. (130,2 mm)
109, Petrol, front		
Number of leaves	11	11
Width of leaves	$2\frac{1}{2}$ in. (63,5 mm)	$2\frac{1}{2}$ in. (63,5 mm)
Static load (vehicle unladen)	750 lb (340 kg)	750 lb (340 kg)
Camber under static load	$2\frac{7}{8}$ in. (73,02 mm)	$2\frac{3}{8}$ in. (60,3 mm)
Free camber	$5\frac{5}{8}$ in. (143 mm)	$5\frac{1}{8}$ in. (130,2 mm)
109, Diesel, front		
Number of leaves	11	11
Width of leaves	$2\frac{1}{2}$ in. (63,5 mm)	$2\frac{1}{2}$ in. (63,5 mm)
Static load (vehicle unladen)	750 lb (340 kg)	750 lb (340 kg)
Camber under static load	$3\frac{3}{8}$ in. (86 mm)	$2\frac{7}{8}$ in. (73,02 mm)
Free camber	$6\frac{1}{4}$ in. (159 mm)	$5\frac{5}{8}$ in. (143 mm)

Hydraulic dampers:

Type	Telescopic, double acting
Mounting	Rubber bushes

SECTION G—STEERING

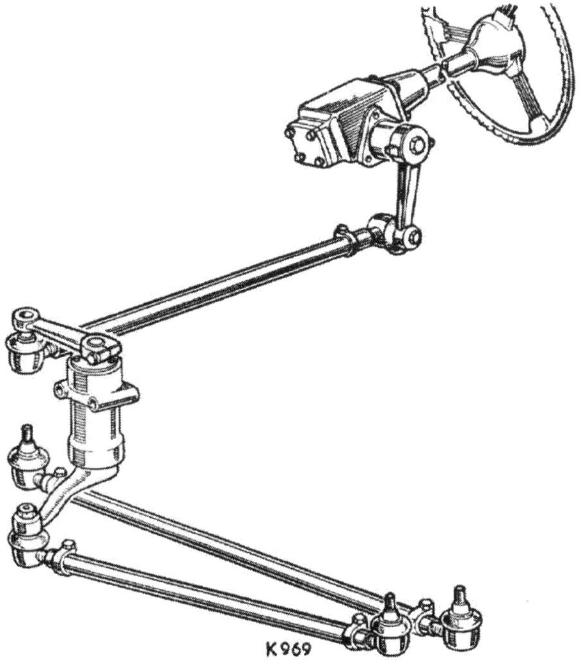

Fig. G1-1. Steering

NOTE: Illustration shows pendant type ball joints, latest type are non-pendant

INDEX—STEERING

Note: A comprehensive, detailed index is included at the end of this manual

Description	Operation No.
Exploded views and description	At beginning of Section
STEERING LINKAGE	
Ball joints	6
Drag link	4
Longitudinal arm	5
Lubrication	6
Relay levers	9
Steering wheel	3
Track rod	4
Wheel alignment	2
STEERING BOX	
Adjustment	7—8
Drop arm	8
Lubrication	7
Steering column	1
	7—8
RELAY UNIT	
Friction damping	9—10
Lubrication	10
Relay levers	1
	9
FAULT DIAGNOSIS	At end of Section
DATA	

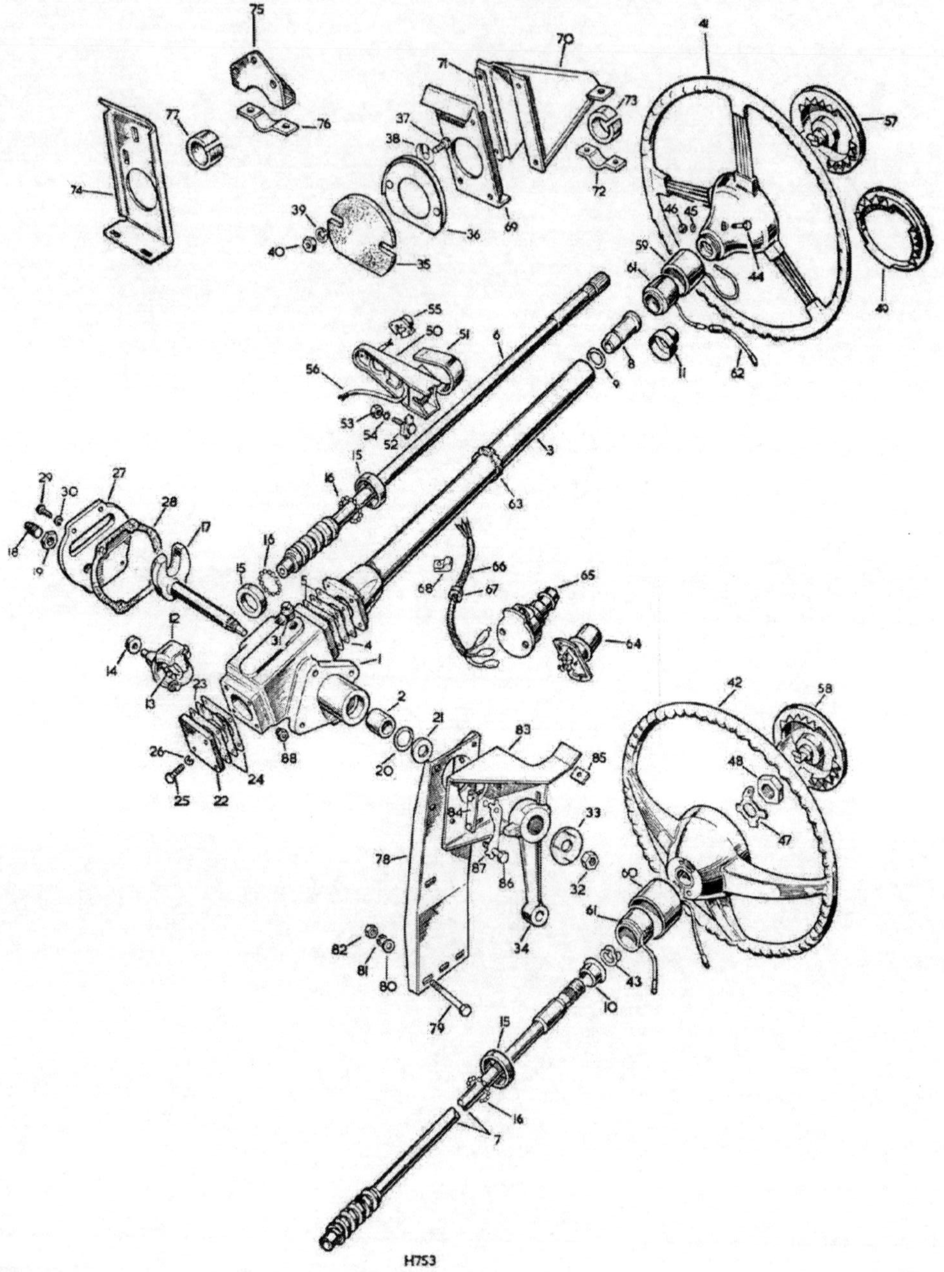

STEERING

Key to layout of steering box

1. STEERING BOX ASSEMBLY
2. Bush for rocker shaft
3. Outer column
4. Joint washer, steel
5. Joint washer, paper
6. Inner column, early type
7. Inner column, latest type
8. Bush for inner column
9. Spring ring for inner column bush
10. Ball bearing for inner column
11. Dust shield for inner column
12. MAIN NUT ASSEMBLY
13. Steel ball ($\frac{3}{8}$ in.) for main nut
14. Roller for main nut
15. Adjustable ball race
16. Steel balls (.280 in.) for adjustable race
17. Rocker shaft
18. Adjuster screw for rocker shaft
19. Locknut for adjuster screw
20. Oil seal for rocker shaft
21. Washer for rocker shaft oil seal
22. End plate
23. Joint washer, steel
24. Joint washer, paper
25. Bolt ($\frac{5}{16}$ in. UNC x $\frac{1}{2}$ in. long) } Fixing end plate
26. Spring washer
27. Side cover plate
28. Joint washer for side cover plate
29. Bolt ($\frac{5}{16}$ in. UNC x $1\frac{1}{16}$ in. long) } Fixing side cover plate
30. Spring washer
31. Oil filler plug
32. Special nut } Fixing drop arm
33. Lock washer
34. Steering drop arm
35. Rubber seal for steering column
36. Cover for steering column seal
37. Screw (2 BA x $\frac{1}{4}$ in. long) } Fixing cover and seal to dash
38. Special washer
39. Spring washer
40. Nut (2 BA)
41. Steering wheel, early type
42. Steering wheel, latest type
43. Special spring washer on inner column for wheel
44. Bolt ($\frac{5}{16}$ in. UNF x 2 in. long) } Fixing early type steering wheel
45. Plain washer
46. Nut ($\frac{5}{16}$ in. UNF)
47. Tag washer } Fixing latest type steering wheel
48. Special nut
49. Steering wheel centre cover, early type
50. Horn push bracket
51. Clip for horn push bracket
52. Yoke assembly for horn push bracket
53. Nut ($\frac{1}{4}$ in. BSF) } Fixing horn push bracket
54. Shakeproof washer
55. Horn push
56. Lead, horn push to junction box
57. Horn push and centre cover for steering wheel, early type
58. Horn push and centre cover for steering wheel, latest type
59. Dust cover and horn contact, early type
60. Dust cover and horn contact, latest type
61. Slip ring complete for horn contact
62. Lead, slip ring to junction box
63. Cable cleat on steering column
64. Dip switch, early type
65. Dip switch, latest type
66. Lead, dip switch to junction box
67. Grommet for lead in toe box floor
68. Clip fixing dip switch lead to floor
69. Support bracket on dash
70. Support bracket for steering column
71. Packing piece for steering column support bracket
72. Clip for steering column
73. Rubber strip for clip
74. Support bracket on dash
75. Clamp, upper, for steering column
76. Clamp, lower, for steering column
77. Rubber strip for clamp
78. Support bracket, steering box to chassis
79. Bolt ($\frac{7}{16}$ in. UNF x $3\frac{1}{4}$ in. long) } Fixing brackets to chassis frame
80. Plain washer, thin
81. Spring washer
82. Nut ($\frac{7}{16}$ in. UNF)
83. Stiffener bracket for steering box } Fixing stiffener bracket to front face of toe box
84. Bolt plate
85. Shim washer
86. Set bolt ($\frac{3}{8}$ in. UNC x $\frac{3}{4}$ in. long) } Fixing steering box to chassis support bracket
87. Locking plate
88. Self-locking nut ($\frac{7}{16}$ in. UNF)

Fig. G1-2. Layout of steering box

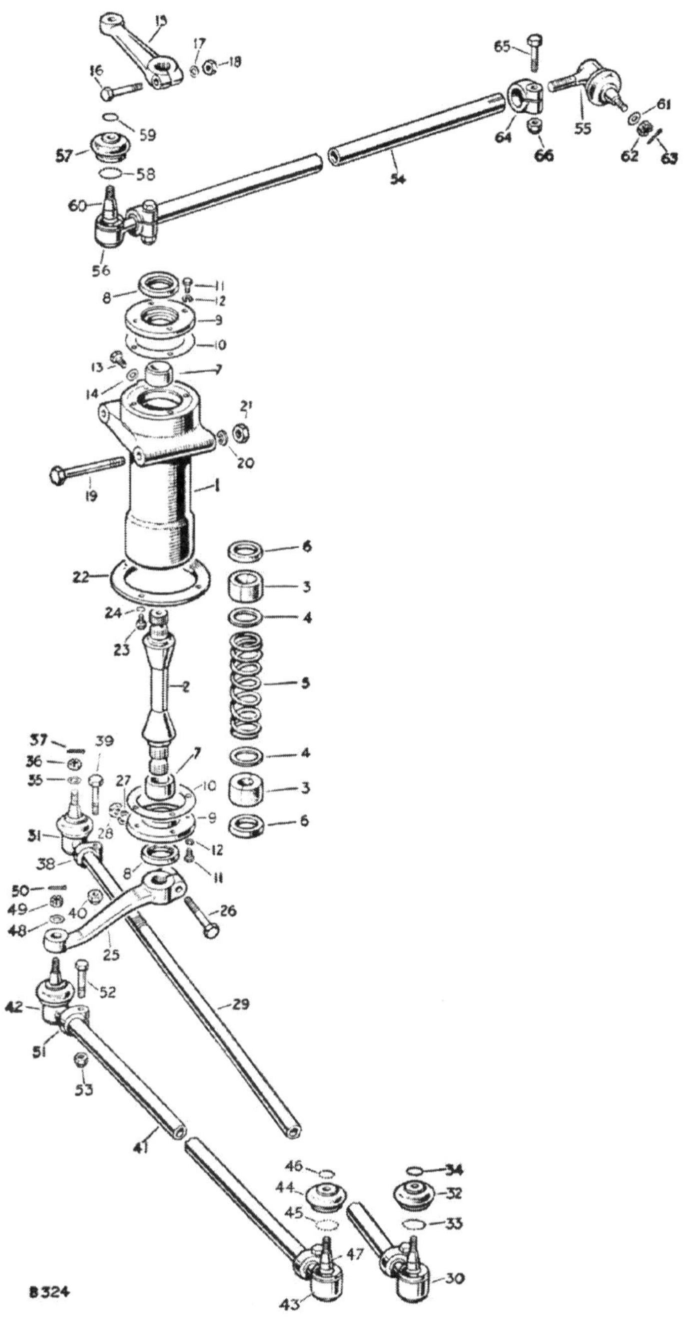

STEERING

Key to layout of steering linkage and relay unit

1	Housing for relay shaft
2	Shaft for steering relay levers
3	Split bush for housing
4	Washer for spring
5	Spring for bushes
6	Thrust washer for shaft
7	Distance piece for shaft
8	Oil seal for shaft
9	Retainer for oil seal
10	Joint washer for retainer
11–12	Fixings for retainer
13	Plug for oil hole
14	Joint washer for plug
15	Relay lever, upper
16–18	Fixings for lever
19–21	Fixings for housing
22	Flange plate for relay mounting
23–24	Fixings for flange plate
25	Relay lever, lower
26–28	Fixings for lever
29	Steering track rod assembly
30	Ball joint assembly RH thread
31	Ball joint assembly LH thread
32	Rubber cover for ball joint
33	Spring ring, cover to body
34	Spring ring and retainer, cover to ball
35–37	Fixings for ball joints
38	Clip for ball joint
39–40	Fixings for ball joint clips
41	Steering drag link assembly
42	Ball joint assembly RH thread
43	Ball joint assembly LH thread
44	Rubber cover for ball joint
45	Spring ring, cover to body
46	Spring ring } Cover to ball
47	Retainer
48–50	Fixings for ball joints
51	Clip for ball joint
52–53	Fixings for ball joint clips
54	Longitudinal steering tube assembly
55	Ball joint assembly RH thread
56	Ball joint assembly LH thread
57	Rubber cover for ball joint
58	Spring ring, cover to body
59	Spring ring } Cover to ball
60	Retainer
61–63	Fixings for ball joints to levers
64	Clip for ball joint
65–66	Fixings for ball joint clips

Fig. G1-3. Layout of steering linkage and relay unit

Section G—Land-Rover

STEERING

Lubrication, steering box and relay unit—Operation G1-1

(For lubrication instructions for steering ball joints, Operation G1-6 refers)

Workshop hand tools:
Spanner sizes: 2 BA, $\frac{7}{16}$ in. AF open end

General

No special provision is made for draining the steering box and relay unit, the lubricating oil normally lasting until time of overhaul. If significant topping up is required, check for oil leaks at joint faces, and at the steering box rocker shaft oil seal, and relay shaft oil seals.

Steering box

1. Lift the bonnet and prop open.
2. Remove the oil filler plug from the top face of the steering box.

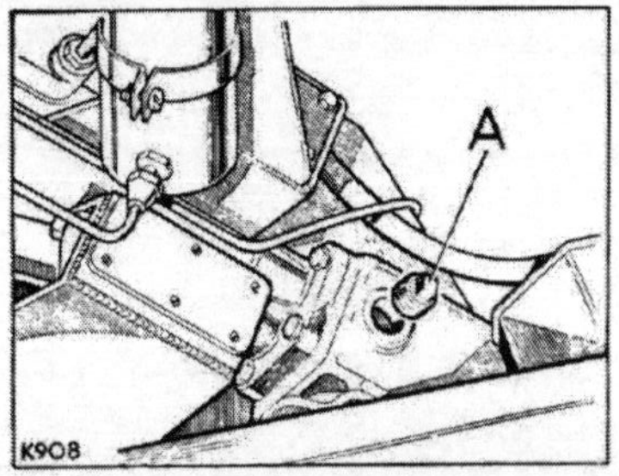

Fig. G1-4. Oil filler hole and plug
A—Oil filler plug

3. Using the correct grade lubricating oil, see Section X, fill the steering box to the bottom of the filler plug hole.
4. Replace the filler plug and close the bonnet.

Steering relay unit

1. Remove the name plate and withdraw the radiator grille.
2. Remove the oil filler plug from the top of the relay unit.

Note: There are two variations of oil filler in use. On the latest type, either of the four bolts securing the relay top cover can be used.

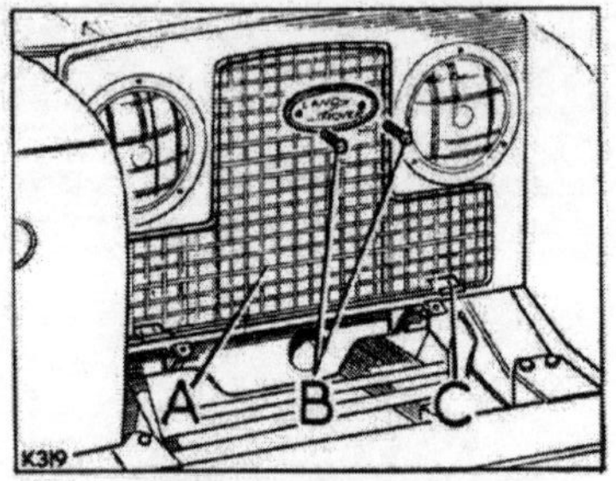

Fig. G1-5. Radiator Grille
A—Radiator grille
B—Fixings for name plate and grille
C—Support brackets

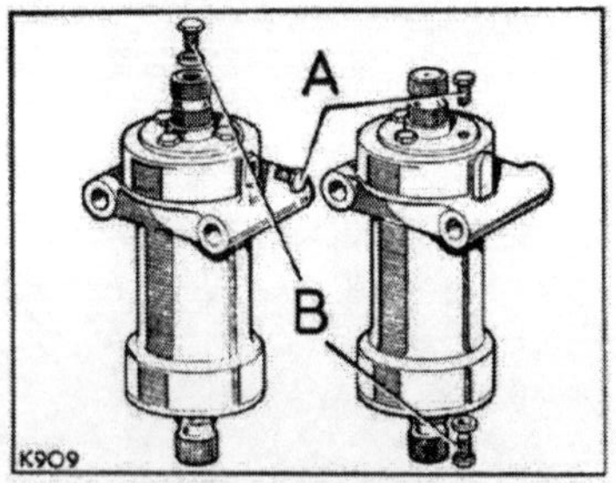

Fig. G1-6. Oil filler and breather plugs, early and latest type
A—Oil filler hole and plug
B—Breather hole and plug on early type. Drain plug on latest type

3. Early type relay unit—Remove the breather plug.
4. Latest type relay unit—Remove a second bolt from the top of the relay unit to provide a breather hole.
5. Using the correct grade lubricating oil, see Section X, fill the relay unit to the bottom of the filler plug hole.
6. Replace filler and breather plugs.
7. Fit the radiator grille and name plate, see Fig. G1-5.

Section G—Land-Rover

STEERING

Front wheel alignment, to adjust—Operation G1-2

Workshop hand tools:
Spanner size: $\frac{7}{16}$ in. AF   Mallet

To check

Toe-in dimension: $\frac{3}{64}$ in. to $\frac{3}{32}$ in. (1,2 mm to 2,4 mm).

Note: No adjustment is provided for caster, camber or swivel pin inclination.

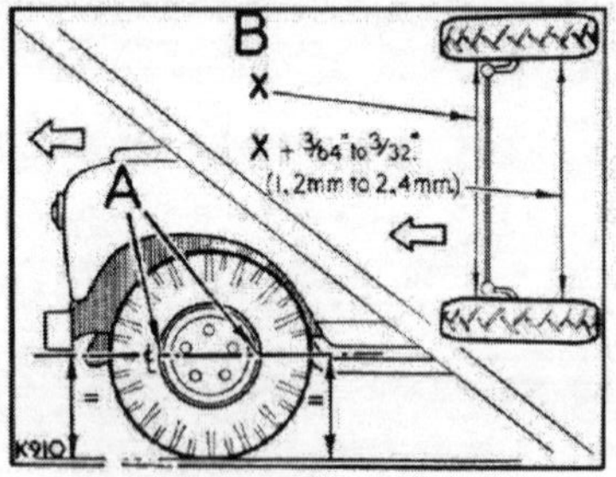

Fig. G1-7. Front wheel toe in
A—Check at horizontal centre line of wheel rim
B—Toe in setting

1. Set the vehicle on level ground with the road wheels in the straight-ahead position, and push it forward a short distance.
2. Measure the toe-in with the aid of a tracking stick or suitable proprietary equipment; it should be $\frac{3}{64}$ in. to $\frac{3}{32}$ in. (1,2 mm to 2,4 mm).
3. If necessary, adjust the toe in as follows:

To adjust

1. Slacken the clamps securing the ball joints at each end of the track rod.

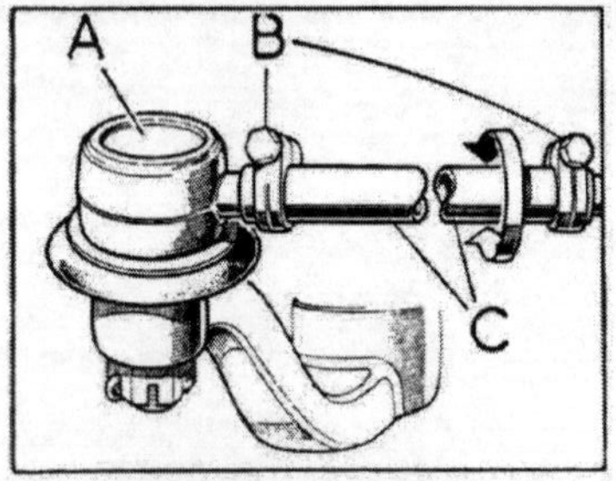

Fig. G1-8. Track rod adjustment
A—Ball joint
B—Clamp for ball joint
C—Track rod, turn as required

2. Turn the track rod to decrease or increase its effective length as necessary, until the toe in is correct.
3. Push the vehicle rearwards turning the steering wheel from side to side to settle the ball joints. Then, with the road wheels in the straight ahead position, push the vehicle forward a short distance.
4. Recheck the toe in. If necessary carry out further adjustment.
5. When the toe in is correct, lightly tap the track rod ball joints in the direction indicated to the maximum of their travel, to ensure full unrestricted movement of the track rod, then secure the ball joint clamps.

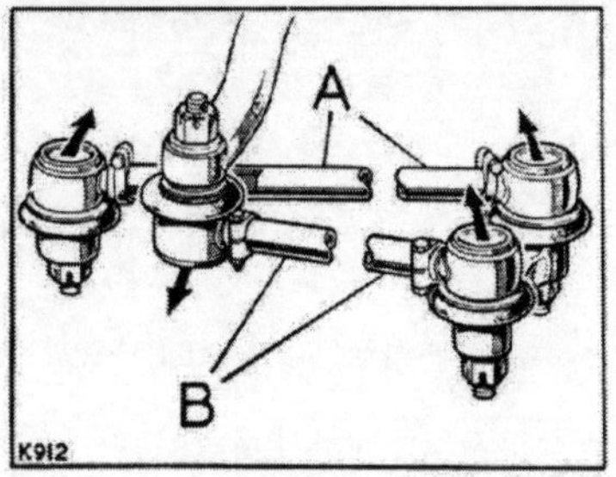

Fig. G1-9. Setting ball joints
A—Track rod
B—Drag link
(Set ball joints as indicated)

STEERING

Steering wheel, remove and refit—Operation G1-3

Workshop hand tools:
Spanner sizes: ½ in. AF, 1 in. AF sockets
Screwdriver (medium)

Note: Two types of steering wheel are in use, utilising different fixings.

To remove early type

1. If the electric horn push is fitted to the steering wheel centre, disconnect the battery to prevent the possibility of an electrical short, then disconnect the horn lead from the snap connector at the dash panel.

2. Disconnect the horn push lead from the snap connector at the dash panel.

3. Prise the centre cover from the steering wheel and disconnect the horn push leads.

4. Remove the fixings and withdraw the steering wheel from the splined column.

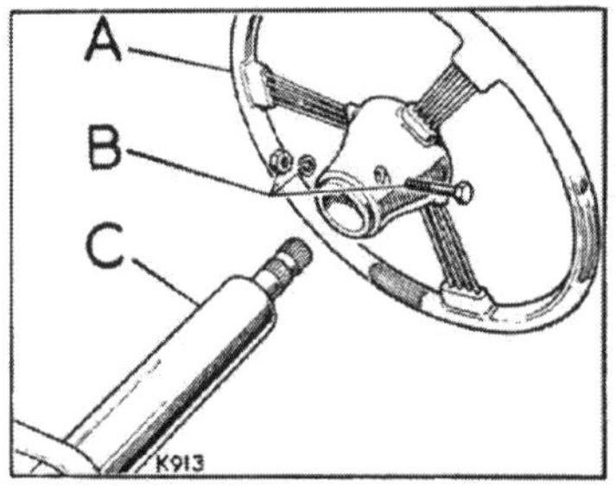

Fig. G1-10. Early type steering wheel
A—Steering wheel
B—Fixings, steering wheel to column
C—Steering column

To remove, latest type

1. Disconnect the battery to prevent the possibility of an electrical short.

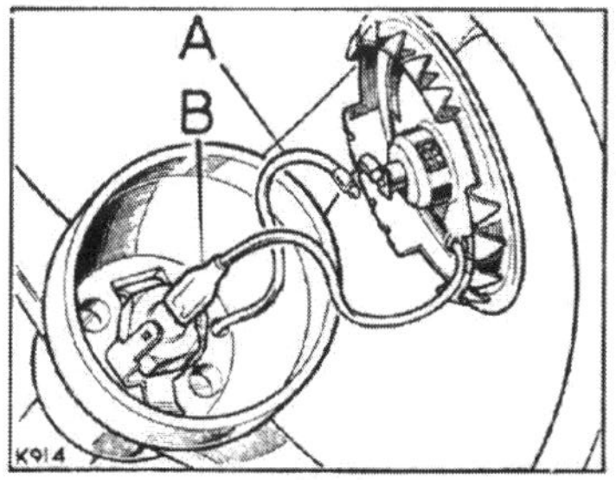

Fig. G1-11. Electrical leads for horn push
A—Connection at horn push
B—Connection at steering wheel

Operation G1-3—continued

2. Disconnect the horn push lead from the snap connector at the dash panel.

3. Prise the centre cover from the steering wheel and disconnect the horn push leads.

4. Remove the fixings and withdraw the steering wheel from the splined column.

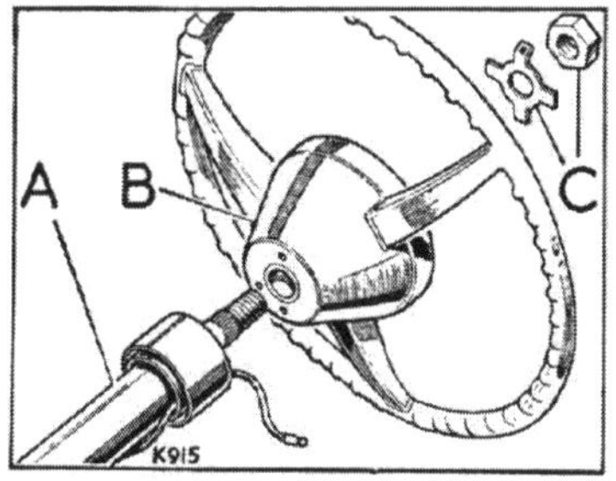

Fig. G1-12. Latest type steering wheel
A—Steering column
B—Steering wheel
C—Fixings, steering wheel to column

To refit, early type

1. Turn the inner steering column lock-to-lock and select the intermediate position (front road wheels straight ahead).

2. Fit the steering wheel with the fixing bolt and nut to the rear and one of the series of spokes pointing forward.

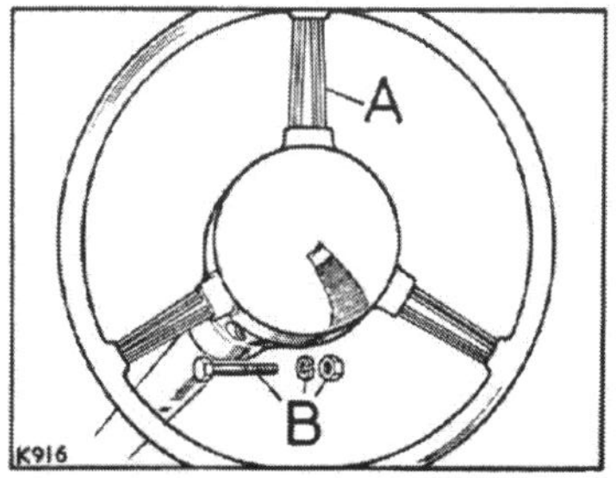

Fig. G1-13. Steering wheel location
A—Spoke facing forward
B—Fixing bolt at rear

3. If the electric horn push is fitted to the steering wheel centre, connect the horn lead to the snap connector at the dash panel.

4. Reconnect the battery.

To refit, latest type

1. Turn the inner steering column lock-to-lock and select the intermediate position (front road wheels straight ahead).

2. Ensure that the special spring washer for the steering wheel is in place on the steering column, then fit the steering wheel with spokes pointing to each side and to the rear. Fit the securing nut, recessed side first, and tighten to a torque figure of 40 lb. ft. (5,4 mkg).

   Note: If the steering wheel securing nut does not have a recess, it should be replaced with the latest recessed type, to ensure that it clears the protruding splines on the inner column and securely clamps the steering wheel.

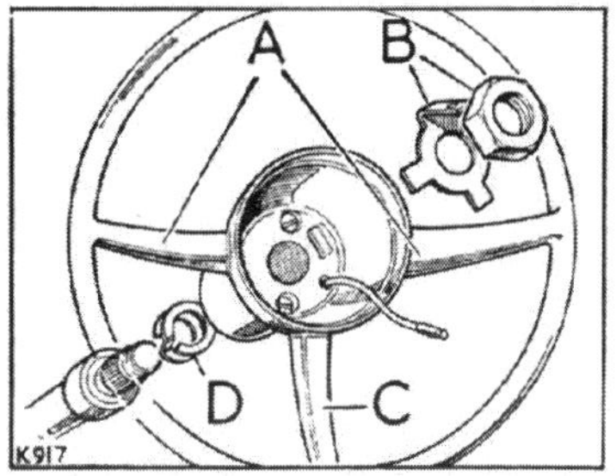

3. Connect the horn push leads to the tag washer and steering wheel centre and fit the centre to the steering wheel, see Fig. G1-11.

4. Connect the horn push lead to the snap connector at the dash panel.

5. Reconnect the battery.

Fig. G1-14. Steering wheel location
A—Spokes facing sideways
B—Fixings for steering wheel
C—Spoke facing rearward
D—Special spring washer

STEERING

Section G—Land-Rover

Steering track rod and drag link, remove and refit—Operation G1-4

(For ball joint servicing instructions, Operation G1-6 refers)

Workshop hand tools:
Spanner sizes: $\frac{7}{8}$ in. BSF, $\frac{7}{16}$ in. AF open end
Pliers, Screwdriver (small)

Special tools:
Tool for extracting ball joints, Part No. 600590

General

From axles numbered:
141107339 88 RHStg
144104520 88 LHStg
151108875 109 RHStg
154103275 109 LHStg onwards

the steering levers are fitted to the bottom of the swivel housings with the ball joints above the levers.

Note: On all models, the ball joint at the relay lever end of the drag link is fitted below the lever.

It is most important that the latest type steering levers are not fitted to an early type housing in the lower position with the existing bolts; the studs detailed above including the special fitting studs 508153 must be fitted. This prevents any tendency for movement between lever and housing which could give rise to premature breakage of the bolts with the possibility of serious damage.

To remove

Note: If the drag link is being removed, jack up the front of the vehicle and remove the front wheel from the side where the drag link is connected to the swivel pin steering lever.

If the track rod is being removed, support the vehicle on stands and remove both front wheels.

1. Remove the fixings from the ball joints at each end of the track rod or drag link, as required.

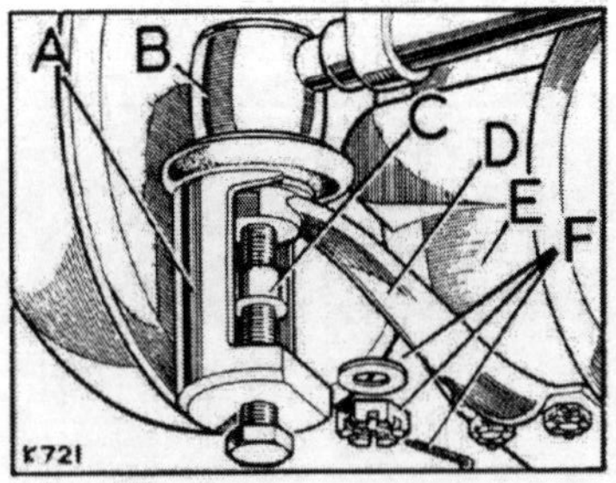

Fig. G1-17. Track rod and drag link connections at swivel pin housings
A—Special tool, Part No. 600590
B—Ball joint
C—Thread protection cap, part of 600590
D—Steering lever
E—Swivel pin housing
F—Fixings, ball joint to steering lever

Fig. G1-15. Early type pendant ball joint

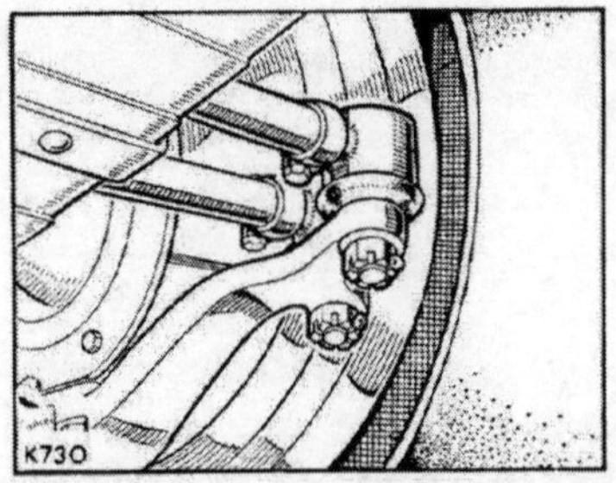

Fig. G1-16. Latest type non-pendant ball joint

Swivel pin and steering levers are not interchangeable as individual items; they can, however, be fitted in pairs provided either the swivel pin housing complete is changed for the latest type, or studs are fitted in the bottom position of the existing swivel pin housing. Studs required are 6 off 508152, 2 off 508153.

STEERING

Section G—Land-Rover

Operation G1-4—continued

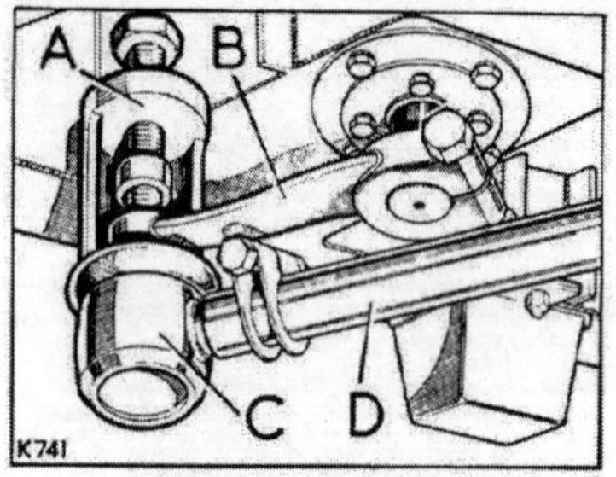

3. If required, slacken the clamps at each end of the track rod or drag link, and unscrew the ball joints, noting that one of the ball joints in each case has a left hand thread.

4. Withdraw the clamps from the track rod or drag link.

To refit

1. Fit the clamps at each end of the track rod or drag link, but do not secure the fixings.

2. Screw the ball joints into the track rod or drag link, noting that one ball joint in each case has a left hand thread.

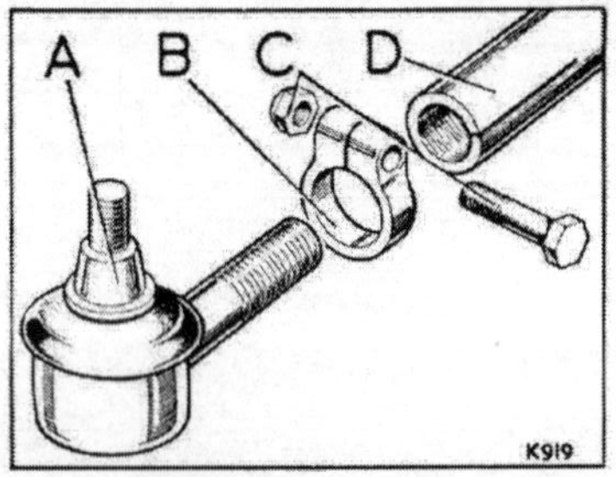

Fig. G1-20. Fitting ball joint
A—Ball joint
B—Clamp
C—Fixings for clamp
D—Track rod or drag link

G1-18. Steering relay connection
A—Special tool, Part No. 600590
B—Lower relay lever
C—Ball joint
D—Steering drag link

2. Using special tool Part No. 600590, extract the ball joints and lift the track rod or drag link clear.

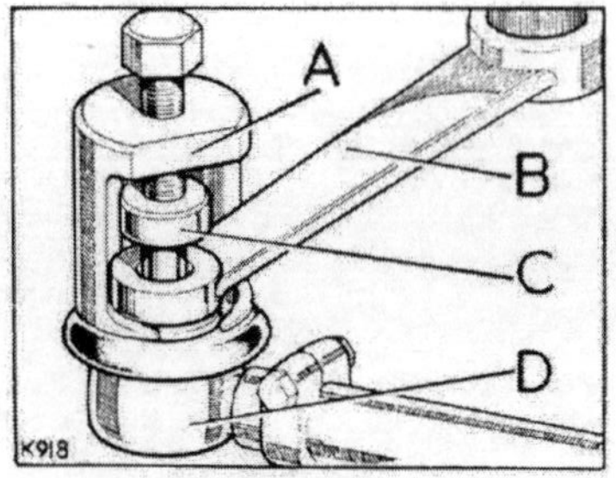

Fig. G1-19. Extracting ball joint
A—Special tool, Part No. 600590
B—Steering lever
C—Thread protection cap (Part of 600590)
D—Ball joint

3. Fit the drag link between the lower relay lever and the steering lever see Fig. G1-18. If necessary, turn the drag link to adjust the overall length, so that the front wheel is in the straight ahead position when the steering wheel is in the intermediate position. Tighten the ball joint fixing nuts to a torque figure of 30 lb. ft. (4.0 mkg).

Section G—Land-Rover STEERING

Operation G1-4—continued

4. Using a mallet, lightly tap the ball joint cups in the direction indicated to the maximum of their travel, to ensure full unrestricted movement of the drag link, then secure both ball joint clamps.

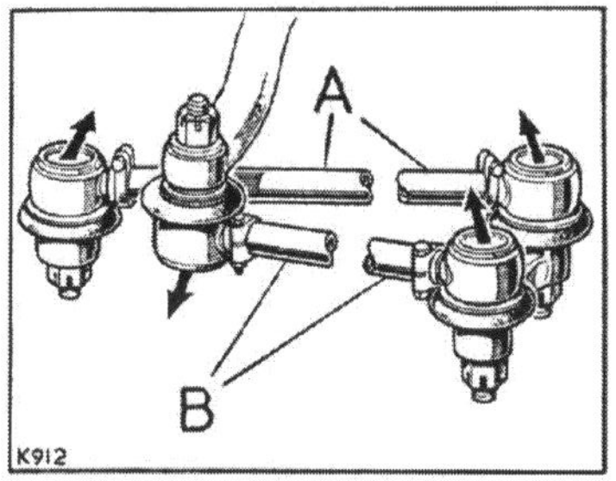

Fig. G1-21. Setting ball joints

A—Track rod
B—Drag link
(Set ball joints as indicated)

5. Fit the track rod between the steering levers, see Fig. G1-17. Tighten the ball joint fixing nuts to a torque figure of 30 lb. ft. (4,0 mkg).

6. Fit the front road wheels.

7. Check, and if necessary, adjust the wheel alignment, Operation G1-2, but do not secure the ball joint clamps.

8. Using a mallet, lightly tap the ball joint cups in the direction indicated to the maximum of their travel, to ensure full unrestricted movement of the track rod, see Fig. G1-21, then secure both ball joint clamps.

Section G—Land-Rover STEERING

Longitudinal steering arm, remove and refit—Operation G1-5

(For ball joint servicing instructions, Operation G1-6 refers)

Workshop hand tools:
Spanner sizes: 7/16 in. BSF, 7/16 in. AF, 1/2 in. AF, 9/16 in. AF, 11/16 in. AF open end
Pliers, Screwdriver (small and large)

Special tools:
Tool for extracting ball joints Part No. 600590

To remove

1. Remove the spare wheel if mounted on the bonnet, disconnect the prop rod and hinge fixings, then lift the bonnet clear.

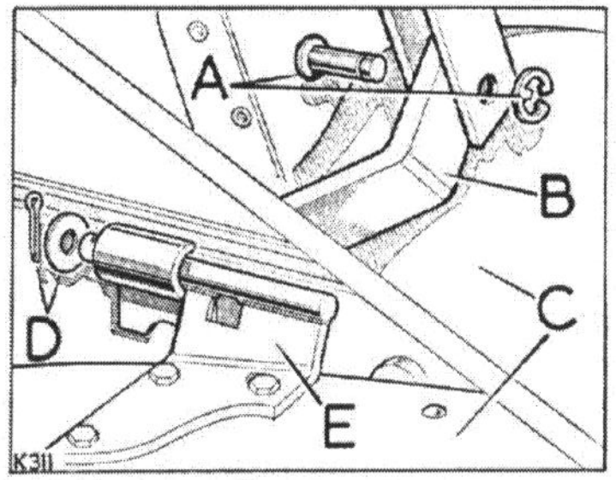

Fig. G1-22. Fixings, bonnet panel

A—Prop rod fixings
B—Prop rod
C—Bonnet panel
D—Hinge fixings, RH side only
E—Bonnet hinge

2. RHStg models only—Remove the air cleaner (see Section A for further details, if required).

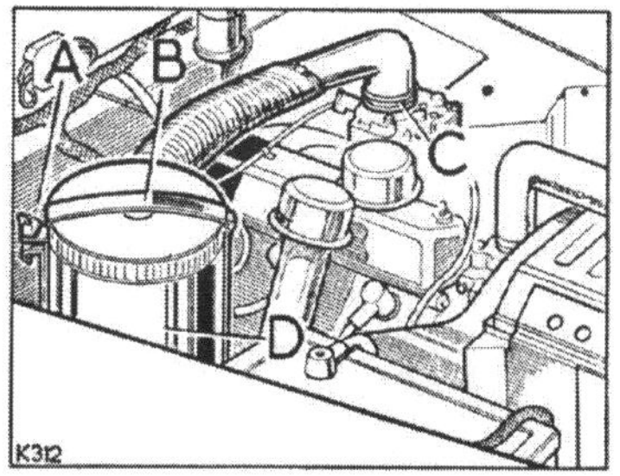

Fig. G1-23. Air cleaner and elbow fixings

A—Retaining strap fixings
B—Retaining strap for air cleaner
C—Elbow fixings
D—Air cleaner

Note: The foregoing operation is not necessary on certain models, where the air cleaner does not obstruct access to the steering box.

3. Remove the name plate and withdraw the radiator grille.

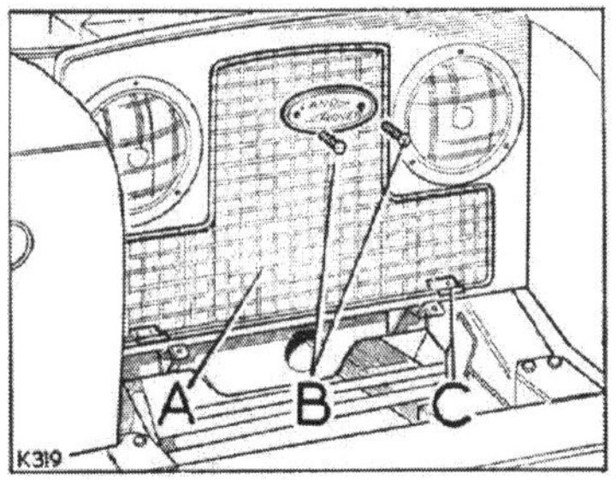

Fig. G1-24. Radiator grille fixings

A—Radiator grille
B—Fixings, for name plate and grille
C—Support brackets

4. Remove the fixings securing the upper relay lever to the relay unit and prise the lever clear.

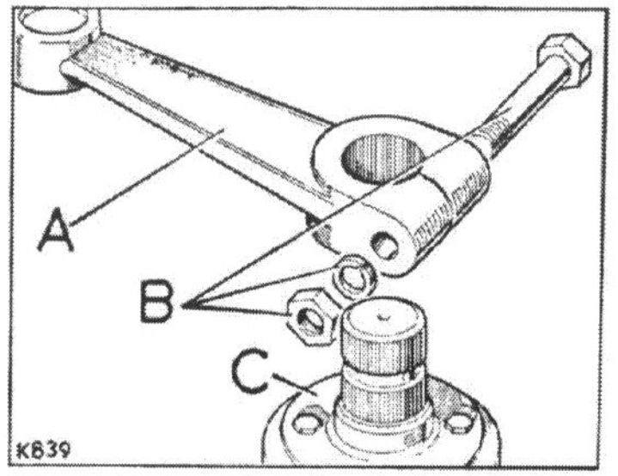

Fig. G1-25. Upper relay lever

A—Relay lever
B—Fixings, lever to relay unit
C—Relay unit

STEERING — Operation G1-5 (continued)

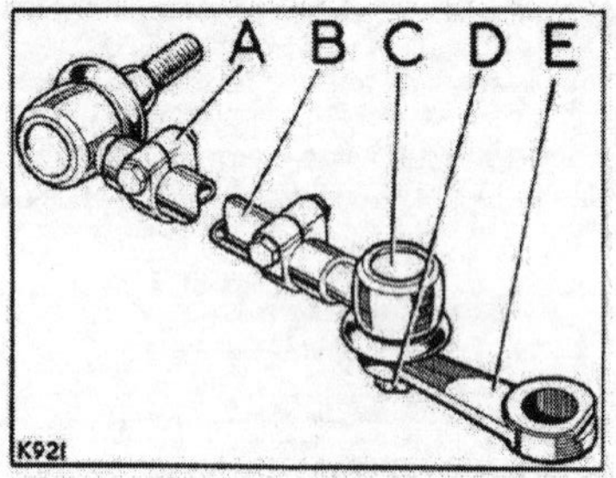

5. Remove the fixings from the ball joint connecting the longitudinal arm to the steering box drop arm.

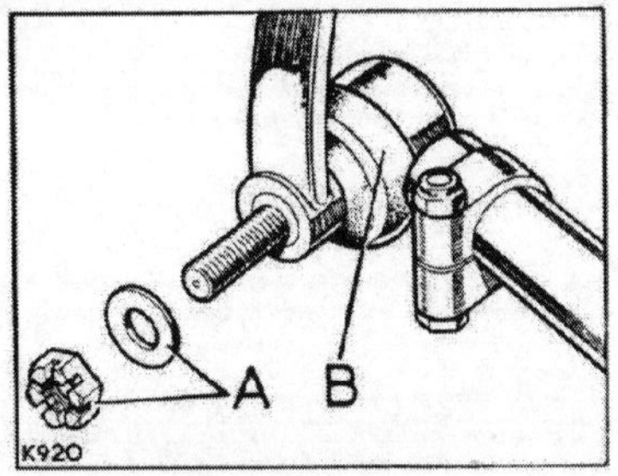

Fig. G1-26. Ball joint fixings
A—Fixings for ball joint
B—Ball joint

6. Using special tool, Part No. 600590, extract the ball joint from the steering box drop arm.
   Note: LHStg models—It may be necessary to remove the exhaust manifold to provide access for the ball joint extractor.

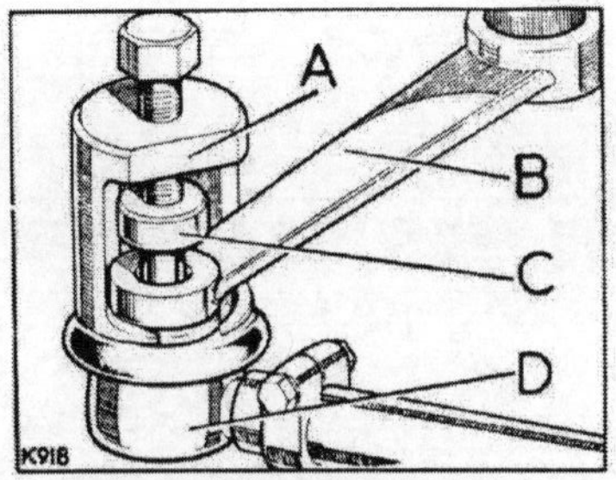

Fig. G1-27. Extracting ball joint
A—Special tool, Part No. 600590
B—Steering drop arm
C—Thread protection cap (part of 600590)
D—Ball joint

7. Manoeuvre the end of the upper relay lever through the aperture in the grille panel, then moving the steering box drop arm fully forward, carefully withdraw the upper relay lever and longitudinal arm assembly.

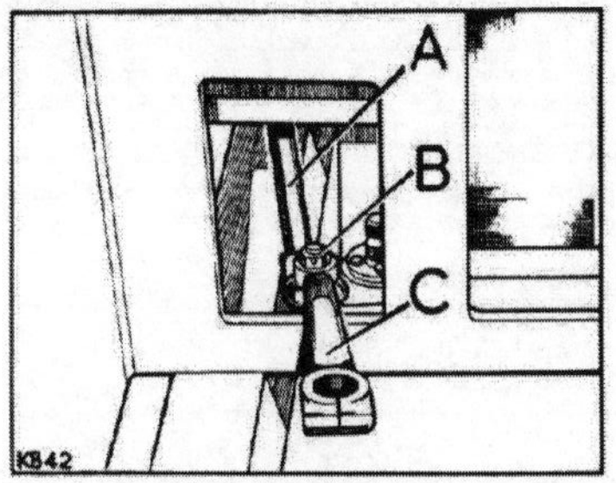

Fig. G1-28. Withdrawing longitudinal arm
A—Longitudinal arm
B—Ball joint
C—Upper relay lever

8. Remove the fixings and extract the ball joint from the upper relay lever.
9. If required, slacken the clamps at each end of the longitudinal arm and unscrew the ball joints, noting that one of the ball joints has a **left hand thread**.
10. Withdraw the clamps from the longitudinal arm.

To refit

1. Fit the clamps at each end of the longitudinal arm, but do not secure the fixings.

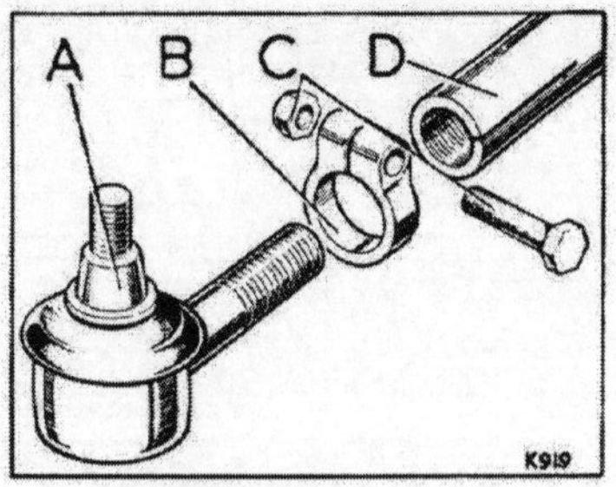

Fig. G1-29. Fitting ball joint
A—Ball joint
B—Clamp
C—Fixings for clamp
D—Longitudinal arm

2. Screw the ball joints into the longitudinal arm, noting that one ball joint has a **left hand thread**.
3. Secure the upper relay lever to the longitudinal arm. The lever may be fitted to either end of the arm. Tighten the ball joint securing nut to a torque figure of 30 lb. ft. (4,0 mkg).
4. Insert the longitudinal arm assembly along the top of the chassis side member, locate and secure the ball joint to the steering box drop arm, see Fig. G1-27. Tighten the ball joint fixing nut to a torque figure of 30 lb. ft. (4,0 mkg).
5. Place the front wheels in the straight ahead position and the steering wheel in the intermediate position, then connect the upper relay lever to the relay unit, the longitudinal arm may require adjusting slightly to align the splines of the relay lever and unit. Tighten the pinch bolt to a torque figure of 55 lb. ft. (7,6 mkg).

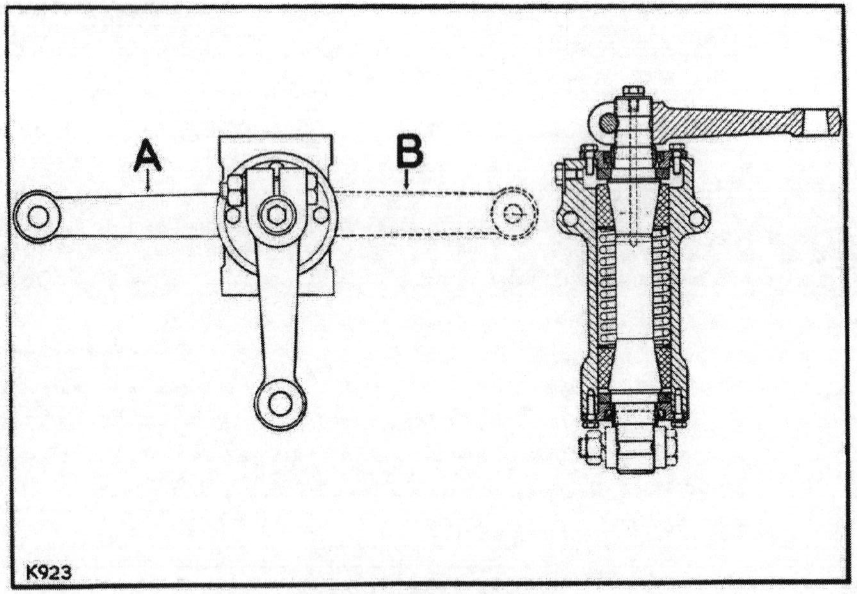

Fig. G1-30. Longitudinal arm assembly
A—Clamp for ball joint
B—Longitudinal arm
C—Ball joint
D—Fixings, ball joint to relay lever
E—Upper relay lever

Fig. G1-31. Location of relay levers
A—Lower relay lever, LHStg models
B—Lower relay lever, RHStg models

STEERING

Operation G1-5—continued

6. Using a mallet, lightly tap the ball joint cups in the direction indicated to the maximum of their travel, to ensure full unrestricted movement of the longitudinal arm, then secure both ball joint clamps.

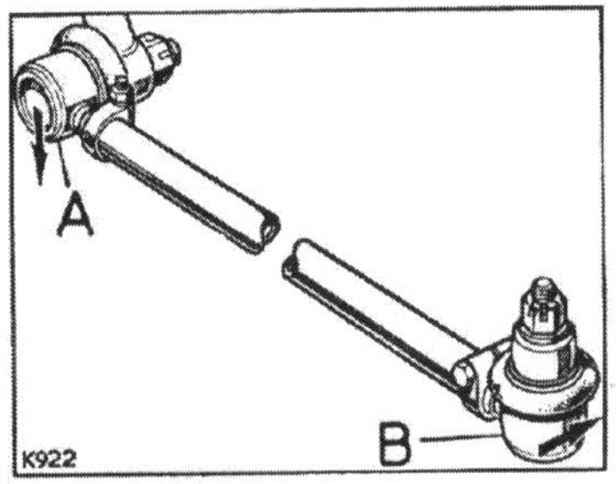

Fig. G1-32. Setting ball joints
A—Ball joint at drop arm
B—Ball joint at relay lever
Set ball joints as indicated

7. Check the steering, lock-to-lock, for correct functioning. If necessary, adjust the overall length of the longitudinal arm by slackening the ball joint clamps and screwing the arm in or out, as required, then secure the clamps.
Caution: DO NOT allow the longitudinal arm to rub the brake pipe. Place the steering in the straight ahead position and check the clearance between the arm and pipe. RHStg models must have 1 in. (25 mm) minimum clearance and LHStg models must have ½ in. (12 mm) minimum clearance. If necessary, bend the brake pipe away from the longitudinal arm to provide the correct clearance.

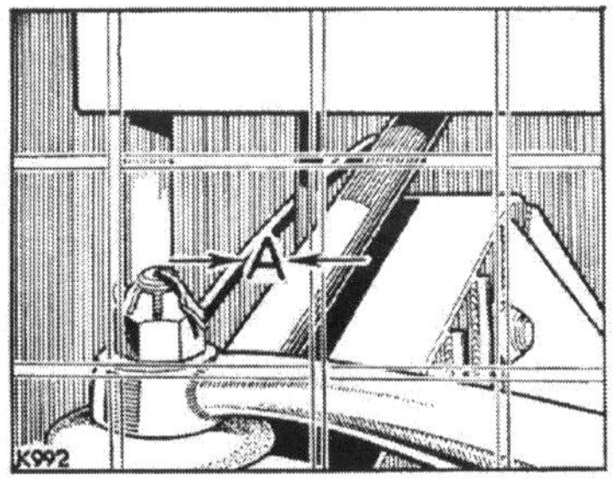

Fig. G1-33. Clearance of brake pipe, RHStg models
A—Ensure that there is 1 in. (25 mm) minimum clearance at this point

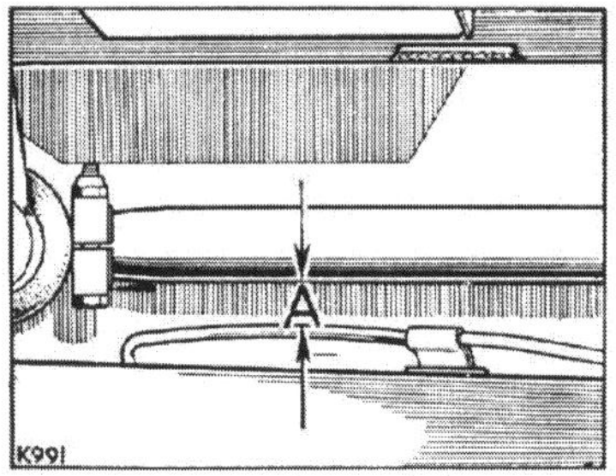

Fig. G1-34. Clearance of brake pipe, LHStg models
A—Ensure that there is ½ in. (12 mm) minimum clearance at this point

8. Fit the radiator grille and name plate, see Fig. G1-23.
9. If removed, fit the air cleaner, see Fig. G1-22.
10. Fit the bonnet, see Fig. G1-24.

Ball joints, to check and lubricate—Operation G1-6

General

The steering ball joints have been designed in such a way as to retain the initial filling of grease for the normal life of the ball joint; however, this applies only if the rubber boot remains in position on the joint. The rubber boots should be checked every 3,000 miles (5,000 km) to ensure that they have not become dislodged or the joint damaged. Should any of the rubber boots be dislodged, proceed as follows:

Procedure

1. Remove the ball joints from the longitudinal arm, track rod and drag link, as required. Operations G1-4 and G1-5.
   Note: If only one ball joint requires attention, it is only necessary to disconnect the applicable end of arm.

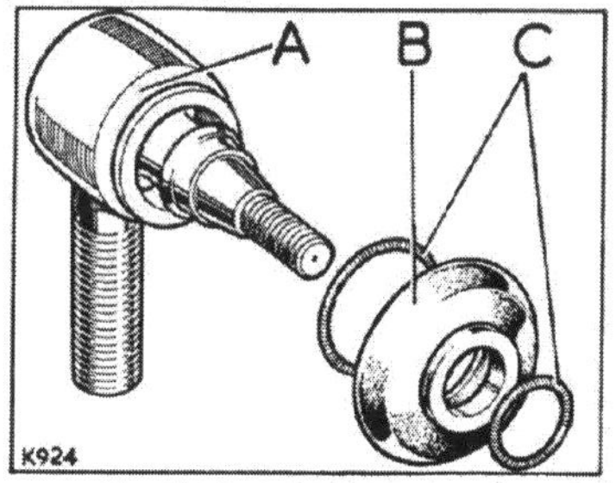

Fig. G1-35. Ball joint and cover
A—Ball joint
B—Rubber cover
C—Spring rings

2. Remove the rubber cover.
3. Thoroughly clean all parts.
4. Place the castle nut upside down on the pin and screw on a few threads, then place the ball joint under a press or between the jaws of a vice and carefully force the pin and ball down against the spring. In this position the interior of the ball joint can be cleaned and lubricated.
5. Apply grease around the taper, and fill the rubber boot.

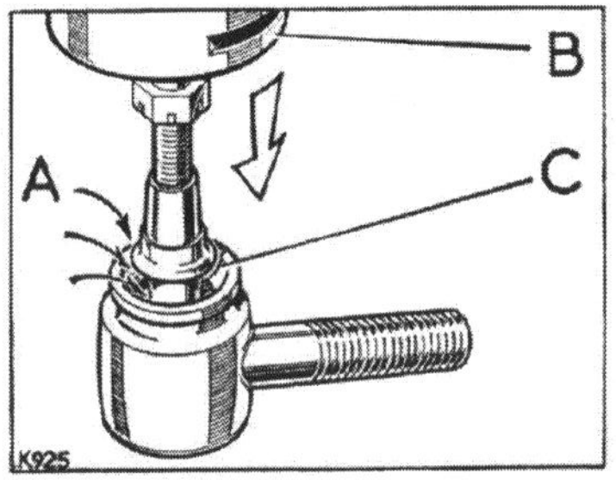

Fig. G1-36. Lubricating ball joint
A—Insert grease as indicated
B—Mandrel press
C—Ball joint

6. Reassemble, using new rubbers and spring rings as required.
7. Fit the ball joints to the vehicle. Operations G1-4 and G1-5.
8. If necessary, adjust the wheel alignment. Operation G1-2.

STEERING

Steering box, remove and refit—Operation G1-7

(For overhaul instructions, Operation G1-8 refers)

Workshop hand tools:
Spanner sizes: 7/16 in. AF, 1/2 in. AF, 9/16 in. AF, 5/8 in. AF, open end, 7/16 in. AF, 1/2 in. AF sockets
Screwdriver (medium)

Special tools:
Tool for extracting steering box drop arm, Part No. 600000

To remove

1. Remove the spare wheel if mounted on the bonnet, disconnect the prop rod and hinge fixings, then lift the bonnet clear.

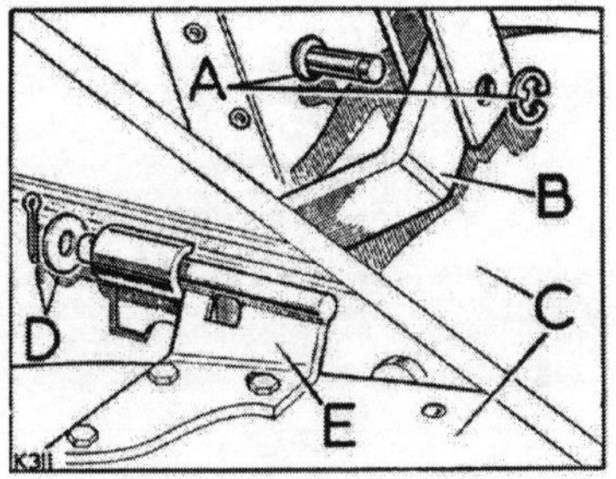

Fig. G1-37. Fixings, bonnet panel
A—Prop rod fixings
B—Prop rod
C—Bonnet panel
D—Hinge fixings, RH side only
E—Bonnet hinge

2. RHStg models only—Remove the air cleaner (see Section A for further details if required).

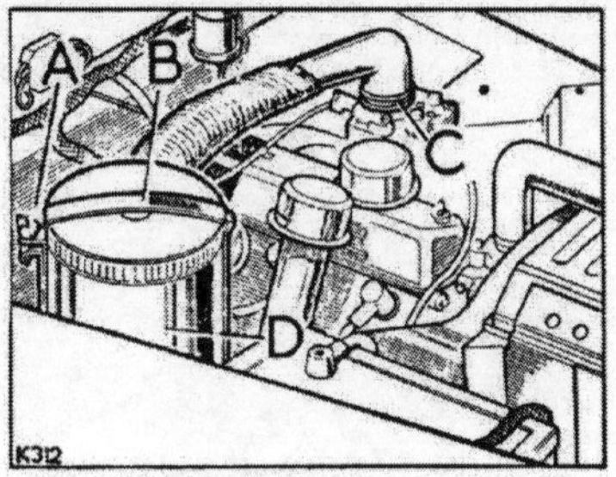

Fig. G1-38. Air cleaner and elbow fixings
A—Retaining strap fixings
B—Retaining strap for air cleaner
C—Elbow fixings
D—Air cleaner

Note: The foregoing operation is not necessary on certain models, where the air cleaner does not obstruct access to the steering box.

3. Remove the name plate and withdraw the radiator grille.

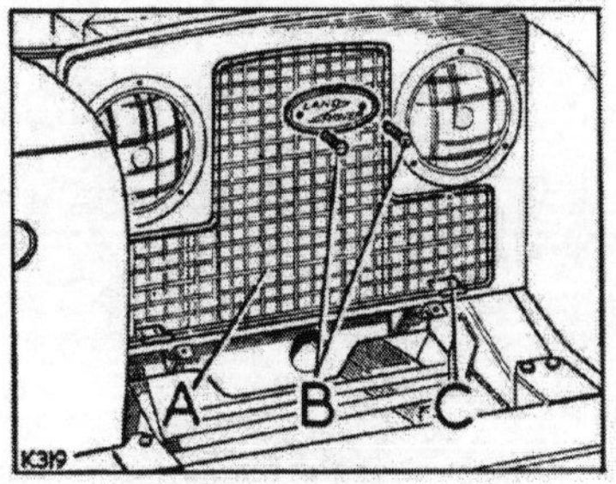

Fig. G1-39. Radiator grille fixings
A—Radiator grille
B—Fixings for name plate and grille
C—Support brackets

4. Remove the steering wheel. Operation G1-3.
5. Remove the longitudinal steering arm. Operation G1-5.

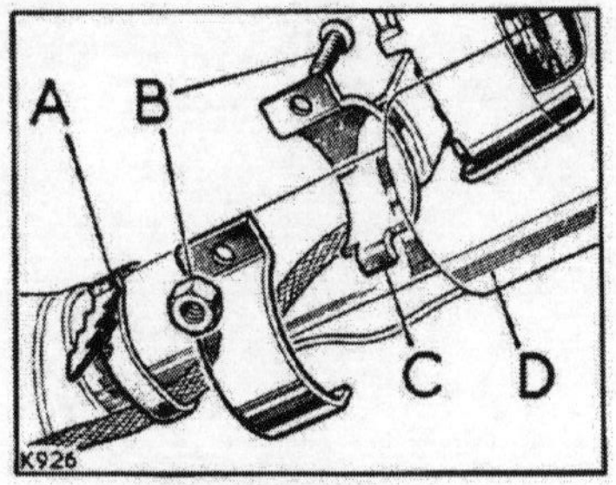

Fig. G1-40. Flasher switch
A—Clip, leads to steering column
B—Fixings, flasher switch
C—Flasher switch
D—Steering column

Operation G1-7—continued

6. Release the flasher switch, or horn push and support bracket on early models, from the steering column. The switch can be placed on the dash panel shelf without disconnecting the leads.
7. Remove the clamp and seal from the steering column and dash support bracket.

Note: On early models, the dash support bracket also forms the top half of the clamp, and the bracket must be removed.

8. LHStg. 2¼ litre petrol engine models only—Disconnect the throttle linkage.

Note: LHStg models fitted with a heat shield at the exhaust manifold. If necessary, remove the heat shield to provide access to the fixings for the steering box stiffener bracket.

9. Remove the fixings between the steering box stiffener bracket and the toe box.

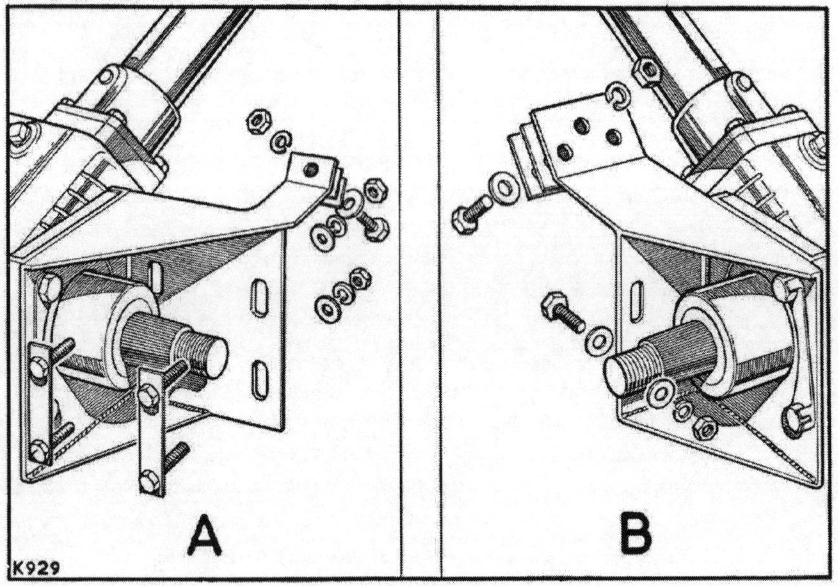

Fig. G1-41. Fixings, stiffener bracket to toe box
A—RHStg models
B—LHStg models

STEERING

Operation G1-7—continued

10. Slacken the fixings at the front road wheel on the steering box side of the vehicle.

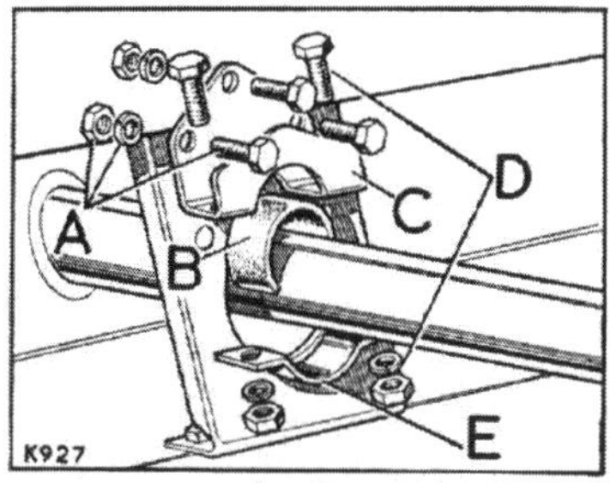

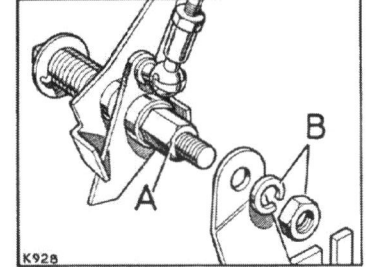

Fig. G1-42. Clamp and seal for steering column
A—Fixings at dash support bracket
B—Seal for clamp
C—Clamp, upper half
D—Fixings, clamp halves
E—Clamp, lower half

11. Jack up the front of the vehicle and support on stands, then remove the road wheel.
12. Remove the steering unit cover box from under the front wing.

Fig. G1-43. Throttle linkage
A—Throttle linkage
B—Fixings

13. Remove the fixings between the support bracket for the steering box and the toe box, wing valance and chassis.

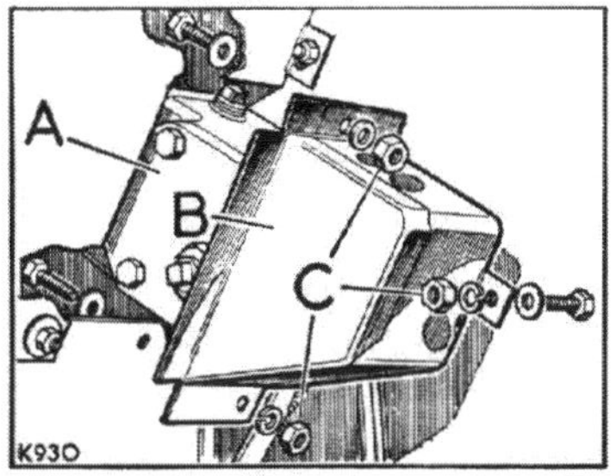

Fig. G1-44. Fixings for cover box
A—Steering box
B—Cover box
C—Fixings at toe box and wing valance

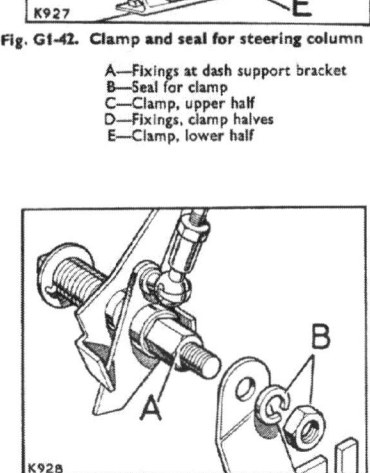

14. Withdraw the steering box and column assembly, complete with the support bracket, stiffener bracket and drop arm, from under the front wing.

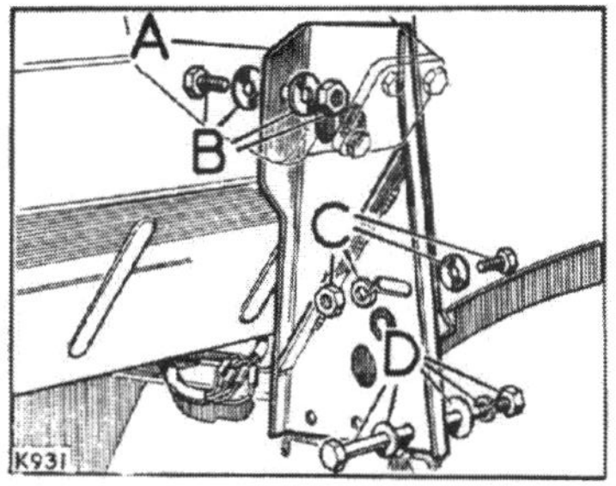

Fig. G1-45. Fixings for support bracket
A—Support bracket
B—Fixings at toe box
C—Fixings at wing valance
D—Fixings at chassis

15. Remove the fixings and extract the drop arm, using special tool Part No. 600000.

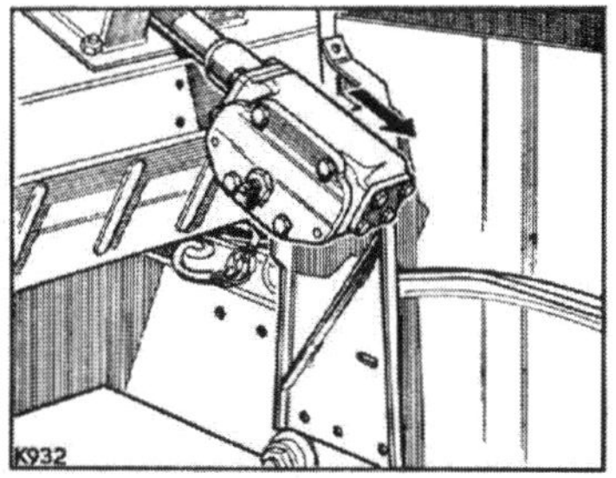

Fig. G1-46. Withdrawing steering box assembly

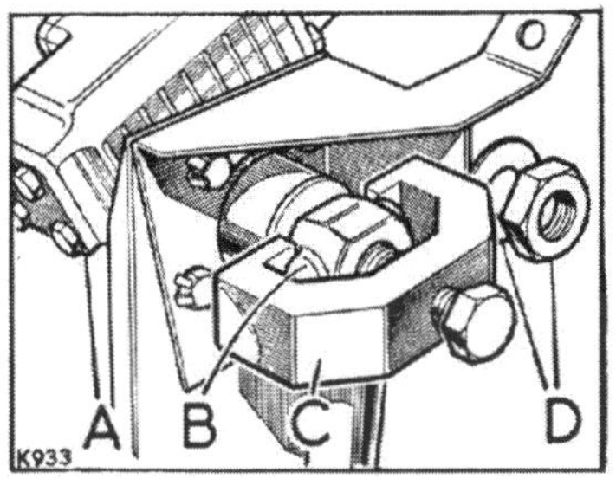

Fig. G1-47. Removing drop arm
A—Steering box
B—Drop arm
C—Special tool Part No. 600000
D—Fixings for drop arm

If required, remove the support and stiffener brackets from the steering box.

Note: The steering box can be overhauled without removing the support and stiffener brackets.

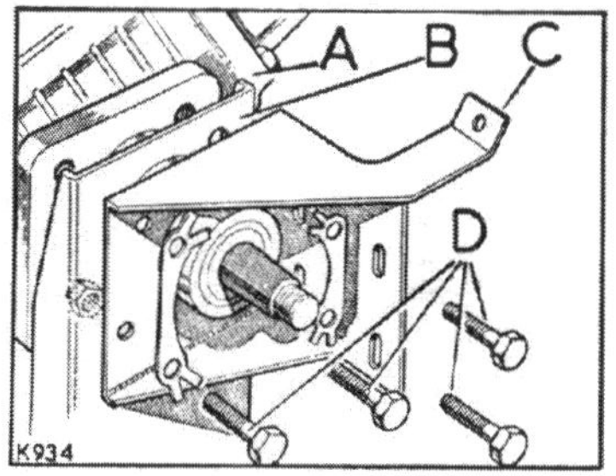

Fig. G1-48. Support and stiffener brackets
A—Steering box
B—Support bracket
C—Stiffener bracket
D—Fixings for brackets

To refit

1. If removed, fit the support and stiffener brackets to the steering box. Tighten the securing bolts to a torque figure of 30 lb ft and engage the lock plates.
2. Locate the steering box and bracket assembly, less drop arm, in position on the vehicle. Retain the support bracket to the chassis, wing valance and toe box, but do not fully tighten the fixings at this stage.
3. Retain the steering box stiffener bracket to the toe box, but do not fully tighten the fixings at this stage. If necessary, fit shim washers between the stiffener bracket and the top face of the toe box to prevent distorting the toe box or bracket.

Caution: During the next item, DO NOT strain the steering column. If necessary, adjust the steering box position, using the slotted fixing holes in the support and stiffener brackets, to obtain a snug fit between the clamp upper half and the steering column, before securing the clamp halves.

Operation G1-7—continued

4. Fit the seal and clamp to the steering column and dash support bracket, see Fig. G1-42.

   Note: On early models, fit the dash support bracket which forms the top half of the clamp.

5. Secure the support and stiffener bracket fixings. Tighten the support bracket to chassis fixing bolts to a torque figure of 15 lb ft (2,0 mkg), see Fig. G1-41 and G1-45.

6. Fit the steering unit cover box, see Fig. G1-44.

7. Fit the road wheel and lower the vehicle to the floor. Fully tighten the road wheel fixings.

8. LHStg, 2¼ litre petrol models only—Connect the throttle linkage, see Fig. G1-43.

9. If removed, fit the heat shield to the exhaust manifold.

10. Fit the flasher switch, or horn push and support bracket on early models, to the steering column, see Fig. G1-40.

11. Fit the steering wheel. Operation G1-3. Latest type steering wheel secured with a nut and tag washer, tighten the nut to a torque figure of 40 lb ft. (5,4 mkg).

12. Fit the steering box drop arm to the longitudinal arm and relay lever assembly. Tighten the ball joint securing nut to a torque figure of 30 lb ft (4,0 mkg).

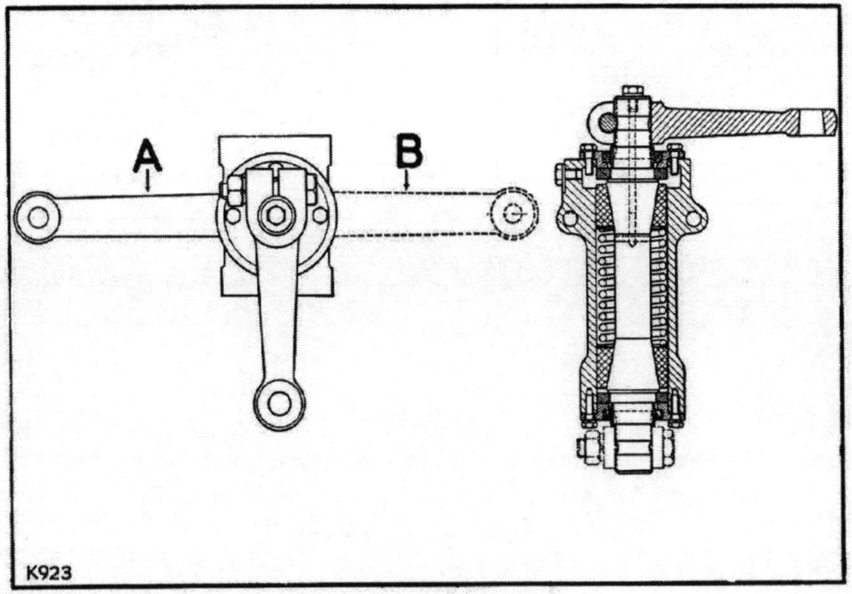

Fig. G1-49. Location of relay levers
A—Lower relay lever, LHStg models
B—Lower relay lever, RHStg models

Operation G1-7—continued

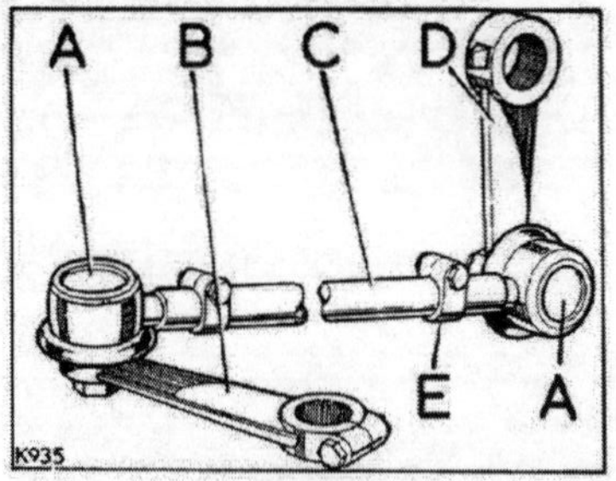

Fig. G1-50. Longitudinal arm assembly
A—Ball joint
B—Relay lever, upper
C—Longitudinal arm
D—Drop arm
E—Clip for ball joint

Fig. G1-51. Drop arm fixings
A—Drop arm
B—Rocker shaft
C—Lockwasher
D—Nut fixing drop arm

13. Insert the longitudinal arm assembly along the top of the chassis side member. Connect the upper relay lever to the relay unit, tighten the pinch bolt to a torque figure of 55 lb ft (7,6 mkg).

14. Place the front wheels in the 'straight ahead' position and the steering wheel in the intermediate position, then fit the drop arm to the rocker shaft. The longitudinal arm may require adjusting slightly to align the splines of the drop arm and rocker shaft. Tighten the drop arm securing nut to a torque figure of 60 to 80 lb ft (8,5 to 11,0 mkg), then engage the lockwasher.

15. Check the steering, lock-to-lock, for correct functioning. If necessary, adjust the overall length of the longitudinal arm assembly by screwing the arm and ball joints in or out, as required.

16. Fit the radiator grille and name plate, see Fig. G1-39.

17. If removed, fit the air cleaner, see Fig. G1-37.

18. Fit the bonnet, see Fig. G1-38.

STEERING

Steering box, overhaul—Operation G1-8

(For removal and refitting instructions, Operation G1-7 refers)

Workshop hand tools:

Spanner sizes: ¾ in. AF, ½ in. AF, ¼ in. AF, ⅝ in. AF, 15/16 in. AF open end
Mallet, Screwdriver (medium)

To dismantle

1. Remove the side cover and drain the oil from the steering box.

Fig. G1-52. Side cover

A—Side cover
B—Fixings for side cover
C—Joint washer for side cover
D—Steering box

2. Lift out the roller for the main nut, and withdraw the rocker shaft.

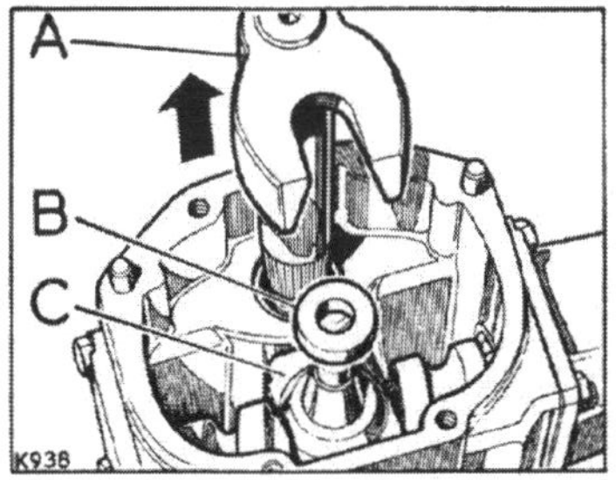

Fig. G1-53. Rocker shaft

A—Rocker shaft
B—Roller for main nut
C—Main nut

3. Hold the outer column in a vice and remove the fixings securing the steering box, then, using a mallet, tap the inner column at the steering wheel end to partially remove the box.

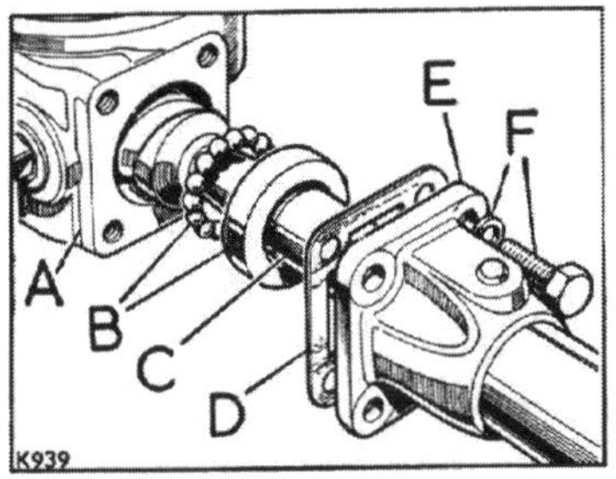

Fig. G1-54. Steering box and column

A—Steering box
B—Bearing, upper, for steering column
C—Inner column
D—Joint washer
E—Outer column
F—Fixings for steering box

4. Withdraw the box and inner column complete. Take care not to loose any of the steel balls from the steering box bearings, or on early models, the dust cover from the top of the steering column.

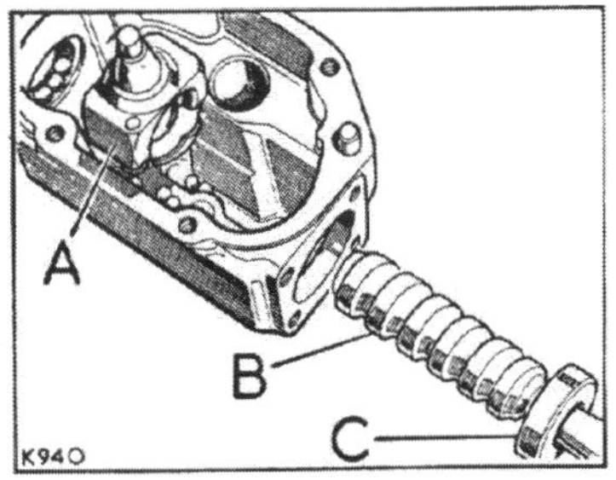

Fig. G1-55. Inner column

A—Main nut
B—Worm shaft
C—Upper ball race

Operation G1-8—continued

5. Rotate the inner column to locate the main nut in the mid-way position on the worm shaft. Then, using a mallet, gently tap the box away from the inner column sufficient to remove the upper ball race. Take care not to loose the steel balls which will be released from the bearings.

6. Wind the worm shaft through the main nut, remove the shaft, main nut and any loose steel balls.

7. Remove the end cover, shims and lower ball race.

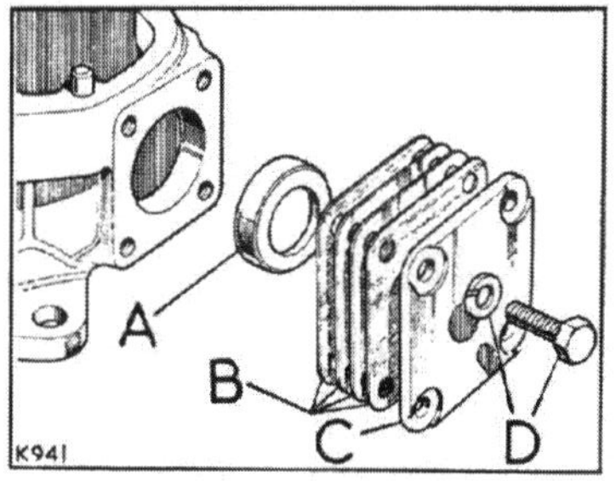

Fig. G1-56. End cover

A—Lower ball race
B—Shims
C—End cover
D—Fixings for end cover

8. Remove the twelve ⅜ in. diameter ball bearings from the main nut and recirculating tube, by tapping the top face of the nut on a wooden block.

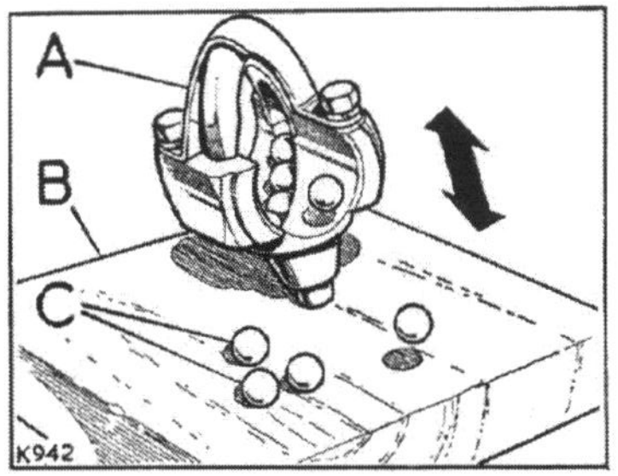

Fig. G1-57. Removing ball bearings from main nut

A—Main nut
B—Wooden block
C—Ball bearings

9. If necessary, remove the retaining washer and oil seal, and press out the rocker shaft bush from the box.

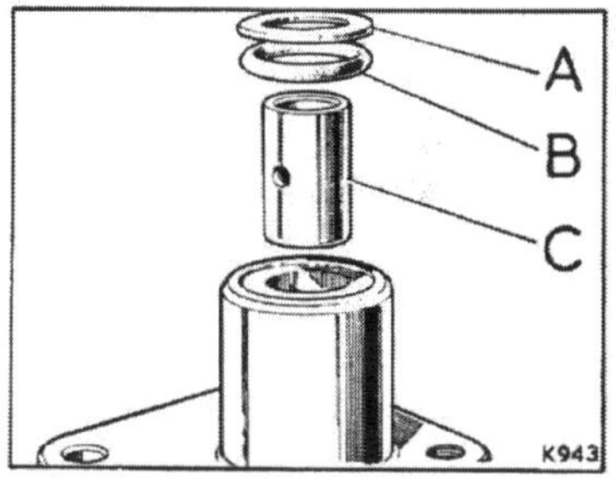

Fig. G1-58. Bush and seal for rocker shaft

A—Retaining washer
B—Oil seal
C—Bush

10. If necessary, remove ball bearing, or on early models the bush and seal, from the top end of the outer column.

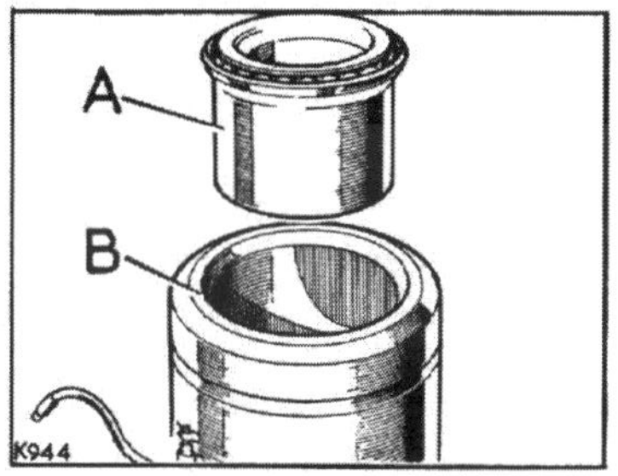

Fig. G1-59. Bearing for outer column

A—Ball bearing
B—Outer column

Page 28-G STEERING Section G—Land-Rover

Operation G1-8—continued

Inspection

1. Examine all components for obvious signs of wear or damage.
2. Examine the main nut ball bearing track for evidence of indentations or scaling.
3. Examine the worm shaft for similar markings. Slight indentations at the extreme end of the shaft can be disregarded as this is a normal wear condition, but if indentations have spread to the middle of the shaft, a new replacement must be fitted.

To assemble

1. Press the ball race, or on early models the bush and seal, into the top of the outer steering column tube.

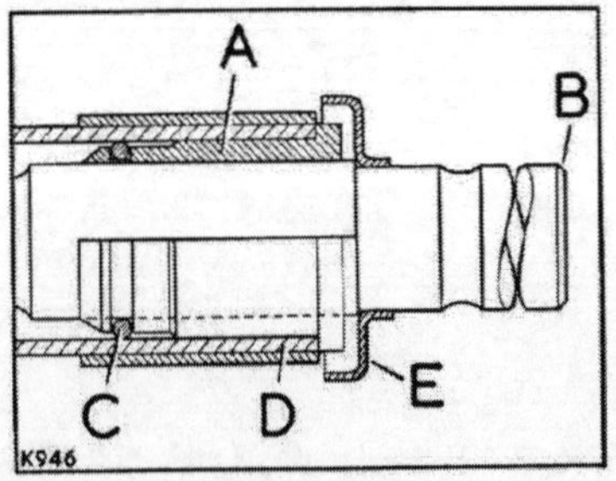

Fig. G1-60. Sectioned view of early type column top

A—Bush
B—Inner column
C—Seal
D—Outer column
E—Dust cover

2. Press the rocker shaft bush into the steering box, then fit the rocker shaft oil seal and retaining washer.
3. Smear both sides of the joint washer with a general purpose grease and place it in position on the flange at the lower end of the outer column, then hold the outer column in a vice, flange end uppermost.

Section G—Land-Rover STEERING Page 29-G

4. Place the upper ball race, less ball bearings, in position on the inner column and slide the inner column into the outer column.

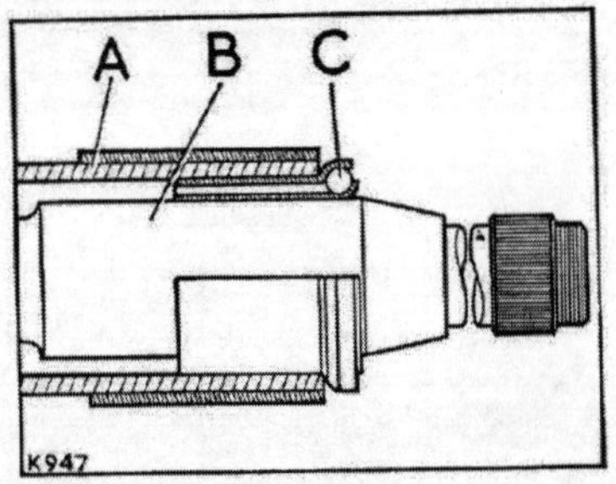

Fig. G1-61. Sectioned view of latest type column top

A—Outer column
B—Inner column
C—Ball bearing

5. Raise the inner steering column slightly, grease the ball race and insert the ten .280 in. diameter steel balls, then lower the inner column again ensuring all balls remain in position and that none have fallen inside the outer column.

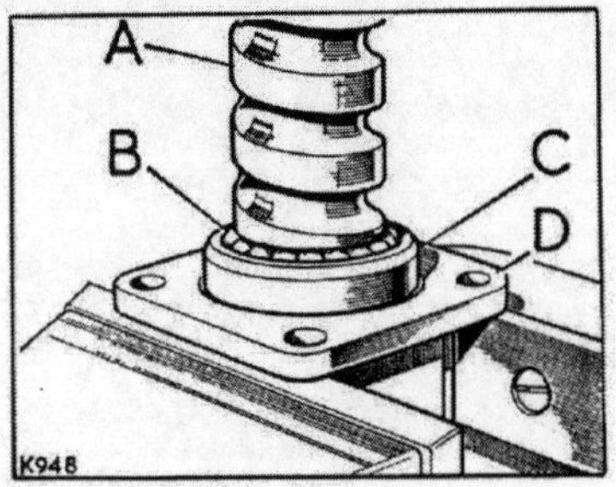

Fig. G1-62. Upper ball race assembly

A—Inner steering column
B—Ball bearings
C—Upper ball race
D—Outer steering column

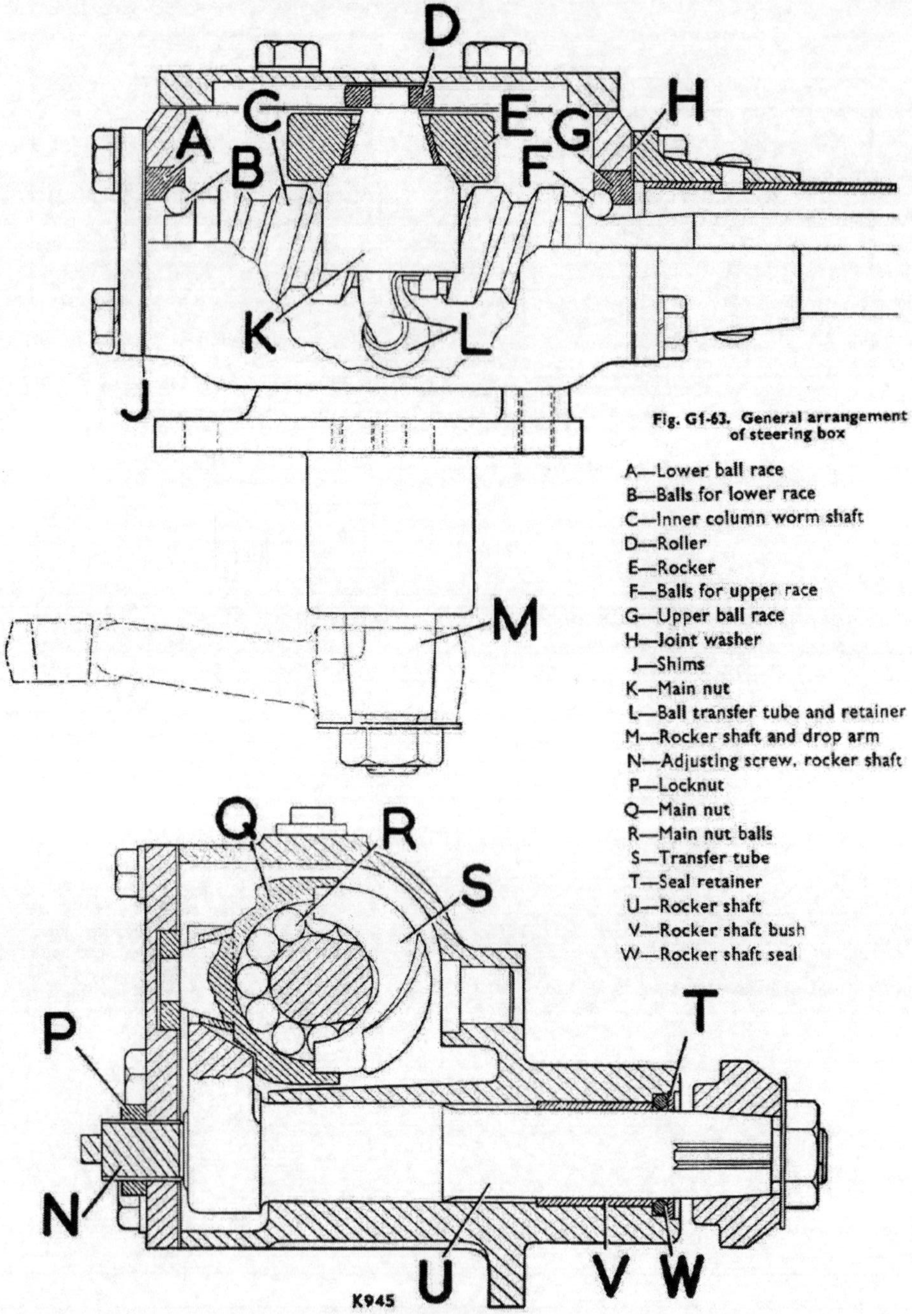

Fig. G1-63. General arrangement of steering box

A—Lower ball race
B—Balls for lower race
C—Inner column worm shaft
D—Roller
E—Rocker
F—Balls for upper race
G—Upper ball race
H—Joint washer
J—Shims
K—Main nut
L—Ball transfer tube and retainer
M—Rocker shaft and drop arm
N—Adjusting screw, rocker shaft
P—Locknut
Q—Main nut
R—Main nut balls
S—Transfer tube
T—Seal retainer
U—Rocker shaft
V—Rocker shaft bush
W—Rocker shaft seal

266

STEERING

Operation G1-8—continued

6. Assemble the twelve ⅜ in. diameter balls into the main nut and retain them in position with grease.

7. Hold the main nut in position inside the steering box and lower the box, oil filler plug end first, together with the main nut over the worm shaft end of the inner column. Carefully rotate the inner column to engage the main nut ensuring that the ball bearings in the main nut are not disturbed.

8. Apply a non-hardening jointing compound to the tapped holes for the steering box to outer column securing bolts, then secure the box to the outer column.

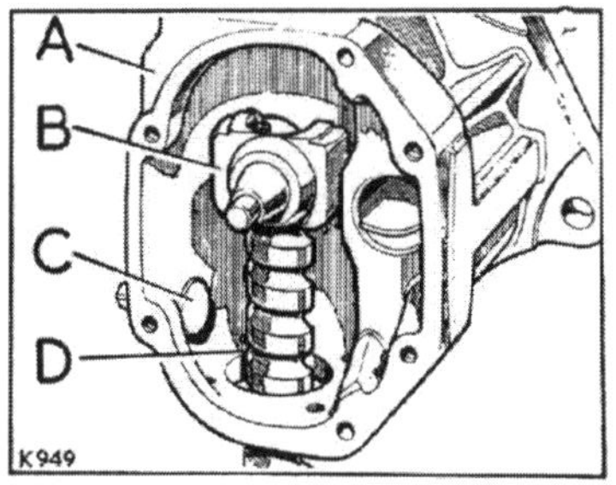

Fig. G1-64. Assembling the main nut
A—Steering box
B—Main nut
C—Oil filler plug
D—Inner steering column

9. Grease the lower ball race and insert the ten 280 in. diameter steel balls. Carefully fit the race into the steering box and locate on the inner column, ensuring that none of the ball bearings are dislodged.

10. Apply a non-hardening jointing compound to the tapped holes in the steering box for the end cover securing bolts, and fit the end cover complete with shims and gaskets. Note that there must be a paper gasket fitted each side of the shims.

11. Move the steering box to the horizontal position and adjust the inner column so that it can be turned by hand but has no end float. Adjust the shim thickness by adding or removing alternate shims and joint washers under the bottom end cover, to achieve this condition.

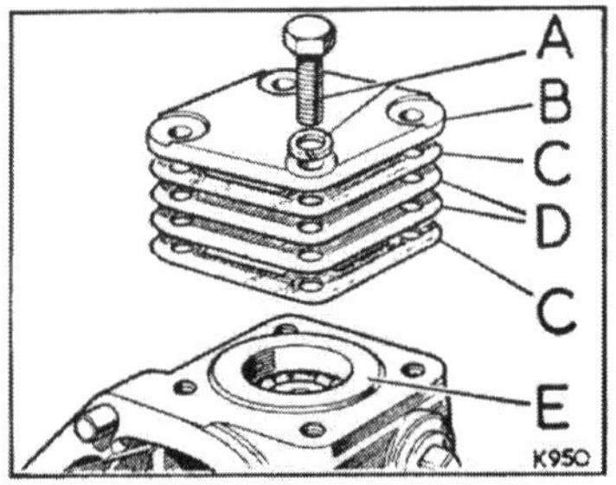

Fig. G1-65. Steering box end cover
A—Fixings for end cover
B—End cover
C—Joint washer
D—Steel shims
E—Lower ball race

12. Smear the side cover joint washer with general purpose grease and locate it in position on the steering box.

13. Fit the rocker shaft, roller and side cover ensuring that the roller is correctly located on the main nut and in the side cover slot.

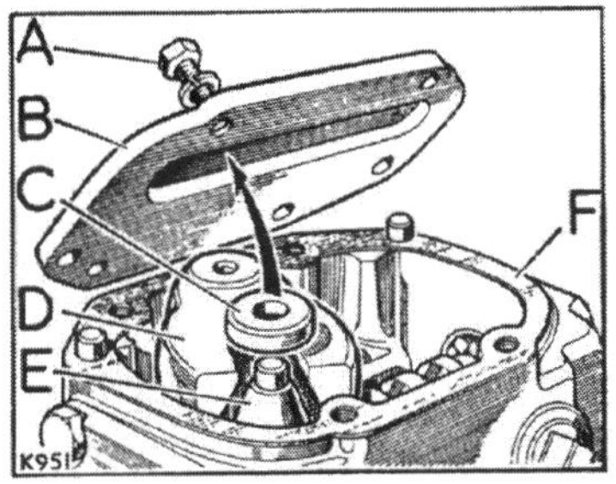

Fig. G1-66. Rocker shaft end side cover
A—Fixings for side cover
B—Side cover
C—Roller for main nut
D—Rocker shaft
E—Main nut
F—Joint washer

Operation G1-8—continued

14. Set the steering in the straight ahead position (mid-way lock-to-lock) and screw the steering box adjuster by hand until there is just no end-float between the adjuster and the rocker shaft, then tighten the adjuster locknut ensuring that the adjuster does not move.

15. Early models only, fit the dust cover to the top of the steering column.

16. Fill the steering box with the correct grade of lubricating oil. Operation G1-1.

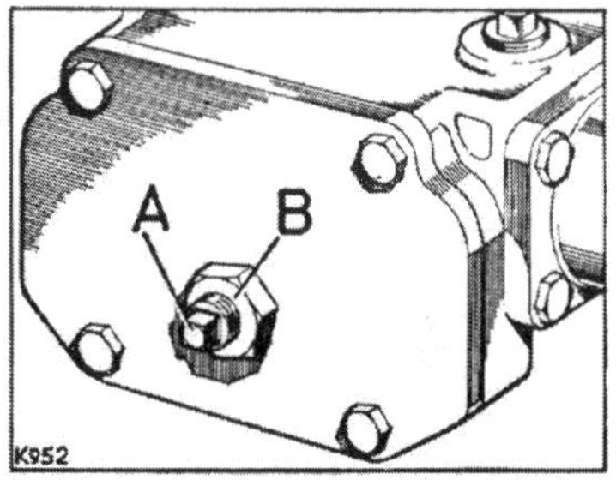

Fig. G1-67. Steering box adjuster
A—Adjuster
B—Locknut

STEERING

Steering relay unit, remove and refit—Operation G1-9
(For overhaul instructions, Operation G1-10 refers)

Workshop hand tools:
Spanner sizes: ½ in. AF, ⅝ in. AF open end, ⅞ in. AF, ⅝ in. AF socket
Screwdriver (medium), Mallet, brass drift

To remove

1. Remove the name plate and withdraw the radiator grille.

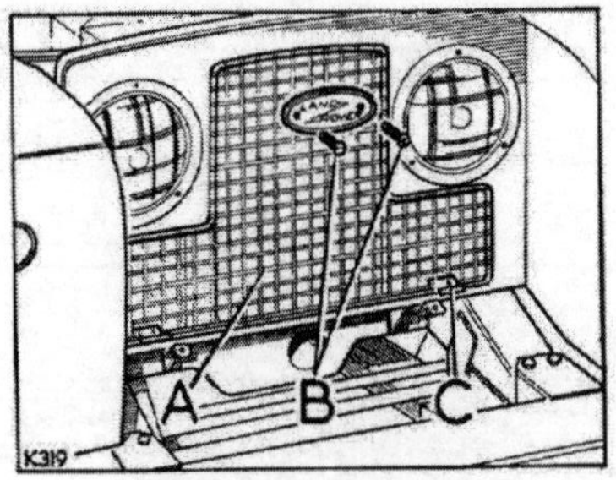

Fig. G1-68. Radiator grille
A—Radiator grille
B—Fixings for name plate and grille
C—Support brackets

2. Remove the fixings securing the upper and lower relay levers to the relay unit and prise the levers clear.

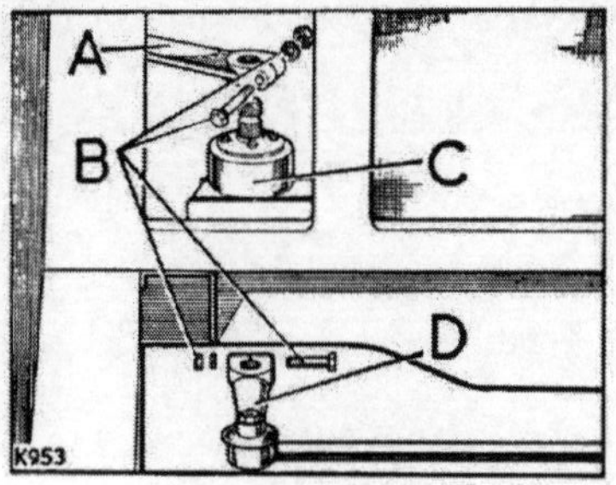

Fig. G1-69. Relay levers
A—Upper relay lever
B—Fixings for relay levers
C—Relay housing
D—Lower relay lever

3. Remove the fixings between the relay housing and the chassis top face.

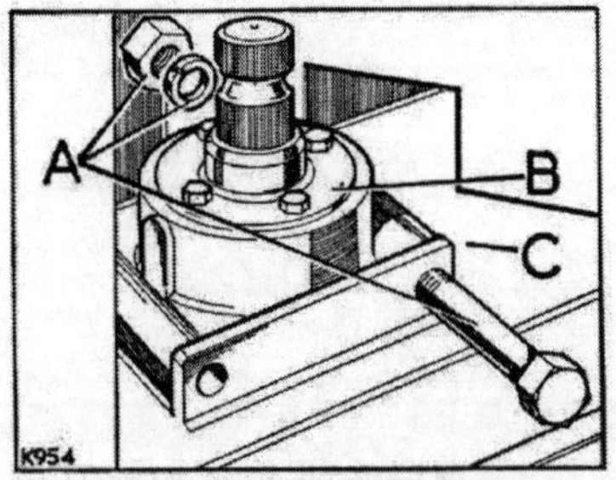

Fig. G1-70. Relay housing top fixings
A—Fixings for relay housing
B—Relay housing
C—Chassis top face

4. Remove the relay mounting flange plate from the underside of the chassis.

Fig. G1-71. Relay mounting flange plate
A—Underside of chassis
B—Flange plate
C—Fixings for flange plate

Note: Before attempting to remove the relay unit, remove any equipment that is mounted directly above and would obstruct relay unit removal.

Operation G1-9—continued

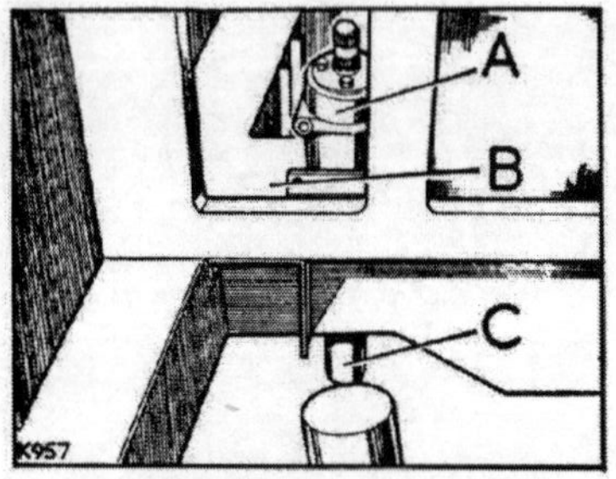

5. Using a brass drift and mallet, drive the relay unit upward to free it from the chassis. If necessary, use penetrating oil between the unit and the chassis.

Fig. G1-72. Removing the relay unit
A—Relay unit
B—Chassis top face
C—Brass drift

To refit

1. Before fitting the relay unit, ensure that it is filled with oil. Operation G1-1.
2. Fit the relay unit to the chassis with the filler plug boss towards the driver's side of the vehicle. The relay unit must be a drive fit in the chassis.
3. Secure the relay unit top fixings, see Fig. G1-70.
4. Fit the relay mounting flange plate to the underside of the chassis, see Fig. G1-71.
5. Fit the upper and lower relay levers to the relay unit. Tighten the relay lever pinch bolts to a torque figure of 55 lb ft (7,6 mkg).

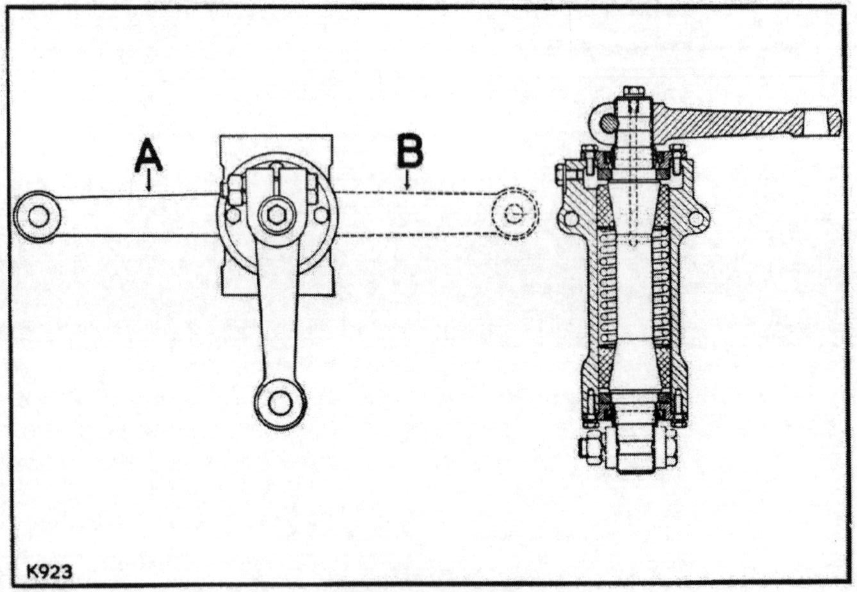

Fig. G1-73. Location of relay levers
A—Lower relay lever, LHStg models
B—Lower relay lever, RHStg models

STEERING

Operation G1-9—continued

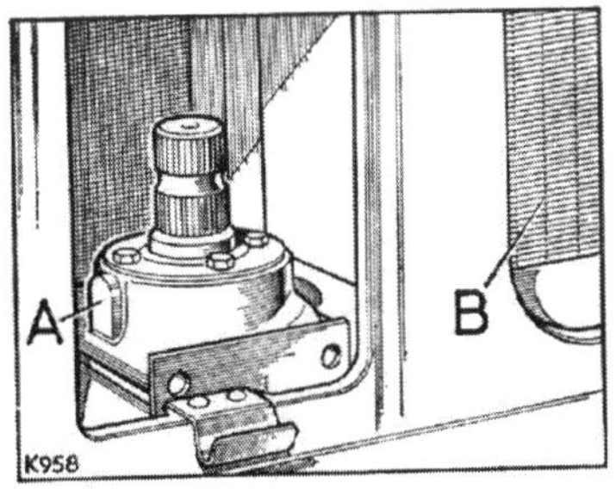

6. Refit any equipment removed to give access to the relay unit during removal.
7. Fit the radiator grille and name plate, see Fig. G1-68.

Fig. G1-74. Relay unit location
A—Boss on relay housing
B—Radiator
(RHStg illustrated. LHStg is symetrically opposite)

Steering relay unit, to overhaul—Operation G1-10

(For removal and refitting instructions, Operation G1-9 refers)

Workshop hand tools:
Spanner size: 2 BA open end
Mallet, 2 in. (50 mm) hose clip

Special tools:
Tool for compressing spring, Part No. 600536

To dismantle

1. Remove the oil filler and breather plugs and drain all the oil from the relay unit.

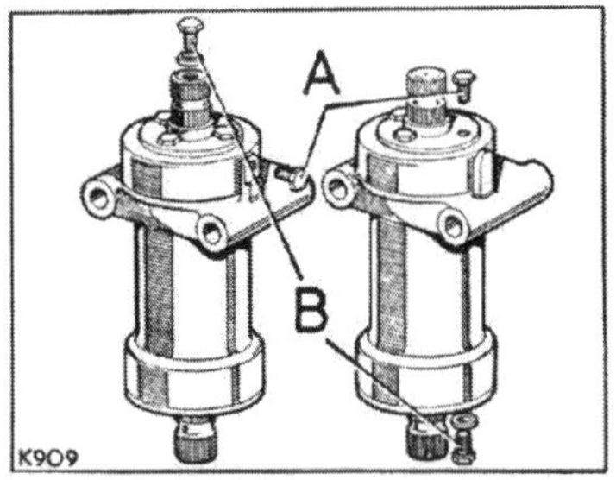

Fig. G1-75. Oil filler and breather plugs, early and latest type
A—Oil filler hole and plug
B—Breather hole and plug on early type.
Drain plug on latest type

2. Remove the bottom oil seal retainer complete with seal and joint washer.

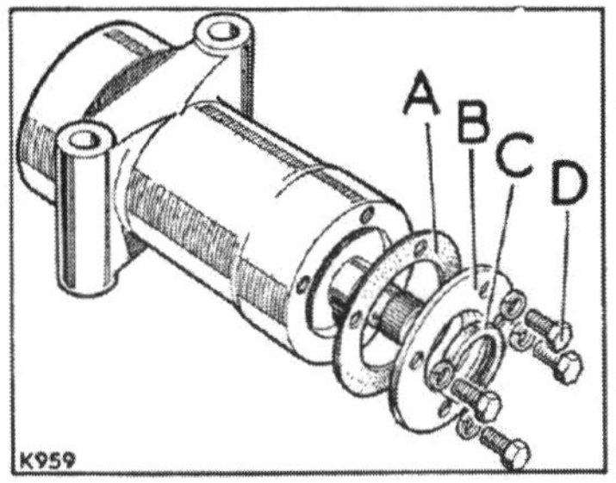

Fig. G1-76. Bottom oil seal retainer
A—Joint washer
B—Oil seal retainer
C—Oil seal
D—Fixings for oil seal retainer

Caution: During the following procedure use extreme care, the relay housing contains a large compressed spring, which is automatically released during dismantling.

2. Cover the bottom end of the shaft by tying a sock to the relay body, then using a mallet, tap out the shaft, thrust washer, spring, fibre bush and plain washer into the sock.

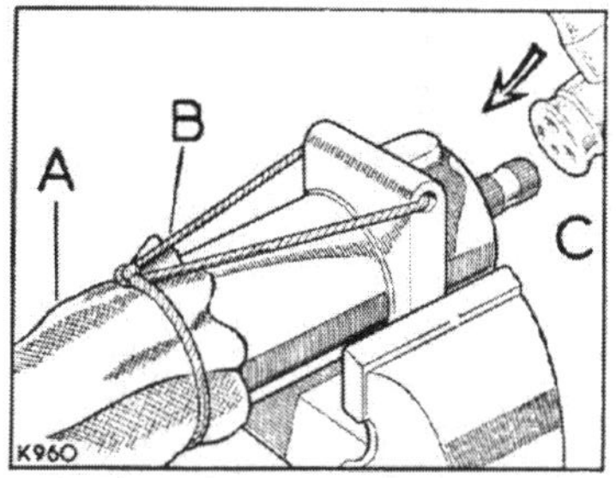

Fig. G1-77. Removing relay shaft
A—Sock covering bottom of housing
B—Tie sock as shown
C—Tap out shaft as indicated

3. Remove the sock and lift out the relay shaft and fittings.

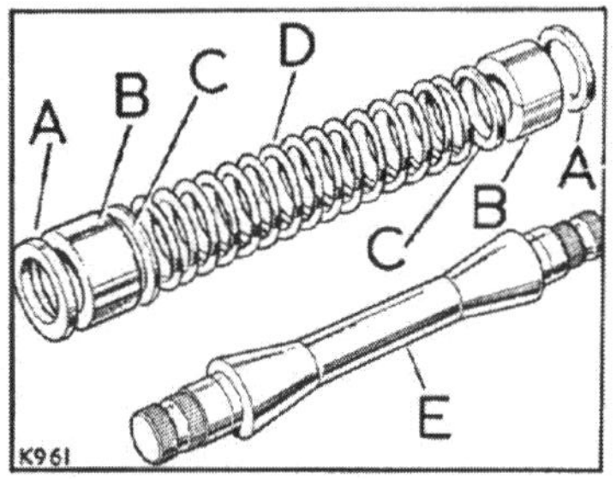

Fig. G1-78. Relay shaft and fittings
A—Thrust washer
B—Split bush
C—Washer for spring
D—Spring
E—Relay shaft

4. Remove the top oil seal retainer complete with seal and joint washer.

STEERING

Section G—Land-Rover

Operation G1-10—continued

Inspection

1. Examine all components for obvious signs of wear or damage and fit new replacements as required.

2. Check the relay shaft at the diameters which form the tracks for the oil seals. Any damage or score marks would cause failure of the oil seals, and a new replacement shaft must be fitted.

   Note: Early type shafts are fitted with distance pieces which can be replaced separately.

3. The free length of the spring should be 7¼ in. (184 mm).

To reassemble

1. If removed, fit the oil seals, lipped side inward, to their retainers, using jointing compound on the outside diameter of the seals.

2. Locate two halves of the split bush on the top cone of the shaft.

3. Insert the assembly of shaft and bush into the housing from the bottom.

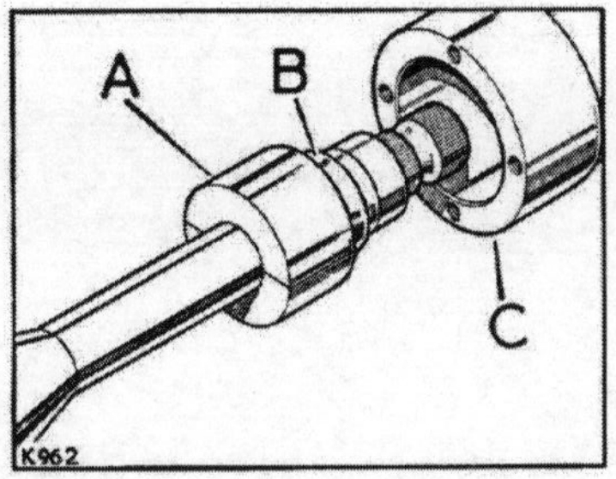

4. Secure the housing and shaft assembly, bottom end uppermost, in a vice with a ¾ in. (19 mm) block under the bottom end of the shaft.

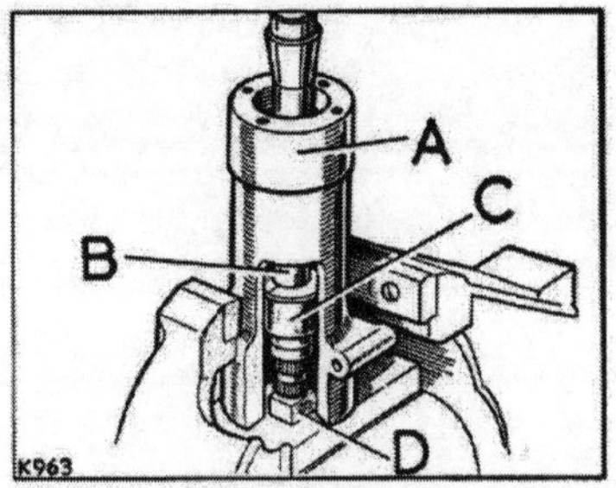

Fig. G1-79. Assembling shaft to housing

A—Split bush
B—Relay shaft top cone
C—Relay housing, bottom end

Fig. G1-80. Housing, shaft and block in position

A—Housing
B—Shaft
C—Split bush halves
D—Block ¾ in. (19 mm) high

5. Insert washer for spring into housing and fit two of the oil seal retainer fixing bolts into the housing diametrically opposite each other.

6. Place the spring in position over the shaft and into the housing.

7. Place washer for spring on the top of the spring.

8. Using special tool Part No. 600536, compress the spring, taking care to ensure that it does not fly out. Turn the tool to lock in position with the keyhole slots under the heads of the bolts.

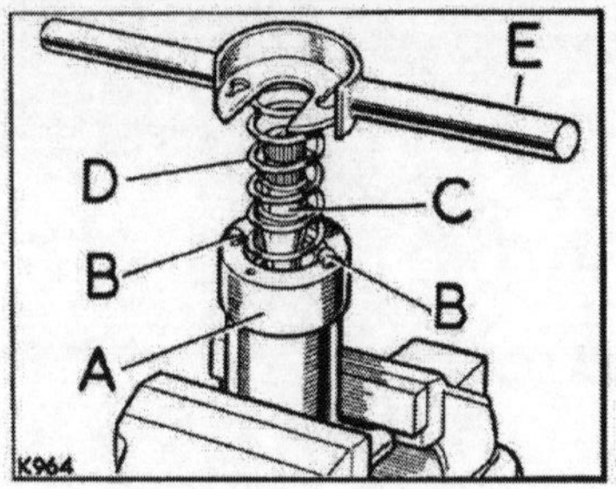

Fig. G1-81. Spring ready to be compressed

A—Housing
B—Bolts for oil seal retainer
C—Shaft
D—Spring
E—Special tool Part No. 600536

Operation G1-10—continued

9. Locate the other split bush in position on the bottom cone of the shaft and secure with a 2 in. (50 mm) hose clip.

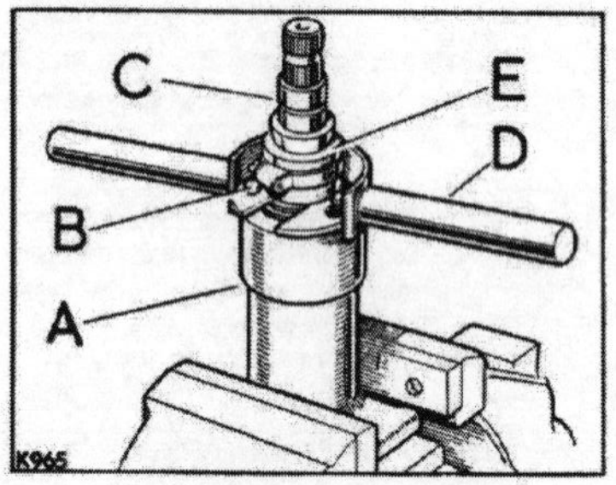

Fig. G1-82. Spring compressed

A—Housing
B—Bolts for oil seal retainer
C—Shaft
D—Special tool, Part No. 600536
E—Split bush secured with 2 in. (50 mm) hose clip

10. Turn the special tool and allow it to clear the bolt heads.

11. Withdraw the tool from between the spring and split bush.

12. Remove the oil seal retainer fixing bolts from the housing.

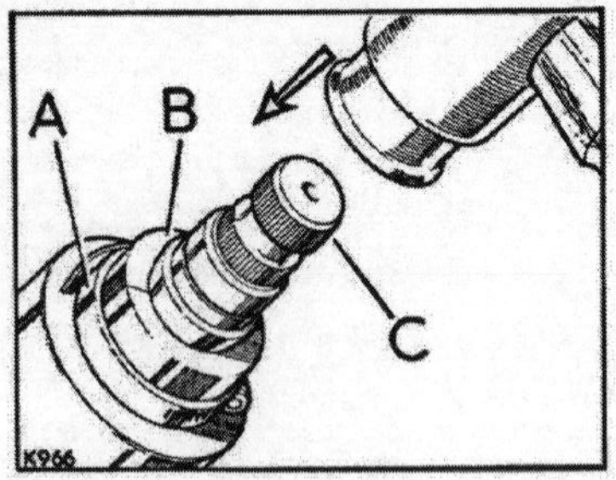

Fig. G1-83. Locating shaft assembly into housing

A—Hose clip
B—Split bush
C—Relay shaft

13. Remove the assembly from the vice, gently tap shaft into position until the split bush has entered the housing for at least half its length.

14. Remove the hose clip and continue to tap the shaft into the housing until the bushes are correctly located in the housing.

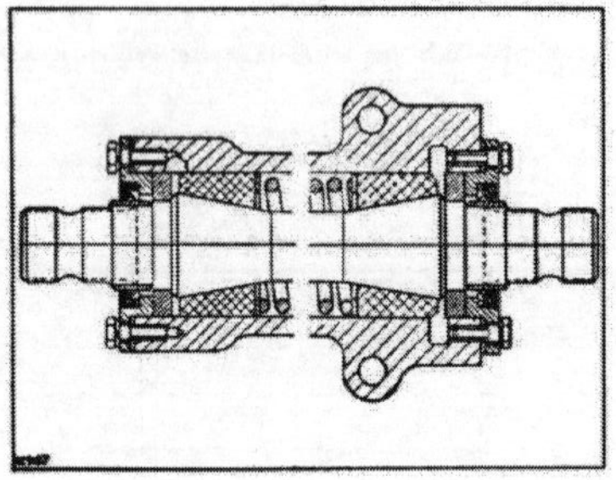

Fig. G1-84. Cross section of steering relay

15. Smear general purpose grease on both sides of the joint washers and fit one to each end of the housing.

16. Fit the thrust washer and oil seal retainer, complete with seal, to bottom end of the housing.

    Note: Latest type relay. Use jointing compound on the threads of the bolt fitted to the breather hole.

17. Using one of the holes in the top of the housing for the oil seal retainer fixing bolts, fill the housing with the correct grade oil, see Section X. Ensure that housing is completely filled.

18. Fit the thrust washer and oil seal retainer, complete with seal to the top of the housing, using jointing compound on the threads of the four securing bolts.

19. Hold the relay unit in a vice, temporarily attach the upper relay lever and use a suitable spring balance to check resistance to rotation of the relay shaft. The resistance, measured on the spring balance, must not be less than 12 lb (5,4 kg) and should not exceed 16 lb (7,3 kg).

Operation G1-10—continued

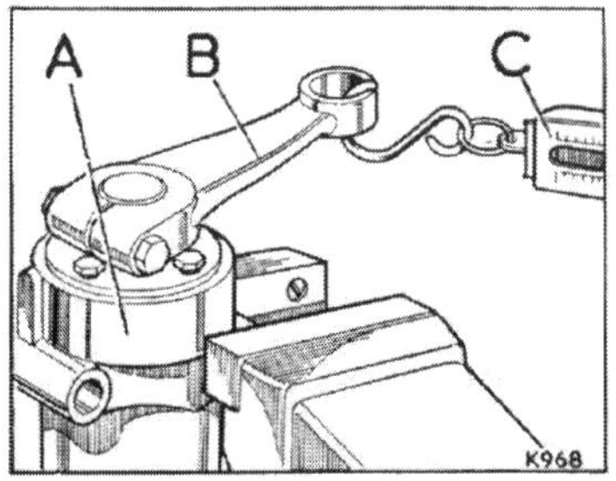

If the resistance is less than 12 lb (5,4 kg), fit a new replacement spring.

If the resistance is excessive, remove the oil seal retainers and thrust washers, then use a suitable piece of tube to push each split bush in turn, clear of its cone and inject lubricating oil. Re-assemble and recheck.

Fig. G1-85. Checking resistance to rotation of relay lever
A—Relay unit
B—Upper relay lever
C—Spring balance

Fault diagnosis—Steering

Steering kick and wheel wobble

A certain amount of wheel kick must be expected over rough surfaces, but if this becomes excessive or if actual wheel wobble is experienced, the following checks must be carried out. Only after these checks have failed to reveal the cause should the swivel pin damping be checked.

1. Ensure that the bolts securing the steering box to its mounting bracket, and the bolts securing the bracket to the frame are tight. Also ensure that the steering box stiffener bracket is fitted.

2. Check the steering box adjustment, Operation G1-8.

3. Check the nut securing the drop arm to the rocker shaft and nuts securing ball joints to track rod and steering arms for tightness.

4. Check the ball joints for alignment and wear. Adjust or renew as necessary.

5. Check the relay top and bottom lever clamp bolt for tightness and check for wear at lever and shaft splines. Rectify any play in the relay unit.

6. The bolts securing the relay to the chassis must be checked for tightness, also the four bolts at the bottom plate for the relay. Check the bolt flanges for cracking and check the fit of the bottom of the relay in the spigot, this must be firm.

7. The nuts and studs securing the steering levers must be checked, and ensure that the one special 'fitting' stud on each side is a tight fit and that it positively locates the arm.

8. Check shock absorber action—replace if weak. Examine the rubber bushes and replace as necessary. Check road spring shackle pins and bushes for wear, check tightness of 'U' bolts. Ensure that the spring location bolt has not sheared and that its seating hole is not elongated.

9. Check all the spring leaves, either side of the centre bolt, for breakage.

10. Check the swivel pin damping (poundage figure), Operation F1-10, and adjust as necessary.

11. Check for badly or unevenly worn tyres. Similar tread pattern tyres should be fitted. Check the tyre pressures, Section R. Check the front wheel alignment, Operation G1-2.

12. While the vehicle is on a ramp or pit, examine the chassis members and axle casings for accident damage.

STEERING

Fault diagnosis—Steering—continued

Symptom	Possible cause	Investigation	Remedy
Excessive looseness or backlash in the steering	Steering rocker shaft incorrectly adjusted or badly worn	Check steering box adjustment, Operation G1-8	Adjust or fit new parts as required
	Steering linkage loose or worn	Check ball joints for security and wear condition	Rectify or renew
	Steering box fixings loose	Check all fixings, see Operation G1-7	Tighten or renew fixings as required
	Swivel pins and bearings loose or worn	Adjust swivel pin damping or dismantle swivel pin housings, see Section F	Adjust or fit new parts as required, lubricate swivel pins on assembly
	Front wheel bearings loose or worn	Check front hub bearings and adjustment, see Section F	Renew and/or adjust hub bearings as required
Tight steering	Low or unequal tyre pressures	Check tyre pressures, see Section R	Adjust as necessary
	Steering box oil level too low	Remove filler plug and check oil level	Replenish as necessary
	Steering rocker shaft adjusted too tightly	Check adjustment, Operation G1-8	Adjust as necessary
	Steering ball joints partially seized or incorrectly set	Check ball joints, ensure rubber boots are in place and joints move freely, Operations G1-4, G1-5 and G1-6	Fit new parts as required. Lubricate ball joints. Set ball joints to ensure maximum travel
	Loss of lubricating oil from relay unit	Remove filler plug and check oil level. Check for damaged oil seals and joint washers	Fit new oil seals and joint washers as required. Replenish lubricating oil
	Swivel pins dry or partially seized	Check swivel pin poundage. Operation F1-10	Adjust and lubricate swivel pins as necessary
Rattle in steering column	Steering rocker shaft incorrectly adjusted or badly worn	Check steering box adjustment, Operation G1-8	Adjust or fit new parts as necessary
Vehicle pulls to one side	Incorrect camber	Check for settled road springs, worn shackle bushes or damage to front axle unit	Renew parts as necessary
	Incorrect or unequal castor or swivel pin inclination	Check front wheel alignment. Check for settled road springs or damage to front axle unit	Adjust wheel alignment and/or fit new parts as required
	Uneven tyre pressures or worn tyres	Check tyre pressures and wear condition, Section R	Fit new tyres and/or adjust pressures
	Dragging brake	Check brake adjustment, Section H	Adjust brakes
	Swivel pin tight	Dismantle and check swivel pins	Fit new parts as required, lubricate swivel pins on assembly
	Tight or dirty front wheel bearings	Remove hubs and check bearings	Fit new parts as required, pack hubs with fresh grease, r-fit and adjust hubs
	Incorrect toe-in of front wheels	Check wheel alignment, Operation G1-2	Adjust as necessary
Vehicle wanders	Incorrect tyre pressures or worn tyres	Check tyre pressures and wear condition, see Section R	Fit new tyres and/or adjust pressures
	Loose axle 'U' bolts	Check 'U' bolt fixings	Securely tighten
	Incorrect toe-in of front wheels	Check wheel alignment, Operation G1-2	Adjust as necessary

Fault diagnosis—Steering—continued

Symptom	Possible cause	Investigation	Remedy
	Tight steering box	Check adjustment, Operation G1-8	Adjust as necessary
	Worn front wheel bearings	Check front hub bearings and adjustment	Renew and/or adjust hub bearings as necessary
	Worn swivel pins and bearings	Dismantle swivel pin housings	Fit new parts as required, lubricate swivel pins on assembly
	Incorrect castor	Check for settled road springs, damage to front suspension and axle unit	Fit new parts as required
	Bent or broken chassis	Check alignment of chassis, Section J	Repair or replace chassis
Wheel wobble	(See notes preceding fault finding chart)		
	Steering column loose at dash	Check fixings	Securely tighten
	Incorrect tyre pressures or worn tyres	Check tyre pressures and wear condition	Fit new tyres and/or adjust pressures
	Eccentric wheels and tyres	Check the tyre concentricity line. Check wheel pressings for damage or distortion	Rectify or renew
	Worn or loose hub bearings	Check bearings and adjustment	Renew and/or adjust hub bearings as necessary
	Worn swivel pins and bearings	Dismantle swivel pin housings	Fit new parts as required, lubricate swivel pins on assembly
	Insufficient damping at swivel pins	Check poundage figure. Operation F1-10	Adjust as necessary
	Insufficient damping at relay unit	Dismantle relay unit	Fit new parts as required
	Loose engine mountings	Check fixings	Securely tighten
	Worn universal joint at axle half shaft	Remove axle half shafts and check	Overhaul universal joints
	Incorrect castor	Check for settled road springs, damage to front suspension and axle unit	Fit new parts as required

STEERING

GENERAL DATA

Type

Re-circulating ball
- Ratio: Straight ahead .. .. 15.6 : 1
- Full lock .. .. 23.8 : 1
- Inner column end-float .. .. Nil
- Rocker shaft end-float .. .. Nil
- Number of turns of steering wheel from lock to lock:
  - 88 and 109 models 3.3
  - 109 1 Ton model 3.75

DETAIL DATA

Relay shaft clearances in bushes .. .. .003 to .0045 (0,08 mm to 0,12 mm)

Longitudinal steering tube

Ball joints:
- Type .. .. Non-adjustable; ⅜ in. Whit (16 TPI) thread
- Tightening torque .. .. 30 lb ft (4 mkg)

Steering relay unit

Bushes:
- Type .. .. Tufnol cones

Spring
- Number of working coils 10
- Free length .. .. 7¼ in. (184 mm)
- Fitted length .. .. 3 in. (72 mm)
- Load at fitted length .. .. 104 lb (47 kg)

Wheel alignment
- Wheel camber .. .. 1½°
- Wheel castor .. .. 3°
- Swivel pin inclination .. .. 7°
- Toe-In .. .. 3/64 in. to 3/32 in. (1,2 mm to 2,4 mm)

SECTION H—BRAKING SYSTEM

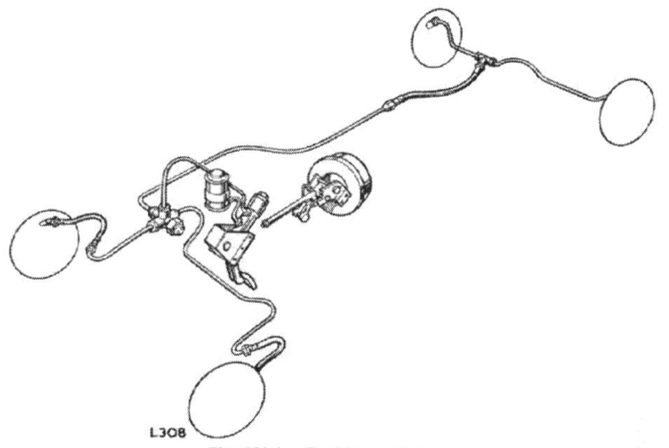

Fig. H1-1. Braking system

INDEX—BRAKING SYSTEM

Note: A comprehensive, detailed index is included at the end of this manual

Description	Operation Number
	At beginning of section
Exploded views and description	1
Bleeding the complete braking system	2
Adjusting the complete braking system	
BRAKE PEDAL ASSEMBLY	
Fluid reservoir	4-4A
Master cylinder	3
MASTER CYLINDER	
'CB' type cylinder	5-6-7-8
'CV' type cylinder	7-8
	5-5A-6-6A
BRAKE ANCHOR PLATES	
10 in. diameter—Front and rear	10
11 in. diameter—Front	10A
11 in. diameter—Rear (Series II)	10B
11 in. diameter—Rear (Series IIA)	10C
Transmission brake	11
Brake shoes	12
Flexible brake pipes	9
TRANSMISSION BRAKE	
Brake shoes	11
Hand brake lever and linkage	12
	13
SERVO UNITS	
Hydraulic type servo	14-15
Mechanical type servo	14A-15A
Exhauster for Diesel engines	16
FAULT DIAGNOSIS	At end of section
DATA	

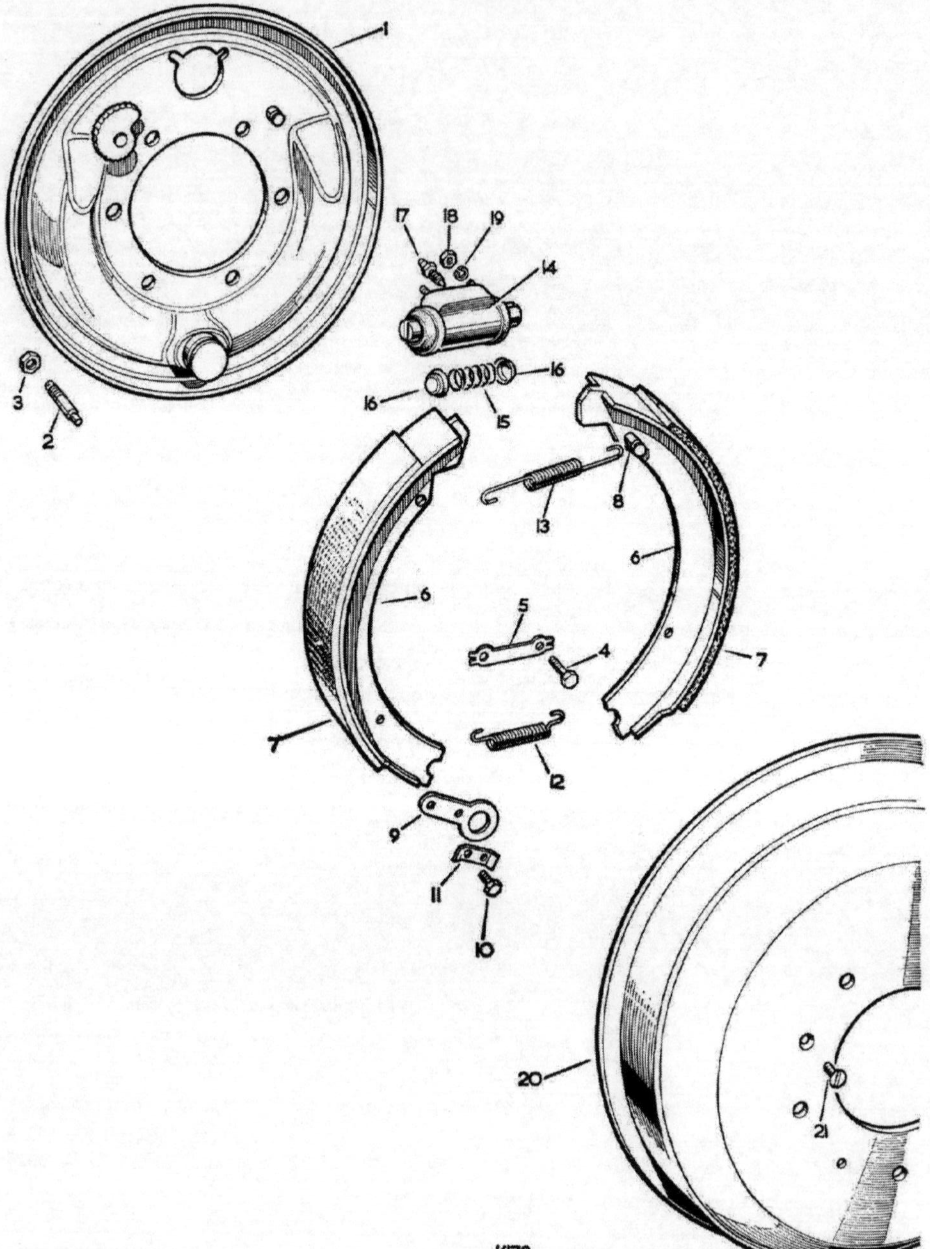

BRAKING SYSTEM

Key to illustration of front and rear wheel brakes, 10 in. diameter, 88 models

1. Brake anchor plate assembly
2. Shoe, steady post
3. Locknut for steady post
4. Set bolt (⅜ in. x 1 in. long) } Fixing front anchor plate to axle case
5. Locker
6. Brake shoe assembly, front and rear
7. Linings complete with rivets, for brake shoe
8. Spring post for brake shoe
9. Anchor for brake shoe
10. Special set screw, fixing anchor
11. Locking plate for bolt
12. Pull-off spring for brake shoe
13. Pull-off spring for leading shoe
14. Wheel cylinder assembly
15. Spring for piston, front
16. Washer for spring, front
17. Bleed screw
18. Special nut } Fixing wheel cylinder
19. Spring washer
20. Brake drum
21. Set screw, fixing brake drum

Fig. H1-2. Front and rear wheel brakes, 10 in. diameter, 88 models

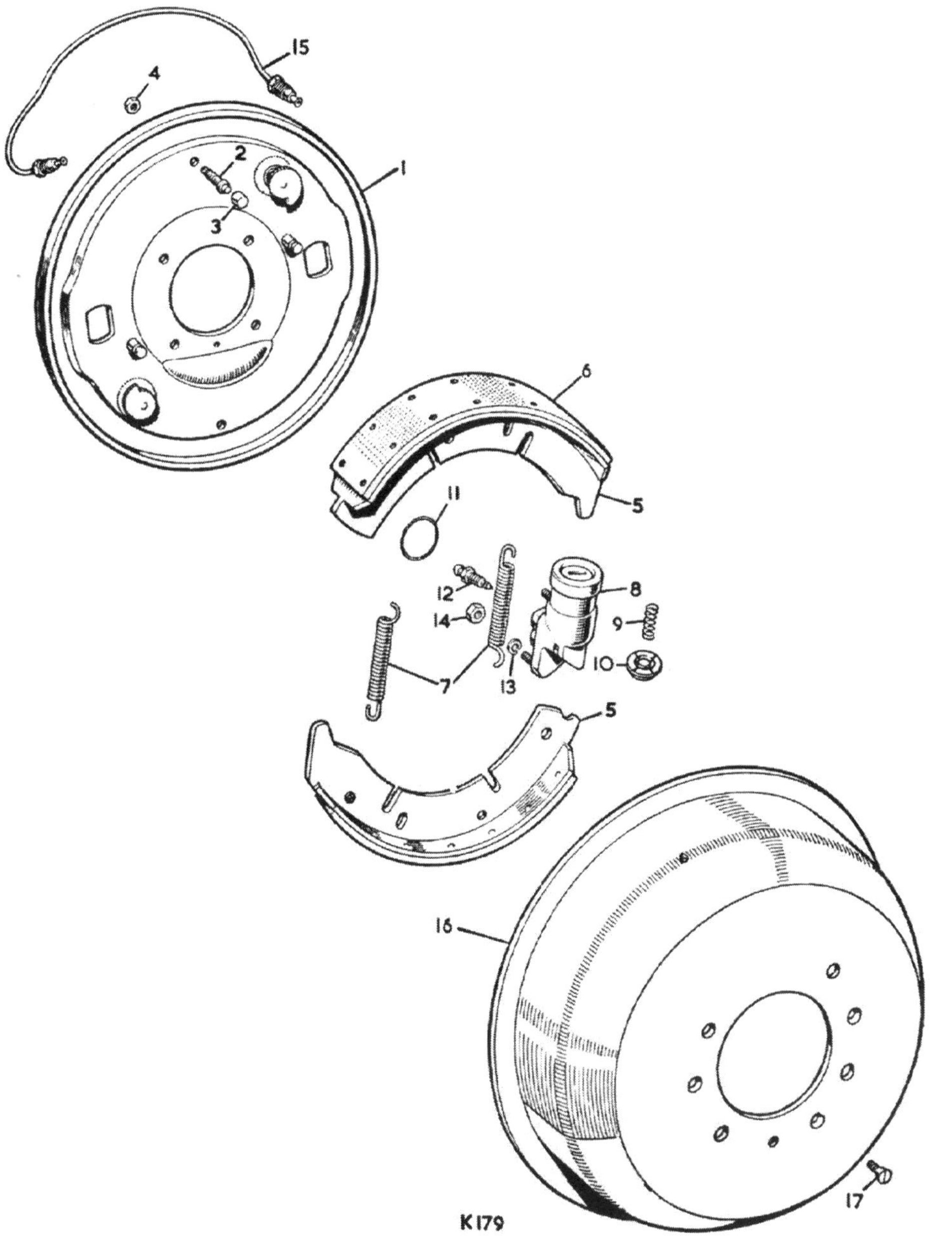

BRAKING SYSTEM

Key to illustration of front wheel brakes, 11 in. diameter, 109 2¼ litre models

1. Brake anchor plate
2. Steady post for brake shoe
3. Bush for steady post
4. Special nut, fixing steady post
5. Brake shoe assembly
6. Lining complete with rivets, for brake shoe
7. Pull-off spring for brake shoe
8. Wheel cylinder assembly
9. Spring (⅝ in. diameter) } For piston
10. Air excluder
11. Sealing ring for cylinder
12. Bleed screw
13. Spring washer } Fixing wheel cylinder
14. Special nut
15. Connecting pipe for wheel cylinder
16. Brake drum
17. Set screw, fixing brake drum

Fig. H1-3. Front wheel brakes, 11 in. diameter, 109 2¼ litre models

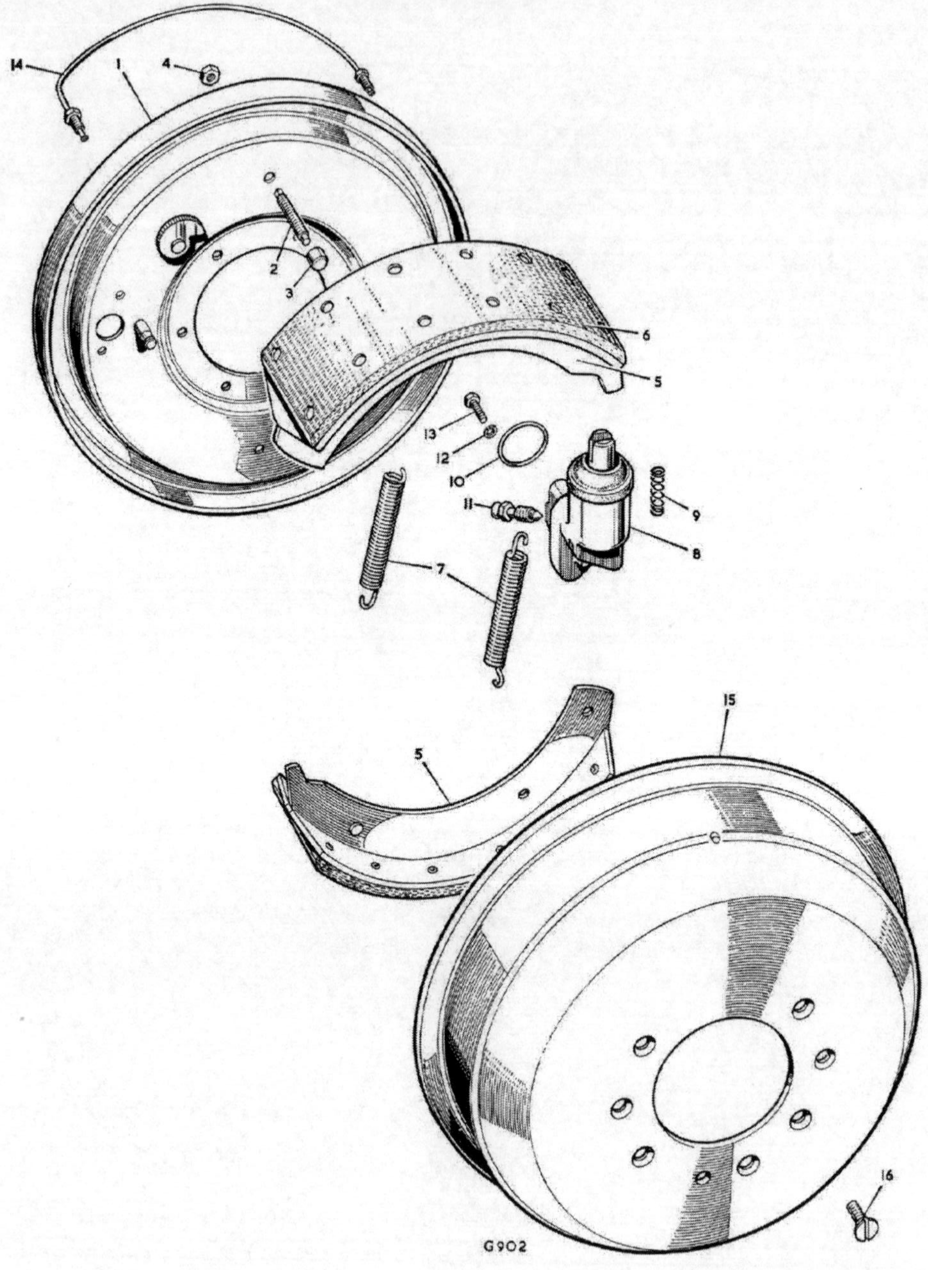

BRAKING SYSTEM

Section H—Land-Rover

Key to illustration of front wheel brakes, 11 in. diameter, 109 2.6 litre models

1. Brake anchor plate, LH front
2. Steady post for brake shoe
3. Bush for steady post
4. Special nut, fixing steady post
5. Brake shoe assembly
6. Lining complete with rivets
7. Pull-off spring for brake shoe
8. Wheel cylinder assembly
9. Spring
10. Sealing ring for cylinder
11. Bleed screw
12. Spring washer } Fixing wheel cylinder
13. Special set bolt }
14. Connecting pipe for wheel cylinder
15. Brake drum
16. Set screw, fixing brake drum

Fig. H1-4. Front wheel brakes, 11 in. diameter, 109 2.6 litre models

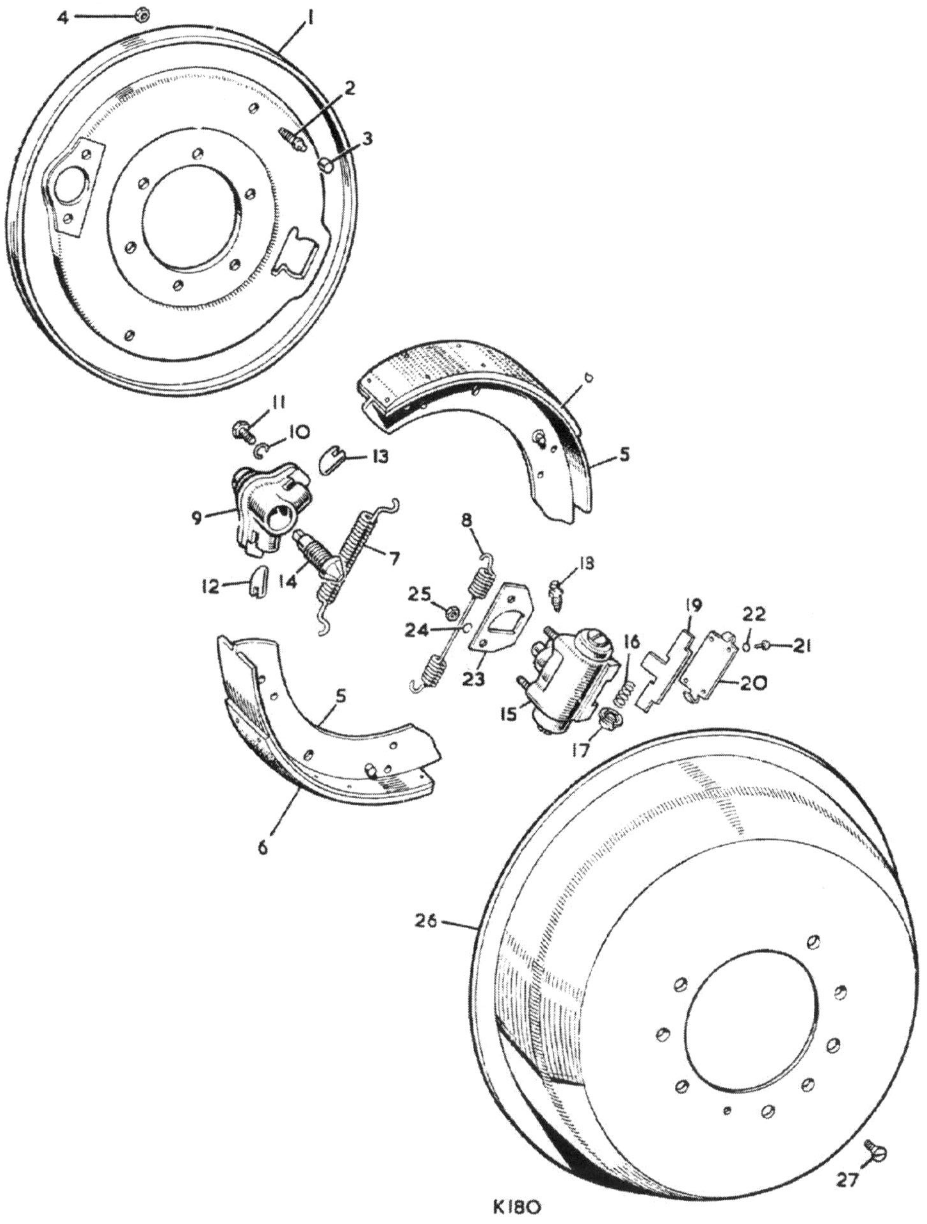

Section H—Land-Rover BRAKING SYSTEM

Key to illustration of rear wheel brakes, 11 in. diameter, 109 series II models

1. Brake anchor plate
2. Steady post for brake shoe
3. Bush for steady post
4. Special nut for steady post
5. Brake shoe assembly
6. Lining complete with rivets, for brake shoe
7. Spring, adjuster end ⎱ For
8. Spring, wheel cylinder end ⎰ brake shoe
9. Adjuster housing
10. Spring washer ⎱ Fixing
11. Special set bolt ⎰ adjuster housing
12. Plunger, LH
13. Plunger, RH
14. Cone for adjuster
15. Wheel cylinder assembly
16. Spring
17. Air excluder
18. Bleed screw
19. Brake shoe abutment plate
20. Retainer for brake shoe abutment plate
21. Screw ⎱ Fixing retainer and
22. Shakeproof washer ⎰ abutment plate
23. Dust cover plate for brake wheel cylinder
24. Spring washer ⎱ Fixing
25. Self-locking nut ⎰ wheel cylinder
26. Brake drum
27. Set screw, fixing brake drum

Fig. H1-5. Rear wheel brakes, 11 in. diameter, 109 Series II models

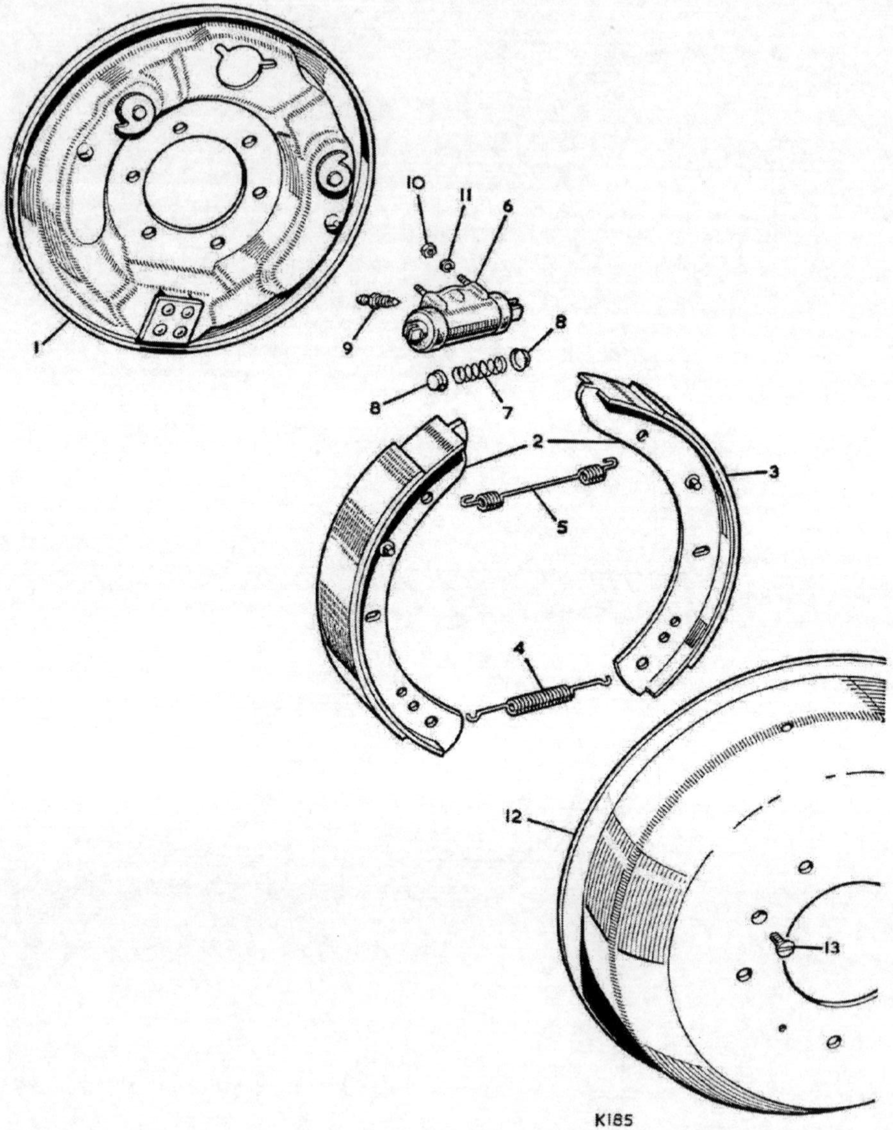

Section H—Land-Rover

BRAKING SYSTEM

Key to illustration of rear wheel brakes, 11 in. diameter, 109 series IIA models

1. Brake anchor plate
2. Brake shoe assembly
3. Lining complete with rivets, for brake shoe
4. Spring, abutment end } For brake shoe
5. Spring, wheel cylinder end
6. Wheel cylinder assembly
7. Spring for piston
8. Washer for spring
9. Bleed screw
10. Special nut } Fixing wheel cylinder
11. Spring washer
12. Brake drum
13. Set screw, fixing brake drum

Fig. H1-6. Rear wheel brakes, 11 in. diameter, 109 Series IIA models

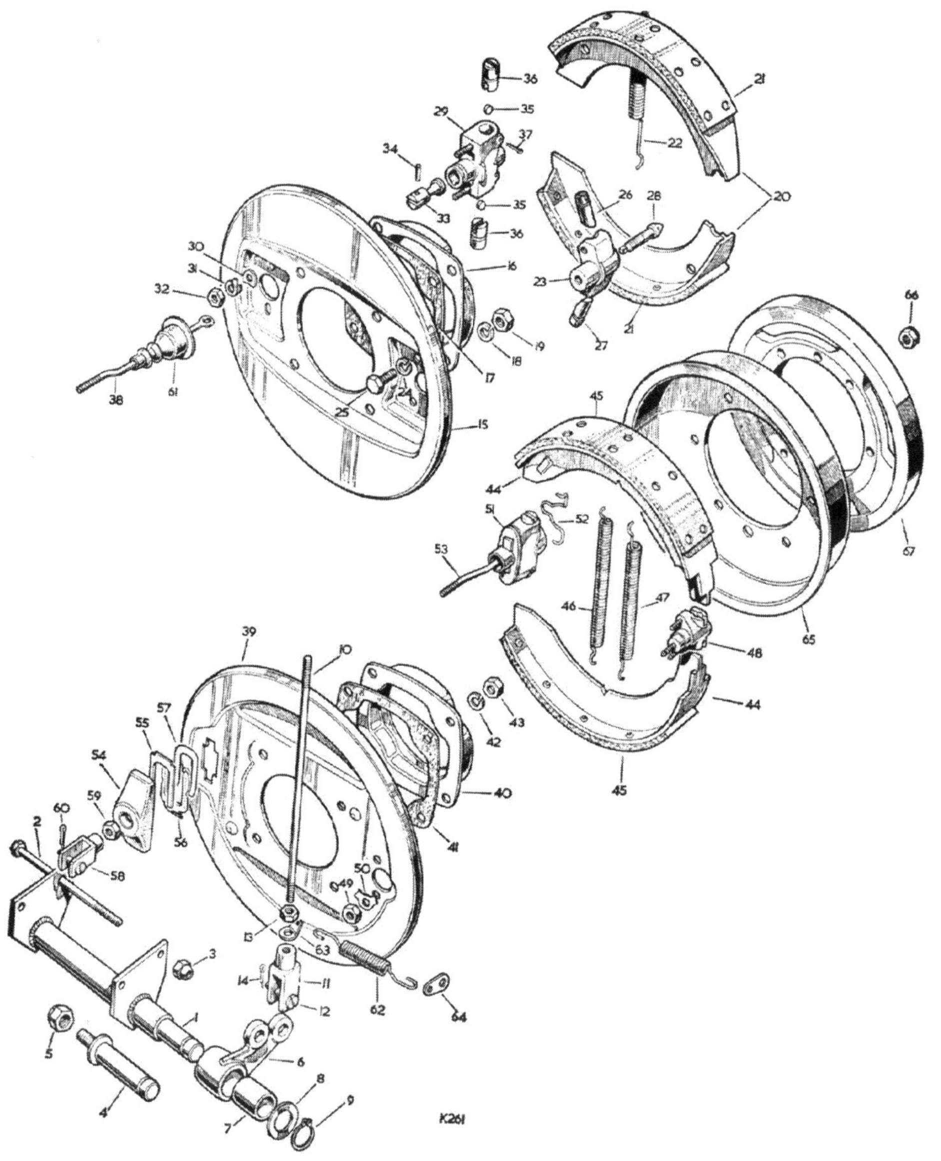

BRAKING SYSTEM

Key to illustration of transmission brake, 10 in. diameter, 88 and 109 models

1. Shaft for hand brake relay lever
2. Bolt (⅜ in. UNF × 4 in. long) — Up to vehicle suffix 'C' inclusive
3. Self-locking nut (⅜ in. UNF) — Fixing shaft to chassis frame
4. Shaft for hand brake relay lever
5. Self-locking nut (⅜ in. UNF) fixing shaft to chassis frame
6. Relay lever assembly for hand brake
7. Bush for relay lever
8. Plain washer — Fixing lever to spindle
9. Circlip
10. Brake rod, relay to hand brake lever
11. Clevis fork end — Fixing brake rod to relay and hand brake lever
12. Clevis pin complete
13. Locknut (⁷⁄₁₆ in. UNF)
14. Split pin
15. Anchor plate, transmission brake
16. Oil catcher for transmission brake
17. Joint washer for oil catcher
18. Spring washer — Fixing anchor plate and oil catcher to speedometer housing
19. Nut (⅜ in. UNF)
20. Brake shoe assembly, boxed pair
21. Lining complete with rivets for shoe
22. Pull-off spring for brake shoe
23. Adjuster housing
24. Spring washer — Fixing adjuster housing
25. Set bolt
26. Plunger, RH
27. Plunger, LH
28. Adjuster cone
29. Expander housing
30. Special washer — Fixing expander housing
31. Spring washer
32. Simmonds nut
33. Expander cone
34. Pin, fixing cone to brake rod
35. Roller for expander
36. Plunger for expander
37. Split pin, fixing plunger
38. Brake rod, expander to relay lever

{ Up to gearboxes numbered: 146000565 156000430 151005187 }

39. Anchor plate, transmission brake
40. Oil catcher for transmission brake
41. Joint washer for oil catcher
42. Spring washer — Fixing anchor plate and oil catcher to speedometer housing
43. Nut (⅜ in. BSF)
44. Brake shoe assembly, boxed pair
45. Lining complete for shoe, boxed pair
46. Pull-off spring, expander end — For brake shoe
47. Return spring, adjuster end
48. Adjuster unit assembly
49. Nut (¼ in. UNF) — Fixing adjuster unit
50. Tab washer
51. Expander unit assembly
52. Clip retaining tappets
53. Brake rod, expander to relay lever
54. Dust cover for expander unit
55. Packing plate
56. Locking plate
57. Retaining spring — Fixing expander unit
58. Clevis complete
59. Locknut (⁷⁄₁₆ in. BSF) — Fixing brake rod to relay lever
60. Split pin
61. Dust cover for brake rod
62. Return spring for brake rod
63. Anchor for spring
64. Anchor for spring, on transfer box
65. Brake drum
66. Self-locking nut (⁵⁄₁₆ in. BSF) fixing brake drum and damper
67. Transmission damper at rear end of gearbox

{ From gearboxes numbered: 146000566 156000431 151005188 onwards }

Fig. H1-7. Transmission brake, 10 in. diameter, 88 and 109 models

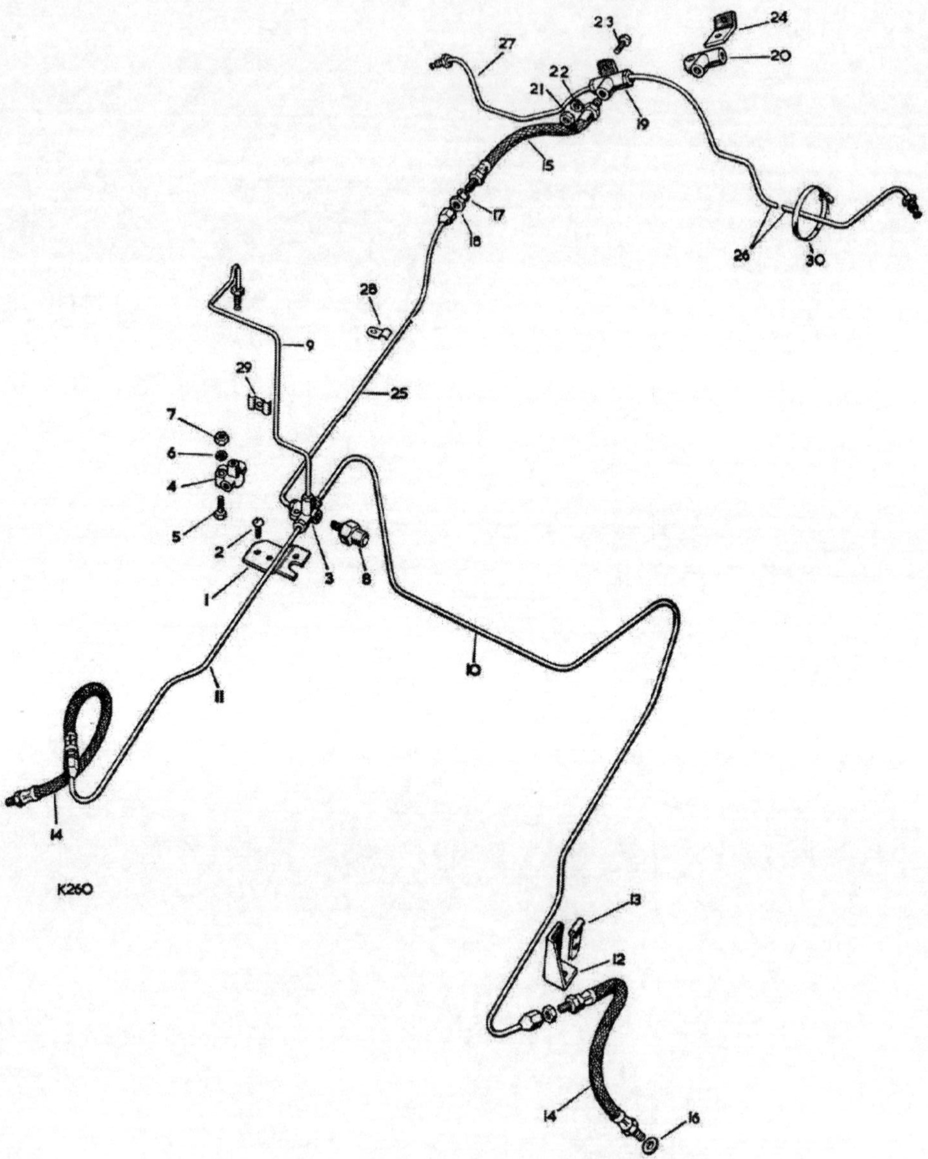

BRAKING SYSTEM

Key to illustration of brake pipes, 88 and 109 2¼ litre models

1. Bracket for junction piece
2. Drive-screw, fixing bracket
3. 5-way junction piece for brake pipes—Up to vehicle suffix 'E' inclusive
4. 4-way junction piece for brake pipes—From vehicle suffix 'F' onwards
5. Bolt (¼ in. UNF x 1¼ in. long) ⎫ Fixing junction piece
6. Spring washer
7. Nut (¼ in. UNF)
8. Stop lamp switch, hydraulic type—Up to vehicle suffix 'E' inclusive
9. Brake pipe, master cylinder to 5-way junction piece
10. Brake pipe, junction piece to LH front
11. Brake pipe, junction piece to RH front
12. Bracket for LH front brake pipe ⎫ 2¼ litre Petrol and Diesel models
13. Clip for LH front brake pipe
14. Hose complete for front wheels
15. Hose complete to rear axle
16. Joint washer for hoses
17. Shakeproof washer ⎫ Fixing hose to bracket
18. Special nut
19. 'T' piece on rear axle, Rover type axles
20. 'T' piece on rear axle, ENV type axle, 109 optional
21. Nut (7/16 in. UNF)
22. Spring washer
23. Bolt (7/16 in. UNF x ¾ in. long)
24. Bracket for 'T' piece, ENV type axle, 109 optional ⎫ Fixing 'T' piece
25. Brake pipe to rear hose
26. Brake pipe, LH rear to 'T' piece
27. Brake pipe, RH rear to 'T' piece
28. Clip, brake pipes to chassis frame
29. Clip, brake and clutch pipes to dash
30. Clip on rear axle for LH pipe

Fig. H1-8. Layout of brake pipes, 88 and 109 2¼ litre models

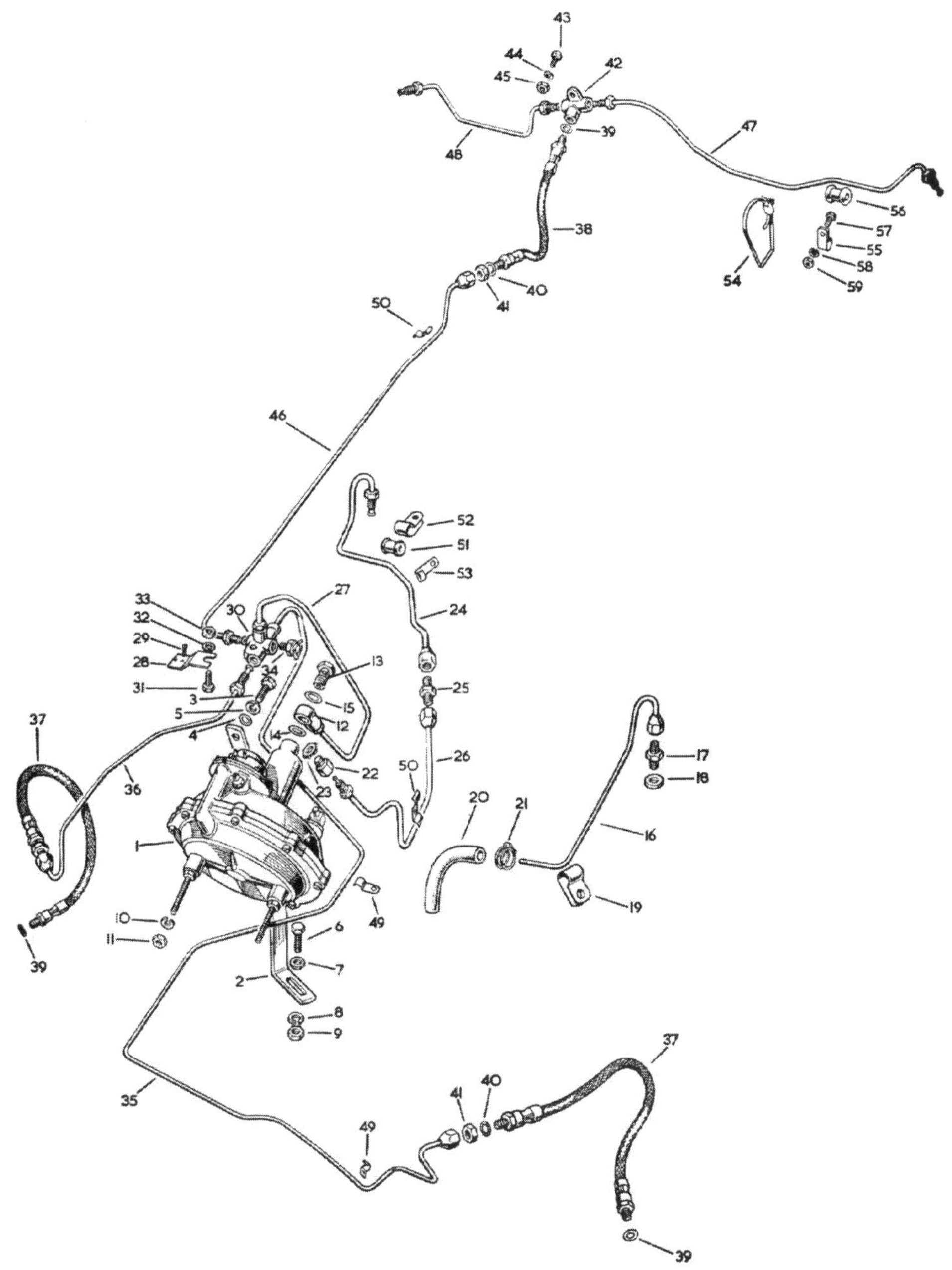

BRAKING SYSTEM

Key to illustration of layout of brake pipes and servo unit, 109 2.6 litre models

1. Brake servo unit
2. Support bracket for brake servo
3. Set bolt (7/16 in. UNC x 5/8 in. long) } Fixing servo to support bracket
4. Plain washer
5. Spring washer
6. Bolt (5/16 in. UNF x 1/2 in. long) } Fixing support bracket to chassis frame
7. Plain washer
8. Spring washer
9. Nut (5/16 in. UNF)
10. Spring washer } Fixing servo to air cleaner support
11. Nut (5/16 in. UNF)
12. Banjo for servo
13. Banjo bolt } Fixing banjo to servo
14. Gasket
15. Gasket
16. Pipe complete, inlet manifold to hose
17. Adaptor } Fixing servo pipe to inlet manifold
18. Gasket
19. Clip, fixing servo pipe to water outlet pipe
20. Rubber hose connecting manifold pipe to servo
21. Clip, fixing rubber hose to pipe and brake servo
22. Adaptor for servo pipe
23. Gasket for adaptor
24. Pipe complete, master cylinder to union
25. Union for pipe
26. Pipe complete, union to servo
27. Pipe complete, brake servo to 5-way piece
28. Bracket for 5-way piece
29. Drive screw, fixing bracket
30. 5-way piece for brake pipes
31. Bolt (1/4 in. UNF x 1 1/4 in. long) } Fixing 5-way piece to support bracket
32. Spring washer
33. Nut (1/4 in. UNF)
34. Stop lamp switch
35. Brake pipe, 5-way to LH front
36. Brake pipe, 5-way to RH front
37. Hose complete for front wheels
38. Hose complete to rear axle
39. Joint washer for hoses
40. Shakeproof washer } Fixing hose to bracket
41. Special nut
42. 'T' piece on rear axle
43. Bolt (5/16 in. UNF x 1/2 in. long) } Fixing 'T' piece
44. Spring washer
45. Nut (5/16 in. UNF)
46. Brake pipe to rear hose
47. Brake pipe, LH rear to 'T' piece
48. Brake pipe, RH rear to 'T' piece
49. Single clip, brake pipes to chassis frame
50. Double clip, brake pipes to chassis frame
51. Grommet
52. Clip } Fixing brake servo pipe to pedal bracket top cover
53. Clip, fixing brake pipe to steering box bracket
54. Clip on rear axle for LH pipe
55. Clip for bush
56. Rubber bush
57. Bolt (2 BA x 1/2 in. long) } Fixing LH axle pipe to chassis frame
58. Spring washer
59. Nut (2 BA)

Fig. H1-9. Layout of brake pipes and servo unit, 109 2.6 litre models

BRAKING SYSTEM

Bleeding complete brake system—Operation H1-1

(For brake adjustment instructions, Operation H1-2 refers)

Workshop hand tools:
Spanner sizes: ⁷⁄₁₆ in. BSF, ⁷⁄₁₆ in. AF, ⅝ in. AF open end
Girling brake adjustment spanner, Girling hose clamp (3 off)

General

The process of removing air from the pipe line and cylinders is known as 'bleeding' and is necessary whenever any part of the system has been disconnected, or the level of fluid in the supply tank has been allowed to fall so low that air has been drawn into the master cylinder.

When seals are worn it is possible for air to enter the wheel cylinders without any sign of leaking fluid and cause a 'spongy' pedal which is the usual indication of bubbles of air in the system.

Use of the Girling Brake Service Hose Clamp considerably facilitates the bleeding procedure by accurate diagnosis of the exact location of air in the system, therefore saving time by (a) locating the hydraulic fault, and (b) saving fluid when servicing the wheel cylinders.

Providing the brake hose is in reasonable condition, damage cannot be caused using the hose clamp, but the use of other tools to clamp the hoses is not recommended as damage may be caused internally to the hose without it being noticed externally.

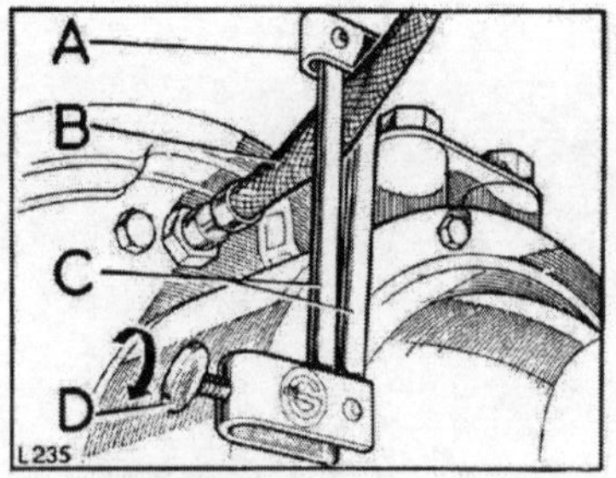

Fig. H1-10. Girling hose clamp

A—Pivot end of clamp
B—Flexible brake pipe
C—Rods
D—Clamp screw

If Girling hose clamps are available, release the clamp screw and fit the clamp so that the hose is between the rods at the pivot end, squeeze the rods together, apply the screw clamp and tighten.

With clamps fitted on the two front and one rear hose the pedal action should be perfect with no indication of 'sponginess'. If under these circumstances a spongy pedal is apparent, a new or overhauled master cylinder assembly must be fitted and bled and the test repeated.

Note: If the system incorporates servo assistance, the servo unit may also require replacement or overhaul, and must in any event be bled.

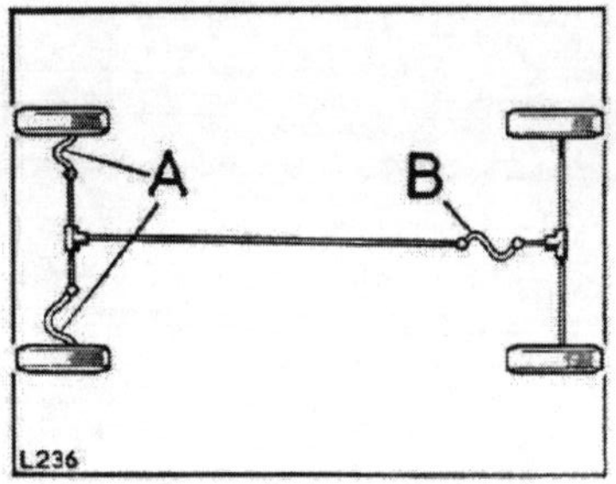

Fig. H1-11. Position of hose clamps

A—Hose clamps at front
B—Hose clamp at rear

If perfect pedal action is obtained with the appropriate three hose clamps in position, remove the rear clamp and if the pedal is spongy, the air must be in the rear cylinders. However, if the pedal action is good, remove first one then the other of the two front clamps, repeating the test until the air is located.

For wheel cylinder servicing only the appropriate hose need be clamped. This keeps the loss of fluid to a minimum and after the service is satisfactorily completed, only the affected parts require bleeding.

It is vital that absolute cleanliness is maintained throughout the entire bleeding operation. Never use a rag of linty texture and ensure that no dirt or grit enters the system—especially at the supply tank. All equipment to be used must be entirely free from petrol, paraffin, or any form of mineral oil, as mineral contamination spreads rapidly in the hydraulic system, causing a dangerous deterioration of the rubber seals.

Operation H1-1—continued

In extreme cases where it is difficult to expel the air from the system, it may be helpful if the front of the vehicle is raised so that the master cylinder is in a horizontal position whilst bleeding the brakes.

To bleed brake system

It is essential to observe strict cleanliness during this operation. Use only fluid of the recommended grade.

1. Check the fluid level in the reservoir and, if necessary, top-up with the recommended grade of fluid, see Section X. This level must be maintained during the operation of bleeding.

Always replace the rubber cap on each bleed-screw to prevent dirt entering the bleed tube during any subsequent bleeding operation.

Never, under any circumstances, use the fluid which has been bled from a system to top-up the supply tank as it may be aerated, have too much moisture content, and/or be contaminated.

There are three main variations of braking system in use, each requiring a different method of bleeding. Take care to identify the system concerned, which will have either a 'CV' (centre valve) or 'CB' (compression barrel) type master cylinder, while a third variant incorporates a servo unit in addition to one of the foregoing master cylinders.

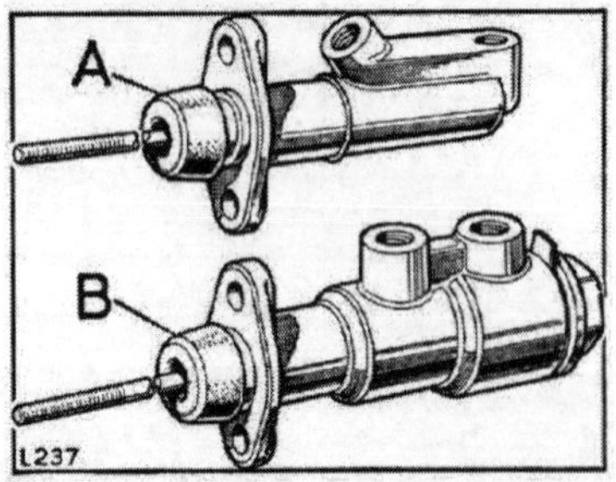

Fig. H1-12. Identification of master cylinders

A—'CV' type
B—'CB' type

Systems fitted with servo assistance

If the system is fitted with a servo unit of the hydraulic type, continue as follows. If the system is fitted with a servo unit of the mechanical type, coupled direct to the brake master cylinder, the servo unit requires no attention and the system must be bled as described for the 'CV' type master cylinder.

1. Do not start the engine before or during the bleeding operation. Residual vacuum in the servo should be destroyed by operating the brake pedal at least six times.

2. Release the pipe nut, a maximum of one turn, at the point where the servo outlet pipe is connected into the original braking system, and pull the pipe end clear of its seat in the fitting. Bleed by operating the brake pedal

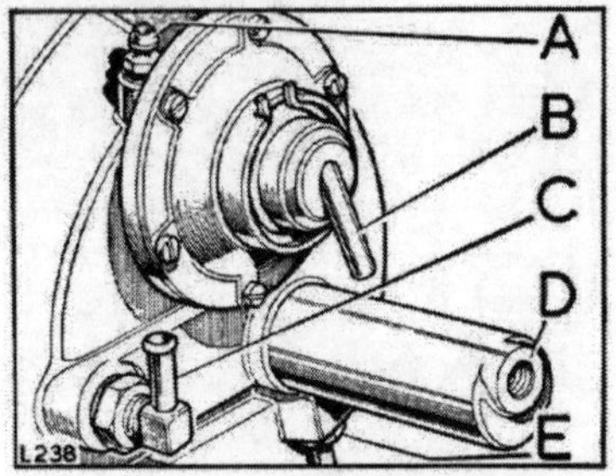

Fig. H1-13. Servo unit pipe connections

A—Brake fluid nipple
B—Air inlet from atmosphere
C—Vacuum hose connection
D—Fluid outlet pipe connection
E—Fluid inlet from master cylinder

IMPORTANT—Systems fitted with 'CB' type master cylinder

If a large proportion of the fluid has been removed from the system, it will be necessary to replenish with new fluid and if possible this should be forced in under pressure, i.e. approximately 14 lb/sq. in. (1 kg/cm²) using Castrol-Girling pressure-filling equipment.

Due to the angled position of the master cylinder, air tends to become trapped at the cap end, behind the seal. This is one of the reasons why it is beneficial to introduce fluid into the system under pressure. Whilst filling, slacken off the fluid outlet pipe connection on the master cylinder. This will help considerably in allowing the air to escape as quickly as possible.

Operation H1-1—continued

It is important that slow pedal movements are made, using only half to three-quarters of the pedal stroke. This will avoid aerating the hydraulic fluid.

4. Bleed until all air is expelled and tighten the pipe nut while the fluid is flowing. This will remove most of the air from the installation without pumping it through the whole system. Cotton waste or rag should be used to absorb waste fluid.

5. Loosen the bleed screw at the top of the servo unit and fit a rubber bleed tube, with the free end submerged in a container of clean brake fluid. Bleed until fluid free from air bubbles is emitted, then tighten the bleed screw at the commencement of a pedal stroke to ensure that air does not enter the system via the bleed screw. DO NOT overtighten—4 to 6 lbs ft (0,55 to 0,8 mkg) torque is sufficient and this can be applied with a short spanner.

All brake systems, continue as follows:

6. Completely slacken off each brake shoe adjuster on all four wheels, to minimise the wheel cylinder volume and reduce the possibility of air being trapped.

7. The system should now be bled commencing at the **wheel cylinder nearest to the master cylinder, continuing with the next nearest wheel cylinder**, so that the final unit is the furthest one away from the master cylinder. Bleed each wheel cylinder in turn as follows:

8. Slacken the bleed screw and fit a bleed tube, with the free end submerged in a container of clean brake fluid. This is to prevent the ingress of air to the system while it is being bled.

9. Operate the brake pedal as follows. If the system employs a 'CV' type master cylinder, the pedal should be pushed down through the full stroke, followed by three short rapid strokes and then the pedal should be allowed to return quickly to its stop with the foot right off. This action should be repeated until the air is dispelled at each bleed screw.

For the 'CB' type master cylinder the action is different; the pedal should be depressed slowly throughout the full stroke and allowed to return slowly; there should be a pause of three or four seconds and the movement repeated until the air is dispelled at each bleed screw.

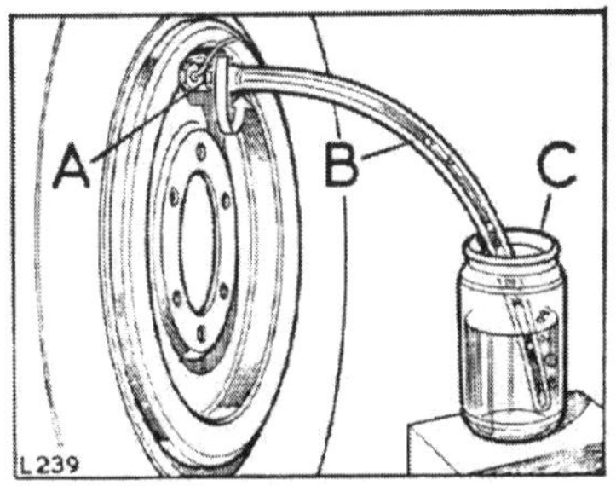

Fig. H1.14. Bleeding wheel cylinders

A—Bleed screw
B—Bleed tube
C—Fluid container

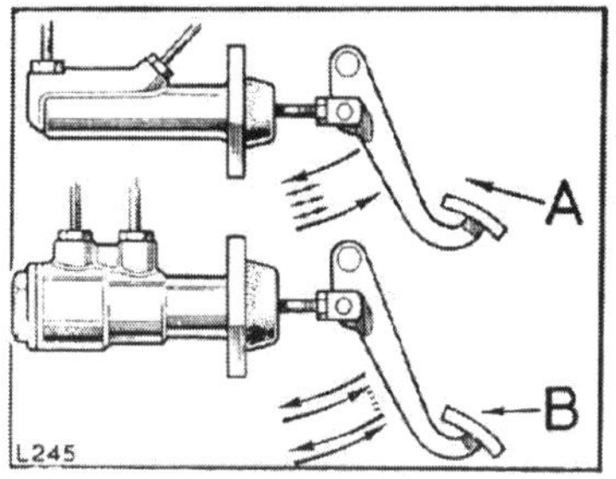

Fig. H1.15. Brake pedal action

A—'CV' type master cylinder
B—'CB' type master cylinder

10. On completion of bleeding each wheel cylinder, before removing the bleed tube, tighten the bleed screw at the commencement of a pedal stroke, to ensure that air does not enter the system via the bleed screw. DO NOT overtighten—4 to 6 lbs ft (0,55 to 0,8 mkg) torque is sufficient and this can be applied with a short spanner.

Note: Any floor mat or other object which may obstruct the full stroke of the pedal, should be removed.

Operation H1-1—continued

11. When bleeding has been completed, hold the brake pedal hard down and check all hydraulic connections and bleed screws for leaks. Fill the master cylinder reservoir to the correct level.

12. Adjust the brakes. Operation H1-2.

13. If the system is fitted with servo assistance:
Hold foot pressure on the brake pedal and start the engine. If the vacuum system is functioning correctly, the pedal will move towards the board. If no movement is felt, the vacuum system is not operating.
Finally, re-bleed the servo unit at the bleed nipple only, as already described.

Adjusting complete brake system—Operation H1·2

(For brake bleeding instructions, Operation H1·1 refers)

Workshop hand tools:
Spanner sizes: $\frac{7}{16}$ in. BSF open end, $\frac{7}{16}$ in. BSF
Girling brake adjustment spanner

General

There are two types of brake shoe adjuster in use; fulcrum type—operated by a square-end adjuster, and snail cam type—operated by a hexagon-end adjuster. Both types of adjuster being located on the rear face of the brake anchor plate.

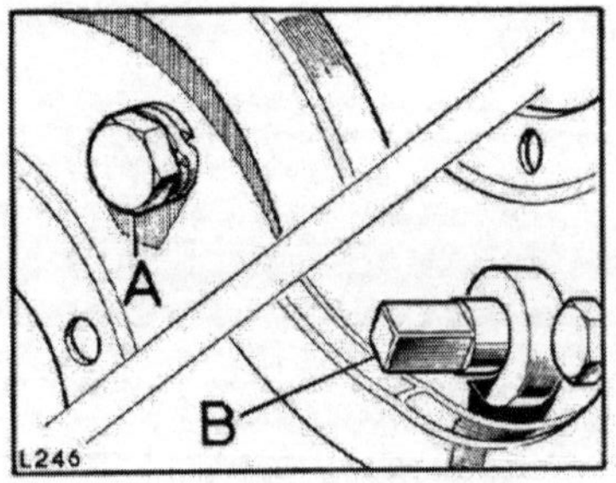

Fig. H1·16. Brake shoe adjusters

A—Snail cam type
B—Fulcrum type

Wheel brake unit, front and rear, 10 in. brakes—88 models

To adjust

Jack-up each wheel in turn. On the back face of the brake anchor plate will be found a hexagon adjustment bolt, which operates a snail cam bearing on the leading shoe. Only one of these is fitted to each wheel brake unit, thereby providing single-point adjustment. Spin the wheel and rotate the adjuster bolt until the brake shoe contacts the drum, then ease the adjuster until the wheel again rotates freely. Repeat for the other three wheels.

Front wheel brake unit, 11 in. brakes—109 models

To adjust

Each shoe is independently set by means of an adjuster operating through a serrated snail cam.

With the front wheels jacked up, ensure that the wheels rotate freely; slacken off the adjusters if necessary by turning anti-clockwise.

Turn the adjuster for each shoe clockwise until the shoe just brushes the brake drum, then slacken off two serrations.

Rear wheel brake unit, 11 in. brakes—109 models Series II

To adjust

The rear brake shoes are adjusted by means of a single adjuster assembly fitted at the lower side of the brake anchor plate which allows the shoes to expand or contract equally.

With the rear wheels jacked up ensure that they rotate freely; slacken the adjuster if necessary, by turning anti-clockwise.

Apply the foot brake to ensure that the shoes are bedded in and turn the adjuster clockwise until the linings brush the brake drum, then slacken adjuster off (anti-clockwise) two clicks.

Rear wheel brake unit, 11 in. brakes—109 models Series IIA

To adjust

Each shoe is independently set by means of an adjuster operating through a serrated snail cam.

With the vehicle jacked up, ensure that the wheels rotate freely; slacken off the adjusters if necessary, by turning anti-clockwise.

Turn the adjuster for each shoe clockwise, until the shoe just brushes the brake drum, then slacken off two serrations.

Transmission brake unit, 10 in. brakes—All models

To adjust

The transmission brake shoes are adjusted by means of a single adjuster assembly which allows the shoes to expand or contract equally.

Turn the adjuster cone until the brake shoes are locked tightly against the drum, then slacken off the cone two clicks; give the brake a firm application to ensure that the shoes have centralised at the expander end. The brake drum should now be free to rotate.

Set the hand brake linkage at the vertical adjuster rod, so that the hand brake has one or two clicks free movement in the 'off' position.

Fluid reservoir, remove and refit—Operation H1·3

(For removal and refitting instructions of the plastic type reservoir secured directly to the master cylinder, Operation H1·5A refers)

Workshop hand tools:
Spanner sizes: $\frac{7}{16}$ in. AF, $\frac{1}{2}$ in. AF open end
Screwdriver (medium)

To remove

1. Lift the bonnet and prop open.
2. Make provision to catch the fluid which will be released, then disconnect the brake and clutch outlet pipes from the fluid reservoir.

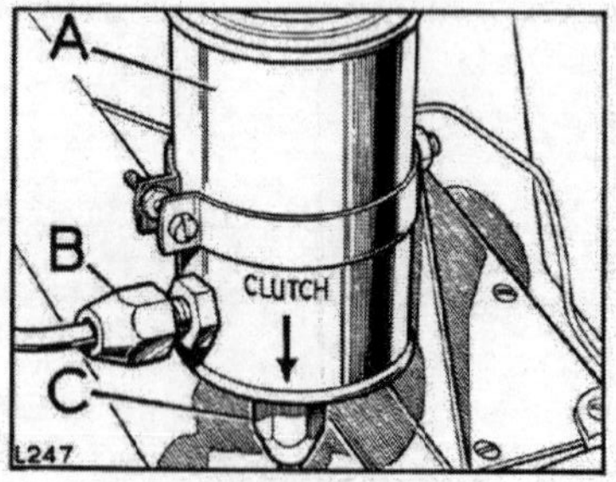

Fig. H1·17. Reservoir outlet pipes

A—Fluid reservoir
B—Brake outlet pipe
C—Clutch outlet pipe

3. Remove the fixings and withdraw the reservoir complete with clamp.

Fig. H1·18. Fixings for reservoir

A—Reservoir and clamp assembly
B—Mounting bracket
C—Fixings for reservoir

4. If required, remove the clamp from the reservoir.

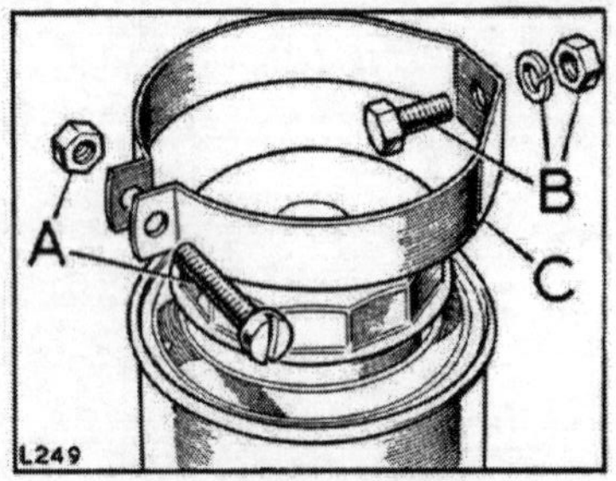

Fig. H1·19. Clamp for reservoir

A—Fixings for clamp
B—Fixings for reservoir
C—Clamp

To refit

1. If removed, fit the clamp and mounting bolt to the reservoir, but do not fully tighten the fixings until the reservoir is positioned on the vehicle.
2. Fit the reservoir in position and secure the fixing, see Fig. H1·18.
3. Connect the brake and clutch outlet pipes to the reservoir and secure the clamp fixings.
4. Replenish the reservoir, using Castrol-Girling Brake and Clutch Fluid.
5. Bleed the complete braking system. Operation H1·1.
6. Bleed the clutch system. Section B.
7. Close the bonnet.

BRAKING SYSTEM

Brake pedal, remove and refit—Operation H1-4

(For removal and refitting instructions for the brake pedal used in conjunction with the Girling mechanical type servo unit, Operation H1-4A refers)

Workshop hand tools:
Spanner sizes: $\frac{7}{16}$ in. AF, $\frac{1}{2}$ in. AF open end
Pliers, screwdriver (medium)

To remove
1. Remove the fluid reservoir. Operation H1-3.
2. Disconnect the inlet and outlet pipes from the brake master cylinder.

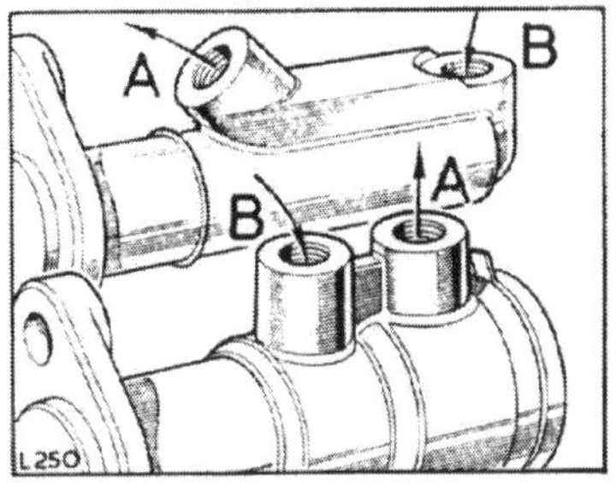

Fig. H1-20. Pipe connections at brake master cylinder

A—Outlet pipe
B—Inlet pipe

Note that connections differ between 'CV' and 'CB' type master cylinders

3. Disconnect the return spring from the brake pedal.
4. Remove the fixings securing the brake pedal bracket to the toe box.

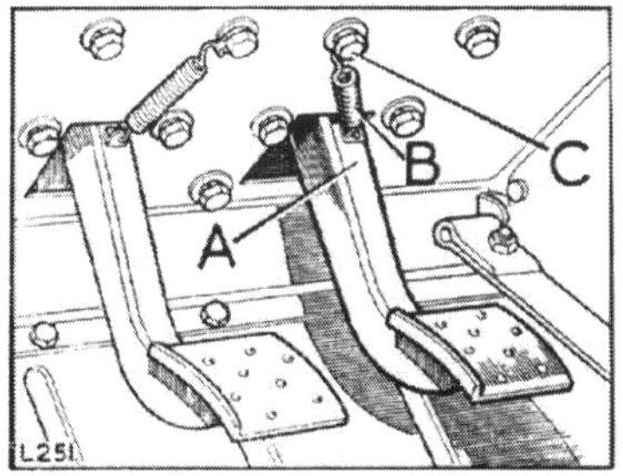

Fig. H1-21. Brake pedal bracket fixings

A—Brake pedal
B—Return spring for pedal
C—Fixings for brake pedal bracket (6 off)

5. Carefully withdraw the brake pedal and bracket assembly from the engine compartment, manoeuvring the pedal through the aperture in the toe box.

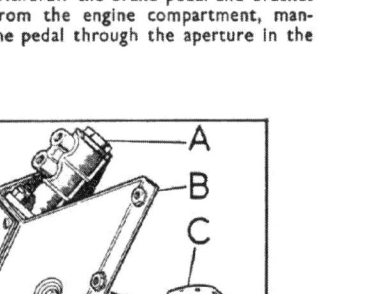

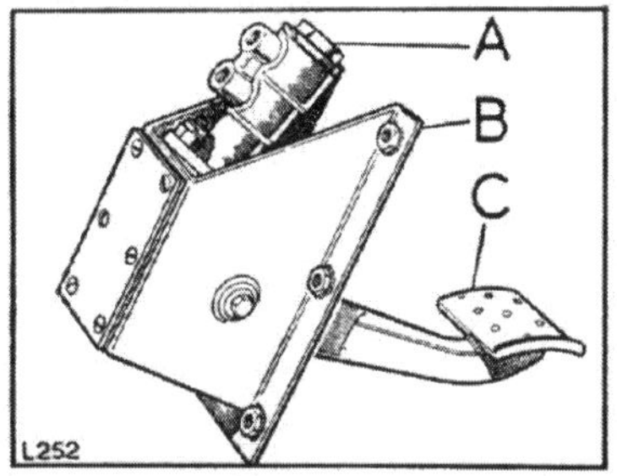

Fig. H1-22. Brake pedal and bracket assembly

A—Master cylinder
B—Bracket for brake pedal
C—Brake pedal

6. Remove the top cover and gasket from the brake pedal bracket.

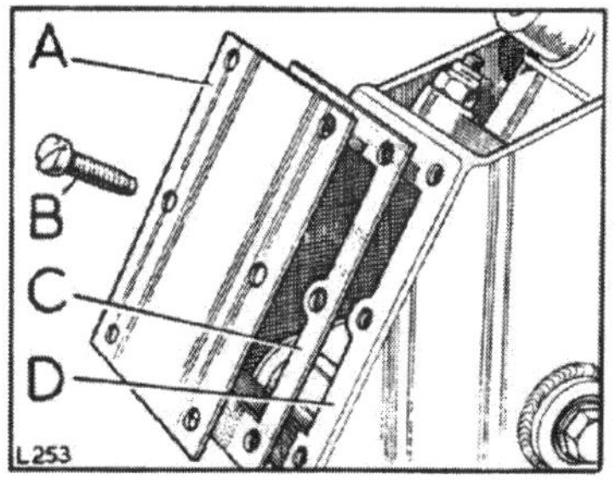

Fig. H1-23. Top cover for brake pedal bracket

A—Top cover
B—Fixings for top cover
C—Gasket
D—Bracket

Operation H1-4—continued

7. Remove the nut and plain washer retaining the master cylinder push rod to the brake pedal trunnion, and push the rod into the master cylinder to clear the trunnion.
8. Using a suitable punch, drift out pin, from the pedal shaft.
9. Remove pedal shaft.

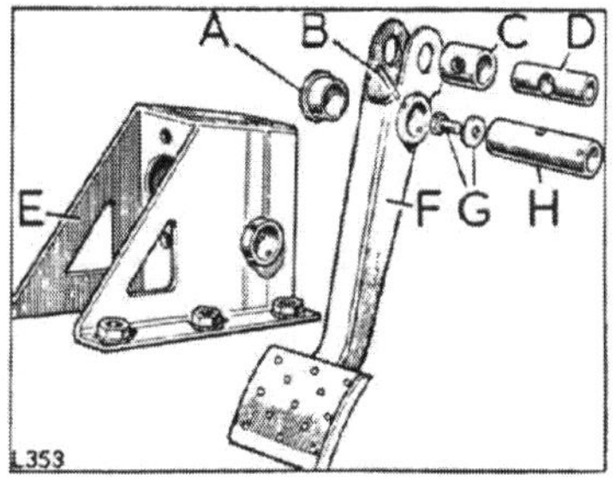

Fig. H1-24. Brake pedal assembly

A—Bush for pedal
B—Pin for pedal shaft
C—Distance piece
D—Trunnion for pedal
E—Bracket for brake pedal
F—Brake pedal
G—Oil plug and washer
H—Shaft for pedal

10. Withdraw the brake pedal complete with bushes and trunnion.
11. If required, remove the bushes, trunnion and distance piece from the brake pedal.

To refit
1. If removed, fit the distance piece, trunnion and bushes to the brake pedal. Lubricate the trunnion and distance piece with general purpose grease on assembly. New pedal bushes must be reamered to .750 in. + .001 in. (15,875 mm + 0,0254 mm).
2. Smear the pedal bushes and shaft with general purpose grease; locate the pedal in position in the bracket and secure with the shaft and pin.
3. Locate the master cylinder push rod through the pedal trunnion and fit the locknut and washer.
4. Remove the oil plug from the pedal shaft; fill the shaft bore with SAE 20 oil, then replace the plug and joint washer.
5. Place the gasket in position on the securing flange of the brake pedal bracket. If necessary, use a little Bostik adhesive to retain the gasket.
6. Carefully locate the brake pedal and bracket assembly in position on the toe box, manoeuvring the pedal through the aperture in the toe box.

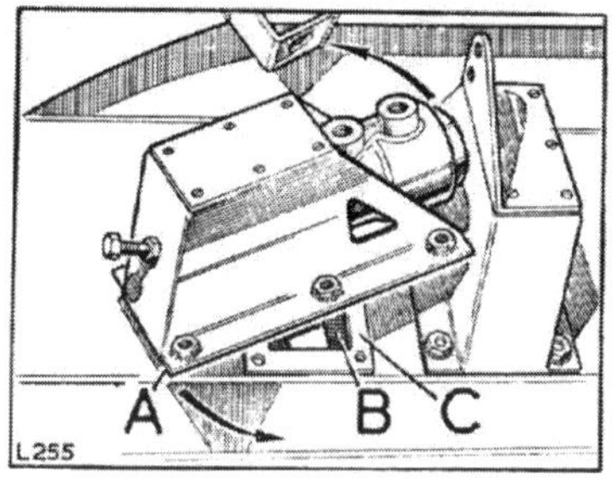

Fig. H1-25. Fitting brake pedal and bracket

A—Brake pedal and bracket
B—Aperture in toe box
C—Gasket

7. Secure the brake pedal and bracket assembly to the toe box, ensuring that the gasket remains in position. See Fig. H1-21.
8. Connect the return spring between the brake pedal and the toe box bracket.
9. Connect the inlet and outlet pipes to the brake master cylinder. See Fig. H1-20.
10. Fit the fluid reservoir. Operation H1-3.

BRAKING SYSTEM

Brake pedal (with Girling mechanical type servo), remove and refit—Operation H1-4A

(For removal and refitting instructions for the brake pedal used in all applications other than above, Operation H1-4 refers)

Workshop hand tools:
Spanner sizes: $\frac{7}{16}$ in. AF, $\frac{1}{2}$ in. AF, $\frac{5}{8}$ in. AF open end
Pliers, hammer, pin punch

To remove

1. Disconnect the electrical lead from the switch fitted to the pedal bracket.
2. Disconnect the outlet pipe from the master cylinder. Fit a blanking plug to the outlet aperture or drain the fluid reservoir, to prevent fluid spillage.

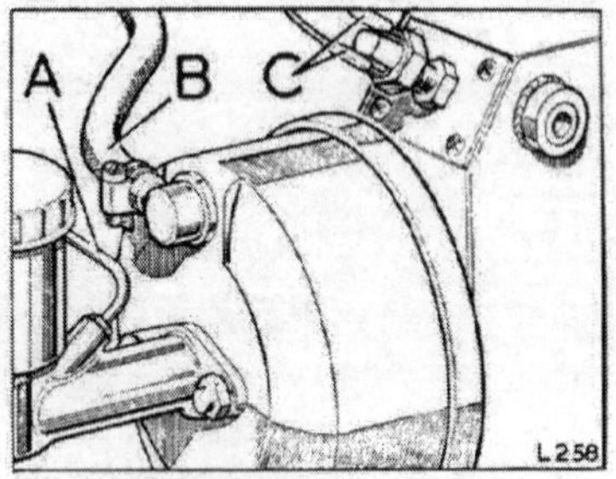

Fig. H1-28. Pipe and lead connections

A—Outlet pipe from master cylinder
B—Vacuum pipe from servo unit
C—Lead from brake switch

3. Disconnect the vacuum pipe from the servo unit.
4. Remove the fixings securing the brake pedal bracket to the toe box.

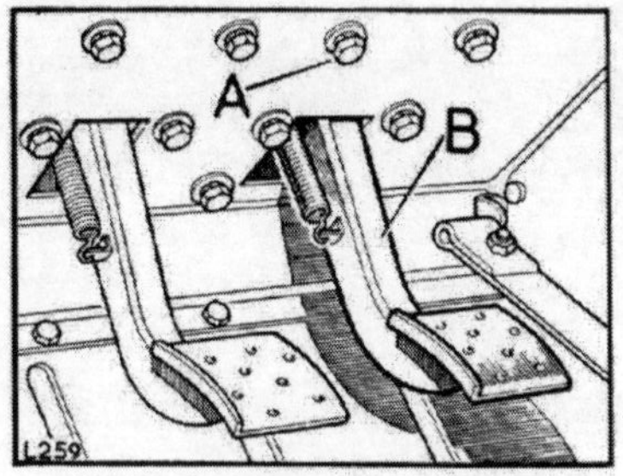

Fig. H1-29. Fixings for brake pedal bracket

A—Fixings (6 off)
B—Brake pedal

5. Carefully withdraw the brake pedal and bracket assembly from the engine compartment, manoeuvring the pedal through the aperture in the toe box.
6. Disconnect the brake pedal return springs.
7. Remove the split pin and pivot pin from the brake pedal to servo coupling.

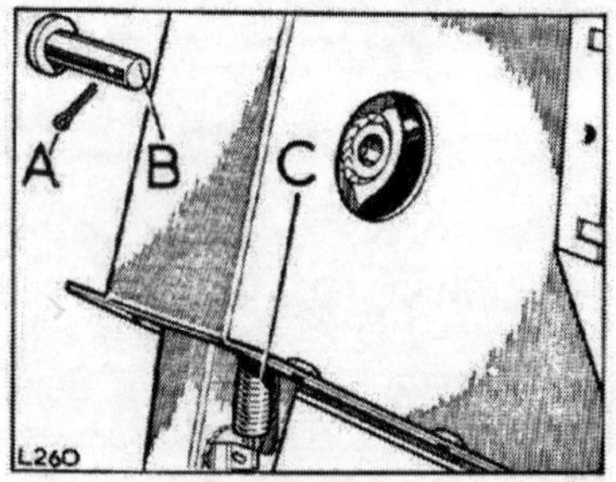

Fig. H1-30. Pedal return spring and servo coupling

A—Split pin, securing pivot
B—Pivot pin for coupling to servo
C—Return springs for brake pedal

8. Using a suitable punch, drift out pin from the pedal shaft.
9. Remove pedal shaft.

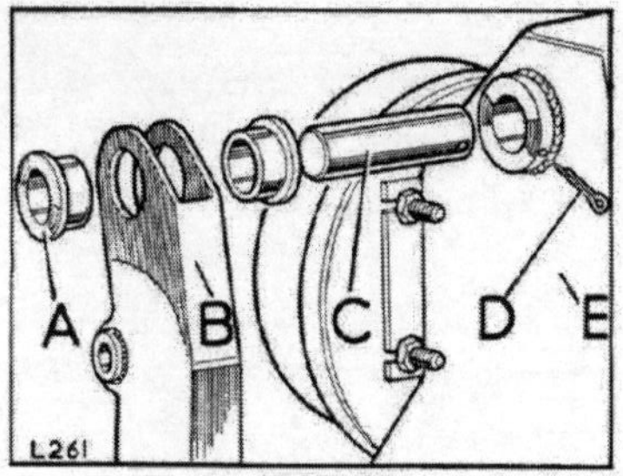

Fig. H1-31. Brake pedal assembly

A—Bush for pedal
B—Brake pedal
C—Shaft for pedal
D—Pin for pedal shaft
E—Bracket for pedal

Operation H1-4—continued

11. Slacken both locknuts on the master cylinder push rod, and adjust the push rod by rotating until there is $\frac{1}{16}$ in. (1.5 mm) free play between the push rod and master cylinder piston, then tighten both locknuts.

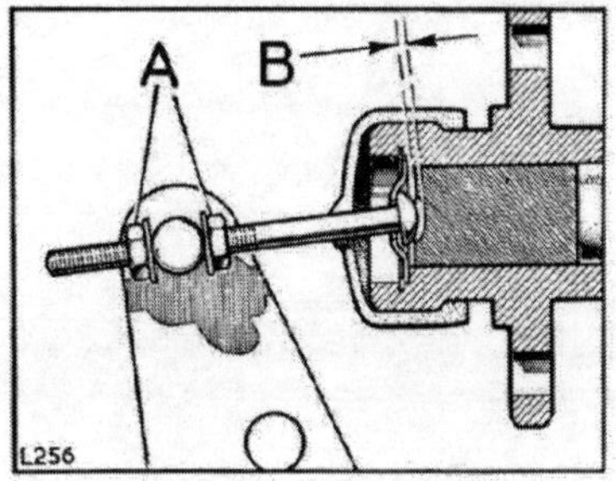

Fig. H1-26. Push-rod setting

A—Locknuts for push rod
B—$\frac{1}{16}$ in. (1.5 mm) free play

12. Bleed the complete braking system, Operation H1-1. Bleed the clutch system, Section B.
13. Re-check and, if necessary, adjust the push rod setting.
14. Fit the top cover and gasket to the brake pedal bracket, see Fig. H1-23.

15. **Brake master cylinder recuperation**

To ensure satisfactory recuperation of brake pedal, check the brake pedal height. The lower edge of the brake pedal should be $6\frac{1}{4}$ in. (158 mm) from the floor. Adjust pedal stop as required. Check brake pedal and ensure there is $\frac{1}{4}$ in. (6 mm) free movement in the brake pedal before pressure is felt. To obtain this it may be necessary to adjust the length of the master cylinder push rod. In addition, examine the trunnion distance piece to see if it is damaged due to crushing.

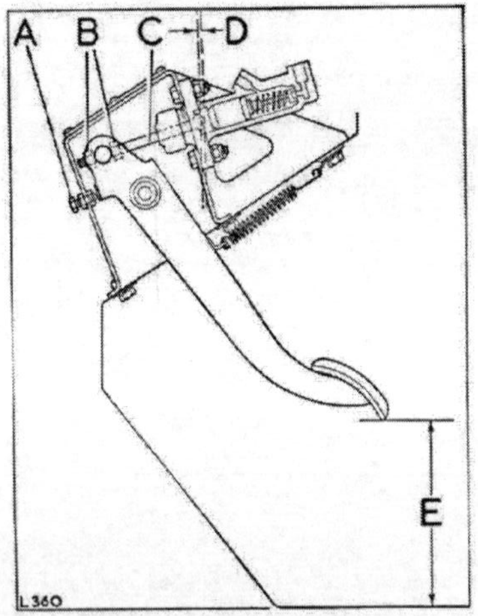

Fig. H1-27. Brake pedal setting

A—Pedal stop
B—Locknuts for master cylinder push rod
C—Master cylinder push rod
D—$\frac{1}{16}$ in. (1.5 mm)
E—Pedal height $6\frac{1}{4}$ in. (158 mm)

BRAKING SYSTEM

Operation H1-4A—continued

10. Withdraw the brake pedal complete with bushes.
11. If required, remove the bushes from the pedal.

To refit

1. If removed, fit the bushes to the brake pedal. New bushes must be reamered to .625 in. + .001 in. (15.875 mm + 0.025 mm).
2. Smear the pedal bushes and shaft with general purpose grease; locate the pedal in position in the bracket and secure with the shaft and pin.
3. Using a new split pin, fit the coupling pin between the pedal and servo unit.
4. Connect the pedal return springs.
5. Apply a waterproof sealant between the joint flanges of the pedal bracket and the toe box. A suitable sealant is 'Seelastrip', manufactured by Expandite Ltd, Chase Road, London NW10.
6. Carefully locate the brake pedal and bracket assembly in position on the toe box, manoeuvring the pedal through the aperture in the toe box, and secure in position. See Fig. H1-29.
7. Connect the vacuum pipe to the servo unit, the fluid outlet pipe to the master cylinder and the electrical lead to the brake pedal switch.
8. Check, and if necessary, adjust the brake pedal switch to operate at ¾ in. to 1 in. (19 mm to 25 mm) of pedal movement.
9. Bleed the complete braking system. Operation H1-1.

Master cylinder (centre valve 'CV' type), remove and refit—Operation H1-5

(For overhaul instructions, Operation H1-6 refers)

(For removal and refitting instructions for the master cylinder used in conjunction with the Girling mechanical type servo unit, Operation H1-5A refers)

Workshop hand tools:
Spanner sizes: 7/16 in. AF, ½ in. AF open end
Pliers, screwdriver (medium)

General

There are two types of master cylinder in use, and care should be taken to correctly identify the unit concerned. A cylinder of the centre valve ('CV') type is normally fitted to 88 vehicles, and a cylinder of the compression barrel ('CB') type is fitted to 109 vehicles. For removal and refitting instructions of the 'CB' type master cylinder, Operation H1-7 refers.

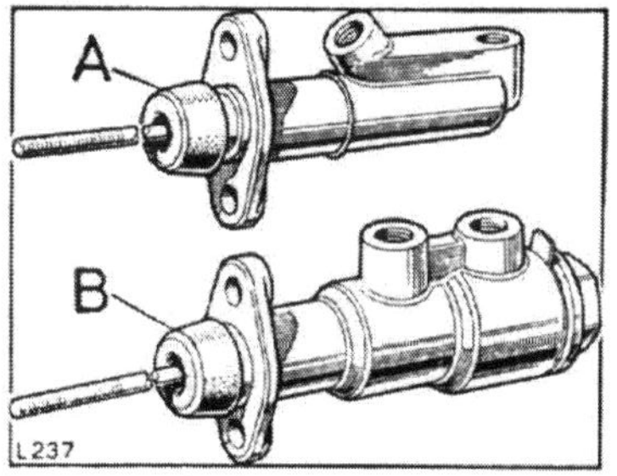

Fig. H1-32. Identification of master cylinders

A—'CV' type master cylinder
B—'CB' type master cylinder

To remove

1. Remove the fluid reservoir. Operation H1-3.
2. Disconnect the inlet and outlet pipes from the brake master cylinder.

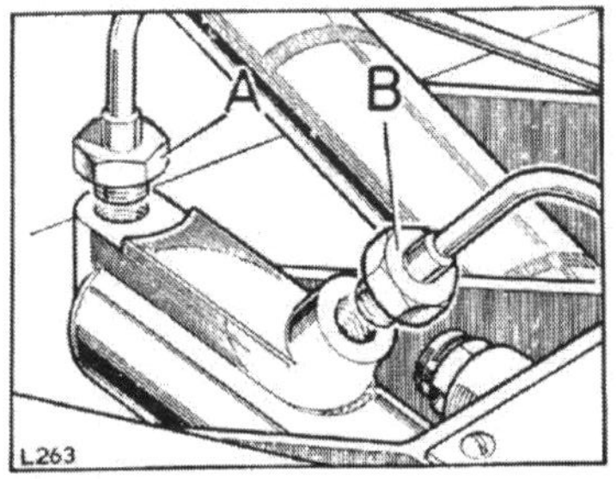

Fig. H1-33. Pipe connections at brake master cylinder

A—Inlet pipe
B—Outlet pipe

3. Remove the top cover and gasket from the brake pedal bracket.

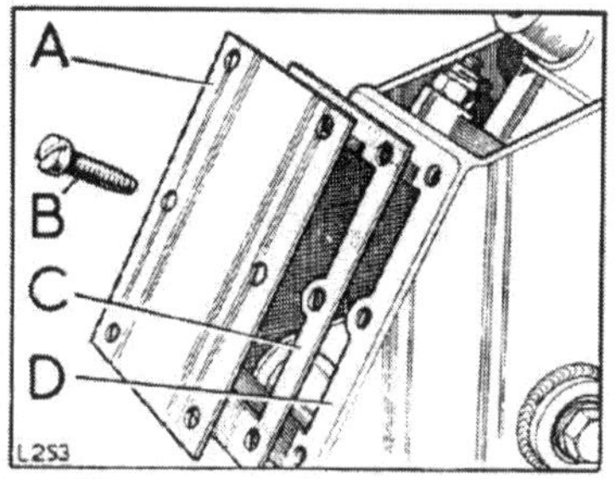

Fig. H1-34. Top cover for brake pedal bracket

A—Top cover
B—Fixings for top cover
C—Gasket
D—Bracket

4. Remove the nut and plain washer securing the master cylinder push rod to the brake pedal trunnion.
5. Remove the fixings and withdraw the master cylinder from the brake pedal bracket.

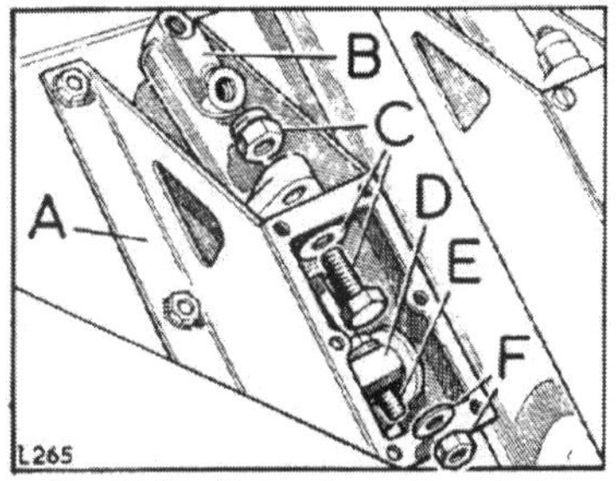

Fig. H1-35. Fixings for master cylinder

A—Bracket for brake pedal
B—Master cylinder
C—Fixings
D—Brake pedal trunnion
E—Push-rod
F—Fixings, push-rod trunnion

BRAKING SYSTEM

Operation H1-5—continued

To refit

1. Fit the master cylinder to the brake pedal bracket. See Fig. H1-35.
2. Connect the inlet and outlet pipes to the master cylinder. See Fig. H1-33.
3. Fit the fluid reservoir. Operation H1-3.
4. Slacken both locknuts on the master cylinder push rod, and adjust the push rod by rotating until there is $\tfrac{1}{16}$ in. (1,5 mm) free play between the push rod and master cylinder piston, then tighten both locknuts.
5. Bleed the complete braking system. Operation H1-1. Bleed the clutch system, Section B.
6. Re-check, and if necessary, adjust the push rod setting.
7. Fit the top cover and gasket to the brake pedal bracket. See Fig. H1-34.

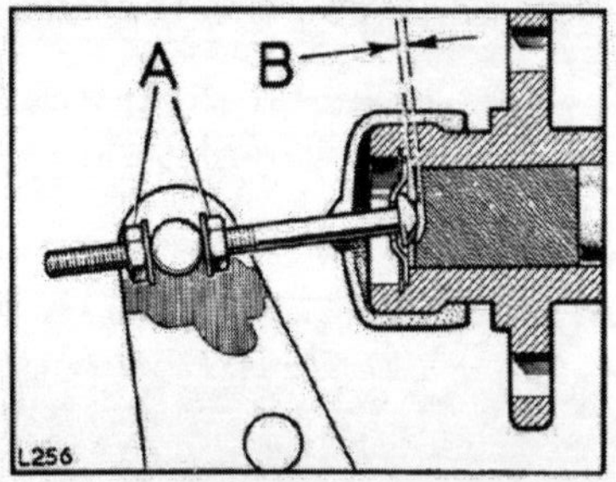

Fig. H1-36. Push rod setting
A—Locknuts for push rod
B—$\tfrac{1}{16}$ in. (1,5 mm) free play

Master cylinder ('CV' type with Girling mechanical type servo unit), remove and refit
Operation H1-5A

(For overhaul instructions, Operation H1-6A refers)
(For removal and refitting instructions for the "CV" type master cylinder used in all applications other than above, Operation H1-5 refers)

Workshop hand tools:
Spanner sizes: $\tfrac{1}{2}$ in. AF, $\tfrac{7}{16}$ in. AF open end, $\tfrac{3}{8}$ in. AF socket
Pliers, long-nosed

To remove

1. Lift the bonnet and prop open.
2. Disconnect the outlet pipe from the brake master cylinder.
3. Remove the fixings and withdraw the master cylinder complete with reservoir.
4. Remove the filler cap from the reservoir and drain all the fluid.
5. Using long-nosed pliers, withdraw the plastic cover from the reservoir adaptor bolt.
6. Remove the adaptor bolt and withdraw the plain washer, reservoir body, and seal. DO NOT attempt to remove the distance piece from the base of the reservoir.

To refit

1. Ensure that the fluid reservoir components are clean.
2. Smear the seal for the reservoir base with Castrol-Girling rubber grease and place it in position.
3. Locate the fluid reservoir in position on the master cylinder, and secure with the plain washer and adaptor bolt. Tighten the adaptor bolt to a torque figure of 20 to 25 lbs ft (2,8 to 3,5 mkg).
4. Push the plastic cover over the head of the adaptor bolt.
5. If removed, fit the gasket to the filler cap.
6. Fit the filler cap to the reservoir.
7. Fit the master cylinder and reservoir assembly to the servo unit. Tighten the master cylinder securing nuts to a torque figure of 16 to 19 lbs ft (2,2 to 2,6 mkg).
8. Connect the outlet pipe to the master cylinder.
9. Bleed the complete braking system. Operation H1-1.

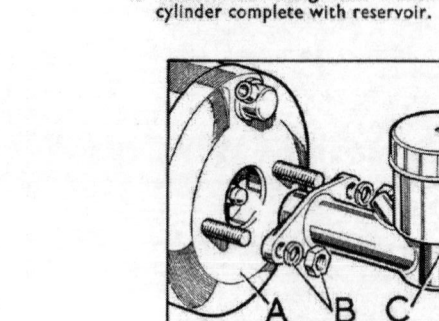

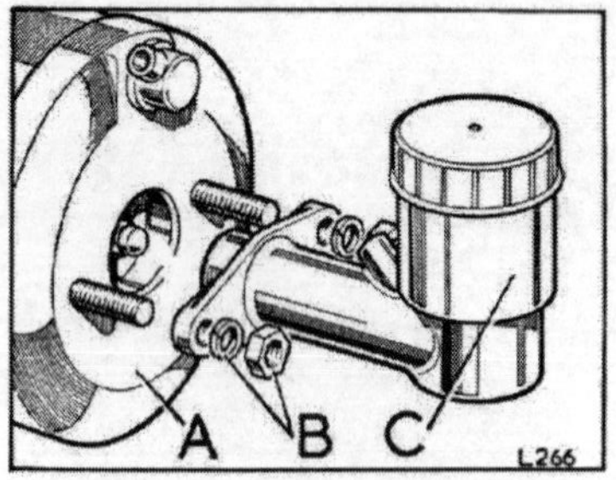

Fig. H1-37. Master cylinder fixings
A—Servo unit
B—Fixings for master cylinder
C—Master cylinder complete with reservoir

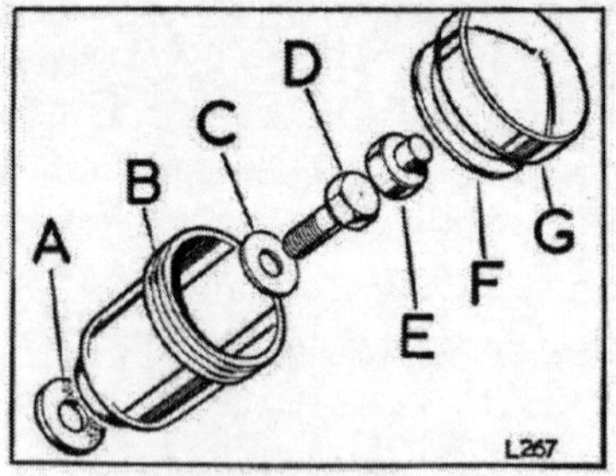

Fig. H1-38. Fluid reservoir
A—Seal, reservoir to master cylinder
B—Reservoir body
C—Plain washer
D—Adaptor bolt
E—Cover for adaptor bolt
F—Gasket for filler cap
G—Filler cap

BRAKING SYSTEM

Master cylinder (centre valve 'CV' type), overhaul—Operation H1-6

(For removal and refitting instructions, Operation H1-5 refers)

(For overhaul instructions for the master cylinder used in conjunction with the Girling mechanical type servo unit, Operation H1-6A refers)

Workshop hand tools:
Spanner size: ½ in. AF
Pliers, screwdriver (small)

General

There are two types of brake master cylinder in use, and care should be taken to correctly identify the unit concerned. A cylinder of the centre valve ('CV') type is normally fitted to 88 vehicles, and a cylinder of the compression barrel ('CB') type is fitted to 109 vehicles. For overhaul instructions of the 'CB' type master cylinder, Operation H1-8 refers.

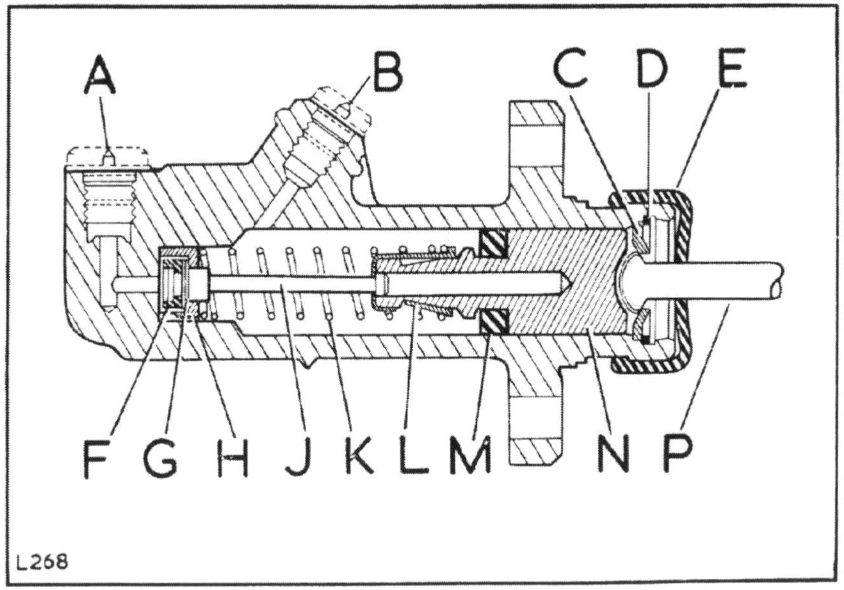

Fig. H1-39. Centre valve ('CV') type master cylinder

A—Inlet port
B—Outlet port
C—Spring washer
D—Circlip
E—Dust cover
F—Valve seal
G—Spring washer
H—Valve spacer
J—Valve stem
K—Return spring
L—Spring retainer
M—Piston seal
N—Piston
P—Push rod

Operation H1-6—continued

3. Withdraw the piston assembly from the master cylinder. If necessary, apply a low air pressure to the outlet port to expel the piston.

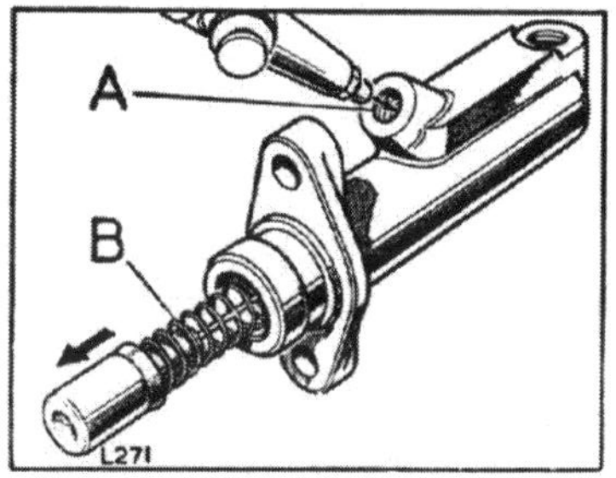

Fig. H1-42. Withdrawing piston assembly

A—Apply low air pressure to outlet port
B—Piston assembly

4. Prise the locking prong of the spring retainer clear of the piston shoulder and withdraw the piston. Remove the piston seal.

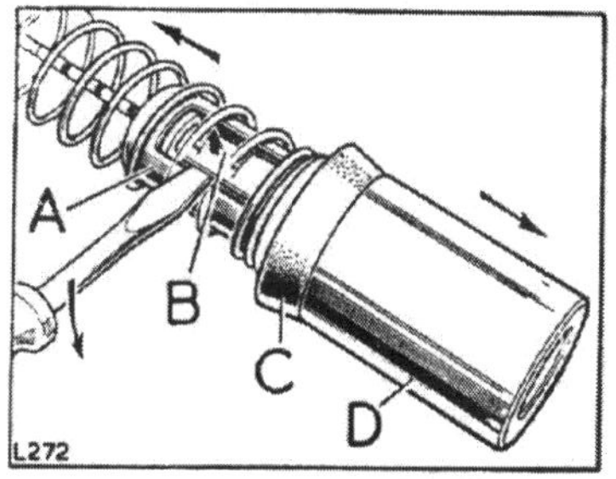

Fig. H1-43. Removing piston

A—Spring retainer
B—Locking prong
C—Seal for piston
D—Piston

To dismantle

1. Remove the plain washer, nut and rubber cover from the push rod.

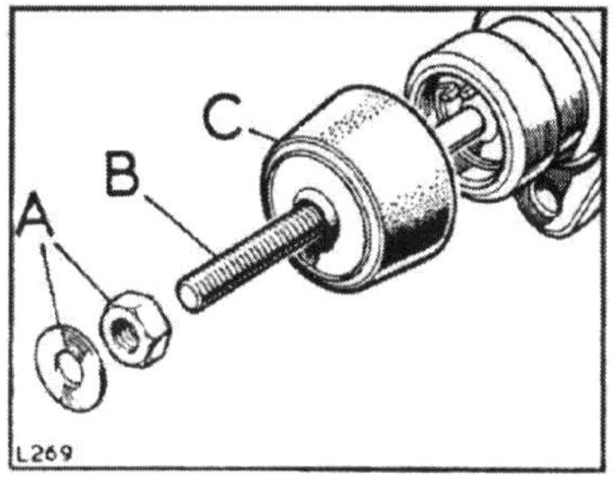

Fig. H1-40. Push rod cover

A—Locknut and washer
B—Push rod
C—Rubber cover

2. Remove the circlip and withdraw the push rod and retaining washer.

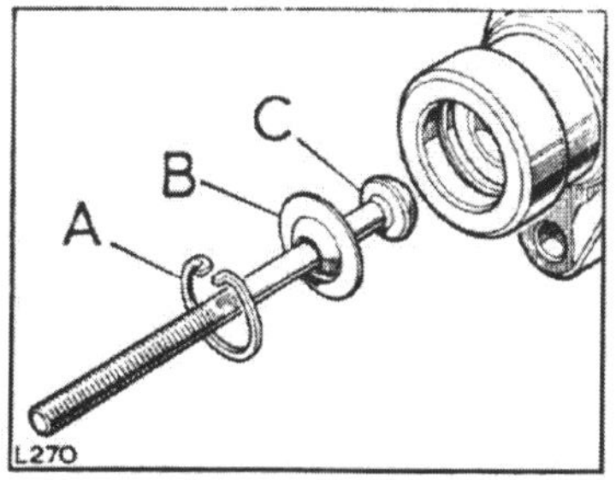

Fig. H1-41. Push rod fixings

A—Circlip
B—Retaining washer
C—Push rod

BRAKING SYSTEM

Section H—Land-Rover

Operation H1-6—continued

5. Compress the spring and position the valve stem to align with the larger hole in the spring retainer. Withdraw the spring and retainer.

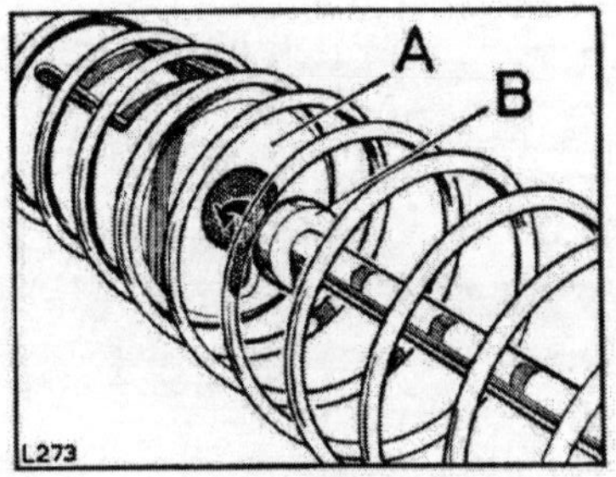

Fig. H1-44. Valve stem to spring retainer location

A—Spring retainer
B—Valve stem

6. Slide the valve spacer over the valve stem. Remove the spring washer and valve seal from the stem.

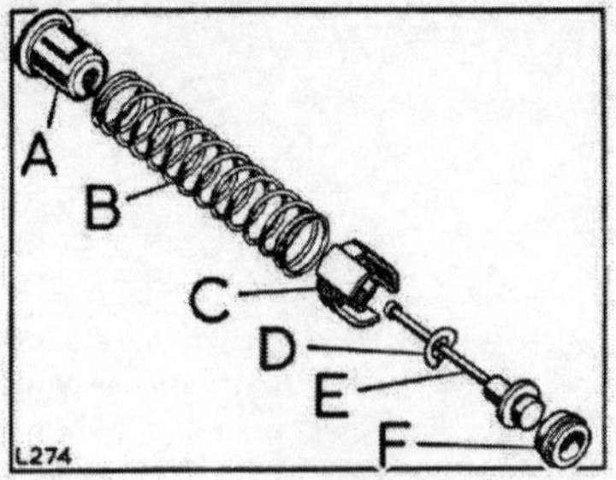

Fig. H1-45. Spring and valve assembly

A—Spring retainer
B—Spring
C—Valve spacer
D—Spring washer
E—Valve stem
F—Valve seal

Inspection

1. Clean all components in Girling cleaning fluid and allow to dry.
2. Examine the cylinder bore and piston, ensure that they are smooth to the touch with no corrosion, score marks or ridges. If there is any doubt, fit new replacements.
3. The seals and dust cover should be replaced with new components. These items are all included in the master cylinder overhaul kit.

To assemble

1. Smear the seals with Castrol-Girling rubber grease and the remaining internal items with Castrol-Girling Brake and Clutch Fluid.
2. Fit the valve seal, flat side first, to the end of the valve stem.
3. Place the spring washer, domed side first, over the small end of the valve stem, then fit the valve spacer, legs first, and the coil spring.

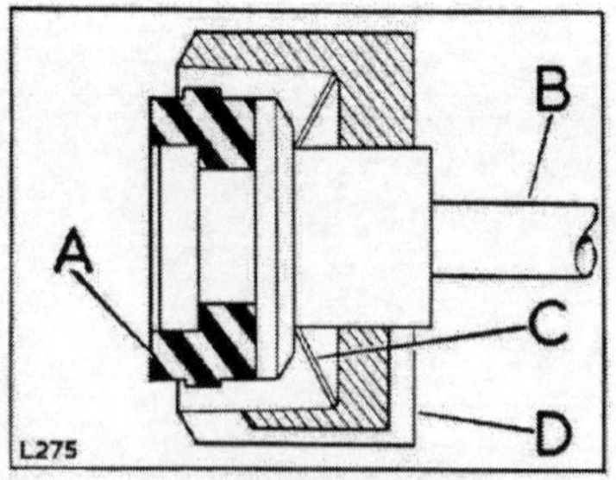

Fig. H1-46. Valve assembly

A—Valve seal
B—Valve stem
C—Spring washer
D—Valve spacer

4. Insert the retainer into the spring and compress until the stem passes through the keyhole and is engaged in the centre. See Fig. H1-44.

BRAKING SYSTEM

Section H—Land-Rover

Operation H1-6—continued

5. Fit the seal, large diameter last, to the piston.
6. Insert the piston into the spring retainer and engage the locking prong.

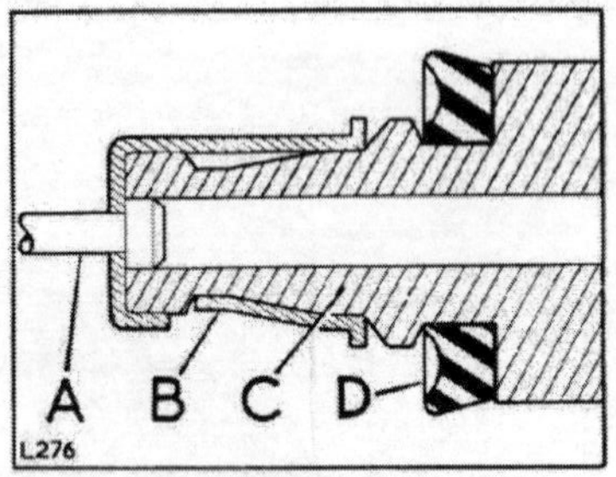

Fig. H1-47. Piston and spring retainer

A—Valve stem
B—Prong in engaged position
C—Piston
D—Seal

7. Smear the piston with Castrol-Girling rubber grease and insert the assembly, valve end first, into the cylinder.
8. Fit the push rod, retaining washer and circlip.

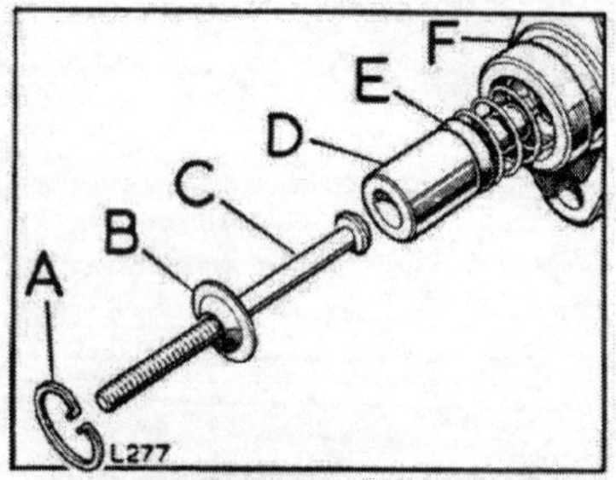

Fig. H1-48. Piston and push rod assembly

A—Circlip
B—Retaining washer
C—Push rod
D—Piston
E—Seal for piston
F—Cylinder

9. Smear liberally the inside of the dust cover with Castrol-Girling rubber grease and fit the cover over the push rod and cylinder.
10. Fit the locknut and washer to the push rod.

BRAKING SYSTEM

Master cylinder ('CV' type with Girling mechanical type servo unit), to overhaul
Operation H1-6A

(For removal and refitting instructions, Operation H1-5A refers)

(For overhaul instructions for the 'CV' type master cylinder used in all applications other than above, Operation H1-6 refers)

Workshop hand tools:
Screwdriver (small)

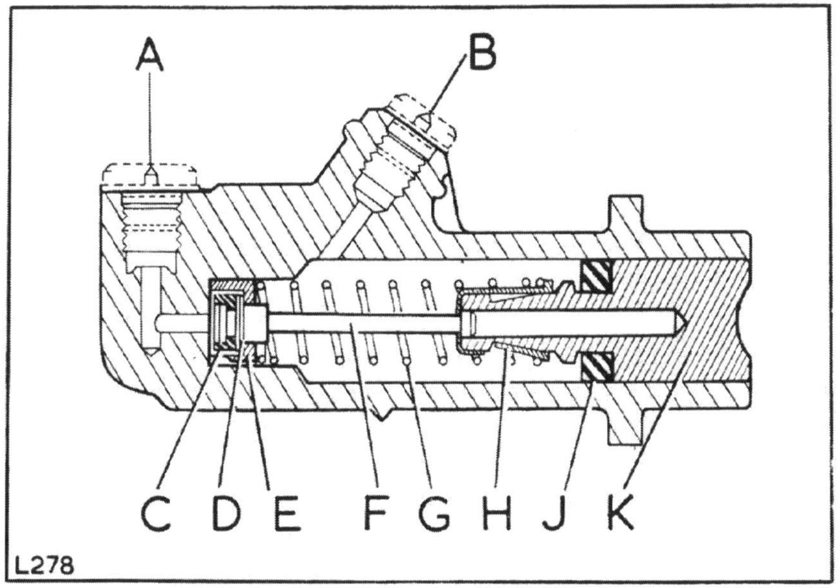

Fig. H1-49. Brake master cylinder components

A—Inlet port
B—Outlet port
C—Valve seal
D—Spring washer
E—Valve spacer
F—Valve stem
G—Return spring
H—Spring retainer
J—Piston seal
K—Piston

Operation H1-6A—*continued*

To dismantle

1. Withdraw the piston assembly from the master cylinder. If necessary, apply a low air pressure to the outlet port to expel the piston.

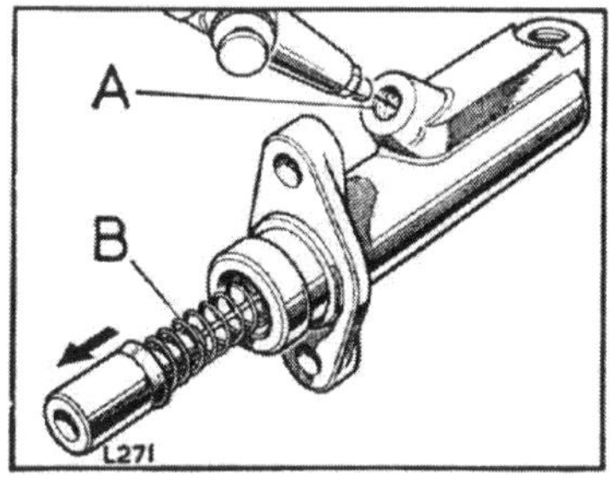

Fig. H1-50. Withdrawing piston assembly

A—Apply low air pressure to outlet port
B—Piston assembly

2. Prise the locking prong of the spring retainer clear of the piston shoulder and withdraw the piston. Remove the piston seal.

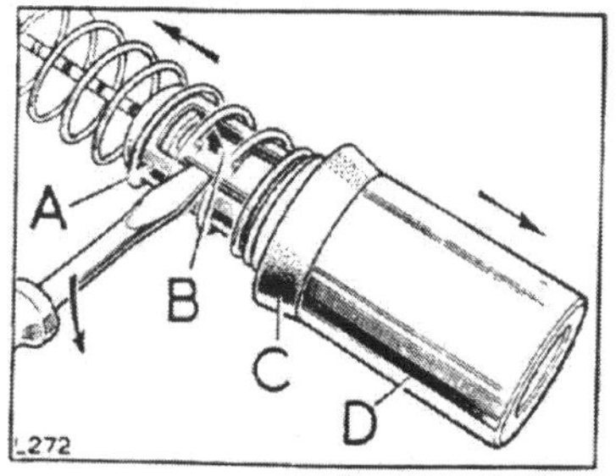

Fig. H1-51. Removing piston

A—Spring retainer
B—Locking prong
C—Seal for piston
D—Piston

3. Compress the spring and position the valve stem to align with the larger hole in the spring retainer. Withdraw the spring and retainer.

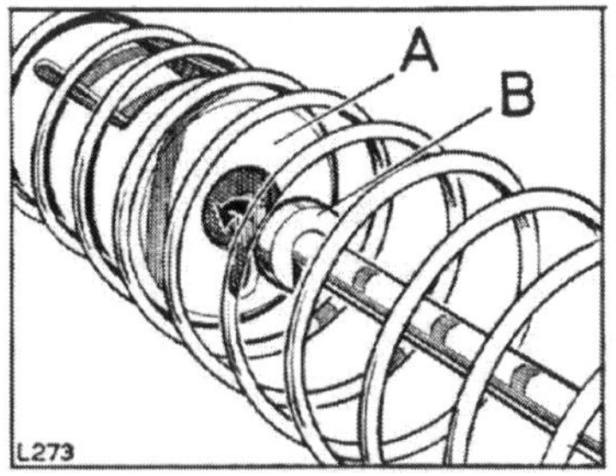

Fig. H1-52. Valve stem to spring retainer location

A—Spring retainer
B—Valve stem

4. Slide the valve spacer over the valve stem. Remove the spring washer and valve seal from the stem.

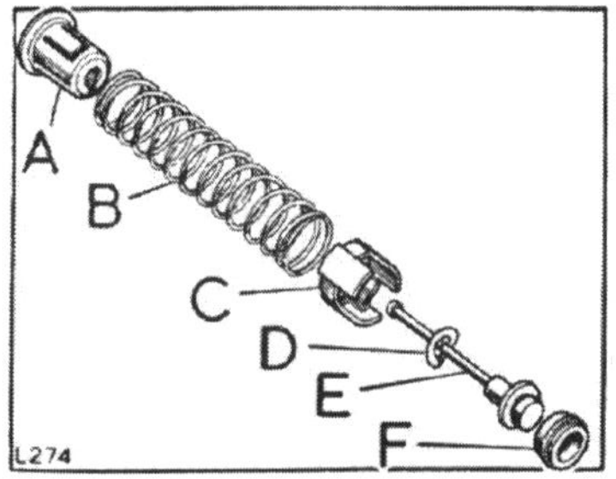

Fig. H1-53. Spring and valve assembly

A—Spring retainer
B—Spring
C—Valve spacer
D—Spring washer
E—Valve stem
F—Valve seal

BRAKING SYSTEM

Operation H1-6A—continued

Inspection

1. Clean all components in Girling cleaning fluid and allow to dry.
2. Examine the cylinder bore and piston. Ensure that they are smooth to the touch with no corrosion, score marks or ridges. If there is any doubt, fit new replacements.
3. The seals should be replaced with new components. These items are all included in the master cylinder overhaul kit.

To assemble

1. Smear the seals with Castrol-Girling rubber grease and the remaining internal items with Castrol-Girling Brake and Clutch Fluid.
2. Fit the valve seal, flat side first, to the end of the valve stem.

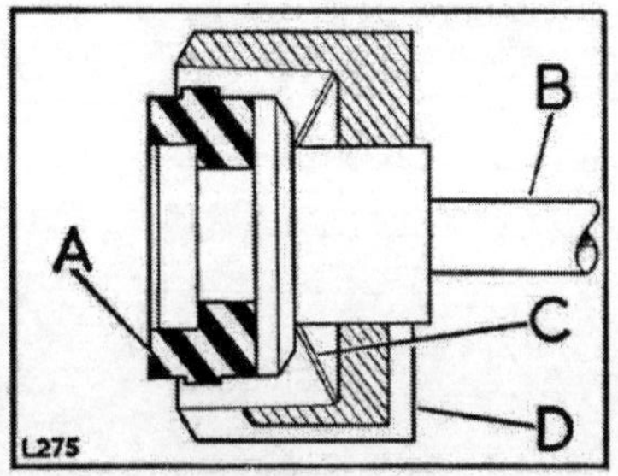

Fig. H1-54. Valve assembly

A—Valve seal
B—Valve stem
C—Spring washer
D—Valve spacer

3. Place the spring washer, domed side first, over the small end of the valve stem, then fit the valve spacer, legs first, and the coil spring.
4. Insert the retainer into the spring and compress until the stem passes through the keyhole and is engaged in the centre. See Fig. H1-52.
5. Fit the seal, large diameter last, to the piston.
6. Insert the piston into the spring retainer and engage the locking prong.

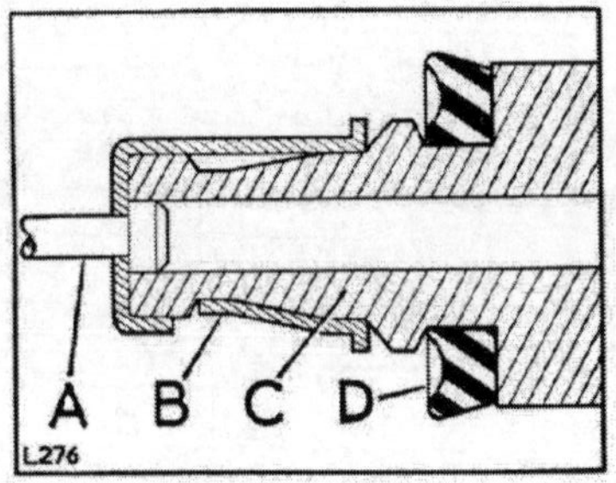

Fig. H1-55. Piston and spring retainer

A—Valve stem
B—Prong in engaged position
C—Piston
D—Seal

7. Smear the piston with Castrol-Girling rubber grease and insert the assembly, valve end first, into the cylinder.
8. Liberally smear Castrol-Girling rubber grease inside the piston end of the master cylinder.

Master cylinder (compression barrel 'CB' type), remove and refit
Operation H1-7

(For overhaul instructions, Operation H1-8 refers)

Workshop hand tools:
Spanner sizes: 7/16 in. AF, 1/2 in. AF open end
Pliers, screwdriver (medium)

General

There are two types of master cylinder in use, and care should be taken to correctly identify the unit concerned. A cylinder of the centre valve ('CV') type is normally fitted to 88 vehicles, and a cylinder of the compression barrel ('CB') type is fitted to 109 vehicles. For removal and refitting instructions of the 'CV' type master cylinder, Operation H1-5 refers.

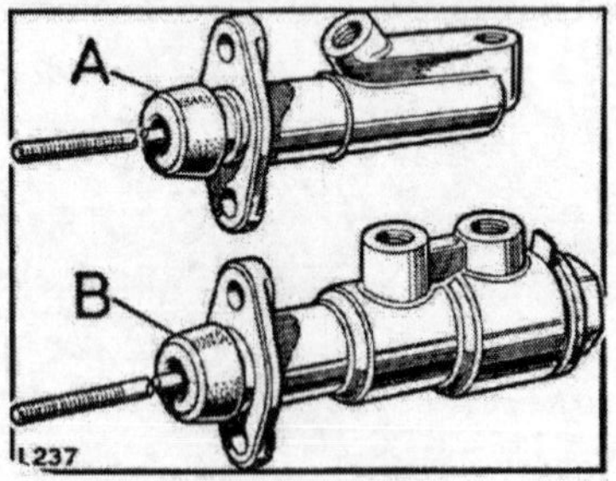

Fig. H1-56. Identification of master cylinders

A—'CV' type master cylinder
B—'CB' type master cylinder

To remove

1. Remove the fluid reservoir, Operation H1-3.
2. Disconnect the inlet and outlet pipes from the brake master cylinder.

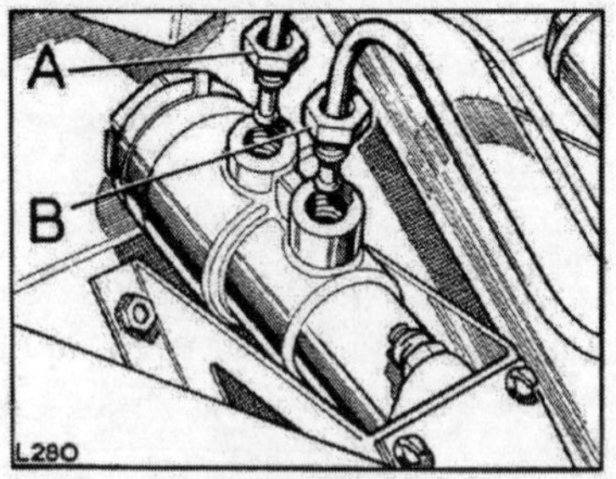

Fig. H1-57. Pipe connections at brake master cylinder

A—Outlet pipe
B—Inlet pipe

3. Disconnect the return spring from the brake pedal.
4. Remove the fixings securing the brake pedal bracket to the toe box.

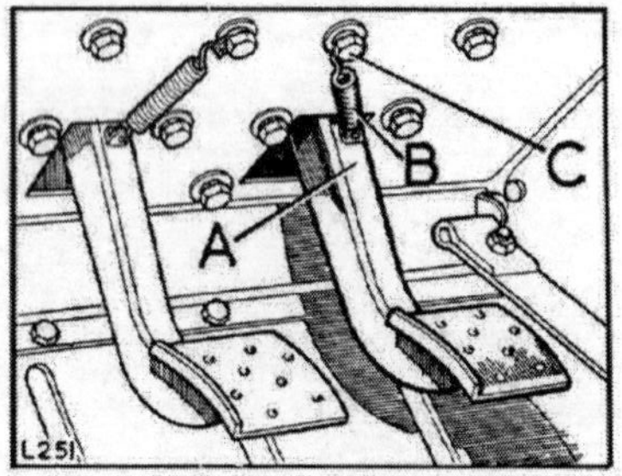

Fig. H1-58. Brake pedal bracket fixings

A—Brake pedal
B—Return spring for pedal
C—Fixings for brake pedal bracket (6 off)

5. Carefully withdraw the brake pedal and bracket assembly from the engine compartment, manoeuvring the pedal through the aperture in the toe box.

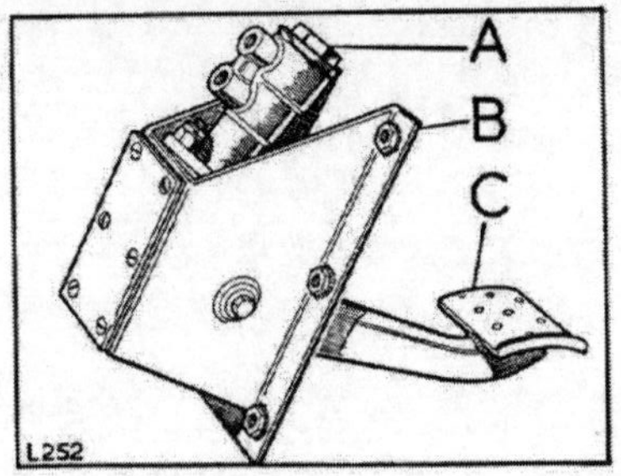

Fig. H1-59. Brake pedal and bracket assembly

A—Master cylinder
B—Bracket for brake pedal
C—Brake pedal

BRAKING SYSTEM

Operation H1-7—continued

6. Remove the top cover and gasket from the brake pedal bracket.

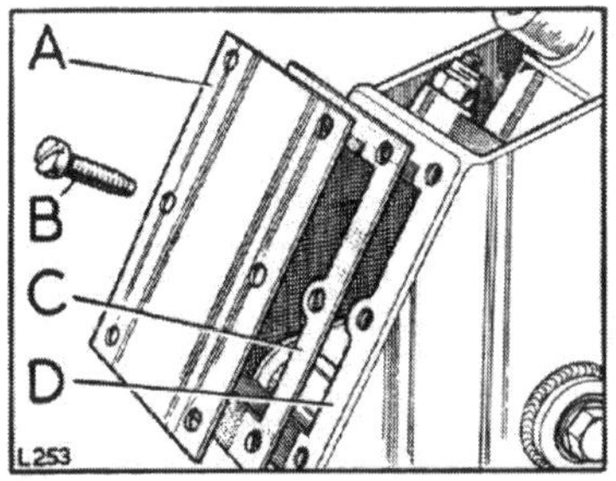

Fig. H1-60. Top cover for brake pedal bracket
A—Top cover
B—Fixings for top cover
C—Gasket
D—Bracket

7. Remove the nut and plain washer retaining the master cylinder push rod to the brake pedal trunnion.

8. Remove the fixings and withdraw the master cylinder from the brake pedal bracket.

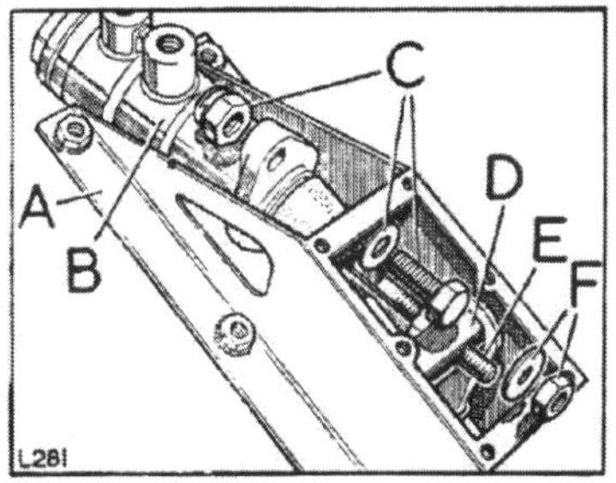

Fig. H1-61. Fixings for master cylinder
A—Bracket for brake pedal
B—Master cylinder
C—Fixings for master cylinder
D—Brake pedal trunnion
E—Push-rod for master cylinder
F—Fixings, push rod to trunnion

Operation H1-7—continued

To refit

1. Fit the master cylinder to the brake pedal bracket. See Fig. H1-61.

2. Place the gasket in position on the securing flange of the brake pedal bracket. If necessary, use a little Bostik adhesive to retain the gasket.

3. Carefully locate the brake pedal and bracket assembly in position on the toe box, manoeuvring the pedal through the aperture in the toe box.

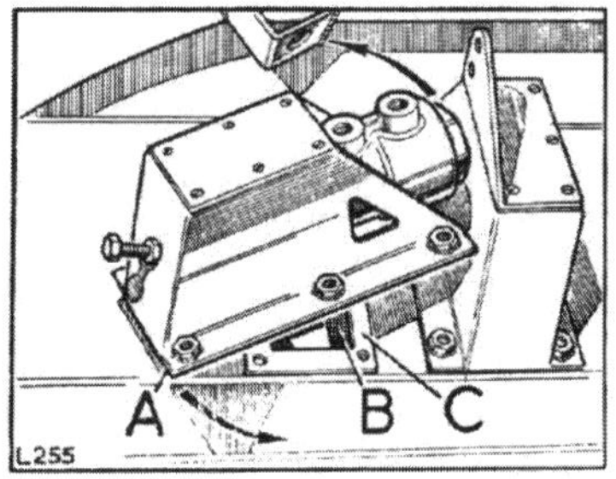

Fig. H1-62. Fitting brake pedal and bracket
A—Brake pedal and bracket
B—Aperture in toe box
C—Gasket

4. Secure the brake pedal and bracket assembly to the toe box, ensuring that the gasket remains in position. See Fig. H1-58.

5. Connect the return spring between the brake pedal and the toe box bracket.

6. Connect the inlet and outlet pipes to the brake master cylinder. See Fig. H1-57.

7. Fit the fluid reservoir. Operation H1-3.

8. Slacken both locknuts on the master cylinder push rod, and adjust the push rod by rotating until there is $\frac{1}{16}$ in. (1.5 mm) free play between the push rod and master cylinder piston, then tighten both locknuts.

9. Bleed the complete braking system. Operation H1-1. Bleed the clutch system, Section B.

10. Recheck, and if necessary, adjust the push rod setting.

11. Fit the top cover and gasket to the brake pedal bracket. See Fig. H1-60.

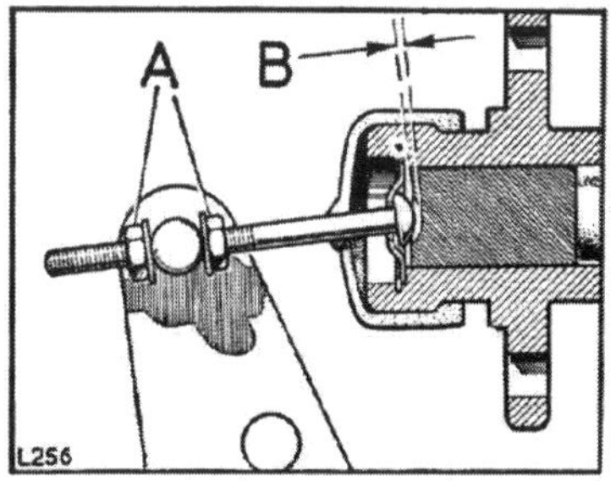

Fig. H1-63. Push-rod setting
A—Locknuts for push rod
B—$\frac{1}{16}$ in. (1.5 mm) free play

BRAKING SYSTEM

Master cylinder (compression barrel 'CB' type), overhaul—Operation H1-8

(For removal and refitting instructions, Operation H1-7 refers)

Workshop hand tools:
Spanner sizes: ½ in. AF, 1¼ in. AF open end
Pliers

General

There are two types of brake master cylinder in use, and care should be taken to correctly identify the unit concerned. A cylinder of the centre valve ('CV') type is normally fitted to 88 vehicles, and a cylinder of the compression barrel ('CB') type is fitted to 109 vehicles. For overhaul instructions of the 'CV' type master cylinder, Operation H1-6 refers.

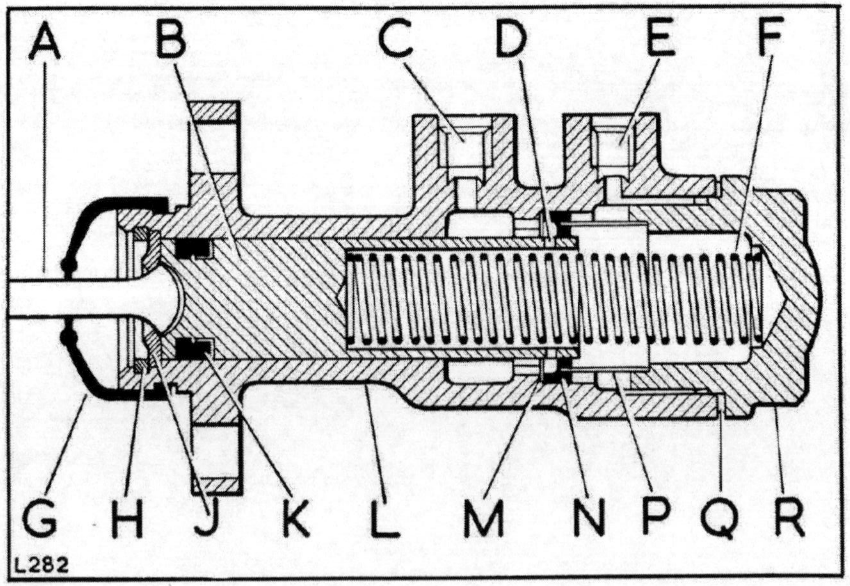

Fig. H1-64. Compression barrel ('CB') type master cylinder

A—Push rod
B—Piston
C—Inlet from reservoir
D—Inlet ports
E—Outlet to wheel cylinders
F—Piston spring
G—Dust cover
H—Circlip
J—Retaining washer
K—End seal
L—Cylinder
M—Shim
N—Recuperating seal
P—Seal support
Q—Gasket
R—End cap

Operation H1-8—continued

To dismantle

1. Remove the plain washer, nut and rubber cover from the push rod.

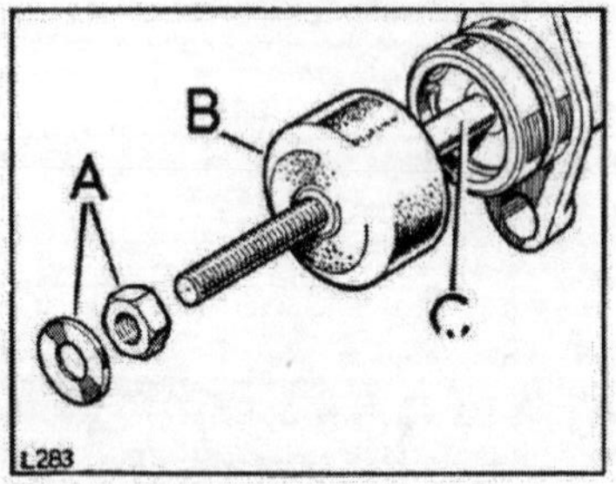

Fig. H1-65. Push-rod cover

A—Locknut and washer
B—Rubber cover
C—Push rod

2. Remove the circlip and withdraw the push rod and retaining washer.

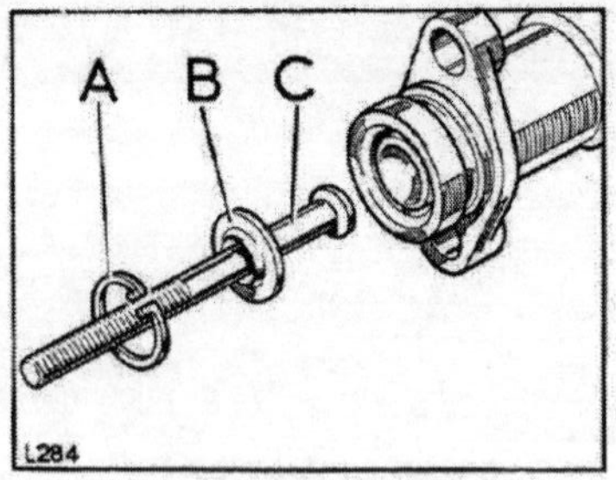

Fig. H1-66. Push rod fixings

A—Circlip
B—Retaining washer
C—Push rod

3. Withdraw the piston and spring from the master cylinder. If necessary, apply a low air pressure to the outlet port to expel the piston.

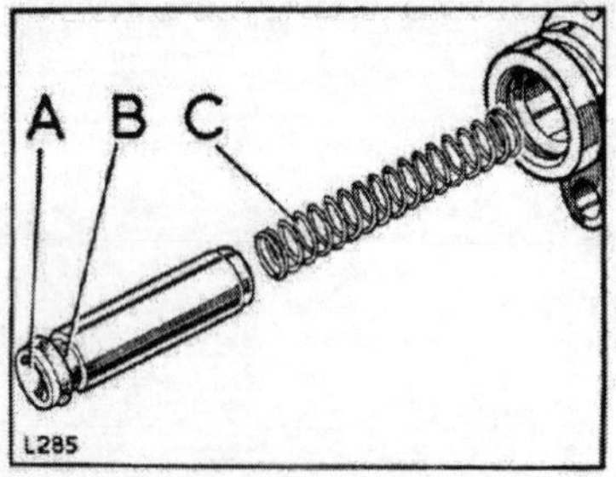

Fig. H1-67. Piston assembly

A—Piston
B—End seal
C—Spring for piston

4. Remove the end cap and gasket from the master cylinder and withdraw the recuperating seal and shim.

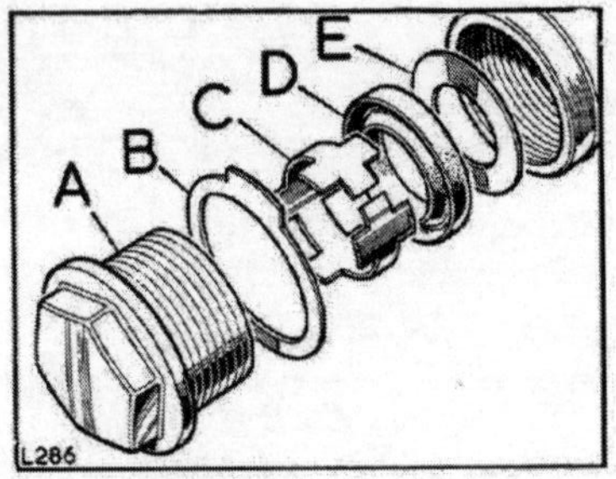

Fig. H1-68. End cap and seal

A—End cap
B—Gasket for end cap
C—Support for seal
D—Recuperating seal
E—Shim

Operation H1-8—continued

5. If required, withdraw the seal support from the end cap.

Inspection

1. Clean all components in Girling cleaning fluid and allow to dry.

2. Examine the cylinder bore and piston; ensure that they are smooth to the touch with no corrosion, score marks or ridges. If there is any doubt, fit new replacements.

3. The seals, seal support, gasket and dust cover should all be replaced with new components. These items are all included in the master cylinder overhaul kit.

To re-assemble

1. Smear the seals with Castrol-Girling rubber grease and the remaining internal items with Castrol-Girling Brake and Clutch Fluid.

2. Fit the end seal, large diameter first, to the push rod end of the piston, ensuring that the inner diameter locates in the first groove.

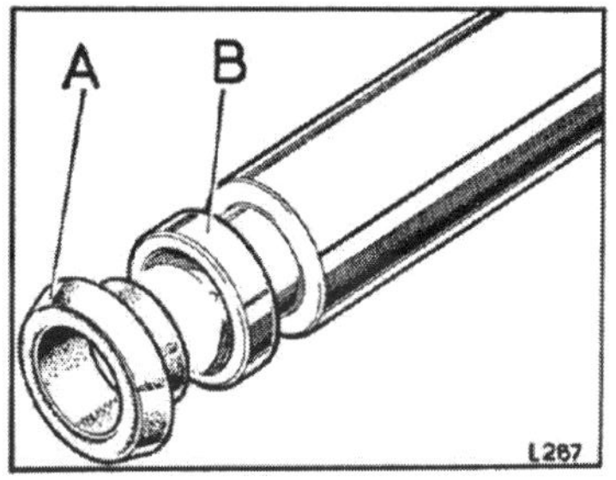

Fig. H1-69. End seal location

A—End seal
B—Push rod end of piston

3. Insert the piston, seal end last, into the push rod end of the cylinder, rotating the piston to ease in the seal.

4. Fit the push rod, retaining washer and circlip.

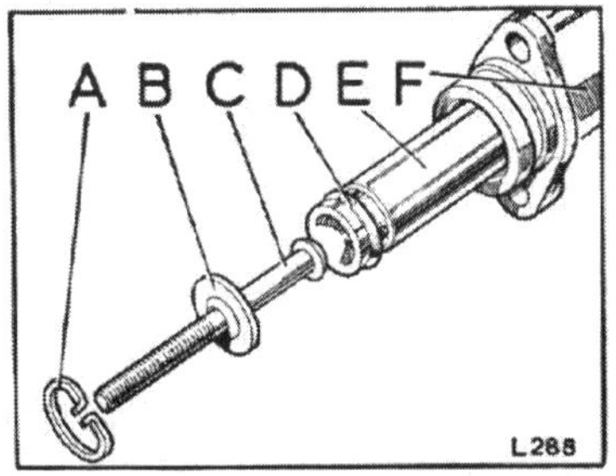

Fig. H1-70. Piston and push rod assembly

A—Circlip
B—Retaining washer
C—Push rod
D—End seal
E—Piston
F—Cylinder

5. Place the shim in the cylinder and locate it over the end of the piston.

Note: Latest type master cylinders have a spigotted plastic washer in place of the shim.

6. Fit the recuperating seal with the back against the shim.

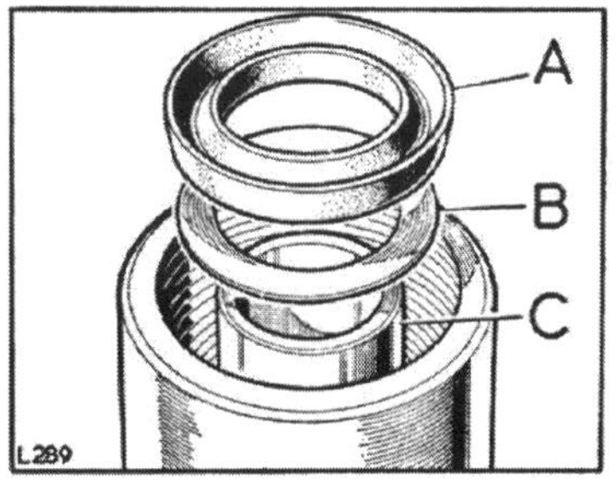

Fig. H1-71. Fitting shim and seal

A—Recuperating seal
B—Shim
C—Piston

Operation H1-8—continued

7. Place the seal support in position.

Note: Two types of seal support are in use. If the support is plastic, locate it into the seal. If it is metal, locate it into the end cap.

8. Fit the spring into the cylinder, locating it into the counter-bore in the piston.

9. Fit the end cap and gasket ensuring that it is securely tightened.

10. Smear liberally the inside of the dust cover with Castrol-Girling rubber grease and fit the cover over the push rod and cylinder.

11. Fit the locknut and washer to the push rod.

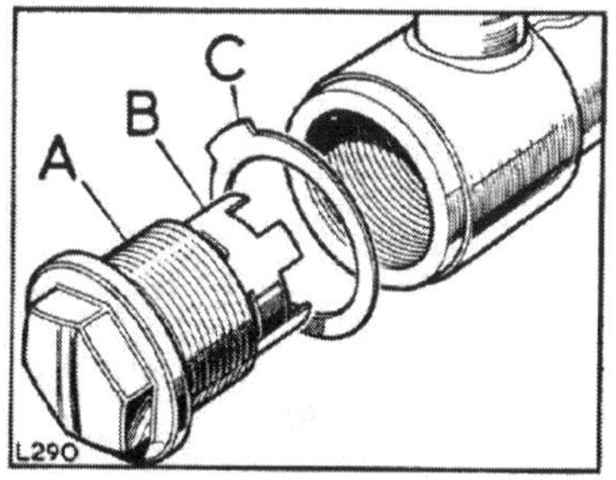

Fig. H1-72. End cap for cylinder

A—End cap
B—Seal support
C—Gasket for end cap

BRAKING SYSTEM

Brake flexible pipes, remove and refit—Operation H1-9

Workshop hand tools:
Spanner sizes: $\frac{9}{16}$ in. AF, $\frac{5}{8}$ in. AF open end

To remove

1. Disconnect the front brake pipe at the connection with the flexible pipe—one each side of the vehicle—and withdraw the flexible pipe from the chassis bracket. Then depress the brake pedal and wedge it in that position to prevent further leakage of brake fluid. When depressing the brake pedal, take precautions to avoid fluid spillage.

2. Unscrew and withdraw the flexible pipe from the brake anchor plate.

3. Disconnect the rear brake pipe at the connection with the flexible pipe and withdraw the flexible pipe from the chassis bracket. Then depress the brake pedal and wedge it in that position to prevent further leakage of brake fluid. When depressing the brake pedal, take precautions to avoid fluid spillage.

4. Unscrew and withdraw the flexible pipe from the brake pipe tee-piece at the rear axle.

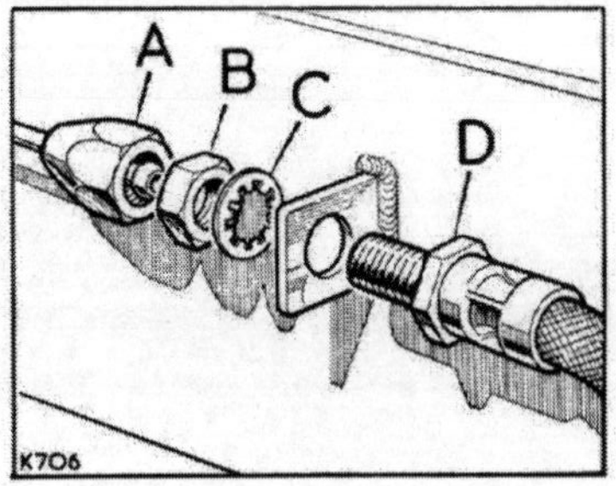

Fig. H1-73. Brake pipe connections

A—Pipe from master cylinder
B—Locknut
C—Shakeproof washer
D—Flexible brake pipe

To refit

1. Fit the front brake flexible pipe, together with a joint washer, to the brake anchor plate.

2. Connect the front brake pipe and flexible pipe coupling. See Fig. H1-73.

3. Fit the rear brake flexible pipe, together with a joint washer, to the tee-piece at the rear axle case.

4. Connect the rear brake pipe and flexible pipe coupling. See Fig. H1-73.

5. Ensure that brake pipes cannot chafe against any adjacent component. If necessary, reposition brake pipes.

6. Bleed the complete brake system. Operation H1-1.

Important: Whenever any section of the pressure pipe system has been removed, a careful check should be made on replacement to ensure that all the connections and joint washers are in good condition. A faulty connection will admit air into the system, so causing poor and 'spongy' braking.

Brake anchor plate, front and rear, 10 in., 88 models, overhaul—Operation H1-10

(For removal and refitting instructions, Operations E1-5 and F1-4 refers)
(For brake shoe relining instructions, Operation H1-12 refers)

Workshop hand tools:
Spanner sizes: $\frac{7}{16}$ in. AF, $\frac{1}{2}$ in. AF, $\frac{11}{16}$ in. AF open end

To dismantle

Note: It is not essential to remove the brake anchor plate from the vehicle; the brake shoe components are accessible after removing the road wheel and brake drum.

1. Turn back the adjuster cam to release the tension of the leading shoe pull-off spring and remove the spring.

2. Remove the trailing shoe anchor plate.

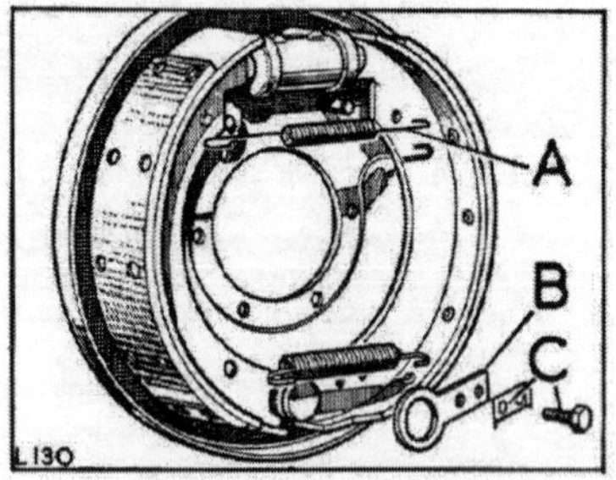

Fig. H1-74. Fixings for brake shoes

A—Spring for leading shoe
B—Anchor for trailing shoe
C—Fixings for anchor

3. Remove the brake shoes together from the pivot end first; part them by disconnecting the return spring.

Note: If the wheel cylinder is not to be removed, e.g., when relining the shoes, it is advisable to use a strong rubber band to retain the cylinder pistons to prevent loss of fluid and admission of air to the system.

4. Disconnect the flexible pipe from the wheel cylinder. If the brake anchor plate is fitted to the vehicle, the flexible pipe MUST FIRST be disconnected at the chassis end. Also take precautions to prevent fluid spillage.

5. Remove the wheel cylinder and detach the rubber dust covers, pistons, seals, seal supports and spring; remove the bleed nipple cover, nipple and ball.

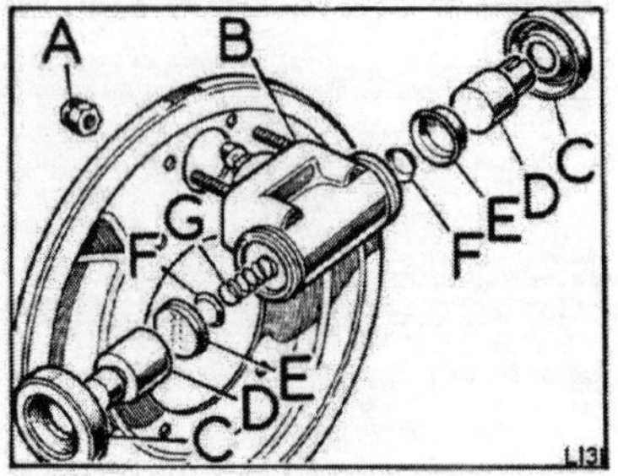

Fig. H1-75. Wheel cylinder

A—Fixings for wheel cylinder
B—Wheel cylinder
C—Dust cover
D—Piston
E—Seal
F—Support for seal
G—Spring

Inspection

1. Clean all components in Girling cleaning fluid and allow to dry.

2. Examine the cylinder bore and pistons. Ensure that they are smooth to the touch with no corrosion, score marks or ridges. If there is any doubt, fit new replacements.

3. The seals and dust covers should be replaced with new components. These items are all included in the wheel cylinder overhaul kit.

4. Examine the brake drum for scoring, ovality and skim if required; standard diameter 10 in. (254 mm). Reclamation limit .030 in. (0,75 mm) oversize on standard diameter.

5. If the brake shoes require relining, refer to Operation H1-12.

BRAKING SYSTEM

Operation H1-10—continued

To assemble

1. Smear the seals and all wheel cylinder internal parts with Castrol-Girling Brake and Clutch Fluid.

2. Fit the bleed ball and nipple. DO NOT overtighten the bleed nipple; 4 to 6 lbs ft (0,55 to 0,8 mkg) torque is sufficient.

3. Assemble the wheel cylinder (see Fig. H1-75) ensuring that the seals are located with their flat back against the piston.

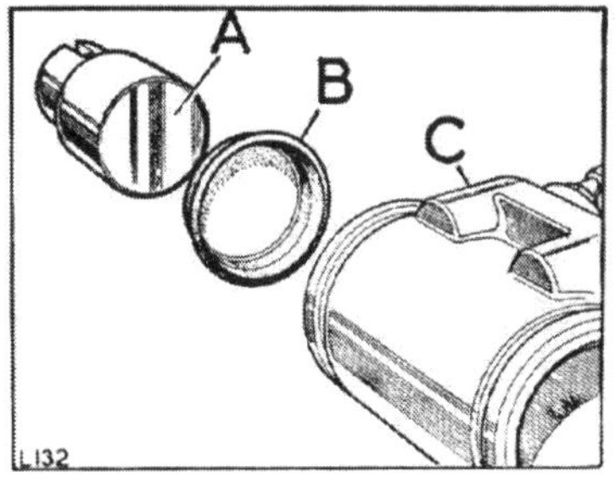

Fig. H1-76. Seal location

A—Piston
B—Seal
C—Wheel cylinder

4. Fit a rubber band around the cylinder to retain the parts, until the brake shoes are in position.

5. Refit the wheel cylinder to the anchor plate.

6. Reconnect the pull-off spring to the brake shoes and fit the shoes at the wheel cylinder end first.

7. Reconnect the leading shoe pull-off spring; replace it with its longest extremity hooked over the post on the shoe web.

8. Replace the trailing shoe anchor plate. See Fig. H1-74.

9. If the brake anchor plate has been removed from the vehicle, refit it together with the hub and brake drum (Operations E1-5 and F1-4) but do not fit the road wheel at this stage.

10. Adjust the brake. Operation H1-2.

11. Early 88 models—If the brake shoe steady posts have been disturbed, they should be reset as follows:

   Screw the posts well back, clear of the shoes. Apply the brakes lightly and turn the drum by hand to centralise the shoes; continue depressing the pedal until the shoes are hard on the drum. Screw in the steady posts until they just contact the shoe webs and secure by means of the locknuts.

   Later 88 models are fitted with anchor plates embodying a pressed projection in place of the shoe steady posts.

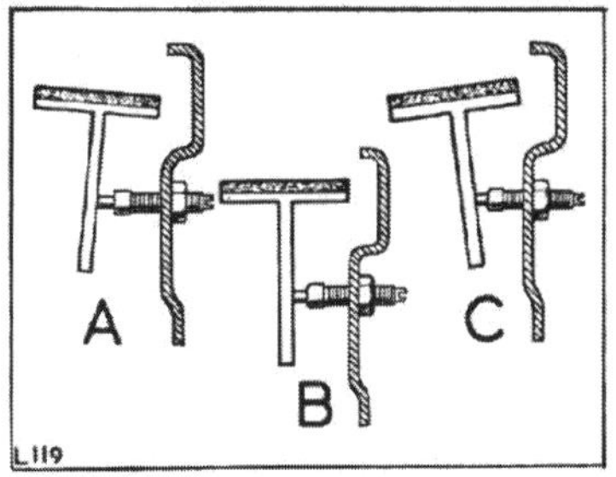

Fig. H1-77. Steady post adjustment

A—Incorrect
B—Correct
C—Incorrect

12. Replace the road wheel.

13. Lower the vehicle from the jack.

14. Bleed the brakes. Operation H1-1.

Brake anchor plate, front, 11 in., 109 models, overhaul—Operation H1-10A

(For removal and refitting instructions, Operation F1-4 refers)
(For brake shoe relining instructions, Operation H1-12 refers)

Workshop hand tools:
Spanner sizes: $\frac{7}{16}$ in. BSF, $\frac{7}{16}$ in. AF, $\frac{1}{2}$ in. AF open end

General

There are two types of 11 in. front brake in use; 4-cylinder engine vehicles are fitted with $2\frac{1}{4}$ in. (57 mm) wide brakes and 6-cylinder engine vehicles are fitted with 3 in. (76 mm) wide brakes. The following instructions cover both types.

To dismantle

Note: It is not essential to remove the brake anchor plate from the vehicle. The brake shoe components are accessible after removing the road wheel and brake drum

1. Release brake shoes and pull-off springs by levering the trailing edge of each shoe away from the wheel cylinders.

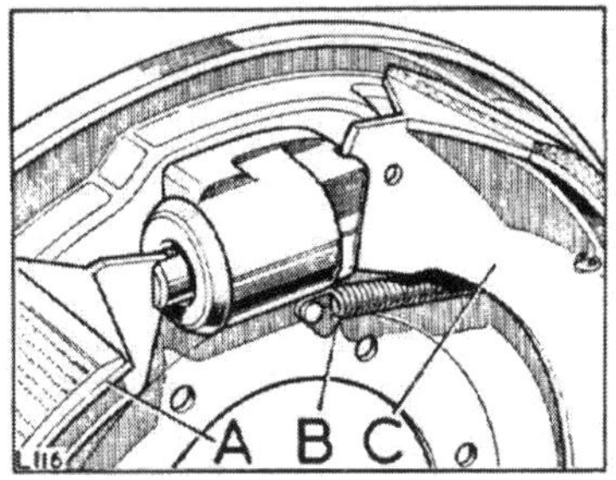

Fig. H1-78. Brake shoe location

A—Leading edge of shoe
B—Pull-off springs
C—Trailing edge of shoe

Note: If the wheel cylinders are not to be removed, e.g., when relining brake shoes, it is advisable to use a strong rubber band to retain the pistons in position and prevent loss of fluid and admission of air to the system.

2. Disconnect flexible pipe and connecting pipe from wheel cylinders. If the brake anchor plate is fitted to the vehicle, the flexible pipe MUST FIRST be disconnected at the chassis end. Also take precautions to prevent fluid spillage.

3. Unscrew securing nuts, then remove wheel cylinders from anchor plate and detach the rubber dust covers, pistons, seals, springs, and where applicable, the seal supports.

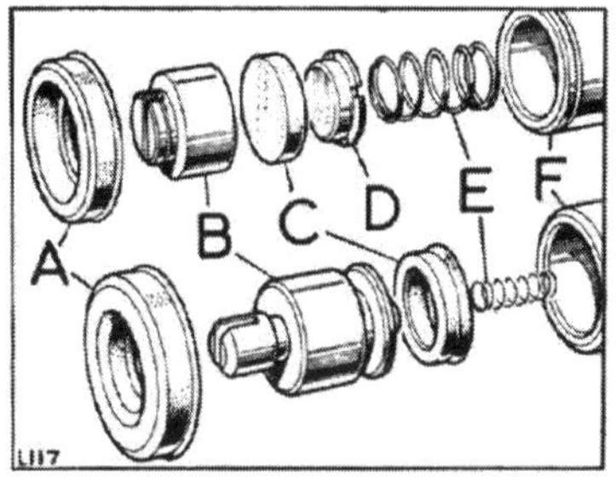

Fig. H1-79. Wheel cylinder components, two types in use

A—Dust cover
B—Piston
C—Seal for piston
D—Support for seal
E—Spring
F—Wheel cylinder

4. Remove the bleed nipple cover and unscrew the nipple.

5. Remove the brake anchor plate and steady posts if necessary.

Inspection

1. Clean all components in Girling cleaning fluid and allow to dry.

2. Examine the cylinder bores and pistons. Ensure that they are smooth to the touch with no corrosion, score marks or ridges. If there is any doubt, fit new replacements.

3. The seals and dust covers should be replaced with new components. These items are included in the wheel cylinder overhaul kit.

4. Examine the brake drum for scoring, ovality and skim if required. Standard diameter: 11 in. $+ .004$ in. (279.4 mm $+ 0,10$ mm). Reclamation limit: .030 in. (0,75 mm) oversize on standard diameter.

Section H—Land-Rover BRAKING SYSTEM

Operation H1-10A—continued

5. If the brake shoes require relining, refer to Operation H1-12.

To assemble

1. Smear the seals and all wheel cylinder internal parts with Castrol-Girling Brake and Clutch Fluid.
2. Fit the bleed nipple. DO NOT overtighten the nipple; 4 to 6 lbs ft (0,55 to 0,8 mkg) torque is sufficient.
3. Assemble the wheel cylinder (see Fig. H1-79) ensuring that the seals are located with their flat backs against the piston.

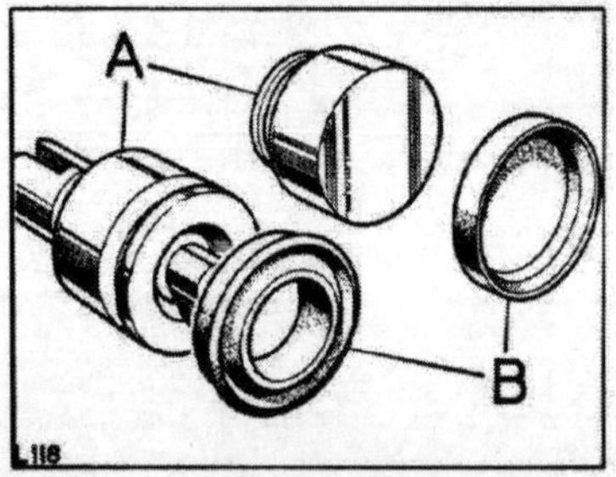

Fig. H1-80. Seal location (two types in use)

A—Piston
B—Seal

4. Fit a rubber band around the cylinder to retain the parts, until the brake shoes are in position.
5. Refit the wheel cylinders to the anchor plate.
6. Reconnect the pull-off springs to the brake shoes and fit the shoes at the wheel cylinder end first.
7. Fit the flexible pipe and connecting pipe to the wheel cylinders.
8. If the brake anchor plate has been removed from the vehicle, refit it together with the hub and drum (Operation E1-5) but do not fit the road wheel at this stage.
9. Adjust the brake. Operation H1-2.
10. If the brake shoe steady posts have been disturbed, they should be reset as follows:
    Screw the posts well back, clear of the shoes. Apply the brakes lightly and turn the drum by hand to centralise the shoes; continue depressing the pedal until the shoes are hard on the drum. Screw in the steady posts until they just contact the shoe webs and secure by means of the locknuts.

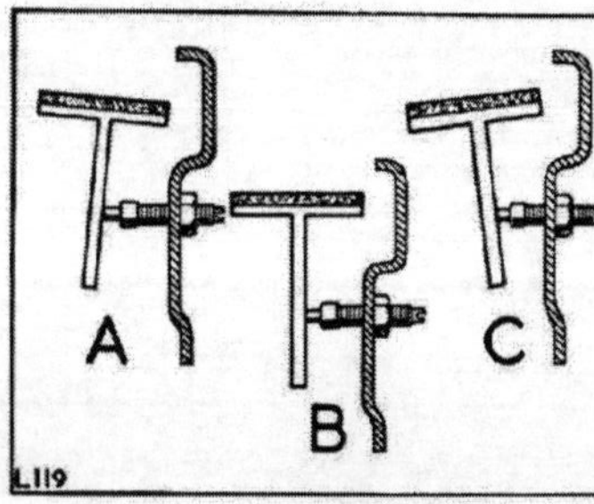

Fig. H1-81. Steady post adjustment

A—Incorrect
B—Correct
C—Incorrect

11. Replace the road wheel.
12. Lower the vehicle from the jack.
13. Bleed the brakes. Operation H1-1.

Brake anchor plate, rear, 11 in., 109 models Series II, overhaul—Operation H1-10B

(For removal and refitting instructions, Operation E1-5 refers)
(For brake shoe relining instructions, Operation H1-12 refers)

Workshop hand tools:
Spanner sizes: $\frac{7}{8}$ in. AF, $\frac{1}{2}$ in. AF, $\frac{7}{16}$ in. AF open end
Screwdriver (medium)

To dismantle

Note: It is not essential to remove the brake anchor plate from the vehicle; the brake shoe components are accessible after removing the road wheel and brake drum.

1. Release the brake shoes and pull-off springs by levering the shoes away from the wheel cylinder.

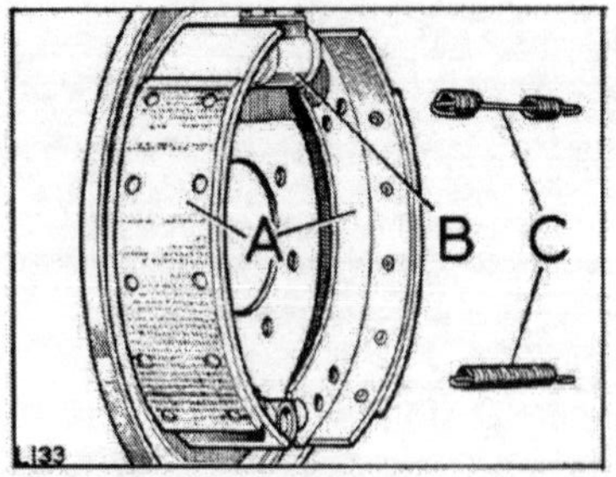

Fig. H1-82. Brake shoe location

A—Brake shoes
B—Wheel cylinder
C—Pull-off springs

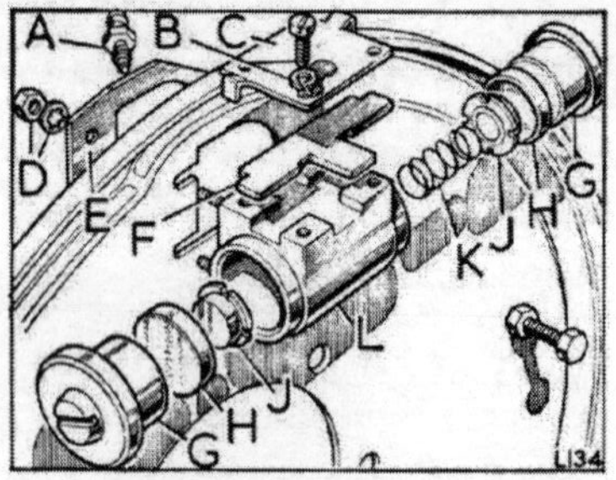

Fig. H1-83. Wheel cylinder components

A—Bleed nipple
B—Fixings for retainer
C—Retainer for abutment plate
D—Fixings for dust cover
E—Dust cover
F—Abutment plate for shoes
G—Piston
H—Seal for piston
J—Support for seal
K—Spring
L—Wheel cylinder

Note: If the wheel cylinders are not to be removed, e.g., when relining brake shoes, it is adviseable to use a strong rubber band to retain the pistons in position and prevent loss of fluid and admission of air to the system.

2. Disconnect the flexible pipe from the wheel cylinder. If the brake anchor plate is fitted to the vehicle, the flexible pipe MUST FIRST be disconnected at the chassis end. Also take precautions to prevent fluid spillage.
3. Remove the securing nuts and withdraw the wheel cylinders from anchor plates, then detach the pistons, seals, air excluders and springs.
4. Remove the securing bolts and withdraw the adjuster assemblies complete with cover plates. Withdraw the plungers and unscrew the adjuster cones.

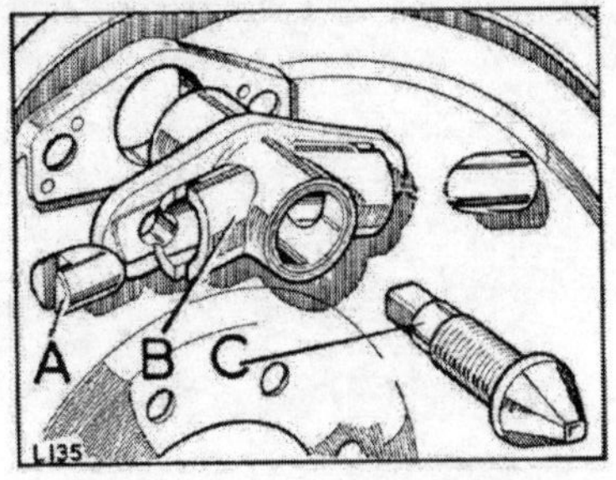

Fig. H1-84. Brake shoe adjuster

A—Plunger (LH and RH)
B—Adjuster housing
C—Cone for adjuster

BRAKING SYSTEM

Operation H1-10B—continued

5. Unscrew the steady posts, with fibre bushes and locknuts.
6. Remove the bleed nipple cover and unscrew the nipple.

Inspection

1. Clean all components in Girling cleaning fluid and allow to dry.
2. Examine the cylinder bore and pistons. Ensure that they are smooth to the touch with no corrosion, score marks or ridges. If there is any doubt, fit new replacements.
3. The seals and dust covers should be replaced with new components. These items are all included in the wheel cylinder overhaul kit.
4. Examine the brake drum for scoring, ovality, and skim if required. Standard diameter: 11 in. + .004 in. (279,4 mm + 0,10 mm). Reclamation limit: .030 in. (0,75 mm) oversize on standard diameter.
5. If the brake shoes require relining, Operation H1-12 refers.

To assemble

1. Smear the seals and all wheel cylinder internal parts with Castrol-Girling Brake and Clutch Fluid.

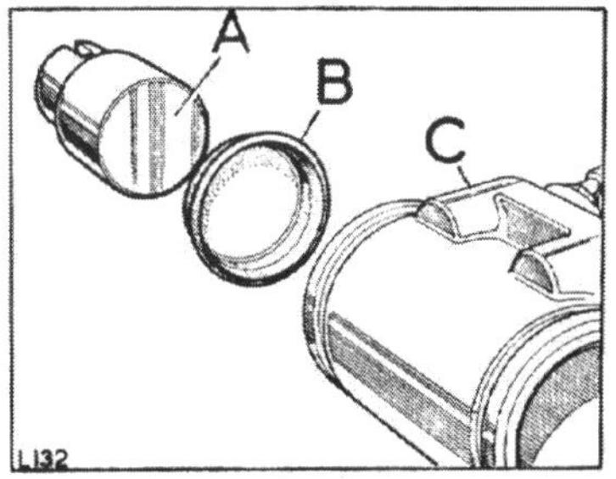

Fig. H1-85. Seal location
A—Piston
B—Seal
C—Wheel cylinder

2. Fit the bleed nipple. DO NOT overtighten the nipple; 4 to 6 lbs ft (0,55 to 0,8 mkg) torque is sufficient.
3. Assemble the wheel cylinder (see Fig. H1-83) ensuring that the seals are located with their flat backs against the piston.
4. Fit a rubber band around the cylinder to retain the parts, until the brake shoes are in position.
5. Refit the wheel cylinder to the anchor plate. Leave the wheel cylinder fixing nuts one turn slack so that the cylinder is free to float on the anchor plate.
6. Fit the flexible pipe to the wheel cylinder.
7. Lubricate the cone and adjuster plungers with graphite grease.
8. Ensure that the plungers are fitted in pairs. This can be checked by placing them end to end; in this position the slots should be parallel to each other.

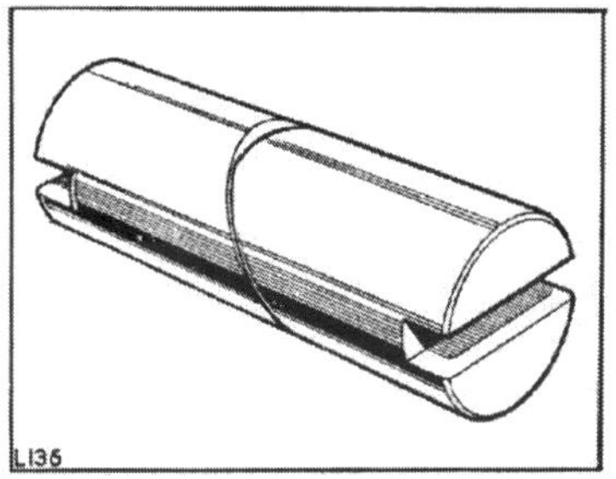

Fig. H1-86. Plungers correctly paired

9. Check that the plungers are fitted to the correct bore in adjuster housing. When the plungers are fitted correctly and forced down on the flats of the adjusting cone, the slot for brake shoe web will be in line with the slots in adjuster housing and the angle of the plunger slot will coincide with the angle of brake shoe web.

Operation H1-10B—continued

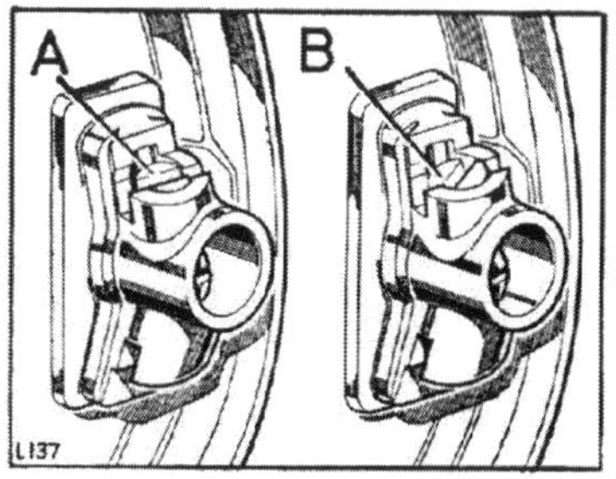

Fig. H1-87. Plunger location
A—Plungers correctly located
B—Plungers incorrectly located

10. Fit the adjuster assembly to the anchor plate. See Fig. H1-84.
11. Reconnect the pull-off springs to the brake shoes and fit the shoes at the wheel cylinder end first. The trailing shoe has the shorter lining and care must be taken to ensure it is not fitted in the leading position.
12. If the brake anchor plate has been removed from the vehicle, refit it together with the hub and drum (Operation F1-4) but do not fit the road wheel at this stage.
13. Adjust the brake. Operation H1-2.
14. If the brake shoe steady posts have been disturbed, they should be reset as follows:
Screw the posts well back clear of the shoes. Apply the brakes lightly and turn the drum by hand to centralise the shoes. Continue depressing the brake pedal until the shoes are hard on the drum. Screw in the steady posts until they just contact the shoe webs and secure by means of the locknuts.

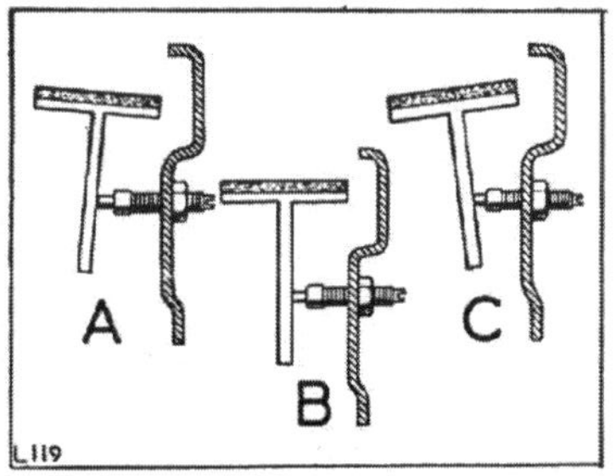

Fig. H1-88. Steady post adjustment
A—Incorrect
B—Correct
C—Incorrect

15. Replace the road wheel.
16. Lower the vehicle from the jack.
17. Bleed the brakes. Operation H1-1.

Brake anchor plate, rear, 11 in., 109 models Series IIA, overhaul—Operation H1-10C

(For removal and refitting instructions, Operation E1-5 refers)
(For brake shoe relining instructions, Operation H1-12 refers)

Workshop hand tools:
Spanner sizes: $\frac{7}{16}$ in. AF, $\frac{1}{2}$ in. AF, $\frac{11}{16}$ in. AF open end

To dismantle

Note: It is not essential to remove the brake anchor plate from the vehicle, the brake shoe components are accessible after removing the road wheel and brake drum.

1. Remove the brake shoes together from the pivot end first and part them by disconnecting the pull-off springs.

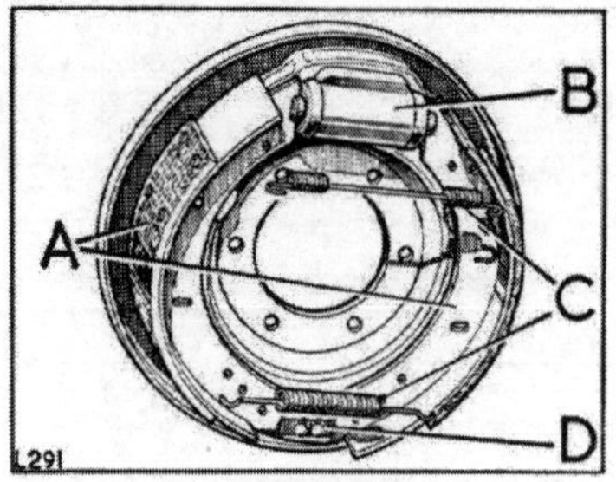

Note: If the wheel cylinder is not to be removed, e.g., when relining the shoes, it is advisable to use a strong rubber band to retain the cylinder pistons to prevent loss of fluid and admission of air to the system.

2. Disconnect the flexible pipe from the wheel cylinder. If the brake anchor plate is fitted to the vehicle, the flexible pipe MUST FIRST be disconnected at the chassis end. Also take precautions to prevent fluid spillage.

3. Remove the wheel cylinder and detach the rubber dust covers, pistons, seals, seal supports and spring. Remove the bleed nipple cover, nipple and ball.

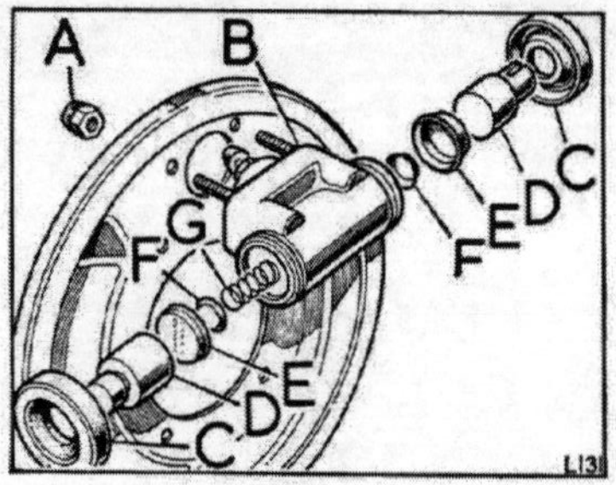

Fig. H1-89. Fixings for brake shoes

A—Brake shoes
B—Wheel cylinder
C—Pull-off spring
D—Pivot for shoes

Fig. H1-90. Wheel cylinder

A—Fixing for wheel cylinder
B—Wheel cylinder
C—Dust cover
D—Piston
E—Seal
F—Support for seal
G—Spring

Inspection

1. Clean all components in Girling cleaning fluid and allow to dry.

2. Examine the cylinder bore and pistons. Ensure that they are smooth to touch with no corrosion, score marks or ridges. If there is any doubt, fit new replacements.

3. The seals and dust covers should be replaced with new components. These items are all included in the wheel cylinder overhaul kit.

4. Examine the brake drum for scoring, ovality, and skim if required. Standard diameter: 11 in. $+ .004$ in. $(279,4$ mm $+ 0,10$ mm$)$. Reclamation limit: .030 in. $(0,75$ mm$)$ oversize on standard diameter.

5. If the brake shoes require relining, Operation H1-12 refers.

Operation H1-10C—continued

To assemble

1. Smear the seals and all wheel cylinder internal parts with Castrol-Girling Brake and Clutch Fluid.

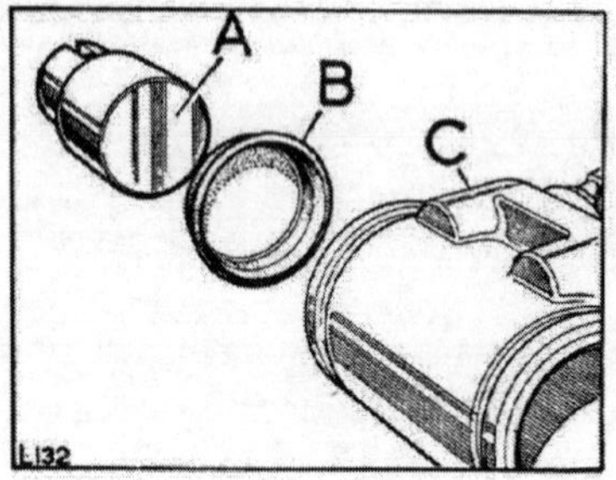

Fig. H1-91. Seal location

A—Piston
B—Seal
C—Wheel cylinder

2. Fit the bleed ball and nipple. DO NOT overtighten the bleed nipple; 4 to 6 lbs ft (0,55 to 0,8 mkg) torque is sufficient.

3. Assemble the wheel cylinder (see Fig. H1-90) ensuring that the seals are located with their flat back against the piston.

4. Fit a rubber band around the cylinder to retain the parts, until the brake shoes are in position.

5. Refit the wheel cylinder to the anchor plate.

6. Reconnect the pull-off spring at the pivot end.

7. Fit brake shoes in position. Fit the pull-off spring at the cylinder end and position the brake shoes at the pivot end and in the wheel cylinder pistons.

8. If the brake anchor plate has been removed from the vehicle, refit it together with the hub and brake drum (Operation F1-4) but do not fit the road wheel at this stage.

9. Adjust the brake. Operation H1-2.

10. Fit the road wheel and lower the vehicle from the jack.

11. Bleed the brakes. Operation H1-1.

BRAKING SYSTEM

Transmission brake, overhaul—Operation H1-11

(For removal and refitting instructions, Operation C1-4 refers)
(For brake shoe relining instructions, Operation H1-12 refers)

Workshop hand tools:
Spanner sizes: ¼ in. Whit, ₇⁄₁₆ in. AF open end
Girling brake adjusting spanner

To dismantle

Note: It is not essential to remove the transmission brake from the vehicle, the brake shoe components are accessible after removing the brake drum, which can be detached from the gearbox output flange and pushed back over the propeller shaft.

1. Remove the brake shoes together with the pull-off springs, separate the shoes by detaching the springs.

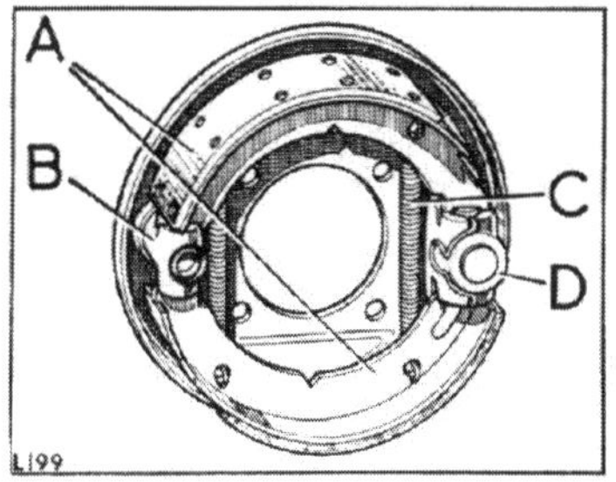

Fig. H1.92. Brake shoe location

A—Brake shoes
B—Adjuster unit
C—Brake shoe pull-off springs
D—Expander unit

2. **Early type.** Remove the clevis, return spring, spring anchor and rubber dust cover from the expander rod and remove the expander housing complete. If necessary, remove the split pins from the expander housing, thus releasing the plungers, steel balls and expander cone; detach the expander rod from the cone.

3. **Late type.** Withdraw the rubber dust excluder and remove the clip securing the expander housing to the anchor plate. Withdraw the expander assembly. If necessary remove the spring clip and withdraw the plungers, steel rollers and operating rod.

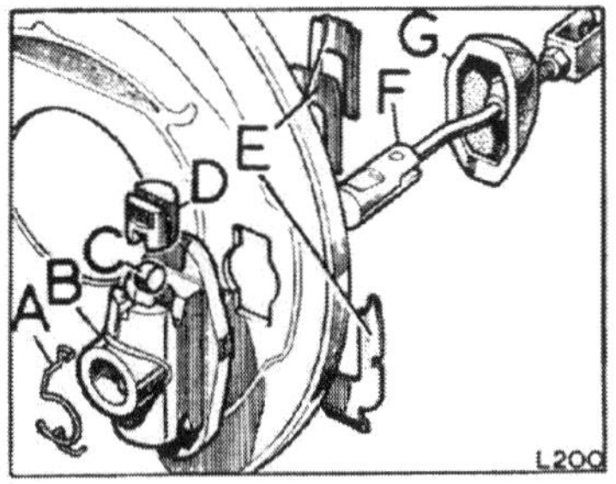

Operation H1-11—continued

4. Remove the adjuster housing; pull out the plungers and unscrew the adjuster cone from the housing.

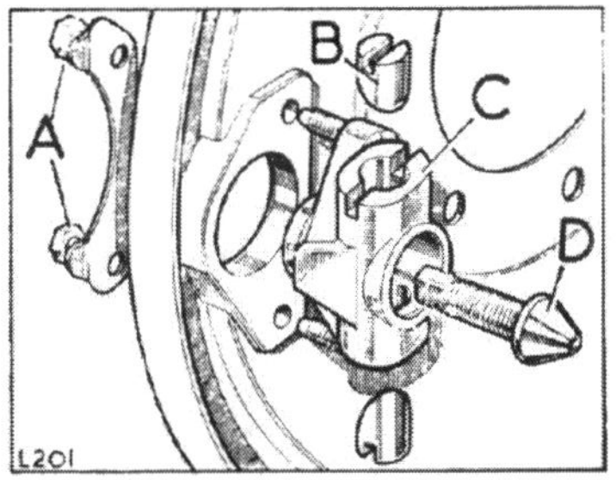

Fig. H1.93. Expander unit

A—Spring clip
B—Housing
C—Roller
D—Plunger
E—Fixings for expander unit
F—Operating rod
G—Rubber dust excluder

Fig. H1.94. Adjuster unit

A—Fixings for adjuster housing
B—Plungers
C—Housing
D—Adjuster cone

Inspection

1. Clean all components in Girling cleaning fluid and allow to dry.

2. Examine all items for obvious signs of wear and replace with new components as necessary. The rollers, plungers and expander are particularly important.

3. Examine the brake drum for scoring, ovality, and skim if required. Standard diameter: 9 in. (228.6 mm). Reclamation limit: .030 in. (0.75 mm) oversize on diameter.

4. If there is any sign of oil contamination on the brake linings, check, and if necessary, replace the output shaft oil seal fitted in the speedometer drive housing, Operation C1-6.

5. If the brake shoes require relining, Operation H1-12 refers.

To assemble

1. Replace the adjuster housing, leaving the securing bolts slack at this stage; screw in the adjuster cone, leaving it in the fully 'off' position.

2. Grease the adjuster plungers and replace them in the housings.

Early type (items 3 to 5)

3. It is essential that the adjuster plungers be replaced in the correct bores of the housings. They are handed, due to the fact that in addition to the adjustment flats being at an angle of 30° when viewed vertically, they are also inclined at an angle of 15° to the plunger axes, owing to the housing bores being similarly inclined. When dismantled the plungers are not readily distinguished, and care must be taken to ensure that handed pairs are fitted.

A quick method of selecting pairs is illustrated. The plungers should be placed end to end with the flats mated exactly, when a correct pair will show the brake shoe slots parallel with each other. If the slots are not in line, both plungers are of the same hand, but this test gives no indication as to which hand, right or left.

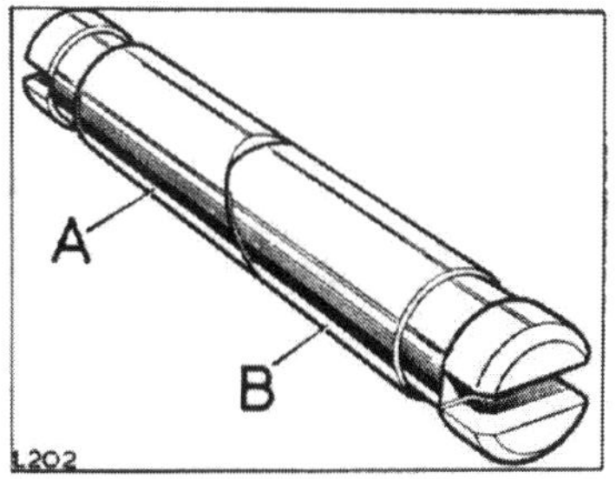

Fig. H1.95. Early type plungers

A—Left-hand plunger
B—Right-hand plunger

4. Having made certain that a correct pair has been chosen, it will still be necessary to make sure that they are fitted in the proper bores, as illustrated, i.e. with the flats of the adjuster cone and plungers face to face; the slots in the ends of the plungers must be in line and vertical (parallel with the anchor plate). In this case, four distinct 'clicks' will be felt for each revolution of the adjuster cone.

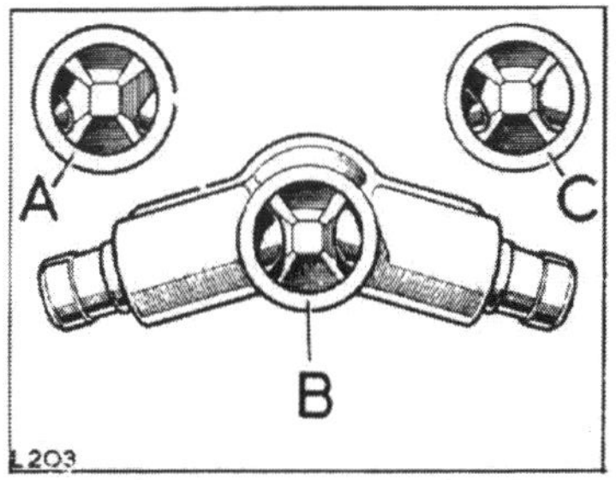

Fig. H1.96. Plunger location

A—Correct pair of plungers in incorrect bore
B—Plungers in correct bores
C—Two right-hand plungers in the housing

BRAKING SYSTEM

Operation H1-11—continued

5. When assembled wrongly, the brake shoes will force the plunger slots into a vertical position, throwing the plunger flat off the flat of the adjuster cone, pushing the plunger approximately 1/16 in. (1,5 mm) out of the housing and so upsetting the centralisation of the shoes.

   It is possible to erect the units incorrectly in three ways:

   (a) RH plunger in LH bore and LH plunger in RH bore.
   In this case it is likely that no 'click' will be felt when adjusting the brake.
   (b) Two LH plungers in the housing.
   (c) Two RH plungers in the housing.
   In both these cases the correct plunger will 'click' on adjustment, thus giving the erroneous impression that the assembly is in order.

Latest type

6. The two plungers are identical and can be fitted in either bore. Align the tapered ends of the plungers with the cone.

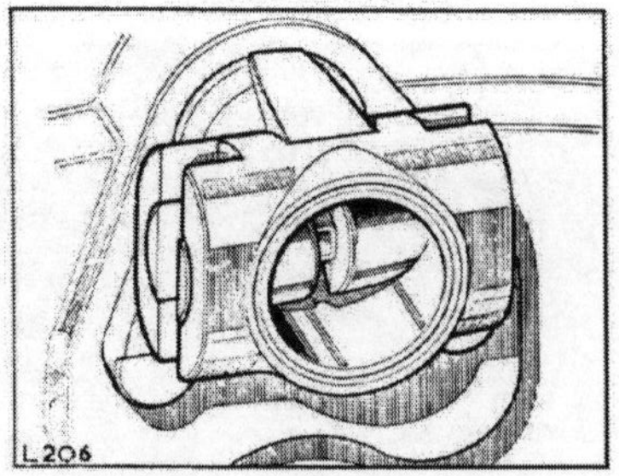

Early type (items 7 to 9)

7. Grease and replace the expander plungers, steel rollers and expander cone in the housing and locate with split pins.

8. Reconnect the expander rod to the brake anchor plate, leaving the Simmonds securing nuts one turn slack. Ensure that the housing is free to float on the anchor plate.

9. Replace the rubber dust cover, spring anchor plate, return spring and clevis on the expander rod.

Late type (items 10 and 11)

10. Grease and replace the plungers, steel rollers and operating rod in the expander housing.

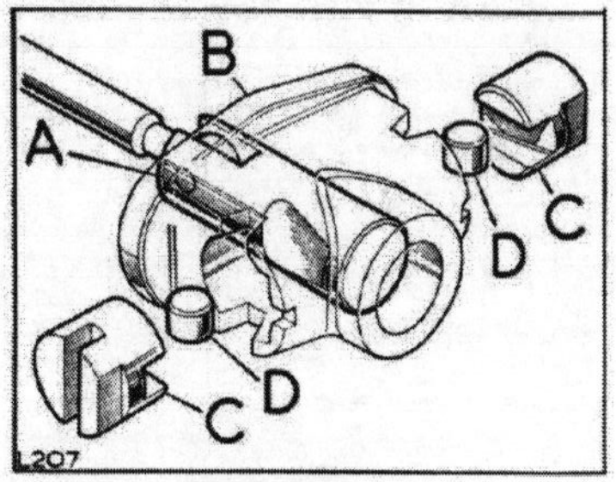

11. Refit the housing to the anchor plate with the spring clip fitted as illustrated. Fit the packing piece, locking plate and retaining spring in the order illustrated, then fit the rubber dust excluder.

12. Refit the brake shoes and pull-off springs together; **Early type**—the half-round slots in the shoe webs should be fitted to the adjuster housing. **Late type**—the fully lined end of the lower shoe must be fitted to the expander housing; the fully lined end of the upper shoe must be fitted to the adjuster housing.

13. If the brake anchor plate has been removed from the vehicle, refit it together with the brake drum and propeller shaft. Operation C1-4.

14. Reconnect the expander rod to the hand brake bell-crank lever.

15. To ensure correct clearance between the brake shoes and drum, turn the adjuster cone until the brake shoes are locked tightly against the drum; tighten the set bolts securing the adjuster housing (these were left slack on assembly) and slacken off the cone two clicks; give the brake a firm application to ensure that the shoes have centralised at the expander end. The brake drum should now be free to rotate.

16. Set the hand brake linkage at the vertical adjuster rod, so that the hand brake has one or two clicks free movement in the 'off' position.

17. Refill the transfer box with oil, 4½ pints (2,5 litres).

Fig. H1-97. Plungers in housing

Fig. H1-98. Expander assembly
A—Operating rod
B—Housing
C—Plunger
D—Roller

Fig. H1-99. Fixings for expander housing
A—Expander housing
B—Packing piece
C—Locking plate
D—Retaining spring

Fig. H1-100. Brake shoe location
A—Expander housing
B—Fully lined ends of brake shoes

BRAKING SYSTEM

Brake shoes, re-line—Operation H1-12

(For removal and refitting instructions, Operations H1-10, 10A, 10B, 10C and H1-11 refer)

Workshop hand tools:
Hammer, chisel (small), pin punch, riveting tools

To reline

1. Remove the old linings from the shoes by shearing the rivets.

    Note: Brake shoes fitted with bonded linings: If the shoes incorporate rivet holes, the bonded linings can be removed and riveted linings can be fitted in their place. If the shoes are not pre-drilled, replacement shoe and lining assemblies must be fitted.

    Important: Use the correct type new linings as detailed in the Parts Catalogue.

2. Attach the new linings to the shoes, commencing at the centre and working outwards, but only peen the rivets sufficient to locate the linings. Then with all the rivets loosely fitted, fully secure, commencing from the centre again.

3. Chamfer both ends of each lining.

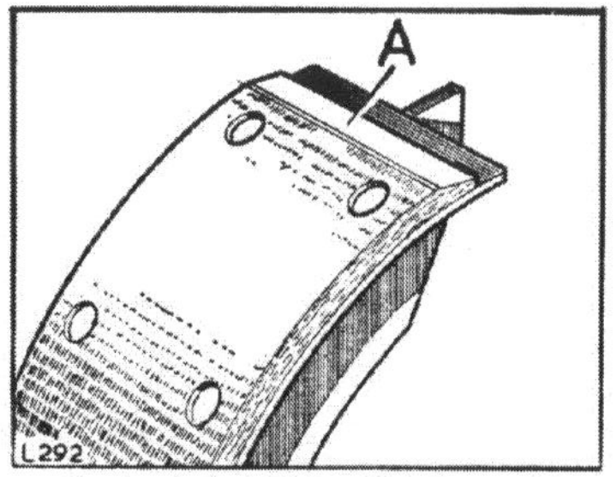

Fig. H1-101. Chamfering brake lining

A—Chamfer

Hand brake lever and linkage, remove and refit—Operation H1-13

Workshop hand tools:
Spanner sizes: ½ in. AF, 7⁄16 in. AF open end
Pliers

To remove

Caution: Before commencing work on the hand brake mechanism, chock the road wheels to prevent the vehicle moving.

Early type—up to vehicle suffix 'C'

RHStg models

1. Remove the centre inspection panel from the seat box.
2. Disconnect the transmission brake expander rod and vertical adjuster rod from the bell-crank lever.
3. Remove the hand brake assembly complete from the vehicle, withdrawing the lever grip carefully through the rubber draught excluder in the front of the seat box.
4. Remove the adjuster rod from the adjuster pin; remove the adjuster pin, thus releasing the brake catch and locating plate.
5. Remove the locating plate.
6. Remove the lever from the ratchet plate.
7. Remove the brake catch from the plunger rod and unscrew the plunger, plunger rod and spring from the brake lever.
8. Remove the bell-crank and spindle complete from the chassis.
9. Remove the bell-crank lever from the spindle.
10. If necessary, press the bush out of the lever.

LHStg models

1. Remove the centre panel from seat box.
2. Disconnect the transmission brake expander rod and vertical adjuster rod from the bell crank lever.
3. Remove the hand brake and cross-shaft complete.
4. Remove the split housing from the cross-shaft support brackets; remove the felt dust seals and self-lubricating bushes supporting the hand brake cross-shaft.
5. Strip the unit as described for RHStg models.
6. Remove the bell crank lever.

To assemble

1. Reverse the sequence of operations detailed for stripping.
2. Renew the bell crank lever bush and spindle if required.
3. LHStg models—The bushes should be greased prior to assembly and new felt seals fitted as required.
4. Set the adjuster rod by means of the locknuts at the adjuster pin, so that the hand brake lever has two ratchet clicks free movement in the 'off' position.

Latest type, from vehicle suffix 'D' onwards
(See Figs. H1-106 and H1-107)

1. From under the vehicle, disconnect the hand brake expander rod from the relay lever.

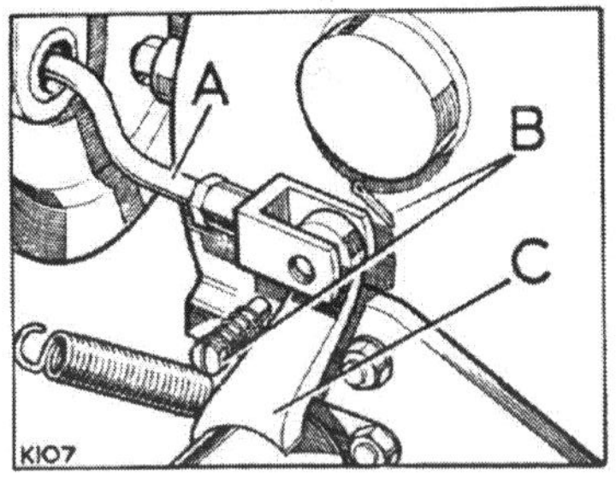

Fig. H1-102. Expander rod

A—Expander rod
B—Fixing, expander rod to relay lever
C—Relay lever

2. Remove the relay lever fixings.
3. LHStg models—Remove the fixings between the hand brake cross-shaft and the RH chassis member.

BRAKING SYSTEM

Operation H1-13—continued

4. Remove the two nuts and spring washers securing the hand brake lever to the chassis.

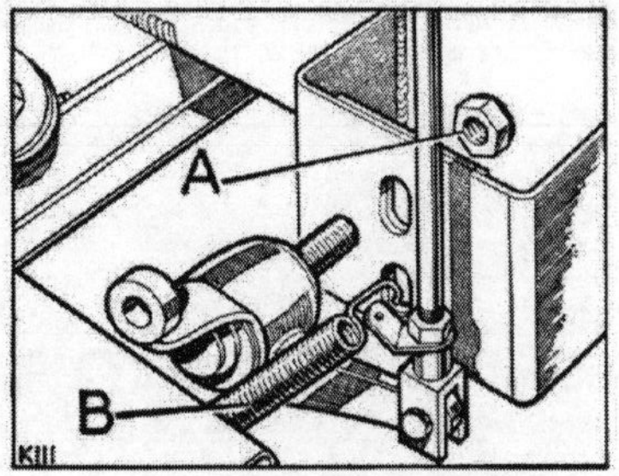

Fig. H1-103. Relay lever fixings

A—Fixings, relay mechanism to chassis
B—Return spring, transmission brake

5. Remove the hand brake assembly complete from the vehicle, withdrawing the lever grip carefully through the rubber draught excluder in the front of the seat box.

LHStg models—To facilitate removal, release the hand brake lever to ratchet fixings and withdraw the cross-shaft and lever separately.

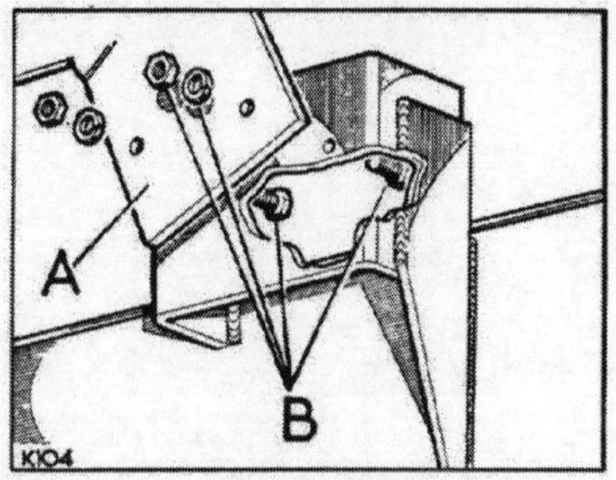

Fig. H1-104. Hand brake lever fixings

A—Mounting bracket for hand brake lever
B—Fixings, hand brake lever to chassis

Operation H1-13—continued

6. LHStg models—If required, remove the split housing from the cross-shaft support brackets; remove the felt dust seals and self-lubricating bushes supporting the hand brake cross-shaft.

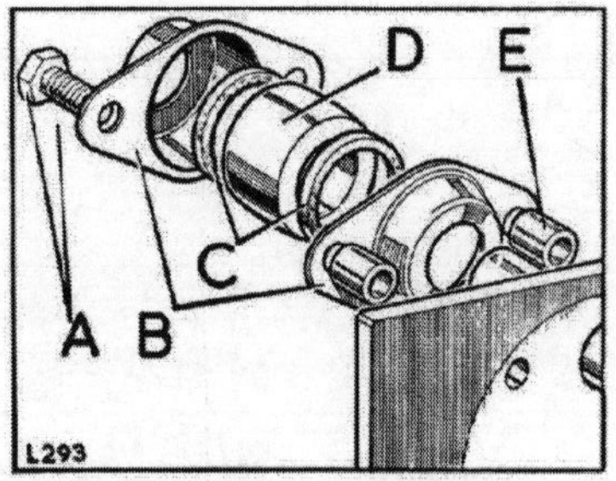

Fig. H1-105. Cross-shaft bearings

A—Fixings for bearing housing
B—Housing for bearing
C—Seal
D—Bearing
E—Distance piece

7. Remove the brake catch pin, catch and distance pieces.
8. RHStg models—Remove the fulcrum pin, ratchet fixings and ratchet from the hand brake lever.
9. Unscrew the plunger and withdraw the spring, washer and the plunger rods.
10. If required, remove the relay lever and spindle. If necessary, press the bush from the lever.

To assemble (See Figs. H1-106 and H1-107)

1. If removed, fit the bush to the relay lever and fit the relay lever and spindle to the chassis.
   Note: The bore size of a new relay lever bush is .7515 in. —.001 in. (19.088 mm —0.0254 mm)
2. Fit the plunger rods, washer, spring and plunger to the hand brake lever.
3. Fit the ratchet and brake catch to the lever, ensuring that the brake catch engages the plunger rod.
   RHStg models—Also fit the pin for the adjuster rod.
4. RHStg models—Fit the hand brake lever to the chassis. See Fig. H1-104.
5. LHStg models—Thoroughly smear the cross-shaft bearings with general purpose grease, assemble the bearings, using new seals, to the support plates. Locate the hand brake lever, cross-shaft and support plate in position. Secure the support plates to the chassis and the cross-shaft to the lever.
6. Connect the adjuster and expander rods to the relay lever. Reconnect the return spring. See Fig. H1-102.
7. Set the hand brake linkage at the vertical adjuster rod, so that the hand brake has one or two clicks free movement in the 'off' position.

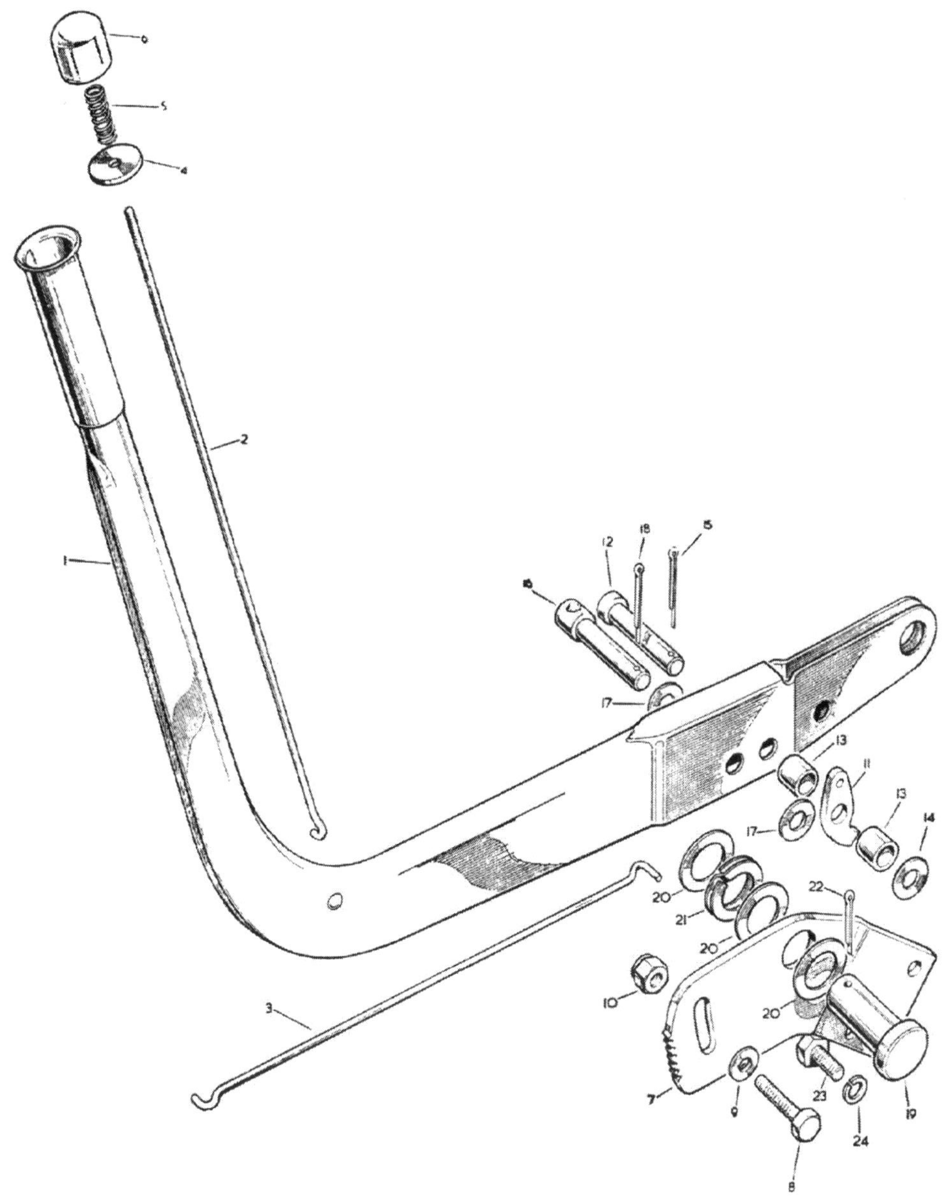

BRAKING SYSTEM

Key to illustration of hand brake lever, RHStg

1. Hand brake lever
2. Plunger rod, upper
3. Plunger rod, lower
4. Washer for plunger spring
5. Spring for plunger rod
6. Plunger
7. Ratchet for hand brake
8. Bolt ($\frac{3}{8}$ in. UNF × 1$\frac{1}{4}$ in. long) } Fixing lever to ratchet
9. Plain washer
10. Self-locking nut ($\frac{3}{8}$ in. UNF)
11. Brake catch } Fixing catch
12. Pin
13. Distance piece
14. Plain washer
15. Split pin
16. Pin for hand brake adjuster rod
17. Plain washer } Fixing pin to hand brake lever
18. Split pin
19. Fulcrum pin for hand brake lever
20. Plain washer } Fixing pin to ratchet and lever
21. Spring washer
22. Split pin
23. Bolt ($\frac{3}{8}$ in. UNF × $\frac{7}{8}$ in. long) } Fixing hand brake lever to chassis frame
24. Spring washer
    Nut ($\frac{3}{8}$ in. UNF)

Fig. H1-106. Hand brake lever, RHStg. From vehicle suffix 'D' onwards

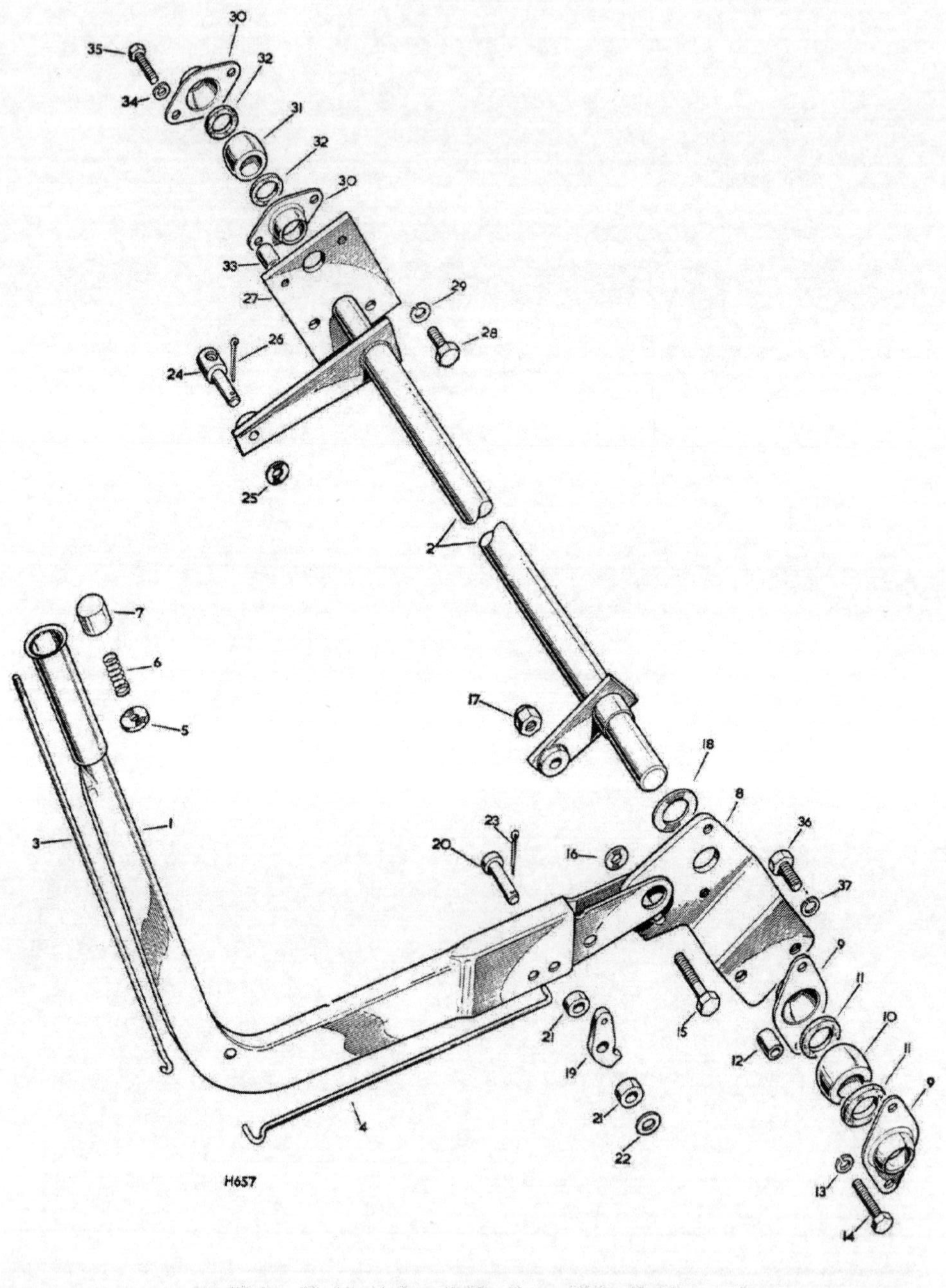

BRAKING SYSTEM

Key to Illustration of hand brake lever, LHStg

1. Hand brake lever
2. Cross-shaft for hand brake
3. Plunger rod, upper
4. Plunger rod, lower
5. Washer for plunger spring
6. Spring for plunger rod
7. Plunger
8. Ratchet for hand brake
9. Housing for cross-shaft bearing
10. Spherical bearing for cross-shaft
11. Felt ring for bearing
12. Distance piece
13. Spring washer
14. Set bolt ($\frac{7}{16}$ in. UNF × $1\frac{1}{8}$ in. long) } Fixing bearing and housing to ratchet
15. Bolt ($\frac{3}{8}$ in. UNF × $1\frac{3}{4}$ in. long) } Fixing lever to ratchet
16. Plain washer
17. Self-locking nut ($\frac{3}{8}$ in. UNF)
18. Plain washer between lever and ratchet
19. Brake catch
20. Pin
21. Distance piece } Fixing catch to lever
22. Plain washer
23. Split pin
24. Pin for hand brake adjuster rod
25. Plain washer } Fixing pin to cross-shaft lever
26. Split pin
27. Support plate for hand brake bearing housing
28. Bolt ($\frac{3}{8}$ in. UNF × $\frac{7}{8}$ in. long) } Fixing support plate to chassis frame
29. Spring washer
30. Nut ($\frac{3}{8}$ in. UNF)
31. Housing for cross-shaft bearing
32. Spherical bearing for cross-shaft
33. Felt ring for bearing
34. Distance piece
35. Spring washer
36. Set bolt ($\frac{5}{16}$ in. BSF × $\frac{7}{8}$ in. long) } Fixing housing and bearing to support plate
37. Bolt ($\frac{5}{16}$ in. UNF × $\frac{7}{8}$ in. long) } Fixing hand brake lever to chassis frame
   Spring washer
   Nut ($\frac{3}{8}$ in. UNF)

Fig. H1-107. Hand brake lever, LHStg. From vehicle suffix 'D' onwards

BRAKING SYSTEM

Servo unit (Clayton Dewandre hydraulic Type,) remove and refit—Operation H1-14

(For overhaul instructions, Operation H1-15 refers)

(For removal and refitting instructions for the Girling mechanical type servo unit, Operation H1-14A refers)

Workshop hand tools
Spanner sizes: $\frac{7}{16}$ in. AF, $\frac{1}{2}$ in. AF, $\frac{11}{16}$ in. AF open end
Screwdriver (medium)

General

Servo assisted brakes are standard on certain models, but are optional on others. When fitted, the servo unit is located in the engine compartment, but the actual position varies with different models.

To remove

1. Disconnect the fluid outlet pipe from the servo unit.
2. Disconnect the fluid inlet pipe from the servo unit. Then depress the brake pedal and wedge it in that position to prevent further leakage of brake fluid. When depressing the brake pedal, take precautions to avoid fluid spillage.

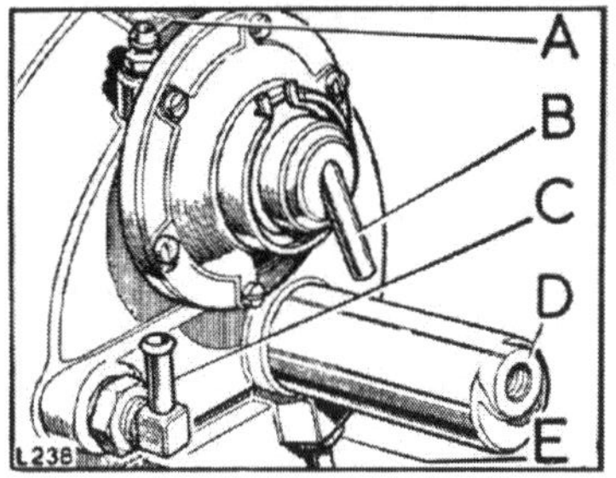

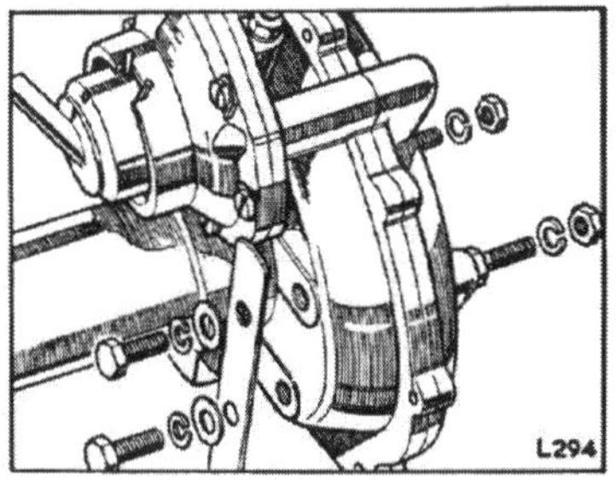

Fig. H1-109. Fixings for servo unit

3. Disconnect the vacuum hose from the servo unit.
4. Remove the fixings and withdraw the servo unit complete.

To refit

1. Locate the servo unit in position, bleed nipple uppermost, and secure the fixings.
2. Connect the fluid inlet and outlet pipes to the servo unit.
3. Connect the vacuum hose to the servo unit and secure the hose clip.
4. Bleed the complete brake system. Operation H1-1.

Fig. H1-108. Servo unit pipe connections

A—Bleed nipple
B—Air inlet (from atmosphere)
C—Vacuum hose connection
D—Fluid outlet pipe connection
E—Fluid inlet pipe connection

Servo unit (Girling mechanical type), remove and refit—Operation H1-14A

(For overhaul instructions, Operation H1-15A refers)

(For removal and refitting instructions for the Clayton Dewandre hydraulic type servo unit, Operation H1-14 refers)

Workshop hand tools:
Spanner sizes: $\frac{1}{2}$ in. AF, $\frac{7}{16}$ in. AF
Pliers (long-nosed)

To remove

1. Remove the brake master cylinder. Operation H1-5A.
2. Disconnect the electrical lead from the switch fitted to the pedal bracket.
3. Disconnect the vacuum pipe from the servo unit.

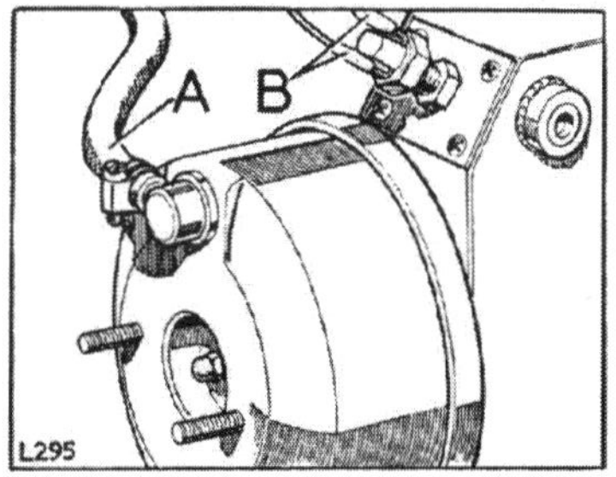

Fig. H1-110. Electrical and vacuum connections

A—Vacuum pipe from servo
B—Electrical lead from brake switch

4. Remove the fixings securing the brake pedal bracket to the toe box.

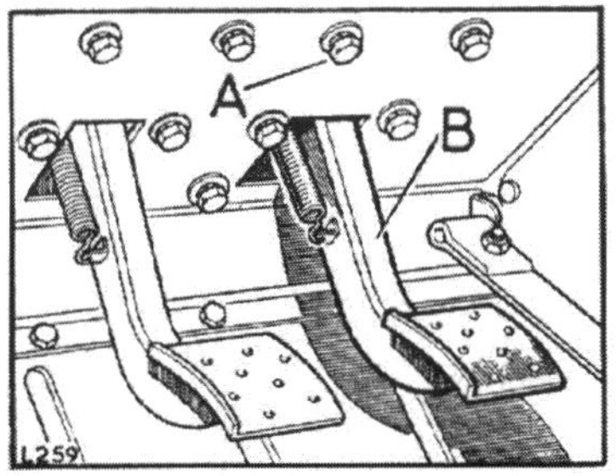

Fig. H1-111. Fixings for brake pedal bracket

A—Fixings (6 off)
B—Brake pedal

5. Carefully withdraw the brake pedal and bracket assembly from the engine compartment, manoeuvring the pedal through the aperture in the toe box.
6. Remove the split pin and pivot pin from the brake pedal to servo coupling.

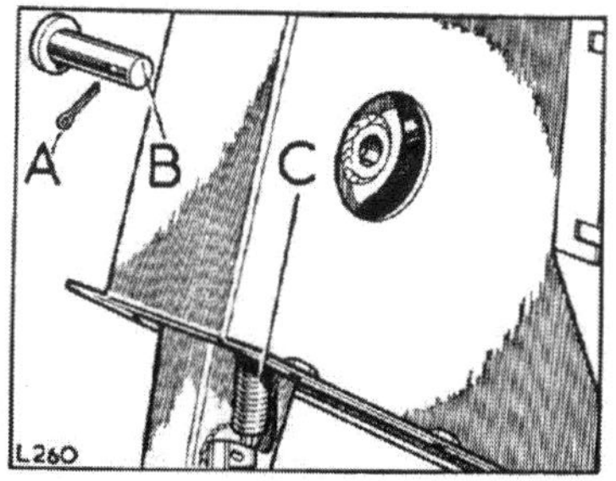

Fig. H1-112. Pedal to servo coupling

A—Split pin, securing pivot
B—Pivot pin for coupling to servo
C—Return springs for brake pedal

7. Remove the fixings and withdraw the servo unit complete from the pedal bracket.

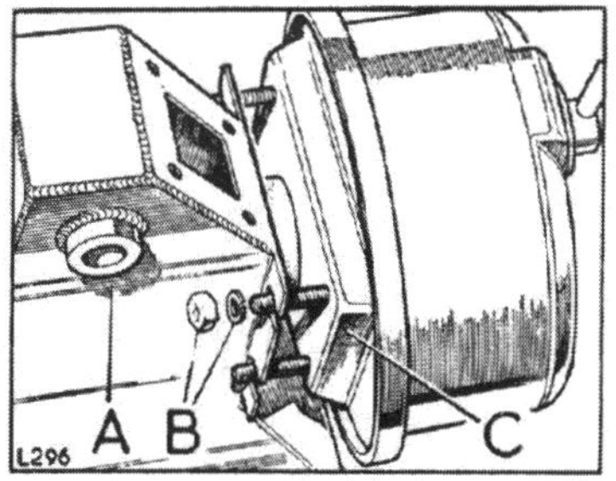

Fig. H1-113. Fixings for servo unit

A—Bracket for brake pedal
B—Fixings for servo unit
C—Servo unit

Operation H1-14A—continued

To refit

1. Secure the servo unit to the brake pedal bracket, with the vacuum connection uppermost.

2. Using a new split pin, fit the coupling pin between the pedal and servo unit.

3. Apply a waterproof sealant between the joint flanges of the pedal bracket and the toe box. A suitable sealant is 'Sealastrip', manufactured by Expandite Ltd, Chase Road, London NW10.

4. Carefully locate the brake pedal and bracket assembly in position on the toe box, manoeuvring the pedal through the aperture in the toe box, and secure in position.

5. Connect the vacuum pipe to the servo unit, and the electrical lead to the brake pedal switch.

6. Fit the brake master cylinder. Operation H1-5A. Tighten the master cylinder securing nuts to a torque figure of 16 to 19 lbs ft (2.2 to 2.6 mkg).

7. Bleed the complete braking system. Operation H1-1.

Servo unit (Clayton Dewandre hydraulic type), overhaul—Operation H1-15

(For removal and refitting instructions, Operation H1-14 refers)

Workshop hand tools:
Spanner sizes: $\frac{7}{16}$ in. AF, $\frac{15}{16}$ in. AF, $1\frac{1}{4}$ in. AF open end
Screwdriver, Pliers

To dismantle

1. Remove the circlip securing the air cleaner and withdraw the cleaner, joint washer, spring and poppet valve.

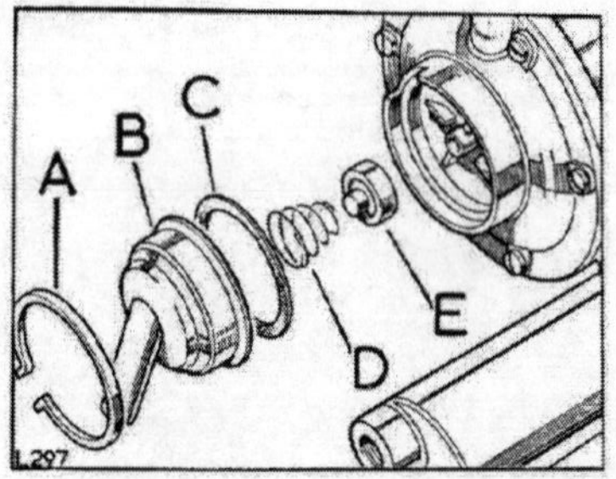

Fig. H1-114. Air cleaner and poppet valve
A—Circlip
B—Air cleaner
C—Joint washer for breather
D—Spring for poppet valve
E—Poppet valve

2. Remove the cover and joint washer from the reaction diaphragm housing and withdraw the spring and the diaphragm assembly.

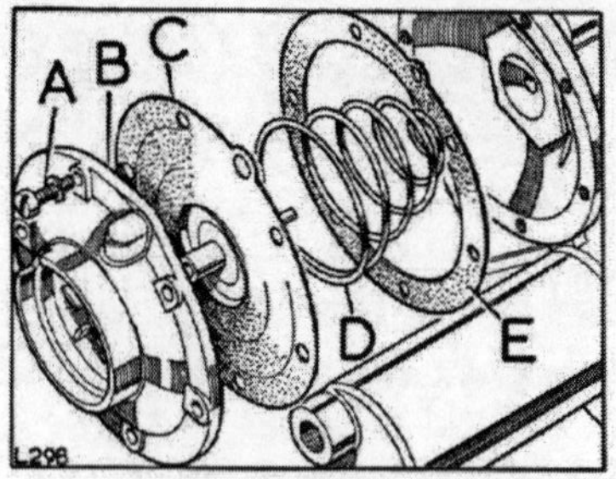

Fig. H1-115. Reaction diaphragm
A—Fixings for cover
B—Cover for reaction diaphragm
C—Reaction diaphragm assembly
D—Spring
E—Joint washer for cover

3. Unscrew the housing for the hydraulic plunger and withdraw the plunger complete with seals. Remove the plunger seals and the 'O' ring from the housing.

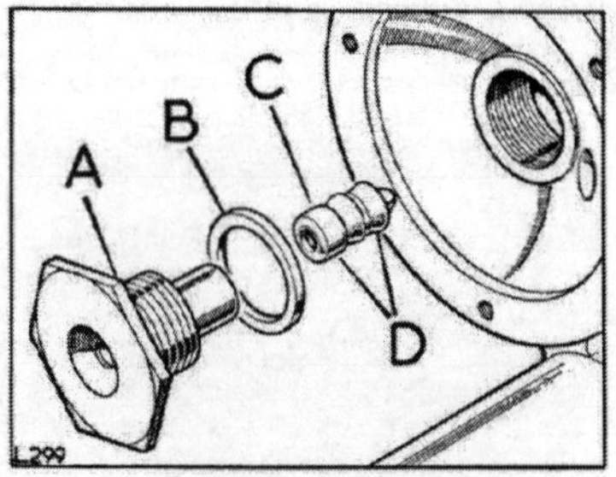

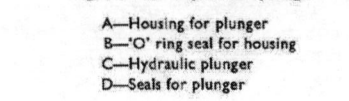

Fig. H1-116. Hydraulic plunger
A—Housing for plunger
B—'O' ring seal for housing
C—Hydraulic plunger
D—Seals for plunger

4. Remove the elbow union and joint washer, and withdraw the spring guide, spring and non-return valve.

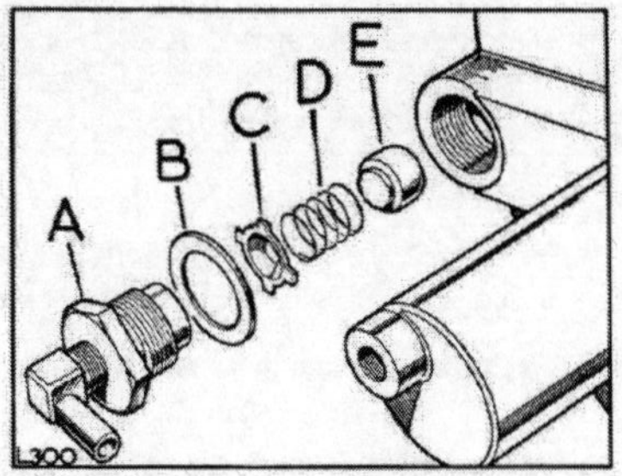

Fig. H1-117. Non-return valve
A—Elbow union
B—Joint washer
C—Spring guide
D—Spring
E—Non-return valve

BRAKING SYSTEM

Operation H1-15—continued

5. Remove the vacuum chamber cover, taking care to retain the connector tube located between the rim of the cover and chamber.

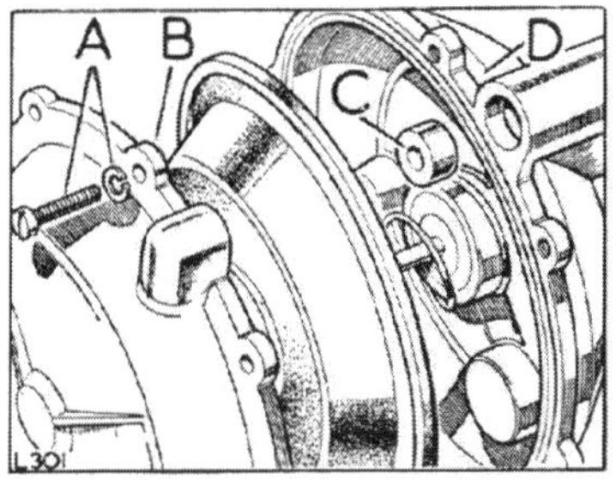

Fig. H1-118. Cover for vacuum chamber

A—Fixings for cover
B—Cover
C—Connector tube
D—Vacuum chamber

6. Withdraw the diaphragm assembly and spring.

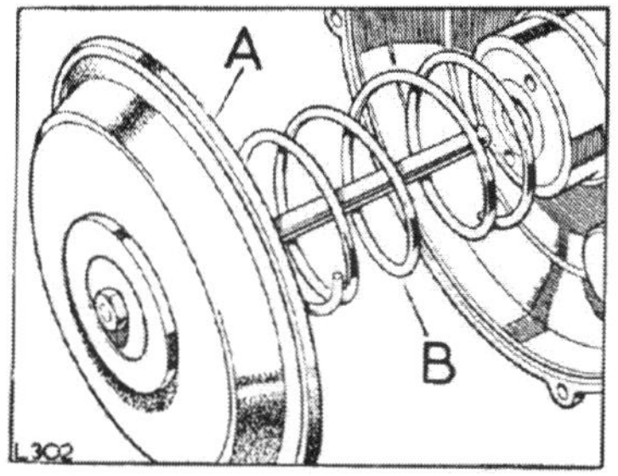

Fig. H1-119. Power diaphragm

A—Diaphragm assembly
B—Spring

7. Using the extractor holes provided, unscrew the push rod housing and withdraw the spring, retaining ring, seal retainer, seal and backing washer.

8. Press the oil seal from the push rod housing.

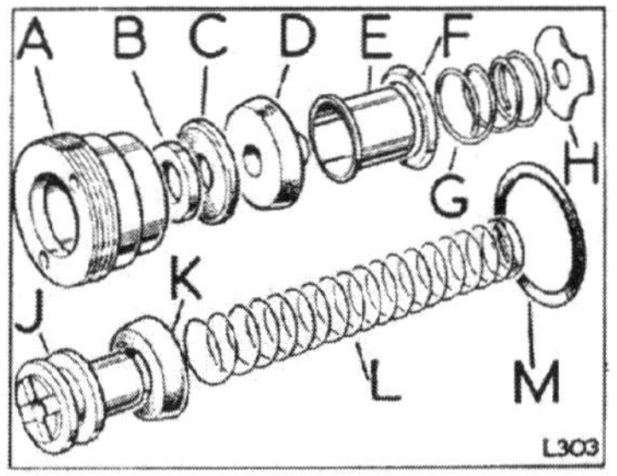

Fig. H1-120. Push rod housing and hydraulic piston

A—Push rod housing
B—Seal for housing
C—Backing washer for seal
D—Seal for push rod
E—Seal retainer
F—Retaining ring for seal
G—Spring, retaining seal
H—Guide washer for push rod
J—Hydraulic piston
K—Seal for piston
L—Spring for hydraulic piston
M—'O' ring seal for cylinder

9. Withdraw the guide washer, hydraulic piston, spring and 'O' ring from the cylinder.

Fig. H1-121. Power diaphragm fixings

A—Fixings for diaphragm
B—Power diaphragm
C—Push rod

10. Remove the seal from the hydraulic piston.
11. Remove the fixings and withdraw the power diaphragm.

Inspection

1. Clean all components in Girling cleaning fluid and allow to dry.
2. Examine the cylinder bore and piston, push rod ball end, non-return valve, poppet valve and hydraulic plunger. Ensure that they are free from corrosion and are not scored or scratched. If there is any doubt, fit new replacements.
3. All seals, joint washers and the diaphragms should be replaced with new components.

To assemble

1. Smear the hydraulic piston seal and the hydraulic plunger seals with Castrol-Girling rubber grease, and the piston, cylinder bore, plunger and plunger bore with Castrol-Girling Brake and Clutch Fluid.

   Important: It is essential that all remaining components are assembled in a perfectly clean and dry condition.

2. Fit the large plain washer to the push rod, followed by the support plate, diaphragm and recessed washer. The support plate and diaphragm must be fitted lipped edge first, and the recessed washer, inner recess first. Secure the assembly.
3. Fit the seal to the groove in the hydraulic piston, with the seal lip towards the small diameter of the piston.
4. Place the 'O' ring seal for the push rod housing into the cylinder.
5. Insert the long spring and the hydraulic piston, small diameter end first, into the cylinder.
6. Press the seal, lipped side inward, into the push rod housing.
7. Insert the fibre washer, chamfered side first, into the push rod housing, followed by the seal (plain side first), seal retainer (flanged end first), seal retaining ring (chamfered side first) and the seal retaining spring.

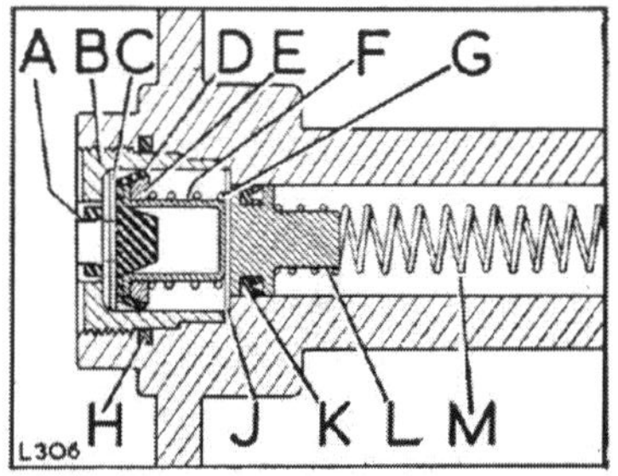

Fig. H1-122. Hydraulic piston assembly

A—Seal for push rod housing
B—Push rod housing
C—Backing washer for seal
D—Seal for push rod
E—Seal retaining ring
F—Seal retainer
G—Spring, retaining seal
H—'O' ring seal for push rod housing
J—Guide washer, three leg
K—Seal for hydraulic piston
L—Hydraulic piston
M—Spring for hydraulic piston

8. Place the three-legged guide washer in position on the hydraulic piston and screw the assembled push rod housing into the cylinder and tighten firmly.
9. Place the spring for the power diaphragm in position in the vacuum chamber, and insert the power diaphragm, locating the push rod into its housing. See Fig. H1-117.
10. Fit the connector tube to the air passage at the rim of the vacuum chamber.
11. Fit the cover to the vacuum chamber, aligning the connecting tube and ensuring that the diaphragm locates in the groove in the vacuum chamber rim. Tighten the fixings evenly and securely. See Fig. H1-118.
12. Locate the spring on to the back of the non-return valve and insert the assembly into its housing in the vacuum chamber. Fit the spring guide, domed side first, followed by the elbow union and joint washer. See Fig. H1-117.

Section H—Land-Rover

Servo unit (Girling mechanical type), overhaul—Operation H1-15A

(For removal and refitting instructions, Operation H1-14A refers)

Workshop hand tools:
Screwdriver (small)

Special tools:
Base plate and lever (see Fig. H1-129)

General

The Girling Supervac is a mechanical servo unit designed to provide power assistance in an exact and controlled manner to the effort applied by the driver's foot to the brake pedal. Vacuum created in the engine inlet manifold is used to suspend in vacuum a diaphragm and by admitting atmospheric pressure to one side of the diaphragm, the force which assists the driver's pedal effort is obtained.

The unit is mounted between the brake pedal and the master cylinder and connected to these parts by push rods. Should a vacuum failure occur, the two push rods act as a single rod; the brakes will therefore work in the conventional manner but more effort will be required on the brake pedal.

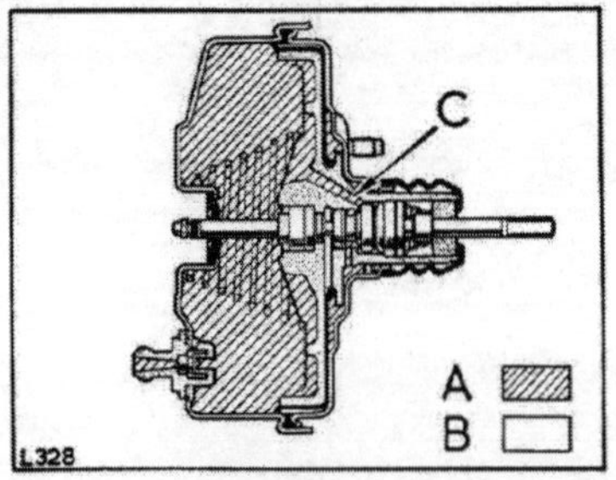

control valve, opening the atmospheric port which is formed between these two parts. Atmospheric pressure then enters the rear shell behind the diaphragm and is assisted by the valve rod in pushing the diaphragm plate forwards and thus the hydraulic push rod actuates the master cylinder plunger.

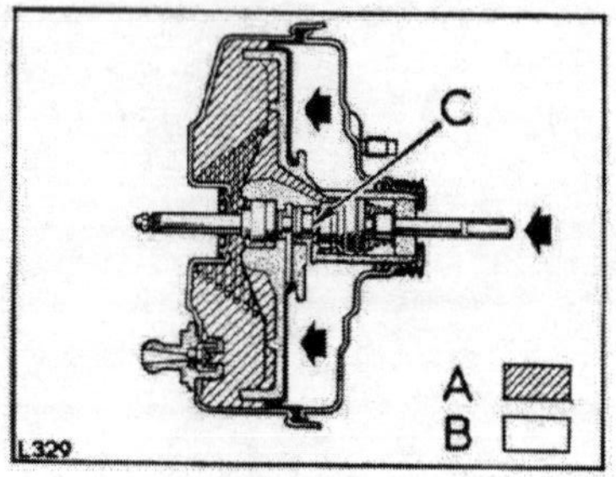

Fig. H1-125. Brake applied
A—Vacuum
B—Air
C—Atmospheric port

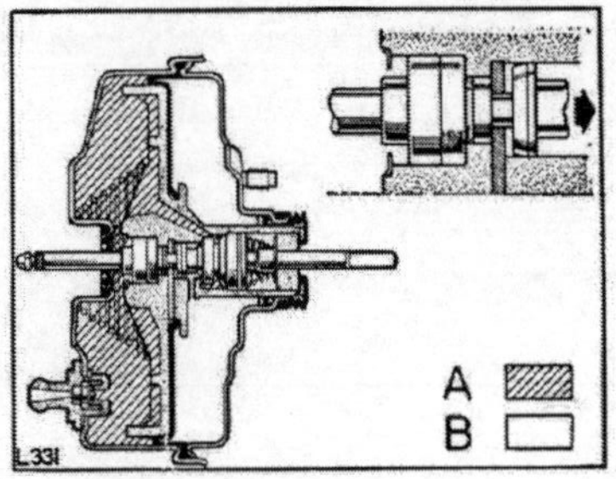

Fig. H1-124. Brake 'off'
A—Vacuum
B—Air
C—Vacuum port

Fig. H1-126. Brake held on
A—Vacuum
B—Air

The diaphragm is fully recuperated and is held against the rear shell by the diaphragm return spring. The valve rod assembly is also fully recuperated by the brake pedal return spring within the diaphragm plate, as far as the stop key, or valve retaining plate will allow. With the valve rod in this position the vacuum port is open and there is a vacuum each side of the diaphragm.

When the brake pedal is depressed, the valve rod assembly moves forward inside the diaphragm plate until the control valve closes the vacuum port; at this junction vacuum is still present on each side of the diaphragm. As the valve rod continues to move forward, the control piston moves away from the

---

Operation H1-15—continued

13. Fit the seals to the hydraulic plunger, with the seal lips towards the cone end of the plunger. See Fig. H1-116.

14. Insert the hydraulic plunger, cone end last, into its housing. Fit the 'O' ring seal to the housing and screw the assembly into the centre of the reaction diaphragm housing. See Fig. H1-116.

15. Place the joint washer in position on the reaction valve housing, ensuring that the hole for the air passage is aligned.

16. Fit the reaction diaphragm assembly, locating the domed end of the vacuum valve into the centre of the hydraulic plunger housing, and ensuring that the air passage hole is aligned.

17. Place the spring in position in the cover for the reaction diaphragm, and fit the cover ensuring that the air passage holes in the cover, diaphragm, joint washer and housing are all aligned. Tighten the fixings evenly and securely. See Fig. H1-115.

18. Locate the poppet valve, flat side inward, and the spring, small end first, into the centre of the reaction diaphragm cover.

19. Fit the gasket and air cleaner to the reaction diaphragm cover, with the inlet pipe positioned so that it will face downwards when on the vehicle. Secure with the circlip. See Fig. H1-114.

20. Fit new sealing washers between the vacuum chamber cover and hexagon shanks of the servo unit mounting studs. Securely tighten the studs.

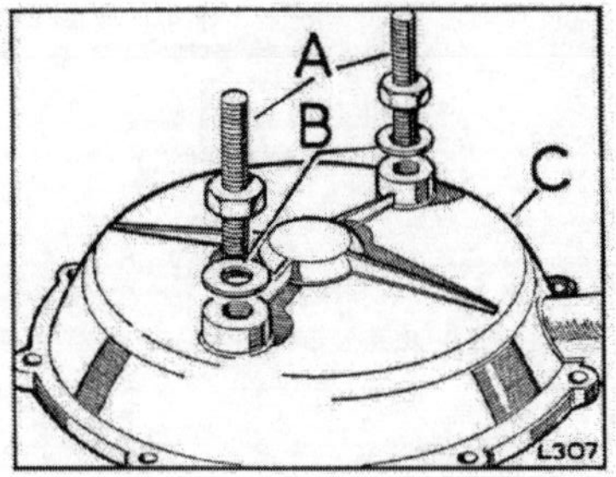

Fig. H1-123. Mounting studs and seals
A—Studs for servo unit mounting
B—Sealing washers for studs
C—Cover for vacuum chamber

BRAKING SYSTEM

Operation H1-15A—continued

When the brake pedal is held on, the diaphragm will momentarily continue to move forward and so compress the outer edges of the reaction disc. This movement causes the centre of the disc to extrude, pressing back the push rod (see insert) and thus closing the atmospheric port. Further movement of the brake pedal either opens the vacuum port or the atmospheric port, depending on whether the brake pedal is released or depressed.

Immediately the brake pedal is released, the vacuum port is opened and the atmospheric pressure in the rear chamber is extracted into the inlet manifold via the non-return valve. The vacuum draws the two halves of the shell together and compresses the diaphragm between the rim of the shells.

To clear the lock on the outer rim, turn the lever anti-clockwise until the recesses in the rim of the shell are in line with the indentations in the front shell. Remove the vacuum hose from the non-return valve and switch off the engine. Depress the operating rod a few times to allow air to enter the unit.

Caution: It is important to press down firmly on top of the unit when atmospheric pressure is allowed to enter, otherwise the diaphragm return spring may cause the two shells to fly apart.

If the halves do not separate immediately, tap the front shell with a hide-faced hammer to break the bond between the shells.

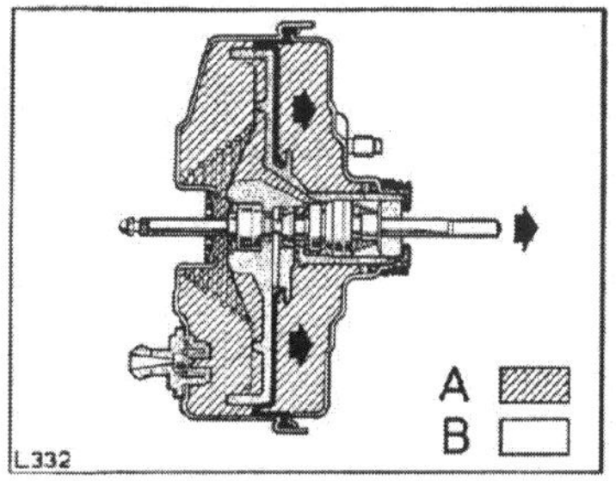

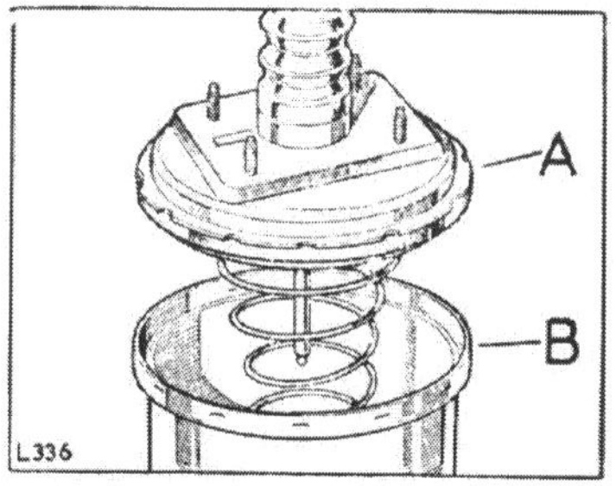

Fig. H1-127. Brake released
A—Vacuum
B—Air

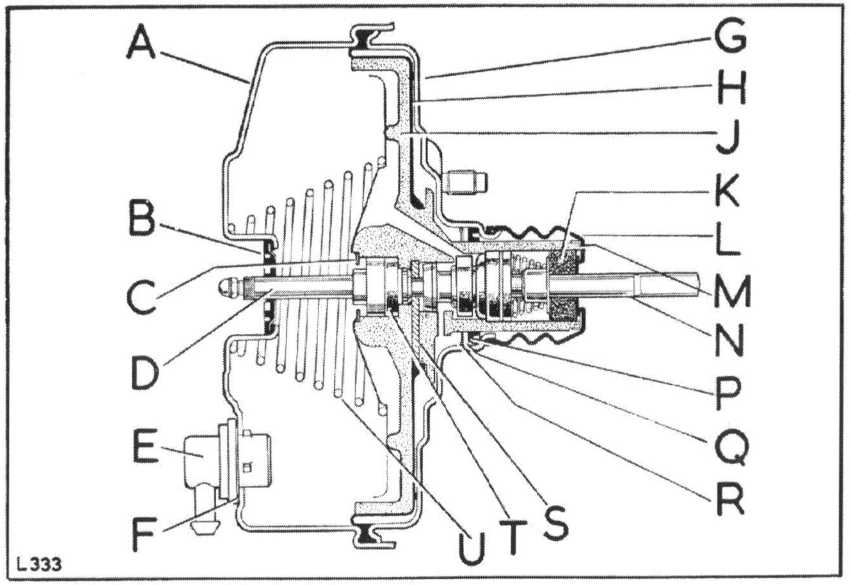

Fig. H1-128. Section view of unit

A—Front shell
B—Seal and plate assembly
C—Retainer sprag washer
D—Hydraulic push rod
E—Non-return valve
F—'O' ring
G—Rear shell
H—Diaphragm
J—Diaphragm plate
K—Filter
L—Dust cover
M—End cap
N—Valve operating rod assembly
P—Seal
Q—Bearing
R—Retainer
S—Valve retaining plate
T—Reaction disc
U—Diaphragm return spring

Operation H1-15A—continued

To dismantle

Special tools, shown in Fig. H1-129 are needed to dismantle and reassemble the unit. Without these tools, it is impossible to separate the two halves of the unit. If the push rod is damaged a new push rod kit is required because, due to an application of Loctite on the bolt threads, the existing push rod cannot be re-adjusted once the height is set. Before commencing to dismantle the unit, scribe a line across the two halves of the shells, as shown, to enable the shells to be reassembled in the same position.

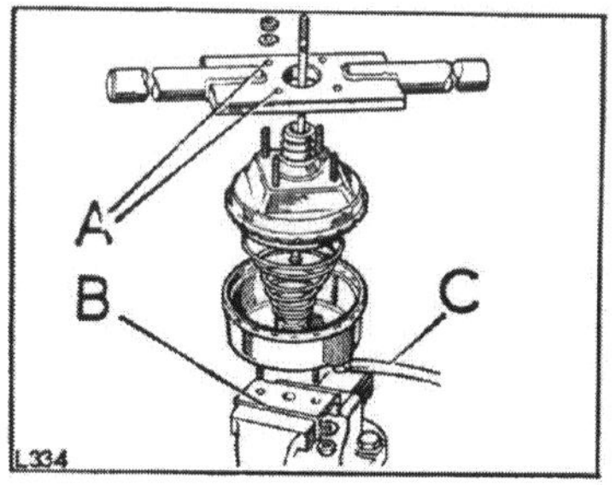

1. To separate the two halves of the assembly, clamp the base plate (Fig. H1-129) in a bench vice. Place the unit on top of this, inserting the studs of the front shell into the holes in the plate, and secure the unit to the plate by two spring washers and nuts.

2. Place the lever on top of the rear shell, locating the studs in the holes in the lever and secure with nuts and washers.

3. Connect one end of a vacuum hose to the non-return valve and the other to the engine inlet manifold. Start the engine. The vacuum draws the two halves of the shell together and compresses the diaphragm between the rim of the shells.

Fig. H1-129. Tools required for overhauling unit
A—Lever with holes drilled to suit the unit being serviced
B—Base plate with holes drilled to suit the unit being serviced
C—Vacuum hose

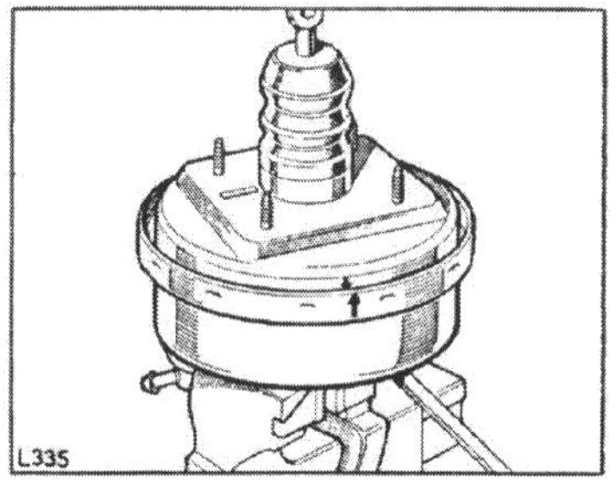

Fig. H1-130. Scribing alignment marks across the two halves of the shell

Fig. H1-131. Removing rear shell
A—Rear shell
B—Front shell

Operation H1-15A—continued

4. Lift off the rear shell and diaphragm return spring. Remove the dust cover, end cap and filter then withdraw the diaphragm and diaphragm plate from the rear shell.

5. To remove the valve rod assembly, remove the diaphragm from the plate, depress the valve rod and shake out the valve retaining plate. The valve rod assembly may now be pulled from the neck of the diaphragm.

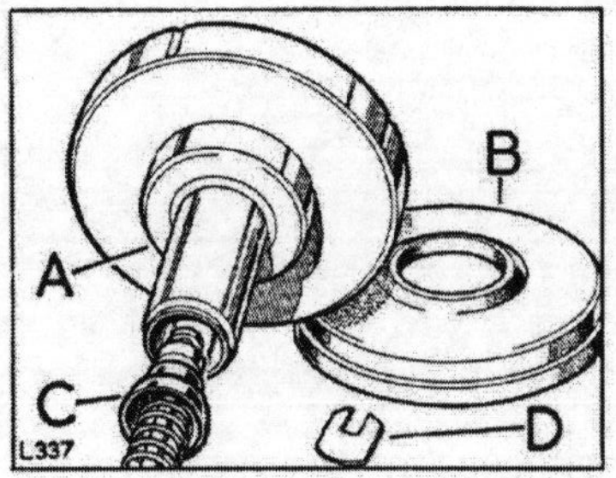

Fig. H1-132. Diaphragm and valve rod assembly

A—Diaphragm plate
B—Diaphragm
C—Valve rod assembly
D—Valve retaining plate

6. The hydraulic push rod is retained by a sprag washer to the diaphragm plate. Use a small screw-driver to ease the washer from the plate and withdraw the push rod and reaction disc.

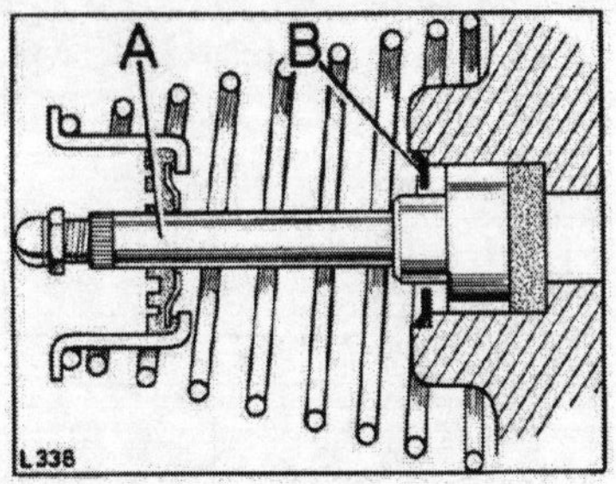

Fig. H1-133. Hydraulic push rod

A—Push rod
B—Sprag washer

7. Remove the seal, bearing and retainer from the neck of the rear shell. Ease out the retainer with a small screwdriver and press out the seal and bearing, but take care not to damage the sealing surface of the shell.

8. Press out the seal and plate assembly from the front shell.

Operation H1-15A—continued

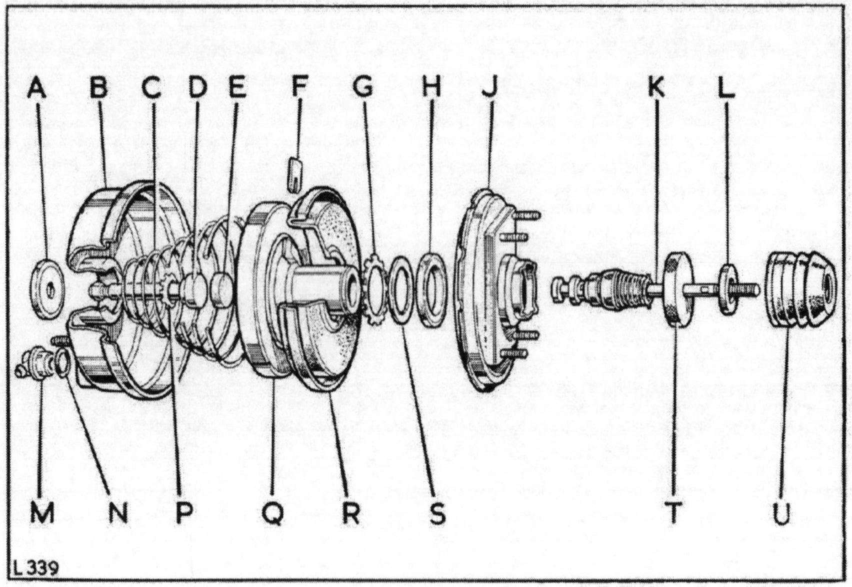

Fig. H1-134. Exploded view of unit

A—Seal and plate assembly
B—Front shell
C—Diaphragm return spring
D—Hydraulic push rod
E—Reaction disc
F—Valve retaining plate
G—Retainer
H—Seal
J—Rear shell
K—Valve operating rod assembly
L—End cap
M—Non-return valve
N—'O' ring
P—Retainer sprag washer
Q—Diaphragm plate
R—Bearing
S—Bearing
T—Filter
U—Dust cover

Operation H1-15A—continued

9. Remove the non-return valve by pulling on the nozzle whilst exerting a side load. If the nozzle is straight, it is easier to remove the valve if the hose is left clipped on. Alternatively, remove the valve by levering with a suitable screwdriver, but care should be taken not to damage the front shell.

The unit is now dismantled and ready for servicing.

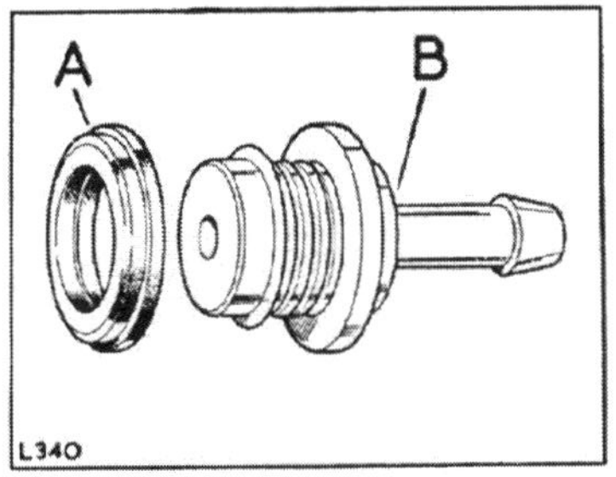

Fig. H1-135. Non-return valve

A—Seal
B—Non-return valve

Inspection

1. Clean all parts with Girling cleaning fluid, making sure that all traces of dirt and grit are removed. Place the cleaned parts on to a clean sheet of paper and allow to dry.

2. Examine all components for obvious signs of wear or damage and fit new replacements as required.

3. Servo overhaul kits are available containing all the components, except the hydraulic push rod, for a normal service overhaul.

To assemble

Important: The two servo greases contained in the overhaul kit must only be used as directed. THEY ARE NOT INTERCHANGEABLE. Considerable damage will be caused to the unit if they are incorrectly used.

1. Smear the seal and bearing with grease No. 64949008, then fit to the rear shell. The flat face of the seal should be adjacent to the bearing and the seal should be pressed firmly into position. Fit the retainer.

2. Smear the reaction disc and the hydraulic push rod with grease No. 64949008 and fit to the diaphragm plate. Refer to Fig. H1-133.

3. Smear grease No. 64949008 to the outer diameter of the diaphragm plate neck and bearing surfaces of the valve plunger. The valve rod assembly should now be inserted into the neck of the diaphragm plate and secured by the valve retaining plate. Fig. H1-132.

4. Lubricate the new grommet for the non-return valve with Girling grease No. 64949009. **Do not use any other lubricant.** Fit the grommet to the front shell and push in the non-return valve.

5. Smear grease No. 64949008 on to the seal and plate assembly. Place the seal and plate assembly over the push rod (with plate side leading) and press into the recess in the front shell.

6. Place the front shell on top of the base plate in the manner used when dismantling the unit. Locate the diaphragm return spring into the front shell. Smear the outer bead of the diaphragm with servo grease No. 64949009 and fit, complete with diaphragm plate, into the rear shell. Place this assembly on top of the spring. Put the lever on top of the unit, locating the studs in the shell into the holes in the lever. Before pressing the rear shell firmly down on the front shell, ensure that the scribed lines will be in alignment. Figs. H1-131 and H1-130.

7. Connect the vacuum hose to the non-return valve and start the engine. Press the two halves firmly together and turn the rear shell clockwise to bring it into the locked position. Remove the vacuum pipe from the non-return valve.

8. Ease the filter over the end of the push rod and press into the neck of the diaphragm plate. Fit the plastic end cap. Ease the dust cover on to the push rod and locate on the lugs of the rear shell.

Important: **The length of the hydraulic push rod should never be altered.** The adjustment bolt threads are coated with Loctite (Grade B) and will strip if moved. If, because of damage, a new push rod is required, setting instructions are included in the push rod kit and not included here as dimensions differ.

Operation H1-15A—continued

To test the unit

1. Check all brakes for locking on, by rapidly applying the brake pedal several times and then checking to see if all wheels are free.

2. Check for vacuum hold by starting the engine and allowing it to run for several minutes to build a working vacuum in the unit.

After ten minutes apply the brake pedal and entry of air into unit should be heard. This means the unit is holding vacuum and is working correctly.

BRAKING SYSTEM

Exhauster for servo unit, Diesel models, overhaul—Operation H1-16

Workshop hand tools:
Spanner size: ¼ in. BSF open end
Screwdriver (medium)

To dismantle

1. Remove the woodruff key from the rotor shaft.
2. Remove the fixings and withdraw the cover and joint washer from the rotor housing.
3. Withdraw the rotor complete with vanes.
4. Prise the oil seal from the rotor housing.
5. Remove the inlet union from the rotor housing.

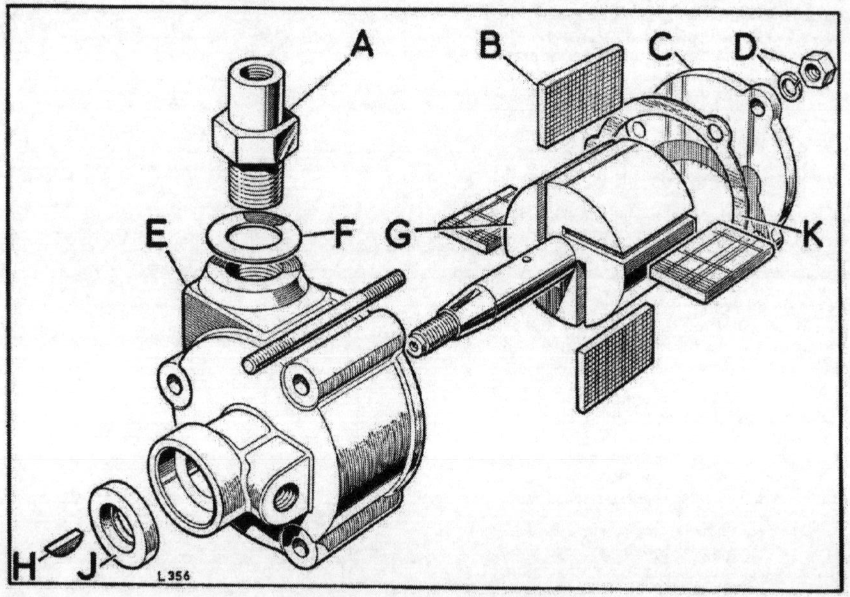

Fig. H1-136. Rotary exhauster

A—Inlet union
B—Vane for rotor
C—Cover for housing
D—Fixings for cover
E—Rotor housing
F—Washer for union
G—Rotor
H—Woodruff key
J—Oil seal
K—Joint washer for cover

BRAKING SYSTEM

Operation H1-16—continued

Inspection

1. Examine the bush in the rotor housing. If there is obvious wear between the bush and the rotor shaft, a new replacement unit complete should be obtained.
2. If the rotor bush is in good condition, check the rotor shaft where it forms a running seat for the oil seal. The surface of the shaft must be free from damage or scratches which would cause seal failure.
3. The rotor vanes, oil seal, joint washer for cover, sealing washer for inlet union and spring washers for fixings should all be replaced with new components. These items are all included in the exhauster repair kit.

To assemble

1. Smear jointing compound on the outside diameter of the oil seal and press the seal, lipped side first, into the rotor housing.
2. Locate the four vanes, radiused edge outward, into the rotor slots; smear the rotor shaft with lubricating oil and insert the rotor into the housing.
3. Using the thickest joint washer from the repair kit, fit the cover to the housing, checking that the rotor turns freely while tightening the cover fixings. If the rotor becomes stiff to turn, add the thin joint washer between the housing and cover. Alternatively, if there is excessive rotor end float, use the thin joint washer only. Tighten the cover fixings evenly and securely.
4. Using the new sealing washer from the repair kit, fit the inlet union to the rotor housing.
5. Fit the woodruff key to the rotor shaft.

BRAKE SYSTEM

Fault diagnosis—Brake system

Symptom	Possible cause	Investigation	Remedy
Spongy pedal action	Air in hydraulic system	If available, use Girling hose clamps to locate air	Bleed the brake system as necessary
	Incorrect adjustment of brake shoes	Check brake shoe adjustment, also if applicable, check brake shoe steady post adjustment	Adjust as necessary
	Swollen rubber components, due to incorrect brake fluid	Check that fluid is Castrol-Girling Crimson Brake and Clutch fluid	Drain the complete brake system, renew the affected parts and replenish with correct fluid
Loss of brake pedal pressure	Leak in brake hydraulic system	Check the brake pipes, master cylinder and wheel cylinders. If available, use Girling hose clamps to locate the leak	Fit new parts as required and bleed the brake system
Hard brake pedal	Incorrect shoe adjustment	Check brake shoe adjustment, also if applicable, check brake shoe steady post adjustment	Adjust as necessary
	Incorrect brake linings	See Parts Catalogue for recommended type	Fit correct linings
	Restriction in master cylinder	Remove and dismantle master cylinder	Fit new parts as required
Binding brake pedal	Loose master cylinder mounting bolts	Check master cylinder fixings to brake pedal bracket. If the vehicle is fitted with a mechanical servo unit, check servo to brake pedal bracket fixings	Securely tighten
	Worn or tight pedal shaft	Apply lubrication via oil hole provided. If still unsatisfactory, remove pedal	Renew worn parts and lubricate during assembly
Brake pedal fails to return	Pedal return spring weak or missing		Fit new spring
	Loose master cylinder mounting bolts	Check master cylinder fixings to pedal bracket. If vehicle is fitted with a mechanical servo unit, check servo to pedal bracket fixings	Securely tighten
	Sticking pedal shaft	Apply lubrication via oil hole provided. If still unsatisfactory, remove pedal	Renew worn parts and lubricate during assembly
Poor brakes	Incorrect brake shoe adjustment	Check brake shoe adjustment, also if applicable, check brake shoe steady post adjustment	Adjust as necessary
	Incorrect master cylinder adjustment	Check push rod for free play	Adjust as necessary
	Water soaked linings		Dry the brake linings by applying the brakes lightly whilst driving
	Glazed or oil contaminated linings	Remove brake drums and inspect linings. Check for brake fluid leakage from wheel cylinders	Fit new linings. Fit new oil seal or wheel cylinder components as necessary
	Incorrect brake linings	See Parts Catalogue for recommended type	Fit correct linings

Fault diagnosis—Brake system—continued

Symptom	Possible cause	Investigation	Remedy
Chattering brakes	Incorrect adjustment of brake shoes	Check brake shoe adjustment, also if applicable, check brake shoe steady post adjustment	Adjust as necessary
	Loose front wheel bearings	Check bearing adjustment and wear condition	Adjust or fit new bearings as required
	High spots on brake drum or distorted drum	Remove drum and check concentricity	Recondition or fit new brake drum and fit new linings as necessary
Grabbing brakes	Incorrect shoe adjustment	Check brake shoe adjustment, also if applicable, check brake shoe steady post adjustment	Adjust as necessary
	Grease, oil or brake fluid soaked linings	Remove brake drums and inspect linings. Check for worn oil seal in hub or fluid leakage from wheel cylinder	Fit new linings. Fit new oil seal or wheel cylinder components as necessary
	Incorrect linings	See Parts Catalogue for recommended type	Fit correct linings
	Scored or cracked drums	Remove drums and inspect	Recondition or replace with new
Side pull	High spots on drum or distorted drum	Remove drum and check concentricity	Recondition or replace with new
	Incorrect shoe adjustment	Check brake shoe adjustment, also if applicable, check brake shoe steady post adjustment	Adjust as necessary
	Incorrect tyre pressures	Check tyre pressures. Section R	Adjust as necessary
	Water and mud in brakes	Clean the brake assemblies, examine drums for scoring, and linings for wear	Fit new parts as necessary
	Clogged or crimped brake hose or pipe	Check flexible hoses. Check all brake pipes for signs of crimping	Clear hose or pipe with air pressure. Fit new hoses or pipes as necessary
	Loose wheel cylinders	Check wheel cylinder fixings	Tighten as necessary
	Mixed types of shoe linings	Check all shoe linings	Fit a set of one of the recommended types of lining
	Excessive wear in brake drum or scored brake drum	Remove drum and inspect	Recondition or fit new drum
Squealing brakes	Shoes binding on steady posts (where applicable)	Check steady post adjustment	Adjust as necessary
	Incorrect linings	See Parts Catalogue for recommended type	Fit correct linings
	Dust or road dirt in drums	Remove drums and clean thoroughly	
	Foreign bodies embedded in brake linings	Remove brake drums and examine linings	If necessary, fit new linings and recondition or renew the brake drum
	Loose wheel cylinders	Check wheel cylinder fixings	Fit new linings
	Sprung or bent brake shoes	Examine brake shoes	Tighten as necessary
			Fit new brake shoes

Fault diagnosis—Brake system—*continued*

Symptom	Possible cause	Investigation	Remedy
	Distorted brake drum	Check drum for concentricity	Recondition or fit new replacement
	Bent brake anchor plate	Examine brake plate	Fit new brake anchor plate
Brakes overheating	Brake shoes in continuous contact with drum	Check brake shoe adjustment	Adjust as necessary
	Incorrect master cylinder adjustment	Check adjustment as described under master cylinder overhaul	Adjust as necessary
	High spots on brake drum	Check brake drum	Recondition or fit new drum
	Dust or road dirt in drums	Remove drums and clean thoroughly	If necessary, fit new linings and recondition or renew brake drum
	Defective master cylinder or swollen rubber components	Remove and dismantle master cylinder	Fit new parts as required
Fading brakes	Poor lining contact	Check brake shoe adjustment	Adjust as necessary
	Incorrect linings	See Parts Catalogue for recommended type	Fit correct linings
	Excessive heat		Fit new linings to brake shoes
One brake drags	Incorrect brake adjustment	Check brake shoe adjustment. Also if applicable, check brake shoe steady post adjustment	Adjust as necessary
	Distorted rubber boots	Remove brake drum and check rubber boots at wheel cylinders	Fit new rubber boots
	Siezed brake shoe	Check that shoes move freely at pivot and wheel cylinder	Free the brake shoe from its anchor and smear the point of seizure lightly with grease
	Seized piston in wheel cylinder	Remove brake drum and check that pistons move freely in cylinders	Fit new wheel cylinder complete
	Weak or broken brake shoe pull-off springs		Fit new springs
	Loose wheel cylinders	Check wheel cylinder fixings	Tighten as necessary
	Distorted brake drum	Check drum for concentricity	Recondition or fit new replacement
	Loose front wheel bearings	Check bearing adjustment and wear condition	Adjust or fit new bearings as required
	Restriction or obstruction in brake pipe	Check all brake pipes for signs of crimping	Clear brake pipe with air pressure. Fit new pipes as necessary
All brakes drag	Incorrect adjustment of brake shoes	Check brake shoe adjustment, also if applicable, check steady post adjustment	Adjust as necessary
	Incorrect master cylinder adjustment	Check push rod for free play	Adjust as necessary
	Distorted rubber boots	Remove brake drums and check rubber boots at wheel cylinders	Fit new rubber boots

Fault diagnosis—Brake system—*continued*

Symptom	Possible cause	Investigation	Remedy
	Weak or broken brake shoe pull-off springs		Fit new springs
	Restriction in master cylinder	Remove and dismantle master cylinder	Fit new parts as required
	Incorrect brake shoe linings (too thick)	See Parts Catalogue for correct type	Fit new linings
Brake locks	Oil or brake fluid soaked linings	Remove brake drum and inspect linings. Check for worn oil seal in hub or fluid leakage from wheel cylinder	Fit new linings. Fit new oil seal or wheel cylinder components as necessary
	Torn or loose linings	Check brake shoe linings for security. Check brake shoes for distortion	Fit new linings and brake shoes as necessary
	Loose wheel cylinders	Check wheel cylinder fixings	Tighten as necessary
	Swollen rubber components	Check wheel cylinders and master cylinder	Fit new components as necessary
Pedal goes to floor board	Lining excessively worn	Remove brake drums and check linings	Fit new linings
	Pedal incorrectly set	Check brake pedal adjustment as detailed under 'Brake pedal, remove and refit'	Adjust as necessary
	Leak in hydraulic system	Check the brake pipes, master cylinder and wheel cylinders. If available, use Girling hose clamps to locate the leak	Fit new parts as required and bleed the brake system
	Air in hydraulic system	If available, use Girling hose clamps to locate the air	Bleed the brake system as necessary
	Loose master cylinder mounting bolts	Check master cylinder fixings to brake pedal bracket. If the vehicle is fitted with a mechanical servo unit, check servo to brake pedal bracket fixings	Securely tighten

DATA

Brakes:

Type	Girling
Operation	Hydraulic

Foot pedal: (except for models fitted with Girling mechanical servo unit)

Fit of bush on pedal shaft	.001 in. to .003 in. (0,02 mm to 0,07 mm)
Bush reamed bore	.751 in. —.0005 in. (19,07 mm —.013 mm)

Foot pedal used with Girling mechanical servo unit:

Fit of bush on pedal shaft	.001 in. to .003 in. (0,02 mm to 0,07 mm)
Bush reamed bore	.625 in. +.001 in. (15,875 mm +0,0254 mm)

Wheel brake unit, front and rear (10 in. brakes):

Lining:	
Length	$8\frac{1}{2}$ in. (215 mm)
Width	$1\frac{1}{2}$ in. (38 mm)
Thickness	$\frac{3}{16}$ in. (4,75 mm)

Brake drum:

Standard diameter	10 in. +.004 in. (254 mm +0,1 mm)
Reclamation limit	.030 in. (0,75 mm) oversize on diameter

Wheel brake unit, front—$2\frac{1}{4}$ litre models (11 in. brakes):

Lining:	
Length	10.45 in. (265 mm)
Width	$2\frac{1}{4}$ in. (57 mm)
Thickness	$\frac{3}{16}$ in. (4,75 mm)

Wheel brake unit, front—2.6 litre models (11 in. brakes):

Lining:	
Length	10.45 in. (265 mm)
Width	3 in. (76 mm)
Thickness	$\frac{3}{16}$ in. (4,75 mm)

Wheel brake unit, rear (11 in. brakes):

Lining:	
Length	8.6 in. (218 mm)
Width	$2\frac{1}{4}$ in. (57 mm)
Thickness	$\frac{3}{16}$ in. (4,75 mm)

Brake drum:

Standard diameter	11 in. +.004 in. (279,4 mm +0,10 mm)
Reclamation limit	.030 in. (0,75 mm) oversize on diameter

Transmission brake:

Lining:	
Length	8.64 in. (219 mm)
Width	$1\frac{3}{4}$ in. (44,5 mm)
Thickness	$\frac{3}{16}$ in. (4,75 mm)

DATA—*continued*

Brake drum:

Standard diameter	9 in. +.004 in. (228,6 mm +0,1 mm)
Reclamation limit	0.30 in. (0,75 mm) oversize on diameter

Master cylinder:

Type (88 models)	Girling CV
Bore	$\frac{3}{4}$ in. (19 mm)
Stroke	$1\frac{1}{2}$ in. (38 mm)
Type (109 models)	Girling CB
Bore	1 in. (25 mm)
Stroke	$1\frac{1}{2}$ in. (38 mm)
Pushrod free movement	$\frac{1}{16}$ in. (1,5 mm)

Master cylinder used with Girling mechanical servo unit:

Type	Girling CV
Bore	1 in. (25 mm)
Stroke	$1\frac{1}{2}$ in. (38 mm)
Pushrod free movement	Not adjustable, pre-set during manufacture

Servo unit (two types in use):

Type	Clayton Dewandre
Operation	Hydraulic slave cylinder
Location	In pipe line between master cylinder and junction to wheel cylinders
Type	Girling 'Supervac' type 38
Operation	Mechanical, acting directly on master cylinder
Location	Mounted on brake pedal bracket in engine compartment

SECTION J—CHASSIS

INDEX—CHASSIS

Note: A comprehensive, detailed index is included at the end of this manual

Description	Operation Number
Chassis frame	1
Front bumper	2
Battery carrier and air cleaner support	3

Frame alignment, to check—Operation J1-1

To check

Figs. J1-2 and J1-3 show the various dimensions that should be used as a guide in checking frame alignment. Fig. J1-1 illustrates the diagonal measurements which may be taken to check the frame for 'squareness'. Extreme care must be taken when checking for malalignment.

When the body is removed, the frame may easily be checked against the measurements in Figs. J1-2 and J1-3. If the body is in position, measurements may be taken with the aid of a plumb-bob and chalk as follows:

1. Place the vehicle on a level floor.
2. Hold the plumb line against one of the measuring points, with the bob slightly above the floor; mark the floor directly beneath the bob.
3. Repeat for other measuring points.
4. Move the vehicle away and measure between the chalk marks.

Care should be taken when measuring diagonals, that exactly corresponding points are used on each side of the frame.

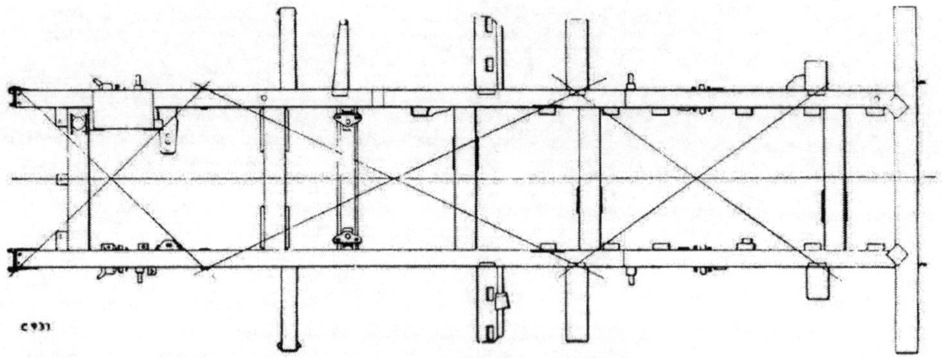

Fig. J1-1. Chassis frame diagonal measurements

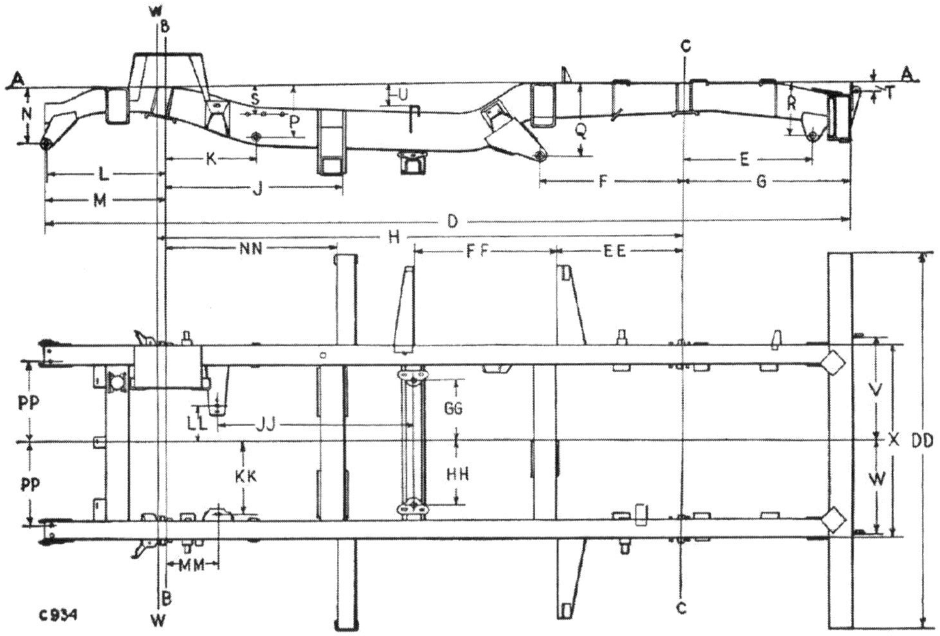

Fig. J1-2. Chassis frame dimensions, 88

AA—Datum line
BB—Front datum
WW—Centre line of front axle
CC—Centre line of rear axle
D—134 $\frac{21}{32}$ in. (3,42 m)
E—21 $\frac{1}{4}$ in. (540 mm)
F—24 in. (610 mm)
G—28 $\frac{5}{64}$ in. (713 mm)
H—88 in. (2,235 m)
J—29 $\frac{1}{4}$ in. (743 mm)
K—14 $\frac{3}{4}$ in. (375 mm)
L—20 in. (508 mm)
M—20 $\frac{37}{64}$ in. (523 mm)
N—9 in. (229 mm)
P—8 $\frac{3}{8}$ in. (213 mm)
Q—11 $\frac{7}{16}$ in. (297 mm)
R—7 $\frac{3}{16}$ in. (182 mm)

S—4 $\frac{3}{4}$ in. (121 mm)
T—1 $\frac{5}{32}$ in. (29 mm)
U—3 $\frac{1}{4}$ in. (83 mm)
V—17 in. (432 mm)
W—15 $\frac{1}{4}$ in. (387 mm)
X—31 in. (787 mm)
DD—60 $\frac{1}{4}$ in. (1,53 m)
EE—21 $\frac{1}{4}$ in. (540 mm)
FF—24 in.* (610 mm)
GG—10 $\frac{1}{8}$ in. $\pm \frac{1}{32}$ in. (257 mm $\pm$0,8 mm)
HH—10 in. $\pm \frac{1}{32}$ in. (254 mm $\pm$0,8 mm)
JJ—32 $\frac{7}{8}$ in. $\pm \frac{1}{32}$ in. (835 mm $\pm$0,8 mm)
KK—11.406 in.** (290 mm)
LL—6 $\frac{9}{16}$ in. (167 mm)
MM—8 in. (203 mm)
NN—28 $\frac{1}{4}$ in. (718 mm)
PP—13 $\frac{1}{16}$ in. $\pm \frac{1}{64}$ in. (332 mm $\pm$0,5 mm)

*23 $\frac{3}{4}$ in. (603 mm) } Early
**11 $\frac{9}{16}$ in. $\pm \frac{1}{32}$ in. (294 mm $\pm$0,8 mm) } models

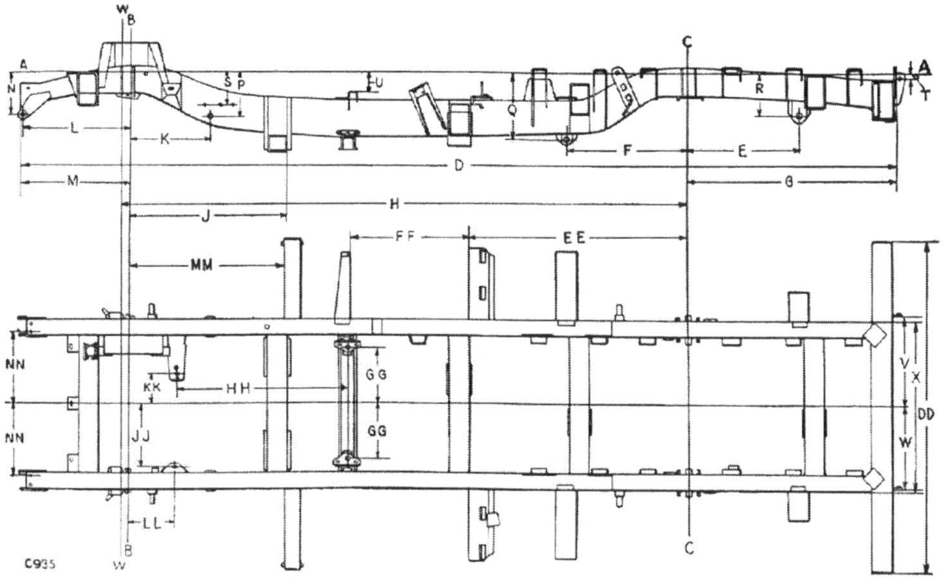

Fig. J1-3. Chassis frame dimensions, 109

AA—Datum line
BB—Front datum
WW—Centre line of front axle
CC—Centre line of rear axle
D—166 $\frac{61}{64}$ in. (4,24 m)
E—21 $\frac{1}{4}$ in. (540 mm)
F—24 in. (610 mm)
G—39 $\frac{3}{8}$ in. (1,00 m)
H—109 in. (2,77 m)
J—29 $\frac{1}{4}$ in. (743 mm
K—14 $\frac{3}{4}$ in. (375 mm)
L—20 in. (508 mm)
M—20 $\frac{37}{64}$ in. (523 mm)
N—9 in. (229 mm)
P—8 $\frac{3}{8}$ in. (213 mm)
Q—11 $\frac{11}{16}$ in. (297 mm)
R—8 $\frac{1}{16}$ in. (205 mm)

S—4 $\frac{3}{4}$ in. (121 mm)
T—1 $\frac{5}{32}$ in. (29 mm)
U—3 $\frac{1}{4}$ in. (83 mm)
V—17 in. (432 mm)
W—15 $\frac{1}{4}$ in. (387 mm)
X—31 in. (787 mm)
DD—60 $\frac{1}{2}$ in. (1,53 m)
EE—42 $\frac{1}{8}$ in. (1,07 m)
FF—24 in.* (610 mm)
GG—10 $\frac{1}{8}$ in. $\pm \frac{1}{32}$ in. (257 mm $\pm$0,8 mm)
HH—32 $\frac{7}{8}$ in. $\pm \frac{1}{32}$ in. (835 mm $\pm$0,8 mm)
JJ—11.406 in.** (290 mm)
KK—6 $\frac{9}{16}$ in. (167 mm)
LL—8 in. (203 mm)
MM—28 $\frac{1}{4}$ in. (718 mm)
NN—13 $\frac{1}{16}$ in. $\pm \frac{1}{64}$ in. (332 mm $\pm$0,50 mm)

*23 $\frac{3}{4}$ in. (603 mm) } Early
**11 $\frac{9}{16}$ in. $\pm \frac{1}{32}$ in. (294 mm $\pm$0,8 mm) } models

CHASSIS — Section J—Land-Rover

Front bumper, to remove and refit—Operation J1-2

Workshop hand tools:
Spanner size: $\frac{7}{16}$ in. AF open end

General

The channel-section front bumper is bolted to the chassis side members, so that it may be removed to facilitate repair after accidental damage.

To remove

1. Remove four nuts, bolts and washers securing the front bumper to the chassis side members.
2. Withdraw the front bumper from the chassis.

To refit

Locate the front bumper in position and secure to the chassis side members, using four bolts with plain washers under their heads and four plain washers and self-locking nuts.

Battery carrier and air cleaner support, to remove and refit—Operation J1-3

Workshop hand tools:
Spanner sizes: $\frac{7}{16}$ in. AF, $\frac{1}{2}$ in. AF open end

General

The battery and air cleaner position varies according to the particular model. In most applications, a combined battery carrier and air cleaner support is located in the RH side of the engine compartment. Diesel-engined models have an additional battery carrier fitted to the LH side of the chassis. Certain six-cylinder engine models have the air cleaner in the engine compartment and the battery carrier mounted on the LH chassis member.

To remove

1. Remove the air cleaner. Section A.
2. Disconnect the battery leads, remove the securing cover and lift the battery clear. Note that there are two batteries and two supports on Diesel vehicles.
3. Remove the battery and air cleaner support from the chassis frame (this action releases the earth leads).

To replace

1. Reverse the removal procedure.

SECTION K—COOLING SYSTEM

Brief description of cooling system

The engine cooling system operates on the conventional thermo-syphon principle, and is impeller pump assisted.

The pump, which carries a fan to assist air flow through the radiator block, is belt driven from the crankshaft pulley.

A thermostat is fitted to ensure rapid engine warm-up. When starting from cold, the thermostat prevents coolant flow through the radiator block until a predetermined temperature has been attained. Upon reaching the operating temperature the thermostat will automatically redirect the coolant flow through the radiator.

The cooling system is designed to operate under pressure, early models at 10 lb/sq in. (0.7 kg/cm²), later models at 9 lb/sq in. (0.6 kg/cm²). The pressure relief valve and also a depression relief valve are incorporated in the radiator filler cap.

On later engines, a semi-sealed cooling system is used in conjunction with an overflow bottle which receives any coolant overflow from the radiator header tank. When the engine is cooling after running, that is, with a depression in the header tank, the coolant trapped in the overflow bottle returns to the header tank.

The coolant level in the system is checked and replenished at the radiator filler cap only. With a cold engine, the correct coolant level is $\frac{1}{2}$ in. to $\frac{3}{4}$ in. (12 mm to 19 mm) below the bottom edge of the filler neck.

There must always be coolant in the overflow bottle sufficient to cover the end of the pipe from the header tank.

Two points are provided for draining the system, a tap at the side of the engine block (RH side for 2.6 litre engines, LH side for 2¼ litre engines) and a drain plug at the base of the radiator block.

Where a heater is fitted, close off the heater supply tap at the engine before draining the system.

Frost precautions

As a thermostat is fitted to the cooling system it is possible for the radiator block to freeze in cold weather even though the engine temperature is quite high, for this reason a good quality glycol-base anti-freeze solution must be used during cold weather.

Coolant system capacities

Bonneted Control Models

Engine Type	Imperial Pints	US Pints	Litres	Anti-freeze Percentage	Frost Precaution
2.6 litre Petrol	20	24	11.2		
2¼ litre Petrol	18	21¼	10.25	33⅓%	−32°C (−25°F)
2¼ litre Diesel	17¼	21	10.0		

INDEX TO OPERATIONS — SECTION K

Description of Listed Operations	Page Number	Operation Number
Thermostat, to overhaul	—	K1-1
Water pump, to overhaul	—	K1-2
Radiator, to replace	—	K1-3
Coolant system, to check	—	K1-4

COOLING SYSTEM

Key to Fig. K1-1. Layout of cooling system components, 4 cylinder models

1. Water pump casing
2. Pump spindle and bearing
3. Hub for fan
4. Carbon ring and seal unit
5. Impeller for pump
6. Spring washer } Locating bearing casing
7. Special set bolt
8. Joint washer for water pump
9. Spring washer } Fixing water pump to front cover
10. Nut
11. Joint washer } For heater return in water outlet pipe
12. Plug (⅜ in. BSP)
13. Thermostat
14. 'O' ring, thermostat to water outlet pipe
15. Water outlet pipe, thermostat to radiator
16. Washer for outlet pipe
17. Set bolt (¼ in. UNF × 2½ in. long) } Fixing outlet pipe to cylinder head
18. Spring washer
19. Hose for by-pass pipe
20. Clip for hose
21. Thermostat, bellows type
    Thermostat, wax type
    'O' ring for thermostat
22. Thermostat housing
23. Joint washer for thermostat housing, upper
24. Water outlet pipe, thermostat to radiator
25. Joint washer for thermostat housing, lower
26. Set bolt (¼ in. UNF × 2½ in. long) } Fixing thermostat housing and outlet pipe to cylinder head
    Set bolt (¼ in. UNF × 2¾ in. long)
27. Spring washer
28. Thermostat by-pass pipe
29. Joint washer for by-pass pipe
30. Set bolt (5/16 in. UNF × 1 in. long) } Fixing by-pass pipe to thermostat housing
31. Spring washer
32. Fan pulley
33. Fan blade
34. Spring washer } Fixing fan blade and pulley to hub
35. Set bolt (¼ in. UNF × ¾ in. long)
36. Fan and dynamo belt

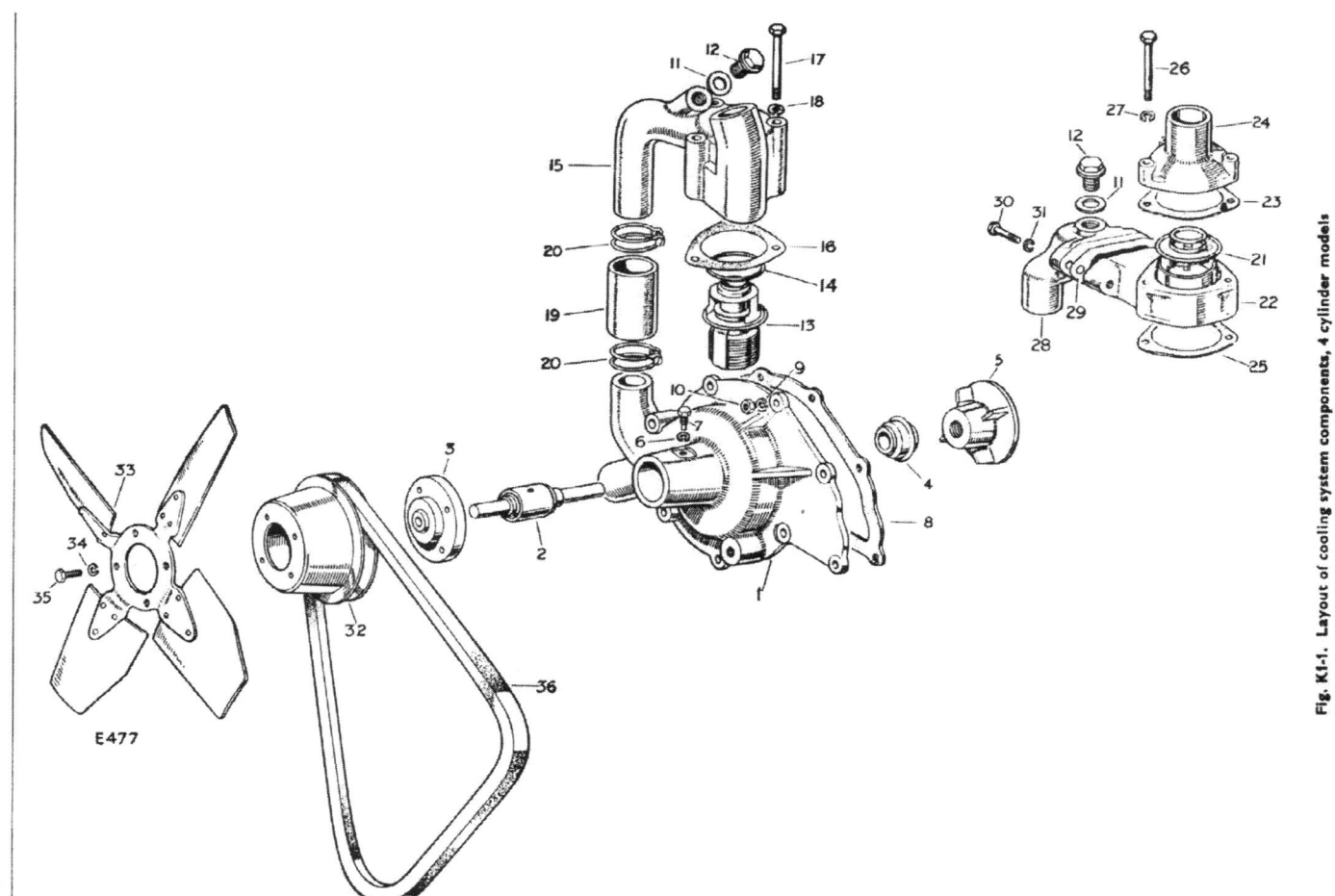

Fig. K1-1. Layout of cooling system components, 4 cylinder models

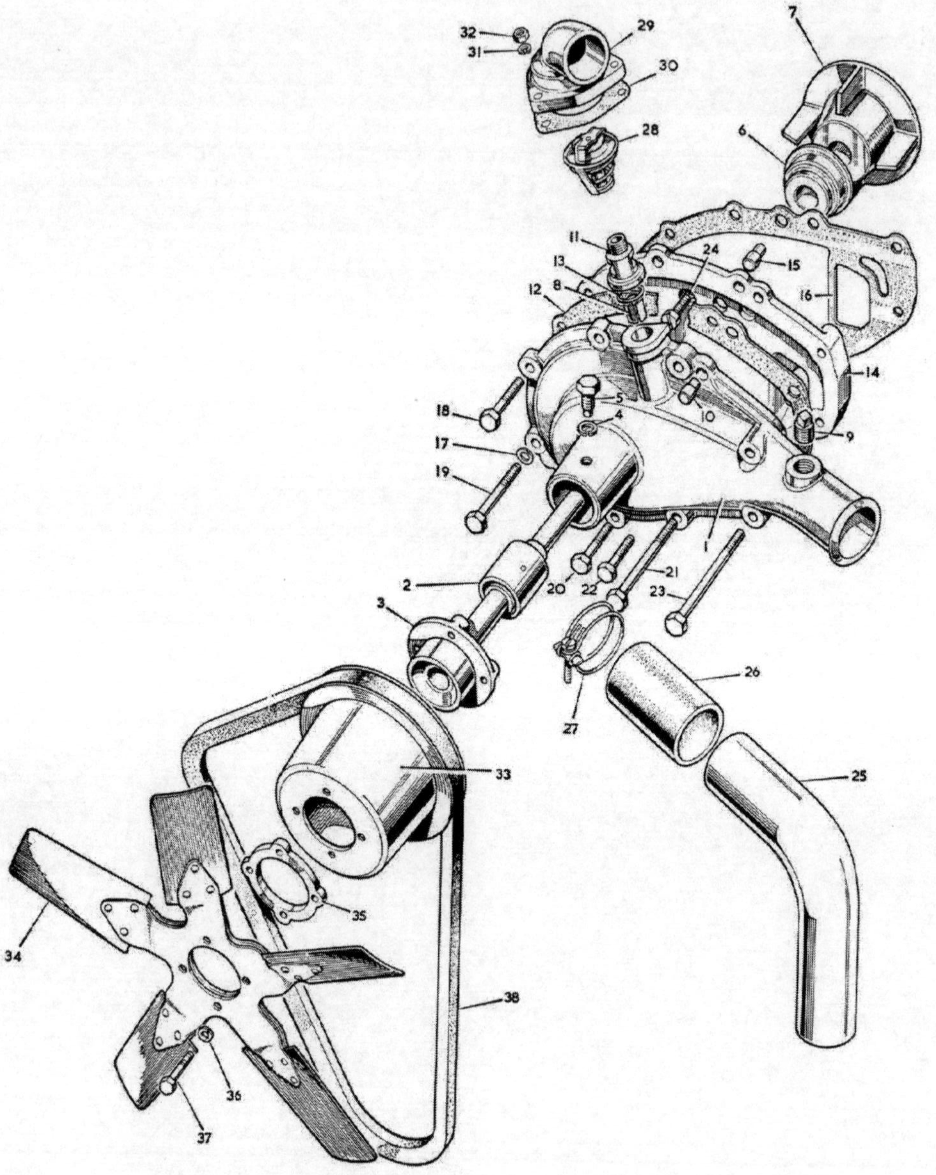

COOLING SYSTEM

Key to Fig. K1-2. Layout of cooling system components, 6 cylinder models

1. Water pump assembly
2. Spindle and bearing complete
3. Hub for fan blade
4. Spring washer ⎤ Locating bearing
5. Special set bolt ⎦ in casing
6. Carbon ring and seal
7. Impeller for pump
8. Tube for thermostat by-pass
9. Plug ($\frac{3}{8}$ in. BSP) for heater adaptor hole in casing
10. Dowel for water pump casing
11. Connector, by-pass to water pump
12. Joint washer for water pump
13. Rubber seal, pump to cylinder head
14. Adaptor for water pump
15. Dowel for adaptor
16. Joint washer for adaptor
17. Spring washer
18. Set bolt ($\frac{1}{4}$ in. UNF × 1 in. long) ⎤
19. Set bolt ($\frac{1}{4}$ in. UNF × 1$\frac{1}{8}$ in. long) ⎥
20. Set bolt ($\frac{1}{4}$ in. UNF × 1$\frac{5}{8}$ in. long) ⎥ Fixing water
21. Set bolt ($\frac{1}{4}$ in. UNF × 2$\frac{1}{4}$ in. long) ⎬ pump and
22. Set bolt ($\frac{1}{4}$ in. UNF × $\frac{7}{8}$ in. long) ⎥ adaptor
23. Set bolt ($\frac{1}{4}$ in. UNF × 2$\frac{1}{4}$ in. long) ⎥ to block
24. Special 'Wedgelok' screw ⎦
25. Inlet pipe for water pump
26. Hose, water inlet pipe to pump
27. Clip, hose to inlet pipe
28. Clip, hose to pump
29. Thermostat, wax type
30. Outlet pipe to radiator
31. Joint washer for water outlet pipe
32. Spring washer ⎤ Fixing pipe to
33. Nut ($\frac{1}{4}$ in. UNF) ⎦ cylinder head
34. Pulley for fan
35. Fan blade
36. Distance piece for fan blade
37. Spring washer ⎤ Fixing pulley
38. Set bolt ($\frac{1}{4}$ in. UNF × 1$\frac{1}{4}$ in. long) ⎬ and blade to hub
39. Fan belt

Fig. K1-2. Layout of cooling system components, 6 cylinder models

COOLING SYSTEM

Thermostat, to overhaul—Operation K1-1

(For removal and refitting details, Section A refers)

Workshop hand tools:
Suitable small rule

General

Two types of thermostat are in use, an early type containing ethyl-alcohol and a later type containing wax. The types are recognisable when removed, see Fig. K1-3 and Fig. K1-4.

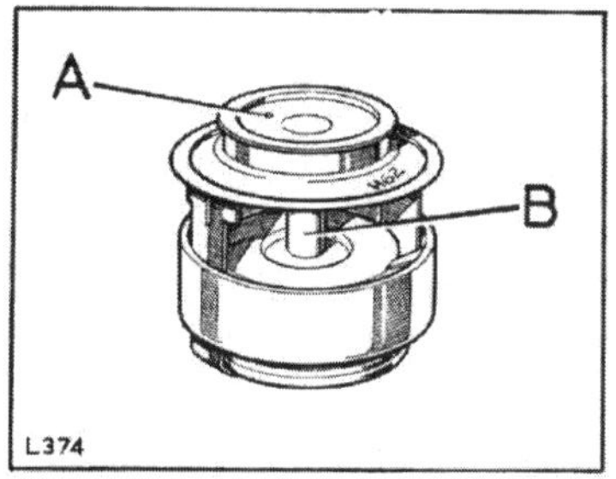

Fig. K1-3. Ethyl-alcohol type thermostat
A—Bleed hole, to prevent airlocks when re-filling system
B—Operating valve

The wax-filled type ensures that pressure fluctuations within the cooling system do not influence the thermostat operation and this type may be fitted to replace the ethyl-alcohol type provided that:

(a) On early 2¼ litre petrol engines a modified water outlet pipe is also fitted.

(b) On early 2¼ litre diesel engines a combined water temperature and oil pressure gauge is also fitted.

Thermostats fitted to Land-Rover engines commence to open at a temperature value of between 70.6°C to 78.5°C (159°F to 173°F) and should be fully open at 90°C (194°F). They are not adjustable.

Thermostats which satisfy the following inspection and functional test are suitable for further use.

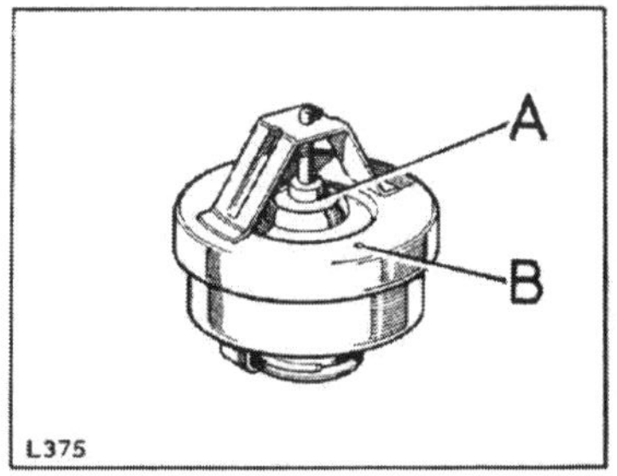

Fig. K1-4. Wax-filled type thermostat
A—Operating valve
B—Bleed hole, to prevent airlocks when re-filling system

Inspection and test, both types of thermostat

1. Examine the thermostat to ensure that it is fully closed.

2. Check the dimension 'B', in Figs. K1-5 or K1-6 as applicable, with the thermostat at ambient temperature.

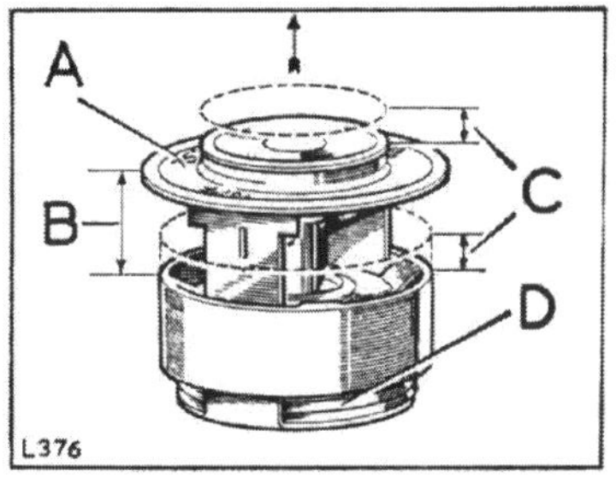

Fig. K1-5. Thermostat operation, ethyl-alcohol type
A—Thermostat opening temperature marked on this face
B—Dimension with thermostat valve closed
C—Dimension ⅜ in. (9.5 mm) approximately when fully open
D—Bellows assembly

Operation K1-1—*continued*

3. Immerse the thermostat in boiling water for a period of 45 to 60 seconds.

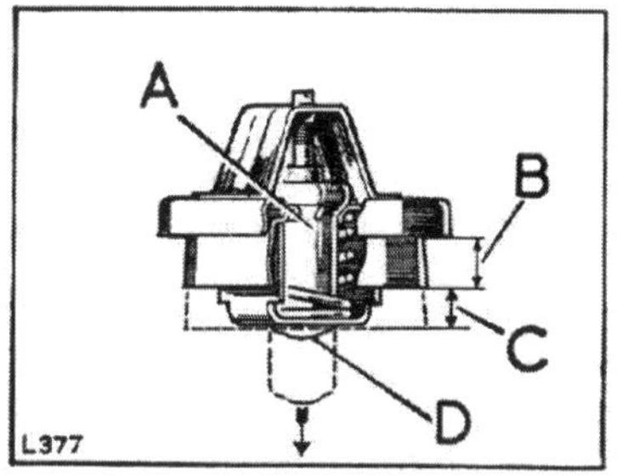

Fig. K1-6. Thermostat operation, wax filled type
A—Wax filled tube
B—Dimension with thermostat valve closed
C—Dimension ⅜ in. (9.5 mm) approximately when fully open
D—Thermostat opening temperature marked on this face

4. With the thermostat immersed, check that the valve has opened by ⅜ in. (9.5 mm) approximately as shown at 'C' in the appropriate illustration.

5. Allow the thermostat to cool to ambient temperature and ensure that the valve has fully returned to its seating.

6. Examine the thermostat for mechanical defects and damage.

Note: Correct engine functioning requires the use of a thermostat in the cooling system.

A thermostat sticking closed will result in engine overheating; sticking open will prevent the required quick warm-up and lead to engine corrosion, wear and to oil contamination.

Therefore do not allow the engine to run continuously without a serviceable thermostat fitted.

COOLING SYSTEM

Water pump, to overhaul—Operation K1-2

(For removal and refitting details, Section A refers)

Workshop hand tools:
Spanner sizes: $\frac{7}{16}$ in. AF open end
Suitable drift, 1 lb hammer, Side-cutting pliers,
Feeler gauges

Special tools:
Suitable hand press

To overhaul

1. Remove the bearing location bolt, place the pump in a soft-jawed vice and drift out the impeller, bearing and spindle as an assembly from the pump body and from hub.

2. Cut through the seal and remove from spindle, insert the spindle into the water pump body, so that the impeller is in the position of the fan pulley. The spindle and bearing may now be drifted out of the impeller.

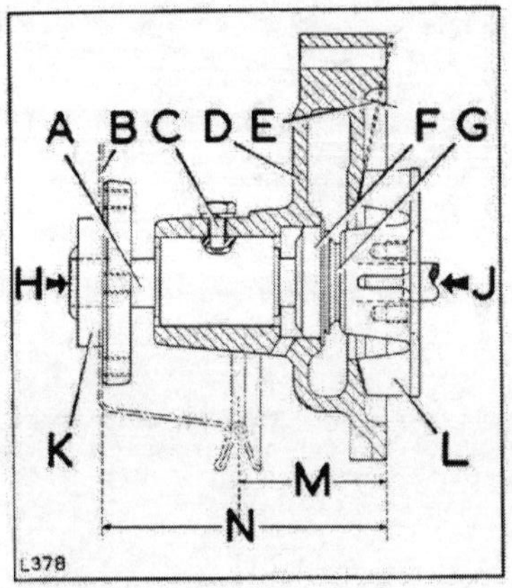

Inspection

1. Examine the spindle and bearing assembly; it need not be renewed if the bearing is satisfactory and the spindle is free from excessive corrosion.

   Clean any corroded portion of the spindle and paint with a suitable chlorinated rubber primer or, alternatively, with a good quality aluminium paint or other anti-corrosive paint.

2. Where a steel deflector washer is fitted to the pump spindle, (later models) check that there is a minimum clearance of .018 in. (0.46 mm) between the washer and the bearing housing face.

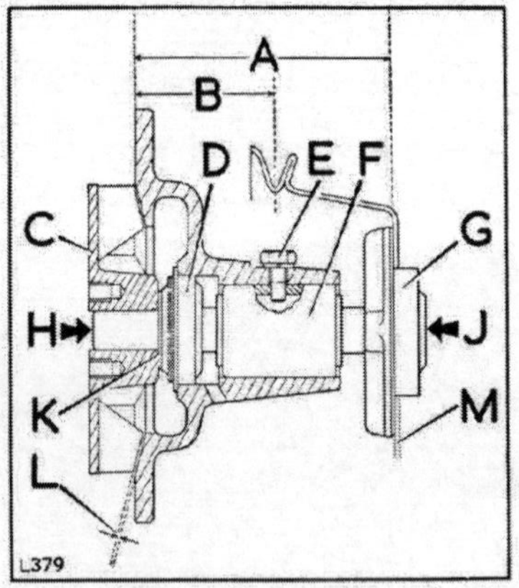

Fig. K1-7. Sectioned view of water pump, 2.6 litre models

A—Pump spindle and bearing
B—Fan belt pulley
C—Bearing location bolt and washer
D—Water pump body
E—Dimension, .025 in. (0.63 mm)
F—Carbon ring and seal assembly
G—Carbon seal faced toward impeller
H—Support here when fitting impeller
J—Support here when fitting hub
K—Fan hub
L—Impeller
M—Dimension, 1.820 in. (46.2 mm)
N—Dimension, 3.820 in. (97.0 mm)

Operation K1-2—continued

To assemble

1. Insert a few drops of thick oil in the location hole in the bearing.

2. Suitably mark the spindle bearing housing and the pump body so that the bearing locating screw holes may be easily aligned during assembly.

3. Fit the spindle and bearing to the pump body and fit the locating screw.

4. Press the fan pulley hub on to the spindle to a set dimension (see Figs. K1-7 and K1-8) measured between the front face of the pulley hub and the mounting face of the water pump casing. When pressing on the hub, support the spindle to avoid load falling on the bearing location bolt.

5. Fit the carbon ring and seal into the bore of the pump body with the carbon ring to the rear.

6. Press the impeller on to the spindle until there is .025 in. (0.63 mm) clearance between the impeller vanes and the pump body face. Check the dimension using feeler gauges. The impeller must be a press fit on the spindle. If the impeller is loose on the spindle, replace either part as necessary.

Fig. K1-8. Cross-section of water pump, 2¼ litre models

A—Dimension, 3.510 in. (89.15 mm)
B—Dimension, 1.930 in. (49.0 mm)
C—Impeller
D—Carbon ring and seal assembly
E—Locating bolt
F—Pump spindle and bearing assembly
G—Fan hub
H—Support here when fitting hub
J—Support here when fitting impeller
K—Carbon seal faced toward impeller
L—Dimension, .025 in. (0.63 mm)
M—Fan belt pulley

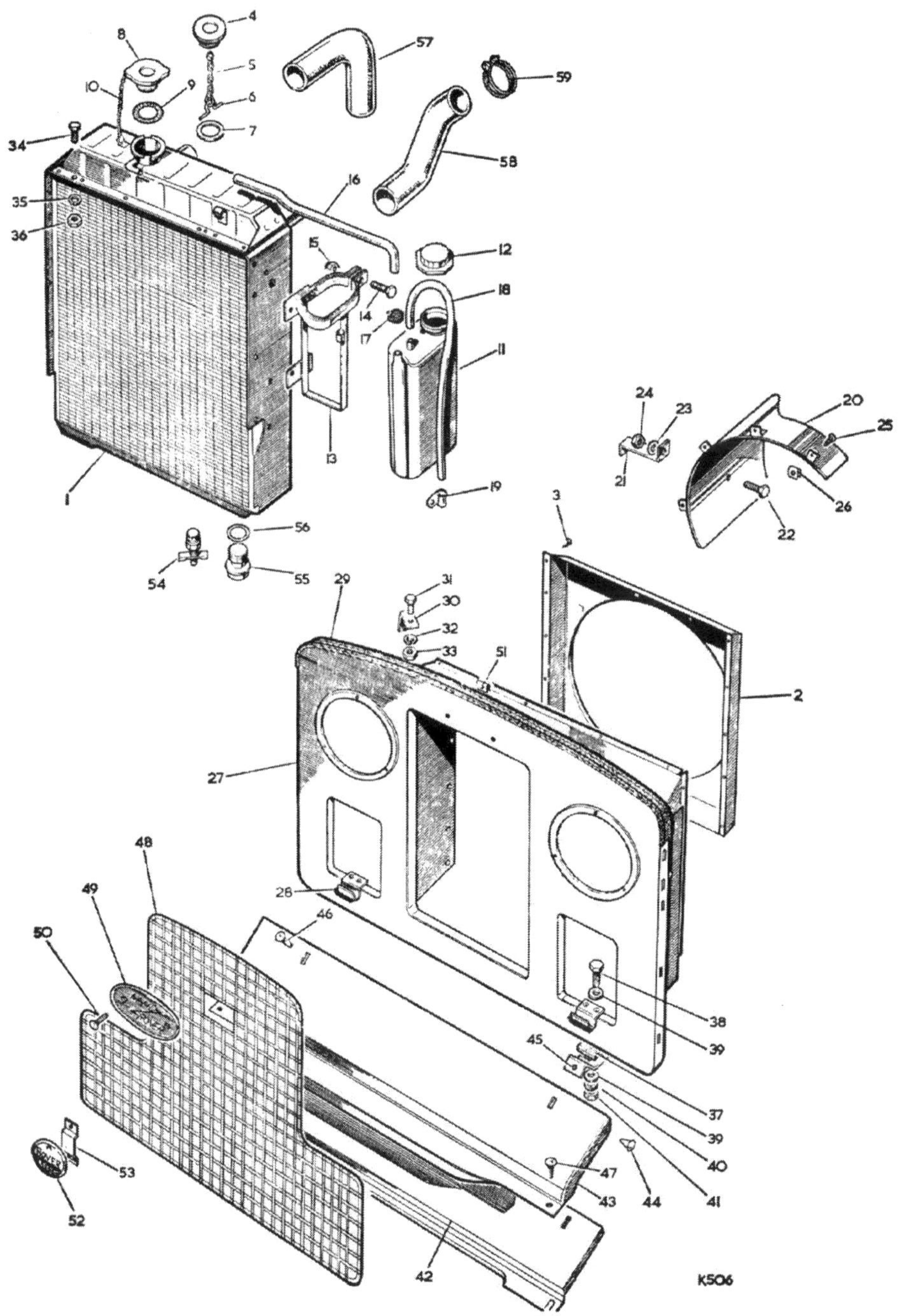

COOLING SYSTEM

Key to Fig. K1-9. Layout of radiator and grille panel

1. Radiator block assembly
2. Fan cowl
3. Drive screw for cowl
4. Filler cap
5. Filler cap chain
6. Retainer for chain
7. Filler cap joint washer
8. Filler cap with overflow bottle provision
9. Joint washer
10. Chain for filler cap
11. Overflow bottle for radiator
12. Cap for overflow bottle
13. Carrier bracket for overflow bottle
14. Bolt ($\frac{1}{4}$ in. UNF × $\frac{7}{8}$ in. long) } Clamping bottle to carrier
15. Self-locking nut ($\frac{1}{4}$ in. UNF)
16. Hose, radiator to overflow bottle
17. Clip, fixing hose
18. Flexible pipe, overflow bottle outlet
19. Clip, fixing outlet pipe
20. Shroud for fan cowl
21. Steady strip for shroud
22. Bolt ($\frac{1}{4}$ in. UNF × $\frac{5}{8}$ in. long) } Fixing steady strip to shroud
23. Spring washer
24. } Shroud fixings
25.
26.
27. Radiator grille panel complete
28. Support clip for grille mesh
29. Bonnet rest strip, 35 in. long
30. Protection plate for headlamp
31. Bolt ($\frac{1}{4}$ in. UNF × $\frac{5}{8}$ in. long) } Fixing plate to grille panel
32. Spring washer
33. Nut ($\frac{1}{4}$ in. UNF)
34. Bolt ($\frac{1}{4}$ in. UNF × $\frac{5}{8}$ in. long) } Fixing radiator block to grille panel
35. Spring washer
36. Nut ($\frac{1}{4}$ in. UNF)
37. Rubber buffer
38. Bolt ($\frac{5}{16}$ in. UNF × $1\frac{1}{2}$ in. long) } Fixing grille panel and front apron bracket to chassis frame
39. Plain washer
40. Spring washer
41. Nut ($\frac{5}{16}$ in. UNF)
42. Front apron panel } Alternatives
43. Front apron panel
44. Rubber buffer for front apron panel
45. Securing bracket for panel
46. Fixings, apron panel to brackets
47. Fixings, apron panel to chassis
48. Grille for radiator
49. 'Land-Rover' nameplate
50. Drive screw } Fixing nameplate and grille to grille panel
51. Spire nut
52. 'Diesel' badge, where applicable
53. Fixing bracket for badge
   Rivet } Fixing bracket and badge to grille
   Lockwasher
54. Drain tap for radiator
55. Drain plug for radiator
56. Joint washer for plug
57. Hose for radiator, top
58. Hose for radiator, bottom
59. Radiator hose clips

Fig. K1-9. Layout of radiator and grille panel

COOLING SYSTEM

Radiator, to replace—Operation K1-3

Workshop hand tools:

Spanner sizes: $\frac{7}{16}$ in. x $\frac{1}{2}$ in. AF open ended (2 off), 2 BA open ended Screwdriver (medium), Pliers

General

1. Cleaning radiator, externally

In the event of the cooling gills of the radiator becoming blocked with dirt, straw, etc., they should be cleaned by means of compressed air or water pressure applied from the rear, so forcing the foreign matter out through the front of the radiator. Never use a metal implement for this purpose or serious damage may result to the radiator core.

2. Internal protection

A sealing pellet, Rover Part No. 601314, may be added to the radiator on earlier models as a protection for the cooling system. Land-Rover models produced after 1st August 1966 have the sealing pellet already added. A bottled version of the pellet and full technical details are obtainable from Messrs. Barrs Motor Products Ltd., 73 Scrubs Lane, London W2, England.

3. Radiator overhaul

Repair is by replacement of the complete radiator block assembly. To replace a radiator, proceed as follows:

To remove

1. Remove the radiator and grille panel complete. Section A.
2. Remove the fixings and detach the radiator block from the grille panel, Fig. K1-9 refers.
3. Remove the drain tap and joint washer from the base of the radiator block.
4. Remove the radiator cap from the radiator filler neck.

To refit

1. Reverse the removal procedure

Cooling system, to check—Operation K1-4

The AC pressure cap and cooling system tester (obtainable from AC Delco Division of General Motors Ltd., Dunstable, Bedfordshire, England) can be used to carry out the following cooling system checks. The equipment is complete with the necessary adaptors.

Pressure cap
Calibration test

Fit cap to tester, then pump up pressure as far as possible. If pressure release is not within the limits marked on the dial, the cap is fatigued and should be replaced.

Leak test

If the cap will not hold pressure for a minimum of 10 seconds it indicates a leaking seal or valve and the cap should be replaced.

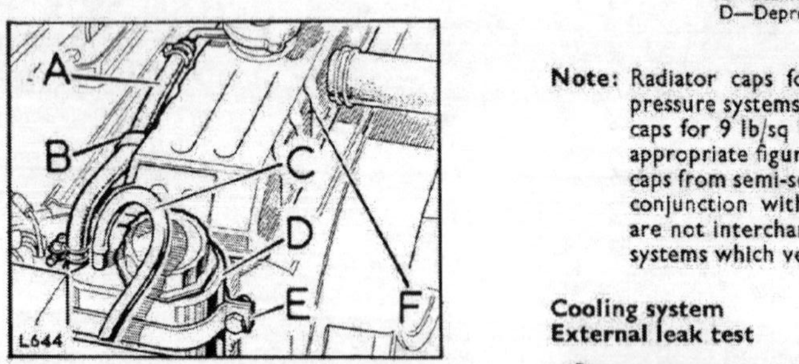

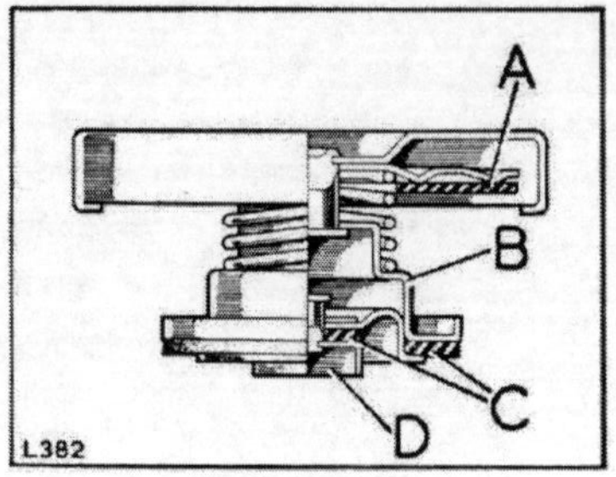

Fig. K1-12. Cross-section view of later type (semi-sealed) radiator cap

A—Additional sealing washer
B—Pressure relief valve
C—Sealing washers
D—Depression valve

Radiator caps for 10 lb/sq in. (0.7 kg/cm²) pressure systems are not interchangeable with caps for 9 lb/sq in. (0.6 kg/cm²) systems. The appropriate figure is marked on the cap. Also, caps from semi-sealed coolant systems (used in conjunction with a coolant overflow bottle) are not interchangeable with the cap used on systems which vent to atmosphere.

Cooling system
External leak test

Remove pressure cap and fit the tester to the radiator. By pumping up the pressure to the poundage indicated on the cap, near actual running conditions can be simulated. If the pressure drops, check all seals and joints for leaks—any leaks will be apparent because the pressure forces the coolant to seep out of any leakage points.

Absence of external leaks may indicate that internal leaks are present.

Blown cylinder head gasket test

Care must be exercised in this test to ensure that the cooling system pressure does not exceed that marked on the cap.

Attach tester to radiator and apply pressure. Start engine and set at a slow tick-over—a blown cylinder head gasket will now show itself by fluctuations in pressure on the tester gauge.

Fig. K1-10. Semi-sealed system with overflow bottle

A—Overflow hose
B—Retaining clip
C—Vent hose
D—Overflow bottle
E—Clamp bracket
F—Radiator

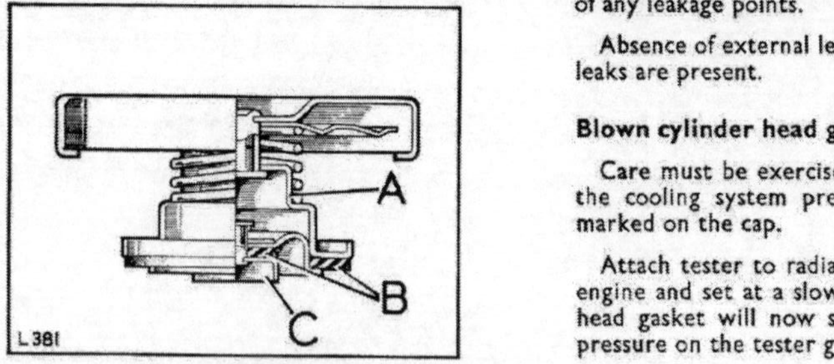

Fig. K1-11. Cross-section view of early type radiator cap

A—Pressure relief valve
B—Sealing washers
C—Depression valve

COOLING SYSTEM DATA

Capacity of cooling system
2¼ litre Diesel	17.5 Imperial pints (10,0 litres)
2¼ litre Petrol	18 Imperial pints (10,25 litres)
2.6 litre Petrol	20 Imperial pints (11,2 litres)

Radiator
Filler cap pressure valve opening pressure:

Early models	10 lb/sq in. (0,7 kg/cm²), cap marked with figure 10
Later models	9 lb/sq in. (0,6 kg/cm²), cap marked with figure 9. No interchangeable with 10 lb/sq in. (0,7 kg/cm²)
Filler cap vacuum valve opening pressure	1 lb/sq in. (0,07 kg/cm²)

Thermostat
Bellows type, alcohol filled—applicable to early 2¼ litre Petrol and 2¼ litre Diesel engines

Opening temperature	161°F to 168°F (71.7°C to 75.6°C)
Fully open at	185°F (85°C)

Wax filled type—applicable to 2.6 litre Petrol and later 2¼ litre Petrol and 2¼ litre Diesel engines

2.6 litre engines:
Opening temperature	161°F to 170°F (71.7°C to 76.7°C)
Fully open at	190°F (87.8°C)

2¼ litre engines:
Opening temperature	159°F to 167°F (70.6°C to 75°C)
Fully open at	185°F (85°C)

Water pump
Type	Centrifugal
Drive	'V' belt
Bearing	Double row ball, sealed on spindle

By-pass type:
2¼ litre models	External
2.6 litre models	Internal

Dimensions between front face of pulley hub and mounting face of pump body:
2¼ litre models	3.513 in. (89,15 mm)
2.6 litre models	3.819 in. (97,0 mm)
Clearance between impeller vanes and pump body, all models	.025 in. (0,63 mm)

Fault diagnosis—Cooling system

Symptom	Possible cause	Investigation	Remedy
A—External leakage	Leakage at hoses and joint faces	Check for loose hose fixings, defective hoses and for leaks at component joint washer	Rectify or replace as necessary
	Water pump seals ineffective	Check for worn and damaged seals. Check mating components for undue wear	Overhaul and replace worn parts as necessary
	Leakage at core plugs	Check for loose plugs	Tighten or replace as necessary
	Damaged radiator seams	Ensure that leakage is from radiator block and not from external connections, drain tap or filler cap	Replace a damaged radiator complete
B—Internal leakage	Defective cylinder head gasket	Check gasket sealing areas for signs of leakage and for damage	Replace gasket. Check engine oil for water contamination, flush and refill as necessary
	Loose cylinder head bolts	Check tightness of fixings using a torque spanner set to correct loading, Section A refers	Retighten in correct sequence to the correct torque loading, Section A refers. Check engine oil for water contamination, flush and refill as necessary
	Cracked cylinder bore	Dismantle and examine	Replace cylinder block
C—Water loss	Overfilling system	Refer to Owner's Instruction Manual for filling instructions	
	Boiling off	Ascertain the cause of engine overheating	Rectify as necessary
	Internal or external leakage	Refer to paragraphs A and B for checks and remedy	
	Restricted radiator or inoperative thermostat	Flush radiator. Check thermostat function	Replace as necessary
	Empty overflow bottle, where fitted	Check if water level in bottle is below end of header tank overflow tube	Replenish coolant until end of tube is fully immersed
	Radiator filler cap or sealing washer defective	Examine sealing washer for defects. Test radiator cap for sealing off	Replace components as necessary
D—Poor circulation	Restriction in system	Check hose runs for crimping. Flush radiator	Rectify as necessary
	Insufficient coolant	Check coolant level in radiator header tank, Section A	Replenish as necessary
	Loose fan belt	Check fan belt tension as described in Section A	Reset belt tension as necessary
	Inoperative thermostat	Check thermostat operation, Section K	Replace as necessary
	Inoperative water pump	Remove pump and examine, Section A	Replace as necessary
E—Corrosion	Infrequent flushing and draining		The cooling system should be drained and flushed at least twice a year
	Incorrect anti-freeze mixture		Use only glycol-based solutions as laid down in Owner's Maintenance Manual

COOLING SYSTEM

Fault diagnosis—Cooling system—continued

Symptom	Possible cause	Investigation	Remedy
E—Corrosion—cont	Excessive impurity in water		Use only clean water, soft if possible (e.g. rainwater)
F—Overheating	Poor circulation	Refer to paragraph D	
	Air locks in system	When refilling the coolant system, always allow a full flow through the coolant drain taps before closing them. Isolate heater, if fitted, before draining system	Clear air lock and replenish
	Air flow through radiator obstructed	Check for foreign matter lodged between radiator fins	Remove matter using air pressure applied from engine side of radiator
	Engine lubrication system faults	Low oil level	Replenish as necessary
		Dirty oil or sludge in system	Flush and replenish, Section A
	Engine settings incorrect	Check fuel distributor pump settings (Diesel) Check ignition timing (Petrol)	Reset as necessary, Section A
		Check valve timing	Reset as necessary, Section A
	Exhaust system faults	Check for choked or damaged exhaust pipes and silencer	Rectify or replace as necessary
	Braking system faults	Check for dragging brakes, Section H	
	Vehicle operating faults	a. Overloading vehicle b. Engine labouring on gradients c. Excessive low gear work d. Excessive engine idling	For these faults the remedy is in the hands of the operator
G—Overcooling	Defective thermostat	Check thermostat operation	Replace as necessary
	Inaccurate temperature gauge (where fitted)	Check by substituting serviceable gauge	Replace as necessary

SECTION L — FUEL SYSTEM

FUEL HANDLING PRECAUTIONS

The following information provides basic precautions which must be observed if petrol (gasoline) is to be handled safely. It also outlines the other areas of risk which must not be ignored.

This information is issued for basic guidance only, and in any case of doubt appropriate enquiries should be made of your local Fire Officer.

GENERAL

Petrol/gasoline vapour is highly flammable and in confined spaces is also very explosive and toxic.

When petrol/gasoline evaporates it produces 150 times its own volume in vapour, which when diluted with air becomes a readily ignitable mixture. The vapour is heavier than air and will always fall to the lowest level. It can readily be distributed throughout a workshop by air current, consequently, even a small spillage of petrol/gasoline is potentially very dangerous.

Always have a fire extinguisher containing FOAM CO_2 GAS, or POWDER close at hand when handling or draining fuel, or when dismantling fuel systems and in areas where fuel containers are stored.

Always disconnect the vehicle battery BEFORE carrying out dismantling or draining work on a fuel system.

Whenever petrol/gasoline is being handled, drained or stored, or when fuel systems are being dismantled all forms of ignition must be extinguished or removed, any head-lamps used must be flameproof and kept clear of spillage.

NO ONE SHOULD BE PERMITTED TO REPAIR COMPONENTS ASSOCIATED WITH PETROL/GASOLINE WITHOUT FIRST HAVING HAD SPECIALIST TRAINING.

FUEL TANK DRAINING

WARNING: PETROL/GASOLINE MUST NOT BE EXTRACTED OR DRAINED FROM ANY VEHICLE WHILST IT IS STANDING OVER A PIT.

Draining or extracting petrol/gasoline from vehicle fuel tank must be carried out in a well ventilated area.

The receptacle used to contain the petrol/gasoline must be more than adequate for the full amount of fuel to be extracted or drained. The receptacle should be clearly marked with its contents, and placed in a safe storage area which meets the requirements of local authority regulations.

WHEN PETROL/GASOLINE HAS BEEN EXTRACTED OR DRAINED FROM A FUEL TANK THE PRECAUTIONS GOVERNING NAKED LIGHTS AND IGNITION SOURCES SHOULD BE MAINTAINED.

FUEL TANK REMOVAL

On vehicles where the fuel line is secured to the fuel tank outlet by a spring steel clip, it is recommended that such clips are released before the fuel line is disconnected or the fuel tank unit is removed. This procedure will avoid the possibility of residual petrol fumes in the fuel tank being ignited when the clips are released.

As an added precaution fuel tanks should have a PETROL/GASOLINE VAPOUR warning label attached to them as soon as they are removed from the vehicle.

FUEL TANK REPAIR

Under no circumstances should a repair to any tank involving heat treatment be carried out without first rendering the tank SAFE, by using one of the following methods:

STEAMING: With the filler cap and tank unit removed, empty the tank. Steam the tank for at least two hours with low pressure steam. Position the tank so that condensation can drain away freely, ensuring that any sediment and sludge not volatised by the steam, is washed out during the steaming process.

BOILING: With the filler cap and tank unit removed, empty the tank. Immerse the tank completely in boiling water containing an effective alkaline degreasing agent or a detergent, with the water filling and also surrounding the tank for at least two hours.

After steaming or boiling a signed and dated label to this effect should be attached to the tank.

INDEX—FUEL SYSTEM

Note: A comprehensive, detailed index is included at the end of this manual

Description	Operation No.
Petrol system—General	Preceding 1
Diesel system—General	Preceding 14
Air cleaner	Section A
CARBURETTER	
Solex	1
Zenith	2
Stromberg	3
SU	4
FUEL PUMP	
Lift pump, mechanical	5
Lift pump, electric	6-7
Distributor pump, Diesel	15 also Section A
FUEL TANK	
Side mounted type	8
Rear mounted type	9
FUEL GAUGE UNIT	
With side mounted fuel tank	10
With rear mounted fuel tank	11
FUEL FILTERS	
Petrol system	12
Diesel system	15
Fuel pipes and hoses	13
Priming the fuel system—Diesel	14
Fuel injectors—Diesel	16
FAULT DIAGNOSIS	At end of Section
DATA	

Petrol fuel system—General notes

Carburetter

There are four types of carburetter in use on the various models in the Land-Rover range. Models fitted with 2¼ litre engines are equipped with either a Solex or Zenith type carburetter, while models fitted with 2.6 litre engines use either a Stromberg or SU type carburetter. Note that the Stromberg type carburetter is manufactured by the Zenith Carburetter Co. Ltd., and carries the manufacturers name, see Fig. L1-1 for identification.

Fuel pump

Two types of fuel pump are in use, all 2¼ litre models have a mechanically operated pump, secured directly to the right-hand side of the engine and driven from the engine camshaft. All models with 2.6 litre engines have an electrically operated pump, mounted on the chassis, RH side.

Fuel filter

All models are equipped with a fuel filter, 2¼ litre engines have a combined filter-sedimenter incorporated with the fuel pump. Models fitted with 2.6 litre engines have a fuel filter mounted on the engine side of the right-hand toe box.

Air cleaner

All details and instructions for air cleaners are included in Section A.

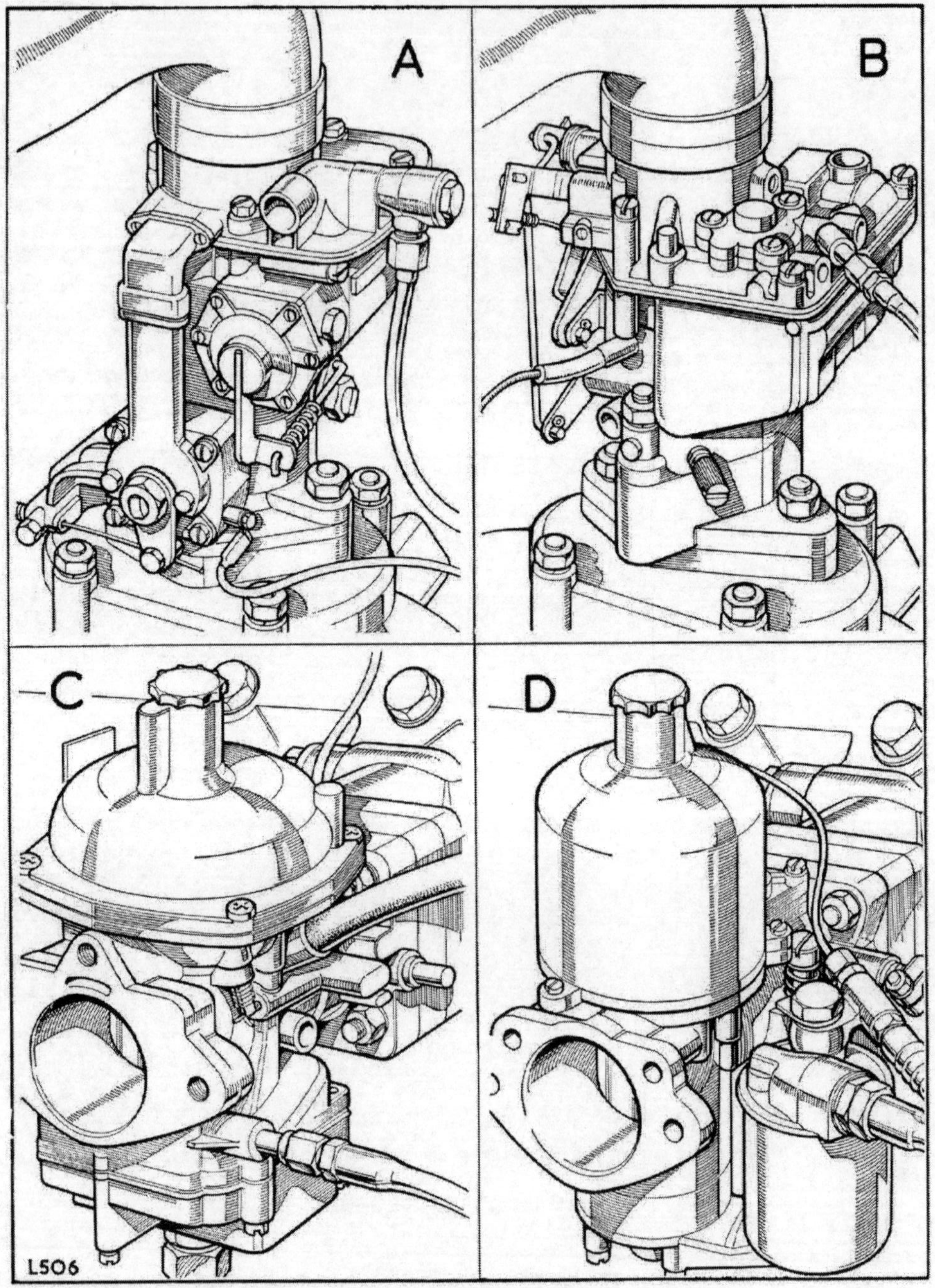

FUEL SYSTEM

Solex carburetter, to overhaul—Operation L1-1

(For removal and refitting instructions, Section A refers)

Workshop hand tools:
Spanner sizes: $\frac{7}{16}$ in. BSF open end, $\frac{3}{8}$ in. AF ring
Screwdriver (medium)

General

The following instructions cover both the SX type 40 PA 105/B and the SX type 40 PA 106 with heater element.

Carburetter, to dismantle

Top cover, to remove

1. Detach top cover from carburetter body.
2. Detach elbow from top cover with distance piece, if fitted.
3. Unscrew fixtures retaining joint washer to top cover and remove.
4. Unscrew needle valve housing.
5. Remove banjo union, filter gauze, washers and bolt.

Fig. L1-1. Carburetter identification

A—Solex   B—Zenith   C—Stromberg   D—SU

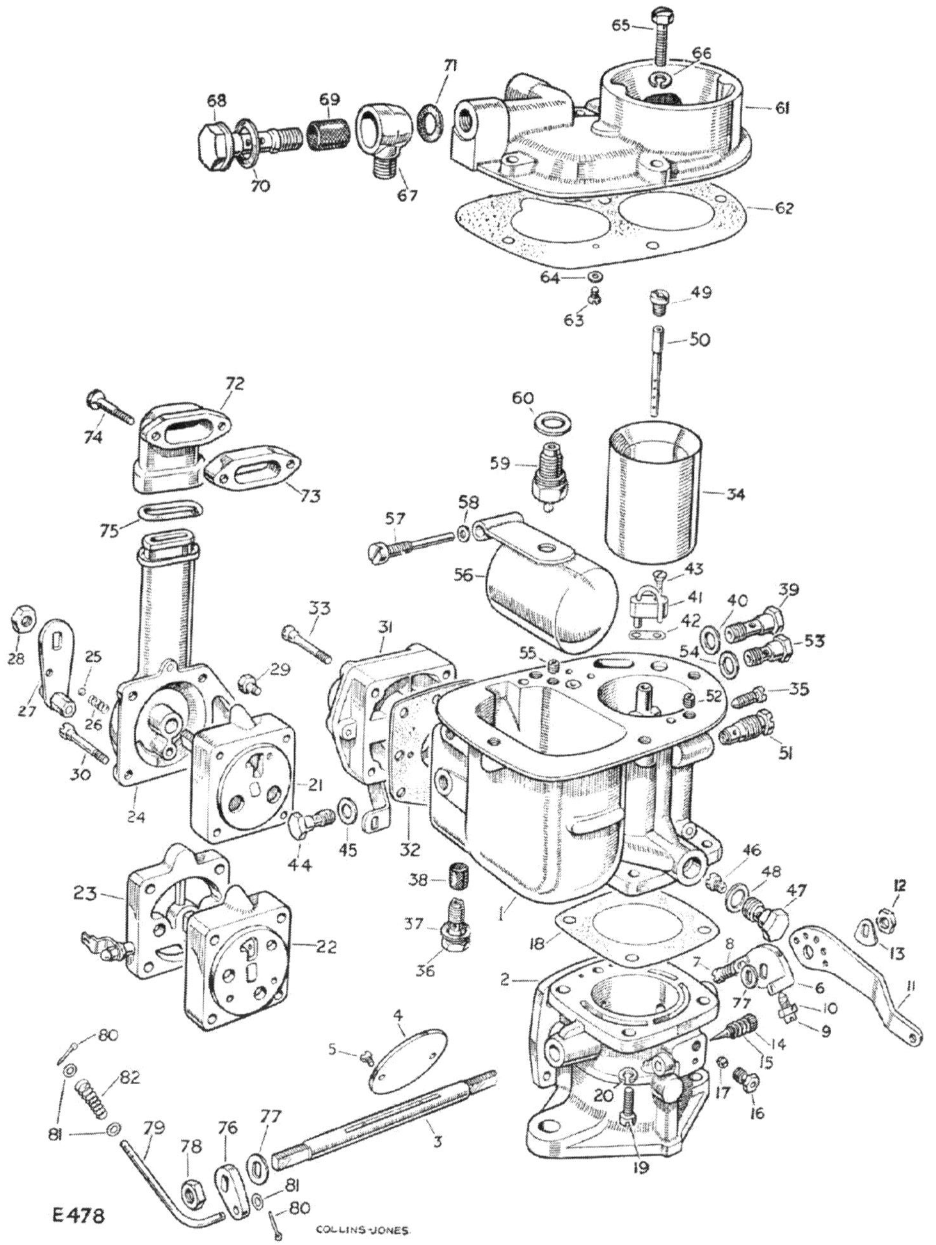

FUEL SYSTEM

Key to Fig. L1-2. Layout of Solex carburetter

1. Carburetter body
2. Throttle chamber
3. Spindle for throttle
4. Butterfly for throttle
5. Special screw fixing butterfly
6. Plate, throttle abutment
7. Special screw — For slow running adjustment
8. Spring
9. Special screw — For throttle stop
10. Locknut
11. Throttle lever
12. Nut fixing throttle lever
13. Lock washer for nut
14. Special screw — For mixture control
15. Spring
16. Screwed union — For suction pipe
17. Olive
18. Joint washer for throttle chamber
19–20. Fixing chamber to carburetter body
21. Starter body and valve, without starter heater element
22. Starter body and valve complete with starter heater element
23. Heater element for starter
24. Cover for starter
25. Ball — For starter valve
26. Spring
27. Lever for starter
28. Nut fixing starter lever
29. Special bolt fixing starter cable
30. Special screw fixing starter body
31. Accelerator pump complete
32. Joint washer for pump
33. Special screw fixing pump
34. Choke tube
35. Special screw fixing choke tube
36. Non-return valve
37. Fibre washer for valve
38. Filter gauze for non-return valve
39. Jet, accelerator pump
40. Fibre washer for jet
41. Pump injector
42. Joint washer for pump injector
43. Special screw fixing injector
44. Economy jet (blank)
45. Joint washer for blank jet
46. Main jet
47. Main jet carrier
48. Fibre washer for carrier
49. Correction jet
50. Emulsion tube
51. Pilot jet
52. Jet air bleed
53. Starter jet, petrol
54. Fibre washer for jet
55. Economy jet
56. Float
57. Spindle for float
58. Copper washer for spindle
59. Needle valve complete
60. Fibre washer for valve
61. Top cover for carburetter
62. Joint washer for top cover
63–64. Fixings—joint washer to top cover
65–66. Fixings—top cover to body
67. Banjo union
68. Special bolt for union
69. Filter gauze for union
70. Fibre washer, large
71. Fibre washer, small
72. Elbow for top cover
73. Distance piece, elbow to top cover
74. Screw fixing elbow to top cover
75. Rubber sealing washer, elbow to starter cover
76. Lever for accelerator pump rod
77. Special washer for lever
78. Nut fixing lever to spindle
79. Control rod for accelerator pump
80. Split pin
81. Plain washer } For control rod
82. Spring

Fig. L1-2. Layout of Solex carburetter

FUEL SYSTEM

Operation L1-1—continued

Throttle chamber, to remove

6. Disconnect control rod for accelerator pump, inserting split pin back into its correct location.

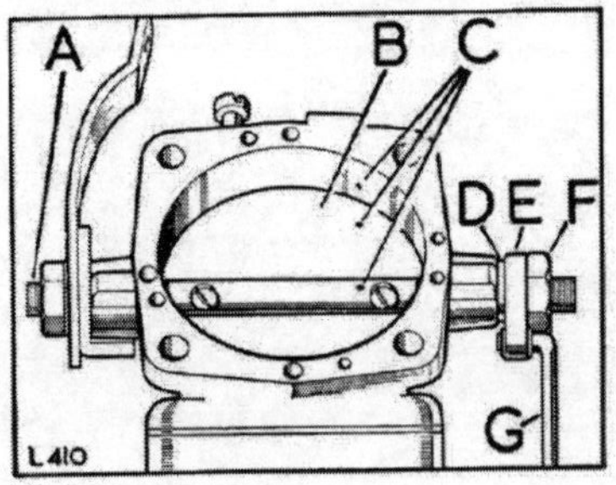

Fig. L1-3. Control rod for accelerator pump and throttle butterfly

A—Spindle for throttle
B—Butterfly for throttle
C—Markings inserted as required
D—Special washer for lever
E—Lever for accelerator pump
F—Nut fixing lever to spindle
G—Control rod for accelerator pump

7. Unscrew volume control screw.
8. Detach throttle chamber from carburetter body.
9. Remove gasket from top of throttle chamber.
10. Mark up throttle butterfly as illustrated and remove butterfly.
11. Withdraw throttle spindle.
12. Remove starter assembly from throttle chamber.
13. Remove starter lever, locating ball and spring.
14. Withdraw starter cover and remove rubber sealing washer.
15. Unclip circlip from starter valve assembly and withdraw heating element assembly if fitted.
16. Withdraw starter valve assembly from starter body.

Carburetter body, to strip

17. Remove bolt retaining float and withdraw float.
18. Remove pump injector.
19. Withdraw choke tube.
20. Remove air connection jet and emulsion tube.
21. Remove economy jet, pilot jet, accelerator pump jet and starter jet.
22. Remove main jet holder and main jet, then non-return valve with filter.

Accelerator pump, to remove

23. Detach accelerator pump from carburetter body and gasket.
24. Remove pump cover assembly.
25. Withdraw pump membrane assembly and pump spring.
26. Twist and withdraw economy valve spring and washer.

Operation L1-1—continued

Inspection and cleaning
Special notes

1. **Carburetter cleaning.**
   When cleaning fuel passages do not use metal tools (files, scrapers, drills, etc.) which could cause dimensional changes in the drillings or jets. Cleaning should be effected using clean fuel and where necessary a moisture-free air blast.

2. **Joint faces.**
   Examine the faces for deep scores which could lead to leakage taking place when assembled, check with straight edge for signs of bow.

3. **Joint gaskets and seals.**
   New gaskets and seals should be used throughout carburetter rebuild. A complete set of gaskets is available for replacement purposes.

4. Examine throttle spindle bushes for wear, if oval or badly worn renew carburetter body.
5. Examine float for puncture or damage and chamber for corrosion, retaining clips for wear.
6. Examine cold start bushes for wear, renew as necessary.
7. Examine accelerator device diaphragm for deterioration and damage, renew.
8. Examine volume control screw for wear and damage.
9. Examine all linkages for wear and lost motion very closely, renew as necessary.

Carburetter, to rebuild
Accelerator pump, to rebuild

1. Fit the economy valve spring and washer to the pump body, turning the economy valve through 90° to secure washer as illustrated.

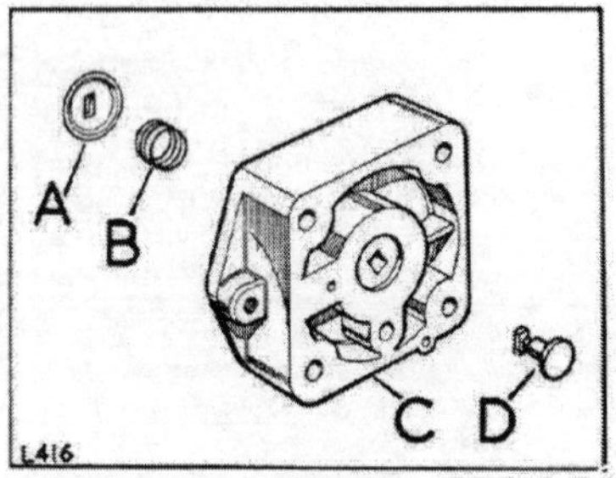

Fig. L1-4. Pump body assembly

A—Economy valve washer
B—Economy valve spring
C—Pump body
D—Economy valve

2. Insert pump spring into body, then place pump membrane into pump cover and secure pump body and pump cover together.
3. Fit pump body gasket to pump body on location peg, then secure accelerator pump to carburetter body as illustration.
4. Fit main jet to main jet holder and fit with washer to carburetter body.

FUEL SYSTEM

Operation L1-1—continued

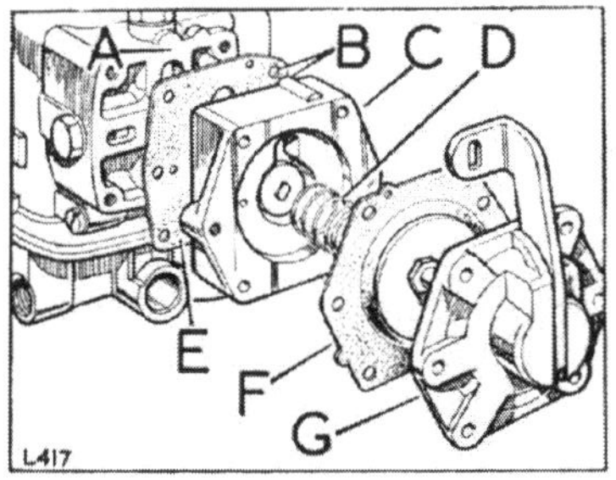

5. Fit pilot jet, accelerator pump jet and starter jet to the illustrated position.
6. Fit the non-return valve and filter to position illustrated.
7. Fit economy petrol jet to its respective position.
8. Fit choke tube, large inside diameter at bottom, then secure.
9. Fit pump injector and washer into carburetter and secure.
10. Insert emulsion tube into its retainer, followed by the air correction jet.
11. Locate float into chamber and retain with spindle.

Starter assembly, to rebuild

12. Fit rubber sealing washer to starter top cover.
13. Insert starter valve into starter body and fit retaining clip.
14. If applicable fit heater element on to starter body as shown.
15. Place starter top cover on starter body over locator, ensuring that valve orifices will align with throttle chamber when assembled. Fit spring and ball in location then retain with starter lever and secure.
16. Secure starter assembly to throttle chamber.

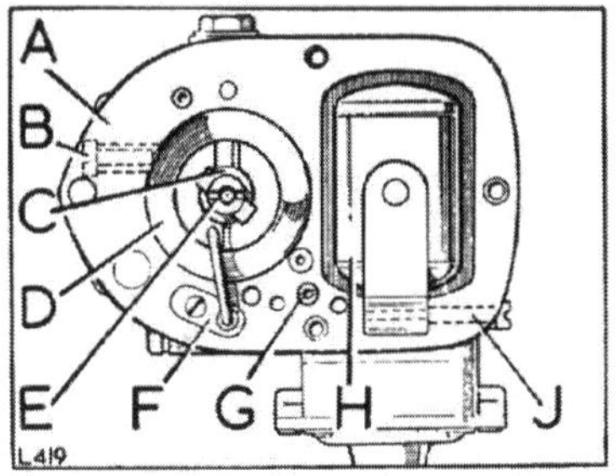

Fig. L1-7. Carburetter top face

A—Carburetter body
B—Choke tube retaining screw
C—Emulsion tube
D—Choke tube
E—Air correction jet
F—Pump injector
G—Economy petrol jet
H—Float
J—Float spindle

Fig. L1-5. Accelerator pump assembly

A—Carburetter body
B—Location peg and hole for pump body to gasket
C—Pump body
D—Pump spring
E—Pump body gasket
F—Pump membrane assembly
G—Top pump cover

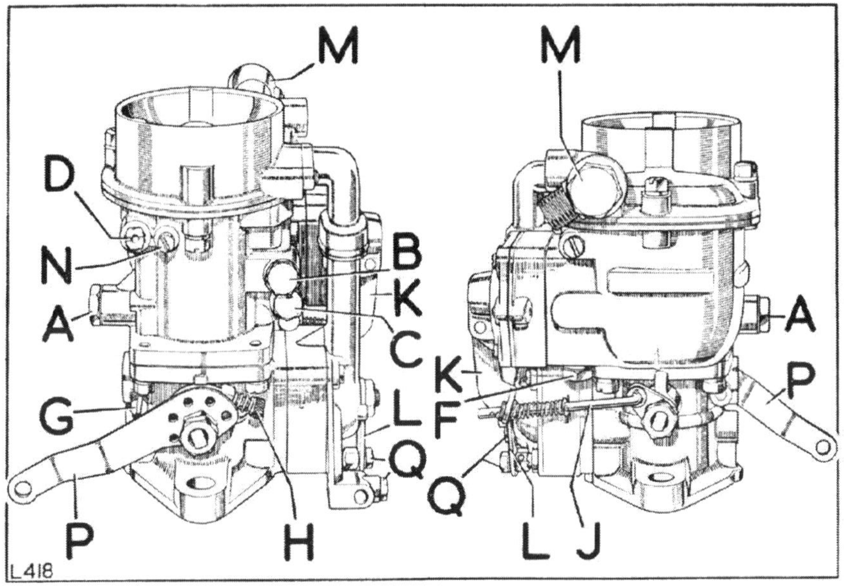

Fig. L1-6. Carburetter jets and controls, without starter heater element

A—Main jet
B—Accelerator pump jet
C—Starter jet, petrol
D—Pilot jet
F—Non-return valve
G—Mixture control
H—Slow running adjustment
J—Pump operating rod
K—Pump operating lever
L—Lever for starter
M—Banjo union
N—Special screw fixing choke tube
P—Throttle lever
Q—Cold start cable clamping bolts

FUEL SYSTEM

Operation L1-1—continued

Carburetter top cover, to rebuild

22. Fit washer on to needle valve and fit assembly into top cover, then test for satisfactory operation.
23. Fit gasket to top cover then secure in place.
24. Assemble banjo union as illustrated and loosely fit to top cover at this stage.
25. Fit elbow for top cover to top cover and secure, if a heater element is fitted to carburetter a distance piece also requires fitting with elbow.
26. Secure top cover to carburetter body.

Accelerator pump operating rod, to adjust

27. Remove the split pin behind the spring and allow the spring to move back along the rod.
28. Slacken the slow running screw right off.
29. With the throttle fully closed and the operating lever just about to operate the pump diaphragm, add washer/s on the end of the rod up to the nearest split pin hole, ensuring that there remains .020 in. (0,5 mm) clearance between the lever and the first washer when the outer split pin is fitted. This clearance ensures that there is no lost movement of the lever travel.
30. Compress the spring and replace the inner split pin.
31. Check that the spring is not coilbound when the throttle is fully open.

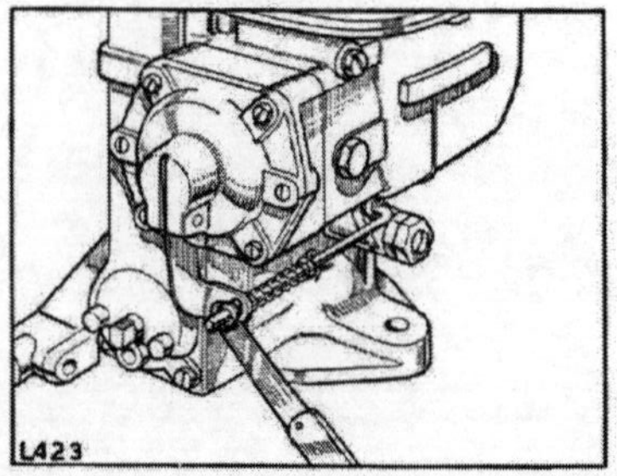

Fig. L1-11. Setting accelerator pump operating rod

Carburetter, to adjust

1. Set mixture control screw one and a half turns from full in position. **DO NOT** overtighten mixture control screw or the fine taper may be damaged.
2. Screw in the slow running screw one complete turn after contacting abutment on throttle chamber.
3. Operate accelerator pedal to ensure that linkage does not stick and throttle lever at carburetter has full travel.
4. Start engine and run until normal operating temperature is attained.
5. Adjust mixture control screw until engine runs smoothly and evenly.
6. Adjust slow running screw to give engine idling speed of 500 rpm.
7. Snap throttle open and shut to ensure that engine does not stall. If stalling occurs, slightly increase slow running speed.

   Note: It may be necessary to alternate slight adjustments between mixture and slow running screws to obtain satisfactory results.

Operation L1-1—continued

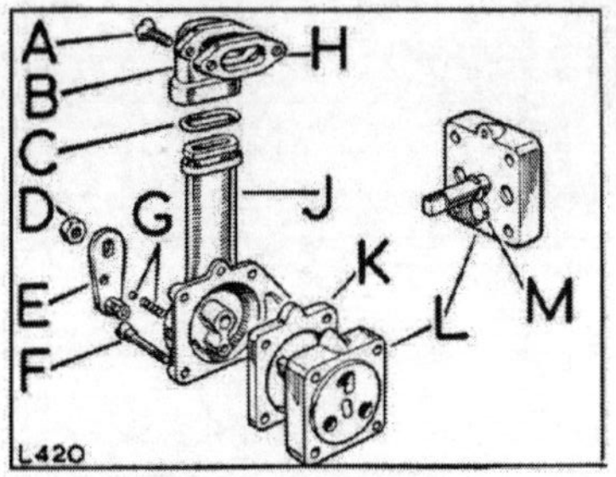

Fig. L1-8. Starter assembly

A—Screw for elbow
B—Elbow
C—Rubber sealing washer
D—Nut fixing starter lever
E—Lever for starter
F—Screw fixing starter body
G—Ball and spring for starter valve
H—Distance piece for elbow
J—Starter top cover
K—Heater element for starter
L—Starter body
M—Locator

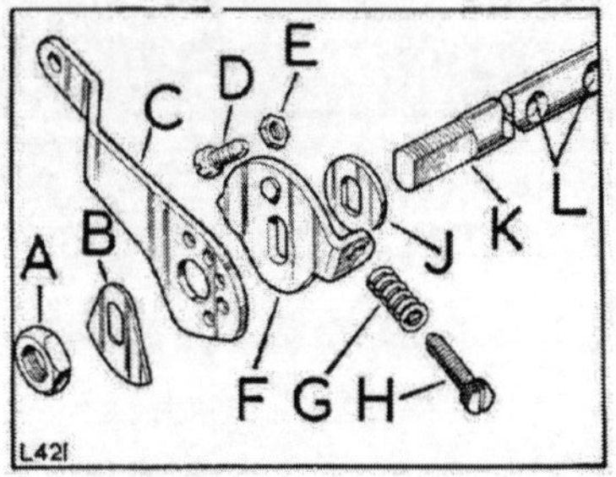

Throttle chamber, to rebuild

17. To assemble throttle linkage, fit throttle spindle abutment plate to spindle, followed by throttle lever and locate on peg. Fit throttle spindle tab washer and nut then secure and lock tab washer as illustrated.
18. Insert throttle spindle into throttle chamber as illustration, then fit throttle butterfly, ensuring chamfered edges mate with chamber wall. Operate throttle butterfly to centralise, then secure and pin-punch screws to prevent rotation.
19. Fit accelerator lever as illustrated, to throttle spindle.
20. Fit throttle chamber gasket, ensuring that it aligns with the holes in carburetter body, then secure carburetter body to throttle chamber, first ensuring that accelerator rod is fitted to pump lever with its spring and split pin.
21. Fit mixture control screw, but do not tighten, then unscrew one and a half turns.

Fig. L1-9. Throttle linkage assembly

A—Spindle nut
B—Spindle nut tab washer
C—Throttle lever
D—Screw } Throttle
E—Nut } stop
F—Abutment plate
G—Spring } Slow
H—Screw } running
K—Throttle spindle
L—Countersunk screw holder
J—Special washer

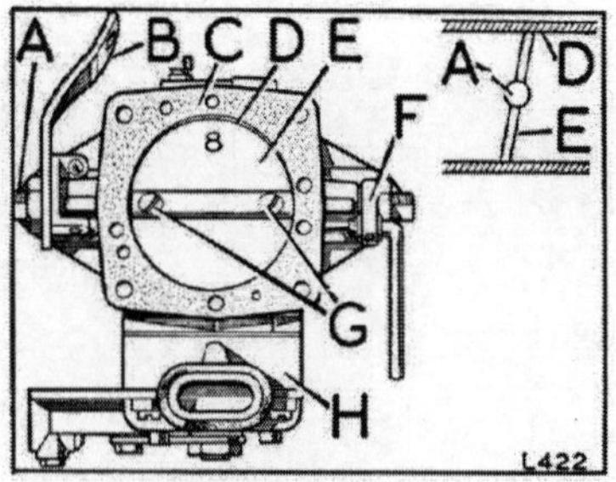

Fig. L1-10. Throttle chamber with butterfly assembly

A—Throttle spindle
B—Throttle lever
C—Throttle chamber gasket
D—Throttle chamber
E—Throttle butterfly
F—Accelerator lever
G—Throttle fixing screws
H—Starter assembly

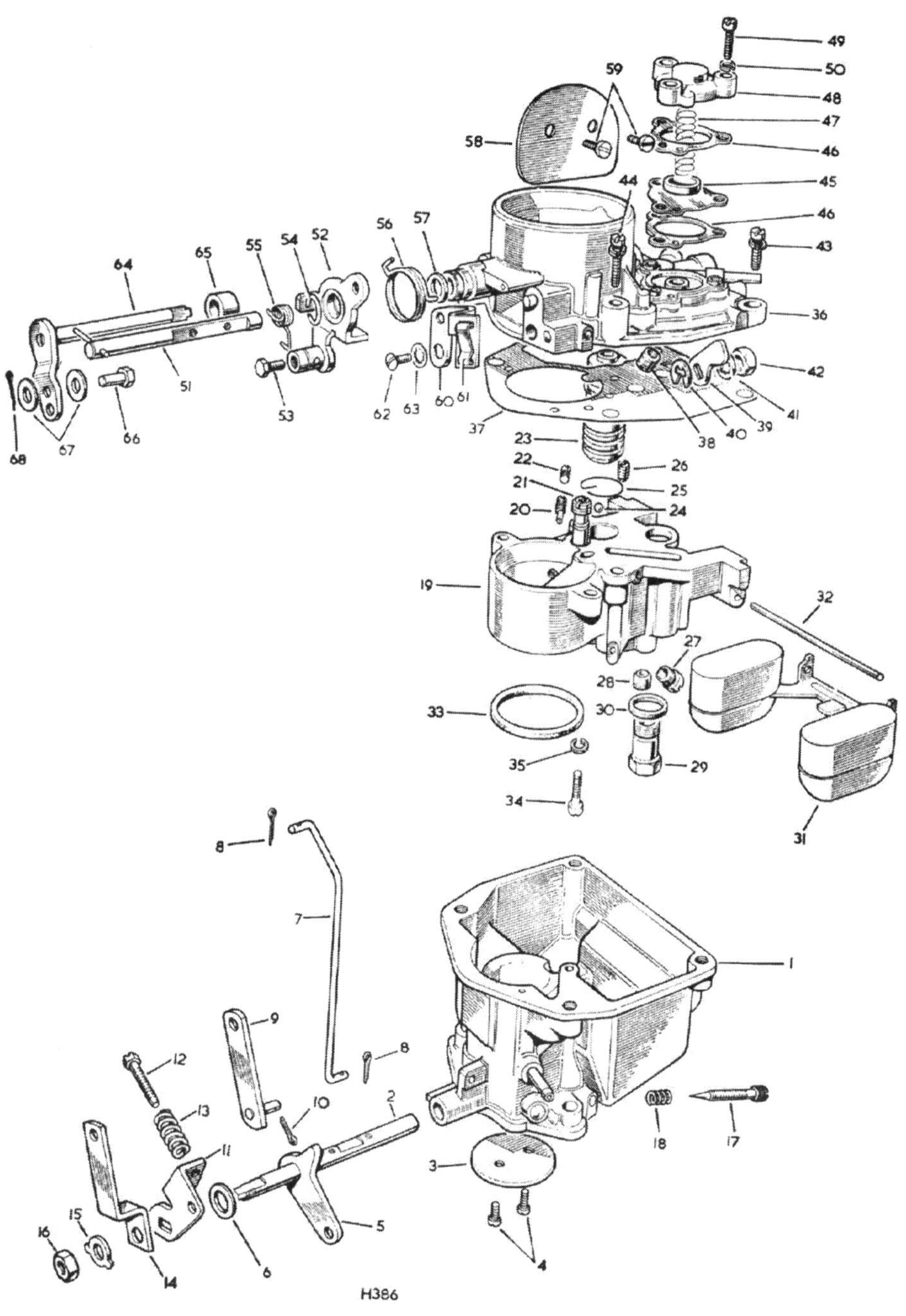

FUEL SYSTEM

Key to illustration of Zenith carburetter

1. Carburetter main body
2. Throttle spindle
3. Butterfly for throttle
4. Special screw fixing butterfly
5. Floating lever on throttle spindle
6. Plain washer on spindle for floating lever
7. Interconnecting link, throttle to choke
8. Split pin fixing link to levers
9. Relay lever, throttle to accelerator pump
10. Split pin fixing relay lever to floating lever
11. Throttle stop and fast idle lever
12. Special screw ⎱ For throttle
13. Spring ⎰ stop
14. Throttle lever
15. Lock washer ⎱ Fixing throttle
16. Special nut ⎰ levers
17. Volume control screw
18. Spring for control screw
19. Emulsion block
20. Pump jet
21. Pump discharge valve
22. Plug for pump jet
23. Piston for accelerator pump
24. Ball for piston
25. Circlip for piston
26. Slow running jet
27. Main jet
28. Enrichment jet
29. Needle valve
30. Special washer (2 mm)
31. Float
32. Spindle for float
33. 'O' ring, emulsion block to body
34. Special screw ⎱ Fixing emulsion
35. Spring washer ⎰ block to body
36. Top cover for carburetter
37. Gasket for top cover
38. Ventilation screw (3.0) for choke
39. Pump lever, internal
40. Retaining ring for pump lever
41. Shakeproof washer ⎫ Fixing
42. Special nut ⎬ pump
43. Screw and spring washer, short ⎱ Fixing top cover
44. Screw and spring washer, long ⎰ to main body
45. Diaphragm for carburetter
46. Gasket for diaphragm
47. Spring for diaphragm
48. Cover for diaphragm
49. Screw ⎱ Fixing
50. Spring washer ⎰ diaphragm cover
51. Spindle and pin for choke lever
52. Lever and swivel for choke
53. Screw for choke lever swivel
54. Circlip fixing choke lever to top cover
55. Spring, small ⎱ For choke
56. Spring, large ⎰ lever
57. Plain washer for choke spindle
58. Butterfly for choke
59. Special screw fixing butterfly
60. Bracket and clip for choke cable
61. Clip for choke bracket
62. Special screw ⎱ Fixing choke bracket to
63. Shakeproof washer ⎰ top cover
64. Spindle and lever for accelerator pump
65. Spacing washer for pump spindle
66. Pin ⎱ Fixing relay
67. Plain washer ⎬ lever to
68. Split pin ⎰ pump lever

Fig. L1-12. Layout of Zenith carburetter

FUEL SYSTEM

Zenith carburetter, to overhaul—Operation L1-2

(For removal and refitting instructions, Section A refers)

Workshop hand tools:
Spanner size: $\frac{7}{16}$ in. AF
Screwdriver (small)

Carburetter, to dismantle

Linkages, to remove

1. Disconnect the interconnecting link.
2. Disconnect accelerator pump spindle lever from throttle relay lever.

Top cover and emulsion block, to separate

3. Detach top cover from carburetter body.
4. Remove float assembly.
5. Remove needle valve housing and needle.
6. Detach emulsion block from carburetter top cover, taking care not to drop the accelerator pump assembly which is now freed.
7. Remove gasket from top cover.

Emulsion block, to dismantle

8. Lift out accelerator pump piston.
9. Remove all jets in emulsion block.
   Note: At the base of the accelerator pump housing bore is a ball inlet valve retained by a circlip, there is no need to remove it.

Carburetter body, dismantling

10. Remove idling volume control screw.
11. Detach adaptor from carburetter body.
12. Mark up (see Fig. L1-19) then remove throttle butterfly disc followed by throttle spindle and linkage if required.
13. Remove the 'O' ring seal from choke venturi tube.

Carburetter top cover

14. Strip down economy valve assembly, taking care not to loose diaphragm spring.
15. Remove, if required, the choke butterfly after marking up. Followed by the choke spindle, taking care to retain the thin washer.
16. Remove spindle and lever for accelerator pump.
17. Remove ventilation screw for choke.

Inspection and cleaning

Special notes

1. **Carburetter cleaning**
   When cleaning fuel passages do not use metal tools (files, scrapers, drills, etc.) which could cause dimensional changes in the drillings or jets. Cleaning should be effected using clean fuel and where necessary a moisture-free air blast.

2. **Joint faces.**
   If the joint faces on the emulsion block, top cover or carburetter body show any signs of distortion or the edges are burred, these faces may be reclaimed by flatting, using fine grade abrasive cloth and a surface plate. Examine the faces for deep scores which would lead to leakage taking place when assembled.

3. **Joint gasket and seals.**
   New gaskets and seals should be used throughout carburetter rebuild. A complete set of gaskets is available for replacement purposes.

4. Examine throttle spindle bushes for wear, if oval or badly worn renew carburetter body.

5. Examine the tapered end of the idling volume screw for wear and damage, renew as required.

Carburetter, to rebuild

Carburetter top cover, rebuild

1. If previously dismantled, insert the choke spindle into its housing and at the same time refit the thin washer. Locate the choke butterfly on the spindle and loosely retain with the two special screws. Operate the butterfly to centralise it on the spindle, then secure the screws and lock them by peening. Engage the spring end on to the choke swivel lever.

2. Fit the economy valve gasket, diaphragm assembly and a further gasket to the top cover upper face, aligning the holes in the gaskets and diaphragm with the drilling in the top cover face.

3. Locate the spring in the seating on the diaphragm assembly, locate the valve cover spigot on the spring free end and align the drilling in the cover casting with the hole in the gasket. Push down on the cover, keeping it square to the diaphragm. Then secure.

Operation L1-2—continued

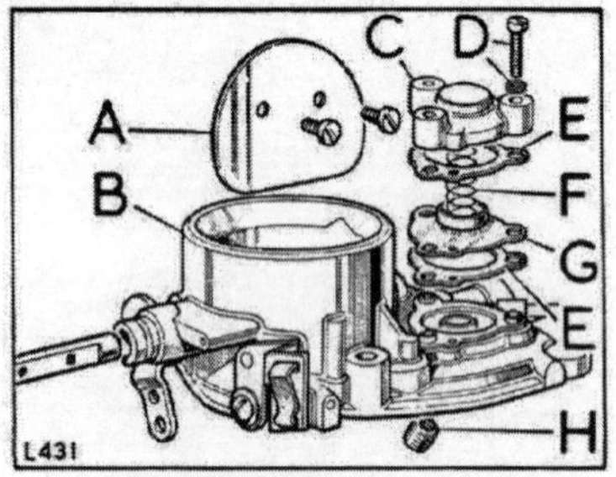

Fig. L1-13. Carburetter top cover details

A—Choke butterfly disc
B—Carburetter top cover
C—Economy valve diaphragm cover
D—Diaphragm cover fixings
E—Diaphragm gaskets
F—Diaphragm spring
G—Diaphragm assembly
H—Ventilation jet

4. Fit the ventilation screw to the angled tapping in the top cover lower face.
5. Fit the spindle and lever for accelerator pump as illustrated.

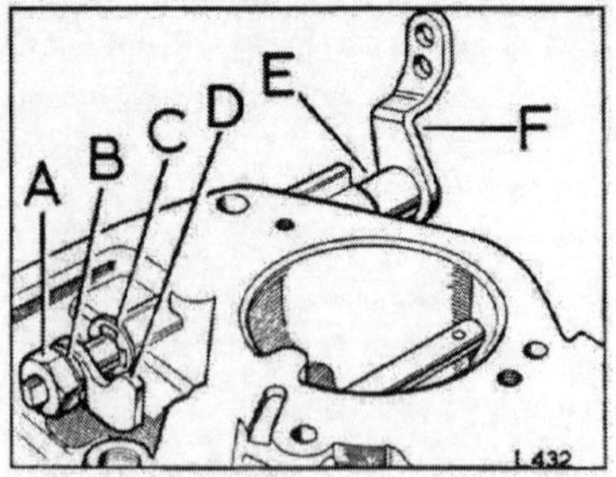

Fig. L1-14. Accelerator spindle assembly

A—Securing nut
B—Shakeproof washer
C—Circlip
D—Accelerator pump arm
E—Distance piece oilite bush
F—Spindle and lever for accelerator pump

Emulsion block, rebuild

6. Fit the blanked off jet and the slow running jet to their respective tappings in the emulsion block upper face, see illustration for positions.
7. Fit the pump jet, followed by the pump jet tapping plug, to the tapping in the side of the emulsion block.
8. Fit the main jet and the enrichment jet into the emulsion block, the enrichment jet into the vertical tapping and the main jet into the angled tapping. The jets are cadmium plated and only plated main and enrichment jets are to be used in this carburetter.

Fitting emulsion block to carburetter top cover

9. Position the gasket on top cover joint face.
10. Apply a thin smear of clean lubricating oil to the accelerator pump piston and assemble. piston first, into its housing bore in the emulsion block.
11. Ensure that the accelerator pump spindle lever is positioned inboard to align with accelerator pump plunger, position emulsion block and accelerator pump assembly on top cover joint face.

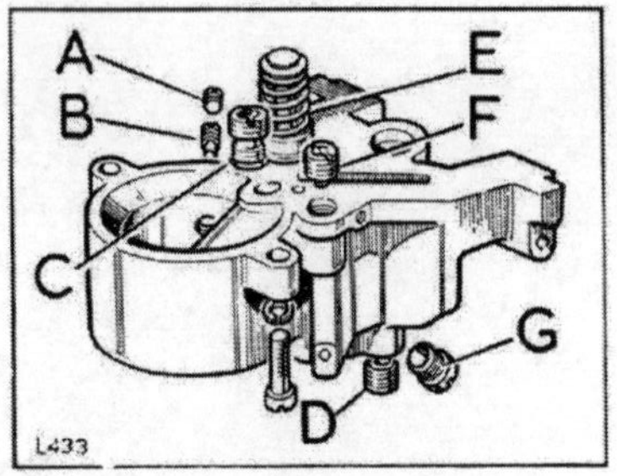

Fig. L1-15. Emulsion block details

A—Plug for pump jet tapping
B—Pump jet
C—Blanked off jet
D—Enrichment jet
E—Accelerator pump piston
F—Slow running jet
G—Main jet

FUEL SYSTEM

Operation L1-2—continued

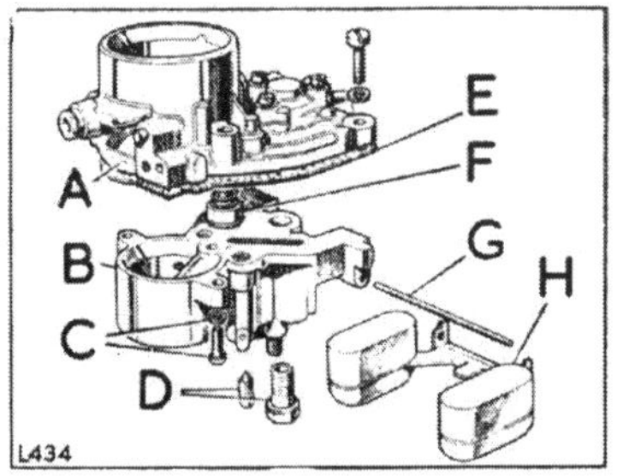

Fig. L1-16. Key to fitting top cover to emulsion block

A—Carburetter top cover
B—Emulsion block
C—Emulsion block attachment screws and washers
D—Needle valve and housing
E—Top cover gasket
F—Accelerator pump piston assembly
G—Hinge pin
H—Float assembly

12. Ensure that the sealing washer for the needle valve housing is in good condition and fit the washer.

13. Fit the needle valve housing and the securing screws into the emulsion block. Do not fully tighten at this stage.

14. Check that the fuel passage drillings in the top cover are clear and not masked by misalignment of the gasket. Now fully tighten the emulsion block securing screw and needle housing.

15. Fit the needle valve into its seating in the needle valve housing. Check for leakage past the assembly by holding the needle valve on to its seating and blowing air into fuel inlet pipe.

Fitting float assembly

16. Position float assembly on to top cover, align pin holes in float carrier and emulsion block flange lugs and secure float carrier with hinge pin.

17. With the needle valve on its seating and the central tongue on the float carrier contacting on the needle valve, measure the distance between the gasket upper face and the highest point on the floats as detailed in the accompanying illustration.

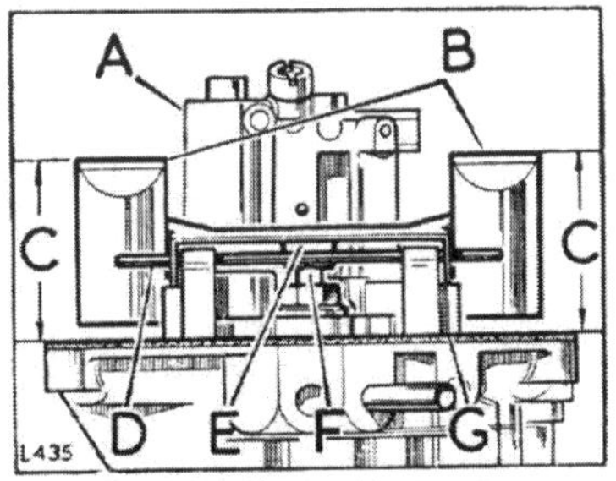

Fig. L1-17. Checking float setting

A—Emulsion block
B—Highest points on floats
C—Dimension to be $1\frac{5}{16}$ in. (33 mm)
D—Hinge pin
E—Central tongue on float carrier
F—Needle valve
G—Gasket

18. The dimension required at this check is $1\frac{5}{16}$ in. (33 mm). Any adjustment must be made by deflecting the central tongue which abuts the needle valve; adjustment must not be made by bending the float carrier arms.

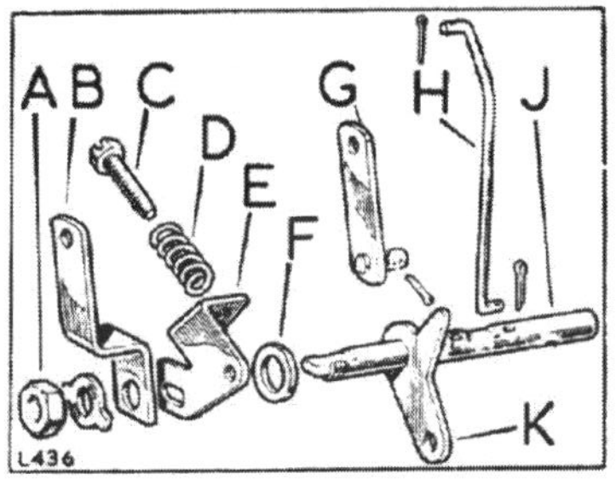

Fig. L1-18. Throttle linkage assembly

A—Lockwasher and securing nut
B—Throttle lever
C—Special screw for throttle stop
D—Spring
E—Throttle stop and fast idle lever
F—Plain washer
G—Relay lever
H—Interconnecting link
J—Throttle spindle
K—Floating lever on throttle spindle

Operation L1-2—continued

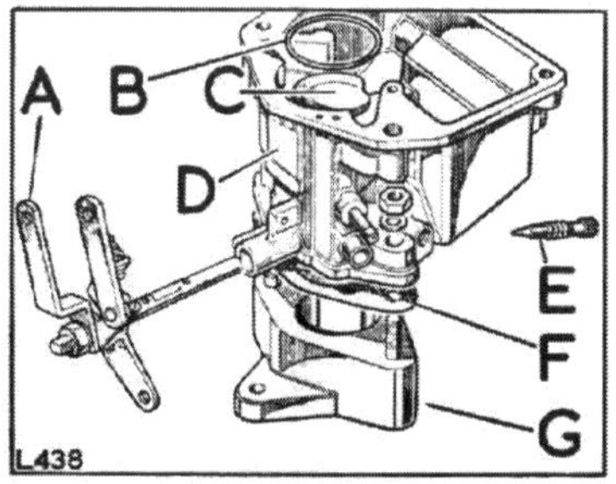

Fig. L1-20. Carburetter body and adaptor

A—Throttle control
B—'O' ring seal
C—Venturi barrel
D—Carburetter body
E—Volume control screw
F—Adaptor gasket
G—Adaptor body

19. Assemble the throttle linkage to the spindle, insert floating lever, plain washer, throttle stop, throttle lever, lock tab and securing nut as illustrated.

20. Fit throttle spindle assembly to carburetter then insert butterfly into spindle, aligning marks previously made, and loosely retain with the two special screws. Operate the butterfly to centralise it on the spindle, then secure the screws and lock them by peening.

21. Fit carburetter adaptor to carburetter body using a new gasket and tighten evenly.

Fitting top cover and emulsion block to carburetter body

22. Fit the 'O' ring seal to the seating around the top end of the venturi barrel. Ensure that the 'O' ring is correctly seated. THIS IS VERY IMPORTANT AS POOR JOINTING WOULD CREATE POOR FUEL CONSUMPTION.

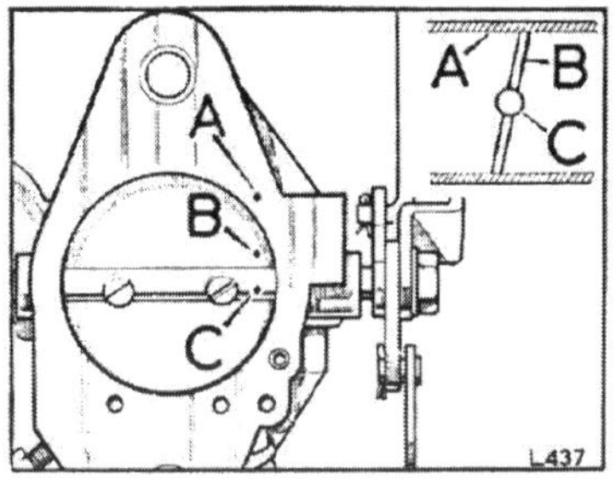

Fig. L1-19. Butterfly assembly

A—Carburetter body marking
B—Butterfly marking
C—Spindle marking

23. Offer up the cover and emulsion block assembly to the carburetter body. Check that the 'O' ring seal around the venturi barrel is holding off the emulsion block, indicated by a small gap between the top cover gasket and carburetter body joint faces. This will ensure a compression seal on the 'O' ring when assembled.

24. Secure the assembly, evenly, to carburetter body. Then replace idling volume control screw.

Carburetter linkage, reconnect

25. Connect the throttle relay lever to the hole furthest from the fulcrum on the accelerator pump spindle lever, using clevis pin, two plain washers and split pin.

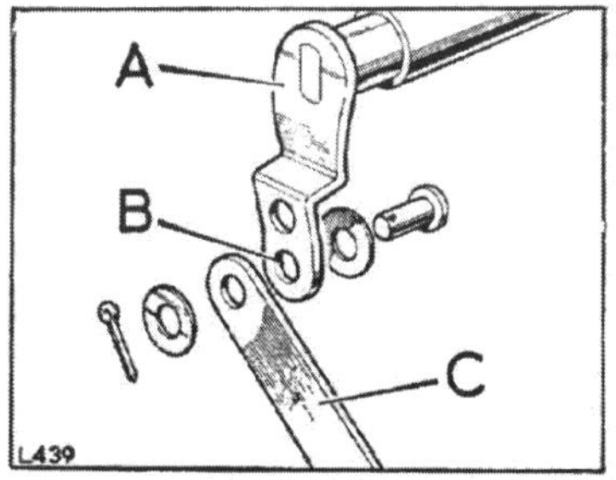

Fig. L1-21. Throttle relay lever position

A—Accelerator pump spindle lever
B—Position of accelerator pump hole
C—Throttle relay lever

FUEL SYSTEM

Operation L1-2—continued

Note: In some applications of the basic carburetter, the hole nearest to the fulcrum is for use only in cold seasons to obtain maximum stroke from the accelerator pump.

26. Fit the interconnecting link between choke operating tab and the floating lever on the throttle spindle and secure with split pins.

Fast-idle interconnection setting

Fully close choke butterfly by actuating choke operating tab. It should be possible to slide a .04 in. diameter (1.25 mm) drill between throttle butterfly edge and the carburetter body. If necessary, bend interconnection link to achieve this condition.

Carburetter, to set and adjust

Before any attempt is made to set the idling speed, a thorough check should be made to ensure that the throttle linkage between the pedal and the carburetter is free and has no tendency to stick, also ensure full throttle operation.

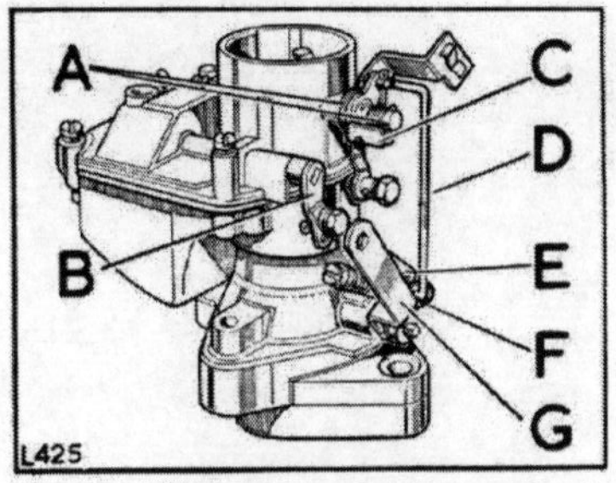

Fig. L1-22. Interconnecting linkage

A—Choke linkage return springs
B—Accelerator pump spindle lever
C—Choke operating tab
D—Interconnecting link
E—Throttle spindle relay lever
F—Throttle spindle floating lever
G—Throttle lever

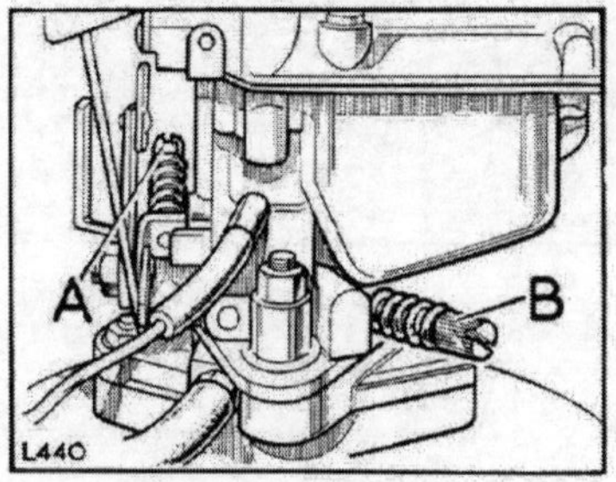

Fig. L1-23. Carburetter slow running adjustment

A—Throttle stop screw
B—Idling volume control screw

1. Start engine and run until warm, denoted by thermostat outlet pipe becoming warm to the touch. Continue running for a further five minutes to thoroughly stabilise engine temperature.

2. Adjust the throttle stop screw to obtain engine idling speed of 500 rpm.

3. Adjust the idling volume control screw until the engine runs smoothly and evenly. Recheck idle speed and correct as necessary. Recheck idling stability. It may be necessary to alternate adjustments between idling volume control screw and throttle stop screw to obtain the required idling setting. The idling volume control screw is then at the setting position required for all engine operating conditions.

To confirm that the setting position selected is correct, turn the volume control screw in and out respectively from the setting position by approximately one-half turn; at these checking positions the engine note will alter and the engine running will become uneven. After checking, return the volume control screw to the correct setting position selected midway between the checking positions.

This page intentionally left blank

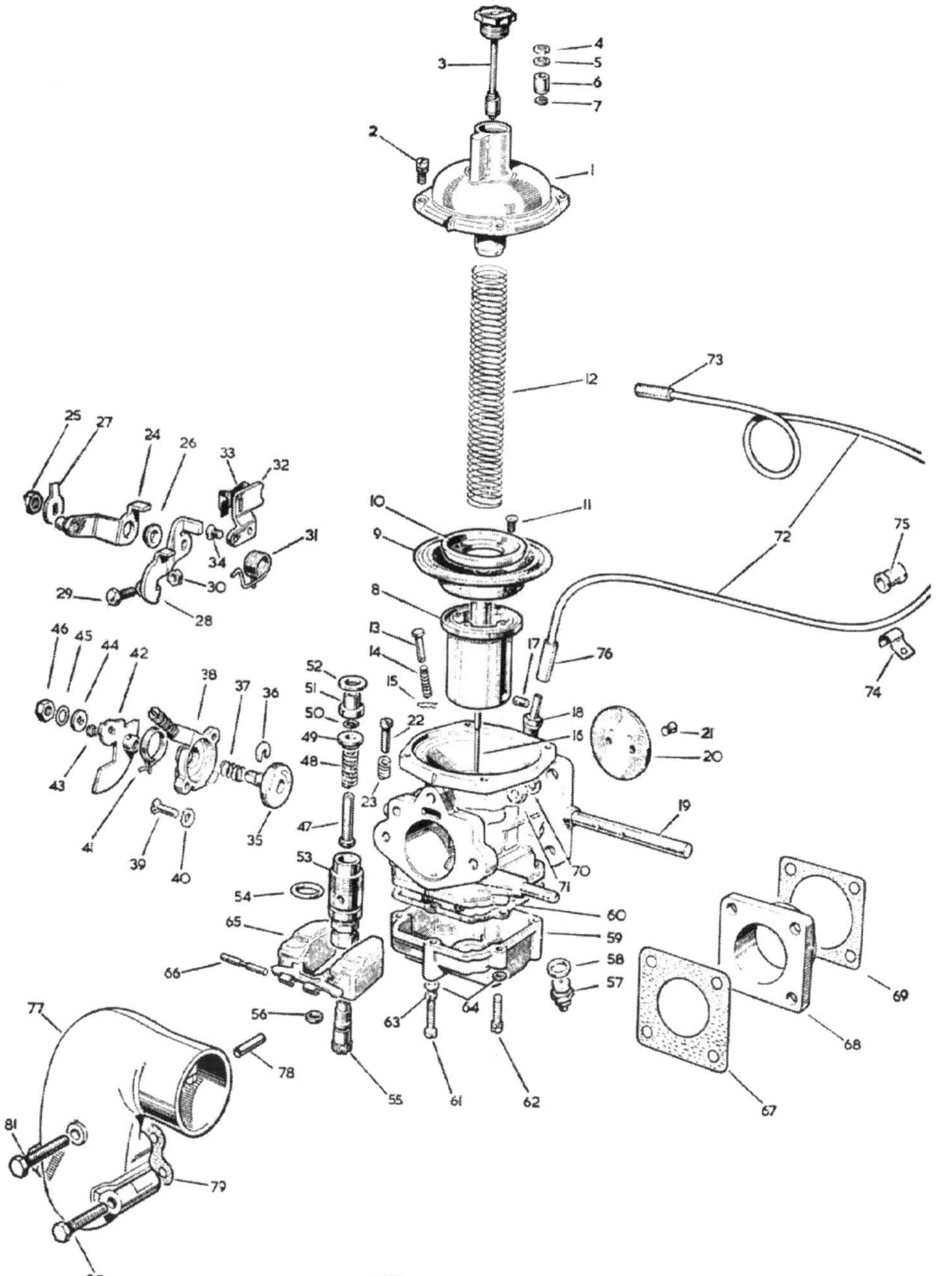

FUEL SYSTEM

Key to illustration of carburetter

1. Top cover for carburetter
2. Special screw and washer fixing top cover
3. Damper and oil cap assembly
4. Special washer, upper
5. Special washer, lower
6. Bush for damper
7. Retaining ring, for damper
8. Air valve, shaft and diaphragm assembly
9. Diaphragm
10. Retaining ring for diaphragm
11. Special screw fixing retaining ring
12. Return spring for air valve
13. Lifting pin for air valve
14. Spring for lifting pin
15. Spring clip for lifting pin
16. Metering needle
17. Locking screw for metering needle
18. Ignition adaptor
19. Throttle spindle
20. Butterfly for throttle
21. Special screw fixing butterfly
22. Throttle stop screw
23. Spring for stop screw
24. Throttle lever
25. Special nut } Fixing throttle levers
26. Special washer
27. Tab washer
28. Throttle stop and fast-idle lever
29. Special screw } For throttle stop
30. Locknut
31. Throttle return spring
32. Bracket and clip for choke cable
33. Clip for choke bracket
34. Special screw fixing choke bracket
35. Cold start spindle
36. Special washer for starter spindle
37. Cold start spring
38. Cover for cold start
39. Special screw } Fixing cover
40. Shakeproof washer
41. Return spring for cam lever
42. Cam lever for cold start
43. Clamping screw for cam lever swivel
44. Spacing washer } Fixing cam lever to cold start spindle
45. Shakeproof washer
46. Special nut
47. Jet orifice
48. Spring
49. Guide bush } For jet orifice
50. 'O' ring
51. Bush
52. Special washer
53. Carrier for jet orifice
54. 'O' ring for carrier
55. Adjusting screw for jet orifice
56. 'O' ring for adjusting screw
57. Needle valve
58. Washer for needle valve
59. Float chamber
60. Gasket for float chamber
61. Special screw, long } Fixing float chamber
62. Special screw, short
63. Spring washer
64. Plain washer
65. Float and arm
66. Spindle for float
67. Joint washer for carburetter
68. Adaptor for carburetter
69. Joint washer for adaptor
70. Spring washer } Fixing carburetter and adaptor to cylinder head
71. Nut ($\frac{5}{16}$ in. UNF)
72. Suction pipe, carburetter to distributor
73. Rubber sleeve, suction pipe to distributor
74. Clip for suction pipe } On engine
75. Rubber grommet for clip
76. Rubber sleeve, suction pipe to carburetter
77. Air inlet elbow assembly
78. Adaptor for top breather hose
79. Joint washer for inlet elbow
80. Set bolt ($\frac{5}{16}$ in. UNC x 2½ in. long) } Fixing elbow to carburetter
81. Set bolt ($\frac{5}{16}$ in. UNC x 3 in. long)

Fig. L1-24. Layout of Stromberg carburetter

Stromberg carburetter (Zenith type 175 CD-2S), to overhaul—Operation L1-3

(For removal and refitting instructions, Section A refers)

Workshop hand tools:
Spanner sizes: ½ in. BSF, ⅝ in. BSF ring, ⅝ in. AF open end
Screwdriver (medium), Phillips screwdriver

Carburetter, to dismantle

Piston assembly, to remove

1. Remove oil cap and damper.
2. Remove top cover and spring.
3. Remove air valve, shaft and diaphragm assembly.

Float chamber, to remove

4. Remove metering needle retained by locking screw.
5. Remove diaphragm from air valve.
6. Detach float chamber from carburetter body with gasket.
7. Remove jet assembly complete, then strip assembly fully.
8. Unclip float and arm with spindle.
9. Remove needle valve and washer from carburetter body.

Carburetter body, to dismantle

10. Remove ignition adaptor from carburetter body.
11. Remove throttle butterfly from the throttle spindle after marking up.

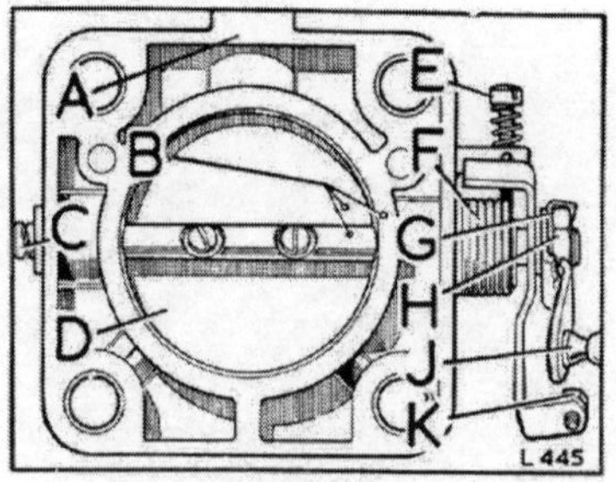

Fig. L1-25. Throttle butterfly assembly

A—Carburetter body
B—Marks to be added during dismantling
C—Throttle spindle
D—Throttle butterfly
E—Fast idle adjusting screw
F—Throttle return spring
G—Tab washer
H—Locknut
J—Throttle lever
K—Throttle stop and fast idle lever

12. Withdraw throttle spindle from carburetter body and strip down throttle linkage if necessary.
13. Remove fast-idle adjusting screw.
14. Detach cold start assembly.
15. Strip cold start assembly.

Inspection and cleaning

Special notes:

1. **Carburetter cleaning.**
   When cleaning fuel passages do not use metal tools (files, scrapers, drills, etc.) which could cause dimensional changes in the drillings or jets. Cleaning should be effected using clean fuel and where necessary a moisture-free air blast.

2. **Joint faces.**
   Examine the faces for deep scores which would lead to leakage taking place when assembled.

3. **Joint gasket and seals.**
   New gaskets and seals should be used throughout carburetter rebuild. A complete set of gaskets is available for replacement purposes.

4. Examine throttle spindle bushes for wear, if oval or badly worn renew carburetter body.

5. Inspect metering needle, it is machined to very close limits and should be handled with care. Examine for wear, bend and twist, renew if necessary.

6. **Diaphragm.**
   In common with other products made from rubber compounds, any contact of the diaphragm with volite cleaners should be avoided, use only CLEAN RAG. Examine for damage and deterioration.

7. Examine float, for puncture or damage and chamber for corrosion, retaining clips for wear.

8. Examine cold start bushes for wear, renew starter cover as necessary.

9. Examine clamping screw for two positions, renew as necessary.

10. Examine lifting pin for air valve for correct operation.

Operation L1-3—continued

Carburetter, to rebuild

Cold start, to rebuild

1. Fit the cold start spring behind the discs and secure with spring retaining clip, ensure discs are able to move easily on spindle.

2. Position cold start return spring on starter cover as illustrated.

3. Offer up cold start spindle assembly to starter cover, paying particular attention to the position of the slots in the disc; refit cam lever then secure in position.

4. Fit the cold start assembly to carburetter body. Then check for ease of operation.

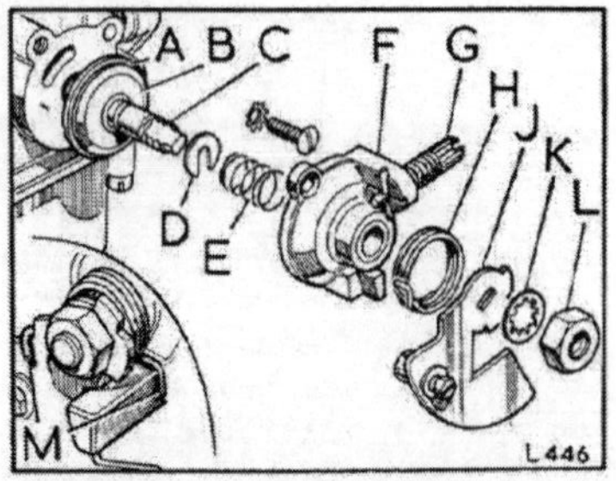

Fig. L1-26. Cold start assembly

A—Cold start outer disc
B—Cold start inner disc
C—Cold start spindle
D—Spring retaining clip
E—Cold start spring
F—Cover for cold start
G—Clamping screw for cam lever swivel
H—Return spring for cam lever
J—Cam lever for cold start
K—Shakeproof washer
L—Locknut
M—Return spring location

Carburetter body, to rebuild

5. Take throttle spindle, with recessed end upwards, fit throttle return spring, throttle stop and idle lever then washer, followed by throttle lever washer, tab washer and locknut. Fully secure assembly and lock tab washer.

6. Insert throttle spindle into throttle flange from the cold start side of carburetter body, fitting the throttle return spring on the fast idle adjusting holder and tension spring half a turn.

7. Fit the throttle butterfly into the throttle lever as previously marked then centralise the throttle butterfly after fitting the retaining screws loosely and actuating the throttle a number of times to align up in the central position. Then tighten securing screws and lock by peening ends of screws.

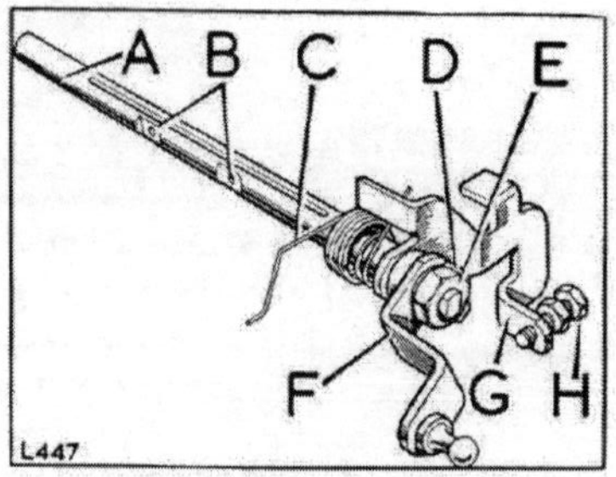

Fig. L1-27. Throttle spindle arrangement

A—Throttle spindle
B—Recess in shaft
C—Throttle return spring
D—Tab washer
E—Locknut
F—Throttle lever
G—Throttle stop and fast idle lever
H—Throttle stop

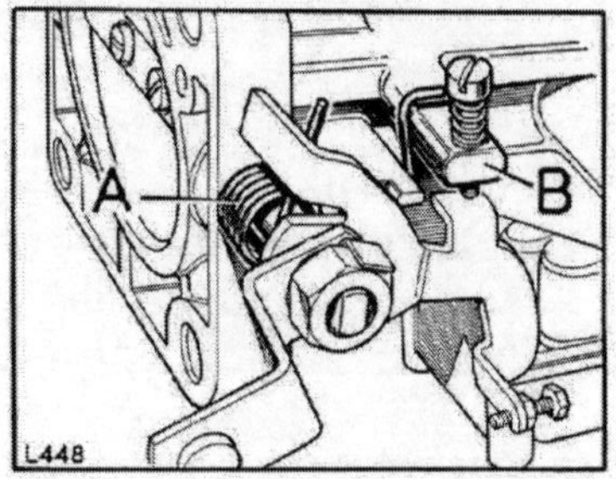

Fig. L1-28. Throttle return spring position

A—Return spring
B—Carburetter body

FUEL SYSTEM

Operation L1-3—continued

8. Fit spring-loaded adjusting screw till it touches the throttle stop and fast-idle lever then turn another one and a half turns.
9. Fit ignition adaptor to carburetter body.

Float chamber, to rebuild

10. Fit needle valve and washer to carburetter body.
11. Fit spindle into float arm then securely clip the spindle into the retaining clips as illustrated.
12. With the needle valve on its seating and the end tab on the float carrier, contacting on the needle valve, measure the distance between the flange face and the highest point on the floats, as illustrated.

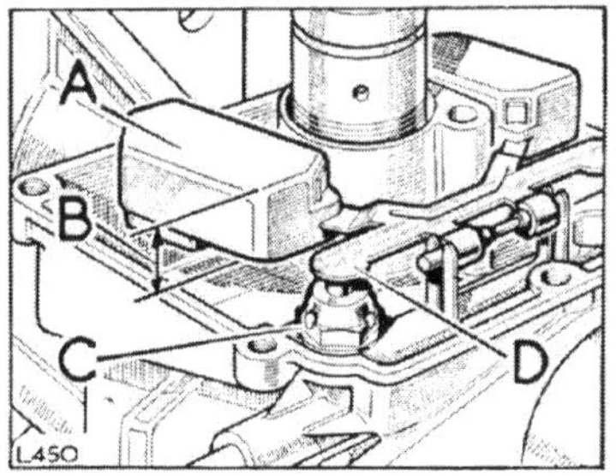

Fig. L1-29. Float level adjustment
A—Float
B—⅝ in. (16 mm)
C—Needle valve
D—Tag

13. The dimension required at this check is 0.67 in. (17 mm) to 0.71 in. (18 mm). Any adjustment must be made by either bending the tag which contacts the end of the needle, or fitting an additional washer under the needle seating arrangement.

   Note: Care should be taken to maintain the tag at right-angles to the needle in the closed position.

14. Fit joint gasket to the float chamber then fit float chamber to the carburetter body, do not fully tighten securing screws at this stage.
15. Fit the three 'O' rings to the jet assembly.
16. Place the spring over the jet orifice followed by the guide bush and bushing which has the 'O' ring fitted in.

17. Place the jet orifice assembly into carrier for jet orifice and insert assembly through float chamber then fully tighten.
18. Fit the adjusting screw for the jet orifice at the bottom of the jet assembly and adjust up until the jet orifice just appears in line with the top of the bushing for jet orifice.

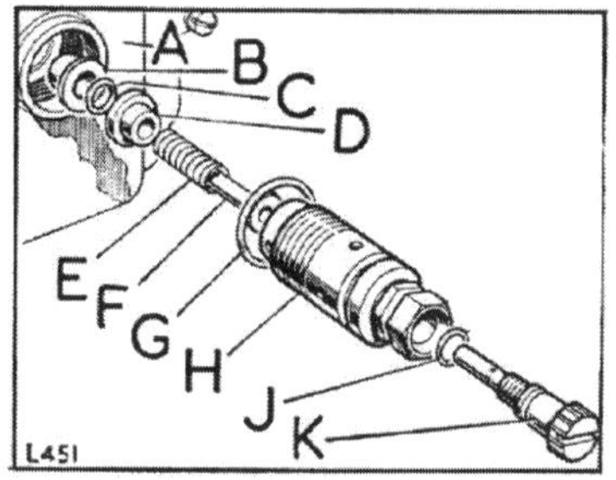

Fig. L1-30. Jet assembly
A—Carburetter body, throttle orifice
B—Bushing for jet orifice
C—'O' ring for bushing for jet orifice
D—Guide bush
E—Spring for jet orifice
F—Jet orifice
G—'O' ring for jet carrier
H—Carrier for jet orifice
J—'O' ring for jet orifice
K—Adjusting screw for jet orifice

Air valve, shaft and diaphragm, to assemble

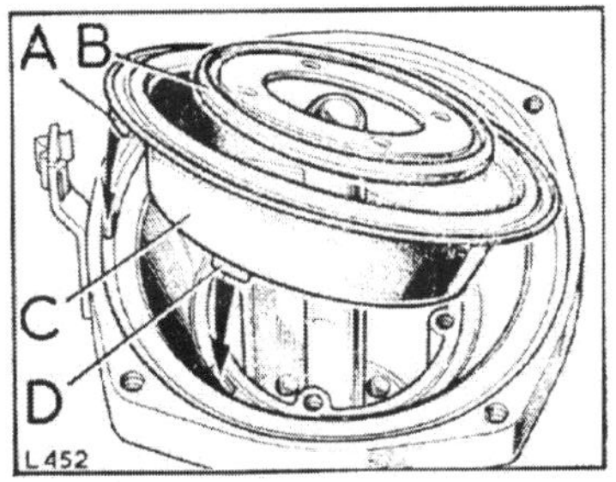

Fig. L1-31. Air vane diaphragm
A—Locating tab, outer
B—Retaining ring for diaphragm
C—Air vane diaphragm
D—Inner locating tab

Operation L1-3—continued

19. Fit the diaphragm to the valve ensuring that the locating tab is inserted in the recess in the air valve then fully secure with retaining ring.
20. Carefully fit the metering needle to the air valve aligning the shoulder of the needle with the top surface of the shaft, as illustrated.

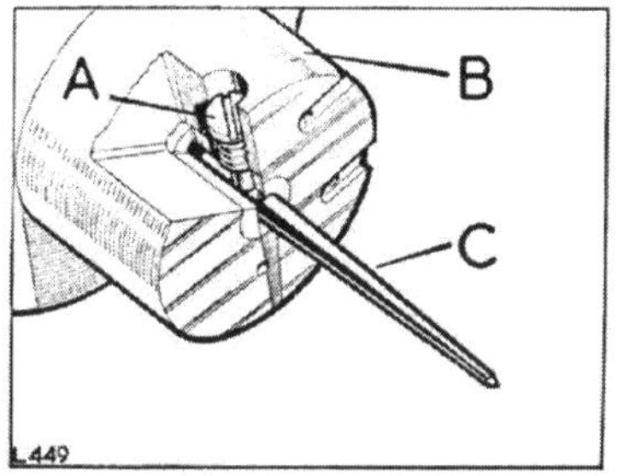

Fig. L1-32. Metering needle position
A—Retaining screw
B—Piston
C—Metering needle

Jet centralisation

Note: The efficient operation of the carburetter depends on the free movement of the air valve and needle in the jet orifice. In the Stromberg there is an annular clearance around the orifice bush which permits the lateral positioning of the bush and jet. Thus it may be clamped up in such a position that the metering needle moves freely in the orifice.

21. Very carefully insert needle into jet orifice and allow it to bottom, if any difficulty is encountered unclamp the jet assembly enough to allow the jet to bottom. In this position ensure that the locating tab on the diaphragm fits into the recess on the carburetter body.
22. Fit the air valve return spring and carburetter top cover, aligning the marks, then secure assembly.
23. Lift the air valve and tighten the jet assembly fully.
24. Slacken off the whole jet assembly approximately half a turn to release jet orifice bush.

25. Allow the air valve to fall; the needle will then enter the orifice and thus automatically centralise it. If necessary, assist the air valve drop by inserting a pencil in the dashpot.
26. Slowly tighten the jet assembly, checking frequently that the needle remains free in the orifice. Check by raising the air valve approximately ¼ in. (6 mm) and allowing it to fall freely. The position should then stop firmly on the bridge.
27. Fill up the dashpot in the air valve to within a ¼ in. (6 mm) of the rod in which the damper operates with SAE 20 engine oil.
28. Fit in the damper assembly and fully secure.

Adjustments

Setting the idle

Two adjustments are used when regulating the idle speed and mixture. The following procedure should be used in setting the throttle adjusting screw which controls the speed, and the jet adjusting screw, which determines the mixture strength.

1. Remove the air cleaner.
2. Remove the damper assembly.
3. Hold the air valve down on the bridge in the throttle bore.
4. Screw up the jet adjustment screw until the jet is felt to come into contact with the underside of the air valve.
5. Turn down the jet adjusting screw three turns.
6. Run the engine till it is thoroughly warm.
7. Adjust the throttle adjusting screw to an idle speed of 500 rpm.

   Note: The idle mixture will be correct when the engine speed is smooth and regular, and by careful and gradual adjustment of the jet adjustment screw, the correct adjustment will be determined.

To check

Lift the air valve ¹⁄₃₂ in. (0.8 mm). If the engine speed rises the mixture is too rich, if the engine stops it is too weak. Correctly adjusted it will remain constant or fall slightly in speed. Turning the orifice adjusting screw into carburetter decreases the mixture strength; unscrewing will enrich.

Operation L1-3—continued

8. Fit the damper assembly.
9. Fit the air cleaner.

Fast-idle adjustment (choke)

1. Operate choke fully.
2. Adjust fast-idle stop screw until engine speed is 1,000 to 1,200 r.p.m.
3. Push choke fully in and ensure that fast-idle stop screw is clear of choke cam lever.

SU carburetter, to overhaul—Operation L1-4

(For removal and refitting instructions, Section A refers)

Workshop hand tools:
Spanner sizes: $\frac{11}{16}$ in. AF, $\frac{7}{16}$ in. AF, $\frac{1}{2}$ in. Whit, $\frac{5}{16}$ in. Whit, $\frac{3}{16}$ in. Whit, 2 BA Screwdriver (medium), Pliers (long nosed)

Carburetter, to dismantle

1. Unscrew oil cap, complete with hydraulic damper and washer, withdraw.
2. Remove suction chamber.
3. Remove piston spring and protection washer from inside piston.
4. Withdraw piston.
5. Slacken needle retaining screw inside of piston and remove needle.
6. Remove double-ended union, fibre washer and gauze filter assembly from top of float chamber.
7. Remove banjo union.
8. Remove float chamber lid, float and joint washer.
9. Remove splined pivot from fork and needle valve.
10. Remove adaptor and gasket from carburetter body.
11. Remove float chamber from base of carburetter body.
12. Remove jet return spring and diaphragm from jet housing and remove jet housing.
13. Remove sliding rod securing screw.
14. Remove jet screw and jet bearing from carburetter body.
15. Remove the slow running adjusting valve complete with spring, dished brass washer and gland.
16. Remove throttle return spring lever from throttle spindle.
17. With butterfly in fully closed position, mark the butterfly with three lines, relative to carburetter body and throttle spindle, to ensure it is refitted in the same position.

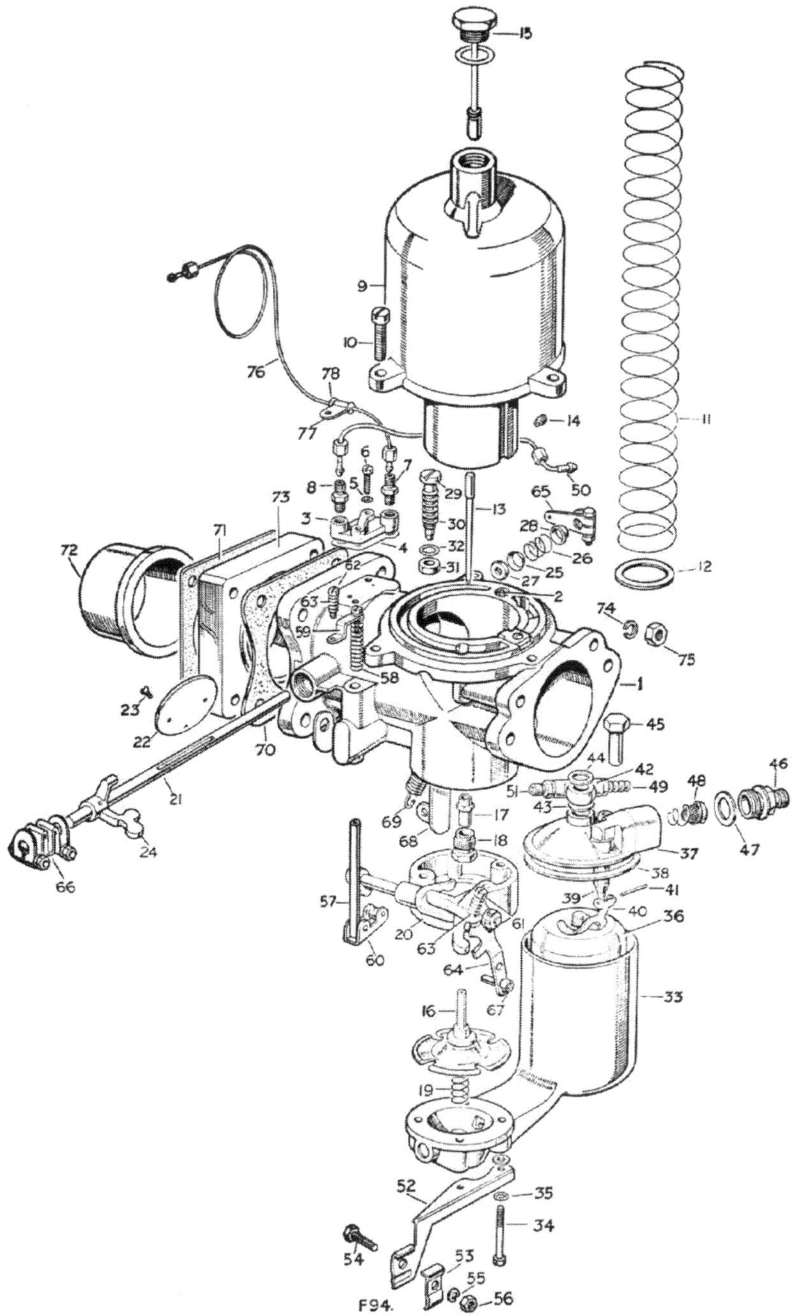

FUEL SYSTEM

Key to layout of SU carburetter

1. Carburetter body
3. Adaptor, ignition and weakening device
4. Gasket for adaptor
5. Shakeproof washer } Fixing adaptor
6. Screw
7. Union for ignition pipe
8. Union for economiser pipe
9. Suction chamber and piston complete
10. Special screw fixing suction chamber
11. Spring for piston (yellow)
12. Thrust washer for suction chamber
13. Needle, SS
14. Special screw fixing needle
15. Oil cap complete
16. Jet complete
17. Jet bearing
18. Jet screw
19. Jet spring
20. Jet housing complete
21. Throttle spindle
22. Throttle butterfly
23. Screw for throttle butterfly
24. Throttle stop
25. Gland washer for throttle spindle, brass
26. Spring for throttle spindle gland
27. Gland washer for throttle spindle, langite
28. Retainer cap for gland washer
29. Slow-running adjusting valve
30. Gland spring for slow running
31. Gland washer for slow running, rubber
32. Brass washer for slow running
33. Float chamber
34. Bolt
35. Shakeproof washer } Fixing float chamber
36. Float
37. Lid for float chamber
38. Joint washer for float chamber lid
39. Needle valve and seat
40. Lever for float
41. Pin for lever
42. Banjo
43. Fibre washer for banjo
44. Aluminium washer for banjo } On float chamber
45. Cap nut fixing banjo
46. Double-ended union for carburetter
47. Washer for union
48. Filter and spring for carburetter body
49. Economiser union for rubber tube
50. Pipe for economiser
51. Union for economiser pipe
57. Sliding rod, roller and cam shoe
58. Spring for sliding rod
59. Top plate
61. Stop screw, bottom
62. Stop screw, top
63. Spring for stop screw
64. Cold start lever
65. Lever for throttle return spring
68. Bracket for throttle return spring
69. Throttle return spring
70. Joint washer for carburetter
71. Joint washer for distance piece
72. Liner for manifold
73. Distance piece for carburetter
74. Spring washer
75. Nut ($\frac{5}{16}$ in. UNF) } Fixing carburetter and distance piece to cylinder head
76. Suction pipe complete
77. Clip for suction pipe } On engine
78. Rubber grommet for clip

Fig. L1-33. Layout of SU carburetter

FUEL SYSTEM

Operation L1-4—continued

4. Examine throttle spindle bushes for wear, if oval or badly worn, renew carburetter body.

5. Inspect metering needle, it is machined to very close limits and should be handled with care. Examine for wear, bend and twist, renew if necessary.

6. **Diaphragm.**
In common with other products made from rubber compounds, any contact of the diaphragm with volite cleaners should be avoided, use only CLEAN RAG. Examine for damage and deterioration.

7. Examine float, for puncture or damage and chamber for corrosion, retaining clips for wear.

8. Examine cold start bushes for wear, renew as necessary.

9. Examine lifting pin for piston for correct operation.

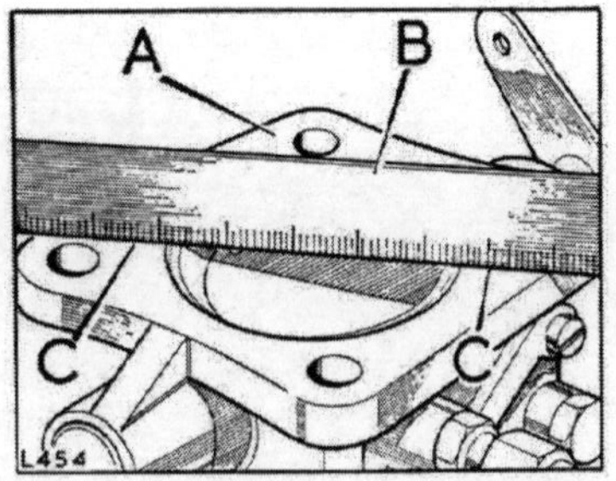

Carburetter, to rebuild

1. Insert carburetter spindle into carburetter body from left to right as viewed from carburetter air intake.

Fig. L1-35. Checking mounting flange
A—Carburetter flange
B—Straight edge
C—Flush fit

2. Insert new langite gland washer for throttle spindle followed by gland brass washer, spring and retainer, using a suitable piece of tubing, into right-hand spindle housing.

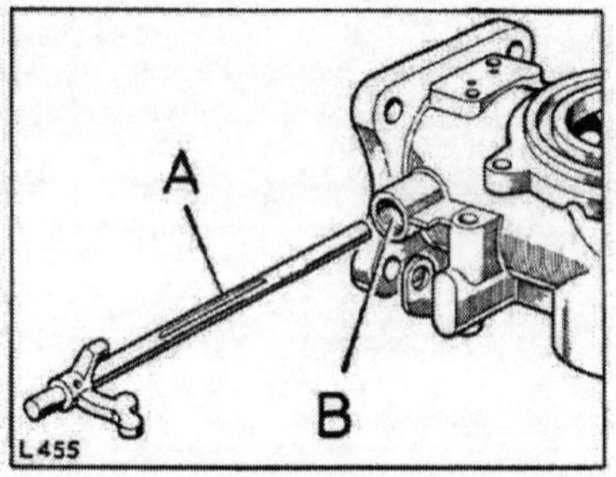

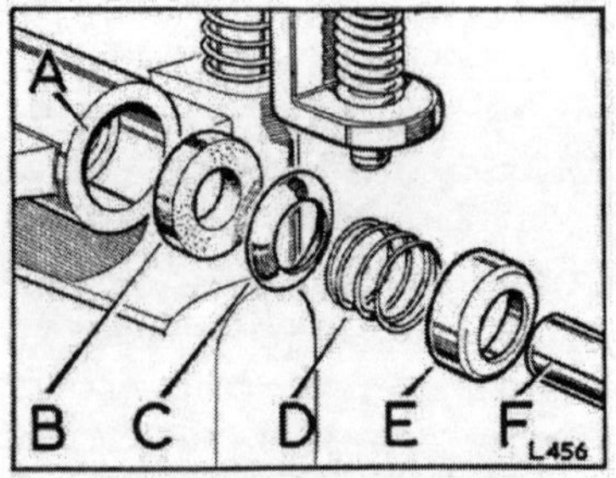

Fig. L1-36. Fitting throttle spindle
A—Spindle
B—Carburetter body

Fig. L1-37. Spindle gland assembly
A—Carburetter body
B—Gland washer, Langite
C—Gland washer, Brass
D—Spring
E—Retainer
F—Spindle

3. Remove spindle and reinsert from right to left, reassemble LH spindle housing gland assembly as item 2.

4. Rotate spindle to the 'fully open' position and insert throttle butterfly ensuring that chamfered edges will slope in the correct direction when closed. Close throttle and insert two securing screws sufficient only to prevent the butterfly from slipping.

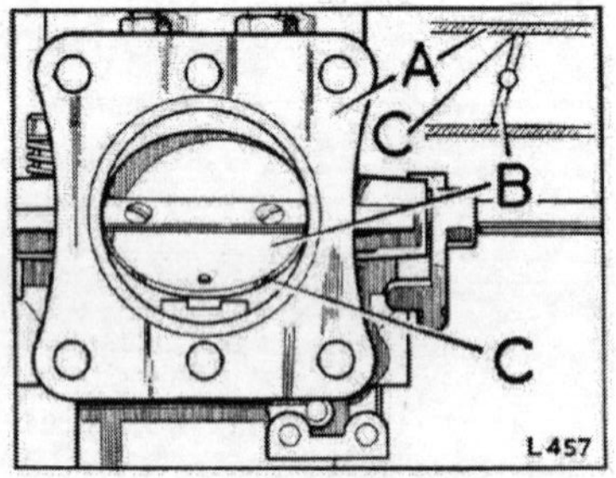

Fig. L1-38. Fitting throttle butterfly
A—Carburetter body
B—Throttle butterfly
C—Chamfered edge

5. Centralise the butterfly by snapping throttle shut several times, allow .015 in. (0,38 mm) minimum clearance between stop lever and body, then tighten screws and spread ends.

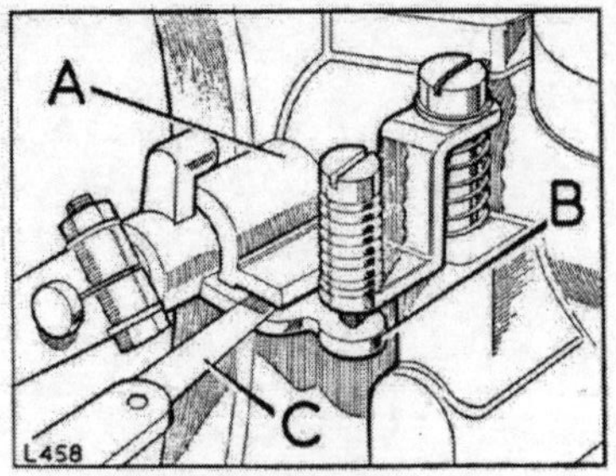

Fig. L1-39. Checking stop lever clearance
A—Carburetter body
B—Stop lever
C—Feeler gauge

FUEL SYSTEM

Operation L1-4—continued

18. With a pair of long-nosed pliers, close split ends of throttle butterfly retaining screws and remove; push out butterfly and withdraw spindle.

19. Lever out gland retainers and remove spring, gland washers and glands from both sides.

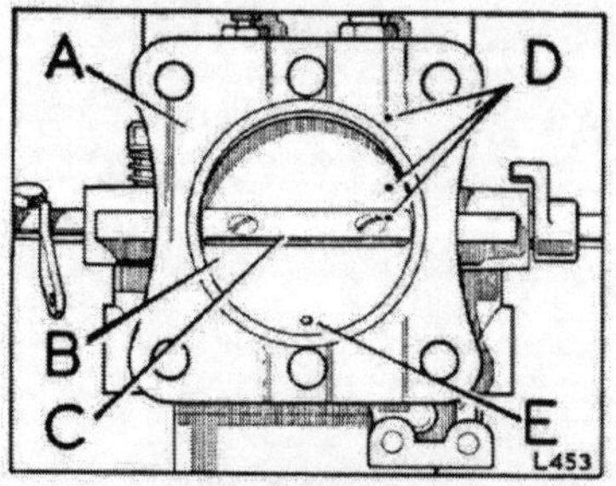

Fig. L1-34. Adding alignment marks to butterfly assembly
A—Carburetter body
B—Throttle butterfly
C—Throttle spindle
D—Aligning marks
E—Hole in throttle butterfly

Inspection and cleaning

Special notes:

1. **Carburetter cleaning.**
When cleaning fuel passages do not use metal tools (files, scrapers, drills, etc.) which could cause dimensional changes in the drillings or jets. Cleaning should be effected using clean fuel and where necessary a moisture-free air blast.

2. **Joint faces.**
Examine the faces for deep scores which would lead to leakage taking place when assembled.

3. **Joint gasket and seals.**
New gaskets and seals should be used throughout carburetter rebuild. A complete set of gaskets is available for replacement purposes.

FUEL SYSTEM

Operation L1-4—continued

6. Refit the throttle return spring lever, but do not fully tighten.
7. Fit needle to piston so that the top of the fitting register is flush with the body of the piston, as illustrated. Secure using a new screw.

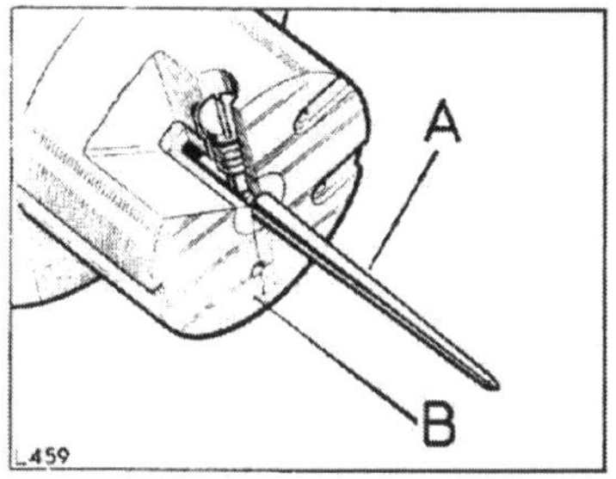

Fig. L1-40. Needle in correct position
A—Needle
B—Piston body

8. Insert the piston into the suction chamber and spin the piston to ensure the needle is not bent.
9. Fit jet bearing short end into the body and retain with the jet securing screw, do not tighten at this stage.

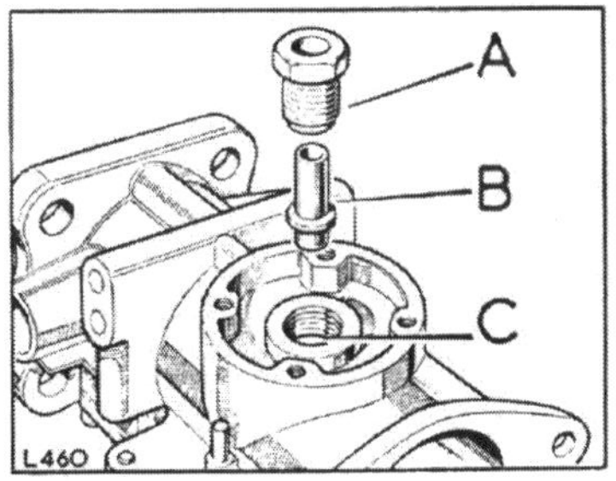

Fig. L1-41. Fitting jet bearing
A—Jet screw
B—Jet bearing
C—Carburetter body

10. Fit piston to carburetter body.
11. Fit thrust washer into body of piston and replace the spring.
12. Fit suction chamber to carburetter body and tighten retaining screws evenly.
13. Invert the carburetter and insert jet and diaphragm assembly, gradually tighten the jet screw ensuring that the needle is not binding on the jet. If the needle is binding, slacken the jet retaining screw and rotate the bearing to free it. Retighten jet retaining screw.
14. Remove jet and fit jet housing to carburetter body.

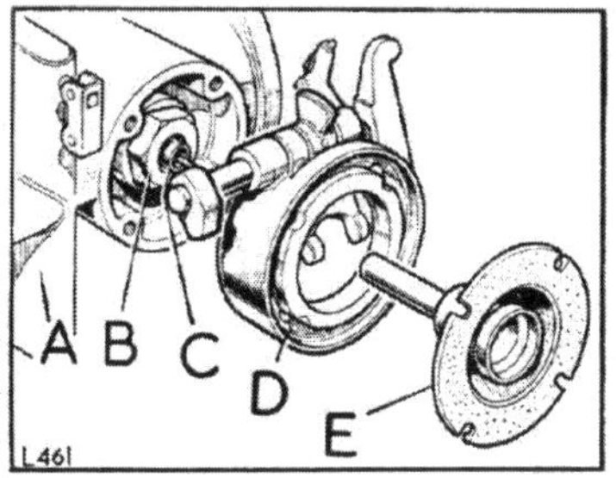

Fig. L1-42. Fitting jet and housing
A—Carburetter body
B—Jet screw
C—Jet bearing
D—Jet housing
E—Jet

15. Insert the jet and align the holes in the diaphragm with those corresponding to them in the jet housing.
16. Fit the jet return spring, float chamber and choke cable bracket plus two distance washers. Do not tighten securing screws at this stage.
17. Ensure that the diaphragm can move to the limit of its travel by operating choke lever, and in this position fully tighten the retaining screws.

Operation L1-4—continued

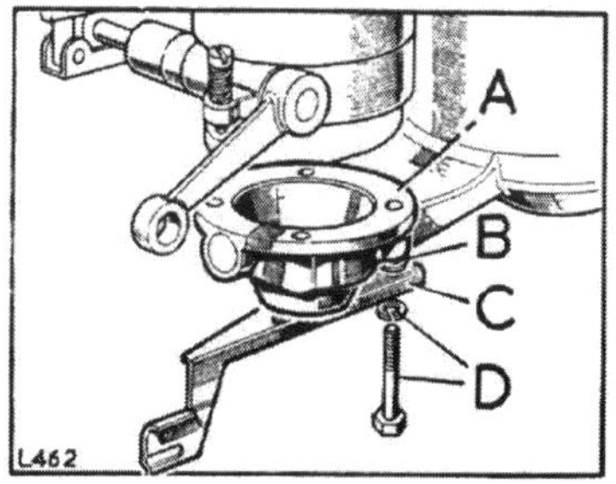

Fig. L1-43. Float chamber and choke bracket assembly
A—Float chamber
B—Distance piece
C—Choke bracket
D—Fixing for bracket

18. Lift piston to its fullest extent by hand, then allow it to fall under its own weight, as the piston comes to rest a distinct click should be heard, if not repeat from item 13, as jet needle is binding.
19. Refit the slow running gland, washer and slow running screw, which should be screwed right in.

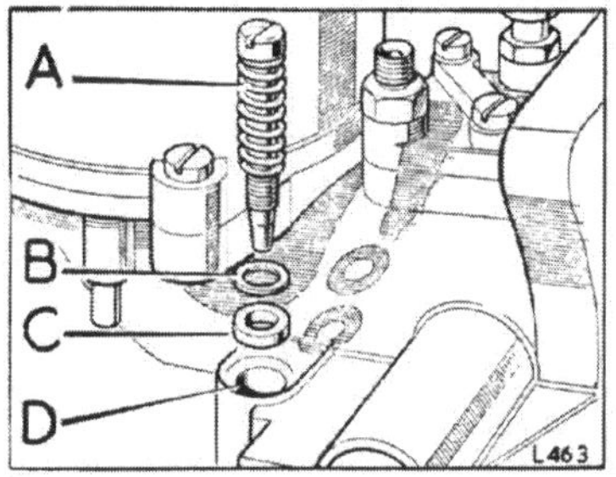

Fig. L1-44. Slow running valve
A—Slow running screw and spring
B—Brass washer
C—Gland washer
D—Carburetter body

20. Fit float into float chamber.
21. Fit gauze filter, fibre washer and union to the float chamber top.
22. Fit needle valve, needle valve fork and splined pivot pin to float chamber top.

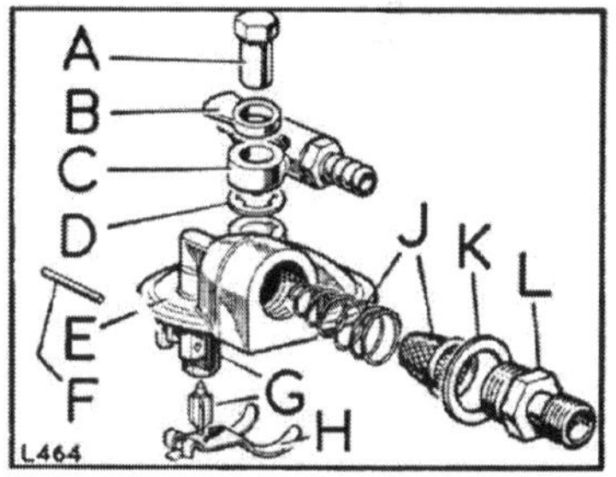

Fig. L1-45. Float chamber lid assembly
A—Cap nut
B—Joint washer, aluminium
C—Banjo unit
D—Joint washer, fibre
E—Lid for float chamber
F—Pin for lever
G—Needle valve and seat
H—Lever for float
J—Filter and spring
K—Joint washer
L—Inlet union

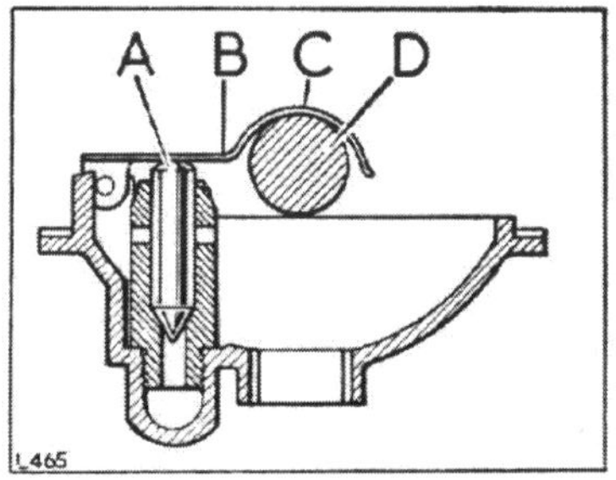

Fig. L1-46. Fitting float level fork
A—Needle valve
B—Point at which fork must be bent
C—Fork
D—$\frac{7}{16}$ in. round bar (11 mm)

FUEL SYSTEM

Operation L1-4—continued

23. Place $\frac{7}{16}$ in. (11 mm) round bar between needle valve fork and float chamber top, ensure that with the bar in position the valve is held on its seat, test by blowing through fuel inlet connection, no air should escape through needle valve. If any adjustments are necessary, bend at point shown in diagram until this condition is attained.
24. Fit float chamber lid washer and banjo union and retain with bolt.
25. Fit gasket to adaptor housing and fit housing to carburetter body.
26. Fit sliding rod, spring and cam shoe with screw.
27. Fill the damper reservoir with SAE 20 engine oil to within $\frac{1}{2}$ in. (12 mm) from the top of the hollow piston rod, replace the cap and fibre washer.

Adjustments

Setting the idle

Two adjustments are used when regulating the idle speed and mixture. The following procedure should be used in setting the throttle adjusting screw which controls the speed, and jet adjusting screw (bottom stop screw), which determines the mixture strength.

1. Remove the air cleaner.
2. Remove the damper assembly.
3. Hold the piston down on the bridge in the throttle bore.
4. Fully slacken the jet adjustment screw by screwing outward until there is free-play at the lever.
5. Screw in the jet adjusting screw one and a half turns.
6. Run the engine till it is thoroughly warm.
7. Adjust the throttle adjusting screw to an idle speed of 500 rpm.

   Note: The idle mixture will be correct when the engine beat is smooth and regular, and by careful and gradual adjustment of the jet adjustment screw, the correct adjustment will be determined.

To check

Lift the piston $\frac{1}{32}$ in. (0.8 mm). If the engine speed rises the mixture is too rich, if the engine stops it is too weak. Correctly adjusted it will remain constant or fall slightly in speed. Turning the jet adjusting screw into carburetter increases the mixture strength; unscrewing will weaken.

8. Fit the damper assembly.
9. Fit the air cleaner.

FUEL SYSTEM

Fuel pump, mechanically driven type, to overhaul—Operation L1-5

(For removal and refitting instructions, Section A refers)

Workshop hand tools:
Spanner size: $\frac{11}{16}$ in. AF
Screwdriver (medium), Pliers

To dismantle

1. Unscrew the nut at base of sediment bowl, move retainer aside, and withdraw the bowl, sealing washer and filter gauze. Care should be taken to avoid damage to filter gauze.
2. Mark the upper and lower halves of pump casing to ensure correct alignment on reassembly.

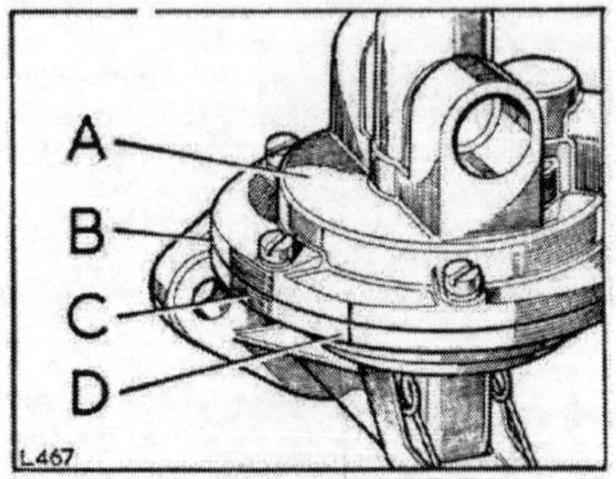

Fig. L1-47. Adding alignment marks

A—Top cover
B—Diaphragm
C—Pump body
D—Alignment marks

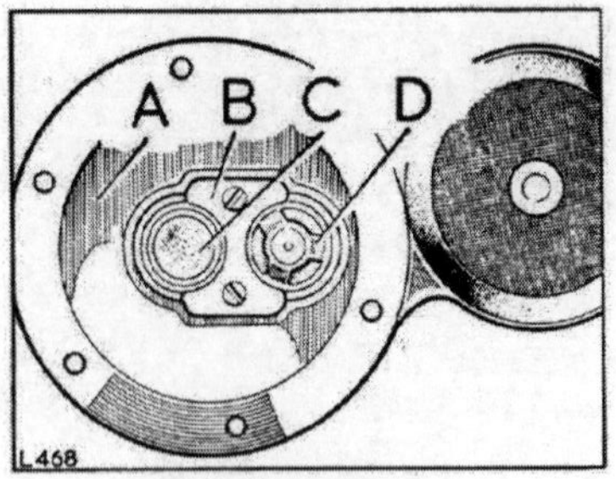

3. Remove top cover fixing screws, and while pressing diaphragm tab against pump body, lift top cover clear.

Fig. L1-48. Pump valves

A—Top cover
B—Retaining plate
C—Outlet valve
D—Inlet valve

4. Remove valve retaining plate and withdraw valves, noting valve positions.
5. Ease the diaphragm from pump body, slightly depress metal part of diaphragm and turn through 90° in either direction, whereon the diaphragm spring will push diaphragm clear.
6. File peening marks from oil seal housing and lever out oil seal and retainer.
7. To remove rocker arm and operating link:

(Early models)
(a) Remove circlips then drift the rocker arm pivot pin from the pump body and withdraw rocker arm, operating link, return spring and plain washers.

(Later models)
(b) Using a small chisel, remove peening from rocker arm retainers, remove retainers, rocker arm, spacing washers, operating link and return spring.

8. It is extremely unlikely that the hand priming mechanism will ever require replacement, but may be removed by filing the hexagon each side of the operating lever and springing the hand lever clear, withdraw the cork washers and hand rocker.

Inspection

1. Clean all parts thoroughly in paraffin.
2. Examine all parts for wear and replace as necessary, observe the following points:

   (a) All gaskets to be renewed.
   (b) Sediment bowl filter disc must be free of damage and fit tightly round inlet neck of upper casing.
   (c) Renew diaphragm assembly if any sign of hardening, cracking or porosity is present.
   (d) Only very slight wear should be tolerated at the rocker arm contact face, pivot pin, operating link and diaphragm pull rod slots.
   (e) Springs should be renewed, but ensure correct type are used.
   (f) Test valves for air tightness, by suction.
   (g) Check upper and lower casing flanges for distortion, using a straight edge.

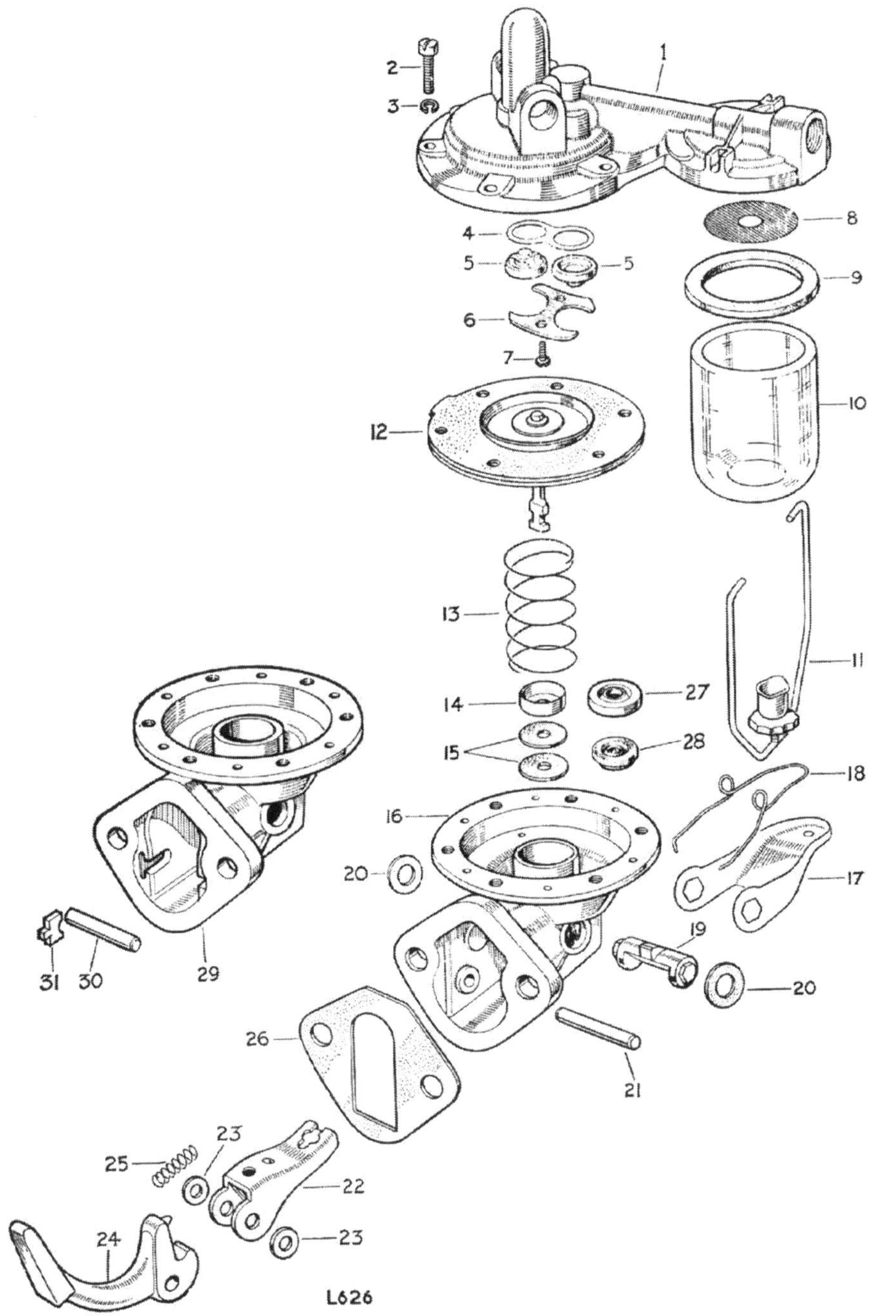
1
2
3
4
5
5
6
7
8
9
10
11
12
13
14
15
16
17
18
19
20
20
21
22
23
23
24
25
26
27
28
29
30
31
L626

Fig. L1-49. Layout of mechanical fuel pump

Key to layout of mechanical fuel pump

1 Top cover	17 Hand priming lever
2 Securing screws	18 Return spring for hand lever
3 Spring washer	19 Hand rocker
4 Valve gasket	20 Cork washers
5 Valves	21 Rocker arm pivot pin, early type
6 Retainer for valves	22 Operating link
7 Screw for retainer	23 Plain washers
8 Gauge filter disc	24 Rocker arm
9 Lock sealing gasket	25 Return spring
10 Sediment bowl	26 Joint washer
11 Bowl retainer	27 Oil seal retainer } Latest type
12 Diaphragm assembly	28 Oil seal } Latest type
13 Diaphragm spring	29 Pump body } Latest type
14 Oil seal retainer } Early type	30 Rocker arm pivot pin } Latest type
15 Sealing washers } Early type	31 Retainer for pivot pin } Latest type
16 Pump body } Early type	

FUEL SYSTEM

Fuel pump (double entry), electrically driven, to remove and refit — Operation L1-6

(For overhaul instructions, Operation L1-7 refers)

Workshop hand tools:
Spanner sizes: 7/16 in. AF, 3/8 in. BSF

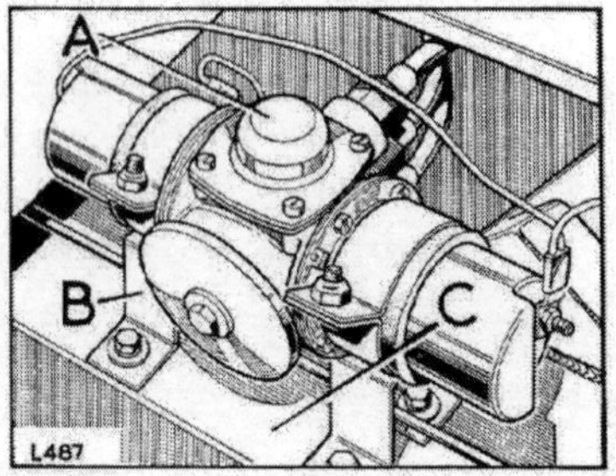

Fig. L1-52. Fuel pump
A—Fuel pump, dual type
B—Bracket fixing fuel pump
C—Chassis frame

Fuel pump, remove

1. Disconnect the battery leads.
2. Lift seat (RH side) and remove seat box panel to expose fuel pump.
3. Disconnect the wiring at the 'Lucar' connectors.
4. Disconnect all pipes from the pump.
5. Remove the pump from the mounting bracket.

Fuel pump, refit

1. Reverse removal procedure.
2. Check pump for correct operation.

Operation L1-5—continued

To rebuild
(Early models)

1. Assemble operating link, rocker arm and spacing washers on a piece of rod .240 in. (6,1 mm) diameter in place of pivot pin.
2. Drive in pivot pin, replacing reduced diameter rod used for assembly location, replace circlips.

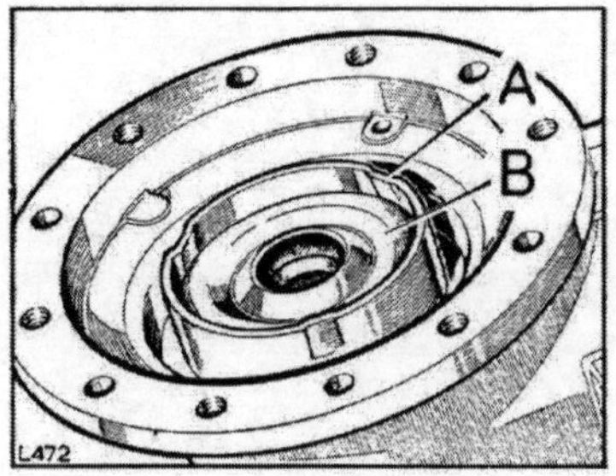

Late models

3. Reassemble rocker arm operating link and spacing washer on to pivot pin and refit to pump body.
4. Tap new retainers into their grooves, hold retainer firmly against pivot pin, peen over the ends of the grooves to ensure they cannot work loose.
   Note: Replacement retainers are slightly shorter than the original to allow for satisfactory fixing in the body.
5. Fit oil seal into retainer and press assembly into oil seal housing, peen over housing flange to retain oil seal assembly, in at least three positions.
6. To refit the diaphragm assembly, hold the pump body with the diaphragm return spring in position, and the rocker arm held outwards. Position the diaphragm over the spring with the flattened end of the pull rod in line with the slot in the operating link. Push the diaphragm inwards and turn lock.
7. Replace the valve gasket, inlet and outlet valve into top cover and secure with the retaining clip.
8. Place top cover assembly in position, aligning the marks made before dismantling. Fit securing screws, but do not tighten at this stage, using hand priming lever, fully depress diaphragm and fully tighten securing screws.

Fig. L1-50. Peening oil seal housing
A—Peen housing in three places
B—Oil seal retainer

Fig. L1-51. Fitting diaphragm
A—Diaphragm
B—Spring
C—Operating link
D—Push inward and turn through 90°

Note: The diaphragm outer edges should be approximately flush with the outer edge of the pump joint faces when fitted, any appreciable protrusion of the diaphragm beyond the joint face edges indicates improper fitment and necessitates the release of the securing screws and refitment in accordance with item 8.

9. Replace filter gauze and neoprene sealing ring, refit retaining clip and position sediment bowl centrally and secure with retaining clip.
   Note: Do not overtighten securing nut, to prevent cracking of sediment bowl.

Fuel pump test: without special equipment

1. Immerse pump in a bath of paraffin and operate rocker arm several times to flush.
2. Hold the pump clear of the bath and continue to operate the rocker arm until the pump is empty, then place a finger over the inlet port and operate rocker arm several times. A distinct suction should be heard when the finger is removed from the inlet port, denoting that a reasonable degree of suction has been developed.
3. Place a finger over the outlet port and again operate the rocker arm. Air pressure should be felt for two to three seconds after rocker movement has ceased. Build up the air pressure in the pump again, and with the finger held firmly over the outlet, submerge the pump completely in the paraffin bath, then observe the joint face edges for signs of air leakage.

FUEL SYSTEM

Fuel pump (double entry), electrically driven, to overhaul—Operation L1-7

(For removal and refitting instructions, Operation L1-6 refers)

Workshop hand tools:
Spanner sizes: 7/16 in. AF, 11/16 in. AF open end
Screwdriver (medium), Feeler gauges

Special tool:
Fork wedge for contact breaker, Part No. 263058

Fuel pump, to dismantle

Electric pump, to strip

1. Remove end cover.
2. Make alignment marks between the magnet housing and the pump body to facilitate reassembly, then remove magnet housing.
3. Ease the diaphragm away from the magnet housing and unscrew in an anti-clockwise direction, taking care to retain the eleven rollers.
4. Remove diaphragm, spring and gasket.
5. Remove spring blade contact.
6. Remove terminal screw and nut.
7. Remove end plate, taking care not to damage earthing lead.
8. Remove condenser.
9. Remove contact pivot pin from spring mechanism.
10. Remove lead washer and terminal screw from end cover.

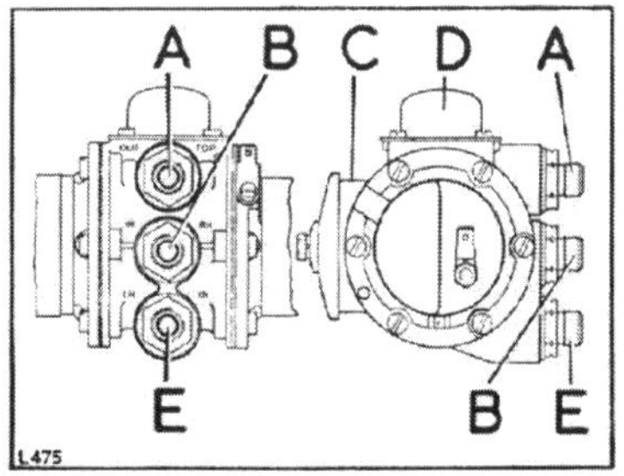

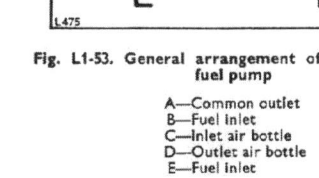

Fig. L1-53. General arrangement of double entry fuel pump

A—Common outlet
B—Fuel inlet
C—Inlet air bottle
D—Outlet air bottle
E—Fuel inlet

Operation L1-7—continued

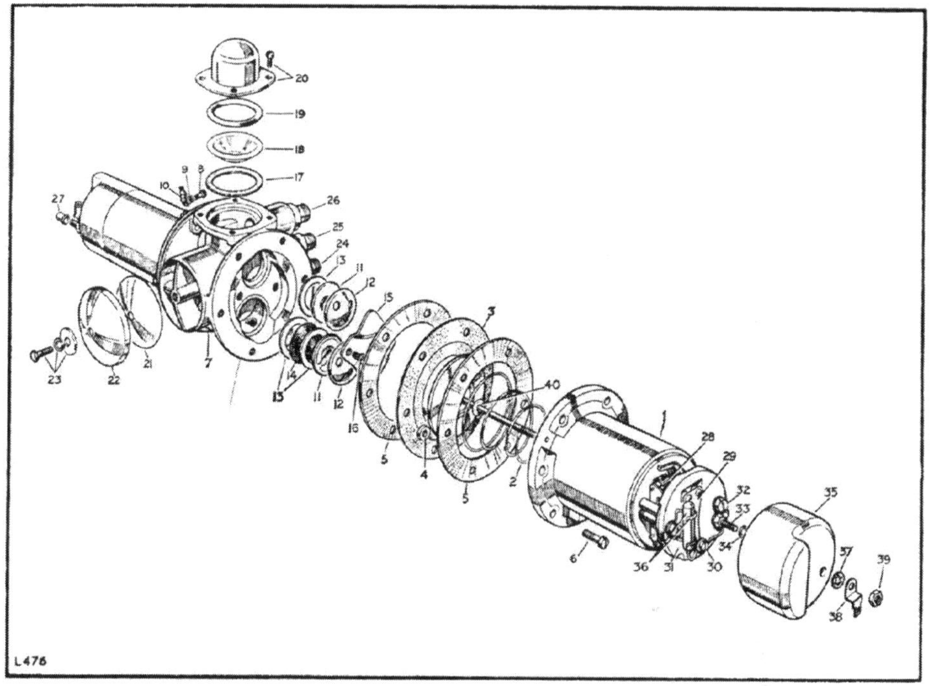

Fig. L1-54. Double entry fuel pump

1. Magnet housing
2. Spring for armature
3. Diaphragm
4. Roller
5. Joint washer
6. Securing screw, body to housing
7. Body
8. Special screw } Earth connection
9. Spring washer
10. Lucar blade
11. Melinex valve assembly
12. Valve cap
13. Sealing washer
14. Fuel filter
15. Clamp plate
16. Clamp plate screws
17. Sealing ring for outlet air bottle
18. Diaphragm for outlet air bottle
19. Rubber sealing ring
20. Outlet air bottle, dome and screw
21. Joint washer for inlet air bottle
22. Cover for inlet air bottle
23. Securing screw and washers
24. Union } Main fuel
25. Union } supply
26. Union for outlet pipe
27. Nylon protection cap
28. Contacts rocker assembly
29. Spring blade contact
30. Anchor screw
31. Moulded end plate
32. Retaining screw for end plate
33. Terminal screw
34. Composition washer
35. End cover
36. Condenser and clip
37. Shakeproof washer
38. Lucar blade
39. Nut
40. Impact washer for armature

FUEL SYSTEM

Operation L1-7—continued

Pump body, to strip

11. Remove the outlet air bottle dome, diaphragm and sealing rings.

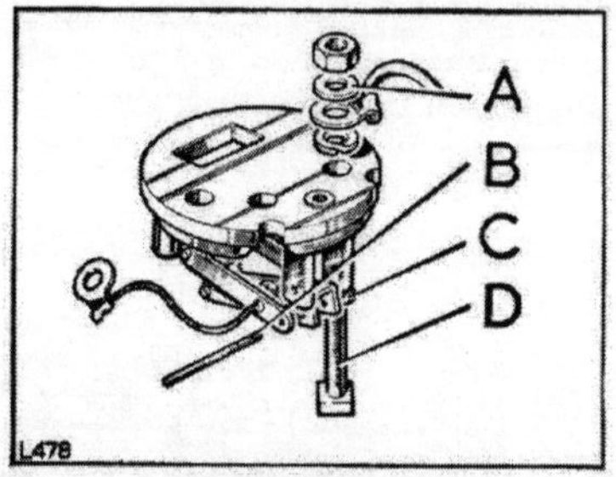

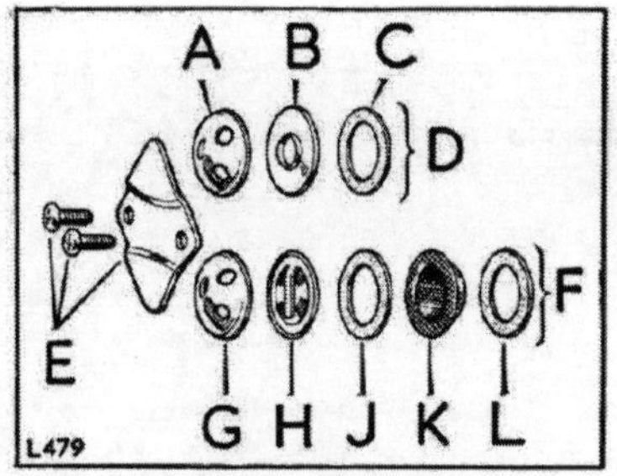

Fig. L1-55. Pivot for contact breaker
A—Lead washer
B—Pivot pin
C—Contact breaker pivot
D—Terminal screw

Fig. L1-56. Layout of valve assembly, double entry type pump
A—Retaining cap
B—Disc valve
C—Cork washer
D—Outlet valve assembly
E—Clamp plate and screw
F—Inlet valve assembly
G—Retaining cap
H—Disc valve
J—Cork washer
K—Filter
L—Cork washer

12. Remove the cover for inlet air bottle and the joint washer.

13. Strip valves:
    Details of one complete valve assembly are given, this arrangement being exactly duplicated in the other section of the pump.
    The outlet valve assembly comprises a Melinex valve disc within a pressed steel cage, and a retaining cap.
    The inlet valve assembly comprises an identical valve which is assembled in the reverse direction, a retaining cap, and a fuel filter.
    Both assemblies have suitable joint washers, and are retained by a single clamping plate which is secured by two self-tapping screws.

14. Remove the three unions and 'O' rings from the pump body.

Inspection and cleaning

1. **Pump body cleaning.**
   Thoroughly clean all internal passageways and chambers with clean fuel.
   Check all flanges for distortion, using a straight edge.

2. Renew diaphragm gaskets and examine all components for wear and damage and renew as necessary.

3. **Electric pump inspection.**
   Renew diaphragm if any signs of deterioration, damage or wear are present.

4. Inspect contact points and renew as necessary.

5. Continuity test magnet assembly.

6. The purpose of the condenser is to prevent arcing of the contact breaker points; if the points are badly burnt, the condenser should be tested and renewed if faulty.

7. Check all electrical wiring for serviceability.

Fuel pump, to assemble

Pump body to assemble (see Fig. L1-54)

1. Fit joint washer for inlet air bottle and cover, then secure.

Operation L1-7—continued

2. Fit gasket, diaphragm for air bottle, sealing ring and outlet air bottle dome, then secure.

3. Fit cork gaskets, valves, fuel filter, valve caps and clamp plate as illustrated, then secure, carefully ensuring that the non-return valves are fitted correctly in opposite directions.

4. Fit inlet and outlet unions and 'O' rings.

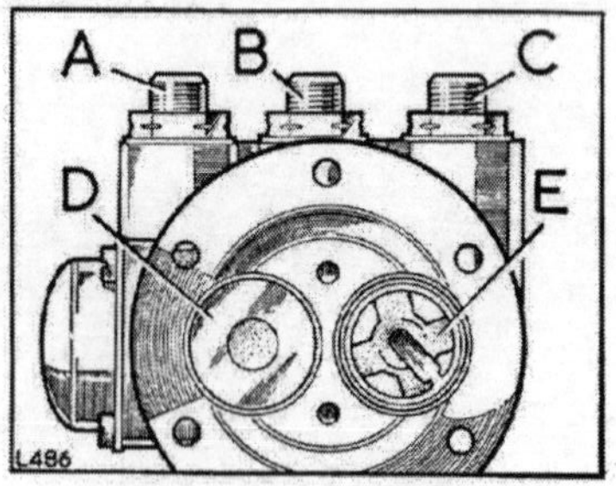

Fig. L1-57. Valve location
A—Outlet   C—Inlet, LH
B—Inlet, RH   D—Outlet valve
E—Inlet valve

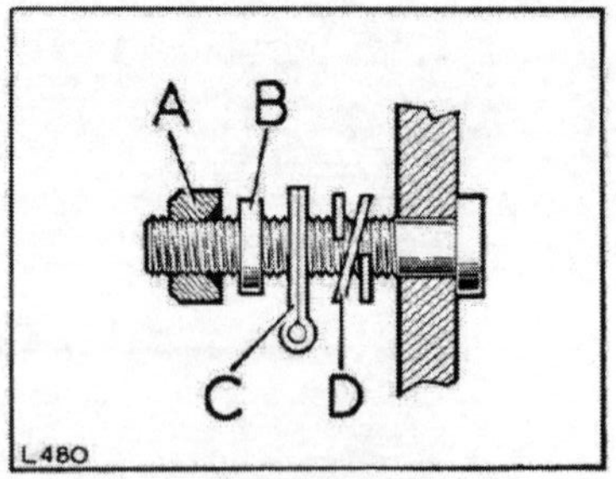

Fig. L1-58. Feed to terminal assembly
A—Countersunk nut
B—Lead washer
C—The tag
D—Spring washer

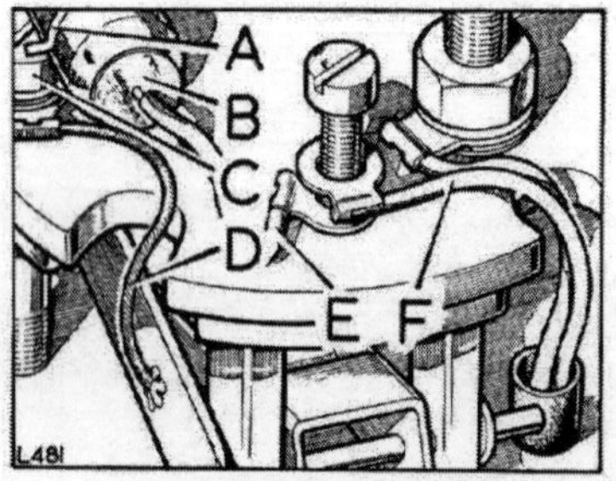

Fig. L1-59. Fitting condenser
A—Clip for condenser
B—Condenser
C—Screw for cover
D—Earth lead
E—Condenser lead
F—Feed lead

Electric pump, to assemble

5. Fit lower contact assembly to end plate with points facing contact aperture by inserting pivot pin, see Fig. L1-55.

6. Locate feed terminal screw into end plate and assemble feed terminal as illustrated; using the larger diameter terminal and a new lead washer.

7. Position end plate assembly on magnet housing then fit and secure with retaining screw nearest to the terminal screw.

8. Assemble condenser clip and earthing clips as illustrated, to the other end plate retaining screw and do not overtighten when securing as the end plate will be cracked.

Magnet assembly

9. Fit the armature return spring with its large diameter towards the coil. The spring must not be stretched or the action of the pump will be affected.

10. Fit the impact washer in the recess of the armature and diaphragm assembly.

11. Screw the armature in through magnet housing to engage nut retained in lower contact assembly for at least six turns.

12. Fit eleven guide rollers in position around the armature.

FUEL SYSTEM

Operation L1-7—continued

16. Place the magnet assembly in position on the pump body, aligning the drain hole at the bottom with the filter plug. Ensure that all the rollers remain in their correct position.

17. Insert the six securing screws but DO NOT tighten at this stage, as it is essential to first stretch the diaphragm to its outermost position using special tool, Part No. 263058.
    Insert the wedged fork of the special tool between the white rollers of the outer rocker and press in under the tips of the inner rocker until it lifts the trunnion in the centre of the inner rocker as far as it will go. Tighten the retaining screws fully, and remove the wedge.
    Note: If a wedge is not available, the diaphragm may be stretched by holding the points in contact, by inserting a matchstick under one of the white fibre rollers and passing a current through the pump; this will excite the magnet, actuate the armature, and so stretch the diaphragm.

18. It is now necessary to check that the top of the contacts inner rocker is in contact with the end face of the magnet housing. If there is a visible gap here, the six screws should be slackened off and then retightened until the correct condition is achieved.

19. Fit the spring blade contact and secure with a screw, together with the condenser and feed leads. The oversize anchor hole in the blade allows the contacts to be positioned so that a wiping action takes place when the pump is operating.

Contact point adjustment

20. Check the position by holding the blade in contact with the pedestal, being careful not to press on the overhanging portion, then ensure that .030 in. (0.75 mm) feeler just slides between the contact stops, as illustrated.

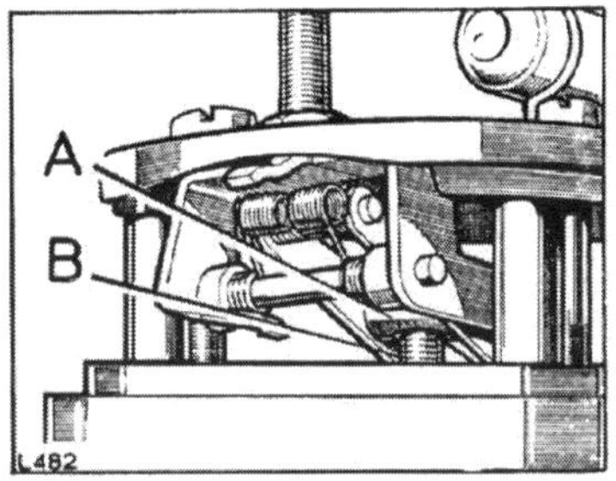

Fig. L1-60. Fitting armature
A—Nut in lower contact assembly
B—Armature

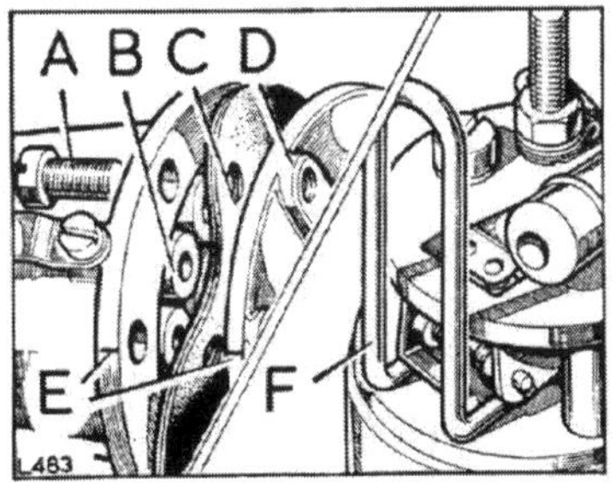

Fig. L1-61. Assembling magnet housing
A—Fixings, magnet housing to pump body
B—Rollers
C—Diaphragm and armature
D—Pump body
E—Alignment marks made previously
F—Special tool, Part No. 263058

13. Hold the magnet assembly in the left hand in an approximately horizontal position. Push the armature in firmly but steadily, with the thumb of the right hand.

14. If the contact breaker throws over, the armature should be screwed in further until it ceases to do so. It should then be unscrewed one-sixth of a turn at a time until a position is found at which the contact breaker just throws over, care being taken to avoid jerking the armature. The armature should then be unscrewed for two-thirds of a turn, i.e. four holes, the setting is then correct—do not forget that this setting must be carried out with the points out of contact.

15. When a new diaphragm is fitted, it is possible that considerable pressure will be required to push the armature right home. If there is any doubt about the point at which the contact throws over, come back one-sixth of a turn.

Fig. L1-62. Checking inner rocker
A—Inner rocker
B—End face of magnet housing

Operation L1-7—continued

Adjustment may be carried out by bending the blade in order to obtain the correct clearance.

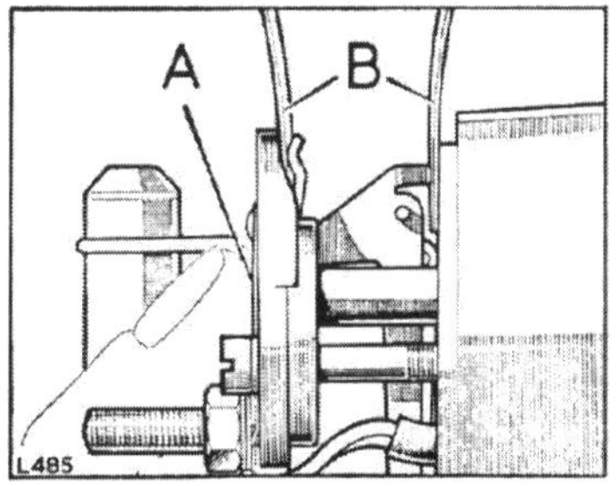

21. Test fuel pump. It is best to use a cut-away cover while testing the pump, as this prevents the hinge pin from falling out, and at the same time makes it possible to observe the action of the contact breaker. The pump should be mounted three feet above the supply tank for testing; either paraffin or petrol may be used. When switched on, the pump should prime itself promptly, and fluid should flow from the outlet union. If the pump outlet is restricted, the pump should slow down gradually, and if completely cut off it should stop for at least 15 seconds.

22. After test procedure refit top cover, Lucar blade and securing nut.

Fig. L1-63. Checking contacts
A—Contact blade
B—Feeler gauges, .030 in. (0.75 mm) minimum clearance

Fuel tank, side mounted type, (Petrol and Diesel models), to remove and refit—Operation L1-8

Workshop hand tools:
Spanner sizes: 2 BA, $\frac{7}{16}$ in. AF, $\frac{1}{2}$ in. AF open end
Screwdriver (medium)

To remove (Fig. L1-64)

1. Disconnect the battery earth lead.
2. Drain fuel into a clean container.
3. Remove RH seat cushion and fold seat squab forward.
4. Disconnect hoses, tank to filler tube and breather hose.
5. Remove cover panel for fuel tank.
6. Disconnect wires at gauge unit.
7. Disconnect fuel supply pipe and for Diesel models, spill return pipes.
8. Support tank and remove tank securing bolts.
9. Lower tank and remove from under the vehicle.

To refit

1. Reverse removal procedure.
2. If the vehicle is a Diesel model, prime the fuel system. Operation L1-14.

Key to layout of side mounted fuel tank, filter and pipes, 2¼ litre Petrol and Diesel models

1. Fuel tank complete
2. Drain plug for petrol tank
3. Joint washer for drain plug
4. Filler cap
5. Joint washer for cap
6. Chain for filler cap
7. Filler tube
8. Extension tube for filler
9. Grommet for fuel tank filler
10. Screw (2 BA × ⅜ in. long) ⎫
11. Plain washer   ⎬ Fixing filler to body side
12. Spring washer   ⎪
13. Nut (2 BA)   ⎭
14. Hose, tank to filler tube
15. Anti-theft grid for filler
16. Clip for hose, bottom
17. Clip for hose, top
18. Breather hose for fuel tank
19. Clip for breather hose
20. Rubber seal for filler pipe
21. Outlet elbow complete for tank
22. Joint washer for outlet and return elbow
23. Spring washer   ⎫ Fixing elbow to tank
24. Screw (3 BA × 9/16 in. long) ⎭
25. Gauge unit for fuel tank
26. Joint washer for gauge unit
27. Spring washer   ⎫ Fixing gauge unit to tank
28. Screw (3 BA × 9/16 in. long) ⎭
29. Bolt (5/16 in. UNF × ¾ in. long) ⎫
30. Plain washer   ⎬ Fixing fuel tank to chassis frame
31. Spring washer   ⎪
32. Nut (5/16 in. UNF)   ⎭
33. Body only
34. Bowl only
35. Gauze for bowl
36. Joint washer for bowl
37. Retainer for bowl
38. Tap and gland complete
39. Special screw for tap
40. Body only
41. Bowl only
42. Gauze for bowl
43. Joint washer for bowl
44. Retainer for bowl
45. Screw cap for retainer
46. Tap and gland complete
47. Bracket for sediment bowl
48. Bolt (¼ in. UNF × 9/16 in. long) ⎫
49. Spring washer   ⎬ Fixing bracket to dash
50. Nut (¼ in. UNF)   ⎭
51. Inlet adaptor for sediment bowl
52. Special nut fixing adaptor and bowl to bracket
53. Outlet union for sediment bowl
54. Petrol pipe complete, tank to bowl
55. Nut   ⎫ Fixing pipe to tank and bowl
56. Nipple ⎭
57. Petrol pipe complete, bowl to pump
58. Nut
59. Nipple ⎫ Fixing pipe to bowl and pump
60. Nut   ⎬
61. Olive   ⎭
62. Flexible fuel pipe complete
63. Fuel pipe complete, flex to carburetter
64. Nipple
65. Nut   ⎫ Fixing pipe to flex and carburetter
66. Nut   ⎬
67. Olive ⎭
68. Fuel pipe retaining bracket
69. Clip for fuel pipes
70. Clip for fuel pipes
71. Bolt (2 BA × ½ in. long) ⎫ Fixing clip and bracket to chassis crossmember
72. Spring washer   ⎬
73. Nut (2 BA)   ⎭
74. Air cleaner
75. Oil container
76. Washer for container
77. Toggle
78. Connection, air cleaner to carburetter
79. Clip fixing connection

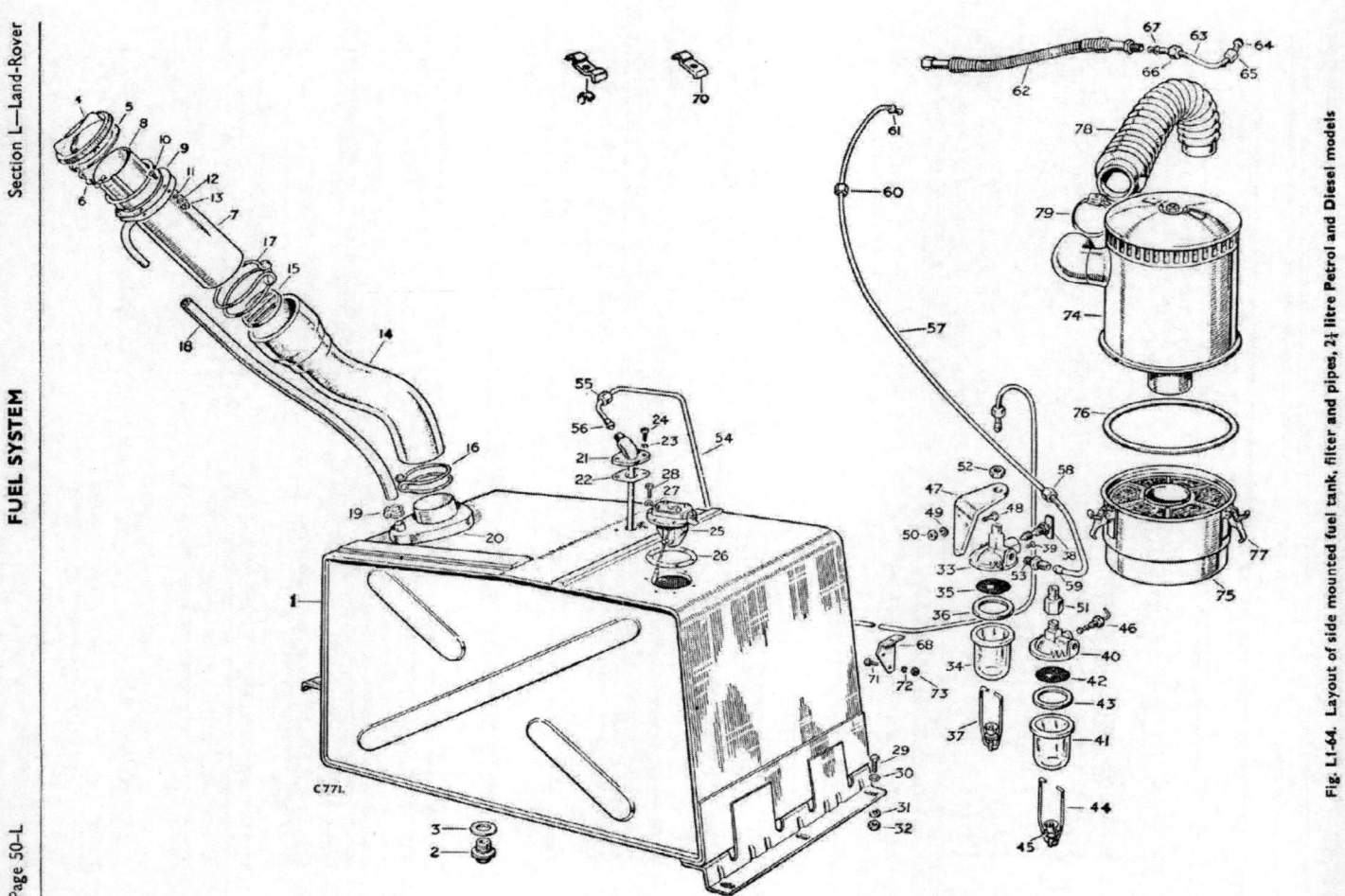

Fig. L1-64. Layout of side mounted fuel tank, filter and pipes, 2¼ litre Petrol and Diesel models

Fuel tank, rear mounted type, (Petrol and Diesel models), to remove and refit—Operation L1-9

Workshop hand tools:
Spanner sizes: $\frac{7}{16}$ in AF, $\frac{9}{16}$ In. AF open end
Screwdriver (medium)

To remove (Fig. L1-65)

1. Disconnect the battery.
2. Drain the fuel into a clean container.
3. Release the clip securing the filler tube hose to the tank.
4. Support the tank and remove the tank securing bolts, then lower the tank sufficient only to give access to the pipes and leads at the tank top.
5. Disconnect the breather and air balance pipes.
6. Disconnect wires at gauge unit.
7. Disconnect the fuel supply pipe, and for Diesel models, the spill return pipe.
8. Lower the tank and remove from under the vehicle.

To refit

1. Reverse the removal procedure.
2. If the vehicle is a Diesel model, prime the fuel system. Operation L1-14.

This page intentionally left blank

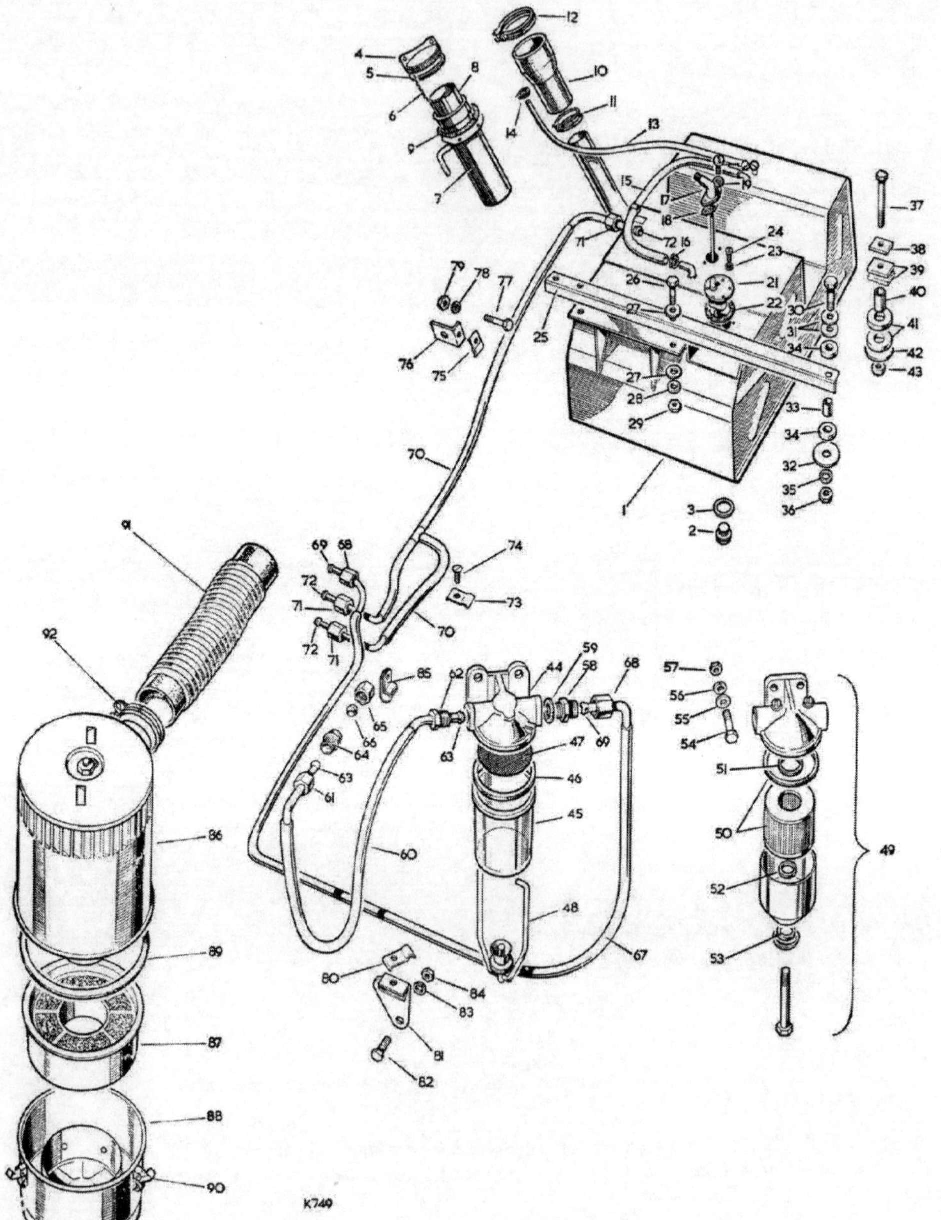

Section L—Land-Rover

FUEL SYSTEM

Key to Fig. L1-65. Layout of rear mounted fuel tank, filter and pipes, 2.6 litre models

1 Fuel tank complete
2 Drain plug } For fuel tank
3 Joint washer
4 Filler cap
5 Joint washer for cap
6 Chain for filler cap
7 Filler tube
8 Extension tube for filler
9 Grommet for fuel tank filler
10 Hose, tank to filler tube
11 Clip for hose, bottom
12 Clip for hose, top
13 Breather hose for fuel tank
14 Clip for breather hose
15 Air balance hose for fuel tank
16 Clip for air balance hose
17 Outlet elbow complete for tank
18 Joint washer for outlet elbow
19 Spring washer } Fixing elbow to tank
20 Screw (3 BA × $\frac{7}{8}$ in. long)
21 Gauge unit for fuel tank
22 Joint washer for gauge unit
23 Spring washer } Fixing gauge unit to tank
24 Set screw (3 BA × $\frac{3}{8}$ in. long)
25 Support for fuel tank
26 Bolt ($\frac{3}{8}$ in. UNF × $\frac{3}{4}$ in. long) } Fixing support to tank
27 Plain washer
28 Spring washer
29 Nut ($\frac{3}{8}$ in. UNF)
30 Bolt ($\frac{3}{8}$ in. UNF × 1$\frac{1}{8}$ in. long) } Fixing front of fuel tank to support and chassis frame
31 Plain washer, small
32 Plain washer, large
33 Distance tube
34 Rubber bush
35 Spring washer
36 Nut ($\frac{3}{8}$ in. UNF)
37 Bolt ($\frac{3}{8}$ in. UNF × 2$\frac{1}{4}$ in. long) } Fixing rear of fuel tank to support and chassis frame
38 Distance piece
39 Distance tube
40 Mounting rubber
41 Plain washer
42 Self-locking nut ($\frac{3}{8}$ in. UNF)
43 Body only
44 Body only
45 Bowl only
46 Joint washer for bowl
47 Gauze for bowl
48 Retainer for bowl
49 Fuel filter complete
50 Element and seal for filter
51 Centre seal, upper
52 Centre seal, lower
53 Seal for centre bolt
54 Bolt ($\frac{1}{4}$ in. UNF × $\frac{7}{8}$ in. long) } Fixing fuel filter to RH toe box
55 Plain washer
56 Spring washer
57 Nut ($\frac{1}{4}$ in. UNF)
58 Double-ended union for filter or bowl
59 Joint washer for union
60 Petrol pipe, nylon, filter or bowl to carburetter
61 Nut, pipe to carburetter union
62 Nut, pipe to filter or bowl
63 Olive
64 Union for petrol pipe
65 Nut } Fixing union to carburetter
66 Olive
67 Petrol pipe, nylon, pump to filter or bowl
68 Nut } Fixing pipe to pump and filter
69 Olive
70 Petrol pipe, nylon, tank to pump
71 Nut } Fixing pipe to pump
72 Olive
73 Clip } Fixing fuel pipe to chassis sidemember
74 Drive screw
75 Clip
76 Bracket
77 Bolt (2 BA × $\frac{5}{8}$ in. long) } Fixing fuel pipe to body support bracket
78 Spring washer
79 Nut (2 BA)
80 Clip
81 Bracket
82 Bolt (2 BA × $\frac{1}{2}$ in. long) } Fixing fuel pipe to chassis crossmember
83 Spring washer
84 Nut (2 BA)
85 Clip fixing fuel pipe to hand brake bracket
86 Air cleaner, AC 7964695
87 Element for air cleaner, AC 7222911
88 Oil container, AC 796469?
89 Washer for container, AC 1574943
90 Toggle, AC 1579211
91 Connection, air cleaner to carburetter adaptor or elbow
92 Clip, fixing connection to air cleaner and adaptor

Fig. L1-65. Layout of rear mounted fuel tank, filter and pipes, 2.6 litre models
Note: This fuel tank is also fitted to 2$\frac{1}{4}$ litre Station Wagon models

Fuel tank gauge unit, (Petrol and Diesel models), side mounted type tank, to remove and refit—Operation L1-10

Workshop hand tools:
Spanner size: $\frac{7}{16}$ in. AF open end
Screwdriver (medium)

To remove (Fig. L1-64)

Before attempting to remove gauge unit ensure that the level of fuel in the tank does not exceed ¾ full.

1. Disconnect battery.
2. Remove RH seat cushion and tank cover panel.
3. Disconnect wires at gauge unit.
4. Mark position of unit in relation to tank.
5. Remove securing screws and lift unit from tank.

To refit

1. Fit new gasket and reverse removal procedure, ensuring correct alignment.

Fuel tank gauge unit, (Petrol and Diesel models), rear mounted type tank, to remove and refit—Operation L1-11

Workshop hand tools:
Spanner sizes: $\frac{7}{16}$ in. AF, $\frac{7}{16}$ in. AF
Screwdriver (medium)

To remove (Fig. L1-65)

1. Remove the fuel tank, Operation L1-9.
2. Mark position of unit in relation to tank.
3. Remove securing screws and lift unit from tank.

To refit

1. Fit new gasket and reverse the removal procedure, ensuring unit is correctly aligned.

Fuel filter, to clean, remove and refit, Petrol models—Operation L1-12

Workshop hand tools:
Spanner sizes: $\frac{7}{16}$ in. AF, $\frac{1}{4}$ in. AF, $\frac{1}{2}$ in. AF, $\frac{5}{8}$ in. AF, $\frac{7}{16}$ in. AF open end

Fuel pump filter and sediment bowl (2¼ litre Petrol)

To remove and clean

1. Unscrew the nut at base of sediment bowl, move the retainer aside and withdraw the bowl, sealing gasket and gauze filter disc. Care must be taken to prevent damage to the filter disc.
2. Clean the bowl and filter disc in petrol, directing a compressed air jet on the gauze to remove any obstinate particles.
3. Examine the cork gasket for filter bowl and renew if signs of deterioration are evident.

To replace

1. Reverse the removal procedure ensuring that the gauze filter disc fits tightly round the inlet neck and is quite undamaged in any way.

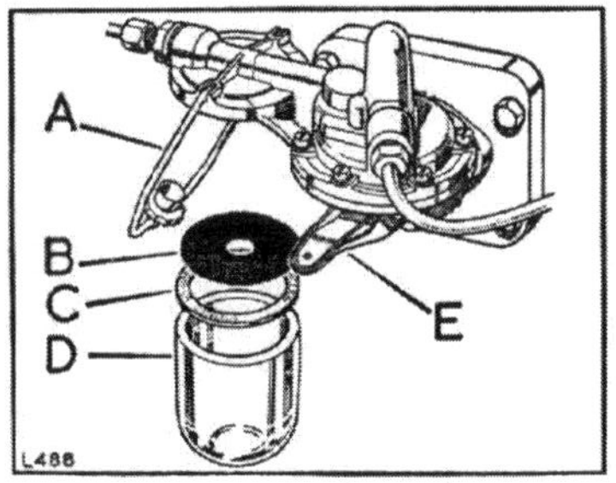

Fig. L1-66. Removing sediment bowl
A—Retainer for sediment bowl
B—Filter gauze
C—Cork gasket.
D—Sediment bowl
E—Hand priming lever

Fuel filter (2.6 litre Petrol models)

There are two types of filter in use, see Fig. L1-65

A—Sediment bowl type filter

To clean

1. Unscrew the nut at base of sediment bowl, move the retainer aside and withdraw the bowl, sealing gasket and gauze filter disc. Care must be taken to prevent damage to the filter disc.
2. Clean the bowl and filter disc in petrol, directing a compressed air jet on the gauze to remove any obstinate particles.
3. Examine the gasket for filter bowl and renew if signs of deterioration are evident.

To replace

1. Reverse the removal procedure ensuring that the gauze filter disc fits tightly round the inlet neck and is quite undamaged in any way.

To remove

1. Disconnect the fuel inlet and outlet pipes from the filter body.
2. Remove the fixings securing filter to toe box and lift clear.

To refit

1. Reverse the removal procedure.

B—Cartridge element type filter

To clean

1. Unscrew the centre bolt and withdraw filter bowl complete with small sealing ring at top of element.
2. Remove and discard filter element.
3. Withdraw the large sealing ring from the underside of the filter body.
4. Wash the filter bowl in clean fuel.
5. Renew the centre sealing rings if their condition is in any way doubtful. A new top sealing ring is supplied with each new element and should always be used.
6. Fit the new element, top sealing rings and refit the bowl.

To remove

1. Disconnect the fuel inlet and outlet pipes from the filter body.
2. Remove the fixings securing filter to toe box and lift clear.

To refit

1. Reverse the removal procedure.

FUEL SYSTEM

Fuel pipes and hoses, (Petrol and Diesel models), to remove and refit—Operation L1-13

Workshop hand tools:
Spanner sizes: 2 BA, 7/16 in. AF, 1/2 in. AF, 9/16 in. AF, 7/16 in. AF open end
Screwdriver (medium)

Filler tube and hose (Figs. L1-64 and L1-65)

To remove

1. Disconnect battery earth lead.
2. Side mounted fuel tank—Remove RH seat cushion and fold seat squab forward. Remove filler hose cover from behind RH seat.
3. Release the upper and lower hose clips securing the filler hose to the filler tube and fuel tank.
4. Release the hose clip securing the breather hose to the filler tube.
5. Remove the fixings securing the filler tube to the body, then withdraw the filler tube and hose.

To refit

1. Refit by reversing the removal procedure.

Breather and air balance pipes (Figs. L1-64 and L1-65)

To remove

1. Disconnect the battery earth lead.
2. Side mounted fuel tank—Remove RH seat cushion and fold seat squab forward. Remove filler hose cover from behind RH seat. Remove upper and lower hose clips and withdraw breather hose.
3. Rear mounted fuel tank—Remove fuel tank, Operation L1-9. Release the clip and withdraw the breather hose from the filler tube. Release the clip and withdraw the air balance hose from the fuel tank.

To refit

1. Reverse the removal procedure, ensuring hose clips are secure.

Fuel supply pipes (Figs. L1-64 and L1-65)

To remove

The fuel supply and spill return pipes comprise short metal pipes, secured to the fuel system units by unions and nuts, interconnected by flexible hoses.

1. Side mounted fuel tank—Remove RH seat cushion and cover for fuel tank.
2. Rear mounted fuel tank—Remove tank, Operation L1-9.
3. Early type flexible hoses—Loosen clips securing the hoses to metal pipes and withdraw hoses.
4. Latest type (black nylon) flexible hoses—Withdraw hoses which are a push fit on the metal pipes.
5. Remove the metal pipes as required.

To refit

1. Refit by reversing the removal procedure.

   Note: Fitting the black nylon type pipes can be facilitated by warming the end immediately prior to fitting. DO NOT use a naked flame near the fuel tank or any components containing fuel.

2. If the vehicle is a Diesel model, prime the fuel system, Operation L1-14.

Diesel fuel system—General notes

General

The first one is fitted in the fuel tank and requires no attention. Early models have a second—a sediment bowl and filter disc—incorporated with the fuel lift pump, the third (second for latest models) is a large self-contained unit mounted on the RH front side of the engine on early models, and on the bulkhead on later vehicles and lastly a small tubular gauze filter is fitted in the injection pump head.

An additional filter is fitted to all export Diesel Land-Rovers. Early models have a paper element type filter mounted on the dash panel, later models have a sedimentor type filter mounted on the right-hand side of the chassis.

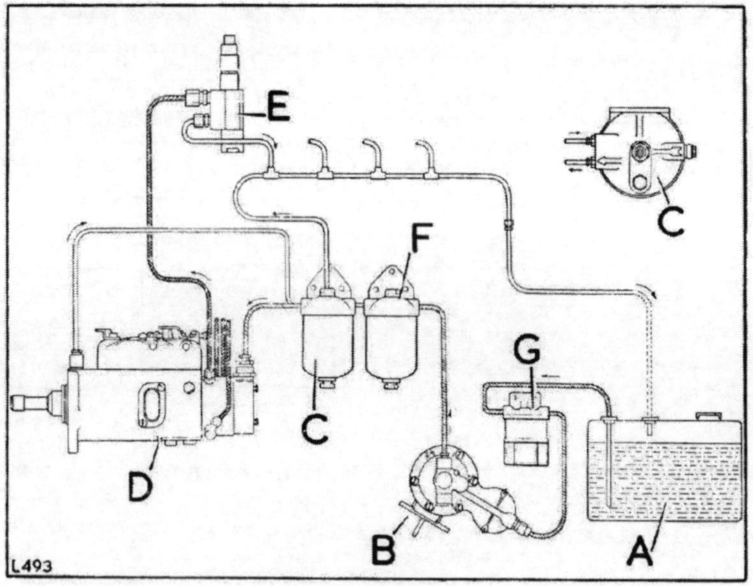

If the injection pump is drained by disconnecting the drain pipe or by running the vehicle until all the fuel has been used, the injection pump must be primed before attempting to restart the engine. To minimise the possibility of inadvertently running out of fuel, a blue fuel level warning light is fitted to the instrument panel which glows when only about two gallons of fuel remain in the tank and remains 'on' until more fuel is added. This device is in addition to the usual fuel contents gauge.

Clean fuel is essential for the efficient operation of the fuel injection pump and injection nozzle assemblies, and for this reason a minimum of three filters are fitted in the system. All export models have four filters.

Diagram of fuel system

A—Fuel tank
B—Fuel pump
C—Main filter
D—Injection pump
E—Injection nozzle
F—Additional filter (early export models)
G—Sedimentor (latest export models)
//////—Low pressure delivery
xxxxxxx—High pressure delivery
====—Excess fuel spill back

Fuel filters

Wear of injection pump, injection nozzle parts and the subsequent loss of power and efficiency is primarily due to the presence of dirt in the fuel.

Filters are situated in the Rover system in a manner calculated to minimise the possibility of foreign matter reaching the injection pump or injection nozzles, but the element in the main filter must be renewed, the sediment bowl and filter gauze on lift pump and the filter gauze in injection pump cleaned, at appropriate intervals. These intervals vary and are dependent on operating conditions, but reference to the Owner's Instruction Manual will provide a guide.

Complete sludging up of the main filter element in an unreasonably short operating period is usually due to an excessive quantity of wax in the fuel. Attention should be paid to the method of storage (where bulk storage is used) and the advice of supplier requested. Never draw fuel from the **lowest** point of a storage tank or barrel for refuelling purposes; the lowest point should only be used for draining off sludge and other impurities which accumulate at the bottom end.

Distributor pump

No attempt should be made to overhaul the distributor pump, as this requires specialised knowledge and equipment outside the scope of this manual. If a distributor pump gives trouble, a new replacement should be fitted. For removal, refitting and setting instructions, Section A refers.

Fuel injectors

Two types of fuel injector are in use, differing mainly in method of fixing to the cylinder head. All injectors have the 'Pintaux' type nozzle which has been developed by CAV for use with the design of cylinder head used on Rover compression ignition engines. This type of nozzle has been found most satisfactory for starting and general running and must be replaced by the same type.

Air cleaner

All details and instructions for air cleaners are included in Section A.

Fuel lift pump

The fuel lift pump is secured directly to the right-hand side of the engine, and is mechanically operated from the engine camshaft. The pump is similar to that used on 2¼ litre Petrol models and complete overhaul instructions are given in Operation L1-5.

This page intentionally left blank

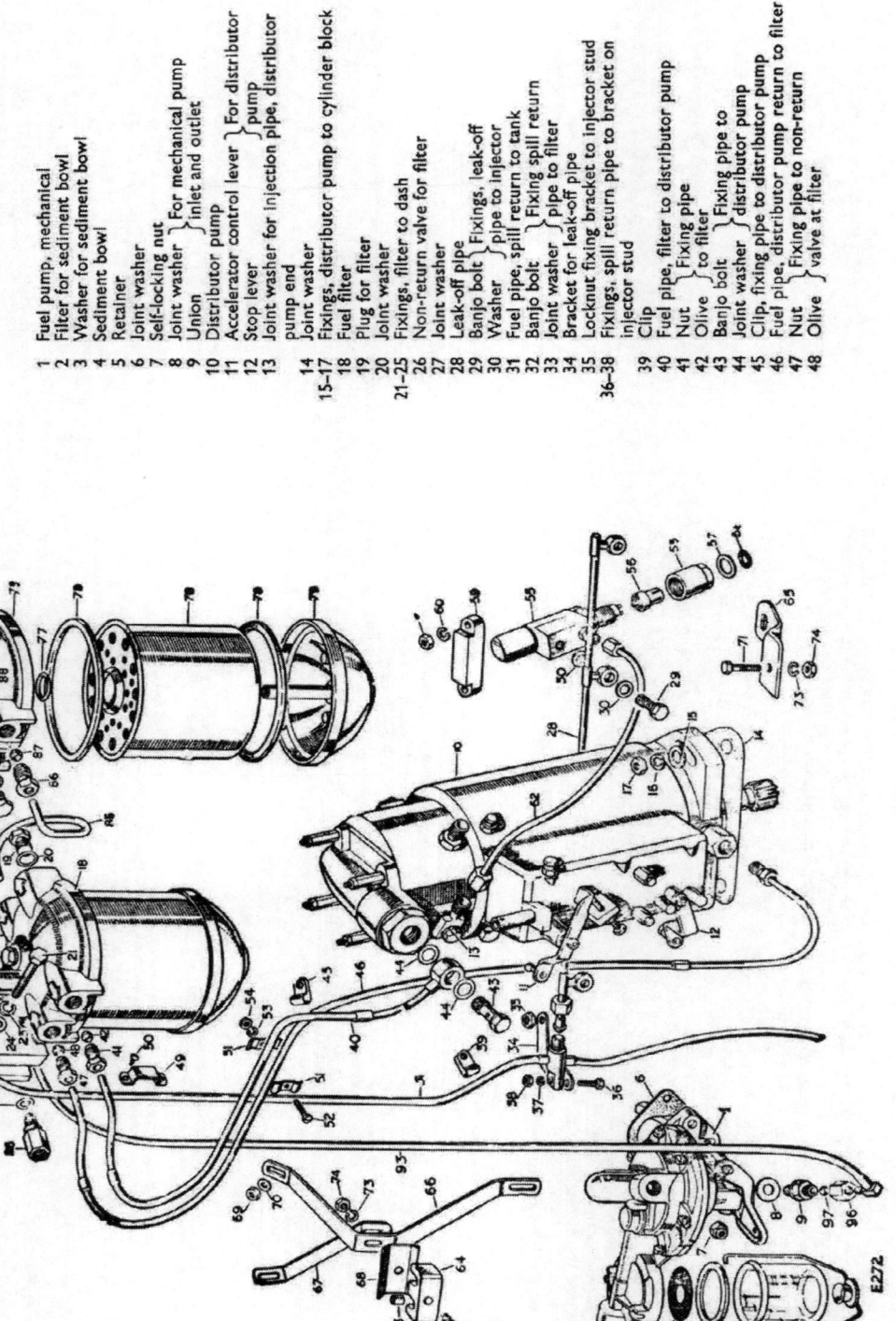

FUEL SYSTEM

Key to Fig. L1-68. General layout of Diesel fuel system, early models

1. Fuel pump, mechanical
2. Filter for sediment bowl
3. Washer for sediment bowl
4. Sediment bowl
5. Retainer
6. Joint washer
7. Self-locking nut
8. Joint washer } For mechanical pump inlet and outlet
9. Union
10. Distributor pump
11. Accelerator control lever
12. Stop lever
13. Joint washer } For distributor pump
14. Joint washer for injection pipe, distributor pump end
15–17. Fixings, distributor pump to cylinder block
18. Fuel filter
19. Plug for filter
20. Joint washer
21–25. Fixings, filter to dash
26. Non-return valve for filter
27. Joint washer
28. Leak-off pipe
29. Banjo bolt } Fixings, leak-off
30. Washer } pipe to injector
31. Fuel pipe, spill return to tank
32. Banjo bolt } Fixing spill return
33. Joint washer } pipe to filter
34. Bracket for leak-off pipe
35. Locknut fixing bracket to injector stud
36–38. Fixings, spill return pipe to bracket on injector stud
39. Clip
40. Fuel pipe, filter to distributor pump
41. Nut } Fixing pipe
42. Olive } to filter
43. Banjo bolt } Fixing pipe to
44. Joint washer } distributor pump
45. Clip, fixing pipe to distributor pump
46. Fuel pipe, distributor pump return to filter
47. Nut } Fixing pipe to non-return
48. Olive } valve at filter
49. Clip
50. Drive screw
51. Double pipe } Fixing distributor pump feed and return pipes together
52–54. Fixings, pipes and clips
55. Injector
56. Nozzle
57. Joint washer, copper } For
58. Joint washer, steel } injector
59. Clamping strip for injector
60–61. Fixings, injector to cylinder head
62. Injector pipe to No. 2 cylinder
63. Damper for injector pipe
64. Shroud
65. Bracket
66. Support strap } For shroud
67. Steady strap
68. Backplate
69–70. Fixings, straps to injector studs
71–74. Fixings, shroud and dampers to backplate, strap and support bracket
75. Fuel filter
76. Element
77. Seal, small } For
78. Seal, large } element
79. Special centre bolt for filter
80. Washer for centre bolt
81. Plug for fuel filter
82. Joint washer
83. Plug for fuel filter, top, leak-off plug
84. Joint washer for leak-off plug
85. Transfer pipe, extra filter to basic filter
86. Nut } Fixing pipe
87. Olive } to filter
88–92. Fixings, filter to dash
93. Fuel pipe, pump to filters
94. Nut } Fixing pipe
95. Olive } to filter
96. Nut } Fixing pipe
97. Olive } to pump

} Additional fuel filter

Fig. L1-68. General layout of Diesel fuel system, early models, twin filters illustrated

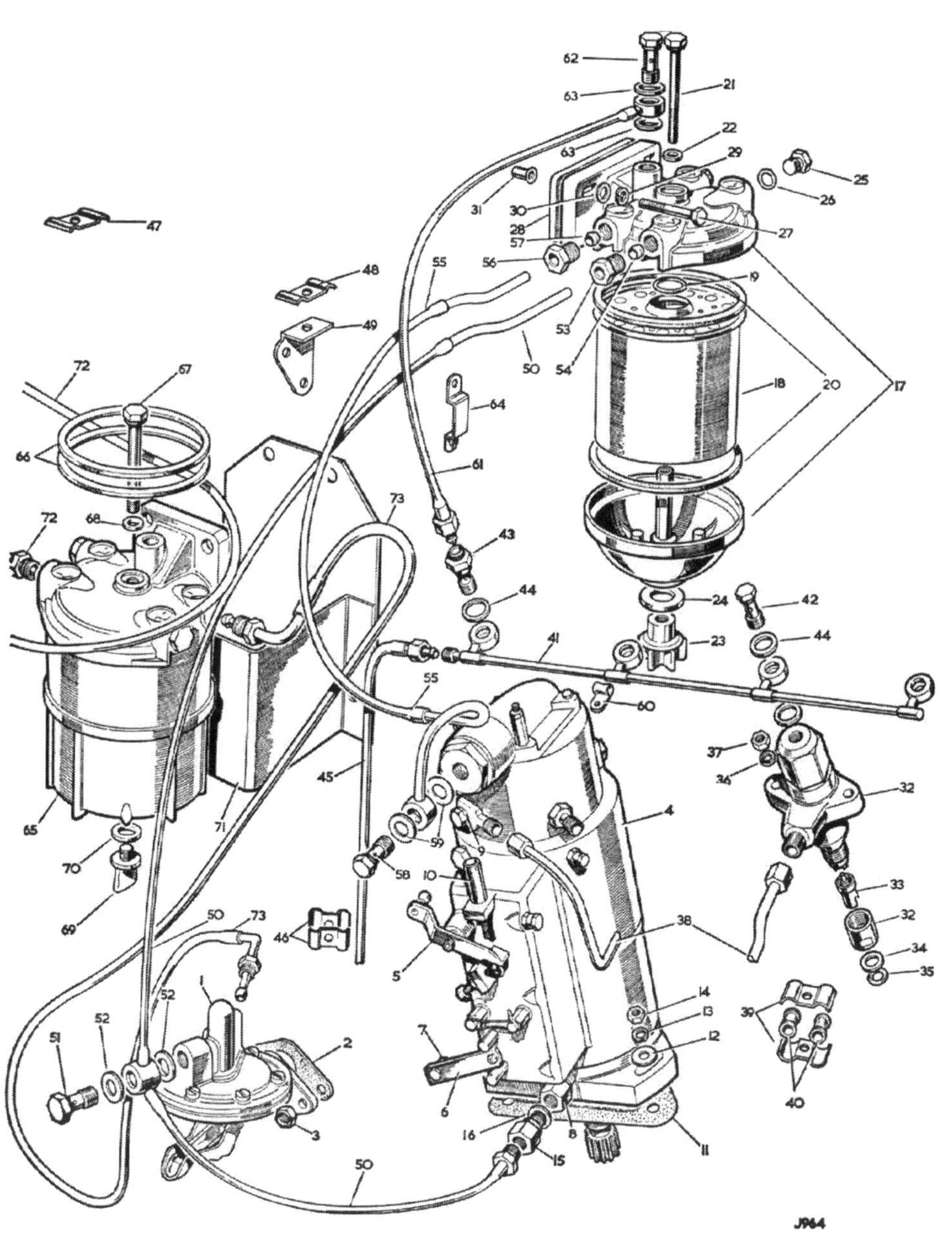

Section L—Land-Rover — FUEL SYSTEM

Key to Fig. L1-69. General layout of Diesel fuel system, latest models

1. Fuel pump, mechanical
2. Joint washer, fuel pump to cylinder block
3. Self-locking nut, fixing fuel pump
4. Distributor pump
5. Accelerator control lever
6. Stop lever
7. Swivel clamp for stop lever
8. Union, fuel pipe connection
9. Joint washer for injection pipe, distributor pump end
10. Sleeve for control lever stop screw
11. Joint washer for distributor pump } For distributor pump
12. Plain washer } Fixing distributor pump to cylinder block
13. Spring washer
14. Nut ($\frac{5}{16}$ in. UNF)
15. Non-return valve for distributor pump
16. Joint washer for non-return valve
17. Fuel filter
18. Element for fuel filter
19. Seal for element, small
20. Seal for element, large
21. Special centre bolt for filter
22. Washer for centre bolt
23. Nylon drain plug for filter
24. Rubber seal for drain plug
25. Plug for filter
26. Joint washer for plug
27. Bolt ($\frac{5}{16}$ in. UNF x $1\frac{5}{8}$ in. long) } Fixing filter to dash
28. Distance plate
29. Spring washer
30. Plain washer
31. Rivnut ($\frac{5}{16}$ in. UNF)
32. Injector complete
33. Nozzle for injector
34. Joint washer for injector, copper
35. Joint washer for injector, steel
36. Spring washer } Fixing injectors to cylinder head studs
37. Nut ($\frac{5}{16}$ in. UNF)
38. Injector pipe to No. 2 cylinder
39. Clamping plate for injector pipe
40. Grommet for injector pipe
41. Spill rail pipe complete
42. Banjo bolt for No. 1, 2 and 3 injectors } Fixing spill rail pipe to injectors
43. Banjo union for No. 4 injector
44. Joint washer for banjo bolt
45. Fuel pipe, spill return to tank
46. Double clip, clamping feed and return pipes together
47. Double clip, fixing feed and return pipes to chassis sidemember
48. Double clip for feed and return pipes
49. Bracket for clip
50. Fuel pipe, mechanical pump and distributor pump to filter
51. Banjo bolt } Fixing fuel pipe to mechanical pump
52. Joint washer
53. Nut } Fixing pipe to filter
54. Olive
55. Fuel pipe, filter to distributor pump
56. Nut } Fixing pipe to filter
57. Olive
58. Banjo bolt } Fixing pipe to distributor pump
59. Joint washer
60. Clip, fixing fuel pipe to distributor pump
61. Fuel pipe filter to spill rail at No. 4 injector
62. Banjo bolt } Fixing fuel pipe to filter
63. Joint washer
64. Double clip, fixing fuel pipes to bulkhead
65. Sedimentor
66. Seal for sedimentor
67. Special centre bolt for sedimentor
68. Washer for centre bolt
69. Drain plug for sedimentor
70. Rubber seal for drain plug
71. Mounting bracket for sedimentor
72. Fuel pipe, tank to sedimentor
73. Fuel pipe, sedimentor to mechanical pump

Fig. L1-69. General layout of Diesel fuel system, latest models

FUEL SYSTEM

Priming the fuel system—Operation L1-14

Workshop hand tools:
Spanner sizes: $\frac{7}{16}$ in. AF, $\frac{7}{16}$ in. AF open end

Priming the fuel system, early type filter

A—When the filter bowl has been cleaned or the paper element changed on **either or both fuel** filters, the system must be primed as follows:

1. Do not attempt to start the engine hoping to draw the fuel through in this way, otherwise the full priming procedure will be necessary.
2. Slacken the air vent screw on the top of the engine filter. See Fig. L1.71.
3. Operate the hand priming lever in the mechanical pump until fuel free from bubbles emerges.
4. Tighten the bleed screw.
5. Operate the hand priming lever once or twice to clear the last bubbles of air into the filter bleed pipe.
6. Start the engine in the normal way and check for leaks.

B—When fuel system has been completely emptied, proceed as follows:

7. Carry out operations above 1 to 5 inclusive.
8. Release air vent screw on distributor pump.
9. Operate the fuel pump hand priming lever until fuel free of air emerges.
10. Retighten the air vent screw.
11. To ensure that all air is exhausted from the pump it may also be necessary to slacken air vent screw in the distributor control cover and repeat items 9 and 10.
12. Start engine in normal way and check for leaks.

C—When distributor pump only has been drained it is only necessary to carry out operations 8 to 12 inclusive.

Ensure that fuel pump lever is on the bottom of the operating cam when priming the fuel system, otherwise maximum movement of the priming lever will not be obtained.

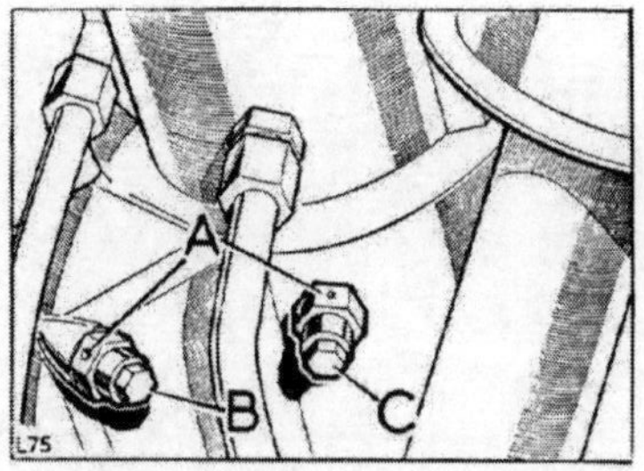

Fig. L1.70. Priming the distributor pump
A—Fuel orifice
B—Air vent screw on distributor
C—Air vent screw on distributor control cover

Priming the fuel system, latest type filters (single or twin filter, or filter and sedimentor system)

A—When the filter bowl has been cleaned or the paper element changed on **either or both fuel** filters, the system must be primed as follows:

When models fitted with a sedimentor have had the water drained only, from the sedimentor bowl, no priming is necessary as the water is replaced by fuel automatically syphoned from the tank. However, if the sedimentor has been dismantled or air has entered the body, then the system must be primed as follows:

1. Do not attempt to start the engine hoping to draw the fuel through in this way, otherwise the full priming procedure will be necessary.
2. Slacken the bleed pipe or air vent screw as the case may be, on the top of the filter which has had the replacement element fitted.
3. Operate the hand priming lever on the mechanical pump, until fuel free from bubbles emerges.
4. Tighten the bleed pipe or air vent screw.
5. Operate the hand priming lever once or twice to clear the last bubbles of air into the filter bleed pipe.
6. Start engine in normal way and check for leaks.

B—When fuel system has been completely emptied proceed as follows:

7. Carry out operations above, 1 to 5 inclusive.
8. Release air vent screw 'B' on distributor body. See Fig. L1.70.

Operation L1-14—continued

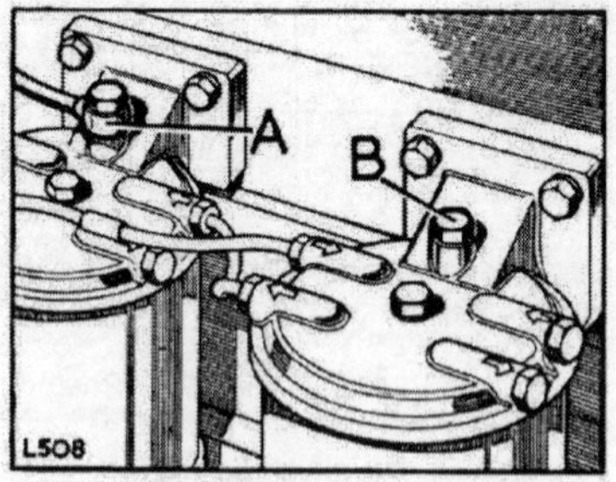

9. Operate the fuel pump hand priming lever until fuel free of air emerges.
10. Retighten the air vent screw.
11. To ensure that all air is exhausted from the pump it may also be necessary to slacken air vent screw 'C' in the distributor control cover and repeat items 9 and 10.
12. Start the engine in the normal way and check for leaks.

C—When distributor pump only has been drained it is only necessary to carry out operations 8 to 12 inclusive.

Always ensure that fuel pump lever is on the bottom of the operating cam when priming the fuel system, otherwise maximum movement of the priming lever will not be obtained.

Fig. L1.71. Air vent on filter
(Twin filter system illustrated)
A—Bleed pipe
B—Air vent screw

FUEL SYSTEM

Fuel filters, to clean, remove and refit, Diesel models—Operation L1-15

Workshop hand tools:
Spanner sizes: $\frac{7}{16}$ in. AF, $\frac{1}{2}$ in. AF, $\frac{5}{8}$ in. AF, $\frac{11}{16}$ in. AF open end

Fuel pump filter and sediment bowl (early models)

To remove and clean

1. Unscrew the nut at base of sediment bowl, move the retainer aside and withdraw the bowl, sealing gasket and gauze filter disc. Care must be taken to prevent damage to the filter disc.
2. Clean the bowl and filter disc in Diesel fuel oil, directing a compressed air jet on the gauze to remove any obstinate particles.
3. Examine the cork gasket for filter bowl and renew if signs of deterioration are evident.

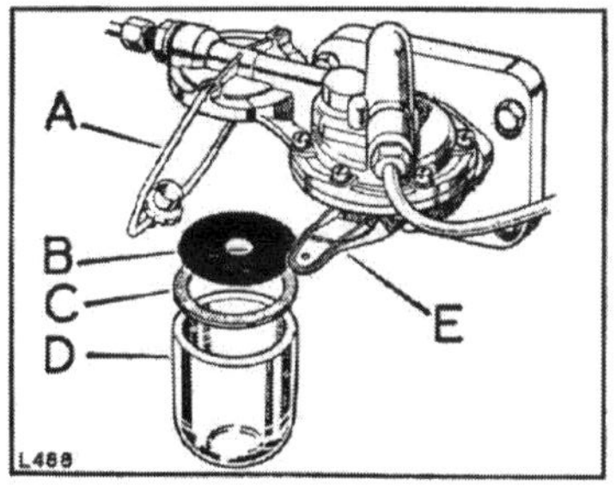

To replace

1. Reverse the removal procedure ensuring that the gauze filter disc fits tightly round the inlet neck and is quite undamaged in any way.

Main filter, early type, engine mounted

To remove

1. Slacken the drain plug at the base of filter container and allow fuel to flow into a suitable receptacle.
2. Disconnect the fuel inlet, outlet and bleed back pipes.
3. Remove the securing bolts and lift the assembly clear.

A non-return valve is incorporated in the excess fuel spill back pipe. It can be removed by disconnecting the union at the top of the filter, and withdrawing the valve complete with holder.

Fig. L1.72. Removing sediment bowl
A—Retainer for sediment bowl
B—Filter gauze
C—Cork gasket
D—Sediment bowl
E—Hand priming lever

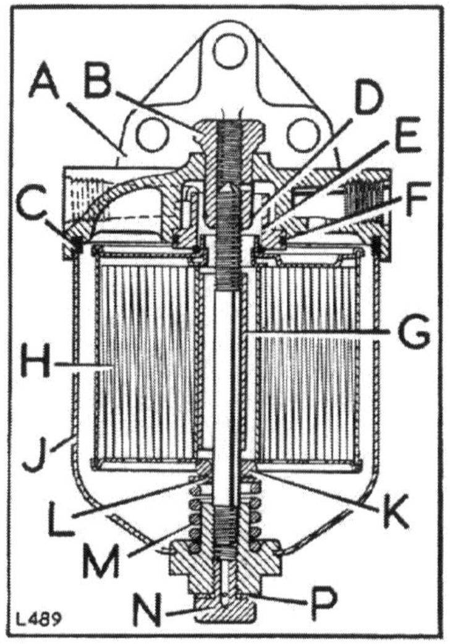

Fig. L1.73. Sectioned view of main fuel filter, early type
A—Housing cover
B—Cap nut
C—Oil seal
D—Circlip
E—Sealing ring
F—Oil seal
G—Location sleeve
H—Element
J—Container
K—Seal
L—Plain washer
M—Spring
N—Drain plug
P—Washer

To remove element, filter in position on vehicle, early type

1. Slacken the plug at base of filter container and allow the fuel to flow into a suitable receptacle.
2. Disconnect the bleed back pipe from the top of filter unit.
3. Unscrew the centre cap nut at top of filter whilst supporting the container.
4. Withdraw the container complete with small sealing ring at top of element and remove the large sealing ring from the underside of filter cover.
5. Discard the filter element, then wash the container thoroughly in fuel oil. Clean the holes in drain plug and boss with a wire. Great care should be taken to ensure that the centre spindle above lower sealing ring is absolutely clean.

To refit

1. Reverse the removal procedure.
2. Prime the fuel system. Operation L1-14.

Operation L1-15—continued

6. Renew the lower sealing ring if its serviceability is in any way doubtful—a new top sealing ring is supplied with each element and should always be used.
7. Examine the large sealing gasket for container and replace if necessary.
8. Fit the new element, top sealing rings, and refit container.
9. Reconnect pipes, tighten drain plug and prime the fuel system. Operation L1-14.

Main filters, late type

The latest type installation can be identified by the black nylon fuel pipes and the fact that the main fuel filter is no longer attached directly to the engine, but is fitted to the dash. The design of the later filter uses the outer casing of the filter element as an extension of the element holder, thus making it impossible to run the vehicle without a filter element in the system.

To renew

1. Support element holder and unscrew the special bolt on the top of the filter; the element holder can now be removed.
2. Remove and discard the used element.
3. Wash the element holder in fuel oil.
4. If necessary, renew both the large rubber washer and the small rubber washer in the filter top, also renew the large rubber washer in the element holder.
5. Push the element on to the filter top spigot, with the perforated holes in the element to the top.
6. Fit the element holder to the bottom of the element and secure with the special bolt.
7. Prime the fuel system. Operation L1-14.

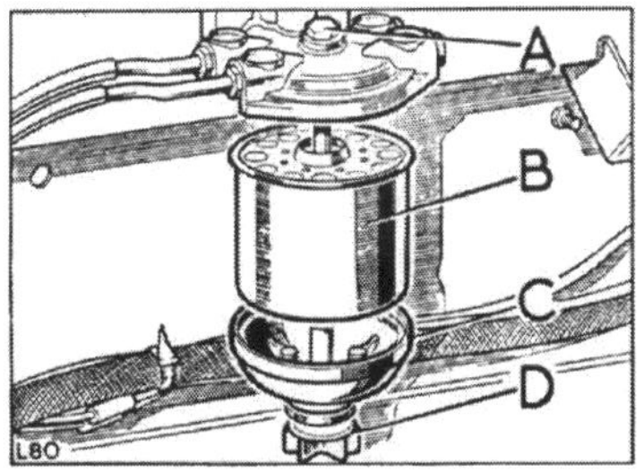

Additional filter

All export models are fitted with an additional fuel filter. Early models have a paper element type fuel filter mounted on the engine side of the dash panel. Latest models have a sedimentor type filter mounted on the RH side chassis member, adjacent to cab door.

Early models

The paper element type fuel filter used on early models is of the same type as the main fuel filter, late type, as already described. The two filters are mounted alongside on the engine side of the dash panel, and the instructions given for the main fuel filter also apply to the additional fuel filter.

Fig. L1.74. Main fuel filter, latest type
A—Element retaining bolt
B—Element
C—Element holder
D—Water drain plug

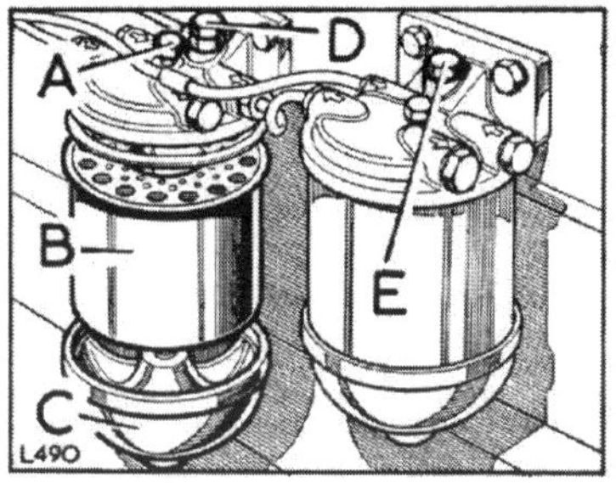

Fig. L1.75. Paper element filter, twin system illustrated
A—Element retaining bolt
B—Element
C—Element holder
D—Bleed pipe
E—Air vent screw

Latest models

The sedimentor increases the working life of the main fuel filter by removing the larger droplets of water and larger particles of foreign matter from the fuel.

FUEL SYSTEM

Operation L1-15—continued

Drain off water as follows:

Slacken off drain plug to allow water to run out.

When pure diesel fuel is emitted, tighten drain plug.

Dismantle and clean as detailed below:

1. Disconnect fuel pipe inlet pipe at sedimentor and raise pipe above level of fuel tank to prevent draining from tank. Support in this position.
2. Support sedimentor bowl and unscrew special bolt on top of unit. The lower chamber, bowl and element can now be removed.
3. Clean all parts in petrol.
4. Fit new oil seals and reverse removal procedure.
5. Prime the system and check for air leaks. Operation L1-14.

To remove

1. Disconnect fuel inlet pipe at sedimentor and raise pipe above level of fuel tank to prevent draining from tank. Support in this position.
2. Drain the sediment trap into a suitable container by unscrewing the drain plug.
3. Remove right-hand floorboard above sediment trap.
4. Disconnect outlet pipe.
5. Remove securing screws and remove sediment trap.

To refit

1. Secure sediment trap to chassis bracket.
2. Reconnect inlet and outlet pipes.
3. Refit right-hand floorboard.
4. Prime fuel system. Operation L1-14.

Injection pump filter

To remove and clean

1. Remove the pipe filter to injection pump.
2. Unscrew the pipe connection from injection pump head and withdraw the filter.
3. Wash the filter in fuel oil and direct an air jet on to it.

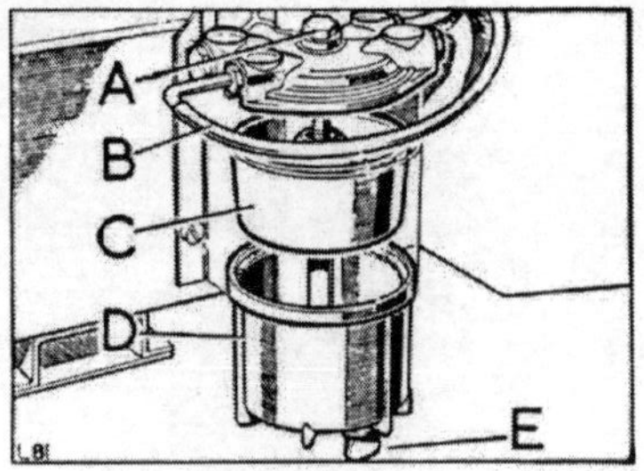

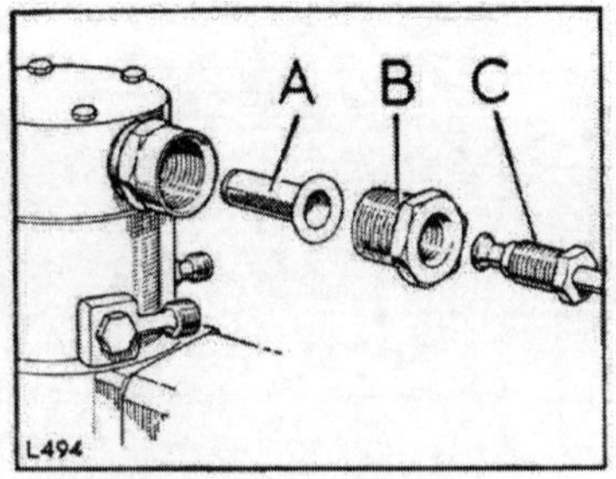

Fig. L1-76. Fuel sedimentor

A—Retainer bolt
B—Inlet pipe
C—Element
D—Bowl
E—Water drain plug

Fig. L1-77. Injection pump filter
A—Filter B—Connection
C—Inlet pipe

To refit

1. Replace the filter and pipe connection and reconnect the feed pipe at main filter end. Operate the lift pump by hand and couple the pipe to injection pump head whilst fuel flows from the pipe.

FUEL SYSTEM

Fuel injectors, Diesel models, to overhaul—Operation L1-16

(For removal and refitting instructions, Section A refers)

Workshop hand tools:
Spanner sizes: ¾ in. AF, 1 in. AF open end

Special tools:
271483 Testing outfit
271482 Spanner for nozzle cap
271484 Cleaning outfit for injectors
276278 Safety can
278181 Tool for flushing injector nozzles
278182 Adaptor for injector

General

The nozzle is a hard working precision made valve, opening approximately 1,800 times a minute at full throttle and it is essential that it is treated with great care at all times.

The 'Pintaux' type nozzle has been developed by CAV for use with the type of cylinder head chosen for Rover CI engines. This type of nozzle has been found most satisfactory for starting and general running and must be replaced by the same type only.

Checking nozzle assemblies on vehicle

When an injection nozzle is considered to be the cause of irregular running and loss of power, a quick check may be made by loosening the fuel feed pipe union nut on each nozzle in turn, whilst the engine is idling and again at approximately 1,000 rpm.

If the injection nozzle assembly being checked has been operating properly, there will be a distinct reduction in rpm accompanied by obvious roughness, but a faulty injection nozzle may make little or no difference to the engine note when its fuel feed pipe is loosened.

Testing nozzle assemblies on vehicle

1. Remove the fuel spill gallery pipe complete, from the injection nozzles, then disconnect the fuel feed pipe (injection pump to nozzle) from the nozzle to be tested and from the injection pump.
2. Release the fixings and withdraw the suspected injection nozzle assembly; reconnect the pipe and nozzle assembly to the injection pump in a position whereby fuel ejection may be observed.
3. Loosen the union nuts securing the remaining fuel pipes to injection nozzles.
4. Whilst the starter turns the engine over, observe the manner in which fuel issues from the nozzle and compare the spray form with section 'A' of Fig. L1-87.

Very little fuel should issue from the main spray hole with the engine turning over at starter speed but a fine spray comparable to that illustrated in section 'A' should be ejected from the auxiliary spray hole. If the ejected fuel is more in the form of a liquid jet or issues from the main pintle hole, then the nozzle and holder assembly should be removed for overhaul and a replacement unit fitted.

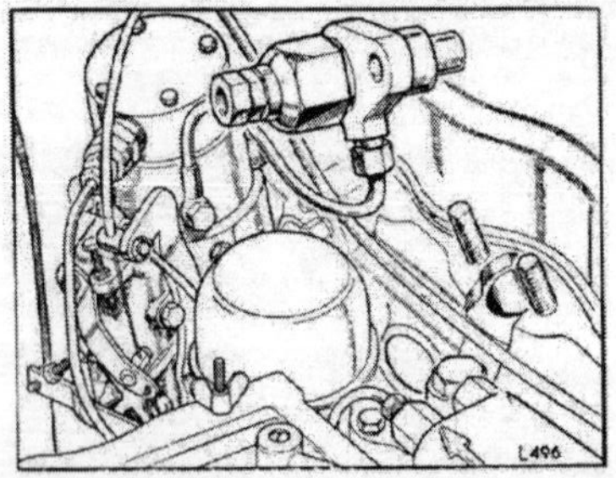

Fig. L1-78. Testing nozzle assemblies on vehicle

Bench testing of injection nozzle and holder assembly

To check a nozzle assembly and ensure that it is functioning correctly, a setting outfit as illustrated is essential. A bench covered with linoleum or non-ferrous sheet metal is most suitable for mounting the outfit; such a surface facilitates the cleanliness essential when checking nozzle parts. Between the bench and setting outfit, a tray, also of non-ferrous metal, should be positioned to prevent spilt fuel spreading. Small containers may be attached to the bench to isolate the component parts of each assembly; these parts are carefully mated by the manufacturers and must **not** be interchanged. Lastly, a small bath with cover, containing Shell calibration fluid for washing components, should be kept conveniently near.

Section L—Land-Rover

FUEL SYSTEM

Operation L1-16—continued

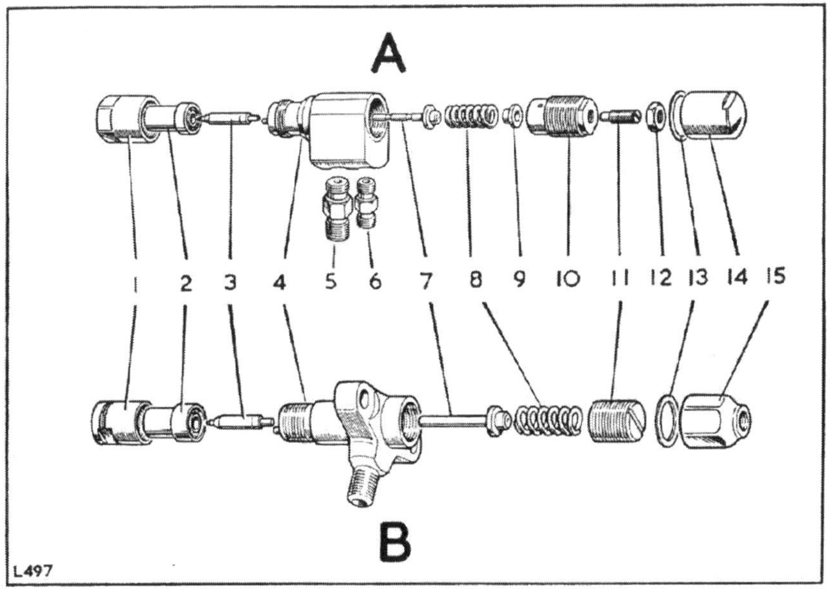

Fig. L1-79. Exploded view of injector nozzle and holder assembly

A—Early type   B—Latest type

1. Cap nut
2. Nozzle valve body
3. Nozzle valve
4. Nozzle holder body
5. Feed pipe union
6. Spill back pipe union
7. Valve spindle and cap
8. Pressure spring
9. Spring cap
10. Pressure sleeve
11. Pressure adjusting screw
12. Locknut—adjusting screw
13. Copper washer
14. Protection cap
15. Combined locknut and end cap

The efficient operation of the injection nozzle assembly is dependent on four main conditions, as follows:

(a) The nozzle valve must open at 135 Ats.
(b) The rate of back leakage must be within 150 to 100 Ats.
(c) Seat tightness must be sufficient to prevent leakage.
(d) Spray form must compare favourably with the illustrations, Fig. L1-87.

Pressure setting, back leakage and seat tightness tests may be made by coupling the injection nozzle and holder assembly direct to the pressure feed pipe on setting outfit, but an adaptor must be fitted between the pipe and injection nozzle and holder assembly when testing spray form. This adaptor, see Fig. L1-86, increases the pressure of fuel to the injection nozzle and holder assembly sufficiently for the main and auxiliary spray form to be determined.

Operation L1-16—continued

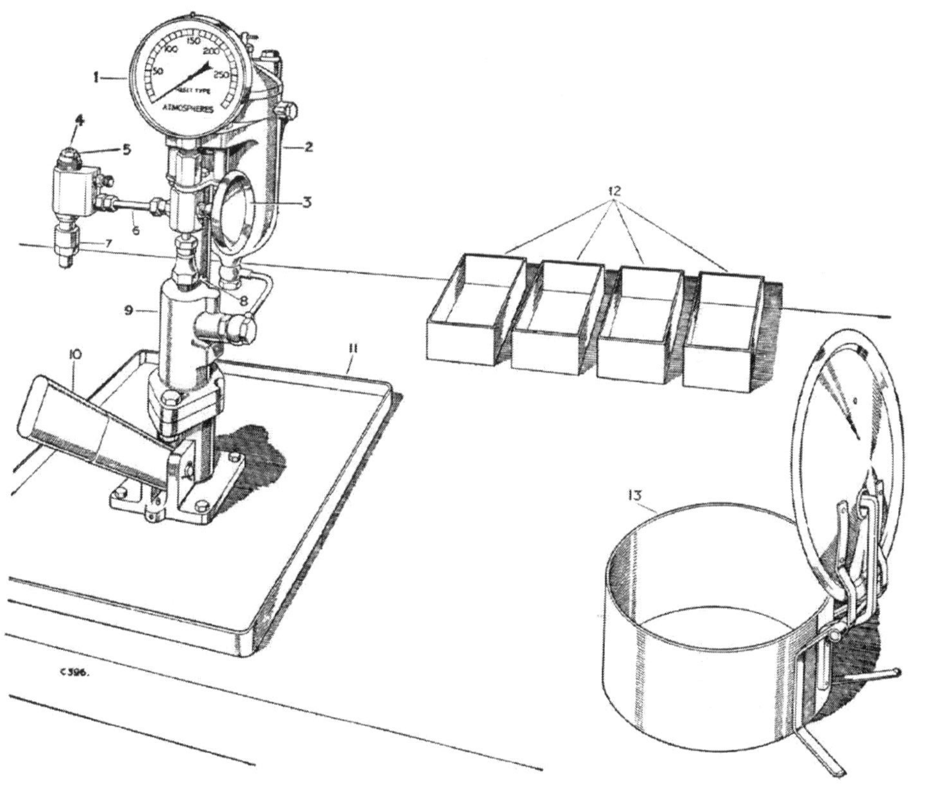

Fig. L1-80. Injection nozzle setting outfit (early type nozzle illustrated)

1. Pressure gauge
2. Fuel container and filtering unit
3. Check valve
4. Nozzle holder injection pressure adjusting screw
5. Locknut for adjusting screw
6. Pressure feed pipe
7. Nozzle cap nut
8. Air vent screw
9. Pump body
10. Operating handle
11. Spill tray
12. Containers for injection nozzle components
13. Cleaning bath

Dismantling and cleaning

A cleaning kit (Part No. 271484) is essential for removing carbon from the component parts of the injection nozzle and holder assembly. The use of special spanners (set Part No. 271482) is recommended.

1. Remove the nozzle holder protection cap and copper washer, unscrew the locknut, pressure adjusting screw and pressure sleeve, then withdraw the spring cap, spring and valve spindle. Unscrew the pipe unions and remove the copper washers. See Fig. L1-79 for variations between early and latest type nozzles.

2. Unscrew the cap nut, then remove the nozzle valve and body.

3. Soak the component parts of the assembly in Shell calibration fluid to loosen carbon deposits, but do **not** allow parts of any one assembly to be interchanged with those of another.

Section L—Land-Rover FUEL SYSTEM

Operation L1-16—continued

4. Brush away all external carbon deposits from component parts with a brass wire brush (Part No. ET068) and replace them in the oil bath.

   Particular care must be exercised when cleaning the pintle and seat of nozzle valve to avoid scratching or scoring, which may result in spray distortion.

5. Clean the three oil feed passages in the nozzle body with a wire or drill of $\frac{1}{16}$ in. (1.5 mm) diameter. Remove the carbon from the annular recess with tool Part No. ET071 and from the valve seat, using tool Part No. ET070, with a rotary motion.

6. Select the appropriate size probe from the pocket of cleaning kit and secure it in the pintle hole cleaner (Part No. ET069). Insert the probe into the bore of nozzle valve body and allow the end to extend through the main fuel outlet, then turn in a rotary manner to remove carbon.

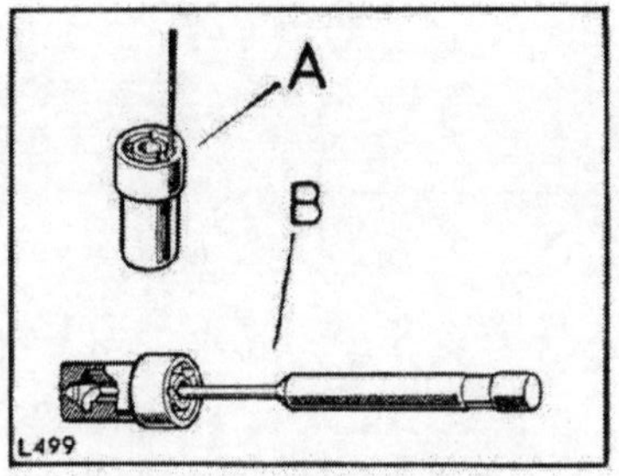

Fig. L1-81. Cleaning nozzle, first stage
A—Cleaning nozzle body oil feed passages
B—Scraping nozzle body annular recess

7. Carbon may be removed from the nozzle valve cone by inserting the valve into tool Part No. ET072 and then rotating it alternatively in a clockwise then anti-clockwise manner whilst pressing the valve inward.

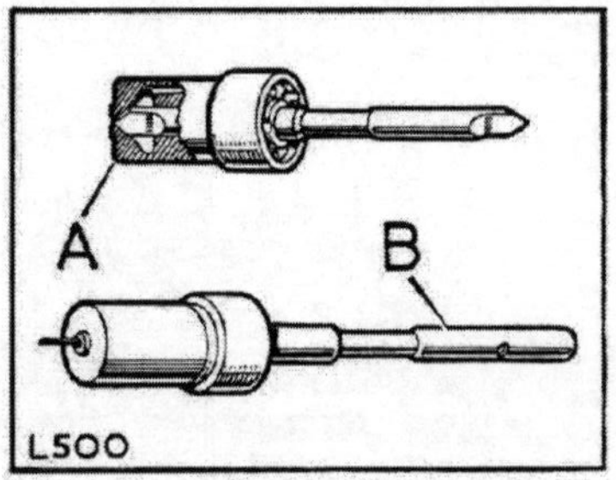

Fig. L1-82. Cleaning nozzle, second stage
A—Removing carbon from valve seat
B—Cleaning Pintaux nozzle hole

If the nozzle is blued or the seating has a dull circumferential ring indicating pitting or wear, the nozzle body and valve should be returned to a CAV Service Agent and replacement parts fitted. See 'Defect Location'.

Do **not** attempt to lap the nozzle valve to body. This process requires special equipment and training.

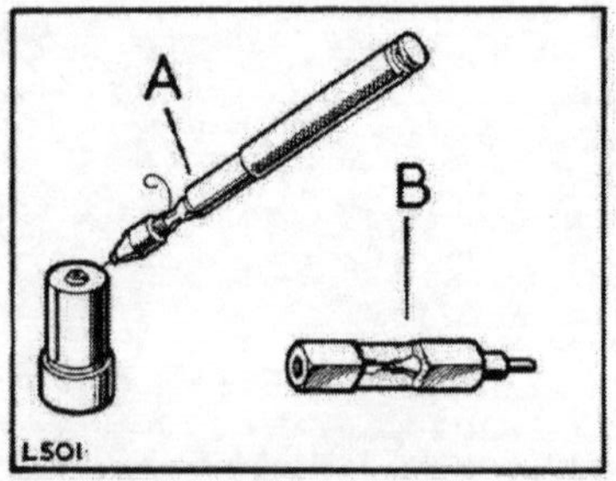

Fig. L1-83. Cleaning the nozzle, third stage
A—Cleaning auxiliary spray hole
B—Removing carbon from nozzle valve cone

Operation L1-16—continued

8. Clean the auxiliary spray hole using Part No. ET120 fitted with probing wire .008 in. (0.20 mm) diameter. Allow $\frac{1}{16}$ in. (2.0 mm) only to extend from the chuck and thus minimise the possibility of the wire bending or breaking while probing. Great care must be taken to prevent breakage of the wire in the hole.

9. With flushing tool ET427 secured to the nozzle testing outfit, fit the nozzle body (spray holes uppermost) to the flushing tool and pump test oil through vigorously. This flushing process is necessary for the removal of any tiny carbon particles which may have become lodged in the body after scraping and probing.

10. Examine the pressure faces of nozzle body and nozzle holder to ascertain their freedom from scoring and scratches. These surfaces must be perfectly smooth. Fit the nozzle to nozzle body and check for freedom of movement.

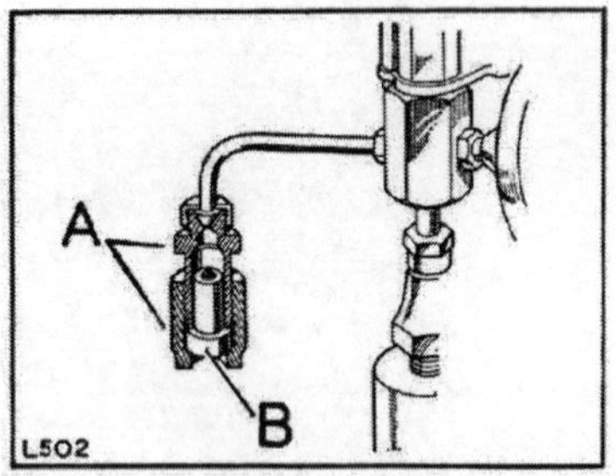

Fig. L1-84. Flushing nozzle body
A—Flushing tool
B—Nozzle body

11. Immerse the nozzle body and valve in the fluid bath and assemble whilst submerged. Wash the remaining components thoroughly and reverse dismantling procedure.

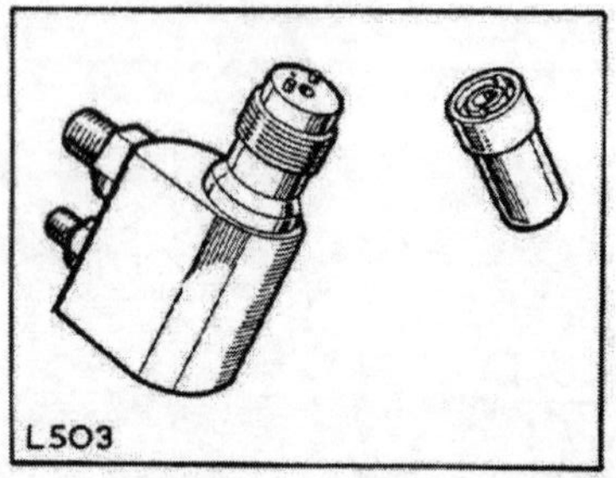

Fig. L1-85. Injector nozzle assembly lapped pressure faces

12. Seat injection nozzle assembly in accordance with the following test procedure.

To test (Fig. L1-80)

Warning: The injection nozzle must **not** be allowed to point towards the operator when spraying and the hands must **never** be allowed to contact the spray, which has great penetrating force.

1. Remove the cap from oil container (2) and fill with 1½ pints (0.8 litre) of Shell callibration fluid.

2. Air vent the system by removing the vent screw (8), allow oil to flow freely for a few seconds and replace the screw whilst the flow continues. Operate the pump handle until oil flows from pipe (6).

3. Connect the injector and holder assembly to the pressure feed pipe with the nozzle pointing downwards. The length and bore of this pipe is important and replacement pipes must be approximately 75 mm (2.8 in.) between the union nuts and of 3 mm (.118 in.) bore.

4. Close the check valve (3) to keep the pressure gauge out of circuit and smartly operate the hand lever (10) several times to expel all air from the system.

Operation L1-16—continued

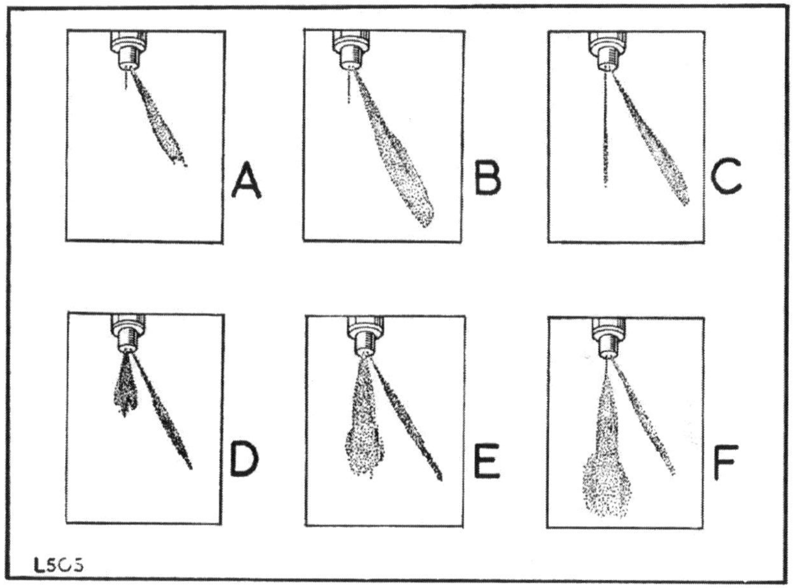

Back leakage test

5. Adjustment is made by removing the cap nut from the nozzle holder, loosening locknut (5) and turning the adjusting screw (4) clockwise to increase and anti-clockwise to decrease the opening pressure.

6. Fit assembled injector to nozzle setting outfit and adjust to open at 160 to 170 atmospheres then pump up to just below this figure, release handle to allow the needle of gauge to fall naturally. Time the pressure drop from 150 atmospheres down to 100 atmospheres.

7. This should be not less than 5 seconds for the original nozzle and not less than 7 seconds if a new one is to be fitted, and not more than 36 seconds for either.

8. Check externally the top and bottom of nozzle cap nut (7) and pressure pipe union nuts for signs of oil leakage. If leakage occurs at the nozzle cap nut, remove the nut and examine the pressure faces of nozzle holders and nozzle body for presence of foreign matter or surface scoring, before tightening further.

A leakproof nozzle assembly with an excessive rate of pressure drop indicates a worn nozzle valve; the nozzle valve and nozzle body should be renewed.

Pressure setting

9. The selected **operational** opening pressure of the nozzle valve is 135 atmospheres. Readjust to this setting in the manner described in item 5.

Seat tightness

10. Wipe the bottom face of the injection nozzle dry and raise the pressure in the system to 125 atmospheres. A slight dampness on the bottom face is permissible, but blob formation or dripping indicates a badly seating valve in which case the assembly should be dismantled for further examination.

Spray form

11. Fuel delivery to the injection nozzle assembly when testing **spray form** must be characteristically similar to fuel delivery under normal operating conditions and to effect these conditions an adaptor (CAV Y7044872) must be fitted between the injection nozzle assembly and the pressure pipe.

The adaptor differs mainly in the cap nut and nozzle valve from the ordinary type of injection nozzle and holder assembly as fitted to the engine; the nozzle valve has no pintle and the cap nut is extended, bored and threaded to receive nozzles for testing.

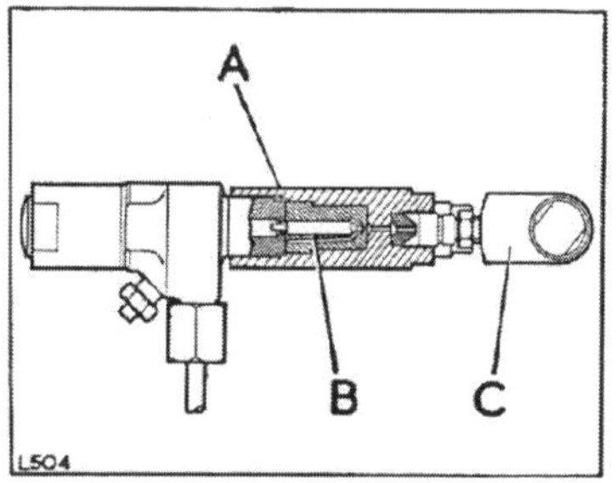

12. Connect the adaptor assembly to the pressure pipe and adjust the opening pressure of the nozzle valve to 220 atmospheres. (See items 4 and 5). Screw the injection nozzle and holder assembly to be tested, into the adaptor and with the check valve closed, operate the handle smartly to expel air from the system.

The auxiliary spray form may be tested at 60 strokes per minute and the main spray at 140. Spray development from starting to running speeds is illustrated, this illustration should be referred to and compared with the spray form of nozzles under test.

Spray formation should be well formed and free from splits or distortion. A slight centre 'core' can be disregarded.

Fig. L1-86. Sectioned view of adaptor (CAV-ET 872)
A—Modified cap nut
B—Nozzle valve (less pintle)
C—Nozzle under test

Fig. L1-87. Injection nozzle spray form development, starting to running conditions

FUEL SYSTEM

Fault diagnosis—Fuel system

The fuel system fault diagnosis is divided into two parts. Part one refers to carburation only and covers all four carburetters used on Land-Rovers. Part two covers general fuel system faults and is applicable to all models.

Part one—carburetter fault diagnosis

Symptom	Possible cause				Check and remedy
	Solex	Zenith	SU and Stromberg	
Difficult starting when cold	Insufficient choke action	Insufficient choke action	Insufficient choke action	Check action of choke unit to ensure that the choke is being applied fully—adjust choke cable
	Fast idle adjustment incorrect	Fast idle adjustment incorrect	Fast idle adjustment incorrect	Check and adjust fast idle setting. Check linkage between choke and throttle for distortion
	Float chamber level too low	Float chamber level too low	Float chamber level too low	Check needle valve for sticking—(closed). Check float level setting. Check inlet connection filter for blockage. Check external fuel system in accordance with fuel system fault diagnosis
	Carburetter flooding	Carburetter flooding	Carburetter flooding	Check needle valve for sticking—(open) Float punctured Fuel pump pressure too high Float level too high
Difficult starting when hot	Choke sticking 'on'	Choke sticking 'on'	Choke sticking 'on'	Check to ensure choke is returning to fully 'off' position, reset as necessary
	Blocked air filter	Blocked air filter	Blocked air filter	Check oil level in air cleaner, Wash out filter gauze in clean petrol and blow with compressed air
	Float chamber level too high	Float chamber level too high	Float chamber level too high	Check float level setting. Check float arms for distortion. Check needle valve for sticking. Punctured float, fuel pump pressure too high
	—	Internal leakage	—	Check 'O' ring around venturi spigot is in good condition
	—	—	Jet tube sticking down (SU)	Check for distortion of jet tube

Fault diagnosis—continued

Symptom	Possible cause				Check and remedy
	Solex	Zenith	SU and Stromberg	
Erratic slow-running or stalling on deceleration	Float level too low	Float level too low	Float level too low	Check float chamber level. Check for needle valve sticking
	—	—	Piston sticking (SU)	Clean piston and suction chamber in clean fuel
	Incorrect slow running setting	Incorrect slow running setting	Incorrect jet setting	Check slow running jet for blockage. Check and reset slow running in accordance with Operation L1-1 or L1-2. Check that the volume control screw conical end is not distorted
	Carburetter air leaks	Carburetter air leaks	Carburetter air leaks	Check throttle spindle and bearings for wear
	Manifold air leaks	Manifold air leaks	Manifold air leaks	Check inlet manifold gasket for leakage. Check inlet manifold for cracks and distortion of mating faces. Check gasket between carburetter and manifold. Check condition of vacuum advance pipe and connections. Check vacuum servo pipes and connections
	—	—	**Damper** oil too thick. No oil in damper	Check and refill to correct level with oil specified
Poor acceleration	Acceleration pump sticking	Acceleration pump sticking	—	Check piston assembly moves freely in its housing and returns under the spring loading
	Ball valve sticking	Ball valve sticking	—	
	Non-return valve sticking	Non-return valve sticking	—	
	Pump diaphragm leaking	—	—	Check accelerator pump cover for signs of fuel leakage indicating a leaking diaphragm
	Pump operating linkage incorrectly adjusted	—	—	Check adjustment of accelerator linkage
	Blocked non-return valve	—	—	Remove jets and discharge tube, wash in clean petrol and clean with compressed air
	Blocked accelerator jet	—	—	
	Discharge tube ball valve seized	—	—	
	—	—	No oil in damper or oil too thin	Check level of oil in damper, and fill to correct level with oil of a viscosity of SAE 20
	—	—	Piston sticking	(SU) Check piston is free, clean chamber and piston assembly with clean petrol (Stromberg) Check diaphragm for signs of cracking or porosity

Fault diagnosis—continued

Symptom	Possible cause			Check and remedy
	Solex	Zenith	SU and Stromberg	
Loss of power	Blocked fuel jets and carburetter drillings	Blocked fuel jets and carburetter drillings	—	Remove and clean all jets using clean petrol and compressed air. Wash carburetter body in clean fuel and clear all drillings with compressed air jet
	See 'Poor acceleration'. Accelerator pumps and linkage			
	Water in fuel	Water in fuel	Water in fuel	If water is present in float chamber, the complete fuel system should be drained, fuel components should be dismantled, inspected for contamination, paying particular attention to sediment bowl and gauze filters
Excessive fuel consumption	Blocked air cleaner	Blocked air cleaner	Blocked air cleaner	Check oil level. Wash out filter gauze in clean petrol
	Incorrectly adjusted carburetter	Incorrectly adjusted carburetter	Incorrectly adjusted carburetter	Check and reset slow running in accordance with carburetter overhaul instructions
	Accelerator linkage incorrectly adjusted	Accelerator linkage incorrectly adjusted	—	Check and reset accelerator linkage
	Float level too high	Float level too high	Float level too high	Check and reset float level
	Worn jets	Worn jets	Worn jets and needle	Check and replace as necessary
	—	—	Incorrect needle	Check needle type
	Choke sticking 'on'	Choke sticking 'on'	Choke sticking 'on'	Check to ensure choke is returning to fully 'off' position, reset as necessary

Part two—general fuel system fault diagnosis

If engine will not start

Check for fuel starvation as follows:

1. With engine cold, remove inlet pipe at carburetter and operate fuel pump priming lever (vehicles with electric fuel pump, switch on ignition), fuel should issue from the pipe in a steady flow.

If fuel is present, check following items:

2. Solex carburetter—check gauze filter for blockage. If necessary, wash in clean fuel.

3. Remove float chamber top cover and test needle valve for sticking closed. Replace as necessary.

4. Solex and Zenith—remove main jet assembly and check for signs of blockage. Clean, using a high pressure air line.

5. SU carburetter—check drilling between float chamber and jet assembly for blockage. Clean, using a high pressure air line.

If fuel is **not** present, check following items:

6. Check fuel tank contents, do not assume gauge reading to be correct. Replenish tank as necessary.

7. Mechanical type fuel pump—remove inlet pipe at fuel pump, place finger over inlet aperture and operate priming lever. A distinct suction should be felt.

If suction is felt, the fault will be either:

(a) Blockage between fuel tank and fuel pump—Check all filters and sediment bowl for blockage. Remove fuel pipes and clear with a high pressure air line.

(b) Air leak in pipes between fuel tank and fuel pump—Check all filters and sediment bowl seals for serviceability and tightness. Check all pipes and connections for damage and security.

(c) Fuel tank air vent blocked—Check air vent pipe is clear.

If no suction is felt—Check sealing washer between sediment bowl and pump. Check filter for blockage. Remove and strip pump, paying particular attention to diaphragm and valve condition, fit new parts as necessary.

8. Electric type fuel pump—disconnect fuel pipe at carburetter and submerge pipe into a suitable container, switch on ignition.

If pump operates normally, then quantity of fuel pumped diminishes, check fuel tank vent for blockage.

If pump output is low accompanied by slow pump action, check suction pipe between tank and pump, also fuel filter and sediment bowl for restrictions. Check fuel pump inlet filter.

9. Electric type fuel pump—if pump does not operate, carry out the following checks:

(a) Disconnect electrical lead from pump and test for supply.

(b) Remove end cover from pump and check that contact breaker points are closed. Test points by placing a piece of wire across points, if the pump begins to operate, the fault is due to dirt corrosion or maladjustment of points.

(c) Remove the inlet pipe connection, if the pump then begins to operate the fault lies in the pipe line between tank and pump.

(d) Check for seized diaphragm and armature assembly. Dismantle pump, check throw-over mechanism. Check armature for seizure.

10. Electric type fuel pump—if pump operation is noisy, submerge pump outlet pipe in a quantity of fuel and switch on ignition. Fuel should be free of air bubbles. If bubbles are present, carry out the following checks:

(a) Check all connections between tank and pump for security.

(b) Check screws securing magnet house to pump body for tightness.

11. Electric type fuel pump—if pump operates with no fuel delivery, carry out the following checks:

(a) Serious air leak on the suction side, check all pipes and connections.

(b) Foreign matter lodged under the fuel pump inlet or outlet valve.

FUEL SYSTEM

DATA

Air cleaner

Type	AC centrifugal
Capacity:	
4-cylinder	1½ Imperial pints; 1.8 US pints; 0.85 litre
6-cylinder	1 Imperial pint; 1.2 US pints; 0.5 litre

Carburetter:

Four carburetters are in use, Solex and Zenith types are used on 2¼ litre models, Zenith/Stromberg and SU types are used on 2.6 litre models. The following are the standard settings, but may vary according to operating conditions.

Make ... **Solex**

Type	PA10-5 and PA10-6
Details	2¼ litre Petrol
Choke size	28
Main jet	125
Correction jet	185
Pilot jet	50
Pump jet	65
Economy jet	Blank
Air bleed jet	1.5
Starter air jet	—
Starter petrol jet	145
Economy system	
Petrol jet	100
Petrol level	⅝ in. ±⅛ in. (16 mm ±3 mm) below float chamber joint face

Carburetter settings which may be advantageous for high altitudes, 2¼ litre Petrol only (Solex carburetter):

Main jet (120)	5,000 ft. to 7,000 ft (1.524 m to 2.134 m)
Main jet (117.5)	7,000 ft. to 9,000 ft. (2.134 m to 2.740 m)
Main jet (115) Pilot jet (45)	9,000 ft to 12,000 ft (2.740 m to 3.655 m)
Main jet (112.5) Pilot jet (45)	12,000 ft to 14,000 ft (3.655 m to 4.268 m)

Make ... **Zenith**

Type	36 IV
Choke size	27 mm
Main jet	125
Enrichment jet	150
Slow running jet (ball type)	60
Pump jet (short stroke outer hole)	65
Part throttle air bleed	3.0
Full throttle air bleed	1.5 drilled
Slow running air bleed	1.4
Spring loaded ball valve in pump circuit	105
Fast idle	1.20
Needle valve	1.75
Needle valve washer	2.00
Fuel level	31–32 mm

Make ... **Zenith/Stromberg**

Type	175 CD 2S
Metering needle	B18362.Z/41
Air valve return spring	B18277.Z
Needle valve	B18353 1.75 mm with 2.0 mm washer 015667
Fast Idle	1.1 mm or No. 57 drill. At edge of throttle
Inter connection setting	
Float height	16 mm to 17 mm

Make ... **SU**

Type	HD 6
Needle	SS
Jet	.100
Float needle valve TI	AUD 9096 assembly
Float needle seating	
Piston spring	Yellow (8 oz)
Economiser	.116
Fast Idling cam	AUC 1298

Fuel filters

Petrol models	Sediment bowl, full flow
Diesel models	Sedimenter, full flow and CAV replaceable element, full flow

Fuel pump

2¼ litre Petrol, Diesel	AC mechanical (not interchangeable)
2.6 litre Petrol	SU electric

Fuel tank

4-cylinder models	10 Imperial gallons; 12 US gallons; 45 litres
6-cylinder models, except Station Wagon	11 Imperial gallons; 13 US gallons; 50 litres
6-cylinder, Station Wagon models	16 Imperial gallons; 19 US gallons; 73 litres

Injection pump, Diesel models

Type	CAV mechanically-governed distributor

Injection nozzle assemblies

Type	CAV Pintaux
Nozzle size	BDNO/SP6209
Opening pressure of nozzle valve	135 Ats
Back leakage rate, 150 to 100 Ats:	
New nozzle	7 seconds
Original nozzle	5 seconds

SECTION M—EXHAUST SYSTEM

INDEX—EXHAUST SYSTEM

Note: A comprehensive, detailed index is included at the rear of this manual

Description	Operation Number
Exploded views and description	At front of Section
Exhaust manifold	1
FRONT EXHAUST PIPE	
4 cylinder models	1
6 cylinder models	2
INTERMEDIATE PIPE	
4 cylinder models	1
6 cylinder models	2
SILENCER AND TAIL PIPE	
4 cylinder models	1
6 cylinder models	2

EXHAUST SYSTEM

Key to illustration of exhaust system for 4 cylinder models

1. Front exhaust pipe complete. 2 litre Petrol and Diesel
2. Front exhaust pipe complete. 88 2½ litre Petrol 1961 onwards
3. Exhaust pipe heat shield, long ⎫
4. Exhaust pipe heat shield, short ⎬ 1958–60 Petrol models
5. Pipe clamp ⎫
6. Bolt (¼ in. UNF x ⅞ in. long) ⎬ Fixing heat shield to front exhaust pipe — Diesel models up to vehicle suffix 'C' inclusive
7. Spring washer ⎬
8. Nut (¼ in. UNF) ⎭
9. Bracket, exhaust manifold to heat shield. Up to engine suffix 'H' inclusive
10. Shield, exhaust manifold. Up to engine suffix 'H' inclusive
11. Bolt (5/16 in. UNF x ¾ in. long) ⎫
12. Plain washer ⎬ Fixing bracket to heat shield
13. Spring washer ⎬
14. Nut (5/16 in. UNF) ⎭
15. Distance washer for heat shield
16. Steady strip for heat shield
17. Bolt (5/16 in. UNC x 1¼ in. long) ⎫ Fixing steady strip, heat shield and distance washer to manifold
18. Plain washer ⎬
19. Spring washer ⎭
20. Bolt (5/16 in. UNC x ⅞ in. long) ⎫ Fixing heatshield and steady strip to manifold — Up to engine suffix 'H' inclusive
21. Plain washer ⎬
22. Spring washer ⎭
23. Bolt (¼ in. UNF x 7/16 in. long) ⎫ Fixing heat shield to steady strip
24. Plain washer ⎬
25. Spring washer ⎭
26. Joint washer for exhaust pipe. Diesel and 2 litre Petrol models
27. Spring washer ⎫ Fixing exhaust pipe to manifold — 2 litre Petrol models
28. Nut (5/16 in. BSF) ⎭
29. Intermediate exhaust pipe. 88 Petrol models 1958–60. Diesel models
30. Silencer complete, RHStg
31. Silencer complete, LHStg
32. Joint washer ⎫
33. Bolt (5/16 in. UNF x 1 in. long) ⎬ Fixing silencer to intermediate pipe
34. Spring washer ⎬
35. Nut (5/16 in. UNF) ⎭
36. Bolt (5/16 in. UNF x 1½ in. long) ⎫ Fixing intermediate pipe to front exhaust pipe
37. Spring washer ⎬
38. Nut (5/16 in. UNF) ⎭
39. Flexible mounting, intermediate exhaust pipe
40. Clamp plate ⎫
41. Distance piece ⎬ Fixing flexible mounting to chassis
42. Bolt (¼ in. UNF x 1 in. long) ⎬
43. Self-locking nut (¼ in. UNF) ⎭
44. Plate for flexible mounting
45. Bolt (¼ in. UNF x 1 in. long) ⎫ Fixing plate to flexible mounting — 88
46. Self-locking nut (¼ in. UNF) ⎭
47. Pipe clamp
48. Bolt (5/16 in. UNF x 1 in. long) ⎫ Fixing pipe clamp to flexible mounting plate
49. Shakeproof washer ⎬
50. Spring washer ⎬
51. Nut (5/16 in. UNF) ⎭
52. Bolt (¼ in. UNF x 1 in. long) ⎫ Fixing pipe clamp to exhaust pipe
53. Spring washer ⎬
54. Nut (¼ in. UNF) ⎭
55. Flexible mounting for tail pipe
56. Distance piece
57. Clamp plate, upper ⎫ Fixing flexible mounting to chassis frame and clamp bracket — 88
58. Packing plate, upper ⎬
59. Packing plate, lower ⎬
60. Clamp plate, lower ⎬
61. Bolt (¼ in. UNF x 1½ in. long) ⎬
62. Plain washer ⎬
63. Self-locking nut (¼ in. UNF) ⎭
64. Pipe clamp bracket, RHStg
65. Pipe clamp bracket, LHStg
66. Saddle for clamp bracket
67. Bolt (5/16 in. UNF x 1 in. long) ⎫ Fixing exhaust pipe to clamp bracket
68. Spring washer ⎬
69. Nut (5/16 in. UNF) ⎭

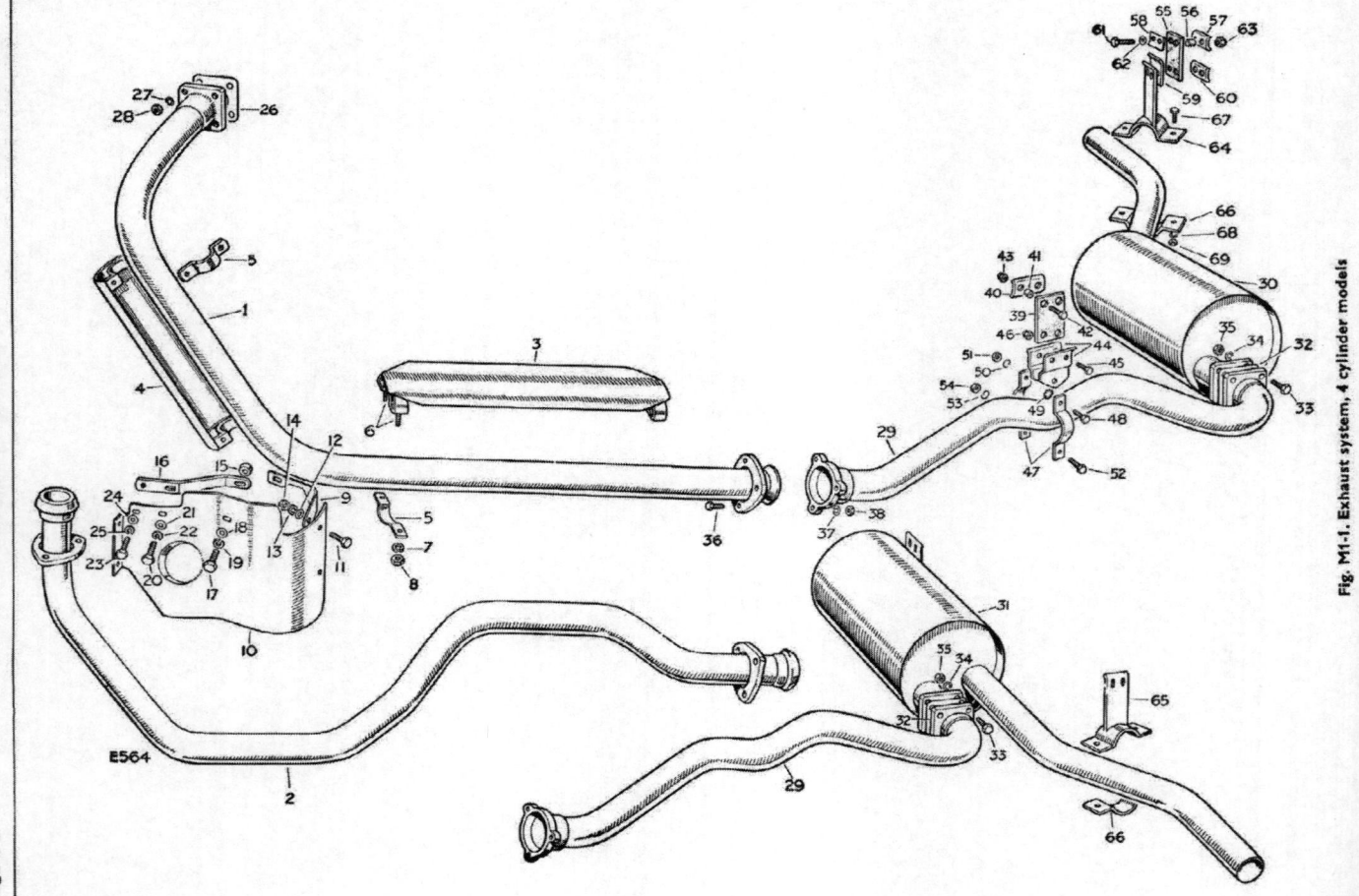

Fig. M1-1. Exhaust system, 4 cylinder models

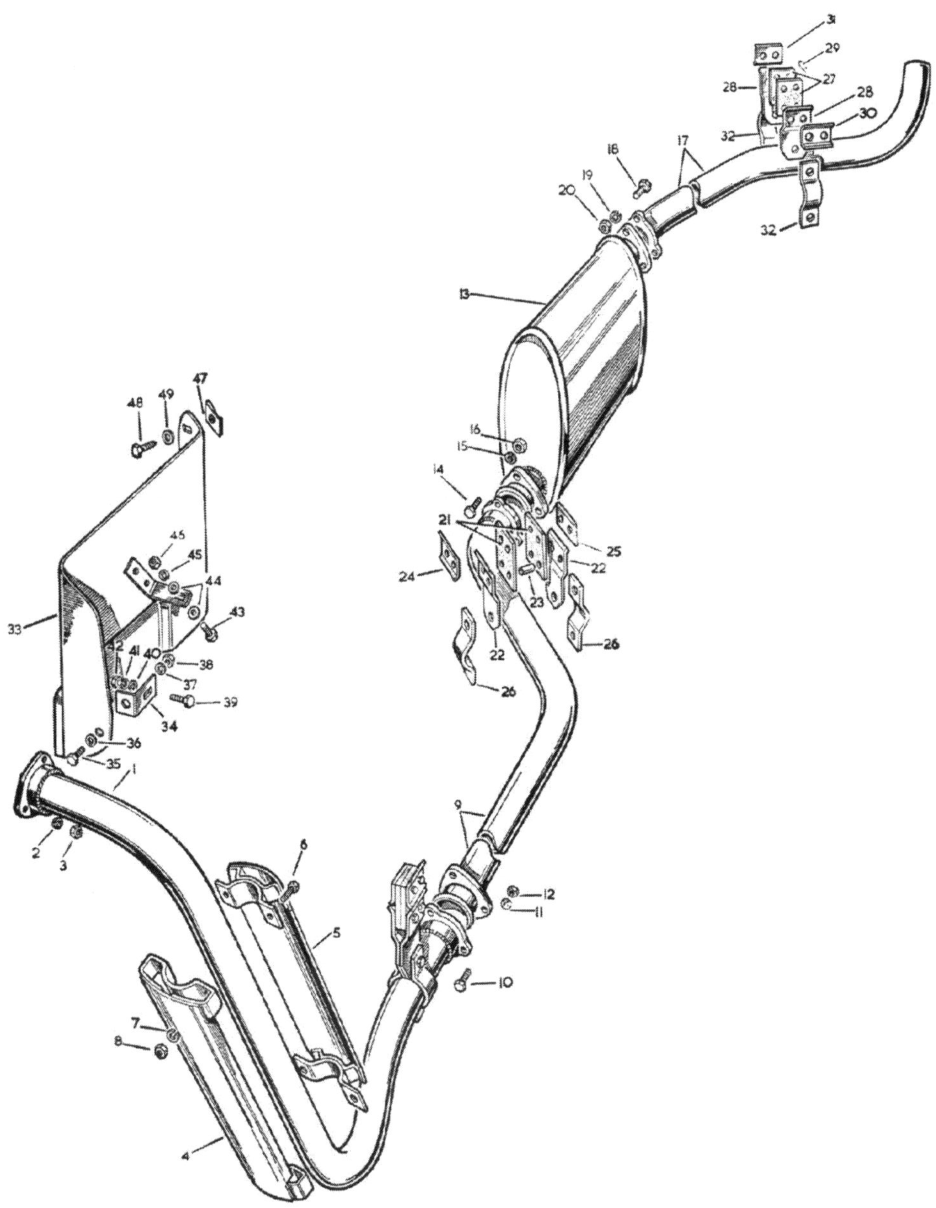

EXHAUST SYSTEM

Key to illustration of exhaust system for 6 cylinder models

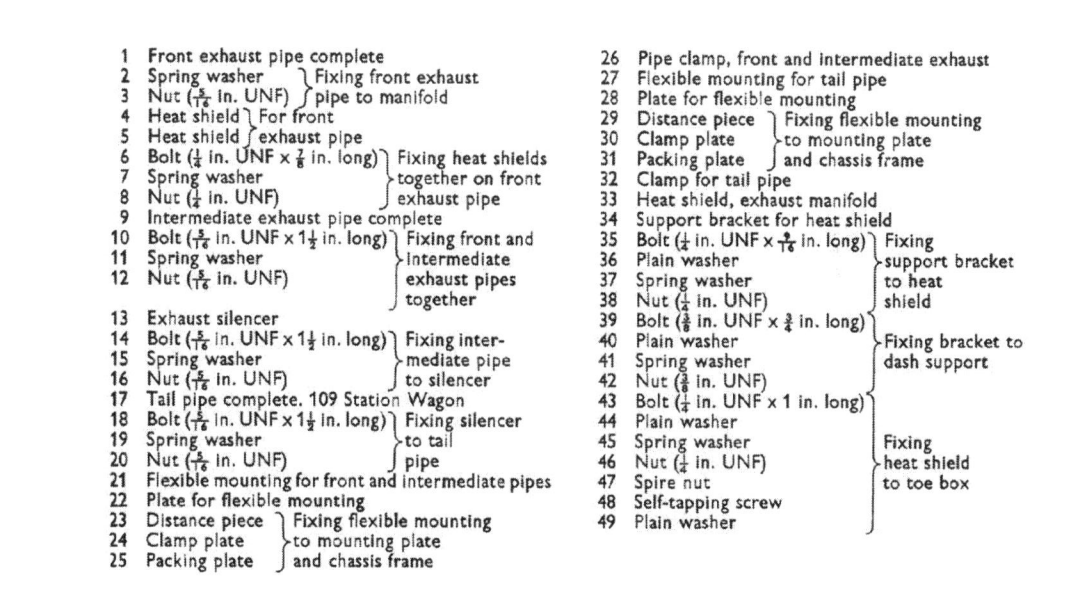

1. Front exhaust pipe complete
2. Spring washer — Fixing front exhaust pipe to manifold
3. Nut ($\frac{7}{16}$ in. UNF)
4. Heat shield — For front exhaust pipe
5. Bolt ($\frac{1}{4}$ in. UNF × $\frac{7}{8}$ in. long) — Fixing heat shields together on front exhaust pipe
6.
7. Spring washer
8. Nut ($\frac{1}{4}$ in. UNF)
9. Intermediate exhaust pipe complete
10. Bolt ($\frac{5}{16}$ in. UNF × 1$\frac{1}{2}$ in. long) — Fixing front and intermediate exhaust pipes together
11. Spring washer
12. Nut ($\frac{5}{16}$ in. UNF)
13. Exhaust silencer
14. Bolt ($\frac{5}{16}$ in. UNF × 1$\frac{1}{2}$ in. long) — Fixing intermediate pipe to silencer
15. Spring washer
16. Nut ($\frac{5}{16}$ in. UNF)
17. Tail pipe complete, 109 Station Wagon
18. Bolt ($\frac{5}{16}$ in. UNF × 1$\frac{1}{2}$ in. long) — Fixing silencer to tail pipe
19. Spring washer
20. Nut ($\frac{5}{16}$ in. UNF)
21. Flexible mounting for front and intermediate pipes
22. Plate for flexible mounting — Fixing flexible mounting to mounting plate and chassis frame
23. Distance piece
24. Clamp plate
25. Packing plate
26. Pipe clamp, front and intermediate exhaust
27. Flexible mounting for tail pipe
28. Plate for flexible mounting — Fixing flexible mounting to mounting plate and chassis frame
29. Distance piece
30. Clamp plate
31. Packing plate
32. Clamp for tail pipe
33. Heat shield, exhaust manifold
34. Support bracket for heat shield
35. Bolt ($\frac{1}{4}$ in. UNF × $\frac{7}{8}$ in. long) — Fixing support bracket to heat shield
36. Plain washer
37. Spring washer
38. Nut ($\frac{1}{4}$ in. UNF)
39. Bolt ($\frac{3}{8}$ in. UNF × $\frac{3}{4}$ in. long) — Fixing bracket to dash support
40. Plain washer
41. Spring washer
42. Nut ($\frac{3}{8}$ in. UNF)
43. Bolt ($\frac{1}{4}$ in. UNF × 1 in. long) — Fixing heat shield to toe box
44. Plain washer
45. Spring washer
46. Nut ($\frac{1}{4}$ in. UNF)
47. Spire nut
48. Self-tapping screw
49. Plain washer

Fig. M1-2. Exhaust system, 6 cylinder models

EXHAUST SYSTEM

Exhaust system, 4 cylinder models, to remove and refit—Operation M1-1

Workshop hand tools:
Spanner sizes: $\frac{5}{16}$ in. BSF, $\frac{7}{16}$ in. AF, $\frac{1}{2}$ in. AF open end

Front exhaust pipe
To remove
1. Remove securing bolts at front exhaust pipe and intermediate pipe joint.
2. Remove nuts and spring washers securing pipe at exhaust manifold.
3. Withdraw the exhaust pipe and joint washer.

To refit
1. Reverse the removal procedure.

Intermediate exhaust pipe
To remove
1. Remove securing bolts at front exhaust pipe and silencer.
2. Remove supporting clamp and withdraw intermediate exhaust pipe.

To refit
1. Reverse the removal procedure, leaving the supporting clamps loose until the pipe has been secured firmly to front exhaust pipe and silencer.

Exhaust silencer (RHStg models only)
To remove
1. Remove the bolts securing intermediate pipe to silencer and release support saddle from silencer tail pipe, keeping silencer supported by hand.
2. Withdraw silencer assembly.

To refit
1. Reverse removal procedure, ensuring that the bolts securing intermediate pipe to silencer are fully tightened before finally clamping the tail pipe support.

Exhaust silencer (LHStg models only)
To remove
1. Remove bolts securing intermediate pipe to silencer.
2. Keeping the silencer supported, release the supporting strap for silencer right-hand side and saddle clamp on tail pipe, then withdraw silencer assembly.

To refit
1. Fit the silencer in position and loosely support by means of supporting strap and saddle clamp.
2. Secure the intermediate pipe to silencer.
3. Finally tighten bolts securing support strap and saddle clamp.

Exhaust system, 6 cylinder models, to remove and refit—Operation M1-2

Workshop hand tools:
Spanner sizes: $\frac{7}{16}$ in. AF, $\frac{1}{2}$ in. AF, $\frac{9}{16}$ in. AF open end

Front exhaust pipe
To remove
1. Remove the securing bolts at the front exhaust pipe and intermediate pipe joint.
2. Remove the securing bolts fixing the front exhaust pipe to the flexible mounting.
3. Remove nuts and spring washers securing pipe at exhaust manifold.
4. Withdraw the exhaust pipe.
5. If required, remove the bolts securing the heat shield to the front exhaust pipe and withdraw the two halves of the shield.

To refit
1. Reverse the removal procedure, leaving the flexible mounting loose until the pipe has been firmly secured to the manifold and intermediate pipe.

Intermediate exhaust pipe
To remove
1. Remove securing bolts at front exhaust pipe and silencer.
2. Remove the securing bolts fixing the intermediate pipe to the flexible mounting and withdraw the intermediate pipe.

To refit
1. Reverse the removal procedure, leaving the flexible mounting loose until the pipe has been firmly secured to front exhaust pipe and silencer.

Exhaust silencer and tail pipe
To remove
1. Remove the bolts securing the intermediate pipe to the silencer and the bolts securing the tail pipe to the flexible mounting, keeping the silencer supported by hand.
2. Withdraw the silencer assembly.
3. If required, remove the bolts securing the tail pipe to the silencer and withdraw tail pipe.

To refit
1. Reverse the removal procedure, ensuring that the bolts securing intermediate pipe to silencer are fully tightened before finally clamping the tail pipe support.

SECTION N—ELECTRICAL EQUIPMENT

INDEX—ELECTRICAL EQUIPMENT

Note: A comprehensive, detailed index is included at the end of this manual

Description	Operation Number
Circuit diagrams	At beginning of Section
Battery	1
Headlamps	2
Side lamps	3
Stop and tail lamps	4
Flasher lamp	5
Rear number plate illumination lamp	6
Stop lamp switch	7
Engine starter switches	8
Dip switch for head amps	9
Flasher switch	10
Flasher unit	11
Ignition coil—Petrol models	12
Distributor—Petrol models	13
Heater plugs—Diesel models	14
Fuse and junction boxes	15
Current voltage regulators	16
Horn push	17
Electric horn	18
Windscreen wiper	19
Starter motor—Petrol models	20
Starter motor—Diesel models	21
Dynamo	22
Alternator output control unit	23
Alternator field isolating relay	24
Alternator warning light control	25
Battery charging system with alternator	26
Alternator	27
Fault Diagnosis	At end of Section
Data	At end of Section

CIRCUIT DIAGRAMS

IMPORTANT

Before commencing any work on the electrical equipment, check the polarity of the system to avoid the possibility of fitting unsuitable components or making wrong connections, resulting in damage.

All 2¼ litre Petrol and Diesel models up to vehicle suffix 'C' inclusive incorporate a **POSITIVE EARTH** electrical system. 2¼ litre Petrol and Diesel models from vehicle suffix 'D' onwards, and all 2.6 litre Petrol models are equipped with a **NEGATIVE EARTH** electrical system.

Caution: When transistorised electrical equipment, such as radios, tachometers, etc., are fitted, it is most important to ensure correct polarity of the electrical connections, otherwise the equipment may be irreparably damaged.

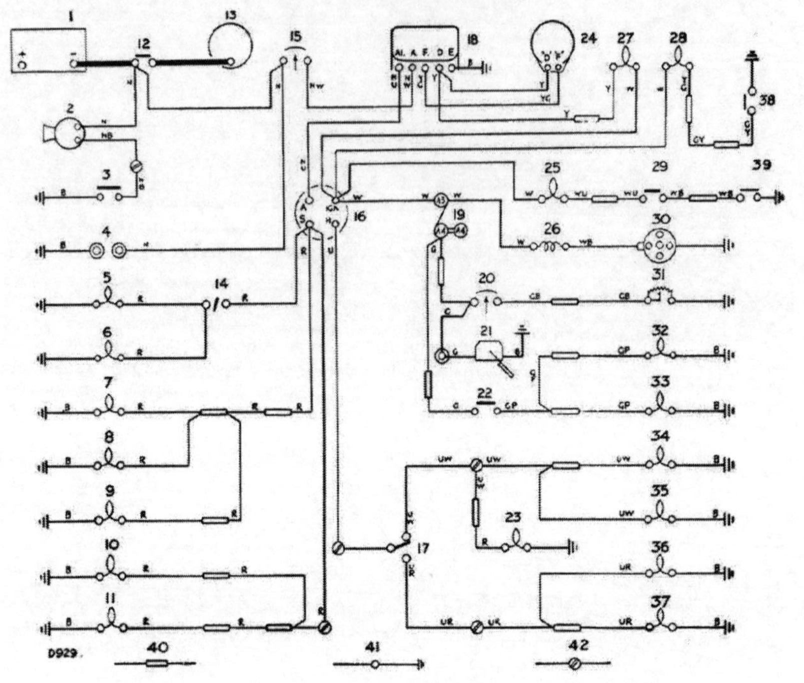

ELECTRICAL EQUIPMENT

Section N—Land-Rover

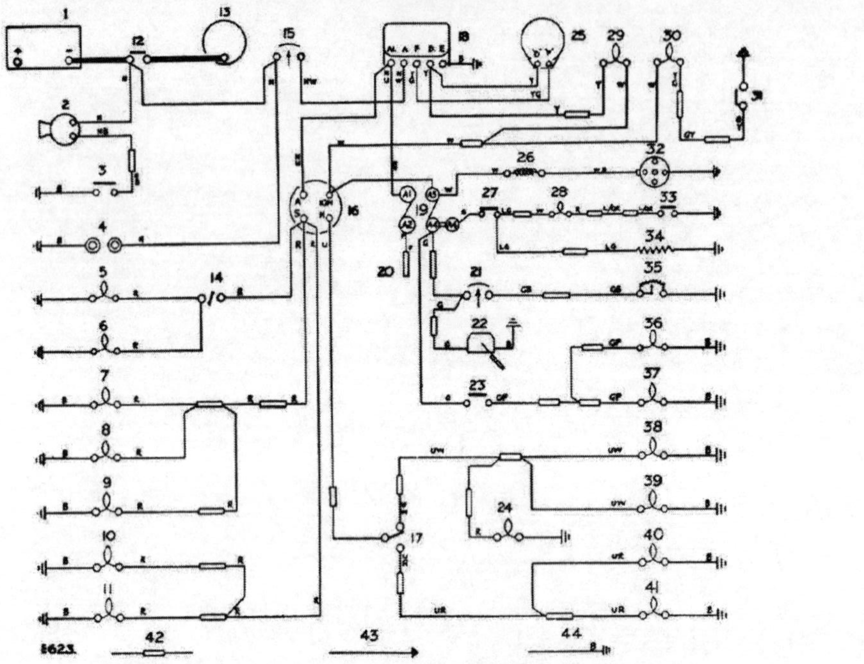

Fig. N1-2. Circuit diagram, 2¼ litre Petrol models, Series IIA, positive earth

1. Battery, 12 volt
2. Horn
3. Horn push button
4. Inspection light sockets
5. Panel illumination
6. Panel illumination
7. Tail light
8. Number plate illumination
9. Tail light
10. Side light
11. Side light
12. Starter switch
13. Starter
14. Panel light switch
15. Ammeter
16. Ignition and lighting switch
17. Headlight dip switch
18. Voltage control box
19. Fuse box
20. To interior lights
21. Fuel gauge
22. Screen wiper, plug and socket
23. Stop light switch
24. Main beam warning light
25. Dynamo
26. Ignition coil
27. Mixture warning light
28. Mixture warning light
29. Charging warning light
30. Oil pressure warning light
31. Oil pressure switch
32. Distributor
33. Mixture thermostat switch
34. Carburetter heater element, optional equipment
35. Gauge, fuel tank
36. Stop light
37. Stop light
38. Headlight, main
39. Headlight, dip
40. Headlight, main
41. Headlight, dip
42. Snap connectors
43. Earth connections via terminals and fixing bolts
44. Earth connections via cables

Key to cable colours

B—Black   G—Green   N—Brown   P—Purple   R—Red   U—Blue
W—White   Y—Yellow   RN—Red with Brown, and so on

When cables have two-colour code letters, the first denotes the main and the latter the tracer. On vehicles to the North American specification, the connections at the lighting switch are such that the sidelamps are extinguished when the headlamps are in use.

ELECTRICAL EQUIPMENT

Section N—Land-Rover

Fig. N1-1. Circuit diagram, 2¼ litre Petrol models, Series II, positive earth

1. Battery, 12 volt
2. Horn
3. Horn push button
4. Inspection light sockets
5. Panel illumination
6. Panel illumination
7. Tail light
8. Number plate illumination
9. Tail light
10. Side light
11. Side light
12. Starter switch
13. Starter
14. Panel light switch
15. Ammeter
16. Ignition and lighting switch
17. Headlight dip switch
18. Voltage control box
19. Fuse box
20. Fuel gauge
21. Screen wiper, plug and socket
22. Stop light switch
23. Main beam warning light
24. Dynamo
25. Ignition coil
26. Charging warning light
27. Mixture warning light
28. Mixture warning light
29. Mixture switch
30. Distributor
31. Fuel gauge, petrol tank
32. Stop light
33. Stop light
34. Headlight, main
35. Headlight, dip
36. Headlight, main
37. Headlight, dip
38. Oil pressure switch
39. Thermostat
40. Snap connectors
41. Earth connections via terminals and fixing bolts
42. Junction box terminals

Key to cable colours

B—Black   G—Green   N—Brown   P—Purple   R—Red   U—Blue
W—White   Y—Yellow   RN—Red with Brown, and so on

When cables have two-colour code letters, the first denotes the main and the latter the tracer. On vehicles to the North American specification, the connections at the lighting switch are such that the sidelamps are extinguished when the headlamps are in use.

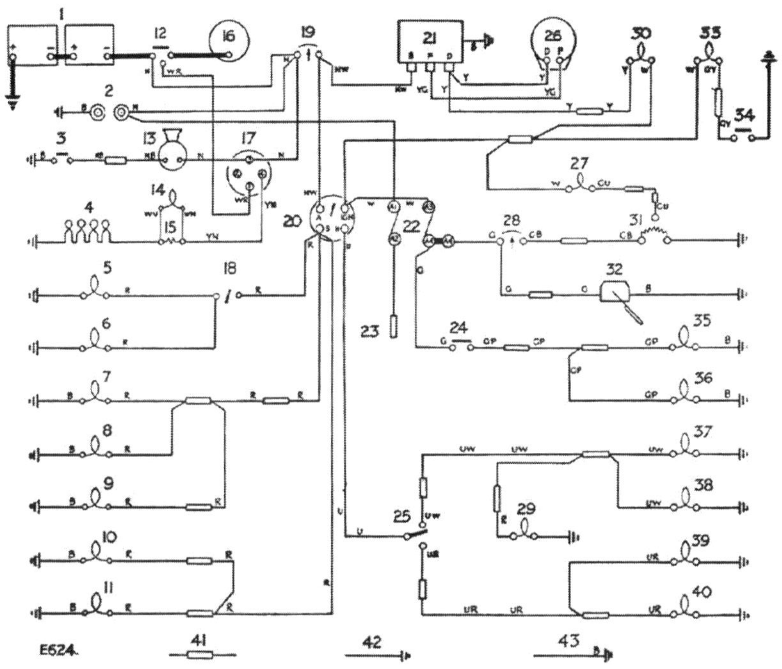

ELECTRICAL EQUIPMENT

Fig. N1-3. Circuit diagram, 2¼ litre Diesel models, Series IIA, positive earth

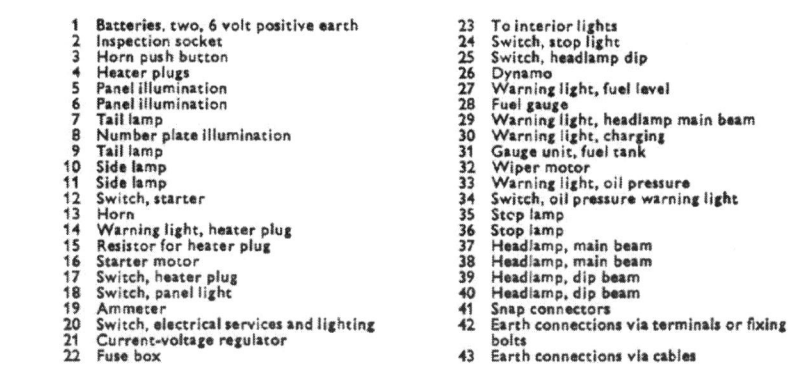

1. Batteries, two, 6 volt positive earth
2. Inspection socket
3. Horn push button
4. Heater plugs
5. Panel illumination
6. Panel illumination
7. Tail lamp
8. Number plate illumination
9. Side lamp
10. Side lamp
11. Horn
12. Switch, starter
13. Horn
14. Warning light, heater plug
15. Resistor for heater plug
16. Starter motor
17. Switch, heater plug
18. Switch, panel light
19. Ammeter
20. Switch, electrical services and lighting
21. Current-voltage regulator
22. Fuse box
23. To interior lights
24. Switch, stop light
25. Switch, headlamp dip
26. Dynamo
27. Warning light, fuel level
28. Fuel gauge
29. Warning light, headlamp main beam
30. Warning light, charging
31. Gauge unit, fuel tank
32. Wiper motor
33. Warning light, oil pressure
34. Switch, oil pressure warning light
35. Stop lamp
36. Stop lamp
37. Headlamp, main beam
38. Headlamp, main beam
39. Headlamp, dip beam
40. Headlamp, dip beam
41. Snap connectors
42. Earth connections via terminals or fixing bolts
43. Earth connections via cables

Key to cable colours

B—Black   G—Green   N—Brown   O—Orange   P—Purple   R—Red
S—Slate   U—Blue   L—Light   W—White   Y—Yellow   RN—Red with Brown

When cables have two-colour code letters, the first denotes the main and the latter the tracer. On vehicles to the North American specification, the connections at the lighting switch are such that the sidelamps are extinguished when the headlamps are in use.

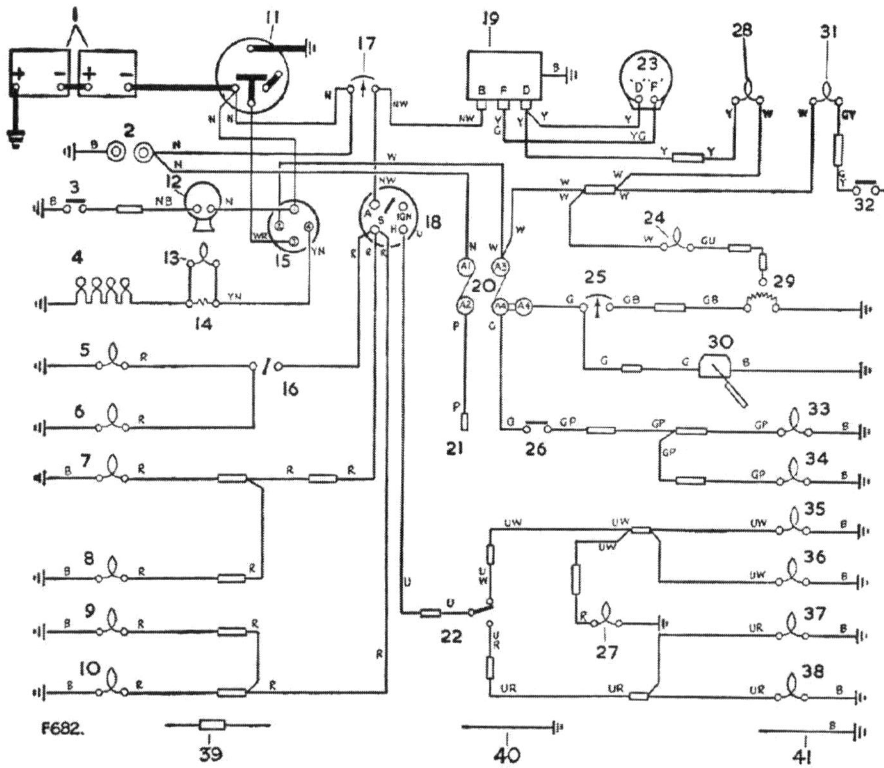

ELECTRICAL EQUIPMENT

Fig. N1-4. Circuit diagram, 'Regular' and 'Long', Diesel models, Series IIA, with combined electrical services, starter and heater plug switch, positive earth

1. Batteries, two, 6 volt positive earth
2. Inspection socket
3. Horn push button
4. Heater plugs
5. Panel illumination
6. Panel illumination
7. Tail and number plate illumination lamp
8. Tail and number plate illumination lamp
9. Side lamp
10. Side lamp
11. Starter motor
12. Horn
13. Warning light, heater plug
14. Resistance for heater plug
15. Electrical services, starter and heater plug switch
16. Switch, panel light
17. Ammeter
18. Lighting switch
19. Current-voltage regulator
20. Fuse box
21. To interior lights
22. Switch, headlamp dip
23. Dynamo
24. Warning light, fuel level
25. Fuel gauge
26. Switch, stop light
27. Warning light, headlamp main beam
28. Warning light, charging
29. Gauge unit, fuel tank
30. Windscreen wiper motor
31. Warning light, oil pressure
32. Switch, oil pressure warning light
33. Stop lamp
34. Stop lamp
35. Headlamp, main beam
36. Headlamp, main beam
37. Headlamp, dip beam
38. Headlamp, dip beam
39. Snap connectors
40. Earth connections via terminals or fixing bolts
41. Earth connections via cables

Key to cable colours

B—Black   G—Green   N—Brown   O—Orange   P—Purple
R—Red   U—Blue   S—Slate   L—Light   W—White   Y—Yellow   RN—Red with Brown

When cables have two-colour code letters, the first denotes the main and the latter colour the tracer colour.

375

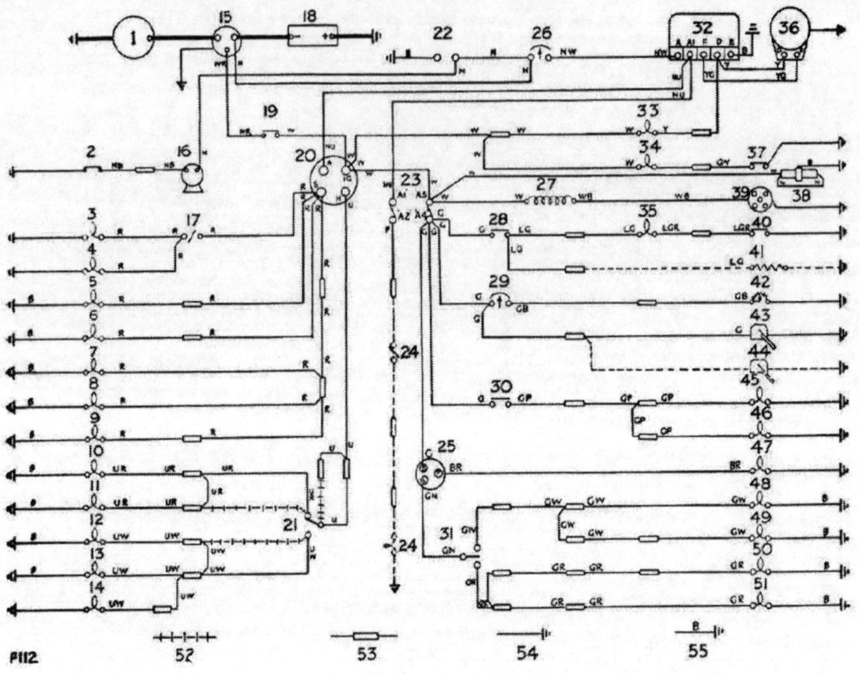

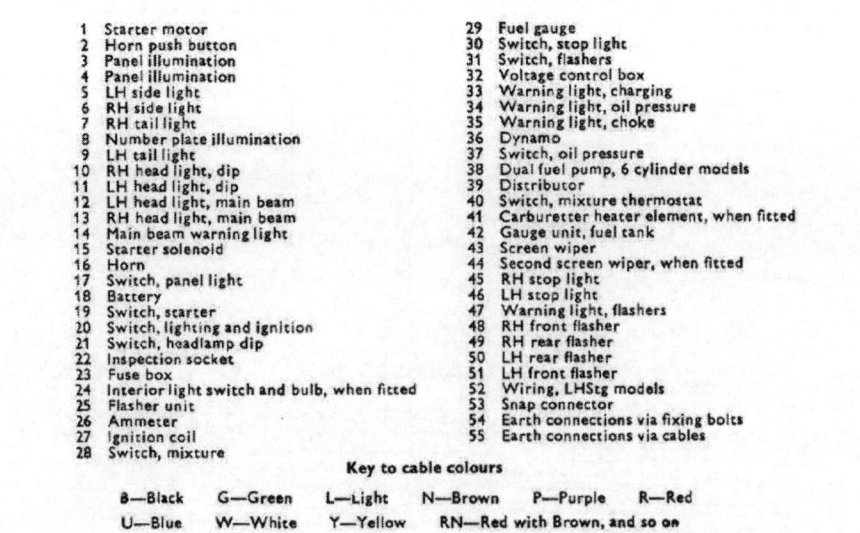

ELECTRICAL EQUIPMENT

Section N—Land-Rover

Fig. N1-5. Circuit diagram, 'Forward Control', Petrol models, Series IIA, positive earth

1. Starter motor
2. Horn push button
3. Panel illumination
4. Panel illumination
5. LH side light
6. RH side light
7. LH tail light
8. RH tail light
9. Number plate illumination
10. RH head light, dip
11. LH head light, dip
12. LH head light, main beam
13. RH head light, main beam
14. Main beam warning light
15. Starter solenoid
16. Horn
17. Switch, panel light
18. Battery
19. Fuse box
20. Switch, starter
21. Switch, lighting and ignition
22. Switch, headlamp dip
23. Inspection socket
24. Interior light switch and bulb, when fitted
25. Snap connector
26. Ammeter
27. Ignition coil
28. Switch, mixture
29. Fuel gauge
30. Switch, stop light
31. Switch, flashers
32. Voltage control box
33. Warning light, charging
34. Warning light, oil pressure
35. Warning light, choke
36. Dynamo
37. Switch, oil pressure
38. Dual fuel pump, 6 cylinder models
39. Distributor
40. Switch, mixture thermostat
41. Carburetter heater element, when fitted
42. Gauge unit, fuel tank
43. Screen wiper
44. Second screen wiper, when fitted
45. RH stop light
46. LH stop light
47. Warning light, flashers
48. RH front flasher
49. RH rear flasher
50. LH rear flasher
51. LH front flasher
52. Wiring, LHStg models
53. Snap connector
54. Earth connections via fixing bolts
55. Earth connections via cables

Key to cable colours

B—Black G—Green L—Light N—Brown P—Purple R—Red
U—Blue W—White Y—Yellow RN—Red with Brown, and so on

When cables have two-colour code letters the first denotes the main and the latter the tracer.

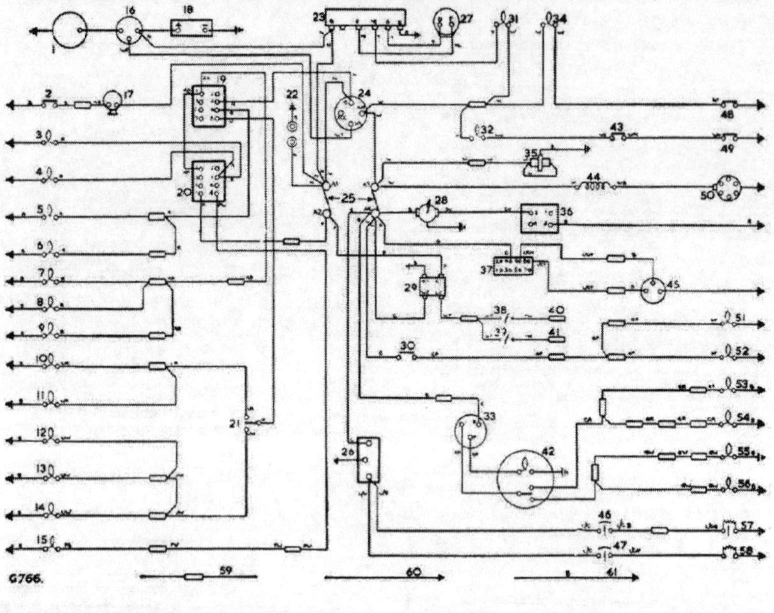

Fig. N1-6. Circuit diagram, North American dollar area, 2.6 litre 109 Station Wagon, LHStg, negative earth

1. Starter motor
2. Horn push
3. Panel illumination
4. Panel illumination
5. Side lamp, RH
6. Side lamp, LH
7. Tail lamp, RH
8. Tail lamp, LH
9. Number plate illumination
10. Headlamp dip, RH
11. Headlamp dip, LH
12. Headlamp main beam, RH
13. Headlamp main beam, LH
14. Headlamp main beam warning light
15. Interior light
16. Starter solenoid
17. Horn
18. Battery
19. Lighting switch
20. Panel and interior light switch
21. Foot dipper switch
22. Inspection lamp socket
23. Voltage regulator
24. Ignition/starter switch
25. Fuses
26. 10 volt stabiliser
27. Dynamo
28. Windscreen wiper motor
29. Snap connector
30. Stop light switch
31. Ignition warning light
32. Choke warning light
33. Direction indicator unit
34. Oil pressure warning light
35. Dual petrol pump
36. Windscreen wiper switch
37. Heater switch
38. Switch for heated windscreen, screen No. 1
39. Switch for heated windscreen, screen No. 2
40. Heated windscreen, screen No. 1
41. Heated windscreen, screen No. 2
42. Direction indicator switch
43. Choke switch
44. Coil
45. Two-speed heater unit
46. Fuel gauge
47. Water temperature gauge
48. Oil pressure switch
49. Choke thermostat
50. Distributor
51. Stop lamp, LH
52. Stop lamp, RH
53. Indicator lamp, LH front
54. Indicator lamp, LH rear
55. Indicator lamp, RH rear
56. Indicator lamp, RH front
57. Fuel tank unit
58. Water temperature transmitter
59. Snap connector
60. Earth connections via terminals or fixing bolts
61. Earth connections made via cables

Cable colour code

B—Black P—Purple R—Red
Y—Yellow U—Blue L—Light
W—White G—Green N—Brown

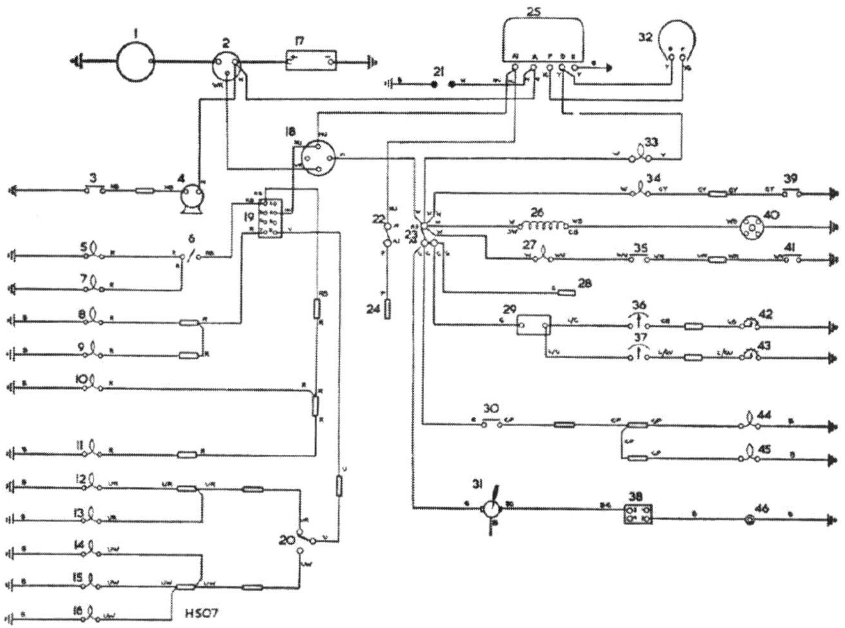

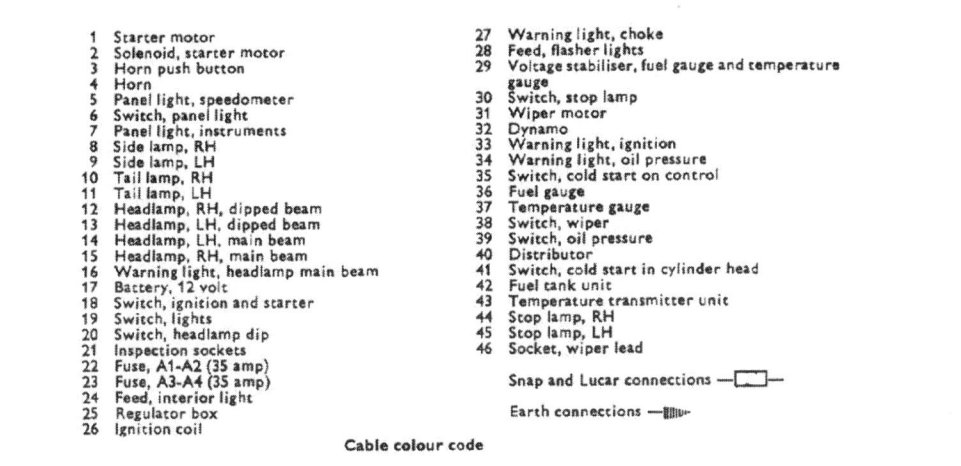

Section N—Land-Rover   ELECTRICAL EQUIPMENT

Fig. N1-7. Circuit diagram, 2¼ litre 'Regular', 'Long' and Station Wagon, Petrol models, negative earth

1. Starter motor
2. Solenoid, starter motor
3. Horn push button
4. Horn
5. Panel light, speedometer
6. Switch, panel light
7. Panel light, instruments
8. Side lamp, RH
9. Side lamp, LH
10. Tail lamp, RH
11. Tail lamp, LH
12. Headlamp, RH, dipped beam
13. Headlamp, LH, dipped beam
14. Headlamp, LH, main beam
15. Headlamp, RH, headlamp main beam
16. Warning light, headlamp main beam
17. Battery, 12 volt
18. Switch, ignition and starter
19. Switch, lights
20. Switch, headlamp dip
21. Inspection sockets
22. Fuse, A1–A2 (35 amp)
23. Fuse, A3–A4 (35 amp)
24. Feed, interior light
25. Regulator box
26. Ignition coil
27. Warning light, choke
28. Feed, flasher lights
29. Voltage stabiliser, fuel gauge and temperature gauge
30. Switch, stop lamp
31. Wiper motor
32. Dynamo
33. Warning light, ignition
34. Warning light, oil pressure
35. Switch, cold start on control
36. Fuel gauge
37. Temperature gauge
38. Switch, wiper
39. Switch, oil pressure
40. Distributor
41. Switch, cold start in cylinder head
42. Fuel tank unit
43. Temperature transmitter unit
44. Stop lamp, RH
45. Stop lamp, LH
46. Socket, wiper lead

Snap and Lucar connections
Earth connections

Cable colour code

B—Black	P—Purple	W—White	R—Red	N—Brown
Y—Yellow	U—Blue	G—Green	L—Light	

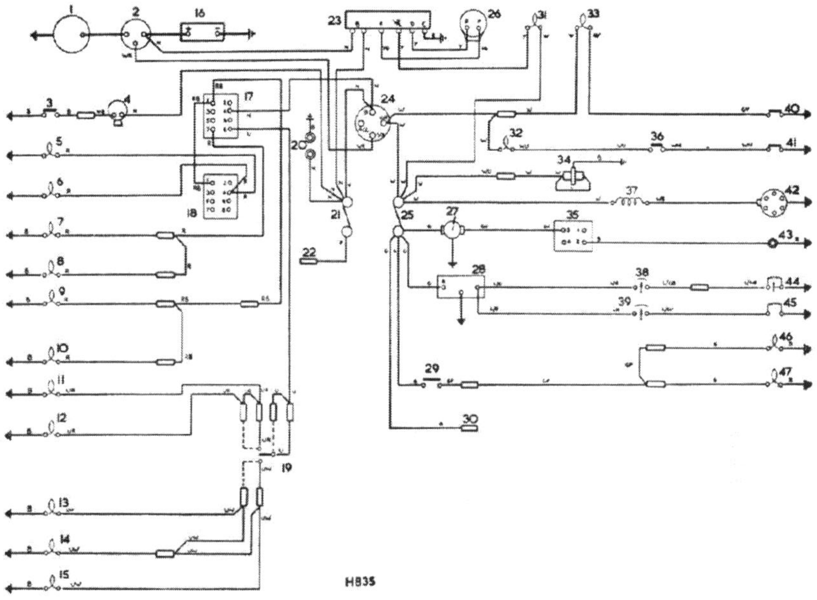

Fig. N1-8. Circuit diagram, 6 cylinder 'Long' and Station Wagon, Petrol models, negative earth

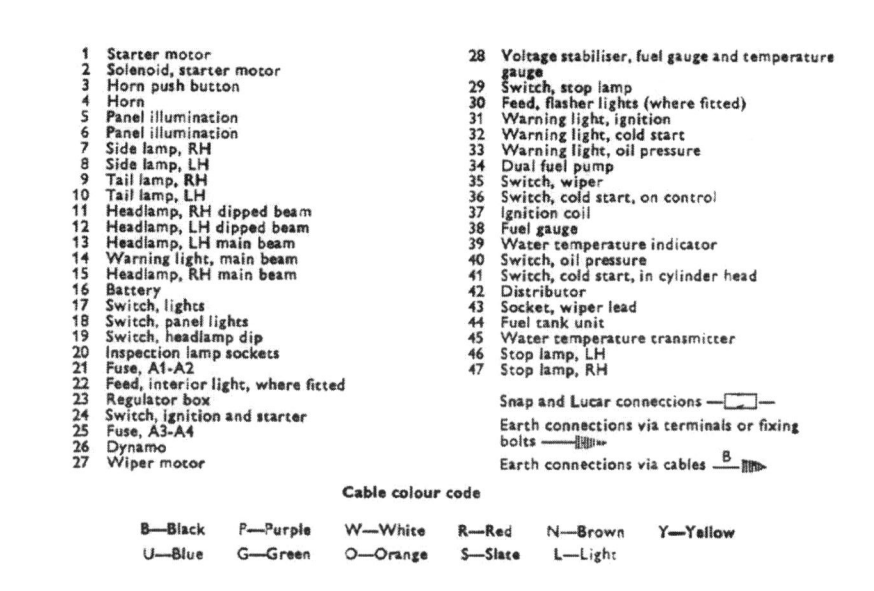

1. Starter motor
2. Solenoid, starter motor
3. Horn push button
4. Horn
5. Panel illumination
6. Panel illumination
7. Side lamp, RH
8. Side lamp, LH
9. Tail lamp, RH
10. Tail lamp, LH
11. Headlamp, RH dipped beam
12. Headlamp, LH dipped beam
13. Headlamp, LH main beam
14. Headlamp, RH main beam
15. Warning light, main beam
16. Battery
17. Switch, panel lights
18. Switch, headlamp dip
19. Inspection lamp sockets
20. Fuse, A1–A2
21. Regulator box
22. Feed, interior light, where fitted
23. Fuse, A3–A4
24. Switch, ignition and starter
25. Dynamo
26. Wiper motor
27. Ignition coil
28. Voltage stabiliser, fuel gauge and temperature gauge
29. Switch, stop lamp
30. Feed, flasher lights (where fitted)
31. Warning light, ignition
32. Warning light, cold start
33. Warning light, oil pressure
34. Dual fuel pump
35. Switch, wiper
36. Switch, cold start, on control
37. Ignition coil
38. Fuel gauge
39. Water temperature indicator
40. Switch, oil pressure
41. Switch, cold start, in cylinder head
42. Distributor
43. Socket, wiper lead
44. Fuel tank unit
45. Water temperature transmitter
46. Stop lamp, LH
47. Stop lamp, RH

Snap and Lucar connections
Earth connections via terminals or fixing bolts
Earth connections via cables

Cable colour code

B—Black	P—Purple	W—White	R—Red	N—Brown	Y—Yellow
U—Blue	G—Green	O—Orange	S—Slate	L—Light	

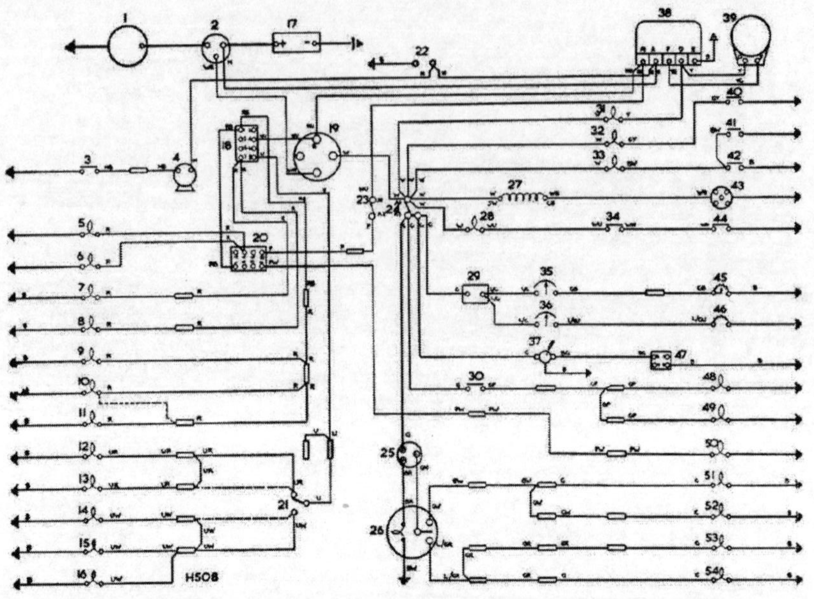

ELECTRICAL EQUIPMENT

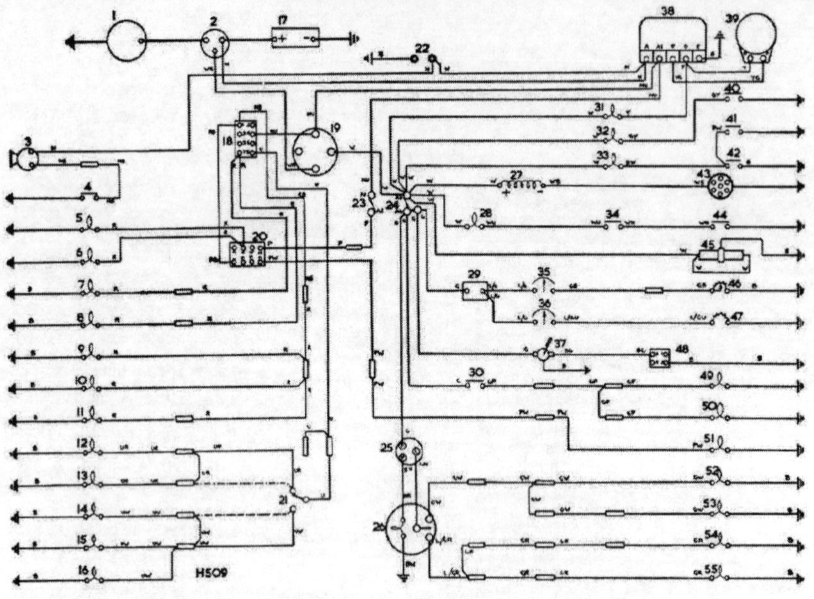

Fig. N1-10. Circuit diagram, 6 cylinder Forward Control, Petrol models, Series IIA, negative earth

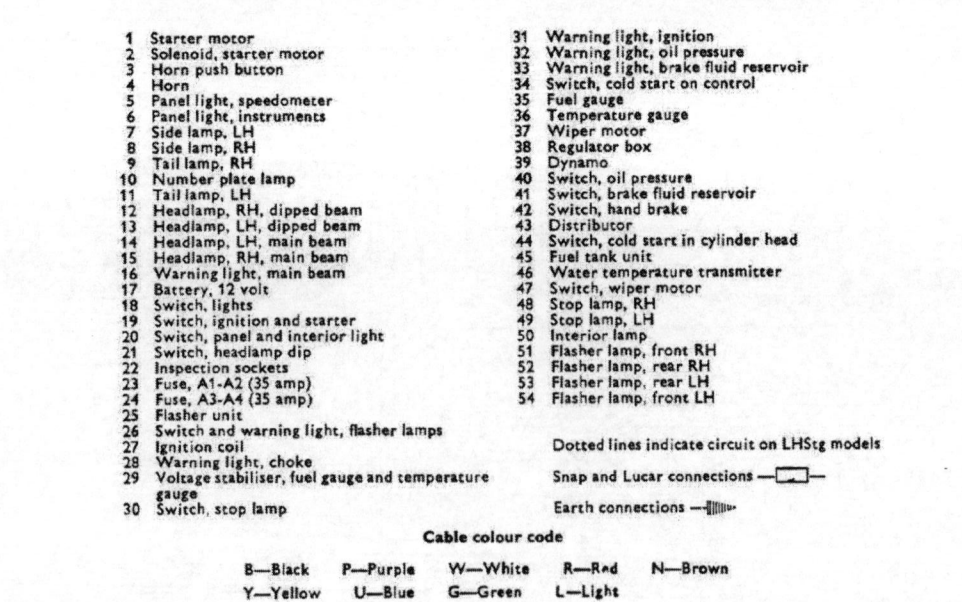

1. Starter motor
2. Solenoid, starter motor
3. Horn
4. Horn push button
5. Panel light, speedometer
6. Panel light, instruments
7. Side lamp, LH
8. Side lamp, RH
9. Tail lamp, LH
10. Number plate lamp
11. Tail lamp, LH
12. Headlamp, RH, dipped beam
13. Headlamp, LH, dipped beam
14. Headlamp, LH, main beam
15. Headlamp, RH, main beam
16. Warning light, main beam
17. Battery, 12 volt
18. Switch, lights
19. Switch, ignition and starter
20. Switch, panel and interior light
21. Switch, headlamp dip
22. inspection sockets
23. Fuse, A1-A2 (35 amp)
24. Fuse, A3-A4 (35 amp)
25. Flasher unit
26. Switch and warning light, flasher lamps
27. Ignition coil
28. Warning light, choke
29. Voltage stabiliser, fuel gauge and water temperature gauge
30. Switch, stop lamp
31. Warning lights, ignition
32. Warning light, oil pressure
33. Warning light, brake fluid reservoir
34. Switch, cold start on control
35. Fuel gauge
36. Temperature gauge
37. Wiper motor
38. Regulator box
39. Dynamo
40. Switch, oil pressure
41. Switch, brake fluid reservoir
42. Switch, brake servo
43. Distributor
44. Switch, cold start in cylinder head
45. Fuel pump
46. Fuel tank unit
47. Water temperature transmitter
48. Switch, wiper motor
49. Stop lamp, RH
50. Stop lamp, LH
51. Interior lamp
52. Flasher lamp, front RH
53. Flasher lamp, rear RH
54. Flasher lamp, rear LH
55. Flasher lamp, front LH

Dotted lines indicate circuit on LHStg models

Snap and Lucar connections

Earth connections

Cable colour code

B—Black   P—Purple   W—White   R—Red   N—Brown
Y—Yellow U—Blue   G—Green   L—Light

ELECTRICAL EQUIPMENT

Fig. N1-9. Circuit diagram, 2¼ litre Forward Control, Petrol models, Series IIA, negative earth

1. Starter motor
2. Solenoid, starter motor
3. Horn
4. Horn push button
5. Panel light, speedometer
6. Panel light, instruments
7. Side lamp, LH
8. Side lamp, RH
9. Tail lamp, LH
10. Number plate lamp
11. Tail lamp, LH
12. Headlamp, RH, dipped beam
13. Headlamp, LH, dipped beam
14. Headlamp, LH, main beam
15. Headlamp, RH, main beam
16. Warning light, main beam
17. Battery, 12 volt
18. Switch, lights
19. Switch, ignition and starter
20. Switch, panel and interior light
21. Switch, headlamp dip
22. inspection sockets
23. Fuse, A1-A2 (35 amp)
24. Fuse, A3-A4 (35 amp)
25. Flasher unit
26. Switch and warning light, flasher lamps
27. Ignition coil
28. Warning light, choke
29. Voltage stabiliser, fuel gauge and temperature gauge
30. Switch, stop lamp
31. Warning light, ignition
32. Warning light, oil pressure
33. Warning light, brake fluid reservoir
34. Switch, cold start on control
35. Fuel gauge
36. Temperature gauge
37. Wiper motor
38. Regulator box
39. Dynamo
40. Switch, oil pressure
41. Switch, brake fluid reservoir
42. Switch, hand brake
43. Distributor
44. Switch, cold start in cylinder head
45. Fuel tank unit
46. Water temperature transmitter
47. Switch, wiper motor
48. Stop lamp, RH
49. Stop lamp, LH
50. Interior lamp
51. Flasher lamp, front RH
52. Flasher lamp, rear RH
53. Flasher lamp, rear LH
54. Flasher lamp, front LH

Dotted lines indicate circuit on LHStg models

Snap and Lucar connections

Earth connections

Cable colour code

B—Black   P—Purple   W—White   R—Red   N—Brown
Y—Yellow U—Blue   G—Green   L—Light

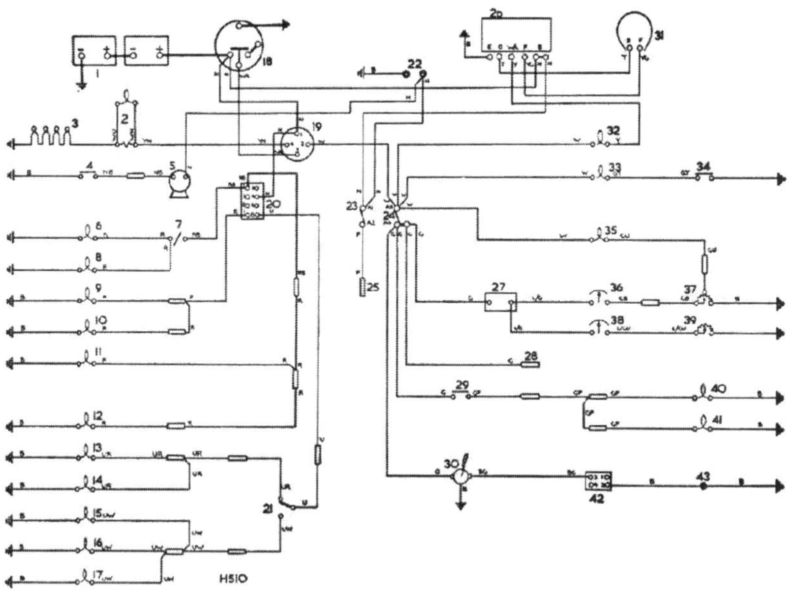

ELECTRICAL EQUIPMENT

Fig. N1-11. Circuit diagram, 2¼ litre 'Regular', 'Long' and Station Wagon, Diesel models, Series IIA, negative earth

1. Batteries, two 6 volt
2. Warning light and resistor, heater plugs
3. Heater plugs
4. Horn push button
5. Horn
6. Panel light, speedometer
7. Switch, panel light
8. Panel light, instrument
9. Side lamp, RH
10. Side lamp, LH
11. Tail lamp, RH
12. Tail lamp, LH
13. Headlamp, RH, dipped beam
14. Headlamp, LH, dipped beam
15. Headlamp, LH, main beam
16. Headlamp, RH, main beam
17. Warning light, headlamp main beam
18. Starter motor
19. Switch, starter-heater plugs
20. Switch, lights
21. Switch, headlamp dip
22. Inspection sockets
23. Fuse, A1–A2 (35 amp)
24. Fuse, A3–A4 (35 amp)
25. Feed, interior light
26. Regulator box
27. Voltage stabiliser, fuel gauge and water temperature gauge
28. Feed, flasher lights
29. Switch, stop lamp
30. Wiper motor
31. Dynamo
32. Warning light, dynamo
33. Warning light, oil pressure
34. Switch, oil pressure
35. Warning light, fuel level
36. Fuel gauge
37. Fuel tank unit
38. Temperature gauge
39. Temperature transmitter unit
40. Stop lamp, RH
41. Stop lamp, LH
42. Switch, wiper motor
43. Socket, wiper lead

Snap and Lucar connections ⬚
Earth connections ⎓

Cable colour code

B—Black P—Purple W—White R—Red N—Brown
Y—Yellow U—Blue G—Green L—Light

ELECTRICAL EQUIPMENT

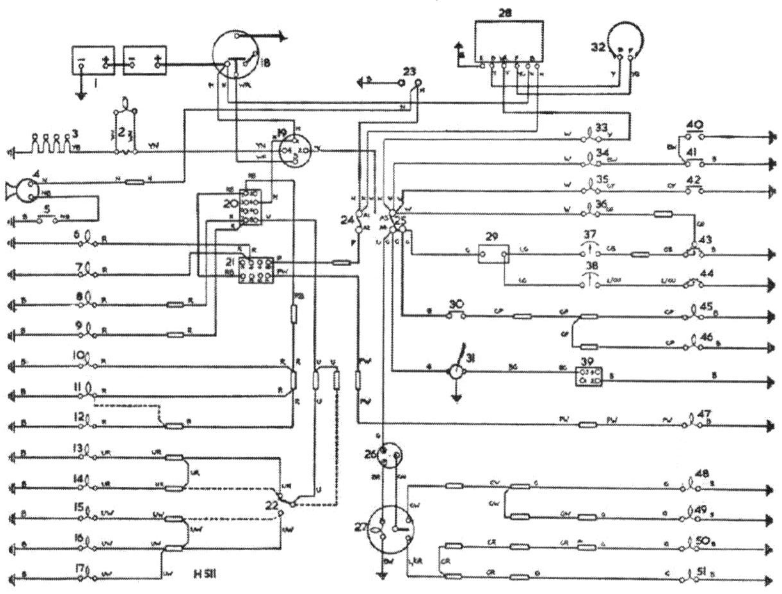

Fig. N1-12. Circuit diagram, 4 cylinder Forward Control, Diesel models, Series IIA, negative earth

1. Batteries, two 6 volt
2. Warning light and resistor, heater plugs
3. Heater plugs
4. Horn push button
5. Horn
6. Panel light, speedometer
7. Switch, panel light
8. Panel light, instrument
9. Side lamp, RH
10. Side lamp, LH
11. Tail lamp, RH
12. Tail lamp, LH
13. Headlamp, RH, dipped beam
14. Headlamp, LH, dipped beam
15. Headlamp, LH, main beam
16. Headlamp, RH, main beam
17. Warning light, main beam
18. Starter motor
19. Switch, starter–heater plugs
20. Switch, lights
21. Switch, panel and interior light
22. Switch, headlamp dip
23. Inspection sockets
24. Fuse, A1–A2 (35 amp)
25. Fuse, A3–A4 (35 amp)
26. Flasher unit
27. Switch and warning light, flasher
28. Regulator box
29. Voltage stabiliser, fuel gauge and temperature gauge
30. Switch, stop lamp
31. Wiper motor
32. Dynamo
33. Warning light, dynamo
34. Warning light, brake fluid reservoir
35. Warning light, oil pressure
36. Warning light, fuel level
37. Fuel gauge
38. Temperature gauge
39. Switch, wiper motor
40. Switch, brake fluid reservoir
41. Switch, brake servo
42. Switch, oil pressure
43. Fuel tank unit
44. Temperature transmitter
45. Stop lamp, RH
46. Stop lamp, LH
47. Interior lamp
48. Flasher lamp, front RH
49. Flasher lamp, rear RH
50. Flasher lamp, rear LH
51. Flasher lamp, front LH

Dotted lines indicate circuit on LHStg models
Snap and Lucar connections ⬚
Earth connections ⎓

Cable colour code

B—Black P—Purple W—White R—Red N—Brown
Y—Yellow U—Blue G—Green L—Light

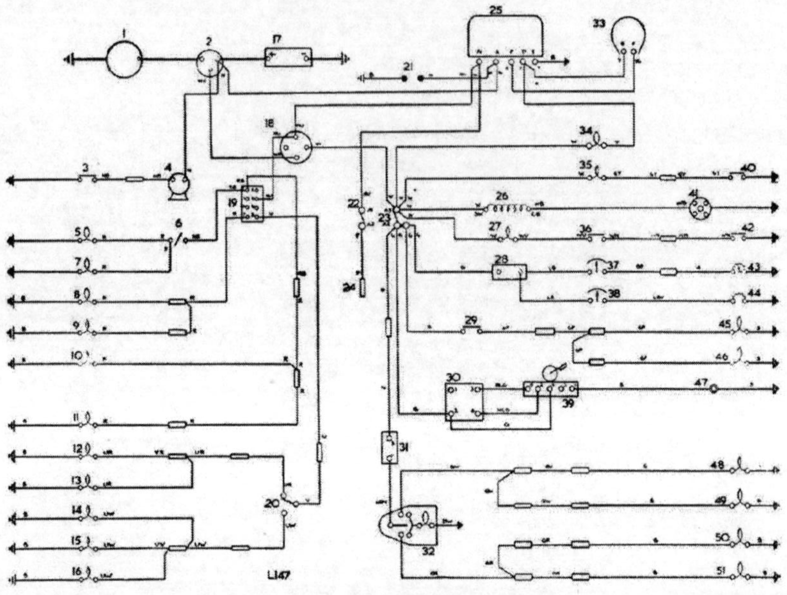

ELECTRICAL EQUIPMENT

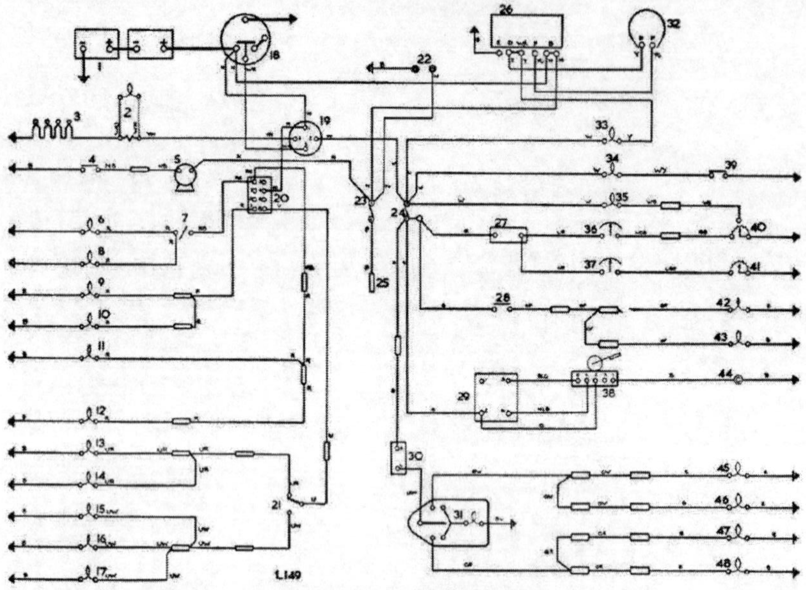

Fig. N1-14. Circuit diagram, 4 cylinder 'Regular', 'Long' and Station Wagon, Diesel models, negative earth, with headlamps mounted in front wings

1. Batteries, two 6 volt
2. Warning light and resistor, heater plugs
3. Heater plugs
4. Horn push button
5. Horn
6. Panel light, speedometer
7. Switch, panel light
8. Panel light, instrument
9. Side lamp, LH
10. Side lamp, RH
11. Tail lamp, RH
12. Tail lamp, LH
13. Headlamp, RH, dipped beam
14. Headlamp, LH, dipped beam
15. Headlamp, LH, main beam
16. Headlamp, RH, main beam
17. Warning light, headlamp main beam
18. Starter motor
19. Switch, starter–heater plugs
20. Switch, lights
21. Switch, headlamp dip
22. Inspection sockets
23. Fuse, A1-A2 (35 amp)
24. Fuse, A3-A4 (35 amp)
25. Feed, interior light
26. Regulator box
27. Voltage stabiliser, fuel gauge and water temperature gauge
28. Switch, stop lamp
29. Switch, wiper motor
30. Indicator unit, flasher
31. Switch and warning light, flasher
32. Dynamo
33. Warning light, dynamo
34. Warning light, oil pressure
35. Warning light, fuel level
36. Fuel gauge
37. Temperature gauge
38. Wiper motor
39. Switch, oil pressure
40. Fuel tank unit
41. Temperature transmitter unit
42. Stop lamp, RH
43. Stop lamp, LH
44. Socket, wiper lead
45. Front flasher, RH
46. Rear flasher, RH
47. Rear flasher, LH
48. Front flasher, LH

Snap and Lucar connections ▬
Earth connections ⋙

Cable colour code

| B—Black | P—Purple | W—White | R—Red | N—Brown |
| Y—Yellow | U—Blue | G—Green | L—Light | |

ELECTRICAL EQUIPMENT

Fig. N1-13. Circuit diagram, 4 cylinder 'Regular', 'Long' and Station Wagon, Petrol models, negative earth, with headlamps mounted in front wings

1. Starter motor
2. Solenoid, starter motor
3. Horn push button
4. Horn
5. Panel light, speedometer
6. Switch, panel light
7. Panel light, instruments
8. Side lamp, RH
9. Side lamp, LH
10. Tail lamp, RH
11. Tail lamp, LH
12. Headlamp, RH, dipped beam
13. Headlamp, LH, dipped beam
14. Headlamp, LH, main beam
15. Headlamp, RH, main beam
16. Warning light, headlamp main beam
17. Battery, 12 volt
18. Switch, ignition and starter
19. Switch, lights
20. Switch, headlamp dip
21. Inspection sockets
22. Fuse, A1-A2 (35 amp)
23. Fuse, A3-A4 (35 amp)
24. Feed, interior light
25. Regulator box
26. Ignition coil
27. Warning light, choke
28. Voltage stabiliser, fuel gauge and temperature gauge
29. Switch, stop lamp
30. Switch, wiper
31. Flasher indicator unit
32. Switch and warning light, flashers
33. Dynamo
34. Warning light, ignition
35. Warning light, oil pressure
36. Switch, cold start on control
37. Fuel gauge
38. Temperature gauge
39. Wiper motor
40. Switch, oil pressure
41. Distributor
42. Switch, cold start in cylinder head
43. Fuel tank unit
44. Temperature transmitter unit
45. Stop lamp, RH
46. Stop lamp, LH
47. Socket, wiper lead
48. Rear flasher, RH
49. Rear flasher, LH
50. Front flasher, LH
51. Front flasher, RH

Snap and Lucar connections ▬
Earth connections ⋙

Cable colour code

| B—Black | P—Purple | W—White | R—Red | N—Brown |
| Y—Yellow | U—Blue | G—Green | L—Light | |

ELECTRICAL EQUIPMENT

Fig. N1-15. Circuit diagram, 6 cylinder 'Long' and Station Wagon, Petrol models, negative earth, with headlamps mounted in front wings

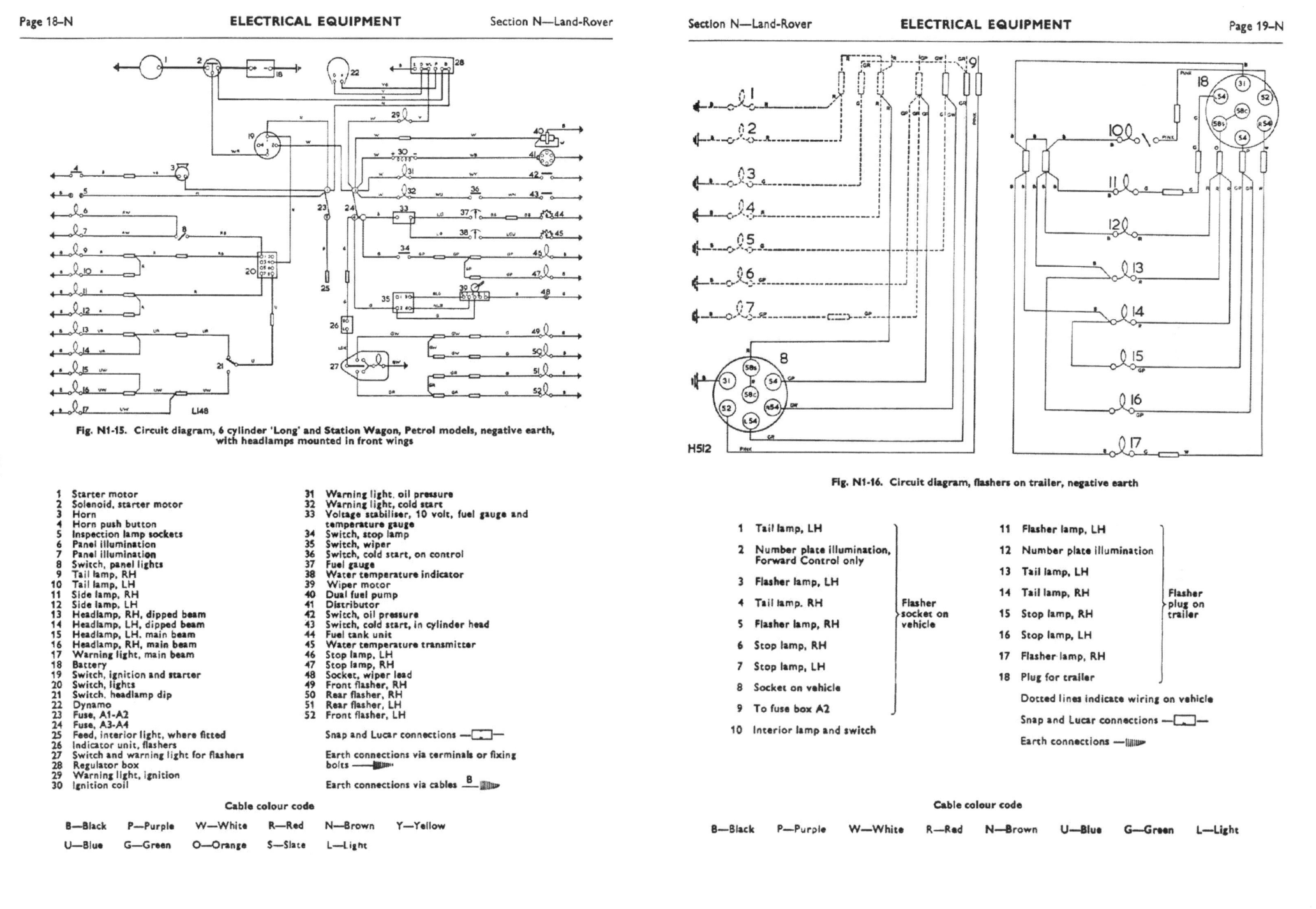

Fig. N1-16. Circuit diagram, flashers on trailer, negative earth

1. Starter motor
2. Solenoid, starter motor
3. Horn
4. Horn push button
5. Inspection lamp sockets
6. Panel illumination
7. Panel illumination
8. Switch, panel lights
9. Tail lamp, RH
10. Tail lamp, LH
11. Side lamp, RH
12. Side lamp, LH
13. Headlamp, RH, dipped beam
14. Headlamp, LH, dipped beam
15. Headlamp, LH, main beam
16. Headlamp, RH, main beam
17. Warning light, headlamp dip
18. Battery
19. Switch, ignition and starter
20. Switch, lights
21. Switch, headlamp dip
22. Dynamo
23. Fuse, A1-A2
24. Fuse, A3-A4
25. Indicator unit, flashers
26. Feed, interior light, where fitted
27. Switch and warning light for flashers
28. Regulator box
29. Warning light, ignition
30. Ignition coil
31. Warning light, oil pressure
32. Warning light, cold start
33. Voltage stabiliser, 10 volt, fuel gauge and temperature gauge
34. Switch, stop lamp
35. Switch, wiper
36. Switch, cold start, on control
37. Fuel gauge
38. Water temperature indicator
39. Wiper motor
40. Dual fuel pump
41. Distributor
42. Switch, oil pressure
43. Switch, cold start, in cylinder head
44. Fuel tank unit
45. Water temperature transmitter
46. Stop lamp, LH
47. Stop lamp, RH
48. Socket, wiper lead
49. Front flasher, RH
50. Rear flasher, RH
51. Rear flasher, LH
52. Front flasher, LH

Snap and Lucar connections
Earth connections via terminals or fixing bolts
Earth connections via cables

Cable colour code

B—Black   P—Purple   W—White   R—Red   N—Brown   Y—Yellow
U—Blue   G—Green   O—Orange S—Slate L—Light

1. Tail lamp, LH
2. Number plate illumination, Forward Control only
3. Flasher lamp, LH
4. Tail lamp, RH
5. Flasher lamp, RH
6. Stop lamp, RH
7. Stop lamp, LH
8. Socket on vehicle
9. To fuse box A2
10. Interior lamp and switch

Flasher socket on vehicle

11. Flasher lamp, LH
12. Number plate illumination
13. Tail lamp, LH
14. Tail lamp, RH
15. Stop lamp, RH
16. Stop lamp, LH
17. Flasher lamp, RH
18. Plug for trailer

Flasher plug on trailer

Dotted lines indicate wiring on vehicle
Snap and Lucar connections
Earth connections

Cable colour code

B—Black   P—Purple   W—White   R—Red   N—Brown   U—Blue   G—Green   L—Light

Batteries, remove, refit and maintenance—Operation N1-1

Workshop hand tools:
Screwdriver (medium)

General

All Petrol engine models are equipped with one 12 volt battery, all Diesel engine models are equipped with two 6 volt batteries connected in series. The batteries are located on the vehicle as follows:

'Regular' and 'Long' 4 cylinder Petrol models—under bonnet at right-hand side.

6 cylinder 'Long' models—under left-hand front seat.

'Regular' and 'Long' Diesel models—one under bonnet at right-hand side, the other under the left-hand seat.

To remove

1. Disconnect the leads, remove the securing frame and lift battery clear (when removing one battery only—Diesel models—always remove the inter-connecting battery lead completely from both batteries).

To refit

1. Reverse removal procedure, taking care to smear the battery terminals with petroleum jelly.

The drive screws securing the battery leads are manufactured from a special non-corrosive metal and must never be replaced with ordinary drive screws, which may cause serious corrosion of the battery terminals.

Battery maintenance

Many cases of poor battery performance are caused by lack of care in their early life; it is extremely important to condition batteries in the early stages of their life in order that they will give adequate performance in service during their later life.

The more compact the battery design the more important it is that conditioning of a new battery should be carried out effectively.

A recharging label, together with the appropriate date, will be found on all new batteries and these instructions must be adhered to.

Dry charge batteries are essential for vehicles in transit over long journeys. Correct charging procedures must be followed when a new dry battery is commissioned. It is not sufficient to fill the dry battery with new electrolyte and then put the battery into service—it is essential that it is properly recharged and the specific gravity of the electrolyte checked.

The correct specific gravity of the electrolyte of a battery in good condition is:

Temperate climate below 80°F (26.5°C)

As commissioned for service (fully charged) specific gravity 1.270 to 1.290. As expected during normal service (½ charged) specific gravity 1.230 to 1.250.

If the specific gravity should read between 1.190 and 1.210 (½ charged), the battery should be bench recharged and a check on the electrical equipment carried out.

Tropical climate above 80°F (26.5°C)

As commissioned for service (fully charged) specific gravity 1.210 to 1.230. As expected during normal service (½ charged) specific gravity 1.170 to 1.190.

If the specific gravity should read between 1.130 and 1.150 (½ charged), the battery should be bench recharged and a check on the electrical equipment carried out.

Check acid level as follows:

1. Wipe all dirt and moisture from the battery top.

2. Remove the filler plugs or manifold lid. If necessary add sufficient distilled water to raise the level to the top of separators. Replace the filler plugs. Avoid the use of a naked light when examining the cells.

In hot climates it will be necessary to top up the battery at more frequent intervals.

In very cold weather it is essential that the vehicle is used immediately after topping up, to ensure that the distilled water is thoroughly mixed with the electrolyte. Neglect of this precaution may result in the distilled water freezing and causing damage to the battery.

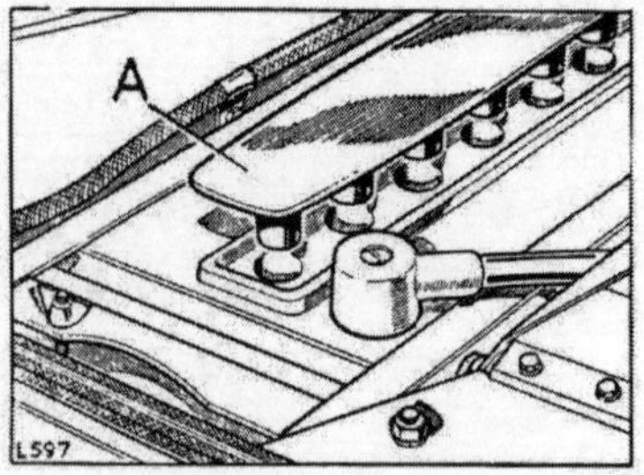

Fig. N1-17. Battery maintenance
A—Manifold lid

Battery terminals

Remove battery terminals, clean, grease and refit. Replace terminal screw, do not overtighten. Do not use the screw for pulling down the terminal.

Battery tests

If the performance of the battery has deteriorated, carry out the following tests to determine its condition and suitability for further service.

1. Hydrometer tests

Measure the specific gravity of the acid in each cell in turn with a hydrometer. To facilitate this measurement being taken, insert a short glass tube into the hydrometer rubber tubing, of a diameter that will pass through one of the apertures in the separator guard. To avoid misleading results, do not take readings immediately after topping up; at least thirty minutes' charging at the normal re-charge rate is required after topping up by each of the cells should be approximately the same; if one cell differs appreciably from the others, an internal fault in that cell is indicated. This will probably be confirmed by the high rate discharge test.

2. High rate discharge test

Note: Latest type batteries it will be seen that there are five small indentations on the battery lid; these coincide with the concealed inter-cell connectors underneath. Two are between and in line with the terminals, and three in line and on the opposite side to the terminals. These indentations must be pierced with a pointed tool to expose the inter-cell connectors and allow the battery to be tested with the high rate discharge tester.

Using a high rate discharge tester, press the pointed prongs firmly against the exposed negative and positive connectors of each cell, and note the readings on the meter. A good cell will maintain a reading of 1.2-1.5 volts for 10 seconds. If the reading rapidly falls off, the cell is probably faulty, in which event a new plate assembly may have to be fitted.

Re-seal the holes with sealing compound after testing.

Key to illustration of head, side and tail lamps. Up to vehicle suffix 'A' inclusive. (Except America dollar area)

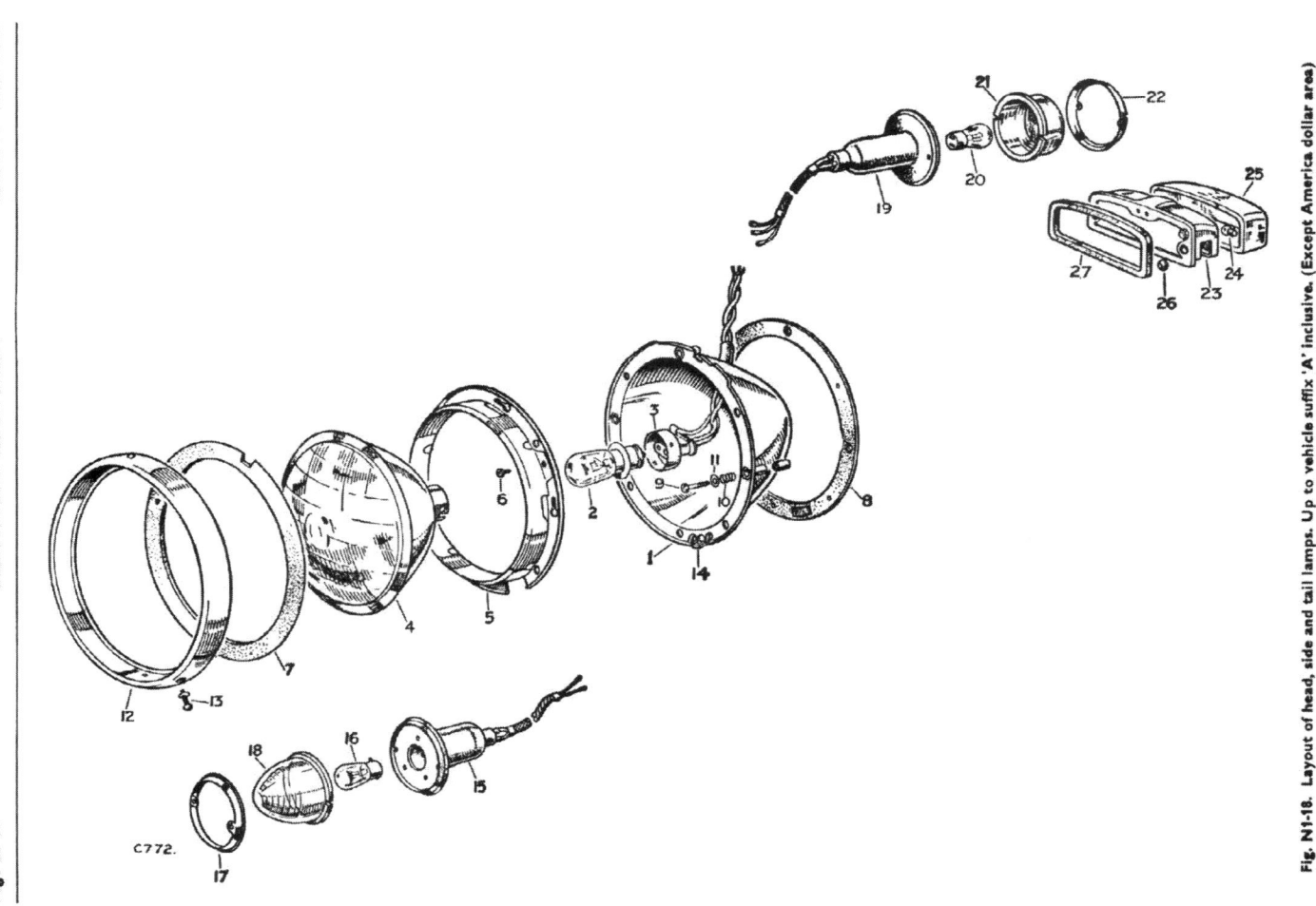

1	Body for headlamp	15	Side lamp body
2	Bulb for headlamp	16	Bulb for side lamp
3	Adaptor for bulb, double contact	17	Bezel
4	Light unit	18	Lens
5	Rim complete for light unit	19	Stop tail lamp body
6	Special screw for light unit rim	20	Bulb for stop tail lamp
7	Rubber gasket for headlamp rim	21	Glass
8	Gasket for body	22	Bezel
9	Special screw ⎫	23	Number plate lamp
10	Spring for screw ⎬ Light unit adjustment	24	Bulb for number plate lamp
11	Cup washer for screw ⎭	25	Glass
12	Rim for headlamp, chrome	26	Rubber grommet
13	Screw ⎫ Retaining	27	Rubber gasket
14	Spire nut ⎬ rim		

Fig. N1-18. Layout of head, side and tail lamps. Up to vehicle suffix 'A' inclusive. (Except America dollar area)

K854

Fig. N1-19 Layout of head, side, tail and flasher lamps. From vehicle suffix 'B' onwards
(Except America dollar area)

Key to illustration of head, side, tail and flasher lamps. From vehicle suffix 'B' onwards (Except America dollar area)

1	Headlamp complete, sealed beam	22	Rubber grommet for wire
2	Headlamp complete	23	Rubber gasket for lamp
3	Bulb for headlamp	24	Stop/tail lamp and rear number plate lamp
4	Light unit, sealed beam	25	Bulb holder, interior
5	Light unit	26	Bulb for lamp
6	Adaptor and leads for headlamp	27	Lens, stop/tail and reflex
7	Rim for light unit	28	Special screw, fixing lens
8	Rim for headlamp, chrome	29	Sleeve for terminal
9	Screw } For light unit adjustment and fitting headlamp to front grille	30	Red rear reflector
10	Spring for screw } For light unit adjustment and fitting headlamp to front grille	31	Spring washer } Fixing reflectors
11	Fibre washer for screw } For light unit adjustment and fitting headlamp to front grille	32	Nut (2 BA) } Fixing reflectors
12	Side lamp complete	33	Flasher unit
13	Bulb holder, interior	34	Self-cancelling switch for flasher, Magnatex
14	Bulb for side lamp	35	Bulb for flasher switch, Magnatex
15	Lens for side lamp	36	Wheel for flasher switch
16	Special screw, fixing lens	37	Front and rear flasher lamp complete
17	Washer for special screw	38	Lens for flasher lamp
18	Sleeve for terminal	39	Special screw, fixing lens
19	Number plate lamp	40	Special washer fixing lens
20	Bulb for number plate lamp	41	Bulb for flasher lamp
21	Lens	42	Bulb holder, interior

K21

Fig. N1-20. Layout of head, side, tail and flasher lamps. (America dollar area)

Key to illustration of head, side, tail and flasher lamps. (America dollar area)

1	Headlamp assembly, sealed beam		23	Bulb for number plate lamp	
2	Light unit for headlamp		24	Lens	For number plate lamp
3	Rim for light unit		25	Gasket for lens	For number plate lamp
4	Rim for headlamps		26	Red rear reflector complete	
5	Gasket for headlamp		27	Flasher unit	
6	Adaptor and leads for light unit		28	Self-cancelling switch for flasher, Magnatex	
7	Side lamp complete		29	Bulb for flasher switch, Magnatex	
8	Bulb for side lamp		30	Wheel for flasher switch	
9	Bulb holder, interior	For side lamp	31	Front flasher lamp	
10	Lens	For side lamp	32	Bulb for front flasher lamp	
11	Rim for lens	For side lamp	33	Bulb holder, interior	
12	Sleeve for terminal	For side lamp	34	Lens for front flasher lamp	
13	Stop/tail lamp complete		35	Chrome rim for lens	
14	Bulb for stop/tail lamp		36	Sleeve for terminal	
15	Bulb holder, interior	For stop/tail lamp	37	Rear flasher lamp complete	
16	Lens	For stop/tail lamp	38	Bulb for rear flasher lamp	
17	Gasket for lens	For stop/tail lamp	39	Bulb holder, interior	
18	Special screw	Fixing lens (for stop/tail lamp)	40	Lens for rear flasher lamp	
19	Special washer	Fixing lens (for stop/tail lamp)	41	Gasket for lens	
20	Sleeve for terminal	For stop/tail lamp	42	Special screw	Fixing lens
21	Grommet for cable entry	For stop/tail lamp	43	Special washer	Fixing lens
22	Number plate lamp complete		44	Grommet for cable entry	

ELECTRICAL EQUIPMENT

Headlamps, to remove, refit and adjust—Operation N1-2

Workshop hand tools:
Screwdriver (medium), Phillips screwdriver (medium)

General

Vehicles which have the headlamps fitted in the radiator grille panel, the RH headlamp is accessible after lifting the bonnet, the LH headlamp is accessible through the radiator grille panel after removing the grille. Vehicles which have the headlamps fitted in the wings, both lamps are accessible after removing the headlamp panel from the wing.

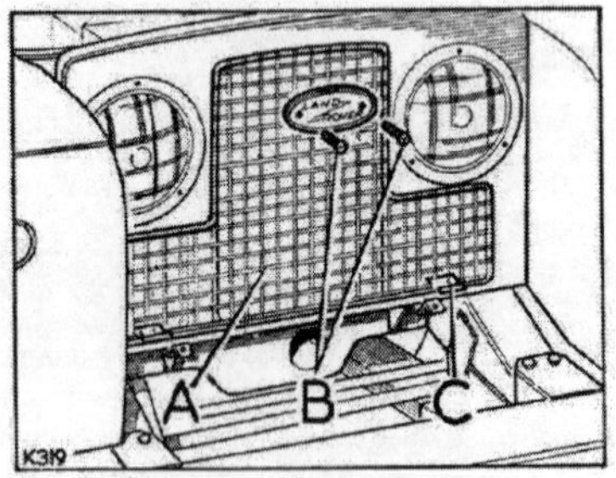

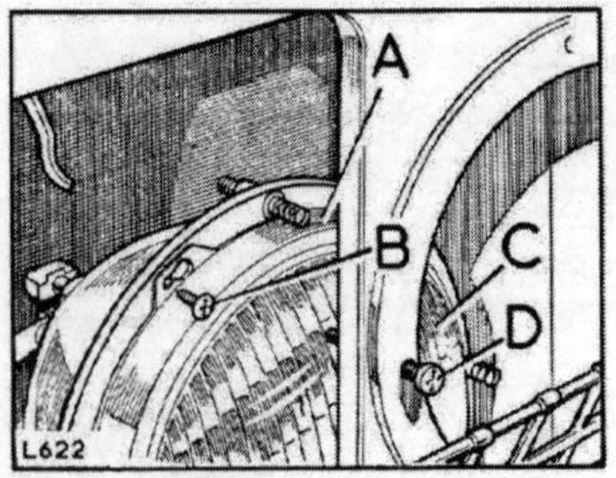

Fig. N1-22. Headlamp light unit replacement

A—Retaining rim
B—Retaining screw for rim
C—Light unit
D—Retaining screw for headlamp

Headlamps mounted in front wings

5. Remove the fixings and withdraw the headlamp bezel from the front wing.

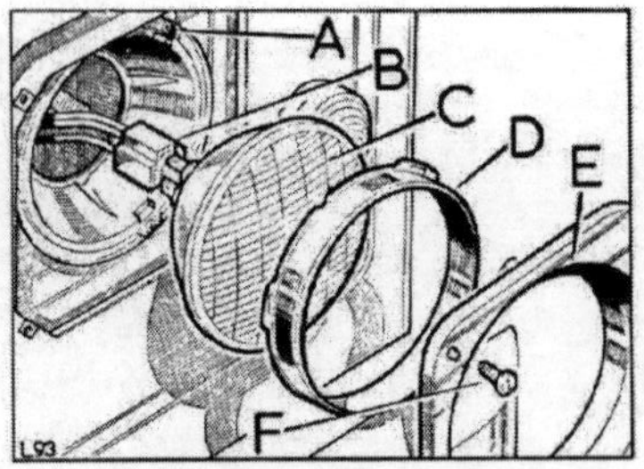

Fig. N1-23. Headlamp light unit replacement

A—Fixings for rim
B—Connector, electrical leads
C—Light unit
D—Rim for headlamp
E—Bezel
F—Fixings for bezel

6. Slacken the three Phillips head screws and turn the headlamp rim to release it from the keyhole slot locations.

Fig. N1-21. Radiator grille

A—Radiator grille
B—Fixings for name plate and grille
C—Support brackets

To replace bulb or light unit

Headlamps mounted in grille panel:

1. RH headlamp—Lift the bonnet and prop open. Remove any equipment mounted above the headlamp which obstructs access.
   LH headlamp—Remove the name plate and withdraw the radiator grille.

2. Bulb type headlamps—Disconnect the snap connectors or plug from the rear of the headlamp and release spring clip. Remove bulb holder; the bulb can then be replaced and the unit assembled.

3. Sealed beam type headlamp—Disconnect snap connectors or plug at the rear and support unit. Unscrew the three Phillips recessed-head screws on grille panel, and lift out sealed beam unit.

4. Fit new sealed beam unit. Reassemble and tighten Phillips recessed-head screws fully.

Replacement bulbs and units

Replacement headlamp bulbs and units—Up to vehicle suffix 'A' inclusive (Except America Dollar area)

Headlamps with bulbs:

RHStg	LU 414, 12 v, 50/40 w
LHStg, except Europe	LU 415, 12 v, 50/40 w
LHStg, Europe except France (early type)	LU 370
LHStg, Europe except France (later type)	LU 410, 12 v, 45/40 w
LHStg, France only	LU 411, 12 v, 45/40 w

Headlamps with sealed beam units:

RHStg	LU 553921
LHStg, except Europe	LU 555447
LHStg, Europe except France (early type)	LU 553940
LHStg, Europe except France (later type)	LU 556452
LHStg, France only	LU 553948

Replacement headlamp bulbs and units—from vehicle suffix 'B' onwards (Except America Dollar area)

Headlamps with bulbs:

LHStg, Europe except France	LU 410, 12 v, 45/40 w
LHStg, France only	LU 411, 12 v, 45/40 w

Headlamps with sealed beam units:

RHStg	LU 54521872
LHStg, except Europe	LU 54522231
LHStg, Europe except Austria	LU 54522683
LHStg, Austria only	LU 54520883

Replacement headlamp unit—America Dollar area

LHStg	LU 54522231

Replacement bulbs for general equipment—All models

Sidelamps	LU 207, 12 v, 6 w
Stop, tail lamps	LU 380, 12 v, 21/6 w
Flasher lamps	LU 382, 12 v, 21 w
Flasher warning lamp	Magnatex GBP, 12 v, 2.2 w
Rear number plate lamp	LU 989, 12 v, 6 w
Instrument panel lights	LU 987, 12 v, 2.2 w MES
Warning lights	LU 987, 12 v, 2.2 w MES
Warning light, brakes, Forward Control models	LU 281, 12 v, 2 w
Warning light, heater plugs, Diesel models	LU 982, 6 v, 1.8 w, MES
Warning light, fuel level, Diesel models	Magnetex GBP, 12 v, 2.8 w. Rover Part No. 560756 Mini-Lamp, 12/14 v, .04 a
Interior light	LU 382, 12 v, 21 w

ELECTRICAL EQUIPMENT

Operation N1-2—continued

7. Lift the headlamp from the wing and withdraw the rubber boot and plug from the rear. Release spring clip and remove bulb.

8. Replace the bulb, engaging its keyway, and re-assemble the unit aligning the cut-aways in the headlamp panel to give access to the beam adjusting screws.

Headlamps to remove and refit

Headlamps mounted in grille panel

1. RH headlamp—Lift the bonnet and prop open. Remove any equipment mounted above the head-lamp which obstructs access.
   LH headlamp—Remove the nameplate and with-draw the radiator grille.

Early type headlamps

2. Disconnect the leads at the snap connectors and remove them from supporting clips.

3. Remove the securing screw from the lower side of rim and ease the rim off from the bottom.

4. Withdraw the dust-excluding rubber.

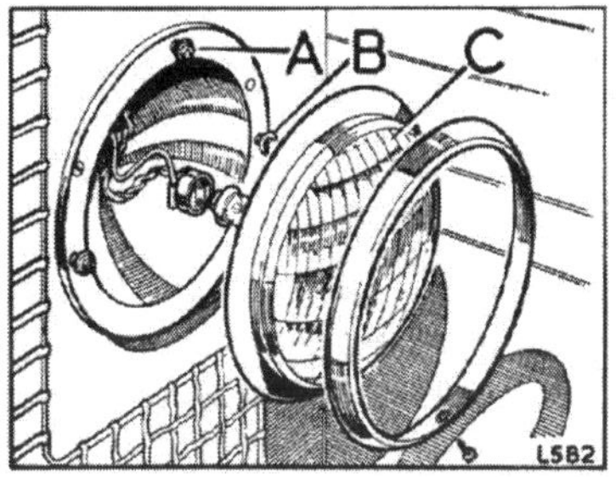

5. Press the light unit against the compression springs of the adjusting screws and turn anti-clockwise to release.

6. Release the bulb contact housing. Remove the bulb if not sealed beam type.

Fig. N1-24. Headlamp, early type
A—Vertical adjustment screw
B—Horizontal adjustment screw
C—Lens

7. Remove the securing screws and withdraw the lamp body complete with leads and rubber gasket.

8. Refit by reversing the removal procedure.

Later type headlamp

9. Disconnect the plug at the rear of the headlamp.

10. Support the headlamp and remove the three Phillips head screws from the grille panel, and lift out the headlamp complete.

11. Refit by reversing the removal procedure.

Headlamps mounted in front wings

12. Remove the fixings and withdraw the headlamp bezel from the front wing.

13. Slacken the three Phillips head screws and turn the headlamp rim to release it from the keyhole slot locations.

14. Lift the headlamp from the wing, withdraw the rubber boot and plug from the rear and lift the headlamp clear.

15. If required remove the headlamp setting screws, detach the tensioning spring and withdraw the rear shell. Remove the fixings and withdraw the headlamp mounting flange and gasket.

16. Refit by reversing the removal procedure.

Headlamp, to adjust

Lamps must be set to comply with local lighting regulations.

Accurate and rapid checking of lamp settings is most easily effected using a beam setter. When such facilities are not available, the lamps can be set by marking off a smooth wall or screen and shining the lamps on it from a distance of 25 ft (7,6 metres).

To adjust, using wall or screen marking

1. Position the vehicle unladen, on level ground 25 ft (7,6 metres) from the wall or screen.

2. Mark the wall or screen as illustrated, the hori-zontal and vertical centre lines must be accurately measured from the vehicle concerned. The mark-ings can be duplicated for setting both headlamps.

Operation N1-2—continued

3. Ensure that the centre line of the vehicle is at right-angles to the wall or screen and that the marked centre lines are in the same planes as the headlamp centre lines.

4. Adjust the beam by turning the adjusting screws (see Fig. N1-24 for grille mounted headlamps. The adjustment screws on wing mounted headlamps are accessible through slots in the headlamp bezel) until the area of concentrated light corres-ponds with the mark on the wall or screen.

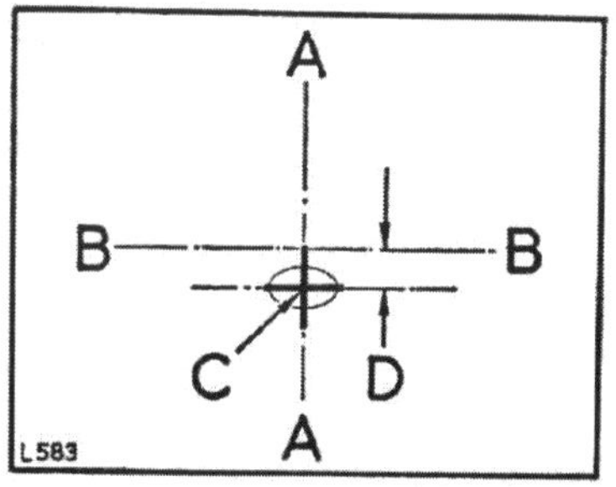

Fig. N1-25. Wall or screen marking for setting headlamp main beam
AA—Vertical centre line of headlamp
BB—Horizontal centre line of headlamp measured from level floor
C—Centre of concentrated area of light
D—2 in. ± 1 in. (50 mm ± 25 mm)

Side lamp, to remove and refit—Operation N1-3

Workshop hand tools:
Screwdriver (small), Screwdriver (Phillips)

To remove (Figs. N1-18, N1-19 and N1-20)

1. Disconnect the leads at the snap connectors, alongside the radiator cowl.
2. Withdraw the rim and lens by removing the securing screws.
3. If required, remove the bulb.
4. Remove the lamp from the wing, by removing the retaining screws, spring washers and nuts.

To refit

1. Reverse the removal procedure, connecting the wiring in accordance with the circuit diagram.
2. Latest type side lamps—Use a small screwdriver to locate the lamp lens into the rubber retainer.

Stop and tail lamp, remove and refit—Operation N1-4

Workshop hand tools:
Screwdriver (small), Screwdriver (Phillips)

To remove (Figs. N1-18, N1-19 and N1-20)

1. Disconnect the tail lamp harness at the snap connectors located beneath the wheel box, adjacent to the chassis frame side member.
2. Remove the screws, washers and nuts, and withdraw the rear lamp cover plate (inside vehicle).
3. Withdraw the tail lamp harness through the rubber grommet in the wheel box.
4. Withdraw the rim and glass by removing the securing screws. If required, remove the bulb.
5. Remove the lamp and harness complete by removing the securing screws.

To refit

1. Reverse the removal procedure, connecting the harness in accordance with the circuit diagram.
2. Latest type stop and tail lamps—Use a small screwdriver to locate the lamp lens into the rubber retainer.

Flasher lamp, to remove and refit—Operation N1-5

Workshop hand tools:
Screwdriver (small), Screwdriver (Phillips)

To remove (Figs. N1-19 and N1-20)

1. Disconnect the leads at the snap connectors alongside the radiator cowl, for the front flasher lamps. Disconnect the leads at the snap connectors located beneath the wheel box adjacent to the chassis side member, for the rear flasher lamps.
2. Remove the fixings screws and withdraw the lens from the rubber retainer.
3. If required, remove the bulb.
4. Remove the lamps from the front wing, by removing the retaining screws, spring washers and nuts.
5. Remove the screws, washers and nuts and withdraw the rear lamp cover plate (inside vehicle).
6. Withdraw the leads—through the wheel box grommet.
7. Remove the lamps from the tail, by removing the retaining drive screws.

To refit

1. Reverse the removal procedure, connecting the wiring in accordance with the appropriate circuit diagram. Use a small screwdriver to locate the lamp lens into the rubber retainer.

Rear number plate illumination lamp, to remove and refit—Operation N1-6

Workshop hand tools:
Spanner size: 2 BA
Screwdriver (medium)

Note: For vehicles which have the number plate lamp incorporated with the stop and tail lamp, refer to the instructions covering the stop and tail lamp.

To remove (Figs. N1-18, N1-19 and N1-20)

1. Disconnect the leads at the snap connectors located beneath the wheel box, adjacent to the chassis frame side member.
2. Remove the screws, washers and nuts and withdraw the rear lamp cover plate (inside vehicle).
3. Withdraw the leads—through the wheel box grommet.
4. Remove the securing screw and withdraw lamp cover. If required, remove the bulb.
5. Withdraw the lamp by removing the securing nuts (inside vehicle).

To refit

1. Reverse removal procedure, connecting the wiring in accordance with the circuit diagram.

ELECTRICAL EQUIPMENT

Stop lamp, to remove and refit—Operation N1-7

Workshop hand tools:
Spanner size: $\frac{7}{16}$ in. AF
Screwdriver (medium)

Hydraulic operated type
To renew

The hydraulic switch is located on the brake pipe five-way piece, at the front RH chassis side member.

1. Disconnect the leads, unscrew switch and remove.
2. Replace by reversing the removal procedure, connecting wires in accordance with the wiring diagram. Minimise loss of brake fluid by fitting new switch immediately.
3. Bleed the brake system. Section H.

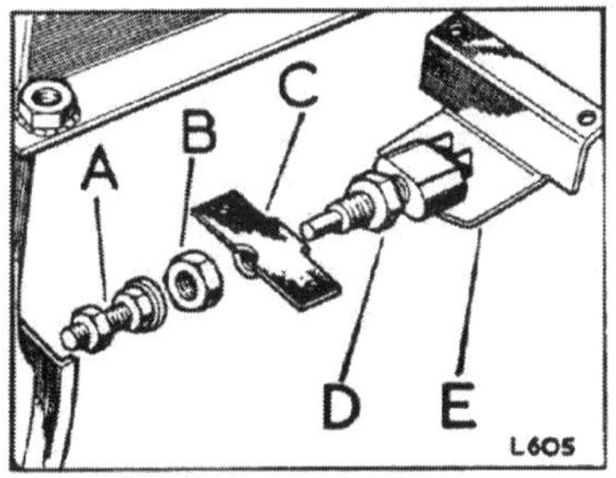

Mechanically operated type
To renew

1. Remove the switch protection plate from the brake pedal bracket.
2. Disconnect the electrical leads from the switch.
3. Depress the brake pedal and remove the end stop from the switch and withdraw the switch from the mounting bracket.
4. Replace by reversing the removal procedure, connecting wire in accordance with the appropriate circuit diagram.
5. If required, set the brake pedal adjuster to give a dimension of 6¼ in. (158 mm) between the lower edge of the pedal foot pad and the floor. See Section H, Operation H1-4.

Mechanically operated switch used with Girling mechanical servo
To renew

1. Disconnect the leads from the stop lamp switch.
2. Release the locknut and unscrew the switch from the brake pedal bracket.
3. Replace by reversing the removal procedure, connecting the leads in accordance with the appropriate circuit diagram.
4. Check, and if necessary, adjust the stop lamp switch to operate at ¾ in. to 1 in. (19 mm to 25 mm) of pedal movement.

Fig. N1-26. Mechanical stop lamp switch

A—Stop adjuster for pedal
B—End stop
C—Mounting bracket for switch
D—Stop lamp switch
E—Protection plate for switch

Engine starter switches, remove and refit—Operation N1-8

Workshop hand tools:
Screwdrivers (small and medium)

General

When removing switches, prior to disconnecting the leads record their colours and relative positions to facilitate refitting.

Petrol models
Early type starter switch (see Section P for ignition switch details)

To remove
1. Disconnect the battery.
2. Disconnect the three leads from the switch.
3. Screw off the switch knob and the locking nut from the switch spindle.
4. Remove the switch from the dash panel.

To refit
Reverse the removal procedure, connecting the wires in accordance with the appropriate circuit diagram.

Latest type combined starter and ignition switch
To remove
1. Disconnect the battery.
2. Remove the screws securing the instrument panel, and draw the panel forward.
3. Disconnect the leads from the starter and ignition switch.
4. Unscrew the chrome locking ring and withdraw the switch.

To refit
Reverse the removal procedure, connecting the leads in accordance with the appropriate circuit diagram. Adjust the locknut so that switch fits flush when secured with locking ring.

Mixture control thermostat switch, Petrol engines
To renew
1. Disconnect the wire from the thermostat switch.
2. Remove the switch from the cylinder head.
3. Check the switch: Contact is made at 51–54°C (124–129°F); contact is broken at 47–53°C (117–127°F).
4. Fit the new switch by reversing the removal procedure.
Renewal of the second switch in the mixture control warning light circuit (at the manual-control) is dealt with in Section P.

Diesel models
Starter and heater plug switch, early type
To remove
1. Disconnect the positive lead from the right-hand battery.
2. Disconnect the leads from the back of the starter switch.
3. Remove the large securing nut from facia side of panel.
4. Withdraw switch.

To refit
1. Reverse removal procedure, connecting leads in accordance with the appropriate circuit diagram.

Starter and heater plug switch, latest type
To remove
1. Disconnect the battery.
2. Remove the screws securing the instrument panel, and draw the panel forward.
3. Disconnect the leads from the starter and heater plug switch.
4. Via the small hole in the body of the switch, depress the barrel lock plunger and remove the barrel.
5. Unscrew the chrome locking ring and withdraw the switch from the rear of the panel.

To refit
Reverse the removal procedure, reconnecting the leads in accordance with the appropriate circuit diagram. Adjust the locknut so that switch fits flush when secured with locking ring.

Key to illustration of general electrical equipment, positive earth system. Series II and IIA models.
Up to vehicle suffix 'C' inclusive

1. Windtone horn
2. Mounting bracket for windtone horn
3. Windscreen wiper motor complete
4. Arm for wiper blade, stud fixing
5. Wiper blade, stud fixing
6. Escutcheon for windscreen wiper motor
7. Rubber seal for escutcheon
8. Battery, dry, 12 volt
10. Voltage regulator box
11. Cover for regulator box
12. Fuse box
13. Cover for fuse box
14. Junction box
15. Resistor for heater plugs
16. Dash harness
17. Headlamp and sidelamp harness
18. Dynamo harness
19. Frame harness
20. Rear crossmember harness
21. Lead, rear number plate lamp
22. Cable, coil to distributor
23. Cable, battery to earth
24. Cable, battery to switch
25. Cable, switch to starter
26. Cable, gearbox to earth
27. Wiper feed lead
28. Plug socket for leads on steering bracket
29. Cap for wiper feed socket
30. Clip for dynamo harness
31. Clip for battery to switch cable
32. Mounting plate for cable clips
33. Cable clip for frame harness, at dash RH
35. Cable clip for frame harness, at junction box
36. Cable clip at LH headlamp
37. Earthing clip for headlamp
38. Earthing clip on rear crossmember
39. Cable clip, fixing harness to dash, RH
40. Cable clip, fixing harness to dash and LH toe box
41. Cable clip on wing valance and toe box
42. Cable clip, fixing harness to RH toe box
43. Cable clip, fixing harness adjacent to junction box
44. Cable clip, fixing dipper and horn leads to RH
45. Clip for rear crossmember harness
48. Cable clip, wiper feed lead
49. Cable clip on fan cowl top baffle
50. Clip, fixing heater switch lead to engine speed control quadrant
51. Cable clip at dash, RH
52. Bowden clip, starter cable to solenoid
53. Cable cleat for engine harness
54. Rubber grommet in dash for wiper motor lead
55. Rubber grommet, main harness, in dash
56. Rubber grommet for side lamp lead
57. Rubber grommet for frame harness
58. Rubber plug for redundant hole
59. Rubber cover for battery terminal

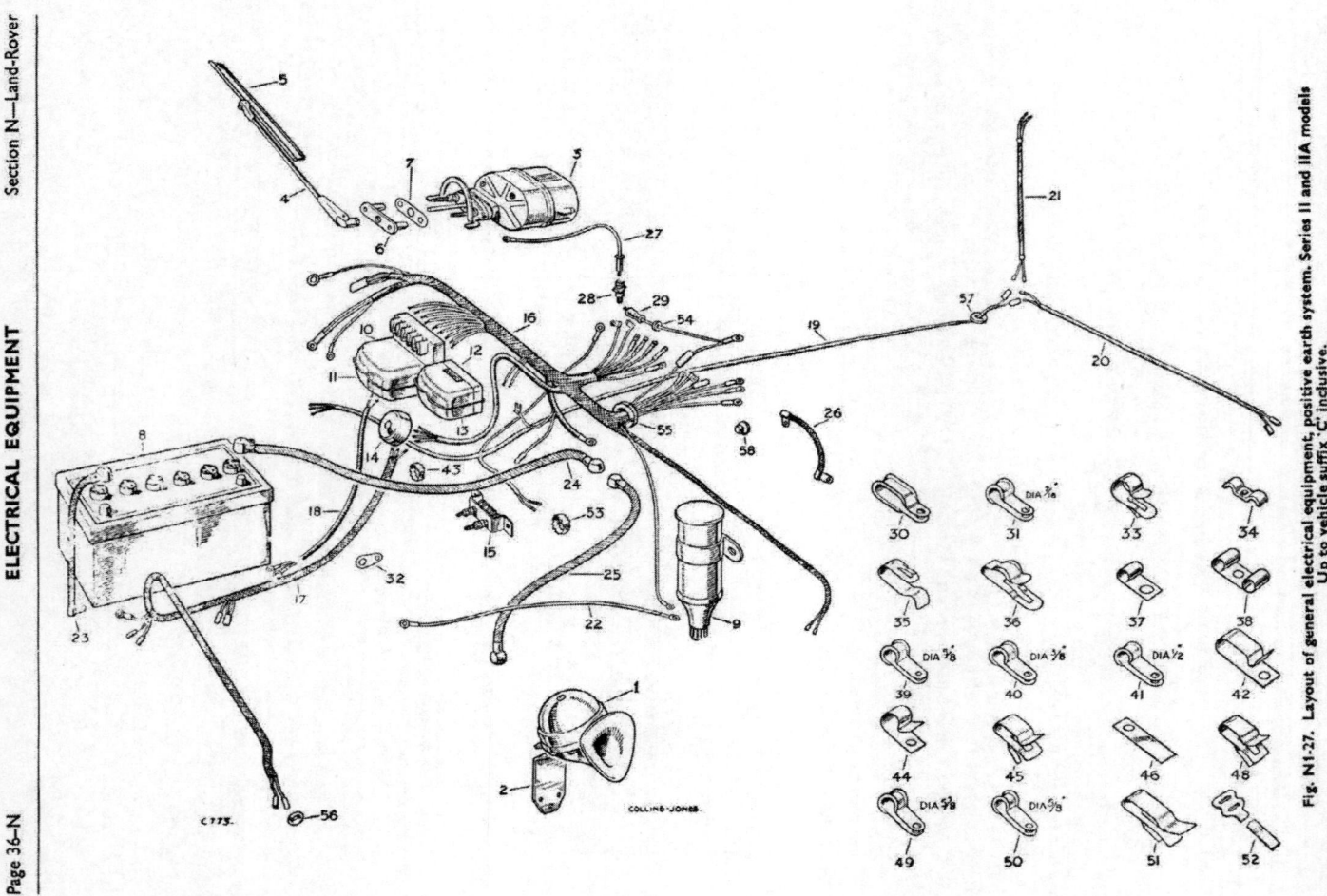

Fig. N1-27. Layout of general electrical equipment, positive earth system. Series II and IIA models. Up to vehicle suffix 'C' inclusive.

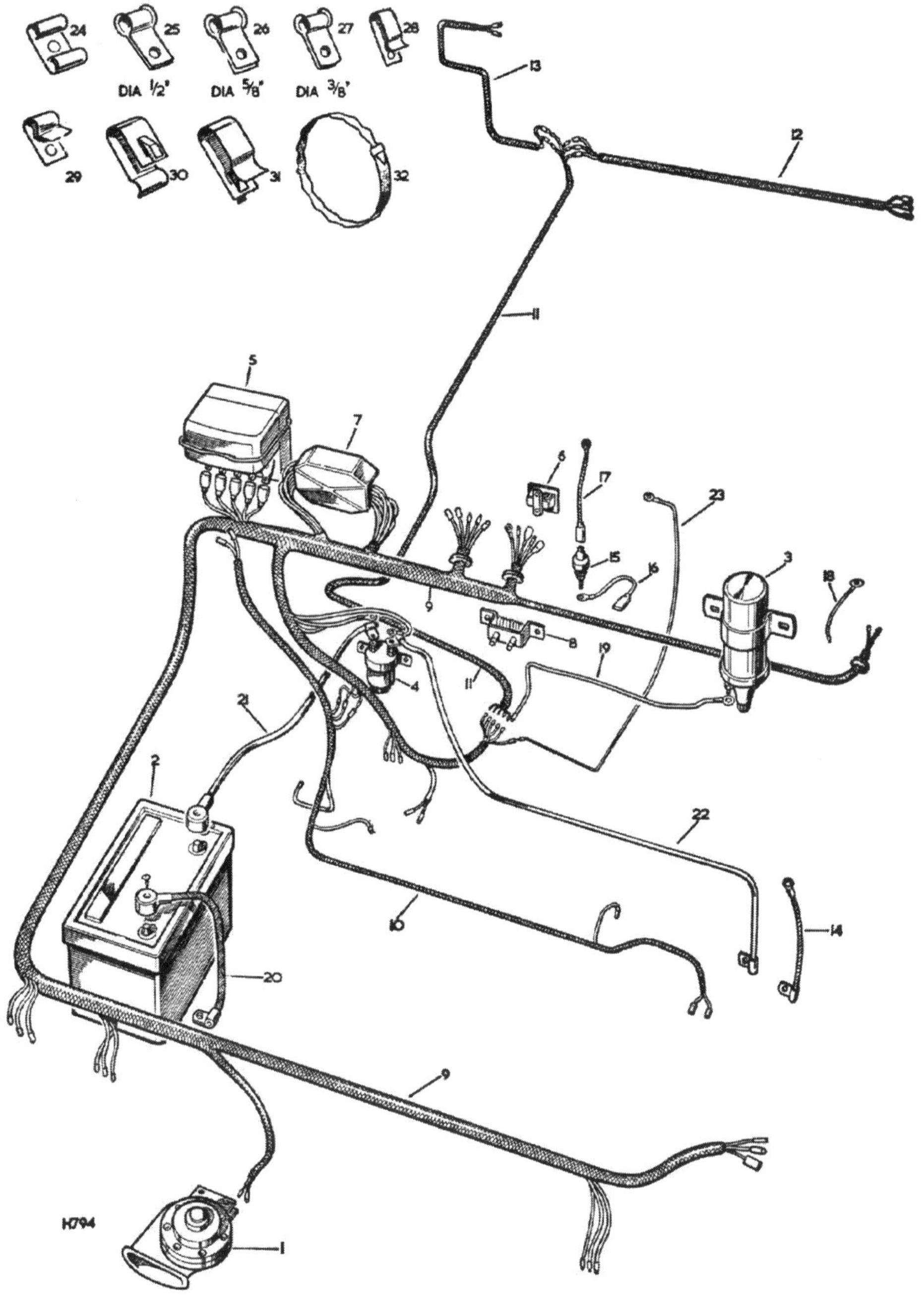

DIA 1/2"
DIA 5/8"
DIA 3/8"
H794

Fig. N1-28. Layout of general electrical equipment, negative earth system. Series IIA 4 cylinder models. From vehicle suffix 'D' onwards

Key to illustration of general electrical equipment, negative earth system. Series IIA 4 cylinder models. From vehicle suffix 'D' onwards

1 Windtone horn, Clearhooter
2 Battery, dry, 12 volt
3 Ignition coil
4 Starter solenoid switch
5 Voltage regulator box
6 Voltage regulator for instruments, 10 volt
7 Fuse box
8 Resistor for heater plugs, KLG
9 Dash harness
10 Dynamo harness
11 Frame harness
12 Rear crossmember harness
13 Lead for rear number plate lamp
14 Lead, starter motor to earth
15 Inhibitor socket for wiper motor leads
16 Lead, wiper switch to inhibitor socket
17 Lead, inhibitor socket to windscreen
18 Lead, wiper motor to earth
19 Cable, coil to distributor, low tension
20 Cable, battery to earth
21 Cable, battery to solenoid switch
22 Cable, solenoid switch to starter
23 Lead for fuel tank unit

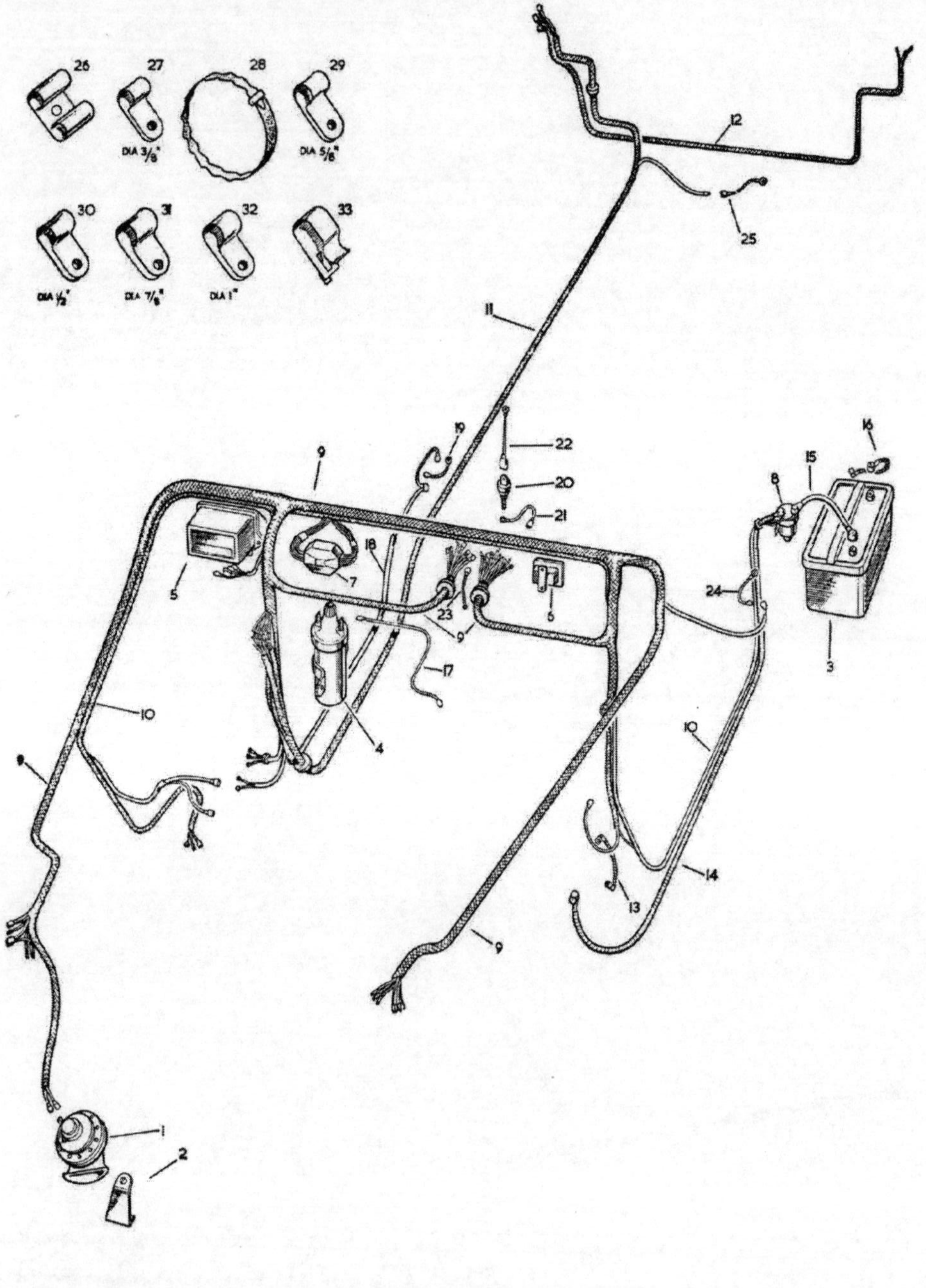

ELECTRICAL EQUIPMENT

Key to illustration of general electrical equipment, negative earth system. 2.6 litre Petrol, 6 cylinder models

1 Windtone horn, complete with bracket
3 Battery, dry, 12 volt
4 Ignition coil
5 Current voltage control box
6 Voltage regulator for instruments
7 Fuse box
8 Starter solenoid switch
9 Dash harness
10 Dynamo harness
11 Frame harness
12 Rear crossmember harness
13 Lead, starter motor to earth
14 Cable, solenoid to starter motor
15 Cable, battery to starter solenoid
16 Cable, battery to earth, negative
17 Cable, coil to distributor, low tension
18 Cable, fuel pump feed
19 Lead, fuel pump to earth
20 Inhibitor socket for wiper motor leads
21 Lead, wiper switch to inhibitor socket
22 Lead, inhibitor socket to windscreen
23 Lead, wiper switch to earth
24 Earth lead for wiper motor
25 Earth lead for fuel tank gauge

Fig. N1-29. Layout of general electrical equipment, negative earth system. 2.6 litre Petrol, 6 cylinder models

ELECTRICAL EQUIPMENT

Dipswitch for headlamp, to remove and refit—Operation N1-9

Workshop hand tools:
Screwdriver (medium)

To remove

1. Disconnect the dipswitch leads at junction box or snap connectors as applicable.
2. Remove the securing screws and withdraw the switch from toe board.

To refit

1. Reverse removal procedure, connecting leads in accordance with the circuit diagram.

Flasher switch, to remove and refit—Operation N1-10

Workshop hand tools:
Screwdriver (small and medium)

To remove

1. Remove the five screws securing the instrument panel to the dash, and ease the panel forward.
2. Disconnect the flasher switch leads from the flasher unit and main harness at the rear of the instrument panel.
3. Withdraw the flasher switch leads through the grommet in the side of the instrument box, and release retaining clips at the dash and steering column.
4. Remove the flasher switch and support bracket from the steering column, and withdraw the switch complete with leads.

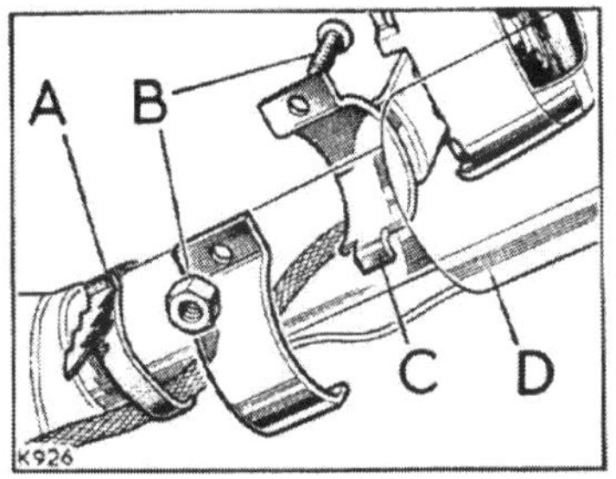

To replace a bulb or wheel in flasher switch

5. Remove the three screws securing the flasher switch cover.
6. Withdraw the bulb from its bayonet fixing.
7. Lift the control lever from the flasher switch.
8. Withdraw the wheel from the pivot shaft.
9. Reassemble by reversing the removal procedure.

To refit flasher switch

1. Reverse the removal procedure, connecting the flasher switch leads in accordance with the appropriate circuit diagram.

Fig. N1-30. Flasher switch
A—Clip, leads to steering column
B—Fixings for flasher switch
C—Flasher switch
D—Steering column

Flasher unit, to remove and refit—Operation N1-11

Workshop hand tools:
Screwdriver (medium)

To remove

1. Remove the five screws securing the instrument panel to the dash, and ease the panel forward.
2. Remove the screw securing the flasher unit, withdraw the leads and lift the flasher unit clear.

To refit

1. Reverse the removal procedure, connecting the leads in accordance with the appropriate circuit diagram.

Ignition coil, to remove and refit—Operation N1-12

Workshop hand tools:
Spanner size: $\frac{7}{16}$ in. AF open end
Screwdriver (medium)

To remove

1. With the ignition switched off, disconnect the high and low tension leads from the coil.
2. 2¼ litre models—Remove the drive screws and shakeproof washers securing the coil to the dash panel, and withdraw coil.
3. 2.6 litre models—Remove the bolts, nuts, plain and spring washers securing the coil to the engine, and withdraw the coil.

To refit

1. Reverse the removal procedure.

ELECTRICAL EQUIPMENT

Distributor, to overhaul—Operation N1-13

(For removal and refitting instructions, Section A refers)

Workshop hand tools:
Spanner size: 4 BA
Screwdriver (medium), Screwdriver (Phillips), Mallet (hide face), Pliers, Feeler gauges

General

The distributors fitted to the 2¼ litre four cylinder engine and the 2.6 litre six cylinder engine, are of the same basic type, with only minor differences such as the cam and distributor cap. The following instructions apply to both four cylinder and six cylinder type distributors.

To dismantle

1. Remove distributor cap and withdraw the rotor arm.
2. Remove the nut, star and plain washer retaining the contact spring and lift off the insulating bush, together with the low tension and capacitor leads.
3. Lift off the moving contact point and the insulating washers from the contact pivot and the spring post.
4. Remove the terminal block from its slot in the distributor body.
5. Remove the set screw, spring and plain washers retaining the fixed contact plate and lift off the fixed contact.
6. Remove the Phillips screw and star washer retaining the capacitor, and lift off the capacitor.
7. Disconnect the spring connecting the vacuum unit to the base plate and withdraw the vacuum unit.
8. Remove the circlip from the micrometer adjusting nut.
9. Remove the ratchet spring plate from the side of the adjusting nut, remove the adjusting nut and coil spring and withdraw the vacuum unit.
10. Remove the two Phillips screws and spring washers securing the base plate to the distributor body and lift off the base plate.
11. Rotate the contact breaker moving plate clockwise to its full extent and withdraw from base plate.
12. Carefully withdraw the two springs from the centrifugal advance unit.
13. Remove the screw from inside the cam and lift off the cam and cam foot, noting the position of the rotor arm slot in relation to the distributor driving dog for assembly purposes.
14. Lift off two weights.
15. Drive out the pin securing the driving dog and remove the dog and brass washer.
16. Remove the action plate and shaft, noting the position and condition of the distance collar beneath the action plate.
17. Remove clamping plate.
18. Using a shouldered mandrel, press out the bush from the body end.
19. Check all parts for wear or damage, and replace as necessary.

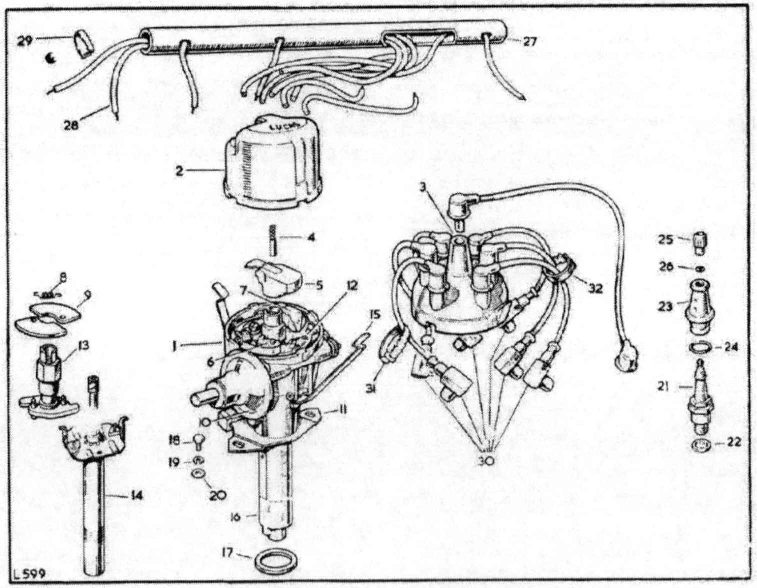

The bearing bush is of sintered copper-iron and must be completely immersed in engine oil for at least 24 hours prior to fitting.

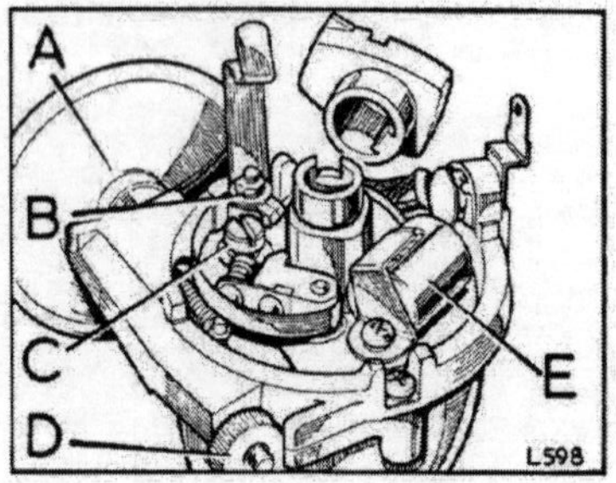

Fig. N1-32. Distributor details

A—Micrometer graduated scale
B—Terminal screw
C—Contact adjustment screw
D—Micrometer adjusting nut
E—Capacitor

Distributor, rebuild

1. Reassemble the distributor by reversing the dismantling instructions.
2. Using the hole in the distributor shank as a guide, drill the bush on one side and remove the frazing.
3. Ensure that the drive shaft rotates freely in the bush.
4. When fitting the centrifugal governor springs, care must be taken not to stretch them.
5. When fully assembled, adjust the contact points to .014 in. to .016 in. (0.35 mm to 0.40 mm).

For ignition timing and distributor adjustment instructions, refer to Section A.

Fig. N1-31. Layout of distributor (6 cylinder version illustrated)

1 Distributor body
2 Distributor cap, early type
3 Distributor cap, latest type
4 Brush and spring for cap
5 Rotor arm
6 Contact points
7 Condenser
8 Auto advance spring, set
9 Auto advance weight
10 Vacuum unit
11 Clamping plate
12 Base plate for contact breaker
13 Cam
14 Shaft and action plate
15 Clip for cover
16 Driving dog
17 Cork washer for distributor housing
18 Set bolt (¼ in. UNF x 1⁄16 in. long) } Fixing distributor to cylinder block
19 Spring washer
20 Plain washer
21 Sparking plug
22 Washer for plug
23 Cover for sparking plug
24 Rubber sealing ring for plug cover
25 Cable nut
26 Washer for cable nut
27 Ignition wire carrier
28 Sparking plug lead set
29 Cable cleat securing No. 1 plug lead and coil leads

ELECTRICAL EQUIPMENT

Heater plugs, Diesel models, to remove, refit and check—Operation N1-14

Workshop hand tools:
Spanner sizes: 2 BA

General

The heater plugs do not require any maintenance. However, if at any time when the heater plugs are in use, the warning light glows very brightly, a short circuit in the system is indicated. No light will indicate an open circuit.

Great care must be taken not to twist the centre terminal when removing heater plug leads.

Fault location on heater plug circuit, plugs in situ

1. Examine the fuse in the fuse box and fit a new replacement if necessary. Refer to the applicable circuit diagram for fuse location.

2. Failure of the warning light bulb will not affect the heater plug circuit, but the bulb should be replaced when conveniently possible. Section P.

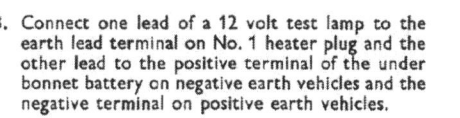

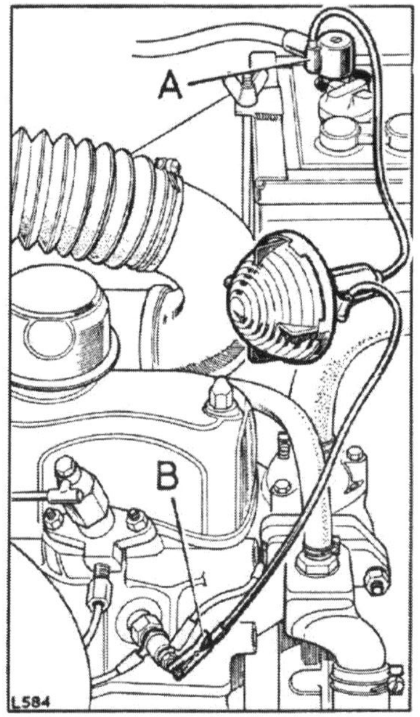

3. Connect one lead of a 12 volt test lamp to the earth lead terminal on No. 1 heater plug and the other lead to the positive terminal of the under bonnet battery on negative earth vehicles and the negative terminal on positive earth vehicles.

4. If the test lamp does not light, a faulty earth lead is indicated.

5. Move the test lamp lead from the heater plug earth lead terminal to the interconnecting lead terminal. If the test lamp remains unlighted, a broken heater plug filament is indicated.

6. Check the remaining plugs in the same manner until the fault is located.

7. If the plugs are proved serviceable, check each terminal of the resistance in the same manner. If the resistance and the output lead are proved to be serviceable, check the input lead and starter switch itself.

Heater plugs, to remove

The shape of the heater plug element and its position in relation to the plug body is important and care must therefore be taken when fitting, removing or cleaning the plug, to avoid distortion or damage to the element.

1. Disconnect the leads from the plugs, avoiding distortion of the central rod. On early heater plugs, use two spanners at each terminal to prevent the central rod or insulating tube twisting.

2. Remove carbon from base of heater plug to avoid possible short circuiting of the element. Do not sandblast.

3. Examine the element for signs of fracture or severe heat attack and the seating for scores. Plugs with fractured elements must be replaced. Where scoring of the seating is sufficient to allow gas leakage or erosion of the element such that a fracture is likely to occur, then a replacement plug must be fitted.

Testing heater plugs when removed from engine

4. Test the plug internal circuit for continuity, by connecting it and a 12 volt side lamp bulb in circuit, to a 12 volt battery.

The inclusion of a bulb in circuit is **essential**.

If the bulb does not light an open circuit is indicated and the heater plug should be replaced with new.

Fig. N1-33. Checking heater plug circuit
A—Battery feed terminal (see text)
B—Earth lead terminal on No. 1 plug

Operation N1-14—continued

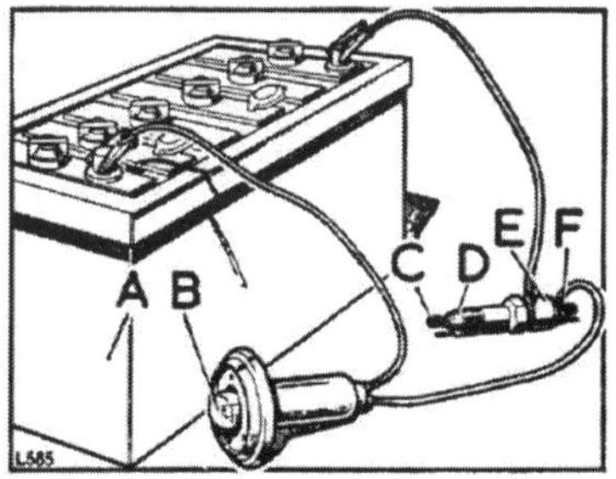

6. Early type heater plugs—Ensure that the shakeproof washers are fitted under the terminal in order to maintain good electrical contact.

7. Refit the heater plugs and tighten to 25 lb/ft (3,4 mkg).

Replace the leads in accordance with the circuit diagram and tighten the terminals. On early type heater plugs, use two spanners at each terminal.

Fig. N1-34. Testing heater plug circuit
A—12 volt battery
B—Bulb (12 v)
C—Element
D—Seating
E—Insulation
F—Terminal nuts

Heater plugs, to refit

5. Ensure that the terminal nuts and threads are clean and that the thread at base of plug is free of carbon.

Resistance, heater plugs

To remove

1. Disconnect the leads from resistance.
2. Remove the securing screws and withdraw the unit.

To refit

1. Reverse the removal procedure.

ELECTRICAL EQUIPMENT

Fuse and junction boxes, to remove and refit—Operation N1-15

Workshop hand tools:
Screwdriver (medium)

Fuses

The fuses are located on the bulkhead under the bonnet. To replace a fuse:

1. The cover should be pulled off.
2. Replace fuse as required:

Fuse number	Fuse protects	Fuse, Amps
A3–A4	Windscreen wiper, fuel tank level unit and stop lights	35
A1–A2	Interior lamps, fog lamps, etc., as applicable	35

Two spare fuses are carried in the fuse box; only 35 amp cartridge type fuses should be used as replacements.

To remove fuse or junction box

1. Disconnect the battery earth lead.
2. Remove the cover from the fuse or junction box, as applicable.
3. Disconnect the leads.
4. Remove the securing screws and withdraw the unit.

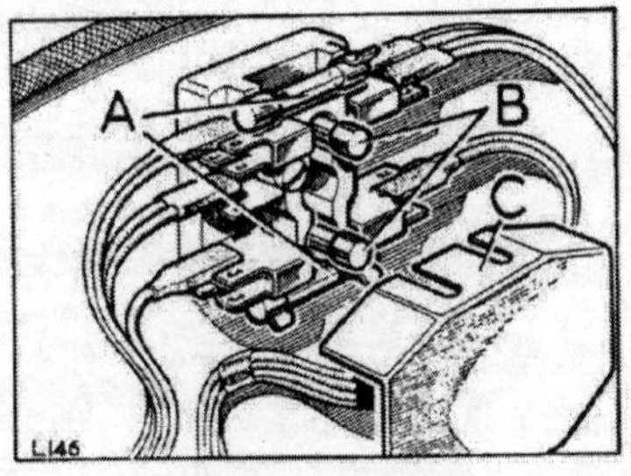

Fig. N1-35. Fuse box
A—Fuses B—Spare fuse

To refit

Reverse the removal procedure, connecting the leads in accordance with the appropriate circuit diagram.

Current voltage regulator, to remove, refit and adjust—Operation N1-16

Workshop hand tools:
Spanner sizes: 2 BA, 4 BA open end and socket
Screwdriver (medium), Feeler gauge

Special tools:
Lucas setting tool No. 54381742 (for RB340 regulator)
Voltmeter, moving coil 0–20 volts
Ammeter 40–0–40 amps

General

There are three types of dynamo and current voltage regulators fitted to Petrol engine models, and two types fitted to Diesel engines, as follows:

Series II 2¼ litre Petrol models
Dynamo type C39 used with current voltage regulator RB106/37182.

Series IIA 2¼ litre Petrol models
Dynamo type C40 used with current voltage regulator RB106/37290.

Series IIA 2.6 litre Petrol models
Dynamo type C42 used with current voltage regulator RB340/37517.

Series II and IIA 2¼ litre Diesel models up to vehicle suffix 'C' inclusive
Dynamo type C40 used with current voltage regulator RB310/37472.

Series IIA 2¼ litre Diesel models from vehicle suffix 'D' onwards
Dynamo type C40 used with current voltage regulator RB340/37387.

It is important that the appropriate dynamos and current voltage regulators are used together as detailed above, otherwise there is a danger of burning out the dynamos.

To remove

1. Disconnect the battery earth lead.
2. Disconnect all wires from the control box.
3. Remove the control box complete.

To refit

1. Reverse the removal procedure, connecting the wiring in accordance with the appropriate circuit diagram.

To check and adjust

A. Current voltage regulator, type RB106

Locating faults on charging circuit

Ensure that the dynamo is functioning correctly and that the batteries are in order, then proceed as follows:

1. Ensure that the wiring between battery and control box is in order by disconnecting the wire from control box terminal 'B' and connecting the end of the wire removed to the negative terminal of a voltmeter. Connect the positive voltmeter terminal to an earthing point on the chassis. If a voltmeter reading is observed, the wiring is in order and the control box must be examined.

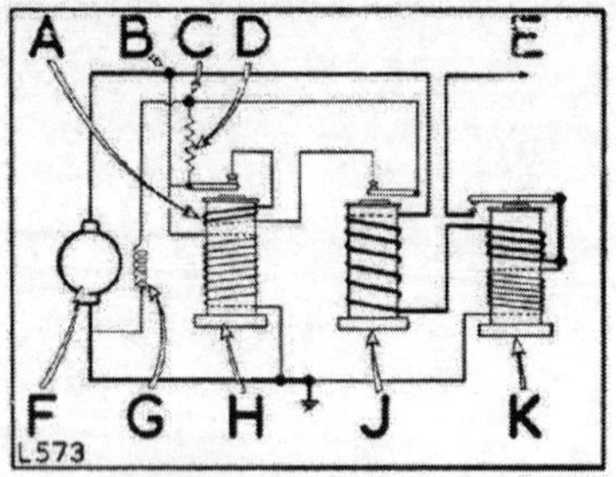

Fig. N1-36. The charging circuit
A—Bucking coil
B—Terminal on control box
C—Terminal on control box
D—Resistor
E—Terminal on control box—to ammeter and battery
F—Armature
G—Field windings
H—Voltage regulator
J—Current regulator
K—Cut-out relay

2. If there is no reading, examine the wiring between battery and control box for defective cables or loose connections.
3. Reconnect the wire to terminal 'B'.

To check

4. Place a piece of paper between the cut-out contacts and connect a moving-coil voltmeter to the 'D' terminal on the regulator and to a good

Operation N1-16—continued

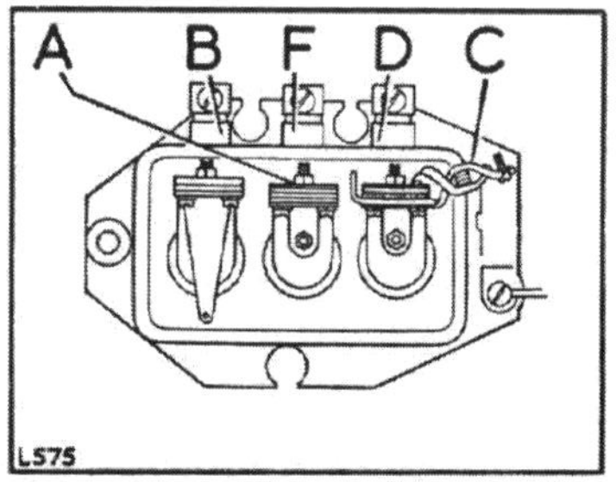

earth (not the one on the regulator box). Start the engine and increase rpm until the voltage remains constant, i.e. the regulator is controlling; the voltmeter reading should be 15.8 to 16.4 volts. If the regulating voltage is not correct, the vehicle should be examined by a qualified electrician. Should the regulator be reading correctly at the commencement of this test, the earth lead of the voltmeter should be transferred to the 'E' connection on the regulator box; the reading should be the same as that obtained with the previous earth. If there is any difference, i.e. the 'E' connection on the regulator gives a lower reading, it will indicate a bad earth on the regulator box.

Regulator adjustments

The regulators are carefully set during manufacture to suit the normal requirements of standard equipment and, in general, further adjustments should not be necessary. However, if the battery does not keep in a charged condition, or if the dynamo output does not fall when the battery is fully charged, it may be advisable to check the settings and readjust if necessary.

Before disturbing any settings, it is preferable to check that a fault in the charging system is not due to a slipping dynamo belt or to a defective battery.

Electrical setting of voltage regulator

5. Disconnect control box terminal 'B'. Connect a first-grade moving-coil 0–20 voltmeter between terminal 'D' and earth.

6. Slowly increase the speed of the engine until the voltmeter needle flicks and steadies. This should occur at a reading between 14.2 and 14.8 volts. If it does not, stop the engine and remove the control box cover.

7. Slacken the adjustment screw locking nut (see illustration) and turn the screw in a clockwise direction to raise the voltage setting, or anti-clockwise to lower the setting. Turn the screw a fraction of a turn only at a time and retighten the locknut.

Repeat this open-circuit voltage test until the correct setting is obtained.
Remake the original connections.

When the dynamo is run at a high speed on open circuit, it builds up a high voltage. Therefore, do not run the

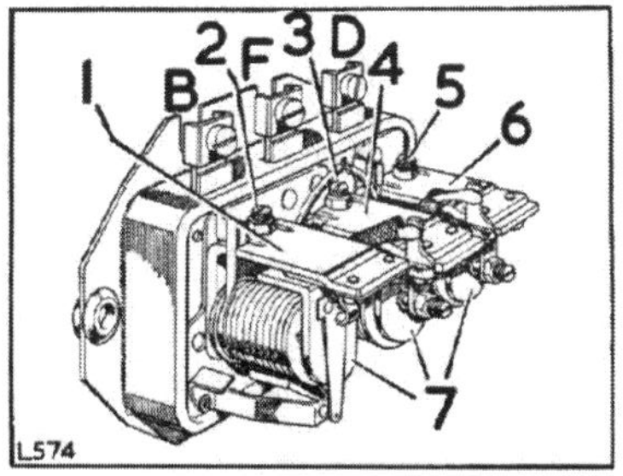

Fig. N1-37. Current voltage regulator

1—Cut-out
2—Cut-out adjusting screw
3—Current adjusting screw
4—Current regulator
5—Voltage adjusting screw
6—Voltage regulator
7—Armature
B—Terminal
F—Terminal
D—Terminal

engine up to more than half throttle or a false voltmeter reading will be obtained. The adjustment should be completed within 30 seconds, otherwise heating of the regulator winding may cause an inaccurate setting to be made.

Electrical setting of current regulator on vehicle

9. When setting the current regulator on the vehicle, the dynamo must be made to develop its maximum rated output, whatever the state of charge of the battery might be at the time of setting. The voltage regulator must therefore be rendered inoperative. To do this, the voltage regulator contacts should be short-circuited with a clip large enough to bridge the outer armature assembly securing screw and the insulated fixed contact bracket, as shown in Fig. N1-38.

10. Disconnect the cable from control box terminal 'B' and connect a first-grade moving-coil 0–40 ammeter between this cable and terminal 'B'. Switch on all lamps and accessories. This will prevent the voltage of the system rising when the engine is started.

noting the instant when the voltmeter reading drops to zero. This should occur between 9.5 and 10.5 volts. If it does not, adjust by carefully bowing the legs of the fixed contact post. Repeat the test and, if necessary, readjust until the armature releases at the voltage specified.

Cleaning contacts

When cleaning the voltage or current regulator contacts, use fine carborundum stone or silicon carbide paper, followed by methylated spirits (denatured alcohol).

When cleaning the cut-out contacts, use a strip of fine glass paper—never carborundum stone or emery cloth.

Mechanical setting of air gaps, voltage and current regulators

All air-gap settings are accurately adjusted before the units leave the factory, and should require no further attention. If, however, an armature is removed for any reason, care must be taken to obtain the correct air-gap settings on reassembly.

14. Slacken the two armature assembly securing screws so that the armature is loosely attached to the regulator frame.

15. Slacken the fixed contact locking nut and unscrew the fixed contact adjustment screw until it is well clear of the armature moving contact.

16. Slacken the voltage (or current) adjustment screw locking nut and unscrew the adjustment screw until it is well clear of the armature tension spring.

17. Using a 0.015 in. thick flat steel gauge, wide enough to cover completely the core face, insert the gauge between the underside of the armature and the copper disc. Take care not to turn up or damage the edge of this disc.

18. Press the armature squarely down against the gauge and retighten the two armature assembly securing screws.

19. With the gauge still in position, screw in the fixed contact adjustment screw until it just touches the armature moving contact. Retighten the locking nut.

20. Carry out the electrical settings, items 5 to 11, as applicable.

Fig. N1-38. Short-circuiting voltage regulator contacts

A—Current regulator adjusting screw
B—Terminal
C—Clip, short-circuiting
D—Terminal
F—Terminal

11. With the dynamo running at approximately 3,000 rpm, the ammeter needle should be steady and indicate a current of 19 amp with a type C39 dynamo, 22 amp with a type C40 dynamo or 30 amp with a type C42 dynamo. If it does not, the unit must be adjusted in a manner similar to that described for the voltage regulator.
Re-make the original connections.

Electrical setting of cut-out relay

12. Connect a first-grade moving-coil 0–20 voltmeter between control box terminal 'D' and earth. Switch on the headlamps and slowly increase the engine speed from zero. Closure of the contacts, indicated by a slight drop in the voltmeter reading, should occur between 12.7 and 13.3 volts. If it does not, the unit must be adjusted in a manner similar to that described for the voltage regulator.

When setting the cut-in voltage at a test bench, a suitable load resistor passing about 6 amperes should be connected between control box terminal 'B' and earth. This will cause the voltmeter needle to flicker at the instant of contact closure.

13. Disconnect the cable from control box terminal 'B'. Connect a first-grade moving-coil 0–20 voltmeter between this terminal and earth. Run the engine up to speed and then slowly decelerate,

ELECTRICAL EQUIPMENT

Operation N1-16—continued

6. Check earth connections, particularly that of the control box.

7. In the event of reported undercharging, ascertain that this is not due to low mileage.

8. Should the control box fail to respond correctly to any adjustment given in the following instructions, it should be exchanged for a factory reconditioned unit.

A special tool, Lucas Part No. 54381742 is required for adjustment of the RB340 control box electrical settings. Checking and adjusting should be completed as rapidly as possible to avoid heating errors.

Voltage regulator, adjust

Ambient Temperature	Voltage Setting RB310	RB340
10°C (50°F)	15.1–15.7	14.9–15.5
20°C (68°F)	14.9–15.5	14.7–15.3
30°C (86°F)	14.7–15.3	14.5–15.1
40°C (104°F)	14.5–15.1	14.3–14.9

9. Disconnect all cables from control box terminal 'B' and tape ends in such a manner that they are still in contact with each other.

10. Connect a first-grade 0–20 moving-coil voltmeter between control box terminal 'D' and a good earthing point.

11. Start the engine and, while observing the voltmeter, gradually speed up to a dynamo speed of 3,000 rpm.

12. The voltmeter pointer should progressively rise to a maximum value, then 'flick' back to a slightly lower reading and remain steady. This is the regulating voltage and should be within the above limits.

13. An unsteady reading of more than ±0.3 volts may be due to unclean contacts. If the reading occurs outside the appropriate limits, an adjustment must be made. In this event, continue as follows:

14. Stop the engine and remove the control box cover.

Early models with type C40 dynamo and RB310 regulator

15. Slacken the adjustment screw locking nut and turn the screw in a clockwise direction to raise the voltage setting, or anti-clockwise to lower the setting. Turn the screw a fraction of a turn only at a time and retighten locknut.

Late models with type C42 dynamo and RB340 regulator

16. Insert the special tool in the voltage regulator and turn the cam a very small amount.
Turning clockwise will increase the voltage setting, and vice-versa.

17. Restart the engine and check the setting, as detailed above.

18. When the dynamo is run at high speed on open circuit it builds up a high voltage. Do not run the engine up to more than half throttle or a false voltage reading will be given. Complete adjustments within 30 seconds as heating of the regulator winding may cause an inaccurate setting to be made.

19. Repeat this procedure as necessary, until the regulating voltage setting lies within the appropriate limits.

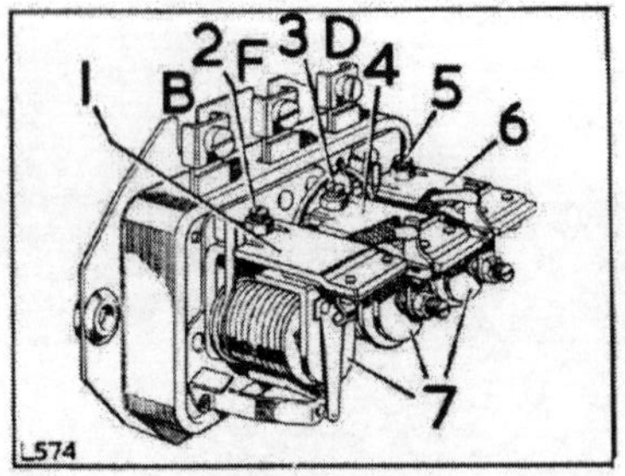

Fig. N1.41. Current voltage regulator, type RB31

1—Cut-out
2—Cut-out adjusting screw
3—Current adjusting screw
4—Current regulator
5—Voltage adjusting screw
6—Voltage regulator
7—Armature
B—Battery
D—Dynamo
F—Field

Operation N1-16—continued

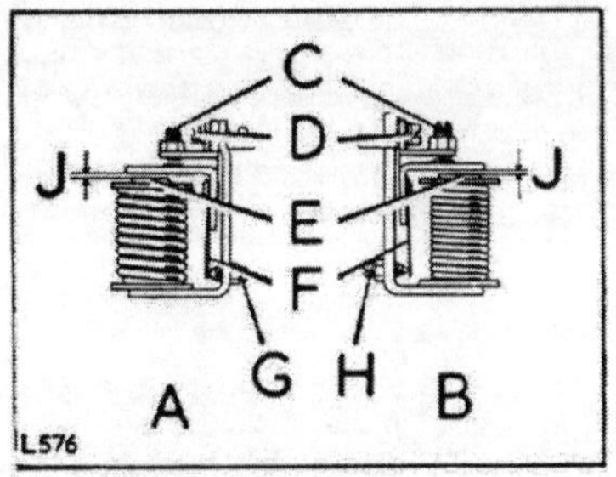

Fig. N1-39. Voltage and current regulators

A—Voltage regulator
B—Current regulator
C—Fixed contact adjustment screws
D—Armature assembly securing screws
E—Cores
F—Armature tension springs
G—Voltage adjustment screws
H—Current adjustment screws
J—.015 in. (0.40 mm)

Setting cut-out relay air-gap

21. Slacken the two armature assembly securing screws so that the armature is loosely attached to the cut-out frame.

22. Slacken the adjustment screw locking nut and unscrew the adjustment screw until it is well clear of the armature tension spring.

23. Press the armature squarely down against the copper-sprayed core face and retighten the two armature assembly securing screws. No gauge is necessary.

24. Press the armature down against the armature back stop and adjust the armature back stop so that a .018 in. (0.5 mm) gap is obtained between the tip of the back stop and the contact blade.

25. Insert a .010 in. (0.25 mm) thick flat steel gauge between the underside of the armature and the copper-sprayed core face. The gauge should be should be just from the side of the core nearest the fixed contact post. The leading edge of the gauge should not be inserted beyond the centre line of the core face. Press the armature down against the core face and check the cut-out contacts. These should be just touching. If necessary, adjust the height of the fixed contact by carefully bowing the legs of the fixed contact post.

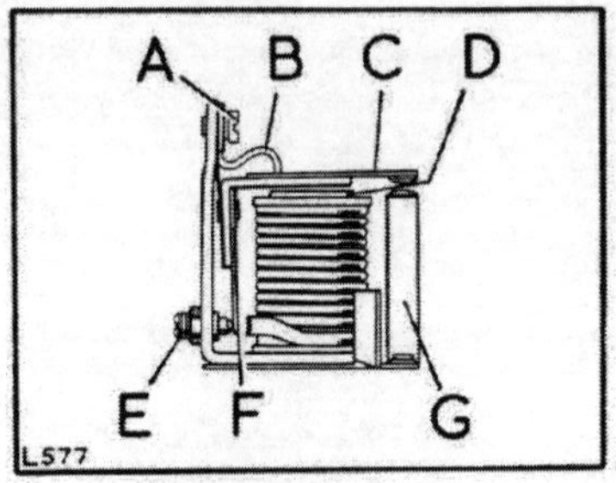

26. Reset the cut-in voltage, items 12 and 13, and lock the adjustment screw.

B. Current voltage regulator, types RB310 and RB340

Control box, adjust

1. Before disturbing any electrical adjustments examine the charging circuit as under to ensure that the fault does not lie outside the control box.

2. Check the battery by substitution or with a hydrometer or heavy discharge tester.

3. Inspect the dynamo driving belt; this should be tensioned to give 7/16 in. to 7/16 in. (8mm to 11 mm) deflection by thumb pressure midway between the fan and crankshaft pulleys.

4. Check the dynamo by substitution or in accordance with Operation N1-22.

5. Inspect the wiring of the charging circuit and carry out continuity test between the dynamo, control box and when fitted, the ammeter.

Fig. N1-40. Cut-out relay

A—Armature assembly securing screw
B—Armature back stop
C—Contact blade
D—Core
E—Adjustment screw
F—Armature tension spring
G—Fixed contact post

ELECTRICAL EQUIPMENT

Operation N1-16—continued

20. Dirty contacts should be cleaned with a fine carborundum stone or silicon carbide paper, followed by methylated spirits. If the contacts setting is disturbed, reset as detailed in Overhaul Instruction (air gap settings), then adjust the electrical settings.

21. When satisfactory, restore the original connections and refit the cover.

Current regulator, adjust

22. The current regulator on-load setting is equal to the maximum rated output of the dynamo, which is:
    Type C40 dynamo—22 amps.
    Type C42 dynamo—30 amps.

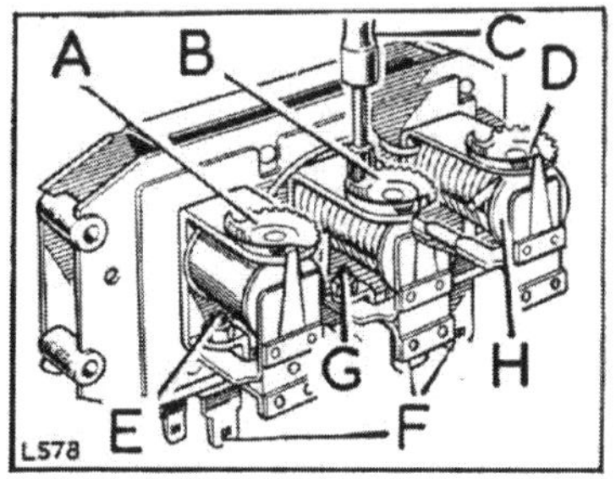

23. The dynamo must be made to develop its maximum rated output, whatever the state of charge of the battery might be at the time of setting. The voltage regulator must therefore be rendered inoperative and this is achieved by shorting-out the voltage regulator contacts.

24. Remove the control box cover with care.

Fig. N1-42. Current voltage regulator, type RB340

A—Adjustment cam of voltage regulator
B—Adjustment cam of current regulator
C—Special setting tool
D—Adjustment cam of cut-out relay
E—Adjustable contact of voltage regulator
F—'Lucar' connection terminals
G—Adjustable contact of current regulator
H—Core face of cut-out relay

Operation N1-16—continued

25. Place a crocodile clip across the voltage regulator fixed contact bracket and the voltage regulator frame, to short-out the contacts.

26. Withdraw the leads from the 'B' terminal of the control box and use a 'jumper lead' to connect the two leads together and to the load side of a first-grade 0–40 moving-coil ammeter.

27. Connect the other side of the ammeter to the 'B' terminal of the control box. It is important that the terminal 'B' carries only the testing ammeter lead.

28. If the battery is well charged switch on an electrical load in excess of the maximum rated output of the dynamo. Start the engine and run the dynamo at 4,500 rpm. Observe ammeter which should be indicating a steady current equal to the maximum rated output of the dynamo.

29. The ammeter pointer should be steady. An unsteady reading (that is one fluctuating more than ± 1 ampere) may be due to unclean contacts which should be cleaned as described for the voltage regulator. If the reading is too high or too low, an adjustment must be made. In this event, continue as follows:

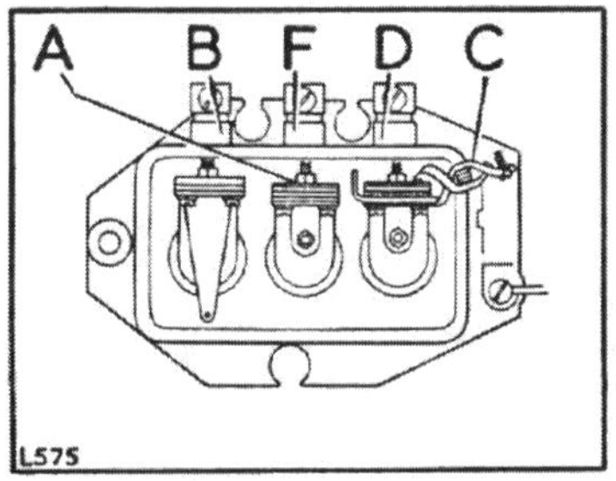

Fig. N1-43. Short-circuiting voltage regulator contacts, type RB310 regulator illustrated

A—Current regulator adjusting screw
B—Terminal
C—Clip, short-circuiting
D—Terminal
F—Terminal

30. Stop the engine for each adjustment. Insert the special tool in the current regulator and turn the cam a very small amount.
    Clockwise rotation will increase the setting and vice-versa.

31. When the setting is satisfactory (i.e. within ± 1 ampere of the maximum output figure for the dynamo), switch off the load and headlamps. Restore the original connections.

32. Refit the control box cover with care.

Cut-in voltage, adjust

Checking and adjusting should be completed as rapidly as possible to avoid heating errors.
Cut-in voltage: 12.7–13.3.
Drop-off voltage: 9.5–11.0.

33. Connect a first-grade 0–20 moving-coil voltmeter between control box terminal 'D' and a good earthing point.

34. Switch on an electrical load, such as the headlamps.

35. Start the engine and slowly increase the engine speed.

36. Observe the voltmeter pointer.

37. Closure of the contacts, indicated by a slight drop in the voltmeter reading, should occur between the limits 12.7–13.3 volts. If the cut-in occurs outside these limits, an adjustment must be made. In this event, continue as follows:

38. Reduce the engine speed below the cut-in value, and remove the control box cover.

39. Insert the special tool in the cut-out relay and turn the cam a small amount in the appropriate direction.
    Clockwise rotation will raise the setting and vice-versa.

40. Repeat the checking and setting procedure as necessary, until the correct setting is obtained.

41. Restore the original connections and refit the cover.

Drop-off voltage, adjust

42. Disconnect the cables from control box at terminal 'B' and tape. Connect a first-grade 0–20 moving-coil voltmeter between this terminal and a good earth on the chassis.

Operation N1-16—continued

43. Start the engine and increase engine speed gradually to approximately one-quarter throttle opening.

44. Slowly decelerate and observe the voltmeter pointer.

45. Opening of the contacts, indicated by the voltmeter pointer dropping to zero, should occur between 9.5–11.0 volts. If the drop-off occurs outside these limits, an adjustment must be made. In this event, continue as follows:

46. Stop the engine and remove the control box cover with care.

47. Adjust the drop-off voltage by carefully bending the fixed contact bracket. Reducing the contact gap will raise the drop-off voltage; increasing the gap will lower the drop-off voltage.

48. Repeat items 43 and 44 and, if necessary, readjust until the correct drop-off setting is obtained.

49. Restore the original connections and refit the control box cover with care.

50. To clean the cut-out relay contacts, use a strip of fine glass paper—never carborundum stone or emery cloth.

Control box overhaul (type RB340)

Air gap settings

All air gap settings are accurately adjusted during production and should require no further attention. However, if it has been found necessary to disturb the original setting it must be readjusted as follows, before the electrical settings can be carried out.

Voltage and current regulators

51. To set the air gap between the bobbin and armature on the voltage and current regulators. Disconnect battery. Use the special tool and turn the adjustment cam to the point giving minimum lift to the armature tensioning spring (that is, fully anti-clockwise).

52. Slacken the adjustable contact locknut and screw back the adjustable contact.

53. Insert a 0.045 in. (1.000 mm) flat feeler gauge between the armature and the core face, taking care not to damage the copper shim. Push the gauge back to the two rivet heads on the under side of the armature.

Operation N1-16—continued

The use of non-magnetic material in the top gap has been discontinued, as from December 1963. When servicing late type units use a feeler gauge of 0.052 in. to 0.056 in. (1.30 mm to 1.40 mm).

54. Screw in the adjustable contact until the gauge is just trapped, that is when it takes a pull of 4 to 5 oz to remove it. Retighten the locknut.

55. Check that narrowest part of back gap, between the armature back face and the frame, on both sides of the armature, is between the limits 0.030 in. to 0.040 in. (0.76 mm to 1.00 mm) with a maximum of 0.010 in. (0.25 mm) taper for current regulator units.

56. Electrical setting of the voltage regulator can now be carried out; leaving the current regulator unit until the cut-out has been adjusted both mechanically and electrically.

Cut-out

57. With the control box cover removed, turn the adjuster to the point giving maximum lift to the armature tensioning spring, that is by turning the adjuster to its fullest extent anti-clockwise.

58. Press the armature squarely down against the copper separation on the core face. Check that the narrowest part of the back gap, between the armature back face and the frame, on both sides of the armature, is from 0.030 in. to 0.040 in. (0.76 mm to 1.00 mm).

59. Insert a 0.015 in. (0.38 mm) flat feeler gauge between the head of the core and the armature using the nearest rivet as a datum. Press the armature down and bend the fixed contact bracket until the two contacts just touch, this is the preliminary setting for contact 'follow through'.

60. Insert a 0.015 in. (0.38 mm) feeler gauge between the head of the core and armature as above. Adjust the armature back stop until it just touches the back of the armature.

61. Check that the top gap, controlled by the back stop and using the nearest rivet as a datum, is from 0.035 in. to 0.045 in. (0.8 mm to 1.1 mm).

62. Proceed with the electrical settings for the cut-out, as detailed.

Horn push, to remove and refit—Operation N1-17

Workshop hand tools:
Screwdriver (medium)

To remove

Bracket mounted type

1. Remove the securing screws and withdraw the horn button and leads.
2. Disconnect the leads if necessary.

Centre type

3. Gently prise out the centre complete from the steering wheel. Disconnect the lead at the snap connector on the centre.
4. Remove the horn button from the centre if necessary.

To refit

1. Reverse the removal procedure.

ELECTRICAL EQUIPMENT

Electric horn, remove, refit and adjust—Operation N1-18

Workshop hand tools:
Spanner sizes:

Horn button

To remove

Bracket mounted type

1. Remove the securing screws and withdraw the horn button and leads.
2. Disconnect the leads if necessary.

Centre type

3. Gently prise out the centre complete from the steering wheel. Disconnect the lead at the snap connector on the centre.
4. Remove the horn button from the centre if necessary.

To refit

1. Reverse the removal procedure.

Electric horn

To remove (Figs. N1-27, N1-28 and N1-29)

The electric horn is mounted behind the radiator grille panel and is accessible after lifting the bonnet, although on certain models, other equipment mounted above the horn must be removed.

1. Disconnect the leads at the snap connectors adjacent to the horn, then remove the securing bolts and withdraw the unit.

To refit

1. Reverse the removal procedure.

Adjustment of horn

Note: Four types of electric horn are in use requiring three methods of adjustment, and care should be taken to refer to applicable instructions.

The horn is adjusted on initial assembly and should not require attention for some considerable time.

Ascertain that horn failure or faulty note is not due to some outside source, such as a discharged battery, loose connections or loose horn mounting, before carrying out any adjustment.

Lucas type horn, to adjust

1. Remove the horn from the vehicle.

Operation N1-18—continued

3. Connect the horn leads to a 12 volt battery and adjust nut (A) until maximum volume is obtained, then lock in position with nut (B). See illustration.
4. Adjust the air gap between armature (C) and the magnet core face (D) to .045 to .050 in. (1.0 to 1,25 mm) by slackening nut (E) and turn the armature (C) clockwise or anti-clockwise until the recommended distance is obtained, then tighten nut (E). The current consumption with horn correctly adjusted is 9 amperes.

Clear Hooters horn (later type, Series IIA models), to adjust

No routine adjustment of the horn is required. Should, however, the note be distorted, proceed as follows:

1. Remove the dome and turn the adjustment screw either clockwise or anti-clockwise.
2. Should this adjustment not produce satisfactory results, the horn should be returned to the manufacturer.

Clear Hooters horn (latest type, Series IIA models), to adjust

The latest type Clear Hooters horn is of all riveted construction and does not have a removable dome. Means of adjustment is provided externally by a special serrated screw adjacent to the cable terminals.

1. Remove the horn from the vehicle.
2. Connect the horn leads to a 12 volt battery and turn the serrated screw anti-clockwise until the horn just fails to sound, then turn it back for approximately one-quarter of a turn.
3. If the foregoing adjustment does not produce satisfactory results, a new replacement should be fitted.

---

2. Remove the dome and dome securing clip, clean the points and adjust them until they are almost touching, then turn the adjusting screw half a turn to increase the gap.
3. If adjustment of the horn does not produce satisfactory results, the horn should be returned to the makers.

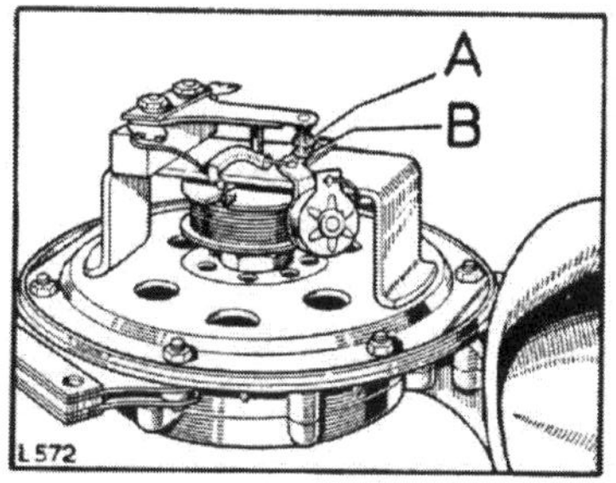

Fig. N1-44. Horn adjustment. Lucas. Series II models
A—Adjustable contact B—Locknut

Clear Hooters horn (early type Series II models), to adjust

1. Remove the horn from the vehicle.
2. Remove the dome and dome clip.

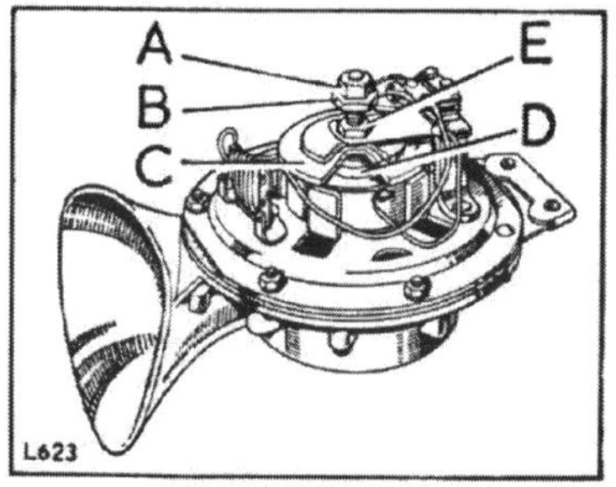

Fig. N1-45. Horn adjustment. Clear Hooters. Series II models
A—Locknut
B—Adjusting nut
C—Armature
D—Magnet core
E—Locknut, armature

Windscreen wiper, to remove and refit—Operation N1-19

Workshop hand tools:
Spanner sizes: 7/16 in. AF, ½ in. AF
Screwdrivers (small and medium)

Early type windscreen wiper, to remove

1. Slacken the wiper arm fixing nut and tap sharply to release the clamp collet, then remove the wiper arm and blade.
2. With the key in lamp switch turned 'off', disconnect the leads from wiper motor.
3. Remove the securing nuts, washers, grommets, wiper blade stop, rubber mounting block and brass bushes, then withdraw the motor.

To refit

1. Reverse removal procedure, but do not lock the wiper arm blade until the sweep is correctly adjusted.

Fig. N1-46. Early type windscreen wiper

This page intentionally left blank

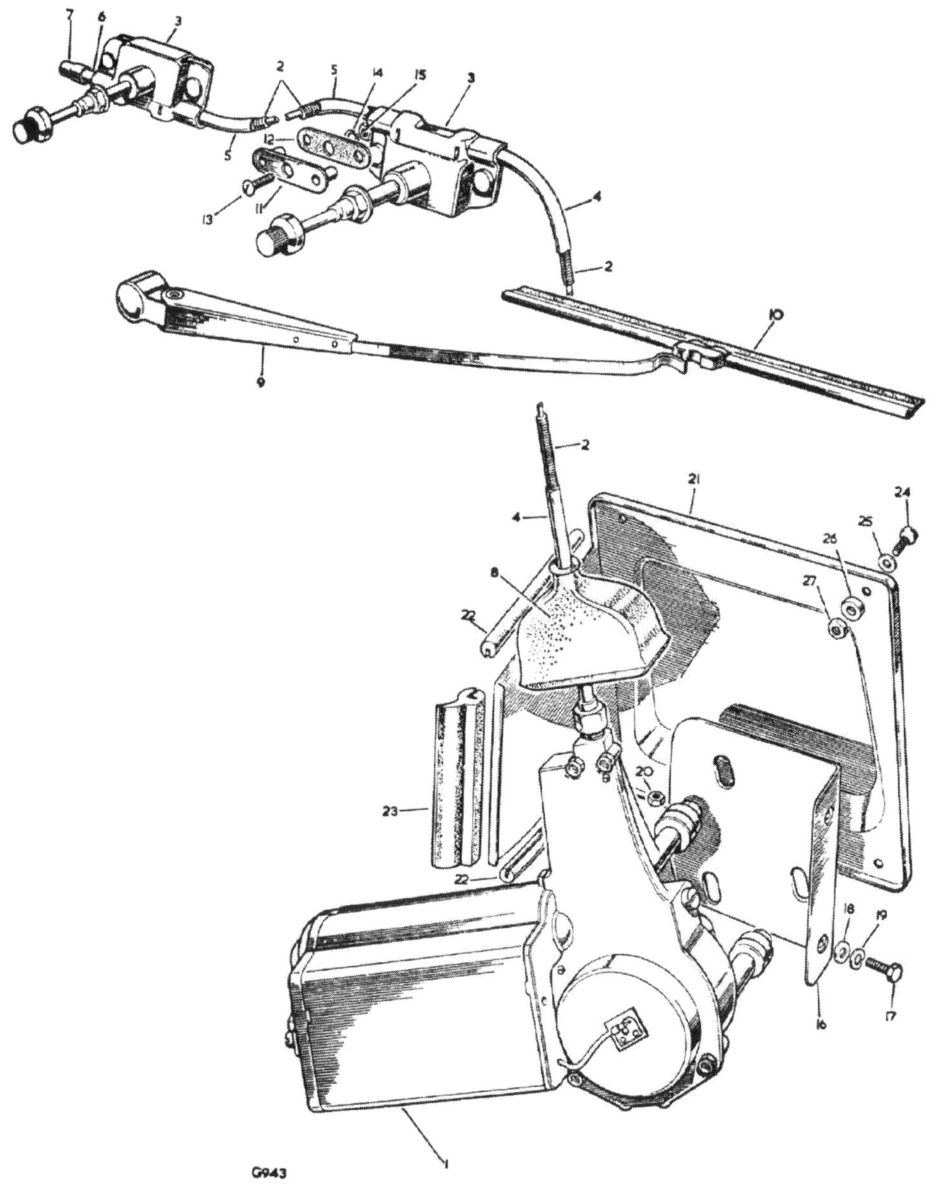

ELECTRICAL EQUIPMENT

Key to illustration of windscreen wiper (Early version of latest type)

1. Windscreen wiper motor complete
2. Flexible drive cable
3. Wheelbox for wiper
4. Outer casing, motor to wheelbox
5. Outer casing, wheelbox to wheelbox
6. Outer casing, wheelbox end
7. Rubber cover for wiper motor in dash
8. Arm for wiper blade, RH
9. Arm for wiper blade, LH
10. Wiper blade
11. Escutcheon for windscreen wiper motor
12. Rubber seal for escutcheon
13. Screw (2 BA x 1⅛ in. long) ⎫ Fixing
14. Spring washer ⎬ redundant
15. Nut (2 BA) ⎭ escutcheon
16. Mounting bracket for wiper motor
17. Bolt (¼ in. UNF x ⅜ in. long) ⎫ Fixing
18. Plain washer ⎬ mounting
19. Spring washer ⎬ bracket to
20. Nut (¼ in. UNF) ⎭ LH glove box
21. Cover plate for wiper motor
22. Rubber finisher ⎫ For cover
23. Rubber seal ⎭ plate
24. Screw (2 BA x ½ in. long) ⎫ Fixing cover plate
25. Plain washer ⎬ to LH glove box
26. Distance washer ⎬
27. Nut (2 BA) ⎭

Fig. N1-47. Layout of windscreen wiper (Early version of latest type)

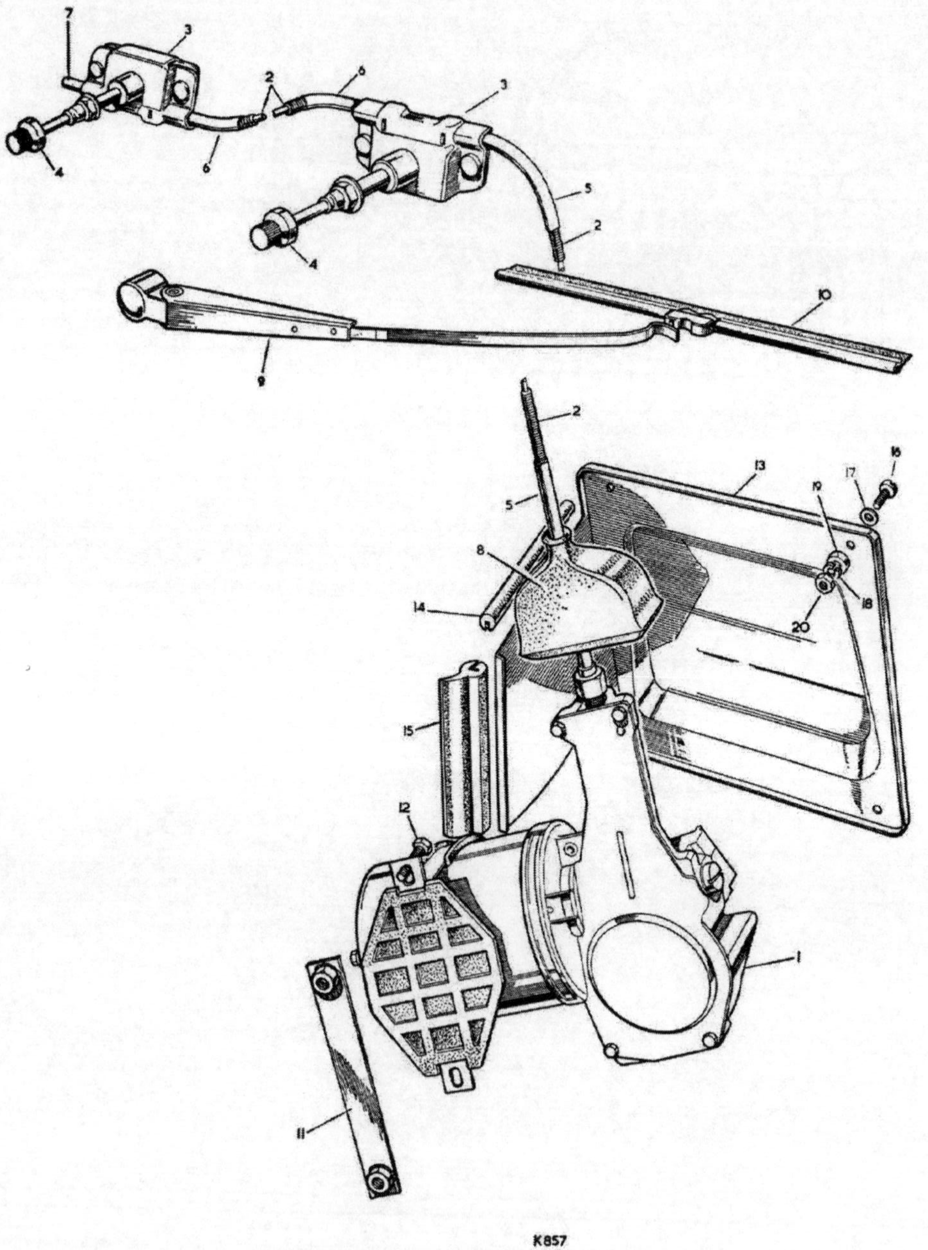

ELECTRICAL EQUIPMENT

Section N—Land-Rover

Key to illustration of windscreen wiper (Latest version of latest type).

1. Windscreen wiper motor complete
2. Flexible drive cable
3. Wheelbox for wiper
4. Spindle and gear for wheelbox
5. Outer casing, motor to wheelbox
6. Outer casing, wheelbox to wheelbox
7. Outer casing, wheelbox end
8. Rubber cover for wiper motor in dash
9. Arm for wiper blade
10. Wiper blade
11. Nut plate for wiper motor
12. Set screw ($\frac{1}{4}$ in. UNF x $\frac{5}{8}$ in. long) fixing wiper motor to dash and nut plate
13. Cover plate for wiper motor
14. Rubber finisher } For cover plate
15. Rubber seal
16. Screw (2 BA x $\frac{5}{8}$ in. long) ⎫
17. Plain washer
18. Spring washer
19. Distance washer
20. Nut (2 BA) ⎭ Fixing cover plate to LH glove box

Fig. N1-48. Layout of windscreen wiper (Latest version of latest type)

Section N—Land-Rover

ELECTRICAL EQUIPMENT

Operation N1-19—continued

Latest type windscreen wiper (two versions in use)

Wiper motor, remove

1. Disconnect battery.
2. Remove wiper blades.
3. Remove dash cover plate, secured by four drive screws.
4. Unscrew nut holding curved tube to wiper motor.

Early version:

5. Remove the four bolts attaching mounting plate to bottom and side of glove box and withdraw wiper motor complete with mounting plate and flexible drive.

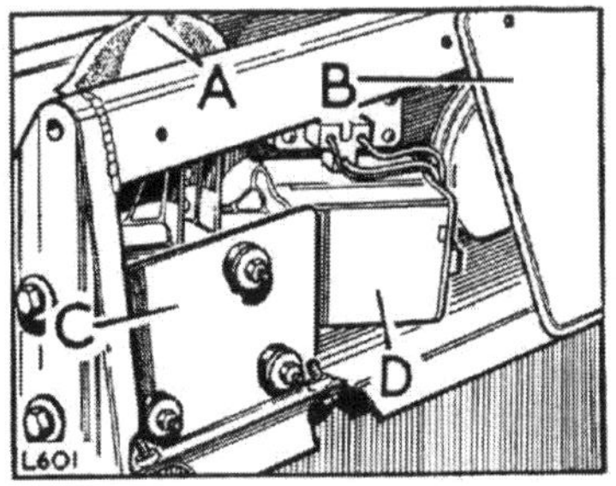

Fig. N1-49. Location of wiper motor in glove box, early version illustrated

A—Rubber cover for wiper
B—Cover for glove box aperture
C—Mounting bracket for wiper
D—Wiper motor

Latest version:

6. Remove the two bolts from the glove box and the nut plate from the engine compartment which secure the wiper motor to the dash panel. Withdraw the wiper motor complete with flexible drive.

Wiper motor, refit

1. Reverse removal procedure.

Wheel box, remove (Latest type windscreen wipers only)

1. Disconnect battery.
2. Remove wiper motor as already described.
3. Remove the six screws securing windscreen lower trim panel and remove panel.
4. Remove the wheel boxes from the body.
5. Remove the outer casings, which are secured to the wheel boxes by two screws.

Wheel box, refit

1. Ensure that the rubber or steel bush is in position on the spindle housing.
2. Lubricate the spindle and spindle gear with Ragosine Listate 225 grease.
3. Place the wheel box over the flexible drive and secure the housing and cover with the two screws. Ensure that the flared ends of the outer casing engage in the slots of the cover in the two outer positions, and the ends of the centre outer casing are on the inside slot to allow for slight transverse adjustment.

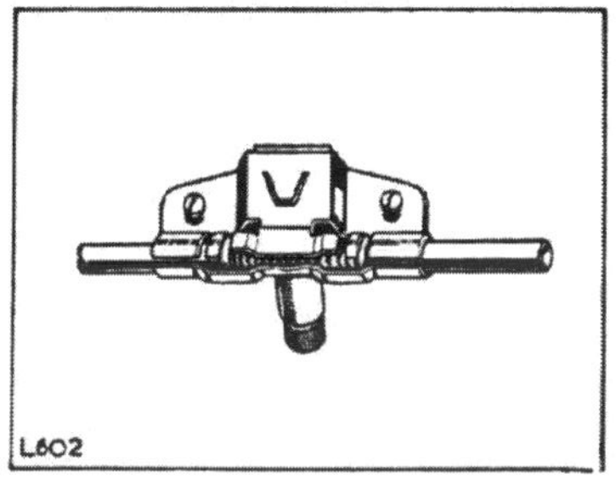

Fig. N1-50. Outer casing in correct position

4. Refit the wheel box and drive assembly to the body.
5. Connect the drive to the motor by reversing removal procedure.
6. Refit trim panel.

Section N—Land-Rover

ELECTRICAL EQUIPMENT

Starter motor, type M418G, 2¼ litre and 2.6 litre Petrol models, to overhaul—Operation N1-20

(For removal and refitting instructions, Section A refers)

Workshop hand tools:
Spanner size: ½ in. BSF open end
Screwdriver (medium), Ohm meter

Special tools:
Clamp (see text)

To dismantle

1. Remove cover band.
2. Lift field brushes from guides.
3. Remove nuts and washers from end cover.
4. Remove the two through bolts.
5. Withdraw commutator end cover.
6. Remove starter yoke from armature assembly.
7. Early starter motors—Remove the split pin and special nut from the armature shaft.
8. Latest starter motors—Using a suitable clamp, see illustration, clamp end collar and compress main spring.
9. Remove the circlip from the armature shaft, then remove the clamp.

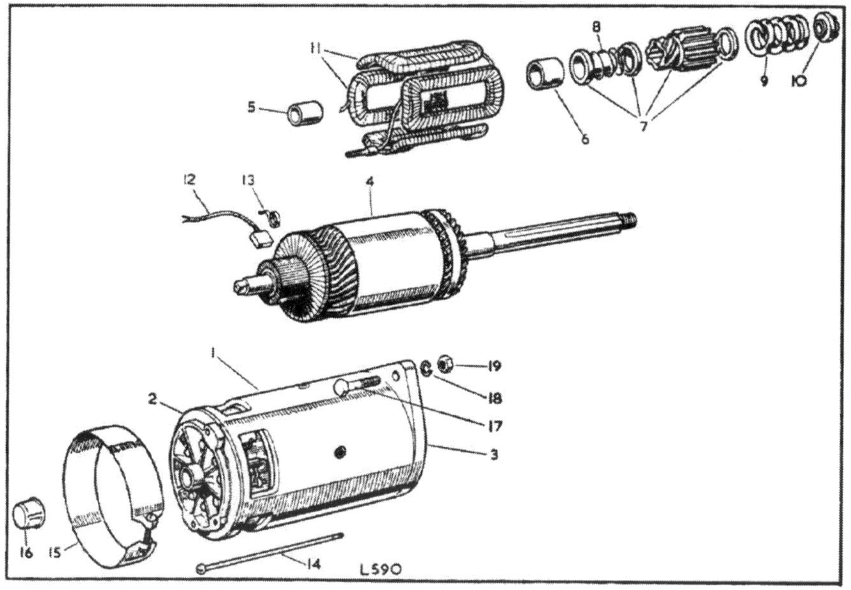

Fig. N1-51. Layout of starter motor, type M418G, 2¼ litre and 2.6 litre Petrol models

1 Yoke
2 Bracket for starter, commutator end
3 Bracket, drive end
4 Armature
5 Bush, commutator end
6 Bush, pinion end
7 Pinion and sleeve
8 Spring for pinion
9 Main spring for pinion
10 Nut for pinion
11 Field coil for starter
12 Brushes for starter motor, set
13 Spring set for brushes
14 Bolt for bracket
15 Cover band
16 Grease cap
17 Bolt (⅜ in. BSF x 1⅜ in. long) } Fixing starter motor to flywheel housing
18 Spring washer
19 Nut (⅜ in. BSF)

ELECTRICAL EQUIPMENT

Operation N1-20—continued

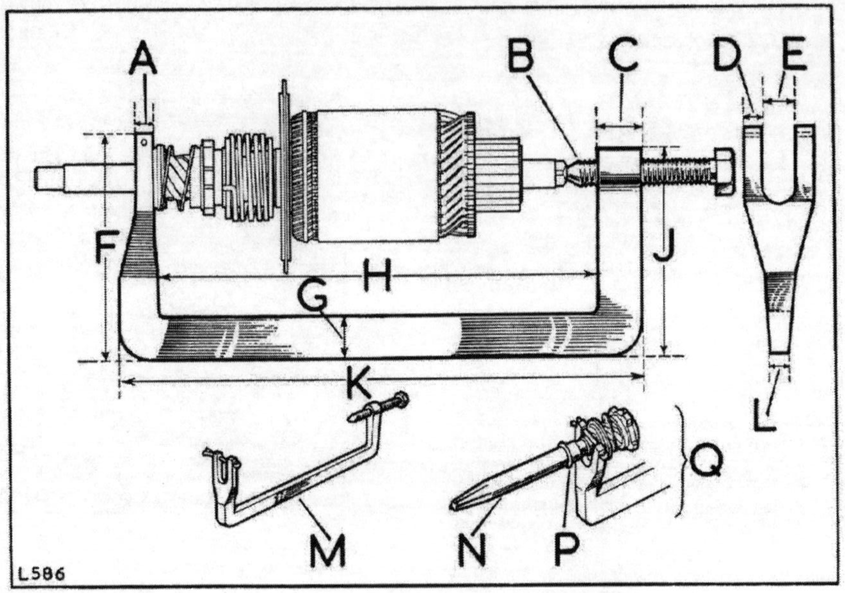

Fig. N1-52. Method of withdrawing and fitting circlip

A—$\frac{7}{16}$ in.
B—$\frac{1}{2}$ in. (12.5 mm) diameter bolt
C—1 in. (25.4 mm)
D—$\frac{3}{8}$ in.
E—$\frac{1}{4}$ in.
F—5 in. (127 mm)
G—$\frac{3}{8}$ in.
H—12 in.
J—4$\frac{1}{2}$ in.
K—14 in.
L—$\frac{3}{4}$ in.
M—Suitable clamp made from wrought iron
N—Tube with internal diameter to suit shaft
P—Circlip
Q—Method of replacing circlip using clamp and tube

10. Withdraw the end collar (latest starter motor), main spring, washer, screwed sleeve and pinion, collar, pinion retaining spring and spring retaining sleeve.

To overhaul

Brushes

1. Check that the brushes move freely in their holders by holding back the brush spring and pulling gently on the flexible connectors. Any tendency to stick should be corrected by cleaning with a petrol-moistened cloth, or in extreme cases by the light use of a smooth file. If a brush is damaged or worn so that it does not make good contact on the commutator, all the brushes must be renewed.

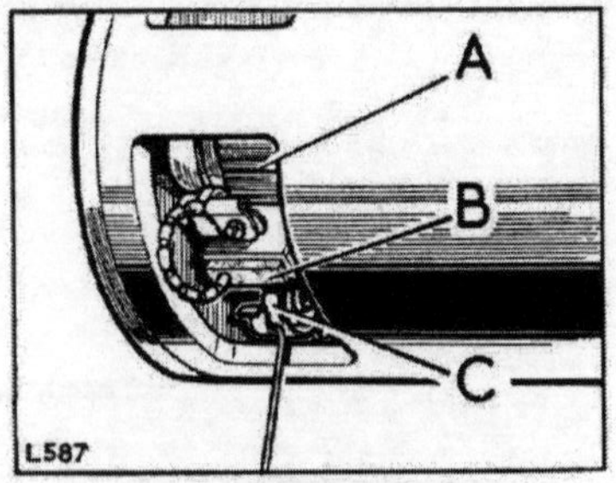

Fig. N1-53. Checking brushes

A—Commutator
B—Brush spring
C—Brush

Operation N1-20—continued

2. Check the tension of the brush springs with a spring balance. The correct tension is 30 to 40 oz (850 to 1134 grammes) and new springs must be fitted if the tension is low.

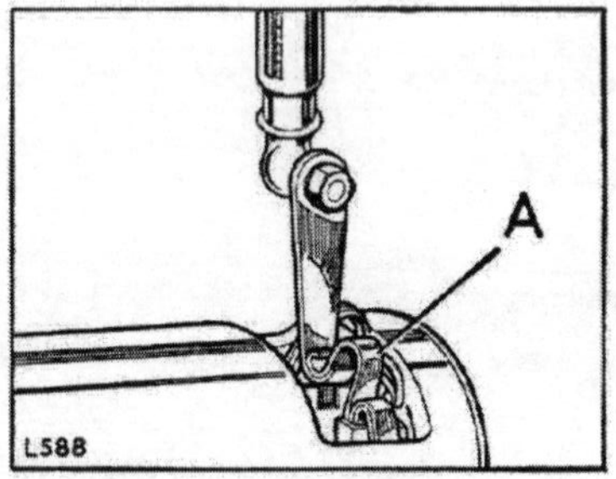

Fig. N1-54. Testing brush spring tension

A—Brush spring

3. When brushes are worn to $\frac{5}{16}$ in. (8.0 mm) in length, new replacements must be fitted.

4. The flexible connectors are soldered or crimped to terminal tags; two are connected to brush boxes, and two are connected to the free ends of the field coils. These flexible connectors must be removed by unsoldering, and the flexible connectors of the new brushes secured in their places by soldering.
The new brushes being pre-formed, 'bedding' to the commutator is unnecessary.

Commutator

5. Clean the commutator with a petrol-moistened cloth. If necessary, rotate the armature and, using fine glass-cloth, remove pits and burned spots from commutator; remove abrasive dust with a dry air blast. If the commutator is badly worn, mount in a lathe, and, using a very sharp tool, take a light cut, taking care not to remove any more metal than necessary. The insulators between the commutator segments must **not** be **Undercut**. Finally, polish with a very fine glass paper.

Armature

6. If the armature is damaged, i.e. 'lifted' conductors' or distorted shaft, a new replacement must be fitted. Never attempt to machine the armature core, or true a distorted armature shaft.

Bearing bushes

If the bearing bushes are worn and allow excessive side play of the armature shaft, new replacements must be fitted.

7. Commutator end bracket bush—Remove brake shoes, thrust washer and Tufnol washer from the end bracket. Screw in a $\frac{9}{16}$ in. tap and withdraw complete with bush.

8. Drive end bracket bush and intermediate bracket bush can be pressed out.

9. New bushes can be fitted using a shouldered mandrel of the same diameter as the shaft.

   Note: Before fitting a new porous bronze bush, it should be completely immersed for 24 hours in clean SAE 30-40 engine oil.
   Porous bronze bushes must **not** be reamered after fitting.

Insulation and continuity checks

If inspection of the armature and field coils of the starter motor do not reveal any faults, it is recommended that the following checks are carried out.

Armature insulation

1. Attach an ohm meter or a 110 volt AC test lamp in series with a 12 volt battery.

2. With two probes attached to the leads check the armature insulation by touching each commutator segment in turn with the other probe attached to the armature shaft.

3. The test lamp should not light up, or if an ohm meter is used, a high reading should be recorded. Should this not be the case, the armature insulation is faulty and a new replacement armature should be fitted.

Armature continuity

4. Indication of an open circuited armature winding will be given by burned commutator segments, this can be confirmed by substitution.

ELECTRICAL EQUIPMENT

Starter motor, type M45G, 2¼ litre Diesel models, to overhaul—Operation N1-21

(For removal and refitting instructions, Section A refers)

Workshop hand tools:
Spanner sizes: 5/16 in. BSF, 3/8 in. AF, 7/16 in. AF, 1/2 in. AF open end
Screwdriver (medium), Feeler gauges, Ohm meter

To dismantle

1. Remove the cover band, hold back the brush springs and lift the brushes from their holders.
2. Disconnect the earthing lead between the lower solenoid terminal and the starter motor casing.
3. Remove the solenoid securing nuts. Withdraw the solenoid from the drive end bracket casting, having **first marked** the solenoid and drive end bracket in relation to one another.
4. Lift the solenoid plunger up and clear of the starter drive engagement lever, and remove.
5. Unscrew and withdraw the two through bolts from the commutator end bracket, and remove bracket from the starter motor yoke.
6. Remove the rubber seal from the drive end bracket.
7. Remove the driving end bracket, complete with armature, drive and intermediate brackets from the yoke.
8. Remove the nut securing the eccentric pin, on which the drive engagement lever pivots, and withdraw pin.
9. Split the armature and intermediate bracket assembly from the drive end bracket and remove the engagement lever.
10. Push back the lock ring cover on the end of the armature shaft and remove the lock ring.
11. Remove the drive assembly, and intermediate bracket from the armature shaft.
    Note the shim(s) behind the intermediate bracket.

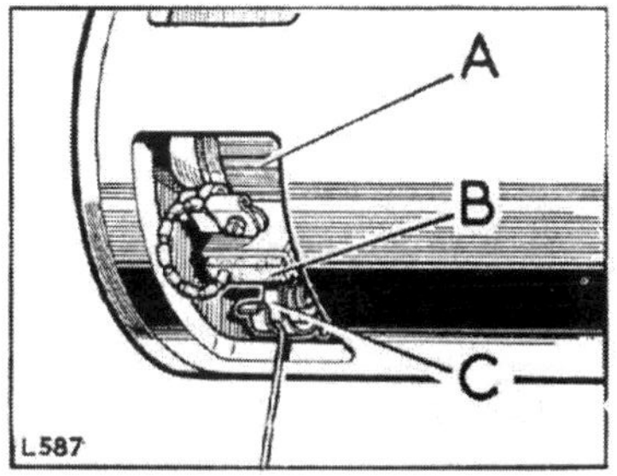

To overhaul

Brushes

1. Check that the brushes move freely in their holders by holding back the brush spring and pulling gently on the flexible connectors. Any tendency to stick should be corrected by cleaning with a petrol-moistened cloth, or in extreme cases by the light use of a smooth file. If a brush is damaged or worn so that it does not make good contact on the commutator, all the brushes must be renewed.

Fig. N1-55. Checking brushes
A—Commutator
B—Brush
C—Brush spring

2. Check the tension of the brush springs with a spring balance. The correct tension is 30 to 40 oz (850 to 1134 grammes) and new springs must be fitted if the tension is low.

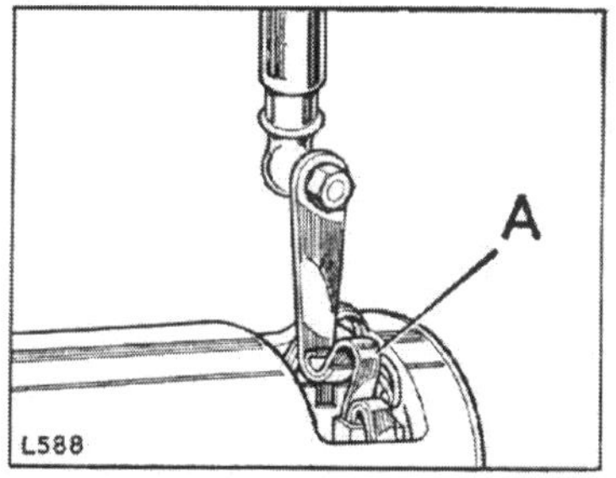

Fig. N1-56. Testing brush spring tension
A—Brush spring

3. When brushes are worn to 9/16 in. (14,3 mm) length, new replacements must be fitted.

Operation N1-20—continued

Field coil continuity

5. Connect a battery and suitable bulb in series with two pointed probes.
6. Place the probes on the field coil brush tappings.
7. The test bulb should light, if not an open circuit is indicated and new replacement field coils should be fitted.
8. If the test bulb does light, proceed with the field coil insulation test.

Field coil insulation

9. Connect an ohm meter or a 110 volt AC test lamp between the terminal post and a clean part of the yoke.
10. Lighting of the test lamp or a low ohmic reading indicates that the field coils are earthed to the yoke and new replacements must be fitted.

To assemble (Fig. N1-51)

1. Refit starter yoke to armature assembly, ensuring that the location peg on the drive end bracket fits into the recess in the yoke.
2. Lift earth brushes up into guides and retain with spring.
3. Fit commutator end cover, ensuring that the earth brush leads do not become trapped between the end cover and the yoke.
4. Fit the two through bolts and spring washers. Tighten the through bolts to a torque figure of 8 lb ft (1,0 mkg).
5. Push down earth brushes on to commutator. The brush spring should act centrally on the brushes.
6. Lift field brush spring with suitable tool, insert field brushes into guides, and allow the springs to act centrally on the brushes.
7. Fit cover band and tighten screw.
8. Fit 'Tufnol' washer, plain washer, spring washer and nut to field coil input post. Loosely attach further spring washer and nut to post.
9. If necessary, fit cover to armature shaft square ended nut.

Key to illustration of starter motor, type M45G, 2¼ litre Diesel models up to engine suffix 'J' inclusive

1. Yoke
2. Bracket, commutator end
3. Bush, commutator end
4. Spring set for brushes
5. Armature
6. Thrust washer, commutator end
7. Bracket for starter, drive end
8. Bush for bracket
9. Bracket for brake
10. Bush for brake bracket
11. Field coil for starter
12. Brushes for starter motor, set
13. Drive assembly for starter motor
14. Rivet for pinion retaining ring
15. Return spring for starter pinion
16. Bush, pinion end
17. Clutch adjusting shim
18. Clutch plates
19. Circlip retaining clutch assembly
20. Lock ring retaining clutch plates
21. Brake shoe complete with springs
22. Driving washer for brake shoe
23. Lock ring retaining brake
25. Cover band for starter
26. Bolt for starter motor
27. Lockwasher for bolt
28. Rubber grommet in drive end bracket
29. Solenoid for starter motor
30. Contact plate for solenoid
31. Base for solenoid
32. Gasket for starter solenoid base
33. Terminal nut for starter solenoid
34. Terminal washer for starter solenoid
35. Terminal screw for solenoid
36. Terminal connector for starter motor
37. Plunger spring for solenoid
38. Bolt ($\frac{7}{16}$ in. UNC × 1¼ in. long)
    Set bolt ($\frac{7}{16}$ in. UNF × 2 in. long) } Fixing starter motor
39. Spring washer
40. Nut ($\frac{7}{16}$ in. UNF)

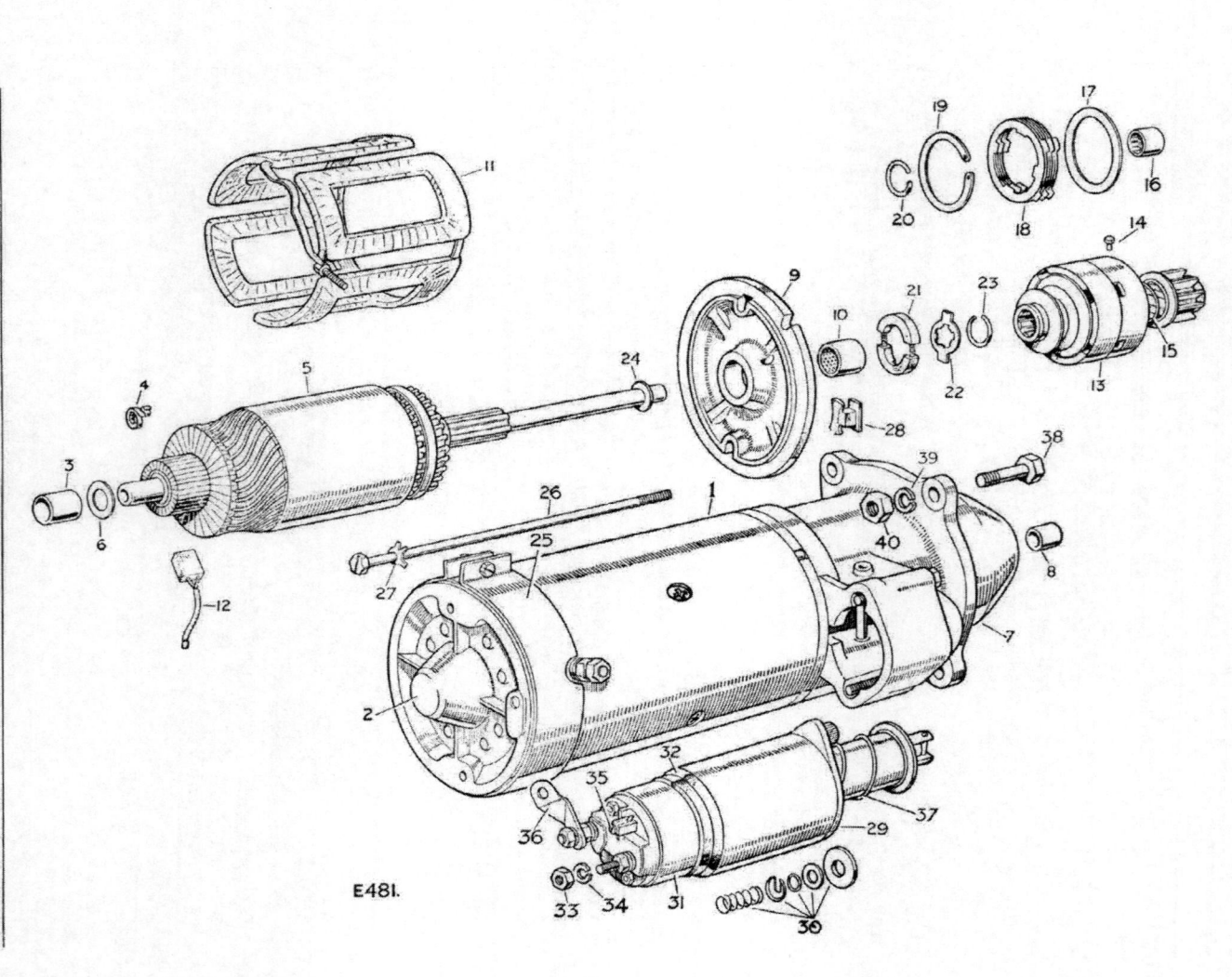

Fig. N1-57. Layout of starter motor, type M45G, 2¼ litre Diesel models up to engine suffix 'J' inclusive

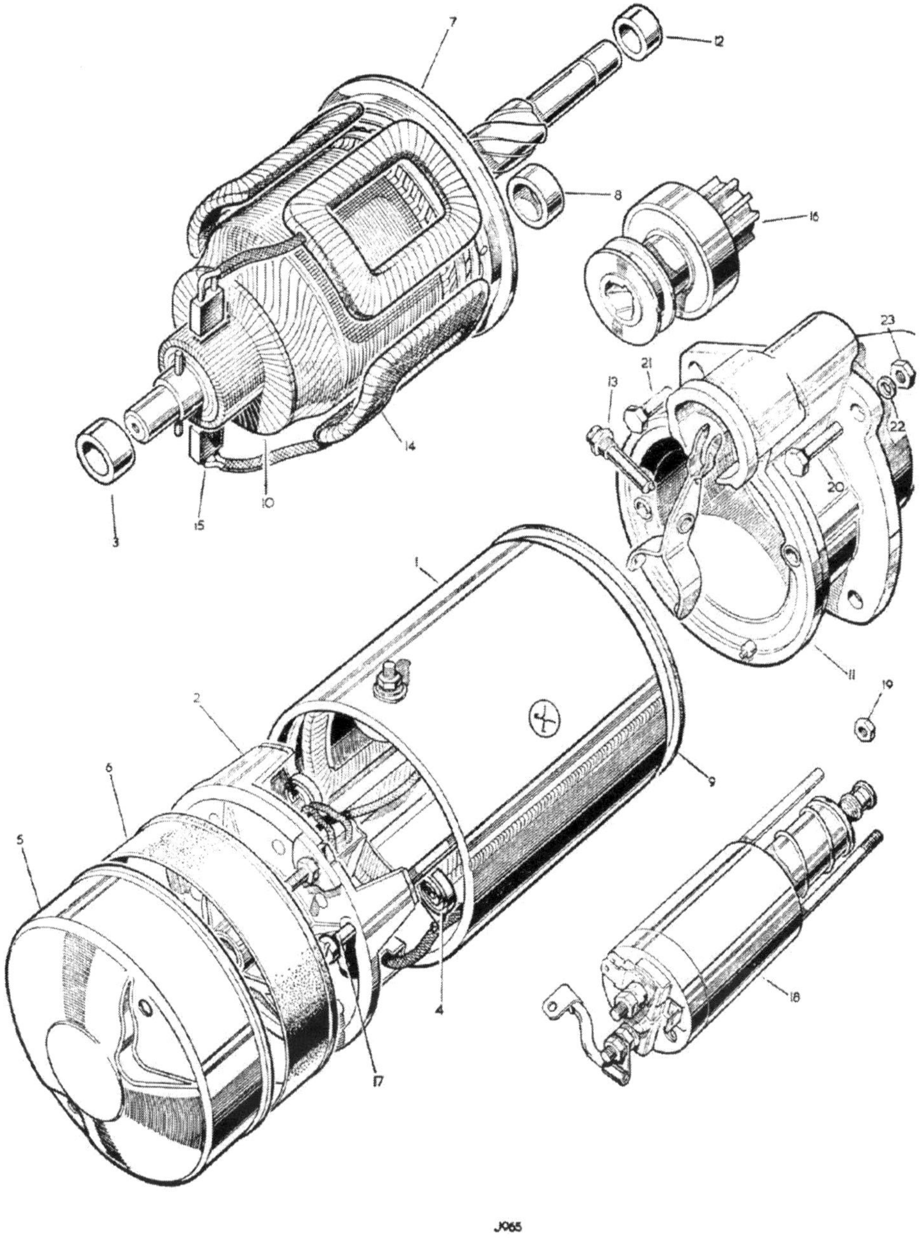

ELECTRICAL EQUIPMENT

Key to illustration of starter motor, type M45G, 2¼ litre Diesel models from engine suffix 'K' onwards

1. Yoke
2. Bracket, commutator end
3. Bush, commutator end
4. Spring set for brushes
5. Cover for starter, commutator end
6. Sealing ring for cover, commutator end
7. Intermediate bracket
8. Bush for bracket
9. Sealing ring for intermediate bracket
10. Armature
11. Bracket for starter, drive end
12. Bush for bracket
13. Pivot pin for starter motor
14. Field coil for starter
15. Brushes for starter motor, set
16. Drive (roller clutch) for starter
17. Bolt for starter motor
18. Solenoid for starter motor
19. Special nut for starter solenoid
20. Bolt ($\frac{7}{16}$ in. UNC x 1¼ in. long) ⎫
21. Set bolt ($\frac{7}{16}$ in. UNF x 2 in. long) ⎬ Fixing starter motor
22. Spring washer
23. Nut ($\frac{7}{16}$ in. UNF) ⎭

Fig. N1-S8. Layout of starter motor, type M45G, 2¼ litre Diesel models from engine suffix 'K' onwards

Operation N1-21—continued

4. The flexible connectors are soldered or crimped to terminal tags; two are connected to brush boxes, and two are connected to the free ends of the field coils. These flexible connectors must be removed by unsoldering, and the flexible connectors of the new brushes secured in their places by soldering.

The new brushes being pre-formed, 'bedding' to the commutator is unnecessary.

Commutator

5. Clean the commutator with a petrol-moistened cloth. If necessary, rotate the armature and, using fine glass-cloth, remove pits and burned spots from commutator; remove abrasive dust with a dry air blast. If the commutator is badly worn, mount in a lathe, and, using a very sharp tool, take a light cut, taking care not to remove any more metal than necessary. The insulators between the commutator segments must not be undercut. Finally, polish with a very fine glass paper.

Armature

6. If the armature is damaged, i.e. 'lifted' conductors, or distorted shaft, a new replacement must be fitted. Never attempt to machine the armature core, or true a distorted armature shaft.

Bearing bushes

If the bearing bushes are worn and allow excessive side play of the armature shaft, new replacements must be fitted.

7. Commutator end bracket bush—Remove brake shoes, thrust washer and 'Tufnol' washer from the end bracket, as applicable. Screw in a $\frac{7}{16}$ in. tap and withdraw complete with bush.

8. Drive end bracket bush and intermediate bracket bush can be pressed out.

9. New bushes can be fitted using a shouldered mandrel of the same diameter as the shaft.

Note: Before fitting a new porous bronze bush, it should be completely immersed for 24 hours in clean SAE 30-40 engine oil.

Porous bronze bushes must not be reamered after fitting.

Roller clutch

This should rotate freely in one direction and lock up in the other. If faulty, a new replacement must be fitted.

Insulation and continuity checks

If inspection of the armature and field coils of the starter motor do not reveal any faults, it is recommended that the following checks are carried out.

Armature insulation

1. Attach an ohm meter or a 110 volt AC test lamp in series with a 12 volt battery.

2. With two probes attached to the leads check the armature insulation by touching each commutator segment in turn with the other probe attached to the armature shaft.

3. The test lamp should not light up, or if an ohm meter is used, a high reading should be recorded. Should this not be the case, the armature insulation is faulty and a new replacement armature should be fitted.

Armature continuity

4. Indication of an open circuited armature winding will be given by burned commutator segments, this can be confirmed by substitution.

Field coil continuity

5. Connect a battery and suitable bulb in series with two pointed probes.

6. Place the probes on the field coil brush tappings.

7. The test bulb should light, if not an open circuit is indicated and new replacement field coils should be fitted.

8. If the test bulb does light, proceed with the field coil insulation test.

Field coil insulation

9. Connect an ohm meter or a 110 volt AC test lamp between the terminal post and a clean part of the yoke.

10. Lighting of the test lamp or a low ohmic reading indicates that the field coils are earthed to the yoke and new replacements must be fitted.

Operation N1-21—continued

Starter solenoid, to test

Tests should be carried out with the solenoid cold. DO NOT attempt to repair a faulty solenoid, fit a new replacement.

The solenoid is composed of two coils, namely, a closing coil, bypassed when the plunger is fully home, and a hold-on coil to retain the plunger in the fully home position.

To test individually, remove existing connections and with the use of a 4 volt DC supply (constant voltage), proceed as below:

Closing coil

1. Connect the supply between the solenoid terminal marked 'S T A' and the smaller centre terminal. This should cause a current of 14.8 to 17.4 amps to pass.

Hold-on coil

2. Connect the supply between the solenoid body and the small centre terminal. This should cause a current of 4.5 to 5.6 amps to pass.

Solenoid contacts

3. Remove the earthing strap, connecting solenoid terminal 'S T A' with the starter yoke.

4. Connect a 10 volt DC supply with a switch in series, to the large terminal marked 'S T A' and the small unmarked terminal.

5. Connect a test lamp, and suitable battery, across the two large solenoid terminals.

6. Insert a stop in the drive end bracket to restrict the pinion travel to out of mesh clearance, normally $\frac{1}{8}$ in. (3 mm). An open ended spanner of approximate size and thickness is suitable, fitted with its jaws embracing the armature shaft extension.

7. Energise the 10 volt supply. The test light bulb should light and remain on, indicating that the solenoid contacts are fully closed.

8. Switch off the 10 volt supply and remove the stop from the armature shaft.

9. Switch on and hold the pinion assembly in the fully engaged position.

10. Switch off. The test lamp should go out, indicating the opening of the solenoid contacts.

To reassemble (Figs. N1-57 and N1-58)

1. Fit shim and intermediate bracket to armature shaft.

2. Lubricate drive assembly with general purpose grease, see Section X, and fit drive assembly to armature shaft.

3. Fit lock ring cover to armature shaft, with recess for lock ring to front.

4. Fit a new lock ring to shaft, and snap lock ring cover over the lock ring.

5. Fit engagement lever to drive end assembly, and fit drive end bracket, ensuring correct location of peg into intermediate bracket.

6. Fit eccentric pin to engagement lever.

7. Fit drive end assembly (drive end bracket, drive assembly and intermediate bracket) to armature shaft assembly ensuring correct location of peg.

8. Fit rubber seal to drive end bracket, ensuring correct location, i.e. plain end of rubber seal to rear, wide lips to yoke body.

9. Locate earth brushes into guides in commutator end bracket, and trap clear with spring.

10. Ensure that the field brushes appear through yoke apertures opposite each other.

11. Fit commutator end bracket to yoke, ensuring that the earth leads do not become trapped between the yoke and the end bracket.

12. If applicable, press down lightly, turn commutator end bracket until brake driving peg aligns with the slots in the brake shoes, and push in.

13. Align location peg between yoke and commutator end bracket.

14. Fit the two through bolts and tighten to a torque figure of 8 lb/ft (1,0 mkg).

15. Fit field brushes, see Fig. N1-55, ensure that spring is in centre of brush in all cases.

16. Turn eccentric pin until the engagement lever is in its lowest and most forward position. Fit solenoid plunger.

Operation N1-21—continued

17. Fit solenoid to drive end bracket, and earthing strap to yoke, aligning location marks made during dismantling.
18. Attach earthing lead to post on yoke.
19. Fit cover band and tighten.

To set solenoid

20. Connect the small unmarked terminal on the solenoid to one side of a 12 volt battery. Using a switch, connect the other side of the battery to a solenoid fixing stud.
21. Close the switch, thus throwing the drive assembly forward into the engaged position. Measure the distance between the pinion and the lock ring cover on the armature shaft.
22. Press the pinion lightly forward, towards the armature, to take up any free play in the engagement linkage. The setting under these conditions should be .005 in. to .015 in. (0,12 mm to 0,40 mm). Adjustment is made by rotating the eccentric pin until the correct clearance is obtained. The adjustment arc is 180° and the head of the arrow marked on pivot pin, should be set only within 90° either side of the cast arrow on the casing. After setting, tighten the securing locknut.

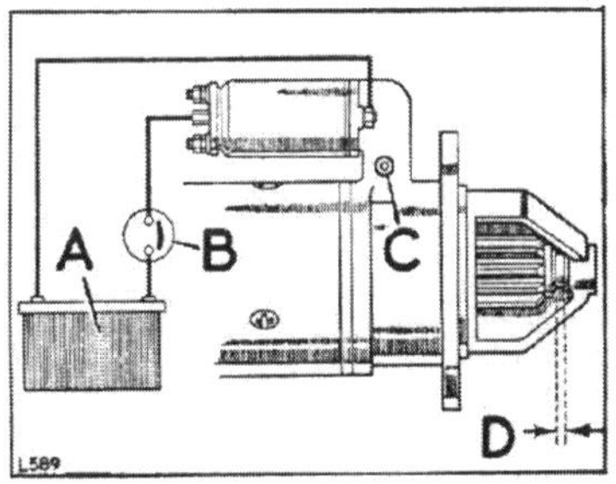

Fig. N1-59. Adjusting pinion clearance with solenoid energised

A—Battery
B—Switch
C—Eccentric pivot pin
D—Clearance 0.005 in. to 0.015 in. (0,12 mm to 0,40 mm)

Dynamo, to overhaul—Operation N1-22

Workshop hand tools:
Spanner size: 11/16 in. AF socket
Screwdrivers (medium and small)

Special tools:
Ammeter, Ohm meter,
Voltmeter 0-20 volt (moving coil)

General

Three types of dynamo are in use, types C39, C40 and C42. The type numbers are stamped on the dynamo yoke (main outer case) to facilitate identification. The following instructions cover all three types, and details of checking the dynamo in situ and when dismantled are included at the end of this operation.

To dismantle

1. Remove fixings and withdraw driving pulley using a suitable extractor.
2. Remove dynamo fan and shims.
3. Remove the through bolts and withdraw the commutator end bracket and fibre thrust washer.
4. Withdraw the driving end bracket complete with armature.

To overhaul

Brushes

1. Lift the brushes up into the brush boxes and secure them there by positioning the brush spring at the side of the brush.
2. Fit the commutator end bracket over the commutator and release the brushes.
3. Check that the brushes move freely in their holders by holding back the brush spring and pulling gently on the flexible connectors. Any tendency to stick should be corrected by cleaning with a petrol-moistened cloth, or in extreme cases by the light use of a smooth file. If a brush is damaged or worn so that it does not make good contact on the commutator, all the brushes must be renewed.

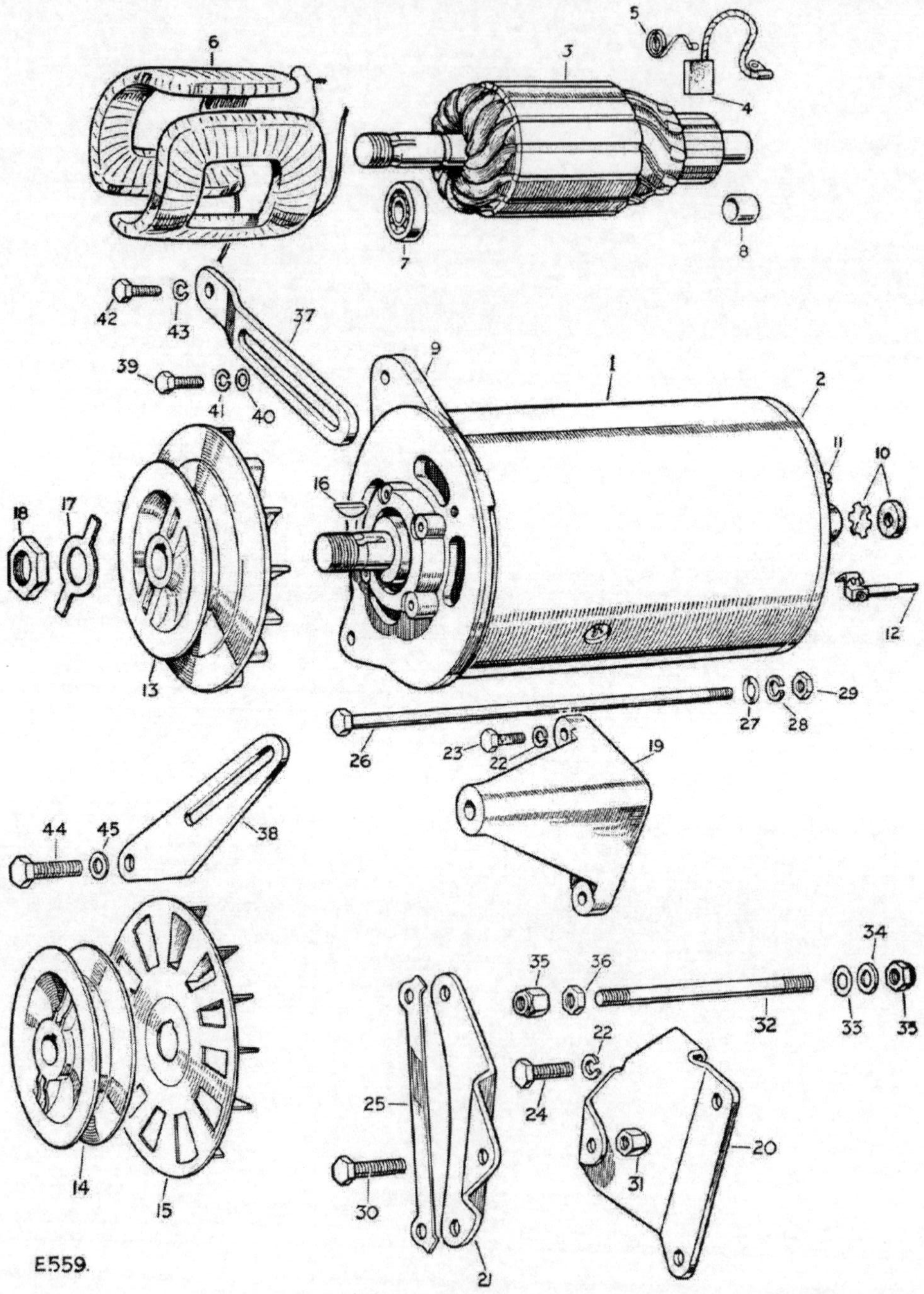

ELECTRICAL EQUIPMENT

Section N—Land-Rover

Key to illustration of dynamo, types C39 and C40

1. Yoke
2. Bracket, commutator end
3. Armature for dynamo
4. Brushes for dynamo, set
5. Spring set for brushes
6. Field coil for dynamo
7. Ball bearing, front
8. Bush, commutator end
9. Bracket, drive end
10. Oiler for dynamo
11. Bolt for bracket
12. Terminal, set
13. Pulley for dynamo
14. Pulley for dynamo
15. Fan for dynamo
16. Woodruff key
17. Lockwasher } Fixing pulley to dynamo
    Spring washer
18. Special nut
19. Anchor bracket for dynamo
20. Support bracket for dynamo
21. Steady bracket for dynamo
22. Spring washer
23. Set bolt ($\frac{5}{16}$ in. UNF x $1\frac{1}{8}$ in. long) } Fixing anchor or support bracket
24. Set bolt ($\frac{5}{16}$ in. UNF x $\frac{5}{8}$ in. long)
25. Locking plate for dynamo bolts
26. Bolt ($\frac{5}{16}$ in. UNF x 7 in. long) } Fixing dynamo to anchor bracket
27. Shim washer
28. Spring washer
29. Nut ($\frac{5}{16}$ in. UNF)
30. Bolt ($\frac{5}{16}$ in. UNF x $1\frac{3}{8}$ in. long) } Fixing dynamo to front support
31. Self-locking nut ($\frac{5}{16}$ in. UNF)
32. Special stud
33. Shim washer
34. Plain washer
35. Self-locking nut ($\frac{5}{16}$ in. UNF) } Fixing dynamo to support bracket
36. Locknut ($\frac{5}{16}$ in. UNF)
37. Adjusting link for dynamo
38. Adjusting link for dynamo
39. Special bolt
40. Plain washer } Fixing adjusting link to dynamo
41. Spring washer
42. Set bolt ($\frac{5}{16}$ in. UNC x $\frac{5}{8}$ in. long) } Fixing adjusting link to front cover
43. Spring washer
44. Bolt ($\frac{5}{16}$ in. UNF x $3\frac{1}{4}$ in. long)
45. Plain washer

Fig. N1-60. Layout of dynamo, types C39 and C40

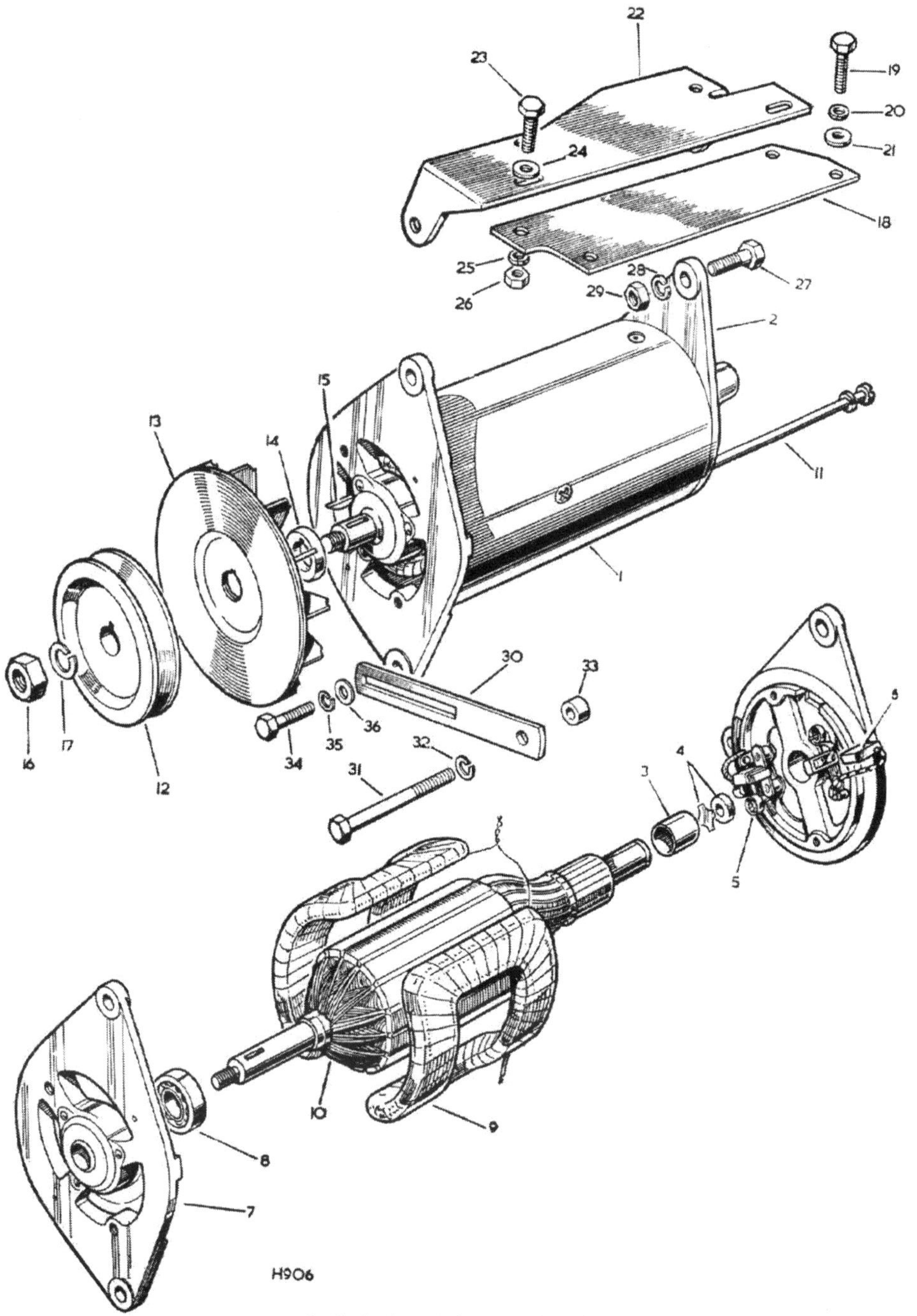

ELECTRICAL EQUIPMENT

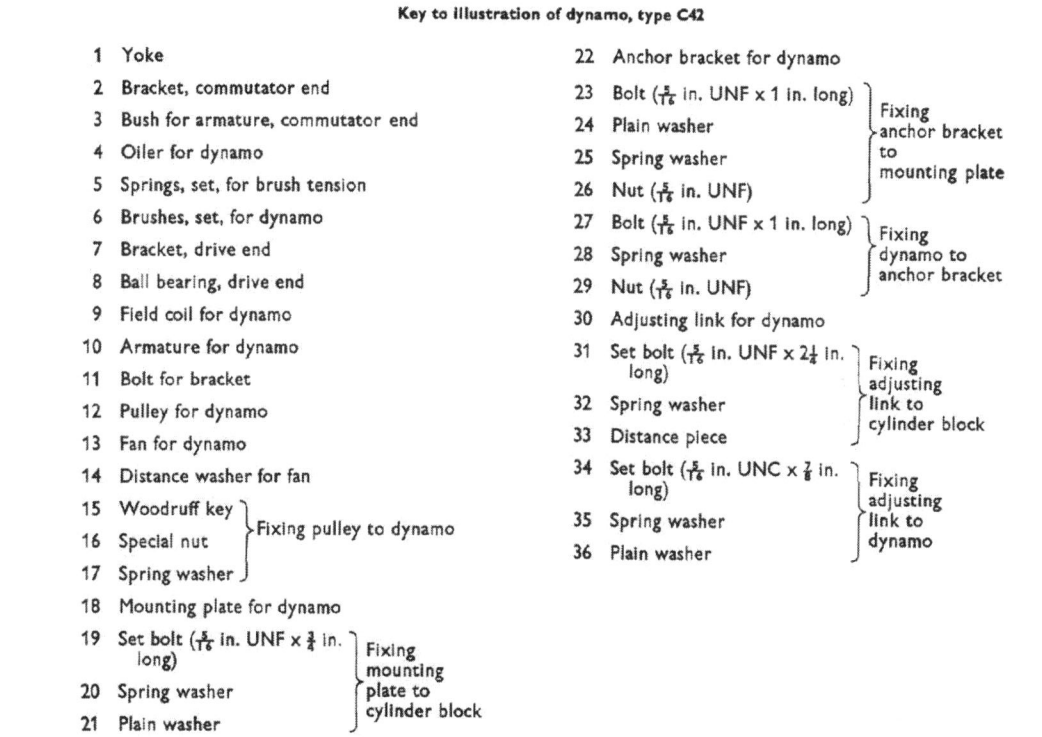

Key to illustration of dynamo, type C42

1. Yoke
2. Bracket, commutator end
3. Bush for armature, commutator end
4. Oiler for dynamo
5. Springs, set, for brush tension
6. Brushes, set, for dynamo
7. Bracket, drive end
8. Ball bearing, drive end
9. Field coil for dynamo
10. Armature for dynamo
11. Bolt for bracket
12. Pulley for dynamo
13. Fan for dynamo
14. Distance washer for fan
15. Woodruff key ⎱ Fixing pulley to dynamo
16. Special nut
17. Spring washer
18. Mounting plate for dynamo
19. Set bolt ($\frac{5}{16}$ in. UNF x $\frac{3}{4}$ in. long) ⎱ Fixing mounting plate to cylinder block
20. Spring washer
21. Plain washer
22. Anchor bracket for dynamo
23. Bolt ($\frac{5}{16}$ in. UNF x 1 in. long) ⎱ Fixing anchor bracket to mounting plate
24. Plain washer
25. Spring washer
26. Nut ($\frac{5}{16}$ in. UNF)
27. Bolt ($\frac{5}{16}$ in. UNF x 1 in. long) ⎱ Fixing dynamo to anchor bracket
28. Spring washer
29. Nut ($\frac{5}{16}$ in. UNF)
30. Adjusting link for dynamo
31. Set bolt ($\frac{5}{16}$ in. UNF x 2$\frac{1}{4}$ in. long) ⎱ Fixing adjusting link to cylinder block
32. Spring washer
33. Distance piece
34. Set bolt ($\frac{5}{16}$ in. UNC x $\frac{7}{8}$ in. long) ⎱ Fixing adjusting link to dynamo
35. Spring washer
36. Plain washer

Fig. N1-61 Layout of dynamo, type C42

ELECTRICAL EQUIPMENT

Operation N1-22—continued

4. Measure brush spring pressures using a spring balance held radially to the commutator.

The maximum spring pressure permissible on a new brush is as follows:

Dynamo type C39—25 ozs (709 grammes).
Dynamo type C40—30 ozs (850 grammes).
Dynamo type C42—33 ozs (940 grammes).

The minimum pressure on a fully worn brush is as follows:

Dynamo type C39—15 ozs (425 grammes).
Dynamo type C40—13 ozs (370 grammes).
Dynamo type C42—16 ozs (450 grammes).

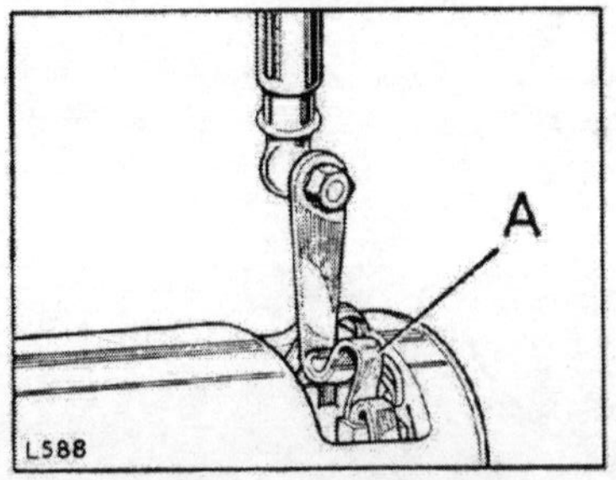

Fig. N1-62. Testing brush spring tension

A—Brush spring

5. To renew brushes, remove screw from mounting block and withdraw lead and brush, and washer. When brushes are worn to a depth of ¼ in. (6,3 mm) new replacements should be fitted.

New brushes are pre-formed and 'bedding' to commutator is not necessary.

Commutator

There are two types of commutator in use, a moulded one and a fabricated type.

A moulded commutator can be recognised by the exposed end being quite smooth, unlike that of the fabricated commutator from which a metal roll-over and an insulating cone protrude.

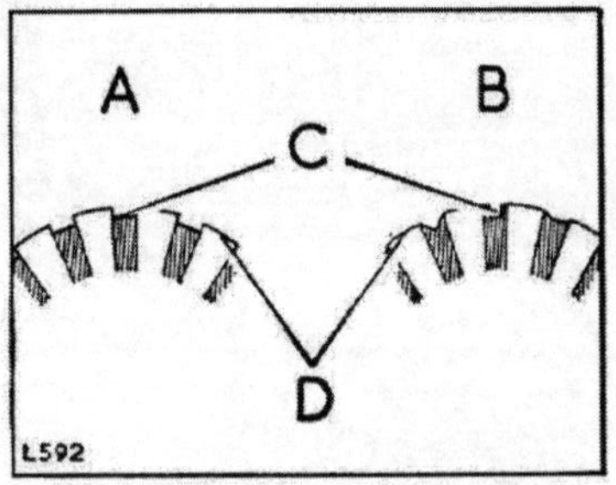

Fig. N1-63. Undercutting commutator insulators

A—Correct C—Insulators
B—Incorrect D—Segments

A moulded commutator can be skimmed to a minimum finished diameter of 1.450 in. (36,83 mm). A moulded commutator can **NOT** be undercut. The insulation slots must be kept clean.

6. Clean the commutator with a petrol-moistened cloth. If necessary, rotate the armature and, using fine glass-cloth, remove pits and burned spots from the commutator; remove abrasive dust with a dry air blast. If the commutator is badly worn, mount in a lathe, and, using a very sharp tool take a light cut, taking care not to remove any more metal than necessary.

Dynamos fitted with fabricated commutator— Undercut the insulators between the segments to a depth of 1/32 in. (0,7 mm) with a hacksaw blade ground to the thickness of the insulator.

Bush for commutator end bracket

7. To replace a bush in the commutator end bracket, screw a ⅝ in. tap squarely into the bush for a few turns and pull out complete with bush.

8. Withdraw felt ring retainer and felt ring, fit new felt ring and replace retainer.

9. Press new bush into commutator end bracket using a shouldered mandrel of the exact diameter of the bush. DO NOT reamer the bush as this would adversely affect its porous surface.

Note: The bush is manufactured from porous bronze, and must be immersed in clean SAE 30 oil for 24 hours prior to fitting.

Operation N1-22—continued

Bearing for drive end bracket

1. To replace bearing in drive end bracket, first remove split distance collar and armature shaft key.

2. Using a suitable press and support plate, press armature shaft out of drive end bracket.

Early type bearing location (items 3 to 10)

3. Remove the screws or drill out the rivets from the bearing retaining plate and withdraw the retaining plate.

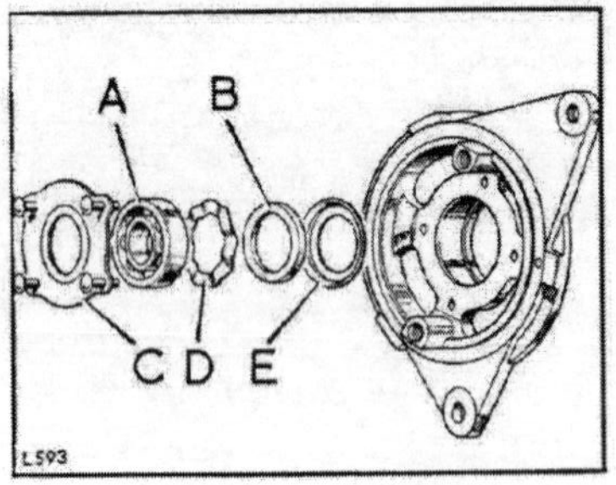

Fig. N1-64. Bearing location, early type

A—Bearing
B—Felt washer
C—Bearing retaining plate
D—Corrugated washer
E—Retaining washer

4. Press the bearing from the end bracket.

5. Remove and clean the corrugated washer and felt ring.

6. Before fitting the replacement bearing, ensure that it is clean and packed with high melting point grease.

7. Refit felt ring and corrugated washer.

8. Press in new bearing.

9. Fit retaining plate and secure rigidly, using screws or rivets as applicable.

10. Press armature through the drive end bracket until the location collar abuts the bearing location then fit split distance collar and armature shaft key.

Latest type bearing location (items 11 to 17)

11. Insert a screwdriver into the extractor notch and remove the circlip.

12. Remove the bearing retaining plate, push out bearing and remove pressure ring, retaining plate and felt ring.

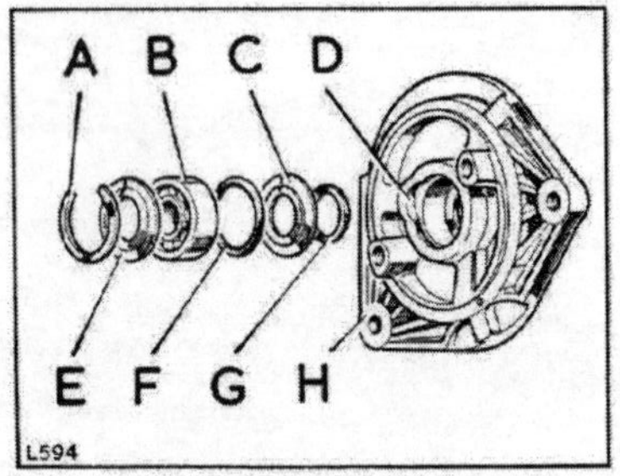

Fig. N1-65. Bearing location, latest type

A—Circlip
B—Bearing
C—Retaining plate for felt ring
D—Circlip extractor notch
E—Bearing retaining plate
F—Pressure ring
G—Felt ring
H—Drive end bracket

13. Renew felt ring and pressure ring and replace with retaining plate in order illustrated.

14. Fit new bearing and bearing retaining plate. The bearing must be packed with high melting point grease, unless it is of the sealed type which are pre-packed during manufacture.

15. Using a suitable hand press, compress the assembly sufficient to allow the circlip to relocate itself.

16. Press the armature through the drive end bracket until location collar abuts the bearing location.

17. Refit split distance collar and armature shaft key.

To assemble (Figs. N1-60 and N1-61)

1. Fit armature and drive end bracket into the yoke, and locate on peg.

2. Fit the fibre washer to commutator end of armature shaft.

ELECTRICAL EQUIPMENT

Operation N1-22—continued

3. Lift the brushes up into the brush boxes and secure them in that position by positioning the brush spring at the side of the brush.

4. Fit the commutator end bracket on the armature shaft until the brush boxes are partly over the commutator. Place a thin screwdriver on top of each brush in turn and press the brush down on the commutator. The brush springs should then position themselves on top of the brushes.

5. Fit the commutator end bracket to the yoke so that the projection on the bracket locates in the slot in the commutator end bracket.

6. Fit the two through bolts.

7. Refit shims removed from behind dynamo fan.

8. Fit dynamo fan and pulley, and secure the fixings.

9. Inject a few drops of any high quality medium viscosity (SAE 30) engine oil into the hole marked 'Oil' at the end of the commutator bearing housing.

Dynamo, to check

In a faulty charging circuit, the dynamo should be checked as follows:

Testing in situ

1. Inspect the driving belt and adjust if necessary.
2. Check terminal connections. Terminal 'D' carries the dynamo output, 'F' the field current.
3. Disconnect the terminal leads and link the terminals with a short length of bare wire.
4. Run engine at idling speed.
5. Attach a 0–20 volt moving-coil voltmeter to one generator terminal, and earth to the yoke.
6. Increase engine rpm gradually. The voltmeter reading should rise rapidly and without fluctuation.
7. If the voltage does not rise rapidly and evenly to the dynamo must be dismantled for detailed examination.

8. If excessive sparking at the commutator is observed in the above test, the armature is faulty and must be changed for a new replacement.

Testing when dismantled

Armature insulation

9. Attach an ohm meter or a 110 volt AC test lamp in series with a 12 volt battery.

10. With two probes attached to the leads, check the armature insulation by touching each commutator segment in turn with the other probe attached to the armature shaft.

11. The test lamp should not light up, or if an ohm meter is used, a high reading should be recorded. Should this not be the case, the armature insulation is faulty and a new replacement armature should be fitted.

Armature continuity

12. Indication of an open circuited armature winding will be given by burned commutator segments, this can be confirmed by substitution.

Field coils

13. To check both the insulation and continuity of the field coils, connect an ohm meter or an ammeter between the field terminal and the yoke, in series with a 12 volt battery.

14. If the field coils are in good order, the following readings should be obtained:

	Field coil resistance (ohms)	Normal ammeter reading (amps)
C39 type dynamo	6.1	2
C40 type dynamo	5.9–6.0	2
C42 type dynamo	4.5	2½

15. An infinity reading on the ohm meter indicates an open circuit and the field coil should be replaced with new. With an ammeter in series, no reading would indicate an open circuit.

16. A low ohm meter reading or a high current reading indicate that the insulation is faulty and new field windings are required.

Alternator output control unit, Model 4TR, to test and adjust—Operation N1-23

Workshop hand tools: Screwdriver
Special tools: Voltmeter, Ammeter

Maintenance

The output control unit does not require any regular maintenance, but the moulded cover should be kept clean, and the terminals checked for tightness.

Control unit, test

1. Before checking and adjusting the control unit it must be established that the alternator and charging circuit wiring are in good order. See Operation N1-26. The battery to control unit wiring, including the 6RA field isolating relay, must also be in good order. See Operation N1-26, item 9. The resistance of this circuit, including the relay, must not exceed 1 ohm. Higher resistance must be traced and remedied.

2. Disconnect the alternator main output lead from the alternator or starter solenoid, and connect an ammeter of 50 amp range in series with the lead and its connection.

3. Connect a voltmeter of 1 per cent accuracy or better between the battery terminals and note the reading with all electrical equipment switched off. If available, use a voltmeter of the suppressed —zero type, reading 12–15 volts.

4. Switch on the side and tail lights to give an electrical load of approximately 2 amperes.

5. Start the engine and run the alternator at approximately 3,000 rpm for at least 8 minutes to ensure the system voltage has stabilised. If the charging current is greater than 10 amperes, continue to run the engine until this figure is reached. The voltmeter should then read 13.9 to 14.3 volts.

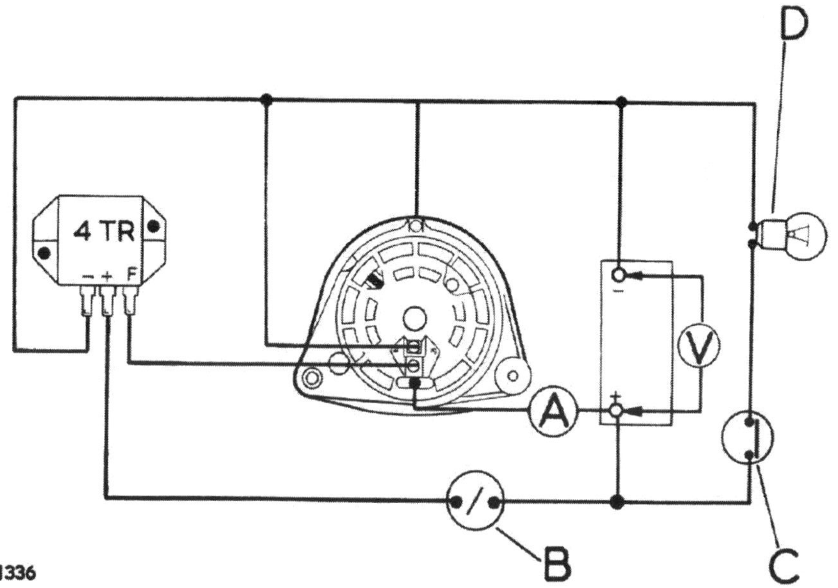

Fig. N1-66. 4TR control unit test circuit

A—Ammeter
B—Field isolating relay
C—Side and tail lamp switch
D—Side and tail lamps
V—Voltmeter

H336

ELECTRICAL EQUIPMENT

Operation N1-23—continued

6. If the reading obtained is stable, but outside these limits, the unit can be adjusted to obtain the correct voltage.

7. If the voltmeter reading remains unchanged at open circuit battery voltage, or increases in an uncontrolled manner, the control unit is faulty and must be replaced.

Control unit, adjust

1. Test control unit as already described.

2. Stop the engine and remove the control unit securing screws, invert the unit and carefully scrape away the sealing compound that conceals the potentiometer adjuster.

3. Start the engine and run the alternator at approximately 3,000 rpm with the voltmeter firmly connected to the battery terminals. Turn the potentiometer adjuster slot clockwise to increase the voltage setting, or counter-clockwise to decrease it. A small movement of the adjuster causes an appreciable difference in the voltage reading.

4. Recheck the setting by stopping the engine, then restarting and running the alternator at 3,000 rpm.

5. Disconnect the voltmeter and ammeter. Reconnect the alternator output lead.

6. Refit the control unit.

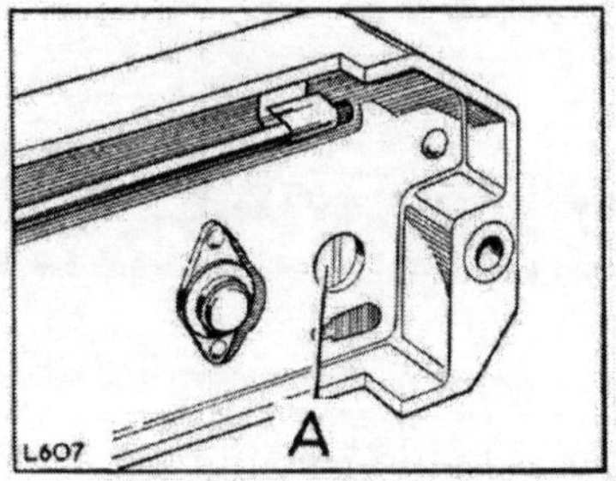

Fig. N1-67. 4TR alternator control, rear view
A—Potentiometer adjuster

Alternator field isolating relay, Model 6RA, to test and adjust—Operation N1-24

Special tools:
Variable DC supply 0-15 volts
Voltmeter, 0-20 volts
Bulb, 12 volts, 1.5 watt

Workshop hand tools:
Screwdriver (medium)
Screwdriver (electrician's)
Pliers, Pliers (long-nosed)

General

The relay has a pair of normally open contacts, is actuated by a continuously rated winding, and has four blade-type terminals, marked C1, C2, W1 and W2.

Terminal C1 is associated with the fixed contact post, C2 with the moving contact; W1 and W2 are the ends of the operating winding. The relay is protected by a metal case secured to the base by gimping.

The relay should be replaced as a unit in the event of failure. Where facilities are available, the case can be removed for checking the contacts, mechanical settings and soldered connections.

Maintenance

Check the tightness of the terminals.

Field isolating relay, test

1. Connect terminals C1 and C2 in series with a 1.5 watt bulb and terminals of a 12 volt battery.

2. Connect terminals W1 and W2 of the relay to the terminals of the battery.

3. The bulb should light when the relay winding between W1 and W2 is energised. If the bulb does not light, the relay winding or contacts are faulty and the relay should be replaced.

Field isolating relay, adjust

1. Prise open the gimping securing the cover to the base.

2. Connect a first grade moving coil voltmeter across the relay operating winding, terminals W1 and W2.

3. Connect a variable direct current supply 0-15 volts to the winding terminals, W1 and W2.

4. Check the cut-in setting by raising the supply voltage from zero. The contacts should close when the voltage is 6.0 to 7.5 volts. The setting is raised by increasing the air gap between the underside of the armature and the bobbin core, and lowered by decreasing the air gap.

5. Check the drop-off setting by raising the voltage to 15 volts then slowly reducing it; the contacts should open at 4.0 volts minimum. The drop-off setting is raised by raising the height of the fixed contact post to increase the contact pressure. The drop-off setting is lowered by lowering the fixed contact post and contact pressure.

6. Disconnect the voltmeter and voltmeter supply.

7. Place the sealing gasket in the case flange and insert the relay assembly. Press the components firmly together and secure at four points by gimping the case lip.

8. Recheck the cut-in and drop-off settings.

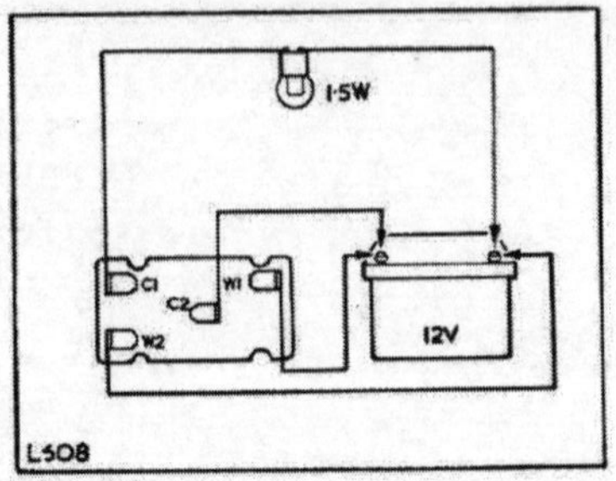

Fig. N1-68. 6RA relay winding and contact test

Alternator warning light control, Model 3AW, to bench test—Operation N1-25

Special tools:
12 volt battery with accessible intercell connections
2.2 watt 12 volt bulb in holder
Three battery connector clips
Three Lucar connections
Watch with second hand

General

The warning light control is a thermally operated relay for controlling the switching on and off of an instrument panel warning light. It is connected to the centre point of one pair of the alternator diodes through terminal 'AL' on the alternator, and to earth. The indication given by the warning light is similar to that provided by the ignition '(no charge)' warning light used with dynamo charging systems.

Warning. Due to the external similarity of the alternator warning light control model 3AW to flasher unit model FL5, a distinctive green label is applied to the aluminium case of model 3AW.

Care must be taken to avoid connecting either of these units into a circuit designed for the other.

Maintenance

Check the tightness of the terminals. Model 3AW is a sealed unit.

Warning light control, test

1. Connect terminal 'E' of the warning light control to the battery negative terminal.
2. Connect the 2.2 watt 12 volt bulb in series with the terminal 'WL' of the warning light control and the positive battery terminal. The bulb should light up immediately. If the bulb does not light up, the warning light control is faulty and must be replaced.
3. With the terminals connected as in 1 and 2 above, connect terminal 'AL' of the warning light control to the 6 volt tapping of the battery. The bulb should go out within five seconds.
4. Transfer the battery connection of terminal 'AL' to the positive battery terminal for ten seconds only. Then quickly transfer it to the battery 2 volt tapping. The bulb should light up within five seconds.
5. If the performance in items 3 and 4 differs appreciably from the test requirements, the unit is faulty and must be replaced.

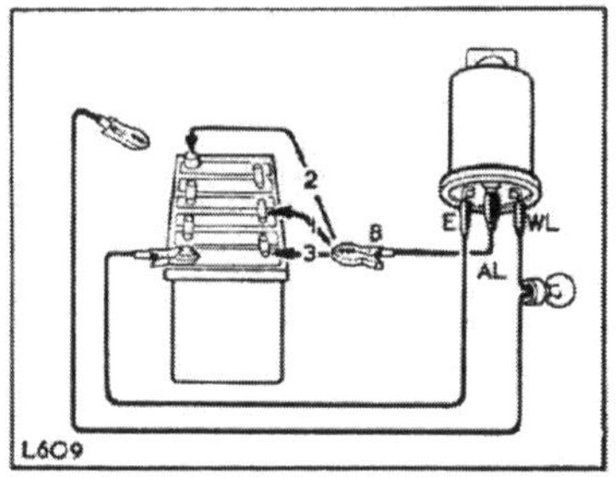

Fig. N1-69. Bench test for warning light control, model 3AW

Connect battery clip 'B' in sequence 1, 2 and 3

Battery charging system, test—Operation N1-26

Special tools:
Ammeter, 0-50 amperes
Extension leads with clips
Voltmeter, 0-15 volts

Charging system, test

1. Check the alternator driving belt for wear and tension. Adjust if necessary.
2. Disconnect the battery negative terminal.
3. Disconnect the 35 amp alternator output lead from the alternator and connect a good quality moving coil ammeter between the output terminal and alternator output lead.
4. Disconnect the leads from the alternator field terminals, and connect them to the battery terminals with the extension leads. Polarity is unimportant.

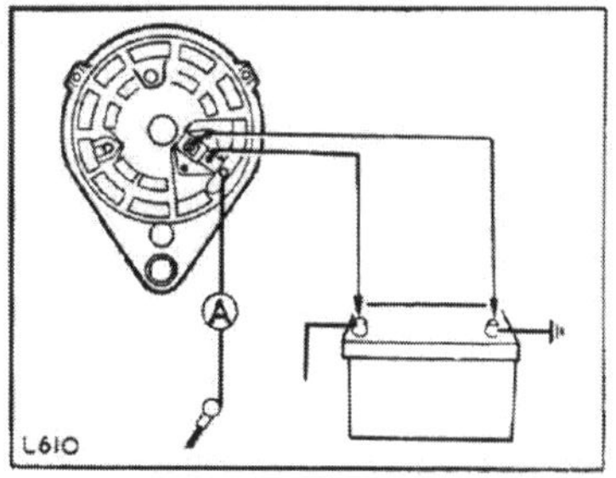

Fig. N1-70. Alternator output test
A—Ammeter

5. Reconnect the battery negative terminal. Start the engine and increase the speed until the alternator is running at approximately 4,000 rpm. The ammeter reading should be approximately 40 amps and if this figure is obtained the alternator and output cable are in order.
6. If a zero or low reading is obtained, check the output circuit and wiring by connecting a voltmeter between the alternator output terminal and the battery positive terminal and noting the reading; then transfer the voltmeter to the alternator frame and the battery negative terminal and noting the reading. If either reading exceeds 0.5 volt there is high resistance in the circuit that must be traced and remedied.

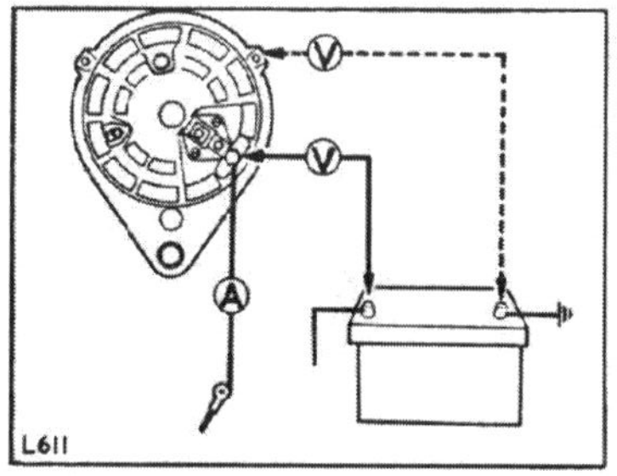

Fig. N1-71. Charging circuit voltage drop test
A—Ammeter   V—Voltmeter

7. If the test in item 6 does not reveal high resistance, and alternator output is low, remove and examine the alternator brush gear. Retest and, if low output persists, replace or overhaul the alternator.
8. If the alternator output is in order, disconnect the battery negative terminal, remove the ammeter and connect the alternator output cable to its terminal. Remove the extension leads from the alternator field cables.
9. Connect the battery negative terminal. Switch on the ignition, and check that battery voltage is applied to the cable ends normally attached to the alternator field terminals by connecting a voltmeter across them. A reading of battery voltage proves that the field isolating relay circuit and wiring is in order. Conversely, a low or zero reading indicates a fault in the field isolating relay associated wiring, or the alternator output control unit. See Operation N1-24 for testing of field isolating relay. Refer to circuit diagram for continuity testing of wiring in the charging system.

ELECTRICAL EQUIPMENT

Alternator, overhaul—Operation N1-27

Workshop hand tools:
Spanner sizes: $\frac{7}{16}$ in. AF, $\frac{1}{2}$ in. AF, $\frac{9}{16}$ in. AF
Screwdriver (electrician's)
Screwdriver (large)
Pliers (long-nosed)

Special tools:
Hand press
Soldering Iron
Ohm meter, Ammeter
Mains AC supply
15 watt 110 volt bulb
1.5 watt 12 volt bulb

For alternator removal, see Section A

Cleaning
Maintain the alternator free from dirt and oil that may collect, particularly around the slip-ring end cover vents.

Lubrication
The bearings are packed with grease during assembly and do not require periodic attention.

Terminal connections
Ensure that all terminal connections are clean and tight.

Alternator, strip

1. Remove the nut and spring washer from the rotor shaft. Withdraw the pulley and fan.
2. Scribe the drive end bracket, lamination pack and slip ring end bracket so that they can be re-assembled in correct angular relation to each other.
3. Remove the three through bolts and washers. Withdraw the drive end bracket and rotor as an assembly from the stator.
4. Remove the Woodruff key and bearing collar. Press out the rotor shaft from the drive end bracket.

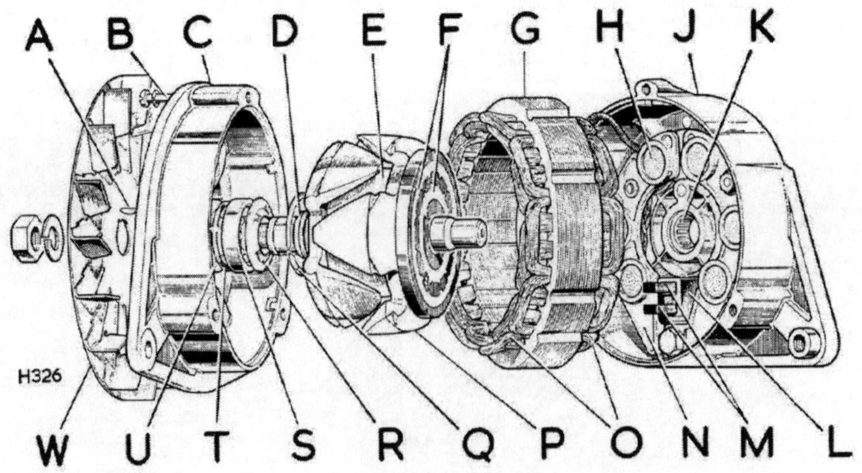

Fig. N1-72. Alternator model 11AC dismantled

A—Woodruff key
B—Through bolt (3)
C—Drive end bracket
D—Jump ring shroud
E—Rotor (field) winding
F—Slip rings
G—Stator laminations
H—Silicon diodes (6)
J—Slip ring end bracket
K—Needle roller bearing
L—Brush box
M—Brushes (2)
N—Diode heat sink (2)
O—Stator winding
P—Rotor
Q—Circlip
R—Bearing retaining plate
S—Ball bearing, drive end
T—'O' ring
U—'O' ring retaining washer
W—Fan

Operation N1-27—continued

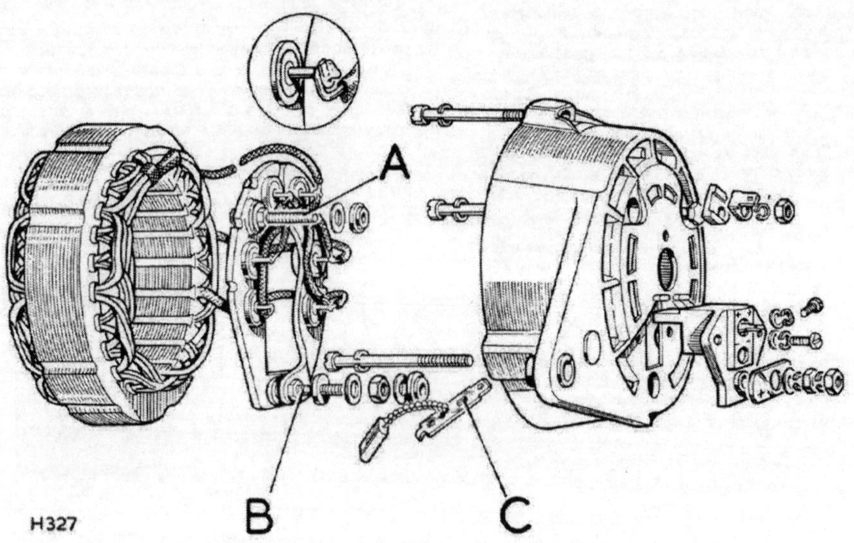

Fig. N1-73. Slip ring end, showing heat sinks withdrawn

A—Warning light terminal 'AL'   B—Output terminal   C—Terminal block retaining tongue

5. Remove the circlip from the drive end bracket and remove the retaining plate. Press out the ball bearing and remove the 'O' ring and retaining washer.
6. Remove the nut, spring washer, 35 amp Lucar blade and plastic strip from the output terminal. Remove the locknut and washer. Remove the two securing screws and washers and withdraw the brush box, noting the two small insulating washers between the brush box and end bracket
7. Close up the retaining tongue at the root of each field terminal blade. Withdraw the brush spring and terminal assemblies from the brush box.
8. Remove the nut and washer from the warning light 'AL' terminal. Lift off the $17\frac{1}{2}$ amp Lucar blade and the insulation bush.
9. Remove the bolt and washer securing the slip ring end bracket to the heat sinks. Withdraw the stator and heat sinks from the end bracket, noting the insulating and plain washers on the 'AL' and output terminal posts.
10. Note the connections of the wires to the diodes, and unsolder the wires, using a pair of long-nosed pliers as a thermal shunt, as in the illustration Great care must be taken to avoid overheating the diodes, or bending the diode pins and the operation should be done as quickly as possible. Remove the nut securing the heat sinks together, and separate the heat sinks, noting the insulation washers.

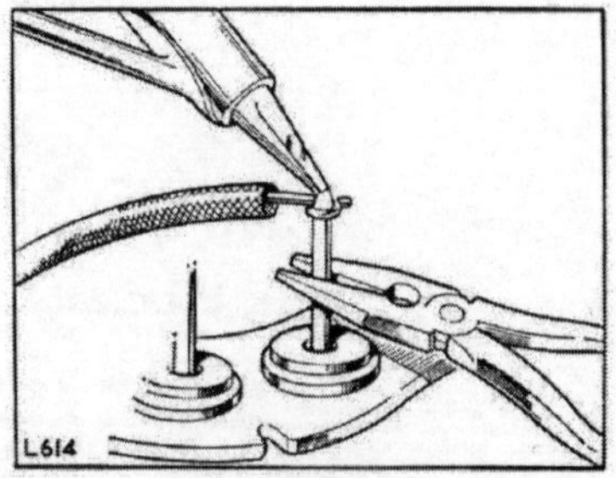

Fig. N1-74. Use of thermal shunt when soldering diode connections

ELECTRICAL EQUIPMENT

Operation N1-27—continued

Inspection and testing of alternator parts

Brushgear

1. Measure the brush length. A new brush is $\frac{5}{8}$ in. (15.9 mm) long; a fully worn brush is $\frac{5}{32}$ in. (4 mm) long, and must be replaced at, or approaching, this length. Brush spring pressures can be checked against the specifications in the technical data.

   Check that the brushes move freely in their holders. Clean the brushes with a petrol-moistened cloth, and lightly polish the brush sides with a smooth file if necessary.

   Note: The brush which bears on the inner slip ring is the positive brush, as the lower linear speed results in reduced mechanical wear and helps to offset the higher rate of electrical wear peculiar to the positive connected brush.

2. **Slip-rings.** The surfaces of the slip rings should be smooth and free from oil. Clean the surfaces with a petrol-moistened cloth, or very fine glass paper if there is evidence of burning. No attempt should be made to machine the slip-rings, as any eccentricity will adversely affect the high speed performance of the alternator.

3. **Rotor.** Test the rotor winding by connecting an ohm meter between the slip rings. The resistance reading should be 3.8 ohms at 68°F.

   An alternative test can be made using a 12 volt battery and large-scale ammeter in series with the winding. The ammeter reading should be approximately 3.2 amperes.

   Test the slip ring/rotor winding insulation by using an AC mains supply and a test lamp in series with a slip-ring and rotor pole. If the lamp lights, the insulation is faulty and the rotor must be replaced.

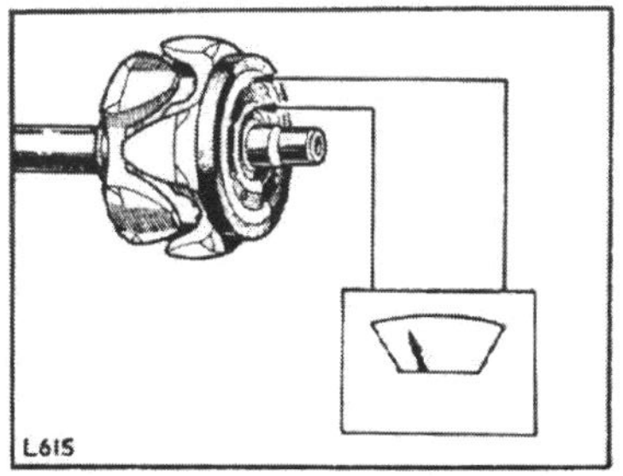

Fig. N1-75. Measuring rotor winding resistance with ohm meter (alternator dismantled)

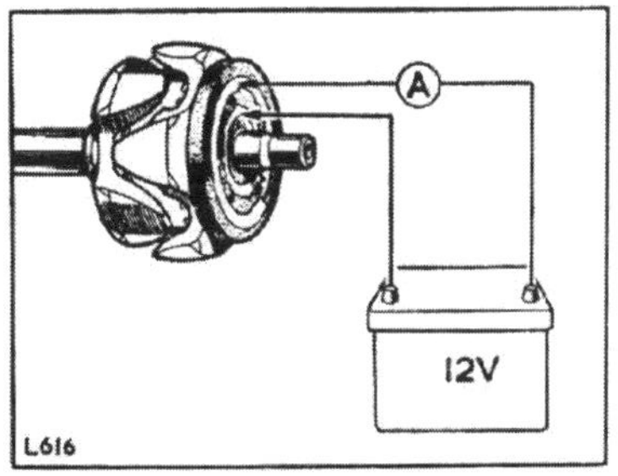

Fig. N1-76. Measuring rotor winding resistance with battery and ammeter (alternator dismantled)

No attempt should be made to machine the rotor poles or true a distorted shaft.

4. **Stator.** Check the continuity of the stator windings with the stator cables separated from the heat sinks. Connect any two of the three stator cables in series with a 1.5 watt test lamp and a 12 volt battery. Repeat the test, replacing one of the two cables by the third cable. Failure of the test lamp to light on either occasion means that part of the stator winding is open-circuit, and the stator must be replaced.

   Test the insulation between the stator coils and lamination pack with an AC mains supply and a bulb in series with any one of the three cable ends and the lamination pack. If the bulb lights, the stator coils are earthing and the stator must be replaced.

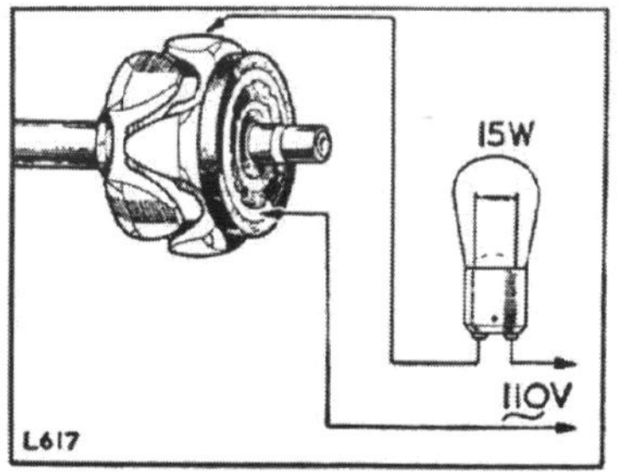

Fig. N1-77. Insulation test of rotor winding

Operation N1-27—continued

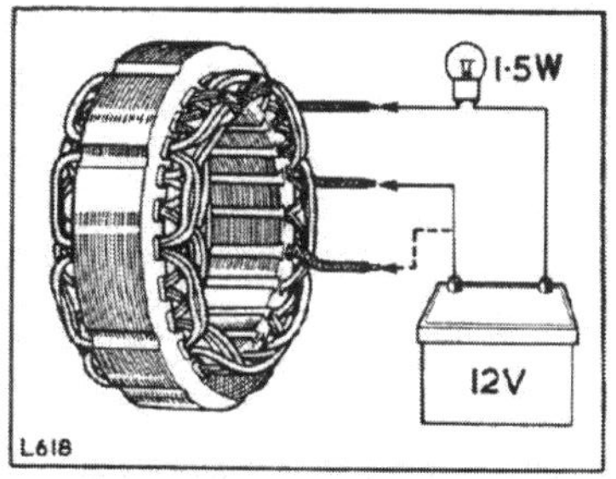

Fig. N1-78. Stator winding continuity test

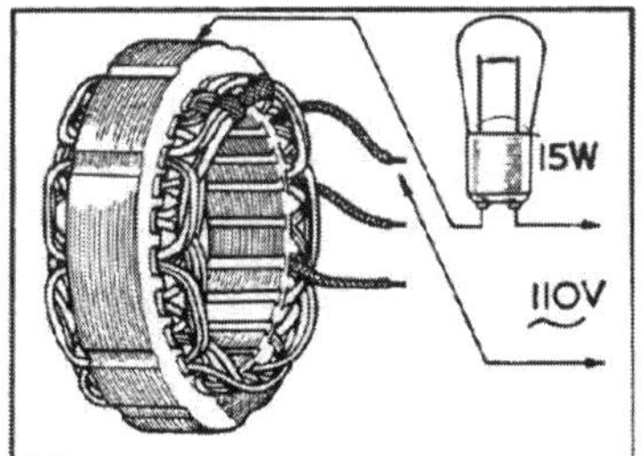

Fig. N1-79. Stator winding insulation test

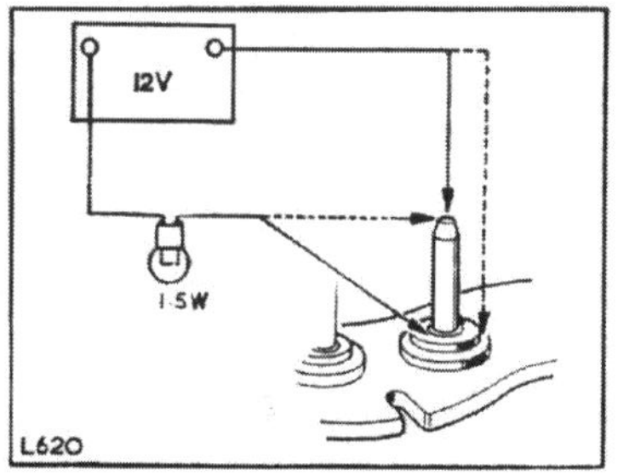

Fig. N1-80. Service test of diodes

WARNING: Ohm meters of the type incorporating a hand-driven generator must never be used for checking diodes.

Bearings. Bearings that are worn to the extent that they allow excessive side movement of the rotor shaft must be renewed. The needle roller bearing in the slip-ring end bracket is not serviced separately, and in the unlikely event that it becomes unserviceable the end bracket must be replaced.

Alternator, assemble

1. Resolder the stator wires to the diodes using M grade 45–55 tin/lead solder. A pair of long-nosed pliers should be used as a thermal shunt, and care must be taken to avoid overheating the diodes or bending the diode pins. Soldering must be carried out as quickly as possible.

Fig. N1-81. Use of thermal shunt when soldering diode connections

Heat sinks and diodes

There are two heat sink assemblies, one of positive polarity and the other negative. Each carries three diodes that are pressed into position. The diodes are not individually replaceable, and if a diode is found defective the heat sink must be replaced.

The diodes can be tested for service purposes with the stator wires separated from the heat sinks. Connect a 12 volt battery and 1.5 watt bulb in series with each diode, and reverse the connections. Current should flow, and the bulb light up, in one direction only. If the bulb lights up in both directions, or does not light up in either, the diode is defective and the heat sink assembly must be replaced.

Accurate measurement of diode resistance requires factory equipment. Since the forward resistance of a diode varies with the voltage applied, no realistic readings can be obtained with battery-powered ohm meters. If a battery ohm meter is used, a good diode will yield infinity in one direction, and some indefinite but much lower reading in the other.

ELECTRICAL EQUIPMENT

Operation N1-27—continued

2. After soldering, the connections must be neatly arranged around the heat sinks to ensure adequate clearance for the rotor, and tacked down with 3 M EC 1022 adhesive where indicated in the illustration. The stator connections must pass through the appropriate notches at the edge of the heat sink.

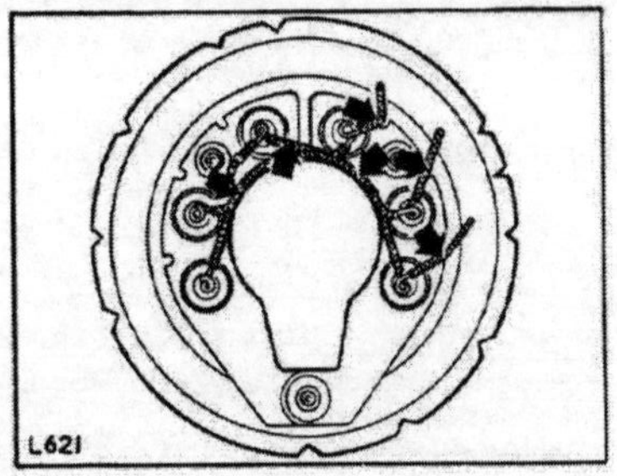

3. Assembly is the reverse of the stripping procedure, observing the torque values given in the Data section. Note the order of the insulation washers between the heat sinks—thick plain washer, thin plain washer and small plain washer.

4. Refit the plain and insulating washers to the 'AL' and output terminal posts before fitting the stator to the slip-ring end bracket.

5. Fit the two small insulating washers under the brush box.

6. To ensure the Lucar terminals of the brushes are properly retained the tongue should be levered up with a fine screwdriver to make an angle of 30° with the terminal blade.

7. Support the inner journal of the drive end bearing when pressing in the rotor shaft. Do not use the bracket as a support for the bearing while fitting the rotor shaft.

8. Align the drive end bracket, lamination pack and slip-ring bracket, and tighten the three bolts evenly. Check that the rotor is quite free in its bearing.

Fig. N1-82. Heat sink cable securing points

Fault diagnosis—Electrical equipment

Symptom	Possible cause	Investigation	Remedy
A—Battery discharged	Incorrect fan belt tension	Check for loose fan belt	Reset as necessary, Section A
	Battery connections faulty	Check for loose and corroded terminal connections	Clean and tighten as necessary
	Battery unserviceable	Check battery condition	Replace as necessary
	Dynamo faults	Check terminal connections for looseness and corrosion	Clean and tighten as necessary
		Check dynamo function	Rectify or replace as necessary
	Voltage regulator faulty	Check regulator and settings	Rectify or replace as necessary
	Faulty circuits	Check horn, ammeter, inspection light and interior light circuits	Rectify or replace as necessary
B—Dynamo output too low	Slipping fan belt	Check fan belt tension setting, Section A	Reset as necessary
			Tighten fixings, Section A
	Dynamo faults	Check for dynamo loose on mountings	Replace as necessary
		Check brushes for excessive wear	Reclaim surface by skimming
		Check commutator for burning and undue wear	Clean surface, using fine grade abrasive cloth
		Check commutator for glazing	Rectify or replace as necessary
	Circuit faults	Dismantle dynamo and check for internal circuit faults	
	Voltage regulator faulty	Check circuit, referring to appropriate circuit diagram	Rectify or replace as necessary
C—Lamps dim at low engine speed	Faulty earth connection	Check regulator and settings and earth	Rectify as necessary
	Battery in low state of charge	Check earthing points of lamps affected and battery	
		Check and remedy as described in paragraph A	
D—Bulbs fail frequently	Battery in low state of charge	Check and remedy as described in paragraph A	
	Voltage regulator faulty	Check regulator and settings	Rectify or replace as necessary
	Loose connections	Check connections in lamps circuit	Clean and tighten as necessary
	Incorrect lamp bulb type	Refer to bulb chart	Fit correct type
E—Horn failure	Faulty connections	Check for loose and dirty connections	Clean and tighten as necessary
	Faulty contact points	Check for burnt or loose contacts	Clean where accessible and adjust as necessary
F—Instrument panel lights fail		Refer to Section P	

Fault diagnosis—Electrical equipment—*continued*

Symptom	Possible cause	Investigation	Remedy
G (a)—Starter motor fails to turn engine (all models)	Stiff engine	Check by turning engine using starting handle	Locate cause and rectify
	Battery in low state of charge	Check by starting engine manually (Petrol models) or substitute a serviceable battery	Recharge battery by period of daylight running or from independent supply
G (b)—Starter motor fails to turn engine Petrol models	Faulty connections in starter circuit	Check for loose, broken or dirty connections at battery, starter and starter switch. Check cables for damage	Rectify as required. Replace damaged cables
	Starter motor faults	Check for greasy, burnt or glazed commutator	Clean or replace as necessary. Skim surface where applicable
		Check brushes for wear, incorrect type and fitting. Check also for sticking in holders and incorrect tensioning	Rectify or replace as necessary
		Check for starter pinion jammed in mesh with flywheel	Rotate squared end of starter shaft to free pinion, using suitable spanner
G (c)—Starter motor fails to operate Diesel models	Batteries discharged	Check state of charge	Recharge batteries
	Starter/heater switch fault	Check for loose wiring at switch	Clean and tighten
		Check switch operation	Replace switch as necessary
	Starter solenoid faulty	Check for loose wiring	Tighten as necessary
		Check for faulty earth connection	Clean and remake connection
		Check solenoid operation	Replace as necessary
	Starter motor faulty	Check for worn brushes and fatigued springs	Replace as necessary
		Check for greasy, burnt or unevenly worn commutator	Clean, using petrol-moistened cloth. Skim surface, where applicable
		Dismantle unit and check for internal fault in circuit	Rectify or replace as necessary
H—Starter operates but does not turn engine	Starter motor fault	Petrol models — Check for starter drive pinion not engaging with flywheel	Clean screwed sleeve and mating parts
		Diesel models — Plate clutch pinion faulty	Rectify or replace as necessary
J—Starter pinion will not disengage from flywheel	Starter motor fault	Petrol models — Check for starter pinion jammed in mesh with flywheel	Rotate squared end of armature shaft until pinion is free. Do not run engine with pinion jammed
		Diesel models — Check for broken return spring in starter	Replace spring

Fault diagnosis—Electrical equipment—*continued*

Symptom	Possible cause	Investigation	Remedy
K—Engine will not fire—Petrol models	Sparking plugs faulty or electrical feed earthing	Check for oily and dirty plugs and for moisture on connections. Check plug gap. Examine plugs for damage to insulation	Clean and reset plug gap. Replace plugs with defective insulation. Dry off all moisture
	Contact breaker faults	Check for dirty and pitted contacts. Check gap	Clean and stone contact pads or replace as necessary. Reset gap to .014 in. to .016 in. (0,35 mm to 0,40 mm)
	Fault in low tension circuit, indicated by no spark occurring between the distributor contact breaker points when separated quickly with ignition 'ON'	Check circuit between battery, coil, distributor, contact breaker and condenser to earth	Examine all ignition cables for damage, ensure sound connections. Check battery terminals, clean and tighten as necessary Replace components as necessary
	Coil or distributor faulty	Remove the lead from the distributor centre terminal and hold the lead end ¼ in. (6 mm) approximately from a suitable metal part of the engine whilst the engine is rotating. If sparks cross the gap regularly, the coil and distributor are functioning satisfactorily	Replace defective components. Ensure that connections from distributor centre lead through carbon brush, rotor arm, distributor segments and plug leads are clean and sound
L—Engine misfires—Petrol models	Contact breaker or condenser faults	Check contact breaker as in paragraph K. Check condenser	Replace components as necessary
	Sparking plug faults	Check sparking plugs as in paragraph K	
	Refer to fault diagnosis in Section A		
M—Engine fails to start from cold—Diesel models	Heater plug fault	Check heater plug circuit	Rectify as necessary
N—Ignition defects—Petrol models	Distributor operation defective. Before commencing investigation, ensure that the ignition timing is correct, Section A refers. Refer also to the ignition system checks described in paragraph K	Check contact breaker points for burning and pitting. Check contact breaker gap	Clean and stone contact pads or replace as necessary. Reset gap
		Check for cracked distributor cap	Replace cap
		Check condenser by substituting a serviceable component	Replace condenser as necessary
		Check rotor arm for pitting and burning	Clean or replace as applicable
		Check for weak or broken contact breaker spring	Replace spring as necessary
		Check for excessive play due to wear in shaft bushes	Replace as necessary

ELECTRICAL EQUIPMENT

Fault diagnosis—Electrical equipment—continued

Symptom	Possible cause	Investigation	Remedy
P—Mixture control warning light fails to glow—engine hot—control pulled out—Petrol models	Electrical circuit defect	Check for broken connections in warning light circuit	Rectify as necessary
		Check for unserviceable warning lamp bulb	Replace as necessary
	Thermostat switch defect	Check switch at cylinder head by substituting a serviceable switch	Replace as necessary
	Mixture control defects	Check for faulty manual switch at mixture control	Replace as necessary
		Check for damaged or broken operating mechanism at switch	Rectify or replace as necessary
Q—Mixture control warning light remains on, engine at running temperature—Petrol models	Mixture control out	Check if manual switch is only partially in	Push control fully in at dash
	Manual switch faulty	Check switch function. Check also for damaged operating mechanism	Replace as necessary
R—Starter operation noisy	Starter loose on mounting	Check fixings at flywheel housing	Tighten as necessary
	Damage to starter or flywheel	Check for starter pinion or flywheel gears chipped or otherwise damaged	Replace as necessary
		Remove armature shaft and examine for bearing wear	Replace as necessary
	Dynamo loose on mounting	Check for loose fixings at dynamo and mounting bracket, where applicable	Tighten as necessary
S—Dynamo operation noisy	Dynamo out of alignment with fan belt	Visually check alignment	Adjust position at dynamo mounting
	Dynamo pulley defect	Check for cracked or damaged pulley	Replace as necessary
	Dynamo internal defect	Check for worn, damaged or defective bearings	Replace as necessary
	Excessive brush noise	Check for rough or dirty commutator, badly seating brushes, insulation between segments requiring cut-back, incorrect brush spring tension, loose brushes and loose field magnets	Rectify or replace as applicable

DATA

System

2¼ litre Petrol and Diesel models up to vehicle suffix 'C' inclusive	POSITIVE EARTH
2¼ litre Petrol and Diesel models from suffix 'D' onwards and all 2.6 litre models	NEGATIVE EARTH

Battery

Petrol models—capacity	Single 12 volt, 58 AH
Diesel models—capacity	Two 6 volt, series connected; 120 AH

Starter motor

Petrol models:
Nominal voltage	12
Starting shaft end float	Zero

Diesel models:
Nominal voltage	12
Starting shaft end float	Zero
Lock torque	26 lb ft (3,5 mkg)
Torque at 1,000 rpm	15 lb ft (2 mkg)

Starter motor drive

Petrol models	Spring loaded pinion and sleeve
Diesel models slip load	Multi-plate clutch 800 to 950 lb/in. (142 to 169 kg/cm

Dynamo

Petrol models, Series II:
Type	C 39/PV 2
Maximum output	19 amps

2¼ litre Petrol and Diesel models, Series IIA:
Type	C 40/1
Maximum output	22 amps

2.6 litre Petrol models:
Type	C 42
Maximum output	30 amps

Control box

2¼ litre Petrol models, Series II: Type	RB 106/37182
2¼ litre Petrol models, Series IIA: Type	RB 106/37290
2.6 litre Petrol models: Type	RB 340/37517
2¼ litre Diesel models, Series II and IIA up to vehicle suffix 'C' inclusive Type	RB 310/37472
2¼ litre Diesel models, Series IIA from vehicle suffix 'D' onwards: Type	RB 340/37387

ELECTRICAL EQUIPMENT

Distributor, Petrol models

Contact breaker gap	.014 in to .016 in. (0,35 mm to 0,40 mm)
Distributor rotation	Clockwise, at drive end
Advance mechanism	Centrifugal/vacuum

Fuses

Quantity	Two
Amperage	35
Protecting A1–A2	Interior lamps, fog lamps, etc., as applicable
A3–A4	Windscreen wiper, fuel tank level unit and stop lights

Heater plugs, Diesel models

Type	Coil element 1–7 volts, 38–42 amps KLG G.F. 210/T or Champion AG 45

Stop lamp switch

Early models	Hydraulic
Latest models	Mechanical

Mixture control thermostat switch, Petrol models

Contact made at	51 to 54°C (124 to 129°F)
Contact broken at	47 to 53°C (117 to 127°F)

Alternator

Type	Lucas 11AC
Nominal voltage	12 volts
Nominal direct current output	43 amperes
Resistance of field coil at 68°F (20°C)	3.8 ohms
Maximum rotor speed	12,500 rpm
Stator phases	3
Stator connection	Star
Number of rotor poles	8
Number of field coils	1
Slip-ring brushes length:	
New	⅝ in. (15,9 mm)
Replace at	5/32 in. (4 mm)
Brush spring tension:	
Load at ¾ in. (19,9 mm)	4 to 5 oz (113 to 142 grms)
Load at ⅖ in. (10,3 mm)	7.5 to 8.5 oz (212 to 241 grms)
Assembly torques, maximum:	
Brushbox fixing screws	10 lb in. (0,115 mkg)
Diode heat sink fixings	25 lb in. (0,288 mkg)
Through bolts	45 to 50 lb in. (0,518 to 0,576 mkg)

Alternator field isolating relay

Nominal voltage	12 volts
Cut-in voltage	6.0 to 7.5 volts
Drop-off voltage	4.0 volts minimum
Resistance of operating winding	76 ohms

Alternator warning light control

Resistance of actuator wire and internal ballast resistor (terminals AL and E)	14 to 16 ohms
Warning light bulb	2.2 watts 12 volts, MES cap

SECTION P—INSTRUMENTS AND CONTROLS

INDEX—INSTRUMENTS AND CONTROLS

Note: A comprehensive, detailed index is included at the end of this manual

Description	Operation Number
	At beginning of Section
Layout of instruments and controls	
Accelerator controls	3
Cut-off control, Diesel models	5
Instruments and switches	1–1A
Mixture control, Petrol models	4
Speedometer drive cable	2
For details of the following items, refer to their respective sections:	
Clutch pedal	Section B
Gearbox controls	Section C
Steering wheel	Section G
Brake pedal	Section H
Windscreen wiper	Section N
Direction indicator switch	Section N
Horn push	Sections G & N
Windscreen ventilator	Section Q
Fault Diagnosis	At end of Section

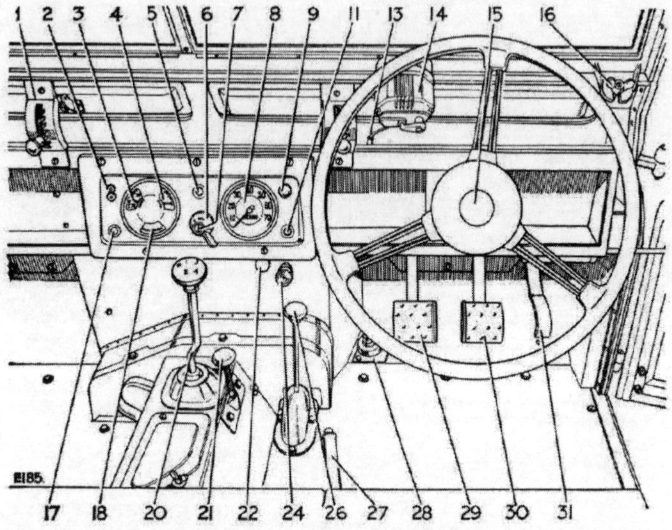

INSTRUMENTS AND CONTROLS

Key to instruments and controls

1. Windscreen ventilator
2. Lead lamp socket
3. Ammeter
4. Fuel level gauge
5. Oil pressure warning light
6. Lamp switch
7. Electrical services or Ignition switch
8. Speedometer
9. Instrument panel light switch
10. Fuel tank warning light (Diesel)
11. Cold start control warning light (Petrol)
12. Heater plug warning light (Diesel)
13. Wiper lead plug
14. Windscreen wiper
15. Horn button
16. Wingnut securing windscreen
17. Charging warning light
18. Headlamp warning light
19. Engine hand speed control (Diesel)
20. Main gear change lever
21. Front wheel drive control
22. Cold start control (Petrol)
23. Engine stop control (Diesel)
24. Starter switch (Petrol)
25. Switch for starter and heater plugs (Diesel)
26. Transfer box lever
27. Hand brake
28. Headlamp dipper switch
29. Clutch pedal
30. Brake pedal
31. Accelerator pedal

Fig. P1-1. Layout of instruments and controls, early Series II and IIA Petrol models

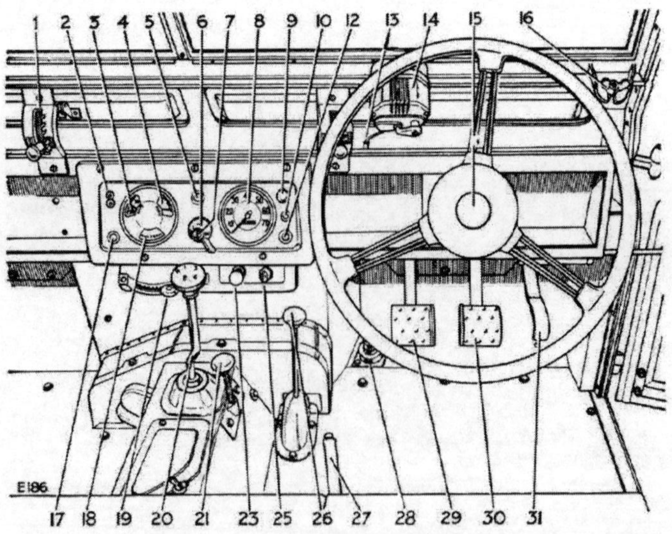

Fig. P1-2. Layout of instruments and controls, early Series II and IIA Diesel models

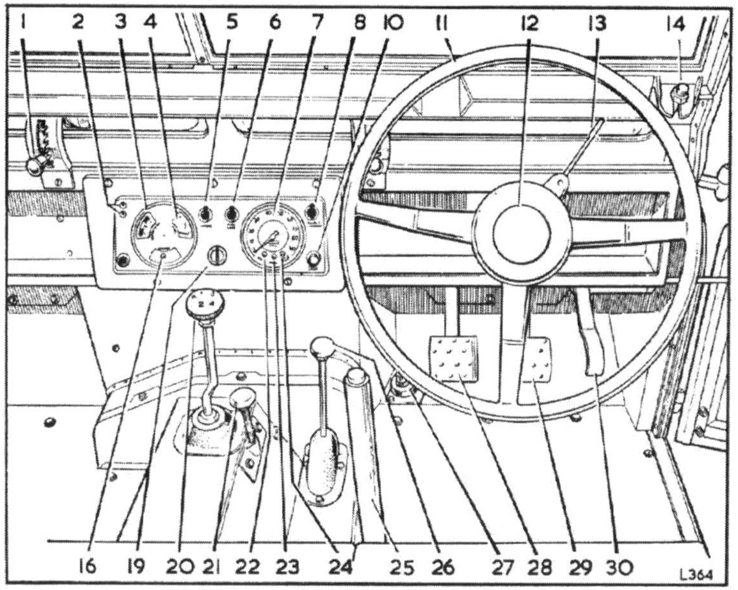

INSTRUMENTS AND CONTROLS

Key to instruments and controls

1. Windscreen ventilator
2. Inspection lamp sockets
3. Water temperature indicator
4. Fuel level indicator
5. Windscreen wiper switch
6. Main light switch
7. Speedometer
8. Panel and interior light switch
9. Engine stop control, Diesel models
10. Cold start control, Petrol models
11. Steering wheel
12. Horn button
13. Direction indicator switch
14. Nut securing windscreen
15. Engine hand speed control, Diesel models
16. Charging warning light
17. Fuel tank level warning light, Diesel models
18. Heater plug and starter switch, Diesel models
19. Ignition and starter switch, Petrol models
20. Main gear change lever (black knob)
21. Four-wheel drive control (yellow knob)
22. Oil pressure warning light
23. Main beam warning light
24. Cold start warning light
25. Hand brake
26. Transfer gear lever (red knob)
27. Headlamp dipper switch
28. Clutch pedal
29. Brake pedal
30. Accelerator pedal

Fig. P1-3. Layout of instruments and controls, latest Series IIA Petrol models

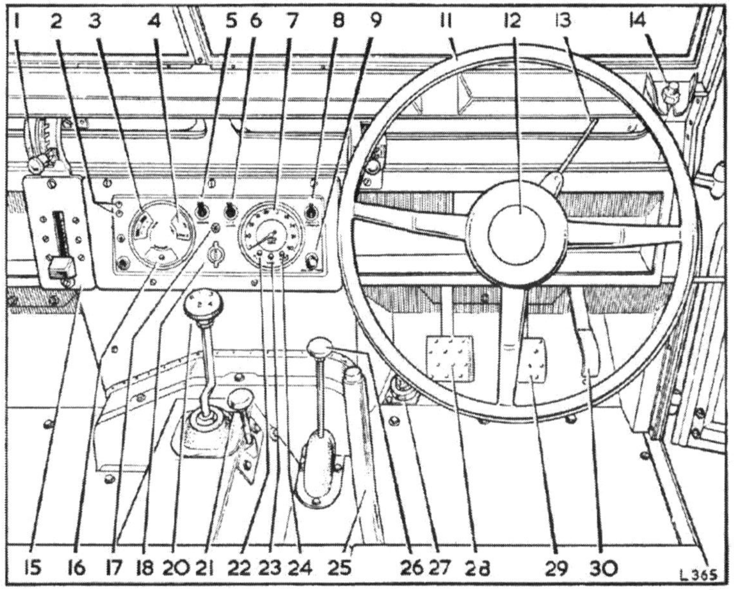

Fig. P1-4. Layout of instruments and controls, latest Series IIA Diesel models

INSTRUMENTS AND CONTROLS

Instruments and switches, POSITIVE EARTH SYSTEM, Series II and IIA models up to vehicle suffix 'C' inclusive, remove and refit—Operation P1-1

Workshop hand tools:
Spanner size: 2 BA
Screwdrivers (medium and small)

To remove

1. Disconnect the battery.
   Diesel—disconnect the positive lead of RH battery.
2. Remove the panel from the dash.
3. Disconnect the speedometer drive cable.
4. Remove the panel light bulb and holder from the speedometer. If necessary, unscrew the bulb from its holder.
5. Remove the speedometer retaining bracket (this action will also release an earth wire) and withdraw the speedometer.
6. Disconnect the wiring from the panel light switch.
7. Unscrew the knob and securing nut from the switch and remove the panel light switch from the panel.
8. Disconnect the wires from the mixture or heater plug warning light.
9. Compress the retaining spring, remove the circlip and withdraw the mixture or heater plug warning light. If necessary, unscrew the bezel from the warning light bakelite holder and withdraw the bulb.
10. Disconnect the wires from the dynamo warning light.
11. Compress the retaining spring, remove the circlip and withdraw the dynamo warning light. If necessary, unscrew the bezel from the warning light bakelite holder and withdraw the bulb.
12. **Diesel**—disconnect the wires from the fuel level warning light, unscrew the lens from the front of instrument panel and withdraw the unit. The bulb may be removed if necessary by easing the smaller diameter of the lamp body from the larger section.
    Diesel—fuel level warning lamp bulb replacement can only be effected by removing the instrument panel.
13. Disconnect the wires from the ignition or auxiliary services and lamp switch.
14. Release the retaining clip and withdraw the ignition or auxiliary services and lamp switch complete.
15. Withdraw the headlamp main beam warning light bulb and holder from the multiple gauge unit. If necessary, unscrew the bulb from its holder.
16. Disconnect the wiring to the ammeter and fuel gauge and withdraw the multiple gauge illumination bulb and holder. If necessary, unscrew the bulb from its holder.
17. Remove the multiple gauge from the panel (this action will also release two earthing wires). The sections of the gauge can be removed separately.
18. Disconnect the wires from the two inspection lamp sockets and withdraw the sockets.
19. Disconnect the wires from the oil pressure warning light.
20. Compress the retaining spring, remove the circlip and withdraw the oil pressure warning light. If necessary, unscrew the bulb from its holder.

To refit

Reverse the removal procedure, connecting the wiring in accordance with the appropriate wiring diagram, Section N. Replacement bulbs are listed in Section N.

Note: Care should be taken when re-connecting the lamp switch wiring on North American vehicles, as it is so arranged that the sidelamps are extinguished when the headlamps are switched on.

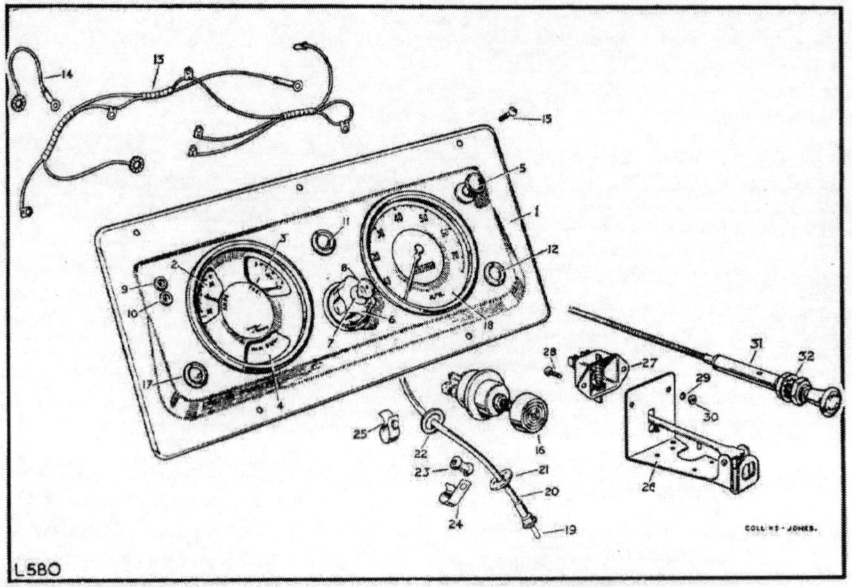

Fig. P1-5. Instruments, POSITIVE EARTH SYSTEM, Series II and IIA models. Up to vehicle suffix 'C' inclusive

1. Instrument panel
2. Ammeter
3. Fuel gauge
4. Warning light for headlamp beam
5. Switch for panel lights
6. Switch for lamps
7. Barrel lock for ignition or electrical services
8. Key for lock
9. Socket for inspection lamp, black
10. Socket for inspection lamp, red
11. Warning light, dynamo*
12. Warning light, mixture or heater plugs
13. Panel harness
14. Lead, ammeter to inspection socket
15. Fixings for instrument panel
16. Starter switch, Petrol models
17. Warning light, oil*
18. Speedometer
19. Cable, inner
20. Cable, outer
21. Retaining plate for cable
22. Rubber grommet, in dash } For speedometer cable
23. Rubber grommet, on cable }
24. Clip } For speedometer cable
25. Clip }
26. Bracket for mixture control ⎫
27. Switch for mixture warning light ⎟ Petrol
28-30. Fixings for switch ⎬ models
31. Mixture control complete ⎟
32. Shakeproof washer for control ⎭

*From late Series II vehicles onwards the position of oil warning light and charging warning light has been interchanged.

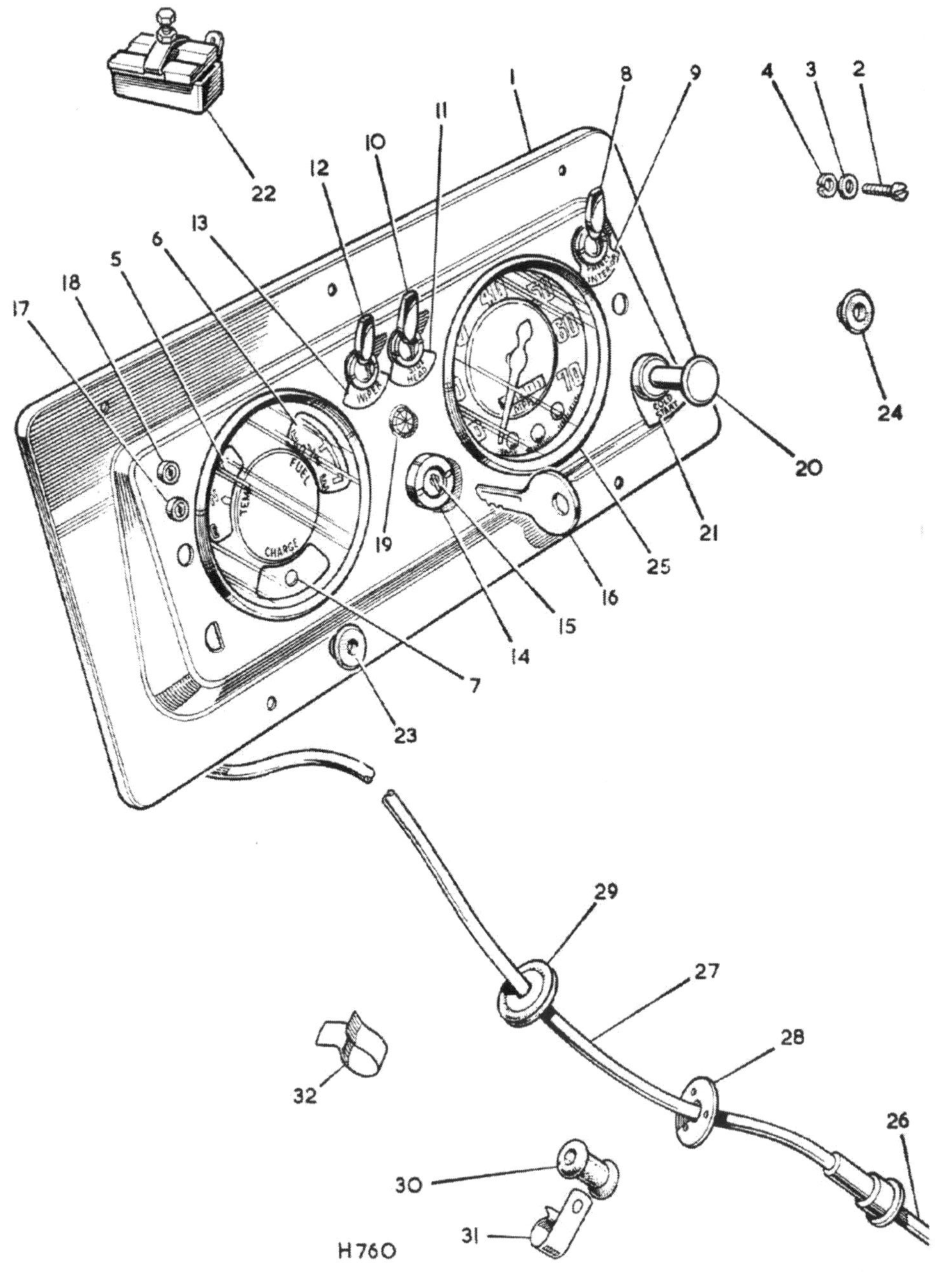

INSTRUMENTS AND CONTROLS

Key to illustration of instruments, negative earth, Series II models from vehicle suffix 'D' onwards

1. Instrument panel
2. Set screw (2 BA x ⅜ in. long) ⎱ Fixing instrument panel
3. Plain washer
4. Spring washer
5. Water temperature gauge
6. Fuel gauge
7. Warning light, charging, red
8. Switch for panel and interior lights
9. Nameplate for switch 'PANEL/INTERIOR'
10. Switch for lamps
11. Nameplate for switch, 'SIDE/HEAD'
12. Switch for wiper motor
13. Nameplate for switch, 'WIPER'
14. Switch for ignition and starter
15. Barrel lock for ignition switch
16. Key for lock
17. Socket for inspection lamp, black
18. Socket for inspection lamp, red
19. Warning light, fuel
20. Cold start control complete
21. Name plate for control, 'COLD START'
22. Switch for cold start warning light
23. Plug, large ⎱ For redundant holes in panel
24. Plug, small ⎰
25. Speedometer and warning lights, mile
26. Cable, inner
27. Cable, outer
28. Retaining plate for cable
29. Rubber grommet, in dash ⎱ For speedometer cable
30. Rubber grommet, on cable ⎰
31. Clip ⎱ For speedometer cable
32. Clip ⎰

Fig. P1-6. Instruments, NEGATIVE EARTH SYSTEM, Series IIA models. From vehicle suffix 'D' onwards

INSTRUMENTS AND CONTROLS

Instruments and switches, NEGATIVE EARTH SYSTEM, Series II and IIA models from vehicle suffix 'D' onwards, remove and refit—Operation P1-1A

Workshop hand tools:
Screwdrivers (medium and small)

To remove

1. Disconnect the battery earth lead.
2. Remove the panel from the dash.
3. Disconnect the speedometer drive cable.
4. Remove the speedometer, oil pressure, main beam and cold start light bulb holders from the speedometer.
5. Remove the speedometer retaining bracket (this action will also release an earth wire) and withdraw the speedometer.
6. Disconnect the wiring from the panel light switch.
7. Unscrew the special securing nut from the switch and remove the panel light switch from the panel.
8. Disconnect the wires from the mixture or heater plug warning light (where fitted).
9. Compress the retaining spring, remove the circlip and withdraw the mixture or heater plug warning light. If necessary, unscrew the bezel from the warning light bakelite holder and withdraw the bulb.
10. Disconnect the leads from the dynamo warning light, water temperature gauge and fuel gauge.
11. Release the three retaining clips and remove the multiple gauge from the panel (this action will also release two earthing wires). The sections of the gauge can be removed separately.
12. **Diesel**—disconnect the leads from the fuel level warning light and withdraw the light and socket.
13. Disconnect the wires from the ignition or auxiliary services and lamp switch.
14. Release the retaining clip and withdraw the ignition or auxiliary services and lamp switch complete.
15. Disconnect the leads from windscreen wiper switch, unscrew the retaining nut and withdraw the switch.
16. Disconnect the leads from the side/headlamp switch, unscrew the retaining nut and withdraw the switch.
17. Disconnect the wires from the two inspection lamp sockets and withdraw the sockets.
18. Disconnect the leads from the instrument voltage stabiliser, and remove stabiliser from panel.

To refit

Reverse the removal procedure, connecting the wiring in accordance with the appropriate wiring diagram, Section N. Replacement bulbs are listed in Section N.

Note: Care should be taken when re-connecting the lamp switch wiring on North American vehicles, as it is so arranged that the sidelamps are extinguished when the headlamps are switched on.

Speedometer drive cable, remove and refit—Operation P1-2

(For removal, refitting and overhaul instructions of the speedometer drive mechanism, Section C refers)

Workshop hand tools:
Spanner size: 2 BA socket
Screwdriver (medium)

To remove

1. Disconnect the battery earth lead.
2. Withdraw the instrument panel clear of the dash.
3. Disconnect the speedometer drive from the speedometer head.
4. Free the cable by withdrawing the end from the dash and pushing the three rubber grommets from the securing clips on the flywheel housing, chassis side member and transfer casing.
5. Disconnect the speedometer cable at the gearbox end. (If necessary, remove the centre seat panel).
6. Withdraw the inner cable from the outer casing.

To refit

1. Thoroughly clean the inner cable and smear suitable grease over its entire length.
2. Insert the cable in the outer casing.
3. Replace the speedometer drive by reversing the removal procedure, care being taken to avoid acute curves. The inner shaft end must be located in the square or slot of the speedometer pinion before the drive is secured to the housing.
4. If the clips holding the securing grommet have been moved, the drive should be correctly positioned before these clips are tightened.

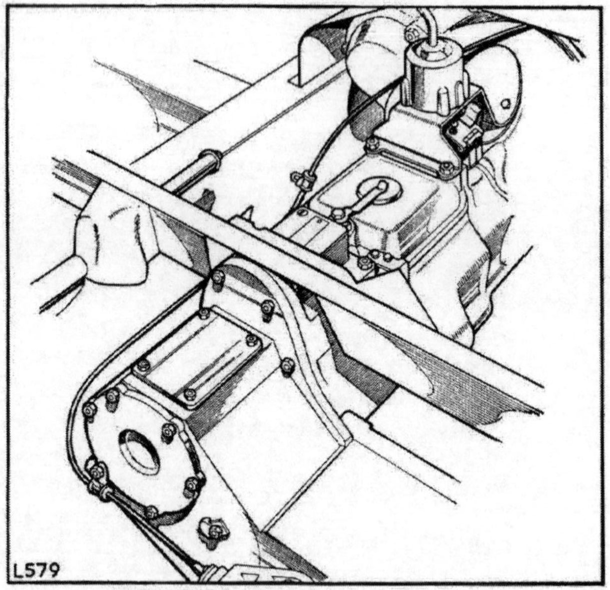

Fig. P1-7. Correct position of speedometer drive cable

Accelerator controls, remove and refit—Operation P1-3

Workshop hand tools:
Spanner sizes: 2 BA, $\frac{7}{16}$ in. AF, $\frac{1}{2}$ in. AF open end
Pliers

General

The accelerator controls vary between different models, the following instructions are generally applicable but reference should be made to exploded views and descriptions of accelerator controls for detail variations.

To remove (see Figs. P1-9, P1-10, P1-11 and P1-12)

1. Remove the throttle return springs.
2. Detach the control rods from the shaft levers.
3. Loosen the clamping bolt, securing lever on accelerator pedal shaft, then withdraw the lever.
4. Remove the accelerator shaft and pedal stop housing.
5. Detach the pedal shaft support bracket from the toe-box and remove the shaft and pedal complete. On LHStg models, the accelerator pedal, pedal shaft and distance piece may be withdrawn without removing the support bracket.
6. Remove the cross-shaft, bracket(s) and distance washers.
7. If necessary, remove the two levers from the cross-shaft.

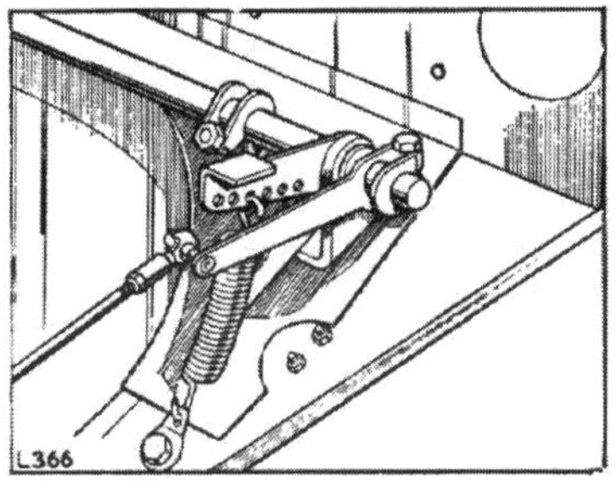

88—2¼ litre Petrol only

8. Remove the accelerator restrictor, if fitted.

On late 88 2¼ litre petrol models an accelerator restrictor is fitted which allows the pedal to be pressed down for three-quarters of its travel with normal pressure, thereafter requiring greater pressure to obtain full throttle.

This device gives a considerable improvement in fuel consumption, and may be fitted to early 88 2¼ litre petrol models if necessary.

To refit

1. Reverse the removal procedure. If disturbed, adjust the lengths of the control rods as necessary.

Hand throttle control—Diesel models

To remove

1. Disconnect the control rod, quadrant to cross-shaft, at the quadrant ball joint, inside vehicle.
2. Remove the securing bolts, quadrant to scuttle.
3. Remove instrument panel and remove securing bolts, quadrant upper bracket to dash bottom centre panel.
4. Withdraw complete unit.

To refit

1. Reverse removal procedure.
2. Check for correct functioning and set the hand speed lever as necessary by adjusting the operational lengths of the control rod, quadrant to cross-shaft.

Fig. P1-8. Accelerator restrictor

Mixture control, Petrol models, remove and refit—Operation P1-4

Workshop hand tools:
Spanner sizes: 2 BA, $\frac{1}{4}$ in. BSF open end
Screwdriver (small)

To remove

A plunger switch is incorporated in the mixture control; it is wired in series with a bi-metal thermostat switch at the rear of the cylinder head and the amber warning light on the instrument panel.

1. Disconnect the battery earth lead.
2. Disconnect the wiring from the mixture control warning light switch.
3. Disconnect the operating wire from the lever at the carburetter.
4. Withdraw the inner wire and knob from the driver's side of the dash.
5. Loosen the screw holding the outer cable at the carburetter.
6. Remove the cold start control outer cable bracket and switch from the dash by removing the securing nut on the driver's side of the dash.
7. If necessary, remove the warning light switch from the bracket.
8. If necessary, remove the control outer cable from the bracket by unscrewing the cable through the securing locknut.

To refit

Reverse the removal procedure, taking care that the carburetter cold start lever is fully closed when the control knob is pushed right in.

Note: For further details of the mixture control warning light system, see Section N.

Cut-off control, Diesel models, remove and refit—Operation P1-5

Workshop hand tools:
Spanner sizes: 2 BA, $\frac{1}{4}$ in. BSF open end
Screwdriver (small)

To remove

1. Disconnect the control cable from the injection pump cut-off lever and outer cable support.
2. Unscrew the securing nut from the engine side of scuttle and withdraw the cut-off control cable complete.

To refit

1. Secure the control to the scuttle and the outer cable to the clamping clip on injection pump; locate the inner cable in the cut-off lever clamping screw, then, pressing the lever firmly downward, tighten the clamping screw.

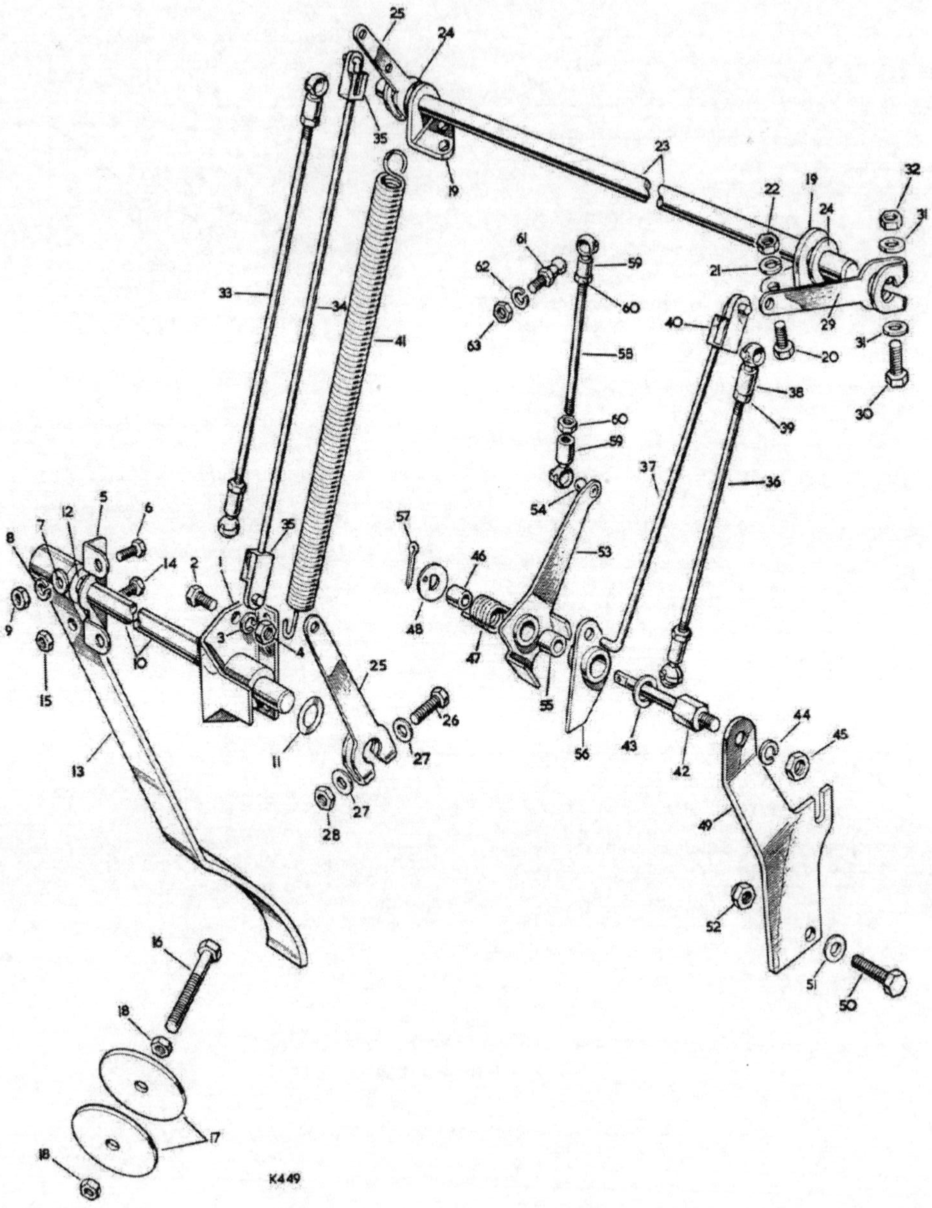

INSTRUMENTS AND CONTROLS

Key to Illustration of accelerator controls, 2¼ litre Petrol models

1. Housing for accelerator shaft and pedal stop
2. Bolt (¼ in. UNF × ½ in. long) } Fixing housing and pedal stop to dash
3. Spring washer
4. Nut (¼ in. UNF)
5. Bracket for accelerator pedal shaft
6. Bolt (¼ in. UNF × ⅝ in. long) } Fixing bracket to dash
7. Plain washer
8. Spring washer
9. Nut (¼ in. UNF)
10. Shaft for accelerator pedal
11. Special washer } On accelerator shaft
12. Plain washer
13. Accelerator pedal
14. Bolt (¼ in. UNF × ⅞ in. long) } Fixing pedal to shaft
15. Nut (⁵⁄₁₆ in. UNF)
16. Bolt (¼ in. UNF × 1¼ in. long) Pedal stop in floor
17. Plain washer
18. Nut (⁵⁄₁₆ in. UNF)
19. Bracket for accelerator cross-shaft, 'L' shaped
20. Bolt (¼ in. UNF × ⅝ in. long) } Fixing bracket to dash
21. Spring washer
22. Nut (¼ in. UNF)
23. Cross-shaft for accelerator
24. Distance washer for lever
25. Lever for accelerator
26. Bolt (¼ in. UNF × 1¼ in. long) } Fixing levers to shaft
27. Plain washer
28. Nut (¼ in. UNF)
29. Lever for cross-shaft
30. Bolt (¼ in. UNF × 1¼ in. long) } Fixing lever to cross-shaft
31. Plain washer
32. Nut (¼ in. UNF)
33. Control rod, pedal shaft to cross-shaft
34. Control rod, pedal shaft to cross-shaft
35. Linkage clip for control rod
36. Control rod, cross-shaft to engine
37. Control rod, cross-shaft to engine
38. Ball joint socket for rods
39. Locknut for socket
40. Linkage clip for control rod, cross-shaft to engine
41. Return spring for pedal
42. Spindle for carburetter bell crank
43. Plain washer } Fixing spindle
44. Spring washer
45. Nut (⅜ in. UNF)
46. Spacer for spindle
47. Torsion spring for bell crank
48. Special washer for torsion spring
49. Bracket for accelerator controls
50. Bolt (⅜ in. UNF × 1 in. long) } Fixing bracket to steering column support bracket
51. Plain washer
52. Self-locking nut (⅜ in. UNF)
53. Carburetter bell crank lever assembly
54. Ball end for lever
55. Bush for bell crank
56. Carburetter relay lever
57. Split pin fixing levers to spindle
58. Control rod, bell crank to carburetter
59. Ball joint } For control rod
60. Locknut (2 BA)
61. Ball end for carburetter lever
62. Spring washer } Fixing ball end to carburetter lever
63. Nut (¼ in. UNF)

Fig. P1-9 Accelerator controls, 2¼ litre Petrol models

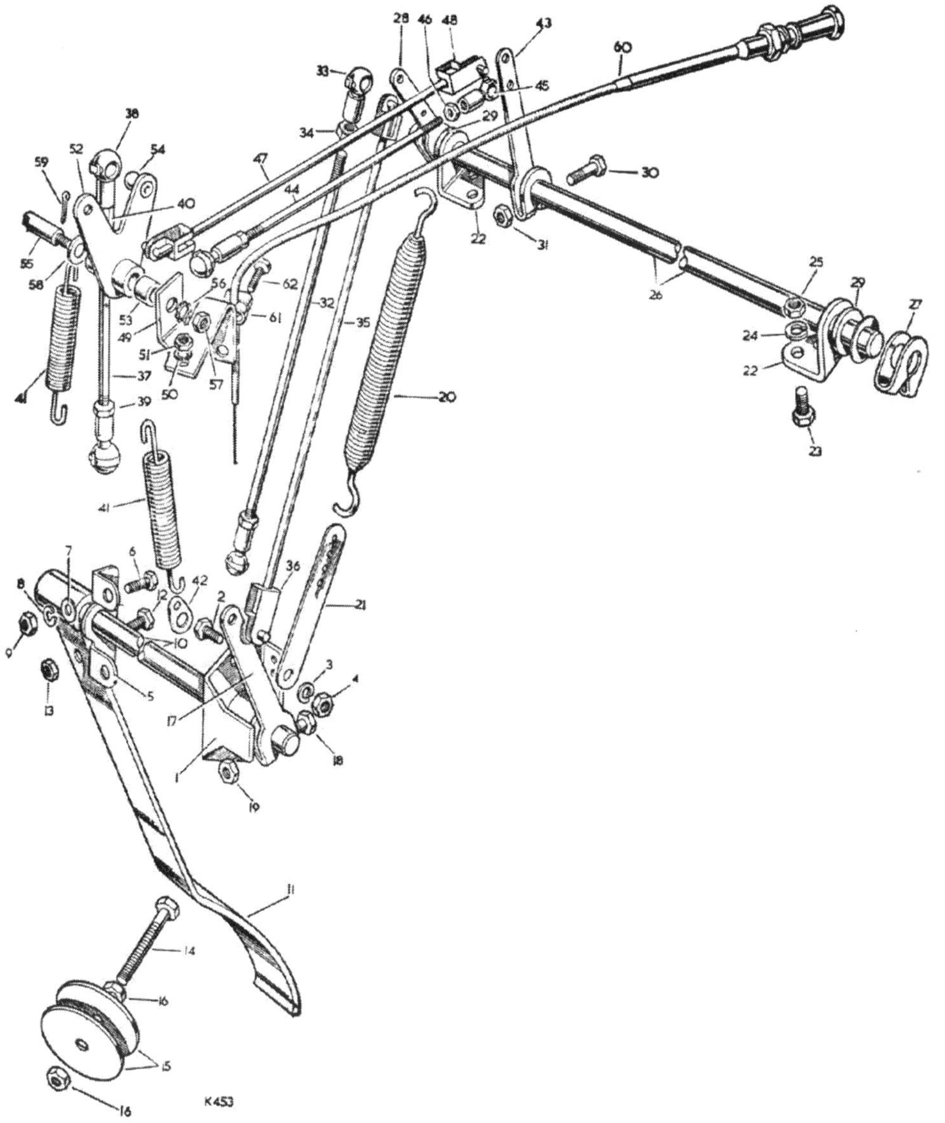

INSTRUMENTS AND CONTROLS

Key to illustration of accelerator controls, 2¼ litre Diesel models

1. Housing for accelerator shaft and pedal stop
2. Bolt (¼ in. UNF × ¾ in. long) } Fixing housing
3. Spring washer } and pedal stop
4. Nut (¼ in. UNF) } to dash
5. Bracket for accelerator pedal shaft
6. Bolt (¼ in. UNF × ⅝ in. long) } Fixing bracket
7. Plain washer } to dash
8. Spring washer
9. Nut (¼ in. UNF)
10. Shaft for accelerator pedal
11. Accelerator pedal
12. Bolt (⁵⁄₁₆ in. UNF × ⅞ in. long) } Fixing pedal
13. Nut (⁵⁄₁₆ in. UNF) } to shaft
14. Bolt (⁵⁄₁₆ in. UNF × 2¼ in. long) } Pedal stop in
15. Plain washer } floor
16. Nut (⁵⁄₁₆ in. UNF)
17. Lever for accelerator on pedal shaft
18. Bolt (¼ in. UNF × 1¼ in. long) } Fixing lever
19. Nut (¼ in. UNF) } to shaft
20. Return spring for pedal
21. Anchor for return spring
22. Bracket for accelerator cross-shaft
23. Bolt (¼ in. UNF × ⅝ in. long) } Fixing
24. Spring washer } brackets
25. Nut (¼ in. UNF) } to dash
26. Accelerator cross-shaft
27. Stop clip for cross-shaft
28. Accelerator lever on cross-shaft from pedal
29. Distance washer for cross-shaft
30. Bolt (¼ in. UNF × 1¼ in. long) } Fixing levers and stop clip to cross-shaft
31. Nut (¼ in. UNF)
32. Control rod, pedal shaft to cross-shaft
33. Ball joint socket } For
34. Locknut (2 BA) } rod
35. Control rod, pedal shaft to cross shaft
36. Linkage clip for control rod
37. Control rod, bell crank to accelerator lever
38. Ball socket
39. Nut (2 BA) } For bell crank control rod
40. Adjuster nut
41. Return spring for accelerator and stop levers on distributor pump
42. Anchor for return spring
43. Accelerator lever on cross-shaft to engine
44. Control rod, cross-shaft to bell crank
45. Ball joint } For
46. Locknut (2 BA) } control rod
47. Control rod, cross-shaft to bell crank
48. Linkage clip for control rod
49. Bracket for bell crank on distributor pump
50. Spring washer } Fixing bracket to
51. Nut (10 UNF) } distributor pump
52. Bell crank complete on distributor pump
53. Bush for bell crank
54. Ball end for bell crank
55. Pin for bell crank
56. Shakeproof washer } Fixing bell crank
57. Nut (¼ in. UNF) } lever to pin
58. Plain washer
59. Split pin
60. 'Engine stop' control
61. Clip } Fixing control outer cable
62. Screw (2 BA × ⅜ in. long) } to abutment bracket on distributor pump

Fig. P1·10. Accelerator controls, 2¼ litre Diesel models

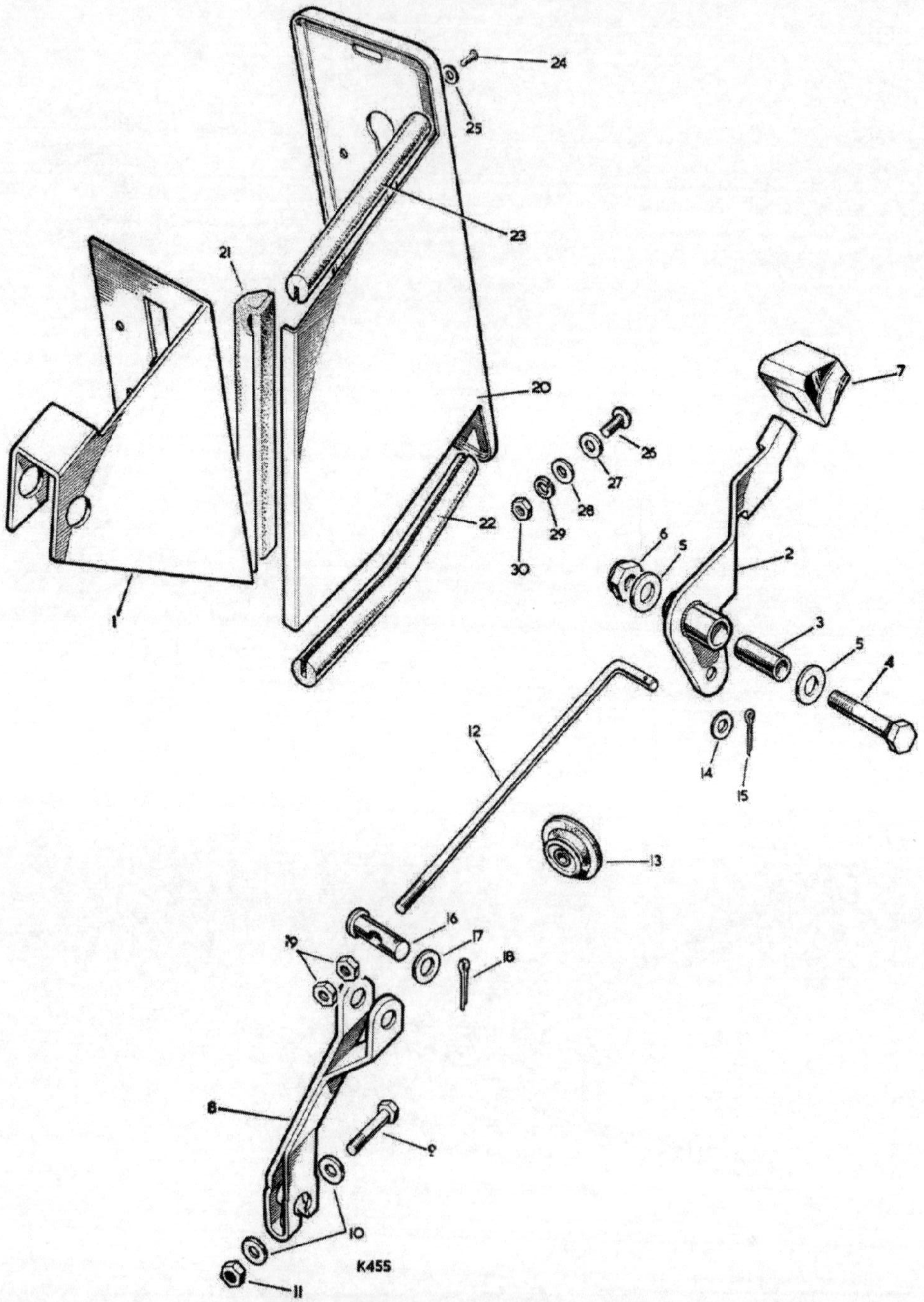

INSTRUMENTS AND CONTROLS

Key to Illustration of hand accelerator, 2¼ litre Diesel models

1. Housing and quadrant for control
2. Lever for control
3. Distance tube for housing
4. Bolt (¼ in. UNF x 1¼ in. long) ⎫ Fixing control lever and tube to housing
5. Plain washer ⎬
6. Self-locking nut (¼ in. UNF) ⎭
7. Knob for lever
8. Operating lever for cross-shaft
9. Bolt (¼ in. UNF x 1⅛ in. long) ⎫ Fixing operating lever to accelerator cross-shaft
10. Plain washer ⎬
11. Nut (¼ in. UNF) ⎭
12. Control rod for engine speed control
13. Grommet in dash for control rod
14. Plain washer ⎫ Fixing control rod to control lever
15. Split pin ⎭
16. Joint pin ⎫ Fixing control rod to operating lever
17. Plain washer ⎬
18. Split pin ⎭
19. Nut (2 BA) fixing control rod to joint pin
20. Mounting panel, LH ⎫ For control housing
    Mounting panel, RH ⎭
21. Rubber seal, rear
22. Rubber finisher, bottom ⎫ For mounting panel
23. Rubber finisher, top ⎭
24. Drive screw ⎫ Fixing mounting panel to control housing
25. Plain washer ⎭
26. Screw (2 BA x ¼ in. long) ⎫ Fixing mounting panel to dash, lower
27. Plain washer ⎬
28. Packing washer ⎬
29. Spring washer ⎬
30. Nut (2 BA) ⎭

Fig. PI-11. Hand accelerator, 2¼ litre Diesel model.

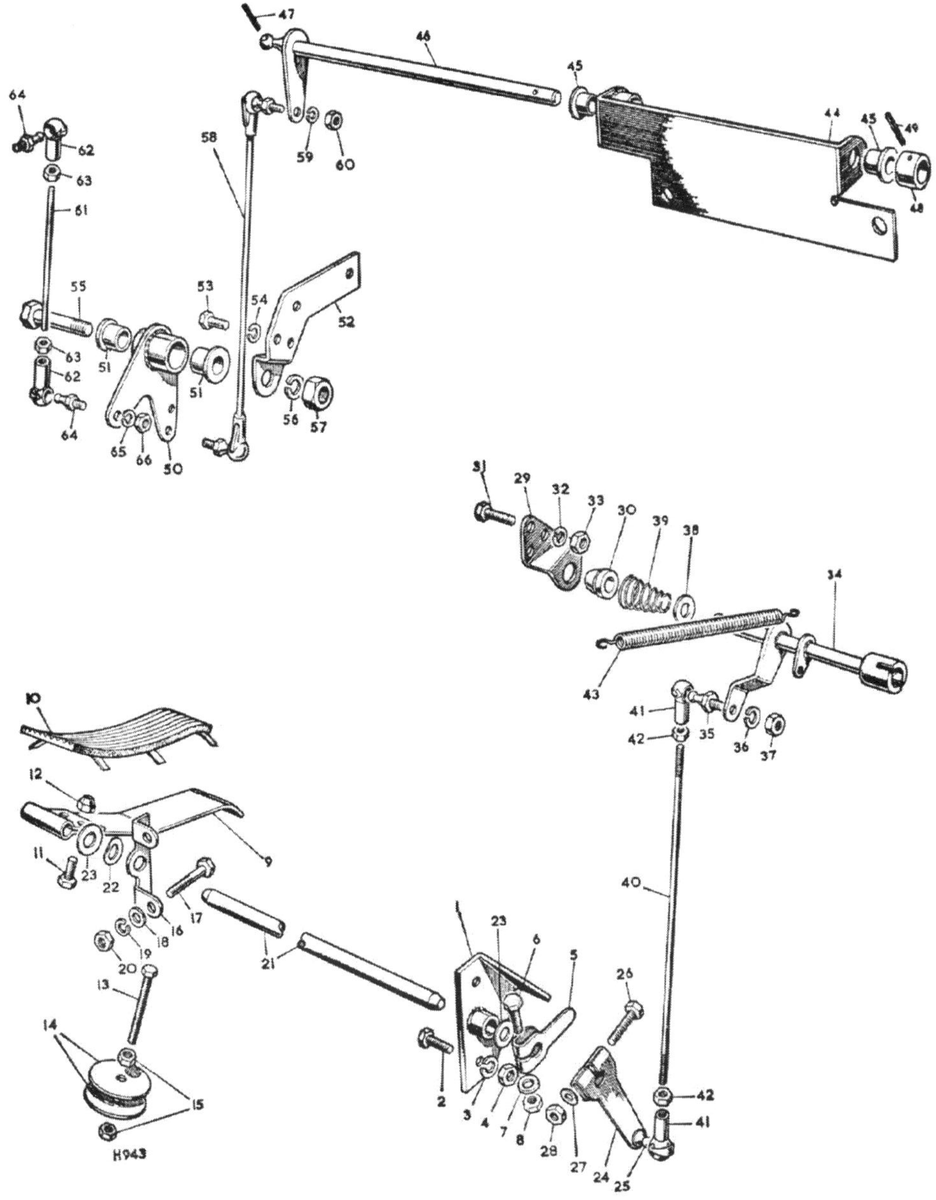

INSTRUMENTS AND CONTROLS

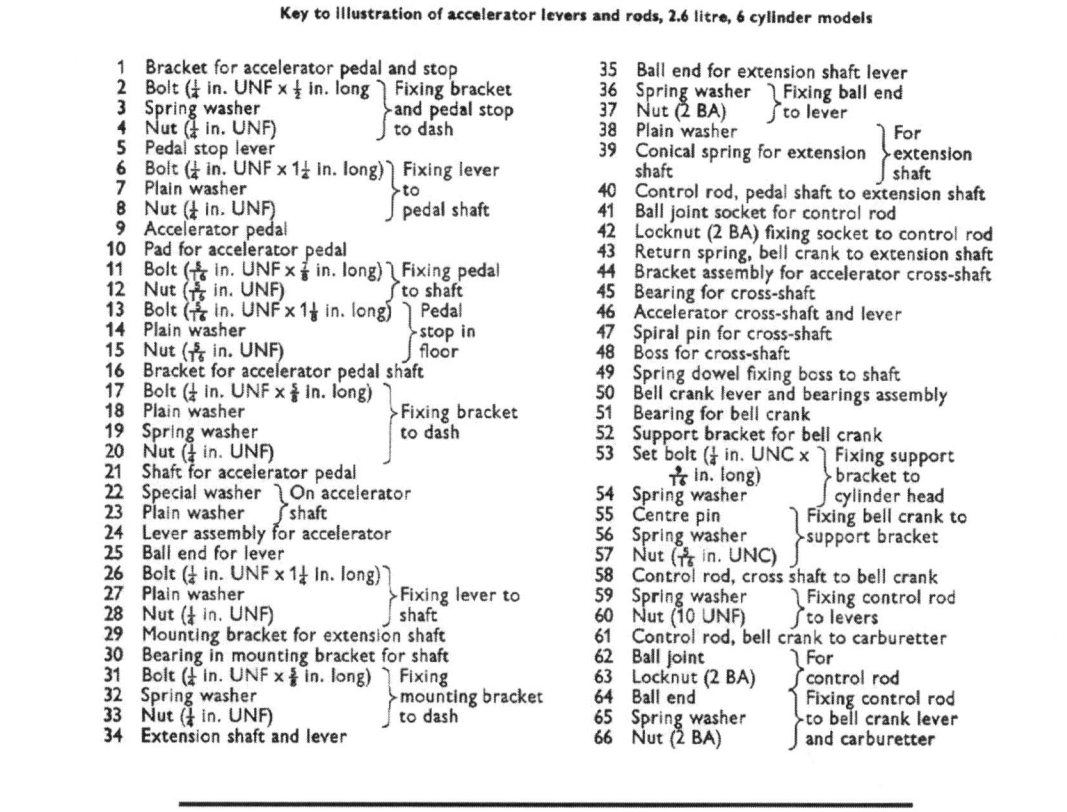

Key to Illustration of accelerator levers and rods, 2.6 litre, 6 cylinder models

1. Bracket for accelerator pedal and stop
2. Bolt (¼ in. UNF × ½ in. long)
3. Spring washer
4. Nut (¼ in. UNF)
5. Pedal stop lever
6. Bolt (¼ in. UNF × 1¼ in. long)
7. Plain washer
8. Nut (¼ in. UNF)
9. Accelerator pedal
10. Pad for accelerator pedal
11. Bolt (⁵⁄₁₆ in. UNF × ⅞ in. long)
12. Nut (⁵⁄₁₆ in. UNF)
13. Bolt (⁵⁄₁₆ in. UNF × 1⅛ in. long)
14. Plain washer
15. Nut (⁵⁄₁₆ in. UNF)
16. Bracket for accelerator pedal shaft
17. Bolt (¼ in. UNF × ⅝ in. long)
18. Plain washer
19. Spring washer
20. Nut (¼ in. UNF)
21. Shaft for accelerator pedal
22. Special washer — On accelerator shaft
23. Plain washer
24. Lever assembly for accelerator
25. Ball end for lever
26. Bolt (¼ in. UNF × 1¼ in. long)
27. Plain washer
28. Nut (¼ in. UNF)
29. Mounting bracket for extension shaft
30. Bearing in mounting bracket for shaft
31. Bolt (¼ in. UNF × ½ in. long)
32. Spring washer
33. Nut (¼ in. UNF)
34. Extension shaft and lever
35. Ball end for extension shaft lever
36. Spring washer — Fixing ball end to lever
37. Nut (2 BA)
38. Plain washer
39. Conical spring for extension shaft
40. Control rod, pedal shaft to extension shaft
41. Ball joint socket for control rod
42. Locknut (2 BA) fixing socket to control rod
43. Return spring, bell crank to extension shaft
44. Bracket assembly for accelerator cross-shaft
45. Bearing for cross-shaft
46. Accelerator cross-shaft and lever
47. Spiral pin for cross-shaft
48. Boss for cross-shaft
49. Spring dowel fixing boss to shaft
50. Bell crank lever and bearings assembly
51. Bearing for bell crank
52. Support bracket for bell crank
53. Set bolt (¼ in. UNC × ⁷⁄₁₆ in. long) — Fixing support bracket to cylinder head; Fixing bell crank to support bracket
54. Spring washer
55. Centre pin
56. Nut (⁷⁄₁₆ in. UNC)
57. Plain washer
58. Control rod, cross shaft to bell crank
59. Spring washer
60. Nut (10 UNF)
61. Control rod, bell crank to carburetter
62. Spring washer — For control rod
63. Ball joint
64. Ball end
65. Spring washer — Fixing control rod to bell crank lever and carburetter
66. Nut (2 BA)

Fault diagnosis—Instruments and controls

Symptom	Possible cause	Investigation	Remedy
Speedometer needle erratic	Loose securing nut at the gearbox rear drive output flange	Remove rear propeller shaft and check nut for security	Securely tighten nut and lock with a new split pin
	Speedometer cable damaged or position of cable incorrect	Check position and condition of inner and outer cables	Reposition or fit new cable as required
	Faulty speedometer head		Fit new speedometer head
	Worn speedometer drive worm and pinion	Remove speedometer drive housing and check worm and pinion	Fit new parts as required

Note: For details of other instruments and warning lights, Section N refers.

Fig. P1-12. Accelerator levers and rods, 2.6 litre, 6 cylinder models

SECTION Q—BODY

INDEX—BODY

Note: A comprehensive, detailed index is included at the end of this manual

Description	Operation Number
Body repairs (welding, rivetting and painting)	At beginning of Section
Bonnet panel	1
Cab	11
Dash panel	8–9
Front floor	6–7
Front wings	3
Hard top	12
Radiator grille	2
Rear body	13
Rear door	15
Safety harness	16
Seat base	10
Side doors	5
Station Wagon top	14
Windscreen	4

Body repairs, general information

With the exception of the radiator grille panel, dash panel, door frames and tail board frame, which are steel, the Land-Rover body is made from a special light magnesium-aluminium alloy known as 'Birmabright', with steel cappings and corner brackets; all steel parts are galvanised.

'Birmabright' was developed for aircraft use, and it is much stronger and tougher than pure aluminium.

It melts at a slightly lower temperature than pure aluminium and will not rust nor corrode under any normal circumstances.

It is work-hardening, and so becomes hard and brittle when hammered, but it is easily annealed.

Exposed to the atmosphere, a hard oxide skin forms on the surface of it.

Panel beating 'Birmabright'

'Birmabright' panels and wings can be beaten out after accidental damage in the same way as sheet steel. However, under protracted hammering the material will harden, and then it must be annealed to prevent the possibility of cracking.

This is quite easily done by the application of heat, followed by slow air-cooling, but as the melting point is low, heat must be applied slowly and carefully. A rough but very useful temperature control is to apply oil to the cleaned surface to be annealed. Play the welding torch on the underside of the cleaned surface and watch for the oil to clear, which it will do quite quickly, leaving the surface clean and unmarked. Then allow to cool naturally in the air, when the area so treated will again be soft and workable. Do not quench with oil or water.

Another method is to clean the surface to be annealed and then rub it with a piece of soap. Apply heat beneath the area, as described above, and watch for the soap stain to clear. Then allow to cool, as for the oil method. When applying the heat for annealing, always hold the torch some little distance from the metal, and move it about, so as to avoid any risk of melting it locally.

Gas welding 'Birmabright'

A small jet must be used, one or two sizes smaller than would be used for welding sheet steel of comparable thickness. For instance, use a No. 2 nozzle for welding 18 swg (.048 in.) sheet, and a No. 3 for 16 swg (.064 in.) sheet. The flame should be smooth, quiet and neutral, though a slightly reducing flame may be used—that is, there may be a slight excess of acetylene. See Fig. Q1-1.

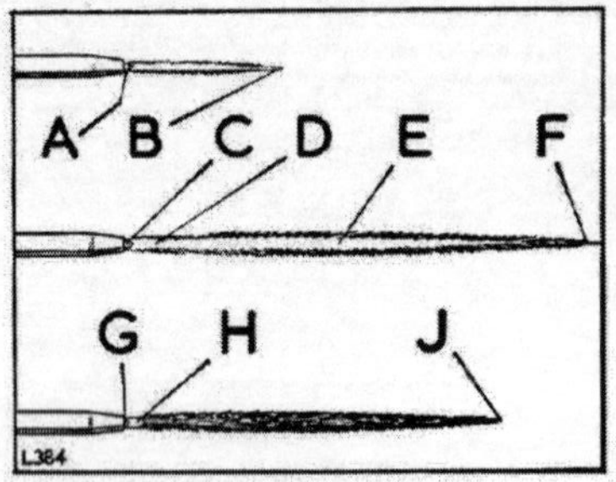

Fig. Q1-1. Welding jet, Oxydising, Neutral Reducing
A—Short pointed inner cone bluish white
B—Bluish envelope
C—Brilliant inner core well defined rounded end
D—Hottest point of flame
E—Blue to orange envelope
F—Nearly colourless
G—Brilliant inner core
H—Feathery white plume
J—Blue to orange envelope

Use only 5 per cent magnesium/aluminium welding rod (5 Mg/A). Sifalumin No. 27 (MG.5 Alloy) (use Sifbronze Special flux with this rod) or a thin strip cut off parent metal—that is to say, a strip cut from an old and otherwise useless 'Birmabright' panel or sheet. Do not use too wide or thick a strip, or trouble may be experienced in making it melt before the material which is being welded.

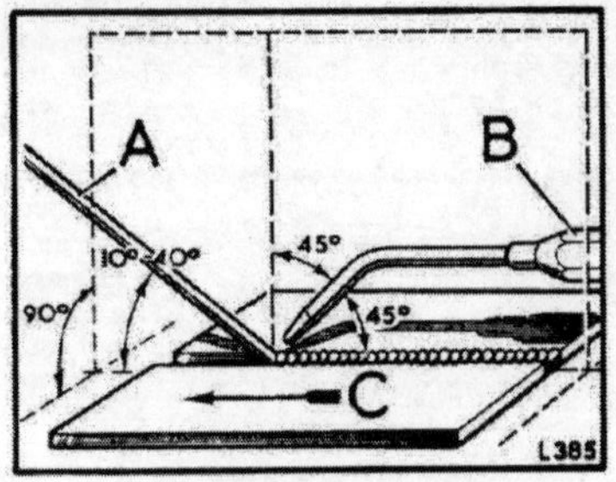

Fig. Q1-2. Method of welding
A—Filler rod
B—Torch
C—Direction of welding

Clean off all grease and paint, dry thoroughly and then clean the edges to be welded, and an area at least half an inch on either side of the weld, with a stiff wire scratch-brush or wire wool. Cleanliness is essential. Also clean the welding rod or strip with wire wool.

A special acid flux must be used, and we recommend Hari-Kari, which is obtainable from:

The Midland Welding Supply Co Ltd,
105 Lakey Lane,
Birmingham 28, England.

or

Sifbronze Special Flux, which is obtainable from:

Suffolk Iron Foundry (1920) Ltd,
Sifbronze Works,
Stowmarket, England.

A small quantity of 'Hari-Kari' may be made into a paste with water, following the directions on the tin, and the paste must be applied to both surfaces to be welded, and also to the rod. In the case of Sifbronze Special Flux use in powder form as directed. Remember that aluminium and its alloys do not show 'red-hot' before melting, and so there is nothing about the appearance of the metal to indicate that it has reached welding temperature. A little experience will enable the operator to gauge this point, but a useful guide is to sprinkle a little sawdust over the work; this will sparkle and char when the right temperature is approached; a piece of dry wood rubbed over the hot metal will sparkle at the point of contact.

As the flux used is highly acid, it is essential to wash it off thoroughly immediately after a weld is completed. The hottest possible water should be used, with wire wool or a scratch-brush. Very hot soapy water is good, because of the alkaline nature of the soap, which will tend to 'kill' the acid.

It is strongly recommended that a few welds are made on scrap metal before the actual repair is undertaken if the operator is not already experienced in welding aluminium and its alloys.

The heat of welding will have softened the metal in the area of the repair, and it may be hardened again by peening with a light hammer. Many light blows are preferable to fewer heavy ones. Use a 'dolly' or anvil behind the work to avoid denting and deformation, and to make the hammering more effective. Filing off surplus metal from the weld will also help to harden the work again.

Welding tears and patching

If a tear extends to the edge of a panel, start the weld from the end away from the edge and also at this point drill a small hole to prevent the crack spreading, then work towards the edge.

When welding a long tear, or making a long welded joint, tack the edges to be welded at intervals of from 2 in. to 4 in. (50 to 100 mm) with spots. This is done by melting the metal at the starting end and fusing into it a small amount of the filler rod, repeating the process at the suggested intervals. After this, weld continuously along the joint from right to left, increasing the speed of the weld as the material heats up.

After the work has cooled, wash off all traces of flux as described above, and file off any excess of build-up metal.

When patching, cut the patch to the correct shape for the hole to be filled, but of such size as to leave a gap of $\frac{1}{32}$ in. between it and the panel all round. Clean the patch and the panel, and then weld as described above. Never apply an 'overlay' patch.

Electric welding

At the Rover Factory the 'Argon-Arc' process is used, and this is very satisfactory, since all atmospheric oxygen is excluded from the weld by the Argon gas shield. For all body repair work normally undertaken by a Distributor's or Dealer's service department, the gas welding method is sufficient and quite satisfactory.

Spot-welding

Spot-welding is largely used in the manufacture of Land-Rover bodies, but this is a process which can only be carried out satisfactorily by the use of the proper apparatus. Aluminium and its alloys are very good conductors of heat and electricity, and thus it is most important to maintain the right conditions for successful spot-welding. The correct current density must be maintained, and so must the 'dwell' of the electrodes. Special spot-welding machines have been developed, but they are expensive, and though the actual work can be carried out by comparatively unskilled labour, supervision and machine maintenance must be in the hands of properly qualified persons.

Riveting

Where both sides of the metal are accessible and it is possible to use an anvil or 'dolly', solid aluminium rivets may be used, with a suitable punch or 'pop' to ensure clean rounded heads on the work. For riveting blind holes, 'pop-rivets' must be used. These are inserted and closed by special 'Lazy-Tong' 'pop-rivet' pliers.

Slightly roughen the surface with emery paper of 100 grit. Apply a suitable primer, such as 'Glasso', as thinly as practicable (too thick a coat may crack or 'craze') then use three coats of filler and finish with the appropriate colour. Unless the initial etcher is used, paint is liable to come away, as it cannot 'key' into the hard oxide of an untreated alloy surface.

Painting

Owing to the hard oxide skin which forms on the surface of the alloy when exposed to the atmosphere, it is necessary to etch a repaired panel before repainting. Degrease the area to be painted by wiping thoroughly with thinners, dry off, and then apply the acid etching medium. A suitable one is 'Deoxidine 125' which is made by ICI Paints Division. After application, wash off thoroughly with hot water, and again dry thoroughly.

Bonnet panel, remove and refit—Operation Q1-1

Workshop hand tools:
Screwdriver (medium), Pliers

To remove

1. Remove the spare wheel from the bonnet panel, if fitted.
2. Remove fixings at prop rod and bonnet hinge.
3. Remove bonnet panel.

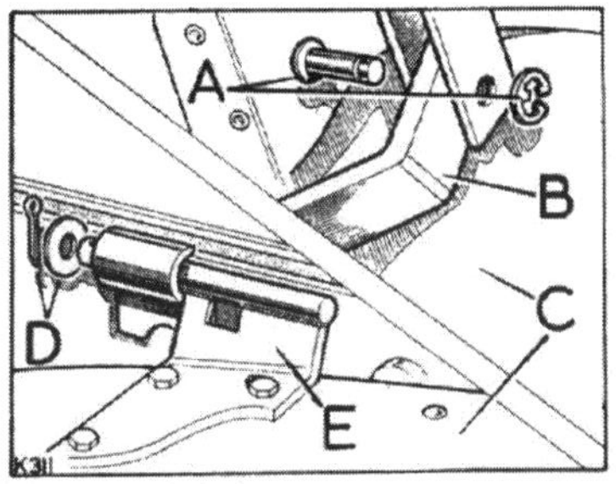

To refit

1. Refit the bonnet panel, using suitable coverings on the wings to avoid damage to paintwork.
2. Refit the spare wheel, if fitted, to bonnet panel.

Fig. Q1-3. Fixings at bonnet panel

A—Prop rod fixings
B—Bonnet prop rod
C—Bonnet panel
D—Bonnet hinge fixings, RH side only
E—Bonnet hinge

BODY

Section Q—Land-Rover

Radiator and grille panel assembly, remove and refit—Operation Q1-2

Workshop hand tools:
Spanner sizes: 7/16 in. x ½ in. AF open ended, 2 off, 2 BA open ended
Screwdriver (medium), Pliers

2¼ litre Petrol and Diesel models:

Refer to Section A for additional detail information.

To remove
1. Remove bonnet. Operation Q1-1.
2. Disconnect battery leads.
3. Remove front apron panel.

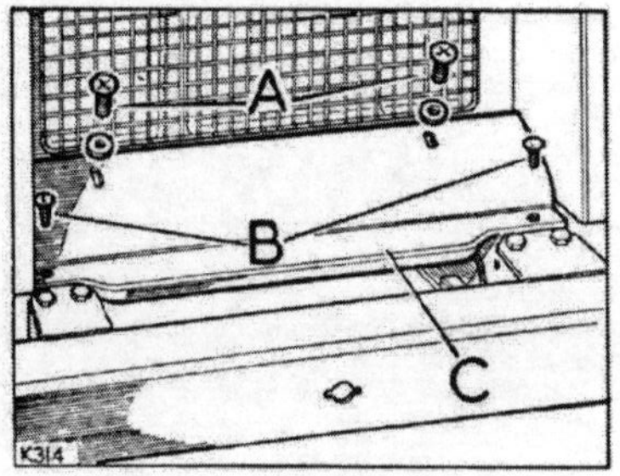

Fig. Q1-4. Apron panel fixings
A—Fixings at cross member brackets
B—Fixings at side members
C—Apron panel

4. Remove nameplate and radiator grille.

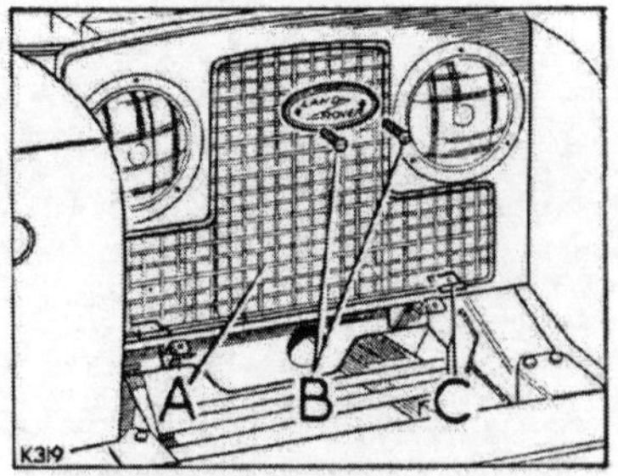

Fig. Q1-5. Radiator grille fixings
A—Radiator grille
B—Fixings for nameplate and grille
C—Support brackets

5. Remove radiator cap, drain off coolant.
6. Remove shroud from radiator fan cowl.
7. Slacken fixings and detach radiator coolant hoses.
8. Remove the fan blades fixings and lower the fan blades to rest on lower part of fan cowl. Remove the fan blades when access is obtained during grille panel removal.

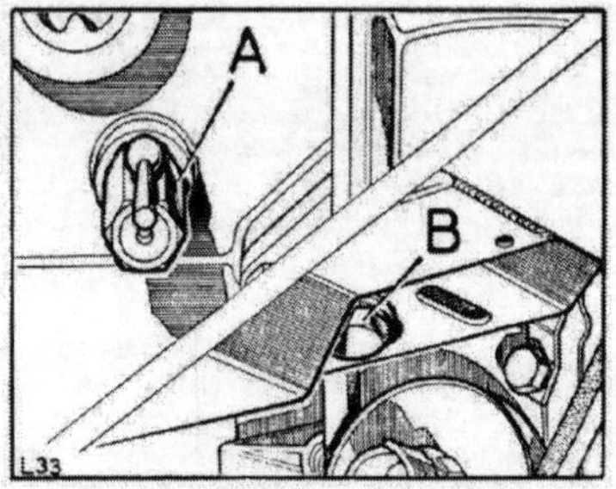

Fig. Q1-6. Coolant drain taps location
A—At engine block, RH side
B—At radiator

9. Disconnect the electrical leads for the front lamps at the snap connectors.
10. Remove the grille panel to front wings fixings, the securing nuts and washers are located in the respective wheelarches.
11. Remove the grille panel fixings at the brackets on the chassis cross member.
12. Carefully withdraw the assembly and the previously released fan blades from the engine compartment.

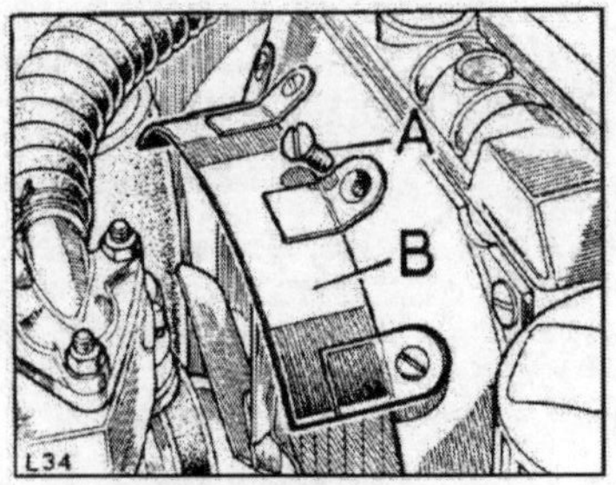

Fig. Q1-7. Fan shroud fixings
A—Fixings for fan shroud
B—Fan shroud

To refit
1. Refit the radiator grille and radiator complete on to the vehicle. Fit the fan blades to the fan pulley before engaging the grille panel fixings. See Figs. Q1-10 and Q1-9 for fixing details.

Operation Q1-2—continued

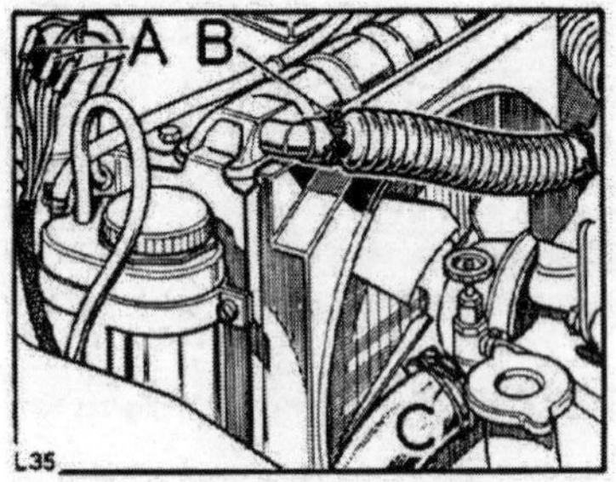

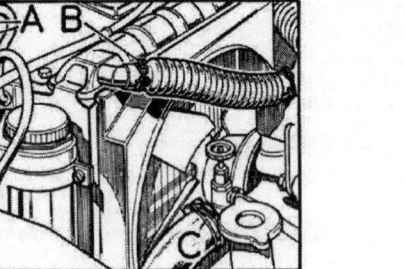

Fig. Q1-8. Coolant hose and lead connectors
A—Snap connectors (3 off each side of vehicle)
B—Fixings at top hose
C—Fixings at bottom hose

2. Make the electrical connections at the snap connectors, referring to Fig. Q1-8 and the appropriate circuit diagram, if necessary, in Section N.
3. Connect the coolant hoses and replenish the engine coolant system, allowing a free flow through the drain taps before closing them. Fig. Q1-8 refers.
4. Refit the front apron panel. Fig. Q1-4 refers.
5. Connect battery lead.
6. Refit the bonnet panel. Operation Q1-1.

Coolant System Capacity
Bonneted Control Models, 2¼ litre Petrol and Diesel

Imperial Pints	U.S. Pints	Litres	Antifreeze	Frost Precaution
18	21¼	10.25	33⅓%	−32°C (−25°F)

Bonneted Control Model, 2.6 Litre Petrol

Imperial Pints	U.S. Pints	Litres	Antifreeze	Frost Precaution
24	29	13.5	33⅓%	−32°C (−25°F)

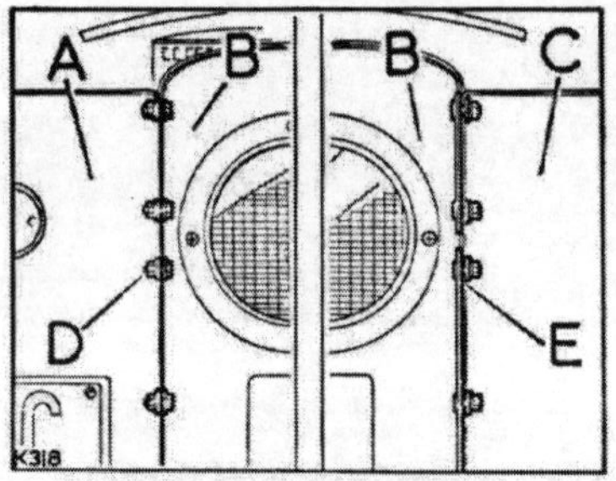

Fig. Q1-9. Radiator grille panel fixings
A—Front wing, RH side
B—Radiator grille panel
C—Front wing, LH side
D—Fixings at wheelarch, RH
E—Fixings at wheelarch, LH

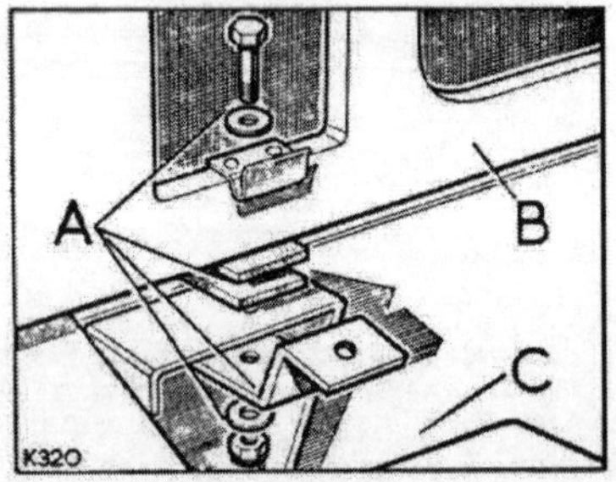

Fig. Q1-10. Fixings at chassis cross member
A—Panel fixings
B—Radiator grille panel
C—Chassis cross member

BODY

Key to illustration of seat base, seats, front floor, wings and bonnet

1. Seat base and floor assembly
2. Tool locker lid
3. Fuel tank cover panel
4. Lid hinge
5. Locker lid hasp
6. Locker lid turnbuckle
7. Centre cover panel
8. Extension panel, at seat base ends
9. Handbrake rubber cover
10. Retainer for rubber cover
11. Handbrake slot cover plate
12. Sill channel LH front
13. Sill channel securing bracket
14. Sill channel mounting bracket, to rear body
15. Front sill panel
16. Rear sill panel
17. Fixing plate for sill panels
18. Front floor complete
19. Inspection cover, for front floor
20. Stud plate for inspection cover wing nut
21. Wing nut, fixing inspection cover
22. Transfer gear lever seal
23. Transfer lever seal retainer
24. Gear lever rubber seal
25. Operating rod cover plate
26. Gearbox cover complete
27. Seat squab
28. Squab spring case
29. Squab frame
30. Buffer, for seat back rest on bracket
31. Seat cushion
32. Cushion spring case
33. Cushion frame
34. Cushion support, outer
35. Seat support, centre
36. Front wing
37. Front panel and registration plate
38. Front wing outer panel
39. Fixing plate, wings to grille panel
40. Wing valance bottom panel
41. Mudshield, front wing
42. Steering unit cover box
43. Front wing stay
44. Bracket, for rear of wing
45. Fixing plate—brackets to dash
46. Mirror
47. Arm for mirror
48. Bonnet top panel
49–50. Bonnet hinges
51. Bonnet catch striker pin
52. Bonnet striker bracket
53. Bonnet control
54. Bonnet prop rod

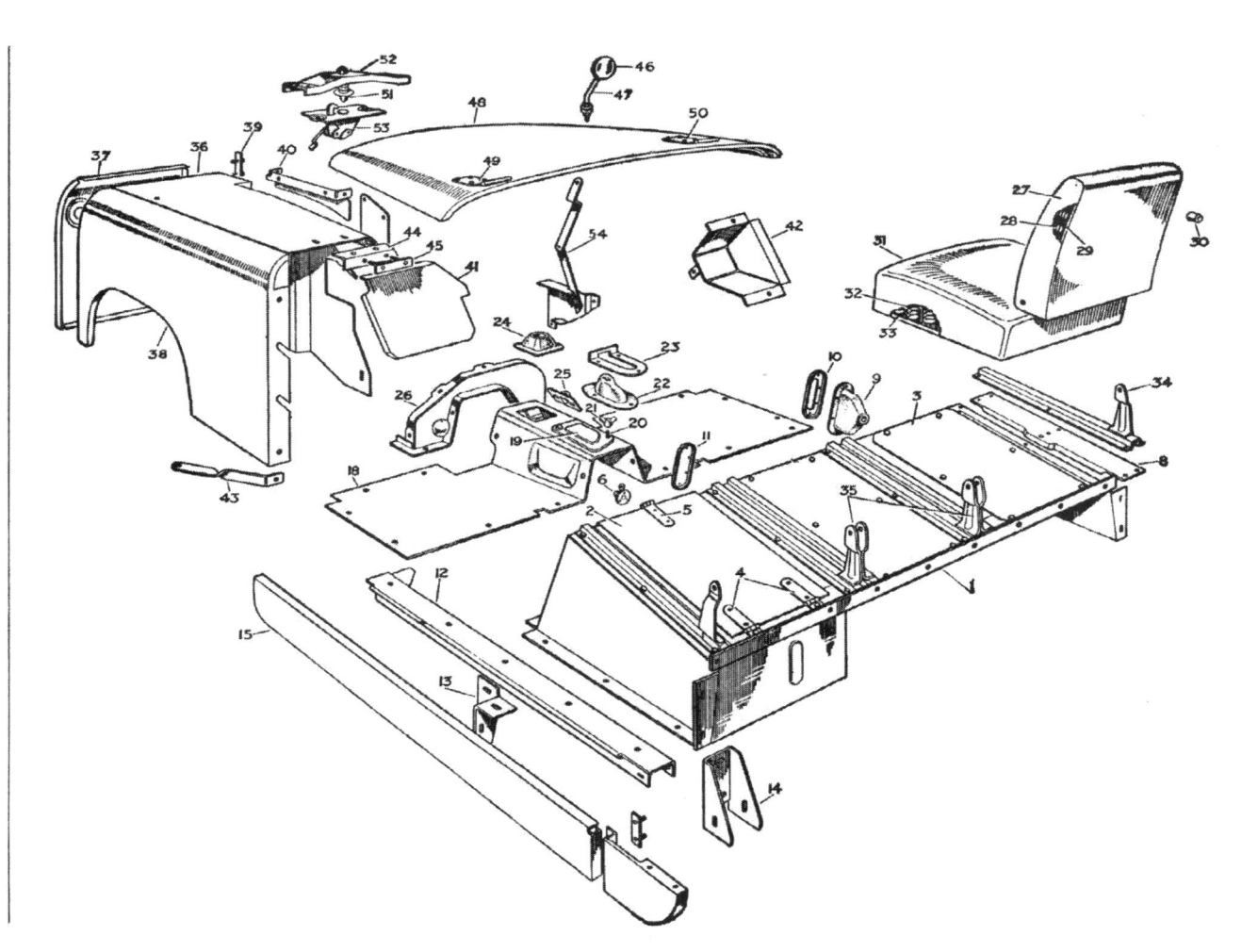

Fig. Q1·11. Layout of seat base, seats, front floor, wings and bonnet

Front wings, to remove and refit—Operation Q1-3

Workshop hand tools:
Spanner sizes: 2 BA, $\frac{7}{16}$ in. AF, $\frac{3}{8}$ in. AF open end and socket

To remove (Fig. Q1-11)

1. Remove the bonnet. Operation Q1-1.
2. Disconnect the side lamp, and if applicable, flasher lamp and head lamp harness at the snap connectors in the engine compartment.
3. Remove the securing bolts and lift the mudshield out from under the wing, Driver's side:remove the steering box mudshield.
4. Using a box spanner, remove the bolts securing the wing to the scuttle pillar.
5. Remove the bolts securing the wing stay and the wing to the sill panel.
6. Remove the bolts securing the wing to the rear wing upper mounting bracket.
7. Remove the bolt securing the wing to the steering column support plate.
8. Remove the bolts securing the wing to the grille panel (on RH wings, this action also releases the bonnet prop bracket).

To refit

1. Reverse the removal procedure

Windscreen, to remove and refit—Operation Q1-4

Workshop hand tools:
Spanner sizes: 2 BA, $\frac{7}{16}$ in. AF, $\frac{3}{8}$ in. AF, $\frac{1}{4}$ in. AF open end
Screwdriver (medium)

Windscreen

To remove (Fig. Q1-12)

1. Remove the cab or hard top. Operation Q1-11 Q1-12 or Q1-14; if a soft hood is fitted, release the front straps from the support stays at the top of the windscreen and disconnect the top drain channels from the windscreens.
2. Early models—remove the windscreen wiper positive lead plug from the socket on the dash panel.
3. Slacken the nuts at the bottom corners of the windscreen.
4. Remove the windscreen pivot bolts and remove the windscreen complete.

To refit

1. Reverse the removal procedure, renewing the windscreen sealing strip if necessary.

Windscreen glass

1. If necessary, remove the windscreen wiper blade; Early models—disconnect the wiper motor earth wire and remove the wiper motor from the windscreen.
2. Withdraw the drive screws securing the retainers round the glass and prise away the retainers; remove the glass or glasses as necessary.
3. Apply sealing strip $\frac{1}{2}$ in. (12 mm) wide, round the outside on both faces of the new glass and fit the glass by reversing the stripping procedure.

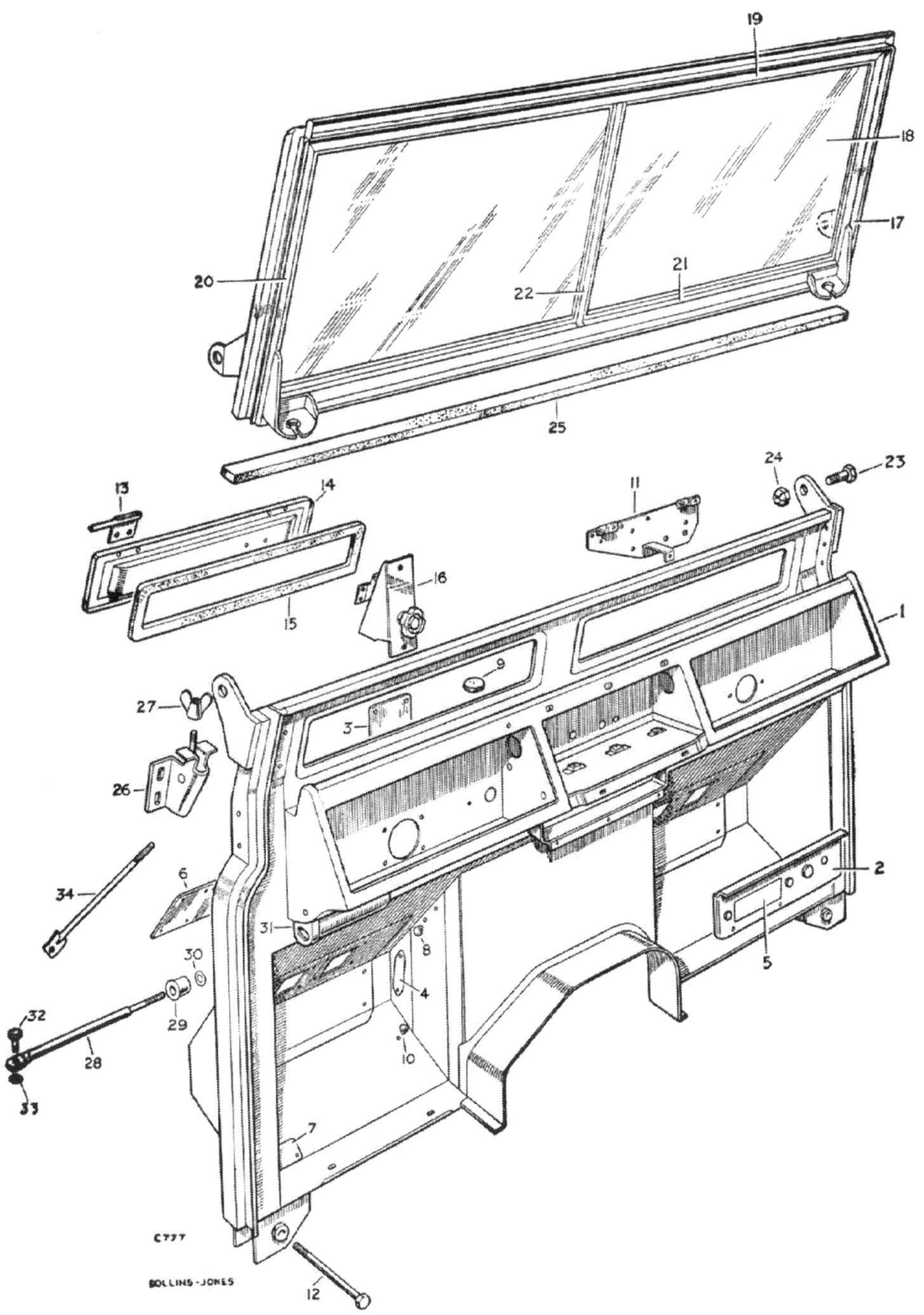

BODY

Key to illustration of dash panel, windscreen and ventilators

1. Dash complete
2. Panel for controls
3. Cover panel for steering cut-out
4. Cover plate for accelerator pedal hole
5. Cover panel for governor cut-out in dash—Petrol models
6. Cover plate for pedal holes
7. Cover plate for dipswitch hole
8. Rubber plug, redundant accelerator holes
9. Rubber grommet for demister holes
10. Rubber plug, redundant accelerator stop holes
11. Mounting plate for pump
12. Tie bolt
13. Ventilator hinge
14. Ventilator lid for dash
15. Sealing rubber for ventilator lids
16. Ventilator control mechanism complete
17. Windscreen complete assembly
18. Glass for windscreen
19. Retainer for windscreen glass, top
20. Retainer for windscreen glass, side
21. Retainer for windscreen glass, bottom
22. Cover for centre strip
23-24. Fixings for windscreen to dash
25. Rubber sealing strip for windscreen
26. Fastener for windscreen, RH
27. Wing nut for fastener
28. Check strap rod
29. Check strap buffer
30. Fixings—buffer to rod
31. Check strap mounting bracket
32-33. Fixings—check strap rod to front door
34. Tie rod

Fig. Q1-12. Layout of dash panel, windscreen and ventilators

Side doors, to remove and refit—Operation Q1-5

Workshop hand tools:
Spanner sizes: 2 BA, $\frac{7}{16}$ in. AF, $\frac{1}{2}$ in. AF open end
Screwdriver (medium), Pliers

Door (Figs. Q1-13 and Q1-14)

To remove

1. Disconnect the door check-strap.
2. Remove the bolts, washers and nuts securing the hinges to the door.
3. Remove the door.

To refit

1. Reverse the removal procedure, renewing sealing rubbers as necessary.

Hinge

To remove

1. The hinges may be stripped by prising back the lock washer tab and removing the special nut and bolt. Care must be taken to ensure that the cone and spring are not lost.

To refit

1. Fit a new lock washer and assemble by reversing the removal procedure.

   Adjust by increasing or lessening the load on the spring by tightening or slackening the special nut, and bend lock tab over to secure assembly.

Door lock

To renew

1. Remove the door lock from the door.
2. If required, remove the striking plate from its support bracket.
3. Renew the lock and plate as necessary and refit by reversing items 1 and 2.
4. Adjust the position of the striking plate as necessary, so that the door draught excluders are slightly compressed.

Special tools:
Tool for locking door handle, Part Number 248877 (early type private locks only)

Sliding window

To renew

1. Move the sliding window to allow access to the screws securing glass run channel—top and bottom—then remove the screws from inside channel.
2. Withdraw the top run channel and sliding window.
3. Renew the bottom run channel if necessary.
4. Fit new parts as necessary and assemble by reversing the removal procedure.

Fixed window

To renew

1. Remove the sliding window.
2. Remove the screws securing front retainer and ease the fixed glass clear of frame.
3. Apply new Prestik sealing strip to window frame, renewing parts as necessary and assemble by reversing the removal procedure.

   Two-piece door only—if necessary, the complete assembly can be removed by removing the nuts, plain washers and spring washers securing the assembly to the door.

This page intentionally left blank

Key to illustration of tailboard, doors and side screens

1. Tailboard assembly
2. Tailboard top capping
3. Tailboard tread plate
4. Tailboard sealing rubber, bottom
5. Tailboard hinge, RH
6. Tailboard hinge, LH
7. Tailboard chain hook
8. Tailboard locking plate
9. Front door assembly
10. Door top capping
11. Hinge complete, upper
12. Hinge complete, lower
13–17. Fixings for door hinge
18. Door lock mounting plate
19. Door lock
20. Washer, handle to cover
21. Handle
22. Door handle bracket
23. Captive plate, door lock mounting to door
24. Seal for door, front upper
25. Seal for door, front lower, dash
26. Seal for door, rear lower
27. Seal for door, bottom, sill
28. Support bracket at door striker
29. Door lock striking plate
30. Side screen assembly
31. Front fixed window
32. Window retainer
33. Rear sliding window
34. Sealing rubber for front edge of sliding window
35. Sealing rubber channel
36. Buffer for sliding window, at top
37–38. Filler strip for windows
39. Top channel
40. Bottom channel
41. Rear channel
42. Sidescreen sealing strip

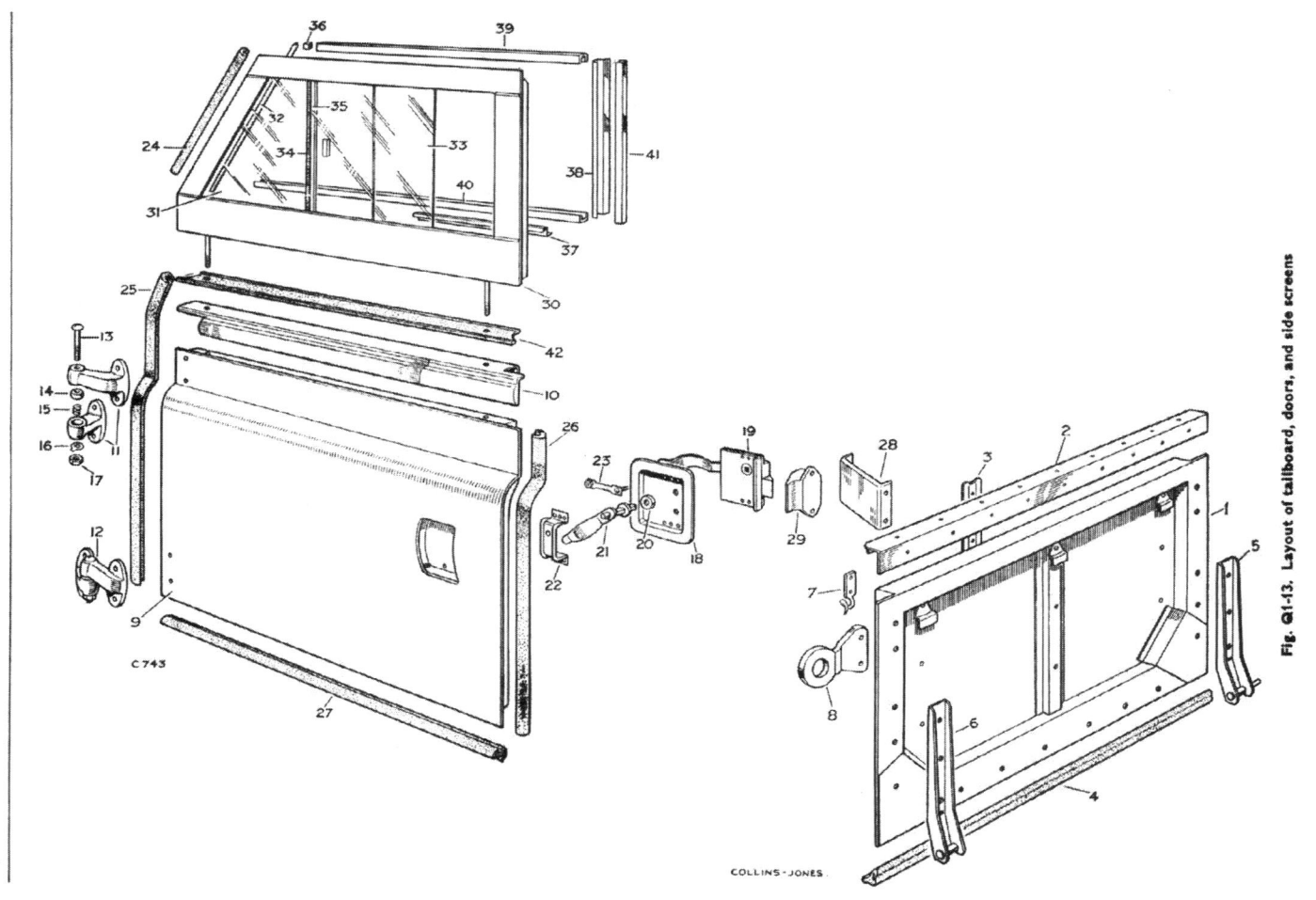

Fig. Q1-13. Layout of tailboard, doors, and side screens

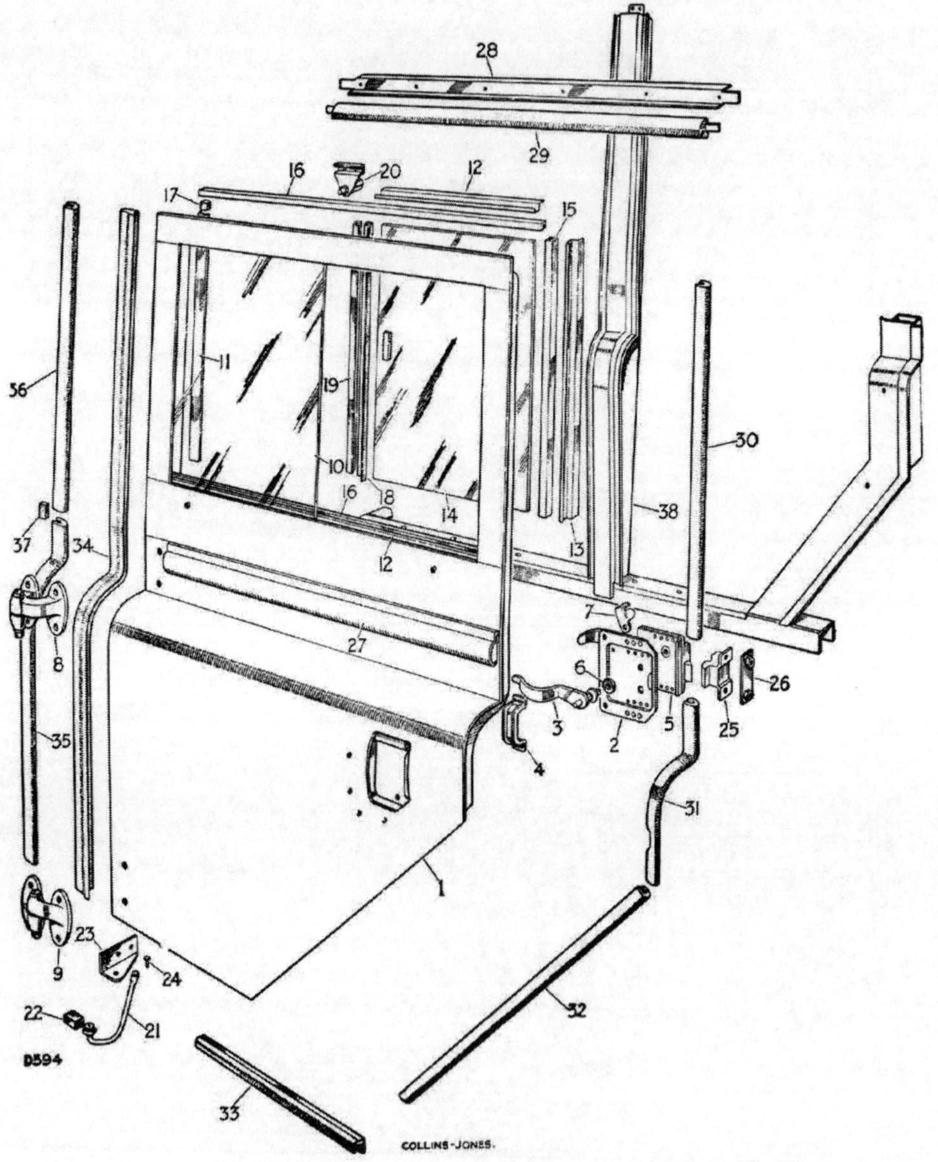

BODY

Key to illustration of rear side doors, 109 Station Wagon

1. Rear side door assembly, LH
2. Mounting plate for door lock
3. Door handle complete, LH
4. Bracket for door handle, outer mounting
5. Door lock complete, LH
6. Sealing washer, handle to cover
7. Locking catch, LH
8. Door hinge, upper LH
9. Door hinge, lower LH
10. Fixed window for sidescreen
11. Retainer for sidescreen, fixed window
12. Filler, top and bottom, for side screen
13. Filler, rear, for sidescreen
14. Sliding window with knob for sidescreen
15. Sliding light channel, rear
16. Sliding light channel, top and bottom
17. Buffer for sidescreen sliding window at top
18. Sealing rubber for sliding glass
19. Retainer for sliding glass sealing rubber
20. Sliding window catch
21. Rod for check strap, LH
22. Buffer for check strap, short
23. Door check bracket, LH, for rear side door
24. Clevis pin
25. Striking plate for rear side door locks
26. Nut plate
27. Waist moulding, rear side door, LH
28. Seal retainer for rear side door, LH top
29. Rubber seal for retainer
30. Door sealing rubber for upper vertical 'D' post
31. Door sealing rubber for lower vertical 'D' post, LH
32. Door sealing rubber for sloping 'D' post
33. Door sealing rubber at rear side sills, bottom
34. Door sealing rubber at 'C' post
35. Door sealing rubber at 'B' post, lower LH
36. Door sealing rubber at 'B' post, upper
37. Filler piece for 'B' post seal
38. Frame for front and rear side doors, LH

Fig. Q1-14. Layout of rear side doors, 109 Station Wagon

Front floor, remove and refit, 2¼ litre models—Operation Q1-6

(For removal and refitting instructions for front floor, 2.6 litre models, Operation Q1-7 refers)

Workshop hand tools:
Spanner sizes: 7/16 In. AF, 7/16 In. BSF open end, 7/16 In. AF socket
Screwdriver (medium)

To remove

1. Unscrew the knob and locknut from the transfer gear lever.
2. Remove the fixings and withdraw the dust cover from the transfer gear lever.
3. Unscrew the knob and locknut from the four-wheel drive lever, and withdraw the spring and ferrule.
4. Remove both halves of the front floor board.
5. Remove the gearbox tunnel cover.
6. Remove the gearbox tunnel front panel.

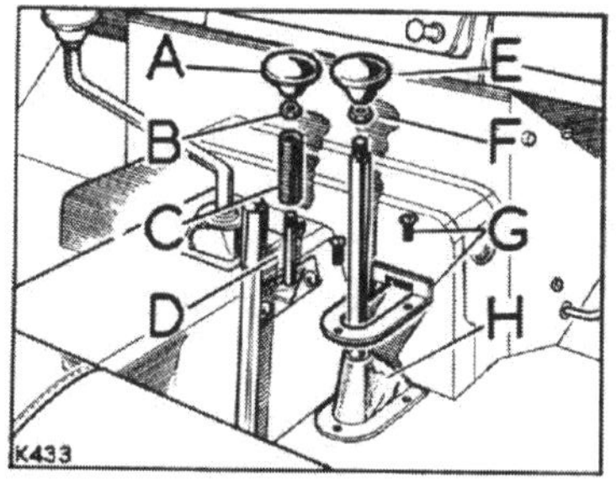

Fig. Q1-15. Four-wheel drive and transfer levers

A—Knob, four-wheel drive lever E—Knob, transfer gear lever
B—Locknut for knob   F—Locknut for knob
C—Spring   G—Fixings for dust cover
D—Ferrule   H—Dust cover

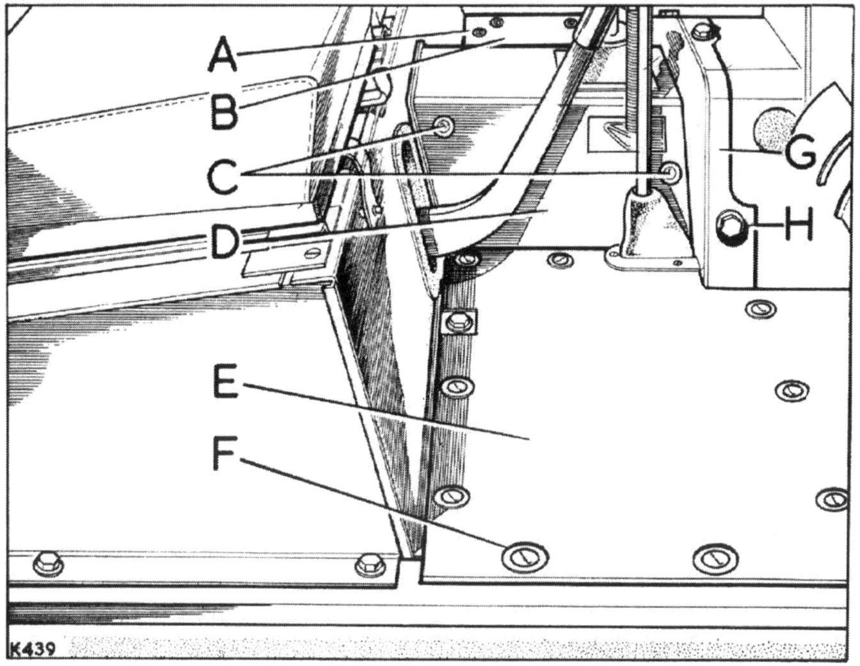

Fig. Q1-16. Front floor

A—Fixings (9 off), left-hand floor board   E—Floor board, right-hand
B—Floor board, left-hand   F—Fixings (12 off), right-hand floor board
C—Fixings (4 off), tunnel cover   G—Front panel for gearbox tunnel cover
D—Gearbox tunnel cover   H—Fixings (4 off), front panel

Operation Q1-6—*continued*

To refit

1. Reverse the removal procedure, using waterproof sealant between the joint flanges of the front floor and the chassis. A suitable sealant is 'Sealastrip', manufactured by Expandite Ltd., Chase Road, London NW 10, England.

2. Adjust the four-wheel drive lever during assembly, as follows: Fit the ferrule, spring and locknut to the lever, depress the lever and adjust the locknut until the compressed spring length is 2 5/16 in. — 1/16 in. (58 mm — 1 mm), then fit the knob and tighten the locknut.

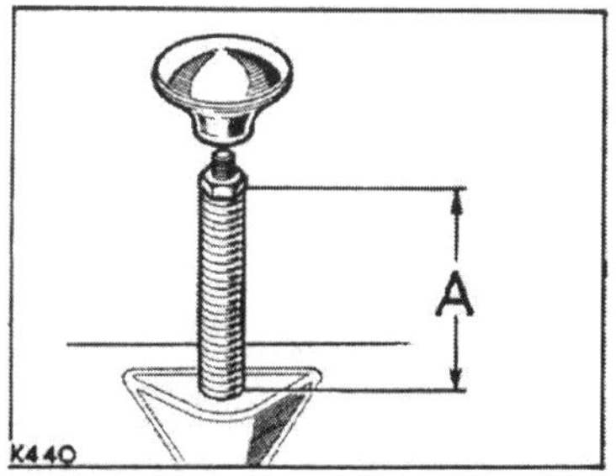

Fig. Q1-17. Adjusting four-wheel drive control lever

A—2 5/16 in. — 1/16 in. (58 mm — 1 mm)

Gearbox tunnel and front panel, 2.6 litre models, remove and refit—Operation Q1-7

(For removal and refitting instructions for front floor, 2¼ litre models, Operation Q1-6 refers)

Workshop hand tools:
Spanner sizes: ⅞ in. AF, ⁷⁄₁₆ in. BSF open end, ⁷⁄₁₆ in. AF socket
Screwdriver (medium)

To remove

1. Unscrew the knob and locknut from the transfer gear lever.
2. Remove the fixings and withdraw the dust cover from the transfer gear lever.
3. Unscrew the knob and locknut from the four-wheel drive lever, and withdraw the spring and ferrule.
4. Remove the gearbox tunnel cover.
5. Remove the gearbox tunnel front panel.

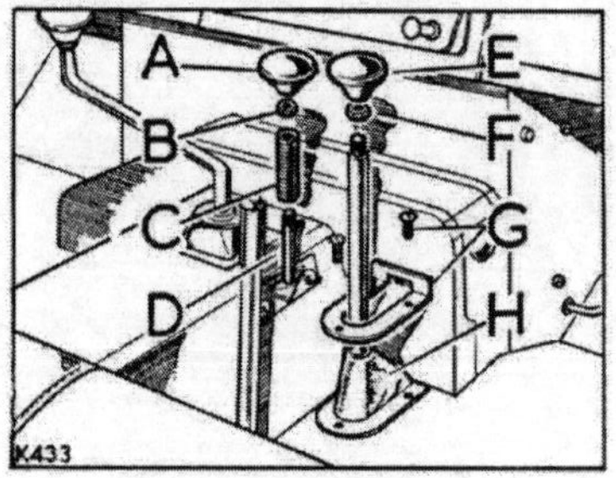

To refit

1. Reverse the removal procedure, using waterproof sealant between the joint flanges of the front floor and the chassis. A suitable sealant is 'Sealastrip', manufactured by Expandite Ltd., Chase Road, London NW 10, England.
2. Adjust the four-wheel drive lever during assembly as follows: Fit the ferrule, spring and locknut to the lever, depress the lever and adjust the locknut until the compressed spring length is 2⁷⁄₁₆ in. —¹⁄₁₆ in. (58 mm — 1 mm), then fit the knob and tighten the locknut.

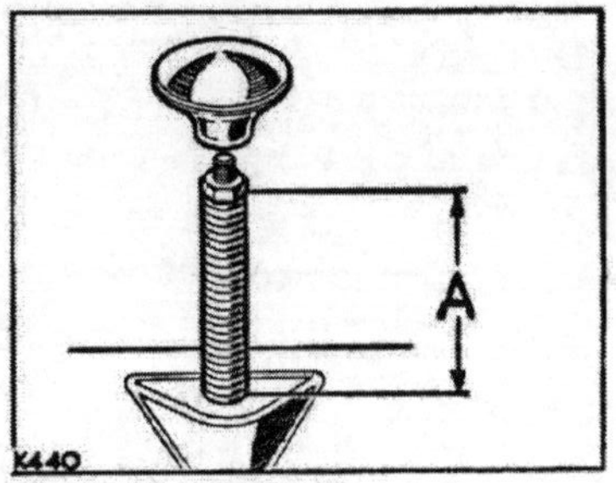

Fig. Q1-18. Four-wheel drive and transfer levers

A—Knob, four-wheel drive lever
B—Locknut for knob
C—Spring
D—Ferrule
E—Knob, transfer gear lever
F—Locknut for knob
G—Fixings for dust cover
H—Dust cover

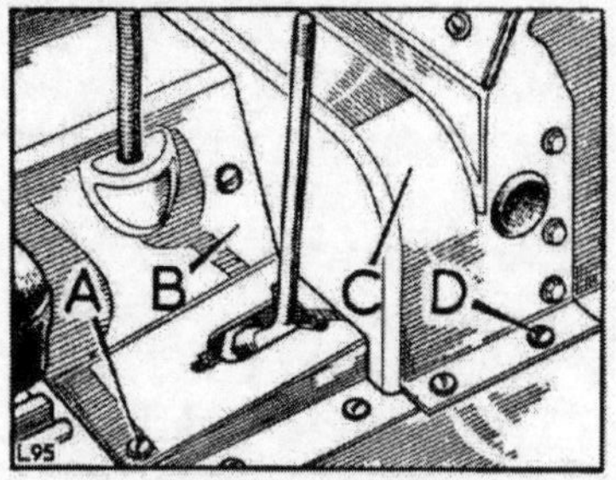

Fig. Q1-19. Front floor

A—Fixings, tunnel cover (9 off)
B—Gearbox tunnel cover
C—Front panel for gearbox tunnel cover
D—Fixings (15 off)

Dash panel, to remove and refit—Operation Q1-8

Workshop hand tools:
Spanner sizes: 2 BA, ⁷⁄₁₆ in. AF, ½ in. AF, ⅜ in. AF open end
Screwdrivers (medium and small), Pliers

General

The following instructions are generally applicable to all models, but individual models may vary slightly, particularly with regard to equipment attached to the dash panel.

To remove (Fig. Q1-12)

1. Disconnect the battery earth lead.
2. Remove the bonnet. Operation Q1-1.
3. Remove the front wings. Operation Q1-3.
4. Remove the windscreen. Operation Q1-4.
5. Remove the front doors. Operation Q1-5.
6. Remove the front floor and gearbox tunnel. Operations Q1-6 or Q1-7.
7. Remove the fixings from the ball joint connecting the longitudinal arm to the steering box drop arm, then using special tool, Part No. 600590, extract the ball joint to release the longitudinal arm.
8. **Petrol models**—disconnect the starter motor lead from the terminal on the switch.
9. **Diesel models**—disconnect the starter/heater plug switch leads from the switch.
10. **Petrol models**—disconnect the high tension wire and the distributor wire from the coil.
11. Disconnect the oil warning light wire from the oil pressure switch.
12. **Petrol models**—disconnect the mixture warning light wire from the switch on the cylinder head.
13. Disconnect the fluid outlet pipes from the brake and clutch master cylinders.
14. Disconnect the clutch jump hose at the bracket on dash.
15. Disconnect the accelerator linkage by disconnecting the control rod, at the carburetter or injection pump.
16. **Diesel models**, or if fitted, 2¼ litre **Petrol**—disconnect the engine hand speed control rod at the cross-shaft by removing the retaining nut and locknut.
17. If fitted, disconnect the heater water pipe hoses, disconnect the leads and remove the heater unit complete.
18. Disconnect the dynamo leads.
19. Disconnect the speedometer drive from the transfer box; release the cable from the clips on the transfer box, the chassis and the flywheel housing.
20. Disconnect the headlamp and horn wires at the junction box on the dash.
21. Part the frame and dash section of the main harness at the snap connectors.
22. **Diesel LHStg**—disconnect the additional filter pipes at the filter.
23. Check that all fuel and brake pipes, electrical leads, controls, etc are disconnected from the dash panel.
24. Remove the bolts securing the steering box support bracket to the chassis; remove the two tie bolts, plain washer and nuts fixing the dash to the chassis; remove the nuts and bolts securing the extremities of the sill panels to the dash. Lift off the dash panel complete.

To strip the dash panel

1. Remove the steering wheel, flasher switch or horn push bracket and steering box. See Section G for details.
2. Lift off the junction box and disconnect the wiring remove the junction box from the dash.
3. Remove the clutch and brake pedal assemblies, master cylinders, pipes, return springs, fluid reservoir. Sections B and H.
4. Remove the steering column support bracket from the dash.
5. Remove the instrument panel, disconnect all instruments and lift the panel clear. See Section P for details.
6. Disconnect the wiring from the control box and the fuse box; remove the mounting plate complete with control box and fuse box.
7. **Petrol models**—disconnect the wiring from the mixture control warning light switch and remove the bracket, switch and mixture control.
8. **Diesel models**—disconnect the wires and remove the heater plug resistance.
9. 2¼ litre **Petrol**—if fitted, remove the hand throttle control; if fitted, remove the engine governor control quadrant assembly.

Fig. Q1-20. Adjusting four-wheel drive control lever

A—2⁷⁄₁₆ in. -¹⁄₁₆ in. (58 mm — 1 mm)

Operation Q1-8—*continued*

10. **Diesel models**—remove the engine hand speed control. Section P.
11. **Petrol models**—disconnect the wiring from the coil and remove the coil from the dash.
Early models—after disconnecting the cables from the starter switch, screw off the starter knob and locknut. Withdraw the switch from the dash.
12. **Diesel models**—disconnect the leads and remove the starter/heater plug switch by removing the large securing nut from facia side of panel.
13. Remove accelerator linkage, Section P; detach the clutch jump hose bracket from the dash.
14. **RHStg models**—detach the pedal shaft bracket from the dash panel complete with shafts and pedals.
15. **LHStg models**—withdraw the pedal shafts complete with pedals and distance pieces.
16. **Diesel LHStg**—remove the additional filter from the dash panel.
17. Remove the dip switch, complete with leads.
18. Remove the windscreen sealing strip. Remove the windscreen fastener catches from the dash panel.
19. Remove the transfer lever instruction plates; remove the rocker shaft access plate.
20. Remove the governor cut-out panel and the pedal hole covers.
21. Remove the ventilators and operating controls. Operation
22. Remove the harness clip.
23. Remove all remaining rubber grommets and plugs; remove the steering column blanking plate and refit it on the new dash panel.
24. Transfer all the dash fittings to the new panel by reversing the removal procedure, referring to appropriate sections and connecting the wiring in accordance with the appropriate wiring diagram. Section N.

To refit

1. Reverse the removal procedure.
2. Connect the wiring in accordance with the appropriate wiring diagram.
3. Adjust the accelerator, mixture or cut-off control and throttle linkage by reference to appropriate sections.
4. Set the road wheels straight ahead and the steering wheel in the midway position between full lock in each direction before securing the longitudinal arm to the steering box drop arm.
5. Bleed the clutch and brake systems. Sections B and H.

Ventilator lid, to remove and refit—Operation Q1-9

Workshop hand tools:
Spanner size: 2 BA open end
Pliers, Screwdriver (medium)

To remove—early type

1. Remove the securing screws and remove one of the ventilator hinges.
2. Remove the securing bolts and disconnect the ventilator panel from the operating control.
3. Withdraw the ventilator. The same procedure applies to either ventilator.
4. If necessary, remove remaining hinges.
5. If necessary, remove the ventilator control.

Late type (Fig. Q1-12)

The hinges of the late type ventilator lids are welded to the dash and the ventilator lids respectively and are therefore not available separately.

6. Remove the pin from the ventilator hinges.
7. Remove the securing bolts and disconnect the ventilator panel from the operating control.
8. Withdraw the ventilator lid. The same procedure applies to the other ventilator.
9. If necessary, remove the ventilator control.

L371

Fig. Q1-21. Ventilator control

To refit—all types

1. Reverse the removal procedure, renewing sealing rubbers as necessary.

BODY

Seat base, remove and refit—Operation Q1-10

Workshop hand tools:
Spanner sizes: $\frac{7}{16}$ in. AF, $\frac{9}{16}$ in. AF open end

To remove

1. Remove the front floor. Operation Q1-6 or Q1-7.
2. Lift out the seat cushions.
3. Release the seat squab retaining straps from the support rail.
4. From under the vehicle, remove the two nuts and spring washers securing the hand brake lever to the chassis.

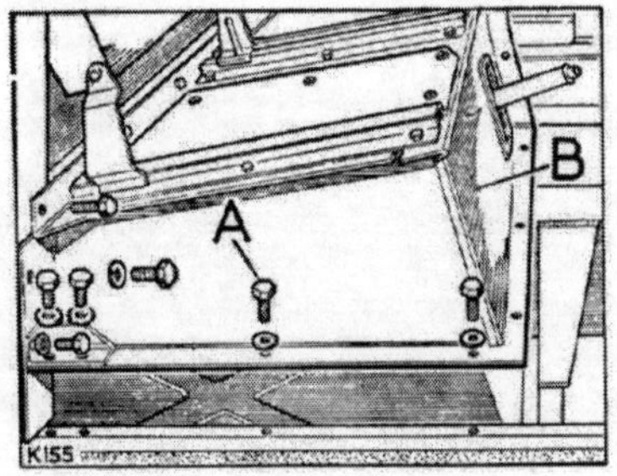

Note: The foregoing operation facilitates seat base removal by allowing the hand brake lever to be manoeuvred, but is not necessary on early models fitted with a short horizontal hand brake lever.

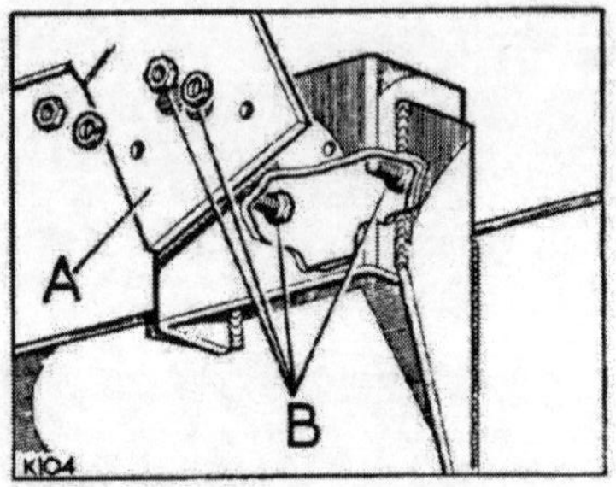

Fig. Q1-22. Seat base
A—Fixings (23 off)   B—Seat base

5. Remove the seat base fixings.
6. Lift out the seat base complete, manoeuvring the hand brake lever through the aperture in the base front.

To refit

Reverse the removal procedure, using waterproof sealant between the joint flanges of the seat base and body. A suitable sealant is 'Sealastrip' manufactured by Expandite Ltd, Chase Road, London, NW 10. Adjust the four-wheel drive control lever. Operation Q1-6.

Fig. Q1-23. Hand brake lever fixings
A—Mounting bracket for hand brake lever
B—Fixings, hand brake lever to chassis

Cab, to remove and refit—Operation Q1-11

Workshop hand tools:
Spanner sizes: 2 BA, $\frac{7}{16}$ in. AF, $\frac{1}{2}$ in. AF open end and sockets
Screwdriver (medium)

Special tools:
Tool for fitting window filler strip, Part Number 262771

Cab
To remove (Fig. Q1-25)

1. Remove the nuts and bolts securing the cab at the windscreen and the nuts securing the cab at the hood sockets.
   88 models: remove the bolts, nuts and washers securing the cab to the cab mounting rail, at the rear body.
   109 models: remove the set bolts and washers securing the cab to the cab mounting brackets, at the rear body.
2. Lift off the cab complete, then remove the roof panel and sealing rubber from the rear panel.
3. Remove the draught excluders and retaining strips from the top of the front door apertures.
4. Remove the rear upper front door seals and the draught pads from the front edge of the side panels.
5. If necessary, remove the rear bottom sealing strip from the back rest panel capping.
6. If necessary, remove the sealing rubber from the front edge of the roof.
7. If necessary, remove all mounting brackets.

To refit
1. Reverse the removal procedure.
2. Renew the back and quarter lights as necessary.

Cab back lights
Sliding light
To renew

1. Withdraw the drive screws securing the bottom channel to the cab rear panel (the drive screws are inside the channel).
2. Remove the 'Phillips' screw, distance piece (two on RH light), special washers and tapped plate securing the catch to the back light.
3. Remove the bottom run channel and sliding back light.
4. If necessary, remove the top run channel.
5. If necessary, remove the catches from the back lights.
6. Renew the rubber sealing strips, fittings and sliding lights as necessary. Refit by reversing the removal procedure.

Quarter light
To renew

1. Prise out the rubber filler strip from the glass weather strip; push the glass and weather strip from the panel aperture.
2. Square off one end of the rubber weather strip, and, starting at the bottom centre, fit the narrow groove of the strip to the panel aperture with the locking groove to the weather side.
3. Force the strip well into the aperture corners, and, allowing about one inch (25 mm) overlap, square off the other end of the moulding. Compress the moulding around its length until the ends can be joined. (This overlap is important, as otherwise a gap will appear between the moulding ends when the glass is fitted).
4. Fit the glass into the moulding, using a flat piece of metal to pull the lip over the glass.
5. Square off one end of the filler strip, and, starting opposite the joint in the moulding, insert the filler strip in the groove in the weather strip by means of the special tool, Part No. 262771. Allowing about $\frac{1}{4}$ in. (6 mm) overlap, square off the end of the filler strip, and force the overlap into the weather strip groove.

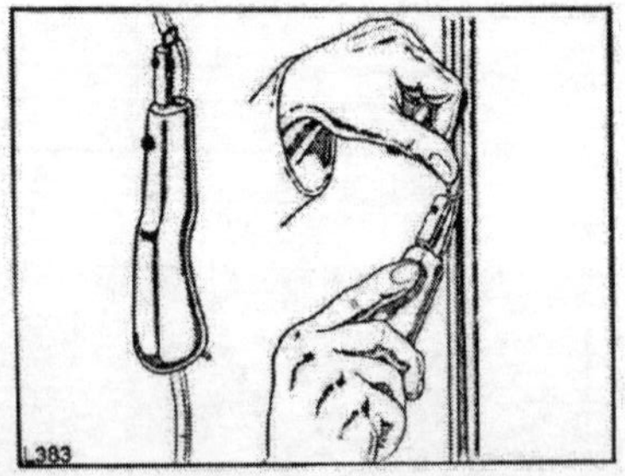

Fig. Q1-24. Fitting filler strip in window weather strip

Cab tropical roof
To remove

1. Remove the screws, spring and plain washers, nuts, distance pieces and rubber washers securing each side of the panel to the roof.
2. Remove the screws, spring, plain and rubber washers and nuts securing the tropical panel stiffeners to the cab roof both at the front and at the back, then lift off the tropical roof panel.

To refit
1. Reverse the removal procedure.

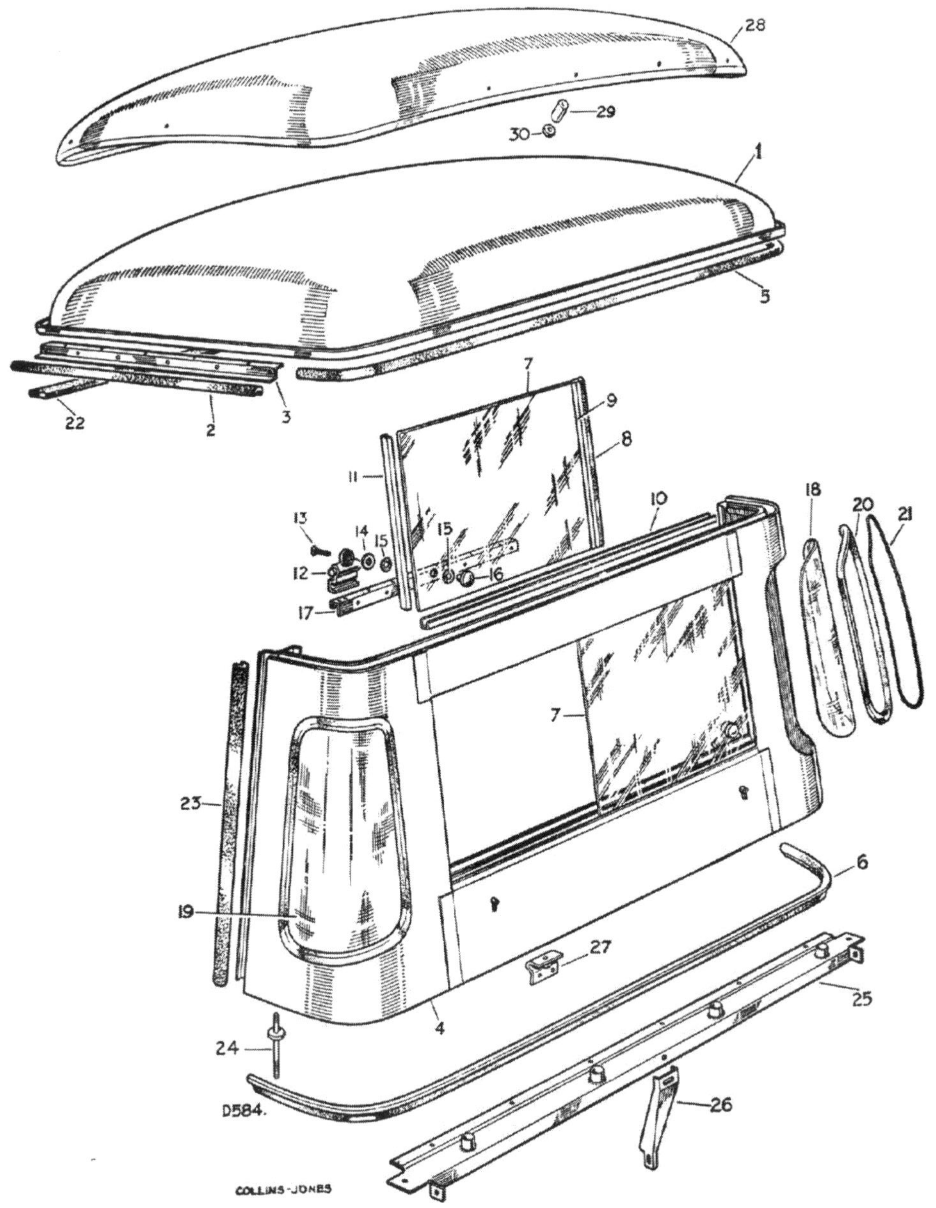

Section Q—Land-Rover   BODY

Key to Illustration of cab and tropical roof

1. Cab roof
2. Sealing rubber, door top
3. Retainer for seal
4. Cab rear panel assembly
5. Rubber seal, roof to back panel, top
6. Rubber seal back panel to rear body
7. Sliding back light
8. Sealing rubber for back light
9. Channel for rubber
10. Channel, top and bottom ⎱ For
11. Channel, sides ⎰ back light
12. Back light catch
13–16. Fixings for catches
17. Runner for sliding back light catch
18. Cab quarter light, RH
19. Cab quarter light, LH
20. Weather strip ⎱ For quarter
21. Sealing strip ⎰ light
22. Sealing rubber, windscreen to roof
23. Sealing rubber, door side
24. Mounting stud
25. Mounting rail for cab
26. Mounting rail support bracket
27. Cab mounting distance piece
28. Cab tropical roof panel
29. Distance piece ⎱ Fixing tropical roof
30. Rubber ⎰ panel to cab roof

Fig. Q1.25. Layout of cab and tropical roof

BODY

Hard top, remove and refit—Operation Q1-12

Workshop hand tools:
Spanner sizes: 2 BA, $\frac{7}{16}$ In. AF, $\frac{1}{2}$ In. AF open end
Screwdriver (medium)

Special tools:
Tool for fitting window filler strip, Part Number 262771

Hard top

To remove (Fig. Q1-26)

1. Remove the nuts, bolts and washers securing the hard top to the windscreen.
2. Remove the set bolts securing the hard top to the front mounting bracket.
3. Remove the nuts, bolts and washers securing the hard top to the centre mounting brackets.
4. Remove the nuts and washers securing the hard top to the rear hood sockets.
5. Remove the nuts, bolts and washers securing the rear mounting brackets to the body. Lift off the hard top complete.

Rear lid

Early type

6. Remove the rear lid by removing the nuts, bolts and washers securing the stays to the side panels, withdraw the split pins and remove the hinge pins. Lift off lid.
7. Remove stays and hinge leaves by removing the securing bolts and washers; if necessary remove glass, as described for the cab quarter light, Operation Q1-11. To remove the lid lock, remove the inner handle by depressing the spring-loaded boss and push out the locking pin.

Late type

8. Remove the rear lid by withdrawing the hinge pins. If necessary remove the split pins securing the stays and remove.
9. If necessary, remove the stay support mounting brackets from the side panels. To remove the lid lock, remove the inner handle by depressing the spring-loaded boss and push out the locking pin.
10. Remove the handle, boss, cap and spring. Withdraw the screws, spring and plain washers and nuts securing the lock to the lid panel; remove the bolts and plain washers securing the bolt guides to the lid panel; remove the outer handle and lift off the lock complete.

Operation Q1-12—continued

11. If necessary, remove the lock bolt sockets from the side panels by removing the securing nuts and bolts. If necessary, remove the rubber seal and retainer from the lower edge of the lid.

Roof panel

8. Remove the roof panel by removing the nuts, bolts and washers securing it to the side panels. If necessary, remove the rubber seal.

Side panels

9. If necessary, remove the glasses. Operation Q1-11.
10. If necessary, remove the seals and retaining strips

To refit

1. Reverse the removal procedure.
2. If removed, replace or renew the seals and retaining strips.
3. If removed, replace or renew the glasses. Operation Q1-11.
4. On assembly of the door handle, it will be necessary to adjust the position of the bolts by slackening the locking nuts, to obtain adequate entry into the sockets.

Hard top window glass

To renew

As some difficulty may be experienced in carrying out this operation, it will be found advantageous, where possible, to remove the panel in which the glass is to be fitted, and lay it flat on a suitable bench or stand.

1. See Operation Q1-11.

Hard top tropical roof

To remove

1. Remove the screws, spring and plain washers, nuts, distance pieces and rubber washers securing each side of the panel to the roof.
2. Remove the screws, spring, plain and rubber washers and nuts securing the tropical panel stiffeners to the hard top roof, both at the front and at the back.
3. Remove the drive screws or shear the pop rivets securing the panel to the hard top stiffeners, and lift off the tropical roof panel.

To refit

1. Reverse the removal procedure.

Tailboard

To remove and refit

1. Release the tailboard keys and drop the tailboard.
2. Unhook the tailboard chains; remove the plain washer, spring washer and split pin from the RH hinge pin and slide out the tailboard to the left.
3. If necessary, remove the tailboard hinges and the chain hooks.
4. Refit by reversing items 1 to 3.

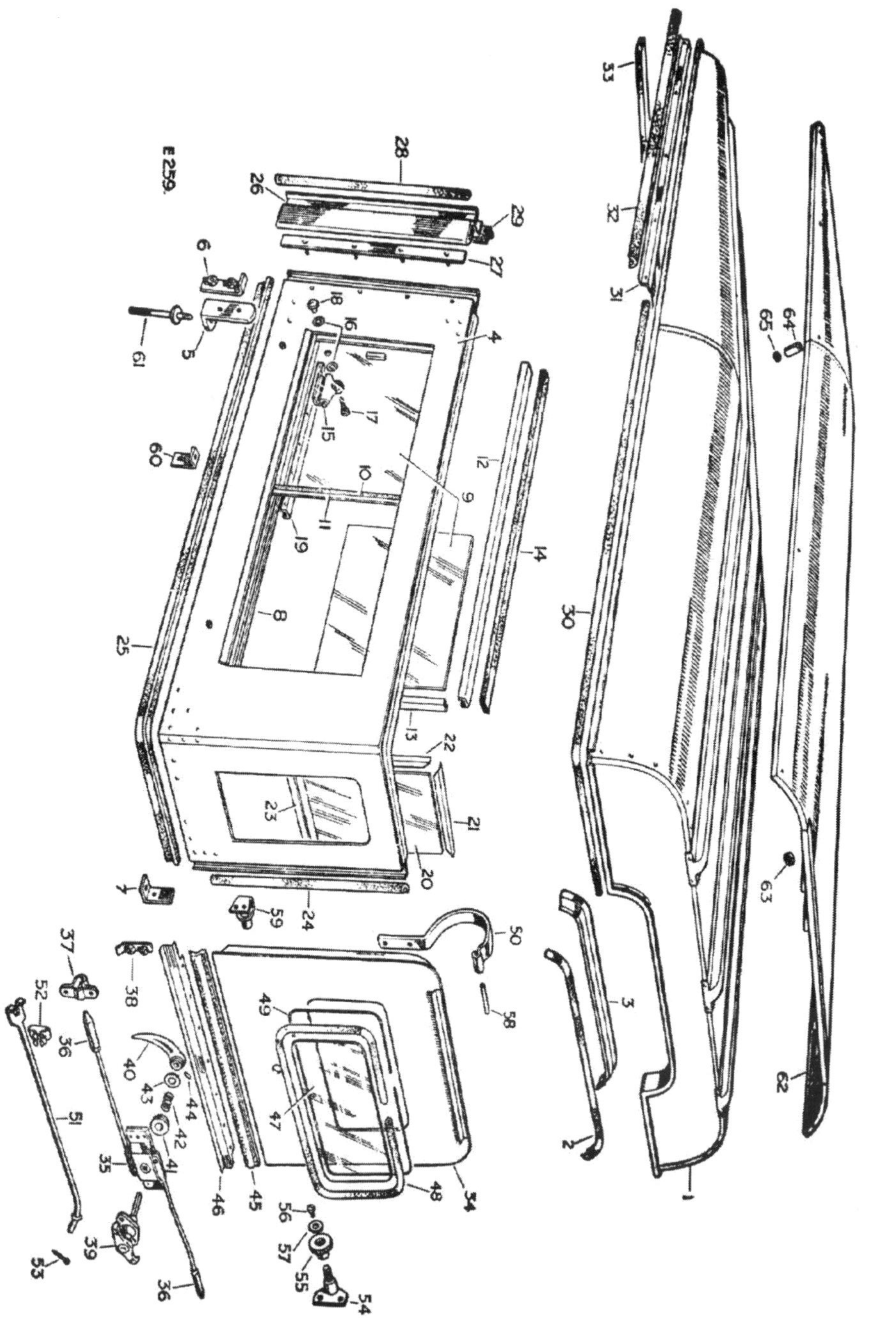

BODY

Key to illustration of hard top with sliding windows

1. Cab roof assembly
2. Rubber seal for roof, rear
3. Seal retainer for roof, rear
4. Side panel assembly, LH
5. Mounting bracket front
6. Nut plate—fixing mounting bracket to body
7. Support bracket at tailboard
8. Drain channel complete for side windows
9. Glass for side window, sliding
10. Sealing rubber for sliding light
11. Channel for sliding light rubber
12. Channel for sliding light, top
13. Channel for sliding light, sides
14. Packing strip for top channel
15. Catch for sliding glass, front
16. Washer for catch
17. Screw fixing front catch
18. Tapped plate for catch
19. Runner for sliding catch
20. Glass for rear end window
21. Retainer for rear end glass upper LH
22. Retainer for rear end glass inner and outer
23. Retainer for rear end glass lower LH
24. Rubber seal for rear lid, side
25. Rubber sealing strip, lower edge to body
26. Capping for front door rear seal, LH
27. Stud plate—fixing cappings to side panel
28. Seal for front door, upper, side
29. Rubber seal at door pillar top and bottom
30. Rubber seal, roof to side
31. Seal retainer for door top, LH
32. Sealing rubber for door top
33. Sealing rubber, windscreen to roof
34. Rear lid assembly
35. Lock complete for rear lid
36. Bolt end for lock
37. Guide for rear lid lock
38. Nut plate
39. Handle for rear lid, outer, locking ⎫ Fixing handle
40. Handle for rear lid, inner ⎭
41. Boss
42. Coil spring
43. Cup for coil spring
44. Locking pin
45. Rubber seal for rear lid, bottom
46. Retainer for bottom seal
47. Glass for rear lid
48. Weather strip for back light
49. Seal strip for weather strip
50. Hinge leaf for rear lid
51. Stay for rear lid
52. Spring clip for rear lid stay
53. Split pin fixing rear lid stay to support
54. Mounting bracket for stay support
55. Locking nut for mounting bracket
56. Screw ⎫ Retaining
57. Plain washer ⎭ locking nut
58. Pin for rear lid hinge
59. Socket for rear lid lock bolt, LH
60. Support bracket, centre, body side
61. Mounting stud—fixing hard top to body
62. Tropical roof panel
63. Rubber washer—fixing roof panel to roof at end of stiffener
64. Distance piece ⎫ Fixing roof to
65. Rubber washer ⎭ panel at sides

Fig. Q1-26. Layout of hard top with sliding windows

Rear body, remove and refit—Operation Q1-13

Workshop hand tools:
Spanner sizes: 2 BA, 4 BA, $\frac{7}{16}$ in. AF, $\frac{1}{2}$ in. AF open end and sockets
Screwdriver (medium)

To remove (Figs. Q1-27 and Q1-28)

1. Remove the hood and hood sticks or the hard top.
2. Remove the spare wheel if fitted in the rear body.
3. **88 models**: remove the seat cushions.
4. **109 models**: tilt forward the squabs.
5. Disconnect the fuel filler and breather hoses.
6. Remove the bolts, washers and nuts securing the rear body to the seat base.
7. Remove the bolts securing the sill channel mounting bracket to the seat base and rear body.
8. Detach the nuts and bolts securing the rear sill panel to the body.
9. **88 models**: detach the wing stays from the chassis members.
10. Remove the nuts and bolts securing the body to the rear cross-member mounting brackets.
11. Remove the rear body complete.
12. If necessary, remove all serviceable parts for fitment to new body.

To refit

1. Reverse the removal procedure.

This page intentionally left blank

Key to illustration of rear body unit, 88 models

1. Side and wheelarch complete RH
2. Side and wheelarch complete LH
3. Rear floor complete
4. Rear floor cross-member and pads
5. Rear floor cross-member mounting pad
6. Rear body front panel
7. Body front panel capping
8. Body top side capping
9. Corner strengthening angle
10. Hood socket complete, rear corner
11. Corner bracket and tailboard cotter
12. Rear protection angle
13. Rear mounting angle
14. Protecting strip at rear of floor
15. Cover panel for rear lamps
16. Spare wheel clamp
17. Clamp reinforcement bracket
18. Spare wheel clamp tie bar
19. Wing nut, fixing spare wheel clamp
20. Spare wheel rubbing strip
21. Tailboard sealing rubber
22. Tailboard rubber buffer
23. Tailboard chain bracket
24. Pin, fixing tailboard chain to bracket
25. Tailboard chain
26. Sleeve for chain
27. Hood strap staple
28. Starting handle and jack handle clip
29. Rear wing stay, front
30. Rear wing stay, rear
31. Fuel filler cowl
32. Fuel filler cover plate
33. 'Land-Rover' name plate
34. Registration plate

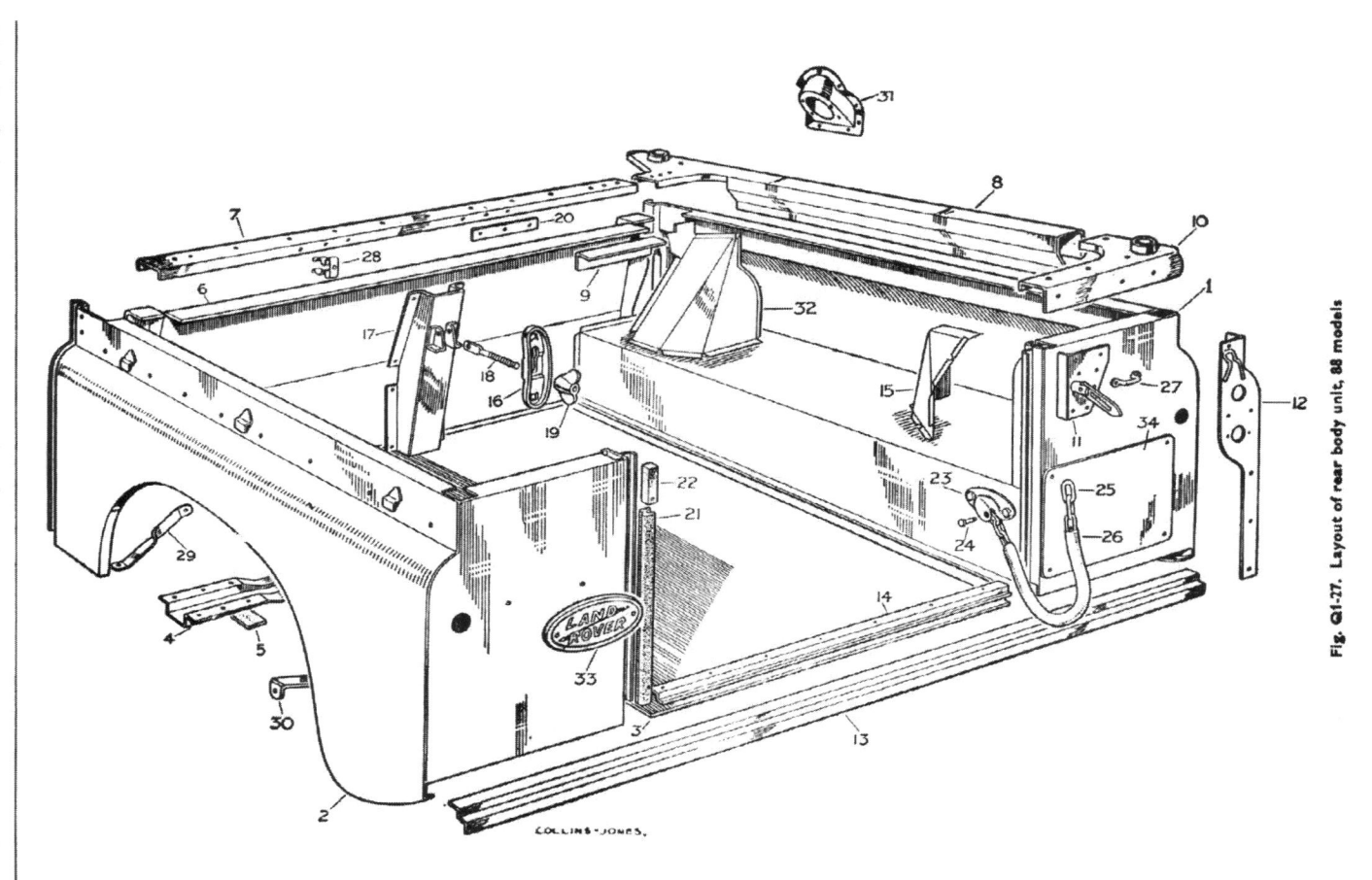

Fig. Q1-27. Layout of rear body unit, 88 models

Key to illustration of rear body unit, 109 models

1. Side and wheelarch complete RH
2. Side and wheelarch complete LH
3. Rear floor complete
4. Rear floor cross-member and pads
5. Rear floor cross-member mounting pad
6. Rear body front panel
7. Rear body front panel capping
8. Body top side capping
9. Corner strengthening angle
10. Hood socket complete, rear corner
11. Rear protection angle
12. Corner bracket and tailboard cotter
13. Protecting strip at rear of floor
14. Rear mounting angle
15. Rear lamp cover panel
16. Spare wheel mounting strengthening member
17. Nut plate
18. Spare wheel housing
19. Spare wheel clamp tie bar
20. Spare wheel clamp
21. Wing nut, fixing spare wheel clamp
22. Cover plate
23. Tailboard sealing rubber
24. Tailboard rubber buffer
25. Tailboard chain bracket
26. Tailboard chain
27. Clevis pin, fixing chain to bracket
28. Sleeve for chain
29. Wheelarch box locker lid
30. Locker lid hinge
31. Locker lid hasp
32. Locker lid turnbuckle
33. Tread plate, wheelarch box top
34. Tread plate, vertical, front panel
35. Tread plate, horizontal, front panel
36. Tread plate for rear floor and wheelarch box sides
37. Starting handle and jack handle clip
38. Fuel filler cover plate
39. Rubber grommet, wheelarch, locker access hole
40. 'Land-Rover' nameplate
41. Registration plate

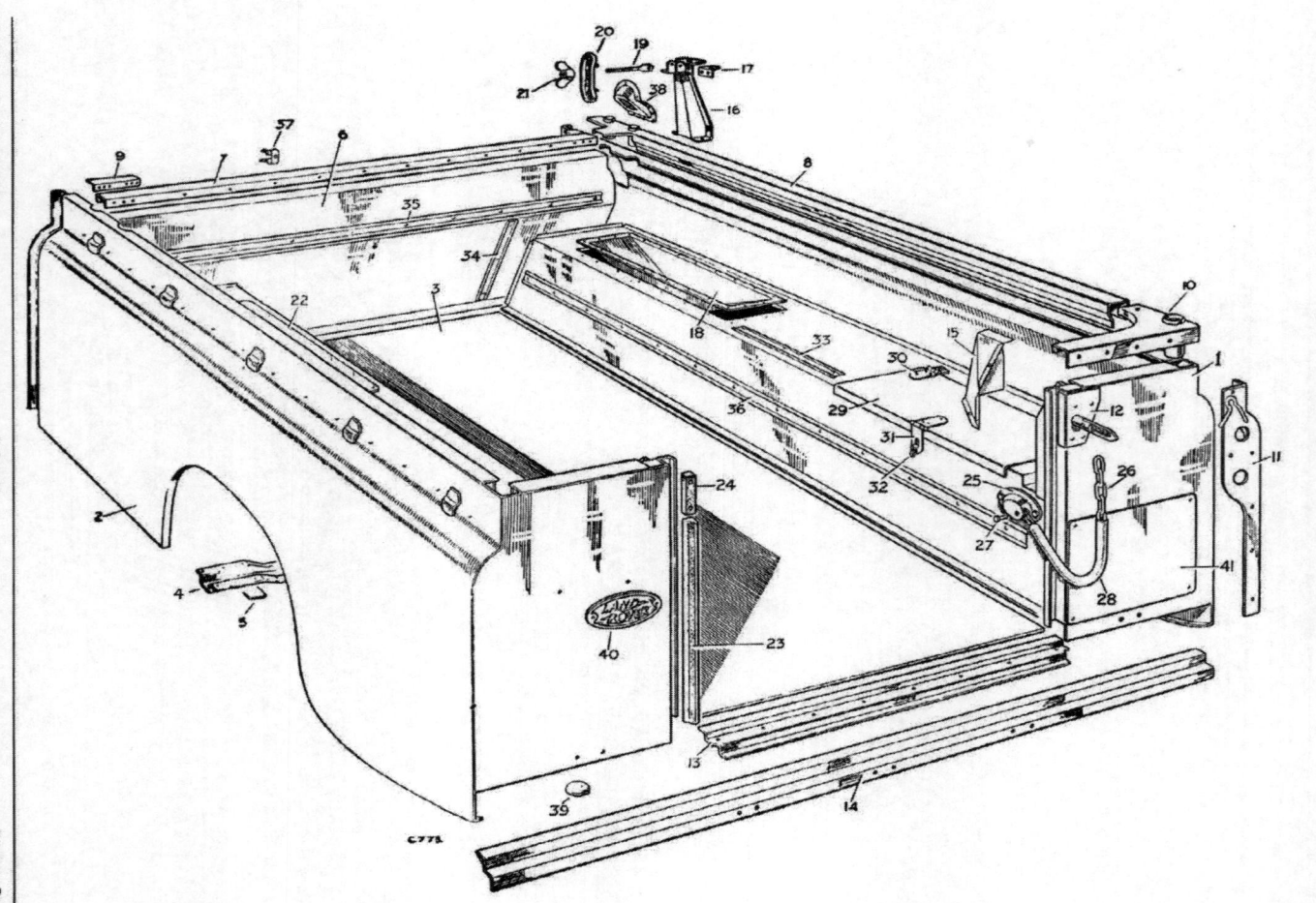

Fig. Q1-28. Layout of rear body unit, 109 models

Station wagon top, to remove and refit—Operation Q1-14

Workshop hand tools:
Spanner sizes: 2 BA, $\frac{7}{16}$ in. AF, $\frac{1}{2}$ in. AF open end
Screwdriver (medium)

To remove (Figs Q1-29, Q1-30 and Q1-31)

1. Remove the rear door.
2. Remove the upper trim.
3. Remove the nuts, bolts and washers securing the hard top to the windscreen.
4. 109 models with four side doors—Remove the bolts securing the hard top to the door pillar.
5. Remove the set bolts securing the hard top to the front mounting bracket.
6. Remove the nuts, bolts and washers securing the hard top to the centre mounting brackets.
7. Remove the nuts and washers securing the hard top to the rear hood sockets.
8. Remove the nuts, bolts and washers securing the rear mounting brackets to the body. Lift off the hard top complete.

Roof panel

9. Remove the roof panel by removing the nuts, bolts and washers securing it to the side panels. If necessary, remove the rubber seal.

Side panels

10. If necessary, remove the glasses as described for the cab. Operation Q1-11.
11. If necessary, remove the seals and retaining strips.

Special tools:
Tool for fitting window filler strip, Part Number 262771

To refit

1. Reverse the removal procedure.
2. If removed, replace or renew the seals and retaining strips.
3. If removed, replace or renew the glasses. Operation Q1-11.
4. On assembly of the door handle, it will be necessary to adjust the position of the bolts by slackening the locking nuts, to obtain adequate entry into the sockets.

Hard top tropical roof

To remove

1. Remove the screws, spring and plain washers, nuts, distance pieces and rubber washers securing each side of the panel to the roof.
2. Remove the screws, spring, plain and rubber washers and nuts securing the tropical panel stiffeners to the hard top roof, both at the front and at the back.
3. Remove the drive screws or shear the pop rivets securing the panel to the hard top stiffeners, and lift off the tropical roof panel.

To refit

1. Reverse the removal procedure.

This page intentionally left blank

Key to illustration of roof and body side panels, 88 Station Wagon

1. Roof and tropical roof panel assembly
2. Tropical roof panel
3. Distance piece
4. Rubber washer
5. Rubber washer
6. Roof ventilator, front
7. Side light for roof
8. Weather strip for side light
9. Filler strip for weather strip
10. Side panel assembly, LH
11. Mounting bracket front
12. Nut plate
14. Capping for front door rear seal LH
15. Stud plate
16. Drain channel complete for side windows
17. Glass for side window, sliding
18. Sealing rubber for sliding light
19. Channel for sliding light rubber
20. Channel for sliding light—top
21. Channel for sliding light—sides
22. Packing strip for top channel
23. Catch for sliding glass, front, overall length 1½ in.
24. Distance piece for catch
25. Washer for catch
26. Screw (2 BA x ⅞ in. long)
27. Tapped plate for catch
28. Runner for sliding catch
29. Glass for rear end window
30. Retainer for rear end glass upper LH
31. Retainer for rear end glass inner and outer
32. Retainer for rear end glass lower LH
33. Seal for front door, upper side
34. Seal at top and bottom for front door, upper side
35. Sealing rubber, lower edge to body
36. Sealing rubber, RH
37. Retainer for front door seal top LH
38. Seal for front door top
39. Rubber seal for canopy
40. Support bracket, centre, body side
41. Mounting stud
42. 'Station Wagon' name plate, front and rear

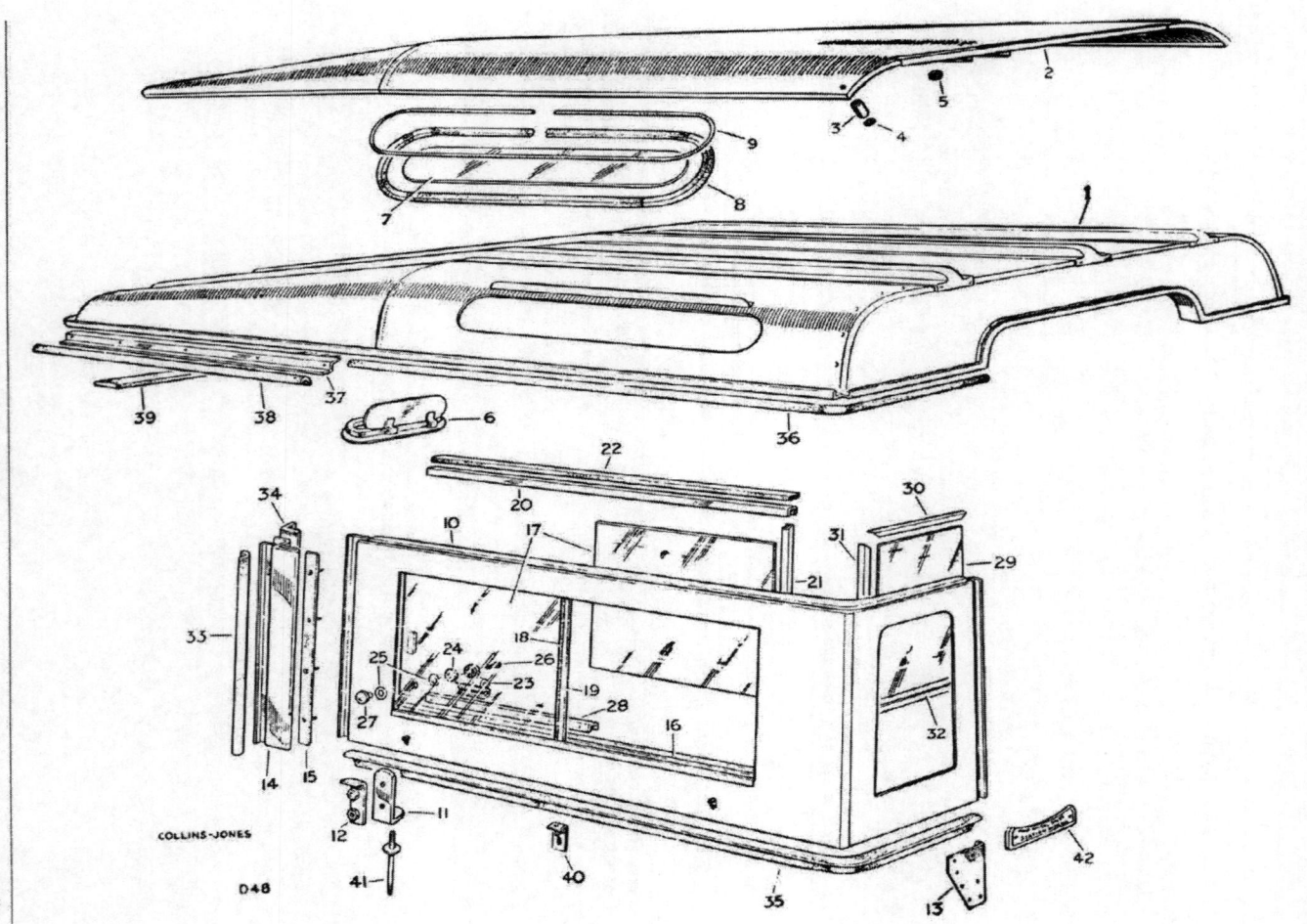

Fig. Q1-29. Layout of roof and body side panels, 88 Station Wagon

Key to illustration of roof and body side panels, 109 Station Wagon

1. Roof complete
2. Tropical roof panel assembly
3. Stiffener, front ⎫ For
4. Stiffener, rear ⎭ roof panel
5. Rubber washer
6. Distance piece
7. Rubber washer
8. Roof ventilator
9. Retainer for roof trim at ventilator
10. Roof side light glass
11. Weather strip for glass
12. Filler strip for weather strip
13. Sealing rubber for roof to windscreen
14. Seal retainer for door top, LH front
15. Seal for retainer
16. Side panel assembly, LH
17. Mounting bracket front
18. Nut plate
19. Capping for 'D' post, LH
20. Stud plate
21. Sealing rubber at top and bottom, upper side, 'D' post pillar
22. Door sealing rubber at 'D' post, upper side
23. Support bracket at tailboard
24. Drain channel complete for side window
25. Glass for side window, sliding
26. Sealing rubber for sliding light
27. Retainer for sliding light rubber
28. Channel for sliding light, top
29. Channel for sliding light, bottom outer
30. Channel for sliding light, side
31. Packing strip for top channel
32. Catch for sliding glass, front overall length 1½ in.
33. Distance piece for catch
34. Washer for catch
35. Screw (2 BA x ⅞ in. long)
36. Tapped plate for catch
37. Runner for sliding catch
38. Glass for rear end window
39. Retainer for rear end glass, upper LH
40. Retainer for rear end glass, inner and outer
41. Retainer for rear end glass, lower LH
42. Sealing rubber, upper to lower body side
43. Sealing rubber, RH
44. Rubber seal, 'BC' post to roof
45. Support bracket, centre body side
46. Mounting stud ($\frac{7}{16}$ UNF)

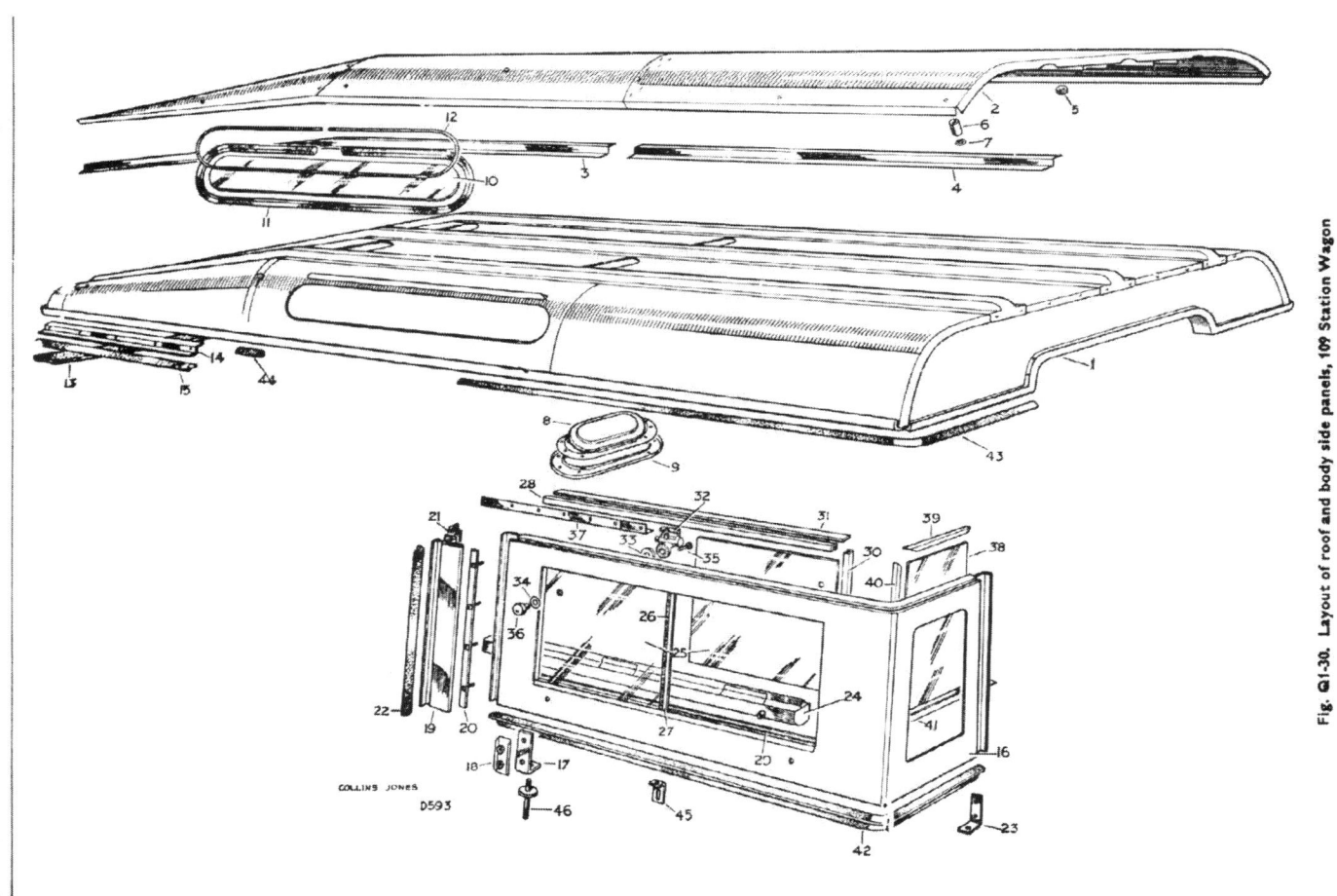

Fig. Q1-30. Layout of roof and body side panels, 109 Station Wagon

Key to illustration of rear body for 109 Station Wagon

1. Body side and wheelarch complete, RH
2. Body side and wheelarch complete, LH
3. Rear floor
4. Cross member and pads for rear floor
5. Mounting pad for rear floor cross member
6. Rear mounting angle
7. Rear corner capping, RH
8. Capping for body top side, RH
9. Rear corner protection angle, RH
10. Lid for rear tool locker
11. Hinge complete
12. Retainer for floor mat, rear end
13. 'Land-Rover' nameplate
14. 'Station Wagon' nameplate
15. Intermediate floor for rear body
16. Cover plate for fuel tank, front
17. Cover plate for fuel tank, rear
18. Tread plate
20. Toe panel complete
21. Sealing rubber, 'BC' post to toe panel
22. Sealing rubber, 'D' post to wheelarch front flange
23. Sill panel, rear, LH
24. Body side lower front extension, LH

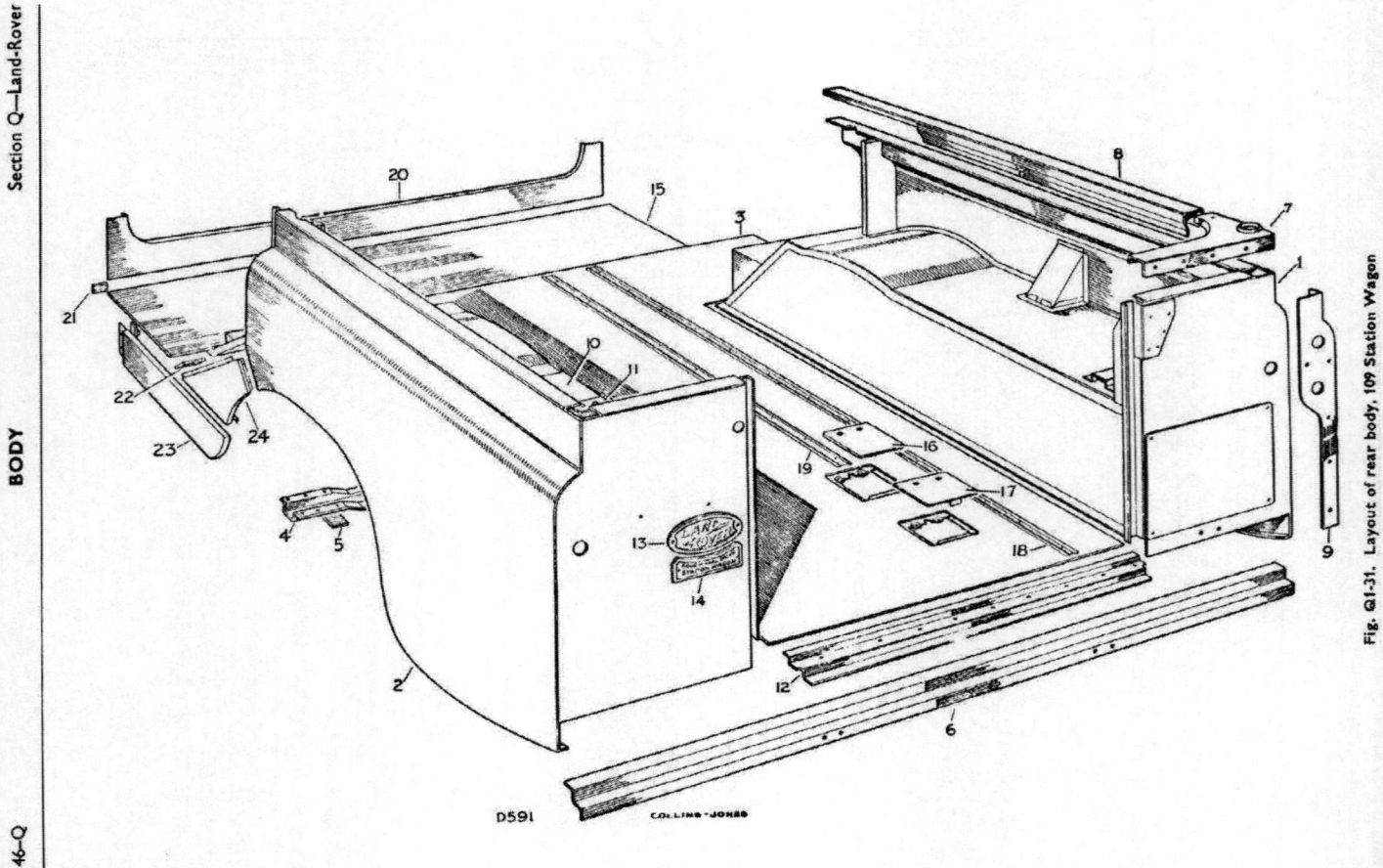

Fig. Q1-31. Layout of rear body, 109 Station Wagon

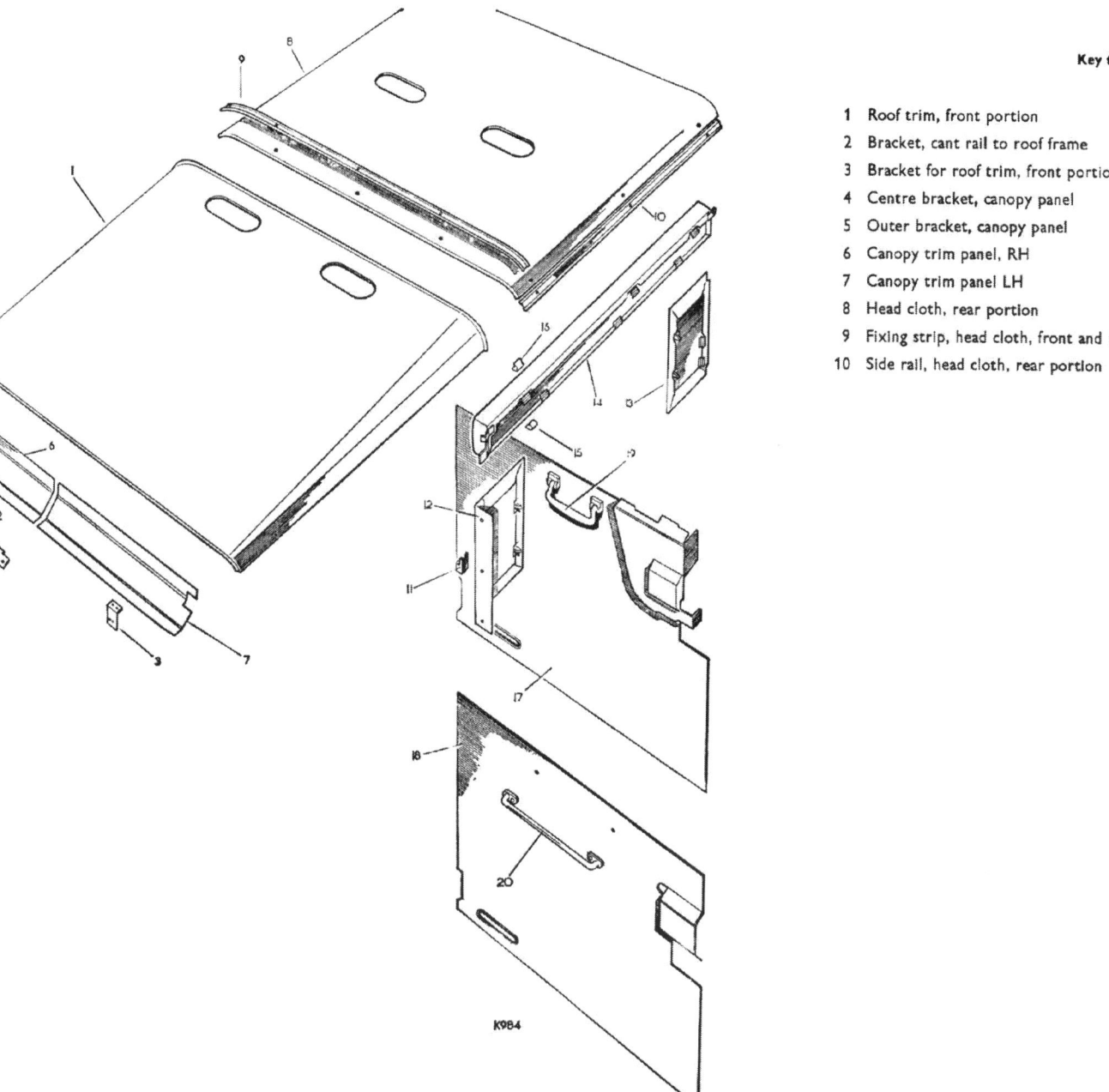

BODY

Key to illustration of trim for 88 Station Wagon

1. Roof trim, front portion
2. Bracket, cant rail to roof frame
3. Bracket for roof trim, front portion
4. Centre bracket, canopy panel
5. Outer bracket, canopy panel
6. Canopy trim panel, RH
7. Canopy trim panel LH
8. Head cloth, rear portion
9. Fixing strip, head cloth, front and rear
10. Side rail, head cloth, rear portion
11. Fixing bracket, RH, sidelight casing, front
12. Sidelight casing, trimmed LH, front
13. Sidelight casing, trimmed, LH rear
14. Roll trim for cant rail, LH
15. Retaining Clip } Fixing roll trim
16. Edge clip
17. Rear door trim casing, GREY
18. Rear door trim casing, GREY
19. Door pull handle
20. Door grab handle

Fig. Q1-32. Layout of trim for 88 Station Wagon

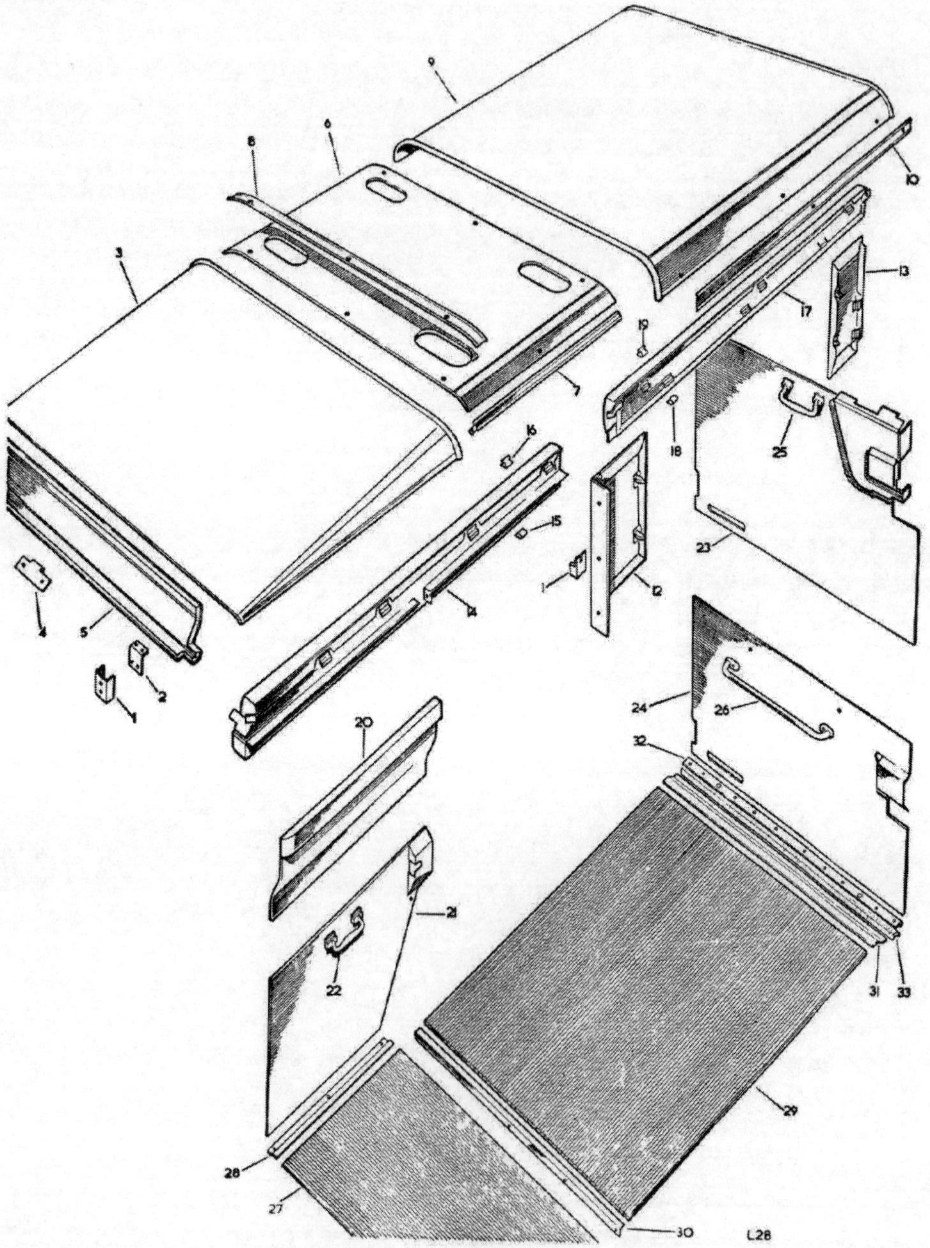

BODY

Key to illustration of trim for 109 Station Wagon

1. Bracket, cant rail to roof frame
2. Bracket for roof trim, front portion
3. Roof trim, front portion
4. Centre bracket for canopy trim panel
5. Canopy trim panel
6. Headcloth, Intermediate
7. Side rail for intermediate headcloth
8. Fixing strip for intermediate headcloth
9. Headcloth, rear
10. Side strip for rear headcloth
11. Fixing bracket, RH sidelight casing, front
12. Sidelight casing, front, LH
13. Sidelight casing, rear, LH
14. Roll trim, cant rail, LH front
15. Retaining clip ⎱ Fixing roll trim
16. Edge clip ⎰
17. Roll trim, cant rail, LH rear
18. Retaining clip ⎱ Fixing roll trim
19. Edge clip ⎰
20. Door trim upper, centre, RH
21. Door trim lower, centre, RH
22. Door pull handle for rear side door
23. Rear door trim casing
24. Rear door trim casing
25. Door pull handle for rear door
26. Door grab handle
27. Intermediate floor rubber mat
28. Retainer for floor mat, intermediate
29. Rear floor rubber mat
30. Retainer for rear floor mat, front end
31. Retainer for seal and rear floor mat, rear end
32. Protection strip for rear door, bottom
33. Sealing rubber for rear door, bottom

Fig. Q1-33. Layout of trim for 109 Station Wagon

Rear door, remove and refit—Operation Q1-15

Workshop hand tools:
Spanner sizes: 2 BA, $\frac{7}{16}$ in. AF, $\frac{1}{2}$ in. AF, $\frac{3}{4}$ in. AF open end
Screwdriver (medium), Pliers

Special tools:
Tool for locking door handle, Part Number 248877 (early type private locks only)

To remove (Fig. Q1-34)

1. If fitted, remove the spare wheel from the rear door.
2. Disconnect the door check strap.
3. Remove the bolts, washers and nuts securing the hinges to the door.
4. Remove the door.
5. Adjust the position of the striking plate as necessary, so that the door draught excluders are slightly compressed.

To refit

1. Reverse the removal procedure, renewing sealing rubbers as necessary.

Hinge

To remove

1. The hinges may be stripped by prising back the lock washer tab and removing the special nut and bolt. Care must be taken to ensure that the cone and spring are not lost.

To refit

1. Fit a new lock washer and assemble by reversing the removal procedure.

   Adjust by increasing or lessening the load on the spring by tightening or slackening the special nut, and bend lock tab over to secure assembly.

Door lock

To renew

1. Remove the door trim.
2. Remove the door lock from the door.
3. If required, remove the striking plate from its support bracket.
4. Renew the lock and plate as necessary and refit by reversing items 1 and 2.

Rear door glass

If required, remove and refit the window glass as described for the cab. Operation Q1-11.

Spare wheel carrier

To remove

1. Remove the spare wheel from the carrier.
2. Remove the door trim.
3. Remove the nuts securing the 'U' bolt, and the screws, nuts and washers securing the wheel stud plate and clamp plate to the door.

To refit

Reverse the removal procedure.

Step for door

To remove

1. Disconnect the return spring from the step.
2. Remove the washer and split pin from one end of the hinge pin, withdraw the hinge pin and step.
3. If required, remove the rivets and screws retaining the mat for the step.

To refit

Reverse the removal procedure.

This page intentionally left blank

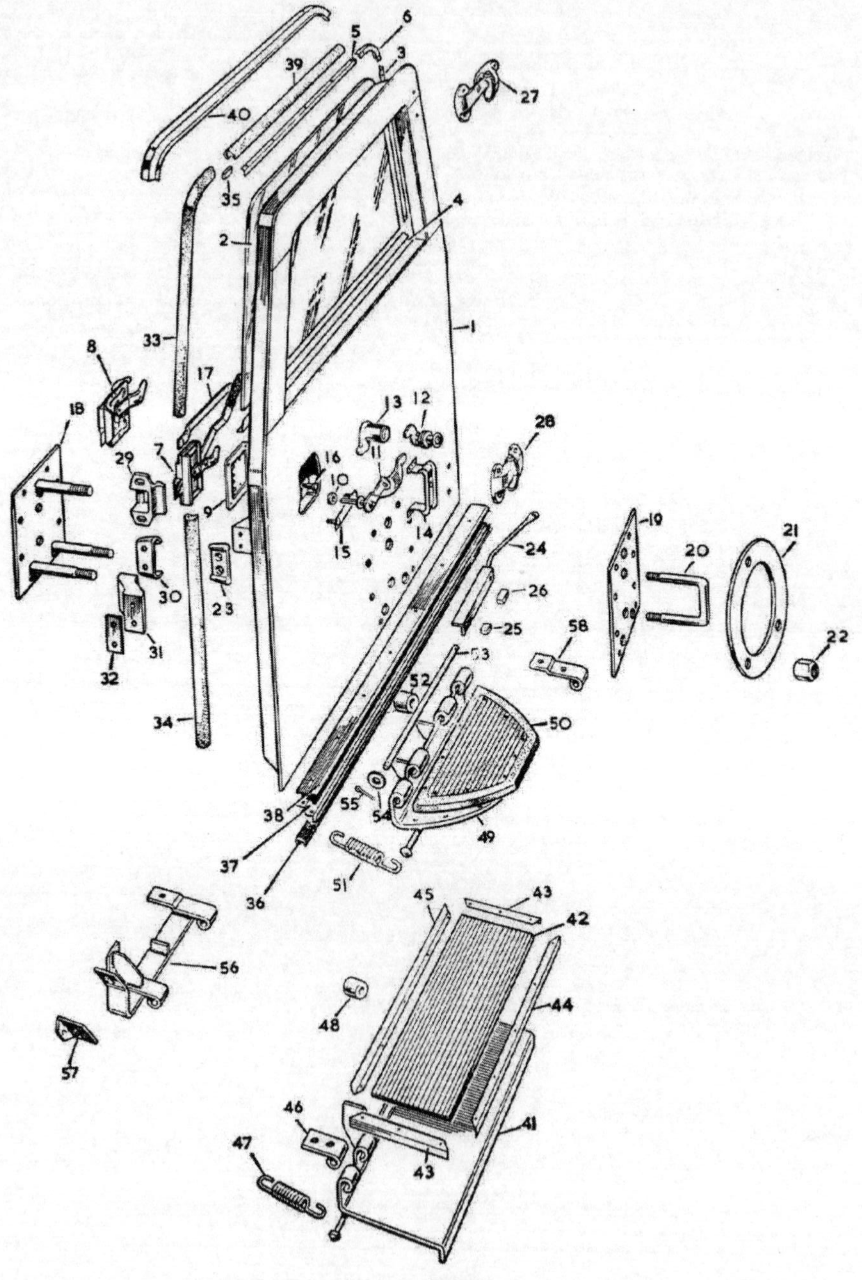

BODY

Key to illustration of rear door, 88 and 109 models

1. Rear door
2. Glass for rear door
3. Retainer for glass, vertical
4. Retainer for glass, bottom
5. Retainer for glass, top
6. Retainer for glass, corners
7. Door lock, mounting and handle assembly
8. Door lock, mounting and handle assembly
9. Mounting plate for door lock
10. Washer, handle to cover
11. Door handle with lock
12. Barrel lock
13. Barrel lock
14. Bracket for door handle
15. Stud plate, door lock, bottom
16. Locking pillar for catch
17. Waist rail lock handle protection strip
18. Wheel stud plate
19. Clamp plate for spare wheel stud Plate
20. 'U' bolt for spare wheel support
21. Retaining plate for spare wheel
22. Hub nut fixing wheel and retaining plate to 'U' bolt
23. Male dovetail
24. Rod for check strap
25. Buffer for check strap, short
26. Buffer for check strap, long
27. Hinge for rear door, upper
28. Hinge for rear door, lower
29. Striking plate
30. Female dovetail
31. Spacer
32. Shim
33. Seal for door sides
34. Seal for door side, LH bottom
35. End filler for seals
36. Seal for rear door, bottom
37. Retainer fixing seal to rear door, bottom
38. Protection strip for rear door, bottom
39. Seal for rear door, top
40. Retainer for rear door seal, top
41. Rear step
42. Rubber mat for step
43. Retainer for rear step, side
44. Retainer for rear step mat, front
45. Retainer for rear step mat, rear
46. Hinge, centre for rear step
47. Spring for rear step
48. Buffer for rear step
49. Rear step
50. Rubber mat for rear step
51. Spring for rear step
52. Buffer for rear step
53. Hinge pin for rear step
54. Plain washer } Fixing hinge pin
55. Split pin
56. Support bracket and hinge centre, LH
57. Anchor bracket for spring
58. Hinge, centre RH

Fig. Q1-34. Layout of rear door, 88 and 109 models.

BODY

Safety harness, remove and refit—Operation Q1-16

Workshop hand tools:
Spanner size: $\frac{7}{16}$ in. AF, $\frac{1}{2}$ in. AF open end and socket
Screwdriver (medium)

To remove

Ensure hands are clean before handling seat straps.

1. Remove the bolt and washer securing the harness at the sill bracket.
2. Remove the nuts and bolts from the harness shackles at the bulkhead.
3. 109 Station wagon—Remove the nuts and bolts from the harness shackle at the 'BC' post.
4. Withdraw the safety harness from the vehicle.
5. Remove the sill bracket and shackle bolts as required.

To refit

1. Fit the adjusting buckle to the sill bracket.

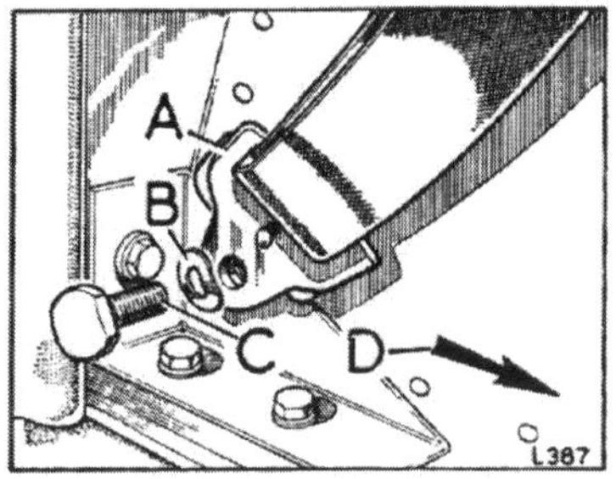

Fig. Q1-35. Showing diagonal strap buckle fitting to sill bracket, right-hand side illustrated

A—Adjusting buckle
B—Wave washer
C—Screw fixing buckle
D—To front of vehicle

Release the two outer front seat squabs and pull forward giving access to safety harness fixing points.

Remove the shackle bolt 'G' from the shackle end 'B' of diagonal shoulder strap 'C' secured with bolt 'A' and locking nut 'D' as illustrated.

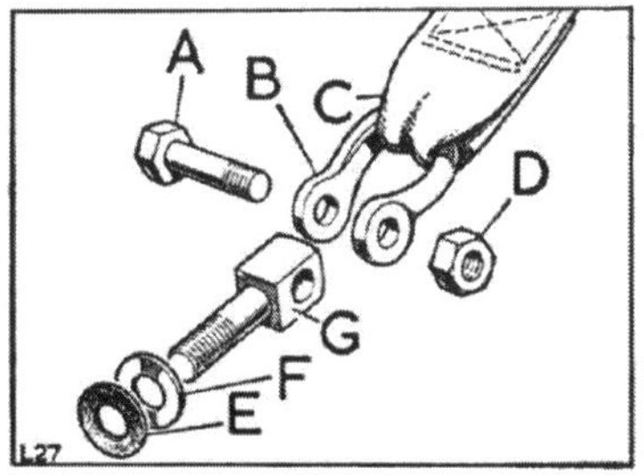

Fig. Q1-36. Shackle end fixings, diagonal and tongue strap ends

A—Bolt
B—Shackle
C—Strap
D—Nut
E—Rubber washer
F—Plain washer
G—Shackle bolt

4. Screw the shackle bolt into the tapped hole in lower bulkhead panel position using rubber washer and plain washer. Tighten the shackle bolt so that it is located as illustrated. The rubber washer allows the shackle bolt to be correctly aligned. Do not over-tighten.
5. Fit the tongue strap shackle to shackle bolt and secure with bolt and nut.

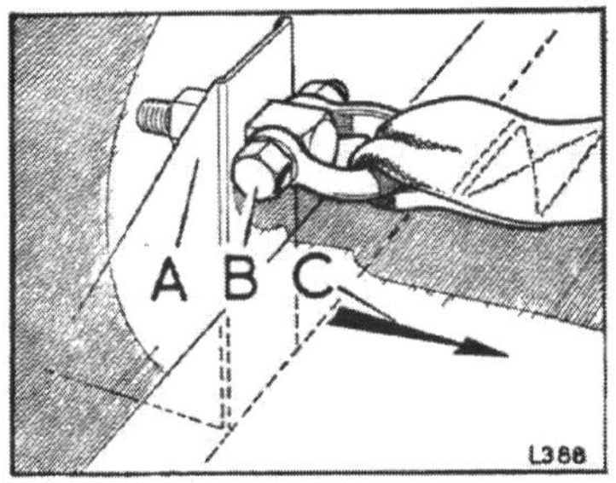

Fig. Q1-37. Tongue strap fixing, lower bulkhead panel, right-hand side illustrated

A—Gusset bracket
B—Shackle fixing bolt
C—To front of vehicle

Operation Q1-16—continued

Early models—Diagonal strap fixing. Except 109 Station Wagon

6. Screw the shackle bolt into the tapped hole in shoulder bracket, rear of seat panel capping using rubber washer and plain washer. Tighten the shackle bolt so that it is located as illustrated in full line. The rubber washer allows the shackle bolt to be correctly aligned. Do not over-tighten.

Late models—Diagonal strap fixing. Except 109 Station Wagon

7. Screw the shackle bolt into the tapped hole in top capping of seat panel, using rubber washer and plain washer. Tighten the shackle bolt, so that it is located as shown in dotted line. The rubber washer allows the shackle bolt to be correctly aligned. Do not over-tighten.

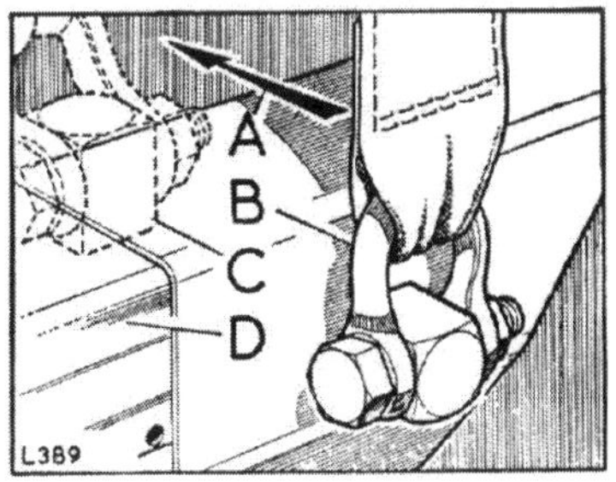

Fig. Q1-38. Diagonal strap fixing, upper bulkhead panel. Except 109 Station Wagon, right-hand side illustrated

A—To front of vehicle
B—Shackle position (early models, in full line)
C—Shackle position (late models, in dotted line)
D—Seat panel capping

109 Station Wagon—Diagonal strap fixing

8. Screw the shackle bolt into the tapped hole in mounting bracket 'B' top of 'BC' post, using rubber washer and plain washer. Tighten the shackle bolt, so that it is located as illustrated. The rubber washer allows the shackle bolt to be correctly aligned. Do not over-tighten.

Fig. Q1-39. Diagonal strap fixing 'BC' post, 109 Station Wagon left-hand side illustrated

A—Shackle fixing bolt
B—Mounting bracket
C—To front of vehicle

9. With the occupant seated in the front seat, the diagonal shoulder strap should pass over the outboard shoulder, as illustrated.

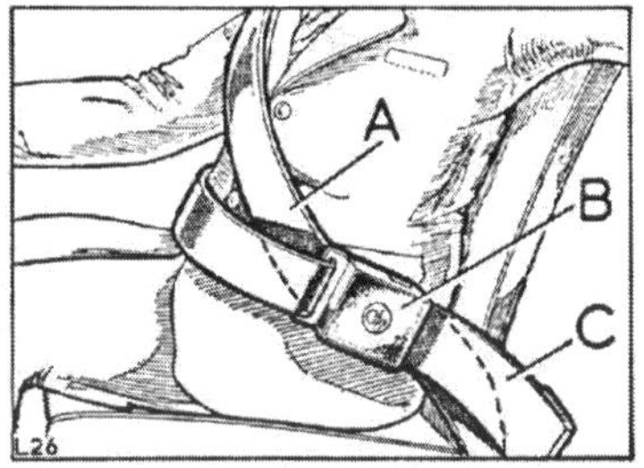

Fig. Q1-40. Showing safety harness in correct position, right-hand side illustrated

A—Diagonal shoulder strap
B—Buckle on shoulder strap
C—Short tongue strap

10. Adjust the position of tongue strap buckle to the position shown, that is, with the buckle as far round the body as possible without actually fouling the seat, by pulling strap 'B' to shorten the tongue strap, as shown.

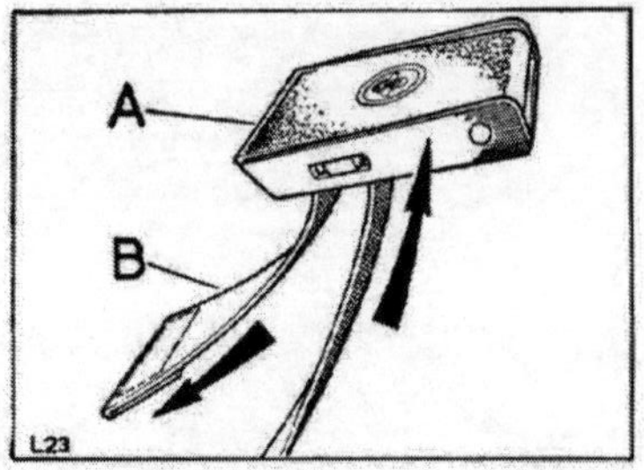

SECTION R—WHEELS AND TYRES

INDEX—WHEELS AND TYRES

Description of Contents	Operation Number
General information	—
Tyres, well base rim wheels, remove and refit ..	R-1
Tyres, divided wheels, remove and refit	R-2
Tyre data	—

General information

1. Factors affecting tyre life

(a) Incorrect tyre pressures.
(b) High average speeds.
(c) Harsh acceleration.
(d) Frequent hard braking.
(e) Warm, dry climatic conditions.
(f) Poor road surfaces.
(g) Impact fractures caused by striking a kerb or loose brick, etc.
(h) Incorrect front wheel alignment. Alignment should be checked periodically and the procedure is described in Section G.

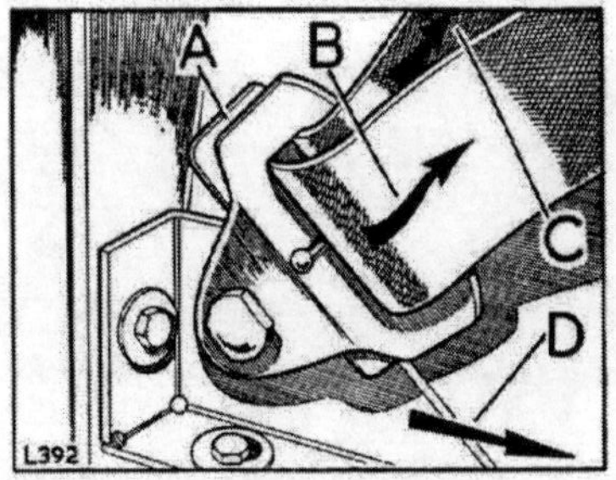

Note: The condition of tyres in use in the United Kingdom must satisfy legal safety requirements and the information given in this Section must be used subject to those requirements where applicable.

2. Changing wheel positions

The road wheels should be changed round at the mileage intervals specified in the Owner's Maintenance Manual as illustrated to equalise tyre wear. At the same time inspect the tyre tread.

Check also for cuts, bulges and exposed ply or cord structure.

When cross-country tyres are used, the 'V' tread should be directed to the front at the top.

Warning: Do not touch the outer ring of nuts on divided type wheels, unless the wheel is removed and the tyre fully deflated, or severe personal injury may result.

Important: As the Land-Rover is fitted with a transmission brake, it is necessary before removing a road wheel to apply the hand brake and engage four-wheel drive.

This will ensure that the hand brake is operative on all four wheels.

Remember to engage two-wheel drive when the road wheel has been replaced.

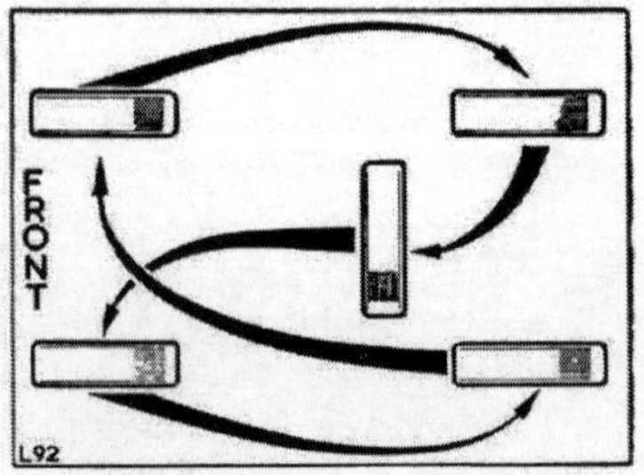

Fig. R1-1. Changing the wheel positions

3. Tyre and inner tube repairs

Minor tyre injuries, such as from nails, require no attention other than removal of the object, but more severe tread or wall cuts require vulcanised repairs.

Avoid the use of gaiters or liners except as a temporary expedient. As 'Butyl' synthetic tubes are used, all repairs must be vulcanised.

4. Tyre pressures and types

Tyre pressures

Maximum tyre life and performance will only be obtained if the tyres are maintained at the correct pressures.

Model		Normal					Emergency soft			
		Load under 550 lb (250 kg)		Load over 550 lb (250 kg)			Load under 550 lb (250 kg)		Load over 550 lb (250 kg)	
		Front	Rear	Front	Rear		Front	Rear	Front	Rear
88 Bonneted Control models 6.00, 6.50 and 7.00 x 16.00	lb/sq in. kg/cm²	25 1,8	25 1,8	25 1,8	30 2,1		15 1,1	15 1,1	15 1,1	20 1,4
7.50 x 16.00	lb/sq in. kg/cm²	25 1,8	25 1,8	25 1,8	30 2,1		12 0,8	12 0,8	12 0,8	20 1,4
109 Bonneted Control and 1 Ton models 7.50 x 16.00	lb/sq in. kg/cm²	25 1,8	25 1,8	25 1,8	36 2,5		15 1,1	15 1,1	15 1,1	26 1,8
9.00 x 16.00	lb/sq in. kg/cm²	20 1,4	20 1,4	20 1,4	30 2,1		10 0,7	10 0,7	10 0,7	20 1,4

Tyre types

To avoid introducing transmission problems when four-wheel drive is engaged, use the same make and type of tyre on all wheels and change wheel positions as specified to equalise tyre wear.

Tyres, well base rim wheels, remove and refit—Operation R1-1

Workshop tools:
Wheelbrace, Valve core key, Suitable tyre levers, Tyre pressure gauge

To remove

Tyres, well base rims (Standard on all models)

1. Remove the valve cap and core (extractor provided in tool kit) and deflate the tyre.
2. Press each bead in turn off its seating. Insert a lever at the valve position and, while pulling on this lever, press the bead into the well, diametrically opposite the valve.
3. Insert a second lever close to the first and prise the bead over the wheel rim. Continue round the bead in small steps until it is completely off the rim.
4. Remove the inner tube and pull the second bead over the rim.

To refit

1. Place the cover over the wheel and press the lower bead over the rim edge into the well.
2. Inflate the Inner tube until it is just rounded out, dust with French chalk, and insert it in the cover, with the white spots near the cover bead coinciding with the black spots on the tube.
3. Press the upper bead into the well diametrically opposite the valve and lever the bead over the rim edge.
4. Push the valve inwards to ensure that the tube is not trapped under the bead, pull it back and inflate the tyre.
5. Visually check the concentricity of the fitting lines on the cover and the rim of the wheel flange. Deflate the tube completely and re-inflate to the correct pressure, to relieve any strains in the tube.

WHEELS AND TYRES

Fault diagnosis—Wheels and tyres

Symptom	Possible cause	Investigation	Remedy
Excessive wear on front tyres	Incorrect tyre pressures	Check tyre pressures	Adjust as necessary
	Failure to rotate tyres		Change position of tyres including spare
	Incorrect toe-in of front wheels	Check wheel alignment, Operation G1-2	Adjust as necessary
	Harsh or unequal brakes	Check brake adjustment, Section H	Adjust as necessary
	Worn swivel pins	Jack up front of vehicle and check swivel pins	Overhaul swivel pin housings
	Incorrectly adjusted brakes	Check brake shoe adjustment, Section H	Adjust as necessary
	Eccentric wheels and tyres	Check tyre concentricity line. Check wheel pressings for damage or distortion	Rectify or renew
	Distorted brake drum	Remove brake drum and check concentricity	Recondition or fit new replacement
	Incorrect camber	Check for settled road springs, damage to front suspension and axle unit	Fit new parts as required
	Fast cornering and/or sustained high speed driving		In the hands of the operator
Excessive wear on rear tyres	Incorrect tyre pressures	Check tyre pressures	Adjust as necessary
	Rear wheel run-out or wobble	Check for loose wheel nuts, damaged wheel or incorrectly fitted tyres	Rectify as necessary
	Rear wheels out of alignment	Check that the rear spring centre dowel is not sheared. Check for a broken rear spring main leaf. Check for a damaged chassis	Rectify as necessary, see Sections E and J
	Harsh and unnecessary use of the brakes or high speed driving		In the hands of the operator
Rattle or noise from wheels	Loose wheel bearings	Check hub bearing adjustment. Sections E and F	Adjust as necessary
	Worn or damaged hub bearings	Remove hub and examine bearings	Fit new bearings
	Brake shoes or anchor plate loose	Remove brake drum and check shoes and anchor plate for security	Tighten fixings
Squeaks from wheels	Wheel stud nuts loose	Examine studs for damage	Tighten wheel nuts
	Lack of lubrication to wheel bearings		Lubricate as described in Sections E and F
	Wheel bearings adjusted too tightly	Check hub bearing adjustments Sections E and F	Adjust as necessary
	Worn or damaged hub bearings	Remove hubs and examine bearings	Fit new bearings

Tyres, divided wheels (early vehicles), remove and refit—Operation R1-2

Workshop tools:
Wheelbrace, Valve core key, Suitable tyre levers, Tyre pressure gauge

To remove

Warning: Do not attempt to remove the outer ring of nuts on divided type wheels unless the wheel is removed and the tyre fully deflated, or severe personal injury may result.

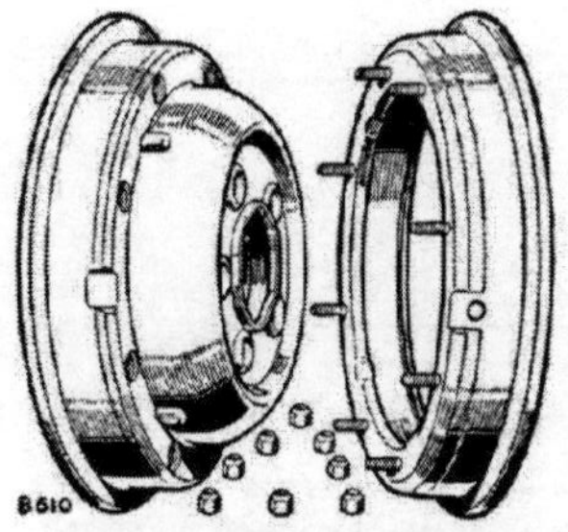

1. Remove the valve cap and core to deflate the tyre.
2. Press each bead in turn away from the flange, using levers and working round the tyre in small steps. Two or three circuits of the tyre may be necessary to free the beads completely.
3. Slacken and remove the clamping nuts. Remove the upper half of the wheel. Push the valve through the lower half of the wheel and remove the cover and tube.

Fig. R1-2. Divided wheel

To refit

1. Thoroughly examine the cover for nails, flints, etc., and ensure that no loose objects have been left inside. Clean the wheel rim flanges and seatings.
2. Inflate the inner tube until it is just rounded out, dust with French chalk and insert it in the cover with the white spots near the cover bead coinciding with the black spots on the tube.
3. Fit the protection flap, starting at the valve position. Make sure that the edges of the flap are not turned over inside the cover and that it lies centrally between the beads. See that the flap fits closely against the tube round the valve.
4. Lay the studded half of the wheel on the floor or bench with the studs pointing upwards. Fit the cover over the wheel and thread the valve through the hole, making sure that it points downwards.
5. Fit the other half of the wheel and tighten the clamping nuts lightly. Finally tighten the nuts using diagonal selection to ensure even tightening. Check that the valve is free and inflate the tyre to the recommended pressure.

Fault diagnosis—Wheels and tyres—*continued*

Symptom	Possible cause	Investigation	Remedy
Squeaks from wheels—cont.	Interference of brake drum with brake shoes	Check the brake drum for distortion and scoring. Check the brake shoes for damage or warping	Rectify or fit new parts as required
Other noises from wheels	Incorrect tyre pressures	Check tyre pressures	Adjust as necessary
	Foreign body embedded in tyre	Examine all tyres	Extract the embedded matter and repair or renew the tyre as necessary
	Variation in tread surface due to patch or damage	Examine all tyres	Fit new tyres as necessary
	Type or condition of tyre tread giving sound similar to gear noise	Ensure that tyres are of the recommended type and fitted correctly. Check tyre wear condition	Fit new tyres of the recommended type as necessary
	Wear in swivel pin housings		See Section E
	Wear in axle half shafts		See Sections E and F
	Wear in differential		
Overheating of wheel bearings	Lack of lubrication to wheel bearings		Lubricate as described in Sections E and F
	Use of a poor quality or incorrect grade of lubricant	See Section X for recommended lubricants	Replenish with correct lubricants
	Wheel bearings adjusted too tightly	Check hub bearing adjustment, Sections E and F	Adjust as necessary
	Worn or damaged wheel bearings	Remove hubs and examine bearings	Fit new bearings as required
	Heat transfer from brake drums due to dragging brakes	Check brake shoe adjustment, Section H	Adjust as necessary
	Excessive use of brakes		In the hands of the operator
	Foreign matter in bearings	Remove hubs and examine bearings	Fit new parts as required

SECTION X—LUBRICANTS AND SERVICING MATERIALS

Recommended lubricants and fluids

These recommendations apply to temperate climates where operational temperatures are above 14°F (–10°C).

Lubricants marked with an asterisk (*) are multigrade oils suitable for all temperature ranges.

Information on oil recommendations for use under extreme winter or tropical conditions can be obtained from your local Rover Distributor or Dealer or the Rover Co. Ltd. Technical Service Department.

COMPONENTS	SAE	BP	CASTROL	DUCKHAM'S	ESSO	MOBIL	REGENT TEXACO-CALTEX	SHELL
Petrol models **Engine, air cleaner and governor**	20W	*BP Super Visco-Static 10W-40	*Castrol GTX	Duckham's Q20-50 Motor Oil	Unifio or Esso Motor Oil 20W/30	Mobiloil Super or Mobiloil Arctic	Havoline 20/20W	*Shell Super Oil 100
Diesel models **Engine and air cleaner**	20W	BP Energol Diesel D20W	Castrol CR1 20	Fleetol HDX 20	Essolube HDX 20W/20	Delvac or Mobiloil Arctic	RPM Delo Special 20-20W	Rotella S or T 20/20W
Gearbox and transfer box **†Differentials and swivel pin housings** **Steering box** **Steering relay unit** **Rear power take-off, pulley unit and capstan winch, hydraulic winch gearbox**	90EP	BP Energol SAE 90EP	Castrol Hypoy	Duckham's Hypoid 90	Esso Gear Oil GP 90/140	Mobilube GX 90	Multigear Lubricant 90	Spirax 90 EP
Hydraulic winch supply tank	—	*BP Super Visco-Static 10W-40	Castrol GTX	Duckham's Q20-50 Motor Oil	Esso Motor Oil 20W/30	Mobiloil Special or Delvex Special	Havoline 20/20W	*Shell Super Oil or Shell Tellus Oil 27
††Lubrication nipples	—	BP Energrease L2	Castrolease LM	Duckham's LB10 Grease	Esso Multi-purpose Grease H	Mobilgrease MP or Mobil-grease Special	Marfak All purpose	Retinax A or Darina AX
Brake and Clutch fluid	Castrol Girling Brake and Clutch Fluid 'Crimson' Specification SAE 70 R3							
Anti-freeze solution	Any anti-freeze solution conforming to British standard No. BS 3152.							

†Rear differential, limited-slip type: Castrol 90EP-LS, Fina Pontonic Plus, Shell Limited-Slip Differential Oil S6721A or Mobilube 46—available in the UK market. Pure Oil TS590, Texaco 3450 or Mobil 46—available in the North America Dollar area

††Use any of these greases where instructions in this manual refer to "general purpose grease"

Recommended jointing compound

'Hylomar' sealing compound SQ 32 M

Capacities

Component	Imperial unit	US unit	Litres
Engine sump oil, 4-cylinder	11 pints	13 pints	6,0
Engine sump oil, 6-cylinder	12 pints	14 pints	6,25
Extra when refilling after fitting new filter, 4-cylinder	1½ pints	1.8 pints	0,85
Extra when refilling after fitting new filter, 6-cylinder	1 pint	1.2 pints	0,5
Air cleaner oil, 4-cylinder	1½ pints	1.8 pints	0,85
Air cleaner oil, 6-cylinder	1 pint	1.2 pints	0,5
Main gearbox oil	2½ pints	3 pints	1,5
Transfer box oil	4½ pints	5½ pints	2,5
Rear differential } Standard and limited	3 pints	3½ pints	1,75
Front differential } slip type	3 pints	3½ pints	1,75
Rear differential } ENV	2⅝ pints	3.1 pints	1,4
Front differential } type	2⅛ pints	2½ pints	1,2
Swivel pin housing oil (each)	1 pint	1,2 pints	0,5
Fuel tank, except 'Long' Station Wagon	10 gallons	12 gallons	45
Fuel tank, 'Long' Station Wagon	16 gallons	19 gallons	73
Cooling system, 4-cylinder, Petrol models	18 pints	21½ pints	10,25
Cooling system, 4-cylinder, Diesel models	17½ pints	21 pints	10,0
Cooling system, 6-cylinder 'Long' models	20 pints	24 pints	11,2
Hydraulic front winch, supply tank	4½ gallons	7½ gallons	20,0
Hydraulic front winch, gearbox	2 pints	2,4 pints	1,0

SECTION Z — TOOLS

General

The following standard and special workshop tools cover all requirements for carrying out the servicing and overhaul procedures detailed in this manual. Standard tools are readily available from tool stockists, special tools are available through the normal Rover spares service.

STANDARD WORKSHOP TOOLS

Socket sets
0 to 6 BA covering all BA sizes
$\frac{7}{16}$ in. to $\frac{7}{8}$ in. Whit covering all BSF and Whitworth sizes
$\frac{7}{16}$ in. to 2 in. AF covering all UNF and UNC sizes

Open-ended spanners, chrome vanadium
0 to 6 BA covering all BA sizes
$\frac{1}{4}$ in. to $\frac{7}{8}$ in. Whit covering all BSF and Whitworth sizes
$\frac{7}{16}$ in. to 1$\frac{1}{4}$ in. AF covering all UNF and UNC sizes

Ring spanners, chrome vanadium
$\frac{1}{4}$ in. to $\frac{7}{8}$ in. Whit covering all BSF and Whitworth sizes
$\frac{7}{16}$ in. to 1$\frac{1}{4}$ in. AF covering all UNF and UNC sizes

Miscellaneous tools and equipment
Cylinder bore measuring equipment
1 Pliers, outer circlip
1 Pliers, inner circlip
1 Pliers, pointed nose
1 Pliers, standard
1 Pin punch
1 Screwdriver, large
1 Screwdriver, medium
1 Screwdriver, small
1 Phillips screwdriver, large
1 Phillips screwdriver, medium
1 Phillips screwdriver, small
1 Stud extractor, $\frac{1}{4}$ in.
1 Stud extractor, $\frac{5}{16}$ in.
1 Stud extractor, $\frac{3}{8}$ in.
1 Copper and plastic-faced mallet, large
1 Adjustable spanner, large
1 Adjustable spanner, small
1 Flat chisel
1 Self-grip wrench
1 Bar and horseshoe magnet
1 Torque wrench registering 150 lbs

1 Set feeler gauges, .0015 in. to .025 in.
1 Hammer, 1 lb
1 Hammer, $\frac{1}{4}$ lb
1 Spring balance, 24 lbs
1 Dial test indicator
1 Inspection lamp
1 Brake bleeding kit
1 Oilcan
1 Hand valve grinder, spring-loaded
1 Rule, 12 in.
1 Carbon slip stone, small
1 Hacksaw frame and blades
1 File, 10 in., flat, rough
1 File, 10 in., flat, smooth
1 File, 10 in., round, rough
1 File, 10 in., round, smooth
1 File, 6 in., pillar
1 File, 6 in., round
1 Set Ease-outs, Nos. 1 to 5
1 Roll of insulating tape
1 Hand drill
1 Voltmeter, moving coil type, calibrated 0–25 volts
1 Ammeter, moving coil type, calibrated 0–40 amps
1 Micrometer, 1 in.
1 Micrometer, 1 in. to 2 in.
1 Micrometer, 2 in. to 3 in.
1 Brass drift, $\frac{1}{2}$ in. diameter
1 Girling brake adjustment spanner
3 Girling hose clamps
1 Lucas setting tool No. 54381742 (Lucas number)

SPECIAL TOOLS

The following list of special tools is arranged in sections conforming to their corresponding sections in the manual. Where a section is not mentioned, no special tools are necessary to carry out the work detailed in that section. The special tool Part numbers are arranged in numerical order within each section.

Symbols used in the text:

*—Essential, must be used when carrying out the particular operation illustrated.

†—Advantageous, these tools will help to give more efficient service when dealing with the operations illustrated.

‡—Required when volume of work justifies use.

SECTION A — ENGINE

Part Number 246650
Press block, cylinder liner*
Essential for fitting liners to 2.6 litre engines

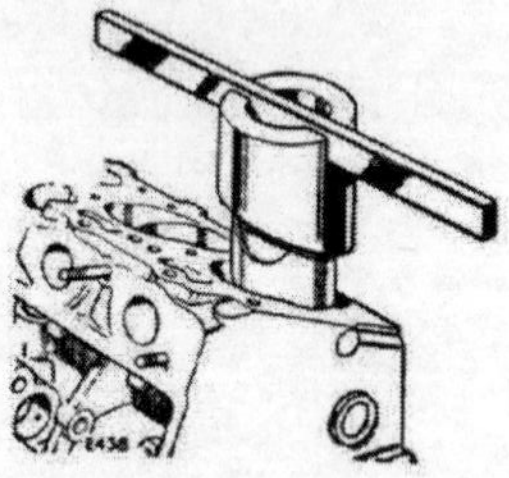

Fig. Z1-1. Cylinder liner press block

Part Number 261288
Jig block, cylinder boring*
Enables the use of standard boring equipment on 2.6 litre engines

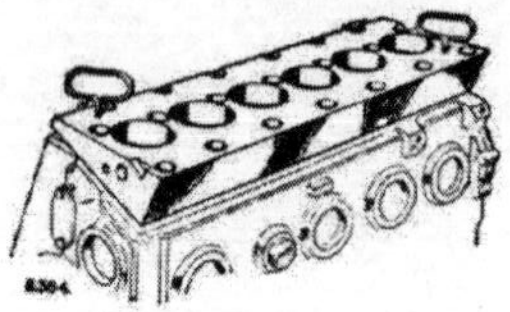

Fig. Z1-2. Reboring jig block

Part Number 262749
Extractor, rocker shafts*
Essential when removing and refitting rockers with engine in position. 2.6 litre engines

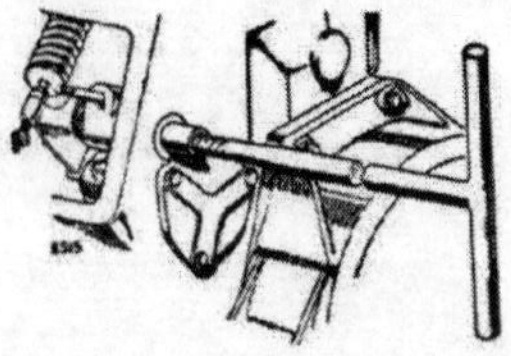

Fig. Z1-3. Extractor, rocker shafts

Part Number 263050
Protection plate for exhaust valve seat removal†
The seat is removed by grinding and breaking, and use of the plate will prevent injury. 2.6 litre engines.

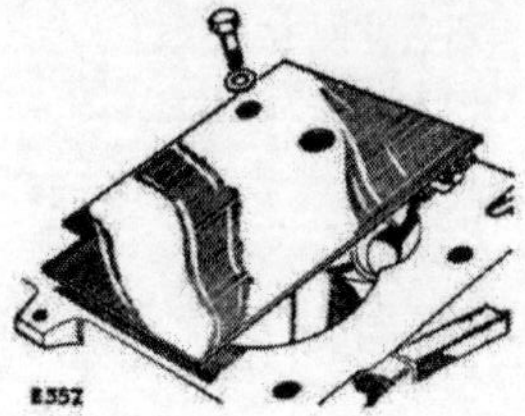

Fig. Z1-4. Protection plate, exhaust valve seat

Part Number 270304
Guides for rear main bearing cap seals†
Provides a leading edge for the rear main seals. 2$\frac{1}{4}$ litre Petrol engines, 2$\frac{1}{4}$ litre Diesel engines, 2.6 litre engines.

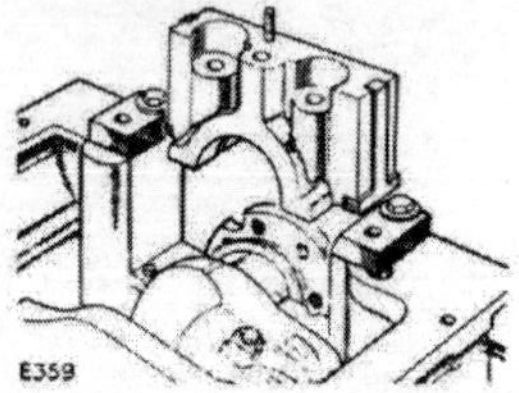

Fig. Z1-5. Guides for rear main bearing cap seals

Part Number 272103
Fitting tool, gudgeon pin ‡
Facilitates refitting of gudgeon pin. 2.6 litre engines.

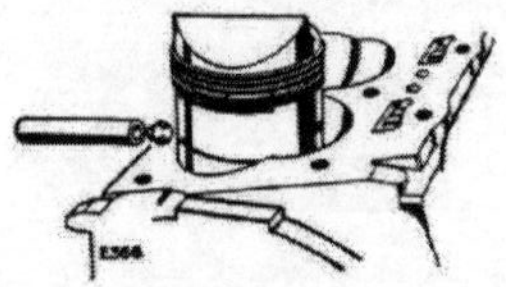

Fig. Z1-6. Gudgeon pin fitting tool

*—Essential   †—Advantageous   ‡—Required when volume of work justifies use

TOOLS

Part Number 274381
Camshaft bearing fitting tool *
Essential when refitting camshaft bearings.
2¼ litre Petrol engines. 2¼ litre Diesel engines

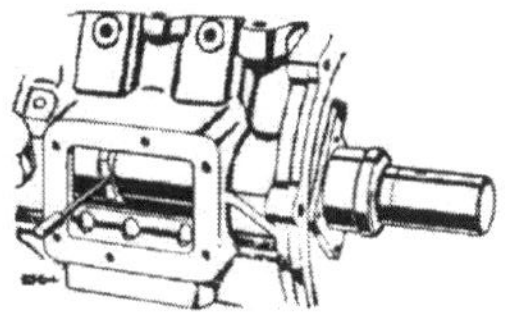

Fig. Z1-7. Camshaft bearing fitting tool

Part Number 274388
Camshaft bearing extractor *
Essential when removing camshaft bearings.
2¼ litre Petrol engines. 2¼ litre Diesel engines.

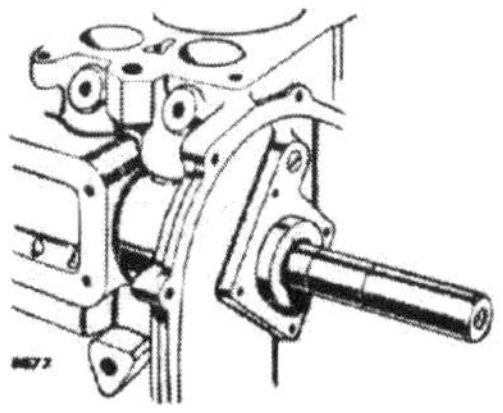

Fig. Z1-8. Camshaft bearing extractor

Part Number 274389
Reamer for camshaft bearings *
Replacement camshaft bearings must be line-bored with this reamer.
2¼ litre Petrol engines. 2¼ litre Diesel engines.

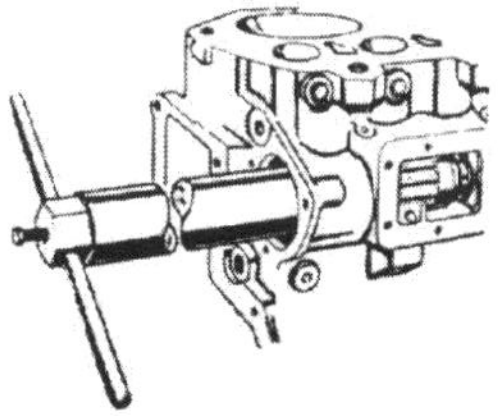

Fig. Z1-9. Camshaft bearing reamer

Part Number 274399
Push rod tube extractor and replacer for 'push rod tube' and 'injector shroud' *
This special drift facilitates push rod tube removal and replacement, and injector shroud fitment.
2¼ litre Diesel engines.

Fig. Z1-10. Push rod tube extractor and injector shroud fitting tool

Part Number 274400
Valve guide removal drift *
Facilitates removal of the valve guide.
2¼ litre Petrol engines. 2¼ litre Diesel engines.

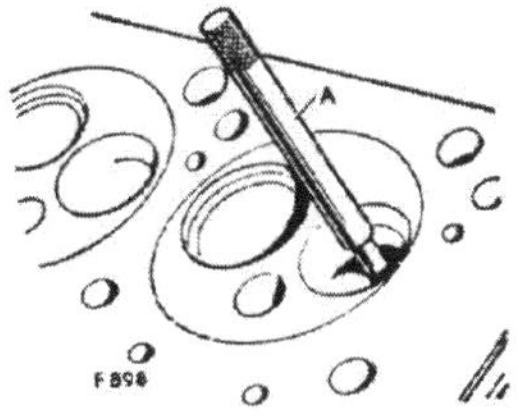

Fig. Z1-11. Valve guide removal drift

Part Number 274401
Valve guide removal drift *
Facilitates removal of the valve guides.
2¼ litre Petrol engines. 2¼ litre Diesel engines.

Fig. Z1-12. Valve guide removal drift

*—Essential   †—Advantageous   ‡—Required when volume of work justifies use

---

Part Number 276102
Valve spring compressor ‡
Suitable for extracting the cotters on both inlet and exhaust valves.
2¼ litre Petrol engines. 2¼ litre Diesel engines. 2.6 litre Diesel engines.

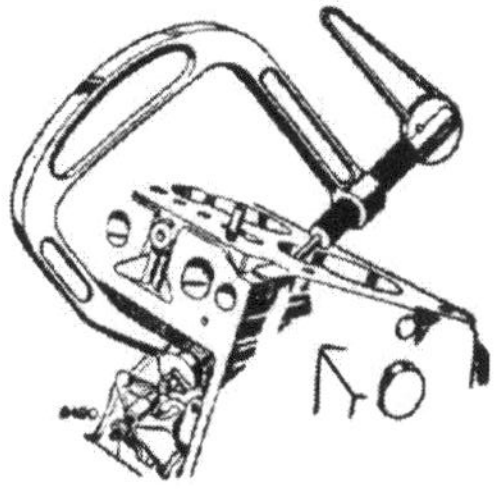

Fig. Z1-13. Valve spring compressor

Part Number 507231
Extractor, chain wheel †
Facilitates chain wheel removal.
2¼ litre Petrol engines. 2¼ litre Diesel engines. 2.6 litre Diesel engines.

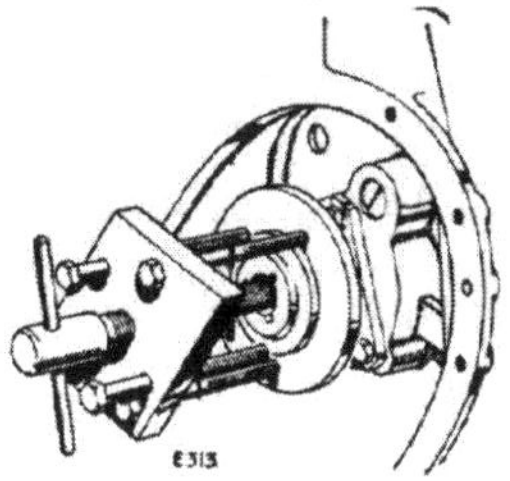

Fig. Z1-14. Extractor, chain wheel

Part Number 530101 (four applications)
Extractor, camshaft ‡
Facilitates camshaft removal.
2¼ litre Petrol engines. 2¼ litre Diesel engines. 2.6 litre Diesel engines.

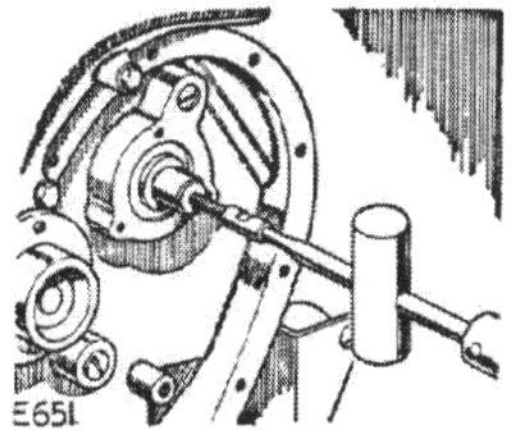

Fig. Z1-15. Extractor, camshaft

Extractor, gudgeon pin ‡
Facilitates removal of gudgeon pin.

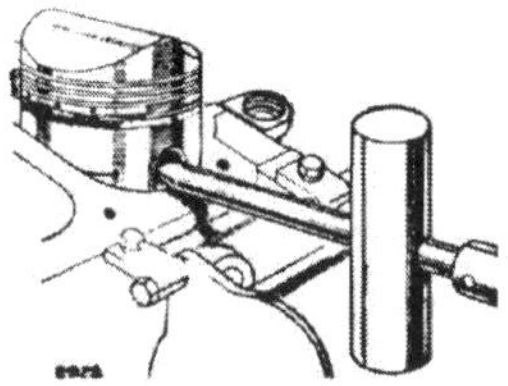

Fig. Z1-16. Gudgeon pin extractor

Tool for pulling in connecting rod bolts ‡
Facilitates the fitting of connecting rod bolts and is supplied with UNF and BSF thread adaptors.

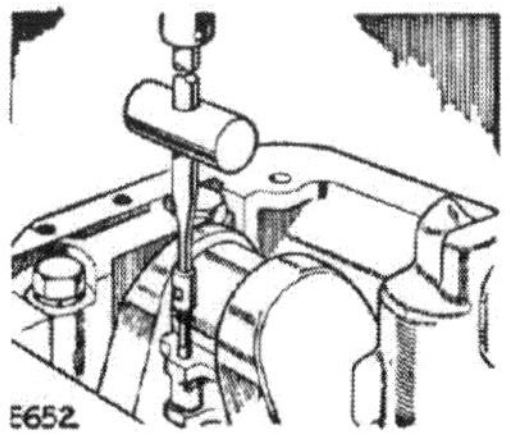

Fig. Z1-17. Fitting tool, connecting rod bolts

Tappet guide extractor and locating tool *
Essential for easy removal of the tappet guide.

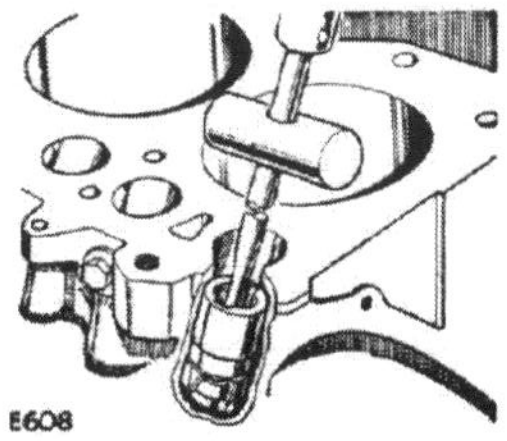

Fig. Z1-18. Tappet guide extractor and locating tool

*—Essential   †—Advantageous   ‡—Required when volume of work justifies use

TOOLS

Part Number 530102
Spanner for starter dog ‡
2¼ litre Petrol engines. 2¼ litre Diesel engines. 2.6 litre engines.

Fig. Z1-19. Starter dog spanner

Part Number 530106
(Many applications, four of which are illustrated)
Bracket for indicator, valve timing ‡
Its use enables the employment of a standard indicator. It has many other applications.
2¼ litre Petrol engines. 2¼ litre Diesel engines. 2.6 litre engines.

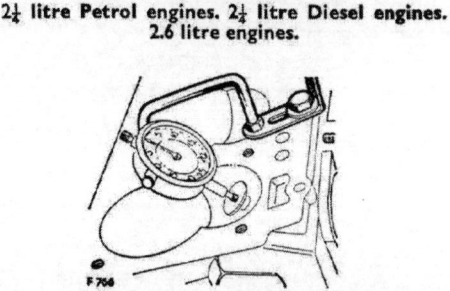

Fig. Z1-20. Indicator bracket, valve timing

Bracket for checking flywheel run-out

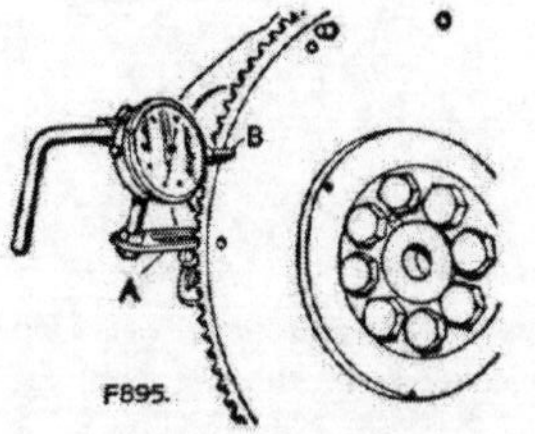

Fig. Z1-21. Bracket for checking flywheel run-out

Bracket for checking crankshaft end-float ‡

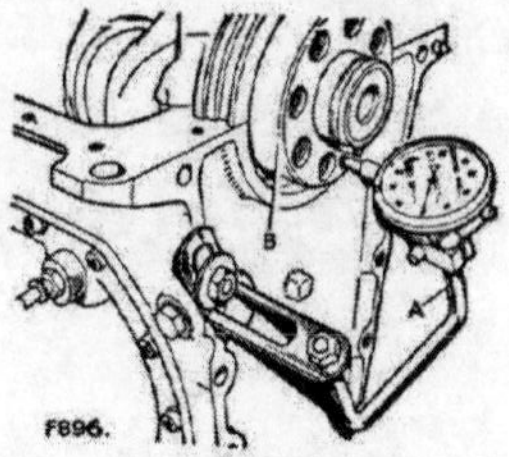

Fig. Z1-22. Bracket for checking crankshaft end-float

Bracket for checking camshaft end-float ‡
Facilitates checking camshaft end-float

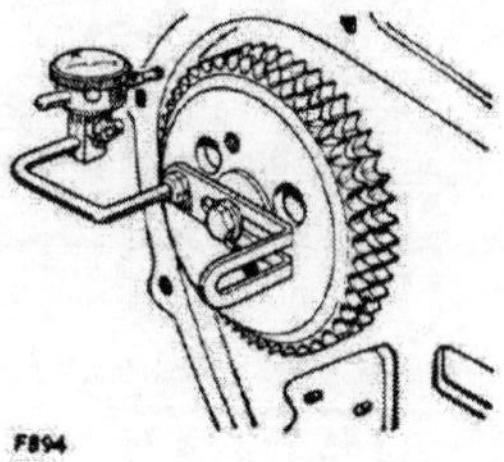

Fig. Z1-23. Bracket for checking camshaft end-float

Part Number 530625
Fitting tool, exhaust valve seat *
The seat insert must be pulled in carefully, to avoid shattering.
2.6 litre engines.

Fig. Z1-24. Fitting tool, exhaust valve seat

Part Number 600959
Fitting tool, exhaust valve guide *
Prevents damage to guide.
2¼ litre Petrol engines. 2¼ litre Diesel engines. 2.6 litre engines.

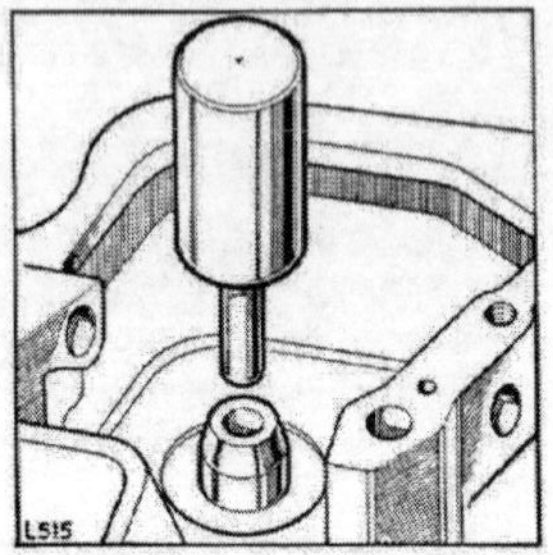

Fig. Z1-25. Fitting tool for exhaust valve guide

Part Number 600963
Engine lifting sling ‡
Facilitates removal and refitting engine.
2¼ litre Petrol engines. 2¼ litre Diesel engines. 2.6 litre engines.

Fig. Z1-26. Engine lifting sling

Part Number 601508
Fitting tool, inlet valve guide *
Prevents damage to guide.
2¼ litre Petrol engines. 2¼ litre Diesel engines. 2.6 litre engines.
Similar to Fig. Z1-25, but varying dimensionally

Part Number 605022
Alignment gauge for clutch plate ‡
Facilitates fitting clutch to engine flywheel.
2¼ litre Petrol engines. 2¼ litre Diesel engines. 2.6 litre engines.

Fig. Z1-27. Alignment gauge for clutch plate

Part Number 605238
Plastigauge for measuring bearing clearance
Provides alternative method of checking engine bearings (now in general use).
2¼ litre Petrol engines. 2¼ litre Diesel engines. 2.6 litre engines.

Fig. Z1-28. Plastigauge for measuring bearing clearance

Part Number 605863
Timing gauge for distributor pump *
Essential for timing distributor pump when fitting pump to engine.
2¼ litre Diesel engines.

Fig. Z1-29. Timing gauge for distributor pump

*—Essential   †—Advantageous   ‡—Required when volume of work justifies use

TOOLS

Part Number 530106
Bracket for indicator, differential backlash ‡
The use of a dial test indicator is the only reliable method of setting backlash.
Also used in Section A—Engine.

Fig. Z1-37. Indicator bracket, differential backlash

Part Number 600299
Gauge for differential pinion setting *
Alternative to Part Number 605004. See Fig. Z1-39.

Part Number 600970
Tool for bearing adjustment, ENV differential

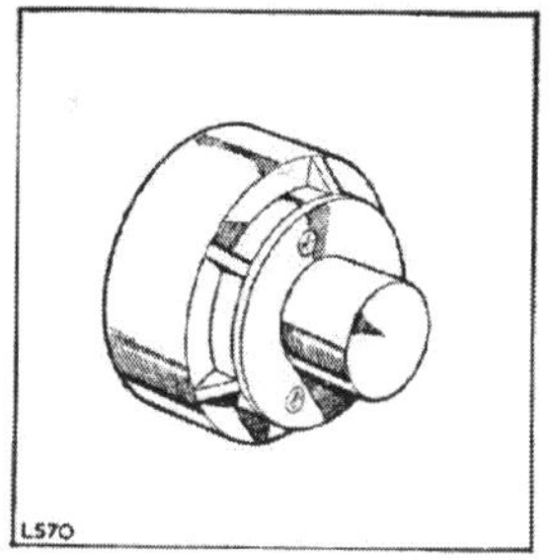

Fig. Z1-38. Tool for bearing adjustment

Part Number 601998
Gauge for differential pinion setting *
Alternative to Part Number 605004. See Fig. Z1-39.

Part Number 262761
Gauge for differential pinion setting *
Alternative to Part Number 605004. See Fig. Z1-39.

Part Number 275870
Axle shaft retaining collar removal and replacement tools *
Essential when removing and replacing axle shaft retaining collar. Supplied with a range of adaptors.

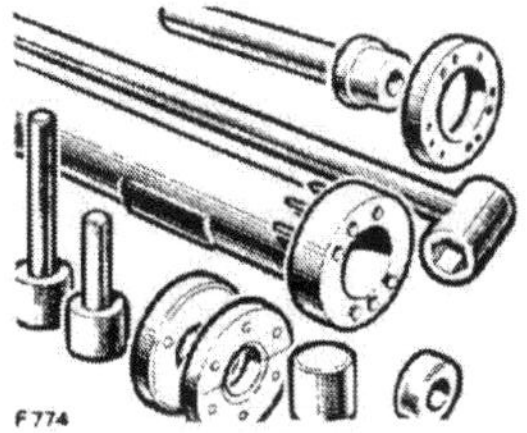

Fig. Z1-35. Axle shaft retaining collar removal tools

Part Number 530105
Spanner, crownwheel locking nuts and differential pinion drive flange ‡
Useful when overhauling the differential.

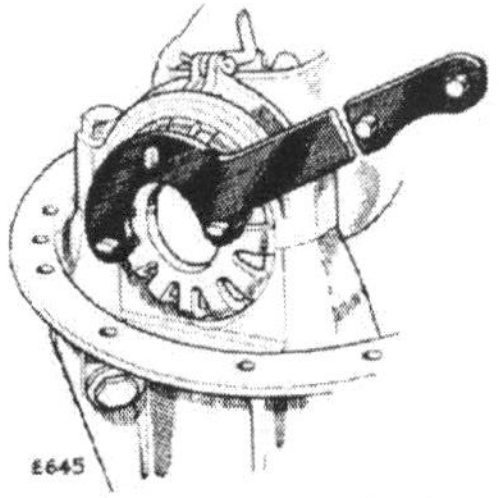

Fig. Z1-36. Spanner, crownwheel locking nuts

*—Essential   ‡—Advantageous   †—Required when volume of work justifies use

---

TOOLS

SECTION B—CLUTCH
Part Number 530103
Gauge plate, clutch release levers †
Clutch lever thrust faces must be set, using these gauges, from the flywheel face.

Fig. Z1-30. Gauge plate, clutch release levers

Part Number 605022
Alignment gauge for clutch
See Fig. Z1-27, Section A—Engine.

SECTION C—GEARBOX
Part Number 243241
Protection cap, gearbox output shaft *
Use of this cap will prevent damage to the shaft thread.

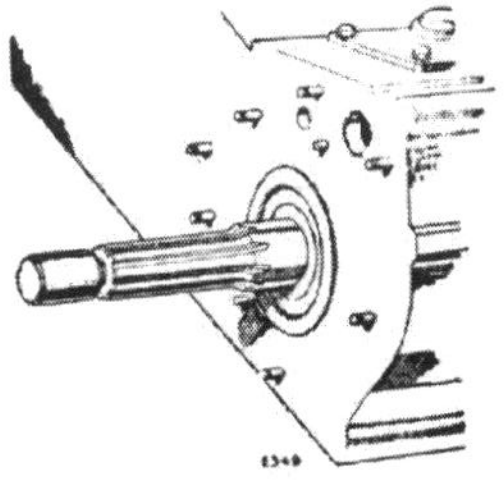

Fig. Z1-31. Protection cap, for gearbox output shaft

Part Number 600300
Spanner for gearbox mainshaft nut *
Essential when removing and replacing gearbox mainshaft nut.

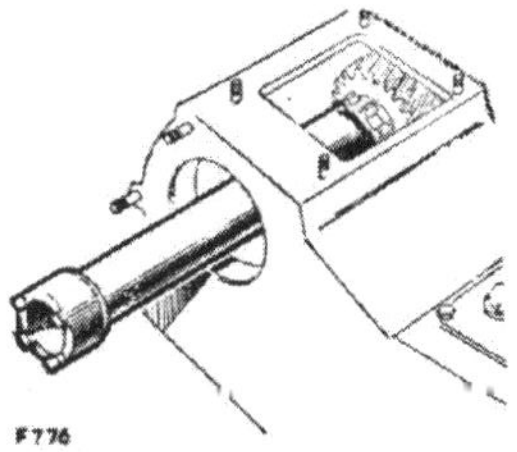

Fig. Z1-32. Spanner for gearbox mainshaft nut

Part Number 605862
Extractor, intermediate shaft, transfer box †
May be used when withdrawing the shaft.

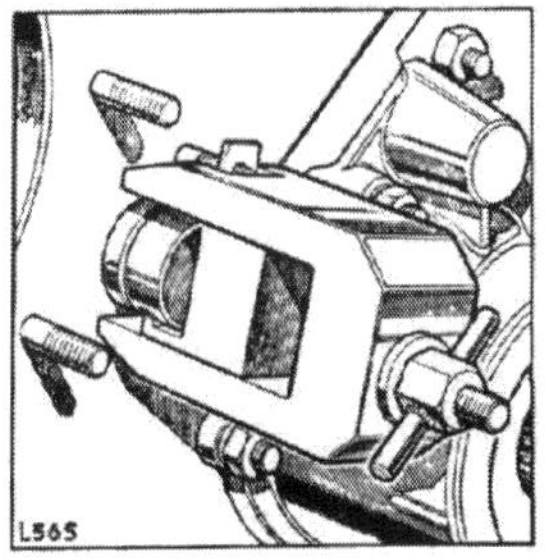

Fig. Z1-33. Extractor for transfer box intermediate shaft

SECTIONS E and F
Part Number 262757
Extractor, differential pinion rear bearing *
Required for differentials with taper roller bearings on the pinion shaft.

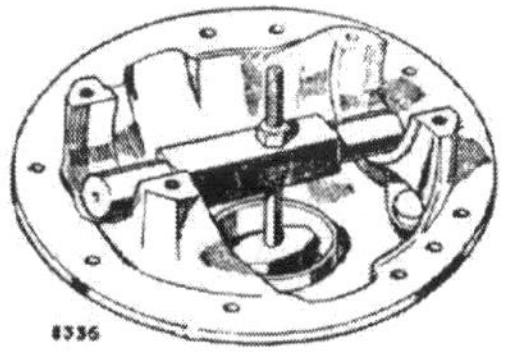

Fig. Z1-34. Pinion bearing extractor

*—Essential   †—Advantageous   ‡—Required when volume of work justifies use

469

Page 10-Z   TOOLS   Section Z—Land-Rover

Part Number 605004
Gauge for differential pinion setting *
Essential for overhauling differential.
Note: Part Number 605004 is the latest gauge, but alternatives mentioned previously may also be used.

Fig. Z1-39. Gauge, differential pinion setting

Part Number 606012
Dummy bearing, differential pinion setting (suffix 'B' axles) *

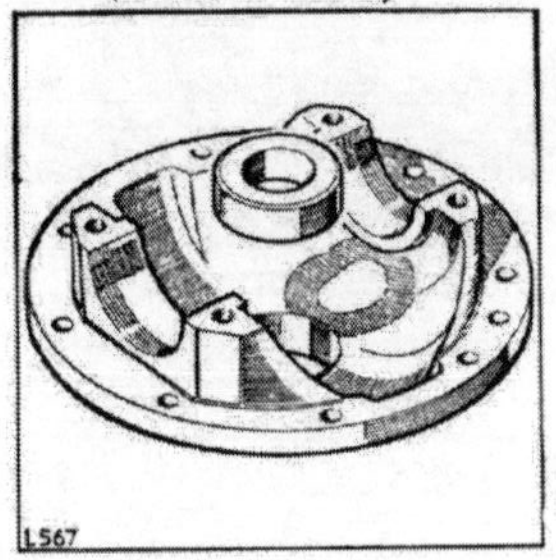

Fig. Z1-40. Dummy bearing, differential setting

Part Number 606019
Dummy bearing, differential pinion setting (suffix 'A' axles) *
Similar to Fig. Z1-40, but varying dimensionally.

Part Number 606435
Spanner for hub bearing nuts *
Essential for removing, fitting and adjusting hubs

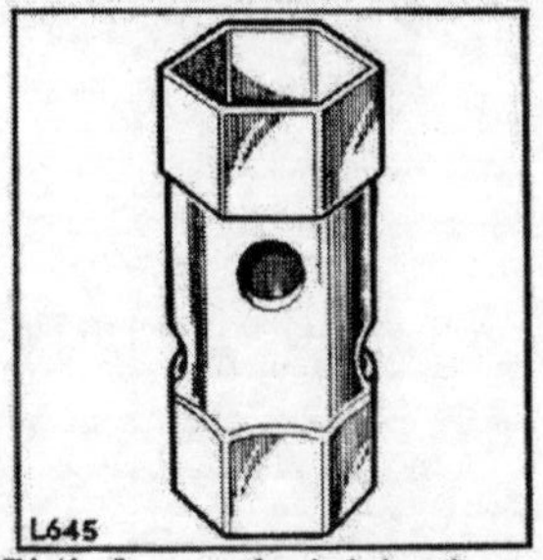

Fig. Z1-41. Spanner for hub bearing nuts

Section Z—Land-Rover   TOOLS

SECTION G—STEERING

Part Number 600000
Extractor for steering drop arm *
Enables drop arm to be removed with steering box in situ.

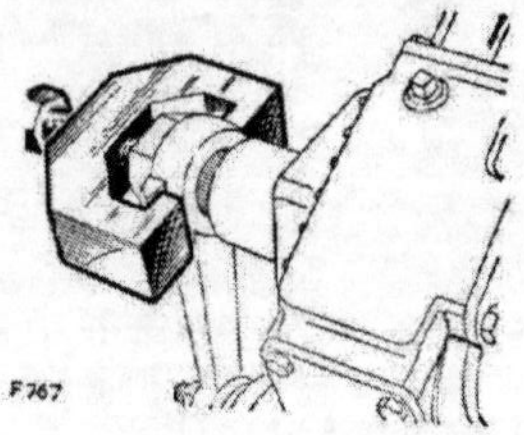

Fig. Z1-42. Extractor for steering drop arm

Part Number 600536
Tool for compressing steering relay spring *
Essential when reassembling the steering relay. Carefully follow the method set out in the Workshop Manual.

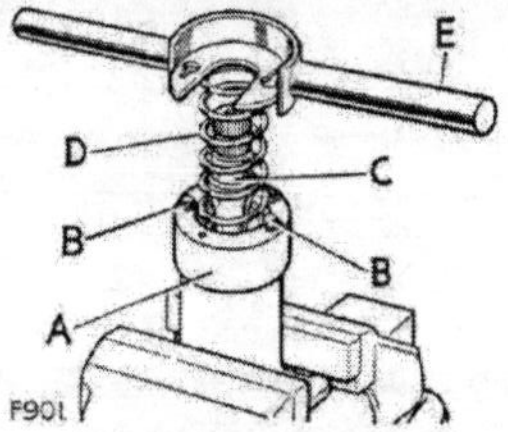

Fig. Z1-43. Tool for compressing steering relay spring

Part Number 600590
Extractor, steering ball joints *
Essential for the easy removal of steering ball joints.

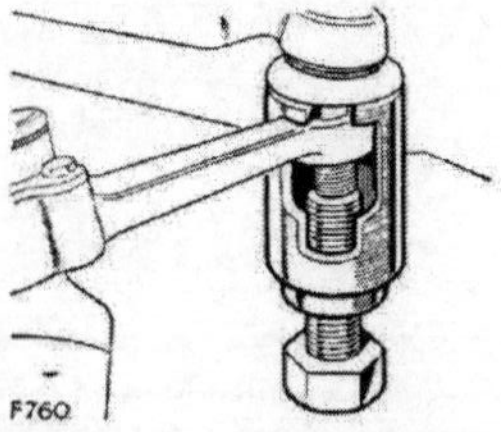

Fig. Z1-44. Extractor, steering ball joints

*—Essential   †—Advantageous   ‡—Required when volume of work justifies use

---

Page 11-Z

Part Number 276278
Safety can *
Provides a fluid reservoir for cleaning nozzle components, fitted with automatic closing lid in the event of fire.

Fig. Z1-48. Safety can

SECTION L—FUEL SYSTEM (DIESEL)

Part Number 271482
Spanner for nozzle cap †
For easy removal of the injector nozzle cap on early type injectors.

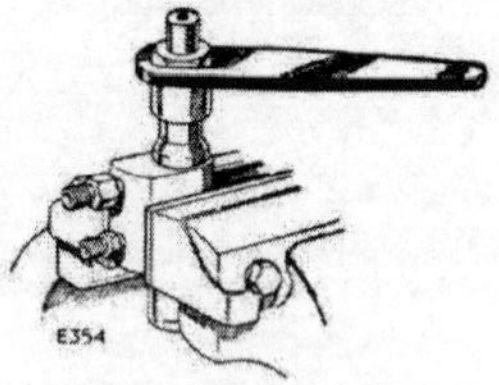

Fig. Z1-45. Nozzle cap spanner

Part Number 271483
Injector nozzle testing and setting outfit *
Essential for testing or setting injector nozzles after overhaul.

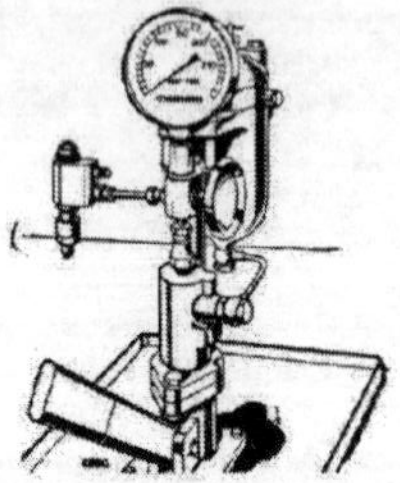

Fig. Z1-46. Injector nozzle testing and setting outfit

Part Number 271484
Injector and nozzle cleaning outfit *
A canvas holdall containing all the tools necessary for cleaning injectors and nozzles.

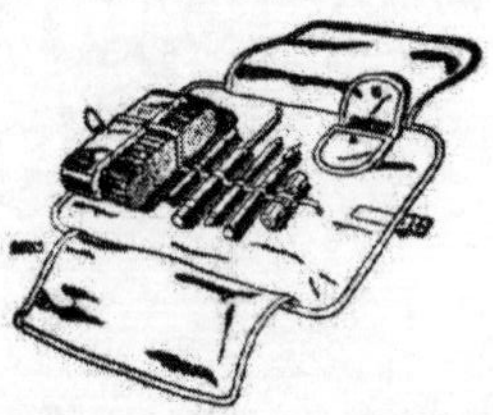

Fig. Z1-47. Injector and nozzle cleaning outfit

Part Number 278181
Flushing tool for injector nozzle *
Essential for flushing the injector nozzle.

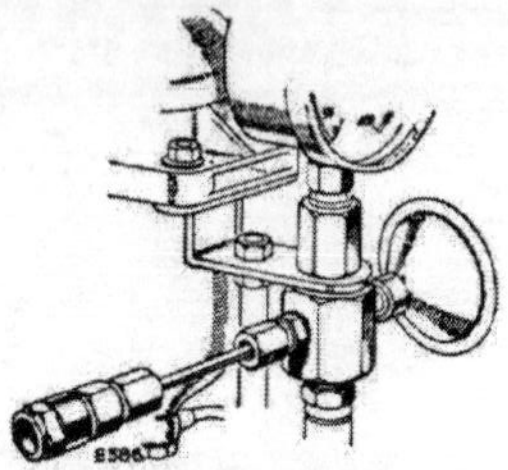

Fig. Z1-49. Injector nozzle flushing tool

Part Number 278182
Adaptor for Pintaux injector *
This adaptor is essential for testing the Pintaux injector.

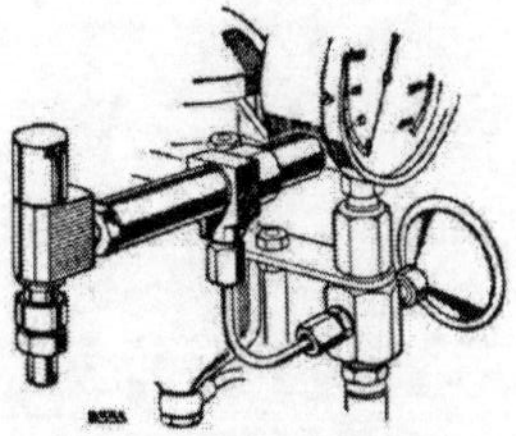

Fig. Z1-50. Injector adaptor

*—Essential   †—Advantageous   ‡—Required when volume of work justifies use

… Section Z—Land-Rover

TOOLS

SECTION N—ELECTRICAL EQUIPMENT

Part Number 263058
Forked wedge, petrol pump ‡

The pump body must be assembled with the diaphragm fully stretched, using this tool.

Note: This tool is required for the electrically driven fuel pump only, and is refered to in Section L

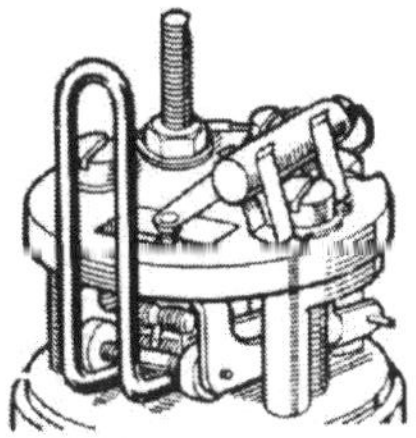

Fig. Z1-51. Forked wedge, petrol pump

SECTION Q—BODY

Part Number 248877
Spanner for locking door handle *

This spanner is essential when fitting or removing the private lock on the Land-Rover.

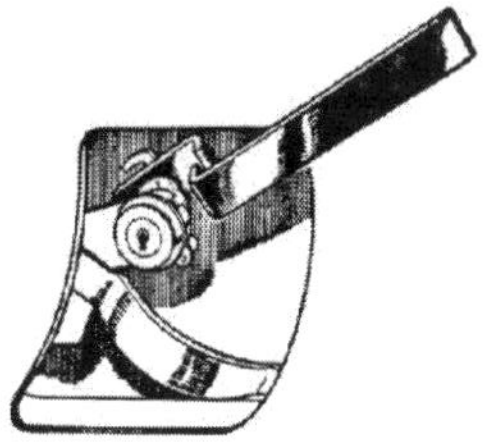

Fig. Z1-52. Door handle spanner

Part Number 262771
Insertion tool, window filler strip *

Essential for fitting weather filler strip, combines a handle projection for strip removal.

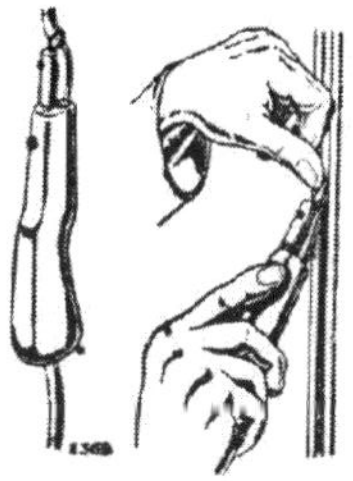

Fig. Z1-53. Filler strip tool

*—Essential †—Advantageous ‡—Required when volume of work justifies use

INDEX

TO

LAND-ROVER WORKSHOP MANUAL

Note: Section letters I, O, S, T, U, V, W, Y are not used

DETAILED INDEX

Description	Remove/Refit	Check/Overhaul
A Accelerator hand control	P1-3	—
Accelerator pedal and linkage	P1-3	—
Accelerator pump, Solex carburetter	L1-1	L1-1
Accelerator pump, Zenith carburetter	L1-2	L1-2
Adjustment, hot spot	—	A1-8
Adjusting tappets, 2¼ litre Petrol	—	A1-19
Adjusting tappets, 2.6 litre Petrol	—	A3-19
Adjusting tappets, 2¼ litre Diesel	—	A2-19
Air cleaner, 2¼ litre Petrol	A1-2	—
Air cleaner, 2.6 litre Petrol	A3-2	—
Air cleaner, 2¼ litre Diesel	A2-2	—
Alternator	A3-10	—
Alternator charging system	—	N1-27
Alternator field isolating relay	—	N1-26
Alternator output control unit	—	N1-24
Alternator warning light control	—	N1-23
Ammeter	—	N1-25
Anchor plate, 10 in. front and rear	P1-1	H1-10
Anchor plate, 11 in. front	E1-5; F1-4	H1-10A
Anchor plate, 11 in. rear, Series II	F1-4	H1-10B
Anchor plate, 11 in. rear, Series IIA	E1-5	H1-10C
Anchor plate, transmission brake	C1-4	H1-11
Apron panel, front, 2¼ litre Petrol	A1-3	—
Apron panel, front, 2.6 litre Petrol	A3-3	—
Apron panel, front, 2¼ litre Diesel	A2-3	—
Axle case breather	E1-2; E1-3A	E1-3; E1-3A
Axle case oil seal, front	F1-4	F1-5
Axle, front	E1-15, F1-18	—
Axle, rear	F1-18	F1-18
Axle shaft, front	F1-19	E1-15
Axle shaft, rear	E1-16	F1-7
Axle stub, front	F1-6	E1-3; E1-3A
Axle stub, rear	E1-2; E1-3A	F1-5
	E1-5	E1-6
B Ball joints, steering linkage	—	G1-6
Battery	N1-1	N1-1
Battery charging system with alternator	—	N1-26
Battery carrier	—	—
Bearing, camshaft, 2¼ litre Petrol	A1-38	A1-38
Bearing, camshaft, 2.6 litre Petrol	A3-36	A3-36
Bearing, camshaft, 2¼ litre Diesel	A2-38	A2-38
Bearing, clutch withdrawal unit	C1-14	C1-15
Bearing, connecting rod, 2¼ litre Petrol	A1-33	A1-34
Bearing, connecting rod, 2.6 litre Petrol	A3-32	A3-33
Bearing, connecting rod, 2¼ litre Diesel	A2-33	A2-34
Bearing, gearbox, layshaft	—	C1-21; C1-25

Description	Remove/Refit	Check/Overhaul
B Bearing, gearbox, front output shaft	C1-9	C1-10
Bearing, gearbox, mainshaft	C1-22	C1-23
Bearing, gearbox, primary pinion	C1-17	C1-17
Bearing, main, 2¼ litre Petrol	A1-35	A1-36
Bearing, main, 2.6 litre Petrol	A3-34	A3-35
Bearing, main, 2¼ litre Diesel	A2-35	A2-36
Bearing, transfer gearbox, intermediate gear	C1-7	C1-8; C1-8A
Bearing, transfer gearbox, mainshaft	—	C1-8; C1-8A
Bearing, transfer gearbox, output shaft	C1-7	C1-8; C1-8A
Belt, fan, 2¼ litre Petrol	A1-10	—
Belt, fan, 2.6 litre Petrol	A3-10	—
Belt, fan, 2¼ litre Diesel	A2-10	—
Bell housing	C1-16	C1-17
Bleeding brake system	—	H1-1
Board, tail	Q1-12	—
Body, rear	Q1-14	—
Body, sides	Q1-13	—
Bonnet	Q1-12	—
Bonnet panel, 2¼ litre Petrol	Q1-1	—
Bonnet panel, 2.6 litre Petrol	A1-1	—
Bonnet panel, 2¼ litre Diesel	A2-1	—
Brake and clutch fluid reservoir	H1-3	—
Brake and clutch supply tank	H1-3	—
Brake cylinder, master, 'CV' type	H1-5	H1-6
Brake cylinder, master, 'CB' type	H1-7	H1-8
Brake cylinder, master, 'CV' type, with servo	H1-5A	H1-6A
Brake cylinder, wheel, 10 in. brakes, front and rear	H1-10	H1-10A
Brake cylinder, wheel, 11 in. brakes, front	H1-10A	H1-10A
Brake cylinder, wheel, 11 in. brakes, rear, Series II	H1-10B	H1-10B
Brake cylinder, wheel, 11 in. brakes, rear, Series IIA	H1-10C	H1-10C
Brake drum, 10 in., front and rear	H1-10	H1-10A
Brake drum, 11 in., front	H1-10A	H1-10A
Brake drum, 11 in., rear, Series II	E1-5	H1-10B
Brake drum, 11 in., rear, Series IIA	E1-5	H1-10C
Brake expander, transmission brake	C1-4	H1-11
Brake drum, hand	H1-11	H1-11
Brake, hand, LHStg	C1-4	H1-11
Brake, hand, RHStg	H1-13	H1-13
Brake pedal	H1-13	H1-13
Brake pedal used with mechanical servo	H1-4	H1-4
Brake pipes	H1-4A	H1-4A
Brake shoe, 10 in. brakes, front and rear	H1-9	—
Brake shoe, 11 in. brakes, front	H1-10	H1-12
Brake shoe, 11 in. brakes, rear, Series II	H1-10A	H1-12
	H1-10B	H1-12

DETAILED INDEX

Description	Operation Number Remove/Refit	Operation Number Check/Overhaul
B		
Brake shoe, 11 in. brakes, rear, Series IIA	H1-10C	H1-12
Brake shoe, transmission brake	H1-11	H1-12
Brake servo unit, hydraulic	H1-14	H1-15
Brake servo unit, mechanical	H1-14A	H1-15A
Brake stop lamps	N1-4	—
Brake stop lamp switch	N1-7	—
Brake, transmission	C1-4	H1-11
Breather box, 2.6 litre Petrol	A3-14	A3-14
Breather, gearbox	C1-2	—
Bumper, front	J1-2	—
C		
Cable harness, headlamp, 2¼ litre Petrol	A1-5	—
Cable harness, headlamp, 2.6 litre Petrol	A3-5	—
Cable harness, headlamp, 2¼ litre Diesel	A2-5	—
Cable, speedometer	P1-2	—
Camshaft, 2¼ litre Petrol	A1-37	A1-37
Camshaft, 2.6 litre Petrol	A3-36	A3-36
Camshaft, 2¼ litre Diesel	A2-37	A2-37
Camshaft bearing, 2¼ litre Petrol	A1-38	A1-38
Camshaft bearing, 2.6 litre Petrol	A3-36	A3-36
Camshaft bearing, 2¼ litre Diesel	A2-38	A2-38
Camshaft chain, 2¼ litre Petrol	A1-27	—
Camshaft chain, 2.6 litre Petrol	A3-25	—
Camshaft chain, 2¼ litre Diesel	A2-27	—
Carburetter, 2¼ litre Petrol	A1-6	L1-1; L1-2
Carburetter, 2.6 litre Petrol	A3-6	L1-3; L1-4
Carburetter, Solex, 2¼ litre Petrol	A1-6	L1-1
Carburetter, Zenith, 2¼ litre Petrol	A1-6	L1-2
Carburetter, Stromberg, 2.6 litre Petrol	A3-6	L1-3
Carburetter, SU, 2.6 litre Petrol	A3-6	L1-4
Casing, transfer box	C1-7	C1-8; C1-8A
Chain, timing, 2¼ litre Petrol	A1-27	—
Chain, timing, 2.6 litre Petrol	A3-25	—
Chain, timing, 2¼ litre Diesel	A2-27	—
Change speed lever, main	C1-11	C1-12
Change speed lever, transfer, 2¼ litre Petrol	A1-4	C1-7
Change speed lever, transfer, 2.6 litre Petrol	A3-4	C1-7
Change speed lever, transfer, 2¼ litre Diesel	A2-4	C1-7
Chassis frame	—	J1-1
Check strap, front door	Q1-5	—
Check strap, rear axle	E1-8	—
Clutch cylinder, master	B1-5	B1-6
Clutch, 2¼ litre Petrol	A1-31	B1-1
Clutch, 2.6 litre Petrol	A3-30	B1-1
Clutch, 2¼ litre Diesel	A2-31	B1-1
Clutch pedal	B1-7	—

DETAILED INDEX

Description	Operation Number Remove/Refit	Operation Number Check/Overhaul
C		
Clutch slave cylinder	B1-3	B1-4
Clutch withdrawal unit	C1-14	C1-15
Coil, ignition, 2¼ litre Petrol	N1-12	—
Coil, ignition, 2.6 litre Petrol	N1-12	—
Connecting rod, 2¼ litre Petrol	A1-33	A1-34
Connecting rod, 2.6 litre Petrol	A3-32	A3-33
Connecting rod, 2¼ litre Diesel	A2-33	A2-34
Connecting rod bearing, 2¼ litre Petrol	A1-33	A1-34
Connecting rod bearing, 2.6 litre Petrol	A3-32	A3-33
Connecting rod bearing, 2¼ litre Diesel	A2-33	A2-34
Control box	N1-16	N1-16
Cover, front, 2¼ litre Petrol	A1-25	—
Cover, front, 2.6 litre Petrol	A3-23	—
Cover, front, 2¼ litre Diesel	A2-25	—
Cover, gearbox	Q1-6; Q1-7	—
Cover, side, 2¼ litre Petrol	A1-14	A1-36
Cover, side, 2.6 litre Petrol	A3-26	A3-35
Cover, side, 2¼ litre Diesel	A2-14	A2-36
Crankshaft, 2¼ litre Petrol	A1-35	—
Crankshaft, 2.6 litre Petrol	A3-34	—
Crankshaft, 2¼ litre Diesel	A2-35	—
Crankshaft bearing oil seal, 2¼ litre Petrol	A1-32	—
Crankshaft bearing oil seal, 2.6 litre Petrol	A3-31	—
Crankshaft bearing oil seal, 2¼ litre Diesel	A2-35	—
Cylinder, brake, master, 'CV' type	H1-5	H1-6
Cylinder, brake, master, 'CB' type	H1-7	H1-8
Cylinder, brake, master, 'CV' type, with servo	H1-5A	H1-6A
Cylinder, brake, wheel, 10 in. brakes, front and rear	H1-10	H1-10
Cylinder, brake, wheel, 11 in. brakes, front	H1-10A	H1-10A
Cylinder, brake, wheel, 11 in. brakes, rear, Series II	H1-10B	H1-10B
Cylinder, brake, wheel, 11 in. brakes, rear, Series IIA	H1-10C	H1-10C
Cylinder block, 2¼ litre Petrol	—	A1-38
Cylinder block, 2.6 litre Petrol	—	A3-37
Cylinder block, 2¼ litre Diesel	—	A2-38
Cylinder head, 2¼ litre Petrol	A1-22	A1-23
Cylinder head, 2.6 litre Petrol	A3-21	A3-22
Cylinder head, 2¼ litre Diesel	A2-22	A2-23
Cylinder liner, 2¼ litre Petrol	A1-38	—
Cylinder liner, 2.6 litre Petrol	A3-37	—
Cylinder liner, 2¼ litre Diesel	A2-38	—
Cylinder reboring, 2¼ litre Petrol	—	A1-38
Cylinder reboring, 2.6 litre Petrol	—	A3-37
Cylinder reboring, 2¼ litre Diesel	—	A2-38
D		
Dash	Q1-8	Q1-9
Data, technical—refer to end of each Section	—	—

473

DETAILED INDEX

Description	Operation Number Remove/Refit	Check/Overhaul
D Decarbonising, 2¼ litre Petrol	—	A1-23
Decarbonising, 2.6 litre Petrol	—	A3-22
Decarbonising, 2¼ litre Diesel	—	A2-23
Diagnosis, fault—refer to end of each Section	—	—
Differential, Rover type	E1-13; F1-16	E1-14
Differential, ENV type	E1-13; F1-16	E1-14A
Dipper switch	N1-9	—
Dipstick, gearbox	C1-2	—
Distributor, 2¼ litre Petrol	A1-18	N1-13
Distributor, 2.6 litre Petrol	A3-18	N1-13
Distributor pump, 2¼ litre Diesel	A2-17	A2-17
Distributor pump timing, 2¼ litre Diesel	—	—
Door hinge	Q1-5	—
Door lock	Q1-5	—
Doors and fittings	Q1-5	—
Door, rear, 88 Station Wagon	Q1-15	—
Door, rear, 109 Station Wagon	Q1-15	—
Door, rear side, 109 Station Wagon	Q1-5	—
Drag link	G1-4	—
Drop arm	G1-7	—
Drum, foot brake	E1-5; F1-4	H1-10, A, B & C
Drum, hand brake	C1-4	H1-11
Dynamo, 2¼ litre Petrol	A1-10	N1-22
Dynamo, 2.6 litre Petrol	A3-10	N1-22
Dynamo, 2¼ litre Diesel	A2-10	N1-22
E Engine hand speed control, Diesel	P1-3	—
Engine, 2¼ litre Petrol	A1-5	—
Engine, 2.6 litre Petrol	A3-5	—
Engine, 2¼ litre Diesel	A2-5	—
Engine, side cover, 2¼ litre Petrol	A1-14	—
Engine, side cover, 2¼ litre Diesel	A2-14	—
Engine stop control, Diesel	P1-5	—
Engine support, front, 2¼ litre Petrol	A1-5	—
Engine support, front, 2.6 litre Petrol	A3-5	—
Engine support, front, 2¼ litre Diesel	A2-5	—
Engine support, rear	C1-3	—
Exhaust manifold, 2¼ litre Petrol	A1-7	A1-8
Exhaust manifold, 2.6 litre Petrol	A3-8	—
Exhaust manifold, 2¼ litre Diesel	A2-8	—
Exhaust pipe and silencer, 2¼ litre	M1-1	—
Exhaust pipe and silencer, 2.6 litre	M1-2	—
Exhaust valve, 2¼ litre Petrol	A1-23	A1-23
Exhaust valve, 2.6 litre Petrol	A3-22	A3-22
Exhaust valve, 2¼ litre Diesel	A2-23	A2-23

Description	Operation Number Remove/Refit	Check/Overhaul
F Fan, 2¼ litre Petrol	A1-3	—
Fan, 2.6 litre Petrol	A3-3	—
Fan, 2¼ litre Diesel	A2-3	—
Fan belt tension, 2¼ litre Petrol	A1-10	—
Fan belt tension, 2.6 litre Petrol	A3-10	—
Fan belt tension, 2¼ litre Diesel	A2-10	—
Filler cap, fuel	L1-8; L1-9	L1-15
Filter, fuel, 2¼ litre Diesel	A2-7	—
Filter, oil, external, 2¼ litre Petrol	A1-16	—
Filter, oil, external, 2.6 litre Petrol	A3-16	—
Filter, oil, external, 2¼ litre Diesel	A2-16	—
Flasher lamp	N1-5	—
Floor, front	Q1-6; Q1-7	—
Floor, front, 2¼ litre Petrol	A1-4	—
Floor, front, 2¼ litre Diesel	A2-4	—
Floor, rear	Q1-13	—
Flywheel, 2¼ litre Petrol	A1-31	A1-39
Flywheel, 2.6 litre Petrol	A3-30	A3-38
Flywheel, 2¼ litre Diesel	A2-31	A2-39
Flywheel housing, 2¼ litre Petrol	A1-32	C1-10
Flywheel housing, 2.6 litre Petrol	A3-31	C1-10
Flywheel housing, 2¼ litre Diesel	A2-32	C1-10
Flywheel reclamation, 2¼ litre Petrol	—	A1-39
Flywheel reclamation, 2.6 litre Petrol	—	A3-38
Flywheel reclamation, 2¼ litre Diesel	—	A2-39
Four wheel drive selector, 2¼ litre Petrol	A1-4	C1-10
Four wheel drive selector, 2.6 litre Petrol	A3-4	C1-10
Four wheel drive selector, 2¼ litre Diesel	A2-4	C1-10
Frame, chassis	—	J1-1
Front apron panel, 2¼ litre Petrol	A1-3	—
Front apron panel, 2.6 litre Petrol	A3-3	—
Front apron panel, 2¼ litre Diesel	A2-3	—
Front bumper	J1-2	—
Front cover, 2¼ litre Petrol	A1-25	—
Front cover, 2.6 litre Petrol	A3-23	—
Front cover, 2¼ litre Diesel	A2-25	—
Front exhaust pipe, 2¼ litre	M1-1	—
Front exhaust pipe, 2.6 litre	M1-2	—
Front shock absorber	F1-11	F1-11
Front wheel alignment	—	G1-2
Front wing	Q1-3	—
Fuel filter, 2¼ litre Diesel	A2-7	L1-15
Fuel filter, Petrol	L1-12	—
Fuel injector, 2¼ litre Diesel	L1-15	L1-16
Fuel pump, 2¼ litre Petrol	A1-13	L1-5

DETAILED INDEX

Description	Remove/Refit	Check/Overhaul
F Fuel pump, electric, 2.6 litre Petrol	L1-6	L1-7
Fuel pump, 2¼ litre Diesel	A2-13	L1-5
Fuel pump, mechanical	A1-13; A2-13	L1-5
Fuel pump, electric	L1-6	L1-7
Fuel sedimenter, 2¼ litre Diesel	L1-15	—
Fuel warning light, Diesel	P1-1; P1-1A	—
Fuse box	N1-15	—
G Gearbox breather	C1-2	—
Gears, main gearbox, layshaft	C1-20	C1-21
Gears, main gearbox, mainshaft	C1-22	C1-23
Gears, transfer box	C1-7	C1-8; C1-8A
Glass, cab	Q1-11	—
Glass, rear door	Q1-15	Q1-11
Glass, side door	Q1-5	Q1-11
Glass, side, hard top	Q1-12	Q1-11
Glass, side, Station Wagon	Q1-14	Q1-11
Glass, windscreen	Q1-4	—
Grille panel, radiator, 2¼ litre Petrol	A1-3	—
Grille panel, radiator, 2.6 litre Petrol	A3-3	—
Grille panel, radiator, 2¼ litre Diesel	A2-3	—
Grille, radiator	Q1-2	—
Gudgeon pin, 2¼ litre Petrol	A1-34	A1-34
Gudgeon pin, 2.6 litre Petrol	A3-33	A3-33
Gudgeon pin, 2¼ litre Diesel	A2-34	A2-34
Guide tappet, 2¼ litre Petrol	A1-24	—
Guide tappet, 2¼ litre Diesel	A2-24	—
H Hand brake lever	H1-13	H1-13
Hand brake, transmission	C1-4	H1-11
Hand control, engine speed, Diesel	P1-3	—
Headlamps	N1-2	N1-2
Heater plugs, Diesel	N1-14	N1-14
Heater plug and starter switch, Diesel	N1-8	—
Horn	A2-23	N1-14
Horn button	N1-18	N1-18
Hot plug, 2¼ litre Diesel	N1-17; G1-3	—
Hot spot adjustment, 2¼ litre Petrol	A2-23	A1-8
Housing, clutch withdrawal	C1-14	C1-15
Housing, front output	C1-9	C1-10
Housing, rear mainshaft bearing	C1-7	C1-8; C1-8A
Housing, swivel pin	F1-9	F1-10
Housing, thermostat, 2¼ litre Petrol	A1-12	—
Housing, thermostat, 2.6 litre Petrol	A3-12	—

DETAILED INDEX

Description	Remove/Refit	Check/Overhaul
Housing, thermostat, 2¼ litre Petrol	A2-12	—
Hub, front	F1-4	F1-5
Hub, rear	E1-5	E1-6
I Ignition timing, 2¼ litre Petrol	—	A1-17
Ignition timing, 2.6 litre Petrol	—	A3-17
Injector, fuel, 2¼ litre Diesel	A2-6	L1-16
Inlet manifold, 2¼ litre Petrol	A1-7	A1-8
Inlet manifold, 2¼ litre Diesel	A2-8	—
Inlet valve, 2¼ litre Petrol	A1-23	A1-23
Inlet valve, 2.6 litre Petrol	A3-22	A3-22
Inlet valve, 2¼ litre Diesel	A2-23	A2-23
Inner tube	R1-1	—
Instruments	P1-1; P1-1A	—
L Lamp, head	N1-2	—
Lamp, number plate	N1-6	—
Lamp, rear	N1-4	—
Lamp, side	N1-3	—
Lamp, stop	N1-4	—
Layshaft	C1-20	C1-21
Level unit, fuel tank, side mounted	L1-10	—
Level unit, fuel tank, rear mounted	L1-11	—
Lever, change speed, main	C1-11	C1-12
Lever, change speed, transfer	C1-7	—
Lever, clutch	B1-9	—
Lever, hand brake	H1-13	H1-13
Lever, hand speed control, Diesel	P1-3	—
Lever, steering	F1-10	—
Lever, steering relay	G1-9	—
Light, warning, instrument panel	P1-1; P1-1A	—
Liner, cylinder, 2¼ litre Petrol	A1-38	—
Liner, cylinder, 2.6 litre Petrol	A3-37	—
Liner, cylinder, 2¼ litre Diesel	A2-38	—
Link, drag	G1-4	—
Lock, door	Q1-5	—
Longitudinal tube, steering	G1-5	—
Lubrication	Section X	—
M Main bearing, crankshaft, 2¼ litre Petrol	A1-35	A1-36
Main bearing, crankshaft, 2.6 litre Petrol	A3-34	A3-35
Main bearing, crankshaft, 2¼ litre Diesel	A2-35	A2-36
Mainshaft, bearing housing, rear	C1-7	C1-8; C1-8A
Mainshaft, gearbox	C1-22	C1-23
Manifold, exhaust, 2¼ litre Petrol	A1-7	—

DETAILED INDEX

Description	Remove/Refit	Check/Overhaul
M Manifold, exhaust, 2.6 litre Petrol	A3-8	—
Manifold, exhaust, 2¼ litre Diesel	A2-8	—
Manifold, inlet, 2¼ litre Petrol	A1-7	A1-8
Manifold, inlet, 2¼ litre Diesel	A2-8	—
Master cylinder, clutch	B1-5	B1-6
Master cylinder, 'CV' type	H1-5	H1-6
Master cylinder, 'CB' type	H1-7	H1-8
Master cylinder, 'CV' type, with servo	H1-5A	H1-6A
Mixture control, Petrol	P1-4	—
Mounting, engine, 2¼ litre Petrol	A1-5	—
Mounting, engine, 2.6 litre Petrol	A3-5	—
Mounting, engine, 2¼ litre Diesel	A2-5	—
N Nozzle, fuel injector, Diesel	A2-6	L1-16
Number plate lamp	N1-6	—
O Oil filter, external, 2¼ litre Petrol	A1-16	—
Oil filter, external, 2.6 litre Petrol	A3-16	—
Oil filter, external, 2¼ litre Diesel	A2-16	—
Oil gallery pipe, 2.6 litre Petrol	A3-21	—
Oil strainer, 2¼ litre Petrol	A1-30	A1-30
Oil strainer, 2.6 litre Petrol	A3-29	A3-29
Oil strainer, 2¼ litre Diesel	A2-30	A2-30
Oil pressure switch	A3-7	—
Output shaft, four wheel drive	P1-1; P1-1A	—
Oil pump, 2¼ litre Petrol	A1-29	—
Oil pump, 2.6 litre Petrol	A3-28	—
Oil pump, 2¼ litre Diesel	A2-29	—
Oil seal, crankshaft bearing, 2¼ litre Petrol	A1-32	—
Oil seal, crankshaft bearing, 2.6 litre Petrol	A3-31	—
Oil seal, crankshaft bearing, 2¼ litre Diesel	A2-32	—
Output shaft, four wheel drive	C1-9	C1-10
P Pedal, accelerator	P1-3	—
Pedal, brake	H1-4	H1-4
Pedal, brake, with mechanical servo	H1-4A	H1-4A
Pedal, clutch	B1-7	L1-5
Petrol pump, mechanical, 2¼ litre	A1-13	L1-7
Petrol pump, electric, 2.6 litre	L1-6	—
Petrol sediment bowl	L1-12	—
Petrol tank, side mounted	L1-8	—
Petrol tank, rear mounted	L1-9	—
Petrol tank level unit, side tank	L1-10	—
Petrol tank level unit, rear tank	L1-11	—
Pipe, brake	H1-9	—

Description	Remove/Refit	Check/Overhaul
P Piston, 2¼ litre Petrol	A1-33	A1-34
Piston, 2.6 litre Petrol	A3-32	A3-33
Piston, 2¼ litre Diesel	A2-33	A2-34
Piston ring, 2¼ litre Petrol	A1-34	A1-34
Piston ring, 2.6 litre Petrol	A3-33	A3-33
Piston ring, 2¼ litre Diesel	A2-34	A2-34
Plug, heater, 2¼ litre Diesel	N1-14	N1-14
Priming fuel system, Diesel	—	L1-14
Propeller shaft, front	D1-2	D1-3
Propeller shaft, rear	D1-2	D1-3
Pump, distributor, 2¼ litre Diesel	A2-17	—
Pump, distributor, timing, 2¼ litre Diesel	—	A2-17
Pump, water, 2¼ litre Petrol	A1-11	K1-2
Pump, water, 2.6 litre Petrol	A3-11	K1-2
Pump, water, 2¼ litre Diesel	A2-11	K1-2
Push rod, tappet, 2¼ litre Petrol	A1-22	—
Push rod, tappet, 2.6 litre Petrol	A3-21	—
Push rod, tappet, 2¼ litre Diesel	A2-22	—
R Radiator grille panel, 2¼ litre Petrol	A1-3	—
Radiator grille panel, 2.6 litre Petrol	A3-3	—
Radiator grille panel, 2¼ litre Diesel	A2-3	—
Rear axle	E1-16	E1-3; E1-3A
Rear axle casing	E1-15	E1-3; E1-3A
Rear axle shaft	E1-2; E1-3A	—
Rear body	Q1-13	—
Rear door	Q1-15	—
Rear side doors	Q1-5	—
Reboring, cylinders, 2¼ litre Petrol	—	A1-38
Reboring, cylinders, 2.6 litre Petrol	—	A3-37
Reboring, cylinders, 2¼ litre Diesel	—	A2-38
Relay unit, steering	G1-9	G1-10
Relief valve, oil, 2¼ litre Petrol	A1-30	—
Relief valve, oil, 2.6 litre Petrol	A3-29	—
Relief valve, oil, 2¼ litre Diesel	A2-30	—
Reverse gear	C1-25	C1-25
Reverse selector shaft, stop	—	C1-13; C1-18
Rings, piston, 2¼ litre Petrol	A1-34	A1-34
Rings, piston, 2.6 litre Petrol	A3-33	A3-33
Rings piston, 2¼ litre Diesel	A2-34	A2-34
Road spring, front	F1-12	F1-13
Road spring, rear	E1-9	E1-10
Road wheel	R1-1; R1-2	—
Rocker shaft, 2¼ litre Petrol	A1-20	—
Rocker shaft, side, 2.6 litre Petrol	A3-26	—

DETAILED INDEX

Description	Remove/Refit	Check/Overhaul
R Rocker shaft, top, 2.6 litre Petrol	A3-20	—
Rocker shaft, 2¼ litre Diesel	A2-20	—
Rod, track	G1-4	—
Roof, cab	Q1-11	—
Roof, hard top	Q1-12	—
Roof, Station Wagon	Q1-14	—
S Seat base	Q1-10	—
Sediment bowl, Petrol	L1-12	—
Sedimenter, Diesel	L1-15	—
Selector, four wheel drive, 2¼ litre Petrol	A1-4	C1-10
Selector, four wheel drive, 2.6 litre Petrol	A3-4	C1-10
Selector, four wheel drive, 2¼ litre Diesel	A2-4	C1-10
Selector shaft adjustment	—	C1-18
Servo unit, hydraulic, brakes	H1-14	H1-15
Servo unit, machanical, brakes	H1-14A	H1-15A
Shackle pin	E1-9; F1-12	E1-10; F1-13
Shaft, front axle	F1-6	F1-7
Shaft, rear axle	E1-2; E1-3A	E1-3; E1-3A
Shaft, gearbox selector	C1-18	C1-19
Shaft, output, four wheel drive	C1-9	C1-10
Shaft, propeller, front	D1-2	D1-3
Shaft, propeller, rear	D1-2	D1-3
Shock absorber	E1-7	E1-7
Shoe, 10 in. brakes, front and rear	H1-10	H1-12
Shoe, 11 in. brakes, front	H1-10A	H1-12
Shoe, 11 in. brakes, rear, Series II	H1-10B	H1-12
Shoe, 11 in. brakes, rear, Series IIA	H1-10C	H1-12
Shoe, transmission brake	H1-11	H1-12
Side lamp	N1-3	—
Side screen	Q1-5	—
Silencer, exhaust, 2¼ litre	M1-1	—
Silencer, exhaust, 2.6 litre	M1-2	—
Slave cylinder, clutch	B1-3	B1-4
Solenoid, starter, 2¼ litre Diesel	N1-21	N1-21
Speedometer	P1-1; P1-1A	—
Speedometer cable	P1-2	—
Spring, road, front	F1-12	F1-13
Spring, road, rear	E1-9	E1-10
Starter motor, 2¼ litre Petrol	A1-9	N1-20
Starter motor, 2.6 litre Petrol	A3-9	N1-20
Starter motor, 2¼ litre Diesel	A2-9	N1-21
Steering ball joints	—	G1-6
Steering box	G1-7	G1-8
Steering box adjustment	—	G1-8

Description	Remove/Refit	Check/Overhaul
Steering column	G1-7	G1-8
Steering drag link	G1-4	—
Steering longitudinal arm	G1-5	—
Steering relay	G1-9	G1-10
Steering track rod	G1-4	—
Steering wheel	G1-3	—
Stop lamp	N1-4	—
Stop lever, Diesel	P1-5	—
Strainer, oil, 2¼ litre Petrol	A1-30	F1-5
Strainer, oil, 2.6 litre Petrol	A3-29	—
Strainer, oil, 2¼ litre Diesel	A2-30	E1-6
Stub axle, front	F1-4	—
Stub axle, rear	E1-5	—
Sump, crankcase, 2¼ litre Petrol	A1-28	—
Sump, crankcase, 2.6 litre Petrol	A3-27	—
Sump, crankcase, 2¼ litre Diesel	A2-28	—
Supply tank, brake and clutch	H1-3	—
Switch, lamps	P1-1; P1-1A	—
Switch, panel lights	P1-1; P1-1A	—
Switch, starter, Petrol	N1-8	—
Switch, starter and heater plug, Diesel	N1-8	—
Switch, stop lamp	N1-7	—
Swivel pins	F1-9	F1-10
T Tailboard	Q1-12	—
Tail lamp	N1-4	—
Tank, brake and clutch supply	H1-3	—
Tank, fuel, side mounted	L1-8	—
Tank, fuel, rear mounted	L1-9	—
Tappet adjustment, 2¼ litre Petrol	—	A1-19
Tappet adjustment, 2.6 litre Petrol	—	A3-19
Tappet adjustment, 2¼ litre Diesel	—	A2-19
Tappet guide, 2¼ litre Petrol	A1-24	—
Tappet guide, 2¼ litre Diesel	A2-24	—
Technical data—refer to end of each Section	—	—
Thermostat, 2¼ litre Petrol	A1-12	K1-1
Thermostat, 2.6 litre Petrol	A3-12	K1-1
Thermostat, 2¼ litre Diesel	A2-12	K1-1
Timing chain, 2¼ litre Petrol	A1-27	—
Timing chain, 2.6 litre Petrol	A3-25	—
Timing chain, 2¼ litre Diesel	A2-27	—
Timing chain tensioner, 2¼ litre Petrol	A1-26	—
Timing chain tensioner, 2.6 litre Petrol	A3-24	—
Timing chain tensioner, 2¼ litre Diesel	A2-26	—
Timing, distributor pump, 2¼ litre Diesel	—	A2-17

477

DETAILED INDEX

Description	Operation Number Remove/Refit	Operation Number Check/Overhaul
T Timing, ignition, 2¼ litre Petrol	—	A1-17
Timing, ignition, 2.6 litre Petrol	—	A3-17
Timing, valve, 2¼ litre Petrol	—	A1-27
Timing, valve, 2.6 litre Petrol	—	A3-25
Timing, valve, 2¼ litre Diesel	—	A2-27
Toe-in, front wheels	—	G1-2
Tools	Section Z	—
Track rod	G1-4	—
Transmission brake	C1-4	H1-11
Tyre, road wheel	R1-1; R1-2	—
U Universal joints, front axle	F1-6	F1-7
Universal joint, propeller shafts	D1-2	D1-3
V Valve guide, exhaust, 2¼ litre Petrol	A1-23	A1-23
Valve guide, exhaust, 2.6 litre Petrol	A3-22	A3-22
Valve guide, exhaust, 2¼ litre Diesel	A2-23	A2-23
Valve guide, inlet, 2¼ litre Petrol	A1-23	A1-23
Valve guide, inlet, 2.6 litre Petrol	A3-22	A3-22
Valve guide, inlet, 2¼ litre Diesel	A2-23	A2-23
Valve seats, 2¼ litre Petrol	A1-23	A1-23
Valve seats, 2.6 litre Petrol	A3-22	A3-22
Valve seats, 2¼ litre Diesel	A2-23	A2-23
Valve timing, 2¼ litre Petrol	—	A1-27
Valve timing, 2.6 litre Petrol	—	A3-25
Valve timing, 2¼ litre Diesel	—	A2-27
Ventilator, windscreen	Q1-9	—
Vertical drive shaft gear, 2¼ litre Petrol	A1-18	—
Vertical drive shaft gear, 2¼ litre Diesel	A2-18	—
Voltage control box	N1-16	—
W Warning light, fuel, Diesel	P1-1; P1-1A	—
Water pump, 2¼ litre Petrol	A1-11	K1-2
Water pump, 2.6 litre Petrol	A3-11	K1-2
Water pump, 2¼ litre Diesel	A2-11	K1-2
Water temperature gauge	P1-1; P1-1A	—
Wheel alignment, front	—	G1-2
Wheel cylinder, 10 in. brakes, front and rear	H1-10	H1-10
Wheel cylinder, 11 in. brakes, front	H1-10A	H1-10A
Wheel cylinder, 11 in. brakes, rear, Series II	H1-10B	H1-10B
Wheel cylinder, 11 in. brakes, rear, Series IIA	H1-10C	H1-10C
Wheel, road	R1-1; R1-2	—

DETAILED INDEX

Description	Operation Number Remove/Refit	Operation Number Check/Overhaul
W Wheel, steering	G1-3	—
Windscreen	Q1-4	—
Windscreen fastener	Q1-4	—
Windscreen wiper	N1-19	—
Windscreen ventilator	Q1-9	—
Wing, front	Q1-3	—
Withdrawal, clutch	C1-14	C1-15

BROOKLANDS BOOKS LAND ROVER PUBLICATIONS

Title	Ref	ISBN
Land Rover Series 1 Workshop Manual	4291	9781783181841
Land Rover Series 1 1948-1953 Parts Catalogue	4051	9781855201194
Land Rover Series 1 1954-1958 Parts Catalogue	4107	9781855201071
Land Rover Series 1 1948-1958 Instruction Manual	4277	9781855207912
Land Rover Series 1 & II Diesel Instruction Manual	4343	9781855201286
Land Rover Series II & IIA Workshop Manual	AKM8159	9781783180295
Land Rover Series II & Early IIA Bonneted Control Parts Catalogue	605957	9781855202382
Land Rover Series IIA Bonneted Control Parts Catalogue	RTC9840CC	9781855202757
Land Rover Series IIA, III & 109 V8 Optional Equipment Parts Catalogue	RTC9842CE	9781855202870
Land Rover Series IIA/IIB Instruction Manual	LSM64IM	9781855201231
Land Rover Series 2A and 3 88 Parts Catalogue Supplement (USA Spec)	606494	9781783180264
Land Rover Series III Workshop Manual	AKM3648	9781855201088
Land Rover Series III Workshop Manual V8 Supplement (edn. 2)	AKM8022	9781855203105
Land Rover Series III 88, 109 & 109 V8 Parts Catalogue	RTC9841CE	9781855202139
Land Rover Series III Owners Manual (handbook) 1971-1978	607324B	9781855201293
Land Rover Series III Owners Manual (handbook) 1979-1985	AKM8155	9781855202269
Military Land Rover (Lightweight) Series II Parts Catalogue	61278	9781855201545
Military Land Rover Series III (L.W.B.) User Handbook	608179	9781855208919
Military Land Rover (Lightweight) Series II User Manual	608180	9781855200159
Land Rover 90/110 & Defender Workshop Manual 1983-1992	SLR621ENWM	9781855202504
Land Rover Defender Workshop Manual 1993-1995	LDAWMEN93	9781783181711
Land Rover Defender 300 Tdi & Supplements Workshop Manual 1996-1998	LRL0097ENGBB	9781855205048
Land Rover Defender Td5 Workshop Manual & Supplements 1999-2006	LRL0410BB	9781855206977
Land Rover Defender Electrical Manual Td5 1999-06 & 300Tdi 2002-2006	LRD5EHBB	9781855206984
Land Rover 110 Parts Catalogue 1983-1986	RTC9863CE	9781855202887
Land Rover Defender Parts Catalogue 1987-2006	STC9021CC	9781855207127
Land Rover 90 • 110 Handbook 1983-1990 MY	LSM0054	9781855204560
Land Rover Defender 90 • 110 • 130 Handbook 1991 MY - Feb. 1994	LHAHBEN93	9781855206502
Land Rover Defender 90 • 110 • 130 Handbook Mar. 1994 - 1998 MY	LRL0087ENG/2	9781855206519
Military Land Rover 90/110 All Variants (Excluding APV & SAS) User Manual	2320-D-122-201	9781855208926
Military Land Rover 90 & 110 2.5 Diesel Engine Versions User Handbook	SLR989WDHB	9781783180233
Military Land Rover Defender XD - Wolf Workshop Manual	2320D128 - 302 522 523 524	9781783180257
Military Land Rover Defender XD - Wolf Parts Catalogue	2320D128711	9781783180240
Land Rover Discovery Workshop Manual 1990-1994 (Petrol 3.5, 3.9, Mpi & Diesel 200 Tdi)	SJR900ENWM	9781855203129
Land Rover Discovery Workshop Manual 1995-1998 (Petrol 2.0 Mpi, 3.9, 4.0 V8 & Diesel 300 Tdi)	LRL0079BB	9781855207332
Land Rover Discovery Series II Workshop Manual 1999-2003 (Petrol 4.0 V8 & Diesel Td5 2.5)	VDR100090/6	9781855208681
Land Rover Discovery 3 2004-2009 TDI Diesel Workshop Manual		9781783182183
Land Rover Discovery 3 2004-2009 V8 4.4 Petrol Workshop Manual		9781783182176
Land Rover Discovery 3 2004-2009 V6 4.0 Petrol Workshop Manual		9781783182169
Land Rover Discovery 3 2004-2009 Chassis and Body Workshop Manual		9781783182152
Land Rover Discovery Parts Catalogue 1989-1998 (2.0 Mpi, 3.5, 3.9 V8 & 200 Tdi & 300 Tdi)	RTC9947CF	9781855206144
Land Rover Discovery Parts Catalogue 1999-2003 (Petrol 4.0 V8 & Diesel Td5 2.5)	STC9049CA	9781855208858
Land Rover Discovery Owners Handbook 1990-1991 (Petrol 3.5 V8 & Diesel 200 Tdi)	SJR820ENHB90	9781855202849
Land Rover Discovery Series II Handbook 1999-2004 MY (Petrol 4.0 V8 & Td5 Diesel)	LRL0459BB	9781855208438
Land Rover Freelander Workshop Manual 1998-2000 (Petrol 1.8 and Diesel 2.0)	LRL0144	9781855206151
Land Rover Freelander Workshop Manual 2001-2003 ON (Petrol 1.8L, 2.5L & Diesel Td4 2.0)	LRL0350ENG/4	9781855208742
Land Rover 101 1 Tonne Forward Control Repair Operation Manual	RTC9120	9781855201392
Land Rover 101 1 Tonne Forward Control Parts Catalogue	608294B	9781855201385
Land Rover 101 1 Tonne Forward Control User Manual	608239	9781855201439
Range Rover Workshop Manual 1970-1985 (Petrol 3.5)	AKM3630	9781855201224
Range Rover Workshop Manual 1986-1989 (Petrol 3.5 & Diesel 2.4 Turbo VM)	SRR660ENWM & LSM180WM	9781783180707
Range Rover Workshop Manual 1990-1994 (Petrol 3.9 V8, 4.2 V6 & Diesel 2.5 200 Tdi)	LHAWMENA02	9781783180691
Range Rover Workshop Manual 1995-2001 (Petrol 4.0, 4.6 V8 & BMW 2.5 Diesel)	LRL0326ENG	9781855207462
Range Rover Workshop Manual 2002-2005 (BMW Petrol 4.4 & BMW 3.0 Diesel)	LRL0477	9781855209046
Range Rover Electrical Manual 2002-2005 JK version (Petrol 4.4 & 3.0 Diesel)	RR02KEMBB	9781855209053
Range Rover Electrical Manual 2002-2005 JSA version (BMW Petrol 4.4)	RR02AEMBB	9781855209060
Range Rover Parts Catalogue 1970-1985 (Petrol 3.5)	RTC9846CH	9781855202528
Range Rover Parts Catalogue 1986-1991 (Petrol 3.5, 3.9 & Diesel 2.4 & 2.5 Turbo VM)	RTC9908CB	9781855202931
Range Rover Parts Catalogue 1992-1994 MY & 95 MY Classic (Petrol 3.9, 4.2 & Diesel 2.5 Turbo VM, 200 Tdi & 300 Tdi)	RTC9961CB	9781855206137
Range Rover Parts Catalogue 1995-2001 MY (Petrol 4.0, 4.6 & BMW 2.5 Diesel)	RTC9970CE	9781855206168
Range Rover Owners Handbook 1970-1980 (Petrol 3.5)	606917	9781855201736
Range Rover Owners Handbook 1981-1982 (Petrol 3.5)	AKM8139	9781855202795
Range Rover Owners Handbook 1983-1985 (Petrol 3.5)	LSM0001HB	9781855202801
Range Rover Owners Handbook 1986-1987 (Petrol 3.5 & Diesel 2.4 Turbo VM)	LSM129HB	9781855202900
Range Rover Owners Handbook 1988-1989 (Petrol 3.5 & Diesel 2.4 Turbo VM)	SRR600EN	9781855202917

Engine Overhaul Manuals for Land Rover & Range Rover

Title	Ref	ISBN
Land Rover 300 Tdi Engine, R380 Manual Gearbox & LT230T Transfer Gearbox Overhaul Manuals	LRL003, 070 & 081	9781855205215
Land Rover Petrol Engine V8 3.5, 3.9, 4.0, 4.2 & 4.6 Overhaul Manual	LRL004 & 164	9781855205284
Land Rover/Range Rover Driving Techniques	LR369	9781855202863
Working in the Wild - Manual for Africa	SMR684MI	9781855202856
Winching in Safety - Complete guide to winching Land Rovers & Range Rovers	SMR699MI	9781855202986

Workshop Manual Owners Edition

Title	ISBN
Land Rover 2 / 2A / 3 Owners Workshop Manual 1959-1983	9780713625127
Land Rover 90 • 110 Workshop Manual 1983-1995 MY Owners Edition 1983-1995	9781855203112
Land Rover Discovery Workshop Manual Owners Edition 1990-1998	9781855207660

www.brooklandsbooks.com

© Content Copyright of Jaguar Land Rover Limited 1968, 1971 and 1975
Brooklands Books Limited 2014 and 2016

This book is published by Brooklands Books Limited and based upon text
and illustrations protected by copyright and first published in 1968, 1971, 1975 by
Jaguar Land Rover Limited and may not be reproduced transmitted or copied by any
means without the prior written permission of Jaguar Land Rover Limited
and Brooklands Books Limited.

Whilst every effort has been made to ensure the accuracy of the particulars in this manual,
neither Brooklands Books Ltd. nor the supplier of this manual shall under any circumstances
be held liable for loss, damage or injury for any inaccuracy or omissions or the consequences thereof.

Brooklands Books Ltd., PO Box 904, Amersham,
Bucks, HP6 9JA, England
www.brooklandsbooks.com

ISBN: 9781783180295   Part No. AKM8159   Ref: LR22AW   4W4/2968

Printed in Great Britain
by Amazon